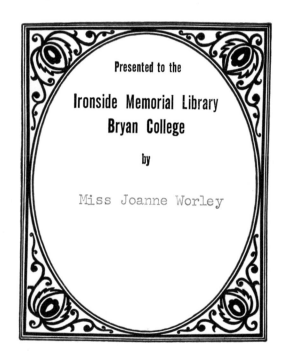

UNDER THE EDITORSHIP OF
ROBERT MORSS LOVETT

CHIEF PATTERNS OF

World

Drama

AESCHYLUS TO ANDERSON

WITH INTRODUCTIONS ON THE HISTORY OF
THE DRAMA AND THE STAGE BY

William Smith Clark II
UNIVERSITY OF CINCINNATI

HOUGHTON MIFFLIN COMPANY
The Riverside Press Cambridge

HOUGHTON MIFFLIN COMPANY
Boston · New York · Chicago · Dallas · Atlanta · San Francisco

The Riverside Press
CAMBRIDGE · MASSACHUSETTS
PRINTED IN THE U.S.A.

Foreword

The drama is one of man's best instruments for quickening his awareness to life. Like all the arts, it aims finally to transform perception into feeling, that is, to create "effects." In the study of the drama, therefore, a main interest, if not the primary one, should be to observe how the playwrights of serious artistic intent, bound as they all have been by the severe limitations of dramatic form as well as of stage production, have shaped and adapted and varied this form to bring about their particular "effects." Hence the present anthology is designed, above everything else, to arouse and cultivate that all-important interest in dramaturgy, the art of dramatic composition, as it has been practiced during the twenty-five centuries of theater in the Western World.

This volume of twenty-nine plays is a selection of the chief patterns of Occidental dramaturgy — a selection which the editor believes to be more representative and inclusive than any hitherto attempted. He is, however, wise enough to know his judgment not infallible and his choice of plays not beyond question. He himself would like to have included a specimen of George Bernard Shaw's craft, but he found that the illustrious Irishman shows no mercy toward lowly anthologists. Shakespeare too has been omitted, because his works are so easily available and so widely read by both students and laymen. In the choice of plays the editor sought, whenever possible, to avoid duplicating the contents of other anthologies, but at no point has he consciously sacrificed dramatic or theatrical quality for a fresh title. *Alcestis*, *The Pot of Gold*, *Andromache*, *The Inspector-General*, *The Admirable Crichton*, *The Silver Box*, *Roll Sweet Chariot*, and *Mary of Scotland* have not previously appeared, it is thought, in any general collection of drama. The translations of *The Pot of Gold* and of *The Life of the Insects* were prepared at the editor's request, and are here printed for the first time. *The Life of the Insects* has never before been published in an English version which reproduces the complete text along with the peculiar stylistic variations of the Czech original. All the plays, even the most recent, have been thoroughly annotated in order to provide an informed enjoyment of every line. With the older drama, the editor has paid especial notice to the stage directions in the conviction that the reader should be helped to visualize a contemporary performance and thus to comprehend for himself the perennial impact of stage conditions upon dramatic form. As further aid three pages of original drawings have been inserted at the appropriate places to illustrate the Greek, the Roman, and the Elizabethan theaters.

Perhaps the most distinctive feature of the present anthology is, however, the series of introductions to the individual plays. These introductions contain a good many little-known facts of biographical and literary significance — for instance, certain of the sources noted for *The Sea-Gull*, *The Admirable Crichton*, and *The Hairy Ape*. The lives of the dramatists have usually been set down in some detail, not only because their careers often hold a notable human interest, but also because their antecedents, early contacts, and life-experiences throw invaluable light on their election and treatment of themes. The introductions, nevertheless, are much more than a set of biographical and critical prefaces. They compose a running history of dramatic and theatrical activity from ancient Greece to present-day America. The almost thirty chapters of this history have been most carefully integrated into what will prove, it is hoped, an entertaining as well as comprehensive narrative. Certainly the drama possesses a more extensive and fascinating record of accomplishment than any other of the arts.

William S. Clark II

Cincinnati, Ohio

Acknowledgments

Grateful acknowledgment is made to the following publishers and authors or their representatives for permission to reprint the plays named:

Anderson House, for "Mary of Scotland," by Maxwell Anderson.

Edward Arnold and Company, for Marshall MacGregor's translation of "The Birds," by Aristophanes.

G. Bell and Sons, Limited, for Robert Bruce Boswell's translation of "Andromache," by Jean Racine, and for C. H. Wall's translation of "The Miser," by Molière, from the Bohn Library Series.

Charles E. Bennett, for his translation of "The Pot of Gold," by Plautus.

Chatto and Windus, for Constance Garnett's translation of "The Sea-Gull," by Anton Chekhov.

Curtis Brown and Company, and Paul Selver, for the latter's translation of "The Life of the Insects," by Josef and Karel Čapek.

E. P. Dutton and Company, Inc., and J. M. Dent and Sons, Limited, for "Naked," by Luigi Pirandello, taken from *Each In His Own Way and Two Other Plays*, translated by Arthur Livingston, published and copyrighted in the United States by E. P. Dutton and Company, Inc., New York.

Samuel French, Inc., for "Roll Sweet Chariot," by Paul Green.

Harvard University Press, for Morris H. Morgan's translation of "Phormio," by Terence.

Houghton Mifflin Company, for Philip M. Hayden's translation of "The Star of Seville," by Lope de Vega.

Oxford University Press, and George Allen and Unwin Limited, for Gilbert Murray's translation of "Alcestis," by Euripides.

Poet Lore, for Paula Green's translation of "Maria Magdalena," by Friedrich Hebbel.

Random House, Inc., for "The Hairy Ape," by Eugene O'Neill.

Random House, Inc., and George Allen and Unwin Limited, for "The Playboy of the Western World," by J. M. Synge.

Charles Scribner's Sons, for "The Admirable Crichton," by J. M. Barrie, "The Silver Box," by John Galsworthy, and Edmund Gosse and William Archer's translation of "Hedda Gabler," by Henrik Ibsen.

Arthur A. Sykes, for his translation of "The Inspector-General," by Nikolai V. Gogol.

Yale University Press, for Clarence W. Mendell's translation of "Prometheus Bound," by Aeschylus.

Contents

Contents

CHIEF PATTERNS OF
World Drama

INTRODUCTION TO
Prometheus Bound

The Beginnings of Drama and Theater in Greece:
Early Attic Tragedy: Aeschylus

THE DRAMA of the Western World had its beginnings in Greece, in the ancient state of Attica, at its capital, Athens. In that city, during the latter half of the sixth century B.C., there arose a combination of communal and esthetic elements which established traditions of dramatic art that have been continued to the present.

Attic drama, in all three of the patterns which the Athenians elevated to the rank of literature — tragedy, comedy, and satyr-play — got its original impulse from the rustic ceremonies at the planting and harvest seasons in honor of Dionysus, the god of wine and vegetation. The spring celebrations developed into the chief festivals of the Attic year. The people of the countryside gathered around rude stone altars set at the foot of hills where the vines grew richly, and worshiped with an abundance of wine their most popular divinity.

The essential feature of the Dionysiac rites always was group singing and dancing, which might be either grave or gay in spirit, according to the ecstatic mood of the celebrants. Forming themselves into choruses, with players of musical instruments in attendance, they sang hymns (called "dithyrambs"), accompanying them by expressive dance movements. Sometimes they wore costumes. The dithyrambs they sang not only rendered praise to Dionysus, but also, like ballads, described his origins, his loves, his exploits. Gradually, as the Dionysiac stories lost their appeal through overmuch repetition, the legends of other gods took their place.

Whether dignified or riotous, these dithyrambic performances originally were simple improvisations, the words and the action all composed on the spur of the moment. In the course of time they lost their extemporary, impromptu character. At the more important centers of Dionysiac worship, contests between choral groups were organized. The songs and dances for such contests came to be divided into fixed types of varying subject matter and sentiment. This process of deliberate instead of impromptu production brought about the separate forms of tragedy, comedy, and satyr-play. Attic drama in all its aspects was the direct offspring of religious enthusiasm, and the chorus was the very heart of its formal expression.

EARLY ATTIC TRAGEDY

Out of a grave and lofty dithyrambic ritual evolved the Attic "*tragoidia*," which means "goat-song." Scholars disagree whether it was so called because the chorus originally clothed themselves in skins of the goat, the sacred animal of Dionysus; or because the statue of Dionysus borne to the scene of celebration was draped in goat-skins; or because a goat originally constituted the prize for the best dithyrambic composition; or because a goat was sacrificed on the altar as an offering to the god at the end of the rites.   Whatever the origin of the term "tragedy," its early pattern is beyond dispute. To the solemn ceremony of song and dance by a dithyrambic chorus of fifty men there were added interludes in which a single actor, with costume and mask, impersonated Dionysus, or in later days, another god or hero.   Sometimes he addressed the chorus; at others, he conversed with its leader; occasionally he spoke in monologue.   Thus, actor and chorus, alternating with each other, enacted an appropriate myth.

For the creation of this first primitive type of tragic drama, tradition has awarded the credit to Thespis, son of Themon, a chorus leader and poet from the Attic town of Icaria. Even if he was not the actual father of the earliest Greek tragedy, certain it is that Thespis in 534 B.C. won the first prize ever awarded for performance of tragedy.

In the spring of that year Pisistratus, famous dictator of Athens (561–528 B.C.), initiated in honor of Dionysus an annual festival known as the City Dionysia, or simply as the Dionysia.   On the southeastern slope of the Acropolis, where a parcel of ground had been set aside for the service of the god, he built a temple and probably laid out, near by, a site for a theater.   In the new festival he introduced as a major feature of the program a contest in tragedy, despite the fact that tragedy then existed as an unpolished and only semi-literary form.   This contest continued to be the leading event of the Dionysia until as late as the second century A.D.

The festival was held at the end of March, when visitors from all parts of the Greek world, especially envoys bearing the yearly tributes from the Athenian allies, crowded the metropolis.   The occasion, therefore, gave opportunity to display the culture of Athens and to intensify patriotism.   No wonder that the Dionysia rose to be the city's outstanding holiday.   Business houses shut down and law courts closed.   Almost all the citizens participated in the festivities.   So important, in fact, did the government deem attendance that toward the close of the fifth century it made provision to pay the daily admission to the contests for any citizen who could not afford the fee of twenty cents.

By 500 B.C. the program of the City Dionysia extended over five or six days.   On the first day there was a magnificent procession with the image of Dionysus, in which marched priests, officials, choral and dramatic groups, and thousands of lay worshipers, all in gala attire.   At night the celebrants escorted the image back to the temple on the Acropolis.   Each day thereafter they brought the image forth to be present at the various contests of the festival.   The second day, and possibly the third, were devoted to dithyrambic contests among male choruses, each consisting of fifty *choreutae* or singers, and each representing one of the ten Attic tribes.   Dramatic competitions occupied the last three days.   Every dramatic poet who wished to strive for the prizes in tragedy had to submit to the chairman of the board of *archons* (or city magistrates) a set of four plays; three tragedies and a satyr-play.   The head *archon* selected three of these sets (or tetralogies), one to be produced each morning of the dramatic festival.   Such a tetralogy took from four to five hours to perform, and the people could not be expected to attend more than one a day.

These annual competitions in tragedy at the City Dionysia enjoyed the most careful supervision and support of the state.   After the *archon* had selected the three contestants, he assigned to each by lot a *choregus*, a wealthy citizen who under Athenian law was required to serve as both patron and business manager.   The duties of the *choregus* were onerous and his expenses large.   He had to select and pay the fifty *choreutae*; board them during the rehearsal period; rent a rehearsal room; hire a *didasculus* or trainer (except in the earlier days when the tragic poets themselves undertook this responsibility), and a pipe-player accompanist; secure all but the leading actors (who at first were provided by the poet and then by the state after the middle of the fifth century); and supply the costumes of both chorus and actors. Clearly the quality of the performance depended upon the generosity of the *choregus*. Fortunate the playwright who obtained a liberal producer, for in Athens, as elsewhere since, fine plays sometimes were spoiled by poor acting and costuming, while second-rate compositions won acclaim by superlative production.

The order of the competing tragic tetralogies was determined by lot, as was the nomination of the five judges. A complicated system of drawing the final jury helped to keep the members' identity a secret. Despite this procedure corruption did appear on occasion, and not infrequently popular applause affected the jury's decision. Any poet who won the public fancy had to be favored, even in Athens of the Golden Age. While all three competitors in tragedy received pecuniary awards on a moderate and sliding scale, only the victor was crowned with a garland of ivy by the presiding *archon*. This officer carried out from year to year another important duty, that of keeping a concise but complete record of the prizewinners and the titles of their plays. Thus he preserved for posterity dramatic annals unique to stage history.

Besides the City Dionysia, plays were acted in Athens at only one other period of the year, the Lenaea, a festival held at the end of January in honor of Dionysus Lenaeus. Though the Lenaea was far older than the Dionysia as a civic celebration, dramatic productions did not receive a place on its program until well into the fifth century, and contests in tragedy not until 433 B.C. Thereafter two poets strove for the prize, each presenting three tragedies but no satyr-play. Though the Lenaea, because of its occurrence in the winter season, never drew more than a few visitors from a distance, it remained for several centuries a family gathering of Athenians invaluable to the cultivation of local dramatic art.

If a modern playgoer could be set down in ancient Athens, he would be surprised, first of all, to discover that he could enjoy his favorite recreation only during these two festivals of January and March. Even more strange, however, would it be for him to find dramatic exhibitions so intimately connected with worship of both gods and country. He would soon learn that the Athenians looked upon these exhibitions as highly significant events in the annual civic routine. The performances combined a solemn religious ceremony and a great state function. Drama for such an occasion was expected to emphasize national currents of thinking and feeling, and to elevate the public mind and character. It had to reflect the grandeur of piety and patriotism. Now to the Athenian imagination the experience of contemporary humanity seemed less exalting, both spiritually and politically, than the legends of Greek divinities and heroes. Hence the Attic tragedians almost invariably chose their stories from that rich store of mythology which was as well known to their audiences as to themselves. Their compositions pictured a super-world remote in time and circumstance but, to the theatergoers of that day, all the more persuasive in its sentiments.

Attic tragedy, like the dramatic art of any age, was shaped also by the architectural characteristics of its theater. These characteristics grew out of the needs which both the religious and popular origins of Athenian drama forced its playhouse to meet. From the outset provision had to be made for a vast audience in democratic assembly, and for a considerable space in which the large dithyrambic chorus could maneuver properly. In so hilly a region as Attica and in so mild a climate the obvious answer to these requirements was an open-air playhouse with an Attic hillside its auditorium, the blue Aegean sky its roof, and the clear Aegean sunlight its "spot." At the bottom of the hillslope could be easily constructed an *orchestra*, a circular dancing-floor of hardened earth with a curb and gutter around its rim, and an altar in its center. On the slope itself a large crowd could be seated in a semicircular amphitheater to view the action on the *orchestra* below. These considerations effected the simple and logical architecture common to the numerous playhouses which came into being throughout Greece during the fifth century.

The site and appearance of the theater at Athens where Thespis scored his first triumph as a tragedian in 534 B.C. cannot now be described. To inaugurate the Dionysia contests in tragedy, Pisistratus may have built an *orchestra* on the southeastern slope of the Acropolis near the temple of Dionysus. At any rate, in 499 B.C. or shortly thereafter, a theater certainly occupied this location, the oldest stage site known in the Occident. Here can still be seen ruins of the *orchestra* of twenty-five centuries ago. This *orchestra*, some sixty-five feet in diameter, was so banked that, as it receded from the Acropolis, its southern edge formed a terrace from six to seven feet higher than the sloping terrain. In the declivity immediately behind the terrace on the south there appeared no scenic background of any kind. A few stage properties, such as a rock or a tomb, were erected for temporary use on that side of the *orchestra* away from the audience. Two ramplike passageways, called *parodoi* and situated on either side of the terrace, provided entrance for both spectators and performers. Whatever dressing rooms the latter possessed at this period must have been placed inconspicuously near the far ends of the ramps. A crude auditorium of wooden bleachers stretched northward up the Acropolis in an extended semicircle with the terminating sides running obliquely to the diameter of the auditorium. The rows of seats near the top may have been cut directly out of the reddish limestone. The seat of greatest honor, the middle one of the row nearest the *orchestra*, was reserved for the priest of Dionysus while other high officials, civil and ecclesiastical, occupied the rest of the front row. The ties between dramatic art, on the one hand, and church and state on the other, have never since been so vividly indicated in the playhouse of any country.

AESCHYLUS

In this original theater on the Acropolis there rose to fame the earliest of the great Greek dramatists, Aeschylus, son of Euphorion. A thinker, poet, and theatrical technician of the first order, Aeschylus brought Attic tragedy to literary and intellectual maturity. The tragic pattern which he created remained the basic design of all subsequent Greek effort. And not only the plays, but also the playwright set a model to succeeding writers. He integrated perfectly the calling of the artist with the duties of a citizen. His chief successors in the Athenian theater did likewise and displayed themselves men of the world as well as poets.

Aeschylus was born about the year 525 B.C. at Eleusis, a village close to Athens, famous over all the Mediterranean area as the originating point of the Eleusinian mysteries — those secret rites in honor of the goddess Demeter which produced a kind of sacred freemasonry among far-flung Greek communities. For a youth these were surroundings charged with the awe and the mystery of religion, and they left their mark upon the mind of Aeschylus. A proud ancestry and moderate wealth inclined him to a conservatism which in his last years caused his voluntary exile. He was nonetheless an ardent patriot, holding public office and engaging in notable military service. At the celebrated battle on the plain of Marathon (490 B.C.), where the Greeks saved Europe from Persian despotism, Aeschylus and his two brothers earned prizes for their valor. According to tradition, he also fought ten years later in the great naval battle off Salamis, a scarcely less important victory for Greek culture.

Engaged as he was in the stirring conflicts of his city-state, at home and abroad, Aeschylus could not help realizing to the full the Athenian heritage. He was qualified to express with peculiar force the essential traditions of his country at the moment when she became the center of world civilization. About 458 B.C. he left Athens permanently to pass the brief remainder of his life at the court of Hiero, dictator of Syracuse in Sicily, where on a former visit he had found a congenial literary circle. In 456, his sixty-ninth year, he died at Gela, Sicily, and was buried with this beautiful epitaph, perhaps of his own phrasing: "Beneath this stone lies Aeschylus, son of Euphorion, the Athenian, who perished in the wheat-bearing land of Gela; of his prowess the grove of Marathon can speak, and the long-haired Persian, who knows it well."

Aeschylus began his career as man of the theater in his early twenties; he is known to have participated in the tragic contest at the Dionysia of 499 B.C. For forty years thereafter he was a prominent figure on the Athenian stage. In the very year of his retirement, 458, he not only won the first prize for tragedy with the *Oresteia*, but also served as *didasculus*, or director, of his own production. An astonishing versatility distinguished his pioneering. He united in his own person almost an entire productional staff — playwright, director, chief actor, chorus trainer, costume designer.

Love of spectacle colored his every effort. His improvements of stage dress resulted in conventionalizing for tragic actors a costume made up of a long robe and a mantle for the shoulders, each garment of bright hue and often gorgeously decorated. The facial masks of cork, linen, or wood, which all performers in the Greek playhouses were accustomed to wear because of ritualistic tradition and theatrical necessity, Aeschylus developed in diversity of type and in expressiveness. The bloody features and snaky locks of the masked Furies in his *Eumenides* produced so startling an effect, it is said, that children fainted and women had hysterics. Perhaps he was also responsible for adding to the paraphernalia of the tragic actors a lofty headdress, called the *onkus*, and a thick-soled wooden boot, the *cothurnus*. These devices heightened the impression of heroic stature in the figures of Attic tragedy.

Aeschylus the chorus trainer and playwright introduced changes of literary as well as theatrical significance. To relieve the choral singers of the heavy burden of memorizing the words, music, dance steps, and stage business for the three tragedies and the satyr-play, which every tragedian was required to present in the annual Dionysia competition, he divided the *choreutae* at his disposal into four groups of twelve each and assigned one group as a chorus for each drama. So effective did this rearrangement prove that twelve continued to be the normal size of the tragic chorus until the middle of the fifth century. To increase the dramatic interest of the three tragedies, he invented the trilogy, three plays linked together by the presentation of successive parts of the same long story. Though he devoted his energies exclusively to this serial form and gained many victories, later dramatists did not imitate his practice, perhaps because it was too difficult.

Of much greater importance, however, than these two innovations was Aeschylus' insertion into the tragic pattern of a second actor. In the crude, one-actor tragedy of Thespis and his followers the leader of the chorus had commonly been employed in addition as a quasi-actor, but of course his speaking was extremely limited in its relation to the *protagonist*, or first performer. No effective struggle between the characters could be depicted. The introduction of a *deuteragonist*, or second performer, permitted for the first time the meeting of conflicting personages face to face and the direct clash of will. Thus, by what appears now an easy and obvious step, but one which in his day artistic ignorance long blocked, Aeschylus made possible full-fledged drama in the dialogue of Attic tragedy.

From four decades of playwriting there have survived intact only seven of Aeschylus' works, although titles or fragments of some seventy more are known. The extant pieces comprise *The Suppliant Maidens* produced *c.* 490 B.C.; *The Persians*, 472 B.C.; *Prometheus Bound*, *c.* 470 B.C.; *The Seven against Thebes*, 467 B.C.; *Agamemnon, The Libation-Bearers, The Furies (Eumenides)*, 458 B.C. The last three plays constitute a trilogy, the solitary specimen of that Athenian species now in existence. This trilogy, often referred to as the *Oresteia* or story of Orestes, is regarded as Aeschylus' most ambitious composition, but it reveals the dramaturgic influence of his younger rival, Sophocles. While all his other works are two-actor dramas, the *Oresteia* requires three actors throughout, after the Sophoclean mode. The same influence also increased the size of the chorus from twelve to fifteen. Therefore, great accomplishment though it is, the *Oresteia* does not represent what the inventive genius of Aeschylus accomplished by itself alone. Nor does the scenic construction of the *Oresteia* conform to the conditions of the earliest theater at Athens, the one in which the master learned his art.

"PROMETHEUS BOUND"

Prometheus Bound, however, displays perfectly the Aeschylean pattern during the era when its author dominated the tragic stage, and before the playhouse on the Acropolis had undergone changes which affected the whole art of stage-setting. This drama typifies Aeschylus' acute "sense of theater" and the pageantry which he founded as a basic tradition of the Greek stage. During the first third of the fifth century he faced an *orchestra* without scenic background. He adapted to it the indefinite site of action in *Prometheus Bound* — merely a crag somewhere in the mountainous desert of the Caucasus. But he achieved a powerful effect of loneliness in the figure of Prometheus starkly outlined on the replica of rock at the rear edge of the bare orchestral space. The play opens and closes skillfully with animated and awesome action. The chaining of Prometheus to the crag catches the immediate attention and sympathy of the spectator by the horrible detail with which it is depicted. Aeschylus made the process of nailing altogether realistic because he employed a wooden dummy for Prometheus at the opening of the play. By thus saving an actor, he could introduce at once two speaking parts, Strength and Hephaestus. Force, it will be noted, is never allowed to speak because of the two-actor convention, and is acted by a mute. Aeschylus himself probably played Hephaestus. After the exit of that character, he took up his position behind the crag to speak thenceforward for Prometheus. Up to the first pause in the dialogue the latter rests strangely dumb.

The disappearance of the Titan at the end of the play forms a stupendous finale calculated to make the audience shudder. A clever bit of stage business accomplished the swift destruction. The six-foot drop in the ground behind the *orchestra* Aeschylus used to his advantage. He arranged for the framework representing the crag to collapse backwards out of sight, and for the gigantic figure of Prometheus to sink into the supposed abyss.

Even the choral parts and the rôle of Oceanus appear to have been worked out for all the visual effect possible. The entrances of the sea-nymphs in wing-shaped chariots, and of Oceanus riding on a griffin, provide novel spectacles. Aeschylus, like every great craftsman in drama, utilized freely the physical devices of his theater for the purposes of art.

Although *Prometheus Bound* was either the first or second member of a trilogy on the story of Prometheus the Fire-Bearer, the loss of the two companion pieces does not impair it in any way as a dramatic entity. So much cannot be said for the three sections of the unique *Oresteia*, for if viewed separately, they lose immeasurably in force and meaning. It is evident that in his earlier trilogies Aeschylus designed a greater independence for the individual parts than in his last masterpiece. Nevertheless, the presentation of a single person in conflict with his destiny, as in *Prometheus Bound*, is by no means so elaborate or accomplished a piece of art as Aeschylus undertook in his *Oresteia*. *Prometheus Bound* at many points comes dangerously close to a *tableau vivant* exhibiting the punishment and fortitude of a revered hero. Yet for that very reason this drama brings into the sharpest relief the statuesque and colossal simplicity which above all else distinguishes Attic tragedy from the modern.

The simplicity of Attic tragedy results, in a measure, from the rigidity of its dramatic architecture. The outline of the tragic structure was fixed by the practice of Aeschylus and others during the first third of the fifth century B.C. No important deviations developed subsequently. Almost all the fundamental points of construction can be discerned in *Prometheus Bound*.

First comes the "prologue" which is the exposition of the situation (ll. 1–131). Then there follows the "*parodos*," the song of the chorus as it files into the *orchestra*. In *Prometheus Bound*, however, Aeschylus, having brought on his chorus swiftly by chariot, substitutes for the entrance song a *kommos* or lyrical exchange between the chorus and Prometheus (ll. 132–205). Such duets are more commonly found inserted as interludes in the dialogue portions of the Attic tragedies.

The next structural division is called the first "*epeisodion*," a passage of dialogue with or without action. Aeschylus varies slightly the normal arrangement by composing this section of *Prometheus Bound* in two parts (ll. 206–90, and ll. 299–408) separated by a choral song (ll. 291–98). Thereafter occurs the first "*stasimon*" or choral song on the *orchestra* (ll. 409–34). Both in the *kommos* and the *stasimon* the chorus accompanies its

singing by a dance movement which breaks the song into passages.   As the chorus circles
from the right to the left of the *orchestra*, it sings the *strophe*; as it returns from the left to
its former position on the right, it sings the *antistrophe*.   The number of these strophic
passages depends entirely on the whim of the dramatic poet.

Following the first *stasimon* is the second *epeisodion* (ll. 435–527); then, in order, the
second *stasimon* (ll. 528–553), the third *epeisodion* (ll. 554–900), the third *stasimon* (ll.
901–26), the fourth *epeisodion* (ll. 927–1113).   *Prometheus Bound* once more departs
from the standard tragic construction at the close, for it does not contain an *exodos*, or
choral recessional after the last *epeisodion*.   The omission is the necessary result of the
abrupt removal of the chorus by the final cataclysm.

In general, the Attic tragic structure is composed of five passages of dialogue which
alternate with the same number of choral parts.   Here is the genesis of the five-act play
which became the accepted form in European drama for many centuries.

The simplicity of Attic tragedy arises, of course, from other structural qualities besides rigidity.   Duration of time and change of scene were limited by the tradition that
a chorus should be on the stage throughout most of the play and that the chorus should
have an evident share in the theatrical proceedings.   It often taxed the ingenuity of the
Attic dramatist to select a group of characters who could be related to the story of the
hero and concerned in his fate.   In *Prometheus Bound* Aeschylus perhaps strains credulity by introducing a chorus of ocean-nymphs who, sorrowed by the Titan's plight, fly to
his side in the rocky wastes of Scythia and finally go down in doom with him.   The continued presence of the chorus forced the playwright usually to keep his action in one general locality and within the apparent confines of a single day.   The strict limitation upon
the number of actors in the Attic drama (a tradition firmly based on economic grounds)
prevented much complexity of story.   Plot assumed the same unity as time and place.
These three unities in combination with the necessarily prominent choral element produced tragedy of stark directness and pronounced lyrical coloring, such as *Prometheus
Bound* conspicuously exemplifies.

The temperament of Aeschylus, however, accentuated the lyric, static tendencies in
Attic tragedy.   The subtle workings of personality and the conflicts of character did not
command his talent.   On the contrary, his creations suggest an intensely reflective mood.
He placed upon Greek tragedy the permanent imprint of the speculative temper.   The
choric odes gave ideal opportunity for him to put to verbal music his profoundest musings on the religious and moral and historical problems related to the mythical groundwork of his drama.   They became in his hands an indispensable instrument for varying
the pitch and tone of the central emotion.

One of the most telling effects of the Aeschylean chorus is the contrasting of two perspectives, the particular and the universal.   The shift from one to the other affords the
poet a recurring chance to balance the views of his hero against the supposed wisdom of
all time.   In *Prometheus Bound* the indignation and self-pity of the "Fire-Bearer to
Man" voice themselves over against the often dark and cold meditations of the chorus.

Not so clearly as elsewhere, and yet clearly enough, does Aeschylus suggest his philosophy, a somber determinism which envisaged a mysterious necessity ruling even the
gods themselves — "Zeus may not shun the fate ordained him."   For men and for demi-
gods too the one thing needful is humility; pride in the sense of insolence remains the un-

forgivable sin.   That way lies ruin for mortals and immortals alike.   Obedience to Law, however inexplicable, stands as the primary principle of the cosmic order.   These speculations on Existence, colored with the poet's gift of imagery, constitute for the thoughtful spectator the pre-eminent appeal in Aeschylean and in Attic tragedy generally.   The intellectual depth and vitality of that drama have never been surpassed, though certain of its subjects have since lost their significance.

Of all the stories which the old Greek plays treated that of *Prometheus Bound* is the most universally significant.   This legend of a god suffering for the sake of mankind has fascinated the imagination of poets in all ages.   Shelley, for example, made a notable attempt in his poem *Prometheus Unbound* to complete the tale of the punishment and final deliverance of the Titan.   The Aeschylean theme of rebellion at divine cruelty awakens both humanity's compassion for the victim and its self-pity in the face of apparent cosmic injustice.   Because *Prometheus Bound* strikes at the very core of human unselfishness on the one hand, and of human egotism on the other, it will remain perennially alive, a signal instance of the ancient Athenian capacity to handle in art the ultimate values of life.

[For a history of the theater and drama of the ancient classic world, see Margarete Bieber, *The History of the Greek and Roman Theater* (1939); for a history of the Greek stage, R. C. Flickinger, *The Greek Theater and Its Drama* (4th ed., 1936); for a study of Greek tragedy, Gilbert Norwood, *Greek Tragedy* (1920); for a critique on Aeschylus, Lewis Campbell, *Tragic Drama in Aeschylus, Sophocles, and Shakespeare* (1904).]

AESCHYLUS

Prometheus Bound

[*Translated by* CLARENCE W. MENDELL]

DRAMATIS PERSONAE

PROMETHEUS, *a Titan*
HEPHAESTUS, *the god of fire*
KRATOS (MIGHT)
BIA (FORCE) } *daemons attendant upon Zeus*
OCEANUS, *the god of oceans*
IO, *daughter of Inachus, a river god*
HERMES, *the winged herald of the gods*
CHORUS *of ocean nymphs*

ARGUMENT

Eons ago a war broke out between the Titans, the primeval deities who were the children of Uranus (Sky) and Gaea (Earth), and the newer gods who dwelt upon Mount Olympus in Thessaly. The Titans favored Cronus, the reigning king, as lord of Heaven, while the Olympians wished to supplant Cronus by his son, Zeus. But one of the Titans, Prometheus, parted from his brothers to support the cause of Zeus. Zeus, once enthroned, displayed enmity against mankind and sought to destroy it. Then, out of pity, Prometheus stole fire from Heaven to bestow it, along with other arts, upon the race of men. These services of the Titan enabled Man to preserve himself, and kindled the wrath of Zeus. The king of the gods had Prometheus fettered to a rocky slope of the Caucasus. Finally the continued rebelliousness of the prisoner led Zeus to shatter the rock with a thunderbolt and hurl Prometheus into an abysmal dungeon within the earth.

The Scene is a barren cliff in Scythia [1]

Enter PROMETHEUS, *a gigantic figure, guarded by* HEPHAESTUS, *and two burly brutes,* KRATOS *and* BIA, *carrying hammers, rivets, bolts, chains, and wedges. They approach the cliff*

Kra. So we are come to the last reach of earth,
To Scythia's shore, a man-forbidden waste;
And thou, Hephaestus, since thou must fulfill

Thy sire's commands, shalt nail this villain here
Unto these jagged cliffs, and bind him fast 5
With bonds unbreakable as adamant.
Thy glory, flame of all-devising fire,
He stole and gave to mortals; for such wrong
He must unto the gods yield punishment,
Learning to love the tyranny of Zeus 10
And cease his benefactions to mankind.
    Heph. Kratos and Bia, God's decree for you
Touches fulfillment, nothing gives you pause.
But I — I dare not, kinsman that he is,[1]
Kinsman and god, bind him perforce to this 15

[1] A vast wild area variously located by the ancients in eastern Europe or western Asia. Aeschylus is thought by most scholars to have had in mind the mountainous region of the Caucasus.

[1] Both Hephaestus and Prometheus were sons of Titans.

Storm-beaten cliff.　And yet, perforce, I must,
For hard it is to slight the Father's word.

Thou of high-towering thoughts, just Themis'
　　son,[1]
Against my will as thine with bonds of brass
Hard to be loosed I'll bind thee to this rock　20
Where man come not, where thou shalt never
　　hear
The voice nor see the form of human kind;
But, scorched beneath the sun's devouring rays,
Shalt yield the bloom of thine immortal flesh.
'Twill be thy joy to see the light of day　25
Hidden behind the star-flecked robe of night.
But quickly day shall follow on the dawn
And ever on the heels of present woe
New woes shall tread, nor has one yet been born
Who can deliver thee.　　　　　　　　　30

　　　　　　　　　　Such is the boon
That thou hast won by fostering mortal man:
God though thou art, yet fearing no god's
　　wrath,
Thou gavest without justice unto men
The treasure of the gods.　Wherefore for-
　　ever　　　　　　　　　　　　　　35
Thou shalt be guardian of this joyless cliff,
Upright and sleepless, bending not the knee.
Many the plaints, many the fruitless cries
That thou shalt utter, for the heart of Zeus
Is hard to bend: new power is ever stern.　40
　　Kra. Let be.　Why dost thou wait and to no
　　　end
Show pity?　Dost not hate the enemy
Of all the gods who gave to man thy boon?
　　Heph. Kinship's a potent bond — and friend-
　　　ship too.
　　Kra. 'Tis true, but canst thou dare to dis-
　　　obey　　　　　　　　　　　　　45
The Father's word?　Weighs not this terror
　　more?
　　Heph. Oh, pitiless and full of boldness thou!
　　Kra. Aye, for I see no cure in pitying him.
Waste not thy strength on what availeth
　　naught.
　　Heph. Oh, craft of mine that I can only hate!

[1] Themis, goddess of justice and order, and daughter of Uranus, is here rather unusually identified as the mother of Prometheus.

　　Kra. Why hate thy craft?　For, speaking
　　　bluntly now,　　　　　　　　　51
These present woes owe nothing to thy craft.
　　Heph. I would some other wielded that same
　　　craft.
　　Kra. All things are hateful save to rule the
　　　gods,
For, briefly spoken, none is free but Zeus.　55
　　Heph. That know I by this present nor deny.
　　Kra. Then haste to put the shackles on this
　　　rogue
Before the Father see thee loitering.
　　　　(HEPHAESTUS, KRATOS, *and* BIA *now*
　　　　　proceed to the work of fettering
　　　　　PROMETHEUS *to the cliff.*
　　Heph. There!　Thou mayst see the shackles
　　　on his hands.
　　Kra. With all thy might then and thy ham-
　　　mer's strength　　　　　　　　60
Make fast his two hands to the rocky cliff.
　　Heph. 'Tis done; nor shall such work be done
　　　in vain.
　　Kra. Give it another twist, a closer fit:
The fellow's shrewd to do the impossible.
　　Heph. This arm is riveted beyond release.　65
　　Kra. Then chain the other fast: so may he
　　　learn
That all his cleverness falls short of Zeus.
　　Heph. In this none but himself can blame
　　　my work.
　　Kra. Now thrust the biting wedge of ada-
　　　mant
Straight through his heart and drive it bravely
　　home.　　　　　　　　　　　70
　　Heph. Alas, Prometheus, for thy woes I
　　　groan.
　　Kra. What, art thou pitying him, an enemy
Of Zeus?　Ere long thou mayst pity thy-
　　self.
　　Heph. Herein thou seest a sight most piti-
　　　able.
　　Kra. I see one reaping his deserts.　Come,
　　　sling　　　　　　　　　　　75
The iron girths around on either side.
　　Heph. It must be done, but urge me not too
　　　far.
　　Kra. I'll urge thee and I'll hound thee on.
　　　Slip down
And force the iron shackles on his legs.

Heph. 'Tis done — how little effort and 'tis
    done.   80
Kra. Then make the anklets fast with pierc-
    ing nails,
For a hard master ordered thee this task.
Heph. Thy tongue is sure as brutal as thy
    face.
Kra. Speak softly if thou wilt, but do not
    blame
My hardness nor the temper of my wrath.   85
Heph. Let us begone: his limbs are fettered
    fast.   (*Exeunt* HEPHAESTUS *and* BIA.
Kra. Now show thine insolence and rob the
    gods
To benefit the creatures of a day!
What can mankind return thee for these woes?
The gods were false that gave to thee thy
    name,   90
Forethinker: for thyself it is that needst
A counselor to save thee from *this* craft.
                    (*Exit* KRATOS.
Prom. Oh, breath of heaven and ye swift-
    winged winds,
Ye springs of water, thou, oh, mother earth,
And all the countless laughter of the waves,   95
Thou sun whence naught is hid — I call you all:
Behold and see how gods torture a god.[1]

Ye may see, ye may see
The grim agony
That is destined to be   100
To eternity.

For such is the pain
That shall ever remain
Through this tyrannous reign
Till Zeus be slain.   105

I groan for a woe that shall never cease.
For where is the end that shall bring release?

What words are these?   I *know* the end of all,
I know the future and no woe shall come
To me unlooked for.   I must bear my fate   110
As best I can, knowing full well that fate
Has power invincible.   Yet in this plight

---

[1] In this soliloquy the actor no doubt paused between
the different lyric sections so that the long passage of
time might be better suggested.

I cannot hold my silence nor yet bear
To speak.   For, giving unto mortal man
His greatest boon, I am bound hand and foot
Unto this fate.   I stole the gift of fire,   116
The source of wisdom, teacher of all arts
To human kind, and for such violence
Am lifted up to pay the penalty.

What sound is that, what breath that comes
    unseen?   120
A god?   A mortal?   Comes some hero here
To this forsaken spot to view my woes?
What other purpose?   Lo, thou seest a god
Bound by a cursed fate, the enemy
Of Zeus, hated of all the sycophants   125
That tread the halls of Zeus, because forsooth
He loved mankind too well.

                  What is this sound
Of beating birds about me?   All the air
Is filled with whirring wings.   I am become
Fearful of all that is.   131

Enter CHORUS *of twelve ocean nymphs in a
             winged chariot*

    Chor.   Fear not, our friendly argosy [1] (Strophe)
Swift fluttering
On eager wing
Comes over lands untraversed else to thee.   135
Hardly the Father's will,
Reluctant to fulfill
Our purpose, sped us wind-borne o'er the sea.

Far in our distant cavern blow on blow
The beating hammers banished maiden fear.   140
Swifter than foot, yet to my heart how slow,
The winged chariot urged its mad career.

    Prom.   Alas, alas, offspring of Tethys' womb,[2]
Children of cunning Tethys, children too
Of him who, issuing from his cavern's gloom,   145
Circles the wide earth round with Ocean's blue.

---

[1] This and all subsequent passages in italics constitute the *sung* portions of the play.

[2] The ocean nymphs, or Oceanides, were the children
of Oceanus, father of all rivers, springs, and seas, and
of his wife, Tethys, daughter of Uranus and Gaea.

These bonds of adamant riveted deep
Behold and ye shall see
How on this cliff unenvied watch I keep
Throughout eternity.   150

Chor. I see, Prometheus — suddenly
           (Antistrophe)
Before mine eyes
The mists arise
Of tears that start unbidden when I see
In everlasting thrall,   155
Nailed to yon craggy wall,
The glorious form of thy divinity.

New stewards lord it in the halls above;
New laws rule heaven, new laws in malice
     wrought.
Zeus reigns with arbitrary might, for love   160
And all the powers of yesterday are naught.

Prom. Would Zeus had banished me beneath
     the earth
To lowest hell, grim Hades' ancient fee.
High monarch o'er the dead, his joyless mirth
Might mock these cruel fetters endlessly.   165

For then no god could feast his eyes in joy
On my grim recompense
Nor laugh to see the almighty Zeus destroy
His peer, in insolence.

Chor. None so hard of heart can be   (Str. 2)
Joys to see thy misery;   171
None but watches sorrowful
None — save Zeus the all-powerful.

Zeus with darkling counsel still
Wreaks his own unbending will;   175
Fearless, knows no mercy he
Till he win satiety. —
Or till by sudden master stroke,
Serfs of heaven strike off the yoke.

Prom. Aye, but that day shall come when heav-
     en's high lord,   180
Bound though I be thus meanly, shall perchance
Have need of me, when of his own accord
He'll beg me to forget his arrogance.

He shall not then beguile with honeyed tongue
My will, nor with his veiled threats dissipate   185
My wrath: till he restore me whence I sprung
And loose my bonds, I'll give him hate for hate.

Chor. Bold of heart and bitter, thou   (Ant. 2)
Brookest not thy head to bow;
Curb nor bit thou'lt tolerate,   190
Stiff-necked, girding at thy fate.

Piercing terror strikes my heart,
Yearning still to take thy part.
Endless years with woes untold
Pledge thee sorrows manifold,   195
For Cronus' son [1] *knows mercy not*
Nor heeds the misery of thy lot.

Prom. Harsh is the tyrant and I know it well:
Justice to him is selfish interest:
But, humbled once from his high citadel,   200
He shall come forth and come at my behest.

For he shall rue this day, his towering rage
Shall vanish wholly in humility:
Peace shall he make — but peace when he engage
Humbly to seek a pact of love with me.   205

Chor. Lead. Unfold thy tale: reveal to us
     the cause
Why Zeus hath seized thee and thus cruelly
Tortures thy being, if so be the tale
Adds not more cruel torture in the telling.
    Prom. Torture it is to speak, yet equal pain
Racks me if I speak not: there's naught but
     woe.   211

When first the gods conceived their mutual hate
And stirred rebellion, eager some to drive
Lord Cronus from his throne that Zeus might
     reign
Forsooth, while other some with equal heat   215
Battled that Zeus might never rule the gods,
I counseled with myself the wisest course:
Sought to win o'er the Titans, sons of earth
And Uranus, to peace; but they disdained
My wiles: with overweening pride they strove
To win untroubled power by violence.   221
Oft had my mother Themis — Gaea too

    [1] Zeus was son of Cronus and Rhea.

They call her: many names, one form are hers —
Revealed to me the future that should be:
How not by power nor might but by the wiles
Of craft should come the prize of majesty.   226
But as I taught them wisdom's better way
They scorned it still as babbling foolishness,
Till I was forced to choose what seemed the
     best
That yet was left, winning my mother's aid,
To range myself confederate with Zeus.   231
My plans they were whereby the yawning
     chasm
Of Tartarus [1] engulfed the ancient-born
Cronus and all his fellows. [2]   Such the aid
That heaven's hard master now rewards in
     full   235
By these soul-rending torments.   Such I ween
The curse of tyrants, ne'er to trust their friends.

But what thou askest, wherefore he decrees
That I should suffer, I will tell thee all.

Once seated on his father's throne, straight-
     way   240
He parceled out to all the lesser gods
Their share of power, but unto wretched
     men
He gave no heed; rather he planned forthwith
To wipe them out incontinent and make
Another race, whereto with one accord   245
All gave consent. I, only I, withstood.
Mine was the courage, 'twas my act alone
Saved man from burial in the deepest black
Of Hades' realm.   This was the villainy
For which I suffer woes hard to endure   250
And piteous to behold.   Mercy I showed
Unto mankind, yet was not deemed myself
Worthy of pity, but with ruthless hate
Am made a spectacle to shame great Zeus.
    Chor. Lead. Steeled against sympathy, rock-
     bound of heart   255
Whoe'er, Prometheus, pities not thy woes.
For I could pray never to have seen thy lot
And, seeing it, am torn with sympathy.
    Prom. Yea, piteous I for my friend to see.

[1] The prison house of Zeus' victims, a region as far beneath Hades, or the Lower World, as Heaven was above the earth.
[2] The Titans.

    Chor. Lead. Thou hast done naught save
     what thy tale recounts?   260
    Prom. I rescued mortals from foreseeing fate.
    Chor. Lead. What cure for such affliction
     didst devise?
    Prom. Blind hopes I taught to spring within
     their hearts.
    Chor. Lead. A mighty boon this gift of thine
     to man.
    Prom. And I bequeathed them too the gift
     of fire.   265
    Chor. Lead. Know mortals then the use of
     gleaming fire?
    Prom. Aye, and shall learn from it all arts to
     know.
    Chor. Lead. On such a charge it is that
     mighty Zeus ——
    Prom. Does me despite nor anywise relents.
    Chor. Lead. Is no bound set unto thy punish-
     ment?   270
    Prom. None, save it seemeth some day good
     to him.
    Chor. Lead. How can it so?   What hope?
     Dost thou not see
That thou hast sinned?   Yet 'tis for me no joy
To say *how* thou hast sinned — nor yet for thee.
Rather shouldst thou be seeking some release.
    Prom. Easy to him whose foot is not en-
     snared   276
The ready counsel and admonishment
For one who suffers.   Well I understood
My act.   Willing I sinned.   No ignorance
I plead.   I willed it, nor deny the deed,   280
For mortals found release, doom for myself.
And yet not such the punishment I dreamed,
To wear my soul out on these towering crags
A lonely dweller in this lonely waste.

But now bewail not my apparent woes: 285
Alight and hear from me the fates foredoomed
That follow after, that ye too may know
The whole.   Yea, grant me this, to sympathize
With one in dire distress; for be assured
Misfortune tarries not in *one* abode.   290
    Chor. Not to unheeding ears
Dost thou proclaim thy fears:
Hence in swift-footed flight
To this wild wind-swept height
Come I in sympathy   295

Hither to thee.
Hence too thy suffering drear
Haste I to hear.

Enter OCEANUS *on a winged sea monster*

Ocean. My leagues-long journey ended, lo, I come,
Prometheus, unto thee, guiding by power   300
Of will alone mine own swift-winged bird.
For I would have thee know that with thy woes
I sympathize. Kinship would teach me so [1]
And more than kinship: there is none beside
That I could wish greater felicity.   305
This will I prove. My nature never is
To speak in flattery. Tell me therefore
How can I help thee? Thou shalt never claim
A friend more worthy than Oceanus.

Prom. What mockery is here? Art thou too come   310
To spy my suffering out? How didst thou dare
To leave thy rock-roofed cavern and the stream
That bears thy name to come unto this land
Of iron-conceiving womb? [2] Didst come expectantly
To view the mummery of my suffering?   315
Lo, what thou seekest: me, the friend of Zeus,
That wrought with him the tyranny of heaven,
And now — thou seest the plight of God's ally.

Ocean. I see, Prometheus, and for all thy wit
I'll bring thee wisdom from the store of time.   320

Learn first to know thyself. Learn to make new
Thy ways, for a new master rules the gods.
If thou in bitterness shalt heavenward hurl
Sharp stinging words, far though he sit apart,
Zeus yet may hear and this thy present plight
Soon seem a mere apprenticeship in woe.   326
Curb then the wrath thou bearest; being outdone,
Beg respite from thy present suffering.
Trite may my wisdom seem to thee, and yet
These are the wages of an insolent tongue.   330

Nor art thou humbled now: thou dost not yield
Before thy present woes but seemest still
To invite yet others. If thou takest me
As counselor thou'lt straightway cease to kick
Against the pricks, knowing that, hard of heart,   335
The tyrant wields his rule mercilessly.

Now I shall go and strive mine uttermost
To loose thee from this sad predicament.
Do thou keep silence: give no more loose rein
Unto thy speech. Or hast thou not perceived
With all thy cunning wit that penalties   341
Are meted out to forward babbling tongues?

Prom. I marvel at thy boldness, being safe
From any charge, that thou hast ventured e'en
To offer help. But trouble not thyself.   345
Never wilt thou persuade him: Zeus is not
Easily won, and in thy quest perchance
Thou mightest, even thou, stumble and fall.

Ocean. Much better is thy wisdom for thy friends
Than for thyself, nor is it by words I judge   350
But by the facts. Yet thou shalt not succeed
To turn me from my purpose, for I boast,
Unhesitant, that Zeus shall grant me this
Petition, to release thee from thy plight.

Prom. For this I praise thee now and evermore: 355
Thou hast abundance of benevolence.
Strive not, however, for thy striving's vain
Nor can avail me aught — if in good faith
Thou dost desire to help. Nay, save thyself.
For if *myself* must suffer, I would not   360
Suffering should come to others. Do I not
Behold with sorrow the unhappy fate
Of Atlas, mine own brother,[1] how upon
The western confines of the world he stands [2]
And holds the pillars of the earth and sky   365

---

[1] Oceanus, like Prometheus, was a son of Gaea.
[2] Iron came to Greece from the north and east of the Black Sea, the vague region of Scythia.

[1] Atlas and Prometheus were both sons of Iapetus and Clymene, according to the ancient legend which Aeschylus is following here for the moment. Atlas joined with the other Titans in the war against Zeus, and hence was condemned by Zeus to bear up earth and heaven on his shoulders.
[2] Atlas was shown the head of Medusa by Perseus and thereupon was changed into the mountain which bears his name. It is located near the pillars of Hercules by the Strait of Gibraltar, the western boundary of the ancient world.

On his broad shoulders, bowed beneath their
     weight?
Him too, the earthborn, from Cilician cave
Who sprung, the monster of a hundred heads,
Typhon,[1] I pity who in violent strife   369
Withstood the immortals: from his horrid jaws
Terror breathes forth: a gorgon-fronted flame
Bursts from his eyes to raze the tyranny
Of Zeus. Yet Zeus with never sleeping shaft
Of hurtling thunder brought his boastings low,
Turning to ashes his high soaring might,   375
His lightning-smitten strength, till now he lies
A useless bulk stretching its helpless length
Along the narrow strait at Aetna's base.[2]
Aloft on Aetna's peak Hephaestus sits,
Beating his iron anvil, whence again   380
The streams of fire shall burst in sudden flow,
With cruel jaws consume the lovely lawns
Of Sicily fair-fruited.[3] So the wrath
Of Typhon vents itself in shafts of fire,
Smitten himself by fiery shafts of Zeus.   385
All this thou knowest, nor hast need of me
To teach thee; save thyself. My present lot
I shall endure until the heart of Zeus
Be pleased to rest from its consuming hate.

     Ocean. Hast thou not heard, Prometheus,
         dost not know   390
That words are healers of hot festering hate?
     Prom. Aye, if the treatment be but oppor-
         tune:
Else it inflames what is malignant now.
     Ocean. But tell me openly, what canst thou
         see
Of danger in the effort I would make?   395
     Prom. Toil to no end, empty simplicity.
     Ocean. Let this disease be mine, for best it is
To *seem* the fool, being in substance wise.
     Prom. Nay, for such crime would then seem
         surely mine.

[1] The youngest of the giant brood of Gaea, who rebelled against Zeus and was imprisoned therefore beneath Mount Aetna, the workshop of Hephaestus. According to ancient belief the earthquakes and eruptions
connected with this peak came from Typhon's efforts to
get free. His name is linked with Cilicia in Asia Minor
because of the old volcano at Arimi there.
[2] The Straits of Messina between Sicily and Italy.
[3] A prophecy of the great eruption of Aetna which occurred in 479 B.C. The devastation was in all probability viewed by Aeschylus at first hand.

     Ocean. Thy words would seem to speed me
         on my way.   400
     Prom. Let not thy pity win thee enmity.
     Ocean. What, from the lord who sits en-
         throned on high?
     Prom. Him must thou honor, else thou too
         shalt mourn.
     Ocean. Thy fate, Prometheus, warns me
         amply there.
     Prom. Begone, begone, nor change thy pres-
         ent mind.   405
     Ocean. I needed not that urging. Even now
My winged charger beats the empty air,
Eager in his own stall to lay him down.
         (*Exit* OCEANUS *on his winged beast.*
     Chor. Thy fate, Prometheus, moves me to the
         heart; (Strophe)
I cannot hold the burning tears that start   410
And flow in pitying stream when I behold
The arbitrary might, the justice cold,
That Zeus wields ever o'er the gods of old.

Great Titan, all the world must mourn for thee,
     (Antistrophe)
For the destruction of thine ancient fee.   415
Through all the regions of the western bound,
Through Asia's realms, wherever man is
     found,
The story of thy injuries shall sound.

Maidens of the Colchian land,[1]   (Str. 2)
Dwellers by the Scythian strand,   420
Maidens of the bow and spear,
Hordes beyond the Maiotic mere,[2]

Flower of Persia's warrior host,   (Ant. 2)
Far beyond the eastern coast,
Hearts untamed in savage might   425
As their own Caucasian height.

One, only one have I known ere now   (Str. 3)
Held in such plight:
Atlas the Titan, bearing his burden,

[1] The Amazons, the famous mythical race of warrior
women, whose chief realm was thought to be Colchis
on the eastern shores of the Black Sea, south of the
Caucasus.
[2] The Sea of Azov, which lies north of the Black Sea,
but which the ancients located vaguely.

Crushed by God's might; [1]   430

And the surge of the sea as it breaks at his feet
    (Ant. 3)
Groans for his fate,
And the deeps of the ocean and hell's dread abyss
Re-echo his hate.

   Prom. Think not that arrogance and stub-
     born will   435
So long have kept me silent: brooding thought
O'erwhelms my heart when I survey my fate.

Yet to these upstart gods who else but I
Laid down the rôles — ah, that *ye* know; no
    more
I'll tell the selfsame tale, but harken ye   440
To this: the story of *man's* suffering,
How without language, witless hitherto,
I gave him mind, the use of intellect,
All, all I'll tell you, witnessing the love
I bore humanity.   445

       First know ye then
That men had eyes and saw not, ears they had
But could not hear. Like figures in a dream
They lived their long lives out; by merest
    chance
All things were done. Never did sun-dried
    brick   450
Or axe-hewn beam rear them a sheltering home.
Nay, in dark caves they dwelt like creeping
    ants,
Crawling through sunless ways. No witness
    sure
Had they of winter's coming or the times
Of flowering summer or of autumn's blaze.   455
Ignorant they of all things till I came
And told them of the rising of the stars
And their dark settings, taught them numbers
    too,
The queen of knowledge. I instructed them
How to join letters, making them their slaves
To serve the memory, mother of the muse.   461
'Twas I that first compelled beneath the yoke
The beasts of burden, thence to be for man
Sharer of all his toil, harnessed the horse
Unto the chariot to obey the rein   465
And be henceforth the pride of opulence.

    [1] See notes on ll. 363 and 364.

I too, I and no other, bade them guide
Sail-driven ships across the boundless sea.

Such were the wise inventions that I found
For human kind, yet have not wit enough   470
To find release from mine own suffering.
   Chor. Lead. Shameful thy treatment. Now,
     perplexed in heart,
A poor physician art thou: fallen thyself
Into disease, thou hast lost heart nor canst
Find for thine own distress the healing drug.
   Prom. Nay, hear me out and thou shalt won-
     der more   476
At all the wonders I have wrought for man.

Greatest I deem is this: if hitherto
Sickness befell, no cure was known on earth,
No strengthening food, no ointment soothing
    pain,   480
No healing draught: man without kindly drugs
Wasted and died. Then *I* came and revealed
The mystery of potions that could cure
Every disease. Nor was this all. I taught
Blind mortals many a sure, unerring way   485
To read the future, what each dream foretold,
How to interpret voices of the air
And portents by the way, the flight of birds,
Wherein lay happiness, where evil lurked,
What elements combined in harmony,   490
And which were hostile, warring evermore
On one another, how to read aright
The smoking entrails, what the gods decreed
The auspicious color of the gall, what shape
Within the lobe, curious, intricate,   495
Augured most happily. I guided man
In all the science of the sacrifice,
To wrap the members in the victim's fat
And read the darkling symbols of the flame.[1]
So I instructed him, and furthermore,   500
Who else but I, delving beneath the earth,
Brought first to light the treasures hidden deep,
The wealth of copper, iron, silver, gold?
None else, I know full well, who would not be
A babbling fool, can claim priority.   505

Wherefore in one short word learn everything:

    [1] The omens and means of divination mentioned in
ll. 486–99 were, of course, all in vogue during Aeschylus'
lifetime.

Prometheus taught *all* arts to human kind.

   Chor. Lead. To human kind give not o'er-
reaching help

And yet forget thyself; for I am sure

That thou shalt even now escape these bonds

And be thyself no lowlier than Zeus.   511

   Prom. Not as thou deemst nor yet does fate
decree

Fulfillment of my lot. But none the less,

Bound as I am beneath ten thousand woes,

I shall escape and rule my destiny —   515

But skill is weaker than necessity.

   Chor. Lead. Who then is helmsman of necessity?

   Prom. The Furies[1] and the unforgetting
Fates.[2]

   Chor. Lead. Is Zeus too subject to the laws
of Fate?

   Prom. Aye, for he shall not 'scape what is
decreed.   520

   Chor. Lead. What is decreed for Zeus save
endless rule?

   Prom. What thou may'st never learn, so ask
it not.

   Chor. Lead. Dreadful, I ween, the fate that
thou wouldst hide.

   Prom. Turn thy thought otherwhere, for in
no wise

Shall this be spoken. 'Tis a secret dread   525

That I must guard. And if I guard it well

I yet shall triumph o'er calamity.

   Chor. Never may Zeus who rules on high

(Strophe)

Counter my will or my hopes defy,

But ever with zeal to the gods' own meal   530

By the shifting sand of the ocean strand

May I come with worshiping cry,

And ever within be pure from sin —

Let not such purpose die.

Sweet to live with the pregnant ray   535

(Antistrophe)

Of hope adown life's flowering way:

Constant joy without alloy —

But I shudder with fear as I trembling hear

Thy lot bereft of day.

For, bold at heart, thou takest the part   540

Of the race of molded clay.

A graceless favor, a helpless boon   (Str. 2)

To a helpless race is given.

Seest thou not the hopeless lot

Of human kind, dream-driven?   545

For never the plan of mortal man

Shall jar the chords of Heaven.

This is the lesson I learn of you,   (Ant. 2)

Foreseer of fallen fame.

Yet once in the happy days gone by   550

I hailed with joy thy name,

When, with ringing peal of the wedding bell,

To thy couch Hesione[1] came.

Enter Io *horned like the moon and distraught
as if pursued by a gadfly*[2]

   Io. What land is here? What race?

In this far place,   555

In rock-hewn fetters held,

By cruel torture felled,

What victim's this I see with furrowed face?

By what dire penalty,

By what grim deviltry   560

Art thou destroyed?

Tell me, I beg of thee,

Whither in misery

Am I convoyed?

Alas, alas!   565

Again the gadfly stings my wretched soul

On to its goal.

Save me, O God!

---

[1] Daughter of Oceanus, whom Prometheus had led
home as bride amid the song of the ocean nymphs.

[2] Io, daughter of Inachus, king of Argos, was beloved
by Zeus. Therefore Hera, his wife, out of jealousy
turned Io into a cow and set Argus, the hundred-eyed
monster, to watch her. Zeus then had Hermes put
Argus to death. Whereupon Hera sent a gadfly to
sting Io and drive her all over the world. Haunted too
by the ghost of Argus, she comes in her wanderings to
the site of Prometheus' punishment.

---

[1] The Erinyes or Eumenides, the avenging deities,
who are represented in Aeschylus' play *Eumenides* as
goddesses with black bodies and serpents in their hair,
sisters of the Fates.

[2] The Moirae, literally the deities who assign to every
man his share, or fate. They were conceived of as three
sisters, Clotho, Lachesis, and Atropus.

The vision of Argus, earth-born, thousand-eyed,
By me defied,   570
I see before me still with threatening rod.
Death even he defies;
With crafty eyes
Pursues me, driven on relentlessly,
Starving across the sands of endless sea.   575

Sounds the song of slumbrous music,
Song of woe from waxen reed.
Woe to me, where lead these wanderings,
Wanderings wide as ocean's mead?

To what end, thou child of Cronus,   580
Hast thou cursed me with thy wooing,
Driven mad with deadly vision
Of the gadfly still pursuing?

Burn me with Hephaestus' fire,
Bury me 'neath earth's abyss,   585
Drown me deep in Ocean's waters:
Grant me, Lord of Heaven, but this.

All sufficient are the wandering,
Winding paths that I have trod,
And the end not yet — Oh, hear me,   590
Hear a maiden's prayer to God.

Prom. I hear the voice of Io, torture-driven,
Inachus' daughter, whose high passion burned
For Zeus himself, till now through endless ways
She knows the hate of Hera's enmity.   595

Io. Whence to thee this hidden knowledge
So to speak my father's name?
Wretched thou as I am wretched
Yet dost know mine utmost shame.

Even that god who unrelenting   600
Tortures me with stinging goads
Thou hast named, who heartless drives me
Wanderer o'er unending roads.

Starving, maddened by the torments
Of another's darkling will,   605
Who of all earth's tortured minions
Could my agony fulfill?

What the end — Oh, thou that seest
Far, if aught thou knowest, speak.

Wisdom hast thou: canst thou fashion   610
Respite that in vain I seek?

Prom. Truly I'll tell thee all that thou
   wouldst know,
No riddles weave, but in a single word
Direct and true, as friend should speak to
   friend.
Prometheus who gave fire to man am I.   615
   Io. Ah, what a boon was there.   Whence
   comes it then,
Valiant Prometheus, that thou sufferest so?
   Prom. This instant past I ceased my sad
   lament.
   Io. Wilt thou not therefore grant this wish
   to me?
   Prom. Ask what thou'lt choose, for *all* thou
   shalt not know.[1]   620
   Io. Tell me but this: who nailed thee to this
   cliff?
   Prom. 'Twas Zeus conceived the deed,
   Hephaestus wrought.
   Io. What was the wrong that earned such
   punishment?
   Prom. Enough that thou shouldst know what
   I have told.   624
   Io. Nay, tell me this beside: what is the end
In store for my most wretched wanderings?
   Prom. Better for thee never to know that
   end.
   Io. Hide not from *me* what 'tis *mine* to en-
   dure.
   Prom. Nay, 'tis no grudging spirit binds my
   tongue.
   Io. Why then delay to speak the utmost
   truth?   630
   Prom. No selfishness: I fear to wound thy
   heart.
   Io. Pray spare me not more than seems sweet
   to me.
   Prom. And thou insist, why, speak I must.
   Hear then.
   Chor. Lead. But not at once.   First grant
   this prayer to me,
To hear her past misfortune, while she tells 635
Her fatal wanderings.   Then be it thine to say
What consummation waits her misery.

[1] A rather obvious device by Aeschylus to prevent
Prometheus from boring the audience with a repetition
of his tale.

Prom. Io, with thee it rests to satisfy
These nymphs, kinswomen of thy sire.[1] 'Tis
    sure
Effort well spent if telling of thy woe   640
But win the compensation of a tear.

Io. I know not how I should refuse and so
In clearest words ye shall most fully hear
What ye desire though the recital bring
Tears to my eyes, picturing yet again   645
The god-sent violence, the utter wreck
Of all my beauty wantonly imposed.
Once, then, to me came stealing endlessly
Into my maiden chamber, whispering
Smooth words, the wandering visions of the
    night.   650
"Thrice happy maiden," so they spake to me,
"Why art thou still a maid? Within thy grasp
"Lies wedlock with the highest, Zeus himself
"Smitten with the shaft of Cypris,[2] burns for
    thee.
"But thou, O maiden, strive not to resist 655
"The couch of Zeus. Nay, of thine own accord
"Forth to the meadow lands of Lerna[3] go
"Where range thy father's cattle. Satisfy
"The longing eyes of Zeus." Night after night
Such dreams haunted me, ill at ease, until 660
I dared at last to tell my father all.
Who straight despatched successive embassies
To Pytho[4] and Dodona,[5] there to learn
What course should please the everlasting
    gods.
The messengers came back; dark oracles, 665
Ambiguous, they brought; but at the last
A clear word came to Inachus, to drive
Me forth from home and country, unrestrained
To wander on the confines of the land.
Else of a surety God's red thunderbolt 670
Should with devouring flame consume his race.
Won by Apollo's words, he drove me forth

And barred me from his home, unwilling he
As I; the bloody bit of Zeus perforce
Compelled him. From that day my human
    form   675
Was changed, my human mind lost 'neath the
    shape
That now thou seest. A horrid heifer, stung
To fury by the gadfly that pursued,
I fled with maddened bounds unreasoning
To Cenchrae's[1] flowing stream, to Lerna's
    spring.   680
But ever and anon relentlessly
The earth-born herdsman Argus guarded me
And with his hundred eyes followed my ways,
Till sudden fate deprived him of his life
Incontinent, and I, beneath the goad 685
Of heaven's scourge, am driven from land to
    land.

The past thou hearest. If thou knowest aught
Of suffering yet to come, I pray thee speak
Nor hope to soothe me with soft pitying words.
For of all evils in this evil world 690
I count the worst false words of sympathy.

Chor. *Alas, alas, have done, have done.*
Would to God I might never know
Such a tale of another's woe:
Hard to behold and hard to bear, 695
Suffering, pain, and fear are there
And the two-edged sword
Of thy cruel word
Strikes my heart with the chill of night.
Alas, alas, have done, have done, 700
For I tremble in horror at Io's plight.

Prom. Too soon thou groanest and art full
    of fear.
Restrain thy pity till thou knowest all.

Chor. Lead. Speak then and tell me, for to
    those in pain
'Tis sweet to know the utmost of their woe.

Prom. Thy first request has now been
    granted thee 706
With labor light for me, for thou didst ask
Of her the history of toils endured.
Now hear the rest: what agony awaits
This maid from Hera's wrath insatiate. 710
And thou, O child of Inachus, consign

---

[1] Inachus, Io's father, was son of Oceanus and therefore brother to the Oceanides.

[2] A surname of Aphrodite, goddess of love, so applied because the island of Cyprus was an outstanding seat of Aphroditean worship.

[3] A district of Argolis in southern Greece, celebrated as the place where Hercules killed the Hydra.

[4] The original name of Delphi, the famous oracle of Apollo, situated on Mount Parnassus in central Greece.

[5] The oldest oracle of Greece, dedicated to Zeus and located in Epirus, to the northwest.

[1] A town in Argolis, south of Argos, the capital, and not far from Lerna.

These words to thine own heart that thou
    mayst know
The end ordained to thy long wandering.
First from this land far toward the rising sun [1]
Thou shalt betake thyself o'er unplowed ways
Unto the Scythian nomads, dwelling high 716
'Neath woven shelters on their high-wheeled
    wains,
Armed with far-shooting bows. Approach
    them not.
Skirting their rock-bound coast, where ever-
    more
Beats the loud sea, fare farther. To the left 720
Swell the rude Chalybes,[2] whose secret is
To temper iron — likewise these avoid,
For they too know not hospitality.
Then shalt thou find that river truly named
Hybristes.[3] Cross it not, for it may not 725
Be crossed, till thou shalt reach the topmost
    peak
Of Caucasus, whose summit belches forth
The torrent's might. Conquer thou must these
    heights
That neighbor with the stars. Then to the
    south
Shalt make thy way, shalt seek the Amazons,
Man-hating host, that in the days to come 731
Shall found their city on the Thermodon [4]
Where cruel Salmydessa spreads her jaws [5]
Welcoming sailors to her fatal maw.
These shall right gladly speed thee on thy
    course.   735
Before thee then, hard by the narrow gates

[1] Prometheus' long story of Io's wanderings, which is given piecemeal hereafter, is an evidence of the strong interest that Aeschylus and the Greeks of his day took in the geography of what was for them a rapidly expanding world. Their imagination had been kindled by reports of strange and distant places. Aeschylus confuses his geography, but doubtless he intended a poetical treatment of the subject.

[2] This race of iron-workers really lived south of the Black Sea, not near Scythia, as Aeschylus pictures.

[3] The "river of violence"; its identity seems uncertain.

[4] A river which flows into the Black Sea on its southeastern shore.

[5] Aeschylus has in mind here the Thracian Bosphorus. The dangerous coast of Thrace immediately to the north was called Salmydessus. But this entrance into the Black Sea is some four hundred miles from the Thermodon.

Of the Maeotic Mere,[1] shall lie a strip
Of narrow isthmus.[2] Boldly must thou leave
This headland: make thy way across the
    strait
Which to unending time shall witness still 740
The legend of thy crossing, named from thee
The Bosphorus.[3] So Europe's desolate steppes
Abandoned, thou shalt win to Asia's plains.[4]

Now wilt thou hold the tyrant of the gods
All powerful, who, lusting to possess   745
This mortal maiden, drives her ruthlessly
Through these mad wanderings. Truly thou
    didst find
A bitter suitor, Io, for thy hand.
Yet all that thou hast heard is scarcely more
Than prelude to thy greater tragedy.   750
   Io. Ah, me, alas!
   Chor. Alas, alas, ah me!
   Prom. Thou dost exclaim in horror, knowing
    part.
What wilt thou do when thou hast learned the
    whole?
   Chor. Lead. Toils then are left for her that
    thou wilt tell?   755
   Prom. A stormy sea of unrelaxing woe.
   Io. What profit then to live? 'Twere better
    far
To hurl myself from this sheer cliff and so
Dashed into bits have done with all my toils.
An easier fate to meet death suddenly   760
Than suffer ill through slowly dragging days.
   Prom. Hardly methinks wouldst thou endure
    my woes
Who am predestined not to die, for death
Would bring some surcease from my suffer-
    ing.
Wherefore no limit has been set by fate   765
Unto my lot, till Zeus shall yield his power.
   Io. Shall Zeus e'er fall from his high tyranny?
   Prom. Such fall, I ween, would bring some
    joy to thee.

[1] The Sea of Azov, to the north of the Black Sea.

[2] The isthmus leading to the Crimea.

[3] The Cimmerian Bosphorus, connecting the Sea of Azov and the Black Sea. The English equivalent of Bosphorus is Ox-ford.

[4] Again Aeschylus confuses the Thracian straits, the boundary between Asia and Europe, with the Cimmerian.

Io. How could it otherwise since 'tis from Zeus
I suffer ill?   770

Prom.   Then hast thou cause for joy.

Io. But who shall dash the scepter from his hand?

Prom. None save himself by his own foolish wit.

Io. How shall that be — if it be safe to tell?

Prom. A marriage he shall make that shall end all.[1]   775

Io. With god or mortal?   Speak if speak ye may.

Prom. What matters that?   It may not yet be told.

Io. And by his consort shall he lose his throne?

Prom. A child she'll bear mightier than his sire.

Io. Can naught deliver him from what impends?   780

Prom. Naught save myself — if I perchance be loosed.

Io. Who shall loose *thee* against the will of Zeus?

Prom. Of thy descendants one shall compass that.

Io. How sayest thou — shall child of mine save thee?

Prom. In the third generation from the tenth.[2]   785

Io. No longer do thy prophecies ring clear.

Prom. Seek not then further to explore thy fate.

Io. Thou wilt not lure me with a promise vain?

Prom. One of two revelations thou must choose.

Io. What are these two?   Explain to me the choice.   790

Prom. So be it.   Choose then which thou'lt have revealed:
Thy future misery or my rescuer.

Chor. Lead. Of these two favors grant the one to me
Nor grudge thy knowledge: unto her relate
The wanderings still to come, to me the man
That shall release thee, satisfying both.   796

Prom. Since thou wilt have it so I'll not oppose
Thy wish but satisfy thy whole desire.
First, Io, unto thee will I reveal
Thy wanderings manifold: engrave them clear
Upon the tablets of thy memory.   801

When thou hast crossed the strait that cleaves in twain
The continents and in thy journey come
Far toward the rising of the flame-faced sun,
Once more the surging ocean must be passed
Till thou approach that gorgon-breeding plain   806
Cisthene,[1] where the ancient Phorcides [2]
Inhabit, maidens three with form of swans.
One eye they share, nor ever does the sun
Look down upon them nor the moon by night.
Hard by, their sisters dwell, the snaky-locked,   811
Man-hating gorgons whom no mortal soul
May look upon and live.   This warning heed,
And hark to further horrors: thou must guard
Thyself against the baying vulture-hounds 815
Of Zeus and after that the griffin [3] host
Of one-eyed Arimaspi; [4] hard beside
The stream of Pluton [5] and its golden glade
They dwell.   Approach them not, for thou must fare
Unto the farthest earth where dusky tribes 820
Live by the sources of the sun whence flows
The river Aethiops.[6]   Along its banks
Proceeding, thou shalt reach the cataract

---

[1] A geographical invention of Aeschylus.

[2] Daughters of Phorcys and Ceto, and sisters of the three Gorgons.   Their names were Pephredo, Enyo, and Dino, sometimes called the Graeae, the "old women."

[3] A creature with the body of a lion and the head and wings of an eagle.

[4] A people in the north of Scythia.

[5] An unidentifiable river, perhaps in the Ural Mountains where gold abounds.

[6] Perhaps the Niger River of central Africa, but the location indicated is far from its true position.

---

[1] A marriage with the sea goddess Thetis, daughter of Nereus and Doris.

[2] Hercules, son of Alcmena and Zeus, released Prometheus after shooting with his bow the eagle which came every day to devour the liver of the fettered Titan.

Whereby the Nile pours from the Bybline hills [1]
Its sacred waters which shall lead thee safe　825
Unto the delta [2] where for thee and thine
A distant, lasting exile is decreed.
If aught of this seem dark or hard to solve,
By questioning thou mayst unravel all;
Leisure is mine ample beyond my need.　830

   Chor. Lead. If there be something further left unsaid
That thou canst yet reveal of Io's fate
Speak on; if all is told, then grant to me
The promised favor thou hast scarce forgot.

   Prom. The goal indeed of all her wanderings
She now has heard, but lest perchance she think　836
'Tis but an idle tale, I shall recount
Her toils ere ever she did reach these shores,
A witness to my words. Yet much thereof
I shall pass by and so narrate forthwith　840
The last course of thy journey. Faring far,
Thy wandering footsteps found the Molossian Plain [3]
About Dodona's fastnesses where stands
The oracle of Zeus that, wondrous wise,
Sounds through the whispering oak leaves; there to thee　845
No longer riddling, spake in accents clear
The consort of great Zeus. [4] (Doth memory
Confirm my words?) Thence, 'neath the gad-fly's sting
Distraught, along the heights that guard the sea
Thou camest unto Rhea's mighty gulf, [5]　850
Whence by the refluent tempest backward borne,
Thou art yet storm-tossed. For all future time
That gulf shall bear the name Ionian [6]
To prove thy journey to posterity.
This then shall be thy surety for the truth　855
Of what I see beyond the visible.

  [1] Another geographical invention by Aeschylus.
  [2] The Nile Delta in Egypt. The word "delta" means three-cornered land, i.e. shaped like the Greek letter delta.
  [3] The Molossians were a tribe in Epirus, inhabiting the district where Dodona was situated.
  [4] Hera.
  [5] The Adriatic Sea. Rhea was the old Greek goddess of fruitfulness.
  [6] The Adriatic was regarded by ancient geographers as a gulf of the Ionian Sea, the body of water which lies between the Greek peninsula and lower Italy.

Now unto both I speak; my story speeds
Unto a common end. A city stands
Where empties forth the river's seven-mouthed stream,
Canopus. [1] There at last in recompense　860
Shall Zeus unto thyself with kindlier hand
Restore thee by his touch: so shalt thou bear
A son called Epaphus, [2] the child of Zeus.
His all the harvests of the delta land
Watered by Nilus. Generations five　865
Shall pass from Epaphus unchronicled
Till fifty daughters of a single sire, [3]
Fleeing unwelcome marriage with their kin,
Shall come to Argos. Swift, with maddened hearts,
Like hawks pursuing birds, shall follow close
Their fifty cousins, eager to compel　871
Forbidden wedlock. God himself shall balk
The suitors of their prey: the land of Greece
Shall welcome them with death stalking by night,
Baptizing in his blood the avenging sword.　875
(Such love I pray fall to mine enemies!)
One maiden only [4] shall desire persuade
To spare her lover; in her softened heart
Her purpose shall be dulled till she fear less
The name of coward than of murderer,　880
And so in Argos found a royal race.
The tale is long, the end is brief and sure:
For from that royal line shall one day come
A wielder of the bow all-powerful
Who shall release me. [5] Such the oracle　885
Mine age-old mother Themis told to me.

  [1] An important city on the coast of Lower Egypt near the most western mouth of the Nile.
  [2] The name means literally "one from the touching."
  [3] The Danaides, daughters of Danaus who was great grandson of Epaphus and twin-brother of Aegyptus. Danaus had been assigned by Belus, his father, to rule over Libya, and Aegyptus over Arabia. The goddess Athene warned Danaus, however, that he and his daughters might expect treachery on the part of the fifty sons of Aegyptus. Hence the Danaides and their father fled to Argos, where subsequently Danaus became king. Thither the sons of Aegyptus pursued them and finally won the Danaides as wives. On the bridal night, however, all the Danaides but one killed their husbands with daggers given them by their father.
  [4] Hypermnestra spared the life of her husband, Lynceus. He later succeeded Danaus as king of Argos.
  [5] Hercules, son of Alcmena, who was descended from the line of Hypermnestra and Lynceus.

Yet how and where, that were too long to tell [1]
Nor would the knowledge profit thee in aught.
  Io. Eleleu! Eleleu! Begins anew
The burning scourge   890
To the utmost verge
Of frenzied madness, where still pursue
The horrors that spring
From the gadfly's sting,
I am driven to prove thy story true.   895

My heart would burst my breast, mine eyes
Roll in bewildering circles; by the breath
Of utter madness I am driven afield.
My tongue unloosed pours forth a babbling sea
Of words that beat like breakers on a beach.
                              (*Exit* Io *furiously.*)

  *Chor. Wise was the seer who spake this
      word,* [2] (Strophe)   901
Weighed in his heart and reasoned there:
Blessed is the man by naught deterred
From seeking his own welfare.

Blessed is he who would not be   905
Rich by grace of the marriage fête,
Wed for the prize of a pedigree
To 'scape from his low estate.

Never of Fate may I be found (Antistrophe)
Sharing the couch of Zeus on high,   910
Never in chains of wedlock bound
To a dweller beyond the sky.

Dreadful the unloved maidenhood
Io won for a wedding dower,
Wandering alone forlorn to brood   915
On Hera's avenging power.

Honored by me shall ever be (Epode)
The marriage that knows not fear,

---

[1] The "how and where" were to form much of the subsequent Prometheus Unbound portion of the Aeschylean trilogy.

[2] Perhaps Pittachus of Mitylene, one of the Seven Wise Men of Greece, who, on being asked whether a man should marry a rich woman of higher rank or a poor woman of equal rank, told the inquirer to go and listen to what the children were saying. The man did so and heard a boy say to his top, "Spin in your own place." He followed this advice of the boy and won contentment.

When twain are one till the journey's done
And the shadows disappear.   920

But never in love may God above
Lure me with lustful eyes:
That were a war that is not war
And a way where no way lies.

For never a mortal maiden yet   925
Hath 'scaped the Almighty's wide-flung net.

  Prom. Verily Zeus even with his stubborn
      heart
Shall one day be brought low: such love he
      craves
As yet shall thrust him from the throne that
      marks
His tyranny. That day shall see fulfilled 930
The malediction that great Cronus hurled
Against the plunderers of his ancient siege.

No god there is who can to him disclose
Escape from this grim fate — not one, save
      me.
I know his end and how it comes; wherefore
Until his hour shall strike, let him sit on, 936
Emboldened by his lofty thunderings,
Wielding the lightning: these shall naught avail
To save him from a fall calamitous,
Fraught with dishonor: such a champion   940
Himself he rears against himself, a foe
Invincible, who shall devise a flame
Mightier than the lightning, drowning all
God's crashing thunder in transcendent din,
Shattering too the spear that shakes the earth,
Poseidon's trident,[1] till by tutelage   946
Of such misfortune, Zeus shall learn to know
How great a gulf lies betwixt king and slave.
  Chor. Lead. Ominous words are these and
      aimed at Zeus.
  Prom. Aye, and shall be fulfilled to my great
      joy.   950
  Chor. Lead. Wouldst have us think that one
      shall master Zeus?
  Prom. Blows worse than that shall be his lot
      to bear.

---

[1] The three-pronged scepter of Poseidon, god of the sea, could cleave rocks or mountains, and stir the depths of the sea or the earth.

Chor. Lead. Canst thou fling forth such
    words untremblingly?
Prom. What should I fear that am not
    doomed to die?
Chor. Lead. Yet he may conjure up more
    poignant woe.   955
Prom. Let him do what he will: I know my
    fate.
Chor. Lead. Wisest are they that worship
    Nemesis.[1]
Prom. Do thine obeisance, cringe and flatter
    him
Who lords it for the instant.   Zeus to me
Is less than nothing.   Let him strut and reign
His little moment as seems best to him.   961
Not long shall be he autocrat in heaven.
But see where comes the messenger of Zeus,
Creature of the new tyrant, sent, I ween,
To carry some new dictates from his lord.   965

Enter HERMES *wearing winged sandals*

Herm. Trickster in words, thou of the sharp-
    ened tongue,
Thou that hast sinned against the gods to give
Honor to mortal men, that didst purloin
Immortal fire, to thee I make address.
The Father bids thee speak explicitly,   970
Abandoning thy riddles, to reveal
The wedlock whence thine idle boasts maintain
His fall shall issue.   Thou, Prometheus, speak,
Nor multiply my journeys; thou canst see
Zeus is not softened by evasive words.   975

Prom. Arrogant is thy word and full of
    pride,
As fits God's menial.   New is the sovereignty
Ye wield in heaven and think to dwell for aye
In painless citadels.   Have I not seen
Ere now two monarchs [2] from those citadels
Hurled headlong?   And the third that rules
    there now   981
I shall behold in swifter, uglier flight
Than those that went before him.   Do I seem

[1] "The Goddess from whom there is no escape"; regarded as a checking power on excessive human happiness.
[2] Uranus, expelled by his son Cronus, and then
Cronus, expelled by his son Zeus.

To cringe and tremble at your upstart gods?
That have I never learned.   So get thee gone
The way thou camest.   For no single whit 986
Of that thou askest shalt thou learn from me.
Herm. Such bursts of stubborn passion in the
    past
Have brought thee to this grievous anchorage.
Prom. Yet be assured that I would never
    change   990
My stormy lot for thy smooth servitude.
Herm. Wouldst choose thy servitude on this
    rude cliff
Rather than be God's trusted messenger?
Prom. Well may he trust thee, for the in-
    solent
Must needs have insolence e'en in their slaves.
Herm. Thou seemst to revel in thy present
    state.   996
Prom. I revel?   Would to God mine enemies
Might revel so — and thou not least of them.
Herm. Am I to blame for thy calamity?
Prom. Nay, *all* the gods do I abominate
Who, faring well, unjustly torture me.   1001
Herm. No trifling madness thine, to trust
    thy words.
Prom. I'll *be* mad, if 'tis mad to hate one's
    foes.
Herm. Thou'd'st be unbearable and thou
    fared'st well.
Prom. Alas!   1005
Herm.   *There* is a word unknown to
    Zeus.
Prom. Time the relentless teaches all things
    well.
Herm. Yet thou hast not yet learned sobri-
    ety.
Prom. Else had I never wrangled with a
    slave.
Herm. It seems thou wilt not do the Father's
    will.   1010
Prom. If I owed aught, to *him* I'd pay my
    debt.
Herm. Thou chidest me as though I were a
    child.
Prom. Art thou then not a child or something
    yet
More witless still if thou dost hope to learn
From me one fragment of the truth?   Be sure
There is no stratagem exists nor force   1016

That Zeus employing can compel my speech
Till he unshackle me these cruel bonds.

Come then the serried lightning flash of Zeus,
Or let him, with the cold white winged snow
And with his earth-born thunderings, con-
    found   1021
All things that are: he shall not bend my will
To tell him whence must come his destined fall.
   Herm. Look well to this, if it be safe for thee.
   Prom. Long since I have looked well; my
      purpose holds.   1025
   Herm. Foolhardy one, have courage even
      now,
Courage to view aright thy present lot.
   Prom. As vain to importune the surging sea.
For know thou this, never in fear of Zeus
Shall I be woman-hearted, raising hands   1030
In prayer effeminate to him I loathe
To loose my bonds. My temper is not such.
   Herm. It seems I speak too much and all for
      naught,
For thou art no whit softened in thy heart
By my appeal, but like a foal new-yoked   1035
Dost champ the bit, fighting against the reins.
Yet 'tis a silly wisdom makes thee hard,
For stubbornness in one who thinks not straight
Of its own self is less than all things else.
But if my words possess no power to move 1040
Give heed at least unto the rising storm
Whose threefold waves of dire calamity
Surge toward thee irresistibly. Know first
That Zeus shall cleave this jagged cliff in twain
With lightning bolt and thunder, plunging thee
Into the stony arms of hell's embrace. 1046
Centuries shall roll by ere thou emerge
Into the light again. And all that while
The winged vulture-hound of Zeus shall tear
Thy helpless body into mighty shreds, 1050
A guest unsummoned, feeding all day long
With bloody jaws upon thy blackened heart.

No end is thine to look for in such plight
Till willingly there come another god [1]

  [1] Chiron, the wisest and justest of the Centaurs, the
mythical race of immortal beings with human heads and
bodies like horses. Chiron, incurably wounded by a
poisoned arrow from the bow of Hercules, was willing to
die in place of Prometheus in order that he might escape
the pain of his wound.

To spell thee in thy misery, himself   1055
Choosing to make his voluntary way
To gleamless Hades and black Tartarus.

Wherefore bethink thee now: no idle boast
Is this but very truth. The mouth of Zeus
Has never learned to lie. He shall fulfill 1060
Each word. But thou, consider well nor deem
A stubborn heart better than wisdom's way.
   Chor. Lead. To me it seems that Hermes
      speaketh well,
In that he bids thee turn from stubbornness
And follow wisdom. Do thou yield to him:
Great shame it is for one so wise to sin. 1066
   Prom. Full well I know this message that he
      speaks
So eagerly. Yet is it no disgrace
For foes to suffer at the hands of foes?
So let it come, the forked flame of fire, 1070
Hurled at my head. Let the wide vault of
      heaven
Be shattered by the thunderbolt and by
The fury of the whirlwind, earth itself
Shaken to its deepest roots, waves of the sea
Confound the constellations in their course.
Down to black Tartarus let angry Zeus 1076
Fling my poor carcass, helpless to resist
The dizzy whirlpool of necessity.
He shall not kill me.
   Herm.   Words of madness these
And frantic counsels. What insanity, 1081
What wild delusion lurks not in that boast?
But ye who suffer with his sufferings
Swiftly begone from this ill-omened spot
Lest indiscriminate destruction fall   1085
Upon you too from heartless thunderbolts.
   Chor. Lead. Give better counsel if thou
      wouldst persuade
My heart, for unendurable the word
Thou speakest. Wouldst thou then dare order
      me   1089
To practice baseness? Nay, I am prepared
With him to suffer all, for I have learned
To hate all traitors: there is not on earth
A thing more wholly foul than treachery.
   Herm. Then see that ye forget not what I
      say,
Nor when the hounds of madness hunt you
      down   1095

Blame it on Fortune.　Never say that Zeus
To unforeseen disaster thrust you forth.
Nay, 'tis your own blind selves.　Fully fore-
　　warned,
Not suddenly nor yet by stealth, shall ye
By your own folly be forever snared　　　1100
Within the toils of madness.　Fare ye well.
　　　　　(*Exit* HERMES.　*The* CHORUS *of ocean*
　　　　　nymphs gather close about PROME-
　　　　　THEUS.
　Prom. No more in empty threat, in very fact
Earth shakes and from beneath earth's shaken
　　crust
The thunders roar, flashes of living fire

Leap forth, cyclonic blasts rear heavenward
The dust of earth and in the vault above　1106
Battalions of the winds with deafening roar
Clash in fierce conflict.　Sky and sea are
　　one,
Confounded utterly.　Such is the shaft
That comes from Zeus to strike my heart with
　　fear.　　　　　　　　　　　　　　　　1110

Oh, holy mother mine, oh, light of heaven,
That sheddest radiance on all things that are,
Thou, thou canst see the injustice of my fate.
　　　　　(PROMETHEUS, *the* CHORUS, *and the*
　　　　　cliff disappear.

A PANORAMIC VIEW OF AN EARLY GREEK THEATER
Drawing based on the theater at Epidauros, c. fourth century B.C.

THE SCENE HOUSE OF THE THEATER AT ATHENS, C. 420 B.C.
A conjectural drawing

INTRODUCTION TO

Electra

The Later Attic Theater and Tragedy: Sophocles

THE LATER ATTIC THEATER

IN 468 B.C. the old master of Attic tragedy, Aeschylus, suffered defeat in the Dionysia competition at the hands of a youthful poet, Sophocles, son of Sophillos. Recognizing the superior craftmanship of this young rival, Aeschylus proceeded to imitate it and to improve his own art. It was, however, in the plays of Sophocles that Attic tragedy reached its height of technical excellence.

Almost simultaneously with the change of ranking among Athens' tragedians, the theater on the Acropolis was remodeled. The hillside was more deeply carved out; the amphitheater enlarged; and, most important of all, the *orchestra* moved fifty feet or so to the north, leaving at its back a level space which belonged to the former orchestral area. On this ground, each year henceforth, was erected a temporary storehouse and dressing-room for the actors, a small wooden structure of one story, called the *skene*, or scene-building. Its unpretentious north front, with a large door in the middle, at once suggested to the Athenian playwrights an ideal background for dramatic action. They quickly shifted from the mode of indefinite scenes to a rather general employment of specified locales, such as the fronts of palaces, temples and houses, or adjoining squares and streets. Before very long Sophocles, more alert than the rest to the new possibilities for scenic effect, went one step further. He introduced movable decorative settings by means of pictorial panels attached to the plain front of the *skene*. Hence Aristotle, the first historian of Greek drama, named Sophocles the founder of the art of scene-painting.

Early in the last quarter of the fifth century further development of the *skene* took place. It still consisted of a wooden superstructure erected every year, but the foundation became a solid stone base. The building grew larger, more elaborate, and more variable in architecture. It occasionally possessed a second story, or sometimes a hut on its roof, in which to house the *mechane*, the crane that raised or lowered the characters whenever they pretended either to ascend toward or descend from the heavens. Moreover, to each end of the *skene* was now added a wing, or *paraskenion*, projecting toward the *orchestra*. These wings formed, in conjunction with the *skene* proper, a space called the *proskenion* (proscenium), similar to a wide and open courtyard.

In the later scene-buildings of the fifth century the arrangement of the doorways for actors' entrances and exits is uncertain. It may well have varied from year to year, or even from day to day, according to the demands of particular productions. Certainly a large doorway, composed in all probability of a pair of doors, continued as in the past to be located at the middle of the scene-building. Often this central door was flanked by smaller doors equidistant between center and wings. The *paraskenia*, on occasion, may have had doors, but whether the latter were on the front toward the *orchestra*, or on the side toward the *proskenion*, or now in one place and now in the other, has not been determined.

SOPHOCLES

All these changes in the staging of Attic drama were spanned by the long life of Sophocles. He was born about 496 B.C. at Colonos, once a village on a lovely hill not far to the northwest of Athens. Here stood the sacred grove of the Eumenides, the divine avengers of the departed. Its presence helped to perpetuate in the community that strong religious traditionalism which ultimately found reflection in the plays of Sophocles. His father, a man with a moderate income from the manufacture of iron or brass products, provided the son with the best educational training. The boy developed into an accomplished musician as well as into a prize-winning student and athlete. These attainments, combined with a handsome physique, brought about, it is said, the selection of Sophocles as leader of a boys' chorus for the Athenian thanksgiving celebration after the victory of Salamis (480 B.C.).

Subsequently Sophocles joined the most intellectual and cultured circle in Athens. There for half a century he enjoyed great prominence in public affairs. About 443 B.C. he held the presidency of the imperial treasury; in 440 he received appointment as a general and served with Pericles in the war against the Samian revolt (440–439); sometime later he had charge of the Greek Confederacy funds; and finally in 413, according to some sources, he became one of the ten commissioners of public safety who ruled Athens after the disastrous expedition to Sicily (415–413). He continued to be a respected elder of the city-state until his death about 406 at the age of ninety.

Like Aeschylus, Sophocles achieved a brilliant career which embraced both statesmanship and art. He participated in the theater of his day with the same zeal that he showed in civic matters. He wrote over one hundred plays, won eighteen victories at the Dionysia, and, it is said, never dropped below second place in sixty years of prize competition. At first he directed and also took part in his own plays, just as did his fellow playwrights, but he seems not to have continued very long in these two lines of activity. Perhaps he gave them up because he did not excel, but more probably because he grew convinced of the desirability of separating the functions of playwriting and production. It is significant that the Athenian dramatists soon followed his example and generally desisted from directing and acting in the second half of the fifth century.

Sophocles accompanied his early success in the play contests with several original contributions to the patterning of Attic tragedy. By 460 B.C. he had made two important innovations. Not content with the prevailing limitation that plays should call for only two actors with speaking parts, he added a third such part. He also changed the size of the chorus from the customary twelve singers to fifteen. This increase permitted a more flexible and symmetrical arrangement of the choral performers. When half-choruses were required, as they were more and more in later tragedy, the numerical balance of the two groups could be maintained while the chorus leader remained apart for solo speaking or singing. Through these changes Sophocles aimed toward a greater complexity both in the dramatic and in the musical elements of the tragic pattern.

No example from the early period of his playwriting has survived. Out of the hundred-odd compositions which he is supposed to have written altogether, the seven extant cover the last two-thirds of his career: *Antigone*, 441 B.C.; *Ajax*, c. 440; *Maidens of Trachis*, c. 435-30; *Oedipus Tyrannus*, c. 429; *Electra*, c. 412-10; *Philoctetes*, 409; *Oedipus at Colonus*, c. 406. These seven pieces reveal a steady development in Sophocles as a dramatic craftsman.

"ELECTRA"

Though *Antigone* and *Oedipus Tyrannus* are perhaps the best known Sophoclean dramas, *Electra* represents that more advanced stage of his art when, in common with Attic tragedy as a whole, he had arrived at a greater dramatic realism. *Electra* also contains the important features which differentiate his plays from those of Aeschylus.

The Sophoclean chorus projects little of the soaring lyricism of which Aeschylus was fond. Sophocles does not try for impressive choric effects, but rather seeks to weave the chorus into the emotional progression of the play and to have it participate directly in the situation. In *Electra* the group of Argive women not only express sympathy with the heroine, but also offer advice.

Sophocles' use of spectacle is more sparing than in Aeschylean tragedy, though he likes tableaux, such as the exposure of Clytemnestra's corpse, flanked by Orestes and Pylades, at the palace door (ll. 1624-25). The exposure was accomplished by means of the *eccyclema*, a platform on wheels which could be swiftly pushed out from the *skene* with the tableau set up on it. Here and usually, however, the spectacle is not an end in itself, but a device to create a particular effect on character.

Sophocles' handling of the three actor technique is far superior to the skill of Aeschylus in the *Oresteia*. To be sure, his three early plays have few scenes with three actors, and even then the three actors never speak together. An increasing freedom in their employment characterizes his later drama. Trio conversations occur in three scenes of *Electra* (ll. 735-893, 1461-1516, 1625-78). By then Sophocles had attained technical mastery and could make the audience conscious of three separate points of view involved in the same situation. Thus his realism reached the peak of complexity possible under the limits imposed by tradition.

Electra surpasses all the other Sophoclean dramas in the popularity of its subject. The famous story of the revenge which Electra and her brother undertook inspired all three of the great Attic tragedians. Since the fifth century B.C. dramatists of Europe and America have constantly chosen the grim legend of the house of Atreus. Eugene O'Neill's massive trilogy in thirteen acts, *Mourning Becomes Electra* (1931), is recent and elaborate proof of the perennial attraction which this ancient Greek tale has held for the playwrights of all nations.

The Attic tragedians varied considerably in their treatments of the Electra story. Aeschylus in his great trilogy, *Oresteia* (458 B.C.), undertakes to depict the emergence of a new order of law and mercy out of the old bloody rule of vengeance. He also presents a long train of action: Agamemnon's homecoming; the murders of Agamemnon, Aegisthus, and Clytemnestra; the near madness of Orestes; his flight to Athens with the avenging Furies in pursuit; his exoneration by the goddess Athena and the Council of Athens; the threat of the Furies to destroy Orestes and Athens; and, at the close, the conversion of the Furies by Athena into kindly guardians of Athenian justice.

Euripides in his single tragedy, *Electra* (413 B.C.), focused attention on Orestes as the unhappy instrument of the gods' revenge. The extent of the action is much briefer, of course, than in the *Orestaia*. The play opens with the reunion of Electra and Orestes years after Agamemnon's death, includes the murders of Aegisthus and then Clytemnestra, and ends with Orestes exiled to Athens and Electra betrothed to Pylades, her brother's friend.

Finally, the *Electra* of Sophocles emphasizes the triumph of retributive justice. He covers the same period of action as Euripides but he introduces the killing of Clytemnestra first and places that of Aegisthus as the play's finale. By reversing the order of these events he gradually builds up the impression that base tyranny has been put down at last.

The version of Sophocles proves him a much less vigorous thinker than Aeschylus. He was more interested in the dramatic fashioning of his story than in the exposition of moral values. He might purify the myths here and there, but he still looked upon them as holy stories to be treated with respect. The original Electra-Orestes narrative in Homer's *Odyssey* pictures the vengeance as a simple act of retribution. Sophocles does not go beyond this traditional attitude. He makes the chorus of Argive women wholly sympathetic to retribution, while he implies that the gods too support the purpose. His is the position of Athenian orthodox piety which commits itself to little more than the comment: "The gods love the modest and hate the wicked."

The genius of Sophocles lay in his art rather than in his philosophy. *Electra* best exhibits his particular craft, excellence in character portrayal. The plot has been carefully designed to illuminate Electra's personality by providing a series of emotions through which she must pass. The scenes correspond and contrast. In them the minor figures serve as foils to present diverse aspects of the heroine. Thus the characters form a related pattern of humanity. First, Electra confronts the chorus; then her sister, Chrysothemis; next, Clytemnestra; then again, Chrysothemis; and finally, Orestes. Each of these persons, representing a varied set of human qualities, draws out Electra in a new direction until the full strength of her character is revealed. The recognition scene between Orestes and Electra (ll. 1207–1357) contains perhaps the subtlest emotional sequence in Greek tragedy. Here is the superb realism of feeling which marks the culmination of Sophocles' artistry.

With this emotional realism he linked idealization of character. Out of the chief men and women in the old myths which he treated he aimed to create the sort of persons whom the loyal Athenian aristocrat *ought* to imagine as heroic characters. He endows Electra with the more usual virtues of courage, piety, filial love, and sisterly affection. In addition, however, he paints her a woman of intelligence and sensitivity who overshadows others by the vigor of her mind and temperament. For Sophocles this combination of judgment and intense feeling qualifies Electra as a great character. In her dignified powerful personality she exemplifies a certain nobility that he would have Athenians emulate.

Yet, according to modern notions, Electra is not the heroine of a thoroughgoing

SOPHOCLES

Electra

[Translated by E. H. PLUMTRE]

DRAMATIS PERSONAE

ORESTES, *son of* AGAMEMNON, *the late king of Argos and Mycenae*
PYLADES, *friend of* ORESTES
ELECTRA
CHRYSOTHEMIS } *sisters of* ORESTES
AEGISTHUS, *husband of* CLYTEMNESTRA
CLYTEMNESTRA, *mother of* ORESTES
Aged ATTENDANT *of* ORESTES, *formerly his guardian*
CHORUS *of Argive women*

ARGUMENT

When Agamemnon, king of the Argives and commander-in-chief of the Greek army, returned to Mycenae from the taking of Troy, his adulterous wife, Clytemnestra, and her paramour, Aegisthus, murdered him within the palace and ruled over the Argives in his stead. They tried also to kill his young son Orestes so that no avenger would be left alive, but Orestes' sister, Electra, secretly sent her brother to Strophius, king of Phocis, her father's friend. She, though filled with hate for Clytemnestra and Aegisthus, had still to dwell in the palace and suffer brutal treatment at their hands. After eight years had passed and Orestes had grown to manhood, he with his good friend Pylades, son of Strophius, in obedience to the oracle of Apollo at Delphi, came to Mycenae to take vengeance upon Agamemnon's murderers. Through careful stratagem Orestes revealed himself to Electra, and then with her connivance gained admittance to the palace to slay separately his mother and Aegisthus. Thus was lifted from the Argive royal line the curse of hatred and revenge which first Pelops, grandfather of Agamemnon, brought upon it.

The Scene is at Mycenae outside the Royal Palace

Enter ORESTES, PYLADES, *and Aged* ATTENDANT

Attend. Now, son of Agamemnon, who of old
Led our great hosts at Troy, 'tis thine to see
What long thou hast desired. For lo! there lies
The ancient Argos,[1] which, with yearning wish,

[1] The ancient capital of Argolis situated on a broad

Thou oft did'st turn to; here the sacred grove 5
Of her who wandered, spurred by ceaseless sting,
Daughter of Inachos:[1] and this, Orestes,

plain in the northeastern part of the Morea Peninsula in southern Greece.

[1] A river-god, the earliest king of Argos. His daughter was Io, the horned moon-maiden, gadfly-driven because of the hate of Hera. See the visit of Io to Prometheus in Aeschylus' *Prometheus Bound*.

tragedy.   She may win admiration, but she does not arouse in the spectator a pity which reaches its peak at the close of the drama.   On the contrary, pity for Electra rises higher in the very early portion of the play where her loneliness and grief are paramount. Gradually her suffering diminishes as her desires move toward fulfillment.   Instead of ultimate catastrophe, she accomplishes her mission of revenge.   The wicked transgressors are punished, and the action concludes on a note of triumphant retribution. How then can this drama be considered tragic?   Certainly *Electra* does not bear out the conventional concept of tragedy as illustrated by *Prometheus Bound*, where the hero is visited with dire misfortune.   It must be remembered, however, that the Athenians originally called all serious drama "tragedy."   Aristotle's writings in the fourth century contain the earliest record of this broad definition.   In chapter six of his *Poetics* he says: "Tragedy, then, is an imitation of an action that is serious, complete, and of a certain magnitude."   An elevated tone rather than a sad conclusion is the essential criterion.   To that Greek view, therefore, Sophocles' *Electra*, with its exhibition of a strong woman emerging from despair into triumph, is perfect tragedy.

[For a critique on Sophocles, see T. B. L. Webster, *An Introduction to Sophocles* (1936).]

Is the wide agora,[1] Lyceian named
In honor of the God who slew the wolves;[2]
Here on the left, the shrine of Hera[3] famed;   10
And where we stand, Mycenae,[4] rich in gold,
Thou look'st upon, in slaughter also rich,
The house of Pelops'[5] line.   Here, long ago,
After thy father's murder, I received thee,
At thy dear sister's hands, to kindred true;   15
And took thee, saved thee, reared thee in my
     home,
To this thy manhood, destined to avenge
Thy father's death.   Now, therefore, O my son,
Orestes, and thou, Pylades, most dear   19
Of all true friends, we needs must quickly plan
What best to do.   For lo!   The sun's bright rays
Wake up the birds to tune their matin songs,
And star-decked night's dark shadows flee
     away;
Ye, then, before ye enter, taking rest,
The roof of living man, hold conference;   25
For as things are, we may not longer on:
The time is come for action.

Ores.   Dearest friend,
Of servants found most faithful, still thou giv'st
Clear tokens of thy nobleness of heart   30
In all that touches us.   For as the steed,
Though he be old, if good blood flows in him,
In danger's hour still loses not his fire,
But pricks his ears, so thou dost urge us on,
And tak'st thyself thy station in the van.   35
Wherefore, I tell thee what my mind approves,
And thou, give heed, full heed, to all my words;
And, if I miss the mark in aught, correct:
For I, when I had reached the Pythian shrine,[6]
That I might learn by what device to wreak   40
My vengeance on my father's murderers,
Heard this from Phoebus,[7] which thou too
     shalt learn,

[1] The market place or public square.
[2] Apollo *Lukeios*, the god of light. *Lukeios* was connected by folk etymology, however, with *lukos*, wolf. Hence, Lyceian Apollo or Apollo the wolf-slayer.
[3] Queen of the Greek divinities and wife of Zeus. This shrine was located about five miles northeast of Argos, and two miles southeast of Mycenae.
[4] The citadel of the Argive kings on high ground some six miles to the north of Argos.
[5] Son of Tantalus and grandfather of Agamemnon.
[6] I.e., shrine of Apollo. He was patron god of Delphi, the older name of which was Pytho.
[7] Phoebus Apollo, i.e., the bright Apollo.

That I myself, unarmed with shield or host,
Should subtly work the righteous deed of blood.
Since then we heard an oracle like this,   45
Do thou go in, whene'er occasion serves,
Within this house, and learn what passes there,
That, knowing all, thou may'st report it well;
Changed as thou art by age and lapse of years,
They will not know thee, nor, with those grey
     hairs,   50
Even suspect thee.   And with this pretence
Go in, that thou a Phocian[1] stranger art,
Come from a man named Phanoteus; for he
Of all their friends is counted most in fame,
And tell them — yea, and add a solemn
     oath —   55
That some fell fate has brought Orestes' death,
In Pythian games,[2] from out the whirling car
Rolled headlong to the earth.   This tale tell
     thou;
And we, first honoring my father's grave,
As the God bade us, with libations pure   60
And tresses from our brow, will then come back,
Bearing the urn well wrought with sides of
     bronze,
Which, thou know'st well, 'mid yonder shrubs
     lies hid,
That we with crafty words may bring to them
The pleasant news that my poor frame is
     gone,   65
Consumed with fire, to dust and ashes turned.
Why should this grieve me, when, by show of
     death,
In truth I safety gain, and win renown?
To me no speech that profits soundeth ill,
For often have I seen men known as wise,   70
Reported dead in words of idle tales,
And then, when fortune brings them home
     again,
Gain more abundant honors.   So I boast
That I, from out this rumor of my death,
Shall, like a meteor, blaze upon my foes.   75
But oh! thou fatherland, ye Gods of home,
Receive me, prosper me in this my way;

[1] I.e., of Phocis, an ancient state between Boeotia and Locris in central Greece.
[2] Similar to the famous Olympian games and celebrated every four years at Delphi in August. They were not instituted, however, until 586 B.C., a date centuries after the supposed period of this drama.

And thou, my father's house (for lo! I come,
Sent by the Gods to cleanse thee righteously),
Send me not back dishonored from the
    land,   80
But lord of ancient wealth, and found at last
Restorer of my race.   So far I've said:
And now, old friend, 'tis thine to watch thy
    task:
We twain go forth.   The true, right time is
    come,
That mightiest master of all works of men.   85
   Elec. (*within*). Woe, woe is me! O misery!
   Attend. (*to* ORES.). I thought, my son, but
    now I heard a cry
As of some hand-maid wailing within doors.
   Ores. And can it be Electra, helpless one?
Shall we remain and listen to her plaint?   90
   Attend. In no wise.   Let us not attempt to do
Aught else before what Loxias [1] bade us do,
And start from that, upon thy father's grave
Pouring the lustral stream.   For this shall bring
Our victory, and strength in all we do.   95
       (*Exeunt* ORESTES, PYLADES, *and At-*
       tendant.

      Enter ELECTRA *from the Palace*

   Elec. O holy light of day, [2]
    And air with earth commensurate,
    Many the wailing songs,
    Many the echoing blow,
    On bosom stained with blood   100
    Thou heardest, when the night
    Of murky darkness ceased;
   And how, in all my vigils of the night
    I wail my hapless sire, [3]
   It knows, the loathèd bed of hated house; —   105
   My sire, whom Ares [4] *fierce and murderous*
   On alien shore [5] *received not as a guest,*
   But she, my mother, [6] *and her paramour,*
   Aegisthus, with the blood-stained hatchet, smote, [7]
    As those that timber fell   110
    Smite down the lofty oak.

   [1] Apollo.
   [2] This and all subsequent passages printed in italics
constitute the *sung* portions of the play.
   [3] Agamemnon.   [4] The god of war.
   [5] I.e., at Troy.   [6] Clytemnestra.
   [7] Between seven and eight years before the opening of
the play.

And thou, my father, hast no pity gained
    From anyone but me,
    Though thou a death hast died
So grievous and so foul to look upon.   115

    But I at least will ne'er
Refrain mine eyes from weeping, while I live,
    Nor yet my voice from wail,
    Not while I see this day,
    And yon bright twinkling stars;   120
    But, like a nightingale
    Of its young brood bereaved,
Before the gates I speak them forth to all.
O house of Hades [1] *and Persephone,* [2]
O Hermes [3] *of the abyss, and thou, dread Curse,* [4]
And ye, Erinnyes, [5] *daughters of the Gods,*   126
    Ye dreaded Ones who look
On all who perish, slain unrighteously,
On all whose bed is stealthily defiled,
Come ye, and help, avenge my father's death;   130
    Send me my brother here,
    For I alone must fail,
Sorrow's great burden in the balance cast.

     Enter CHORUS *of Argive women*

   Chor. O child, Electra dear,   (*Strophe*)
Child of a mother guilty above all,   135
Why dost thou ever wear thyself away
    In ceaseless, wailing cry,
For him thy father, Agamemnon, slain,
Long years ago by godless subtlety,
    Thy mother's, steeped in guile,   140
    By coward hand betrayed?
    May he who did the deed
    (If this my wish be right)
    Perish for evermore!
   Elec. Offspring of noble souls,   145
    Ye come to soothe my woes;
   I know it, yea, I comprehend it all,
    Nothing escapes my ken;
And yet I will not leave my task undone,

   [1] Pluto, king of the lower world and brother of Zeus.
   [2] Queen of the lower world and daughter of Demeter.
   [3] The conductor of the departed spirits to the lower
world.
   [4] The curse uttered by Agamemnon against his murderers.
   [5] The Furies, or the avenging spirits who bring retribution upon lawbreakers.

Nor cease to wail my hapless father's fate.   150
Ye then who give me every token kind
    Of true affection's bond,
    Leave me, I pray, ah! leave
    To vent my sorrow thus.
   Chor. And yet with groans and prayers,   155
                      (Antistrophe)
From Hades' pool, where all that live must go,
Thy sire thou can'st not raise, but passest on,
    Lamenting ceaselessly,
    From evil one might bear
To woe that baffles every remedy,   160
Where respite from our sorrows there is none.
    Why, why, I ask, dost thou
    Still in thy spirit seek
    Those evils hard to bear?
   Elec. Childish and weak is he   165
    Who learneth to forget
The parents that have perished miserably;
    Far better pleaseth me
The wailing one who "Itys, Itys," mourns,[1]
The bird heartbroken, messenger of Zeus.[2]   170
Ah, Niobe![3] *with all thy countless woes*
    I count thee still divine,
    Who in thy tomb of rock
    Weepest for evermore.
   Chor. Not unto thee alone,   (Str. 2)   175
    My child, of those that live
    Have grief and sorrow come;
Nor sufferest thou ought more than those within
With whom thou sharest home and kith and kin,
Iphianassa and Chrysothemis;[4]   180
And one is mourning in a youth obscure
    Yet happy, too, in part,

---

[1] The Greek ear heard the cry of "Itys" in the song of the nightingale. Itys, son of Tereus, king of Thrace, was slain in revenge for his father's cruelty to Philomela, daughter of Pandion, king of Athens. Tereus attacked Philomela and then tore her tongue out. Zeus, taking pity on the outraged maiden, changed Philomela into a nightingale. Hence the nightingale ever wails for Itys.

[2] I.e., the harbinger of spring. The nightingale appears in Attica about the end of March.

[3] Niobe, daughter of Tantalus, married Amphion, king of Thebes. Later she boasted her children were more numerous and goodly than those of Leto, mother of Apollo and Artemis. Then Leto's children in wrath slew Niobe's progeny. She, going to Phrygia to mourn her loss, was turned into a rock by Zeus and still continued to weep.

[4] Sisters of Electra.

Whom one day the Mycenians' glorious land
Shall welcome as the heir of noble race,
    Coming to this our soil,   185
    As sent by grace of Zeus,
    Orestes, come at last.
   Elec. Ah! Him I wait for with unwearied
    hope,
    And go, ah! piteous fate!
    Childless, unwedded still;   190
    My cheeks are wet with tears,
And still I bear an endless doom of woe.
    And he, alas! forgets
All he has met with, all that I had taught.
    What message goes from me   195
That is not mocked? for still he yearns to come,
    And yet he deigneth not.
Yearn though he may, to show himself to us.
   Chor. Take heart, my child, take heart;
                      (Ant. 2)
    Mighty in heaven He dwells,   200
    Zeus, seeing, guiding all:
Resign to Him the wrath that vexes sore.
And as for them, the foes whom thou dost hate,
Nor grieve too much, nor yet forget them quite;
    Time is a calm and patient Deity: 205
    For neither he who dwells
Where oxen graze on far Crisaean shore,
The boy who sprang from Agamemnon's loins,[1]
    Lives heedless of thy woe;
    Nor yet the God who reigns   210
    By Acheron's dark shore.[2]
   Elec. And yet the larger portion of my life
    Is gone without a hope,
    And I am all too weak,
Who waste away in orphaned loneliness,   215
    Whom no dear husband loves,
But, like an alien stranger in the house,
    I do my task unmeet,
And tend the chambers where my father dwelt,
    In this unseemly guise,   220
And stand at tables all too poorly filled.
   Chor. Sad was his voice in that his homeward
    march,   (Str. 3)

---

[1] Orestes was dwelling supposedly in Phocis, where also was located the district of Crisa in the close vicinity of Delphi.

[2] Hades or Pluto, who as king of the dead became their avenger. The realm of Pluto extended along the banks of the river Acheron in the lower world.

And sad when that sharp blow
(There in his father's couch,)
Of brazen axe went straight; [1]   225
Guile was it that devised,
And lust that struck the blow,
Engendering foully foulest form of sin,
   Whether it was a God,
   Or one of mortal men,   230
   That did the deed of guilt.
  Elec. Ah, day of all that ever came to me,
   Most horrible by far!
O night! O sufferings, strange as wonderful,
   Of banquets foul and dark!   235
Dread forms of death which he, my father, saw
   Wrought out by their joint hands,
Who, traitorous, murdered him who was my
   life,
   And so brought death to me.
May He who dwelleth on Olympus high,   240
   God, the Almighty One,
Give them for this to groan all grievously;
And ne'er may they in prosperous days rejoice,
   Who did such deeds as this.
  Chor. Take heed, take heed, and utter speech
   no more.   (Ant. 3)   245
   Hast thou no thought from whence,
   Into what evils dread,
   Sorrows thou mak'st thine own,
   Thou fallest piteously?
For thou hast reaped excess of misery,   250
   Still brooding over war
   In thine unquiet heart;
   With kings 'tis ill to strive.
  Elec. I was sore vexed with evils dire, yea. dire;
I know it well; my wrath escapes me not.   255
   Yet in this hard, hard fate,
I will not cease from uttering woe on woe,
   While life still holds me here.
For who is there, companions kind and true,
From whom to learn the speech that profiteth,   260
   Whose thoughts befit the time?
Leave me, oh, leave me, friends that fain would
   soothe,
For these my woes as endless shall be known,
And never from my wailings shall I cease,
   Nor pause to count my tears.   265

---

[1] Clytemnestra and Aegisthus murdered Agamemnon as he reposed at a banquet on the royal couch, the Greek fashion on such formal occasions.

  Chor. And yet, in pure goodwill I speak to
   thee,   (Epode)
   As mother faithful found,
   Not to heap ills on ills.
  Elec. What limit is there then to misery?
What? Is it noble to neglect the dead?   270
   Where has this custom grown?
   May I ne'er share their praise,
Nor, should I come to any form of good,
   Dwell with it peaceably,
If I should stay my wailing sorrow's wings,   275
   And leave my father shamed?
For if the dead, as dust and nothing found,
   Shall lie there in his woe,
   And they shall fail to pay
   The penalty of blood,   280
Then should all fear of Gods from earth decay,
And all men's worship prove a thing of nought.
  Chor. Lead. I came, my child, in earnest zeal
   for thee
And for myself. But if I speak not well,   284
Have thou thy way, and we will follow thee.
  Elec. I feel some shame, ye women, if I seem
To over-weary you with many tears:
But hard compulsion forces me to this,
Therefore bear with me. What maid nobly
   born,
Seeing a father's sorrows, would not do   290
As I am doing, — sorrows which, by night
As well as day, I see bud forth and bloom,
In nowise wither, — I who, first of all
Have on my mother's part, yes, hers who bore
   me,
Found deadliest hate; and then, in this my
   house,   295
Companion with my father's murderers,
I bow to them, and at their hands receive,
Or suffer want. And next, I pray thee, think
What kind of days I pass, beholding him,
Aegisthus, sitting on my father's throne,   300
And seeing him wear all his kingly robes,
And pouring forth libations on the hearth
Where his hands slew him; last, and worst of
   all,
I see that murderer in my father's couch,
With her, my wretched mother, if that name
Of mother I may give to one who sleeps   306
With such an one as he; and she is bold,
And lives with that adulterer, fearing not

The presence of Erinnyes, but, as one
Who laughs in what she does, she notes the day
In which she slew my father in her guile,   311
And on it forms her choral band, and slays
Her sheep each month, as victims to the Gods
That give deliverance; I, poor hapless one,
Beholding it, (ah misery!) within   315
Bewail, and pine, and mourn the fatal feast,
Full of all woe, that takes my father's name, —
I by myself alone. I dare not weep,
Not even weep, as fain my heart would wish;
For she, that woman, noble but in words,   320
Heaps on my head reproaches such as these:
"O impious, hateful mood! Has death deprived
Thee only of a father? Do none else
Feel touch of sorrow? Evil fate be thine,
And never may the Gods that reign below   325
Free thee from wailing!" So she still reviles;
But when she hears one speak Orestes' name,
As one day coming, then in maddened rage
She comes and screams, "And art not thou the cause?
And is not this thy deed, who, stealing him,
Orestes, from my hands, hast rescued him?   331
But know that thou shalt pay full price for this."
So does she howl, and he too eggs her on,
That spouse of hers as noble, standing near,
That utter coward, that mere mischief, he   335
Who with the help of women wages war.
And I, who wait Orestes evermore
To come and stop these evils, waste away;
For he, still ever meaning to effect
Some great achievement, brings to nothingness
All my hopes here, and all hopes far away.   341
At such a time, my friends, there is no room
For self-control or measured reverence;
Ills force us into choosing words of ill.

    Chor. Lead. Tell us, I pray, if thus thou
      speakest out,   345
Aegisthus being near, or gone from home.
    Elec. From home, most surely; do not dream
      that I,
If he were near, had ventured out of doors;
But, as it happens, he is gone a-field.
    Chor. Lead. So much the more would I take
      heart to hold   350
My converse with thee, if indeed 'tis so.

    Elec. Yes, he is gone. Ask thou whate'er
      thou wilt.
    Chor. Lead. Well, then, I ask thee of thy
      brother first,
Comes he, or stays he still? I fain would
      know.
    Elec. He speaks of coming; yet he nothing
      does.   355
    Chor. Lead. One who works great things oft
      is slow in them.
    Elec. I was not slow when I did save his life.
    Chor. Lead. Take heart. Right noble he, to
      help his friends.
    Elec. I trust, or else I had not lived till
      now.
    Chor. Lead. Not one word more; for coming
      from the house   360
I see thy sister, of one father born,
And of one mother, fair Chrysothemis;
And in her hand she brings sepulchral gifts,[1]
Such as are offered to the souls that sleep.

    Enter from the Palace CHRYSOTHEMIS,
      bearing funeral offerings

    Chrys. What plaint is this thou utterest,
      sister dear,   365
Here at the outlet of the palace gates?
And wilt not learn the lessons time would
      teach
To yield no poor compliance to a wrath
That is but vain? This much myself I know;
I grieve at what befalls us. Had I strength,
I would show plainly what I think of them;   371
But now it seems most wise in weather foul,
To slack my sail, and make no idle show
Of doing something when I cannot harm;
And on this wise I wish thee too to act;   375
While yet I grant that what thou think'st is
      just,
Not what I say. But if I wish to live
In freedom, I must bow to those that rule.
    Elec. Strange is it thou, who callest such
      a man
Thy father, should'st forget him, and should'st
      care   380
For such a mother. All this good advice
Thou giv'st to me is not thine own but hers,

    [1] These commonly consisted of milk, honey, and oil.

Thy lesson learnt by rote.   Take then thy
    choice;
Or thou hast lost thy reason, or, if sane,   384
Thou hast no memory of thy dearest friends,
Who said'st but now, that, had'st thou strength
    enough,
Thou would'st make plain the hate thou hast
    for them;
And yet when I am working to avenge
Thy father, wilt not join me, and would'st fain
Turn me aside from action. Is there not   390
In this, besides all else, a coward's heart?
Tell me (yea, hear) what profit should I have
Were I to cease from tears? Do I not live?
In evil case I own, and yet for me
Enough; and these I vex, and so I give   395
Due honor to the dead, — if they can be
Or pleased or thankful. Thou, with that thy
    hate,
Hatest in words, and yet in act dost live
In friendship with thy father's murderers.
Never would I, no, not though one should bring
To me the gifts which thou rejoicest in,   401
Give way to them.   No! Let thy board be
    spread
With dainties rich, and let thy life be full;
My only food be this, to spare myself   404
What most would pain. I covet not thy place,
Nor, wert thou wise, would'st thou. But, as it
    is,
When thou might'st be the child of noblest
    father,
Choose to be called thy mother's.   Thus shalt
    thou
To most men seem contemptible and base,
Forsaking thy dead father and thy friends.   410
    Chor. Lead. By all the Gods, I pray thee,
        cease from wrath;
In both your words, some profit may be found,
If thou from her would'st learn, and she from
    thee.
    Chrys. I, O my friends, am somewhat used
        to hear
Her words; nor had I now recurred to them,
But that I heard of evil drawing near,   416
Which soon shall stop her long protracted
    wails.
    Elec. Tell then this dreadful evil. Hast thou
        aught

To tell me more than what I suffer now,
I will resist no longer.   420
    Chrys.   All I know
Myself, I'll tell thee; for their purpose is,
Unless thou ceasest from thy wailings loud,
To send thee where thou never more shalt see
The light of day, but in a dungeon cave,   425
Immured alive, beyond your country's bounds,
Shalt sing thy song of sorrow.   Take good heed,
And do not, when thou sufferest, all too late,
Cast then the blame on me.   Be wise in time.
    Elec. And is it thus they have decreed to
        treat me?   430
    Chrys. Beyond all doubt, when home
        Aegisthus comes.
    Elec. If this be all, would God he may come
        soon.
    Chrys. What evil prayer is this, poor sister
        mine?
    Elec. That he may come, if this his purpose
        be.
    Chrys. What would'st thou suffer?   Whither
        turn thy thoughts?   435
    Elec. To flee as far as may be from you all.
    Chrys. Hast thou no care for this thy present
        life?
    Elec. A goodly life for men to wonder at!
    Chrys. So might it be, if thou would'st
        wisdom learn.
    Elec. Teach me no baseness to the friends
        I love.   440
    Chrys. I teach not that, yet kings must be
        obeyed.
    Elec. Fawn as thou wilt; thy fashion is not
        mine.
    Chrys. Yet is it well through rashness not to
        fall.
    Elec. If fall we must, we'll fall our father
        helping.
    Chrys. Our father, so I deem, will pardon
        this.   445
    Elec. These words will win due praises from
        the vile.
    Chrys. Wilt thou not yield and hearken to
        my words?
    Elec. Not so; ne'er may I be so reft of sense.
    Chrys. I then will go the way that I was sent.
    Elec. And whither goest thou?   Whose the
        gifts thou bring'st?   450

Chrys. Mother to father bids me pour
  libations.

Elec. How say'st thou? To the man whom
  most she hates?

Chrys. "The man she slew" — 'Tis that
  thou fain would'st say.

Elec. Who gave this counsel? Who has
  this approved?

Chrys. 'Tis, as I think, some terror of the
  night.   455

Elec. Gods of my fathers! Be ye with me
  now!

Chrys. And does this terror give thee confidence?

Elec. If thou would'st tell the vision, I should
  know.

Chrys. I know it not, but just in briefest tale.

Elec. Ah, tell me that; brief words ere now
  have laid   460
Men low in dust, and raised them up again.

Chrys. A rumor runs that she our father's
  presence
(Yes, thine and mine) a second time to light
Saw coming, and he stood upon the hearth,
And took the sceptre which he bore of old, 465
Which now Aegisthus bears, and fixed it there,
And from it sprang a sucker fresh and strong,
And all Mycenae rested in its shade.
This tale I heard from some one who was
  near
When she declared her vision to the Sun;[1] 470
But more than this I heard not, save that she
Now sends me hither through that fright of
  hers.
        (ELECTRA, *wild and impassioned, is
          about to speak.*
And now by all the Gods of kith and kin,
I pray thee, hearken to me; do not fall
Through lack of counsel; if thou turn'st me
  back,   475
In trouble sore thou'lt seek me yet again.

Elec. Ah, sister dear, of what thy hands do
  bear
Put nothing on the tomb; for nature's law
Forbids it as unholy thus to bring

----

[1] The Sun God, Helios, was called upon to dispel the
terrifying dreams of darkness or to reveal lurking danger
foreshadowed perhaps by an evil dream. An altar to
Helios stood by the road from Argos to Mycenae.

Funereal offerings, lustral[1] waters pour,   480
From wife unfriendly, on a father's grave.
No! cast them to the rivers, hide them deep
In dust where never aught of them shall come
To where my father sleeps; but when she dies,
Let them be stored below as gifts for her. 485
For, surely, were she not the boldest found
Among all women, ne'er would she have poured
These hateful offerings o'er the man she slew.
Think, if the dead who sleeps in yonder tomb
Will welcome kindly gifts like these from her,
By whom, most foully slain as hated foe,   491
His feet and hands were lopped off shamefully,
Who wiped upon his head the blood-stained
  knife,
As if to purge the guilt. And dost thou think
To bring these gifts redeeming her from
  guilt?   495
Not so. Nay, put them by, and then do
  thou,
Cutting the highest locks that crown thy head,
Yea, and mine also, poor although I be,
(Small offering, yet 'tis all the store I have,)
Give to him, yes, this lock, untrimmed, un-
  meet   500
For suppliant's vow, and this my girdle, decked
With no gay fringe. And ask thou, falling low,
That he will come to us in mood of grace,
From out the earth, a helper 'gainst our foes,
And that his son, Orestes, with a hand   505
Victorious, trample upon those his foes,
In fullest life returning, so that we
Hereafter may with gifts more bounteous come
To deck his grave than those we offer now.
I think, for one, I surely think that he   510
Has sent these dark, unsightly dreams to her;
But be this as it may, my sister, come
And do this service, for thyself and me,
Nor less for him, of all men most beloved,
Our father, now in Hades slumbering.   515

Chor. Lead. The maiden speaks with filial
  reverence;
And thou, dear friend, if thou art wise, wilt do
What so she counsels.

Chrys.   I will do it then.
It is not meet with two to wrangle still,   520
Debating of the right, but haste and act.
But if I thus essay this enterprise,

----

[1] Purifying.

By all the Gods, my friends, be hushed and
    still;
For if my mother hears it, well I trow
That what I dare will end full bitterly.   525
           (*Exit* CHRYSOTHEMIS.
   Chor. *If wisdom fail me not,*   (Strophe)
As seer misled by doubtful auguries,
    And wanting counsel wise,
She comes, true augur with foreshadowing tread,
    Vengeance, with hands that bear   530
    The might of righteousness:
She comes, my child, full soon, in hot pursuit.
And through my veins there springs a courage
    new,
    Hearing but now these dreams
    That come with favoring gale;   535
For he, thy father, king of all Hellenes,
    Will not forget for aye,
Nor will that hatchet with its double edge,
    Wrought out in bronze of old,
    Which laid him low in death   540
    With vilest contumely.

    And She shall also come,   (Antistrophe)
Dread form, with many a foot, and many a hand,
    Erinnys [1] *shod with brass,*
Who lieth still in ambush terrible: 545
    For there has come to those
    For whom it was not right,
The hot embrace of marriage steeped in blood,
Of evil omen, bed and bride alike;
    But, above all, this thought   550
    Fills heart and soul, that ne'er
The boding sign will come unblamed to those
    Who did the deed, or shared;
Lo! men can find no prophecies in dreams,
    Nor yet in words divine,   555
    Unless it gain its goal,
    This vision of the night.

    Ah, in the olden time,   (Epode)
Thou chariot race of Pelops, perilous,
How did'st thou come to this our father-land   560
    In long-enduring gloom?
For since he slept beneath the waters deep,
    Poor Myrtilus, who fell,
Cast headlong from the chariot bright with gold,
    Both root and branch destroyed,   565

    [1] One of the avenging Furies.

There has not left our master's lordly house
    All shame and ignominy. [1]

    Enter CLYTEMNESTRA, *followed by an*
             ATTENDANT

  Clytem. Thou, as it seems, dost take thine
    ease abroad,
Aegisthus being absent, who has charged
That thou should'st not, being seen without the
    gates,   570
Disgrace thy friends. But now, since he is
    gone,
For me thou little carest. Yea, thou say'st
Full many a time to many men, that I
Am over-bold, and rule defying right,
Insulting thee and thine. But I disclaim   575
All insult, and but speak of thee the ill
I hear so often from thee. Evermore,
Thy father, and nought else, is thy pretext;
As that he died by me.... By me? Right well
I know 'tis true. That deed deny I not,   580
For Justice seized him, 'twas not I alone;
And thou should'st aid her, wert thou wise of
    heart,
Since that thy father, whom thou mournest
    still,
Alone of all the Hellenes had the heart
To sacrifice thy sister to the Gods,[2]   585
Although, I trow, his toil was less than mine,

    [1] Oenomaüs, king of Pisa in Elis, promised his daughter, Hippodameia, to the suitor who should defeat him in a chariot race. With the help of Myrtilus, charioteer of Oenomaüs, young Pelops defeated the king in a race and won his daughter. Then Pelops, either because he was unwilling to reward Myrtilus or because he suspected him of loving Hippodameia, threw Myrtilus headlong into the sea. As the charioteer sank beneath the waves, he uttered a curse on Pelops and all his line. This curse proved the starting point of evils subsequently visited upon Pelops' house.
    [2] When Agamemnon and his brother, Menelaus, went forth with the Greek fleet to attack Troy and bring back Helen, Menelaus' wife stolen by Paris, son of Priam, king of Troy, the goddess Artemis became angry and stopped the wind from blowing off the Boeotian coast. Thus the fleet lay becalmed at Aulis many days. Finally, Calchas the prophet announced that Agamemnon must sacrifice his daughter, Iphigenia, to Artemis before the fleet could sail for Troy. The king then did offer up the maiden at Aulis; the wind came up; and the Greek ships departed.

And little knew he of my travail-pangs.
And now I ask thee, tell me for whose sake
He slew her? "For the Argives," sayest thou?
They had no right to seek my daughter's death;
But if he killed mine for another's sake,   591
His brother Menelaüs', should he not
Be righteously requited? Had not he
Two sons, who it was fit should die far more
Than this my daughter, seeing they were born
Of father and of mother for whose sake   596
The armament went forth? Or was it so
That Hades had a special lust to feast
Upon my children rather than on hers?
Or was it that her father cast aside,   600
Cold-blooded, hard, all yearning for my child,
Yet cared for Menelaüs? Was he not
In this a reckless father found, and base?
I answer, Yes, though thou refuse assent;
And she that died would say it, could she speak.
I then feel no remorse for what is done;   606
But if I seem to thee as base in heart,
First judge thou right, then blame thy next of
    kin.
   Elec. This time, at least, thou wilt not say
    that I,
Being first to vex, then heard these words from
    thee;   610
But, if thou giv'st me leave, I fain would plead
For him who died, and for my sister too.
   Clytem. I give thee leave. Had'st thou thus
    spoken always,
To list to thee had given me less annoy.
   Elec. Thus speak I then to thee — Thou
    say'st thy hand   615
Did slay my father! Is there aught of shame
Than this more shameful, whether thou can'st
    urge,
Or not, the plea of justice? But I say
Thou did'st not justly slay him, but wast led
By vile suggestion of the coward base   620
Who now lives with thee. Next, I pray thee,
    ask
The huntress Artemis what guilt restrained
The many winds in Aulis; or my voice
Shall tell thee; for from her thou may'st not
    learn.   624
My father once, as I have heard the tale,
Taking his sport within the holy grove
The Goddess calls her own, had raised a deer,

Dappled, and antlered, and in careless mood
Boasted loudly at the death.[1] And therefore
    she,
Leto's fair daughter, in her wrath detained   630
The Achaeans that my father might perforce
Slay his own daughter, in the balance weighed
Against that quarry. Thus the matter stood
As to that offering. Other means were none
To free the army, or for homeward voyage,   635
Or yet for Ilion.[2] Therefore sore constrained
And struggling, hardly at the last he wrought
The act of sacrifice, and not through love
For Menelaüs. But had it been so,
Had he done this with wish to profit him,   640
(For I will take thy premiss,) ought he then
To die by thine hand? Why, what right is
    this?
See to it, giving men a law like this,
If thou but cause fresh trouble to thyself,   644
And change of purpose bringing late regret;
For, should we evermore take blood for blood,
Thou would'st fall first, if thou did'st get thy
    due.
See to it well, lest thus thy vain pretence
Be found as nought. For tell me, if thou wilt,
In recompense for what dost thou now do   650
Deed of all deeds most shameful, who dost
    sleep
With that red-handed felon who with thee
Murdered my father, and to him dost bear
New children, while thou castest out from thee
Those born before, right seed of righteous
    sire?   655
How shall I praise these deeds? or wilt thou say
That thus thou takest vengeance for thy child?
Basely enough, if thou should'st say it. Lo!
It is not good to wed an enemy,   659
E'en in a daughter's cause. But since to speak
A word of counsel is not granted us,
Though thou dost love to speak all words of ill,
That "we revile a mother;" — yet I look
On thee as more his mistress than my mother,
Living a woeful life, by many ills   665
Encompassed which proceed from thee, and
    him,
The partner of thy guilt. That other one,

[1] Agamemnon, according to the legend, boasted that
he had surpassed Artemis in skill of chase.
[2] Troy.

My poor Orestes, hardly 'scaped from thee,
Drags on a weary life. Full oft hast thou
Charged me with rearing him to come at last
A minister of vengeance; and I own,   671
Had I but strength, be sure of this, 'twere done.
For this then, even this, proclaim aloud
To all men, as thou wilt, that I am base,
Or foul of speech, or full of shamelessness: 675
For if I be with such things conversant,
Then to thy breeding I bring no disgrace.

   Chor. Lead. I see she breathes out rage —
     but whether right
Be on her side, for this no care I see.

   Clytem. And why should I give heed to one
     like her,   680
Who thus her mother scorns? And at her age!
Does she not seem to thee as one prepared
To go all lengths, and feel no touch of shame?

   Elec. Know well, I do feel shame for all I do,
Though thou think'st otherwise, and well I
     know   685
I do things startling, most unmeet for me;
But thy fixed hate and these thy deeds perforce
Constrain me still to do them. Still it holds,
Base deeds by base are learnt and perfected.

   Clytem. Thou shameless creature! I then,
     and my words,   690
And my deeds too, they make thee prate too
     much.

   Elec. Thou sayest it, not I; for thou dost do
The deed: and deeds will find their fitting words.

   Clytem. Now by my mistress Artemis, I
     swear,
For this thy daring thou shalt pay in full 695
When back Aegisthus comes.

   Elec.   Now look you there!
Thou'rt swayed by fury, though thou gav'st
     me leave
To speak whate'er I would, and can'st not
     learn
To play a listener's part!   700

   Clytem.   And wilt thou not
Give leave to do my rites with clamor hushed,
Seeing that I let thee speak thy whole mind
     out?

   Elec. I let thee, bid thee, do them. Charge
     not thou
My lips with folly. Now, I speak no more. 705
     (*Retires toward the Palace.*

   Clytem. Do thou then, my attendant, bring
     the gifts
Of many fruits, that I may breathe my prayers
To this our King for respite from the fears
Which now possess me.
     (*Advances to the altar in the center of
     the orchestra.*

          Hear, O Phoebus, Thou   710
Our true deliverer, hear my secret speech;
For this my prayer is not among my friends,
Nor is it fit to bring it all to light,
While she is near me still, lest in her mood
Of envy, and with cry of many tongues,   715
She spread the vain report through all the
     town;
But hear thou me; for thus I make my prayer;
The vision which I looked on in the night
Of doubtful dreams, grant me, Lyceian king,
If they are good, their quick accomplishment;
If adverse, send them on mine adversaries; 721
And if there be that wish, by craft and guile,
To hurl me from the wealth I now enjoy,
Suffer them not, but ever let me live
With life unharmed, and sway the Atreidae's
     house,   725
And these their sceptres, dwelling with the
     friends
Whom now I dwell with, passing prosperous
     days
With all my children, who nor hatred bring
Nor bitter sorrow. This, Lyceian king,
Apollo, hear all pitiful, and grant   730
To all of us, as we implore thee now;
All else, though I be silent, I will deem
Thou, being a God, dost know. One well may
     think
The sons of Zeus see all things.

   Enter the Aged ATTENDANT *of* ORESTES

   Attend.   Might I know, 735
Ye ladies, if these dwellings that I see
Are those of King Aegisthus?

   Chor. Lead.   Even so!
Thou guessest well, O stranger.

   Attend.   Am I right 740
In once more guessing that his wife stands
     here?
For sure her mien bespeaks her sovereignty.

Chor. Lead. Right, more than ever. Lo, she
standeth there.
    Attend. All hail, O queen; I bring thee tid-
ings good,
Thee and Aegisthus also, from a friend.   745
    Clytem. I hail the omen; but I fain would
know
This first, what man has sent thee here to us.
    Attend. The Phocian Phanoteus, discharging
thus
A weighty task.
    Clytem.   And what its nature, pray?   750
Tell me, O stranger; for right well I know
Thou from a friend wilt bring us friendly words.
    Attend. Orestes. . . . He is dead. That word
tells all.
    Elec. O wretched me! This day I perish too.
    Clytem. What say'st thou, stranger?
What? . . .   755
Heed not her words.
    Attend. Orestes . . . He is dead — I say again.
    Elec. Ah me! I perish utterly. All's lost.
    Clytem. Look thou to what concerns thee.
But do thou, (*to the* ATTENDANT)
O stranger, tell us truly how he died.   760
    Attend. For this end was I sent; and I will
tell
All as it happened. He then journeyed forth
To those great games which Hellas counts her
pride,
To join the Delphic contests;[1] and he heard
The herald's voice, with loud and clear com-
mand,   765
Proclaim, as coming first, the chariot race:
And so he entered radiant, every eye
Admiring as he passed. And in the race
He equalled all the promise of his form   769
In those his rounds, and so with noblest prize
Of conquest left the ground. And, summing
up
In fewest words what many scarce could tell,
I know of none in strength and act like him;
But one thing know, for having won the prize
In all the five-fold forms of race which
they,   775
The umpires, had proclaimed for those that ran
The ground's whole length and back, he then
was hailed,

[1] The same as the Pythian games. See note to l. 57.

Proclaimed an Argive, and his name Orestes,
His son who once led Hellas' glorious host,
The mighty Agamemnon. So far well.   780
But when a God will injure, none can 'scape,
Strong though he be. For lo! another day,
When, as the sun was rising, came the race
Swift-footed, of the chariot and the horse,
He entered there, with many charioteers;   785
One an Achaean,[1] one from Sparta, two
From Libya,[2] who with four-horsed chariots
came,
And he with these, with swift Thessalian mares,
Came as the fifth; a sixth with bright bay
colts
Came from Aetolia;[3] and the seventh was born
In far Magnesia;[4] and the eighth, by race   791
An Aenian,[5] with white horses; and the ninth
From Athens came, the city built of God;[6]
Last, a Boeotian,[7] tenth in order, came,
And made the list complete. And so they
stood —   795
When the appointed umpires fixed by lot,
And placed the cars in order; and with sound
Of brazen trump they started. Cheering all
Their steeds at once, they shook the reins, and
then
The course was filled with all the clash and
din   800
Of rattling chariots, and the dust rose high;
And all commingled, sparing not the goad,
That each might pass his neighbour's axle-
trees,
And horses' hot, hard breathings; for their
backs
And chariot-wheels were white with foam, and
still   805
The breath of horses smote them; and he, come

[1] Achaea, the northwestern portion of the Morea
Peninsula in southern Greece.
[2] The section of north African coast just west of
Egypt.
[3] The southwestern portion of central Greece, lying
opposite Achaea on the other side of the Corinthian
Gulf.
[4] The eastern coastal tract of Thessaly in central
Greece.
[5] One of a tribe in the south of Thessaly.
[6] Note the patriotic puff which would win the favor
of the theater audience.
[7] Boeotia, the ancient state adjoining Attica on the
west and north.

Just where the last stone marks the course's
    goal,
Turning the corner sharp, and, letting go
The right hand trace-horse, pulled the nearer
    in;   809
And so at first the chariots keep their course;
But then the unbroken colts the Aenian owned
Rush at full speed, and, turning headlong back,
Just as they closed their sixth round or their
    seventh,
Dash their heads right against the chariot
    wheels
Of those who came from Barcae.¹ And from
    thence,   815
From that one shock, each on the other crashed,
They fell o'erturned, and Crissa's spacious
    plain
Was filled with wreck of chariots. Then the
    man
From Athens, skilled and wily charioteer,
Seeing the mischief, turns his steeds aside,   820
At anchor rides, and leaves the whirling surge
Of man and horse thus raging. Last of all,
Keeping his steeds back, waiting for the end,
Orestes came. And when he sees him left,
His only rival, then, with shaken rein,   825
Urging his colts, he follows, and they twain
Drove onward both together, by a head,
Now this, now that, their chariots gaining
    ground;
And all the other rounds in safety passed.
Upright in upright chariot still he stood,   830
Ill-starred one; then the left rein letting loose
Just as his horse was turning, unawares
He strikes the furthest pillar, breaks the spokes
Right at his axle's centre, and slips down
From out his chariot, and is dragged along, 835
With reins dissevered. And, when thus he fell,
His colts tore headlong to the ground's mid-
    space:
And when the host beheld him fallen thus
From off the chariot, they bewailed him sore,
So young, so noble, so unfortunate,   840
Now hurled upon the ground, and now his
    limbs
To heaven exposing. Then the charioteers
Full hardly keeping back the rush of steeds,

¹ A town in ancient Libya about fifty miles from the
coastal colony of Cyrene.

Freed the poor corpse so bloody, that not one
Of all his friends would know him, and his
    body   845
They burnt upon the pyre; and now they bear,
The chosen of the Phocians that have come,
In a poor urn of bronze, a mighty form
Reduced to these sad ashes, that for him
May be a tomb within his fatherland.   850
Such is my tale, full sad, I trow, to hear,
But unto those who saw it as we saw,
The greatest of all evils I have known.
    Chor. Lead. Woe, woe! So perish, root and
        branch, it seems,
The race of those our lords of long ago.   855
    Clytem. O Zeus! What means this ... Shall
        I say, good news?
Or fearful, yet most gainful? Still 'tis sad
If by my sorrows I must save my life.
    Attend. Why does my tale, O queen, thus
        trouble thee?
    Clytem. Wondrous and strange the force of
        motherhood!   860
Though wronged, a mother cannot hate her
    children.
    Attend. We then, it seems, are come to thee
        in vain.
    Clytem. Nay, not in vain. How could it be
        in vain?
Since thou bring'st proofs that he is dead, who,
        born
Child of my heart, from breasts that gave him
        suck   865
Then turned aside, and dwelt on foreign soil
In banishment; and since he left our land
Ne'er came to see me, but with dreadful words,
His father's death still casting upon me,
Spake out his threats; so that nor day nor
        night   870
I knew sweet sleep, but still the sway of Time
Led on my life, as one condemned to death.
But now, (for lo! this day has stopped all
        fear
From her and him, for she was with me still,
The greater mischief, sucking out my life,   875
My very heart's blood:) now, for all her threats,
We shall live on and pass our days in peace.
    Elec. Ah, wretched me! for now I can but
        mourn,
Orestes, at thine evil case, thus dying,

By this thy mother scorned.   Can this be
    well?   880

Clytem. Not so with thee.   For him what is
    is well.

Elec. Hear this, thou Power, avenging him
    who died!

Clytem. Right well she heard, and what she
    heard hath wrought.

Elec. Heap scoff on scoff; thou'rt fortune's
    darling now.

Clytem. Thou and Orestes, will ye check me
    now?   885

Elec. We, we are checked, and far from
    checking thee.

Clytem. (to Attendant). Thou would'st deserve much praise, if thou hast checked,
O stranger, that loud cry of many tongues.

Attend. And may I then depart, my task
    being done?

Clytem. Nay, nay; thou would'st not then
    fare worthily   890
Of me, or of the friend that sent thee here;
Come in, and leave this girl to cry without,
And wail her own misfortunes and her friends'.

    (*Exeunt* CLYTEMNESTRA *and* ATTEND-
    ANT *into the Palace.*

Elec. And does she seem to you, that hateful
    one,
As one who grieves in bitter pain of heart,   895
To wail and weep full sorely for her son
Who died so sadly?   Nay, (ah, wretched me!)
She wends her way exulting.   Ah, Orestes!
Dear brother, in thy death thou slayest me;
For thou art gone, bereaving my poor heart
Of all the little hope that yet remained,   901
That thou would'st come, a living minister
Of vengeance for thy father and for me,
Me miserable.   Now whither shall I turn?
For now I am indeed alone, bereaved   905
Of thee and of my father.   Now once more
I must live on in bondage unto those
Of all mankind most hateful far to me,
My father's murderers.   Goes it well with me?
But I at least through all the time to come   910
Will not dwell with them, but at this their gate,
All reckless, friendless, waste away my life;
And then, if one of those that dwell within
Is wroth with this, why, let him slay me
    straight;

I'll thank him, if he kill me; should I live   915
There is but sorrow; wish for life is none.

Chor. Where then the bolts of Zeus, (Strophe)
    And where the glorious Sun,
      If, seeing deeds like these,
      They hold their peace, and hide?   920

Elec. (sobbing). Alas, ah me, ah woe!

Chor. My child, why weepest thou?

Elec. Fie on it, fie, . . .

Chor. Lead. Hush, hush, be not too bold.

Elec. Thou wilt but break my heart.   925

Chor. Lead.   *What meanest thou?*

Elec. If thou suggestest any hope from those
So clearly gone to Hades, then on me,
Wasting with sorrow, thou wilt trample more.

Chor. And yet I know that King Amphia-
    raüs [1]   (Antistrophe)   930
Was taken in the toils of golden snare,
By woman's craft, and now below the earth . . .

Elec. (sobbing). Ah me! ah me!

Chor.   *He reigns in fullest life.*

Elec. Fie on it, fie.   935

Chor. Lead.   *Yes, fie indeed; for she,*
Fell traitress. . . .

Elec.   *Perished, you would say?*

Chor. Lead.   *E'en so.*

Elec. I know, I know it.   One was left to care
For him who suffered.   None is left to me;   940
For he who yet remained is snatched away.

Chor. Most piteous thou, and piteous is thy
    lot.   (Str. 2)

Elec. That know I well, too well,
In this my life, which through the months runs
    on,   945
    Filled full of grievous fears,
    And bitter, hateful ills.

Chor. We saw what thou dost mourn.

Elec. Cease, cease, to lead me on
    Where now not one is left. . . .   950

Chor. Lead. What say'st thou?   What?

---

[1] Seer and warrior of Argos, he opposed the expedition
of Polyneices against Thebes, foreseeing a fatal outcome,
but he was induced finally by his treacherous wife, Eri-
phyle, to join the enterprise.   When in the subsequent
rout of the Argives he was fleeing toward the river Is-
menus near Thebes, a sudden earthquake swallowed
him up along with his chariot.   Then his son, Alcmaeon,
avenged the father's death by slaying the guilty Eri-
phyle.   Thereafter Amphiaraüs became honored as an
earth-god.

Elec. Where not one helper comes,
From all the hopes of common fatherhood
*   And stock of noble sire.*
Chor. Death is the lot of all.   (Ant. 2)   955
Elec. What?   Is it all men's lot
*   In that fierce strife of speed,*
To fall, as he fell, by an evil fate,
*   In severed reins entangled?*
Chor. Wondrous and dark that doom.   960
Elec. I trow it was, if in a strange land, he,
*   Without my helping hands . . .*
Chor. Lead. Oh, horror! horror!
Elec. Was buried with no sepulture from us,
*   Nor voice of wailing.*   965

Enter CHRYSOTHEMIS, *running eagerly*

Chrys. In pure delight, dear sister, thus I
    rush,
My maiden grace abandoning, to come
With swiftest foot; for lo!   I bring great joy
And respite from the ills thou long hast borne,
And still did'st wail.   970
Elec.   And whence can'st thou have found
Help for my woes where healing there is none?
Chrys. Orestes comes at last.   Count this
    as sure,
Hearing my words, as that thou see'st me here.
Elec. What!   Art thou mad, poor wretch,
    and so dost mock   975
At thine own sorrows, and at mine as well?
Chrys. Nay!   By our father's hearth, I do
    not speak
These things in scorn, but say that he is come.
Elec. Ah, wretched me!   And whose word
    is it then
That thou hast heard with such credulity?   980
Chrys. I, of myself, no other, clearest proof
Have seen, and therefore I believe this thing.
Elec. What hast thou seen, poor soul; what
    caught thy gaze,
That thou art fevered with this flameless fire?
Chrys. Now by the Gods!   I pray thee, list
    to me,   985
That thou may'st know if I be sane or mad.
Elec. Tell then thy tale, if thou find joy in it.
Chrys. And I will tell each thing of all I saw;
For when I came where stands our father's
    tomb

Time-honored, on the summit of the mound
I see the marks of flowing streams of milk   991
New poured, and lo! my father's bier was
    crowned
With garlands of all flowers that deck the
    fields;
And, seeing it, I wondered, and looked round,
Lest any man should still be hovering
    near;   995
And when I saw that all the place was calm,
I went yet nearer to the mound, and there
I saw upon the topmost point of all
A tress of hair, fresh severed from the head.
And when poor I beheld it, in my soul   1000
A once-familiar image stirs the thought
That here I saw a token true from him
Whom most I love, Orestes.   In my hands
I take it, uttering no ill-omened cries,
But straight mine eyes were filled with tears of
    joy;   1005
And then and now I know with equal faith
This precious gift can come from none but
    him;
Whose work else could it be save mine or thine?
And I, I know, have had no hand in it,
Nor yet hast thou; how else, when thou'rt
    forbid   1010
E'en to the Gods to go from 'neath this roof
Except at cost of tears?   Nor does her heart,
Our mother's, love to do such things as these;
Nor could she, doing it, have 'scaped our view.
No!   These tomb-offerings from Orestes
    come.   1015
Take courage, sister dear!   The same drear
    fate
Stands not for ever to the same men comrade:
Till now it frowned on us; but lo! to-day
Shall be of countless good the harbinger.
Elec. Ah me!   How much thy madness
    moves my pity!   1020
Chrys. What!   Speak I not a thing that
    gives thee joy?
Elec. Thou know'st not where thou art in
    fact or thought.
Chrys. How can I not know what I clearly
    saw?
Elec. He, thou poor soul, is dead, and with
    him goes   1024
All hope of safety.   Think no more of him.

Chrys. Ah, wretched me! From whom hast
    thou heard this?
Elec. From one who stood hard by when he
    was killed.
Chrys. And where is he? Strange wonder
    thrills through me.
Elec. Within, our mother's not unwelcome
    guest.
Chrys. Ah me! And yet what man was it
    that left   1030
These many offerings at my father's grave?
Elec. I for my part must think that some
    one placed them,
Memorials of Orestes who is dead.
Chrys. Ah me! I hastened, joyous, with my
    tale,   1034
Not knowing in what depths of woe we were;
And now, when I have come, I find at once
My former woes, with fresh ones in their
    train.
Elec. So stands it with thee. But if thou
    wilt list
To me, thou shalt cast off this weight of woe.
Chrys. What! shall I ever bring the dead to
    life?   1040
Elec. I meant not that: I am not quite so
    mad.
Chrys. What bidd'st thou, then, that I can
    answer for?
Elec. That thou should'st dare to do what I
    shall bid.
Chrys. Well! If it profit, I will not refuse.
Elec. See! without labor nothing prospers
    well.   1045
Chrys. I see, and I with all my strength will
    work.
Elec. Hear, then, what I am purposed to
    perform.
Thou knowest, e'en thou, that we behold no
    more
The presence of our friends, but Hades dark
Has snatched them, and we twain are left
    alone.   1050
And I, as long as I still heard and deemed
My brother strong and living, still had hopes
That he would come to avenge our father's
    death;
But now that he is gone I look to thee,   1054
That thou flinch not, with me thy sister here,

From slaying him, Aegisthus, whose hand
    wrought
Our father's murder; for I may not hide
Aught of my mind from thee. How long, how
    long
Dost thou wait dully, looking to what hope
As yet remaining, when for thee is nought   1060
But grief, as robbed of all thy father's wealth,
And sorrow that thou waxest old till now,
Without or marriage-bed or marriage-song?
And cherish thou no hope that thou shalt gain
Or this or that. Aegisthus is not blind,   1065
To let our progeny, or mine or thine,
Spring up or grow, to be his certain harm.
But, if thou wilt to my advice give heed,
First, thou shalt gain the praise of reverence
    due   1070
Both from our father, who now sleeps below,
And from our brother; next, thou shalt be
    called,
As thou wast born, free, noble, and shalt gain
Befitting marriage. All men love to look
On deeds of goodness. Dost not see full clear
All the fair fame thou'lt gain for thee and
    me,   1075
If thou obey my counsels? Who, seeing us,
Or citizen or stranger, will not greet us
With praises such as these? "Behold, my
    friends,
Those sisters twain, who saved their father's
    house,
And on their foes who walked in pride of
    strength,   1080
Regardless of their lives, wrought doom of
    death!
These all must love, these all must reverence;
These in our feasts, and when the city meets
In full assemblage, all should honor well,
For this their manly prowess." Thus will
    all   1085
Speak of us, so that fame we shall not miss,
Living or dying. Do but hear me, dear one.
Toil for thy father, for thy brother work;
Free me from all my evils, free thyself,   1089
Knowing this, that living basely is for those
Who have been born of noble stock most base.
Chor. Lead. Forethought at such a crisis is
    for those
Who speak and those that hear, the best ally.

Chrys. And she, O women, ere she spoke,
    had kept   1094
(Had she not chanced to be of mind diseased)
That cautious reverence which she keeps not
    now.
(*To* ELEC.) What hast thou seen that thou
    dost arm thyself
In such foolhardy rashness, and dost call
On me to help thee?   Wilt thou never see?
Lo, thou wast born a woman, not a man,   1100
And art less strong than those thine enemies.
And their good fortune prospers every day,
While ours falls off, and doth to nothing come.
Who, plotting to attack a man like that,   1104
Shall pass unscathed, unvexed by bitter woe?
Take heed lest we who fare but badly now
Should fare yet worse, if any hear thy speech;
For nothing does it help or profit us,
Gaining fair fame, a shameful death to die;
Yet death is not the worst, but when one
    seeks   1110
To die, and fails e'en that poor gain to win.
Come, I implore thee, and before thou work
Our utter ruin, and our house lay waste,
Restrain thine anger.   What thou now hast
    said
I will keep secret, and no ill result   1115
From this shall come.   But thou, be wise at
    last,
Powerless thyself, to yield before the strong.
    Chor. Lead. Yes, hearken thou!   No gain
        that men can reap
Surpasses forethought and wise-counselled
    mind.
    Elec. Thou hast said nought unlooked for.
        Well I knew   1120
That thou would'st none of all I urged on thee.
Well! I alone, with my own hands, must do
This deed: for void we will not leave it now.
    Chrys. (*ironically*). Would thou had'st had
        this spirit then, when he,
Our father, died!   Great things thou then
    had'st wrought.   1125
    Elec. My nature was the same, though weak
    my mind.
    Chrys. (*ironically again*). Strive, then, to
    have such mind for evermore.
    Elec. Thou giv'st advice as one who will not
    help.

Chrys. 'Tis fit that they who do ill, ill should
    fare.   1129
Elec. I praise thy wit; thy cowardice I hate.
Chrys. Soon I shall have to hear, while thou
    dost praise.
Elec. Thou at my hands shalt never suffer
    that.
Chrys. The long, long future must on this
    decide.
Elec. Away! away!   Thou hast no power to
    help.
Chrys. I have; but thou hast lost the power
    to learn.   1135
Elec. Go then.   Tell all to that thy mother
    there.
Chrys. I do not hate thee with a hate like
    that.
Elec. Yet think to what a shame thou lead-
    est me.
Chrys. No, 'tis not shame, but forethought
    for thy good.
Elec. Must I then follow what thou deemest
    just?   1140
Chrys. When thou art wise, then thou shalt
    take the lead.
Elec. 'Tis strange one speaking well should
    err greatly.
Chrys. Thou hast said well the ill thou
    mak'st thine own.
Elec. What?   Seem I not to thee to speak
    the right?
Chrys. There is a time when even right may
    harm.   1145
Elec. I do not choose to live by laws like that.
Chrys. If this thou dost, thou'lt one day give
    me praise.
Elec. And I will do it, nothing scared by thee.
Chrys. And is it so?   Wilt thou not change
    thy plans?
Elec. Not so; then evil counsel nought is
    worse.   1150
Chrys. Thou seem'st to care for nought of
    all I speak.
Elec. Long since I planned it; 'tis no new
    device.
Chrys. I then must needs depart; thou dar-
    est not
To praise my words, nor I these moods of
    thine.

Elec. Go, then, within: I ne'er will follow
    thee;   1155
No! not though thou should'st wish it eagerly.
To hunt a shadow is a madman's sport.
    Chrys. Nay, then! If thou dost think thou
    reasonest well,
So reason. When thou find'st thyself in
    grief,
Then thou wilt praise my counsels.   1160
        (*Exit* CHRYSOTHEMIS *into the Palace.*

    Chor. Why, when we see on high   (Strophe)
    The birds for wisdom famed [1]
Caring to nourish those from whom they spring,
    From whom they found support,
    Why fail we to requite   1165
    Like boon on equal scale?
But, lo! by Zeus' glaring lightning flash,
    By Themis [2] throned on high,
Not long shall we escape our chastisement.
Ah, Voice that to the central depths of earth   1170
    Dost bear our human deeds,
    Lift up thy wailing speech
To those of Atreus' sons who sleep below,
    Telling of foulest shame,
    Unmeet for choral song.   1175

    Long since their house is sick   (Antistrophe)
    With sorrow's pain, and now
Their children's strife no more may be appeased
    By kindly intercourse.
    Electra, left alone,   1180
    Sails on a troubled sea
Still wailing evermore, with piteous cry,
    The father whom she loved,
Like nightingale whose song is fraught with
    woe
Nor has she any shrinking fear of death,   1185
    Ready to close her eyes
    In darkness as of night
If only she the Erinnys pair [3] destroy.
    Who lives there true in soul
    To noble stock as she?   1190

[1] The storks, who in their care of the older birds displayed the Greek ideal of filial reverence.

[2] Wife of Zeus and also a Titaness, mother of Prometheus.

[3] Clytemnestra and Aegisthus, who, though intensely evil, were yet the instruments of divine vengeance upon the house of Pelops for all its earlier misdeeds.

    None of the great and good   (Str. 2)
    Would lose his ancient name,
And stain his glory by a wretched life.
So thou, my child, my child, did'st choose the fate,
    The fate which all bewail,   1195
    And, having warred with ill,
    Did'st gain, in one brief word,
The good report of daughter wise and best.

    May'st thou, in might and wealth,   (Ant. 2)
    Prevail o'er those thy foes,   1200
As much as now thou liv'st beneath their hands;
For I have found thee, not in high estate
    Wending thy way, yet still,
    In love and fear of Zeus,
    Gaining the foremost prize   1205
In all the laws that best and greatest are.

Enter ORESTES *and* PYLADES, *followed by two
or three Attendants bearing a funeral urn*

    Ores. And did we then, ye women, hear
    aright?
And do we rightly journey where we wish?
    Chor. Lead. What dost thou search? And
    wherefore art thou come?
    Ores. This long time past I seek Aegisthus'
    home.   1210
    Chor. Lead. Thou comest right, and blame-
    less he who told thee.
    Ores. And which of you would tell to those
    within
The longed-for coming of our company?
    Chor. Lead. (*pointing to* ELEC.). She, if 'tis
    fit to call the nearest one.
    Ores. Go then, O maiden, go and tell them
    there,   1215
That certain men from Phocis seek Aegisthus.
    Elec. Ah, wretched me! It cannot be ye
    bring
Clear proofs of that dire rumor which we
    heard?
    Ores. I know not of thy rumor; Strophius
    old   1219
Charged me to bring the news about Orestes.
    Elec. What is it, stranger? Fear creeps
    through my veins.
    Ores. We bring, as thou dost see, in one
    small urn,

All that is left, poor relics of the dead.
   Elec. Ah, me! And this is it! 'Twould
     seem I gaze   1224
On that same burden, clear and close at hand.
   Ores. If thou dost weep Orestes' hapless fate,
Know that this urn doth all his body hold.
   Elec. Ah, stranger! Now by all the Gods, I
     pray,
If this urn hold him, give it in mine hands,
That I my fate and that of all my kin   1230
May wail and weep with these poor ashes here.
   Ores. (*to his Attendants*). Bring it, and give it
     her, whoe'er she be:
At least she does not ask it as in hate,
But is perchance a friend, or near in blood.
   Elec. (*taking the urn in her hands*). O sole
     memorial of his life whom most   1235
Of all alive I loved! Orestes mine,
With other thoughts I sent thee forth than
     these
With which I now receive thee. Now, I bear
In these my hands what is but nothingness;
But sent thee forth, dear boy, in bloom of
     youth.[1]   1240
Ah, would that I long since had ceased to live
Before I sent thee to a distant shore,
With these my hands, and saved thee then from
     death!
So had'st thou perished on that self-same day,
And had a share in that thy father's tomb.
But now from home, an exile in a land   1246
That was not thine, without thy sister near,
So did'st thou die, and I, alas, poor me!
Did neither lay thee out with lustral rites   1249
And loving hands, nor bear thee, as was meet,
Sad burden, from the blazing funeral pyre;
But thou, poor sufferer, tended by the hands
Of strangers, comest, in this paltry urn,
In paltry bulk. Ah, miserable me!
For all the nurture, now so profitless,   1255
Which I was wont with sweetest toil to give
For thee, my brother. Never did she love,
Thy mother, as I loved thee; nor did they
Who dwell within there nurse thee, but 'twas I,
And I was ever called thy sister true;   1260
But now all this has vanished in a day

---

   [1] Orestes, born before Agamemnon went to Troy,
must have been at least eleven or twelve years old when
Electra sent him to Phocis.

In this thy death; for, like a whirlwind, thou
Hast passed, and swept off all. My father
     falls;
I perish; thou thyself hast gone from sight;
Our foes exult. My mother, wrongly named,
For mother she is none, is mad with joy,   1266
Of whom thou oft did'st send word secretly
That thou would'st come and one day show
     thyself
A true avenger. But thine evil fate,   1269
Thine and mine also, hath bereaved me of thee,
And now hath sent, instead of that dear form,
This dust, this shadow, vain and profitless.
          Woe, woe is me!
   O piteous, piteous corpse!
   Thou dearest, who did'st tread   1275
     (Woe, woe is me!)
   Paths full of dread and fear,
   How hast thou brought me low,
Yea, brought me very low, thou dearest one!
Therefore receive thou me to this thine home,
Ashes to ashes, that with thee below   1281
I may from henceforth dwell. When thou wast
     here
I shared with thee an equal lot, and now
I crave in dying not to miss thy tomb;
For those that die I see are freed of grief.   1285
   Chor. Lead. Thou, O Electra, take good heed,
     wast born
Of mortal father, mortal, too, Orestes;
Yield not too much to grief. To suffer thus
Is common lot of all.
   Ores. (*trembling*). Ah, woe is me!   1290
What shall I say? Ah, whither find my way
In words confused? I fail to rule my speech.
   Elec. What grief disturbs thee? Wherefore
     speak'st thou thus?
   Ores. Is this Electra's noble form I see?
   Elec. That self-same form, and sad enough
     its state.   1295
   Ores. Alas, alas, for this sad lot of thine!
   Elec. Surely thou dost not wail, O friend,
     for me?
   Ores. O form most basely, godlessly misused!
   Elec. Thy words ill-omened fall on none but
     me.   1299
   Ores. Alas, for this thy life of lonely woe!
   Elec. Why, in thy care for me, friend, groan-
     est thou?

Ores. How little knew I of my fortune's ills!

Elec. What have I said to throw such light on them?

Ores. Now that I see thee clad with many woes.

Elec. And yet thou see'st but few of all mine ills. 1305

Ores. What could be sadder than all this to see?

Elec. This, that I sit at meat with murderers.

Ores. With whose? What evil dost thou mean by this?

Elec. My father's; next, I'm forced to be their slave.

Ores. And who constrains thee to this loathèd task? 1310

Elec. My mother she is called, no mother like.

Ores. How so? By blows, or life with hardships full?

Elec. Both blows and hardships, and all forms of ill.

Ores. And is there none to help, not one to check?

Elec. No, none. Who was ... thou bringest him as dust. 1315

Ores. O sad one! Long I pitied as I gazed!

Elec. Know, then, that thou alone dost pity me.

Ores. For I alone come suffering woes like thine.

Elec. What? Can it be thou art of kin to us?

Ores. If these are friendly, I could tell thee more. 1320

Elec. Friendly are they; thou'lt speak to faithful ones.

Ores. Put by that urn, that thou may'st hear the whole.

Elec. Ah, by the Gods, O stranger, ask not that.

Ores. Do what I bid thee, and thou shalt not err.

Elec. Nay, by thy beard, of that prize rob me not. 1325

Ores. I may not have it so.

Elec.   Ah me, Orestes,
How wretched I, bereaved of this thy tomb!

Ores. Hush, hush such words: thou hast no cause for wailing.

Elec. Have I no cause, who mourn a brother's death? 1330

Ores. Thou hast no call to utter speech like this.

Elec. Am I then deemed unworthy of the dead?

Ores. Of none unworthy. This is nought to thee.

Elec. Yet if I hold Orestes' body here ...

Ores. 'Tis not Orestes' save in show of speech. 1335

Elec. Where, then, is that poor exile's sepulchre?

Ores. Nay, of the living there's no sepulchre.

Elec. What say'st thou, boy?

Ores.   No falsehood what I say.

Elec. And does he live? 1340

Ores.   He lives, if I have life.

Elec. What? Art thou he?

Ores.   Look thou upon this seal,
My father's once, and learn if I speak truth.

Elec. O blessed light! 1345

Ores.   Most blessed, I too own.

Elec. O voice! And art thou come?

Ores.   No longer learn
Thy news from others.

Elec.   And I have thee here, 1350
Here in my grasp?

Ores.   So may'st thou always have me!

Elec. O dearest friends, my fellow-citizens,
Look here on this Orestes, dead indeed 1354
In feigned craft, and by that feigning saved.

Chor. Lead. We see it, daughter; and at what has chanced
A tear of gladness trickles from our eyes.

Elec. *O offspring, offspring of a form most dear,*
Ye came, ye came at last,
Ye found us, yea, ye came, 1360
Ye saw whom ye desired.

Ores. *Yes, we are come. Yet wait and hold thy peace.*

Elec. *What now?*

Ores. *Silence is best, lest some one hear within.*

Elec. *Nay, nay. By Artemis,* 1365
The ever-virgin One,[1]
I shall not deign to dread

[1] The goddess of wild nature, the virgin huntress, who is associated with the moon.

Those women there within,
With worthless burden still
Cumbering the ground.   1370
  Ores. *See to it, for in women too there lives*
The strength of battle. Thou hast proved it well.
  Elec. (sobbing). *Ah, ah! Ah me!*
There thou hast touched upon a woe unveiled,
    That knows no healing, no,   1375
    Nor ever may be hid.
  Ores. *I know it well. But, when occasion bids,*
Then should we call those deeds to memory.
  Elec. *All time for me is fit,*
    Yea, all, to speak of this,   1380
    With wrath as it deserves;
Till now I had scant liberty of speech.
  Ores. *There we are one. Preserve, then, what*
    thou hast.
  Elec. *And what, then, shall I do?*
  Ores.   *When time serves not,*   1385
    Speak not o'ermuch.
  Elec.   *And who then worthily,*
    Now thou art come, would choose
    Silence instead of speech?
For lo! I see thee now unlooked, unhoped for.
  Ores. *Then thou did'st see me here,*   1391
    When the Gods urged my coming.
  Elec.   *Thou hast said*
What mounts yet higher than thy former boon,
    If God has sent thee forth   1395
    To this our home; I deem
    The work as Heaven's own deed.
  Ores. *Loth am I to restrain thee in thy joy,*
And yet I fear delight o'ermasters thee.   1399
  Elec. *O thou who after many a weary year*
    At last hast deigned to come,
    (Oh, coming of great joy!)
    Do not, thus seeing me
    Involved in many woes, . . .   1404
  Ores. *What is it that thou ask'st me not to do?*
  Elec. *Deprive me not, nor force me to forego*
The joy supreme of looking on thy face.
  Ores. *I should be wroth with others who would*
    force thee.
  Elec. *Dost thou consent, then?*
  Ores.   *How act otherwise?*   1410
  Elec. *Ah, friends, I heard a voice*
Which never had I dreamt would come to me;
Then I kept in my dumb and passionate mood,
    Nor cried I, as I heard;

But now I have thee; thou hast come to me   1415
With face most precious, dear to look upon,
Which e'en in sorrow I can ne'er forget.
  Ores. *All needless words pass over. Tell me*
    not
My mother's shame, nor how Aegisthus drains
My father's wealth, much wastes, and scatters
    much;   1420
Much speech might lose occasion's golden hour;
But what fits in to this our present need,
That tell me, where, appearing or concealed,
We best shall check our boasting enemies,
In this our enterprise; so when we twain   1425
Go to the palace, look to it, that she note not,
Thy mother, by thy blither face, our coming,
But mourn as for that sorrow falsely told.
When we have prospered, then shalt thou have
    leave
Freely to smile, and joy exultingly.   1430
  Elec. Yes, brother dear! Whatever pleaseth
    thee,
That shall be my choice also, since my joy
I had not of mine own, but gained from thee,
Nor would I cause thee e'en a moment's pain,
Myself to reap much profit. I should fail,
So doing, to work His will who favors us.   1436
What meets us next, thou knowest, dost thou
    not?
Aegisthus, as thou hearest, gone from home;
My mother there within, of whom fear not
Lest she should see my face look blithe with
    joy;   1440
For my old hatred eats into my soul,
And, since I've seen thee, I shall never cease
To weep for very joy. How could I cease,
Who in this one short visit looked on thee
Dead, and alive again? Strange things to-day
Hast thou wrought out, so strange that should
    there come   1446
My father, in full life, I should not deem
'Twas a mere marvel, but believe I saw him.
But, since thou com'st on such an enterprise,
Rule thou as pleases thee. Were I alone,   1450
I had not failed of two alternatives,
Or nobly had I saved myself, or else
Had nobly perished.
  Ores.   Silence now is best;
I hear the steps of some one from within,   1455
As if approaching.

Elec. (*in a loud voice*).　Enter in, my friends,
On many grounds, and chiefly that ye bring,
What none will send away, yet none receive
With any touch of pleasure.　　　　　1460

Enter Aged ATTENDANT *of* ORESTES *from the Palace*

Attend.　　　　　　　　O ye fools,
And blind, bereaved of counsel, care ye now
No longer for your lives? or is there not
Your mother-wit still with you?　Know ye not
Ye stand — I say not on the very verge,　1465
But in the ills — the greatest ills themselves?
Had I not chanced long since to keep my watch
Just at the gate, your doings had been known
There, in the house, before your forms were
　　seen.
But, as it is, I guarded against this;　1470
And now, set free from all this flood of talk,
Free from this girl's insatiate burst of joy,
Go ye within.　In such a deed delay
Is evil, and 'tis time to end with it.
Ores.　How stand things there for me to go
　　within?　　　　　　　　　　　1475
Attend.　Right well! for none is found who
　　knows thee there.
Ores.　'Twould seem that thou hast told of
　　me as dead.
Attend.　Know thou art here as one to Hades
　　gone.
Ores.　Do they rejoice in this?　What words
　　were said?
Attend.　When all is o'er, I'll tell thee.　As it
　　is,　　　　　　　　　　　　1480
All is well with them, even what is ill.
Elec.　Who is this, brother?　Tell me, by the
　　Gods.
Ores.　Dost thou not know?
Elec.　　　　　　I call him not to mind.
Ores.　Know'st thou not him whose hands
　　thou gav'st me to?　　　　　　1485
Elec.　To whom?　What say'st thou?
Ores.　　　　　　Even he, who brought me
Through thy wise forethought, to the Phocian
　　plain.
Elec.　What?　Is this he, whom only, out of
　　many,　　　　　　　　　　1489
I faithful found when they our father slew?

Ores.　'Tis he: waste no more words in ques-
　　tioning.
Elec.　O blessed light, O thou preserver sole
Of Agamemnon's house, how cam'st thou here?
And art thou he who then did rescue him　1494
And me from many sorrows?　O dear hands,
And thou that did'st thy feet's glad ministry,
How was it that so long thou stayed'st with me,
And yet did'st 'scape my ken, did'st not ap-
　　pear,
But did'st in words destroy me, bringing acts
Most full of joy?　Hail, O my father, hail,
(For sure, I think I see a father's face,)　1501
Hail, once again, and know that this one day
Above all men I hated thee and loved.
Attend.　This is enough, methinks.　What
　　lies between
Full many a day and many a circling night
Shall show thee plain, Electra.　　　1506
(*To* ORES. *and* PYL.)　But you twain,
There standing by, I call to act, for now
The time is come.　Now Clytemnestra sits
Alone.　Now no man is within.　Think
　　well,　　　　　　　　　　1510
If ye hold back, that ye will have to fight
With these and others craftier far than they.
Ores.　No longer is it time for lengthened
　　speech,
My Pylades, but with swift foot to press　1514
Within, when first we have adored the shrines
Of all the ancestral Gods who guard these
　　gates.
　　　　(*Exeunt* ORESTES *and* PYLADES *into
　　　　the Palace.*
Elec.　O King Apollo, hear them graciously,
And hear me also, who of what I had
Have stood before thee with a liberal hand;
And now Lyceian king, Apollo, hear;　1520
With all I have I kneel, pray, supplicate;
Be Thou the gracious helper of our plans,
And show to all men how the Gods bestow
Their due rewards on all impiety.
　　　　　　　　(*Exit into the Palace.*
Chor.　*See ye, where Ares,*[1]　*breathing slaughter
　　still,*　　　　　　(Strophe)　1525
　　　Speeds on his onward way,
　　　Slaughter that none may check;
E'en at this very hour, beneath the roof,
　　[1] God of war, and son of Zeus and Hera.

They go who track all evil deeds of guile,
   The hounds whom none escape;   1530
And lo! my soul's dream doth not tarry long,
   Floating in wild suspense;

For now beneath the roof-tree he has passed,
              (Antistrophe)
   The avenger of the dead,
   Treading with subtle feet,   1535
E'en to his father's high ancestral halls,
And in his hands bears slaughter newly edged;
   And Hermes, Maia's[1] son,
Hiding their counsel, leads them to the goal,
   Leads on, and tarries not.   1540

Enter ELECTRA *from the Palace*

Elec. *Now, dearest friends, the men stand*
   there within,[2]
And do their deed. But hush: In silence wait.
   Chor. How is't? What do they?
   Elec.   *She prepares an urn*
For sepulture, and those two stand hard by 1545
   Chor. Why did'st thou rush without?
   Elec.   *To stand on guard,*
That so Aegisthus, if he home return,
May not escape our notice.
   Clytem. (within).   *Woe! Oh, woe!* 1550
   O house bereaved of friends,
   And full of them that slay!
   Elec. A cry goes up within; friends, hear ye
   not?
   Chor. I heard what none should hear, ah
   misery!
And shuddered listening.   1555
   Clytem. (within). *Ah me! Ah me! Woe,*
   Woe!
Aegisthus, where art thou?
   Elec.   *Ha! List again,*
I hear a bitter cry.
   Clytem. (within). *My son, my son,*   1560
Have pity on thy mother!
   Elec.   *Thou had'st none*
On him, nor on the father that begat him.

---

[1] The eldest and most beautiful of the Pleiades, who were the seven daughters of Atlas and Pleione.
[2] Ll. 1541–1597 form a peculiarly complicated *kommos*, or lyric interlude, sung in alternating parts; for several different actors, as well as the invisible Clytemnestra, alternate with the chorus.

Chor. O land! O miserable race! Thy doom
Each day is "perish, perish utterly."   1565
   Clytem. (within). *Ah! I am smitten.*
   Elec.   *Smite her yet again,*
If thou hast strength for it.
   Clytem. (within).   *Ah, blow on blow!*
   Elec. Would that Aegisthus shared them.
   Chor.   *Yes. The curse* 1570
Is now fulfilled. The buried live again;
For they who died long since now drain in turn
The blood of those that slew them.

Enter ORESTES *and* PYLADES *from the Palace*

         See! They come; 1575
And lo! their crimsoned hands drip drops of gore
Poured out to Ares; and I dare not blame.
   Elec. How fare ye now, Orestes?
   Ores.   *All within*
Is well, if well Apollo prophesied.   1580
   Elec. And is she dead, vile wretch?
   Ores.   *Yes. Fear thou not,*
Thy mother's mood shall e'er shame thee again.
   Chor. Hush! For I see Aegisthus full in
   sight.
   Elec.   *Back, back, ye boys!* 1585
   Ores. And where see ye this man?
   Elec. He from the suburbs comes upon us now,
Rejoicing.
   Chor.   *Go, full speed, behind the doors,*
That ye, one work well done, may yet again. . . .
   Ores. Take courage, we will act. . . .   1590
   Elec.   *Now speed thy plans.*
   Ores. I then am gone.
     (Exeunt ORESTES *and* PYLADES *into*
     the Palace.
   Elec.   *What meets us next is mine.*
   Chor. 'Twere good to speak to this man in his
   ear   1595
But few words, very gently, that he rush
Into the hidden struggle of his doom.

Enter AEGISTHUS

Aegis. Who knows of you where they, from
   Phocis come,
May now be found, who bring, they tell me,
   news   1599
That our Orestes has breathed out his last,

In wreck of chariot-storm? (*To* ELEC.) Thee,
    thee, I ask —
Yes, thee, still wont to be of old so brave.
As I suppose it touches thee the most,
So thou, knowing most, may'st tell me what I
    seek.
    Elec. I know. How else? Could I then
    stand aloof   1605
From that dear chance of those who most are
    mine?
    Aegis. Where are the strangers, then? Tell
    this to me.
    Elec. Within; for they have found a loving
    hostess.
    Aegis. And did they say distinctly he was
    dead?
    Elec. Ah no! They showed him, not in
    words alone.   1610
    Aegis. And is he here, that we may see him
    plain?
    Elec. 'Tis here, a most unwelcome sight to
    see.
    Aegis. Against thy wont thou giv'st me joy
    indeed.
    Elec. Thou may'st rejoice, if this be ground
    of joy.
    Aegis. I bid you hush, and open wide the
    gates,   1615
That all of Argos and Mycenae see.
So, if there be that once were lifted up,
With hopes they had, vain hopes they fixed on
    him.
Now seeing him dead, they may receive my
    curb,
And, finding me their master, sense may gain,
Without coercion.   1621
    Elec.   Yea, my task indeed
Is done; for I at last have wisdom gained,
To work with those more mighty.

The doors of the Palace are thrown open, and dis-
    close ORESTES *and* PYLADES *standing by*
    the dead body of CLYTEMNESTRA, *covered*
    with a sheet and a veil over the face

    Aegis.   Lo, I see,   1625
O Zeus, a form that lies there, fallen low,
Not without wrath of Heaven (should that
    word stir
Heaven's jealousy, I wish it all unsaid).

Withdraw the veil which hides the face, that I
To kindred blood may pay the meed of
    tears.   1630
    Ores. Do thou uplift it. 'Tis thy task, not
    mine,
To look on this, and kindly words to speak.
    Aegis. Thou giv'st good counsel, and I list
    to thee.
(*To* ELEC.) And thou, if yet she tarries in the
    house,
Call Clytemnestra.   1635
    Ores. (*as* AEGISTHUS *lifts the veil*). Here she
    lies before thee!
Seek her not elsewhere.
    Aegis.   Oh, what sight is this!
    Ores. Whom fearest thou? Who is't thou
    dost not know?
    Aegis. Into whose snares, whose closely-
    tangled mesh,   1641
Have I, poor victim, fallen?
    Ores.   See'st not yet
That thou did'st greet the living as the dead?
    Aegis. Ah me! I catch thy words. It needs
    must be
This is Orestes who now speaks to me.   1645
    Ores. Wert thou then tricked, who dost di-
    vine so well?
    Aegis. I then am lost, woe's me! yet let me
    speak
One little word.
    Elec.   Give him no leave to speak,
By all the Gods, my brother, nor to spin   1650
His long discourse. When men are plunged in
    ills,
What gain can one who stands condemned to
    die
Reap from delay? No, slay him out of hand,
And, having slain him, cast him forth, to find
Fit burial at their hands from whom 'tis
    meet   1655
That he should have it, far away from view.
Thus only shall I gain a remedy
For all the evils of the years gone by.
    Ores. (*to* AEGIS.). Go thou within, and
    quickly. Now our strife
Is not of words, but for thy life itself.   1660
    Aegis. Why dost thou force me in? If this
    be right,
What need of darkness? Why not slay at once?

Ores. Give thou no orders, but where thou
    did'st slay
My father, go, that thou too there may'st
    die.
Aegis. Is it then doomed this house should
    see the ills   1665
Of Pelops' line, both present and to come?
Ores. Yes, thine: of that, at least, I'm pro-
    phet true.
Aegis. The skill thou boastest came not from
    thy sire.
Ores. Still thou dost bandy many idle words,
And length'nest out the way. Move on. 1670
Aegis.   Lead thou.
Ores. Not so. Thou must go first.

Aegis.   Dost think I'll flee?
Ores. Thou must not die the death thou
    would'st desire;
I needs must make it bitter. Doom like
    this   1675
Should fall on all who dare transgress the laws,
The doom of death. Then wickedness no more
Would multiply its strength.

    (*Exeunt* ELECTRA, ORESTES, *and* AE-
       GISTHUS *into the Palace, and the*
       doors close.

Chor. O seed of Atreus, after many woes,
Thou hast come forth, thy freedom hardly won,
By this emprise made perfect!   1681
                    (*Exeunt.*

INTRODUCTION TO

Alcestis

Euripides: The Decline of Attic Tragedy: Alcestis and the Attic Satyr-Play

EURIPIDES

THE brilliant accomplishments of Aeschylus and Sophocles in Attic tragedy temporarily obscured the genius of a third master, Euripides. Probably not until the last decade of his life did Athenians fully realize that they had in their midst another tragedian worthy to rank with his two great predecessors. From that time on, however, his reputation rose steadily throughout the ancient world until a century after his death it surpassed that of Aeschylus and Sophocles.

Euripides, son of Mnesarchides and Clito, was born on the island of Salamis in 480 B.C., presumably upon the very day of the great battle there between the Greek and Persian fleets. His parents were people of means and high social standing in the town of Phlya, about six miles northeast of Athens. He enjoyed the usual education of privileged Athenian youth, which included athletics, and he seems to have excelled in boxing. He began life as a painter, so it is said, but soon he must have shifted his professional interest to dramatic poetry. In 455 B.C. — when Aeschylus was just dead, Sophocles forty years old, and Euripides twenty-five — the latter was permitted for the first time to compete in the tragedy contest, but got only the third and lowest prize.

Success, in fact, came slowly. It was fifteen years before Euripides carried off the first prize at the Dionysia. After another long interval of twelve years, he won his second victory in 428 with *Hippolytus*. During the remainder of his career he secured the first prize on two or three occasions. One of his victories took place after his death when his youngest son, Euripides, produced a trio of the father's last tragedies.

Of Euripides' private life and character little is known with certainty. Unlike the two other great tragedians he apparently took small part in public affairs. He may have served as an Athenian ambassador to Sicily subsequent to the disastrous expedition of 413 B.C. He seems to have confined himself pretty much to his literary work. According to several historians, he had a habit of retiring now and then to a cave on Salamis which offered a lovely vista towards the sea. There he would spend the days in meditation and writing. An earnest student, he owned what was for the Athens of that period a very large private library. His circle of acquaintance included prominent thinkers like Anaxagoras and Socrates. Yet none of them could claim him as a follower, for he drew his ideas from many sources. His philosophical turn of mind was so well recognized that contemporaries spoke of him as the "Stage Philosopher."

Despite his concentration on a literary career Euripides was no more prolific a playwright than Aeschylus or Sophocles. Records of seventy-four Euripidean dramas exist. Nineteen of his plays have come down to modern times in complete form — more than survive of Aeschylus and Sophocles together. This large number tells its own story of Euripides' relative popularity. Among his chief extant works are the following: *Alcestis*, 438 B.C.; *Medea*, 431; *Hippolytus*, 428; *The Trojan Women*, c. 415; *Iphigenia among the Taurians*, c. 414; *Electra*, c. 413; *Iphigenia in Aulis*, c. 405; *The Bacchae*, c. 405; *Cyclops*. The last named is the only complete specimen of the Attic satyr drama known. None of Euripides' very early plays remain. On the other hand, the very late compositions have survived in large measure. When viewed in chronological order, his extant writings do not give evidence of any such consistent advancement in dramatic art as is to be observed in the work of Aeschylus and Sophocles.

Toward the end of his life Euripides went to Macedonia, where King Archelaus treated him with great distinction. Whether he went on invitation, or as a result of some unpleasant experience in Athens cannot ever be settled. At all events he died in Macedonia during the year 406 B.C. His death came about by a sad accident. One day when he had gone walking by himself in the woods near the city, the king came out hunting with his dogs. As soon as they were released to search for game, they darted off, came upon Euripides, attacked, and killed him before the royal party arrived on the scene. Though the Athenians sent an embassy to bring his body back to Greece, the Macedonians refused to give it up and buried it near Arethusa. The Athenians then erected a cenotaph to Euripides on the great road from Athens to its seaport, Piraeus.

THE DECLINE OF ATTIC TRAGEDY

It is a strange coincidence that Sophocles and Euripides should die in the same year, 406 B.C. With their passing the decline of the Athenian tragic stage began. Already the religious significance originally attached to Attic tragedy had nearly disappeared. Soon the tradition became wholly secular, while the content degenerated into sentimental melodrama. During the fifth century the prize plays had never been performed more than once at Athens, except for an occasional repetition of an Aeschylean tragedy in honor of the pioneer master. So poor, however, grew the fare of new plays provided by the Athenian tragedians in the fourth century that the festival programs had to be filled out regularly by revivals of the old tragedies. For this purpose a play of Euripides was selected in three successive years, 342–340 B.C., and reproduced at the Dionysia. This is but one of many records concerning that decadent custom. Significantly enough, not a single Attic tragedy written subsequent to 400 B.C. was saved for posterity.

By the second century B.C. the tragic pattern had changed to such an extent that the element of the chorus was entirely discarded. Despite this revolutionary innovation, tragedy at Athens continued to wane until it disappeared altogether about the beginning of the fifth century A.D. For eight centuries it died a slow death after one century of brilliant flowering.

"ALCESTIS" AND THE ATTIC SATYR-PLAY

Of all the extant plays by Euripides *Alcestis* is the oldest and the most distinctive. It was written as the fourth play of a tragic tetralogy, the three others being *The Cretan Women*, *Alcmaeon at Psophis*, and *Telephus*. This group won the second prize at the Dionysia of 438 B.C., where Sophocles emerged the first-prize victor with plays now unknown.

The rule for the Dionysia contest was that after the three tragedies proper there should follow as a kind of dramatic relief a fourth play of quite different type, called a "satyr-play." Euripides, however, composed *Alcestis* to take the place, in his tetralogy, of the customary satyr-play. This was a rare but not unique dramatic experiment among the Attic playwrights. *Alcestis*, however, is the only surviving example. Its unusual pattern arises from the special rôle which it had to play on the festival program.

Alcestis, to be sure, contains the more notable characteristics of Euripides' tragic design. His prologues do not start the action so much as relate the preceding events in the story which forms the play's subject. They are opened with long speeches, delivered usually by a character who is little evident in the subsequent scenes. In *Alcestis* the god Apollo performs this function and then does not enter again.

The conclusion of an Euripidean drama generally comes about through the notorious device of *deus ex machina*, that is, the arbitrary introduction of a god from heaven to cut the knot, so to speak. In *Alcestis* the god, Heracles (or Hercules), does not appear direct from on high, but he does intervene and save Admetus from the loss of his wife.

The rôle of the chorus is even more lyrical in the tragedy of Euripides than in that of Aeschylus. Euripides almost turns the choral songs into *entr'acte* music. In many of his pieces the beauty of these odes constitutes the outstanding feature. They represent at their best the meditations of a deeply poetic spirit impressed with life's uncertainty. The choral recessional in *Alcestis* sets forth a typical Euripidean sentiment about human fortunes. In this sentiment there lurks a mild disillusionment.

In spite of these tragic characteristics, *Alcestis* exhibits the most unusual pattern in all Attic serious drama. Even the ancient Greeks perceived its marked individuality. One of their critics left behind this apt comment: "The play is somewhat satyr-like. It ends in rejoicing and gladness contrary to the convention of tragedy." There is no doubt that the traditions of Attic satyr drama much influenced Euripides in his shaping of *Alcestis*.

The Attic satyr-play descended directly from one type of dithyrambic performance at the folk festivals in honor of Dionysus. In this type the chorus sang and danced, dressed in the garb of satyrs. Fantastic-looking creatures, half-human, half-animal, the satyrs were the joyous undisciplined attendants of Dionysus. The choral singers who impersonated such beings wore pointed ears, and goatskin loincloths with horse-tails attached at the rear, and no other clothing. Exuberant buffoonery characterized both the songs and the actions of the satyr chorus.

From these primitive dramatic elements Pratinas sometime late in the sixth century B.C. developed the satyr-play. He abbreviated the part of the satyr chorus, but still allowed the choral singing to predominate. He introduced a slight plot in the shape of a humorous saga about Dionysus, and made the god the chief speaker-actor. The diction somewhat imitated the tragic style. The burlesque tone of the whole performance rendered such language properly absurd.

In the Dionysia of 501 B.C. the satyr-play became established as the finale of the long tragic programs. The Athenian audience welcomed with relief the antics of the satyrs and the jovial simplicity of the plot. Thereafter the satyr-play, like tragedy, underwent further development. Other heroes supplanted Dionysus, as numerous myths which tragedy drew on were gradually appropriated for the satyr-play too. Heracles especially proved an ideal satyric or reveling hero.   By a process of gradual refining the action and the dialogue lost most of whatever brutality and lewdness they once possessed.   At the same time the satyr-play still retained the burlesque character of heroic farce.

Certain elements in *Alcestis* were clearly derived from the satyr-plays.   One of the chief characters in Euripides' composition is Heracles, the heroic reveler of satyr drama. His jovial behavior and talk with the manservant (ll. 842–73) are particularly in keeping with that conception of him.   He shows himself a hearty fellow throughout, never the refined actor of conventional tragedy.   Another character from the satyric world is Thanatos (or Death) who appears not as a mighty god but as a mere sheriff from Hades, a kind of bogeyman whom Heracles, the great killer, rejoices in destroying.

The plot of *Alcestis* Euripides borrowed from a lost satyr-play by Phrynichus.   It was a fantastic and grotesque saga of immortality by special privilege, of battling with Death, and of resurrection from the dead — perfect raw material for a gross and boisterous drama.   *Alcestis*, however, while preserving the main details of the old story, presents the whole affair in a new and refined light.

Though Euripides refined the material of the Alcestis saga by subjecting it to sensitive psychological judgment, the satyr-play tradition greatly affected his treatment of the characters.   He had to take into account the nature of the piece for which *Alcestis* was to be substituted.   It would not be appropriate to supply a wholly serious drama.   He might handle his characters with sympathy and yet he must make them somewhat amusing.   He proceeded therefore with a faint touch of satire.   The portrait of Admetus most clearly illustrates this fundamental tone.   The king soon reveals himself as an egoist, an unconscious hypocrite, an impulsive, hospitable, sentimental person. Euripides, always kindly, exposes Admetus thoroughly in the scenes with Pheres and Alcestis, but does not permit him to become downright ridiculous.   Toward the end of the play, in fact, the king commands a moderate respect because of the self-discovery he seems to have achieved.   Yet the total impression of the man provokes a mild smile. Pheres, a proud, stubborn old aristocrat, tenacious of life, and Heracles, a lusty fighter and blustering guest, both bring forth a gentle chuckle.   Even the lovely Alcestis is amusing in her unreflective devotion, her businesslike arranging of her husband's and her children's future, and her traces of wifely jealousy.

This quality of delicate amusement dominates the whole play.   There are, of course, moments of pathos as when the children of Admetus bid farewell to their mother and she then dies.   Nevertheless, a light touch of irony plays over these apparently serious scenes.   Euripides does not intensify unduly his character effects; at the same time he does suggest the underlying comedy of his personages.   It is the normal, but absurd mixture of nobility and pettiness, of intelligence and stupidity, which makes them essentially interesting creatures.

The fascinating characterization obscures the incredibility of the plot.   The combination of fantasy and psychological realism, blended with thoughtful humor, gives a peculiar charm to *Alcestis*.   The Greeks, with somewhat rigid notions of form, perhaps found it a strange play.   Modern taste forgets the strangeness and delights in the vitality of its drama.

[For critiques on Euripides, see Gilbert Murray, *Euripides and His Age* (1912); W. N. Bates, *Euripides* (1930).]

EURIPIDES

Alcestis

[*Translated by* GILBERT MURRAY]

DRAMATIS PERSONAE

APOLLO

THANATOS (DEATH)

HERACLES (HERCULES)

ADMETUS, *King of Pherae*

ALCESTIS, *his wife*

PHERES, *father of* ADMETUS, *formerly king*

TWO CHILDREN, *son and daughter of* ADMETUS

A MAN SERVANT

A HANDMAID

CHORUS *of Elders of Pherae*

ARGUMENT

Phoebus Apollo had by the nymph Coronis a son, Asclepius, who became the god of medicine and healing. Asclepius presumed to transgress divine law and to raise from the dead a mortal, Hippolytus, who came to life in Italy. In anger Zeus struck down Asclepius with a thunderbolt forged by the Cyclops. Whereupon Apollo, enraged at the part which these Titans had played in the death of his son, slew them. For this deed of revenge Zeus condemned Apollo to descend from Olympus, lay his godhead aside, and serve for an appointed time as herdsman to Admetus, King of Pherae in Thessaly. Sometime after Apollo had completed his term of service with him, Admetus married Alcestis, daughter of Pelias, King of Iolcus, but on his wedding day he offended the goddess Artemis and was doomed to die. Now Apollo, grateful for the kind treatment of his former master, came to his assistance, reconciled him with Artemis, and secured from the Fates this boon for Admetus: that when his hour of death should come, they should accept in ransom for his life the life of whosoever should have previously consented to die in his place. None of Admetus' kin, however, would offer to be his ransom. Then Alcestis, in accord with the Greek ideal of wifely devotion, pledged herself to die for her husband. Finally the fateful day arrived when she must render up her life, and Death made his appearance at the palace to obtain his victim. But in this very hour Heracles, son of Zeus, stopped his journeying to seek hospitality from Admetus. For his host he wrought a great deliverance and turned mourning into joy.

The Scene represents the Palace or ancient Castle of ADMETUS *near Pherae* [1] *in Thessaly*

Enter from the Castle APOLLO, *radiant, as god of sunlight. He turns and looks back at the Castle*

Apol.[2] Admetus' House! 'Twas here I bowed my head
Of old, and chafed not at the bondman's bread,
Though born in heaven. Aye, Zeus to death had hurled
My son, Asclepius, Healer of the World,
Piercing with fire his heart; and in mine ire   5
I slew his Cyclop [3] churls, who forged the fire.
Whereat Zeus cast me forth to bear the yoke
Of service to a mortal. To this folk
I came, and watched a stranger's herd for pay,
And all his house I have prospered to this day.
For innocent was the Lord I chanced upon   11
And clean as mine own heart, King Pheres' son,
Admetus. Him I rescued from the grave,
Beguiling the Grey Sisters [4] till they gave
A great oath that Admetus should go free,   15
Would he but pay to Them Below in fee
Another living soul. Long did he prove
All that were his, and all that owed him love,
But never a soul he found would yield up life
And leave the sunlight for him, save his wife:
Who, even now, down the long galleries   21
Is borne, death-wounded; for this day it is
She needs must pass out of the light and die.
And, seeing the stain of death must not come nigh
My radiance, I must leave this house I love.   25
   But ha! The Headsman of the Pit, above
Earth's floor, to ravish her! Aye, long and late
He hath watched, and cometh at the fall of fate.

[1] One of the most ancient cities of Thessaly; it was situated not far from the famous Mount Pelion in the southeast corner of Pelasgiotis. The modern town of Velestino stands on its site; the remains of Pherae's walls are still to be seen.

[2] In all but two of his extant plays Euripides begins with a monologue, put in the mouth of one of the dramatis personae or of some other person, and explaining the position of affairs when the play opens.

[3] The Cyclops were three Titans who derived their name from the single, round eye in the middle of their foreheads.

[4] The three Fates, Clotho, Lachesis, and Atropos, whom Apollo is said to have intoxicated and then persuaded to his will.

Enter from the side THANATOS, *a crouching black-haired and winged figure, carrying a drawn sword. He starts in revulsion on seeing* APOLLO

Than. Aha!
Why here? What mak'st thou at the gate,   30
Thou Thing of Light? Wilt overtread
The eternal judgment, and abate
And spoil the portions of the dead?
'Tis not enough for thee to have blocked
In other days Admetus' doom   35
With craft of magic wine, which mocked
The three grey Sisters of the Tomb;
   But now once more
I see thee stand at watch, and shake
That arrow-armèd hand to make   40
This woman thine, who swore, who swore,
To die now for her husband's sake.
Apol. Fear not.
I bring fair words and seek but what is just.
Than. (*sneering*). And if words help thee not, an arrow must?   45
Apol. 'Tis ever my delight to bear this bow.
Than. And aid this house unjustly? Aye, 'tis so.
Apol. I love this man, and grieve for his dismay.
Than. And now wilt rob me of my second prey!
Apol. I never robbed thee, neither then nor now.   50
Than. Why is Admetus here then, not below?
Apol. He gave for ransom his own wife, for whom . . .
Than. (*interrupting*). I am come; and straight will bear her to the tomb.
Apol. Go, take her. — I can never move thine heart.
Than. (*mocking*). To slay the doomed? — Nay; I will do my part.   55
Apol. No. To keep death for them that linger late.
Than. (*still mocking*). 'Twould please thee, so? . . . I owe thee homage great.
Apol. Ah, then she may yet . . . she may yet grow old?
Than. (*with a laugh*). No! . . . I too have my rights, and them I hold.

Apol. 'Tis but one life thou gainest either-
    wise.   60
Than. When young souls die, the richer is
    my prize.
Apol. Old, with great riches they will bury
    her.
Than. Fie on thee, fie! Thou rich-man's
    lawgiver!
Apol. How? Is there wit in Death, who
    seemed so blind?
Than. The rich would buy long life for all
    their kind.   65
Apol. Thou wilt not grant me, then, this
    boon? 'Tis so?
Than. Thou knowest me, what I am: I tell
    thee, no!
Apol. I know gods sicken at thee and men
    pine.
Than. Begone! Too many things not
    meant for thine   69
Thy greed hath conquered; but not all, not all!
Apol. I swear, for all thy bitter pride, a fall
Awaits thee. One even now comes conquering
Towards this house, sent by a southland king
To fetch him four wild coursers, of the race
Which rend men's bodies in the winds of
    Thrace.   75
This house shall give him welcome good, and he
Shall wrest this woman from thy worms and
    thee,
So thou shalt give me all, and thereby win
But hatred, not the grace that might have been.
    (*Exit* APOLLO.
Than. Talk on, talk on! Thy threats shall
    win no bride   80
From me. — This woman, whatsoe'er betide,
Shall lie in Hades' house. Even at the word
I go to lay upon her hair my sword.[1]
For all whose head this grey sword visiteth   84
To death are hallowed and the Lords of death.
    (*Exit into the Castle.*

Enter the CHORUS *of Elders of Pherae*

Chor. Lead. Quiet, quiet, above, beneath! [2]

---

[1] I.e., like the priest officiating at a sacrifice, who cuts
off a lock of the victim's hair before the commencement
of the actual sacrifice.

[2] The passages throughout this play in italics were the
sung portions.

1 Eld. The house of Admetus holds its breath.
2 Eld. And never a King's friend near,
To tell us either of tears to shed
For Pelias' daughter,[1] crowned and dead;   90
Or joy, that her eyes are clear.
Bravest, truest of wives is she
That I have seen or the world shall see.

Divers Cits. (conversing). —[2] *Hear ye no sob,*
    or noise of hands   (Strophe)
    Beating the breast? No mourners' cries   95
    For one they cannot save?
— Nothing: and at the door there stands
    No handmaid. — Help, O Paian;[3] rise,
    O star beyond the wave!

— Dead, and this quiet? No, it cannot be   100
— Dead, dead! — Not gone to burial secretly!
— Why? I still fear: what makes your speech so
    brave?
— Admetus cast that dear wife to the grave
    Alone, with none to see?

— I see no bowl of clear spring water.   105
    (Antistrophe)
    It ever stands before the dread
    Door where a dead man rests.[4]
— No lock of shorn hair![5] Every daughter
    Of woman shears it for the dead.
    No sound of bruisèd breasts!   110

— Yet 'tis this very day . . . — This very day?
— The Queen should pass and lie beneath the
    clay.
— It hurts my life, my heart! — All honest
    hearts
    Must sorrow for a brightness that departs,
    A good life worn away.   115
Lead. To wander o'er leagues of land, (Str. 2)
To search over wastes of sea,

---

[1] Alcestis.

[2] The dashes here and hereafter in the choral sections
indicate new speakers.

[3] "O Healer," a cry for help and an epithet of Apollo.

[4] It was customary for the Greeks to place an earthen
vessel of spring water before the door of the house
wherein a dead body was lying, so that those who visited there might sprinkle themselves on leaving and so
avoid pollution from the corpse.

[5] A lock of hair was hung up at the vestibule of the
house in token of affliction within.

Where the Prophets of Lycia stand,
Or where Ammon's daughters three
Make runes in the rainless sand,[1]   120
   For magic to make her free —
     Ah, vain! for the end is here;
     Sudden it comes and sheer.
What lamb on the altar-strand
   Stricken shall comfort me?   125
2 Eld. Only, only one, I know: (Ant. 2)
   Apollo's son was he,[2]
Who healed men long ago.
   Were he but on earth to see,
She would rise from the dark below   130
   And the gates of eternity.
     For men whom the Gods had slain
     He pitied and raised again;
Till God's fire laid him low,
   And now, what help have we?   135
Others. All's done that can be.   *Every vow*
                       (Epode)
Full paid; and every altar's brow
Full crowned with spice of sacrifice.
No help remains nor respite now.

Enter from the Castle a HANDMAID, *almost
in tears*

Lead. But see, a handmaid cometh, and the
    tear   140
Wet on her cheek! What tiding shall we
    hear? . . .
Thy grief is natural, daughter, if some ill
Hath fallen today. Say, is she living still
Or dead, your mistress? Speak, if speak you
    may.
Maid. Alive. No, dead. . . . Oh, read it
    either way.   145
Lead. Nay, daughter, can the same soul live
    and die?
Maid. Her life is broken; death is in her eye.
Lead. Poor King, to think what she was, and
    what thou!
Maid. He never knew her worth. . . . He
    will know it now.

Lead. There is no hope, methinks, to save
    her still?   150
Maid. The hour is come, and breaks all hu-
    man will.
Lead. She hath such tendance as the dying
    crave?
Maid. For sure: and rich robes ready for her
    grave.
Lead. 'Fore God, she dies high-hearted, aye,
    and far
In honor raised above all wives that are! 155
Maid. Far above all! How other? What
    must she,
Who seeketh to surpass this woman, be?
Or how could any wife more shining make
Her lord's love, than by dying for his sake?
But thus much all the city knows. 'Tis
    here,   160
In her own rooms, the tale will touch thine ear
With strangeness. When she knew the day
    was come,
She rose and washed her body, white as foam,
With running water; then the cedarn press 164
She opened, and took forth her funeral dress
And rich adornment. So she stood arrayed
Before the Hearth-Fire of her home, and
    prayed:
"Mother,[1] since I must vanish from the day,
This last, last time I kneel to thee and pray;
Be mother to my two children![2] Find some
    dear   170
Helpmate for him, some gentle lord for her.
And let not them, like me, before their hour
Die; let them live in happiness, in our
Old home, till life be full and age content."
To every household altar then she went   175
And made for each his garland of the green
Boughs of the wind-blown myrtle,[3] and was
    seen
Praying, without a sob, without a tear.
She knew the dread thing coming, but her clear
Cheek never changed: till suddenly she fled
Back to her own chamber and bridal bed: 181

---

[1] Sometimes a sick person could be saved, it was thought, by appealing to an oracle, such as that of Apollo at Patara on the coast of Lycia in southern Asia Minor, or that of Zeus Ammon in an oasis of the great Libyan desert, northern Africa.

[2] Asclepius.

[1] Hestia or Vesta ("hearth-fire") was goddess of the hearth and often addressed as "mother."

[2] A boy, Eumelus, and a girl, Perimele.

[3] The myrtle was associated regularly with funeral ceremonies, both as altar decoration and as chaplet for the dead.

Then came the tears and she spoke all her
    thought.
  "O bed, whereon my laughing girlhood's
    knot
Was severed by this man, for whom I die,
Farewell! 'Tis thou ... I speak not bit-
    terly ...   185
'Tis thou hast slain me. All alone I go
Lest I be false to him or thee. And lo,
Some woman shall lie here instead of me —
Happier perhaps; more true she cannot be."
  She kissed the pillow as she knelt, and wet
With flooding tears was that fair coverlet.   191
  At last she had had her fill of weeping; then
She tore herself away, and rose again,
Walking with downcast eyes; yet turned before
She had left the room, and cast her down once
    more   195
Kneeling beside the bed. Then to her side
The children came, and clung to her and cried,
And her arms hugged them, and a long good-
    bye
She gave to each, like one who goes to
    die.
The whole house then was weeping, every slave
In sorrow for his mistress. And she gave   201
Her hand to all; aye, none so base was there
She gave him not good words and he to her.
  So on Admetus falls from either side   204
Sorrow. 'Twere bitter grief to him to have died
Himself; and being escaped, how sore a woe
He hath earned instead — Ah, some day he
    shall know!

Lead. Surely Admetus suffers, even to-day,
For this true-hearted love he hath cast
    away?

Maid. He weeps; begs her not leave him
    desolate,   210
And holds her to his heart — too late, too late!
She is sinking now, and there, beneath his eye
Fading, the poor cold hand falls languidly,
And faint is all her breath. Yet still she fain
Would look once on the sunlight [1] — once
    again   215
And never more. I will go in and tell
Thy presence. Few there be, will serve so well

---

[1] The sun was the last object on which the ancient
Greeks wished their eyes to rest as a final act of religious
observance.

My master and stand by him to the end.
But thou hast been from olden days our
    friend.

        (*The* MAID *goes into the Castle.*

Chor. 3 Eld. O Zeus,   (Strophe)   220
    What escape and where
      From the evil thing?
    How break the snare
      That is round our King?
2 Eld. Ah list!   225
    One cometh? ... No
    Let us no more wait;
    Make dark our raiment
      And shear this hair.
Lead. Aye, friends!   230
    'Tis so, even so.
    Yet the gods are great
    And may send allayment.
      To prayer, to prayer!
All (praying). O Paian wise!   235
Some healing of this home devise, devise!
Find, find. ... Oh, long ago when we were blind
  Thine eyes saw mercy ... find some healing
    breath!
Again, O Paian, break the chains that bind;
  Stay the red hand of Death!   240

Lead. Alas!   (Antistrophe)
    What shame, what dread,
      Thou Pheres' son,
    Shalt be harvested
      When thy wife is gone!   245
2 Eld. Ah me;
    For a deed less drear
    Than this thou ruest
      Men have died for sorrow;
      Aye, hearts have bled.   250
3 Eld. 'Tis she;
    Not as men say dear,
      But the dearest, truest,
    Shall lie ere morrow
      Before thee dead!   255
All. But lo! Once more!
She and her husband moving to the door!
Cry, cry! And thou, O land of Pherae, hearken!
  The bravest of women sinketh, perisheth,
Under the green earth, down where the shadows
    darken,   260
  Down to the House of Death!

During the last words ADMETUS *and* ALCESTIS
have entered from the Castle. ALCESTIS *is
supported by her handmaids and followed
by her two children*

Lead. And who hath said that Love shall bring
    More joy to man than fear and strife?
I knew his perils from of old,
I know them now, when I behold   265
    The bitter faring of my King,
Whose love is taken, and his life
    Left evermore an empty thing.
Alc. O Sun, O light of the day that falls!
O running cloud that races along the sky! 270
    Adm. They look on thee and me, as stricken
    twain,
Who have wrought no sin that God should have
    thee slain.
    Alc. Dear Earth, and House of sheltering
    walls,
And wedded homes of the land where my
    fathers lie!
    Adm. Fail not, my hapless one. Be strong,
    and pray   275
The o'er-mastering Gods to hate us not alway.
    Alc. (*faintly, her mind wandering*). A boat
    two-oared, upon water; I see, I see.
And the Ferryman of the Dead,[1]
His hand that hangs on the pole, his voice that
    cries;
"Thou lingerest; come.   Come quickly, we
    wait for thee."   280
    He is angry that I am slow; he shakes his
    head.
    Adm. Alas, a bitter boat-faring for me,
My bride ill-starred. — Oh, this is misery!
    Alc. (*as before*). Drawing, drawing!   'Tis
    some one that draweth me . . .
To the Palaces of the Dead.   285
So dark.   The wings, the eyebrows and ah, the
    eyes![2] . . .
    Go back!   God's mercy!   What seekest
    thou?   Let me be! . . .
(*Recovering*) Where am I?   Ah, and what paths
    are these I tread?

[1] Charon, the old boatman in peasant's cap and
sleeveless tunic, who ferried the souls of the dead across
the river Styx to the kingdom of Hades.
[2] This strange figure, apparently, is Thanatos, who is
invisible to ordinary human eyes.

    Adm. Grievous for all who love thee, but for
    me   289
And my two babes most hard, most solitary.
    Alc. Hold me not; let me lie. —
I am too weak to stand; and Death is near,
And a slow darkness stealing on my sight.
    My little ones, good-bye.
Soon, soon, and mother will be no more
    here. . . .   295
Good-bye, two happy children in the light.
    Adm. Oh, word of pain, oh, sharper ache
    Than any death of mine had brought!
For the Gods' sake, desert me not,
For thine own desolate children's sake.   300
Nay, up!   Be brave.   For if they rend
    Thee from me, I can draw no breath;
    In thy hand are my life and death,
Thine, my belovèd and my friend!
    Alc. Admetus, seeing what way my fortunes
    lie,   305
I fain would speak with thee before I die.
I have set thee before all things; yea, mine own
Life beside thine was naught.   For this alone
I die. . . . Dear Lord, I never need have died.
I might have lived to wed some prince of
    pride,   310
Dwell in a king's house. . . . Nay, how could I,
    torn
From thee, live on, I and my babes forlorn?
I have given to thee my youth — not more nor
    less,
But all — though I was full of happiness.
Thy father and mother both — 'tis strange to
    tell —   315
Had failed thee, though for them the deed was
    well,
The years were ripe, to die and save their son,
The one child of the house: for hope was none,
If thou shouldst pass away, of other heirs.
So thou and I had lived through the long
    years,   320
    Both.   Thou hadst not lain sobbing here alone
For a dead wife and orphan babes. . . . Tis
    done
Now, and some God hath wrought out all his
    will.
    Howbeit I now will ask thee to fulfill
One great return-gift — not so great withal
As I have given, for life is more than all; 326

But just and due, as thine own heart will tell.
For thou hast loved our little ones as well
As I have.... Keep them to be masters here
In my old house; and bring no stepmother   330
Upon them. She might hate them. She might be
Some baser woman, not a queen like me,
And strike them with her hand. For mercy, spare
Our little ones that wrong. It is my prayer....
They come into a house: they are all strife   335
And hate to any child of the dead wife....
Better a serpent than a stepmother!
    A boy is safe. He has his father there
To guard him. But a little girl! (*Taking the*
    LITTLE GIRL *to her*) What good   339
And gentle care will guide thy maidenhood?
What woman wilt thou find at father's side?
One evil word from her, just when the tide
Of youth is full, would wreck thy hope of love.
And no more mother near, to stand above
Thy marriage-bed, nor comfort thee pain-tossed   345
In travail, when one needs a mother most!
Seeing I must die.... 'Tis here, across my way,
Not for the morrow, not for the third day,
But now — Death, and to lie with things that were.
    Farewell. God keep you happy. — Husband dear,   350
Remember that I failed thee not; and you,
My children, that your mother loved you true.
    Lead. Take comfort. Ere thy lord can speak, I swear,
If truth is in him, he will grant thy prayer.
    Adm. He will, he will! Oh, never fear for me.   355
Mine hast thou been, and mine shalt ever be,
Living and dead, thou only. None in wide
Hellas [1] but thou shalt be Admetus' bride.
No race so high, no face so magic-sweet   359
Shall ever from this purpose turn my feet.
And children ... if God grant me joy of these,
'Tis all I ask; of thee no joys nor ease
He gave me. And thy mourning I will bear
Not one year of my life but every year,
    [1] Greece.

While life shall last.... My mother I will know   365
No more. My father shall be held my foe.
They brought the words of love but not the deed,
While thou hast given thine all, and in my need
Saved me. What can I do but weep alone,
Alone alway, when such a wife is gone? ...   370
    An end shall be of revel, and an end
Of crowns and song and mirth of friend with friend,
Wherewith my house was glad. I ne'er again
Will touch the lute nor ease my heart from pain
With pipes of Afric.[1] All the joys I knew,   375
And joys were many, thou hast broken in two.
Oh, I will find some artist wondrous wise
Shall mould for me thy shape, thine hair, thine eyes,
And lay it in thy bed; and I will lie   379
Close, and reach out mine arms to thee, and cry
Thy name into the night, and wait and hear
My own heart breathe: "Thy love, thy love is near."
A cold delight; yet it might ease the sum
Of sorrow.... And good dreams of thee will come
Like balm. 'Tis sweet, even in a dream, to gaze
On a dear face, the moment that it stays.   386
    O God, if Orpheus' [2] voice were mine, to sing
To Death's high Virgin [3] and the Virgin's King,[4]
Till their hearts failed them, down would I my path
Cleave, and naught stay me, not the Hound of Wrath,[5]   390
Not the grey oarsman of the ghostly tide,[6]

    [1] The wood out of which Greek flutes were commonly made came from the lotus, a plant which grew especially in Libya, northern Africa.
    [2] The bard and prophet, Orpheus, went down to the Lower World to win back his wife, Eurydice. Hades and Persephone, spellbound by his music, granted that Eurydice should return to earth, on condition that Orpheus should go before his wife, playing his harp, and should never look back. Just at the end of the journey he looked back, and Eurydice vanished.
    [3] Persephone.
    [4] Hades.
    [5] Cerberus, the many-headed dog which guards the entrance to Hades' kingdom.
    [6] Charon.

Till back to sunlight I had borne my bride.

But now, wife, wait for me till I shall come
Where thou art, and prepare our second home.
These ministers in that same cedar sweet   395
Where thou art laid will lay me, feet to feet,
And head to head, oh, not in death from thee
Divided, who alone art true to me!

Lead. This life-long sorrow thou hast sworn,
I too,   399
Thy friend, will bear with thee. It is her due.

Alc. Children, ye heard his promise? He
will wed
No other woman nor forget the dead.

Adm. Again I promise. So it shall be done.

Alc. (*giving the children into his arms one
after the other*). On that oath take my
daughter: and my son.

Adm. Dear hand that gives, I accept both
gift and vow.   405

Alc. Thou, in my place, must be their mother
now.

Adm. Else were they motherless — I needs
must try.

Alc. My babes, I ought to live, and lo, I die.

Adm. And how can I, forlorn of thee, live on?

Alc. Time healeth; and the dead are dead
and gone.   410

Adm. Oh, take me with thee to the dark below,
Me also!

Alc.   'Tis enough that one should go.

Adm. O Fate, to have cheated me of one so
true!

Alc. (*her strength failing*). There comes a
darkness: a great burden, too.   415

Adm. I am lost if thou wilt leave me....
Wife! Mine own!

Alc. I am not thy wife; I am nothing. All
is gone.

Adm. Thy babes! Thou wilt not leave
them. — Raise thine eye.

Alc. I am sorry ... But good-bye, children;
good-bye.   420

Adm. Look at them! Wake and look at
them!

Alc.   I must go.

Adm. What? Dying!

Alc.   Farewell, husband! (*She dies.*

Adm. (*with a cry*). Ah!... Woe, woe!   425

Lead. Admetus' Queen is dead!

(*While* ADMETUS *is weeping silently,
and the* CHORUS *veil their faces, the*
LITTLE BOY *runs up to his dead
Mother.*

Little Boy.[1] Oh, what has happened? Mummy has gone away,
And left me and will not come back any
more!
Father, I shall be lonely all the day....

Look! Look! Her eyes ... and her arms
not like before,   430
How they lie ...
Mother! Oh, speak a word!
Answer me, answer me, Mother! It is I.
I am touching your face. It is I, your little
bird.

Adm. (*recovering himself and going to the
Child*). She hears us not, she sees us not.
We lie   435
Under a heavy grief, child, thou and I.

Little Boy. I am so little, Father, and lonely
and cold
Here without Mother. It is too hard....
And you,
Poor little sister, too.
       Oh, Father!   440
Such a little time we had her. She might have
stayed
On till we all were old ...
Everything is spoiled when Mother is dead.

(*The* LITTLE BOY, *sobbing, is taken
away, with his Sister, into the Castle.*

Lead. My King, thou needs must gird thee
to the worst.
Thou shalt not be the last, nor yet the first,   445
To lose a noble wife. Be brave, and know
To die is but a debt that all men owe.

Adm. I know. It came not without doubts
and fears,

---

[1] Euripides employs children for dramatic pathos far
more frequently than any other Greek dramatist. In
three plays, besides *Alcestis*, he has them speak, and in
four others he employs children as mute figures. The
speech of Eumelus here is curiously stylized. Euripides
intends him to speak in the stately tragic diction of
adult characters mixed with a few words of child-lan-
guage at appropriate moments. It is a hybrid style
difficult to make convincing and even more difficult to
translate.

This thing.   The thought hath poisoned all my
    years.
    Howbeit, I now will make the burial due   450
To this dead Queen.   Be assembled, all of you;
And, after, raise your triumph-song to greet
This pitiless Power that yawns beneath our feet.
    Meantime let all in Thessaly who dread
My sceptre join in mourning for the dead   455
With temples sorrow-shorn and sable weed.
Ye chariot-lords, ye spurrers of the steed,[1]
Shear close your horses' manes!   Let there be
    found
Through all my realm no lute, nor lyre, nor
    sound
Of piping, till twelve moons are at an end.   460
For never shall I lose a closer friend,
Nor braver in my need.   And worthy is she
Of honor, who alone hath died for me.

> (*The body of* ALCESTIS *is carried into
>   the Castle by mourners;* ADMETUS
>   *follows it.*

Chor. Daughter of Pelias, fare thee well,
> (Strophe)
May joy be thine in the Sunless Houses!   465
For thine is a deed which the Dead shall tell
Where a King black-browed[2] in the gloom
>   *carouses;*
> *And the cold grey hand at the helm and oar[3]*
> *Which guideth shadows from shore to shore,*
Shall bear this day o'er Tears that Well,[4]   470
A Queen of women, a spouse of spouses.

Minstrels many shall praise thy name
> (Antistrophe)
With lyre full-strung and with voices lyreless,
When Mid-Moon riseth, an orbèd flame,
> *And from dusk to dawning the dance is tire-*
>   *less;*   475
> *And Carnos cometh to Sparta's call,*
> *And Athens shineth in festival;[5]*

---

[1] Thessaly was famous among the Greek states for its
cavalry.   Its plains bred the finest horses in Greece.
[2] Hades.
[3] Charon.
[4] The lake that spreads out from Acheron, the River
of Sorrows.
[5] Alcestis is to be celebrated hereafter at certain full-
moon feasts in Athens and Sparta, especially at the
Carneia, a great Spartan festival held at the full-moon
in the month Carneios (August–September).

For thy death is a song, and a fullness of
*   fame,*
> *Till the heart of the singer is left desireless.*
Lead. Would I could reach thee, oh,   (Str. 2)
> *Reach thee and save, my daughter,*   481
> *Starward from gulfs of Hell,*
> *Past gates, past tears that swell,*
> *Where the weak oar climbs thro'*
> *The night and the water!*   485
2 Eld. Belovèd and lonely one,
> *Who feared not dying:*
> *Gone in another's stead*
> *Alone to the hungry dead:*
> *Light be the carven stone*   490
> *Above thee lying!*
3 Eld. Oh, he who should seek again
> *A new bride after thee,*
> *Were loathed of thy children twain,*
> *And loathed of me.*   495
Lead. Word to his mother sped,   (Ant. 2)
> *Praying to her who bore him;*
> *Word to his father, old,*
> *Heavy with years and cold;*
> *"Quick, ere your son be dead!*   500
> *What dare ye for him?"*
2 Eld. Old, and they dared not; grey,
> *And they helped him never!*
> *'Twas she, in her youth and pride,*
> *Rose up for her lord and died.*   505
> *Oh, love of two hearts that stay*
> *One-knit for ever....*
3 Eld. 'Tis rare in the world!   God send
> *Such bride in my house to be;*
> *She should live life to the end,*   510
> *Not fail through me.*

As the song ceases there enters a stranger, walking
*   strongly, but travel-stained, dusty, and tired.*
*   His lion-skin and club show him to be* HER-
ACLES

Her. Ho, countrymen!   To Pherae am I come
By now?   And is Admetus in his home?
    Lead. Our King is in his house, Lord Her-
        acles. —
But say, what need brings thee in days like
    these   515
To Thessaly and Pherae's wallèd ring?

Her. A quest I follow for the Argive King.[1]

Lead. What prize doth call thee, and to what far place?

Her. The horses of one Diomede, in Thrace.[2]

Lead. But how ... ?　Thou know'st not? Is he strange to thee?　520

Her. Quite strange.　I ne'er set foot in Bistony.

Lead. Not without battle shalt thou win those steeds.

Her. So be it!　I cannot fail my master's needs.

Lead. 'Tis slay or die, win or return no more.

Her. Well, I have looked on peril's face before.　525

Lead. What profit hast thou in such manslaying?

Her. I shall bring back the horses to my King.

Lead. 'Twere none such easy work to bridle them.

Her. Not easy?　Have they nostrils breathing flame?

Lead. They tear men's flesh; their jaws are swift with blood.　530

Her. Men's flesh!　'Tis mountain wolves', not horses' food!

Lead. Thou wilt see their mangers clogged with blood, like mire.

Her. And he who feeds such beasts, who was his sire?

Lead. Arês, the war-lord of the Golden Targe.[3]

Her. Enough! — This labor fitteth well my large　535

Fortune, still upward, still against the wind.

How often with these kings of Arês' kind

Must I do battle?　First the dark wolf-man,

Lycaon; then 'twas he men called The Swan;[1]

And now this man of steeds! ... Well, none shall see　540

Alcmena's son[2] turn from his enemy.

Lead. Lo, as we speak, this land's high governor,

Admetus, cometh from his castle door.

Enter ADMETUS *from the Castle*

Adm. Zeus-born of Perseid line,[3] all joy to thee!

Her. Joy to Admetus, Lord of Thessaly!　545

Adm. Right welcome were Joy! — But thy love I know.

Her. But why this mourning hair, this garb of woe?

Adm. (*in a comparatively light tone*).　There is a burial I must make today.[4]

Her. God keep all evil from thy children!

Adm.　　　　　　　　　　Nay,　550

My children live.

Her.　　　　　　Thy father, if 'tis he,

Is ripe in years.

Adm.　　　　　　He liveth, friend, and she

Who bore me.　555

Her.　　　　　　Surely not thy wife?　'Tis not Alcestis?

Adm. (*his composure a little shaken*).　Ah; two answers share my thought,

Questioned of her.

Her.　　　　　　Is she alive or dead?　560

Adm. She is, and is not; and my heart hath bled

Long years for her.

Her.　　　　　　I understand no more.

Thy words are riddles.

Adm.　　　　　Heard'st thou not of yore　565

The doom that she must meet?

---

[1] It had been the doom of Heracles (Hercules) to be subject to his kinsman, Eurystheus, king of Argos. The latter had imposed twelve labors upon Heracles. When he had accomplished them he was to receive immortality.　Seven he had already achieved, and he was now on his way to undertake the eighth.　Heracles knew Admetus well because he had entertained him more than once in Argos.

[2] Diomedes, son of Ares, the war-god, was the savage king of the Bistones in Thrace.　He had trained his horses to eat human flesh and threw wayfarers to them for food.

[3] Golden Shield.

[1] Heracles had slain Lycaon, the Wolf-hero, and Cycnus, the Swan-hero, both of them sons of Ares.

[2] Alcmena was the mother of Heracles.

[3] Heracles was son of Zeus and great-grandson of Perseus on his mother's side.

[4] Admetus is anxious throughout the subsequent scene to conceal from Heracles the death of Alcestis, so that he may keep the son of Zeus as a guest and carry out the proper rites of hospitality.　Admetus' strong regard for hospitality is *the* virtue for which he was to be rewarded finally.

Her.   I know thy wife
Has sworn to die for thee.

Adm.   And is it life,   569
To live with such an oath hung o'er her head?

Her. (relieved). Ah,
Weep not too soon, friend. Wait till she be
     dead.

Adm. He dies who is doomed to die; he is
     dead who dies.

Her. The two are different things in most
     men's eyes.

Adm. Decide thy way, lord, and let me de-
     cide   575
The other way.

Her.   Who is it that has died?
Thou weepest.

Adm.   'Tis a woman. It doth take   579
My memory back to her of whom we spake.

Her. A stranger, or of kin to thee?

Adm.   Not kin,
But much beloved.

Her.   How came she to be in
Thy house to die?   585

Adm.   Her father died, and so
She came to us, an orphan, long ago.

Her. (as though about to depart). 'Tis sad.
I would I had found thee on a happier day.

Adm. Thy words have some intent: what
     wouldst thou say?   590

Her. I must find harbor with some other
     friend.

Adm. My prince, it may not be! God never
     send
Such evil!

Her.   'Tis great turmoil, when a guest
Comes to a mourning house.   595

Adm.   Come in and rest.
Let the dead die!

Her.   I cannot, for mere shame,
Feast beside men whose eyes have tears in
     them.

Adm. The guest-rooms are apart where thou
     shalt be.   600

Her. Friend, let me go. I shall go grate-
     fully.

Adm. Thou shalt not enter any door but
     mine.
(To an Attendant) Lead in our guest. Unlock
     the furthest line

Of guest-chambers; and bid the stewards
     there   604
Make ready a full feast; then close with care
The midway doors. 'Tis unmeet, if he hears
Our turmoil or is burdened with our tears.

     (The Attendant leads HERACLES *into the
         Castle.*

Lead. How, master? When within a thing
     so sad
Lies, thou wilt house a stranger? Art thou mad?

Adm. And had I turned the stranger from
     my door,   610
Who sought my shelter, hadst thou praised me
     more?
I trow not, if my sorrow were thereby
No whit less, only the more friendless I.
And more, when bards tell tales, were it not
     worse
My house should lie beneath the stranger's
     curse?   615
Now he is my sure friend, if e'er I stand
Lonely in Argos, in a thirsty land.

Lead. Thou callest him thy friend; how didst
     thou dare
Keep hid from him the burden of thy care?

Adm. He never would have entered, had he
     known   620
My grief. — Aye, men may mock what I have
     done,
And call me fool. My house hath never
     learned
To fail its friend, nor seen the stranger spurned.

     *(*ADMETUS *goes into the Castle.*

Chor. Oh, a House that loves the stranger,
                           (Strophe)
    And a House for ever free!   625
And Apollo, the Song-changer,
    Was a herdsman in thy fee; [1]
       Yea, a-piping he was found,
       Where the upward valleys wound,
   To the kine from out the manger   630
       And the sheep from off the lea,
       And love was upon Othrys [2] *at the sound.*

---

[1] Apollo had served as a herdsman to Admetus before
his marriage to Alcestis. At that time, when singing
and harping as a shepherd god, he had gathered the wild
beasts around him just as did Orpheus.

[2] The mountain range to the south of Pherae, a range
which abounded in forests.

And from deep glens unbeholden

                      (Antistrophe)

  Of the forest to his song
There came lynxes streaky-golden,   635
  There came lions in a throng,
  Tawny-coated, ruddy-eyed,
  To that piper in his pride;
And shy fawns he would embolden,
  Dappled dancers, out along   640
  The shadow by the pine-tree's side.

And those magic pipes a-blowing   (Str. 2)
  Have fulfilled thee in thy reign
By thy Lake [1] *with honey flowing,*
  By thy sheepfolds and thy grain;   645
  Where the Sun turns his steeds
  To the twilight, all the meads
Of Molossus [2] *know thy sowing*
  And thy ploughs upon the plain.
Yea, and eastward thou art free   650
  To the portals of the sea,
And Pelion, [3] *the unharbored, is but minister to*
  thee.

He hath opened wide his dwelling   (Ant.2)
  To the stranger, though his ruth
For the dead was fresh and welling,   655
  For the loved one of his youth.
  'Tis the brave heart's cry:
  "I will fail not, though I die!"
Doth it win, with no man's telling,
  Some high vision of the truth?   660
  We may marvel. Yet I trust,
  When man seeketh to be just
And to pity them that wander, God will raise him
  from the dust.

As the song ceases the doors of the Castle are
  thrown open and ADMETUS *comes before*
  them: a great funeral procession is seen mov-
  ing out

---

[1] Lake Boibeïs across the plain of Pherae to the north-east.

[2] Epirus; so called because the Molossi were one of the three chief tribes in that mountainous land to the west of Thessaly.

[3] The famous mountain extending along the steep harborless coast of Magnesia in eastern Thessaly.

Adm. Most gentle citizens, our dead is here
Made ready; and these youths to bear the
  bier   665
Uplifted to the grave-mound and the urn.
Now, seeing she goes forth never to return,
Bid her your last farewell, as mourners may.

       (*The procession moves forward past him.*

Lead. Nay, lord; thy father, walking old and
  grey;
And followers bearing burial gifts and brave
Gauds, which men call the comfort of the
  grave.   671

Enter from the side PHERÊS *with followers*
      bearing robes and gifts

Pher. I come in sorrow for thy sorrow, son.
A faithful wife indeed thou hast lost, and one
Who ruled her heart. But, howso hard they be,
We needs must bear these griefs. — Some gifts
  for thee   675
Are here.... Yes; take them. Let them go
  beneath
The sod. We both must honor her in death,
Seeing she hath died, my son, that thou mayst
  live
Nor I be childless. Aye, she would not give
My soul to a sad old age, mourning for thee.
Methinks she hath made all women's life to
  be   681
A nobler thing, by one great woman's deed.
  Thou saviour of my son, thou staff in need
To our wrecked age, farewell! May some good
  life   684
Be thine still in the grave. — Oh, 'tis a wife
Like this man needs; else let him stay unwed!

       (*The old man has not noticed* ADME-
       TUS's *gathering indignation.*

Adm. I called not thee to burial of my dead,
Nor count thy presence here a welcome thing.
My wife shall wear no robe that thou canst
  bring,
Nor needs thy help in aught. There was a
  day   690
We craved thy love, when I was on my way
Deathward — thy love, which bade thee stand
  aside
And watch, gray-bearded, while a young man
  died!

And now wilt mourn for her? Thy fatherhood!
Thou wast no true begetter of my blood, 695
Nor she my mother who dares call me child.
Oh, she was barren ever; she beguiled
Thy folly with some bastard of a thrall.
Here is thy proof! This hour hath shown me
    all
Thou art; and now I am no more thy son. 700
'Fore God, among all cowards can scarce be
    one
Like thee. So grey, so near the boundary
Of mortal life, thou wouldst not, durst not, die
To save thy son! Thou hast suffered her to do
Thine office, her, no kin to me nor you, 705
Yet more than kin! Henceforth she hath all
    the part
Of mother, yea, and father in my heart.
    And what a glory had been thine that day,
Dying to save thy son — when, either way,
Thy time must needs be brief. Thy life has
    had 710
Abundance of the things that make men glad;
A crown that came to thee in youth; a son
To do thee worship and maintain thy throne —
Not like a childless king, whose folk and lands
Lie helpless, to be torn by strangers' hands.
    Wilt say I failed in duty to thine age; 716
For that thou hast let me die? Not so; most
    sage,
Most pious I was, to mother and to thee;
And thus ye have paid me! Well, I counsel ye,
Lose no more time. Get quick another son
To foster thy last years, to lay thee on 721
Thy bier, when dead, and wrap thee in thy pall.
I will not bury thee. I am, for all
The care thou hast shown me, dead. If I have
    found
Another, true to save me at the bound 725
Of life and death, that other's child am I,
That other's fostering friend, until I die.
    How falsely do these old men pray for death,
Cursing their weight of years, their weary
    breath!
When Death comes close, there is not one that
    dares 730
To die; age is forgot and all its cares.
    Lead. Oh, peace! Enough of sorrow in our
    path
Is strewn. Thou son, stir not thy father's wrath.

Pher. My son, whom seekest thou ... some
    Lydian thrall,
Or Phrygian,[1] bought with cash? ... to affright
    withal 735
By cursing? I am a Thessalian, free,
My father a born chief of Thessaly;
And thou most insolent. Yet think not so
To fling thy loud lewd words at me and go.
    I got thee to succeed me in my hall, 740
I have fed thee, clad thee. But I have no call
To die for thee. Not in our family,
Not in all Greece, doth law bid fathers die
To save their sons. Thy road of life is thine,
None other's, to rejoice at or repine. 745
All that was owed to thee by us is paid.
My throne is thine. My broad lands shall be
    made
Thine, as I had them from my father.... Say,
How have I wronged thee? What have I kept
    away?
"Not died for thee?" ... I ask not thee to die.
    Thou lovest this light: shall I not love it,
    I? ... 751
'Tis age on age there, in the dark; and here
My sunlit time is short, but dear; but dear.
    Thou hast fought hard enough. Thou
    drawest breath
Even now, long past thy portioned hour of
    death, 755
By murdering her ... and blamest my faint heart,
Coward, who hast let a woman play thy part
And die to save her pretty soldier! Aye,
A good plan, surely! Thou needst never die;
Thou canst find alway somewhere some fond
    wife 760
To die for thee. But, prithee, make not strife
With other friends, who will not save thee so.
Be silent, loving thine own life, and know
All men love theirs! ... Taunt others, and
    thou too
Shalt hear much that is bitter, and is true. 765
    Lead. Too much of wrath before, too much
    hath run
After. Old man, cease to revile thy son.
    Adm. Speak on. I have spoken.... If my
    truth of tongue

[1] Many of the Greek slaves were captives from Lydia
and Phrygia, countries of western and central Asia
Minor respectively.

Gives pain to thee, why didst thou do me
    wrong?
Pher. Wrong? To have died for thee were
    far more wrong.   770
Adm. How can an old life weigh against a
    young?
Pher. Man hath but one, not two lives, to
    his use.
Adm. Oh, live on; live, and grow more old
    than Zeus!
Pher. Because none wrongs thee, thou must
    curse thy sire?
Adm. I blest him. Is not life his one desire?
Pher. This dead, methinks, is lying in *thy*
    place.   776
Adm. A proof, old traitor, of thy cowardli-
    ness!
Pher. Died she through me? . . . That thou
    wilt hardly say.
Adm. (*almost breaking down*). O God!   779
Mayst thou but feel the need of me some day!
Pher. Go forward; woo more wives that
    more may die.
Adm. As thou wouldst not! Thine is the
    infamy.
Pher. This light of heaven is sweet, and
    sweet again.
Adm. Thy heart is foul. A thing unmeet
    for men.
Pher. Thou laugh'st not yet across the old
    man's tomb.   785
Adm. Dishonored thou shalt die when
    death shall come.
Pher. Once dead, I shall not care what tales
    are told.
Adm. Great Gods, so lost to honor and so
    old!
Pher. *She* was not lost to honor: she was
    blind.
Adm. Go! Leave me with my dead. . . .
    Out from my mind!   790
Pher. I go. Bury the woman thou hast
    slain. . . .
Her kinsmen yet may come to thee with plain
Question. Acastus[1] hath small place in good
Men, if he care not for his sister's blood.
    (PHERES *goes off, with his Attendants.*
    ADMETUS *calls after him as he goes.*

[1] The brother of Alcestis.

Adm. Begone, begone, thou and thy bitter
    mate!   795
Be old and childless — ye have earned your
    fate —
While your son lives! — For never shall ye be
From henceforth under the same roof with
    me. . . .
Must I send heralds and a trumpet's call
To abjure thy blood? Fear not, I will send
    them all. . . .   800
    (PHERES *is now out of sight;* ADMETUS
    *drops his defiance and seems like a
    broken man.*
But we — our sorrow is upon us; come
With me, and let us bear her to the tomb.

Chor. *Ah me!*
Farewell, unfalteringly brave!
  Farewell, thou generous heart and true!   805
  May Pluto [1] *give thee welcome due,*
And Hermes [2] *love thee in the grave.*
Whate'er of blessèd life there be
  For high souls to the darkness flown,
  Be thine for ever, and a throne   810
Beside the crowned Persephonê.[3]

*The funeral procession has formed and moves
    slowly out, followed by* ADMETUS *and the*
    CHORUS.[4] *The stage is left empty, till a side
    door of the Castle opens and there comes out
    a* SERVANT, *angry and almost in tears*
Serv. Full many a stranger and from many a
    land
Hath lodged in this old castle, and my hand
Served them; but never has there passed this
    way
A scurvier ruffian than our guest today.   815
He saw my master's grief, but all the more
In he must come, and shoulders through the
    door.
And after, think you he would mannerly
Take what was set before him? No, not he!
If, on this day of trouble, we left out   820
Some small thing, he must have it with a shout.

[1] The god of the Lower World; also called Hades.
[2] The conductor of the dead to Hades.
[3] The queen of the Lower World and Pluto's wife.
[4] It is extremely rare in Greek tragedy for the Chorus
to leave the stage altogether in the middle of a play.

Up, in both hands, our vat of ivy-wood
He raised, and drank the dark grape's burning
    blood,
Strong and untempered, till the fire was red
Within him; then put myrtle round his head
And roared some noisy song. So had we
    there   826
Discordant music. He, without a care
For all the affliction of Admetus' halls,
Sang on; and, listening, one could hear the
    thralls
In the long gallery weeping for the dead. 830
  We let him see no tears. Our master made
That order, that the stranger must not know.
  So here I wait in her own house, and do
Service to some black thief, some man of prey;
And she has gone, has gone for ever away. 835
I never followed her, nor lifted high
My hand to bless her; never said good-bye....
I loved her like my mother. So did all
The slaves. She never let his anger fall
Too hard. She saved us alway.... And this
    wild beast   840
Comes in our sorrow when we need him least!

During the last few lines HERACLES *has entered,
    unperceived by the* SERVANT. *He has evi-
    dently bathed and changed his garments and
    drunk his fill, and is now reveling, a gar-
    land of flowers on his head. He frightens
    the* SERVANT *a little from time to time during
    the following speech*

  Her. Friend, why so solemn and so cranky-
    eyed?
'Tis not a henchman's office, to show pride
To his betters. He should smile and make
    good cheer.
  There comes a guest, thy lord's old comrade,
    here;   845
And thou art all knitted eyebrows, scowls and
    head
Bent, because somebody, forsooth, is dead!
  Come close! I mean to make thee wiser.
    (*The* SERVANT *reluctantly comes close.*
        So.
Dost comprehend things mortal, how they
    grow?...
(*To himself*) I suppose not. How could he?...

Look this way!   850
Death is a debt all mortal men must pay;
Aye, there is no man living who can say
If life will last him yet a single day.
On, to the dark, drives Fortune; and no force
Can wrest her secret nor put back her
    course....   855
  I have told thee now. I have taught thee.
    After this
  Eat, drink, make thyself merry. Count the
    bliss
Of the one passing hour thine own; the rest
Is Fortune's. And give honor chiefliest
To our lady Cypris,[1] giver of all joys   860
To man. 'Tis a sweet goddess. Otherwise,
Let all these questions sleep and just obey
My counsel.... Thou believest all I say?
I hope so.... Let this stupid grieving be;
Rise up above thy troubles, and with me   865
Drink in a cloud of blossoms. By my soul,
I vow the sweet plash-music of the bowl
Will break thy glumness, loose thee from the
    frown
Within. Let mortal man keep to his own
Mortality, and not expect too much.   870
  To all your solemn dogs and other such
Scowlers — I tell thee truth, no more nor
    less —
Life is not life, but just unhappiness.
    (*He offers the wine-bowl to the* SER-
      VANT, *who avoids it.*
  Serv. We know all this. But now our for-
    tunes be
Not such as ask for mirth or revelry.   875
  Her. A woman dead, of no one's kin; why
    grieve
So much? Thy master and thy mistress live.
  Serv. Live? Man, hast thou heard nothing
    of our woe?
  Her. Yes, thy lord told me all I need to
    know.
  Serv. He is too kind to his guests, more kind
    than wise.   880
  Her. Must I go starved because some
    stranger dies?

[1] Aphrodite or Venus, who after her birth was said to
have gone to Cyprus, the large island in the eastern
Mediterranean. There one of her chief temples was
established.

Serv. Some stranger? — Yes, a stranger verily!

Her. (*his manner beginning to change*). Is this
some real grief he hath hid from me?

Serv. Go, drink, man! Leave to us our
master's woes.

Her. It sounds not like a stranger. Yet,
God knows... 885

Serv. How should thy revelling hurt, if that
were all?

Her. Hath mine own friend so wronged me
in his hall?

Serv. Thou camest at an hour when none
was free

To accept thee. We were mourning. Thou
canst see

Our hair, black robes... 890

Her. (*suddenly, in a voice of thunder*). Who is
it that is dead?

Serv. Alcestis, the King's wife.

Her. (*overcome*). What hast thou said?

Alcestis?... And ye feasted me withal!

Serv. He held it shame to turn thee from his
hall. 895

Her. Shame! And when such a wondrous
wife was gone!

Serv. (*breaking into tears*). Oh, all is gone, all
lost, not she alone!

Her. I knew, I felt it, when I saw his tears,

And face, and shorn hair.[1] But he won mine
ears 899

With talk of the strange woman and her rite

Of burial. So in mine own heart's despite

I crossed his threshold and sat drinking — he

And I old friends! — in his calamity.

Drank, and sang songs, and revelled, my head
hot

With wine and flowers!... And thou to tell
me not, 905

When all the house lay filled with sorrow, thou!

(*A pause; then suddenly*) Where lies the
tomb? — Where shall I find her now?

Serv. (*frightened*). Close by the straight
Larissa[2] road. The tall

White marble showeth from the castle wall.

Her. O heart, O hand, great doings have ye
done 910

[1] Shorn hair was a sign of mourning.

[2] An important Thessalian town northwest of Pherae
and capital of the district Pelasgiotis.

Of old: up now, and show them what a son

Took life that hour, when she of Tiryns' sod,

Electryon's daughter,[1] mingled with her God!

I needs must save this woman from the shore

Of death and set her in her house once more,

Repaying Admetus' love.... This Death, this
black 916

And wingèd Lord of corpses, I will track

Home. I shall surely find him by the grave

A-hungered, lapping the hot blood they gave

In sacrifice. An ambush: then, one spring,

One grip! These arms shall be a brazen
ring, 921

With no escape, no rest, howe'er he whine

And curse his mauled ribs, till the Queen is
mine!

Or if he escape me, if he come not there

To seek the blood of offering, I will fare 925

Down to the Houses without Light, and bring

To Her we name not and her nameless King

Strong prayers, until they yield to me and send

Alcestis home, to life and to my friend:

Who gave me shelter, drove me not away 930

In his great grief, but hid his evil day

Like a brave man, because he loved me well.

Is one in all this land more hospitable,

One in all Greece? I swear no man shall say

He hath cast his love upon a churl away! 935

(*He goes forth, just as he is, in the direction of the grave. The* SERVANT
*watches a moment and goes back into
the hall.*)

The stage is empty; then ADMETUS *and the*
CHORUS *return*

Adm.   Alas!
Bitter the homeward way,
        Bitter to seek
    A widowed house; ah me,
Where should I fly or stay, 940
        Be dumb or speak?
    Would I could cease to be!

Despair, despair!
My mother bore me under an evil star.

[1] Alcmena, daughter of Electryon, king of Tiryns, an
ancient city southeast of Argos. She was beloved of
Zeus, though married to Amphitryon, and bore to the
god a son, Heracles.

I envy them that are perished; my heart is
    there.   945
It dwells in the Sunless Houses, afar, afar.

I take no joy in looking upon the light;
    No joy in the feel of the earth beneath my
        tread.
The Slayer hath taken his hostage; the Lord of
    the Dead   949
    Holdeth me sworn to taste no more delight.
(*He throws himself on the ground in despair.*

Each member of the CHORUS *speaks his line
    severally, as he passes* ADMETUS, *who is
    heard sobbing at the end of each line.*

Chor. — *Advance, advance;*
        Till the house shall give thee cover.
    — *Thou hast borne heavy things*
        And meet for lamentation.
    — *Thou hast passed, hast passed,*   955
        Thro' the deepest of the River.
    — *Yet no help comes*
        To the sad and silent nation.
— *And the face of thy belovèd, it shall meet
    thee never, never!*
Adm. Ye wrench my wounds asunder.
    Where   960
Is grief like mine, whose wife is dead?
My wife, whom would I ne'er had wed,
Nor loved, nor held my house with her....

Blessed are they who dare to dwell
    Unloved of woman! 'Tis but one   965
Heart that they bleed with, and alone
Can bear their one life's burden well.

No young shall wither at their side,
    No bridal room be swept by death....
Aye, better man should draw his breath   970
For ever without child or bride.
Chor. (*as before*). — *'Tis Fate, 'tis Fate:*
        *She is strong and none shall break
            her.*
    — *No end, no end,*
        Wilt thou lay to lamentations?   975
    — *Endure and be still:*
        Thy lamenting will not wake her.
    — *There be many before thee,*
        Who have suffered and had patience.

— *Though the face of Sorrow changeth, yet
    her hand is on all nations.*   980
Adm. The garb of tears, the mourner's cry:
    Then the long ache when tears are past!...
Oh, why didst hinder me to cast
This body to the dust and die
With her, the faithful and the brave?   985
    Then not one lonely soul had fled,
    But two great lovers, proudly dead,
Through the deep waters of the grave.
Lead. A friend I knew,
        In whose house died a son,   990
    Worthy of bitter rue,
        His only one.
    His head sank, yet he bare
    Stilly his weight of care,
        Though grey was in his hair   995
        And life nigh done.
Adm. Ye shapes that front me, wall and
    gate,
How shall I enter in and dwell
Among ye, with all Fortune's spell
Dischanted? Aye, the change is great.   1000

That day I strode with bridal song
    Through lifted brands of Pelian pine;[1]
    A hand belovèd lay in mine;
And loud behind a revelling throng

Exalted me and her, the dead.   1005
    They called us young, high-hearted; told
    How princes were our sires of old,
And how we loved and we must wed....

For those high songs, lo, men that moan,
    And raiment black where once was white;
    Who guide me homeward in the night,   1011
On that waste bed to lie alone.
    2 Eld. It breaks, like strife,
        Thy long peace, where no pain
        Had entered; yet is life,   1015
            Sweet life, not slain.
    A wife dead; a dear chair
    Empty: is that so rare?
    Men live without despair
        Whose loves are ta'en.   1020

[1] Mount Pelion, famous for its pine trees, overlooked
Iolcus, where Alcestis lived as a maiden. These Pelian
mountain pines supplied appropriate arboral decorations
at her wedding ceremonies.

Adm. (*erect and facing them*). Behold, I
    count my wife's fate happier,
Though all gainsay me, than mine own. To
    her
Comes no more pain for ever; she hath rest
And peace from all toil, and her name is blest.
But I am one who hath no right to stay   1025
Alive on earth; one that hath lost his way
In fate, and strays in dreams of life long
    past. . . .
Friends, I have learned my lesson at the last.
    I have my life. Here stands my house. But
    now
How dare I enter in? Or, entered, how   1030
Go forth again? Go forth, when none is there
To give me a parting word, and I to her? . . .
    Where shall I turn for refuge? There
    within,
The desert that remains where she hath been
Will drive me forth, the bed, the empty
    seat   1035
She sat in; nay, the floor beneath my feet
Unswept, the children crying at my knee
For mother; and the very thralls will be
In sobs for the dear mistress that is lost.
    That is my home! If I go forth, a host   1040
Of feasts and bridal dances, gatherings gay
Of women, will be there to fright me away
To loneliness. Mine eyes will never bear
The sight. They were her friends; they played
    with her.   1044
    And always, always, men who hate my name
Will murmur: "This is he who lives in shame
Because he dared not die! He gave instead
The woman whom he loved, and so is fled
From death. He counts himself a man withal!
And seeing his parents died not at his call   1050
He hates them, when himself he dared not
    die!"
    Such mocking beside all my pain shall I
Endure. . . . What profit was it to live on,
Friend, with my grief kept and mine honor
    gone?
    Chor. I have sojourned in the Muse's land,
                              (Strophe)
    Have wandered with the wandering star,   1056
Seeking for strength, and in my hand
    Held all philosophies that are;
Yet nothing could I hear nor see

Stronger than That Which Needs Must Be.   1060
No Orphic rune, no Thracian scroll,
    Hath magic to avert the morrow;[1]
No healing all those medicines brave
Apollo to the Asclepiad gave;
Pale herbs of comfort in the bowl   1065
    Of man's wide sorrow.

She hath no temple, she alone,   (Antistrophe)
    Nor image where a man may kneel;
No blood upon her altar-stone
    Crying shall make her hear nor feel.   1070
I know thy greatness; come not great
Beyond my dreams, O Power of Fate!
Aye, Zeus himself shall not unclose
    His purpose save by thy decerning.
The chain of iron, the Scythian sword,   1075
It yields and shivers at thy word;
Thy heart is as the rock, and knows
    No ruth, nor turning.
                (CHORUS *turn to* ADMETUS.

Her hand hath caught thee; yea, the keeping
                         (Str. 2)
    Of iron fingers grips thee round.   1080
Be still. Be still. Thy noise of weeping
    Shall raise no lost one from the ground.
Nay, even the Sons of God are parted
    At last from joy, and pine in death. . . .
Oh, dear on earth when all did love her,   1085
Oh, dearer lost beyond recover:
Of women all the bravest-hearted
    Hath pressed thy lips and breathed thy breath.

Let not the earth that lies upon her   (Ant. 2)
    Be deemed a grave-mound of the dead.   1090
Let honor, as the Gods have honor,
    Be hers, till men shall bow the head,
And strangers, climbing from the city
    Her slanting path, shall muse and say:
"This woman died to save her lover,   1095
And liveth blest, the stars above her:
Hail, Holy One, and grant thy pity!"
    So pass the wondering words away.

    Lead. But see, it is Alcmenas's son once more,
My lord King, cometh striding to thy door.

---

[1] Orpheus was supposed to have inscribed magical
sayings or charms on certain tablets in Thrace.

Enter HERACLES; *his dress is as in the last scene, but shows signs of a struggle.   Behind come two Attendants, guiding between them a veiled Woman, who seems like one asleep or unconscious.   The Woman remains in the background while* HERACLES *comes forward*

Her. Thou art my friend, Admetus; there-
    fore bold   1101
And plain I tell my story, and withhold
No secret hurt. — Was I not worthy, friend,
To stand beside thee; yea, and to the end
Be proven in sorrow if I was true to thee? 1105
And thou didst tell me not a word, while she
Lay dead within; but bid me feast, as though
Naught but the draping of some stranger's
    woe
Was on thee. So I garlanded my brow
And poured the gods drink-offering, and but
    now   1110
Filled thy death-stricken house with wine and
    song.
Thou hast done me wrong, my brother; a great
    wrong
Thou hast done me. But I will not add more
    pain
In thine affliction. — Why I am here again,
Returning, thou must hear. I pray thee, take
And keep yon woman for me till I make 1116
My homeward way from Thrace, when I have
    ta'en
Those four steeds and their bloody master slain.
And if — which heaven avert! — I ne'er should
    see
Hellas again, I leave her here, to be   1120
An handmaid in thy house. No labor small
Was it that brought her to my hand at all.
I fell upon a contest certain Kings
Had set for all mankind, sore buffetings
And meet for strong men, where I staked my
    life   1125
And won this woman. For the easier strife
Black steeds were prizes; herds of kine were
    cast
For heavier issues, fists and wrestling; last,
This woman.... Lest my work should all
    seem done
For naught, I needs must keep what I have
    won;   1130
So prithee take her in. No theft, but true

Toil, won her.... Some day thou mayst
    thank me, too.
  Adm. 'Twas in no scorn, no bitterness to
    thee,
I hid my wife's death and my misery.
Methought it was but added pain on pain.
If thou shouldst leave me, and roam forth
    again   1136
Seeking another's roof. And, for mine own
Sorrow, I was content to weep alone.
  But, for this damsel, if it may be so,   1139
I pray thee, Lord, let some man, not in woe
Like mine, take her. Thou hast in Thessaly
Abundant friends.... 'Twould wake sad
    thoughts in me.
How could I have this damsel in my sight
And keep mine eyes dry? Prince, why wilt
    thou smite
The smitten? Griefs enough are on my
    head.   1145
  Where in my castle [1] could so young a maid
Be lodged — her veil and raiment show her
    young:
Here, in the men's hall? I should fear some
    wrong.
'Tis not so easy, Prince, to keep controlled
My young men. And thy charge I fain would
    hold   1150
Sacred. — If not, wouldst have me keep her in
The women's chambers... where my dead
    hath been?
How could I lay this woman where my bride
Once lay? It were dishonor double-dyed.
These streets would curse the man who so be-
    trayed   1155
The wife who saved him for some younger
    maid;
The dead herself... I needs must worship her
And keep her will.
        (*During the last few lines* ADMETUS *has
        been looking at the veiled Woman and,
        though he does not consciously recog-*

[1] The castle is divided into two main parts: a large public hall where the men live during the day and sleep at night, and a private region, ruled by the queen and centering in the royal bed-chamber. If the "veiled woman" were taken into this harem, so to speak, even if Admetus had no word with her, the Greek world outside would likely assume the worst and consider it a dishonorable situation.

nize her, feels a strange emotion over-
mastering him. He draws back.

　　　　Aye. I must walk with care. . . .
O woman, whosoe'er thou art, thou hast 1160
The shape of my Alcestis; thou art cast
In mould like hers. . . . Oh, take her from mine
　　eyes!
In God's name! (HERACLES *signs to the Attend-*
　　　　ants to take ALCESTIS *away again.*
　　　　She stays veiled and unnoticing in
　　　　the background.

　　　　　　　　I was fallen, and in this wise
Thou wilt make me deeper fall. . . . Meseems,
　　meseems,　　　　　　　　　　　1164
There in her face the loved one of my dreams
Looked forth. — My heart is made a turbid
　　thing,
Craving I know not what, and my tears spring
Unbidden. — Grief I knew 'twould be; but how
Fiery a grief I never knew till now.

Lead. Thy fate I praise not. Yet, what gift
　　soe'er　　　　　　　　　　　1170
God giveth, man must steel himself and bear.

Her. (*drawing* ADMETUS *on*). Would God, I
　　had the power, 'mid all this might
Of arm, to break the dungeons of the night,
And free thy wife, and make thee glad again!

Adm. Where is such power? I know thy
　　heart were fain;　　　　　　　　1175
But so 'tis writ. The dead shall never rise.

Her. Chafe not the curb, then: suffer and be
　　wise.

Adm. Easier to give such counsel than to keep.

Her. Who will be happier, shouldst thou
　　always weep?

Adm. Why, none. Yet some blind longing
　　draws me on . . .　　　　　　　1180

Her. 'Tis natural. Thou didst love her that
　　is gone.

Adm. 'Tis that hath wrecked, oh more than
　　wrecked, my life.

Her. 'Tis certain: thou hast lost a faithful
　　wife.

Adm. Till life itself is dead and wearies me.

Her. Thy pain is yet young. Time will
　　soften thee.　　　　　　　　　1185
　　(*The veiled Woman begins dimly, as*
　　　　though in a dream, to hear the words
　　　　spoken.

Adm. Time? Yes, if time be death.

Her. 　　　　　　　Nay, wait; and some
Woman, some new desire of love, will come.

Adm. (*indignantly*). Peace!
How canst thou? Shame upon thee!　1190

Her. 　　　　　　　　Thou wilt stay
Unwed for ever, lonely night and day?

Adm. No other bride in these void arms shall
　　lie.

Her. What profit will thy dead wife gain
　　thereby?

Adm. Honor; which finds her wheresoe'er
　　she lies.　　　　　　　　　　　1195

Her. Most honorable in thee: but scarcely
　　wise!

Adm. God curse me, if I betray her in her
　　tomb!

Her. So be it! . . .
And this good damsel, thou wilt take her home?

Adm. No, in the name of Zeus, thy father!
　　No!　　　　　　　　　　　　　1200

Her. I swear, 'tis not well to reject her so.

Adm. 'Twould tear my heart to accept her.

Her. 　　　　　　　　Grant me, friend,
This one boon! It may help thee in the end.

Adm. Woe's me!　　　　　　　　1205
Would God thou hadst never won those vic-
　　tories!

Her. Thou sharest both the victory and the
　　prize.

Adm. Thou art generous. . . . But now let
　　her go.

Her. 　　　　　She shall,　　　　1209
If go she must. Look first, and judge withal.
　　(*He takes the veil off* ALCESTIS.

Adm. (*steadily refusing to look*). She must. —
　　And thou, forgive me!

Her. 　　　　　　　　Friend, there is
A secret reason why I pray for this.

Adm. (*surprised, then reluctantly yielding*).
I grant thy boon then — though it likes me ill.

Her. 'Twill like thee later. Now . . . but do
　　my will.　　　　　　　　　　　1215

Adm. (*beckoning to an Attendant*). Take her;
　　find her some lodging in my hall.

Her. I will not yield this maid to any thrall.

Adm. Take her thyself and lead her in.

Her. 　　　　　　　　　I stand　　1219
Beside her; take her; lead her to thy hand.

(He brings the Woman close to ADME-
TUS, *who looks determinedly away.
She reaches out her arms.*

Adm. I touch her not. — Let her go in!

Her.   I am loth
To trust her save to thy pledged hand and oath.
        (He lays his hand on ADMETUS'S
        shoulder.

Adm. *(desperately).* Lord, this is violence . . .
        wrong . . .

Her.   Reach forth thine hand   1225
And touch this comer from a distant land.

Adm. *(holding out his hand without looking).*
Like Perseus when he touched the Gorgon,[1]
        there!

Her. Thou hast touched her?

Adm. *(at last taking her hand).* Touched her?
        . . . Yes.

Her. *(a hand on the shoulder of each).* Then
        cling to her;   1230
And say if thou hast found a guest of grace
In God's son, Heracles! Look in her face;
Look; is she like . . . ?
        *(*ADMETUS *looks and stands amazed.*
            Go, and forget in bliss
Thy sorrow!

Adm. O ye Gods! What meaneth this? 1235
A marvel beyond dreams! The face . . . 'tis
        she;
Mine, verily mine! Or doth God mock at
        me
And blast my vision with some mad surmise?

Her. Not so. This is thy wife before thine
        eyes.

Adm. *(who has recoiled in his amazement).*
Beware! The dead have phantoms that they
        send . . .   1240

Her. Nay; no ghost-raiser hast thou made
        thy friend.

Adm. My wife . . . she whom I buried?

Her.   I deceive
Thee not; nor wonder thou canst scarce believe.

Adm. And dare I touch her, greet her, as
        mine own   1245

Wife living?

Her.   Greet her. Thy desire is won.

Adm. *(approaching with awe).* Belovèd eyes;
        belovèd form; O thou
Gone beyond hope, I have thee, I hold thee
        now?

Her. Thou hast her: may no god begrudge
        your joy.   1250

Adm. *(turning to* HERACLES*).* O lordly con-
        queror, Child of Zeus on high,
Be blessèd! And may He, thy sire above,
Save thee, as thou alone hast saved my love!
        (He kneels to HERACLES, *who raises
        him.*
But how . . . how didst thou win her to the
        light?

Her. I fought for life with Him I needs must
        fight.   1255

Adm. With Death thou hast fought! But
        where?

Her.   Among his dead
I lay, and sprang and gripped him as he fled.

Adm. *(in an awed whisper, looking towards*
        ALCESTIS*).* Why standeth she so still?
        No sound, no word!

Her. She hath dwelt with Death. Her voice
        may not be heard   1260
Ere to the Lords of Them Below she pay
Due cleansing, and awake on the third day.[1]
(To the Attendants) So; guide her home.
        (They lead ALCESTIS *to the doorway.*
            And thou, King, for the rest
Of time, be true; be righteous to thy guest,
As he would have thee be. But now farewell!
My task yet lies before me, and the spell   1266
That binds me to my master; forth I fare.

Adm. Stay with us this one day! Stay but
        to share
The feast upon our hearth!

Her.   The feasting day   1270
Shall surely come; now I must needs away.
        *(*HERACLES *departs.*

[1] Alcestis, having died, had been consecrated to the powers of the Lower World. She was thus under a ban and considered polluted. Among the Greeks it was not lawful for one under pollution to speak till after purification. Hence, by this ingenious excuse of ritualistic propriety, Euripides can manage to keep his Alcestis silent to the end of the play and to employ a mute for her rôle in the concluding scene.

[1] Medusa, of snaky locks and terrible aspect, would turn to stone any who looked upon her face. Perseus, son of Zeus and Danaë, finally succeeded in circumventing her fatal power by looking at the reflection of her face in his shield. Thus he was able to attack and slay her.

Adm. Farewell! All victory attend thy name
And safe home-coming!
                Lo, I make proclaim
To the Four Nations [1] and all Thessaly;
A wondrous happiness hath come to be: 1275
Therefore pray, dance, give offerings and make
    full
Your altars with the life-blood of the Bull!
For me . . . my heart is changed; my life shall
    mend

[1] Thessaly had been divided since very early Greek times into four districts or kingdoms.

Henceforth.   For surely Fortune is a friend.
    (*He goes with* ALCESTIS *into the Castle.*
Chor. There be many shapes of mystery;   1280
   And many things God brings to be,
     Past hope or fear.
   And the end men looked for cometh not,
   And a path is there where no man thought.
    So hath it fallen here.[1]   1285

[1] This concluding choral passage represents a poetic reflection which Euripides was fond of using to close his dramas. The almost identical lines form the endings of his *Andromache, Bacchae, Helena,* and *Medea.*

INTRODUCTION TO

The Birds

The Beginnings of Comedy in Attica: Attic Old and Middle Comedy: Aristophanes

THE BEGINNINGS OF COMEDY IN ATTICA

ATTIC COMEDY, like Attic tragedy, had its origin in the choral songs and dances of the folk festivals held each year in honor of Dionysus. The celebrations from which comedy grew, however, were gay and boisterous, and the lyrics of the chorus had a humorous, and sometimes a licentious character. The term "comedy" comes from *komoidia* meaning the song of the *Komos* or troop of Dionysian revelers.

In the course of time, the members of the reveling chorus, for the purpose both of hiding their identity and of hilarious impersonation, disguised themselves as animals — cocks, foxes, and the like — or human types — warriors, old men, etc. At first the songs were impromptu, but later they were prepared by a poet. Then the chorus or the leader of the chorus began to insert between the lyrics improvised satirical remarks directed against certain bystanders or well-known individuals of the vicinity. Such remarks to the audience gradually became an established convention of short addresses, or one longer address, which contained mocking, often scurrilous, attacks on contemporary personages.

To be a full-fledged dramatic form, however, these comic performances of choral singing and lampooning required at least one distinct actor who should engage in dialogue. That kind of dramatic comedy seems to have arisen in Attica during the first half of the sixth century B.C. Some creative spirits at Athens, headed perhaps by a writer named Susarion, brought about an amalgamation of the songs, gibes, and mumming of the Dionysian revel chorus with the farcical skits so popular in the neighboring Doric city of Megara on the isthmus of Corinth. The Doric farce supplied a loose series of ludicrous scenes plus an actor dressed in a grotesque mask and a short jerkin. The jerkin had outlandishly heavy padding on the stomach and the posteriors. The actor cracked jests, carried on humorous conversation with the chorus or its leader, and on the whole behaved like a clown. He subsequently acquired a colleague whose presence resulted in more elaborate repartee and more dramatic action. Meanwhile the comic purpose remained, as a rule, the burlesquing of prominent persons or current affairs.

About 560 B.C. volunteer performances of comedy made their appearance at the Athenian January festival, the Lenaea. These continued to be given at the Lenaea for over a century before the state bestowed formal sanction on them. Even though the state proved extremely slow to support the comedy acted during this festival, comedy always overshadowed tragedy there. The early Lenaean productions took place near the temple of Dionysus Lenaeus in the hollow between the Acropolis and the Areopagus.   When the permanent theater on the Acropolis had been completed, they were transferred thither.

At the Dionysia, the March festival, volunteer comic pieces began about 500 B.C., but the state did not institute official competitions in comedy until 486.   The arrangements concerning financial subsidy, acting personnel, prizes, and judges followed those which already existed for the tragic contests.   State supervision fixed the comic chorus, hitherto variable in size, at twenty-four singers.   That number allowed for two sufficient half-choruses such as were commonly desired to offer comic contrasts either in costume or song.

ATTIC OLD AND MIDDLE COMEDY

The Dionysia contests and the emphasis on form prevalent in tragedy rather tardily influenced the art of the comic plays.   Their construction had been traditionally informal because for a long time the Athenians had not viewed comedy as drama of lasting literary significance.   By the middle of the fifth century B.C., however, a moderate fixity of pattern had evolved.   The resulting type is now called Attic Old Comedy.

The father of the species may be regarded as Cratinus (c. 490–c. 420 B.C.), who won his first victory at the Dionysia of 452 B.C.   Like Aeschylus in tragedy a half-century earlier, Cratinus achieved so definite an intellectual and literary finish in his writings that at once they set up traditions.   Imitating the custom of tragedy, he arranged for three acting rôles.   He strengthened structural unity by utilizing a connecting idea for his entire composition.   Finally, he widened the area of comic themes by the occasional burlesquing of old myths, popular fantasies, and fads, in addition to the usual ridiculing of politics and personalities.

Though none of the plays by Cratinus have survived, the more important features of the pattern which he popularized for comedy can be outlined: (1) the prologue, an opening scene with buffoonery and jesting between two or three actors; (2) the *parodos* or entrance song of the chorus, a group of twenty-four men in colorful or grotesque costume; (3) the *agon* or contest, an argumentative scene in which the actors present opposing points of view on some issue of the day; (4) the *parabasis* or address to the audience, an elaborate song by the chorus after the exit of the actors; (5) the episodic section, a series of short scenes by the actors with interspersed songs by the chorus; (6) the *exodos* or choral recessional.   Throughout the play the dialogue is in verse of varying meters, except for scattered remarks in prose.   This general pattern clearly owes more than a little to the example of tragic drama.

The one great successor of Cratinus in Attic Old Comedy was Aristophanes, who produced his first play in 427 B.C.   For the next forty years he ruled the Athenian comic stage and brought it to the summit of its art.

Before Aristophanes' career ended in the second decade of the third century B.C., Attic comedy passed into a new stage of development.   The end of the long Peloponnesian War in 404 B.C. stimulated in Athens a change of atmosphere to which comic drama inevitably responded.   The Athenians began to lose their intense interest in the discussion of public questions as liberty diminished and censorship increased.   Enthusiasm for personal and political satire waned.   In the face of this shifting attitude, comedy gave up bit by bit the ancient methods of lampoon and invective.   It confined its caricature more and more to mythology, literature, philosophy, and manners.

The outward form of comedy also underwent revision. Just as in tragedy, so too in the comic drama popular taste dictated a steadily greater subordination of the choral and lyric elements. The *parabasis*, which once had been the most distinguished feature of comic poetry, soon disappeared, and the other parts for the chorus were much reduced.

Evidence of these changes in subject matter and design may be observed in Aristophanes' last play, *Plutus*, produced in 388 B.C. It is little more than a whimsical allegory on the theme of wealth, with slight satire upon individuals or the state of the country. No *parabasis* appears, and the choral odes are missing, probably because they were improvisations at the original performance.

Thus Attic Old Comedy early in the fourth century B.C. passed into what is now termed Middle Comedy. This second type continued until about the time of Alexander the Great's accession to the Macedonian throne in 336 B.C., by which date the political independence of Athens had been thoroughly crushed. Other than *Plutus* no specimen of Attic Middle Comedy remains. The oblivion which has descended upon it is no doubt well deserved. The mental vigor and lyric beauty of Athenian comic art were, for the most part, lost when the Old Comedy passed away.

ARISTOPHANES

The greatest writer not only of Attic comedy but of comic drama of the ancient classical world, was Aristophanes. So far did his works surpass those of other comedians in Attica during the fifth and fourth centuries that the Athenians took the pains to preserve the texts of his plays alone. Even his contemporaries recognized his genius as one of the choicest expressions of Attic civilization. It is said that shortly after Aristophanes' death, Dionysius, dictator of Syracuse (430–367 B.C.), asked the philosopher Plato (431–351 B.C.) to give him a description of Athenian culture. In answer to the request Plato sent him the works of Aristophanes.

The son of Philippos and Zenodora, Aristophanes was born about 447 B.C., probably at Athens. Of his family nothing is known except that his father owned property on the island of Aegina to the south of Attica. He was writing plays for production as early as 427, when he would have been about twenty years old. The heyday of his career roughly coincided with the period of the famous Peloponnesian War (431–404 B.C.) which almost exhausted the material and spiritual resources of Athens. As an anti-imperialist, he was bitterly opposed to the imperialistic aims of the conflict. His early plays attacked without mercy the leading figure of the war party, Cleon, a notorious demagogue. The latter became an arch-enemy who made several attempts in the courts to have Aristophanes declared an alien and therefore liable to deportation as an undesirable.

After the War Aristophanes continued to create comedy, but his efforts showed a steady decline in power. Like his beloved city-state, he had spent himself during the long struggle. Strangely enough, the date of his death has not been recorded. It occurred presumably at Athens subsequent to 388 B.C., the year of his last work. After his passing Plato composed this charming epitaph:

"The Graces, seeking an imperishable sanctuary, found the soul of Aristophanes."

During his forty years of playwriting Aristophanes averaged one play a year. Only eleven now survive.   Several of his productions came out under the assumed names of Callistratus or Philonides, but the identity of the author could never be long concealed. The chief of his extant pieces, with the details of production and content, are as follows:

The Knights — 424 B.C. — first prize at the Lenaea — a satire of war policy.
The Clouds — 423 B.C. — third place at the Dionysia — a satire of Socrates, the Sophists, and the new education.
The Birds — 414 B.C. — second prize at the Dionysia — a comic fantasy.
Lysistrata — 411 B.C. — a satire of war policy.
The Frogs — 405 B.C. — first prize at the Lenaea — a satire of contemporary tragedians, especially of Euripides.

This partial list of Aristophanes' comic achievements at least suggests the broad domain over which his mind ranged.   An immense intellectual vitality possessed him. He dealt with the entire sweep of contemporary Athenian life and thought: events, personages, gossip, customs, art, literature, education, philosophy, and, above all, politics, domestic and foreign.   Whatever in his metropolitan world afforded subject for ridicule lay within the scope of his dramatic interests.

All this medley of current topics was approached with a vast sense of fun mixed with an uncompromising spirit of criticism.   For Aristophanes, denunciation went hand in hand with laughter.   He felt constant indignation at the folly and vice in Athens, whether personal or social.   He was, however, a moralist of the highest type; one governed by pre-eminent good sense.   He attacked the craze for imperialism because it meant war and dictatorial government.   He opposed the educational program of the Sophists because it developed only mental agility and not true wisdom.   He assailed the tendencies in tragic style as illustrated by Euripides because they failed to elevate human character and emotion.

A man of strong and consistent principles, he could not avoid partisanship.   He supported the conservatism of the old aristocratic group.   The new movements in politics, philosophy, and literature all pointed toward decadence, the breakdown of freedom, integrity, and simplicity.   A corrupted Athens, he thought, must return to the standards of that vigorous generation to which she owed her democracy and her greatness, the generation of the "noble Aeschylus."   Thus Aristophanes aimed to purify the public taste by reviving the former healthy and honest views of his community.

Yet he was much more than a conservative moralist turned playwright.   High spirits, wit, lyricism, and fancy colored his satire.   In one and the same composition he could display the paradoxical qualities of the diverting buffoon and the delicate poet.   Comic ideas, however, rather than comic characterization inspired his dramatic imagination. His stage consisted of a series of caricatures framed in fantasy.

The many-sided genius of Aristophanes found its perfect medium in the flexible pattern of Attic Old Comedy and the hodgepodge of humorous, critical, and aesthetic appeals therein.   Faced with extraordinarily few restrictions he could create his play as an elaborate, fantastic, satiric joke, decorated with choral song and spectacle.   His comedy therefore became a unique blend of pantomime, burlesque, extravaganza, and musical farce.   It was a drama so dependent upon the peculiar artistic conditions of an era that it could have no later counterpart.   The comic opera of Gilbert and Sullivan bears but a feeble resemblance to the magnificent mosaic of dramatic effects which the comedy of Aristophanes must have achieved in the open-air theater at Athens.

"THE BIRDS"

Of all Aristophanic comedy *The Birds* is the most unusual and ageless. No serious motif drawn from contemporary politics or tastes underlies the surface drollery and fantasy. Unlike other plays by Aristophanes, it is an extravaganza pure and simple. Because its humor, therefore, depends only to a slight degree upon the personalities and life of the day, *The Birds* appeals to the modern taste perhaps more than any other of his works. Yet, for the very same reason, the Athenians did not accord the piece the loudest applause upon its original performance. It lost the first prize to a play filled with allusions to affairs of the moment. The Attic audience did not judge for posterity.

The Birds was acted in March, 414 B.C. For the previous year or two Athens had been filled with excitement over its imperialistic ventures. In the summer of 415 the most formidable Greek armament ever known had set forth against Sicily. Alcibiades (450–404 B.C.) had led the state to cherish great schemes of conquest. First Sicily, then Carthage, and finally the Peloponnese were to be subdued. Athens should emerge as lord of the Hellenic world. Dreams of unparalleled power and prosperity spread among the city populace. Aristophanes saw in this contemporary psychology the opportunity for a light and ludicrous caricature.

As a result he shaped *The Birds* to represent an amusing allegory of the Utopian hopes of the moment. Two old Athenians, Euelpides and Peithetaerus, weary of the city's life, make their way to the kingdom of the birds, where the Hoopoo is king. From him they hope to learn of a quiet, easy-going existence somewhere. Before the Hoopoo has given an answer to their query, Peithetaerus thinks of a brilliant scheme for making the birds lords of mankind and rulers of the universe in place of the gods. The birds hold a council, adopt the plan of Peithetaerus, and set about its accomplishment under his guidance. They enclose the mid-space between Heaven and Earth with an enormous wall. Here they erect a new city, Cloud-cuckoo-rise, garrisoned and guarded by birds so that no communication can exist between the gods and their worshipers on earth. After a while Prometheus comes to the new Utopia and informs Peithetaerus that the gods, deprived of the savors from the sacrifices on earth, are being starved. He advises Peithetaerus to push his claims against the gods. Next, Heracles, Poseidon, and another god appear as envoys to make a treaty. They finally agree that Peithetaerus is to receive the handmaid of Zeus, Basileia (Sovereignty), in marriage. He goes to Heaven and returns with his bride to Cloud-cuckoo-rise, where the bird-chorus greets them as the new lords of the universe.

The structure of *The Birds* adheres to the broad pattern of Attic Old Comedy already described. For no two compositions, however, did Aristophanes employ quite the same construction. In this play the prologue extends to l. 321. There is no true *parodos* or entrance song of the chorus, because the singers, dressed as birds, come on in most effective separate entrances. The entrance section also includes the attack of the birds on the two men. The third division, the *agon*, which contains the argument or plan, includes ll. 493–923. From here on the structure grows unusually complicated because Aristophanes inserts, instead of the usual single one, two *parabases* or lyric

addresses by the chorus to the audience.   The songs are separated by episodic material.
The first and longer *parabasis* occurs between ll. 924 and 1085; the other, between
ll. 1375 and 1440.   Thereafter the episodic portion of the play is much more extensively
and dramatically developed than is customary in Aristophanic comedy.   A genuine
climax results from the bargaining between Peithetaerus and the gods.   The denouement follows in the *exodos* (ll. 2108–80).

The Birds exhibits all of Aristophanes' brilliance as a comedian.   The whole conception of the bird kingdom, of the stratagem against the gods, and of the latter's relin-
quishment of sovereignty to avoid starvation, constitutes fun-making of the highest
order.   What an inimitable piece of whimsical imagination is this Aristophanic universe
which lasts for a rainbow moment like the soap bubble blown by a child!   The charm of
that universe grows out of many elements: the colorful extravagance in the costuming
and behavior of the chorus of two dozen different birds; the lovely choral lyrics, especially the hymn on the bird family (l. 932 ff.); the witty burlesque, such as the skit of the
perennial versifier (l. 1190 ff.); and the delightful buffoonery, like the scene (l. 1871 ff.)
between Peithetaerus and Prometheus with his muffler and parasol.   Thus, throughout
the play, rollicking humor, critical perception, and poetic fancy are all fused together.
It is this combination of the most eminent and diverse qualities which distinguishes
The Birds as a product of superlative comic genius.

[For a study of Greek comedy, see Gilbert Norwood, *Greek Comedy* (1931); for a study of Aristophanes, L. E. Lord, *Aristophanes, His Plays and His Influence* (1925).]

ARISTOPHANES

The Birds

[Translated by MARSHALL MACGREGOR*]*

DRAMATIS PERSONAE

(In the order of their appearance)

EUELPIDES
PEITHETAERUS } *elderly Athenians*

TROCHILUS, *a bird-servant of the* HOOPOO

HOOPOO, *formerly Tereus*

NIGHTINGALE, *formerly Procne, wife of the*
    HOOPOO

CHORUS OF BIRDS

A PRIEST

A POET

A PROPHET

METON, *a mathematician and surveyor*

A GOVERNMENT INSPECTOR

A CONSTITUTIONAL LAWYER

TWO BIRD-MESSENGERS

IRIS

A THIRD BIRD-MESSENGER

AN INTENDING PARRICIDE

CINESIAS, *a dithyrambic poet*

A BLACKMAILER

PROMETHEUS

POSEIDON

HERCULES

A DANUBIAN GOD

SOVEREIGNTY, *a mute character, bride of*
    PEITHETAERUS

Bird-Attendants, Bird-Courtiers

The SCENE *is a wild rocky region, a thicket in the background*

Enter two elderly Athenians, PEITHETAERUS *and* EUELPIDES, *the former carrying a crow, the latter a jackdaw. They solemnly cross and recross the stage in opposite directions, their attention riveted on the birds in their hands*

Euel. (*addressing his jackdaw*). Straight where the tree shows — that, you mean, 's the track?

Pei. (*to his crow*). Curse and confound you! (*To* EUEL.) Here, she's croaking "Back."

Euel. Pfff! Up and down, and down and up we go,

We'll die of tramping idly to and fro.

Pei. Oh what a fool, to let a crow beguile   5
Me into footing weary mile on mile!

Euel. Oh what a dolt, to let a daw impose
On me to wear the nails right off my toes!

Pei. Where in the world we are I'm far from clear.

Euel. Could you contrive to make your home from here?   10

Pei. From here? 'T would baffle Execestides.[1]
Oh Hell!

Euel.   *You* can go there, Sir, if you please.

Pei. Crazy Philocrates,[2] who has a name
For game and poultry, has made *us* his game.
These were the guides, he said, to take us on   16
To Tereus,[3] now Sir Bird of Birdlington,

---

[1] An alien from Caria in southwest Asia Minor, who became notorious at Athens for his cleverness in passing himself off as an Athenian citizen and thus finding a home country. He is satirized again in ll. 1050 and 1917.

[2] An Athenian dealer in wild birds, which he exposed on earthenware trays.

[3] Pandion, King of Athens, had two daughters, Procne and Philomela. Tereus of Thrace married Procne and outraged Philomela. In revenge the sisters

And sold that daw for two pence, full of tricks
As Tharraleides' son,[1] this crow for six.
But how to peck, it seems, is all they know.   20
   Euel. (*to daw*). *Now* what are you agape for?
     Can we go
Over the precipice?   There's no road there.
   Pei. (*peering over the rocks*). Not, I'll be
     bound, a footpath anywhere.
   Euel. Hasn't the crow a hint to give us now?
   Pei. She isn't croaking what she did, I'll
     vow.   25
   Euel. What does she say about the toad then?
   Pei.   Say?
Just that she'll gnaw my fingers all away.
   Euel. Isn't it monstrous?   Each of us pre-
     pared
And full of zeal to be a gallows-bird,   30
And yet we can't contrive to find the way.
(*He addresses himself directly to the audience.*)
We're sick, good Sirs here present at our play,
With the reverse of Sacas'[2] malady.
He is no citizen, but strives to be.
We with all rights of birth and blood indued 35
Equal to any, whom none ever shoo'd
Out of our land, hot-foot away have flown.
Not that we hate our city.   She, we own,
Great in prosperity and bliss has waxed,
And everyone within her's free-ly taxed.   40
Cicalas[3] twitter for a month or two
On twigs and sprays, and men at Athens do
The same on lawsuits all their whole lives
     through.
That's why we're footing it upon our feet,
With basket, pot, and myrtle boughs com-
     plete,[4]   45

killed Itys, son of Tereus by Procne, and served him up
for his father's dinner.   Outraged by this act Tereus
pursued the two women to punish them.   But by the
latter's prayer the gods changed all three into birds:
Tereus into a hoopoo; Procne into a nightingale; Philomela into a swallow.
   [1] An unidentified Athenian.
   [2] Acestor, a contemporary poet, who was nicknamed
"Sacas" because of his supposed Scythian (i.e. Thracian) ancestry.   He, like Execestides, got himself on
the roll of Athenian citizens, though an alien.
   [3] Cicadas or locusts.   Their singing in the branches
of trees and shrubs was a favorite topic of the Greek
poets, such as Homer and Hesiod.
   [4] These were the accoutrements necessary for a Greek
pilgrim to carry in order to make the proper sacrificial
ceremony.

Searching around to find a snug retreat
To live in the remainder of our days.
And so, to make inquiries, now our way's
To Tereus the hoopoo, if in his flight
Such city anywhere has crossed his sight.   50
   Pei. (*who during* EUELPIDES' *explanation to
     the audience has been indulging in "busi-
     ness" with his crow*).   I say!
   Euel.   Hello!
   Pei.   Ever so long my crow
'S been pointing up.
   Euel.   My daw, it seems, would show 55
Me something too by gaping from below.
There must be birds up there — there *are*, I'll
     vow.
We'll soon discover, if we make a row.
   Pei. I'll tell you.   Bang your leg against the
     rock.
   Euel. *You* bang your *head* — it'll cause
     twice the shock.   60
   Pei. Well, get a stone and knock then.
   Euel.   That I'll do.
     (*He takes a stone and, knocking on the
     rock, calls loudly.*
House!   House!
   Pei.   What's this?   A *house* d'you
     call the Hoopoo?
Hoospoo, not *House*, you should have called
     out, when   65
You knocked.
   Euel.   Well, *Hoospoo!*   Must I knock
     again?
(*More loudly*) *Hoospoo!*

A small bird with an enormous gaping beak, the
   TROCHILUS,[1] *issues from the thicket.* PEI-
   THETAERUS *and* EUELPIDES *tumble about
   the stage in terror, allowing the crow and daw
   to escape*

   Troch.   Who's there?   Who'd with
     my master speak?
   Euel. Heaven bless and save us!   What a
     frightful beak!   70
   Troch. (*in dismay at seeing men*). Woe's me!
     Alack!   Two fowlers here — our curse.

   [1] The dunlin or plover-page, a shore bird.   The name
"trochilus" means "runner" and refers to the manner
of its movement on the ground.

Pei. It *is* a monster—and its speech is worse.

Troch. You'll die.

Pei.   No ... We're not men.

Troch.   What may you be?   75

Pei. A bird, in Libya [1] native, Shakiknee.

Troch. (*turning to* EUELPIDES). And what may this bird be then? (EUELPIDES *hesitates.*) Can't you speak?

Euel. A tell-tale tit from Lydia,[2] Bowelsweak.

Troch. Nonsense.   80

Euel. (*pointing to ordure at his feet*). There's that will vouch the truth you seek.

Pei. What, in Heaven's name, are *you*, pray? What's *your* stock?

Troch. I am a servant-bird.

Pei.   A fighting cock
That lost, you mean?   85

Troch.   No, it was Master who,
When changed to a hoopoo, prayed that I too
Might be a bird to serve his every need.

Pei. A bird must have his servant then? Indeed!

Troch. His having been a man accounts for that.   90
Suppose he fancies a Phalerian sprat;[3]
Off with a pot to fetch the sprats desired!
It's soup he wants, a bowl and spoon required;
Off for a spoon!

Pei. The Scurrier-bird! Quite so.   95
I'll tell you what, Sir Scurrier-bird. Pray go
And call your Master.

Troch.   He's just had a heap
Of gnats and myrtle-berries, and's asleep.

Pei. No matter, wake him.   100

Troch.   He'll be vexed, I know,
But, as you make a point of it, I'll go.
           (*Re-enters the thicket.*

Euel. (*looking after the retreating* TROCHILUS). Curse you, you nearly made me die of fright.
Now here's ill luck — my daw gone out of sight
In terror.   105

Pei.   Oh you cowardly creature, you!
You let him go in a panic.

[1] A large district in northern Africa, adjoining Egypt on the west.

[2] The western portion of Asia Minor.

[3] Small herrings from Phalerum, the most easterly of the harbors of Athens.

Euel.   Is it true
You held your crow fast, when you fell and roared?

Pei. Of course.   110

Euel.   Where *is* she?

Pei. (*shortly*). Spread her wings and soared.

Euel. You held her fast though. (*With mock obeisance*) Hail, my Hero Lord!

Hoo. (*within the thicket, grandiloquently*). Ope now my boughs, that straight I may appear.

The HOOPOO [1] *enters from the thicket.* PEITHE-TAERUS *and* EUELPIDES *are convulsed with laughter at his dilapidated appearance*

Euel. Preserve us, Heaven! What creature have we here?   115
What sort of plumes are these? Three crests — how queer!

Hoo. Who is it seeks me?

Euel.   Heaven's chastising staff,
I think, has hit you hard.

Hoo.   You do not laugh   120
That thus I plume myself? Time was, Sirs, when
I was a MAN.

Pei. (*apologetically*). No, it's not you.

Hoo.   What then?

Pei. Your beak looks funny, but (*bursting again into laughter*) excuse us, please.   125

Hoo. It's the outrageous fashion Sophocles
Treats ME, ME TEREUS, in his tragedies.[2]

Pei. You're Tereus? Really now! Peacock or bird?

Hoo. A bird.

Pei.   Why then, your feathers — what's occurred?   130

Hoo. I have been moulting.

[1] A European bird of wide distribution, about the size of a large thrush, with a handsome crest a slender decurved bill, and striking plumage of cinnamon and black. Of course the Hoopoo of this scene possesses none of his species' usual impressiveness; he is indeed almost featherless.

[2] Sophocles had written a tragedy called *Tereus*, in the last episode of which he had doubtless presented Tereus as transformed into a hoopoo in accordance with the myths.

Pei.   Through an illness, eh?

Hoo. No, in the winter-time it is the way

Of birds to shed old feathers and grow new.

Tell me, who are you?   135

Pei.   We? Just mortals two.

Hoo. Your country is —?

Pei.   The land of gallant ships.

Hoo. Not Baillies are you?

Euel.   No, the sort that skips,   140

Leg-baillies.

     Hoo.   What? There too they sow that

     seed?

Euel. You'd find, if you were short, a bit at

     need.

Hoo. What quest is it has brought you to this

     spot?

Pei. We wish to have your counsel.   145

Hoo.   Touching what?

Pei. Once on a time you were a man — like

us,

A time when into debt you ran — LIKE US,

But on all payment put a ban — *LIKE US.*

Then later you became a bird and flew   150

Over all lands and seas the whole world through.

What man or bird knows is all known to you.

That's why we've come to seek your aid.

     Maybe

You know a downy spot somewhere, where we

Could snuggle, as in blankets, cosily.   155

     Hoo. (*in surprise*). You want a greater town

     than Rugged Screes?

Pei. No, one that better with our type

     agrees.

Hoo. *Bon ton* you want, it's patent, some-

     thing *chic.*

Euel. Chic! Not at all. And *bon bons* make

     me sick.

Hoo. What city would you count a place of

     bliss?   160

Pei. One where the greatest worry would be

     this: —

First thing a knock upon the door there'd be.

A friend to ask me, "Promise solemnly

You'll join our wedding feast today. Now, do.

Dress and come early. Bring the children

     too.   165

Don't disappoint me, please, or see you stay

At home likewise, when troubles come my

     way."

Hoo. These *are* sad troubles that attract

     your mind.

(*To* EUELPIDES) And you?

Euel.   Oh, I like that kind too.   170

Hoo.   What kind?

Euel. I'd like a place where sire of blooming

     maid

Would greet me furiously with this tirade: —

"A nice thing this, Fitz-Sparks! You meet my

     girl   174

Fresh from her dancing class, all frill and curl,

And don't accost, kiss, clasp, have joy of her,

And you and I friends, as our fathers were!"

Hoo. Unhappy man, such miseries to crave!

There's such a city where the Red Sea's wave

Rolls, happy ——   180

Euel.   No, no rolling wave, I pray,

For us, where in the morning one fine day

Up pops the Athens mail-boat with the —

     POLICE.

Pei. Can't you inform us of a spot in Greece?

Hoo. Why wouldn't Scabz in Elis ¹ suit your

     case?   185

Euel. Why? Bless me, though I've never

     seen the place,

I hate it — it suggests Melanthius' face.²

Hoo. There's Locris ³ now, Opuntians ⁴

     might be found

Convenient too.

     Euel.   Not for a thousand pound   190

I'd be *A. Puncheon* ⁵ — not on any ground.

What's life here with the Birds like? Smooth

     and rough.

You know it all.

¹ This country, on the west coast of the Peloponnesus, the southern peninsula of Greece, contained a town called Lepreus, i.e., "leprous"—hence "Scabz" here. In 420 B.C. Elis contracted an alliance with the Athenians. Therefore this reference may have been intended as a compliment to Athens' relatively new allies, whose envoys no doubt were viewing this play at the Great Dionysia.

² Melanthius, a contemporary tragic poet obnoxious to Aristophanes, apparently had a scabby face and was thought to be leprous.

³ A state in central Greece to the northwest of Attica.

⁴ The people living in northwestern Locris along the coast facing the island of Euboea.

⁵ The Greek name here is "Opuntius." Aristophanes calls the man "the one-eyed crow" in l. 1643. He was apparently a common informer.

Hoo.   The days pass well enough,
For, first, there is no use for purses here.   195
   Euel. Then life's base coin must mostly disappear.
   Hoo. In myrtle-berried gardens fair we feed
On thyme and orange-blooms and poppyseed.
   Euel. Why surely that's the life that bridegrooms lead!
   Pei. Hi! Hi!   200
I see a mighty scheme, that brings the birds
Vast power, if you'll but listen to my words.
   Hoo. Listen — to what?
   Pei.   To what? This first, forbear   204
To fly and gawk here, there and everywhere.
It's not good form. Suppose a man inquires
Where we come from, down yonder, of the
     fliers,
"What bird is that?" Cockman, be sure, 'll cry,
"A Man-bird, shifty creature, quick to fly,
Now here, now there, but not long anywhere."
   Hoo. Aye, that's a hit thrust shrewdly home,
     I swear.   211
What then?
   Pei.   Combine and found a city.
   Hoo.   What?
We found a city! We, the birds! Oh, rot!   215
   Pei. Indeed! It's *you* whose words are far
     from wise.
Look down.
   Hoo.   I'm looking.
   Pei.   Now then raise your eyes.
   Hoo. Yes.   220
   Pei.   Twist your neck around.
   Hoo.   So obviously
Its dislocation will be good for me.
   Pei. You see something?
   Hoo. Yes, clouds, of course, and sky.   225
   Pei. This is the birds' SITE, that you won't
     deny.
   Hoo. SITE? In what way?
   Pei.   Their region, as it were.
It's VISITED, a general thoroughfare,
And so, of course, the name of SITE must
     bear.
But once you've settled there and walled it
     round,   231
CI–TY instead of SITE it will be found,
And men shall be as locusts in your power,

And gods like Melians [1] with hunger cower.
   Hoo. Why?   235
   Pei. Surely twixt the Earth and them's the
     Air.
So just as, if a mission we prepare
To Pytho,[2] from Boeotia we ask then
Free passage, so with offerings from men
To gods, unless *they* pay the proper dues,   240
Passage to thighbones' savor you'll refuse
Chaos by law being yours alone to use.
   Hoo. Hurrah! Hurrah!
By Earth, I swear, by trap and springe and net,
I've never heard a prettier notion yet.   245
In setting up your CITY count on me,
Provided that the other birds agree.
   Pei. But who'll explain the project to them?
   Hoo.   You.
They understand Greek now, they used not to;
I've taught them, though it took some time to
     do.   251
   Pei. And how'll you call a meeting?
   Hoo.   Easily.
I'll step at once into this brake you see
And there arouse my Nightingale. Then we
Will summon them — they've but to hear our
     cry,   256
And they'll be here as fast as they can fly.
   Pei. Come, my dear bird, don't tarry then,
     but make,
I beg of you, all speed into the brake   259
And there forthwith your Nightingale [3] awake.

The Hoopoo *retires into the thicket,[4] where he
arouses the* Nightingale *in the following
address*

*Hoo. Wake, Mistress, wake, from slumber cease,
The strains of sacred song release,*

[1] The inhabitants of Melos, an island in the southwestern Aegean, whom the Athenians besieged in 416 B.C. during the Peloponnesian War and reduced to submission by starvation.

[2] The ancient oracle of Apollo at Delphi in Phocis, a country northwest of Attica. The Athenians could not communicate by land with Delphi, except through the adjoining state of Boeotia.

[3] Procne, the transformed wife of Tereus.

[4] Perhaps Aristophanes had the Hoopoo retire into the thicket — on the stage, of course, the scene house — before the beginning of his serenade, so that a more qualified singer might perform behind the scene.

The dirge that from thy lips divine
Pours forth for Itys,[1] *thine and mine,*
   The liquid melody that thrills   265
     Thy golden throat.
Through leaf-tressed briony thy cry
Uprises clear to Zeus on high,
Where golden-haired Apollo hears,
And straight responsive to thy tears,   270
   His ivory lyre Olympus fills
     With dulcet note.
Then, as they thread the dance's maze,
   The gods upraise
In unison their holy lays.[2]   275
     (*There follows the* NIGHTINGALE'S
     song, a solo on the flute, performed
     behind the scene by the flutist.

Pei. Great Heaven, the notes that from the
   bird's throat pour!
With melody the brake's all honeyed o'er.
Euel. I say ——
Pei.   Be quiet, can't you?
Euel.   Why, what's wrong?   280
Pei. Now it's the Hoopoo's turn to sing his
   song.
   Hoo. (*sings off*).
Hoo-poopoopoo-poopoopoo-poopoopoo-poop!
Come come, draw ye nigh, draw ye nigh!
Feathered comrades, hither fly!
Ye to whom the farmer's field   285
Grain and seed must ever yield,
   As ye wing your way,
   Swiftly in thousands piping soft your lay;
Who in the furrow still
Around the new-turned earth-clod twitter shrill
   With voices sweet,   291
   Tweet-a-weet, Tweet-a-weet, Tweet-a-weet,
     Tweet-a-weet;
Who in the gardens on the ivy boughs
And branches house,
Mountain-birds, strawberry-tits, olive-peckers
   all,   295
Come flying at my call,
   Quick!
Tr-o, To-tr-o, To-to-to, Twick!
Who devour stinging gnats, where the fens' waters
   flow

Down the runnels, ye who haunt where the lush
   grasses grow,   300
Who Marathon's[1] *fair meadow know,*
   Come, and thou, francolin, francolin, too
   With thy plumes' many a hue;
Ye with the halcyons through the air cleaving,
Where briny Ocean his bosom is heaving,   305
Come, I have news that ye should be receiving,
   Slender-necked birds now of every feather
   Assemble together.
Here is one with new perspective,
New objective,   310
   High for wit his reputation,
   Gather now for consultation,
Quick! Quick! Quick! Quick!
Toro-toroto-rotoro-twick
Keek-abow, Keek-abow,   315
To-rotoro-toroto-rolili-lick.
   Pei. D' you see one coming?
   Euel.   No, by Heaven, not I,
Although I'm scanning all agape the sky.
   Pei. (*dejectedly*). Lost labor then, that in the
   brake Hoopoo   320
Has set up such a curlew's hullabaloo.

A solitary bird, the leader of the chorus, enters the
   Orchestra. From the thicket the HOOPOO *re-*
   appears upon the stage

   Bird. Torotwick! Torotwick!
   Pei. (*excitedly at sight of the bird*). Look!
   Look there! At last one's coming.
Over yonder! Don't you see?
   Euel. By the Lord, a bird! What is it?
   Peacock? No, it cannot be.   325
   Pei. Here's the very one to tell us. I'll in-
   quire. (*To the* HOOPOO) What's that
   bird there?
   Hoo. That's a bird you seldom see, belonging
   to a species rare,
Nesting in the fens.
   Pei.   A fine bird, on my word!
   He gleams like flame.
   Hoo. Yes, of course he does. It's natural, as
   flam-ingo is his name.   330

[1] The famous plain on the east coast of Attica, where
the Athenians defeated the Persians in 490 B.C.

---

[1] The butchered son of Procne and Tereus. See note
to l. 17.
[2] All subsequent passages in italics are *sung*.

A second bird enters the Orchestra

Euel. Oh, I say!

Pei.   Why what's the matter?

Euel. Here's another, (*pointing*) there you are.

Pei. Yes, begad it is.

Hoo.   He also usually nests afar.   335
Save at sacred, festive seasons he is known to very few
And derives his name from Turkey.

Euel.   Turkey! Bless me, is that true?
Turkey! Then why ever has he failed to bring plum-pudding too?

A third bird enters

Pei. Goodness gracious! Here's another bird that looks as if he's dyed.   340
What the —! So you're not the only hoopoo
There's this one beside
Who's a hoopoo also.

Hoo. Well, he's son of Philocles' hoopoo,[1]
I'm the father of his father,[2] as one might remark to you —
"Callias, son of Hipponicus, who himself is Callias' son."[3]   345

Euel. Callias is it? How he's moulting!
Why, his plumes are nearly done!

Hoo. Well, you see his stock's a good one, so blackmailers strip him bare
And at plucking him the women too contrive to do their share.

[1] A tragic poet, Philocles, a contemporary of Aristophanes, also produced a play on the theme of Tereus and evidently exhibited the transformation of the hero into a hoopoo.

[2] A suggestion that Philocles plagiarized the drama of Sophocles called *Tereus*.

[3] The custom of naming the eldest son after his grandfather and of thereby alternating the family names was prevalent at Athens, notably in this noble and wealthy family, who enjoyed the hereditary role of torchbearer at the Eleusinian Mysteries, the most exclusive of Athenian religious rites. The elder Callias mentioned here was fined a large sum in 449 B.C. for taking bribes in connection with the peace treaty he concluded with Persia. Callias the younger was a rank profligate. In his house Plato laid the scene of *Protagoras*, and Xenophon the historian, the scene of *Symposium*.

A fourth bird enters

Pei. Here again's another coming, with a crest too. Tell us how
This one is addressed among you.   350

Hoo.   That's the glut-hen coming now.

Pei. It's Cleonymus,[1] it must be. He's the glutton, all agree.

Euel. No, it can't be. This bird hasn't lowered his crest and turned to flee.

Pei. Can you tell us what this waving plume upon these birds attests?
Is it a race with helms upon their heads, cuirasses on their chests?   355

Hoo. No, they're like the Carians, who to gain protection mount their crests.[2]

The other birds of the chorus come flocking in

Pei. Goodness gracious! Don't you see them? How the deuce their numbers grow!
Birds and Birds!

Euel.   Great Heaven, preserve us!
Clouds of Birds! Hello, hello!
They're so dense they hide the entrance as they flutter to and fro.   360

Hoo. (*pointing*). Here's the Partridge, over yonder you the God-wit will descry,
Look this way, you'll see the Mallard — and the Halcyon passing by.

Euel. Yes, and who is that behind her?

Hoo.   That? The Shaver.

Euel.   Really! Then   365
You've a Shaver.

Hoo.   Yes, to Birds he's what the Barber is to Men.
Here's the Owl.

Euel.   Who brought an owl to Athens? Labor lost again![3]

[1] Aristophanes frequently attacked this Athenian contemporary; in the *Knights*, as a glutton; in the *Wasps*, as a demagogue; and here, as both a glutton and a coward.

[2] The people of Caria in western Asia Minor were the first to use crests on helmets.

[3] Owls were so numerous in Athens that the saying "carrying owls to Athens" became the equivalent of the English "carrying coals to Newcastle."

Hoo. Jay and Pigeon, Lark and Heron, Kestrel, Thyme-finch, Hawk, Cuckoo, 370
Kite and Redpoll with Woodpecker, Cushat-dove and Ring-dove too,
Diving Fantail, Coot and Vine-tit, Scarletfoot and Crimson Mew.

> (*The chorus hop twittering to and fro about the Orchestra, eventually forming up into lines facing the stage.*

Euel. Oh, what a flock of birds! Hello!
And blackbirds also. Oh! Oh! Oh!
How they hop and twitter, trying each the other to outcrow! 375
Are they meaning mischief, think you? Oh their bills are gaping, see!
And their eyes are glaring at us.

Pei. The idea had struck me.

Chor. (*excitedly*). Wh-wh-wh-wh-wh-wh-where
> Sojourns my summoner? 380
> Whither his way doth he wend?

Hoo. *Waiting here I've been this long while like a tried and trusty friend.*

Chor. Wh-wh-wh-wh-wh-wh-what
> Tidings for me hast thou got,
> That shall enrapture my breast? 385

Hoo. *Sound, safe, sweet and profitable, in the common interest —*
Men have come, two subtle sages, here to seek me in my nest.

Chor. Where? How?
> Sayst thou —?

Hoo. *That from men there have arrived here two that aged are and wise,* 390
And have brought the embryo of an elephantine enterprise.

Chor. What a crime! In all my lifetime there has been none like it, none,
How d'you say —?

Hoo. *Now wait a moment, don't be scared.*

Chor. What have you done? 395

Hoo. *Welcomed men who have a passion to consort with us who fly.*

Chor. You have done this thing?

Hoo. I've done it and am glad, I don't deny.

Chor. And they're present here among us?

Hoo. Yes, they're here as much as I. 400

> (*The* Chorus *at this avowal break into a passionate outburst.*

Chor. Ha! Ha!
Treachery! Villainy! Our friend erstwhile
> Who ranged our plain,
> Who ate our grain,
Proves traitor vile. 405
> *False to the Birds' Time-honored ordinance,*
> *False to his solemn, sworn allegiance.*
He's lured me to a trap, ah me! a helpless prey
Of wicked foe, who's sought to take my life away
E'en from his natal day. 410

Chor. Lead. With the bird we'll settle later, for the present he can wait,
But the two old men to Justice we will forthwith dedicate,
To be torn and rent asunder.

Pei. That appears to seal our fate.

Euel. You're to blame, it's all your fault we're in this awful misery. 415
What did you bring me away from home for?

Pei. Why, to keep me company.

Euel. Floods of tears, you mean, to shed here.

Pei. That remark is hardly wise.
How'll you do it once the birds' bills have deprived you of your eyes? 420

Chor. (*preparing to attack*). Ho! Ho!
On now! Set on! On and attack the foe!
> Around them close,
> Till with the blows
Of wings blood flow! 425
> *Both shall today bewail their sorry fate,*
> *And with their flesh our eager bills shall sate.*
Nor mountain shadow casts, nor cloud obscures the sky,
Not gray sea-billow heaves, whereunto they shall fly
And our revenge defy. 430

Chor. Lead. Ho! We'll peck them and we'll pluck them. Now's no time for holding back.
Where's the Company-commander? 'Vance the right wing to attack!

Euel. (*in terror*). There, you see! Where can I run to? Oh, poor me!

Pei. Hi! Stand your ground.

Euel. To be torn in pieces by them? 435

Pei. Do you fancy that you've found
Means of 'scaping from their clutches?

Euel. No, I don't.

Pei.   I'll tell you what
We must do — stand fast and fight them, and
     for arms take each a pot.   440
Euel. Take a pot! What use'll that be?
Pei.   Ne'er an "owl" will come our way.[1]
Euel. Look at those with crooked talons!
Pei.   That's a game that two can play,
Plant your toasting-fork before you, prongs on
     top.   445
Euel.   And for my eyes?
Pei. Get a pipkin or a saucer and a helmet
     improvise.

     (EUELPIDES *and* PEITHETAERUS *busy
     themselves procuring their novel ar-
     mor from their luggage.*

Euel. It's a notion marks you master of the
     military art.
At ingenious devices you'd give Nicias[2] a start.
Chor. Lead. Hullabaloo! Fix beaks and at
     'em! On, away and do your worst! 450
Maul them, tear them, thrash them, skin them,
     smite the pot and smash it first!

     (*The attack is delivered and repulsed.*

Hoo. (*interposing between the assailants and
     the assailed*). Why, you vilest of all
     creatures, do you mean to take the life
Of two men who've never harmed you, and in
     foolish, furious strife
Rend them limb from limb asunder — kith and
     kindred of my wife?
Chor. Lead. Shall we spare them? Then the
     wolf shall in our breasts compassion
     move.   455
Where on foes more foul and bitter shall we
     birds our vengeance prove?
Hoo. If, although to all appearance they are
     foes, at heart they're friends
And have come here to inform you what to your
     advantage tends —
Chor. Lead. (*interrupting angrily*). How
     should *they* inform or show us our ad-
     vantage, who of yore

[1] There have been many attempts to explain this
remark. Perhaps the most satisfactory is that the
pilgrim's pot contained lighted fire which the owl as the
bird of night would shun.
[2] Sole commander of the Athenian expedition against
Sicily. At the time of the production of *The Birds*,
Alcibiades, his colleague, had been recalled. Nicias
was noted as a military tactician.

On our fathers and grandfathers waged exter-
     minating war?   460
Hoo. But it's wisdom's way to gather knowl-
     edge even from a foe.
For example, to Precaution all their preserva-
     tion owe.
Yet, while friends can never teach it, foemen
     do — and quickly too.
Obviously from their foemen, not from friends,
     the cities drew
Hints to build the beetling wall, the battleship
     that queens the seas,   465
And this knowledge 'tis preserves their homes,
     belongings, families.
Chor. (*after consultation*). *We agree to wait
     and listen first to hear what they advise.
It's as well to do so. Foemen may sometimes sug-
     gest what's wise.*
Pei. (*to* EUEL.). *Look, their rage, it seems,
     abates. Retire by numbers* — ONE,
     TWO, THREE.

     (*They solemnly retire up the stage.*

Hoo. (*to* CHORUS). *It's the course that's just
     and honest, and a favor due to me.*   470
*Chor. In the past we've never quarreled, now
     we mustn't disagree.*
*Pei. Now their passion's growing colder.
Ground your pipkins and your pot,
But our toasting-forks we'll shoulder
And on sentry-duty trot   475
Up and down our pitcher-fences,
Since for flight there no pretense is.*

     (PEITHETAERUS *and* EUELPIDES *move,
     forks on shoulder, up and down be-
     hind their improvised defenses of
     crockery, passing and repassing each
     other.*

*Euel. Oh, indeed! And, if they slay us,
Can you tell me where they'll lay us?*
Pei. Where the nation crowns with glory   480
*Those who fall in combat gory.
To the Generals I and you
Will explain how here we cherished
Gallant hearts and nobly perished
In the Battle of Bird's-Eye-View.   485
Chor. Lead.* (*to* CHORUS *in approved military
     fashion*).
*'Shun! Ground rages! So let 'em cool
There by your angers, according to rule*

Taught in the orthodox military school.
  Ready there, steady there,
    Till we enquire,   490
  Who they are, whence they are,
  What they desire.
(*To* HOOPOO) I say, Hoopoo, a word with you!
  Hoo. A word with me? Now what's to do?
  Chor. Lead. Who are these men, and what's
    their race?   495
  Hoo. Wise Hellas is their native place.
  Chor. Lead. And what is there, that can
    bring
Here to us up above
Such a pair?
  Hoo.   'Tis their love   500
Of you and life upon the wing.
Fain they'd dwell in your land
Yours for aye, heart and hand.
  Chor. Lead. Really?
And for their love what ground appears?   505
  Hoo. You'll scarce, I think, believe your ears.
  Chor. Lead. He sees some profit that he'll
    here secure
Worth stopping for, that makes him sure
To conquer foe and succor friend,
If with the Birds his life he blend?   510
  Hoo. He speaks of high prosperity
Nor words describe nor thought has known.
    Convincingly
What's here, what's there
What's everywhere,   515
He proves is yours, and yours alone.
  Chor. Lead. (*after an astonished pause*). Is he
    diseased in the brain?
  Hoo. Never a man was more sane.
  Chor. Lead. Then he is cunning of heart?
  Hoo. Never a fox was more smart.   520
Craft's his trade, a perfect blade
He'll cut more than hot butter.
  Chor. Lead. Oh bid him speak without delay!
I long to hear him. What you say
Has set me all aflutter.   525
  Hoo. (*to servants* XANTHIAS *and* MANO-
    DORUS). Come you and you, collect
    this armory
And hang it in the chimney, where you see
The stock-pot hanging and good luck with ye!
    (*The servants gather up the crockery,*
    and the HOOPOO *turns to* PEITHETAERUS.

And you expound and state the reasons why
I've summoned them to meet.   530
  Pei.   By Heaven, not I,
Save under that same covenant and deed,
To which the Monkey and his wife agreed,
The Cutler viz. All biting to be barred,
Low hitting, gouging ——   535
  Chor. Lead. (*pointing*). *This?* Oh that's
    too hard.
Refused.
  Pei. No, eyes — it's those I want to guard.
  Chor. Lead. Oh, that's agreed then.
  Pei.   Swear it on your oath.   540
  Chor. Lead. I swear it, as I'd win the votes of
    both
Judges and audience all.
  Pei.   So shall it be.
  Chor. Lead. Forsworn I'd have — a bare ma-
    jority.
  Pei. (*in the manner of a Commander-in-Chief*).
    NOTICE TO MEN AT ARMS. THE
    PRESENT STRESS   545
BEING PAST, EACH WILL RETURN TO
    HIS ADDRESS.
FOR FUTURE ORDERS SEE THE PUBLIC
    PRESS.
  Chor. Nature created Man ever in every way
A thing of cunning. Still you can say your say,
For, perhaps, you may   550
  Reveal some profit that you descry for me,
  Or loftier majesty
I'm too unintellectual to see.
Now the scheme, that you're setting afoot, to all
    declare.
For if blessing it chance to bear,   555
In that blessing my friends all alike shall share.
  Chor. Lead. Come, we beg you, disclose the
    design you propose
And are here to effect. Have no fear.
Not a finger upon you we'll lay till you've done.
  To the truce we will strictly adhere.   560
  Pei. Egad I'm aquiver my speech to deliver.
I've mixed and made ready the dough.
By nothing I'm barred from now kneading it
    hard.
Hi, my lad, bring a garland,[1] and go
Fetch some water to wash me my hands.   565

[1] It was an Athenian custom for a speaker at a feast
or a public occasion to wear a wreath on his head.

Euel.   Oh begosh!
    Does this mean it's a dinner or no?
Pei. (*aside to* EUELPIDES). Not a bit. What
    for ages my brain-power engages
Is how to discover a lie,
A great big one and fat, which will lay them all
    flat,   570
While their souls into splinters will fly.
(*To the Birds, with an air of patronizing sym-*
    pathy) Such a grief my heart wrings for
    you Birds who were kings.
Chor. Lead. (*in surprise*). We were Kings!
    Kings of what?
Pei.   Everything.
Whatsoever there be, Kings of him, Kings of
    me,   575
Kings of Zeus the Olympians's King.
For in order of birth Cronus,[1] Titans,[2] the
    Earth
Must all yield pride of place to the Bird.
Euel. What! The Earth?
Pei. Yes, exact-ly I'm stating the fact. 580
Euel. Well, egad, it's a fact I'd not heard.
Pei. There's a deal *you* don't know. You are
    lacking in go
And in Esop[3] you haven't read far,
Who distinctly declared that the lark was the
    bird
First created of all things that are.   585
She was born before Earth, and then, after her
    birth,
Her poor father to sickness succumbed.
Earth still was to seek, she had waked him a
    week,
And the problem her faculties numbed.
Not a place had she, where she her sire could
    inter,   590
So she made him a grave in her head.
Euel. The result, I remark, is the sire of the
    lark
Rests at Headingly now that he's dead.
Pei. If you're prior by birth to the gods and
    the Earth,
The conclusion, all people must own,   595

[1] The youngest of the Titans, ruler of the world before
Zeus.
[2] The children of Gaea, the Earth, and primeval
gods in Greek myth.
[3] A Greek author of animal fables, who rose to fame
about the middle of the sixth century B.C.

Can but be that to you as the eldest is due
    Both by custom and justice the throne.
Euel. It's a matter that speaks for itself.
    Now our beaks
We must all keep remarkably fine.
To the woodpecker straight Zeus must yield up
    his state   600
And the scepter, its symbol, resign.
Pei. The original sway and predominance
    lay
With the Birds, not the Gods, it is clear.
Of mankind they were kings. There are nu-
    merous things
Whence the truth of my words will appear.
First, an obvious case, take the cock and the
    place   606
He once held upon Persia's throne,
The first king and the best long before all the
    rest,
Megabazus,[1] Darius — were known.
And so lasting the fame of his reign that his
    name   610
Is the Persian-bird down to this date.
Euel. That's the reason he struts now so
    proudly and puts
On his turban straight up on his pate.
Quite unique is his style of thus wearing his tile
And a proof of his old royal state.   615
Pei. And so vast was his strength and so
    spread through the length
And the breadth of the earth, that you know
Still today, through his power in the past, at
    the hour
Of the dawn he has only to crow,
And, although they're asleep, from their beds
    all will leap   620
To their work, Potter, Tanner, and Smith,
Men who wait upon bather-ers, who toil at the
    lathe,
Turning lyres and targes therewith.
Boots are laced and away ere the breaking of
    day,
Euel. I know all about that to my cost. 625
Through a cock'rel that crew I a beautiful new
Woolen cloak most unhappily lost.

[1] One of the generals of Darius, king of Persia, 521–
485 B.C. After the Persian conquest of the Black Sea
region in 506 Darius left him behind to subdue Macedonia and Thrace.

At a christening party I got a bit hearty.
    Then on me a drowsiness grew.
To the country of dreams I'd just passed,
        when, it seems,   630
    Before dinner-time this fellow crew.
But *I* took it for warning that daylight was
        dawning
    And straight was for Halimus [1] bound.
I had just put my nose through the gate when
        the blows
    Of a club sent me flat to the ground.   635
There I wallow and sprawl and for help start
        to bawl —
    But no trace of my cloak could be found.
Pei. 'Twas the Kite of the day who held
        sovereign sway
    Over Greece as its ruler supreme.
Chor. Lead. Over Greece?   640
Pei.   Yes, it's plain it was during his
        reign
That the custom which still we esteem
Of saluting the bird first began.
    Euel.   On my word!
    There was one that one day crossed my sight,
So obeisance I paid and with head backward
        laid   646
I was gazing up watching his flight,
When a sixpence I'd popped in my mouth
        somehow dropped
    Down my throat. I'd no supper that night.
Pei. And the Cuckoo again a great kingdom
        had then,   650
    All of Egypt, Phoenicia too,
He had only to call "Cuckoo," "Cuckoo," and
        all
    In the fields without further to do
Upon harvest intent all their energies bent
    Toward reaping their barley and wheat. 655
    Euel. Yes, of course, that is why on occasion
        they cry,
    "Cuckoo, Jew,[2] to the field turn your feet."
Pei. With so stringent a hand did the Birds
        hold command,

[1] An Attic village on the coast near Peiraeus, port
of Athens. Thucydides, the noted historian, came
from there.
[2] So called here in coarse humor, because as mythical
king of the circumcised Egyptians and Phoenicians he
can be jocularly associated in the Greek mind with
other circumcised peoples such as the Jews.

That if mortal was suffered to be
On the throne, as we're told, Menelaus and
        bold   660
    Agamemnon [1] were, always you'd see
On his scepter a bird ready perched and pre-
        pared
    To take so much per cent of each fee.
Euel. Now of *that*, I declare, I was *quite* un-
        aware.
    And, indeed, I had thought it absurd   665
That each time at the play when he'd some-
        thing to say
    Priam [2] always came on with a bird.
But, of course, it was there with an eye to a
        share
    In the bribes that Lysicrates [3] got.
Pei. Then there's Zeus to whom now all as
        sovereign bow   670
    — It's the strangest thing this of the lot —
Though as king he may stand, on his head in
        command
    Sits an eagle perched high over all,
While his daughter Athen-a an owl owns as
        queen,
    And a hawk holds Apollo in thrall.   675
Euel. What you say's quite correct. What's
        the cause you detect
    That assigns to the birds such a place?
Pei. When a victim men slay in the regular
        way
    Of a god to win favor and grace,
In *his* hands they will put all the *viscera*.[4] But
    The first portion's consumed by the *bird*. 681
There was no man of yore who by God ever
        swore,
    But all called you to witness their word.
Still today Lampon's [5] use is to swear by the
        goose,

[1] The famous sons of Atreus, king of Mycenae in
southern Greece. They were the leaders of the Greeks
in the Trojan War. In ancient times an eagle was a
common ornament for the top of royal scepters.
[2] The luckless king of Troy who lost his country to
the Greeks.
[3] An unidentified Athenian contemporary of Aristophanes.
[4] Entrails.
[5] A prominent Athenian soothsayer and oracle monger, whom Aristophanes mentions again in l. 1282. His
oath was "by the goose" instead of the more usual "by
Zeus."

When he's telling another a lie,   685
For thus holy and great all accounted your state
In the centuries that have gone by.
(*Cumulatively, without pausing for breath*) But as Fashion now rules, you are slaves, asses, fools,
And with pebbles today they will drive you away,
Just like folk who're insane, then on temples again   690
Every fowler's snare for the birds of the air,
Now he's liming his twigs, now his springes he rigs,
Cunning nooses and nets to entrap you he sets,
And he ties you when caught up in lots to be bought,
And they poke you and pat you to feel if you're fat,   695
And suppose you excuse them for this, they refuse
You the RIGHT TO BE TOASTED AND SERVED UP AS ROASTED,
But with cheese grated fine, olive oil they'll combine
And some spices to taste, then they beat to a paste,
Adding vinegar, which makes deliciously rich
Kind of sauce — this they do and then pour over you   701
From a pot, scalding hot,
Just as though you were rough fit-for-pigs sort of stuff.
Chor. (*deeply stirred by* PEITHETAERUS' *recital of their wrongs*). *It's a terrible, terrible tale, friend, that you now disclose.*
See, from my eyes a torrent of teardrops flows.
Oh, how base were those,   706
    Whose sires bequeathed them honors like these, and they
    Have left their sons today
    Thus to live in a menial way!
But salvation has come to us. Hail to Fortune blest   710
And benign! For to you, our guest,
Everyone now entrusts himself and all his — nest.
Chor. Lead. Come, at once here and now make it plain to us how
We must act. For to live were in vain,

Save the Kingship we've lost, whatsoever it cost,
Or by hook or by crook we regain.   716
Pei. Very well, I'll disclose the design I propose.
In the first place, all creatures that fly
One vast city shall found and shall raise right around
All the space 'twixt the earth and the sky
A great wall of burnt brick, just as high and as thick   721
As the wall around Babylon built.
Euel. Oh ye builders of Babel! It sounds like a fable
To make the soul shudder and wilt.
Pei. Then as soon as your wall is complete, you must call   725
Upon Zeus your old sway to restore.
Let's assume he's declined to accede and his mind
Doesn't instantly change, then a war
You'll declare, a crusade, against him to be made,
And on gods an embargo you'll lay.   730
The restraint you'll inflict is that *ensibus strictis* [1]
No more in the old-fashioned way
Through your realm they shall go to the earth down below
With the women the devil to play,
Alope and Alcmen-a and Tyndarus' Queen. [2]
Or if any *must* journey beyond   736
Your terrain, an appeal shall be lodged and your seal
Set thereon place his weapon IN BOND.
To mankind too likewise you must send and apprise
Them the birds once again, as of yore,   740
Are their kings, to whom they must their sacrifice pay
First and foremost henceforth evermore.
To the gods by your grace is allowed second place,
But provided that offerings due
To a god shall be paid with a sacrifice made
To the bird who's related thereto.   746

[1] With swords drawn.
[2] These women were mistresses of the gods. Alope bore Hippothoön to Poseidon; Alcmena, Hercules to Zeus; Tyndarus' queen, Semele, Dionysus to Zeus.

If the goddess of love tribute claim, to the dove
  Man will fittingly corn dedicate;
If the god of the sea gets a sheep there must be
  Corn therewith to the duck consecrate;   750
If one makes sacrifice unto Hercules, nice
  Honeyed cakes are the cormorant's claim;
If one pay offering unto Zeus who is *King*,
  It's the bull-finch 'mongst birds has that
    name;
To the bull-finch, therefore, a bull-gnat in his
    gore   755
  First must wallow, ere Zeus have his meed.
Euel. I'm charmed with the notion. A gnat
  in an ocean
Of blood! Pooh, Zeus' thunders indeed!
Chor. Lead. Why however will men count us
  deities when
Hither, thither we flutter and fly   760
And they've every cause to regard us as daws?
Pei. Nonsense, Hermes, you'll hardly deny,
Is a god, yet we know He is wingèd. And so
Are a great many others besides.
There is Vict'ry, we're told, has her pinions of
    gold,   765
  And on golden wings Love also rides.
Iris,[1] often compared to a fluttering bird
  By old Homer, on pinions must soar,
And, of course, there are wings to the bolt that
    Zeus flings
  Mid the thunderstorm's echoing roar.   770
Chor. Lead. But suppose they're so dull as to
  reckon as null,
And to think that Olympus on high
Is the true dwelling place of the gods' happy
  race?
Pei. Then in clouds rooks and sparrows shall
  fly
To devour all the seed of the crops which
  they need   775
For the good of the body and soul.
Then to Demeter[2] they, when they're hungry,
  can pray
To entreat her to grant them a dole.
Euel. And she'll tell them, I'll swear, she has
  nothing to spare,
As we're told by our FOODSTUFFS' CON-
  TROL.   780

  [1] The messenger goddess, especially of Zeus and Hera.
  [2] The "Corn-Mother," the goddess of agriculture.

Pei. And the eyes of their sheep and the oxen
  they keep
For their plowing we'll rob of their sight
With the bills of the crows, as a test to disclose
  Which opinion is wrong and which right.
Phoebus *must* have a chance his repute to en-
  hance   785
  As a healer. He pockets the fees.
Euel. Oh, no, no! It's not fair. I've a poor
  little pair
And I really must — sell them first, *please*.
Pei. But suppose they receive you as gods
  and believe
Cronus, Earth, Life, Poseidon[1] are YOU,
Then, of course, you will see that all blessings
  there be   791
  Are their lot.
Chor. Lead.   Tell me one thing I'll do.
Pei. First the locusts that loot every tender
  young shoot
Shall no longer the vines devastate.   795
Owls and kestrels — a corps they will need
  and no more
Very quickly to settle their fate.
Then the grubs and the flies on fig-leaves gor-
  mandize
Till they eat every tittle and jot,
But in one or two brushes a squadron of
  thrushes   800
Will make a clean sweep of the lot.
Chor. Lead. Yes but how make men rich?
  It is riches of which
Above everything else they have need.
Pei. When they seek aid divine at oracular
  shrine
Birds will give them an excellent lead.   805
Birds will counsel the seer, making perfectly clear
  When success trading ventures will crown,
And no merchant there'll be drowned through
  shipwreck at sea
Any longer.
Chor. Lead.   And why won't they drown?
Pei. Everyone who applies to a shrine to
  advise   811
Will be warned by a bird what to do.
For example, "Don't sail, it will soon blow a
  gale,"
"Put to sea and great gain will ensue."

  [1] The god of the sea.

Euel. I'm for buying a ship and then ho! For
    a trip   815
And for trading! I won't stay with you.
Pei. Then there's silver and gold that was
    hidden of old.
Now the birds will the places declare.
It is obvious they know them well. All men say,
"There is none of my treasure aware,   820
But secure from all eyes snugly hidden it lies,
Though, it may be, a little bird knows."
Euel. I have finished with trade. I'm for
    buying a spade
And I'll Earth's buried treasures disclose.
Chor. Lead. Yes, but health is a dower that is
    not in our power,   825
Because health is the gods' to bestow.
Pei. But whenever a man's doing well,
    people can
Say "It's well with him" fairly, you know.
If a man's doing ill, not a single soul will
Say he's well in the midst of his woe.   830
Chor. Lead. Yes, but how to contrive to
    maintain men alive?
'Tis the gods' to concede or deny.
Must they then breathe their last ere their
    childhood is passed?
Pei. Not at all, for the birds will supply
Them with years, fifteen score.   835
Chor. Lead. Fifteen *what?* From whose store?
Pei. From whose store? Why, of course,
    from their own,
For men come and men go, but no raucous-
    voiced crow
Less than five generations has known.
Euel. Hip, hooroo! Hip, hurrah! Birds are
    fitter by far   840
Than is Zeus for the sovereign's throne.
Pei. Birds are fitter by far? Why they *cer-
tainly* are.
To begin with it's plain we need build them no
    fane
With its walls and its floors made of marble,
    and doors
That will dazzle the sight with their gold's
    glittering light,   845
But the thicket and brake they their temple
    will make,
Or if any demand an abode that's more grand,
A mere tree will suffice for a great edifice.

And to Delphi no more nor to Libya's shore
To make offerings we'll roam, but we'll just
    stop at home,   850
Mid the olives we'll stand and the arbutes,[1] a
    hand
Filled with groats[2] or with wheat, and the
    birds we'll entreat,
Our arms thus extending, to bless us by sending
In response to our prayer of all good things a
    share.
And they'll straightway attend to our prayer
    and they'll send   855
Us a lot on the spot
In return for the hay seed or two that we pay.
Chor. Lead. You my bitterest foe but a mo-
    ment ago
Now I hail as my kindliest friend,
And I'll never, no never, my purpose dissever
From yours, but on you I'll depend.   861
    With joy-filled heart I hear you, and de-
    clare
    This solemn vow that here and now I
    swear —
    If firm alliance 'gainst the gods with me
    You'll make in pious, frank sincerity,   865
    Your heart at one with mine, ere long I'll
    tear
    From them the scepter — MINE — which
    now they bear.
Tasks of physical force, as a matter of course,
    Are *our* pleasure and duty to do,
But whatever we find makes a call on the mind,
    We are leaving entirely to *you.*   871
Hoo. Well, now's no time for dozing drowsily,
For shilly-shallying and "Wait-and-see."
Act, and at once, we must. And first it's best
That you should visit me in my poor nest   875
Beneath my humble roof of twigs and straws,
And — how must I address you?
Pei.   That'll cause
No trouble — Talkemover.
Hoo. Yes, and (*pointing to* EUELPIDES) he?
Pei. Cockcertainson of Sheepspate.   881
Hoo.   Glad to see
You both.
Pei.   We're much obliged.

[1] Strawberry trees, a common European shrub of
considerable height.
[2] Hulled kernels of oats.

Hoo.   Come in now, pray.   885
Pei. Let's go along. (*To* HOOPOO) You show us in.
Hoo.   This way.
    (*The* HOOPOO *makes to enter the thicket.* PEITHETAERUS, *following with* EUELPIDES, *stops suddenly and calls after* HOOPOO.
    Pei. But — what's the word? Back-water! Here, I say!
Let's see, explain to us. How'll we get on
With you, when you have wings and we have none?   890
    Hoo. All right.
    Pei.   But look, in Esop there's a lot
Of talk about a fox, who, when she'd got
An eagle for a partner, wished she'd not.[1]
    Hoo. Don't be alarmed. There's a nice little root;   895
One nibble, and straight out your wings will shoot.
    Pei. Oh then let's go along. (*To the* ATTENDANTS) Here, Thomas, you
And William just bring in our luggage too.
    Chor. Lead. (*calling after them*). Hi! A moment, just wait for a moment, please.
    Hoo. (*turning*). State your request.   900
    Chor. Lead.   Take the strangers away.
To enjoy, as is due, a good luncheon with you,
But the bird, whose melodious lay
To the Muses is dear, fetch and leave with us here,
That she make us all merry and gay.   905
    Pei. Oh yes, *do* grant them this request they make,
And bring the bird out from the reedy brake.
    Euel. Yes, bring her out here, please, and do not fail,
That we as well may see the Nightingale.
    Hoo. Well what you both desire I needs must do.   910
(*Calls into the brake.*) Come, Procne, let the strangers look at you.

[1] The Eagle built her nest in a lofty tree; the Fox made its home in a thicket at the foot of that tree. Each proceeded to raise a family. But one day, in the absence of the Fox, the Eagle, desirous of food for her nestlings and herself, bore off the Fox's cubs to her nest, where they provided a meal for the eagle family.

The flute-girl, gaily dressed and wearing a mouth-piece, enters with her flute

    Pei. Oh priceless Heaven! What a lovely bird!
How soft and fresh and fair!
    Euel.   Upon my word
There's where I'd gladly find myself ensnared.   915
    Pei. Covered with gold too, like a dainty miss!
    Euel. Another thing I fancy is a kiss!
    Pei. You, fool, just mark her beak of skewers, I beg.
You'd have to treat her as you would an egg,   920
And first, to kiss her face, remove the shell.
    Hoo. Come now.
    Pei.   Lead on then, and may all be well!
    (*The* CHORUS *welcome in their opening lines the Nightingale-flute-girl, who joins them in order to provide the musical accompaniment.*
    Chor. Bird I love, bird of gold,
Whom dearest of all I hold,   925
    In song, in life my companion, hail!
    Greeting I give thee, Nightingale,
    Here, before my eyes, now.
Sweet the sounds thou dost ever bring,
Tune thy flute to the notes of Spring,   930
Let the anapaests straight outring
    In the usual wise now.
           (Turning and facing the audience)
O mankind, ye who pass like the leaves and the grass,
    Ye whose lifetime is brief and obscure,
Vain Creations of clay, wingless things of a day,
    Strengthless shadows that cannot endure,   936
Ye who nothing avail, wretched mortals and frail
    As the phantoms in slumber revealed,
Come, to us now attend who have life without end
    Nor to Age nor to Death ever yield,   940
Who abide in the skies where supreme we devise
    Our eternal, immortal decrees;
We the truth will declare of the regions of Air,
    We will teach you the family trees
Of the birds and the Clods, of the Rivers and Gods,
    Of great Chaos and Erebus.[1] *Crammed*   946
[1] Son of Chaos. The name signifies "darkness."

With this knowledge by us you can tell Prodicus [1]
    He may take himself off and be damned,
There were Chaos and Night and broad Tartarus,
    light —
    Lacking Erebus black as the tomb.   950
But the Earth was not there nor the Heavens nor
    the Air.
    Then in Erebus' infinite womb
First a wind-egg was laid by the sable-winged maid,
    To wit, Night. So the seasons were told,
And at length there was hatched out a chick never
    matched   955
    With his wings all aglitter with gold,
Yet sturdy, and fast as the eddying blast.
    It was Love setting all things aflame.
With winged Chaos he wed on broad Tartarus' bed
    And to light out of darkness we came.   960
We the birds of the Air their first progeny were.
    But no race of immortals was found,
Until Love with desire set creation on fire
    And all things in communion bound.
'Twas this passion to wed that in time duly led
    To the birth of the skies and the sea,   966
Of the Earth and eternal blest beings supernal,
    From which you will gather that we
Far surpass in our birth, as we do in our worth,
    All the gods whom ye worship and fear.   970
There is plenty to prove we are children of Love.
    We have wings, we to lovers are dear.
Many fair ones who spurned their admirers have
    turned,
    When their beauty was full in its flower,
And have sought their embrace — a result you
    must trace   975
    To the birds and their wonderful power.
For their lovers prevail with the gift of a quail,
    Or a redcap, a cock or a goose.
And in all that to men's most important, again
    We the birds are of manifest use.   980
'Tis from us that they learn all the seasons in turn,
    Summer, Winter, the Autumn, the Spring,
It is time, it is plain, to sow seed, when the crane
    To far Libya [2] *cawing takes wing.*

[1] A prominent Sophist philosopher and teacher, a native of the island of Ceos near Attica, who lectured throughout Greece.

[2] In autumn the crane flies southward across the Mediterranean to Libya, the coastland of Africa opposite Greece.

Then the sailor unships his stout rudder and slips
    Into sleep which his weariness cures,   986
And a coat for Bill Sikes [1] *must be made, for he*
    likes,
    If he's cold, to appropriate yours.
Next in turn comes the Kite after this into sight
    And declares a new season is nigh,   990
When the sheep you must shear in the youth of
    the year.
    Then when "Look, there's a swallow" men cry,
You're aware it is well your thick ulster to sell
    And to purchase a light, fancy vest.
For advice you don't go to Apollo and Co.,   995
    Since you know that the birds are the best.
You must aye have the word first of all from a bird,
    Ere you make any venture in life,
Be it business and trade with a deal to be made,
    Or a woman becoming a wife.   1000
As a bird *you esteem whatsoever you deem*
    Of the future a token and sign.
Is a sound in the air? It's a bird *you will swear.*
    Someone sneezes, a bird *you divine.*
What you meet on your way, what you happen
    to say,   1005
    Servants, donkeys, as birds *you will class.*
Thus as prophets and seers it most plainly appears
    That Apollo himself we surpass.

If as deities we are accepted, you'll see
    How the songster and seer, how the times of
    the year,   1010
Chilly winter, the stir of the soft summer air,
Mellow autumn, the spring as our blessings we'll
    bring,
For you won't find us proud flying off to a cloud,
As does Zeus, there to perch, leaving you in the
    lurch,
But we'll hover above and exhibit our love   1015
To yourselves and your sons and your sons' little
    ones.
    Both good health and great wealth,
Peace, and plenty, success, laughter, youth, happi-
    ness,
Song, dance, feasting we'll shower, and the cream
    of our dower
    Will be Birds' whey and curds.   1020

[1] I.e., a thief. Bill Sikes, a thief and ruffian of the worst sort, is a prominent character in Dickens' *Oliver Twist*. Aristophanes names a notorious robber, Orestes.

You will actually tire of the things men desire,
  As they pour down galore,
Such abundant excess one and all will possess.

Songstress of the brake,
  Tweet — Tweetaweet — Tweetaweet — Tweet-
    aweet — Twick.   1025
    Note with note so subtly blending,
    Ever my comrade upon me attending,
  Tweetaweet — Tweetaweet — Twick.
Where the pines in the glens on the hilltops their
    green tresses shake.
  Tweetaweet — Tweetaweet — Twick.   1030
    There my golden throat trills to the Queen of
      the hills,
    Songs wherewith dancing they greet her who
      love her,
    And strains that are sacred to Pan I discover.
  Tititit — Tititit — Tititit — Tick.
Hither, thither bee-like winging   1035
  Phrynichus [1] *ever would browse on my*
    flowers.
  Their honey 'tis dowers
With its sweetness all his singing.

If there's any, Sirs, among you who henceforth
    would joyously
Weave the web of life in Birdland, he should join
    our company.   1040
Everything that here in Athens Custom has pro-
    claimed as vile,
Is with us the Birds accounted the most honorable
    style.
Here, for instance, thrashing fathers Custom holds
    a dire disgrace,
But in Birdland Honor's code demands you peck
    your father's face,
Butting into him and shouting, "Put your spurs
    up, if you'll fight."   1045
If a servant by his master's been tattooed for tak-
    ing flight,
He with us the style and title shall possess of
    speckled grouse.
If a man was born in Phrygia next to Spintha-
    rus' [2] *old house,*

[1] The chief Attic tragedian between Thespis and
Aeschylus, and as a poet, celebrated especially for the
beauty of his choruses.

[2] A tragic poet from Heraclea on the coast of the
Black Sea, who like Philemon and Execestides, men-

A Phrypigeon with Philemon [1] *he can balance*
    pedigrees.
If a slave there be from Caria, such as Execesti-
    des, [2]   1050
He shall get him grandforef(e)athers and (h)en-
    franchized he shall be;
And if Peisias' son [3] *with outlaws to betray the*
    gates agree
For a bribe, he like a true chick of the old cock,
    must have place
As a gold-filch, for to filch gold is in Birdland no
    disgrace.

  Thus Swans in harmony   1055
    Tweet — Tweetaweet — Tweetaweet —
      Tweetaweet — Twick
    With their wings in concert beating
    Raised to Apollo their chorus of greeting
  Tweetaweet — Tweetaweet — Twick
On the banks where the waters of Hebrus [4]
    sweep by to the sea.   1060
  Tweetaweet — Tweetaweet — Twick.
    Through the clouds upon high, thrills their
      note to the sky.
    Crouched lie the wild beasts, a strange, soft
      emotion
    Lulls them, a windless calm hushes the
      ocean.
  Tititit — Tititit — Tititit — Tick.   1065
Rings Olympus with their voices,
    Gods start with wonder, and Graces and
      Muses,
    Each, as she uses,
Loud with answ'ring strain rejoices.

There is nothing that for profit and for pleasure
    can compare   1070
With a pair of wings. For instance, some of you,
    who're sitting there,

tioned hereafter, illegally secured recognition as an
Athenian citizen, but later had his name struck from the
rolls.

[1] Presumably an alien poet from Asia Minor, but his
identity obscure.

[2] See l. 11.

[3] Of neither Peisias or his son is there any extant information.

[4] The principal river of Thrace, which rises in the
mountains and flows southward into the Aegean. The
Hebrus was connected frequently with legends of Dionysus.

Have perhaps been bored and hungry, while the
*   tragedies were played.*
Now if wings you'd had, aloft you might have
*   soared and homeward made*
For a hearty lunch, returning here to see the Com-
*   edies.*[1]
Then if Mr. Busybowels were impelled to seek his
*   ease,*   1075
He would not befoul his linen, but would fly away,
*   and when*
He'd discharged his wind and burthen, back on
*   wings would haste again.*
Or suppose you loved a lady who'd forgot her mar-
*   riage vows,*
And before you in the front row unsuspecting sat
*   her spouse,*
Wings would swiftly waft you to her, with what
*   rapture you would meet,*   1080
Have your joy of her and fly back, softly settling in
*   your seat.*
Growing wings — there's nothing like it. Those
*   Diitrephes* [2] *can flap*
Are but like the straw and wicker, which about a
*   flask you wrap;*
Yet he's soared to captain armies, both of foot and
*   horsemen too,*
And today a Horse-Cock-Buff he cackles Cock-a-
*   doodle-doo.*   1085

PEITHETAERUS *and* EUELPIDES *re-enter*
grotesquely winged

Pei. (examining himself and his companion).
So this is this. (*Laughing heartily*)
Egad, I've never met
Anything so absurd to look at yet.
Euel. What are you laughing at?
Pei.   Those quills you boast.
D'you know what you with wings resemble
    most?   1090

[1] These lines are good evidence that at the Athenian state festivals the dramatic contests included in the forenoon one tragic trilogy plus a satyr play, and in the afternoon one comedy.

[2] A rapacious and unprincipled busy-body, who made his fortune in the manufacture of wicker flasks and finally got himself elected a general in the Athenian cavalry. Apparently he lost his life in the return from the barbarous massacre of the Beotian town, Myca-lessus, which he carried out a little over a year after the production of *The Birds.*

The scamped sketch of a goose a penny buys.
Euel. And you a blackbird tonsured basin-
    wise.
Pei. These shafts, as Aeschylus remarks,
    have flown
"Not upon others' pinions, but our own." [1]
Euel. What's to be done now?   1095
Pei.   First of all, we'll name
The city as becomes its size and fame.
Then make the gods an offering.
Euel.   I agree.
Pei. Think now, what shall our city's title
    be?   1100
Euel. There's that great Spartan name that
    you might give
And style it (*lisping*) Lathadaemon.[2]
Pei.   As I live,
I'll not. What? Lath — *my* city? For a bed
I'd have no laths, but mattress-springs in-
    stead.   1105
Euel. What shall we call it?
Pei.   Something that implies
This lofty, airy realm of clouds and skies,
Highly inflated.
Euel. H'm. (*Thinks and has an inspira-*
    tion.) CLOUDCUCKOORISE!   1110
Pei. (*with excited approval*) Hurrah! Hur-
    rah!
A really great and glorious name you've found.
CLOUDCUCKOORISE — the place where,
    I'll be bound,
Theagenes has most of his estate
And Aeschines [3] his all?   1115
Euel.   Yes, and its great
Possession 's Phlegra,[4] where the gods' strong
    blow
Shattered the Giants' — braggadocio.
Pei. A smart affair, our city. Who'll be
    hailed   1119
Its guardian god with holy vestment veiled?

[1] A line from an Aeschylean drama on the Myrmi-dons, now extant in fragment only.

[2] I.e., Lacedaemon, the Peloponnesian state of which Sparta was the capital.

[3] Theagenes and Aeschines were two needy Athenian braggarts, contemporaries of Aristophanes, who became notorious for their perpetual boasting of wealth which lay only in the clouds.

[4] The volcanic plain along the coast of Campania in Italy, where the gods were thought to have killed and buried the giants in a great battle of primeval time.

Euel. That's been Athena's [1] role. Why make a change?

Pei. Our social system it would disarrange.
Our god a woman who war's weapons plies,
And Cleisthenes [2] concerned with hooks and eyes!

Euel. Who then will guard our city's banks and rocks? 1125

Pei. A bird belonging to the race of *Cocks,*
Accounted generally smart and quick,
Ares [3] employed him.

Euel.   Gracious Sovereign Chick! 1129
He is the god to guide where rocks are thick.

Pei. Now for *your* part. Off with you to the Air
And help the builders who are working there;
Strip off your coat, fetch mortar, knead the clay,
Take hods up ladders, fall off on the way, 1134
Post sentries, bank the fire, and on your round
To see the guards are all awake, sleep sound,
Accredit representatives to go
To gods above and down to men below,
Report for further orders.

Euel. (*indignantly*). Don't *you* stir. 1140
For further orders — damn you.

Pei. (*persuasively*).   Go, good sir,
Without your presence all will be at odds.

                    (*Exit* EUELPIDES.

My part's to sacrifice to our new gods.
I'll have the priest for technicalities. 1145
(*Calls.*) Within! A basket and a chalice, please.

Enter in procession PRIEST *and* ATTENDANTS *with implements of sacrifice and an extremely meager goat as victim*

Chor. (singing while procession enters).
    Now here's a plan, which I can
    Welcome greatly, that in stately
        Solemn column
    They shall tender thanks, and render 1150
    Up a beast in sacrifice
    (It should bring us something nice).

[1] Pallas Athene, the patron goddess of Athens.
[2] An Athenian contemporary frequently assailed for his gross effeminacy.
[3] The god of war. The Greeks often called the cock "the chick of Ares."

Ring out the shout, that Delphi knows,
While Chaeris [1] nigh in concert blows.
    (*A flute-player, attired as a crow, plays his instrument discordantly.*

Pei. (*who has busied himself during the song arranging the sacrifice, is annoyed by the raucous notes*). Stop! (*Looks up and sees the crow fluting in professional style.*)
Why, what's *this?* God bless me! Is it true? 1155
I've seen in my time much that's strange and new,
But not a flutist-crow — with mouthpiece too!
(*Turning to the* PRIEST) Your office, priest.
Pay our new gods their right.

Pri. Yes. Where's the basket and the acolyte?
(*In professional style*) Your prayers are requested to the Avine Hearth, and to the Hawk, 1160
Guardian of the Hearth — and to all the Olympian Birds — to all the Olympian Birdesses —

Pei. (*rendering the responses*). Hail to thee, Hawk of Sunium, [2] Lord of Storkington!

Pri. And to Swan of Pytho and of Delos [3] — and to Leto, [4] mother of Quail —
And to Linnetean Artemis —

Pei. Colaenean no more, but Linnetean Artemis. [5] 1165

Pri. And to Phrygian Sabazius [6] — and to Sparrow, mighty mother of gods and men —

[1] An Athenian piper whose presence at sacrificial feasts was particularly unwelcome to Aristophanes. He is satirized in two other of the latter's comedies.
[2] An epithet for Poseidon, who was worshiped at Sunium, the promontory at the southern end of Attica.
[3] An epithet for Apollo, whom the swans transported from his birthplace on Delos, an island in the Aegean, to his sanctuary at Pytho or Delphi in Phocis.
[4] The mother of Apollo by Zeus. She, to escape the persecution of Hera, went to Delos or Ortygia, the "quail island," to give birth to Apollo. Some say that Leto took the form of a quail in order to reach the island.
[5] Twin sister of Apollo, who was worshiped in eastern Attica as Artemis Colaenis from the name of an ancient Attican hero, Colaenus, builder of a shrine to her.
[6] The great nature god of Phrygia, Asia Minor; akin to the Greek Dionysus.

Pei. O Sparrow, Cybele,[1] Queen, mother of
Cleocritus![2]

Pri. That they grant unto the Cloudcuckoorisians —

Health and salvation — unto them and unto
the Chians.[3]

Pei. How nicely it always ends with "and
unto the Chians"!   1170

Pri. And this we beg of the Hero-Birds —
and of the Hero-Birds'-sons — of Coot and of
Spoonbill — of Bloodfinch and of Capercailzie
— of Peacock and Reedwarbler — of Teal and
of Bittern — of Heron and of Oyster-   1175
Catcher — of Tit and of Blackpoll — of . . .

> (*The Birds flock thickly towards the
> stage in answer to the* PRIEST'S
> *prayer, and* PEITHETAERUS, *recog-
> nizing the scant dimensions of his
> offering, is alarmed.*

Pei. (*interrupting*). Stop, damn you, stop
inviting them! Good Lord,

What sort of feast, you fool, will *this* afford

Your vultures and sea-eagles? Don't you
see

One kite could whirl it off quite easily?   1180

Out of the way, you and your fillets! Shoo!

I'll see what I without your help can do.

> (*He drives the* PRIEST *off the stage and
> himself assumes the sacred office.*

Chor. (*during* PEITHETAERUS' *new preparations*).

> A second strain once again
> Therefore troll I reverent, holy,
> Sing to bring you   1185
> To your portals all the Immortals.
> (*One alone will quite suffice
> To consume the sacrifice.
> At least the beast to me seems thin,
> In fact, compact of bone and skin.*) 1190

Pei. (*his preparations completed, opening the
service*). To the Bird-gods let us sacrifice and pray. . . .

A POET *enters — singing*

Poet. *Cloudcuckoorise's glorious name,
O Muse, acclaim
In such strains as suit thy fame.*

Pei. Where is this creature from? (*To*
POET) Who are you? Say.   1195

Poet (*singing*). *O honey-tongued songs I
chant, with swift subvention*

Serving the Muses (confidentially), *Homer's, I'd
mention*

And beg your attention.

Pei. The reason for your jacket's *vents*,
that's clear.

But why the devil, Poet, are you here?   1200

Poet. I have made songs for your Cloudcuckoorise,

Manifold songs, composed in wondrous wise.

> (*He produces one bundle of Ms. after an-
> other.*)

Maidens' chorales — after Simonides,[1] —

Pei. (*waving away the proffered Mss.*). And
how long is it since you finished
these?

Poet. For years and years I've sung this
city's fame.   1205

Pei. And I this moment christening the same

And giving to the newborn babe its name!

Poet. (*singing*). *Nay but swift doth the voice
of Muses speed,[2]*

As the flash of a racing steed.

Etna's father and founder,[3] named   1210

Like the off'ring thrice-holy acclaimed,

Grant to my prayer whatsoe'er

Thou'lt graciously incline

Thy head to mark as mine.   1214

Pei. Here is a pest will worry us, I know,

Unless we make it worth his while to go.

> (*Looks round and addresses an* ATTENDANT.

Come, you've a jerkin and a tunic too.

Off with it, it's the learned poet's due.

---

[1] The great nature goddess of Phrygia; akin to the
Greek Rhea.

[2] A monstrous and ungainly Athenian, whom Aristophanes in his *Frogs* ridicules again.

[3] The people of Chios, a large island off the coast of
Asia Minor, which had remained an ever faithful ally of
Athens amid the changing fortunes of the Pelopon-
nesian War then going on.

[1] One of the chief Greek lyric poets (556–467 B.C.),
especially celebrated for the sweetness and polish of his
choral odes.

[2] The seven lines of the Poet's song are quoted from
Pindar, the greatest of the Greek writers of odes and
hymns (c. 522–442 B.C.).

[3] Hiero, tyrant of Syracuse in Sicily (478–467 B.C.),
who re-colonized the town of Cabana at the foot of
Mount Aetna and called it Aetna.

(*To the* POET) The jerkin's yours. The cold
   has made you blue.
   Poet (*singing*). *O with good will the affection-*
    ate Muse   1220
Accepteth, nor doth refuse.
Yet in thy heart I'd have thee weigh
That which Pindar doth say.
   Pei. The fellow doesn't mean to go away.
   Poet. (*singing*). *Far, afar upon Scythia's*[1]
    marge[2]   1225
Straton[3] *roams at large,*
  And of shuttle-tossed vestments ne'er a one
  possesseth.
An inglorious fame a shirtless jacket oppresseth.
Notice, pray, what I say.   1229
   Pei. I note your wishes on the tunic fall.
(*To* ATTENDANT) Off with it. Bards have
   claims upon us all.
Here, take it and be off.
   Poet.   Lo! I am gone.
I go to sing your city's benison. (*Exit singing.*
Of her, O gold-enthroned one, sing 1235
Quivering, shivering.
In the infinite fields that the snowflakes whip
Sojourned I. Hip! Hip! HIP!
   Pei. (*looking after the* POET). *You* needn't
   fear a shivering attack
With that nice little tunic on your back. 1240
A nuisance that I didn't contemplate.
Fancy his having heard about our State!
(*To an* ATTENDANT) Sprinkle the holy water
   round again.
(*Solemnly*). Silence now ——
   Prophet (*entering suddenly*). Hold, from
   sacrifice refrain.   1245
   Pei. (*annoyed*). Who're *you?*
   Pro.   Me? I'm a prophet.
   Pei.   Damn you then!
   Pro. (*in a shocked voice*). Sir! Sir! Com-
   temn not the gods' gift to men.
An oracle of Bacis[4] has a clear   1250
Bearing upon Cloudcuckoorise.

[1] A vast bare wild land, most probably to the east of
the Black Sea.
[2] The five lines of this speech are a further quotation
from Pindar.
[3] A fictitious personage.
[4] An ancient seer of Boeotia, whose oracles had been
commended in the then recently published history of
Greece by Herodotus.

   Pei.   It's queer
You weren't inspired to tell me this before
I founded it.
   Pro.   By Heaven's will I forbore. 1255
   Pei. Well, the best thing's to hear the proph-
   et's lore.
   Pro. (*reciting*). Soon as the hoary crow for
   her house-mate the gray greeteth,
E'en in that self-same spot where Corinth with
   Sicyon[1] meeteth —
   Pei. Corinth? Why, what concern can I
   have there?   1259
   Pro. Bacis was speaking darkly of the Air.
(*Reciting*) Slaughter a white-fleeced ram to
   Pandora,[2] piously praying,
Then to the man who hath first declared to
   thee this I am saying,
Give new shoes and a spotless robe, thus his
   guerdon paying.
   Pei. Are shoes included?   1264
   Pro. Take the book and look (*offering it*).
(*Reciting*) Give him the wine-cup; with
   flesh of the victim his hand shall be
   filled.
   Pei. Is victim's flesh included?
   Pro.   Take the book and look.
(*Reciting*) This if thou dost, holy youth, ac-
   cording as I have willed,
Thou shalt an eagle become in the clouds.
   But if gifts thou deniest,   1270
Never as eagle, nor dove, nor as woodpecker
   even, thou fliest.
   Pei. That's there — included?
   Pro.   Take the book and look.
   Pei. (*decidedly*). Then there's an absolute
   discrepancy   1274
With what Apollo once declared to *me* ——
(*Reciting*) If at a rite sacrificial a liar, who
   was not invited,
Causes annoyance, thereto by the lust of his
   belly incited,
Meetly shall he with assault on the space twixt
   his flanks be requited.
   Pro. (*annoyed*). You're trifling with me.
   Pei.   Take the book and look. 1280
(*Reciting*) Strike thou and spare not — nor

[1] Sicyon and Corinth are adjacent districts in the
northeastern Peloponnesus.
[2] The first woman on earth.

eagle that soareth where scarcely the eye
sees,
No, not if Lampon [1] himself it shall be, or the
great Diopeithes.[2]

Pro. That's there — included?

Pei.　　　　　Take the book and look.
To the devil with you!　Go!　　　1285
　　　(*He assaults and drives him off.*

Pro.　　　　Help!　Mercy!　Spare!

Pei. Cut off now with your prophecies elsewhere!　　　　　(*Exit* PROPHET.

Enter a mathematician, METON,[3] *with a number
of instruments for surveying and measuring*

Met. (*importantly*).　I've come to you.

Pei. (*aside*).　　　Again!　A second pest!
(*To* METON *with a lordly air*)　What aim do
　you pursue?　What form of quest?　1290
What means, what boots it, that thus here you
　fare?

Met. (*rapidly, filled with enthusiasm for his
　project*).　I wish to make a survey of
　your Air
Dividing it by acres ——

Pei.　　　　　In Heaven's name,
Who *are* you?　　　　　1295

Met.　　　Meton.　I'm a man of fame
In Greece and in Colonus.[4]

Pei.　　　　　And those tools
You've there with you?

Met.　　Oh, these are Air footrules.　1300
Air, it is clear, in general design
Resembles an extinguisher.　Align
This curving rule, therefore, above it — so,
Insert the compasses — you follow? [5]

Pei. (*bewildered*).　　　No.　1305

---

[1] See note on l. 684.

[2] Another Athenian soothsayer, satirized also in
Aristophanes' *Knights* and *Wasps*, whom some considered a fanatic and others an impostor.

[3] A celebrated Athenian astronomer of the day, who
in 432 B.C. had announced a new calendar of nineteen
years, afterward called the Metonic cycle.

[4] An eminence in the great Athenian Agora, or market place, whereon Meton, apparently not long before
the production of *The Birds*, had set up a water-clock.

[5] Aristophanes, deliberately of course, presents
Meton spouting mathematical nonsense on the ancient
problem of squaring the circle.

Met. Align the straight rule, and I'll have
　its size.
Your circle's squared, see; on the center lies
The Market, and straight in from near and far
Roads run right to the middle, as a star
Shines circular itself, and yet may strew　1310
Straight beams all round it.

Pei.　　　　Thales [1] number two!
Meton?

Met. Yes.　　　　　1314

Pei.　　　I'm your friend, you will allow?
　　　　　(METON *nods assent.*
Well, be advised by me and toddle — *now.*

Met. But what's the danger?

Pei.　　　　　Pains and penalties
For aliens, as at Sparta.[2]　Add to these
Blows flying through the town.　　　1320

Met. (*aghast*).　　　What!　Civil War?

Pei. Oh no.

Met.　　　Well, what?

Pei.　　　　A general movement for
The swishing of all folk who swank and
　spout.　　　　　1325

Met. Then I'll be moving.

Pei.　　　　Yes, I should.　I doubt
If you'll escape in time.　Why, look!　They're
　nigh.　　　　(*Thrashes him.*

Met. (*endeavoring to escape*).　Lord help me!

Pei.　　Well I told you, didn't I?　1330
Go size yourself up somewhere else — good-
bye.　　　　　(*Exit* METON.

*Enter a Government Official, come to inspect the
newly established city*

Inspector. Where are the Consuls?

Pei. (*aside*).　　Who's this haughty Bey? [3]

Ins. I've come as State-Inspector to survey
Cloudcuckoorise.　　　　　1335

Pei.　　　　Inspector, did you say?
Who sent you?

Ins.　　　Birdman passed a rotten bill
To do it.

---

[1] One of the Seven Sages of Greece (c. 636–c. 546
B.C.), and one of the founders in Greece of the study of
philosophy and mathematics.

[2] Strangers could be expelled by mere executive order
without any legal hearing.

[3] Commissioner.

Pei.   If your fee is paid, you will   1340
Leave without troubling us?
    Ins.   Of course, dear sir.
The House is sitting and I should be there.
I have a deal for Pharnaces ¹ to square.
    Pei. I'll pay and you can go.   Here, take
        your fees.   (*Thrashes him.* 1345
    Ins. Bless me, what's this?
    Pei.   A sitting on Pharnaces.
    Ins. Strike an INSPECTOR!   Take care
what you do.
    Pei. Be off! (*Throws his despatch cases after
him.*)   And your official boxes too!
                (*Exit* INSPECTOR.
Monstrous!   Inspectors here in the city's
    street   1350
Before its consecration is complete!

Enter a CONSTITUTIONAL LAWYER *with a num-*
   ber of documents, from one of which he is
   reading

    Cons. Law. If a Cloudcuckoorisian commit
    an offence against an Athenian ——
    Pei. Damn it, what document is that you've
    got?
    Cons. Law. I deal in Constitutions.   I've a
    lot
Of laws to sell you.   1355
    Pei.   For example, what?
    Cons. Law. (*reading*). The following weights,
measures and Parliamentary Acts shall be those
of the Cloudcuckoorisians, according to the use
and wont of the Ohohians ——   1360
    Pei. The Howlhowlians shall be yours with-
    out delay.   (*Thrashes him.*
    Cons. Law. Here, what's to do?
    Pei.   Go, take your laws away.
I'll make you rue those laws of yours today.

The CONSTITUTIONAL LAWYER *is driven off at
   one side of the stage.   At the other the* IN-
   SPECTOR *reappears*

    Ins. I cite Peithetaerus to appear in court in
    April on a charge of outrageous con-
    duct ——   1365

¹ Persian satrap or governor of the northwest provinces of Asia Minor at this period.

    Pei. (*sarcastically, not knowing where the
    voice comes from*).   Now really! (*See-
    ing the* INSPECTOR) Hello! *You're*
    still here, are you?
         (*Rushes at him and drives him off.*
    Cons. Law. (*reappearing on opposite side of
    stage and reading from one of his laws*).
Anyone maltreating the Authorities and
not accepting, under the statute ——
    Pei. Curse and confound it!   And *you're*
    still here, too?
         (*Rushes at him and drives him off.*
    Ins. (*reappearing*).   I'll ruin you with thou-
    sand-pounder writs.
    Pei. And I'll smash your despatch cases to
    bits.   1370
         (*Rushes at him and drives him off.*
    Cons. Law. (*reappearing*).   D'you mind the
    night you fouled the statue, eh?
    Pei. (*dashing towards him as he escapes*).
    Bah!   Catch him, someone!   Don't
    run away.
       (*Returning he gathers up his discarded
        instruments of sacrifice and ad-
        dresses his* ATTENDANTS.
Come, we'll stop here no longer, but begin
Our offering of the goat again within.
               (*Exeunt omnes.*

    Chor. Lo, to me all-surveying,   1375
    All-supreme, are mortals paying
    Sacrifice, favors praying.
      Watch I keep o'er all Earth's places,
    Fruits and flowers save and cherish.
    By my bill doomed to perish   1380
      All the fell, cruel races;
    They that, where young buds sprout,
    Gluttonously hold their rout,
      Settling here, settling there,
      Branch and bough stripping bare.   1385
    Doomed to me too those whose savage
    Onsets fragrant gardens ravage.
      All that crawls, all that stings,
      Neath the blows of my wings
    Stricken lies,   1390
    In its gore weltering dies.
Always, everywhere, you hear it publicly pro-
    claimed today —
"Hundred pounds' reward to any who shall well
    and truly slay

Diagoras of Melos.[1] Likewise hundred pounds'
    reward per head
Will be paid for slaughtered tyrants. (N.B.
    THEY'RE ALREADY DEAD.)" 1395
Now in public proclamations we desire to have
    our say —
"Hundred pounds' reward to any who shall well
    and truly slay
Philocrates [2] surnamed Sparrovian. Or, for his
    arrest alive,
Half a thousand." Tits he's vending at a penny
    a bunch of five.
Thrushes he inflates for public view (Ah! how the
    insult hurts!) 1400
And in Blackbirds' nostrils too he feathers cun-
    ningly inserts.
Pigeons also he will capture, coop within a nar-
    row room,
Make them from within a net decoy their fellows
    to their doom.
Hear then, hear our proclamation. And if any-
    one there be
Who has birds he keeps in cages, we command he
    set them free. 1405
If you do not as we bid you, then the Birds shall
    force employ,
And in Birdland you in your turn shall be held
    for a decoy.
    Happy who wear the feather!
    Nor our upper nor our nether
    Limbs we wrap in chill weather. 1410
      So if stifling heats betide me,
    Though their rays far may follow,
    In the mead's bosomed hollow
    Leaves and flowers safely hide me,
    When beneath noontide's glow 1415
    Harmonies wondrous flow,
      As the Sun's frenzy fires
      All the shrill cicala-choirs.

Through the winter caves' recesses 1419
Give me warmth and Nymphs' caresses
    And in Spring myrtle's white
    Berries I eat, Maids' delight,
    And I browse
    Gardens where Graces house.
Just a word now with the Judges in relation to
    the Prize. 1425
If to us it is awarded, for them all we shall devise
Every blessing — bounties better far than ever
    Paris [1] won.
First there's that to which the wishes of all Judges
    mostly run —
Guinea [2]-fowls you'll ne'er be short of (those, I
    mean, the Mint has bred),
But their home they'll make among you, in your
    purses lay their bed; 1430
Snugly brooding there you'll find them and small
    change for you they'll hatch.
Add to this too that your houses with cathedral
    fanes will match.
For we Birds will duly roof them technically after
    Wren.[3]
Should you get a petty office under Government,
    and then
Not object if to your fingers something sticks,
    we'll send you claws 1435
Like a Kite has. If you dine out, we'll provide
    capacious craws.
Yes, but should you give your verdict for our
    rivals, have a care!
Forge yourselves those little covers that you see
    the statues wear.[4]
For when spick and span you're tricked out, if a
    cover you have not,
Just revenge that moment taking every Bird shall
    shoot his shot. 1440

---

[1] Surnamed "the Atheist," because of his attacks on the popular religion and especially upon the Eleusinian Mysteries. Finally he was accused of impiety, and fearing the result of a trial, he fled from Athens just previous to the performance of this play. Inscriptions similar to the one here were actually erected in Athens and perhaps in the vicinity.

[2] See note on l. 14.

[1] Son of the Trojan king, Priam; the youth to whom Aphrodite gave Helen, the fairest of women, because he adjudged that goddess the loveliest of the deities.

[2] A pun on the English gold coin, a "guinea," worth twenty-one shillings.

[3] A pun on the name of the famous English architect, Christopher Wren (1632–1723), who built St. Paul's Cathedral, London.

[4] The Greeks surmounted many of their statues with little moon-shaped disks of bronze to protect them from the birds.

PEITHETAERUS, *having succeeded in offering his sacrifice without interruption within, re-enters and addresses the* CHORUS *grandiloquently*

Pei. Birds, our sacrifices promise fair.
But what is this? How now? No messenger
From the wall to tell us how it passes there?
                       (*Pauses.*
Ah, here comes one panting like a race-winner.

A MESSENGER *enters breathless with haste*

Mess. Where is he? Wh-where is he?
     Wh-wh-where,   1445
Where's Peithetaerus, chief in command?
Pei.   Hello!
Mess. Your wall is built, it's all complete.
Pei.   Bravo!
Mess. Splendid, magnificent, past comparison;   1450
So broad it stands, Proxenides of Boastington
And Theagenes [1] with steeds, huge as that one
Of Troy,[2] to their chariots harnessed might drive
Atop of it past each other.
Pei.   Sakes alive! 1455
Mess. Its height — this is the measurement that I
Made for myself — AN HUNDRED FATHOMS.[3]
Pei. Why,
That *is* a heightness! Who built it so high?
Mess. Birds, none beside. Egyptian laborer   1460
Toiled not, nor stonemason, nor carpenter,
But all themselves they marvelously wrought.
From Libya thrice ten thousand cranes have brought
Foundation stones, which down their throats they'd slipped.[4]

---

[1] Two notorious Athenian braggarts. For Theagenes cf. ll. 1114–15 and note.
[2] The unique Wooden Horse which had hidden within its body a whole troop of Greek cavalry.
[3] I.e., six hundred feet, twice the height of the famous Wall of Babylon.
[4] An allusion to the Greek popular belief that the cranes in their migrations from the Libyan shore of North Africa swallowed pebbles as ballast to steady themselves over the Mediterranean.

These into shape by the Ruffs' bills were
    chipped.[1]   1465
For bricklayers ten thousand storks there were,
While water from below into the air
Curlews and other river-birds would bear.
Pei. Who fetched the clay?
Mess.   Herons in hods,[2] nor spilled   1470
A drop.
Pei. What, hods? How did they get them filled?
Mess. That, Sir, was managed in most skill-ful way.
Geese drove their feet like spades into the clay
And laid upon each hod its load complete. 1475
Pei. What feat is there beyond the reach of feet?
Mess. Aye and the ducks their aprons round them drew [3]
And carried bricks, while up the swallows flew,
Trowel behind,[4] like unto children, bore, 1479
While clay they carried in their beaks before.
Pei. Why, after this, hire laborers for pay?
Let's see — the wooden portions, who were they
Who fashioned those? Birds?
Mess.   Joiners of great skill,
Woodpeckers, made the gates, using the bill
For axe and saw. From their resounding
    blows   1486
Clamor, as of a vessel building, rose.
Now gated all with gates, bolted and barred
It stands, and all around is under guard,
Sentries, inspections, challenges — every-
    where   1490
Is watch and ward, and in the towers the flare
Stands ready. Now to wash me will I bend
My footsteps. To the rest yourself attend.
                        (*Exit.*
(PEITHETAERUS, *completely staggered by the messenger's news, reels about holding his head in his hands.*

---

[1] The rasping note of the Ruff sounds like the scraping and grating of a stonemason's chisel.
[2] The heron in flight stretches its legs behind and upturns its feet in such a way as to suggest hod-shaped appendages.
[3] The neck of the mallard duck has a white ring which recalls the white apron around the mason's waist.
[4] The tail, which on the nest the swallow often uses with a pressing motion to maintain balance.

Chor. Lead. Hi! What's to do? Are you
    amazed that we
Had the wall built with such celerity?   1495
   Pei. By Heaven, I *am.* It merits my sur-
    prise.
It bears to me the genuine look of — lies.
                       (*Pauses.*)
But look! A guard from there with news I spy
Coming hither hotfoot, daggers in his eye.

A second MESSENGER *enters shouting wildly*

   Mess. Oho! Oho! Oho! Oho! Oho!
    Oho!   1500
   Pei. What's to do *now?*
   Mess.   An outrage has been done!
One of the Olympian gods lately run
The gauntlet of the day-guard — daws they
    were —
Flying unmarked through the gates into the
    Air.   1505
   Pei. What a foul, wicked, monstrous thing
    to do!
What god was it?
   Mes.   That we don't know. He flew,
We know.
   Pei.   The patrols then! Quick, the way
    he went!   1510
Send them upon his track at once.
   Mess.   We've sent
Thirty thousand hawks, mounted and armed
    with bows;
In hot pursuit each bird with talons goes,
Kestrel and vulture, eagle, owl and kite;   1515
With stir and whir of wings in furious flight
The air's aquiver. Thus the god they pursue
Nor is he far away, but nigh to you
Already.
   Pei.   Ho, now! Slings and bows there!
    Bring   1520
Me bows and slings! Come, all who serve your
    King,
Shoot! Hit! A sling there, someone! Ho!
    A sling!
      (*The stage is filled with the stir and
        bustle of preparation, while the*
        CHORUS *chants.*)
   Chor. War, an ineffably
       Terrible war's begun;

    Gods are at strife with me,   1525
       On guard everyone.
    Lest within Erebus' cloud —
       Compassed child, the Air,
    God enter unallowed
       Taking us unaware.   1530
       Keep sharp lookout
       All round about.
*For hark! The voice of whirring wings doth cry
Aloud some deity is soaring nigh.*

Enter IRIS, *flying* [1]

   Pei. (*shouting*). Where — where — Where
    are you flying to? Hi! Stop!   1535
Halt! Not a movement! Let your pinions
    drop!   (IRIS *stops poised in the air.*
Who're you? Whence are you flying? What's
    your race?
   Iris. I'm from Olympus, the Gods' dwelling
    place.
   Pei. What name d'you bear? Bonnet or
    Barquentine? [2]
   Iris. Iris the fleet.   1540
   Pei.   China or Home,[3] d'you mean?
   Iris (*astonished*). Why, what —?
   Pei.   A gamecock will by my request
Fly up and straight arrest her.
   Iris.   ME? ARREST? 1545
Why, what the mischief's this?
   Pei.   You shall pay dear.
      (IRIS *is arrested and brought down to
        the stage opposite* PEITHETAERUS.)
   Iris. This *is* extraordinary!
   Pei.   How came you here,
Vile rogue, within our rampart? Through
    which gate?   1550
   Iris. That, on my solemn oath, I cannot
    state.
   Pei. (*to* CHORUS *and* ATTENDANTS). You
    hear her, how she fences with me, eh?

---

[1] The goddess is swung on and suspended by the
mechane or crane located on the roof of the scene-
house.

[2] I.e., "Are you a head-dress or a schooner?" It
must be remembered that in the performance, Iris with
her long flowing robes and her streaming beribboned
hair would look, while flying across the stage, not unlike
a ship under full sail.

[3] A pun: China or Home *fleet*, i.e., squadron.

(*To* Iris)   You saw the Daws' Commanders?
     Won't you say?
The Storks have viséed you?
   Iris.   Plague take it!   What ——   1555
   Pei. They haven't?
   Iris.   Are you *right?*
   Pei.   Your ticket's not
Been punched in person by an officer?
   Iris (*indignantly*).   Fellow!   *My* ticket's not
     been punched, I'll swear.   1560
   Pei. And flying thus in secret then you came
Through Chaos, where you have no rightful
     claim?
   Iris. Where, if not there, must gods their
     courses steer?
   Pei. I don't know where they must.   They
     mustn't HERE.
Your presence now's a crime.   Why, don't you
     see,   1565
Strictly by right already dead you'd be.
Never an Iris death so merited.
   Iris. But I *can't* die.
   Pei.   No matter, YOU'D BE DEAD.
No better shall we be, methinks, than clods,
If, while the rest obey us, you the gods   1571
Shall misconduct yourselves, nor own that now
You to your betters in your turn must bow.
Tell us the port to which you waft your prow.
   Iris. The port?   To men my father bade me
     wing   1575
To urge them pay the gods due offering
Of sheep and oxen on the altar slain,
With savor fill the streets ——
   Pei.   What gods?   Explain.
   Iris. What gods?   Why us, who in the
     heavens abide.   1580
   Pei. Gods are you?
   Iris.   Yes.   What god is there beside?
   Pei. BIRDS now are gods.   To BIRDS
     must men make use
Of sacrifices, not, by Zeus, to Zeus.
   Iris (*in mock tragic fashion*).   Rash fool!
     Rash fool!   To anger do not stir   1585
The heart of the gods.   For Justice shall not
     spare,
But with Zeus' mattock hurl thy race to doom.
Licymnian [1] bolts mid the smoke's flame-shot

---

[1] Licymnius, the half-brother of Alcmena, the mother of Hercules, was slain by the latter's son. The allusion

loom
Thee and thy enfolding chambers shall con-
     sume.
   Pei. (*imperatively*).   Here, listen!   Drop this
     fluster-bluster-blow.   1590
                (Iris *moves impatiently.*
Be quiet!   I'm no Lydian, you know,
Or Phrygian to be scared by bugaboo.
D'you know, if Zeus annoys me, what I'll do?
(*In burlesque imitation of* Iris' *manner and lan-
     guage*)   With flame-fraught eagles I will
     burn his halls   1594
To blackened ash, and eke Amphion's [1] walls,
Firepolls I'll launch against him to the skies,
Thousand on thousand, all in martial wise
Panoplied in leopard-skins.   I fancy he
With but *one* Firepoll once had difficulty. [2]
If *you* annoy me, then you too shall smart, 1600
The servant ere her lord — I'll play *my* part,
So Iris' self shall wonder how I am
So old, and yet like battleship can ram.
   Iris. Wretch, may your swol'n boasts burst
     themselves and you!
   Pei. Away this minute!   Quick!   Pack,
     whack!   Shoo, shoo!   1605
   Iris. My sire will crush you, who his power
     defy.
   Pei. (*in feigned terror*).   Oh dear!   I'm lost!
     Fly somewhere else and try
Zeus' thunderbolts on one less old than I.
                   (*Exit* Iris.

   Chor.   *Ramparted round we are.*
           Gods of the race divine   1610

---

here is to a tragedy by Euripides, *Licymnius* (now lost),
wherein lightning destroys somebody or something.
This line and the next are probably near-quotation of
Euripidean language, which Aristophanes loved to
ridicule.

[1] Son of Zeus and Antiope, queen of Thebes. He
with his twin-brother Zethus sacked Thebes after their
mother had been treated with great cruelty there. They
then fortified the city with a wall.   It is told that when
Amphion, an expert player of the lyre, sounded his instrument, the stones moved from the ground and
formed the wall of their own accord.

[2] In Greek "firepoll" is "porphyrion."   One of the
most formidable of the ancient Giants who fought the
Gods was named Porphyrion.   He attempted to throw
the island of Delos at the Gods, it is said, but Zeus
threw a thunderbolt at him and Hercules completed his
destruction with arrows.

Now shall no longer fare
Across this city of mine.
Smoke of the sacrifice
Up to Olympus' floor
Out of the Earth shall rise   1615
Through my domain no more.

Pei. Strange — that messenger we sent to men,
If he is never to return again.

Enter a MESSENGER *bearing a crown*

Mess. O Peithetaerus, O blessed one, O wise,
O famed, O wise, O cunning to devise,   1620
O triply-blessed, O — (*appealingly*) wind me up.
Pei.   What's this?
Mess. Now all the peoples hail thee Prince of Bliss,
Crown thee for wisdom with this golden crown ——   (*Crowns him.*
Pei. I'm much obliged. What wins me this renown?   1625
Mess. Founder of this famed City of the Air,
Thou know'st not how much honor is thy share
'Mongst men, how many passion for this land.
Ere yet this city thy creative hand   1629
Had fashioned, Lacedaemon was men's craze.
Hairy they went and hungry, foul, with ways
Like Socrates, and carried clubs. But now
Bird-crazy are they, joyously they bow
To every fashion that the Birds dictate.
At dawn, soon as they wake from slumber, straight   1635
Each flutters off, just as we do, to *try* [1]
For bread; as we do, to the *sage* he'll fly
And there find food wherewith to pack his *bill*.
So patent their Bird-craziness, their will
Full oft is to be called by a Bird-name,   1640
One of them was styled *Partridge* (he's a lame
Huckster [2]); Menippus they as *Swallow* [3] know;
Opuntius' title is the one-eyed *Crow*,[1]
And Chaerephon's [2] is *Bat, Lark* Philocles'.[3]
Ibis Lycurgus', *Goose-fox* Theagenes'.[4]   1645
Syracosius [5] was called *Jay*, and Meidias [6] bore
The name of *Quail*, as like to one that sore-
Ly stricken leaves the ring with addled brains.
From all, in passion for the Birds, rose strains
Wherein they hymned a swallow or a dove,
For ducks, hens, geese loudly proclaimed their love,   1651
For wings, for feathers, for a bit of fluff.
Thus 'tis with them. To thee one word's enough.
They'll come in thousands hither to demand
The uplifting feather and the clutching hand.   1655
Feathers provide these immigrants to dress. . . .
    Pei. (*interrupting in great excitement*). Then now's no longer time for idleness.
Ho there! Away now straight with right good will,
With feathers every box and basket fill.
James, when they're filled, will bring them here to me,   1660
And I'll receive our citizens to be.
    (*Exeunt* ATTENDANTS. *Bustle and confusion.*
    Chor. O *full soon will the voice of mankind acclaim*
    Our city's popularity,
    If Fortune show us charity.
For with love for our city all men are aflame.
    Pei. (*to servants within*). *Be quick, do what I told you!*   1666
    Chor. There is nobody need fear
    That he'll lack what he wants here.
There are Wisdom and Passion and Graces divine,

---

[1] This and the two following underlined words bear double meanings, the second of which in every case refers to legal procedure. Aristophanes is satirizing the litigious habits of the Athenians in his day.

[2] An allusion to the partridge's habit of feigning lameness on being surprised with her young in order to draw attention away from them.

[3] As a blacksmith in Athens, Menippus attended to that important portion of a horse, the hollow of its foot, which to the Greek eye resembled the shape of the swallow; hence the appellation here.

[1] See l. 188 and note.

[2] A pupil of Socrates, finally banished in 404 B.C.

[3] See l. 343 and note.

[4] See ll. 1115 and 1452 and notes.

[5] A noisy legislator frequently satirized by the Athenian comic writers.

[6] An Athenian quail-breeder, who evidently possessed a dazed look such as the quail had in the old Greek game of quail-filliping. In this game the bird was placed on a board within a ring and then struck sharply on the head to see if it would flinch and back out of the ring, or not.

And the eyes of fair Peace with soft tenderness
    shine   1670
In blessing to enfold you.
    Pei. (*to servant who is hastening in and out*).
      How slow you are!   Ho, bustle now!
Come hurry, scurry, hustle now!
    Chor. *Hi, be quick there!   A basket with feath-
ers filled.*
(*To* PEITHETAERUS.) *Just go and set him jogging
Like this, look! with a flogging,*   1676
For he's slow as a donkey unless he's well milled.
    Pei.   *He is a worthless creature.*
    Chor. *As a wise preparation
Make a classification*   1680
*Into birds of the ocean, of omen, and song,
And be sure to prescribe for them plumes that
belong*
            To each man's leading feature.
    Pei. Now, by the Kestrels, I'll not let
    you go   1684
Scot free, when you're so dilatory and slow.
              (*Beats him.*

Enter an intending PARRICIDE, *singing*

    Parr. *On eagle's wings would I soar through
the Air,
Would wing my flight high over the gray bil-
lows, where
Never comes the harvester.*
    Pei. Our messenger's report, it seems, proves
    true.   1689
See, someone comes — and sings of eagles too.
    Parr. (*smacking his lips in anticipation*).
    Plpp!
What's sweeter than to fly on wings above?
With birds and all their ways I'm deep in love.
I'm all aflutter, mad for them, my craze
Is to live with you, I adore your ways.   1695
    Pei. Which ways d'you mean?   The birds
    have not a few.
    Parr. All — but particularly that with you
Biting and strangling is a father's due.
    Pei. Yes, we do reckon that it shows good
    blood
To thrash one's father in one's chickenhood.
    Parr. That's just why I've migrated here.
    I'm hot   1701
To choke my father and get all he's got.

    Pei. But there's a law to which we birds
    submit,
That in the ANCIENT CODE OF STORKS
    is writ —
"A father stork, who has maintained his brood
Till they are fledged with due solicitude,   1706
Thereafter shall receive from them his food."
    Parr. (*disgustedly*). A pretty profit that for
    me to reap
From coming — father on my hands to keep!
    Pei. (*consolingly*). No gain at all.   But as
    your coming's stirred   1710
My sympathy, I'll "fledge an orphan bird."
I'll just give you a hint, my boy — it's nought
To hurt, but what in *my* young days they
    taught.
DON'T STRIKE YOUR FATHER.   Here's
    a wing [1] for you,
And, in the other hand, a cock's spur [2] too. 1715
Fancy that here a cock's proud comb [3] you
    wear —— (*putting feathers in his hair*)
Now join the army, earn your pay and fare,
Let father live, and, as a fighting man,
Straight Thracewards fly and there fight all
    you can.[4]
    Parr. Upon my life, I like what you advise,
I'll do as you suggest.   1721
    Pei.   Then you'll be wise.
            (*Exit the intending* PARRICIDE.

Enter CINESIAS,[5] *a dithyrambic poet, singing*

    Cin.   *Up, up do I fly
      On high to the sky,
        Soaring on pinions light.*   1725
      *I am wafted along
      Ever new paths of song —*

[1] I.e., as a shield.   [2] I.e., as a sword
[3] I.e., as a helmet.
[4] This whole speech and its accompanying business is
a parody of a ceremony that the audience had recently
observed.   At the opening of the Great Dionysia a
band of youths in shining armor were led forward and
proclaimed by a herald to be orphans of Athenian war
veterans, who had been supported during childhood by
the state and had now been invested with the martial
equipment of an adult citizen.   Then, in full regalia
still, this band sat in the front row of the theater.
[5] A contemporary Athenian poet much in vogue, but
much ridiculed too by the wits for his spindling figure
and his lyrical bathos.

Pei. This needs a cargo-load of plumes to preen.

Cin.   *My heart quails not,*
     Limb fails not,   1730
     But with all zest
     Press the quest.

Pei. (*in mock tragic vein*). Good-day, Cinesias, the green-and-lean.

What does your bow-legs' rolling hither mean?

Cin.   *Oh I would be a Nightingale*   1735
     Shrill sweet melody making!

Pei. (*prosaically*). Let singing be and plainly say your say.

Cin. I would be winged by you and fly away
Up to the Clouds there preludes to inflate,
NOVEL, SNOW–SMITTEN, AIR–EXAGI-
     TATE.   1740

Pei. The Clouds? Could anyone find preludes *there?*

Cin. 'Tis upon them our art hangs poised in air.

Dithyrambic verses of a brilliant sheen
Are AIRY, MURKY, FLAME–FLECKED-
     AZURINE,
FEATHER–EXAGITATE.   You'll see I'm
     right.   (*Prepares to sing.*   1745

Pei. No, no, I won't.

Cin.   Yes, yes when I recite.
I'll scour the whole air for you in my flight ——
(*Sings*)   *Ye couriers of air, ye*
     Who phantom-like fare, ye   1750
     With ominous note
     In your slender throat ——

Pei. Easy O!

Cin. (*rapidly*). *If I could leap*
     Over the deep   1755
     Where the winds keep
     Blustering and blowing ——

Pei. (*making a whip*). I'll see *your* blustering is put to sleep.

Cin. *Now to the South neath the Sun's arrows burning,*
Now from the South to the North my feet turning,   1760
Through the harborless ocean of air my path churning ——

(*To* Peithetaerus, *eyeing his preparations*)
That's nice, old man; it shows your skill innate.

Pei. (*flogging him*). Don't you enjoy being
— FEATHER–EXAGITATE?

Cin. This to the Cyclic poet,[1] this to ME,
Whom people quarrel over ceaselessly!   1765

Pei. Won't you stop here and train for Giddiman
A fliers' choir to represent the clan
Of Monkeymen?

Cin.   You mock me, yes you do.
But I'll not rest — I warn you that it's true —
Till winged I shall have coursed the whole
     air through.   (*Exit.*   1771

Enter a Blackmailer *warbling*

Bla. *Birds who nothing possess,*
Feathers your dress
     Spangled with many a hue,
O thou many-hued, slender-wingèd swallow!

Pei. This is no petty evil that's astir.   1776
Here comes another quavering an air.

Bla. (*singing*). *Aye thou many-hued, slender-wingèd swallow!*

Pei. His catch on "swallow" has his coat in view,
Transparently it wants them — plenty too.[2]

Bla. Where's he who wings the folk who visit here?   1781

Pei. You see him. Pray make your requirements clear.

Bla. Wings, I require, wings, wings. Don't ask me twice.

Pei. (*pointing to his ragged cloak*). What, are you off to Tweedtown in a trice?

Bla. Oh no. I practice blackmailing (I've made   1785
The isles my special sphere) ——

Pei. (*interrupting*).   A glorious trade!

---

[1] At the Dionysia there were not only contests in tragedy and comedy, but also in dithyrambs or cyclic choruses, i.e., choral singing and dancing combined. Each of the ten Athenian tribes presented a competing chorus for the prize of a bull. Cinesias boasts here that he is in demand as a dithyrambic writer for these contests.

[2] Since the blackmailer's costume was tattered and torn, and hence little protection against the cold of the current season, Peithetaerus suggests that the blackmailer's invocations of the swallow grow out of his longing for spring and warmer weather. The swallow was always the Athenian harbinger of spring.

Bla. —— and litigation. I want wings to scare
The cities with writ-servings everywhere.
　Pei. Will wings make you serve writs more
　　skillfully?　　　　　　　　　　　　1790
　Bla. No, but from plaguing pirates I'll be
　　free.
I'll swallow lots of lawsuits and again,
Thus ballasted, fly homeward with the crane.
　Pei. What! *This* is the profession you
　　pursue?
You blackmail foreigners, a youth like you?
　Bla. I don't know how to dig, what must
　　I do?　　　　　　　　　　　　　　1796
　Pei. But surely there are decent jobs which
　　could
Afford a man like you a livelihood
By honest means rather than law-and-lies.
　Bla. (*impatiently*). My good sir, make me
　　winged, and not wise.　　　　　　1800
　Pei. Now by my words I do so.
　Bla.　　　　　　　　What, by speech
You'd put a man on wings?
　Pei.　　　　　　　　It's thus that each
And every one is winged.　　　　　　1805
　Bla.　　　　　　　　　　Thus?
　Pei.　　　　　　　Yes, you've heard
The talk lads' fathers, when they have a
　word
About them in the barbers' shops, employ —
"Grandison's talk has put wings on my
　boy.　　　　　　　　　　　　　　1810
He's flying straight to drive a coach-and-
　pair."
The stage, another says, is *his* boy's flair,
His senses taking wing are all in air.
　Bla. Words give them wings?
　Pei.　　　　　　Precisely, as I state,
Words are the means the mind to elevate　1816
And lift a man. So it's my wish with words
Of good advice to wing you like the birds,
And turn you to some honest work.
　Bla.　　　　　　　　Not ME.　1820
　Pei. What then?
　Bla.　　　　　I'll not disgrace my pedigree.
Our family profession is BLACKMAIL.
Come give me light, swift feathers, wing and
　tail,
Kestrel's or hawk's, that citing to appear　1825

In court a foreigner, my charge made HERE,
I fly back THERE.[1]
　Pei.　　　　　　I think I follow you.
You mean — before he comes, the case is
　through,
Gone, by default, to you.　　　　　　1830
　Bla.　　　　　　　You follow quite.
　Pei. Then while *he* takes a boat HERE, *you*
　take flight
THERE, to distrain his goods.
　Bla.　　　　　　　　You have it pat.
HERE — THERE, just like a top.　　1835
　Pei.　　　　　　　　I follow *that*,
A top, yes. In Corcyra [2] by-the-bye
They use this pretty means to make things fly.
　　　　　　　　　　　(*Produces a whip.*
　Bla. (*alarmed*). O dear me! That's a whip.
　Pei.　　　　　No, means of flight,　1840
Whereby today I'll make you *to*(*ho*)*p* all right.
　　　　　　　　　　　　(*Thrashes him.*
　Bla. O dear! O —!
　Pei.　　　　Go, get out of this, take wing,
Pack yourself off, you damnable vile thing.
Bitter you'll find your crooked-craft-at-law.
　　　　　　　(*Exit* BLACKMAILER.　1845
(*Addresses his* ATTENDANTS.) Let's gather up
　the feathers and withdraw.
　　　　　　　　　　　　(*Exeunt omnes.*
　Chor. Many strange and novel places,
　　Many wondrous marvels we,
　　Where our pinions waft us, see.
In the far and fearsome spaces,　　　1850
Miles from Pluckytown, in Thrace is
　Found a tree, CLEONYMY.[3]

　Very difficult to class,
　Just a wretched, useless mass,
In fine weather accusations　　　　　1855
It will bear and litigations,
But, when tempests shake the nations,
　Strew the fields with fallen — shields.

[1] This blackmailer is chiefly a process-server in suits
where the defendants were overseas residents of Athenian ally states, who had to travel to Athens for the
trial of their cases.
[2] Now Corfu; a large island off the coast of Epirus
(Albania), famous in ancient times for its double-
thonged scourges of great size.
[3] The Cleonymus tree, a bit of Aristophanic invention
again. Cleonymus was a pestilent demagogue whom
the comedian had satirized in two other of his plays.

There's a realm the sun's beams scorning
  And a spot nigh to it, where   1860
  Lights are all extremely rare.
Men and heroes in the morning
Here consort, but evening's warning
  Is BEWARE AND COME NOT THERE.

It's a dangerous thing to do.   1865
  For Bill Sikes's hero crew
People's pates then set to cracking,
Strip them bare, and with a whacking
From their cudgels send them packing,
  Tanned like hide all down the side.   1870

Enter PROMETHEUS *stealthily. He is com-*
  pletely muffled up [1] and carries a parasol

Prom. Oh dear, I must take care Zeus doesn't
    see.
Where's Peithetaerus?
Pei. (*entering*). Why what —— Gracious me!
Who's this muffled with weepers? [2]
Prom.   Do you spy   1875
A god behind me there?
Pei. (*looking*).   None meets my eye.
Who are you?
Prom.   Do you know the time of day?
Pei. The time? A little after noon. I say,
Who *are* you?   1881
Prom.   Is it luncheon time or past?
Pei. (*disgustedly*). I'm sick of you.
Prom.   The weather — overcast
Is it or cloudless?   1885
Pei.   You can go and cry
Your eyes out.
Prom.   Then I'll lay my weepers by.
                    (*Unmuffles his face.*
Pei. (*loudly and enthusiastically*). My dear
    Prometheus!
Prom. (*in a whisper mysteriously*). Stop!
    Stop! Please don't shout!   1890
Pei. (*surprised*). What is it?
Prom. (*whispering*).   Hush! Don't bawl
    my name about!
It'll be my ruin, if Zeus sees me here.
I want to make how things up there stand clear.

[1] So heavily muffled that he can hear nothing said to
him in the ensuing scene.
[2] Black veil of mourning.

Just take this parasol, and hold it — so, 1895
Above me, then the gods won't see below.
                    (*Arranges the parasol.*
  Pei. (*delightedly*). Ha ha! Ha ha!
A brilliant thought in true Promethean vein.
Slip under quick and boldly all explain.
  Prom. (*solemnly*). Listen.   1900
  Pei.   I'm listening. Speak, what's this
    affair?
  Prom. (*in emphatic staccato*). Zeus' — days
    — are — ended.[1]
  Pei.   When — did — it — occur?
  Prom. The very hour you settled in the
    Air.
No one on Earth now pays the gods sublime
Their sacrifice, nor ever since that time   1906
To us ascends the thigh bones' savory reek.
We keep a Thesmophorian fast [2] and seek
In vain for off'rings. As Illyrians do,
So the Barbarian gods, a famished crew,   1910
Scream they'll descend and quickly make Zeus
    rue,
Save he provide ports open for receipt
Of plentiful supplies of sausage meat.
  Pei. Other gods are there, north by some
    degrees,
Barbarians?   1915
  Prom.   Yes, Barbarians — one of these
Is family god to Execestides.[3]
  Pei. And these Barbarian gods — they have
    a name,
Have they?
  Prom.   A name? Damubians.[4]   1920
  Pei.   The same,
Of course, from whom our saying "Damn you"
    came.
  Prom. Precisely. One thing's sure, I tell
    you. Zeus
Will join in sending here to beg a truce
With the Damubians of the hinterland.   1925
Never you grant it, unless Zeus shall hand

[1] Cf. with this colloquy the scene between Prometheus and Io in *Prometheus Bound.*
[2] The Thesmophorian festival, in honor of Demeter
Thesmophorus ("the bringer of law"), was celebrated
at Athens annually in October by the women exclusively. The festival lasted five days, and on the third
day the celebrants fasted.
[3] See l. 11 and note.
[4] A fictitious name, of course.

The Birds the scepter back, and as their head
You receive SOVEREIGNTY from him to wed.
  Pei. Who's SOVEREIGNTY?
  Prom.   A maiden passing fair.   1930
The thunderbolt of Zeus is in her care
And every single thing — wise policies,
Wise statutes, Moderation, Docks and Quays,
Bad language, Paymasters, ten-bob[1]-a-
    day ——
  Pei. He leaves *all* in her care then?   1935
  Prom.   As I say.
Secure HER from him and supreme you reign.
That's what I've come on purpose to explain.
The FRIEND OF MAN has always been my
    rôle.
  Pei. You've been the one salvation of his —
    coal.   1940
  Prom. The Gods I've always *hated*, you'll
    agree.
  Pei. No love was lost between you certainly.
  Prom. I'm just the DEVIL to hate them.
    Now, away!
My parasol, that, if Zeus sees, he may
Think I'm a débutante at Church Parade.   1945
  Pei. And here's a Dorothy-bag,[2] as suits a
    maid.   (*Exeunt.*
  *Chor. There's a deep pool, where to keep cool
    Natives all protect their polls* [3]
    With their feet for parasols.
Socrates with souls departed   1950
There consorts, and broken-hearted
  Came Peisander [4] *there to seek*
  For a spirit fled out of sight.
He'd a camel-lambkin [5] *(this use*
Is prescribed) and, like Odysseus,[6]   1955
Cut its throat and then retired.
From below, as it expired,
  Chaerephon [7] *rose with a squeak.*

  [1] English colloquialism for "shilling."
  [2] A small handbag.   [3] Heads.
  [4] Presumably a notorious coward in Athens of that day.
  [5] A huge lamb.
  [6] In Book XI of the *Odyssey* he goes to the Underworld to visit the departed seer Teiresias. In order to
see the latter, he must summon up the souls of the dead
by cutting the throat of a sheep in the sacrificial blood-
pit. This he did, and the spirits rose around him in
horrible array, but he stood his ground until the soul he
wanted appeared. Peisander, on the contrary, fled
away in fright.
  [7] See l. 1644 and note.

Enter AMBASSADORS *from the gods,* POSEIDON,
    HERCULES *and a* DAMUBIAN

  Pos. Here is the City of Cloudcuckoorise,
To which our mission is, before our eyes.   1960
(*To the* DAMUBIAN) How now, what's *this,*
    Sir? Wear your cloak like that?
Why don't you make it sit as mine has sat?
    (*The* DAMUBIAN *tries to rearrange his cloak.*
What, Idiot? Oh you born Makemuddle, you!
Democracy, what *will* you bring us to,   1964
When gods elect to represent them — THAT?
    (*Approaches and arranges the dress of*
      the DAMUBIAN, *who fidgets uneasily.*
Be still, confound you. You, I tell you flat,
Are far the most barbarian god I've seen.
Now, Hercules, what shall we do?
  Her.   I mean,
Just as I said, to wring the fellow's neck,   1970
Whoe'er he is, who's put the gods in check.
  Pos. But, my good Sir, we were empowered
    to treat
For peace.
  Her. That makes the wringing twice as sweet.
    (*During this colloquy* PEITHETAERUS,
      realizing the arrival and composition
      of the Embassy, has had a fire, cook-
      ing implements, and food brought on-
      to the stage, and now feigns to be en-
      grossed in the preparation of a meal.
  Pei. (*to* ATTENDANTS). Give me the cheese-
    grater — and I'll require   1975
The spice — and bring the cheese — and poke
    the fire.
  Pos. (*importantly*). We three immortals
    courteously greet
The mortal.
  Pei. (*dissembling knowledge of their presence*).
    Now I'll have to spice the meat.
  Her. What meat is this?   1980
  Pei. (*ostentatiously busy without looking up*).
    Foul, revolutionary
Conspirators against Democracy,
Judged guilty of high treason.
  Her.   So you strew
Spice on them first?   1985
  Pei. (*looking up and feigning great surprise*).
    What, Hercules? It's you?
How now?

Pos. (*intervening with great dignity*). We are
the gods' emissaries
Touching cessation of hostilities ——
Servant (*interrupting*). The oil has all run
out, the cruse is dry!   1990
Pei. (*in dismay*). And fowl requires a plen-
tiful supply!
Pos. (*continuing*). To us this present war has
brought no gain,
And you, if friendly to us, would have rain
To swell your standing pools and waterways,
And all your lives would pass as halcyon
days.   1995
On all these issues we have plenary powers.
Pei. Well, as at first it was no fault of
ours
The war began, so now, if you agree,
Late as it is, to act with justice, we   1999
Are willing to make terms. This our demand —
Zeus must resign the scepter from his hand
Back to the Birds, and so let Peace be made.
If you accept this, I'll have luncheon laid.
Her. (*promptly and decidedly*). I'm fully sat-
isfied and I say Yes.
Pos. Idiot! You fool and glutton you,
what's this?   2005
Deprive your father would you of his throne?
Pei. Come, come, you gods will really, you
must own,
Increase your power, if Birds hold sway below.
At present mortals skulking, as you know,
'Neath the clouds' cover take your names in
vain.   2010
But, with the Birds allied to you, it's plain,
When mortal takes an oath "By Crow and
Zeus,"
The Crow, to pay him for the oath's abuse,
Will swoop down suddenly and blind his eye.
Pos. Sense, by my mother's son, I can't
deny.   2015
Her. I think so too.
Pos. (*to* DAMUBIAN). And you?
Dam.   Yayighsayaye.
Pei. You see? He too approves. Now let
me tell
A second way in which we'll serve you well.
Suppose a man who's promised he would
make   2021
A god an offering, then proceeds to fake

Excuses — "Gods can wait" — too mean to
pay,
We'll exact payment.
Pos.   Let's see, in what way?
Pei. When he is counting out his coin in
rows,   2026
Or sitting in the bath without his clothes,
A kite will swoop and snatch, ere he's aware,
The value of two sheep, the god's due share.
Her. I vote the Birds receive from us again
Forthwith the scepter.   2031
Pos.   Ask the Damubian then.
Her. (*threateningly, brandishing his club*).
Damubian, d'you want trouble?
Dam.   No-me-u
Klubknockee.   2035
Her. (*to* POSEIDON). Yes, he says it's quite
his view.
Pos. Then, if you both approve, I do so too.
Her. (*to* PEITHETAERUS). I say, about the
scepter — we agree.
Pei. A second point has just occurred to me.
Hera [1] to Zeus I readily resign,   2040
But the girl Sovereignty must now be mine
To marry.
Pos. (*shortly*). It's not peace you have at
heart.
Come, we'll return.
Pei.   I don't mind when you start.   2045
See that the gravy's sweet, cook; that's your
part.
Her. Great heavens, Poseidon! What are
you coming to?
War — for one woman! What possesses you?
Pos. What shall we do then?
Her.   Do? Of course agree.   2050
Pos. Poor wretch, he's duping you. Why,
don't you see
You're injuring yourself? If Zeus release
His hold upon the throne before decease,
You're pauperized. With you possession lies
Of all Zeus leaves behind him, when he dies.
Pei. Oh dear! I'm shocked that he should
trick you so.   2056
Come here, I'll tell you something you should
know.
(*Confidentially*) Your uncle, my poor fellow, 's
making game.

[1] The wife of Zeus, queen of the gods.

To what's your father's you've no scrap of
     claim,
That's *law*. You're bastard, not legitimate.
   Her. I bastard! What d'you mean? 2061
   Pei.   Just what I state.
Your mother was an alien.[1] Why, think you
Athena's[2] title would be sound and true,
A daughter's, were there lawful male issue?
   Her. Suppose my father, dying, made me
     heir   2066
By deed of gift?
   Pei.   It's void, the laws declare.
Poseidon there, who's prompting you, will be
The first to claim your father's property, 2070
Urging that, as blood-brother, it's his right.
Listen to Solon's[3] law which I'll recite —
"There being lawful issue, a bastard shall have
     no right of kin.
In default of lawful issue property shall be
     divided among the next of kin."
   Her. Then nothing that my father leaves can
     go   2075
To me?
   Pei. No, as he lives, it can't. D'you know
Whether he's put you on the voters' list?
   Her. No. I'd long wondered how my name
     was missed.
   Pei. (*very confidentially and persuasively*).
     Why glare assault and battery at the
     sky?   2080
Join *us*, I'll make you tyrant, I'll supply
Deep draughts of pigeon's milk, when you are
     dry.
   Her. (*loudly*). Touching the girl, again I
     take the view
Your claim is just, and herewith give her you.
   Pei. And your vote is?   2085
   Pos.   Against, with all my heart.
   Pei. And you, Damubian? To decide's
     your part.
   Dam. Glubbly gurrllie michty Sovereignno
Give Birdee.
   Her. We've to yield her, he says so. 2090

[1] The mother of Hercules was Alcmena, queen of
Thebes. As a mortal she was, of course, an alien in the
realm of the gods.
[2] Pallas Athene, daughter of Zeus.
[3] The great Athenian legislator (c. 638–c. 558 B.C.),
whose law actually still remained in force at the time of
The Birds, worded very nearly as stated here.

   Pos. By Heaven, if that is what he means to
     say,
He says it as the swallows say "Away."
   Pei. Why then he means "Don't say the
     swallows nay."
   Pos. Conclude your compact for the war to
     cease.
Since you are set on it, I'll hold my peace.
   Her. We are prepared to grant all you de-
     mand.   2096
Come with us now to Heaven, and your own
     hand
Shall receive Sovereignty and all things there.
   Pei. And these birds killed to serve for
     wedding fare
Just in the nick of time!   2100
   Her.   Suppose I stay
And watch them cooking, while you're all
     away.
   Pos. And watch them cooking! Blow your-
     self out tight,
You mean. COME WITH US.
   Her. (*going reluctantly*).   I'd have been
     all right.   2105
   Pei. (*to* ATTENDANTS). Fetch me gay garb.
     I claim my bride tonight.   (*Exeunt.*
   Chor. In Blackliars cursed Paul Pryers[1]
     Haunt the lawcourts, rogues who still
     With the tongue the belly fill.
Tongue they use if seed they're sowing, 2110
Tongue at harvest time for mowing,
     Tongue to pluck the ripened bunch.
     Whence they be's a mystery.
Foggs and Dodsons[2] they, whose fashion
Thus to make their belly's ration 2115
Out of tongue has spread the notion
That to tongue a strict devotion
     Must by all be paid — AT LUNCH.

Enter a MESSENGER *who harangues in*
mock tragic manner

   Mes. O happy, happy race, ye feathered
     Birds,
Blest with all blessings, blest beyond all words,

[1] I.e., impudent, meddlesome people; so called from a
chief character in John Poole's comedy *Paul Pry* (1825).
[2] Messrs. Dodson and Fogg were two unprincipled
lawyers in Dickens' *The Pickwick Papers* (1838).

Welcome your royal lord to his rich home. 2121
He comes.   No star set in Heaven's golden
      dome
Can match its ray 'gainst his refulgent beam,
No, not the Sun's own glittering far-flung
      gleam
So radiant glows, as doth the beauteous grace
Ineffable lighten in his mistress' face.   2126
The thunderbolt he wields, Zeus' winged shaft,
To Heaven's high arch strange, fragrant odors
      waft,
Fair vision, incense-smoke's curled canopy
Floats on the breezes fluttering tremblingly.
Lo, where he comes!   The Muses' lips un-
      seal   2131
With sacred song to greet and wish him weal.

Enter PEITHETAERUS, *who is splendidly at-*
tired and invested with the attributes of
Zeus, and is accompanied by SOVEREIGNTY
and ATTENDANTS

  Chor. Lead.   Back, there, divide, give them
      room, stand aside,
  So — flutter about
Him, blessed with all blessings, within and
      without.   2135
  O look, what beauty!   Look, what loveli-
      ness!
Greeting we give thee, who bringest thy bride
      our city to bless.
  O how great, O how great, are the blessings
      that wait
  The Bird race through the grace   2139
Of this man!   Bridal lays in his honor upraise,
With nuptial song pay to him honor today
And to her whom you see with him come —
      Sovereignty.
  Chor. Once on a day with Hera wed
  He who sits on Olympus' throne,
  Whom the gods as their sovereign own, 2145
      And as to his bed
      The maid they led,
  The Fates in unison cried, O!
  O Hail!   Hail to the bride, O! [1]

[1] To the Greek the sanctity of all marriage ties was
derived from the great primeval marriage of Zeus and
Hera.   Hence the continual allusion to them in this
marriage hymn.

All in his pride with his gold wings, see, 2150
Love sits holding the tautened rein,
Guiding the steeds as they forward strain,
      O happy she'll be
      Whose squire is he,
Hera, there by his side, O!   2155
O Hail!   Hail to the bride, O!
  Chor. Lead.   With delight do I hear your
      sweet notes ringing clear,
And my heart swells with joy.   Now your
      voices employ
To proclaim how his sway Earth's deep thun-
      ders obey,
And how Zeus to him yields the dread weapons
      he wields,   2160
Flaming   and   gleaming   'mid   lightnings
      streaming.
  Chor. Dread golden glare of the lightning
      flashes,
Javelin of flame immortal,
Thunder that 'neath the Earth rumbles and
      crashes
Or roars from the storm-cloud's portal, 2165
Weapons to make the world quiver —
His they are now, (to SOVEREIGNTY) THOU
      the giver.
Sovereignty, see, hath her place by his side, O!
O Hail!   Hail to the bride, O!
  Pei. Come, join ye in the wedding train 2170
      Feathery fellow-mates o' mine.
      Now we seek the couch divine
      Where Zeus with Hera erst has lain.

  Come, Fortune smiles, my happy bride.
  Put thy hand forth, clasp my wing. 2175
  So, leaning on me, dance and sing,
  And lightly thus thy steps I'll guide.

All. Hip-ip-ip-ip!   Hurrah!   Hurrah!
  Cheer for the Conqueror, Cheer on cheer,
  Divinity without a peer!   2180

(*Exeunt omnes singing and dancing*
through the Orchestra.   The strains
"Once on a day with Hera wed"
and "Dread golden glare of the
lightning flashes" are heard more
and more faintly as the procession
passes out of sight.

INTRODUCTION TO

The Pot of Gold

*The Spread of Attic Tragedy and Comedy to Rome: The Early Roman
Theater: Roman Tragedy: Early Roman Comedy and Plautus*

THE SPREAD OF ATTIC TRAGEDY AND COMEDY TO ROME

EVEN BEFORE Aeschylus died in 456 B.C. certain of his plays had been performed in the new theater at Syracuse, Sicily. Within a few decades the prize-winning tragedies of the Athenian festivals were regularly being produced at various Greek centers throughout the Mediterranean world. During the fourth and well into the third century B.C. the Attic tragedy, especially of Euripides and his successors, enjoyed frequent performance in the Hellenic communities of southern Italy and Sicily.

Attic comedy, however, spread far more slowly to these regions, because of their strong local forms of comic entertainment. When Attic comedy did transplant itself at the beginning of the third century B.C., it was not the Old Comedy of *The Birds*, nor even the Middle Comedy of Aristophanes' last years, but a third type called the New Comedy. This new form flourished in Attica from about 336 B.C. (when Alexander the Great completed Macedon's dictatorship over Athens and all Greece) down to 250 B.C. Containing neither the satire of personages and public affairs so characteristic of Aristophanic drama, nor the literary satire of Middle Comedy, it drew its materials almost entirely from private life. It became in essence a comedy of manners which caricatured familiar types or classes rather than individuals.

The types were, of course, common in the everyday world of the Athenian citizen — for example, the stern father, the talkative woman, the wayward son, the upstart, the courtesan, the tricky slave, and the braggart soldier. Special masks and make-up belonged to each type. The braggart soldier had either black hair and dark complexion, or blond head and fair skin. The country fellow possessed tanned cheeks, wide lips, flat nose, and black hair coiled on the crown of his head. Thus the audience could identify at first sight the character rôle which each actor was playing.

The plotting, as well as the characterization, of the New Comedy differed much from that of the Old. The rather loose, haphazard action in the Old Comedy was supplanted by a sequence of scenes closely connected by cause and effect. The result was a compact and complicated intrigue such as the older Attic comedy never displayed. While the structure of the plots improved, the content grew more restricted. Fantasy was altogether neglected in the face of an enthusiasm for supposedly lifelike situations. The themes represented, for the greater part, a monotonous repetition of love affairs. One of the most frequent plots depicted a young man wanting to marry his former mistress, his father opposed to the match on the grounds that she was an alien courtesan, and finally, the discovery of the young woman's respectable native birth, which removed parental opposition.

The patterning of the New Comedy departed in other important respects from Old Comedy. For a long time the chorus had been found a distinct hindrance in the development of comedy toward an imitation of private and domestic experiences. At last the New Comedy relegated the chorus to a place quite outside the dramatic action. The choral performers no longer stood in the orchestra throughout the play, but came on solely to break up the action at the proper intervals by offering *entr'acte* entertainment. The *entr'actes* as often consisted of vaudeville and specialty dancing as of musical numbers.

The changing function of the comic chorus effected a reduction in its size to only seven men. Simultaneously the speaking parts in the comedy proper were increased to four, and even five, from the strict limitation of three which existed in Old and Middle Comedy. The larger allowance of actors permitted, in turn, a more extensive *dramatis personae* and a more involved plot.

The finest writer of the New Comedy was Menander, born in 342 B.C. at Athens of a wealthy aristocratic family. His parents provided him with the best of education and acquaintance. The writer of the celebrated Greek character sketches, Theophrastus (?–*c*. 287 B.C.), acted as one of his tutors, while from youth he had the famous philosopher Epicurus (*c*. 342–270 B.C.) as a warm friend. The most important influence, however, came from his uncle Alexis, a well-known author of Middle Comedy. The latter taught his nephew about playwriting and started him as a comedian at the age of twenty.

During the thirty years of his career, which were all spent at Athens, Menander wrote over one hundred plays. He achieved a tremendous popularity, though strangely enough he won only eight first prizes in the festival competitions. Stranger still, his comedies were not well preserved. Mere scattered fragments existed until the late nineteenth century when from the rubbish heaps of a Roman town in Egypt there came to light considerable portions of three plays, *The Woman of Samos*, *The Shorn Lady*, and *The Arbitration*. These mutilated works represent the only extant specimens of Attic New Comedy, the general pattern of which has already been described. Menander's drama differs only in the superior quality of its artistry and language.

After Menander's death in 291 B.C. the Athenians, it is said, erected a statue of him in the theater on the Acropolis. His fame soon reached to the far corners of the Mediterranean world. He gradually gained a reputation not merely for comic art but for literary excellence. His brilliant epigrammatic style inspired quotation on a vast scale. These quotations found their way into the works of many ancient writers, even into the New Testament. Paul's first epistle to the Corinthians (chap. xv, v. 33) contains one of Menander's maxims: "Evil communications corrupt good manners."

The plays of Menander comprised the cream of the Attic New Comedy which spread to Sicily and southern Italy at the opening of the third century B.C. After the Roman capture of Tarentum, the chief center of Greek culture in Italy, in 272 B.C., a deep interest in Greek civilization arose at Rome. The study of Greek literature and art became the vogue, though up to that time Roman cultivation of these fields had been very slight. The only Roman drama had consisted in the occasional performances of *saturae*, merry little scenes from daily life, composed in verse, done with music, and possessed of no continuity.   The opportunity was ripe for Attic tragedy and comedy to make their way to Rome and to replace this crude form of dramatic art.

It remained for a Greek of Tarentum, Livius Andronicus, finally to bring the highly finished drama of Athens upon the Roman stage.   As a boy he had been taken captive to Rome in 272, sold as a slave to a certain Livius, educated, and then made a freedman.   With his command of both Greek and Latin he proceeded to translate or adapt from the Greek two plays, a comedy and a tragedy.   Their performance in 240 B.C. at the *iudi Romani* (Roman games), the September festival in honor of Jupiter, marked the first exhibition of regular plays in Rome.   From that year onward the acting of Latin plays, modeled on Greek originals, formed one of the secular side shows to this festival.   The Roman stage had at length been born out of Attic tragedy and comedy.

THE EARLY ROMAN THEATER

The number of the Roman public games where the production of plays occurred steadily rose.   Early in the second century B.C., dramatic representations were taking place not only at the four great festival periods in April, July, September, and November, but also at the celebrations connected with dedications, triumphs, and funerals. Rome at this time had as many as forty holidays when stage entertainments might be given.

All the games or celebrations had sponsors who through their provision of amusement courted popularity.   The sponsor, upon deciding to include plays on the program, made his arrangements with the manager of a theatrical troupe.   The manager, often an actor as well as a producer, was usually a freedman, but at least the majority of his company were slaves.   From the earliest days the Romans maintained a deep prejudice against the profession of acting.   Citizens of free birth almost never engaged in any sort of theatrical enterprise.   This prejudice must be accounted an important obstacle to any pronounced creative effort in dramatic art among the high class Romans.

The manager, as well as the sponsor, took great pains to insure the success of the plays given at the games.   The financial reward of the manager depended on the sponsor's opinion of the popular applause.   The actors in turn received payment from the manager according to the response which they drew.   He would beat the lesser actors (the slaves) if he thought they had done poorly.   The manager assumed the responsibility of selecting the plays to be produced, though often, no doubt, he submitted his choices to the sponsor.   The decisions hinged on the sole consideration of winning public favor.

Public favor, however, always proved fickle.   The audiences consisted largely of the lower classes who had paid little or nothing for the privilege of attendance.   Admission fees were scarcely ever charged for the performances, because the sponsors desired primarily to secure the approbation of the common people, a miscellaneous rabble that shouted or hooted as the whim moved.   They did not hesitate to leave the performance in a group if they believed more attractive entertainment available elsewhere.   In 165 B.C. at the April festival games, when Terence's comedy *Hecyra* was being acted, the spectators heard that boxing and rope-dancing were going on near by.   Thereupon they deserted the not too exciting comedy, and its acting came to an abrupt end.

Dramatic performances must have taken place not later than noon, for they concluded before the principal Roman meal eaten in mid-afternoon. When the production began, the manager, coming forward, announced the title of the play, the author, and the Greek source. The absence of a handbill program necessitated such a prologue. Few, if any, in the audience could have had any previous knowledge in regard to the dramatic offering for that particular day.

The theatergoers at Rome for several centuries attended plays under primitive conditions. The Roman Senate remained continually hostile to stage exhibitions on the ground that they encouraged a taste for luxury and corrupted youth. The Senate prevented the building of any permanent theaters until 55 B.C. when Pompey the Great constructed a huge stone theater in the Campus Martius patterned after the existing Greek models in southern Italy. Previous to that date the so-called theaters were temporary affairs, located on open spaces near temples or on other public grounds. The architectural construction which they involved was always taken down after each period of performance. At first, theaters consisted of no more than a wooden stage-platform, called the *pulpitum;* the *scaena,* a wooden wall for background to the platform; and the *cavea,* a place without seats, usually sloping ground, where the audience could sit or stand. The level space of the *cavea* close to the platform was later reserved for senators and other distinguished persons, who sat on wooden benches. Later still, wooden bleachers filled the *cavea* so that all the spectators might be seated. In all cases, these early Roman theaters must be imagined as relatively small, holding hundreds of persons where the Athenian theater held thousands.

The shallow stage-platform, the *pulpitum,* represented a street, while the wooden rear wall, the *scaena,* suggested the fronts of houses on the street. The ends of the *pulpitum* provided, by means of steps, exits to, or entrances from localities at a distance. The side on the audience's right led to the center of the city and the forum; that on the left, to the country and the sea. The *scaena* usually contained three doors, just as did the front of the *skene* in the Athenian theater. Each of these doors could indicate a different house, or two of them might belong to the same dwelling. One door, kept ajar, might serve on occasion as the open end of a supposed alley, a common place of concealment for one of the characters. The doors were never allowed to open to disclose an interior, since there was not enough space back of the *scaena.* All conversations, therefore, had to be carried on in the open or at the house-door. On account of such limitations in staging the Roman playwrights did not attempt to depart from their Greek models by utilizing interior scenes. Theirs had to remain a drama of the thoroughfare, the market place, and the threshold, quite identical in this respect with its forebears in Attic tragedy and comedy.

ROMAN TRAGEDY

Roman tragedy, instituted by Livius Andronicus in 240 B.C., remained always very much as he had set it forth — a frank imitation of Attic tragedy both in pattern and content. Indeed many of the Roman writers attempted little more than free Latin translations of Aeschylus, Sophocles, Euripides, and a few lesser figures, with the omission of the choral material. Ennius (239–169 B.C.) and Accius (170–*c.* 86 B.C.), the two leading tragedians before the downfall of the Republic, wrote plays upon the Attic model with titles such as *Atreus*, *Ajax*, and *Phoenix*, though they also undertook some Roman historical themes like *The Sabine Women* and *Brutus*.

All this Roman tragedy has perished, with the single exception of the plays of Lucius Annaeus Seneca, the most original and influential of the tragic writers. Son of the rhetorician Marcus Annaeus Seneca, he was born at Cordova, Spain, near the beginning of the Christian era. In childhood he removed to Rome, where he got an excellent education in rhetoric and philosophy. Under the emperors, Caligula and Claudius, he served as a member of the Roman Senate, but in 41 A.D. he was exiled by political chicanery to Corsica. Eight years later Agrippina, wife of Claudius, got him recalled to become tutor for her son Nero, who later became emperor. During the first years of the latter's reign Seneca exercised great influence. Then Nero grew jealous of Seneca's power, accused him of conspiracy against the throne, and compelled him to commit suicide in 65 A.D.

Seneca wrote nine or ten tragedies on the legends used by Aeschylus, Sophocles, and Euripides: for example, *Agamemnon*, *Medea*, *Oedipus*, *The Trojan Women*. Yet he did not imitate slavishly the pattern of their drama. He intended his compositions not as stage plays, but as pieces for elocutionists to read aloud. It is highly improbable that they were ever acted in Rome, since they are altogether too slow moving to have attracted a Roman audience. Indeed the Senecan tragedies are the natural product of a rhetorician and philosopher, with tedious dialogues which are almost sermons, colored by Stoic philosophy, and expressed in bombastic language. The characterizations lack all subtlety and sensibility. The various dramatic devices of the Greeks, such as the messenger and the departed spirit or ghost, Seneca introduced with mechanical obtuseness. At best the plays are ponderous, crude, and rather distant imitations of Attic tragedy.

Despite the primitiveness of his dramatic art Seneca exerted a powerful influence in the development of English tragedy during Shakespeare's youth. Senecan drama was much read and produced in the English schools and universities. A complete English edition of the *Ten Tragedies of Seneca* appeared in 1582. Every budding playwright made acquaintance with the Roman tragedian either in Latin or in English translation. He provided at a needy moment a considerable number of appealing features in the way of dramatic content, structure, and style: the revenge motif, the ghost, murder and other horrible butchery, insanity, the explicit division into five acts, sententious and moralizing passages, and above all else, elaborate oratorical phraseology. The high-flown poetry of Shakespearean speech is mainly the refinement of Senecan rhetoric. Thus through the sole medium of this now unread Roman tragedian some faint touches of the Attic tragedy of Aeschylus, Sophocles, and Euripides were conveyed to the genius of Shakespeare.

EARLY ROMAN COMEDY AND PLAUTUS

Roman comedy, as well as Roman tragedy, owed its establishment to Livius Andronicus. After producing his first comic drama at the Roman games in 240 B.C., he continued for many years to translate and adapt specimens of Attic New Comedy. By the time of his death in 204 B.C. many other writers had followed his example and had thoroughly popularized in Rome this Greek comedy of manners and domestic intrigue. To its material, however, they had begun to add a definite Roman flavor, so that the resulting product was often a curious mixture of Greek and Roman life.

The outward pattern of Roman comic drama imitated rather closely the structural and stylistic features of its Greek sources. The Roman comedians, like the Greek, took no account of act divisions in the modern sense. They visualized the action of their plays as continuous. If pauses in the performance were desired, the theatrical manager, not the playwright, determined their place and number. During intermissions of this sort a flute-player or a dancer entertained the audience. The act divisions to be noted now in the texts of the Roman comedies were put in long after the original composition. They represent conformity to the tradition of late classical scholarship that all drama should have acts and that five should be the proper number.

The Roman comedians, however, did recognize scene divisions as a regular structural device. The entrance or exit of one or more characters marked the transition from one scene to the next, but no pause or break in the action needed to occur at this point. If after the exit of one or several persons only a very brief dialogue or soliloquy ensued before the entrance of a new character, then the intervening short scene was not considered a scene in the technical sense.

The scenes of Roman comedy, as in Greek, were composed entirely in *verse*, though the verse varied with the type of scene. The scenes consisted of two classes: (1) the *spoken*, (2) the *sung*. The first, known as *diverbia* or dialogues, was carried on like ordinary conversation with no musical accompaniment. The second group, the *cantica*, included two subtypes: (*a*) scenes declaimed or chanted with musical accompaniment on the flute, like the "recitative" of a modern opera; (*b*) lyrical monologues sung to the tune of the flute and accompanied by gestures or dancing. In these lyrical monologues the actor himself sometimes did not sing but merely performed appropriate "business" while a boy slave near the flutist sang the verses. Despite their variety of style all the scenes of Roman comedy belonged to the genus of poetry. Hence the Romans, like the Greeks, spoke of their comedians as comic poets.

The most brilliant of the early Roman comic poets was Titus Maccius Plautus, whose plays are the oldest surviving drama of Rome. Plautus, born of poor but free parents at Sarsina in the Umbrian district of northern Italy about 254 B.C., came as a youth to Rome. There he found eventual employment as an artisan connected with theatrical productions. With his savings he attempted to set up in business away from Rome, but failed and returned to the capital to work in a baker's mill. His former associations with the stage, however, caused him to experiment on the side with dramatic composition. When about thirty years old, he succeeded in persuading a theatrical manager to perform one or several of his plays. Immediate success enabled him to give up his menial occupation and to devote himself to playwriting. During the forty years until his death in 184 B.C. his output is reported to have reached the extraordinary total of one hundred and thirty comedies. Twenty have come down to the present. The most important are *Amphitruo* (Amphitryon), *Aulularia* (The Pot of Gold), *Captivi* (The Captives), *Menaechmi* (The Twin Brothers), and *Miles Gloriosus* (The Boastful Soldier).

The comedies of Plautus were all derived from plays in the Greek New Comedy, chiefly those of Menander, Diphilus, and Philemon. They faithfully reproduced even the details of the originals. Plautus retained the references to Greek social customs, dress, coinage, places, and marine life, as well as the Greek scene of action and the

A ROMAN THEATER OF THE TIMES OF PLAUTUS AND TERENCE
A conjectural drawing

dramatis personae. The actors of his plays wore the typical make-ups, the low-heeled light shoe ("sock"), and the *pallium* or short cloak of the Greek comic stage, though they did not wear masks as was done in Attica. On the whole, Plautine comedy did not attempt to transform its foreign background.

Yet, while so many of the externals were manifestly Greek, Roman elements did appear. Allusions to Roman geography, law, government, customs, business, pastimes, and history, were frankly inserted by Plautus alongside the Greek material. An amusing topsy-turvydom of descriptive fact is the consequence, though the greater part of his audience probably never noticed the point, and therefore were never amused.

More important, however, than this minor infusion of Roman coloring, is the distinctly native treatment Plautus gave to plot and dialogue. His problem was to interest a crowd of people of limited refinement. He had to make the play clear to these restless "lowbrows" and keep them in good humor. No dramatic *finesse* or polished style of language suited them. Plautus knew well the folk drama which then was all the rage with the Roman populace, the short Atellan farces with their horseplay and broad humor. They had been welcomed to Rome from the south of Italy about the time that Plautus turned playwright. In fact, as a bit of Plautine humor, he seems to have given himself a middle name after one of the prominent stock figures in this Atellan farce: Maccus, the glutton and braggart. Consideration of the popular taste, therefore, impelled him to coarsen his Greek models. Their intrigues he preserved, but he made the action more lively and boisterous. He introduced roguery and imposture, beatings, scolding matches, gross depictions of eating, drinking, and love-making. Through these physical incidents and through verbal means he created a rollicking and obvious humor. Disputations, loud retorts, puns, and coarse jests were his frequent devices to provoke laughter. All in all, it was a comedy of simple robust wit and constant movement, one perfectly adapted to the average Roman audience. With his accurate judgment of the public taste, and with dramatic talents to match it, Plautus quite rightly became the most popular dramatist that Rome ever produced.

His popularity did not end with Rome. In England of the sixteenth century Plautus enjoyed immense fame. The English school boys and university men commonly acted as well as studied his plays. Plautine drama was set up as *the* model for Elizabethan writers of comedy. Shakespeare at the outset of his career used the *Menaechmi* as the basis for *The Comedy of Errors*. The influence of Plautus extended to France in the seventeenth century, when the great Molière borrowed heavily from him. In Germany of the eighteenth century Lessing was much indebted to the work of the noted Roman comedian. Even in recent years he has afforded inspiration. During the season of 1937–38 the Theater Guild presented in New York a very successful comedy by S. N. Behrman, *Amphitryon 38*, the lineage of which traces back to the *Amphitruo* of Plautus. These instances of continued indebtedness testify to the perennial fertility of his comic invention. Because of that genius he has been an outstanding force in the development of world comedy.

"THE POT OF GOLD"

Aulularia or *The Pot of Gold* is one of Plautus' most interesting plays, and perhaps too little appreciated. It contains all the characteristics of his farce-comedy: (1) a rapidly developed situation with an even more rapid *denouement* by a faithful and clever slave, Strobilus; (2) type characters, like the old female servant, Staphyla, and the wealthy middle-aged bachelor, Megadorus; (3) humor of physical action, such as the beatings of Staphyla and Congrio by Euclio; (4) broad wit from the talk of servants — Anthrax, Congrio, and Strobilus, all of whom play on words and utter with surprising ease the most apt, though occasionally suggestive, comparisons; (5) colorful passages of satire on contemporary living, similar to Megadorus' long speech on spendthrift wives and modern luxury (Act III, Scene 10, l. 39 ff.).

Certain features of dramatic exposition in *The Pot of Gold* are very typical of Plautine technique.   The prologue by the Household God, relating the circumstances which have led up to the play, corresponds to similar opening addresses in all the comedies of Plautus though sometimes they are given by an actor or a "Prologus," rather than by a god. This device descended to Roman comedy by way of Greek New Comedy from the *prologos* or opening section in Euripidean tragedy, of which *Alcestis* affords a good example.   Other expository instruments which Plautus perhaps developed more fully than previous playwrights are the "aside" and what might be called the informing monologue.   A particularly excellent example of the latter is in Act V, Scene 1, where Strobilus enters and informs the audience all the details of his capture of the pot.   Both these contrivances are highly artificial and crude, but the Roman audience did not worry about primitive dramatic technique as long as they kept abreast of the situation. Thanks to classical example, the contrivances in question long remained part of general dramatic practice, certainly until the nineteenth century.

The distinguishing quality of *The Pot of Gold*, however, is not the intrigue, as in many comedies by Plautus, but the characterization of Euclio, the miserly old man.   As Plautine plots go, the intrigue is relatively undeveloped.   The emphasis in this play falls on the portrayal of the central character, the owner of the pot.   Upon the depiction of Euclio, Plautus bestowed far more than his usual skill in drawing persons.   The mental quirks of the miser, his nervousness over the safety of the pot under the hearth, and his suspicion of the motives of every move made in his direction, are handled with such dramatic deftness that the type caricature is almost obliterated in the spontaneity of Euclio's absurd behavior.   Touches of individuality deepen the portrait here and there, as when he appears hugging his pot and says that he has just knocked the cock's head off, for scratching around the hearth where the pot was buried.   Then he adds with whimsical irritation that the cooks had probably bribed the cock to find the money (Act III, Scene 9, l. 8 ff.).   Here, at least, there are traces of individual reaction.   At such points Plautus displays a psychological interest that rises above his prevailing farcical bent.

The Pot of Gold stands out among his plays for this tendency toward the richer comedy of character.   Indeed Molière was so far impressed with the portraiture of Euclio that he built one of the great French comedies, *The Miser*, upon the dramatic foundation which Plautus laid in *The Pot of Gold*.   A comparison of these two dramas vividly illuminates the distinction between "high" and "low" comedy.   The genius seen in *The Pot of Gold* is vigorous but confessedly limited in the depth of its comic motivations.

[For a study of Roman comedy and Plautus, see Paul Nixon, *Plautus* (1916); Gilbert Norwood, *Plautus and Terence* (1932); F. A. Wright, *Three Roman Poets* (1938).]

TITUS MACCIUS PLAUTUS

The Pot of Gold [1]

[*Translated by* CHARLES E. BENNETT]

DRAMATIS PERSONAE

THE HOUSEHOLD GOD, *who speaks the Prologue*	ANTHRAX ⎫
EUCLIO, *an aged Athenian*	CONGRIO ⎭ *cooks*
MEGADORUS, *uncle of* LYCONIDES	EUNOMIA, *mother of* LYCONIDES
LYCONIDES, *a young Athenian*	PHAEDRIA, *daughter of* EUCLIO
STROBILUS, *slave of* MEGADORUS *and* LYCONIDES	STAPHYLA, *an old woman, servant of* EUCLIO
PYTHODICUS, *slave of* MEGADORUS	*Flute-Girls, Tradesmen, Flogging-Slaves*

The Scene is a street in Athens, before the houses of EUCLIO and MEGADORUS,
and the Temple of Faith

PROLOGUE

Spoken by the GUARDIAN SPIRIT *of the Household*

That none may wonder what my name and state,
In discourse brief this tale I shall relate.
I am the Spirit of this household here
Whence you have seen me come.   For many a year
This house has shelter'd me; grandsire and sire   5
Of him who tends its hearth have kept the fire
That shines upon me.   But with earnest prayer,
Unknown to all, the grandsire to my care
Consign'd a hoard of gold, well hid beside
The midmost hearth, and begg'd, whate'er betide,   10
That I should guard it in his stead.   When stole
Death's sleep upon him, still his niggard soul
Would ne'er disclose the secret to the son
He left behind, but as his life had run
Through all its years, prefer'd to leave his heir   15
A dower of penury than to declare
Existence of the treasure.   Acres scant
Of land he left him, that in toil and want
Might bring him mean subsistence.   When he died
Who charg'd me with the hoard of gold, I tried   20
To test his son, whether in any wise
His honor toward me might the higher rise
Than that his sire had paid — but scanter still
The reverence giv'n, and less and less the will
To worship.   So in turn at length did I   25
Toward him.   And in good time he came to die.

He left this heir who dwells here now — like son,
Like sire, like grandsire. Of his line but one
Is left, a daughter; she with every day
Makes offering to me — now a chaplet gay,   30
Or wine, or incense, or somewhat beside.
'Tis out of love for her I've come to guide
This Euclio to the treasure, that a dower
Might be at hand against her marriage hour,
Should he so wish; for she has been betray'd   35
By a youth of finest lineage, who, 'tis said,
Knows whom he has wrong'd, whereas she does not know
His name, nor does her father, Euclio,
Yet know of her disgrace. I'll bring this day
A white-hair'd gentleman across the way,   40
Our neighbor here, to bargain for her hand,
With this in view, as you may understand,
That he who wrong'd her may with greater ease
Wed her himself. This oldster, if you please,
Who is to seek her for his wife, will prove   45
The uncle of that youth who in the grove
Of Ceres ravish'd her in dead of night
At the goddess' festival.¹ But now, in quite
His usual way, here's our old man about
His daily row; he's throwing the old crone out   50
Lest she detect the secret. I'm believing
He wants to see if his gold is safe from thieving.

ACT I

SCENE 1

EUCLIO *appears in the doorway, energetically*
driving out STAPHYLA

Euc. Out with you! Out, I say! By heaven,
     you *will*
Go hence, you pryabout, with bulging eyes
That spy on everything!
Sta.   Why beat me, pray,
Who've misery enough?   5
Euc.   That you may know
Yet more of misery, and being accurst
Live out a life accurst, as is your due.
Sta. But why thus drive me from the house,
     I say?
Euc. Must I show cause to you, you whip-
     crop? Here!   10

Back from that doorway! — Look you, how she
     creeps!
But know you what's the case with you? If
     once
I get my hands on some good club or whip
I'll speed that tortoise-pace of yours!
Sta.   Alas!   15
Would that the gods would drive me to the
     rope!
Better to hang than slave as I must do
In such a household.
Euc.   Harkye, how the hag
Is muttering to herself! By heaven, you jade,
I'll gouge those eyes clean out — and then we'll
     see   21
If you'll still spy upon me and my doings!
Off with you! (*Pushing her*) More! — Still
     more! Stop! Stand you there!

---

¹ The reference is probably to the Thesmophoria, a festival of the Greek harvest goddess, Demeter (the Roman Ceres), celebrated by women in commemoration of the search by Demeter for her lost daughter, Persephone, or Proserpina, who was carried off by Pluto. The major portion of the celebration took place at night, without lights.

Now by the gods, if you but dare to stir
A finger's breadth, yea, or a nail's width even,
From that one spot, or if you look around   26
Before I order you, I swear by heaven
I'll hand you to the hangman then and there
To practise on! (*To himself*) I know in very
    sooth
I've never seen a creature more accurst   30
Than this old crone; and sore I fear her, too,
Lest secretly she cheat me unaware,
Or smell the place, confound her, where the
    gold
Is hid, since she, it seems, has eyes i' the back
As well as the front o' her head. — But now I'll
    go   35
And see if all my gold is still untouch'd
As I have hid it, for it keeps me rack'd
With utter misery with every moment.
                      (*He goes inside.*

SCENE 2

STAPHYLA, *alone*

Sta. So help me heaven, I cannot conceive
What blight or madness I may say has fallen
Upon my master; in so strange a wise
Ten times a day he oft will drive me forth
From out the house. I' faith, I do not know   5
What craziness has got him in its grasp.
Whole nights he watches, and by day he sits
For days on end at home, for all the world
Like some lame cobbler. Nor can I devise   9
How longer I may hide the shame that's come
Upon my master's daughter, since her time
Is near at hand. There's nothing better now
For me, I fancy, than to tie my neck
Into a halter noose, and hanging high
Make of myself a dangling letter "I."   15

SCENE 3

Enter EUCLIO, *from his house*

Euc. (*to himself*). Now that my mind has
    eas'd itself, at length
I go out of my house, since I have seen
That all is safe within. (*To* STAPHYLA) You,
    there, return
Into the house at once, and keep sharp watch
On all within.   5

Sta.   Keep watch on what, forsooth?
Is it lest someone take the house away?
For here in our house naught is left as spoil
For thieves, so full is it of emptiness
And cobwebs.   10
Euc.   Yea, a marvel 'tis, indeed,
That for your sake Jove does not make of me
King Philip or Darius![1] Threefold spawn
Of witches! — Bah! — Those very cobwebs 'tis
I'd have you watch for me. I'm poor, I know,
But I endure it; what the gods may bring   16
I take with thankfulness. Now go within,
And shut the door. I shall be back anon.
Take care meanwhile to let no stranger in.
Sta. But what if someone asks for fire?   20
Euc.   I want
The fire put out, that none may have excuse
To ask you for it. For if it's kept alive
'Tis you who'll be extinguish'd on the instant.
Say too the water has run out, if one   25
Should seek it. And in like wise knife or axe,
Pestle or mortar, gear the neighbors aye
Are asking loan of, say that thieves have come
And clean'd them out. In short, while I'm
    away
I want no one admitted to my house.   30
Nay, this I tell you, too — e'en Lady Luck,
Should she present herself, don't let her in!
Sta. I' faith, that lady takes good care, I
    think,
Never to cross our threshold; though she lives
Next door, she's never yet set foot inside.   35
Euc. Now hold your tongue, and go.
Sta.   I'll hold my tongue
And go at once.
Euc.   See that you close the door
And draw both bolts. I shall return anon.   40
               (STAPHYLA *goes inside.*
I'm troubl'd sore in mind that I must leave
My house. I' faith, 'tis much against my will
I go at all. But yet I know full well
What I'm about. The master of our ward
Has made announcement of a shilling dole   45
To every citizen. If I forego
My share, and ask not for it, all forthwith
Will be suspecting I have gold at home.
For likely 'tis that no man who is poor   49

---

[1] Philip, king of Macedonia, and Darius, king of Persia, are taken as types of rich and powerful monarchs.

Would scorn e'en such a trifle, and would fail
To claim his dole.   For now, while I take pains
To hide my wealth from all men, lest they
    know,
They seem to know, in my despite, and all
Salute me with a greater deference
Than they had shown before.   They notice
    me,   55
They stop me, take my hand, inquire my state
Of health, my business, what I am about,
But now I'll go where I was bound.   That
    done,
I'll hasten home with all the speed I may.

      (*Exit* Euclio, *in the direction of the
      Forum.*

ACT II

Scene 1

Eunomia *and* Megadorus *come out of*
Megadorus' *house in earnest conversation*

Eun. I'd have you think, my brother, that
    I speak
These words straight from a loyal heart that
    craves
Your welfare, as befits a sister's love;
Albeit I'm well aware we womenfolk
Are oft accounted irksome.   For with right   5
We all are branded chatterers; and in fact
'Tis said that neither in this present day
Nor any age has there been ever found
One woman who was dumb.   Yet there is this
I'd have you ponder, brother — I stand next
Of kin to you, as you to me; and hence   11
'Tis fitting I should counsel give to you,
And you in turn to me, on what we judge
Of mutual interest, nor hold it back
Or keep it silent through some sense of fear;   15
Nay, rather I should share my thoughts with
    you,
And you likewise with me.   And 'tis for this
I've brought you here apart, outside the house,
That I might here discuss with you somewhat
Of import to yourself.   20
    Meg.   Give me your hand,
O best of women!
    Eun.   Where, or who, I pray,
Is this your "best of women"?

    Meg.   'Tis yourself. 25
Eun. Oh, say you so?
    Meg.   Only your own denial
Will call forth mine.
    Eun.   But you should speak the truth.
No woman, brother, can be rated best: 30
'Tis only one is worse than other.
    Meg.   Aye,
Your thought is mine.   On that I am resolv'd
Ne'er to gainsay you, sister.
    Eun.   Lend, I pray, 35
Your ear.
    Meg. 'Tis yours; your servant I
At your command, if you have aught to crave.
    Eun. A matter that I deem of much import
And much to your advantage, this I come 40
To bring to your attention.
    Meg.   You but act,
Dear sister, in your usual way.
    Eun.   This lies
Close to my heart.   45
    Meg.   What is it, sister?
    Eun.   This!
May everlasting blessings be your lot:
To keep your line —
    Meg.   God grant it! 50
    Eun.   'Tis my wish
That you bring home a wife.
    Meg.   Oh, oh! I'm ruin'd!
    Eun. How so?
    Meg.   Alas! Your words, my sister, beat
My poor brains out.   You utter stones. 56
    Eun.   Well, well!
Do this one thing your sister bids.
    Meg.   So be
It suits my liking, 'twill be done. 60
    Eun.   'Twill be
For your best good.
    Meg.   To die before the day
I marry, yes.   If you would have me wed
On these conditions, then I'll take a wife: 65
Let her who comes tomorrow be carried out
Tomorrow's morrow.   On these terms who is it
You wish to give?   I yield.   Prepare the rites.
    Eun. I can provide you, brother, with a wife
Who'll bring an ample dower.   Her years
    perhaps 70
Are just a thought too many — in fact her age
Is quite distinctly "middle" for a woman.

If you'll but say the word I'll ask for her.

Meg. You don't object, of course, if I in turn
Ask you a question?   75

Eun.   Ask it, if you like.

Meg. Suppose a man well on in years should
    wed
A wife beyond her prime, and chance to breed
By her a child of his old age and hers;
Doubt you the name "Posthumus," all pre-
    par'd,   80
Is ready for such offspring? Nay, I'll spare
And ease this labor for you, sister. I,
By God's good grace, and my forefathers' too,
Have wealth enough; this high estate, this
    pride,
These lavish dowers, acclaim of servile crowds,
Imperious orders, ivory-spangl'd cars,   86
Rich mantles, purple garments, I confess
I have no jot of patience with — things all
That by their sheer extravagance bring men
To naught but wretched misery.   90

Eun. (pointedly).   Tell me, pray,
Who is the lady whom you'd like to take
For wife?

Meg.   I'll tell you. Know you Euclio,
Our poor and aged neighbor here?   95

Eun.   I know him,
And not a bad sort, neither, by my troth.

Meg. His maiden daughter's hand it is I
    wish
The promise of. — No words, my dear. I know
What you would say: she's poor. But being
    poor   100
She suits me.

Eun.   May the gods be kind.

Meg.   You speak
My wish as well.

Eun. What more? Wish you for aught?

Meg. Nay. Fare you well.   106

Eun.   And you, my brother.

Meg.   Now
I'll go meet Euclio if he's within.   109
But look, he hastens home, I know not whence.

SCENE 2

Enter EUCLIO

Euc. (to himself). I felt it in my bones 'twas
    all for naught

That I was going, before I left the house;
Hence I was loth to go. For not a man
Of all our wardsmen came, nor show'd his face
The master of the ward, whose duty 'twas   5
To portion out the dole. I make all haste
Therefore to be at home; for though I'm here,
My mind is there.

Meg.   The best of health to you,
And fortune also, Euclio.   10

Euc.   God's grace
To you too, Megadorus.

Meg.   And how fares
The world with you? You're well, I hope, and
    quite
As you might wish?   15

Euc. (aside). It's not for naught, forsooth,
A rich man speaks a poor so fair. Right now
This fellow knows that I've got gold — that's
    why
His greeting's courteous.

Meg.   You're well, you say? 20

Euc. Troth, not so well in fiscal matters —
    no.

Meg. I' faith, if you've a mind at peace,
    enough
Is yours to live a good life on.

Euc. (aside).   'Od's blood!   24
The hag's been hinting to him about the gold —
It's clear the murder's out. I'll lop her tongue
And dig her eyes out once I get myself
Inside the house!

Meg.   Why speak you to yourself?

Euc. I mourn my poverty. I have a daugh-
    ter   30
Of age for marriage, yet unblest with dower
And so unsought, nor can I find the means
To wed her.

Meg.   Hold your peace, be of good cheer,
Friend Euclio. She shall be wed; my aid   35
Shall serve you. If you've need of aught,
    speak out,
Command me, pray.

Euc. (aside).   His promise holds a threat:
He brings a stone in one hand, while he shows
The bread in t'other. I put no trust in him   40
Who, being rich, brims o'er with graciousness
To him who's poor; for when he lays his hand
Upon the poor man's back, he's loading him
With some new damage. Well I know, forsooth,

These leeches who when they have touch'd a
    thing   45
Will never let it go.
    Meg.   Lend me your ear
A moment, Euclio, an't be you may.
I'd lay before you a concern we share
In common.   50
    Euc. (*aside*). Ah! Woe's me! My gold
    indoors
Is filch'd. He wants, I'm sure of it, to come
To compromise with me. I'll go within
And track it.   (*Starts toward his house.*
    Meg.   Whither go you?   55
    Euc.   I'll return
Upon the instant. There's somewhat inside
I must attend to.   (*He goes in.*
    Meg.   Faith, 'tis my belief
That when I front him with his daughter's name
And my desire to wed her, he'll suppose   61
He's being mock'd at. Surely there is none
In all the world more penny wise than he
For all his poverty.
    Euc. (*coming out of his house*). The gods are
    with me.   65
But what a scare was mine! Before I stepp'd
Indoors, I well-nigh died of fright. (*Aloud*)
    I'm now
Return'd, and at your service, Megadorus.
    Meg. Accept my thanks. I pray you that
    on what
I shall inquire of you anon you speak   70
Without reluctance.
    Euc.   So it be a matter
Whereon I choose to speak.
    Meg.   Pray, tell me then,
What think you of the stock from which I'm
    sprung?   75
    Euc. Good.
    Meg.   What of my own standing?
    Euc.   Excellent.
    Meg. And conduct?
    Euc.   Neither bad nor censurable.   80
    Meg. Know you the number of my years?
    Euc.   I know
That they are goodly, like your wealth.
    Meg.   I' faith,
At any rate I've always counted you,   85
As I do now, a citizen unsway'd
By guile or evil thought.

    Euc. (*aside*).   He smells the gold.
(*Aloud*) What would you of me now?
    Meg.   Since you know me   90
And I know you, what manner of man you
    are,
'Tis this — and may it blessing bring to me,
To you and to your daughter — I now ask
Your daughter as my wife. Give me your word
That it shall be so.   95
    Euc.   Hoity toity, sir!
This deed of yours suits not your usual acts;
You laugh at me, a poor man, innocent
Of guile toward you and yours. For ne'er in
    act
Nor yet in word have I deserv'd of you   100
Such things as now you do.
    Meg.   Upon my word
I neither come to laugh at you, nor deem
That you have earn'd it.
    Euc.   Why then do you ask 105
My daughter's hand?
    Meg.   That through me you may find
A happier lot, as I through you and yours.
    Euc. This, Megadorus, is my thought, that
    you
Are rich, a man of rank, while I am poor, 110
Yes, poorest of the poor. Now should I give
My daughter's hand to you, I'd think of you
As ox, myself as ass: when I was yok'd
With you, and fail'd to bear the load with you
In equal portion, I, the ass, would lie   115
Prone in the mud, while you, the ox, would
    look
On me with no whit more of deference
Than had I ne'er been born. So should I find
You less than just, and my own kind dispos'd
To laugh at me, nor should I find, wher.
    once   120
We had been parted, stabling sure with either:
The asses' teeth would tear me, and the oxen
Would gore me with their horns. — Great risk
    it is
To pass from ass to ox-kind.
    Meg.   But the best 125
Is to unite yourself as close as may be
With those who are best. Do you accept this
    match —
Listen to me — and promise her to me.
    Euc. But there is naught to give as dower.

Meg.   Forego it.   130
So be she comes whole-soul'd, she's dower'd
    enough.
   Euc. I say this lest you might suppose I've
    found —
Well, treasures, let us say.
   Meg.   I know — no need
Of explanation. Promise her.   135
   Euc.   So be it.
       (*Starts suddenly, and looks around.*
So help me Jove! Can I be ruin'd already?
   Meg. What ails you, pray?
   Euc. What was that noise? — like iron —?
   Meg. (*laughing*). I've order'd men to spade
    my garden there.   140
        (*Euclio runs off into his house.*
But where's the fellow? He's run off and left
No word behind. 'Twould seem he's irk'd with
   me
Because he sees I crave his friendship. — Well,
He's of a piece with other men — the rich
Goes forth to seek the favor of the poor,   145
The poor man fears to face him, and the thing
Is bungl'd through embarrassment. But when,
Too late, the chance is lost, he wishes for 't.
   Euc. (*coming out of the house, addressing*
    STAPHYLA, *who is inside*).
By heaven, if I don't give you up and have
Your tongue torn out by the roots, I order you
With my full warranty to turn me o'er   151
To any wayside butcher to be gelded!
   Meg. I' faith, I see you deem me, Euclio,
Fit man to sport with in my hoary age,
A view I scarce deserve.   155
   Euc.   No, by my troth,
It's not that, Megadorus, I am not
A sporting man — I've not the means.
   Meg.   How now?
Do you then promise me your daughter's
   hand?   160
   Euc. I do so promise.
   Meg.   May the gods bestow
Their blessing on 't.
   Euc.   Aye, may the gods so do.
But look you well that you remember this: 165
That we've agreed my daughter has no dower!
   Meg. I've that in mind.
   Euc.   But I'm aware how men
Of your sort oft confuse the issue: what   169

Was bargain'd is no bargain, while no bargain
Becomes a bargain, according to your pleasure.
   Meg. You'll find no cause for quarrel in my
   dealing.
But is there aught of reason why the rites
Shall not be held this day?
   Euc.   Nay, best of reasons   175
Therefor.
   Meg. I'll go then, and prepare. Need you
My further service here?
   Euc.   Only for this:
Go with good luck.   180
   Meg.   Ho, Strobilus, make haste
To follow me to market. — Speed your pace!
               (*Exit.*
   Euc. He's off. Immortal gods, I conjure
   you!
How gold buys grace! I cannot but believe
He's got some wind of this my treasure
   here   185
Within my house. 'Tis that he's thirsting for;
'Tis that has made him set upon this match.

SCENE 3

EUCLIO *alone. Going to the door of the house,*
   he opens it, and calls to STAPHYLA *within*

   Euc. Now where are you, who've blabb'd it
   out to all
The neighbors round that I will give
A dower to my daughter? — Staphyla, ho!
I'm calling you! D'ye hear? Make haste in
   there
And wash the pots and pans — clean, too!
   I've pledg'd   5
To wed my daughter. On this very day
She's to be giv'n to Megadorus here.

Enter STAPHYLA *from the house*

   Sta. Heaven prosper it. But, good Lord!
   it can't be done —
It's all too sudden!
   Euc.   Hold your tongue, and go!   10
Be sure all's ready when I come from town.
And shut the house up — I'll be back anon.
               (*Exit.*
   Sta. What now am I to do? There's ruin
   close

At hand for us — myself and master's daugh-
ter.
For both her shame and her confinement stand
Upon the very point of currency.   16
All that till now had been conceal'd and hid
Can be no more. — I'll go within, that there
My master's orders may be fully done
When he returns.   Alas! I fear 'tis mine   20
To drink a bitter potion for my wine.
                              (*She goes inside.*

ACT III

Scene i

STROBILUS, ANTHRAX, *and* CONGRIO *enter from
the market-place, with Flute-Girls and
a number of Tradesmen carrying provisions*

Stro. My master, when he'd done his mar-
keting
And hired these cooks and flute-girls at the
stalls,
Bade me divide the viands half by half
In equal shares.
Anth.   By God, I'll tell you straight 5
You'll not split *me!* But if you'd have me go
To any place whole as I am, I'm ready.
Con. A pretty punk, and modest, by my
troth!
Time was when you'd not balk at being split.
Stro. Nay, Anthrax, you mistake my sense;
'twas quite   10
In other wise I spoke. This is the day
My master's to be married.
Anth.   And to whom?
Whose daughter?
Stro.   Euclio's — his neighbor here.   15
That's why he order'd half this food I've got
Given to him — one cook, one flute-girl like-
wise.
Anth. You mean you take one half to him,
and half
Goes home with you?
Stro.   Exactly.   20
Anth.   How is that?
The old man could not even stand the expense
Of his own daughter's wedding?
Stro.   Pish!

Anth.   What's wrong? 25
Stro. What's wrong, you ask? A pumice
stone will prove
Less dry than that old skinflint.
Anth.   Say you so?
Stro. Be your own judge.   Why, he's forever
crying
For aid from gods and men, and wailing all 30
Is lost, himself in ruin, whene'er perchance
The smoke escapes between the rafters. —
Why,
He never sleeps until he first has tied
A bag beneath his gullet.
Anth.   Why, pray tell?   35
Stro. That he may lose no breath in sleeping.
Anth.   Ha!
And I suppose he stops up t'other end
As well, lest he lose wind in sleeping.
Stro.   There 40
'Tis just as fair I credit you as you
Should credit me.
Anth.   So be. I'll take your word for 't.
Stro. And know you furthermore how 'tis
with him?
I swear it hurts him ever to throw away   45
The water when he washes.
Anth.   But, I pray,
Think you 'tis possible that we might beg
Or borrow from this hoary-head a talent
To buy our freedom with?   50
Stro.   Nay, by my troth,
He'd never even give you loan of hunger
Were you to ask it. Why, a few days since
The barber cut his nails, and what did he 54
But gather up the parings and take 'em home.
Anth. In sooth, a three-skinn'd skinflint, by
your tell.
Stro. Oh, so you think he's grasping, and
his life
Is niggardly? Attend to this. A kite
A few days since snatch'd up some trifling bit
Of food or other. Behold him posting off 60
A-blubbering to the praetor.[1] There with tears
And loud lamentings he put in a plea

---

[1] A Roman magistrate, a part of whose duty it was to
administer justice. It is to be noted that here and in
other parts of the play Plautus refers to Roman officials,
even though the scene, as in the original Greek play, is
laid at Athens.

To have the kite on bail. — Oh, there are
    scores
Of other things that I could tell you of,
Had I but time enow. — But which of you 65
Is cleverer? Tell me.
    Con.   I — far better I.
    Stro. A cook I'm after, not a thief.
    Con.   Save you,
'Tis as a cook I mean.   70
    Stro. (*to* ANTHRAX). And what say you?
    Anth. I'm as you see me.
    Con.   He's a weekly cook:
One day a week he cooks — he's regular!
    Anth. What? You three-letter'd knave,[1]
    you thief — you dare   75
To throw abuse at me?
    Con.   I do indeed,
You triple spawn of thieves!
    Stro.   Now hold your tongue,
And which is fatter of the lambs take in 80
To our house here.
    Con.   So be.
    Stro.   Nay, Congrio,
Your lamb is this one. (*Pointing to* EUCLIO's
    house) Take it indoors there.
(*To Flute-Girls and certain of the Tradesmen*)
And do you follow him. The rest of you 85
Come this way to our house.
    Con.   But, by my troth,
You've not divided fair. The lamb they've got
Is much the fattest.
    Stro.   Well then, you'll be giv'n 90
The fattest flute-girl. You there, Phrygia, go
With him. And you, Eleusium, just step
Indoors at our house here.
    Con.   What, Strobilus, 94
You crafty knave, have you maroon'd me here
With this old pinch-fist, where if I should ask
For aught, I'll ask myself to hoarseness ere
One thing is furnish'd me?
    Stro.   'Tis folly, yea,
And thanklessness as well, to do a service 100
Where service comes to naught.
    Con.   How say you so?
    Stro. You ask? First, then, in yonder house
There's no confusion. If you've need of aught

---

[1] Notorious thieves were often branded with the letters FUR, the Latin word for "Thief."

Bring it with you from home, nor lose your
    pains   105
By asking for 't. But here in our house all
Is in a turmoil — numerous retinue,
Fine gear, gold, garments, costly silver ware.
If aught's lost here — (I know, of course, *your*
    hands
Would ne'er touch aught — that's kept away
    from them!)   110
It may be said: "The cooks have filch'd it;
    ho!
Seize, bind and beat them! Clap them in the
    hold!"
But you'll have none of that, since there'll be
    naught
For you to pilfer. — Follow me this way.
    Con. I follow.   115
    Stro. (*knocking at the door of* EUCLIO's *house*).
          Ho there, Staphyla, come out.
Undo the door.
    Sta. (*from within*). Who calls there?
    Stro.   Strobilus.

SCENE 2

Enter STAPHYLA

    Sta. What would you?
    Stro.   That you take these cooks inside,
This flute-girl too. 'Tis Megadorus bade
Me take these things to Euclio.
    Sta.   Hm! Ceres is it 5
Your honoring with this wedding, Strobilus?
    Stro. Why so?
    Sta.   Because I see no wine brought in.
    Stro. 'Twill be here soon, when he gets back
    from town.
    Sta. There's no wood in the place.   10
    Con.   You've rafters, eh?
    Sta. Of course.
    Con.   You've wood then. Spare
    yourself the pains
Of seeking it outside.
    Sta.   What would you, scum? 15
Though fire's your trade, would you be asking
    us
To burn our house down for a dinner's sake,
Or for your paltry hire?
    Con.   I don't ask that,
Of course.

Stro.   Take them inside.
Sta.   Here, follow me.
> (*They follow her inside, and* STROBILUS
> *goes with the others into the house of*
> MEGADORUS.)

SCENE 3

Enter PYTHODICUS, *from the house of*
MEGADORUS

Pyth. Be at your tasks there.   I'll step in
     and see
What's toward with the cooks; for keeping
     watch
On them this day 's in truth a proper task.
Unless I'd have them ply their trade below
Down in the hold, and thence, when all is
     done,   5
Draw up the food in baskets.   But e'en so,
Should they be minded to devour the food
They'd cook'd below, the high would go unfed,
The low be feasted.   But I'm wasting words
As I had naught to do, when such a pack   10
Of thieves is in the house.   I'll hie me back.
> (*He goes back into the house.*)

SCENE 4

Enter EUCLIO, *with a few straggling garlands
in his hand*

Euc. At length I got to screw my courage up
To spread myself at this my daughter's wed-
     ding.
I make the rounds of markets, ask the
     price
Of fish.   They tell me it is dear; lamb too
Is dear, and beef, veal, cod and pork —   5
All dear.   And what has made them still more
     dear,
I've not a copper.   So I came away
A-boil because I'd naught wherewith to
     buy.
Thus did I baulk those filthy knaves.   And
     then
On my way back I fell to thinking: "Now   10
If on a feastday you will squander aught,
You'll want on work-days, so you be not
     saving."

And when I'd brought this excellent reasoning
     home
To heart and belly, so my mind as well
Came round to my opinion, that 'twas meet   15
I make my daughter's marriage with the least
I might expend.   Now I have bought this bit
Of frankincense, these chaplets too withal,
To set upon the hearth as offering
Unto our Lar, that he be pleas'd to grant   20
A happy marriage to my daughter. — Ha!
Why do I see our house wide open? — Hark!
There's noise within!   Can I be robb'd?
     Woe's me!
Con. (*speaking from within*).   Go ask the
     neighbors for a bigger pot
If you can find one.   This one is too small;   25
It cannot hold it.
Euc.   Woe! I'm ruin'd quite!
The gold's being carried off; my pot it is
They've got their hands on!   All is up with me
Unless I haste to run at topmost speed   30
Within the house here.   (*Stopping, and ex-
     tending his hands in an attitude of sup-
     plication*)   Help and save, I pray,
Apollo, one whom thou hast help'd before
In time of need.   Pierce with thy vengeful
     shafts
The plunderers of my treasure. — But why
     hold
My running, lest I perish on the instant?   35
> (*He runs into the house.*)

SCENE 5

Enter ANTHRAX, *from the house of*
MEGADORUS

Anth. (*speaking to slaves within*).
You, Dromio, scale the fish.   Machaerio,
Do you bone well the lamprey and the conger.
I'll ask the loan from neighbor Congrio here
Of a baking-pan.   You there, if you've got
     sense,
Will pluck that capon for me twice as clean   5
As any tweezer'd dancer. — But what's to-
     ward?
What bedlam's this I hear next door?   I' faith,
The cooks, I ween, are at their usual tricks.
I'll run indoors before the row spreads further.
> (*He goes into the house.*)

SCENE 6

CONGRIO *runs hastily from* EUCLIO'S
house

Con. Ho! friends and countrymen, towns-
men and neighbors,
All strangers too, make way, that I may flee!
Clear all the streets! Never until today
Have I gone out to cook in such a den
Of Bacchants [1] at their revels. What a rain 5
Of sticks they shower'd upon my wretched
back,
And on my kitchen-boys! I'm one big ache,
And well-nigh dead to boot, so thoroughly
This ancient made a proving-ground of me,
And in such wise has driv'n us all outside, 10
Myself and them, with sticks upon our backs
For burden. Nowhere have I seen, forsooth,
In all the world more lavish dole of wood.

    (*Sees* EUCLIO *about to come out of his
house.*

Alack! here's sorry ruin for me. The den
Of Bacchants opes. The devil himself comes
forth; 15
He follows us. — I know what I must do —
My master taught me a good trick or two.

SCENE 7

EUCLIO *rushes out of his house, driving before
him the Cooks and the Flute-Girl*

Euc. (*to* CONGRIO *and the others, who are
running off*). Come back! Where run
you now? Hold there, I say!
Con. Why shout you thus, you dolt?
Euc.   Because I'll give
Your names this instant to the triumvirs. [2]
Con. Why, pray? 5
Euc.   You've got a knife.
Con.   As well befits
A cook.
Euc. Why did you threaten me?

---

[1] Female worshipers of Bacchus, whose rites were
characterized by unrestrained emotional expression as
they reveled over the mountains in wild dances.

[2] The *Triumviri Capitales*, Roman magistrates whose
duty it was to track criminals, examine prisoners under
authorization of the higher magistrates, inspect prisons,
and superintend the carrying out of capital sentences
and corporal punishment.

Con.   And now   Egad, 10
'Twas badly done, I think, it was not thrust
Between your ribs.
Euc.   There's not a man alive
A bigger knave than you, nor one whose head
I'd bring down mischief on with greater pleas-
ure. 15
Con. 'Faith, though you hold your tongue,
that's clear as day:
The thing's its own attest: I'm softer now
From all your basting than a catamite. [1]
But by what right do you lay hands on me,
You beggar's spawn? 20
Euc. What right? You ask? Good sooth,
Just let me ——   (*Starts to strike* CONGRIO.
Con.   By my faith, 'tis at your peril
An this head should feel aught.
Euc.   Troth, I know not 25
What may be afterward; just now your head
Feels somewhat! But what business, pray,
had you
In my house, in my absence, without orders?
Answer me that.
Con.   Hold your tongue, then. Know 30
We came to cook for the wedding.
Euc.   What the plague
Is it to you whether I eat my meat
Plain raw or cook'd, unless you chance to be
My guardian? 35
Con. This I want to know. Will you,
Or will you not permit us to prepare
The dinner here?
Euc.   'Tis my wish, too, to know
If what is mine at home will be unharm'd. 40
Con. If only I get off with what is mine
That I brought here, I'll have me no regrets
At quitting yours.
Euc.   I know — no need to preach;
I know your ways. 45
Con.   Why is it that you bar
Our cooking dinner here? What have we done?
What said that has displeas'd you?
Euc.   Ask you that,
You scurvy villain, who've been making free 50
With every corner of my house, and nos'd
In every cupboard? If you'd kept your place
Beside the hearth where 'twas your business to,
You'd want a broken head. What you have got

---

[1] A male prostitute; here, a symbol of effeminacy.

You've earn'd.   And now, that you may know
   my will,   55
If you move one step nearer to that door
Unless I say the word, I'll make of you
A sorry wretch indeed. — You know my mind.
                (*He goes inside.*
   Con. Where go you?   Here!   Come back!
     So love me well
Laverna,[1] an you order not my pots   60
Return'd to me at once, I'll cry you down
To all and sundry, here before the house.
What now?   I' faith, 'twas on no lucky day
I travell'd here. — A groat was promis'd me;
I've more need now of physick than of fee. 65

SCENE 8

Enter EUCLIO, *from his house, with the pot
of money hidden under his cloak*

   Euc. (*to himself*). This, by my faith, wher-
    ever I may go,
Shall go with me — I'll carry it myself,
Nor ever trust it to that place again
To run such risk of forfeit.   4
(*To* CONGRIO *and his assistants*) Now then, go
Inside, all of you, cooks and flute-girl. — Aye,
Take, an it please, a pack of menials;
Cook, ply your office, bustle all you will.
   Con. In good time 'tis, forsooth, when you
    have fill'd
Their heads with cudgel-cracks.   10
   Euc.   Be off.   Your hands
Were hired here, not your mouth.
   Con.   Look you, old man,
I'll seek accounting, mark me, for those
   blows!
I let myself for cooking, not for basting.   15
   Euc. Aye, have the law on me! — Irk me no
    more.
Go cook the dinner, or begone forthwith
To black perdition!
   Con.   Just my wish for you!
     (*He goes into the house, taking the cooks
     and the Flute-Girl.*

[1] The Roman patroness of thieves.

SCENE 9

EUCLIO, *alone*

   Euc. He's off.   Immortal gods, a man
    who's poor
Is rash indeed when he would undertake
To deal with men of wealth.   As even now
This Megadorus here has plagu'd me sore
In feigning 'twas in deference to me   5
He sent these cooks here, with a plain intent
That they might purloin this (*hugging the pot*),
   a poor man's all.
And quite in keeping, too, my dunghill-cock
Within the house (the old hag's pet it was)
Had well-nigh been my ruin; for all around   10
The spot where this was buried he made forth
To scratch wi' his claws.   What need of words?
   My gorge
Rose up.   I seiz'd a stick, and knock'd the
   head
Clean off the cock, a thief caught in the act.
I' faith, 'tis my belief the cooks had pledg'd   15
Reward to him should he uncover it.   Ha!
I stole a march on them.   What need of words?
A pretty cock-fight that, in sooth.   But
   see,
Here comes my neighbor Megadorus home   19
From the market-place.   I dare not pass him by
Without accosting him — I'll wait him here.
     (*He retires toward the end of the stage,
     close to his door.*

SCENE 10

Enter MEGADORUS *at a distance*

   Meg. I've shar'd with many friends this
    plan of mine
Anent this match, and they have naught but
   praise
For Euclio's daughter, saying 'twas sagely done
And with good sense.   'Tis my opinion too
That if all other men of means might hold   5
The selfsame course, and take unto themselves
As wives the undower'd daughters of the poor,
So would our state find greater harmony,
And less of envy be our lot than now.
For wives would stand in fear of discipline   10
Far more than now, and we their husbands live
At less expense.   For the majority

Of folk this rule is sound, but some there be,
A lesser part, who would rebel — those kings
Of avarice whose grasping minds and souls
No law or praetor could set curb upon.   16
"But," one will say, "how will those haughty
    dames
Both rich and dower'd be wed, if such a law
Be laid down for the poor ones?" — Let them
    wed
Whome'er they please, so there be naught of
    dower   20
To bear them company. If this were done,
They'd win them better manners to be-
    stow
In lieu of dower than now they bring. In
    sooth,
I'll warrant mules, whose price today o'ertops
The cost of horses, would be cheaper far   25
Than Gallic geldings.
    Euc. (*aside*).   Aye, so love me Jove,
As I lend willing ear to this discourse.
Right handsomely he pleads the cause of thrift.
    Meg. (*to himself*). No wife would then be
        saying: "I'd have you know   30
I brought a dower far greater than your wealth;
'Tis only fair, forsooth, I should be giv'n
Purple and gold, maid-servants, carriage-
    mules,
Mule-drivers, lackeys, page-boys, carriages
To ride in."   35
    Euc. (*aside*). What a keen and practis'd eye
He has for ways of wives! I'd have him made
Prefect of women's manners.
    Meg. (*to himself*).   Nay, what's more,   39
Go where you will, you'll find more rigs in town
Than wagons in the country. But e'en this
Is sheer felicity beside the day
When creditors ask for payment. At your
    door
There stands the cleaner, sempstress, jeweller,
The woolen-draper, flouncer, tunic-maker,   45
Dyers in red and violet and flesh,
Sleeve-fitters, perfumers and linen-drapers,
Shoemakers, squatting cobblers, slipper-mak-
    ers;
The sandal-stitchers stand there, mallow-
    dyers,
Hairdressers push their claims, and menders
    theirs.   50

Then come the bodice-fitters, kirtle-makers.
You think them all paid off; they yield their
    place,
And lo, three hundred others hound you,
    pack'd
Within your hall — purse-makers, weavers,
    lace   54
And casket-makers. They're let in and paid.
No sooner rid of them, than saffron-dyers
Come stalking in, or there's some wretched
    pest
That's always seeking somewhat.
    Euc. (*aside*).   I'd accost him
Did I not fear he'd stop his discourse short   60
Upon the ways of women. For the nonce
I'll let it be.
    Meg. (*to himself*). When all this money's
        paid
These gewgaw-mongers, then at last there
    comes
The tax-collector, and presents his claim   65
For payment. Off you go in haste to make
Appointment with your banker, while at
    home
The agent waits, half starv'd, but hopeful still
His money will be paid. But when at last
The banker's made his reckoning, 'tis found   70
You're overdrawn already, and the hopes
The agent held must be again put off
To another day. These, then, and more be-
    sides
Of irksome ills and outlays beyond bearing   74
Attend on goodly dowers. So she who comes
Undower'd is in her husband's power; the
    dower'd
Condemn their husbands to sheer loss and ruin.
But see, my marriage-kinsman's standing here
Before the house. — How do you, Euclio?
    Euc. Right gladly I've devour'd each single
        word   80
Of your discourse.
    Meg.   You heard me?
    Euc.   Everything,
From the beginning.
    Meg. (*looking him up and down*). Still, in
        my opinion,   85
'Twere more becoming should you show your-
    self
More tidy for your daughter's wedding.

Euc.   Those
Who match their luster to their circumstance,
Their splendor to their means, will ne'er forget
Whence they are sprung. So neither by myself
Nor any poor man else is aught set out   92
At home beyond what's evident to all.
    Meg. Nay, surely there's enough. And may
        God's grace
Still have it so, and prosper more and more
That which you now possess.   96
    Euc. (*aside*).   I like me not
That word "That which you now possess."
He knows I've got this just as well as I;
The old hag'd let it out.   100
    Meg.   But why retire
Alone and leave our council thus?
    Euc.   I' faith,
I had in mind to bring a well-earn'd charge
Against you.   105
    Meg.   What is toward?
    Euc.   You ask what's toward?
You, who have fill'd, to my bedevilment,
Each several corner of my house with thieves?
You, who have brought inside my walls a pack
Of half a thousand cooks, with six hands each,
Vile spawn of Geryon,[1] whom Argus'[2] self,   112
That all-ey'd monster once by Juno set
To spy on Jupiter, were he to watch,
Could ne'er keep eyes on? And a flute-girl,
        too,   115
Who all alone could drink clean dry for me
The fountain of Pirene,[3] were 't to flow
With wine. Then those provisions —
    Meg.   By my troth,
There's plenty for a legion. Why, I sent   120
A whole lamb even.
    Euc.   Than which lamb I vow
There's not in all the world a beast more
        quaint.
    Meg. How say you "quaint"?
    Euc.   Why, it's acquaint with grief;
That's why it's lean — it's naught but skin and
        bone.   126

E'en though it's still alive you can inspect
Its entrails when the sun shines through. It's
        clear
As any Punic lanthorn.[1]
    Meg.   But 'twas fit   130
For killing when I bought it.
    Euc.   Then you'd best
Take steps to have it carried off for burying.
It's dead by now, I doubt not.
    Meg.   Euclio,   135
I wish this day to have a drinking bout
With you.
    Euc. Nay, by my troth, I must not drink.
    Meg. But I'll have brought one cask of ripe
        old wine
From my house.   140
    Euc.   'Faith, I'll none of it. I'm set
On drinking naught but water.
    Meg. (*jocosely*).   As I live
I'll have you well bedrench'd this day who're
        bent
On drinking water.   145
    Euc. (*aside*).   Well I know his scheme:
He aims to muddle me with wine, and then
To shift the place of this I carry here.
I'll look to that. I'll hide it in some spot
Without. I'll make him lose both wine and
        pains.   150
    Meg. Unless you need me further, I'll go
        bathe,
That I may sacrifice. (*He goes into the house.*
    Euc. (*taking the pot from under his cloak, and
        caressing it*). I' faith, you pot,
You've many enemies, you and the gold
That's in your keeping! Now it suits me
        best   155
To take you, precious pot, to Faith's own shrine
And hide you there with care. Faith, I am
        known
To thee and thou to me. Change not thy
        name, I pray,
If I trust this unto thy care. — I come to thee,
Sweet Faith, secure in thy fidelity.   160
        (*He goes into the Temple of Faith.*

---

[1] A giant, slain by Hercules. He was reputed to have
three heads and a triple body, hence six hands.
[2] A fabled giant with a hundred eyes, set by Juno to
watch Io, beloved of Jupiter, after Io, at Juno's instance, had been transformed into a white heifer.
[3] A spring of Corinth in southern Greece.

[1] The flame-guard of Roman lanterns was made of
horn, scraped thin, and bent to form a cylinder. The
Punic or Carthaginian horn imported from northern
Africa was more transparent than any other, hence
much in demand.

ACT IV

SCENE 1

Enter STROBILUS

Stro. A faithful servant's duty 'tis to do
As I do now, nor hold his master's word
A plague or trouble to him. For in truth
That servant who's resolv'd with right good will
To serve his master it behooves to act   5
Betimes for him, but tardily for self.
E'en sleeping, let him sleep in consciousness
That he is servant. But who serves, as I,
A man in love, and sees his master yield
To love's obsession, this, methinks, must be   10
His task, for safety's sake to hold him back,
Nor urge him on whither his bent would lead.
As boys who'd learn to swim make shift to lie
Upon a float of bulrushes, that so,
Their labor lessen'd, they may move their hands   15
And swim with greater ease, so do I think
A servant well may make himself a buoy
Unto his lovelorn master, that his aid
May bear him up, lest like a sounding-lead
He sink straight to the bottom. Let him learn   20
His master's will, that eyes be quick to read
What brow would fain declare. Whate'er he bids,
That let him haste to do with greater speed
Than swiftest racing-horses. He who keeps
An eye to this will shun for his own back   25
The sentence of the ox-hide, nor by dint
Of private toil will bring to chains
A lustrous polish. Now my master loves
The daughter of this Euclio, a man
Of slender means. Just now word has been brought   30
That she's been giv'n to Megadorus here.
He's sent me here to spy, that what may hap
He may be privy to. Now I'll sit here,
Without distrust, beside the sacred altar,
And from this vantage point I'll cast an eye   35
Both here and there, and judge what they're about.

(*He sits down by the altar, and on seeing* EUCLIO *hides behind it.*)

SCENE 2

Enter EUCLIO, *from the Temple*

Euc. Sweet Faith, be it thy care ne'er to discover
To any mortal that my gold is there.
No fear have I that 'twill be found, so well
Is it conceal'd within its hiding-place.   40
In sooth he'll have a pretty booty there,
Should any man lay hands upon my pot
Weigh'd down with gold. But I entreat thee, Faith,
Forbid thou that. Now I'll go wash myself
That I may make a proper sacrifice,   45
Nor bring delay to my new kinsman here;
But when he sends to fetch her he may take
My daughter home forthwith. Now once again,
And yet once more, O Faith, do thou take care
That I may have again my pretty pot   50
In safety from thy temple. To thy faith
Have I consign'd my gold. Here in thy grove
And in thy holy temple is it laid.

(*He goes into the house.*)

Stro. (*coming out from behind the altar*). Immortal gods, what deed is this I hear
This fellow tell of, how he's hidden here   55
Within this very shrine of Faith a pot
Brimful of gold? Prithee, beware you, Faith,
How you show more fidelity to him
Than me! And he, as I may well surmise,
Is father of the girl my master loves.   60
I'll get me in. I'll search the temple through
And see if anywhere I come upon
The gold, while he's engag'd. And if I find it —
O Goddess Faith, I'll surely offer thee
A gallon jug of honey'd wine, i' faith I will —
And drink it up myself when I have done.   66

(*He goes back behind the altar.*)

SCENE 3

Enter EUCLIO, *from his house*

Euc. (*to himself*). 'Twas not for naught, forsooth, that raven croak'd
Just now upon the left. He scratch'd the ground
And caw'd withal. At once my heart began

To play the jester, and to leap about
Within my breast. But why do I delay   5
To run? (*He discovers* STROBILUS, *and drags
him from behind the altar.*
    Come out, you muckworm! You
    who've crept
Just now from out the earth; a moment since
You're nowhere to be found, and now you're
    seen
You'll die for 't. By my faith, you juggling
    knave,   10
I'll give you welcome in no gentle fashion!
    (*He begins to beat him.*
    Stro. Hold! What the cursed plague is
    ailing you?
What would you with me, dotard? Why lay on
And maul me thus? Why plaster me with
    blows?
    Euc. You whipping-post, you dare to ask?
    No thief,   15
But thrice-dy'd thief!
    Stro.   What have I thiev'd from you?
    Euc. Just give it back, I say.
    Stro.   What would you, pray,
I give you back?   20
    Euc.   You ask?
    Stro.   I've taken naught
That's yours.
    Euc. Then give me back what you have
    filch'd
That's yours. You'll not?   25
    Stro.   Not what?
    Euc.   Don't ever think
You'll run away with it!
    Stro.   What is't you want?
    Euc. Come, lay it down.   30
    Stro.   'Tis you, methinks, old man,
Who would "lay down."
    Euc.   Nay, drop it, and have done
With quibbling. I'm not trifling now.
    Stro.   What, pray,   35
Should I be dropping? Why not call its name,
Whatever 'tis? I' faith, I've neither stol'n
Nor touch'd a thing.
    Euc. Show me your hands.
    Stro.   Why there!   40
See, here they are.
    Euc.   I see them. Come now, show
The third hand too.

    Stro. (*aside*).   Sprites, frenzy, madness, all
Have seiz'd this greybeard! (*Aloud*) Do you
    wrong to me?   45
    Euc. Aye, and a great one, I confess, for that
I hang you not. But that too shall be done
Upon the instant if you'll not confess.
    Stro. But what shall I confess?
    Euc.   What 'twas you took   50
Away from here.
    Stro.   But damn me if I've taken
Aught that is yours — (*aside*) and if I don't
    wish now
I'd taken it!   54
    Euc.   Come now, shake out your cloak.
    Stro. Glad to oblige. (*He shakes his cloak.*
    Euc.   You haven't got it there
Under your tunic?
    Stro.   Search me where you will.
    Euc. (*aside*). Aha! how civilly the rascal
    speaks   60
To throw me off the track. (*Aloud*) I know
    your tricks!
Show me again your right hand.
    Stro.   There you are!
    Euc. And now the left.
    Stro.   I'll show you both at once.   65
    (*He does so.*
    Euc. Enough, I'll leave off searching. Give
    it me.
    Stro. Give what?
    Euc. You're talking nonsense. There's no
    doubt
You've got it there.
    Stro.   *I've* got it? Pray, got what?   70
    Euc. Nay, I'll not say. You want to hear.
    Give back
Whate'er you have that's mine.
    Stro.   I' faith, you're mad.
You've search'd me at your pleasure, yet
    you've found
Nothing of yours about me.   75
    Euc. (*starting*).   Stop! Who's that?
Who was that other with you there inside?
Troth, I am ruin'd. He's rummaging within;
If I let this one go, he'll off at once.
I've search'd him through and through — He's
    not a thing.   80
Be off, then, where you will. May Jupiter
And all the gods confound you!

Stro. (*aside*).   He bespeaks
A proper gratitude!
   Euc.   I'll in here now   85
And get my hands this instant on the throat
Of that ally of yours. — What, not yet gone?
Off with you there!
   Stro.   I'm off.
   Euc.   And look you well   90
You never come into my sight again.
             (*He goes into the Temple.*

SCENE 4

STROBILUS, *alone*

   Stro. Would I were rather dead outright, by
     death
Most miserable, that fail to set this day
An ambush for this greybeard. Well I know
He'll never dare to hide the gold here now!   4
He'll take it with him otherwhere, and change
Its hiding-place. But hark! there's noise
     within.
The doors are opening. See, he's coming forth
And bringing out the gold. I'll step aside
Meanwhile, and hide me here beside the
     door.
             (*He conceals himself near the door.*

SCENE 5

Enter EUCLIO, *from the Temple, carrying the pot*

   Euc. 'Twas my belief the faith I had repos'd
In Faith was safety's self; she well-nigh made
A pretty fool of me. Had I not had
The raven's aid I had been ruin'd quite.
I wish with all my heart he'd come again,   5
This bird who warn'd me, that I might bestow
A few kind words upon him. (I'd as lief
Give him somewhat to eat — as lose 't out-
     right.)
I'm thinking now of some secluded spot
Where I might hide this. — There's a lonely
     grove,   10
Haunt of Sylvanus,[1] just outside the walls,
Set thick with willows. There I'll find a spot.
I'll trust Sylvanus where I trust not Faith.
             (*He goes out.*

[1] An old Italic deity of woods and groves.

   Stro. (*reappearing from his hiding-place*).
Good! Excellent! The gods are my salva-
     tion!
I'll run there first and climb some tree, and
     thence   15
I'll spy just where the old fool hides his gold.
Although my master bade me to remain,
I'll rather risk a flogging, if with gain.
             (*He hurries out.*

SCENE 6

Enter LYCONIDES *and* EUNOMIA, *from the house of* MEGADORUS

   Lyc. You have the story, mother; well as I
You know the case of Euclio's daughter. Now
I beg you, mother, o'er and o'er again,
As I have begg'd ere now, that you inform
My uncle of my deed.   5
   Eun.   You know yourself
That your desire is mine, and I have hope
That I'll persuade my brother of it. The
     case
Is good, if what you say is true — that you
Have wrong'd the damsel in a drunken fit.   10
   Lyc. But, mother, could I lie, before your
     face?
        (PHAEDRIA, *in the pangs of labor, cries
         out, in* EUCLIO'S *house.*
   Ph. I die, my nurse! My pains are coming
     on!
   Lyc. Ah, mother, there's a surer proof for
     you.
She cries aloud — she's in the pangs of labor.
   Eun. Come in with me, my son, to meet my
     brother   15
And win from him that which you beg of
     me.
   Lyc. Go, and I follow on the instant.
            (EUNOMIA *goes into the house.*
Strange, what's become of Strobilus, my slave.
I bade him wait me here. I'm of the mind
That if he's aiding me, 'tis scarcely just   20
I should be angry with him. I'll go in
Where council's held upon my very life.
            (*He goes into the house.*

ACT V

SCENE 1

Enter STROBILUS, with the pot of money

Stro. I, by myself, o'ertop in wealth this day
The Griffins, dwellers in the Hills of Gold!
Those other kings I make no reckoning of —
Mere beggars they — King Philip now am I!
O Beauteous day! For when I got me hence, 5
I reach'd there much the first, and long before
I hid me in a tree, and spied from thence
Where the old man hid the gold. Once he had
    gone
I clamber'd down, I dug, and found this pot
Fill'd full of gold. Then from that spot I
    mark'd 10
The old man coming back. He saw me not,
For that I turn'd aside out of the path.
But hist! He comes this way himself. I'll hie
Me home and hide my treasure high and dry.
    (*He goes into the house of* MEGADORUS.

SCENE 2

*Enter EUCLIO, tearing his hair and wringing
his hands*

Euc. I'm lost, I'm ruin'd, slain! Where
    shall I run?
Where not run? Catch him, catch him!
    Whom, or who?
I know naught, see naught, walk with blinded
    eyes,
Nor where I go, nor where I am or who
Know I for certain. (*To the audience*)
    Pray you, lend your aid.
I crave, entreat you, point me out the man 6
Who's filch'd it. (*To one of the spectators*)
    What say *you?* I'm quite dispos'd
To trust you, since you have an honest face.
(*To the audience as a whole*)
What is 't? Why do you laugh? I know you
    all;
I know there's many thieves among you —
    men 10
Who hide themselves with whiten'd clothes
    and sit
Like honest folk. What? None of them has
    got it?

You've been the death of me. But tell me
    then,
Who *is* 't has got it? You don't know? Alas!
What misery is mine! In utter woe 15
I perish utterly. In sorry guise
I go, so much of grief this day has brought,
So much of groaning and of misery,
Yea, poverty and hunger. None in all
The world is more acquaint with grief than I.
For what avails my life, when I have lost 21
So much of gold I'd been at pains to guard?
Now others lick their chops at this my loss
And my distress. — 'Tis more than I can bear!
    (*He runs about, crying and wringing
    his hands.*

SCENE 3

*Enter LYCONIDES, from the house of
MEGADORUS*

Lyc. What man is this that here before our
    house
Laments and moans with loud complaining?
    Why,
'Tis Euclio, I fancy. All is lost!
The murder's out; he knows, I'm sure of it,
His daughter's brought to bed. I'm all at sea
Whether to go or stay, face him or fly. 6
What shall I do? I' faith, I do not know.
Euc. Who speaks here?
Lyc.   I, a wretch indeed.
Euc.   Nay, I,
And wretchedly undone, so great a load 11
Of woe and grief is mine.
Lyc.   Be of good cheer.
Euc. How can I, pray?
Lyc.   Because that deed that galls
Your soul was mine, and I confess it. 16
Euc.   Ha!
What hear I from you?
Lyc.   Truth.
Euc.   What ill, young man,
Have I deserv'd of you, that you should do 21
So base a deed, that brings down utter ruin
On me and on my children?
Lyc.   'Twas a god
That was my prompter — he entic'd me to it.
Euc. How so? 26
Lyc. I've sinn'd, that I confess, and know

I merit censure. Hence I come to you
To beg you'll brook it, and will grant me pardon.

    Euc. How dar'd you touch that which was
        not your own?   30

    Lyc. What would you then? 'Tis done, nor
        can it be
Undone. 'Tis my belief the gods have will'd
it,
For had they will'd it not, 'twould not be done,
I'm sure of it.

    Euc.   But my belief it is   35
The gods have will'd I lay you by the heels
Here in my house.

    Lyc.   Don't say it!

    Euc.   What business, then,   39
Had you to touch what's mine against my will?

    Lyc. Because I did it sway'd, to my own hurt,
By wine and love.

    Euc.   Monster of impudence,
To think you dare to come to me with words
Like these! Out on you, say I. For if this   45
Be lawful and deserving of excuse,
Then let us openly, in broad daylight,
Filch from great dames their golden trinkets —
    aye,
And being caught excuse ourselves with plea
That we were drunk, and did it out of love! 50
Too cheap are wine and love, in very truth,
If any toss-pot or love-smitten blade
Have leave to do whate'er he's minded to
And run no risk of forfeit.

    Lyc.   But I'm come   55
Of my own will to crave your clemency
For this my want of sense.

    Euc.   He likes me not
Who, having sinn'd, seeks warrant for his sin.
You knew you had no right thereto — 'twas
    meet   60
You keep your hands off.

    Lyc.   What I've dar'd to touch
I'll not begrudge to keep.

    Euc.   What? Would you keep
What's mine against my will?   65

    Lyc.   Against your will
I do not ask it; but 'tis my opinion
I have a claim thereto. And what is more,
You'll find yourself, friend Euclio, ere long
My claim's a just one.   70

    Euc.   Nay, so help me heaven,
I'll drag you to the praetor, and I'll serve
A writ on you unless you give me back —

    Lyc. Give what back, pray?

    Euc.   That which you filch'd from me.

    Lyc. I filch'd from you? Where, pray? Or
    what?   76

    Euc.   For love
Of Jove, what innocence!

    Lyc.   Unless, indeed,
You tell me what you're asking of.   80

    Euc.   My pot,
My pot of gold, I say, I'm asking back,
Which you confess'd to me you've stol'n.

    Lyc.   I' faith,
I've neither said nor done so.   85

    Euc.   You deny it?

    Lyc. I do deny it flat. It's past my ken
Or comprehension what it means, this gold
Or pot of yours.

    Euc.   Give me that pot you took   90
From the forest of Sylvanus. Hand it over!
I'd liefer give you half. Thief though you
    are,
I'll not be hard on you. Come, give it here!

    Lyc. You're mad to call me thief. 'Twas
        somewhat else   94
I thought you'd come to knowledge of, a thing
That touches me. 'Twas on this deep concern
Of mine I wish'd to speak you at your leisure,
If so be you are free.

    Euc.   But tell me then
On your good faith, have you not stol'n the
    gold?   100

    Lyc. On my good faith, I've not.

    Euc.   Nor know who 'tis
Who took it?

    Lyc.   On my good faith, No, to this
As well.   105

    Euc. But if you learn who pilfer'd it
You'll tell me of it?

    Lyc.   I will.

    Euc.   And take no share
Thereof, nor shelter give the thief?   110

    Lyc.   I promise.

    Euc. But what if you deceive me?

    Lyc.   Then may Jove
Do with me what he will.

    Euc.   I am content.   115

Come then, say what you wish.
Lyc.   If you know me
But ill, and what my lineage, Megadorus
Is uncle to me, Antimachus was my father,
Lyconides my name, my mother's call'd   120
Eunomia.
    Euc.   I know the family.   Now
What would you?   This I want to know.
    Lyc.   You have
A daughter of your own?   125
    Euc.   Aye, there at home.
    Lyc. You have, as I believe, bestow'd her
    hand
Upon my uncle.
    Euc.   You've the fact complete.
    Lyc. Now he has bidden me to announce to
    you   130
Refusal of her.
    Euc.   Refusal?   When all stands
In readiness, the wedding rites prepar'd?
Immortal gods and goddesses, I pray,
Confound him, one and all, on whose account
I've lost this day my gold — oh misery!   136
    Lyc. Be of good cheer, and bless him rather.
    Now —
And may it find a good and happy issue
For you and for your daughter — May the
    gods
Bring blessing on it — say it after me.   140
    Euc. (*doubtfully*). The gods bring blessing
    on't.
    Lyc.   And unto me
The gods bring blessing likewise.   Hear me
    now.
No man who opes his heart unto a fault
Is of so little worth that he would feel   145
No sense of shame, nor strive to clear himself.
Now I entreat you, Euclio, if I
In thoughtlessness have wrought what's less
    than just   148
To you or to your daughter, that you grant
Forgiveness for 't, and give me her as wife
As law provides.   I own that I have wrong'd
Your daughter at the feast of Ceres, spurr'd
By wine and by the urge of youth.
    Euc.   Woe's me!
What monstrous deed is this I hear of you?
    Lyc. What need of wailing thus, when I have
    made   156

A grandsire of you on the very day
Your daughter's to be wed?   For she's been
    brought
To bed the ninth month after — calculate
If so it please you.   And 'tis this has led   160
My uncle in my favor to present
His own refusal.   Go indoors, I beg,
And ask if all is not as I've declar'd.
    Euc. O utter misery!   Such mass of woe
Has stuck me fast on ruin.   I'll within   165
And learn what truth is in it.
                 (*He goes into the house.*
    Lyc.   I follow you
At once.   (*To himself*) Now does this matter
    seem to near
A haven of safety.   But I know not where
To say my servant Strobilus may be.   170
I'll wait him here a little; and thereupon
I'll follow him.   Meanwhile I'll give him
    leisure
To search my doings from the nurse who
    waits
Upon his daughter; she's aware of all.

Scene 4

Enter Strobilus, *at a distance*

    Stro. (*to himself*).   Immortal gods, what store
    of great delights
You've shower'd on me!   I've got a four-
    pound pot
Chock-full of gold.   What man so rich as I?
Who in all Athens do the gods now smile on
With greater favor?   5
    Lyc. (*to himself*).   Of a truth, I seem'd
To hear just now the voice of someone speak-
    ing.
    Stro. Ha!   See I not my master?
    Lyc.   Is it not
My servant Strobilus I see?   10
    Stro.   'Tis he himself.
    Lyc. None other 'tis for sure.
    Stro.   I'll speak to him.
    Lyc. I'll go and meet him.   I believe he's
    been
To see the grandam, as I bade, the nurse   15
Of Euclio's daughter.
    Stro.   Why not speak my mind
And say I've found this plunder?   In return

I'll beg of him to set me free. I'll go
And speak to him. (*Aloud*) I've found — 20
  Lyc.   What have you found?
  Stro.   Not that which boys cry out they've
found in a bean!
  Lyc.   You trifle with me, then, as you are
     wont?
  Stro.   Hold, master, I'll speak out. Hear
     me, I pray.
  Lyc.   Come, out with it!   25
  Stro.   Master, I've found today
Enormous riches.
  Lyc.   Where?
  Stro.   A four-pound pot,
I say, fill'd full of gold.   30
  Lyc.   What deed is this
I hear of you?
  Stro.   Under the very nose
Of this old Euclio I lifted it.
  Lyc.   But where's the gold?   35
  Stro.   Home, in my box. And now
I beg you'll set me free.
  Lyc.   What? Set you free,
You pyramid of mischief?
  Stro.   Cry you mercy, 40
My master. I'm aware what you're about.
I've tried you cleverly, in sooth. You aim'd
To get it from me. What then would you
     do,
Suppose I'd found it?
  Lyc.   Nay, you can't make good
Your foolery. Come, give up the gold.   46
  Stro.   What? I?
Give up the gold?
  Lyc.   Aye, give it up, I say,
That it may be return'd to him.   50
  Stro.   But whence?
Where shall I get it?
  Lyc.   From that box of yours
You swore just now 'twas in.
  Stro.   'Faith, 'tis my wont 55
To prattle nonsense. 'Twas that way I spoke.
  Lyc. (*seizing him*).   But know you what —
  Stro.   Kill me outright, I say;
I' faith, you'll never get it hence of me.[1]

---

[1] The original text of the play from this point to the
end has been lost. The acrostic summary which is
prefixed to the play reveals that Lyconides obtained the
gold, and returned it to Euclio, who presented it to him

  Lyc.   I'll have it will you nill you, when I've
     stretch'd   60
You on the rack, and drawn your ruptur'd guts.
But why delay to rush upon the jaws
Of this vile gallows-bird, and drive his breath
To seek a nether exit? Will you give it
Or no?   65
  Stro.   I'll give it.
  Lyc.   But I'll have it now,
Not presently.
  Stro.   I'll give it to you now;
But let me get my breath, I beg of you.   70
          (LYCONIDES *lets him go.*
Aha! What was it now you wanted me
To give you, master?
  Lyc.   Know you not, you knave?
Dare you withhold from me the four-pound
     pot
Of gold you swore just now that you had
     stol'n?   75
What ho! Where are the flogging-men?
  Stro.   But, master,
Hear you a word or two.
  Lyc.   I'll not. Ho there!
Ho, floggers, hither! I've a task for you. 80

SCENE 5

Enter two Flogging-Slaves

  Slave.   What is it?
  Lyc.   I'd have you put the chains in order.
  Stro.   Hear me, I beg; then you may have
     me bound
To your heart's content.
  Lyc.   I'll hear, but speed the matter. 5
  Stro.   If now you have me tortur'd unto
     death,
See how you profit. First, you count the loss
Of me your slave; then, what you most desire
You cannot have. But had you tempted
     me   9
With freedom's precious bait, by now your wish
Would be fulfill'd. Nature has borne all men

as a marriage portion with his daughter. A number of
attempts to complete the play have been made from
time to time, none wholly satisfactory. In the interest
of continuity the translator has included a rendering of
the supplement written by Antonius Codrus Urceus, a
learned scholar and professor at Bologna, as the best of
available efforts at making the play complete.

In freedom, and all men by nature crave
Sweet liberty.   But slavery is worse
Than any evil, any mishap else;
And whom Jove hates, him first he makes a
          slave.   15
   Lyc. Your words lack not in sense.
   Stro.   Now hear the rest.
Our age has bred o'ergrasping monsters, men
It is my wont to name Harpagos, Harpies,
And Tantali,[1] poor mid the greatest wealth 20
And thirsty mid the waters of the sea.
No riches are enough for them — not those
Of Midas[2] or of Croesus,[3] nor can all
The wealth of Persia fill their hellish maw.
Now masters treat their slaves with harshness;
          slaves   25
Obey their masters with reluctance.   Thus
On neither side is justice done.   Their stores,
Kitchens and larders do these aged cribs
Lock with a thousand keys, and scarce can
          brook
To have them left unto their lawful heirs. 30
Meanwhile a pilfering host of sneaking slaves,
Two-fac'd and sly, run off with stores lock'd up
With keys past numbering; they filch, devour,
And lick them clean, vile knaves that ne'er
          disclose
Their myriad pilferings, e'en on the cross. 35
So evil slaves take vengeance on their state
With laughter and with jesting.   Thus I hold
That liberality makes faithful slaves.
   Lyc. Well spoken that, but not in sparing
          words

---

[1] These names are all synonyms for persons of excessive greed. *Harpago* in Latin means literally a grappling-hook.   The Harpies, greedy monsters with bodies of vultures and human countenances, are frequently referred to in ancient literature as snatching up and carrying off food just as it was about to be eaten.   Tantalus was a wealthy king of Sipylus in Phrygia, Asia Minor, whose offense against the gods is variously reported.   His punishment consisted in his being immersed in water up to his chin, while over his head hung a branch of luscious fruit.   Whenever he lowered his head to drink, the water receded, and the branch of fruit always sprang up just beyond his reach.   Thus he became the symbol of unsatisfied greed.

[2] A king of Phrygia, gifted through the favor of Dionysus with the power of turning to gold whatever he touched.

[3] A fabulously rich king of Lydia, also in Asia Minor.

As you had promis'd.   But if I set you free, 40
Will you give back that which I'm asking for?
   Stro. I'll give it back; but I'd have witnesses.
Your pardon, Master, but I trust you little.
   Lyc. A hundred if you will, it's naught to
          me.
   Stro. (*going to the door of* MEGADORUS' *house*).
Ho, Megadorus, you, Eunomia, too,   45
Attend, I pray, an 't please.   Come out.
The business over, you'll return anon.

SCENE 6

Enter MEGADORUS *and* EUNOMIA

   Meg. Who calls us?   Ah, Lyconides.
   Eun.   You too,
Eh, Strobilus?   What's toward?   Speak, both
          of you.
   Lyc. The matter's brief.
   Meg.   What is it?   5
   Stro.   I call you both
As witnesses.   If I bring here at once
A four-pound pot of gold, and hand it over
To one Lyconides, the said Lyconides
Contracts to set me free and bid me stand 10
In my own right.   (*To* LYCONIDES) Do you so
          promise?
   Lyc.   Aye,
I promise.
   Stro.   Heard ye this what he has said?
   Meg. We have so heard it.   15
   Stro.   Swear by Jupiter.
   Lyc. What straits I'm come to through another's guilt!
This is too much!   But yet I'll do his bidding.
   Stro. Hark you, our class is not the trusting
          kind.
The writs are sign'd, a dozen witnesses   20
Are present, clerk makes note of time and
          place —
There's found a pleader to deny 'twas done.
   Lyc. But let me get this over with dispatch.
   Stro. (*handing him a stone*).   Here, take this
          stone.   You know the proper phrase.
   Lyc. (*rapidly repeating the formula*).   "If with
          my knowledge I deceive you, so   25
May Jupiter eject me from his grace,
The town and castle safe, as I now cast
This stone." — Have I convinc'd you now?

Stro.   Enough.
I go to bring the gold.   30
    Lyc.   Go you with speed
Of Pegasus, and burn the road returning.
                    (*Exit* STROBILUS.
A heaviness unto a decent man
Is any meal-mouth'd slave who seeks to be
More knowing than his master. Let him go
This Strobilus, to freedom, and withal   36
To sheer perdition, so he bring to me
The pot full of pure gold, that I may lift
My kinsman Euclio from grief to joy,
And win his daughter's favor, now she's
    brought   40
To bed from my abuse of her. But lo,
Yon comes my Strobilus well-heel'd. Me-
    thinks
He brings the pot. Aye, surely, 'tis the pot
He's carrying.
    Stro.   Lyconides, I bring   45
The find I promis'd you, the four-pound pot
Of gold. Have I been long?
    Lyc.   Beyond a doubt.
    (*He puts his hand into the pot, and
    takes out some of the money.*)
O ye immortal gods, what do I see?
What hold? Six hundred Philips, yes, there's
    thrice   50
Or four time that. But let's call Euclio
Without delay. (*He goes to the door of* EU-
    CLIO'S *house.*) Ho, Euclio, Euclio!
    Euc. (*appearing at the window*). What is it?
    Lyc. Come down to us. The gods have
    will'd
That you be sav'd. We've got the pot!   55
    Euc.   You've got it?
Or make you sport of me?
    Lyc.   It's here, I say.
Now if you can, fly hither.
    Euc. (*coming out of the door*). O mighty
    Jove,   60
O Household Lar,[1] Queen Juno, Hercules

[1] The Lares were the guardian spirits of the Roman
household. Their images were kept near the hearth,
where they became the center of family worship. They
are frequently associated with the Penates, or gods of
the pantry and storehouse. It is the *Lar Familiaris*, or
chief guardian spirit of Euclio's house, who speaks the
Prologue to the play.

My treasurer! At last you've come to pity
A poor old man. (*Takes the pot in his arms.*)
    Oh, with what joyful arms
I clasp you, pot of mine, your aged friend,
And welcome you with kisses! Not enough 65
A thousand warm embraces. O my hope,
Sweet heart of mine, that scatters all my grief!
    Lyc. I've always thought that lack of gold
    was worst,
For boys, and men and old folk. Indigence
Drives boys to mischief, men to theft, the old
To beggary. But much worse it is,   71
I see it now, to overload ourselves
With gold beyond our needs. Alas! what woes
Did Euclio suffer from the pot he lost
A short while since.   75
    Euc.   To whom shall I return
Appropriate thanks? The gods, who have re-
    gard
For honest folk? My friends, right-minded
    men?
Or unto both? Rather to both, I think.
And first of all to you, Lyconides,   80
Fountain and author of so great a boon.
So I present you with this pot of gold,
Accept it with good grace — I'd have it yours,
This and my daughter with it, here in presence
Of Megadorus and his sister, your good mother,
Eunomia.   86
    Lyc.   Now both is grace receiv'd
And grace return'd, as you have well deserv'd,
Good Euclio, most welcome as my kin.
    Euc. Nay, I shall deem the favor well repaid
If you accept with grace my gift and me.   91
    Lyc. I do accept, and wish my house to be
Your house as well.
    Stro.   But, master, don't forget
What still remains, that I am to be free.   95
    Lyc. You've well reminded me. Be you
    then free
As you deserve, my Strobilus. And now
Prepare indoors our interrupted feast.
    Stro. (*coming forward*). Spectators, Euclio,
    the miserly,
Has chang'd his natural bent, and suddenly
Become the soul of generosity.   101
So too do you, and if our play has found
Favor with you, let loud applause go round.
                    (*Exeunt.*

INTRODUCTION TO

Phormio

Later Roman Comedy: Terence

LATER ROMAN COMEDY

PLAUTUS had been a man of the theater and had developed Roman comedy to fit popular taste.   In contrast, his most notable successor, Publius Terentius Afer, or Terence, as he is commonly known, was a man of letters who introduced into comedy artistic refinement for the purpose of pleasing a small audience of cultivated Romans.   The taste of this class had, since the death of Plautus in 184 B.C., become dominated by admiration of Greek literature and art.   Sentiment turned strongly toward a close imitation of the works of Greek genius.   Therefore, as one of the comic poets who catered to the literarily-minded aristocrats, Terence proceeded to reproduce Attic New Comedy in a fashion more strict and more finished than Plautus had ever attempted.

With the writings of Terence the development of Roman comedy ceased.   The plays of both Plautus and Terence continued to be performed with some frequency, but new comic drama seldom appeared.   By the first century B.C. the writing of true comedy had virtually stopped.   After the opening of the Christian era the works of the two masters, though often appreciated as closet drama, made their way onto the Roman stage only at rare intervals.

Comedy survived no better than tragedy the growing degeneracy of dramatic taste at Rome.   The theaters under the emperors were given over more and more to indecent farces and pantomimes, acrobatics, ballet, juggling, replicas of land and sea battles, animal baitings, horse races, or gladiatorial combats.   Regular drama of any kind had been almost obliterated by the time that the Lombards, descending into Italy at the middle of the sixth century A.D., put an end to theatrical entertainments at Rome.

TERENCE

Terence was born probably of African-Phoenician parentage about 190 B.C. in or near the ancient metropolis of northern Africa, Carthage.   As a child slave he somehow reached Rome where M. Terentius Lucanus, a Roman senator, bought him.   After educating Terence like a freeman, the senator gave him his freedom in consequence of the youth's unusual gifts and personal attractiveness.   He also helped Terence to gain admittance to the circle of younger aristocrats presided over by Scipio Africanus the Younger (185–129 B.C.).   To this coterie who desired to foster Greek culture and arts in Roman life, Terence looked for patronage when he undertook the profession of comic poet.   He read his compositions aloud to the Scipionic circle and secured valuable criticism from them.

That assistance matured Terence's literary art rapidly and started him early on a career in the Roman theater.   In 166 B.C., when he was not over twenty-four years old, the Aediles as official sponsors accepted his comedy, *Andria* (*Woman of Andros*), for performance at the April Megalensian games.   During the next half-dozen years he became an outstanding playwright in Rome by exhibiting the following new plays:

Hecyra (*The Husband's Mother*), at the Megalensian games, 165 B.C.

Heauton Timorumenos (*The Self-Tormentor*), at the Megalensian games, 163 B.C.

Eunuchus (*The Eunuch*), at the Megalensian games, 161 B.C.

Phormio, at the Roman games in September, 161 B.C.

Adelphoe (*The Brothers*), at the funeral games of Aemilius Paulus, 160 B.C.

Three or four of these plays certainly had second or even third performances within a few years after their first appearance.   For all the presentations Lucius Ambivius Turpio, the most skillful producer of the time, acted as manager.   His management had much to do with the success of the Terentian comedies during the author's lifetime.   In general, however, they did not win from the public anything like the popularity which Plautine drama enjoyed.   *Hecyra*, for example, had to be given a third production before an audience would listen to the entire piece.

In 160 B.C. Terence voyaged to Greece in order to secure a richer background for his writing of comedy upon the Greek model.   There he made translations of certain plays by Menander, which he intended to bring out later at Rome.   On his way home in 159 B.C. he lost his life, apparently by some accident at sea.   Thus abruptly his career came to an end when he was but thirty years of age.

The comedies of Terence both in content and manner present a more exact imitation of Attic comedy, especially that of Menander, than do the plays of Plautus.   Terence followed Menander rather than Plautus in allowing the love intrigue to monopolize the dramatic interest of all his plays.   As a result, his characters are more faintly drawn than those of Plautus and less interesting.   They have about them an air of urbanity and worldly wisdom which makes them nearer akin to the Greek than the Plautine personages.   In their dialogue Terence frequently tried to reproduce the refined and reflective tone of Menander.   He replaced the striking incongruities and the exuberant humor of Plautus with a certain elegance of action and feeling.   His comedies reveal not a strongly jocose playwright, but a finished writer of mixed sentiments.

Terence's plays when read as closet drama in the century or two after his death gained a popularity which far exceeded that of their original stage appearance.   The Roman critics like Cicero (106–43 B.C.) and Horace (65–8 B.C.) praised his comedy for its polished style.   This same quality caused the Middle Ages to cherish and study Terence's works alone out of all ancient dramatic literature.   In the tenth century A.D. a certain nun in Saxony, Hrosvitha, composed as a literary exercise some short moralistic plays in Latin after the Terentian style.   She, like others of her time, was interested in the plays as models of rhetoric and not as expressions of dramatic art.

Terence's influence since the Renaissance, however, has grown from the fertility of his plots.   In England and France of the seventeenth and eighteenth centuries playwrights often copied his dramatic situations.   Molière drew on *The Brothers* for his *School of Husbands* (1661) and on *Phormio* for his *Impostures of Scapin* (1671).   Sir Charles Sedley refashioned *The Eunuch* into a London comedy, *Bellamira* (1687).   Sir Richard Steele in the early eighteenth century based a large portion of his notable piece,

The Conscious Lovers (1723), upon Terence's *Woman of Andros*. The writers of fiction later utilized the stories of his plays. Perhaps the most recent example is Thornton Wilder's novel, *The Woman of Andros* (1930), the very title of which suggests the source of its indebtedness.

"PHORMIO"

In *Phormio* Terence departed from his common practice in two respects. First, he did not go to Menander for his inspiration, but to Apollodorus of Carystus, a minor writer of Attic New Comedy. Second, he constructed the play in question from a single Greek work instead of putting together parts of several compositions.

Otherwise *Phormio* represents the most characteristic combination of qualities to be found in Terentian comedy. It contains the usual narrative of a socially irregular passion which ends, by the discovery of a long-lost daughter, in a marriage satisfactory to all concerned. The characters constitute a customary group: two fathers, two sons, a parasite, a clever servant, a nurse, etc. No one is particularly distinguished as an individual, not even the parasite, Phormio, who is the mainspring of the plot, nor the clever servant, Geta, who brings about the denouement. The scenes are less lively and colorful than in Plautus. Argument largely replaces repartee. Serious and sententious comment by the worldly wise characters occurs now and again, such as Hegio's remark: "Many men of many minds; many birds of many kinds; each man has his own point of view" (Act III, ll. 268–70). Dialogue as well as action displays a consistent moderateness of emotional tone.

Phormio therefore lacks the comic vigor of Plautine comedy. Its effects are built up more gradually and handled more quietly. The scene (Act III, ll. 70–280) in which Phormio tries to upset Demipho's attitude in the presence of Demipho's advisers, and then Demipho turns to them for advice only to be the more bewildered, rises to a fine climax of humor. The humor, however, depends not so much upon outward action as upon the appeal to reflection. Hence Terence's comedy often moves in the direction of "high comedy." Yet it does not finally gain its effects through character. Terence's creative fancy focused upon ingenious plot contrivance. The interplay of incidents and motives done in skillful sequence called forth his best talent. The manipulation of the two fathers, Demipho and Chremes, by Phormio and Geta is admirably conceived and executed. In this comedy of intrigue lies the dramatic strength of *Phormio*. For such artfulness of plotting Terence surpassed Plautus and became the teacher of subsequent generations of European comedians.

[For a critique of Terence, see Gilbert Norwood, *The Art of Terence* (1923).]

PUBLIUS TERENTIUS AFER ("TERENCE")

Phormio

[*Translated by* MORRIS H. MORGAN]

DRAMATIS PERSONAE

DAVOS, *a slave*
GETA, *slave of* DEMIPHO
ANTIPHO, *a young man, son of* DEMIPHO
PHÆDRIA, *a young man, son of* CHREMES
DEMIPHO, *an old man*
PHORMIO, *a parasite*

HEGIO
CRATINUS } *advisers of* DEMIPHO
CRITO
DORIO, *a slave-trader*
CHREMES, *an old man,* DEMIPHO'S *brother*
SOPHRONA, *an old nurse*
NAUSISTRATA, *a matron, wife of* CHREMES
A Cantor

The Scene is at Athens

ACT I

A street leading on the right to the market-place, on the left to the port. At the back, the houses of CHREMES (L.), DEMIPHO (C.), *and* DORIO (R.).

Enter DAVOS, R.

Dav. My particular friend and countryman, Geta, came to see me yesterday. I had been owing him some small balance of cash on account a good while, and he asked me to get it together. I've got it together, and I'm 5 bringing it to him now. The fact is, I'm told that his master's son has got married; it's for the girl, I suppose, that he's scraping this testimonial together. How unfair it is that poor folks should always be adding something 10 to rich people's piles! Now here's Geta; — the poor fellow's been saving up out of his rations a pint at a time, and hardly that, cheating his own belly, and now my lady'll spoil him of it all without ever thinking what a lot of 15 work it took to get it. Then besides they'll strike him for another testimonial when she has a baby; and then another too when the baby has a birthday, and another when it gets initiated. The mother, of course, will 20 walk off with it all, and the child will be only an excuse for the gift. But don't I see Geta?

Enter GETA *from* DEMIPHO'S

Geta (*looking back*). If e'er a red-head asks for me —
Dav. Here he is. That'll do. 25
Geta. Ha! Why, Davos, you were the very man I wanted to meet.
Dav. (*handing him the bag*). There you are! Take it; it's good money. You'll find the total comes to what I owe you. 30
Geta. Thank you. I'm obliged to you for not forgetting it.
Dav. Particularly as things go nowadays. Why, it's come to such a pass that you're expected to feel very much obliged when a 35 man pays you a debt. But what makes you so glum?
Geta. Me? Oh, you don't know what a fright and what danger we are in!
Dav. Why! what's the matter? 40
Geta. You shall hear, — that is, provided you can keep mum.

Dav. Get out, will you, you simpleton. When you've seen that a man's to be trusted in a matter of money, are you afraid to trust   45 him with words? Why, what should I gain by deceiving you there?

Geta. Well, then, listen.

Dav. I'm at your service.

Geta. Davos, do you know our old gen-   50 tleman's elder brother Chremes?

Dav. Of course I do.

Geta. And his son Phædria?

Dav. As well as I know you.

Geta. The two old fellows happened to   55 start out at the same time, — Chremes on a trip to Lemnos,[1] and our governor to Cilicia[2] to see an old friend. He had enticed the old man over by letters, promising him all but mountains of gold.   60

Dav. Him, with already so much and to spare?

Geta. Never mind; it is his nature to.

Dav. Oh, if only *I* had been a millionaire!

Geta. Well, when the two old gentlemen   65 set out, they left me here with their sons as a sort of guardian.

Dav. O Geta, Geta! No soft job you had there.

Geta. I've found that out — by experi-   70 ence. I see now that my guardian angel was out of sorts with me when I was left behind. I started in by opposition; but, to make a long story short, I found that being true to the old man was the ruination of my back.   75

Dav. Just what I was thinking; it's folly, you know, kicking against the pricks.

Geta. So I began to do everything they wanted, and to comply with all their wishes.

Dav. You understand how to carry your   80 pigs to the best market.

Geta. Our fellow didn't make any trouble at first; but Phædria there, — the first thing he did was to pick up a pretty little harp-lady, and he fell desperately in love with her. She   85 belonged to the lowest sort of a slave-trader, and we hadn't a penny to give him, — the old gentlemen had looked out for that. So the

only thing left for Phædria to do was to feast his eyes on her, tag at her heels, take her   90 down to the singing school, and see her home. My young master and I, having nothing to do, devoted ourselves to Phædria. Now there was a barber's shop just across the street from the school she went to, and there we pretty   95 generally used to wait until it was time for her to go home. One day, as we were sitting there, a young fellow came up, all in a flood of tears. Surprise on our part, — we asked what was up. "I never knew so well before," cried he,   100 "what a wretched, crushing burden it is to be poor. I've just seen near here a poor girl be-wailing her dead mother, who lay buried over opposite. She hadn't with her a well-wisher or friend or relative helping with the funeral,   105 except one lone woman. It was pitiable. The girl herself was a beauty." In short, he stirred us all up, and Antipho cried out, "Shall we go and see her?" and somebody else, "I move we do, — let's go, — show us the way,   110 please." We start; we're there; we take a look. The girl *was* a beauty, and you could put it all the more strongly because she hadn't any artificial fallals to make her so. Hair di-sheveled — feet bare — she all frowsy —   115 weeping — meanly dressed; in fact, if she hadn't been the very essence of beauty, all this would have eclipsed her beauty. The young fellow who was in love with the harp-lady only said, "She's very pretty"; but my young   120 master ——

Dav. I know without being told; he fell in love with her.

Geta. Rather! See how it turns out. The very next day he went straight to the old   125 woman; begged that he might have her. But she refused, and said he wasn't doing the proper thing; "for the girl was an Athenian, a good girl of good stock. If he wanted to marry her, it could be done in the regular legal way;   130 but if he meant anything else, no." My master didn't know what to do; on the one hand he longed to marry the girl, on the other he was afraid of his father, who was gone abroad.

Dav. Wouldn't his father have given   135 him leave when he came home?

Geta. What, he! give leave to marry a girl

---

[1] An island of the northern Aegean formerly belonging to Greece, now to Italy.

[2] An old Roman province in southern Asia Minor.

without a dowry and of unknown family? Never in the world.

Dav. Well, what happened in the end? 140

Geta. What happened? There's a parasite of the name of Phormio — a cheeky fellow — blast him!

Dav. Why, what's he been up to?

Geta. He supplied the scheme which I 145 am going to describe. "There's a law," says he, "that orphan girls must marry their next of kin, and by the same law the kinsmen are obliged to marry them. Now, I'll say that you're her kinsman, and I'll bring a suit 150 against you. I'll pretend that I was a friend of the girl's father. We shall come into court. Who her father was, and who her mother, and how she is related to you, I'll make all that up. It will be good and easy for me, for you 155 won't disprove any of the charges, and so of course I shall win. Your father will come home; that means a lawsuit against me. But what do I care for that? The girl will be ours anyhow."   160

Dav. A jolly piece of cheek!

Geta. Antipho agreed — 'twas done — off we went — got beaten — he married her.

Dav. What *are* you telling me?

Geta. Just what you hear.   165

Dav. Oh, Geta, what will become of you?

Geta. By the powers I don't know that; but one thing I do know, which is, that "bravely we'll bear the burden fortune brings."

Dav. I like that; that's taking it like a 170 little man.

Geta. I've no hope in anybody but myself.

Dav. Good again!

Geta. I suppose I must go to somebody who will beg me off in this style: "Do let him 175 off just this once; but if he is ever guilty again, I won't say a word," — all but adding, "Kill him, for all me, when I've once got away."

Dav. What about the harp-lady's 180 chaperon? How's he getting on?

Geta. So, so. Pretty poorly.

Dav. Hasn't much to give, perhaps?

Geta. Nothing at all but unadulterated hope.

Dav. His father home yet or not? 185

Geta. Not yet.

Dav. Well, how long before you expect your own old man?

Geta. I don't know for sure, but I'm told that a letter has come from him which has 190 been taken to the custom-house; I'll go after it.

Dav. Can't do anything more for you, Geta, can I?

Geta. Only take care of yourself. (*Exit* DAVOS, R.) Hi! boy! is nobody ever 195 coming? (*Enter a slave.*) Take this, and give it to Dorcium.   (*Gives him the bag, and exit* L.

ACT II

Enter ANTIPHO *and* PHÆDRIA *from the house of* CHREMES

Ant. Oh, Phædria, to think that it has come to this, that I should be afraid of my own father whenever I think of his coming home! He wishes nothing but my good. If I hadn't been so thoughtless, I should be waiting for his 5 coming with joy.

Phæd. Why, what's the matter?

Ant. Matter, you accomplice in my bold scheme? Oh, how I wish it had never occurred to Phormio to urge me to it, and that he 10 hadn't driven me, when I was in the heat of my passion, to take this step, which was the beginning of all my troubles! I shouldn't have got the girl, of course, and that would have made me wretched for some days; but still, I 15 shouldn't be suffering this everlasting anxiety all the time, —

Phæd. Yes, yes.

Ant. Constantly expecting that he will soon be here to break up this marriage of mine. 20

Phæd. Other men are wretched because they haven't got the object of their love, but you're unhappy because you've got too much of it. You're embarrassed with bliss, Antipho. But I tell you that your position is one to be 25 coveted and desired. Bless me, for the chance to be so long with her I love I'm ready to pay down my life. Only just reckon up all that I'm suffering from privation and all that you're enjoying in possession! To say nothing of 30 your having got a well-born lady without any expense, and of having the wife of your choice publicly acknowledged, and without any scandal! Here you are perfectly happy except for one thing, — a temper to bear it all with 35 equanimity. If you had to deal with a slave-trader like that one of mine, then you'd find out! But that's the way almost all of us are made; we're dissatisfied with our own lot.

Ant. On the contrary, Phædria, it seems 40 to me that you are the lucky man. You're still perfectly free to make up your mind to your liking, — to keep your sweetheart or to give her up. But I, unluckily, have got into such a fix that I can neither keep mine nor let 45 her go either. But what's here? Isn't this Geta I see running up this way? It's the very man. Oh, dear me, I'm dreadfully frightened about the news he may be bringing!   (*They retire.*

Enter GETA *hastily from the port*

Geta. You're done for, Geta, unless you 50 find some way out and mighty quick! Such troubles threaten you all of a sudden and you're so unprepared. I don't see how to dodge them or how to get myself out of this fix. Our reckless doings can't possibly be concealed any 55 longer.

Ant. (*aside*). Why in the world is the man come in such a fright?

Geta. Besides, I've only a minute to think of it; master's close by. 60

Ant. (*aside*). What's this trouble?

Geta. Once he's heard of it, how shall I head off his fury? Talk? 'T would set him afire. Silence? Merely egging him on. Clear myself? Might as well wash a brick. Oh, 65 dear me! I'm frightened on my own account, and then I'm in torture when I think of Antipho. He's the man I'm sorry for. I'm afraid for his sake now, and it's he that keeps me here. Why, if it were not for him, I should have 70 seen to myself easily enough, and got even with the old man for his anger. I should just have got some traps together, and then taken to my heels straight out of here.

Ant. (*aside*). Why, what's this he's 75 plotting about running away or stealing?

Geta. But where shall I find Antipho? Which way shall I go to look for him?

Phæd. (*aside*). He's talking about you.

Ant. (*aside*). I dread some great misfor- 80 tune from this news.

Phæd. (*aside*). Oh, dear!

Geta. I'll go on home. That's where he is generally.

Phæd. (*aside*). Let's call the fellow back. 85

Ant. Stop where you are!

Geta. Ha! pretty peremptory, don't care who you are!

Ant. Geta!

Geta. It's the very man I wanted to find. 90

Ant. Out with your news, for mercy's sake; and, if you can, dispatch it in one word.

Geta. I will.

Ant. Speak out.

Geta. Just now, down at the post — 95

Ant. My —

Geta. You've hit it.

Ant. I'm a dead man!

Phæd. Whew!

Ant. What shall I do? 100

Phæd. What's this you say?

Geta. That I saw his father, your uncle.

Ant. Now how am I to find a way out of this sudden catastrophe, dear, dear me? Why, life isn't worth living, if it's my fate to be torn 105 away from you, Phanium.

Geta. Well, if that's so, Antipho, there's all the more need of being wide awake. Fortune favors the brave.

Ant. I'm all abroad! 110

Geta. But that's just where you mustn't be now, Antipho; for your father will think you guilty if he sees you frightened.

Phæd. That's true.

Ant. I can't change my nature. 115

Geta. Suppose you had to do something still harder, what then?

Ant. As I can't do this, I could do that still less.

Geta. It's no use, Phædria; it's all over. 120 Why waste our time here for nothing? I'm off.

Phæd. And I too (*going*).

Ant. For mercy's sake! Suppose I make believe? Will this do?   (*Strikes an attitude.*

Geta. Silly! 125

Ant. But just look at my face. There! is that satisfactory?

Geta. No.

Ant. How about this?

Geta. Pretty fair.   130

Ant. And this?

Geta. That will do. Keep that, and look out that you answer him word for word, tit for tat, so that he shan't rout you with harsh language while he's in a passion.   135

Ant. I understand.

Geta. Say you were forced into it, against your will.

Phæd. By the law — by the court.

Geta. Do you catch on? But who's   140 that old man I see down the street? It's the governor!

Ant. I can't face him

Geta. Here! what are you doing? Where are you going, Antipho? Wait, say.   145

Ant. I know myself and my own fault. I leave Phanium and my own life in your hands.
                                        (*Runs off*, R.

Phæd. What's going to be done now, Geta?

Geta. You'll get a wigging pretty soon, and I shall be strung up and whipped, if I'm   150 not mistaken. But we ought to do ourselves, Phædria, just what we were advising Antipho.

Phæd. None of your "oughts." Just give me your orders what I'm to do.

Geta. Do you remember what you said   155 long ago when we started in with this affair, about protecting ourselves from trouble, — that the other side's case was just, easy, sure to win, the best in the world?

Phæd. Yes, I remember.   160

Geta. Well, now's the time for that very plea, or, if possible, for a better and one more cunning still.

Phæd. I'll do my best.

Geta. You go up to him first, and I'll   165 stay here in ambush as a reserve force, in case you fail.

Phæd. Very well.   (GETA *retires*.

Enter DEMIPHO, L.

Dem. What, what, what! Antipho's got married, has he, without my consent?   170 As for my authority, — well, never mind authority, — but only think of his having no regard even for my displeasure! Not a bit ashamed, either. Oh, what a monstrous thing! Oh, Geta, Geta, you rare adviser!   175

Geta (*aside*). In for it at last!

Dem. Now what will they say to me? What excuse will they find? I wonder very much.

Geta (*aside*). Oh, I shall find one; you needn't worry about that.   180

Dem. Is this what he'll say: "I did it against my will; the law forced me to it." Yes, yes; I admit it.

Geta. You old dear!

Dem. But with his eyes open, without   185 a word, to give up the case to the other side! Did the law force him to that?

Phæd. (*aside*). Ah, that's a hard nut!

Geta (*aside*). I'll crack it, though; let me alone for that!   190

Dem. It's taken me so unawares, — it's so past belief that I can't tell what to do. I'm so much exasperated that I can't compose my mind to think it over. Well, the fact is, when everything is most successful with you, 195 then's the time to reflect how to bear the brunt of trouble, — your son's bad conduct, your wife's death, your daughter's illness; — these things happen to everybody, they can happen to you, so there shouldn't be anything 200 surprising in them; but everything that surprises you by ending well, you can set down as so much clear gain.

Geta (*aside*). Ha, Phædria! It's past belief how much more of a sage I am than my   205 master. I *have* reflected on all the troubles that master's return will bring upon *me*, — grinding to do at the mill, floggings to get, fetters to wear, set to work on the farm. Not a single one of them will take me by sur- 210 prise. But everything that surprises me by ending well, I shall set down as so much clear gain. But why don't you step up to him and address him politely to begin with?

Dem. There's my nephew Phædria, I   215 see, coming to meet me.

Phæd. How do you do, uncle?

Dem. How do you do? But where's Antipho?

Phæd. You've got back safe, —   220

Dem. Yes, yes; but answer my question.

Phæd. He's well — he's here; but has everything gone to your liking?

Dem. I wish it had, indeed.

Phæd. Why, what's the matter?   225

Dem. What a question, Phædria! This is a fine marriage that you've cooked up here while I was away!

Phæd. Holloa! are you angry with him for that?   230

Geta (aside). Fine acting!

Dem. And shouldn't I be angry with him? Why, I'm just aching to get a sight of him, so that he may find out once for all how he's turned his good-natured old father into a   235 perfect savage!

Phæd. But he hasn't done anything to make you angry, uncle.

Dem. Now just look at that! Birds of a feather! They're all in it! When you   240 know one, you know all.

Phæd. It isn't so.

Dem. When A's in trouble, B turns up to make excuses for him; and when it's B, then up comes A. They go partners in it.   245

Geta (aside). The old man's drawn a fine sketch of their proceedings without knowing it.

Dem. If it wasn't so, you wouldn't be taking his part, Phædria.

Phæd. Well, uncle, if it is a fact that   250 Antipho has done a wrong, regardless of his interests or reputation, I have nothing to say against his suffering as he has deserved. But if somebody took advantage of his own cunning to lay a snare for our youthful innocence   255 and has caught us in it, is it our fault or that of the judges? You know what a habit they have of robbing the rich from envy, and giving to the poor from pity.

Geta (aside). If I didn't know the case,   260 I should believe that he was telling the truth.

Dem. Is there a judge alive who can possibly know your rights when you don't answer a word yourself, like that son of mine?

Phæd. He behaved like a young man of   265 good breeding. When we got into court, he couldn't speak his piece; his modesty struck him quite dumb then and there.

Geta (aside). Bravo, you! but shall I not address the old man at once? (*Going for-*   270

ward.) Good-day, master. I'm glad you've got home safe.

Dem. Ha, ha! fine guardian, good-day, main stay of my house; it was in your charge that I left my son when I went away.   275

Geta. I've heard you blaming us all for ever so long when we didn't deserve it, and I least of anybody. Why, what would you have had me do in the matter? The laws don't allow a man who's a slave to plead, and he can't give   280 evidence either.

Dem. I waive all that, and I admit this, too, that the boy was afraid and unsuspecting. I grant that you are a slave. But no matter how near a relative she was, he needn't have   285 married her; no, no. You should have given her a dowry, as the law directs, and let her look out for another husband. On what account, then, did he prefer to bring home a pauper?   290

Geta. It wasn't on account, — it was cash down that was wanted.

Dem. He should have got it somewhere or other.

Geta. Somewhere or other? Nothing   295 easier to say!

Dem. On interest, at the worst, if on no other terms.

Geta. Bless my soul! Pretty fine talk! As if anybody would have trusted him, with   300 you alive!

Dem. No, no; it shan't be so; it can't be. What! let her stay on as his wife a single day? This is no case for kindness. But I want to have that man pointed out to me, or to   305 be shown where he lives.

Geta. You mean Phormio?

Dem. The woman's next friend.

Geta. I'll bring him here at once.

Dem. Where's Antipho now?   310

Geta. Out.

Dem. Go and look for him, Phædria, and bring him here.

Phæd. I'll make a bee line.

(*Exit to* DORIO'S.)

Geta (aside). Yes, to Pamphila's.   315

(*Exit* R.)

Dem. As for me, I'll turn in home and pay my respects to my household gods, and then go on 'Change and call some friends to stand by me in this affair, so that I shan't be unprepared in case of Phormio's coming. 320

(Exit to his house.

ACT III

Enter PHORMIO *and* GETA, R.

Phor. And so you say he's gone off in a fright at his father's return?

Geta. Exactly.

Phor. Phanium left all by herself?

Geta. Just so. 5

Phor. And the old man boiling.

Geta. Precisely.

Phor. Then, Phormio, the whole responsibility rests on you; you mixed this mess, and now you've got to eat it all yourself. Brace 10 up!

Geta. For mercy's sake, Phormio!

Phor. Supposing he asks —

Geta. You're our only hope!

Phor. See here, what if he retorts — 15

Geta. You drove the boy to it.

Phor. There, that'll do, I fancy.

Geta. Come to the rescue!

Phor. Trot out your old man, for I've got my plans all marshaled in my head. 20

Geta. What are you going to do?

Phor. What, indeed, except let Phanium stay here, clear Antipho of this charge, and turn the whole current of the old man's wrath on to myself? 25

Geta. Oh, you brave, kind man! but what I'm often afraid of, Phormio, is that all this courage may land you in the stocks at last.

Phor. Oh, no, not at all; I've tried it; I know where to set my feet. How many fellows 30 do you think I've beaten to death before today? Yet come, did you ever hear of anybody bringing a suit against me for assault and battery?

Geta. How does it come about?

Phor. It's because we never set traps 35 for the hawks and kites that really hurt us; it's only for birds that don't hurt that traps are set. There's something to be made out of them, but on others it's only time thrown away. Other people have their dangers, from one source 40 or another, — people something can be got out of; but everybody knows that I've got nothing to lose. But perhaps you'll say that they'll convict me and take me home to hold me there. Oh, no; they don't want to keep a raven- 45 ous fellow like me; they don't want to do good for evil, and that's where they're wise, I think.

Geta. Well, he can't ever thank you as much as you deserve.

Phor. Not quite so. Nobody ever can 50 thank his *patron* as much as he deserves. Think of it! You come scot free to his dinner, all perfumed and shining from the bath, with a heart free from care, when he's drowned with worry and eaten up with expenses. While 55 everything's done to your liking, he's snarling. You can laugh, drink your wine before him, take the higher seat; and then a puzzling banquet's spread.

Geta. What's that? 60

Phor. That's when you're puzzled what to help yourself to first. Now, when you come to reckon up how nice all this is and how much it costs, aren't you obliged to think your host a god incarnate right before your eyes? 65

Geta. Here's the old man; mind what you're about; the first onset is always the fiercest. If you stand that, you may afterwards make play as you like.

Enter DEMIPHO *and his advisers*, R.

Dem. Did you ever hear of a more in- 70 sulting piece of injustice done to anybody than this to me? Stand by me, I beg of you.

Geta (aside). He's in a passion.

Phor. (to GETA *aside).* Mind your cue now; I'm going to touch him up pretty quick. 75 *(Aloud, to* GETA.*)* Great heavens! Does Demipho actually *deny* that Phanium's related to him? What! Demipho says this girl's no relation?

Geta. He says not. 80

Phor. And that he doesn't know who her father was?

Geta. He says not.

Dem. I fancy this is the very man I was talking about. Follow me. 85

Phor. Because the poor thing is left in poverty, her father is disowned and she herself is abandoned. Only see what avarice does!

Geta. You'll hear what you won't like if you insinuate anything wrong about my mas- 90 ter.

Dem. Oh, what impudence! Why, he's come to take the initiative by accusing me!

Phor. I've no reason at all to be angry with the young fellow for not knowing her 95 father; of course he was a man pretty well along, poor, working for his living, generally keeping in the country, where my father let him have a farm to cultivate. The old fellow used often to tell me how this kinsman of 100 his neglected him. But what a fine man he was! the best *I* ever saw in all my life.

Geta. I hope you'll ever see yourself such as you describe him.

Phor. You be hanged! No; if I hadn't 105 esteemed him as I did, I should never have got into a quarrel with your people, all on account of this girl that your master's slighting now in this ungentlemanlike way.

Geta. Will you persist in slandering my 110 master behind his back, you dirty dog?

Phor. Serves him right.

Geta. Still more of it, you jail-bird?

Dem. Geta ——

Geta. You extortioner, you law-shark! 115

Dem. Geta!

Phor. (*aside*). Answer him.

Geta. Whom have we here? Oh!

Dem. Hold your tongue!

Geta. Why, he's been insulting you all 120 day long behind your back, — insults that don't fit you and do fit him.

Dem. Avast there! Hold on! Young man (*to* PHORMIO), to begin with, I want to ask you this, with your kind permission, if you will 125 be good enough to answer me: Explain to me who this friend of yours was you're talking about, and how he said that I was related to him.

Phor. There you are, fishing; as if you 130 didn't know.

Dem. Didn't know?

Phor. Yes.

Dem. I say I don't; but you, who say I do, just jog my memory. 135

Phor. What, man! not know your own cousin?

Dem. You're killing me. Tell me his name.

Phor. His name; of course.

Dem. Why don't you speak? 140

Phor. (*aside*). By the powers, I'm a goner! I've forgotten the name.

Dem. What's that you say?

Phor. (*aside to* GETA). Geta, just prompt me if you recollect the name that was 145 given at the time. (*Aloud*) No, I won't tell you. You're here to pump me, as if you didn't know it yourself.

Dem. What! Pumping you?

Geta (*aside to* PHORMIO). Stilpo. 150

Phor. And then again, what do I care? It's Stilpo.

Dem. Whom did you say?

Phor. Stilpo, I tell you; you knew him.

Dem. I didn't know him either, and I 155 never had a relative of such a name.

Phor. So, so? Don't you feel abashed before these gentlemen? Yet if he had left a property worth ten talents ——

Dem. Oh, confound you! 160

Phor. You'd be the very first with a tip-top memory to trace your ancestry all the way from grandfather and great-grandfather.

Dem. Very likely, as you say. Well, when I came forward I should have stated how 165 she was related to me. Now, you do the same. Come, how is she related?

Geta. Bravo, master, well done! and you, sir, look out for yourself.

Phor. My duty was to explain it to the 170 court, and I did so with perfect clearness. If it wasn't true, why didn't your son disprove it on the spot?

Dem. You talk to me about my son? Why, I can't find words to describe his stupidity. 175

Phor. Well, then, you who are so wise, go to the magistrates and make them try the same case all over again for you. For you talk as though you were sole lord paramount in these parts and the only man alive entitled to a 180 second trial of the same case.

Dem. Though I have been unjustly treated, still, rather than go to law or have to listen to you — here, just as if she really were related,

take these five ducats, the dowry that the   185
law directs, and carry her away.

Phor. Ha! ha! ha! you sweety!

Dem. What's the matter? There's nothing
wrong in my demand, is there? Am I not to
get the benefit of what is the law of the   190
land?

Phor. Does the law direct you, I'd like to
know, to pay her and send her off like a courtesan? Or was it to prevent a freeborn lady from
doing anything to disgrace herself through   195
poverty that the law directs to give her to her
nearest kinsman to live with him? And that's
just what you're preventing.

Dem. Yes, to her nearest kinsman. But
how do we come in, or on what grounds?   200

Phor. Oh, dear! "don't open a case that's
closed," as the saying goes.

Dem. Don't open it? On the contrary, I'll
never rest until I've seen it through.

Phor. Silly of you.   205

Dem. You just let me alone.

Phor. In short, Demipho, I've nothing to do
with you. It was your son that lost the suit,
not you; for your time for marrying was gone
long ago.   210

Dem. You can take him as saying all that I
say now; if he doesn't I'll shut him and his wife
out of my house.

Geta (*aside*). He's in a passion.

Phor. You'd better do the same thing   215
with yourself.

Dem. So you're ready to take a stand against
me in everything, are you, you ill-starred
wretch?

Phor. (*aside to* GETA). He's afraid   220
of us, though he tries hard to conceal it.

Geta (*aside to* PHORMIO). Your first moves
are well made.

Phor. (*aloud*). Why not put up with what
you must put up with? That will be in   225
keeping with your reputation, and we shall be
friends.

Dem. What! I seek your friendship, or wish
to see or hear of you?

Phor. If you make it up with her, you'll   230
have somebody to cheer your old age; think of
your time of life.

Dem. Keep her to cheer yourself.

Phor. Do moderate your angry passions.

Dem. See here! enough said. If you only   235
don't hurry and take that woman away, I'll
throw her out of doors. That's my last word,
Phormio.

Phor. And if you lay a finger on her in any
way unbefitting a lady, I'll bring a smash-   240
ing suit against you. That's my last word,
Demipho. (*Aside to* GETA.) Here! if you need
me for anything, you'll find me at home.

Geta. All right!

(*Exit* PHORMIO, R.

Dem. What worry and trouble my son   245
does give me by involving himself and me in
this marriage! And he doesn't come to let me
see him either, so that at least I might know
what he has to say about the matter, or what
he thinks. Off with you! see whether he   250
has got home yet.

Geta. Yes.

(*Exit to house of* DEMIPHO.

Dem. (*to his advisers*). You see in what a
state things are. Now what am I to do? Tell
me, Hegio.   255

Heg. I? I move Cratinus does, if you please.

Dem. Well, speak, Cratinus.

Crat. Do you mean me?

Dem. Yes sir.

Crat. I should like to have you act for   260
the interests of your house. Now this is the
way it seems to me; it's all right and proper
that what your son has done in your absence
should be put back entirely as it was, and you
will carry that point. That's what I say.   265

Dem. Now, Hegio, it's your turn to speak.

Heg. I believe that he has spoken advisedly;
but this is the way of it; many men of many
minds, many birds of many kinds; each man
has his own point of view. Now it doesn't   270
seem to me that what the law has done can be
undone; and it's discreditable to try it.

Dem. Well, Crito?

Crit. I vote we take time to think it over;
it's important.   275

Heg. We can't do anything more for you,
can we?

Dem. You have done finely. (*Exeunt advisers* R.) I'm much more bewildered than before.   280

Enter GETA, *from* DEMIPHO'S *house*

Geta. They say he hasn't come in.

Dem. I must wait for my brother. I'll follow the advice which he gives me in the matter. I'll go down to the port to find out when he's to come home.   (*Exit* L.   285

Geta. And I'll go look for Antipho, so that he may know how things are. But, halloa! I see him coming in the nick of time.

Enter ANTIPHO, R.

Ant. Well, Antipho, you and your panic have much to answer for. The idea of   290 your having made off and left your very life in other people's keeping! Did you suppose that others would attend to your business better than you would yourself? No, no; however it was about the rest, you certainly ought   295 to have taken care of that girl of yours at home, to prevent her from getting into trouble from her trust in you. All she has and all she hopes for, poor thing, hinge on you alone now.

Geta. And really, master, we too have   300 been finding fault with you behind your back for leaving us.

Ant. You're the very man I was looking for.

Geta. But for all that we haven't failed you a bit.   305

Ant. For heaven's sake, tell me how my fate and fortunes stand. My father hasn't got wind of anything?

Geta. Not yet.

Ant. Any prospect for the future?   310

Geta. I don't know.

Ant. Oh, dear!

Geta. But Phædria has never ceased his efforts for you.

Ant. That's nothing new in him.   315

Geta. Then Phormio, too, has shown the man of energy in this as in everything else.

Ant. Why, what has he done?

Geta. He's bluffed the angry old man with talk.   320

Ant. Oh, bravo, Phormio!

Geta. And I did what I could myself.

Ant. My dear Geta, I'm much obliged to you all.

Geta. The opening moves were made   325 as I have described; all's quiet up to the present time, and your father is going to wait until your uncle comes home.

Ant. Why for him?

Geta. He said he wanted to act in this   330 case according to his advice.

Ant. Oh, Geta, how I do dread to see my uncle come home safe and sound! For life and death, I find, depend on his single voice.

Geta. Here comes Phædria.   335

Ant. Where, pray?

Geta. There, coming out from his playground.

Enter PHÆDRIA *and* DORIO *from* DORIO'S *house*

Phæd. Do listen to me, Dorio, for pity's sake!   340

Dor. No, I won't.

Phæd. Just a minute.

Dor. Why won't you let me alone?

Phæd. But listen to what I have to say.

Dor. No; I'm tired of hearing the same   345 thing a thousand times.

Phæd. But now I'm going to say something which you will like to hear.

Dor. Speak out then. I'm listening.

Phæd. Can't I prevail on you to wait   350 just these three days? Why, where are you going now?

Dor. I wondered whether you had anything new to bring forward.

Ant. (*aside*). Oh, dear! I'm afraid this   355 slave-trader may be —

Geta (*aside*). Hoist with his own petar? I'm afraid so, too.

Phæd. You don't believe me yet, eh?

Dor. You're a mind reader!   360

Phæd. But if I give you my word?

Dor. Stuff!

Phæd. You'll have reason to call your kindness a fine investment.

Dor. Words, words.   365

Phæd. Believe me, you'll be glad you did it. It's true, by heaven!

Dor. Moonshine!

Phæd. Just try the experiment; it's not for long.   370

Dor. Always singing the same old song!

Phæd. I'll call you my kinsman, — father, — friend —

Dor. Nonsense!

Phæd. To think of your being so hard   375 and unbending that neither pity nor prayers can soften you!

Dor. And to think of your being so unreasonable and impudent, Phædria, as to lead me on with gilded promises, and so get my slave   380 girl for nothing!

Ant. (*aside*). What a pity!

Phæd. Oh, dear me! he's got the better of me.

Geta (*aside*). How they both do live up   385 to their own characters.

Phæd. Think of all this trouble happening to me at the very time when Antipho is full of another worry of his own.

Ant. (*coming forward*). Why, Phædria,   390 what is all this?

Phæd. Oh, Antipho, you luckiest of men!

Ant. I?

Phæd. Yes; for the girl you love is in your own keeping, and you've never had occa-   395 sion to struggle with such a difficulty as mine.

Ant. In my own keeping?   Not quite so; I'm "holding a wolf by the ears," as the old saying is.

Dor. That's just how I feel about him.   400

Ant. Halloa!   Act up to your rôle of slave-trader!   Has he been doing anything?

Phæd. He?   Been behaving like a barbarian; he's sold my Pamphila.

Ant. What!   Sold her?   405

Geta. You don't say so!   Sold her?

Phæd. Yes, he's sold her.

Dor. What an outrage, to sell a girl bought with my own money!

Phæd. And I can't prevail on him to   410 wait for me and to put off keeping his promise to the man for only three days, while I am getting the money promised me by my friends. If I don't pay it by that time, you needn't wait for me an hour longer.   415

Dor. Still dinning it into me?

Ant. It's no long time he asks for.   Come, consent.   He'll return the kindness with a hundred per cent interest.

Dor. Fine talk!   420

Ant. Will you let Pamphila be carried away from this town, and can you bear to see such a pair of lovers torn asunder?

Dor. Of course I can't any more than you.

Geta. Heaven send you what you de-   425 serve!

Dor. I have been putting up for some months against my will with your promising and not performing and your whimpering; but now I've got the opposite of all this.   I   430 have found a man who pays and doesn't cry about it.   Make way for your betters.

Ant. But, by heaven, if I remember rightly, there was a day set on which you were to pay him?   435

Phæd. There was.

Dor. I don't deny it, do I?

Ant. Has it come yet?

Dor. No, but today has come in ahead of it.

Ant. Aren't you ashamed to be such a   440 fraud?

Dor. Not a bit if it is for my gain.

Geta. Oh, you dunghill!

Phæd. Look here, Dorio, is this the right way to behave?   445

Dor. It's my way; if you like me, take me as you find me.

Ant. And you cheat him like this?

Dor. On the contrary, Antipho, it's he who is cheating me: for he knew all along that   450 I was the sort of man I am; but I supposed that he was different.   He's taken me in, but to him I am exactly what I was before.   But never mind; this is what I'll do.   A soldier man has promised to pay me the money tomorrow   455 morning; now, Phædria, if you bring it to me before he does, I'll follow my regular rule, that he is the better man who is first to come down with the cash.   Good-bye.   (*Exit*, R.

Phæd. What shall I do?   Where am I   460 to find the money for him in such a hurry, when I've less than nothing myself, poor fellow?   It was promised to me, if I could only have begged these three days out of him!

Ant. Shall we let him be made so un-   465 happy, Geta, after he has just helped me, as you tell me, in such a friendly way?   Why not try to return his kindness now when it's needed?

Geta. I know of course it's only the fair thing to do. 470

Ant. Come, then, you are the only man who can save him.

Geta. What can I do?

Ant. Find the money.

Geta. I want to; but where? Tell me 475 that.

Ant. My father's here.

Geta. I know he is, but what of it?

Ant. Oh, a word to the wise is quite enough.

Geta. That's it, hey? 480

Ant. That's it.

Geta. And a fine suggestion, too, by cracky! Get out, won't you? Isn't it triumph enough if I get off from your marriage with a whole skin without your telling me, when I'm 485 in the stocks already, to try to get hanged for his sake?

Ant. There's truth in what he says.

Phæd. What, Geta, am I a mere stranger to all of you? 490

Geta. I suppose not; but isn't it enough that the old man is so very angry with us all now, without our prodding him still more, so as to leave us no chance to cry off?

Phæd. And shall another man carry 495 her off to foreign parts before my very eyes? Ah me! Well, then, you two, talk to me and look your fill on me while you may, Antipho, and while I'm here.

Ant. What do you mean? What are 500 you going to do? Out with it.

Phæd. Wherever in the world she's carried, I'm resolved to follow, or to die in the attempt.

Geta. Heaven bless your efforts; go slow, though. 505

Ant. Do see whether you can help him in any way.

Geta. Any way? But what way?

Ant. Try to think of something, for mercy's sake. Don't let him do anything, great 510 or small, Geta, that shall make us sorry when it's too late.

Geta. I am trying. (*A pause.*) Well, he's all right, I think; but really I'm afraid there'll be trouble. 515

Ant. Never fear; we'll share it with you, good or bad.

Geta. Tell me; how much money do you need?

Phæd. Only thirty ducats. 520

Geta. Thirty? Whew! She's pretty dear, Phædria.

Phæd. No, not at all; she's cheap.

Geta. Well, well. I'll see that it's found, and give it to you. 525

Phæd. Oh, you are a trump!

Geta. Take yourself off.

Phæd. I need it at once.

Geta. You shall have it at once; but I need Phormio to help me in this business. 530

Ant. He's all ready; lay on him boldly any load you like; he'll carry it off. He's a friend indeed to a friend.

Geta. Let's hurry to him then.

Ant. You don't need any help from me, 535 do you?

Geta. No. You go home and comfort that poor girl, for I know she's in there now half dead with fright. What! waiting?

Ant. There's nothing I shall be so glad 540 to do. (*Exit to* DEMIPHO'S.

Phæd. How are you going to manage this affair?

Geta. I'll tell you on the way; only take yourself out of this. (*Exeunt,* R. 545

ACT IV

Enter DEMIPHO *and* CHREMES, L.

Dem. Well, Chremes, did you bring your daughter with you, what you went to Lemnos for?

Chre. No.

Dem. Why not? 5

Chre. Why, when her mother saw that I kept staying and staying on in Athens, and the girl was grown up and couldn't be neglected any longer, she set out, they told me, bag and baggage, to come and find me. 10

Dem. Then why, I want to know, did you stay there so long when you heard that?

Chre. 'Gad, I was kept there by illness.

Dem. How so? What illness?

Chre. What illness? Old age is illness 15 enough in itself. But the skipper who brought

them told me that they reached here safe and
sound.

Dem. Have you heard what has happened
to my son in my absence, Chremes?   20

Chre. That's just what makes me so undecided in my plans. For if I offer her in marriage to any outsider, I must tell the whole
story of how and by whom I came to be her
father. As for you, I knew that you were   25
as loyal to me as I am to myself. But if a
stranger seeks alliance with me, he will hold his
tongue just so long as we are close friends with
one another; but if he breaks with me, then he
will know more than he ought to know.   30
And I'm afraid my wife may get an inkling of
all this. If she does, the only thing left for me
to do is to give myself a shake and leave the
house; for I'm all I've got in the world.

Dem. I know that is so; that's what   35
makes me so anxious, and I shall never weary
of making every effort to perform my promise
for you.

Enter GETA, R.

Geta (*aside*). A shrewder fellow than Phormio I never saw in my born days. I went   40
to tell him that money was wanted and how it
was to be got. I had hardly told him half the
story when he understood it all, — began to
laugh, congratulated me, asked where the old
man was. Then he thanked heaven that   45
now he had a chance to show that he was as
much of a friend to Phædria as to Antipho.
I told the fellow to wait on 'Change, and said
that I would bring the old man there. Halloa!
here he is. Who's that on the other side?   50
Oh my! Phædria's father's come home. Lubber that I am, what was I afraid of? Was it
because I've got two to trick instead of one?
It's handier, I think, to have two strings to
your bow. I'll try to get the money from   55
the man I meant originally. If he gives it, all
right; if nothing can be done with him, then
I'll attack this newcomer.

Enter ANTIPHO, *unobserved*, R.

Ant. (*aside*). I'm expecting Geta back every
minute. Why, there's my uncle standing   60

with my father. Dear me! how I do fear what
father may be driven to by his coming!

Geta. I'll go up. Why! our good friend
Chremes! How do you do?

Chre. How do you do, Geta?   65

Geta. I'm delighted to see you back safe.

Chre. Dare say.

Geta. How goes it? Do you find many surprises here, as usual when a man comes home?

Chre. A good many.   70

Geta. To be sure. Have you heard what's
happened to Antipho?

Chre. The whole story.

Geta (*to* DEMIPHO). You told him, then?
What an outrageous thing, Chremes, to   75
be taken in in this way.

Chre. Just what I was telling him.

Geta. But on thinking it all over carefully, by
the powers I believe I've found a way out of it.

Chre. What, Geta?   80

Dem. What's your way out?

Geta. When I left you I happened to meet
Phormio.

Chre. Who's Phormio?

Dem. The man who was her —   85

Chre. I see.

Geta. I thought I had better find out his real
feelings, so I buttonholed the fellow. "Phormio," says I, "why not try to settle these matters that are between us with good feeling,   90
rather than with bad? My master is a gentleman, and he is shy of lawsuits. But, by the
powers, all his friends have just been advising
him with one voice to turn the girl out of
doors!"   95

Ant. (*aside*). Now what can he be starting
on, or how will he end this blessed day?

Geta. "But, you'll say, won't the law punish
him if he turns her out? He's looked into
that already, and I tell you, you'll have to   100
sweat for it, if you begin on a man like him.
He's that eloquent! But come, suppose he is
beaten: at the worst it's only money that's at
stake, and not his life." When I saw that
the fellow was shaken by this talk, "Here   105
we are by ourselves," says I; "come now, say
what you want in cash for yourself to release
my master from this lawsuit, she to make herself scarce, and you to give no trouble."

Ant. (*aside*). Can he be in his sober 110 senses?

Geta. "The fact is, I am certain that if you name anything that's at all fair and reasonable, there won't be three words between you. He's such a kind-hearted man." 115

Dem. Who gave you orders to say that?

Chre. No, no; he couldn't have better brought about just what we want.

Ant. (*aside*). I'm a dead man!

Dem. Go on and finish. 120

Geta. At first the fellow was wild.

Chre. Tell us what he asked.

Geta. Oh, a great deal too much.

Chre. How much? Speak.

Geta. If you'd offer a great talent — 125

Dem. A great big D, you mean! What! has the fellow no shame?

Geta. Just what I said to him. "Look here," said I; "suppose he were marrying off an only daughter of his own; he hasn't 130 gained much by not having one himself if somebody else's turns up for him to portion." Well, to be brief, and omitting all his silly talk, this was finally his last word: "From the very first," says he, "I have wanted to marry 135 my old friend's daughter myself, as was proper; for I saw how disagreeable it would be for her, a poor girl, married only to be a rich man's slave. But, to tell you the honest truth, I needed a wife who should bring me a 140 little something to pay off what I owe; yes, and even after all that's passed, if Demipho is willing to give as much as I am getting with the girl to whom I am engaged, there's nobody in the world whom I should like better for a wife." 145

Ant. (*aside*). I can't make out whether he's acting from stupidity or mischief, from design or off his guard.

Dem. But suppose he owes body and soul?

Geta. "My farm," said he, "is mort- 150 gaged for ten ducats."

Dem. Well, well; let him marry her. I'll pay it.

Geta. "Then my house for another ten."

Dem. Whew! it's too much! 155

Chre. Don't make a row. You can get those ten of me.

Geta. "Then there's a lady's maid to be bought for my wife; then I need a little more furniture, and some cash to spend on the 160 wedding. Put down ten more for this," says he.

Dem. Then let him bring hundreds and hundreds of lawsuits against me. I won't give him a penny. What! that dirty fellow to get 165 the laugh on me again?

Chre. Pray be quiet. I'll pay it myself. All you've got to do is to make your son marry the girl we wish.

Ant. (*aside*). Oh, dear me! you've 170 been the death of me, Geta, with your tricks.

Chre. She is turned out for my sake, and so it's fair for me to be the loser.

Geta. "Let me know as soon as you 175 can," says he, "if they are going to give her to me, so that I may get rid of this other girl, and not be kept in doubt; for her people have agreed to pay me the dowry down at once." 180

Chre. Let him have the money at once, break the engagement with them, and marry her.

Dem. Yes, and may bad luck go with her.

Chre. Fortunately, I have just brought 185 the money with me now, the rents from my wife's estates in Lemnos. I'll take it out of that, and tell my wife that you needed it.

(*Exeunt* DEMIPHO *and* CHREMES *to* CHREMES'S.

Ant. (*coming forward*). Geta!

Geta. Halloa! 190

Ant. What have you done?

Geta. Cleaned the old gentlemen out of their cash.

Ant. Is that all?

Geta. By the powers, I don't know; it 195 was all I was told to do.

Ant. What, you rogue! I ask you one thing, and you answer another?

Geta. Why, what are you talking about?

Ant. What am I talking about? Here 200 I am actually reduced to the rope, and it's all your doing? May all the gods and goddesses up above and down below make the worst sort of an example of you! Well, well; if you want to succeed in a thing, leave it to this fel- 205 low, who can bring you out of smooth sailing straight on to a rock! Why, what could have been worse than to lay your finger on this sore and to mention my wife? Here's my father made to hope that he can cast her off. 210 Come now, what follows? Suppose Phormio gets the dowry and has to marry her, what then?

Geta. But he won't marry her.

Ant. Oh, no! But when they ask the 215 money back, then of course he'll prefer to go to jail for my sake.

Geta. There isn't any story in the world, Antipho, that can't be spoiled in the telling. Now you're leaving out all the good side 220 and telling only the bad. Now, then, hear the other side. Suppose now he gets the money: he will have to marry her, as you say; I admit that; — but they'll give him a little time anyhow to get ready for the wedding, to send 225 out the invitations, and to offer sacrifice. Meanwhile Phædria's friends will give him the money which they have promised, and Phormio will pay back the dowry out of that.

Ant. On what ground? What can he 230 say?

Geta. What a question! "Since my engagement I've had so many bad omens. A strange black dog trotted straight into my front hall; a snake fell down from the roof 235 through the rain hole; a hen has crowed; the clairvoyant forbade it, the soothsayer won't let me. Besides, to take up anything new before the winter sets in," — that's the strongest reason in the world. That's the way it 240 will be.

Ant. I only hope it may.

Geta. May? It shall. Look to me for that. There's your father coming out. Go tell Phædria that we've got the money. 245
(*Exit* ANTIPHO, R.

Enter DEMIPHO *and* CHREMES, *from* CHREMES'S

Dem. Do be quiet, I say. I'll take care he doesn't play me any trick. I'll never let the money go from me helter-skelter without having witnesses. I'll have it understood to whom I am giving it and why I give it. 250

Geta (*aside*). How cautious he is, where he hasn't any call to be.

Chre. That's just what you ought to do; but make haste, while he's still in the mood for it. If that other girl is more pressing, perhaps 255 he'll leave us in the lurch.

Geta (*aside*). You've hit the very point.

Dem. (*to* GETA). Take me to him, then.

Geta. I'm ready.

Chre. When you have attended to that, 260 go over to my wife's to get her to call on the girl before she goes away. Let her tell the girl, to prevent her from being angry, that we are marrying her to Phormio, and that he is a better match for her, because she knows 265 him better; and that we have done our duty, too, and given her as large a dowry as he asked for.

Dem. What the plague does that matter to you? 270

Chre. A good deal, Demipho. It's not enough for you to do your duty if the world doesn't approve of what you've done. I want this to take place of her own free will, so that she shan't be saying that we drove her out. 275

Dem. Well, I can bring all that about myself.

Chre. But a woman's the best hand to deal with a woman.

Dem. I'll ask her, then.
(*Exeunt* DEMIPHO *and* GETA, R.

Chre. I wonder now where I can find 280 those women?

Enter SOPHRONA *from the house of*
DEMIPHO

Soph. What shall I do? Where am I to find a friend in my distress? Whom shall I consult? Where get help? I'm afraid my mistress may come to grief from following my 285 advice; the young man's father takes all this so hard, I hear.

Chre. (*aside*). Why, who's this old woman that's come out of my brother's house so excited? 290

Soph. It was our poverty that drove me to it, though I knew such a marriage was a shaky thing, to provide that at least she might be sure of a living in the mean time.

Chre. (*aside*). Upon my word, unless 295 my mind's going or my eyesight's bad, that's my own daughter's nurse that I see there.

Soph. And we can't track out —

Chre. (*aside*). What shall I do?

Soph. Her father —   300

Chre. (*aside*). Shall I go and speak to her, or stay where I am until I know better what she is saying?

Soph. If only I could find him, there's nothing I should be afraid of.   305

Chre. It's the very woman. I'll speak to her.

Soph. Who's this talking here?

Chre. Sophrona!

Soph. Calling me by name, too.   310

Chre. Look at me.

Soph. Oh, good gracious! can this be Stilpo?

Chre. No!

Soph. What? No?

Chre. Come over here a little, away 315 from that door, Sophrona, please, and don't call me by that name any more.

Soph. Why not? for mercy's sake, aren't you the man you always said you were?

Chre. Hush!   320

Soph. What is there in this door that you're afraid of?

Chre. I've got a savage wife caged up in there. As for that name, it was a wrong one which I took in those days, so that you 325 shouldn't let the truth leak out without meaning to, and my wife find it out some way or other.

Soph. Law me, that's just why we poor women have never been able to find you. 330

Chre. But tell me, what have you to do with the people whose house you just came out from? Where are the ladies?

Soph. Oh, dear me!

Chre. Hey? What's the matter? Aren't 335 they alive?

Soph. Your daughter is; but her mother, poor thing, died of grief.

Chre. Too bad!

Soph. And so I, being only a lone lorn 340 old woman, whom nobody knew, did my best and got the girl married to the young gentleman who lives in here.

Chre. To Antipho?

Soph. Certainly; the very man.   345

Chre. What! has he got two wives?

Soph. For pity's sake, no; she's the only one he has.

Chre. What about the other who is called his relative?   350

Soph. Why, it's she, of course.

Chre. What's that you say?

Soph. It was a put-up job, — the only way by which her lover might get her without a dowry.   355

Chre. Heaven help us! how often things do turn out by haphazard which you'd scarcely dare to wish for! Here I've come home and found my daughter married to the very man I wanted and just as I wanted it! The 360 very thing that we were both trying with all our might to bring about, he has taken the greatest trouble to do all by himself without any trouble of ours.

Soph. Well now, just see what's to be 365 done next. The young man's father has arrived, and they say that he is bitterly opposed to it.

Chre. There's no danger at all. But, by heaven and earth, don't let anybody find 370 out that she is my daughter.

Soph. Nobody shall from me.

Chre. Follow me; you shall hear the rest inside.   (*Exeunt to* DEMIPHO's.

ACT V

Enter DEMIPHO *and* GETA, R.

Dem. It's all our own fault that people find it pays them to be rogues; it's because we are too anxious to be called kind and generous. "Enough is as good as a feast," says the proverb. Wasn't it enough to be injured by 5 him that we must actually go and throw him a sop in the way of money, to give him something to live on until he can work up some other outrage?

Geta. Perfectly true.   10

Dem. Nowadays people who make right wrong get rewarded.

Geta. True enough.

Dem. So it proves that we've made a stupid mess of it with him!   15

Geta. Well, if only we get out of it by his marrying her —

Dem. Why, is there any question about that?

Geta. I swear, I don't know but that   20 he may change his mind, considering the kind of fellow he is.

Dem. Bless me! What! Change his mind?

Geta. I don't know about it. I'm only saying "supposing."   25

Dem. That's what I'll do, what my brother advised: I'll bring his wife here to talk with that girl. Geta, you go ahead and tell her that Nausistrata is coming.

(*Exit to* CHREMES'S.

Geta. Phædria's money is found and   30 all's quiet with the lawsuit. We've looked out that the bride shan't be sent off for the present. Now, what next? What's to be done? Sticking in the same rut still? Robbing Peter to pay Paul, Geta? You've put off the evil   35 day for now, but there's a crop of whippings growing if you don't look out ahead. I'll go home and tell Phanium that she mustn't be afraid of Phormio or of Nausistrata's talk.

(*Exit to* DEMIPHO'S.

Enter DEMIPHO *and* NAUSISTRATA *from* CHREMES'S

Dem. Come, then, Nausistrata, with   40 your usual good nature make her feel kindly towards us, so that she may do of her own accord what must be done.

Naus. I will.

Dem. You'll be aiding me now with   45 your good offices, just as you helped me a while ago with your purse.

Naus. You're quite welcome; and upon my word, it's my husband's fault that I can do less than I might well do.   50

Dem. Why, how is that?

Naus. Because he takes wretched care of my father's honest savings; he used regularly to get two silver talents [1] from those estates.

[1] The silver talent of ancient Athens was worth 6000 drachmas or about $1450.

How much better one man is than an-   55 other!

Dem. Two talents, do you say?

Naus. Yes, two talents, and when prices were much lower than now.

Dem. Whew!   60

Naus. What do you think of that?

Dem. Oh, of course —

Naus. I wish I'd been born a man. I'd soon show you —

Dem. Oh yes, I'm sure.   65

Naus. The way —

Dem. Pray, do save yourself up for her, lest she may wear you out; she's young, you know.

Naus. I'll do as you tell me. But there's my husband coming out of your house.   70

Enter CHREMES

Chre. Ha! Demipho, has the money been paid him yet?

Dem. I saw to it at once.

Chre. I wish it hadn't been. (*Aside*) Oh, dear! there's my wife. I had almost said   75 too much.

Dem. What makes you wish it hadn't, Chremes?

Chre. No matter now.

Dem. What have you been about?   80 Have you told her why we are bringing Nausistrata?

Chre. I've attended to it.

Dem. Well, what does she say?

Chre. She's not to be taken away.   85

Dem. Why isn't she?

Chre. Because they're heart to heart.

Dem. What's that to us?

Chre. A good deal. Besides I have found out that she really is related to us.   90

Dem. What? You're raving.

Chre. You'll find it's so. I'm not speaking at random. I've recollected.

Dem. Are you in your right mind?

Naus. Oh, for mercy's sake! take care   95 not to hurt a relative.

Dem. She isn't one.

Chre. Don't say that. Her father went by another name; that's how you made a mistake.   100

Dem. Didn't she know who her father was?

Chre. Oh, yes.

Dem. What made her call him something else?

Chre. Won't you ever stop insisting, 105 and take in what I mean?

Dem. But if you don't tell me anything?

Chre. (*aside to* DEMIPHO). You'll ruin me!

Naus. I wonder what it all is.

Dem. By heaven, I'm sure I don't 110 know.

Chre. Do you want to know the truth? Then, so help me God, there isn't a man in the world nearer of kin to her than you and I.

Dem. Great heavens! Let's go straight 115 to her. If it's so, I want us all to know it alike — or if it isn't so.

Chre. Oh, dear!

Dem. What's the matter?

Chre. To think of your trusting me so 120 little!

Dem. You want me to believe it, then? You want me to consider it settled? Very well, have it so. But then, what's to be done with the other girl, *our friend's* daughter? 125

Chre. Oh, that's all right.

Dem. Shall we drop her, then?

Chre. Why not?

Dem. And this one is to stay?

Chre. Yes. 130

Dem. You can go, then, Nausistrata.

Naus. Good gracious, I think it is better for all concerned that she should stay, than to have it as you first intended; for she seemed to me a very lady-like thing when I saw her. 135

(*Exit* NAUSISTRATA *to* CHREMES'S.

Dem. Now, what is the meaning of this business?

Chre. Has she shut the door yet?

Dem. Yes.

Chre. O Lord! heaven does smile on us! 140 I've found my daughter married to your son!

Dem. Bless me! how can that be?

Chre. This place isn't safe enough to tell the story in.

Dem. Well, come indoors, then. 145

Chre. Look here, I don't want our sons to get an inkling of this. (*Exeunt to* DEMIPHO'S.

Enter ANTIPHO, R.

Ant. However things are going with me, I'm glad that my cousin has succeeded in getting what he wants. What a nice thing it is 150 to conceive such desires that you can satisfy them by simple means when things go wrong! No sooner has he got the money than he's freed from anxiety; but here I am, unable to get out of these troubles by any means whatever, 155 but what I'm in terror if it's kept quiet, and disgraced if it comes out. I shouldn't be coming home now if there wasn't some hope of my having her. But where can I find Geta?

Enter PHORMIO, R.

Phor. (*aside*). I've received the money 160 and handed it over to the trader. I've taken away the girl and arranged that Phædria may have her for his own; she's been emancipated. Now there's only one thing left over for me to see to, and that is to get time from the 165 old gentlemen to make a spree of it. I propose to take some days off.

Ant. Why, there's Phormio. Say!

Phor. Say what?

Ant. What's Phædria going to do now? 170 How does he propose to spend his honeymoon?

Phor. He's going to take his turn at playing your part.

Ant. What part is that?

Phor. To run away from his father. 175 And he requests you in return to play his and plead his cause for him. The fact is, he is going to my house for a little spree. I shall tell the old gentlemen that I am going down to Sunium to the fair, to buy that lady's 180 maid that Geta talked about; then they won't think I'm squandering their money when they don't see me here. But there's a noise at your front door.

Ant. See who is coming out. 185

Phor. It's Geta.

Enter GETA *from* DEMIPHO'S

Geta. Oh Fortune! oh Lucky Fortune! With what blessings and how suddenly have

you loaded my master Antipho with your
kindness today!   190

Ant. (*aside*). Why, what can he mean?

Geta. And unloaded all us friends of his of
fear! But here I am dilly-dallying instead of
loading up my shoulder with my cloak and
hurrying off to find him, so that he may   195
learn all that's happened.

Ant. (*aside to* PHORMIO). You can't make
out what he is talking about, can you?

Phor. (*aside*). Nor you either?

Ant. (*aside*). Not a bit.   200

Phor. (*aside*). No more can I.

Geta. I'll start and go to the slave-trader's;
they're there now.

Ant. Halloa, Geta!

Geta. There you are! Always the way!   205
Called back just when you have started running.

Ant. Geta!

Geta. Keeping it up, begad! Well, you
shan't ever beat me with your insolence.   210

Ant. Wait, won't you?

Geta. Oh, go get yourself thrashed!

Ant. That's just what will happen to you in
a minute if you don't stop, you knave!

Geta (*aside*). He must know me pretty   215
well — to threaten me with a thrashing. Why,
is it the man I am after or not? It is the very
man. Up to him on the spot.

Ant. What's the matter?

Geta. Oh you most blessed man in all the   220
world! I tell you, Antipho, there's no denying
that you're the only man whom heaven loves.

Ant. I should like to be; but I should like to
have you tell me why I'm to think so.

Geta. Is it enough if I set you all drip-   225
ping down with joy?

Ant. You'll be the death of me.

Phor. Away with your promises and out
with your news!

Geta. What! you here too, Phormio?   230

Phor. Yes, but why don't you go ahead?

Geta. Well, then, listen. After we had paid
you the money on 'Change, we started straight
home; then master sent me over to see your
wife.   235

Ant. What for?

Geta. I'll leave that out; it's nothing to do

with the case, Antipho. Just as I was entering
my lady's chamber, Mida, her slave boy, ran
up to me, caught me by the cloak behind   240
and pulled me back. I looked round and
asked him what he was stopping me for. He
said that there was no admission to his mistress. "Sophrona has just brought in the old
man's brother Chremes and he's in there   245
now with the ladies," says he. When I heard
that, I went up softly on tiptoe, stood still, held
my breath and put my ear against the door;
and I began to listen, trying to catch their
talk so fashion.   250

Phor. Bravo, Geta!

Geta. Whereupon I heard a most beautiful
piece of business; so much so that by cracky,
I nearly shouted for joy.

Ant. What was it?   255

Geta. Well, what do you think?

Ant. I don't know.

Geta. But it's most marvelous! Your uncle
has proved to be your wife Phanium's father.

Ant. What's that you say?   260

Geta. He lived with her mother at Lemnos
unbeknownst.

Phor. You're dreaming! As if the girl
wouldn't know her own father!

Geta. Oh well, depend upon it, Phor-   265
mio, there's some reason for that; but do you
think that I, outside of the door, could understand everything that went on between them
inside?

Ant. Yes, and I have had an inkling   270
of this story, too.

Geta. Yes, and I'll give you something to
make you believe still more. After a while
your uncle came out here, and soon after that
he went in again with your father. They   275
both said that you were allowed to keep her.
Finally I was sent to look you up and bring you
home.

Ant. Why don't you drag me off then?
What are you waiting for?   280

Geta. I'll do it mighty quick.

Ant. Good-bye, my dear Phormio.

Phor. Good-bye, Antipho. God bless me,
this is a good thing. I'm glad of it.

(*Exeunt* ANTIPHO *and* GETA *to* DEMI-
PHO'S.

Phor. What an unexpected piece of 285 good luck for these boys! And now I have a fine chance to take the old gentlemen in, and to rid Phædria of his worry about the money, so that he shan't have to beg it of any of his fellows. For this very same money, 290 given already, shall be his outright in spite of all their opposition. The facts have shown me how to force them to it. I must now put on a new air and change my expression. I'll withdraw into this alley close by 295 and show myself to them from there when they come out. I shan't go to the fair as I pretended. (*Withdraws*, R.

Enter DEMIPHO *and* CHREMES *from* DEMIPHO'S

Dem. I am grateful and thankful to the gods, brother, and they deserve it, since 300 all this has turned out so well for us today.

Chre. Isn't she a thorough lady though, as I told you?

Dem. Through and through. We must now find Phormio as soon as possible and get 305 our thirty ducats away from him before he makes ducks and drakes of them.

Phor. (*coming forward*). I'll just see whether Demipho is at home, so as to —

Dem. Ah, we were just going to see 310 you, Phormio.

Phor. On the same old errand, perhaps?

Dem. Yes, to be sure.

Phor. I supposed so. But what made you think it necessary to come? 315

Dem. Oh pooh!

Phor. Did you think I wouldn't do what I had once undertaken? See here, however poor I may be, there's one thing I've always been particular about, and that is to keep my 320 word. And so I came to tell you this, Demipho, that I'm all ready. Give me my wife whenever you wish. I have put off all my other business, and properly enough, too, when I saw how very bent you were upon 325 it.

Dem. But Chremes here has persuaded me not to give her to you. "Why, what will Mrs. Grundy say," says he, "if you do that? Awhile

ago, when you could have done it de- 330 cently, you didn't release her. To turn her out now, divorced, is an outrage." In fact, his arguments were all pretty much the same that you urged against me yourself awhile ago face to face. 335

Phor. You're making game of me in a pretty high and mighty way.

Dem. How's that?

Phor. How's that? Why, because I shan't be able to marry that other girl now. For 340 how could I have the face to go back to the woman after slighting her?

Chre. (*aside to* DEMIPHO). "Besides I see that Antipho doesn't want to let her leave him" — say that. 345

Dem. Besides I see that my son doesn't at all want to let the woman leave him. So come over to the bank, please, and have that money transferred to me again, Phormio.

Phor. What! after I have already paid 350 it round among my different creditors?

Dem. What's to be done then?

Phor. If you will give me the lady as you promised, I will marry her; but if you really want her to stay with you, Demipho, 355 why the dowry must stay with me. It isn't fair that I should be the loser through the means of you two; for it was out of regard for you that I broke off with the other lady who was to bring me just as large a dowry. 360

Dem. You be hanged with your high-toned talk, you vagabond! Do you suppose that we don't know you and your doings?

Phor. You're making me angry.

Dem. So you'd marry her, would you, 365 if we gave her to you?

Phor. Try it on.

Dem. Yes, so that my son might live with her in your house; that was your scheme.

Phor. What are you talking about, 370 pray?

Dem. Come, hand over my money.

Phor. Not much; you hand over my wife.

Dem. Walk straight into court then.

Phor. Look here, if you are going to 375 keep on being troublesome —

Dem. What are you going to do about it?

Phor. I? Perhaps you two think that I'm

the protector of undowried women only; but
I'm in the habit of protecting dowried　380
ones too.

Chre. What's that to us?

Phor. Oh, nothing.　But I knew a woman
round here whose husband married —

Chre. Ha!　385

Dem. What's the matter?

Phor. Another wife at Lemnos —

Chre. I'm done for!

Phor. By whom he had a daughter; is bringing her up, too, on the sly.　390

Chre. I'm as good as buried.

Phor. I'm just going to tell her all about it.

Chre. For heaven's sake, don't!

Phor. Oh, you were the man, were you?

Dem. What game he's making of us!　395

Chre. We let you off scot free.

Phor. Oh, bosh!

Chre. Well, what would you have?　We let
you off with the money that you've got.

Phor. Oh, yes!　Why the deuce are　400
you making game of me with your silly, childish shilly-shallying?　"I won't, I will, and I
will, I won't," — one after the other; "take it
— give it back" — say a thing and unsay it;
make a bargain one minute and break it　405
off the next.

Chre. (*aside*).　How or where did he ever
come to find this out?

Dem. (*aside*).　I don't know; but I'm sure I
didn't tell anybody.　410

Chre. (*aside*).　A perfect miracle, as I hope to
live!

Phor. (*aside*).　I've put a spoke in his
wheel.

Dem. See here, is this rascal going to　415
rob us of all this money and laugh in our very
faces?　By heaven, I'll die the death first!
(*Aside to* CHREMES)　Make ready to be bold
and have your wits about you.　You see your
little peccadillo has got out and you can't　420
hide it from your wife any longer.　The easiest
way to get it forgiven, Chremes, is for us to tell
her ourselves what she is sure to hear from
others.　And then we shall be able to revenge
ourselves at our ease upon this dirty　425
fellow.

Phor. (*aside*).　My goodness!　I'm in a fix

if I don't look out for myself.　They are
making at me with the air of prize-fighters.

Chre. (*aside*).　But I'm afraid we can't　430
make her forgive me.

Dem. (*aside*).　Courage, Chremes!　I'll bring
you back into her good graces, on the strength
of this, that the woman by whom you had this
child is out of the way.　435

Phor. That's the way you deal with me, is
it?　A cunning attack enough!　It's not for
his good that you've stirred me up, Demipho, by heaven!　Aha! when you've been
carrying on abroad after your own sweet　440
will without any regard for yonder noble lady,
but on the contrary, insulting her in this
strange fashion, would you come now with
prayers to wash away your sin?　Why, I'll set
her so afire against you with this story　445
that you shan't put her out though you actually dissolve away in tears.

Dem. Was ever a man so impudent!　Why
doesn't the government transport the knave
to some desert island?　450

Chre. I'm reduced to such a state that I
don't know what to do with him.

Dem. I do, then.　Let's go to law.

Phor. To law?　To *her*, if you don't
mind.　455

Chre. Follow him up; hold on to him while I
call the slaves out.

Dem. I can't all by myself; run and help
me.

Phor. Here's one suit for assault and　460
battery against you!

Dem. Go to law, then!

Phor. And another for you, Chremes.

Chre. Hurry him off!

Phor. That's it, hey?　Why, then, I　465
must use my voice — Nausistrata!　Come out
here!

Chre. Stop his dirty mouth; just see how
strong he is.

Phor. I say, Nausistrata!　470

Dem. Hold your tongue, won't you?

Phor. Hold my tongue?

Dem. If he doesn't come along, hit him in
the belly with your fists.

Phor. Gouge out an eye if you like;　475
but I shall soon have a fine revenge.

Enter NAUSISTRATA *from* CHREMES'S

Naus. Who's calling me? Why, husband, what's this disturbance about, for mercy's sake?

Phor. Halloa! what's struck you so 480 dumb now?

Naus. Who is this fellow? Won't you answer me?

Phor. He answer you! When by heaven he doesn't know who he is himself! 485

Chre. Don't believe anything the fellow says.

Phor. Go and touch him; if he's not cold all over, you may murder me.

Chre. It's nothing at all. 490

Naus. Well, then, what is he talking about?

Phor. You shall soon find out — just listen.

Chre. Are you going to believe him?

Naus. For mercy's sake, what should I believe when he hasn't said anything? 495

Phor. The poor wretch is raving mad with fear.

Naus. Upon my word, it's not for nothing that you are so frightened.

Chre. I frightened? 500

Phor. All right, then. As you're afraid of nothing, and as what I say is nothing, just tell her yourself.

Dem. What! tell it for you, you scoundrel?

Phor. Oho you! you've done finely for 505 your brother, of course!

Naus. Won't you tell me, husband?

Chre. But —

Naus. But what?

Chre. There's no need of telling. 510

Phor. Not for you of course, but she ought to know. In Lemnos —

Naus. Ah! what's that you say?

Chre. Won't you hold your tongue?

Phor. Behind your back — 515

Chre. Oh dear me!

Phor. He married another wife.

Naus. God forbid, my dear man!

Phor. It's true.

Naus. Alas! I'm undone! 520

Phor. And by her he's already had one daughter, too, without your dreaming of it.

Chre. What shall I do?

Naus. Oh heavens! what a wicked, shameful thing! 525

Phor. Do? You're done for!

Naus. Was there ever anything more infamous! When it comes to their wives, they're old enough forsooth! Demipho, I appeal to you, for I am sick of talking to this 530 creature. This was the meaning, was it, of all those constant trips and long stays at Lemnos? This was the low prices that reduced our rents there?

Dem. For my part, Nausistrata, I 535 don't say that he doesn't deserve to be blamed in this matter, but it is a fault that may be pardoned.

Phor. Might as well talk to the dead.

Dem. The fact is, it was not that he 540 didn't care for you or that he disliked you. His affair with this woman was about fifteen years ago, once when he had drunk too much, and that was how this girl came to be born; he never went near the woman after- 545 wards; she is dead and out of the way; that was the only stumbling-block left. And so I beg of you that you will bear this patiently, as you act in other things.

Naus. Patiently — why should I? I 550 certainly do want to have an end of it all, I'm so wretched; but how could I expect that? Can I count on his sinning less as he grows older? He was an old man even then, if it's old age that makes men 555 virtuous. Do my own looks or my years make me more attractive now than I was then, Demipho? Come, what can you offer to make me expect or trust that this won't happen again? 560

Phor. All who desire to attend the funeral of Chremes, now's the time! That's the way I'll give it to 'em! Now come on, whoever wants to stir up Phormio! I'll ruin him as completely as I have Chremes. 565

Dem. Don't be so angry; calm yourself, Nausistrata.

Phor. Yes, yes, let him back into your good graces; he's been punished enough to satisfy me. And she's got something to din into 570 his ears just as long as he lives.

Naus. I deserved it, then, I suppose. Why

should I, at this late day, Demipho, rehearse what a wife I've been to him?

Dem. I know it all as well as you do.   575

Naus. Do you think I've deserved this treatment?

Dem. Never in the world. But what's done cannot be undone by reproaches. Do forgive him. He begs pardon, — he owns up, —   580 he offers to atone. What more can you want?

Phor. (*aside*). Really now, before she pardons him I must look out for myself and Phædria. (*Aloud*) See here, Nausistrata, just listen to me before you answer him off-   585 hand.

Naus. What is it?

Phor. I got thirty ducats out of him by a trick, and gave them to your son. He bought his mistress with them from her owner.   590

Chre. Hey! what's that you say?

Naus. Do you think it's so very bad for a young fellow like your son to have one mistress, when here you are yourself with two wives? Have you no sense of shame?   595 How can you have the face to scold him for it? Answer me that.

Dem. He shall do everything you wish.

Naus. Well, to let you know my decision, I neither pardon him nor promise anything   600 nor make any answer at all, before seeing my son. I leave the whole thing to his judgment. I'll do whatever he tells me.

Phor. You are a wise woman, Nausistrata.

Naus. Does that satisfy you?   605

Dem. Certainly.

Chre. (*aside*). Upon my word, I get out of it pretty finely, and better than I expected.

Naus. (*to* Phormio). Please to tell me your name.   610

Phor. Phormio, a friend of your house, by heaven, and particularly of your son Phædria.

Naus. Well, Phormio, after this I'll do and say for you whatever you like as well as I can, upon my word I will.   615

Phor. That's very kind of you.

Naus. I'm sure you have deserved it.

Phor. Do you want to begin by giving me a pleasure today, Nausistrata, and to make your husband's eyes ache at the same time?   620

Naus. Yes.

Phor. Then invite me to dinner.

Naus. Certainly, I invite you.

Dem. Let us go in, then.

Naus. Well, but where is Phædria, who   625 is to decide between us?

Phor. I'll bring him here.

Cantor.[1] Farewell, and give us your applause.

(*Exeunt,* Phormio, R., *the others to* Chremes's.

[1] The *cantor* was the person who sang the lyrical monologues. It was customary for him to come forward at the close of the performance and ask, on behalf of the actors, for the audience's applause.

INTRODUCTION TO

The Second Shepherds' Play

The Religious Drama of Medieval Europe:
The Miracle Play in England

THE RELIGIOUS DRAMA OF MEDIEVAL EUROPE

WITH the break-up of the corrupted Roman stage in the sixth century drama virtually disappeared from western Europe for several hundred years. These were, in truth, the Dark Ages of theatrical art. Before the end of the ninth century, however, the Christian Church, which had actively encouraged the death of the ancient drama, provided the beginnings of a new dramatic tradition.

This new drama of medieval Europe, like that of Attica fifteen hundred years previous, sprang from religious devotion and ceremony. The Christian clergy desired to deepen the faith of the common people who could not fully appreciate the Latin ritual of the church services. Therefore, first at the Easter festival and later at Christmas, they introduced into the services a simple acting out of the appropriate episodes from the life of Christ: on Easter, the coming of the three Marys to the sepulcher; and, on Christmas, the search for the Holy Child by the three shepherds. These dramatized scenes (termed "liturgical plays" because they were inserted into the service or liturgy) were given in the chancel of the church by the priests, who in part chanted, and in part spoke the Latin dialogue composed chiefly of scriptural passages.

The congregations of unlettered folk welcomed the little plays in the midst of the long Mass. Popular delight soon led to the expansion of the Easter and Christmas dramas. At Easter, Mary Magdalene lingered behind the other Marys on their departure from the tomb and had a meeting with Christ in the guise of a gardener. Then, as a later addition, Peter and John made their appearance, one racing the other to the sepulcher. At Christmas a similar development took place. After the scene of the shepherds the three Magi were exhibited in gorgeous array, bringing expensive gifts to the cradle of the Christ-child. Subsequently, the Magi were shown visiting Herod on their way to Bethlehem. He fell into a rage and hurled the Book of the Prophets to the ground when he heard the Magi's news of the birth of the King of Kings.

In course of time liturgical plays were acted at other services than those of Christmas and Easter. They began to depict not only the life of Christ, but further stories from the Bible and from the lives of the Christian saints. Legends of St. Nicholas, for example, inspired numerous playlets for his feast day, December 6th. The dialogue in this liturgical drama gradually changed from Latin to the vernacular. With that shift the last hindrance to complete popular enjoyment was removed.

The dramatizations at Christmas and Easter especially grew into a series of scenes so extensive that in many churches they occupied the choir, the center of the nave, and the transepts.   The congregations were crowded into the aisles and forced to relocate themselves for each scene.   The productions eventually became too elaborate to maintain as adjuncts to the regular order of worship.   The throngs of spectators increased until they could be no longer handled properly within the church edifices.

The inevitable consequence of these conditions was that the ecclesiastical authorities had to separate the dramatic performances from the church services, and move the plays outdoors.   The cathedral porch and steps, or the churchyard, served as the stage. Laymen began to take part alongside the clergy.   The days of acting the "miracle plays," as the religious plays now were called, came to be community holidays.   Farmers and villagers traveled into the larger villages and towns as spectators.   Merrymaking of all sorts accompanied the playgoing.   For the people in general the miracle plays rapidly turned into secular shows.

The Church realized by this time that the drama which it had nurtured for purposes of religious instruction had developed into a great agency of public amusement.   Hence it quickly relinquished the rôle of guardian to secular auspices.   In the thirteenth century the miracle plays as a popular lay institution spread over all western Europe.   During the three succeeding centuries they formed an essential part of the life and entertainment of medieval Italy, Spain, France, Germany, and England.

THE MIRACLE PLAY IN ENGLAND

The miracle plays under secular sponsorship flourished in England as they did nowhere else.   The rich development there resulted from the enthusiastic support of the craft guilds in the towns.   The town guilds were powerful trade unions which took over the patronage of religious drama for reasons of business as well as of pleasure.   Like modern chambers of commerce they saw in the production of plays an opportunity to advertise themselves and to boost local trade.

At York, Chester, Coventry, and other centers, the guilds joined together to institute a series or cycle of plays which presented the more important stories of the Old and New Testaments from the Creation to the Last Judgment.   The cycles of the various towns differed greatly in length.   That of York, the most elaborate known, ultimately consisted of over fifty plays; that of Chester, one of the oldest, contained but twenty-five. The playwrights continued to be members of the clergy, since in most communities they constituted the only persons qualified.   The Church also provided an ideal holiday season for the outdoor cycle performances.   Late in the thirteenth century it established the great festival in honor of the Eucharist, Corpus Christi Day, which fell either toward the end of May or early in June.   Here at the height of the English spring the country folk could combine a holy pilgrimage and a vacation trip to town.

The guild production of the miracle play cycles became highly organized.   In the larger towns the town corporation finally assumed supervision of the guilds' activities in connection with the dramatic festivals.   The York corporation in the fifteenth century took care of play scripts from one year to the next, conducted trials for the aspiring actors under the chairmanship of the mayor, and issued proclamations by official crier to announce its Corpus Christi plays.   Both at York and elsewhere each play in the cycle was assigned to a single guild or a pair, depending on the size of the guilds.   A certain appropriateness of craft to cycle episode usually determined the assignments.   Thus the shipwrights of York played the building of Noah's ark; the goldsmiths, the adoration of gift-bearing Magi. At Chester the water carriers represented the Deluge, while in Coventry the tailors and shearmen acted the episodes of the nativity and the slaughter of the innocents.

The guild or guilds responsible for a particular play had to furnish everything necessary for its production, from scripts to actors, and to underwrite all expenses by a levy on the members. In 1490 the Smiths of Coventry expended for their play on the trial and crucifixion of Christ a total of sixty-seven shillings, perhaps about seventy-five dollars at present values. Costuming of a rather lavish kind formed a large item of expense. At Coventry in 1501, Mary, the mother of Jesus, wore a new crown of gold and silver which cost forty-three shillings (fifty dollars, say). Stage properties seem to have been similarly costly on occasion. Approximately five dollars was paid for the making of a gorgeous lily which the angel Gabriel carried in a Coventry play of 1540. Stage effects were often attempted with like elaborateness. In *The Salutation and Conception* of the "N town" cycle there occurs this complicated spectacle: "the Holy Ghost descends with three beams [of light] to Our Lady; the Son of the Godhead, next, with three beams, to the Holy Ghost; the Godly Father, with three beams, to the Son; and so enter all three into her bosom." All in all it is clear that the guilds spent liberally for a colorful setting forth of their miracle plays. The pageantry no doubt had much to do with the popular enjoyment of the performances.

The guilds incurred expense in other ways too. They paid fees to their members for acting. They also exacted fines if the actors neglected rehearsals or failed to learn their parts on time. The fees to the players were evidently fixed with an eye for the dignity rather than the difficulty of the parts undertaken. In a sixteenth century Coventry cycle "God" received the princely sum of 3 *s.* 6 *d.* (about five dollars today); three "white souls" and three "black souls," 1 *s.* 8 *d.* each; two "worms of conscience," 8 *d.* each; but the man who did the "cock-crowing," only 4 *d.* In addition to fees, the players often had to be supplied with refreshments, as at Norwich where Noah and his family required "wine when the ship went about."

The staging of the miracle plays in cycles by the guilds initiated an unique method of production. Since large crowds of people must be accommodated all day long for a comfortable viewing of many different plays, the guilds adopted a processional type of performance. Each play in the cycle was staged on its own movable platform, a broad and long wagon called a "pageant." The term "pageant," however, soon denoted not merely the stage vehicle, but also the play exhibited upon it. According to Archdeacon Robert Rogers of Chester, sixteenth-century eye-witness, the pageant-wagon consisted of a two-story wooden scaffold set upon four wheels. It was "a high-place made like a house with two rooms," but "all open on the top." In the lower room, curtained off from the public gaze, the actors "apparelled and dressed themselves; and in the higher room they played." Members of the guild, usually the apprentices or the journey-men, pulled the pageant-wagon.

Early in the morning of the festival day, or days, on which the cycle of miracle drama was to be presented, the wagon of the first pageant proceeded to the first of the "stations" established around the town. The stations were sites of performance selected for their convenience to all concerned, perhaps a public square, or a street junction, or a town gate. After the first pageant had been given before the crowd gathered at the first station, the wagon was wheeled to the second station. There the actors repeated their play before a new audience at the same time that the second pageant in the cycle was being shown at the first station. By this processional method every spectator who held his place from dawn to dusk usually saw presented before him as many plays as the guilds had prepared for acting on that day. Sometimes darkness put a stop to production before the entire cycle had been completed. When Queen Margaret with her lords and ladies visited Coventry on Corpus Christi Day in 1456 to watch the guild plays, "she saw then all the pageants played save Doomsday, which might not be played for lack of day." To avoid this kind of disappointment Chester and some other towns spread their cycles over several days.

The cycle productions called forth the same interest and effort from the community at large as the festival performances at Athens had done in the time of Aeschylus. More significant than this parallel, however, was the fundamental difference of dramatic taste between the two periods and peoples. The Greeks revealed an instinctive liking for unity of effect. The ruder populace of medieval England had little concern for artistry of feeling; it cared primarily for emotional vigor, let the methods of expression be what they might. Hence the serious devotional spirit of the Biblical stories and of the saints' legends was by no means strictly preserved in the miracle play cycles. Some of the plays do exhibit an attitude of reverence throughout — for instance, *Abraham and Isaac* in the so-called Brome version of this Biblical situation. This piece dramatizes with simple pathos the story of the pious father commanded to sacrifice his trustful and innocent son. More frequently, however, the cycle plays contain side by side the sacred and the secular, the serious and the comic. Immediately after God has solemnly rebuked Cain for killing Abel, Cain exchanges jests and then blows with his ploughboy, Pikeharness. Again, Noah and his wife, a true village scold, tussle with each other in front of the ark, while God's deluge is wiping sinful mankind from the face of the earth. The coarse language and the horseplay in such scenes meant no deliberate irreverence in the minds of the actors or of the audience. The prevalent crudity of sentiment and manners, and the mirthful atmosphere surrounding the religious festivals combined to induce this peculiar medley of the holy and the burlesque in the English religious drama generally.

"THE SECOND SHEPHERDS' PLAY"

The most interesting and dramatic of the English miracle plays now known is *The Second Shepherds' Play*, so entitled because it was found in an old manuscript at Towneley Hall, Yorkshire, as the second of two plays on the birth of Christ and the adoration of the shepherds. The Towneley manuscript, containing thirty-two plays in all, represents the cycle of pageants acted probably by the guilds of Wakefield, a large market town in southern Yorkshire. The play texts date from the fourteenth century, and may have been composed for the guilds by monks in the neighboring abbey of Woodkirk. Whoever the authors were, they gave Wakefield the liveliest cycle of any English metropolis.

The unidentified writer of *The Second Shepherds' Play* demonstrated an inventive capacity far beyond that of other composers of the miracle drama. He did not simply expand the Biblical narrative; he made it an appendage to a situation of his own originating. The secular main plot distinguishes *The Second Shepherds' Play* from all other miracle plays. The story of Mak the sheep-stealer is a homely comic sketch from shepherd life on the Yorkshire moors six hundred years ago. The first scene with the three shepherds meeting and complaining of their fortunes offers a glimpse into the harsh living conditions of the English countrymen, such as cannot be discovered elsewhere in the early drama. Every one of the five rustic characters is given at least a touch of individuality: Coll weather-beaten; Gyb hen-pecked; Daw roguish and shrewd; Mak a clever, lazy scamp; Gill a contriving slut. The realism of the characterization and the speech turns the simple farce of the sheep-stealing intrigue into a refreshing, though crude, specimen of folk comedy.

The dramatization of the tale of the Nativity is attached to the play of the sheep-stealing almost as if it were an afterthought. The Biblical episodes form a violent antithesis to the comedy which has preceded. Even though the scene at the stable is gently moving in its naïveté, still the tender piety of the shepherds before the Christ Child with their terms of endearment — "my sweeting," "little tiny mop," "little day-star" — contrasts strangely with their temper during the earlier scenes. This incongruity of tone between the native and the Biblical portions of *The Second Shepherds' Play* reflects the untutored taste typical of English audiences everywhere up to the middle of the sixteenth century.

Imagine an audience gathered in a cobbled market-place of medieval Wakefield for a guild performance of *The Second Shepherds' Play*. Rows of narrow, gabled, stone houses, the windows of which are filled with peering faces, surround the square teeming with a motley humanity. On one side there stand bleachers occupied by well-dressed gentlefolk, country squires, military officers, prelates in clerical robes, and other persons of means and position. All about in the street, farmers, villagers, clerks, yeomen, parish priests and monks in gowns, townsmen and women of low estate, vagabonds of every sort, children of all ages, have crowded toward a two-floored wagon slung high on its wheels. The actors climb up the ladder from their dressing room on the lower level and enter one by one to the upper floor as the performance of *The Second Shepherds' Play* gets under way upon its "multiple stage." The limited area of the pageant platform represents four different locales: the moors near Wakefield, Mak's cottage, the hillside near Bethlehem, and the stable with the holy manger. One end of the platform serves as the moors and, later, as the hillside, while the other end does for Mak's cottage and, later, for the stable. At this end there is situated the cradle in which Mak hides the sheep. The cradle subsequently becomes the manger for the Holy Child. The characters move from one end of the platform to the other according to the locale demanded. There is a rather primitive quality about the acting of these craftsmen players and about their method of staging, but fortunately the childlike imagination of the Wakefield spectators transforms the whole into a splendid spectacle of dramatic art.

[For the history of medieval drama in Europe see E. K. Chambers, *The Medieval Stage* (2 vols., 1903); for an account of early English religious plays, K. L. Bates, *The English Religious Drama* (latest edition, 1921), A. W. Pollard, *English Miracle Plays, Moralities, and Interludes* (latest edition, 1923).]

The Second Shepherds' Play

DRAMATIS PERSONAE

FIRST SHEPHERD, COLL
SECOND SHEPHERD, GIB
THIRD SHEPHERD, DAW
MAK

GILL, MAK'S *wife*
AN ANGEL
MARY

The Scene is the Yorkshire moors, and then Bethlehem

The FIRST SHEPHERD *enters*

1 Shep. Lord, but this weather is cold, and
  I am ill wrapped!
Nigh dazed, were the truth told, so long have I
  napped;
My legs under me fold; my fingers are
  chapped —
With such like I don't hold, for I am all lapt
    In sorrow. 5
In storms and tempest,
Now in the east, now in the west,
Woe is him has never rest
    Midday nor morrow!

But we wretched shepherds that walk on the
  moor, 10
In faith we're nigh at hand to be put out of
  door.
No wonder, as it doth stand, if we be poor,
For the tilth of our land lies fallow as the floor,
    As ye ken.
We're so burdened and banned, 15
Over-taxed and unmanned,
We're made tame to the hand
    Of these gentry men.

Thus they rob us of our rest, our Lady them
  harry!
These men bound to their lords' behest, they
  make the plough tarry, 20
What men say is for the best, we find the contrary, —
Thus are husbandmen oppressed, in point to
  miscarry,

    In life,
Thus hold they us under
And from comfort sunder. 25
It were great wonder,
    If ever we should thrive.

For if a man may get an embroidered sleeve or
  a brooch now-a-days,
Woe is him that may him grieve, or a word in
  answer says!
No blame may he receive, whatever pride he
  displays; 30
And yet may no man believe one word that he
  says,
    Not a letter.
His daily needs are gained
By boasts and bragging feigned,
And in all he's maintained 35
    By men that are greater.

Proud shall come a swain [1] as a peacock may
  go,
He must borrow my wain,[2] my plough also,
Then I am full fain to grant it ere he go.
Thus live we in pain, anger, and woe 40
    By night and day!
He must have it, if he choose,
Though I should it lose,
I were better hanged than refuse,
    Or once say him nay! 45

It does me good as I walk thus alone
Of this world for to talk and to make my
  moan.

[1] Squire.   [2] Wagon.

To my sheep will I stalk, and hearken anon,
There wait on a balk,[1] or sit on a stone.
     Full soon,   50
For I trow, pardie,[2]
True men if they be,
We shall have company,
     Ere it be noon.

(*The* First Shepherd *goes to one side.*

    The Second Shepherd *enters*

2 *Shep.* Ben'cite[3] and Dominus!   What
    may this mean?   55
Why fares the world thus!   The like often
    we've seen!
Lord, but it is spiteful and grievous, this
    weather so keen!
And the frost so hideous — it waters mine
    een![4]
     That's no lie!
Now in dry, now in wet,   60
Now in snow, now in sleet,
When my shoes freeze to my feet,
     It's not all easy!

But so far as I ken, wherever I go,   64
We wretched wedded men suffer mickle[5]
    woe,
We have sorrow once and again, it befalls oft
    so.
Seely Capel, our hen, both to and fro
     She cackles,
But if she begins to croak,
To grumble or cluck,   70
Then woe be to our cock,
     For he is in the shackles!

These men that are wed have not all their
    will;
When they're full hard bestead, they sigh
    mighty still;
God knows the life they are led is full hard and
    full ill,   75
Nor thereof in bower or bed may they speak
    their will,
     This tide.[6]

[1] Ridge between ploughed furrows.
[2] By God.   [3] Bless me!   [4] Eyes.
[5] Much.   [6] Time.

My share I have found,
Know my lesson all round,
Wo is him that is bound,   80
     For he must it abide!

But now late in men's lives (such a marvel to me
That I think my heart rives such wonders to
    see,
How that destiny drives that it should so be!)
Some men will have two wives and some men
    three   85
     In store.
Some are grieved that have any,
But I'll wager my penny
Woe is him that has many,
     For he feels sore!   90

But young men as to wooing, for God's sake
    that you bought,
Beware well of wedding, and hold well in
    thought,
"Had I known" is a thing that serves you
    nought.
Much silent sorrowing has a wedding home
    brought,
     And grief gives,   95
With many a sharp shower —
For thou mayest catch in an hour
What shall taste thee full sour
     As long as one lives!

For — if ever read I epistle! — I have one by
    my fire,   100
As sharp as a thistle, as rough as a briar,
She has brows like a bristle and a sour face by
    her;
If she had once wet her whistle, she might sing
    clearer and higher
     Her pater-noster;
She is as big as a whale,   105
She has a gallon of gall, —
By him that died for us all,
     I wish I had run till I had lost her!

    1 Shep. God over look the row! Like a
        deaf man ye stand.
    2 Shep. Yea, sluggard, the devil thy maw
        burn with his brand!   110
Didst see aught of Daw?

1 Shep.   Yea, on the pastureland
I heard him blow just before; he comes nigh at
　　hand
　　　Below there.
Stand still.
　2 Shep.   Why?
　1 Shep. For he comes, hope I.   115
　2 Shep. He'll catch us both with some lie
　　Unless we beware.

The THIRD SHEPHERD *enters, at first without seeing them*

3 Shep. Christ's cross me speed and St.
　Nicholas!
Thereof in sooth I had need, it is worse than it
　　was.
Whoso hath knowledge, take heed, and let the
　　world pass,   120
You may never trust it, indeed, — it's as brittle
　　as glass,
　　　As it rangeth.
Never before fared this world so,
With marvels that greater grow,
Now in weal, now in woe,   125
　　And everything changeth.

There was never since Noah's flood such floods
　　seen,
Winds and rains so rude and storms so keen;
Some stammered, some stood in doubt, as I
　　ween.[1] —
Now God turn all to good, I say as I mean! 130
　　For ponder
How these floods all drown
Both in fields and in town,
And bear all down,
　　And that is a wonder!   135

We that walk of nights our cattle to keep,
We see startling sights when other men sleep.
　　　(*Catches sight of the others.*
Yet my heart grows more light — I see shrews [2]
　　a-peep.
Ye are two tall wights [3] — I will give my sheep
　　A turn, below.   140
But my mood is ill-sent;
As I walk on this bent,[4]

　　¹ Believe.   ² Knaves.   ³ Stout fellows.   ⁴ Moor.

I may lightly repent,
　　If I stub my toe.

Ah, Sir, God you save and my master sweet!
A drink I crave, and somewhat to eat.   146
　1 Shep. Christ's curse, my knave, thou'rt a
　　lazy cheat!
　2 Shep. Lo, the boy lists to rave! Wait till
　　later for meat,
　　　We have eat it.
Ill thrift on thy pate!   150
Though the rogue came late,
Yet is he in state
　　To eat, could he get it.

　3 Shep. That such servants as I, that sweat
　　and swink,[1]   154
Eat our bread full dry gives me reason to think.
Wet and weary we sigh while our masters wink,[2]
Yet full late we come by our dinner and drink —
　　But soon thereto
Our dame and sire,
When we've run in the mire,   160
Take a nip from our hire,[3]
　　And pay slow as they care to.

But hear my oath, master, since you find fault
　　this way,
I shall do this hereafter — work to fit my
　　pay;
I'll do just so much, sir, and now and then
　　play,   165
For never yet supper in my stomach lay
　　In the fields.
But why dispute so?
Off with staff I can go.
"Easy bargain," men say,   170
　　"But a poor return yields."

　1 Shep. Thou wert an ill lad for work to ride
　　wooing
From a man that had but little for spending.
　2 Shep. Peace, boy, I bade! No more jan-
　　gling,
Or I'll make thee full sad, by the Heaven's
　　King,   175
　　　With thy gauds![4]
Where are our sheep, boy? Left lorn?

　¹ Labor.   ² Sleep.   ³ Wages.   ⁴ Tricks.

3 Shep. Sir, this same day at morn,
I them left in the corn
   When they rang Lauds.[1]   180

They have pasture good, they cannot go wrong.
   1 Shep. That is right.   By the Rood,[2] these
   nights are long!
Ere we go now, I would someone gave us a
   song.
   2 Shep. So I thought as I stood, to beguile us
   along.
   3 Shep.   I agree.   185
   1 Shep. The tenor I'll try.
   2 Shep. And I the treble so high.
   3 Shep. Then the mean shall be I.
     How ye chant now, let's see!
                   (They sing.

Then enters MAK *clad in a cloak over his smock*

   Mak. Now, Lord, by thy seven names' spell,
   that made both moon and stars on
   high,   190
Full more than I can tell, by thy will for me,
   Lord, lack I.
I am all at odds, nought goes well — that oft
   doth my temper try.
Now would God I might in heaven dwell, for
   there no children cry,
   So still.[3]
   1 Shep. Who is that pipes so poor?   195
   Mak. Would God ye knew what I endure!
   1 Shep. Lo, a man that walks on the moor,
   And has not all his will!

   2 Shep. Mak, whither dost speed?   What
   news do you bring?
   3 Shep. Is he come?   Then take heed each
   one to his thing.   200
          (Takes the cloak from MAK.
   Mak. What!   I am a yeoman — since
   there's need I should tell you — of the
   King.
That self-same, indeed, messenger from a great
   lording,
   And the like thereby.
Fie on you!   Go hence

Out of my presence!   205
I must have reverence,
   And you ask "who am I!"

   1 Shep. Why dress ye it up so quaint?[1]
   Mak, ye do ill!
   2 Shep. But, Mak, listen, ye saint,[2] I believe
   what ye will!
   3 Shep. I trow the knave can feint, by the
   neck the devil him kill!   210
   Mak. I shall make complaint, and you'll all
   get your fill,
     At a word from me —
And tell your doings, forsooth!
   1 Shep. But, Mak, is that truth?
Now take out that southern tooth[3]   215
     And stick in a flea!
   2 Shep. Mak, the devil be in your eye, verily!
   to a blow I'd fain treat you.
   3 Shep. Mak, know you not me?   By God,
   I could beat you!

   Mak. God keep you all three!   Me thought
   I had seen you — I greet you,
Ye are a fair company!
   1 Shep.   Oh, now you remem-
   ber, you cheat, you!   220
   2 Shep.   Shrew, jokes are cheap!
When thus late a man goes,
What will folk suppose? —
You've a bad name, God knows,
     For stealing of sheep!   225

   Mak. And true as steel am I, all men know
   and say,
But a sickness I feel, verily, that grips me hard,
   night and day.
My belly is all awry, it is out of play —
   3 Shep. "Seldom doth the Devil lie dead by
   the way —"
   Mak.   Therefore   230
Full sore am I and ill,
Though I stand stone still;
I've not eat a needle
     This month and more.

---

[1] Morning church services directly after Matins.
[2] Cross.   [3] Steadily.

[1] Strangely.   [2] The term used ironically here.
[3] "Now get rid of that southern dialect."   Mak has
been using South of England speech in order to deceive
them.

1 Shep. How fares thy wife, by my hood,
    how fares she, ask I?   235
Mak. Lies asprawl, by the Rood, lo, the fire
    close by,
And a house-full of home-brewed she drinks
    full nigh —
Ill may speed any good thing that she will try
    Else to do! —
Eats as fast as may be,   240
And each year there'll a day be
She brings forth a baby,
      And some years two.

But were I now kinder, d'ye hear, and far
    richer in purse,
Still were I eaten clear out of house and home,
    sirs.   245
And she's a foul-favored dear, see her close, by
    God's curse!
No one knows or may hear, I trow, of a worse,
    Not any!
Now will ye see what I proffer? —
To give all in my coffer,   250
Tomorrow next to offer
      Her head-mass penny.[1]

2 Shep. Faith, so weary and worn is there
    none in this shire.
I must sleep, were I shorn of a part of my
    hire.
3 Shep. I'm naked, cold, and forlorn, and
    would fain have a fire.   255
1 Shep. I'm clean spent, for, since morn, I've
    run in the mire.
      Watch thou, do!
2 Shep. Nay, I'll lie down hereby,
For I must sleep, truly.
3 Shep. As good a man's son was I,   260
      As any of you!
        (*They prepare to lie down.*

But, Mak, come lie here in between, if you
    please.
Mak. You'll be hindered, I fear, from talk-
    ing at ease,
      Indeed!   (*Yields and lies down.*
From my top to my toe,   265
Manus tuas commendo,

[1] Money for her burial service.

Poncio Pilato,[1]
      Christ's cross me speed!

*Then he rises, when the shepherds are
asleep, and speaks:*

Now 'twere time a man knew, that lacks what
    he'd fain hold,
To steal privily through then into a fold,   270
And then nimbly his work do — and be not too
    bold,
For his bargain he'd rue, if it were told
      At the ending
Now 'twere time their wrath to tell! —
But he needs good counsel   275
That fain would fare well,
      And has but little for spending.

But about you a circle as round as a moon,
        (*Draws a magic circle.*
Till I have done what I will, till that it be noon,
That ye lie stone still, until I have done;   280
And I shall say thereto still, a few good words
    soon
      Of might:
Over your heads my hand I lift.
Out go your eyes!   Blind be your sight!
But I must make still better shift,   285
      If it's to be right.

Lord, how hard they sleep — that may ye all
    hear!
I never herded sheep, but I'll learn now, that's
    clear.
Though the flock be scared a heap, yet shall I
    slip near.   (*Captures a sheep.*
Hey — hitherward creep!   Now that betters
    our cheer   290
      From sorrow.
A fat sheep, I dare say!
A good fleece, swear I may!
When I can, then I'll pay,
      But this I will borrow!   295

MAK *goes to his house, and knocks at
the door*

Ho, Gill, art thou in?   Get us a light!
    Gill. Who makes such a din at this time of
    night?

[1] "Into thy hands, Pontius Pilate, I commend my
spirit": a jocular misquotation, of course, of Scripture.

I am set for to spin, I think not I might
Rise a penny to win!   Curses loud on them
     light
        Trouble cause!   300
A busy house-wife all day
To be called thus away!
No work's done, I say,
        Because of such small chores!

   Mak. The door open, good Gill.   See'st
     thou not what I bring?   305
   Gill. Draw the latch, an thou will.   Ah,
     come in, my sweeting!
   Mak. Yea, thou need'st not care didst thou
     kill me with such long standing!
   Gill. By the naked neck still thou art likely
     to swing.
   Mak.   Oh get away!
I am worthy of my meat,   310
For at a pinch I can get
More than they that swink and sweat
       All the long day.

Thus it fell to my lot, Gill!   Such luck came
     my way!
   Gill. It were a foul blot to be hanged for it
     some day.   315
   Mak. I have often escaped, Gillot, as risky
     a play.
   Gill. But "though long goes the pot to the
     water," men say,
     "At last
Comes it home broken."
   Mak. Well know I the token,   320
But let it never be spoken —
       But come and help fast!

I would he were slain, I would like well to
     eat,
This twelvemonth was I not so fain to have
     some sheep's meat.
   Gill. Should they come ere he's slain and
     hear the sheep bleat —   325
   Mak. Then might I be ta'en.   That were a
     cold sweat!
       The door —
Go close it!
   Gill.   Yes, Mak, —
For if they come at thy back —

   Mak. Then might I suffer from the whole
     pack   330
       The devil, and more!

   Gill. A good trick have I spied, since thou
     thinkest of none,
Here shall we him hide until they be gone —
In my cradle he'll bide — just you let me
     alone —
And I shall lie beside in childbed and groan.
   Mak.   Well said!   336
And I shall say that this night
A boy child saw the light.
   Gill. Now that day was bright
       That saw me born and bred!   340

This is a good device and a far cast.
Ever a woman's advice gives help at the last!
I care not who spies!   Now go thou back
     fast!
   Mak. Save I come ere they rise, there'll
     blow a cold blast!
       I will go sleep.   345

      MAK *goes back to the moor, and pre-*
         pares to lie down

Still sleeps all this company,
And I shall slip in privily
As it had never been I
       That carried off their sheep.

   1 Shep. *Resurrex a mortruis!* [1]   Reach me a
     hand!   350
Judas carnas dominus!   I can hardly stand!
My foot's asleep, by Jesus, and my mouth's
     dry as sand.
I thought we had laid us full nigh to England!
   2 Shep.   Yea, verily!
Lord, but I have slept well.   355
As fresh as an eel,
As light do I feel,
       As leaf on the tree.

   3 Shep. Ben'cite be herein!   So my body is
     quaking,
My heart is out of my skin with the to-do it's
     making.   360

[1] Mock Latin here and in the following line.

Who's making all this din, so my head's set to
    aching.
To the doer I'll win! Hark, you fellows, be
    waking!
      Four we were —
See ye aught of Mak now?
    1 Shep. We were up ere thou.   365
    2 Shep. Man, to God I vow,
      Not once did he stir.

    3 Shep. Methought he was lapt in a wolf's
      skin.
    1 Shep. So many are wrapped now —
      namely within.
    3 Shep. When we had long napped, me-
      thought with a gin [1]   370
A fat sheep he trapped, but he made no din.
    2 Shep.   Be still!
Thy dream makes thee mad,
It's a nightmare you've had.
    1 Shep. God bring good out of bad,   375
      If it be his will!
    2 Shep. Rise, Mak, for shame! Right long
      dost thou lie.
    Mak. Now Christ's Holy Name be with us
      for aye!
What's this, by Saint James, I can't move
    when I try.
I suppose I'm the same. Oo-o, my neck's lain
    awry   380
      Enough, perdie —
Many thanks! — since yester even.
Now, by Saint Stephen,
I was plagued by a sweven,[2]
      Knocked the heart of me.   385

I thought Gill begun to croak and travail full
    sad,
Well-nigh at the first cock, with a young lad
To add to our flock. Of that I am never glad,
I have "tow on my rock [3] more than ever I
    had."
      Oh, my head!   390
A house full of young banes —
The devil knock out their brains!
Wo is him many gains,
      And thereto little bread.

[1] A trick.   [2] A dream.
[3] Flax on my distaff, i.e., more to take care of.

I must go home, by your leave, to Gill, as I
    thought.   395
Prithee look in my sleeve that I steal naught.
I am loath you to grieve, or from you take
    aught.
    3 Shep. Go forth — ill may'st thou thrive!
      (*Mak goes.*) Now I would that we
      sought
      This morn,
That we had all our store.   400
    1 Shep. But I will go before.
Let us meet.
    2 Shep.   Where, Daw?
    3 Shep. At the crooked thorn.

They go out. MAK *enters and knocks at his door*

    Mak. Undo the door, see who's here! How
      long must I stand?
    Gill. Who's making such gear? Now "walk
      in the wenyand." [1]   405
    Mak. Ah, Gill, what cheer? It is I, Mak,
      your husband.
    Gill. Then may we "see here the devil in a
      band,"
      Sir Guile!
Lo, he comes with a note
As he were held by the throat.   410
And I cannot devote
      To my work any while.

    Mak. Will ye hear the pother she makes to
      get her a gloze [2] —
Naught but pleasure she takes, and curls up
    her toes.
    Gill. Why, who runs, who wakes, who comes,
      who goes,   415
Who brews, who bakes, what makes me hoarse,
    d'ye suppose!
      And also,
It is ruth [3] to behold,
Now in hot, now in cold,
Full woeful is the household   420
      That no woman doth know!

But what end hast thou made with the shep-
    herds, Mak?

[1] In the waning of the moon, i.e., an unlucky season.
[2] An excuse.   [3] Pitiful.

Mak. The last word that they said when I
    turned my back
Was they'd see that they had of their sheep all
    the pack.
They'll not be pleased, I'm afraid, when they
    their sheep lack,   425
    Perdie.
But how so the game go,
They'll suspect me, whether or no,
And raise a great bellow,
    And cry out upon me.   430

But thou must use thy sleight.
    Gill. Yea, I think it not ill.
I shall swaddle him aright in my cradle with
    skill.
Were it yet a worse plight, yet a way I'd find
    still.
    (GILL *meanwhile swaddles the sheep
    and places him in the cradle.*
I will lie down forthright.   Come tuck me up.
Mak.   That I will.
Gill.   Behind!   435
    (MAK *tucks her in at the back.*
If Coll come and his marrow,[1]
They will nip us full narrow.
    Mak. But I may cry out "Haro,"
    The sheep if they find.

Gill. Hearken close till they call — they will
    come anon.   440
Come and make ready all, and sing thou
    alone —
Sing lullaby, thou shalt, for I must groan
And cry out by the wall on Mary and John
    Full sore.
Sing lullaby on fast,   445
When thou hear'st them at last,
And, save I play a shrewd cast,
    Trust me no more.

The Shepherds enter on the moor and meet

3 Shep. Ah, Coll, good morn!   Why sleepest
    thou not?
1 Shep. Alas, that ever I was born!   We
    have a foul blot.   450
A fat wether have we lorn.
    [1] Mate.

3 Shep.   Marry, God for-
    bid, say it not!
2 Shep. Who should do us that scorn?   That
    were a foul spot.
1 Shep.   Some shrew.[1]
I have sought with my dogs
All Horbury Shrogs,[2]   455
And of fifteen hogs
    Found I all but one ewe.

3 Shep. Now trust me, if you will, by Saint
    Thomas of Kent.[3]
Either Mak or Gill their aid thereto lent!
    1 Shep. Peace, man, be still!   I saw when he
    went.   460
Thou dost slander him ill.   Thou shouldest re-
    pent
    At once, indeed!
    2 Shep. So may I thrive, perdie,
Should I die here where I be,
I would say it was he   465
    That did that same deed!

3 Shep. Go we thither, quick sped, and run
    on our feet,
I shall never eat bread till I know all complete!
    1 Shep. Nor drink in my head till with him
    I meet.
    2 Shep. In no place will I bed until I him
    greet,   470
    My brother!
One vow I will plight,
Till I see him in sight,
I will ne'er sleep one night
    Where I do another!   475

They go to MAK'S *house.* MAK, *hearing them
coming, begins to sing lullaby at the top of his
voice, while* GILL *groans in concert.*
3 Shep. Hark the row they make!   List our
    sire there croon!
1 Shep. Never heard I voice break so clear
    out of tune.
Call to him.
2 Shep.   Mak, wake there!   Undo your
    door soon!

    [1] Rascal.   [2] Horbury Thickets, near Wakefield.
[3] Saint Thomas à Becket, whose tomb and shrine are
at Canterbury Cathedral in Kent.

Mak. Who is that spake as if it were noon,
     Aloft?[1]   480
Who is that, I say?
     3 Shep. Good fellows, if it were day —
                  (*Mocking* MAK.
     Mak. As far as ye may,
         Kindly, speak soft;

O'er a sick woman's head in such grievous
     throes!   485
I were liefer dead than she should suffer such
     woes.
     Gill. Go elsewhere, well sped. Oh, how my
     pain grows —
Each footfall ye tread goes straight through
     my nose
         So loud, woe's me!
     1 Shep.   Tell us, Mak, if ye may,   490
How fare ye, I say?
     Mak. But are ye in this town today —
         Now how fare ye?

Ye have run in the mire and are wet still a bit,
I will make you a fire, if ye will sit.   495
A nurse I would hire — can you help me in it?
Well quit is my hire — my dream the truth hit —
         In season.
I have bairns, if ye knew,
Plenty more than will do,   500
But we must drink as we brew,
         And that is but reason.

I would ye would eat ere ye go. Methinks that
     ye sweat.
     2 Shep. Nay, no help could we know in
     what's drunken or eat.
     Mak. Why, sir, ails you aught but good,
     though?   504
     3 Shep.   Yea, our sheep that we get
Are stolen as they go; our loss is great.
     Mak.   Sirs, drink!
Had I been there,
Some one had bought it sore, I swear.
     1 Shep. Marry, some men trow that ye were,
     And that makes us think!   511

     2 Shep. Mak, one and another trows it
     should be ye.
[1] Loudly.

     3 Shep. Either ye or your spouse, so say we.
     Mak. Now if aught suspicion throws on Gill
     or me,
Come and search our house, and then may ye
     see   515
         Who had her —
If I any sheep got,
Or cow or stot;[1]
And Gill, my wife, rose not,
         Here since we laid her.   520

As I am true and leal,[2] to God, here I pray
That this is the first meal that I shall eat this
     day.
     1 Shep. Mak, as may I have weal, advise
     thee, I say —
"He learned timely to steal that could not say
     nay."
     Gill. Me, my death you've dealt!   525
Out, ye thieves, nor come again,
Ye've come just to rob us, that's plain.
     Mak. Hear ye not how she groans amain —
         Your hearts should melt!

     Gill. From my child, thieves, begone. Go
     nigh him not, — there's the door!   530
     Mak. If ye knew all she's borne, your hearts
     would be sore.
Ye do wrong, I you warn, thus to come in before
A woman that has borne — but I say no more.
     Gill.   Oh, my middle — I die!
I vow to God so mild,   535
If ever I you beguiled,
That I will eat this child
         That doth in this cradle lie!

     Mak. Peace, woman, by God's pain, and cry
     not so.
Thou dost hurt thy brain and fill me with
     woe.   540
     1 Shep. I trow our sheep is slain. What
     find ye two, though?
Our work's all in vain. We may as well go.
         Save clothes and such matters
I can find no flesh
Hard or nesh,[3]   545
Salt nor fresh,
         Except two empty platters.
[1] Steer.   [2] Loyal.   [3] Soft.

Of any "cattle" but this, tame or wild, that we
     see,
None, as may I have bliss, smelled as loud as
     he.
     Gill. No, so God joy and bliss of my child
          may give me!   550
     1 Shep. We have aimed amiss; deceived, I
          trow, were we.
     2 Shep.   Sir, wholly each one.
Sir, Our Lady him save!
Is your child a knave? [1]
     Mak. Any lord might him have,   555
          This child, for his son.

When he wakes, so he grips, it's a pleasure to
     see.
     3 Shep. Good luck to his hips, and blessing,
          say we!
But who were his gossips, [2] now tell who they
     be?
     Mak. Blest be their lips —
               (*Hesitates, at a loss.*
     1 Shep. (*aside*).   Hark a lie
          now, trust me!   560
     Mak.   So may God them thank,
Parkin and Gibbon Waller, I say,
And gentle John Horn, in good fey [3] —
He made all the fun and play —
          With the great shank. [4]   565

     2 Shep. Mak, friends will we be, for we are
          at one.
     Mak. We! — nay, count not on me, for
          amends get I none.
Farewell, all three!   Glad 'twill be when ye're
     gone!
          (*The* SHEPHERDS *go out of the house.*
     3 Shep. "Fair words there may be, but love
          there is none
          This year."   570
     1 Shep. Gave ye the child anything?
     2 Shep. I trow, not one farthing.
     3 Shep. Fast back I will fling.
          Await ye me here.
          (DAW *goes back.   The other* SHEP-
          HERDS *turn and follow him slowly,
          entering while he is talking with* MAK.

[1] A boy.   [2] His godparents.
[3] Good faith.   [4] With the long legs.

     3 Shep. Mak, I trust thou'lt not grieve, if I
          go to thy child.   575
     Mak. Nay, great hurt I receive, — thou
          hast acted full wild.
     3 Shep. Thy bairn 'twill not grieve, little
          day-star so mild.
Mak, by your leave, let me give your child
          But six-pence.
               (*Goes to cradle, and starts to draw
               away the covering.*
     Mak. Nay, stop it — he sleeps!   580
     3 Shep. Methinks he peeps —
     Mak. When he wakens, he weeps;
          I pray you go hence!
               (*The other* SHEPHERDS *return.*

     3 Shep. Give me leave him to kiss, and lift
          up the clout. [1]   584
What the devil is this? — he has a long snout!
     1 Shep. He's birth-marked amiss.   We
          waste time hereabout.
     2 Shep. "A weft [2] that ill-spun is, comes
          ever foul out."   (*Sees the sheep.*
          Aye — so!
He is like to our sheep!
     3 Shep. Ho, Gib, may I peep?   590
     1 Shep. I trow "Nature will creep
          Where it may not go." [3]

     2 Shep. This was a quaint gaud [4] and a far
          cast.
It was a high fraud.
     3 Shep.   Yea, sirs, that was't.
Let's burn this bawd, and bind her fast.   595
"A false scold," by the Lord, "will hang at the
     last!"
          So shalt thou!
Will ye see how they swaddle
His four feet in the middle!
Saw I never in the cradle   600
          A horned lad ere now!

     Mak. Peace, I say!   Tell ye what, this to-do
          ye can spare!   (*Pretending anger.*
It was I him begot and yon woman him bare.
     1 Shep. What the devil for name has he got?
     Mak? — Lo, God, Mak's heir!

[1] Cloth.   [2] Woof.   [3] May not walk.
[4] Clever device.

2 Shep. Come, joke with him not.   Now,
    may God give him care,   605
        I say!
Gill. A pretty child is he
As sits on a woman's knee,
A dilly-down, perdie,
        To make a man gay.   610

3 Shep. I know him by the earmark — that
    is a good token.
Mak. I tell you, sirs, hark, his nose was
    broken —
Then there told me a clerk he'd been mis-
    spoken.[1]
1 Shep. Ye deal falsely and dark; I would
    fain be wroken.[2]
        Get a weapon, — go!   615
Gill. He was taken by an elf,
I saw it myself.
When the clock struck twelve,
        Was he mis-shapen so.

2 Shep. Ye two are at one, that's plain, in all
    ye've done and said.   620
1 Shep. Since their theft they maintain, let
    us leave them dead!
Mak. If I trespass again, strike off my head!
At your will I remain.
3 Shep.   Sirs, take my counsel instead.
        For this trespass
We'll neither curse nor wrangle in spite,   625
Chide nor fight,
But have done forthright,
        And toss him in canvas.

(*They toss* MAK *in one of* GILL'S *can-
    vas sheets till they are tired.   He dis-
    appears groaning into his house.*

The SHEPHERDS *pass over to the moor on the
    other side of the stage.*

1 Shep. Lord, lo! but I am sore, like to burst,
    in back and breast.   629
In faith, I may no more, therefore will I rest.
2 Shep. Like a sheep of seven score he
    weighed in my fist.
To sleep anywhere, therefore seemeth now best.
3 Shep.   Now I you pray,
On this green let us lie.

    [1] Bewitched.   [2] Revenged.

1 Shep. O'er those thieves yet chafe I.   635
3 Shep. Let your anger go by, —
        Come do as I say.

As they are about to lie down THE ANGEL *ap-
    pears and sings "Gloria in excelsis."   Then
    he speaks:*

Angel. Rise, herdsmen gentle, attend ye, for
    now is he born
From the fiend that shall rend what Adam had
    lorn,   639
That warlock[1] to shend,[2] this night is he born,
God is made your friend now on this morn.
        Lo! thus doth he command —
Go to Bethlehem, see
Where he lieth so free,[3]
In a manger full lowly   645
        'Twixt where twain beasts stand.
                    (THE ANGEL *goes.*

1 Shep. This was a fine voice, even as ever I
    heard.
It is a marvel, by St. Stephen, thus with dread
    to be stirred.
2 Shep. 'Twas of God's Son from heaven he
    these tidings averred.
All the wood with a levin,[4] methought, at his
    word   650
        Shone fair.
3 Shep. Of a Child did he tell,
In Bethlehem, mark ye well.
1 Shep. That this star yonder doth spell[5] —
        Let us seek him there.   655

2 Shep. Say, what was his song — how it
    went, did ye hear?
Three breves to a long[6] —
3 Shep.   Marry, yes, to my ear
There was no crotchet wrong, naught it lacked
    and full clear!
1 Shep. To sing it here, us among, as he
    nicked[7] it, full near,
        I know how —   660
2 Shep. Let's see how you croon!
Can you bark at the moon?

    [1] Devil.   [2] Overthrow.   [3] So noble.
    [4] A flash of lightning.   [5] Betoken.
    [6] Three short notes to one long note.   [7] Trilled.

3 Shep. Hold your tongues, have done!
      Hark after me now!   (*They sing.*

2 Shep. To Bethlehem he bade that we
      should go.   665
I am sore afraid that we tarry too slow.
      3 Shep. Be merry, and not sad — our song's
      of mirth not of woe,
To be forever glad as our meed may we know,
      Without noise.
      1 Shep. Hie we thither, then, speedily, 670
Though we be wet and weary,
To that Child and that Lady! —
      We must not lose those joys!

2 Shep. We find by the prophecy — let be
      your din! —
David and Isaiah, and more that I mind me
      therein,   675
They prophesied by clergy, that in a virgin,
Should he alight and lie, to assuage our sin,
      And slake it,
Our nature, from woe,
For it was Isaiah said so,   680
"Ecce virgo
      Concipiet" [1] a child that is naked.

3 Shep. Full glad may we be and await that
      day
That lovesome one to see, that all mights doth
      sway.   684
Lord, well it were with me, now and for aye,
Might I kneel on my knee some word for to say
      To that child.
But the angel said
In a crib was he laid,
He was poorly arrayed,   690
      Both gracious and mild.

1 Shep. Patriarchs that have been and
      prophets beforne,
They desired to have seen this child that is
      born.
They are gone full clean, — that have they lorn.
We shall see him, I ween, ere it be morn, 695
      For token.[2]

      [1] "Behold, a virgin shall conceive."   See *Isaiah* VII.
14.
      [2] Proof.

When I see him and feel,
I shall know full well,
It is true as steel,
      What prophets have spoken,   700

To so poor as we are that he would appear,
First find and declare by his messenger.
      2 Shep. Go we now, let us fare, the place is
      us near.
      3 Shep. I am ready and eager to be there;
      let us together with cheer
      To that bright one go.   705
Lord, if thy will it be,
Untaught are we all three,
Some kind of joy grant us, that we
      Thy creatures, comfort may know!

*They enter the stable and adore the in-
fant Saviour*

      1 Shep. Hail, thou comely and clean one!
      Hail, young Child!   710
Hail, Maker, as I mean, from a maiden so
      mild!
Thou hast harried, I ween, the warlock so
      wild, —
The false beguiler with his teen [1] now goes be-
      guiled.
      Lo, he merries,[2]
Lo, he laughs, my sweeting!   715
A happy meeting!
Here's my promised greeting, —
      Have a bob [3] of cherries!

2 Shep. Hail, sovereign Saviour, for thou
      hast us sought!
Hail, noble nursling and flower, that all things
      hast wrought!   720
Hail, thou, full of gracious power, that made
      all from nought!
Hail, I kneel and I cower!   A bird have I
      brought
      To my bairn from far.
Hail, little tiny mop! [4]
Of our creed thou art the crop,   725
I fain would drink in thy cup,
      Little day-star!

      [1] Woe.   [2] He is merry.   [3] A bunch.
      [4] Darling.

3 Shep. Hail, darling dear one, full of God-
head indeed!
I pray thee be near, when I have need.
Hail, sweet is thy cheer! My heart would
    bleed   730
To see thee sit here in so poor a weed,[1]
    With no pennies.
Hail, put forth thy dall,[2]
I bring thee but a ball,
Keep it, and play with it withal,   735
    And go to the tennis.

Mary. The Father of Heaven this night,
    God omnipotent,
That setteth all things aright, his Son hath he
    sent.
My name he named and did light on me ere
    that he went.

[1] Dress.
[2] Hand.

I conceived him forthright through his might
    as he meant,   740
    And now he is born.
May he keep you from woe!
I shall pray him do so.
Tell it, forth as ye go,
    And remember this morn.   745

    1 Shep. Farewell, Lady, so fair to behold
With thy child on thy knee!
    2 Shep. But he lies full cold!
Lord, 'tis well with me! Now we go, behold!
    3 Shep. Forsooth, already it seems to be told
Full oft!   750
    1 Shep. What grace we have found!
    2 Shep. Now are we won safe and sound.
    3 Shep. Come forth, to sing are we bound.
    Make it ring then aloft!
         (They depart singing.

Here ends the play of the Shepherds.

INTRODUCTION TO

Nice Wanton

The Morality Play: The Interlude and John Heywood:
The Moral Interlude

THE MORALITY PLAY

TOWARD THE END of the fourteenth century, when the miracle plays were being enthusiastically produced throughout western Europe, another type of drama with a similar
religious intent made its appearance. This new form, termed "moral play" or "morality," lived for some two hundred years alongside the miracle drama and, like the latter,
served to focus the attention of the public upon the doctrines of the Christian faith.
Then during the last quarter of the sixteenth century both the morality and the miracle
play disappeared as popular dramatic entertainment.

While the miracle play had its roots in the historical literature of the Christian church,
the morality grew out of the ethical teachings of the clergy and flourished on the love for
allegory which had permeated medieval culture both on the Continent and in England.
The new species of drama possessed what the miracle play lacked, a well-defined universal conflict. Furthermore, it was a conflict which brought the theater closer, than heretofore, to the ordinary mortal. The morality treated of the perennial struggle in man's
life between good and evil, and of the relation of this warfare to the Christian salvation
of man's soul. Any story of sinful mankind which might be allegorized to point a lesson
about human conduct qualified as a proper subject for a morality. The characters, for
the most part, represented personifications of abstract qualities, that is, of virtues and
vices.

The struggle between mere abstractions certainly would have constituted forbidding
material for popular drama in any other age. The authors of the early English moralities evidenced, however, little fear of boring their public, for they wrote heavy,
didactic pieces three or four times as long as the average miracle play. Yet they usually
took pains to introduce a few moments of amusing spectacle. In *The Castle of Perseverance* (c. 1425), for example, Belial (Satan) makes his entrance to assault the Castle
with pipes of burning gunpowder attached to his hands and ears and rump. Despite
such lively moments this oldest of the extant moralities is a tedious dramatization of
the battle between the Seven Deadly Sins and the Seven Cardinal Virtues over the
soul of Mankind (*Humanum Genus*), a battle only ended when Christ's mercy saves
Mankind at the last judgment.

The most artistic of the full-fledged moralities is *Everyman*, written by an anonymous
churchman in the late years of the fifteenth century and thereafter widely known on the
Continent as well as in England. The play depicts "how the High Father of Heaven
sendeth Death to summon every creature to come and give account of their lives in this
world." Everyman, when thus summoned, finds to his dismay that his earthly friends,

Goods, Fellowship, Kindred, Cousin, Beauty, Strength, Knowledge, Discretion, refuse
to accompany him to the bar of God's judgment. Only Good Deeds is willing to make
the journey beyond this world, but the presence of Good Deeds gives assurance of heavenly salvation to Everyman as he descends into the grave at the close. Though the
dramatic action in *Everyman* is slight, it is so movingly expressed that the play has been
revived again and again on the twentieth-century stage of Europe and America. Perhaps the most notable production was given on both sides of the Atlantic in the 1920's
by Max Reinhardt with Alexander Moissi, the renowned German actor, in the title rôle
of Everyman.

Such wholly serious moralities as *Everyman* did not please the English populace any
more than did those miracle plays which were unrelieved by humor. The same rude
audiences demanded their ethical lessons seasoned with dashes of comedy. The element of comic realism, therefore, soon increased in the morality texts, especially in the
parts of the vices. These latter became established as merry fellows, and their rôle
eventually conventionalized as "the Vice," a clown and trickster. The morality *Mankind* (c. 1475) includes a certain Titivillus who, horribly arrayed like a devil, plays
pranks on Mankind while the latter is tilling his field. Titivillus steals away first Mankind's sack of seed corn and then his spade. Antics such as these certainly obscured the
moral instruction, but they lightened otherwise dull plays and made them continue to be
acceptable as popular amusements.

The earlier productions of the morality plays were open-air community affairs presented on a stationary platform or, in some cases, as *The Castle of Perseverance*, on a circular series of small stages. Conditions of dramatic entertainment, however, changed
so rapidly in England during the fifteenth century that the original community character of the morality performances was much affected. This type of play became the
chief vehicle for acting on the part of the many troupes of players (men and boys only),
who began at this period to travel about the country. Some of the troupes secured the
patronage of noblemen and then were known by the name of their patron; as, for example, "the Earl of Oxford's Players" and "the Earl of Derby's Players." Indeed, before
1500, King Henry VII had initiated the custom of retaining a small body of male actors
as members of the royal household. The sovereign's troupe also took to the road when
the court had no desire for their services. These professional groups, when playing in
the houses of aristocratic patrons, acted on a rough platform in the banqueting hall with
perhaps a screen and a door available. When touring towns and villages, they set up a
stage in a square, or on a green, or, best of all sites for their purpose, in the open courtyard of an inn.

The fifteenth-century morality *Mankind* is an interesting illustration of a play composed definitely for inn-yard performance. The opening speaker addresses the "sover-
eigns that sit," that is, the better class of spectators seated in the balconies running
around the yard; and then he speaks to the "brethren that stand right up," who are the
rabble milling about the yard. Halfway through the play, after a loud explosion set off
by "the Vice," Titivillus, the actors declare an intermission and proceed among the
audience to take up a collection. With remuneration safely in hand the company then
resume production and give the onlookers their money's worth of buffoonery and didacticism.

THE INTERLUDE AND JOHN HEYWOOD

The dramatic performances in private halls and the "road shows" by professional troupes created a need for plays strictly limited in length and in cast, and avowedly entertaining. The "interlude" evolved as an answer to these new conditions. It was a play which could be acted in an hour or less by some half-dozen players, if the parts were doubled properly. By the sixteenth century almost all kinds of brief drama, from morally edifying tales to *fabliaux* or droll stories, were called in England "interludes."

The secularization of the interlude and its transformation into an intellectual or a humorous skit was accomplished by John Heywood (1497?–1580?), the first notable English playwright. Through his marriage in 1523 Heywood joined the family circle of Sir Thomas More (1478–1535), famous scholar and author of *Utopia*, who was also very fond of theatricals. Heywood in his later twenties held a court post as singer and musician. Subsequently he had charge of a singing school of boys (perhaps the choir school of St. Paul's Cathedral), and introduced his boys in dramatic entertainments at court. By 1533 he had written four or five interludes which quite possibly were acted on a private outdoor stage erected by his father-in-law, John Rastell the printer, near the latter's house in Finsbury Fields, London. The most dramatic of Heywood's skits is *A Merry Play between Johan Johan, the husband, Tyb, his wife, and Sir Johan, the priest*. This "merry play" treats of the deception practiced upon a hen-pecked husband by his wife and her lover, the parish-priest. The farce is vigorously conceived and rises steadily to a climax of effrontery. Another of Heywood's interludes, *The Play of the Weather*, offers a more original humor in its situation. Nine characters, ranging from a merchant to a little boy, one by one urge Jupiter to send them weather suited to their own particular needs or desires. At the end the play points out with pleasing whimsey the moral that men would make a mess of rain, wind, and sunshine, if they had the power of governing these elements.

THE MORAL INTERLUDE

The didactic tradition, which even Heywood in his *Play of the Weather* could not altogether escape, forever dominated the interludes, so that the large majority may be more properly called "moral interludes." In no small measure the English schools contributed to the preservation of the moralizing character of the interlude. Dramatic entertainment grew to be a common school activity during the first quarter of the sixteenth century. The schools seized upon the moral interlude as an ideal stage vehicle, because it could expound under a diverting guise the theme of the straight and narrow path, whether applied to conduct or to study. Many of the moral interludes therefore owed their birth to academic theatricals.

Though the didacticism in these interludes remained strong, the allegorizing greatly declined. Individual personages came to occupy a fairly prominent share of the *dramatis personae*. The so-called allegorical characters developed into more or less humanized figures. The moral interlude *Hickscorner* (c. 1513) even takes its title from the one character in its cast with an individual name. Hickscorner, the fool who has said in his heart, "There is no God," fills, strangely enough, a rôle quite secondary to that of his two dissolute companions, Freewill and Imagination. With Hickscorner forgotten at the last, these two are converted to righteousness by Perseverance and Contemplation.

The play's vitality lies in the narration by the three roisterers of their racy experiences. Hickscorner, for instance, has paid a visit to the unique "land of Rumbelow, three miles out of Hell." However pious the author of this moral interlude, he possessed an intimate acquaintance with the seamy side of life in the sixteenth century and created a far more vivid impression of fleshly adventure than of spiritual devotion. He was but one of a long line of playwrights who have contradicted their purpose by making virtue less interesting than vice.

"NICE WANTON"

Of all the moral interludes that with the most dramatic merit is *Nice Wanton*, printed at London in 1560 but composed perhaps ten or twenty years earlier. This "pretty interlude" on child training and human wantonness illustrates the trend toward individualized characters and realistic situations. The allegorical survives only in the names of Iniquity, Baily Errand, and Worldly Shame. The characters themselves belong to the stock type of "the Vice." Colorful touches of actuality enliven the action, such as the game of craps between Ismael, Dalila, and Iniquity (ll. 211–31), and the amusing attempt by Baily Errand to bribe Daniel, the judge, at the trial of Ismael (ll. 350–61). Unlike most of the morality drama *Nice Wanton* is full of incident.

Its superiority to other plays of the same class is most noticeable, however, in its more artistic construction. Something of a plot really develops during the course of six distinct and varied scenes. The exposition moves awkwardly, but steadily to a catastrophe and then to a conclusion of repentance.

The punishment meted out to Ismael and Dalila, the wayward brother and sister, seems today rather overdrawn, and the priggishness of Barnabas quite intolerable. Yet these extravagances in delineation did not disturb the less sophisticated audience of four hundred years ago. *Nice Wanton*, acted with spirit by masters and boys in a school hall, proved a lively preachment on youthful disobedience and parental indulgence. Drama in England of the mid-sixteenth century was not expected to approach any higher level of art.

[For further study of the morality drama and its production, see E. K. Chambers, *The Medieval Stage* (2 vols., 1903), W. R. Mackenzie, *The English Moralities* (1914); for a critique on the comic elements in the moralities and interludes, C. M. Gayley, *An Historical View of the Beginnings of English Comedy* in *Representative English Comedies*, Vol. I (1903); for a critique on John Heywood, A. W. Pollard, *John Heywood* in *Representative English Comedies*, Vol. I (1903).]

A Pretty Interlude Called
Nice Wanton [1]

Wherein you may see	Early sharp that will be thorn; [2]
Three branches of an ill tree:	Soon ill that will be naught;
The mother and her children three,	To be naught, better unborn;
Two naught, and one goodly.	Better unfed than naughtily taught.

Ut magnum magnos, pueros puerilia docent. [3]

Personages [4]

THE MESSENGER	INIQUITY
BARNABAS	BAILY [8] ERRAND
ISMAEL [5]	XANTIPPE [9]
DALILA [6]	WORLDLY SHAME
EULALIA [7]	DANIEL, THE JUDGE [10]

THE PROLOGUE

The Messenger. [11] The prudent prince, Solomon, doth say,
"He that spareth the rod, the child doth hate"; [12]
He would youth should be kept in awe alway
By correction in time at reasonable rate,

To be taught to fear God and their parents obey,   5
To get learning and qualities, [13] thereby to maintain
An honest quiet life, correspondent alway
To God's law and the king's; for it is certain

If children be nursed in idleness and ill
And brought up therein, it is hard to restrain   10
And draw them from natural wont [14] evil,
As here in this interlude ye shall see plain

[1] An entertaining playlet called "Lewd Wayward Youth."
[2] The worthless thornbush grows sharp points early.
[3] Just as a great matter instructs adults, so small things teach the young.
[4] The characters all bear tag-names which suggest their intended natures.
[5] The name of the outcast son of Abraham (see *Genesis* XVI. 12).
[6] The name of the woman who discovered from Samson the secret of his strength and then betrayed him to the Philistines (see *Judges* XVI).
[7] "Fair speech."   [8] Bailiff.
[9] The name of the shrewish wife of the famous Greek philosopher, Socrates.
[10] The name of the good judge who invokes the law against the evil accusers of the chaste matron in the Apocryphal narrative of *Susannah and the Elders*.   The Apocrypha, or noncanonical books of the Bible were commonly published in early Protestant Bibles between the Old and the New Testaments.
[11] So called from the character *Nuntius* (Messenger), who often appeared in the Latin plays then well known, and who acted as reporter of events offstage.   Here, however, he merely reports the subject of the play and the moral.
[12] A rephrasing of *Proverbs* XIII. 24.   [13] Virtues.   [14] Customary.

By two children brought up wantonly in play,
    Whom the mother doth excuse when she should chastise.
They delight in dalliance and mischief alway;
    At least they end their lives in miserable wise.   16

The mother, persuaded by Worldly Shame
    That she was the cause of their wretched life,
So pensive, so sorrowful for their death she became,
    That in despair she would slay herself with a knife.   20

Then her son, Barnabas — by interpretation,
    The son of comfort — her ill purpose to stay,
By the Scriptures he giveth her godly consolation;
    And so concludeth.   All these parts will we play.   (*Exit.*

BARNABAS *cometh*

Barn. My master in my lesson yesterday   25
    Did recite this text of *Ecclesiasticus*: [1]
"Man is prone to evil from his youth," did he
    say;
    Which sentence may well be verified in
    us —

Myself, my brother, and sister Dalila,
    Whom our parents to their cost to school
    do find.[2]   30
I tarry for them here; time passeth away,
    I lose my learning; they ever loiter be-
    hind.

If I go before, they do me threat
    To complain to my mother; she for their
    sake,
Being her tender tiddlings,[3] will me beat.   35
    Lord, in this perplexity, what way shall
    I take?

What will become of them?   Grace God them
    send [4]
To apply their learning and their manners
    amend!

ISMAEL *and* DALILA *come in singing:*

    Here we come! and here we love!
    And here we will abide, abide-a!   40

Barn. Fie, brother, fie! and specially you,
    sister Dalila!
Soberness becometh maids alway.
    Dal. What, ye dolt!   Ye be ever in one song!
    Ism. Yea, sir, it shall cost you blows ere it
    be long!
    Barn. Be ye not ashamed the truants to
    play,   45
Losing your time and learning, and that every
    day?
Learning bringeth knowledge of God and
    honest living to get.
    Dal. Yea, marry,[1] I warrant you, Master
    Hodypeke! [2]
    Barn. Learn apace, sister, and after to spin
    and sew,   49
And other honest housewifely points to know.

    Ism. Spin, quoth he?   Yea, by the mass,
    and with your heels up-wind,[3]
For a good mouse-hunt is cat after kind.[4]
    Barn. "Lewd speaking corrupteth good
    manners," St. Paul doth say.[5]
Come, let us go, if you will to school this day.
I shall be shent [6] for tarrying so long.   55
        (BARNABAS *goeth out.*
    Ism. Go, get thee hence, thy mouth full of
    horse-dung!
Now, pretty sister, what sport shall we devise?

---

[1] The Apocryphal book of wisdom.   [2] Support.
[3] Spoiled darlings.   [4] God send them grace.

[1] By the Virgin Mary.   [2] Blockhead.
[3] I.e., kick up your heels, be sportive.
[4] I.e., the proper kind of sport is to follow after one's
own nature, to give free play to one's impulses.
[5] *I Corinthians* XV. 33.   [6] Punished.

Thus palting [1] to school, I think us unwise;
In summer die for thirst, in winter for cold,
And still to live in fear of a churl — who
    would?   60
  Dal. Not I, by the mass! I had rather he
  hanged were
Than I would sit quaking like a mome [2] for
  fear.

I am sun-burned in summer, in winter the
  cold
    Maketh my limbs [3] gross and my beauty
    decay.   64
If I should use it [4] as they would I should,
    I should never be fair woman, I dare
    say.

  Ism. No, sister, no! but I can tell
    Where we shall have good cheer,
Lusty companions two or three,
    At good wine, ale and beer.   70

  Dal. Oh, good brother, let us go;
I will never go more to school.
Shall I never know
What pastime meaneth?
Yes, I will not be such a fool.   75
  Ism. Have with thee, Dalila!
                  (*They sing.*
    Farewell our school!
    Away with book and all!
            (*They cast away their books.*
    I will set my heart
    On a merry pin,[5]   80
    Whatever shall befall!
            (*They go out singing.*

        Enter EULALIA

  Eul. Lord, what folly is in youth!
    How unhappy be children now-a-days!
And, the more pity, to say the truth,
    Their parents maintain them in evil ways,
    Which is a great cause that the world
    decays,   86
For children brought up in idleness and play
Unthrifty and disobedient continue alway.

A neighbor of mine hath children hereby, 89
    Idle, disobedient, proud, wanton and nice.[1]
As they come by, they do shrewd turns daily;
    Their parents so to suffer them, surely be
    not wise.
    They laugh me to scorn when I tell them
    mine advice;
I will speak to their elders and warn them
    neighborly.   94
Never in better time! — their mother is hereby.

        Enter XANTIPPE

  Eul. God save you, gossip! [2] I am very fain
    That you chance now to come this way;
I long to talk with you a word or twain,
    I pray you take it friendly that I shall say.
    Ismael, your son, and your daughter,
    Dalila,   100
Do me shrewd [3] turns, daily more and more,
Chide and beat my children — it grieveth me
  sore.

They swear, curse and scold, as they go by the
  way,
    Giving others ill example to do the same,
To God's displeasure, and their hurt another
    day.   105
    Chastise them for it, or else you be to
    blame!

  Xant. Tush! tush! If you have no more
    than that to say,
You may hold your tongue and get you away.
Alas! poor souls, they sit a' school all day
In fear of a churl; and if a little they play, 110
He beateth them like a devil. When they
  come home,
Your mistresship would have me lay on.
If I should beat them so oft as men complain,
By the mass! within this month I should make
  them lame.

  Eul. Be not offended, I pray you; I must
    say more.   115
    Your son is suspect light-fingered to be;
Your daughter hath nice tricks three or four;

---

  [1] Hastening.   [2] Dunce.   [3] Features.
  [4] Behave.   [5] Note.

  [1] Lewd.   [2] Good friend.
  [3] Mischievous.

See to it in time, lest worse you do see.
He that spareth the rod, hateth the child
   truly;
Yet Solomon sober correction doth mean,   120
Not to beat and bounce them to make them
   lame.

   Xant. God thank you, mistress, I am well
    at ease!
(*Aside*) Such a fool to teach me, preaching as
   she please!
Dame, you belie them deadly; I know plain,
Because they go handsomely, you disdain.[1] 125
   Eul. Then on the other as well would I
    complain;[2]
But your other son is good, and no thank to
   you!
These will you make naught, by sweet Jesu!

   Xant. Eulalia, my children naught?   You
    lie!
By your malice they shall not set a fly.   130
I have but one mome, in comparison of his
   brother —
Him the fool praiseth, and despiseth the other.
   Eul. Well, Xantippe, better in time than too
    late!
Seeing you take it so, here my leave I take.
                          (*Exit.*

   Xant. Marry, good leave have you, the great
    God be with you!   135
   My children or I be curst, I think;
They be complained on wherever they go,
   That for their pleasure they might drink;
Nay, by this the poor souls be come from school
   weary.   139
I will go get them meat[3] to make them merry.
                          (*Exit.*

INIQUITY, ISMAEL, *and* DALILA *come in*
       together singing:

Iniq. Lo! lo! here I bring her.
Ism. What is she, now you have her?

   Dal. I, lusty minion[1] lover?
Iniq. For no gold will I give her.
All together. Welcome my honey ay.   145
Iniq. Oh my heart!   (*Here he speaketh.*
   This wench can sing
And play her part.
   Dal. I am yours (and you mine), with all
    my heart.

   Iniq. By the mass, it is well sung!   150
Were you not sorry you were a maid so long?
   Dal. Fie, Master Iniquity! fie! I am a maid
    yet.
   Ism. No, sister, no; your maidenhead is sick.
Iniq. That knave, your brother, will be a
   blab still,
Surely, Dalila, you can say as much by him, if
   you will!   155
   Dal. By him, quoth he?   He hath whores
   two or three.
But [2] I tell your minion Doll, by God's body —
It skilleth not,[3] she doth hold[4] you as much.
   Ism. You lie falsely, she will play me no
   such touch.[5]
   Dal. Not she! Yes, to do your heart good!
I could tell you who putteth a bone in your
   hood.[6]   161
   Ism. Peace, whore! or you bear me a box on
   the ear.
   Dal. Here is mine ear, knave, strike and
   thou dare!   (*He strikes her.*
(*To* INIQ.) To suffer him thus you be no
   man!

If you will not revenge me, I will find one!   165
To set so little by me you were not wont.
Well, it is no matter! Though you do, *ceteri
   nolunt.*[7]
   Iniq. Peace, Dalila! Speak ye Latin, poor
   fool?
   Dal. No, no, but a proverb I learned at
   school.
   Ism. Yea, sister, you went to school till you
   were past grace.   170

---

[1] Take offense.
[2] I.e., if I had really taken offense, then I should complain of Barnabas as well.
[3] Food.

[1] Darling.   [2] If.
[3] It makes no difference.   [4] Wager.
[5] She will test me in no such way.
[6] Who is unfaithful to you.
[7] The others will be unwilling to have it that way.

Dal. Yea, so didst thou, by thy knave's face!

Iniq. Well, no more ado; let all this go.

We kinsfolk must be friends; it must be so.

Come on! come on! come on!

Here they be that will do us all good.   175

        (He casteth dice on the board.

Ism. If you use it long, your hair will grow
    through your hood.

Iniq. Come on, knave, with Christ's curse!

I must have some of the money

Thou hast picked out of thy father's purse. 179

Dal. He, by the mass, if he can get his purse

Now and then, he maketh it by half the
    worse.

Ism. I defy you both, whore and knave!

Iniq. What, you princock,[1] begin you to
    rave?

Come on!

Dal.   Master Iniquity, by your leave,

I will play a crown or two here by your sleeve.

Ism. Then be you servant to a worshipful
    man;   186

Master Iniquity — a right name, by Saint
    John!

Dal. What can you say by Master Iniquity?

I love him and his name most heartily.

Iniq. God a mercy, Dalila, good luck, I
    warrant thee!   *(He kisseth her.* 190

I will shrive[2] you both by-and-by.

Ism. Come on, but first let us have a song.

Dal. I am content, so that it be not long.

        *(*INIQUITY *and* DALILA *sing.*

    Iniq. Goldilocks,

    She must have knocks,   195

        Or else I do her wrong.

    Dal. When you have your will,

    You were best lie still,

        The winter nights be long.

    Iniq. When I nay may   200

    Another assay,

        I will take it for no wrong.

    Dal. Then, by the rood,

    A bone in your hood

        I shall put ere it be long.   205

Ism. She matcheth you, sirrah!

---

[1] Coxcomb.

[2] Impose a punishment — i.e., by dicing your money away from you.

Iniq. By God's blood, she is the best whore
    in England!

Dal. It is knavishly praised, give me your
    hand.

Iniq. I would thou had such another.

Ism. By the mass, rather than forty pound,
    brother.   210

Iniq. Here, sirs, come on;[1] seven!

        (They set[2] him.

        Eleven, at all!

Ism. Do you nick[3] us? be-knave your
    noodle!

Iniq. Ten mine!

Ism.   Six mine!   *(Casteth dice.*

Have at it, and it were for all my father's kin!

It is lost, by His wounds! and ten to one! 215

Iniq. Take the dice, Dalila; cast on!

Dal. Come on; five!

        (She casteth, and they set.

        Thrive at fairest!

Ism. Gup, whore! and I at rest.   *(He loseth.*

By God's blood, I ween[4] God and the devil
    be against me!

Iniq. If th'one forsake thee, th'other will
    take thee.   220

Ism. Then is he a good fellow; I would not
    pass,

So that I might bear a rule in hell, by the mass,

To toss firebrands at these pennyfathers'[5]
    pates.

I would be porter and receive them at the gates.

In boiling lead and brimstone I would seethe
    them each one.   225

The knaves have all the money, good fellows
    have none!

Dal. Play, brother; have you lost all your
    money now?

Ism. Yea, I thank that knave and such a
    whore as you!

'Tis no matter; I will have money, or I will
    sweat.

By God's blood, I will rob the next I meet! 230

Yea, and it be my father!   *(He goeth out.*

---

[1] Iniquity hereupon takes out a pair of dice and invites the other two to play a game of craps.

[2] Wager.

[3] Beat by throwing a "nick" — in this case, an **eleven**.

[4] Believe.

[5] Skinflints.

Iniq. Thou boy! by the mass, you will climb the ladder![1]
Ah, sirrah, I love a wench that can be wily;
She perceived my mind with a twink of mine eye.[2]
If we two play booty on[3] any man,   235
We will make him as bare as Job[4] anon.
Well, Dalila, let's see what you have won!
Dal. Sir, I had ten shillings when I began,
And here is all, every farthing. (*They tell[5] it.*
Iniq. You lie like a whore! you have won a pound.   240
Dal. Then the devil strike me to the ground!
Iniq. I will feel your pocket, by your leave, mistress!
Dal. Away, knave; not mine, by the mass!
Iniq. Yes, by God, and give you this to boot!
(*He giveth her a box.*
Dal. Out, horeson[6] knave, I beshrew[7] thy heart-root!   245
Wilt thou rob me and beat me, too?
Iniq. In the way of correction, but a blow or two.
Dal. Correct thy dogs! thou shalt not beat me!
I will make your knave's flesh cut, I warrant thee.
You think I have no friends? Yes, I have in store   250
A good fellow or two — perchance more.
Yea, by the mass, they shall box you for this gear![8]
A knave I found thee; a knave I leave thee here!
(*She goeth out.*
Iniq. Gup, whore! Do you hear this jade?[9]
Loving when she is pleased;   255
When she is angry, thus shrewd.
Thief brother, sister whore —
Two grafts of an ill tree!
I will tarry no longer here;
Farewell, God be with ye!   260
(*He goeth out.*

A long interval

[1] Mount the gallows.
[2] I.e., Dalila cheated Ismael when Iniquity gave her the wink.
[3] Plot to rob.
[4] He lost all his possessions (see *Job* I. 21).
[5] Count.   [6] Scurvy.   [7] Curse.   [8] Trick.
[9] A line to the audience; a familiar device in the early English plays.

DALILA *cometh in ragged, her face hid or disfigured, halting[1] on a staff*

Dal. Alas, wretched wretch that I am!
Most miserable caitiff that ever was born!
Full of pain and sorrow, crooked and lame,
Stuffed with diseases, in this world forlorn!

My sinews be shrunken, my flesh eaten with pocks,   265
My bones full of aches and great pain;
My head is bald, that bare yellow locks;
Crooked I creep to the earth again;

Mine eye-sight is dim; my hands tremble and shake;
My stomach abhorreth all kind of meat;
For lack of clothes great cold I take;   271
When appetite serveth, I can get no meat;

Where I was fair and amiable of face,
Now am I foul and horrible to see,
All this I have deserved for lack of grace,   275
Justly for my sins, God doth plague me.

My parents did tiddle[2] me — they were to blame —
Instead of correction, in ill did me maintain.
I fell to naught, and shall die with shame!
Yet all this is not half of my grief and pain.

The worm of my conscience, that shall never die,   281
Accuseth me daily more and more.
So oft have I sinned wilfully
That I fear to be damned forevermore.

Enter BARNABAS

Barn. What woeful wight[3] art thou, tell me,   285
That here most grievously dost lament?
Confess the truth, and I will comfort thee
By the word of God Omnipotent.
Although your time ye have misspent,
Repent and amend while ye have space,   290
And God will restore you to health and grace.

[1] Limping.   [2] Spoil.   [3] Man.

Dal. To tell you who I am, I dare not for
    shame;
    But my filthy living hath brought me in
    this case.
Full oft for my wantonness you did me blame,
    Yet to take your counsel I had not the
    grace.   295

To be restored to health, alas, it is past,
    Disease hath brought me into such decay!
Help me with your alms while my life doth last,
    That, like a wretch as I am, I may go my
    way.
    Barn. Show me your name, sister, I you
    pray,   300
And I will help you now at your need:
Both body and soul will I feed.

Dal. You have named me already, if I durst
    be so bold.
    Your sister Dalila, that wretch I am.
My wanton, nice toys[1] you knew of old —   305
    Alas, brother, they have brought me to
    this shame!

When you went to school, my brother and I
    would play,
    Swear, chide, and scold with man and
    woman;
To do shrewd turns our delight was alway;
    Yet were we tiddled, and you beaten now
    and then.   310

Thus our parents let us do what we would,
    And you, by correction, they kept under
    awe;
When we grew big, we were sturdy and bold,
    By father and mother we set not a straw.

Small matter for me, I am past!   315
    But your brother and mine is in great
    jeopardy,
In danger to come to shame at the last,
    He frameth his living so wickedly.

Barn. Well, sister, I ever feared you would
    be nought,   319
    Your lewd behaviors sore grieved my heart.

[1] Diversions.

To train you to goodness all means have I
    sought,
    But in vain; yet will I play a brotherly
    part,

For the soul is more precious, most dearly
    bought
    With the blood of Christ dying therefore,
To save it first a means must be sought   325
    At God's hand by Christ, man's only
    Savior.

Consider, Dalila, God's fatherly goodness,
    Which for your good hath brought you in
    this case,
Scourged you with his rod, of pure love doubt-
    less,
    That once knowing yourself, you might
    call for grace.   330

You seem to repent, but I doubt whether
    For your sins or for the misery you be in.
Earnestly repent for your sin rather,
    For these plagues be but the reward of sin.

But so repent that you sin no more,   335
    And then believe with steadfast faith
That God will forgive you forevermore
    For Christ's sake, as the Scripture saith.

As for your body, if it be curable,
    I will cause to be healed, or during your
    life   340
I will clothe you and feed you as I am able.
    Come, sister, go with me; you have need
    of relief.   *(They go.*

The judge DANIEL, INIQUITY, BAILY ERRAND
    come in; the judge sitteth down

Dan. As a judge of the country here am I
    come,
    Sent by the King's Majesty[1] justice to do,
Chiefly to proceed in judgment of a felon; 345
    I tarry for the verdict of the quest[2] ere I
    go.
    Go, Baily; know whether they be all
    agreed or no;

[1] Cf. l. 545 and note.   [2] Jury.

If they be so, bid them come away,
And bring their prisoner; I would hear what
    they say.

    Baily. I go, my lord, I go, too soon for one,
He is like to play a cast [1] will break his neck-
    bone.   351
I beseech your lordship be good to him;
The man is come of good kin.
        *(He telleth him in his ear, that all [2] may
        hear.*
If your lordship would be so good to me
As for my sake to set him free,   355
I could have twenty pound in a purse;
Yea, and your lordship a right fair horse,
Well worth ten pound.
    Dan. Get thee away, thou hell-hound!
If you were well examined and tried,   360
Perchance a false knave you would be spied.
        *(*INIQUITY *goeth out; the judge speaketh
        still.*
Bribes, saith Solomon, blind the wise man's
    sight,[3]
That he can not see to give judgment right.
Should I be a briber?   Nay; he shall have the
    law,
As I owe to God and the king obedience and
    awe.   365
        (They bring ISMAEL *in, bound like a
        prisoner.   The jury comes also.*
        INIQUITY *whispers to* ISMAEL.
    Iniq. You be tied fair enough for running
    away;
If you do not after me, you will be hanged, I
    dare say.
If thou tell no tales, but hold thy tongue,
I will set thee at liberty ere it be long,
Though thou be judged to die anon.[4]   370
    Judge. Come on, sirs, I pray you, come on.
Be you all agreed in one?
        (One of them speaketh for the quest.
    Juror. Yea, my lord, everyone.
    Judge. Where Ismael was indicted by twelve
    men
    Of felony, burglary, and murder,   375

[1] Make a throw of the dice (a figurative meaning intended in this case).
[2] I.e., all of the audience.
[3] Cf. *Proverbs* XVII. 23.   [4] At once.

As the indictment declareth how, where, and
    when —
Ye heard it read to you lately, in order —
You, with the rest — I trust, all true men —
Be charged upon your oaths to give verdict
    directly   379
Whether Ismael thereof be guilty or not guilty.
        (One for the quest.
    Juror. Guilty, my lord, and most guilty.
    Iniq. (*to* ISMAEL). Wilt thou hang, horeson
    noddy? [1]
    Judge (*to* ISMAEL). The Lord have mercy
    upon thee!
    Iniq. (*to* ISMAEL). Tush, hold thy tongue,
    and I warrant thee!

    Judge (*to* ISMAEL). Thou shalt go to the
    place [2] thou camest fro,[3]   385
    Till tomorrow nine of the clock there to
    remain;
To the place of execution then shalt thou go,
    There be hanged to death; and after,
    again,
    Being dead, for example to be hanged in
    a chain.
Take him away, and see it be done,   390
At your peril, that may fall thereupon!

    Ism. Though I be judged to die, I require [4]
    respite,
For the king's advantage in things I can recite.
    Iniq. Away with him, he will speak but of
    spite.
    Judge. Well, we will hear you say what you
    can;   395
But see that you wrongfully accuse no man.
    Ism. I will belie no man, but this I may say:
Here standeth he that brought me to this way.
    Iniq. My lord, he lieth like a damned knave;
The fear of death doth make him rave.   400
    Ism. His naughty company and play at dice
Did me first to stealing entice;
He was with me at robberies, I say it to his
    face;
Yet can I say more in time and place.
    Iniq. (*aside*). Thou hast said too much, I
    beshrew thy horeson's face! —   405

[1] Scurvy fool.   [2] I.e., the prison.
[3] From.   [4] Beg.

Hang him, my lord, out of the way;
The thief careth not what he doth say.
(*Aside*) Let me be hangman, I will teach him a sleight; [1]
For fear of talking I will strangle him straight. —
Tarry here that list, for I will go.   410
                (*He would go.*)
  Judge. No, no, my friend, not so!
I thought always you should not be good,
And now it will prove, I see, by the rood! [2]
Take him and lay him in irons strong.
We will talk with you more ere it be long. 415
   (*They take him in a halter;* [3] *he fighteth with them.*)
  Iniq. He that layeth hands on me in this place,
I lay my brawling-iron [4] on his face!
By God's blood, I defie thy worst!
If thou shouldest hang me, I were accurst.[5]
I have been at as low an ebb as this, 420
And quickly aloft again, by Gisse! [6]
I have more friends than ye think I have;
I am entertained of all men like no slave.
Yea, within this month, I may say to you, 424
I will be your servant, and your master, too —
Yea, creep into your breast! Will you have it so?
  Judge. Away with them both! lead them away!
At his death, tell me what he doth say;
For then, belike, he will not lie. 429
  Iniq. I care not for you both; no, not a fly!
            (*They lead them out.*)
  Judge. If no man have here more matter to say,
I must go hence some other way.
                (*He goeth out.*)

Enter WORLDLY SHAME

  Worldly Shame. Ha! ha! though I come in rudely, be not aghast!
I must work a feat in all the haste.
I have caught two birds; I will set [7] for the dame; 435

If I catch her in my clutch, I will her tame!
Of all this while know ye not my name?
I am right worshipful Master Worldly Shame.
The matter that I come now about
Is even this, I put you out of doubt: 440
There is one Xantippe, a curst shrew —
I think all the world doth her know —
Such a jade she is and so curst a quean [1]
She would outscold the devil's dame, I ween.
Sirs, this fine woman had babes three: 445
Twain the dearest darlings that might be —
Ismael and fair Dalila, these two;
With the lout Barnabas I have nothing to do.
All was good that these tiddlings do might —
Swear, lie, steal, scold, or fight, 450
Card, dice, kiss, clip,[2] and so forth.
All this our Mammy would take in good worth.
Now, sirs, Dalila, my daughter, is dead of the pocks,[3]
And my son hanged in chains and waveth his locks.
These news will I tell her, and the matter so frame 455
That she shall be thine own, Master Worldly Shame.
Ha, ha, ha!

XANTIPPE *cometh in*

  Peace, peace! she cometh hereby.
I spoke no word of her, no, not I!
Oh Mistress Xantippe, I can tell you news;
  The fair wench, your dear daughter Dalila, 460
Is dead of the pocks, taken at the stews; [4]
  And thy son Ismael, that pretty boy,
Whom, I dare say, you loved very well,
Is hanged in chains, every man can tell.

Every man saith thy daughter was a strong [5] whore, 465
  And thy son a strong thief and a murderer, too;
It must needs grieve you wondrous sore
  That they died so shamefully, both two.

---

[1] Trick.   [2] Cross.
[3] A hangman's rope.   [4] Sword.
[5] I.e., I'll be damned if you shall hang me.
[6] By Jesus.   [7] Lay a trap.

[1] Slattern.   [2] Embrace.   [3] Syphilis.
[4] Houses of prostitution.   [5] Utter, absolute.

Men will taunt you and mock you, for they say
    now   469
The cause of their death was even very you.

Xant. I the cause of their death!
         (*She would swoon.*
Worldly Shame. Will ye swoon? the devil
    stop thy breath!

Thou shalt die, I trow, with more shame;
    I will get me hence out of the way;
If the whore should die, men would me blame —
    That I killed her, knaves should say.   476
         (*Exit.*

Xant. Alas, alas, and weel-a-way!
    I may curse the time that I was born!
Never woman had such fortune, I dare say;
    Alas, two of my children be forlorn![1]   480

My fair daughter Dalila is dead of the pocks;
    My dear son Ismael hanged up in chains —
Alas, the wind waveth his yellow locks!
    It slayeth my heart and breaketh my
    brains!

Why should God punish and plague me so sore,
    To see my children die so shamefully?   486
I will never eat bread in this world more;
    With this knife will I slay myself by-and-
    by!
         (*She would stick herself with a knife.*

Enter BARNABAS

Barn. Beware what ye do! fie, mother, fie!
    Will ye spill[2] yourself for your own of-
    fense,   490
And seem forever to exclude God's mercy?
    God doth punish you for your negligence;
    Wherefore take his correction with pa-
    tience
And thank him heartily that, of his goodness,
He bringeth you in knowledge of your trespass.

For when my brother and sister were of young
    age,   496
    You saw they were given to idleness and
    play,

Would apply no learning but live in outrage,
    And men complained on them every day;
    You winked at their faults and tiddled
    them alway;   500
By maintenance they grew to mischief and ill;
So, at last, God's justice did them both spill.

In that God preserved me, small thank to you!
    If God had not given me special grace
To avoid evil and do good — this is true —   505
    I had lived and died in as wretched case
    As they did, for I had both suffrance[1] and
    space;
But it is an old proverb — you have heard it, I
    think —
That[2] God will have see, shall not wink.[3]

Yet in this we may all take comfort: 510
    They took great repentance, I heard say;
And, as for my sister, I am able to report
    She lamented for her sins to her dying day.
    To repent and believe I exhorted her
    alway.
Before her death she believed that God, of his
    mercy,   515
For Christ's sake, would save her eternally.

If you do even so, you need not despair,
    For God will freely remit your sins all.
Christ hath paid the ransom; why should you
    fear?
    To believe this and do well, to God for
    grace call;   520
    All worldly cares let pass and fall;
And thus comfort my father, I pray you
    heartily!
I have a little to say, I will come by-and-by.
         (XANTIPPE *goeth out.*
Right gentle audience, by this interlude you
    may see[4]
    How dangerous it is for the frailty of
    youth,   525
Without good governance, to live at liberty.
    Such chances as these oft happen, of truth;
    Many miscarry, it is the more ruth,

---

[1] Entirely lost.   [2] Kill.

[1] Permission.   [2] Whomsoever.
[3] Shut his eyes.
[4] At this point Barnabas begins to speak what is really
the epilogue.

By negligence of their elders and not taking
    pain   529
In time good learning and qualities to attain.

Therefore exhort I all parents to be diligent
    In bringing up their children, yea, to be
      circumspect;
Lest they fall to evil, be not negligent,
    But chastise them before they be sore in-
      fect;
    Accept their well-doing, in ill them reject.
A young plant ye may plait [1] and bow as ye
    will;   536
Where it groweth strong, there will it abide
    still:

Even so by children — in their tender age
    Ye may work them like wax to your own
      intent;
But if ye suffer them long to live in outrage,
    They will be sturdy and stiff, and will not
      relent.   541
    O ye children, let your time be well spent;

[1] Twine.

Apply your learning and your elders obey;
It will be your profit another day.
                     (He kneeleth down.
Now for the Queen's Royal Majesty [1] let us
    pray,   545
That God, in whose hands is the heart of
    all queens,
May endue Her Highness with godly puissance
    alway,
    That Her Grace may long reign and pros-
      per in all things,
    In God's word and justice may give light
      to all queens.
Let us pray for the Honorable Council and
    Nobility,   550
That they may always counsel in wisdom with
    tranquillity.
God save the Queen, the Realm, and Com-
    monalty!
            (He maketh a curtsy and goeth out.

[1] I.e., Queen Elizabeth. The original prayer, however, would have been for the King, Edward VI, since,
according to the evidence of ll. 344 and 393, the interlude was written during a king's reign.

INTRODUCTION TO

Edward the Second

The Growth of English Drama under Queen Elizabeth: Classical and Italian Influences: The Organization of Elizabethan Actors and Troupes: The Early London Theaters and Audiences: The University Wits: Marlowe and the Chronicle History Play

THE GROWTH OF ENGLISH DRAMA UNDER QUEEN ELIZABETH

THE influence of the Christian Church fell more and more faintly upon English play-writing as the sixteenth century ran its course. Early in the long reign of Queen Elizabeth, 1558–1603, the sacred and didactic elements of the medieval dramatic tradition were entirely replaced by what was secular and entertaining. Thereafter theatrical entertainment attained a richness comparable to that at Athens during the half-century when Aeschylus, Sophocles, Euripides, and Aristophanes flourished. The dramatic art of England, however, made the more remarkable growth within the same span of time. The first years of the Elizabethan era still saw in performance the naïve, structureless miracle and morality plays; the last years witnessed the production of Shakespeare's subtle, patterned tragedy of *Hamlet*. So rapid an advance to intellectual and aesthetic maturity stands unparalleled in the history of the world theater.

The rapidity of the advance owed much to the strong taste for drama among almost all ranks of Elizabethans. Only the more straight-laced of the clergy and of the middle class, who formed the backbone of Puritanism, decried playgoing on the grounds that it bred disorder, prodigality, and irreligion. In places of learning and high society, mimetic activity flowered as it never has since in any country. The boys' schools, the colleges at Oxford and Cambridge, the London inns-of-court or law clubs, all became hotbeds of dramatic creativeness. The Queen supported with enthusiasm yearly seasons of court theatricals, usually in the Christmas–New Year holidays and again just before Lent. Her liking redoubled the interest of the nobility in stage pastimes, public as well as private. This approbation of the sovereign and the aristocracy developed the theater of Elizabethan England into a national institution.

CLASSICAL AND ITALIAN INFLUENCES

Important new sources of literary culture also speeded the refining of Elizabethan dramatic art. When the revival of classical learning which gave to Europe the Renaissance reached England about the opening of the sixteenth century, it brought in its wake the study of the plays of ancient Rome. English schoolboys and collegians had introduced into their reading the tragedies of Seneca and the comedies of Plautus and Terence. Performance of the Roman drama by the students soon followed. Then schoolmasters and university men began to try their hands at plays in Latin which imitated the Roman patterns. By the middle of the century they were composing their imitations in English with a native background.

The classical models afforded to the fast-growing but immature English drama an inspiration which could never have been gained from the outgrown religious plays. The strict differences in tone and content between Roman tragedy and comedy made for clearer ideas of dramatic propriety. The Roman observance of the so-called "three unities" of time, place, and action pointed out the value of more careful structure. Though the Elizabethan playwrights did not ever practice these unities much, they did borrow as their standard the Roman design of five acts. Roman comedy provided fresh types of character, such as the witty servant; and new plot devices, such as mistaken identity. Seneca furnished the concept of heroic tragedy, that is, the fall of persons of high estate into misfortune and death. His example also initiated the motive of revenge, the character of the ghost, and the rhetorical style. Thus the Roman dramatists contributed a wealth of subject matter as well as a sense of form.

English adaptation of the classical patterns seems to have been tried first in the field of comedy. The earliest known effort of this nature is *Ralph Roister Doister* by Nicholas Udall, headmaster at Eton from 1534 to 1541, and at Westminster School, London, from 1554 to 1556. He wrote his comedy for performance probably by the Westminster schoolboys, who may have taken it to court where they had the honor of acting every year. Udall's title character, Ralph Roister Doister, resembles the *miles gloriosus*, or the boastful soldier, in Plautus' comedy of that name. Like Plautus, Udall divided his play into five acts, and employed a single exterior setting, a London street upon which open the houses of the chief characters. The plot, considerably lacking in matter, centers upon Ralph's laughable courtship of the already affianced Dame Custance. In this enterprise he is led on by the clever Matthew Merrygreek, a prototype of the parasite in Roman comedy. Such farcical situations as the misreading of Ralph's love letter and the battle with kitchen utensils still appeal sufficiently after four hundred years to cause the sporadic production of *Ralph Roister Doister* in academic circles on both sides of the Atlantic.

The tendency to amalgamate Roman and English comic elements is more fully illustrated by *Gammer Gurton's Needle*, a play originally acted at Christ's College, Cambridge, about the same time as *Ralph Roister Doister*. More crude and coarse than the latter, this piece of university drama is set in an English village and has characters who use rural dialect. What little of plot it has is concerned with the absurd search for Gammer (Dame) Gurton's lost needle. Its hiding place turns out to be the seat of her hired man's trousers! Classical influence hardly extends beyond the five-act construction.

English tragedy in imitation of the Roman did not appear presumably until after Elizabeth had ascended the throne. The oldest survival is *Gorboduc*, or *Ferrex and Porrex*, written in 1561 by Thomas Sackville (1536–1608) and Thomas Norton (1532–84), two aristocratic youths in one of London's law clubs. This tragic drama won immediate distinction largely because the students of the Inner Temple presented it before the Queen and her court on the evening of January 18, 1561–62. The plot of *Gorboduc* comes from a legend of ancient Britain, in which the division of the kingdom by the old king, Gorboduc, between his two sons, Ferrex and Porrex, brings on family strife, murders, and finally, civil war. Sackville and Norton closely copied the features of

Senecan tragedy — the division into five acts; the speech by a "chorus," really a commentator between the acts; the bloody action in which the violence is all off-stage; the use of a messenger as a narrator; and the declamatory, often sententious dialogue with frequent long speeches. The most notable feature in *Gorboduc*, however, is the blank verse, or unrhymed iambic pentameter, in which the characters talk. This form of verse, borrowed from contemporary Italian poetry, had never before been employed in English drama. So pleasing did the innovation prove that within a few years blank verse established itself as the standard medium of English tragedy and continued as such up to the end of the nineteenth century.

Elizabethan drama was indebted to Italy for a great deal more than blank verse. Italian *novelli* (tales) and romances, either in the original or in translation, supplied endless stories for English plots. Hence many a play of the period had its setting in Italy or in some other Mediterranean locale. What was perhaps the earliest Elizabethan romantic comedy derived its material from Italian fiction. It was a bourgeois "road play" of the 1560's, entitled "an excellent and pleasant comedy termed after the name of the Vice, *Common Conditions*, drawn out of the most famous history of Galiarbus, Duke of Arabia." This comedy abounds with colorful scenes of pirates, tinkers, sailors, lords and ladies, who move back and forth between Arabia, Phrygia, and a Mediterranean isle. The earliest English tragedy of romantic love, *Gismund of Salerne*, grew out of one of the tales in the famous Italian classic, the *Decameron* by Boccaccio. It is a grim drama of passion, wherein a father kills his daughter's lover, the daughter poisons herself, and the father commits suicide — all these events taking place in front of the audience. When the students of the Inner Temple staged *Gismund of Salerne* in the winter of 1568, they, as typical Elizabethans, doubtless luxuriated in its horrors.

Italian drama too exerted an influence on Elizabethan playwriting. The most noted Italian author of the early sixteenth century, Ludovico Ariosto (1474–1533), wrote among other works a comedy of the Plautine mold, *I Suppositi*. It was translated under the title of *Supposes* by George Gascoigne (?1542–?1577), while a student at the Inner Temple, and there produced in 1566. Gascoigne's play is filled with disguises and mistaken identities. From its complex intrigue Shakespeare drew his sub-plot for *The Taming of the Shrew*. But the outstanding contribution of *Supposes* is the prose form of its dialogue. All previous English comedy, including *Ralph Roister Doister* and *Gammer Gurton's Needle*, had been composed in some sort of verse. Gascoigne's dialogue evidenced so much more ease and wit that it opened the way to the regular use of prose in Elizabethan comedy. That convention has persisted on the English stage ever since.

THE ORGANIZATION OF ELIZABETHAN ACTORS AND TROUPES

The emergence of acting as a recognized profession and of the theater as an organized business constituted another important force behind the quick development of Elizabethan drama. For close to a century, actors had been banding themselves into companies under the nominal patronage of various noblemen who assumed a degree of responsibility for the good conduct of their "servants." Players needed the protection of these "masters," because otherwise they ran in constant danger of prosecution as irresponsible vagrants. Not until 1572, when the licensing of players was inaugurated, did acting gain complete recognition as an occupation in the sight of the law. From 1573 onwards the Privy Council, the royal cabinet of ministers, undertook regulation of theatrical enterprise in or near London by issuing "patents" to certain approved troupes and by placing control of actors and productions in the hands of the Master of the Revels, a royal officer of long standing. Hostile to the encouragement of theatricals, the London city fathers attempted to challenge the power of the Privy Council within municipal limits and to enforce strict, sometimes prohibitory measures regarding stage productions. After more than a decade of unsuccessful legislation, however, the London Council ceased any vigorous opposition.

As soon as the companies acting in London had been given an official status, their number and character came to be more or less stabilized. They were divided into two distinct categories: (1) the boys' companies, two in number, recruited from the choir schools of the Royal Chapel and of St. Paul's Cathedral respectively; (2) the adult companies, usually numbering about a half-dozen, who went by the name of their patron. During the earlier years of Elizabeth's reign the troupes of boys were only semi-professional groups under adult directors who trained them for occasional performances, chiefly at court. Later, when they occupied permanent playhouses, they took on a somewhat more professional character with their director really a commercial producer. The adult troupes evolved into shareholding corporations with a manager (also a part-owner) who attended to the maintenance of the personnel and to the purchase of play scripts, costumes, and stage properties. The more important members of a company usually held the shares and were designated as "sharers"; the subordinate members worked on salary; and the inexperienced were affiliated as apprentices.

The Elizabethan world of acting was altogether a man's world. English custom would not countenance actresses until 1660, though women participated in the masques, elaborate private entertainments of singing and dancing along with dialogue. On the regular stage boys of graceful physique and soprano voice took the feminine parts. Every adult company included a handful of such boys. Their playing, though often talented, never compensated for the lack of women. Female characterization had to be limited to suit the boy actor. Playwrights were forced to draw such conventional patterns of womanhood as youths could depict plausibly. Thus the prohibition of actresses imposed a serious restriction upon English dramatic art in its golden age.

THE EARLY LONDON THEATERS AND AUDIENCES

The development of Elizabethan drama, however, required theaters more than actresses. The occasional atmosphere of innyards and halls could not satisfy for long the demands of the growing national pastime. In 1576, exactly two hundred years before the American Declaration of Independence, the first two English theaters were built in London.

Their erection at once brought into existence a theatrical situation peculiar to London of the sixteenth and seventeenth centuries. Two types of playhouse emerged: (1) the "public" playhouse, a building with an open-air stage, where the theatergoer paid his admission fee on entrance; (2) the "private" playhouse, a structure entirely roofed, to which admittance was gained by advance subscription. This method of collecting the charges rendered the building and its enterprise "private" before the law and therefore not liable to interference from the local authorities. The division into public and private theaters survived till the general shut-down at the outbreak of civil war in 1642. In the beginning it produced two distinct, though not mutually exclusive, audiences who cared for different kinds of dramatic fare.   Subsequent to the Elizabethan period these distinctions of audience and taste broke down to some extent, but they remained sufficient to induce a larger variety in the dramatic output than if they had not existed at all.

The earlier of the two pioneer theaters was a public playhouse located by its builder, James Burbage, north of London proper in order to escape the jurisdiction of the unfriendly city council.   Its site in Finsbury Fields beyond Bishop's Gate lay amid the public recreation area.   Burbage, a carpenter by trade but in 1576 a member of the leading adult company, the Earl of Leicester's, secured capital from his father-in-law, John Braynes, a grocer, so that he might engage in a new sort of venture.   He proceeded to put up a superior auditorium for stage exhibitions and then persuaded his company to lease it.   Burbage's playhouse immediately received the name of "The Theatre" because it featured what the Elizabethans, following classical terminology, often called a "theater," that is, a stage.   They rarely, if ever, used the single word "theater" to mean a playhouse.

Burbage modeled The Theatre for the most part after the regular innyard playhouses of London, such as the Bull, the Bell, and the Cross Keys, where doubtless he often acted.   These improvised theaters consisted of a rectangular yard, surrounded by two or three galleries.   The yard had a covered entranceway at each end.   The passage at the front end served as a door of admission for the spectators who intended to stand. Those who desired to pay an extra fee for better accommodations went through the inn to take seats in the galleries.

A temporary stage was set up in the rear entranceway, with a curtain hung before the opening.   The drawing of this curtain permitted that part of the platform located within the passage to be used for an interior scene or for a setting with elaborate "props." The space further back in the passage formed the dressing-room of the actors.   The part of the gallery just above the acting platform provided an upper stage which could represent a balcony or the top of a city wall.

All these structural arrangements of the innyard Burbage reproduced in The Theatre, with one exception.   He made his building of a circular shape identical with the bear-baiting amphitheaters or "rings" which already existed in London.   The round wooden auditorium with its thatch-roofed tier of three galleries enclosed a large yard known as the "pit."   All the galleries had bleacher-like seats, but the pit accommodated standees only.   The first gallery contained box compartments or "rooms" for occupancy by the more elite.   Admission to the playhouse, including the pit, cost 1d. (about 20¢ today); to the first gallery, 2d. additional; to the other galleries, 1d. additional.   Takers at the stairways collected the gallery fees.   In accordance with old innyard custom, a large proportion, if not all, of the gallery fees went to the owner of the building, while the acting company took the admission receipts.

The stage of The Theatre was a large platform raised four to five feet above the ground and equipped with several trap doors.   It jutted well out into the pit so that the spectators there, "the groundlings," surrounded the platform on three sides.   The actors performed literally in the midst of their audience.   Though in the beginning the stage may have been without cover, sooner or later a "shadow" was constructed over it, probably with two high pillars as supports at the forecorners of the stage.   The latter possessed no drop-curtain of any sort, but in the center of the wall at the rear of the

THE SWAN PLAYHOUSE, LONDON, C. 1600

Drawing based on a contemporary sketch by Johannes De Witt

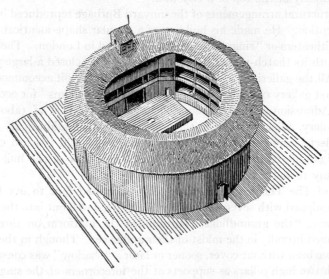

"THE THEATRE," LONDON, C. 1576

Drawing based on a conjectural model by W. S. Clark

stage a pair of curtains, termed variously "the arras," "the traverse," "the hangings," closed off a small room.   With the curtains drawn this inner stage could be utilized for interior settings like the study in Marlowe's *Dr. Faustus* and the burial vault in *Romeo and Juliet*.   To the right and to the left of the curtained room a regular stage door led into the "tiring-house."   There the actors had dressing-rooms and places for storing costumes and properties.   The architectural background of the main stage constituted the front of the tiring-house.

The second story of the tiring-house front corresponded with the first, namely, a curtained space in the center and a door to either side.   The doors, however, opened on a narrow balustraded gallery which ran along probably the entire front and projected over the stage.   This gallery, ten to twelve feet from the stage floor, proved an ideal balcony for a Romeo to scale with a makeshift rope.   The upper curtained room fulfilled a number of different functions.   It served as an upper stage interior whenever the play so demanded.   Certainly in the later years of The Theatre it was used by the playhouse musicians who performed before or during the stage piece.   Also it may have been occupied as a kind of stage box by distinguished personages and their guests.   At any rate what came to be called "the lord's room" was located somewhere in the second story of the tiring-house.

The third story occasionally represented a "heaven" or "heavens," from which divinities descended.   A crane thrust out through a door in the front of the tiring-house lowered these deities on "thrones," a procedure strongly reminiscent of the appearance of the gods on the ancient Athenian stage.

Still higher up, a small tower-like structure, the "hut," surmounted the tiring-house. From a pole on top of the hut there flew the house flag of The Theatre on every day of performance.   This was the chief means of informing the public that acting of a play could be assured for a given afternoon.   Inclement weather, periods of plague, or censorship often rendered production uncertain.   Through a window of the hut a trumpeteer blew at intervals three blasts to time the start of the play for the gathering spectators.   Performances usually began about two o'clock.   Early in the seventeenth century the hour of opening seems to have been moved to 2.30 or even 3 P.M.

The spectators who gathered at The Theatre included a fair cross-section of London's inhabitants.   They formed a rather democratic assemblage, for at least in the pit nobility, gentry, and commoners rubbed shoulders with one another.   Men vastly predominated, but a considerable number of women with male escorts sat in the lower galleries.   This varied audience's taste in dramatic entertainment was more than a little determined by the boisterous atmosphere of a playhouse where the cracking and eating of nuts threatened to drown out the actors' voices.   The prevailing temper approached that of the crowd at an outdoor circus.   The run of the spectators sought excitement and laughter; they were not at all interested in "problem drama" as it is now known. The sensational effects of battles, murders, and madness, of storms, ghosts, and magic delighted these playgoers.   They loved the flow of language as well as of action.   An extraordinary zest for words caused them to enjoy on the stage wit, poetry, bombast, and indeed every nuance of speech.   After all, what they looked for in the theater was a reflection of their vigorous and colorful era.

The nature of the stage at The Theatre helped much toward the exploitation of vigor and color in the plays given there.   Since little in the way of scenery was ever placed on the main stage, it represented successively whatever location a play required — woods, seashore, city square, or bedchamber. However extreme the changes of scene, they necessitated no halt in the acting. When a play called for the inner stage with its definite picture, the set could be made ready ahead of time. The drawing of the curtain took so brief a moment that no perceptible delay occurred. This flexibility of staging enabled an Elizabethan performance to display far more continuity and verve than the conventional modern performance. In fact, the rapid tempo of Elizabethan production would startle the average spectator today. Shakespeare did not much exaggerate when in *Romeo and Juliet* he called the playing of an ordinary five-act drama "this two hours' traffic of our stage."

The dearth of scenery, properties, and lighting effects, on the other hand, forced the playwright to have his characters' lines define the time and setting of the various scenes. Hence many a speech in an Elizabethan drama abounds with descriptive color. Romeo in parting from Juliet paints the beauty of the dawn breaking over the Capulet garden. Such purple passages on the actors' lips were greeted by the Elizabethan audience with enthusiasm.

The absence of any drop-curtain resulted in diverse bits of pageantry on the stage. Corpses always had to be carried out, those of the nobility conveyed in state by the "bearers of the dead." Witness at the close of *Hamlet* the funeral march in honor of the prince. The numerous scenes of royal audience had to be concluded with an elaborate processional to the stage doors. Scenes of crowded festivity often ended with a "going-out song" to cover the departure of the guests from the stage. These and similar devices of clearing the stage added no little color to the performance.

In its main architectural arrangements, its stage methods, and the character of its audience The Theatre typified all the public playhouses in London before England's Civil War. The parent institution of 1576 established theatrical traditions that were not essentially altered during three-quarters of a century. The second public theater, The Curtain, followed within a year on a near-by site in Finsbury Fields. The obscurity of its subsequent history suggests that it never achieved much popularity with the theater-going public. For ten or twelve years The Theatre carried on without a serious rival, reaching its heyday between 1583 and 1591 when the "Queen's Men" who received royal pensions and liveries acted there in most of the best contemporary drama.

During the last decade of the century the public playhouses multiplied while at the same time the center of the theatrical district shifted from north of London southward across the Thames River to the Bankside. Here, near the bear-baiting rings and houses of ill-fame, Philip Henslowe, famous manager of the Lord Admiral's company, led off in building The Rose as a home for his troupe. A few years afterwards The Swan was erected somewhat further to the west. Then in 1598 Richard Burbage, manager and leading actor of the Lord Chamberlain's company, tore down The Theatre, which he had inherited from his father, so that he might have material for a new playhouse on the Bankside. Not far to the south of The Rose, his chief competitor, he finished in 1599 The Globe, the theatrical birthplace of Shakespeare's greatest plays. Not to be outdone, Henslowe at once designed a larger and finer structure with a square instead of the conventional round auditorium. He dared a further innovation by abandoning the Bankside for a better-class location west of Finsbury Fields and north of Cripplegate. The opening of The Fortune there in 1600 completed the century-end boom in theater construction.

The public playhouses, however, had not been the only type of theater in London since the erection of The Theatre in 1576. Burbage's venture led Richard Farrant, the deputy master of the Royal Chapel choir-school, to start during the same year a theater in the well-to-do southwest corner of the city. The upper floor of a building belonging to the former Blackfriars monastery Farrant converted into a large hall with a raised platform at one end. Doors opened from this platform into dressing and property rooms backstage. Large candelabra on the walls furnished the illumination, but this artificial lighting possessed no more flexibility than that of the open-air auditoriums. The Blackfriars auditorium had neither galleries nor a place for standing. All spectators were seated on covered benches arranged probably in a rising tier. The audience included, for the most part, noblemen, courtiers, and citizens of high position. Such an exclusive and wealthy group liked the distinction of subscribing in advance to a season of performances at the high rate of four to sixpence per play. Thus Farrant could launch his enterprise as a "private" theater which took in no money at the door and therefore might not be interfered with by local officials.

For actors he trained the best of the Chapel choir-boys. They acted their plays in Blackfriars at irregular intervals during the fall and winter. Each of their repertoire they usually repeated at court soon after the original Blackfriars performance. Because of this close association with the court, the Blackfriars productions followed the method of simultaneous staging used in the theatricals there but never in the public playhouses. Multiple scenery in the shape of "players' houses" was placed about the stage with little regard to the ensemble effect or the perspective. The houses were frames of wood and painted canvas variously designed to represent arbors, castles, palaces, etc. They were supplemented by a free use of smaller properties like caves, rocks, wells, and thrones. Since these scenic decorations at the Blackfriars far exceeded the pictorial suggestiveness of the public stages, they served as an important drawing card for the boys' performances.

THE UNIVERSITY WITS

It was at the Blackfriars theater that there rose to prominence the first of the "university wits," a coterie of brilliant college-bred youths who during the 1580's turned playwriting into a profession and caused Elizabethan drama to come of age. In the summer of 1583 the Earl of Oxford, an ardent patron of drama, took over the Blackfriars playhouse in order to promote a more vigorous program of entertainment there. He appointed as director his literary protégé, John Lyly (?1554–1606), an Oxford University graduate. Lyly already had won a reputation from his fictional best-seller, *Euphues, or the Anatomy of Wit* (1578), but he had had no experience with drama or its production. Nothing daunted, he organized a fresh company of boy actors, the cream of both the Chapel and St. Paul's choir-schools. Then during the ensuing fall and winter he wrote and produced with much success two original plays, *Alexander, Campaspe, and Diogenes;* and *Sappho and Phao*. His highly stylized prose, his mixture of classical learning and poetic fancy, and his situations of romantic sentiment at once affected the contemporary drama. Lyly's plays instituted the soon-to-be-popular pattern of the double plot, the sub-plot of which is loosely connected with the main one and is often carried on by a contrasting set of characters. In *Campaspe* the main plot consists of the triangular love affair involving Alexander the Great, his lovely captive Campaspe, and the painter

Apelles, while the eccentric life and talk of the philosopher Diogenes, who lives in a tub, makes up the sub-plot. Though stilted in structure and development, *Campaspe* in its literary finish marked a great advance over current plays.

In the spring of 1584 the Blackfriars theater closed on account of litigation, not to open again until 1600. The closing forced the Oxford troupe of boys to disband, and Lyly to give up his career as a producer. About 1587 or 1588 he began to write plays for the boy actors of St. Paul's choir-school to perform on their stage and then at court. The director of "the Paul's boys," Henry Evans, was conducting at the school a more or less private theater. The best of Lyly's four or five compositions for this enterprise were *Endymion, the Man in the Moon* (1588), a fantasy compounded of mythology and allegory; and *Mother Bombie* (1590), a comedy of intrigue on Latin lines. *Endymion* includes a charming scene, where a band of fairies hover over the brawny, dull Corsites drowsing on a bank of moonwort, sing several delicate lyrics, and cast a magic spell upon him. This scene must have inspired Shakespeare to the memorable scenes in *Midsummer Night's Dream* between Bottom and the fairies.

Early in 1591 "the Paul's boys" were compelled to cease acting because their performances had touched on controversial topics. Their demise ended Lyly's playwriting, for he had been too long associated exclusively with boy actors and genteel audiences to accommodate his talents to the more robust demands of The Theatre or The Rose. Despite the limited scope of his endeavor, John Lyly contributed much to the elevation of Elizabethan drama in both theme and material.

Another of the "wits" to gain fame by way of the Blackfriars theater was George Peele (?1558–?1596), an Oxford man like Lyly. After coming up from the university to London about 1581, for fifteen years he lived with moderate success the none too savory life of the young Elizabethan who was making literature his fortune. He composed his first play, a pastoral called *The Arraignment of Paris*, for a boys' company at the Blackfriars, probably the one under Lyly's direction in the winter of 1583–84. Peele introduced a clever and profitable twist to his dramatic version of the story about Paris and the Golden Apple by having Diana, the judge of the beauty contest, award the prize to neither of the contesting goddesses, but to the "wondrous nymph" Elizabeth. Such a flattering tribute to the Queen roused, of course, great applause at the court performance.

After his initial success on the private stage, Peele proceeded to do all his subsequent playwriting for the adult troupes in the public theaters. A "pleasant, conceited comedy" entitled *The Old Wives Tale* (c. 1592) emerged as his single piece of distinction, one which helped to enlarge the Elizabethan world of romantic humor. It is a quaint and satiric fantasy in one long act leading from reality to romance, only to ridicule the latter in a lively spirit. Three jolly rustics have lost their way in a dark wood. They meet Clunch, a smith, on his way home. He conducts them to his cottage, where Madge, his wife, after supper starts to entertain the guests with a tale. Suddenly the characters of her tale come to life on the stage and begin to enact the old woman's story in front of her and her visitors. The play then turns into a melange of fairy tale material including a sorcerer, a giant, a ghost, a braggart soldier, two furies, a church warden, harvest-men, lost youths and maidens, enchantments and other magical happenings. Peele intended his absurdly supernatural melodrama to burlesque the extravagant romancing in the popular plays of the moment. Thus *The Old Wives Tale* became the first of a long line of dramatic literary satires on the English stage.

One of Peele's fellow "wits" in London was Robert Greene (1558–92), who on the title-pages of his works boasted that he held a Master of Arts from both Cambridge and Oxford. Greene's short life contained more color than even his autobiographical fiction imparted. After he had spent his wife's dowry on a Continental tour without her, he deserted both her and her child. Then in London he embarked on the paradoxical career of Bohemianism and want, of fame and obscurity, so typical of Elizabethan playwrights. He took for a mistress the sister of Cutting Ball, notorious London thief. Either in irony or vain hope he named the offspring of this union "Fortunatus." Between 1587 and 1592, despite riotous living, he kept busy turning out prose tracts, romances, and plays. On a late August evening of 1592 he had supper with another "wit," Thomas Nashe (1567–1601), in a tavern where they ate a quantity of pickled herrings and drank much wine. The strain of this repast caused Greene to fall into a stupor, from which he never fully recovered. While ill on his bed at a shoemaker's house, he composed a last pamphlet, *Greene's Groatsworth of Wit Bought with a Million of Repentance*, in which his penitence did not prevent him from one more jealous attack on a rival dramatist. This, the earliest known allusion to Shakespeare, upbraids him as "an upstart crow beautified in our feathers, that, with his tiger's heart wrapt in a player's hide, supposes he is as well able to bombast out a blank verse as the best of you; and is ... in his own conceit the only Shakescene in a country." Very early in September Greene died unattended by relative or friend. The shoemaker's wife buried him with a wreath on his head in accordance with his dying wish. That wreath was the last gesture of a proud, vain man who felt that the Elizabethan world would never do honor to him any more than it did to its other dramatic poets.

Greene's significance to Elizabethan drama lay in his development of romantic setting and of female characterization. *The Honorable History of Friar Bacon and Friar Bungay* (1589–90) and *The Scottish History of James IV* (c. 1591) most clearly demonstrate his talent. In the first play the main plot deals with the rivalry in magical powers between the two English friars, Bacon and Bungay, and later between Bacon and the German necromancer, Vandermast. The wooing of Margaret, the gamekeeper's daughter, by Lacy, Earl of Lincoln, and Edward, Prince of Wales, constitutes the sub-plot. Greene mingled three worlds — the aristocratic, the rural, the supernatural — so that kings consort with commoners, nobles marry the low born, while devils and spirits walk the earth. Such a medley of the pretty and the grotesque, of the lyrical and the humorous, soon characterized much of Elizabethan romantic comedy. Greene's peculiar gift to the latter, however, was the idyllic atmosphere of life and love in the English countryside. The center of his pastoral idyl is Margaret, "the lovely maid of Fressingfield" with "golden hair," "sparkling eyes," and "lily arms" — an Elizabethan dream of unsophisticated female grace. In Margaret, Greene drew the stage original for a succession of idealized young women whom later playwrights created as heroines.

James IV displays a formula of romantic comedy similar to that of *Friar Bacon* with an interweaving of the same three worlds. Oberon, King of the Fairies, replaces the magicians. The name and the rôle caught the attention of Shakespeare and were introduced a second time to Elizabethan audiences in *Midsummer Night's Dream*. The love triangle of *James IV* reverses the situation of *Friar Bacon*, for instead of two men attracted to one woman, one man, James, King of Scotland, is torn between two women — his wife, Dorothea, and Ida, daughter of a Scottish lord. An interesting variation on the pastoral idyl is supplied by the wanderings of the lonely Dorothea before her restoration to her husband's arms. Disguised as a man she travels about the country with her dwarf and maidservant, Nano. The circumstances probably suggested to Shakespeare the scenes in *As You Like It* where the lovelorn Rosalind accompanied by Celia roams in disguise through the Forest of Arden. With his fair, tender heroines, Dorothea and Margaret, Greene played up for the first time on the English stage both the charm and the romantic nature of woman. The conception which he held, at least for dramatic purposes, is well expressed toward the close of *Friar Bacon* in the Earl of Sussex' *bon mot* concerning women: "Be they never so near God, yet they love to die in a man's arms."

Lyly, Peele, and Greene devoted themselves almost entirely to the creation of comedy, but others of their literary set in London turned to tragedy, in which little of consequence had developed since *Gorboduc* (1562). The earliest of these writers in the tragic vein was Thomas Kyd (?1558–94), a native of London who never enjoyed a university training, though he was a close associate of the "university wits." Less is known about him than about any one else in that group. His importance to the history of English drama rests wholly upon one play, *The Spanish Tragedy* (c. 1585–87), which became the most popular tragedy on the English stage before 1600. It set the vogue for one of the outstanding types in Elizabethan and seventeenth century drama, the tragedy of blood and revenge. From the much respected Seneca, Kyd borrowed the theme of revenge and the crude framework of an induction and act-end chorus played by the ghost of the slain Spanish courtier, Andrea, and by the Spirit of Revenge. Kyd, however, outdid Seneca by working up a plot of revenge upon revenge, whereby Hieronimo, Marshal of Spain, avenges the murder of his son, Horatio, after the latter has avenged Andrea's death by making his slayer a prisoner of war. In his series of revengeful actions Kyd, aware of the Elizabethan fondness for bloody scenes, disregarded Seneca's avoidance of violence on the stage and arranged ten deaths in sight of the audience, including outdoor strangling at night, public hanging, shooting from ambush, murder by means of theatrical trickery, and suicide after the biting off of the tongue.

Of all the English playwrights prior to Shakespeare, the author of *The Spanish Tragedy* possessed by far the keenest sense of "theater." His play moves with steadily rising tension through a well-constructed sequence of varied incident to the melodramatic climax of Hieronimo's court play, when the chief characters not yet dead meet death. In each scene no opportunity for effective stage business is overlooked. For instance, when Hieronimo enters lamenting the loss of his son and crying out for evidence of the murderer, at the precise moment when he voices his wish for clues, a letter falls in front of him on the stage. Kyd taught Shakespeare, as well as lesser lights, many items of theatrical technique, such as the bloody handkerchief as a reminder of violence, the *meditative* soliloquy, the reading of a book before a soliloquy, the play within a play, and madness real or pretended.

More valuable, however, than Kyd's flair for theatricalism was the subtlety of characterization which he achieved in Hieronimo, an absolutely new kind of stage hero for London theatergoers. He is sensitive, thoughtful, inclined to indecision — a man whose hesitancies result from an inner weighing of considerations. Stricken with grief until on the verge of mental breakdown, he then hits upon madness as the very ruse to further his designs of revenge. For Kyd, dramatic tragedy is not merely a conflict with circumstance, but a struggle of wits and a suffering of the spirit. Hieronimo personifies the new psychological element which Kyd thus early introduced into Elizabethan tragic drama. His emphasis in that direction exerted a strong influence on Shakespeare, so strong, in fact, that the latter's hero, Hamlet, is a direct descendant of Hieronimo, while the play *Hamlet*, derives many of its features from *The Spanish Tragedy*. Without Thomas Kyd one of the world's dramatic masterpieces would never have assumed its present pattern.

MARLOWE AND THE CHRONICLE HISTORY PLAY

Kyd's sole rival in the writing of tragedy was the greatest of the university wits, Christopher Marlowe. Of all the dramatists of the Elizabethan age none perhaps cut quite so romantic a figure as "Kit" Marlowe, the victim of murder in his thirtieth year when at the height of his fame. He was born the son of a shoemaker in the old cathedral town of Canterbury on February 6, 1564, only two months before the birth of Shakespeare. At fifteen he entered the select King's School, Canterbury, as a scholarship boy, an unusual honor for a tradesman's son. Because he seemed a promising student, he received a further scholarship to attend Corpus Christi College, Cambridge, where he took his B.A. in 1584. He continued study there for a Master of Arts, but on the verge of completing his course he got infected with the prevailing spirit of political intrigue. Plots and counter-plots were going on in circles domestic as well as foreign. Queen Elizabeth had to spy not only on the Spanish and the French, but also on her own ministers, while the latter in turn had had to keep secret track of each other's designs. Marlowe left College in February, 1587, to act as a government agent, perhaps at Rheims, a center of the Papist plotting against England. During the ensuing summer the Cambridge university authorities, at the insistence of the Privy Council, took the extraordinary action of granting Marlowe his M.A. *in absentia*. In the fall of 1587 he returned to London to join the growing coterie of young authors. For the next five years, much of the time on the move, he engaged in three major activities — writing for the stage, espionage, and bachelor brawling. The brawling sometimes grew out of his theatrical connections, but more often out of his undercover affiliations. No doubt the uncertain, rather exciting occupation of secret agent helped to satisfy a restless and ambitious nature. Marlowe seems to have hoped for a major rôle in some matter that the great ones of the government, like his patron, Sir Thomas Walsingham, might have in the making.

In September, 1589, Marlowe and another agent, Thomas Watson, duelled in Hog Lane, London, with a third spy, whom Watson finally stabbed to death. For his part in this fracas Marlowe suffered confinement in the foul Newgate prison for two weeks. About 1591 or 1592 he shared lodgings for a while with Thomas Kyd, toward whom he seems to have acted with deliberate bravado. He apparently disturbed the more cautious Kyd by his riotous behavior and radical remarks, especially on religion. When Kyd during the first months of 1593 found himself in trouble over some allegedly dangerous papers, he informed on Marlowe and caused the latter's arrest on May 20 for atheistical views. Marlowe then broke bail by fleeing to Deptford in Kent, whence he evidently planned to seek refuge with influential persons in Scotland. On May 30, however, at Eleanor Bull's tavern in Deptford he met with two government agents, Robert Poley and Ingram Frizer. That night, after hours of talking and drinking in their private room, the three men got into an altercation. Whether the brawl was premeditated by Poley and Frizer in order to do Marlowe in or was simply a sudden flare-up of intoxicated wits, remains an unsettled question. At any rate, Frizer in self-defense, so he claimed, drew a dagger and stabbed Marlowe through the brain. Thus in a death scene as bloody and ignoble as any out of Elizabethan tragedy, England's leading dramatist of the day made his exit. Yet the event shocked a callous public so slightly that all the details were at once forgotten, to continue lost from literary history until 1925.

Marlowe probably undertook the composition of his first play about 1586 while still a student at Cambridge. His "aspiring mind," to use Marlowe's own phrase, disdained the "jigging veins of rhyming mother-wits" for the high calling of tragedy. Fired by Machiavelli's idea of the Prince or superman, which had excited the imagination of people all over Renaissance Europe, Marlowe discarded the conventional tragic pattern based on Seneca and conceived a fresh formula with the sweep of the epic in it. Poet rather than psychologist, he aimed to present the splendid passion of the superman's career. His maiden effort, *Tamburlaine the Great*, took London by storm when the Lord Admiral's company first performed it in the fall of 1587. Huge Edward Alleyn, who became the greatest Elizabethan tragedian, won his spurs in the title-rôle. Audiences marveled at the length, the grandeur, and the poetry of Marlowe's tragedy. It was the first English drama to consist of two parts, each a five-act play which required a separate day of performance. These ten acts exhibit the amazing rise of the Scythian shepherd to be a world conqueror, and also to be the lover of the "divine Zenocrate"; and then the speedy decline of all his fortune, first in Zenocrate's death and later in his own. The inevitable enemy of every man without exception struck down Tamburlaine despite his arrogant pretence to a special destiny. The last words of the dying hero voice Marlowe's sense of the tragedy: "Tamburlaine the Scourge of God *must* die." Mortality, not justice, is the decisive force or fate.

Many of the scenes in *Tamburlaine the Great* are striking, though often horrible in line with the conqueror's ruthless character. The most audacious touch of stage business, which provoked allusions for a century after, is the entrance of the captured Turkish emperor, Bajazeth, in a cage drawn by two Moors. Taken out of the cage like a circus animal, he is forced to prostrate himself so that Tamburlaine may use him as a footstool to mount his throne. The splendor of Marlowe's drama, however, comes not merely from such spectacles of triumph, but from the "high astounding terms" with which Tamburlaine threatens the world and pays tribute to the beautiful Zenocrate. A lyric magnificence suffuses the dialogue from beginning to end. Marlowe transformed the hitherto stilted medium of blank verse into a vehicle of music and color. Throughout every scene he created a pageantry of words so gorgeous that his "immortal flowers of poesy" enrapture and confuse the senses of any spectator. The latter listens quite forgetful of the savage warrior himself when Tamburlaine breaks forth into sweet musings on

> Our souls, whose faculties can comprehend
> The wondrous architecture of the world,
> And measure every wandering planet's course.

No such sheer richness of speech had ever before been heard on the English stage and only rarely has it been heard since Marlowe and his pupil, Shakespeare.

The tremendous success of *Tamburlaine the Great* encouraged Marlowe to write within a year a second tragedy, *The Tragical History of Dr. Faustus*, in which Alleyn could again star. He dramatized the career of another strong-willed man ambitious for power — in this case, power that comes from craft rather than brute force. The play reproduces the high points in the Renaissance legend of the German scholar, Dr. Faustus, who sold his soul to the devil for twenty-four years' unrestricted exercise of magic. Though *Dr. Faustus*, too, is little more than a loose series of scenes, Marlowe advanced upon his art in *Tamburlaine the Great* by offering glimpses of a moral struggle within the mind of the hero. Faustus grows aware that he has turned from a scholar into a worldly trickster. Marlowe, however, depended too much upon a primitive, morality play technique of having a Good and a Bad Angel strive for mastery over Faustus. In the final brief scene where Faustus faces the devil's approach the agony of his conscience comes out with full force through a great soliloquy. Other than this last moment of tragedy *Dr. Faustus* contains but a few scattered passages of superlative poetry to alleviate the generally mediocre level of its drama. No lovelier lines can be found in any English play than Faustus' tribute to Helen of Troy,

> O thou art fairer than the evening air
> Clad in the beauty of a thousand stars.

Marlowe's next play, *The Famous Tragedy of the Rich Jew of Malta*, which the Lord Admiral's company produced a year or so after *Dr. Faustus*, gave Alleyn a third chance to play an outstanding part, that of Barabas the Jew. Once more Marlowe chose as his theme the ambition for power, but his exposition marks a clear decline in dramatic art. At the opening of the play Barabas is a man to command respect for his desire to lead his race, and for his devotion to an only daughter, Abigail; a devotion similar to Shylock's for Jessica in *The Merchant of Venice*. Then he develops rapidly into a cheap, brutal villain at the same time that the play deteriorates into melodrama and horror. The concluding scene is a climax of the grotesque. Barabas drops through a false floor into a boiling cauldron far below and suffers the terrible death he had prepared for his enemies. Despite the absence of tragic elevation in its outcome *The Jew of Malta* delighted London audiences until well into the seventeenth century.

In the space of some three years Marlowe had scored three outstanding hits on the stage and had arrived at the top of his profession. Each succeeding play, however, showed that he was tiring of tragedy which concentrated on the superman's failure to win the world of his ambition. Furthermore he was ripening slowly as a playwright and was subduing little by little the urge to rhetoric and lyricism in favor of a more dramatic style. No matter how successful, therefore, his drama of egocentric wills had proved with the public, to Marlowe himself in 1591 a new pattern of tragedy appealed more. He found at hand a type still undeveloped but growing in favor. The world-wide expansion of English trade and travel during the first two decades of Elizabeth's reign had awakened an intensely national sentiment. This sentiment in turn had fostered a widespread interest in English history. The thrilling victory of the English fleet over the great Spanish Armada in the summer of 1588 accentuated the enthusiasm for the national past. Even before this momentous event the London playwrights had begun to cater to the patriotic fervor of the common people at the public theaters by dramatizing portions of the English chronicles. Most of the historical plays before 1590 have not survived, chiefly because they were written by obscure or anonymous authors. The best extant specimen of this early group is *The Famous Victories of Henry V*, extremely popular in its day. Though some of the scenes reveal lively touches of character, the characterization of persons of high rank reduces them to the level of the middle class citizens with whom the average London playgoer could be expected to feel most in sympathy. Like the characters, the situations are handled without close attention to historical plausibility. Dramatic structure amounts to little more than a chronological sequence of heterogeneous scenes. These traits of artistic inferiority typified the chronicle history play up to 1591.

In choosing at this date the chronicle history as the pattern of his new tragedy, Marlowe took up an established favorite. He, however, improved very much upon all previous achievements of the kind. Indeed, *The Troublesome Reign and Lamentable Death of Edward the Second* is Marlowe's finest piece of dramaturgy, though it did not stir such interest at its premiere as his earlier plays. Perhaps the absence of Alleyn from the king's rôle may have made for a less impressive performance. Marlowe had broken off relations with the Lord Admiral's company and sold his fourth play to the Earl of Pembroke's troupe for production in 1592.

The theme of *Edward the Second* is quite the reverse of the subject which previously had monopolized its author's concern. Instead of a strong-willed hero pitted against an external stronger force, a weakling encompasses his own defeat. From Holinshed's *Chronicle of England* (1577) and Stow's *Annals of England* (1580) Marlowe took the story of the king who allowed his affection for a foppish youth, Gaveston, to alienate his barons and to bring about his eventual abdication and murder. Marlowe's development of the situation, however, betrays the deficient conception of tragedy common to his earlier plays also. He fashioned such self-centered heroes that the spectator cannot feel for them a complete respect and sympathy. King Edward's downfall may be attended by most pitiable circumstances but it does not convey that sense of profound loss which great tragic art produces.

The excellence of *Edward the Second* arises from the varied touches of characterization combined with a dramatic concentration of historical material. Marlowe did not confine himself to the delineation of one or two major figures as he had in the past. His blank verse had grown so supple that it was capable of suggesting any distinction of personality desired. He breathed some semblance of individuality into a score or more of persons ranging from a king and his favorite to a poor man and a murderer. Sometimes the characters paint their own portraits in a colorful exchange of remarks, as when in Act II, Scene 1, Young Spencer advises Baldock how to be a courtier. On the other hand, at the close of Act I (ll. 402–19) Marlowe has Young Mortimer deliver for the information of the spectator a brilliant sketch of the dapper Gaveston at court. Yet with all his increased talent for character study Marlowe could not create an interesting woman. Queen Isabella is quite as disappointingly neutral as his previous heroines.

Around a large galaxy of historical individuals Marlowe built an interesting and coherent drama. With great skill he selected and adapted the often disconnected events of Edward the Second's reign, 1307–27, so that they form a single plot with a proper catastrophe; with equal skill he compressed the action dispersed over some twenty-five years so that it all seems to occur without interruption and within a year. A conflict between two protagonists, the irresolute monarch and the resolute Young Mortimer "that scorns the world," is worked up step by step to a fine climax in the last act. Two scenes of unusual pathos portray first Edward's spiritual downfall and then his physical one. The first scene of Act V traces with keen insight the torture wrought upon the king's mind by the forced surrender of his crown, while the fifth scene depicts the ignominy and agony which the king suffers during his last hours. In this latter scene (ll. 58–69) Edward gives utterance to the depth of his misery with the most poignant speech Marlowe ever wrote. The superb restraint and simplicity make it surpass the more gorgeous passages of poetry in *Tamburlaine* and *Dr. Faustus*.

The tragic power with which Marlowe endowed history in *Edward the Second* is the more remarkable because Marlowe found absolutely no precedent of careful plotting in chronicle history plays. His refinement of the type resulted in a dramatic pattern which the budding genius of Shakespeare exploited during the next four or five years. Shakespeare paid *Edward the Second* a notable tribute when about 1594 he decided to dramatize the reign of Richard II. He clearly modeled his Richard on Marlowe's Edward, though of course his king is a richer study in personality. Shakespeare also constructed the conflict in *Richard II* along much the same lines as that in *Edward the Second*, even imitating the latter's two highlights, the abdication and the dungeon-murder scenes. Perhaps he recognized that Marlowe's play is the most excellent example of sheer dramatic exposition among English plays prior to his own.

[For detailed description of Elizabethan theaters and their staging, see W. J. Lawrence, *The Physical Conditions of the Elizabethan Public Playhouse* (1927), *The Elizabethan Playhouse and Other Studies* (two series, 1912 and 1913), *Pre-Restoration Stage Studies* (1927); and J. Q. Adams, *Shakespearean Playhouses* (1917); for all aspects of Elizabethan theatricals, E. K. Chambers, *The Elizabethan Stage* (4 vols., 1923); for Seneca's relation to England, J. W. Cunliffe, *The Influence of Seneca on Elizabethan Tragedy* (1907); for a critique on pre-Shakespearean drama, C. F. Tucker Brooke, *The Tudor Drama* (1911); for Marlowe, J. E. Bakeless, *Christopher Marlowe, the Man in his Time* (1937), and F. S. Boas, *Christopher Marlowe: a Biographical and Critical Study* (1940).]

CHRISTOPHER MARLOWE

The Troublesome Reign and Lamentable Death of Edward the Second

DRAMATIS PERSONAE

KING EDWARD THE SECOND

PRINCE EDWARD, *his son, afterwards King Edward the Third*

EDMUND, EARL OF KENT, *half-brother to King Edward the Second*

PIERCE DE GAVESTON, *afterwards Earl of Cornwall*

ARCHBISHOP OF CANTERBURY

BISHOP OF COVENTRY

BISHOP OF WINCHESTER

GUY, EARL OF WARWICK

THOMAS, EARL OF LANCASTER

AYMER, EARL OF PEMBROKE

EDMUND, EARL OF ARUNDEL

HENRY, EARL OF LEICESTER

SIR THOMAS BERKELEY

ROGER, LORD MORTIMER, *the* elder

ROGER, LORD MORTIMER, *the* younger, *his nephew*

HUGH, LORD SPENCER, *the* elder

HUGH, LORD SPENCER, *the* younger, *his son*

ROBERT BALDOCK

HENRY DE BEAUMONT

SIR WILLIAM TRUSSEL

SIR THOMAS GURNEY

SIR JOHN MATREVIS

LIGHTBORN

SIR JOHN OF HAINAULT

LEVUNE

RICE AP HOWELL

JAMES

Abbot, Monks, Herald, Lords, Poor Men, Mower, Champion, Messengers, Soldiers, and Attendants

QUEEN ISABELLA, *wife to King Edward the Second*

Niece *to King Edward the Second, daughter to the Earl of Gloucester*

Ladies

ACT I

SCENE 1. *A street in Westminster, London*

Enter GAVESTON,[1] *reading on a letter that was brought him from the King*

Gaveston. "My father is deceas'd! Come, Gaveston,
And share the kingdom with thy dearest friend."
Ah! words that make me surfeit with delight!
What greater bliss can hap to Gaveston

Than live and be the favorite of a king!   5
Sweet prince, I come; these, these thy amorous lines
Might have enforc'd me to have swum from France,
And, like Leander,[1] gasp'd upon the sand,
So [2] thou would'st smile, and take me in thine arms.
The sight of London to my exil'd eyes   10
Is as Elysium to a new-come soul;
Not that I love the city, or the men,
But that it harbors him I hold so dear —
The king, upon whose bosom let me die,[3]

---

[1] The son of a French knight and the boon friend of Edward II while still a prince. Edward I had banished Gaveston in February, 1307, because of his bad influence, but Edward II recalled him on ascending the throne in July, 1307.

[1] A legendary Greek youth who swam the Hellespont nightly to visit Hero, his beloved.

[2] Provided that.   [3] Swoon.

And with the world be still at enmity.   15
What need the arctic people love starlight,
To whom the sun shines both by day and night?
Farewell base stooping to the lordly peers!
My knee shall bow to none but to the king.
As for the multitude, that are but sparks   20
Rak'd up in embers of their poverty; —
Tanti.[1] I'll fawn first on the wind
That glanceth at my lips, and flyeth away.

Enter three Poor Men

But how now, what are these?

    Poor Men. Such as desire your worship's
      service.   25
    Gav. What canst thou do?
    1 P. Man. I can ride.
    Gav. But I have no horses. — What art thou?
    2 P. Man. A traveler.
    Gav. Let me see: thou would'st do well   30
To wait at my trencher[2] and tell me lies at
    dinner time;
And as I like your discoursing, I'll have you. —
And what art thou?
    3 P. Man. A soldier that hath serv'd against
    the Scot.
    Gav. Why, there are hospitals[3] for such
    as you.   35
I have no war, and therefore, sir, begone.
    3 P. Man. Farewell, and perish by a sol-
    dier's hand,
That would'st reward them with an hospital.
    Gav. (aside). Ay, ay, these words of his
    move me as much
As if a goose should play the porpentine,[4]   40
And dart her plumes, thinking to pierce my
    breast.
But yet it is no pain to speak men fair;
I'll flatter these, and make them live in hope. —
You know that I came lately out of France,
And yet I have not view'd my lord the king;   45
If I speed well, I'll entertain you all.
    All. We thank your worship.
    Gav. I have some business: leave me to
    myself.
    All. We will wait here about the court.
    Gav. Do. *(Exeunt the* Poor Men.*)* These
    are not men for me: 50

[1] So much for them.   [2] Wooden plate.
[3] Almshouses.   [4] Porcupine.

I must have wanton[1] poets, pleasant wits,
Musicians, that with touching of a string
May draw the pliant King which way I please.
Music and poetry is his delight;
Therefore I'll have Italian masks[2] by night,   55
Sweet speeches, comedies, and pleasing shows;
And in the day, when he shall walk abroad,
Like sylvan nymphs my pages shall be clad;
My men, like satyrs[3] grazing on[4] the lawns,
Shall with their goat-feet dance an antic hay.[5]
Sometime a lovely boy in Dian's shape,[6]   61
With hair that gilds the water as it glides,
Crownets[7] of pearl about his naked arms,
And in his sportful hands an olive tree,[8]   64
To hide those parts which men delight to see,
Shall bathe him in a spring; and there hard by,
One like Actaeon[9] peeping through the grove
Shall by the angry goddess be transform'd,
And running in the likeness of an hart
By yelping hounds pull'd down, and seem to
    die; —   70
Such things as these best please his majesty,
My lord. — Here comes the King, and the
    nobles
From the parliament. I'll stand aside. *(Retires.*

Enter KING EDWARD II,[10] LANCASTER, the
    ELDER MORTIMER, YOUNG MORTIMER;[11]
    EDMUND, EARL OF KENT,[12] GUY, EARL OF
    WARWICK, *and Attendants*

    K. Edw. Lancaster!   75
    Lan. My lord.

[1] Amorous.
[2] Masquerade performances accompanied by dancing and music became popular in sixteenth-century England as a fashion imported in large measure from Italy.
[3] Figures part man and part goat.
[4] Straying over.   [5] Grotesque country dance.
[6] In the guise of the goddess Diana.
[7] Bracelets.   [8] Olive branch.
[9] A huntsman of Greek legend, who, having surprised Diana bathing in a spring, was transformed by the angry goddess into a deer, and was then pursued and killed by his own hounds.
[10] Born in April, 1284, the son of Edward I and Eleanor of Castile, he became king in July, 1307.
[11] The Mortimers were powerful barons on the Welsh border, who in history had nothing to do with the opposition to Gaveston.
[12] Born in 1301, the son of Edward I and his second wife, Margaret of France, he had no historical connection with the Gaveston affair.

Gav. (aside). That Earl of Lancaster do I
　　abhor.
K. Edw. Will you not grant me this? —
　　(Aside) In spite of them
I'll have my will; and these two Mortimers,
That cross me thus, shall know I am displeas'd.
E. Mor. If you love us, my lord, hate
　　Gaveston.　　　　　　　　　　　80
Gav. (aside). That villain Mortimer! I'll
　　be his death.
Y. Mor. Mine uncle here, this earl, and I
　　myself
Were sworn to your father at his death,
That he [1] should ne'er return into the realm;
And know, my lord, ere I will break my oath,
This sword of mine, that should offend your
　　foes,　　　　　　　　　　　　86
Shall sleep within the scabbard at thy need,
And underneath thy banners march who will,
For Mortimer will hang his armor up.
Gav. (aside). Mort Dieu! [2]　　　　90
K. Edw. Well, Mortimer, I'll make thee
　　rue [3] these words.
Beseems it thee to contradict thy king?
Frown'st thou thereat, aspiring Lancaster?
The sword shall plane the furrows of thy brows,
And hew these knees that now are grown so
　　stiff.　　　　　　　　　　　　95
I will have Gaveston; and you shall know
What danger 'tis to stand against your king.
Gav. (aside). Well done, Ned!
Lan. My lord, why do you thus incense
　　your peers,
That naturally would love and honor you　100
But for that base and obscure Gaveston?
Four earldoms have I, besides Lancaster —
Derby, Salisbury, Lincoln, Leicester, —
These will I sell, to give my soldiers pay,
Ere Gaveston shall stay within the realm;　105
Therefore, if he be come, expel him straight.
Kent. Barons and earls, your pride hath
　　made me mute;
But now I'll speak, and to the proof,[4] I hope.
I do remember, in my father's days,　　109
Lord Percy of the north, being highly mov'd,
Braved Mowbery in presence of the king;

For which, had not his highness lov'd him well,
He should have lost his head; but with his look
The undaunted spirit of Percy was appeas'd,
And Mowbery and he were reconcil'd:　115
Yet dare you brave the king unto his face? —
Brother, revenge it, and let these their heads
Preach upon poles, for trespass of their tongues.
War. O, our heads!
K. Edw. Ay, yours; and therefore I would
　　wish you grant —　　　　　　　120
War. Bridle thy anger, gentle Mortimer.
Y. Mor. I cannot, nor I will not; I must
　　speak. —
Cousin,[1] our hands I hope shall fence our heads,
And strike off his that makes you threaten
　　us.　　　　　　　　　　　　124
Come, uncle, let us leave the brain-sick king,
And henceforth parley with our naked swords.
E. Mor. Wiltshire [2] hath men enough to save
　　our heads.
War. All Warwickshire will love [3] him for
　　my sake.
Lan. And northward Gaveston hath many
　　friends. —　　　　　　　　　129
Adieu, my lord; and either change your mind,
Or look to see the throne, where you should sit,
To float in blood; and at thy wanton [4] head,
The glozing [5] head of thy base minion [6] thrown.
　　(Exeunt all except KING EDWARD,
　　　　KENT, GAVESTON, *and Attendants.*
K. Edw. I cannot brook these haughty
　　menaces.
Am I a king, and must be overrul'd? —　135
Brother, display my ensigns in the field;
I'll bandy [7] with the barons and the earls,
And either die or live with Gaveston.
Gav. I can no longer keep me from my lord.
　　　　　　　　　　(Comes forward.
K. Edw. What, Gaveston! welcome! — Kiss
　　not my hand —　　　　　　　140
Embrace me, Gaveston, as I do thee.
Why should'st thou kneel? Know'st thou not
　　who I am?
Thy friend, thyself, another Gaveston!

---

[1] I.e., Gaveston.
[2] Lit., God's death: — an old French oath.
[3] Regret.　　[4] Irrefutably.

[1] Kinsman.
[2] A county in south central England.
[3] Used in ironic sense.
[4] Flighty.　　　[5] Flattering.
[6] Favorite.　　　[7] Contend.

Not Hylas was more mourn'd of Hercules,[1]
Than thou hast been of me since thy exile.
  Gav. And since I went from hence, no soul
        in hell   146
Hath felt more torment than poor Gaveston.
  K. Edw. I know it. — Brother, welcome
        home my friend.
Now let the treacherous Mortimers conspire,
And that high-minded [2] Earl of Lancaster:
I have my wish, in that I joy thy sight;   151
And sooner shall the sea o'erwhelm my land,
Than bear the ship that shall transport thee
        hence.
I here create thee Lord High Chamberlain,
Chief Secretary to the state and me,   155
Earl of Cornwall, King and Lord of Man.
  Gav. My lord, these titles far exceed my
        worth.
  Kent. Brother, the least of these may well
        suffice
For one of greater birth than Gaveston.
  K. Edw. Cease, brother, for I cannot brook [3]
        these words.   160
Thy worth, sweet friend, is far above my
        gifts.
Therefore, to equal it, receive my heart.
If for these dignities thou be envied,
I'll give thee more; for, but to honor thee,
Is Edward pleas'd with kingly regiment.[4] 165
Fear'st thou [5] thy person?   Thou shalt have
        a guard.
Wantest thou gold?   Go to my treasury.
Wouldst thou be lov'd and fear'd?   Receive
        my seal;
Save or condemn, and in our name command
Whatso thy mind effects,[6] or fancy likes,   170
  Gav. It shall suffice me to enjoy your love,
Which whiles I have, I think myself as great
As Caesar riding in the Roman street,
With captive kings at his triumphant car.

[1] When Hercules went with Jason and other Greek
heroes in search of the Golden Fleece, he took with him
a youth named Hylas.   The expedition touched at
Mysia on the coast of Asia Minor, where Hylas landed
to secure a supply of water.   At the well the nymphs,
infatuated by his beauty, drew him down into the
water.   On his disappearance Hercules made a frantic
search but never heard more than an echo of his voice.
  [2] Arrogant.   [3] Endure.   [4] Rule.
  [5] Fear'st thou for.   [6] Desires.

Enter the BISHOP OF COVENTRY

  K. Edw. Whither goes my lord of Coventry
        so fast?   175
  B. of Cov. To celebrate your father's
        exequies.[1]
But is that wicked Gaveston return'd?
  K. Edw. Ay, priest, and lives to be reveng'd
        on thee,
That wert the only cause of his exile.
  Gav. 'Tis true; and but for reverence of
        these robes,   180
Thou should'st not plod one foot beyond this
        place.
  B. of Cov. I did no more than I was bound
        to do;
And, Gaveston, unless thou be reclaim'd,
As then I did incense the parliament,   184
So will I now, and thou shalt back to France.
  Gav. Saving your reverence, you must
        pardon me.
  K. Edw. Throw off his golden miter,[2] rend
        his stole,[3]
And in the channel [4] christen him anew.
  Kent. Ah, brother, lay not violent hands on
        him!
For he'll complain unto the see of Rome.   190
  Gav. Let him complain unto the see of
        hell;
I'll be reveng'd on him for my exile.
  K. Edw. No, spare his life, but seize upon
        his goods.
Be thou lord bishop and receive his rents,
And make him serve thee as thy chaplain.   195
I give him thee — here, use him as thou wilt.
  Gav. He shall to prison, and there die in
        bolts.
  K. Edw. Ay, to the Tower,[5] the Fleet,[6] or
        where thou wilt.
  B. of Cov. For this offense, be thou accurst
        of God!
  K. Edw. Who's there?   Convey this priest
        to the Tower.   200

  [1] Burial rites.
  [2] The bishop's crown.
  [3] The bishop's outer vestment, a band hung around
the neck and over the shoulders.
  [4] Street-gutter.
  [5] The Tower of London on the Thames River.
  [6] The Fleet Prison, built in the eleventh century.

B. of Cov. True, true.[1]

K. Edw. But in the meantime, Gaveston, away,

And take possession of his house and goods.

Come, follow me, and thou shalt have my guard

To see it done, and bring thee safe again.

  Gav. What should a priest do with so fair a house?   206

A prison may best beseem his holiness.

                         (*Exeunt.*

SCENE 2. *London, near the King's palace*

Enter on one side both the MORTIMERS; *on the other*, WARWICK *and* LANCASTER

War. 'Tis true, the bishop is in the Tower,

And goods and body given to Gaveston.

  Lan. What! will they tyrannize upon the church?

Ah, wicked king! accursed Gaveston!

This ground, which is corrupted with their steps,   5

Shall be their timeless [2] sepulchre or mine.

  Y. Mor. Well, let that peevish Frenchman guard him sure;

Unless his breast be sword-proof he shall die.

  E. Mor. How now! why droops the Earl of Lancaster?

  Y. Mor. Wherefore is Guy of Warwick discontent?   10

  Lan. That villain Gaveston is made an earl.

  E. Mor. An earl!

  War. Ay, and besides Lord Chamberlain of the realm,

And Secretary too, and Lord of Man.

  E. Mor. We may not, nor we will not suffer this.   15

  Y. Mor. Why post we not from hence to levy men?

  Lan. "My Lord of Cornwall" now at every word!

And happy is the man whom he vouchsafes,[3]

For vailing [4] of his bonnet, one good look.   19

Thus, arm in arm, the king and he doth march

Nay more, the guard upon his lordship waits

And all the court begins to flatter him.

  War. Thus leaning on the shoulder of the king,

He nods and scorns and smiles at those that pass.

  E. Mor. Doth no man take exceptions at [1] the slave?   25

  Lan. All stomach [2] him, but none dare speak a word.

  Y. Mor. Ah, that bewrays [3] their baseness, Lancaster!

Were all the earls and barons of my mind,

We'll hale him from the bosom of the king,

And at the court-gate hang the peasant up,   30

Who, swoln with venom of ambitious pride,

Will be the ruin of the realm and us.

Enter the ARCHBISHOP OF CANTERBURY *and an Attendant*

  War. Here comes my lord of Canterbury's grace.

  Lan. His countenance bewrays [4] he is displeas'd.

  A. of Cant. (*to Attendant*). First were his [5] sacred garments rent and torn,   35

Then laid they violent hands upon him; next

Himself imprisoned, and his goods asseiz'd.[6]

This certify the Pope; — away, take horse,

                (*Exit Attendant.*

  Lan. My lord, will you take arms against the king?

  A. of Cant. What need I?   God himself is up in arms,   40

When violence is offered to the church.

  Y. Mor. Then will you join with us, that be his [7] peers,

To banish or behead that Gaveston?

  A. of Cant. What else, my lords? for it concerns me near;

The bishopric of Coventry is his.   45

---

[1] The Bishop senses an ironic meaning in the King's word, "convey," for it meant in Elizabethan slang "steal."

[2] Untimely.   [3] Upon whom he bestows.

[4] Doffing.

[1] Express objections against.

[2] Feel resentment toward.

[3] Betrays.

[4] See note to l. 27.

[5] I.e., the Bishop of Coventry's.

[6] Seized.

[7] I.e., the King's.

Enter QUEEN ISABELLA

Y. Mor. Madam, whither walks your
    majesty so fast?
Q. Isab. Unto the forest,[1] gentle Mortimer,
To live in grief and baleful discontent;
For now my lord the king regards me not,
But dotes upon the love of Gaveston.   50
He claps [2] his cheeks, and hangs about his neck,
Smiles in his face, and whispers in his ears;
And when I come he frowns, as who should say,
"Go whither thou wilt, seeing I have
    Gaveston."
  E. Mor. Is it not strange that he is thus
    bewitch'd?   55
  Y. Mor. Madam, return unto the court
    again.
That sly inveigling Frenchman we'll exile,
Or lose our lives; and yet, ere that day come,
The king shall lose his crown; for we have
    power,
And courage too, to be reveng'd at full.   60
  A. of Cant. But yet lift not your swords
    against the king.
  Lan. No; but we will lift Gaveston from
    hence.
  War. And war must be the means, or he'll
    stay still.
  Q. Isab. Then let him stay; for rather than
    my lord
Shall be oppress'd by civil mutinies,   65
I will endure a melancholy life,
And let him frolic with his minion.
  A. of Cant. My lords, to ease all this, but
    hear me speak: —
We and the rest, that are his counsellors,
Will meet, and with a general consent   70
Confirm him banishment with our hands and
    seals.
  Lan. What we confirm the king will frus-
    trate.
  Y. Mor. Then may we lawfully revolt from
    him.
  War. But say, my lord, where shall this
    meeting be?
  A. of Cant. At the New Temple.[3]   75

  Y. Mor. Content.
  A. of Cant. And, in the meantime, I'll en-
    treat you all
To cross to Lambeth,[1] and there stay with
    me.
  Lan. Come then, let's away.
  Y. Mor. Madam, farewell!   80
  Q. Isab. Farewell, sweet Mortimer, and, for
    my sake,
Forbear to levy arms against the king.
  Y. Mor. Ay, if words will serve; if not, I
    must.   (*Exeunt.*

SCENE 3. *A street in Westminster, London*

Enter GAVESTON *and* KENT

  Gav. Edmund, the mighty Prince of Lan-
    caster,
That hath more earldoms than an ass can
    bear,
And both the Mortimers, two goodly men,
With Guy of Warwick, that redoubted knight,
Are gone toward Lambeth — there let them
    remain!
        (*Exeunt.*

SCENE 4

Enter LANCASTER, WARWICK, PEMBROKE, *the*
ELDER MORTIMER, YOUNG MORTIMER, *the*
ARCHBISHOP OF CANTERBURY, *and At-
tendants*

  Lan. Here is the form of Gaveston's exile:
May it please your lordship to subscribe your
    name.
  A. of Cant. Give me the paper.
    (*He subscribes, as do the others after
    him.*
  Lan. Quick, quick, my lord; I long to write
    my name.
  War. But I long more to see him banish'd
    hence.   5
  Y. Mor. The name of Mortimer shall fright
    the king,
Unless he be declin'd [2] from that base peasant.

---

[1] A figurative remark, = "into seclusion."   [2] Pats.
[3] Knight Templar buildings to the south of Fleet
Street toward the Thames.

[1] The Archbishop's palace on the south bank of the
Thames opposite Westminster.
[2] Turned away.

Enter KING EDWARD, GAVESTON, *and* KENT

K. Edw. What, are you mov'd that Gaveston
sits here? [1]
It is our pleasure; we will have it so.
    Lan. Your grace doth well to place him by
        your side,   10
For nowhere else the new earl is so safe.
    E. Mor. What man of noble birth can brook
        this sight?
Quam male conveniunt! [2]
See what a scornful look the peasant casts!
    Pem. Can kingly lions fawn on creeping ants?
    War. Ignoble vassal, that like Phaeton [3] 16
Aspir'st unto the guidance of the sun!
    Y. Mor. Their downfall is at hand, their
        forces down;
We will not thus be fac'd [4] and over-peer'd. [5]
    K. Edw. Lay hands on that traitor Morti-
        mer!   20
    E. Mor. Lay hands on that traitor Gaveston!
    Kent. Is this the duty that you owe your
        king?
    War. We know our duties — let him know
        his peers.
    K. Edw. Whither will you bear him? Stay,
        or ye shall die.
    E. Mor. We are no traitors; therefore
        threaten not.   25
    Gav. No, threaten not, my lord, but pay
        them home!
Were I a king —
    Y. Mor. Thou villain, wherefore talk'st thou
        of a king,
That hardly art a gentleman by birth?
    K. Edw. Were he a peasant, being my
        minion,   30
I'll make the proudest of you stoop to him.
    Lan. My lord, you may not thus disparage [6]
        us. —
Away, I say, with hateful Gaveston!

[1] I.e., beside the King's seat.
[2] How ill they go together!
[3] Son of Helios the sun god, he arrogantly sought his
father's permission to drive the sun chariot. The horses
got out of his control and began to draw the chariot
toward the earth. Zeus then struck him dead with a
lightning bolt.
[4] Bullied.   [5] Looked down on.
[6] Degrade.

    E. Mor. And with the Earl of Kent that
        favors him.
        (*Attendants remove* KENT *and* GAVESTON.
    K. Edw. Nay, then, lay violent hands upon
        your king.   35
Here, Mortimer, sit thou in Edward's throne;
Warwick and Lancaster, wear you my crown.
Was ever king thus over-rul'd as I?
    Lan. Learn then to rule us better, and the
        realm.
    Y. Mor. What we have done, our heart-blood
        shall maintain.   40
    War. Think you that we can brook this
        upstart pride?
    K. Edw. Anger and wrathful fury stops my
        speech.
    A. of Cant. Why are you mov'd? Be pa-
        tient, my lord,
And see what we your counsellors have done.
    Y. Mor. My lords, now let us all be resolute,
And either have our wills, or lose our lives. 46
    K. Edw. Meet you for this, proud overdaring
        peers?
Ere my sweet Gaveston shall part from me,
This isle shall fleet [1] upon the ocean,
And wander to the unfrequented Inde. [2]   50
    A. of Cant. You know that I am legate to
        the Pope.
On your allegiance to the see of Rome,
Subscribe, as we have done, to his exile.
    Y. Mor. Curse [3] him, if he refuse; and then
        may we
Depose him and elect another king.   55
    K. Edw. Ay, there it goes! but yet I will
        not yield.
Curse me, depose me, do the worst you can.
    Lan. Then linger not, my lord, but do it
        straight.
    A. of Cant. Remember how the bishop was
        abus'd!
Either banish him that was the cause thereof,
Or I will presently discharge these lords   61
Of duty and allegiance due to thee.
    K. Edw. (*aside*). It boots [4] me not to
        threat; I must speak fair. —
The legate of the Pope will be obey'd.

[1] Float.   [2] India.
[3] Excommunicate; remove from church membership.
[4] Avails.

My lord, you shall be Chancellor of the
    realm;   65
Thou, Lancaster, High Admiral of our fleet;
Young Mortimer and his uncle shall be earls;
And you, Lord Warwick, President of the
    North;
And thou, of Wales. If this content you not,
Make several kingdoms of this monarchy,   70
And share it equally amongst you all,
So I may have some nook or corner left,
To frolic with my dearest Gaveston.
    A. of Cant. Nothing shall alter us, we are
    resolv'd.
    Lan. Come, come, subscribe.   75
    Y. Mor. Why should you love him whom the
    world hates so?
    K. Edw. Because he loves me more than all
    the world.
Ah, none but rude [1] and savage-minded men
Would seek the ruin of my Gaveston;
You that be noble-born should pity him.   80
    War. You that are princely-born should
    shake him off.
For shame subscribe, and let the lown [2] depart.
    E. Mor. Urge him, my lord.
    A. of Cant. Are you content to banish him
    the realm?
    K. Edw. I see I must, and therefore am
    content.   85
Instead of ink, I'll write it with my tears.
                      (Subscribes.
    Y. Mor. The king is love-sick for his minion.
    K. Edw. 'Tis done; and now, accursed hand,
    fall off!
    Lan. Give it me; I'll have it publish'd in
    the streets.
    Y. Mor. I'll see him presently [3] despatch'd
    away.   90
    A. of Cant. Now is my heart at ease.
    War.   And so is mine.
    Pem. This will be good news to the common
    sort.
    E. Mor. Be it or no, he shall not linger here.
          (Exeunt all except KING EDWARD.
    K. Edw. How fast they run to banish him I
    love!
They would not stir, were it to do me good.   95
Why should a king be subject to a priest?

Proud Rome! that hatchest such imperial
    grooms,
For these thy superstitious taper-lights,
Wherewith thy antichristian churches blaze,
I'll fire thy crazed buildings, and enforce   100
The papal towers to kiss the lowly ground!
With slaughtered priests make Tiber's [1] channel
    swell,
And banks rais'd higher with their sepulchres!
As for the peers, that back the clergy thus,
If I be king, not one of them shall live.   105

              Re-enter GAVESTON

    Gav. My lord, I hear it whispered every-
    where,
That I am banish'd, and must fly the land.
    K. Edw. 'Tis true, sweet Gaveston — O!
    were it false!
The legate of the Pope will have it so,
And thou must hence, or I shall be depos'd.   110
But I will reign to be reveng'd of them;
And therefore, sweet friend, take it patiently.
Live where thou wilt, I'll send thee gold enough;
And long thou shalt not stay, or if thou
    dost,
I'll come to thee; my love shall ne'er decline.
    Gav. Is all my hope turn'd to this hell of
    grief?   116
    K. Edw. Rend not my heart with thy too
    piercing words:
Thou from this land, I from myself am
    banish'd.
    Gav. To go from hence grieves not poor
    Gaveston;
But to forsake you, in whose gracious looks
The blessedness of Gaveston remains,   121
For nowhere else seeks he felicity.
    K. Edw. And only this torments my
    wretched soul
That, whether I will or no, thou must depart.
Be governor of Ireland in my stead,   125
And there abide till fortune call thee home.
Here take my picture, and let me wear thine;
            (They exchange pictures.
O, might I keep thee here as I do this,
Happy were I! but now most miserable!
    Gav. 'Tis something to be pitied of a king.

[1] Barbarous.   [2] Low-born fellow.   [3] At once.

[1] The famous river in Rome.

K. Edw. Thou shalt not hence — I'll hide
  thee, Gaveston.   131
 Gav. I shall be found, and then 'twill grieve
  me more.
K. Edw. Kind words and mutual talk makes
  our grief greater;
Therefore, with dumb embracement, let us
  part. —
Stay, Gaveston, I cannot leave thee thus. 135
 Gav. For every look, my lord drops down a
  tear.
Seeing I must go, do not renew my sorrow.
 K. Edw. The time is little that thou hast to
  stay,
And, therefore, give me leave to look my fill.
But come, sweet friend, I'll bear thee on thy
  way.   140
 Gav. The peers will frown.
 K. Edw. I pass [1] not for their anger. —
  Come let's go;
O that we might as well return as go.

    Enter QUEEN ISABELLA [2]

 Q. Isab. Whither goes my lord?
 K. Edw. Fawn not on me, French strumpet!
  Get thee gone!   145
 Q. Isab. On whom but on my husband
  should I fawn?
 Gav. On Mortimer! with whom, ungentle
  queen —
I say no more. Judge you the rest, my lord.
 Q. Isab. In saying this, thou wrong'st me,
  Gaveston.
Is't not enough that thou corrupt'st my lord,
And art a bawd to his affections,[3]   151
But thou must call mine honor thus in ques-
  tion?
 Gav. I mean not so; your grace must pardon
  me.
 K. Edw. Thou art too familiar with that
  Mortimer,
And by thy means is Gaveston exil'd; 155
But I would wish thee reconcile the lords,
Or thou shalt ne'er be reconcil'd to me.

 [1] Care.
 [2] Daughter of Philip IV, King of France (1285–1314),
she married Edward II in Boulogne on January 25,
1308, at the age of fifteen.
 [3] Fancies.

 Q. Isab. Your highness knows it lies not in
  my power.
 K. Edw. Away then! touch me not. —
  Come, Gaveston.
 Q. Isab. Villain! 'tis thou that robb'st me
  of my lord.   160
 Gav. Madam, 'tis you that rob me of my
  lord.
 K. Edw. Speak not unto her; let her droop
  and pine.
 Q. Isab. Wherein, my lord, have I deserv'd
  these words?
Witness the tears that Isabella sheds,
Witness this heart, that, sighing for thee,
  breaks,   165
How dear my lord is to poor Isabel.
 K. Edw. And witness Heaven how dear
  thou art to me!
There weep; for till my Gaveston be repeal'd,
Assure thyself thou com'st not in my sight.
    (*Exeunt* EDWARD *and* GAVESTON.
 Q. Isab. O miserable and distressed queen!
Would, when I left sweet France and was em-
  bark'd,   171
That charming [1] Circes,[2] walking on the waves,
Had chang'd my shape, or at the marriage-
  day
The cup of Hymen [3] had been full of poison,
Or with those arms that twin'd about my neck
I had been stifled, and not liv'd to see 176
The king my lord thus to abandon me!
Like frantic Juno [4] will I fill the earth
With ghastly murmur of my sighs and cries;
For never doted Jove on Ganymede [5] 180
So much as he on cursed Gaveston.
But that will more exasperate his wrath;
I must entreat him, I must speak him fair,
And be a means to call home Gaveston.
And yet he'll ever dote on Gaveston; 185
And so am I for ever miserable.

 [1] Exercising charms or spells.
 [2] Circe, a sorceress of Greek mythology, who, according to Ovid's *Metamorphoses*, xiv, 48 ff., walked over the
waves when she went to enchant the sea nymph Scylla.
 [3] The Greek god of marriage.
 [4] The wife of Jove.
 [5] A shepherd boy of Phrygia, Asia Minor, who on account of his beauty was carried off to Mt. Olympus as a
cup-bearer for the gods. There he became the favorite
of Jove, the ruler of the gods.

Re-enter LANCASTER, WARWICK, PEMBROKE,
   the ELDER MORTIMER, *and* YOUNG MORTI-
   MER

Lan. Look where the sister of the King of
   France
Sits wringing of her hands, and beats her
   breast!
War. The king, I fear, hath ill-entreated [1]
   her.
Pem. Hard is the heart that injures such a
   saint.   190
Y. Mor. I know 'tis 'long of Gaveston she
   weeps.
E. Mor. Why? He is gone.
Y. Mor.   Madam, how fares your grace?
Q. Isab. Ah, Mortimer! now breaks the
   king's hate forth,
And he confesseth that he loves me not.
Y. Mor. Cry quittance, madam, then; and
   love not him.   195
Q. Isab. No, rather will I die a thousand
   deaths!
And yet I love in vain; — he'll ne'er love me.
Lan. Fear ye not, madam; now his minion's
   gone,
His wanton humor will be quickly left.
Q. Isab. O never, Lancaster! I am enjoin'd
To sue upon you all for his repeal;   201
This wills my lord, and this must I perform,
Or else be banish'd from his highness' presence.
Lan. For his repeal? Madam, he comes not
   back,   204
Unless the sea cast up his shipwrack'd body.
War. And to behold so sweet a sight as that,
There's none here but would run his horse to
   death.
Y. Mor. But, madam, would you have us
   call him home?
Q. Isab. Ay, Mortimer, for till he be restor'd,
The angry king hath banish'd me the court;
And, therefore, as thou lov'st and tend'rest
   me,   211
Be thou my advocate unto these peers.
Y. Mor. What! would ye have me plead for
   Gaveston?
E. Mor. Plead for him he that will, I am
   resolv'd.

[1] Ill-treated.

Lan. And so am I, my lord.   Dissuade the
   queen.   215
Q. Isab. O Lancaster! let him dissuade the
   king,
For 'tis against my will he should return.
War. Then speak not for him, let the peasant
   go.
Q. Isab. 'Tis for myself I speak, and not for
   him.
Pem. No speaking will prevail,[1] and there-
   fore cease.   220
Y. Mor. Fair queen, forbear to angle for
   the fish
Which, being caught, strikes him that takes it
   dead;
I mean that vile torpedo,[2] Gaveston,
That now, I hope, floats on the Irish seas.
Q. Isab. Sweet Mortimer, sit down by me
   awhile,   225
And I will tell thee reasons of such weight
As thou wilt soon subscribe to his repeal.
Y. Mor. It is impossible; but speak your
   mind.
Q. Isab. Then thus, — but none shall hear
   it but ourselves.
      (*Talks to* YOUNG MORTIMER *apart.*
Lan. My lords, albeit the queen win Morti-
   mer,   230
Will you be resolute, and hold with me?
E. Mor. Not I, against my nephew.
Pem. Fear not, the queen's words cannot
   alter him.
War. No? Do but mark how earnestly she
   pleads!
Lan. And see how coldly his looks make
   denial!   235
War. She smiles; now for my life his mind is
   chang'd!
Lan. I'll rather lose his friendship, I, than
   grant.
Y. Mor. Well, of necessity it must be so.
My lords, that I abhor base Gaveston,
I hope your honors make no question,   240
And therefore, though I plead for his repeal,
'Tis not for his sake, but for our avail;
Nay for the realm's behoof, and for the king's.

[1] Avail.
[2] The fish called the electric-ray, which delivers an
electric shock on contact.

Lan. Fie, Mortimer, dishonor not thyself!
Can this be true, 'twas good to banish him?
And is this true, to call him home again?   246
Such reasons make white black, and dark night
     day.
     Y. Mor. My lord of Lancaster, mark the
     respect.[1]
Lan. In no respect can contraries be true.
     Q. Isab. Yet, good my lord, hear what he
     can allege.   250
War. All that he speaks is nothing; we are
     resolv'd.
     Y. Mor. Do you not wish that Gaveston
     were dead?
     Pem. I would he were!
     Y. Mor. Why, then, my lord, give me but
     leave to speak.
     E. Mor. But, nephew, do not play the
     sophister.[2]   255
     Y. Mor. This which I urge is of a burning
     zeal
To mend the king, and do our country good.
Know you not Gaveston hath store of gold,
Which may in Ireland purchase him such
     friends
As he will front the mightiest of us all?   260
And whereas [3] he shall live and be belov'd,
'Tis hard for us to work his overthrow.
     War. Mark you but that, my lord of Lan-
     caster.
     Y. Mor. But were he here, detested as he is,
How easily might some base slave be suborn'd [4]
To greet his lordship with a poniard,   266
And none so much as blame the murderer,
But rather praise him for that brave attempt,
And in the chronicle enrol his name
For purging of the realm of such a plague!
     Pem. He saith true.   271
     Lan. Ay, but how chance this was not done
     before?
     Y. Mor. Because, my lords, it was not
     thought upon.
Nay, more, when he shall know it lies in us
To banish him, and then to call him home,   275
'Twill make him vail [5] the top-flag of his pride,
And fear to offend the meanest nobleman.

[1] The motive.
[2] Do not use sophistical or fallacious arguments.
[3] Where.   [4] Incited secretly.   [5] Lower.

     E. Mor. But how if he do not, nephew?
     Y. Mor. Then may we with some color [1]
     rise in arms;
For howsoever we have borne it out,   280
'Tis treason to be up against the king.
So we shall have the people of [2] our side,
Which for his father's sake lean to the king,
But cannot brook a night-grown mushroom,
Such a one as my lord of Cornwall is,   285
Should bear us down of the nobility.
And when the commons and the nobles join,
'Tis not the king can buckler [3] Gaveston;
We'll pull him from the strongest hold he hath.
My lords, if to perform this I be slack,   290
Think me as base a groom [4] as Gaveston.
     Lan. On that condition, Lancaster will grant.
     War. And so will Pembroke and I.
     E. Mor. And I.   294
     Y. Mor. In this I count me highly gratified,
And Mortimer will rest at your command.
     Q. Isab. And when this favor Isabel forgets,
Then let her live abandon'd and forlorn. —
But see, in happy time, my lord the king,
Having brought the Earl of Cornwall on his
     way,   300
Is new return'd. This news will glad him much,
Yet not so much as me. I love him more
Than he can Gaveston; would he lov'd me
But half so much, then were I treble-blest.

Re-enter KING EDWARD, *mourning, with* BEAU-
MONT *and other Attendants*

     K. Edw. He's gone, and for his absence thus
     I mourn.   305
Did never sorrow go so near my heart
As doth the want of my sweet Gaveston;
And could my crown's revenue bring him back,
I would freely give it to his enemies,
And think I gain'd, having bought so dear a
     friend.   310
     Q. Isab. Hark! how he harps upon his minion.
     K. Edw. My heart is as an anvil unto sorrow,
Which beats upon it like the Cyclops'[5] hammers,
And with the noise turns up my giddy brain,

[1] Pretext.   [2] On.   [3] Shield.   [4] Servant.
[5] Mythological one-eyed giants who assisted at the
forges in the workshop of Vulcan, the fire-god, under
Mt. Etna in Sicily.

And makes me frantic for my Gaveston.   315
Ah! had some bloodless [1] Fury [2] rose from hell,
And with my kingly scepter struck me dead,
When I was forc'd to leave my Gaveston!

   Lan. Diablo! [3] What passions call you these?

   Q. Isab. My gracious lord, I come to bring
    you news.   320

   K. Edw. That you have parley'd with your
    Mortimer!

   Q. Isab. That Gaveston, my lord, shall be
    repeal'd. [4]

   K. Edw. Repeal'd! The news is too sweet
    to be true!

   Q. Isab. But will you love me, if you find it
    so?   324

   K. Edw. If it be so, what will not Edward do?

   Q. Isab. For Gaveston, but not for Isabel.

   K. Edw. For thee, fair queen, if thou lov'st
    Gaveston.
I'll hang a golden tongue [5] about thy neck,
Seeing thou hast pleaded with so good success.

   Q. Isab. No other jewels hang about my
    neck   330
Than these, [6] my lord; nor let me have more
   wealth
Than I may fetch from this rich treasury.
O how a kiss revives poor Isabel!

   K. Edw. Once more receive my hand; and
    let this be
A second marriage 'twixt thyself and me.   335

   Q. Isab. And may it prove more happy than
    the first!
My gentle lord, bespeak these nobles fair,
That wait attendance for a gracious look,
And on their knees salute your majesty.

   K. Edw. Courageous Lancaster, embrace
    thy king!   340
And, as gross vapors perish by the sun,
Even so let hatred with thy sovereign's smile.
Live thou with me as my companion.

   Lan. This salutation overjoys my heart.

   K. Edw. Warwick shall be my chiefest
    counsellor: 345

[1] Pale-faced.
[2] The avenging goddess who punished crime.
[3] The devil!
[4] Recalled.
[5] A golden piece of jewelry shaped like a tongue was not an uncommon ornament in the sixteenth century.
[6] The King's arms.

These silver hairs will more adorn my court
Than gaudy silks, or rich embroidery.
Chide me, sweet Warwick, if I go astray.

   War. Slay me, my lord, when I offend your
    grace.

   K. Edw. In solemn triumphs, and in public
    shows,   350
Pembroke shall bear the sword before the
   king.

   Pem. And with this sword Pembroke will
    fight for you.

   K. Edw. But wherefore walks young Morti-
    mer aside?
Be thou commander of our royal fleet;
Or, if that lofty office like [1] thee not,   355
I make thee here Lord Marshal of the realm.

   Y. Mor. My lord, I'll marshal so your ene-
    mies,
As England shall be quiet, and you safe.

   K. Edw. And as for you, Lord Mortimer of
    Chirke, [2]   359
Whose great achievements in our foreign war
Deserves no common place nor mean reward,
Be you the general of the levied troops,
That now are ready to assail the Scots.

   E. Mor. In this your grace hath highly
    honored me,
For with my nature war doth best agree.   365

   Q. Isab. Now is the King of England rich
    and strong,
Having the love of his renowned peers.

   K. Edw. Ay, Isabel, ne'er was my heart so
    light.
Clerk of the crown, direct our warrant forth
For Gaveston to Ireland. — Beaumont, fly
As fast as Iris [3] or Jove's Mercury. [4]   371

   Beau. It shall be done, my gracious lord.
                           (*Exit.*

   K. Edw. Lord Mortimer, we leave you to
    your charge.
Now let us in, and feast it royally.   374
Against our friend the Earl of Cornwall comes,
We'll have a general tilt and tournament;
And then his marriage shall be solemniz'd.

[1] Please.
[2] Seat of residence on the border between Shropshire and Wales.
[3] The messenger of the goddess Juno.
[4] The messenger of Jove.

For wot [1] you not that I have made him sure [2]
Unto our cousin,[3] the Earl of Gloucester's heir?

    Lan. Such news we hear, my lord.   380

    K. Edw. That day, if not for him, yet for
        my sake,
Who in the triumph [4] will be challenger,
Spare for no cost; we will requit your love.

    War. In this, or aught, your highness shall
        command us.

    K. Edw. Thanks, gentle Warwick: come,
        let's in and revel.   385

        (*Exeunt all except the* MORTIMERS.

    E. Mor. Nephew, I must to Scotland; thou
        stayest here.
Leave now t'oppose thyself against the king.
Thou seest by nature he is mild and calm,
And seeing his mind so dotes on Gaveston,
Let him without controlment have his will. 390
The mightiest kings have had their minions:
Great Alexander loved Hephestion; [5]
The conquering Hercules for Hylas wept; [6]
And for Patroclus [7] stern Achilles droopt:
And not kings only, but the wisest men: 395
The Roman Tully [8] lov'd Octavius; [9]
Grave Socrates, wild Alcibiades.[10]
Then let his grace, whose youth is flexible,
And promiseth as much as we can wish,
Freely enjoy that vain, light-headed earl; 400
For riper years will wean him from such toys.

    Y. Mor. Uncle, his wanton humor grieves
        not me;
But this I scorn, that one so basely born
Should by his sovereign's favor grow so pert,
And riot it with the treasure of the realm.
While soldiers mutiny for want of pay, 406

He wears a lord's revenue on his back,
And Midas-like,[1] he jets [2] it in the court,
With base outlandish cullions [3] at his heels,
Whose proud fantastic liveries make such
    show   410
As if that Proteus,[4] god of shapes, appear'd.
I have not seen a dapper Jack so brisk;
He wears a short Italian hooded cloak
Larded with pearl, and, in his Tuscan cap,[5]
A jewel of more value than the crown.   415
While others walk below, the king and he
From out a window laugh at such as we,
And flout our train, and jest at our attire.
Uncle, 'tis this that makes me impatient.

    E. Mor. But, nephew, now you see the king
        is chang'd.   420

    Y. Mor. Then so am I, and live to do him
        service:
But whiles I have a sword, a hand, a heart,
I will not yield to any such upstart.
You know my mind; come, uncle, let's away.

        (*Exeunt.*

ACT II

SCENE I. *A hall in the castle of the* EARL OF
GLOUCESTER

Enter YOUNG SPENCER *and* BALDOCK

    Bald. Spencer, seeing that our lord th' Earl
    of Gloucester's dead,[6]
Which of the nobles dost thou mean to serve?

    Y. Spen. Not Mortimer, nor any of his side
Because the king and he are enemies.
Baldock, learn this of me, a factious [7] lord
Shall hardly do himself good, much less us;

---

[1] Know.   [2] Betrothed him.

[3] Niece, i.e., Margaret de Clare, daughter of the Earl
of Gloucester.

[4] Tournament.

[5] The intimate friend and companion of Alexander
the Great, King of Macedon (356–323 B.C.).

[6] See note to Scene i, l. 144.

[7] Friend of Achilles, who, fighting in the latter's
armor, was killed by Hector, the Trojan champion.

[8] Marcus *Tullius* Cicero, Roman statesman (106–
43 B.C.).

[9] Augustus Caesar (63 B.C.–14 A.D.), the first Roman
emperor.

[10] Athenian politician and general (450–404 B.C.),
who had the philosopher Socrates (469–399 B.C.) as his
counsellor.

[1] Midas, a mythical king of Phrygia in Asia Minor
was given by the god Dionysus the power of turning to
gold all that he touched.

[2] Struts.   [3] Base foreign fellows.

[4] The sea-god who could change his shape at will.

[5] Italian fashions of dress were much affected in
Marlowe's day. Tuscany is the province of north central Italy in which Florence is located.

[6] The Earl of Gloucester actually died in 1295, many
years before Gaveston's execution. Neither Spencer
nor Baldock were historically connected with the Earl's
retinue. The Spencers lived on the Welsh border
Robert Baldock became Lord Chancellor of England
c. 1322 through the Spencers' influence.

[7] Given to dissension.

But he that hath the favor of a king,
May with one word advance us while we live.
The liberal Earl of Cornwall is the man   9
On whose good fortune Spencer's hope depends.
    Bald. What, mean you then to be his fol-
      lower?
    Y. Spen. No, his companion; for he loves me
      well,
And would have once preferr'd [1] me to the king.
    Bald. But he is banish'd; there's small hope
      of him.
    Y. Spen. Ay, for a while; but, Baldock,
      mark the end.   15
A friend of mine told me in secrecy
That he's repeal'd, and sent for back again;
And even now a post came from the court
With letters to our lady [2] from the king;
And as she read she smil'd, which makes me
    think   20
It is about her lover Gaveston.
    Bald. 'Tis like enough; for since he was exil'd
She neither walks abroad, nor comes in sight.
But I had thought the match had been broke
    off,
And that his banishment had chang'd her
    mind.   25
    Y. Spen. Our lady's first love is not wavering;
My life for thine, she will have Gaveston.
    Bald. Then hope I by her means to be pre-
      ferr'd,
Having read unto her since she was a child.
    Y. Spen. Then, Baldock, you must cast the
      scholar off,   30
And learn to court it like a gentleman.
'Tis not a black coat and a little band,[3]
A velvet-cap'd coat, fac'd before with serge,
And smelling to a nosegay all the day,
Or holding of a napkin in your hand,   35
Or saying a long grace at a table's end,
Or making low legs [4] to a nobleman,
Or looking downward with your eyelids close,
And saying, "Truly, an't [5] may please your
    honor,"

Can get you any favor with great men; [1]   40
You must be proud, bold, pleasant, resolute,
And now and then stab, as occasion serves.
    Bald. Spencer, thou know'st I hate such
      formal toys,
And use them but of mere hypocrisy.
Mine old lord whiles he liv'd was so precise,[2]   45
That he would take exceptions at my buttons,
And being like pin's heads, blame me for the
    bigness;
Which made me curate-like in mine attire,
Though inwardly licentious enough
And apt for any kind of villainy.   50
I am none of these common pedants, I,
That cannot speak without *propterea quod*.[3]
    Y. Spen. But one of those that saith *quan-*
      doquidem,[4]
And hath a special gift to form a verb.[5]
    Bald. Leave off this jesting, here my lady
      comes.   55

Enter KING EDWARD'S *Niece*

    Niece. The grief for his exile was not so much
As is the joy of his returning home.
This letter came from my sweet Gaveston: —
What need'st thou, love, thus to excuse thy-
    self?
I know thou couldst not come and visit me.   60
(*Reads*) "I will not long be from thee, though
    I die."
This argues the entire love of my lord;
(*Reads*) "When I forsake thee, death seize on
    my heart":
But stay thee here where Gaveston shall sleep.
          (*Puts the letter into her bosom.*
Now to the letter of my lord the king. —   65
He wills me to repair unto the court,
And meet my Gaveston. Why do I stay,

---

[1] Recommended.
[2] The daughter of the Earl of Gloucester, Margaret
de Clare.
[3] Narrow strip of trimming around the collar.
[4] Bows.
[5] If it.

[1] Ll. 32–40 constitute a satirical portrait of the Elizabethan Puritan scholar who sought preferment as a
domestic chaplain in some nobleman's household.
[2] Puritanical.
[3] A formal, pedantic Latin phrase meaning "because."
[4] Elegant, cultivated Latin phrase also meaning
"because."
[5] To say a thing in the right way. — Spencer is gently
poking fun at Baldock's pretensions to gentlemanly
polish in speech.

Seeing that he talks thus of my marriage-day?
Who's there? Baldock!
See that my coach be ready, I must hence.   70
   Bald. It shall be done, madam.
   Niece. And meet me at the park-pale pres-
     ently.   (*Exit* BALDOCK.
Spencer, stay you and bear me company,
For I have joyful news to tell thee of.
My lord of Cornwall is a-coming over,   75
And will be at the court as soon as we.
   Y. Spen. I knew the king would have him
     home again.
   Niece. If all things sort out as I hope they
     will,
Thy service, Spencer, shall be thought upon.
   Y. Spen. I humbly thank your ladyship. 80
   Niece. Come, lead the way; I long till I am
     there.   (*Exeunt.*

SCENE 2. *The Great Hall in Tynemouth* [1]
Castle

Enter KING EDWARD, QUEEN ISABELLA, KENT,
LANCASTER, YOUNG MORTIMER, WAR-
WICK, PEMBROKE, *and Attendants*

   K. Edw. The wind is good, I wonder why he
     stays;
I fear me he is wrack'd [2] upon the sea.
   Q. Isab. Look, Lancaster, how passionate
     he is,
And still his mind runs on his minion!
   Lan. My lord, —   5
   K. Edw. How now! what news?   Is Gaves-
     ton arriv'd?
   Y. Mor. Nothing but Gaveston! — What
     means your grace?
You have matters of more weight to think
   upon;
The King of France sets foot in Normandy.
   K. Edw. A trifle! we'll expel him when we
     please.   10
But tell me, Mortimer, what's thy device [3]
Against the stately triumph we decreed?
   Y. Mor. A homely one, my lord, not worth
     the telling.

   [1] An old port at the mouth of the Tyne on the northeast coast of England.
   [2] Wrecked.
   [3] A painting on a shield with a motto attached.

   K. Edw. Pray thee let me know it.
   Y. Mor. But, seeing you are so desirous, thus
     it is: 15
A lofty cedar-tree, fair flourishing,
On whose top-branches kingly eagles perch,
And by the bark a canker [1] creeps me up,
And gets into the highest bough of all:
The motto, *Aeque tandem*.[2]   20
   K. Edw. And what is yours, my lord of
     Lancaster?
   Lan. My lord, mine's more obscure than
     Mortimer's.
Pliny [3] reports there is a flying fish
Which all the other fishes deadly hate,
And therefore, being pursued, it takes the air:
No sooner is it up, but there's a fowl   26
That seizeth it; this fish, my lord, I bear:
The motto this: *Undique mors est*.[4]
   K. Edw. Proud Mortimer! ungentle [5] Lan-
     caster!
Is this the love you bear your sovereign?   30
Is this the fruit your reconcilement bears?
Can you in words make show of amity,
And in your shields display your rancorous
   minds!
What call you this but private libeling
Against the Earl of Cornwall and my brother?
   Q. Isab. Sweet husband, be content, they all
     love you.   36
   K. Edw. They love me not that hate my
     Gaveston.
I am that cedar, shake me not too much;
And you the eagles; soar ye ne'er so high,
I have the jesses [6] that will pull you down;
And *Aeque tandem* shall that canker cry   41
Unto the proudest peer of Britany.
Though thou compar'st him to a flying fish,
And threatenest death whether he rise or fall,
'Tis not the hugest monster of the sea,   45

   [1] Cankerworm.
   [2] Equally high, at last.   By implication, Gaveston,
the cankerworm, will rise in the end to a place of equal
power with Edward, the eagle.
   [3] Roman naturalist and writer (23–79 A.D.).   He does
not, however, make any such report in his famous
Natural History.
   [4] On all sides is death.   [5] Rude.
   [6] Short straps of leather, silk, or other material, which
were permanently fastened around the legs of a trained
hawk, so that a leash could be easily attached.

Nor foulest harpy [1] that shall swallow him.

Y. Mor. (*aside to the Nobles*). If in his absence thus he favors him,
What will he do whenas he shall be present?

Lan. (*aside to* Y. MOR.). That shall we see;
look where his lordship comes.

Enter GAVESTON

K. Edw. My Gaveston!   50
Welcome to Tynemouth! Welcome to thy
friend!
Thy absence made me droop and pine away;
For, as the lovers of fair Danae,[2]
When she was lock'd up in a brazen tower,
Desir'd her more, and wax'd outrageous,   55
So did it fare with me; and now thy sight
Is sweeter far than was thy parting hence
Bitter and irksome to my sobbing heart.

Gav. Sweet lord and king, your speech
preventeth [3] mine,
Yet have I words left to express my joy: 60
The shepherd nipt with biting winter's rage
Frolics not more to see the painted [4] spring,
Than I do to behold your majesty.

K. Edw. Will none of you salute my
Gaveston?

Lan. Salute him? yes. Welcome, Lord
Chamberlain!   65

Y. Mor. Welcome is the good Earl of Cornwall!

War. Welcome, Lord Governor of the Isle
of Man!

Pem. Welcome, Master Secretary!

Kent. Brother, do you hear them?

K. Edw. Still will these earls and barons use
me thus.   70

Gav. My lord, I cannot brook these injuries.

Q. Isab. (*aside*). Aye me, poor soul, when
these begin to jar.

K. Edw. Return it to their throats, I'll be
thy warrant.

---

[1] Hideous winged creature with a woman's head.

[2] Daughter of the king of Argos, Acrisius, who locked
her up in a brazen tower because of a prophecy that her
child would kill her father. She had only one lover,
however, — Jupiter. He visited her in the form of a
shower of gold.

[3] Anticipates.

[4] I.e., painted with flowers.

Gav. Base, leaden earls, that glory in your
birth,
Go sit at home and eat your tenants' beef;   75
And come not here to scoff at Gaveston,
Whose mounting thoughts did never creep so low
As to bestow a look on such as you.

Lan. Yet I disdain not to do this for you.
(*Draws his sword and offers to stab*
GAVESTON.

K. Edw. Treason! treason! where's the
traitor?   80

Pem. Here! here!

K. Edw. Convey hence Gaveston; they'll
murder him.

Gav. The life of thee shall salve this foul
disgrace.

Y. Mor. Villain! thy life, unless I miss mine
aim. (*Wounds* GAVESTON.

Q. Isab. Ah! furious Mortimer, what hast
thou done?   85

Y. Mor. No more than I would answer, were
he slain.
(*Exit* GAVESTON *with Attendants.*

K. Edw. Yes, more than thou canst answer,
though he live.
Dear shall you both abye [1] this riotous deed.
Out of my presence! Come not near the court.

Y. Mor. I'll not be barr'd the court for
Gaveston.   90

Lan. We'll hale him by the ears unto the
block.

K. Edw. Look to your own heads; his is sure
enough.

War. Look to your own crown, if you back
him thus.

Kent. Warwick, these words do ill beseem
thy years.

K. Edw. Nay, all of them conspire to cross
me thus;   95
But if I live, I'll tread upon their heads
That think with high looks thus to tread me
down.
Come, Edmund, let's away and levy men,
'Tis war that must abate these barons' pride.
(*Exeunt* KING EDWARD, QUEEN ISA-
BELLA, *and* KENT.

War. Let's to our castles, for the king is
mov'd.   100

---

[1] Pay the penalty for.

Y. Mor. Mov'd may he be, and perish in his
 wrath!
Lan. Cousin, it is no dealing with him now,
He means to make us stoop by force of arms;
And therefore let us jointly here protest,[1]
To persecute that Gaveston to the death. 105
 Y. Mor. By heaven, the abject villain shall
 not live!
War. I'll have his blood, or die in seeking it.
Pem. The like oath Pembroke takes.
Lan. And so doth Lancaster.
Now send our heralds to defy[2] the king; 110
And make the people swear to put him down.

Enter a Messenger

Y. Mor. Letters! From whence?
Mess. From Scotland, my lord.
    (Gives letters to MORTIMER.
Lan. Why, how now, cousin, how fares all
 our friends?
Y. Mor. My uncle's taken prisoner by the
 Scots. 115
Lan. We'll have him ransom'd, man; be of
 good cheer.
Y. Mor. They rate his ransom at five thou-
 sand pound.
Who should defray the money but the king,
Seeing he is taken prisoner in his wars?
I'll to the king. 120
Lan. Do, cousin, and I'll bear thee company.
War. Meantime, my lord of Pembroke and
 myself
Will to Newcastle[3] here, and gather head.[4]
 Y. Mor. About it then, and we will follow
 you.
Lan. Be resolute and full of secrecy. 125
War. I warrant[5] you.
    (Exit with PEMBROKE.
Y. Mor. Cousin, and if he will not ransom
 him,
I'll thunder such a peal into his ears,
As never subject did unto his king.
 Lan. Content, I'll bear my part — Holla!
 who's there? 130

---

[1] Vow. [2] Renounce allegiance to.
[3] A few miles up the river Tyne from Tynemouth.
[4] Gather forces.
[5] Assure or promise.

Enter Guard

Y. Mor. Ay, marry, such a guard as this
 doth well.
Lan. Lead on the way.
Guard. Whither will your lordships?
Y. Mor. Whither else but to the king. 134
Guard. His highness is dispos'd to be alone.
Lan. Why, so he may, but we will speak to
 him.
Guard. You may not in, my lord.
Y. Mor. May we not?

Enter KING EDWARD *and* KENT

K. Edw. How now!
What noise is this? Who have we there? Is't
 you?   *(Turns to go.* 140
 Y. Mor. Nay, stay, my lord, I come to bring
 you news;
Mine uncle's taken prisoner by the Scots.
K. Edw. Then ransom him.
Lan. 'Twas in your wars; you should ransom
 him.
Y. Mor. And you shall ransom him, or
 else —— 145
Kent. What! Mortimer, you will not
 threaten him?
K. Edw. Quiet yourself, you shall have the
 broad seal
To gather[1] for him thoroughout the realm.
Lan. Your minion Gaveston hath taught
 you this.
Y. Mor. My lord, the family of the Morti-
 mers 150
Are not so poor, but, would they sell their
 land,
'Twould levy men enough to anger you.
We never beg, but use such prayers as these.
 K. Edw. Shall I still be haunted[2] thus?
 Y. Mor. Nay, now you're here alone, I'll
 speak my mind. 155
Lan. And so will I, and then, my lord, fare-
 well.
 Y. Mor. The idle triumphs, masques, las-
 civious shows,
And prodigal gifts bestow'd on Gaveston,

---

[1] I.e., the great seal of royal authority to gather alms.
[2] Followed persistently.

Have drawn thy treasury dry, and made thee
    weak;   159
The murmuring commons overstretched are.[1]
  Lan. Look for rebellion, look to be depos'd.
Thy garrisons are beaten out of France,
And, lame and poor, lie groaning at the gates.
The wild O'Neill,[2] with swarms of Irish kerns,[3]
Lives uncontroll'd within the English pale[4]   165
Unto the walls of York the Scots made road,[5]
And unresisted drave away rich spoils.
  Y. Mor. The haughty Dane commands the
    narrow seas,[6]
While in the harbor ride thy ships unrigg'd.
  Lan. What foreign prince sends thee am-
    bassadors?   170
  Y. Mor. Who loves thee, but a sort[7] of
    flatterers?
  Lan. Thy gentle queen, sole sister to Valois,[8]
Complains that thou hast left her all forlorn.
  Y. Mor. Thy court is naked, being bereft of
    those   174
That make a king seem glorious to the world;
I mean the peers, whom thou should'st dearly
    love.
Libels are cast again[9] thee in the street;
Ballads and rhymes made of thy overthrow.
  Lan. The Northern borderers seeing their
    houses burnt,
Their wives and children slain, run up and
    down,   180
Cursing the name of thee and Gaveston.

[1] Common people are overstrained. — The "are" is
the editor's emendation for the word lost out of the
original text. Other editors emend with "hath" or
"break."
[2] The O'Neills were Irish chieftains famous for their
resistance to the English in the sixteenth century, but
not so prominent earlier.
[3] Light-armed foot soldiers.
[4] The district around Dublin which was kept fairly
safe for English settlers.
[5] Raid.
[6] I.e., the English Channel. — None of these references, however, to Irish, Scots, or Danes are in close
accordance with the events of Edward II's time or of
Marlowe's.
[7] A set.
[8] Isabella was sister to Charles IV of France, the last
of the Capet line. The first Valois king, Philip VI, was
her cousin, but he ascended the throne after Edward II
had died.
[9] Defamatory pamphlets are scattered against.

  Y. Mor. When wert thou in the field with
    banner spread,
But once? and then thy soldiers marcht like
    players,
With garish robes, not armor; and thyself,   184
Bedaub'd with gold, rode laughing at the rest,
Nodding and shaking of thy spangled crest,
Where women's favors hung like labels[1] down.
  Lan. And therefore came it, that the fleer-
    ing[2] Scots,
To England's high disgrace, have made this
    jig:[3]   189
"Maids of England, sore may you mourn, —
For your lemans[4] you have lost at Bannocks-
    bourn,[5] —
    With a heave and a ho!
What weeneth the King of England,
So soon to have won Scotland? —
    With a rombelow!"[6]   195
  Y. Mor. Wigmore shall fly,[7] to set my uncle
    free.
  Lan. And when 'tis gone, our swords shall
    purchase more.
If ye be mov'd, revenge it as you can;
Look next to see us with our ensigns spread.
             (*Exit with* YOUNG MORTIMER.
  K. Edw. My swelling heart for very anger
    breaks!   200
How oft have I been baited by these peers,
And dare not be reveng'd, for their power is
    great!
Yet, shall the crowing of these cockerels
Affright a lion? Edward, unfold thy paws,
And let their lives' blood slake thy fury's
    hunger.   205
If I be cruel and grow tyrannous,
Now let them thank themselves, and rue too
    late.
  Kent. My lord, I see your love to Gaveston
Will be the ruin of the realm and you,   209

[1] Slips of paper or parchment for affixing a seal to a
document.
[2] Veering.   [3] Lively, mocking song.   [4] Sweethearts.
[5] The Battle of Bannockburn, where the Scots under
Robert Bruce defeated the English, did not take place
until June, 1314, two years after Gaveston's death.
[6] A meaningless word coined by sailors for their
rowing-song refrains.
[7] I.e., Wigmore Castle (Young Mortimer's estate)
shall be sold.

For now the wrathful nobles threaten wars,
And therefore, brother, banish him for ever.

   K. Edw. Art thou an enemy to my Gaveston?

   Kent. Ay, and it grieves me that I favored
him.

   K. Edw. Traitor, begone! whine thou with
Mortimer.

   Kent. So will I, rather than with Gaveston.

   K. Edw. Out of my sight, and trouble me
no more!   216

   Kent. No marvel though thou scorn thy
noble peers,

When I thy brother am rejected thus.

   K. Edw. Away!   (*Exit* KENT.

Poor Gaveston, that has no friend but me,   220

Do what they can, we'll live in Tynemouth
here,

And, so I walk with him about the walls,

What care I though the earls begirt us round? —

Here comes she that is cause of all these jars.

Enter QUEEN ISABELLA *with* KING EDWARD'S
Niece, *two Ladies,* GAVESTON, BALDOCK,
and YOUNG SPENCER

   Q. Isab. My lord, 'tis thought the earls are
up in arms.   225

   K. Edw. Ay, and 'tis likewise thought you
favor him.[1]

   Q. Isab. Thus do you still suspect me without cause?

   Niece. Sweet uncle! speak more kindly to
the queen.

   Gav. My lord, dissemble with her, speak her
fair.

   K. Edw. Pardon me, sweet, I forgot myself.   230

   Q. Isab. Your pardon is quickly got of Isabel.

   K. Edw. The younger Mortimer is grown
so brave,[2]

That to my face he threatens civil wars.

   Gav. Why do you not commit him to the
Tower?

   K. Edw. I dare not, for the people love him
well.   235

   Gav. Why, then we'll have him privily made
away.

[1] I.e., Young Mortimer.
[2] Presumptuous.

   K. Edw. Would Lancaster and he had both
carous'd

A bowl of poison to each other's health!

But let them go, and tell me what are these?

   Niece. Two of my father's servants whilst
he liv'd, —   240

Mayst please your grace to entertain them
now.

   K. Edw. Tell me, where wast thou born?
What is thine arms?[1]

   Bald. My name is Baldock, and my gentry

I fetcht from Oxford, not from heraldry.

   K. Edw. The fitter art thou, Baldock, for
my turn.   245

Wait on me, and I'll see thou shalt not want.

   Bald. I humbly thank your majesty.

   K. Edw. Knowest thou him, Gaveston?

   Gav.   Ay, my lord;

His name is Spencer, he is well allied;[2]

For my sake, let him wait upon your grace;

Scarce shall you find a man of more desert.   251

   K. Edw. Then, Spencer, wait upon me; for
his sake

I'll grace thee with a higher style[3] ere long.

   Y. Spen. No greater titles happen unto me,

Than to be favored of your majesty.   255

   K. Edw. Cousin, this day shall be your
marriage-feast.

And, Gaveston, think that I love thee well

To wed thee to our niece, the only heir

Unto the Earl of Gloucester late deceas'd.[4]

   Gav. I know, my lord, many will stomach[5]
me,   260

But I respect[6] neither their love nor hate.

   K. Edw. The headstrong barons shall not
limit me;

He that I list to favor shall be great.

Come, let's away; and when the marriage
ends,

Have at the rebels, and their 'complices!   265

                    (*Exeunt.*

[1] Coat-of-arms.
[2] Of good family.
[3] Title.
[4] The niece was not "the only heir," for she had two
sisters. The Earl of Gloucester was not "late deceas'd," for he had died in 1295. His wife had been
Joan of Acre, sister of Edward II.
[5] See note to Act I, Sc. 2, l. 26.
[6] Pay attention to.

SCENE 3. *Near Tynemouth Castle*

Enter KENT, LANCASTER, YOUNG MORTIMER,
    WARWICK, PEMBROKE, *and others*

Kent. My lords, of love to this our native
    land
I come to join with you and leave the king; [1]
And in your quarrel and the realm's behoof
Will be the first that shall adventure life.
    Lan. I fear me, you are sent of policy, [2]   5
To undermine us with a show of love.
    War. He is your brother, therefore have we
    cause
To cast [3] the worst, and doubt of your revolt.
    Kent. Mine honor shall be hostage of my
    truth;
If that will not suffice, farewell, my lords.   10
    Y. Mor. Stay, Edmund; never was Plan-
    tagenet
False to his word, and therefore trust we thee.
    Pem. But what's the reason you should
    leave him now?
    Kent. I have inform'd the Earl of Lancaster.
    Lan. And it sufficeth. Now, my lords,
    know this,   15
That Gaveston is secretly arriv'd,
And here in Tynemouth frolics with the king.
Let us with these our followers scale the walls,
And suddenly surprise them unawares.
    Y. Mor. I'll give the onset.
    War.   And I'll follow thee.   20
    Y. Mor. This tottered [4] ensign of my an-
    cestors,
Which swept the desert shore of that dead sea
Whereof we got the name of Mortimer, [5]
Will I advance upon these castle-walls.
Drums, strike alarum, raise them from their
    sport,   25
And ring aloud the knell of Gaveston!
    Lan. None be so hardy as to touch the
    king;
But neither spare you Gaveston nor his friends.
                             (*Exeunt.*

---

[1] In history Kent's alliance with the rebellious nobles
came sometime after Gaveston's death.
[2] By stratagem.   [3] Expect.   [4] Tattered.
[5] The traditional derivation was from the Latin
"Mortuum Mare," i.e., "Dead Sea." Actually the
name comes from a village of Normandy, France,
"Mortemer," whence the family migrated to England.

SCENE 4. *The same*

Enter KING EDWARD *and* YOUNG SPENCER

    K. Edw. O tell me, Spencer, where is
    Gaveston?
    Spen. I fear he is slain, my gracious lord.
    K. Edw. No, here he comes; now let them
    spoil and kill.

Enter QUEEN ISABELLA, KING EDWARD'S
    Niece, GAVESTON, *and Nobles*

Fly, fly, my lords, the earls have got the hold; [1]
Take shipping and away to Scarborough; [2]   5
Spencer and I will post away by land.
    Gav. O stay, my lord, they will not injure you.
    K. Edw. I will not trust them; Gaveston,
    away!
    Gav. Farewell, my lord.
    K. Edw. Lady, farewell.   10
    Niece. Farewell, sweet uncle, till we meet
    again.
    K. Edw. Farewell, sweet Gaveston; and
    farewell, niece.
    Q. Isab. No farewell to poor Isabel thy
    queen?
    K. Edw. Yes, yes, for Mortimer, your lover's
    sake. (*Exeunt all but* QUEEN ISABELLA.
    Q. Isab. Heavens can witness I love none
    but you!   15
From my embracements thus he breaks away.
O that mine arms could close this isle about,
That I might pull him to me where I would!
Or that these tears that drizzle from mine eyes
Had power to mollify his stony heart,   20
That when I had him we might never part.

Enter LANCASTER, WARWICK, YOUNG MORTI-
    MER, *and others.* *Alarums* [3]

    Lan. I wonder how he scap'd!
    Y. Mor.   Who's this? The queen!
    Q. Isab. Ay, Mortimer, the miserable queen,
Whose pining heart her inward sighs have
    blasted,

---

[1] Castle.
[2] An old port to the south of Tynemouth on the Yorkshire coast.
[3] The signals of drum and trumpet commonly used
on the Elizabethan stage to indicate the approach of
hostilities.

And body with continual mourning wasted.   25
These hands are tir'd with haling of my lord
From Gaveston, from wicked Gaveston,
And all in vain; for, when I speak him fair,
He turns away, and smiles upon his minion.

   Y. Mor. Cease to lament, and tell us where's
     the king?   30
   Q. Isab. What would you with the king?
     Is't him you seek?
   Lan. No, madam, but that cursed Gaveston.
Far be it from the thought of Lancaster
To offer violence to his sovereign.
We would but rid the realm of Gaveston: 35
Tell us where he remains, and he shall die.

   Q. Isab. He's gone by water unto Scar-
     borough;
Pursue him quickly, and he cannot scape;
The king hath left him, and his train is small.

   War. Foreslow [1] no time, sweet Lancaster;
     let's march.   40
   Y. Mor. How comes it that the king and he
     is parted?
   Q. Isab. That this your army, going several
     ways,
Might be of lesser force; and with the power
That he intendeth presently to raise,
Be easily suppress'd; therefore be gone.   45

   Y. Mor. Here in the river rides a Flemish
     hoy; [2]
Let's all aboard, and follow him amain.

   Lan. The wind that bears him hence will
     fill our sails.
Come, come aboard, 'tis but an hour's sailing.

   Y. Mor. Madam, stay you within this castle
     here.   50
   Q. Isab. No, Mortimer, I'll to my lord the
     king.
   Y. Mor. Nay, rather sail with us to Scar-
     borough.
   Q. Isab. You know the king is so suspicious,
As if he hear I have but talk'd with you,
Mine honor will be call'd in question;   55
And therefore, gentle Mortimer, be gone.

   Y. Mor. Madam, I cannot stay to answer
     you,
But think of Mortimer as he deserves.
     (*Exeunt all except* QUEEN ISABELLA.

[1] Waste.
[2] Fishing sloop.

   Q. Isab. So well hast thou deserv'd, sweet
     Mortimer,
As Isabel could live with thee for ever!   60
In vain I look for love at Edward's hand,
Whose eyes are fix'd on none but Gaveston;
Yet once more I'll importune him with prayers.
If he be strange [1] and not regard my words,
My son and I will over into France,   65
And to the king my brother there complain,
How Gaveston hath robb'd me of his love:
But yet I hope my sorrows will have end,
And Gaveston this blessed day be slain. (*Exit.*

SCENE 5. *Near Scarborough*

Enter GAVESTON, *pursued*

   Gav. Yet, lusty lords, I have escap'd your
     hands,
Your threats, your 'larums, and your hot pur-
     suits;
And though divorced from King Edward's eyes,
Yet liveth Pierce of Gaveston unsurpris'd, [2]   4
Breathing, in hope (*malgrado* [3] all your beards,
That muster rebels thus against your king),
To see his royal sovereign once again.

Enter WARWICK, LANCASTER, PEMBROKE,
YOUNG MORTIMER, *Soldiers,* JAMES, *and
other Attendants of* PEMBROKE

   War. Upon him, soldiers, take away his
     weapons.
   Y. Mor. Thou proud disturber of thy coun-
     try's peace,
Corrupter of thy king, cause of these broils,   10
Base flatterer, yield! and were it not for shame,
Shame and dishonor to a soldier's name,
Upon my weapon's point here shouldst thou
     fall,
And welter in thy gore.
   Lan.   Monster of men!
That, like the Greekish strumpet,[4] train'd [5] to
     arms   15
And bloody wars so many valiant knights;
Look for no other fortune, wretch, than death!
Kind Edward is not here to buckler thee.

[1] Unresponsive.   [2] Uncaptured.
[3] In spite of.   [4] I.e., Helen of Troy.
[5] Enticed.

War. Lancaster, why talk'st thou to the
    slave?   19
Go, soldiers, take him hence, for, by my sword,
His head shall off.   Gaveston, short warning
Shall serve thy turn; it is our country's cause
That here severely we will execute
Upon thy person.   Hang him at a bough.
    Gav. My lord! —
    War.   Soldiers, have him away; —   25
But for thou wert the favorite of a king,
Thou shalt have so much honor at our hands —[1]
    Gav. I thank you all, my lords: then I per-
    ceive,
That heading is one, and hanging is the other,
And death is all.

Enter EARL OF ARUNDEL

    Lan.   How now, my lord of Arundel?   30
    Arun. My lords, King Edward greets you
    all by me.
    War. Arundel, say your message.
    Arun.   His majesty,
Hearing that you had taken Gaveston,
Entreateth you by me, yet but he may
See him before he dies; for why,[2] he says,   35
And sends you word, he knows that die he shall;
And if you gratify his grace so far,
He will be mindful of the courtesy.
    War. How now?
    Gav. Renowmed[3] Edward, how thy name
Revives poor Gaveston!
    War.   No, it needeth not;   40
Arundel, we will gratify the king
In other matters; he must pardon us in this.
Soldiers, away with him!
    Gav.   Why, my lord of Warwick,
Will not these delays beget my hopes?
I know it, lords, it is this life you aim at,   45
Yet grant King Edward this.
    Y. Mor.   Shalt thou appoint
What we shall grant?   Soldiers, away with him!
Thus we'll gratify the king:
We'll send his head by thee; let him bestow
His tears on that, for that is all he gets   50
Of Gaveston, or else his senseless trunk.

---

[1] I.e., Gaveston shall have a gentleman's execution by
beheading instead of a criminal's, by hanging.
[2] Because.   [3] Renowned.

    Lan. Not so, my lords, lest he bestow more
    cost
In burying him than he hath ever earn'd.
    Arun. My lords, it is his majesty's request,
And in the honor of a king he swears,   55
He will but talk with him, and send him back.
    War. When? can you tell?   Arundel, no; we
    wot
He that the care of his realm remits,[1]
And drives his nobles to these exigents[2]
For Gaveston, will, if he sees him once,   60
Violate any promises to possess him.
    Arun. Then if you will not trust his grace in
    keep,[3]
My lords, I will be pledge for his return.
    Y. Mor. 'Tis honorable in thee to offer this;
But for we know thou art a noble gentleman,
We will not wrong thee so, to make away   66
A true man for a thief.
    Gav. How mean'st thou, Mortimer?   That
    is over-base.
    Y. Mor. Away, base groom, robber of king's
    renown!   69
Question with thy companions and thy mates.
    Pem. My Lord Mortimer, and you, my lords,
    each one,
To gratify the king's request therein,
Touching the sending of this Gaveston,
Because his majesty so earnestly
Desires to see the man before his death,   75
I will upon mine honor undertake
To carry him, and bring him back again;
Provided this, that you my lord of Arundel
Will join with me.
    War.   Pembroke, what wilt thou do?
Cause yet more bloodshed?   Is it not enough
That we have taken him, but must we now   81
Leave him on "had I wist,"[4] and let him go?
    Pem. My lords, I will not over-woo your
    honors,
But if you dare trust Pembroke with the
    prisoner,
Upon mine oath, I will return him back.   85
    Arun. My lord of Lancaster, what say you
    in this?

---

[1] Gives up.   [2] Extreme measures.
[3] In custody.
[4] "Had I known," — a common exclamation among
those who repent of their actions too late.

Lan. Why, I say, let him go on Pembroke's
    word.
Pem. And you, Lord Mortimer?
Y. Mor. How say you, my lord of Warwick?
War. Nay, do your pleasures, I know how
    'twill prove.   90
Pem. Then give him me.
Gav.   Sweet sovereign, yet I come
To see thee ere I die.
    War. (*aside*).   Yet not perhaps,
If Warwick's wit and policy prevail.
    Y. Mor. My lord of Pembroke, we deliver
    him you;   94
Return him on your honor. — Sound, away!
      (*Exeunt all except* PEMBROKE, ARUN-
      DEL, GAVESTON, JAMES, *and other*
      Attendants of PEMBROKE.
Pem. My lord Arundel, you shall go with me.
My house is not far hence; out of the way
A little, but our men shall go along.
We that have pretty wenches to our wives,
Sir, must not come so near and baulk their lips.
    Arun. 'Tis very kindly spoke, my lord of
    Pembroke;   101
Your honor hath an adamant[1] of power
To draw a prince.
    Pem.   So, my lord. Come hither, James:
I do commit this Gaveston to thee,   104
Be thou this night his keeper; in the morning
We will discharge thee of thy charge. Be gone.
    Gav. Unhappy Gaveston, whither goest thou
    now?
      (*Exit with* JAMES *and the other At-*
      tendants.
    Horse-boy. My lord, we'll quickly be at Cob-
    ham.[2]   (*Exeunt.*

ACT III

SCENE 1. *The Yorkshire country*

Enter GAVESTON *mourning,* JAMES *and other*
Attendants of PEMBROKE

Gav. O treacherous Warwick! thus to wrong
    thy friend.
James. I see it is your life these arms pursue.

[1] Magnet.
[2] A village of Kent in southeastern England. — The
reference is wholly ungeographical, for the spot is close
to two hundred miles from Scarborough.

Gav. Weaponless must I fall, and die in
    bands?[1]
O! must this day be period[2] of my life,
Center[3] of all my bliss? An[4] ye be men,   5
Speed to the king.

Enter WARWICK *and his company*

War.   My lord of Pembroke's men,
Strive you no longer — I will have that
    Gaveston.
    James. Your lordship does dishonor to your-
    self,
And wrong our lord, your honorable friend.
    War. No, James, it is my country's cause I
    follow.   10
Go, take the villain; soldiers, come away.
We'll make quick work. Commend me to your
    master,
My friend, and tell him that I watch'd it well.
Come, let thy shadow[5] parley with King
    Edward.
    Gav. Treacherous earl, shall I not see the
    king?   15
    War. The king of Heaven, perhaps; no other
    king.
Away!
      (*Exeunt* WARWICK *and his men with*
      GAVESTON.
    James. Come, fellows, it booted not[6] for us
    to strive,
We will in haste go certify[7] our lord. (*Exeunt.*

SCENE 2. *Near Boroughbridge, Yorkshire*

Enter KING EDWARD *and* YOUNG SPENCER,
BALDOCK, *and Nobles of the* KING'S *side,*
and Soldiers with drums and fifes

K. Edw. I long to hear an answer from the
    barons
Touching my friend, my dearest Gaveston.
Ah! Spencer, not the riches of my realm
Can ransom him! Ah, he is mark'd to die!
I know the malice of the younger Mortimer,   5
Warwick I know is rough, and Lancaster
Inexorable, and I shall never see

[1] Bonds.   [2] End.   [3] Lowest point.
[4] If.   [5] Ghost.   [6] It was of no avail.
[7] Inform.

My lovely Pierce, my Gaveston again!
The barons overbear me with their pride.

    Y. Spen. Were I King Edward, England's
      sovereign,   10
Son to the lovely Eleanor of Spain,
Great Edward Longshanks'[1] issue, would I
    bear
These braves,[2] this rage, and suffer uncon-
    troll'd
These barons thus to beard me in my land,
In mine own realm? My lord, pardon my
    speech: 15
Did you retain your father's magnanimity,[3]
Did you regard the honor of your name,
You would not suffer thus your majesty
Be counterbuff'd of your nobility.[4]
Strike off their heads, and let them preach on
    poles!   20
No doubt, such lessons they will teach the rest,
As by their preachments they will profit much,
And learn obedience to their lawful king.

    K. Edw. Yea, gentle Spencer, we have been
      too mild,
Too kind to them; but now have drawn our
    sword,   25
And if they send me not my Gaveston,
We'll steel[5] on their crest, and poll their tops.[6]

    Bald. This haught[7] resolve becomes your
      majesty,
Not to be tied to their affection,[8]   29
As though your highness were a schoolboy still,
And must be aw'd and govern'd like a child.

Enter the ELDER SPENCER, *with his truncheon*[9]
and Soldiers

    E. Spen. Long live my sovereign, the noble
      Edward,
In peace triumphant, fortunate in wars!

    K. Edw. Welcome, old man, com'st thou in
      Edward's aid?
Then tell thy prince of whence, and what thou
    art.   35

    E. Spen. Lo, with a band of bowmen and of
      pikes,
Brown bills and targeteers,[1] four hundred
    strong,
Sworn to defend King Edward's royal right,
I come in person to your majesty,
Spencer, the father of Hugh Spencer there,   40
Bound to your highness everlastingly,
For favor done, in him, unto us all.

    K. Edw. Thy father, Spencer?

    Y. Spen.   True, an it like your grace,
That pours, in lieu of all your goodness shown,
His life, my lord, before your princely feet.   45

    K. Edw. Welcome ten thousand times, old
      man, again.
Spencer, this love, this kindness to thy king,
Argues thy noble mind and disposition.
Spencer,[2] I here create thee Earl of Wiltshire,
And daily will enrich thee with our favor,   50
That, as the sunshine, shall reflect o'er thee.
Beside, the more to manifest our love,
Because we hear Lord Bruce doth sell his land,[3]
And that the Mortimers are in hand[4] withal,
Thou shalt have crowns[5] of us t' outbid the
    barons: 55
And, Spencer, spare them not, but lay it on.
Soldiers, a largess,[6] and thrice welcome all!

    Y. Spen. My lord, here comes the queen.

Enter QUEEN ISABELLA *and her son* PRINCE
EDWARD, *and* LEVUNE, *a Frenchman*

    K. Edw. Madam, what news?

    Q. Isab. News of dishonor, lord, and discon-
      tent.   60
Our friend Levune, faithful and full of trust,
Informeth us, by letters and by words,
That Lord Valois our brother, King of France,
Because your highness hath been slack in
    homage,

---

[1] Nickname for Edward I, who had unusually long legs.
[2] Insults.   [3] Haughty courage.
[4] Be stopped by your nobles.
[5] Strike with the sword.   [6] Cut off their heads.
[7] Lofty.   [8] Desire.   [9] Staff.

[1] Men with bronzed halberds and men with shields.
[2] I.e., Young Spencer. — Historically no such title was ever given him.
[3] Lord William de Bruce had Welsh borderlands near the properties of the Mortimers. These lands he sold in 1321 to Young Spencer much to the displeasure of the Mortimers.
[4] In negotiation.
[5] Coins valued at five shillings.
[6] Liberal gift.

Hath seized Normandy into his hands.   65
These be the letters, this the messenger.

   K. Edw. Welcome, Levune. Tush, Sib,[1] if
     this be all
Valois and I will soon be friends again. —
But to my Gaveston; shall I never see,
Never behold thee now? — Madam, in this
     matter,   70
We will employ you and your little son;
You shall go parley with the king of France.[2]
Boy, see you bear you bravely to the king,
And do your message with a majesty.

   P. Edw. Commit not to my youth things of
     more weight   75
Than fits a prince so young as I to bear,
And fear not, lord and father, Heaven's great
     beams
On Atlas' shoulder shall not lie more safe,
Than shall your charge committed to my trust.

   Q. Isab. Ah, boy! this towardness makes thy
     mother fear   80
Thou art not mark'd to many days on earth.

   K. Edw. Madam, we will that you with
     speed be shipp'd,
And this our son; Levune shall follow you
With all the haste we can despatch him hence.
Choose of our lords to bear you company,   85
And go in peace; leave us in wars at home.

   Q. Isab. Unnatural wars, where subjects
     brave their king;
God end them once! My lords, I take my leave,
To make my preparation for France.
           (*Exit with* PRINCE EDWARD.

Enter ARUNDEL

   K. Edw. What, Lord Arundel, dost thou
     come alone?   90

   Arun. Yea, my good lord, for Gaveston is
     dead.

   K. Edw. Ah, traitors! have they put my
     friend to death?
Tell me, Arundel, died he ere thou cam'st,
Or didst thou see my friend to take his death?

   [1] Kinswoman, — hence, here, "wife."
   [2] This embassy actually took place in 1325, while the
territorial conflict with France had started in 1322.
Yet these matters are announced almost simultaneously with the death of Gaveston (see l. 91 below),
which occurred in June, 1312.

   Arun. Neither, my lord; for as he was sur-
     pris'd,[1]   95
Begirt with weapons and with enemies round,
I did your highness' message to them all;
Demanding him of them, entreating rather,
And said, upon the honor of my name,
That I would undertake to carry him   100
Unto your highness, and to bring him back.

   K. Edw. And tell me, would the rebels deny
     me that?

   Y. Spen. Proud recreants!

   K. Edw.   Yea, Spencer, traitors all.

   Arun. I found them at the first inexorable;
The Earl of Warwick would not bide the hear-
     ing,   105
Mortimer hardly; Pembroke and Lancaster
Spake least: and when they flatly had denied,
Refusing to receive me pledge for him,
The Earl of Pembroke mildly thus bespake:
"My lords, because our sovereign sends for
     him,   110
And promiseth he shall be safe return'd,
I will this undertake, to have him hence,
And see him re-delivered to your hands."

   K. Edw. Well, and how fortunes that he
     came not?

   Y. Spen. Some treason, or some villainy, was
     cause.   115

   Arun. The Earl of Warwick seiz'd him on
     his way;
For being delivered unto Pembroke's men,
Their lord rode home thinking his prisoner safe;
But ere he came, Warwick in ambush lay,
And bare him to his death; and in a trench   120
Strake off his head, and march'd unto the camp.

   Y. Spen. A bloody part, flatly 'gainst law
     of arms!

   K. Edw. O shall I speak, or shall I sigh and
     die!

   Y. Spen. My lord, refer your vengeance to
     the sword
Upon these barons; hearten up your men;   125
Let them not unreveng'd murder your friends!
Advance your standard, Edward, in the field,
And march to fire them from their starting
     holes.[2]

   [1] Captured.
   [2] To smoke them (as if they were hunted animals)
from the holes in which they have taken refuge.

K. Edw. (*kneeling*). By earth, the common
    mother of us all,   129
By Heaven, and all the moving orbs thereof,
By this right hand, and by my father's sword,
And all the honors 'longing to my crown,
I will have heads and lives for him, as many
As I have manors, castles, towns, and towers!—
                            (*Rises.*
Treacherous Warwick! traitorous Mortimer!
If I be England's king, in lakes of gore   136
Your headless trunks, your bodies will I trail,
That you may drink your fill, and quaff in
    blood,
And stain my royal standard with the same,
That so my bloody colors may suggest   140
Remembrance of revenge immortally
On your accursed traitorous progeny,
You villains, that have slain my Gaveston!
And in this place of honor and of trust,
Spencer, sweet Spencer, I adopt thee here: 145
And merely of our love we do create thee
Earl of Gloucester, and Lord Chamberlain,[1]
Despite of times, despite of enemies.
    Y. Spen. My lord, here's a messenger from
    the barons.
Desires access unto your majesty.   150
    K. Edw. Admit him near.

Enter the Herald *from the Barons, with his coat
of arms*

    Her. Long live King Edward, England's
    lawful lord!
    K. Edw. So wish not they, I wis,[2] that sent
    thee hither.
Thou com'st from Mortimer and his 'complices,
A ranker rout[3] of rebels never was.   155
Well, say thy message.
    Her. The barons up in arms, by me salute
Your highness with long life and happiness;
And bid me say, as plainer[4] to your grace,
That if without effusion of blood   160
You will this grief have ease and remedy,
That from your princely person you remove
This Spencer, as a putrifying branch,

That deads[1] the royal vine, whose golden leaves
Empale[2] your princely head, your diadem, 165
Whose brightness such pernicious upstarts dim,
Say they; and lovingly advise your grace,
To cherish virtue and nobility,
And have old servitors in high esteem,   169
And shake off smooth dissembling flatterers.
This granted, they, their honors, and their lives,
Are to your highness vow'd and consecrate.
    Y. Spen. Ah, traitors! will they still display
    their pride?
    K. Edw. Away, tarry no answer, but be gone!
Rebels, will they appoint their sovereign 175
His sports, his pleasures, and his company?
Yet, ere thou go, see how I do divorce
               (*Embraces* SPENCER.
Spencer from me. — Now get thee to thy lords,
And tell them I will come to chastise them
For murdering Gaveston; hie thee, get thee
    gone!   180
Edward with fire and sword follows at thy heels.
                     (*Exit* Herald.
My lords, perceive you how these rebels swell?
Soldiers, good hearts, defend your sovereign's
    right,
For now, even now, we march to make them
    stoop.
Away!   185
                     (*Exeunt.*

SCENE 3. *The battlefield at Boroughbridge,
Yorkshire*[3]

*Alarums, excursions,[4] a great fight, and a retreat
sounded, within*

Enter KING EDWARD, *the* ELDER SPENCER,
YOUNG SPENCER, *and Noblemen of the*
KING's *side*

    K. Edw. Why do we sound retreat?   Upon
    them, lords!
This day I shall pour vengeance with my sword
On those proud rebels that are up in arms
And do confront and countermand their king.

---

    [1] Young Spencer secured this office in 1322, but he
never got the Gloucester earldom.
    [2] I know.   [3] Crowd.
    [4] Complainer or plaintiff.

    [1] Kills.   [2] Encircle.
    [3] Marlowe condenses the military engagements be-
tween King Edward and the rebellious nobles during
1321–22 into this one battle of Boroughbridge fought on
March 16, 1322.
    [4] Passages of small bodies of soldiers across the stage.

Y. Spen. I doubt it not, my lord, right will
     prevail.   5
E. Spen. 'Tis not amiss, my liege, for either
     part
To breathe awhile; our men, with sweat and
     dust
All chokt well near, begin to faint for heat;
And this retire [1] refresheth horse and man.
     Y. Spen. Here come the rebels.   10

Enter YOUNG MORTIMER, LANCASTER, WAR-
WICK, PEMBROKE, *and others*

Y. Mor. Look, Lancaster, yonder is Edward
Among his flatterers.
     Lan.   And there let him be
Till he pay dearly for their company.
     War. And shall, or Warwick's sword shall
     smite in vain.
     K. Edw. What, rebels, do you shrink and
     sound retreat?   15
     Y. Mor. No, Edward, no; thy flatterers faint
and fly.
     Lan. Thou'd best betimes forsake them, and
     their trains,[2]
For they'll betray thee, traitors as they are.
     Y. Spen. Traitor on thy face, rebellious
     Lancaster!
     Pem. Away, base upstart, brav'st thou
     nobles thus?   20
     E. Spen. A noble attempt and honorable
     deed,
Is it not, trow ye, to assemble aid,
And levy arms against your lawful king!
     K. Edw. For which ere long their heads shall
     satisfy,
T' appease the wrath of their offended king.   25
     Y. Mor. Then, Edward, thou wilt fight it to
     the last,
And rather bathe thy sword in subjects' blood,
Than banish that pernicious company?
     K. Edw. Ay, traitors all, rather than thus
     be brav'd,
Make England's civil towns huge heaps of
     stones,   30
And ploughs to go about our palace-gates.
     War. A desperate and unnatural resolution!
Alarum! to the fight!

   [1] Retreat.   [2] Plots.

St. George [1] for England, and the barons' right!
     K. Edw. Saint George for England, and
     King Edward's right!   35
     (*Alarums. Exeunt the two parties
     severally.*

SCENE 4. *The same*

Enter KING EDWARD *and his followers, with the
Barons and* KENT, *captives*

     K. Edw. Now, lusty lords, now, not by
     chance of war,
But justice of the quarrel and the cause,
Vail'd is your pride; methinks you hang the
     heads,
But we'll advance [2] them, traitors. Now 'tis
     time
To be aveng'd on you for all your braves,[3]   5
And for the murder of my dearest friend,
To whom right well you knew our soul was knit,
Good Pierce of Gaveston, my sweet favorite.
Ah, rebels! recreants! you made him away.
     Kent. Brother, in regard of [4] thee, and of
     thy land,   10
Did they remove that flatterer from thy
     throne.
     K. Edw. So, sir, you have spoke; away,
     avoid our presence!   (*Exit* KENT.
Accursed wretches, was't in regard of us,
When we had sent our messenger to request
He might be spar'd to come to speak with
     us,   15
And Pembroke undertook for his return,
That thou, proud Warwick, watch'd the
     prisoner,
Poor Pierce, and headed him 'gainst law of
     arms?
For which thy head shall overlook the rest,
As much as thou in rage outwent'st the rest.
     War. Tyrant, I scorn thy threats and men-
     aces;   21
'Tis but temporal [5] that thou canst inflict.
     Lan. The worst is death, and better die to
     live
Than live in infamy under such a king.

   [1] Not adopted as England's patron saint until the
reign of Edward III (1327–77).
   [2] Raise.   [3] Insults.   [4] Out of regard for.
   [5] I.e., bodily punishment.

K. Edw. Away with them, my lord of Win-
    chester! [1]   25
These lusty leaders, Warwick and Lancaster,
I charge you roundly — off with both their
    heads! [2]
Away!
    War. Farewell, vain world!
    Lan.   Sweet Mortimer, farewell.
    Y. Mor. England, unkind to thy nobility,
Groan for this grief, behold how thou art
    maim'd!   31
    K. Edw. Go take that haughty Mortimer to
    the Tower,
There see him safe bestow'd; and for the rest,
Do speedy execution on them all.
Begone!   35
    Y. Mort. What, Mortimer! can ragged
    stony walls
Immure thy virtue that aspires to Heaven?
No, Edward, England's scourge, it may not be;
Mortimer's hope surmounts his fortune far.
    (*The captive Barons are led off.*
    K. Edw. Sound drums and trumpets! March
    with me, my friends,   40
Edward this day hath crown'd him king anew.
    (*Exeunt all except* YOUNG SPENCER,
        LEVUNE, *and* BALDOCK.
    Y. Spen. Levune, the trust that we repose
    in thee,
Begets the quiet of King Edward's land.
Therefore begone in haste, and with advice
Bestow that treasure on the lords of France, 45
That, therewith all enchanted, like the guard
That suffered Jove to pass in showers of gold
To Danaë,[3] all aid may be denied
To Isabel, the queen, that now in France
Makes friends, to cross the seas with her young
    son,   50
And step into his father's regiment.
    Levune. That's it these barons and the subtle
    queen
Long levell'd [4] at.
    Bal.   Yea, but, Levune, thou seest
These barons lay their heads on blocks together;

What they intend, the hangman frustrates
    clean.   55
    Levune. Have you no doubt, my lords, I'll
    clap [1] so close [2]
Among the lords of France with England's gold,
That Isabel shall make her plaints in vain,
And France shall be obdurate with her tears.
    Y. Spen. Then make for France amain;
    Levune, away!   60
Proclaim King Edward's wars and victories.
                     (*Exeunt.*

ACT IV

SCENE I. *Near the Tower of London on the
Thames*

Enter KENT

    Kent. Fair blows the wind for France; blow
    gentle gale,
Till Edmund be arriv'd for England's good!
Nature, yield to my country's cause in this.
A brother? No, a butcher of thy friends!
Proud Edward, dost thou banish me thy pres-
    ence? [3]   5
But I'll to France, and cheer the wronged
    queen,
And certify what Edward's looseness is.
Unnatural king! to slaughter noblemen
And cherish flatterers! Mortimer, I stay   9
Thy sweet escape:stand gracious,gloomy night,
To his device.

Enter YOUNG MORTIMER, *disguised*

    Y. Mor.   Holla! who walketh there?
Is't you, my lord?
    Kent.   Mortimer, 'tis I;
But hath thy potion wrought so happily?
    Y. Mor. It hath, my Lord; the warders all
    asleep,   14
I thank them, gave me leave to pass in peace.
But hath your grace got shipping unto France?
    Kent. Fear it not.   (*Exeunt.*

---

[1] I.e., the elder Spencer, who in history received this title from the parliament of 1322.
[2] The Earl of Warwick really died a natural death in 1315.
[3] See note to Act II, Sc. 2, l. 53.   [4] Aimed.

[1] I.e., bargain. "To clap" really means "to strike each other's hands in token of a bargain."
[2] So secretly.
[3] Historically Kent was neither banished nor connected with Mortimer's escape from the Tower in 1323.

SCENE 2. QUEEN ISABELLA'S *lodgings in Paris*

Enter QUEEN ISABELLA *and her son* PRINCE EDWARD

Q. Isab. Ah, boy! our friends do fail us all
    in France.
The lords are cruel, and the king [1] unkind;
What shall we do?
    P. Edw.   Madam, return to England,
And please my father well, and then a fig   4
For all my uncle's friendship here in France.
I warrant you, I'll win his highness quickly;
'A loves me better than a thousand Spencers.
    Q. Isab. Ah, boy, thou art deceiv'd, at least
    in this,
To think that we can yet be tun'd together;
No, no, we jar too far. Unkind Valois!   10
Unhappy Isabel! when France rejects,
Whither, oh! whither dost thou bend thy steps?

Enter SIR JOHN *of* HAINAULT

Sir J. Madam, what cheer?
    Q. Isab.   Ah! good Sir John of Hainault,
Never so cheerless, nor so far distrest.
    Sir J. I hear, sweet lady, of the king's un-
    kindness;   15
But droop not, madam; noble minds contemn
Despair. Will your grace with me to Hainault,[2]
And there stay time's advantage with your son?
How say you, my lord, will you go with your
    friends,
And share of all our fortunes equally?   20
    P. Edw. So pleaseth the queen, my mother,
    me it likes.
The King of England, nor the court of France,
Shall have me from my gracious mother's side,
Till I be strong enough to break a staff;[3]
And then have at the proudest [4] Spencer's head.
    Sir J. Well said, my lord.   26
    Q. Isab. O, my sweetheart, how do I moan
    thy wrongs,
Yet triumph in the hope of thee, my joy!

Ah, sweet Sir John! even to the utmost verge
Of Europe, or the shore of Tanais,[1]   30
Will we with thee to Hainault — so we will: —
The marquis [2] is a noble gentleman;
His grace, I dare presume, will welcome me.
But who are these?

Enter KENT *and* YOUNG MORTIMER

Kent.   Madam, long may you live,
Much happier than your friends in England
    do!   35
    Q. Isab. Lord Edmund and Lord Mortimer
    alive!
Welcome to France! The news was here, my
    lord,
That you were dead, or very near your death.
    Y. Mor. Lady, the last was truest of the
    twain;
But Mortimer, reserv'd for better hap,   40
Hath shaken off the thraldom of the Tower,
And lives t' advance your standard, good my
    lord.
    P. Edw. How mean you? An the king, my
    father, lives?
No, my Lord Mortimer, not I, I trow.
    Q. Isab. Not, son! why not? I would it
    were no worse.   45
But, gentle lords, friendless we are in France.
    Y. Mor. Monsieur le Grand, a noble friend
    of yours,
Told us, at our arrival, all the news:
How hard the nobles, how unkind the king
Hath show'd himself; but, madam, right makes
    room   50
Where weapons want; and, though a many
    friends
Are made away, away, as Warwick, Lancaster,
And others of our party and faction;
Yet have we friends, assure your grace, in
    England
Would cast up caps, and clap their hands for
    joy,   55
To see us there, appointed [3] for our foes.

---

[1] I.e., the king of France, Isabella's brother.
[2] A district now located in northeast France and southwest Belgium.
[3] I.e., a lance.
[4] Then attack the extremely proud.

[1] Don River in southeastern Russia; a river which the English of Marlowe's day looked upon as the boundary line between Europe and Asia.
[2] William, Count of Hainault, brother of Sir John.
[3] All fitted out.

Kent. Would all were well, and Edward well
     reclaim'd,
For England's honor, peace, and quietness.
     Y. Mor. But by the sword, my lord, 't must
     be deserv'd,[1]
The king will ne'er forsake his flatterers.   60
     Sir J. My lord of England, sith [2] th' un-
     gentle king
Of France refuseth to give aid of arms
To this distressed queen his sister here,
Go you with her to Hainault.   Doubt ye not,
We will find comfort, money, men, and friends
Ere long, to bid the English king a base.[3]   66
How say, young prince?   What think you of
     the match?
     P. Edw. I think King Edward will outrun
     us all.
     Q. Isab. Nay, son, not so; and you must not
     discourage   69
Your friends, that are so forward [4] in your aid.
     Kent. Sir John of Hainault, pardon us, I pray;
These comforts that you give our woful queen
Bind us in kindness all at your command.
     Q. Isab. Yea, gentle brother; and the God
     of heaven   74
Prosper your happy motion,[5] good Sir John.
     Y. Mor. This noble gentleman, forward in
     arms,
Was born, I see, to be our anchor-hold.
Sir John of Hainault, be it thy renown,
That England's queen and nobles in distress,
Have been by thee restor'd and comforted.   80
     Sir J. Madam, along, and you my lords,
     with me,
That England's peers may Hainault's welcome
     see.   (*Exeunt.*

SCENE 3. *A room in the royal palace at
Westminster, London*

Enter KING EDWARD, ARUNDEL, *the* ELDER *and*
YOUNGER SPENCER, *with others*

     K. Edw. Thus after many threats of wrath-
     ful war,
Triumpheth England's Edward with his friends;

[1] Earned.   [2] Since.
[3] "To bid a base" means "to challenge."   The term
comes from the game, "prisoner's base."
[4] Eager.   [5] Proposal.

And triumph, Edward, with his friends un-
     controll'd!
My lord of Gloucester, do you hear the news?
     Y. Spen. What news, my lord?   5
     K. Edw. Why, man, they say there is great
     execution
Done through the realm; my lord of Arundel,
You have the note, have you not?
     Arun. From the Lieutenant of the Tower,
     my lord.
     K. Edw. I pray let us see it. (*Takes the
     note.*)   What have we there?   10
Read it, Spencer.
     (*Hands the note to* YOUNG SPENCER
     who reads the names.
Why, so; they bark'd apace a month ago:
Now, on my life, they'll neither bark nor bite.
Now, sirs, the news from France?   Gloucester,
     I trow
The lords of France love England's gold so well
As Isabella gets no aid from thence.   16
What now remains?   Have you proclaim'd, my
     lord,
Reward for them can bring in Mortimer?
     Y. Spen. My lord, we have; and if he be in
     England,
'A will be had ere long, I doubt it not.   20
     K. Edw. If, dost thou say?   Spencer, as true
     as death,
He is in England's ground; our portmasters
Are not so careless of their king's command.

Enter a Messenger

How now, what news with thee?   From
     whence come these?
     Mess. Letters, my lord, and tidings forth of
     France; —   25
To you, my lord of Gloucester, from Levune.
     (*Gives letters to* YOUNG SPENCER.
     K. Edw. Read.
     Y. Spen. (*reads*).
"My duty to your honor premised, &c., I
have, according to instructions in that behalf,
dealt with the King of France his lords,   30
and effected that the queen, all discontented
and discomforted, is gone: whither, if you ask,
with Sir John of Hainault, brother to the
marquis, into Flanders.   With them are gone

Lord Edmund, and the Lord Mortimer, 35
having in their company divers of your nation,
and others; and, as constant report goeth, they
intend to give King Edward battle in England,
sooner than he can look for them.   This is all
the news of import.   40
    Your honor's in all service, LEVUNE."
    K. Edw. Ah, villains! hath that Mortimer
escap'd?
With him is Edmund gone associate?
And will Sir John of Hainault lead the round? [1]
Welcome, a' [2] God's name, madam, and your
son;   45
England shall welcome you and all your rout.
Gallop apace, bright Phoebus, through the sky,
And dusky night, in rusty iron car,
Between you both shorten the time, I pray,
That I may see that most desired day   50
When we may meet these traitors in the field.
Ah, nothing grieves me but my little boy
Is thus misled to countenance their ills.
Come, friends, to Bristow, [3] there to make us
strong;
And, winds, as equal be to bring them in, 55
As you injurious were to bear them forth!
                       (*Exeunt.*

SCENE 4. *Near Harwich* [4]

Enter QUEEN ISABELLA, *her son* PRINCE ED-
WARD, KENT, YOUNG MORTIMER, *and* SIR
JOHN *of* HAINAULT

    Q. Isab. Now, lords, our loving friends and
countrymen,
Welcome to England all, with prosperous
winds! [5]
Our kindest friends in Belgia [6] have we left,
To cope [7] with friends at home; a heavy case
When force to force is knit, and sword and
glaive [8]   5
In civil broils make kin and countrymen
Slaughter themselves in others, and their sides

With their own weapons gor'd!   But what's
the help?
Misgoverned kings are cause of all this wrack; [1]
And, Edward, thou art one among them all, 10
Whose looseness hath betray'd thy land to
spoil,
Who made the channels [2] overflow with blood.
Of thine own people patron shouldst thou be,
But thou ——   14
    Y. Mor. Nay, madam, if you be a warrior,
You must not grow so passionate in speeches.
Lords,
Sith that we are by sufferance of Heaven
Arriv'd and armed in this prince's right,
Here for our country's cause swear we to him
All homage, fealty, and forwardness; [3]   21
And for the open wrongs and injuries
Edward hath done to us, his queen and land,
We come in arms to wreck it [4] with the sword;
That England's queen in peace may repossess
Her dignities and honors; and withal   26
We may remove these flatterers from the king,
That havocs [5] England's wealth and treasury.
    Sir J. Sound trumpets, my lord, and forward
let us march.
Edward will think we come to flatter him.   30
    Kent. I would he never had been flattered
more.   (*Exeunt.*

SCENE 5. *Near Bristol*

Enter KING EDWARD, BALDOCK, *and* YOUNG
SPENCER, *flying about the stage*

    Y. Spen. Fly, fly, my lord! the queen is
over-strong;
Her friends do multiply, and yours do fail.
Shape we our course to Ireland, there to
breathe.
    K. Edw. What! was I born to fly and run
away,   4
And leave the Mortimers conquerors behind?
Give me my horse, and let's reinforce our
troops:
And in this bed of honor die with fame.
    Bald. O no, my lord, this princely resolution
Fits not the time; away! we are pursu'd.
                       (*Exeunt.*

---

[1] The dance.   [2] In.
[3] Bristol, an old port in the west of England on the
Severn Channel.
[4] The first important port on the east coast of England north of London.
[5] The landing of the Queen and her retinue happened
on September 25, 1326.
[6] The Netherlands.   [7] Battle.   [8] Lance.

[1] Destruction.   [2] Gutters.   [3] Zeal.
[4] Work destruction on it.   [5] Works havoc with.

Enter KENT, *with sword and target*

Kent. This way he fled, but I am come too
    late.   10
Edward, alas! my heart relents for thee.
Proud traitor, Mortimer, why dost thou chase
Thy lawful king, thy sovereign, with thy sword?
Vile wretch! and why hast thou, of all un-
    kind,[1]   14
Borne arms against thy brother and thy king?
Rain showers of vengeance on my cursed head,
Thou God, to whom in justice it belongs
To punish this unnatural revolt!
Edward, this Mortimer aims at thy life!
O fly him, then! But, Edmund, calm this rage,
Dissemble, or thou diest; for Mortimer   21
And Isabel do kiss, while they conspire;
And yet she bears a face of love forsooth.
Fie on that love that hatcheth death and hate!
Edmund, away! Bristow to Longshanks' blood
Is false. Be not found single for suspect:[2]   26
Proud Mortimer pries near unto thy walks.

Enter QUEEN ISABELLA, PRINCE EDWARD,
    YOUNG MORTIMER, *and* SIR JOHN *of*
    HAINAULT

Q. Isab. Successful battle gives the God of
    kings
To them that fight in right and fear his wrath.
Since then successfully we have prevailed,   30
Thanks be Heaven's great architect, and you.
Ere farther we proceed, my noble lords,
We here create our well-beloved son,
Of love and care unto his royal person,
Lord Warden of the realm, and sith the fates
Have made his father so unfortunate,   36
Deal you, my lords, in this, my loving lords,
As to your wisdoms fittest seems in all.
    Kent. Madam, without offense, if I may ask,
How will you deal with Edward in his fall?   40
    P. Edw. Tell me, good uncle, what Edward
    do you mean?
    Kent. Nephew, your father; I dare not call
    him king.
    Y. Mor. My lord of Kent, what needs these
    questions?

[1] Altogether unnatural.
[2] Found alone because of the suspicion against you.

'Tis not in her controlment, nor in ours,
But as the realm and parliament shall please,
So shall your brother be disposed of. —   46
I like not this relenting mood in Edmund.
        (*Aside to the* QUEEN.
Madam, 'tis good to look to him betimes.
    Q. Isab. My lord, the Mayor of Bristow
    knows our mind.
    Y. Mor. Yea, madam, and they scape not
    easily   50
That fled the field.
    Q. Isab.   Baldock is with the king,
A goodly chancellor, is he not, my lord?
    Sir J. So are the Spencers, the father and
    the son.
    Kent. This Edward is the ruin of the realm.

Enter RICE AP HOWELL *and the Mayor of*
    Bristol, with the ELDER SPENCER *prisoner,*
    and Attendants

Rice. God save Queen Isabel, and her
    princely son!   55
Madam, the mayor and citizens of Bristow,
In sign of love and duty to this presence,
Present by me this traitor to the state,
Spencer, the father to that wanton Spencer,
That, like the lawless Catiline of Rome,[1]   60
Reveled in England's wealth and treasury.
    Q. Isab. We thank you all.
    Y. Mor.   Your loving care in this
Deserveth princely favors and rewards.
But where's the king and the other Spencer fled?
    Rice. Spencer the son, created Earl of
    Gloucester,   65
Is with that smooth-tongu'd scholar Baldock
    gone
And shipt but late for Ireland with the king.
    Y. Mor. (*aside*). Some whirlwind fetch them
    back or sink them all! —
They shall be started thence, I doubt it not.
    P. Edw. Shall I not see the king my father
    yet?   70
    Kent. (*aside*). Unhappy's Edward, chas'd
    from England's bounds.

[1] Lucius Sergius Catalina, a Roman senator, along
with other desperate men conspired against the Republic of Rome, but their plot was foiled by Cicero.
Catalina was slain in 62 B.C.

Sir J. Madam, what resteth,[1] why stand you
   in a muse?[2]

Q. Isab. I rue my lord's ill-fortune; but alas!
Care of my country call'd me to this war.

Y. Mor. Madam, have done with care and
   sad complaint;   75
Your king hath wrong'd your country and
   himself,
And we must seek to right it as we may.
Meanwhile, have hence this rebel to the block.[3]
Your lordship cannot privilege your head.

E. Spen. Rebel is he that fights against his
   prince;   80
So fought not they that fought in Edward's
   right.

Y. Mor. Take him away, he prates.
     (*Exeunt Attendants with the* ELDER
     SPENCER.
               You, Rice ap Howell,
Shall do good service to her majesty,
Being of countenance in your country here,
To follow these rebellious runagates.[4]   85
We in meanwhile, madam, must take advice
How Baldock, Spencer, and their complices
May in their fall be followed to their end.
                     (*Exeunt.*

SCENE 6. *A room in Neath Abbey, Glamorgan-*
     shire, Wales

Enter the ABBOT, *Monks,* KING EDWARD,
   YOUNG SPENCER, *and* BALDOCK, *the three*
   latter disguised

Abbot. Have you no doubt, my lord; have
   you no fear;
As silent and as careful we will be,
To keep your royal person safe with us,
Free from suspect[5] and fell invasion[6]
Of such as have your majesty in chase,   5
Yourself, and those your chosen company,
As danger of this stormy time requires.

K. Edw. Father, thy face should harbor no
   deceit.
O! hadst thou ever been a king, thy heart,
Pierced deeply with sense of my distress,   10

---

[1] Remains to be done.   [2] In revery.
[3] The elder Spencer was beheaded at Bristol in October, 1326.
[4] Runaways.   [5] Suspicion.   [6] Cruel attack.

Could not but take compassion of my state.
Stately and proud, in riches and in train,
Whilom[1] I was, powerful, and full of pomp:
But what is he whom rule and empery[2]
Have not in life or death made miserable?   15
Come, Spencer; come, Baldock, come, sit down
   by me;
Make trial now of that philosophy,
That in our famous nurseries of arts
Thou suck'dst from Plato and from Aristotle.
Father, this life contemplative is Heaven.   20
O that I might this life in quiet lead!
But we, alas! are chas'd; and you, my friends,
Your lives and my dishonor they pursue.
Yet, gentle monks, for treasure, gold, nor fee,
Do you betray us and our company.   25

Monks. Your grace may sit secure, if none
   but we
Do wot of your abode.

Y. Spen.   Not one alive; but shrewdly I
   suspect
A gloomy fellow in a mead below.
'A gave a long look after us, my lord;   30
And all the land I know is up in arms,
Arms that pursue our lives with deadly hate.

Bald. We were embark'd for Ireland,
   wretched we!
With awkward winds and sore tempests driven
To fall on shore, and here to pine in fear   35
Of Mortimer and his confederates.

K. Edw. Mortimer! who talks of Mortimer?
Who wounds me with the name of Mortimer,
That bloody man? Good father, on thy lap
Lay I this head, laden with mickle[3] care.   40
O might I never open these eyes again!
Never again lift up this drooping head!
O never more lift up this dying heart!

Y. Spen. Look up, my lord. — Baldock, this
   drowsiness
Betides no good; here even we are betray'd.   45

Enter, with Welsh hooks,[4] RICE AP HOWELL,
   a Mower, *and the* EARL OF LEICESTER

Mow. Upon my life, these be the men ye
   seek.

---

[1] Formerly.   [2] Empire.   [3] Much.
[4] Cutting instruments with a hook-shaped point, a cross-piece below the blade, and a long handle.

Rice. Fellow, enough. — My lord, I pray be short,
A fair commission warrants what we do.

   Leices. The queen's commission, urged by Mortimer;
What cannot gallant Mortimer with the queen? —   50
(*Aside*) Alas! see where he sits, and hopes unseen
T' escape their hands that seek to reave[1] his life.
Too true it is, *Quem dies vidit veniens superbum,*
Hunc dies vidit fugiens jacentem.[2] —
But, Leicester, leave to grow so passionate.[3]
Spencer and Baldock, by no other names,[4]   56
I arrest you of high treason here.
Stand not on[5] titles, but obey th' arrest;
'Tis in the name of Isabel the queen.
My lord, why droop you thus?   60

   K. Edw. O day, the last of all my bliss on earth!
Center of all misfortune! O my stars,
Why do you lour unkindly on a king?
Comes Leicester, then, in Isabella's name
To take my life, my company from me?   65
Here, man, rip up this panting breast of mine,
And take my heart in rescue of my friends!

   Rice. Away with them!

   Y. Spen.   It may become thee yet
To let us take our farewell of his grace.

   Abbot (aside). My heart with pity earns[6] to see this sight, —   70
A king to bear these words and proud commands.

   K. Edw. Spencer, ah, sweet Spencer, thus then must we part?

   Y. Spen. We must, my lord, so will the angry Heavens.

   K. Edw. Nay, so will hell and cruel Mortimer;
The gentle Heavens have not to do in this.   75

   Bald. My lord, it is in vain to grieve or storm.

Here humbly of your grace we take our leaves;
Our lots are cast; I fear me, so is thine.

   K. Edw. In Heaven we may, in earth ne'er shall we meet;   79
And, Leicester, say, what shall become of us?

   Leices. Your majesty must go to Killingworth.[1]

   K. Edw. Must! it is somewhat hard, when kings *must* go.

   Leices. Here is a litter[2] ready for your grace,
That waits your pleasure, and the day grows old.

   Rice. As good be gone, as stay and be benighted,   85

   K. Edw. A litter hast thou? Lay me in a hearse.
And to the gates of hell convey me hence;
Let Pluto's[3] bells ring out my fatal knell,
And hags howl for my death at Charon's[4] shore,
For friends hath Edward none but these[5] and these,[6]   90
And these must die under a tyrant's sword.

   Rice. My lord, be going; care not for these,
For we shall see them shorter by the heads.[7]

   K. Edw. Well, that shall be, shall be: part we must!   94
Sweet Spencer, gentle Baldock, part we must!
Hence feigned weeds! unfeigned are my woes;
             (*Throws off his disguise.*
Father, farewell! Leicester, thou stay'st for me,
And go I must. Life, farewell, with my friends.
        (*Exeunt* KING EDWARD *and* LEICESTER.

   Y. Spen. O! is he gone? Is noble Edward gone?
Parted from hence, never to see us more?   100
Rent,[8] sphere of Heaven! and, fire, forsake thy orb!
Earth, melt to air! gone is my sovereign,
Gone, gone, alas! never to make return.

---

[1] Snatch away.
[2] Whom the dawn saw proud, evening saw thus prostrate. (Seneca, *Thyestes*, ll. 613–14.)
[3] Cease to grow so compassionate.
[4] I.e., without recital of full names.
[5] Do not wait for.
[6] Grieves.

[1] Kenilworth in Warwickshire, central England.
[2] A curtained couch mounted on shafts for carrying by porters.
[3] God of the lower world of departed spirits.
[4] The ferryman on the River Styx in the lower world.
[5] The abbot and monks.
[6] Spencer and Baldock.
[7] I.e., by beheading.   [8] Rend.

Bald. Spencer, I see our souls are fleeted [1]
   hence;
We are depriv'd the sunshine of our life: 105
Make for a new life, man; throw up thy eyes,
And heart, and hand to Heaven's immortal
   throne;
Pay nature's debt with cheerful countenance;
Reduce we all our lessons unto this:
To die, sweet Spencer, therefore live we all;
Spencer, all live to die, and rise to fall.   111

   Rice. Come, come, keep these preachments
till you come to the place appointed.   You,
and such as you are, have made wise work in
England.   Will your lordships away?   115

   Mow. Your lordship, I trust, will remember
   me?

   Rice. Remember thee, fellow! what else?
Follow me to the town.   (*Exeunt*.

ACT V

Scene 1.   *A room in Kenilworth Castle*

Enter King Edward, Leicester, *the* Bishop
   of Winchester, *and* Trussel

   Leices. Be patient, good my lord, cease to
   lament,
Imagine Killingworth Castle were your court,
And that you lay for pleasure here a space,
Not of compulsion or necessity.

   K. Edw. Leicester, if gentle words might
   comfort me,   5
Thy speeches long ago had eas'd my sorrows;
For kind and loving hast thou always been.
The griefs of private men are soon allay'd,
But not of kings.   The forest deer, being
   struck,
Runs to an herb [2] that closeth up the wounds;
But, when the imperial lion's flesh is gor'd,   11
He rends and tears it with his wrathful paw,
Highly scorning that the lowly earth
Should drink his blood, mounts up into the air.
And so it fares with me, whose dauntless mind
The ambitious Mortimer would seek to curb,
And that unnatural queen, false Isabel,   17
That thus hath pent and mew'd me in a prison;
For such outrageous passions cloy my soul,

[1] Fled.
[2] I.e., dittany, sometimes called pepperwort.

As with the wings of rancor and disdain   20
Full often am I soaring up to Heaven,
To plain me [1] to the gods against them both.
But when I call to mind I am a king,
Methinks I should revenge me of my wrongs,
That Mortimer and Isabel have done.   25
But what are kings, when regiment [2] is gone,
But perfect shadows in a sunshine day?
My nobles rule, I bear the name of king;
I wear the crown, but am controll'd by them,
By Mortimer, and my unconstant queen,   30
Who spots my nuptial bed with infamy;
Whilst I am lodg'd within this cave of care,
Where sorrow at my elbow still attends,
To company [3] my heart with sad laments,
That bleeds within me for this strange ex-
   change.   35
But tell me, must I now resign my crown,
To make usurping Mortimer a king?

   B. of Win. Your grace mistakes; it is for
   England's good,
And princely Edward's right we crave the
   crown.

   K. Edw. No, 'tis for Mortimer, not Ed-
   ward's head;   40
For he's a lamb, encompassed by wolves,
Which in a moment will abridge his life.
But if proud Mortimer do wear this crown,
Heavens turn it to a blaze of quenchless fire!
Or like the snaky wreath of Tisiphon,[4]   45
Engirt the temples of his hateful head;
So shall not England's vine [5] be perished,
But Edward's name survives, though Edward
   dies.

   Leices. My lord, why waste you thus the
   time away?
They stay your answer; will you yield your
   crown?   50

   K. Edw. Ah, Leicester, weigh how hardly I
   can brook
To lose my crown and kingdom without cause;
To give ambitious Mortimer my right,
That like a mountain overwhelms my bliss,   54
In which extreme my mind here murdered is.
But what the heavens appoint, I must obey!

[1] Complain.   [2] Governance.   [3] Accompany.
[4] Tisiphone, one of the Furies, from whose head
snakes hung like hair.
[5] I.e., the emblematic vine on the English royal crown.

Here, take my crown; the life of Edward too;
(Takes off the crown.
Two kings in England cannot reign at once.
But stay awhile, let me be king till night,
That I may gaze upon this glittering crown;   60
So shall my eyes receive their last content,[1]
My head, the latest honor due to it,
And jointly both yield up their wished right.
Continue ever thou celestial sun;
Let never silent night possess this clime: 65
Stand still you watches of the element;[2]
All times and seasons, rest you at a stay,
That Edward may be still fair England's king!
But day's bright beam doth vanish fast away,
And needs I must resign my wished crown.   70
Inhuman creatures! nurs'd with tiger's milk!
Why gape you for your sovereign's overthrow!
My diadem I mean, and guiltless life.
See, monsters, see, I'll wear my crown again!
(Puts on the crown.
What, fear you not the fury of your king?   75
But, hapless Edward, thou art fondly[3] led;
They pass[4] not for thy frowns as late they did,
But seek to make a new-elected king;
Which fills my mind with strange despairing
thoughts,
Which thoughts are martyred with endless
torments,   80
And in this torment comfort find I none,
But that I feel the crown upon my head;
And therefore let me wear it yet awhile.
   Trus. My lord, the parliament must have
present news,
And therefore say, will you resign or no?   85
(The KING *rageth.*
   K. Edw. I'll not resign, but whilst I live —
Traitors, be gone and join with Mortimer!
Elect, conspire, install, do what you will;
Their blood and yours shall seal these treacher-
ies!
   B. of Win. This answer we'll return, and so
farewell. *(Starts to go with* TRUSSEL. 90
   Leices. Call them again, my lord, and speak
them fair;
For if they go, the prince shall lose his right.
   K. Edw. Call thou them back, I have no
power to speak.

[1] Satisfaction.   [2] Sky.
[3] Foolishly.   [4] Care.

   Leices. My lord, the king is willing to resign.
   B. of Win. If he be not, let him choose.   95
   K. Edw. O would I might, but heavens and
earth conspire
To make me miserable!   Here receive my
crown: —
Receive it?   No, these innocent hands of mine
Shall not be guilty of so foul a crime.
He of you all that most desires my blood,   100
And will be call'd the murderer of a king,
Take it.   What, are you mov'd?   Pity you
me?
Then send for unrelenting Mortimer,
And Isabel, whose eyes, being turn'd to steel,
Will sooner sparkle fire than shed a tear.   105
Yet stay, for rather than I'll look on them,
Here, here!
(Gives the crown.
   Now, sweet God of Heaven,
Make me despise this transitory pomp,
And sit for aye enthronized in Heaven!
Come, death, and with thy fingers close my
eyes,   110
Or if I live, let me forget myself.
   B. of Win. My lord —
   K. Edw. Call me not lord; away — out of
my sight!
Ah, pardon me: grief makes me lunatic!
Let not that Mortimer protect my son;[1]   115
More safety is there in a tiger's jaws,
Than his embracements.   Bear this to the
queen,
Wet with my tears, and dried again with sighs;
(Gives a handkerchief.
If with the sight thereof she be not mov'd,
Return it back and dip it in my blood.   120
Commend me to my son, and bid him rule
Better than I.   Yet how have I transgress'd,
Unless it be with too much clemency?
   Trus. And thus most humbly do we take our
leave.   124
   K. Edw. Farewell. —
(Exeunt the BISHOP OF WINCHESTER
and TRUSSEL.
   I know the next news that they bring
Will be my death; and welcome shall it be;
To wretched men, death is felicity.

[1] I.e., be Lord Protector to my son during his minority.

Enter BERKELEY, *who gives a paper to*
              LEICESTER

Leices. Another post! what news brings
    he?

K. Edw. Such news as I expect — come,
    Berkeley, come,
And tell thy message to my naked breast.   130

Berk. My lord, think not a thought so vil-
    lainous
Can harbor in a man of noble birth.
To do your highness service and devoir,[1]
And save you from your foes, Berkeley would
    die.

Leices. My lord, the council of the queen
    commands   135
That I resign my charge.

K. Edw. And who must keep me now?
    Must you, my lord?

Berk. Ay, my most gracious lord; so 'tis
    decreed.

K. Edw. (*taking the paper*). By Mortimer,
    whose name is written here!   139
Well may I rend his name that rends my heart!
                  (*Tears it.*
This poor revenge has something eas'd my
    mind.
So may his limbs be torn, as is this paper!
Hear me, immortal Jove, and grant it too!

Berk. Your grace must hence with me to
    Berkeley[2] straight.

K. Edw. Whither you will; all places are
    alike,   145
And every earth is fit for burial.

Leices. Favor him, my lord, as much as lieth
    in you.

Berk. Even so betide my soul as I use him.

K. Edw. Mine enemy hath pitied my estate,
And that's the cause that I am now remov'd.

Berk. And thinks your grace that Berkeley
    will be cruel?   151

K. Edw. I know not; but of this am I as-
    sured,

[1] Duty.
[2] Berkeley Castle, Gloucestershire, near the Severn
River, almost halfway between Gloucester and Bristol.
— The abdication of Edward II took place in January,
1327, while his transfer to Berkeley was not carried out
until April.

That death ends all, and I can die but once.
Leicester, farewell!

Leices. Not yet, my lord; I'll bear you on
    your way.   155
                  (*Exeunt.*

SCENE 2.   *A room in the royal palace at
Westminster, London*

Enter QUEEN ISABELLA *and* YOUNG
           MORTIMER

Y. Mor. Fair Isabel, now have we our de-
    sire;
The proud corrupters of the light-brain'd
    king
Have done their homage to the lofty gallows,
And he himself lies in captivity.
Be rul'd by me, and we will rule the realm.   5
In any case take heed of childish fear,
For now we hold an old wolf[1] by the ears,
That, if he slip, will seize upon us both,
And grip the sorer,[2] being gript himself.
Think therefore, madam, that imports us
    much   10
To erect your son with all the speed we may,
And that I be protector over him;
For our behoof will bear the greater sway
Whenas a king's name shall be under writ.

Q. Isab. Sweet Mortimer, the life of Isabel,
Be thou persuaded that I love thee well,   16
And therefore, so the prince my son be safe,
Whom I esteem as dear as these mine eyes,
Conclude against his father what thou wilt,
And I myself will willingly subscribe.   20

Y. Mor. First would I hear news that he
    were depos'd,
And then let me alone to handle him.

Enter Messenger

Letters! from whence?

Mess.   From Killingworth, my lord.

Q. Isab. How fares my lord the king?

Mess. In health, madam, but full of pensive-
    ness.   25

Q. Isab. Alas, poor soul, would I could ease
    his grief!

[1] I.e., England.
[2] The more fiercely.

Enter the BISHOP OF WINCHESTER *with the crown*

Thanks, gentle Winchester.   (*To the* Messenger.)   Sirrah, be gone.
               (*Exit* Messenger.

B. of Win. The king hath willingly resign'd his crown.

Q. Isab. O happy news! send for the prince, my son.

B. of Win. Further, or [1] this letter was seal'd, Lord Berkeley came,   30
So that he now is gone from Killingworth;
And we have heard that Edmund laid a plot
To set his brother free, no more but so.
The lord of Berkeley is so pitiful [2]   34
As Leicester that had charge of him before.

Q. Isab. Then let some other be his guardian.

Y. Mor. Let me alone, here is the privy seal.
       (*Exit the* BISHOP OF WINCHESTER.
(*To Attendants within*) Who's there? — Call hither Gurney and Matrevis. —
To dash the heavy-headed Edmund's drift,[3]
Berkeley shall be discharg'd, the king remov'd,
And none but we shall know where he lieth.   41

Q. Isab. But, Mortimer, as long as he survives,
What safety rests for us, or for my son?

Y. Mor. Speak, shall he presently be dispatch'd and die?

Q. Isab. I would he were, so 'twere not by my means.   45

Enter MATREVIS *and* GURNEY

Y. Mor. Enough. —
Matrevis, write a letter presently
Unto the lord of Berkeley from ourself
That he resign the king to thee and Gurney;
And when 'tis done, we will subscribe our name.   50

Mat. It shall be done, my lord.

Y. Mor.   Gurney.

Gur.   My lord.

Y. Mor. As thou intend'st to rise by Mortimer,
Who now makes Fortune's wheel turn as he please,

Seek all the means thou canst to make him droop,
And neither give him kind word nor good look.

Gur. I warrant you, my lord.   56

Y. Mor. And this above the rest: because we hear
That Edmund casts [1] to work his liberty,
Remove him still [2] from place to place by night,
Till at the last he come to Killingworth,   60
And then from thence to Berkeley back again;
And by the way, to make him fret the more,
Speak curstly [3] to him, and in any case
Let no man comfort him; if he chance to weep,
But amplify his grief with bitter words.   65

Mat. Fear not, my lord, we'll do as you command.

Y. Mor. So now away; post thitherwards amain.[4]

Q. Isab. Whither goes this letter? To my lord the king?
Commend me humbly to his majesty,
And tell him that I labor all in vain   70
To ease his grief, and work his liberty;
And bear him this as witness of my love.
              (*Gives a ring.*

Mat. I will, madam.   (*Exit with* GURNEY.

Enter PRINCE EDWARD *and* KENT *talking with him*

Y. Mor. Finely dissembled.   Do so still, sweet queen.
Here comes the young prince with the Earl of Kent.   75

Q. Isab. Something he whispers in his childish ears.

Y. Mor. If he have such access unto the prince,
Our plots and stratagems will soon be dash'd.

Q. Isab. Use Edmund friendly, as if all were well.

Y. Mor. How fares my honorable lord of Kent?   80

Kent. In health, sweet Mortimer. How fares your grace?

Q. Isab. Well, if my lord your brother were enlarg'd.[5]

[1] Plans.   [2] Constantly.   [3] Harshly.
[4] At full speed.   [5] Set free.

[1] Before.   [2] As full of pity.   [3] Plot.

Kent. I hear of late he hath depos'd himself.

Q. Isab. The more my grief.

Y. Mor.   And mine.

Kent. (*aside*).   Ah, they do dissemble!

Q. Isab. Sweet son, come hither, I must talk
    with thee.   85

Y. Mor. You being his uncle, and the next of
blood,

Do look to be protector o'er the prince.

Kent. Not I, my lord; who should protect
   the son,

But she that gave him life? I mean the queen.

P. Edw. Mother, persuade me not to wear
   the crown: 90

Let him be king — I am too young to reign.

Q. Isab. But be content, seeing 'tis his highness' pleasure.

P. Edw. Let me but see him first, and then
   I will.

Kent. Ay, do, sweet nephew.

Q. Isab. Brother, you know it is impossible.

P. Edw. Why, is he dead?   96

Q. Isab. No, God forbid!

Kent. I would those words proceeded from
   your heart.

Y. Mor. Inconstant Edmund, dost thou
   favor him,

That wast the cause of his imprisonment? 100

Kent. The more cause have I now to make
   amends.

Y. Mor. (*aside to* Q. Isab.). I tell thee, 'tis
   not meet that one so false

Should come about the person of a prince. —

My lord, he hath betray'd the king his brother,

And therefore trust him not.   105

P. Edw. But he repents, and sorrows for it
   now.

Q. Isab. Come, son, and go with this gentle
   lord and me.

P. Edw. With you I will, but not with
   Mortimer.

Y. Mor. Why, youngling, 'sdain'st thou so
   of Mortimer?

Then I will carry thee by force away.   110

P. Edw. Help, uncle Kent! Mortimer will
   wrong me.

Q. Isab. Brother Edmund, strive not; we
   are his friends;

Isabel is nearer than the Earl of Kent.

Kent. Sister, Edward is my charge, redeem
   him.

Q. Isab. Edward is my son, and I will keep
   him.   115

Kent. Mortimer shall know that he hath
   wrong'd me! —

(*Aside*) Hence will I haste to Killingworth
   Castle,

And rescue aged [1] Edward from his foes.

To be reveng'd on Mortimer and thee.

   (*Exeunt on one side* QUEEN ISABELLA,
   PRINCE EDWARD, *and* YOUNG MOR-
   TIMER; *on the other,* KENT.

SCENE 3. *Near Kenilworth Castle*

Enter MATREVIS *and* GURNEY *and Soldiers,*
with KING EDWARD

Mat. My lord, be not pensive, we are your
   friends;

Men are ordain'd to live in misery,

Therefore come, — dalliance dangereth [2] our
   lives.

K. Edw. Friends, whither must unhappy
   Edward go?

Will hateful Mortimer appoint no rest?   5

Must I be vexed like the nightly bird,

Whose sight is loathsome to all winged fowls?

When will the fury of his mind assuage?

When will his heart be satisfied with blood?

If mine will serve, unbowel straight this breast,

And give my heart to Isabel and him;   11

It is the chiefest mark they level at.[3]

Gur. Not so, my liege, the queen hath given
   this charge

To keep your grace in safety;

Your passions make your dolors[4] to increase.

K. Edw. This usage makes my misery to increase.   16

But can my air [5] of life continue long

When all my senses are annoy'd with stench?

Within a dungeon England's king is kept,

Where I am starv'd for want of sustenance. 20

My daily diet is heart-breaking sobs,

That almost rents [6] the closet of my heart.

---

[1] The deposed king was forty-three years old.
[2] Delay endangers.   [3] Aim at.
[4] Your intense feelings make your woes.
[5] Breath.   [6] See note to Act IV, Sc. 6, l. 101.

Thus lives old Edward not reliev'd by any,
And so must die, though pitied by many.
O, water, gentle friends, to cool my thirst,   25
And clear my body from foul excrements!

  Mat. Here's channel water,[1] as our charge
     is given.
Sit down, for we'll be barbers to your grace.

  K. Edw. Traitors, away! What, will you
     murder me,
Or choke your sovereign with puddle water?

  Gur. No; but wash your face, and shave
     away your beard,   31
Lest you be known and so be rescued.

  Mat. Why strive you thus? Your labor is
     in vain!

  K. Edw. The wren may strive against the
     lion's strength,
But all in vain: so vainly do I strive   35
To seek for mercy at a tyrant's hand.

     (*They wash him with puddle water,
      and shave his beard away.*

Immortal powers! that knows the painful cares
That wait upon my poor distressed soul,
O level [2] all your looks upon these daring men,
That wrongs their liege and sovereign, Eng-
     land's king!   40
O Gaveston, 'tis for thee I am wrong'd;
For me, both thou and both the Spencers died!
And for your sakes a thousand wrongs I'll take.
The Spencers' ghosts, wherever they remain,
Wish well to mine; then tush, for them I'll die.

  Mat. 'Twixt theirs and yours shall be no
     enmity.   46
Come, come away; now put the torches out,
We'll enter in by darkness to Killingworth.

Enter KENT

  Gur. How now, who comes there?

  Mat. Guard the king sure: it is the Earl of
     Kent.   50

  K. Edw. O gentle brother, help to rescue me!

  Mat. Keep them asunder; thrust in the king.

  Kent. Soldiers, let me but talk to him one
     word.

  Gur. Lay hands upon the earl for this as-
     sault.

[1] Gutter water.
[2] See note to l. 12.

  Kent. Lay down your weapons, traitors!
     Yield the king!   55

  Mat. Edmund, yield thou thyself, or thou
     shalt die.

  Kent. Base villains, wherefore do you gripe [1]
     me thus?

  Gur. Bind him and so convey him to the
     court.

  Kent. Where is the court but here? Here is
     the king;
And I will visit him; why stay you me?   60

  Mat. The court is where Lord Mortimer
     remains;
Thither shall your honor go; and so farewell.

     (*Exeunt* MATREVIS *and* GURNEY,
      with KING EDWARD.

  Kent. O miserable is that commonweal,
Where lords keep courts, and kings are lockt
     in prison!

  Sol. Wherefore stay we? On, sirs, to the
     court!   65

  Kent. Ay, lead me whither you will, even to
     my death,
Seeing that my brother cannot be releas'd.[2]

                       (*Exeunt.*

SCENE 4. *A hall in the royal palace at Westminster, London*

Enter YOUNG MORTIMER, *alone*

  Y. Mor. The king must die, or Mortimer
     goes down;
The commons now begin to pity him.
Yet he that is the cause of Edward's death,
Is sure to pay for it when his son's of age;
And therefore will I do it cunningly.   5
This letter, written by a friend of ours,[3]
Contains his death, yet bids them save his life.

                       (*Reads.*

"*Edwardum occidere nolite timere, bonum est:*
Fear not to kill the king, 'tis good he die."
But read it thus, and that's another sense: 10
"*Edwardum occidere nolite, timere bonum est:*

[1] Seize.
[2] It was really in 1330 that the Earl of Kent, thinking
Edward II still secretly alive, plotted to restore him to
the throne. Mortimer had Kent beheaded for this
treason on March 19. Marlowe has brought forward
the whole affair three years.
[3] The Bishop of Hereford.

Kill not the king, 'tis good to fear the worst."
Unpointed [1] as it is, thus shall it go,
That, being dead, if it chance to be found,
Matrevis and the rest may bear the blame,
And we be quit that caus'd it to be done. 16
Within this room is lock'd the messenger
That shall convey it, and perform the rest;
And by a secret token that he bears,
Shall he be murdered when the deed is done. —
Lightborn, come forth!   21

Enter LIGHTBORN

Art thou as resolute as thou wast?
   Light. What else,[2] my lord? And far more
     resolute.
   Y. Mor. And hast thou cast [3] how to ac-
     complish it?
   Light. Ay, ay, and none shall know which
     way he died.   25
   Y. Mor. But at his looks, Lightborn, thou
     wilt relent.
   Light. Relent! ha, ha! I use much to relent.
   Y. Mor. Well, do it bravely, and be secret.
   Light. You shall not need to give instruc-
     tions;
'Tis not the first time I have kill'd a man. 30
I learn'd in Naples how to poison flowers;
To strangle with a lawn [4] thrust through the
     throat;
To pierce the windpipe with a needle's point;
Or whilst one is asleep, to take a quill
And blow a little powder in his ears;   35
Or open his mouth and pour quicksilver down.
And yet I have a braver [5] way than these.
   Y. Mor. What's that?
   Light. Nay, you shall pardon me; none shall
     know my tricks.
   Y. Mor. I care not how it is, so it be not
     spied.   40
Deliver this to Gurney and Matrevis.
                      (Gives letter.
At every ten mile end thou hast a horse.
Take this. *(Gives money.)* Away! and never
     see me more.
   Light. No?

---

[1] Unpunctuated.   [2] Why otherwise.
[3] Planned.   [4] A strip of fine linen.
[5] Finer.

   Y. Mor. No;   45
Unless thou bring me news of Edward's death.
   Light. That will I quickly do. Farewell,
     my lord.   *(Exit.*
   Y. Mor. The prince I rule, the queen do I
     command,
And with a lowly congé [1] to the ground,
The proudest lords salute me as I pass;   50
I seal, I cancel, I do what I will.
Fear'd am I more than lov'd; — let me be
     fear'd,
And when I frown, make all the court look pale.
I view the prince with Aristarchus' [2] eyes,
Whose looks were as a breeching [3] to a boy. 55
They thrust upon me the protectorship,
And sue to me for that that I desire.
While at the council-table, grave enough,
And not unlike a bashful puritan,
First I complain of imbecility,[4]   60
Saying it is *onus quam gravissimum*,[5]
Till being interrupted by my friends,
Suscepi that *provinciam* [6] as they term it;
And to conclude, I am Protector now.
Now is all sure: the queen and Mortimer 65
Shall rule the realm, the king; and none rule us.
Mine enemies will I plague, my friends ad-
     vance;
And what I list command who dare control?
Major sum quam cui possit fortuna nocere.[7]
And that this be the coronation-day,   70
It pleaseth me, and Isabel the queen.
                   (Trumpets within.
The trumpets sound, I must go take my place.

Enter the young KING, QUEEN ISABELLA, *the*
   ARCHBISHOP OF CANTERBURY, *Champion,*
   and Nobles

   A. of Cant. Long live King Edward, by the
     grace of God
King of England and Lord of Ireland!
   Cham. If any Christian, Heathen, Turk, or
     Jew,   75

---

[1] Bow.
[2] A famous Greek grammarian and schoolmaster of
the second century B.C.
[3] Whipping.   [4] Incapacity.
[5] An extremely heavy burden.
[6] I have undertaken that office.
[7] I am greater than fortune can injure.

Dares but affirm that Edward's not true king,
And will avouch his saying with the sword,
I am the champion that will combat him.

Y. Mor. None comes, sound trumpets.
               (*Trumpets sound.*

K. Edw. Third.   Champion, here's to
thee.[1]

Q. Isab. Lord Mortimer, now take him to
your charge.   80

Enter Soldiers, with KENT *prisoner*

Y. Mor. What traitor have we there with
blades and bills?[2]

Sol. Edmund, the Earl of Kent.

K. Edw. Third.   What hath he done?

Sol. 'A would have taken the king away
perforce,
As we were bringing him to Killingworth.

Y. Mor. Did you attempt this rescue, Edmund? Speak.   85

Kent. Mortimer, I did; he is our king,
And thou compell'st this prince to wear the
crown.

Y. Mor. Strike off his head! he shall have
martial law.[3]

Kent. Strike off my head! Base traitor, I
defy thee!

K. Edw. Third. My lord, he is my uncle, and
shall live.   90

Y. Mor. My lord, he is your enemy, and
shall die.

Kent. Stay, villains!

K. Edw. Third. Sweet mother, if I cannot
pardon him,
Entreat my Lord Protector for his life.

Q. Isab. Son, be content; I dare not speak a
word.   95

K. Edw. Third. Nor I, and yet methinks I
should command;
But, seeing I cannot, I'll entreat for him —
My lord, if you will let my uncle live,
I will requite it when I come to age.

[1] The king's champion regularly appeared at English coronation banquets until 1821. The new sovereign always drank a toast to the champion out of a silver-gilt cup, and then gave the cup to him as a fee.

[2] With swords and bill-hooks (a cutting weapon with a hooked-end to the blade).

[3] I.e., be treated according to the laws of war.

Y. Mor. 'Tis for your highness' good, and
for the realm's. —   100
How often shall I bid you bear him hence?

Kent. Art thou king? Must I die at thy
command?

Y. Mor. At our command. — Once more
away with him.

Kent. Let me but stay and speak; I will not
go.
Either my brother or his son is king,   105
And none of both them thirst for Edmund's
blood:
And therefore, soldiers, whither will you hale
me?
       (*They hale* KENT *away, and carry him
to be beheaded.*

K. Edw. Third. What safety may I look for
at his hands,
If that my uncle shall be murdered thus?

Q. Isab. Fear not, sweet boy, I'll guard thee
from thy foes;   110
Had Edmund liv'd, he would have sought thy
death.
Come, son, we'll ride a-hunting in the park.

K. Edw. Third. And shall my uncle Edmund ride with us?

Q. Isab. He is a traitor; think not on him;
come.   (*Exeunt.*

SCENE 5.   *A room in Berkeley Castle.*

Enter MATREVIS *and* GURNEY

Mat. Gurney, I wonder the king dies not,
Being in a vault up to the knees in water,
To which the channels[1] of the castle run,
From whence a damp continually ariseth.
That were enough to poison any man,   5
Much more a king brought up so tenderly.

Gur. And so do I, Matrevis: yesternight
I opened but the door to throw him meat,
And I was almost stifled with the savor.[2]

Mat. He hath a body able to endure   10
More than we can inflict: and therefore now
Let us assail his mind another while.

Gur. Send for him out thence, and I will
anger him.

Mat. But stay, who's this?

[1] Drains.

[2] Smell.

Enter LIGHTBORN

Light.   My Lord Protector greets you.
                                         (*Gives letter.*)
Gur. What's here? I know not how to con-
    strue it.   15
Mat. Gurney, it was left unpointed for the
    nonce; [1]
"*Edwardum occidere nolite timere,*" [2]
That's his meaning.
Light. Know ye this token? I must have
    the king.   (*Gives token.*)
Mat. Ay, stay awhile, thou shalt have an-
    swer straight. —   20
(*Aside*) This villain's sent to make away
    the king.
Gur. (*aside*). I thought as much.
Mat. (*aside*).   And when the murder's
    done,
See how he must be handled for his labor.
"*Pereat iste!*" [3] Let him have the king. —
What else? Here is the keys, this is the lake, [4]
Do as you are commanded by my lord.   26
Light. I know what I must do. Get you
    away.
Yet be not far off, I shall need your help;
See that in the next room I have a fire,
And get me a spit, and let it be red-hot.   30
Mat. Very well.
Gur.   Need you anything besides?
Light. What else? A table and a feather-
    bed.
Gur. That's all?
Light. Ay, ay; so, when I call you, bring it in.
Mat. Fear not thou that.   35
Gur. Here's a light, to go into the dungeon.
            (*Gives a light, and then exit with*
                  MATREVIS.
Light. So now
Must I about this gear; [5] ne'er was there any
So finely handled as this king shall be.   39
Foh! here's a place indeed, with all my heart!
            (*Opens a door and discovers* KING
                  EDWARD.
K. Edw. Who's there? What light is that?
    Wherefore com'st thou?

[1] Purposely.   [2] See Act V, Sc. 4, ll. 8–12.
[3] Let this man perish.   [4] Underground dungeon.
[5] Affair.

Light. To comfort you, and bring you joyful
    news.
K. Edw. Small comfort finds poor Edward in
    thy looks.
Villain, I know thou com'st to murder me.
Light. To murder you, my most gracious
    lord!   45
Far is it from my heart to do you harm.
The queen sent me to see how you were used,
For she relents at this your misery:
And what eyes can refrain from shedding tears,
To see a king in this most piteous state?   50
K. Edw. Weep'st thou already? List awhile
    to me
And then thy heart, were it as Gurney's is,
Or as Matrevis', hewn from the Caucasus,
Yet will it melt, ere I have done my tale.
This dungeon where they keep me is the sink
Wherein the filth of all the castle falls.   56
Light. O villains!
K. Edw. And there in mire and puddle have
    I stood
This ten days' space; and, lest that I should
    sleep,
One plays continually upon a drum.   60
They give me bread and water, being a king;
So that, for want of sleep and sustenance,
My mind's distempered, and my body's
    numb'd,
And whether I have limbs or no I know not.
O, would my blood dropp'd out from every
    vein,   65
As doth this water from my tattered robes.
Tell Isabel, the queen, I look'd not thus,
When for her sake I ran at tilt in France,
And there unhors'd the Duke of Cleremont.
Light. O speak no more, my lord! this breaks
    my heart.   70
Lie on this bed, and rest yourself awhile.
                              (*Bed discovered.* [1])

K. Edw. These looks of thine can harbor
    nought but death:
I see my tragedy written in thy brows.

[1] I.e., curtains to the inner stage are drawn to reveal
the bed. — The stage direction is supplied by the present editor. The only alternative to this "business"
would be the conveyance of a bed upon the stage by attendants during the previous conversation between
Lightborn and the King. Such an arrangement, however, is a less likely Elizabethan practice.

Yet stay awhile; forbear thy bloody hand,
And let me see the stroke before it comes,   75
That even then when I shall lose my life,
My mind may be more steadfast on my God.
    Light. What means your highness to mistrust me thus?
    K. Edw. What mean'st thou to dissemble with me thus?
    Light. These hands were never stain'd with innocent blood,   80
Nor shall they now be tainted with a king's.
    K. Edw. Forgive my thought for having such a thought.
One jewel have I left; receive thou this.
                  (Gives jewel.
Still fear I, and I know not what's the cause,
But every joint shakes as I give it thee.   85
O, if thou harbor'st murder in thy heart,
Let this gift change thy mind, and save thy soul!
Know that I am a king: O, at that name
I feel a hell of grief!   Where is my crown?
Gone, gone! and do I remain alive?   90
    Light. You're overwatch'd,[1] my lord; lie down and rest.
    K. Edw. But that grief keeps me waking, I should sleep;
For not these ten days have these eye-lids clos'd.
Now as I speak they fall, and yet with fear.
Open again.   O wherefore sitt'st thou here?   95
    Light. If you mistrust me, I'll begone, my lord.
    K. Edw. No, no, for if thou mean'st to murder me,
Thou wilt return again, and therefore stay.
    Light. He sleeps.
    K. Edw. *(waking).* O let me not die yet!
Stay, O stay a while!   100
    Light. How now, my lord?
    K. Edw. Something still buzzeth in mine ears,
And tells me if I sleep I never wake;
This fear is that which makes me tremble thus.
And therefore tell me, wherefore art thou come?   105
    Light. To rid thee of thy life. — Matrevis, come!

[1] Exhausted by staying awake.

    K. Edw. I am too weak and feeble to resist: —
Assist me, sweet God, and receive my soul!

        Enter MATREVIS

    Light. Run for the table.   *(Exit* MATREVIS.
    K. Edw. O spare me, or despatch me in a trice.   110
        *(*MATREVIS *and* GURNEY *bring in a table.*
    Light. So, lay the table down, and stamp on it,
But not too hard, lest that you bruise his body.
        *(*KING EDWARD *is murdered, crying out.*
    Mat. I fear me that this cry will raise the town,
And therefore, let us take horse and away.   114
    Light. Tell me, sirs, was it not bravely [1] done?
    Gur. Excellent well: take this for thy reward.
        (Then GURNEY *stabs* LIGHTBORN *dead.*
Come, let us cast the body in the moat,
And bear the king's to Mortimer our lord:
Away!   *(Exeunt with the bodies.*

    SCENE 6. *A hall in the royal palace at Westminster, London*

    Enter YOUNG MORTIMER *and* MATREVIS

    Y. Mor. Is't done, Matrevis, and the murderer dead?
    Mat. Ay, my good lord; I would it were undone!
    Y. Mor. Matrevis, if thou now growest penitent
I'll be thy ghostly father; [2] therefore choose,
Whether thou wilt be secret in this,   5
Or else die by the hand of Mortimer.
    Mat. Gurney, my lord, is fled, and will, I fear,
Betray us both, therefore let me fly.
    Y. Mor. Fly to the savages!   9
    Mat. I humbly thank your honor.   *(Exit.*
    Y. Mor. As for myself, I stand as Jove's huge tree,[3]
And others are but shrubs compar'd to me.
All tremble at my name, and I fear none;
Let's see who dare impeach me for his death?

[1] Finely.   [2] Thy priest.   [3] I.e., the oak.

Enter QUEEN ISABELLA

Q. Isab. Ah, Mortimer, the king my son
     hath news   15
His father's dead, and we have murdered him!
    Y. Mor. What if he have? The king is yet
     a child.
    Q. Isab. Ay, but he tears his hair, and wrings
     his hands,
And vows to be reveng'd upon us both.
Into the council-chamber he is gone,   20
To crave the aid and succor of his peers.
Ay me! see here he comes, and they with him.
Now, Mortimer, begins our tragedy.

Enter KING EDWARD THE THIRD, *Lords
and Attendants*

    1 Lord. Fear not, my lord, know that you
     are a king.
    K. Edw. Third. Villain! —   25
    Y. Mor. How now, my lord!
    K. Edw. Third. Think not that I am frighted
     with thy words!
My father's murdered through thy treachery;
And thou shalt die, and on his mournful hearse [1]
Thy hateful and accursed head shall lie,[2]   30
To witness to the world, that by thy means
His kingly body was too soon interr'd.
    Q. Isab. Weep not, sweet son!
    K. Edw. Third. Forbid me not to weep, he
     was my father;
And, had you lov'd him half so well as I,   35
You could not bear his death thus patiently.
But you, I fear, conspir'd with Mortimer.
    1 Lord. Why speak you not unto my lord
     the king?
    Y. Mor. Because I think scorn to be accus'd.
Who is the man dare say I murdered him?   40
    K. Edw. Third. Traitor! in me my loving
     father speaks,
And plainly saith, 'twas thou that murd'redst
     him.
    Y. Mor. But has your grace no other proof
     than this?

    [1] Coffin.
    [2] The murder of Edward II occurred in September,
1327, but Mortimer was not executed for treason until
three years later on November 30, 1330.

    K. Edw. Third. Yes, if this be the hand of
     Mortimer.   (*Shows letter.*
    Y. Mor. (*aside*). False Gurney hath betray'd
     me and himself.   45
    Q. Isab. (*aside*). I fear'd as much; murder
     cannot be hid.
    Y. Mor. It is my hand; what gather you by
     this?
    K. Edw. Third. That thither thou didst send
     a murderer.
    Y. Mor. What murderer? Bring forth the
     man I sent.
    K. Edw. Third. Ah, Mortimer, thou knowest
     that he is slain;   50
And so shalt thou be too. — Why stays he here?
Bring him unto a hurdle,[1] drag him forth;
Hang him, I say, and set his quarters up;
But bring his head back presently to me.
    Q. Isab. For my sake, sweet son, pity Mor-
     timer!   55
    Y. Mor. Madam, entreat not, I will rather die,
Than sue for life unto a paltry boy.
    K. Edw. Third. Hence with the traitor! with
     the murderer!
    Y. Mor. Base Fortune, now I see, that in
     thy wheel
There is a point, to which when men aspire,   60
They tumble headlong down: that point I
     touch'd,
And, seeing there was no place to mount up
     higher,
Why should I grieve at my declining fall? —
Farewell, fair queen; weep not for Mortimer,
That scorns the world, and, as a traveler,   65
Goes to discover countries yet unknown.
    K. Edw. Third. What! suffer you the traitor
     to delay?
       (YOUNG MORTIMER *is taken away by
         1 Lord and Attendants.*
    Q. Isab. As thou receivedst thy life from me,
Spill not the blood of gentle Mortimer!
    K. Edw. Third. This argues that you spilt
     my father's blood,   70
Else would you not entreat for Mortimer.
    Q. Isab. I spill his blood? No!
    K. Edw. Third. Ay, madam, you; for so the
     rumor runs.

    [1] A sled used to draw criminals to the place of execu-
tion.

Q. Isab. That rumor is untrue; for loving
    thee,
Is this report rais'd on poor Isabel.   75
    K. Edw. Third. I do not think her so un-
    natural.
    2 Lord. My lord, I fear me it will prove
    too true.
    K. Edw. Third. Mother, you are suspected
    for his death,
And therefore we commit you to the Tower [1]
Till farther trial may be made thereof;   80
If you be guilty, though I be your son,
Think not to find me slack [2] or pitiful.
    Q. Isab. Nay, to my death, for too long have
    I liv'd
Whenas my son thinks to abridge [3] my days.
    K. Edw. Third. Away with her, her words
    enforce these tears,   85
And I shall pity her if she speak again.
    Q. Isab. Shall I not mourn for my beloved
    lord,
And with the rest accompany him to his grave?
    2 Lord. Thus, madam, 'tis the king's will
    you shall hence.
    Q. Isab. He hath forgotten me; stay, I am
    his mother.   90

[1] Historically Queen Isabella suffered no confinement
nor any other punishment.
[2] Lax.   [3] Shorten.

    2 Lord. That boots [1] not; therefore, gentle
    madam, go.
    Q. Isab. Then come, sweet death, and rid
    me of this grief. (*Exit with Attendants.*

Re-enter 1 Lord, with the head of YOUNG
    MORTIMER

    1 Lord. My lord, here is the head of Mortimer.
    K. Edw. Third. Go fetch my father's hearse,[2]
    where it shall lie;
And bring my funeral robes.
            (*Exeunt Attendants.*
            Accursed head,   95
Could I have rul'd thee then, as I do now,
Thou had'st not hatch'd this monstrous
    treachery! —
Here comes the hearse; help me to mourn, my
    lords.

*Re-enter Attendants with the hearse and
    funeral robes*

Sweet father, here unto thy murdered ghost
I offer up this wicked traitor's head;   100
And let these tears, distilling from mine eyes,
Be witness of my grief and innocency.
                  (*Exeunt.*

[1] Avails.   [2] See note to l. 29.

INTRODUCTION TO

The Shoemakers' Holiday

Shakespeare and Elizabethan Drama in 1600: Thomas Dekker and the
Romantic Comedy of Local Color

SHAKESPEARE AND ELIZABETHAN DRAMA IN 1600

BETWEEN the death of Marlowe in 1593 and the end of the century, an amazing productivity characterized Elizabethan drama. The two leading theatrical companies, the Lord Chamberlain's under Richard Burbage and the Lord Admiral's under Philip Henslowe, were performing new plays in extraordinary numbers. The London producers had to meet a constant demand for fresh programs, because the limited size of the theatergoing public did not render the system of the "run" profitable. According to Henslowe's *Diary* he alone produced in the six years before 1600 some one hundred and twenty new pieces of drama, a majority of which were never printed and therefore soon lost. The huge turnover in plays during this period attracted a multitude of new writers to supply the market. Among these William Shakespeare (1564–1616), who had become attached to Burbage's troupe in 1594, rose to be the outstanding figure. By 1600 he had to his credit about twenty compositions in the multifarious fields of tragedy, comedy, chronicle history, and romantic drama. No contemporary playwright could even approach him in versatility or depth.

The secret of Shakespeare's greatness lay in the art with which he put new wine into old bottles. Shakespeare was at bottom a time-server, and yet one of such quality that his achievement will live for all time. He thoroughly absorbed the instruction of his important predecessors, Lyly, Peele, Greene, Kyd, and Marlowe. Then his comprehensive genius developed their contributions in accordance with stage fashion and personal whim. Felicitous language, deft contrivance, and psychological insight soon made him the acknowledged master of his profession, but these gifts did not set in motion new dramatic currents. Neither his play patterns, nor his technique, nor his ideology departed from existing traditions. His talent simply did not run toward innovation. For that reason he influenced only a little the drama of his immediate age.

THOMAS DEKKER AND THE ROMANTIC COMEDY OF LOCAL COLOR

As the seventeenth century dawned the brilliance of Shakespeare did not entirely overshadow the work of several promising novices in the theater. One of the newcomers was Thomas Dekker (c. 1570–c. 1632), a London youth of humble background and little formal schooling. By 1598 he had become one of Henslowe's hack playwrights, adept at tinkering with the scripts which the Lord Admiral's company were to act. During the next five years Henslowe's *Diary* evidences that Dekker put his hand to at least forty-one plays, of which less than a handful were solely his own. Throughout his career he worked to a very large extent at collaboration or revision.

In 1601 John Marston, another rising dramatist, persuaded Dekker to join his "war" against Ben Jonson, a controversy of literary personalities which had amused London theatergoers since 1598. Elizabethan audiences and actors rather abetted the "poets" in quarrels which to the modern taste appear childish. Marston and Dekker proceeded to compose for performance at The Globe a play with the title of *Satiromastix*, in which Jonson is lampooned as an ignorant poetaster. So effective did their ridicule prove that the crusty Jonson withdrew from further attack and the notorious "War of the Poets" ceased.

Two years later Dekker attained some prominence for his part in the lavish entertainments which London offered to welcome the new sovereign, James I. From that time on the events of Dekker's life still on record are few and relatively unimportant. He began to experience great difficulty in making both ends meet. After all, he obtained from Henslowe only a pound or two (about $50 to $100 today) for each job of revision or collaboration, and not often more than three or four pounds for a play of his own making. The Elizabethans loved the stage, but they felt no concern for the meager rewards of those who furnished their stage fare. Dekker kept falling into debtors' prison, from which Henslowe bailed him out again and again in order that the useful fellow might be able to continue finishing off scripts for the Henslowe troupe to perform.

In 1609 Dekker published *The Gull's Hornbook*, a delightful volume of satire on the habits of the London "gull" or foolish gallant. This little primer abounds in intimate, colorful touches on life in Elizabethan London. The chapter entitled "How a Gallant should behave himself in a Playhouse" contains entertaining and invaluable comment about playhouse manners in Shakespeare's heyday.

Only a very few of the numerous plays with which Dekker's name is associated still deserve attention. His two earliest surviving pieces, both acted at "The Rose" in 1599, are *The Pleasant Comedy of Old Fortunatus*, an agreeable fantasy on the legend of the wishing hat, and *The Shoemakers' Holiday*. In 1604–05 Dekker's only noteworthy serious composition, *The Honest Whore*, came out in two parts, in the first of which Thomas Middleton had a share. This remains one of the more provocative and moving tragedies of the early seventeenth century, though its main theme of marital infidelity takes on rather stark aspects in certain scenes. At about the same period Dekker, with the aid of John Webster, brought forth *Westward Ho* and *Northward Ho*, two comedies of the London lower world, which are interesting chiefly for their local color. Five years later Dekker collaborated again with Middleton in *The Roaring Girl*, or *Moll Cutpurse*, an unusual and sentimental portrait of a female thief who plays patron saint to the distressed. The remainder of his career produced no efforts of particular merit.

This cursory survey of Dekker's playwriting shows him a competent and versatile dramatist but one lacking the genius of his greatest contemporaries. *The Shoemakers' Holiday* stands out as the happiest expression of Dekker's art. According to Henslowe's *Diary* it seems to have taken only six weeks to write, from about May 30, 1599, to July 15. On the latter date Henslowe paid Dekker the munificent sum of three pounds for the completion of his script. A current and popular work of fiction, *The Gentle Craft* (1598) by Thomas Deloney, inspired Dekker to rework some of its contents into a play. This volume of three stories concerning shoemakers furnished the groundwork of Dekker's plot. He took over without change the story of Simon Eyre the master shoemaker who, advised to a lucky speculation by one of his foreign journeymen, Dutch

Hans, gained wealth and became Sheriff and then Lord Mayor of London. From Deloney's story of the royal shoemakers, Crispine and Crispianus, Dekker, substituting other character names, borrowed the romance of the Earl of Lincoln's son and the Lord Mayor's daughter. The suggestion for the affair involving Ralph, his wife Jane, and Master Hammon, came from that portion of Deloney's tale about Eyre and his journeymen shoemakers, in which one of the latter, French John, courts Mrs. Eyre's maid Florence, only to have his suit stopped by the return from France of his supposedly dead wife. Though Dekker drew heavily on Deloney for plot material, he displayed much originality in his adroit linking of young Lacy's doings with the Eyre establishment.

After the manner of Robert Greene, Dekker patterned the love idyl of Lacy and "the fair-cheeked Rose" with its glimpses of the countryside at Old Ford. The triumph of their pure devotion over all obstacles harks back to the affair between another Lacy and his Margaret in Greene's *Friar Bacon and Friar Bungay*.

The fine humanitarianism which *The Shoemakers' Holiday* pictures alike in the London aristocrats, the solid citizens, and the tradespeople was calculated to please all sections of the audience at The Rose. Dekker's whole drama occurs in a world going on exactly as human sentiment would like. The business man wins the highest political office in his community as the result of his honesty and philanthropy; the upstanding young man gets the lovely girl of his choice in spite of parents and rivals; and the brave war veteran comes in safety home to a wife sorely tried but ever true. Such sunny romancing has a timeless appeal.

To conventional romantic comedy Dekker introduced, however, a new comic element of local color. The hearty communal spirit of "the City," the mercantile center of London, had never been presented before in Elizabethan drama. Dekker's sympathetic intimacy with the life of London's lower classes well qualified him to express the robust humor of its tradefolk. He created as lovable a character as the English stage has ever seen in swaggering Simon Eyre with his inexhaustible stream of epithets and his genial familiarity toward both high and low. The boisterous gaiety of "mad Sim" and of his "merry Hyperboreans" — Firk, Hodge, Ralph, and the apprentices — must infect any audience. *The Shoemakers' Holiday* remains not only one of the most refreshing of older English plays, but also a still charming holiday in the living theater, as attested by the success of Orson Welles' production at the Mercury Theater, New York, in the winter of 1938.

[For studies of Dekker, see Mary L. Hunt, *Thomas Dekker: a study* (1911); Kate L. Gregg, *Thomas Dekker: a study in economic and social background* (1924); A. F. Lange, *The Shoemakers' Holiday* edited with a critical essay in *Representative English Comedies* (C. M. Gayley, ed.), vol. 3 (N.D.).]

THOMAS DEKKER

The Shoemakers' Holiday

DRAMATIS PERSONAE

KING HENRY V
THE EARL OF CORNWALL
SIR HUGH LACY, EARL OF LINCOLN
ROWLAND LACY, *sometime*
  disguised as HANS,⎫ *his nephews*
ASKEW,⎭
SIR ROGER OATELEY, *Lord Mayor of London*
Master HAMMON,⎫
Master WARNER,⎬ *citizens of London*
Master SCOTT,⎭
SIMON EYRE, *the shoemaker*
ROGER, *commonly*
  called HODGE,⎫
FIRK,⎬ EYRE'S *journeymen*
RALPH DAMPORT,⎭

LOVELL, *a courtier*
DODGER, *servant to the* EARL OF LINCOLN
A Dutch Skipper
A Boy

ROSE, *daughter of* SIR ROGER
SYBIL, *her maid*
MARGERY, *wife of* SIMON EYRE
JANE, *wife of* RALPH

Courtiers, attendants, officers, soldiers, hunters, shoemakers, apprentices, servants

The Scene is London and Old Ford

ACT I

SCENE 1. *A street in London*

Enter the LORD MAYOR *and the* EARL
OF LINCOLN

Lincoln. My lord mayor, you have sundry
  times
Feasted myself and many courtiers more;
Seldom or never can we be so kind
To make requital of your courtesy.
But leaving this, I hear my cousin[1] Lacy   5
Is much affected to[2] your daughter Rose.
  L. Mayor. True, my good lord, and she loves
  him so well
That I mislike her boldness in the chase.
  Linc. Why, my lord mayor, think you it
  then a shame,

To join a Lacy with an Oateley's name?   10
  L. Mayor. Too mean is my poor girl for his
  high birth;
Poor citizens must not with courtiers wed,
Who will in silks and gay apparel spend
More in one year than I am worth, by far;
Therefore your honor need not doubt[1] my girl.
  Linc. Take heed, my lord, advise you what
  you do!   16
A verier unthrift[2] lives not in the world,
Than in my cousin; for I'll tell you what:
'Tis now almost a year since he requested
To travel countries for experience;   20
I furnished him with coins, bills of exchange,
Letters of credit, men to wait on him,
Solicited my friends in Italy
Well to respect him.   But to see the end,   24

---

[1] A term applied to any kinsman; here, nephew.
[2] Very fond of.

[1] Not be concerned about.
[2] A greater spendthrift.

Scant had he journeyed through half Germany,
But all his coin was spent, his men cast off,
His bills embezzled,[1] and my jolly coz,[2]
Ashamed to show his bankrupt presence here,
Became a shoemaker in Wittenberg,[3]
A goodly science for a gentleman   30
Of such descent! Now judge the rest by this:
Suppose your daughter have a thousand pound,
He did consume me more in one half year;
And make him heir to all the wealth you have,
One twelvemonth's rioting will waste it all. 35
Then seek, my lord, some honest citizen
To wed your daughter to.
  L. Mayor. I thank your lordship.
(*Aside*) Well, fox, I understand your subtilty —
As for your nephew, let your lordship's eye 40
But watch his actions, and you need not fear,
For I have sent my daughter far enough.
And yet your cousin Rowland might do well,
Now he hath learned an occupation;
And yet I scorn to call him son-in-law. 45
  Linc. Ay, but I have a better trade for him.
I thank his Grace,[4] he hath appointed him
Chief colonel of all those companies
Mustered in London and the shires about,
To serve his highness in those wars of France.
See where he comes! —   51

Enter Lovell, Lacy, *and* Askew

    Lovell, what news with you?
  Lov. My Lord of Lincoln, 'tis his highness'
  will,
That presently [5] your cousin ship for France
With all his powers; [6] he would not for a mil-
  lion,   55
But they should land at Dieppe [7] within four
  days.
  Linc. Go certify his grace, it shall be done.
      (*Exit* Lovell.

[1] Squandered. [2] Cousin. — See note to l. 5.
[3] An old town in Saxony, Prussia, famed as the birth-place of the Protestant Reformation, and, to Dekker's public, as the home of Faustus in Marlowe's popular *Dr. Faustus.*
[4] I.e., His Majesty King Henry V, who was then campaigning against the French. His campaign ended with the decisive victory of Agincourt in 1415.
[5] Immediately. [6] Troops.
[7] A French port on the English Channel.

Now, cousin Lacy, in what forwardness
Are all your companies?
  Lacy. All well prepared. 60
The men of Hertfordshire lie at Mile-end,[1]
Suffolk and Essex train in Tothill-fields,[2]
The Londoners and those of Middlesex,
All gallantly prepared in Finsbury,[3] 64
With frolic spirits long for their parting hour.
  L. Mayor. They have their imprest,[4] coats,
  and furniture; [5]
And, if it please your cousin Lacy come
To the Guildhall,[6] he shall receive his pay;
And twenty pounds besides my brethren [7]
Will freely give him, to approve our loves 70
We bear unto my lord, your uncle here.
  Lacy. I thank your honor.
  Linc. Thanks, my good lord mayor.
  L. Mayor. At the Guildhall we will expect [8]
  your coming.   (*Exit.*
  Linc. To approve your loves to me? No,
  subtilty!   75
Nephew, that twenty pound he doth bestow
For joy to rid you from his daughter Rose.
But, cousins both, now here are none but
  friends,
I would not have you cast an amorous eye
Upon so mean a project as the love 80
Of a gay, wanton, painted citizen.
I know, this churl even in the height of scorn
Doth hate the mixture of his blood with thine.
I pray thee, do thou so! Remember, coz,
What honorable fortunes wait on thee. 85
Increase the king's love, which so brightly
  shines,
And gilds thy hopes. I have no heir but thee,—
And yet not thee, if with a wayward spirit
Thou start from the true bias [9] of my love.
  Lacy. My lord, I will for honor, not desire
Of land or livings, or to be your heir, 91
So guide my actions in pursuit of France,
As shall add glory to the Lacies' name.

[1] Open fields to the east of the old city of London.
[2] To the west of old London.
[3] Finsbury Fields, to the north of the city, where the earliest playhouses were located.
[4] Advance pay. [5] Equipment.
[6] The townhall in which the craft guilds held their joint gatherings.
[7] I.e., the city aldermen. [8] Await.
[9] Inclination.

Linc. Coz, for those words here's thirty
    portagues,[1]
And, nephew Askew, there's a few for you. 95
Fair Honor, in her loftiest eminence,
Stays in France for you, till you fetch her
    thence.
Then, nephews, clap swift wings on your de-
    signs.
Begone, begone, make haste to the Guildhall;
There presently I'll meet you. Do not stay:
Where honor beckons shame attends de-
    lay.   (*Exit.* 101
    Askew. How gladly would your uncle have
    you gone!
    Lacy. True, coz, but I'll o'erreach his policies.[2]
I have some serious business for three days,
Which nothing but my presence can dis-
    patch.   105
You, therefore, cousin, with the companies,
Shall haste to Dover; there I'll meet with you:
Or, if I stay past my prefixéd [3] time,
Away for France; we'll meet in Normandy.
The twenty pounds my lord mayor gives to me
You shall receive, and these ten portagues, 111
Part of mine uncle's thirty. Gentle coz,
Have care to our great charge; I know, your
    wisdom
Hath tried itself in higher consequence.[4]
    Askew. Coz, all myself am yours: yet have
    this care,   115
To lodge in London with all secrecy;
Our uncle Lincoln hath, besides his own,
Many a jealous eye, that in your face
Stares only to watch means for your disgrace.
    Lacy. Stay, cousin, who be these?   120

Enter SIMON EYRE, *his wife* MARGERY,
HODGE, FIRK, JANE, *and* RALPH *with a piece* [5]

    Eyre. Leave whining, leave whining! Away
with this whimp'ring, this puling, these blubb-
b'ring tears, and these wet eyes! I'll get thy
husband discharg'd, I warrant thee, sweet
Jane; go to!   125
    Hodge. Master, here be the captains.

---

[1] Gold pieces of Portuguese coinage, worth between
twenty and twenty-five dollars each.
[2] Schemes.   [3] Appointed.
[4] In matters of importance.   [5] A gun.

    Eyre. Peace, Hodge; husht, ye knave, husht!
    Firk. Here be the cavaliers and the colonels,
master.
    Eyre. Peace, Firk; peace, my fine Firk! 130
Stand by with your pishery-pashery,[1] away!
I am a man of the best presence; I'll speak to
them, an [2] they were Popes. — Gentlemen,
captains, colonels, commanders! Brave men,
brave leaders, may it please you to give 135
me audience. I am Simon Eyre,[3] the mad
shoemaker of Tower Street;[4] this wench with
the mealy mouth [5] that will never tire, is my
wife, I can tell you; here's Hodge, my man and
my foreman; here's Firk, my fine firking [6] 140
journeyman, and this is blubbered Jane. All
we come to be suitors for this honest Ralph.[7]
Keep him at home, and as I am a true shoemaker and a gentleman of the gentle craft,[8]
buy spurs yourself, and I'll find ye boots 145
these seven years.
    Marg. Seven years, husband?
    Eyre. Peace, midriff,[9] peace! I know what
I do. Peace!
    Firk. Truly, master cormorant, you 150
shall do God good service to let Ralph and his
wife stay together. She's a young new-married
woman; if you take her husband away from her
a-night, you undo her; she may beg in the day-
time; for he's as good a workman at a 155
prick and an awl as any is in our trade.
    Jane. O let him stay, else I shall be undone!
    Firk. Aye, truly, she shall be laid at one side
like a pair of old shoes else, and be occupied for
no use.   160

---

[1] Stop your prattle.   [2] If.
[3] Eyre is pronounced "air." The historic Simon
Eyre was first an upholsterer and later a draper. He
became Sheriff of London in 1434 (the year in which
Roger Oateley, a grocer, was Lord Mayor) and then
Lord Mayor in 1445. He died in 1459.
[4] The street leading from the Tower of London westward into the center of the old city.
[5] With the soft-spoken tongue.   [6] Frisky.
[7] Pronounced, and often spelled in the original text,
"Rafe."
[8] Because St. Hugh, who lived according to tradition
in the latter half of the third century, was once be-
friended by journeymen shoemakers, he called them
"gentlemen of the gentle craft."
[9] Diaphragm. — A satiric reference to Margery's
corpulence.

Lacy. Truly, my friends, it lies not in my power;
The Londoners are pressed,[1] paid, and set forth
By the lord mayor; I cannot change a man.

Hodge. Why, then you were as good be a corporal as a colonel, if you cannot dis- 165 charge one good fellow; and I tell you true, I think you do more than you can answer, to press a man within a year and a day of his marriage.[2]

Eyre. Well said, melancholy Hodge; 170 gramercy,[3] my fine foreman.

Marg. Truly, gentlemen, it were ill done for such as you, to stand so stiffly against a poor young wife; considering her case, she is new-married, but let that pass. I pray, deal 175 not roughly with her; her husband is a young man, and but newly entered, but let that pass.

Eyre. Away with your pishery-pashery, your pols[4] and your edipols![5] Peace, midriff; silence, Cicely Bumtrinket![6] Let your 180 head[7] speak.

Firk. Yea, and the horns[8] too, master.

Eyre. Too soon, my fine Firk, too soon! Peace, scoundrels! See you this man? Captains, you will not release him? Well, 185 let him go; he's a proper shot,[9] let him vanish! Peace, Jane, dry up thy tears, they'll make his powder dankish.[10] Take him, brave men; Hector of Troy was an hackney[11] to him, Hercules and Termagant[12] scoundrels, Prince 190 Arthur's Round-table — by the Lord of Ludgate[13] — ne'er fed such a tall,[14] such a dapper

swordsman; by the life of Pharaoh, a brave, resolute swordsman! Peace, Jane! I say no more, mad knaves. 195

Firk. See, see, Hodge, how my master raves in commendation of Ralph!

Hodge. Ralph, th' art a gull,[1] by this hand, an thou goest not.

Askew. I am glad, good Master Eyre, it is my hap 200
To meet so resolute a soldier.
Trust me, for your report and love to him,
A common slight regard shall not respect him.[2]

Lacy. Is thy name Ralph?

Ralph.   Yes, sir. 205

Lacy.   Give me thy hand;
Thou shalt not want, as I am a gentleman.
Woman, be patient; God, no doubt, will send
Thy husband safe again; but he must go,
His country's quarrel says it shall be so. 210

Hodge. Th' art a gull, by my stirrup,[3] if thou dost not go. I will not have thee strike thy gimlet into these weak vessels; prick thine enemies, Ralph.

Enter DODGER

Dodger. My lord, your uncle on the Tower-hill 215
Stays with the lord mayor and the aldermen,
And doth request you with all speed you may,
To hasten thither.

Askew.   Cousin, let's go.

Lacy. Dodger, run you before, tell them we come. — (*Exit* DODGER. 220
This Dodger is mine uncle's parasite,[4]
The arrant'st varlet that e'er breathed on earth;
He sets more discord in a noble house
By one day's broaching[5] of his pickthank[6] tales,
Than can be salved[7] again in twenty years,
And he, I fear, shall go with us to France, 226
To pry into our actions.

Askew. Therefore, coz,
It shall behove you to be circumspect.

---

[1] Drafted.

[2] There was a Biblical law that a newly wed man should be free at home for one year. See *Deuteronomy,* xxiv, 5.

[3] Many thanks.

[4] A mild oath formed by a contraction of the name of the Latin god Pollux.

[5] The same kind of exclamation, from the Latin phrase meaning "by Pollux."

[6] Margery's maid. Cf. Act II, Sc. 3.   [7] I.e., Eyre.

[8] The husband whose wife has been unfaithful was symbolized by the Elizabethans as wearing horns on his head.

[9] Good marksman.   [10] Damp.   [11] Hireling.

[12] An imaginary Mohammedan god, depicted in the early morality plays as a blustering character.

[13] The name of Lud, a legendary king of Britain, was given to one of the gates in the ancient city wall of London.

[14] Brave.

[1] Fool.

[2] I.e., he shall receive special consideration.

[3] The strap by which the shoemaker steadies his last on his knee.

[4] Toady.   [5] Utterance.   [6] Tattling.   [7] Cured.

Lacy. Fear not, good cousin. — Ralph, hie
to your colors.   230
                (*Exeunt* LACY *and* ASKEW.
Ralph. I must, because there's no remedy;
But, gentle master and my loving dame,
As you have always been a friend to me,
So in mine absence think upon my wife.
Jane. Alas, my Ralph.   235
Marg.   She cannot speak for weeping.
Eyre. Peace, you crack'd [1] groats,[2] you mus-
tard tokens,[3] disquiet not the brave soldier.
Go thy ways, Ralph!
Jane. Aye, aye, you bid him go; what   240
shall I do when he is gone?
Firk. Why, be doing with me or my fellow
Hodge; be not idle.
Eyre. Let me see thy hand, Jane. This fine
hand, this white hand, these pretty fingers 245
must spin, must card, must work; work, you
bombast [4] cotton-candle [5]-quean; [6] work for
your living, with a pox to you.[7] — Hold thee,
Ralph, here's five sixpences for thee; fight for
the honor of the gentle craft, for the gen- 250
tlemen shoemakers, the courageous cordwainers,[8] the flower of St. Martin's,[9] the mad knaves
of Bedlam, Fleet Street, Tower Street and
Whitechapel; [10] crack me the crowns of the
French knaves; a pox on them, crack   255
them; fight, by the lord of Ludgate; fight, my
fine boy!
Firk. Here, Ralph, here's three twopences;
two carry into France, the third shall wash our
souls at parting, for sorrow is dry. For   260
my sake, firk [11] the *Basa-mon-cues*.[12]

[1] I.e., worthless.
[2] Old English coins worth four pence each.
[3] Tokens given to a purchaser of mustard, which were
of no value until a large number had been accumulated.
Then they could be turned in for a small refund.
[4] Cotton, or cotton padding.
[5] Candle with a cotton wick.
[6] Wench. — The entire phrase implies that Jane is a
delicate, pampered creature.
[7] Plague take you.
[8] Workers in cordovan leather.
[9] The parish of St. Martin's Le Grand, a center of the
shoemaking trade.
[10] Other centers of the craft in the east part of the old
city.
[11] Beat.
[12] The "kiss-my-tails." — A corrupt and insulting
phrase for the Frenchmen.

Hodge. Ralph, I am heavy [1] at parting; but
here's a shilling for thee. God send [2] thee to
cram thy slops [3] with French crowns, and thy
enemies' bellies with bullets.   265
Ralph. I thank you, master, and I thank
you all.
Now, gentle wife, my loving, lovely Jane,
Rich men, at parting, give their wives rich
    gifts,
Jewels and rings to grace their lily hands.
Thou know'st our trade makes rings for
    women's heels: 270
Here take this pair of shoes, cut out by Hodge,
Stitch'd by my fellow Firk, seam'd by myself,
Made up and pink'd [4] with letters for thy
    name.
Wear them, my dear Jane, for thy husband's
    sake,
And every morning when thou pull'st them
    on,   275
Remember me, and pray for my return.
Make much of them; for I have made them so
That I can know them from a thousand mo.[5]
Drums sound. Enter the LORD MAYOR, *the*
EARL OF LINCOLN, LACY, ASKEW, DODGER,
and soldiers. They pass over the stage;
RALPH *falls in amongst them;* FIRK *and the*
rest cry "Farewell," etc., and so exeunt.

ACT II

SCENE I. *The garden of the* LORD MAYOR'S
country house at Old Ford [6]

Enter ROSE, *alone, making a garland*

Rose. Here sit thou down upon this flow'ry
    bank
And make a garland for thy Lacy's head.
These pinks, these roses, and these violets,
These blushing gilliflowers, these marigolds,
The fair embroidery of his coronet,   5
Carry not half such beauty in their cheeks,
As the sweet count'nance of my Lacy doth.
O my most unkind father! O my stars,
Why lower'd you so at my nativity,

[1] Sad.   [2] Grant.   [3] Breeches.
[4] Decorated with little holes.   [5] More.
[6] A suburb to the northeast of old London; now
within the city.

To make me love, yet live robb'd of my love?
Here as a thief am I imprisoned   11
For my dear Lacy's sake within those walls,
Which by my father's cost were builded up
For better purposes.   Here must I languish
For him that doth as much lament, I know,   15
Mine absence, as for him I pine in woe.

Enter SYBIL

Sybil. Good morrow, young mistress.   I am
sure you make that garland for me, against [1] I
shall be Lady of the Harvest.
Rose. Sybil, what news at London?   20
Sybil. None but good; my lord mayor, your
father, and master Philpot, your uncle, and
Master Scot, your cousin, and Mistress Frig-
bottom by Doctors' Commons,[2] do all, by my
troth, send you most hearty commenda-   25
tions.[3]
Rose. Did Lacy send kind greetings to his
love?
Sybil. O yes, out of cry,[4] by my troth.   I
scant [5] knew him; here 'a [6] wore a scarf;   30
and here a scarf, here a bunch of feathers, and
here precious stones and jewels, and a pair of
garters, — O, monstrous! like one of our yellow
silk curtains at home here in Old Ford House
here, in Master Bellymount's chamber.   35
I stood at our door in Cornhill, look'd at him,
he at me indeed, spake to him, but he not to
me, not a word; marry gup,[7] thought I, with
a wanion![8]   He passed by me as proud —
Marry foh! are you grown humorous,[9]   40
thought I; and so shut the door, and in I
came.
Rose. O Sybil, how dost thou my Lacy
      wrong!
My Rowland is as gentle as a lamb,
No dove was ever half so mild as he.   45
Sybil. Mild? yea, as a bushel of stamped
crabs.[10] He looked upon me as sour as ver-

juice.[1]   Go thy ways, thought I; thou may'st
be much in my gaskins,[2] but nothing in my
netherstocks.[3] This is your fault, mistress,   50
to love him that loves not you; he thinks
scorn to do as he's done to; but if I were as you,
I'd cry, "Go by, Jeronimo, go by!" [4]
I'd set mine old debts against my new driblets,
And the hare's foot against the goose gib-
      lets,[5]   55
For if ever I sigh, when sleep I should take,
Pray God I may lose my maidenhead when I
      wake.
Rose. Will my love leave me then, and go to
      France?
Sybil. I know not that, but I am sure I see
him stalk before the soldiers.   By my   60
troth, he is a proper [6] man; but he is proper
that proper doth.   Let him go snick up,[7]
young mistress.
Rose. Get thee to London, and learn per-
      fectly,
Whether my Lacy go to France, or no.   65
Do this, and I will give thee for thy pains
My cambric apron and my Romish [8] gloves,
My purple stockings and a stomacher.
Say, wilt thou do this, Sybil, for my sake?
Sybil. Will I, quoth 'a? [9] At whose suit?   70
By my troth, yes, I'll go.   A cambric apron,
gloves, a pair of purple stockings, and a stom-
acher!   I'll sweat in purple, mistress, for you;
I'll take anything that comes a' God's name.
O rich! a cambric apron!   Faith, then have   75
at "up tails all." [10] I'll go jiggy-joggy to Lon-
don, and be here in a trice, young mistress.
                              (*Exit.*

Rose. Do so, good Sybil.   Meantime
      wretched I
Will sit and sigh for his lost company.   (*Exit.*

[1] Juice of green fruit.   [2] Breeches.
[3] Tights. — The gist of Sybil's rather vulgar remark
is that the gentleman and she may be acquainted
slightly, but certainly not intimately.
[4] A popular phrase from Thomas Kyd's famous
"hit," *The Spanish Tragedy*, Act IV, Sc. 5. — Sybil's
advice is to dismiss Lacy.
[5] Again in proverbial language Sybil counsels Rose to
risk a new love.
[6] Handsome.   [7] Go hang.
[8] From Rome.   [9] Says she?
[10] A boisterous card game; also a rollicking tune. —
Sybil's meaning is, "then for a high old time."

---

[1] In anticipation of the time when.
[2] The buildings of the College of Doctors of Civil
Law, south of St. Paul's Cathedral in the center of old
London.
[3] Regards.   [4] Beyond measure.
[5] Hardly, scarcely.   [6] He.   [7] Go on with you.
[8] A vengeance!   [9] Temperamental.
[10] Crushed crabapples.

SCENE 2. *A street in London*

Enter ROWLAND LACY, *dressed like a Dutch shoemaker*

Lacy. How many shapes have gods and
    kings devised,
Thereby to compass their desired loves!
It is no shame for Rowland Lacy, then,
To clothe his cunning with the Gentle Craft,
That, thus disguised, I may unknown possess
The only happy presence of my Rose.   6
For her have I forsook my charge in France,
Incurred the king's displeasure, and stirred up
Rough hatred in mine uncle Lincoln's breast.
O love, how powerful art thou, that canst
    change   10
High birth to baseness, and a noble mind
To the mean semblance of a shoemaker!
But thus it must be. For her cruel father,
Hating the single union of our souls,
Has secretly convey'd my Rose from London,
To bar me of her presence; but I trust,   16
Fortune and this disguise will further me
Once more to view her beauty, gain her sight.
Here in Tower Street with Eyre the shoemaker
Mean I a while to work; I know the trade,   20
I learnt it when I was in Wittenberg.
Then cheer thy hoping spirits, be not dismay'd,
Thou canst not want: do Fortune what she can,
The gentle craft is living for a man.   (*Exit.*

SCENE 3. *Before* EYRE'S *house*

Enter EYRE, *making himself ready*

Eyre. Where be these boys, these girls, these
drabs,[1] these scoundrels? They wallow in the
fat brewis [2] of my bounty, and lick up the
crumbs of my table, yet will not rise to see my
walks cleansed. Come out, you powder-   5
beef [3] queans! What, Nan! what, Madge
Mumble-crust! [4] Come out, you fat midriff-
swag-belly-whores, and sweep me these ken-
nels [5] that the noisome stench offend not the
noses of my neighbors. What, Firk, I say!   10

---

[1] Slatterns.   [2] Broth.   [3] Corned-beef.
[4] A popular appellation borrowed from the name of
the old nurse in Nicholas Udall's comedy, *Ralph Roister
Doister*.
[5] Gutters.

What, Hodge! Open my shop windows! What,
Firk, I say!

Enter FIRK

Firk. O master, is't you that speak bandog [1]
and Bedlam [2] this morning? I was in a dream,
and mused what madman was got into the   15
street so early. Have you drunk this morning
that your throat is so clear?
Eyre. Ah, well said, Firk; well said, Firk.
To work, my fine knave, to work! Wash thy
face, and thou't be more blest.   20
Firk. Let them wash my face that will eat it.
Good master, send for a sousewife,[3] if you'll
have my face cleaner.

Enter HODGE

Eyre. Away, sloven! avaunt, scoundrel! —
Good-morrow, Hodge; good-morrow, my   25
fine foreman.
Hodge. O master, good-morrow; y'are an
early stirrer. Here's a fair morning. — Good-
morrow, Firk, I could have slept this hour.
Here's a brave day towards.[4]   30
Eyre. Oh, haste to work, my fine foreman,
haste to work.
Firk. Master, I am dry as dust to hear my
fellow Roger talk of fair weather; let us pray
for good leather, and let clowns and plough-   35
boys and those that work in the fields pray for
brave days. We work in a dry shop; what care
I if it rain?

Enter MARGERY

Eyre. How now, Dame Margery, can you see
to rise? Trip and go, call up the drabs,   40
your maids.
Marg. See to rise? I hope 'tis time enough,
'tis early enough for any woman to be seen
abroad. I marvel how many wives in Tower
Street are up so soon. Gods me, 'tis not   45
noon, — here's a yawling! [5]
Eyre. Peace, Margery, peace! Where's
Cicely Bumtrinket, your maid? She has a

---

[1] Like a chained dog.   [2] Like a madman.
[3] A woman who sells pickled-pork.
[4] In prospect.   [5] Howling.

privy fault, she farts in her sleep. Call the quean up; if my men want shoethread, I'll 50 swinge her in [1] a stirrup.

Firk. Yet that's but a dry beating; here's still a sign of drought.

Enter LACY, *disguised, singing*

Lacy. Der was een bore van Gelderland,
    Frolick sie byen;   55
He was als dronck he cold nyet stand,
    Upsolce sie byen.
Tap eens de canneken,
Drincke, schone mannekin.[2]

Firk. Master, for my life, yonder's a 60 brother of the gentle craft; if he bears not Saint Hugh's bones,[3] I'll forfeit my bones; he's some uplandish [4] workman: hire him, good master, that I may learn some gibble-gabble; 'twill make us work the faster.   65

Eyre. Peace, Firk! A hard world! Let him pass, let him vanish; we have journeymen enow.[5] Peace, my fine Firk!

Marg. Nay, nay, y' are best follow your man's counsel; you shall see what will come 70 on't. We have not men enow, but we must entertain every butter-box; [6] but let that pass.

Hodge. Dame, 'fore God, if my master follow your counsel, he'll consume little beef. He shall be glad of men an he can catch them. 75

Firk. Aye, that he shall.

Hodge. 'Fore God, a proper man, and I warrant, a fine workman. Master, farewell; dame, adieu; if such a man as he cannot find work, Hodge is not for you.   (*Offers to go.* 80

Eyre. Stay, my fine Hodge.

---

[1] Beat her with.
[2] A song in pseudo-Dutch as follows:
    There was a boor from Gelderland,
      Jolly they be;
    He was so drunk he could not stand,
      Dead drunk they be.
    Draw once the cannikin,
    Drink, pretty mannikin.
[3] After St. Hugh's martyrdom the shoemakers secretly secured his bones, which he had bequeathed to them, and made them into the tools of their trade. Ever since the shoemaker's tools have been called "St. Hugh's bones."
[4] From the country.   [5] Enough.
[6] I.e., Dutchman.

Firk. Faith, an your foreman go, dame, you must take a journey to seek a new journeyman; if Roger remove, Firk follows. If Saint Hugh's bones shall not be set a-work, I may prick 85 mine awl in the walls, and go play. Fare ye well, master; good-bye, dame.

Eyre. Tarry, my fine Hodge, my brisk foreman! Stay, Firk! — (*To* MARGERY) Peace, pudding-broth! By the Lord of Ludgate, 90 I love my men as my life. Peace, you gallimaufry! [1] — Hodge, if he want work, I'll hire him. One of you to him; stay — he comes to us.

Lacy. Goeden dach, meester, ende u vro oak.[2]

Firk. Nails, if I should speak after him 95 without drinking, I should choke. And you, friend Oake, are you of the Gentle Craft?

Lacy. Yaw, yaw, ik bin den skomawker.[3]

Firk. Den skomaker, quoth 'a! And hark you, skomaker, have you all your tools, a 100 good rubbing-pin, a good stopper, a good dresser, your four sorts of awls, and your two balls of wax, your paring knife, your hand and thumb-leathers, and good St. Hugh's bones to smooth up your work?   105

Lacy. Yaw, yaw; be niet voryeard. Ik hab all de dingen voour mack skooes groot and cleane.[4]

Firk. Ha, ha! Good master, hire him; he'll make me laugh so that I shall work more in mirth than I can in earnest.   110

Eyre. Hear ye, friend, have ye any skill in the mystery [5] of cordwainers?

Lacy. Ik weet niet wat yow seg; ich verstaw you niet.[6]

Firk. Why, thus, man. (*Imitates by* 115 *gesture a shoemaker at work.*) Iche verste u niet, quoth 'a.[7]

Lacy. Yaw, yaw, yaw; ick can dat wel doen.[8]

Firk. Yaw, yaw! He speaks yawing like a jackdaw that gapes to be fed with cheese- 120 curds. Oh, he'll give a villainous pull at a can of double-beer; but Hodge and I have the

---

[1] Hodge-podge.
[2] Good-day, master, and you, goodwife, too.
[3] Yes, yes, I am a shoemaker.
[4] Yes, yes; don't be afraid. I have everything to make shoes big and little.
[5] Craft.
[6] I don't know what you say; I don't understand you.
[7] I don't understand you, says he.
[8] Yes, yes, yes; I can do that well.

vantage, we must drink first, because we are
the eldest journeymen.

Eyre. What is thy name?   125

Lacy. Hans — Hans Meulter.

Eyre. Give me thy hand; th' art welcome.
— Hodge, entertain him; Firk, bid him welcome; come, Hans. Run, wife, bid your maids,
your trullibubs,[1] make ready my fine 130
men's breakfasts. To him, Hodge!

Hodge. Hans, th' art welcome; use thyself
friendly, for we are good fellows; if not, thou
shalt be fought with, wert thou bigger than a
giant.   135

Firk. Yea, and drunk with, wert thou Gar-
gantua.[2] My master keeps no cowards, I tell
thee. — Ho, boy, bring him an heel-block,
here's a new journeyman.

Enter a Boy

Hans. O, ich wersto you; ich moet een 140
halve dossen cans betaelen; here, boy, nempt dis
skilling; tap eens freelicke.[3]   (*Exit Boy.*

Eyre. Quick, snipper-snapper, away! Firk,
scour thy throat; thou shalt wash it with
Castilian [4] liquor.   145

Re-enter Boy

Come, my last of the fives,[5] give me a can.
Have to thee, Hans; here, Hodge; here, Firk;
drink, you mad Greeks, and work like true
Trojans, and pray for Simon Eyre, the shoemaker. — Here, Hans, and th' art wel- 150
come.

Firk. Lo, dame, you would have lost a good
fellow that will teach us to laugh. This beer
came hopping in well.

Marg. Simon, it is almost seven.   155

[1] I.e., your good-for-nothings.

[2] A gluttonous giant who is the hero of Rabelais'
satirical romance of the same name, a French classic of
the sixteenth century.

[3] Oh, I understand you; I must pay for half a dozen
cans; here, boy, take this shilling; draw once freely.

[4] Eyre means "Castalian." Castalia was a spring on
Mt. Parnassus, Greece, sacred to Apollo and the Muses.
Hence its waters were looked upon as sources of in-
spiration.

[5] An allusion to the Boy's small size, since a number
five last is quite small.

Eyre. Is't so, Dame Clapper-dundgeon?[1]
Is't seven a clock, and my men's breakfast not
ready? Trip and go, you sous'd conger,[2] away!
Come, you mad Hyperboreans;[3] follow me,
Hodge; follow me, Hans, come after, my 160
fine Firk; to work a while, and then to breakfast.   (*Exit.*

Firk. Soft! Yaw, yaw, good Hans, though
my master have no more wit but to call you
afore me, I am not so foolish to go be- 165
hind you, I being the elder journeyman.

(*Exeunt.*

SCENE 4. *A field near Old Ford*

Halloaing within. Enter WARNER *and*
HAMMON, *dressed like hunters*

Ham. Cousin, beat every brake, the game's
          not far;

This way with winged feet he fled from death,
Whilst the pursuing hounds, scenting his steps,
Find out his highway to destruction.
Besides, the miller's boy told me even now, 5
He saw him take soil,[4] and he halloaed him,
Affirming him to have been so embost [5]
That long he could not hold.

Warn.   If it be so, 9
'Tis best we trace these meadows by Old Ford.

A noise of hunters within. Enter a Boy

Ham. How now, boy? Where's the deer?
Speak, saw'st thou him?

Boy. O yea; I saw him leap through a hedge,
and then over a ditch, then at my lord mayor's
pale, over he skipt me, and in he went me, 15
and "holla" the hunters cried, and "there, boy;
there, boy!" But there he is, a' mine honesty.

Ham. Boy, Godamercy. Cousin, let's away;
I hope we shall find better sport today.

(*Exeunt.*

[1] Margery is so called because her tongue makes as
much noise as the wooden cover of a beggar's clap-dish.

[2] Pickled conger-eel.

[3] Mythological people of the far north, who live in the
strange state of perpetual happiness.

[4] Take cover.

[5] Exhausted.

SCENE 5. *The park of the* LORD MAYOR'S *house at Old Ford*

Sounds of hunting within.　Enter ROSE *and* SYBIL

Rose.　Why, Sybil, wilt thou prove a forester?

Sybil.　Upon some, no.　Forester?　Go by; no, faith, mistress.　The deer came running into the barn through the orchard and over the pale;[1] I wot well, I lookt as pale as a new 　5 cheese to see him.　But whip, says Goodman Pinclose, up with his flail, and our Nick with a prong, and down he fell, and they upon him, and I upon them.　By my troth, we had such sport; and in the end we ended him; his 　10 throat we cut, flay'd him, unhorn'd him, and my lord mayor shall eat of him anon, when he comes.　　　　　　　　(*Horns sound within.*

Rose.　Hark, hark, the hunters come; y' are best take heed,

They'll have a saying to you for this deed.　15

Enter HAMMON, WARNER, *Boy, and Huntsmen*

Ham.　God save you, fair ladies.

Sybil.　Ladies!　O gross![2]

Warn.　Came not a buck this way?

Rose.　　　　　　　　No, but[3] two does.

Ham.　And which way went they?　Faith, we'll hunt at those.　　　　　　　　20

Sybil.　At those?　Upon some, no.　When, can you tell?

Warn.　Upon some, aye.

Sybil.　　　　　　　　Good Lord!

Warn.　　　　　　Wounds!　Then farewell!

Ham.　Boy, which way went he?　　　25

Boy.　　　　　　This way, sir, he ran.

Ham.　This way he ran indeed, fair Mistress Rose;

Our game was lately in your orchard seen.

Warn.　Can you advise, which way he took his flight?

Sybil.　Follow your nose; his horns will guide you right.　　　　　　　　30

Warn.　T' art a mad wench.

Sybil.　　　　　　O, rich!

Rose.　　　　　　　　Trust me, not I.

It is not like that the wild forest-deer

Would come so near to places of resort;　35
You are deceiv'd, he fled some other way.

Warn.　Which way, my sugar-candy, can you show?

Sybil.　Come up, good honeysops, upon some, no.

Rose.　Why do you stay, and not pursue your game?

Sybil.　I'll hold my life, their hunting-nags be lame.　　　　　　　　40

Ham.　A deer more dear is found within this place.

Rose.　But not the deer, sir, which you had in chase.

Ham.　I chas'd the deer, but this dear chaseth me.

Rose.　The strangest hunting that ever I see. But where's your park?　　　　　45

　　　　　　(*She offers to go away.*

Ham.　　　　　　'Tis here: O stay!

Rose.　Impale[1] me, and then I will not stray.

Warn.　They wrangle, wench; we are more kind than they.

Sybil.　What kind of hart[2] is that dear heart you seek?

Warn.　A hart, dear heart.　　　50

Sybil.　　　　　　Who ever saw the like?

Rose.　To lose your heart, is 't possible you can?

Ham.　My heart is lost.

Rose.　　　　　　Alack, good gentleman!

Ham.　This poor lost heart would I wish you might find.　　　　　　　55

Rose.　You, by such luck, might prove your hart a hind.[3]

Ham.　Why, Luck had horns,[4] so have I heard some say.

Rose.　Now, God, an 't be his will, send Luck into your way.

Enter the LORD MAYOR *and Servants*

L. Mayor.　What, Master Hammon?　Welcome to Old Ford!

Sybil (*aside to* WARNER).　God's pittikins,[5] hands off, sir!　Here's my lord.　　60

[1] Fence.　　[2] Stag deer.　　[3] A doe.
[4] Dame Fortune's horn of plenty, or cornucopia.
[5] God's little pities.

---

[1] Fence.　　[2] O stupid!　　[3] Only.

L. Mayor. I hear you had ill luck, and lost
your game.

Ham. 'Tis true, my lord.

L. Mayor.   I am sorry for the same.
What gentleman is this?

Ham.   My brother-in-law. 65

L. Mayor. Y' are welcome both; sith [1] For-
tune offers you
Into my hands, you shall not part from hence,
Until you have refreshed your wearied limbs.
Go, Sybil, cover the board! — You shall be
guest
To no good cheer, but even a hunter's feast. 70

Ham. I thank your lordship. — (*Aside to*
WARNER) Cousin, on my life,
For our lost venison I shall find a wife.

L. Mayor. In, gentlemen; I'll not be absent
long.— (*Exeunt all but the* LORD MAYOR.
This Hammon is a proper gentleman,
A citizen by birth, fairly allied;   75
How fit an husband were he for my girl!
Well, I will in, and do the best I can,
To match my daughter to this gentleman.

                                  (*Exit.*

ACT III

SCENE I. *A room in* EYRE'S *house*

Enter HANS (LACY *in disguise*), HODGE,
FIRK, *and a Dutch Skipper*

Skip. Ick sal yow wat seggen, Hans; dis skip,
dat comen from Candy, is al vol, by Got's sacrament, van sugar, civet, almonds, cambrick, end
alle dingen, towsand towsand ding. Nempt it,
Hans, nempt it vor v meester. Daer be de 5
bils van laden. Your meester Simon Eyre sal
hae good copen. Wat saggen yow, Hans? [2]

Firk. Wat seggen de reggen, de copen slopen [3]
— laugh, Hodge, laugh!

Hans. Mine liever broder Firk, bringt 10
Meester Eyre tot det signe vn Swannekin; daer

sal yow finde dis skipper end me. Wat seggen
yow, broder Firk? Doot it, Hodge.[1] Come,
skipper. (*Exeunt* HANS *and the Skipper.*

Firk. Bring him, quoth you? Here's no 15
knavery, to bring my master to buy a ship
worth the lading of two or three hundred thousand pounds. Alas, that's nothing; a trifle, a
bauble, Hodge.

Hodge. The truth is, Firk, that the mer- 20
chant owner of the ship dares not show his
head, and therefore this skipper that deals for
him, for the love he bears Hans, offers my
master Eyre a bargain in the commodities.
He shall have a reasonable day of pay- 25
ment; he may sell the wares by that time, and
be an huge gainer himself.

Firk. Yea, but can my fellow Hans lend my
master twenty porpentines [2] as an earnest
penny? [3]   30

Hodge. Portuguese,[4] thou wouldst say; here
they be, Firk; hark, they jingle in my pocket
like St. Mary Overy's [5] bells.

Enter EYRE *and* MARGERY

Firk. Mum, here comes my dame and my
master. She'll scold, on my life, for loi- 35
tering this Monday; but all's one, let them all
say what they can, Monday's our holiday.

Marg. You sing, Sir Sauce, but I beshrew
your heart.
I fear, for this your singing we shall smart.

Firk. Smart for me, dame; why, dame, 40
why?

Hodge. Master, I hope you'll not suffer my
dame to take down [6] your journeymen.

Firk. If she take me down, I'll take her up; [7]
yea, and take her down too,[8] a button-hole 45
lower.

Eyre. Peace, Firk; not I, Hodges; by the
life of Pharaoh, by the Lord of Ludgate, by
this beard, every hair whereof I value at a

---

[1] Since.

[2] I'll tell you what, Hans; this ship, which comes
from Candy [Crete, an island in the eastern Mediter-
ranean], is all full, by God's sacrament, of sugar, civet,
almonds, cambric, and everything, a thousand thousand
things. Take it, Hans, take it for your master. There
are the bills of lading. Your master Simon Eyre shall
have a good bargain. What do you say, Hans?

[3] Firk's playfully imitative jargon.

[1] My dear brother Firk, bring Master Eyre to the
sign of the Swan [a tavern in Old Fish Street, not far
away]; there you shall find this skipper and me. What
do you say, brother Firk? Do it, Hodge.

[2] Cant phrase for pounds.

[3] Down payment.   [4] See note to Act I, l. 94.

[5] The church at the south end of London Bridge.
"Overy" is a contraction of "over-the-river."

[6] Cheat.   [7] Seize her.   [8] Humble her too.

king's ransom, she shall not meddle with 50 you. — Peace, you bombast-cotton-candle-quean;[1] away, queen of clubs;[2] quarrel not with me and my men, with me and my fine Firk; I'll firk[3] you, if you do.

Marg. Yea, yea, man, you may use me 55 as you please; but let that pass.

Eyre. Let it pass, let it vanish away; peace! Am I not Simon Eyre? Are not these my brave men, brave shoemakers, all gentlemen of the Gentle Craft? Prince am I none, yet 60 am I nobly born, as being the sole son of a shoe-maker. Away, rubbish! vanish, melt; melt like kitchen-stuff.[4]

Marg. Yea, yea, 'tis well; I must be called rubbish, kitchen-stuff, for a sort[5] of 65 knaves.

Firk. Nay, dame, you shall not weep and wail in woe for me. Master, I'll stay no longer; here's an inventory of my shop-tools. Adieu, master; Hodge, farewell. 70

Hodge. Nay, stay, Firk; thou shalt not go alone.

Marg. I pray, let them go; there be more maids than Mawkin, more men than Hodge, and more fools than Firk. 75

Firk. Fools? Nails! if I tarry now, I would my guts might be turned to shoe-thread.

Hodge. And if I stay, I pray God I may be turned to a Turk, and set in Finsbury[6] for boys to shoot at. — Come, Firk. 80

Eyre. Stay, my fine knaves, you arms of my trade, you pillars of my profession. What, shall a tittle-tattle's words make you forsake Simon Eyre? — Avaunt, kitchen-stuff! Rip, you brown-bread Tannikin;[7] out of my 85 sight! Move me not! Have not I ta'en you from selling tripes in Eastcheap,[8] and set you in my shop, and made you hail-fellow with Simon Eyre, the shoemaker? And now do you deal thus with my journeymen? Look, 90

---

[1] See notes to Act I, l. 247.
[2] I.e., queen of the apprentices, whose ordinary weapon was the club.
[3] Beat.　　[4] Greasy refuse from the kitchen.
[5] Pack.
[6] See note to Act I, l. 64.
[7] Get a move on, you common little Dutchwoman.
[8] A street near the Thames and Tower Street much frequented by fish-mongers.

you powder-beef-quean, on the face of Hodge, here's a face for a lord.

Firk. And here's a face for any lady in Christendom.

Eyre. Rip, you chitterling,[1] avaunt! — 95 Boy! (*Enter Boy.*) Bid the tapster of the Boar's Head fill me a dozen cans of beer for my journeymen.

Firk. A dozen cans? O brave! Hodge, now I'll stay. 100

Eyre (*aside to the Boy*). An the knave fills any more than two, he pays for them. (*Aloud as the Boy goes out*) A dozen cans of beer for my journeymen. (*Re-enter Boy.*) Here, you mad Mesopotamians,[2] wash your livers 105 with this liquor. Where be the odd ten? (*Aside*) No more, Madge, no more. — Well said.[3] Drink and to work! — What work dost thou, Hodge? What work?

Hodge. I am a-making a pair of shoes 110 for my lord mayor's daughter, Mistress Rose.

Firk. And I a pair of shoes for Sybil, my lord's maid. I deal with her.

Eyre. Sybil? Fie, defile not thy fine work-manly fingers with the feet of kitchen- 115 stuff and basting-ladles. Ladies of the court, fine ladies, my lads, commit their feet to our appareling; put gross work to Hans. Yark[4] and seam, yark and seam!

Firk. For yarking and seaming let me 120 alone, I come to't.

Hodge. Well, master, all this is from the bias.[5] Do you remember the ship my fellow Hans told you of? The skipper and he are both drinking at the Swan. Here be the 125 Portuguese to give earnest. If you go through with it, you cannot choose but be a lord at least.

Firk. Nay, dame, if my master prove not a lord, and you a lady, hang me. 130

Marg. Yea, like enough, if you may loiter and tipple[6] thus.

Firk. Tipple, dame? No, we have been

---

[1] Little sausage.
[2] The people living in Asia between the Tigris and Euphrates Rivers, the country now called Iraq. — The name is used here only as a bit of outlandish jargon.
[3] Well done.　　[4] Pull the stitch tight.
[5] Aside from the business.　　[6] Sip drinks.

bargaining with Skellum [1] Skanderbag,[2] Can-you-Dutch-spreaken [3] for a ship of silk   135
cypress,[4] laden with sugar-candy?

Enter the Boy with a velvet coat and an alder-
man's gown.   Eyre puts them on

Eyre. Peace, Firk; silence, Tittle-tattle!
Hodge, I'll go through with it.   Here's a seal-ring, and I have sent for a guarded [5] gown and
a damask cassock.[6]   See where it comes;   140
look here, Maggy; help me, Firk; apparel me,
Hodge; silk and satin, you mad Philistines,[7]
silk and satin.

Firk. Ha, ha, my master will be as proud as
a dog in a doublet, all in beaten [8] damask   145
and velvet.

Eyre. Softly, Firk, for rearing of the nap,[9]
and wearing threadbare my garments.   How
dost thou like me, Firk?   How do I look, my
fine Hodge?   150

Hodge. Why, now you look like yourself,
master.   I warrant you, there's few in the city,
but will give you the wall,[10] and come upon you
with [11] the Right Worshipful.

Firk. Nails, my master looks like a   155
threadbare cloak new turned and dressed.
Lord, Lord, to see what good raiment doth!
Dame, dame, are you not enamored?

Eyre. How say'st thou, Maggy, am I not
brisk?[12]   Am I not fine?   160

Marg. Fine? By my troth, sweetheart, very
fine! By my troth, I never liked thee so well
in my life, sweetheart; but let that pass.   I

warrant, there be many women in the city have
not such handsome husbands, but only   165
for their apparel; but let that pass too.

Enter Hans and the Skipper

Hans. Godden day, mester.   Dis be de skipper
dat heb de skip van marchandice; de commodity
ben good; nempt it, master, nempt it.[1]

Eyre. Godamercy, Hans; welcome,   170
skipper.   Where lies this ship of merchandise?

Skip. De skip ben in revere; dor be van sugar,
civet, almonds, cambrick, and a towsand towsand
tings, gotz sacrament; nempt it, mester: ye sal heb
good copen.[2]   175

Firk. To him, master!   O sweet master!
O sweet wares! Prunes, almonds, sugar-candy,
carrot-roots, turnips, O brave fatting meat!
Let not a man buy a nutmeg but yourself.

Eyre. Peace, Firk!   Come, skipper, I'll   180
go aboard with you. — Hans, have you made
him drink?

Skip. Yaw, yaw, ic heb veale gedrunck.[3]

Eyre. Come, Hans, follow me.   Skipper,
thou shalt have my countenance in the   185
city.   (*Exeunt.*

Firk. "*Yaw, heb veale gedrunck,*" quoth 'a.
They may well be called butter-boxes, when
they drink fat veal and thick beer too.   But
come, dame, I hope you'll chide us no   190
more.

Marg. No, faith, Firk; no, perdy, Hodge.
I do feel honor creep upon me, and which is
more, a certain rising in my flesh; but let that
pass.   195

Firk. Rising in your flesh do you feel, say
you?   Aye, you may be with child, but why
should not my master feel a rising in his flesh,
having a gown and a gold ring on?   But you
are such a shrew, you'll soon pull him   200
down.

Marg. Ha, ha! prithee, peace!   Thou

---

[1] Scoundrel.
[2] Iskander Bey or Beg (Prince Alexander), the Turk-ish name of George Castorita (1403–68), who led the Albanian struggle for independence from Turkish rule.
[3] Can-you-speak-Dutch. — Firk is here copying Eyre in his use of outlandish jargon.
[4] Very fine black silk cloth.
[5] Decorated along the edges.
[6] Long, loose-fitting, silk outer robe.
[7] The people occupying the southwest coast of Pales-tine in Biblical times.
[8] Stamped.
[9] For fear of roughening the pile (of the velvet).
[10] I.e., give you precedence. — In Elizabethan Lon-don the streets not only had no sidewalks, but they were full of mucky filth.   The pedestrian nearest the wall, therefore, had the driest and cleanest route.
[11] Approach you with the title of.   [12] Spruce.

[1] Good day, master.   This is the skipper that has the ship of merchandise; the profit is good; take it, master, take it.
[2] The ship is in the river; there is sugar, civet, al-monds, cambric, and a thousand thousand things, by God's sacrament; take it, master: you shall have a good bargain.
[3] Yes, yes, I have drunk much.

mak'st my worship laugh; but let that pass.
Come, I'll go in; Hodge prithee, go before me;
Firk, follow me.   205

Firk. Firk doth follow: Hodge, pass out in
state.   (*Exeunt.*

SCENE 2.   *A room in the* EARL OF LIN-
COLN'S *house at London*

Enter the EARL OF LINCOLN *and* DODGER

Linc. How now, good Dodger, what's the
news in France?

Dodger. My lord, upon the eighteenth day
of May
The French and English were prepar'd to fight;
Each side with eager fury gave the sign
Of a most hot encounter.   Five long hours   5
Both armies fought together; at the length
The lot of victory fell on our side.
Twelve thousand of the Frenchmen that day
died,
Four thousand English, and no man of name
But Captain Hyam and young Ardington,   10
Two gallant gentlemen, I knew them well.

Linc. But Dodger, prithee, tell me, in this
fight
How did my cousin Lacy bear himself?

Dodger. My lord, your cousin Lacy was not
there.

Linc. Not there?   15

Dodger.   No, my good lord.

Linc.   Sure, thou mistakest.
I saw him shipp'd, and a thousand eyes beside
Were witnesses of the farewells which he gave,
When I, with weeping eyes, bid him adieu.   20
Dodger, take heed.

Dodger.   My lord, I am advis'd [1]
That what I spake is true: to prove it so,
His cousin Askew, that supplied his place,
Sent me for him from France, that secretly   25
He might convey himself thither.

Linc.   Is't even so?
Dares he so carelessly venture his life
Upon the indignation of a king?
Has he despis'd my love, and spurn'd those
favors   30
Which I with prodigal hand pour'd on his head?
He shall repent his rashness with his soul;

   [1] Assured.

Since of my love he makes no estimate,
I'll make him wish he had not known my hate.
Thou hast no other news?   35

Dodger.   None else, my lord.

Linc. None worse I know thou hast. —
Procure the king
To crown his giddy brows with ample honors,
Send him chief colonel, and all my hope
Thus to be dash'd! But 'tis in vain to grieve,
One evil cannot a worse relieve.   41
Upon my life, I have found out his plot;
That old dog, Love, that fawn'd upon him so,
Love to that puling [1] girl, his fair-cheek'd Rose,
The lord mayor's daughter, hath distracted him,
And in the fire of that love's lunacy   46
Hath he burnt up himself, consum'd his credit,
Lost the king's love, yea, and I fear, his life,
Only to get a wanton to his wife.
Dodger, it is so.   50

Dodger.   I fear so, my good lord.

Linc. It is so — nay, sure it cannot be!
I am at my wits' end.   Dodger!

Dodger.   Yea, my lord.

Linc. Thou art acquainted with my neph-
ew's haunts,   55
Spend this gold for thy pains; go seek him out.
Watch at my lord mayor's — there if he live,
Dodger, thou shalt be sure to meet with him.
Prithee, be diligent. — Lacy, thy name
Liv'd once in honor, now 'tis dead in shame. —
Be circumspect.   61

Dodger. I warrant you, my lord.   (*Exeunt.*

SCENE 3.   *A room in the* LORD MAYOR'S
house at London

Enter the LORD MAYOR *and* SCOTT

L. Mayor. Good Master Scott, I have been
bold with you,
To be a witness to a wedding-knot
Betwixt young Master Hammon and my
daughter.
O, stand aside; see where the lovers come.

Enter HAMMON *and* ROSE

Rose. Can it be possible you love me so?   5
No, no, within those eyeballs I espy

   [1] Childish, silly.

Apparent likelihoods of flattery.
Pray now, let go my hand.

Ham.   Sweet Mistress Rose,
Misconstrue not my words, nor misconceive
Of my affection, whose devoted soul   11
Swears that I love thee dearer than my heart.

Rose. As dear as your own heart?   I judge it
     right,
Men love their hearts best when they're out of
     sight.

Ham. I love you, by this hand.   15

Rose.   Yet hands off now!
If flesh be frail, how weak and frail's your
     vow!

Ham. Then by my life I swear.

Rose.   Then do not brawl;
One quarrel loseth wife and life and all.   20
Is not your meaning thus?

Ham.   In faith, you jest.

Rose. Love loves to sport; therefore leave
     love, y' are best.

L. Mayor (aside). What? Square they,[1]
     Master Scott?

Scott (aside). Sir, never doubt,   25
Lovers are quickly in, and quickly out.

Ham. Sweet Rose, be not so strange [2] in
     fancying me.
Nay, never turn aside, shun not my sight;
I am not grown so fond,[3] to fond [4] my love
On any that shall quit [5] it with disdain;   30
If you will love me, so — if not, farewell.

L. Mayor (advancing). Why, how now, lov-
     ers, are you both agreed?

Ham. Yes, faith, my lord.

L. Mayor. 'Tis well, give me your hand.
Give me yours, daughter. — How now, both
     pull back?   35
What means this, girl?

Rose.   I mean to live a maid.

Ham. (aside). But not to die one; pause, ere
     that be said.

L. Mayor. Will you still cross me, still be
     obstinate?

Ham. Nay, chide her not, my lord, for doing
     well: 40
If she can live an happy virgin's life,
'Tis far more blessed than to be a wife.

----

[1] Do they quarrel?   [2] Coy.
[3] Foolish.   [4] Found.   [5] Requite.

Rose. Say, sir, I cannot; I have made a vow,
Whoever be my husband, 'tis not you.

L. Mayor. Your tongue is quick; but Master
     Hammon, know,   45
I bade you welcome to another end.

Ham. What, would you have me pule [1] and
     pine and pray,
With "lovely lady," "mistress of my heart,"
"Pardon your servant," and the rimer play,
Railing on Cupid and his tyrant's-dart;   50
Or shall I undertake some martial spoil,
Wearing your glove at tourney and at tilt,
And tell how many gallants I unhorsed —
Sweet, will this pleasure you?

Rose.   Yea, when wilt begin?   55
What, love rimes, man?   Fie on that deadly
     sin!

L. Mayor. If you will have her, I'll make
     her agree.

Ham. Enforcéd love is worse than hate to
     me.
(Aside) There is a wench keeps shop in the
     Old Change,
To her will I; it is not wealth I seek,   60
I have enough, and will prefer her love
Before the world. — My good lord mayor,
     adieu.
Old love for me, I have no luck with new.
                                        (*Exit.*

L. Mayor. Now, mammet,[2] you have well
     behaved yourself,   64
But you shall curse your coyness if I live. —
Who's within there?   See you convey your
     mistress
Straight to th' Old Ford!   I'll keep you
     straight enough.
Fore God, I would have sworn the puling girl
Would willingly accept of Hammon's love;
But banish him, my thoughts! — Go, minion,[3]
     in!   (*Exit* ROSE.   70
Now tell me, Master Scott, would you have
     thought
That Master Simon Eyre, the shoemaker,
Had been of wealth to buy such merchandise?

Scott. 'Twas well, my lord, your honor and
     myself
Grew partners with him; for your bills of lading
Show that Eyre's gains in one commodity   76

----

[1] Whimper.   [2] Doll.   [3] Creature.

Rise at the least to full three thousand pound
Besides like gain in other merchandise.
L. Mayor. Well, he shall spend some of his
    thousands now,
For I have sent for him to the Guildhall.   80

Enter EYRE

See, where he comes.   Good-morrow, Master
    Eyre.
Eyre. Poor Simon Eyre, my lord, your shoe-
    maker.
L. Mayor. Well, well, it likes yourself [1] to
    term you so.

Enter DODGER

Now, Master Dodger, what's the news with
    you?
Dodger. I'd gladly speak in private to your
    honor.   85
L. Mayor. You shall, you shall. — Master
    Eyre and Master Scott,
I have some business with this gentleman;
I pray, let me entreat you to walk before
To the Guildhall; I'll follow presently.
Master Eyre, I hope ere noon to call you
    sheriff.   90
Eyre. I would not care, my lord, if you
    might call
Me King of Spain. — Come, Master Scott.
            (*Exeunt* EYRE *and* SCOTT.
L. Mayor. Now, Master Dodger, what's the
    news you bring?
Dodger. The Earl of Lincoln by me greets
    your lordship,
And earnestly requests you, if you can,   95
Inform him where his nephew Lacy keeps.
L. Mayor. Is not his nephew Lacy now in
    France?
Dodger. No, I assure your lordship, but dis-
    guised
Lurks here in London.
    L. Mayor.   London?   Is't even so? 100
It may be; but upon my faith and soul,
I know not where he lives, or whether he lives;
So tell my Lord of Lincoln. — Lurks in Lon-
    don?

[1] It is pleasing to you.

Well, Master Dodger, you perhaps may start
    him; [1]
Be but the means to rid [2] him into France, 105
I'll give you a dozen angels [3] for your pains;
So much I love his honor, hate his nephew.
And, prithee, so inform thy lord from me.
Dodger. I take my leave.   (*Exit* DODGER.
L. Mayor. Farewell, good Master Dodger.
Lacy in London?   I dare pawn my life,   111
My daughter knows thereof, and for that cause
Denied young Master Hammon in his love.
Well, I am glad I sent her to Old Ford.
God's Lord, 'tis late; to Guildhall I must hie;
I know my brethren [4] stay my company.   116
                                      (*Exit.*

SCENE 4.   *Before* EYRE'S *house*

Enter FIRK, MARGERY, HANS, *and* HODGE

Marg. Thou goest too fast for me, Roger.
O, Firk!
Firk. Ay, forsooth.
Marg. I pray thee, run — do you hear? —
run to Guildhall, and learn if my husband,   5
Master Eyre, will take that worshipful vocation
of Master Sheriff upon him.   Hie thee, good
Firk.
Firk. Take it?   Well, I go; and he should
not take it, Firk swears to forswear him.   10
Yes, forsooth, I go to Guildhall.
Marg. Nay, when?   Thou art too compen-
dious [5] and tedious.
Firk. O rare, your excellence is full of elo-
quence.   (*Aside*) How like a new cart-   15
wheel my dame speaks,[6] and she looks like an
old musty ale-bottle [7] going to scalding.
Marg. Nay, when?   Thou wilt make me
melancholy.
Firk. God forbid your worship should   20
fall into that humor!   I run.   (*Exit.*

[1] Drive him from cover.   [2] Dispatch.
[3] Gold coins worth in Dekker's day about ten shillings or $2.50.
[4] I.e., the aldermen.
[5] Brief. — Margery, as wife of the sheriff, is trying
out a vocabulary befitting her new position.   Her fresh
learning contradicts her meaning!
[6] Because a new cart-wheel operates with lack of
ease, and so does Margery.
[7] I.e., a leather one.

Marg. Let me see now, Roger and Hans.

Hodge. Ay, forsooth, dame — mistress, I should say, but the old term so sticks to the roof of my mouth, I can hardly lick it off. 25

Marg. Even what thou wilt, good Roger; dame is a fair name for any honest Christian; but let that pass. How dost thou, Hans?

Hans. Mee tanck you, vro.[1]

Marg. Well, Hans and Roger, you see, 30 God hath blest your master, and, perdy, if ever he comes to be Master Sheriff of London — as we are all mortal — you shall see, I will have some odd thing or other in a corner for you; I will not be your back-friend;[2] but let that 35 pass. Hans, pray thee, tie my shoe.

Hans. Yaw, ic sal, vro.

Marg. Roger, thou know'st the length of my foot; as it is none of the biggest, so I thank God, it is handsome enough; prithee, let 40 me have a pair of shoes made, cork,[3] good Roger, wooden heel[4] too.

Hodge. You shall.

Marg. Art thou acquainted with never a farthingale-maker,[5] nor a French hood- 45 maker? I must enlarge my bum,[6] ha, ha! How shall I look in a hood, I wonder! Perdy, oddly, I think.

Hodge (aside). As a cat out of[7] a pillory.[8] — Very well, I warrant you, mistress. 50

Marg. Indeed, all flesh is grass;[9] and, Roger, canst thou tell where I may buy a good hair?

Hodge. Yes, forsooth, at the poulterer's[10] in Gracious Street.[11]

Marg. Thou are an ungracious wag; 55 perdy, I mean a false hair for my periwig.

Hodge. Why, mistress, the next time I cut my beard, you shall have the shavings of it; but they are all true hairs.

---

[1] Well, I thank you, mistress.   [2] False friend.
[3] I.e., cork-soled shoes, such as ladies of the nobility wear.
[4] I.e., high-heeled — the fashionable type.
[5] Maker of hoop skirts.   [6] Buttocks.   [7] In.
[8] The French hood framed the wearer's face much as the pillory encircled the head of its victim.
[9] A Biblical saying from *I Peter*, 1: 24.
[10] Poultry shop. — Hodge pretends to think that Margery wants a "hare."
[11] Colloquial name for Grace Church Street, which ran to the north end of London Bridge.

Marg. It is very hot, I must get me a 60 fan or else a mask.

Hodge (aside). So you had need, to hide your wicked face.

Marg. Fie upon it, how costly this world's calling is; perdy, but that it is one of the 65 wonderful works of God, I would not deal with it.[1] Is not Firk come yet? Hans, be not so sad, let it pass and vanish, as my husband's worship says. 69

Hans. Ick bin vrolicke, lot see yow soo.[2]

Hodge. Mistress, will you drink[3] a pipe of tobacco?

Marg. Oh, fie upon it, Roger, perdy! These filthy tobacco-pipes are the most idle slavering baubles that ever I felt. Out upon it! 75 God bless us, men look not like men that use them.

Enter RALPH, *being lame*

Hodge. What, fellow Ralph? Mistress, look here, Jane's husband! Why, how now, lame? Hans, make much of him, he's a 80 brother of our trade, a good workman, and a tall[4] soldier.

Hans. You be welcome, broder.

Marg. Perdy, I knew him not. How dost thou, good Ralph? I am glad to see thee 85 well.

Ralph. I would to God you saw me, dame, as well
As when I went from London into France.

Marg. Trust me, I am sorry, Ralph, to see thee impotent.[5] Lord, how the wars have 90 made him sunburnt! The left leg is not well; 'twas a fair gift of God the infirmity took not hold a little higher, considering thou camest from France; but let that pass.

Ralph. I am glad to see you well, and I rejoice 95
To hear that God hath blest my master so
Since my departure.

Marg. Yea, truly, Ralph, I thank my Maker; but let that pass.

---

[1] I.e., part with my face.
[2] I'm happy, let's see you so.
[3] Smoke.   [4] Brave.
[5] Incapacitated.

Hodge. And, sirrah Ralph, what news, what news in France?   101
Ralph. Tell me, good Roger, first, what
    news in England?
How does my Jane?   When didst thou see my
    wife?
Where lives my poor heart?   She'll be poor
    indeed,
Now I want limbs to get whereon to feed.   105
Hodge. Limbs?   Hast thou not hands, man?
Thou shalt never see a shoemaker want bread,
though he have but three fingers on a hand.
Ralph. Yet all this while I hear not of my
    Jane.
Marg. O Ralph, your wife, —perdy, we   110
know not what's become of her.   She was here
a while, and because she was married, grew
more stately [1] than became her; I check'd [2]
her, and so forth; away she flung, never returned, nor said bye nor bah; and, Ralph,   115
you know, "ka me, ka thee." [3]   And, so as I
tell ye —— Roger, is not Firk come yet?
Hodge. No, forsooth.
Marg. And so, indeed, we heard not of her,
but I hear she lives in London; but let that   120
pass.   If she had wanted, she might have
opened her case to me or my husband, or to
any of my men; I am sure, there's not any of
them, perdy, but would have done her good
to his power.   Hans, look if Firk be   125
come.
Hans. Yaw, ik sal, vro. [4]   (*Exit.*
Marg. And so, as I said — but, Ralph, why
dost thou weep?   Thou knowest that naked
we came out of our mother's womb, and   130
naked we must return; [5] and, therefore, thank
God for all things.
Hodge. No, faith, Jane is a stranger here;
but, Ralph, pull up a good heart, I know thou
hast one.   Thy wife, man, is in London;   135
one told me, he saw her a while ago very brave [6]
and neat; we'll ferret her out, an London hold
her.

Marg. Alas, poor soul, he's overcome with
sorrow; he does but as I do, weep for the   140
loss of any good thing.   But, Ralph, get thee
in, call for some meat and drink, thou shalt
find me worshipful towards thee.
Ralph. I thank you, dame; since I want
    limbs and lands,
I'll trust to God, my good friends, and these
    my hands.   145

Enter HANS *and* FIRK *running*

Firk. Run, good Hans! O Hodge, O mistress!
Hodge, heave up thine ears; mistress, smug up [1]
your looks; on with your best apparel; my
master is chosen, my master is called, nay,
condemn'd by the cry [2] of the country to   150
be sheriff of the city for this famous year now
to come.   And, time now being, a great many
men in black gowns were askt for their voices [3]
and their hands, and my master had all their
fists about his ears presently, and they   155
cried, "Aye, aye, aye, aye" — and so I came
away ——
Wherefore without all other grieve
    I do salute you, Mistress Shrieve. [4]
Hans. Yaw, my mester is de groot man,   160
de shrieve. [5]
Hodge. Did I not tell you, mistress?   Now
I may boldly say: Good-morrow to your
worship.
Marg. Good-morrow, good Roger.   I   165
thank you, my good people all. — Firk, hold
up thy hand: here's a three-penny piece for
thy tidings.
Firk. 'Tis but three-half-pence, I think.   Yes,
'tis three-pence, I smell the rose. [6]   170
Hodge. But, mistress, be rul'd by me, and do
not speak so pulingly. [7]
Firk. 'Tis her worship [8] speaks so, and not
she.   No, faith, mistress, speak me in the old
key: "To it, Firk"; "there, good Firk";   175
"ply your business, Hodge"; "Hodge, with a

---

[1] Grand.   [2] Rebuked.
[3] A proverbial phrase meaning "I serve you as you
serve me."
[4] Yes, I will, mistress.
[5] Another Biblical quotation, from *Job* 1: 21.
[6] Smartly dressed.

[1] Spruce up.   [2] Vote.   [3] Votes.   [4] Sheriff.
[5] Yes, my master is the great man, the sheriff.
[6] The silver threepence bore the head of Queen Elizabeth, and a rose on the obverse side.
[7] Simperingly.
[8] I.e., Margery in her rôle of the sheriff's wife.

full mouth"; "I'll fill your bellies with good cheer, till they cry twang."

Enter EYRE *wearing a gold chain*

Hans. See, myn liever broder, heer compt my meester.[1]   180

Marg. Welcome home, Master Shrieve; I pray God continue you in health and wealth.

Eyre. See here, my Maggy, a chain, a gold chain for Simon Eyre. I shall make thee a lady; here's a French hood for thee; on 185 with it, on with it! dress thy brows with this flap of a shoulder of mutton,[2] to make thee look lovely. Where be my fine men? Roger, I'll make over my shop and tools to thee; Firk, thou shalt be the foreman; Hans, thou 190 shalt have an hundred for twenty.[3] Be as mad knaves as your master Sim Eyre hath been, and you shall live to be sheriffs of London. — How dost thou like me, Margery? Prince am I none, yet am I princely born. Firk, 195 Hodge, and Hans!

All Three. Aye, forsooth, what says your worship, Master Sheriff?

Eyre. Worship and honor, you Babylonian knaves, for the gentle craft. But I forgot 200 myself, I am bidden by my lord mayor to dinner to Old Ford; he's gone before, I must after. Come, Madge, on with your trinkets! Now, my true Trojans, my fine Firk, my dapper Hodge, my honest Hans, some device,[4] 205 some odd crotchets,[5] some morris,[6] or such like, for the honor of the gentle shoemakers. Meet me at Old Ford, you know my mind. Come, Madge, away. Shut up the shops, knaves, and make holiday.   210

                (*Exeunt* EYRE *and* MARGERY.

Firk. O rare! O brave! Come, Hodge; follow me, Hans;
We'll be with them for a morris-dance.
                         (*Exeunt.*

[1] See, my dear brothers, here comes my master.
[2] I.e., the French hood, which was dark-colored material trimmed with white wool or light-colored fur.
[3] I.e., for the twenty "Portagues" which Hans lent to purchase the ship's merchandise.
[4] Entertainment.
[5] Odd tricks.
[6] Morris dance.

SCENE 5. *A room in the* LORD MAYOR'S *house at Old Ford*

Enter the LORD MAYOR, ROSE, EYRE, MARGERY *in a French hood,* SYBIL, *and other servants*

L. Mayor. Trust me, you are as welcome to Old Ford
As I myself.
  Marg.   Truly, I thank your lordship.
L. Mayor. Would our bad cheer were worth the thanks you give.   4
Eyre. Good cheer, my lord mayor, fine cheer! A fine house, fine walls, all fine and neat.
L. Mayor. Now, by my troth, I'll tell thee, Master Eyre,
It does me good, and all my brethren,
That such a madcap fellow as thyself
Is ent'red into our society.   10
Marg. Aye, but, my lord, he must learn now to put on gravity.
Eyre. Peace, Maggy, a fig for gravity! When I go to Guildhall in my scarlet gown, I'll look as demurely as a saint, and speak as gravely as a justice of peace, but now I am 15 here at Old Ford, at my good lord mayor's house, let it go by, vanish, Maggy, I'll be merry; away with flip-flap,[1] these fooleries, these gulleries. What, honey? Prince am I none, yet am I princely born. What says 20 my lord mayor?
L. Mayor. Ha, ha, ha! I had rather than a thousand pound, I had an heart but half so light as yours.
Eyre. Why, what should I do, my lord? 25 A pound of care pays not a dram of debt. Hum, let's be merry, whiles we are young; old age, sack and sugar will steal upon us, ere we be aware.

The First Three Men's Song [2]

O the month of May, the merry month of May,
  So frolic, so gay, and so green, so green, so green!   31
O, and then did I unto my true love say:
  "Sweet Peg, thou shalt be my summer's queen!

[1] An allusion probably to Margery's French hood.
[2] Song for three male voices.

"Now the nightingale, the pretty nightingale,
  The sweetest singer in the forest's choir, 35
Entreats thee, sweet Peggy, to hear thy true
    love's tale;
  Lo, yonder she sitteth, her breast against a
    brier.

"But O, I spy the cuckoo, the cuckoo, the
    cuckoo;
  See where she sitteth: come away, my joy;
Come away, I prithee! I do not like the cuckoo
  Should sing where my Peggy and I kiss and
    toy." 41

O the month of May, the merry month of May,
  So frolic, so gay, and so green, so green, so
    green!
And then did I unto my true love say:
  "Sweet Peg, thou shalt be my summer's
    queen!" 45

  L. Mayor. It's well done. — Mistress Eyre,
pray, give good counsel to my daughter.
  Marg. I hope Mistress Rose will have the
grace to take nothing that's bad.
  L. Mayor. Pray God she do; for i' faith,
    Mistress Eyre, 50
I would bestow upon that peevish [1] girl
A thousand marks [2] more than I mean to give
    her
Upon condition she'd be ruled by me.
The ape still crosseth me. There came of late
A proper gentleman of fair revenues, 55
Whom gladly I would call son-in-law:
But my fine cockney [3] would have none of
    him. —
(*To* ROSE) You'll prove a coxcomb [4] for it, ere
    you die;
A courtier, or no man, must please your eye.
  Eyre. Be ruled, sweet Rose: th' art ripe 60
for a man. Marry not with a boy that has no
more hair on his face than thou hast on thy
cheeks. A courtier? Wash, go by! stand not
upon pishery-pashery; those silken fellows are
but painted images, outsides, outsides, 65

  [1] Silly.
  [2] A mark of silver was worth about two-thirds of a
pound or about $3.25.
  [3] Spoiled darling.   [4] Fool.

Rose; their inner linings are torn. No, my fine
mouse, marry me with a gentleman grocer like
my lord mayor, your father; a grocer is a sweet
trade; plums, plums. Had I a son or daughter
should marry out of the generation and 70
blood of the shoemakers, he should pack; what,
the Gentle Trade is a living for a man through
Europe, through the world.
  (*A noise within of a tabor* [1] *and a pipe.*
  L. Mayor. What noise is this?
  Eyre. O my lord mayor, a crew of good 75
fellows that for love to your honor are come
hither with a morris-dance. — Come in, my
Mesopotamians, cheerily.

Enter HODGE, HANS, RALPH, FIRK, *and other
  shoemakers, in a morris; after a little dancing the* LORD MAYOR *speaks*

  L. Mayor. Master Eyre, are all these shoe-
makers?
  Eyre. All cordwainers, my good lord mayor.
  Rose (*aside*). How like my Lacy looks yond'
shoemaker! 81
  Hans (*aside*). O that I durst but speak unto
my love!
  L. Mayor. Sybil, go fetch some wine to make
these drink.
You are all welcome.
  All.   We thank your lordship.
  (ROSE *takes a cup of wine and goes to*
    HANS.
  Rose. For his sake whose fair shape thou
    represent'st, 86
Good friend, I drink to thee.
  Hans. Ic bedancke, good frister. [2]
  Marg. I see, Mistress Rose, you do not want
judgment; you have drunk to the properest [3]
man I keep. 91
  Firk. Here be some have done their parts to
be as proper as he.
  L. Mayor. Well, urgent business calls me
back to London.
Good fellows, first go in and taste our cheer;
And to make merry as you homeward go, 96
Spend these two angels in beer at Stratford-
  Bow.

  [1] Small drum.   [2] I thank you, good miss.
  [3] Handsomest.

Eyre. To these two, my mad lads, Sim Eyre adds another; then cheerily, Firk; tickle it, Hans, and all for the honor of shoemakers.

　　　(*All the shoemakers go dancing out.*

L. Mayor. Come, Master Eyre, let's have
　　your company.　　　(*Exeunt.*　101

Rose. Sybil, what shall I do?

Sybil.　　　　Why, what's the matter?

Rose. That Hans the shoemaker is my love
　　Lacy,
Disguised in that attire to find me out.　105
How should I find the means to speak with him?

Sybil. What, mistress, never fear; I dare venture my maidenhead to nothing, and that's great odds, that Hans the Dutchman, when we come to London, shall not only see and　110 speak with you, but in spite of all your father's policies steal you away and marry you. Will not this please you?

Rose. Do this, and ever be assured of my love.

Sybil. Away, then, and follow your father to London, lest your absence cause him to　116 suspect something:
　　Tomorrow, if my counsel be obeyed,
　　I'll bind you prentice to the Gentle Trade.

　　　　　　　　　　(*Exeunt.*

ACT IV

Scene i. *A street in London*

Jane *discovered in a seamster's shop,*[1] *working. Enter at a door* Hammon, *muffled; he stands aloof*

Ham. Yonder's the shop, and there my fair
　　love sits.
She's fair and lovely, but she is not mine.
O, would she were!　Thrice have I courted her,
Thrice hath my hand been moistened with her
　　hand,　　　　　　　　　　　　　　4
Whilst my poor famished eyes do feed on that
Which made them famish.　I am infortunate;
I still love one, yet nobody loves me.
I muse[2] in other men what women see,
That I so want!　Fine Mistress Rose was coy,
And this too curious![3]　Oh, no, she is chaste,　10

[1] The curtains of the inner stage draw apart to reveal the shop and Jane within.
[2] Wonder.　　[3] Too fastidious.

And for[1] she thinks me wanton, she denies
To cheer my cold heart with her sunny eyes.
How prettily she works!　Oh, pretty hand!
Oh, happy work!　It doth me good to stand
Unseen to see her.　Thus I oft have stood　15
In frosty evenings, a light burning by her,
Enduring biting cold, only to eye her.
One only look hath seemed as rich to me
As a king's crown; such is love's lunacy.
Muffled I'll pass along, and by that try　20
Whether she know me.

Jane.　　　　Sir, what is 't you buy?
What is 't you lack, sir, calico or lawn,
Fine cambric shirts, or bands, what will you
　　buy?

Ham. (*aside*). That which thou wilt not sell.
　　Faith, yet I'll try. —　　　　　25
How do you sell this handkerchief?

Jane.　　　　　　Good cheap.[2]

Ham. And how these ruffs?

Jane.　　　　　　Cheap too.

Ham.　　　　　And how this band?　30

Jane. Cheap too.

Ham.　　　　All cheap, how sell you
　　then this hand?

Jane. My hands are not to be sold.

Ham.　　　　　　To be given then!
Nay, faith, I come to buy.　　　　35

Jane.　　　　But none knows when.

Ham. Good sweet, leave work a little while;
　　let's play.

Jane. I cannot live by keeping holiday.

Ham. I'll pay you for the time which shall
　　be lost.

Jane. With me you shall not be at so much
　　cost.　　　　　　　　　40

Ham. Look, how you wound[3] this cloth, so
　　you wound me.

Jane. It may be so.

Ham.　　　　'Tis so.

Jane.　　　　　　What remedy?

Ham. Nay, faith, you are too coy.　　45

Jane.　　　　　Let go my hand.

Ham. I will do any task at your command;
I would let go this beauty, were I not
In mind to disobey you by a power
That controls kings: I love you!　　　50

[1] And because.　　[2] At a bargain.
[3] I.e., by cutting it with her scissors.

Jane.   So, now part.

Ham. With hands I may, but never with my
    heart.

In faith, I love you.

Jane.   I believe you do.

Ham. Shall a true love in me breed hate in
    you?   55

Jane. I hate you not.

Ham.   Then you must love.

Jane.   I do.

What are you better now?   I love not you.

Ham. All this, I hope, is but a woman's fray,

That means, "Come to me," when she cries,
    "Away!"   61

In earnest, mistress, I do not jest,

A true chaste love hath ent'red in my breast.

I love you dearly, as I love my life,

I love you as a husband loves a wife;   65

That, and no other love, my love requires.

Thy wealth, I know, is little; my desires

Thirst not for gold.   Sweet, beauteous Jane,
    what's mine

Shall, if thou make myself thine, all be thine.

Say, judge, what is thy sentence, life or death?

Mercy or cruelty lies in thy breath.   71

Jane. Good sir, I do believe you love me
    well;

For 'tis a silly conquest, silly pride

For one like you — I mean a gentleman —

To boast that by his love-tricks he hath brought

Such and such women to his amorous lure;   76

I think you do not so, yet many do,

And make it even a very trade to woo.

I could be coy, as many women be,

Feed you with sunshine smiles and wanton looks,

But I detest witchcraft; say that I   81

Do constantly believe you constant have ——

Ham. Why dost thou not believe me?

Jane.   I believe you;   84

But yet, good sir, because I will not grieve you

With hopes to taste fruit which will never fall,

In simple truth this is the sum of all:

My husband lives, at least, I hope he lives.

Prest was he to these bitter wars in France;

Bitter they are to me by wanting him.   90

I have but one heart, and that heart's his due.

How can I then bestow the same on you?

Whilst he lives, his I live, be it ne'er so poor,

And rather be his wife than a king's whore.

Ham. Chaste and dear woman, I will not
    abuse thee,   95

Although it cost my life, if thou refuse me.

Thy husband, prest for France, what was his
    name?

Jane. Ralph Damport.

Ham. Damport? — Here's a letter sent

From France to me, from a dear friend of
    mine,   100

A gentleman of place; here he doth write

Their names that have been slain in every fight.

Jane. I hope death's scroll contains not my
    love's name.

Ham. Cannot you read?

Jane.   I can.   105

Ham.   Peruse the same.

To my remembrance such a name I read

Amongst the rest.   See here.

Jane.   Ay me, he's dead!

He's dead!   If this be true, my dear heart's
    slain!   110

Ham. Have patience, dear love.

Jane.   Hence, hence!

Ham.   Nay, sweet Jane,

Make not poor sorrow proud with these rich
    tears.

I mourn thy husband's death, because thou
    mourn'st.   115

Jane. That bill is forg'd; 'tis sign'd by
    forgery.

Ham. I'll bring thee letters sent besides to
    many,

Carrying the like report: Jane, 'tis too true.

Come, weep not: mourning, though it rise from
    love,

Helps not the mourned, yet hurts them that
    mourn.   120

Jane. For God's sake, leave me.

Ham.   Whither dost thou turn?

Forget the dead, love them that are alive;

His love is faded, try how mine will thrive.

Jane. 'Tis now no time for me to think on
    love.   125

Ham. 'Tis now best time for you to think
    on love,

Because your love lives not.

Jane.   Though he be dead,

My love to him shall not be buried;

For God's sake, leave me to myself alone.   130

Ham. 'Twould kill my soul, to leave thee
          drown'd in moan.
Answer me to my suit, and I am gone;
Say to me yea or no.
     Jane.   No.
     Ham.   Then farewell! 135
One farewell will not serve, I come again;
Come, dry these wet cheeks; tell me, faith,
          sweet Jane,
Yea or no, once more.
     Jane.   Once more I say no;
Once more be gone, I pray; else will I go. 140
     Ham. Nay, then, I will grow rude, by this
          white hand,
Until you change that cold "no"; here I'll stand
Till by your hard heart ——
     Jane.   Nay, for God's love, peace!
My sorrows by your presence more increase.
Not that you thus are present, but all grief 146
Desires to be alone; therefore in brief
Thus much I say, and saying bid adieu:
If ever I wed man, it shall be you.
     Ham. O blessed voice! Dear Jane, I'll urge
          no more,   150
Thy breath hath made me rich.
     Jane.   Death makes me poor. (*Exeunt.*

SCENE 2. HODGE'S *shop*

Enter HODGE, *at his shop-board*, RALPH, FIRK,
     HANS, *and a Boy at work* [1]

All. Hey, down a down, down derry.
Hodge. Well said, my hearts; ply your work
today, we loit'red yesterday; to it pell-mell,
that we may live to be lord mayors, or alder-
men at least.   5
Firk. Hey, down a down, derry.
Hodge. Well said, i' faith! How say'st thou,
Hans, doth not Firk tickle it? [2]
Hans. Yaw, mester. [3]
Firk. Not so neither, my organ-pipe 10
squeaks this morning for want of liquoring.
Hey, down a down, derry!
Hans. Forware, Firk, tow best un jolly young-

ster. — Hort 'ee, mester, ic bid yo cut me un pair
vampres vor Mester Jeffre's boots. [1]   15
Hodge. Thou shalt, Hans.
Firk. Master!
Hodge. How now, boy?
Firk. Pray, now you are in the cutting vein,
cut me out a pair of counterfeits, [2] or else 20
my work will not pass current; hey, down a
down!
Hodge. Tell me, sirs, are my cousin Mistress
Priscilla's shoes done?
Firk. Your cousin? No, master; one 25
of your aunts, [3] hang her; let them alone.
Ralph. I am in hand with them; [4] she gave
charge that none but I should do them for her.
Firk. Thou do for her? Then 'twill be a
lame doing, and that she loves not. Ralph, 30
thou might'st have sent her to me, in faith, I
would have yarked and firked your Priscilla.
Hey, down a down, derry. This gear [5] will not
hold.
Hodge. How say'st thou, Firk, were we 35
not merry at Old Ford?
Firk. How, merry! Why, our buttocks went
jiggy-joggy like a quagmire. Well, Sir Roger
Oatmeal, [6] if I thought all meal of that nature,
I would eat nothing but bagpuddings.   40
Ralph. Of all good fortunes my fellow Hans
had the best.
Firk. 'Tis true, because Mistress Rose drank
to him.
Hodge. Well, well, work apace. They 45
say, seven of the aldermen be dead, or very sick.
Firk. I care not, I'll be none.
Ralph. No, nor I; but then my Master Eyre
will come quickly to be lord mayor.

Enter SYBIL

Firk. Whoop, yonder comes Sybil.   50
Hodge. Sybil, welcome i' faith; and how dost
thou, mad wench?

----

[1] The shoemakers enter and work upon the inner
stage, the curtains of which remain drawn from the preceding shop scene.
[2] Make it go.
[3] Yes, master.

[1] Truly, Firk, you are a jolly youngster. — Listen,
master, I pray you cut me a pair of vamps for Master
Jeffrey's boots.
[2] Patterns. — A play on words is intended in connection with "pass current."
[3] Mistresses.   [4] I am at work on them.
[5] Business.
[6] A play on the Lord Mayor's name, Oateley.

Firk. Sib-whore,[1] welcome to London.

Sybil. Godamercy, sweet Firk; good lord, Hodge, what a delicious shop you have got! 55 You tickle it, i' faith.

Ralph. Godamercy, Sybil, for our good cheer at Old Ford.

Sybil. That you shall have, Ralph.

Firk. Nay, by the mass, we had tickling 60 cheer, Sybil; and how the plague dost thou and Mistress Rose and my lord mayor? I put the women in first.

Sybil. Well, Godamercy; but God's me, I forget myself, where's Hans the Fleming? 65

Firk. Hark, butter-box, now you must yelp out some *spreken*.[2]

Hans. Wat begaie you? Vat vod you, frister?[3]

Sybil. Marry, you must come to my young mistress, to pull on her shoes you made last. 70

Hans. Vare ben your egle fro, vare ben your mistris?[4]

Sybil. Marry, here at our London house in Cornhill.   74

Firk. Will nobody serve her turn but Hans?

Sybil. No, sir. Come, Hans, I stand upon needles.[5]

Hodge. Why, then, Sybil, take heed of pricking.

Sybil. For that let me alone. I have a 80 trick in my budget. Come, Hans.

Hans. Yaw, yaw, ic sall meete yo gane.[6]

(*Exeunt* HANS *and* SYBIL.

Hodge. Go, Hans, make haste again. Come, who lacks work?

Firk. I, master, for I lack my breakfast; 85 'tis munching-time, and past.

Hodge. Is 't so? Why, then, leave work, Ralph. To breakfast! Boy, look to the tools. Come, Ralph; come, Firk.   (*Exeunt.*

SCENE 3. *Before* HODGE'S *shop*

Enter a Serving-man

Serv. Let me see, now, the sign of the Last in Tower Street. Mass, yonder's the house. What, haw! Who's within?

[1] Another bit of word-play. "Sib" means "kin to."
[2] Some words.
[3] What do you want? What would you, girl?
[4] Where is your noble lady; where is your mistress?
[5] I am in a hurry.   [6] Yes, yes, I'll go with you.

Enter RALPH

Ralph. Who calls there? What want you, sir?   5

Serv. Marry, I would have a pair of shoes made for a gentlewoman against tomorrow morning. What, can you do them?

Ralph. Yes, sir, you shall have them. But what length's her foot?   10

Serv. Why, you must make them in all parts like this shoe; but, at any hand,[1] fail not to do them, for the gentlewoman is to be married very early in the morning.

Ralph. How? By this shoe must it be 15 made? By this? Are you sure, sir, by this?

Serv. How, by this? Am I sure, by this? Art thou in thy wits? I tell thee, I must have a pair of shoes, dost thou mark me? A pair of shoes, two shoes, made by this very shoe, 20 this same shoe, against tomorrow morning by four o'clock. Dost understand me? Canst thou do 't?

Ralph. Yes, sir, yes — Ay, ay! — I can do 't. By this shoe, you say? I should know this 25 shoe. Yes, sir, yes, by this shoe, I can do 't. Four o'clock, well. Whither shall I bring them?

Serv. To the sign of the Golden Ball in Watling Street; enquire for one Master Hammon, a gentleman, my master.   30

Ralph. Yea, sir; by this shoe, you say?

Serv. I say, Master Hammon at the Golden Ball; he's the bridegroom, and those shoes are for his bride.

Ralph. They shall be done by this shoe; 35 well, well, Master Hammon at the Golden Shoe — I would say, the Golden Ball; very well, very well. But I pray you, sir; where must Master Hammon be married?

Serv. At Saint Faith's Church, under 40 Paul's.[2] But what's that to thee? Prithee, dispatch those shoes, and so farewell. (*Exit.*

Ralph. By this shoe, said he. How am I amazed
At this strange accident! Upon my life,
This was the very shoe I gave my wife, 45
When I was pressed for France; since when, alas!

[1] By all means.
[2] A parish church beneath the choir of St. Paul's Cathedral.

I never could hear of her: 'tis the same,
And Hammon's bride no other but my Jane.

Enter FIRK

Firk. 'Snails,[1] Ralph, thou hast lost thy part
of three pots, a countryman of mine gave 50
me to breakfast.
   Ralph. I care not; I have found a better thing.
   Firk. A thing? Away! Is it a man's thing,
or a woman's thing?
   Ralph. Firk, dost thou know this shoe? 55
   Firk. No, by my troth; neither doth that
know me! I have no acquaintance with it,
'tis a mere stranger to me.
   Ralph. Why, then I do; this shoe, I durst be
     sworn,
Once covered the instep of my Jane. 60
This is her size, her breadth, thus trod my love;
These true-love knots I pricked; I hold my life,
By this old shoe I shall find out my wife.
   Firk. Ha, ha! Old shoe, that wert new!
How a murrain[2] came this ague-fit of fool- 65
ishness upon thee?
   Ralph. Thus, Firk: even now here came a
     serving-man:
By this shoe would he have a new pair made
Against tomorrow morning for his mistress,
That's to be married to a gentleman. 70
And why may not this be my sweet Jane?
   Firk. And why may'st not thou be my sweet
ass? Ha, ha!
   Ralph. Well, laugh and spare not! But the
     truth is this:
Against tomorrow morning I'll provide 75
A lusty[3] crew of honest shoemakers,
To watch the going of the bride to church.
If she prove Jane, I'll take her in despite[4]
From Hammon and the devil, were he by.
If it be not my Jane, what remedy? 80
Hereof I am sure, I shall live till I die,
Although I never with a woman lie. (*Exit.*
   Firk. Thou lie with a woman, to build
nothing but Cripplegates![5] Well, God sends

---

[1] God's nails.   [2] Plague.   [3] Valiant.
[4] Defiance.
[5] A pun on Ralph's lameness. Cripplegate in the old
London wall was so called because cripples begged
there.

fools fortune, and it may be, he may light 85
upon his matrimony[1] by such a device; for
wedding and hanging goes by destiny. (*Exit.*

SCENE 4. *A room in the* LORD MAYOR'S
house in London

Enter HANS *and* ROSE, *arm in arm*

   Hans. How happy am I by embracing thee!
Oh, I did fear such cross mishaps did reign
That I should never see my Rose again.
   Rose. Sweet Lacy, since fair opportunity
Offers herself to further our escape, 5
Let no too over-fond esteem of me
Hinder that happy hour. Invent the means,
And Rose will follow thee through all the
     world.
   Hans. Oh, how I surfeit with excess of joy,
Made happy by thy rich perfection! 10
But since thou pay'st sweet interest to my
     hopes,
Redoubling love on love, let me once more
Like to a bold-faced debtor crave of thee,
This night to steal abroad, and at Eyre's house,
Who now by death of certain aldermen 15
Is mayor of London, and my master once,
Meet thou thy Lacy, where in spite of change,
Your father's anger, and mine uncle's hate,
Our happy nuptials will we consummate.

Enter SYBIL

   Sybil. Oh God, what will you do, mis- 20
tress? Shift for yourself, your father is at hand!
He's coming, he's coming! Master Lacy, hide
yourself in my mistress! For God's sake, shift
for yourselves!
   Hans. Your father come! Sweet Rose, what
     shall I do? 25
Where shall I hide me? How shall I escape?
   Rose. A man, and want wit in extremity?
Come, come, be Hans still, play the shoemaker,
Pull on my shoe.
   Hans. Mass, and that's well remembered.

Enter the LORD MAYOR

   Sybil. Here comes your father. 31

---

[1] I.e., his wife.

Hans. Forware, metresse, 'tis un good skow;
it sal vel dute, or ye sal neit betallen.[1]

Rose. Oh God, it pincheth me; what will
you do? 　　　　35

Hans (aside). Your father's presence pincheth, not the shoe.

L. Mayor. Well done; fit my daughter well,
and she shall please well.

Hans. Yaw, yaw, ick weit dat well; for- 40
ware, 'tis un good skoo, 'tis gimait van neitz
leither: se ever, mine here.[2]

Enter a Prentice

L. Mayor. I do believe it. — What's the
news with you?

Prentice. Please you, the Earl of Lincoln at
the gate
Is newly lighted,[3] and would speak with you.

L. Mayor. The Earl of Lincoln come to
speak with me? 　　　　46
Well, well, I know his errand. Daughter
Rose,
Send hence your shoemaker, dispatch, have
done!
Syb, make things handsome! Sir boy, follow
me. 　　　　(*Exit with the Prentice.*

Hans. Mine uncle come! Oh, what may
this portend? 　　　　50
Sweet Rose, this of our love threatens an
end.

Rose. Be not dismay'd at this; whate'er
befall,
Rose is thine own. To witness I speak
truth,
Where thou appoint'st the place, I'll meet with
thee.
I will not fix a day to follow thee, 　　　　55
But presently[4] steal hence. Do not reply:
Love, which gave strength to bear my father's
hate,
Shall now add wings to further our escape.
　　　　　　　　　　　　(*Exeunt.*

[1] Truly, mistress, 'tis a good shoe; it will do, or you
shall not pay for it.

[2] Yes, yes, I know that well; truly, 'tis a good shoe,
'tis made of neat's leather: see here, sir.

[3] Dismounted.

[4] Immediately.

SCENE 5. *The same*

Enter the LORD MAYOR *and the* EARL OF
Lincoln

L. Mayor. Believe me, on my credit, I speak
truth:
Since first your nephew Lacy went to France
I have not seen him. It seem'd strange to me,
When Dodger told me that he stay'd behind,
Neglecting the high charge the king imposed.

Lincoln. Trust me, Sir Roger Oateley, I did
think 　　　　6
Your counsel had given head to this attempt,
Drawn to it by the love he bears your child.
Here I did hope to find him in your house;
But now I see mine error, and confess, 　　　　10
My judgment wrong'd you by conceiving so.

L. Mayor. Lodge in my house, say you?
Trust me, my lord,
I love your nephew Lacy too too dearly,
So much to wrong his honor; and he hath
done so,
That first gave him advice to stay from France.
To witness I speak truth, I let you know 　　　　16
How careful I have been to keep my daughter
Free from all conference or speech of him;
Not that I scorn your nephew, but in love
I bear your honor, lest your noble blood 　　　　20
Should by my mean worth be dishonored.

Lincoln (aside). How far the churl's tongue
wanders from his heart! —
Well, well, Sir Roger Oateley, I believe you, 23
With more than many thanks for the kind love
So much you seem to bear me. But, my lord,
Let me request your help to seek my nephew,
Whom if I find, I'll straight embark for France.
So shall your Rose be free, my thoughts at
rest,
And much care die which now lies in my breast.

Enter SYBIL

Sybil. Oh Lord! Help, for God's sake! 30
My mistress; oh, my young mistress!

L. Mayor. Where is thy mistress? What's
become of her?

Sybil. She's gone, she's fled!

L. Mayor. Gone! Whither is she fled? 35

Sybil. I know not, forsooth; she's fled out of

doors with Hans the shoemaker; I saw them scud,[1] scud, scud, apace, apace!

L. Mayor. Which way? What, John![2] Where be my men? Which way?   40

Sybil. I know not, an it please your worship.

L. Mayor. Fled with a shoemaker? Can this be true?

Sybil. Oh Lord, sir, as true as God's in Heaven.   45

Lincoln. Her love turn'd shoemaker? I am glad of this.

L. Mayor. A Fleming butter-box, a shoemaker!
Will she forget her birth, requite my care
With such ingratitude? Scorn'd she young Hammon   50
To love a honniken,[3] a needy knave?
Well, let her fly. I'll not fly after her.
Let her starve, if she will: she's none of mine.

Lincoln. Be not so cruel, sir.

Enter FIRK *with shoes*

Sybil.   I am glad she's scapt.   55

L. Mayor. I'll not account of her as of my child.
Was there no better object for her eyes,
But a foul drunken lubber, swill-belly,
A shoemaker? That's brave![4]

Firk. Yea, forsooth; 'tis a very brave   60 shoe, and as fit as a pudding.[5]

L. Mayor. How now, what knave is this? From whence comest thou?

Firk. No knave, sir. I am Firk the shoemaker, lusty Roger's chief lusty journey-   65 man, and I have come hither to take up the pretty leg of sweet Mistress Rose, and thus hoping your worship is in as good health, as I was at the making hereof,[6] I bid you farewell, yours, Firk.   70

L. Mayor. Stay, stay, Sir Knave!

Lincoln. Come hither, shoemaker!

Firk. 'Tis happy the knave is put before the

shoemaker, or else I would not have vouchsafed to come back to you. I am moved, for I stir.

L. Mayor. My lord, this villain calls us   76 knaves by craft.

Firk. Then 'tis by the gentle craft, and to call one knave gently, is no harm. Sit your worship merry![1] Syb, your young mis-   80 tress — (*Aside*) I'll so bob[2] them, now my Master Eyre is lord mayor of London.

L. Mayor. Tell me, sirrah, whose man are you?

Firk. I am glad to see your worship so   85 merry. I have no maw to this gear,[3] no stomach as yet to a red petticoat.   (*Pointing to* SYBIL.

Lincoln. He means not, sir, to woo you to his maid,
But only doth demand whose man you are.

Firk. I sing now to the tune of Rogero.[4]   90 Roger, my fellow, is now my master.

Lincoln. Sirrah, know'st thou one Hans, a shoemaker?

Firk. Hans, shoemaker? Oh yes, stay, yes, I have him. I tell you what, I speak it in   95 secret: Mistress Rose and he are by this time — no, not so, but shortly are to come over one another[5] with "Can you dance the shaking of the sheets?"[6] It is that Hans — (*Aside*) I'll so gull these diggers![7]   100

L. Mayor. Know'st thou, then, where he is?

Firk. Yes, forsooth; yea, marry!

Lincoln. Canst thou, in sadness[8] ——

Firk. No, forsooth, no, marry!

L. Mayor. Tell me, good honest fellow, where he is,   105
And thou shalt see what I'll bestow on thee.

Firk. Honest fellow? No, sir; not so, sir; my profession is the gentle craft; I care not for seeing, I love feeling; let me feel it here; *aurium tenus*,[9] ten pieces of gold; *genuum*   110

---

[1] Run swiftly.
[2] The Mayor is calling to a servant outside.
[3] Low fellow.
[4] Fine — in a sarcastic sense.
[5] Firk pretends to take the Mayor's remark literally as applying to the shoes.
[6] The making of the shoes.

[1] May your worship be merry!
[2] Fool.
[3] No appetite for this business.
[4] A popular tune of the day.
[5] Approach one another.
[6] Another well-known tune.
[7] Fool these delvers after information.
[8] In seriousness.
[9] Up to the ears. — Firk is playing again on words, pretending "aurium" to be the Latin for "pieces of gold" and "tenus" to stand for "ten."

tenus,[1] ten pieces of silver; and then Firk is
your man — (*aside*) in a new pair of stretchers.[2]

    L. Mayor. Here is an angel,[3] part of thy
    reward,
Which I will give thee; tell me where he is.

    Firk. No point.[4] Shall I betray my 115
brother? No! Shall I prove Judas to Hans?
No! Shall I cry treason to my corporation?
No, I shall be firkt and yerkt then. But give
me your angel; your angel shall tell you.

    Lincoln. Do so, good fellow; 'tis no hurt 120
to thee.

    Firk. Send simpering Syb away.

    L. Mayor. Huswif,[5] get you in. (*Exit* SYBIL.

    Firk. Pitchers have ears, and maids have
wide mouths; but for Hans Prauns, upon 125
my word, tomorrow morning he and young mistress Rose go to this gear, they shall be married
together, by this rush,[6] or else turn Firk to a
firkin of butter, to tan leather withal.

    L. Mayor. But art thou sure of this? 130

    Firk. Am I sure that Paul's steeple is a hand-
ful higher than London Stone,[7] or that the
Pissing-Conduit [8] leaks nothing but pure
Mother Bunch? [9] Am I sure I am lusty Firk?
God's nails, do you think I am so base to 135
gull you?

    Lincoln. Where are they married? Dost
thou know the church?

    Firk. I never go to church, but I know the
name of it; it is a swearing church — stay 140
a while, 'tis — aye, by the mass, no, no — 'tis —
ay, by my troth, no, nor that; 'tis — ay, by my
faith, that, that, 'tis, ay, by my Faith's Church
under Paul's Cross. There they shall be knit
like a pair of stockings, in matrimony; 145
there they'll be inconie.[10]

    [1] Up to the knees.
    [2] Firk is punning on the double meaning of the word:
(1) shoe-stretchers; (2) lies.
    [3] Gold coin worth about $2.50. [4] Not at all. [5] Wench.
    [6] Rushes were used as floor coverings both in resi-
dences and on the playhouse stages.
    [7] An ancient stone to mark the center from which the
Roman roads radiated over England.
    [8] A small conduit in Cornhill, yet a well-known land-
mark.
    [9] I.e., pure water. — Mother Bunch had been a fa-
mous dispenser of ale, but in time her ale grew "slimy."
Then it became a byword for "very thin drink."
    [10] A rare sight.

    Lincoln. Upon my life, my nephew Lacy
    walks
In the disguise of this Dutch shoemaker.

    Firk. Yes, forsooth.

    Lincoln. Doth he not, honest fellow? 150

    Firk. No, forsooth; I think Hans is nobody
but Hans, no spirit.

    L. Mayor. My mind misgives me now, 'tis so
indeed.

    Lincoln. My cousin speaks the language,
knows the trade.

    L. Mayor. Let me request your company,
my lord;
Your honorable presence may, no doubt, 155
Refrain their headstrong rashness, when myself
Going alone perchance may be o'erborne.
Shall I request this favor?

    Lincoln.   This, or what else.[1]

    Firk. Then you must rise betimes,[2] for 160
they mean to fall to their hey-pass and repass,[3]
pindy-pandy, which hand will you have,[4] very
early.

    L. Mayor. My care shall every way equal
    their haste. 164
This night accept your lodging in my house,
The earlier shall we stir, and at Saint Faith's
Prevent this giddy hare-brained nuptial.
This traffic of hot love shall yield cold gains;
They ban [5] our loves, and we'll forbid their
    banns.[6]   (*Exit.*

    Lincoln. At Saint Faith's Church thou say'st?

    Firk. Yes, by their troth. 171

    Lincoln. Be secret, on thy life. (*Exit.*

    Firk. Yes, when I kiss your wife! Ha, ha,
here's no craft in the Gentle Craft. I came
hither of purpose with shoes to Sir Roger's 175
worship, whilst Rose, his daughter, be cony-
catched [7] by Hans. Soft now; these two gulls
will be at Saint Faith's Church tomorrow morning, to take Master Bridegroom and Mistress
Bride napping, and they, in the meantime, 180

    [1] Whatever else you wish.
    [2] Early.
    [3] Terms used by conjurers.
    [4] Terms used in the children's game of handy-dandy.
— All Firk's jargon simply alludes to the exchange of
marriage vows.
    [5] Curse.
    [6] Church notice of a proposed marriage.
    [7] Be stolen away.

shall chop up [1] the matter at the Savoy.[2] But
the best sport is, Sir Roger Oateley will find my
fellow lame Ralph's wife going to marry a gentleman, and then he'll stop her instead of his
daughter. Oh, brave! there will be fine   185
tickling sport. Soft now, what have I to do?
Oh, I know; now a mess of shoemakers meet at
the Woolsack in Ivy Lane. to cozen [3] my gentleman of lame Ralph's wife, that's true.

    Alack, alack!   190
    Girls, hold out tack! [4]
    For now smocks for this jumbling
    Shall go to wrack.   (*Exit.*

ACT V

SCENE I. *A room in* EYRE'S *house*

Enter EYRE, MARGERY, HANS, *and* ROSE

Eyre. This is the morning, then, say, my
bully, my honest Hans, is it not?

Hans. This is the morning that must make us
two happy or miserable; therefore, if you ——

Eyre. Away with these ifs and ans, Hans, 5
and these et caeteras! By mine honor, Rowland Lacy, none but the king shall wrong thee.
Come, fear nothing, am not I Sim Eyre? Is not
Sim Eyre lord mayor of London? Fear nothing, Rose; let them all say what they can;   10
dainty, come thou to me — laughest thou?

Marg. Good my lord, stand her friend in
what thing you may.

Eyre. Why, my sweet Lady Madgy, think
you Simon Eyre can forget his fine Dutch   15
journeyman? No, vah! Fie, I scorn it, it shall
never be cast in my teeth, that I was unthank-
ful. Lady Madgy, thou had'st never covered
thy Saracen's head [5] with this French flap, nor
loaden thy bum with this farthingale ('tis   20
trash, trumpery, vanity); Simon Eyre had
never walked in a red petticoat,[6] nor wore a
chain of gold, but for my fine journeyman's

Portuguese.[1] — And shall I leave him? No!
Prince am I none, yet bear a princely mind.   25

Hans. My lord, 'tis time for us to part from
hence.

Eyre. Lady Madgy, Lady Madgy, take two
or three of my pie-crust-eaters, my buff-jerkin [2]
varlets, that do walk in black gowns at   30
Simon Eyre's heels; take them, good Lady
Madgy; trip and go, my brown queen of periwigs,[3] with my delicate Rose and my jolly Rowland to the Savoy; see them linked, countenance [4] the marriage; and when it is done,   35
cling, cling together, you Hamborow [5] turtle-
doves. I'll bear you out, come to Simon Eyre;
come, dwell with me, Hans, thou shalt eat
minced-pies and marchpane.[6] Rose, away,
cricket; trip and go, my Lady Madgy, to   40
the Savoy; Hans, wed, and to bed; kiss, and
away! Go, vanish!

Marg. Farewell, my lord.

Rose. Make haste, sweet love.

Marg. She'd fain the deed were done.   45

Hans. Come, my sweet Rose; faster than
deer we'll run.   (*Exeunt all but* EYRE.

Eyre. Go, vanish, vanish! Avaunt, I say!
By the Lord of Ludgate, it's a mad life to be a
lord mayor; it's a stirring life, a fine life, a   50
velvet life, a careful life. Well, Simon Eyre,
yet set a good face on it, in the honor of Saint
Hugh. Soft, the king this day comes to dine
with me, to see my new buildings; his majesty
is welcome, he shall have good cheer, deli-   55
cate cheer, princely cheer. This day, my fellow
prentices of London come to dine with me too;
they shall have fine cheer, gentlemanlike cheer.
I promised the mad Cappadocians,[7] when we
all served at the Conduit together,[8] that   60
if ever I came to be mayor of London, I would
feast them all, and I'll do't, I'll do't, by the life
of Pharaoh; by this beard, Sim Eyre will be no

---

[1] Finish up.
[2] Savoy Chapel, connected with the hospital or alms-
house of the same name near the Thames.
[3] Cheat.
[4] Defend or protect your clothes.
[5] An allusion to the ferocious-looking head so called
on many London signs of the day.
[6] The robe of the Lord Mayor.

[1] The gold coins lent by Hans.
[2] Military leather-jacket.
[3] Margery, as Lord Mayoress, can now be attended
by footmen wearing periwigs.
[4] Witness.   [5] Hamburg.
[6] A fancy cake made of almond paste.
[7] The people of an ancient Roman province in Asia
Minor. Here, the apprentices.
[8] The apprentices as one of their duties had to draw
water for their masters at the conduits.

flincher. Besides, I have procured that upon every Shrove Tuesday, at the sound of the 65 pancake-bell,[1] my fine dapper Assyrian lads shall clap up [2] their shop windows, and away. This is the day, and this day they shall do't, they shall do't. 69

Boys, that day are you free, let masters care, And prentices shall pray for Simon Eyre.

(*Exit.*

SCENE 2. *A street near St. Faith's Church*

Enter HODGE, FIRK, RALPH, *and five or six shoemakers, all with cudgels or such weapons*

Hodge. Come, Ralph; stand to it, Firk. My masters, as we are the brave bloods of the shoemakers, heirs apparent to Saint Hugh, and perpetual benefactors to all good fellows, thou shalt have no wrong; were Hammon a king of 5 spades,[3] he should not delve in thy close without thy sufferance.[4] But tell me, Ralph, art thou sure 'tis thy wife?

Ralph. Am I sure this is Firk? This morning, when I stroked [5] on her shoes, I looked 10 upon her, and she upon me, and sighed, asked me if ever I knew one Ralph. Yes, said I. For his sake, said she — tears standing in her eyes — and for thou art somewhat like him, spend this piece of gold. I took it; my lame leg 15 and my travel beyond sea made me unknown. All is one for that; I know she's mine.

Firk. Did she give thee this gold? O glorious glittering gold! She's thine own, 'tis thy wife, and she loves thee; for I'll stand to 't, 20 there's no woman will give gold to any man, but she thinks better of him than she thinks of them she gives silver to. And for Hammon, neither Hammon nor hangman shall wrong thee in London. Is not our old master Eyre 25 lord mayor? Speak, my hearts.

---

[1] On Shrove Tuesday, the last day before Lent, the apprentices had their annual holiday. Early on that day the parish bells of the city rang as a signal for the start of the feasting and merry-making. Since pancakes were a popular substitute for meat, this signal came to be termed the "pancake-bell."
[2] Shut up with board shutters.
[3] I.e., apprentices — an allusion to their "clubs."
[4] Dig in thy private ground without thy permission.
[5] Fitted.

All. Yes, and Hammon shall know it to his cost.

Enter HAMMON, *his Serving-man,* JANE, *and others*

Hodge. Peace, my bullies; yonder they come.

Ralph. Stand to 't, my hearts. Firk, 30 let me speak first.

Hodge. No, Ralph, let me. — Hammon, whither away so early?

Ham. Unmannerly, rude slave, what's that to thee? 35

Firk. To him, sir? Yes, sir, and to me, and others. Good-morrow, Jane, how dost thou? Good Lord, how the world is changed with you! God be thanked!

Ham. Villains, hand off! How dare you 40 touch my love?

All. Villains? Down with them! Cry clubs [1] for pretences!

Hodge. Hold, my hearts! — Touch her, Hammon? Yea, and more than that: we'll 45 carry her away with us. — My masters and gentlemen, never draw your bird-spits; [2] shoemakers are steel to the back, men every inch of them, all spirit.

All of Hammon's side. Well, and what of 50 all this?

Hodge. I'll show you. — Jane, dost thou know this man? 'Tis Ralph, I can tell thee; nay, 'tis he in faith, though he be lam'd by the wars. Yet look not strange, but run to him, 55 fold him about the neck and kiss him.

Jane. Lives then my husband? Oh, God, let me go!

Let me embrace my Ralph.

Ham.   What means my Jane?

Jane. Nay, what meant you, to tell me he was slain? 60

Ham. Pardon me, dear love, for being misled.

(*To* RALPH) 'Twas rumor'd here in London thou wert dead.

Firk. Thou seest he lives. — Lass, go, pack home with him. —

Now, Master Hammon, where's your mistress, your wife?

---

[1] The rallying cry of the London apprentices.
[2] A derisive term for swords.

Serv. 'Swounds, master, fight for her! 65
Will you thus lose her?

All. Down with that creature! Clubs!
Down with him!

Hodge. Hold, hold!

Ham. Hold, fool! — Sirs, he shall do no
wrong. 70
Will my Jane leave me thus, and break her
faith?

Firk. Yea, sir! She must, sir! She shall,
sir! What then? Mend it!

Hodge. Hark, fellow Ralph, follow my counsel: set the wench in the midst, and let her 75
choose her man, and let her be his woman.

Jane. Whom shall I choose? Whom should
my thoughts affect
But him whom Heaven hath made to be my
love?
Thou art my husband, and these humble weeds
Make thee more beautiful than all his wealth.
Therefore, I will but put off this attire, 81
Returning it into the owner's hand,
And after ever be thy constant wife.

Hodge. Not a rag, Jane! The law's on our
side: he that sows in another man's ground, 85
forfeits his harvest. Get thee home, Ralph;
follow him, Jane; he shall not have so much as
a busk-point [1] from thee.

Firk. Stand to that, Ralph; the appurtenances are thine own. Hammon, look 90
not at her!

Serv. O, swounds, no!

Firk. Blue coat,[2] be quiet, we'll give you a
new livery else; we'll make Shrove Tuesday
Saint George's Day [3] for you. Look not, 95
Hammon, leer not! I'll firk you! For thy
head now, one glance, one sheep's eye, anything, at her! Touch not a rag, lest I and my
brethren beat you to clouts.[4]

Serv. Come, Master Hammon, there's 100
no striving here.

---

[1] The lacing which fastened the end of a busk. A
busk was a strip of wood or whalebone used to stiffen
the front of a corset.

[2] I.e., servant, because blue liveries were the fashionable apparel for menservants.

[3] April 23, the "blue coats'" holiday. — Firk threatens to give the man a blue coat now by a thorough beating.

[4] Rags.

Ham. Good fellows, hear me speak; and,
honest Ralph,
Whom I have injured most by loving Jane,
Mark what I offer thee: here in fair gold
Is twenty pound, I'll give it for thy Jane; 105
If this content thee not, thou shalt have more.

Hodge. Sell not thy wife, Ralph; make her
not a whore.

Ham. Say, wilt thou freely cease thy claim
in her,
And let her be my wife? 110

All.   No, do not, Ralph.

Ralph. Sirrah Hammon, Hammon, dost thou
think a shoemaker is so base to be a bawd to
his own wife for commodity? Take thy gold,
choke with it! Were I not lame, I would 115
make thee eat thy words.

Firk. A shoemaker sell his flesh and blood?
O indignity!

Hodge. Sirrah, take up your pelf, and be
packing. 120

Ham. I will not touch one penny, but in
lieu
Of that great wrong I offered thy Jane,
To Jane and thee I give that twenty pound.
Since I have fail'd of her, during my life,
I vow, no woman else shall be my wife. 125
Farewell, good fellows of the gentle trade:
Your morning mirth my mourning day hath
made. (*Exit* HAMMON *and his party.*

Firk (*to the Serving-man*). Touch the gold,
creature, if you dare! Y'are best be trudging.
(*Exit Serving-man.*) — Here, Jane, take 130
thou it. Now let's home, my hearts.

Hodge. Stay! Who comes here? Jane, on
again with thy mask!

Enter the EARL OF LINCOLN, *the* LORD
MAYOR, *and servants*

Lincoln. Yonder's the lying varlet mockt
us so. 135

L. Mayor. Come hither, sirrah!

Firk. I, sir? I am sirrah? You mean me,
do you not?

Lincoln. Where is my nephew married?

Firk. Is he married? God give him joy, 140
I am glad of it. They have a fair day, and the
sign is in a good planet, Mars in Venus.

L. Mayor. Villain, thou toldst me that my daughter Rose
This morning should be married at Saint Faith's;
We have watch'd there these three hours at the least,   145
Yet see we no such thing.

Firk. Truly, I am sorry for't; a bride's a pretty thing.

Hodge. Come to the purpose. Yonder's the bride and bridegroom you look for, I hope. 150
Though you be lords, you are not to bar by your authority men from women, are you?

L. Mayor. See, see, my daughter's maskt.

Lincoln.   True, and my nephew,
To hide his guilt, counterfeits him lame.   155

Firk. Yea, truly; God help the poor couple, they are lame and blind.

L. Mayor. I'll ease her blindness.

Lincoln.   I'll his lameness cure.

Firk. Lie down, sirs, and laugh! My   160
fellow Ralph is taken for Rowland Lacy, and Jane for Mistress Damask Rose. This is all my knavery.

L. Mayor. What, have I found you, minion?

Lincoln.   O base wretch!   165
Nay, hide thy face, the horror of thy guilt
Can hardly be washt off. Where are thy powers?[1]
What battles have you made? O yes, I see,
Thou fought'st with Shame, and Shame hath conquer'd thee.
This lameness will not serve.   170

L. Mayor.   Unmask yourself.

Lincoln. Lead home your daughter.

L. Mayor.   Take your nephew hence.

Ralph. Hence! 'Swounds, what mean you?
Are you mad? I hope you cannot enforce   175
my wife from me. Where's Hammon?

L. Mayor. Your wife?

Lincoln. What, Hammon?

Ralph. Yea, my wife; and, therefore, the proudest of you that lays hands on her   180
first, I'll lay my crutch 'cross his pate.

Firk. To him, lame Ralph! Here's brave sport!

Ralph. Rose call you her? Why, her name is Jane. Look here else; do you know her   185
now?   (*Unmasking* JANE.

[1] Troops.

Lincoln. Is this your daughter?

L. Mayor.   No, nor this your nephew.
My Lord of Lincoln, we are both abus'd
By this base, crafty varlet.   190

Firk. Yea, forsooth, no varlet; forsooth, no base; forsooth, I am but mean; no crafty neither, but of the gentle craft.

L. Mayor. Where is my daughter Rose?
Where is my child?   195

Lincoln. Where is my nephew Lacy married?

Firk. Why, here is good lac'd mutton,[1] as I promist you.

Lincoln. Villain, I'll have thee punisht for this wrong.   200

Firk. Punish the journeyman villain, but not the journeyman shoemaker.

Enter DODGER

Dodger. My lord, I come to bring unwelcome news.
Your nephew Lacy and your daughter Rose
Early this morning wedded at the Savoy,   205
None being present but the lady mayoress.
Besides, I learnt among the officers,
The lord mayor vows to stand in their defense
'Gainst any that shall seek to cross the match.

Lincoln. Dares Eyre the shoemaker up-   210
hold the deed?

Firk. Yes, sir, shoemakers dare stand in a woman's quarrel, I warrant you, as deep as another, and deeper too.

Dodger. Besides, his grace today dines with the mayor;   215
Who on his knees humbly intends to fall
And beg a pardon for your nephew's fault.

Lincoln. But I'll prevent him! Come, Sir Roger Oateley;
The king will do us justice in this cause.
Howe'er their hands have made them man and wife,   220
I will disjoin the match, or lose my life.

          (*Exeunt the* EARL OF LINCOLN, *the*
               LORD MAYOR, DODGER, *and servant.*

Firk. Adieu, Monsieur Dodger! Farewell, fools! Ha, ha! Oh, if they had stayed, I would

[1] "Lac'd" is a pun on "Lacy-ed." "Mutton" was a slang term for a whore. Firk's remark is a bold gibe at the Earl, who is a Lacy.

have so lambed [1] them with flouts! O heart, my codpiece-point [2] is ready to fly in pieces 225 every time I think upon Mistress Rose; but let that pass, as my lady mayoress says.

Hodge. This matter is answered. Come, Ralph; home with thy wife. Come, my fine shoemakers, let's go to our master's, the 230 new lord mayor, and there swagger this Shrove Tuesday. I'll promise you wine enough, for Madge keeps the cellar.

All. O rare! Madge is a good wench.

Firk. And I'll promise you meat 235 enough, for simp'ring Susan keeps the larder. I'll lead you to victuals, my brave soldiers; follow your captain. O brave! Hark, hark!

                    (*Bell rings.*

All. The pancake-bell rings, the pancake-bell!
Trilill, my hearts! 240

Firk. O brave! O sweet bell! O delicate pancakes! Open the doors, my hearts, and shut up the windows! keep in the house, let out the pancakes! Oh, rare, my hearts! Let's march together for the honor of Saint 245 Hugh to the great new hall [3] in Gracious Street-corner, which our master, the new lord mayor, hath built.

Ralph. O the crew of good fellows that will dine at my lord mayor's cost today! 250

Hodge. By the Lord, my lord mayor is a most brave man. How shall prentices be bound to pray for him and the honor of the gentlemen shoemakers! Let's feed and be fat with my lord's bounty. 255

Firk. O musical bell, still! O Hodge, O my brethren! There's cheer for the heavens: venison-pasties walk up and down piping hot, like sergeants; beef and brewis [4] comes marching in dry-vats,[5] fritters and pancakes come 260 trowling [6] in in wheelbarrows; hens and oranges hopping in porters'-baskets, collops [7] and eggs in scuttles, and tarts and custards come quavering in in malt-shovels.

[1] Pounded (i.e., with words).
[2] The lace on the peculiar flap which was worn at the front of Elizabethan tight breeches.
[3] The Leadenhall. The historic building was erected by Eyre in 1419, fifteen years before he was Sheriff of London.
[4] Broth.   [5] Casks.   [6] Rolling.   [7] Rashers of bacon.

Enter more prentices

All. Whoop, look here, look here! 265

Hodge. How now, mad lads, whither away so fast?

First Pren. Whither? Why, to the great new hall, know you not why? The lord mayor hath bidden all the prentices in London 270 to breakfast this morning.

All. Oh, brave shoemaker, oh, brave lord of incomprehensible good fellowship! Whoo! Hark you! The pancake-bell rings.

               (*Cast up caps.*

Firk. Nay, more, my hearts! Every 275 Shrove Tuesday is our year of jubilee; and when the pancake-bell rings, we are as free as my Lord Mayor; we may shut up our shops, and make holiday. I'll have it called Saint Hugh's Holiday. 280

All. Agreed, agreed! Saint Hugh's Holiday.

Hodge. And this shall continue for ever.

All. Oh, brave! Come, come, my hearts! Away, away!

Firk. O eternal credit to us of the 285 Gentle Craft!
March fair, my hearts! Oh, rare! (*Exeunt.*

SCENE 3. *A street in London*

Enter the KING *and his train, who pass over the stage*

King. Is our lord mayor of London such a gallant?

Noble. One of the merriest madcaps in your land.
Your grace will think, when you behold the man,
He's rather a wild ruffian than a mayor.
Yet thus much I'll ensure your majesty, 5
In all his actions that concern his state,[1]
He is as serious, provident, and wise,
As full of gravity amongst the grave,
As any mayor hath been these many years.

King. I am with child,[2] till I behold this huff-cap.[3] 10
But all my doubt is, when we come in presence,
His madness will be dashed clean out of countenance.

[1] Office.   [2] I continue impatient.   [3] Swaggerer.

Noble. It may be so, my liege.

King.   Which to prevent
Let some one give him notice, 'tis our pleasure
That he put on his wonted merriment.   16
Set forward!

All.   On afore! (*Exeunt*

SCENE 4. *The Leadenhall* [1]

Enter EYRE, HODGE, FIRK, RALPH, *and other
shoemakers, all with napkins on their
shoulders*

Eyre. Come, my fine Hodge, my jolly gentlemen shoemakers; soft, where be these can-
nibals, these varlets, my officers? Let them all
walk and wait upon my brethren; for my meaning is, that none but shoemakers, none but   5
the livery of my company shall in their satin
hoods wait upon the trencher of my sovereign.

Firk. O my lord, it will be rare!

Eyre. No more, Firk; come, lively! Let
your fellow prentices want no cheer; let   10
wine be plentiful as beer, and beer as water.
Hang these penny-pinching fathers, that cram
wealth in innocent lambskins.[2] Rip, knaves,
avaunt! Look to my guests!

Hodge. My lord, we are at our wits' end   15
for room; those hundred tables will not feast
the fourth part of them.

Eyre. Then cover me those hundred tables
again, and again, till all my jolly prentices be
feasted. Avoid, Hodge! Run, Ralph!   20
Frisk about, my nimble Firk! Carouse me
fathom-healths [3] to the honor of the shoemakers. Do they drink lively, Hodge? Do
they tickle it,[4] Firk?

Firk. Tickle it? Some of them have   25
taken their liquor standing so long that they
can stand no longer; but for meat, they would
eat it, and they had it.

Eyre. Want they meat? Where's this swag-
belly, this greasy kitchen-stuff cook? Call   30
the varlet to me! Want meat? Firk, Hodge,

[1] The great hall newly built on the corner of Cornhill
and Grace Church Street by Eyre. See Act V, Sc. 2,
ll. 246-47. It is now a market site.

[2] I.e., wallets which hold lambskin documents, such
as deeds, wills, etc.

[3] Drink for me capacity healths.

[4] Make merry.

lame Ralph, run, my tall men, beleaguer the
shambles,[1] beggar all Eastcheap, serve me
whole oxen in chargers,[2] and let sheep whine
upon the tables like pigs for want of good   35
fellows to eat them. Want meat? Vanish,
Firk! Avaunt, Hodge!

Hodge. Your lordship mistakes my man
Firk; he means, their bellies want meat, not
the boards; for they have drunk so much,   40
they can eat nothing.

The Second Three Men's Song

Cold's the wind, and wet's the rain,
    Saint Hugh be our good speed:
Ill is the weather that bringeth no gain,
    Nor helps good hearts in need.   45
Trowl [3] the bowl, the jolly nut-brown bowl,
    And here, kind mate, to thee:
Let's sing a dirge for Saint Hugh's soul,
    And down it merrily.

Down a down hey down a down,   50
    Hey derry derry, down a down!
        (*Close with the tenor boy:*
Ho, well done; to me let come!
Ring compass, gentle joy.[4]

Trowl the bowl, the nut-brown bowl,
    And here, kind mate, to thee: etc.   55
    (*Repeat as often as there be men to
        drink; at last, when all have drunk,
        this verse:*)
Cold's the wind, and wet's the rain,
    Saint Hugh be our good speed:
Ill is the weather that bringeth no gain,
    Nor helps good hearts in need.

Enter HANS, ROSE, *and* MARGERY

Marg. Where is my lord?   60

Eyre. How now, Lady Madgy?

Marg. The king's most excellent majesty is
new come; he sends me for thy honor; one of his
most worshipful peers bade me tell thou must
be merry, and so forth; but let that pass.   65

[1] Besiege the butcher shops.   [2] Large platters.

[3] Pass around.

[4] Complete the circle, sweet love; i.e., send the drink
around.

Eyre. Is my sovereign come? Vanish, my tall shoemakers, my nimble brethren; look to my guests, the prentices. Yet stay a little! How now, Hans? How looks my little Rose?

Hans. Let me request you to remember me. I know, your honor easily may obtain   71 Free pardon of the king for me and Rose, And reconcile me to my uncle's grace.

Eyre. Have done, my good Hans, my honest journeyman; look cheerily! I'll fall upon   75 both my knees, till they be as hard as horn, but I'll get thy pardon.

Marg. Good my lord, have a care what you speak to his grace.

Eyre. Away, you Islington [1] whitepot! [2]   80 hence, you hopper-arse! you barley-pudding, full of maggots! you broiled carbonado! [3] avaunt, avaunt, avoid, Mephistophiles! [4] Shall Sim Eyre learn to speak of you, Lady Madgy? Vanish, Mother Miniver-cap; [5] vanish, go,   85 trip and go; meddle with your partlets [6] and your pishery-pashery, your flews [7] and your whirligigs; go, rub, [8] out of mine alley! Sim Eyre knows how to speak to a Pope, to Sultan Soliman, [9] to Tamburlaine, [10] an he were   90 here, and shall I melt, shall I droop before my sovereign? No, come, my Lady Madgy! Follow me, Hans! About your business, my frolic free-booters! Firk, frisk about, and about, and about, for the honor of mad Simon Eyre, lord mayor of London.   96

Firk. Hey, for the honor of the shoemakers!
                        (*Exeunt.*

---

[1] A suburb to the northwest of old London.
[2] A dish, made of milk, eggs, and sugar, baked in a pot — a kind of baked custard.
[3] A steak cut crossways and broiled on coals.
[4] A well-known character to Elizabethans, the agent of the Devil in Marlowe's *Dr. Faustus.*
[5] A cap trimmed or lined with miniver fur, a special white fur.
[6] Ruffs for the neck.
[7] Flaps (of the French hood, probably).
[8] Obstruction: a term in bowling.
[9] Solyman the Magnificent, Turkish emperor (1496–1566).
[10] Mongol warrior, later emperor (*c.* 1333–1405), who was made famous to the Elizabethans through Marlowe's popular tragedy in ten acts, *Tamburlaine the Great.*

SCENE 5. *The same*

A long flourish, or two. Enter the KING, *Nobles,* EYRE, MARGERY, LACY, ROSE. LACY *and* ROSE *kneel*

King. Well, Lacy, though the fact was very foul Of your revolting from our kingly love And your own duty, yet we pardon you. Rise both, and, Mistress Lacy, thank my lord mayor For your young bridegroom here.   5

Eyre. So, my dear liege, Sim Eyre and my brethren, the gentlemen shoemakers, shall set your sweet majesty's image cheek by jowl by Saint Hugh for this honor you have done poor Simon Eyre. I beseech your grace, pardon   10 my rude behavior; I am a handicraftsman, yet my heart is without craft; I would be sorry at my soul, that my boldness should offend my king.

King. Nay, I pray thee, good lord mayor, be even as merry   15 As if thou wert among thy shoemakers; It does me good to see thee in this humor.

Eyre. Say'st thou me so, my sweet Dioclesian? [1] Then, humph! [2] Prince am I none, yet am I princely born. By the Lord of   20 Ludgate, my liege, I'll be as merry as a pie. [3]

King. Tell me, in faith, mad Eyre, how old thou art.

Eyre. My liege, a very boy, a stripling, a younker; [4] you see not a white hair on my   25 head, not a gray in this beard. Every hair, I assure thy majesty, that sticks in this beard, Sim Eyre values at the King of Babylon's ransom, Tamar Cham's [5] beard was a rubbing brush to't: yet I'll shave it off, and stuff   30 tennis-balls with it, [6] to please my bully [7] king.

King. But all this while I do not know your age.

Eyre. My liege, I am six and fifty year old, yet I can cry humph! with a sound heart   35

---

[1] Diocletian, Roman emperor (284–305 A.D.), in whose reign the martyrdom of St. Hugh occurred.
[2] Hurrah!   [3] Magpie.   [4] Youngster.
[5] Timur Khan, or Tamburlaine.
[6] The balls of the Elizabethan game of tennis were stuffed with hair.
[7] Gallant.

for the honor of Saint Hugh. Mark this old
wench, my king; I danced the shaking of the
sheets with her six and thirty years ago, and
yet I hope to get two or three young lord
mayors, ere I die. I am lusty still, Sim 40
Eyre, still. Care and cold lodging brings white
hairs. My sweet Majesty, let care vanish, cast
it upon thy nobles, it will make thee look always young like Apollo, and cry humph! Prince
am I none, yet am I princely born. 45

King. Ha, ha! Say, Cornwall, didst thou
ever see his like?

Cor. Not I, my lord.

Enter the Earl of Lincoln *and the (now
former)* Lord Mayor

King.   Lincoln, what news with you?
Lincoln. My gracious lord, have care unto
     yourself, 50
For there are traitors here.
All.   Traitors? Where? Who?
Eyre. Traitors in my house? God forbid!
Where be my officers? I'll spend my soul, ere
my king feel harm. 55
King. Where is the traitor, Lincoln?
Lincoln.   Here he stands.
King. Cornwall, lay hold on Lacy! — Lin-
     coln speak,
What canst thou lay unto thy nephew's charge?
Lincoln. This, my dear liege: your Grace, to
     do me honor, 60
Heaped on the head of this degenerate boy
Desertless [1] favors; you made choice of him
To be commander over powers in France.
But he ——
King. Good Lincoln, prithee, pause a while!
Even in thine eyes I read what thou wouldst
     speak. 66
I know how Lacy did neglect our love,
Ran himself deeply, in the highest degree,
Into vile treason ——
Lincoln.   Is he not a traitor? 70
King. Lincoln, he was; now have we par-
     doned him.
'Twas not a base want of true valor's fire,
That held him out of France, but love's
     desire.

[1] Undeserved.

Lincoln. I will not bear his shame upon my
     back.
King. Nor shalt thou, Lincoln; I forgive you
     both. 75
Lincoln. Then, good liege, forbid the boy to
     wed
One whose mean birth will much disgrace his
     bed.
King. Are they not married?
Lincoln.   No, my liege.
Both.   We are. 80
King. Shall I divorce them then? O be it
     far
That any hand on earth should dare untie
The sacred knot, knit by God's majesty;
I would not for my crown disjoin their hands
That are conjoin'd in holy nuptial bands. 85
How say'st thou, Lacy, wouldst thou lose thy
     Rose?
Lacy. Not for all India's wealth, my sov-
     ereign.
King. But Rose, I am sure, her Lacy would
     forego?
Rose. If Rose were askt that question, she'd
     say no.
King. You hear them, Lincoln? 90
Lincoln.   Yea, my liege, I do
King. Yet canst thou find i' th' heart to
     part these two?
Who seeks, besides you, to divorce these lovers?
L. Mayor. I do, my gracious lord, I am her
     father.
King. Sir Roger Oateley, our last mayor
     I think? 95
L. Mayor. The same, my liege.
King.   Would you offend Love's laws?
Well, you shall have your wills, you sue to me
To prohibit the match. Soft, let me see ——
You both are married, Lacy, art thou not? 100
Lacy. I am, dread sovereign.
King.   Then, upon thy life
I charge thee, not to call this woman wife.
L. Mayor. I thank your grace.
Rose.   O my most gracious lord! 105
         (*Kneels*
King. Nay, Rose, never woo me; I tell you
     true,
Although as yet I am a bachelor,
Yet I believe I shall not marry you.

Rose. Can you divide the body from the soul,
Yet make the body live?　　　　　　　　110
King.　　　　　　　Yea, so profound?
I cannot, Rose, but you I must divide.
This fair maid, bridegroom, cannot be your
　　bride.
Are you pleas'd, Lincoln? Oateley, are you
　　pleas'd?
Both. Yes, my lord.　　　　　　　115
King.　　　　Then must my heart be eas'd;
For, credit me, my conscience lives in pain,
Till these whom I divorc'd, be join'd again.
Lacy, give me thy hand; Rose, lend me thine!
Be what you would be! Kiss now! So, that's
　　fine.　　　　　　　　　　120
At night, lovers, to bed! — Now, let me see,
Which of you all mislikes this harmony.
　L. Mayor. Will you then take from me my
　　child perforce?
　King. Why tell me, Oateley: shines not
　　Lacy's name
As bright in the world's eye as the gay beams
Of any citizen?　　　　　　　　126
　Lincoln.　　　　Yea, but, my gracious lord,
I do mislike the match far more than he;
Her blood is too too base.
　King.　　　　　Lincoln, no more.　130
Dost thou not know that love respects no
　　blood,
Cares not for difference of birth or state?
The maid is young, well born, fair, virtuous,
A worthy bride for any gentleman.
Besides, your nephew for her sake did stoop
To bare necessity, and, as I hear,　　136
Forgetting honors and all courtly pleasures,
To gain her love, became a shoemaker.
As for the honor which he lost in France,
Thus I redeem it: Lacy, kneel thee down! —
Arise, Sir Rowland Lacy! Tell me now,　141
Tell me in earnest, Oateley, canst thou chide,
Seeing thy Rose a lady and a bride?
　L. Mayor. I am content with what your grace
　　hath done.
　Lincoln. And I, my liege, since there's no
　　remedy.　　　　　　　　145
　King. Come on, then, all shake hands: I'll
　　have you friends;
Where there is much love, all discord ends.
What says my mad lord mayor to all this love?

　Eyre. O my liege, this honor you have done
to my fine journeyman here, Rowland　150
Lacy, and all these favors which you have
shown to me this day in my poor house, will
make Simon Eyre live longer by one dozen of
warm summers more than he should.
　King. Nay, my mad lord mayor, that shall
　　be thy name,　　　　　　　155
If any grace of mine can length thy life,
One honor more I'll do thee; that new building,
Which at thy cost in Cornhill is erected,
Shall take a name from us; we'll have it called
The Leadenhall, because in digging it　160
You found the lead that covereth the same.
　Eyre. I thank your majesty.
　Marg.　　　　　God bless your grace!
　King. Lincoln, a word with you!

　　　Enter HODGE, FIRK, RALPH, *and more*
　　　　　　shoemakers

　Eyre. How now, my mad knaves? Peace,
　　speak softly, yonder is the king.　165
　King. With the old troop which there we
　　keep in pay,
We will incorporate a new supply.
Before one summer more pass o'er my head,
France shall repent England was injured.　169
What are all those?
　Lacy.　　　　All shoemakers, my liege,
Sometime [1] my fellows; in their companies
I lived as merry as an emperor.
　King. My mad lord mayor, are all these
shoemakers?　　　　　　　　175
　Eyre. All shoemakers, my liege; all gentlemen of the Gentle Craft, true Trojans, courageous cordwainers; they all kneel to the shrine
of holy Saint Hugh.　　　　　　179
　All the Shoemakers. God save your majesty!
　King. Mad Simon, would they anything
with us?
　Eyre. Mum, mad knaves! Not a word! I'll
do't; I warrant you. — They are all beggars,
my liege; all for themselves, and I for　185
them all, on both my knees do entreat, that for
the honor of poor Simon Eyre and the good
of his brethren, these mad knaves, your grace
would vouchsafe some privilege to my new
　　[1] Formerly.

Leadenhall, that it may be lawful for us to   190
buy and sell leather there two days a week.

King. Mad Sim, I grant your suit, you shall
    have patent
To hold two market-days in Leadenhall,
Mondays and Fridays, those shall be the times.
Will this content you?   195

All.   Jesus bless your grace!

Eyre. In the name of these my poor brethren shoemakers, I most humbly thank your
grace.   But before I rise, seeing you are in the
giving vein and we in the begging, grant   200
Sim Eyre one boon more.

King. What is it, my lord mayor?

Eyre. Vouchsafe to taste of a poor banquet
that stands sweetly waiting for your sweet
presence.   205

King. I shall undo thee, Eyre, only with
    feasts;
Already have I been too troublesome;
Say, have I not?

Eyre. O my dear king, Sim Eyre was taken
unawares upon a day of shroving,[1] which   210
I promised long ago to the prentices of London.

    [1] Merrymaking.

For, an't please your highness, in time past,
I bare the water-tankard, and my coat
Sits not a whit the worse upon my back;
And then, upon a morning, some mad boys,
It was Shrove Tuesday, even as 'tis now,   216
Gave me my breakfast, and I swore then by
the stopple[1] of my tankard, if ever I came to
be lord mayor of London, I would feast all the
prentices.   This day, my liege, I did it,   220
and the slaves had an hundred tables five times
covered; they are gone home and vanished;
Yet add more honor to the Gentle Trade,
Taste of Eyre's banquet, Simon's happy
    made.

King. Eyre, I will taste of thy banquet, and
    will say,   225
I have not met more pleasure on a day.
Friends of the Gentle Craft, thanks to you all,
Thanks, my kind lady mayoress, for our
    cheer. —
Come, lords, a while let's revel it at home!
When all our sports and banquetings are done,
Wars must right wrongs which Frenchmen
    have begun.   (*Exeunt.*   231

    [1] Stopper.

INTRODUCTION TO
Epicoene, or The Silent Woman

Ben Jonson and His Rise to Fame: The Blackfriars Playhouse and the War of the Theaters: The Masque and English Stage Setting: Jonson's Heyday and Decline: The Comedy of Humors

BEN JONSON AND HIS RISE TO FAME

BEFORE Thomas Dekker wrote *The Shoemakers' Holiday* in the romantic vein of traditional Elizabethan comedy, another young dramatist, Ben Jonson, had introduced London theatergoers to a new species of comedy that was destined to influence the English stage for the next century. Jonson became one of the most distinctive personalities ever connected with playwriting in England, and her first poet-laureate.

The love of learning and common sense, which colored Jonson's entire career as a man of letters, descended to him from his forebears in Annandale, Scotland (the birthplace of Thomas Carlyle in the eighteenth century). Jonson himself was born not in Scotland, but at London in 1572 or 1573, a month after his father, a clergyman, had died. His mother subsequently married a bricklayer, whose trade Ben learned in boyhood and practiced as a young man. Henslowe, the theatrical manager, once in scorn referred to him as "Benjamin Jonson, bricklayer."

In his early teens Jonson attracted the notice of William Camden, master of Westminster School, and gained admittance as a scholarship student there. The learned Camden so steeped his receptive pupil in classical culture that years later Jonson asserted he owed to his mentor "all that I am in arts, all that I know." Jonson never attended any university, but Camden's training enabled him to develop into a man of outstanding erudition.

After the completion of his study at Westminster about 1589 Jonson went through a period of most varied experiences. He served as a soldier in the Netherlands; he did bricklaying around London; he married and left a woman whom he called "a shrew, yet honest"; and he belonged to a troupe of strolling players. The year 1597 saw him, like Dekker, an actor and playwright in the employ of Henslowe.

On a September day of 1598 Jonson's characteristic pugnacity got him into a duel with one of Henslowe's better actors, Gabriel Spencer. He killed his adversary in Hogsden Fields near The Theatre and The Curtain. The ability to read and write qualified him to plead under ancient law the benefit of clergy and thus to avoid hanging. He nevertheless suffered brief confinement in Tyburn prison, and the branding of a "T" on his left thumb.

Sometime before his quarrel with Spencer Jonson had fallen out with Henslowe and the Lord Admiral's Men. Hence he had sold to the Lord Chamberlain's company the play he had recently completed. An ancient but very doubtful tradition has claimed that only Shakespeare's intervention induced the manager, Burbage, to purchase this new comedy, entitled *Every Man in his Humour*. It is a fact that Shakespeare played a rôle in the original production at The Curtain — the only definite record of Shakespeare's acting. The performance of *Every Man in his Humour* in the season of 1598-99 brought Jonson instant fame as innovator of a fresh comic pattern.

THE BLACKFRIARS PLAYHOUSE AND THE WAR OF THE THEATERS

During the following year Jonson precipitated the famous "War of the Poets" or "War of the Theaters" with the first of a series of "comical satires" upon contemporary playwrights and actors. This composition, *Every Man out of his Humour*, ridiculed especially the rising dramatist, John Marston (?1575-1634), who had drawn a humorous portrait of Jonson in a play of the previous winter.

Jonson's second and third comical satires, *Cynthia's Revels* and *Poetaster*, connected him with the most important theatrical development of the day. In September, 1600, Henry Evans, who during the 1580's had directed a boys' troupe at a private playhouse in the Blackfriars district, leased from Burbage another Blackfriars building which recently had been fitted as a theater. Evans planned to repeat his former enterprise in a neighboring location. He had procured a royal license not only to organize a company, "The Children of the Chapel," composed of choirboys from the royal chapel and elsewhere, but even to draft such boys for acting. With a group of fifteen to twenty picked youths he opened the second private theater in Blackfriars during the fall of 1600. The price scale of seats, sixpence to a shilling (about $1 to $2 today), set a new high for London and guaranteed an exclusive clientele.

The musical proclivities of the boys led Evans to institute in the Blackfriars productions vocal and instrumental numbers between the acts. These *entr'acte* programs initiated the breakdown of the Elizabethan custom of continuous performance. By the 1620's pauses between the acts regularly occurred at the public as well as at the private theaters. Dramatists sometimes took advantage of the pauses to stir the audience to greater suspense, as Middleton and Rowley did in *The Changeling* (*c.* 1623), where during an act interval the villain comes out on the stage to hide a sword which he is to use in the next act.

Desirous for other novelties besides music to advertise his new venture, Evans added Jonson's comical satire to the repertoire of the Chapel Children. *Cynthia's Revels*, one of the Blackfriars plays in 1600, presented invidious comparisons between the boy actors and the adult players on the "common stages." *Poetaster* during 1601 contained more slurs upon the public theaters. One of the characters, Histrio, a supposed actor on the "common stage," is made to boast that "we have as much ribaldry in our plays as can be... All the sinners in the suburbs [i.e., the inmates of the Bankside disorderly houses] come and applaud our actions daily." Jonson's slamming of his rivals, both playhouses and playwrights, set the city agog. Audiences flocked to Blackfriars. The boys' performances grew so popular in 1601 and 1602 that they quite overshadowed the activity of the adult troupes. The situation provoked Shakespeare in the players' scene of *Hamlet* to voice a protest through Rosencrantz: "There is, sir, an aery [nest] of children, little eyases [nestlings], that cry out on the top of question, and are most tyrannically clapped for't: these are now the fashion, and so berattle the common stages — so they call them — that many wearing rapiers [i.e., fashionable society] are afraid of goose-quills [i.e., the dramatists' pens], and dare scarce come thither [i.e., to the Globe Theater]." The popularity of the Chapel Children, however, soon waned. By 1608 they had to disband and turn over their Blackfriars playhouse to the Globe actors for use as a winter home.

The War of the Theaters came to an end before Queen Elizabeth's death in 1603. The new monarch, James I, at once emphasized royal patronage of all stage groups. He created the Chapel Children the "Children of the Queen's Revels," while he assigned the principal adult companies to the direct protection of various members of the royal family. The Lord Chamberlain's Men became the King's Men; the Lord Admiral's, the Prince's Men; and the Earl of Worcester's, the Queen's Men. Thus the members of a profession which at the opening of Elizabeth's reign had possessed no legal standing had now risen to be the servants of royalty. From this time on, as political divisions in England deepened, the sentiment of the acting profession inevitably ran in favor of the king, and the theater in general looked more and more toward the court party for its support.

THE MASQUE AND ENGLISH STAGE SETTING

The accession of King James to the throne started Jonson off on a new line of literary endeavor — the writing of court entertainments called masques. Though a by-form of drama quite divorced from the popular theater, they ultimately exerted a very considerable effect upon the progress of English stage production. The masque arose from the older masked revels of the English nobility. Staged amid the torches and candles of a great hall, it combined sumptuous costumes, dances, songs, and recitation into a loose kind of show upon a fanciful theme. Jonson invested the masque with a literary and dramatic value not hitherto realized. His first creation, *The Masque of Blackness*, on its court performance in January, 1605, aroused tremendous enthusiasm. A veritable rage for this species of amusement seized high society. The thousands of dollars expended on masques annually over the next thirty-five years provoked the Puritans and the lower classes to bitter condemnation of the aristocracy.

Jonson's inventiveness and his poetic skill established him for twenty-five years as without a peer in the writing of masques. His greatest innovation appeared first in *The Masque of Queens* (1609). He inserted, as a contrast to the customary high-flown fancy, an "antimasque," a comic portion in which "antick" characters carried out ludicrous or grotesque dances and dialogue. This device of relief entered prominently into succeeding development of the masque.

The main responsibility for the production of Jonson's court entertainments did not fall upon him, but upon the talented royal architect, Inigo Jones. Jones had learned the last word on scenic representation by an extended investigation of theatrical art in Italy at the turn of the century. He constructed in the playhouse at Whitehall Palace a stage which was framed by an ornate proscenium arch and equipped with a painted front curtain. His first shows, like *The Masque of Blackness* (1605), employed as pictorial background a single "perspective." Then Jones began to experiment with various forms of movable scenery until finally in 1640 he evolved for Davenant's masque, *Salmacida Spolia*, a series of wing and back flats which permitted four complete changes of the stage picture plus partial variations in setting.

The masque stage with its movable scenes, proscenium, and curtain, provided the model for the so-called "picture-stage" in the London theaters erected after the Civil War. Even before the closing of the playhouses in 1642, however, the scenic effects of the masques influenced the staging at the private theaters. Sir John Suckling's *Aglaura*, acted at Blackfriars around Christmas, 1637, "had some scenes to it which in those days were only used at Masques," so a contemporary reported. There are similar records of "scenes" in productions of the late 1630's at the other two private playhouses — The Phoenix, or The Cockpit in Drury Lane, built in 1617; and Salisbury Court, built in 1629. The movement for regular scenery on the popular stage was well under way when national disturbance intervened. The restoration of theatrical prosperity in the 1660's brought the movement to a successful conclusion. Thus the Jonson-Jones court masques led in half a century to the beginnings of modern scenic art in the English theater.

JONSON'S HEYDAY AND DECLINE

When in 1604 Jonson commenced the writing of entertainments for King James and his courtiers, he did not turn aside from his labors for the playgoing public. On the contrary, he achieved his principal dramatic successes during the following decade. In 1606 the King's Men acted Jonson's best-known comedy, *Volpone, or The Fox*, a merciless exposure of avarice. The rich but miserly Volpone (Fox), feigning mortal illness, offers his estate to the highest bidder among several grasping persons — a lawyer, Voltore (Vulture); an old gentleman, Corbaccio (Big Crow); and a merchant, Corvino (Little Crow). He then orders his valet Mosca to announce that Volpone has died and has made Mosca heir. In the end, however, Volpone, to prevent Mosca's acquisition of all his property, has to reveal their rascality in court. The law imprisons both rogues, confiscates the wealth of Volpone, and also punishes his dupes for their greed.

Four years after *Volpone* Jonson put forth his next comedy, *Epicoene, or The Silent Woman*. The London background of *Epicoene* marked an important departure from Jonson's previous practice. He had laid the scenes of his first two comic masterpieces in Italy, *Every Man in his Humour* at Florence, and *Volpone* at Venice. Subsequent to *Epicoene* he revised *Every Man in his Humour* and made it a drama of London life. Yet Jonson was strangely slow in realizing the far greater conviction which the native background would give to his comic theory that "no country's mirth is better than our own." His eventual adoption of local settings represented the tardy triumph of common sense over learning.

The Alchemist, Jonson's fourth important comedy, made its appearance on the Globe stage in 1610. It portrays the shrewd methods of the London fakirs in chemistry and magic, who mulcted a variety of persons, both foolish and vicious, by the ancient lure of much for little. Certain scenes contain an extraordinary amount of professional information, proof of Johnson's intimacy with the more disreputable circles in his metropolis. Such intimacy probably accentuated his natural tendency to indignation over human vice and corruption.

After another lapse of four years, Jonson produced his last notable drama, *Bartholomew Fair*. This most famous of London carnivals presented a human circus filled with excesses and wickedness. Jonson reveled in the rich opportunity for satire of hypocrisy mixed with vulgarity. He lashed especially his pet enemies, the Puritans. In Zeal-of-the-Land Busy, and the Littlewits who circle about him, he created the most strik-ing of all his multifarious caricatures.

Bartholomew Fair marked the virtual exhaustion of Jonson's dramatic inspiration. For over ten years thereafter he brought forth no plays at all. He himself must have recognized that his playwriting had come to a turning point, because in 1616 he did what no other dramatist at that date would have considered doing. He published a care-fully edited and collected edition of his plays, poetry, and masques. The master Shake-speare had just died without taking thought for the preservation of his work. Proud Ben Jonson did not intend to make that mistake.

Shakespeare's death opened the way for Jonson to be acknowledged the greatest of living English authors. The publication of the big folio volume of his writings helped at once to confirm the estimate. Before the end of 1616, King James created the post of poet laureate and awarded it to Jonson in recognition of his literary pre-eminence. Two years later the sovereign bestowed upon him the reversion of the office of the Master of the Revels, a position which would have given him charge of all stage enter-tainment at court and made him censor of all productions in the London theaters. He would have delighted in such powers, but did not live long enough to assume the office.

By the summer of 1618, inactivity was palling on Jonson. He therefore carried out a unique venture for a man of letters in his day — a journey on foot to Scotland, the country of his forebears. Edinburgh, the Scottish capital, granted him the freedom of the city in an impressive welcome. Scotland's leading poet, William Drummond, en-tertained him for some weeks at Hawthornden on the edge of the lovely Lammermoor Hills south of Edinburgh. Drummond's notes on his distinguished guest's conversation about literature and writers have preserved for posterity the peculiar mixture of learning, judgment, and arrogance which formed the essential Ben Jonson.

After his return from the Scottish tour, Jonson set up his court in various London taverns, "The Sun," "The Dog," "The Triple Inn," and especially "The Devil," whose upper room, known as the Apollo, bore on its walls in letters of gold some of his own sayings. There at "lyric feasts," as Robert Herrick (1591–1674) called them, Jonson presided, the dictator of English letters. The goodly company of "The Tribe of Ben" listened affectionately to his reminiscences, to his literary loves and hates, but above all, to his inimitable wit in verse which, so Herrick testified, "outdid the meat, outdid the frolic wine."

In 1625 Jonson lost through death his good patron, King James I. In expectation of less generous favor from the new king, Charles I, Jonson resumed the writing of plays, producing four within the next eight years without one success. John Dryden well termed these pieces "Jonson's dotages." During the same period an intense quarrel broke out between Jonson and his old friend, Inigo Jones, over court prefer-ments. In 1628 he got the post of Chronologer to the City of London, but later lost it because a paralytic stroke prevented the fulfillment of his duties. By the early 1630's he had declined into a broken-down, testy veteran of a past literary epoch. On August 6, 1637, he died. England honored him with burial in Westminster Abbey, and with an epitaph which has echoed through three centuries: "O rare Ben Jonson."

THE COMEDY OF HUMORS

The most significant of all Ben Jonson's varied accomplishments was his comedy of humors. Though hating Puritans, he had their moralistic and reforming temper. He preferred the dramatic art which undertook the instruction of erring humanity. This had been a leading object of classical comedy ever since the great Aristophanes in Athens. Jonson endorsed Cicero's view that comedy should be "the imitation of life, the mirror of custom, the image of truth, a thing throughout pleasant and ridiculous, and *accommodated to the correction of manners.*" The prevalence of romance in English comedy at the end of the sixteenth century therefore seemed to him irrelevant and absurd. He determined to develop the satiric as the dominant element.

The theory of human personality which had grown out of medieval science suggested to Jonson a new formula for satiric characterization. The physiology of the Middle Ages had taught that "humors," the moistures or fluids in the blood operating through the brain, determined a man's nature. An excess of one humor, or a change in that balance of humors which maintained normality, was believed to cause eccentricity of one kind or another, such as irritability, melancholy, dullness, or timidity. The eccentricities also came to be termed, like their causes, humors. With these notions Jonson proceeded to renovate the principle of type figures (crotchety fathers or clever slaves, for example), which Plautus and Terence had practiced. The essence of each of Jonson's characters was supposed to be a humor, which he defined "as when some one peculiar quality doth possess a man, that it doth draw all his affects, his spirits, and his powers, in their confluctions, all to run one way." Jonson could not resist sometimes, however, the temptation to exhibit, instead of a ruling bias of temperament or interest, a mere oddity of speech or dress or manners: — to take his own examples, a London fop's "wearing a pied feather, . . . a yard of shoe-tie, or the Switzers knot on his French garters."

The novel pattern of Jonson's comedy was described to perfection by the title to his maiden work, *Every Man in his Humour.* It aimed to "sport with human follies" by an exhibition of "every man in his humor" — a satirical parade of contemporary eccentrics. Downright is "a plain [i.e., plain spoken] squire"; Stephen, "a country gull" or dupe; Captain Bobadill, a bragging and cowardly gallant; and so on. Jonson ridiculed these current and minor types of man's frailty with good-natured scorn. In his later comedies he tended to depict the more serious vices and to make the satire more biting. The corrective impulse apparently took a deeper hold upon him the longer he wrote for the stage.

Jonson's comedy of humors influenced to some degree almost all English comedy during the reigns of James I and Charles I. The closest imitation came from Philip Massinger (1583–1640), a playwright with a moralistic bent similar to Jonson's. Massinger's finest comedy, *A New Way to Pay Old Debts* (c. 1625), includes minor characters, such as Greedy, Furnace, Marrall, and Tapwell, who belong to the Jonson line of humors. The chief personage, Sir Giles Overreach, an extortioner, develops into an incredible monster. He finally suffers the melodramatic doom of madness. *A New Way to Pay Old Debts*, though a popular vehicle for star actors as recent as Walter Hampden, clearly lacks the perception and balance of Jonson's satire. No other of the old English dramatists could raise indignation to such a fine art as Ben Jonson.

"EPICOENE"

Epicoene, or The Silent Woman, is the brightest of all Jonson's comedies. A spirit of playfulness unusual to him pervades its scenes, perhaps because he was composing a drama for performance by child actors during holiday revels. A well-known actor, Nathaniel Field (1587–1633), whom Jonson had tutored in Horace and other classical authors, organized late in 1609 a fresh company of boy players, known as "Children of Her Majesty's Revels." Field fitted up some kind of private playhouse in the old monastic precincts of Whitefriars adjoining the Blackfriars district on the west, but lying outside the city wall. His good friend Jonson wrote *Epicoene* for production at his new theater in January, 1610, before an audience of aristocrats and smart society. *Epicoene* continued a great favorite on the London stage until the Civil War. After the reopening of the theaters in 1660 it had frequent revivals until well into the eighteenth century.

The plot materials of *Epicoene* represent the mixture of learning and observation usual in all Jonson's comedies. He borrowed the device of the nervous misanthrope's marriage to a quiet-tongued woman who turns into a scold from a story by Libanius (314–91), a teacher of rhetoric at Constantinople, whose declamations were much read by Elizabethan scholars. Jonson gave to the story a new conclusion which he took from Plautus's comedy *Casina*, where a supposed bride is discovered to be of the male sex. Other Roman works, Ovid's *Art of Love* and Juvenal's *Satires*, supplied most of the talk by the gallants, Dauphine, Clerimont, and Truewit, on women. Truewit's duping of the two gulls, Daw and La-Foole, into a near quarrel (Act IV, Scene 5) Jonson adapted from Shakespeare's *Twelfth Night* (Act III, Scene 4), where Sir Toby Belch incites Viola and Sir Andrew Aguecheek to a reluctant duel in Olivia's garden. Finally, one of the absurd fads among London's female inhabitants suggested the inclusion of the "college ladies" with their pretensions of sophistication.

From these mixed sources Jonson contrived a well-knit plot which evidences the discipline of his classical studies. Few plays of his day show such a strict use of the classical unities of time, place, and action. *Epicoene* opens in mid-morning and closes by mid-afternoon of the same day. All the events occur in neighboring places within a single district of London. The plot carefully develops act by act its complications until the last scene of Act V, when the climax comes off with the surprising discovery of Epicoene's identity.

Jonson's veneration for classical example even went so far that he arranged the scene divisions of his plays in conformity with the late classical convention in the texts of Plautus and Terence. This convention required a new scene after any entrance or exit which gave to the existing scene a turn, however slight. Though Jonson's arrangement of scenes is merely a literary device without the least effect on his dramatic pattern, it is proof of his independence as a writer. No other English dramatist of note ever copied the classical scheme of scenes.

Jonson in his own age won high recognition as a poet, especially as a lyricist. The twentieth century seldom remembers him as the author of the love song which it often enjoys, "Drink to me only with thine eyes." *Epicoene* contains one of Jonson's finest lyrics, one which is among the most famous of old English lyrics, "Still to be neat, still to be dressed" (Act I, Scene 1, ll. 111–22). It is peculiarly deft and graceful in phrase, with neither a word superfluous nor one out of keeping with the total effect.   The very perfection of its literary finish, however, suggests a certain lack of spontaneity in Jonson's muse, as if he carved out his poems with expert deliberation.

The characters in *Epicoene* represent a typical set of Jonsonian humors derived from current humanity.   Several of the people possess more than one humor.   Mrs. Otter, for example, displays three obsessions: to lord it over her spouse, to dwell upon dreams and their significance, and to affect the smart society dame.   Perhaps the most interesting personages are the "college ladies," Lady Haughty, Lady Centaure, and Mistress Mavis, with their strangely modern airs.   In them Jonson might well be taking off the ultra-sophisticated females of the leisure class in urban Europe and America.   The twentieth century has seen such women, who, tiring of conventional domesticity and wanting to assert a masculine freedom in their social behavior, set up apartments where they may entertain male admirers.   *Epicoene* reveals that neither the urge nor the method are as recent in origin as might be thought.

The most distinguished element in *Epicoene* is Jonson's theatrical wit.   It proceeds from a skillful creation of stage situations which exploit the comic weaknesses of the characters.   Jonson provided the openings and then allowed his characters to get themselves involved in absurdity.   In the first scene of Act V, Daw and La-Foole, as timid in their relations with women as in everything else, desire to convince Clerimont that they "know what's what," as they say.   He leads them on from one invention of experience to another, each growing more ridiculous than the last.   Finally their stories come to a preposterous climax in the claim of intimacy with the supposed bride, Epicoene.   Thus these two fops by their own testimony lay bare the complete folly of their humor.

The tone of the ridicule in *Epicoene* shows Jonson the satirist in his most pleasant vein. He implied his concern over the failures of man as *homo sapiens*, man endowed with wisdom, but he did not allow the Moroses, the Daws, the Lady Haughtys to sour his mind.   Without venom he painted these misanthropes and silly men about town and empty-headed feminists as grotesques.   Theirs are the more moderate vices of irrationality.   Though Jonson nonetheless despised them, he kept his judgment restrained and his reproof gay.   *Epicoene*, in consequence, is a still entertaining demonstration by a great lover of reason that mankind under manifold guises is forever playing the fool.

[For critiques on Ben Jonson, see C. H. Herford and Percy Simpson, *Ben Jonson; edited with introduction and notes* (6 vols. 1925–38), and Mina Kerr, *The Influence of Ben Jonson on English Comedy* (1912); for the "War of the Theaters," J. H. Penniman, Introduction to *Poetaster* and *Satiromastix* in the Belles Lettres Series; for the masque, Enid Welsford, *The Court Masque* (1927), and A. Nicoll, *Stuart Masques and the Renaissance Stage* (1937).]

BEN JONSON

Epicoene,

OR

The Silent Woman

DRAMATIS PERSONAE

MOROSE, *a gentleman that loves no noise*
SIR DAUPHINE EUGENIE, *a knight, his nephew*
NED CLERIMONT, *a gentleman, his friend*
TRUEWIT, *another friend*
SIR JOHN DAW, *a knight*
SIR AMOROUS LA-FOOLE, *another knight*
THOMAS OTTER, *a land and sea captain*
CUTBEARD, *a barber*
MUTE, *one of* MOROSE'S *servants*
Parson
Page to CLERIMONT

EPICOENE, *supposed the* Silent Woman
LADY HAUGHTY,
LADY CENTAURE, } *ladies collegiates*
MISTRESS MAVIS,
MISTRESS OTTER, *the*
  captain's wife,
MISTRESS TRUSTY, } *pretenders*
LADY HAUGHTY'S
  woman,
Pages, servants, etc.

The Scene is London

PROLOGUE

Truth says, of old the art of making plays
Was to content the people; and their praise
Was to the poet money, wine, and bays.

But in this age, a sect of writers are,
That, only, for particular likings care,
And will taste nothing that is popular.   5

With such we mingle neither brains nor breasts;
Our wishes, like to those make public feasts,
Are not to please the cook's taste but the guests'.

Yet, if those cunning palates hither come,   10
They shall find guests' entreaty, and good room;
And though all relish not, sure there will be some,

That, when they leave their seats, shall make them say,
Who wrote that piece, could so have wrote a play,
But that he knew this was the better way.   15

For, to present all custard, or all tart,
And have no other meats to bear a part,
Or to want bread, and salt, were but coarse art.

The poet prays you then, with better thought
To sit; and, when his cates [1] are all in brought,   20
Though there be none far-fet, there will dear-bought,

Be fit for ladies: some for lords, knights, 'squires;
Some for your waiting-wench, and city-wires; [2]
Some for your men, and daughters of Whitefriars.[3]

Nor is it, only, while you keep your seat   25
Here, that his feast will last; but you shall eat
A week at ord'naries,[4] on his broken meat:
     If his muse be true,
     Who commends her to you.

ANOTHER PROLOGUE

The ends of all, who for the scene do write,
Are, or should be, to profit and delight.
And still't hath been the praise of all best times,
So persons were not touch'd, to tax the crimes.
Then, in this play, which we present tonight,   5
And make the object of your ear and sight,
On forfeit of yourselves, think nothing true:

Lest so you make the maker to judge you.
For he knows, poet never credit gained
By writing truths, but things, like truths, well feigned.   10
If any yet will, with particular sleight
Of application, wrest what he doth write;
And that he meant, or him, or her, will say:
They make a libel, which he made a play.

ACT I

SCENE I. *A room in* CLERIMONT'S *house.*

Enter CLERIMONT, *making himself ready,*
followed by his page

   Cler. Have you got the song yet perfect, I gave you, boy?

   Page. Yes, sir.

   Cler. Let me hear it.

   Page. You shall, sir; but i'faith let nobody   5 else.

   Cler. Why, I pray?

   Page. It will get you the dangerous name of a poet in town, sir; besides me a perfect deal of ill-will at the mansion you wot [5] of, whose   10 lady is the argument of it; where now I am the welcomest thing under a man that comes there.

[1] Sweetmeats.   [2] City-dames wearing dresses stiffened and shaped by wires.
[3] Women of Whitefriars, the district between Fleet Street and the Thames River in the heart of London where pickpockets, gamblers, prostitutes, rascals and debtors of both sexes sought refuge from the law. The garbs in that area were distinctly Bohemian.
[4] Public eating-houses.   [5] Know.

Cler. I think; and above a man too, if the truth were racked out of you.

Page. No, faith, I'll confess before, sir. 15 The gentlewomen play with me, and throw me on the bed, and carry me in to my lady: and she kisses me with her oiled face, and puts a peruke on my head; and asks me an [1] I will wear her gown? and I say no: and then she hits me a 20 blow o' the ear, and calls me Innocent! and lets me go.

Cler. No marvel if the door be kept shut against your master, when the entrance is so easy to you — well, sir, you shall go there 25 no more, lest I be fain to seek your voice in my lady's rushes,[2] a fortnight hence. Sing, sir.

(*Page sings.*

Enter TRUEWIT

True. Why, here's the man that can melt away his time and never feels it! What between his mistress abroad and his ingle [3] at 30 home, high fare, soft lodging, fine clothes, and his fiddle; he thinks the hours have no wings, or the day no post-horse. Well, sir gallant, were you struck with the plague [4] this minute, or condemned to any capital punishment tomor- 35 row, you would begin then to think, and value every article of your time, esteem it at the true rate, and give all for it.

Cler. Why, what should a man do?

True. Why, nothing; or that which, 40 when 'tis done, is as idle. Hearken after the next horse-race, or hunting-match, lay wagers, praise Puppy, or Peppercorn, White-foot, Franklin; swear upon Whitemane's [5] party; speak aloud, that my lords may hear you; 45 visit my ladies at night, and be able to give them the character of every bowler or better on the green.[6] These be the things wherein your fashionable men exercise themselves, and I for company. 50

Cler. Nay, if I have thy authority, I'll not leave yet. Come, the other are considerations,

when we come to have gray heads and weak hams, moist eyes and shrunk members. We'll think on 'em then; and we'll pray and fast. 55

True. Ay, and destine only that time of age to goodness, which our want of ability will not let us employ in evil!

Cler. Why, then 'tis time enough.

True. Yes; as if a man should sleep all 60 the term,[1] and think to effect his business the last day. O, Clerimont, this time, because it is an incorporeal thing, and not subject to sense, we mock ourselves the fineliest out of it, with vanity and misery indeed! not seeking an 65 end of wretchedness, but only changing the matter still.

Cler. Nay, thou'lt not leave now ——

True. See but our common disease! [2] with what justice can we complain, that great 70 men will not look upon us, nor be at leisure to give our affairs such dispatch as we expect, when we will never do it to ourselves? nor hear, nor regard ourselves?

Cler. Foh! thou hast read Plutarch's 75 morals, now, or some such tedious fellow; and it shews so vilely with thee! 'fore God, 'twill spoil thy wit utterly. Talk to me of pins, and feathers, and ladies, and rushes,[3] and such things: and leave this Stoicity [4] alone, till thou 80 mak'st sermons.

True. Well, sir; if it will not take, I have learned to lose as little of my kindness as I can; I'll do good to no man against his will, certainly. When were you at the college? 85

Cler. What college?

True. As if you knew not!

Cler. No, faith, I came but from court yesterday.

True. Why, is it not arrived there yet, 90 the news? A new foundation, sir, here in the town, of ladies, that call themselves the collegiates, an order between courtiers and country-madams, that live from their husbands; and give entertainment to all the wits, and 95 braveries [5] of the time, as they call them: cry down, or up, what they like or dislike in a brain

---

[1] If.   [2] The common floor-covering at the time.

[3] Boy-favorite.

[4] The plague, or black death, steadily virulent in seventeenth-century London.

[5] A noted race-horse of the day.   [6] Bowling green.

[1] Term of court, lasting in London about three weeks four times a year.

[2] Failing.   [3] Trifles.   [4] Stoical indifference.

[5] Beaux.

or a fashion, with most masculine, or rather hermaphroditical authority; and every day gain to their college some new probationer.   100

Cler. Who is the president?

True. The grave and youthful matron, the Lady Haughty.

Cler. A pox of her autumnal face, her pieced beauty! there's no man can be admitted till   105 she be ready, now-a-days, till she has painted, and perfumed, and washed, and scoured, but the boy, here; and him she wipes her oiled lips upon, like a sponge. I have made a song (I pray thee hear it) on the subject. (*Page sings.*   110

Still to be neat, still to be drest,
As you were going to a feast;
Still to be powdered, still perfumed;
Lady, it is to be presumed,
Though art's hid causes are not found,   115
All is not sweet, all is not sound.

Give me a look, give me a face,
That makes simplicity a grace;
Robes loosely flowing, hair as free:
Such sweet neglect more taketh me,   120
Than all the adulteries [1] of art;
They strike mine eyes, but not my heart.

True. And I am clearly on the other side: I love a good dressing before any beauty o' the world. O, a woman is then like a deli-   125 cate garden; nor is there one kind of it; [2] she may vary every hour; take often counsel of her glass, and choose the best. If she have good ears, show them; good hair, lay it out; good legs, wear short clothes; a good hand, discover   130 it often: practice any art to mend breath, cleanse teeth, repair eye-brows; paint, and pro- fess it.

Cler. How! publicly?

True. The doing of it, not the manner: 135 that must be private. Many things that seem foul in the doing, do please done. A lady should, indeed, study her face, when we think she sleeps; nor, when the doors are shut, should men be enquiring; all is sacred within,   140 then. Is it for us to see their perukes put on, their false teeth, their complexion, their eye-

brows, their nails? You see gilders will not work, but inclosed. They must not discover how little serves, with the help of art, to   145 adorn a great deal. How long did the canvas hang afore Aldgate? [1] Were the people suf- fered to see the city's Love and Charity, while they were rude stone, before they were painted and burnished? No; no more should   150 servants [2] approach their mistresses, but when they are complete and finished.

Cler. Well said, my Truewit.

True. And a wise lady will keep a guard al- ways upon the place, that she may do   155 things securely. I once followed a rude fellow into a chamber, where the poor madam, for haste, and troubled, snatched at her peruke to cover her baldness; and put it on the wrong way.

Cler. O prodigy!   160

True. And the unconscionable knave held her in compliment an hour with that reverst face, when I still looked when she should talk from the t'other side.   164

Cler. Why, thou shouldst have relieved her.

True. No, faith, I let her alone, as we'll let this argument, if you please, and pass to an- other. When saw you Dauphine Eugenie?

Cler. Not these three days. Shall we go to him this morning? He is very melan-   170 choly, I hear.

True. Sick of the uncle, is he? I met that stiff piece of formality, his uncle, yesterday, with a huge turban of night-caps on his head, buckled over his ears.   175

Cler. Oh, that's his custom when he walks abroad. He can endure no noise, man.

True. So I have heard. But is the disease [3] so ridiculous in him as it is made? They say he has been upon divers treaties with the fish-   180 wives and orange-women; and articles pro- pounded between them: marry, the chimney- sweepers will not be drawn in.

[1] Adulterations or corruptions.   [2] I.e., of dressing.

[1] The east gate of the old London city wall. On the city side of this gate, rebuilt in 1606, stood statues of Peace and Charity, copied from the figures on ancient Roman coins dug up when the new gate foundations were made.

[2] Lovers.

[3] Eccentricity. The uncle, Morose, could endure none of the street-cries uttered by the tradespeople of London.

Cler. No, nor the broom-men:[1] they stand out stiffly. He cannot endure a costard- 185 monger,[2] he swoons if he hear one.

True. Methinks a smith should be ominous.

Cler. Or any hammer-man.[3] A brasier[4] is not suffered to dwell in the parish, nor an armorer. He would have hanged a pew- 190 terer's prentice once upon a Shrove-tuesday's riot,[5] for being of that trade, when the rest were quit.[6]

True. A trumpet should fright him terribly, or the hautboys. 195

Cler. Out of his senses. The waights[7] of the city have a pension of[8] him not to come near that ward. This youth practiced on him one night like the bell-man; and never left till he had brought him down to the door with a 200 long sword; and there left him flourishing with the air.

Page. Why, sir, he hath chosen a street to lie in so narrow at both ends, that it will receive no coaches, nor carts, nor any of these com- 205 mon noises: and therefore we that love him, devise to bring him in such as we may, now and then, for his exercise, to breathe him. He would grow resty else in his ease: his virtue would rust without action. I entreated a 210 bearward,[9] one day, to come down with the dogs of some four parishes that way, and I thank him he did; and cried his games under master Morose's window: till he was sent crying away, with his head made a most bleeding spec- 215 tacle to the multitude. And, another time, a fencer marching to his prize, had his drum most tragically run through, for taking that street in his way at my request. 219

True. A good wag! How does he for the bells?

Cler. Oh, in the Queen's time, he was wont to go out of town every Saturday at ten o'clock,

or on holy day eves. But now, by reason of the sickness, the perpetuity of ringing has made him devise a room, with double walls and 225 treble ceilings; the windows close shut and caulked: and there he lives by candle-light. He turned away a man, last week, for having a pair of new shoes that creaked. And this fellow waits on him now in tennis-court socks, or 230 slippers soled with wool: and they talk each to other in a trunk. See, who comes here!

SCENE 2. *The same.*

Enter SIR DAUPHINE EUGENIE

Daup. How now! what ail you, sirs? dumb?

True. Struck into stone, almost, I am here, with tales o' thine uncle. There was never such a prodigy heard of.

Daup. I would you would once lose this 5 subject, my masters, for my sake. They are such as you are, that have brought me into that predicament I am with him.

True. How is that?

Daup. Marry, that he will disinherit me; 10 no more. He thinks, I and my company are authors of all the ridiculous acts and monuments are told of him.

True. 'Slid, I would be the author of more to vex him; that purpose deserves it: it gives 15 thee law of plaguing him. I'll tell thee what I would do. I would make a false almanack, get it printed; and then have him drawn out on a coronation day to the Tower-wharf,[1] and kill him with the noise of the ordnance. Dis- 20 inherit thee! He cannot, man. Art not thou next of blood, and his sister's son?

Daup. Ay, but he will thrust me out of it, he vows, and marry.

True. How! That's a more portent.[2] 25 Can he endure no noise, and will venture on a wife?

Cler. Yes: why thou art a stranger, it seems, to his best trick, yet. He has employed a fellow this half year all over England to 30

---

[1] Sellers of brooms.   [2] Apple or fruit venders.
[3] A hooper of barrels, or shoer of horses, or artificer in metals.
[4] A brass worker.
[5] On this festival day, the Tuesday before the first Wednesday in Lent, the apprentices took the law very often into their own hands and did all sorts of violent mischief.
[6] Acquitted.   [7] Serenaders.   [8] From.
[9] Bear warden, a keeper of a bear which is to be tormented by dogs in a bear-baiting.

---

[1] The anniversary of the royal coronation was a gala-day with much noisy celebration. The cannon outside the walls of old London Tower on the bank of the Thames were always fired off.
[2] A greater amazing feat.

hearken him out a dumb woman; be she of any form, or any quality, so she be able to bear children: her silence is dowry enough, he says.

True. But I trust to God he has found none.

Cler. No; but he has heard of one that's 35 lodged in the next street to him, who is exceedingly soft-spoken; thrifty of her speech; that spends but six words a day. And her he's about now, and shall have her.

True. Is't possible! Who is his agent 40 in the business?

Cler. Marry, a barber, one Cutbeard; an honest fellow, one that tells Dauphine all here.

True. Why you oppress me with wonder: a woman, and a barber, and love no noise! 45

Cler. Yes, faith. The fellow trims him silently, and has not the knack [1] with his sheers or his fingers: and that continence in a barber he thinks so eminent a virtue, as it has made him chief of his counsel. 50

True. Is the barber to be seen, or the wench?

Cler. Yes, that they are.

True. I prithee, Dauphine, let's go thither.

Daup. I have some business now: I cannot, i'faith. 55

True. You shall have no business shall make you neglect this, sir: we'll make her talk, believe it; or, if she will not, we can give out at least so much as shall interrupt the treaty; we will break it. Thou art bound in con- 60 science, when he suspects thee without cause, to torment him.

Daup. Not I, by any means. I'll give no suffrage to't. He shall never have that plea against me, that I opposed the least phan- 65 t'sy of his. Let it lie upon my stars to be guilty, I'll be innocent.

True. Yes, and be poor, and beg; do, innocent: [2] when some groom of his has got him an heir, or this barber, if he himself cannot. 70 Innocent! — I prithee, Ned, where lies she? Let him be innocent still.

Cler. Why, right over against the barber's; in the house where Sir John Daw lies.

True. You do not mean to confound me!

Cler. Why? 76

[1] Does not make a clacking sound. This was a common habit of Elizabethan barbers.
[2] Fool.

True. Does he that would marry her know so much?

Cler. I cannot tell.

True. 'Twere enough of imputation to 80 her with him.

Cler. Why?

True. The only talking [1] sir in the town! Jack Daw! and he teach her not to speak! — God be wi' you. I have some business too. 85

Cler. Will you not go thither, then?

True. Not with the danger to meet Daw, for mine ears.

Cler. Why, I thought you two had been upon very good terms. 90

True. Yes, of keeping distance.

Cler. They say, he is a very good scholar.

True. Ay, and he says it first. A pox on him, a fellow that pretends only to learning, buys titles, and nothing else of books in him! 95

Cler. The world reports him to be very learned.

True. I am sorry the world should so conspire to belie him.

Cler. Good faith, I have heard very 100 good things come from him.

True. You may; there's none so desperately ignorant to deny that: would they were his own! God be wi' you, gentlemen.

(*Exit hastily.*

Cler. This is very abrupt! 105

Scene 3. *The same.*

Daup. Come, you are a strange open man, to tell everything thus.

Cler. Why, believe it, Dauphine, Truewit's a very honest fellow.

Daup. I think no other: but this frank 5 nature of his is not for secrets.

Cler. Nay, then, you are mistaken, Dauphine: I know where he has been well trusted, and discharged the trust very truly, and heartily. 10

Daup. I contend not, Ned; but with the fewer a business is carried, it is ever the safer. Now we are alone, if you'll go thither, I am for you.

Cler. When were you there? 15

[1] Talkative.

Daup. Last night: and such a Decameron [1] of sport fallen out! Boccace never thought of the like. Daw does nothing but court her; and the wrong way. He would lie with her, and praises her modesty; desires that she would talk 20 and be free, and commends her silence in verses; which he reads, and swears are the best that ever man made. Then rails at his fortunes, stamps, and mutines,[2] why[3] he is not made a counselor, and called to affairs of state. 25

Cler. I prithee let's go. I would fain partake this. — Some water, boy.   (*Exit Page.*

Daup. We are invited to dinner[4] together, he and I, by one that came thither to him, Sir La-Foole. 30

Cler. Oh, that's a precious mannikin![5]

Daup. Do you know him?

Cler. Ay, and he will know you too, if e'er he saw you but once, though you should meet him at church in the midst of prayers. He is 35 one of the braveries,[6] though he be none of the wits. He will salute a judge upon the bench, and a bishop in the pulpit, a lawyer when he is pleading at the bar, and a lady when she is dancing in a masque, and put her out. He 40 does give plays, and suppers, and invites his guests to them, aloud, out of his window, as they ride by in coaches. He has a lodging in the Strand for the purpose: or to watch when ladies are gone to the china-houses,[7] or the 45 Exchange,[8] that he may meet them by chance, and give them presents, some two or three hundred pounds' worth of toys, to be laughed at. He is never without a spare banquet, or sweetmeats in his chamber, for their women to 50 alight at, and come up to for a bait.

Daup. Excellent! He was a fine youth last night; but now he is much finer! What is his Christian name? I have forgot.

---

[1] I.e., such a collection. In 1353 the Italian writer Boccaccio published his celebrated collection of a hundred tales under the title of "Decameron."
[2] Mutinies, rebels.   [3] Because.
[4] The fashionable dinner hour was noon or a little before.
[5] Little man.   [6] Gallants.
[7] Shops exhibiting Chinese merchandise, resorts of fashionable society at this time.
[8] The New Exchange in the Strand, opened in 1609. It became at once a fashionable bazaar and rendezvous.

Re-enter Page

Cler. Sir Amorous La-Foole. 55

Page. The gentleman is here below that owns that name.

Cler. 'Heart, he's come to invite me to dinner, I hold my life.

Daup. Like enough: prithee, let's have 60 him up.

Cler. Boy, marshal him.

Page. With a truncheon,[1] sir?

Cler. Away, I beseech you. (*Exit Page.*) — I'll make him tell us his pedigree now; and 65 what meat he has to dinner; and who are his guests; and the whole course of his fortunes; with a breath.

SCENE 4. *The same.*

Enter SIR AMOROUS LA-FOOLE

La-F. 'Save, dear Sir Dauphine! honored Master Clerimont!

Cler. Sir Amorous! you have very much honested[2] my lodging with your presence.

La-F. Good faith, it is a fine lodging: 5 almost as delicate a lodging as mine.

Cler. Not so, sir.

La-F. Excuse me, sir, if it were in the Strand, I assure you. I am come, Master Clerimont, to entreat you to wait upon two 10 or three ladies, to dinner, today.

Cler. How, sir! Wait upon them? Did you ever see me carry dishes?

La-F. No, sir, dispense with me;[3] I meant, to bear them company. 15

Cler. Oh, that I will, sir: the doubtfulness of your phrase, believe it, sir, would breed you a quarrel once an hour, with the terrible boys,[4] if you should but keep them fellowship a day.

La-F. It should be extremely against my 20 will, sir, if I contested with any man.

Cler. I believe it, sir. Where hold you your feast?

La-F. At Tom Otter's, sir.

Daup. Tom Otter! what's he? 25

---

[1] The sheriff's staff of authority.
[2] Honored.   [3] Pardon me.
[4] A riotous set of young bucks who haunted the London streets at all hours.

La-F. Captain Otter, sir; he is a kind of gamester, but he has had command both by sea and by land.

Daup. O, then he is *animal amphibium*? [1]

La-F. Ay, sir: his wife was the rich china- 30 woman,[2] that the courtiers visited so often; that gave the rare entertainment.   She commands all at home.

Cler. Then she is captain Otter.

La-F. You say very well, sir; she is my 35 kinswoman, a La-Foole by the mother-side, and will invite any great ladies for my sake.

Daup. Not of the La-Fooles of Essex?

La-F. No, sir, the La-Fooles of London.

Cler. (*aside*). Now, he's in.[3]   40

La-F. They all come out of our house, the La-Fooles of the north, the La-Fooles of the west, the La-Fooles of the east and south — we are as ancient a family as any is in Europe — but I myself am descended lineally of the 45 French La-Fooles — and, we do bear for our coat [4] yellow, or *or*,[5] checker'd *azure*,[6] and *gules*,[7] and some three or four colors more, which is a very noted coat, and has, sometimes, been solemnly worn by divers nobility of our house 50 — but let that go, antiquity is not respected now. — I had a brace of fat does sent me, gentlemen, and half a dozen of pheasants, a dozen or two of godwits, and some other fowl, which I would have eaten, while they are good, and 55 in good company: — there will be a great lady or two, my Lady Haughty, my Lady Centaure, Mistress Dol Mavis — and they come o' purpose to see the silent gentlewoman, Mistress Epicoene, that honest Sir John Daw has 60 promised to bring thither — and then, Mistress Trusty, my lady's woman, will be there too, and this honorable knight, Sir Dauphine, with yourself, Master Clerimont — and we'll be very merry, and have fiddlers, and dance. — I 65 have been a mad wag in my time, and have spent some crowns since I was a page in court, to my Lord Lofty, and after, my lady's gentle-

man-usher,[1] who got me knighted in Ireland, since it pleased my elder brother to die. — 70 I had as fair a gold jerkin [2] on that day, as any worn in the island voyage,[3] or at Cadiz,[4] none dispraised; and I came over in it hither, showed myself to my friends in court, and after went down to my tenants in the country, and 75 surveyed my lands, let new leases, took their money, spent it in the eye o' the land [5] here, upon ladies: — and now I can take up [6] at my pleasure.

Daup. Can you take up ladies, sir?   80

Cler. O, let him breathe, he has not recovered.

Daup. Would I were your half in that commodity!

La-F. No, sir, excuse me: I meant money, which can take up anything.   I have an- 85 other guest or two, to invite, and say as much to, gentlemen.   I'll take my leave abruptly, in hope you will not fail — Your servant.   (*Exit.*

Daup. We will not fail you, Sir precious La-Foole; but she shall, that your ladies come 90 to see, if I have credit afore, Sir Daw.

Cler. Did you ever hear such a wind-sucker,[7] as this?

Daup. Or such a rook [8] as the other, that will betray his mistress to be seen! Come, 95 'tis time we prevented it.

Cler. Go.   (*Exeunt.*

ACT II

SCENE 1. *A room in* MOROSE'S *house.*

Enter MOROSE, *with a tube in his hand,*
followed by MUTE

Mor. Cannot I, yet, find out a more compendious [9] method, than by this trunk, to save my servants the labor of speech, and mine ears

---

[1] A creature of two natures.
[2] Proprietress of a china-shop.
[3] Now, he's started.
[4] I.e., the fool's coat.   The household fools of aristocratic families had worn a garb of motley color.
[5] Gold.   [6] Blue.   [7] Red.

---

[1] A man-servant who waited upon ladies chiefly.
[2] Gold-embroidered doublet.
[3] The voyage of Sir Francis Drake in 1585 to the West Indies, where San Domingo was captured.
[4] The expedition of the Earl of Essex and of Lord Admiral Howard against Cadiz in 1596, when the Spanish fleet was burnt and the city sacked.
[5] I.e., London.   [6] Borrow.
[7] An unserviceable breed of hawk, but, figuratively, a tiresome windy fellow.
[8] I.e., a fool.   The rook was considered a stupid bird.
[9] Expeditious.

the discords of sounds? Let me see: all discourses but my own afflict me; they seem 5 harsh, impertinent, and irksome. Is it not possible, that thou shouldst answer me by signs, and I apprehend thee, fellow? Speak not, though I question you. You have taken the ring off from the street door, as I bade you? 10 Answer me not by speech, but by silence; unless it be otherwise. (MUTE *makes a leg.*[1]) — Very good. And you have fastened on a thick quilt, or flock-bed,[2] on the outside of the door; that if they knock with their daggers, or 15 with brick-bats, they can make no noise? — But with your leg, your answer, unless it be otherwise. (MUTE *makes a leg.*) — Very good. This is not only fit modesty in a servant, but good state and discretion in a master. And 20 you have been with Cutbeard the barber, to have him come to me? (MUTE *makes a leg.*) — Good. And, he will come presently? Answer me not but with your leg, unless it be otherwise; if it be otherwise, shake your head, or shrug. 25 (MUTE *makes a leg.*) — So! Your Italian and Spaniard are wise in these: and it is a frugal and comely gravity. How long will it be ere Cutbeard come? Stay; if an hour, hold up your whole hand, if half an hour, two fingers; if 30 a quarter, one; (MUTE *holds up a finger bent.*) — Good: half a quarter? 'tis well. And have you given him a key, to come in without knocking? (MUTE *makes a leg.*) — Good. And is the lock oiled, and the hinges, today? (MUTE *makes* 35 *a leg.*) — Good. And the quilting of the stairs no where worn out and bare? (MUTE *makes a leg.*) — Very good. I see, by much doctrine, and impulsion,[3] it may be effected; stand by. The Turk, in this divine discipline, is ad- 40 mirable, exceeding all the potentates of the earth; still waited on by mutes; and all his commands so executed; yea, even in the war, as I have heard, and in his marches, most of his charges and directions given by signs, and 45 with silence: an exquisite art! and I am heartily ashamed, and angry oftentimes, that the princes of Christendom should suffer a barbarian to transcend them in so high a point of

---

[1] Makes a bow.
[2] A bed filled with short wool fibers.
[3] Incitement.

felicity. I will practice it hereafter. (*A* 50 *horn winded within.*) — How now? Oh! oh! what villain, what prodigy of mankind is that? Look. (*Exit* MUTE.) — (*Horn again.*) — Oh! cut his throat, cut his throat! what murderer, hell-hound, devil can this be? 55

Re-enter MUTE

Mute. It is a post from the court ——
Mor. Out, rogue! and must thou blow thy horn too?
Mute. Alas, it is a post from the court, sir, that says, he must speak with you, pain of 60 death ——
Mor. Pain of thy life, be silent!

SCENE 2. *The same.*

Enter TRUEWIT *with a post-horn, and a halter in his hand*

True. By your leave, sir; — I am a stranger here: — Is your name Master Morose? Is your name Master Morose? Fishes![1] Pythagoreans[2] all! This is strange. What say you, sir? Nothing! Has Harpocrates[3] been 5 here with his club,[4] among you? Well, sir, I will believe you to be the man at this time: I will venture upon you, sir. Your friends at court commend them to you, sir ——
Mor. O men! O manners! was there ever 10 such an impudence?[5]
True. And are extremely solicitous for you, sir.
Mor. Whose knave are you?
True. Mine own knave, and your com- 15 peer, sir.
Mor. Fetch me my sword ——
True. You shall taste the one half of my

---

[1] I.e., dumb as fishes.
[2] The followers of the Greek philosopher, Pythagoras (sixth century B.C.), kept their doctrines and observances a deep secret.
[3] The Egyptian god of the sun, said to have been born with his finger on his lip, indicative of secrecy and mystery.
[4] Harpocrates was sometimes identified with the Greek god Heracles (Hercules), who was always pictured with a club.
[5] An impudent fellow.

dagger, if you do, groom; and you the other, if you stir, sir: Be patient, I charge you, 20 in the king's name, and hear me without insurrection. They say, you are to marry; to marry! do you mark, sir?

Mor. How then, rude companion!

True. Marry, your friends do wonder, 25 sir, the Thames being so near, wherein you may drown, so handsomely; or London-bridge, at a low fall,[1] with a fine leap, to hurry you down the stream; or, such a delicate steeple in the town, as Bow,[2] to vault from; or, a braver 30 height, as Paul's:[3] Or, if you affected to do it nearer home, and a shorter way, an excellent garret-window into the street; or, a beam in the said garret, with this halter (*shows him the halter*) — which they have sent, and desire, 35 that you would sooner commit your grave head to this knot, than to the wedlock noose; or, take a little sublimate, and go out of the world like a rat; or a fly, as one said, with a straw in your arse: any way, rather than follow this gob- 40 lin Matrimony. Alas, sir, do you ever think to find a chaste wife in these times? now? when there are so many masques, plays, Puritan preachings, mad folks,[4] and other strange sights to be seen daily, private and public? If 45 you had lived in King Etheldred's time, sir, or Edward the Confessor,[5] you might, perhaps, have found one in some cold country hamlet, then, a dull frosty wench, would have been contented with one man: now, they will as soon 50 be pleased with one leg, or one eye. I'll tell you, sir, the monstrous hazards you shall run with a wife.

Mor. Good sir, have I ever cozened[6] any friends of yours of their land? bought their 55 possessions? taken forfeit of their mortgage?

---

[1] I.e., when the rapids under the arches of the old bridge were slight.

[2] St. Mary le Bow in Cheapside, an ancient and famous church destroyed in the fire of 1666.

[3] The old St. Paul's Cathedral burnt in 1666.

[4] Jonson's catalogue of spectacles in contemporary London brings together a strange diversity of entertainment, at all of which in his opinion scandalous behavior was apparent.

[5] Edward the Confessor (1004-1066) was noted for his sanctity, and canonized in 1161. His father was Etheldred II, or the Unready (968-1016).

[6] Cheated.

begged a reversion from them? bastarded their issue? What have I done, that may deserve this?

True. Nothing, sir, that I know, but 60 your itch of marriage.

Mor. Why, if I had made an assassinate upon your father, vitiated[1] your mother, ravished your sisters ——

True. I would kill you, sir, I would kill 65 you, if you had.

Mor. Why, you do more in this, sir: it were a vengeance centuple, for all facinorous[2] acts that could be named, to do that you do.

True. Alas, sir, I am but a messenger: 70 I but tell you, what you must hear. It seems your friends are careful after your soul's health, sir, and would have you know the danger: (but you may do your pleasure for all them, I persuade not, sir). If, after you are married, 75 your wife do run away with a vaulter,[3] or the Frenchman that walks upon ropes, or him that dances the jig, or a fencer for his skill at his weapon; why it is not their fault, they have discharged their consciences; when you 80 know what may happen. Nay, suffer valiantly, sir, for I must tell you all the perils that you are obnoxious[4] to. If she be fair, young and vegetous,[5] no sweetmeats ever drew more flies; all the yellow doublets and great roses[6] in the 85 town will be there. If foul and crooked, she'll be with them, and buy those doublets and roses, sir. If rich, and that you marry her dowry, not her, she'll reign in your house as imperious as a widow. If noble, all her 90 kindred will be your tyrants. If fruitful, as proud as May, and humorous[7] as April; she must have her doctors, her midwives, her nurses, her longings every hour; though it be for the dearest morsel of man. If learned, 95 there was never such a parrot; all your patrimony will be too little for the guests that must be invited to hear her speak Latin and Greek; and you must lie with her in those languages

---

[1] Violate the chastity of.   [2] Infamous.

[3] Entertainers who did all sorts of leaping either on the ground or on horseback.

[4] Liable.   [5] Vigorous.

[6] The London gallants were then notorious for their bright costumes and the decorative roses on their shoes.

[7] Capricious.

too, if you will please her. If precise,[1] 100
you must feast all the silenced brethren,[2] once
in three days; salute the sisters; entertain the
whole family, or wood [3] of them; and hear long-
winded exercises, singings and catechisings,
which you are not given to, and yet must 105
give for; to please the zealous matron your wife,
who for the holy cause, will cozen you over and
above. You begin to sweat, sir! but this is not
half, i'faith: you may do your pleasure, notwithstanding, as I said before: I come not 110
to persuade you. (MUTE *is stealing away.*) —
Upon my faith, master serving-man, if you do
stir, I will beat you.

Mor. Oh, what is my sin! what is my sin!

True. Then, if you love your wife, or 115
rather dote on her, sir; Oh, how she'll torture
you, and take pleasure in your torments! You
shall lie with her but when she lists; she will not
hurt her beauty, her complexion; or it must be
for that jewel, or that pearl, when she 120
does: every half hour's pleasure must be bought
anew, and with the same pain and charge you
wooed her at first. Then you must keep what
servants she please; what company she will;
that friend must not visit you without her 125
license; and him she loves most, she will seem
to hate eagerliest, to decline your jealousy; or,
feign to be jealous of you first; and for that
cause go live with her she-friend, or cousin [4]
at the college, that can instruct her in all 130
the mysteries of writing letters, corrupting
servants, taming spies; where she must have
that rich gown for such a great day; a new one
for the next; a richer for the third; be served in
silver; have the chamber filled with a suc- 135
cession of grooms, footmen, ushers, and other
messengers; besides embroiderers, jewelers,
tire-women,[5] sempsters,[6] feathermen,[7] perfumers; whilst she feels not how the land drops
away, nor the acres melt; nor foresees the 140
change, when the mercer [8] has your woods for
her velvets; never weighs what her pride costs,

sir; so she may kiss a page, or a smooth chin,
that has the despair of a beard: be a states-
woman, know all the news, what was done 145
at Salisbury,[1] what at the Bath,[2] what at court,
what in progress;[3] or, so she may censure poets,
and authors, and styles, and compare them;
Daniel [4] with Spenser,[5] Jonson with the t'other
youth, and so forth: or be thought cun- 150
ning in controversies, or the very knots of divinity; and have often in her mouth the state of
the question; and then skip to the mathematics,
and demonstration: and answer in religion to
one, in state to another, in bawdry to a third.

Mor. Oh, oh! 156

True. All this is very true, sir. And then
her going in disguise to that conjurer,[6] and
this cunning woman: [7] where the first question
is, how soon you shall die? next, if her 160
present servant [8] love her? next, if she shall
have a new servant? and how many? which of
her family would make the best bawd, male or
female? what precedence she shall have by her
next match? and sets down the answers, 165
and believes them above the scriptures. Nay,
perhaps she'll study the art.

Mor. Gentle sir, have you done? Have you
had your pleasure of me? I'll think of these
things. 170

True. Yes, sir: and then comes reeking home
of vapor [9] and sweat, with going afoot, and lies
in a month of a new face, all oil and birdlime,[10]
and rises in asses' milk, and is cleansed with a
new fucus: [11] God be wi' you, sir. One 175
thing more, which I had almost forgot. This
too, with whom you are to marry, may have
made a conveyance of her virginity afore hand,
as your wise widows do of their states, before
they marry, in trust to some friend, sir: 180

---

[1] A Puritan.
[2] The Nonconformist or Puritan clergy had been
silenced by a royal edict of 1604.
[3] Crowd.   [4] Lover.   [5] Milliners.
[6] Dressmakers.   [7] Feathermakers.
[8] Dealer in textiles.

[1] Fashionable horse races at Salisbury.
[2] A leading resort of society, where there were many
mineral hot baths.
[3] In royal tours about the country.
[4] Samuel Daniel (1562–1619), a well-known poet of
the time.
[5] Edmund Spenser (1552–99), author of the famous
epic, *The Faerie Queene.*
[6] The quack spiritualists of Elizabethan days.
[7] Fortune teller.
[8] Suitor.   [9] Wind.
[10] Sticky salve for beautifying the face.
[11] Cosmetic or facial paint.

Who can tell? Or if she have not done it yet, she may do, upon the wedding-day, or the night before, and antedate you cuckold. The like has been heard of in nature. 'Tis no de- 185 vised, impossible thing, sir. God be wi' you: I'll be bold to leave this rope with you, sir, for a remembrance. — Farewell, Mute! (*Exit.*

Mor. Come, have me to my chamber: but first shut the door. (TRUEWIT *winds the horn without.*) Oh, shut the door, shut the 190 door! Is he come again?

Enter CUTBEARD

Cut. 'Tis I, sir, your barber.

Mor. Oh, Cutbeard, Cutbeard, Cutbeard! here has been a cutthroat with me: help me in to my bed, and give me physic with thy 195 counsel.   (*Exeunt.*

SCENE 3. *A room in* SIR JOHN DAW'S *house.*

Enter DAW, CLERIMONT, DAUPHINE, *and* EPICOENE

Daw. Nay, an she will, let her refuse at her own charges;[1] 'tis nothing to me, gentlemen: but she will not be invited to the like feasts or guests every day.

Cler. Oh, by no means, she may not re- 5 fuse — to stay at home, if you love your reputa- tion: 'Slight, you are invited thither o' purpose to be seen, and laughed at by the lady of the college, and her shadows.[2] (*Aside to* EPI.) This trumpeter hath proclaim'd you. 10

Daup. (*aside to* EPI.). You shall not go; let him be laughed at in your stead, for not bring- ing you: and put him to his extemporal[3] faculty of fooling and talking loud, to satisfy the com- pany. 15

Cler. (*aside to* DAUP.). He will suspect us; talk aloud. — Pray, Mistress Epicoene, let's see your verses; we have Sir John Daw's leave; do not conceal your servant's merit, and your own glories. 20

---

[1] Her own risk.
[2] Uninvited persons who may come with an invited guest to a dinner.
[3] Extemporaneous.

Epi. They'll prove my servant's glories, if you have his leave so soon.

Daup. His vain-glories, lady!

Daw. Show them, show them, mistress; I dare own them. 25

Epi. Judge you, what glories.

Daw. Nay, I'll read them myself too: an author must recite his own works. It is a madrigal[1] of Modesty. —
Modest and fair, for fair and good are near
        Neighbors, howe'er. 31

Daup. Very good.

Cler. Ay, is't not?

Daw. No noble virtue ever was alone,
        But two in one. 35

Daup. Excellent!

Cler. That again, I pray, Sir John.

Daup. It has something in't like rare wit and sense.

Cler. Peace. 40

Daw. No noble virtue ever was alone,
        But two in one.
Then, when I praise sweet modesty, I praise
        Bright beauty's rays:
And having praised both beauty and modesty,
        I have praised thee. 46

Daup. Admirable!

Cler. How it chimes, and cries tink in the close, divinely!

Daup. Ay, 'tis Seneca.[2] 50

Cler. No, I think 'tis Plutarch.[3]

Daw. The dor[4] on Plutarch and Seneca! I hate it: they are mine own imaginations, by that light. I wonder those fellows have such credit with gentlemen. 55

Cler. They are very grave[5] authors.

Daw. Grave asses! mere essayists: a few loose sentences, and that's all. A man would talk so, his whole age: I do utter as good things every hour, if they were collected and ob- 60 served, as either of them.

Daup. Indeed, Sir John!

Cler. He must needs; living among the wits and braveries too.

---

[1] A short, pastoral, love poem.
[2] Lucius Annaeus Seneca (4 B.C.–A.D. 65), Roman poet and moralist.
[3] Greek biographer and moralist (*c.* 46–120 A.D.).
[4] The drone, or perhaps the fool — a mock oath.
[5] Serious, profound.

Daup. Ay, and being president of them,   65
as he is.

Daw. There's Aristotle, a mere commonplace fellow; Plato, a discourser; Thucydides[1]
and Livy,[2] tedious and dry; Tacitus,[3] an entire
knot; sometimes worth the untying, very   70
seldom.

Cler. What do you think of the poets, Sir
John?

Daw. Not worthy to be named for authors.
Homer, an old tedious, prolix ass, talks of   75
curriers, and chines of beef; Virgil of dunging of
land, and bees; Horace, of I know not what.

Cler. I think so.

Daw. And so, Pindarus,[4] Lycophron,[5] Anac-
reon,[6] Catullus,[7] Seneca the tragedian,   80
Lucan,[8] Propertius,[9] Tibullus,[10] Martial,[11] Juvenal,[12] Ausonius,[13] Statius,[14] Politian,[15] Valerius
Flaccus,[16] and the rest ——

Cler. What a sack full of their names he has
got!   85

Daup. And how he pours them out! Politian
with Valerius Flaccus!

Cler. Was not the character right of him?

Daup. As could be made, i'faith.

Daw. And Persius,[17] a crabbed coxcomb,   90
not to be endured.

[1] Athenian historian (B.C. 471–400).

[2] Titus Livius (B.C. 59–A.D. 17), Roman historian.

[3] Publius Cornelius Tacitus (A.D. 55?–after 117),
Roman historian.

[4] Greek lyric poet (B.C. 522–448?).

[5] Greek tragic poet (B.C. third century).

[6] Greek lyric poet (B.C. 563?–478).

[7] Gaius Valerius Catullus (B.C. 87–54), Roman poet.

[8] Marcus Annaeus Lucanus (A.D. 39–65), Roman poet.

[9] Sextus Propertius (B.C. 50?–15?), Roman poet.

[10] Albius Tibullus (B.C. 54–*c.* 18), Roman elegiac poet.

[11] Marcus Valerius Martialis (A.D. 40?–102?), Roman
epigrammatist.

[12] Decimus Junius Juvenalis (A.D. *c.* 60–*c.* 140),
Roman satirist.

[13] Decimus Magnus Ausonius (A.D. 310–394), Roman
poet.

[14] Publius Papinius Statius (A.D. 45–96), Roman epic
poet.

[15] Angelus Politianus (1454–94), an Italian humanist
and epigrammatist.   His inclusion is a humorous
anachronism.

[16] Roman epic poet, died A.D. 90.

[17] Aulus Persius Flaccus (A.D. 34–62), Roman satirist.

Daup. Why, whom do you account for
authors, Sir John Daw?

Daw. Syntagma juris civilis;[1] Corpus juris
civilis; Corpus juris canonici;[2] the king of   95
Spain's bible ——

Daup. Is the king of Spain's bible an author?

Cler. Yes, and Syntagma.

Daup. What was that Syntagma, sir?

Daw. A civil lawyer, a Spaniard.   100

Daup. Sure, Corpus was a Dutchman.

Cler. Ay, both the Corpuses, I knew 'em:
they were very corpulent authors.

Daw. And then there's Vatablus,[3] Pomponatius,[4] Symancha:[5] the other are not to   105
be received, within the thought of a scholar.

Daup. (*aside*). 'Fore God, you have a simple
learned servant, lady — in titles.

Cler. I wonder that he is not called to the
helm, and made a counselor.   110

Daup. He is one extraordinary.

Cler. Nay, but in ordinary: to say truth, the
state wants such.

Daup. Why that will follow.

Cler. I muse a mistress can be so silent   115
to the dotes[6] of such a servant.

Daw. 'Tis her virtue, sir.   I have written
somewhat of her silence too.

Daup. In verse, Sir John?

Cler. What else?   120

Daup. Why, how can you justify your own
being of a poet, that so slight all the old poets?

Daw. Why, every man that writes in verse
is not a poet; you have of the wits that write
verses, and yet are no poets: they are poets   125
that live by it, the poor fellows that live by it.

Daup. Why, would not you live by your
verses, Sir John?

Cler. No, 'twere pity he should.   A knight
live by his verses! he did not make them   130
to that end, I hope.

[1] A hodgepodge of Greek and Latin.   *Syntagma* =
corpus, body or compilation.   Hence, the compilation of
civil law.

[2] The compilation of canon or ecclesiastical law.

[3] François Vatable (d. 1517), a noted French scholar
of Hebrew.

[4] Petrus Pomponatius (1462–1524), a famous Italian
professor of philosophy.

[5] Jacobus Simancas (Didacus), a Spanish professor of
law, and bishop, of the later sixteenth century.

[6] Qualifications.

Daup. And yet the noble Sidney [1] lives by his, and the noble family not ashamed.

Cler. Ay, he profest himself; but Sir John Daw has more caution: he'll not hinder his 135 own rising in the state so much. Do you think he will? Your verses, good Sir John, and no poems.

Daw. Silence in woman, is like speech in man;
           Deny't who can.   140

Daup. Not I, believe it: your reason, sir.

Daw.   Nor is't a tale,
That female vice should be a virtue male,
Or masculine vice a female virtue be:
         You shall it see   145
         Prov'd with increase;
I know to speak, and she to hold her peace.
Do you conceive me, gentlemen?

Daup. No, faith; how mean you "with increase," Sir John?   150

Daw. Why, with increase is, when I court her for the common cause of mankind, and she says nothing, but *consentire videtur*; [2] and in time is *gravida*.[3]   154

Daup. Then this is a ballad of procreation?

Cler. A madrigal of procreation; you mistake.

Epi. Pray give me my verses again, servant.

Daw. If you'll ask them aloud, you shall.
      (*Walks aside with the papers.*

SCENE 4. *The same.*

Enter TRUEWIT *with his horn*

Cler. See, here's Truewit again! — Where hast thou been, in the name of madness, thus accoutered with thy horn?

True. Where the sound of it might have pierced your sense with gladness, had you 5 been in ear-reach of it. Dauphine, fall down and worship me; I have forbid the banns, lad: I have been with thy virtuous uncle, and have broke the match.

Daup. You have not, I hope.   10

True. Yes, faith; and thou shouldst hope otherwise, I should repent me: this horn got me entrance; kiss it. I had no other way to get in, but by feigning to be a post; but when I got in once, I proved none, but rather the contrary, turned him into a post, or a stone, or 15 what is stiffer, with thundering into him the incommodities of a wife, and the miseries of marriage. If ever Gorgon [1] were seen in the shape of a woman, he hath seen her in my 20 description: I have put him off o' that scent forever. — Why do you not applaud and adore me, sirs? Why stand you mute? Are you stupid? You are not worthy of the benefit.

Daup. Did not I tell you? Mischief! —— 25

Cler. I would you had placed this benefit somewhere else.

True. Why so?

Cler. 'Slight, you have done the most inconsiderate, rash, weak thing, that ever man 30 did to his friend.

Daup. Friend! If the most malicious enemy I have, had studied to inflict an injury upon me, it could not be a greater.

True. Wherein, for God's sake? Gentle- 35 men, come to yourselves again.

Daup. But I presaged thus much afore to you.

Cler. Would my lips had been soldered when I spake on't! 'Slight, what moved you to 40 be thus impertinent?

True. My masters, do not put on this strange face to pay my courtesy; off with this vizor. Have good turns done you, and thank 'em this way!   45

Daup. 'Fore heaven, you have undone me. That which I have plotted for, and been maturing now these four months, you have blasted in a minute: Now I am lost, I may speak. This gentlewoman was lodged here by me o' 50 purpose, and, to be put upon my uncle, hath profest this obstinate silence for my sake; being my entire friend, and one that for the requital of such a fortune as to marry him, would have made me very ample conditions; where 55 now, all my hopes are utterly miscarried by this unlucky accident.

Cler. Thus 'tis when a man will be ignorantly officious, do services, and not know his why; I wonder what courteous itch possest you. 60

---

[1] Sir Philip Sidney (1554–86), well-known Elizabethan sonneteer and author of the prose romance, *Arcadia*.
[2] Seems to consent.   [3] Pregnant.

[1] Female goddesses with horrible aspects and snaky locks.
[2] Pretense.

You never did absurder part in your life, nor a greater trespass to friendship or humanity.

Daup. Faith, you may forgive it best; 'twas your cause principally.

Cler. I know it; would it had not.   65

Enter CUTBEARD

Daup. How now, Cutbeard! what news?

Cut. The best, the happiest that ever was, sir. There has been a mad gentleman with your uncle this morning (*seeing* TRUEWIT) — I think this be the gentleman — that has   70 almost talked him out of his wits, with threatening him from marriage ——

Daup. On, I prithee.

Cut. And your uncle, sir, he thinks 'twas done by your procurement; therefore he   75 will see the party you wot of presently; and if he like her, he says, and that she be so inclining to dumb [1] as I have told him, he swears he will marry her today, instantly, and not defer it a minute longer.   80

Daup. Excellent! beyond our expectation!

True. Beyond our expectation! By this light, I knew it would be thus.

Daup. Nay, sweet Truewit, forgive me.

True. No, I was *ignorantly officious, im-*   85 *pertinent*; this was the *absurd, weak part.*

Cler. Wilt thou ascribe that to merit now, was mere fortune!

True. Fortune! mere providence. Fortune had not a finger in't. I saw it must neces-   90 sarily in nature fall out so: my genius is never false to me in these things. Show me how it could be otherwise.

Daup. Nay, gentlemen, contend not; 'tis well now.   95

True. Alas, I let him go on with *inconsider-ate*, and *rash*, and what he pleased.

Cler. Away, thou strange justifier of thyself, to be wiser than thou wert, by the event!

True. Event! by this light, thou shalt   100 never persuade me, but I foresaw it as well as the stars themselves.

Daup. Nay, gentlemen, 'tis well now. Do you two entertain Sir John Daw with discourse, while I send her away with instructions.   105

[1] Dumbness.

True. I'll be acquainted with her first, by your favor.

Cler. Master Truewit, lady, a friend of ours.

True. I am sorry I have not known you sooner, lady, to celebrate this rare virtue   110 of your silence.

(*Exeunt* DAUP., EPI., *and* CUTBEARD.

Cler. Faith, an you had come sooner, you should have seen and heard her well celebrated in Sir John Daw's madrigals.

True. (*advancing to* DAW). Jack Daw,   115 God save you! when saw you La-Foole?

Daw. Not since last night, Master Truewit.

True. That's a miracle! I thought you two had been inseparable.

Daw. He's gone to invite his guests.   120

True. 'Odso! 'tis true! What a false memory have I towards that man! I am one: [1] I met him even now, upon that he calls his delicate fine black horse, rid into foam, with posting from place to place, and person to person,   125 to give them the cue ——

Cler. Lest they should forget?

True. Yes. There was never poor captain took more pains at a muster to show men, than he, at this meal, to show friends.   130

Daw. It is his quarter-feast, sir.

Cler. What! do you say so, Sir John?

True. Nay, Jack Daw will not be out, [2] at the best friends he has, to the talent of his wit. Where's his mistress, to hear and applaud   135 him? Is she gone?

Daw. Is Mistress Epicoene gone?

Cler. Gone afore, with Sir Dauphine, I warrant, to the place.

True. Gone afore! that were a manifest   140 injury, a disgrace and a half; to refuse him at such a festival-time as this, being a bravery,[3] and a wit too!

Cler. Tut, he'll swallow it like cream: he's better read in Jure civili,[4] than to esteem   145 anything a disgrace, is offer'd him from a mistress.

Daw. Nay, let her e'en go; she shall sit alone, and be dumb in her chamber a week together, for John Daw, I warrant her. Does she   150 refuse me?

[1] I.e., one of his guests.   [2] Be forgetful.
[3] A gallant.   [4] Civil law.

Cler. No, sir, do not take it so to heart; she does not refuse you, but a little neglects you. Good faith, Truewit, you were to blame, to put it into his head, that she does refuse him.   155

True. Sir, she does refuse him palpably, however you mince it. An I were as he, I would swear to speak ne'er a word to her today for't.

Daw. By this light, no more I will not.

True. Nor to anybody else, sir.   160

Daw. Nay, I will not say so, gentlemen.

Cler. (*aside to* Truewit). It had been an excellent happy condition for the company, if you could have drawn him to it.

Daw. I'll be very melancholy, i'faith.   165

Cler. As a dog, if I were as you, Sir John.

True. Or a snail, or a hog-louse: I would roll myself up for this day; in troth, they should not unwind me.

Daw. By this pick-tooth,[1] so I will.   170

Cler. 'Tis well done: He begins already to be angry with his teeth.

Daw. Will you go, gentlemen?

Cler. Nay, you must walk alone, if you be right melancholy, Sir John.   175

True. Yes, sir, we'll dog you, we'll follow you afar off.   (*Exit* Daw.

Cler. Was there ever such a two yards of knighthood measured out by time, to be sold to laughter?   180

True. A mere talking mole, hang him! No mushroom was ever so fresh. A fellow so utterly nothing, as he knows not what he would be.

Cler. Let's follow him: but first let's go   185 to Dauphine, he's hovering about the house to hear what news.

True. Content.   (*Exeunt.*

SCENE 5. *A room in* Morose's *house.*

Enter Morose *and* Mute, *followed by* Cutbeard *with* Epicoene

Mor. Welcome, Cutbeard! draw near with your fair charge: and in her ear softly entreat her to unmask. (Epi. *takes off her mask.*) — So! Is the door shut? (Mute *makes a leg.*) —

[1] Toothpicks were an indispensable item of the gallant's paraphernalia, and their use in public an important part of his etiquette.

Enough. Now, Cutbeard, with the same   5 discipline I use to my family, I will question you. As I conceive, Cutbeard, this gentlewoman is she you have provided, and brought, in hope she will fit me in the place and person of a wife? Answer me not but with your leg,   10 unless it be otherwise. (Cut. *makes a leg.*) — Very well done, Cutbeard. I conceive, besides, Cutbeard, you have been pre-acquainted with her birth, education, and qualities, or else you would not prefer her to my acceptance, in   15 the weighty consequence of marriage. (Cut. *makes a leg.*) — This I conceive, Cutbeard. Answer me not but with your leg, unless it be otherwise. (Cut. *bows again.*) — Very well done, Cutbeard. Give aside now a little,   20 and leave me to examine her condition, and aptitude to my affection. (*Goes about her and views her.*) — She is exceeding fair, and of a special good favor; a sweet composition or harmony of limbs; her temper of beauty   25 has the true height of my blood. The knave hath exceedingly well fitted me without: I will now try her within. — Come near, fair gentlewoman; let not my behavior seem rude, though unto you, being rare, it may haply appear   30 strange. (Epicoene *curtsies.*) Nay, lady, you may speak, though Cutbeard and my man might not; for of all sounds, only the sweet voice of a fair lady has the just length of mine ears. I beseech you, say, lady; out of the   35 first fire of meeting eyes, they say, love is stricken: do you feel any such motion suddenly shot into you, from any part you see in me? ha, lady? (Epi. *curtsies.*) — Alas, lady, these answers by silent curtsies from you are too   40 courtless and simple. I have ever had my breeding in court; and she that shall be my wife, must be accomplished with courtly and audacious ornaments.[1] Can you speak, lady?

Epi. (*softly*). Judge you, forsooth.   45

Mor. What say you, lady? Speak out, I beseech you.

Epi. Judge you, forsooth.

Mor. On my judgment, a divine softness! But can you naturally, lady, as I enjoin   50 these by doctrine and industry, refer yourself to the search of my judgment, and, not taking

[1] Spirited manners.

pleasure in your tongue, which is a woman's chiefest pleasure, think it plausible to answer me by silent gestures, so long as my speeches 55 jump right [1] with what you conceive? (EPI. *curtsies.*) — Excellent! divine! if it were possible she should hold out thus! — Peace, Cutbeard, thou art made forever, as thou hast made me, if this felicity have lasting: but I 60 will try her further. Dear lady, I am courtly, I tell you, and I must have mine ears banqueted with pleasant and witty conferences,[2] pretty girds,[3] scoffs, and dalliance in her that I mean to choose for my bed-phere.[4] The ladies in 65 court think it a most desperate impair[5] to their quickness of wit, and good carriage, if they cannot give occasion for a man to court 'em; and when an amorous discourse is set on foot, minister as good matter to continue it, as him- 70 self: And do you alone so much differ from all them, that what they, with so much circumstance, affect and toil for, to seem learned, to seem judicious, to seem sharp and conceited, you can bury in yourself with silence, and 75 rather trust your graces to the fair conscience of virtue, than to the world's or your own proclamation?

Epi. (*softly*). I should be sorry else.

Mor. What say you, lady? Good lady, 80 speak out.

Epi. I should be sorry else.

Mor. That sorrow doth fill me with gladness. O Morose, thou art happy above mankind! pray that thou mayest contain thyself. I 85 will only put her to it once more, and it shall be with the utmost touch and test of their sex. But hear me, fair lady; I do also love to see her whom I shall choose for my heifer,[6] to be the first and principal in all fashions, precede 90 all the dames at court by a fortnight, have council of tailors, lineners, lace-women, embroiderers: and sit with them sometimes twice a day upon French intelligences,[7] and then come forth varied like nature, or oftener than 95 she, and better by the help of art, her emulous servant. This do I affect: and how will you be able, lady, with this frugality of speech, to give the manifold but necessary instructions, for that bodice, these sleeves, those skirts, 100 this cut, that stitch, this embroidery, that lace, this wire,[1] those knots, that ruff, those roses, this girdle, that fan, the t'other scarf, these gloves? Ha! what say you, lady?

Epi. (*softly*). I'll leave it to you, sir. 105

Mor. How, lady? Pray you rise a note.

Epi. I leave it to wisdom and you, sir.

Mor. Admirable creature! I will trouble you no more: I will not sin against so sweet a simplicity. Let me now be bold to print 110 on those divine lips the seal of being mine. — Cutbeard, I give thee the lease of thy house free; thank me not but with thy leg. (CUTBEARD *shakes his head.*) — I know what thou wouldst say, she's poor, and her friends 115 deceased. She has brought a wealthy dowry in her silence, Cutbeard; and in respect of her poverty, Cutbeard, I shall have her more loving and obedient, Cutbeard. Go thy ways, and get me a minister presently, with a soft 120 low voice, to marry us; and pray him he will not be impertinent, but brief as he can; away: softly, Cutbeard. (*Exit* CUT.) — Sirrah, conduct your mistress into the dining-room, your new mistress. (*Exit* MUTE, *followed by* 125 EPI.) — O my felicity! how shall I be revenged on mine insolent kinsman, and his plots to fright me from marrying! This night I will get an heir, and thrust him out of my blood, like a stranger. He would be knighted, for- 130 sooth, and thought by that means to reign over me; his title must do it: No, kinsman, I will now make you bring me the tenth lord's and the sixteenth lady's letter, kinsman; and it shall do you no good, kinsman. Your knight- 135 hood itself shall come on its knees, and it shall be rejected; it shall be sued for its fees to execution, and not be redeemed; it shall cheat at the twelve-penny ordinary,[2] it [3] knighthood for its diet, all the term-time, and tell tales 140 for it in the vacation to the hostess; or it knighthood shall do worse, take sanctuary in

---

[1] Agree exactly.   [2] Confidences.
[3] Taunts.   [4] Bedfellow.
[5] Obstacle.   [6] Yoke-mate.
[7] News of French fashions.

[1] Material to stiffen parts of the dress, especially the skirt.
[2] A tavern which served a twelve-penny dinner.
[3] Dialectical form of *its*; here, *your*.

Cole-harbor,[1] and fast. It shall fright all its friends with borrowing letters; and when one of the fourscore hath brought it knighthood 145 ten shillings, it knighthood shall go to the Cranes,[2] or the Bear at the Bridge-foot,[3] and be drunk in fear; it shall not have money to discharge one tavern-reckoning, to invite the old creditors to forbear it knighthood, or the 150 new, that should be, to trust it knighthood. It shall be the tenth name in the bond to take up the commodity [4] of pipkins and stone-jugs: and the part thereof shall not furnish it knighthood forth for the attempting of a baker's 155 widow, a brown baker's [5] widow. It shall give it knighthood's name for a stallion, to all gamesome citizens' wives, and be refused, when the master of a dancing-school, or how do you call him, the worst reveller in the town is 160 taken: it shall want clothes, and by reason of that, wit, to fool to lawyers. It shall not have hope to repair itself by Constantinople, Ireland, or Virginia;[6] but the best and last fortune to it knighthood shall be to make Dol Tear- 165 sheet, or Kate Common a lady, and so it knighthood may eat. (*Exit.*

SCENE 6. *A lane, near* MOROSE'S *house.*

Enter TRUEWIT, DAUPHINE, *and* CLERIMONT

True. Are you sure he is not gone by?

Daup. No, I staid in the shop ever since.

Cler. But he may take the other end of the lane.

Daup. No, I told him I would be here at 5 this end: I appointed him hither.

True. What a barbarian it [7] is to stay then!

Daup. Yonder he comes.

Cler. And his charge left behind him, which is a very good sign, Dauphine. 10

[1] Cold Harbor, near the Thames, a retreat for debtors, gamblers, etc.
[2] A tavern on Upper Thames Street.
[3] A famous tavern just below old London Bridge on the Surrey or south side of the Thames.
[4] Borrow money by accepting goods instead of cash as the loan.
[5] A baker of brown bread, the coarsest and cheapest kind.
[6] Investments in the Turkish (Trading) Company; the 1605 settlement in Ulster, Ireland; the 1607 and 1609 colonization ventures in Virginia.   [7] I.e., he.

Enter CUTBEARD

Daup. How now, Cutbeard! Succeeds it, or no?

Cut. Past imagination, sir, *omnia secunda*;[1] you could not have pray'd to have had it so well. *Saltat senex,*[2] as it is in the proverb; 15 he does triumph in his felicity, admires the party! he has given me the lease of my house too! and I am now going for a silent minister to marry them, and away.

True. 'Slight! get one of the silenced 20 ministers;[3] a zealous brother would torment him purely.[4]

Cut. Cum privilegio,[5] sir.

Daup. O, by no means; let's do nothing to hinder it now: when 'tis done and finished, 25 I am for you, for any device of vexation.

Cut. And that shall be within this half hour, upon my dexterity, gentlemen. Contrive what you can in the mean time, *bonis avibus.*[6]
(*Exit.*

Cler. How the slave doth Latin it! 30

True. It would be made a jest to posterity, sirs, this day's mirth, if ye will.

Cler. Beshrew his heart that will not, I pronounce.

Daup. And for my part. What is it? 35

True. To translate [7] all La-Foole's company, and his feast thither, today, to celebrate this bride-ale.[8]

Daup. Ay, marry; but how will't be done?

True. I'll undertake the directing of all 40 the lady-guests thither, and then the meat must follow.

Cler. For God's sake, let's effect it; it will be an excellent comedy of affliction, so many several noises. 45

Daup. But are they not at the other place, already, think you?

[1] All good fortune.
[2] The old man dances.
[3] I.e., Non-Conformist ministers, who had been stopped from preaching. Jonson is fond of satirizing their religious zeal.
[4] Intensely.
[5] Duly authorized.
[6] My good fellows.
[7] Transport.
[8] Bridal feast.

True. I'll warrant you for the college-honors: one of their faces has not the priming color laid on yet, nor the other her smock sleek'd.   50

Cler. O, but they'll rise earlier than ordinary to a feast.

True. Best go see, and assure ourselves.

Cler. Who knows the house?

True. I'll lead you. Were you never   55 there yet?

Daup. Not I.

Cler. Nor I.

True. Where have you lived then? Not know Tom Otter!   60

Cler. No: for God's sake, what is he?

True. An excellent animal, equal with your Daw or La-Foole, if not transcendant;[1] and does Latin it as much as your barber: He is his wife's subject; he calls her princess, and at   65 such times as these follows her up and down the house like a page, with his hat off, partly for heat, partly for reverence. At this instant he is marshaling of his bull, bear, and horse.

Daup. What be those, in the name   70 of Sphynx?

True. Why, sir, he has been a great man at the Bear-garden[2] in his time; and from that subtle sport has ta'en the witty denomination of his chief carousing cups. One he calls   75 his bull, another his bear, another his horse. And then he has his lesser glasses, that he calls his deer and his ape; and several degrees of them too; and never is well, nor thinks any entertainment perfect, till these be brought   80 out, and set on the cupboard.

Cler. For God's love! — We should miss this, if we should not go.

True. Nay, he has a thousand things as good, that will speak him[3] all day. He   85 will rail on his wife, with certain common places, behind her back; and to her face ——

Daup. No more of him. Let's go see him, I petition you.

(*Exeunt.*

---

[1] Superior.

[2] The Bear Garden in Southwark on the Bankside opposite to London was a famous and long-lived amphitheater for the exhibition of bear- and bull-baiting.

[3] I.e., to him.

ACT III

SCENE I. *A room in* OTTER'S *house.*

Enter CAPTAIN OTTER *with his cups, and*
MRS. OTTER

Ott. Nay, good princess, hear me *pauca verba.*[1]

Mrs. Ott. By that light, I'll have you chained up, with your bull-dogs and bear-dogs, if you be not civil the sooner. I'll send you to kennel,   5 i'faith. You were best bait me with your bull, bear, and horse. Never a time that the courtiers or collegiates come to the house, but you make it a Shrove-tuesday![2] I would have you get your Whitsuntide[3] velvet cap, and   10 your staff in your hand, to entertain them: yes, in troth, do.

Ott. Not so, princess, neither; but under correction, sweet princess, give me leave. — These things I am known to the courtiers by: It is   15 reported to them for my humor, and they receive it so, and do expect it. Tom Otter's bull, bear, and horse is known all over England, *in rerum natura.*[4]

Mrs. Ott. 'Fore me, I will *na-ture* them   20 over to Paris-garden,[5] and *na-ture* you thither too, if you pronounce them again. Is a bear a fit beast, or a bull, to mix in society with great ladies? think in your discretion, in any good policy.   25

Ott. The horse then, good princess.

Mrs. Ott. Well, I am contented for the horse; they love to be well horsed, I know: I love it myself.

Ott. And it is a delicate fine horse this: 30 *Poetarum Pegasus.*[6] Under correction, princess, Jupiter did turn himself into a — *taurus,* or bull, under correction, good princess.

---

[1] A few words.

[2] The Tuesday just before Lent, and a day of much merrymaking.

[3] Whitsunday, the seventh Sunday after Easter. On every holy-day English law required the wearing of a cap.

[4] In the natural course of events.

[5] The oldest of the bear-baiting rings on the Bankside.

[6] The Muse of the Poets.

Enter TRUEWIT, CLERIMONT, *and* DAUPHINE
at the back of the stage

Mrs. Ott. By my integrity, I'll send you over to the Bank-side: I'll commit you to the 35 master of the Garden, if I hear but a syllable more. Must my house or my roof be polluted with the scent of bears and bulls, when it is perfumed for great ladies? Is this according to the instrument,[1] when I married you? that 40 I would be princess, and reign in mine own house; and you would be my subject, and obey me? What did you bring me, should make you thus peremptory? Do I allow you your half-crown a day, to spend where you will, 45 among your gamesters, to vex and torment me at such times as these? Who gives you your maintenance, I pray you? Who allows you your horse-meat[2] and man's meat? your three suits of apparel a year? your four pair of 50 stockings, one silk, three worsted? your clean linen, your bands and cuffs, when I can get you to wear them? — 'Tis marle[3] you have them on now. — Who graces you with courtiers or great personages, to speak to you out of their 55 coaches, and come home to your house? Were you ever so much as looked upon by a lord or a lady, before I married you, but on the Easter or Whitsun-holidays? and then out at the banqueting-house window, when Ned Whiting 60 or George Stone[4] were at the stake?

True. For God's sake, let's go stave her off him.

Mrs. Ott. Answer me to that. And did not I take you up from thence, in an old greasy 65 buff-doublet, with points, and green velvet sleeves, out at the elbows? You forget this.

True. She'll worry him, if we help not in time. *(They come forward.*

Mrs. Ott. Oh, here are some of the gal- 70 lants! Go to, behave yourself distinctly,[5] and with good morality; or, I protest, I'll take away your exhibition.[6]

---

[1] Contract.
[2] Food for your horses.
[3] 'Tis a marvel.
[4] Two common names of baited bears, who were called after the names of their owners.
[5] Properly.
[6] Allowance.

SCENE 2. *The same.*

True. By your leave, fair Mistress Otter, I'll be bold to enter these gentlemen in your acquaintance.

Mrs. Ott. It shall not be obnoxious, or difficil,[1] sir. 5

True. How does my noble captain? Is the bull, bear, and horse in *rerum natura* still?

Ott. Sir, *sic visum superis.*[2]

Mrs. Ott. I would you would but intimate[3] them, do. Go your ways in, and get toasts 10 and butter made for the woodcocks:[4] that's a fit province for you. *(Drives him off.*

Cler. Alas, what a tyranny[5] is this poor fellow married to!

True. Oh, but the sport will be anon, 15 when we get him loose.

Daup. Dares he ever speak?

True. No Anabaptist[6] ever railed with the like license: but mark her language in the mean time, I beseech you. 20

Mrs. Ott. Gentlemen, you are very aptly come. My cousin, Sir Amorous, will be here briefly.[7]

True. In good time, lady. Was not Sir John Daw here, to ask for him, and the company?

Mrs. Ott. I cannot assure you, Master 26 Truewit. Here was a very melancholy knight in a ruff, that demanded my subject for somebody, a gentleman, I think.

Cler. Ay, that was he, lady. 30

Mrs. Ott. But he departed straight, I can resolve[8] you.

Daup. What an excellent choice phrase this lady expresses in.

True. Oh, sir, she is the only authentical 35 courtier, that is not naturally bred one, in the city.

Mrs. Ott. You have taken that report upon trust, gentlemen.

True. No, I assure you, the court gov- 40 erns it so, lady, in your behalf.

Mrs. Ott. I am the servant of the court and courtiers, sir.

---

[1] Difficult.   [2] Thus it pleased the gods.
[3] Announce.   [4] Simpletons.   [5] Tyrant.
[6] A Non-Conformist sect noted for their ranting.
[7] Shortly.   [8] Assure.

True. They are rather your idolaters.

Mrs. Ott. Not so, sir.   45

Enter CUTBEARD

Daup. How now, Cutbeard! any cross?[1]

Cut. O no, sir, *omnia bene.*[2] 'Twas never better on the hinges; all's sure. I have so pleased him with a curate, that he's gone to't almost with the delight he hopes for soon.   50

Daup. What is he[3] for a vicar?

Cut. One that has catched a cold, sir, and can scarce be heard six inches off; as if he spoke out of a bulrush that were not picked, or his throat were full of pith: a fine quick fellow,   55 and an excellent barber[4] of prayers. I came to tell you, sir, that you might *omnem movere lapidem,*[5] as they say, be ready with your vexation.

Daup. Gramercy, honest Cutbeard! be   60 thereabouts with thy key, to let us in.

Cut. I will not fail you, sir; *ad manum.*[6]
                                        (*Exit.*

True. Well, I'll go watch my coaches.

Cler. Do; and we'll send Daw to you, if you meet him not.   (*Exit* TRUEWIT. 65

Mrs. Ott. Is Master Truewit gone?

Daup. Yes, lady, there is some unfortunate business fallen out.

Mrs. Ott. So I adjudged by the physiognomy of the fellow that came in; and I had a   70 dream last night too of the new pageant,[7] and my lady mayoress, which is always very ominous to me. I told it my Lady Haughty t'other day, when her honor came hither to see some China stuffs;[8] and she expounded it out of   75 Artemidorus,[9] and I have found it since very true. It has done me many affronts.

Cler. Your dream, lady?

Mrs. Ott. Yes, sir, anything I do[10] but

[1] Hitch, obstacle.   [2] All is well.
[3] Whom has he considered.   [4] Curtailer.
[5] To turn the stone over, i.e., to upset the whole business.   [6] At your service.
[7] Pageants were always given to celebrate the induction of a new Lord Mayor and his wife.
[8] Merchandise from China, then very fashionable.
[9] A Greek interpreter of dreams, living in the second century A.D.
[10] I would do anything.

dream of the city. It stained me a damask   80 table-cloth, cost me eighteen pound, at one time; and burnt me a black satin gown, as I stood by the fire, at my Lady Centaure's chamber in the college, another time. A third time, at the lords' masque, it dropt all my wire   85 and my ruff with wax candle, that I could not go up to the banquet. A fourth time, as I was taking coach to go to Ware, to meet a friend, it dashed me a new suit all over (a crimson satin doublet, and black velvet skirts) with a   90 brewer's horse, that I was fain to go in and shift[1] me, and kept my chamber a leash of days[2] for the anguish of it.

Daup. These were dire mischances, lady.

Cler. I would not dwell in the city, an   95 'twere so fatal to me.

Mrs. Ott. Yes, sir; but I do take advice of my doctor to dream of it as little as I can.

Daup. You do well, Mistress Otter.

Enter SIR JOHN DAW, *and is taken aside by* CLERIMONT

Mrs. Ott. Will it please you to enter the   100 house farther, gentlemen?

Daup. And your favor, lady: but we stay to speak with a knight, Sir John Daw, who is here come. We shall follow you, lady.

Mrs. Ott. At your own time, sir. It   105 is my cousin, Sir Amorous, his feast ——

Daup. I know it, lady.

Mrs. Ott. And mine together. But it is for his honor, and therefore I take no name of it, more than of the place.   110

Daup. You are a bounteous kinswoman.

Mrs. Ott. Your servant, sir.   (*Exit.*

SCENE 3. *The same.*

Cler. (*coming forward with* DAW). Why, do not you know it, Sir John Daw?

Daw. No, I am a rook if I do.

Cler. I'll tell you, then; she's married by this time. And, whereas you were put in the   5 head, that she was gone with Sir Dauphine, I assure you, Sir Dauphine has been the noblest, honestest friend to you, that ever gentleman of

[1] Change clothes.   [2] A space of three days.

your quality could boast of. He has discovered
the whole plot, and made your mistress so   10
acknowledging, and indeed so ashamed of her
injury to you, that she desires you to forgive
her, and but grace her wedding with your presence today — She is to be married to a very
good fortune, she says, his uncle, old   15
Morose; and she willed me in private to tell
you, that she shall be able to do you more
favors, and with more security now than before.

Daw. Did she say so, i'faith?

Cler. Why, what do you think of me,   20
Sir John? Ask Sir Dauphine.

Daw. Nay, I believe you. — Good Sir
Dauphine, did she desire me to forgive her?

Daup. I assure you, Sir John, she did.

Daw. Nay, then, I do with all my heart,   25
and I'll be jovial.

Cler. Yes, for look you, sir, this was the
injury to you. La-Foole intended this feast to
honor her bridal day, and made you the property to invite the college ladies, and prom-   30
ise to bring her; and then at the time she would
have appeared, as his friend, to have given you
the dor.[1] Whereas now, Sir Dauphine has
brought her to a feeling of it, with this kind of
satisfaction, that you shall bring all the   35
ladies to the place where she is, and be very
jovial; and there, she will have a dinner, which
shall be in your name: and so disappoint La-
Foole, to make you good again, and, as it were,
a saver in the main.[2]   40

Daw. As I am a knight, I honor her; and forgive her heartily.

Cler. About it then presently. Truewit is
gone before to confront the coaches, and to
acquaint you with so much, if he meet you.   45
Join with him, and 'tis well. —

Enter SIR AMOROUS LA-FOOLE

See; here comes your antagonist; but take you
no notice, but be very jovial.

La-F. Are the ladies come, Sir John Daw,
and your mistress? (*Exit* DAW.) — Sir   50
Dauphine! you are exceeding welcome, and

honest Master Clerimont. Where's my cousin?
Did you see no collegiates, gentlemen?

Daup. Collegiates! do you not hear, Sir
Amorous, how you are abused?   55

La-F. How, sir!

Cler. Will you speak so kindly to Sir John
Daw, that has done you such an affront?

La-F. Wherein, gentlemen? Let me be a
suitor to you to know, I beseech you.   60

Cler. Why, sir, his mistress is married today
to Sir Dauphine's uncle, your cousin's neighbor,
and he has diverted all the ladies, and all your
company thither, to frustrate your provision,
and stick a disgrace upon you. He was   65
here now to have enticed us away from you too:
but we told him his own, I think.

La-F. Has Sir John Daw wronged me so
inhumanely?

Daup. He has done it, Sir Amorous,   70
most maliciously and treacherously: but, if
you'll be ruled by us, you shall quit him,[1] i'faith.

La-F. Good gentlemen, I'll make one,[2] believe it. How, I pray?

Daup. Marry, sir, get me your pheas-   75
ants, and your godwits,[3] and your best meat,
and dish it in silver dishes of your cousin's
presently; and say nothing, but clap me a clean
towel about you, like a sewer;[4] and, bare-
headed, march afore it with a good confi-   80
dence ('tis but over the way, hard by), and
we'll second[5] you, where you shall set it on the
board, and bid them welcome to't, which shall
show 'tis yours, and disgrace his preparation
utterly: and for your cousin, whereas she   85
should be troubled here at home with care of
making and giving welcome, she shall transfer
all that labor thither, and be a principal guest
herself; sit ranked with the college-honors, and
be honored, and have her health drunk as   90
often, as bare[6] and as loud as the best of them.

La-F. I'll go tell her presently. It shall be
done, that's resolved. (*Exit.*)

Cler. I thought he would not hear it out, but
'twould take him.   95

---

[1] To have made you the fool.
[2] One who wins as much as he loses in a dicing game.

[1] Get revenge upon him.
[2] Join in the scheme.
[3] A species of marsh bird.
[4] Wrap my clean towel about you, like a waiter.
[5] Assist.   [6] As bare-headed.

Daup. Well, there be guests and meat now; how shall we do for music?

Cler. The smell of the venison, going through the street, will invite one noise [1] of fiddlers or other.   100

Daup. I would it would call the trumpeters hither!

Cler. Faith, there is hope: they have intelligence of all feasts. There's good correspondence [2] betwixt them and the London   105 cooks: 'tis twenty to one but we have them.

Daup. 'Twill be a most solemn day for my uncle, and an excellent fit of mirth for us.

Cler. Ay, if we can hold up the emulation betwixt Foole and Daw, and never bring   110 them to expostulate.[3]

Daup. Tut, flatter them both, as Truewit says, and you may take their understandings in a purse-net.[4] They'll believe themselves to be just such men as we make them, neither   115 more nor less. They have nothing, not the use of their senses, but by tradition.

Re-enter LA-FOOLE, *like a sewer*

Cler. See! Sir Amorous has his towel on already. Have you persuaded your cousin?

La-F. Yes, 'tis very feasible: she'll do   120 anything, she says, rather than the La-Fooles shall be disgraced.

Daup. She is a noble kinswoman. It will be such a pestling device,[5] Sir Amorous; it will pound all your enemy's practices to   125 powder, and blow him up with his own mine, his own train.

La-F. Nay, we'll give fire, I warrant you.

Cler. But you must carry it privately, without any noise, and take no notice by any   130 means ——

Re-enter CAPTAIN OTTER

Ott. Gentlemen, my princess says you shall have all her silver dishes, *festinate*:[6] and she's

gone to alter her tire [1] a little, and go with you ——   135

Cler. And yourself too, Captain Otter?

Daup. By any means, sir.

Ott. Yes, sir, I do mean it: but I would entreat my cousin Sir Amorous, and you, gentlemen, to be suitors to my princess, that I may carry my bull and my bear, as well as my horse.

Cler. That you shall do, Captain Otter.   142

La-F. My cousin will never consent, gentlemen.

Daup. She must consent, Sir Amorous,   145 to reason.

La-F. Why, she says they are no decorum [2] among ladies.

Ott. But they are *decora*,[3] and that's better, sir.   150

Cler. Ay, she must hear argument. Did not Pasiphaë, who was a queen, love a bull? and was not Calisto, the mother of Arcas, turned into a bear, and made a star, Mistress Ursula, in the heavens?   155

Ott. O God! that I could have said as much! I will have these stories painted in the Beargarden, *ex Ovidii metamorphosi*.[4]

Daup. Where is your princess, captain? Pray, be our leader.   160

Ott. That I shall, sir.

Cler. Make haste, good Sir Amorous.

(*Exeunt.*

SCENE 4. *A room in* MOROSE'S *house.*

Enter MOROSE, EPICOENE, *Parson, and* CUTBEARD

Mor. Sir, there's an angel [5] for yourself, and a brace of angels for your cold. Muse not at this manage of my bounty. It is fit we should thank fortune, double to nature,[6] for any benefit she confers upon us; besides, it is your   5 imperfection, but my solace.

---

[1] Company.   [2] Friendly intimacy.   [3] Explain.
[4] A net the mouth of which can be drawn tight by cords.
[5] A device with the disintegrating effect of a pestle.
[6] Hasten.

[1] Attire.   [2] Seemly exhibit.   [3] Ornaments.
[4] Out of Ovid's *Metamorphoses*. Publius Ovidius Naso (43 B.C.–17 A.D.) wrote a collection of legends of "metamorphoses" or transformations, which was an extremely popular work in Jonson's day.
[5] A gold coin worth ten shillings, or about $2.50.
[6] I.e., thank fortune twice, where you would thank a natural cause only once.

Par. (*speaking as if having a cold*). I thank your worship; so it is mine, now.

Mor. What says he, Cutbeard?

Cut. He says, *praesto*,[1] sir, whensoever 10 your worship needs him, he can be ready with the like. He got this cold with sitting up late, and singing catches with cloth-workers.[2]

Mor. No more. I thank him.

Par. God keep your worship, and give 15 you much joy with your fair spouse! — uh! uh! uh!

Mor. Oh, oh! stay, Cutbeard! Let him give me five shillings of my money back. As it is bounty to reward benefits, so it is equity to 20 mulct injuries. I will have it. What says he?

Cler. He cannot change it, sir.

Mor. It must be changed.

Cut. (*aside to Parson*). Cough again.

Mor. What says he? 25

Cut. He will cough out the rest, sir.

Par. Uh, uh, uh!

Mor. Away, away with him! Stop his mouth! Away! I forgive it.

(*Exit* Cut. *thrusting out the Parson.*

Epi. Fie, Master Morose, that you will 30 use this violence to a man of the church.

Mor. How!

Epi. It does not become your gravity, or breeding, as you pretend, in court, to have offered this outrage on a waterman, or any 35 more boisterous creature, much less on a man of his civil coat.

Mor. You can speak then!

Epi. Yes, sir.

Mor. Speak out, I mean. 40

Epi. Ay, sir. Why, did you think you had married a statue, or a motion[3] only? one of the French puppets, with the eyes turned with a wire? or some innocent[4] out of the hospital, that would stand with her hands thus, and 45 a plaise[5] mouth, and look upon you?

Mor. O immodesty! a manifest woman! What, Cutbeard!

Epi. Nay, never quarrel with Cutbeard, sir; it is too late now. I confess it doth bate 50 somewhat of the modesty I had, when I writ simply maid: but I hope I shall make it a stock still competent to the estate and dignity of your wife.

Mor. She can talk! 55

Epi. Yes, indeed, sir.

Enter Mute

Mor. What sirrah! None of my knaves there? Where is this impostor Cutbeard?

(Mute *makes signs.*

Epi. Speak to him, fellow, speak to him! I'll have none of his coacted,[1] unnatural 60 dumbness in my house, in a family where I govern. (*Exit* Mute.

Mor. She is my regent already! I have married a Penthesilea,[2] a Semiramis;[3] sold my liberty to a distaff. 65

Scene 5. *The same.*

Enter Truewit

True. Where's Master Morose?

Mor. Is he come again! Lord have mercy upon me!

True. I wish you all joy, Mistress Epicoene, with your grave and honorable match. 5

Epi. I return you the thanks, Master Truewit, so friendly a wish deserves.

Mor. She has acquaintance, too!

True. God save you, sir, and give you all contentment in your fair choice, here! Be- 10 fore, I was the bird of night to you, the owl;[4] but now I am the messenger of peace, a dove, and bring you the glad wishes of many friends to the celebration of this good hour.

Mor. What hour, sir? 15

True. Your marriage hour, sir. I commend your resolution, that, notwithstanding all the dangers I laid afore you, in the voice of a night-

---

[1] At once.
[2] The London cloth-workers, or weavers, came from the Netherlands or France, and were noted for their skill at "catches" or part songs.
[3] Marionnette.   [4] Idiot.
[5] Wry, twisted-looking.

[1] Compulsory.
[2] Queen of the Amazons, mythical race of female warriors.
[3] Mythical Assyrian queen, who founded Babylon and conquered much of western Asia and northeastern Africa for her empire.
[4] I.e., the bird of ill omen.

crow, would yet go on, and be yourself. It shows you are a man constant to your own 20 ends, and upright to your purposes, that would not be put off with left-handed [1] cries.

Mor. How should you arrive at the knowledge of so much?

True. Why, did you ever hope, sir, com- 25 mitting the secrecy of it to a barber, that less than the whole town should know it? You might as well have told it the conduit,[2] or the bake-house, or the infantry [3] that follow the court, and with more security. Could your 30 gravity forget so old and noted a remnant, as, *lippis et tonsoribus notum?* [4] Well, sir, forgive it yourself now, the fault, and be communicable with your friends. Here will be three or four fashionable ladies from the college to visit 35 you presently, and their train of minions and followers.

Mor. Bar my doors! bar my doors! Where are all my eaters? [5] my mouths, now? —

Enter Servants

Bar up my doors, you varlets!   40

Epi. He is a varlet that stirs to such an office. Let them stand open. I would see him that dares move his eyes toward it. Shall I have a *barricado* [6] made against my friends, to be barr'd of any pleasure they can bring in 45 to me with their honorable visitation?

           (Exeunt Servants.

Mor. O Amazonian impudence!

True. Nay, faith, in this, sir, she speaks but reason; and, methinks, is more continent than you. Would you go to bed so presently, 50 sir, afore noon? A man of your head and hair should owe more to that reverend ceremony, and not mount the marriage-bed like a town-bull, or a mountain-goat; but stay the due season; and ascend it then with religion and 55

fear. Those delights are to be steeped in the humor and silence of the night; and give the day to other open pleasures, and jollities of feasting, of music, of revels, of discourse: we'll have all, sir, that may make your Hymen [1] 60 high and happy.

Mor. O my torment, my torment!

True. Nay, if you endure the first half hour, sir, so tediously, and with this irksomeness; what comfort or hope can this fair gentle- 65 woman make to herself hereafter, in the consideration of so many years as are to come.

Mor. Of my affliction. Good sir, depart, and let her do it alone.

True. I have done, sir.   70

Mor. That cursed barber.

True. Yes, faith, a cursed wretch indeed, sir.

Mor. I have married his cittern,[2] that's common to all men. Some plague above the plague ——   75

True. All Egypt's ten plagues.[3]

Mor. Revenge me on him!

True. 'Tis very well, sir. If you laid on a curse or two more, I'll assure you he'll bear them. As, that he may get the pox with 80 seeking to cure it, sir; or, that while he is curling another man's hair, his own may drop off; or, for burning some male-bawd's lock, he may have his brain beat out with the curling iron.[4]

Mor. No, let the wretch live wretched. 85 May he get the itch, and his shop so lousy, as no man dare come at him, nor he come at no man!

True. Ay, and if he would swallow all his balls [5] for pills, let not them purge him. 90

Mor. Let his warming-pan be ever cold.

True. A perpetual frost underneath it, sir.

Mor. Let him never hope to see fire again.

True. But in hell, sir.

---

[1] Ill-omened.

[2] A news center, because a motley crowd gathered to draw water.

[3] The lower order of hangers-on.

[4] "To be known to barbers is to be known to everybody." The Latin here is a partial quotation from Horace, *Satires*, 1.7.3.

[5] Servants.

[6] Barricade.

[1] I.e., marriage. Hymen was the Greek god of marriage.

[2] This musical instrument was to be found in every London barber shop. Customers could play on it while waiting to be served.

[3] The famous plagues visited upon the Egyptians when Pharoah would not let the Hebrews depart into the Promised Land.

[4] Hair-dressings of various forms of curls were popular with fashionable gentlemen of the day.

[5] I.e., balls of soap.

Mor. His chairs be always empty, his 95 scissors rust, and his combs mold in their cases.

True. Very dreadful that! And may he lose the invention, sir, of carving lanterns in paper.

Mor. Let there be no bawd carted that year, to employ a basin of his: [1] but let him be 100 glad to eat his sponge for bread.

True. And drink lotium to it, and much good do him.

Mor. Or, for want of bread.

True. Eat ear-wax, sir. I'll help you. 105 Or, draw his own teeth, and add them to the lute-string.[2]

Mor. No, beat the old ones to powder, and make bread of them. 109

True. Yes, make meal of the mill-stones.

Mor. May all the botches and burns that he has cured on others break out upon him.

True. And he now forget the cure of them in himself, sir; or, if he do remember it, let him have scraped all his linen into lint for't, 115 and have not a rag left him for to set up with.

Mor. Let him never set up again, but have the gout in his hands forever! — Now, no more, sir.

True. O, that last was too high set; you 120 might go less with him, i'faith, and be revenged enough: as, that he be never able to new paint his pole ——[3]

Mor. Good sir, no more, I forgot myself.

True. Or, want credit to take up with a 125 comb-maker ——

Mor. No more, sir.

True. Or, having broken his glass in a former despair, fall now into a much greater, of ever getting another —— 130

Mor. I beseech you, no more.

True. Or, that he never be trusted with trimming of any but chimney-sweepers ——

Mor. Sir ——

---

[1] Prostitutes and other infamous persons were often punished by being dragged through the London streets tied to a cart. Usually a mob preceded the cart, beating metal basins and pots to create a din and call out spectators.

[2] The barber of Jonson's time not only was a hairdresser, but he cleaned ears, carried on dentistry, and undertook varied surgical operations.

[3] Every barber had his pole set up before his shop and painted red and white.

True. Or, may he cut a collier's throat 135 with his razor, by chance-medley,[1] and yet be hanged for't.

Mor. I will forgive him, rather than hear any more. I beseech you, sir.

SCENE 6. *The same.*

Enter DAW, *introducing* LADY HAUGHTY, LADY CENTAURE, MRS. MAVIS, *and* MRS. TRUSTY

Daw. This way, madam.

Mor. O, the sea breaks in upon me! another flood! an inundation! I shall be overwhelmed with noise. It beats already at my shores. I feel an earthquake in myself for't. 5

Daw. 'Give you joy, mistress.

Mor. Has she servants too!

Daw. I have brought some ladies here to see and know you. My Lady Haughty — (*as he presents them severally,* EPICOENE *kisses them.*) This my Lady Centaure — Mistress Dol 10 Mavis — Mistress Trusty, my Lady Haughty's woman. Where's your husband? Let's see him: can he endure no noise? Let me come to him.

Mor. What nomenclator [2] is this! 15

True. Sir John Daw, sir, your wife's servant, this.

Mor. A Daw, and her servant! Oh, 'tis decreed, 'tis decreed of me, an [3] she have such servants. 20

(*He starts to go.*)

True. Nay, sir, you must kiss the ladies; you must not go away, now: they come toward you to seek you out.

Hau. I'faith, Master Morose, would you steal a marriage thus, in the midst of so many 25 friends, and not acquaint us? Well, I'll kiss you, notwithstanding the justice of my quarrel: you shall give me leave, mistress, to use a becoming familiarity with your husband. 29

Epi. Your ladyship does me an honor in it, to let me know he is so worthy your favor: as you have done both him and me grace to visit so unprepared a pair to entertain you.

---

[1] Pure chance.

[2] Caller of names.

[3] 'Tis fated for me, if.

Mor. Compliment! compliment!

Epi. But I must lay the burden of that 35
upon my servant here.

Hau. It shall not need, Mistress Morose; we
will all bear, rather than one shall be opprest.

Mor. I know it: and you will teach her the
faculty, if she be to learn it. 40
  (*Walks apart while the rest talk.*

Hau. Is this the silent woman?

Cen. Nay, she has found her tongue since she
was married, Master Truewit says.

Hau. Oh, Master Truewit! 'save you. What
kind of creature is your bride here? She 45
speaks, methinks!

True. Yes, madam, believe it, she is a gentlewoman of very absolute [1] behavior, and of a
good race.

Hau. And Jack Daw told us she could 50
not speak!

True. So it was carried in plot, madam, to
put her upon this old fellow, by Sir Dauphine,
his nephew, and one or two more of us: but
she is a woman of an excellent assurance, 55
and an extraordinary happy wit and tongue.
You shall see her make rare sport with Daw ere
night.

Hau. And he brought us to laugh at her!

True. That falls out often, madam, that 60
he that thinks himself the master-wit, is the
master-fool. I assure your ladyship, ye cannot
laugh at her.

Hau. No, we'll have her to the college: An
she have wit, she shall be one of us, shall 65
she not, Centaure? We'll make her a collegiate.

Cen. Yes, faith, madam, and Mavis and she
will set up a side. [2]

True. Believe it, madam, and Mistress
Mavis, she will sustain her part. 70

Mav. I'll tell you that, when I have talked
with her, and tried her.

Hau. Use her very civilly, Mavis.

Mav. So I will, madam.
  (*Whispers to* EPI.

Mor. (*aside*). Blessed minute! that they 75
would whisper thus ever!

True. In the mean time, madam, would but
your ladyship help to vex him a little: you know

[1] Perfect.
[2] I.e., will become partners in a game of cards.

his disease, talk to him about the wedding ceremonies, or call for your gloves,[1] or —— 80

Hau. Let me alone. Centaure, help me.
— Master bridegroom, where are you?

Mor. (*aside*). O, it was too miraculously good
to last!

Hau. We see no ensigns of a wedding 85
here; no character of a bridal: where be our
scarves and our gloves? I pray you, give them
us. Let us know your bride's colors, and
yours at least.[2] 89

Cen. Alas, madam, he has provided none.

Mor. Had I known your ladyship's painter,
I would.

Hau. He has given it you, Centaure, i'faith.
But do you hear, Master Morose? a jest will
not absolve you in this manner. You that 95
have sucked the milk of the court, and from
thence have been brought up to the very strong
meats and wine of it; been a courtier from the
biggen to the night-cap,[3] as we may say, and
you to offend in such a high point of cere- 100
mony as this, and let your nuptials want all
marks of solemnity! How much plate have
you lost today (if you had but regarded your
profit), what gifts, what friends, through your
mere rusticity! 105

Mor. Madam ——

Hau. Pardon me, sir, I must insinuate your
errors to you; no gloves? no garters?[4] no
scarves? no epithalamium?[5] no masque?[6]

Daw. Yes, madam, I'll make an epi- 110
thalamium, I promise my mistress; I have begun it already: will your ladyship hear it?

Hau. Ay, good Jack Daw.

Mor. Will it please your ladyship command
a chamber, and be private with your 115
friend? You shall have your choice of rooms to

[1] Gloves, scarfs, and fancy ribbons were regularly
given to the wedding-guests at this period.
[2] The bride and groom chose a particular color of
ribbon as their own. Then their friends wore this color
in their honor.
[3] From the infant's cap to the old man's cap: i.e.,
all your life.
[4] At the wedding the bride was lavishly gartered with
ribbons, which, as soon as the ceremony was over,
the young men tried to strip from her.
[5] Formal wedding song.
[6] Dramatic entertainment with music, dancing, and
costuming.

retire to after: my whole house is yours. I know it hath been your ladyship's errand into the city at other times, however now you have been unhappily diverted [1] upon me; but I shall 120 be loth to break any honorable custom of your ladyship's. And therefore, good madam ——

Epi. Come, you are a rude bridegroom, to entertain ladies of honor in this fashion.

Cen. He is a rude groom indeed. 125

True. By that light you deserve to be grafted and have your horns reach from one side of the island to the other.[2] — Do not mistake me, sir; I but speak this to give the ladies some heart again, not for any malice to you. 130

Mor. Is this your bravo, ladies?

True. As God help me, if you utter such another word, I'll take mistress bride in, and begin to you in a very sad cup; do you see? Go 134 to, know your friends, and such as love you.

Scene 7. *The same.*

Enter Clerimont, *followed by a number of Musicians*

Cler. By your leave, ladies. Do you want any music? I have brought you variety of noises.[3] — Play, sirs, all of you.

    (*To the Musicians, who strike up all together.*)

Mor. O, a plot, a plot, a plot, a plot, upon me! this day I shall be their anvil to work 5 on, they will grate me asunder. 'Tis worse than the noise of a saw.

Cler. No, they are hair, rosin, and guts: I can give you the receipt.

True. Peace, boys! 10

Cler. Play! I say.

True. Peace, rascals! (*To* Mor.) You see who's your friend now, sir: take courage, put on a martyr's resolution. Mock down all their attemptings with patience: 'tis but a day, 15 and I would suffer heroically. Should an ass exceed me in fortitude? No. You betray

your infirmity with your hanging dull ears, and make them insult: bear up bravely, and constantly. (La-Foole *passes over the stage as* 20 *a sewer,*[1] *followed by servants carrying dishes, and* Mistress Otter.) — Look you here, sir, what honor is done you unexpected by your nephew; a wedding-dinner come, and a knight-sewer before it, for the more reputation: and fine Mistress Otter, your neighbor, in the rump 25 or tail of it.

Mor. Is that Gorgon, that Medusa [2] come! hide me, hide me.

True. I warrant you, sir, she will not transform you. Look upon her with a good 30 courage. Pray you entertain her, and conduct your guests in. No! — Mistress bride, will you entreat in the ladies? Your bridegroom is so shame-faced, here. 34

Epi. Will it please your ladyship, madam?

Hau. With the benefit of your company, mistress.

Epi. Servant, pray you perform your duties.

Daw. And glad to be commanded, mistress.

Cen. How like you her wit, Mavis? 40

Mav. Very prettily, absolutely well.

Mrs. Ott. 'Tis my place. (*Tries to go ahead.*)

Mav. You shall pardon me, Mistress Otter.

Mrs. Ott. Why, I am a collegiate.

Mav. But not in ordinary.[3] 45

Mrs. Ott. But I am.

Mav. We'll dispute that within.

    (*Exeunt Ladies.*)

Cler. Would this had lasted a little longer.

True. And that they had sent for the heralds.[4] 50

Enter Captain Otter

— Captain Otter! what news?

Ott. I have brought my bull, bear, and horse, in private, and yonder are the trumpeters without, and the drum, gentlemen.

    (*The drum and trumpets sound within.*

---

[1] Turned aside.

[2] I.e., be widely advertised as a husband whose wife is unfaithful. Horns on the head were the accepted symbol of the cuckolded man.

[3] E.g., harps, lutes, fiddles, trumpets, drums. Such a variety of noise was common at weddings.

---

[1] I.e., head server or butler.

[2] The mythical goddess of horrible appearance and snaky locks.

[3] In actual and constant attendance.

[4] The heralds at arms, the royal trumpeters, blew upon their horns to attract the populace and then announced important news.

Mor. O, o, o!   55
Ott. And we will have a rouse [1] in each of them, anon, for bold Britons, i'faith.

                 (*They sound again.*

Mor. O, o, o!   (*Exit hastily.*
All. Follow, follow, follow!   (*Exeunt.*

ACT IV

SCENE I. *A room in* MOROSE'S *house.*

Enter TRUEWIT *and* CLERIMONT

True. Was there ever poor bridegroom so tormented? or man, indeed?

Cler. I have not read of the like in the chronicles of the land.

True. Sure, he cannot but go to a place   5
of rest, after all this purgatory.

Cler. He may presume it, I think.

True. The spitting, the coughing, the laughter, the sneezing, the farting, dancing, noise of the music, and her masculine and loud   10
commanding, and urging the whole family, makes him think he has married a fury.

Cler. And she carries it up bravely.

True. Ay, she takes any occasion to speak: that's the height on't.   15

Cler. And how soberly Dauphine labors to satisfy him, that it was none of his plot!

True. And has almost brought him to the faith, in the article. Here he comes. —

Enter SIR DAUPHINE

Where is he now? what's become of him,   20
Dauphine?

Daup. O, hold me up a little, I shall go away in the jest [2] else. He has got on his whole nest of night-caps, and locked himself up in the top of the house, as high as ever he can climb   25
from the noise. I peeped in at a cranny, and saw him sitting over a cross-beam of the roof, like him on the saddler's horse in Fleet-street, upright: and he will sleep there.

Cler. But where are your collegiates?   30

Daup. Withdrawn with the bride in private.

True. Oh, they are instructing her in the col-

---

[1] Toast.
[2] I shall die laughing.

---

lege-grammar. If she have grace with them, she knows all their secrets instantly.

Cler. Methinks the Lady Haughty looks   35
well today, for all my dispraise of her in the morning. I think I shall come about to thee [1] again, Truewit.

True. Believe it, I told you right. Women ought to repair the losses time and years   40
have made in their features, with dressings. And an intelligent woman, if she know by herself the least defect, will be most curious [2] to hide it: and it becomes her. If she be short, let her sit much, lest, when she stands, she   45
be thought to sit. If she have an ill [3] foot, let her wear her gown the longer, and her shoe the thinner. If a fat hand, and scald [4] nails, let her carve the less, [5] and act [6] in gloves. If a sour breath, let her never discourse fasting, [7] and   50
always talk at her distance. If she have black and rugged [8] teeth, let her offer the less at laughter, especially if she laugh wide and open.

Cler. Oh, you shall have some women, when they laugh, you would think they brayed,   55
it is so rude and ——

True. Ay, and others, that will stalk in their gait like an ostrich, and take huge strides. I cannot endure such a sight. I love measure in the feet, and number in the voice: they are   60
gentlenesses, that oftentimes draw no less than the face.

Daup. How camest thou to study these creatures so exactly? I would thou wouldst make me a proficient.   65

True. Yes, but you must leave to live [9] in your chamber, then, a month together upon Amadis de Gaul, [10] or Don Quixote, [11] as you are wont; and come abroad where the matter is frequent, [12] to court, to tiltings, public   70
shows and feasts, to plays, and church some-

---

[1] I shall side with thee.   [2] Most careful.
[3] Ill-shaped.   [4] Shabby.
[5] Women usually did the carving at family tables.
[6] Gesticulate.   [7] I.e., while she is fasting.
[8] Uneven.   [9] Leave off living.
[10] An immensely popular Spanish romance of the period, a tale of the adventures of the illegitimate son of Perion, King of Gaul, and Elisena, Princess of Brittany.
[11] The famous satiric romance by Cervantes, the first part of which came out at Madrid in 1605.
[12] The evidence is abundant.

times: thither they come to show their new tires[1] too, to see, and to be seen. In these places a man shall find whom to love, whom to play with, whom to touch once, whom to 75 hold ever. The variety arrests his judgment. A wench to please a man comes not down dropping from the ceiling, as he lies on his back droning[2] a tobacco-pipe. He must go where she is. 80

Daup. Yes, and be never the nearer.

True. Out, heretic! That diffidence makes thee worthy it should be so.

Cler. He says true to you, Dauphine.

Daup. Why? 85

True. A man should not doubt to overcome any woman. Think he can vanquish them, and he shall: for though they deny, their desire is to be tempted. Penelope herself cannot hold out long.[3] Ostend, you saw, was taken at last.[4] 90 You must persevere and hold to your purpose. They would solicit us, but that they are afraid. Howsoever, they wish in their hearts we should solicit them. Praise them, flatter them, you shall never want eloquence or trust: even 95 the chastest delight to feel themselves that way rubbed. With praises you must mix kisses too: if they take them, they'll take more — though they strive, they would be overcome. 99

Cler. Oh, but a man must beware of force.

True. It is to them an acceptable violence, and has oft-times the place of the greatest courtesy. She that might have been forced, and you let her go free without touching, though then she seem to thank you, will 105 ever hate you after; and glad in the face, is assuredly sad at the heart.

Cler. But all women are not to be taken all ways.

True. 'Tis true; no more than all birds, 110

---

[1] Attires.   [2] Puffing.

[3] Penelope, the faithful wife of Odysseus (Ulysses), was beset by suitors when her husband was thought lost on his travels after the Trojan War. She announced that she would make no choice until she had completed a funeral robe for her father-in-law, Laërtes. Then each night she unraveled secretly what she had knitted during the day.

[4] The Spanish captured this Belgian port on the English Channel on September 8, 1604, after a siege of three years and ten weeks.

or all fishes. If you appear learned to an ignorant wench, or jocund to a sad, or witty to a foolish, why she presently begins to mistrust herself. You must approach them in their own height, their own line; for the contrary 115 makes many, that fear to commit themselves to noble and worthy fellows, run into the embraces of a rascal. If she love wit, give verses, though you borrow them of a friend, or buy them, to have good. If valor, talk of your sword, 120 and be frequent in the mention of quarrels, though you be staunch in fighting. If activity, be seen on your barbary[1] often, or leaping over stools,[2] for the credit of your back. If she love good clothes or dressing, have your learned 125 council about you every morning, your French tailor, barber, linener, etc. Let your powder, your glass, and your comb be your dearest acquaintance. Take more care for the ornament of your head, than the safety; and wish the 130 commonwealth rather troubled, than a hair about you. That will take her. Then, if she be covetous and craving, do you promise anything, and perform sparingly; so shall you keep her in appetite still. Seem as you would 135 give, but be like a barren field, that yields little; or unlucky dice to foolish and hoping gamesters. Let your gifts be slight and dainty, rather than precious. Let cunning be above cost. Give cherries at time of year,[3] or apricots; and 140 say, they were sent you out of the country, though you bought them in Cheapside.[4] Admire her tires: like her in all fashions; compare her in every habit to some deity; invent excellent dreams to flatter her, and riddles; or, 145 if she be a great one,[5] perform always the second parts to her: like what she likes, praise whom she praises, and fail not to make the household and servants yours, yea the whole family, and salute them by their names ('tis but light 150 cost, if you can purchase them so), and make

---

[1] Barbary horse, a fashionable breed from the coast of north Africa.

[2] A common form of exercise among London gallants, which aroused frequent derision.

[3] Cherries in season.

[4] The chief shopping street of old London. It ran from the east to the north corner of St. Paul's Church-Yard.

[5] A lady of position.

her physician your pensioner, and her chief woman. Nor will it be out of your gain to make love to her too, so she follow, not usher her lady's pleasure. All blabbing[1] is taken 155 away, when she comes to be a part of the crime.

Daup. On what courtly lap hast thou late slept, to come forth so sudden and absolute a courtling?

True. Good faith, I should rather 160 question you, that are so hearkening after[2] these mysteries. I begin to suspect your diligence, Dauphine. Speak, art thou in love in earnest?

Daup. Yes, by my troth, am I; 'twere 165 ill dissembling before thee.

True. With which of them, I prithee?

Daup. With all the collegiates.

Cler. Out on thee! We'll keep you at home, believe it, in the stable, an[3] you be such 170 a stallion.

True. No; I like him well. Men should love wisely, and all women; some one for the face, and let her please the eye; another for the skin, and let her please the touch; a third for 175 the voice, and let her please the ear; and where the objects mix, let the senses so too. Thou would'st think it strange, if I should make them all in love with thee afore night!

Daup. I would say, thou hadst the 180 best philtre[4] in the world, and couldst do more than madam Medea,[5] or Doctor Foreman.[6]

True. If I do not, let me play the mountebank for my meat, while I live, and the bawd for my drink. 185

Daup. So be it, I say.

SCENE 2. *The same.*

Enter OTTER, *with his three cups,* DAW, *and* LA-FOOLE

Ott. O lord, gentlemen, how my knights and I have mist you here!

Cler. Why, captain, what service, what service?

Ott. To see me bring up my bull, bear, 5 and horse[1] to fight.

Daw. Yes, faith, the captain says we shall be his dogs to bait them.

Daup. A good employment.

True. Come on, let's see your course, 10 then.

La-F. I am afraid my cousin will be offended, if she come.

Ott. Be afraid of nothing. — Gentlemen, I have placed the drum and the trumpets, 15 and one to give them the sign when you are ready. Here's my bull for myself, and my bear for Sir John Daw, and my horse for Sir Amorous. Now set your foot to mine, and yours to his, and —— 20

La-F. Pray God my cousin come not.

Ott. St. George, and St. Andrew,[2] fear no cousins.[3] Come, sound, sound! (*Drum and trumpets sound.*) *Et rauco strepuerunt cornua cantu.*[4] (*They drink.* 25

True. Well said, captain, i'faith; well fought at the bull.

Cler. Well held at the bear.

True. Low, low! captain.

Daup. Oh, the horse has kicked off his 30 dog already.

La-F. I cannot drink it, as I am a knight.

True. Ods so! off with his spurs, somebody.

La-F. It goes against my conscience. My cousin will be angry with it. 35

Daw. I have done mine.

True. You fought high and fair, Sir John.

Cler. At the head.

Daup. Like an excellent bear-dog.

Cler. You take no notice of the business, 40 I hope?

Daw. Not a word, sir; you see we are jovial.

---

[1] Tattling.   [2] Seeking so much information about.
[3] If.   [4] Love potion.
[5] The outstanding enchantress of Greek myth; the daughter of the king of Colchis, who by her magic helped her lover, Jason, steal the Golden Fleece out of her father's kingdom.
[6] Dr. Simon Foreman (1552–1611), London's famous quack-doctor and conjurer.

[1] These are his three drinking-cups of various sizes, either shaped or painted to represent the bull, bear, and horse. This whole scene is a silly parody on bull- and bear-baiting, favorite popular pastimes. The animals chained to stakes were worried by bull-dogs.
[2] The patron saints of England and Scotland, recently reconciled, so to speak, by the union of the two kingdoms under James I in 1603.
[3] No kinsmen.
[4] And the trumpets sounded a loud blast.

Ott. Sir Amorous, you must not equivocate. It must be pulled down, for all my cousin.

Cler. 'Sfoot,[1] if you take not your drink, 45 they'll think you are discontented with something; you'll betray all, if you take the least notice.

La-F. Not I; I'll both drink and talk, then.

Ott. You must pull the horse on his knees, 50 Sir Amorous; fear no cousins. *Jacta est alea.*[2]

True. Oh, now he's in his vein, and bold. The least hint given him of his wife now, will make him rail[3] desperately.

Cler. Speak to him of her. 55

True. Do you, and I'll fetch her to the hearing of it.   (*Exit.*

Daup. Captain He-Otter, your She-Otter is coming, your wife.

Ott. Wife! buz! *titivilitium!*[4] There's 60 no such thing in nature. I confess, gentlemen, I have a cook, a laundress, a house-drudge, that serves my necessary turns, and goes under that title; but he's an ass that will be so uxorious to tie his affections to one circle. 65 Come, the name dulls appetite. Here, replenish again; another bout. (*Fills the cups again.*) Wives are nasty, sluttish animals.

Daup. Oh, captain.

Ott. As ever the earth bare, *tribus verbis.*[5] 70 — Where's Master Truewit?

Daw. He's slipt aside, sir.

Cler. But you must drink and be jovial.

Daw. Yes, give it me.

La-F. And me too. 75

Daw. Let's be jovial.

La-F. As jovial as you will.

Ott. Agreed. Now you shall have the bear, cousin, and Sir John Daw the horse, and I'll have the bull still. Sound, Tritons[6] of the 80 Thames! (*Drum and trumpets sound again.*) *Nunc est bibendum, nunc pede libero*——[7]

Mor. (*entering above*).[8] Villains, murder-

ers, sons of the earth, and traitors, what do you there? 85

Cler. Oh, now the trumpets have waked him, we shall have his company.

Ott. A wife is a scurvy clogdogdo,[1] an unlucky thing, a very foresaid bear-whelp, without any good fashion or breeding, *mala* 90 *bestia.*[2]

Enter TRUEWIT *with* MRS. OTTER, *at the back of the stage*

Daup. Why did you marry one then, captain?

Ott. A pox! — I married with six thousand pound, I was in love with that. I ha' 95 not kissed my Fury these forty weeks.

Cler. The more to blame you, captain.

True. (*aside*). Nay, Mistress Otter, hear him a little first.

Ott. She has a breath worse than my 100 grandmother's, *profecto.*[3]

Mrs. Ott. O treacherous liar! kiss me, sweet Master Truewit, and prove him a slandering knave.

True. I'll rather believe you, lady. 105

Ott. And she has a peruke that's like a pound of hemp, made up in shoe-threads.

Mrs. Ott. O viper, mandrake![4]

Ott. O most vile face! and yet she spends me forty pound a year in mercury and 110 hogs-bones.[5] All her teeth were made in the Blackfriars,[6] both her eyebrows in the Strand, and her hair in Silverstreet.[7] Every part of the town owns a piece of her. 114

Mrs. Ott. (*coming forward*). I cannot hold.[8]

Ott. She takes herself asunder still when

---

[1] God's foot.   [2] Chance has been overthrown.

[3] Utter insolent and reproachful words.

[4] Good-for-nothing.

[5] I.e., three true words, namely, "nasty, sluttish animals."

[6] Subordinate sea deities, who blew shell-trumpets to calm the waves.

[7] Now it ought to be drunk, now foot-loose——

[8] I.e., in the gallery overlooking the stage.

[1] A ridiculous term coined by Otter, meaning "a dog's clog."

[2] An evil beast.   [3] Truly.

[4] A plant with a forked root somewhat like the human figure. It was believed to be alive and to shriek so fearfully on being uprooted that the hearers went mad.

[5] Mercury, i.e., quicksilver, and hog's bones were often used as cosmetics.

[6] The jocular implication is that his wife's teeth are very dark in color and therefore might well have come from this locality.

[7] Further far-fetched jokes on the names of the localities mentioned.

[8] Restrain myself.

she goes to bed, into some twenty boxes; and
about next day noon is put together again,
like a great German clock:[1] and so comes forth,
and rings a tedious larum to the whole   120
house, and then is quiet again for an hour,
but for her quarters[2] —— Have you done me
right, gentlemen?

Mrs. Ott. (*falling upon him, and beating him*).
No, sir, I'll do you right with my quarters,
with my quarters.   125

Ott. O, hold, good princess.

True. Sound, sound!

(*Drum and trumpets sound.*

Cler. A battle, a battle!

Mrs. Ott. You notorious stinkardly bearward,[3] does my breath smell?   130

Ott. Under correction, dear princess. —
Look to my bear and my horse, gentlemen.

Mrs. Ott. Do I want teeth, and eyebrows,
thou bull-dog?

True. Sound, sound still.   135

(*The drum and trumpets sound again.*

Ott. No, I protest, under correction ——

Mrs. Ott. Ay, now you are under correction,
you protest: but you did not protest before
correction, sir. Thou Judas, to offer to betray
thy princess! I'll make thee an example ——

(*Beats him.*

Enter from above MOROSE *with his long sword*

Mor. I will have no such examples in   141
my house, Lady Otter.

Mrs. Ott. Ah! ——

(MRS. OTTER, DAW, *and* LA-FOOLE
run off.

Mor. Mistress Mary Ambree,[4] your examples are dangerous. — Rogues, hell-   145
hounds,[5] Stentors![6] out of my doors, you sons

[1] The German clocks of the day were notorious for
their complexity and poor time-keeping.

[2] I.e., the strikings for the quarter-hours.

[3] See note to Act I, Sc. 1, l. 211.

[4] A female warrior in the siege of Ghent in 1584.
Popular songs and ballads made her a well-known
heroine.

[5] There was a widespread belief that the Devil had
dogs who hunted down game for him.

[6] Stentor was the Greek herald whose voice, as loud as
fifty men shouting together, often is mentioned in
Homer's tale of the Trojan War.

of noise and tumult, begot on an ill May-day,[1]
or when the galley-foist[2] is afloat to Westminster! (*Drives out the musicians.*) A trumpeter could not be conceived but then.   150

Daup. What ails you, sir?

Mor. They have rent my roof, walls, and all
my windows asunder, with their brazen
throats.

(*Exit.*

True. Best follow him, Dauphine.   155

Daup. So I will.

(*Exit.*

Cler. Where's Daw and La-Foole?

Ott. They are both run away, sir. Good
gentlemen, help to pacify my princess, and
speak to the great ladies for me. Now   160
must I go lie with the bears this fortnight, and
keep out of the way, till my peace be made, for
this scandal she has taken. Did you not see
my bull-head, gentlemen?

Cler. Is't not on, captain?   165

True. No; but he may make a new one,
by that is on.

Ott. Oh, here it is. An you come over,
gentlemen, and ask for Tom Otter, we'll go
down to Ratcliff,[3] and have a course[4] i'   170
faith, for all these disasters. There is *bona
spes*[5] left.

True. Away, captain, get off while you are
well.

(*Exit* OTTER.

Cler. I am glad we are rid of him.   175

True. You had never been, unless we had
put his wife upon him. His humor is as tedious
at last, as it was ridiculous at first. (*Exeunt.*

SCENE 3. *A large lobby in*
MOROSE'S *house.*

Enter LADY HAUGHTY, MISTRESS OTTER,
MAVIS, DAW, LA-FOOLE, CENTAURE, *and*
EPICOENE

Hau. We wondered why you shrieked so,
Mistress Otter.

Mrs. Ott. O lord, madam, he came down

[1] A day of noisy celebration.

[2] The state barge which brought the new lord mayor
to Westminster to take his oath of office.

[3] A village down the Thames about a mile from
London Tower.

[4] Drink.   [5] Good hope.

with a huge long naked weapon in both his
hands, and looked so dreadfully! Sure   5
he's beside himself.

Mav. Why, what made you there, Mistress
Otter?

Mrs. Ott. Alas, Mistress Mavis, I was
chastising my subject, and thought noth-   10
ing of him.

Daw. Faith, mistress, you must do so too:
learn to chastise. Mistress Otter corrects her
husband so, he dares not speak but under
correction.   15

La-F. And with his hat off to her: 'twould
do you good to see.

Hau. In sadness, 'tis good and mature
counsel; practice it, Morose. I'll call you
Morose[1] still now, as I call Centaure and   20
Mavis; we four will be all one.

Cen. And you'll come to the college, and
live with us?

Hau. Make him give milk and honey.

Mav. Look how you manage him at   25
first, you shall have him ever after.

Cen. Let him allow you your coach, and
four horses, your woman, your chamber-maid,
your page, your gentleman-usher, your French
cook, and four grooms.   30

Hau. And go with us to Bedlam,[2] to the
china-houses,[3] and to the Exchange.[4]

Cen. It will open the gate to your fame.

Hau. Here's Centaure has immortalized
herself, with taming of her wild male.   35

Mav. Ay, she has done the miracle of the
kingdom.

Enter CLERIMONT and TRUEWIT

Epi. But, ladies, do you count it lawful to
have such plurality of servants, and do them
all graces?[5]   40

Hau. Why not? Why should women deny
their favors to men? Are they the poorer or
the worse?

Daw. Is the Thames the less for the dyers'
water, mistress?   45

La-F. Or a torch for lighting many torches?

True. Well said, La-Foole; what a new one
he has got!

Cen. They are empty losses women fear in
this kind.   50

Hau. Besides, ladies should be mindful of
the approach of age, and let no time want his
due use. The best of our days pass first.

Mav. We are rivers, that cannot be called
back, madam: she that now excludes her   55
lovers, may live to lie a forsaken beldame,[1] in
a frozen bed.

Cen. 'Tis true, Mavis: and who will wait
on us to coach then? Or write, or tell us the
news then, make anagrams of our names,   60
and invite us to the cockpit,[2] and kiss our hands
all the play-time, and draw their weapons for
our honors?

Hau. Not one.

Daw. Nay, my mistress is not alto-   65
gether unintelligent[3] of these things; here be
in presence have tasted[4] of her favors.

Cler. What a neighing hobby-horse[5] is this!

Epi. But not with intent to boast them
again, servant. — And have you those   70
excellent receipts, madam, to keep yourselves
from bearing of children?

Hau. Oh yes, Morose: how should we
maintain our youth and beauty else? Many
births of a woman make her old, as many   75
crops make the earth barren.

SCENE 4. *The same.*

Enter MOROSE and DAUPHINE

Mor. O my cursed angel, that instructed me
to this fate!

Daup. Why, sir?

---

[1] A prevalent feminine mode to address one another
after the manner of men.

[2] The Hospital of St. Mary of Bethlehem, established
in 1547 as an asylum for lunatics. Situated to the
northeast of the old city outside Bishopsgate, it was a
fashionable place of visitation.

[3] The chinaware shops, another fashionable resort.

[4] The Royal Exchange, a shopping center for high
society.

[5] Favors.

[1] Old woman.

[2] The pits for cock-fighting were frequented even by
the king and court.

[3] Unacquainted.

[4] In attendance those who have tasted.

[5] What a talkative fool.

Mor. That I should be seduced by so foolish a devil as a barber will make!   5

Daup. I would I had been worthy, sir, to have partaken your counsel; you should never have trusted it to such a minister.

Mor. Would I could redeem it with the loss of an eye, nephew, a hand, or any other   10 member.

Daup. Marry, God forbid, sir, that you should geld yourself, to anger your wife.

Mor. So it would rid me of her! — and, that I did supererogatory[1] penance in a   15 belfry, at Westminster-hall,[2] in the cockpit, at the fall of a stag,[3] the Tower-wharf — what place is there else? — London-bridge, Paris-garden,[4] Billinsgate,[5] when the noises are at their height, and loudest. Nay, I would   20 sit out a play, that were nothing but fights at sea, drum, trumpet, and target.

Daup. I hope there shall be no such need, sir. Take patience, good uncle. This is but a day, and 'tis well worn too now.   25

Mor. Oh, 'twill be so forever, nephew, I foresee it, forever. Strife and tumult are the dowry that comes with a wife.

True. I told you so, sir, and you would not believe me.   30

Mor. Alas, do not rub those wounds, Master Truewit, to blood again: 'twas my negligence. Add not affliction to affliction. I have perceived the effect of it, too late, in Madam Otter.   35

Epi. How do you, sir?

Mor. Did you ever hear a more unnecessary question? As if she did not see! Why, I do as you see, empress, empress.

Epi. You are not well, sir; you look   40 very ill: something has distemper'd you.

Mor. O horrible, monstrous impertinencies! would not one of these have served, do you think, sir? Would not one of these have served?   45

True. Yes, sir; but these are but notes of female kindness, sir; certain tokens that she has a voice, sir.

Mor. Oh, is it so! Come, an't be no otherwise —— What say you?   50

Epi. How do you feel yourself, sir?

Mor. Again that!

True. Nay, look you, sir, you would be friends with your wife upon unconscionable terms; her silence.   55

Epi. They say you are run mad, sir.

Mor. Not for love, I assure you, of you; do you see?

Epi. O lord, gentlemen! lay hold on him, for God's sake. What shall I do? Who's   60 his physician, can you tell, that knows the state of his body best, that I might send for him? Good sir, speak; I'll send for one of my doctors else.

Mor. What, to poison me, that I might   65 die intestate, and leave you possest of all!

Epi. Lord, how idly he talks, and how his eyes sparkle! he looks green about the temples! do you see what blue spots he has!

Cler. Ay, 'tis melancholy.[1]   70

Epi. Gentlemen, for Heaven's sake, counsel me. Ladies! — Servant, you have read Pliny[2] and Paracelsus;[3] ne'er a word now to comfort a poor gentlewoman? Ay me, what fortune had I, to marry a distracted man!   75

Daw. I'll tell you, mistress ——

True. (*aside to Cler.*). How rarely she holds it up!

Mor. What mean you, gentlemen?

Epi. What will you tell me, servant?   80

Daw. The disease in Greek is called μανια, in Latin *insania, furor, vel ecstasis melancholica,*[4] that is, *egressio,*[5] when a man *ex melancholico evadit fanaticus.*[6]

Mor. Shall I have a lecture read upon me   85 alive?

---

[1] Extra.
[2] A noisy place on account of the law courts and the shops of stationers, booksellers, toy merchants, etc.
[3] At such an event, much hurrahing, blowing of horns, and the like.
[4] A famous bear-baiting spot in Southwark on the south bank of the Thames.
[5] The fish wharf, notorious for noisy and foul language.

[1] Melancholia.
[2] A noted Roman writer of natural science in the first century A.D.
[3] A German-Swiss scientist and lecturer (1493–1541), who advanced the study of medicine and alchemy.
[4] Insanity, madness, or the frenzy of melancholia.
[5] Outburst.
[6] From a state of melancholia attempts to escape frantically.

Daw. But he may be but *phreneticus*[1] yet, mistress; and *phrenetis* is only *delirium*, or so.

Epi. Ay, that is for the disease, servant; but what is this to the cure? We are sure enough of the disease. 90

Mor. Let me go.

True. Why, we'll entreat her to hold her peace, sir.

Mor. Oh no, labor not to stop her. She is like a conduit-pipe, that will gush out with more force when she opens again. 95

Hau. I'll tell you, Morose, you must talk divinity[2] to him altogether, or moral philosophy. 100

La-F. Ay, and there's an excellent book of moral philosophy, madam, of Reynard the Fox, and all the beasts, called Doni's Philosophy.[3]

Cen. There is indeed, Sir Amorous La- 105 Foole.

Mor. O misery!

La-F. I have read it, my lady Centaure, all over, to my cousin here.

Mrs. Ott. Ay, and 'tis a very good book 110 as any is, of the moderns.

Daw. Tut, he must have Seneca read to him, and Plutarch, and the ancients; the moderns are not for this disease.

Cler. Why, you discommended them 115 too, today, Sir John.

Daw. Ay, in some cases: but in these they are best, and Aristotle's *Ethics*.

Mav. Say you so, Sir John? I think you are deceived; you took it upon trust. 120

Hau. Where's Trusty, my woman? I'll end this difference. I prithee, Otter, call her. Her father and mother were both mad, when they put her to me.

Mor. I think so. — Nay, gentlemen, I 125 am tame. This is but an exercise, I know, a marriage ceremony, which I must endure.

Hau. And one of them, I know not which,

was cured with the Sick Man's Salve,[1] and the other with Green's Groat's-worth of 130 Wit.[2]

True. A very cheap cure, madam.

Enter TRUSTY

Hau. Ay, 'tis very feasible.

Mrs. Ott. My lady called for you, Mistress Trusty: you must decide a controversy. 135

Hau. Oh, Trusty, which was it you said, your father, or your mother, that was cured with the Sick Man's Salve?

Trus. My mother, madam, with the Salve.

True. Then it was the sick woman's 140 salve?

Trus. And my father with the Groat's-worth of Wit. But there was other means used: we had a preacher that would preach folk asleep still; and so they were pre- 145 scribed to go to church, by an old woman that was their physician, thrice a week ——

Epi. To sleep?

Trus. Yes, forsooth: and every night they read themselves asleep on those books. 150

Epi. Good faith, it stands with great reason. I would I knew where to procure those books.

Mor. Oh!

La-F. I can help you with one of them, Mistress Morose, the Groat's-worth of Wit.

Epi. But I shall disfurnish you, Sir Amorous: can you spare it? 157

La-F. O yes, for a week, or so; I'll read it myself to him.

Epi. No, I must do that, sir; that must 160 be my office.

Mor. Oh, oh!

Epi. Sure he would do well enough, if he could sleep.

Mor. No, I should do well enough, if 165 you could sleep. Have I no friend that will make her drunk, or give her a little laudanum,[3] or opium?

---

[1] Delirious.

[2] Theology.

[3] La-Foole confuses two different well-known works of the time: an old epic tale called *The History of Reynard the Fox*, and *Doni's Moral Philosophy*, an Italian version of a collection of Persian beast fables, which Sir Thomas North translated into English in 1605.

[1] A moralistic tract first published in 1561 by Thomas Bacon, a Calvinist preacher (1511–67).

[2] Another moralistic pamphlet, written just before his death by Robert Greene the playwright (1560–92) and published in 1596.

[3] In this case, the tincture of opium.

True. Why, sir, she talks ten times worse in her sleep. 170

Mor. How!

Cler. Do you not know that, sir? Never ceases all night.

True. And snores like a porpoise.

Mor. O redeem me, fate; redeem me, 175 fate! For how many causes may a man be divorced, nephew?

Daup. I know not, truly, sir.

True. Some divine must resolve you in that, sir, or canon-lawyer.[1] 180

Mor. I will not rest, I will not think of any other hope or comfort, till I know.

(*Exit with* DAUPHINE.

Cler. Alas, poor man!

True. You'll make him mad indeed, ladies, if you pursue this. 185

Hau. No, we'll let him breathe now, a quarter of an hour or so.

Cler. By my faith, a large truce!

Hau. Is that his keeper, that is gone with him? 190

Daw. It is his nephew, madam.

La-F. Sir Dauphine Eugenie.

Cen. He looks like a very pitiful knight ——

Daw. As can be. This marriage has put him out of all. 195

La-F. He has not a penny in his purse, madam.

Daw. He is ready to cry[2] all this day.

La-F. A very shark; he set me in the nick[3] t'other night at Primero.[4] 200

True. How these swabbers[5] talk!

Cler. Ay, Otter's wine has swell'd their humors above a springtide.

Hau. Good Morose, let's go in again. I like your couches exceeding well; we'll go lie 205 and talk there.

(*Exeunt all but* EPI., TRUE., CLER.

Epi. (*starting to go out*). I wait on you, madam.

True. (*stopping her*). 'Slight, I will have

[1] The divine will advise on the theological aspects of the matter, and the canon lawyer on the ecclesiastical law involved.

[2] Beg.   [3] Won the wager.

[4] A very old game of cards combining features of poker, euchre, and seven-up.

[5] Dolts.

them as silent as signs, and their post too, 210 ere I have done. Do you hear, lady-bride? I pray thee now, as thou art a noble wench, continue this discourse of Dauphine within; but praise him exceedingly: magnify him with all the height of affection thou canst; — I 215 have some purpose in't: and but beat off these two rooks, Jack Daw and his fellow, with any discontentment, hither, and I'll honor thee forever.

Epi. I was about it here. It angered 220 me to the soul, to hear them begin to talk so malapert.[1]

True. Pray thee perform it, and thou winn'st me an idolater to thee everlasting. 224

Epi. Will you go in and hear me do't?

True. No, I'll stay here. Drive them out of your company, 'tis all I ask; which cannot be any way better done, than by extolling Dauphine, whom they have so slighted.

Epi. I warrant you; you shall expect 230 one of them presently. (*Exit.*

Cler. What a cast of kestrils[2] are these, to hawk after ladies, thus!

True. Ay, and strike at such an eagle as Dauphine. 235

Cler. He will be mad when we tell him. Here he comes.

SCENE 5. *The same.*

Re-enter DAUPHINE

Cler. O sir, you are welcome.

True. Where's thine uncle?

Daup. Run out of doors in his night-caps, to talk with a casuist about his divorce. It works admirably. 5

True. Thou wouldst have said so, an thou hadst been here! The ladies have laugh'd at thee most comically, since thou went'st, Dauphine.

Cler. And asked, if thou wert thine 10 uncle's keeper.

True. And the brace of baboons answer'd, Yes; and said thou wert a pitiful poor fellow, and didst live upon posts, and hadst nothing but three suits of apparel, and some few 15

[1] Boldly.

[2] Pair of degenerate hawks.

benevolences that the lords gave thee to fool to them, and swagger.

Daup. Let me not live, I'll beat them: I'll bind them both to grand-madam's bed-posts, and have them baited[1] with monkies.   20

True. Thou shalt not need, they shall be beaten to thy hand, Dauphine. I have an execution to serve upon them, I warrant thee, shall serve; trust my plot.

Daup. Ay, you have many plots! so you   25 had one to make all the wenches in love with me.

True. Why, if I do it not yet afore night, as near as 'tis, and that they do not every one invite thee, and be ready to scratch for   30 thee, take the mortgage of my wit.

Cler. 'Fore God, I'll be his witness thou shalt have it, Dauphine: thou shalt be his fool forever, if thou dost not.

True. Agreed. Perhaps 'twill be the   35 better estate. Do you observe this gallery, or rather lobby, indeed? Here are a couple of studies, at each end one: here will I act such a tragi-comedy between the Guelphs and the Ghibellines,[2] Daw and La-Foole —   40 which of them comes out first, will I seize on; — you two shall be the chorus behind the arras,[3] and whip out between the acts and speak — If I do not make them keep the peace for this rem- nant of the day, if not of the year, I have   45 failed once —— I hear Daw coming: hide, and do not laugh, for God's sake. (*They withdraw.*)

Re-enter DAW

Daw. Which is the way into the garden, trow?

True. Oh, Jack Daw! I am glad I have   50

[1] Harassed.

[2] The two contending parties in the Italian states from the thirteenth to the seventeenth century. The Guelphs were the popular party supporting the inde- pendence of the Pope; the Ghibellines, the aristocratic faction supporting the rule of the German emperors over Italy.

[3] Tapestry hangings covered the walls in the homes of the higher classes. They were attached to wooden frames, between which and the wall itself there was space enough to permit a person to hide. — On the stage, the arras was the particular hangings which closed off the inner stage and constituted a favorite means of concealment.

met with you. In good faith, I must have this matter go no further between you: I must have it taken up.

Daw. What matter, sir? Between whom?

True. Come, you disguise it: Sir Amor-   55 ous and you. If you love me, Jack, you shall make use of your philosophy now, for this once, and deliver me your sword. This is not the wedding the Centaurs were at,[1] though there be a she one here. (*Takes* DAW'S   60 *sword.*) The bride has entreated me I will see no blood shed at her bridal: you saw her whisper me erewhile.

Daw. As I hope to finish Tacitus,[2] I in- tend no murder.   65

True. Do you not wait for Sir Amorous?

Daw. Not I, by my knighthood.

True. And your scholarship too?

Daw. And my scholarship too.

True. Go to, then I return you your   70 sword, and ask you mercy; but put it not up, for you will be assaulted. I understood that you had apprehended it, and walked here to brave[3] him; and that you had held your life contemptible in regard of your honor.   75

Daw. No, no; no such thing, I assure you. He and I parted now, as good friends as could be.

True. Trust not you to that visor. I saw him since dinner with another face: I have   80 known many men in my time vexed with losses, with deaths, and with abuses; but so offended a wight[4] as Sir Amorous, did I never see or read of. For taking away his guests, sir, today, that's the cause; and he declares   85 it behind your back with such threatenings and contempts —— He said to Dauphine, you were the arrant'st ass —

Daw. Ay, he may say his pleasure.

True. And swears you are so protested   90 a coward, that he knows you will never do

[1] Pirithoüs, King of the Lapithae in Thessaly, invited to his wedding with Deidamia the Centaurs, another Thessalian people shaped half like horses, half like men. The Centaurs, inflamed by wine, attempted to seize the bride and other maidens, but were beaten off by Theseus and the Lapithae.

[2] Famous Roman historian (?55–?117 A.D.).

[3] Oppose.

[4] Man, creature.

him any manly or single right; and therefore he will take his course.

Daw. I'll give him any satisfaction, sir — but fighting.   95

True. Ay, sir: but who knows what satisfaction he'll take: blood he thirsts for, and blood he will have; and whereabouts on you he will have it, who knows but himself?

Daw. I pray you, Master Truewit, be   100 you a mediator.

True. Well, sir, conceal yourself then in this study till I return. (*Puts him into the study.* [1]) Nay, you must be content to be lock'd in; for, for mine own reputation, I would not   105 have you seen to receive a public disgrace, while I have the matter in managing. Ods so, here he comes; keep your breath close, that he do not hear you sigh. — In good faith, Sir Amorous, he is not this way; I pray you   110 be merciful, do not murder him; he is a Christian, as good as you: you are armed as if you sought revenge on all his race. Good Dauphine, get him away from this place. I never knew a man's choler so high, but he   115 would speak to his friends, he would hear reason. — Jack Daw, Jack! asleep!

Daw (*within*). Is he gone, Master Truewit?

True. Ay; did you hear him?

Daw. O god, yes!   120

True. What a quick ear fear has!

Daw (*coming out of the study*). But is he so armed, as you say?

True. Armed! did you ever see a fellow set out to take possession? [2]   125

Daw. Ay, sir.

True. That may give you some light to conceive of him; but 'tis nothing to the principal. Some false brother in the house has furnished him strangely; or, if it were out   130 of the house, it was Tom Otter.

Daw. Indeed he's a captain, and his wife is his kinswoman.

True. He has got somebody's old two-hand sword, to mow you off at the knees; and   135 that sword hath spawn'd such a dagger! —

[1] The study must be imagined behind one of the stage doors.

[2] I.e., possession of an estate likely to be contested by force.

But then he is so hung with pikes, halberds, petronels,[1] calivers,[2] and muskets, that he looks like a justice of peace's hall;[3] a man of two thousand a-year is not cessed[4] at so   140 many weapons as he has on. There was never fencer challenged at so many several foils.[5] You would think he meant to murder all St. Pulchre parish.[6] If he could but victual himself for half a-year in his breeches,[7] he is   145 sufficiently armed to over-run a country.

Daw. Good lord! what means he, sir? I pray you, Master Truewit, be you a mediator.

True. Well, I'll try if he will be appeased with a leg or an arm; if not you must die once.   150

Daw. I would be loth to lose my right arm, for writing madrigals.[8]

True. Why, if he will be satisfied with a thumb or a little finger, all's one to me. You must think, I'll do my best.   155

Daw. Good sir, do.

(TRUEWIT *puts* DAW *in the study again.*
Cler. (*coming forward with* DAUPHINE). What hast thou done?

True. He will let me do nothing, he does all afore; he offers his left arm.

Cler. His left wing for a Jack Daw.   160

Daup. Take it by all means.

True. How! maim a man forever, for a jest? What a conscience hast thou!

Daup. 'Tis no loss to him; he has no employment for his arms, but to eat spoon-   165 meat.[9] Beside, as good maim his body as his reputation.

True. He is a scholar and a wit, and yet he does not think so. But he loses no reputation with us; for we all resolved[10] him an   170 ass before. To your places again.

[1] A portable firearm resembling a large horse-pistol.

[2] Another type of portable firearm.

[3] Such a hall often contained official weapon museums.

[4] A man of two thousand pounds (about ten thousand dollars) per year is not assessed, etc. In Jonson's time the wealthier the man the larger his armory would be.

[5] Fencing weapons with blunted points.

[6] St. Sepulchre's Parish in Farringdon, to the northwest of old London, was a district of evil reputation.

[7] Great breeches, large trunk hose which could be swelled, might be stuffed with food instead of cloth padding.   [8] Love poems of a pastoral character.

[9] Spoon-food, liquid or semi-liquid victuals.

[10] Judged.

Cler. I pray thee, let be me in at the other a little.

True. Look, you'll spoil all; these be ever your tricks.   175

Cler. No, but I could hit of some things that thou wilt miss, and thou wilt say are good ones.

True. I warrant you. I pray forbear, I'll leave it off, else.

Daup. Come away, Clerimont.   180

(DAUP. *and* CLER. *withdraw as before.*

Enter LA-FOOLE

True. Sir Amorous!

La-F. Master Truewit.

True. Whither were you going?

La-F. Down into the court to make water.

True. By no means, sir; you shall   185
rather tempt your breeches.

La-F. Why, sir?

True. Enter here, if you love your life.

(*Opens the door of the other study.*

La-F. Why? why?

True. Question till your throat be cut,   190
do: dally till the enraged soul find you.

La-F. Who is that?

True. Daw it is: will you in?

La-F. Ay, ay, I'll in: what's the matter?

True. Nay, if he had been cool enough   195
to tell us that, there had been some hope to atone you;[1] but he seems so implacably enraged!

La-F. 'Slight, let him rage! I'll hide myself.   200

True. Do, good sir. But what have you done to him within, that should provoke him thus? You have broke[2] some jest upon him afore the ladies.

La-F. Not I, never in my life, broke   205
jest upon any man. The bride was praising Sir Dauphine, and he went away in snuff,[3] and I followed him; unless he took offense at me in his drink erewhile, that I would not pledge all the horse full.[4]   210

True. By my faith, and that may be; you

[1] Bring you together amicably.
[2] Cracked.   [3] In a sudden fit of anger.
[4] Drink a toast with a full cup (the cup shaped like or decorated with a horse).

remember well: but he walks the round[1] up and down, through every room o' the house, with a towel in his hand, crying, "Where's La-Foole? Who saw La-Foole?" And when   215
Dauphine and I demanded the cause, we can force no answer from him, but — "O revenge, how sweet art thou! I will strangle him in this towel" — which leads us to conjecture that the main cause of his fury is, for   220
bringing your meat today, with a towel about you, to his discredit.

La-F. Like enough. Why, an he be angry for that, I'll stay here till his anger be blown over.   225

True. A good becoming resolution, sir; if you can put it on[2] o' the sudden.

La-F. Yes, I can put it on: or, I'll away into the country presently.

True. How will you go out of the house,   230
sir? He knows you are in the house, and he'll watch this se'ennight, but he'll have you: he'll outwait a sergeant[3] for you.

La-F. Why, then I'll stay here.

True. You must think how to victual   235
yourself in time then.

La-F. Why, sweet Master Truewit, will you entreat my cousin Otter to send me a cold venison pasty, a bottle or two of wine, and a chamber-pot?   240

True. A stool were better, sir, of Sir Ajax his invention.[4]

La-F. Ay, that will be better, indeed; and a pallet to lie on.

True. O, I would not advise you to   245
sleep by any means.

La-F. Would you not, sir? Why, then I will not.

True. Yet, there's another fear —

La-F. Is there! what is't?   250

True. No, he cannot break open this door with his foot, sure.

[1] Makes the circuit.
[2] You can take it upon yourself.
[3] A sergeant-at-law, well known for persistence in searching out offenders and bringing them to court.
[4] A gibing allusion to *The Metamorphosis of Ajax*, a small treatise on the improvement of domestic sanitation, which was published in 1596 by Sir John Harington (1561–1612). For this work Queen Elizabeth temporarily banished him from court.

La-F. I'll set my back against it, sir. I have a good back.

True. But then if he should batter. 255

La-F. Batter! if he dare, I'll have an action of battery against him.

True. Cast you the worst. He has sent for powder already, and what he will do with it, no man knows: perhaps blow up the 260 corner of the house where he suspects you are. Here he comes; in quickly. (*Thrusts in* LA-FOOLE *and shuts the door.*) — I protest, Sir John Daw, he is not this way: what will you do? Before God, you shall hang no 265 petard[1] here: I'll die rather. Will you not take my word? I never knew one but would be satisfied. — Sir Amorous (*speaking through the key-hole*), there's no standing out: he has made a petard of an old brass pot, to force 270 your door. Think upon some satisfaction, or terms to offer him.

La-F. (*within*). Sir, I'll give him any satisfaction: I dare give any terms.

True. You'll leave it to me then? 275

La-F. Ay, sir: I'll stand to any conditions.

True. (*beckoning forward* CLER. *and* DAUP.). How now, what think you, sirs? Were't not a difficult thing to determine which of these two feared most?

Cler. Yes, but this fears the bravest: 280 the other a whiniling[2] dastard, Jack Daw! But La-Foole, a brave heroic coward! and is afraid in a great look and a stout accent; I like him rarely.

True. Had it not been pity these two 285 should have been concealed?

Cler. Shall I make a motion?

True. Briefly: for I must strike while 'tis hot.

Cler. Shall I go fetch the ladies to the 290 catastrophe?

True. Umph! ay, by my troth.

Daup. By no mortal means. Let them continue in the state of ignorance, and err still; think them wits and fine fellows, as they 295 have done. 'Twere sin to reform them.

True. Well, I will have them fetched, now I think on't, for a private purpose of mine: do,

Clerimont, fetch them, and discourse to them all that's past, and bring them into the 300 gallery here.

Daup. This is thy extreme vanity, now: thou think'st thou wert undone, if every jest thou mak'st were not published.

True. Thou shalt see how unjust thou 305 art presently. Clerimont, say it was Dauphine's plot. (*Exit* CLERIMONT.) Trust me not, if the whole drift be not for thy good. There is a carpet in the next room, put it on, with this scarf over thy face, and a cushion on 310 thy head, and be ready when I call Amorous. Away! (*Exit* DAUPHINE.) John Daw!

(*Goes to* DAW's *study and brings him out.*

Daw. What good news, sir?

True. Faith, I have followed and argued with him hard for you. I told him you 315 were a knight, and a scholar, and that you knew fortitude did consist *magis patiendo quam faciendo, magis ferendo quam feriendo.*[1]

Daw. It doth so indeed, sir.

True. And that you would suffer, I 320 told him: so at first he demanded by my troth, in my conceit, too much.

Daw. What was it, sir?

True. Your upper lip, and six of your foreteeth. 325

Daw. 'Twas unreasonable.

True. Nay, I told him plainly, you could not spare them all. So after long argument *pro* and *con*,[2] as you know, I brought him down to your two butter-teeth,[3] and them he 330 would have.

Daw. Oh, did you so? Why, he shall have them.

True. But he shall not, sir, by your leave. The conclusion is this, sir: because[4] you 335 shall be very good friends hereafter, and this never to be remembered or upbraided; besides, that he may not boast he has done any such thing to you in his own person; he is to come here in disguise, give you five kicks in 340 private, sir, take your sword from you, and lock

---

[1] Place no explosive charge.
[2] Whindling, whimpering.

[1] More in suffering than in doing, more in enduring than in beating.
[2] For and against.
[3] Two middle teeth of the upper jaw.
[4] In order that.

you up in that study during pleasure: which will be but a little while, we'll get it released presently.

Daw. Five kicks! he shall have six,   345 sir, to be friends.

True. Believe me, you shall not over-shoot yourself, to send him that word by me.

Daw. Deliver it, sir; he shall have it with all my heart, to be friends.   350

True. Friends! Nay, an he should not be so, and heartily too, upon these terms, he shall have me to enemy while I live. Come, sir, bear it bravely.

Daw. O lord, sir, 'tis nothing.   355

True. True: what's six kicks to a man that reads Seneca?[1]

Daw. I have had a hundred, sir.

Enter above[2] CLERIMONT *with all the ladies*

True. Sir Amorous!

Re-enter DAUPHINE, *disguised*

No speaking one to another, or rehearsing   360 old matters.

Daw (*as* DAUP. *kicks him*). One, two, three, four, five. I protest, Sir Amorous, you shall have six.

True. Nay, I told you, you should not   365 talk. Come give him six, an he will needs. (DAUPHINE *kicks* DAW *again.*) — Your sword. (*Takes* DAW's *sword.*) Now return to your safe custody; you shall presently meet afore the ladies, and be the dearest friends one to   370 another. (*Puts* DAW *into the study.*) — Give me the scarf now, thou shalt beat the other bare-faced. Stand by. (DAUPHINE *retires, and* TRUEWIT *goes to the other study and releases* LA-FOOLE.) — Sir Amorous!

La-F. What's here! A sword?   375

True. I cannot help it, without I should take the quarrel upon myself. Here he has sent you his sword ——

La-F. I'll receive none on't.

True. And he wills you to fasten it   380 against a wall, and break your head in some few several places against the hilts.[1]

La-F. I will not: tell him roundly. I cannot endure to shed my own blood.

True. Will you not?   385

La-F. No. I'll beat it against a fair flat wall, if that will satisfy him: if not, he shall beat it himself, for Amorous.

True. Why, this is strange starting off, when a man undertakes for you! I offer'd   390 him another condition; will you stand to that?

La-F. Ay, what is't?

True. That you will be beaten in private.

La-F. Yes, I am content, at the blunt.[2]

True. Then you must submit yourself   395 to be hoodwinked in this scarf, and be led to him, where he will take your sword from you, and make you bear a blow over the mouth *gules*,[3] and tweaks by the nose *sans nombre*.[4]

La-F. I am content. But why must   400 I be blinded?

True. That's for your good, sir; because, if he should grow insolent upon this, and publish it hereafter to your disgrace (which I hope he will not do), you might swear safely, and   405 protest, he never beat you, to your knowledge.

La-F. Oh, I conceive.

True. I do not doubt but you'll be perfect good friends upon't, and not dare to utter an ill thought one of another in future.   410

La-F. Not I, as God help me, of him.

True. Nor he of you, sir. If he should (*binds his eyes*). — Come, sir. (*Leads him forward.*) — "All hid,"[5] Sir John!

Enter DAUPHINE, *and tweaks him by the nose*

La-F. O, Sir John, Sir John! Oh, o-o-o-   415 o-o-Oh ——

True. Good Sir John, leave tweaking, you'll

---

[1] The tragedies of the Roman playwright, Lucius Annaeus Seneca (?4 B.C.–65 A.D.), were long and heavy reading.

[2] I.e., in the gallery of the second story of the tiring house, overlooking the stage.

[1] Projecting transverse guards to the sword handle.

[2] With the flat of the sword.

[3] Colored red, i.e., by the blow.

[4] Without number, countless.

[5] The well-known signal in an old children's game similar to hide-and-seek.

blow his nose off. — 'Tis Sir John's pleasure, you should retire into the study. (*Puts him in again. Exeunt from above* CLERIMONT *and all the ladies*.) — Why, now you are friends. 420 All bitterness between you, I hope, is buried; you shall come forth by and by, Damon and Pythias[1] upon't,[2] and embrace with all the rankness of friendship that can be. — I trust, we shall have them tamer in their lan- 425 guage hereafter. Dauphine, I worship thee. — God's will, the ladies have surprised us!

SCENE 6. *The same.*

Enter LADY HAUGHTY, LADY CENTAURE, MRS. MAVIS, MRS. OTTER, EPICOENE, *and* TRUSTY

Hau. Centaure, how our judgments were imposed on by these adulterate knights!

Cen. Nay, madam, Mavis was more deceived than we; 'twas her commendation uttered them[3] in the college. 5

Mav. I commended but their wits. madam, and their braveries.[4] I never looked toward their valors.

Hau. Sir Dauphine is valiant, and a wit too, it seems. 10

Mav. And a bravery[5] too.

Hau. Was this his project?

Mrs. Ott. So Master Clerimont intimates, madam.

Hau. Good Morose, when you come to 15 the college, will you bring him with you? He seems a very perfect gentleman.

Epi. He is so, madam, believe it.

Cen. But when will you come, Morose?

Epi. Three or four days hence, madam, 20 when I have got me a coach and horses.

Hau. No, tomorrow, good Morose; Centaure shall send you her coach.

Mav. Yes, faith, do, and bring Sir Dauphine with you. 25

Hau. She has promised that, Mavis.

Mav. He is a very worthy gentleman in his exteriors, madam.

Hau. Ay, he shows he is judicial in his clothes. 30

Cen. And yet not so superlatively neat as some, madam, that have their faces set in a brake.[1]

Hau. Ay, and have every hair in form.

Mav. That wear purer[2] linen than our- 35 selves, and profess more neatness than the French hermaphrodite!

Epi. Ay, ladies, they, what they tell one of us, have told a thousand; and are the only thieves of our fame, but think to take us 40 with that perfume, or with that lace, and laugh at us unconscionably when they have done.

Hau. But Sir Dauphine's carelessness[3] becomes him.

Cen. I could love a man for such a nose. 45

Mav. Or such a leg.

Cen. He has an exceeding good eye, madam.

Mav. And a very good lock.

Cen. Good Morose, bring him to my chamber first. 50

Mrs. Ott. Please your honors to meet at my house, madam.

True. (*aside to* DAUP.). See how they eye thee, man! They are taken, I warrant thee.

Hau. (*coming forward*). You have un- 55 braced[4] our brace[5] of knights here, Master Truewit.

True. Not I, madam; it was Sir Dauphine's engine:[6] who, if he have disfurnish'd[7] your ladyship of any guard or service by it, is 60 able to make the place good again in himself.

Hau. There is no suspicion of that, sir.

Cen. God so, Mavis, Haughty is kissing.

Mav. Let us go too, and take part.

(*They come forward.*

Hau. But I am glad of the fortune (be- 65 side the discovery of two such empty caskets) to gain the knowledge of so rich a mine of virtue as Sir Dauphine.

---

[1] Two famous friends of Greek legend. Pythias was condemned to die for plotting against the life of Dionysius, dictator of Syracuse in Sicily. To permit Pythias to say farewell to his kindred, Damon offered himself as a hostage. When Pythias returned to liberate Damon at the last moment, Dionysius so much admired the behavior of the two men as perfect friends that he let both go free.

[2] As a result of it.

[3] Advertised them as acceptable.

[4] Fine attire.   [5] Gallant.

[1] I.e., in an immovable expression.   [2] Daintier.

[3] Unstudied or unaffected appearance.   [4] Disarmed

[5] Pair.   [6] Plot.   [7] Deprived.

Cen. We would be all glad to style him of our friendship, and see him at the college.   70

Mav. He cannot mix with a sweeter society, I'll prophesy; and I hope he himself will think so.

Daup. I should be rude to imagine otherwise, lady.   75

True. (*aside to* Daup.). Did not I tell thee, Dauphine! Why, all their actions are governed by crude opinion, without reason or cause; they know not why they do anything; but, as they are informed, believe, judge, praise, con- 80 demn, love, hate, and in emulation one of another, do all these things alike. Only they have a natural inclination sways them generally to the worst, when they are left to themselves. But pursue it, now thou hast them.   85

Hau. Shall we go in again, Morose?

Epi. Yes, madam.

Cen. We'll entreat Sir Dauphine's company.

True. Stay, good madam, the interview of the two friends, Pylades and Orestes:[1] I'll 90 fetch them out to you straight.

Hau. Will you, Master Truewit?

Daup. Ay, but noble ladies, do not confess in your countenance, or outward bearing to them, any discovery of their follies, that we may 95 see how they will bear up again, with what assurance and erection.

Hau. We will not, Sir Dauphine.

Cen. Mav. Upon our honors, Sir Dauphine.   100

True. (*going to the first study*). Sir Amorous, Sir Amorous! The ladies are here.

La-F. (*within*). Are they?

True. Yes; but slip out by and by, as their backs are turned, and meet Sir John here, 105 as by chance, when I call you. (*Goes to the other study.*) — Jack Daw.

Daw (*within*). What say you, sir?

True. Whip out behind me suddenly, and no anger in your looks to your adversary.   110 Now, now!

(LA-FOOLE *and* DAW *come out of their studies, and salute each other.*

[1] Pylades, son of the king of Phocis, and Orestes, son of Agamemnon, king of Argolis, were cousins and intimate friends. See Sophocles' *Electra* and the introduction thereto.

La-F. Noble Sir John Daw, where have you been?

Daw. To seek you, Sir Amorous.

La-F. Me! I honor you.   115

Daw. I prevent you, sir.

Cler. They have forgot their rapiers.

True. Oh, they meet in peace, man.

Daup. Where's your sword, Sir John?

Cler. And yours, Sir Amorous?   120

Daw. Mine! my boy had it forth to mend the handle, e'en now.

La-F. And my gold handle was broke too, and my boy had it forth.

Daup. Indeed, sir! — How their ex- 125 cuses meet!

Cler. What a consent there is in the handles!

True. Nay, there is so in the points too, I warrant you.   130

SCENE 7. *The same.*

Enter MOROSE, *with two drawn swords in his hands*

Mrs. Ott. Oh me! madam, he comes again, the madman! Away!

(*Ladies,* DAW, *and* LA-FOOLE, *run off.*

Mor. What make these naked weapons here, gentlemen?

True. Oh sir! here hath like to have been 5 murder since you went; a couple of knights fallen out about the bride's favors! We were fain to take away their weapons; your house had been begg'd[1] by this time else.

Mor. For what?   10

Cler. For manslaughter, sir, as being accessory.

Mor. And for her favors?

True. Ay, sir, heretofore, not present — Clerimont, carry them their swords now.   15 They have done all the hurt they will do.

(*Exit* CLER. *with the two swords.*

Daup. Have you spoke with the lawyer, sir?

Mor. Oh no! There is such a noise in the court, that they have frighted me home with more violence than I went! Such speak- 20 ing and counter-speaking, with their several voices of citations, appellations, allegations,

[1] Confiscated.

certificates, attachments, intergatories,[1] references, convictions, and afflictions indeed, among
the doctors [2] and proctors,[3] that the noise   25
here is silence to't, a kind of calm midnight!

True. Why, sir, if you would be resolved indeed, I can bring you hither a very sufficient
lawyer, and a learned divine, that shall enquire
into every least scruple for you.   30

Mor. Can you, Master Truewit?

True. Yes, and are very sober, grave persons,
that will dispatch it in a chamber, with a
whisper or two.

Mor. Good sir, shall I hope this benefit   35
from you, and trust myself into your hands?

True. Alas, sir! Your nephew and I have
been ashamed and oft-times mad, since you
went, to think how you are abused. Go in,
good sir, and lock yourself up till we call   40
you; we'll tell you more anon, sir.

Mor. Do your pleasure with me, gentlemen;
I believe in you, and that deserves no delusion.
          (*Exit.*

True. You shall find none, sir; — but heaped,
heaped plenty of vexation.   45

Daup. What wilt thou do now, Wit?

True. Recover me hither Otter and the
barber, if you can, by any means, presently.

Daup. Why? To what purpose?

True. O, I'll make the deepest divine,   50
and gravest lawyer, out of them two for him——

Daup. Thou canst not, man; these are waking dreams.

True. Do not fear me. Clap but a civil
gown with a welt [4] on the one, and a canon-   55
ical cloak with sleeves on the other, and give
them a few terms in their mouths, if there come
not forth as able a doctor and complete a parson, for this turn, as may be wished, trust not
any election: and I hope, without wrong-   60
ing the dignity of either profession, since they
are but persons put on,[5] and for mirth's sake, to
torment him. The barber smatters Latin, I
remember.

Daup. Yes, and Otter too.   65

True. Well then, if I make them not wrangle
out this case to his no comfort, let me be thought
a Jack Daw or La-Foole or anything worse. Go
you to your ladies, but first send for them.

Daup. I will.   70
          (*Exeunt.*

ACT V

SCENE I. *A room in* MOROSE'S *house.*

Enter LA-FOOLE, CLERIMONT, *and* DAW

La-F. Where had you our swords, Master
Clerimont?

Cler. Why, Dauphine took them from the
madman.

La-F. And he took them from our boys,   5
I warrant you.

Cler. Very like, sir.

La-F. Thank you, good Master Clerimont.
Sir John Daw and I are both beholden [1] to you.

Cler. Would I knew how to make you so,   10
gentlemen!

Daw. Sir Amorous and I are your servants,
sir.

Enter MRS. MAVIS

Mav. Gentlemen, have any of you a pen and
ink? I would fain write out a riddle in   15
Italian, for Sir Dauphine to translate.

Cler. Not I, in troth, lady; I am no scrivener.[2]

Daw. I can furnish you, I think, lady.
          (*Exeunt* DAW *and* MRS. MAVIS.

Cler. He has it in the haft of a knife, I believe.

La-F. No, he has his box of instruments.   20

Cler. Like a surgeon!

La-F. For the mathematics: his square, his
compasses, his brass pens, and black-lead, to
draw maps of every place and person where he
comes.   25

Cler. How, maps of persons!

La-F. Yes, sir, of Nomentack [3] when he was

---

[1] Interrogatories, i.e., questions put in writing.
[2] Lawyers with the doctoral degree.
[3] Lawyers licensed to practice especially in the admiralty and ecclesiastical courts.
[4] Put but a civil lawyer's gown with fur border.
[5] Characters assumed.

[1] Obliged.
[2] A lawyer's assistant, noted for dishonest practices.
[3] An Indian chief brought to London from Virginia about this period.

here, and of the prince of Moldavia,[1] and of his
Mistress Epicoene.

Re-enter DAW

Cler. Away! he hath not found out her   30
latitude, I hope.

La-F. You are a pleasant gentleman, sir.

Cler. Faith, now we are in private, let's
wanton it a little, and talk waggishly. — Sir
John, I am telling Sir Amorous here, that   35
you two govern the ladies wherever you come;
you carry the feminine gender afore you.

Daw. They shall rather carry us afore them,
if they will, sir.

Cler. Nay, I believe that they do, withal   40
— but that you are the prime men in their
affections, and direct all their actions ——

Daw. Not I; Sir Amorous is.

La-F. I protest, Sir John is.

Daw. As I hope to rise in the state, Sir   45
Amorous, you have the person.

La-F. Sir John, you have the person, and the
discourse too.

Daw. Not I, sir. I have no discourse — and
then you have activity beside.   50

La-F. I protest, Sir John, you come as high
from Tripoly[2] as I do, every whit: and lift as
many joint stools,[3] and leap over them, if you
would use[4] it.

Cler. Well, agree on't together, knights;   55
for between you, you divide the kingdom or
commonwealth of ladies' affections: I see it, and
can perceive a little how they observe[5] you,
and fear you, indeed. You could tell strange
stories, my masters, if you would, I know.   60

Daw. Faith, we have seen somewhat, sir.

La-F. That we have — velvet petticoats,
and wrought[6] smocks, or so.

Daw. Ay, and ——

Cler. Nay, out with it, Sir John; do not   65

[1] A former principality in southeastern Europe, now a
part of northern Roumania.

[2] A jesting phrase commonly used in connection with
some feat of indoor jumping.

[3] Stools with jointed parts; folding stools. Lifting of
such stools in quantity was an indoor sport of the time.

[4] Practice.

[5] Pay deference to.

[6] Carefully worked by hand.

envy your friend the pleasure of hearing, when
you have had the delight of tasting.

Daw. Why — a —— Do you speak, Si
Amorous.

La-F. No, do you, Sir John Daw.   7

Daw. I'faith, you shall.

La-F. I'faith, you shall.

Daw. Why, we have been ——

La-F. In the great bed at Ware[1] together i
our time. On, Sir John.   7

Daw. Nay, do you, Sir Amorous.

Cler. And these ladies, with you, knights?

La-F. No, excuse us, sir.

Daw. We must not wound reputation.

La-F. No matter — they were these, or   8
others. Our bath cost us fifteen pounds when
we came home.

Cler. Do you hear, Sir John? You shall te
me but one thing truly, as you love me.

Daw. If I can, I will, sir.   8

Cler. You lay in the same house with th
bride here?

Daw. Yes, and conversed with her hourly, sir

Cler. And what humor is she of? Is sh
coming and open, free?   9

Daw. O, exceeding open, sir. I was her se
vant,[2] and Sir Amorous was to be.

Cler. Come, you have both had favors fron
her: I know, and have heard so much.

Daw. O no, sir.   9

La-F. You shall excuse us, sir; we must nc
wound reputation.

Cler. Tut, she is married now, and you can
not hurt her with any report; and therefor
speak plainly: how many times, i'faith?   1c
Which of you led first? Ha!

La-F. Sir John had her maidenhead, indeec

Daw. Oh, it pleases him to say so, sir; bu
Sir Amorous knows what's what, as well.

Cler. Dost thou, i'faith, Amorous?   1c

La-F. In a manner, sir.

Cler. Why, I commend you, lads. Littl
knows Don[3] Bridegroom of this; nor shall h
for me.

[1] A notorious piece of ancient furniture, twelve fe
square and capable of holding twenty to twenty-fo
persons.

[2] Lover.

[3] Master; a term of disparagement.

Daw. Hang him, mad ox!   110

Cler. Speak softly; here comes his nephew, with the Lady Haughty: he'll get the ladies from you, sirs, if you look not to him in time.

La-F. Why, if he do, we'll fetch them home again, I warrant you.   115

(*Exit with* DAW. CLERIMONT *walks aside.*

SCENE 2. *The same.*

Enter DAUPHINE *and* LADY HAUGHTY

Hau. I assure you, Sir Dauphine, it is the price and estimation of your virtue only, that hath embarked me to this adventure; and I could not but make out to tell you so: nor can I repent me of the act, since it is always an   5 argument of some virtue in ourselves, that we love and affect[1] it so in others.

Daup. Your ladyship sets too high a price on my weakness.

Hau. Sir, I can distinguish gems from   10 pebbles ——

Daup. (*aside*). Are you so skillful in stones?

Hau. And howsoever I may suffer in such a judgment as yours, by admitting equality of rank or society with Centaure or Mavis ——

Daup. You do not, madam; I perceive   16 they are your mere foils.

Hau. Then are you a friend to truth, sir. It makes me love you the more. It is not the outward, but the inward man that I affect.   20 They are not apprehensive of an eminent perfection, but love flat and dully.

Cen. (*within*). Where are you, my Lady Haughty?

Hau. I come presently, Centaure. — My   25 chamber, sir, my page shall show you; and Trusty, my woman, shall be ever awake for you: you need not fear to communicate anything with her, for she is a Fidelia.[2] I pray you wear this jewel for my sake, Sir Dauphine ——

Enter CENTAURE

Where's Mavis, Centaure?   31

Cen. Within, madam, a-writing. I'll follow you presently: I'll but speak a word with Sir Dauphine.   (*Exit* LADY HAUGHTY.

[1] Have affection for.   [2] Faithful woman.

Daup. With me, madam?   35

Cen. Good Sir Dauphine, do not trust Haughty, nor make any credit to her[1] whatever you do besides. Sir Dauphine, I give you this caution,[2] she is a perfect courtier, and loves nobody but for her uses; and for her uses she   40 loves all. Besides, her physicians give her out to be none o' the clearest,[3] whether she pay them or no, heaven knows; and she's above fifty too, and pargets![4] See her in a forenoon. Here comes Mavis, a worse face than she!   45 You would not like this by candle-light.

Re-enter MAVIS

If you'll come to my chamber one o' these mornings early, or late in an evening, I'll tell you more. Where's Haughty, Mavis?

Mav. Within, Centaure.   50

Cen. What have you there?

Mav. An Italian riddle for Sir Dauphine — you shall not see it, i'faith, Centaure. (*Exit* CENTAURE.) Good Sir Dauphine, solve it for me: I'll call for it anon.   (*Exit.*   55

Cler. (*coming forward*). How now, Dauphine! how dost thou quit[5] thyself of these females?

Daup. 'Slight, they haunt me like fairies, and give me jewels here; I cannot be rid of them.

Cler. Oh, you must not tell, though.[6]   60

Daup. Mass, I forgot that: I was never so assaulted. One loves for virtue, and bribes me with this — (*shows the jewel*) — another loves me with caution, and so would possess me; a third brings me a riddle here: and all are   65 jealous, and rail each at other.

Cler. A riddle! pray let me see it.   (*Reads.*

Sir Dauphine, I chose this way of intimation for privacy. The ladies here, I know, have both hope and purpose to make a collegiate and   70 servant of you. If I might be so honored, as to appear at any end of so noble a work, I would enter into a fame[7] of taking physic tomorrow, and continue it four or five days, or longer, for your visitation.   MAVIS.   75

[1] Credit her in anything.   [2] Warning.
[3] None too clear of bodily faults.
[4] Paints her face.   [5] Rid.
[6] To tell anyone of a fairy's gift made it void.
[7] Begin the infamy.

By my faith, a subtle one! Call you this a riddle? What's their plain-dealing, trow?

Daup. We lack Truewit to tell us that.

Cler. We lack him for somewhat else too: his knights reformadoes [1] are wound up as high 80 and insolent as ever they were.

Daup. You jest.

Cler. No drunkards, either with wine or vanity, ever confessed such stories of themselves. I would not give a fly's leg in balance 85 against all the women's reputations here, if they could be but thought to speak truth: and for the bride, they have made their affidavit against her directly —— 89

Daup. What, that they have lain with her?

Cler. Yes; and tell times and circumstances, with the cause why, and the place where. I had almost brought them to affirm that they had done it today.

Daup. Not both of them? 95

Cler. Yes, faith; with a sooth [2] or two more I had effected it. They would have set it down under their hands.

Daup. Why, they will be our sport, I see, still, whether we will or no. 100

Scene 3. *The same.*

Enter Truewit

True. O, are you here? Come, Dauphine; go call your uncle presently: I have fitted my divine and my canonist,[3] dyed their beards and all. The knaves do not know themselves, they are so exalted and altered. Preferment 5 changes any man. Thou shalt keep one door and I another, and then Clerimont in the midst, that he may have no means of escape from their cavilling, when they grow hot once again. And then the women, as I have given the bride 10 her instructions, to break in upon him in the l'envoy.[4] Oh, 'twill be full and twanging! [5] Away! fetch him. (*Exit* Dauphine.

[1] Deprived of their position, i.e., as gallants admired by the ladies.

[2] Cajoling word.

[3] Canon lawyer. Canon law was the law administered by the ecclesiastical courts, which continued in England until 1857. These courts had entire jurisdiction over matrimonial matters.

[4] The conclusion.   [5] Complete and sudden.

Enter Otter *disguised as a divine, and* Cutbeard *as a canon lawyer*

Come, master doctor, and master parson, look to your parts now, and discharge them 15 bravely;[1] you are well set forth,[2] perform it as well. If you chance to be out,[3] do not confess it with standing still, or humming, or gaping one at another; but go on, and talk aloud and eagerly; use vehement action, and only re- 20 member your terms, and you are safe. Let the matter go where it will: you have many will do so. But at first be very solemn and grave, like your garments, though you lose [4] yourselves after, and skip out like a brace of jugglers 25 on a table. Here he comes: set your faces, and look superciliously, while I present you.

Re-enter Dauphine *with* Morose

Mor. Are these the two learned men?

True. Yes, sir; please you salute them.

Mor. Salute them! I had rather do any- 30 thing, than wear out time so unfruitfully, sir. I wonder how these common forms, as "God save you," and "You are welcome," are come to be a habit in our lives, or "I am glad to see you!" when I cannot see what the profit 35 can be of these words, so long as it is no whit better with him whose affairs are sad and grievous, that he hears this salutation.

True. 'Tis true, sir; we'll go to the matter then. — Gentlemen, master doctor, and 40 master parson, I have acquainted you sufficiently with the business for which you are come hither; and you are not now to inform yourselves in the state of the question, I know. This is the gentleman who expects your resolu- 45 tion, and therefore, when you please, begin.

Ott. Please you, master doctor.

Cut. Please you, good master parson.

Ott. I would hear the canon-law speak first.

Cut. It must give place to positive divin- 50 ity, sir.

Mor. Nay, good gentlemen, do not throw me into circumstances. Let your comforts arrive quickly at me, those that are. Be swift in

[1] Well.   [2] Attired.

[3] Forget your lines.   [4] Forget.

affording me my peace, if so I shall hope 55
any. I love not your disputations, or your
court-tumults. And that it be not strange to
you. I will tell you: My father, in my education, was wont to advise me, that I should always collect and contain [1] my mind, not 60
suffering it to flow loosely; that I should look
to what things were necessary to the carriage [2]
of my life, and what not; embracing the one
and eschewing [3] the other: in short, that I
should endear myself to rest,[4] and avoid 65
turmoil; which now is grown to be another
nature to me. So that [5] I come not to your
public pleadings, or your places of noise; not
that I neglect those things that make for the
dignity of the commonwealth; but for the 70
mere avoiding of clamors and impertinences of
orators, that know not how to be silent. And
for the cause of noise, am I now a suitor to you.
You do not know in what a misery I have been
exercised this day, what a torrent of evil! 75
My very house turns round with the tumult! I
dwell in a windmill: the perpetual motion is
here, and not at Eltham.[6]

True. Well, good master doctor, will you
break the ice? Master parson will wade 80
after.

Cut. Sir, though unworthy, and the weaker,
I will presume.

Ott. 'Tis no presumption, *domine* [7] doctor.

Mor. Yet again! 85

Cut. Your question is: For how many causes
a man may have *divortium legitimum*, a lawful
divorce? First, you must understand the
nature of the word, divorce, *a divertendo* —— [8]

Mor. No excursions upon words, good 90
doctor; to the question briefly.

Cut. I answer then, the canon law affords
divorce but in few cases; and the principal is in
the common case, the adulterous case: But
here are *duodecim impedimenta*, twelve 95
impediments, as we call them, all which do not

---

[1] Hold in check.   [2] Conduct.
[3] Avoiding.   [4] Grow fond of calmness.
[5] Hence.
[6] A town in Kent, southeast of London, where a contrivance pretending to perpetual motion was located.
[7] Sir. All holders of bachelor's degrees were allowed
the title of "dominus."
[8] By digressing.

---

dirimere contractum, but *irritum reddere matrimonium*, as we say in the canon law, *not take
away the bond, but cause a nullity therein.*

Mor. I understood you before: good sir, 100
avoid your impertinency of translation.

Ott. He cannot open this too much, sir, by
your favor.

Mor. Yet more!

True. Oh, you must give the learned 105
men leave, sir. — To your impediments, master
doctor.

Cut. The first is *impedimentum erroris.*

Ott. Of which there are several species.

Cut. Ay, as *error personae.* 110

Ott. If you contract yourself to one person,
thinking her another.

Cut. Then, *error fortunae.*

Ott. If she be a beggar, and you thought her
rich. 115

Cut. Then, *error qualitatis.*

Ott. If she prove stubborn or head-strong,
that you thought obedient.

Mor. How! is that, sir, a lawful impediment?
One at once, I pray you, gentlemen. 120

Ott. Ay, *ante copulam*, but not *post copulam*,
sir.

Cut. Master parson says right. *Nec post
nuptiarum benedictionem.* It doth indeed but
irrita reddere sponsalia, annul the con- 125
tract; after marriage it is of no obstancy.[1]

True. Alas, sir, what a hope are we fallen
from by this time!

Cut. The next is *conditio*: if you thought her
free born, and she prove a bond-woman, 130
there is impediment of estate and condition.

Ott. Ay, but, master doctor, those servitudes
are *sublatae* [2] now, among us Christians.

Cut. By your favor, master parson ——

Ott. You shall give me leave, master 135
doctor.

Mor. Nay, gentlemen, quarrel not in that
question; it concerns not my case: pass to the
third.

Cut. Well then, the third is *votum*: [3] if 140
either party have made a vow of chastity. But
that practice, as master parson said of the

---

[1] Impediment.
[2] Conditions of servitude are abandoned.
[3] Vow of celibacy.

other, is taken away among us, thanks be to
discipline.[1]   The fourth is *cognatio*;[2] if the persons be of kin within the degrees.   145

Ott. Ay: do you know what the degrees are,
sir?

Mor. No, nor I care not, sir; they offer me no
comfort in the question, I am sure.

Cut. But there is a branch of this im-   150
pediment may, which is *cognatio spiritualis*:[3] if
you were her godfather, sir, then the marriage
is incestuous.

Ott. That comment is absurd and superstitious, master doctor: I cannot endure it.   155
Are we not all brothers and sisters, and as much
akin in that, as godfathers and goddaughters?

Mor. O me! to end the controversy, I never
was a godfather, I never was a godfather in my
life, sir.   Pass to the next.   160

Cut. The fifth is *crimen adulterii*;[4] the known
case.   The sixth, *cultus disparitas*, difference of
religion: Have you ever examined her, what religion she is of?

Mor. No, I would rather she were of   165
none, than be put to the trouble of it.

Ott. You may have it done for you, sir.

Mor. By no means, good sir; on to the rest:
shall you ever come to an end, think you?

True. Yes, he has done half, sir. — On   170
to the rest. — Be patient, and expect, sir.

Cut. The seventh is, *vis*:[5] if it were upon
compulsion or force.

Mor. O no, it was too voluntary, mine; too
voluntary.   175

Cut. The eighth is, *ordo*;[6] if ever she have
taken holy orders.

Ott. That's superstitious too.

Mor. No matter, master parson; would she
would go into a nunnery yet.   180

Cut. The ninth is, *ligamen*;[7] if you were
bound, sir, to any other before.

Mor. I thrust myself too soon into these
fetters.

Cut. The tenth is, *publica honestas*;[8]   185
which is *inchoata quaedam affinitas*.[9]

---

[1] Church rules of conduct.   [2] Kinship.
[3] Spiritual affinity.
[4] Commission of adultery.
[5] Force.   [6] Order.   [7] Bond.   [8] Public honor.
[9] Some incomplete connection or affinity.

Ott. Ay, or *affinitas orta ex sponsalibus*;[1] and
is but *leve impedimentum*.[2]

Mor. I feel no air of comfort blowing to me,
in all this.   190

Cut. The eleventh is, *affinitas ex fornicatione*.[3]

Ott. Which is no less *vera affinitas*,[4] than the
other, master doctor.

Cut. True, *quae oritur ex legitimo matri-
monio*.[5]   195

Ott. You say right, venerable doctor: and
*nascitur ex eo, quod per conjugium duae personae
efficiuntur una caro* —— [6]

True. Hey-day, now they begin!

Cut. I conceive you, master parson: *ita*   200
*per fornicationem aeque est verus pater, qui sic
generat* —— [7]

Ott. Et vere filius qui sic generatur —— [8]

Mor. What's all this to me?

Cler. Now it grows warm.   205

Cut. The twelfth and last is, *si forte coire
nequibis*.[9]

Ott. Ay, that is *impedimentum gravissimum*:[10]
it doth utterly annul, and annihilate, that.   If
you have *manifestam frigiditatem*,[11] you   210
are well, sir.

True. Why, there is comfort come at length,
sir.   Confess yourself but a man unable, and
she will sue to be divorced first.

Ott. Ay, or if there be *morbus perpetuus*,   215
et insanabilis;[12] as *paralysis, elephantiasis*, or
so ——

Daup. Oh, but *frigiditas* is the fairer way,
gentlemen.

Ott. You say troth, sir, and as it is in   220
the canon, master doctor ——

Cut. I conceive you, sir.

Cler. Before he speaks!

---

[1] Affinity born of betrothal.
[2] Light impediment.
[3] Affinity arising from fornication.
[4] A true affinity.
[5] The one which arises from legal marriage.
[6] It arises from that which through the marriage the
two persons bring forth.
[7] Thus through fornication there is always a true
father, who indeed generates.
[8] And a true child who is indeed generated.
[9] If coition shall be clearly impossible.
[10] Most serious impediment.
[11] Manifest impotence.
[12] Permanent and incurable disease.

Ott. That a boy, or child, under years, is not fit for marriage, because he cannot *reddere*   225 *debitum.*[1] So your *omnipotentes* ——

True. (aside to OTTER). Your *impotentes*, you whoreson lobster!

Ott. Your *impotentes*, I should say, are *minime apti ad contrahenda matrimonium.*[2] 230

True. Matrimonium! we shall have most unmatrimonial Latin with you: *matrimonia*, and be hanged.

Daup. You put them out, man.

Cut. But then there will arise a doubt,   235 master parson, in our case, *post matrimonium:*[3] that *frigiditate praeditus*[4] — do you conceive me, sir?

Ott. Very well, sir.

Cut. Who cannot *uti uxore pro uxore*,   240 may *habere eam pro sorore.*[5]

Ott. Absurd, absurd, absurd, and merely apostatical!

Cut. You shall pardon me, master parson, I can prove it.   245

Ott. You can prove a will, master doctor; you can prove nothing else. Does not the verse of your own canon say, *Haec socianda vetant connubia, facta retractant?*[6]

Cut. I grant you; but how do they   250 *retractare*, master parson?

Mor. Oh, this was it I feared.

Ott. In aeternum,[7] sir.

Cut. That's false in divinity, by your favor.

Ott. 'Tis false in humanity to say so.   255 Is he not *prorsus inutilis ad thorum?*[8] Can he *praestare fidem datam?*[9] I would fain know.

Cut. Yes; how if he do *convalere?*[10]

Ott. He cannot *convalere*, it is impossible.

True. Nay, good sir, attend the learned   260 men; they'll think you neglect them else.

Cut. Or, if he do *simulare* himself *frigidum, odio uxoris,*[11] or so?

Ott. I say, he is *adulter manifestus*[1] then.

Daup. They dispute it very learnedly, i'faith.

Ott. And *prostitutor uxoris;*[2] and this is   266 positive.

Mor. Good sir, let me escape.

True. You will not do me that wrong, sir?

Ott. And, therefore, if he be *manifeste*   270 *frigidus,*[3] sir ——

Cut. Ay, if he be *manifeste frigidus*, I grant you ——

Ott. Why, that was my conclusion.

Cut. And mine too.   275

True. Nay, hear the conclusion, sir.

Ott. Then, *frigiditatis causa* —— [4]

Cut. Yes, *causa frigiditatis* ——

Mor. O, mine ears!

Ott. She may have *libellum divortii*[5]   280 against you.

Cut. Ay, *divortii libellum* she will sure have.

Mor. Good echoes, forbear.

Ott. If you confess it. ——

Cut. Which I would do, sir ——   285

Mor. I will do any thing.

Ott. And clear myself *in foro conscientiae* —— [6]

Cut. Because you want indeed ——

Mor. Yet more!

Ott. Exercendi potestate.[7]   290

SCENE 4. *The same.*

EPICOENE *rushes in, followed by* LADY HAUGHTY, LADY CENTAURE, MRS. MAVIS, MRS. OTTER, DAW, *and* LA-FOOLE

Epi. I will not endure it any longer. Ladies, I beseech you, help me. This is such a wrong as never was offered to poor bride before: upon her marriage-day to have her husband conspire against her, and a couple of mer-   5 cenary companions to be brought in for form's sake, to persuade a separation! If you had blood or virtue in you, gentlemen, you would not suffer such earwigs[8] about a husband, or scorpions to creep between man and wife.   10

Mor. Oh the variety and changes of my torment!

---

[1] Annul the obligation.
[2] Less apt to contract matrimony.
[3] After matrimony.
[4] Aforementioned impotence.
[5] Use a wife for a wife may have her for a sister.
[6] They forbid these following marriage ties; if made they retract.   [7] To eternity.
[8] Henceforth useless for the marriage bed.
[9] Keep his pledged word.   [10] Recover.
[11] Pretend himself impotent, out of dislike for his wife.

[1] Plain adulterer.	[2] Prostituter.
[3] Clearly impotent.	[4] By reason of impotence.
[5] Writing of divorce.	[6] In the court of conscience.
[7] Exercising power.	[8] Whisperers of insinuations.

Hau. Let them be cudgeled out of doors by our grooms.

Cen. I'll lend you my footman.　15

Mav. We'll have our men blanket them in the hall.

Mrs. Ott. As there was one at our house, madam, for peeping in at the door.

Daw. Content, i'faith.　20

True. Stay, ladies and gentlemen; you'll hear before you proceed?

Mav. I'd have the bridegroom blanketed too.

Cen. Begin with him first.　25

Hau. Yes, by my troth.

Mor. O mankind [1] generation!

Daup. Ladies, for my sake forbear.

Hau. Yes, for Sir Dauphine's sake.

Cen. He shall command us.　30

La-F. He is as fine a gentleman of his inches, madam, as any is about the town, and wears as good colors when he lists. [2]

True. Be brief, sir, and confess your infirmity; she'll be a-fire to be quit of you, if 35 she but hear that named once, you shall not entreat her to stay: she'll fly you like one that had the marks [3] upon him.

Mor. Ladies, I must crave all your pardons ——　40

True. Silence, ladies.

Mor. For a wrong I have done to your whole sex, in marrying this fair and virtuous gentlewoman ——

Cler. Hear him, good ladies.　45

Mor. Being guilty of an infirmity, which, before I conferred with these learned men, I thought I might have concealed ——

True. But now being better informed in his conscience by them, he is to declare it, and 50 give satisfaction, by asking your public forgiveness.

Mor. I am no man, ladies.

All. How!

Mor. Utterly unabled in nature, by 55 reason of frigidity, to perform the duties, or any the least office of a husband.

Mav. Now out upon him, prodigious creature!

Cen. Bridegroom uncarnate!　60

Hau. And would you offer it to a young gentlewoman?

Mrs. Ott. A lady of her longings?

Epi. Tut, a device, a device, this! it smells rankly, ladies. A mere comment of his 65 own.

True. Why, if you suspect that, ladies, you may have him searched ——

Daw. As the custom is, by a jury of physicians.　70

La-F. Yes, faith, 'twill be brave.

Mor. O me, must I undergo that?

Mrs. Ott. No, let women search him, madam; we can do it ourselves.

Mor. Out on me! worse.　75

Epi. No, ladies, you shall not need, I'll take him with all his faults.

Mor. Worst of all!

Cler. Why then, 'tis no divorce, doctor, if she consent not?　80

Cut. No, if the man be *frigidus*, it is *de parte uxoris,* [1] that we grant *libellum divortii,* in the law.

Ott. Ay, it is the same in theology.

Mor. Worse, worse than worst!　85

True. Nay, sir, be not utterly disheartened; we have yet a small relic of hope left, as near as our comfort is blown out. Clerimont, produce your brace of knights. What was that, master parson, you told me *in errore* 90 *qualitatis,* [2] e'en now? — (*Aside*) Dauphine, whisper [3] the bride, that she carry it as if she were guilty, and ashamed.

Ott. Marry, sir, *in errore qualitatis* (which master doctor did forbear to urge), if she 95 be found *corrupta,* that is, vitiated or broken up, that was *pro virgine desponsa,* espoused for a maid ——

Mor. What then, sir?

Ott. It doth *dirimere contractum,* and 100 *irritum reddere* too. [4]

True. If this be true, we are happy again,

---

[1] Mannish; violent.
[2] Pleases.
[3] I.e., marks of the plague, which was a frightfully contagious disease in seventeenth-century London.

[1] On behalf of the wife.　[2] In an error of quality.
[3] Whisper to.
[4] Dissolve the contract, and render it as if it had never existed.

sir, once more. Here are an honorable brace of knights, that shall affirm so much.

Daw. Pardon us, good Master 105 Clerimont.

La-F. You shall excuse us, Master Clerimont.

Cler. Nay, you must make it good now, knights, there is no remedy; I'll eat no 110 words for you, nor no men: you know you spoke it to me.

Daw. Is this gentleman-like, sir?

True. (*aside to* DAW). Jack Daw, he's worse than Sir Amorous; fiercer a great deal. 115 — (*Aside to* LA-FOOLE) Sir Amorous, beware, there be ten Daws in this Clerimont.

La-F. I'll confess it, sir.

Daw. Will you, Sir Amorous, will you wound reputation? 120

La-F. I am resolved.

True. So should you be too, Jack Daw: what should keep you off? She's but a woman, and in disgrace: he'll be glad on't.

Daw. Will he? I thought he would 125 have been angry.

Cler. You will dispatch, knights; it must be done, i' faith.

True. Why, an it must, it shall, sir, they say: they'll ne'er go back. — (*Aside to* 130 DAW *and* LA-FOOLE) Do not tempt his patience.

Daw. Is it true indeed, sir?

La-F. Yes, I assure you, sir.

Mor. What is true, gentlemen? What 135 do you assure me?

Daw. That we have known your bride, sir ——

La-F. In good fashion. She was our mistress, or so —— 140

Cler. Nay, you must be plain, knights, as you were to me.

Ott. Ay, the question is, if you have *carnaliter*,[1] or no?

La-F. Carnaliter! what else, sir? 145

Ott. It is enough; a plain nullity.

Epi. I am undone, I am undone!

Mor. Oh, let me worship and adore you, gentlemen!

Epi. I am undone. (*Weeps.* 150

[1] In the carnal manner.

Mor. Yes, to my hand, I thank these knights. Master parson, let me thank you otherwise. (*Gives him money.*

Cen. And have they confessed?

Mav. Now out upon them, informers! 155

True. You see what creatures you may bestow your favors on, madams.

Hau. I would except against them as beaten knights,[1] wench, and not good witnesses in law. 160

Mrs. Ott. Poor gentlewoman, how she takes it!

Hau. Be comforted, Morose, I love you the better for't.

Cen. So do I, I protest. 165

Cut. But, gentlemen, you have not known her since *matrimonium*?

Daw. Not today, master doctor.

La-F. No, sir, not today.

Cut. Why, then I say, for any act be- 170 fore, the *matrimonium* is good and perfect; unless the worshipful bridegroom did precisely, before witness, demand, if she were *virgo ante nuptias*.[2]

Epi. No, that he did not, I assure you, 175 master doctor.

Cut. If he cannot prove that, it is *ratum conjugium*,[3] notwithstanding the premises; and they do no way *impedire*.[4] And this is my sentence, this I pronounce. 180

Ott. I am of master doctor's resolution too, sir; if you made not that demand *ante nuptias*.

Mor. O my heart! wilt thou break? wilt thou break? This is worst of all worst worsts that hell could have devised! Marry a whore, 185 and so much noise!

Daup. Come, I see now plain confederacy in this doctor and this parson, to abuse a gentleman. You study[5] his affliction. I pray be gone, companions. — And, gentlemen, 190 I begin to suspect you for having parts with them. — Sir, will it please you hear me?

[1] Take exception to their appearance as witnesses, because they are beaten knights. According to ancient English usage, knights defeated in the lists could never be admitted as witnesses.
[2] Virgin before the nuptials.
[3] Valid marriage.
[4] Hinder.
[5] I.e., plot to increase.

Mor. Oh, do not talk to me; take not from me the pleasure of dying in silence, nephew.

Daup. Sir, I must speak to you. I have 195 been long your poor despised kinsman, and many a hard thought has strengthened you against me: but now it shall appear if either I love you or your peace, and prefer them to all the world beside. I will not be long 200 or grievous to you, sir. If I free you of this unhappy match absolutely, and instantly, after all this trouble, and almost in your despair, now ——

Mor. It cannot be. 205

Daup. Sir, that you be never troubled with a murmur of it more, what shall I hope for, or deserve of you?

Mor. Oh, what thou wilt, nephew! Thou shalt deserve [1] me, and have me. 210

Daup. Shall I have your favor perfect [2] to me, and love hereafter?

Mor. That, and anything beside. Make thine own conditions. My whole estate is thine; manage it, I will become thy ward. 215

Daup. Nay, sir, I will not be so unreasonable.

Epi. Will Sir Dauphine be mine enemy too?

Daup. You know I have been long a suitor to you, uncle, that out of your estate, 220 which is fifteen hundred a-year, you would allow me but five hundred during life, and assure the rest upon me after; to which I have often, by myself and friends, tendered you a writing to sign, which you would never 225 consent or incline to. If you please but to effect [3] it now ——

Mor. Thou shalt have it, nephew: I will do it, and more.

Daup. If I quit [4] you not presently, [5] 230 and forever, of this cumber, [6] you shall have power instantly, afore all these, to revoke your act, and I will become whose slave you will give me to, forever.

Mor. Where is the writing? I will seal 235 to it, that, or to a blank, and write thine own conditions.

Epi. O me, most unfortunate, wretched gentlewoman!

Hau. Will Sir Dauphine do this? 240

Epi. Good sir, have some compassion on me.

Mor. Oh, my nephew knows you, belike; away, crocodile! [1]

Cen. He does it not sure without good ground. 245

Daup. Here, sir. (*Gives him the parchment.*)

Mor. Come, nephew, give me the pen; I will subscribe to anything, and seal to what thou wilt, for my deliverance. Thou art my restorer. Here, I deliver it thee as my deed. 250 If there be a word in it lacking, or writ with false orthography, I protest before heaven I will not take the advantage.

(*Returns the parchment.*)

Daup. Then here is your release, sir. (*Takes off* EPICOENE'S *peruke and other disguises.*) You have married a boy, a gentleman's 255 son, that I have brought up this half year at my great charges, and for this composition, [2] which I have now made with you. — What say you, master doctor? This is *justum impedimentum*, [3] I hope, *error personae*? [4] 260

Ott. Yes, sir, *in primo gradu.* [5]

Cut. In primo gradu.

Daup. I thank you, good Doctor Cutbeard and Parson Otter. (*Pulls their false beards and gowns off.*) You are beholden [6] to 265 them, sir, that have taken this pains for you and my friend, Master Truewit, who enabled [7] them for the business. Now you may go in and rest; be as private as you will, sir. I'll not trouble you, till you trouble me with your 270 funeral, which I care not how soon it come (*Exit* MOROSE.) — Cutbeard, I'll make your lease good. Thank me not, but with your leg, [8] Cutbeard. — And Tom Otter, your princess shall be reconciled to you. — How 275 now, gentlemen, do you look at me?

Cler. A boy!

Daup. Yes, Mistress Epicoene.

True. Well, Dauphine, you have lurched your friends of the better half of the garland, [9] by concealing this part of the plot: but 280

---

[1] Deserve recompense from.   [2] Assured.   [3] Do.
[4] Relieve.   [5] At once.   [6] Encumbrance.

[1] Hypocrite.   [2] Agreement.
[3] A legal impediment.   [4] An error of person.
[5] Of the first degree.   [6] Indebted.
[7] Prepared.   [8] Except with your bow.
[9] Cheated your friends of the better half of the victory.

ACT V, SCENE 4

much good do it thee, thou deserv'st it, lad. And, Clerimont, for thy unexpected bringing these two to confession, wear my part of it freely. Nay, Sir Daw and Sir La-Foole, 285 you see the gentlewoman that has done you the favors! We are all thankful to you, and so should the woman-kind here, specially for lying on[1] her, though not with her! You meant so, I am sure. But that we have 290 stuck it upon you today, in your own imagined persons, and so lately, this Amazon, the champion of the sex, should beat you now thriftily, for the common slanders which ladies receive from such cuckoos as you are. 295 You are they that, when no merit or fortune can make you hope to enjoy their bodies, will yet lie with their reputations, and make their fame[2] suffer. Away, you common moths of these, and all ladies' honors. Go, travel 300

[1] About.   [2] Honor.

to make legs and faces, and come home with some new matter to be laughed at; you deserve to live in an air as corrupted as that wherewith you feed rumor. (*Exeunt* DAW *and* LA-FOOLE.) — Madams, you are mute, 305 upon this new metamorphosis! But here stands she that has vindicated your fames.[1] Take heed of such *insectae*[2] hereafter. And let it not trouble you, that you have discovered any mysteries[3] to this young gentleman: 310 he is almost of years, and will make a good visitant within this twelvemonth.[4] In the mean time, we'll all undertake for his secrecy, that can speak so well of his silence. — (*Coming forward*) Spectators, if you like this 315 comedy, rise cheerfully, and now Morose is gone in, clap your hands. It may be, that noise will cure him, at least please him.   (*Exeunt.*

[1] Reputations.   [2] Insects.   [3] Secrets.
[4] A humorous allusion to the extreme youthfulness of the boy who acted the part of Epicoene.

INTRODUCTION TO
The Maid's Tragedy

Shakespeare and the Decline in English Tragedy after 1600: The Romantic Drama of Beaumont and Fletcher: Jacobean and Caroline Tragedy

SHAKESPEARE AND THE DECLINE IN ENGLISH TRAGEDY AFTER 1600

ENGLISH tragedy, like English comedy, began to show signs of a major change in the first years of the seventeenth century. During that period Shakespeare reached the summit of his genius in four of the world's dramatic masterpieces — *Hamlet* (*c.* 1601), *Othello* (*c.* 1604), *King Lear* (*c.* 1605), and *Macbeth* (*c.* 1606). The four plays exhibit a tragic pattern with the following highlights: (1) a theme of fatal passion excluding love as a primary motive; (2) an outstanding personality as the center of the dramatic action; (3) a vital weakness in the hero's character as the paramount cause of catastrophe; (4) the conflict within the hero as the main source of the sense of tragedy. By means of these four features Shakespeare raised the melodramatic plot of his era to the level of high tragedy. Shakespeare's lofty pattern, however, did not determine the course of English tragedy in the Jacobean and Caroline periods (the reigns of James I and Charles I respectively), because it represented a final expression of *Elizabethan* spiritual aspiration. The intellectual and moral vigor which produced that aspiration had considerably weakened before Elizabeth's death. The influence of King James's dissipated court only accelerated the trend. The first and the most important indications of decadence on the stage made their appearance in tragedy.

As early as 1603 Thomas Heywood (?1575–1648) reflected the less robust taste of the theater audiences in his popular play, *A Woman Killed with Kindness*. The very title suggests artificiality of situation and feeling. A certain Mrs. Frankford is persuaded to infidelity by Master Wendoll, a friend of her husband. Frankford imposes "a mild sentence" upon his wife by sending her to a lonely house where she repentantly languishes away. She finally dies overwhelmed by her husband's kindness after he has arrived and pardoned her with a kiss. Heywood's preposterous story discloses a growing demand for more unusual treatments of the love theme. The simple, fresh romance of the Romeo-and-Juliet type had declined in appeal. Its pure, if naïve, sentiment was being replaced by an insidious sentimentality. *A Woman Killed with Kindness* pandered to this falsifying of emotion. The fatal pining of Mrs. Frankford is a mere tear-compelling artifice. No more maudlin conclusion could have been devised than the deathbed finale where the expiring heroine and her husband and friends would make the spectator believe that, after forgiveness of infidelity, dying is such *sweet* sorrow. Thus Heywood by spurious emotionalizing fed the sentimentalism of the new age.

A Woman Killed with Kindness was but a foreshadowing of the developments in

English tragedy during the next decade. Within that short space the London stage moved under the sway of the court aristocracy. Their taste discouraged the use of native bourgeois atmosphere such as Heywood's tragedy had featured, but intensified the emotional tendencies apparent in his drama. Interest in love became a preoccupation with lust, sex, and the social code. The inclination toward sentimentality deepened into a desire for sensationalism. Pathos had to be spiced with novelty for jaded appetites.

THE ROMANTIC DRAMA OF BEAUMONT AND FLETCHER

The first dramatic pattern to embody the likings of the Jacobean élite resulted from one of the most famous collaborations in stage history. About 1608 or 1609 two young gentlemen of London, Francis Beaumont and John Fletcher, set up bachelor quarters together on the Bankside near the Globe playhouse. Both came from well-to-do families with many connections in fashionable society. Beaumont, son of Justice Francis Beaumont, a Leicestershire squire of illustrious lineage, was born about 1584. After attending Pembroke College, Oxford, he began in 1600 a legal career at the Inner Temple, London. The Temple's ancient tradition as a nursery of literary and theatrical effort attracted him, however, more than the law. Within six or seven years he had attained some notice as a poet and dramatist.

Fletcher, son of Richard Fletcher, later Bishop of London, and cousin of the two well-known Jacobean poets, Giles and Phineas Fletcher, was born in 1579 at Rye, Sussex, where his father then occupied a rectory. In 1591 he entered Corpus Christi College, Cambridge, but when his father assumed the London bishopric in 1595, he left college to enjoy the more colorful life of the metropolis. Though he already had tried his hand at play-writing he won no notice before he joined forces with Beaumont.

Their partnership flourished until Beaumont married in 1613 and retired from authorship to be a country gentleman in Kent. Fletcher continued his career with prolific successes in both tragedy and comedy. He wrote not only alone, but also in collaboration with the leading playwrights of the day, including Shakespeare, whose *Henry VIII* and *The Two Noble Kinsmen* owe much to him. Fletcher's popularity surpassed that of any living dramatist when the plague at London put a sudden end to his life in August, 1625. Beaumont had died on March 6, 1616, a month before Shakespeare's decease. Shakespeare was laid away in Stratford Church without public honors, but Beaumont was buried in Westminster Abbey as one of England's distinguished poets.

During the four or five years in which Beaumont and Fletcher lived and wrote together they produced for their actor-neighbors at the Globe, the King's company, a trio of notable plays — *Philaster* (c. 1609–10), *The Maid's Tragedy* (c. 1610–11), and *A King and No King* (c. 1611). The first and last of these pieces are tragi-comedy or near-tragedy. Their plots take the main characters to the brink of misfortune or frustration, and then in the closing act restore them to contentment. In *Philaster* the discovery at the last moment that a supposed boy-attendant, Bellario, is really a woman, saves the match between Arethusa and Philaster. In *A King and No King* another last minute revelation makes it possible for the lovesick king, Arbaces, to marry his supposed sister, Panthea, and thus to continue on a throne which is rightfully hers.

The Maid's Tragedy contains, instead of any sudden averting of catastrophe, four fatalities in the last act.

All three of these Beaumont and Fletcher plays employ a formula of extravagant romance suited to a polite and worldly audience. The major action develops from the amorous interests of kings and courtiers in distant countries like Sicily or Iberia. Political intrigue forms a minor but noticeable element in the situation. The *dramatis personae* include a more or less stock group of characters, such as the lovelorn court lady, the lascivious maid-in-waiting, the testy counselor, the bluff soldier, and the gallant prince.

Love in one form or another dominates the Beaumont and Fletcher environment. The purely sentimental side appears in the person of the loving, but not loved, maiden, like Aspatia in *The Maid's Tragedy*. More commonly, however, love is treated in its physical aspects, legitimate or illegitimate. The note of sex desire runs through many a scene, where the woman speaks as frankly as the man. Yet, strangely enough, a strict code controls the conduct of this lax society. Woman's virtue and man's honor must be jealously guarded — at least in public. A suspected threat to either provokes immediate agitation, for reputation lies at stake. Considerations of honor or virtue on occasion clash with those of love or friendship, and cause surprising turns of situation. In *Philaster* the hero, who has just become betrothed to his beloved Arethusa, suddenly hears an accusation of her lack of virtue. He at once starts to kill himself, because for him, honor demands nothing less than the ending of his life. This unreasonable sensibility characterizes the chief Beaumont and Fletcher characters.

Excessive emotionalism leading to unexpected incident produced the kind of excitement which the public now craved most. Beaumont and Fletcher, therefore, concentrated on swift-moving scenes colored by exaggerated feelings. They substituted for the lyrical wordy manner of Elizabethan and Shakespearean tragedy a more nervous, direct speech with less poetic coloring. The more subtle qualities of style, character, and emotion were sacrificed for immediate effectiveness in the theater. The Beaumont and Fletcher plays at once became the last word in serious drama. Even Shakespeare may have been influenced by the new fashion in his romantic plays, *Cymbeline* (c. 1609–10) and *The Winter's Tale* (c. 1610–11). Indeed, up to the middle of the eighteenth century the works of Beaumont and Fletcher continued more popular on the stage than any other English drama written before the Civil War.

JACOBEAN AND CAROLINE TRAGEDY

The Beaumont and Fletcher sensationalism assumed more extreme forms as Jacobean and Caroline tragedy decayed with the times. Sensationalistic appeal developed in two directions: (1) physical thrills; (2) sensual passion.

The plays of the first type exploited violence, horror, and gloom. *The Duchess of Malfi* by John Webster (?1575–?1625) pointed the way as early as 1614. Webster's celebrated tragedy depicts the cruel fate of an Italian duchess who takes her steward, Antonio, as a husband. Her brothers, disgusted at the marriage, torture and finally murder her through their villainous tool, Bosola. *The Duchess of Malfi* abounds in all sorts of sensational devices — scenes in the dark, echoes, murder, poison, madmen, fake pictures, corpses, and a dead man's hand. The murder of the duchess is preceded by a lengthy series of horrors which culminate in the killing of her maid and the strangling of her children before her eyes. The pathos with which Webster tried to surround the character of the duchess does not conceal the melodrama.

The tragedies of James Shirley (1596–1666), the last important playwright of the Caroline period, mark the climax of the trend toward violence and horror. *The Traitor* (1631) and *The Cardinal* (1641) depend upon inhuman and depraved intrigues in a court society given over to lust and bloodthirstiness. The element of pathos has almost disappeared. Shirley's only objective seems the representation of "a heap of tragedies" (to use his phrase); that is, a heap of dead persons.

The second line of sensationalism in Jacobean and Caroline tragedy developed from the erotic vein in the Beaumont and Fletcher drama. Later treatment of the love motif manifested an increasing delight in unwholesome and abnormal passion. John Ford (1586–?1640) accomplished the most effective poeticizing of sensualism. *'Tis Pity She's a Whore* (c. 1624) deals with the incestuous feelings of a brother and sister, Giovanni and Annabella. Ford delineates in polished verse the mental and physical torture of this young pair because of their illicit affection. The play's title well reveals Ford's distorted concept of the pity appropriate to tragic drama.

Thus English tragedy in the writings of Shirley and Ford arrived at complete degeneracy before the Civil War. Shirley's brutality and Ford's morbidity trace back, however, to the spiritual decadence which the romanticism of Beaumont and Fletcher heralded.

"THE MAID'S TRAGEDY"

The Maid's Tragedy exhibits more skillfully than any other play by Beaumont and Fletcher the dramatic components which pleased the courtly taste of their age. The opening act introduces the palace atmosphere congenial to the Jacobean aristocracy. The celebration of the wedding night of Evadne and Amintor by a masque (Act I, Scene 2) imitates a frequent occasion among "persons of quality." The masque in *The Maid's Tragedy*, though briefer and less complicated, embraces all the delicate fancy and lyricism of the masques which Ben Jonson and Inigo Jones staged at court once or twice a year. This Beaumont and Fletcher masque, however, did not call for the rich scenery customary on the court stage.

The dual handling of love which was so instrumental in establishing the Beaumont and Fletcher vogue forms a prominent feature of *The Maid's Tragedy*. Sex desire not only brings about the main conflict, that between Evadne, Amintor, and the King, but it permeates the conversation at many points. The scenes connected with the retiring of Amintor and Evadne on their wedding night, and with their rising on the next day (Act II, Scene 1, and Act III, Scene 1), serve no other purpose than that of giving opportunity for suggestive comment on the marital tie.

Yet amorous passion is strangely mixed with amorous sentimentality. The melancholy of "the wronged Aspatia" runs through the play as a minor refrain. The scene in which she converses with two other maidens about men and love (Act II, Scene 2, ll. 1–90) performs the sole function of toying with sadness. The death of this deserted young woman at the hands of Amintor, her former lover (Act V, Scene 3, l. 125), offers the final touch of exaggeration to the pathos of "the maid's tragedy."

Amintor and his friend, Melantius, exemplify the temperamental nature of Beaumont and Fletcher's heroes.   Their emotions are as volatile as those of the proverbial woman. They affect a punctilious regard for honor which transcends considerations both of friendship and of love.   Their extravagant unreasonable behavior is well illustrated by the scene where they almost come to tears and then to blows (Act III, Scene 2, ll. 56–305).

The rapid changes of attitude on the part not merely of the heroes, but of the other characters in *The Maid's Tragedy*, beget situations of theatrical excitement.   Beaumont and Fletcher's ingenious devising of turns and counter-turns, as in the scene of Evadne's repentance (Act IV, Scene 1), distracts attention from the false intensity of feeling and conduct.   *The Maid's Tragedy*, lacking as it is in spiritual plausibility and elevation, cannot be compared to Shakespeare's high tragedy.   Nevertheless, among older English tragic plays, it is one of the best-designed specimens of what stage producers now call "sure-fire theater."

[For a critique on Shakespeare and tragedy, see A. C. Bradley, *Shakespearean Tragedy* (1904); for critiques on Beaumont and Fletcher, Baldwin Maxwell, *Studies in Beaumont, Fletcher, and Massinger* (1939), and C. M. Gayley, *Beaumont, the Dramatist* (1914); for appraisal of tendencies and playwrights in English tragedy, 1600–1640, F. E. Schelling, *Elizabethan Drama* (1908), and Henry W. Wells, *Elizabethan and Jacobean Playwrights* (1939).]

FRANCIS BEAUMONT AND JOHN FLETCHER

The Maid's Tragedy

DRAMATIS PERSONAE

KING
LYSIPPUS, *brother to the* KING
AMINTOR
MELANTIUS ⎫
DIPHILUS ⎭ *brothers to* EVADNE
CALIANAX, *father to* ASPATIA
CLEON ⎫
STRATO ⎭ *gentlemen*
DIAGORAS, *a servant to* CALIANAX

EVADNE, *wife to* AMINTOR
ASPATIA, *troth-plight wife to* AMINTOR
ANTIPHILA ⎫
OLYMPIAS ⎬ *waiting gentlewomen to* ASPATIA
DULA, *a lady attendant on* EVADNE

Lords, Ladies, Gentlemen, Servants, etc.

Masquers: NIGHT, CYNTHIA, NEPTUNE, AEOLUS,
    Sea Gods, Winds

The Scene is Rhodes [1]

ACT I

SCENE 1. *A room in the royal palace.*

Enter CLEON, STRATO, LYSIPPUS,
and DIPHILUS

Cle. The rest are making ready, sir.
Lys. So let them; there's time enough.
Diph. You are the brother to the King, my
    lord;
We'll take your word.
Lys. Strato, thou hast some skill in poetry;
What think'st thou of a masque?   Will it be
    well?   6
Stra. As well as masques can be.
Lys.   As masques can be!
Stra. Yes; they must commend their king,
    and speak in praise   9
Of the assembly, bless the bride and bridegroom
In person of some god; they're tied to rules
Of flattery.
Cle.   See, good my lord, who is returned!

Enter MELANTIUS

Lys. Noble Melantius, the land by me
Welcomes thy virtues home to Rhodes;   15

[1] A large island in the Aegean Sea.

Thou that with blood abroad buyest us our
    peace!
The breath of kings is like the breath of gods;
My brother wished thee here, and thou art here.
He will be too kind, and weary thee
With often welcomes; but the time doth give
    thee   20
A welcome above his or all the world's.
Mel. My lord, my thanks; but these
    scratched limbs of mine
Have spoke my love and truth unto my friends,
More than my tongue e'er could.   My mind's
    the same
It ever was to you: where I find worth,   25
I love the keeper till he let it go,
And then I follow it.
Diph.   Hail, worthy brother!
He that rejoices not at your return
In safety is mine enemy forever.   30
Mel. I thank thee, Diphilus.   But thou art
    faulty:
I sent for thee to exercise thine arms
With me at Patria; [1] thou cam'st not, Diphilus;
'Twas ill.
Diph.   My noble brother, my excuse   35

[1] Probably the ancient port of Patrae or Patras in the
Peloponnesian or Morea Peninsula of Greece.

Is my king's strict command, — which you,
　my lord,
Can witness with me.
　　Lys.　　　　　　'Tis most true, Melantius;
He might not come till the solemnities
Of this great match were past.　　　　　　40
　　Diph.　　　　　　Have you heard of it?
　　Mel.　Yes, and have given cause to those
　　that here
Envy my deeds abroad to call me gamesome:
I have no other business here at Rhodes.
　　Lys.　We have a masque tonight, and you
　　must tread　　　　　　45
A soldier's measure.[1]
　　Mel.　These soft and silken wars are not for
　　me:
The music must be shrill and all confused
That stirs my blood; and then I dance with
　　arms.
But is Amintor wed?　　　　　　50
　　Diph.　　　　　　This day.
　　Mel.　All joys upon him! for he is my friend.
Wonder not that I call a man so young my friend:
His worth is great; valiant he is and temperate;
And one that never thinks his life his own, 55
If his friend need it.　When he was a boy,
As oft as I returned (as, without boast,
I brought home conquest), he would gaze
　　upon me
And view me round, to find in what one limb
The virtue [2] lay to do those things he heard; 60
Then would he wish to see my sword, and feel
The quickness [3] of the edge, and in his hand
Weigh it: he oft would make me smile at this.
His youth did promise much, and his ripe years
Will see it all performed. —　　　　　65

Enter ASPATIA, *passing by*

　　　　　　　　　Hail, maid and wife!
Thou fair Aspatia, may the holy knot,
That thou hast tied today, last till the hand
Of age undo it! may'st thou bring a race
Unto Amintor, that may fill the world　　70
Successively with soldiers!
　　Asp.　　　　　　My hard fortunes
Deserve not scorn, for I was never proud
When they were good.　　(*Exit* ASPATIA.

[1] A stately dance.　　[2] Power.　　[3] Keenness.

　　Mel.　　　　　　How's this?　75
　　Lys.　You are mistaken, sir; she is not mar-
　　ried.
　　Mel.　You said Amintor was.
　　Diph.　'Tis true; but ——
　　Mel.　　　　　　Pardon me; I did receive
Letters at Patria from my Amintor,　　80
That he should marry her.
　　Diph.　　　　　　And so it stood
In all opinion long; but your arrival
Made me imagine you had heard the change.
　　Mel.　Who hath he taken then?　　85
　　Lys.　　　　　　A lady, sir,
That bears the light above her,[1] and strikes
　　dead
With flashes of her eye; the fair Evadne,
Your virtuous sister.
　　Mel.　　　　Peace of heart betwixt them!　90
But this is strange.
　　Lys.　　　　The King, my brother, did it
To honor you; and these solemnities
Are at his charge.
　　Mel.　'Tis royal, like himself.　But I am sad
My speech bears so unfortunate a sound　96
To beautiful Aspatia.　There is rage
Hid in her father's breast.　Calianax
Bent long against me; and he should not think,
Could I but call it back, that I would take　100
So base revenges, as to scorn the state
Of his neglected daughter.　Holds he still
His greatness with the King?
　　Lys.　　　　　　Yes.　But this lady
Walks discontented, with her watery eyes　105
Bent on the earth.　The unfrequented woods
Are her delight; where, when she sees a bank
Stuck full of flowers, she with a sigh will tell
Her servants what a pretty place it were
To bury lovers in; and make her maids　110
Pluck 'em, and strow her over like a corpse.
She carries with her an infectious grief,
That strikes all her beholders: she will sing
The mournful'st things that ever ear hath
　　heard,　　　　　　114
And sigh, and sing again; and when the rest
Of our young ladies, in their wanton blood,[2]
Tell mirthful tales in course,[3] that fill the room

[1] I.e., that is of greater distinction than Aspatia.
[2] Their playful moods.
[3] In turn, one after another.

With laughter, she will, with so sad a look,
Bring forth a story of the silent death
Of some forsaken virgin, which her grief   120
Will put in such a phrase, that, ere she end,
She'll send them weeping one by one away.

Mel. She has a brother under my command,
Like her; a face as womanish as hers;
But with a spirit that hath much outgrown   125
The number of his years.

Enter AMINTOR

Cle.   My lord the bridegroom!

Mel. I might run fiercely, not more hastily,
Upon my foe. I love thee well, Amintor;
My mouth is much too narrow for my heart;
I joy to look upon those eyes of thine;   131
Thou art my friend, but my disordered speech
Cuts off my love.

Amin.   Thou art Melantius;
All love is spoke in that. A sacrifice,   135
To thank the gods Melantius is returned
In safety! Victory sits on his sword,
As she was wont: may she build there and dwell;
And may thy armor be, as it hath been,
Only thy valor and thine innocence!   140
What endless treasures would our enemies give,
That I might hold thee still[1] thus!

Mel.   I am poor
In words; but credit me, young man, thy
      mother
Could do no more but weep for joy to see thee
After long absence: all the wounds I gave   146
Fetched not so much away, nor all the cries
Of widowèd mothers. But this is peace,
And that was war.

Amin.   Pardon, thou holy god   150
Of marriage-bed, and frown not, I am forced,
In answer of such noble tears as those,
To weep upon my wedding-day!

Mel. I fear thou art grown too fickle; for I
      hear
A lady mourns for thee; men say, to death;   155
Forsaken of thee; on what terms[2] I know not.

Amin. She had my promise; but the King
      forbade it,
And made me make this worthy change, thy
      sister,

[1] Ever.   [2] Under what circumstances.

Accompanied with graces above her;
With whom I long to lose my lusty youth,   160
And grow old in her arms.

Mel.   Be prosperous!

Enter a Messenger

Mess. My lord, the masquers rage[1] for you.

Lys.   We are gone. —
Cleon, Strato, Diphilus!   165

Amin. We'll all attend you. —
      (*Exeunt* LYSIPPUS, CLEON, STRATO,
      DIPHILUS, *and the Messenger.*
                We shall trouble you
With our solemnities.

Mel.   Not so, Amintor:
But if you laugh at my rude carriage   170
In peace, I'll do as much for you in war,
When you come thither. Yet I have a mistress
To bring to your delights; rough though I am,
I have a mistress, and she has a heart
She says; but, trust me, it is stone, no better;
There is no place that I can challenge in't.   176
But you stand still, and here my way lies.
                (*Exeunt.*

SCENE 2. *A hall in the royal palace.*

Enter CALIANAX *with* DIAGORAS

Cal. Diagoras, look to the doors better, for
shame! you let in all the world, and anon the
King will rail at me. Why, very well said.[2]
By Jove, the King will have the show i' th'
court.   5

Diag. Why do you swear so, my lord? You
know he'll have it here.

Cal. By this light, if he be wise, he will not.

Diag. And if he will not be wise, you are
forsworn.   10

Cal. One must sweat his heart out with
swearing, and get thanks on no side. I'll be
gone, look to't who will.

Diag. My lord, I shall never keep them out!
Pray, stay; your looks will terrify them.   15

Cal. My looks terrify them, you coxcombly[3]
ass, you! I'll be judged by all the company
whether thou hast not a worse face than I.

[1] Grow impatient.   [2] Well done.
[3] Silly.

Diag. I mean, because they know you and your office.[1] 20

Cal. Office! I would I could put it off! I am sure I sweat quite through my office.[2] I might have made room at my daughter's wedding: they ha' near killed her amongst them; and now I must do service for him that 25 hath forsaken her. Serve that will! (*Exit.*

Diag. He's so humorous[3] since his daughter was forsaken! (*Knock within.*) Hark, hark! there, there! so, so! codes, codes![4] What now? 30

Mel. (*within*). Open the door.

Diag. Who's there?

Mel. (*within*). Melantius.

Diag. I hope your lordship brings no troop with you; for, if you do, I must return them.[5] 35
(*Opens the door.*

Enter MELANTIUS *and a Lady*

Mel. None but this lady, sir.

Diag. The ladies are all placed above,[6] save those that come in the King's troop; the best of Rhodes sit there; and there's room.

Mel. I thank you, sir. — When I have 40 seen you placed, madam, I must attend the King; but, the masque done, I'll wait on you again.

Diag. (*opening another door*). Stand back there! — Room for my Lord Melantius! (*Exeunt* MELANTIUS *and Lady.*) — Pray, bear 45 back: this is no place for such youths and their trulls.[7] Let the doors shut again. — No? — Do your heads itch? I'll scratch[8] them for you. (*Closes the door.*) — So, now thrust and hang. (*Knocking within.*) — Again! who is't now? 50 — I cannot blame my Lord Calianax for going away; would he were here! He would run raging among them, and break a dozen wiser heads than his own in the twinkling of an eye.— What's the news now? 55

One (*within*). I pray you, can you help me to the speech of the master-cook?

---

[1] Position.   [2] Robe of office.   [3] Temperamental.
[4] Probably a corruption of "gods, gods!"
[5] Turn them back.
[6] I.e., in the gallery. — The gallery was on the second floor of the tiring house, overlooking the stage.
[7] Wenches.   [8] Crack.

Re-enter CALIANAX

Diag. If I open the door, I'll cook some of your calves-heads. Peace, rogues! (*Knocking within.*) — Again! who is't? 60

Mel. (*within*). Melantius.

Cal. Let him not in.

Diag. Oh, my lord, I must. (*Opens the door.*) — Make room there for my lord. — Is your lady placed? 65

Re-enter MELANTIUS

I thank you. — My Lord Calianax, well met. Your causeless hate to me I hope is buried.

Cal. Yes, I do service for your sister here, That brings my own poor child to timeless[1] death. She loves your friend Amintor, such another 70 False-hearted lord as you.

Mel.   You do me wrong, A most unmanly one, and I am slow In taking vengeance; but be well advised.

Cal. It may be so. — Who placed the lady there 75 So near the presence of the King?

Mel.   I did.

Cal. My lord, she must not sit there.

Mel.   Why?

Cal. The place is kept for women of more worth. 80

Mel. More worth than she! It misbecomes your age And place to be thus womanish: forbear! What you have spoke I am content to think The palsy shook your tongue to.

Cal.   Why, 'tis well, 85 If I stand here to place men's wenches.

Mel.   I Shall quite forget this place, thy age, my safety, And, through all, cut that poor sickly week Thou hast to live away from thee. 90

Cal. Nay, I know you can fight for your whore.

Mel. Bate me[2] the King, and, be he flesh and blood, 'A lies that says it! Thy mother at fifteen Was black and sinful to her.

---

[1] Untimely.   [2] Leave out.

Diag.　　　　　　　　Good my lord — 95
Mel. Some god pluck threescore years from
　　that fond [1] man,
That I may kill him, and not stain mine honor!
It is the curse of soldiers that in peace
They shall be braved by such ignoble men
As, if the land were troubled, would with
　　tears　　　　　　　　　　　　　　100
And knees beg succor from 'em. Would that
　　blood,
That sea of blood, that I have lost in fight
Were running in thy veins, that it might make
　　thee
Apt to say less, or able to maintain,
Should'st thou say more! This Rhodes, I see,
　　is nought　　　　　　　　　　　　105
But a place privileged to do men wrong.
Cal. Ay, you may say your pleasure.

Enter AMINTOR

Amin.　　　　　　　　What vile injury
Has stirred my worthy friend, who is as slow
To fight with words as he is quick of hand? 110
Mel. That heap of age, which I should
　　reverence
If it were temperate; but testy years
Are most contemptible.
Amin.　　　　　　　　Good sir, forbear.
Cal. There is just such another as your-
　　self.　　　　　　　　　　　　　　115
Amin. He will wrong you, or me, or any man,
And talk as if he had no life to lose,
Since this our match. The King is coming in;
I would not for more wealth than I enjoy
He should perceive you raging. He did
　　hear　　　　　　　　　　　　　　120
You were at difference now, which hastened
　　him.　　　　　　(*Hautboys play within.*
Cal. Make room there!

Enter the KING, EVADNE, ASPATIA, *Lords, and Ladies*

King. Melantius, thou art welcome, and my
　　love
Is with thee still; but this is not a place
To brabble [2] in. — Calianax, join hands. 125

[1] Foolish.　　[2] Squabble.

Cal. He shall not have mine hand.
King.　　　　　　　　This is no time
To force you to't. I do love you both. —
Calianax, you look well to your office. —
And you, Melantius, are welcome home. — 130
Begin the masque.
Mel. Sister, I joy to see you and your choice;
You looked with my eyes when you took that
　　man:
Be happy in him!　　　　(*Recorders* [1] *play.*
Evad.　　　Oh, my dearest brother, 135
Your presence is more joyful than this day
Can be unto me!

THE MASQUE

NIGHT *rises in mists*

Night. Our reign is come; for in the quenching
　　sea
The sun is drowned, and with him fell the Day.
Bright Cynthia,[2] hear my voice! I am the
　　Night,　　　　　　　　　　　　140
For whom thou bear'st about thy borrowed light:
Appear! no longer thy pale visage shroud,
But strike thy silver horns quite through a cloud,
And send a beam upon my swarthy face,
By which I may discover all the place　　145
And persons, and how many longing eyes
Are come to wait on our solemnities.

Enter CYNTHIA

How dull and black am I! I could not find
This beauty [3] without thee, I am so blind:
Methinks they show like to those eastern
　　streaks,　　　　　　　　　　　　150
That warn us hence before the morning breaks.
Back, my pale servant! for these eyes know how
To shoot far more and quicker rays than thou.
Cynth. Great queen, they be a troop for whom
　　alone
One of my clearest moons I have put on; 155
A troop, that looks as if thyself and I
Had plucked our reins in and our whips laid by,
To gaze upon these mortals, that appear
Brighter than we.
Night.　　　　Then let us keep 'em here; 160
And never more our chariots drive away,
But hold our places and outshine the Day.

[1] Flageolets.
[2] I.e., the moon goddess.
[3] I.e., the beauty of the court ladies who form the
audience on the stage and in the gallery.

Cynth. Great queen of shadows, you are pleased
    to speak
Of more than may be done: we may not break
The gods' decrees; but, when our time is come,   165
Must drive away, and give the Day our room.
Yet, whilst our reign lasts, let us stretch our power
To give our servants one contented hour,
With such unwonted solemn grace and state,
As may forever after force them hate   170
Our brother's glorious beams, and wish [1] the Night
Crowned with a thousand stars and our cold light:
For almost all the world their service bend
To Phoebus,[2] and in vain my light I lend,
Gazed on unto my setting from my rise   175
Almost of none but of unquiet eyes.
    Night. Then shine at full, fair queen, and by thy
    power
Produce a birth, to crown this happy hour,
Of nymphs and shepherds; let their songs discover,
Easy and sweet, who is a happy lover;   180
Or, if thou woo't,[3] then call thine own Endymion [4]
From the sweet flowery bank he lies upon,
On Latmus' brown, thy pale beams drawn away,
And of his long night let him make this day.
    Cynth. Thou dream'st, dark queen; that fair boy
    was not mine,   185
Nor went I down to kiss him.   Ease and wine
Have bred these bold tales: poets, when they rage,[5]
Turn gods to men, and make an hour an age.
But I will give a greater state and glory,
And raise to time a nobler memory   190
Of what these lovers are. — Rise, rise, I say,
Thou power of deeps, thy surges laid away,
Neptune, great king of waters, and by me
Be proud to be commanded!

NEPTUNE rises

Nept.   Cynthia, see,   195
Thy word hath fetched me hither: let me know
Why I ascend.
    Cynth.   Doth this majestic show
Give thee no knowledge yet?
    Nept.   Yes, now I see   200
Something intended, Cynthia, worthy thee.
Go on; I'll be a helper.
    Cynth.   Hie thee, then,
And charge the Wind fly from his rocky den,

Let loose his subjects; only Boreas,[1]   205
Too foul for our intentions as he was,
Still keep him fast chained: we must have none here
But vernal blasts and gentle winds appear,
Such as blow flowers and through the glad boughs
    sing
Many soft welcomes to the lusty spring;   210
These are our music.   Next, thy watery race
Bring on in couples (we are pleased to grace
This noble night), each in their richest things
Your own deeps or the broken vessel brings.
Be prodigal, and I shall be as kind   215
And shine at full upon you.
    Nept.   Oh, the wind-
Commanding Aeolus! [2]

Enter AEOLUS out of a rock

    Aeol.   Great Neptune!
    Nept.   He.   220
    Aeol. What is thy will?
    Nept.   We do command thee free
Favonius [3] and thy milder winds, to wait
Upon our Cynthia; but tie Boreas strait: [4]
He's too rebellious.   225
    Aeol.   I shall do it.
    Nept.   Do.   (*Exit* AEOLUS.
    Aeol. (*within*). Great master of the flood and all
    below,
Thy full command has taken. — Oh, the Main!
Neptune!   230
    Nept. Here.

Re-enter AEOLUS, followed by FAVONIUS and
other Winds

    Aeol.   Boreas has broke his chain,
And, struggling with the rest, has got away.
    Nept. Let him alone, I'll take him up at sea;
I will not long be thence.   Go once again,   235
And call out of the bottoms of the main
Blue Proteus [5] and the rest; charge them put on
Their greatest pearls, and the most sparkling stone
The beaten [6] rock breeds; tell this night is done
By me a solemn honor to the Moon: 240
Fly, like a full sail.
    Aeol.   I am gone.   (*Exit.*
    Cynth.   Dark Night,
Strike a full silence, do a thorough right
To this great chorus, that our music may   245
Touch high as Heaven, and make the east break day
At midnight.   (*Music.*

---

    [1] Wish for.   [2] The sun god.   [3] Wilt.
    [4] A beautiful shepherd boy on Mt. Latmus in Caria,
Asia Minor, who was beloved by the moon goddess and
thrown into an unbroken slumber that she might caress
him nightly without interference.
    [5] I.e., when they are seized by a burst of inspiration.

---

    [1] The North Wind.   [2] The god of the winds.
    [3] The West Wind.   [4] Tight.
    [5] The sea god who is the color of the ocean.
    [6] I.e., sea-beaten.

FIRST SONG

during which PROTEUS *and other sea-deities
enter from below*

Cynthia, to thy power and thee
    We obey.
Joy to this great company!   250
    And no day
Come to steal this night away,
    Till the rites of love are ended,
And the lusty bridegroom say,
    "Welcome, light, of all befriended!"   255

Pace out, you watery powers below;
    Let your feet,
Like the galleys when they row,
    Even beat.
Let your unknown measures, set   260
    To the still winds, tell to all
That gods are come, immortal, great,
    To honor this great nuptial.
      (*The Masquers dance a measure.*[1]

SECOND SONG

Hold back thy hours, dark Night, till we have done;
    The Day will come too soon: 265
Young maids will cure thee, if thou steal'st away,
And leav'st their losses open to the day:
    Stay, stay, and hide
    The blushes of the bride.

Stay, gentle Night, and with thy darkness cover 270
    The kisses of her lover;
Stay, and confound her tears and her shrill cryings,
Her weak denials, vows, and often-dyings;
    Stay, and hide all:
    But help not, though she call.   275
      (*The Masquers dance another measure.*

Nept. Great queen of us and heaven, hear what
    I bring
To make this hour a full one.
Cynth.   Speak, sea's king.
Nept. The tunes my Amphitrite [2] joys to have,
When she will dance upon the rising wave,   280
And court me as she sails. My Tritons, play
Music to lay a storm! I'll lead the way.

THIRD SONG

To bed, to bed! Come, Hymen, lead the bride,
And lay her by her husband's side;

---

[1] A stately dance.
[2] His wife, the daughter of Nereus and Doris.

Bring in the virgins every one,   285
    That grieve to lie alone;
That they may kiss while they may say a maid;
Tomorrow 'twill be other kissed and said.
    Hesperus, be long a-shining,
    Whilst these lovers are a-twining.   290
    (*The Masquers dance another measure,
    which Neptune leads.*

Aeol. (*within*). Ho, Neptune!
Nept.   Aeolus!

Re-enter AEOLUS

Aeol.   The sea goes high,
Boreas hath raised a storm: go and apply
Thy trident; else, I prophesy, ere day   295
Many a tall ship will be cast away.
Descend with all the gods and all their power,
To strike a calm.
Cynth.   We thank you for this hour:
My favor to you all. To gratulate   300
So great a service, done at my desire,
Ye shall have many floods, fuller and higher
Than you have wished for; and no ebb shall dare
To let the Day see where your swellings are.
Now back unto your governments in haste,   305
Lest your proud charge should swell above the
    waste, [1]
And win upon [2] the island.
Nept.   We obey.
    (NEPTUNE *descends and the sea-gods.
    Exeunt* AEOLUS *and all the Winds.*
Cynth. Hold up thy head, dead Night; see'st
    thou not Day?
The east begins to lighten: I must down,   310
And give my brother place.
Night.   Oh, I could frown
To see the Day, the Day that flings his light
Upon my kingdom and contemns old Night!
Let him go on and flame! I hope to see   315
Another wild-fire in his axle-tree,[3]
And all fall drenched.[4] But I forget. — Speak,
    queen:
Day grows on; I must no more be seen.
Cynth. Heave up thy drowsy head again, and see
A greater light, a greater majesty,   320
Between our set [5] and us! Whip up thy team:

---

[1] I.e., sea-coast.
[2] Overflow.
[3] The charioteer Phaeton's mad driving of the horses
of the Sun may burn out the axles of the chariot.
[4] Drowned.
[5] Setting.

The day breaks here, and yon sun-flaring stream [1]
Shot from the south. Which way wilt thou go?
    Say.
  Night. I'll vanish into mists.
  Cynth.   I into Day. (*Exeunt.* 325

          Finis Masque

  King. Take lights there! — Ladies, get the
    bride to bed. —
(*To* EVADNE) We will not see you laid.[2]— Good
    night, Amintor;
We'll ease you of that tedious ceremony.
Were it my case, I should think time run slow.
If thou be'st noble, youth, get me a boy, 330
That may defend my kingdoms from my foes.
  Amin. All happiness to you!
  King.   Good night, Melantius.
                      (*Exeunt.*

ACT II

SCENE I. *The anteroom to* EVADNE'S *bedchamber
    in the royal palace.*

    Enter EVADNE, ASPATIA, DULA, *and
         other ladies*

  Dula. Madam, shall we undress you for this
    fight?
The wars are nak'd that you must make tonight.
  Evad. You are very merry, Dula.
  Dula.   I should be
Far merrier, madam, if it were with me 5
As it is with you.
  Evad.   How's that?
  Dula.   That I might go
To bed with him wi' th' credit that you do.
  Evad. Why, how now, wench?   10
  Dula.   Come, ladies, will you help?
  Evad. I am soon undone.
  Dula.   And as soon done:
Good store of clothes will trouble you at both.
  Evad. Art thou drunk, Dula?   15
  Dula.   Why, here's none but we.
  Evad. Thou think'st belike there is no
    modesty
When we're alone.
  Dula. Ay, by my troth, you hit my thoughts
    aright.

  [1] Ray.   [2] I.e., put to bed.

  Evad. You prick me, lady.   20
  1 Lady.   'Tis against my will.
  Dula. Anon you must endure more and lie
    still;
You're best to practice.
  Evad.   Sure, this wench is mad.
  Dula. No, faith, this is a trick that I have
    had   25
Since I was fourteen.
  Evad.   'Tis high time to leave it.
  Dula. Nay, now I'll keep it till the trick
    leave me.
A dozen wanton words put in your head
Will make you livelier in your husband's bed.
  Evad. Nay, faith, then take it.[1]   31
  Dula.   Take it, madam! Where?
We all, I hope, will take it that are here.
  Evad. Nay, then I'll give you o'er.
  Dula.   So will I make 35
The ablest man in Rhodes, or his heart, ache.
  Evad. Wilt take my place tonight?
  Dula.   I'll hold your cards
Against any two I know.
  Evad.   What wilt thou do? 40
  Dula. Madam, we'll do't, and make 'em
    leave play too.
  Evad. Aspatia, take her part.
  Dula.   I will refuse it:
She will pluck down a side; [2] she does not use it.[3]
  Evad. Why do I, prithee? [4]   45
  Dula.   You will find the play
Quickly, because your head lies well that way.
  Evad. I thank thee, Dula. Would thou
    couldst instill
Some of thy mirth into Aspatia!
Nothing but sad thoughts in her breast do
    dwell: 50
Methinks a mean betwixt you would do well.
  Dula. She is in love: hang me, if I were so,
But I could run my country.[5] I love too
To do those things that people in love do.
  Asp. It were a timeless [6] smile should prove
    my cheek: 55
It were a fitter hour for me to laugh,

  [1] I.e., take the trick (as in cards).
  [2] She will cause the loss of the game to her side.
  [3] She is not accustomed to the game.
  [4] Why am I accustomed, tell me?
  [5] I could make things run.   [6] Untimely.

When at the altar the religious priest
Were pacifying the offended powers
With sacrifice, than now.   This should have
    been
My rite; and all your hands have been em-
    ployed   60
In giving me a spotless offering
To young Amintor's bed, as we are now
For you.   Pardon, Evadne: would my worth
Were great as yours, or that the King, or he,
Or both, thought so!   Perhaps he found me
    worthless: 65
But till he did so, in these ears of mine,
These credulous ears, he poured the sweetest
    words
That art or love could frame.   If he were false,
Pardon it, heaven! and, if I did want
Virtue, you safely may forgive that too;   70
For I have lost none that I had from you.
    Evad.   Nay, leave this sad talk, madam.
    Asp.   Would I could!
Then should I leave the cause.
    Evad.   See, if you have not spoiled all Dula's
    mirth!   75
    Asp.   Thou think'st thy heart hard; but, if
    thou be'st caught,
Remember me; thou shalt perceive a fire
Shot suddenly into thee.
    Dula.   That's not so good; let 'em shoot
anything but fire, I fear 'em not.   80
    Asp.   Well, wench, thou may'st be taken.
    Evad.   Ladies, good night: I'll do the rest
    myself.
    Dula.   Nay, let your lord do some.
    Asp. (singing).   Lay a garland on my hearse
    Of the dismal yew —
    Evad.   That's one of your sad songs, madam.
    Asp.   Believe me, 'tis a very pretty one.   86
    Evad.   How is it, madam?
    Asp. (singing)
      Lay a garland on my hearse
      Of the dismal yew;
    Maidens, willow-branches bear;   90
      Say I died true.
    My love was false, but I was firm
      From my hour of birth:
    Upon my buried body lie
      Lightly, gentle earth!   95
    Evad.   Fie on't, madam! the words are so

strange, they are able to make one dream of
hobgoblins. — "I could never have the power"
— sing that, Dula.
    Dula (singing)
    I could never have the power   100
      To love one above an hour,
    But my heart would prompt mine eye
      On some other man to fly.
      Venus, fix mine eyes fast,
Or, if not, give me all that I shall see at last!
    Evad.   So, leave me now.   106
    Dula.   Nay, we must see you laid.
    Asp.   Madam, good night.   May all the
    marriage-joys
That longing maids imagine in their beds
Prove so unto you!   May no discontent   110
Grow 'twixt your love and you! but, if there do,
Inquire of me, and I will guide your moan;
Teach you an artificial [1] way to grieve,
To keep your sorrow waking.   Love your lord
No worse than I: but, if you love so well, 115
Alas, you may displease him! so did I.
This is the last time you shall look on me. —
Ladies, farewell.   As soon as I am dead,
Come all and watch one night about my hearse;
Bring each a mournful story and a tear,   120
To offer at it when I go to earth;
With flattering ivy clasp my coffin round;
Write on my brow my fortune; let my bier
Be borne by virgins, that shall sing by course [2]
The truth of maids and perjuries of men.   125
    Evad.   Alas, I pity thee.
    All.   Madam, good night.   (*Exit* EVADNE.
    1 Lady.   Come, we'll let in the bridegroom.
    Dula (opening the door).   Where's my lord?

Enter AMINTOR

    1 Lady.   Here, take this light.   130
    Dula.   You'll find her in the dark.
    1 Lady.   Your lady's scarce a-bed yet; you
    must help her.
    Asp.   Go, and be happy in your lady's love.
May all the wrongs that you have done to me
Be utterly forgotten in my death!   135
I'll trouble you no more; yet I will take
A parting kiss, and will not be denied.
                    (*Kisses* AMINTOR

---

[1] Artful.   [2] By turns.

You'll come, my lord, and see the virgins weep
When I am laid in earth, though you yourself
Can know no pity.   Thus I wind myself   140
Into this willow-garland,[1] and am prouder
That I was once your love, though now refused,
Than to have had another true to me.
So with my prayers I leave you, and must try
Some yet unpracticed way to grieve and die.
   Dula. Come, ladies, will you go?   146
   All.   Good night, my lord.
   Amin. Much happiness unto you all! —
             (*Exeunt* DULA *and Ladies*.
I did that lady wrong.   Methinks, I feel   149
A grief shoot suddenly through all my veins;
Mine eyes rain: this is strange at such a time.
It was the King first moved me to't; but he
Has not my will in keeping.   Why do I
Perplex myself thus?   Something whispers me,
Go not to bed.   My guilt is not so great   155
As mine own conscience, too sensible,[2]
Would make me think; I only brake a promise,
And 'twas the King that forced me.   Timorous
   flesh,
Why shak'st thou so?   Away, my idle fears!

Re-enter EVADNE

(*Aside*) Yonder she is, the luster of whose eye
Can blot away the sad remembrance   161
Of all these things. — Oh, my Evadne, spare
That tender body; let it not take cold!
The vapors of the night will not fall here.
To bed, my love: Hymen[3] will punish us   165
For being slack performers of his rites.
Camest thou to call me?
   Evad.   No.
   Amin.   Come, come, my love,
And let us lose ourselves to one another.   170
Why art thou up so long?
   Evad.   I am not well.
   Amin. To bed then; let me wind thee in
   these arms
Till I have banished sickness.
   Evad.   Good my lord,
I cannot sleep.   176
   Amin.   Evadne, we will watch;
I mean no sleeping.

   [1] A symbol of rejected love.   [2] Sensitive.
   [3] The god of marriage.

   Evad.   I'll not go to bed.
   Amin. I prithee, do.   180
   Evad.   I will not for the world.
   Amin. Why, my dear love?
   Evad.   Why! I have sworn I will not.
   Amin. Sworn!
   Evad.   Ay.   185
   Amin.   How? Sworn, Evadne!
   Evad. Yes, sworn, Amintor; and will swear
   again,
If you will wish to hear me.
   Amin. To whom have you sworn this?
   Evad. If I should name him, the matter were
   not great.   190
   Amin. Come, this is but the coyness of a
   bride.
   Evad. The coyness of a bride!
   Amin.   How prettily
That frown becomes thee!
   Evad.   Do you like it so?
   Amin. Thou canst not dress thy face in
   such a look   196
But I shall like it.
   Evad.   What look likes[1] you best?
   Amin. Why do you ask?
   Evad. That I may show you one less pleasing
   to you.   200
   Amin. How's that?
   Evad. That I may show you one less pleasing
   to you.
   Amin. I prithee, put thy jests in milder looks;
It shows as thou wert angry.
   Evad.   So perhaps
I am indeed.   206
   Amin.   Why, who has done thee wrong?
Name me the man, and by thyself I swear,
Thy yet-unconquered self, I will revenge thee!
   Evad. Now I shall try thy truth.   If thou
   dost love me,   210
Thou weigh'st not any thing compared with me:
Life, honor, joys eternal, all delights
This world can yield, or hopeful people feign,
Or in the life to come, are light as air
To a true lover when his lady frowns,   215
And bids him "do this."   Wilt thou kill this
   man?
Swear, my Amintor, and I'll kiss the sin
Off from thy lips.

   [1] Pleases.

Amin.   I wo' not swear, sweet love,
Till I do know the cause.   220
    Evad.   I would thou wouldst.
Why, it is thou that wrong'st me; I hate thee;
Thou should'st have killed thyself.
    Amin. If I should know that, I should
        quickly kill
The man you hated.   225
    Evad.   Know it, then, and do't.
    Amin. Oh, no! what look soe'er thou shalt
        put on
To try my faith, I shall not think thee false;
I cannot find one blemish in thy face,
Where falsehood should abide. Leave,[1] and
    to bed.   230
If you have sworn to any of the virgins
That were your old companions to preserve
Your maidenhead a night, it may be done
Without this means.
    Evad.   A maidenhead, Amintor,
At my years!   236
    Amin.   Sure she raves; this cannot be
Her natural temper. — Shall I call thy maids?
Either thy healthful sleep hath left thee long,
Or else some fever rages in thy blood.   240
    Evad. Neither, Amintor: think you I am
        mad,
Because I speak the truth?
    Amin.   Is this the truth?
Will you not lie with me tonight?   244
    Evad.   Tonight!
You talk as if you thought I would hereafter.
    Amin. Hereafter! yes, I do.
    Evad.   You are deceived.
Put off amazement, and with patience mark
What I shall utter, for the oracle   250
Knows nothing truer: 'tis not for a night
Or two that I forbear thy bed, but ever.
    Amin. I dream. Awake, Amintor!
    Evad.   You hear right:
I sooner will find out the beds of snakes,   255
And with my youthful blood warm their cold
    flesh,
Letting them curl themselves about my limbs,
Than sleep one night with thee. This is not
    feigned,
Nor sounds it like the coyness of a bride.   259
    Amin. Is flesh so earthly to endure all this?

[1] Leave off, desist.

Are these the joys of marriage? — Hymen, keep
This story (that will make succeeding youth
Neglect thy ceremonies) from all ears;
Let it not rise up, for thy shame and mine
To after-ages: we will scorn thy laws,   265
If thou no better bless them. Touch the heart
Of her that thou hast sent me, or the world
Shall know this: not an altar then will smoke
In praise of thee; we will adopt us sons;
Then virtue shall inherit, and not blood.   270
If we do lust, we'll take the next we meet,
Serving ourselves as other creatures do;
And never take note of the female more,
Nor of her issue. (*Aside*) I do rage in vain;
She can but jest. — Oh, pardon me, my love!
So dear the thoughts are that I hold of thee,
That I must break forth. Satisfy my fear;   277
It is a pain, beyond the hand of death,
To be in doubt. Confirm it with an oath,
If this be true.   280
    Evad.   Do you invent the form;
Let there be in it all the binding words
Devils and conjurers can put together,
And I will take it. I have sworn before,
And here by all things holy do again,   285
Never to be acquainted with thy bed!
Is your doubt over now?
    Amin. I know too much; would I had
        doubted still!
Was ever such a marriage-night as this? —
You powers above, if you did ever mean   290
Man should be used thus, you have thought a
    way
How he may bear himself and save his honor:
Instruct me in it; for to my dull eyes
There is no mean, no moderate course to run;
I must live scorned or be a murderer.   295
Is there a third? — Why is this night so calm?
Why does not Heaven speak in thunder to us,
And drown her voice?
    Evad.   This rage will do no good.
    Amin. Evadne, hear me. Thou hast ta'en
        an oath,   300
But such a rash one that to keep it were
Worse than to swear it. Call it back to thee;
Such vows as that never ascend to Heaven;
A tear or two will wash it quite away.
Have mercy on my youth, my hopeful youth,
If thou be pitiful! for, without boast,   306

This land was proud of me. What lady was
    there,
That men called fair and virtuous in this isle,
That would have shunned my love? It is in
    thee
To make me hold this worth. Oh, we vain men,
That trust all our reputatiön   311
To rest upon the weak and yielding hand
Of feeble woman! But thou art not stone;
Thy flesh is soft, and in thine eyes doth dwell
The spirit of love; thy heart cannot be hard.
Come, lead me from the bottom of despair 316
To all the joys thou hast; I know thou wilt;
And make me careful lest the sudden change
O'ercome my spirits.
    Evad.   When I call back this oath,
The pains of hell environ me!   321
    Amin. I sleep, and am too temperate. Come
    to bed!
Or by those hairs, which, if thou hadst a soul
Like to thy locks, were threads for kings to wear
About their arms ——   325
    Evad.   Why, so perhaps they are.
    Amin. I'll drag thee to my bed, and make
    thy tongue
Undo this wicked oath, or on thy flesh
I'll print a thousand wounds to let out life.
    Evad. I fear thee not: do what thou darest
    to me!   330
Every ill-sounding word or threatening look
Thou showest to me will be revenged at full.
    Amin. It will not sure, Evadne?
    Evad. Do not you hazard that.   334
    Amin.   Ha' ye your champions?
    Evad. Alas, Amintor, think'st thou I forbear
To sleep with thee, because I have put on
A maiden's strictness? Look upon these cheeks,
And thou shalt find the hot and rising blood
Unapt for such a vow. No; in this heart   340
There dwells as much desire and as much will
To put that wish'd act in practice as ever yet
Was known to woman; and they have been
    shown
Both. But it was the folly of thy youth
To think this beauty, to what hand soe'er 345
It shall be called, shall stoop to any second.
I do enjoy the best, and in that height
Have sworn to stand or die. You guess the
    man.

    Amin. No; let me know the man that wrongs
    me so,
That I may cut his body into motes,   350
And scatter it before the northern wind.
    Evad. You dare not strike him.
    Amin.   Do not wrong me so:
Yes, if his body were a poisonous plant
That it were death to touch, I have a soul
Will throw me on him.   356
    Evad.   Why, 'tis the King.
    Amin.   The King!
    Evad. What will you do now?
    Amin.   'Tis not the King!
    Evad. What did he make this match for,
    dull Amintor?   361
    Amin. Oh, thou hast named a word, that
    wipes away
All thoughts revengeful! In that sacred name,
"The King," there lies a terror. What frail
    man   364
Dares lift his hand against it? Let the gods
Speak to him when they please: till when, let us
Suffer and wait.
    Evad. Why should you fill yourself so full
    of heat,
And haste so to my bed? I am no virgin.
    Amin. What devil put it in thy fancy, then,
To marry me?   371
    Evad.   Alas, I must have one
To father children, and to bear the name
Of husband to me, that my sin may be
More honorable!   375
    Amin.   What strange thing am I!
    Evad. A miserable one; one that myself
Am sorry for.
    Amin.   Why, show it then in this:
If thou hast pity, though thy love be none, 380
Kill me; and all true lovers, that shall live
In after ages crossed in their desires,
Shall bless thy memory, and call thee good,
Because such mercy in thy heart was found,
To rid [1] a lingering wretch.   385
    Evad.   I must have one
To fill thy room again, if thou wert dead;
Else, by this night, I would! I pity thee.
    Amin. These strange and sudden injuries
    have fallen
So thick upon me, that I lose all sense   390

    [1] Dispatch.

Of what they are.   Methinks, I am not
    wronged;
Nor is it aught, if from the censuring world
I can but hide it.   Reputation,
Thou art a word, no more! — But thou hast
    shown
An impudence so high, that to the world   395
I fear thou wilt betray or shame thyself.
    Evad.   To cover shame, I took thee; never
    fear
That I would blaze [1] myself.
    Amin.   Nor let the King
Know I conceive he wrongs me; then mine
    honor   400
Will thrust me into action: *that* [2] my flesh
Could bear with patience.   And it is some
    ease
To me in these extremes, that I knew this
Before I touched thee; else, had all the sins
Of mankind stood betwixt me and the King,
I had gone through 'em to his heart and
    thine.   406
I have lost one desire: 'tis not his crown
Shall buy me to thy bed, now I resolve [3]
He has dishonored thee.   Give me thy hand;
Be careful of thy credit, and sin close; [4]   410
'Tis all I wish.   Upon thy chamber-floor
I'll rest tonight, that morning visitors
May think we did as married people use;
And prithee, smile upon me when they come,
And seem to toy, as if thou hadst been
    pleased   415
With what we did.
    Evad.   Fear not; I will do this.
    Amin.   Come, let us practice; and, as wan-
    tonly
As ever loving bride and bridegroom met,
Let's laugh and enter here.   420
    Evad.   I am content.
    Amin.   Down, all the swellings of my
    troubled heart!
When we walk thus entwined, let all eyes see
If ever lovers better did agree.
                   (*Exeunt.*

[1] Blazon, proclaim abroad.
[2] I.e., the King's ignorance of the fact that Amintor
realizes the true situation.
[3] Realize.
[4] In secret.

SCENE 2. ASPATIA'S *room in the house of*
         CALIANAX.

Enter ASPATIA, ANTIPHILA, *and* OLYMPIAS

    Asp.   Away, you are not sad! force it no
    further.
Good gods, how well you look!   Such a full
    color
Young bashful brides put on: sure, you are new
    married!
    Ant.   Yes, madam, to your grief.
    Asp.   Alas, poor wenches!   5
Go, learn to love first; learn to lose yourselves;
Learn to be flattered, and believe and bless
The double tongue that did it; make a faith
Out of the miracles of ancient lovers,
Such as spake truth and died in't; and, like me,
Believe all faithful, and be miserable.   11
Did you ne'er love yet, wenches? — Speak,
    Olympias:
Thou hast an easy temper, fit for stamp.
    Olym.   Never.
    Asp.   Nor you, Antiphila?   15
    Ant.   Nor I.
    Asp.   Then, my good girls, be more than
    women, wise;
At least be more than I was; and be sure
You credit any thing the light gives life to,
Before a man.   Rather believe the sea   20
Weeps for the ruined merchant, when he roars;
Rather, the wind courts but the pregnant sails,
When the strong cordage cracks; rather, the sun
Comes but to kiss the fruit in wealthy autumn,
When all falls blasted.   If you needs must love
(Forced by ill fate), take to your maiden-
    bosoms   26
Two dead-cold aspics,[1] and of them make lovers.
They cannot flatter nor forswear; one kiss
Makes a long peace for all.   But man —
Oh, that beast, man!   Come, let's be sad, my
    girls: —   30
That down-cast of thine eye, Olympias,
Shows a fine sorrow. — Mark, Antiphila;
Just such another was the nymph Oenone's [2]
When Paris brought home [3] Helen.   (*To* OLYM.)
    Now, a tear;

[1] Asps.
[2] Wife of Paris, whom he abandoned for Helen.
[3] I.e., to Troy.

And then thou art a piece expressing fully 35
The Carthage queen,[1] when from a cold sea-
rock,
Full with her sorrow, she tied fast her eyes
To the fair Trojan ships; and, having lost them,
Just as thine eyes do, down stole a tear. —
Antiphila,
What would this wench do, if she were Aspatia?
Here she would stand, till some more pitying
god 41
Turned her to marble. (*To* OLYM.) 'Tis
enough,[2] my wench.
(*To* ANT.) Show me the piece of needlework
you wrought.
  Ant. Of Ariadne,[3] madam?
  Asp. Yes, that piece. — 45
This should be Theseus; h'as a cozening[4] face.—
You meant him for a man?
  Ant. He was so, madam.
  Asp. Why, then, 'tis well enough. — Never
look back;
You have a full wind and a false heart, The-
seus. — 50
Does not the story say his keel was split,
Or his masts spent, or some kind rock or other
Met with his vessel?
  Ant. Not as I remember.
  Asp. It should ha' been so. Could the gods
know this, 55
And not, of all their number, raise a storm?
But they are all as evil. (*Looking at the needle-
work*) This false smile
Was well expressed; just such another caught
me. —
(*To* THESEUS) You shall not go so. —
Antiphila, in this place work a quicksand, 60
And over it a shallow, smiling water,
And his ship ploughing it; and then a Fear:
Do that Fear to the life, wench.
  Ant. 'Twill wrong the story.
  Asp. 'Twill make the story, wronged by
wanton[5] poets, 65

Live long and be believed. But where's the
lady?
  Ant. There, madam.
  Asp. Fie, you have missed it here, Anti-
phila;
You are much mistaken, wench.
These colors are not dull and pale enough 70
To show a soul so full of misery
As this sad lady's was. Do it by me,[1]
Do it again by me, the lost Aspatia;
And you shall find all true but the wild island.[2]
Suppose I stand upon the sea-beach now, 75
Mine arms thus, and mine hair blown with the
wind,
Wild as that desert; and let all about me
Tell that I am forsaken. Do my face
(If thou hadst ever feeling of a sorrow)
Thus, thus, Antiphila: strive to make me look
Like Sorrow's monument; and the trees about
me, 81
Let them be dry and leafless; let the rocks
Groan with continual surges; and behind me
Make all a desolation. See, see, wenches,
A miserable life[3] of this poor picture! 85
  Olym. Dear madam!
  Asp. I have done. Sit down; and let us
Upon that point fix all our eyes, that point
there.
Make a dull silence, till you feel a sudden sad-
ness
Give us new souls. 90

Enter CALIANAX

  Cal. The King may do this, and he may not
do it:
My child is wronged, disgraced. — Well, how
now, huswives?
What, at your ease! is this a time to sit still?
Up, you young lazy whores, up, or I'll swinge
you!
  Olym. Nay, good my lord — 95
  Cal. You'll lie down shortly. Get you in,
and work!
What, are you grown so resty[4] you want heats?
We shall have some of the court-boys heat you
shortly.

---

[1] Dido, who fell in love with the Trojan hero, Aeneas,
on his stop at Carthage. He sailed away toward Italy
without reciprocating her love.
[2] I.e., I've done enough teasing.
[3] Daughter of Minos, King of Crete. She fled to
the island of Naxos with Theseus after he had slain the
Minotaur. There he deserted her.
[4] Deceitful. [5] Playful, light-hearted.

[1] Fashion it after me. [2] I.e., Naxos.
[3] Miserable living model. [4] Lazy, sluggish.

Ant. My lord, we do no more than we are
  charged:
It is the lady's pleasure we be thus;   100
In grief she is forsaken.
  Cal.   There's a rogue [1] too.
A young dissembling slave! — Well, get you
  in. —
I'll have a bout with that boy. 'Tis high
  time
Now to be valiant: I confess my youth   105
Was never prone that way. What, made an
  ass!
A court stale! [2] Well, I will be valiant,
And beat some dozen of these whelps; I will!
And there's another of 'em, a trim cheating
  soldier,[3]
I'll maul that rascal; h'as out-braved me
  twice: 110
But now, I thank the gods, I am valiant. —
Go, get you in. — I'll take a course with all.
                              (*Exeunt.*

ACT III

SCENE I. *The anteroom to* EVADNE'S
          bedchamber.

Enter CLEON, STRATO, *and* DIPHILUS

Cle. Your sister is not up yet.
  Diph. Oh, brides must take their morning's
rest; the night is troublesome.
  Stra. But not tedious.
  Diph. What odds, he has not my sister's   5
maidenhead tonight?
  Stra. None; it's odds against any bride-
groom living, he ne'er gets it while he lives.
  Diph. Y'are merry with my sister; you'll
please to allow me the same freedom with   10
your mother.
  Stra. She's at your service.
  Diph. Then she's merry enough of herself;
she needs no tickling. Knock at the door.
  Stra. We shall interrupt them.   15
  Diph. No matter; they have the year before
them. — Good morrow, sister. Spare yourself
today; the night will come again.

[1] I.e., Amintor.
[2] Laughing stock.
[3] I.e., Melantius.

Enter AMINTOR

  Amin. Who's there? my brother! I'm no
readier yet.[1] Your sister is but now up.   20
  Diph. You look as you had lost your eyes
tonight: I think you ha' not slept.
  Amin. I'faith I have not.
  Diph. You have done better, then.
  Amin. We ventured for a boy; when he is
  twelve,   25
A' shall command against the foes of Rhodes.
Shall we be merry?
  Stra. You cannot; you want sleep.
  Amin.   'Tis true; — (*aside*) but she,
As if she had drunk Lethe, or had made   30
Even with heaven, did fetch so still a sleep,
So sweet and sound ——
  Diph.   What's that?
  Amin.   Your sister frets
This morning, and does turn her eyes upon me,
As people on their headsman. She does chafe,
And kiss, and chafe again, and clap my cheeks!
She's in another world.
  Diph. Then I had lost: I was about to lay [2]
You had not got her maidenhead tonight.   40
  Amin. (*aside*). Ha! does he not mock me? —
          Y'ad lost indeed;
I do not use [3] to bungle.
  Cle.   You do deserve her.
  Amin. (*aside*). I laid my lips to hers, and
          that wild breath,
That was so rude and rough to me last night,
Was sweet as April. I'll be guilty too,   46
If these be the effects.

Enter MELANTIUS

  Mel. Good day, Amintor; for to me the name
Of brother is too distant: we are friends,
And that is nearer.   50
  Amin.   Dear Melantius!
Let me behold thee. Is it possible?
  Mel. What sudden gaze is this?
  Amin.   'Tis wondrous strange!
  Mel. Why does thine eye desire so strict
  a view   55

[1] I'm not yet any more fully dressed.
[2] Wager.
[3] I am not used.

Of that it knows so well? There's nothing here
That is not thine.

Amin.   I wonder much, Melantius,
To see those noble looks, that make me think
How virtuous thou art; and, on the sudden,
'Tis strange to me thou shouldst have worth
      and honor;   61
Or not be base, and false, and treacherous,
And every ill. But ——

Mel. (*at a loss to understand*). Stay,[1] stay,
      my friend;
I fear this sound will not become our loves.   65
No more; embrace me.

Amin.   Oh, mistake me not!
I know thee to be full of all those deeds
That we frail men call good; but by the course
Of nature thou shouldst be as quickly changed
As are the winds; dissembling as the sea,   71
That now wears brows as smooth as virgins' be,
Tempting the merchant to invade his face,
And in an hour calls his billows up,
And shoots 'em at the sun, destroying all   75
'A carries on him. (*Aside*) Oh, how near am I
To utter my sick thoughts.

Mel. But why, my friend, should I be so by
      nature?

Amin. I have wed thy sister, who has
      virtuous thoughts
Enough for one whole family; and it is strange
That you should feel no want.   81

Mel. Believe me, this is compliment too
      cunning for me.

Diph. What should I be then by the course
      of nature,
They having both robbed me of so much virtue?

Stra. Oh, call the bride, my Lord Amintor,
That we may see her blush, and turn her eyes
      down.   86
It is the prettiest sport!

Amin.   Evadne!

Evad. (*within*).   My lord?

Amin. Come forth, my love;   90
Your brothers do attend, to wish you joy.

Evad. (*within*). I am not ready[2] yet.

Amin.   Enough, enough.

Evad. (*within*). They'll mock me.   94

Amin.   Faith, thou shalt come in.

[1] Stop.
[2] Dressed.

Enter EVADNE

Mel. Good morrow, sister. He that under-
      stands
Whom you have wed need not to wish you
      joy;
You have enough: take heed you be not proud.

Diph. Oh, sister, what have you done?

Evad. I done! why, what have I done?   100

Stra. My Lord Amintor swears you are no
      maid now.

Evad. Pish!

Stra.   I' faith, he does.

Evad.   I knew I should be mocked.

Diph. With a truth.   105

Evad.   If 'twere to do again,
In faith I would not marry.

Amin. (*aside*). Nor I, by Heaven!

Diph.   Sister, Dula swears
She heard you cry two rooms off.   110

Evad.   Fie, how you talk.

Diph. Let's see you walk, Evadne. By my
      troth,
Y'are spoiled.

Mel. Amintor!

Amin. (*startled*). Ha!   115

Mel. Thou art sad.

Amin. Who, I? I thank you for that.
Shall Diphilus, thou and I sing a catch?[1]

Mel. How!

Amin. Prithee, let's.   120

Mel. Nay, that's too much the other way.

Amin. I'm so lightened with my happiness
— How dost thou, love? Kiss me.

Evad. I cannot love you; you tell tales of me.

Amin. Nothing but what becomes us. —
      Gentlemen,   125
Would you had all such wives, and all the
      world,
That I might be no wonder! Y'are all sad:
What, do you envy me? I walk, methinks,
On water, and ne'er sink, I am so light.

Mel. 'Tis well you are so.   130

Amin. "Well"! how can I be other,
When she looks thus? — Is there no music
      there?
Let's dance.

Mel.   Why, this is strange, Amintor!

[1] A popular song for three or more voices.

Amin. I do not know myself; yet I could
   wish   135
My joy were less.
  Diph. I'll marry too, if it will make one thus.
  Evad. Amintor, hark.
  Amin. What says my love? I must obey.
  Evad. (*aside*). You do it scurvily, 'twill be
   perceived.   140

Enter KING *and* LYSIPPUS

  Cleo. My lord, the King is here.
  Amin.   Where?
  Stra.   And his brother.
  King. Good morrow, all! —   144
Amintor, joy on joy fall thick upon thee! —
And, madam, you are altered since I saw you;
I must salute you; you are now another's.
How liked you your night's rest?
  Evad.   Ill, sir.
  Amin.   Indeed,
She took but little.   151
  Lys.   You'll let her take more,
And thank her too, shortly.
  King. Amintor, wert thou truly honest[1] till
Thou wert married?   155
  Amin.   Yes, sir.
  King.   Tell me, then, how shows
The sport unto thee?
  Amin.   Why, well.
  King.   What did you do?
  Amin. No more, nor less, than other couples
use;   161
You know what 'tis; it has but a coarse name.
  King. But, prithee, I should think, by her
   black eye,
And her red cheek, she should be quick[2] and
   stirring
In this same business; ha?   165
  Amin.   I cannot tell;
I ne'er tried other, sir; but I perceive
She is as quick as you delivered.[3]
  King. Well, you'll trust me then, Amintor,
   to choose
A wife for you again?   170
  Amin.   No, never, sir.
  King. Why, like you this so ill?
  Amin.   So well I like her.

[1] Chaste.   [2] Lively.   [3] Reported.

For this I bow my knee in thanks to you,
And unto Heaven will pay my grateful tribute
Hourly; and do hope we shall draw out   176
A long contented life together here,
And die both, full of gray hairs, in one day:
For which the thanks is yours. But, if the
   powers
That rule us please to call her first away,
Without pride spoke, this world holds not a
   wife   181
Worthy to take her room.
  King (*aside*). I do not like this. — All for-
   bear the room,
But you, Amintor, and your lady.
        (*Exeunt all but the* KING, AMINTOR,
          and EVADNE.
I have some speech with you, that may concern
Your after-living well.   186
  Amin. (*aside*). 'A will not tell me that he lies
   with her!
If he do, something heavenly stay my heart,
For I shall be apt to thrust this arm of mine
To acts unlawful!   190
  King.   You will suffer me
To talk with her, Amintor, and not have
A jealous pang?
  Amin.   Sir, I dare trust my wife
With whom she dares to talk, and not be
   jealous.   (*Retires.* 195
  King. How do you like Amintor?
  Evad.   As I did, sir.
  King. How's that?
  Evad. As one that, to fulfill your will and
   pleasure,   199
I have given leave to call me wife and love.
  King. I see there is no lasting faith in sin;
They that break word with heaven will break
   again
With all the world, and so dost thou with me.
  Evad. How, sir?   204
  King.   This subtle woman's ignorance
Will not excuse you: thou hast taken oaths,
So great, methought they did not well become
A woman's mouth, that thou wouldst ne'er
   enjoy
A man but me.
  Evad.   I never did swear so; 210
You do me wrong.
  King.   Day and night have heard it.

Evad. I swore indeed that I would never love
A man of lower place; but, if your fortune
Should throw you from this height, I bade you
    trust   215
I would forsake you, and would bend to him
That won your throne: I love with my ambi-
    tion,
Not with my eyes. But, if I ever yet
Touched any other, leprosy light here
Upon my face! which for your royalty   220
I would not stain!
    King. Why, thou dissemblest, and it is in me
To punish thee.
    Evad.   Why, it is in me, then,
Not to love you, which will more afflict   225
Your body than your punishment can mine.
    King. But thou hast let Amintor lie with
    thee.
    Evad. I ha' not.
    King.   Impudence! he says himself so.
    Evad. 'A lies.   230
    King.   'A does not.
    Evad.   By this light, he does,
Strangely and basely! and I'll prove it so:
I did not only shun him for a night,
But told him I would never close with him.
    King. Speak lower; 'tis false.   236
    Evad.   I am no man
To answer with a blow; or, if I were,
You are the King. But urge me not; 'tis most
    true.
    King. Do not I know the uncontrollèd
    thoughts   240
That youth brings with him, when his blood is
    high
With expectation and desire of that
He long hath waited for? Is not his spirit,
Though he be temperate, of a valiant strain
As this our age hath known? What could
    he do,   245
If such a sudden speech had met his blood,
But ruin thee forever, if he had not killed thee?
He could not bear it thus: he is as we,
Or any other wrongèd man.
    Evad.   It is dissembling.
    King. Take him! farewell: henceforth I am
    thy foe;   251
And what disgraces I can blot thee with look
for.

    Evad. Stay, sir! — Amintor! — You shall
    hear. — Amintor!
    Amin. (*coming forward*). What, my love?
    Evad. Amintor, thou hast an ingenious [1]
    look,   255
And shouldst be virtuous: it amazeth me
That thou canst make such base malicious lies!
    Amin. What, my dear wife?
    Evad.   "Dear wife!" I do despise thee.
Why, nothing can be baser than to sow   260
Dissension amongst lovers.
    Amin.   Lovers! who?
    Evad. The King and me —
    Amin.   Oh, God!
    Evad. Who should live long, and love with-
    out distaste,   265
Were it not for such pickthanks [2] as thyself.
Did you lie with me? Swear now, and be
    punished
In hell for this!
    Amin. (*aside*). The faithless sin I made
To fair Aspatia is not yet revenged;   270
It follows me. — I will not lose a word
To this vile woman: but to you, my King,
The anguish of my soul thrusts out this truth,
Y' are a tyrant! and not so much to wrong
An honest man thus, as to take a pride   275
In talking with him of it.
    Evad.   Now, sir, see
How loud this fellow lied!
    Amin. You that can know to wrong, should
    know how men
Must right themselves. What punishment is
    due   280
From me to him that shall abuse my bed?
Is it not death? nor can that satisfy,
Unless I show how nobly I have freed myself.
    King. Draw not thy sword; thou knowest I
    cannot fear
A subject's hand; but thou shalt feel the weight
Of this, if thou dost rage.   286
    Amin.   The weight of that!
If you have any worth, for heaven's sake, think
I fear not swords; for, as you are mere man,
I dare as easily kill you for this deed,   290
As you dare think to do it. But there is
Divinity about you, that strikes dead
My rising passions: as you are my king,

    [1] Ingenuous, innocent.   [2] Tattletales.

I fall before you, and present my sword
To cut mine own flesh, if it be your will.
Alas, I am nothing but a multitude   296
Of walking griefs!   Yet, should I murder you,
I might before the world take the excuse
Of madness: for, compare my injuries,
And they will well appear too sad a weight
For reason to endure: but, fall I first   301
Amongst my sorrows, ere my treacherous hand
Touch holy things!   But why (I know not
     what
I have to say), why did you choose out me
To make thus wretched?   There were thou-
     sands, fools   305
Easy to work on, and of state enough,
Within the island.
    Evad.   I would not have a fool;
It were no credit for me.   309
    Amin.   Worse and worse!
Thou, that darest talk unto thy husband thus,
Profess thyself a whore, and, more than so,
Resolve to be so still! — It is my fate
To bear and bow beneath a thousand griefs,
To keep that little credit with the world. —
But there were wise ones too; you might have
     ta'en   316
Another.
    King.   No: for I believed thee honest,[1]
As thou wert valiant.
    Amin.   All the happiness   320
Bestowed upon me turns into disgrace.
Gods, take your honesty again, for I
Am loaden with it! — Good my lord the King,
Be private[2] in it.   324
    King.   Thou mayst live, Amintor,
Free as thy king, if thou wilt wink at this,
And be a means that we may meet in secret.
    Amin. A bawd!   Hold, hold, my breast! A
     bitter curse
Seize me, if I forget not all respects[3]
That are religious, on another word   330
Sounded like that;[4] and through a sea of sins
Will wade to my revenge, though I should call
Pains here and after life upon my soul!
    King. Well, I am resolute[5] you lay not with
     her;
And so I leave you.   (*Exit.*   335

[1] Virtuous.   [2] Secret.   [3] Considerations.
[4] I.e., God.   [5] Convinced.

    Evad.   You must needs be prating;
And see what follows!
    Amin.   Prithee, vex me not:
Leave me; I am afraid some sudden start
Will pull a murther on me.   340
    Evad.   I am gone;
I love my life well.   (*Exit.*
    Amin.   I hate mine as much.
This 'tis to break a troth!   I should be glad,
If all this tide of grief would make me mad.
          (*Exit.*

SCENE 2. *A room in the royal palace.*

Enter MELANTIUS

    Mel.   I'll know the cause of all Amintor's
     griefs,
Or friendship shall be idle.[1]

Enter CALIANAX

    Cal.   O Melantius,
My daughter will die!
    Mel.   Trust me, I am sorry: 5
Would thou hadst ta'en her room![2]
    Cal.   Thou art a slave,
A cut-throat slave, a bloody treacherous slave!
    Mel. Take heed, old man; thou wilt be
     heard to rave,
And lose thine offices.   10
    Cal.   I am valiant grown
At all these years, and thou art but a slave!
    Mel. Leave!
Some company will come, and I respect   14
Thy years, not thee, so much, that I could wish
To laugh at thee alone.
    Cal.   I'll spoil your mirth:
I mean to fight with thee. (*Throwing his cloak
     aside, and drawing his sword*)   There
     lie, my cloak.
This was my father's sword, and he durst fight.
Are you prepared?   21
    Mel.   Why wilt thou dote thyself
Out of thy life?   Hence, get thee to bed,
Have careful looking-to, and eat warm things,
And trouble not me: my head is full of thoughts
More weighty than thy life or death can be.   26

[1] Be an empty term.
[2] Place.

Cal. You have a name in war, where you
    stand safe
Amongst a multitude; but I will try
What you dare do unto a weak old man
In single fight. You'll give ground, I fear. 30
Come, draw.
    Mel. I will not draw, unless thou pull'st thy
    death
Upon thee with a stroke. There's no one
    blow
That thou canst give hath strength enough to
    kill me.
Tempt me not so far, then: the power of earth
Shall not redeem thee.   36
    Cal. (*aside*).   I must let him alone:
He's stout and able; and, to say the truth,
However I may set a face and talk,
I am not valiant. When I was a youth,   40
I kept my credit with a testy trick [1]
I had 'mongst cowards, but durst never fight.
    Mel. I will not promise to preserve your life,
If you do stay.
    Cal. (*aside*). I would give half my land 45
That I durst fight with that proud man a
    little.
If I had men to hold him, I would beat him
Till he asked me mercy.
    Mel.   Sir, will you be gone?
    Cal. (*aside*). I dare not stay; but I will go
    home and beat   50
My servants all over for this.   (*Exit.*
    Mel.   This old fellow haunts me;
But the distracted carriage of mine Amintor
Takes deeply on me. I will find the cause:
I fear his conscience cries he wronged Aspatia.

Enter AMINTOR

    Amin. (*aside*). Men's eyes are not so subtle
    to perceive   56
My inward misery: I bear my grief
Hid from the world. How art thou wretched
    then?
For aught I know, all husbands are like me,
And every one I talk with of his wife   60
Is but a well dissembler of his woes,
As I am. Would I knew it! for the rareness
Afflicts me now.

    [1] A trick of showing testiness, of being easily angered.

    Mel.   Amintor, we have not
Enjoyed our friendship of late, for we were wont
To change [1] our souls in talk.   66
    Amin. Melantius, I can tell thee
A good jest of Strato and a lady the last day.
    Mel. How was't?
    Amin.   Why, such an odd one!   70
    Mel.   I have longed
To speak with you; not of an idle jest
That's forced, but of matters you are bound to
    utter to me.
    Amin. What is that, my friend?
    Mel.   I have observed your words 75
Fall from your tongue
Wildly; and all your carriage
Like one that strove to shew his merry mood,
When he were ill disposed. You were not wont
To put such scorn into your speech, or wear 80
Upon your face ridiculous jollity.
Some sadness sits here, which your cunning
    would
Cover o'er with smiles, and 'twill not be.
What is it?
    Amin. A sadness here! What cause 85
Can fate provide for me to make me so?
Am I not loved through all this isle? The King
Rains greatness on me. Have I not received
A lady to my bed, that in her eye
Keeps mounting fire, and on her tender cheeks
Inevitable [2] color, in her heart   91
A prison for all virtue? Are not you,
Which is above all joys, my constant friend?
What sadness can I have? No; I am light, 94
And feel the courses of my blood more warm
And stirring than they were. Faith, marry too;
And you will feel so unexpressed [3] a joy
In chaste embraces that you will indeed
Appear another.
    Mel.   You may shape, Amintor, 100
Causes to cozen [4] the whole world withal,
And yourself too; but 'tis not like a friend
To hide your soul from me. 'Tis not your
    nature
To be thus idle. I have seen you stand 104
As you were blasted 'midst of all your mirth,
Call thrice aloud, and then start, feigning joy
So coldly! — World, what do I here? A friend

    [1] Exchange, communicate.   [2] Irresistible.
    [3] Inexpressible.   [4] Deceive.

Is nothing.   Heaven, I would ha' told that man
My secret sins! I'll search an unknown land,
And there plant friendship; all is withered here.
Come with a compliment! [1]   I would have
  fought,   111
Or told my friend 'a lied, ere soothed [2] him so.—
Out of my bosom! [3]

 Amin. But there is nothing.

 Mel. Worse and worse! farewell: 115
From this time have acquaintance, but no
  friend.

 Amin. Melantius, stay: you shall know what
  that is.

 Mel. See, how you played with friendship!
  be advised [4]
How you give cause unto yourself to say
You ha' lost a friend.   120

 Amin. Forgive what I ha' done;
For I am so o'ergone with injuries
Unheard of, that I lose consideration
Of what I ought to do, — Oh! — Oh!

 Mel. Do not weep. What is't? 125
May I once but know the man
Hath turned my friend thus!

 Amin. I had spoke at first,
But that —

 Mel. But what? 130

 Amin. I held it most unfit
For you to know. Faith, do not know it yet.

 Mel. Thou see'st my love, that will keep
  company
With thee in tears; hide nothing, then, from me;
For when I know the cause of thy distemper,
With mine old armor I'll adorn myself, 136
My resolution, and cut through thy foes,
Unto thy quiet, till I place thy heart
As peaceable as spotless innocence.
What is it?   140

 Amin. Why, 'tis this — it is too big
To get out — let my tears make way awhile.

 Mel. Punish me strangely, heaven, if he
  scape
Of life or fame, that brought this youth to this!

 Amin. Your sister —   145

 Mel. Well said.

 Amin. You'll wish't unknown,
When you have heard it.

[1] Act with ceremonious expression!
[2] Humbugged. [3] Confidence. [4] Warned.

 Mel. No.

 Amin. Is much to blame, 150
And to the King has given her honor up,
And lives in whoredom with him.

 Mel. How is this?
Thou art run mad with injury indeed;
Thou couldst not utter this else. Speak again;
For I forgive it freely; tell thy griefs. 156

 Amin. She's wanton: I am loath to say, a
  whore,
Though it be true.

 Mel. Speak yet again, before mine anger
  grow
Up beyond throwing down: what are thy griefs?

 Amin. By all our friendship, these. 161

 Mel. What, am I tame?
After mine actions, shall the name of friend
Blot all our family, and stick the brand
Of whore upon my sister, unrevenged? 165
My shaking flesh, be thou a witness for me,
With what unwillingness I go to scourge
This railer, whom my folly hath called friend!—
I will not take these basely: thy sword 169
    (*Draws his sword.*
Hangs near thy hand; draw it, that I may whip
Thy rashness to repentance; draw thy sword!

 Amin. Not on thee, did thine anger go as
  high
As troubled waters. Thou shouldst do me ease
Here and eternally, if thy noble hand
Would cut me from my sorrows. 175

 Mel. This is base
And fearful.[1] They that use to utter lies
Provide not blows but words to qualify [2]
The men they wronged. Thou hast a guilty
  cause.

 Amin. Thou pleasest me; for so much more
  like this   180
Will raise my anger up above my griefs,
(Which is a passion easier to be borne,)
And I shall then be happy.

 Mel. Take, then, more
To raise thine anger: 'tis mere cowardice 185
Makes thee not draw; and I will leave thee
  dead,
However. But if thou art so much pressed
With guilt and fear as not to dare to fight,

[1] Cowardly.
[2] Moderate.

I'll make thy memory loathed, and fix a
　　scandal
Upon thy name forever.　　　　　　　　190
　　Amin. (*drawing his sword*). Then I draw,
As justly as our magistrates their swords
To cut offenders off. I knew before
'Twould grate your ears; but it was base in you
To urge a weighty secret from your friend, 195
And then rage at it. I shall be at ease,
If I be killed; and, if you fall by me,
I shall not long outlive you.
　　Mel.　　　　　　　　　　Stay awhile.
(*Aside*) The name of friend is more than family,
Or all the world besides: I was a fool.　201
Thou searching human nature, that didst wake
To do me wrong, thou art inquisitive,
And thrustest me upon questions that will take
My sleep away! Would I had died, ere known
This sad dishonor! — Pardon me, my friend!
　　　　　　　　　　(*Sheathes his sword.*
If thou wilt strike, here is a faithful heart;
Pierce it, for I will never heave my hand
To thine. Behold the power thou hast in me!
I do believe my sister is a whore,　　　210
A leprous one. Put up thy sword, young man.
　　Amin. How should I bear it, then, she being
　　　　so?
I fear, my friend, that you will lose me shortly;
　　　　　　　　　　(*Sheathes his sword.*
And I shall do a foul act on myself,
Through these disgraces.　　　　　　215
　　Mel.　　　　　　　Better half the land
Were buried quick [1] together. No, Amintor;
Thou shalt have ease. Oh, this adulterous
　　　King,
That drew her to't! Where got he the spirit
To wrong me so?　　　　　　　　220
　　Amin.　　　　What is it, then, to me,
If it be wrong to you?
　　Mel.　　　　　　Why, not so much.
The credit of our house is thrown away.
But from his iron den I'll waken Death, 225
And hurl him on this King. My honesty [2]
Shall steel my sword; and on its horrid [3] point
I'll wear my cause, that shall amaze the eyes
Of this proud man, and be too glittering
For him to look on.　　　　　　　230
　　Amin.　　　I have quite undone my fame.
　　[1] Alive.　　[2] Virtue.　　[3] Bristling.

　　Mel. Dry up thy watery eyes,
And cast a manly look upon my face;
For nothing is so wild as I, thy friend,
Till I have freed thee. Still this swelling breast
I go thus from thee, and will never cease 23
My vengeance till I find thy heart at peace.
　　Amin. It must not be so. Stay. (*Aside*
　　　Mine eyes would tell
How loth I am to this; but, love and tears,
Leave me awhile! for I have hazarded　24
All that this world calls happy. — Thou has
　　　wrought
A secret from me, under name of friend,
Which art could ne'er have found nor tortur
　　　wrung
From out my bosom. Give it me again;
For I will find it, wheresoe'er it lies,　　24
Hid in the mortal'st part. Invent a way
To give it back.
　　Mel.　　　　Why would you have it back
I will to death pursue him with revenge.
　　Amin. Therefore I call it back from thee
　　　for I know　　　　　　　　　25
Thy blood so high, that thou wilt stir in this,
And shame me to posterity. Take to th
　　　weapon!　　　　　(*Draws his sword*
　　Mel. Hear thy friend, that bears more year
　　　than thou.
　　Amin. I will not hear: but draw, or I —
　　Mel.　　　　　　　　Amintor! 25
　　Amin. Draw, then; for I am full as resolut
As fame and honor can enforce me be:
I cannot linger. Draw!
　　Mel. (*drawing his sword*). I do. But is no
My share of credit equal [hurt] with thine,
If I do stir?　　　　　　　　　26
　　Amin.　　　No; for it will be called
Honor in thee to spill thy sister's blood,
If she her birth abuse, and on the King
A brave revenge; but on me, that have walked
With patience in it, it will fix the name　26
Of fearful cuckold. Oh, that word! Be quick
　　Mel. Then, join with me.
　　Amin.　　　　　I dare not do a sin
Or else I would. Be speedy.　　　27
　　Mel. Then, dare not fight with me; for that'
　　　a sin.
(*Aside*) His grief distracts him. — Call th
　　　thoughts again,

And to thyself pronounce the name of friend,
And see what that will work. I will not
    fight.
  Amin. You must.   275
  Mel. (*sheathing*). I will be killed first.
    Though my passions
Offered the like to you, 'tis not this earth
Shall buy my reason to it. Think awhile,
For you are (I must weep when I speak that)
Almost beside yourself.   280
  Amin. (*sheathing*). Oh, my soft temper!
So many sweet words from thy sister's mouth,
I am afraid would make me take her to
Embrace, and pardon her. I am mad in-
    deed,
And know not what I do. Yet have a care
Of me in what thou dost.   286
  Mel.   Why, thinks my friend
I will forget his honor? or, to save
The bravery of our house, will lose his fame,
And fear to touch the throne of majesty?
  Amin. A curse will follow that; but rather
    live   291
And suffer with me.
  Mel.   I will do what worth
Shall bid me, and no more.
  Amin.   Faith, I am sick,
And desperately, I hope; yet, leaning thus, 296
I feel a kind of ease.
  Mel.   Come, take again
Your mirth about you.
  Amin.   I shall never do't.
  Mel. I warrant you; look up; we'll walk
    together;   301
Put thine arm here; all shall be well again.
  Amin. Thy love (Oh, wretched!) ay, thy
    love, Melantius;
Why, I have nothing else.
  Mel.   Be merry, then. (*Exeunt.*

Enter MELANTIUS *again*

  Mel. This worthy young man may do
    violence   306
Upon himself; but I have cherished him
As well as I could, and sent him smiling from
    me,
To counterfeit again. Sword, hold thine edge;
My heart will never fail me. —   310

Enter DIPHILUS

            Diphilus!
Thou com'st as sent.[1]
  Diph.   Yonder has been such laughing.
  Mel. Betwixt whom?
  Diph.   Why, our sister and the King;
I thought their spleens would break; they
    laughed us all   316
Out of the room.
  Mel. They must weep, Diphilus.
  Diph.   Must they?
  Mel.   They must.
Thou art my brother; and, if I did believe 321
Thou hadst a base thought, I would rip it
    out,
Lie where it durst.
  Diph.   You should not; I would first
Mangle myself and find it.   325
  Mel.   That was spoke
According to our strain.[2] Come, join thy hands,
And swear a firmness to what project I
Shall lay before thee.   329
  Diph.   You do wrong us both;
People hereafter shall not say there passed
A bond, more than our loves, to tie our lives
And deaths together.
  Mel. It is as nobly said as I would wish.
Anon I'll tell you wonders: we are wronged.
  Diph. But, I will tell you now, we'll right
    ourselves.   336
  Mel. Stay not: prepare the armor in my
    house;
And what friends you can draw unto our
    side,
Not knowing of the cause, make ready too.
Haste, Diphilus, the time requires it, haste! —
           (*Exit* DIPHILUS.
I hope my cause is just; I know my blood 341
Tells me it is; and I will credit it.
To take revenge, and lose myself withal,
Were idle,[3] and to scape impossible,
Without I had the fort, which (misery!)
Remaining in the hands of my old enemy 346
Calianax — but I must have it. See
Where he comes shaking by me!

---

[1] As if sent for.
[2] Our heritage.
[3] Foolish.

Enter CALIANAX, *passing across the stage*

                          Good my lord,
Forget your spleen to me: I never wronged you,
But would have peace with every man.   351
   Cal. (stopping).   'Tis well;
If I durst fight, your tongue would lie at quiet.
   Mel. Y'are touchy without all cause.
   Cal.   Do, mock me.
   Mel. By mine honor, I speak truth.   356
   Cal.   Honor! where is't?
   Mel. See, what starts [1] you make
Into your idle hatred, to [2] my love
And freedom to [3] you. I come with resolution
To obtain a suit of you.   361
   Cal.   A suit of me!
(Sarcastically) 'Tis very like it should be
   granted, sir.
   Mel. Nay, go not hence.   364
'Tis this: you have the keeping of the fort,
And I would wish you, by the love you ought
To bear unto me, to deliver it
Into my hands.
   Cal.   I am in hope thou art mad,
To talk to me thus.   370
   Mel.   But there is a reason
To move you to it: I would kill the King,
That wronged you and your daughter.
   Cal.   Out, traitor!
   Mel. Nay, but stay: I cannot scape, the deed
   once done,   375
Without I have this fort.
   Cal.   And should I help thee?
Now thy treacherous mind betrays itself.
   Mel. (drawing his sword). Come, delay me
   not;
Give me a sudden answer, or already   380
Thy last is spoke! Refuse not offered love
When it comes clad in secrets.
   Cal. (aside).   If I say
I will not, he will kill me; I do see't   384
Writ in his looks; and should I say I will,
He'll run and tell the King. — I do not shun
Your friendship, dear Melantius; but this cause
Is weighty: give me but an hour to think.
   Mel. (sheathing his sword). Take it.
(Aside) I know this goes unto the King;   390
But I am armed.   *(Exit.*

   [1] Sallies.   [2] Against.   [3] For.

   Cal.   Methinks I feel myself
But twenty now again. This fighting fool
Wants policy.[1] I shall revenge my girl,   394
And make her red [2] again. I pray my legs
Will last that pace that I will carry them:
I shall want breath before I find the King.
                         (Exit.

ACT IV

SCENE I. EVADNE'S *chamber in the royal
palace.*

Enter MELANTIUS *to* EVADNE *and her ladies*

   Mel. Save you!
   Evad.   Save you, sweet brother.
   Mel. In my blunt eye, methinks, you look,
   Evadne —
   Evad. Come, you would make me blush.
   Mel.   I would, Evadne;   5
I shall displease my ends else.
   Evad.   You shall, if you
Commend me; I am bashful. Come, sir, how do
I look?   9
   Mel. I would not have your women hear me
Break into commendation of you; 'tis not
Seemly.
   Evad. Go, wait me in the gallery.
                      (Exeunt ladies.
Now speak.
   Mel. I'll lock the door first. *(Locks the door.*
   Evad.   Why?   16
   Mel. I will not have your gilded things,
   that dance
In visitation with their Milan skins,[3]
Choke up my business.
   Evad. You are strangely disposed, sir.   20
   Mel. Good madam, not to make you merry.
   Evad. No; if you praise me, 'twill make me
   sad.
   Mel. Such a sad commendation I have for
   you.
   Evad. Brother, the court hath made you
   witty,
And learn to riddle.   25

   [1] Lacks craft.   [2] Red-cheeked, healthy.
   [3] I.e., perfumed skins. — A figurative usage suggested
by the fact that fashionable gloves or "skins" often
came from Milan and were perfumed.

Mel. I praise the court for't: has it learned [1]
   you nothing?
Evad. Me!
Mel.   Ay, Evadne; thou art young and
   handsome,
A lady of a sweet complexion,
And such a flowing carriage,[2] that it cannot   30
Choose but inflame a kingdom.
  Evad.   Gentle brother!
Mel. 'Tis yet in thy repentance, foolish
   woman,
To make me gentle.
  Evad.   How is this?   35
Mel.   'Tis base;
And I could blush, at these years, through all
My honored scars, to come to such a parley.
  Evad. I understand ye not.
Mel.   Ye dare not, fool!   40
They that commit thy faults fly the remem-
   brance.
  Evad. My faults, sir! I would have you
   know, I care not
If they were written here, here in my forehead.
  Mel. Thy body is too little for the story,
The lusts of which would fill another woman,
Though she had twins within her.[3]   46
  Evad.   This is saucy:
Look you intrude no more; there lies your way.
  Mel. Thou art my way, and I will tread
   upon thee,
Till I find truth out.   50
  Evad.   What truth is that you look for?
  Mel. Thy long-lost honor. Would the gods
   had set me
Rather to grapple with the plague, or stand
One of their loudest bolts!   Come, tell me
   quickly,
Do it without enforcement, and take heed   55
You swell me not above my temper.
  Evad.   How, sir!
Where got you this report?
  Mel.   Where there was people,
In every place.   60
  Evad.   They and the seconds of it
Are base people: believe them not: they lied.

---

[1] Taught.   [2] Graceful bearing.
[3] The record of thy lusts would cover with writing
not only thy body, but another woman's whole body
too, even if it were distended by her bearing of twins.

Mel. Do not play with mine anger, do not,
   wretch!   (*Takes hold of her*.
I come to know that desperate fool that drew
   thee
From thy fair life: be wise, and lay him open.
  Evad. Unhand me, and learn manners! such
   another   66
Forgetfulness forfeits your life.
  Mel. Quench me this mighty humor,[1] and
   then tell me
Whose whore you are; for you are one, I
   know it.
Let all mine honors perish but I'll find him,   70
Though he lie locked up in thy blood!   Be
   sudden;
There is no facing it; [2] and be not flattered.
The burnt air, when the Dog [3] reigns, is not
   fouler
Than thy contagious name, till thy repentance
(If the gods grant thee any) purge thy sickness.
  Evad. Begone! you are my brother; that's
   your safety.   76
  Mel. I'll be a wolf first: 'tis, to be thy
   brother,
An infamy below the sin of coward.
I am as far from being part of thee
As thou art from thy virtue: seek a kindred   80
'Mongst sensual beasts, and make a goat thy
   brother;
A goat is cooler. Will you tell me yet?
  Evad. If you stay here and rail thus, I shall
   tell you
I'll ha' you whipped.   Get you to your com-
   mand,
And there preach to your sentinels, and tell
   them   85
What a brave man you are: I shall laugh at you.
  Mel. Y'are grown a glorious whore! Where
   be your fighters?
What mortal fool durst raise thee to this daring,
And I alive! By my just sword, h'ad safer
Bestrid a billow when the angry north   90
Ploughs up the sea, or made Heaven's fire his
   foe!
Work me no higher. Will you discover yet?

---

[1] Cease this high-handed attitude.
[2] No bluffing it out.
[3] The Dog Star, Sirius, supposed to cause the heat
of midsummer dog days.

Evad. The fellow's mad. Sleep, and speak
　　sense.

Mel. Force my swoln heart no further;
　　I would save thee.
Your great maintainers are not here; they dare
　　not.　　　　　　　　　　　　　　　　95
Would they were all, and armed! I would
　　speak loud;
Here's one should thunder to 'em. Will you
　　tell me?
Thou hast no hope to scape. He that dares
　　most,
And damns away his soul to do thee service,
Will sooner snatch meat from a hungry lion
Than come to rescue thee. Thou hast death
　　about thee.　　　　　　　　　　　　101
H'as undone thine honor, poisoned thy virtue,
And, of a lovely rose, left thee a canker.[1]

Evad. Let me consider.

Mel. 　　　　Do, whose child thou wert,
Whose honor thou hast murdered, whose grave
　　opened,　　　　　　　　　　　　106
And so pulled on the gods that, in their justice,
They must restore him flesh again, and life,
And raise his dry bones to revenge this scandal.

Evad. The gods are not of my mind; they
　　had better　　　　　　　　　　　110
Let 'em lie sweet still in the earth; they'll stink
　　here.

Mel. Do you raise mirth out of my easiness?
Forsake me, then, all weaknesses of nature
That make men women. Speak, you whore,
　　speak truth,　　(*Draws his sword.* 114
Or, by the dear soul of thy sleeping father,
This sword shall be thy lover. Tell, or I'll kill
　　thee;
And, when thou hast told all, thou wilt de-
　　serve it.

Evad. You will not murder me?

Mel. No; 'tis a justice, and a noble one, 119
To put the light out of such base offenders.

Evad. (*calling*). Help!

Mel. By thy foul self, no human help shall
　　help thee,
If thou criest! When I have killed thee, as I
Have vowed to do, if thou confess not, naked
As thou hast left thine honor will I leave
　　thee,　　　　　　　　　　　　　125

[1] A dog-rose, a wild-rose.

That on thy branded flesh the world may read
Thy black shame and my justice. Wilt thou
　　bend yet?

Evad. Yes.

Mel. 　　Up, and begin your story.　　129

Evad. 　　　　Oh, I am miserable!

Mel. 'Tis true, thou art. Speak truth still.

Evad. I have offended: noble sir, forgive
　　me!

Mel. With what secure slave?

Evad. 　　　　　Do not ask me, sir;
Mine own remembrance is a misery　　135
Too mighty for me.

Mel. 　　　　　Do not fall back again:
My sword's unsheathed yet.

Evad. 　　　　　What shall I do? 139

Mel. Be true, and make your fault less.

Evad. 　　　　　　I dare not tell.

Mel. Tell, or I'll be this day a-killing thee.

Evad. Will you forgive me, then?

Mel. Stay; I must ask mine honor first.
I have too much foolish nature in me:　　145
Speak.

Evad. Is there none else here?

Mel. None but a fearful conscience; that's
　　too many.
Who is't?

Evad. Oh, hear me gently! It was the King.

Mel. No more. — (*Sheathing his sword*) My
　　worthy father's and my services　　151
Are liberally rewarded! King, I thank thee!
For all my dangers and my wounds thou hast
　　paid me
In my own metal: these are soldiers' thanks! —
How long have you lived thus, Evadne?　155

Evad. 　　　　　　Too long.

Mel. Too late you find it. Can you be very
　　sorry?

Evad. Would I were half as blameless!

Mel. Evadne, thou wilt to thy trade again.

Evad. First to my grave.　　　　　　160

Mel. 　　Would gods thou hadst been so blest!
Dost thou not hate this King now? Prithee
　　hate him:
Couldst thou not curse him? I command thee,
　　curse him;
Curse till the gods hear, and deliver him
To thy just wishes. Yet I fear, Evadne, 165
You had rather play your game out.

Evad.   No; I feel
Too many sad confusions here, to let in
Any loose flame hereafter.
    Mel. Dost thou not feel, amongst all those,
        one brave anger,   170
That breaks out nobly, and directs thine arm
To kill this base King?
    Evad.   All the gods forbid it!
    Mel. No, all the gods require it; they are
Dishonored in him.   175
    Evad. 'Tis too fearful.
    Mel. Y'are valiant in his bed, and bold
        enough
To be a stale whore, and have your madam's
        name
Discourse for grooms and pages; and hereafter,
When his cool majesty hath laid you by,   180
To be at pension with some needy sir
For meat and coarser clothes: thus far you
        know
No fear.   Come, you shall kill him.
    Evad.   Good sir!
    Mel. An 'twere to kiss him dead, thou'dst
        smother him: 185
Be wise, and kill him.   Canst thou live, and
        know
What noble minds shall make thee, see thyself
Found out with every finger, made the shame
Of all successions,[1] and in this great ruin
Thy brother and thy noble husband broken?
Thou shalt not live thus.   Kneel, and swear to
        help me,   191
When I shall call thee to it; or, by all
Holy in heaven and earth, thou shalt not live
To breathe a full hour longer; not a thought!
Come, 'tis a righteous oath.   Give me thy hands,
And, both to heaven held up, swear, by that
        wealth   196
This lustful thief stole from thee, when I say it,
To let his foul soul out.
    Evad.   Here I swear it;   (*Kneels.*
And, all you spirits of abusèd ladies,   200
Help me in this performance!
    Mel. (*raising her*). Enough.   This must be
        known to none
But you and I, Evadne; not to your lord,
Though he be wise and noble, and a fellow
Dares step as far into a worthy action   205

    [1] Succeeding generations.

As the most daring, ay, as far as justice.
Ask me not why.   Farewell.   (*Exit.*
    Evad. Would I could say so to my black
        disgrace!
Oh, where have I been all this time?   How
        friended,
That I should lose myself thus desperately,   210
And none for pity show me how I wandered?
There is not in the compass of the light
A more unhappy creature: sure, I am mon-
        strous;
For I have done those follies, those mad mis-
        chiefs,
Would dare[1] a woman.   Oh, my loaded soul,
Be not so cruel to me; choke not up   216
The way to my repentance!

Enter AMINTOR

                        Oh, my lord!
    Amin. How now?
    Evad. My much-abusèd lord!   (*Kneels.*
    Amin.   This cannot be!   221
    Evad. I do not kneel to live; I dare not
        hope it;
The wrongs I did are greater.   Look upon me,
Though I appear with all my faults.
    Amin.   Stand up.   225
This is a new way to beget more sorrow:
Heaven knows I have too many.   Do not
        mock me:
Though I am tame, and bred up with my
        wrongs,   228
Which are my foster-brothers, I may leap,
Like a hand-wolf,[2] into my natural wildness,
And do an outrage: prithee, do not mock me.
    Evad. My whole life is so leprous, it infects
All my repentance.   I would buy your pardon,
Though at the highest set, even with my life —
That slight contrition, that's no sacrifice   235
For what I have committed.
    Amin.   Sure, I dazzle;[3]
There cannot be a faith in that foul woman
That knows no god more mighty than her
        mischiefs.
Thou dost still worse, still number on thy
        faults,   240

    [1] Daunt, frighten.   [2] Tame wolf.
    [3] I am become confused.

To press my poor heart thus.   Can I believe
There's any seed of virtue in that woman
Left to shoot up, that dares go on in sin
Known, and so known as thine is? Oh, Evadne!
Would there were any safety [1] in thy sex,   245
That I might put a thousand sorrows off,
And credit thy repentance! but I must not.
Thou hast brought me to that dull calamity,
To that strange misbelief of all the world
And all things that are in it, that I fear   250
I shall fall like a tree, and find my grave,
Only rememb'ring that I grieve.
    Evad.   My Lord,
Give me your griefs; you are an innocent,   254
A soul as white as Heaven; let not my sins
Perish your noble youth.   I do not fall here
To shadow,[2] by dissembling with my tears
(As all say women can) or to make less
What my hot will hath done, which Heaven
    and you
Know to be tougher than the hand of time   260
Can cut from man's remembrance; no, I do not;
I do appear the same, the same Evadne,
Dressed in the shames I lived in, the same
    monster.
But these are names of honor to [3] what I am;
I do present myself the foulest creature,   265
Most poisonous, dangerous, and despised of
    men,
Lerna [4] e'er bred, or Nilus.[5]   I am hell,
Till you, my dear lord, shoot your light into
    me,
The beams of your forgiveness; I am soul-sick,
And wither with the fear of one condemned,
Till I have got your pardon.   271
    Amin.   Rise, Evadne.
Those heavenly powers that put this good into
    thee
Grant a continuance of it!   I forgive thee:
Make thyself worthy of it; and take heed,
Take heed, Evadne, this be serious.   276
Mock not the powers above, that can and dare
Give thee a great example of their justice

[1] Any quality of giving confidence.
[2] I do not come here to obscure.
[3] In comparison with.
[4] The lake or swamp near Argos in southern Greece,
where the Hydra, the monster with nine heads, lived.
[5] The Nile River in Egypt.

To all ensuing eyes, if thou play'st
With thy repentance, the best sacrifice.   280
    Evad. I have done nothing good to win belief,
My life hath been so faithless. All the creatures
Made for Heaven's honors have their ends, and
    good ones,
All but the cozening crocodiles, false women.
They reign here like those plagues, those killing
    sores,   285
Men pray against; and, when they die, like tales
Ill told and unbelieved, they pass away
And go to dust forgotten. But, my lord,
Those short days I shall number to my rest
(As many must not see me) shall, though too
    late,   290
Though in my evening, yet perceive I will,
Since I can do no good, because a woman,
Reach constantly at something that is near it.
I will redeem one minute of my age,
Or, like another Niobe,[1] I'll weep,   295
Till I am water.
    Amin.   I am now dissolved;
My frozen soul melts.   May each sin thou
    hast
Find a new mercy!   Rise; I am at peace.
Hadst thou been thus, thus excellently good,
Before that devil-king tempted thy frailty,   301
Sure thou hadst made a star.   Give me thy
    hand:
From this time I will know thee; and, as far
As honor gives me leave, be thy Amintor.   304
When we meet next, I will salute thee fairly,
And pray the gods to give thee happy days.
My charity shall go along with thee,
Though my embraces must be far from thee.
I should ha' killed thee, but this sweet re-
    pentance
Locks up my vengeance: for which thus I kiss
    thee —   310
The last kiss we must take: and would to
    Heaven
The holy priest that gave our hands together
Had given us equal virtues!   Go, Evadne.

[1] Mythological queen of Thebes, whose pride in her
numerous children prompted an ungracious comparison
of herself with the goddess Leto who had only two.
The latter, Apollo and Artemis, proceeded to avenge
their mother by slaying all Niobe's children. Zeus
completed the punishment by turning Niobe into stone,
in which form she still wept over her loss.

The gods thus part our bodies.   Have a care
My honor falls no farther: I am well, then.   315
    Evad.   All the dear joys here, and above
       hereafter,
Crown thy fair soul!   Thus I take leave, my
       lord;
And never shall you see the foul Evadne,
Till she have tried all honored means that may
Set her in rest and wash her stains away.   320
                      (*Exeunt.*

SCENE 2.   *A hall in the royal palace.*
Hautboys[1] *play within.   A banquet discovered.*[2]

    Enter the KING *and* CALIANAX

    King.   I cannot tell how I should credit this
From you, that are his enemy.
    Cal.   I am sure
He said it to me; and I'll justify it
What way he dares oppose — but[3] with my
       sword.   5
    King.   But did he break, without all circum-
       stance,[4]
To you, his foe, that he would have the fort,
To kill me, and then scape?
    Cal.   If he deny it,
I'll make him blush.   10
    King.   It sounds incredibly.
    Cal.   Ay, so does everything I say of late.
    King.   Not so, Calianax.
    Cal.   Yes, I should sit
Mute, whilst a rogue with strong arms cuts
       your throat.   15
    King.   Well, I will try him; and, if this be true,
I'll pawn my life I'll find it; if't be false,
And that[5] you clothe your hate in such a lie,
You shall hereafter dote in your own house,
Not in the court.   20
    Cal.   Why, if it be a lie,
Mine ears are false, for I'll be sworn I heard it.
Old men are good for nothing; you were best
Put me to death for hearing, and free him
For meaning it.   You would ha' trusted me   25
Once; but the time is altered.

   [1] Oboes.
   [2] I.e., the curtains are drawn apart to show on the
inner stage a table set out with a banquet.
   [3] Except.
   [4] Did he broach the subject, without any occasion.
   [5] If.

    King.   And will still,
Where I may do with justice to the world.
You have no witness?
    Cal.   Yes, myself.   30
    King.   No more,
I mean, there were that heard it?
    Cal.   How? no more?
Would you have more?   Why, am not I enough
To hang a thousand rogues?   35
    King.   But so you may
Hang honest men too, if you please.
    Cal.   I may!
'Tis like I will do so: there are a hundred
Will swear it for a need too, if I say it.   40
    King.   Such witnesses we need not.
    Cal.   And 'tis hard
If my word cannot hang a boisterous knave.
    King.   Enough. — (*Calling*) Where's Strato?

           Enter STRATO

    Stra.   Sir?   45
    King.   Why, where's all the company?   Call
       Amintor in;
Evadne.   Where's my brother? and Melantius?
Bid him come too; and Diphilus.   Call all
That are without there.   (*Exit* STRATO.) — If
       he should desire
The combat of you, 'tis not in the power   50
Of all our laws to hinder it, unless
We mean to quit[1] 'em.
    Cal.   Why, if you do think
'Tis fit an old man and a councillor   54
To fight for what he says, then you may grant it.

Enter AMINTOR, EVADNE, MELANTIUS, DIPHI-
     LUS, LYSIPPUS, CLEON, STRATO, *and*
     DIAGORAS

    King.   Come, sirs! — Amintor, thou art yet
       a bridegroom,
And I will use thee so; thou shalt sit down. —
Evadne, sit; — and you, Amintor, too;
This banquet is for you, sir. — Who has
       brought
A merry tale about him, to raise laughter   60
Amongst our wine?   Why, Strato, where art
       thou?

   [1] Abandon.

Thou wilt chop out [1] with them unseasonably,
When I desire 'em not.

Stra.   'Tis my ill luck, sir, so to spend them,
then.

King.   Reach me a bowl of wine. — Melan-
tius, thou   65
Art sad.

Amin.   I should be, sir, the merriest here,
But I ha' ne'er a story of mine own
Worth telling at this time.

King.   Give me the wine. —   70
Melantius, I am now considering
How easy 'twere for any man we trust
To poison one of us in such a bowl.

Mel.   I think it were not hard, sir, for a knave.

Cal. (*aside*).   Such as you are.   75

King.   I' faith, 'twere easy.   It becomes us
well
To get plain-dealing men about ourselves,
Such as you all are here. — Amintor, to thee;
And to thy fair Evadne!   (*Drinks.*

Mel. (*apart to* CAL.).   Have you thought   80
Of this, Calianax?

Cal.   Yes, marry, have I.

Mel.   And what's your resolution?

Cal.   Ye shall have it,
Soundly, I warrant you.   85

King.   Reach to Amintor, Strato.

Amin.   Here, my love;
            (*Drinks, and then hands the cup to*
            EVADNE.
This wine will do thee wrong, for it will set
Blushes upon thy cheeks; and, till thou dost
A fault, 'twere pity.   90

King.   Yet I wonder much
Of the strange desperation of these men,
That dare attempt such acts here in our state:
He could not scape that did it.

Mel.   Were he known,   95
Unpossible.

King.   It would be known, Melantius.

Mel.   It ought to be.   If he got then away,
He must wear all our lives upon his sword:
He need not fly the island; he must leave   100
No one alive.

King.   No; I should think no man
Could kill me, and scape clear, but that old
man.

    [1] Burst out.

Cal.   But I! heaven bless me!   I! should I,
my liege?

King.   I do not think thou wouldst; but yet
thou mightst,   105
For thou hast in thy hands the means to scape,
By keeping of the fort. — He has, Melantius,
And he has kept it well.

Mel.   From cobwebs, sir,
'Tis clean swept: I can find no other art   110
In keeping of it now: 'twas ne'er besieged
Since he commanded.

Cal.   I shall be sure
Of your good word: but I have kept it safe
From such as you.   115

Mel.   Keep your ill temper in:
I speak no malice; had my brother kept it,
I should ha' said as much.

King.   You are not merry.
Brother, drink wine.   Sit you all still. —
            (*Aside*) Calianax,   120
I cannot trust this: I have thrown out words,
That would have fetched warm blood upon the
cheeks
Of guilty men, and he is never moved;
He knows no such thing.

Cal.   Impudence may scape,   125
When feeble virtue is accused.

King.   'A must,
If he were guilty, feel an alteration
At this our whisper, whilst we point at him:
You see he does not.   130

Cal.   Let him hang himself:
What care I what he does?   This he did say.

King.   Melantius, you can easily conceive
What I have meant; for men that are in fault
Can subtly apprehend when others aim   135
At what they do amiss: but I forgive
Freely before this man: heaven do so too!
I will not touch thee, so much as with shame
Of telling it.   Let it be so no more.

Cal.   Why, this is very fine!   140

Mel.   I cannot tell
What 'tis you mean; but I am apt enough
Rudely to thrust into an ignorant fault.
But let me know it: happily [1] 'tis nought
But misconstruction; and, where I am clear,
I will not take forgiveness of the gods,   146
Much less of you.

    [1] Probably.

King.   Nay, if you stand so stiff,
I shall call back my mercy.

Mel.   I want smoothness   150
To thank a man for pardoning of a crime
I never knew.

King. Not to instruct your knowledge, but
    to show you
My ears are everywhere; you meant to kill me,
And get the fort to scape.   155

Mel.   Pardon me, sir,
My bluntness will be pardoned.   You preserve
A race of idle people here about you,
Facers [1] and talkers, to defame the worth
Of those that do things worthy.   The man that
       uttered this   160
Had perished without food, be't who it will,
But for this arm, that fenced him from the foe:
And if I thought you gave a faith to this,
The plainness of my nature would speak more.
Give me a pardon (for you ought to do't)   165
To kill him that spake this.

Cal. (aside).   Ay, that will be
The end of all: then I am fairly paid
For all my care and service.

Mel.   That old man,   170
Who calls me enemy, and of whom I
(Though I will never match my hate so low)
Have no good thought, would yet, I think,
       excuse me,
And swear he thought me wronged in this.

Cal.   Who, I?
Thou shameless fellow! didst thou not speak
       to me   176
Of it thyself?

Mel.   O, then, it came from him!

Cal. From me! who should it come from but
       from me?

Mel. Nay, I believe your malice is enough:
But I ha' lost my anger. — Sir, I hope   181
You are well satisfied.

King.   Lysippus, cheer
Amintor and his lady. — (*To* Amin.) There's
       no sound
Comes from you; I will come and do't myself.

Amin. You have done already, sir, for me,
I thank you.   186

King. Melantius, I do credit this from him,
How slight soe'er you make't.

    [1] Braggarts.

Mel.   'Tis strange you should.

Cal. 'Tis strange 'a should believe an old
       man's word,   190
That never lied in's life!

Mel.   I talk not to thee. —
Shall the wild words of this distempered man,
Frantic with age and sorrow, make a breach
Betwixt your majesty and me?   'Twas wrong
To hearken to him; but to credit him,   196
As much at least as I have power to bear.
But pardon me — whilst I speak only truth,
I may commend myself — I have bestowed
My careless blood [1] with you, and should be
       loath   200
To think an action that would make me lose
That and my thanks too.   When I was a boy,
I thrust myself into my country's cause,
And did a deed that plucked five years from
       time,
And styled me man then.   And for you, my
       King,   205
Your subjects all have fed by virtue of
My arm — this sword of mine hath ploughed
       the ground —
And reaped the fruit in peace;
And you yourself have lived at home in ease.
So terrible I grew, that without swords   210
My name hath fetched you conquest: and my
       heart
And limbs are still the same; my will as great
To do you service.   Let me not be paid
With such a strange distrust.

King.   Melantius,   215
I held it great injustice to believe
Thine enemy, and did not; if I did,
I do not; let that satisfy. — What, struck
With sadness all?   More wine!

Cal.   A few fine words   220
Have overthrown my truth.   Ah, th'art a
       villain!

Mel. (aside). Why, thou wert better let me
       have the fort:
Dotard, I will disgrace thee thus forever;
There shall no credit lie upon thy words:
Think better, and deliver it.   225

Cal.   My liege,
He's at me now again to do it. — Speak;
Deny it, if thou canst. — Examine him

    [1] I have shed my blood for you without stint.

Whilst he is hot; for, if he cool again,
He will forswear it.   230
    King.   This is lunacy,
I hope, Melantius.
    Mel.   He hath lost himself
Much since his daughter missed the happiness
My sister gained; and, though he call me foe,
I pity him.   236
    Cal.   Pity!   A pox upon you!
    Mel.   Mark his disordered words: and, at the
      masque,
Diagoras knows, he raged and railed at me,
And called a lady "whore," so innocent   240
She understood him not.   But it becomes
Both you and me too to forgive distraction:
Pardon him, as I do.
    Cal.   I'll not speak for thee,
For all thy cunning. — If you will be safe,   245
Chop off his head; for there was never known
So impudent a rascal.
    King.   Some that love him,
Get him to bed.   Why, pity should not let
Age make itself contemptible; we must be   250
All old.   Have him away.
    Mel.   Calianax,
The king believes you; come, you shall go home,
And rest; you ha' done well. — (*Aside*) You'll
      give it up,
When I have used you thus a month, I hope.
    Cal.   Now, now, 'tis plain, sir; he does move
      me still.   256
He says, he knows I'll give him up the fort,
When he has used me thus a month.   I am mad,
Am I not, still?
    All.   Ha, ha, ha!   260
    Cal.   I shall be mad indeed, if you do thus.
Why should you trust a sturdy fellow there
That has no virtue in him (all's in his sword)
Before me?   Do but take his weapons from him,
And he's an ass; and I am a very fool,   265
Both with 'em and without 'em, as you use me.
    All.   Ha, ha, ha!
    King.   'Tis well, Calianax: but, if you use
This once again, I shall entreat some other
To see your offices be well discharged. —   270
Be merry, gentlemen. — It grows somewhat
    late.
Amintor, thou wouldst be abed again.
    Amin.   Yes, sir.

    King.   And you, Evadne. — Let me take
Thee in my arms, Melantius, and believe   275
Thou art, as thou deservest to be, my friend
Still and forever. — Good Calianax,
Sleep soundly; it will bring thee to thyself.
        (*Exeunt all except* MELANTIUS *and*
        CALIANAX.
    Cal. (*aside*).   Sleep soundly!   I sleep soundly
    now, I hope;
I could not be thus else. — How dar'st thou
    stay   280
Alone with me, knowing how thou hast used me?
    Mel.   You cannot blast me with your tongue,
    and that's
The strongest part you have about you.
    Cal.   I
Do look for some great punishment for this;
For I begin to forget all my hate,   286
And take't unkindly that mine enemy
Should use me so extraordinarily scurvily.
    Mel.   I shall melt too, if you begin to take
Unkindnesses: I never meant you hurt.   290
    Cal.   Thou'lt anger me again.   Thou wretched
    rogue,
Meant me no hurt!   Disgrace me with the King!
Lose all my offices!   This is no hurt,
Is it?   I prithee, what dost thou call hurt?
    Mel.   To poison men, because they love me
    not;   295
To call the credit of men's wives in question;
To murder children betwixt me and land: [1]
This I call hurt.
    Cal.   All this thou think'st is sport;
For mine is worse.   But use thy will with me;
For, betwixt grief and anger, I could cry.   301
    Mel.   Be wise, then, and be safe; thou may'st
    revenge —
    Cal.   Ay, o' the King; I would revenge of thee.
    Mel.   That you must plot yourself.
    Cal.   I am a fine plotter.
    Mel.   The short is, I will hold thee with the
    King   306
In this perplexity, till peevishness
And thy disgrace have laid thee in thy grave;
But, if thou wilt deliver up the fort,
I'll take thy trembling body in my arms   310
And bear thee over dangers.   Thou shalt hold
Thy wonted state.

   [1] I.e., children who stand between me and land

Cal.   If I should tell the King,
Canst thou deny't again?

Mel.   Try, and believe.   315

Cal. Nay, then, thou canst bring anything
    about.
Melantius, thou shalt have the fort.

Mel.   Why, well.
Here let our hate be buried; and this hand
Shall right us both.   Give me thy aged breast
To compass.   321

Cal.   Nay, I do not love thee yet;
I cannot well endure to look on thee;
And, if I thought it were a courtesy,
Thou shouldst not have it.   But I am dis-
    graced;   325
My offices are to be ta'en away;
And, if I did but hold this fort a day,
I do believe the King would take it from me,
And give it thee, things are so strangely carried.
Ne'er thank me for't; but yet the King shall
    know   330
There was some such thing in't I told him of,
And that I was an honest man.

Mel.   He'll buy
That knowledge very dearly.

Re-enter DIPHILUS

                    Diphilus,   335
What news with thee?

Diph.   This were a night indeed
To do it in: the King hath sent for her.

Mel. She shall perform it, then. — Go,
    Diphilus,
And take from this good man, my worthy friend,
The fort; he'll give it thee.   341

Diph.   Ha' you got that?

Cal. Art thou of the same breed? canst thou
    deny
This to the King too?

Diph.   With a confidence   345
As great as his.

Cal.   Faith, like enough.

Mel. Away, and use him kindly.

Cal.   Touch not me;
I hate the whole strain.[1] If thou follow me   350
A great way off, I'll give thee up the fort;
And hang yourselves.

    [1] Family.

Mel.   Begone.

Diph.   He's finely wrought! [1]
    (*Exeunt* CALIANAX *and* DIPHILUS.

Mel. This is a night, spite of astronomers,[2]
To do the deed in.   I will wash the stain   356
That rests upon our house off with his blood.

Enter AMINTOR

Amin. Melantius, now assist me: if thou
    be'st
That which thou say'st, assist me.   I have lost
All my distempers, and have found a rage   360
So pleasing!   Help me.

Mel. (*aside*).   Who can see him thus,
And not swear vengeance? — What's the
    matter, friend?

Amin. Out with thy sword; and, hand in
    hand with me,
Rush to the chamber of this hated King,   365
And sink him with the weight of all his sins
To hell forever.

Mel.   'Twere a rash attempt,
Not to be done with safety.   Let your reason
Plot your revenge, and not your passion.   370

Amin. If thou refusest me in these extremes,
Thou art no friend.   He sent for her to me;
By heaven, to me, myself! and I must tell ye,
I love her as a stranger: there is worth
In that vile woman, worthy things, Melantius;
And she repents.   I'll do't myself alone,   376
Though I be slain.   Farewell.

Mel. (*aside*).   He'll overthrow
My whole design with madness. — Amintor,
Think what thou dost: I dare as much as
    valor;   380
But 'tis the King, the King, the King, Amintor,
With whom thou fightest! — (*Aside*) I know
    he's honest,[3]
And this will work with him.

Amin.   I cannot tell
What thou hast said; but thou hast charmed
    my sword   385
Out of my hand, and left me shaking here,
Defenseless.

Mel.   I will take it up for thee.

    [1] Tenderly concerned!
    [2] Astrologers.
    [3] Loyal.

Amin. What a wild beast is uncollected
    man![1]
The thing that we call honor bears us all   390
Headlong unto sin, and yet itself is nothing.
    Mel. Alas, how variable are thy thoughts!
    Amin. Just like my fortunes. I was run to
    that
I purposed to have chid thee for. Some plot,
I did distrust, thou hadst against the King,   395
By that old fellow's carriage. But take heed;
There's not the least limb growing to a king
But carries thunder in it.
    Mel.   I have none
Against him.   400
    Amin.   Why, come, then; and still re-
    member
We may not think revenge.
    Mel. I will remember. (*Exeunt.*

ACT V

Scene i. *The King's bedchamber.*

Enter Evadne *and a Gentleman of the
Bedchamber*

    Evad. Sir, is the King abed?
    Gent.   Madam, an hour ago.
    Evad. Give me the key, then, and let none
    be near;
'Tis the King's pleasure.
    Gent. I understand you, madam; would
    'twere mine!   5
I must not wish good rest unto your ladyship.
    Evad. You talk, you talk.
    Gent. 'Tis all I dare do, madam; but the King
Will wake, and then, methinks —
    Evad. Saving your imagination, pray, good
    night, sir.   10
    Gent. A good night be it, then, and a long
    one, madam.
I am gone.   (*Exit.*
    Evad. The night grows horrible; and all
    about me
Like my black purpose. Oh, the consciënce
Of a lost virtue, whither wilt thou pull me?   15
To what things dismal as the depth of hell
Wilt thou provoke me? Let no woman dare
From this hour be disloyal, if her heart be flesh,

[1] Man with his mind disordered.

If she have blood and can fear. 'Tis a daring
Above that desperate fool's that left his peace,
And went to sea to fight: 'tis so many sins,   21
An age cannot repent 'em; and so great,
The gods want mercy for. Yet I must through
    'em:
I have begun a slaughter on my honor;
And I must end it there. (*Draws the curtains,
    discovering the* King *abed.*[1]) 'A sleeps.
    O God!   25
Why give you peace to this untemperate beast,
That hath so long transgressed you? I must
    kill him;
And I will do it bravely: the mere joy
Tells me, I merit in it. Yet I must not
Thus tamely do it as he sleeps — that were   30
To rock him to another world: my vengeance
Shall take him waking, and then lay before him
The number of his wrongs and punishments.
I'll shape his sins like Furies, till I waken
His evil angel, his sick consciënce,   35
And then I'll strike him dead. — King, by your
    leave.   (*Ties his arms to the bed.*
I dare not trust your strength; your grace and I
Must grapple upon even terms no more. —
So, if he rail me not from my resolution,   39
I shall be strong enough. — My lord the King!
My lord! — 'A sleeps, as if he meant to wake
No more. — My lord! — Is he not dead al-
    ready? —
Sir! My lord!
    King. Who's that?
    Evad.   Oh, you sleep soundly, sir.   45
    King.   My dear Evadne,
I have been dreaming of thee; come to bed.
    Evad. I am come at length, sir; but how
    welcome?
    King. What pretty new device is this,
    Evadne?
What, do you tie me to you? By my love,   50
This is a quaint one. Come, my dear, and
    kiss me;
I'll be thy Mars; to bed, my queen of love:
Let us be caught together, that the gods may
    see
And envy our embraces.

[1] Evadne opens the curtains to the inner stage and
discloses the King lying on a bed immediately behind
them.

Evad.　　　　　　　　Stay, sir, stay;　55
You are too hot, and I have brought you physic
To temper your high veins.

King. Prithee, to bed, then; let me take it
　　warm;
There thou shalt know the state of my body
　　better.

Evad. I know you have a surfeited foul body;
And you must bleed.　　　(*Draws a knife.*　61

King.　　　　　　　　Bleed!

Evad. Ay, you shall bleed. Lie still; and if
　　the devil,
Your lust, will give you leave, repent. This
　　steel
Comes to redeem the honor that you stole,　65
King, my fair name; which nothing but thy
　　death
Can answer to the world.

King.　　　　　　How's this, Evadne?

Evad. I am not she; nor bear I in this breast
So much cold spirit to be called a woman:　70
I am a tiger; I am anything
That knows not pity. Stir not: if thou dost,
I'll take thee unprepared, thy fears upon thee,
That make thy sins look double, and so send
　　thee
(By my revenge, I will!) to look [1] those tor-
　　ments　　　　　　　　　75
Prepared for such black souls.

King. Thou dost not mean this; 'tis impos-
　　sible;
Thou art too sweet and gentle.

Evad.　　　　　　　No, I am not:
I am as foul as thou art, and can number　80
As many such hells here. I was once fair,
Once I was lovely; not a blowing rose
More chastely sweet, till thou, thou, thou, foul
　　canker,[2]
(Stir not) didst poison me. I was a world of
　　virtue,
Till your cursed court and you (hell bless you
　　for't)　　　　　　　　85
With your temptations on temptations
Made me give up mine honor; for which, King,
I am come to kill thee.

King.　　　　　　No!

Evad.　　　　　　　I am.　　90

---

[1] Look for.
[2] Canker worm.

King.　　　　　　　　Thou are not!
I prithee speak not these things: thou art gentle,
And wert not meant thus rugged.

Evad.　　　　　　Peace, and hear me.
Stir nothing but your tongue, and that for mercy
To those above us; by whose lights I vow　96
Those blessèd fires [1] that shot to see our sin,
If thy hot soul had substance with thy blood,
I would kill that too; which, being past my steel,
My tongue shall reach. Thou art a shameless
　　villain;　　　　　　　100
A thing out of the overcharge of nature,
Sent, like a thick cloud, to disperse a plague
Upon weak catching [2] women; such a tyrant,
That for his lust would sell away his subjects,
Ay, all his heaven hereafter!　　　105

King.　　　　　　Hear, Evadne,
Thou soul of sweetness, hear! I am thy King.

Evad. Thou art my shame! Lie still; there's
　　none about you,
Within [3] your cries; all promises of safety
Are but deluding dreams. Thus, thus, thou
　　foul man,　　　　　　　110
Thus I begin my vengeance!　(*Stabs him.*

King.　　　　　　Hold, Evadne!
I do command thee hold!

Evad.　　　　　　I do not mean, sir,
To part so fairly with you; we must change [4]
More of these love-tricks yet.　　　116

King.　　　　　What bloody villain
Provoked thee to this murder?

Evad.　　　　　　Thou, thou monster.

King. Oh!　　　　　　　120

Evad. Thou kept'st me brave [5] at court, and
　　whored me, King;
Then married me to a young noble gentleman,
And whored me still.

King.　　　　　Evadne, pity me!

Evad. Hell take me, then! This for my lord
　　Amintor!　　(*Stabs him again.*　125
This for my noble brother! And this stroke
For the most wronged of women!
　　　　　　　(*Stabs him mortally.*

King.　　　　　　Oh! I die.　　(*Dies.*

Evad. Die all our faults together! I forgive
　　thee.　　　　　　　(*Exit.*

---

[1] I.e., shooting stars.　　[2] Susceptible.
[3] Within reach of.　　[4] Exchange.
[5] In splendid state.

Enter two Gentlemen of the Bedchamber

1 Gent. Come, now she's gone, let's enter;
the King expects it, and will be angry.   131
2 Gent. 'Tis a fine wench; we'll have a snap
at her one of these nights, as she goes from him.
1 Gent. Content. How quickly he had done
with her! I see kings can do no more   135
that way than other mortal people.
2 Gent. How fast he is! I cannot hear him
    breathe.
1 Gent. Either the tapers give a feeble light
Or he looks very pale.
2 Gent.   And so he does: 140
Pray Heaven he be well! let's look. — Alas!
He's stiff, wounded, and dead! Treason,
    treason!
1 Gent. Run forth and call.
2 Gent. (*calling*). Treason, treason! (*Exit.*
1 Gent.   This will be laid on us: 145
Who can believe a woman could do this?

Enter Cleon *and* Lysippus

Cleon. How now! where's the traitor?
1 Gent. Fled, fled away; but there her woeful
    act
Lies still.
Cleon. Her act? a woman!   150
Lys.   Where's the body?
1 Gent. There.
Lys. Farewell, thou worthy man! There
    were two bonds
That tied our loves, a brother and a king,   154
The least of which might fetch a flood of
    tears;
But, such the misery of greatness is,
They have no time to mourn; then, pardon me!
Sirs, which way went she?

Enter Strato

Stra.   Never follow her;
For she, alas! was but the instrument.   160
News is now brought in that Melantius
Has got the fort, and stands upon the wall,
And with a loud voice calls those few that pass
At this dead time of night, delivering
The innocence of this act.   165

Lys.   Gentlemen,
I am your King.
Stra.   We do acknowledge it.
Lys. I would I were not! Follow, all; for this
Must have a sudden stop.   (*Exeunt.* 170

SCENE 2. *Before the fort.*

Enter Melantius, Diphilus, *and* Calianax
on the walls of the fort [1]

Mel. If the dull people can believe I am
    armed
(Be constant, Diphilus), now we have time
Either to bring our banished honors home
Or create new ones in our ends.
Diph.   I fear not;   5
My spirit lies not that way. — Courage,
    Calianax!
Cal. Would I had any! you should quickly
    know it.
Mel. Speak to the people; thou art eloquent.
Cal. 'Tis a fine eloquence to come to the
    gallows:
You were born to be my end; the devil take
    you!   10
Now must I hang for company. 'Tis strange
I should be old and neither wise nor valiant.

Lysippus, Diagoras, Cleon, Strato, *and*
Guard enter below

Lys. See where he stands, as boldly confident
As if he had his full command about him.
Stra. He looks as if he had the better cause,
    sir;   15
Under your gracious pardon, let me speak it!
Though he be mighty-spirited, and forward
To all great things, to all things of that
    danger
Worse men shake at the telling of, yet certainly
I do believe him noble, and this action   20
Rather pulled on than sought: his mind was
    ever
As worthy as his hand.
Lys.   'Tis my fear too.
Heaven forgive all! — Summon him, lord Cleon.
Cle. Ho, from the walls there!   25

[1] I.e., on the gallery of the second story of the
tiringhouse, overlooking the stage.

Mel.   Worthy Cleon, welcome:
We could a wished you here, lord; you are
    honest.
    Cal. (aside). Well, thou art as flattering a
    knave, though
I dare not tell thee so —
    Lys. Melantius!   30
    Mel.   Sir?
    Lys. I am sorry that we meet thus; our old
    love
Never required such distance. Pray to heaven,
You have not left yourself, and sought this
    safety   34
More out of fear than honor! You have lost
A noble master; which your faith, Melantius,
Some think might have preserved: yet you
    know best.
    Cal. (aside). When time was [1] I was mad!
    Some that dares fight,
I hope will pay this rascal.
    Mel. Royal young man, those tears look
    lovely on thee: 40
Had they been shed for a deserving one,
They had been lasting monuments. Thy
    brother,
Whilst he was good, I called him King, and
    served him
With that strong faith, that most unwearied
    valor,   44
Pulled people from the farthest sun to seek him,
And beg his friendship: I was then his soldier.
But since his hot pride drew him to disgrace me,
And brand my noble actions with his lust,
(That never-cured dishonor of my sister,
Base stain of whore, and, which is worse,   50
The joy to make it still so) like myself,
Thus I have flung him off with my allegiance;
And stand here mine own justice, to revenge
What I have suffered in him, and this old man
Wronged almost to lunacy.   55
    Cal.   Who, I?
You would draw me in. I have had no wrong;
I do disclaim ye all.
    Mel.   The short is this.
'Tis no ambition to lift up myself   60
Urgeth me thus; I do desire again
To be a subject, so [2] I may be free:
If not, I know my strength, and will unbuild

[1] Once upon a time.   [2] Provided that.

This goodly town. Be speedy, and be wise,
In a reply.   65
    Stra. Be sudden, sir, to tie
All up again. What's done is past recall,
And past you to revenge; and there are thou-
    sands
That wait for such a troubled hour as this.
Throw him the blank.   70
    Lys.   Melantius, write in that
Thy choice: my seal is at it.
          (*Throws* MELANTIUS *a paper*.
    Mel. It was our honors drew us to this act,
Not gain; and we will only work our pardons.
    Cal. Put my name in too.   75
    Diph.   You disclaimed us all
But now,[1] Calianax.
    Cal.   That is all one; [2]
I'll not be hanged hereafter by a trick:
I'll have it in.   80
    Mel.   You shall, you shall. —
Come to the back gate, and we'll call you King,
And give you up the fort.
    Lys.   Away, away! (*Exeunt.*

SCENE 3. *An anteroom to* AMINTOR'S *apartments.*

Enter ASPATIA, *in man's apparel*

Asp. This is my fatal hour. Heaven may
    forgive
My rash attempt, that causelessly hath laid
Griefs on me that will never let me rest,
And put a woman's heart into my breast.
It is more honor for you that I die;   5
For she that can endure the misery
That I have on me and be patient too
May live and laugh at all that you can do.

Enter a Servant

God save you, sir!
    Ser. And you, sir! What's your business?
    Asp. With you, sir, now; to do me the fair
    office   11
To help me to your lord.
    Ser.   What, would you serve him?

[1] Only a moment ago.   [2] That makes no difference.

Asp. I'll do him any service; but, to haste,[1]
For my affairs are earnest; I desire   15
To speak with him.
    Ser. Sir, because you are in such haste, I
       would
Be loth delay you longer: you cannot.
    Asp. It shall become you, though, to tell
       your lord.
    Ser.   Sir, he will speak with nobody;
But in particular, I have in charge,   21
About no weighty matters.[2]
    Asp.   This is most strange.
Art thou gold-proof? There's for thee; help
     me to him.   (*Gives money.*
    Ser. Pray be not angry, sir: I'll do my best.
                         (*Exit.*
    Asp. How stubbornly this fellow answered
     me!   26
There is a vile dishonest trick in man
More than in woman. All the men I meet
Appear thus to me; are harsh and rude,
And have a subtilty in everything,   30
Which love could never know; but we fond
     women
Harbor the easiest and the smoothest thoughts,
And think all shall go so. It is unjust
That men and women should be matched
     together.

         Enter AMINTOR *and the Servant*

    Amin. Where is he?   35
    Ser.   There, my lord.
    Amin.   What would you, sir?
    Asp. Please it your lordship to command
     your man
Out of the room, I shall deliver things
Worthy your hearing.   40
    Amin.   Leave us.
                     (*Exit Servant.*
    Asp. (*aside*).   Oh, that that shape
Should bury falsehood in it!
    Amin.   Now your will, sir.
    Asp. When you know me, my lord, you
     needs must guess   45
My business; and I am not hard to know;

    [1] Make haste.
    [2] I.e., but especially, so I have been instructed, will he
speak to no one on any important matter.

For, till the chance of war marked this smooth
     face
With these few blemishes,[1] people would call
     me
My sister's picture, and her mine. In short,
I am brother to the wronged Aspatia.   50
    Amin. The wronged Aspatia! Would thou
     wert so too
Unto the wronged Amintor! Let me kiss
That hand of thine, in honor that I bear
Unto the wronged Aspatia. Here I stand
That did it. Would he could not![2] Gentle
     youth,   55
Leave me; for there is something in thy looks
That calls my sins in a most hideous form
Into my mind; and I have grief enough,
Without thy help.
    Asp.   I would I could with credit!   60
Since I was twelve years old, I had not seen
My sister till this hour I now arrived:
She sent for me to see her marriäge —
A woful one! but they that are above
Have ends in everything. She used few words,
But yet enough to make me understand   66
The baseness of the injuries you did her.
That little training I have had is war:
I may behave myself rudely in peace;
I would not, though. I shall not need to tell
     you   70
I am but young, and would be loth to lose
Honor, that is not easily gained again.
Fairly I mean to deal: the age is strict
For single combats; and we shall be stopped,
If it be published. If you like your sword,   75
Use it; if mine appear a better to you,
Change; for the ground is this, and this the time
To end our difference.   (*Draws.*
    Amin.   Charitable youth,
If thou be'st such, think not I will maintain   80
So strange a wrong: and, for thy sister's sake,
Know, that I could not think that desperate
     thing
I durst not do; yet, to enjoy this world,
I would not see her; for, beholding thee,
I am I know not what. If I have aught   85
That may content thee, take it, and begone;

    [1] I.e., she is made up with artificial scars on her face
    [2] I.e., would that he who wronged Aspatia could not
stand here.

For death is not so terrible as thou;
Thine eyes shoot guilt into me.

Asp.   Thus, she swore,
Thou wouldst behave thyself, and give me
    words   90
That would fetch tears into my eyes; and so
Thou dost indeed. But yet she bade me watch
Lest I were cozened,[1] and be sure to fight
Ere I returned.

Amin.   That must not be with me.   95
For her I'll die directly; but against her
Will never hazard it.

Asp.   You must be urged.
I do not deal uncivilly with those
That dare to fight; but such a one as you   100
Must be used thus.   (*Strikes him.*

Amin.   I prithee, youth, take heed.
Thy sister is a thing to me so much
Above mine honor, that I can endure   104
All this — Good gods! a blow I can endure —
But stay not, lest thou draw a timeless[2] death
Upon thyself.

Asp.   Thou art some prating fellow;
One that hath studied out a trick to talk,
And move soft-hearted people. To be kicked,
                         (*Kicks him.*
Thus to be kicked. (*Aside*) Why should he be
    so slow   111
In giving me my death?

Amin.   A man can bear
No more, and keep his flesh. Forgive me, then!
I would endure yet, if I could. Now show   115
                       (*Draws.*
The spirit thou pretendest, and understand
Thou hast no hour to live.
       (*They fight;* ASPATIA *is wounded.*
           What dost thou mean?
Thou canst not fight: the blows thou mak'st
    at me
Are quite besides;[3] and those I offer at thee,
Thou spread'st thine arms, and tak'st upon
    thy breast,   121
Alas, defenseless!

Asp.   I have got enough,
And my desire. There is no place so fit
For me to die as here.   (*Falls.* 125

[1] Deceived.
[2] Untimely.
[3] Quite to one side.

Enter EVADNE, *her hands bloody, with a knife*

Evad. Amintor, I am loaden with events,
That fly to make thee happy; I have joys,
That in a moment can call back thy wrongs,
And settle thee in thy free state again.
It is Evadne still that follows thee,   130
But not her mischiefs.

Amin. Thou canst not fool me to believe
    again;
But thou hast looks and things so full of news,
That I am stayed.

Evad. Noble Amintor, put off thy amaze,[1]
Let thine eyes loose, and speak. Am I not
    fair?   136
Looks not Evadne beauteous with these rites
    now?
Were those hours half so lovely in thine eyes
When our hands met before the holy man?
I was too foul within to look fair then.   140
Since I knew ill, I was not free till now.

Amin. There is presage of some important
    thing
About thee, which, it seems, thy tongue hath
    lost.
Thy hands are bloody, and thou hast a knife.

Evad. In this consists thy happiness and
    mine.   145
Joy to Amintor! for the King is dead.

Amin. Those have most power to hurt us,
    that we love;
We lay our sleeping lives within their arms.
Why, thou hast raised up mischief to his height,
And found one to out-name[2] thy other faults;
Thou hast no intermission of thy sins   151
But all thy life is a continued ill.
Black is thy color now, disease thy nature.
Joy to Amintor! Thou hast touched a life,
The very name of which had power to chain
Up all my rage and calm my wildest wrongs.

Evad. 'Tis done; and, since I could not find
    a way   157
To meet thy love so clear as through his life,
I cannot now repent it.

Amin. Couldst thou procure the gods to
    speak to me,   160
To bid me love this woman and forgive,
I think I should fall out with them. Behold,

[1] Amazement.   [2] Surpass.

Here lies a youth whose wounds bleed in my
    breast,
Sent by a violent fate to fetch his death   164
From my slow hand! And, to augment my woe,
You now are present, stained with a king's
    blood
Violently shed. This keeps night here,
And throws an unknown wilderness [1] about me.

Asp. Oh, oh, oh!

Amin.   No more; pursue me not.

Evad.   Forgive me, then,   171
And take me to thy bed: we may not part.
                        (*Kneels.*

Amin. Forbear, be wise, and let my rage go
    this way.

Evad. 'Tis you that I would stay, not it.

Amin.   Take heed;
It will return with me.   176

Evad.   If it must be,
I shall not fear to meet it. Take me home.

Amin. Thou monster of cruelty, forbear!

Evad. For Heaven's sake, look more calm!
    Thine eyes are sharper   180
Than thou canst make thy sword.

Amin.   Away, away!
Thy knees are more to me than violence.
I am worse than sick to see knees follow me
For that I must not grant. For heaven's sake,
    stand.   185

Evad. Receive me, then.

Amin.   I dare not stay thy language:
In midst of all my anger and my grief,
Thou dost awake something that troubles me,
And says, I loved thee once. I dare not stay;
There is no end of woman's reasoning.   191
                     (*Leaves her.*

Evad. (*rising*). Amintor, thou shalt love me
    now again:
Go; I am calm. Farewell, and peace forever!
Evadne, whom thou hatest, will die for thee.
                   (*Stabs herself.*

Amin. I have a little human nature yet,
That's left for thee, that bids me stay thy hand.
                 (*Returns near her.*

Evad. Thy hand was welcome, but it came
    too late.   197
Oh, I am lost! the heavy sleep makes haste.
                     (*Dies.*

[1] Wildness.

Asp. Oh, oh, oh!

Amin. This earth of mine doth tremble, and
    I feel   200
A stark affrighted motion in my blood;
My soul grows weary of her house, and I
All over am a trouble to myself.
There is some hidden power in these dead
    things,
That calls my flesh unto 'em; I am cold: 205
Be resolute, and bear 'em company.
There's something yet, which I am loath to
    leave:
There's man enough in me to meet the fears
That death can bring; and yet would it were
    done!
I can find nothing in the whole discourse   210
Of death, I durst not meet the boldest way;
Yet still, betwixt the reason and the act,
The wrong I to Aspatia did stands up; [1]
I have not such another fault to answer: 214
Though she may justly arm herself with scorn
And hate of me, my soul will part less troubled,
When I have paid to her in tears my sorrow:
I will not leave this act unsatisfied,
If all that's left in me can answer it.

Asp. Was it a dream? There stands Amintor
    still;   220
Or I dream still.

Amin. How dost thou? Speak; receive my
    love and help.
Thy blood climbs up to his old place again;
There's hope of thy recovery.

Asp. Did you not name Aspatia?   225

Amin.   I did.

Asp. And talked of tears and sorrow unto
    her?

Amin. 'Tis true; and, till these happy signs
    in thee
Stayed my course, it was thither I was going.

Asp. Thou art there already, and these
    wounds are hers: 230
Those threats I brought with me sought not
    revenge,
But came to fetch this blessing from thy hand:
I am Aspatia yet.

Amin. Dare my soul ever look abroad again?

Asp. I shall sure live, Amintor; I am well;
A kind of healthful joy wanders within me.   236

[1] Stands out.

Amin. The world wants [1] lives to excuse thy
    loss;
Come, let me bear thee to some place of help.
  Asp. Amintor, thou must stay; I must rest
    here;
My strength begins to disobey my will.   240
How dost thou, my best soul?   I would fain
    live
Now, if I could: wouldst thou have loved me,
    then?
  Amin. Alas,
All that I am's not worth a hair from thee!
  Asp. Give my thine hand; mine hands grope
    up and down,   245
And cannot find thee; I am wondrous sick:
Have I thy hand, Amintor?
  Amin. Thou greatest blessing of the world,
    thou hast.
  Asp. I do believe thee better than my sense.
Oh, I must go! farewell!   (*Dies.* 250
  Amin. She swoons. — Aspatia! — Help! for
    God's sake, water,
Such as may chain life ever to this frame! —
Aspatia, speak! — What, no help yet? I fool;
I'll chafe her temples. Yet there's nothing
    stirs:
Some hidden power tell her, Amintor calls,
And let her answer me! — Aspatia, speak! 256
I have heard, if there be any life, but bow
The body thus, and it will show itself.
Oh, she is gone! I will not leave her yet.
Since out of justice we must challenge nothing,
I'll call it mercy, if you'll pity me,   261
You heavenly powers, and lend forth some few
    years
The blessed soul to this fair seat again!
No comfort comes; the gods deny me too.
I'll bow the body once again. — Aspatia! —
The soul is fled forever; and I wrong   266
Myself, so long to lose her company.
Must I talk now? Here's to be with thee, love!
          (*Stabs himself.*

Enter a Servant

  Ser. This is a great grace to my lord, to have
the new king come to him: I must tell him he is
entering. — O God! — Help, help!   271
  [1] Lacks.

Enter Lysippus, Melantius, Calianax,
  Cleon, Diphilus, *and* Strato

  Lys. Where's Amintor?
  Ser.   Oh, there, there!
  Lys. How strange is this!
  Cal.   What should we do here? 275
  Mel. These deaths are such acquainted [1]
    things with me,
That yet my heart dissolves not. May I stand
Stiff here forever! Eyes, call up your tears!
This is Amintor: heart, he was my friend;
Melt! now it flows. — Amintor, give a word
To call me to thee.   281
  Amin. Oh!
  Mel. Melantius calls his friend Amintor. Oh,
Thy arms are kinder to me than thy tongue!
Speak, speak!   285
  Amin. What?
  Mel. That little word was worth all the
    sounds
That ever I shall hear again.
  Diph.   Oh, brother,
Here lies your sister slain! You lose yourself
In sorrow there.   291
  Mel.   Why, Diphilus, it is
A thing to laugh at, in respect of this:
Here was my sister, father, brother, son;
All that I had. — Speak once again; what youth
Lies slain there by thee?   296
  Amin.   'Tis Aspatia.
My last is said. Let me give up my soul
Into thy bosom.   (*Dies.*
  Cal. What's that? What's that? Aspatia!
  Mel.   I never did 301
Repent the greatness of my heart till now;
It will not burst at need.
  Cal.   My daughter dead here too!
And you have all fine new tricks to grieve;
But I ne'er knew any but direct crying. 306
  Mel. I am a prattler: but no more.
        (*Offers* [2] *to stab himself.*
  Diph.   Hold, brother!
  Lys. Stop him.
  Diph. Fie, how unmanly was this offer in you!
Does this become our strain? [3]   311

  [1] Familiar.
  [2] Attempts.
  [3] Family.

Cal. I know not what the matter is, but
I am grown very kind, and am friends with you
all now. You have given me that among you
will kill me quickly; but I'll go home, and live
as long as I can.   (*Exit.* 316

Mel. His spirit is but poor that can be kept
From death for want of weapons.
Is not my hands a weapon sharp enough
To stop my breath? Or, if you tie down those,
I vow, Amintor, I will never eat,   321
Or drink, or sleep, or have to do with that
That may preserve life! This I swear to keep.

Lys. Look to him, though, and bear those
    bodies in.[1]
May this a fair example be to me   325
To rule with temper;[2] for on lustful kings
Unlooked-for sudden deaths from God are
    sent;
But cursed is he that is their instrument.
                  (*Exeunt.*

---

[1] This command was a common and necessary device
for clearing the curtainless stage of the dead or the
wounded before the end of the scene.

[2] Temperance, moderation.

INTRODUCTION TO

The Star of Seville

The Rise of the Spanish "Comedia": The Theater in Renaissance Spain:
Lope de Vega

THE RISE OF THE SPANISH "COMEDIA"

THE drama of Spain, like that of England, had its beginnings during the later Middle Ages in short plays, or *autos*, based upon Biblical stories, the lives of the saints, and the doctrines of the Christian Church. Performance was confined largely to the Corpus Christi festival in May, and took place more commonly in the streets than in the churches. The trade guilds of the larger towns, just as in England, produced these religious or moral plays until the latter part of the sixteenth century when municipal or royal authorities took over the responsibility. Thereafter, for another hundred and fifty years, the *autos sacramentales* flourished at the Corpus Christi season in city theaters as well as in the open air.

Late in the fifteenth century, however, the nobility and the wealthy of the Spanish cities began to sponsor private theatricals in their palaces. Dramatic entertainment for such occasions needed to be amusing and secular. This need initiated the development of a peculiarly Spanish species of drama, the *comedia*.

The earliest important effort in the direction of a native dramatic type came from Juan del Encina (?1468–?1529). While in the service of the Duke of Alba at Toledo from 1492 to 1500, he composed comic pieces with contemporary characters, idiomatic speech, and popular situations. His *Auto del repelon* ("Sketch of the Brawl"), for example, depicts a lively clash between some shepherds and a group of students from the city of Salamanca.

Lope de Rueda (?1510–65), the first known theatrical manager in Spain, hastened the final development of the *comedia* as a strictly national form of drama. Originally a goldsmith of Seville, he turned author as well as head of a company of strolling actors, and from about 1550 to 1565 he presented comedies of literary merit both in palaces and squares all over the country. His career securely established the professional dramatist on the Spanish stage.

The *comedia* attained its artistic maturity near the close of the sixteenth century at the hands of Lope de Vega (1562–1635). As perfected by him, the *comedia* is not to be identified with the English "comedy." The *comedia* must be in three acts with dialogue in verse. It may contain any kind of dramatic material whatsoever — fantastic, realistic, historical, mythological — or a mixture of several kinds. Finally, and most important, it may have either a tragic or a comic effect, but is not confined to either. The latitude of subject matter and emotional objectives permitted to the *comedia* distinguishes it as a unique type of world drama.

THE THEATER IN RENAISSANCE SPAIN

At the same time that Lope de Vega was perfecting the *comedia* Spain was undergoing a great expansion of theatrical activity. Seville, Valencia, Toledo, Valladolid, and Madrid abounded in dramatic entertainment furnished by professional troupes who toured from city to city. Six to eight companies had royal licenses to act; many others carried on without official authority. Before the end of the sixteenth century all the troupes contained female performers. The presence of women on the Spanish stage encouraged a strong emphasis upon romantic gallantry in the drama of the period.

Permanent playhouses came into existence at the new Spanish capital of Madrid very shortly after the first public theaters had appeared in England. Madrid, like London, however, contained for many years only two playhouses — the "Corral de la Cruz" opened in 1579, and the "Corral del Principe" opened in 1583. Both were built by charitable brotherhoods as means of raising money for their hospitals and asylums. Forty per cent of the admission fees always went for these and other philanthropic enterprises. By 1600 the patronage of the two Madrid playhouses had grown so heavy that the income for charity ran to $40,000 or $50,000 in a theatrical season.

The season extended from September to June, but the theaters closed in the spring during the six weeks of Lent. Performances usually took place on Tuesday, Thursday, Sunday, and then in addition, on feast days or holidays. The selection of plays for the week was announced by posters and by street criers. The doors of the theaters opened at noon, though the acting did not start until 4 P.M., or 2 P.M. in the dead of winter. Persons of wealth and position often sent their servants to hold seats. The masters could put in appearance just as the musicians were about to sing the customary prelude to the afternoon's program.

Before the musical prelude, the spectators entertained themselves in buying fruits, confections, and drinks from vendors who passed around among the audience. After the musicians had sung their ballad, one of the actors spoke a *loa*, a nonsensical prologue sometimes related to the *comedia* of the day, but composed especially to entertain the women and the lower class in the audience. Then the *comedia* followed, with some light entertainment in the two intermissions between acts — a short farce by two actors, a ballad with music, and a dance. The *comedia* always concluded with a dance and song. Thus the daily bills of fare included varied features to please all tastes. The program lasted from two to three hours, depending on the numbers offered.

The Madrid playhouse was first termed "corral" or "yard," because it was in fact a large courtyard enclosed by the backs of rows of houses. The rectangular, open-air court, called the *patio*, resembled the Elizabethan "pit." The sides of the *patio* were walled like house exteriors, with recessed porches stretching along the ground level, and with a series of grated windows in the two or three upper stories. The porches contained bleachers priced at about 35 cents per seat where middle class citizens sat with their veiled wives. The grated windows screened the boxes which the nobles and the wealthy occupied. They usually took their boxes by season subscriptions running from $800 to $1200. A box for a single performance sold for about $9.

The front of the *patio* near the stage contained chairs or rows of benches popular with the gallants and well-to-do bachelors, who paid about 75 cents for the privilege of occupying a prominent location. The admission fee of about 45 cents, levied on all the spectators, entitled to standing room in the *patio* behind the benches. The *mosqueteros*, or standees, constituted a rough and boisterous rabble. They voiced approval at any time in the program by shouting "Victor!" When displeased, they whistled, hissed, or pelted the actors with fruit.

All unescorted females had to sit in a large, covered gallery facing the stage at the rear of the *patio*. This gallery, the *cazuela* ("stewing-pan"), had its entrance direct from the street. A guard at the door kept out any straying men, and kept order within, for the motley crowd of gallery women, like the *mosqueteros* below, sometimes raised a riot with rattles and keys, or threw orange peels and small cucumbers upon the stage.

The stage was a very wide and shallow platform without a front curtain. A roofing of canvas protected both the platform and the benches in the *patio*. Painted canvas also closed in the sides and back of the stage. The rear wall displayed the same arrangements as in the Elizabethan playhouse. Two doors flanked a curtained recess which might represent a bed-chamber, cave, or tent. A raised gallery, running along the back of the stage, served as a balcony, a battlement, a tower, or a mountain peak.

Stage decorations at first were crude and meager, if present at all. By the second decade of the seventeenth century, however, painted scenery, in the shape of cardboard or canvas models of rocks, trees, gardens, castles, and the like, frequently supported performances. Even so, many changes of setting in the plays were not accompanied by changes in the stage scenery. The poverty of scenic effects in the Spanish theaters until the 1630's accounts for the practice of more or less unlocalized action in the drama before that time.

LOPE DE VEGA

The "father" of the *comedia* and the most striking literary personality of the Spanish Golden Age was Lope Félix de Vega Carpio, born at Madrid on November 25, 1562, a year and a half before Shakespeare. These two men, the foremost playwrights of Spain and England, brought the dramatic art of their respective nations to full flower at the same moment — one of the outstanding coincidences in the history of the world theater. Lope's career, however, surpassed that of his great English contemporary not only in length but also in variety and romance.

Like Shakespeare, Lope descended from humble, country stock. His parents, embroiderers at Madrid, had come from the *vega*, or valley, of Carriedo in the mountains of Asturia, a far northwestern province. When the Bishop of Avila sent Lope as a needy, orphaned, but worthy lad to the University of Alcala at the age of fifteen, he already had run away from school on a vagabond tour of Spain, enlisted as a soldier against the Portuguese, become adept at poetry, music, dancing, fencing, and appeared a more likely gallant than priest. Tiring of the University in 1582, he joined the successful naval expedition to the Azores. On return he entered the service of a Madrid nobleman, began to write plays, and quickly formed profitable connections with the prominent actor-manager, Jeronimo Velazquez. The latter's married daughter, Elena, soon lost her heart to Lope, who for several years celebrated her in his stage ballads. Then in 1587 he quarreled with the Velazquez family, lampooned the father, and incurred a libel suit. The suit resulted in his exile from Castile for two years, and from Madrid for eight.

Not at all daunted by so heavy a reverse Lope shortly eloped with the daughter of a well-known courtier. Then almost at once he left her to take part in the Spanish Armada which set off against England at the end of May, 1588. His galleon, the *San Juan*, escaped destruction in the mighty battle of the English Channel, sailed on around the British Isles, and got back safely to Cadiz. During this exciting six months' voyage he calmly absorbed himself in the composition of a fanciful epic, *The Beauty of Angelica*.

During the next quarter of a century Lope, under the patronage of a succession of noblemen, resided by turns at Toledo, Seville, and Madrid. Year by year his play-writing went on with mounting successes. His large earnings eventually gave him a position of affluence and independence. By the early 1600's all Spain acknowledged his leadership of the national drama. In 1609 the Madrid Academy of Letters, the most exclusive cultural body in the country, invited him to deliver a lecture on his craft. He composed for the occasion a metrical address, entitled *The New Art of Making Plays in This Age*, in which he unashamedly pictured himself as the people's dramatist, who listened to the applause of the crowd paying for his comedies rather than to the authoritative precepts of Plautus and Terence. Yet he knew very well that the theater audiences in autocratic Spain took their cue from the affectations of the nobility. His drama therefore never failed to idealize the court and the upper classes in general.

In 1598 Lope had married the daughter of a wealthy Madrid meat packer, but in 1613 he lost her by death. Meanwhile he developed an intimacy with a noted actress, Micaela de Lujan, by whom he had four children. Perhaps contrition for his waywardness prompted him in 1614 to take holy orders along with the impressive clerical titles of "Familiar of the Holy Office of the Inquisition" and "Doctor of Theology in the *Collegium Sapientiae* of Rome."

Lope's assumption of priesthood did not long interrupt his pursuit of love. Within the next several years he contracted two notorious liaisons — one of short duration with a mad actress, and one of long standing with a young married lady of Madrid, Doña Maria, who remained devoted to him until her passing in 1632. Three years later, on August 27, 1635, he ended a colorful life of passion and piety. As a scholar, cavalier, poet, novelist, critic, exile, soldier of fortune, priest, and Don Juan with untold conquests, Lope de Vega had mirrored in himself the paradoxical qualities of his dynamic era.

An incredible productivity marked Lope's literary endeavor. He wrote in abundance all sorts of poetry from sonnets to epics, from burlesque pieces to religious meditations. In prose he composed short comic tales, pastorals, romances, an autobiographical novel, and a history of the Roman Church in Japan. The theater, however, inspired his most prolific and successful efforts. His full-length plays ran to a total of at least 1500 (of which between 400 and 500 have survived) in addition to countless hundreds of religious *autos*, interludes, and *loas*, or prologues. These dramatic compositions often were turned out at amazing speed. Lope boasted that he finished more than 100 of his *comedias* in a day apiece. Once completed, playscripts rarely underwent revision at his hands. His concern, like Shakespeare's, was for performance, not publication.

In his quest for stage material Lope explored the Bible, the saints' legends, the writings of the Church Fathers, classical and medieval mythology, Greek and Roman literature, the historical chronicles of Europe and Asia, the chivalric romances, the Italian *novelli*, and world affairs of his own century. Out of this rich background he fashioned *comedias* of every description. For example, *The Sheep Well* presents in serious vein a peasant uprising. *Madrid Steel*, a so-called "cape-and-sword" *comedia*, deals frivolously with the love intrigues of the urban upper class. *The Gardener's Dog* is a romantic comedy with a Neapolitan setting. *The Crown of Otún* portrays the sad downfall of King Ottokar of Bohemia in his struggle to be Holy Roman Emperor.

The tremendous range of Lope's subject matter and dramatic treatment established for the *comedia* a tradition of wide diversity in content and mood. He also set up the further tradition of vigorous plot invention. He made the *comedia* utterly conform to the Spanish audience's taste for a story-telling drama. The *comedia* never freed itself from the predominance of action which relegated character portrayal to a minor place in the design.

Lope de Vega left so strong a stamp upon the drama of Spain that neither its form nor substance changed during the next two hundred years. At the same time its artistic vitality greatly declined. Pedro Calderón de la Barca (1600–81), a playwright of more intellectual bent than Lope and a finer stylist in verse, did postpone the decadence of the *comedia* for half a century. His most famous play, *Life Is a Dream*, is an unusual philosophical fantasy about the purifying power of a dream upon a young ruler's lust for cruelty. Calderón's pleasing but conventional "cape-and-sword" *comedias*, however, exerted the more powerful influence in other European countries during the seventeenth and eighteenth centuries. The death of their author closed the great cycle in the Spanish theater which the Renaissance had opened one hundred years before.

"THE STAR OF SEVILLE"

No *comedia* generally attributed to Lope de Vega is better known than *The Star of Seville*, probably one of his later compositions, written about 1622 or 1623. It belongs to that group of his plays which depicted a fanciful heroic age of Spanish monarchy in the spirit of the popular legends. Though King Sancho IV of Castile was an historical figure of the thirteenth century, none of the events in *The Star of Seville* has any connection with his reign. Sheer poetic invention created this tale of the beautiful Sevillian lady, the knightly lover, and the infatuated monarch.

The Star of Seville delightfully exemplifies Lope's flamboyant drama of love and honor. The primary interest lies in the succession of ingenious situations which arise from the adroit manipulations of a feudal and romantic code. The facile plotting conforms to Lope's ideal of a first act exposing the cause for conflict, of a second contriving unexpected complications, and of a third concealing the solution until the very last moment. Indeed the most effective touch of art in *The Star of Seville* is the surprising ending where Sancho and Stella, whose betrothal to one another now has the king's blessing, mutually agree to abandon their prospective marriage.

Despite their artificiality and their often stiff, rhetorical speech, Lope's characters with their chivalric sentiments impart to the play a peculiar charm. *The Star of Seville* possesses that lighthearted atmosphere of aristocratic gallantry which forms the unique distinction of the Spanish *comedia*.

[For the Spanish *comedia*, see James Fitzmaurice-Kelly, *A New History of Spanish Literature* (1926); for the Renaissance stage in Spain, H. A. Rennert, *The Spanish Stage in the Time of Lope de Vega* (1909); for Lope de Vega, H. A. Rennert, *The Life of Lope de Vega* (1904).]

LOPE DE VEGA

The Star of Seville

[Translated in prose by PHILIP M. HAYDEN*]*

DRAMATIS PERSONAE

KING SANCHO THE BOLD
DON ARIAS, *confidant of the* KING
DON PEDRO DE GUZMAN ⎱ *chief alcaldes*
FARFAN DE RIVERA ⎰
DON GONZALO DE ULLOA, *the Cid of Cordova*
FERNAN PEREZ DE MEDINA, *Captain*
DON SANCHO ORTIZ ⎱ *councilors*
BUSTOS TABERA ⎰
IÑIGO OSORIO

DON MANUEL
PEDRO DE CAUS, *Governor of the Prison of Triana*
CLARINDO, *Gracioso, servant to* DON SANCHO
STELLA, *the Star of Seville*
TEODORA, *servant*
MATILDE, *slave*
Attendants, Servants, Musicians, People

The Scene is at Seville in the late Middle Ages

ACT I

SCENE I. *A room in the palace.*

Enter the KING, DON ARIAS, DON PEDRO DE GUZMAN, *and* FARFAN DE RIVERA

King. My welcome in Seville has greatly pleased me, and I perceive I am indeed the sovereign monarch in Castile; my reign dates from this day, since this day Seville receives me and does me honor; for it is clear and 5 evident, and an accepted law, that no man could be king in Castile who did not reign in Seville. I shall not be content if I do not reward the munificence of my reception, and the splendor of my entrance. My court shall 10 have its seat within these walls, and marvel not that the Castilian court should make its seat in Seville, for I shall reign in Castile, while I reign in Seville.

D. Ped. We, the chief alcaldes [1] of the 15 city, kiss your feet in gratitude, for we receive your favors in her name. Jurors and councilmen gladly offer you their wealth and loyalty, and the council is in accord, provided only that the chartered rights of this your city do not 20 suffer.

[1] Judges.

King. I am much pleased —

D. Ped. Grant us your hand to kiss.

King. — that in receiving me you have borne yourselves like the men you are, and 25 I believe that with your support I shall make myself king of Gibraltar, which sleeps in fancied security upon the Columns,[1] and if fortune favors me I shall make myself remembered.

Far. With loyalty the people of Seville 30 will serve Your Highness in this lofty enterprise, offering their lives as one.

Ari. His Majesty feels it so, and is well pleased with you and your desire.

King. Men of Seville, I believe you and 35 so declare. Go with God. *(Exeunt the alcaldes*

Ari. My lord, how like you Seville?

King. Much; for today I am truly king.

Ari. She will deserve your favor, Sire, and win it more from day to day. 40

King. Surely; for so rich and fair a city, as I live longer in it, will be admired at leisure.

Ari. The beauty and the grandeur of its streets — I know not if Augustus saw the like in Rome, or had such wealth. 45

King. And her ladies, divinely fair, why do

[1] The Pillars of Hercules, the two promontories which Hercules was said to have set on the Strait of Gibraltar

you not mention them? How can you limit or describe their attributes and radiance? Tell me, why are you not aflame in the light of such glories? 50

Ari. Doña Leonor de Ribera seemed heaven itself, for in her countenance shone the light of the springtime sun.

King. She is too pale. A sun with rays of ice is little worth, for it chills instead of 55 warming. I want a burning sun, not freezing.

Ari. The one who threw you roses is Doña Mencia Coronel.

King. A handsome dame, but I saw others lovelier. 60

Ari. The two lively damsels at the next window were Doña Ana and Doña Beatriz Megia, sisters through whom day gains fresh splendors.

King. Ana is but a vulgar name for one, 65 and Beatriz for the other, lonely like the phœnix, because unequaled.

Ari. Does good fortune or ill attend even upon a name?

King. In love — and do not wonder at 70 it — names unusual, and indicating quality and breeding, are a magnet to a man.

Ari. The pale, auburn-haired. . . .

King. Tell me not her name. The pale lady with auburn hair will be marble and 75 bronze, and your descriptions weary me as you continue. One I saw there full of grace, whom you have left unmentioned; for you have noted only the blonde, and not the raven-haired. Who is she who on her balcony drew my 80 attention, and to whom I doffed my hat? Who is she whose two eyes flash lightning like Jove's thunder-bolts, and sent their deadly rays into my heart, unknowing of their power? One who, though dark, outshone the sun? 85 In tresses of night she eclipsed the orb of day; her beauty obscured its rays.

Ari. I have it, Sire.

King. Choose the loveliest of them all, for that is she. 90

Ari. They call her the Star of Seville.

King. If she is fairer than the sun, why slight her thus? But Seville does not esteem her, seeing her daily. Sun she shall be called, since she is a sun that revives and kindles. 95

Ari. Her name is Doña Stella Tabera, and Seville, in homage, calls her its star.

King. And it might call her its sun.

Ari. Her brother hopes to marry her in Seville, as well he may. 100

King. Her brother's name?

Ari. Bustos Tabera, and he is councilor in Seville, in saying which I bear tribute to his quality.

King. And is he married? 105

Ari. He is not married, for in the Sevillian firmament he is the sun, if Stella is his sister, and Star and Sun are in conjunction.

King. My guiding star brought me to Seville, and I find great joy in it, if it is as 110 brilliant as I hope. All will go well with me, under such a star. What means, Don Arias, will you find, for me to see her and to speak with her?

Ari. You shall find her a friendly star, 115 in spite of the Sun. Heap honors upon her brother, for the most rigid honor yields to honors. Favor him, for favors can overcome and conquer the impossible. If you give to him, and he receives, he binds himself, 120 and sees himself obliged to requite what you have given; for he graves in bronze who accepts favors.

King. Let him be summoned, and take measures likewise that the following 125 night I may see Stella in her house. O vision that inflames my inmost soul. (*Exit* ARIAS.

Enter DON GONZALO, *in mourning*

Gonz. I kiss your highness' feet.

King. Rise, Gonzalo. On this day of joy, why do you come so sad? 130

Gonz. My father is no more.

King. I have lost a valiant captain.

Gonz. And the frontier remains without defender.

King. Yes, a heroic commander has 135 departed. Grieving I listen to you.

Gonz. Sire, the frontier of Archidona [1] has suffered a great loss, and since there can be found no equal to his valor, and since I have

---

[1] A town in Malaga province, southern Spain, near the border of Granada.

inherited the honored name of the great　140
general, I implore your majesty not to permit
another to receive the post now vacant.

King. There is sufficient proof that his valor
lives again in you.　Lament your father's
death, and while you are in mourning　145
and in sorrow, rest in my court.

Gonz. Fernan Perez de Medina comes with
the same request, and thinks his services may
claim the baton, for in fact he has been ten
years captain, and with his sword has　150
stained with ruby hue the pearly walls of Granada.[1]　Hence my diligence.

King. I will consider it; for if I must make
this decision, I wish to weigh the matter.

Enter FERNAN PEREZ DE MEDINA

Fer. I fear, O king, that I arrive too　155
late.　I kiss your feet, and then...

King. You may present your homage, Fernan Perez, with a tranquil mind.　The office is
still in my hands, and such a post will not be
given without consulting first yourself　160
and others of high credit in the kingdom who
being bulwarks in themselves will be advisers
concerning Archidona.　Go, and rest.

Gonz. This memorial I leave with you, my
lord.　165

Fer. And I leave mine, which is the crystal
mirror of my valor, in which my nature can be
seen, pure, accomplished, loyal.

Gonz. Mine is crystal too, and shows the
clearness of my claim.　170

(*Exeunt* FERNAN *and* GONZALO.

Enter ARIAS *and* BUSTOS

Ari. Here, my lord, is Bustos Tabera.

Bust. Perturbed you see me at your feet, my
lord, for so it is natural for the vassal to be
confused in presence of his king; I am for this
reason and by the common lot perturbed,　175
but twice perturbed, because this undreamt-of
favor hath further agitated me.

King. Rise.

Bust. Nay, this is my place.　If kings should
be adored like saints upon an altar, my　180
place is here.

[1] The famous old capital of Granada province, southern Spain.

King. You are a gallant gentleman.

Bust. Of that I have shown proof in Spain.
But, Sire, I crave but such advancement as is
due me.　185

King. Then cannot I advance you?

Bust. The laws of God and man give power
to kings, but forbid the vassal to be presumptuous; for he, my lord, must keep his wishes
within bounds.　So I, seeing this law　190
transgressed, limit my ambition to my lawful
aspirations.

King. What man ever did not desire to become greater?

Bust. If I were greater, I should be　195
covered now; but if I am Tabera, Tabera must
stand uncovered.

King (*aside to* ARIAS).　A strange philosophy
of honor!

Ari. (*aside to* KING).　A caprice novel　200
and unexampled.

King. I do not desire, Tabera, upon my life,
that you stand covered before I have advanced you, and given you a proof of my affection.　And thus it is my will that you　205
cease to be Tabera, and become General of
Archidona, for your heroism shall be the defense of that frontier.

Bust. But, Sire, in what war have I ever
served you?　210

King. Even in the occupations of peace,
Bustos, I see you so capable of defending my
lands, that I give you preference over these,
whose memorials show such services.　Here in
my presence read and decide: the candi-　215
dates are three — yourself and these two; see
what competitors you have.

Bust. (*reads*): "Most noble King, Don Gonzalo de Ulloa entreats your majesty to grant
him the post of captain general of the　220
frontier of Archidona, inasmuch as my father
died in battle, after serving you more than
fourteen years, rendering notable services to
God in behalf of your crown.　I implore justice,
etc."　If Don Gonzalo has inherited the　225
valor of his father, I name him for the place.

King. Read the other memorial.

Bust. (*reads*): "Most noble king, Fernan
Perez de Medina has been a soldier twenty
years in the service of your father, and de-　230
sires to serve you with his arm and sword, on

Spanish or on foreign soil. Ten years he has been captain in the plain of Granada, and three years a prisoner, in close confinement, for which reasons, and by his sword, in 235 which he places all his claim, he by this memorial asks the baton of general of the fields of Archidona."

King. Recite your claims.

Bust. I have no service to relate to 240 second a request, or justify a favor. I could recall the noble exploits of my ancestors, the banners captured, the castles conquered; but, Sire, they had their reward, and I cannot reap the glory for their services. Justice, to 245 deserve the name, must be well ordered, for it is a sacred boon divine, suspended by a hair. Justice requires that this post be given to one of these two men, for if you give it me, you do injustice. Here in Seville, my Lord, I 250 have no claim upon you, for in the wars I was a soldier, in peace, a councilor. In truth Fernan Perez de Medina merits the honor, for his age is worthy of the frontier post; Don Gonzalo is young, and a nobleman of Cordova; 255 him you can make a captain.

King. Then it shall be as you desire.

Bust. I desire only what is right and in accord with justice, to give to those who serve their due reward. 260

King. Enough. You put me to shame with your good counsels.

Bust. They are mirrors of truth, and so in them you see your true self.

King. You are a noble gentleman, and 265 I desire your attendance in my chamber and in my palace, for I wish to have you near me. Are you married?

Bust. My Lord, I am the protector of a sister, and will not marry, until I have 270 given her a husband.

King. I will give her a better one, Bustos. Her name?

Bust. Doña Stella.

King. To a star, if she be fair, I know 275 not what husband to give, except the sun.

Bust. I wish only a man, Sire, for Stella. She is not a heavenly star.

King. I will unite her to one who is worthy of her. 280

Bust. In her name I thank you, Sire.

King. I will give her, Bustos, a husband suited to her rank. Inform your sister that her marriage is in my care, and that I shall dower her. 285

Bust. Now, Sire, I pray you tell me on what business you have called me; for your summons agitated me.

King. You are right, Tabera, I summoned you for an affair of Seville, and wished to 290 talk with you first before discussing it. But peace and leisure are before us and we will treat it later. From today attend me in my chamber and my palace. Go with God.

Bust. I kiss your feet. 295

King. I embrace you, noble councilor.

Bust. (*aside*). Such favor passes my understanding, and I am filled with misgiving. To love me and to honor me without knowing me seems rather to attack my honor than to 300 favor me.   (*Exit.*

King. The man is keen of mind; as wise as he is honorable.

Ari. I have no patience with these men of honor. How many, Sire, have been so, 305 until occasion meets them! Yes, all are occasionally wise, but not all, my lord, on all occasions. Today the breath of slander reaches him who denounced another yesterday; and the law which he invoked is invoked anon 310 on him. If he puts his honor in the balance, you can put in the other your favors and your gifts, your praises and your privity.

King. In secret I intend to see this woman in her house. For she is a sun, and has 315 inflamed me, although she seems a star. Let Spain say what it will, a blinded king, I follow the Star of Seville.

        (*Exeunt the* KING *and* ARIAS.

SCENE 2.   *A room in* TABERA'S *house.*

Enter DON SANCHO, DOÑA STELLA,
MATILDE, *and* CLARINDO

San. Angel of heaven, when will you be mine, when will you free from this restraint the passion that I feel for you? Like a sun you rise, dispensing radiance from coral lips formed for love: — when will you turn the pale 5

dew that drops from my eyes to pearls that
may deck the peaceful joys of our souls?

Stel. If time kept pace with my desires, its
giant strides should outstrip the sun; Seville
should celebrate my sweet submission,   10
and your happy love should cease to envy
the tender turtle dove, which, softly coo-
ing, makes its nest amid a thousand favoring
branches.

San. Ah, how gratefully my heart re-   15
ceives these sighings! My soul yearns for the
noblest gifts of fame, to lay them at your feet.

Stel. I ask only for life, to join it to yours.

San. Oh, sweet Stella, clothed in love and
light!   20

Stel. Ah! Can life endure such love?

San. Oh charms divine, lodestar to my dazzled eyes!

Clar. (*to* MATILDE). Why should not we,
like our masters, utter a few sweet sighs,   25
soft as finest cambric?

San. Be quiet, knave!

Clar. We're dumb. (*To* MATILDE.) Ah!
Sleek filly! Despair of my existence!

Mat. Oh, low-born suitor! Your poetics   30
smack of the currycomb.

Clar. Oh, my love!

Mat. Oh, happy man!

Clar. What leper ever heaved such sighs!

San. What does your brother say?   35

Stel. That when the papers are made out and
signed, the marriage may proceed; and that
there shall be but a few days' delay, while he
makes the arrangements.

San. He'll bring my love to despera-   40
tion; delay is torment for it. Would we might
wed today, lest fortune change before tomorrow!

Stel. If delay continues, speak to my
brother.   45

San. Speak I will, for I shall die if this persists.

Clar. Bustos Tabera comes.

Enter BUSTOS

Bust. Sancho, my friend!

Stel. Heavens! What is this?   50

San. Such sadness? You?

Bust. Sadness and joy are cause of my dismay. Stella, leave us alone.

Stel. God help me! Delay has turned
against me.   (*Exit.*   55

Bust. Sancho Ortiz de las Roelas, . . .

San. Do you no longer call me brother?

Bust. A steed beyond control sweeps me on
unspurred. Know that the king sent for me;
God is my witness that I know not why,   60
for though I asked him, yet he told me not.
Unasked, he was about to make me general
of Archidona, and indeed, had I not resisted,
would have given me the royal commission.
Finally he made me . . .   65

San. Proceed, for all of this is joy. Tell me
your sadness, explain your grief.

Bust. He attached me to his suite.

San. And he did well.

Bust. We come now to the pain.   70

San. (*aside*). I foresee sorrow here for me.

Bust. He told me not to seek a match for
Stella; that should be his care; and he preferred
that he should dower her, not I, and give her a
husband of his choosing.   75

San. You said that you were sad and joyful
too, but I alone am sad; for you attain to honors,
and I reap only pains. Leave with me your
grief, and keep your joy, for in the king's
suite, and with a brilliant marriage for   80
your sister, it is natural for you to be merry.
But you break the law of friendship, for you
should have told the king your sister was already promised.   84

Bust. It was all so strange, and my head so
troubled, that I did not find the chance to say
it.

San. Being so, shall my marriage not take
place?

Bust. I will return and inform the king   90
that the agreements and the writings are all
made, and the contract will then stand, for his
authority will not disregard your just claim.

San. But if the king should turn the law,
who can constrain him if guided by self-   95
interest or pleasure?

Bust. I will speak to him, and you as well;
for then, in my confusion, I did not tell him
of our agreement.

San. Would that my griefs might kill   100

me! I said indeed that fortune stands not a moment steadfast, and that sorrow and weeping cast their shadow on our joys. And if the king should wish to do us wrong?

Bust. Sancho Ortiz, the king's the king. 105 Be silent and have patience. (*Exit.*

San. In such a plight, who can have patience, and forbear? Oh, tyrant, come to thwart my happy marriage, applauded though you be in Seville, may your people drive 110 you from your kingdom of Castile! Well do you deserve the name of Sancho the Bold by the acts I learn of now, if you win the name by tyranny! But God will break your plans — may He drive you from your kingdom of 115 Castile! I'll leave Seville, and go to Gibraltar, to seek death in the battle-front.

Clar. Methinks we'll find it nearer than Gibraltar!

San. Loving Stella the fair, why is my 120 love so ill-starred? But my star is unfavorable, and her influence works my unhappiness!

Clar. A shooting star, mayhap.

San. May you be banished from your kingdom of Castile! (*Exeunt.* 125

SCENE 3. *A street in Seville, showing entrance to* TABERA'S *house.*

Enter the KING, DON ARIAS, *and Suite*

King. Announce that I am here.

Ari. They are informed, and Don Bustos Tabera is already at the door to greet you, Sire.

Enter BUSTOS

Bust. What an honor, and what conde- 5 scension! Your highness in my house!

King. I was strolling in disguise to see the city, and they told me as we passed, this was your house; and I would see it, for they say it is most beautiful. 10

Bust. It is the house of a simple esquire.

King. Let us go in.

Bust. Sire, 'tis fit for my humble station, but not for you; for so great a lord it is too small. And it will not be well received in Seville, 15 when they know you came to visit me.

King. I come not for your house, Tabera, but for you.

Bust. My lord, you do me great honor. But if you come for me, it is not meet that I 20 obey you; for it would be uncourtly, that the king should come to the vassal, and the vassal permit it and consent to it. I am your servant and your vassal, and it is fitting that I come to you in the palace, if you wish to honor 25 me. For favors may become affronts, when open to suspicion.

King. Suspicion? Of what?

Bust. It will be said, though it be false, you came to my house to see my sister; and 30 her good name, however well established, might come in question; for honor is a crystal clear — a breath may tarnish it.

King. Since I am here, I wish to speak with you of matters of importance. Let us go in. 35

Bust. It shall be upon the way, with your permission. My house is not in order.

King (*aside to* ARIAS). He makes great opposition.

Ari. (*aside to the* KING). Take him away, 40 and I will stay behind and speak to her for you.

King. Speak low, that he may not hear you. The fool puts all his honor in his ears.

Ari. The weight will break them.

King (*to* BUSTOS). So be it; I would not 45 see your house against your will.

Bust. Sire, at Stella's marriage you shall see it suitably adorned.

Ari. Bring up the coach.

King. Bustos, you'll ride upon the step. 50

Bust. I'll go on foot, with your permission.

King. The coach is mine, and I give orders here.

Ari. The carriage waits.

King. Drive to the palace. 55

Bust. (*aside*). Great favors these! The king does me much honor: please God it be for good. (*Exeunt.* *Manet* ARIAS.

Enter STELLA *and* MATILDE

Stel. What do you say, Matilde?

Mat. It was the king, my lady. 60

Ari. It was he, and it is not the first time a king was guided by a star. He came to your

house to do homage to your charms; for if
he is king of Castile, you are the queen of
beauty. The King Don Sancho, whom 65
for his unconquered prowess, the public, and
the Moors who tremble at his name, have
called The Bold, saw at a balcony your divine
beauty, which rivals Aurora in her palace,
when, hailed by drowsy birds mid roses 70
and lilies, and weeping at the wakening, she
scatters garlands of pearls. He ordered me
to offer you the riches of Castile, though riches
be but little for such charms. Accept his will,
for if you do accept it, and reward it, you 75
shall be the Sun of Seville, where you have been
the Star. He will give you towns and cities,
whereof you shall be Duchess, and he will wed
you to a Duke, whereby you will crown the
glory of your ancestors, and bring honor to 80
the name of Tabera. What say you?

Stel. What do I say? See!

                 (*She turns her back.*

Ari. Hold! Wait!

Stel. To such ignoble message, my back gives
a reply.   (*Exit.* 85

Ari. A noble pair! I marvel at them both.
The austerity of Rome survives in them in
Seville. It seems impossible for the king to
outwit and conquer them, but strength and persistence level mountains and split rocks. 90
I'll speak to this servant, for gifts are gates to
favor with the Portias and Lucrecias. Are
you the servant of the house?

Mat. Servant I am, by force.

Ari. By force?   95

Mat. I am a slave.

Ari. A slave!

Mat. Deprived of blessed liberty, and subject both to prison and to death.

Ari. I'll have the king release you, and 100
give you with your freedom, a thousand ducats
rent, if you will do his will.

Mat. For liberty and gold, there is no crime
that I'll not undertake. What is there I can
do? I'll do it if I can.   105

Ari. You'll give the king admittance to the
house tonight.

Mat. He shall find the doors all open, if you
but keep your promise.

Ari. Before he enters, I will give you a 110

letter from the king, in his own hand and signed
by him.

Mat. Then I'll put him in Stella's very bed
tonight.

Ari. What time does Bustos come?   115

Mat. Each night he's out till dawn. He has
a lady, and this distraction often costs men
dear.

Ari. What time do you think the king
should come?   120

Mat. Let him come at eleven, for then she
will be in bed.

Ari. Take this emerald as pledge of the
favors that await you.   (*Exeunt.*

SCENE 4.   *A room in the palace.*

Enter IÑIGO OSORIO, BUSTOS TABERA *and*
DON MANUEL, *with golden keys*

Man. I congratulate your lordship on the
key, and the dignity it represents. May you
win the honors you desire.

Bust. Would I might repay his majesty the
honor that he does me, undeserved.   5

Iñi. 'Tis not beyond your merit. Be assured, the king makes no mistake.

Bust. The key he's given me admits me to his
paradise; although thus elevated I fear a fall
to earth; for he has granted me abruptly 10
all these honors and I foresee that he who gives
thus hastily may change as suddenly.

Enter ARIAS

Ari. You may retire, gentlemen. The king
intends to write.

Man. Let's go and seek amusement for 15
the night.   (*Exeunt.*

Enter the KING

King. You say I shall enjoy her charms tonight, Don Arias?

Ari. The little slave is wholly won.

King. Castile shall raise a statue to her. 20

Ari. You are to give her a document.

King. Prepare it, Arias. I shall not hesitate to sign, for my love impels it.

Ari. In faith, the little slave is useful.

King. 'Tis the sun in heaven she pro- 25
cures for me, in the Star of Seville.
(*Exeunt* KING *and* ARIAS.

ACT II

SCENE I. *Street before* TABERA'S *house.*

Enter the KING, DON ARIAS, *and* MATILDE

Mat. Alone; it will be safer, for all are now
at rest.
King. And Stella?
Mat. She is sleeping, and the room is dark.
King. Although my promise might suf- 5
fice, here, woman, is the paper, with your lib-
erty therein. I will give another slave to
Bustos.
Ari. And the money and all is included in it.
Mat. I kiss your feet. 10
Ari. All alike, my lord, yield to their interest.
King. What joy divine to be a king!
Ari. Who can resist it?
King. To be more secret, I'll go up alone.
Ari. You risk yourself alone, my lord? 15
King. Now, tell me: although I risk myself,
and though it be not safe — is not the king at
hand? Begone.
Ari. Where shall I wait?
King. Not in the street; some nook 20
where I can find you.
Ari. I'll enter in Saint Mark's. (*Exit.*
King. What time will Bustos come?
Mat. He always comes when the birds salute
the dawn. And till he comes, the door is 25
open.
King. My love impels me to this high ad-
venture.
Mat. Follow me, your highness; the passage
is in darkness. (*Exeunt.* 30

Enter BUSTOS, DON MANUEL, *and*
DON IÑIGO

Bust. Here is my house.
Iñi. Farewell.
Bust. It is early for me.
Man. You need not go farther.
Bust. 'Tis well. 35
Iñi. We two have a certain visit still to
make.

Bust. Did Feliciana please your fancy?
Man. Tomorrow at the palace, my good 40
friend, we will speak of her, for she is a
figure worthy of all praise. (*Exeunt.*
Bust. I'm early home to bed. The house is
dark. No page is at the door. Ho! Lujan,
Osorio, Juan, Andres! They're all asleep.
Justine! Ines! The maids are sleeping 45
too. Matilde! The slave also has surrendered. Sleep is the god and master of her
senses. (*Exit* BUSTOS.

SCENE 2. *A room in the house.*

Enter MATILDE *and the* KING

Mat. I think that was my master calling.
I am lost.
King. Did you not say he came at dawn?
Mat. Woe is me!

Enter BUSTOS. *The* KING *wraps himself in
his cloak*

Bust. Matilde! 5
Mat. O God! I cannot face him.
King (*aside to* MATILDE). Have no fear.
(*Exit* MATILDE.
Bust. Who's there?
King. A man.
Bust. A man, at this hour? And in 10
my house? His name!
King. Stand back.
Bust. You lack in courtesy, and if you pass,
it shall be by the point of this sword; for al-
though this house is sacred, I'll profane it. 15
King. Lower your sword.
Bust. What! Lower it, when my sister's
room is thus profaned? Tell me your name,
or I will kill you here.
King. I am a person of importance. 20
Let me pass.
Bust. This house is mine, and I command in
it.
King. Let me pass; observe, I am a man of
rank, and though I have come to your 25
house, my intent is not to attack your honor,
but to increase it.
Bust. Is honor thus increased?
King. Your honor is in my care.

Bust. A better defender is this sword. 30
And if you seek my honor, why do you come
disguised? Do you conceal yourself to hon-
or me? Do you hide yourself to do me service? Let your fear convince you how true it is
that no one who gives honor need bring 35
shame with it. Draw, or by Heaven, I'll kill you!

King. Rash provocation!

Bust. I'll kill you here and now, or you'll kill
me.

King. I'll tell him who I am. Hold! I 40
am the king.

Bust. You lie! The king, seeking my shame,
alone, disguised, and unattended? It cannot be, and you insult your king, since you accuse him of a fault that is the depth of 45
baseness. What? The king outrage his vassal?
This angers me still more. For this I'll kill
you, in spite of all resistance. Offending me,
lay not such charges against His Majesty,
for well you know the laws of God and 50
man condemn to just chastisement him who
fancies or suspects unworthy conduct in his
king.

King. What strange persistence! Man, I
say I am the king. 55

Bust. Still less do I believe it, for the name
of king is here, but not the deeds. The king
is he who seeks my honor, and you seek my
dishonor.

King (*aside*). He is both fool and 60
boor. What shall I do.

Bust. (*aside*). It is the king, disguised. There
is no doubt. I'll let him pass, and later learn
if he has wronged me. My soul is roused to
anger and to fury, for honor is a thing that 65
he who gives may also take away. — Pass,
whoever you may be, and next time do not defame the king, nor call yourself the king, wretch,
when you have to blush for your acts. Know
that the king my master, the dread of 70
Africa, is most Christian and most holy, and
you insult his name. He has entrusted to me
the key to his house, and could not come without a key to mine, when he has given me his.
And do not offend the law; remember 75
that he is an honorable man. This I say to
you, and I spare you because you feigned
to be the king. Marvel not to see me loyal,

though offended, for 'tis a vassal's obligation
to respect the name. Thus will he learn 80
to be ruler of the honor of his vassals, and
cease to wrong them against God's law and
man's.

King. I can no more; I choke with shame
and anger. Fool! You let me go because 85
I feigned to be the king? Then let me tell
you that because I said so, I'll go out thus
from here. (*He draws.*) For if I win to freedom
because I called myself the king, and you respect
the name, I'll act the king, and you'll re- 90
spect his deeds. (*They fight.*) Die, villain, for
here the name of king gives power to me; the
king will kill you.

Bust. My honor rules me more than any
king. 95

Enter Servants with lights

Serv. What's this?

King. I'll make escape before I'm recognized. I leave this offended ruffian, but I
will have revenge. (*Exit.*

Serv. Your enemy has fled. 100

Bust. Follow him! Chastise him! ... No,
let him go, we'll give the enemy a bridge of
silver. Give a light to Matilde, and do you
withdraw. (*They give her one and exeunt.*

Bust. (*aside*). She has betrayed me, for 105
she hangs her head in shame. I will obtain the
truth with a cunning lie. — Close the door.
I am about to kill you. The king has told
me all.

Mat. If he has not kept the secret, 110
how can I in my unhappy state do so, my
lord? All the king has told you is the truth.

Bust. (*aside*). Now I shall learn the damage
to my honor. — So then you gave the king admittance? 115

Mat. He promised me my freedom, and for
that I brought him to this place, as you have
seen.

Bust. And does Stella know aught of this?

Mat. I think her wrath would have 120
consumed me, had she heard my plot.

Bust. That is certain, for if her light were
dimmed, she'd be no star.

Mat. Her radiance suffers neither shadow

nor eclipse, and her light is clear and 125
bright as of the sun. The king but reached
her room, and entered, giving me this paper,
and you behind him.

Bust. What? The king gave you this paper?

Mat. With a thousand ducats [1] rent, 130
and liberty.

Bust. A noble gift, at the expense of my
honor! Well does he honor and advance
me! Come with me.

Mat. Where do you take me? 135

Bust. You are going where the king may
see you, for thus I fulfill the law and obligation that rests upon me.

Mat. Ah, unhappy slave!

Bust. Though the king sought to eclipse 140
her, the fame shall not be lost in Spain of the
Star of Seville. (*Exeunt* BUSTOS *and* MATILDE.

SCENE 3. *A street leading to the palace.*

Enter the KING *and* ARIAS

King. And that is what befell me.

Ari. You would go in alone.

King. He was so mad and bold as to insult
me; for I know he recognized me. He drew
upon me with equivocal words and 5
though I contained myself a time, the natural
resentment born in every man broke down the
dignity my rank demands. I attacked him,
but they came with lights who would have told
the truth that they imagined, had I not 10
turned my back fearing to be recognized. And
so I come; you see, Arias, what befell me with
Bustos Tabera.

Ari. Let him pay for his offense with death;
behead him, let the rising sun shine on 15
his just punishment, for in the boundaries of
Spain there is no law but your desire.

King. To execute him publicly, Arias, is
error great.

Ari. You will have sufficient pretext; 20
for he is councilor of Seville, and the wisest
and most prudent, Sire, still commits some
crime, a prey to power and ambition.

King. He is so circumspect and prudent,
that he has no guilt. 25

[1] A gold ducat was worth about $2.25; a silver one,
half this amount.

Ari. Then have him killed in secret, Sire.

King. That might be done, but to whom can
I entrust the secret?

Ari. To me.

King. I do not wish to endanger you. 30

Ari. Then I will find you a man, courageous
and valiant soldier, and distinguished nobleman as well, before whom the Moor has trembled in the strong fortress of Gibraltar, where
he has been many times victorious cap- 35
tain, and was never conquered. Today in Seville they give him first rank among the brave
and gallant, for he is the glory of the soldier's
trade.

King. What is his name? 40

Ari. Sancho Ortiz de las Roelas, called besides the Cid of Andalusia. [1]

King. Summon him to me at once, for dawn
approaches.

Ari. Come to bed. 45

King. What bed can tempt him who is offended, and in love? Call the man at once.

Ari. What form is that, that hangs upon the
palace, swinging in the wind?

King. A form, you say? What can 50
it be?

Ari. There must be reason for it.

King. See what it is.

Ari. The little slave, with her paper in her
hands. 55

King. What cruelty!

Ari. And what a crime!

King. I'll kill the brother and the sister, too,
if Seville shows sedition.

Ari. Have her cut down at once, and 60
secretly give her a decent burial. Such bold
effrontery! Tabera must die.

(*Exeunt the* KING *and* ARIAS.

SCENE 4. *A room in* TABERA'S *house.*

Enter BUSTOS *and* STELLA

Stel. What do I hear?

Bust. Close the door.

Stel. Hardly does the sleepy sun, shod with
sapphires, leave the palace of Aurora, and

[1] Andalusia is the name given to the southern portion
of Spain, in which are located Seville, Granada, Cordova, Malaga, and other provinces.

you rouse me from my bed, alone, troubled,　5
and afflicted? You are agitated and perturbed! Tell me, have you seen some fault,
in which I am concerned?

Bust. You can tell me if there has been
such.　　　　　　　　　　　　　　　10

Stel. I? What do you say? Are you mad?
Tell me, have you lost your mind? I, a fault?
Nay, you have committed one in saying so,
for only to question is a crime against me. Do
you not know me? Know you not who　15
I am? In my mouth have you ever heard
words not in keeping with the honor with
which I guard my tongue? And if you have
seen nothing that can testify against me, what
fault can I have done?　　　　　　　　20

Bust. I do not speak without occasion.

Stel. Without occasion?

Bust. Alas! Stella!... for this night and
in this house ...

Stel. Speak, for if I should be guilty, I　25
offer myself at once for punishment. What
happened in this house this night?

Bust. This night was the epicycle of the sun,
for this night my Stella's star declined.

Stel. No astrologics in dealing with　30
questions of honor! Speak plainly, and leave
the sun in its five zones, for though my name
be Stella, the sun does not control me.

Bust. When the discordant tones of the bell
of Cuevas sounding in the sky marked　35
the middle of the night, I entered the house,
and found in it, and near your very room, the
king alone and in disguise.

Stel. What say you?

Bust. I speak the truth. Ask your-　40
self, Stella, why the king could have come to
my house alone at such an hour, if he came not
for Stella. Matilde was with him: I heard her
step, for then my honor was alert and keen.
I drew, and said: "Who's there?" "A　45
man," he answered. I advanced upon him,
and he retreating, said he was the king. And
although I recognized him at once, I pretended not to know him, for Heaven willed to
give me torment. He attacked me like an　50
angry and offended monarch, for a king who
attacks in anger fails not in valor. Pages came
with lights, and then he turned his back lest he

be seen, and was not recognized by any. I questioned the slave, and she, without need　55
of torture, confessed the truth. The king gave
her her freedom, signed in a paper that he
wrote, chief witness in the case, in which his
guilt stood clear. I took her from the house at
once, lest her infected breath sow dishonor　60
within these walls. I seized her at the door,
and placing her upon my shoulders, made my
way to the palace, and for her crime I hanged
her from the railings; for I'd have the king
know that if he is a Tarquin, I will be a　65
Brutus. Now you know all, Stella. Our honor
is in danger. I am forced to leave you, and
must give you a husband. Sancho Ortiz it
shall be, for in his care you will be delivered
from the designs of the king, and I can go　70
my way in peace.

Stel. Oh, Bustos, give me your hand for the
service you have done me.

Bust. It must be today, and till I see you
wed to him, keep silence, for my honor　75
is at stake.

Stel. O joy, my love! Thou art mine at last,
and shalt not escape again. And yet, who
knows the end from the beginning, if between
the cup and the lip the sage feared dan-　80
ger?　　　　　　(*Exeunt* STELLA *and* BUSTOS.

SCENE 5. *A room in the palace.*

Enter ARIAS, *and the* KING, *with two
papers*

Ari. Sanchos Ortiz de las Roelas is waiting
in the antechamber.

King. All of love is trickery, and pity
takes hold upon me. In this paper I have
sealed his name and fate, and in this I say　5
that I command his death: in this fashion the
killer will be safeguarded. Have him come
in. Then draw the bolt and do you remain
without.

Ari. Without?　　　　　　　　　10

King. Yes; for I wish him to see that I alone
am in the secret. Thus my desire conceives
the vengeance more assured.

Ari. I'll call him.　　　　　　(*Exit.*

King. I fear this is no glorious or lofty　15
token of my love.

Enter SANCHO ORTIZ

San. I kiss your feet.

King. Rise, I would not humble you, rise.

San. My Lord.

King (*aside*). A noble youth. 20

San. My lord, it is not strange that I should be confused, being no courtier, nor yet orator.

King. Why, tell me: What see you in me? 25

San. Majesty and valor; and in fine I see in you God's image, since the king is his embodiment; and I believe in you, as I do in Him. I submit myself here, great king, to your imperial will. 30

King. What is your state?

San. Never so honored as I am today.

King. I applaud your wisdom and your zeal. Now, since you will be anxious, and eager to learn why I have summoned you, 35 I'll tell you, and will see if I have in you as well a valiant soldier. My interest demands the killing of a man, in secret, and this task I mean to trust to you, for I prefer you to all others in the city. 40

San. Is he guilty?

King. He is.

San. Then, why a secret murder for a culprit? You may, in justice, publicly effect his death, without killing him in secret; for 45 thus you do accuse yourself, accusing him, since men will think you cause his death unjustly. If this poor man has but a slight offense, my lord, I ask you pardon him.

King. Sancho Ortiz, you are not here as 50 advocate for him, but executioner. And since I order it, hiding the hand that strikes, it must be that it interests my honor to kill him thus. Does he who has attacked my person merit death? 55

San. By fire.

King. And if his crime was that?

San. My lord, I would demand his death at once, and if 'tis so, then I will give it, though he were my brother, and hesitate 60 no more.

King. Give me your hand upon it.

San. And with it my soul and faith.

King. You can kill him, taking him unawares. 65

San. My lord, I am Roela and a soldier, would you make me a traitor? I, kill by treachery! Face to face I'll kill him, where Seville may see, in street or market place. For none can excuse him who kills and does 70 not fight; and he who dies by treachery fares better than the one who kills. He who lives thus proclaims his perfidy to all he meets.

King. Kill him as you like. You bear this paper signed by me, as guarantee, in which 75 it states that I have pardoned any crime you do. Read. (*He gives him a paper.*)

San. It reads thus (*reads*):

"*Sancho Ortiz*, At once for me and in my name give death to him this paper indicates. 80 I act through you, and if you be disturbed, I promise you hereby that I shall free you.

"*I the King.*"

I am amazed Your Majesty should think so meanly of me. I, a promise! a paper! 85 My loyalty trusts more in you than it. If your words have effect to move the hills, and carry out whate'er they say, give me your promise, Sire, and then I need no paper. Destroy it, for without it death is better 90 sought than with it, since to some degree the paper casts discredit on your word. (*He tears it.*) Without a paper, Sire, we'll pledge ourselves, and promise, I to avenge you, you to protect me. If so it be, we need no docu- 95 ments which are an obstacle. I go at once to execute your will, and only ask you, as reward, the woman whom I choose, as wife.

King. Be she a duchess of Castile, I give her to you. 100

San. May you regain the Moorish throne! May your glorious possessions reach the sea, and even to the pole!

King. Your excellent service, Sancho, shall be rewarded. In this paper is the name 105 of the man who is to die. (*Gives him the paper.*) And when you open it, be not dismayed. I have heard it said in Seville, he is brave.

San. That we shall see hereafter.

King. We two alone this secret know. 110 I need not say, be prudent, act, and keep your counsel. (*Exit*

Enter CLARINDO

Clar. I have sought you, my lord, bearing good news. I ask a guerdon for your dearest wish fulfilled.   115

San. You come in good spirits.

Clar. Does your heart not divine the guerdon?   (*Gives him a paper.*)

San. From whom is this?

Clar. From Stella, who was fairer and   120 lovelier than the sun. She ordered me to give you this paper and ask a guerdon.

San. For what?

Clar. For the marriage, which is to take place at once.   125

San. What do you say? This joy will kill me. What! Stella will be mine? The glorious radiance of Aurora is for me? And I may hope that the sun's golden rays will bathe in floods of light our former griefs?   130
    (*Reads.*

"*My husband:* The happy day so long desired has arrived. My brother seeks you, to crown my life, and to reward you. If you accord, seek him at once and lose no time.
    Your Stella."   135

Oh, fairest maid! What height may I not reach with such a star! Advise my steward of the happy bond which I assume. Let him bring forth at once the liveries reserved for this event, and let my servants and pages put   140 on their hats adorned with finest plumes. And if you claim a guerdon, take this hyacinth. I would give even the sun, if it were mounted in a ring.

Clar. May you outlive the very stones,   145 and cling like ivy to your bride! Nay, since I love you so, may you live longer than a fool!
    (*Exit.*

San. I will seek Bustos, for I am tormented with hope and eagerness. But with this marriage and my joy, I had forgot the king.   150 It was not right. The paper is unsealed; I'll see who is it must be killed.   (*Reads.*

"*Sancho,* he whom you must kill is Bustos Tabera."

Heaven help me! Is this his will? After   155 joy, disaster! All this life is but a game of chance, the cards ill shuffled and leading

to reverse and ruin, for it's all in gains and losses, like a game of cards. I won at first, but now my luck has changed, and turned   160 the card to give me death. Did I read aright? But I should not have read it, if the paper said not so. I'll look again. (*Reads.*) "Sancho, he whom you must kill is Bustos Tabera." I am undone. What shall I do? For I   165 have given my promise to the king, and I shall lose his sister.... Sancho Ortiz, it must not be; Bustos shall live! — But it is not right that my desire constrain my honor. Bustos shall die! Bustos must die! — But hold,   170 fierce hand! Bustos must live, shall live! — But I cannot obey my honor, if I yield to love. — But who can resist the force of love? — 'Tis better that I die or go away, so that I serve the king, and he may live. — But I must do   175 the king's will. (*Reads.*) "Sancho, he whom you must kill is Bustos Tabera." — But if the king kills him because of Stella, and seeks to honor her? If for Stella he kills him! Then he shall not die because of her. I will offend   180 him and defend her. — But I am a gentleman, and must not do that which I will, but what I ought. — What is my duty? To obey the law that takes precedence. — But there is no law that forces me to this — But yes, there   185 is, for though the king be wrong, he is accountable to God. My mad love must give way, for though it cost me cruel grief, to obey the king is right: Bustos must die, shall die! None may rightly say: Bustos must live, shall live!   190 Forgive me, beloved Stella, but O the sacrifice, to renounce you and become your enemy. What shall I do? Can I do otherwise?

Enter BUSTOS TABERA

Bust. Brother, I am blessed by fate in finding you.   195

San. (*aside*). And I am cursed by fate in meeting you, for you seek me to give me life, but I seek you to kill you.

Bust. Brother, the hour has come for your desired marriage.   200

San. (*aside*). The hour of all my grief, I'd better say. O God! Was ever man in such despair? That I should have to kill the man

I most have loved! to renounce his sister! to
lose all that I hold dear! 205

Bust. By contract you are already wed to
Stella.

San. I meant to marry her, but now it may
not be, although you grant it.

Bust. Do you know me, and address me thus?

San. Because I know you, I speak 211
thus, Tabera.

Bust. If you know me to be Tabera, how dare
you use such words?

San. I speak because I know you. 215

Bust. You know my birth, my blood, and
valor; and virtue, which is honor, for without it honor never was: and I am aggrieved,
Sancho.

San. But less than I. 220

Bust. How so?

San. To have to speak with you.

Bust. If you cast reflection on my honor or
my faith, you basely lie, and here I do maintain
it. (*He draws.* 225

San. What have you to maintain, villain?
(*Aside*) Forgive me, love; the king's excess
has made me mad, and none may resist me
now. (*They fight.*

Bust. You've killed me; stay your hand. 230

San. Ah! I am beside myself and wounded
you unknowing. But now I beg you, brother,
since I have regained my sense, to kill me.
Sheathe your sword within my breast, and
open passage for my soul. 235

Bust. Brother, I leave my Stella in your care.
Farewell. (*He dies.*

San. O cruel sword! O bloody, savage
murder! Since thou hast taken half my life,
complete thy work, that my soul may 240
expiate this other wound.

Enter two alcaldes, PEDRO *and* FARFAN

Ped. What's this? Hold your hand.

San. Why stay me if I've killed one dear to
me?

Far. O what confusion! 245

Ped. What is this?

San. I have killed my brother. I am a
Cain in Seville, since in cruel vengeance I
killed an innocent Abel. You see him; kill me

here, for since he dies through me I seek 250
to die through him.

Enter ARIAS

Ari. What's this?

San. A cruel violence, for such is the effect in
man of promises fulfilled, and purest loyalty.
Tell the king my master that Sevillians 255
keep their promises by acts, as you see here;
and for them they offend the stars, and know
no brother.

Ped. Has he killed Bustos Tabera?

Ari. O what a rash deed! 260

San. Seize me, take me prisoner, for it is
right that he who kills should die. See what
a cruel deed love made me undertake, for it
has forced me to kill him, and has forced me
to die. Now through him I come to ask 265
the death he owes to me.

Ped. Take him a prisoner to Triana, for
the city is in confusion.

San. O Bustos Tabera, my friend!

Far. The man has lost his mind. 270

San. Gentlemen, let me bear away the cold
form, bathed in its noble blood, for so I shall
support him, and will give him for a space the
life that I have taken.

Ped. He's mad. 275

San. If I have violated friendship, I have
kept the law, and that, sir, is to be king; and
that, sir, is not to be king. Understand me,
or understand me not, for I'll be silent. I
killed him, there is no denying, but I will 280
not answer why; let another tell the reason,
for I confess I killed him.

(*They take him and exeunt.*

SCENE 6. *A room in* TABERA'S *house.*

Enter STELLA *and* TEODORA

Stel. I know not if I dressed me well, for I
did dress in haste. Give me the mirror, Teodora.

Teo. You have but to regard within yourself,
my lady, for there is no glass that tells 5
such truths, nor shows the image of such
beauty.

Stel. My face is flushed, my color warm.

Teo. Your blood, my lady, has mounted to your cheek, 'twixt fear and modesty, to 10 celebrate your joy.

Stel. It seems to me already that I see my husband come, his face all wreathed in smiles, with soft caress to take my hand; — I seem to hear him utter a thousand tender words, 15 and that my soul on hearing leaps into my eyes, and takes possession of them. O happy day! O my guiding star!

Teo. I hear a knock. (*Drops mirror.*) The envious mirror fell. (*She picks it up.*) 20 The glass within the frame of one light made a thousand.

Stel. Did it break?

Teo. Yes, my lady.

Stel. 'Tis well, for I await the mirror, 25 Teodora, in which my eyes will see another self, and since I shall have such a mirror, let this one break, for I would not have this serve as mirror when he comes.

Enter CLARINDO *in gala dress*

Clar. This dress announces joy and 30 happiness, for my plumes already proclaim the wedding. I gave the paper to my master, and he gave this ring for guerdon.

Stel. Then I will change this guerdon for you. Give it me, and take this diamond. 35

Clar. The stone is split in two; it is for melancholy; they say that hyacinths have this complaint, although they lose it. It's split in two.

Stel. What matter that 'tis broken! 40 The very jewels feel my joy and happiness. O happy day! O my guiding star!

Teo. I hear people in the courtyard.

Clar. I think I hear the guests upon the stairs. 45

Stel. How can I bear my joy?... But what is this?

Enter the two alcaldes with TABERA'S *body*

Ped. Disaster and sorrow are the lot of man; for life is a sea of tears. Don Bustos Tabera is dead. 50

Stel. O hostile fate!

Ped. One consolation still remains to you, which is that the murderer, Sancho Ortiz de las Roelas, is a prisoner, and that he will suffer the penalty tomorrow without fail. 55

Stel. Leave me, O cruel men, for in your words you bear the torments of hell. My brother dead, and killed by Sancho Ortiz! Can one pronounce these words, or listen to them, and not die? I must be stone, for 60 I am still alive. O fateful day! O my guiding star! But if you have human pity, kill me.

Ped. Her grief dements her, and well may.

Stel. Unhappy is my star! My brother is dead, and Sancho Ortiz killed him, and 65 broke three hearts in one! Leave me, for I'm lost indeed. (*Starts to go.*)

Ped. She's desperate.

Far. Unhappy maid!

Ped. Follow her. 70

Clar. My lady...

Stel. Leave me, wretch, henchman of that murderer! Now, since all is ended, I'll end my life as well. Unhappy day! O my guiding star! (*Exeunt.*

ACT III

SCENE I. *A room in the palace.*

Enter the KING, *the two alcaldes,* DON ARIAS

Ped. He confesses that he killed him, but he will not confess why.

King. Does he not say what impelled him?

Far. He only answers "I do not know."

Ari. Great mystery! 5

King. Does he say whether there was provocation?

Ped. In no wise, my lord.

Ari. What obstinate temerity!

Far. He says he killed him, but he 10 knows not if 'twas right. He only confesses that he killed him, because he swore to kill him.

Ari. He must have given provocation.

Ped. He says not so.

King. Go back and speak to him for me, 15 and say that I demand his plea. Tell him I am his friend, but I will be his enemy in rigorous punishment. Let him declare on what provocation he killed Bustos Tabera, and give in

summary phrase the reason for the crime, 20
rather than meet death in obstinacy. Let him
say who ordered him, or on whose account he
killed him, or what incitement moved him to
this act; that on this condition I will show him
mercy, else he must prepare to die.   25

Ped. 'Tis that he most desires; his grief has
made him mad: after a deed so odious, so barbarous and cruel, he is bereft of reason.

King. Does he complain of any man?

Far. No, Sire. He takes counsel only of   30
his grief.

King. Rare and noble courage.

Far. He is silent on the crimes of others, and
blames himself alone.

King. Never in the world were two such   35
men; as I perceive their valor, it astounds me
more and more. Tell him from me to name
who caused the death or urged him to it; and
warn him that he should declare it, though
'twere the king. If he do not confess at   40
once, tomorrow on the scaffold he shall serve
as warning to Seville.

Ari. I go.   (*Exeunt alcaldes and* ARIAS.

Enter DON MANUEL

Man. Doña Stella begs permission to kiss
your hand.   45

King. Who prevents her?

Man. The citizens, my lord.

King. She measures her act with reason.
Give me a chair, and let her enter now.

Man. I'll go for her.   (*Exit.* 50

King. She will come radiant with beauty,
like the star that appears in heaven after a
storm.

Enter DON MANUEL, STELLA, *and people*

Man. She is here, beautiful as the sun, but
a sun whose summer radiance has turned   55
cold as stone.

Stel. Don Sancho, most Christian and illustrious monarch of Castile, famous for your exploits, celebrated for virtue: an unhappy star,
her bright rays veiled in mourning, in   60
dark clouds gathered by weeping, comes to implore justice; not, however, that you adminis-

ter it, but that you leave my vengeance in my
hands. I would not dry my eyes, for drowned
in tears, my grief commands respect. I   65
loved my brother Tabera, whose concerns are
now of heaven, where he treads the starry
streets of paradise. As a brother he protected
me, and I obeyed him as a father, and respected his commands. I lived in happi-   70
ness with him, and sheltered from the sun,
though its beams but rarely assailed my window. Seville envied our mutual affection, and
all believed we were twin stars reduced to one.
A cruel hunter bends his bow upon my   75
brother, and ends our happiness. I have lost
my brother, I have lost my husband, I am left
alone. And you do not hasten to your royal
duty, from which none has released you! Justice, Sire! Give me the murderer, fulfill 80
the law in this; let me pass judgment on him.

King. Be comforted, and dry your eyes, else
will my palace burst in flame, for stars are
tears of the sun, as each of its rays is topaz.
Let Aurora gather her riches in them, if   85
the new-born sun gives her the time, and let
heaven treasure them, for 'tis not right that
they be squandered here. Take this ring, it
will open the castle of Triana for you. Let
them deliver him to you, and be to him the   90
cruel tigress of Hircanian [1] cliffs; — although
the storks in flight urge us to pity and to weak
compassion, for it is true, surprising though it
be, that birds and beasts confound man's savagery.   95

Stel. In this case, Sire, severity's a virtue, for if in me were silver and gold, I'd
tear them from my head, and cover my face
with ugliness, though 'twere by burning coals.
If one Tabera's dead, another lives, and   100
if Tabera's shame is in my face, my hands
shall tear my flesh till it strike terror to the
hardest heart.   (*Exeunt all but the* KING.

King. If they deliver Sancho Ortiz to her,
I believe she'll slay him with her own   105
hands. Can God permit such cruelty to be in
form so fair and wonderful! See what a deed
mad passion doth commit: I did incite Sancho

[1] Hyrcania, a district of Asia, anciently located southeast of the Caspian Sea and reputed to be desert and
rough country.

Ortiz, and now I give him up, for love treads under foot the royal purple and promul- 110 gates his decrees at his own pleasure.   (*Exit.*

SCENE 2. *A prison.*

Enter SANCHO, CLARINDO, *and musicians*

San. Have you not made some verses on my fate, Clarindo?

Clar. Who would write verses, my lord, when poetry is so ill paid? At the festival in the market-place, many asked verses 5 from me, and later seeing me in the streets, would say to me, as if I were a tailor, or re-pairer, "Is not the compliment finished?" and urged me to more haste than for a mend-ed doublet. And had I not been hungry, 10 I'd have excelled Anaxagoras [1] in silence, and would have made a jest of Greek and Latin genius.

Enter the alcaldes and ARIAS

Ped. Enter.

Clar. I believe these men have come, 15 my lord, to inform you of your sentence.

San. (*to Musicians*). Then quickly begin a song. Now is death welcome, and I wish by singing to give evidence of my content. Be-sides, I'd show them my fortitude, and 20 that death itself has no power to move me.

Clar. Admirable courage! What better could a drunken Teuton do, his soul steeped in oldest wine?

Mus. (*sing*).

　　　　Since my unhappy fate 25
　　　　Consists in living,
　　　　So long as death delays,
　　　　It stays my dying.

Clar. An excellent enigma that they 29 sing!

San. A timely sentiment.

Mus.

　　　　There's naught in life like death
　　　　For one who lives a-dying.

Ped. Is this a time for music, sir?

San. Why, what better entertainment 35 in their misery can prisoners have?

[1] A famous Greek philosopher, *c.* 500–428 B.C.

Far. Can one be entertained by music when death threatens him hourly, and when he mo-mentarily awaits the sentence of his harsh judgment? 40

San. I am a swan, and sing before I die.

Far. The time has come.

San. I kiss your hands and feet, for the news you give me. O blessed day of my desire!

Ped. Sancho Ortiz de las Roelas, do 45 you confess you killed Bustos Tabera?

San. Yes, I declare it here aloud. Seek bar-barous punishments, invent new tortures, that shall make Spain forget Phalaris [1] and Max-entius. 50

Far. Then did you kill him unprovoked?

San. I killed him; that I do confess. The cause, since I have kept it secret, if there be any man who knows it, let him tell; for I know not why he died, I only know I killed 55 him without knowing.

Ped. It seems a treachery to kill him with-out cause.

San. He certainly gave cause, since he is dead. 60

Ped. To whom?

San. To him who brought me where I am, to this extremity.

Ped. Who is it?

San. I cannot tell, because he charged 65 me secrecy. And if I acted like a king, I will keep silence like one, and to put me to death, you need but know that I have killed him, without demanding why.

Ari. Señor Sancho Ortiz, I come to you 70 in the king's name, to ask that you confess, at his request, who caused this mad disorder. If you did it for friends, for women, or for rela-tives, or for some man in power, some grandee of this realm, and if you have from him 75 some paper, safeguard, or agreement, written or signed by his hand, show it at once, and thereby do your duty.

San. If I do so, my lord, I shall not do my duty. Say to His Majesty, my friend, 80 that I fulfill my promise, and if he is Don Sancho the Bold I bear the same name. Tell him that I may have had a paper, but he in-

[1] A cruel tyrant of Sicily in the sixth century B.C. He roasted many persons alive in a brazen bull.

sults me when he asks for papers, having seen them torn. I killed Bustos Tabera, and 85 though I might free myself now, I will not, because I know I break a promise. I keep my promise like a king, and I have done that I did promise, and he should do the same who also promises. Let him now act whose obli- 90 gation is to speak, for I fulfilled my obligation in action.

Ari. If you can justify yourself by a word, 'tis madness to refuse it.

San. I am who I am, and being who 95 I am, I avenge myself by my silence, and I defy one who keeps silence. And who is who he is, let him act as who he is, and so we shall both act as befits us.

Ari. I'll say that to His Majesty. 100

Ped. Sancho Ortiz, you have done a thing most ill advised, and you have acted rashly.

Far. You have offended the municipality of Seville, and exposed your life to her severity, your neck to her just vengeance. 105

(*Exeunt the alcaldes and* ARIAS.

Clar. Is it possible that you accept such insults?

San. I consent that men should punish me, and Heaven confound me: and already, Clar- 110 indo, it begins. Do you not hear a confused clamor? The air's aflame with thunderbolts and lightning: one sweeps upon me like a serpent, describing swift curves of fire.

Clar. I think that he has lost his wits. I'll follow his humor. 115

San. How I burn!

Clar. How I broil!

San. Did the bolt strike you too?

Clar. Do you not see me in ashes?

San. God save us! 120

Clar. Yes, my lord, I am the ashes of a fagot.

San. We are now in the other world.

Clar. In hell, I think.

San. In hell, Clarindo? Why say you 124 so?

Clar. Because I see in yonder castle, my lord, a thousand lying tailors.

San. You rightly say we're there; for Pride is burning upon yon tower formed of the arrogant and haughty; there I see Ambition 130 drinking a river of fire.

Clar. And farther on there is a legion of cabmen.

San. If coaches pass through here, they'll wreck the place. But if this is hell, why 135 do we see no lawyers?

Clar. They won't receive them, lest they bring lawsuits here.

San. If there are no lawsuits here, hell's not so bad. 140

Clar. Aha! There is the tyrant Honor, bearing a crowd of fools, who suffer for honor.

San. I'll join them. — Honor, an honorable fool comes to be your servant, for not violating your laws. — Friend, you have done 145 badly, for true honor consists today in having none. Dost seek me yonder, and for a thousand centuries I've been dead! Seek wealth, my friend, for wealth is honor. What did you do? — I sought to keep a promise. — You 150 make me laugh. Do you keep promises? You seem a simpleton, for not to keep a promise is a noble act these days. — I promised to kill a man, and raging killed him, though he was my friend. — Bad! 155

Clar. At least not good!

San. At least not good. Put him in prison, and condemn him for a fool. — Honor, I lost his sister, and now I suffer in that I did fight him. — No matter. 160

Clar. God help me! If I let him continue further, he will be mad entirely. I will invent a trick. (*He shouts.*

San. Who calls? Who calls?

Clar. It is the dog Cerberus who calls, 165 the porter of this palace. Do you not know me?

San. Methinks I do.

Clar. And who are you?

San. A man of honor.

Clar. What! In here! Begone. 170

San. What say you?

Clar. Go out at once; this place is not for men of honor. Seize him, and take him bound to the other world, to the prison of Seville, on the wind, but bandage his eyes, that he 175 may fly without fear. — Now his eyes are covered. — Now let the lame devil on his shoulders take him there at a leap. — At a leap? I am content. — Go, and take also his companion by the hand. (*Gives him a whirl, and re-* 180 *leases him.*) — Now you are in the world, my friend. God be with you, as with me.

San. God, said he?

Clar. Yes, my lord, for this devil, before he was one, was a baptized Christian, and 185 is a Gallego[1] of Caldefrancos.

San. It seems to me that I am waking from a trance. God help me! O Stella! How wretched is my fate without you! But since I caused your grief, I deserve my punish- 190 ment.

Enter the Governor of the prison and STELLA, *veiled*

Stel. Deliver me the prisoner at once.

Gov. Here is the prisoner, my lady, and as the king commands me, I deliver him to your hands. Señor Sancho Ortiz, His Majesty 195 commands us to deliver you to this lady.

Stel. Sir, come with me.

San. I welcome your compassion, if it is to kill me, for I desire death.

Stel. Give me your hand and come. 200

Clar. Does it not seem enchantment?

Stel. Let no one follow us. (*Exeunt.*

Clar. 'Tis well. In faith, we're traveling well, from hell to Seville, and from Seville to hell! Please God this Star reveal herself 205 as Venus! (*Exit.*

SCENE 3. *Outside the prison.*

Enter STELLA, *covered with her cloak,* SANCHO

Stel. Now I have placed you at liberty. Go with God, Sancho Ortiz, and remember that I have been merciful and compassionate. Go with God! Go. You are free. Why do you linger? Why look you so? Why hesitate? 5 He who delays is wasting time. Go, for a horse awaits you on which you can escape; the serv- ant has money for the journey.

San. Madame, I kiss your feet.

Stel. Go, for there is no time to lose. 10

San. With heavy heart I go. May I not know who has liberated me, that I may give thanks for such mercy?

[1] A Galician, one who lives in Galicia, at the extreme northwest corner of Spain.

Stel. A woman; I wish you well, for I give you liberty, having it in my discretion. 15 Go with God.

San. I will not pass from here, except you tell me who you are, or let me see your face.

Stel. I cannot now.

San. I wish to repay you for my life, 20 and freedom: I must know to whom I owe such obligation, acknowledging this debt.

Stel. I am a woman of noble birth, and more- over, the one who loves you best, and whom you love least. Go with God. 25

San. I will not go if you do not uncover.

Stel. That you may go, I am...

(*Uncovers.*

San. Stella, star of my soul!

Stel. A star I am, that guides you, the omen of your life. Go, for thus does love o'er- 30 come the force of sternness, for as I love you, so am I to you a favoring Star.

San. You! resplendent and fair, in presence of your mortal enemy! You! Such pity for me! Treat me more cruelly, for here pity 35 is cruelty, for pity is punishment. Have me put to death, seek not so generously to do me harm with good, when good is to my harm. Give liberty to one who killed your brother! It is not right that I should live, since he 40 met death through me. And it is right that one who thus lost a friend should lose you too. In freedom now I thus deliver myself to death, for if I were a prisoner, how should I ask for death? 45

Stel. My love is finer and stronger, and so I give you life.

San. Then I will go to death, since 'tis your will to free me, for if you act as who you are, I have to act my part. 50

Stel. Why do you die?

San. To avenge you.

Stel. For what?

San. For my treachery.

Stel. 'Tis cruelty. 55

San. 'Tis justice.

Stel. There is no plaintiff.

San. Love is plaintiff.

Stel. 'Tis to offend me.

San. 'Tis to love you. 60

Stel. How do you prove it?

San. By dying.
Stel. Nay, you insult me.
San. By living.
Stel. Hear me.   65
San. There is nothing to be said.
Stel. Where are you going?
San. I go to die, since by my life I offend
you.
Stel. Go, and leave me.   70
San. It is not well.
Stel. Live, and take your freedom.
San. It is not right.
Stel. Why do you die?
San. It is my pleasure.   75
Stel. 'Tis cruelty.
San. 'Tis honor, too.
Stel. Who accuses you?
San. Your disdain.
Stel. I have none.   80
San. I am unmoved.
Stel. Are you in your senses?
San. I am in my honor, and I offend you
by living.
Stel. Then, madman, go and die, for I   85
will also die.

(Exeunt on opposite sides.)

SCENE 4.   *A room in the palace.*

Enter the KING *and* ARIAS

King. And so he'll not confess that I commanded him to kill?
Ari. I ne'er saw bronze more firm. His
whole intent is to deny. He said at last that
he has fulfilled his obligation, and that it is   5
right that he to whom he owed the obligation
now keep his word.
King. He hopes to force me by his silence.
Ari. Indeed he has constrained you.
King. He has fulfilled his promise, and   10
I am sore perplexed not to be able to keep
the word I gave him in a moment of anger.
Ari. You cannot evade a promise given, for
if an ordinary man must keep it, in a king's
mouth it becomes law, and all must bow   15
before the law.
King. 'Tis true, when the law is interpreted
by natural right.
Ari. It is an obligation. The vassal does
not question the law of the king; the vassal   20
can only execute the law, blindly and unques-
tioning; and it is for the king to take thought.
In this instance you did give it in a paper, and
since he executed it without the paper, you
are bound to fulfill to him the law you   25
made in ordering him to kill Bustos Tabera;
for had it not been by your command, he had
not killed him.
King. Then must I say that I ordered his
death, and used such cruelty to one who   30
never offended me? What will the council of
Seville say of me, Arias, when it sees I was the
cause? And what will be said in Castile when
Don Alonso there already calls me tyrant, and
the Roman pontiff attacks me with his cen- 35
sure? Perchance he will take up my nephew's
claims, and his support assures them. I fail
in my desires likewise, I see, if I let Sancho die,
and that is baseness. What shall I do?
Ari. Your Highness may with flattery   40
win the alcaldes, and ask them that by exile
Sancho Ortiz pay for his crime and grievous
fault, suppressing greater rigors; thus do you
intercede for him. You may make him general on some frontier, and so you reward   45
him with a laurel crown.
King. You say well; but if Doña Stella, to
whom I gave my ring, has already wreaked
vengeance on him, what shall we do then?
Ari. All shall be put in order. I will   50
go in your name and seize her person alleging
your order, and will bring her alone and secretly to the palace. Here you may win her
to your design; and to persuade her, you may
marry her to some grandee of the court, for 55
her virtue and her rank deserve a noble husband.
King. How I repent my weakness, Arias!
The sage well says that he alone is wise who is
upon occasion prudent, as on occasion stern.
Go now and take Stella, since by her   60
capture you free me from my perplexity. And
to placate her I will marry her to a Duke of
Castile, and could I give my throne, would
put her in my place, for such a brother and
sister merit immortal glory.   65
Ari. The people of this city dim the glory
of Rome.

(Exit ARIAS.

Enter the Governor of the prison

Gov. I kiss Your Highness' feet.

King. Pedro de Caus, what occasion brings you to my feet? 70

Gov. Sire, this ring, engraved with your arms, is it not Your Majesty's?

King. Yes, this is pardon and safeguard for any crime you may have done.

Gov. O mighty king, there came with 75 it to Triana a woman closely veiled, saying that Your Highness ordered Sancho Ortiz be delivered her. I referred your mandate to the guards, together with the ring, and all were of opinion that he be delivered. I released 80 him, but shortly Sancho Ortiz, like a madman, with loud cries, begs that the castle gate be opened. "I will not do the king's command," he said, "and wish to die, for it is right that he who kills should die." I refused admit- 85 tance, but he shouted so I was obliged to open. He entered, and in joy he waits for death.

King. I never saw such noble or such Christian folk as in this city. Bronze, marble, statues, may be silent. 90

Gov. The woman says, my lord, she gave him freedom, and he would not accept it, when he knew she was the sister of Bustos Tabera, whom he put to death.

King. What you say now astounds me 95 all the more, their magnanimity passes nature. She when she should be most vindictive, forgives, and frees him; and he to reward her generous soul, returned to die. If their deeds go further, they will be immortalized in rec- 100 ords of eternity. Do you, Pedro de Caus, bring me Don Sancho in my carriage to the palace, with strictest secrecy, avoiding noise or guards.

Gov. I go to do your bidding.

(*Exit.*

Enter a servant

Serv. The two chief alcaldes desire to 105 see Your Majesty.

King. Tell them to enter, with their wands of office. (*Exit servant.*) Now if I can I'll keep my word to Sancho Ortiz, without revealing my deed of cruelty. 110

Enter the alcaldes

Ped. Sire, the guilt is proved; the case requires sentence.

King. Pronounce it. I only beg you, since you are the guardians of the state, to consider justice, and clemency oft favors it. San- 115 cho Ortiz is councilor of Seville, and if he who is dead was also councilor, the one claims mercy, if the other calls for vengeance.

Far. Sire, we are alcaldes of Seville, and her confidence and honor repose on us to- 120 day. These staves represent your imperial authority, and if they fail to honor your divine right, they offend your person. Held upright, they look to God, and if they are bent or lowered, they look to man, and deflect- 125 ing, they lose their heavenly function.

King. I ask not that you deflect them, but that equity be done in justice.

Ped. Sire, the source of our authority is Your Majesty. On your command de- 130 pend our hopes. Spare his life; you may pardon him, since kings are accountable to none. God creates kings, and God transfers the crown of sovereignty from Saul to David.

King. Go in, and weigh the sentence 135 that you give for penalty, and let Sancho Ortiz go to execution as the laws require. (*Aside*) You, Pedro de Guzman, listen to a word apart.

Ped. What is Your Highness' will?

King. By putting Sancho to death, my 140 dear Don Pedro, you do not restore life to the dead. May we not avoid the extreme penalty, and exile him to Gibraltar, or Granada, where in my service he may find a voluntary death? What say you? 145

Ped. That I am Don Pedro de Guzman, and I am at your feet. Yours is my life, and my possessions and my sword.

King. Embrace me, Don Pedro de Guzman. I did expect no less from a noble heart. 150 Go with God; send Farfan de Rivera to me. (*Aside*) Flattery levels mountains.

Far. You see me at your feet.

King. Farfan de Rivera, it grieved me that Sancho Ortiz should die, but now it is 155 proposed that death be changed to exile, and it will be longer, since it will be for life. I need your opinion to decide a matter of so great importance.

Far. Your Highness may command 160 Farfan de Rivera without reserve, for my loyalty has no reserve in serving you.

King. In truth you are Rivera, in whom the flowers of virtue spring, to adorn and attend you. Go with God. (*Exeunt alcaldes.*) 165 Well have I labored. Now, Sancho Ortiz escapes death, and my promise is saved without becoming known. I will have him go as general to some frontier, whereby I exile and reward him. 170

Re-enter alcaldes

Ped. Now the sentence is signed, and it remains only to submit it to Your Majesty.

King. Such noble lords as you will have made it, I doubt not, as I desired.

Far. Our boast is loyalty. 175

King (*reads the sentence*). "Our finding and decision is that he be publicly beheaded." Is this the sentence that you bring me signed? Thus, traitors, do you keep your promise to your king? Zounds! 180

Far. When this wand is laid aside, the lowest of your subjects, as you see, will keep his promise with his life or arms. But with it in hand, let none commit offense in act or words, for human empire, for earth or heaven. 185

Ped. Give us your orders as subjects, but as chief alcaldes, ask not unjust things, for then we bear our wands; as vassals we're without them. And the Council of Seville is what it is. 190

King. Enough; 'tis well, for all of you put me to shame.

Enter ARIAS and STELLA

Ari. Stella is now here.

King. Don Arias, what shall I do? What is your counsel in such great confusion? 195

Enter the Governor, SANCHO ORTIZ, and CLARINDO

Gov. Sancho Ortiz is before you.

San. Great king, why do you not end my

sufferings with death, my misfortunes with your condemnation? I killed Bustos Tabera, kill me; he who kills must die. Show 200 mercy, Sire, by executing justice.

King. Wait! Who ordered you to kill him?

San. A paper.

King. From whom? 205

San. Could the paper speak, 'twould tell, that is clear and evident; but papers torn give but confused reply. I only know I killed the man I most did love, because I promised. But here at your feet Stella awaits my death in 210 atonement, and still is her vengeance incomplete.

King. Stella, I have determined your marriage with a noble of my house, young, gallant, a prince of Castile, and lord of Salva. 215 And in return for this, we ask his pardon, which may not justly be refused.

Stel. Sire, if I am married, let Sancho Ortiz go free. I renounce my vengeance.

San. And so you give me pardon, be- 220 cause His Highness marries you?

Stel. Yes, for that I pardon you.

San. And are you thus avenged for my offense?

Stel. And satisfied. 225

San. Then that your hopes may be fulfilled, I consent to live, although I wished to die.

King. Go with God.

Far. Look what you do, my lord, for this is to offend Seville, and he must die. 230

King (*to* ARIAS). What shall I do? These people anger and dismay me.

Ari. Speak.

King. Men of Seville, put me to death, for I was cause of this murder. I ordered 235 him to kill, and this suffices to discharge him.

San. My honor awaited only this avowal, for the king ordered me to kill him, and I had not committed an act so cruel, had the king not ordered it. 240

King. I declare that this is true.

Far. Then is Seville content, for since you ordered he be put to death, no doubt he gave you cause.

King. The nobility of Seville leaves 245 me in wonder.

San. I will depart to exile, when Your Majesty fulfills another promise that you gave me.

King. I'll keep it.   250

San. I said that you should give to me for wife the woman I should ask.

King. So it was.

San. I ask for Stella.

Stel. Sancho Ortiz, I am promised.   255

San. Promised?

Stel. Yes.

San. Woe is me.

King. Stella, this was my promise; I am king and must fulfill it.   What do you say?   260

Stel. Your will be done.   I am his.

San. I am hers.

King. And now, what lacks?

San. Harmony.

Stel. Which we shall never find in life   265 together.

San. I say the same, and therefore I release you from your word.

Stel. And I release your word; for always to see the murderer of my brother at my   270 bed and board, would give me too much pain.

San. And me too much, to be forever with the sister of him I killed unjustly, loving him like my soul.

Stel. Then we are free?   275

San. Yes.

Stel. So then farewell.

San. Farewell.

King. Wait.

Stel. Sire, I cannot take for husband   280 a man who killed my brother, though I love him and adore him.   (*Exit.*

San. And I, Sire, because I love her, it is not just that I should marry her.

King. What nobility!   285

Ari. What constancy!

Clar. Madness it seems to me.

King. I marvel at these people.

Ped. Such are the people of Seville.

King. I intend to give her a husband,   290 and such as she deserves.

Clar. And now Lope consecrates to you this tragedy, giving eternal fame to the Star of Seville, whose marvelous history is writ on tablets of bronze.   295

(*Exeunt.*

INTRODUCTION TO

The Miser

The Early Drama and Stage in France: Molière and His Theater:
Molière's High Comedy

THE EARLY DRAMA AND STAGE IN FRANCE

IN FRANCE, as elsewhere in Europe, the drama originated with the Biblical and saints' plays presented as an adjunct to the services of the medieval churches. By the opening of the fifteenth century, however, the production of this sacred drama in the larger French towns had come under lay control. Groups of citizens, chiefly artisans or tradesmen, organized themselves into theatrical societies, called *confréries*. As purveyors of dramatic amusement the *confréries* corresponded to the trade guilds of England and Spain. Every year they produced cycles of plays on the Old and New Testaments, on the Acts of the Apostles, or on the Virgin Mary. The cycle performances commonly were interspersed with pantomimes and farces to add variety to the entertainment.

The productions of the *confréries* took place either in a public square, as at Valenciennes and Mons, or in a large hall, as at Paris. The usual type of setting consisted in numerous "mansions" — that is, booths or structural sets representing specific locales — arranged in a series to the sides and rear of an open acting-place. On this "multiple stage," Heaven, Noah's Ark, The Temple of Jerusalem, Herod's Palace, and Bethlehem's Fields appeared alongside a Garden of Eden gaudy with flowers and fruits, and a Hell-mouth "made like a great gargoyle which opens and closes." Lavish scenery, costuming, and mechanical effects changed the often tedious drama into colorful spectacle. The method of simultaneous setting passed over to the professional stage of seventeenth-century Paris and lasted up to the 1650's.

The oldest of the theatrical fraternities was the Confrérie de la Passion at Paris, licensed by the King in 1402 to act religious plays. In 1548, on account of supposedly scandalous treatment of sacred material, a royal edict permitted the Confrérie hereafter to present only "decent and lawful" secular works. The society then built in the St. Denis quarter of Paris the Hôtel de Bourgogne, France's first playhouse and her sole one for almost a century. There the Confrérie performed medieval types of drama and exercised a virtual monopoly over Parisian theatricals until about 1598, when it ceased to be a producing organization. Thenceforth the Hôtel de Bourgogne was leased to troupes of actors visiting Paris.

During the second half of the sixteenth century regular companies with female players in their personnel began to stroll through the French provinces. They acted at the houses of the nobility, in town halls and squares, upon almost bare platforms. Their meager repertoires contained tragedies crudely imitative of Seneca, tragicomedies of romantic intrigue, and coarse farces. The impoverished and disturbed condition of the country, together with the frequent opposition of officials and ecclesiastics, rendered professional strolling a precarious career. The outstanding troupe of the period, the Comédiens du Roi, or King's Players, had their Parisian debut in 1599 at the Hôtel de Bourgogne. They rented this theater with increasing regularity during the subsequent thirty years. Finally in 1629 they concluded a permanent lease.

Meanwhile dramatic art in France had advanced very slowly. The civil disturbances of the early seventeenth century caused Paris to lag far behind London and Madrid in material well-being and general culture. The polite world of the French capital had not yet taken up the theater. Hence the profession of playwriting did not much attract authors of literary talent. When Shakespeare and Lope de Vega were raising to the peak of excellence the drama of their respective nations, France was producing her first professional playwright, Alexandre Hardy (?1575–?1631). His prolific output of all the then popular forms — "regular" tragedies, tragicomedies, and pastorals or plays of shepherd romance — won him during his lifetime pre-eminence in his own country, but proved him immeasurably inferior to the best dramatists of England and Spain.

In 1630 a second troupe of actors settled permanently at Paris. After playing in various halls used for court tennis, they reconstructed one of these buildings and opened the Théâtre du Marais on December 31, 1634. Some years later a third company, Italian comedians exclusively, established themselves in the city.

This expansion of theatrical enterprise in Paris accompanied a great change of attitude toward drama and the stage. The dictatorship set up in 1624 by Cardinal Richelieu (1585–1642) inaugurated an era of peace, order, and economic progress. Intense social and intellectual fermentation resulted. The idea of *politesse* or refinement took strong hold of high society. *Salons* for the cultivation of manners and the arts sprang up. The drama came to be regarded as the leading form of *belles lettres*. Plays were read aloud at the *salons* where dramatic technique formed a subject for critical discussion. Even the best circles began to frequent the theater.

Though many high-ranking churchmen vehemently opposed the drama, Richelieu showed a deep interest in all phases of that art. He encouraged gifted poets to write for the stage, pensioned prominent dramatists and actors, gave private performances of new plays, and in 1641 completed at the new Cardinal's Palace the finest playhouse of seventeenth-century France. In that year also he prompted Louis XIII to bestow upon the company at the Hôtel de Bourgogne the title of the Troupe Royale together with an annual subsidy of $3000. At the same time the King granted an equal subsidy to the Italian comedians and one of $1500 to the troupe of the Théâtre du Marais. This governmental support continued under Louis XIV (1643–1715), whose prime minister (1643–61), Cardinal Mazarin, cared for dramatics quite as much as Richelieu.

MOLIÈRE AND HIS THEATER

The French stage therefore was flourishing under generous royal patronage when on the evening of October 24, 1658, in the guard hall of the old Louvre Palace, there occurred a performance which quite changed the complexion of theatrical affairs in Paris. A troupe fresh from the provinces scored an extraordinary triumph before Louis XIV and a crowd of notables with a farcical afterpiece, *The Love-Sick Doctor*, written by the director, Molière. The play and Molière's acting in it immediately stirred the King to admiration. Louis decreed that Molière's company should be called the Troupe de Monsieur ("Monsieur" being the title of the King's brother) and that they should use for half of each week the Hôtel du Petit Bourbon, the playhouse of the Italian buffoons. Thus Molière almost overnight became a figure of prominence in the capital of France.

Molière's success, however, had been long in the making. He was baptized on January 15, 1622, as Jean Baptiste Poquelin, the son of a wealthy Parisian furniture dealer and decorator. From 1637 to 1641 he attended the most distinguished school in the city, the Jesuit Collège de Clermont. Then he rejected the family desire that he should succeed to his father's business and to his father's court post of "valet-upholsterer," a kind of gentleman-in-waiting. Yet, for a year or so, he carried out his father's duties and made the king's bed while Louis XIII campaigned in the south of France. In 1643 he decided upon acting as his profession. Under the stage name of Molière he proceeded to associate himself with a well-known actress, Madeleine Béjart, and her two brothers, in the organization of the Illustre Théâtre. The new company during its brief existence of 1644–45 tried two different tennis courts in Paris, but enjoyed so little prosperity that in the summer of 1645 Molière's father had to bail him out of debtor's prison. Toward the end of the same year he left the capital along with the three Béjarts to join a provincial troupe. Elected its director about 1650, Molière brought it up to first place among the strolling groups. For twelve years he carried on as a barnstorming actor, manager, and playwright. When he returned to Paris in 1658, he had become a disciplined showman who believed that it was the theater's first object to excite and amuse.

From his opening production at the Hôtel du Petit Bourbon Molière won popularity with a repertoire largely of comedy. *Les Précieuses Ridicules* (*The Ridiculous, Affected Ladies*), his gay one-act play of 1659, caused a sensation. Its satire of the *salon* affectations in behavior, dress, speech, and learning, which "country cousins" aped as fashionable, conveyed a note of social criticism such as French comedy never before had exhibited. Louis XIV, delighted with this new comic vein, by a public gift of $750 announced Molière more than ever the King's man.

Royal favor rescued Molière from a serious predicament in the autumn of 1660. His rivals at the two other Parisian theaters hastened the government's demolition of the Hôtel du Petit Bourbon, hoping to deprive him of a suitable stage in Paris. He, however, turned the tables by securing the commodious Théâtre du Palais Royal which Richelieu had built. It opened under Molière's management in January, 1661. Six months later his first full-length play in Paris, *The School for Husbands*, achieved a "hit" with its sprightly portrayal of middle-aged tyranny outwitted by youthful love.

A companion piece, *The School for Wives*, attained a similar triumph during the following year.

With his theater now a lucrative business Molière, still a bachelor at forty, began to pay heed to his personal life. On February 20, 1662, he ventured into a romantic marriage with twenty-year old Armande, sister to his fellow trouper of longest standing, Madeleine Béjart. The attractive, high-spirited Armande, who had literally grown up in his troupe, had developed under his tutelage into so talented an actress that he henceforth wrote a leading part for her in every play. Their marriage, because of the disparity in age and mental endowment, may not have turned out a true comradeship, but it certainly did not darken his subsequent life.

Serious illness befell Molière in 1666, and again the next year. The symptoms pointed toward consumption. Despite physical disability his genius worked at its height in the years between 1666 and 1672. First came *The Misanthrope*, a portrait of a forthright man, Alceste, whose excessive disgust of the follies in the world about him prevents him from compromise even for the sake of marriage. Two months after *The Misanthrope* Molière brought forth *The Doctor In Spite of Himself*, a rollicking play in which a certain Sganarelle, compelled unexpectedly to act the quack-doctor, finds such profit in the quackery that he decides to pursue it as a business. *The Miser* in 1668 marked a return to sharper satire. Molière soon pursued the same mode in *Tartuffe*, which caricatured religious hypocrisy in the person of the pietistic, scheming "friend of the family." *Tartuffe* not only aroused a furor of misunderstanding, but gained for its author the undying hatred of many prominent churchmen. A certain cleric asserted that "Monsieur de Molière is one of the most dangerous enemies to the Church of Jesus Christ that this century or the world has produced." Undeterred by such abuse, he kept on ridiculing. In 1670 the social ambitions of the *nouveaux riches* supplied the target of *The Would-be Gentleman*, a good-humored portrait of the dull and inept Monsieur Jourdain who longs for culture and social grace. Two years later the pretensions of lightheaded blue-stockings to knowledge of literature and science afforded the subject for another devastating comedy, *The Learned Women*.

During the winter of 1672-73 Molière's health began to fail badly. Nevertheless, when his friend Boileau urged him to relinquish his theatrical responsibilities, he stoutly retorted: "It is a matter of honor with me not to quit the stage." On February 17, 1673, his condition seemed so critical that his wife and friends urged him not to undertake a performance, but the veteran leader, thinking only of his troupe, insisted: "I have fifty poor workmen who will be deprived of bread if I do not play." That afternoon, while he was acting in his latest composition, *The Imaginary Invalid*, hemorrhages started. Late in the evening he died, attended only by a sister of mercy, because no priest would administer confession to the creator of *Tartuffe*. The parish rector denied his body burial in the neighborhood cemetery. Even after the personal intercession of the King the funeral of France's greatest dramatist had to be conducted secretly at the dead of night. A silent, torchlit procession of friends bore him to a last resting-place on Montmartre, the perennial refuge of artists.

Molière's workshop remained to his dying hour the Théâtre du Palais Royal. Here, before an enthusiastic sovereign and citizens of all ranks, comedy arrived at a brilliance of performance which probably has never been surpassed. Richelieu's large and ornate, though not sumptuous, playhouse furnished the most attractive facilities of any professional theater then existing in France. The auditorium was a lofty, rectangular hall, about seventy feet long and sixty wide, with four big chandeliers of crystal to provide illumination. The stage stood at one end of the hall behind an ornamented proscenium frame. Three galleries, divided into compartments, ran along each side. High society occupied the two lower rows of gold-decorated boxes, while people of small means inhabited the plain top gallery. The front part of the hall, the "parterre," containing no seats, accommodated those who could afford merely standing room. Artisans, clerks, soldiers, lackeys, and idlers gathered there. Behind the parterre rose an amphitheater which filled the entire rear of the hall. The more well-to-do of the middle class occupied this section. Some thirty to forty spectators, chiefly young aristocrats or city dandies, were allowed to sit behind railings on the two sides of the stage. They now and then annoyed the players by silly or offensive remarks. A "full house" at the Théâtre du Palais Royal indicated an audience of about one thousand.

Yet Molière's brilliant regime rarely attracted a full house because the scale of admission prices was much higher than in the London and Madrid theaters of the later seventeenth century. Standing room in the parterre ordinarily cost about fifty cents; a place in the third gallery, seventy-five cents, or in the upper boxes, one dollar; a seat in the amphitheater, two dollars; a chair in the lower boxes or on the stage, three dollars. Prices always doubled, and sometimes multiplied even more, on the occasion of a new play, or of a play with extraordinary scenery and "machines."

Molière's troupe as a rule performed on Sundays, Tuesdays, and Fridays. Though performances were advertised by posters and by street-criers to begin at 3 P.M., they more often got under way a half-hour to an hour late. Diversion before the play and between the acts was afforded by musicians in a box adjacent to the stage. At these same times orange girls went about the house hawking their wares of sweetmeats, fruits, and cooling drinks. The afternoon's production opened with the announcement of coming attractions by the "orator," usually Molière himself.

The productions of Molière's day, except those of the special "machine plays," attempted little by way of pictorial effect. Candelabra suspended from the roof by pulley and chains gave poor and inflexible lighting on the stage. A unique proscenium curtain with which Richelieu in 1641 had equipped the Théâtre du Palais Royal seems never to have been employed by Molière. Without a front curtain neither he nor the other managers could undertake tableaux, or "discoveries" such as the Elizabethans accomplished by means of their inner stage. A single set of flats, representing a palace apartment, customarily served for tragedy. Comedy rarely called for more than an interior or an exterior scene. If both were required, then one was located at the front and the other at the rear of the stage with a drop curtain between. The one set which Molière used in *The Miser* represented a room opening on a garden at the back. The only furnishings, according to the original property list, consisted of a table, a chair, a writing-desk, and two candles burning on the table in Act V. Such utter simplicity of setting is a far cry from the elaborate scenic art developing in the London productions of the same period. French taste still subordinated stage decoration to dramatic action.

MOLIÈRE'S HIGH COMEDY

Comedy, as distinguished from farce, suffered a tardy development in France. Until about 1630 the French playwrights hardly paid it serious attention. Then, after studying Plautus, Terence, and Italian Renaissance comedy, they commenced to put forth imitations in growing numbers. During the 1650's the leading dramatists, like Paul Scarron (1610–60) and Philippe Quinault (1635–88), made comedy the most popular of the dramatic forms. The majority of their works copied Roman, Italian, or Spanish plays of intrigue and romance. A few dealt rather tentatively with the manners and the characters of the day. Molière's *Les Précieuses Ridicules* in 1659 effected, however, the ascendancy of comedy with social pointing. The immense success of this brief satire on contemporary life determined the future objective of Molière's art. He soon affirmed that "the business of comedy is to represent in a general way all the defects of men, and particularly those of our own age."

Molière's age indeed offered the perfect subject for the comic spirit. French society under Louis XIV, so immersed in the game called "progress," mirrored with extraordinary clarity the follies, the vanities, and the lusts of men. Though Molière, in the rôle of showman to the King, often exercised his remarkable versatility upon farces, ballet-drama, and gay interludes for royal fêtes, he inevitably returned to the absurdities of contemporary humanity and their exposure. Critical comedy, which, to use his words, painted "the manners of the time without aiming at individuals," most fully satisfied his artistic ambition. Unlike Ben Jonson, his chief predecessor in critical comedy, he never wrote with rancor or indignation. The combination of intelligence and good-heartedness kept his comic sense pure. Not even ill health, the enmities of professional rivals, or the attacks of religious bigots could disturb Molière's equanimity. Perhaps the long experience in trouping led him to view mankind as an incurable child, to be corrected a little, but, above all, to be entertained. His plays from first to last reveal a thoughtful but gay detachment.

Molière wrought this detached comedy with the aid of a rich stock-in-trade which he had accumulated during his long connection with the stage. His playwriting gives evidence of a broad acquaintance with comic literature, ancient and modern. Molière studied for years the Italian *commedia dell' arte* and its players, whose sparkling theatricalism he esteemed. His sharing with them the stage of both the Hôtel du Petit Bourbon and the Théâtre du Palais Royal resulted in unforgettable impressions. The lively caricatures, the prankishness, the mobility of the *commedia dell' arte* encouraged his natural tendencies. Thus, like Jonson, Molière borrowed heavily out of both past and present, but transformed the borrowings into a new comic type. Yet he much surpassed Jonson's drama in vitality as well as deftness. His characterizations possess a fundamental humanity which Jonson's never acquired. Molière therefore achieved the truer "high" comedy, that is, comedy developed more from personality than from situation. His output of high comedy remains unexcelled by any other writer. The modern theater of Europe and America finds Molière's plays quite as fresh as those of Shakespeare. Ever since the 1660's they have contributed to the comic drama of countless authors not only in France, but in England, Russia, and other countries. This imperishable universality in Molière's art entitles him to be accounted among the greatest dramatists of all time.

"THE MISER"

The Miser had its premiere on September 9, 1668, with Molière as the avaricious Harpagon, Molière's wife as Marianne, and his sister-in-law, Madeleine Béjart, as Frosine. Though the comedy did not prove an immense success on this occasion, it rose to high popularity before Molière's death. From the founding of the French national theater, the Comédie Française, at Paris in 1680, *The Miser* has continued one of the three Molière favorites there. Harpagon has grown so notorious a stage figure that his name is now a by-word for miser.

The Miser well illustrates Molière's habit of picking up the materials for his comedy all over the literary landscape. In that trait he closely resembles Shakespeare. *The Pot of Gold* by Plautus has been regularly mentioned as the basis of *The Miser*. Plautus' comedy furnished (1) the hoarder who has a treasure box hidden in his garden; (2) the robbery of the box by a servant; and (3) several farcical incidents, such as the confusion between Harpagon and Valère over the daughter and the box (Act V, Scene 3). Two contemporary French comedies, however, provided a much larger share of both the situations and the characters. They, rather than *The Pot of Gold*, may have originally suggested the subject of the miser foiled. Chappuzeau's *The Miser Duped, or The Intriguing Lady* (1663) presented a miser in love, and an intriguing woman, who, like Frosine, conspires with a young couple against the miser. *The Beautiful Pleader* (1655) by Boisrobert depicted a wealthy miser who lends money at usurious rates, keeps his establishment and his horses on meager rations, quarrels with an extravagant son, and remains miser to the last. The same play also supplied the marriages of the miser's son and daughter to a sister and brother respectively, as well as the situation in which the miser and his son unexpectedly face one another in the money-lending arrangements. Molière therefore is considerably more indebted to this contemporary comedy than to *The Pot of Gold*. A half-dozen other French plays of his period contributed many other minor details. All this medley of borrowed stuff he refined and blended into a work of distinct originality.

The formal features of *The Miser*, as of Jonson's *Epicoene*, are largely derived from Roman comedy. The five acts and the so-called "*liaison*" or "linking" of the scenes within the act imitate the practice of Plautus and Terence. The dialogue, in following the Italian mode of prose, departs from Molière's usual custom in high comedy. *The Misanthrope* and *Tartuffe*, for example, employ verse after the manner of the ancients. *The Miser* adheres to the classical unities of place and time by limiting action to one locale and to the space of a few hours.

The classical unity of action, however, is not carefully observed. The plot primarily revolves about the marriages of the miser's children. Nevertheless much of the second, third, and fourth acts does not treat of these matters. Molière seems to have sought no more than a loose unifying of the various scenes through their common connection with the protagonist. Other weaknesses in design may be noted. The opening scene between Valère and Élise, the most stilted and dull in *The Miser*, starts the play off badly. Then the denouement of Act V, Scene 5, wherein Valère and Marianne are revealed as Anselme's children, repeats the sudden and arbitrary unravelings at the end of the Roman comedies. It is a solution unworthy of Molière's talent.

The Miser's many brilliant moments of comedy quite overshadow these few blemishes. The play abounds in remarks of inimitable humor, such as La Flèche's memorandum on the stuffed lizard, "a pleasing curiosity to hang on the ceiling of a room" (Act II, Sc. 1, ll. 148–49), or Harpagon's comment when Mr. Simon tells him of the borrower's pledge that his father shall die before eight months, "That is something" (Act II, Sc. 2, l. 20). As for the action, it runs the whole range of comic appeals. Cléante's prank of bestowing Harpagon's diamond on Marianne (Act III, Sc. 12) is an admirable bit of surprise. Harpagon in getting the truth out of Cléante about Marianne (Act IV, Sc. 3) entertains by his clever contrivance. The scene where Cléante in front of Harpagon pays his respects to Marianne (Act III, Sc. 11) provokes amusement because of the irony in the situation. But comedy of character, concentrated on Harpagon, forms the core of *The Miser*. Molière much enlarged the figure of the mean and cowardly hoarder found in *The Pot of Gold*. Harpagon, though obsessed by greed, exhibits a rounded and impressive personality. He is a man of business, shrewd, hard, lively in speech and action, and ingenious enough to trap his son. He also discloses himself an egotist, proud of his appearance and susceptible to praise. His behavior in the face of Frosine's blandishments (Act II, Sc. 6), mixed as it is with the vanity and selfishness of old age, constitutes a masterly scene of human comicality. *The Miser's* entire portrayal of the childishness beneath Harpagon's front of avarice exemplifies Molière's high comedy at its best.

[For the early French drama and stage, see Frederick Hawkins, *Annals of the French Stage from its Origin*, etc. (2 vols., 1884); for the French drama and theater after 1600, H. C. Lancaster, *A History of French Dramatic Literature in the Seventeenth Century* (3 pts. in 6 vols., 1929–   ); for Molière, John Palmer, *Molière* (1930).]

JEAN BAPTISTE POQUELIN ("MOLIÈRE")

The Miser

[*Translated by* C. H. WALL]

DRAMATIS PERSONAE

HARPAGON,[1] *father to* CLÉANTE, *in love with* MARIANNE

CLÉANTE, HARPAGON'S *son, lover to* MARIANNE

VALÈRE, *son to* ANSELME, *and lover to* ÉLISE

ANSELME, *father to* VALÈRE *and* MARIANNE

MASTER SIMON, *broker*

MASTER JACQUES, *cook and coachman to* HARPAGON

LA FLÈCHE, *valet to* CLÉANTE

BRINDAVOINE ⎱ *lackeys to* HARPAGON
LA MERLUCHE ⎰

A MAGISTRATE *and his Clerk*

ÉLISE, *daughter to* HARPAGON

MARIANNE, *daughter to* ANSELME

FROSINE, *an intriguing woman*

DAME CLAUDE, *servant to* HARPAGON

The Scene is at Paris, in HARPAGON'S *house*

ACT I

SCENE I [2]

Enter VALÈRE *and* ÉLISE

Valère. What, dear Élise! you grow sad after having given me such dear tokens of your love; and I see you sigh in the midst of my joy! Can you regret having made me happy? and do you repent of the engagement which my love has 5 forced from you?

Élise. No, Valère, I do not regret what I do for you; I feel carried on by too delightful a power, and I do not even wish that things should be otherwise than they are. Yet, to 10 tell you the truth, I am very anxious about the consequences; and I greatly fear that I love you more than I should.

Valère. What can you possibly fear from the affection you have shown me? 15

Élise. Everything; the anger of my father,

---

[1] A Greek word, latinized by Plautus, meaning "a rapacious person."

[2] The scene throughout is a room opening on a garden at the back.

the reproaches of my family, the censure of the world, and, above all, Valère, a change in your heart! I fear that cruel coldness with which your sex so often repays the too warm 20 proofs of an innocent love.

Valère. Alas! do not wrong me thus; do not judge of me by others. Think me capable of everything, Élise, except of falling short of what I owe to you. I love you too much 25 for that; and my love will be as lasting as my life!

Élise. Ah! Valère, all men say the same thing; all men are alike in their words; their actions only show the difference that exists 30 between them.

Valère. Then why not wait for actions, if by them alone you can judge of the truthfulness of my heart? Do not suffer your anxious fears to mislead you, and to wrong me. Do not let 35 an unjust suspicion destroy the happiness which is to me dearer than life; but give me time to show you by a thousand proofs the sincerity of my affection.

Élise. Alas! how easily do we allow our- 40

selves to be persuaded by those we love. I believe you, Valère; I feel sure that your heart is utterly incapable of deceiving me, that your love is sincere, and that you will ever remain faithful to me. I will no longer doubt that 45 happiness is near. If I grieve, it will only be over the difficulties of our position, and the possible censures of the world.

Valère. But why even this fear?

Élise. Oh, Valère! if everybody knew 50 you as I do, I should not have much to fear. I find in you enough to justify all I do for you; my heart knows all your merit, and feels, moreover, bound to you by deep gratitude. How can I forget that horrible moment 55 when we met for the first time? Your generous courage in risking your own life to save mine from the fury of the waves; your tender care afterwards; your constant attentions and your ardent love, which neither time nor 60 difficulties can lessen! For me you neglect your parents and your country; you give up your own position in life to be a servant of my father! How can I resist the influence that all this has over me? Is it not enough to jus- 65 tify in my eyes my engagement to you? Yet, who knows if it will be enough to justify it in the eyes of others? and how can I feel sure that my motives will be understood?

Valère. You try in vain to find merit in 70 what I have done; it is by my love alone that I trust to deserve you. As for the scruples you feel, your father himself justifies you but too much before the world; and his avarice and the distant way in which he lives with his chil- 75 dren might authorize stranger things still. Forgive me, my dear Élise, for speaking thus of your father before you; but you know that, unfortunately, on this subject no good can be said of him. However, if I can find my parents, 80 as I fully hope I shall, they will soon be favorable to us. I am expecting news of them with great impatience; but if none comes I will go in search of them myself.

Élise. Oh no! Valère, do not leave me, 85 I entreat you. Try rather to ingratiate yourself in my father's favor.

Valère. You know how much I wish it, and you can see how I set about it. You know the skillful maneuvers I have had to use in 90 order to introduce myself into his service; under what a mask of sympathy and conformity of tastes I disguise my own feelings to please him; and what a part I play to acquire his affection. I succeed wonderfully well, and 95 I feel that to obtain favor with men, there are no better means than to pretend to be of their way of thinking, to fall in with their maxims, to praise their defects, and to applaud all their doings. One need not fear to overdo it, 100 for however gross the flattery, the most cunning are easily duped; there is nothing so impertinent or ridiculous which they will not believe, provided it be well seasoned with praise. Honesty suffers, I acknowledge; but when 105 we have need of men, we may be allowed without blame to adapt ourselves to their mode of thought; and if we have no other hope of success but through such stratagem, it is not after all the fault of those who flatter, but the 110 fault of those who wish to be flattered.

Élise. Why do you not try also to gain my brother's good-will, in case the servant should betray our secret?

Valère. I am afraid I cannot humor 115 them both. The temper of the father is so different from that of the son that it would be difficult to be the confidant of both at the same time. Rather try your brother yourself; make use of the love that exists between you to 120 enlist him in our cause. I leave you, for I see him coming. Speak to him, sound him, and see how far we can trust him.

Élise. I greatly fear I shall never have the courage to speak to him of my secret. 125

(*Exit* VALÈRE.

SCENE 2

Enter CLÉANTE

Cléante. I am very glad to find you alone, sister. I longed to speak to you and to tell you a secret.

Élise. I am quite ready to hear you, brother. What is it you have to tell me? 5

Cléante. Many things, sister, summed up in one word — love.

Élise. You love?

Cléante. Yes, I love. But, before I say more, let me tell you that I know I depend on my 10 father, and that the name of son subjects me to his will; that it would be wrong to engage ourselves without the consent of the authors of our being; that heaven has made them the masters of our affections, and that it is our 15 duty not to dispose of ourselves but in accordance to their wish; that their judgment is not biased by their being in love themselves; that they are, therefore, much more likely not to be deceived by appearances, and to judge 20 better what is good for us; that we ought to trust their experience rather than the passion which blinds us; and that the rashness of youth often carries us to the very brink of dangerous abysses. I know all this, my sister, and I 25 tell it you to spare you the trouble of saying it to me, for my love will not let me listen to anything, and I pray you to spare me your remonstrances.

Élise. Have you engaged yourself, 30 brother, to her you love?

Cléante. No, but I have determined to do so; and I beseech you once more not to bring forward any reason to dissuade me from it.

Élise. Am I such a very strange person, 35 brother?

Cléante. No, dear sister; but you do not love. You know not the sweet power that love has upon our hearts; and I dread your wisdom.

Élise. Alas! my brother, let us not speak 40 of my wisdom. There are very few people in this world who do not lack wisdom, were it only once in their lifetime; and if I opened my heart to you, perhaps you would think me less wise than you are yourself. 45

Cléante. Ah! would to heaven that your heart, like mine . . .

Élise. Let us speak of you first, and tell me whom it is you love.

Cléante. A young girl who has lately 50 come to live in our neighborhood, and who seems made to inspire love in all those who behold her. Nature, my dear sister, has made nothing more lovely; and I felt another man the moment I saw her. Her name is Marianne, 55 and she lives with a good, kind mother, who is almost always ill, and for whom the dear girl

shows the greatest affection. She waits upon her, pities and comforts her with a tenderness that would touch you to the very soul. 60 Whatever she undertakes is done in the most charming way; and in all her actions shine a wonderful grace, a most winning gentleness, an adorable modesty, a . . . ah! my sister, how I wish you had but seen her. 65

Élise. I see many things in what you tell me, dear brother; and it is sufficient for me to know that you love her for me to understand what she is.

Cléante. I have discovered, without their 70 knowing it, that they are not in very good circumstances, and that, although they live with the greatest care, they have barely enough to cover their expenses. Can you imagine, my sister, what happiness it must be to im- 75 prove the condition of those we love; skillfully to bring about some relief to the modest wants of a virtuous family? And think what grief it is for me to find myself deprived of this great joy through the avarice of a father, and for 80 it to be impossible for me to give any proof of my love to her who is all in all to me.

Élise. Yes, I understand, dear brother, what sorrow this must be to you.

Cléante. It is greater, my sister, than 85 you can believe. For is there anything more cruel than this mean economy to which we are subjected? this strange penury in which we are made to pine? What good will it do us to have a fortune if it only comes to us when we are 90 not able to enjoy it; if now to provide for my daily maintenance I get into debt on every side; if both you and I are reduced daily to beg the help of tradespeople in order to have decent clothes to wear? In short, I wanted to 95 speak to you that you might help me to sound my father concerning my present feelings; and if I find him opposed to them, I am determined to go and live elsewhere with this most charming girl, and to make the best of what 100 Providence offers us. I am trying everywhere to raise money for this purpose; and if your circumstances, dear sister, are like mine, and our father opposes us, let us both leave him, and free ourselves from the tyranny in which 105 his hateful avarice has for so long held us.

Élise. It is but too true that every day he gives us more and more reason to regret the death of our mother, and that . . .

Cléante. I hear his voice. Let us go a   110 little farther and finish our talk. We will afterwards join our forces to make a common attack on his hard and unkind heart.

(*Exeunt* Élise *and* Cléante.

SCENE 3

Enter Harpagon *and* La Flèche

Harpagon. Get out of here, this moment; and let me have no more of your prating. Now then, be gone out of my house, you sworn pickpocket, you veritable gallows' bird.

La Flèche (*aside*). I never saw anything   5 more wicked than this cursed old man; and I truly believe, if I may be allowed to say so, that he is possessed with a devil.

Harpagon. What are you muttering there between your teeth?   10

La Flèche. Why do you send me away?

Harpagon. You dare to ask me my reasons, you scoundrel? Out with you, this moment, before I give you a good thrashing.

La Flèche. What have I done to you?   15

Harpagon. Done this, that I wish you to be off.

La Flèche. My master, your son gave me orders to wait for him.

Harpagon. Go and wait for him in the   20 street, then; out with you; don't stay in my house, straight and stiff as a sentry, to observe what is going on, and to make your profit of everything. I won't always have before me a spy on all my affairs; a treacherous scamp,   25 whose cursed eyes watch all my actions, covet all I possess, and ferret about in every corner to see if there is anything to steal.

La Flèche. How the deuce could one steal anything from you? Are you a man likely   30 to be robbed when you put every possible thing under lock and key, and mount guard day and night?

Harpagon. I will lock up whatever I think fit, and mount guard when and where I   35 please. Did you ever see such spies as are set upon me to take note of everything I do?

(*Aside*) I tremble for fear he should suspect something of my money. (*Aloud*) Now, aren't you a fellow to give rise to stories about my   40 having money hid in my house?

La Flèche. You have some money hid in your house?

Harpagon. No, scoundrel! I do not say that. (*Aside*) I am furious! (*Aloud*) I   45 only ask if out of mischief you do not spread the report that I have some?

La Flèche. Oh! What does it matter whether you have money, or whether you have not, since it is all the same to us?   50

Harpagon (*raising his hand to give* La Flèche *a blow*). Oh! Oh! You want to argue, do you? I will give you, and quickly too, some few of these arguments about your ears. Get out of the house, I tell you once more.   54

La Flèche. Very well; very well. I am going.

Harpagon. No, wait; are you carrying anything away with you?

La Flèche. What can I possibly carry away?

Harpagon. Come here, and let me see. Show me your hands.   60

La Flèche. There they are.

Harpagon. The others.

La Flèche. The others?

Harpagon. Yes.

La Flèche. There they are.   65

Harpagon (*pointing to* La Flèche's *breeches*) Have you anything hid in here?

La Flèche. Look for yourself.

Harpagon (*feeling the knees of the breeches*) These wide kneebreeches are convenient receptacles of stolen goods; and I wish a pair of them had been hanged.   70

La Flèche (*aside*). Ah! how richly such a man deserves what he fears, and what joy it would be to me to steal some of his . . .

Harpagon. Eh?

La Flèche. What?   75

Harpagon. What is it you talk of stealing?

La Flèche. I say that you feel about everywhere to see if I have been stealing anything.

Harpagon. And I mean to do so too.

(*Feels in* La Flèche's *pockets.*

La Flèche. Plague take all misers and   80 all miserly ways!

Harpagon. Eh? What do you say?

La Flèche. What do I say?

Harpagon. Yes. What is it you say about misers and miserly ways?   85

La Flèche. I say plague take all misers and all miserly ways.

Harpagon. Of whom do you speak?

La Flèche. Of misers.   89

Harpagon. And who are they, these misers?

La Flèche. Villains and stingy wretches!

Harpagon. But what do you mean by that?

La Flèche. Why do you trouble yourself so much about what I say?

Harpagon. I trouble myself because I   95 think it right to do so.

La Flèche. Do you think I am speaking about you?

Harpagon. I think what I think; but I insist upon your telling me to whom you speak   100 when you say that.

La Flèche. To whom I speak? I am speaking to the inside of my hat.

Harpagon. And I will, perhaps, speak to the outside of your head.   105

La Flèche. Would you prevent me from cursing misers?

Harpagon. No; but I will prevent you from prating and from being insolent. Hold your tongue, will you?   110

La Flèche. I name nobody.

Harpagon. Another word, and I'll thrash you.

La Flèche. He whom the cap fits, let him wear it.   115

Harpagon. Will you be silent?

La Flèche. Yes; much against my will.

Harpagon. Ah! ah!

La Flèche (*showing* HARPAGON *one of his doublet pockets*). Just look, here is one more pocket. Are you satisfied?   120

Harpagon. Come, give it up to me without all that fuss.

La Flèche. Give you what?

Harpagon. What you have stolen from me.

La Flèche. I have stolen nothing at all from you.   126

Harpagon. Are you telling the truth?

La Flèche. Yes.

Harpagon. Good-bye, then, and now you may go to the devil.   130

La Flèche (*aside*). That's a nice way of dismissing anyone.

Harpagon. I leave it to your conscience, remember!   (*Exit* LA FLÈCHE.

SCENE 4

HARPAGON *alone*

Harpagon. This rascally valet is a constant vexation to me; and I hate the very sight of the good-for-nothing cripple. Really, it is no small anxiety to keep by one a large sum of money; and happy is the man who has all his cash   5 well invested, and who needs not keep by him more than he wants for his daily expenses. I am not a little puzzled to find in the whole of this house a safe hiding-place. Don't speak to me of your strong boxes, I will never trust   10 to them. Why, they are just the very things thieves set upon!

SCENE 5

Enter ÉLISE *and* CLÉANTE *who talk together at the back of the stage*

HARPAGON (*thinking himself alone*). Meanwhile, I hardly know whether I did right to bury in my garden the ten thousand crowns which were paid to me yesterday. Ten thousand crowns in gold is a sum sufficiently ...   5 (*Aside, on perceiving* ÉLISE *and* CLÉANTE *whispering together*) Good heavens! I have betrayed myself; my warmth has carried me away. I believe I spoke aloud while reasoning with myself. (*To* CLÉANTE *and* ÉLISE) What do you want?   10

Cléante. Nothing, father.

Harpagon. Have you been here long?

Élise. We have only just come.

Harpagon. Did you hear? ...

Cléante. What, father?   15

Harpagon. There! ...

Cléante. What?

Harpagon. What I was just now saying.

Cléante. No.

Harpagon. You did. I know you did.   20

Élise. I beg your pardon, father, but we did not.

Harpagon. I see well enough that you overheard a few words. The fact is, I was only talking to myself about the trouble one 25 has nowadays to raise any money; and I was saying that he is a fortunate man who has ten thousand crowns in his house.

Cléante. We were afraid of coming near you, for fear of intruding. 30

Harpagon. I am very glad to tell you this, so that you may not misinterpret things, and imagine that I said that it was I who have ten thousand crowns.

Cléante. We do not wish to interfere in 35 your affairs.

Harpagon. Would that I had them, these ten thousand crowns!

Cléante. I should not think that ...

Harpagon. What a capital affair it 40 would be for me.

Cléante. There are things ...

Harpagon. I greatly need them.

Cléante. I fancy that ...

Harpagon. It would suit me exceedingly well. 46

Élise. You are ...

Harpagon. And I should not have to complain, as I do now, that the times are bad.

Cléante. Dear me, father, you have no 50 reason to complain; and everyone knows that you are well enough off.

Harpagon. How? I am well enough off! Those who say it are liars. Nothing can be more false; and they are scoundrels who 55 spread such reports.

Élise. Don't be angry.

Harpagon. It is strange that my own children betray me and become my enemies.

Cléante. Is it being your enemy to say 60 that you have wealth?

Harpagon. Yes, it is. Such talk and your extravagant expenses will be the cause that some day thieves will come and cut my throat, in the belief that I am made of gold. 65

Cléante. What extravagant expenses do I indulge in?

Harpagon. What! Is there anything more scandalous than this sumptuous attire with which you jaunt it about the town? I was 70 remonstrating with your sister yesterday, but you are still worse. It cries vengeance to

heaven; and were we to calculate all you are wearing, from head to foot, we should find enough for a good annuity. I have told you 75 a hundred times, my son, that your manners displease me exceedingly; you affect the marquis terribly, and for you to be always dressed as you are, you must certainly rob me.

Cléante. Rob you? And how? 80

Harpagon. How should I know? Where else could you find money enough to clothe yourself as you do?

Cléante. I, father? I play: and as I am very lucky, I spend in clothes all the money I win. 85

Harpagon. It is very wrong. If you are lucky at play, you should profit by it, and place the money you win at decent interest, so that you may find it again some day. I should like to know, for instance, without mentioning 90 the rest, what need there is for all these ribbons with which you are decked from head to foot, and if half a dozen tags are not sufficient to fasten your breeches. What necessity is there for anyone to spend money upon wigs, when 95 we have hair of our own growth, which costs nothing? I will lay a wager that, in wigs and ribbons alone, there are certainly twenty pistoles spent, and twenty pistoles brings in at least eighteen livres six sous eight deniers 100 per annum, at only eight per cent interest.[1]

Cléante. You are quite right.

Harpagon. Enough on this subject; let us talk of something else. (*Aside, noticing* CLÉANTE *and* ÉLISE, *who make signs to one another*) I believe they are making signs 105 to one another to pick my pocket. (*Aloud*) What do you mean by those signs?

Élise. We are hesitating as to who shall speak first, for we both have something to tell you.

Harpagon. And I also have something 110 to tell you both.

Cléante. We wanted to speak to you about marriage, father.

Harpagon. The very thing I wish to speak to you about. 115

Élise. Ah! my father!

Harpagon. What is the meaning of that ex-

---

[1] A pistole, a gold coin equal to eleven livres, was then worth about four dollars. A livre contained twenty sous, and a sou twelve deniers.

clamation? Is it the word, daughter, or the thing itself that frightens you?

Cléante. Marriage may frighten us 120 both according to the way you take it; and our feelings may perhaps not coincide with your choice.

Harpagon. A little patience, if you please. You need not be alarmed. I know what 125 is good for you both, and you will have no reason to complain of anything I intend to do. To begin at the beginning. (*To* CLÉANTE) Do you know, tell me, a young person, called Marianne, who lives not far from here? 130

Cléante. Yes, father.

Harpagon. And you?

Élise. I have heard her spoken of.

Harpagon. Well, my son, and how do you like the girl? 135

Cléante. She is very charming.

Harpagon. Her face?

Cléante. Modest and intelligent.

Harpagon. Her air and manner?

Cléante. Perfect, undoubtedly. 140

Harpagon. Do you not think that such a girl well deserves to be thought of?

Cléante. Yes, father.

Harpagon. She would form a very desirable match? 145

Cléante. Very desirable.

Harpagon. That there is every likelihood of her making a thrifty and careful wife?

Cléante. Certainly.

Harpagon. And that a husband might 150 live very happily with her?

Cléante. I have not the least doubt about it.

Harpagon. There is one little difficulty; I am afraid she has not the fortune we might 155 reasonably expect.

Cléante. Oh, my father, riches are of little importance when one is sure of marrying a virtuous woman.

Harpagon. I beg your pardon. Only 160 there is this to be said: that if we do not find as much money as we could wish, we may make it up in something else.

Cléante. That follows as a matter of course.

Harpagon. Well, I must say that I am 165 very much pleased to find that you entirely agree with me, for her modest manner and her gentleness have won my heart; and I have made up my mind to marry her, provided I find she has some dowry. 170

Cléante. Eh!

Harpagon. What now?

Cléante. You are resolved, you say ... ?

Harpagon. To marry Marianne.

Cléante. Who? you? you? 175

Harpagon. Yes, I, I, I. What does all this mean?

Cléante. I feel a sudden dizziness, and I must withdraw for a little while.

Harpagon. It will be nothing. Go 180 quickly into the kitchen and drink a large glass of cold water, it will soon set you all right again.

(*Exit* CLÉANTE.

SCENE 6

HARPAGON, ÉLISE

Harpagon. There goes one of your effeminate fops, with no more stamina than a chicken. That is what I have resolved for myself, my daughter. As to your brother, I have thought for him of a rich widow, of whom I heard 5 this morning; and you I shall give to Mr. Anselme.

Élise. To Mr. Anselme?

Harpagon. Yes, a staid and prudent man, who is not above fifty, and of whose riches 10 everybody speaks.

Élise (curtseying). I have no wish to marry, father, if you please.

Harpagon (imitating ÉLISE). And I, my little girl, my darling, I wish you to marry, if you 15 please.

Élise (curtseying again). I beg your pardon, my father.

Harpagon (again imitating ÉLISE). I beg your pardon, my daughter. 20

Élise. I am the very humble servant of Mr. Anselme, but (*curtseying again*) with your leave, I shall not marry him.

Harpagon. I am your very humble servant, but (*again imitating* ÉLISE) you will marry 25 him this very evening.

Élise. This evening?

Harpagon. This evening.

Élise (*curtseying again*). It cannot be done, father.   30

Harpagon (*imitating* ÉLISE). It will be done.

Élise. No.

Harpagon. Yes.

Élise. No, I tell you.

Harpagon. Yes, I tell you.   35

Élise. You will never force me to do such a thing.

Harpagon. I will force you to it.

Élise. I had rather kill myself than marry such a man.   40

Harpagon. You will not kill yourself, and you will marry him. But did you ever see such impudence? Did ever anyone hear a daughter speak in such a fashion to her father?

Élise. But did ever anyone see a father   45 marry his daughter after such a fashion?

Harpagon. It is a match against which nothing can be said, and I am perfectly sure that everybody will approve of my choice.

Élise. And I know that it will be ap-   50 proved of by no reasonable person.

Harpagon (*seeing* VALÈRE). There is Valère coming. Shall we make him judge in this affair?

Élise. Willingly.   55

Harpagon. You will abide by what he says?

Élise. Yes, whatever he thinks right, I will do.

Harpagon. Agreed.

SCENE 7

Enter VALÈRE

Harpagon. Valère, we have chosen you to decide who is in the right, my daughter or I.

Valère. It is certainly you, Sir.

Harpagon. But have you any idea of what we are talking about?   5

Valère. No, but you could not be in the wrong; you are reason itself.

Harpagon. I want to give her tonight, for a husband, a man as rich as he is good; and the hussy tells me to my face that she scorns to   10 take him. What do you say to that?

Valère. What do I say to it?

Harpagon. Yes.

Valère. Eh! eh!

Harpagon. What?   15

Valère. I say that I am, upon the whole, of your opinion, and that you cannot but be right; yet, perhaps, she is not altogether wrong; and . . .

Harpagon. How so? Mr. Anselme is an   20 excellent match; he is a nobleman, and a gentleman too; of simple habits, and extremely well off. He has no children left from his first marriage. Could she meet with anything more suitable?   25

Valère. It is true. But she might say that you are going rather fast, and she ought to have at least a little time to consider whether her inclination could reconcile itself to . . .

Harpagon. It is an opportunity I must   30 not allow to slip through my fingers. I find an advantage here which I should not find elsewhere, and he agrees to take her without dowry.

Valère. Without dowry?   35

Harpagon. Yes.

Valère. Ah! I have nothing more to say. A more convincing reason could not be found; and she must yield to that.   39

Harpagon. It is a considerable saving to me.

Valère. Undoubtedly; this admits of no contradiction. It is true that your daughter might represent to you that marriage is a more serious affair than people are apt to believe; that the happiness or misery of a whole life depends   45 on it, and that an engagement which is to last till death ought not to be entered into without great consideration.

Harpagon. Without dowry!

Valère. That must of course decide   50 everything. There are certainly people who might tell you that on such occasions the wishes of a daughter are no doubt to be considered, and that this great disparity of age, of disposition, and of feelings might be the   55 cause of many an unpleasant thing in a married life.

Harpagon. Without dowry!

Valère. Ah! it must be granted that there is no reply to that; who in the world could   60 think otherwise? I do not mean to say but that there are many fathers who would set a much higher value on the happiness of their daughter than on the money they may have to give for their marriage; who would not like 65 to sacrifice them to their own interests, and who would, above all things, try to see in a marriage that sweet conformity of tastes which is a sure pledge of honor, tranquillity and joy; and that . . .   70

Harpagon. Without dowry!

Valère. That is true; nothing more can be said. Without dowry. How can anyone resist such arguments?   74

Harpagon (aside, looking towards the garden). Ah! I fancy I hear a dog barking. Is anyone after my money? (*To* VALÈRE) Stop here, I'll come back directly.   (*Exit* HARPAGON.

SCENE 8
ÉLISE, VALÈRE

Élise. Surely, Valère, you are not in earnest when you speak to him in that manner?

Valère. I do it that I may not vex him, and the better to secure my ends. To resist him boldly would simply spoil everything.   5 There are certain people who are only to be managed by indirect means, temperaments averse from all resistance, restive natures whom truth causes to rear, who always kick when we would lead them on the right   10 road of reason, and who can only be led by a way opposed to that by which you wish them to go. Pretend to comply with his wishes; you are much more likely to succeed in the end, and . . .   15

Élise. But this marriage, Valère?

Valère. We will find some pretext for breaking it off.

Élise. But what pretext can we find if it is to be concluded tonight?   20

Valère. You must ask to have it delayed, and must feign some illness or other.

Élise. But he will soon discover the truth if they call in the doctor.

Valère. Not a bit of it. Do you imagine 25 that a doctor understands what he is about? Nonsense! Don't be afraid. Believe me, you may complain of any disease you please, the doctor will be at no loss to explain to you from what it proceeds.   30

SCENE 9
Enter HARPAGON

Harpagon (alone, at the back of the stage). It was nothing, thank heaven!

Valère (not seeing HARPAGON). In short, flight is the last resource we have left us to avoid all this; and if your love, dear Élise, is as strong as . . . (*seeing* HARPAGON) Yes, a 5 daughter is bound to obey her father. She has no right to inquire what a husband offered to her is like, and when the most important question, "without dowry," presents itself, she should accept anybody that is given her.   10

Harpagon. Good; that was beautifully said!

Valère. I beg your pardon, Sir, if I carry it a little too far, and take upon myself to speak to her as I do.

Harpagon. Why, I am delighted, and I 15 wish you to have her entirely under your control. (*To* ÉLISE) Yes, you may run away as much as you like. I give him all the authority over you that heaven has given me, and I will have you do all that he tells you.   20

Valère. After that, resist all my expostulations, if you can.   (*Exit* ÉLISE.

SCENE 10
HARPAGON, VALÈRE

Valère. I will follow her, Sir, if you will allow me, and will continue the lecture I was giving her.

Harpagon. Yes, do so; you will oblige me greatly.   5

Valère. She ought to be kept in with a tight hand.

Harpagon. Quite true, you must . . .

Valère. Do not be afraid; I believe I shall end by convincing her.   10

Harpagon. Do so, do so. I am going to take a short stroll in the town, and I will come back again presently.

Valère (going towards the door through which ÉLISE *left, and speaking as if it were to her).* Yes, money is more precious than anything 15 else in the world, and you should thank heaven that you have so worthy a man for a father. He knows what life is. When a man offers to marry a girl without a dowry, we ought to look no farther. Everything is comprised 20 in that, and "without dowry" compensates for want of beauty, youth, birth, honor, wisdom, and probity.

Harpagon. Ah! the honest fellow! he speaks like an oracle. Happy is he who can se- 25 cure such a servant! (*Exeunt.*

ACT II

SCENE I

Enter CLÉANTE *and* LA FLÈCHE

Cléante. How now, you rascal! where have you been hiding? Did I not give you orders to...?

La Flèche. Yes, sir, and I came here re- solved to wait for you without stirring, but 5 your father, that most ungracious of men, drove me into the street in spite of myself, and I well nigh got a good drubbing into the bargain.

Cléante. How is our affair progressing? 10 Things are worse than ever for us, and since I left you, I have discovered that my own father is my rival.

La Flèche. Your father in love?

Cléante. It seems so; and I found it very 15 difficult to hide from him what I felt at such a discovery.

La Flèche. He meddling with love! What the deuce is he thinking of? Does he mean to set everybody at defiance? And is love 20 made for people of his build?

Cléante. It is to punish me for my sins that this passion has entered his head.

La Flèche. But why do you hide your love from him? 25

Cléante. That he may not suspect anything, and to make it more easy for me to fall back, if need be, upon some device to prevent this marriage. What answer did you receive?

La Flèche. Indeed, Sir, those who borrow 30 are much to be pitied, and we must put up with strange things when, like you, we are forced to pass through the hands of the usurers.

Cléante. Then the affair won't come off?

La Flèche. Excuse me; Mr. Simon, the 35 broker who was recommended to us, is a very active and zealous fellow, and says he has left no stone unturned to help you. He assures me that your looks alone have won his heart.

Cléante. Shall I have the fifteen thousand 40 francs which I want?

La Flèche. Yes, but under certain trifling conditions, which you must accept if you wish the bargain to be concluded.

Cléante. Did you speak to the man who 45 is to lend the money?

La Flèche. Oh! dear no. Things are not done in that way. He is still more anxious than you to remain unknown. These things are greater mysteries than you think. His 50 name is not by any means to be divulged, and he is to be introduced to you today at a house provided by him, so that he may hear from yourself all about your position and your family; and I have not the least doubt 55 that the mere name of your father will be sufficient to accomplish what you wish.

Cléante. Particularly as my mother is dead, and they cannot deprive me of what I inherit from her. 60

La Flèche. Well, here are some of the con- ditions which he has himself dictated to our go-between for you to take cognizance of, before anything is begun.

"Supposing that the lender is satisfied 65 with all his securities, and that the borrower is of age and of a family whose property is ample, solid, secure, and free from all in- cumbrances, there shall be drawn up a good and correct bond before as honest a no- 70 tary as it is possible to find, and who for this purpose shall be chosen by the lender, because he is the more concerned of the two that the bond should be rightly executed."

Cléante. There is nothing to say against 75 that.

La Flèche. "The lender, not to burden his conscience with the least scruple, does not wish to lend his money at more than five and a half per cent." 80

Cléante. Five and a half per cent? By Jove, that's honest! We have nothing to complain of.

La Flèche. That's true.

"But as the said lender has not in hand   85
the sum required, and as, in order to oblige
the borrower, he is himself obliged to borrow
from another at the rate of twenty per cent,
it is but right that the said first borrower shall
pay this interest, without detriment to   90
the rest; since it is only to oblige him that the
said lender is himself forced to borrow."

Cléante. The deuce! What a Jew! what a
Turk we have here! That is more than
twenty-five per cent.   95

La Flèche. That's true; and it is the remark I made. It is for you to consider the
matter before you act.

Cléante. How can I consider? I want the
money, and I must therefore accept   100
everything.

La Flèche. That is exactly what I answered.

Cléante. Is there anything else?

La Flèche. Only a small item.

"Of the fifteen thousand francs which   105
are demanded, the lender will only be able to
count down twelve thousand in hard cash;
instead of the remaining three thousand, the
borrower will have to take the chattels, clothing, and jewels, contained in the follow-   110
ing catalogue, and which the said lender has
put in all good faith at the lowest possible."

Cléante. What is the meaning of all that?

La Flèche. I'll go through the catalogue: —
"Firstly: — A fourpost bedstead, with   115
hangings of Hungary lace very elegantly
trimmed with olive-colored cloth, and six
chairs and a counterpane to match; the whole
in very good condition, and lined with soft red
and blue shot-silk. Item: — the tester   120
of good pale pink Aumale serge, with the
small and the large fringes of silk."

Cléante. What does he want me to do with
all this?

La Flèche. Wait.   125
"Item: — Tapestry hangings representing
the loves of Gombaud and Macée.[1] Item:
— A large walnut table with twelve columns or turned legs, which draws out at
both ends, and is provided beneath with   130
six stools."

[1] The hero and heroine of an old French comic pastoral tale.

Cléante. Hang it all! What am I to do
with all this?

La Flèche. Have patience.

"Item: — Three large matchlocks in-   135
laid with mother-of-pearl, with rests to correspond. Item: — A brick furnace with two
retorts and three receivers, very useful to those
who have any taste for distilling."

Cléante. You will drive me crazy.   140

La Flèche. Gently!

"Item: — A Bologna lute with all its strings,
or nearly all. Item: — A pigeon-hole table
and a draught-board, and a game of mother
goose, restored from the Greeks, most   145
useful to pass the time when one has nothing
to do. Item: — A lizard's skin, three feet and
a half in length, stuffed with hay, a pleasing
curiosity to hang on the ceiling of a room.
The whole of the above-mentioned ar-   150
ticles are really worth more than four thousand five hundred francs,[1] and are reduced
to the value of a thousand crowns[2] through the
considerateness of the lender."

Cléante. Let the plague choke him with   155
his considerateness, the wretch, the cut-throat
that he is! Did ever anyone hear of such
usury? Is he not satisfied with the outrageous
interest he asks that he must force me to take,
instead of the three thousand francs, all   160
the old rubbish which he picks up? I shan't
get two hundred crowns for all that, and yet
I must bring myself to yield to all his wishes;
for he is in a position to force me to accept
everything, and he has me, the villain,   165
with a knife at my throat.

La Flèche. I see you, Sir, if you'll forgive
my saying so, on the highroad followed by
Panurge[3] to ruin himself — taking money in
advance, buying dear, selling cheap, and   170
cutting your corn while it is still grass.[4]

[1] I.e., about $1800. The franc was then worth about
40¢.

[2] I.e., about $1200. The crown (*écu*) was then worth
about $1.20.

[3] The roguish companion of Pantagruel, the jolly
drunkard giant in the satirical romance *Pantagruel* by
François Rabelais (1495–1553).

[4] These are Rabelais' own phrases to describe the
behavior of Panurge after he had been made governor
of Salmygondin by Pantagruel. See Book III, chap. 2
of the romance.

Cléante. What would you have me do? It
is to this that young men are reduced by the
accursed avarice of their fathers; and people
are astonished after that, that sons long 175
for their death.

La Flèche. No one can deny that yours
would excite against his meanness the most
quiet of men. I have not, thank God, any inclination gallows-ward, and among my 180
colleagues whom I see dabbling in various
doubtful affairs, I know well enough how to
keep myself out of hot water, and how to
keep clear of all those things which savor ever
so little of the ladder; but to tell you the 185
truth, he almost gives me, by his ways of going on, the desire of robbing him, and I should
think that in doing so I was doing a merito-
rious action.

Cléante. Give me that memorandum 190
that I may have another look at it.

SCENE 2

Enter HARPAGON *and* MR. SIMON (CLÉANTE
and LA FLÈCHE *at the back of the stage*)

Mr. Simon. Yes, Sir; it is a young man who
is greatly in want of money; his affairs force
him to find some at any cost, and he will
submit to all your conditions.

Harpagon. But are you sure, Mr. Simon, 5
that there is no risk to run in this case? and
do you know the name, the property, and the
family of him for whom you speak?

Simon. No; I cannot tell you anything for
certain, as it was by mere chance that I 10
was made acquainted with him; but he will tell
you everything himself, and his servant has
assured me that you will be quite satisfied
when you know who he is. All I can tell you
is that his family is said to be very wealthy, 15
that he has already lost his mother, and that
he will pledge you his word, if you insist upon
it, that his father will die before eight months
are passed.

Harpagon. That is something. Charity, 20
Mr. Simon, demands of us to gratify people
whenever we have it in our power.

Simon. Evidently.

La Flèche (*aside to* CLÉANTE, *on recognizing*

MR. SIMON). What does this mean? Mr.
Simon talking with your father! 25

Cléante (*aside to* LA FLÈCHE). Has he been
told who I am, and would you be capable of
betraying me?

Simon (*to* CLÉANTE *and* LA FLÈCHE). Ah!
you are in good time! But who told you 30
to come here? (*To* HARPAGON.) It was
certainly not I who told them your name and
address; but I am of opinion that there is no
great harm done; they are people who can be
trusted, and you can come to some under- 35
standing together.

Harpagon. What!

Simon (*showing* CLÉANTE). This is the
gentleman who wants to borrow the fifteen
thousand francs of which I have spoken to you.

Harpagon. What! miscreant! is it you 41
who abandon yourself to such excesses?

Cléante. What! father! is it you who stoop
to such shameful deeds?

　　(MR. SIMON *runs away, and* LA
　　　FLÈCHE *hides himself.*

SCENE 3

HARPAGON, CLÉANTE

Harpagon. It is you who are ruining yourself
by loans so greatly to be condemned!

Cléante. So it is you who seek to enrich
yourself by such criminal usury!

Harpagon. And you dare, after that, to 5
show yourself before me?

Cléante. And you dare, after that, to show
yourself to the world?

Harpagon. Are you not ashamed, tell me,
to descend to these wild excesses, to rush 10
headlong into frightful expenses, and disgracefully to dissipate the wealth which your
parents have amassed with so much toil?

Cléante. And are you not ashamed of dis-
honoring your station by such dealings, of 15
sacrificing honor and reputation to the insatiable desire of heaping crown upon crown,
and of outdoing the most infamous devices
that have ever been invented by the most
notorious usurers? 20

Harpagon. Get out of my sight, you repro-
bate; get out of my sight!

Cléante. Who is the more criminal in your opinion: he who buys the money of which he stands in need, or he who obtains, by un- 25 fair means, money for which he has no use?

Harpagon. Begone, I say, and do not provoke me to anger. (*Exit* CLÉANTE.) After all, I am not very much vexed at this adventure; it will be a lesson to me to keep a better 30 watch over all his doings.

SCENE 4

Enter FROSINE

Frosine. Sir.

Harpagon. Wait a moment, I will come back and speak to you. (*Aside*) I had better go and see a little after my money. (*Exit.*

SCENE 5

Enter LA FLÈCHE

La Flèche (*without seeing* FROSINE). The adventure is most comical. Hidden somewhere he must have a large store of goods of all kinds, for the list did not contain one single article which either of us recognized. 5

Frosine. Hallo! is it you, my poor La Flèche? How is it we meet here?

La Flèche. Ah! ah! it is you, Frosine; and what have you come to do here?

Frosine. What have I come to do? Why! 10 what I do everywhere else, busy myself about other people's affairs, make myself useful to the community in general, and profit as much as I possibly can by the small talents I possess. Must we not live by our wits in this world? 15 and what other resources have people like me but intrigue and cunning?

La Flèche. Have you, then, any business with the master of this house?

Frosine. Yes. I am transacting for him 20 a certain small matter for which he is pretty sure to give me a reward.

La Flèche. He give you a reward! Ah! ah! Upon my word, you will be 'cute if you ever get one, and I warn you that ready money 25 is very scarce hereabouts.

Frosine. That may be, but there are certain services which wonderfully touch our feelings.

La Flèche. Your humble servant; but as yet you don't know Harpagon. Harpagon 30 is the human being of all human beings the least humane, the mortal of all mortals the hardest and closest. There is no service great enough to induce him to open his purse. If, indeed, you want praise, esteem, kindness, 35 and friendship, you are welcome to any amount; but money, that's a different affair. There is nothing more dry, more barren, than his favor and his good grace, and "give" is a word for which he has such a strong dislike that he 40 never says, "I give," but "I lend you a good morning."

Frosine. That's all very well; but I know the art of fleecing men. I have a secret of touching their affections by flattering 45 their hearts, and of finding out their weak points.

La Flèche. All useless here. I defy you to soften, as far as money is concerned, the man we are speaking of. He is a Turk on that 50 point, of a Turkishness to drive anyone to despair, and we might starve in his presence and never a peg would he stir. In short, he loves money better than reputation, honor, and virtue, and the mere sight of anyone 55 making demands upon his purse sends him into convulsions; it is like striking him in a vital place, it is piercing him to the heart, it is like tearing out his very bowels! And if . . . But here he comes again, I leave 60 you. (*Exit.*

SCENE 6

Enter HARPAGON

Harpagon (*aside*). All is as it should be. (*To* FROSINE) Well, what is it, Frosine?

Frosine. Bless me, how well you look! You are the very picture of health.

Harpagon. Who? I? 5

Frosine. Never have I seen you looking more rosy, more hearty.

Harpagon. Are you in earnest?

Frosine. Why! you have never been so young in your life; and I know many a man 10 of twenty-five who looks much older than you do.

Harpagon. And yet, Frosine, I have passed threescore.

Frosine. Threescore! Well, and what 15 then? You don't mean to make a trouble of that, do you? It's the very flower of manhood, the threshold of the prime of life.

Harpagon. True; but twenty years less would do me no harm, I think. 20

Frosine. Nonsense! You've no need of that, and you are of a build to last out a hundred.

Harpagon. Do you really think so?

Frosine. Decidedly. You have all the 25 appearance of it. Hold yourself up a little. Ah! what a sign of long life is that line there straight between your two eyes!

Harpagon. You know all about that, do you? 30

Frosine. I should think I do. Show me your hand. Dear me, what a line of life there is there!

Harpagon. Where?

Frosine. Don't you see how far this line 35 goes?

Harpagon. Well, and what does it mean?

Frosine. What does it mean? There ... I said a hundred years; but no, it is one hundred and twenty I ought to have said. 40

Harpagon. Is it possible?

Frosine. I tell you, they will have to kill you, and you will bury your children and your children's children.

Harpagon. So much the better! And 45 what news of our affair?

Frosine. Is there any need to ask? Did ever anyone see me begin anything and not succeed in it? I have, especially for matchmaking, the most wonderful talent. There 50 are no two persons in the world I could not couple together: and I believe that, if I took it into my head, I could make the Grand Turk marry the Republic of Venice.[1] But we had, to be sure, no such difficult thing to 55 achieve in this matter. As I know the ladies

[1] The Turks and the Venetians were old and notorious enemies. After a war of twenty years, the Turks took the rich Mediterranean island of Crete away from Venice in 1669, the year following the *première* of this play.

very well, I told them every particular about you; and I acquainted the mother with your intentions towards Marianne since you saw her pass in the street and enjoy the fresh 60 air out of her window.

Harpagon. What did she answer...?

Frosine. She received your proposal with great joy; and when I told her that you wished very much that her daughter should come 65 tonight to assist at the marriage contract which is to be signed for your own daughter, she assented at once, and entrusted her to me for the purpose.

Harpagon. You see, Frosine, I am obliged 70 to give some supper to Mr. Anselme, and I should like her to have a share in the feast.

Frosine. You are quite right. She is to come after dinner to pay a visit to your daughter; then she means to go from here 75 to the fair, and return to your house just in time for supper.

Harpagon. That will do very well; they shall go together in my carriage, which I will lend them. 80

Frosine. That will suit her perfectly.

Harpagon. But I say, Frosine, have you spoken to the mother about the dowry she can give her daughter? Did you make her understand that under such circumstances 85 she ought to do her utmost and to make a great sacrifice? For, after all, one does not marry a girl without her bringing something with her.

Frosine. How something! She is a girl 90 who will bring you a clear twelve thousand francs a year!

Harpagon. Twelve thousand francs a year?

Frosine. Yes! To begin with, she has been nursed and brought up with the strictest 95 notions of frugality. She is a girl accustomed to live upon salad, milk, cheese, and apples, and who consequently will require neither a well served-up table, nor any rich broth, nor your everlasting peeled barley; none, in 100 short, of all those delicacies that another woman would want. This is no small matter, and may well amount to three thousand francs yearly. Besides this, she only cares for simplicity and neatness; she will have 105 none of those splendid dresses and rich jewels, none of that sumptuous furniture in which girls like her indulge so extravagantly; and this item is worth more than four thousand francs per annum. Lastly, she has the 110 deepest aversion to gambling; and this is not very common nowadays among women. Why, I know of one in our neighborhood who lost at least twenty thousand francs this year. But let us reckon only a fourth of that sum. 115 Five thousand francs a year at play and four thousand in clothes and jewels make nine thousand; and three thousand francs which we count for food, does it not make your twelve thousand francs? 120

Harpagon. Yes, that's not bad; but, after all, that calculation has nothing real in it.

Frosine. Excuse me; is it nothing real to bring you in marriage a great sobriety, to inherit a great love for simplicity in dress, 125 and the acquired property of a great hatred for gambling?

Harpagon. It is a farce to pretend to make up a dowry with all the expenses she will not run into. I could not give a receipt for 130 what I do not receive; and I must decidedly get something.

Frosine. Bless me! you will get enough; and they have spoken to me of a certain country where they have some property, 135 of which you will be master.

Harpagon. We shall have to see to that. But, Frosine, there is one more thing that makes me uneasy. The girl is young, you know; and young people generally like 140 those who are young like themselves, and only care for the society of the young. I am afraid that a man of my age may not exactly suit her taste, and that this may occasion in my family certain complications that would 145 in nowise be pleasant to me.

Frosine. Oh, how badly you judge her! This is one more peculiarity of which I had to speak to you. She has the greatest detestation to all young men, and only likes old 150 people.

Harpagon. Does she?

Frosine. I should like you to hear her talk on that subject; she cannot bear at all the sight of a young man, and nothing delights 155 her more than to see a fine old man with a venerable beard. The oldest are to her the most charming, and I warn you beforehand not to go and make yourself any younger than you really are. She wishes for one 160 sixty years old at least; and it is not more than six months ago that on the very eve of being married she suddenly broke off the match on learning that her lover was only fifty-six years of age, and did not put on spectacles to 165 sign the contract.

Harpagon. Only for that?

Frosine. Yes; she says there is no pleasure with a man of fifty-six; and she has a decided affection for those who wear spectacles. 170

Harpagon. Well, this is quite new to me.

Frosine. No one can imagine how far she carries this. She has in her room a few pictures and engravings, and what do you imagine they are? An Adonis,[1] a Cephalus,[2] a 175 Paris,[3] an Apollo?[4] Not a bit of it! Fine portraits of Saturn,[5] of King Priam,[6] of old Nestor,[7] and of good father Anchises[8] on his son's shoulders.

Harpagon. That's admirable. I should 180 never have guessed such a thing; and I am pleased to hear that she has such taste as this. Indeed, had I been a woman, I should never have loved young fellows.

Frosine. I should think not. Fine 185 trumpery indeed, these young men, for any one to fall in love with. Fine jackanapes and puppies for a woman to hanker after. I should like to know what relish anyone can find in them! 190

Harpagon. Truly, I don't understand it myself, and I cannot make out how it is that some women dote so on them.

[1] A legendary Greek youth of great beauty, beloved by Aphrodite (Venus).
[2] A youthful Greek hunter, beloved by Eos, goddess of the dawn.
[3] The handsome prince of Troy, who stole Helen.
[4] The superb-looking god of the sun.
[5] The elderly Roman god of seed-sowing.
[6] The old king of Troy.
[7] The king of Pylus who joined the Greek expedition against Troy.
[8] The aged father of Aeneas, the Trojan founder of Rome.

Frosine. They must be downright idiots. Can anyone be in his senses who thinks 195 youth amiable? Can those curly-pated coxcombs be men, and can one really get attached to such animals?

Harpagon. Exactly what I say every day! With their effeminate voices, their three 200 little bits of a beard turned up like cat's whiskers, their tow wigs,[1] their flowing breeches and open breasts!

Frosine. Yes, they are famous guys compared with yourself. In you we see some- 205 thing like a man. There is enough to satisfy the eye. It is thus that one should be made and dressed to inspire love.

Harpagon. Then you think I am pretty well?   210

Frosine. Pretty well! I should think so; you are charming, and your face would make a beautiful picture. Turn round a little, if you please. You could not find anything better anywhere. Let me see you walk. 215 You have a well-shaped body, free and easy, as it should be, and one which gives no sign of infirmity.

Harpagon. I have nothing the matter to speak of, I am thankful to say. It is only 220 my cough, which returns from time to time.[2]

Frosine. That is nothing, and coughing becomes you exceedingly well.

Harpagon. Tell me, Frosine, has Marianne seen me yet? Has she not noticed me 225 when I passed by?

Frosine. No, but we have had many conversations about you. I gave her an exact description of your person, and I did not fail to make the most of your merit, and to 230 show her what an advantage it would be to have a husband like you.

Harpagon. You did right, and I thank you very much for it.

Frosine. I have, Sir, a small request to 235 make to you. I am in danger of losing a lawsuit for want of a little money (HARPAGON *looks grave*), and you can easily help me with it, if you have pity upon me. You cannot

[1] Wigs made of flax fibers.
[2] Molière is alluding here to his own habitual infirmity, which finally brought about his death.

imagine how happy she will be to see 240 you. (HARPAGON *looks joyful*.) Oh! how sure you are to please her, and how sure that antique ruff of yours is to produce a wonderful effect on her mind. But, above all, she will be delighted with your breeches fastened 245 to your doublet with tags; that will make her mad after you, and a lover who wears tags will be most welcome to her.

Harpagon. You send me into raptures, Frosine, by saying that.   250

Frosine. I tell you the truth, Sir; this lawsuit is of the utmost importance for me. (HARPAGON *looks serious again*.) If I lose it, I am forever ruined; but a very small sum will save me. I should like you to have 255 seen the happiness she felt when I spoke of you to her. (HARPAGON *looks pleased again*.) Joy sparkled in her eyes while I told her of all your good qualities; and I succeeded, in short, in making her look forward with the great- 260 est impatience to the conclusion of the match.

Harpagon. You have given me great pleasure, Frosine, and I assure you I . . .

Frosine. I beg of you, Sir, to grant me the little assistance I ask of you. (HARPAGON 265 *again looks grave*.) It will put me on my feet again, and I shall feel grateful to you forever.

Harpagon. Good-bye; I must go and finish my correspondence.

Frosine. I assure you, Sir, that you 270 could not help me in a more pressing necessity.

Harpagon. I will see that my carriage is ready to take you to the fair.

Frosine. I would not importune you so if I were not compelled by necessity.   275

Harpagon. And I will see that we have supper early, so that nobody may be ill.

Frosine. Do not refuse me the service, I beg of you. You can hardly believe, Sir, the pleasure that . . .   280

Harpagon. I must go; somebody is calling me. We shall see each other again by and by.   (*Exit.*

Frosine (*alone*). May the fever seize you, you stingy cur, and send you to the devil 285 and his angels! The miser has held out against all my attacks, but I must not drop the negotiation; for I have the other side,

and there, at all events, I am sure of a good
reward.   (*Exit.* 290

ACT III

SCENE 1

Enter HARPAGON, CLÉANTE, ÉLISE, VALÈRE,
DAME CLAUDE (*holding a broom*), MASTER
JACQUES, BRINDAVOINE, *and* LA MER-
LUCHE

Harpagon. Here, come here, all of you; I
must give you orders for by and by, and
arrange what each one will have to do. Come
nearer, Dame Claude; let us begin with you.
(*Looking at her broom*) Good; you are ready 5
armed, I see. To you I commit the care of
cleaning up everywhere; but, above all, be careful not to rub the furniture too hard, for fear of
wearing it out. Besides this, I put the bottles
under your care during supper, and if any 10
one of them is missing, or if anything gets
broken, you will be responsible for it, and pay
it out of your wages.

Jacques (*aside*). A shrewd punishment that.

Harpagon (*to* DAME CLAUDE). Now you 15
may go.   (*Exit* DAME CLAUDE.

SCENE 2

HARPAGON, CLÉANTE, ÉLISE, VALÈRE, MASTER
JACQUES, BRINDAVOINE, LA MERLUCHE

Harpagon. To you, Brindavoine, and to
you, La Merluche, belongs the duty of washing the glasses, and of giving to drink, but only
when people are thirsty, and not according to
the custom of certain impertinent lackeys, 5
who urge them to drink, and put the idea into
their heads when they are not thinking about
it. Wait until you have been asked several
times, and remember always to have plenty
of water.   10

Jacques (*aside*). Yes; wine without water
gets into one's head.

La Merluche. Shall we take off our smocks,
Sir?

Harpagon. Yes, when you see the guests 15
coming; but be very careful not to spoil your
clothes.

Brindavoine. You know, Sir, that one of the
fronts of my doublet is covered with a large
stain of oil from the lamp.   20

La Merluche. And I, Sir, that my breeches
are all torn behind, and that, saving your
presence . . .

Harpagon (*to* LA MERLUCHE). Peace! Turn
carefully towards the wall, and always 25
face the company. (*To* BRINDAVOINE, *showing him how he is to hold his hat before his
doublet, to hide the stain of oil*) And you,
always hold your hat in this fashion when you
wait on the guests.

(*Exeunt* BRINDAVOINE *and* LA MERLUCHE.

SCENE 3

HARPAGON, CLÉANTE, ÉLISE, VALÈRE,
MASTER JACQUES

Harpagon. As for you, my daughter, you
will look after all that is cleared off the table,
and see that nothing is wasted; this care is very
becoming to young girls. Meanwhile get
ready to welcome my lady-love, who is com- 5
ing this afternoon to pay you a visit, and will
take you off to the fair with her. Do you
understand what I say?

Élise. Yes, father.   (*Exit.*

SCENE 4

HARPAGON, CLÉANTE, VALÈRE, MASTER
JACQUES

Harpagon. And you, my young dandy of a
son, to whom I have the kindness of forgiving
what happened this morning, mind you don't
receive her coldly, or show her a sour face.

Cléante. Receive her coldly! And why 5
should I?

Harpagon. Why? why? We know pretty
well the ways of children whose fathers marry
again, and looks they give to those we call
stepmothers. But if you wish me to forget 10
your last offense, I advise you, above all things,
to receive her kindly, and, in short, to give her
the heartiest welcome you can.

Cléante. To speak the truth, father, I cannot promise you that I am very happy to 15
see her become my stepmother; but as to

receiving her properly, and as to giving her a kind welcome, I promise to obey you in that to the very letter.

Harpagon. Be careful you do, at least.   20

Cléante. You will see that you have no cause to complain.

Harpagon. You will do wisely.

                      (*Exit* CLÉANTE.

SCENE 5

HARPAGON, VALÈRE, MASTER JACQUES

Harpagon. Valère, you will have to give me your help in this business. Now, Master Jacques, I kept you for the last.

Jacques. Is it to your coachman, Sir, or to your cook you want to speak, for I am both   5 the one and the other?

Harpagon. To both.

Jacques. But to which of the two first?

Harpagon. To the cook.

Jacques. Then wait a minute, if you   10 please.

         (JACQUES *takes off his stable-coat and appears dressed as a cook.*

Harpagon. What the deuce is the meaning of this ceremony?

Jacques. Now I am at your service.

Harpagon. I have engaged myself, Mas-   15 ter Jacques, to give a supper tonight.

Jacques (*aside*). Wonderful!

Harpagon. Tell me, can you give us a good supper?

Jacques. Yes, if you give me plenty   20 of money.

Harpagon. The deuce! Always money! I think they have nothing else to say except money, money, money! Always that same word in their mouth, money! They al-   25 ways speak of money! It's their pillow companion, money!

Valère. Never did I hear such an impertinent answer! Would you call it wonderful to provide good cheer with plenty of money?   30 Is it not the easiest thing in the world? The most stupid could do as much. But a clever man should talk of a good supper with little money.   34

Jacques. A good supper with little money?

Valère. Yes.

Jacques (*to* VALÈRE). Indeed, Mr. Steward, you oblige me greatly by telling me your secret, and also, if you like, by filling my place as cook; for you keep on meddling here,   40 and want to be everything.

Harpagon. Hold your tongue. What shall we want?

Jacques. Ask that of Mr. Steward, who will give you good cheer with little money.   45

Harpagon. Do you hear? I am speaking to you, and expect you to answer me.

Jacques. How many will there be at your table?

Harpagon. Eight or ten; but you must   50 only reckon for eight. When there is enough for eight, there is enough for ten.

Valère. That is evident.

Jacques. Very well, then; you must have four tureens of soup and five side dishes;   55 soups, entrees...

Harpagon. What! do you mean to feed a whole town?

Jacques. Roast...

Harpagon (*clapping his hand on* JACQUES' *mouth*). Ah! Wretch! you are eating up   60 all my substance.

Jacques. Entremets...

Harpagon (*again putting his hand on* JACQUES' *mouth*). More still?

Valère (*to* JACQUES). Do you mean to kill everybody? And has your master invited   65 people in order to destroy them with over-feeding? Go and read a little the precepts of health, and ask the doctors if there is anything so hurtful to man as excess in eating.

Harpagon. He is perfectly right.   70

Valère. Know, Master Jacques, you and people like you, that a table overloaded with eatables is a real cut-throat; that, to be the true friends of those we invite, frugality should reign throughout the repast we give, and   75 that according to the saying of one of the ancients,[1] "We must eat to live, and not live to eat."

Harpagon. Ah! How well the man speaks! Come near, let me embrace you for this   80

[1] A saying similar to this was attributed to Socrates by the Greek historian Plutarch (?46–?120 A.D.).

last saying. It is the finest sentence that I have ever heard in my life: "We must live to eat, and not eat to live." No; that isn't it. How do you say it?

Valère. That we must eat to live, and not 85 live to eat.

Harpagon (to JACQUES). Yes. Do you hear that? (*To* VALÈRE) Who is the great man who said that?

Valère. I do not exactly recollect his 90 name just now.

Harpagon. Remember to write down those words for me. I will have them engraved in letters of gold over the mantel-piece of my dining-room. 95

Valère. I will not fail. As for your supper, you had better let me manage it. I will see that it is all as it should be.

Harpagon. Do so.

Jacques. So much the better; all the 100 less work for me.

Harpagon (to VALÈRE). We must have some of those things of which it is not possible to eat much, and that satisfy directly. Some good fat beans, and a pâté¹ well stuffed 105 with chestnuts.

Valère. Trust to me.

Harpagon. Now, Master Jacques, you must clean my carriage.

Jacques. Wait a moment; this is to the 110 coachman. (*Puts on his coat.*) You say . . .

Harpagon. That you must clean my carriage, and have my horses ready to drive to the fair.

Jacques. Your horses! Upon my word, 115 Sir, they are not at all in a condition to stir. I won't tell you that they are laid up, for the poor things have got nothing to lie upon, and it would not be telling the truth. But you make them keep such rigid fasts that they 120 are nothing but phantoms, ideas, and mere shadows of horses.

Harpagon. They are much to be pitied. They have nothing to do.

Jacques. And because they have nothing 125 to do, must they have nothing to eat? It would be much better for them, poor things,

¹ Pie.

to work much and eat to correspond. It breaks my heart to see them so reduced; for, in short, I love my horses; and when I 130 see them suffer, it seems as if it were myself. Every day I take the bread out of my own mouth to feed them; and it is being too hard-hearted, Sir, to have no compassion upon one's neighbor. 135

Harpagon. It won't be very hard work to go to the fair.

Jacques. No, Sir. I haven't the heart to drive them; it would go too much against my conscience to use the whip to them in the 140 state they are in. How could you expect them to drag a carriage? They have not even strength enough to drag themselves along.

Valère. Sir, I will ask our neighbor, Picard, to drive them; particularly as we shall 145 want his help to get the supper ready.

Jacques. Be it so. I had much rather they should die under another's hand than under mine.

Valère. Master Jacques is mightily 150 considerate.

Jacques. Mr. Steward is mightily indispensable.

Harpagon. Peace.

Jacques. Sir, I can't bear these flatteries, 155 and I can see that, whatever this man does, his continual watching after the bread, wine, wood, salt, and candles, is done but to curry favor and to make his court to you. I am indignant to see it all; and I am sorry 160 to hear every day what is said of you; for, after all, I have a certain tenderness for you; and, except my horses, you are the person I like most in the world.

Harpagon. And I would know from you, 165 Master Jacques, what it is that is said of me.

Jacques. Yes, certainly, Sir, if I were sure you would not get angry with me.

Harpagon. No, no; never fear.

Jacques. Excuse me, but I am sure 170 you will be angry.

Harpagon. No, on the contrary, you will oblige me. I should be glad to know what people say of me.

Jacques. Since you wish it, Sir, I will 175 tell you frankly that you are the laughing-

stock of everybody; that they taunt us everywhere by a thousand jokes on your account,
and that nothing delights people more than
to make sport of you, and to tell stories 180
without end about your stinginess. One says
that you have special almanacks printed,
where you double the ember days[1] and vigils,
so that you may profit by the fasts to which
you bind all your house; another, that 185
you always have a ready-made quarrel for your
servants at Christmas time or when they
leave you, so that you may give them nothing.
One tells a story how not long since you pro-
secuted a neighbor's cat because it had 190
eaten up the remainder of a leg of mutton;
another says that one night you were caught
stealing your horses' oats, and that your
coachman — that is, the man who was before
me — gave you, in the dark, a good sound 195
drubbing, of which you said nothing. In
short, what is the use of going on? We can go
nowhere but we are sure to hear you pulled to
pieces. You are the butt and jest and by-
word of everybody; and never does any- 200
one mention you but under the names of
miser, stingy, mean, niggardly fellow and
usurer.

Harpagon (beating JACQUES). You are a
fool, a rascal, a scoundrel, and an imperti- 205
nent wretch.

Jacques. There, there! Did not I know
how it would be? You would not believe me.
I told you I should make you angry if I spoke
the truth. 210

Harpagon. Learn how to speak. (*Exit.*

SCENE 6

VALÈRE, MASTER JACQUES

Valère (laughing). Well, Master Jacques,
your frankness is badly rewarded, I fear.

Jacques. S'death! Mr. Upstart, you who
assume the man of consequence, it is no business of yours as far as I can see. Laugh 5
at your cudgeling when you get it, and don't
come here and laugh at mine.

[1] Days set aside for prayer and fasting in each of the
four seasons of the year.

Valère. Ah! Master Jacques, don't get into
a passion, I beg of you.

Jacques (aside). He is drawing in his 10
horns. I will put on a bold face, and if he is
fool enough to be afraid of me, I will pay him
back somewhat. (*To* VALÈRE) Do you know,
Mr. Grinner, that I am not exactly in a laughing humor, and that if you provoke me too 15
much, I shall make you laugh after another
fashion.

(*Pushes* VALÈRE *toward the back of
the stage, threatening him.*

Valère. Gently, gently.

Jacques. How gently? And if it does not
please me to go gently? 20

Valère. Come, come! What are you
about?

Jacques. You are an impudent rascal.

Valère. Master Jacques...

Jacques. None of your Master Jacques 25
here! If I take up a stick, I shall soon make
you feel it.

Valère. What do you mean by a stick?
(*Drives back* JACQUES *in his turn.*

Jacques. No; I don't say anything about
that. 30

Valère. Do you know, Mr. Conceit, that
I am a man to give you a drubbing in good
earnest?

Jacques. I have no doubt of it.

Valère. That, after all, you are nothing 35
but a scrub of a cook?

Jacques. I know it very well.

Valère. And that you don't know me
yet?

Jacques. I beg your pardon. 40

Valère. You will beat me, you say?

Jacques. I only spoke in jest.

Valère. I don't like your jesting, and (*beating*
JACQUES) remember that you are but a sorry
hand at it. 45

(*Exit.*

Jacques (alone). Plague take all sincerity;
it is a bad trade. I give it up for the future,
and will cease to tell the truth. It is all very
well for my master to beat me; but as for
that Mr. Steward, what right has he to 50
do it? I will be revenged on him if I can.

SCENE 7

Enter MARIANNE and FROSINE

Frosine. Do you know if your master is at home?

Jacques. Yes, he is indeed; I know it but too well.

Frosine. Tell him, please, that we are 5
here.   (*Exit* JACQUES.

SCENE 8

MARIANNE, FROSINE

Marianne. Ah! Frosine, how strange I feel, and how I dread this interview!

Frosine. Why should you? What can you possibly dread?

Marianne. Alas! can you ask me? Can 5
you not understand the alarms of a person about to see the instrument of torture to which she is to be tied?

Frosine. I see very well that to die agreeably, Harpagon is not the torture you 10
would embrace; and I can judge by your looks that the fair young man you spoke of to me is still in your thoughts.

Marianne. Yes, Frosine; it is a thing I do not wish to deny. The respectful visits he 15
has paid at our house have left, I confess, a great impression on my heart.

Frosine. But do you know who he is?

Marianne. No, I do not. All I know is that he is made to be loved; that if things 20
were left to my choice, I would much rather marry him than any other, and that he adds not a little to the horrible dread that I have of the husband they want to force upon me.

Frosine. Oh yes! All those dandies are 25
very pleasant, and can talk agreeably enough, but most of them are as poor as church mice; and it is much better for you to marry an old husband, who gives you plenty of money. I fully acknowledge that the senses somewhat 30
clash with the end I propose, and that there are certain little inconveniences to be endured with such a husband; but all that won't last; and his death, believe me, will soon put you in a position to take a more pleasant 35
husband, who will make amends for all.

Marianne. Oh, Frosine! What a strange state of things that, in order to be happy, we must look forward to the death of another. Yet death will not fall in with all the pro- 40
jects we make.

Frosine. You are joking. You marry him with the express understanding that he will soon leave you a widow; it must be one of the articles of the marriage contract. It would 45
be very wrong in him not to die before three months are over. Here he is himself.

Marianne. Ah! dear Frosine, what a face!

SCENE 9

Enter HARPAGON

Harpagon (*to* MARIANNE). Do not be offended, my fair one, if I come to you with my glasses on. I know that your beauty is great enough to be seen with the naked eye; but, still, it is with glasses that we look 5
at the stars, and I maintain and uphold that you are a star, the most beautiful star in the land of stars. — Frosine, she does not answer, and, it seems to me, shows no joy at the sight of me. 10

Frosine. It is because she is still quite awestruck, and young girls are always shy at first, and afraid of showing what they feel.

Harpagon (*to* FROSINE). You are right. (*To* MARIANNE) My pretty darling, there is 15
my daughter coming to welcome you.

SCENE 10

Enter ÉLISE

Marianne. I am very late in acquitting myself of the visit I owed you.

Élise. You have done what I ought to have done. It was for me to have come and seen you first. 5

Harpagon. You see what a great girl she is; but ill weeds grow apace.

Marianne (*aside to* FROSINE). Oh, what an unpleasant man!

Harpagon (*to* FROSINE). What does my 10
fair one say?

Frosine. That she thinks you perfect.

Harpagon. You do me too much honor, my adorable darling.

Marianne (aside). What a dreadful crea- 15 ture!

Harpagon. I really feel too grateful to you for these sentiments.

Marianne (aside). I can bear it no longer.

SCENE II

Enter CLÉANTE, VALÈRE, *and* BRINDAVOINE

Harpagon. Here is my son, who also comes to pay his respects to you.

Marianne (aside to FROSINE). Oh, Frosine! what a strange meeting! He is the very one of whom I spoke to you.   5

Frosine (to MARIANNE). Well, that is extraordinary.

Harpagon. You are surprised to see that my children can be so old; but I shall soon get rid of both of them.   10

Cléante (to MARIANNE). Madam, to tell you the truth, I little expected such an event; and my father surprised me not a little when he told me today of the decision he had come to.

Marianne. I can say the same thing. It 15 is an unexpected meeting; and I certainly was far from being prepared for such an event.

Cléante. Madam, my father cannot make a better choice, and it is a great joy to me to have the honor of welcoming you here. At 20 the same time, I cannot say that I should rejoice if it were your intention to become my stepmother. I must confess that I should find it difficult to pay you the compliment; and it is a title, forgive me, that I cannot wish 25 you to have. To some this speech would seem coarse, but I feel that you understand it. This marriage, Madam, is altogether repugnant to me. You are not ignorant, now that you know who I am, how opposed it is to all 30 my own interests, and with my father's permission I hope you will allow me to say that, if things depended on me, it would never take place.

Harpagon (aside). What a very imperti- 35 nent speech to make; and what a confession to make to her!

Marianne. And as my answer, I must tell you that things are much the same with me, and that, if you have any repugnance in 40 seeing me your stepmother, I shall have no less in seeing you my stepson. Do not believe, I beg of you, that it is of my own will that this trouble has come upon you. I should be deeply grieved to cause you the least 45 sorrow, and unless I am forced to it by a power I must obey, I give you my word that I will never consent to a marriage which is so painful to you.

Harpagon. She is right. A foolish 50 speech deserves a foolish answer. I beg your pardon, my love, for the impertinence of my son. He is a silly young fellow, who has not yet learnt the value of his own words.

Marianne. I assure you that he has 55 not at all offended me. I am thankful, on the contrary, that he has spoken so openly. I care greatly for such a confession from him, and if he had spoken differently, I should feel much less esteem for him.   60

Harpagon. It is very kind of you to excuse him thus. Time will make him wiser, and you will see that his feelings will change.

Cléante. No, father, they will never change; and I earnestly beg of you, Madam, to be- 65 lieve me.

Harpagon. Did ever anybody see such folly? He is becoming worse and worse.

Cléante. Would you have me false to my inmost feelings?   70

Harpagon. Again! Change your manners, if you please.

Cléante. Very well, since you wish me to speak differently. Allow me, Madam, to take for a moment my father's place; and for- 75 give me if I tell you that I never saw in the world anybody more charming than you are; that I can understand no happiness to equal that of pleasing you, and that to be your husband is a glory, a felicity, I should 80 prefer to the destinies of the greatest princes upon earth. Yes, Madam, to possess you is, in my mind, to possess the best of all treasures; to obtain you is all my ambition. There is nothing I would not do for so precious a 85 conquest, and the most powerful obstacles. . . .

Harpagon. Gently, gently, my son, if you please.

Cléante. These are complimentary words which I speak to her in your name.   90

Harpagon. Bless me! I have a tongue of my own to explain my feelings, and I really don't care for such an advocate as you. ... Here, bring us some chairs.

Frosine. No; I think it is better for us   95 to go at once to the fair, in order to be back earlier, and have plenty of time for talking.

Harpagon (*to* BRINDAVOINE). Have the carriage ready at once.   (*Exit* BRINDAVOINE.

SCENE 12

HARPAGON, MARIANNE, ÉLISE, CLÉANTE, VALÈRE, FROSINE

Harpagon (*to* MARIANNE). I hope you will excuse me, my dear, but I forgot to order some refreshments for you, before you went out.

Cléante. I have thought of it, father, and have ordered to be brought in here some   5 baskets of China oranges, sweet citrons, and preserves, which I sent for in your name.

Harpagon (*aside to* VALÈRE). Valère!

Valère (*aside to* HARPAGON). He has lost his senses!   10

Cléante. You are afraid, father, that it will not be enough? I hope, Madam, that you will have the kindness to excuse it.

Marianne. It was by no means necessary.

Cléante. Did you ever see, Madam, a   15 more brilliant diamond than the one my father has upon his finger?

Marianne. It certainly sparkles very much.

Cléante (*taking the diamond off his father's finger*). You must see it near.

Marianne. It is a beautiful one; it pos-   20 sesses great luster.

Cléante (*stepping before* MARIANNE, *who wants to restore it*). No, Madam, it is in hands too beautiful; it is a present my father gives you.

Harpagon. I?

Cléante. Is it not true, father, that you   25 wish her to keep it for your sake?

Harpagon (*aside to his son*). What?

Cléante (*to* MARIANNE). A strange question

indeed! He is making me signs that I am to force you to accept it.   30

Marianne. I would not ...

Cléante (*to* MARIANNE). I beg of you. ... He would not take it back.

Harpagon (*aside*). I am bursting with rage!

Marianne. It would be ...   35

Cléante (*still hindering* MARIANNE *from returning it*). No; I tell you, you will offend him.

Marianne. Pray ...

Cléante. By no means.

Harpagon (*aside*). Plague take ...

Cléante. He is perfectly shocked at your   40 refusal.

Harpagon (*aside to his son*). Ah! traitor!

Cléante (*to* MARIANNE). You see he is in despair.

Harpagon (*aside to his son, threatening him*). You villain!   45

Cléante. Really, father, it is not my fault. I do all I can to persuade her to accept it; but she is obstinate.

Harpagon (*in a rage, aside to his son*). Rascal!

Cléante. You are the cause, Madam, of   50 my father scolding me.

Harpagon (*aside with the same looks*). Scoundrel!

Cléante (*to* MARIANNE). You will make him ill; for goodness' sake, hesitate no longer.   55

Frosine (*to* MARIANNE). Why so much ceremony? Keep the ring, since the gentleman wishes you to.

Marianne (*to* HARPAGON). I will keep it now, Sir, in order not to make you angry, and I   60 shall take another opportunity of returning it to you.   (*Exit* CLÉANTE.

SCENE 13

HARPAGON, MARIANNE, ÉLISE, VALÈRE, FROSINE, BRINDAVOINE

Brindavoine. Sir, there is a gentleman here who wants to speak to you.

Harpagon. Tell him that I am engaged, and that I cannot see him today.

Brindavoine. He says he has some money   5 for you.

Harpagon (*to* MARIANNE). Pray, excuse me;
I will come back directly.

(HARPAGON *and* BRINDAVOINE *start to go.*)

SCENE 14

Enter CLÉANTE *and* LA MERLUCHE

La Merluche (*coming in running, and throwing*
HARPAGON *down*). Sir . . .

Harpagon. Oh! he has killed me.

Cléante. What's the matter, father? Have
you hurt yourself?

Harpagon. The wretch must have been　5
bribed by some of my debtors to break my neck.

Valère (*to* HARPAGON). There is nothing
serious.

La Merluche (*to* HARPAGON). I beg your pardon, Sir; I thought I had better run fast to　10
tell you . . .

Harpagon. What?

La Merluche. That your two horses have lost
their shoes.　　　　　　　　　　　　　14

Harpagon. Take them quickly to the smith.

Cléante. In the meantime, father, I will do
the honors of the house for you, and take this
lady into the garden, where lunch will be
brought.

(*Exeunt* CLÉANTE, MARIANNE, ÉLISE,
FROSINE, *and* LA MERLUCHE.

SCENE 15

HARPAGON, VALÈRE

Harpagon. Valère, look after all this; and
take care, I beseech you, to save as much of it
as you can, so that we may send it back to the
tradesman again.

Valère. I will.　　　　　　(*Exit.*　5

Harpagon (*alone*). Miscreant! do you mean
to ruin me?

ACT IV

SCENE 1

Enter CLÉANTE, MARIANNE, ÉLISE, *and*
FROSINE

Cléante. Let us come in here; we shall be
much better. There is no one about us that
we need be afraid of, and we can speak openly.

Élise. Yes, Madam, my brother has told me
of the love he has for you. I know what　5
sorrow and anxiety such trials as these may
cause, and I have the greatest sympathy for you.

Marianne. I feel it a great comfort in my
trouble to have the sympathy of a person like
you, and I entreat you, Madam, ever to　10
retain for me a friendship so capable of softening the cruelty of my fate.

Frosine. You really are both very unfortunate not to have told me of all this before. I
might certainly have warded off the blow,　15
and not have carried things so far.

Cléante. What could I do? It is my evil
destiny which has willed it so. But you, fair
Marianne, what have you resolved to do?
What resolution have you taken?　　　20

Marianne. Alas! Is it in my power to take
any resolution? And, dependent as I am, can
I do anything else except form wishes?

Cléante. No other support for me in your
heart? Nothing but mere wishes? No　25
pitying energy? No kindly relief? No active
affection?

Marianne. What am I to say to you? Put
yourself in my place, and judge what I can
possibly do. Advise me, dispose of me, I　30
trust myself entirely to you, for I am sure that
you will never ask of me anything but what is
modest and seemly.

Cléante. Alas! to what do you reduce me
when you wish me to be guided entirely　35
by feelings of strict duty and of scrupulous
propriety?

Marianne. But what would you have me do?
Even if I were, for you, to divest myself of the
many scruples which our sex imposes on us,　40
I have too much regard for my mother, who has
brought me up with great tenderness, for me to
give her any cause of sorrow. Do all you can
with her. Strive to win her. I give you leave
to say and do all you wish; and if anything　45
depends upon her knowing the true state of my
feelings, by all means tell her what they are;
indeed I will do it myself if necessary.

Cléante. Frosine, dear Frosine, will you not
help us?　　　　　　　　　　　　　50

Frosine. Indeed, I should like to do so, as

you know. I am not naturally unkind. Heaven has not given me a heart of flint, and I feel but too ready to help when I see young people loving each other in all earnestness 55 and honesty. What can we do in this case?

Cléante. Try and think a little.

Marianne. Advise us.

Élise. Invent something to undo what you have done. 60

Frosine. Rather a difficult piece of business. (*To* MARIANNE) As far as your mother is concerned, she is not altogether unreasonable, and we might succeed in making her give to the son the gift she reserved for the father. (*To* 65 CLÉANTE) But the most disheartening part of it all is that your father is your father.

Cléante. Yes, so it is.

Frosine. I mean that he will bear malice if he sees that he is refused, and he will be in no 70 way disposed afterwards to give his consent to your marriage. It would be well if the refusal could be made to come from him, and you ought to try by some means or other to make him dislike you, Marianne. 75

Cléante. You are quite right.

Frosine. Yes, right enough, no doubt. That is what ought to be done; but how in the world are we to set about it? Wait a moment. Suppose we had a somewhat elderly woman 80 with a little of the ability which I possess, and able sufficiently well to represent a lady of rank, by means of a retinue made up in haste, and of some whimsical title of a marchioness or viscountess, whom we would suppose to come 85 from Lower Brittany. I should have enough power over your father to persuade him that she is a rich woman, in possession, besides her houses, of a hundred thousand crowns in ready money; that she is deeply in love with him, 90 and that she would marry him at any cost, were she even to give him all her money by the marriage contract. I have no doubt he would listen to the proposal. For certainly he loves you very much, my dear, but he loves 95 money still better. When once he has consented to your marriage, it does not signify much how he finds out the true state of affairs about our marchioness.

Cléante. All that is very well made up. 100

Frosine. Leave it to me; I just remember one of my friends who will do beautifully.

Cléante. Depend on my gratitude, Frosine, if you succeed. But, dear Marianne, let us begin, I beg of you, by gaining over your 105 mother; it would be a great deal accomplished if this marriage were once broken off. Make use, I beseech you, of all the power that her tenderness for you gives you over her. Display without hesitation those eloquent 110 graces, those all-powerful charms with which Heaven has endowed your eyes and lips; forget not, I beseech you, those tender entreaties, those loving caresses to which, I feel, nothing could be refused. 115

Marianne. I will do all I can, and will forget nothing.

SCENE 2

Enter HARPAGON *at the back of the stage*

Harpagon (*aside, and without being seen*). Ah! ah! my son is kissing the hand of his intended stepmother, and his intended stepmother does not seem much averse to it! Can there be any mystery in all this? 5

Élise. Here comes my father.

Harpagon (*coming forward*). The carriage is quite ready, and you can start when you like.

Cléante. Since you are not going, father, allow me to take care of them. 10

Harpagon. No, stop here; they can easily take care of themselves, and I want you.

(*Exeunt* MARIANNE, ÉLISE, *and* FROSINE.

SCENE 3

HARPAGON, CLÉANTE

Harpagon. Well, now, all consideration of stepmother aside, tell me what do you think of this lady?

Cléante. What do I think of her?

Harpagon. Yes, what do you think of her 5 appearance, her figure, her beauty and intelligence?

Cléante. So, so.

Harpagon. But still?

Cléante. To tell you the truth, I did not   10
find her such as I expected.   Her manner is
that of a thorough coquette, her figure is rather
awkward, her beauty very middling, and her
intelligence of the meanest order.   Do not suppose that I say this to make you dislike   15
her; for if I must have a stepmother, I like the
idea of this one as well as of any other.

Harpagon. You spoke to her just now, nevertheless . . .

Cléante. I paid her several compliments   20
in your name, but it was to please you.

Harpagon. So then you don't care for her?

Cléante. Who? I? Not in the least.

Harpagon. I am sorry for it, for that puts an
end to a scheme which had occurred to me.   25
Since I have seen her here, I have been thinking
of my own age; and I feel that people would find
fault with me for marrying so young a girl.
This consideration had made me determine to
abandon the project, and as I had de-   30
manded her in marriage, and had given her my
promise, I would have given her to you if it
were not for the dislike you have for her.

Cléante. To me?

Harpagon. To you.   35

Cléante. In marriage?

Harpagon. In marriage.

Cléante. It is true she is not at all to my taste;
but, to please you, father, I will bring myself
to marry her, if you please.   40

Harpagon. If I please! I am more reasonable than you think. I don't wish to compel
you.

Cléante. Excuse me! I will make an attempt
to love her.   45

Harpagon. No, no; a marriage cannot be
happy where there is no love.

Cléante. That, my father, will, perhaps, come
by and by, and it is said that love is often the
fruit of marriage.   50

Harpagon. No, it is not right to risk it on the
side of the man, and there are some troublesome
things I don't care to run the chance of.   If
you had felt any inclination for her, you should
have married her instead of me, but as it   55
is, I will return to my first intention and marry
her myself.

Cléante. Well, father, since things are so, I

had better be frank with you, and reveal our
secret to you.   The truth is that I have   60
loved her ever since I saw her one day on the
promenade.   I intended to ask you today to let
me marry her, and I was only deterred from it
because you spoke of marrying her, and because
I feared to displease you.   65

Harpagon. Have you ever paid her any
visits?

Cléante. Yes, father.

Harpagon. Many?

Cléante. Yes, considering how long we   70
have been acquainted.

Harpagon. You were well received?

Cléante. Very well, but without her knowing
who I was; and that is why Marianne was so
surprised when she saw me today.   75

Harpagon. Have you told her of your love,
and of your intention of marrying her?

Cléante. Certainly, and I also spoke a little
to the mother on the subject.

Harpagon. Did she kindly receive your   80
proposal for her daughter?

Cléante. Yes, very kindly.

Harpagon. And does the daughter return
your love?

Cléante. If I can believe appearances,   85
she is certainly well disposed towards me.

Harpagon (*aside*). Well! I am glad to have
found out this secret; it is the very thing I
wanted to know. (*To* CLÉANTE) Now, look
here, my son, I tell you what. You will   90
have, if you please, to get rid of your love for
Marianne, to cease to pay your attentions to a
person I intend for myself, and to marry very
soon the wife I have chosen for you.

Cléante. So, father, it is thus you de-   95
ceive me! Very well, since things are come to
such a pass, I openly declare to you that I shall
not give up my love for Marianne.   No! understand that henceforth there is nothing from
which I shall shrink in order to dispute   100
her with you; and if you have on your side the
consent of the mother, perhaps I shall have
some other resources left to aid me.

Harpagon. What, rascal! You dare to
trespass on my grounds?   105

Cléante. It is you who trespass on mine.
I was the first.

Harpagon. Am I not your father, and do you not owe me respect?

Cléante. There are things in which chil- 110 dren are not called upon to pay deference to their fathers; and love is no respecter of persons.

Harpagon. My stick will make you know me better. 115

Cléante. All your threatenings are nothing to me.

Harpagon. You will give up Marianne?

Cléante. Never!

Harpagon. Bring me my stick. Quick, 120 I say! my stick!

SCENE 4

Enter MASTER JACQUES

Jacques. Hold! hold! Gentlemen, what does this mean? What are you thinking of?

Cléante. I don't care a bit for it.

Jacques (to CLÉANTE*).* Ah! Sir, gently.

Harpagon. He dares to speak to me with 5 such impudence as that!

Jacques (to HARPAGON*).* Ah! Sir. I beg of you.

Cléante. I shall keep to it.

Jacques (to CLÉANTE*).* What! to your father?

Harpagon. Let me do it. 11

Jacques (to HARPAGON*).* What! to your son? To me it's different.

Harpagon. I will make you judge between us, Master Jacques, so that you may see 15 that I have right on my side.

Jacques. Willingly. (*To* CLÉANTE) Go a little farther away.

(CLÉANTE *goes to the other end of the stage.*

Harpagon. There is a young girl I love and want to marry, and the scoundrel has the 20 impudence to love her also, and wants to marry her in spite of me.

Jacques. Oh! he is wrong.

Harpagon. Is it not an abominable thing to see a son who does not shrink from becom- 25 ing the rival of his father? And is it not his bounden duty to refrain from interfering with my love?

Jacques. You are quite right; stop here, and let me go and speak to him. 30

Cléante (to JACQUES, *as he approaches*). Very well; if he wants to make you a judge between us, I have no objection. I care little who it is, and I don't mind referring our quarrel to you.

Jacques. You do me great honor. 35

Cléante. I am in love with a young girl who returns my affection, and who receives kindly the offer of my heart; but my father takes it into his head to disturb our love by asking her in marriage. 40

Jacques. He certainly is wrong.

Cléante. Is it not shameful for a man of his age to think of marrying? I ask you if it is right for him to fall in love? and ought he not now to leave that to younger men? 45

Jacques. You are quite right; he is not serious. Let me speak a word or two to him. (*He goes back to* HARPAGON.) Really, your son is not so extravagant as you think, and is amenable to reason. He says that he is conscious 50 of the respect he owes you, and he only got angry in the heat of the moment. He will willingly submit to all you wish if you will only promise to treat him more kindly than you do, and will give him in marriage a person to 55 his taste.

Harpagon. Ah! tell him, Master Jacques, that he will obtain everything from me on those terms, and that, except Marianne, I leave him free to choose for his wife whomsoever he 60 pleases.

Jacques. Leave that to me. (*He goes to* CLÉANTE.) Really, your father is not so unreasonable as you make him out to me; and he tells me that it is your violence which irritated 65 him. He only objects to your way of doing things and is quite ready to grant you all you want, provided you will use gentle means and will give him the deference, respect, and submission that a son owes to his father. 70

Cléante. Ah! Master Jacques, you can assure him that if he grants me Marianne, he will always find me the most submissive of men, and that I shall never do anything contrary to his pleasure. 75

Jacques (going back to HARPAGON). It's all right; he consents to what you say.

Harpagon. Nothing could be better.

Jacques (*returning to* CLÉANTE). It's all settled; he is satisfied with your promises.   80

Cléante. Heaven be praised!

Jacques. Gentlemen, you have nothing to do but to talk quietly over the matter together; you are agreed now, and yet you were on the point of quarreling through want of 85 understanding each other.

Cléante. My poor Jacques, I shall be obliged to you all my life.

Jacques. Don't mention it, Sir.

Harpagon. You have given me great 90 pleasure, Master Jacques, and deserve a reward. (HARPAGON *feels in his pocket,* JACQUES *holds out his hand, but* HARPAGON *only pulls out his handkerchief.*) Go; I will remember it, I promise you.

Jacques. I thank you kindly, Sir. (*Exit.* 95

SCENE 5

HARPAGON, CLÉANTE

Cléante. I beg your pardon, father, for having been angry.

Harpagon. It is nothing.

Cléante. I assure you that I feel very sorry about it.   5

Harpagon. I am very happy to see you reasonable again.

Cléante. How very kind of you so soon to forget my fault.

Harpagon. One easily forgets the faults 10 of children when they return to their duty.

Cléante. What! you are not angry with me for my extravagant behavior?

Harpagon. By your submission and respectful conduct you compel me to forget my anger.

Cléante. I assure you, father, I shall for- 16 ever keep in my heart the remembrance of all your kindness.

Harpagon. And I promise you that, in future, you will obtain all you like from me.   20

Cléante. Oh, father! I ask nothing more; it is sufficient for me that you give me Marianne.

Harpagon. What?

Cléante. I say, father, that I am only too thankful already for what you have done, 25 and that when you give me Marianne, you give me everything.

Harpagon. Who talks of giving you Marianne?

Cléante. You, father.   30

Harpagon. I?

Cléante. Yes.

Harpagon. What! is it not you who promised to give her up?

Cléante. I! give her up?   35

Harpagon. Yes.

Cléante. Certainly not.

Harpagon. Did you not give up all pretensions to her?

Cléante. On the contrary, I am more de- 40 termined than ever to have her.

Harpagon. What, scoundrel! again?

Cléante. Nothing can make me change my mind.

Harpagon. Let me get at you again, wretch!

Cléante. You can do as you please.   46

Harpagon. I forbid you ever to come within my sight.

Cléante. As you like.

Harpagon. I abandon you.   50

Cléante. Abandon me.

Harpagon. I disown you.

Cléante. Disown me.

Harpagon. I disinherit you.

Cléante. As you will.   55

Harpagon. I give you my curse.

Cléante. I want none of your gifts.

(*Exit* HARPAGON.

SCENE 6

Enter from the garden LA FLÈCHE *with a money box*

La Flèche. Ah! Sir, you are just in the nick of time. Quick! follow me.

Cléante. What is the matter?

La Flèche. Follow me, I say. We are saved.

Cléante. How?   5

La Flèche. Here is all you want.

Cléante. What?

La Flèche. I have watched for this all day.

Cléante. What is it?

La Flèche. Your father's treasure that I 10 have got hold of.

Cléante. How did you manage it?

La Flèche. I will tell you all about it. Let us be off. I can hear him calling out.

(*Exeunt* CLÉANTE *and* LA FLÈCHE.

SCENE 7

Enter HARPAGON, *from the garden, rushing in without his hat, and shouting*

Harpagon. Thieves! thieves! assassins! murder! Justice, just heavens! I am undone; I am murdered; they have cut my throat; they have stolen my money! Who can it be? What has become of him? What shall I do to 5 find him? Where shall I run? Where shall I not run? Is he not here? Who is this? Stop! (*To himself, taking hold of his own arm*) Give me back my money, wretch.... Ah!... it is myself.... My mind is wandering, and I know 10 not where I am, who I am, and what I am doing. Alas! my poor money! my poor money! my dearest friend, they have bereaved me of thee; and since thou art gone, I have lost my support, my consolation, and my joy. All is ended 15 for me, and I have nothing more to do in the world! Without thee it is impossible for me to live. It is all over with me; I can bear it no longer. I am dying; I am dead; I am buried. Is there nobody who will call me from the 20 dead, by restoring my dear money to me, or by telling me who has taken it? Ah! what is it you say? It is no one. Whoever has committed the deed must have watched carefully for his opportunity, and must have chosen the 25 very moment when I was talking with my miscreant of a son. I must go. I will demand justice, and have the whole of my house put to the torture — my maids and my valets, my son, my daughter, and myself too. (*He looks* 30 *around at the audience.*) What a crowd of people are assembled here! Everyone seems to be my thief. I see no one who does not rouse suspicion in me. Ha! what are they speaking of there? Of him who stole my money? What noise 35 is that up yonder? Is it my thief who is there? (*To the audience*) For pity's sake, if you know anything of my thief, I beseech you to tell me. Is he hiding there among you? They all look at me and laugh. We shall see that they 40 all have a share in the robbery. Quick! magis-trates, police, provosts, judges, racks, gibbets, and executioners! I will hang everybody, and if I do not find my money, I will hang myself afterwards. 45

ACT V

SCENE 1

Enter HARPAGON *and a Police Officer*

Officer. Leave that to me. I know my business. Thank heaven! this is not the first time I have been employed in finding out thieves; and I wish I had as many bags of a thousand francs as I have had people hanged. 5

Harpagon. Every magistrate must take this affair in hand; and if my money is not found, I shall call justice against justice itself.

Officer. We must take all needful steps. You say there was in that box ... ? 10

Harpagon. Ten thousand crowns [1] in cash.

Officer. Ten thousand crowns!

Harpagon. Ten thousand crowns.

Officer. A considerable theft.

Harpagon. There is no punishment 15 great enough for the enormity of the crime; and if it remain unpunished, the most sacred things are no longer secure.

Officer. In what coins was that sum?

Harpagon. In good louis d'or [2] and pis- 20 toles [3] of full weight.

Officer. Whom do you suspect of this robbery?

Harpagon. Everybody. I wish you to take into custody the whole town and suburbs. 25

Officer. You must not, if you trust me, frighten anybody, but must use gentle means to collect evidence, in order afterwards to proceed with more rigor for the recovery of the sum which has been taken from you. 30

SCENE 2

Enter MASTER JACQUES

Jacques (turning back to the door by which he came in). I am coming back. Have his throat cut at once; have his feet singed; put him in

---

[1] About $12,000. See footnote on p. 479.
[2] A gold coin worth between $4 and $4.75.
[3] A gold coin then valued at about $4.

boiling water, and hang him up to the ceiling.

Harpagon. What! Him who has robbed me?

Jacques. I was speaking of a sucking pig 5
that your steward has just sent me; and I want
to have it dressed for you after my own fancy.

Harpagon. This is no longer the question;
and you have to speak of something else to this
gentleman. 10

Officer (*to* JACQUES). Don't get frightened.
I am not a man to cause any scandal, and matters will be carried on by gentle means.

Jacques (*to* HARPAGON). Is this gentleman
coming to supper with you? 15

Officer. You must, in this case, my good man,
hide nothing from your master.

Jacques. Indeed, Sir, I will show you all I
know, and will treat you in the best manner I
possibly can. 20

Officer. That's not the question.

Jacques. If I do not give as good fare as I
should like, it is the fault of your steward, who
has clipped my wings with the scissors of his
economy. 25

Harpagon. Rascal! We have other matters
to talk about than your supper; and I want you
to tell me what has become of the money which
has been stolen from me.

Jacques. Some money has been stolen 30
from you?

Harpagon. Yes, you rascal! And I'll have
you hanged if you don't give it me back again.

Officer (*to* HARPAGON). Pray, don't be hard
upon him. I see by his looks that he is an 35
honest fellow, and that he will tell you all you
want to know without going to prison. Yes,
my friend, if you confess, no harm shall come
to you, and you shall be well rewarded by your
master. Some money has been stolen from 40
him, and it is not possible that you know
nothing about it.

Jacques (*aside*). The very thing I wanted in
order to be revenged of our steward. Ever
since he came here, he has been the favor- 45
ite, and his advice is the only one listened to.
Moreover, I have forgotten neither the cudgeling of today nor ...

Harpagon. What are you muttering about
there? 50

Officer (*to* HARPAGON). Leave him alone. He

is preparing himself to satisfy you; I told you
that he was an honest fellow.

Jacques. Sir, since you want me to tell you
what I know, I believe it is your steward 55
who has done this.

Harpagon. Valère?

Jacques. Yes.

Harpagon. He who seemed so faithful to me!

Jacques. Himself. I believe that it is 60
he who has robbed you.

Harpagon. And what makes you believe it?

Jacques. What makes me believe it?

Harpagon. Yes. 64

Jacques. I believe it ... because I believe it.

Officer. But you must tell us the proofs you
have.

Harpagon. Did you see him hanging about
the place where I had put my money?

Jacques. Yes, indeed. Where was your 70
money?

Harpagon. In the garden.

Jacques. Exactly; I saw him loitering about
in the garden; and in what was your money?

Harpagon. In a box. 75

Jacques. The very thing. I saw him with a
box.

Harpagon. And this box, what was it like?
I shall soon see if it is mine.

Jacques. What it was like? 80

Harpagon. Yes.

Jacques. It was like ... like a box.

Officer. Of course. But describe it a little,
to see if it is the same.

Jacques. It was a large box. 85

Harpagon. The one taken from me is a small
one.

Jacques. Yes, small if you look at it in that
way; but I call it large because of what it contains. 90

Harpagon. And what color was it?

Jacques. What color?

Officer. Yes.

Jacques. Of a color ... of a certain color ...
Can't you help me to find the word? 95

Harpagon. Ugh!

Jacques. Red; isn't it?

Harpagon. No, gray.

Jacques. Ha! yes, reddish-gray! That's
what I meant. 100

Harpagon. There is no doubt about it, it's my box for certain. Write down his evidence, Sir! Heavens! whom can we trust after that? We must never swear to anything, and I believe now that I might rob my own self. 105

Jacques (*to* HARPAGON). There he is coming back, Sir. I beg of you not to go and tell him that it was I who let it all out, Sir.

SCENE 3

Enter VALÈRE

Harpagon. Come, come near, and confess the most abominable action, the most horrible crime, that was ever committed.

Valère. What do you want, Sir?

Harpagon. What, wretch! you do not 5 blush for shame after such a crime?

Valère. Of what crime do you speak?

Harpagon. Of what crime do I speak? Base villain, as if you did not know what I mean! It is in vain for you to try to hide it; the thing 10 is discovered, and I have just heard all the particulars. How could you thus abuse my kindness, introduce yourself on purpose into my house to betray me, and to play upon me such an abominable trick? 15

Valère. Sir, since everything is known to you, I will neither deny what I have done nor will I try to palliate it.

Jacques (*aside*). Oh! oh! Have I guessed the truth? 20

Valère. I intended to speak to you about it, and I was watching for a favorable opportunity; but, as this is no longer possible, I beg of you not to be angry, and to hear my motives.

Harpagon. And what fine motives can 25 you possibly give me, infamous thief?

Valère. Ah! I do not deserve these names. I am guilty towards you, it is true; but, after all, my fault is pardonable.

Harpagon. How pardonable? A pre- 30 meditated trick, and such an assassination as this!

Valère. I beseech you not to be so angry with me. When you have heard all I have to say, you will see that the harm is not so great as 35 you make it out to be.

Harpagon. The harm not so great as I make

it out to be! What! my heart's blood, scoundrel!

Valère. Your blood, Sir, has not fallen 40 into bad hands. My rank is high enough not to disgrace it, and there is nothing in all this for which reparation cannot be made.

Harpagon. It is, indeed, my intention that you should restore what you have taken 45 from me.

Valère. Your honor, Sir, shall be fully satisfied.

Harpagon. Honor is not the question in all this. But tell me what made you commit 50 such a deed?

Valère. Alas! do you ask it?

Harpagon. Yes, I should rather think that I do.

Valère. A god, Sir, who carries with him 55 his excuses for all he makes people do. Love.

Harpagon. Love?

Valère. Yes.

Harpagon. Fine love that! fine love, indeed! the love of my gold! 60

Valère. No, Sir, it is not your wealth that has tempted me, it is not that which has dazzled me; and I swear never to pretend to any of your possessions, provided you leave me what I have.

Harpagon. In the name of all the devils, 65 no, I shall not leave it to you. But did anyone ever meet with such villainy! He wishes to keep what he has robbed me of!

Valère. Do you call that a robbery?

Harpagon. If I call that a robbery? A 70 treasure like that!

Valère. I readily acknowledge that it is a treasure, and the most precious one you have. But it will not be losing it to leave it to me. I ask you on my knees to leave in my posses- 75 sion this treasure so full of charms; and if you do right, you will grant it to me.

Harpagon. I will do nothing of the kind. What in the world are you driving at?

Valère. We have pledged our faith to 80 each other, and have taken an oath never to forsake one another.

Harpagon. The oath is admirable, and the promise strange enough!

Valère. Yes, we are engaged to each 85 other forever.

Harpagon. I know pretty well how to disengage you, I assure you of that.

Valère. Nothing but death can separate us.   90

Harpagon. You must be devilishly bewitched by my money.

Valère. I have told you already, Sir, that it is not self-interest which has prompted me to what I have done. It was not that 95 which prompted my heart; a nobler motive inspired me.

Harpagon. We shall hear presently that it is out of Christian charity that he covets my money! But I will put a stop to all this, 100 and justice, impudent rascal, will soon give me satisfaction.

Valère. You will do as you please, and I am ready to suffer all the violence you care to inflict upon me, but I beg of you to believe, 105 at least, that if there is any harm done, I am the only one guilty, and that your daughter has done nothing wrong in all this.

Harpagon. I should think not! It would be strange, indeed, if my daughter had a share 110 in this crime. But I will have that treasure back again, and you must confess to what place you have carried it off.

Valère. I have not carried it off, and it is still in your house.   115

Harpagon (aside). O my beloved box! (*To* VALÈRE) My treasure has not left my house?

Valère. No, Sir.

Harpagon. Well, then, tell me, have you taken any liberties with...?   120

Valère. Ah! Sir, you wrong us both; the flame with which I burn is too pure, too full of respect.

Harpagon (aside). He burns for my box.

Valère. I had rather die than show the 125 least offensive thought; I found too much modesty and too much purity for that.

Harpagon (aside). My cash-box modest!

Valère. All my desires were limited to the pleasures of sight, and nothing criminal 130 has profaned the passion those fair eyes have inspired me with.

Harpagon (aside). The fair eyes of my cash-box! He speaks of it as a lover does of his mistress.   135

Valère. Dame Claude knows the whole truth, and she can bear witness to it.

Harpagon. Hallo! my servant is an accomplice in this affair?

Valère. Yes, Sir, she was a witness to 140 our engagement; and it was after being sure of the innocence of my love that she helped me to persuade your daughter to engage herself to me.

Harpagon. Ah! (*Aside*) Has the fear 145 of justice made him lose his senses? (*To* VALÈRE) What rubbish are you talking about my daughter?

Valère. I say, Sir, that I found it most difficult to make her modesty consent to 150 what my love asked of her.

Harpagon. The modesty of whom?

Valère. Of your daughter; and it was only yesterday that she could make up her mind to sign our mutual promise of marriage. 155

Harpagon. My daughter has signed a promise of marriage?

Valère. Yes, Sir, and I have also signed.

Harpagon. O heavens! another misfortune!

Jacques (to the Officer). Write, Sir, write. 160

Harpagon. Aggravation of misery! Excess of despair! (*To the Officer*) Sir, discharge your duty, and draw me up an indictment against him as a thief and a suborner.

Jacques. As a thief and a suborner. 165

Valère. These are names which I do not deserve, and when you know who I am...

SCENE 4

Enter ÉLISE, MARIANNE, *and* FROSINE

Harpagon. Ah! guilty daughter! unworthy of a father like me! is it thus that you put into practice the lessons I have given you? You give your love to an infamous thief, and engage yourself to him without my consent! But 5 you shall both be disappointed. (*To* ÉLISE) Four strong walls will answer for your conduct in the future; (*to* VALÈRE) and good gallows, impudent thief, shall do me justice for your audacity.   10

Valère. Your anger will be no judge in this affair, and I shall at least have a hearing before I am condemned.

Harpagon. I was wrong to say gallows; you shall be broken alive on the wheel.   15

Élise (*kneeling to her father*). Ah! my father, be more merciful, I beseech you, and do not let your paternal authority drive matters to extremes. Do not suffer yourself to be carried away by the first outburst of your anger, 20 but give yourself time to consider what you do. Take the trouble of inquiring about him whose conduct has offended you. He is not what you imagine, and you will think it less strange that I should have given myself to him, when 25 you know that without him you would long ago have lost me forever. Yes, father, it is he who saved me from the great danger I ran in the waters, and to whom you owe the life of that very daughter who ...   30

Harpagon. All this is nothing; and it would have been much better for me if he had suffered you to be drowned rather than do what he has done.

Élise. My father, I beseech you, in the 35 name of paternal love, grant me ...

Harpagon. No, no. I will hear nothing, and justice must have its course.

Jacques (*aside*). You shall pay me for the blows you gave me.   40

Frosine. What a perplexing state of affairs!

Scene 5

Enter ANSELME

Anselme. What can have happened, Mr. Harpagon? You are quite upset.

Harpagon. Ah, Mr. Anselme, you see in me the most unfortunate of men; and you can never imagine what vexation and disorder 5 is connected with the contract you have come to sign! I am attacked in my property; I am attacked in my honor; and you see there a scoundrel and a wretch who has violated the most sacred rights, who has introduced 10 himself into my house as a servant in order to steal my money, and seduce my daughter.

Valère. Who ever thought of your money about which you rave?

Harpagon. Yes; they have given each 15 other a promise of marriage. This insult concerns you, Mr. Anselme; and it is you who

ought to be plaintiff against him, and who at your own expense ought to prosecute him to the utmost, in order to be revenged.   20

Anselme. It is not my intention to force anybody to marry me, and to lay claim to a heart which has already bestowed itself; but as far as your interests are concerned, I am ready to espouse them as if they were my own.

Harpagon. This is the gentleman, an 26 honest officer, who has promised that he will omit nothing of what concerns the duties of his office. (*To the Officer, showing* VALÈRE) Charge him, Sir, as he ought to be, and make mat- 30 ters very criminal.

Valère. I do not see what crime they can make of my passion for your daughter, nor the punishment you think I ought to be condemned to for our engagement; when it is known 35 who I am. ...

Harpagon. I don't care a pin for all those stories, and the world is full, nowadays, of those pretenders to nobility, of those impostors, who take advantage of their obscurity and 40 deck themselves out insolently with the first illustrious name that comes into their head.

Valère. Know that I am too upright to adorn myself with a name which is not mine, and that all Naples can bear testimony to my birth! 45

Anselme. Softly! Take care of what you are about to say. You speak before a man to whom all Naples is known, and who can soon see if your story is true.

Valère (*proudly putting on his hat*). I am 50 not the man to fear anything; and if all Naples is known to you, you know who was Don Thomas d'Alburci.

Anselme. Certainly; I know who he is, and few people know him better than I do.   55

Harpagon. I care neither for Don Thomas nor Don Martin.

    (*Seeing two candles burning, he blows one out.*)

Anselme. Have patience and let him speak; we shall soon know what he has to say of him.

Valère. That it is to him that I owe my birth.

Anselme. To him?   61

Valère. Yes.

Anselme. Nonsense; you are laughing. Try and make out a more likely story, and don't

pretend to shelter yourself under such a　65
piece of imposture.

Valère. Consider your words better before
you speak; it is no imposture, and I say nothing
here that I cannot prove.

Anselme. What! You dare to call your-　70
self the son of Don Thomas d'Alburci?

Valère. Yes, I dare to do so; and I am ready
to maintain the truth against anyone, whoever
he may be.

Anselme. This audacity is marvelous.　75
Learn to your confusion that it is now at least
sixteen years ago since the man of whom you
speak died in a shipwreck at sea with his wife
and children, when he was trying to save their
lives from the cruel persecutions which　80
accompanied the troubles at Naples, and which
caused the banishment of several noble families.

Valère. Yes; but learn to your confusion that
his son, seven years of age, was, with a servant,
saved from the wreck by a Spanish vessel　85
and that this son is he who now speaks to you.
Learn that the captain of that ship, touched
with compassion at my misfortune, loved me;
that he had me brought up as his own son, and
that the profession of arms has been my　90
occupation ever since I was fit for it; that lately
I heard that my father is not dead, as I thought
he was; that, passing this way to go and find
him out, an accident, arranged by heaven,
brought to my sight the charming Élise;　95
that the sight of her made me a slave to her
beauty, and that the violence of my love and
the harshness of her father made me take the
resolution to come into his house disguised as a
servant, and to send someone else to look　100
after my parents.

Anselme. But what other proofs have you
besides your own words that all this is not a
story invented by you out of a single true fact?

Valère. What proofs? The captain of　105
the Spanish vessel; a ruby seal which belonged
to my father; an agate bracelet which my
mother put upon my arm; and old Pedro, that
servant who was saved with me from the wreck.

Marianne. Alas! I can answer here for　110
what you have said; that you do not deceive us;
and all you say clearly tells me that you are my
brother.

Valère. You my sister?

Marianne. Yes, my heart was touched　115
as soon as you began to speak; and our mother,
who will be delighted at seeing you, often told
me of the misfortunes of our family. Heaven
spared us also in that dreadful wreck; but our
life was spared at the cost of our liberty,　120
for my mother and myself were taken up by
pirates from the wreck of our vessel. After ten
years of slavery a lucky event gave us back to
liberty, and we returned to Naples, where we
found all our property sold, and could hear　125
no news of our father. We embarked for
Genoa, where my mother went to gather what
remained of a family estate which had been
much disputed. Leaving her unjust relatives,
she came here, where she has lived but a　130
weary life.

Anselme. O heaven! how wonderful are thy
doings, and how true it is that it only belongs
to thee to work miracles! Come to my arms,
my children, and share the joy of your　135
happy father!

Valère. You are our father?

Marianne. It was for you that my mother
wept?

Anselme. Yes, my daughter; yes, my　140
son; I am Don Thomas d'Alburci, whom
heaven saved from the waves, with all the
money he had with him, and who, after sixteen
years, believing you all dead, was preparing,
after long journeys, to seek the consola-　145
tions of a new family in marrying a gentle and
virtuous woman. The little security there was
for my life in Naples has made me abandon the
idea of returning there, and having found the
means of selling what I had, I settled here　150
under the name of Anselme. I wished to forget
the sorrows of a name associated with so many
and great troubles.

Harpagon (*to* ANSELME). He is your son?

Anselme. Yes.　155

Harpagon. That being so, I make you responsible for the ten thousand crowns that he
has stolen from me.

Anselme. He steal anything from you!

Harpagon. Yes.　160

Valère. Who said so?

Harpagon. Master Jacques.

Valère (*to* JACQUES). You say that?

Jacques. You see that I am not saying anything.   165

Harpagon. He certainly did. There is the
officer who has received his deposition.

Valère. Can you really believe me capable of
such a base action?

Harpagon. Capable or not capable, I   170
must find my money.

SCENE 6

Enter CLÉANTE *and* LA FLÈCHE

Cléante. Do not grieve for your money,
father, and accuse anyone. I have news of it,
and I come here to tell you that if you consent
to let me marry Marianne, your money will
be given back to you.   5

Harpagon. Where is it?

Cléante. Do not trouble yourself about that.
It is in a safe place, and I answer for it; everything depends on your resolve. It is for you
to decide, and have the choice either of   10
losing Marianne or your cash-box.

Harpagon. Has nothing been taken out?

Cléante. Nothing at all. Is it your intention
to agree to this marriage, and to join your
consent to that of her mother, who leaves   15
her at liberty to do as she likes?

Marianne (*to* CLÉANTE). But you do not
know that this consent is no longer sufficient,
and that heaven has given me back a brother
(*pointing to* VALÈRE) at the same time   20
that it has given me back a father (*pointing to*
ANSELME); and you have now to obtain me
from him.

Anselme. Heaven, my dear children, has not
restored you to me that I might oppose   25
your wishes. Mr. Harpagon, you must be
aware that the choice of a young girl is more
likely to fall upon the son than upon the
father. Come, now, do not force people to
say to you what is unnecessary, and con-   30
sent, as I do, to this double marriage.

Harpagon. In order for me to be well
advised, I must see my box.

Cléante. You shall see it safe and sound.

Harpagon. I have no money to give my   35
children in marriage.

Anselme. Never mind, I have some; do not
let this trouble you.

Harpagon. Do you take upon yourself to
defray the expenses of these two weddings?   40

Anselme. Yes, I will take this responsibility
upon myself. Are you satisfied?

Harpagon. Yes, provided you order me a
new suit of clothes for the wedding.

Anselme. Agreed! Let us go and enjoy   45
the blessings this happy day brings us.

Officer. Stop, Sirs, stop; softly, if you please.
Who is to pay me for my writing?

Harpagon. We have nothing to do with
your writing.   50

Officer. Indeed! and yet I do not pretend
to have done it for nothing.

Harpagon (*showing* JACQUES). There is a
fellow you can hang in payment!

Jacques. Alas! what is one to do? I   55
receive a good cudgeling for telling the truth,
and now they would hang me for lying.

Anselme. Mr. Harpagon, you must forgive
him this piece of imposture.   59

Harpagon. You will pay the officer then?

Anselme. Let it be so. Let us go quickly,
my children, to share our joy with your
mother!

Harpagon. And I to see my dear box!

(Exeunt.

INTRODUCTION TO

Andromache

*The Rise of French Tragedy: Corneille: Racine
and French Classical Tragedy*

THE RISE OF FRENCH TRAGEDY

FRENCH TRAGEDY came into existence at the middle of the sixteenth century. A group of learned poets, calling themselves the Pléïade, initiated at Paris a movement to create a national literature modeled after the works of the Greek and Roman writers. In 1552 a member of the Pléïade, Étienne Jodelle (1532–73), entertained King Henry II and his court with the first French tragedy, *Cléopâtre Captive*. Jodelle and his more distinguished follower, Robert Garnier (1534–90), fashioned their drama after the pattern of Seneca, but modified the pattern to fit the classical unities of action, place, and time, as practiced in Renaissance Italy. These pioneer French compositions were lifeless verse plays filled with lengthy monologues, descriptions, narratives, and choruses. Such tragedy lacked all popular appeal and hence attained no more than a private recitation or performance.

The leading French dramatist of the early seventeenth century, Alexandre Hardy (?1575–?1631), tried to inject more vitality into the tragic species. He abolished the chorus, neglected the structural unities, and inserted more incident. Yet his plays remained wooden and rhetorical. Consequently the French stage all but abandoned production of tragedy until the revival of so-called "classical" drama in the 1630's.

This revival proceeded from a desire for reform on the part of the more refined and critical among Parisian high society. They wished to see rationalization, concentration, and discipline applied to the French drama as well as to the other phases of French culture. They disliked the looseness of form prevalent in contemporary playwriting. They craved relief from the absurd illusions of the "multiple scenery" then current on the stage. The classical observance of highly unified action, place, and time seemed to offer the best possible means of securing both intensity and order in dramaturgy. Soon the cry went up for the strict adoption of the "Three Unities" in tragedy.

CORNEILLE

To that cry Jean Mairet (1604–86) made the first response in 1634 with his tragedy *Sophonisbe*. Its demonstration of the "Three Unities" aroused so great an enthusiasm that another prominent dramatist, Pierre Corneille (1606–84), followed Mairet's example in *The Cid*, one of the masterpieces of French dramatic literature. The production of *The Cid* in January, 1637, proved an epoch-making event, for the success of Corneille's play set up a pattern of tragedy which ruled the French stage until the rebellion of Victor Hugo (1802–85) two hundred years later.

Corneille retained from classical and Renaissance tragedy the wholly serious plot, the five-act structure, the characters of high social position, the lofty style, and the dialogue in verse. He used native Alexandrine (or hexameter) couplets as the most desirable French equivalent of the classical meter. Most of the physical action he placed off stage as in classical drama, while his fidelity to the "Three Unities" led him to concentrate on a single line of conflict and to limit the action to one day in one locality. The outstanding and original feature of Corneille's pattern, however, is the transposing of all the essential action to the plane of the mind. Thus he evolved a kind of drama which reconciled the popular taste for variety and movement with the desire of the critical for inner dramatic unity. The major excitement of his tragedy springs from mental tension, the tension of warring sentiments and volitions. This tension is continually apparent in connection with the important characters.

Corneille preferred to exhibit his leading individuals possessed of a determined will which triumphantly exercises itself against the natural passions as well as against other persons of equal will. In *The Cid* he depicted a pair of lovers who, though constantly fluctuating between love and honor, never permit love to overcome honor. Don Rodrique, the young Spanish warrior, kills the father of his beloved Chimène rather than permit his own father to go unavenged. Chimène, duty-bound to vindicate her murdered father's honor, plots the death of Rodrique, the man she loves. Then Rodrique defeats Chimène's champion in order to save her from an unhappy marriage to the latter. Finally, Chimène refuses her hand to Rodrique, because he is her father's murderer. This depiction of illustrious personages resolutely struggling to act with honor is repeated by Corneille in his subsequent tragedies, *Horace* (1640), *Cinna* (1640), and *Polyeucte* (1642). Though none of these plays even approached the immense success of *The Cid*, the influence of their so-called "heroic" sentiment spread to England and helped ultimately to shape the "heroic plays" of the Restoration period there.

RACINE AND FRENCH CLASSICAL TRAGEDY

With the swift decline of Corneille's genius tragedy in France entered upon several decades of inferior creativeness. By the 1660's, when Molière was in the first flush of his fame, comedy had quite eclipsed its sister art on the Parisian stage. Then a new genius, Racine, appeared to elevate tragedy once more and to take his place alongside Molière as a master dramatist of France.

Jean Racine, born in December, 1639, at La Ferté-Milon, a small town near Paris, was the only son of a petty tax-collector. An orphan at the age of four, he came under the care of his grandmother, a very religious woman belonging to the active Jansenist sect. This sect believed in a simple but rigid discipline, and in no compromise with "the world." Racine's family connections with Jansenism haunted him all his life. In 1655 he went to the famous Jansenist abbey at Port-Royal, a few miles out of Paris. Here he found austere piety combined with devotion to humane letters. The paradoxical character of this Port-Royal training bred in him a conflict of ideals which took years to come to a head. The instruction in Greek language and culture excited his special enthusiasm. He acquired an intimacy with Greek drama such as no other European playwright of the century enjoyed.

In 1658 Racine moved to Paris to live with an uncle, a well-to-do business man. Soon he was exploring the worldly society which his uncle's connections opened up to him. An acquaintance with Jean de La Fontaine (1621–95), the famous writer of fables, introduced Racine to a lively circle of artistic folk. He played, to use his words to La Fontaine, "a gay bird with you, and the other gay birds, your cronies." His Aunt Agnes remonstrated from Port-Royal about associating with players "whose name is abominable to everyone who has the slightest degree of piety." These stage friends inspired him to compose during 1660 and 1661 two plays, both of which met rejection from the theatrical directors. At the same time some poetic effusions brought him a little reputation in the salons, but incited his Aunt Agnes to dispatch what he termed "excommunication after excommunication." The really disturbing fact, however, to him was that his present career in Paris pointed to no visible means of support.

He therefore accepted the invitation of another uncle, vicar-general at Uzès, a town near Nîmes in southern France, to study theology there with a view to gaining a sinecure in the Church. When more than a year had elapsed without a sign of the promised clerical office, Racine gave up hope and returned to Paris during the winter of 1662–63. His sojourn at Uzès, however, had not been without its value. The experience gave him opportunity to study mankind, women in particular, from a detached position, and to brood upon the intensity of human passions. He wrote in 1662 to a friend that "in this country you do not see any *amours médiocres*. All passions are extreme here, and the people of this town, who are rather easygoing in other matters, involve themselves more violently in their love affairs than they do in any other place in the world." These observations hint that the problem of *amour-passion* (i.e., ardent romantic passion), later the theme of his finest plays, laid deep hold on his fancy from this time forward.

Back at Paris in 1663, he settled down to a literary career. He re-established his former connections with theatrical people, with Molière especially. The latter produced in 1664 Racine's latest composition, *The Thebaide*. Though it stirred little interest, Molière in the following year put on the boards another play by Racine, *Alexander the Great*. The poor performance by Molière's company, whose forte, of course, was comedy, provoked Racine to an indefensible move. He secretly arranged for immediate production of *Alexander the Great* by Molière's rivals at the Hôtel de Bourgogne. Furthermore, he persuaded the beautiful Marquise Du Parc, whose acting of the heroine's part had delighted him, to transfer her talents to the Hôtel de Bourgogne. These maneuvers naturally put an end to the friendship with Molière.

A second notable enmity resulted for Racine from *Alexander the Great*. He read this play to the "grand old man of tragedy," Pierre Corneille, for an advance opinion on its worth. Corneille is reported to have given judgment that the composition, though containing some fine poetry, showed no gift for tragedy. The young playwright, stung to the quick, afterward took every possible occasion to attack Corneille. Racine's pride continued to stir up hostility till the day of his retirement from the theatrical world.

His interest in the charming Marquise Du Parc blossomed into a *grande passion*. The liaison brought him into touch with the lurid underworld of Parisian high society. His mistress lived on intimate terms with the vicious Catherine des Hayes who presided over that underworld. It must have afforded a spectacle of pride, jealousy, hate, and desire, which deeply gripped Racine's imagination. His glimpses into the darker regions of the human heart, more perhaps than the affair with Du Parc, inspired him to compose in 1666–67 a brilliant carnival of love and hate, *Andromache*. This new piece, far superior to all previous French tragedies, caused the capital to acclaim its author the greatest tragedian of his nation.

In 1670 he scored another resounding triumph with *Berenice*. The performance of the new young actress La Champmeslé in the title rôle roused him to his second *grande passion*. She led him a merry life. In 1671 La Champmeslé was reported "having delightful suppers — regular high jinks" at the fashionable suburb of St. Germain in company with Racine and his most recent companion, Nicolas-Despréaux (1636–1711), the renowned satirist. Much collaboration of a professional nature, however, accompanied the gaiety between the actress and her dramatist-lover. She played with distinction the leads in all his subsequent creations: *Bajazet* (1672), *Mithridates* (1673), *Iphigenia* (1674), and *Phaedra* (1677).

Phaedra marked a turning-point both in Racine's art and in his career. For the first time a heroine of his expressed a sense of sin and remorse in relation to her passion. This inclusion of moral consciousness as a tragic factor in Phaedra's struggle hinted at an impending change in Racine's outlook. Then, at the premiere on New Year's Day, 1677, his many enemies purchased large blocks of box seats to keep them vacant and afterward hissed throughout the performance. Two days later they packed the rival theater to applaud a new play which they had hired to be written on the same subject. Racine fell into despair. Opposition of this sort eventually would ruin his income and his reputation. His affair with La Champmeslé had broken up. He felt a growing repugnance for the whole order of his past life. When, in the spring of 1677, Louis XIV offered him the post of royal historiographer, he saw the means of escape and accepted. His acceptance meant the close of his career as a professional dramatist.

In June Racine married a Parisian lawyer's daughter, a pious lady, the possessor of a large dowry, but of so little literary taste that she is said never to have read a single one of her husband's plays. He now abandoned both his actor friends and his theatergoing. He gave himself over to an orderly domestic routine. Reconciliation with the Jansenists at Port-Royal completed his spiritual revolution. Religious devotion superseded the old worldliness. One of his contemporaries dryly observed that "he loves God now the way he used to love his mistresses."

The next twenty years for Racine passed busily, but quietly. He wrote history, waited on the King in various capacities, and dabbled in court patronage on behalf of the Jansenists. He returned briefly to his old occupation of playwriting when Madame de Maintenon, the King's mistress, requested "some kind of moral or historic poem from which love should be entirely banished," as a stage vehicle for her St. Cyr schoolgirls. A flaring-up of the old love caused him to compose two operatic, Biblical tragedies, *Esther* (1689) and *Athaliah* (1691). For some time thereafter his intimacy with the King grew closer than ever. Then about 1697 the relations cooled perceptibly from uncertain, but probably political, causes. In the fall of 1698 a painful illness seized the already despondent Racine. After six months of suffering he died on April 21, 1699, and was buried in his old school at Port-Royal. According to the monument there, "he followed for some time the ways of the world, but God showed him His grace."

The ways of the world had impelled Racine to undertake the revitalizing of a French tragedy which had lost public favor. He faced a self-indulgent and romance-ridden audience that spent a good deal of its time in the pursuit of secret passions. This audience desired a tragic drama which should satisfy its morbid curiosity about the human heart. For such drama Racine possessed the two needed capacities, craftsmanship and sensibility.   The craftsmanship proceeded from an instinct for form, supplemented by the study of Greek drama and art. The perturbations of the author's passionate nature yielded the sensibility.

Racine's craftsmanship refined the pattern of Corneille's tragedy in several important respects. The strictest possible observance of the "Three Unities" is employed in order to intensify the mental tensions. The action is confined to one scene and to a few hours. Only the last moments before the catastrophe are presented. Thus the drama concentrates to the maximum on the crisis of the situation.

In addition to these refinements of Corneille's pattern, Racine introduced a compositional method similar to that found in music. Not only the play as a whole, but also each individual scene and act displays a deliberate emotional progression akin to the musical principle of counterpoint. The emotions alternate, oppose, and blend in evident designs. Both pianissimo passages and climaxes are skillfully placed. But over and above the variety and modulation there stands a dominating passion which preserves the unity of theme. This "musical" structure, because it permits impressive histrionic effects, has been a notable reason for Racine's continued popularity with the French actors.

Racine also improved upon Corneille's tragedy in regard to characterization. His protagonists are more emotionally complex. They are also more evenly balanced between instinct and will, desire and duty. Their sensitiveness and constant wavering lead to stratagems, feints, and reversals of decision. This complicated series of reactions makes possible an endless variety of purely psychological situations. Racine's plays come to resemble chess games with mentalities as the pawns.

The most significant, however, of the developments in Racine's tragedy is the impassioned tone. He substituted emotionalism for admiration, a drama of sensibility for Corneille's drama of heroism. Resolute males give way to temperamental females as mainsprings of the action. The struggle concerns man the creature of the natural passions, the victim of love and jealousy in particular. The outstanding characters are "great lovers." *Amour-passion* becomes the central theme. Tragedy consists in the victory of passion over reason.

Thus Racine perfected the ideal tragedy for his audience — a tragedy which dissected the subtleties of the human heart with the severe economy of classical form. He took delight in his contrivance of intensity out of simplicity. "A crowd of incidents has always been the refuge of poets who have never felt their genius rich and strong enough to hold attention through five acts by a simple action, sustained by the violence of the passions, the beauty of the sentiments, and the elegance of the expression," he asserted. The taste not only of France but of all Europe soon applauded Racine's art as the perfect model for tragedy and maintained that view into the nineteenth century. At that point the remarkable order and compactness of his structure bore fruit in the "well-made plays" of the French dramatists, Scribe and Sardou, and thence in the works of Ibsen.

Nevertheless, Racine cannot challenge the supremacy of Shakespeare the tragedian in either depth or vitality. Shakespeare highlights man's strength amid weakness in order to convey aspiration along with compassion. Racine concentrates on man's weakness to invoke only compassion. His drama of sensibility, moreover, is at bottom a dry art. The dissecting of emotions tends to atrophy through lack of contrast. Characters never develop wholeness of being when external manifestations of personality are prevented. A mixture of physical action with mental, such as Shakespearean tragedy richly provides, always results in superior dramatic vitality.

Racine's tragedy, therefore, requires for its appreciation an intellectual and critical temper. Its excellence lies less in interpretation than in treatment. Only a love of formal beauty can enjoy properly the unique discipline of design which Racine imposes on the violent heart of man. He stands out as the foremost exponent of classical structure in the later European drama.

"ANDROMACHE"

Andromache, Racine's first real success on the Parisian stage, had its premiere sometime in November, 1667, perhaps on the 17th, when there was a performance in the Queen's apartment. Its public triumph occurred at the playhouse with which Racine was always affiliated after his quarrel with Molière in 1665, the Hôtel de Bourgogne. Though the latter could not compare in size or pretentiousness with Molière's Théâtre du Palais Royal, it boasted a century-old tradition and the presence of the King's troupe. The long and narrow hall, dingily lighted by candelabra, contained a main floor or "parterre" without seats, and a low stage with a balustrade across it. Two rows of boxes lined each side of the hall. Prominent officials and families had more or less permanent occupancy of certain ones in the lower tier. Their names appeared in decorated scrolls on the box fronts. Despite such aristocratic touches, the crude old playhouse really offered a strange contrast to the splendid dress of the audience.

Andromache is an excellent representative specimen of Racine's art. He drew the outline of external events from Book III of Vergil's *Aeneid*, but the essential mental drama is his peculiar invention. His favorite theme of *amour-passion* stands revealed in all its emotional magnificence — the despair and the exaltation, the criminality and the selflessness. The persistent fluctuations of feeling in each character keep the mental tension undiminished to the last scene. Hermione's remark to Orestes about Pyrrhus typifies the continual ebb-and-flow: "Unless he dies today, tomorrow I may love him" (Act IV, ll. 165–66). Love exasperated by jealousy, Racine's most explosive combination of sentiments, finally engulfs three of the four protagonists in a finale of rage and violence. The spectator comes away from the cataclysm, echoing for each of the other lovers Orestes' question: "Was reason's light extinguished in my heart?" (Act V, l. 188). The tragedy of *Andromache*, as always with Racine, is that passion triumphs wholesale over reason.

The steadfast, tender Andromache, the most appealing of all Racine's heroines, alone survives the turmoil. The play takes its title from her, because she serves as the pivot of the action and gives unity to a plot woven of two strands. Her policy toward Pyrrhus determines, from point to point, Hermione's attitude toward Orestes. Andromache's final decision brings on the catastrophe through Hermione. The latter's rôle, though the less crucial, is the more colorful. Racine endows her with the greater passionateness. He not only assigns her the larger number of scenes, but leaves her on the stage until nearly the close. Her last scene is a grand display of emotionalism, reaching its apex in the renowned line to Orestes, a master stroke of irony and irrationality, "Who bade you do it?" (Act V, l. 161). Andromache, on the other hand, leaves the stage for good in Act IV, Scene 1, a gently moving scene. It is no wonder, therefore, that more recent actresses who have starred in *Andromache*, such as the great Rachel and Sarah Bernhardt, have preferred the part of Hermione. This rôle, next to Racine's Phaedra, is recognized as the greatest in all French tragedy.

The two males, the amorous Pyrrhus and the neurotic Orestes, disclose far less forceful characters than the two women. More interesting, however, than most of Racine's men, they form with Andromache and Hermione the best-balanced group of personages in any Racine tragedy. His heroes tend to be rather puerile, indecisive creatures. Perhaps they suffer from "a mediocre goodness," as their creator defined it in excuse. He took only sufficient pains with his male characters to render them passable foils for his females.

The skillful delineation of feminine sensibility in *Andromache* demonstrates Racine's peculiar forte. This play with its pair of contrasting women and their lovers constitutes his most ambitious canvas. It is a notable drama of the human passions, combining great psychological ingenuity with elegance of form.

[For a study of earlier French tragedy and of Racine, see A. F. B. Clark, *Jean Racine* (1939).]

JEAN RACINE

Andromache

[*Translated by* ROBERT BRUCE BOSWELL]

DRAMATIS PERSONAE

ANDROMACHE, *widow of* HECTOR, *captive of*
    PYRRHUS
PYRRHUS, *son of* ACHILLES, *king of Epirus*
ORESTES, *son of* AGAMEMNON
HERMIONE, *daughter of* HELEN, *betrothed to*
    PYRRHUS

PYLADES, *friend of* ORESTES
CLEONE, *friend of* HERMIONE
CEPHISSA, *friend of* ANDROMACHE
PHOENIX, *tutor of* ACHILLES, *and afterwards of*
    PYRRHUS
Attendants of ORESTES

The Scene is a hall in the palace of Pyrrhus at Buthrotum, a town of Epirus *

ACT I

SCENE 1

Enter ORESTES *and* PYLADES

Ores. Yes, since I find again a friend so true,
My fortune 'gins to wear another face;
Already seems her wrath to have been soothed,
Permitting us to meet each other here.
Who would have thought that this detested
    coast   5
Would first present you to Orestes' eyes;
And, lost six months and more, you should be
    found
Where in Epirus Pyrrhus holds his court?
   Pyl. Thanks be to Heav'n, that has de-
    tain'd my steps
So oft, and seem'd to shut me out from
    Greece,   10
Since that disastrous day when winds and
    waves
Scatter'd our vessels almost in the sight
Of this Epirus. How I mourn'd and wept,
Myself an exile, for Orestes' fate;
Dreading for him ever some danger new,   15
Some sorrow that my friendship could not
    share!

That melancholy most of all I fear'd
Which I have seen so long your soul o'ercloud;
I fear'd that Heav'n might grant you cruel aid,
And offer what you ever sought — a tomb.   20
But now I see you, and, if I may dare
To say it, happier fortune brings you here:
This stately train that on your steps attends
Looks not like that of wretch who seeks his
    death.
   Ores. Alas! Who knows what fortune is my
    guide?   25
Love bids me seek a cruel mistress here;
But I am ignorant of Fate's decrees,
Whether 'tis life or death that I shall find.
   Pyl. Is then your soul so bound in slavery,
That for Love's sake alone you care to
    live?   30
What spell constrains you to those fires again,
The tortures you have suffer'd all forgot?
Will she,[1] who would not listen to your pray'rs
At Sparta, in Epirus prove more kind?

---

[1] Hermione, daughter of Menelaus, king of Sparta,
and of Helen of Troy, and cousin to Orestes. The
latter had wooed her in Sparta, but Menelaus promised
her to Pyrrhus for services rendered in the war against
the Trojans.

---

* The northwesternmost district of ancient Greece with its coastline on the Adriatic Sea.

Ashamed of having utter'd vows so vain,   35
You should despise her; speak no more of her.
Your words deceived me.
   Ores.   I deceived myself.
O'erwhelm not, friend, a wretch who clings to
   you:
Have I from you e'er hidden heart's desire?   40
You knew my flame fresh born, my earliest
   sighs:
When Menelaus pledged his daughter's hand
To Pyrrhus, the avenger of his race,
You witness'd my despair; since then you've
   seen
How I have dragg'd my chains from sea to
   sea.   45
I saw you, pitying my forlorn estate,
Ready to follow me where'er I went;
Checking my madness in its wild career,
You saved me from myself from day to day.
But when, distracted by my fears, I thought   50
Hermione was lavishing her charms
On Pyrrhus, well you know how, fill'd with
   wrath,
I strove to make forgetfulness repay
Her scorn.   I made you think, and thought
   myself,
The victory achieved; deem'd passion changed
To hatred, and, disparaging her charms,   56
Abhorr'd her harshness, and defied her eyes
To raise the tender feelings I had crush'd.
In that deceitful calm I came to Greece,
And found her princes muster'd to withstand 60
A danger, and no mean one, that appear'd
Fraught with fresh troubles.   Eagerly I join'd
Their ranks, and hoped in war to find release
From other cares, that, former strength re-
   gain'd,
My heart would lose all memory of love.   65
But mark with me how persecuting Fate
Entrapp'd me in the snare I thought to shun.
On every side I heard murmurs and threats
Raised against Pyrrhus from the whole of
   Greece,
Complaining that, forgetful of his blood   70
And promise, at his court he rears her foe,
Astyanax, the young ill-fated son
Of Hector, relic of so many kings
Buried 'neath Troy.   To save the babe from
   death,

Andromache, as I have heard, deceived   75
Wily Ulysses, while another child,
Torn from her arms, was slaughter'd in his
   stead.
They say Hermione has fail'd to charm
My rival, that elsewhere his heart and crown
He offers.   Menelaus, loath to trust   80
The rumor, is sore vex'd at long delay.
The cause of his displeasure is to me
A source of secret triumph, yet at first
I deem'd it but a feeling of revenge,
A thought that flatter'd pride. But soon I found
The fair tormentor had resumed her place   86
Within my heart; the smoldering fire revived,
I felt my hatred melt and disappear,
Or rather felt my love had never ceased.
Soliciting support from all the Greeks,   90
To Pyrrhus I was sent, and here I am.
My mission is to try if I can wrest
This infant from his arms, who, while he lives,
Brings fear to many.   Happy shall I be,
If I can carry off, not Hector's son,   95
But my princess!   Nor fancy that my flame,
Fann'd by repression, can extinguished be
By any peril.   All resistance proved
To be in vain, I blindly yield myself
To Passion's sway; I love Hermione,   100
Am come to win her, fly with her, or die.
Pyrrhus you know; what think you he will do?
Tell me what passes in his court, and what
Within his heart.   Still to Hermione
Is he enslaved?   Will he restore the prize 105
Of which he robb'd me?
   Pyl.   Should I promise that,
I should deceive you; not with his consent
Shall she be yours.   Not that he seems much
   pleased
T' have won her; Hector's widow [1] fires his
   heart   110
With warmer passion, but she proves unkind,
And hitherto has paid his love with hate,
Tho' daily he attempts in every way
To bind her stubborn will or rouse her fears.
From her he hides her boy, threatens his life,
Then fain would dry the tears he forced to flow
Hermione has seen a hundred times   115
Her lover's wrath submit to sue again,

      [1] Andromache, mother of Astyanax.

And offer humbly oft-rejected vows,
With troubled sighs of mingled love and rage.
You must not then expect that I can tell　121
Th' emotions of a heart so ill controll'd.
In its distraction he may wed, perchance,
The one he scorns, and lose the one he loves.
　　Ores. But tell me how Hermione beholds
Her charms contemn'd, the marriage rites
　　　delay'd.　　　　　　　　　　　126
　　　Pyl. To all appearance she would seem, my
　　　lord,
Disdainful of her suitor's fickleness,
And thinks that, anxious to be reconciled,
He'll soon entreat her to take back his heart.
To me indeed she has her grief reveal'd;　131
She mourns in secret his indifference;
Ready to leave him, still she always stays,
And sometimes calls Orestes to her aid.
　　Ores. Ah, if I thought so, Pylades, full soon
Would I go, cast myself ——　　　　136
　　Pyl.　　　　　　　Fulfill your task;
Wait on the King, and tell him that all Greece
Is banded against Hector's son.　So far
From giving up the child of her she loves,　140
Their hatred will but make his heart more fond;
All efforts made to part them will the more
Unite them.　Urge your mission, and its end
Must fail.　He comes.
　　Ores.　　　　　Prepare her then to see　145
A lover who comes hither but for her.
　　　　　　　　　　　(*Exit* PYLADES.

SCENE 2

Enter PYRRHUS *and* PHOENIX

　　Ores. Ere by my voice all Greece addresses
　　　you,
Let me express my pleasure in her choice
Of me, and at beholding face to face
Achilles' offspring, conqueror of Troy.　150
Yes, we admire your exploits like his own;
Before him Hector fell, Troy before you;
Your daring and success alike have shown
Achilles' son alone can fill his place.
But what he never would have done, with pain
We see you do, giving unhappy Troy　156
Fresh pow'r to injure, letting pity move
Your heart with fatal touch, prolonging feud
Already waged so long.　Do you forget

The might of Hector?　We remember still　160
What blood he cost us; at his very name
Widows and orphans tremble; not a home
But calls for vengeance on this son of his,[1]
For father or for husband lost thro' him.
Who knows what harm this child may one day
　　　work?　　　　　　　　　　165
Perchance he may come down upon our ports,
As we have seen his sire do, burn our ships,
And, fire in hand, pursue them o'er the waves.
Sir, shall I dare to tell you what I think?
You fear what recompense your cares may
　　　meet,　　　　　　　　　　170
And lest this serpent, in your bosom nursed,
May punish you one day for sheltering him.
Be the desire of Greece then satisfied,
Secure your life by wreaking her revenge;
Destroy a dangerous foe, who will on you　175
Practice the sword hereafter to be used
Against her.
　　Pyr.　　　Greece alarms herself too much
On my behalf.　By more important cares
I thought her moved, and that such envoy
　　　brought　　　　　　　　　　180
Some grander project than I yet have heard.
Who would suppose that Agamemnon's son
Would deign to intervene in this affair:
Or that all Greece, after such triumphs won,
Could thus conspire against an infant's life?
To whom am I to make the sacrifice?　186
Greece may no longer claim his life as hers;
Or is it not allow'd to me, alone
Of all the Greeks, to treat as I may please　189
A captive won by lot?　When 'neath the walls
Of smoking Troy the victors, blood besprent,
The spoil divided, to my share there fell
Andromache and Hector's infant son;
Ulysses made the cup of misery
O'erflow for Hecuba;[2] to Argos went　195
Cassandra[3] with your sire.[4]　Have I controll'd
Them or their captives, or presumed to claim
The fruit of their brave deeds?　They fear the
　　　day
When Hector shall revive — his son may take
My life if his be spared.　Such caution shows
Care in excess.　Misfortunes so remote　201
Are quite beyond my ken.　I see proud Troy

---

[1] Astyanax.　　　　[2] Wife of Priam, king of Troy.
[3] Daughter of Priam.　　　　[4] Agamemnon.

As once she was, mother of heroes, queen
Of Asia, crown'd with tow'rs; and then I see
How she fell headlong, how she prostrate lies;
For walls but heaps of ashes I behold —   206
A river that runs blood, forsaken fields,
A child in chains; and little can I think
That Troy, so fallen, meditates revenge.
If it were sworn that Hector's son should die,
Why did we let a year pass o'er his head?   211
Why could we not have slain him in the arms
Of Priam? Troy might well have been his tomb
No less than that of others. Age and Youth
Pleaded alike in vain their weakness then;   215
War's frenzy and night's darkness, worse than
    we,
Left no distinctions to our murderous swords.
My rage was fierce as that of any there
Against the vanquish'd. But should cruelty
Outlive one's fury? Can I in cool blood,   220
Discarding pity, slaughter a poor child?
No, Sir; let Greece hunt up some other prey,
Efface elsewhere all vestiges of Troy:
My enmity is finish'd, and what war
Has spared Epirus safely shall preserve.   225
    Ores. You know, my lord, full well what
        cunning trick
Brought to the sword a false Astyanax
Instead of Hector's son. It is not Troy
Nor Trojans, it is Hector they pursue;   229
Greece tracks the father's footsteps in the son;
The wrath his bloodshed kindled must in blood
Be quench'd, and none but Hector's can avail;
E'en to Epirus will they follow it:
Prevent them.
    Pyr.   No, the challenge I accept   235
With joy, and in Epirus let them seek
A second Troy: while hatred makes them class
With foes the friend who brought them victory.
Greece will not then for the first time requite
Unjustly all Achilles' services;   240
Once Hector profited, the day may come
When Hector's son shall profit in his turn.
    Ores. So Greece in you finds a rebellious son!
    Pyr. Have I then conquer'd only to depend
On her?   245
    Ores.   Hermione will check your course;
Between her father and yourself her eyes
Will interpose.
    Pyr.   She may be dear to me,

And yet I need not be her father's slave   250
Because I love her. Time may reconcile
Honor, perchance, with what affection claims.
Meanwhile fair Helen's daughter you may see,
I know what tie of blood links you and her.[1]
No longer will I keep you after that;   255
Go, say that I refuse what Greece demands.
                    (*Exit* ORESTES.

SCENE 3
PYRRHUS, PHOENIX

    Phoe. Thus then you send him to his
        mistress' feet!
    Pyr. Long for the princess has his passion
        burn'd,
They say.   259
    Phoe. What if that fire should be revived,
His heart be giv'n to her, and hers to him?
    Pyr. Let them love, Phoenix! She may take
        her leave
With my consent. Ay, let th' enamor'd pair
Go back to Sparta; not a port shall bar
Their exit. Let her spare me more constraint!
    Phoe. My lord!   266
    Pyr.   I'll bare my soul another time;
Andromache approaches.

SCENE 4
Enter ANDROMACHE and CEPHISSA

    Pyr.   Is it I,
Madam, you seek? May I indulge a hope
So pleasing?   271
    Andr.   I was passing to the place
That holds my son, permitted once a day
To see the only being left to me
Of Troy and Hector: and I have not yet   275
Wept with him, no, nor held him in my arms
A moment.
    Pyr.   Greece, if her alarm tells truth,
Will give you other causes soon for tears.
    Andr. What is this terror that has struck
        her heart?   280
Has then some Trojan managed to escape?
    Pyr. Not yet extinguish'd is the hatred felt
For Hector. And they dread his son.
    Andr.   Their fear   284

---

[1] Hermione and Orestes were first cousins.

Has found a worthy object! He, poor child,
Yet knows not Hector for his sire, nor you
For master!

    Pyr.   All the same, the Greeks demand
His blood, and Agamemnon's son is here
To urge his punishment.   290

    Andr.   Will you pronounce
Sentence so hard? My interest in him
Is his sole crime; it is not that they fear
He will avenge his father, but will dry
His mother's tears. He would have filled the
     place   295
Of sire and husband. I must lose them all,
And at your hand.

    Pyr.   Weep not, I have refused
To do their bidding, tho' they threaten war;
Shall they again with twice five hundred ships
Set sail, to force you to give up your son;   301
Tho' all the blood that Helen caused to flow
Must be the price, and, after ten years' war,
My palace sink in flames, I falter not,
And with my own will I defend his life.   305
But 'mid these perils, suffer'd for your sake,
Will you refuse to grant a kinder look?
Press'd on all sides, and hated by the Greeks,
Must I still strive against your cruelty?
My arm is at your service: may I hope   310
You will accept the heart's devotion too?
Let not your champion have to reckon you
Among the number of his enemies.

    Andr.   Think what you do, my lord, what
     Greece will say.   314
Can soul so great as yours such weakness show?
You would not have your generous purpose pass
For the mere madness of a lovesick swain.
How can you wish a captive sad as I
To love you — I, who cannot bear myself?
Can eyes that sorrow haunts have charms for
     you,   320
Doom'd by yourself to everlasting tears?
No, no; respect your captive's misery,
Relieve the wretched, to a mother's arms
Restore a son, withstand the cruelty
Of all the Greeks, nor make my heart the price
Of succor; and, at need against my will,   326
Protect him. That were conduct that befits
Achilles' son.

    Pyr.   What! Is your wrath still hot?
Shall hatred and the punishment it prompts

Ne'er cease? Much woe I doubtless caused,
     and Troy   331
Has seen this hand dyed crimson with your
     blood,
A hundred times. But, smitten by the shafts
From Beauty's eyes, have I not dearly paid
For all their tears, and long since learn'd
     remorse?   335
I suffer all the ills I gave to Troy;
Vanquish'd and taken prisoner, with regrets
Loaded, consumed with fires more fierce than
     those
I kindled. Such anxiety, such tears,   339
Such restless longings — was I e'er so harsh
As you are now? Have you not punish'd me
Indeed enough? Nay, let our common foes
Unite us. Tell me only I may hope,
I give you back your son, will be to him
A father, and will teach him to avenge   345
His country. I myself will punish Greece
For your calamities and mine. One look
Shall give me strength for all. Troy shall revive,
E'en from her ashes; sooner than its siege
Lasted, her walls shall rise, your son be crown'd
Her king.   351

    Andr.   I care not for such glory now,
That prospect pleased me while his father lived.
Troy's sacred walls [1] that Hector could not save
May never hope to see our faces more.   355
My lord, the wretched are content with less;
'Tis exile only that these tears demand.
Far from the Greeks, ay, too, and far from you,
Let me go hide my son, and mourn my loss.
Your love inflames their hatred against us;
Return to Helen's daughter, oh, return!   361

    Pyr. That can I not. Then why distress me
     more?
How may a heart that's yours be giv'n to her?
I know that she was promised its command,
I know she hither came to reign as queen;   365
Fate to Epirus brought you both alike,
Her to impose the chains of slavery,
And you to wear them. But I took no pains
To please her. Seeing how your charms prevail
And hers are scorn'd, it might be rather thought
That she is captive here, and you are queen.
Ah, how a single sigh, of all I breathe   372

----

[1] Sacred because built by the gods Apollo and Neptune.

For you, would carry joy if giv'n to her!

Andr. How should they not be welcome?
Can she e'er
Forget the services that you have wrought?
Hector and Troy are names that do not cause
A shudder, nor is all her tenderness　　377
Devoted to the dead. Ah, what a loss
Was mine, bitter to think on! Slaying him,
Your father made himself immortal, gain'd
The crown of all his glory, and my tears　381
Have made you both renown'd.

Pyr.　　　　　　　　It needs must be
That I obey you, Madam, and forget.　384
Nay, hate you. Love has been too violent
To change its course to mere indifference.
Be well assured, the heart henceforth that loves
No more with passion must with fury hate.
Nought will I in my righteous anger spare;　389
The son shall answer for the mother's scorn;
Greece asks his life: why should I always stoop
To save th' ungrateful? I'll do so no more.

Andr. Alas, then he must die! His mother's
tears
His sole protection, and his innocence —
And yet, perchance, so wretched is my lot,　395
His death may lift this load of misery.
Life and its woes I bore but for his sake;
To follow him will bring me to his sire.
Thus reunited, thanks to you, my lord,
We three shall ——　　　　　　　　400

Pyr.　　　　Madam, go and see your son;
The sight of him may teach your heart to shun
The path to which your anger beckons you.
I'll choose another hour to learn my fate.
Think how to save him, while you clasp him
close.　　　　　(*Exeunt.* 405

ACT II

Scene i

Enter Hermione *and* Cleone

Herm. Yes, he shall see me, since you'll have
it so;
That pleasure will I grant him once again.
Soon Pylades will bring him; but were I
To use my judgment, it should not be so.

Cleo. What evil lurks there in the sight of
him?　　　　　　　　　　　　5
Say, is he not the same Orestes still

For whose return you sigh'd a hundred times,
Whose love and constancy has been the theme
Of your regret?

Herm.　　　　Paid with ingratitude!　10
That love it is which makes his presence here
Repugnant; shame for me, triumph for him,
To see my misery so like his own!
Is that the proud Hermione, he'll say,　14
Lo, she who scorn'd me once herself despised!
The wretch who on her heart set price so high
Learns in her turn the pangs of outraged love!
Oh, Heav'ns!

Cleo.　　Dispel these most unworthy fears:
Too deeply has he felt your pow'r to charm.
He comes to urge his love, not to insult,　21
He brings a heart from which he cannot blot
Your image. But you have not told me yet
What writes your sire.

Herm.　　　　　If Pyrrhus still delays,　25
And if he will not let the Trojan die,
My father bids me with the Greeks depart.

Cleo. 'Tis well: then hear Orestes. You at
least
May finish that which Pyrrhus has begun;
You must forestall him to obtain success.　30
Have you not told me that you hated him?

Herm. Hate him, Cleone? Can just pride do
less,
When he forgets the favor freely giv'n?
That heart was treacherous which I learn'd to
love;
Too dear he was, not to be hated now!　35

Cleo. Fly from him then, and since you are
beloved ——

Herm. Ah, let my rage have time to grow
more strong;
Leave me to guard myself against my foe.
Cleone, it is terrible to part,
And he will force me to it but too well,　40
The faithless wretch!

Cleo.　　　Wait you for some new wrong?
To love his slave, before your very eyes!
What more can make him odious, if not that?
What greater insult can he offer yet?　45
Had he known how, he would have left undone
Nothing that could displease you.

Herm.　　　　　　　Why provoke
Fresh torture? I would fain disguise the truth.
Try to believe not what your eyes have seen;

Think that my love is banish'd; give me joy 51
That I have conquer'd, and my heart is steel'd
Against its weakness. Make me think so too.
You'ld have me fly; there's nought to hinder it,
Let us depart, and leave him to enjoy   55
A conquest that degrades him; to his slave
Himself submissive. Let us fly! But what
If Faith and Duty should reclaim his heart,
If he should crave his pardon at my feet,
And Love have pow'r to make him all my own?
But no, he only seeks to humble me.   61
Yet let us stay to mar their happiness,
Finding some pleasure still in spoiling theirs;
Or, making him renounce his solemn pledge,
Render him guilty in the eyes of Greece. 65
Already have I drawn upon the son
Their anger; I would have them ask of him
The mother too, and so those pangs repay
Which she has made me feel. Let her lose him,
Nay, let him cause her death.   70
  Cleo.   Think you that she,
Whose eyes run down with tears, can pleasure find
In trying to supplant you, that, bow'd down
With grief, she courts her persecutor's love?
What signs have shown her anguish soothed
    thereby?   75
Why is her soul then plunged in misery?
Why 'gainst a favor'd lover so severe?
  Herm. Ah, I have lent too credulous an ear
To faithless vows, and utter'd what I felt.
I saw no danger in sincerity,   80
My eyes unguarded let their secret out,
And my own heart pleaded his cause too well.
What woman would not have declared her love,
As I did, trusting to his solemn oaths?
Did his eye scorn me then, as it does now? 85
You cannot but remember all combined
To aid his suit — my family avenged,
The joy of Greece, our vessels charged with
    spoils
From Troy, his father's exploits by the son's
Eclipsed, his passion deem'd to pass my
    own,   90
My heart — Yes, and his fame e'en dazzled you;
E'er he betray'd me, all of you conspired
To that same end. Enough; if Pyrrhus has,
I have not ceased to feel; Orestes' heart
Is noble as his deeds, and he can love   95

Without return. — Ay, and perhaps can make
Himself beloved. I'll see him.
  Cleo.   Look, he comes.
  Herm. Ah me! I had not thought he was so
  nigh.

SCENE 2

Enter ORESTES

  Herm. Sir, shall I think some tender traces
  left   100
Of former Love prompt you to visit me,
In my distress, or is it Duty's voice,
And that alone, which urges you to come?
  Ores. Such is the fatal blindness of my heart,
Known to you well, that I am destined still 105
To come, and come again, to worship you,
In spite of all my vows to come no more.
To see you will, I know, reopen wounds;
Each step that brings me near makes me for-
    sworn;   109
I know it, and I blush thereat. But Heav'n,
That saw how our last parting wrung my heart,
Be witness how I strove to free myself,
By certain death, from oath so hard to keep
And ceaseless torture; how to savage tribes,
Whose gods are only pleased with human blood,
I offer'd life; they shut their temple doors, 116
Sparing to take such willing sacrifice.
To you at length I come, and from your eyes
Must seek the Death that shuns my close pur-
    suit,
And their indifference shall end despair; 120
They need but cut the last fond cord of hope
To bring the fatal hour for which I yearn,
They need but say what they have said be-
    fore —
Said always. For a year past, that has been
My only aim: be yours the victim's blood 125
That Scythians [1] might have spilt instead of
    you,
Had any so relentless there been found.
  Herm. Have done, Sir, with these accents of
  despair;
With matters more momentous you are
  charged.

---

[1] A wild savage race supposed by the Greeks to inhabit the distant regions of southern Russia near the Black Sea or the Caucasus.

Why talk of Scythia, or my cruelty?   130
Think of the many kings you represent.
And must their vengeance on your transports
     hang?
Is it Orestes' blood that they demand?
Discharge the office they imposed on you.   134
   Ores. Pyrrhus refuses, and my task is done.
Madam, he sends me back.   Some other pow'r
Makes him defend the cause of Hector's son.
     Herm. False and forsworn!
     Ores.   So, ready to depart,
My own fate at your lips I come to learn.   140
Ere utter'd, your reply I think I hear,
That you detest me in your secret heart.
     Herm. What always so unjust?   Why will
         your grief
Forever of my enmity complain?
How have I shown the harshness that you
     blame   145
So often?   'Twas obedience to my sire
That brought me hither; but who knows if I
Have not been sick at heart since then, and
     shared
Alarms no less than yours?   I may have shed,
In this Epirus, bitter tears.   And none   150
Can say I have not sometimes wish'd you here,
Despite my duty.
     Ores.   Wish'd me here!   Oh, joy! —
But can it be to me that you address
These heavenly words?   Open your eyes, and
     see   155
Orestes, upon whom they frown'd so long.
     Herm. Yes, you — who first taught them to
         know their pow'r,
Whose love with their attractions grew, whose
     worth
I could not but esteem, and who have had   159
My sighs, and whom indeed I fain would love.
     Ores. I understand how hopeless is my lot;
Your heart is giv'n to Pyrrhus, and to me
Vain wishes.
     Herm.   Ah, you need not envy him,
Unless you crave my hatred.   165
     Ores.   Yes; for then
Love well might follow from a source opposed;
I cannot please you whom you fain would love,
But, if you wish'd to hate me, Love alone   169
Would be obey'd, and I should win your heart.
Ye gods! Such worship, and such tender love —

Speak they not for me, could you lend an ear?
Your voice alone supports a prior claim
For Pyrrhus, it may be against your will,
Against his, certainly; for in his soul   175
He hates you, loves another ——
     Herm.   Who has dared
To tell you that he scorns me?   Have his looks
And words reveal'd it?   Think you that my
     eyes   179
Can light no lasting fire, but soon must rouse
Contempt?   Perhaps more favorable judge
May somewhere else be found.
     Ores.   'Tis well to taunt
Me thus!   Am I the one who scorns your
     charms?
Have you not tried my constancy enough?   185
Am I a witness that your eyes lack pow'r?
Despise them?   Ah, how gladly would they see
My rival so despise them as do I!
     Herm. What care I, Sir, whether he loves or
     hates?
Go, and against a rebel arm all Greece;   190
Pay him the price of disobedience;
Go, let them make this land a second Troy!
Will you say now, my heart is giv'n to him?
     Ores. Madam, do more, and come to Greece
     yourself.
Will you remain here as a hostage? Come;   195
To every heart let your fair eyes appeal,
Till common hatred prompts our joint attack.
     Herm. What if he wed Andromache mean-
     while?
     Ores. Madam!
     Herm.   What deep disgrace must then be
     mine,   200
To have this Phrygian [1] woman hold my place!
     Ores. And yet you hate him!   Madam, own
     the truth;
We cannot shut Love's fires within the breast,
Our very eyes betray us — silence, speech;
And fires we hide in vain burst forth more
     fierce.   205
     Herm. Your mind is prepossess'd, I see it
     well,
And spreads a deadly venom o'er my words,
In every argument detects deceit,
And thinks my hatred prompted by my love.

[1] Troy lay in Phrygia, the northwest district of Asia
Minor.

I must explain myself, and you shall act   210
Accordingly.   You know 'twas Duty led
My footsteps hither, and detains me here;
I cannot leave till Pyrrhus or my sire
Compel me.   Make my father understand
The foe of Greece will form no marriage bond
With us; between the Trojan and myself   216
Make Pyrrhus choose, which he will keep, and which
Dismiss.   Farewell.   I wait but his consent
To follow you.
(Exeunt Hermione and Cleone.

SCENE 3

Orestes alone

Ores.   Yes, you will follow me,   220
No doubt of that.   Already his consent
Is sure, nor need I fear that Pyrrhus wants
To keep you, for he has no eyes forsooth
Save for his dear Andromache, all else   224
Irksome, and seeks some pretext that may part
Himself and you.   One word, and all is done!
What joy to rob Epirus of a prize
So rare!   Troy's relics she may save, and keep
Unharm'd brave Hector's widow and his son,
And thousand others; 'tis enough for me,   230
That, ne'er again to see thee or thy prince,
Hermione departs.
Good Fortune brings
Him hither.[1]   To such charms, Love, close his
    eyes.

SCENE 4

Enter Pyrrhus and Phoenix

Pyr.   I have sought you, Sir,   235
To own that in a fit of violence
I fought against your reasons.   Since I went,
Their justice and their force have shown them-
    selves.
I feel, like you, that I have thwarted Greece,
My father's efforts, and, indeed, my own,   240
In aiding Troy, frustrating all achieved
Both by Achilles and myself; nor now
Do I condemn resentment which was based
On solid ground.   Your victim soon shall be

---

[1] Orestes sees Pyrrhus approaching — hence the abrupt change in his soliloquizing at this point.

At your disposal.   245
Ores.   By this firm resolve,
Prudent as firm, a caitiff's blood buys peace.
Pyr. And to assure you further, I consent
To wed Hermione, the pledge of peace
Forever.   Such a pleasing spectacle   250
Can have no better witness here than you,
Who represent all Greece, and most her sire,
For in yourself his brother lives again.
Go to her, tell her that tomorrow morn
I will receive her at your hands with peace.   255
Ores. (aside). Great gods!   (Exit Orestes.

SCENE 5

Pyrrhus, Phoenix

Pyr. Well, Phoenix, has Love won the day?
Say, do your eyes refuse to know me still?
Phoe. I see you as you were; that righteous
    wrath
Restores you to the Greeks and to yourself.   260
No more the plaything of a servile flame,
'Tis Pyrrhus, 'tis Achilles' son, and more
His rival, who at last obeys the laws
Of honor, and a second triumph wins
O'er Troy.   265
Pyr.   Say rather that my victory
Begins today when I can feel its joy,
And my heart, lifted from its low estate,
Seems to have triumph'd o'er a thousand
    foes
In crushing love.   Think, Phoenix, what a host
Of troubles I avoid that follow close   271
On passion; how content to sacrifice
Duty and friendship, danger I despised,
Courting destruction from the arms of Greece,
Might I but win a single look of love.   275
Phoe. I bless, my lord, the kind severity
Which gives you back ——
Pyr.   See how she treated me!
I thought that, when the mother's fears were
    roused,
She would have yielded for her infant's sake,
Disarm'd by his caresses, but I found   281
No signs of weakness mingled with her tears.
Embitter'd by her woes, more fierce she seem'd
Each time the name of Hector pass'd her lips.
Oft as I promised to protect her son,   285
"'Tis Hector," she would say, as in her arms

She held him, "his those eyes, that mouth, the
    heart
Already bold. My husband I embrace
In this his image." Does she think that I
Will let her keep him thus to feed her love   290
For Hector?
    Phoe.   Such were doubtless the return
That she would make. But leave her now.
    Pyr.   I see
How consciousness of beauty flatters her,   295
And makes her proudly wait, despite my wrath,
To see me at her knees. Rather at mine
I'll see her crouch in vain; eternal hate
Parts Hector's widow and Achilles' son!
    Phoe. Then speak of her no more to me, my
      liege.   300
Go, see Hermione; and at her feet
Be your sole thought her pleasure, and forget
What's past. Prepare her for the nuptial rites
Yourself, nor to a rival leave that task
Who loves her but too well.   305
    Pyr.   Think you she will
Be jealous if I wed Hermione?
    Phoe. What, harping on the Trojan woman
      still!
What matters it to you if vex'd or glad?
What spell attracts you tow'rds her, in despite
Of your own will?   311
    Pyr.   I have not told her all
I meant to say; I show'd but half the rage
I feel; she knows not what a bitter foe
She has in me. Let us return and flout   315
Her vengeance, to my hatred give full scope,
And see her pride and beauty in the dust.
Come.
    Phoe. Go and cast yourself before her, Sir,
Go swear that in your heart you love her still,
And so encourage her to scorn you more!   321
    Pyr. I see you think my heart, ready to find
Excuses, hankers after her, and seeks
Atonement.   324
    Phoe.   Yes, you love her. That's enough.
    Pyr. Love her, forsooth, who hates me all
      the more,
The more she's flatter'd! Friendless, with no
    hope
But over me! A stranger, ay, a slave!
I can destroy her son, perhaps I ought.   329
To her I give that son, myself, my throne;

And in her treacherous heart can gain no rank
Better than that of persecutor! No,
No, I have sworn it, my revenge is sure,
And shall for once her hatred justify;
Her infant I abandon, let her shed   335
What tears she may, call me whatever name
Anguish can prompt! Ah, what a sight, today,
Her eyes will see! Phoenix, 'twill be her
    death,
And I shall cause it, yea, myself shall hold
The dagger to her breast!   340
    Phoe.   Why blazon it
Abroad? Too highly did you rate your
    strength
Some hours ago.
    Pyr.   Pardon the tenderness
Of an old wound. You need not fear it,
    match'd   345
With my resentment; 'tis the final spark
Of love extinct. I'll follow your advice:
Must I give up her son, and must I see
The princess?
    Phoe. Yes, Sire; and with humble vows   350
Assure her ——
    Pyr. What I promised, I'll perform.
                                 (*Exeunt.*

ACT III

SCENE I

Enter ORESTES *and* PYLADES

    Pyl. My friend, restrain this most imprudent
    rage:
You are no more yourself, I know you not.
Let me ——
    Ores. No, no, your counsel comes too late,
The voice of Reason only wearies me.   5
I must cut short the torture of this life.
I'll bear her hence, or perish. My resolve
Is taken, and I'll execute the same:
Yes, that I will.
    Pyl.   By all means be it so;   10
I sanction that. But, still, think where you
    are;
To show your hand is but to court defeat;
Learn to disguise your feelings, calm your rage;
Bid your eyes keep the secret of your heart.
These guards, these very walls, each breath of
    air   15

Serve Pyrrhus, and yet more Hermione;
Hide your resentment with most care from her.
Why did you seek her, in the name of Heav'n,
In such a state?

Ores.   I knew not what I did; 20
Master'd by rage, I may have gone so far
As to vent open threats against them both.

Pyl. And what fruit did that fit of passion
    bear?

Ores. Was not the blow sufficient to distract
The coolest, and drive reason from her seat? 25
Tomorrow he will wed Hermione,
And from my hand receive her, as a mark
Of honor. Sooner may it with his blood ——

Pyl. You blame him for a purpose he pur-
    sues
In desperation. Rather, pity him   30
As I do you: his tortures are as great.

Ores. Nay, I know well, he laughs at my
    despair;
He scorn'd her till he knew her loved by me,
Her charms were lost upon him but for that;
He takes her but to tear her from my arms. 35
Gods! when already I had deem'd her won,
Prepared to leave his sight forevermore;
Her heart, divided between love and hate,
But waited his refusal to become
My own. Her eyes were open'd, and her
    ears   40
Hearken'd to me with pity. One word more,
And sure success.

Pyl.   You think so?

Ores.   Ay, her wrath
Was hot against the wretch.   45

Pyl.   Never more loved!
Had Pyrrhus giv'n her up, do you suppose
No other pretext would have held her back?
Let not her charms beguile you more, but fly
From her forever, rather than attempt   50
To carry off a Fury who detests
Your love, and would embitter all your life
With vain regret, having so nearly gain'd
Her dearest object.

Ores.   'Tis that very thought 55
Urges me on. All things would smile on her,
And nought but bootless rage be mine, com-
    pell'd
To seek oblivion far from her, once more
An exile. No, those torments she must share

Which I have borne too long alone. Enough 60
Of being pitied. She shall, in her turn,
Feel what it is to fear me, weep with woe,
And call me cruel, e'en as I did her!

Pyl. Thus as a ravisher Orestes crowns
His embassy!   65

Ores.   What matter, Pylades?
Greece shall not wreak revenge at my expense,
Nor an ungrateful princess mock my tears.
How will our country's praises profit me,
When jeer'd at in Epirus as a fool?   70
What would you? To confess the truth, I feel
My innocence a heavy load to bear.
When did the gods before prove so perverse
As to pursue the guiltless, and leave crime
Unpunish'd? Wheresoe'er I turn my eyes,   75
I see around me troubles that condemn
Their justice. Let me earn their wrath,
    deserve
Their hatred, eat the fruit if I must pay
The penalty of crime. But why draw down
Their anger on yourself, when aimed at me? 80
My friendship has procured you harm enough;
Leave me alone to guilt and misery.
Dear Pylades, your pity warps your sense;
Avoid the dangers that encompass me.
Convey to Greece the infant given up   85
By Pyrrhus. Go!

Pyl.   We'll carry off his bride!
A brave heart faces peril without fear.
Where love leads, friendship follows, and can
    act
As boldly. Let us arm your company   90
With zeal; our fleet is ready, and the breeze
Invites us. Every winding passage dark
I know; the sea washes these palace walls,
And by a secret way this very night
Your prize shall be conducted to your ship. 95

Ores. Dear friend, I trespass on your love
    too far;
Those griefs, that you alone could pity, beg
Forgiveness for a wretch, who loses all
He sets his heart on; hated by the world
He hates himself. But under happier stars 100
I, in my turn ——

Pyl.   Do not betray yourself;
Before the blow conceal your purpose, that
Is all I ask; till then forget your wrongs,
Forget your love. But see, she comes.   105

Ores.   Go, friend,
Answer for her as I will for myself.
                                        (*Exit* PYLADES.

SCENE 2

Enter HERMIONE *and* CLEONE

Ores. Well, Madam, you have won, thanks
  to my care:
I have seen Pyrrhus, and your marriage now
Will soon take place.   110
  Herm.   So I am told, and you
Were seeking me that I might be prepared.
  Ores. And will you not reject these tardy
    vows?
  Herm. Who would have fancied Pyrrhus
    faithful still?
That passion could have been delay'd so
    long   115
From bursting into flame, and its return
Should linger till I was about to leave him?
I'll think with you, 'tis Greece he dreads; not
    love
But prudence moves him; o'er your soul my
    eyes
Had pow'r more absolute.   120
  Ores.   No, no; 'tis love,
I cannot doubt it; and your eyes have wrought
All that they wish'd, nor would displease him
    now.
  Herm. What can I do, Sir, when my faith is
    pledged?
Rob him of what it was not I who gave?   125
The star that rules a princess is not love,
No other glory than obedience left
For her. Yet I was going, and you saw
How I made duty yield to your desire.
  Ores. Ah, cruel one, you knew — But every
    heart   130
Is free to follow its own choice, and yours
Was at your own disposal; and if giv'n,
I had no right to claim it as my own.
And yet I hoped; but Fortune more than you
I blame, and why should I your patience
    try   135
With vain complaints? Act as your duty
    bids,
Mine is to spare you words of sad reproach.
                                        (*Exit* ORESTES.

SCENE 3

HERMIONE, CLEONE

  Herm. Did you expect his wrath to be so
    mild?
  Cleo. A silent sorrow need not be for that
Less fatal. As the cause of his own woe   140
I pity him the more; 'tis his own stroke
That slays him. How long has your marriage
    been
In preparation? When Orestes spoke,
Pyrrhus declared himself.
  Herm.   You think 'tis fear?   145
Fear! And of whom? Those who for twice
    five years
Fled before Hector, and, Achilles lost,
Crouch'd in alarm within their burning ships,
And who, but for his son, would have left Troy
Unpunish'd, and foregone a fruitless quest! 150
Why should he fight against himself? Whate'er
He does, he wishes; if he marries me,
He loves me. Let Orestes, if he will,
Charge me with all his sorrows, better cheer
Awaits me than his sighs. Pyrrhus returns! 155
Ah, dear Cleone, what a rapturous thought!
Know you his exploits? Have you heard them
    told,
Too many to be number'd? And himself,
So brave, so charming, and so faithful too
As shown at last, his glory nothing lacks.   160
Think ——
  Cleo. Hide your feelings! Look, your rival
    comes,
To cast her troubles, doubtless, at your feet.
  Herm. Ah, 'tis too soon to check this flood
    of joy!
Let us begone; what should I say to her?   165

SCENE 4

Enter ANDROMACHE *and* CEPHISSA

  Andr. Why fly you, Madam? Is it not a
    sight
To please you, Hector's widow at your knees,
Weeping? But not with tears of jealousy
I come, nor do I envy you the heart
Surrender'd to your charms. A cruel hand   170
Robb'd me of him whom only I admired.
Love's flame was lit by Hector long ago,

With him it was extinguish'd in the tomb.
But he has left a son. Some day you'll know
How closely to one's heart a son can cling; 175
But you will never know, I wish it not,
How keen the pang when danger threatens
    him,
And they would take him from you, all that's
    left
To soothe a blighted heart. Ah, when worn
    out
With ten long years of war, the Trojans
    sought 180
Your mother's life, on Hector I prevail'd
To succor her. O'er Pyrrhus you have pow'r
As I had then o'er Hector. Can they dread
The infant he has left? Him let me hide
In some far distant isle. And they may
    trust 185
My fears to keep him there, taught but to
    weep
With me.

Herm. I feel for you, but duty holds
My tongue tied, when my sire declares his
    will:
It is by him that Pyrrhus' wrath is stirr'd. 190
But who can bend him better than yourself?
His soul has long been subject to your eyes;
Make him pronounce the word, and I'll consent.
    (*Exeunt* HERMIONE *and* CLEONE.)

SCENE 5

ANDROMACHE, CEPHISSA

Andr. How scornfully did she refuse my
    prayer!

Ceph. Accept her counsel. See him, as she
    says: 195
One look of yours may Greece and her con-
    found ——
But, look, he seeks you of his own accord.

SCENE 6

Enter PYRRHUS and PHOENIX

Pyr. (*to* PHOE.). Where is the princess?
    Said you not that she
Was here?

Phoe. I thought so. 200

Andr. (*to* CEPH.). Now you see what pow'r

My eyes have over him!

Pyr. (*to* PHOE.). What says she?

Andr. (*to* CEPH.). All
Is lost! 205

Phoe. (*to* PYR.). Hermione is gone, and we
Will follow.

Ceph. (*to* ANDR.). Speak! Why obstinately
    dumb?

Andr. Has he not promised them my child?

Ceph. But not 210
Given him up.

Andr. Vain are my tears, his death
Is certain.

Pyr. (*to* PHOE.). How her pride disdains to
    look
My way! 215

Andr. (*to* CEPH.). I should but irritate him
    more.
Let us retire.

Pyr. (*to* PHOE.). Come, Hector's son shall be
Yielded to Greece.

Andr. (*throwing herself at* PYRRHUS' *feet*).
Stop, Sire. What will you do? 220
Give up the son? Why not the mother
    then?
Where is the kindness that you swore to me
So lately? Can I touch no chord at least
Of pity? Does this sentence bar all hope
Of pardon? 225

Pyr. Phoenix knows my word is pledged.

Andr. No dangers were too great for you to
    brave
On my behalf!

Pyr. Blind then, I now can see.
Your wishes might have won his pardon
    once; 230
You ne'er so much as ask'd it. Now you come
Too late.

Andr. Full well you understood, my lord,
The sigh that fear'd repulse. Forgive the
    trace
Of pride, that died not with my royal rank, 235
And made me shrink from importunity.
My lord, you know, had it not been for you,
Andromache would never have embraced
A master's knees.

Pyr. No, in your secret soul 240
You hate me, scorn to owe me anything.
This son, the only object of your care,

You would have loved him less, had he been
    saved
Thro' me. You hate me with a bitter scorn,
You hate me more than all the Greeks to-
    gether.   245
Enjoy at leisure such a noble rage.
Come, Phoenix.
    Andr.   I will go where Hector's gone.
    Ceph. Madam ——
    Andr.   What further can I say to him?   250
The author of my woes, he knows them all.
(*To* PYR.) See to what state you have re-
    duced me, Sire!
I've seen my father slain, our walls enwrapt
In flames, and all our family cut off,
My husband's bloody corpse dragg'd thro' the
    dust,   255
His only son reserved for chains with me.
For his sake I endure to live a slave.
Yea, more, this thought has sometimes brought
    relief,
That Fate has fix'd my place of exile here;
The son of many kings beneath your sway   260
Is happier as a slave than he could be
Elsewhere, and I had hoped his prison walls
Might be a place of refuge. Priam found
Achilles could respect his fallen state;[1]
I thought his son more generous still. That
    trust,   265
My Hector, pardon, when I deem'd thy foe
Too noble to commit a dastard's crime!
Ah, would he but allow us to abide
Where for thine ashes I have raised a tomb,
And, ending there his hatred and our woes,   270
Divide us not from thy beloved remains!
    Pyr. Go, and await me, Phoenix.
                             (*Exit* PHOENIX.

SCENE 7

PYRRHUS, ANDROMACHE, CEPHISSA

    Pyr.   Madam, stay.
Your tears may yet win back this cherish'd son.
Yes, I regret that, moving you to weep,   275
I arm'd you with a weapon 'gainst myself;
I thought I could have brought more hatred
    here.

[1] Priam begged Achilles for Hector's body and was
granted it so that the Trojan hero could be buried with
proper funeral rites.

You might at least consent to look at me:
See, are my eyes those of an angry judge,
Whose pleasure 'tis to cause you misery?   280
Why force me to be faithless to yourself?
Now for your son's sake let us cease to hate.
'Tis I who urge you, save the child from death.
Must sighs of mine beg you to spare his life?
And must I clasp your knees to plead for
    him?   285
Once more, but once, save him and save
    yourself.
I know what solemn vows for you I break,
What hatred I bring down upon myself.
Hermione shall go, and on her brow
For crown I set a burning brand of shame: 290
And in the fane deck'd for her marriage rites
Her royal diadem yourself shall wear.
This offer, lady, is no longer one
You can afford to scorn. Perish or reign!
A year's contempt has made me desperate,   295
Nor can I any longer live in doubt,
Harass'd by fears and mingling threats with
    groans.
To lose you is to die — 'tis death to wait.
I leave you to consider, and will come   299
To bring you to the temple where this child
My fury shall destroy before your eyes,
Or where in love I crown you as my queen.
                           (*Exit* PYRRHUS.

SCENE 8

ANDROMACHE, CEPHISSA

    Ceph. Is't not as I foretold? In spite of
    Greece,
You are still mistress of your destiny.
    Andr. Alas, that it should be as you have
    said!   305
I have no choice but to condemn my son.
    Ceph. That were to stretch fidelity too far.
Excess of virtue may be fraught with guilt.
Hector himself would urge a milder course.
    Andr. Pyrrhus in Hector's place! I loathe
    the thought.   310
    Ceph. Think of his son, torn from your arms
    by force;
More than aught else his shade would blush
    at that.
It would not shame him that your conqueror

Should reinstate you in your royal rank,
Trample your foes beneath his feet in wrath,
Forget that fierce Achilles was his sire,   316
And frustrate all his exploits.

  Andr.   How can I
Cease to remember them, tho' he forget?
Hector's unburied corpse, dishonor'd, dragg'd
Around the walls of Troy? His father slain
Before mine eyes, and grasping as he fell   322
The altar stain'd with his own blood? That
    night,
That cruel night, think how its horrors brought
Eternal night to Troy! Recall the look   325
Of Pyrrhus, crossing in the lurid light
Our burning threshold; how his eyeballs
    glared,
My fallen brothers [1] spurn'd beneath his tread,
Kindling the carnage, dyed from head to foot
With gore! Canst hear the victor's shouts,
    the groans   330
From dying lips, as fire and sword rush on?
Canst see Andromache's despair, and how
Pyrrhus confronts her with those frightful
    deeds
Wherewith he won his glory? There behold
The husband you would give me! No, my
    friend,   335
I will not be th' accomplice of his crimes.
His latest victim let him make of me,
And I without a murmur will submit.

  Ceph. Then let us go and see your son
    expire;
Your presence only do they wait for. How   340
You shudder!

  Andr.   Yes, remembrance sends a pang
That pierces deep. What! See him perish too,
My only joy, on whom my Hector stamp'd
His image, token of the love I lost!   345
Ah me! I call to mind the day he sought
Achilles, fatal day for him. He press'd
His boy to his courageous heart, and said,
Drying my tears — "Dear wife, I know not
    how
Fate may decide the fight to which I go.   350
I leave you this my son, a faithful pledge;
And should he lose his father, be to him
Father and mother both; if you hold dear

  [1] Really Hector's brothers, Andromache's brothers-in-law. Her own seven brothers were slain by Achilles.

The happiness we shared, then show to him
How much you loved me." Shall that pre-
    cious blood   355
Be shed before my eyes, his line extinct
With him? Ah, cruel King, must my offense
Be counted his? He has not hated thee,
Nor yet reproach'd thee with his kinsmen's
    death,
Resenting not the ills he cannot feel.   360
Yet thou must die, my son, unless I turn
The sword aside that hangs above thy head.
The choice is mine; and shall I let it fall?
No, never can I suffer thee to die.
Let us find Pyrrhus. No, Cephissa, go,   365
Find him for me.

  Ceph.   What shall I say to him?

  Andr. Tell him a mother loves her son
    enough ——
But has he sworn indeed to slay the child?
Can passion make Pyrrhus so merciless?   370

  Ceph. Madam, in fury he will soon return.

  Andr. Then go, assure him ——

  Ceph.   Of your faith, or what?

  Andr. Alas! have I that promise still to
    give?
O ashes of my husband and my sire!   375
How dearly must I buy thy life, my son!
Come, let us go.

  Ceph.   Whither? With what resolve?

  Andr. To Hector's tomb, there to consult
    his will.   (*Exeunt.*

ACT IV

SCENE I

Enter ANDROMACHE *and* CEPHISSA

  Ceph. My lady, 'tis your husband, doubt it
    not;
'Tis Hector works this miracle in you!
Surely he wishes Troy should rise again
Under that son whose life he bids you guard.
Pyrrhus has promised you the boy. Just
    now   5
You heard him say he waits but for your word
To make him yours; and you may trust his
    love.
Your heart contents him; father, scepter,
    friends,

He recks them not, if you will reign o'er him
And o'er his people.   Does he then deserve 10
Hatred?   Indignant, he confronts the Greeks,
And pities the poor babe no less than you,
Guards him from outrage, and withstands their
    rage,
Exposing his own life to shelter his.   14
But all is ready.   You have promised ——
    Andr.   Yes,
I will be there.   Let us go see my son.
    Ceph. Why in such haste?   No one forbids
      you now
To visit him; therewith be satisfied,
And soon your tenderness shall have full scope
In many a fond and unrestrain'd caress.   21
Will it not bring you joy to rear your babe
No longer for a life of slavery,
But to revive the glories of his line?
    Andr. Cephissa, 'tis the last time I shall
      see   25
My child.
    Ceph.   Why, what is this?
    Andr.   O my dear friend,
With whom my soul should wear no mask,
    for you
Have proved in all my trouble faithful still, 30
I hoped you knew me better than to deem
Myself so faithless found as to betray
The husband who within my heart survives,
That, caring not how much I vex'd the dead,
I should think only of my own repose.   35
Is that to keep my promise made so oft
To Hector's ashes?   But I am obliged
To save his son.   Pyrrhus, on wedding me,
Vows to protect him — I may trust his word.
I know his nature, violent but sincere;   40
He will do more, Cephissa, than he said.
And I rely too on the wrath of Greece,
Her hatred will on Hector's son bestow
A father.   Since a victim is required
I will assure to Pyrrhus all that's left   45
Of life to me, and by most sacred bonds
Indissolubly bind him to my boy.
But straightway shall this hand with fatal
    stroke
Sever the chord of life no longer true,
And so preserve me stainless, and yet pay   50
Pyrrhus his due, nor fail in what I owe
To son and husband, ay, and to myself.

This is the harmless plot my love suggests,
Or rather Hector's spirit.   So, alone,
Him and my sires I join.   Close you mine
    eyes.   55
    Ceph. Ah, if you die, think not that I will
    live.
    Andr. Nay, I forbid you, friend, to follow
    me.
My only treasure to your care I trust:
You lived for me, live now for Hector's son.
Sole guardian of the hopes of fallen Troy,   60
Her royal line requires your constant care.
Watch Pyrrhus well, and make him keep his
    faith;
If he shall need it, speak to him of me.
Remind him I consented to be his
Before my death, teach him to prize that
    bond   65
And blot out all resentment from his soul;
That, leaving him my son, I show'd how much
I valued him.   And to that son make known
The heroes of his race; direct his steps
To follow them; tell him of all their fame,   70
Of what they did rather than what they were.
Dwell on his father's virtues day by day,
And sometimes whisper of a mother's love.
But of avenging me he must not dream;
His master's friendship let him strive to win.
Regarding his high birth with modesty,   76
Let him remember, tho' of Hector's blood,
Troy lives in him alone; and for his sake,
In one day, I lay down life, hatred, love!
    Ceph. Alas!   80
    Andr. You must not come with me, unless
Your heart is brave and can command your
    tears.
Cephissa, dry your eyes.   I hear a step.
Remember your great trust.   Hermione
Approaches; let us shun her violence.   85
                  (*Exeunt.*

SCENE 2

Enter HERMIONE *and* CLEONE

    Cleo. This silence, Madam, fills me with
    surprise;
You utter not a word; this cruel slight
Seems not to ruffle your tranquillity!
Tamely you suffer such a rude rebuff   89

Who shudder'd but to hear your rival's name!
You who could scarce endure without despair
The passing glance that Pyrrhus cast on her!
He weds her, makes her partner of his throne,
And plights the troth so lately giv'n to you;
Yet still your lips are dumb, your tongue
    disdains   95
T' upbraid the traitor with deserved reproach!
I fear what such a fatal calm forebodes!
It would be better far ——
   Herm.   You sent for him,
Is it not so?   100
   Cleo.   Orestes will be here,
And, as you may believe, will place himself
Wholly at your disposal, without hope
Of recompense.   Your eyes are sure enough
To charm him.   See, he enters.   105

        SCENE 3
      Enter ORESTES

   Ores.   Can it be
That I, for once, in seeking you obey
Your bidding, or has false hope flatter'd me?
Have you indeed wish'd me to come to you?
Shall I believe your eyes, at last disarm'd,   110
Will ——
   Herm.   I would know whether you love
    me, Sir.
   Ores. Love you! Great gods! My vows too
    hard to keep,
My flight, return, reverence that curb'd re-
    proach,
My dark despair, my eyes all drown'd in
    tears: 115
What witness will you, if you trust not these?
   Herm. I trust them all; avenge me.
   Ores.   Let us go,
My mistress, and once more set Greece on fire.
This arm shall make your name renown'd;
    and you   120
Shall rival Helen, I the King of Men.
Let us revive the miseries of Troy
Here in Epirus, and our fathers' fame
Eclipse.   Yes, I am ready; let us start.
   Herm. No, let us stay, nor carry these
    affronts   125
So far.   What! crown the insults of my foes,
And wait elsewhere to wreak a slow revenge!

Resign myself to the arbitrament of war,
That after all might fail to vindicate
My wrongs! I will have all Epirus weep   130
When I depart.   Avenge me in an hour,
Or not at all.   Delay — and you refuse.
Haste to the temple.   You must slay ——
   Ores.   Ay, whom?
   Herm. Pyrrhus.   135
   Ores.   The King?
   Herm.   Your hatred hesitates?
Run quickly thither, lest I call you back.
Speak not of duties I would fain forget,
Nor will I hear a word in his defense,   140
And least from you.
   Ores.   From me! Your tenderness
Has stamp'd his crime too deeply on my soul.
Let us take vengeance, but by other means;
Become his foes, but not his murderers,   145
And with the arms of justice ruin him.
Shall I for answer to the Greeks bring back
His head? And have I taken on myself
This charge from them, to turn assassin? No.
In Heaven's name let Greece the challenge
    meet,   150
And crush'd beneath her hatred let him die.
The name of king is sacred, and the brow ——
   Herm. Is not my sentence then enough for
    you?
That my offended dignity demands
A victim to be offer'd to myself?   155
That if you quell the tyrant you shall have
Me for reward? That I hate him whom once
I loved? Yes, I confess it, he knew how
To win my heart; whether my father's will
Or inclination moved me matters not.   160
Act on that knowledge.   Tho' he broke his
    vows,
Tho' with just horror I regard his crime,
Yet, while he lives, fear I may still forgive.
Distrust my wavering wrath, till death removes
The monster.   For unless he dies today,   165
Tomorrow I may love him.
   Ores.   Then must death
Prevent his pardon.   How shall I proceed?
Can I so soon avenge your injuries?
Where lies the path that leads him to his
    doom?   170
I have but just set foot upon this soil,
And you would have me overturn the State,

And slay the King; and for his punishment
You grant me but a day; no, not an hour.
It must be done before his people's eyes;　175
My victim to the altar shall be brought.
No longer I demur, I will but go
And view th' appointed place of sacrifice:
This night I do your bidding, and he dies!

Herm. Meanwhile today he weds Andro-
　　mache;　　　　　　　　　　　　　180
Already in the shrine his throne is set,
His crime accomplish'd, and my shame con-
　firm'd.
Why should you wait? He offers you his life;
No guards attend him to this festival,
He makes them all encircle Hector's son,　185
And gives himself to my avenger's arm.
Will you then of his life take greater care
Than he does? Arm my followers, with your
　　Greeks;
Stir up your friends; on mine you may rely.
Me he betrays, fools you, and scorns us all.
Surely their hatred is as great as mine,　191
The Trojan woman's husband loath to spare.
Speak, and my foe cannot escape your hands,
Or rather they will strike him dead themselves.
Lead or be led by this their noble rage;　195
Dyed with the faithless wretch's blood, return;
Thus only can you gain my heart. Now go.

Ores. But, Madam, think ——

Herm.　　　　　　This really passes bounds,
Your scruples grate upon my angry mood.　200
I show the way to win Hermione,
And make Orestes happy; but I see
He will do nought to earn her, only whine
Forever. Go; boast of your constancy
Elsewhere, and leave me to avenge myself.　205
My weak concessions fill my soul with shame;
One day of such refusals is too much,
When all is ready for the marriage rite:
And where you dare not venture, I will go
Alone, find means t' approach my enemy,　210
And stab the heart I could not touch with love.
Then shall my blood-stain'd hands, turn'd on
　　myself,
Unite our destiny in spite of him:
And, traitor tho' he be, 'twill be more sweet
For me to die with him than live with you.　215

Ores. No, I will rob you of that dismal joy;
He shall not die but by Orestes' hand.

Yes, by my arm your enemies shall fall,
And you shall then reward me, if you will.

Herm. Go. Leave your future fortune in
　my care.　　　　　　　　　　　　220
Let all your ships be ready for our flight.

　　　　　　　　　　　　(*Exit* ORESTES.

SCENE 4
HERMIONE, CLEONE

Cleo. Think, Madam, ere your ruin you
　　invoke ——

Herm. Ruin or no, I mean to have revenge.
I doubt, whatever promises be made,
The trust reposed on others than myself:　225
The guilt of Pyrrhus does not scorch his eyes
As it does mine; my stroke would be more sure.
To be my own avenger would be sweet,
To stain this fair arm with the traitor's blood,
And, to increase my pleasure and his pain,　230
To hide my rival from his dying gaze!
What if Orestes fail to let him know
He dies a victim sacrificed to me!
Go, find and tell him to inform the wretch
He owes his death to me, and not to Greece.　235
Run, dear Cleone, my revenge is balk'd,
If he should die unconscious that his doom
Proceeds from me.

Cleo.　　　　　I will obey you. — Ah!
What do I see? Who would have fancied it?
The King himself!　　　　　　　　241

Herm.　　　　　Follow Orestes straight,
He must do nought till he sees me again!

　　　　　　　　　　　　(*Exit* CLEONE.

SCENE 5
Enter PYRRHUS *and* PHOENIX

Pyr. You are surprised that I should seek
　　you here,
And my approach disturbs your colloquy.　245
I do not come arm'd with unworthy wiles,
No feign'd excuse shall gloss the wrong I do:
My heart condemns me with no doubtful
　　voice,
Nor can I urge a plea I know is false.
I wed a Trojan woman. Yes, I own　　250
The faith I plight to her was giv'n to you.
I might remind you that our fathers form'd

These ties at Troy without consulting us,
And we were bound together by no love
Or choice of ours; but 'tis enough for me   255
That I submitted. My ambassadors
Made you the promise of my heart and hand;
So far from wishing to revoke the pledge,
I willingly confirm'd it; you, with them,
Came hither, and, altho' another eye   260
Already had subdued me and forestall'd
Your sway, that passion did not make me
     pause,
And I resolved still to be true to you.
I welcomed you as queen, and, till this day,
I thought my oath would hold the place of
     love.   265
But love prevail'd, and, by a fatal stroke,
Andromache has won the heart she hates:
Each drawn by th' other in our own despite,
We hasten to the altar, there to swear
Union forever. Blame me as you may   270
For traitor: tho' a willing one, I grieve
To prove defaulter; nor do I presume
To check the just resentment that relieves
Myself as much as you. Call me forsworn,
I fear your silence more than your reproach;
Wrung by the secret witness in my heart,   276
The less you say the more I feel my guilt.
     Herm. Sir, this confession, stripp'd of all
     deceit,
Shows that at least you to yourself are just;
And, tho' resolved to snap this solemn tie,   280
Crime makes you in your own eyes criminal.
Yet, after all, why should a conqueror stoop
To common honesty that keeps its word?
No, perfidy for you has secret charms;
You seek me but to glory in your shame;   285
Unhinder'd by your duty or your oath,
A maid of Greece and then a dame of Troy
Attract your fickle fancy, flying off,
Returning, and then leaving me once more;
Crowning in turn the princess and the slave,
Making Troy bow to Greece, and Greece to
     Troy!   291
Thus acts a heart that's master of itself,
Heroic, and no slave of promises!
Your bride might be displeased were I to stint
Such honey'd terms as wretch and perjurer.   295
You came to look whether my face were pale,
And then to mock my sorrow in her arms.

You would be glad if I would follow her
In tears; but one day has brought joy enough.
You need not seek new titles to renown,   300
Those that you have may well suffice your
     greed,
The aged sire of Hector smitten down
Dying before the eyes of all his kin,
While your sword, thrust into his feeble heart,
Seeks the few frozen drops that linger there;
Troy all in flames, plunged in a sea of blood;
Your hand too cut Polyxena's fair throat,[1]   307
A cruel sight that Greece herself condemn'd.
Such glorious deeds claim fit acknowledgment.
     Pyr. I know full well to what excess of
     rage   310
Revenge for Helen's rape transported me:
To you, her child, I might impute the blood
That I have shed; but be the past forgot.
I thank high Heaven that your indifference
Sanctions a happier passion in my breast.   315
My heart, too ready to torment itself,
Should know you better, and excuse its change.
Madam, I did you wrong to feel remorse;
Can one be faithless who was never loved?
You have not tried to keep me bound to
     you: 320
Fearing to injure, it may be that I
Serve you. No sympathy unites our hearts;
'Twas duty that I follow'd, as did you:
You never loved me in reality.
     Herm. I never loved you! What then did
     I do?   325
For you our native princes I despised,
Sought you myself in your remotest realms;
Still am I here, tho' you have proved untrue,
And all my Greeks my weakness view with
     shame.   329
I have commanded them to hide my wrongs;
In secret I awaited your return
To duty; trusting whether soon or late,
You would bring back a heart I claim'd as
     mine.
I loved you tho' inconstant; could I more   334
If faithful found? E'en while your cruel lips
Calmly announce the death of all my hopes,
I doubt if I have ceased to love you yet.
But if it must be so, and Heav'n in wrath

[1] Pyrrhus made a sacrifice of Polyxena, daughter of
Priam and Hecuba, on Achilles' tomb.

Reserves for other eyes the pow'r to charm,
Complete this marriage; but at least refrain
From forcing me to witness my disgrace. 341
Listen, for this may be my last appeal;
Let one day pass, tomorrow you shall wed ——
You answer nought? Ah, faithless wretch,
  'tis clear
You count those moments lost you spend
  with me! 345
Impatient your enchantress to behold
Once more, you grudge with others to con-
  verse:
With her your heart inspires each word, each
  look.
Escape where you are free, I hold you not
From going; swear as you have sworn to
  me. 350
Go, and profane the majesty of Heav'n,
The justice of the gods, who'll ne'er forget
How those same oaths have bound you to
  myself.
Haste, to their altars take that perjured heart;
There dread to meet Hermione once more.
               (*Exit* HERMIONE.

SCENE 6

PYRRHUS, PHOENIX

Phoe. My lord, you heard her: be upon your
  guard, 356
Beware the vengeance of a baffled love
Inflamed to fury, arm'd with the support
Of Greece that is the champion of her cause:
Orestes loves her still, perchance that prize —
Pyr. Andromache awaits me. Guard her
  son!   (*Exeunt.* 361

ACT V

SCENE 1

Enter HERMIONE *alone*

Herm. Where am I? and what is it I have
  done?
What yet remains? What rage possesses me?
How thro' these halls I roam irresolute,
Devour'd with grief, and know not if I love
Or hate! His eye at parting seem'd to freeze
My soul, nor did he ever feign to pity; 6

No, not a moment's tenderness or sorrow;
His heart refused to grant a single groan.
Deaf to my sighs, 'mid all my anguish calm,
My tears awoke no sympathy in him. 10
And yet I mourn his loss! And for a crown
Of sorrow, still this weak heart throbs for him.
I tremble at the blow so soon to fall,
Forget revenge, and almost pardon him!
But no, my sentence shall not be revoked: 15
Perish the traitor, since he's dead to me!
Triumphantly he laughs my wrath to scorn,
And thinks this tempest will dissolve in tears,
That, always feeble and irresolute, 19
With one hand I'll ward off the other's blows:
Past kindness makes him deem it measure-
  less.
But other thoughts, rather, his mind engross:
The traitor in his triumph little cares
Whether the absent wish him life or death,
And leaves to me this dire perplexity. 25
One stroke shall end it; at Orestes' hand
He meets the death he ought to have foreseen,
Which he himself has forced me to desire.
What! Is it I then who pronounce his doom?
And must he die because Hermione 30
Has loved him? He whose oft-repeated deeds
Gave ever fresh delight when heard again,
To whom in secret I had link'd my lot
Ere to the fatal contract we were bound?
Have I then cross'd so many lands and seas, 35
And come so far, only to dig his grave,
To be his murderer? Ah, ere he dies ——

SCENE 2

Enter CLEONE

Herm. What have I done, Cleone? Have
  you aught
To tell me? Where is Pyrrhus?
Cleo.   At the height 40
Of love and happiness; proudest of men,
I saw him to the temple lead his bride,
His latest conquest: in his eye there shone
The light of joy and hope. Gazing on her,
He seem'd to drink intoxicating draughts. 45
Andromache, 'midst all the glad acclaim,
Bore in her heart sad memories of Troy;
Incapable alike of love and hate,
Submissive, she nor murmur'd nor rejoiced.

Herm. And Pyrrhus?　Carried he his bold
　affront　　　　　　　　　　　　　　50
To th' end?　Observed you well his counte-
　nance?
Seem'd he to taste calm pleasure unalloy'd?
Did he not hither cast a single look?
Tell me, Cleone, did you meet his eye?
And did he blush when he perceived you
　there?　　　　　　　　　　　　　　55
Show'd he with troubled brow a sense of guilt,
Or did his pride support him to the last?

Cleo.　He noticed nothing; and his safety
　seem'd,
With honor's voice, forgotten like yourself.
Heedless of those who follow, friends or foes,　60
He hastens onward to Love's wish'd-for goal.
Round Hector's son he has bestow'd his
　guards,
And fancies danger threatens him alone.
Phoenix has him in charge, who to a fort
Far from the temple and the palace brings　65
The child, whose safety seems the only care
That Pyrrhus knows.

Herm.　　　The wretch shall die!　What said
Orestes?

Cleo.　　　He has enter'd with his men　70
The temple.

Herm.　　　Is he ready to avenge
My wrongs?

Cleo.　　　I know not.

Herm.　　　What, you know not!　Will
Orestes too prove false?　　　　　　　76

Cleo.　　　He worships you;
But with a thousand scruples of remorse
Contending, now to Honor he gives heed,
And now to Love.　In Pyrrhus he respects　80
The throne, Achilles, and Achilles' son.
He fears the wrath of Greece and all the world;
But more than all, he said, he fears himself.
As victor he would bring the traitor's head,
But not as an assassin, odious name!　　　85
At last he enter'd, knowing not if thence
He should go forth blood guilty, or a mere
Spectator.

Herm.　　No; their triumph he will watch
Without the wish to strike a jarring note.　90
I know what scruples make his courage blench;
The coward fears to die, and fears nought else.
My mother stoop'd not to a single prayer,

Yet in her cause all Greece rose up in arms.
Her eyes, thro' ten years' war, saw twenty
　kings,　　　　　　　　　　　　　95
Whose names she scarcely knew, die for her sake:
While I but ask death to a perjurer,
Charging a lover to avenge my wrongs,
And so to win me at no risk to him;
I give myself, and yet I am refused!　　100
Go to, my own arm must for justice strike.
Let cries of pain thro' all the temple ring;
Their fatal bridal shall in bloodshed end,
And but one moment see them man and wife.
Nor shall my fury halt to choose its prey,　105
Orestes shall as Pyrrhus be to me;
And if by death I purchase my revenge,
I'll gladly die in such good company!

SCENE 3

Enter ORESTES

Ores. Madam, 'tis over, and your will is done;
Yes, at the altar now the traitor yields　110
His life.

Herm.　Is Pyrrhus dead?

Ores.　　　He breathes his last,
Our Greeks have blotted out his guilt in blood.
I gave my promise, tho' this plot to me　115
Appear'd too horrible.　With hasty steps
I sought the temple, when I found our men
Had to the very altar crept unseen
Amid the crowd. With countenance unchanged,
Pyrrhus perceived me, and his courage seem'd
Warm'd at the sight; Greece, in my person
　braved,　　　　　　　　　　　　121
Lending fresh glory to his nuptial rites.
Proudly he raised on high the diadem,
And placed it on the Trojan woman's brow
With his own hand, saying: "I give to you
My crown, and plight my troth; reign o'er my
　realms　　　　　　　　　　　　126
And o'er myself; your son shall find in me
A father's love; may Heav'n confirm the vow
I make to you his mother, and his foes　129
Be mine.　I hail him as the King of Troy."
Applause resounded as he spake these words,
Answer'd by cries of wrath from Grecian
　throats.
They throng'd around the traitor where he
　stood,

So that I found no place to strike, for each   134
Vied with his neighbor who should lay him low.
Cover'd with blood, vainly he sought escape
From countless blows, and at the altar fell.
Thence passing thro' the terror-stricken crowds,
I came, to bring my princess to the port.
There will our friends, their hands with
    slaughter red,   140
Be with us soon.   My promise is fulfill'd.
   Herm. What have they done?
   Ores.   If their excess of zeal
Has marr'd your vengeance, pardon them for
    that.   144
You would have had me be the first to strike,
That he might feel it was for you he died;
But 'twas my ardor prompted them to act;
For your sake, and yours only, were they
    brought
Within the temple; you may justly claim
As sacrificed to you the life they took,   150
As agents of the vengeance you had plann'd.
   Herm. Traitor, be silent, nor impute to me
The crime which brands you coward.   Let the
    Greeks
Applaud the impious act.   Go; I disown
Your cruelty and you, who have destroy'd   155
The noblest of mankind this fatal day.
Did no compunction visit your fell hearts
To check such slaughter?   Who made you the
    judge
To sentence him to death? What was his crime?
What right had you to slay him?   Tell me that!
Who bade you do it?   161
   Ores.   Heav'ns! It was you yourself,
Just now, upon this spot, the order gave.
   Herm. You should have paid no heed to
    love bereft   164
Of reason, but have read my deeper thoughts.
Saw you not while I raved distractedly,
My heart belied whatever words I spoke?
E'en had I meant them, you should have
    refused,
A hundred times repeated, such a wish: 169
Ask'd me again before the blow was struck,
And then return'd, or rather shunn'd my sight.
You should have let me wreak my own revenge.
What lured you hither, hateful to mine eyes?
Behold what bitter fruit your love has borne!
You bring me all the ills that follow you: 175

Your embassy it was, fatal to both,
That to my rival made his thoughts incline,
He might have else admitted me to share
His heart again, or feign'd at least to love.
Go you, in this Epirus I will stay.   180
Greece and my Spartan home I here renounce,
Yea, all my family; enough for me
That they have bred a monster like yourself!
      (*Exeunt* HERMIONE *and* CLEONE.

SCENE 4
ORESTES *alone*

   Ores. Was that Hermione I saw and heard?
She for whom flow'd the blood that I have shed?
Did she not call me traitor, murderer?   186
Am I Orestes?   And is Pyrrhus slain?
Was reason's light extinguish'd in my heart
That I should kill a king whom I revere,
In one day violate a sovereign's rights,   190
An envoy's office, and all human ties,
Profane the altars where he stood at bay,
And turn a sacrilegious regicide?
And all for one who knows no gratitude,
Who made me vow to slay him, or she ne'er 195
Would see me more.   When I have done the
    task
Her fury set, she taunts me with his blood!
She loves him!   As a monster looks on me!
Far from mine eyes forever she withdraws, 199
And in her thankless flight leaves me for hire
Names of reproach, incurr'd to please her rage!

SCENE 5
Enter PYLADES *and Soldiers of* ORESTES

   Pyl. We must depart, and leave this palace,
    Sir;
Or be content never to leave at all.
Our Greeks defend the gate one moment more,
Ere our pursuers' forces grow too strong. 205
All here obey Andromache's commands,
They treat her as their queen, and us as foes:
And she herself, stubborn while Pyrrhus lived,
All duties of a faithful widow pays,
And urges vengeance, haply all the more 210
That Hector's shade too claims the blood of
    Greece.
Let us not wait, then, till they hem us round;

Our men will join us, and, while all the crowd
Still gaze and gape upon Hermione,
We may pass thro' in safety. Come this way.

Ores. No, friends; it is Hermione I fain   216
Would follow, her last sentence can I not
Survive. Go; let me expiate my crime.

Pyl. Hermione! Forget her. Would you
     still,
The instrument and object of her rage,   220
Invite fresh insult e'en among the dead?
And, because she dies, must you perish too?

Ores. She dies! Ye gods, what is it that I
     hear?

Pyl. Did you not know? We met her, as we
     came;
With hurrying feet, and frenzy in her eyes,   225
She sought the temple, and found Pyrrhus borne
By soldiers whom his blood to vengeance
     roused:
Doubtless that sight stirr'd madness too in her.
We saw her, as we stood above the gate,
O'er Pyrrhus bending low, dagger in hand;   230
Then, eyes uplifting, plunge it in her breast,
And fall.

Ores. Ah, Heav'n has been pleased t' inflict
Woes worse than I had look'd for! Never
     turn'd
One moment from relentless punishment,   235
The gods have made my agony supreme,
And found delight devising miseries,
That I might serve as an example meet
Of wrath celestial, born to wretchedness.   239
Well, I have drain'd the cup, and die content.
Where are the lovers? To complete my joy,
Let me be drown'd in blood, their own and mine.

Let me behold them as they both expire
And three hearts be united, that were long
Discordant ——   245
     But what thickness of black night
Enshrouds me suddenly! What horror thrills
Thro' all my frame, with no way of escape!
Thank heav'n! I see a glimmering light. 'Tis
     blood,
Streams of red blood all round me!   250
Pyl.   Ah, my lord!

Ores. What, Pyrrhus! Must I meet thee
     everywhere?
How has my hated rival 'scaped his wounds?
Hold, I have yet a stroke reserved for thee.
But what is this? Hermione, with arms   255
Encircling, tears him from the threaten'd blow!
Ye gods! What frightful looks she casts on me!
Serpents and fiendish faces dog her steps.
Why are your hands outstretch'd, Furies of
     Hell?
Whom do these snakes, that hiss above your
     heads,   260
Threaten to sting? What means this horrid
     train?
Come ye to bear me to eternal night?
So be it, to your rage Orestes yields.
But no, leave vengeance to Hermione;
'Twere better that she tear me limb from limb,
Yea, and devour the heart I offer her!   266

Pyl. Friends, he has lost his senses. While
     there's time,
Let's take advantage of this fit, and save
The prince. Our efforts will be vain if once   269
His madness here with consciousness return.

                    (*Exeunt.*

INTRODUCTION TO
The Man of Mode,
OR
Sir Fopling Flutter

The Rebirth of the Stage in Restoration England: The Restoration "Heroic Play" and Tragedy: The Restoration Comedy of Manners: Sir George Etherege: The Restoration Theaters and "Picture-Stage"

THE REBIRTH OF THE STAGE IN RESTORATION ENGLAND

IN SEPTEMBER, 1642, the English Parliament, seeing the gathering clouds of conflict between Cavaliers and Puritans, banned stage plays and closed the playhouses to avert "the Wrath of God." During the next eighteen years of civil war and of Puritan commonwealth, theatrical performances (for the most part, brief farces called "drolls") took place surreptitiously in London and vicinity. Dramatic composition virtually ceased.

The restoration of Charles II as king in May, 1660, effected an immediate rebirth of the English stage. The new sovereign, while exiled in France and the Low Countries, had shown a great enthusiasm for dramatic entertainments. Consequently playwrights, players, and producers now hastened to secure the patronage of a monarch whose personal knowledge of their arts was to exceed that of any ruler in the history of the world's theater. Within a few months two troupes of actors — the King's Company and the Duke's Company (so called from its sponsorship by Charles II's brother, James, Duke of York) — received royal licenses and indefinite monopoly over stage amusement within London. Since the theaters of Jacobean and Caroline days had fallen more or less to ruin, two tennis-court buildings were converted into playhouses. Legitimate theatricals got fully under way by the winter of 1660–61.

Playwriting followed close upon renewed production, but the output of fresh plays was for some years insufficient to meet the demands of the revived repertory system. Among the old dramatists Beaumont and Fletcher, Jonson, and Shirley won most applause. Their works dominated the programs at both the Theatre Royal and the Duke's Theatre until well toward the end of the 1660's.

THE RESTORATION "HEROIC PLAY" AND TRAGEDY

Under such circumstances the new drama of the Restoration era obviously could not break altogether from the past; rather it brought to fruition several tendencies already visible on the stage in the reigns of James I and Charles I. The serious plays of Beaumont and Fletcher had focused some attention upon the *motif* of love and honor in conflict, as in *The Maid's Tragedy*. John Ford (1586–?1640) subsequently developed this theme in tragic intensity for his piece, *The Broken Heart* (c. 1629), while Sir William

D'Avenant (1606–68) treated it more happily but no less seriously in *Love and Honor* (1634). Thus the struggle of the passion of love with the ethical demands of honor or virtue had established itself in the dramatic taste of English polite society before the Civil War. Thereafter, for almost two decades, the imagination of this society, scattered though its members were throughout England, Ireland, and the Continent, uniformly subsisted upon the chivalric epics of Italian and French poets, the enormous French prose romances, and the heroic drama of Corneille and his imitators. All this literary material emphasized one common subject, love versus honor.

When, therefore, dramatic composition was once more resumed in England and was directed chiefly to the approbation of a king and his court, the epic or heroic theme of love versus honor inevitably formed the warp and woof of the Restoration serious dramas and caused them to be termed "heroic plays." Because of King Charles's admiration for the rimed verse of contemporary French tragedy, the new English plays imitated that fashion by employing riming couplets in their dialogue. The most famous of the heroic plays was *The Conquest of Granada* (1670) by John Dryden (1631–1700). This stirring drama, in two parts of five acts each, concerns a Spanish warrior, Almanzor, who performs superhuman feats of valor to win finally the hand of Almahide, a paragon of honor. The absurd extravagance of the language, the sentiments, and the action in Dryden's creation provoked George Villiers, Duke of Buckingham (1628–87) to a hilarious parody of the heroic species, entitled *The Rehearsal*, which held the boards consistently from its premiere in 1671 down into the eighteenth century.

Not long after the appearance of Buckingham's satire, the classical restraint of Racine and the poetic dignity of Shakespeare began to attract the notice of the jaded heroic practitioners and to temper their childish bombast. A fresh, though very slight, vitality crept into tragedy. Blank verse replaced the heroic couplet. Dryden's *All For Love* (1677), based on the story of Antony and Cleopatra, attempted an amalgamation of Racine and Shakespeare. Though it is perhaps the most notable tragedy written between 1620 and 1820 (when Shelley wrote *The Cenci*), *All For Love* is only notable because of the astonishing repetitiousness of tragic patterns on the London stage for these two centuries. In 1682 Dryden's nearest rival as a tragedian, Thomas Otway (1652–85), brought forth *Venice Preserved*, a piece in a definitely Shakespearean-Elizabethan mold with subtler delineation of character and mood than *All For Love*. Whatever the relative merits of the two plays, there can be no question that they mutually evidence the enfeebled state of the English tragic muse during the later seventeenth century.

THE RESTORATION COMEDY OF MANNERS

Not only the serious but also the comic plays of the Restoration had their antecedents in currents of dramatic taste visible for several decades previous. The humor of Jonson dealt primarily with human eccentricity and remained always corrective. This vein of comedy continued quite vigorous, though of no outstanding merit, into the reign of Charles II, at which time Thomas Shadwell (1640–92), a devoted admirer of Jonson, gained a large reputation for his "humors" style in such plays of contemporary setting as *Epsom Wells* (1672), *The Squire of Alsatia* (1688), and *Bury Fair* (1689). However successful these pieces on the stage, their mood is rather pre-Restoration and their art retrogressive.

The deeper course of the comic spirit in English drama subsequent to Jonson was turning ever so slowly but steadily from sheer satire of human folly and vice to a more playful mimicry of men's deeds.   As the playhouse audiences grew increasingly aristocratic in the days of Charles I, high society and its foibles came to be a more and more appealing topic for genial amusement.   James Shirley, the leading playwright of the 1630's, portrayed in *The Lady of Pleasure* (1635) the gaiety, affectation, and flippant talk of fashionable London folk, from frivolous dowagers to sophomoric college boys. Though it is by no means free from the older didacticism, *The Lady of Pleasure* does offer incontrovertible proof that a new trend of mirroring the *beau monde* had set in before the Civil War.

While that English *beau monde* lived in exile, Molière arose to fame in Paris.   He presented his comic drama, with its fling at *salon* modes, before English *emigrés* as well as before Louis XIV and his court.   *Les Précieuses Ridicules* (1659) made an indelible impression on the English literary aristocracy, but at this juncture its comic pattern was merely stimulating rather than revolutionary.   With or without Molière's influence, English comedy would have moved in the direction of the comedy of contemporary manners.   Native tradition had been pointing toward that type.   Finally the urbane character of the Restoration playhouse audience demanded it.   In this social fact lies the reason for the pre-eminent vitality of that new comedy.   It soon attained an artistic vigor which set it up as the one distinctive contribution of English playwriting to world drama between the seventeenth and the twentieth century.

From the beginning the Restoration theater took shape as a class institution.   The playgoing public constituted a mere handful of the inhabitants of London.   Two playhouses of some six to seven hundred seats each did only a fair business in the earlier and more prosperous years of that period.   By 1682 they found business so poor that they amalgamated into one producing organization.   This, the United Company, operated at the Theatre Royal in Drury Lane, the only legitimate theater open in London between 1682 and 1695.   What the Restoration audience, however, lacked in size it made up in its strong sense of social solidarity.   For the men of title, the city gallants, the fawning politicians, the ladies of fashion, the *demi-mondaines*, the mistresses of the great, and the motley crew of male hangers-on — for all these, who composed the bulk of the playgoers, the Court provided a core to existence and formed a common tie among them.   They frowned upon intruders into their little world of the theater.   Samuel Pepys, an official in the Navy Office, whose diary offers an incomparable miniature of London life between 1660 and 1670, on more than one occasion recorded disgustedly encounters with tradespeople and other "low persons" in the playhouse balconies.   His disdainful attitude typified the snobbery of the vast majority in the audience.   They felt themselves a perfect microcosm, presided over by a sovereign of no mean attainments and united by a fixed code of taste.   No national theater before or since has been supported by so homogeneous a community of patrons.

It is easy to exaggerate the undeniable licentiousness of that microcosm, for the expression of its lust in life and in literature was so unbridled as to make for permanent notoriety.   The *Diary* of John Evelyn (1620–1706) testifies, however, to the enthusiasm with which a goodly number of persons in high station pursued hobbies in the arts and sciences.   Serious intellectual and cultural interests were stirring amid the libertinism of the age. Yet Restoration polite society easily forgave the sins of any member whose deportment proved comely and whose mind agile. The chief sanction of conduct was not morality but style. Style outwardly concluded in civility or gallantry; style within culminated in wit.

Early in the new era there evolved an amoral, polished, and rapier-edged temper, at once conducive to the creation of a dramatic pattern in its own likeness. For the first time since Shakespeare the English stage turned to pure comedy. The art of pure comedy, more than any other kind of art, must attend to the moment, to its tone and its idiom. Without censoriousness pure comedy seeks to record from age to age the amusing, yet fleeting, image of man's constant incongruity. In the Restoration comedy of manners men and women are observed allowing life to appear as if it were a refined series of attitudes. For them modishness has killed freedom, wit superseded sentiment. The comic essence, therefore, consists in the ironic contemplation of the incongruity of human passion with its cool and studied expression. Hence such drama should be viewed not for soundness or unsoundness in ethical implications, but rather for vitality in artistry. The sense of Life is the be-all and the end-all.

Although the comedy of manners continued vigorous until the opening of the eighteenth century, the number of its authors remained small and their playwriting limited. The outstanding Restoration contributors, Sir George Etherege (?1635–1691), William Wycherley (1641–1715), William Congreve (1670–1729), and Sir John Vanbrugh (1664–1726), created only about a dozen comedies in all. Each one of this playwriting quartet possessed a somewhat individual vein of comic treatment, though in general their plays agree on the dramatic essentials. Wycherley's laughter exceeds the others' in scorn and cynicism. *The Plain Dealer* (1676), usually thought to be his masterpiece, lies nearer to the Jonson school in its Puritanical tone of satire on immorality and infidelity and legal injustice. *Love in a Wood* (1671) and *The Country Wife* (1675) better display the Wycherley comedy of manners. Vanbrugh, the least creative of the four playwrights, secured his reputation with *The Relapse* (1696), in which appeared the long-lived stage character, Lord Foppington. Congreve, the contemporary of Vanbrugh, won instant fame with *Love for Love* (1695) and then surpassed the achievement with *The Way of the World* (1700), often adjudged the finest example of Restoration comedy. Certainly this play, with Millamant, the most fascinating of the Restoration modish heroines, and with a repartee of brilliant finesse, constituted a fitting climax to the manners tradition. Shortly after the turn of the century the tradition began to succumb to the perverted taste of a growing middle-class audience, and before long had been obliterated by the rising tide of sentimentalism. The foundation, however, had been laid to one of the patterns for which the English drama has become especially famous.

SIR GEORGE ETHEREGE

The founder of the pure comedy of manners in England was Sir George Etherege, whose first effort in that direction preceded any other by a half-dozen years. Etherege's ancestry and birth are still shrouded in some uncertainty, as is his career up to March, 1664, when his maiden composition, *The Comical Revenge*, was acted at the Duke's Theatre. The popular favor which greeted this piece opened to him at the age of about thirty the society of the gayest of the gay rakes about the court — Sir Charles Sedley, the Earl of Rochester, and the Earl of Dorset. A second play from Etherege's pen, *She Would If She Could*, the Duke's Company produced in February, 1667–68, but it did not win the approbation which its lively picture of fashionable London haunts and flirtations deserved. Later in the same year its author went to Constantinople as secretary to the Embassy in Turkey. After some three years of dull living there, he returned to London and his beloved group of titled playboys, who were still racketing about the town. Sometime later he settled down long enough to write another comedy, his masterpiece, *The Man of Mode*, which came out at the Duke's Theatre in March, 1675–76.

Early in the following summer occurred an escapade illustrative of the riotous conduct in which Etherege and his aristocratic cronies sometimes indulged. One Sunday night in June at Epsom Wells, a fashionable rendezvous, a group of gallants, among them Etherege, were tossing some fiddlers in a blanket for refusing to play. A certain barber, a bystander, got mixed up in the fracas, and, to extricate himself, offered to bring the gallants to the loveliest woman in Epsom. He led them to the constable's house, where they beat upon the door and cried for entrance. When the constable would not open, they broke in and beat him severely. Before the brawling had ceased, the town watch, who had finally come on the scene, mortally wounded one of the gallants with a pike.

About 1680 Etherege married a rich London widow, and at approximately the same period he received knighthood. James II, upon his accession in 1685, appointed Etherege minister to the Diet at Ratisbon (Regensburg), Bavaria, whither he went shortly without his wife. In the provincial Bavarian city, this "ornament of London society" spent between three and four tedious years. His diplomatic career there had to be terminated in February, 1689, when William III's assumption of the English crown caused a shake-up throughout the governmental services. Etherege hastened to France where his royal patron had taken refuge, and died at Paris early in 1691.

Of his residence in Ratisbon Etherege has left a vivid record in his *Letterbook*. This volume of correspondence (1685–89) gives an account of daily living more detailed and picturesque than that available for any other poet or dramatist of the century. The portrait which emerges from that account typifies a thoroughly London-bred Restoration gallant still true to his mode when on foreign soil. Etherege's Ratisbon entourage included not only valets and lackeys, and a French-trained cook, but also a fencing and a dancing master, both of whom he kept occupied. A pack of greyhounds took him often afield hunting for hares. He "bungled away now and then a morning at tennis." Frequently games of ombre with the ladies whiled away the time, as well as gentle flirtations either indoors or in his garden. A household orchestra of four pieces rendered for him the latest musical airs, which he took pains to procure regularly from Paris and London. Now and then a bout of gaming or drinking with some of the stupid diplomatic corps, or an assignation with an undelectable "lady of pleasure," enlivened the evenings. The more shocking he could make his diversion in the eyes of the staid German aristocracy whom he detested, the greater joy the dashing English diplomat took in his amusement.

His most successful venture in this direction came off about a year after his arrival at Ratisbon. A certain Nuremburg actress, comely but of doubtful virtue, was playing in the city and regularly was invited to dine by Etherege, who would send his coach for Julia after the stage performance. Such open attentions to a mere player by a man of official prominence infuriated the Germans. A band of young aristocrats, led by Baron de Sensheim, determined to put an end to the business. On a November evening of 1686 they gathered noisily in front of Etherege's house and awaited the departure of Julia. Etherege took up their challenge with spirit and prepared a brave convoy for his coach and the lady guest — "two footmen marching before with pistols ready cocked in one hand and flambeaux in the other; the damsel with a man and a musketoon followed after in the coach which was guarded on each side by two persons, and behind by three more all well furnished with swords and pistols." Thus guarded, the actress passed through the principal streets to the accompaniment of "hooting and hollowing" on the part of the Baron's troop. These latter, in a last touch of derision as the lady neared home, began to cry in unison that "great was the Diana of the English Envoye!"

The surviving glimpses of Etherege's colorful personality explain why his admiring contemporaries called him "gentle George," that is, "genteel George." For them, as for posterity, he was the perfect specimen of Restoration gallantry, the ideal "wit." Of himself he wrote: "I must confess I am a fop in my heart;... I have been so used to affectation that without the help of the air of the court what is natural cannot touch me. You see what we get by being polished as we call it." Concerned though he was to be a fine gentleman rather than a man of letters, he never tired of turning a witty sentence. His letters from Ratisbon displayed the same facility in pregnant epigrammatic statement as his dramatic compositions of earlier days. Listen to the fluent brilliance of his gossip to an old London friend:

> Notwithstanding the ebbing and the flowing in the flesh, my mind is a kind of lake and has the same standing pleasures it had in London: wine and women.... The town is too little to hide us, and the liberty of talking is too great, so that poor lovers, like hares in relieving time, are fain to clicket up and down in the gardens at midnight.... Here are two very handsome young ladies, but their unconscionable price is marriage; nevertheless were I as capable of a *belle passion* as some at my age are, they would have cost me many a billet and much time in tying my cravat at 'em, but I cannot think of laying a siege.... I wear flannel, Sir, wherefore pray talk to me no more of poetry.

With what cadence and pictorial grace the pen runs on — a seemingly effortless style!

So finished a prose talent combined with a debonair wit to produce in Etherege the exact genius fitted to inaugurate the new English comedy of manners. He was so much a part of the world which the Restoration audience delighted to see mirrored, and yet withal so aware of its comical affectation, that a slight spurring of his fancy (it could hardly have been anything more, for he lived always under the sway of what he called "a noble laziness of mind") could bring the microcosm of high society to the stage with just the exaggeration necessary for artistic effect. His depictions of people and places in *The Man of Mode* had so great an illusion of contemporaneity about them that the spectators of this play for years argued over the identities of the characters, even down to the shoemaker and the orangewoman. For Dorimant at least three identifications were warmly supported!

In fidelity to the human scene Etherege certainly surpassed his nearest rival in comedy, Congreve. This is only one manifestation of Etherege's greater dramatic sensibility. His conceptions of scene in *The Man of Mode* reveal more dynamic qualities — a larger variety of action and a clearer differentiation in speakers' style. Congreve's best work, *The Way of the World*, excels in a certain intellectuality of tone and in verbal exquisiteness. His treatment, however, gives the impression of being a skillful and conscious distillation of those life elements which Etherege first exhibited. There is pristine force in Etherege's drama: it suggests an immediacy between its art and the reality.

THE RESTORATION THEATERS AND "PICTURE-STAGE"

The comedies of Etherege were designed for a playhouse and a stage which bore little resemblance to those in the days of Jonson, and Beaumont and Fletcher. The resumption of dramatic activity in 1660 brought about great changes in theatrical architecture. The new Restoration playhouses were rectangular structures, entirely roofed over and topped by a cupola of large dimensions for ventilation. Their long and narrow auditoriums had for illumination candelabra of wax tapers which could be lighted or snuffed only by hand. The Duke's Theatre in Dorset Garden, where *The Man of Mode* was originally acted in 1676, had been built five years before under the supervision of the famous architect, Sir Christopher Wren. It cost £9000, and established in size and luxury a record which remained well into the eighteenth century. Its interior, one hundred feet long and fifty-seven feet wide, was ornamented with gilded and figured pilasters. Rows of "benches without back boards," arranged in semicircular fashion, occupied the pit. At the rear of this amphitheater rose a circle of seven boxes holding twenty persons each. Here in the center box sat the king whenever he attended a performance. Over the first tier of boxes projected a second circle of identical size, and above the latter, an upper gallery or "paradise" with merely rows of benches, the cheapest seats in the house. A green carpeting covered all the seats in the pit and in the two box circles, and added a decorative effect which Continental visitors, who were unused to such a luxury, always commented upon.

But the most revolutionary feature of this Duke's Theatre as of all the Restoration theaters was the new "picture-stage," so called from the fact that now for the first time the English playhouse stage offered scenery as a definite pictorial background to the acting, while its architecture gave framing to the action. In the Restoration picture-stage the theory and arrangement of the orthodox twentieth-century stage had its beginning. Since then the outline of principles and of design has never altered essentially. A proscenium arch, equipped with a curtain which could rise and fall, divided the acting platform into a front and a rear stage. A music loft, where the theater orchestra played, jutted out over the stage from above the middle of the proscenium. Because of the poor acoustics in the rectangular auditoriums the actors had to be brought toward the audience as far as possible. Hence the front stage, termed the "apron," was thrust forward into the pit. Two entrance doors, with boxes above, opened upon the apron from each side and thus caused a large portion of the acting to take place on the deep front stage. Even so, complaints of inability to hear recur constantly in annals of the time.

The rear stage held all the scenery. Not far behind the proscenium were located the painted canvas frames, or "flats," which constituted the "scenes," as they were generally denoted. These flats moved laterally in grooves on the stage floor, and were drawn on and off by hand. For the most part the scenery must have featured crude interior or exterior "perspectives." Three kinds of scene appear in use: (1) a single flat running across the entire stage; (2) a pair of flats meeting in the center of the stage to form one perspective; (3) a combination of side-wings and rear flat to depict an elaborate setting with a distant prospect. Shifts of scenic location on the Restoration stage rarely involved the proscenium curtain, which, if utilized at all, was only employed at the act breaks. Usually this curtain rose at the opening of the performance after the prologue and fell at the close before the epilogue.

Changes of scenery, in general, occurred in full view of the audience and were accomplished by "scene-drawing"; that is, the removal of a flat (or pair of flats) to expose another perspective behind — or the process might be exactly reversed. In any case, the scene-drawing immediately changed the locality of the subsequent action. Thus actors could be at once transported from one spot to another without leaving the stage. The players also might make their entrance to a new locale not through the doors on the apron, but by being "discovered" when flats were drawn apart. Act IV, Scene 1 of *The Man of Mode* offers an interesting example of this convention. At the start of the act the scene in place was drawn off, and as the flats were parting, the actors, now exposed to view, came through the parted scene downstage out to the apron. In so doing they suggested to the Restoration audience that they had moved from the ball room of Lady Townley's house (formerly behind the closed flats) to her drawing-room, where the ensuing dialogue took place.

To the more sophisticated taste of the twentieth century, Restoration stage methods, like Elizabethan ones, often appear naïve and amusing. The grotesque compromises in scenic effect which the Restoration spectator faced resulted, of course, from the embryonic state of the art of pictorial staging during the later seventeenth century. The imagination of the theatergoer was compelled to dwell about halfway between the unlimited scenic flexibility of Elizabethan production and the constricted literalness of modern stage realism.

THE MAN OF MODE

The Man of Mode marks a great advance over Etherege's previous two plays and exhibits an artistic climax appropriate to the end of his playwriting career. Spiritedly he has presented what he called "the harmless lust of the town," from morning in a gallant's bedchamber until evening when all the world meets in St. James's Park at High Mall. The dialogue, whether of high or of low, reveals a sure and lively style; again and again it scintillates with pointed wit. Yet its really distinctive quality (for brilliance of repartee commonly arises in the best of Restoration comedy) is the occasional touch of delicate and airy fancy, of sensuous imagery; as when Medley describes the mouth of Harriet Woodvil: "pretty, pouting lips, with a little moisture ever hanging on them, that look like the Provins rose fresh on the bush, ere the morning sun has quite drawn up the dew" (Act I, Scene 1, ll. 171-75).

Etherege, however, was far more than a stylist in his descriptive talent; with dramatic effectiveness he inserted idylls of fashionable behavior, such as the scene in the third act when Young Bellair and Harriet take off the flirtatious posturing of a gallant and a lady with a fan.   They imitate the mode so perfectly that they hoodwink their respective parents into thinking they are in love with one another.   Thus the surface comedy takes on a vein of deeper humor.   Etherege's pictorial ability reaches its height in the characterizations.   The colors in his painting are always bright; the figures never wooden, not even "the ill-fashion'd Fellows" in the Mall.   The "Man of Mode," Sir Fopling Flutter, though not the first of Restoration stage fops, became the most attractive and famous, and fostered a goodly progeny.   An amiable coxcomb utterly absorbed in costume and deportment, he is therefore kept by Etherege from seeking the heart or hand of any lady.   His creator allows him a little dalliance by the way; but to the very end Etherege wisely preserved him in character and had him remark in departure, "No one woman is worth the loss of a cut in a caper" (Act V, Scene 2, ll. 482–83).

The treatment of the hero and heroine, Dorimant and Harriet, is equally sound in its psychology.   Though each has struck fire in the other's breast, Etherege knew that they are too intelligent and worldly-wise to rush into each other's arms without a longer probation for their sentiments.   He did not, therefore, arrange the conventional betrothal as a closing episode.   Rather the spectator is left quite properly uncertain whether Dorimant's dawning passion will draw him eventually to court Harriet in the country, to which she is returning.   It is a master stroke of lifelike plotting, though a disappointing dénouement to those who desire all destinies decided at the fall of the curtain.   But Etherege's finest touch is the changing tone which creeps into the sparring of Harriet and Dorimant.   The hard, brittle repartee at the start of the courtship gradually shifts to a final conversation in which a certain tenderness hovers over the words of both.   The restraint of feeling is admirably handled.   In the closing moments of *The Man of Mode* Etherege played a deeper note of emotion and understanding than any other Restoration comedy contains.

[For a history of the Restoration theater and drama, see Allardyce Nicoll, *A History of Restoration Drama* (second edition, 1928); for critiques on Restoration comedy, John Palmer, *The Comedy of Manners* (1913), and Bonamy Dobrée, *Restoration Comedy* (1924); for an account of Etherege's life and work, H. F. B. Brett-Smith, Introduction to *The Dramatic Works of Sir George Etherege* (2 vols., 1927).]

SIR GEORGE ETHEREGE

The Man of Mode,

OR

Sir Fopling Flutter

DRAMATIS PERSONAE

Gentlemen

MR. DORIMANT
MR. MEDLEY
OLD BELLAIR
YOUNG BELLAIR
SIR FOPLING FLUTTER

Gentlewomen

LADY TOWNLEY, *sister of* OLD BELLAIR
EMILIA, *companion of* LADY TOWNLEY
MRS. LOVEIT, DORIMANT'S *former mistress*
BELLINDA, *friend of* DORIMANT
LADY WOODVILL, *a country gentlewoman*
HARRIET, *daughter of* LADY WOODVILL

Waiting-Women

PERT
BUSY

MR. SMIRK, *a parson*
HANDY, *valet-de-chambre to* MR. DORIMANT
SWEARING TOM, *a shoemaker*
FOGGY NAN, *an orange-woman*
Three Slovenly Bullies
Two Chairmen
Pages, Footmen, etc.

The Scene is at London in the 1670's

PROLOGUE

BY SIR CAR SCROOPE, BARONET [1]

Like dancers on the ropes poor poets fare,
Most perish young, the rest in danger are;
This, one would think, should make our authors wary,
But, gamester like, the giddy fools miscarry.
A lucky hand or two so tempts 'em on,　　　　　　5
They cannot leave off play till they're undone.
With modest fears a muse does first begin,
Like a young wench newly enticed to sin;
But tickled once with praise, by her good will,
The wanton fool would never more lie still.　　　　10
'Tis an old mistress you'll meet here tonight,
Whose charms you once have looked on with delight.

---

[1] Sir Car Scroop, Scroope, or Scrope (1649–80), was a well-known gallant and amateur poet at the court of Charles II.

But now of late such dirty drabs have known ye,
A muse o'th' better sort's ashamed to own ye.
Nature well drawn, and wit, must now give place   15
To gaudy nonsense and to dull grimace;
Nor is it strange that you should like so much
That kind of wit, for most of yours is such.
But I'm afraid that while to France we go, ⎫
To bring you home fine dresses, dance, and show, ⎬   20
The stage, like you, will but more foppish grow. ⎭
Of foreign wares, why should we fetch the scum,
When we can be so richly served at home?
For, Heav'n be thanked, 'tis not so wise an age
But your own follies may supply the stage.   25
Tho' often plowed, there's no great fear the soil
Should barren grow by the too frequent toil;
While at your doors are to be daily found
Such loads of dunghill to manure the ground.
'Tis by your follies that we players thrive,   30
As the physicians by diseases live;
And as each year some new distemper reigns,
Whose friendly poison helps t'increase their gains,
So among you there starts up every day
Some new, unheard-of fool for us to play.   35
Then, for your own sakes be not too severe,
Nor what you all admire at home, damn here;
Since each is fond of his own ugly face,
Why should you, when we hold it, break the glass?

ACT I

SCENE I. *A dressing-room. A table covered with a toilet; clothes laid ready.*

Enter DORIMANT *in his gown and slippers, with a note in his hand, made up, repeating verses*

Dor. Now for some ages had the pride of Spain
Made half the sun shine on the world in vain.[1]
(*Then looking on the note, he reads*) "For Mrs. Loveit" — What a dull, insipid thing is a billet-doux written in cold blood, after the   5
heat of the business is over! It is a tax upon good nature which I have here been laboring to pay, and have done it, but with as much regret as ever fanatic paid the Royal Aid[2] or

church duties. 'Twill have the same fate,   10
I know, that all my notes to her have had of late; 'twill not be thought kind enough. 'Faith, women are i'the right when they jealously examine our letters, for in them we always first discover our decay of passion.   15
— Hey! Who waits?

Enter HANDY

Han. Sir —
Dor. Call a footman.
Han. None of 'em are come yet.
Dor. Dogs! Will they ever lie snoring   20
abed till noon?
Han. 'Tis all one, sir; if they're up, you indulge 'em so, they're ever poaching after whores all the morning.
Dor. Take notice henceforward: who's   25
wanting in his duty, the next clap he gets, he shall rot for an example. — What vermin are those chattering without?

---

[1] Ll. 1–2 of a poem, "Upon a War with Spain and a Fight at Sea," by Edmund Waller (1606–87), the dean of the Restoration court poets.
[2] Tax.

Han. Foggy [1] Nan, the orange-woman, and Swearing Tom, the shoemaker.   30

Dor. Go, call in that over-grown jade with the flasket of guts before her; [2] fruit is refreshing in a morning.   (*Exit* HANDY.

(*Reads:*

It is not that I love you less
Than when before your feet I lay — [3] 35

Enter ORANGE-WOMAN *and* HANDY

How now, double tripe, what news do you bring?

Or.-Wom. News! Here's the best fruit has come to town t'year; gad, I was up before four o'clock this morning and bought all the   40 choice i'the market.

Dor. The nasty refuse of your shop.

Or.-Wom. You need not make mouths at it; I assure you, 'tis all culled ware.

Dor. The citizens buy better on a holi-   45 day in their walk to Totnam. [4]

Or.-Wom. Good or bad, 'tis all one; I never knew you commend anything. Lord! would the ladies had heard you talk of 'em as I have done! (*Sets down the fruit.*) Here, bid   50 your man give me an angel. [5]

Dor. (*to* HANDY). Give the bawd her fruit again.

Or.-Wom. Well, on my conscience, there never was the like of you! — God's my   55 life, I had almost forgot to tell you there is a young gentlewoman lately come to town with her mother, that is so taken with you.

Dor. Is she handsome?

Or.-Wom. Nay, gad, there are few finer   60 women, I tell you but so — and a hugeous fortune, they say. — Here, eat this peach. It comes from the stone; 'tis better than any Newington [6] y'have tasted.

Dor. (*taking the peach*). This fine wom-   65

an, I'll lay my life, is some awkward, ill-fashioned country toad who, not having above four dozen of black hairs on her head, has adorned her baldness with a large, white fruz, [1] that she may look sparkishly in the fore-   70 front of the King's box at an old play.

Or.-Wom. Gad, you'd change your note quickly if you did but see her.

Dor. How came she to know me?

Or.-Wom. She saw you yesterday at   75 the Change. [2] She told me you came and fooled with the woman at the next shop.

Dor. I remember there was a mask observed me, indeed. Fooled, did she say?

Or.-Wom. Aye; I vow she told me   80 twenty things you said, too, and acted with her head and with her body so like you ——

Enter MEDLEY

Med. Dorimant, my life, my joy, my darling sin! How dost thou?

Or.-Wom. Lord, what a filthy trick   85 these men have got of kissing one another!
                (*She spits.*

Med. Why do you suffer this cartload of scandal to come near you and make your neighbors think you so improvident to need a bawd?

Or.-Wom. (*to* DORIMANT). Good, now   90 we shall have it; you did but want [3] him to help you! Come, pay me for my fruit.

Med. Make us thankful for it, huswife. Bawds are as much out of fashion as gentlemen-ushers; [4] none but old formal ladies use the   95 one, and none but foppish old stagers employ the other. Go, you are an insignificant brandy bottle.

Dor. Nay, there you wrong her; three quarts of Canary [5] is her business.   100

Or.-Wom. What you please, gentlemen.

Dor. To him! give him as good as he brings.

Or.-Wom. Hang him, there is not such another heathen in the town again, except it be the shoemaker without.   105

---

[1] Fat; or dull.

[2] That over-sized wench with the tub of guts on the front of her.

[3] Ll. 1–2 of Waller's poem, "The Self-Banished."

[4] A London suburban district of the period, frequented by the lower middle class.

[5] An old gold coin worth in the Restoration era about ten shillings.

[6] A noted orchard district in Kent, south of London.

[1] Wig of curled hair.

[2] The New Exchange, an arcade of fashionable shops in the Strand.

[3] Need.

[4] Male attendants to a lady.

[5] I.e., Canary Islands wine.

Med. I shall see you hold up your hand at the bar next sessions for murder, huswife; that shoemaker can take his oath you are in fee with the doctors to sell green fruit to the gentry, that the crudities may breed diseases.   110

Or.-Wom. (*to* DORIMANT). Pray, give me my money.

Dor. Not a penny! When you bring the gentlewoman hither you spoke of, you shall be paid.   115

Or.-Wom. The gentlewoman! the gentlewoman may be as honest[1] as your sisters for aught I know. — Pray, pay me, Mr. Dorimant, and do not abuse me so; I have an honester way of living — you know it.   120

Med. Was there ever such a restive bawd!

Dor. Some jade's tricks she has, but she makes amends when she's in good humor. (*To the* ORANGE-WOMAN) Come, tell me the lady's name and Handy shall pay you.   125

Or.-Wom. I must not; she forbid me.

Med. (*to* DORIMANT). That's a sure sign she would have you.

Dor. Where does she live?

Or.-Wom. They lodge at my house.   130

Med. Nay, then she's in a hopeful way.

Or.-Wom. Good Mr. Medley, say your pleasure of me, but take heed how you affront my house! — God's my life, in a hopeful way!

Dor. Prithee, peace! What kind of   135 woman's the mother?

Or.-Wom. A goodly, grave gentlewoman. Lord, how she talks against the wild young men o' the town! As for your part, she thinks you an arrant devil; should she see you,   140 on my conscience she would look if you had not a cloven foot.

Dor. Does she know me?

Or.-Wom. Only by hearsay; a thousand horrid stories have been told her of you,   145 and she believes 'em all.

Med. By the character this should be the famous Lady Woodvill and her daughter Harriet.

Or.-Wom. (*aside*). The devil's in him   150 for guessing, I think.

Dor. Do you know 'em?

Med. Both very well; the mother's a great

admirer of the forms and civility of the last age.   155

Dor. An antiquated beauty may be allowed to be out of humor at the freedoms of the present. This is a good account of the mother; pray, what is the daughter?

Med. Why, first, she's an heiress —   160 vastly rich.

Dor. And handsome?

Med. What alteration a twelvemonth may have bred in her I know not, but a year ago she was the beautifullest creature I ever saw: 165 a fine, easy, clean shape; light brown hair in abundance; her features regular; her complexion clear and lively; large, wanton eyes; but above all, a mouth that has made me kiss it a hundred times in imagination; teeth   170 white and even, and pretty, pouting lips, with a little moisture ever hanging on them, that look like the Provins[1] rose fresh on the bush, ere the morning sun has quite drawn up the dew.   175

Dor. Rapture! mere[2] rapture!

Or.-Wom. Nay, gad, he tells you true, she's a delicate creature.

Dor. Has she wit?

Med. More than is usual in her sex,   180 and as much malice. Then she's as wild as you would wish her, and has a demureness in her looks that makes it so surprising.

Dor. Flesh and blood cannot bear this and not long to know her.   185

Med. I wonder what makes her mother bring her up to town; an old doting keeper cannot be more jealous of his mistress.

Or.-Wom. She made me laugh yesterday; there was a judge came to visit 'em, and   190 the old man she told me did so stare upon her, and when he saluted her, smacked so heartily. Who would think it of 'em?

Med. God a-mercy,[3] Judge!

Dor. Do 'em right; the gentlemen of   195 the long robe[4] have not been wanting by their good examples to countenance the crying sin o' the nation.

---

[1] Chaste.

[1] A town situated about 50 miles southeast of Paris, and noted for its roses.
[2] Pure.   [3] Thanks! Literally, God have mercy!
[4] Legal profession.

Med. Come, on with your trappings; 'tis later than you imagine.   200

Dor. Call in the shoemaker, Handy.

Or.-Wom. Good Mr. Dorimant, pay me. Gad, I had rather give you my fruit than stay to be abused by that foul-mouthed rogue; what you gentlemen say, it matters not   205 much, but such a dirty fellow does one more disgrace.

Dor. Give her ten shillings — and be sure you tell the young gentlewoman I must be acquainted with her.   210

Or.-Wom. Now do you long to be tempting this pretty creature? Well, heavens mend you!

Med. Farewell, bog! [1]

(*Exeunt* ORANGE-WOMAN *and* HANDY. Dorimant, when did you see your *pis-*   215 *aller*,[2] as you call her — Mrs. Loveit?

Dor. Not these two days.

Med. And how stand affairs between you?

Dor. There has been great patching of late, much ado; we make a shift to hang to-   220 gether.

Med. I wonder how her mighty spirit bears it.

Dor. Ill enough, on all conscience; I never knew so violent a creature.   225

Med. She's the most passionate in her love and the most extravagant in her jealousy of any woman I ever heard of. What note is that?

Dor. An excuse I am going to send her for the neglect I am guilty of.   230

Med. Prithee, read it.

Dor. No; but if you will take the pains, you may.

Med. (*reads*).

"I never was a lover of business, but now I have a just reason to hate it, since it   235 has kept me these two days from seeing you. I intend to wait upon you in the afternoon, and in the pleasure of your conversation forget all I have suffered during this tedious absence."   240
This business of yours, Dorimant, has been with a vizard [3] at the playhouse; I have had an eye on you. If some malicious body should

[1] Farewell, saucy!   [2] Last resource.
[3] Masked woman.

betray you, this kind note would hardly make your peace with her.   245

Dor. I desire no better.

Med. Why, would her knowledge of it oblige you?

Dor. Most infinitely; next to the coming to a good understanding with a new mistress,   250 I love a quarrel with an old one. But the devil's in't! There has been such a calm in my affairs of late, I have not had the pleasure of making a woman so much as break her fan, to be sullen, or forswear herself, these   255 three days.

Med. A very great misfortune. Let me see; I love mischief well enough to forward this business myself. I'll about it presently, and though I know the truth of what you've   260 done will set her a-raving, I'll heighten it a little with invention, leave her in a fit o' the mother,[1] and be here again before y'are ready.

Dor. Pray stay; you may spare yourself the labor. The business is undertaken al-   265 ready by one who will manage it with as much address, and I think with a little more malice than you can.

Med. Who i' the devil's name can this be!

Dor. Why, the vizard — that very   270 vizard you saw me with.

Med. Does she love mischief so well as to betray herself to spite another?

Dor. Not so neither, Medley. I will make you comprehend the mystery. This   275 mask, for a farther confirmation of what I have been these two days swearing to her, made me yesterday at the playhouse make her a promise before her face utterly to break off with Loveit, and, because she tenders [2] my reputation   280 and would not have me do a barbarous thing, has contrived a way to give me a handsome occasion.

Med. Very good.

Dor. She intends about an hour before   285 me, this afternoon, to make Loveit a visit and, having the privilege by reason of a professed friendship between 'em, to talk of her concerns.

Med. Is she a friend?

Dor. Oh, an intimate friend!   290

Med. Better and better; pray proceed.

[1] Hysterical passion.   [2] Esteems.

Dor. She means insensibly to insinuate a discourse of me and artificially [1] to raise her jealousy to such a height that, transported with the first motions of her passion, she 295 shall fly upon me with all the fury imaginable as soon as ever I enter. The quarrel being thus happily begun, I am to play my part, confess and justify all my roguery, swear her impertinence and ill-humor make her in- 300 tolerable, tax her with the next fop that comes into my head, and in a huff march away — slight her and leave her to be taken by whosoever thinks it worth his time to lie down before her. 305

Med. This vizard is a spark and has a genius that makes her worthy of yourself, Dorimant.

Enter HANDY, *the* Shoemaker, *and a* Footman

Dor. (*to the* Footman). You rogue, there, who sneak like a dog that has flung down a dish! if you do not mend your waiting, I'll uncase 310 you and turn you loose to the wheel of fortune. — Handy, seal this and let him run with it presently. (*Gives* HANDY *the letter*.
(*Exit the* Footman.

Med. Since you're resolved on a quarrel, why do you send her this kind note? 315

Dor. To keep her at home in order to the business. (*To the* Shoemaker) How now, you drunken sot?

Shoe. 'Zbud, you have no reason to talk; I have not had a bottle of sack of yours in 320 my belly this fortnight.

Med. The orange-woman says your neighbors take notice what a heathen you are, and design to inform a bishop and have you burned for an atheist. 325

Shoe. Damn her, dunghill, if her husband does not remove her, she stinks so, the parish intends to indict him for a nuisance.

Med. I advise you like a friend; reform your life. You have brought the envy of the 330 world upon you by living above yourself. Whoring and swearing are vices too genteel for a shoemaker.

Shoe. 'Zbud, I think you men of quality will grow as unreasonable as the women. 335

[1] Artfully.

You would engross [1] the sins of the nation; poor folks can no sooner be wicked but they're railed at by their betters.

Dor. Sirrah, I'll have you stand i' the pillory for this libel! 340

Shoe. Some of you deserve it, I'm sure; there are so many of 'em that our journeymen nowadays, instead of harmless ballads, sing nothing but your damned lampoons.

Dor. Our lampoons, you rogue! 345

Shoe. Nay, good master, why should not you write your own commentaries as well as Cæsar?

Med. The rascal's read, I perceive.

Shoe. You know the old proverb — ale 350 and history.

Dor. Draw on my shoes, sirrah.

Shoe. (*obeying*). Here's a shoe!

Dor. Sits with more wrinkles than there are in an angry bully's forehead! 355

Shoe. 'Zbud, as smooth as your mistress's skin does upon her! So; strike your foot in home. 'Zbud, if e'er a monsieur of 'em all make more fashionable ware, I'll be content to have my ears whipped off with my own paring 360 knife.

Med. And served up in a ragout instead of coxcombs to a company of French shoemakers for a collation.

Shoe. Hold, hold! Damn 'em — 365 caterpillars! Let 'em feed upon cabbage. — Come, master, your health this morning's next my heart now. (*Holds out his hand for money.*

Dor. Go! Get you home and govern your family better! Do not let your wife 370 follow you to the alehouse, beat your whore, and lead you home in triumph.

Shoe. 'Zbud, there's never a man i'the town lives more like a gentleman with his wife than I do. I never mind her motions; [2] she 375 never inquires into mine. We speak to one another civilly, hate one another heartily, and because 'tis vulgar to lie and soak [3] together, we have each of us our several [4] settle-bed.

Dor. (*to* MEDLEY). Give him half a 380 crown.

Med. Not without he will promise to be bloody drunk.

[1] Monopolize. [2] Actions. [3] Steep in drink. [4] Separate.

Shoe. "Tope"'s the word i'the eye of the world.[1] (*To* HANDY) For my master's 385 honor, Robin.[2]

Dor. Do not debauch my servants, sirrah.

Shoe. I only tip him the wink; he knows an alehouse from a hovel.   (*Exit* Shoemaker.

Dor. (*to* HANDY). My clothes, quickly. 390

Med. Where shall we dine today?

Enter YOUNG BELLAIR

Dor. Where you will; here comes a good third man.

Young Bel. Your servant, gentlemen.

Med. Gentle sir, how will you answer 395 this visit to your honorable mistress? 'Tis not her interest you should keep company with men of sense who will be talking reason.

Young Bel. I do not fear her pardon, do you but grant me yours for my neglect of late. 400

Med. Though y'ave made us miserable by the want of your good company, to show you I am free from all resentment, may the beautiful cause of our misfortune give you all the joys happy lovers have shared ever since the 405 world began.

Young Bel. You wish me in heaven, but you believe me on my journey to hell.

Med. You have a good strong faith, and that may contribute much towards your sal- 410 vation. I confess I am but of an untoward constitution, apt to have doubts and scruples, and in love they are no less distracting than in religion. Were I so near marriage, I should cry out by fits as I ride in my coach, "Cuck- 415 old, cuckold!" with no less fury than the mad fanatic does "Glory!" in Bethlem.[3]

Young Bel. Because religion makes some run mad, must I live an atheist?

Med. Is it not great indiscretion for a 420 man of credit, who may have money enough on his word, to go and deal with Jews, who for little sums make men enter into bonds and give judgments?[4]

[1] I.e., "tope"'s the word for a gentleman to use.
[2] Here the shoemaker goes through the motions of drinking Dorimant's health.
[3] The hospital of St. Mary of Bethlehem near Bishopsgate, a hospital for lunatics since 1400.
[4] Assignments of property.

Young Bel. Preach no more on this 425 text. I am determined, and there is no hope of my conversion.

Dor. (*to* HANDY, *who is fiddling about him*). Leave your unnecessary fiddling; a wasp that's buzzing about a man's nose at dinner is not more troublesome than thou art.   430

Han. You love to have your clothes hang just, sir.

Dor. I love to be well dressed, sir, and think it no scandal to my understanding.

Han. Will you use the essence, or 435 orange-flower water?[1]

Dor. I will smell as I do today, no offense to the ladies' noses.

Han. Your pleasure, sir.   (*Exit* HANDY.

Dor. That a man's excellency should 440 lie in neatly tying of a ribband[2] or a cravat! How careful's nature in furnishing the world with necessary coxcombs!

Young Bel. That's a mighty pretty suit of yours, Dorimant.   445

Dor. I am glad't has your approbation.

Young Bel. No man in town has a better fancy in his clothes than you have.

Dor. You will make me have an opinion of my genius.   450

Med. There is a great critic, I hear, in these matters lately arrived piping hot from Paris.

Young Bel. Sir Fopling Flutter, you mean?

Med. The same.   455

Young Bel. He thinks himself the pattern of modern gallantry.

Dor. He is indeed the pattern of modern foppery.

Med. He was yesterday at the play, 460 with a pair of gloves up to his elbows, and a periwig more exactly curled than a lady's head newly dressed for a ball.

Young Bel. What a pretty lisp he has!

Dor. Ho! that he affects in imitation 465 of the people of quality of France.

Med. His head stands, for the most part, on one side, and his looks are more languishing than a lady's when she lolls at stretch in her coach or leans her head carelessly against 470 the side of the box i' the playhouse.

[1] Perfume of orange extract.   [2] Ribbon.

Dor. He is a person indeed of great acquired follies.

Med. He is like many others, beholding to his education for making him so eminent 475 a coxcomb. Many a fool had been lost to the world had their indulgent parents wisely bestowed neither learning nor good breeding on 'em.

Young Bel. He has been, as the spark- 480 ish word is, "brisk upon the ladies" already. He was yesterday at my Aunt Townley's and gave Mrs. Loveit a catalogue of his good qualities under the character of "a complete gentleman," who, according to Sir Fop- 485 ling, ought to dress well, dance well, fence well, have a genius for love letters, an agreeable voice for a chamber, be very amorous, something discreet, but not overconstant.

Med. Pretty ingredients to make an 490 accomplished person!

Dor. I am glad he pitched upon Loveit.

Young Bel. How so?

Dor. I wanted a fop to lay to her charge, and this is as pat as may be. 495

Young Bel. I am confident she loves no man but you.

Dor. The good fortune were enough to make me vain, but that I am in my nature modest.

Young Bel. (*whispers*). Hark you, 500 Dorimant. (*Aloud*) With your leave, Mr. Medley; 'tis only a secret concerning a fair lady.

Med. Your good breeding, sir, gives you too much trouble; you might have whispered without all this ceremony. 505

Young Bel. (*to* DORIMANT). How stand your affairs with Bellinda of late?

Dor. She's a little jilting baggage.

Young Bel. Nay, I believe her false enough, but she's ne'er the worse for your purpose; 510 she was with you yesterday in a disguise at the play.

Dor. There we fell out and resolved never to speak to one another more.

Young Bel. The occasion? 515

Dor. Want of courage to meet me at the place appointed. These young women apprehend loving as much as the young men do fighting, at first; but once entered, like them too, they all turn bullies straight. 520

Enter HANDY

Han. (*to* YOUNG BELLAIR). Sir, your man without desires to speak with you.

Young Bel. Gentlemen, I'll return immediately. (*Exit* YOUNG BELLAIR.

Med. A very pretty fellow this. 525

Dor. He's handsome, well bred, and by much the most tolerable of all the young men that do not abound in wit.

Med. Ever well dressed, always complaisant, and seldom impertinent. You and he are 530 grown very intimate, I see.

Dor. It is our mutual interest to be so: it makes the women think the better of his understanding, and judge more favorably of my reputation; it makes him pass upon 535 some for a man of very good sense, and I upon others for a very civil person.

Med. What was that whisper?

Dor. A thing which he would fain have known, but I did not think it fit to tell him; it 540 might have frightened him from his honorable intentions of marrying.

Med. Emilia — give her her due — has the best reputation of any young woman about the town who has beauty enough to 545 provoke detraction. Her carriage is unaffected, her discourse modest — not at all censorious nor pretending, like the counterfeits of the age.

Dor. She's a discreet maid, and I be- 550 lieve nothing can corrupt her but a husband.

Med. A husband?

Dor. Yes, a husband. I have known many women make a difficulty of losing a maidenhead, who have afterwards made none 555 of making a cuckold.

Med. This prudent consideration I am apt to think has made you confirm poor Bellair in the desperate resolution he has taken.

Dor. Indeed, the little hope I found 560 there was of her, in the state she was in, has made me by my advice contribute something towards the changing of her condition.

Enter YOUNG BELLAIR

Dear Bellair! By heavens, I thought we had lost thee; men in love are never to be 565 reckoned on when we would form a company.

Young Bel. Dorimant, I am undone; my man has brought the most surprising news i' the world.

Dor. Some strange misfortune has be- 570 fallen your love?

Young Bel. My father came to town last night and lodges i' the very house where Emilia lies.

Med. Does he know it is with her you 575 are in love?

Young Bel. He knows I love, but knows not whom, without some officious sot has betrayed me.

Dor. Your Aunt Townley is your con- 580 fidant and favors the business.

Young Bel. I do not apprehend any ill office from her. I have received a letter, in which I am commanded by my father to meet him at my aunt's this afternoon. He tells me 585 farther he has made a match for me and bids me resolve to be obedient to his will or expect to be disinherited.

Med. Now's your time, Bellair. Never had lover such an opportunity of giving a 590 generous proof of his passion.

Young Bel. As how, I pray?

Med. Why, hang an estate, marry Emilia out of hand, and provoke your father to do what he threatens. 'Tis but despising a 595 coach, humbling yourself to a pair of goloshes,[1] being out of countenance when you meet your friends, pointed at and pitied wherever you go by all the amorous fops that know you, and your fame will be immortal. 600

Young Bel. I could find in my heart to resolve not to marry at all.

Dor. Fie, fie, that would spoil a good jest and disappoint the well-natured town of an occasion of laughing at you. 605

Young Bel. The storm I have so long expected hangs o'er my head and begins to pour down upon me. I am on the rack and can have no rest till I'm satisfied in what I fear. — Where do you dine? 610

Dor. At Long's or Locket's.[2]

Med. At Long's let it be.

[1] Overshoes with wooden soles.
[2] Fashionable taverns for the gallants of London.

Young Bel. I'll run and see Emilia and inform myself how matters stand. If my misfortunes are not so great as to make me 615 unfit for company, I'll be with you.

(*Exit* YOUNG BELLAIR.

Enter a Footman *with a letter*

Foot. (*to* DORIMANT). Here's a letter, sir.

Dor. The superscription's right: "For Mr. Dorimant."

Med. Let's see — the very scrawl and 620 spelling of a true-bred whore.

Dor. I know the hand; the style is admirable, I assure you.

Med. Prithee, read it.

Dor. (*reads*).

"I told a you you dud not love me, if 625 you dud, you wou'd have seen me again ere now. I have no money and am very Mallicolly. Pray send me a Guynie to see the Operies.

Your Servant to Command, 630
Molly"

Med. Pray, let the whore have a favorable answer, that she may spark it [1] in a box and do honor to her profession.

Dor. She shall, and perk up i' the face 635 of quality. — Is the coach at the door?

Han. You did not bid me send for it.

(*Offers to go out.*

Dor. Eternal blockhead! Hey, sot —

Han. Did you call me, sir?

Dor. I hope you have no just exception 640 to the name, sir?

Han. I have sense, sir.

Dor. Not so much as a fly in winter. — How did you come, Medley?

Med. In a chair. 645

Foot. You may have a hackney coach if you please, sir.

Dor. I may ride the elephant if I please, sir. Call another chair and let my coach follow to Long's. 650

(*Exeunt* DORIMANT *and* MEDLEY *singing*, "Be calm, ye great parents," etc.[2]

[1] Play the belle.
[2] An unidentified song of the day.

ACT II

Scene 1. Lady Townley's *house.*

Enter Lady Townley *and* Emilia

Lady Town. I was afraid, Emilia, all had been discovered.

Emil. I tremble with the apprehension still.

Lady Town. That my brother should take lodgings i' the very house where you lie! 5

Emil. 'Twas lucky we had timely notice to warn the people to be secret. He seems to be a mighty good-humored old man.

Lady Town. He ever had a notable smirking way with him. 10

Emil. He calls me "rogue," tells me he can't abide me, and does so bepat me.

Lady Town. On my word, you are much in his favor then!

Emil. He has been very inquisitive, I 15 am told, about my family, my reputation, and my fortune.

Lady Town. I am confident he does not i' the least suspect you are the woman his son's in love with. 20

Emil. What should make him, then, inform himself so particularly of me?

Lady Town. He was always of a very loving temper himself; it may be he has a doting fit upon him — who knows? 25

Emil. It cannot be!

Enter Young Bellair

Lady Town. Here comes my nephew. — Where did you leave your father?

Young Bel. Writing a note within. Emilia, this early visit looks as if some kind jeal- 30 ousy would not let you rest at home.

Emil. The knowledge I have of my rival gives me a little cause to fear your constancy.

Young Bel. My constancy! I vow ——

Emil. Do not vow. Our love is frail as 35 is our life and full as little in our power — and are you sure you shall outlive this day?

Young Bel. I am not; but when we are in perfect health, 'twere an idle thing to fright ourselves with the thoughts of sudden death. 40

Lady Town. Pray, what has passed between you and your father i' the garden?

Young Bel. He's firm in his resolution, tells me I must marry Mrs. Harriet, or swears he'll marry himself and disinherit me. When 45 I saw I could not prevail with him to be more indulgent, I dissembled an obedience to his will, which has composed his passion and will give us time — and, I hope, opportunity — to deceive him. 50

Enter Old Bellair *with a note in his hand*

Lady Town. Peace, here he comes!

Old Bel. Harry, take this and let your man carry it for me to Mr. Fourbe's[1] chamber — my lawyer i' the Temple.[2] (*Exit* Young Bellair.) (*To* Emilia) Neighbor, a dod! I am glad 55 to see thee here. — Make much of her, sister; she's one of the best of your acquaintance. I like her countenance and her behavior well; she has a modesty that is not common i' this age — a dod, she has! 60

Lady Town. I know her value, brother, and esteem her accordingly.

Old Bel. (*aside*). Advise her to wear a little more mirth in her face; a dod, she's too serious.

Lady Town. The fault is very excusable 65 in a young woman.

Old Bel. Nay, a dod, I like her ne'er the worse. A melancholy beauty has her charms. I love a pretty sadness in a face, which varies now and then, like changeable colors, into 70 a smile.

Lady Town. Methinks you speak very feelingly, brother.

Old Bel. I am but five and fifty, sister, you know — an age not altogether unsensible. 75 — (*To* Emilia) Cheer up, sweetheart! I have a secret to tell thee may chance to make thee merry. We three will make collation together anon; i' the meantime, mum — I can't abide you! Go, I can't abide you. 80

Enter Young Bellair

Harry, come! You must along with me to my Lady Woodvill's. — (*To the ladies*) I'm going to slip the boy at a mistress.

---

[1] "Fourbe" means "cheat."

[2] A group of buildings in the heart of old London, occupied by one of the law societies.

Young Bel. At a wife, sir, you would say.

Old Bel. You need not look so glum, sir; 85
a wife is no curse when she brings the blessing
of a good estate with her. But an idle town
flirt, with a painted face, a rotten reputation,
and a crazy fortune, a dod! is the devil and all,
and such a one I hear you are in league 90
with.

Young Bel. I cannot help detraction, sir.

Old Bel. Out! A pize [1] o' their breeches,
there are keeping-fools [2] enough for such flaunting baggages, and they are e'en too good 95
for 'em. (*To* EMILIA) Remember 'night.
Go; you're a rogue, you're a rogue! Fare you
well, fare you well! — Come, come, come
along, sir! (*Exeunt* OLD *and* YOUNG BELLAIR.

Lady Town. On my word, the old man 100
comes on apace. I'll lay my life he's smitten.

Emil. This is nothing but the pleasantness
of his humor.

Lady Town. I know him better than you.
Let it work; it may prove lucky. 105

Enter a Page

Page. Madam, Mr. Medley has sent to
know whether a visit will not be troublesome
this afternoon.

Lady Town. Send him word his visits never
are so. (*Exit* Page. 110

Emil. He's a very pleasant man.

Lady Town. He's a very necessary man
among us women; he's not scandalous i' the
least, perpetually contriving to bring good
company together, and always ready to 115
stop up a gap at ombre.[3] Then, he knows all
the little news o' the town.

Emil. I love to hear him talk o' the intrigues.
Let 'em be never so dull in themselves, he'll
make 'em pleasant i' the relation. 120

Lady Town. But he improves things so much
one can take no measure of the truth from him.
Mr. Dorimant swears a flea or a maggot is not
made more monstrous by a magnifying glass
than a story is by his telling it. 125

[1] Pox; i.e., a plague on, etc.
[2] I.e., keepers of mistresses.
[3] A card game of Spanish origin, usually played by
three persons, and very popular at this period.

Enter MEDLEY

Emil. Hold, here he comes.

Lady Town. Mr. Medley.

Med. Your servant, madam.

Lady Town. You have made yourself a
stranger of late. 130

Emil. I believe you took a surfeit of ombre
last time you were here.

Med. Indeed, I had my belly full of that
termagant, Lady Dealer. There never was so
insatiable a carder,[1] an old gleeker [2] 135
never loved to sit to't like her. I have played
with her now at least a dozen times till she's
worn out all her fine complexion and her
tower [3] would keep in curl no longer.

Lady Town. Blame her not, poor wo- 140
man, she loves nothing so well as a black ace.[4]

Med. The pleasure I have seen her in when
she has had hope in drawing for a matadore.[5]

Emil. 'Tis as pretty sport to her as persuading masks off is to you, to make discov- 145
eries.

Lady Town. Pray, where's your friend Mr.
Dorimant?

Med. Soliciting his affairs; he's a man of
great employment — has more mistresses 150
now depending than the most eminent lawyer
in England has causes.[6]

Emil. Here has been Mrs. Loveit so uneasy
and out of humor these two days.

Lady Town. How strangely love and 155
jealousy rage in that poor woman!

Med. She could not have picked out a devil
upon earth so proper to torment her; h'as made
her break a dozen or two fans already, tear half
a score points [7] in pieces, and destroy hoods 160
and knots [8] without number.

Lady Town. We heard of a pleasant serenade he gave her t'other night.

[1] Gamester.
[2] Card player. Gleek was another popular game for
three people.
[3] Headdress of hair piled up high.
[4] The ace of spades, the highest trump in ombre; or
the ace of clubs, the third highest.
[5] The deuce of a black trump suit, or the seven of a
red one.
[6] Cases.   [7] Lace kerchiefs.
[8] Bows of ribbon.

Med. A Danish serenade with kettle-drums and trumpets.　165

Emil. Oh, barbarous!

Med. What! You are of the number of the ladies whose ears are grown so delicate since our operas [1] you can be charmed with nothing but *flute doux* [2] and French hautboys.[3]　170

Emil. Leave your raillery, and tell us is there any new wit come forth — songs or novels?

Med. A very pretty piece of gallantry, by an eminent author, called *The Diversions*　175 *of Brussels*,[4] very necessary to be read by all old ladies who are desirous to improve themselves at questions and commands, blindman's buff, and the like fashionable recreations.

Emil. Oh, ridiculous!　180

Med. Then there is *The Art of Affectation*, written by a late beauty of quality, teaching you how to draw up your breasts, stretch out your neck, to thrust out your breech, to play with your head, to toss up your nose,　185 to bite your lips, to turn up your eyes, to speak in a silly, soft tone of a voice, and use all the foolish French words that will infallibly make your person and conversation charming — with a short apology at the latter end　190 in the behalf of young ladies who notoriously wash and paint though they have naturally good complexions.

Emil. What a deal of stuff you tell us!

Med. Such as the town affords, mad-　195 am. The Russians, hearing the great respect we have for foreign dancing, have lately sent over some of their best balladines,[5] who are now practicing a famous ballet which will be suddenly [6] danced at the Bear Garden.[7]　200

Lady Town. Pray, forbear your idle stories,

and give us an account of the state of love as it now stands.

Med. Truly, there have been some revolutions in those affairs — great chopping　205 and changing among the old, and some new lovers whom malice, indiscretion, and misfortune have luckily brought into play.

Lady Town. What think you of walking into the next room and sitting down before　210 you engage in this business?

Med. I wait upon you, and I hope (though women are commonly unreasonable) by the plenty of scandal I shall discover, to give you very good content, ladies.　(*Exeunt.*　215

SCENE 2. MRS. LOVEIT'S *dressing-room.*

Enter MRS. LOVEIT *and* PERT, *her maid.*
MRS. LOVEIT *puts up a letter, then draws out a pocket-glass and looks in it*

Mrs. Lov. Pert.

Pert. Madam?

Mrs. Lov. I hate myself, I look so ill today.

Pert. Hate the wicked cause on't, that base man Mr. Dorimant, who makes you tor-　5 ment and vex yourself continually.

Mrs. Lov. He is to blame, indeed.

Pert. — To blame to be two days without sending, writing, or coming near you, contrary to his oath and covenant! 'Twas to much　10 purpose to make him swear! I'll lay my life there's not an article but he has broken — talked to the vizards i' the pit, waited upon the ladies from the boxes to their coaches, gone behind the scenes, and fawned upon those　15 little insignificant creatures, the players. 'Tis impossible for a man of his inconstant temper to forbear, I'm sure.

Mrs. Lov. I know he is a devil, but he has something of the angel yet undefaced in　20 him, which makes him so charming and agreeable that I must love him, be he never so wicked.

Pert. I little thought, madam, to see your spirit tamed to this degree, who banished　25 poor Mr. Lackwit but for taking up another lady's fan in your presence.

Mrs. Lov. My knowing of such odious fools

---

[1] Not opera of the Italian type, but a hybrid variety with dialogue and singing mixed, got under way at London in the early sixteen-seventies and was the last word in modish entertainment.

[2] An obsolete kind of flute.　[3] Oboes.

[4] This book, and *The Art of Affectation* mentioned in Medley's next speech, are both his inventions.

[5] Ballet dancers.　[6] Shortly.

[7] A notorious resort in the Bankside, Southwark, across the Thames River from the old city limits of London. From the sixteenth century bear- and bull-baiting, cock- and dog-fighting, and like pastimes, had taken place there regularly.

contributes to the making of me love Dorimant the better.   30

Pert. Your knowing of Mr. Dorimant, in my mind, should rather make you hate all mankind.

Mrs. Lov. So it does — besides himself.

Pert. Pray, what excuse does he make   35 in his letter?

Mrs. Lov. He has had business.

Pert. Business in general terms would not have been a current excuse for another. A modish man is always "very busy" when   40 he is in pursuit of a new mistress.

Mrs. Lov. Some fop has bribed you to rail at him. He had business; I will believe it, and will forgive him.

Pert. You may forgive him anything,   45 but I shall never forgive him his turning me into ridicule, as I hear he does.

Mrs. Lov. I perceive you are of the number of those fools his wit has made his enemies.

Pert. I am of the number of those he's   50 pleased to rally, madam, and if we may believe Mr. Wagfan and Mr. Caperwell, he sometimes makes merry with yourself too, among his laughing companions.

Mrs. Lov. Blockheads are as malicious   55 to witty men as ugly women are to the handsome; 'tis their interest, and they make it their business to defame 'em.

Pert. I wish Mr. Dorimant would not make it his business to defame you.   60

Mrs. Lov. Should he, I had rather be made infamous by him than owe my reputation to the dull discretion of those fops you talk of.

Enter BELLINDA

— Bellinda!   (*Running to her.*

Bel. My dear!   65

Mrs. Lov. You have been unkind of late.

Bel. Do not say unkind, say unhappy.

Mrs. Lov. I could chide you. Where have you been these two days?

Bel. Pity me rather, my dear, where I   70 have been so tired with two or three country gentlemen, whose conversation has been more unsufferable than a country fiddle.

Mrs. Lov. Are they relations?

Bel. No; Welsh acquaintance I made   75 when I was last year at St. Winifred's.[1] They have asked me a thousand questions of the modes and intrigues of the town, and I have told 'em almost as many things for news that hardly were so when their gowns were in   80 fashion.

Mrs. Lov. Provoking creatures! How could you endure 'em?

Bel. (*aside*). Now to carry on my plot. Nothing but love could make me capable   85 of so much falsehood. 'Tis time to begin, lest Dorimant should come before her jealousy has stung her. (*Laughs, and then speaks on.*) I was yesterday at a play with 'em, where I was fain to show 'em the living, as the man at   90 Westminster [2] does the dead: "That is Mrs. Such-a-one, admired for her beauty; that is Mr. Such-a-one, cried up for a wit; that is sparkish Mr. Such-a-one, who keeps reverend Mrs. Such-a-one, and there sits fine Mrs.   95 Such-a-one who was lately cast off by my Lord Such-a-one."

Mrs. Lov. Did you see Dorimant there?

Bel. I did, and imagine you were with him and have no mind to own it.   100

Mrs. Lov. What should make you think so?

Bel. A lady masked in a pretty dishabille, whom Dorimant entertained with more respect than the gallants do a common vizard.

Mrs. Lov. (*aside*). Dorimant at the   105 play entertaining a mask! Oh, heavens!

Bel. (*aside*). Good!

Mrs. Lov. Did he stay all the while?

Bel. Till the play was done and then led her out, which confirms me it was you.   110

Mrs. Lov. Traitor!

Pert. Now you may believe he has business, and you may forgive him, too.

Mrs. Lov. Ingrateful, perjured man!

Bel. You seem so much concerned, my   115 dear, I fear I have told you unawares what I had better have concealed for your quiet.

Mrs. Lov. What manner of shape had she?

Bel. Tall and slender. Her motions were

---

[1] St. Winifred's Well, a resort in Flintshire, Wales.

[2] The official guide who showed visitors around the tombs of Westminster Abbey even as early as the seventeenth century.

very genteel; certainly she must be some　120
person of condition.

Mrs. Lov. Shame and confusion be ever in
her face when she shows it!

Bel. I should blame your discretion for loving that wild man, my dear, but they say　125
he has a way so bewitching that few can defend their hearts who know him.

Mrs. Lov. I will tear him out from mine or
die i' the attempt.

Bel. Be more moderate.　130

Mrs. Lov. Would I had daggers, darts, or
poisoned arrows in my breast, so I could but
remove the thoughts of him from thence!

Bel. Fie, fie! your transports are too violent,
my dear; this may be but an accidental　135
gallantry, and 'tis likely ended at her coach.

Pert. Should it proceed farther, let your
comfort be, the conduct Mr. Dorimant affects
will quickly make you know your rival, ten to
one let you see her ruined, her reputation　140
exposed to the town — a happiness none will
envy her but yourself, madam.

Mrs. Lov. Whoe'er she be, all the harm I
wish her is, may she love him as well as I do
and may he give her as much cause to　145
hate him.

Pert. Never doubt the latter end of your
curse, madam.

Mrs. Lov. May all the passions that are
raised by neglected love — jealousy, in-　150
dignation, spite, and thirst of revenge — eternally rage in her soul as they do now in mine.

(*Walks up and down with a distracted air.*

Enter a Page

Page. Madam, Master Dorimant —

Mrs. Lov. I will not see him.

Page. I told him you were within,　155
madam.

Mrs. Lov. Say you lied — say I'm busy;
shut the door! — Say anything!

Page. He's here, madam.

Enter DORIMANT

Dor.
They taste of death who do at heaven arrive;
But we this paradise approach alive.[1]　161

---

[1] Waller's poem, "Of Her Chamber," ll. 1–2.

(*To* MISTRESS LOVEIT) What, dancing "The
Galloping Nag"[1] without a fiddle? (*Offers to
catch her by the hand. She flings away and
walks on, he pursuing her.*) I fear this rest-
lessness of the body, madam, proceeds　165
from an unquietness of the mind. What unlucky accident puts you out of humor? — A
point ill washed, knots spoiled i' the making
up, hair shaded awry, or some other little
mistake in setting you in order?　170

Pert. A trifle, in your opinion, sir, more inconsiderable than any you mention.

Dor. Oh, Mrs. Pert! I never knew you
sullen enough to be silent; come, let me know
the business.　175

Pert. The business, sir, is the business that
has taken you up these two days. How have
I seen you laugh at men of business, and now
to become a man of business yourself!

Dor. We are not masters of our affec-　180
tions; our inclinations daily alter. Now we love
pleasure, and anon we shall dote on business.
Human frailty will have it so, and who can
help it?

Mrs. Lov. Faithless, inhuman, barba-　185
rous man —

Dor. (*aside*). Good! Now the alarm
strikes.

Mrs. Lov. — Without sense of love, of honor,
or of gratitude, tell me, for I will know,　190
what devil masked she was you were with at
the play yesterday?

Dor. Faith, I resolved as much as you,
but the devil was obstinate and would not
tell me.　195

Mrs. Lov. False in this as in your vows to
me! You do know.

Dor. The truth is, I did all I could to
know.

Mrs. Lov. And dare you own it to my　200
face? Hell and furies!

(*Tears her fan in pieces.*

Dor. Spare your fan, madam; you are growing hot and will want it to cool you.

Mrs. Lov. Horror and distraction seize you!
Sorrow and remorse gnaw your soul, and　205
punish all your perjuries to me!　(*Weeps.*

---

[1] A popular country dance.

Dor.

So thunder breaks the cloud in twain
And makes a passage for the rain.[1]
(*Turning to* BELLINDA) Bellinda, you are the
devil that has raised this storm; you were   210
at the play yesterday and have been making
discoveries to your dear.

Bel. You're the most mistaken man i' the
world.

Dor. It must be so, and here I vow re-   215
venge; resolve to pursue and persecute you more
impertinently than ever any loving fop did
his mistress, hunt you i' the Park,[2] trace you
i' the Mall,[3] dog you in every visit you make,
haunt you at the plays and i' the drawing-   220
room, hang my nose in your neck and talk to
you whether you will or no, and ever look upon
you with such dying eyes till your friends grow
jealous of me, send you out of town, and the
world suspect your reputation. (*In a*   225
lower voice) At my Lady Townley's when we
go from hence. (*He looks kindly on* BELLINDA.

Bel. I'll meet you there.

Dor. Enough.

Mrs. Lov. Stand off! (*Pushing* DORI-   230
MANT *away*) You sha' not stare upon her so.

Dor. Good; there's one made jealous already.

Mrs. Lov. Is this the constancy you vowed?

Dor. Constancy at my years? 'Tis not   235
a virtue in season; you might as well expect
the fruit the autumn ripens i' the spring.

Mrs. Lov. Monstrous principle!

Dor. Youth has a long journey to go,
madam; should I have set up my rest [4]   240
at the first inn I lodged at, I should never
have arrived at the happiness I now enjoy.

Mrs. Lov. Dissembler, damned dissembler!

Dor. I am so, I confess. Good nature and
good manners corrupt me. I am honest   245
in my inclinations, and would not, wer't not to
avoid offense, make a lady in years believe I
think her young — willfully mistake art for
nature — and seem as fond of a thing I am
weary of as when I doted on't in earnest.   250

Mrs. Lov. False man!

Dor. True woman!

Mrs. Lov. Now you begin to show yourself.

Dor. Love gilds us over and makes us show
fine things to one another for a time, but   255
soon the gold wears off and then again the
native brass appears.

Mrs. Lov. Think on your oaths, your vows,
and protestations, perjured man!

Dor. I made 'em when I was in love.   260

Mrs. Lov. And therefore ought they not to
bind? Oh, impious!

Dor. What we swear at such a time may be a
certain proof of a present passion, but to say
truth, in love there is no security to be   265
given for the future.

Mrs. Lov. Horrid and ingrateful! Begone,
and never see me more!

Dor. I am not one of those troublesome coxcombs who, because they were once well   270
received, take the privilege to plague a woman
with their love ever after. I shall obey you,
madam, though I do myself some violence.

(*Offers to go and* MRS. LOVEIT *pulls
him back.*)

Mrs. Lov. Come back! You sha' not go!
Could you have the ill-nature to offer it?   275

Dor. When love grows diseased, the best
thing we can do is to put it to a violent death.
I cannot endure the torture of a ling'ring and
consumptive passion.

Mrs. Lov. Can you think mine sickly?   280

Dor. Oh, it is desperately ill. What worse
symptoms are there than you being always
uneasy when I visit you, your picking quarrels with me on slight occasions, and in my
absence kindly listening to the imperti-   285
nences of every fashionable fool that talks to
you?

Mrs. Lov. What fashionable fool can you
lay to my charge?

Dor. Why, the very cock-fool of all   290
those fools — Sir Fopling Flutter.

Mrs. Lov. I never saw him in my life but
once

---

[1] The source of this couplet remains unlocated.

[2] I.e., Hyde Park.

[3] A gravel walk in St. James's Park, constructed by
Charles II in the early 1660's as an enclosure for playing his favorite game of "pall mall," a game in which a
large wooden ball is driven by a mallet through a series
of hoops set in an alley. This gravel walk soon became a fashionable rendezvous. See Act III, Scene 3.

[4] Abode.

Dor. The worse woman you, at first sight to put on all your charms, to entertain him　295 with that softness in your voice, and all that wanton kindness in your eyes you so notoriously affect when you design a conquest.

Mrs. Lov. So damned a lie did never malice yet invent.　Who told you this?　300

Dor. No matter.　That ever I should love a woman that can dote on a senseless caper, a tawdry French ribband, and a formal cravat!

Mrs. Lov. You make me mad.

Dor. A guilty conscience may do　305 much.　Go on — be the game-mistress o' the town, and enter[1] all our young fops as fast as they come from travel.

Mrs. Lov. Base and scurrilous!

Dor. A fine mortifying reputation 'twill　310 be for a woman of your pride, wit, and quality!

Mrs. Lov. This jealousy's a mere pretense, a cursed trick of your own devising. — I know you.

Dor. Believe it and all the ill of me you　315 can, I would not have a woman have the least good thought of me, that can think well of Fopling.　Farewell!　Fall to, and much good may you do with your coxcomb.

Mrs. Lov. Stay!　Oh stay! and I will　320 tell you all!

Dor. I have been told too much already.　(*Exit.*

Mrs. Lov. Call him again!

Pert. E'en let him go — a fair riddance.　325

Mrs. Lov. Run, I say!　Call him again!　I will have him called!

Pert. The devil should call him away first, were it my concern.　(*Exit.*

Bel. He's frightened me from the　330 very thoughts of loving men.　For heaven's sake, my dear, do not discover[2] what I told you! I dread his tongue as much as you ought to have done his friendship.

Enter PERT

Pert. He's gone, madam.　335

Mrs. Lov. Lightning blast him!

Pert. When I told him you desired him to come back, he smiled, made a mouth at me, flung into his coach, and said —

Mrs. Lov. What did he say?　340

Pert. "Drive away!" and then repeated verses.

Mrs. Lov. Would I had made a contract to be a witch when first I entertained this greater devil — monster — barbarian!　I could　345 tear myself in pieces.　Revenge — nothing but revenge can ease me!　Plague, war, famine, fire — all that can bring universal ruin and misery on mankind, with joy I'd perish to have you in my power but this moment!　(*Exit.*

Pert. Follow, madam; leave her not in　351 this outrageous passion!　(*Gathers up the things.*

Bel. He's given me the proof which I desired of his love, but 'tis a proof of his ill-nature too. I wish I had not seen him use her so.　355

I sigh to think that Dorimant may be
One day as faithless and unkind to me.

(*Exeunt.*

ACT III

SCENE I. LADY WOODVILL'S *lodgings.*

Enter HARRIET *and* BUSY, *her woman*

Busy. Dear madam, let me see that curl in order.

Har. Let me alone; I will shake 'em all out of order.

Busy. Will you never leave this wildness?　5

Har. Torment me not.

Busy. Look! there's a knot falling off.

Har. Let it drop.

Busy. But one pin, dear madam.

Har. How do I daily suffer under thy　10 officious fingers!

Busy. Ah, the difference that is between you and my Lady Dapper!　How uneasy she is if the least thing be amiss about her!

Har. She is indeed most exact; nothing　15 is ever wanting to make her ugliness remarkable.

Busy. Jeering people say so.

Har. Her powdering, painting, and her patching never fail in public to draw the　20 tongues and eyes of all the men upon her.

Busy. She is, indeed, a little too pretending.

Har. That women should set up for beauty

---

[1] Initiate.　　[2] Reveal.

as much in spite of nature as some men have done for wit!   25

Busy. I hope without offense one may endeavor to make one's self agreeable.

Har. Not when 'tis impossible. Women then ought to be no more fond of dressing than fools should be of talking; hoods and mod-   30 esty, masks and silence — things that shadow and conceal — they should think of nothing else.

Busy. Jesu! Madam, what will your mother think is become of you? For heaven's   35 sake go in again!

Har. I won't.

Busy. This is the extravagant'st thing that ever you did in your life, to leave her and a gentleman who is to be your husband.   40

Har. My husband! Hast thou so little wit to think I spoke what I meant when I overjoyed her in the country with a low curtsey and "What you please, madam; I shall ever be obedient"?   45

Busy. Nay, I know not, you have so many fetches.[1]

Har. And this was one to get her up to London — nothing else, I assure thee.

Busy. Well, the man, in my mind, is a   50 fine man.

Har. The man indeed wears his clothes fashionably and has a pretty, negligent way with him, very courtly and much affected; he bows, and talks, and smiles so agreeably   55 as he thinks.

Busy. I never saw anything so genteel.

Har. Varnished over with good breeding, many a blockhead makes a tolerable show.

Busy. I wonder you do not like him.   60

Har. I think I might be brought to endure him, and that is all a reasonable woman should expect in a husband; but there is duty i' the case, and like the haughty Merab
I find much aversion in my stubborn
    mind,   65
Which is bred by being promised and designed.[2]

---

[1] Stratagems.

[2] Merab, the elder daughter of Saul, who promised her to David and then gave her to Adriel (*I Samuel* XVIII. 17–19). In his epic poem, *Davideis*, first pub-

Busy. I wish you do not design your own ruin! I partly guess your inclinations, madam — that Mr. Dorimant —

Har. Leave your prating, and sing   70 some foolish song or other.

Busy. I will, the song you love so well ever since you saw Mr. Dorimant.

Song

When first Amintas charmed my heart,
My heedless sheep began to stray;   75
The wolves soon stole the greatest part,
And all will now be made a prey.

Ah, let not love your thoughts possess,
'Tis fatal to a shepherdess;
The dang'rous passion you must shun,   80
Or else like me be quite undone.

Har. Shall I be paid down by a covetous parent for a purchase? I need no land; no, I'll lay myself out all in love. It is decreed ——

Enter YOUNG BELLAIR

Young Bel. What generous resolution   85 are you in making, madam?

Har. Only to be disobedient, sir.

Young Bel. Let me join hands with you in that ——

Har. With all my heart. I never   90 thought I should have given you mine so willingly. Here I, Harriet ——

Young Bel. And I, Harry ——

Har. Do solemnly protest ——

Young Bel. And vow ——   95

Har. That I with you ——

Young Bel. And I with you ——

Both. Will never marry.

Harriet. A match!

Young Bel. And no match! How do   100 you like this indifference now?

Har. You expect I should take it ill, I see.

Young Bel. 'Tis not unnatural for you women to be a little angry; you miss a con-

---

lished in 1656 but still very fashionable in the 1660's and 1670's, Abraham Cowley (1618–67) depicted Merab as a haughty lady. Harriet paraphrases ll. 705–06 of the *Davideis*, Book III.

quest, though you would slight the poor 105
man were he in your power.

Har. There are some, it may be, have an
eye like Bart'lomew [1] — big enough for the
whole fair; but I am not of the number, and
you may keep your gingerbread. 'Twill 110
be more acceptable to the lady whose dear
image it wears, sir.

Young Bel. But I confess, madam, you came
a day after the fair.

Har. You own, then, you are in love? 115

Young Bel. I do.

Har. The confidence is generous, and in return I could almost find in my heart to let you
know my inclinations.

Young Bel. Are you in love? 120

Har. Yes, with this dear town, to that degree I can scarce endure the country in land-
scapes and hangings.

Young Bel. What a dreadful thing 'twould
be to be hurried back to Hampshire! 125

Har. Ah, name it not!

Young Bel. As for us, I find we shall agree
well enough. Would we could do something
to deceive the grave people!

Har. Could we delay their quick pro- 130
ceeding, 'twere well. A reprieve is a good step
towards the getting of a pardon.

Young Bel. If we give over the game, we are
undone. What think you of playing it on
booty? [2] 135

Har. What do you mean?

Young Bel. Pretend to be in love with one
another! 'twill make some dilatory excuses we
may feign, pass the better.

Har. Let us do't, if it be but for the 140
dear pleasure of dissembling.

Young Bel. Can you play your part?

Har. I know not what it is to love, but I
have made pretty remarks [3] by being now and
then where lovers meet. Where did you 145
leave your gravities?

Young Bel. I' th' next room! Your mother
was censuring our modern [4] gallant.

<hr>

[1] An allusion to the rolling, staring eyes of the puppets in the many shows at Bartholomew Fair, formerly
held each year in Smithfield, London. Enamored
swains at the fair bought gingerbread cakes of fancy
design to present to their lady loves.

[2] Dishonestly. [3] Observations. [4] Ordinary.

Enter OLD BELLAIR *and* LADY WOODVILL

Har. Peace! Here they come; I will lean
against this wall and look bashfully down 150
upon my fan, while you, like an amorous spark,
modishly entertain me.

Lady Wood. (to OLD BELLAIR). Never go
about to excuse 'em; come, come, it was not so
when I was a young woman. 155

Old Bel. A dod, they're something disrespect-
ful ——

Lady Wood. Quality was then considered
and not rallied by every fleering fellow.

Old Bel. Youth will have its jest — a 160
dod, it will.

Lady Wood. 'Tis good breeding now to be
civil to none but players and Exchange
women; [1] they are treated by 'em as much
above their condition as others are below 165
theirs.

Old Bel. Out! A pize on 'em; talk no
more! The rogues ha' got an ill habit of pre-
ferring beauty no matter where they find it.

Lady Wood. See your son and my 170
daughter; they have improved their acquaintance since they were within.

Old Bel. A dod, methinks they have! Let's
keep back and observe.

Young Bel. (to HARRIET). Now for a 175
look and gestures that may persuade 'em I am
saying all the passionate things imaginable —

Har. Your head a little more on one side.
Ease yourself on your left leg and play with
your right hand. 180

Young Bel. Thus, is it not?

Har. Now set your right leg firm on the
ground, adjust your belt, then look about you.

Young Bel. A little exercising will make me
perfect. 185

Har. Smile, and turn to me again very sparkish.

Young Bel. Will you take your turn and be
instructed?

Har. With all my heart! 190

Young Bel. At one motion play your fan,
roll your eyes, and then settle a kind look
upon me.

Har. So!

<hr>

[1] Shop-women in the New Exchange.

Young Bel. Now spread your fan, look 195 down upon it, and tell[1] the sticks with a finger.

Har. Very modish!

Young Bel. Clap your hand up to your bosom, hold down your gown, shrug a little, draw up your breasts, and let 'em fall 200 again gently, with a sigh or two ——

Har. By the instructions you give, I suspect you for one of those malicious observers who watch people's eyes, and from innocent looks make scandalous conclusions. 205

Young Bel. I know some, indeed, who out of mere love to mischief are as vigilant as jealousy itself, and will give you an account of every glance that passes at a play and i' th' Circle.[2]

Har. 'Twill not be amiss now to seem a 210 little pleasant.

Young Bel. Clap your fan, then, in both your hands — snatch it to your mouth — smile — and with a lively motion fling your body a little forwards. So! Now spread 215 it — fall back on the sudden — cover your face with it and break out into loud laughter. Take up! look grave and fall a-fanning of yourself. — Admirably well acted!

Har. I think I am pretty apt at these 220 matters.

Old Bel. (*to* LADY WOODVILL). A dod, I like this well!

Lady Wood. This promises something.

Old Bel. Come! there is love i' th' case 225 — a dod there is, or will be. — (*To* HARRIET) What say you, young lady?

Young Bel. All in good time, sir; you expect we should fall to and love as game-cocks fight, as soon as we are set together? A dod, 230 you're unreasonable!

Old Bel. A dod, sirrah, I like thy wit well.

Enter a Servant

Serv. The coach is at the door, madam.

Old Bel. Go! get you and take the air together. 235

Lady Wood. Will not you go with us?

Old Bel. Out, a pize! A dod, I ha' business

[1] Count.
[2] The Ring in Hyde Park, where the most fashionable society paraded.

and cannot. We shall meet at night at my sister Townley's.

Young Bel. (*aside*). He's going to 240 Emilia. I overheard him talk of a collation.[1]

(*Exeunt.*

SCENE 2.   LADY TOWNLEY'S *drawing-room.*

Enter LADY TOWNLEY, EMILIA, *and* MR. MEDLEY

Lady Town. I pity the young lovers we last talked of, though to say truth their conduct has been so discreet they deserve to be unfortunate.

Med. Y'have had an exact account, from 5 the great lady i' th' box down to the little orange wench.

Emil. You're a living libel — a breathing lampoon. I wonder you are not torn in pieces.

Med. What think you of setting up an 10 office of intelligence for these matters? The project may get money.

Lady Town. You would have great dealings with country ladies.

Med. More than Muddiman[2] has with 15 their husbands.

Enter BELLINDA

Lady Town. Bellinda, what has been become of you? We have not seen you here of late with your friend Mrs. Loveit.

Bel. Dear creature, I have left her but 20 now so sadly afflicted!

Lady Town. With her old distemper, jealousy?

Med. Dorimant has played her some new prank. 25

Bel. Well, that Dorimant is certainly the worst man breathing.

Emil. I once thought so.

Bel. And do you not think so still?

Emil. No, indeed! 30

Bel. Oh, Jesu!

[1] Luncheon.
[2] Henry Muddiman (1629–92), whose "news-letters" were subscribed to by hundreds of clients all over England, especially by the country gentry.

Emil. The town does him a great injury, and I will never believe what it says of a man I do not know again, for his sake.

Bel. You make me wonder.   35

Lady Town. He's a very well-bred man.

Bel. But strangely ill-natured.

Emil. Then, he's a very witty man.

Bel. But a man of no principles.

Med. Your man of principles is a very   40 fine thing, indeed.

Bel. To be preferred to men of parts by women who have regard to their reputation and quiet. Well, were I minded to play the fool, he should be the last man I'd think   45 of.

Med. He has been the first in many ladies' favors, though you are so severe, madam.

Lady Town. What he may be for a lover, I know not; but he's a very pleasant ac-   50 quaintance, I am sure.

Bel. Had you seen him use Mrs. Loveit as I have done, you would never endure him more ——

Emil. What, has he quarreled with her   55 again?

Bel. Upon the slightest occasion; he's jealous of Sir Fopling.

Lady Town. She never saw him in her life but yesterday, and that was here.   60

Emil. On my conscience, he's the only man in town that's her aversion. How horribly out of humor she was all the time he talked to her!

Bel. And somebody has wickedly told   65 him ——

Emil. Here he comes.

Enter DORIMANT

Med. Dorimant! you are luckily come to justify yourself. — Here's a lady ——

Bel. Has a word or two to say to you   70 from a disconsolate person.

Dor. You tender [1] your reputation too much, I know, madam, to whisper with me before this good company.

Bel. To serve Mrs. Loveit I'll make a   75 bold venture.

[1] Cherish.

Dor. Here's Medley — the very spirit of scandal.

Bel. No matter!

Emil. 'Tis something you are unwilling   80 to hear, Mr. Dorimant.

Lady Town. Tell him, Bellinda, whether he will or no.

Bel. (aloud). Mrs. Loveit ——

Dor. Softly! these are laughers; you   85 do not know 'em.

Bel. (to DORIMANT *apart).* In a word, y'ave made me hate you, which I thought you never could have done.

Dor. In obeying your commands.   90

Bel. 'Twas a cruel part you played. How could you act it?

Dor. Nothing is cruel to a man who could kill himself to please you. Remember five o'clock tomorrow morning!   95

Bel. I tremble when you name it.

Dor. Be sure you come!

Bel. I sha' not.

Dor. Swear you will!

Bel. I dare not.   100

Dor. Swear, I say!

Bel. By my life — by all the happiness I hope for ——

Dor. You will.

Bel. I will!   105

Dor. Kind!

Bel. I am glad I've sworn. I vow, I think I should ha' failed you else!

Dor. Surprisingly kind! In what temper did you leave Loveit?   110

Bel. Her raving was prettily over, and she began to be in a brave way of defying you and all your works. Where have you been since you went from thence?

Dor. I looked in at the play.   115

Bel. I have promised, and must return to her again.

Dor. Persuade her to walk in the Mall this evening.

Bel. She hates the place and will not   120 come.

Dor. Do all you can to prevail with her.

Bel. For what purpose?

Dor. Sir Fopling will be here anon; I'll prepare him to set upon her there before me. 125

Bel. You persecute her too much — but I'll do all you'll ha' me.

Dor. (*aloud*). Tell her plainly 'tis grown too dull a business; I can drudge no longer.

Emil. There are afflictions in love, 130 Mr. Dorimant.

Dor. You women make 'em, who are commonly as unreasonable in that as you are at play. Without the advantage be on your side, a man can never quietly give over 135 when he's weary.

Med. If you would play without being obliged to complaisance, Dorimant, you should play in public places.

Dor. Ordinaries[1] were a very good thing 140 for that, but gentlemen do not of late frequent 'em. The deep play is now in private houses.

(BELLINDA *starts to leave.*)

Lady Town. Bellinda, are you leaving us so soon?

Bel. I am going to the Park with 145 Mrs. Loveit, madam. (*Exit.*

Lady Town. This confidence[2] will go nigh to spoil this young creature.

Med. 'Twill do her good, madam. Young men who are bred up under practicing 150 lawyers prove the abler counsel when they come to be called to the bar themselves.

Dor. The town has been very favorable to you this afternoon, my Lady Townley; you used to have an *embarras*[3] of chairs and 155 coaches at your door, an uproar of footmen in your hall, and a noise of fools above here.

Lady Town. Indeed, my house is the general rendezvous, and next to the playhouse is the common refuge of all the young, 160 idle people.

Emil. Company is a very good thing, madam, but I wonder you do not love it a little more chosen.

Lady Town. 'Tis good to have an uni- 165 versal taste; we should love wit, but for variety be able to divert ourselves with the extravagancies of those who want it.

Med. Fools will make you laugh.

Emil. For once or twice, but the repe- 170 tition of their folly after a visit or two grows tedious and unsufferable.

Enter a Page

Page. Sir Fopling Flutter, madam, desires to know if you are to be seen.

Lady Town. Here's the freshest fool 175 in town, and one who has not cloyed you yet. — Page!

Page. Madam?

Lady Town. Desire him to walk up.

Dor. Do not fall on him, Medley, and 180 snub him. Soothe him up in his extravagance; he will show the better.

Med. You know I have a natural indulgence for fools and need not this caution, sir.

Enter SIR FOPLING FLUTTER *with his* Page *after him*

Sir Fop. Page, wait without. (*To* LADY 185 TOWNLEY) Madam, I kiss your hands. I see yesterday was nothing of chance; the *belles assemblées*[1] form themselves here every day. (*To* EMILIA) Lady, your servant. — Dorimant, let me embrace thee! Without lying, I 190 have not met with any of my acquaintance who retain so much of Paris as thou dost — the very air thou hadst when the marquise mistook thee i' th' Tuileries[2] and cried, "Hey, Chevalier!" and then begged thy par- 195 don.

Dor. I would fain wear in fashion as long as I can, sir; 'tis a thing to be valued in men as well as baubles.

Sir Fop. Thou art a man of wit and un- 200 derstandst the town. Prithee, let thee and I be intimate; there is no living without making some good man the confidant of our pleasures.

Dor. 'Tis true! but there is no man so improper for such a business as I am. 205

Sir Fop. Prithee, why hast thou so modest an opinion of thyself?

Dor. Why, first, I could never keep a secret in my life; and then, there is no charm so infal-

---

[1] Taverns where regular meals were served.
[2] Intimacy.
[3] Crush.

[1] Fashionable gatherings.
[2] The palace of Louis XIV in Paris near the Louvre. It is no longer in existence.

libly makes me fall in love with a woman   210
as my knowing a friend loves her. — I deal
honestly with you.

Sir Fop. Thy humor's very gallant, or let me
perish! I knew a French count so like you!

Lady Town. Wit, I perceive, has more   215
power over you than beauty, Sir Fopling, else
you would not have let this lady stand so long
neglected.

Sir Fop. (*to* EMILIA). A thousand pardons,
madam; some civilities due of course upon   220
the meeting a long absent friend.   The *éclat* ¹ of
so much beauty, I confess, ought to have
charmed me sooner.

Emil. The *brilliant* ² of so much good language, sir, has much more power than the   225
little beauty I can boast.

Sir Fop. I never saw anything prettier than
this high work on your *point d'Espagne.*³

Emil. 'Tis not so rich as *point de Venise.*⁴

Sir Fop. Not altogether, but looks   230
cooler and is more proper for the season. —
Dorimant, is not that Medley?

Dor. The same, sir.

Sir Fop. Forgive me, sir; in this *embarras* ⁵
of civilities I could not come to have you   235
in my arms sooner.   You understand an equi-
page⁶ the best of any man in town, I hear.

Med. By my own you would not guess it.

Sir Fop. There are critics who do not write,
sir.   240

Med. Our peevish poets will scarce allow it.

Sir Fop. Damn 'em, they'll allow no man
wit who does not play the fool like themselves and show it!   Have you taken notice of
the *calèche* ⁷ I brought over?   245

Med. Oh, yes!   It has quite another air
than the English makes.

Sir Fop. 'Tis as easily known from an
English tumbril⁸ as an Inns-of-Court man ⁹
is from one of us.   250

Dor. True; there is a *bel air* ¹⁰ in *calèches* as
well as men.

---

¹ Dazzling effect.   ² Sparkle.   ³ Spanish lace.
⁴ Venetian lace.   ⁵ See l. 155 and note.
⁶ You know how to manage a retinue of servants.
⁷ Light carriage open.   ⁸ Heavy wagon.
⁹ Lawyer.
¹⁰ Stylish air.

Med. But there are few so delicate to observe it.

Sir Fop. The world is generally very   255
grossier ¹ here, indeed.

Lady Town. He's very fine.

Emil. Extreme proper.²

Sir Fop. A slight suit I made to appear in
at my first arrival — not worthy your   260
consideration, ladies.

Dor. The pantaloon is very well mounted.

Sir Fop. The tassels are new and pretty.

Med. I never saw a coat better cut.

Sir Fop. It makes me show long-   265
waisted, and, I think, slender.

Dor. That's the shape our ladies dote on.

Med. Your breech, though, is a handful too
high, in my eye, Sir Fopling.

Sir Fop. Peace, Medley, I have wished   270
it lower a thousand times, but a pox on't! 'twill
not be.

Lady Town. His gloves are well fringed,
large, and graceful.

Sir Fop. I was always eminent for   275
being *bien ganté.*³

Emil. He wears nothing but what are
originals of the most famous hands in Paris.

Sir Fop. You are in the right, madam.

Lady Town. The suit?   280

Sir Fop. Barroy.⁴

Emil. The garniture? ⁵

Sir Fop. Le Gras.

Med. The shoes?

Sir Fop. Piccar.   285

Dor. The periwig?

Sir Fop. Chedreux.

Lady Town. }
Emil.   }   The gloves?

Sir Fop. Orangerie! ⁶   You know the smell,
ladies.   Dorimant, I could find in my   290
heart for an amusement to have a gallantry
with some of our English ladies.

Dor. 'Tis a thing no less necessary to con-

---

¹ Vulgar; unmannered.
² Extremely elegant.
³ Well-gloved.
⁴ The four French names which Sir Fopling cites in
quick succession were those of Parisian merchants outstanding in their respective lines of goods.
⁵ Trimming.
⁶ Perfumed with orange.

firm the reputation of your wit than a duel will be to satisfy the town of your courage.   295

Sir Fop. Here was a woman yesterday ——

Dor. Mistress Loveit?

Sir Fop. You have named her!

Dor. You cannot pitch on a better for your purpose.   300

Sir Fop. Prithee, what is she?

Dor. A person of quality, and one who has a rest of reputation enough to make the conquest considerable; besides, I hear she likes you too.   305

Sir Fop. Methought she seemed, though, very reserved and uneasy all the time I entertained her.

Dor. Grimace and affectation! You will see her in the Mall tonight.   310

) *Sir Fop.* Prithee, let thee and I take the air together.

Dor. I am engaged to Medley, but I'll meet you at Saint James's and give you some information upon the which you may regu-   315 late your proceedings.

Sir Fop. All the world will be in the Park tonight. Ladies, 'twere pity to keep so much beauty longer within doors and rob the Ring of all those charms that should adorn it.   320 —— Hey, page!

Enter Page

See that all my people be ready.   (*Exit* Page. —— Dorimant, *au revoir*.   (*Exit*.

Med. A fine, mettled coxcomb.

Dor. Brisk and insipid.   325

Med. Pert and dull.

Emil. However you despise him, gentlemen, I'll lay my life he passes for a wit with many.

Dor. That may very well be; Nature   330 has her cheats, stums[1] a brain, and puts sophisticate dullness often on the tasteless multitude for true wit and good humor. Medley, come!

Med. I must go a little way; I will meet   335 you i' the Mall.

Dor. I'll walk through the garden thither. —— (*To the women*) We shall meet anon and bow.

---

[1] Renews by giving a false impression of sparkle.

Lady Town. Not tonight. We are engaged about a business the knowledge of which   340 may make you laugh hereafter.

Med. Your servant, ladies.

Dor. "*Au revoir*," as Sir Fopling says.

(*Exeunt* DORIMANT *and* MEDLEY.

Lady Town. The old man will be here immediately.   345

Emil. Let's expect[1] him i' th' garden.

Lady Town. "Go! you are a rogue."

Emil. "I can't abide you."[2]   (*Exeunt*.

SCENE 3. *The Mall.*

Enter HARRIET *and* YOUNG BELLAIR, *she pulling him*

Har. Come along.

Young Bel. And leave your mother?

Har. Busy will be sent with a hue and cry after us, but that's no matter.

Young Bel. 'Twill look strangely in me.   5

Har. She'll believe it a freak of mine and never blame your manners.

Young Bel. (*looking back, off stage*). What reverend acquaintance is that she has met?

Har. A fellow-beauty of the last king's   10 time, though by the ruins you would hardly guess it.

(*Exeunt* HARRIET *and* YOUNG BELLAIR.

Enter DORIMANT, *who crosses the stage and passes out*

Enter HARRIET *and* YOUNG BELLAIR

Young Bel. By this time your mother is in a fine taking.[3]

Har. If your friend Mr. Dorimant were   15 but here now, that she might find me talking with him!

Young Bel. She does not know him, but dreads him, I hear, of all mankind.

Har. She concludes if he does but speak   20 to a woman, she's undone —— is on her knees every day to pray Heaven defend me from him.

Young Bel. You do not apprehend[4] him so much as she does?

---

[1] Wait for.   [2] See Act II, ll. 80, 97.
[3] In much excitement.   [4] Fear.

Har. I never saw anything in him that   25
was frightful.

Young Bel. On the contrary, have you not
observed something extreme delightful in his
wit and person?

Har. He's agreeable and pleasant, I   30
must own; but he does so much affect being so,
he displeases me.

Young Bel. Lord, madam! all he does and
says is so easy and so natural!

Har. Some men's verses seem so to the   35
unskillful, but labor i' the one and affectation in the other to the judicious plainly appear.

Young Bel. I never heard him accused of
affectation before.   40

Enter DORIMANT *and stares upon her*

Har. It passes on the easy town, who are
favorably pleased in him to call it humor.
(*Exeunt* YOUNG BELLAIR *and* HARRIET.

Dor. 'Tis she! it must be she — that lovely
hair, that easy shape, those wanton eyes, and
all those melting charms about her mouth   45
which Medley spoke of! I'll follow the lot-
tery and put in for a prize with my friend
Bellair.   (*Exit* DORIMANT *repeating*
In love the victors from the vanquished fly;
They fly that wound, and they pursue that die.[1]

Enter YOUNG BELLAIR *and* HARRIET; *and
after them,* DORIMANT, *at a distance*

Young Bel. Most people prefer Hyde   51
Park to this place.

Har. It has the greater reputation, I confess; but I abominate the dull diversions there
— the formal bows, the affected smiles,   55
the silly by-words and amorous tweers[2] in
passing. Here one meets with a little conversation now and then.

Young Bel. These conversations have been
fatal to some of your sex, madam.   60

Har. It may be so; because some who
want temper[3] have been undone by gaming,
must others who have it wholly deny themselves the pleasure of play?

Dor. (*coming up gently and bowing to her*).
Trust me, it were unreasonable, madam.   65

Har. (*giving a start and looking grave*). Lord,
who's this?

Young Bel. Dorimant.

Dor. (*aside*). Is this the woman your father
would have you marry?   70

Young Bel. It is.

Dor. Her name?

Young Bel. Harriet.

Dor. I am not mistaken; she's handsome.

Young Bel. Talk to her; her wit is better   75
than her face. We were wishing for you but
now.

Dor. (*to* HARRIET). Overcast with seriousness o'the sudden! A thousand smiles were
shining in that face but now; I never saw   80
so quick a change of weather.

Har. (*aside*). I feel as great a change within;
but he shall never know it.

Dor. You were talking of play, madam.
Pray, what may be your stint?[1]   85

Har. A little harmless discourse in public
walks, or at most an appointment in a box,
barefaced, at the playhouse. You are for
masks and private meetings, where women engage for all they are worth, I hear.   90

Dor. I have been used to deep play, but I
can make one at small game when I like my
gamester well.

Har. And be so unconcerned you'll ha' no
pleasure in't.   95

Dor. Where there is a considerable sum to
be won, the hope of drawing people in makes
every trifle considerable.

Har. The sordidness of men's natures, I
know, makes 'em willing to flatter and   100
comply with the rich, though they are sure
never to be the better for 'em.

Dor. 'Tis in their power to do us good, and
we despair not but at some time or other they
may be willing.   105

Har. To men who have fared in this town
like you, 'twould be a great mortification to
live on hope. Could you keep a Lent for a
mistress?

---

[1] The last couplet of Waller's poem "To a Friend, of
the Different Success of their Loves."
[2] Leers.   [3] Self-control.

[1] Limit of loss set by a gamester before playing.

Dor. In expectation of a happy Easter   110
and, though time be very precious, think forty
days well lost to gain your favor.

Har. Mr. Bellair, let us walk; 'tis time to
leave him.   Men grow dull when they begin to
be particular.   115

Dor. Y'are mistaken; flattery will not ensue,
though I know you're greedy of the praises
of the whole Mall.

Har. You do me wrong.

Dor. I do not. As I followed you, I ob-   120
served how you were pleased when the fops
cried, "She's handsome — very handsome!
By God, she is!" and whispered aloud your
name.   The thousand several forms you put
your face into, then, to make yourself   125
more agreeable!   How wantonly you played
with your head, flung back your locks, and
looked smilingly over your shoulder at 'em!

Har. I do not go begging the men's, as you
do the ladies', good liking, with a sly   130
softness in your looks and a gentle slowness
in your bows as you pass 'em — as thus, sir.
(*Acts him.*)   Is not this like you?

Enter LADY WOODVILL *and* BUSY

Young Bel. Your mother, madam.
(*Pulls* HARRIET; *she composes herself.*
Lady Wood. Ah, my dear child Harriet!   135
Busy (*aside*).   Now is she so pleased with
finding her again she cannot chide her.

Lady Wood. Come away!

Dor. 'Tis now but high Mall, madam — the
most entertaining time of the evening.[1]   140

Har. I would fain see that Dorimant,
mother, you so cry out of for a monster; he's
in the Mall, I hear.

Lady Wood. Come away then!   The plague
is here and you should dread the infection.   145

Young Bel. You may be misinformed of the
gentleman.

Lady Wood. Oh, no!   I hope you do not
know him.   He is the prince of all the devils in
the town — delights in nothing but in   150
rapes and riots!

Dor. If you did but hear him speak, madam!

_____
[1] I.e., the very height of the fashionable period.

Lady Wood. Oh, he has a tongue they say
would tempt the angels to a second fall.

Enter SIR FOPLING *with his equipage, six*
Footmen *and a* Page

Sir Fop. Hey! Champagne, Norman,   155
La Rose, La Fleur, La Tour, La Verdure! —
Dorimant ——

Lady Wood. Here, here he is among this
rout! — He names him!   Come away, Harriet;
come away!   160
(*Exeunt* LADY WOODVILL, HARRIET,
BUSY, *and* YOUNG BELLAIR.

Dor. This fool's coming has spoiled all;
she's gone.   But she has left a pleasing image
of herself behind that wanders in my soul — it
must not settle there.   164

Sir Fop. What reverie is this?   Speak, man!

Dor. Snatcht from myself, how far behind
Already I behold the shore![1]

Enter MEDLEY

Med. Dorimant, a discovery!   I met with
Bellair.

Dor. You can tell me no news, sir; I know all.

Med. How do you like the daughter?   171

Dor. You never came so near truth in your
life as you did in her description.

Med. What think you of the mother?

Dor. Whatever I think of her, she   175
thinks very well of me, I find.

Med. Did she know you?

Dor. She did not; whether she does now or
no, I know not.   Here was a pleasant scene
toward,[2] when in came Sir Fopling, mus-   180
tering up his equipage, and at the latter end
named me and frightened her away.

Med. Loveit and Bellinda are not far off; I
saw 'em alight at St. James's.

Dor. Sir Fopling! Hark you, a word or   185
two. (*Whispers.*)   Look you do not want assurance.

Sir Fop. I never do on these occasions.

Dor. Walk on; we must not be seen together.
Make your advantage of what I have   190

_____
[1] Ll. 3–4 of Waller's poem, "Of Loving at First Sight."
[2] Developing.

told you.   The next turn you will meet the lady.

Sir Fop. Hey!   Follow me all!

(*Exit* SIR FOPLING *and his equipage.*

Dor. Medley, you shall see good sport anon between Loveit and this Fopling.   195

Med. I thought there was something toward, by that whisper.

Dor. You know a worthy principle of hers?

Med. Not to be so much as civil to a man who speaks to her in the presence of him   200 she professes to love.

Dor. I have encouraged Fopling to talk to her tonight.

Med. Now you are here, she will go nigh to beat him.   205

Dor. In the humor she's in, her love will make her do some very extravagant thing doubtless.

Med. What was Bellinda's business with you at my Lady Townley's?   210

Dor. To get me to meet Loveit here in order to an *éclaircissement.*[1] I made some difficulty of it and have prepared this rencounter to make good my jealousy.

Med. Here they come!   215

Enter MRS. LOVEIT, BELLINDA, *and* PERT

Dor. I'll meet her and provoke her with a deal of dumb civility in passing by, then turn short and be behind her when Sir Fopling sets upon her —

See how unregarded now   220
That piece of beauty passes.[2]

(*Exeunt* DORIMANT *and* MEDLEY.

Bel. How wonderful respectfully he bowed!

Pert. He's always over-mannerly when he has done a mischief.

Bel. Methought, indeed, at the same   225 time he had a strange, despising countenance.

Pert. The unlucky look, he thinks, becomes him.

Bel. I was afraid you would have spoken to him, my dear.   230

[1] An understanding.
[2] Ll. 1–2 of "Sonnet I" by Sir John Suckling (1609–42), a Caroline court poet still fashionable among the Restoration aristocracy.

Mrs. Lov. I would have died first. He shall no more find me the loving fool he has done.

Bel. You love him still?

Mrs. Lov. No!

Pert. I wish you did not.   235

Mrs. Lov. I do not, and I will have you think so.   What made you hale me to this odious place, Bellinda?

Bel. I hate to be hulched up[1] in a coach; walking is much better.   240

Mrs. Lov. Would we could meet Sir Fopling now!

Bel. Lord, would you not avoid him?

Mrs. Lov. I would make him all the advances that may be.   245

Bel. That would confirm Dorimant's suspicion, my dear.

Mrs. Lov. He is not jealous; but I will make him so, and be revenged a way he little thinks on.   250

Bel. (*aside*). If she should make him jealous, that may make him fond of her again. I must dissuade her from it. — Lord, my dear, this will certainly make him hate you.

Mrs. Lov. 'Twill make him uneasy,   255 though he does not care for me. I know the effects of jealousy on men of his proud temper.

Bel. 'Tis a fantastic remedy; its operations are dangerous and uncertain.

Mrs. Lov. 'Tis the strongest cordial we   260 can give to dying love. It often brings it back when there's no sign of life remaining. But I design not so much the reviving his, as my revenge.

Enter SIR FOPLING *and his equipage*

Sir Fop. Hey! Bid the coachman   265 send home four of his horses and bring the coach to Whitehall;[2] I'll walk over the Park. Madam, the honor of kissing your fair hand is a happiness I missed this afternoon at my Lady Townley's.   270

Mrs. Lov. You were very obliging, Sir Fopling, the last time I saw you there.

Sir Fop. The preference was due to your

[1] Hunched-up.
[2] The royal palace on the east side of St. James's Park, destroyed by fire in 1698.

wit and beauty. — Madam, your servant;
there never was so sweet an evening.   275

Bel. 'T has drawn all the rabble of the town
hither.

Sir Fop. 'Tis pity there's not an order
made that none but the *beau monde* [1] should
walk here.   280

Mrs. Lov. 'Twould add much to the beauty
of the place. See what a sort [2] of nasty fellows
are coming.

Enter four ill-fashioned fellows, singing

"''Tis not for kisses alone,'' [3] etc.

Mrs. Lov. Fo! Their periwigs are   285
scented with tobacco so strong ——

Sir Fop. It overcomes our pulvilio [4] — methinks I smell the coffee-house they come from.

1st Man. Dorimant's convenient, [5] Madam
Loveit.   290

2d Man. I like the oily buttock [6] with her.

3d Man. What spruce prig [7] is that?

1st Man. A caravan [8] lately come from Paris.

2d Man. Peace! they smoke. [9]

(*They sing again:*
"There's something else to be done," etc.   295
(*All of them coughing, exeunt singing.*

Enter DORIMANT *and* MEDLEY

Dor. They're engaged.

Med. She entertains him as if she liked him!

Dor. Let us go forward — seem earnest in
discourse and show ourselves; then you shall
see how she'll use him.   300

Bel. Yonder's Dorimant, my dear.

Mrs. Lov. I see him. (*Aside*) He comes
insulting, [10] but I will disappoint him in his expectation. (*To* SIR FOPLING) I like this
pretty, nice humor of yours, Sir Fopling.   305
(*Aside to* BELLINDA) With what a loathing eye
he looked upon those fellows!

Sir Fop. I sat near one of 'em at a play today

[1] High society.   [2] Gang.
[3] L. 5 of a current popular song, "Tell me no more
you love." In l. 295 the singing starts at l. 7 of the
same song.
[4] Sachet powder.   [5] Mistress.   [6] Sleek-figured whore.
[7] Fastidious dandy.   [8] A dupe; a gull.
[9] "Catch on."   [10] Exulting.

and was almost poisoned with a pair of cordovan [1] gloves he wears.   310

Mrs. Lov. Oh, filthy cordovan! How I hate
the smell!   (*Laughs in a loud, affected way.*

Sir Fop. Did you observe, madam, how their
cravats hung loose an inch from their necks
and what a frightful air it gave 'em?   315

Mrs. Lov. Oh, I took particular notice of one
that is always spruced up with a deal of dirty
sky-colored riband.

Bel. That's one of the walking flageolets [2]
who haunt the Mall o'nights.   320

Mrs. Lov. Oh, I remember him; he's a hollow tooth [3] enough to spoil the sweetness of an
evening.

Sir Fop. I have seen the tallest walk the
streets with a dainty pair of boxes [4]   325
neatly buckled on.

Mrs. Lov. And a little foot-boy at his heels,
pocket-high, with a flat cap, a dirty face ——

Sir Fop. And a snotty [5] nose.

Mrs. Lov. Oh, odious! — There's many   330
of my own sex with that Holborn equipage [6]
trig [7] to Gray's Inn Walks [8] and now and then
travel hither on a Sunday.

Med. She takes no notice of you.

Dor. Damn her! I am jealous of a   335
counter-plot!

Mrs. Lov. Your liveries are the finest, Sir
Fopling — Oh, that page! that page is the
prettili'st dressed — they are all Frenchmen?

Sir Fop. There's one damned English   340
blockhead among 'em; you may know him by
his mien.

Mrs. Lov. Oh, that's he — that's he! What
do you call him?

Sir Fop. Hey — I know not what to   345
call him ——

[1] Cordovan leather was made from horsehide.
[2] I.e., men shaped like flageolets; hence, tall and thin.
A flageolet is closely related to a piccolo flute.
[3] A sap head.   [4] Overshoes.   [5] Dirty.
[6] Holborn, in the heart of old London, was inhabited
chiefly by merchants and hence unfashionable in its
modes. Thus, "a Holborn equipage" means a bourgeois retinue of tradesmen admirers.
[7] Walk briskly; trip.
[8] Gray's Inn, one of the four Inns-of-Court or law
societies, was located between Holborn and Theobald's
Road. Its gardens and walks, laid out by Francis
Bacon, were a popular place for promenading.

Mrs. Lov. (*to* Footman). What's your name?

Foot. John Trott, madam.

Sir Fop. Oh, unsufferable! Trott, 350 Trott, Trott! There's nothing so barbarous as the names of our English servants. — What countryman are you, sir?

Foot. Hampshire, sir.

Sir Fop. Then Hampshire be your 355 name. — Hey, Hampshire!

Mrs. Lov. Oh, that sound — that sound becomes the mouth of a man of quality!

Med. Dorimant, you look a little bashful on the matter. 360

Dor. She dissembles better than I thought she could have done.

Med. You have tempted her with too luscious a bait. She bites at the coxcomb.

Dor. She cannot fall from loving me, to 365 that.

Med. You begin to be jealous in earnest.

Dor. — Of one I do not love.

Med. You did love her.

Dor. The fit has long been over. 370

Med. But I have known men fall into dangerous relapses when they found a woman inclining to another.

Dor. (*aside*). He guesses the secret of my heart. I am concerned but dare not 375 show it, lest Bellinda should mistrust all I have done to gain her.

Bel. (*aside*). I have watched his look and find no alteration there. Did he love her, some signs of jealousy would have appeared. 380

Dor. (*approaching*). I hope this happy evening, madam, has reconciled you to the scandalous Mall. We shall have you now hankering here ¹ again ——

Mrs. Lov. Sir Fopling, will you walk? 385

Sir Fop. I am all obedience, madam.

Mrs. Lov. Come along then, and let's agree to be malicious on all the ill-fashioned things we meet.

Sir Fop. We'll make a critique on the 390 whole Mall, madam.

Mrs. Lov. Bellinda, you shall engage ² ——

Bel. To the reserve of ³ our friends, my dear.

¹ Lingering here in expectation.   ² Take part.
³ With the exception of.

Mrs. Lov. (*to* SIR FOPLING). No, no exceptions. 395

Sir Fop. We'll sacrifice all to our diversion ——

Mrs. Lov. All — all ——

Sir Fop. All.

Bel. All? Then let it be. 400

(*Exeunt* SIR FOPLING, MRS. LOVEIT, BELLINDA, *and* PERT, *laughing.*

Med. Would you had brought some more of your friends, Dorimant, to have been witnesses of Sir Fopling's disgrace and your triumph.

Dor. 'Twere unreasonable to desire 405 you not to laugh at me; but pray, do not expose me to the town this day or two.

Med. By that time you have hope to have regained your credit?

Dor. I know she hates Fopling and 410 only makes use of him in hope to work on me again. Had it not been for some powerful considerations which will be removed tomorrow morning, I had made her pluck off this mask and show the passion that lies pant- 415 ing under.

Enter a Footman

Med. Here comes a man from Bellair with news of your last adventure.

Dor. I am glad he sent him. I long to know the consequence of our parting. 420

Foot. Sir, my master desires you to come to my Lady Townley's presently and bring Mr. Medley with you. My Lady Woodvill and her daughter are there.

Med. Then all's well, Dorimant. 425

Foot. They have sent for the fiddles and mean to dance. He bid me tell you, sir, the old lady does not know you, and would have you own yourself ¹ to be Mr. Courtage. They are all prepared to receive you by 430 that name.

Dor. That foppish admirer of quality, who flatters the very meat at honorable tables and never offers love to a woman below a lady-grandmother? 435

¹ Pretend.

Med. You know the character you are to act, I see.

Dor. This is Harriet's contrivance — wild, witty, lovesome, beautiful, and young! [1] —— Come along, Medley.   440

Med. This new woman would well supply the loss of Loveit.

Dor. That business must not end so; before tomorrow's sun is set I will revenge and clear it. And you and Loveit, to her cost, shall find, I fathom all the depths of womankind.   446

(Exeunt.

ACT IV

Scene i. Lady Townley's *drawing-room.*

The scene opens with fiddlers playing a country dance.

Enter Dorimant, Lady Woodvill, Young Bellair, *and* Mrs. Harriet, Old Bellair *and* Emilia, Mr. Medley *and* Lady Townley, *as having just ended the dance*

Old Bel. So, so, so — a smart bout! a very smart bout, a dod!

Lady Town. How do you like Emilia's dancing, brother?

Old Bel. Not at all — not at all!   5

Lady Town. You speak not what you think, I am sure.

Old Bel. No matter for that; go, bid her dance no more. It don't become her — it don't become her! Tell her I say so. (*Aside)* 10 A dod, I love her!

Dor. (*to* Lady Woodvill). All people mingle nowadays, madam, and in public places women of quality have the least respect showed 'em.

Lady Wood. I protest you say the truth, 15 Mr. Courtage.

Dor. Forms and ceremonies, the only things that uphold quality and greatness, are now shamefully laid aside and neglected.

Lady Wood. Well, this is not the wo- 20

[1] Dorimant, with Waller's verses again running in his mind, is consciously misquoting l. 14 of the poem "Of the Danger His Majesty . . . Escaped in the Road at St. Andrews," where Waller refers to Edward IV as "Fierce, Goodly, Valiant, Beautiful, and Young."

men's age. Let 'em think what they will, lewdness is the business now; love was the business in my time.

Dor. The women, indeed, are little beholding [1] to the young men of this age; they're 25 generally only dull admirers of themselves, and make their court to nothing but their periwigs and cravats, and would be more concerned for the disordering of 'em, tho' on a good occasion, than a young maid would be for the tum- 30 bling of her head or handkercher.

Lady Wood. I protest you hit 'em.

Dor. They are very assiduous to show themselves at court, well dressed, to the women of quality, but their business is with the stale 35 mistresses of the town, who are prepared to receive their lazy addresses by industrious old lovers who have cast 'em off and made 'em easy.

Har. (*to* Medley). He fits my mother's humor so well, a little more and she'll dance 40 a kissing dance with him anon.

Med. Dutifully observed, madam.

Dor. (*to* Lady Woodvill). They pretend to be great critics in beauty. By their talk you would think they liked no face, and yet 45 can dote on an ill one if it belong to a laundress or a tailor's daughter. They cry, "A woman's past her prime at twenty, decayed at four-and-twenty, and unsufferable at thirty."

Lady Wood. Unsufferable at thirty! 50 That they are in the wrong, Mr. Courtage, at five-and-thirty, there are living proofs enough to convince 'em.

Dor. Aye, madam. There's Mrs. Setlooks, Mrs. Droplip, and my Lady Loud; show 55 me among all our opening buds a face that promises so much beauty as the remains of theirs.

Lady Wood. The depraved appetite of this vicious age tastes nothing but green fruit, 60 and loathes it when 'tis kindly [2] ripened.

Dor. Else so many deserving women, madam, would not be so untimely neglected.

Lady Wood. I protest, Mr. Courtage, a dozen such good men as you would be enough to 65 atone for that wicked Dorimant and all the under [3] debauchees of the town. (Harriet, Emilia, Young Bellair, Medley, *and* Lady

[1] Indebted.   [2] Naturally.   [3] Lesser.

TOWNLEY *break out into laughter*.) — What's the matter here?

Med. A pleasant mistake, madam, that 70 a lady has made, occasions a little laughter.

Old Bel. Come, come; you keep 'em idle! They are impatient till the fiddles play again.

Dor. You are not weary, madam?

Lady Wood. One dance more; I cannot 75 refuse you, Mr. Courtage. (*They dance. After the dance* OLD BELLAIR, *singing and dancing, comes up to* EMILIA.

Emil. You are very active, sir.

Old Bel. A dod, sirrah! when I was a young fellow I could ha' capered up to my woman's gorget.[1]   80

Dor. (*to* LADY WOODVILL). You are willing to rest yourself, madam?

Lady Town. (*to* MEDLEY). We'll walk into my chamber and sit down.

Med. Leave us Mr. Courtage; he's 85 a dancer, and the young ladies are not weary yet.

Lady Wood. We'll send him out again.

Har. If you do not quickly, I know where to send for Mr. Dorimant.   90

Lady Wood. This girl's head, Mr. Courtage, is ever running on that wild fellow.

Dor. 'Tis well you have got her a good husband, madam; that will settle it.

(*Exeunt* LADY TOWNLEY, LADY WOOD-
VILL, *and* DORIMANT.

Old Bel. (*to* EMILIA). A dod, sweetheart, 95 be advised and do not throw thyself away on a young, idle fellow.

Emil. I have no such intention, sir.

Old Bel. Have a little patience; thou shalt have the man I spake of. A dod, he loves 100 thee and will make a good husband — but no words!

Emil. But, sir —

Old Bel. No answer — out a pize, peace! and think on't.   105

Enter DORIMANT

Dor. Your company is desired within, sir.

Old Bel. I go, I go!   Good Mr. Courtage,

---

[1] I.e., Old Bellair could have kicked as high as his partner's neck. A gorget was a ruff worn about the neck of a lady of fashion.

fare you well! — (*To* EMILIA) Go, I'll see you no more!

Emil. What have I done, sir?   110

Old Bel. You are ugly! you are ugly! — Is she not, Mr. Courtage?

Emil. (*to* DORIMANT). Better words or I shan't abide you.

Old Bel. Out a pize; a dod, what does 115 she say?   Hit her a pat for me there.

(*Exit* OLD BELLAIR.

Med. You have charms for the whole family.

Dor. You'll spoil all with some unseasonable jest, Medley.

Med. You see I confine my tongue and 120 am content to be a bare spectator, much contrary to my nature.

Emil. Methinks, Mr. Dorimant, my Lady Woodvill is a little fond of you.

Dor. Would her daughter were!   125

Med. It may be you may find her so.   Try her — you have an opportunity.

Dor. And I will not lose it.   Bellair, here's a lady has something to say to you.

Young Bel. I wait upon her.   Mr. 130 Medley, we have both business with you.

Dor. Get you all together then.   (*To* HARRIET) That demure curtsey is not amiss in jest, but do not think in earnest it becomes you.

Har. Affectation is catching, I find — 135 from your grave bow I got it.

Dor. Where had you all that scorn and coldness in your look?

Har. From nature, sir; pardon my want of art.   I have not learnt those softnesses 140 and languishings which now in faces are so much in fashion.

Dor. You need 'em not; you have a sweetness of your own if you would but calm your frowns and let it settle.   145

Har. My eyes are wild and wandering like my passions, and cannot yet be tied to rules of charming.

Dor. Women, indeed, have commonly a method of managing those messengers of 150 love.   Now they will look as if they would kill, and anon they will look as if they were dying. They point and rebate their glances,[1] the better to invite us.

---

[1] I.e., they make their glances lively, and then dull.

Har. I like this variety well enough,   155
but hate the set face that always looks as if it
would say, "Come, love me" — a woman who
at plays makes the *doux yeux* [1] to a whole
audience and at home cannot forbear 'em to
her monkey.   160

Dor. Put on a gentle smile and let me see
how well it will become you.

Har. I am sorry my face does not please you
as it is, but I shall not be complaisant and
change it.   165

Dor. Though you are obstinate, I know 'tis
capable of improvement and shall do you justice, madam, if I chance to be at Court when
the critics of the Circle pass their judgment;
for thither you must come.   170

Har. And expect to be taken in pieces, have
all my features examined, every motion cen-
sured, and on the whole be condemned to be
but pretty, or a beauty of the lowest rate.
What think you?   175

Dor. The women, nay, the very lovers who
belong to the drawing-room, will maliciously
allow you more than that. They always grant
what is apparent, that they may the better be
believed when they name concealed faults   180
they cannot easily be disproved in.

Har. Beauty runs as great a risk exposed at
Court as wit does on the stage, where the ugly
and foolish all are free to censure.

Dor. (*aside*). I love her and dare not   185
let her know it; I fear she has an ascendant
o'er me and may revenge the wrongs I have
done her sex. (*To her*) Think of making a
party, madam, love will engage.

Har. You make me start! I did not   190
think to have heard of love from you.

Dor. I never knew what 'twas to have a
settled ague yet, but now and then have had
irregular fits.

Har. Take heed; sickness after long   195
health is commonly more violent and dangerous.

Dor. (*aside*). I have took the infection from
her, and feel the disease now spreading in me.
(*To her*) Is the name of love so frightful that
you dare not stand it?   200

Har. 'Twill do little execution out of your
mouth on me, I'm sure.

[1] Casts amorous glances.

Dor. It has been fatal ——

Har. To some easy women, but we are not
all born to one destiny. I was informed   205
you used to laugh at love and not make it.

Dor. The time has been, but now I must
speak ——

Har. If it be on that idle subject, I will put
on my serious look, turn my head care-   210
lessly from you, drop my lip, let my eyelids
fall and hang half o'er my eyes — thus —
while you will buzz a speech of an hour long
in my ear, and I answer never a word. Why
do you not begin?   215

Dor. That the company may take notice
how passionately I make advances of love!
And how disdainfully you receive 'em.

Har. When your love's grown strong enough
to make you bear being laughed at, I'll   220
give you leave to trouble me with it; till then
pray forbear, sir.

Enter SIR FOPLING *and others in masks*

Dor. What's here — masquerades?

Har. I thought that foppery had been left
off, and people might have been in private   225
with a fiddle.

Dor. 'Tis endeavored to be kept on foot still
by some who find themselves the more acceptable the less they are known.

Young Bel. This must be Sir Fopling.   230

Med. That extraordinary habit shows it.

Young Bel. What are the rest?

Med. A company of French rascals whom he
picked up in Paris and has brought over to be
his dancing equipage on these occasions.   235
Make him own himself; a fool is very troublesome when he presumes he is incognito.

Sir Fop. (*to* HARRIET). Do you know me?

Har. Ten to one but I guess at you.

Sir Fop. Are you women as fond of a   240
vizard as we men are?

Har. I am very fond of a vizard that covers
a face I do not like, sir.

Young Bel. Here are no masks, you see, sir,
but those which came with you. This   245
was intended a private meeting; but because
you look like a gentleman, if you will discover

yourself and we know you to be such, you shall be welcome.

Sir Fop. (*pulling off his mask*). Dear 250 Bellair!

Med. Sir Fopling! How came you hither?

Sir Fop. Faith, as I was coming late from Whitehall, after the King's *couchée*,[1] one of my people told me he had heard fiddles at my 255 Lady Townley's, and ——

Dor. You need not say any more, sir.

Sir Fop. Dorimant, let me kiss thee.

Dor. Hark you, Sir Fopling —— (*Whispers.*

Sir Fop. Enough, enough, Courtage. — 260 A pretty kind of young woman that, Medley. I observed her in the Mall — more *éveillée*[2] than our English women commonly are. Prithee, what is she?

Med. The most noted coquette in 265 town. Beware of her.

Sir Fop. Let her be what she will, I know how to take my measures. In Paris the mode is to flatter the prude, laugh at the *faux-prude*, make serious love to the *demi-prude*, and 270 only rally with the coquette.[3] Medley, what think you?

Med. That for all this smattering of mathematics, you may be out in your judgment at tennis. 275

Sir Fop. What a *coq-à-l'âne*[4] is this? I talk of women and thou answer'st tennis.

Med. Mistakes will be for want of apprehension.

Sir Fop. I am very glad of the ac- 280 quaintance I have with this family.

Med. My lady truly is a good woman.

Sir Fop. Ah, Dorimant — Courtage, I would say — would thou hadst spent the last summer in Paris with me! When thou 285 wert there, La Corneus and Sallyes[5] were the only habitués we had: a comedian would have

been a *bonne fortune*.[1] No stranger ever passed his time so well as I did some months before I came over. I was well received in a dozen 290 families where all the women of quality used to visit; I have intrigues to tell thee more pleasant than ever thou read'st in a novel.

Har. Write 'em, sir, and oblige us women. Our language wants such little stories. 295

Sir Fop. Writing, madam, 's a mechanic part of wit. A gentleman should never go beyond a song or a billet.[2]

Har. Bussy was a gentleman.

Sir Fop. Who, d'Ambois?[3] 300

Med. Was there ever such a brisk blockhead!

Har. Not d'Ambois, sir, but Rabutin[4] — he who writ the loves of France.

Sir Fop. That may be, madam; many gentlemen do things that are below 'em. Damn 305 your authors, Courtage; women are the prettiest things we can fool away our time with.

Har. I hope ye have wearied yourself tonight at Court, sir, and will not think of fooling with anybody here. 310

Sir Fop. I cannot complain of my fortune there, madam. — Dorimant ——

Dor. Again!

Sir Fop. Courtage — a pox on't! I have something to tell thee. When I had made 315 my court within, I came out and flung myself upon the mat under the state[5] i' th' outward room, i' th' midst of half a dozen beauties who were withdrawn "to jeer among themselves," as they called it. 320

Dor. Did you know 'em?

Sir Fop. Not one of 'em, by heavens! — not I; but they were all your friends.

Dor. How are you sure of that?

Sir Fop. Why, we laughed at all the 325

---

[1] Reception held by a sovereign at the hour of retiring for the night.

[2] Sprightly.

[3] A *faux-prude* is a falsely prudish woman, while a *demi-prude* is a woman halfway between the falsely prudish and the coquette.

[4] Mixture of nonsense.

[5] Mesdames Corneul and Selles were minor figures in the French literary world of that period.

---

[1] A piece of good luck, a "good catch."

[2] A brief personal letter, a note.

[3] Sir Fopling's French veneer fails him here as elsewhere, and he confuses the subject of Harriet's fashionable reference with a stage character long known to English playgoers, Louis de Clermont d'Amboise, Sieur de Bussy (1549–79). This Bussy was the hero of a tragedy by George Chapman, *Bussy D'Ambois* (1607), still a popular play in the Restoration period.

[4] Roger de Rabutin, Comte de Bussy (1618–93), the then fashionable author of the *Histoire Amoureuse des Gaules*, a collection of love tales.

[5] Large canopy.

town — spared nobody but yourself. They found me a man for their purpose.

Dor. I know you are malicious, to [1] your power.

Sir Fop. And faith, I had occasion to 330 show it, for I never saw more gaping fools at a ball or on a birthday.

Dor. You learned who the women were?

Sir Fop. No matter; they frequent the drawing-room.   335

Dor. And entertain themselves pleasantly at the expense of all the fops who come there.

Sir Fop. That's their bus'ness. Faith, I sifted [2] 'em, and find they have a sort of wit among them — Ah, filthy!   340
                    (*Pinches a tallow candle.*

Dor. Look, he has been pinching the tallow candle.

Sir Fop. How can you breathe in a room where there's grease frying! Dorimant, thou art intimate with my lady; advise her for 345 her own sake and the good company that comes hither, to burn wax lights.

Har. What are these masquerades who stand so obsequiously at a distance?

Sir Fop. A set of balladines [3] whom I 350 picked out of the best in France and brought over with a *flute-douce* [4] or two — my servants. They shall entertain you.

Har. I had rather see you dance yourself, Sir Fopling.   355

Sir Fop. And I had rather do it — all the company knows it — but madam ——

Med. Come, come, no excuses, Sir Fopling.

Sir Fop. By heavens, Medley ——

Med. Like a woman I find you must 360 be struggled with, before one brings you to what you desire.

Har. (*aside*). Can he dance?

Emil. And fence and sing too, if you'll believe him.   365

Dor. He has no more excellence in his heels than in his head. He went to Paris a plain, bashful English blockhead, and is returned a fine undertaking [5] French fop.

Med. I cannot prevail.   370

[1] To the limit of.   [2] Examined.
[3] Ballet dancers.   [4] An old type of flute.
[5] Enterprising, i.e., bold.

Sir Fop. Do not think it want of complaisance, madam.

Har. You are too well bred to want that, Sir Fopling. I believe it want of power.

Sir Fop. By heavens, and so it is! I 375 have sat up so damned late and drunk so cursed hard since I came to this lewd town, that I am fit for nothing but low dancing now — a *corant*, a *bourrée*, or a *menuet*.[1] But St. André [2] tells me, if I will but be regular, in one month 380 I shall rise again. (*Endeavors at a caper.*) — Pox on this debauchery!

Emil. I have heard your dancing much commended.

Sir Fop. It had the good fortune to 385 please in Paris. I was judged to rise within an inch as high as the Basque [3] in an entry [4] I danced there.

Har. (*to* EMILIA). I am mightily taken with this fool; let us sit. — Here's a seat, Sir 390 Fopling.

Sir Fop. At your feet, madam; I can be nowhere so much at ease. — By your leave, gown.

Har. }
Emil. } Ah, you'll spoil it!

Sir Fop. No matter; my clothes are 395 my creatures. I make 'em to make my court to you ladies. — Hey! *Qu'on commence.*[5] (*The Servants dance.*) To an English dancer, English motions. I was forced to entertain [6] this fellow,[7] one of my set miscarrying.[8] — Oh, 400 horrid! Leave your damned manner of dancing and put on the French air. Have you not a pattern before you? — Pretty well! — Imitation in time may bring him to something.

After the dance, enter OLD BELLAIR, LADY WOODVILL, *and* LADY TOWNLEY

Old Bel. Hey, a dod, what have we 405 here — a mumming? [9]

[1] Stately square dances done without "capers" or high kicks.
[2] A popular French dancer in London at this period.
[3] Probably some noted contemporary Parisian dancer from the Basque country of southwest France.
[4] A dance done as an interlude in an entertainment.
[5] Start it up.
[6] Engage, hire.   [7] I.e., Trott.
[8] Meeting with misfortune.
[9] An old English form of acting in disguise.

Lady Wood. Where's my daughter — Harriet?

Dor. Here, here, madam! I know not but under these disguises there may be dan- 410 gerous parks; I gave the young lady warning.

Lady Wood. Lord! I am much obliged to you, Mr. Courtage.

Har. Lord, how you admire this man!

Lady Wood. What have you to except 415 against him?

Har. He's a fop.

Lady Wood. He's not a Dorimant — a wild extravagant fellow of the times.

Har. He's a man made up of forms and 420 commonplaces sucked out of the remaining lees of the last age.

Lady Wood. He's so good a man that, were you not engaged ——

Lady Town. You'll have but little night 425 to sleep in.

Lady Wood. Lord, 'tis perfect day.

Dor. (*aside*). The hour is almost come I appointed Bellinda, and I am not so foppishly in love here to forget. I am flesh and 430 blood yet.

Lady Town. I am very sensible,[1] madam.
(*Bowing.*

Lady Wood. Lord, madam! (*Bowing in turn.*

Har. Look! in what a struggle is my poor mother yonder! 435

Young Bel. She has much ado to bring out the compliment.

Dor. She strains hard for it.

Har. See, see! her head tottering, her eyes staring, and her under lip trembling —— 440

Dor. Now — now she's in the very convulsions of her civility. (*Aside*) 'Sdeath, I shall lose Bellinda! I must fright her hence; she'll be an hour in this fit of good manners else. (*To* LADY WOODVILL) Do you not know 445 Sir Fopling, madam?

Lady Wood. I have seen that face — Oh, heavens! 'tis the same we met in the Mall! How came he here?

Dor. A fiddle, in this town, is a kind of 450 fop-call; no sooner it strikes up but the house is besieged with an army of masquerades straight.

Lady Wood. Lord, I tremble, Mr. Cour-

[1] Appreciative.

tage! For certain, Dorimant is in the company. 455

Dor. I cannot confidently say he is not. You had best be gone. I will wait upon you; your daughter is in the hands of Mr. Bellair.

Lady Wood. I'll see her before me. — Harriet, come away. 460

Young Bel. (*calls*). Lights! lights!
(*Goes out with* LADY WOODVILL *and* HARRIET.

Lady Town. Light, down there!   (*Exit.*

Old Bel. A dod, it needs not ——

Dor. (*to the* Servant *entering*). Call my Lady Woodvill's coach to the door quickly. 465
(*Exit.*

Old Bel. Stay, Mr. Medley. Let the young fellows do that duty; we will drink a glass of wine together. 'Tis good after dancing. — What mumming spark is that?
(*Points at* SIR FOPLING.

Med. He is not to be comprehended in 470 few words.

Sir Fop. Hey, La Tour!

Med. Whither away, Sir Fopling?

Sir Fop. I have bus'ness with Courtage.

Med. He'll but put the ladies into their 475 coach and come up again.

Old Bel. In the meantime I'll call for a bottle.   (*Exit.*

Enter YOUNG BELLAIR

Med. Where's Dorimant?

Young Bel. Stol'n home. He has had 480 business waiting him there all this night, I believe, by an impatience I observed in him.

Med. Very likely; 'tis but dissembling drunkenness, railing at his friends, and then the kind soul will embrace the blessing 485 and forget the tedious expectation.

Sir Fop. I must speak with him before I sleep.

Young Bel. (*to* MEDLEY). Emilia and I are resolved on that business. 490

Med. Peace, here's your father.

Enter OLD BELLAIR *and a* Butler *with a bottle of wine*

Old Bel. The women are all gone to bed. — Fill, boy. Mr. Medley, begin a health.

Med. (*whispers*). To Emilia!

Old Bel. Out a pize! she's a rogue and   495
I'll not pledge you.

Med. I know you will.

Old Bel. A dod, drink it then!

Sir Fop. Let us have the new bacchic.

Old Bel. A dod, that is a hard word.   500
What does it mean, sir?

Med. A catch or drinking song.

Old Bel. Let us have it then.

Sir Fop. Fill the glasses round and draw up
in a body.   Hey, music!   505
(*They sing:*

The pleasures of love and the joys of good wine
To perfect our happiness, wisely we join.
We to beauty all day
Give the sovereign sway
And her favorite nymphs devoutly obey.   510
At the plays we are constantly making our
        court,
And when they are ended we follow the sport
To the Mall and the Park,
Where we love till 'tis dark.
Then sparkling champagne   515
Puts an end to their reign;
It quickly recovers
Poor languishing lovers;
Makes us frolic and gay, and drowns all our
        sorrow.
But alas! we relapse again on the morrow.   520
    Let every man stand
    With his glass in his hand,
And briskly discharge at the word of command:
        Here's a health to all those
        Whom tonight we depose!   525
Wine and beauty by turns great souls should
        inspire;
Present all together — and now, boys, give fire!
(*They drink.*

Old Bel. A dod! a pretty business and very
merry.

Sir Fop. Hark you, Medley; let you   530
and I take the fiddles and go waken Dorimant.

Med. We shall do him a courtesy, if it be
as I guess.   For after the fatigue of this night
he'll quickly have his belly full and be glad of
an occasion to cry, "Take away, Handy!"   535

Young Bel. I'll go with you, and there we'll
consult about affairs, Medley.

Old Bel. (*looks on his watch*).   A dod, 'tis
six o'clock!

Sir Fop. Let's away then.   540

Old Bel. Mr. Medley, my sister tells me you
are an honest man — and a dod, I love you.
Few words and hearty — that's the way with
old Harry, old Harry.

Sir Fop. (*to his Servants*).   Light your   545
flambeaux.[1]   Hey!

Old Bel. What does the man mean?

Med. 'Tis day, Sir Fopling.

Sir Fop. No matter; our serenade will look
the greater.   (*Exeunt omnes.*   550

SCENE 2.   DORIMANT'S *lodging.   A table, a
    candle, toilet articles, etc.;* HANDY, *tying
    up linen.*

Enter DORIMANT *in his gown, and* BELLINDA

Dor. Why will you be gone so soon?

Bel. Why did you stay out so late?

Dor. Call a chair,[2] Handy.   (*Exit* HANDY.)
— What makes you tremble so?

Bel. I have a thousand fears about me.   5
Have I not been seen, think you?

Dor. By nobody but myself and trusty
Handy.

Bel. Where are all your people?

Dor. I have dispersed 'em all on sleeve-   10
less[3] errands.   What does that sigh mean?

Bel. Can you be so unkind to ask me?
(*Sighs.*)   Well — were it to do again ——

Dor. We should do it, should we not?

Bel. I think we should — the wickeder   15
man you, to make me love you so well. — Will
you be discreet now?

Dor. I will.

Bel. You cannot.

Dor. Never doubt it.   20

Bel. I never will expect it.

Dor. You do me wrong.

Bel. You have no more power to keep a
secret than I had not to trust you with it.

Dor. By all the joys I have had and   25
those I keep in store ——

Bel. — You'll do for my sake, what you
never did before.

Dor. By that truth thou hast spoken, a wife

---

[1] Torches.   [2] A sedan-chair.   [3] Fruitless.

shall sooner betray herself to her husband.   30

Bel. Yet I had rather you should be false in this than in another thing you promised me.

Dor. What's that?

Bel. That you would never see Loveit more but in public places — in the Park, at 35 Court, and plays.

Dor. 'Tis not likely a man should be fond of seeing a damned old play when there is a new one acted.

Bel. I dare not trust your promise.   40

Dor. You may ——

Bel. This does not satisfy me. You shall swear you never will see her more.

Dor. I will, a thousand oaths. By all ——

Bel. Hold! You shall not, now I think 45 on't better.

Dor. I will swear!

Bel. I shall grow jealous of the oath and think I owe your truth to that, not to your love.   50

Dor. Then, by my love; no other oath I'll swear.

Enter HANDY

Han. Here's a chair.

Bel. Let me go.

Dor. I cannot.   55

Bel. Too willingly, I fear.

Dor. Too unkindly feared. When will you promise me again?

Bel. Not this fortnight.

Dor. You will be better than your word. 60

Bel. I think I shall. Will it not make you love me less? (*Starting; fiddles without.*) — Hark, what fiddles are these?

Dor. Look out, Handy.

(HANDY *goes out and returns.*

Han. Mr. Medley, Mr. Bellair, and Sir 65 Fopling; they are coming up.

Dor. How got they in?

Han. The door was open for the chair.

Bel. Lord, let me fly!

Dor. Here! here down the back stairs! 70 I'll see you into your chair.

Bel. No, no! Stay and receive 'em. — And be sure you keep your word and never see Loveit more. Let it be a proof of your kindness.   75

Dor. It shall. — Handy, direct her. (*Kissing her hand*) Everlasting love go along with thee.   (*Exeunt* BELLINDA *and* HANDY.

Enter YOUNG BELLAIR, MEDLEY, *and* SIR FOPLING

Young Bel. Not abed yet?

Med. You have had an "irregular fit,"[1] 80 Dorimant?

Dor. I have.

Young Bel. And is it off already?

Dor. Nature has done her part, gentlemen; when she falls kindly to work, great cures 85 are effected in little time, you know.

Sir Fop. We thought there was a wench in the case, by the chair that waited. Prithee, make us a *confidence.*[2]

Dor. Excuse me.   90

Sir Fop. Le sage[3] Dorimant! — Was she pretty?

Dor. So pretty she may come to keep her coach and pay parish duties if the good humor of the age continue.   95

Med. And be of the number of the ladies kept by public-spirited men for the good of the whole town.

Sir Fop. (*dancing by himself*). Well said, Medley.   100

Young Bel. See Sir Fopling dancing!

Dor. You are practicing and have a mind to recover, I see.

Sir Fop. Prithee, Dorimant, why hast thou not a glass hung up here? A room is the 105 dullest thing without one.

Young Bel. Here is company to entertain you.

Sir Fop. But I mean in case of being alone. In a glass a man may entertain himself.

Dor. The shadow of himself, indeed.   110

Sir Fop. Correct the errors of his motions and his dress.

Med. I find, Sir Fopling, in your solitude you remember the saying of the wise man, and study yourself.   115

Sir Fop. 'Tis the best diversion in our retirements. Dorimant, thou art a pretty fellow and wear'st thy clothes well, but I never saw thee have a handsome cravat. Were they

[1] See p. 573, l. 194.   [2] Tell us the secret.
[3] The prudent.

made up like mine, they'd give another 120 air to thy face. Prithee, let me send my man to dress thee but one day. By heavens, an Englishman cannot tie a ribbon.

Dor. They are something clumsily fisted——

Sir Fop. I have brought over the pret- 125 tiest fellow that ever spread a toilet. He served some time under Merille,[1] the greatest *genie*[2] in the world for a *valet-de-chambre.*[3]

Dor. What, he who formerly belonged to the Duke of Candale?[4] 130

Sir Fop. The same, and got him his immortal reputation.

Dor. Y'have a very fine brandenburg[5] on, Sir Fopling.

Sir Fop. It serves to wrap me up after 135 the fatigue of a ball.

Med. I see you often in it, with your periwig tied up.

Sir Fop. We should not always be in a set dress; 'tis more *en cavalier*[6] to appear 140 now and then in a *deshabillé.*[7]

Med. Pray, how goes your business with Loveit?

Sir Fop. You might have answered yourself in the Mall last night. Dorimant, did 145 you not see the advances she made me? I have been endeavoring at a song.

Dor. Already!

Sir Fop. 'Tis my *coup d'essai*[8] in English — I would fain have thy opinion of it. 150

Dor. Let's see it.

Sir Fop. Hey, page, give me my song. — Bellair, here; thou hast a pretty voice — sing it.

Young Bel. Sing it yourself, Sir Fopling.

Sir Fop. Excuse me. 155

Young Bel. You learnt to sing in Paris.

Sir Fop. I did — of Lambert,[9] the greatest

master in the world. But I have his own fault, a weak voice, and care not to sing out of[1] a *ruelle.*[2] 160

Dor. (*aside*). A *ruelle* is a pretty cage for a singing fop, indeed.

Young Bel. (*reads the song*):

How charming Phyllis is, how fair!
Ah, that she were as willing
To ease my wounded heart of care, 165
And make her eyes less killing.
I sigh, I sigh, I languish now,
And love will not let me rest;
I drive about the Park and bow,
Still as I meet my dearest. 170

Sir Fop. Sing it! sing it, man; it goes to a pretty new tune which I am confident was made by Baptiste.[3]

Med. Sing it yourself, Sir Fopling; he does not know the tune. 175

Sir Fop. I'll venture. (*Sings.*

Dor. Aye, marry! now 'tis something. I shall not flatter you, Sir Fopling; there is not much thought in't, but 'tis passionate and well turned. 180

Med. After the French way.

Sir Fop. That I aimed at. Does it not give you a lively image of the thing? Slap[4] down goes the glass, and thus we are at it.

Dor. It does, indeed. I perceive, Sir 185 Fopling, you'll be the very head of the sparks who are lucky in compositions of this nature.

Enter SIR FOPLING'S Footman

Sir Fop. La Tour, is the bath ready?

Foot. Yes, sir.

Sir Fop. Adieu donc, mes chers.[5] (*Exit.* 190

Med. When have you your revenge on Loveit, Dorimant?

Dor. I will but change my linen and about it.

Med. The powerful considerations which hindered, have been removed then? 195

---

[1] The chief confidant of the Duke of Candale.
[2] Genius.
[3] Gentleman-in-waiting.
[4] Duc de Candale (1627–58), grandson of Henry IV of France, and a prominent figure at the court of Louis XIV.
[5] A type of dressing gown named after Brandenburg, the Prussian center of woolen manufacture.
[6] Gallant, fashionable.   [7] Dishabille.
[8] First endeavor.
[9] Michel Lambert (1610–96), a favorite musician at the court of Louis XIV.

[1] Except at.
[2] A morning reception held in the bedchamber or anteroom by both French and English ladies of fashion.
[3] Jean Baptiste Lully (1633–87), Italian composer who introduced opera to the court of Louis XIV.
[4] Suddenly.
[5] Farewell, then, my good friends.

Dor. Most luckily this morning. You must along with me; my reputation lies at stake there.

Med. I am engaged to Bellair.

Dor. What's your business?

Med. Ma-tri-mony, an't like you.   200

Dor. It does not, sir.

Young Bel. It may in time, Dorimant. What think you of Mrs. Harriet?

Dor. What does she think of me?

Young Bel. I am confident she loves   205 you.

Dor. How does it appear?

Young Bel. Why, she's never well but when she's talking of you — but then, she finds all the faults in you she can. She laughs at   210 all who commend you — but then, she speaks ill of all who do not.

Dor. Women of her temper betray themselves by their over-cunning. I had once a growing love with a lady who would always quar-   215 rel with me when I came to see her, and yet was never quiet if I stayed a day from her.

Young Bel. My father is in love with Emilia.

Dor. That is a good warrant for your proceedings. Go on and prosper; I must to   220 Loveit. Medley, I am sorry you cannot be a witness.

Med. Make her meet Sir Fopling again in the same place and use him ill before me.

Dor. That may be brought about, I   225 think. I'll be at your aunt's anon and give you joy, Mr. Bellair.

Young Bel. You had not best think of Mrs. Harriet too much; without church security there's no taking up there.   230

Dor. I may fall into the snare too. But ——
The wise will find a difference in our fate;
You wed a woman, I a good estate.   (*Exeunt.*

SCENE 3. *The street before* MRS. LOVEIT'S *house.*

Enter the Chairmen *with* BELLINDA; *the men set down the chair and open it.* BELLINDA *starting*

Bel. (*surprised*). Lord, where am I? — in the Mall? Whither have you brought me?

1 Chair. You gave us no directions, madam.

Bel. (*aside*). The fright I was in made me forget it.   5

1 Chair. We use to carry a lady from the Squire's hither.

Bel. (*aside*). This is Loveit's: I am undone if she sees me. — Quickly, carry me away!

1 Chair. Whither, an't like your honor?   10

Bel. Ask no questions ——

Enter LOVEIT'S Footman

Foot. Have you seen my lady, madam?

Bel. I am just come to wait upon her.

Foot. She will be glad to see you, madam. She sent me to you this morning to desire   15 your company, and I was told you went out by five o'clock.

Bel. (*aside*). More and more unlucky!

Foot. Will you walk in, madam?

Bel. I'll discharge my chair and follow.   20 Tell your mistress I am here. (*Exit* Footman.) Take this. (*Gives the* Chairmen *money*.) And if ever you should be examined, say you took me up in the Strand over against the Exchange, as you will answer it to Mr. Dorimant.   25

Chair. We will, an't like your honor.
(*Exeunt* Chairmen.

Bel. Now to come off, I must on —

In confidence and lies some hope is left;
'Twere hard to be found out in the first theft.
(*Exit.*

ACT V

SCENE I. MRS. LOVEIT'S *dressing-room.*

Enter MRS. LOVEIT *and* PERT, *her woman*

Pert. Well, in my eyes Sir Fopling is no such despicable person.

Mrs. Lov. You are an excellent judge.

Pert. He's as handsome a man as Mr. Dorimant, and as great a gallant.   5

Mrs. Lov. Intolerable! Is't not enough I submit to his impertinences, but I must be plagued with yours too?

Pert. Indeed, madam ——

Mrs. Lov. 'Tis false, mercenary mal-   10 ice ——

Enter her Footman

Foot. Mrs. Bellinda, madam.
Mrs. Lov. What of her?
Foot. She's below.
Mrs. Lov. How came she?   15
Foot. In a chair; Ambling Harry brought her.
Mrs. Lov. (aside). He bring her? His chair stands near Dorimant's door and always brings me from thence. — Run and ask him where he took her up. Go! There is no truth 20 in friendship neither. Women, as well as men — all are false — or all are so to me, at least.
                              (Exit Footman.
Pert. You are jealous of her, too?
Mrs. Lov. You had best tell her I am. 'Twill become the liberty you take of late. This 25 fellow's bringing of her, her going out by five o'clock — I know not what to think.

Enter BELLINDA

Bellinda, you are grown an early riser, I hear.
Bel. Do you not wonder, my dear, what made me abroad so soon?   30
Mrs. Lov. You do not use to be so.
Bel. The country gentlewomen I told you of (Lord, they have the oddest diversions!) would never let me rest till I promised to go with them to the markets this morning to eat 35 fruit and buy nosegays.
Mrs. Lov. Are they so fond of a filthy nosegay?
Bel. They complain of the stinks of the town, and are never well but when they 40 have their noses in one.
Mrs. Lov. There are essences and sweet waters.
Bel. Oh, they cry out upon perfumes, they are unwholesome; one of 'em was falling 45 into a fit with the smell of these *narolii*.[1]
Mrs. Lov. Methinks in compliance you should have had a nosegay, too.
Bel. Do you think, my dear, I could be so loathsome, to trick myself up with carna- 50 tions and stock gillyflowers? I begged their pardon and told them I never wore anything but orange flowers and tuberose. That which

[1] Neroli, or essence of orange flowers.

made me willing to go, was a strange desire I had to eat some fresh nectarines.   55
Mrs. Lov. And had you any?
Bel. The best I ever tasted.
Mrs. Lov. Whence came you now?
Bel. From their lodgings, where I crowded out of a coach and took a chair to come 60 and see you, my dear.
Mrs. Lov. Whither did you send for that chair?
Bel. 'Twas going by empty.
Mrs. Lov. Where do these country- 65 women lodge, I pray?
Bel. In the Strand over against the Exchange.
Pert. The place is never without a nest of 'em. They are always, as one goes by, 70 fleering [1] in balconies or staring out of windows.

Enter Footman

Mrs. Lov. (to the Footman). Come hither!
                              (Whispers.
Bel. (aside). This fellow by her order has been questioning the chairmen. I threatened 'em with the name of Dorimant; if they 75 should have told truth, I am lost forever.
Mrs. Lov. — In the Strand, said you?
Foot. Yes, madam; over against the Exchange.   *(Exit* Footman.
Mrs. Lov. She's innocent, and I am 80 much to blame.
Bel. (aside). I am so frightened my countenance will betray me.
Mrs. Lov. Bellinda, what makes you look so pale?   85
Bel. Want of my usual rest and jolting up and down so long in an odious hackney.

Footman returns

Foot. Madam, Mr. Dorimant.
Mrs. Lov. What makes him here?
Bel. (aside). Then I am betrayed, in- 90 deed. He's broken his word and I love a man that does not care for me!
Mrs. Lov. Lord, you faint, Bellinda!

[1] Jeering.

Bel. I think I shall — such an oppression here on the sudden.   95

Pert. She has eaten too much fruit, I warrant you.

Mrs. Lov. Not unlikely.

Pert. 'Tis that lies heavy on her stomach.

Mrs. Lov. Have her into my chamber,   100 give her some surfeit water,[1] and let her lie down a little.

Pert. Come, madam, I was a strange[2] devourer of fruit when I was young — so ravenous ——   105

(*Exeunt* BELLINDA *and* PERT *leading her off.*)

Mrs. Lov. Oh, that my love would be but calm awhile, that I might receive this man with all the scorn and indignation he deserves!

Enter DORIMANT

Dor. Now for a touch of Sir Fopling to begin with. — Hey, page, give positive order   110 that none of these people stir.   Let the *canaille*[3] wait as they should do.   Since noise and nonsense have such powerful charms,

I, that I may successful prove,
Transform myself to what you love.[4]   115

Mrs. Lov. If that would do, you need not change from what you are.   You can be vain and loud enough.

Dor. But not with so good a grace as Sir Fopling. — "Hey, Hampshire!" — Oh,   120 that sound, that sound becomes a man of quality!

Mrs. Lov. Is there a thing so hateful as a senseless mimic?

Dor. He's a great grievance to all who,   125 like yourself, madam, love to play the fool in quiet.

Mrs. Lov. A ridiculous animal, who has more of the ape than the ape has of the man in him!   130

Dor. I have as mean an opinion of a sheer mimic as yourself; yet were he all ape, I should prefer him to the gay, the giddy, brisk, insipid, noisy fool you dote on.

---

[1] Charged or soda water.   [2] Remarkable.
[3] Rabble.
[4] Ll. 5–6 of Waller's poem "To the Mutable Fair."

Mrs. Lov. Those noisy fools, however   135 you despise 'em, have good qualities which weigh more (or ought at least) with us women than all the pernicious wit you have to boast of.

Dor. That I may hereafter have a just value for their merit, pray, do me the favor to   140 name 'em.

Mrs. Lov. You'll despise 'em as the dull effects of ignorance and vanity; yet I care not if I mention some.   First, they really admire us, while you at best but flatter us well.   145

Dor. Take heed!   Fools can dissemble too.

Mrs. Lov. They may, but not so artificially as you.   There is no fear they should deceive us. — Then, they are assiduous, sir; they are ever offering us their service, and always   150 waiting on our will.

Dor. You owe that to their excessive idleness.   They know not how to entertain themselves at home, and find so little welcome abroad they are fain to fly to you who   155 countenance 'em, as a refuge against solitude they would be otherwise condemned to.

Mrs. Lov. Their conversation, too, diverts us better.

Dor. Playing with your fan, smelling   160 to your gloves, commending your hair, and taking notice how 'tis cut and shaded after the new way ——

Mrs. Lov. Were it sillier than you can make it, you must allow 'tis pleasanter to laugh   165 at others than to be laughed at ourselves, though never so wittily.   Then, though they want skill to flatter us, they flatter themselves so well they save us the labor.   We need not take that care and pains to satisfy 'em of   170 our love, which we so often lose on you.

Dor. They commonly, indeed, believe too well of themselves, and always better of you than you deserve.

Mrs. Lov. You are in the right.   They   175 have an implicit faith in us which keeps 'em from prying narrowly into our secrets and saves us from the vexatious trouble of clearing doubts which your subtle and causeless jealousies every moment raise.   180

Dor. There is an inbred falsehood in women, which inclines 'em still to them whom they may most easily deceive.

Mrs. Lov. The man who loves above his quality does not suffer more from the in- 185 solent impertinence of his mistress than the woman who loves above her understanding does from the arrogant presumptions of her friend.

Dor. You mistake the use of fools; they 190 are designed for properties,[1] and not for friends. You have an indifferent stock of reputation left yet. Lose it all like a frank gamester on the square; 'twill then be time enough to turn rook[2] and cheat it up again on a good, 195 substantial bubble.[3]

Mrs. Lov. The old and the ill-favored are only fit for properties, indeed, but young and handsome fools have met with kinder fortunes.

Dor. They have — to the shame of 200 your sex be it spoken! 'Twas this, the thought of this, made me by a timely jealousy endeavor to prevent the good fortune you are providing for Sir Fopling. But against a woman's frailty all our care is vain. 205

Mrs. Lov. Had I not with a dear experience bought the knowledge of your falsehood, you might have fooled me yet. This is not the first jealousy you have feigned, to make a quarrel with me, and get a week to throw away 210 on some such unknown, inconsiderable slut as you have been lately lurking with at plays.

Dor. Women, when they would break off with a man, never want th' address[4] to turn the fault on him. 215

Mrs. Lov. You take a pride of late in using me ill, that the town may know the power you have over me, which now (as unreasonably as yourself) expects that I (do me all the injuries you can) must love you still. 220

Dor. I am so far from expecting that you should, I begin to think you never did love me.

Mrs. Lov. Would the memory of it were so wholly worn out in me, that I did doubt it, too! What made you come to disturb my 225 growing quiet?

Dor. To give you joy of your growing infamy.

Mrs. Lov. Insupportable! Insulting devil!

This from you, the only author of my 230 shame! This from another had been but justice; but from you, 'tis a hellish and inhuman outrage. What have I done?

Dor. A thing that puts you below my scorn, and makes my anger as ridiculous as you 235 have made my love.

Mrs. Lov. I walked last night with Sir Fopling.

Dor. You did, madam; and you talked and laughed aloud, "Ha, ha, ha!" — Oh, 240 that laugh! that laugh becomes the confidence of a woman of quality.

Mrs. Lov. You who have more pleasure in the ruin of a woman's reputation than in the endearments of her love, reproach me 245 not with yourself — and I defy you to name the man who can lay a blemish on my fame.

Dor. To be seen publicly so transported with the vain follies of that notorious fop, to me is an infamy below the sin of prostitution 250 with another man.

Mrs. Lov. Rail on! I am satisfied in the justice of what I did; you had provoked me to't.

Dor. What I did was the effect of passion, whose extravagancies you have been will- 255 ing to forgive.

Mrs. Lov. And what I did was the effect of a passion you may forgive if you think fit.

Dor. Are you so indifferent grown?

Mrs. Lov. I am. 260

Dor. Nay, then 'tis time to part. I'll send you back your letters you have so often asked for. — I have two or three of 'em about me.

Mrs. Lov. Give 'em me.

Dor. You snatch as if you thought I 265 would not. There! and may the perjuries in 'em be mine if e'er I see you more!

(*Offers to go; she catches him.*

Mrs. Lov. Stay!

Dor. I will not.

Mrs. Lov. You shall. 270

Dor. What have you to say?

Mrs. Lov. I cannot speak it yet.

Dor. Something more in commendation of the fool? — Death, I want patience; let me go!

Mrs. Lov. I cannot. (*Aside*) I can 275 sooner part with the limbs that hold him. — I hate that nauseous fool; you know I do.

[1] As peculiarities or freaks.   [2] Turn cheat.
[3] Deception.
[4] Skill.

Dor. Was it the scandal you were fond of then?

Mrs. Lov. Y'had raised my anger equal   280
to my love — a thing you ne'er could do before,
and in revenge I did — I know not what I did.
Would you would not think on't more!

Dor. Should I be willing to forget it, I shall
be daily reminded of it; 'twill be a com-   285
monplace for all the town to laugh at me, and
Medley, when he is rhetorically drunk, will
ever be declaiming on it in my ears.

Mrs. Lov. 'Twill be believed a jealous spite.
Come, forget it.   290

Dor. Let me consult my reputation; you are
too careless of it. (*Pauses.*) You shall meet
Sir Fopling in the Mall again tonight.

Mrs. Lov. What mean you?

Dor. I have thought on it, and you   295
must. 'Tis necessary to justify my love to the
world. You can handle a coxcomb as he deserves when you are not out of humor, madam.

Mrs. Lov. Public satisfaction for the wrong
I have done you? This is some new de-   300
vice to make me more ridiculous.

Dor. Hear me!

Mrs. Lov. I will not.

Dor. You will be persuaded.

Mrs. Lov. Never!   305

Dor. Are you so obstinate?

Mrs. Lov. Are you so base?

Dor. You will not satisfy my love?

Mrs. Lov. I would die to satisfy that; but
I will not, to save you from a thousand   310
racks, do a shameless thing to please your vanity.

Dor. Farewell, false woman!

Mrs. Lov. Do — go!

Dor. You will call me back again.

Mrs. Lov. Exquisite fiend, I knew you   315
came but to torment me!

Enter BELLINDA *and* PERT

Dor. (*surprised*). Bellinda here!

Bel. (*aside*). He starts and looks pale! The
sight of me has touched his guilty soul.

Pert. 'Twas but a qualm, as I said — a   320
little indigestion; the surfeit water did it,
madam, mixed with a little *mirabilis*.[1]

[1] A fashionable strong drink made of spirits of wine
and spices. Ladies often carried it about with them.

Dor. (*aside*). I am confounded, and cannot
guess how she came hither!

Mrs. Lov. 'Tis your fortune, Bellinda,   325
ever to be here when I am abused by this
prodigy of ill-nature.

Bel. I am amazed to find him here. How
has he the face to come near you?

Dor. (*aside*). Here is fine work towards!   330
I never was at such a loss before.

Bel. One who makes a public profession of
breach of faith and gratitude — I loathe the
sight of him.

Dor. (*aside*). There is no remedy; I   335
must submit to their tongues now, and some
other time bring myself off as well as I can.

Bel. Other men are wicked; but then, they
have some sense of shame. He is never well
but when he triumphs — nay, glories to   340
a woman's face in his villainies.

Mrs. Lov. You are in the right, Bellinda, but
methinks your kindness for me makes you concern yourself too much with him.

Bel. It does indeed, my dear. His bar-   345
barous carriage[1] to you yesterday made me
hope you ne'er would see him more, and the
very next day to find him here again, provokes
me strangely. But because I know you love
him, I have done.   350

Dor. You have reproached me handsomely,
and I deserve it for coming hither; but ——

Pert. You must expect it, sir. All women
will hate you for my lady's sake.

Dor. (*aside to* BELLINDA). Nay, if she   355
begins too, 'tis time to fly; I shall be scolded
to death else. (*Aloud*) I am to blame in some
circumstances, I confess; but as to the main,
I am not so guilty as you imagine. I shall seek
a more convenient time to clear myself.   360

Mrs. Lov. Do it now. What impediments
are here?

Dor. I want time, and you want temper.

Mrs. Lov. These are weak pretenses.

Dor. You were never more mistaken in   365
your life; and so farewell. (DORIMANT *flings off.*

Mrs. Lov. Call a footman, Pert, quickly; I
will have him dogged.

Pert. I wish you would not, for my quiet
and your own.   (*Exit.* 370

[1] Behavior.

Mrs. Lov. I'll find out the infamous cause of all our quarrels, pluck her mask off, and expose her bare-faced to the world!

Bel. (*aside*).   Let me but escape this time, I'll never venture more.   375

Mrs. Lov. Bellinda, you shall go with me.

Bel. I have such a heaviness hangs on me with what I did this morning, I would fain go home and sleep, my dear.

Mrs. Lov. Death and eternal dark-   380 ness! I shall never sleep again.   Raging fevers seize the world and make mankind as restless as I am!   (*Exit.*

Bel. I knew him false and helped to make him so.   Was not her ruin enough to   385 fright me from the danger?   It should have been, but love can take no warning.   (*Exit.*

SCENE 2. LADY TOWNLEY'S *house.*

Enter MEDLEY, YOUNG BELLAIR, LADY TOWN-
LEY, EMILIA, *and* SMIRK, *a* Chaplain

Med. Bear up, Bellair, and do not let us see that repentance in thine we daily do in married faces.

Lady Town. This marriage will strangely surprise my brother when he knows it.   5

Med. Your nephew ought to conceal it for a time, madam, since marriage has lost its good name.   Prudent men seldom expose their own reputations till 'tis convenient to justify their wives.   10

Old Bel. (*without*).   Where are you all there? Out! a dod, will nobody hear?

Lady Town. My brother! Quickly, Mr. Smirk, into this closet; you must not be seen yet!   (SMIRK *goes into the closet.*   15

Enter OLD BELLAIR *and* LADY TOWNLEY'S
Page

Old Bel. Desire Mr. Fourbe to walk into the lower parlor; I will be with him presently. (*To* YOUNG BELLAIR) Where have you been, sir, you could not wait on me today?

Young Bel. About a business.   20

Old Bel. Are you so good at business?   A dod, I have a business too, you shall dispatch out of hand, sir. — Send for a parson, sister; my Lady Woodvill and her daughter are coming.   25

Lady Town. What need you huddle up things [1] thus?

Old Bel. Out a pize! youth is apt to play the fool, and 'tis not good it should be in their power.   30

Lady Town. You need not fear your son.

Old Bel. H'has been idling this morning, and a dod, I do not like him.   (*To* EMILIA) How dost thou do, sweetheart?

Emil. You are very severe, sir — mar-   35 ried in such haste.

Old Bel. Go to, thou'rt a rogue, and I will talk with thee anon. [2]   Here's my Lady Woodvill come.

Enter LADY WOODVILL, HARRIET, *and* BUSY

Welcome, madam; Mr. Fourbe's below   40 with the writings.

Lady Wood. Let us down and make an end then.

Old Bel. Sister, show the way.   (*To* YOUNG BELLAIR, *who is talking to* HARRIET) Harry, your business lies not there yet.   Excuse   46 him till we have done, lady, and then, a dod, he shall be for thee.   Mr. Medley, we must trouble you to be a witness.

Med. I luckily came for that purpose,   50 sir.   (*Exeunt* OLD BELLAIR, YOUNG BEL-
LAIR, LADY TOWNLEY, *and* LADY
WOODVILL.

Busy. What will you do, madam?

Har. Be carried back and mewed up [3] in the country again — run away here — anything rather than be married to a man I do not   55 care for!   Dear Emilia, do thou advise me.

Emil. Mr. Bellair is engaged, you know.

Har. I do, but know not what the fear of losing an estate may fright him to.

Emil. In the desperate condition you   60 are in, you should consult with some judicious man.   What think you of Mr. Dorimant?

Har. I do not think of him at all.

Busy. She thinks of nothing else, I am sure.

[1] Why need you do things hastily?
[2] Soon.   [3] Confined.

Emil. How fond your mother was of   65
Mr. Courtage!

Har. Because I contrived the mistake to
make a little mirth, you believe I like the man.

Emil. Mr. Bellair believes you love him.

Har. Men are seldom in the right when   70
they guess at a woman's mind. Would she
whom he loves, loved him no better!

Busy (*aside*). That's e'en well enough, on all
conscience.

Emil. Mr. Dorimant has a great deal   75
of wit.

Har. And takes a great deal of pains to show
it.

Emil. He's extremely well fashioned.

Har. Affectedly grave, or ridiculously   80
wild and apish.

Busy. You defend him still against your
mother!

Har. I would not, were he justly rallied, but
I cannot hear anyone undeservedly railed   85
at.

Emil. Has your woman learned the song you
were so taken with?

Har. I was fond of a new thing; 'tis dull at
a second hearing.   90

Emil. Mr. Dorimant made it.

Busy. She knows it, madam, and has made
me sing it at least a dozen times this morning.

Har. Thy tongue is as impertinent as thy
fingers.   95

Emil. You have provoked her.

Busy. 'Tis but singing the song and I shall
appease her.

Emil. Prithee, do.

Har. She has a voice will grate your   100
ears worse than a cat-call, and dresses so ill
she's scarce fit to trick up a yeoman's daughter
on a holiday.

BUSY *sings:*

SONG

BY SIR C. S.[1]

As Amoret with Phyllis sat,
One evening on the plain,   105
And saw the charming Strephon wait
To tell the nymph his pain;

[1] Sir Car Scroope, who wrote the prologue.

The threat'ning danger to remove,
She whispered in her ear,
"Ah, Phyllis, if you would not love,   110
This shepherd do not hear!

"None ever had so strange an art,
His passion to convey
Into a list'ning virgin's heart,
And steal her soul away.   115

"Fly, fly betimes, for fear you give
Occasion for your fate."
"In vain," said she; "in vain I strive!
Alas, 'tis now too late."

Enter DORIMANT

Dor. Music so softens and disarms the
mind ——   120

Har. That not one arrow does resistance
find.[1]

Dor. Let us make use of the lucky minute,
then.

Har. (*aside, turning from* DORIMANT). My
love springs with my blood into my face;   125
I dare not look upon him yet.

Dor. What have we here? The picture of
celebrated beauty giving audience in public to
a declared lover?

Har. Play the dying fop and make the   130
piece complete, sir.

Dor. What think you if the hint were well
improved — the whole mystery of making love
pleasantly designed and wrought in a suit of
hangings?[2]   135

Har. 'Twere needless to execute fools in
effigy who suffer daily in their own persons.

Dor. (*aside to* EMILIA). Mrs. Bride, for such
I know this happy day has made you ——

Emil. (*aside*). Defer the formal joy   140
you are to give me, and mind your business
with her. (*Aloud*) Here are dreadful preparations, Mr. Dorimant — writings sealing, and
a parson sent for.

Dor. To marry this lady?   145

Busy. Condemned she is, and what will be-

[1] This couplet is the sixth in Waller's poem "On My
Lady Isabella Playing on the Lute."

[2] In a series of wall tapestries.

come of her I know not, without you generously engage in a rescue.

Dor. In this sad condition, madam, I can do
no less than offer you my service.   150

Har. The obligation is not great; you are
the common sanctuary for all young women
who run from their relations.

Dor. I have always my arms open to receive
the distressed, but I will open my heart   155
and receive you where none yet did ever enter.
You have filled it with a secret; might I but
let you know it ——

Har. Do not speak it if you would have me
believe it.   Your tongue is so famed for   160
falsehood, 'twill do the truth an injury.

                    (*Turns away her head.*

Dor. Turn not away, then, but look on me
and guess it.

Har. Did you not tell me there was no credit
to be given to faces? — that women now-   165
adays have their passions as much at will as
they have their complexions, and put on joy
and sadness, scorn and kindness, with the
same ease they do their paint and patches?
Are they the only counterfeits?   170

Dor. You wrong your own while you suspect my eyes.   By all the hope I have in you,
the inimitable color in your cheeks is not more
free from art than are the sighs I offer.

Har. In men who have been long hard-   175
ened in sin, we have reason to mistrust the first
signs of repentance.

Dor. The prospect of such a heaven will
make me persevere and give you marks that
are infallible.   180

Har. What are those?

Dor. I will renounce all the joy i have in
friendship and in wine, sacrifice to you all the
interest I have in other women ——

Har. Hold!   Though I wish you de-   185
vout, I would not have you turn fanatic.   Could
you neglect these a while and make a journey
into the country?

Dor. To be with you, I could live there and
never send one thought to London.   190

Har. Whate'er you say, I know all beyond
Hyde Park's a desert to you, and that no gallantry can draw you farther.

Dor. That has been the utmost limit of
my love; but now my passion knows no   195
bounds, and there's no measure to be taken of
what I'll do for you from anything I ever did
before.

Har. When I hear you talk thus in Hampshire, I shall begin to think there may   200
be some little truth enlarged upon.

Dor. Is this all? — Will you not promise me?

Har. I hate to promise; what we do then is
expected of us and wants much of the welcome
it finds when it surprises.   205

Dor. May I not hope?

Har. That depends on you and not on me,
and 'tis to no purpose to forbid it.

                    (*Turns to* BUSY.

Busy. Faith, madam, now I perceive the
gentleman loves you, too; e'en let him   210
know your mind and torment yourselves no
longer.

Har. Dost think I have no sense of modesty?

Busy. Think, if you lose this you may never
have another opportunity.   215

Har. May he hate me (a curse that frightens
me when I speak it), if ever I do a thing against
the rules of decency and honor.

Dor. (*to* EMILIA).   I am beholding to you
for your good intentions, madam.   220

Emil. I thought the concealing of our marriage from her might have done you better
service.

Dor. Try her again.

Emil. What are you resolved, madam? 225
The time draws near.

Har. To be obstinate and protest against
this marriage.

Enter LADY TOWNLEY *in haste*

Lady Town. (*to* EMILIA).   Quickly! quickly!
let Mr. Smirk out of the closet.   230

                    (SMIRK *comes out.*

Har. A parson!   Had you laid him in here?

Dor. I knew nothing of him.

Har. Should it appear you did, your opinion
of my uneasiness may cost you dear.

Enter OLD BELLAIR, YOUNG BELLAIR, MED-
LEY, *and* LADY WOODVILL

Old Bel. Out a pize!   The canonical   235

hour [1] is almost past.   Sister, is the man of God come?

Lady Town. He waits your leisure.

Old Bel. (*to* SMIRK).   By your favor, sir. — A dod, a pretty spruce fellow!   What 240 may we call him?

Lady Town. Mr. Smirk — my Lady Bigot's chaplain.

Old Bel. A wise woman; a dod, she is.   The man will serve for the flesh as well as the 245 spirit.   (*To* SMIRK)   Please you, sir, to commission a young couple to go to bed together a-God's name. — Harry!

Young Bel. Here, sir.

Old Bel. Out a pize!   Without your 250 mistress in your hand!

Smirk. Is this the gentleman?

Old Bel. Yes, sir.

Smirk. Are you not mistaken, sir?

Old Bel. A dod, I think not, sir.   255

Smirk. Sure, you are, sir?

Old Bel. You look as if you would forbid the banns, Mr. Smirk.   I hope you have no pretension to the lady?

Smirk. Wish him joy, sir; I have done 260 the good office today already.

Old Bel. Out a pize!   What do I hear!

Lady Town. Never storm, brother; the truth is out.

Old Bel. How say you, sir?   Is this 265 your wedding day?

Young Bel. It is, sir.

Old Bel. And a dod, it shall be mine too. (*To* EMILIA)   Give me your hand, sweetheart. — What dost thou mean?   Give me thy 270 hand, I say. (EMILIA *kneels and* YOUNG BELLAIR.

Lady Town. Come, come! give her your blessing.   This is the woman your son loved and is married to.

Old Bel. Ha! cheated! cozened! and by 275 your contrivance, sister!

Lady Town. What would you do with her? She's a rogue and you can't abide her.

Med. Shall I hit her a pat for you, sir?

Old Bel. A dod, you are all rogues, and 280 I never will forgive you.

---

[1] I.e., noon.   English canon or church law allowed marriages to be performed only between eight and twelve o'clock in the morning.

Lady Town. Whither?   Whither away?

Med. Let him go and cool awhile.

Lady Wood. (*to* DORIMANT).   Here's a business broke out now, Mr. Courtage; I am 285 made a fine fool of.

Dor. You see the old gentleman knew nothing of it.

Lady Wood. I find he did not.   I shall have some trick put upon me if I stay in this 290 wicked town any longer. — Harriet!   Dear child, where art thou?   I'll into the country straight.

Old Bel. A dod, madam, you shall hear me first.   295

Enter MRS. LOVEIT *and* BELLINDA

Mrs. Lov. Hither my man dogged him.

Bel. Yonder he stands, my dear.

Mrs. Lov. (*aside*).   I see him, and with him the face that has undone me.   Oh, that I were but where I might throw out the anguish 300 of my heart!   Here, it must rage within and break it.

Lady Town. Mrs. Loveit!   Are you afraid to come forward?

Mrs. Lov. I was amazed to see so much 305 company here in the morning.   The occasion sure is extraordinary.

Dor. (*aside*).   Loveit and Bellinda!   The devil owes me a shame today and I think never will have done paying it.   310

Mrs. Lov. Married, dear Emilia?   How am I transported with the news!

Har. (*to* DORIMANT).   I little thought Emilia was the woman Mr. Bellair was in love with. I'll chide her for not trusting me with 315 the secret.

Dor. How do you like Mrs. Loveit?

Har. She's a famed mistress of yours, I hear.

Dor. She has been on occasion.

Old Bel. (*to* LADY WOODVILL).   A dod, 320 madam, I cannot help it.

Lady Wood. You need make no more apologies, sir.

Emil. (*to* MRS. LOVEIT).   The old gentleman's excusing himself to my Lady 325 Woodvill.

Mrs. Lov. Ha, ha, ha! I never heard of anything so pleasant!

Har. (*to* DORIMANT). She's extremely overjoyed at something.   330

Dor. At nothing. She is one of those hoit-
ing [1] ladies who gaily fling themselves about
and force a laugh when their aching hearts are
full of discontent and malice.

Mrs. Lov. O Heaven! I was never so   335
near killing myself with laughing. — Mr. Dorimant, are you a brideman?

Lady Wood. Mr. Dorimant! — Is this Mr.
Dorimant, madam?

Mrs. Lov. If you doubt it, your daugh-   340
ter can resolve you, I suppose.

Lady Wood. I am cheated too — basely
cheated!

Old Bel. Out a pize! what's here? More
knavery yet?   345

Lady Wood. Harriet! On my blessing come
away, I charge you!

Har. Dear mother, do but stay and hear me.

Lady Wood. I am betrayed and thou art
undone, I fear.   350

Har. Do not fear it; I have not, nor never
will, do anything against my duty. Believe
me, dear mother — do!

Dor. (*to* MRS. LOVEIT). I had trusted you
with this secret but that I knew the vio-   355
lence of your nature would ruin my fortune —
as now unluckily it has. I thank you, madam.

Mrs. Lov. She's an heiress, I know, and very
rich.

Dor. To satisfy you, I must give up   360
my interest wholly to my love. Had you been
a reasonable woman, I might have secured 'em
both and been happy.

Mrs. Lov. You might have trusted me with
anything of this kind — you know you   365
might. Why did you go under a wrong name?

Dor. The story is too long to tell you now.
Be satisfied, this is the business; this is the
mask [2] has kept me from you.

Bel. (*aside*). He's tender of my honor,   370
though he's cruel to my love.

Mrs. Lov. Was it no idle mistress, then?

Dor. Believe me, a wife to repair the ruins
of my estate, that needs it.

Mrs. Lov. The knowledge of this   375

----

[1] Wanton or boisterous.   [2] Masked woman.

makes my grief hang lighter on my soul, but
I shall never more be happy.

Dor. Bellinda!

Bel. Do not think of clearing yourself with
me; it is impossible. Do all men break   380
their words thus?

Dor. Th' extravagant words they speak in
love. 'Tis as unreasonable to expect we should
perform all we promise then, as do all we
threaten when we are angry. When I   385
see you next ——

Bel. Take no notice of me, and I shall not
hate you.

Dor. How came you to Mrs. Loveit?

Bel. By a mistake the chairmen made,   390
for want of my giving them directions.

Dor. 'Twas a pleasant one. We must meet
again.

Bel. Never!

Dor. Never?   395

Bel. When we do, may I be as infamous
as you are false.

Lady Town. Men of Mr. Dorimant's character always suffer in the general opinion of
the world.   400

Med. You can make no judgment of a witty
man from the common fame, considering the
prevailing faction, madam.

Old Bel. A dod, he's in the right.

Med. Besides, 'tis a common error   405
among women to believe too well of them they
know, and too ill of them they don't.

Old Bel. A dod, he observes well.

Lady Town. Believe me, madam, you will
find Mr. Dorimant as civil a gentleman   410
as you thought Mr. Courtage.

Har. If you would but know him better ——

Lady Wood. You have a mind to know him
better? Come away! You shall never   415
see him more.

Har. Dear mother, stay!

Lady Wood. I won't be consenting to your
ruin.

Har. Were my fortune in your   420
power ——

Lady Wood. Your person is.

Har. Could I be disobedient, I might take
it out of yours and put it into his.

Lady Wood. 'Tis that you would be 425
at? — You would marry this Dorimant?

Har. I cannot deny it; I would, and never
will marry any other man.

Lady Wood. Is this the duty that you
promised? 430

Har. But I will never marry him against
your will.

Lady Wood. (*aside*). She knows the way to
melt my heart. (*Aloud*) Upon yourself light
your undoing! 435

Med. (*to* OLD BELLAIR). Come, sir, you have
not the heart any longer to refuse your blessing.

Old Bel. A dod, I ha' not. — Rise, and God
bless you both! Make much of her, Harry;
she deserves thy kindness. (*To* EMILIA) 440
A dod, sirrah, I did not think it had been in
thee!

Enter SIR FOPLING *and his* Page

Sir Fop. 'Tis a damned windy day. Hey,
page, is my periwig right?

Page. A little out of order, sir. 445

Sir Fop. Pox o' this apartment! It wants
an antechamber to adjust oneself in. (*To* MRS.
LOVEIT) Madam, I came from your house,
and your servants directed me hither.

Mrs. Lov. I shall give order hereafter 450
they shall direct you better.

Sir Fop. The great satisfaction I had in
the Mall last night has given me much disquiet
since.

Mrs. Lov. 'Tis likely to give me more 455
than I desire.

Sir Fop. (*aside*). What the devil makes her
so reserved? (*Aloud*) — Am I guilty of an
indiscretion, madam?

Mrs. Lov. You will be — of a great 460
one — if you continue your mistake, sir.

Sir Fop. Something puts you out of humor?

Mrs. Lov. The most foolish, inconsiderable
thing that ever did.

Sir Fop. Is it in my power? 465

Mrs. Lov. — To hang or drown it. Do one
of 'em and trouble me no more.

Sir Fop. So *fière*? *Serviteur, madame.*[1] —
Medley, where's Dorimant?

[1] So haughty? At your service, madam.

Med. Methinks the lady has not made 470
you those advances today she did last night,
Sir Fopling.

Sir Fop. Prithee, do not talk of her!

Med. She would be a *bonne fortune.*[1]

Sir Fop. Not to me at present. 475

Med. How so?

Sir Fop. An intrigue now would be but a
temptation to me to throw away that vigor
on one, which I mean I shall shortly make my
court to the whole sex in a ballet. 480

Med. Wisely considered, Sir Fopling.

Sir Fop. No one woman is worth the loss
of a cut[2] in a caper.

Med. Not when 'tis so universally designed.

Lady Wood. Mr. Dorimant, everyone 485
has spoke so much in your behalf that I can no
longer doubt but I was in the wrong.

Mrs. Lov. There's nothing but falsehood and
impertinence in this world! All men are villains or fools! Take example from my 490
misfortunes, Bellinda; if thou wouldst be
happy, give thyself wholly up to goodness.

Har. (*to* MRS. LOVEIT). Mr. Dorimant has
been your God Almighty long enough; 'tis time
to think of another. 495

Mrs. Lov. Jeered by her! — I will lock myself up in my house and never see the world
again.

Har. A nunnery is the more fashionable
place for such a retreat, and has been the 500
fatal consequence of many a *belle passion.*[3]

Mrs. Lov. Hold, heart, till I get home!
Should I answer, 'twould make her triumph
greater. (*Is going out.*

Dor. Your hand, Sir Fopling —— 505

Sir Fop. Shall I wait upon you, madam?

Mrs. Lov. Legion of fools, as many devils
take thee! (*Exit.*

Med. Dorimant, I pronounce thy reputation clear; and henceforward when I 510
would know anything of woman, I will consult
no other oracle.

Sir Fop. Stark mad, by all that's handsome!
— Dorimant, thou hast engaged me in a pretty
business. 515

[1] A "good catch."
[2] A flick of the feet by a dancer.
[3] Love affair.

Dor. I have not leisure now to talk about it.

Old Bel. Out a pize! what does this man of mode do here again?

Lady Town. He'll be an excellent entertainment within, brother, and is luckily come 520 to raise the mirth of the company.

Lady Wood. Madam, I take my leave of you.

Lady Town. What do you mean, madam?

Lady Wood. To go this afternoon part of my way to Hartley —— 525

Old Bel. A dod, you shall stay and dine first! Come, we will all be good friends, and you shall give Mr. Dorimant leave to wait upon you and your daughter in the country.

Lady Wood. If his occasions bring him 530 that way, I have now so good an opinion of him, he shall be welcome.

Har. To a great rambling, lone house that looks as if it were not inhabited, the family's so small. There you'll find my mother, an 535 old lame aunt, and myself, sir, perched up on chairs at a distance in a large parlor, sitting moping like three or four melancholy birds in a spacious volery.[1] Does not this stagger your resolution? 540

[1] Bird-house.

Dor. Not at all, madam. The first time I saw you you left me with the pangs of love upon me, and this day my soul has quite given up her liberty.

Har. This is more dismal than the 545 country! Emilia, pity me, who am going to that sad place. Methinks I hear the hateful noise of rooks already — *Kaw, kaw, kaw!* There's music in the worst cry in London, "My dill and cowcumbers to pickle!"[1] 550

Old Bel. Sister, knowing of this matter, I hope you have provided us some good cheer.

Lady Town. I have, brother, and the fiddles, too.

Old Bel. Let 'em strike up, then; the 555 young lady shall have a dance before she departs. (*All dance.*)

(*After the dance*) So! Now we'll in and make this an arrant[2] wedding-day. (*To the pit*)

> And if these honest gentlemen rejoice, 560
> A dod, the boy has made a happy choice.

(*Exeunt omnes.*

[1] An old and notable London street cry. Joseph Addison wrote in 1711 that it "is not heard above two months" of the year (see *The Spectator*, no. 251).

[2] Out-and-out.

THE EPILOGUE

By Mr. Dryden

Most modern wits such monstrous fools have shown,
They seemed not of heaven's making, but their own.
Those nauseous harlequins in farce may pass,
But there goes more to a substantial ass.
Something of man must be exposed to view 5
That, gallants, it may more resemble you.
Sir Fopling is a fool so nicely writ,
The ladies would mistake him for a wit;
And when he sings, talks loud, and cocks,[1] would cry,
"Ay now, methinks he's pretty company, 10
So brisk, so gay, so traveled, so refined!"
As he took pains to graft upon his kind.[2]
True fops help nature's work and go to school,
To file and finish God A'mighty's fool.
Yet none Sir Fopling him, or him, can call; 15
He's knight o' th' shire, and represents ye all.
From each he meets, he culls whate'er he can;

[1] Swaggers.
[2] Because he took pains to improve upon his natural endowments.

Legion's his name, a people in a man.
His bulky folly gathers as it goes,
And, rolling o'er you, like a snowball grows.   20
His various modes, from various fathers follow;
One taught the toss,[1] and one the new French wallow.[2]
His sword-knot, this; his cravat, this, designed;
And this, the yard-long snake [3] he twirls behind.
From one the sacred periwig he gained,   25
Which wind ne'er blew, nor touch of hat prophaned.
Another's diving bow he did adore,
Which with a shog [4] casts all his hair before,
Till he with full decorum brings it back,
And rises with a water spaniel's shake.   30
As for his songs (the ladies' dear delight),
Those sure he took from most of you who write.
Yet every man is safe from what he feared,
For no one fool is hunted from the herd.

[1] Throwing up the head with a peculiar jerk.
[2] Rolling walk.
[3] The tail of the periwig.
[4] Shake, jerk.

INTRODUCTION TO

The School for Scandal

*The Drama of Eighteenth-Century England: Sheridan and Social
Comedy: The Drury Lane Theater*

THE DRAMA OF EIGHTEENTH-CENTURY ENGLAND

EIGHTEENTH-CENTURY ENGLAND exhibited the paradox of a drama declining in the face
of a growing enthusiasm for the theater. The middle classes, for the first time since the
days of Queen Elizabeth, resorted to the playhouses in large numbers. As a result the
eighteenth-century audiences were far more mixed in character than those of the
Restoration period. They rapidly developed a fondness for the less literary forms of
dramatic entertainment; they doted on both Italian and native opera as much for the
colorful production as for the music. The Haymarket Opera House, opened at London
in 1708, enjoyed a flourishing business. Serious opera eventually begot a rage for comic
or ballad opera. John Gay (1685–1732) first perfected the type in *The Beggar's Opera*
(1728), a theatrical sensation in its own era and a piece still popular in the twentieth
century. Pantomimes and burlesque skits also became such a craze that toward the
end of the eighteenth century they had to be incorporated into the daily bill of the legitimate playhouses. In addition, the fad for intricate stage "machines" and spectacles
(such as Drury Lane's famous house of stone blocks which collapsed on the outbreak
of a fire within) almost bankrupt the theater managements. All these stage sidelines
diminished the appreciation of pure dramatic art and accelerated the deterioration of
the eighteenth-century playgoers' taste.

Even the cult of Shakespeare which reached its climax in the Stratford Jubilee Festival
of 1769 could not prevent the inevitable deterioration. The idolizing of the great master
only served to cover up the superficiality of the contemporary drama. Although the
roots of that superficiality run far back into the seventeenth century, the immediate
cause was the sentimentalism introduced around 1700 by middle-class influences. This
sentimentalism weakened further the already feeble spirit of tragedy. During the entire
eighteenth century playwrights futilely experimented with a variety of external methods
to inject a new intensity into tragedy, when all the time they themselves suffered from
a shallow or false emotionality. Joseph Addison (1672–1719) in *Cato* (1713) attempted
a tone of classical restraint and a structure based on the "Three Unities." Nicholas
Rowe (1674–1718) tried in *Jane Shore* (1714) to imitate Elizabethan dramatic material
and Shakespearean forms. George Lillo (1693–1739), in order to bring tragedy closer
to the experience of its audience, dispensed with both classicism and Shakespeare in
The London Merchant (1731), a prose dramatization of a "moral" ballad about a Lon-

don clerk. John Home (1722–1808), a Scotsman, imposed Shakespearean dramaturgy on the romanticized local history and landscape contained in his *Douglas* (1756). No one of these four plays, the outstanding tragedies of their age, succeeded in establishing a tradition. English tragedy merely drifted through the eighteenth century to emerge at the end in a Gothic melodrama of "drear forests, ruin'd aisles, and haunted towers."

Sentimentalism enfeebled tragedy; it perverted comedy. It substituted gravity and tenderness for laughter and ridicule. Comedy became genteel instead of witty, moralized instead of critical. So lively and notable a play as *The Beaux' Stratagem* (1707) by George Farquhar (?1678–1707) exhibits a highly sentimental touch in the reform of its rakish hero by love for the virtuous heiress he had intended to swindle. It remained, however, for another Irishman, Sir Richard Steele (1672–1729), to complete the sentimentalizing of comic drama. *The Conscious Lovers* (1722), a tale of "conscious honor" finally united to "conscious innocence," fully illustrates Goldsmith's famous definition of a sentimental comedy; namely, a comedy "in which the virtues of private life are exhibited rather than the vices exposed; and the distresses rather than the faults of mankind make our interest." Steele in his prologue exhorted the audience "with breeding to refine the age, to chasten wit, and moralize the stage." Following Steele's lead, later writers of sentimental comedy, like Hugh Kelly (1739–77) in his *False Delicacy* (1768), employed the stage as "a school of morality." Richard Cumberland (1732–1811), though less tearful in his tremendous success, *The West Indian* (1771), stressed the soft-hearted humanitarianism that was associated with the sentimental formula. His hero, Belcour, must be revealed at the close as a man possessing, "through the veil of some irregularities, a heart beaming with benevolence, an animated nature fallible but not incorrigible." Thus, for half a century all English comedy continued to forget its birthright by upholding the conviction, expressed as early as 1704 by Steele, that "laughter's a distorted passion."

Against that conviction the genial Irishman, Oliver Goldsmith (1728–74), voiced the first prominent protest. His *Essay on the Theater* (1772), really an attack on sentimental comedy, pleaded that genteelness should be done away with and that gaiety be restored. Goldsmith even went so far as to assert in reference to comedy that "low life and middle life are entirely its object." The times, he said, call for "laughing and even low comedy." Not content, however, merely to talk of the need, he undertook to meet it by writing *She Stoops to Conquer*, a play of rollicking humor which has held the stage ever since.

SHERIDAN AND SOCIAL COMEDY

The unexpectedly enthusiastic reception of *She Stoops to Conquer* in March, 1773, persuaded still another Irishman, Richard Brinsley Sheridan, to challenge, as he said, "the goddess of the woeful countenance — the sentimental Muse." The son of Thomas Sheridan, former actor-manager of the Theater Royal in Dublin, and of Frances Le Fanu, a Dublin authoress, Richard Sheridan came to playwriting by natural inheritance. Born at Dublin on October 30, 1751, he moved to England with his parents in 1758. After eight years of schooling at Harrow, he joined his father, now a widower in London. The Sheridans in 1770 took up residence at Bath, smart West-of-England spa, where the father assumed management of the playhouse. The dashing, handsome

Richard cut a gay figure among the smart set. A lovely singer in the city, Elizabeth Linley, soon captivated him. Mr. Linley did not look with favor upon young Sheridan as a suitor. At the same time a worthless rival secretly threatened to abduct Miss Linley. In desperation, Sheridan spirited her away to a French convent. He returned to England, won a duel over his rival, and then married his lady-love on April 13, 1773. The young couple settled in London with almost no funds. During that same spring *She Stoops to Conquer* was the "hit" of the year. Sheridan, casting about for means of revenue, decided to write a similarly bright comedy in which the romantic circumstances of his own marriage should constitute some of the plot material.

Sheridan's resolution gave birth to that still popular comedy, *The Rivals*. The premiere in January, 1775, bestowed immediate fame upon its author and checked for the moment the domination of sentimentalism. Once more English comic drama expressed the properly critical attitude toward mankind. *The Rivals* exposed for laughter human foibles, for example, Mrs. Malaprop's "nice derangement of epitaphs." Lydia Languish's books of sensibility and Bob Acres' "sentimental swearing" burlesque the fashion of sentimentalism. Yet the playwright himself yielded to that very mode in creating the mawkish sub-plot of Falkland and Julia.

Sheridan within the year followed his first triumph with a second, *The Duenna*, a comic opera. These successes confirmed him in the ambition for a career connected with the theater. The chance to fulfill this ambition came in June, 1776, when the illustrious David Garrick (1717–79) retired from the management of the Drury Lane Theater. Sheridan, with the help of his father-in-law and friends, took over the ownership. He installed his father as stage manager, his wife as keeper of accounts, and his father-in-law as musical director. During the following season he increased his popularity with *A Trip to Scarborough* and *The School for Scandal*, his masterpiece of social comedy. Contemporaries now recognized him as a leading man of letters. The exclusive Literary Club in 1777 elected Sheridan to membership at the instigation of their dictator, Dr. Samuel Johnson (1709–84), who praised him for "the two best comedies of the age." Two years later Sheridan scored another "hit" with *The Critic*, a dramatic burlesque on current fashions and persons, chiefly the sentimentalists. This production marked the virtual conclusion of his playwriting.

Apparently tired of the theatrical world, Sheridan directed his ambition toward politics; won election to Parliament in 1780 as a Whig; served in 1782 as Under-Secretary of State, and in 1783 as Secretary to the Treasury; then, on the defeat of the Whig Ministry in 1784, returned to the House of Commons. He headed the prosecution of Warren Hastings, governor of Bengal Province, British India, before the House of Lords. This extraordinary trial, extending from 1788 to 1795, gave Sheridan ample opportunity to exhibit his magnificent oratory, as when he held the House tense for seven hours without a break. Though Hastings was acquitted, his prosecutor emerged the greatest speaker of an age which included such orators as Edmund Burke (1729–97).

Sheridan's decline began in 1794 when the rebuilding of the Drury Lane Theater loaded him with a huge debt. He was always thereafter in trouble over money matters. His lifelong fondness of gay living gradually turned into serious dissipation. Friends deserted him because of his increasingly loose and extravagant habits. In 1809 the destruction of the Drury Lane Theater by fire left him completely bankrupt. Three years later he lost his seat in Parliament. Then poverty and obscurity descended. Nevertheless, after his death on July 7, 1816, he was buried with much pomp in the Poet's Corner of Westminster Abbey. England at the last honored a man of brilliant talents, the finest writer of comedy in eighteenth-century Europe.

Sheridan's drama marked only a brief flare-up of the true comic spirit. His social satire did not win contemporary taste away from sentimentalism. The old tradition again ruled the stage a few months after his unmerciful ridicule of it in *The Critic* (1779). The prologue to Sophia Lee's *The Chapter of Accidents* (1780), a very popular comedy, announces "a serio-comic play — sunshine and shower" with "smiling in tears" and "sentiment." Eighteenth-century England preferred in its drama feelings to reason, sensibility to irony. Sheridan could not prevail against what the era chose to term "nature — eternal nature."

THE DRURY LANE THEATER

The Drury Lane Theater, which became in the year of American Independence Sheridan's own property, was at that date one of the two legitimate playhouses permitted to London by the Licensing Act of 1737, an act in force until 1843. Its rival, the Covent Garden Theater, built in 1732, did not differ markedly in size or arrangements. Both playhouses considerably exceeded the dimensions of their Restoration predecessors. Drury Lane, standing on its original site of 1674, had been much remodeled in 1762 to seat about two thousand persons. The architectural plan of stage and auditorium in general remained unaltered. The stage "apron," however, had been shortened a little. The lower (i.e., the one nearer the pit) of the two doors on each side of the apron had been converted into a box. In compensation, a door had been added on each side just inside the proscenium.

Though the lighting of the auditorium by candles remained as crude as in the Restoration, Garrick's visit to France in 1765 had brought about much improvement in the stage illumination. He had introduced footlights in the shape of oil lamps, and replaced the chandeliers, which formerly hung over the stage, with a row of candles attached to the inside of the proscenium.

Methods of staging and the character of the "scenes" had changed little since Restoration days despite the great advances in stage decoration on the Continent. Scene painting, however, had developed into an activity for artists of recognized ability. A few interior sets composed of flats with *lateral* side-wings may have been introduced toward the end of the century in very elaborate productions. Certainly none of Sheridan's plays enjoyed such a set during his heyday. A 1778 print of the screen scene (Act IV, Sc. 3) in *The School for Scandal* at Drury Lane exhibits two pairs of pillared side-wings backed by a flat depicting a library wall with bookshelves and window. Scenery continued to serve as a mere decorative background for the acting, because the actors, in order to be heard, played almost entirely outside the proscenium on the apron. Meanwhile, Continental stages, having no apron, made the acting and the scene merge in one harmonious perspective. English practice was not to attain that degree of artistry until the abolition of stage apron and doors about the middle of the nineteenth century.

Performances began at 6 to 6.30 P.M. Notices of the daily offerings were published in the newspapers as well as distributed by handbills. Changes of program frequently occurred without any advance warning to the playgoers. Seat prices continued at the approximate scale which existed in the Restoration period; namely, $2 for boxes, $1.25 for the pit, 75 cents for the "middle" gallery, and 50 cents for the upper. This scale ran somewhat higher than in the public theaters on the Continent.

The boxes were occupied, of course, by the élite. Other fashionable and intellectual persons sat in the pit, the so-called "critics" in the front rows. The middle classes, by far the largest element, thronged the "middle" gallery and the gallery behind the pit on a level with the lowest tier of boxes. The poorer folk, as always, climbed to the upper gallery, sometimes called the "paradise" as in France. All in all, the Drury Lane audience represented a cross-section of English society.

"THE SCHOOL FOR SCANDAL"

When all ranks of this audience applauded *The School for Scandal* on its opening night, few of them realized what severe labor its composition had caused Sheridan. He undertook to incorporate into the new play two earlier unfinished pieces, *The Slanderers* and *The Teazles*, and found much revamping of plot necessary. Though the structure still wants smoothness at certain points, the tying together of the various strands of plot in the screen scene (Act IV, Sc. 3) is masterly. Sheridan kept everyone, including himself, on edge over the completion of the script. The actors had to rehearse their parts piecemeal, for the copy reached their hands only section by section. When the author sent the last sheet to Drury Lane, he appended at the bottom: "Finished at last, thank God!" The prompter, Hawkins, wrote below: "Amen!"

The School for Scandal's premiere came off on May 8, 1777. David Garrick, still a popular idol though retired from the stage, wrote the prologue. He sat on this occasion at the front of the pit, the cynosure of all eyes, and gave the cues for applause by stamping his foot loudly. The house, crowded with London's elect, experienced a tumultuous evening. Only Richard Cumberland, the noted writer of sentimental comedy, sat stiffly in his stage box without cracking a smile.

Sheridan's genius accomplished in *The School for Scandal* a skillful distillation of literary influences, the chief of which were Molière, Restoration comedy, and sentimentalism. Molière suggested the "school" title, but, what is far more important, he offered instruction in the development of comic situations filled with dramatic irony. The auctioning of the family portraits to Uncle Oliver (Act IV, Sc. 1) and the famed screen scene are superlative. Both the satire of fashionable society and the scenes of witty repartee, such as the verbal sparring of the Teazles in Act III, Scene 1, are reminiscent of Restoration comedy. Sheridan, however, removed all traces of indecency from the Restoration wit and softened its temper. A certain geniality underlies even the sharpest moment of satire. This new tone was an undoubted effect of sentimentalism. The sentimental influence is much more apparent, however, in the treatment of the Surface brothers. Though Joseph with his pretense of good intention is an obvious caricature of the sentimentalist, Sheridan grossly exaggerates his hypocrisy to make him a villain, a foil for the honorable Charles. Charles is the typical hero of the sentimental plays — a good-hearted, generous, rakish fellow, who in the end can be altogether reformed by the love of a sweet, virtuous girl.

The mild tincture of sentimentalism in Sheridan's comedy does not seriously affect its vitality. He does not attempt to develop unforgettable individuals; he rather aims to portray through representative characters unforgettable traits in human nature. We forget Sheridan's scandalmongers; we cannot forget his gorgeous bits of scandal-mongering, such as the last meeting of the "school" to discuss Sir Peter's fate (Act V, Sc. 2). These glimpses of the universal and ageless traits in mankind, added to the vivacious dialogue and the imperishably humorous situations, confer upon *The School for Scandal* a perennial freshness. It is not only the finest English drama between the Restoration and the end of the nineteenth century, but a comedy of unique character in the rich tradition of social comedy.

[For a history of the drama and theater in the eighteenth century, see A. Nicoll, *A History of Early 18th Century Drama* (1929), and *A History of Late 18th Century Drama* (1927); for sentimentalism in the drama, Ernest Bernbaum, *The Drama of Sensibility* (1925); for Sheridan, W. Fraser Rae, *Sheridan, a Biography* (2 vols., 1896).]

RICHARD BRINSLEY SHERIDAN
The School for Scandal

DRAMATIS PERSONAE

SIR PETER TEAZLE	ROWLEY	LADY TEAZLE
SIR OLIVER SURFACE	MOSES	MARIA
JOSEPH SURFACE	TRIP	LADY SNEERWELL
CHARLES SURFACE	SNAKE	MRS. CANDOUR
CRABTREE	CARELESS	
SIR BENJAMIN BACKBITE	SIR HARRY BUMPER [1]	

The Scene is London in the 1770's

PROLOGUE

WRITTEN BY MR. GARRICK [2]

A School for Scandal! tell me, I beseech you,
Needs there a school this modish art to teach you?
No need of lessons now, the knowing think;
We might as well be taught to eat and drink.
Caused by a dearth of scandal, should the vapors   5
Distress our fair ones — let them read the papers;
Their powerful mixtures such disorders hit;
Crave what you will — there's *quantum sufficit.*[3]
"Lord!" cries my Lady Wormwood (who loves tattle,
And puts much salt and pepper in her prattle),   10
Just ris'n at noon, all night at cards when threshing
Strong tea and scandal — "Bless me, how refreshing!
"Give me the papers, Lisp — how bold and free! (*sips*)
"'*Last night Lord L. (sips) was caught with Lady D.*'
"For aching heads what charming sal volatile![4] (*sips*)   15
"'*If Mrs. B. will still continue flirting,*
"'*We hope she'll* DRAW, *or we'll* UNDRAW *the curtain.*'
"Fine satire, poz[5] — in public all abuse it,
"But, by ourselves (*sips*), our praise we can't refuse it.
"Now, Lisp, read you — there, at that dash and star."[6]   20
"Yes, ma'am — '*A certain lord had best beware,*

---

[1] "Sir Toby Bumper" in some early editions of the play.
[2] David Garrick (1717–79), the most famous actor of the eighteenth century and the predecessor of Sheridan as manager of the Drury Lane Theatre.
[3] A sufficient amount: a pharmacist's phrase.   [4] Ammonia smelling salts.
[5] Positively.
[6] London newspapers of the time, when printing scandal, often gave only initials followed by a dash or by asterisks.

"'*Who lives not twenty miles from Grosvenor Square:* [1]
"'*For should he Lady W. find willing,*
"'*Wormwood is bitter'* — Oh, that's me, the villain!
"Throw it behind the fire, and never more   25
"Let that vile paper come within my door."
Thus at our friends we laugh, who feel the dart;
To reach our feelings, we ourselves must smart.
Is our young bard so young, to think that he
Can stop the full spring-tide of calumny?   30
Knows he the world so little, and its trade?
Alas! the devil's sooner raised than laid.
So strong, so swift, the monster there's no gagging:
Cut Scandal's head off, still the tongue is wagging.
Proud of your smiles once lavishly bestow'd,   35
Again your young Don Quixote takes the road;
To show his gratitude he draws his pen,
And seeks this hydra,[2] Scandal, in his den.
For your applause all perils he would through —
He'll fight — that's write — a cavalliero [3] true,   40
Till every drop of blood — that's ink — is spilt for you.

ACT I

SCENE 1.   LADY SNEERWELL'S *house.*

LADY SNEERWELL *discovered at the dressing-table;* SNAKE *drinking chocolate*

Lady Sneer. The paragraphs, you say, Mr. Snake, were all inserted?

Snake. They were, madam; and as I copied them myself in a feigned hand, there can be no suspicion whence they came.   5

Lady Sneer. Did you circulate the report of Lady Brittle's intrigue with Captain Boastall?

Snake. That's in as fine a train as your ladyship could wish. In the common course of things, I think it must reach Mrs.   10 Clackitt's ears within four-and-twenty hours; and then, you know, the business is as good as done.

Lady Sneer. Why, truly, Mrs. Clackitt has a very pretty talent, and a great deal of in-   15 dustry.

Snake. True, madam, and has been tolerably successful in her day. To my knowledge she has been the cause of six matches being broken off, and three sons disinherited; of four   20 forced elopements, and as many close confinements; nine separate maintenances, and two divorces. Nay, I have more than once traced her causing a *Tête-à-Tête* in the *Town and Country Magazine,*[1] when the parties, perhaps,   25 had never seen each other's face before in the course of their lives.

Lady Sneer. She certainly has talents, but her manner is gross.

Snake. 'Tis very true. She generally   30 designs well, has a free tongue, and a bold invention; but her coloring is too dark, and her outlines often extravagant. She wants that delicacy of tint, and mellowness of sneer, which distinguishes your ladyship's scandal.   35

Lady Sneer. You are partial, Snake.

Snake. Not in the least; everybody allows that Lady Sneerwell can do more with a word or a look than many can with the most labored detail, even when they happen to have a   40 little truth on their side to support it.

Lady Sneer. Yes, my dear Snake; and I am no hypocrite to deny the satisfaction I reap

---

[1] A fashionable London locale near Hyde Park.
[2] A many-headed monster of classical myth.
[3] A knight.

[1] A fashionable periodical of the day, which featured "Memoirs," or imaginary conversations, accompanied by a "Tête-à-Tête," a picture portraying the converser in vignette.

from the success of my efforts. Wounded myself in the early part of my life by the en- 45 venomed tongue of slander, I confess I have since known no pleasure equal to the reducing others to the level of my own injured reputation.

Snake. Nothing can be more natural. 50 But, Lady Sneerwell, there is one affair in which you have lately employed me, wherein, I confess, I am at a loss to guess your motives.

Lady Sneer. I conceive you mean with respect to my neighbor, Sir Peter Teazle, 55 and his family?

Snake. I do. Here are two young men, to whom Sir Peter has acted as a kind of guardian since their father's death; the elder possessing the most amiable character, and univer- 60 sally well spoken of; the younger, the most dissipated and extravagant young fellow in the kingdom, without friends or character: the former an avowed admirer of your ladyship, and apparently your favorite; the latter 65 attached to Maria, Sir Peter's ward, and confessedly beloved by her. Now, on the face of these circumstances, it is utterly unaccountable to me, why you, the widow of a city knight,[1] with a good jointure, should not 70 close with the passion of a man of such character and expectations as Mr. Surface; and more so why you should be so uncommonly earnest to destroy the mutual attachment subsisting between his brother Charles and 75 Maria.

Lady Sneer. Then at once to unravel this mystery, I must inform you that love has no share whatever in the intercourse between Mr. Surface and me. 80

Snake. No!

Lady Sneer. His real attachment is to Maria, or her fortune; but finding in his brother a favored rival, he has been obliged to mask his pretensions, and profit by my assistance. 85

Snake. Yet still I am more puzzled why you should interest yourself in his success.

Lady Sneer. How dull you are! Cannot you surmise the weakness which I hitherto, through shame, have concealed even from you? 90

[1] A merchant who has been knighted because of some public benefaction or service.

Must I confess that Charles, that libertine, that extravagant, that bankrupt in fortune and reputation, that he it is for whom I'm thus anxious and malicious, and to gain whom I would sacrifice everything? 95

Snake. Now, indeed, your conduct appears consistent; but how came you and Mr. Surface so confidential?

Lady Sneer. For our mutual interest. I have found him out a long time since. I 100 know him to be artful, selfish, and malicious; in short, a sentimental knave; while with Sir Peter, and indeed with all his acquaintance, he passes for a youthful miracle of prudence, good sense, and benevolence. 105

Snake. Yes; yet Sir Peter vows he has not his equal in England; and above all, he praises him as a man of sentiment.

Lady Sneer. True; and with the assistance of his sentiment and hypocrisy, he has 110 brought Sir Peter entirely into his interest with regard to Maria; while poor Charles has no friend in the house, though, I fear, he has a powerful one in Maria's heart, against whom we must direct our schemes. 115

Enter Servant

Serv. Mr. Surface.

Lady Sneer. Show him up. (*Exit* Servant.

Enter JOSEPH SURFACE

Jos. My dear Lady Sneerwell, how do you do today? Mr. Snake, your most obedient.

Lady Sneer. Snake has just been rally- 120 ing me on our mutual attachment; but I have informed him of our real views. You know how useful he has been to us, and, believe me, the confidence is not ill placed.

Jos. Madam, it is impossible for me to 125 suspect a man of Mr. Snake's sensibility and discernment.

Lady Sneer. Well, well, no compliments now; but tell me when you saw your mistress, Maria; or, what is more material to me, 130 your brother.

Jos. I have not seen either since I left you; but I can inform you that they never meet.

Some of your stories have taken a good effect on Maria.   135

Lady Sneer. Ah! my dear Snake! the merit of this belongs to you; but do your brother's distresses increase?

Jos. Every hour. I am told he has had another execution in the house yesterday.   140 In short, his dissipation and extravagance exceed anything I have ever heard of.

Lady Sneer. Poor Charles!

Jos. True, madam; notwithstanding his vices, one can't help feeling for him. Poor   145 Charles! I'm sure I wish it were in my power to be of any essential service to him; for the man who does not share in the distresses of a brother, even though merited by his own misconduct, deserves ——   150

Lady Sneer. Oh, Lud! you are going to be moral, and forget that you are among friends.

Jos. Egad, that's true! I'll keep that sentiment till I see Sir Peter; however, it certainly is a charity to rescue Maria from such a   155 libertine, who, if he is to be reclaimed, can be so only by a person of your ladyship's superior accomplishments and understanding.

Snake. I believe, Lady Sneerwell, here's company coming; I'll go and copy the   160 letter I mentioned to you. Mr. Surface, your most obedient.

Jos. Sir, your very devoted. (*Exit* SNAKE. Lady Sneerwell, I am very sorry you have put any further confidence in that fellow.   165

Lady Sneer. Why so?

Jos. I have lately detected him in frequent conference with old Rowley, who was formerly my father's steward, and has never, you know, been a friend of mine.   170

Lady Sneer. And do you think he would betray us?

Jos. Nothing more likely; take my word for't, Lady Sneerwell, that fellow hasn't virtue enough to be faithful even to his own   175 villainy. Ah! Maria!

Enter MARIA

Lady Sneer. Maria, my dear, how do you do? What's the matter?

Maria. Oh! there is that disagreeable lover of mine, Sir Benjamin Backbite, has just   180 called at my guardian's, with his odious uncle, Crabtree; so I slipped out, and ran hither to avoid them.

Lady Sneer. Is that all?

Jos. If my brother Charles had been   185 of the party, madam, perhaps you would not have been so much alarmed.

Lady Sneer. Nay, now you are severe; for I dare swear the truth of the matter is, Maria heard *you* were here. But, my dear, what   190 has Sir Benjamin done, that you would avoid him so?

Maria. Oh, he has done nothing; but 'tis for what he has said: his conversation is a perpetual libel on all his acquaintance.   195

Jos. Ay, and the worst of it is, there is no advantage in not knowing him; for he'll abuse a stranger just as soon as his best friend; and his uncle's as bad.

Lady Sneer. Nay, but we should make   200 allowance; Sir Benjamin is a wit and a poet.

Maria. For my part, I confess, madam, wit loses its respect with me, when I see it in company with malice. What do you think, Mr. Surface?   205

Jos. Certainly, madam; to smile at the jest which plants a thorn in another's breast is to become a principal in the mischief.

Lady Sneer. Pshaw! there's no possibility of being witty without a little ill nature: the   210 malice of a good thing is the barb that makes it stick. What's your opinion, Mr. Surface?

Jos. To be sure, madam; that conversation, where the spirit of raillery is suppressed, will ever appear tedious and insipid.   215

Maria. Well, I'll not debate how far scandal may be allowable; but in a man, I am sure, it is always contemptible. We have pride, envy, rivalship, and a thousand motives to depreciate each other; but the male slanderer   220 must have the cowardice of a woman before he can traduce one.

Enter Servant

Serv. Madam, Mrs. Candour is below, and if your ladyship's at leisure, will leave her carriage.   225

Lady Sneer. Beg her to walk in. (*Exit Servant.*) Now, Maria, here is a character to your taste; for though Mrs. Candour is a little talkative, everybody allows her to be the best-natured and best sort of woman. 230

Maria. Yes, with a very gross affectation of good nature and benevolence, she does more mischief than the direct malice of old Crabtree.

Jos. I' faith that's true, Lady Sneerwell: whenever I hear the current running 235 against the characters of my friends, I never think them in such danger as when Candour undertakes their defense.

Lady Sneer. Hush! here she is!

Enter MRS. CANDOUR

Mrs. Can. My dear Lady Sneerwell, 240 how have you been this century? Mr. Surface, what news do you hear? though indeed it is no matter, for I think one hears nothing else but scandal.

Jos. Just so, indeed, ma'am. 245

Mrs. Can. Oh, Maria! child, what, is the whole affair off between you and Charles? His extravagance, I presume; the town talks of nothing else.

Maria. Indeed! I am very sorry, 250 ma'am, the town is not better employed.

Mrs. Can. True, true, child; but there's no stopping people's tongues. I own I was hurt to hear it, as I indeed was to learn, from the same quarter, that your guardian, Sir 255 Peter, and Lady Teazle have not agreed lately as well as could be wished.

Maria. 'Tis strangely impertinent for people to busy themselves so.

Mrs. Can. Very true, child; but what's 260 to be done? People will talk; there's no preventing it. Why, it was but yesterday I was told Miss Gadabout had eloped with Sir Filigree Flirt. But, Lord! there's no minding what one hears; though, to be sure, I had 265 this from very good authority.

Maria. Such reports are highly scandalous.

Mrs. Can. So they are, child; shameful! shameful! But the world is so censorious, no character escapes. Lord, now who would 270 have suspected your friend, Miss Prim, of an

indiscretion? Yet such is the ill-nature of people, that they say her uncle stopped her last week, just as she was stepping into the York diligence with her dancing-master. 275

Maria. I'll answer for't there are no grounds for that report.

Mrs. Can. Ah, no foundation in the world, I dare swear: no more, probably, than for the story circulated last month, of Mrs. Fes- 280 tino's affair with Colonel Cassino; though, to be sure, that matter was never rightly cleared up.

Jos. The license of invention some people take is monstrous indeed. 285

Maria. 'Tis so; but, in my opinion, those who report such things are equally culpable.

Mrs. Can. To be sure they are; tale-bearers are as bad as the tale-makers; 'tis an old observation, and a very true one. But what's 290 to be done, as I said before? How will you prevent people from talking? Today, Mrs. Clackitt assured me, Mr. and Mrs. Honeymoon were at last become mere man and wife, like the rest of their acquaintance. She 295 likewise hinted that a certain widow, in the next street, had got rid of her dropsy and recovered her shape in a most surprising manner. And at the same time, Miss Tattle, who was by, affirmed that Lord Buffalo had dis- 300 covered his lady at a house of no extraordinary fame; and that Sir Harry Bouquet and Tom Saunter were to measure swords on a similar provocation. But, Lord, do you think I would report these things? No, no! tale-bearers, 305 as I said before, are just as bad as the talemakers.

Jos. Ah, Mrs. Candour, if everybody had your forbearance and good nature!

Mrs. Can. I confess, Mr. Surface, I 310 cannot bear to hear people attacked behind their backs; and when ugly circumstances come out against our acquaintance, I own I always love to think the best. By-the-bye, I hope 'tis not true that your brother is absolutely 315 ruined?

Jos. I am afraid his circumstances are very bad indeed, ma'am.

Mrs. Can. Ah! I heard so; but you must tell him to keep up his spirits; everybody al- 320

most is in the same way — Lord Spindle, Sir
Thomas Splint, Captain Quinze, and Mr.
Nickit — all up,[1] I hear, within this week; so if
Charles is undone, he'll find half his acquaint-
ance ruined too, and that, you know, is a   325
consolation.

Jos. Doubtless, ma'am; a very great one.

Enter Servant

Serv. Mr. Crabtree and Sir Benjamin Backbite.   (*Exit.*

Lady Sneer. So, Maria, you see your   330
lover pursues you; positively you sha'n't escape.

Enter CRABTREE *and* SIR BENJAMIN
BACKBITE

Crab. Lady Sneerwell, I kiss your hand.
Mrs. Candour, I don't believe you are acquainted with my nephew, Sir Benjamin Backbite? Egad! ma'am, he has a pretty wit,   335
and is a pretty poet too; isn't he, Lady Sneerwell?

Sir Benj. O fie, uncle!

Crab. Nay, egad, it's true; I back him at
a rebus or a charade against the best   340
rhymer in the kingdom. Has your ladyship
heard the epigram he wrote last week on Lady
Frizzle's feather catching fire? Do, Benjamin,
repeat it, or the charade you made last night
extempore at Mrs. Drowzie's conversa-   345
zione.[2] Come now; your first is the name of a
fish, your second a great naval commander,
and ——

Sir Benj. Uncle, now — pr'ythee ——

Crab. I' faith, ma'am, 'twould surprise   350
you to hear how ready he is at all these fine sort
of things.

Lady Sneer. I wonder, Sir Benjamin, you
never publish anything.

Sir Benj. To say truth, ma'am, 'tis   355
very vulgar to print; and as my little productions are mostly satires and lampoons on particular people, I find they circulate more by
giving copies in confidence to the friends of the

[1] All "sold up," i.e., arrested for debt.
[2] A social gathering for the discussion of literary and
artistic topics; such affairs were fashionable then as
later.

parties. However, I have some love   360
elegies, which, when favored with this lady's
smiles, I mean to give the public.

                           (*Bows to* MARIA.

Crab. 'Fore heaven, ma'am, they'll immor-
talize you! You will be handed down to posterity, like Petrarch's Laura, or Waller's   365
Sacharissa. [1]

Sir Benj. Yes, madam, I think you will like
them, when you shall see them on a beautiful
quarto page, where a neat rivulet of text shall
meander through a meadow of margin.   370
'Fore Gad, they will be the most elegant things
of their kind!

Crab. But, ladies, that's true. Have you
heard the news?

Mrs. Can. What, sir, do you mean the   375
report of ——

Crab. No, ma'am, that's not it. Miss
Nicely is going to be married to her own footman.

Mrs. Can. Impossible!   380

Crab. Ask Sir Benjamin.

Sir Benj. 'Tis very true, ma'am; everything
is fixed, and the wedding liveries bespoke.

Crab. Yes; and they do say there were pressing reasons for it.   385

Lady Sneer. Why, I have heard something of
this before.

Mrs. Can. It can't be, and I wonder anyone
should believe such a story, of so prudent a
lady as Miss Nicely.   390

Sir Benj. Oh, Lud! ma'am, that's the very
reason 'twas believed at once. She has always been so cautious and so reserved, that
everybody was sure there was some reason for
it at bottom.   395

Mrs. Can. Why, to be sure, a tale of scandal
is as fatal to the credit of a prudent lady of her
stamp, as a fever is generally to those of the
strongest constitutions. But there is a sort of
puny, sickly reputation, that is always   400
ailing, yet will outlive the robuster characters
of a hundred prudes.

[1] Laura, the heroine of the famous sonnet cycle by
Francesco Petrarca (1304–74), the first great Italian
poet. Sacharissa, actually Lady Dorothy Sydney, to
whom Edmund Waller (1606–87) addressed many love
poems.

Sir Benj. True, madam, there are valetudinarians in reputation as well as constitution; who, being conscious of their weak part, 405 avoid the least breath of air, and supply their want of stamina by care and circumspection.

Mrs. Can. Well, but this may be all a mistake. You know, Sir Benjamin, very trifling circumstances often give rise to the most 410 injurious tales.

Crab. That they do, I'll be sworn, ma'am. Did you ever hear how Miss Piper came to lose her lover and her character last summer at Tunbridge?[1] Sir Benjamin, you remem- 415 ber it?

Sir Benj. Oh, to be sure! The most whimsical circumstance.

Lady Sneer. How was it, pray?

Crab. Why, one evening, at Mrs. 420 Ponto's assembly, the conversation happened to turn on the breeding Nova Scotia sheep in this country. Says a young lady in company, " I have known instances of it, for Miss Letitia Piper, a first cousin of mine, had a Nova 425 Scotia sheep that produced her twins." "What!" cries the Lady Dowager Dundizzy (who you know is as deaf as a post), "has Miss Piper had twins?" This mistake, as you may imagine, threw the whole company into a fit of 430 laughter. However, 'twas the next morning everywhere reported, and in a few days believed by the whole town, that Miss Letitia Piper had actually been brought to bed of a fine boy and a girl; and in less than a week 435 there were some people who could name the father, and the farm-house where the babies were put to nurse.

Lady Sneer. Strange, indeed!

Crab. Matter of fact, I assure you. 440 Oh, Lud! Mr. Surface, pray is it true that your uncle, Sir Oliver, is coming home?

Jos. Not that I know of, indeed, sir.

Crab. He has been in the East Indies a long time. You can scarcely remember him, 445 I believe? Sad comfort, whenever he returns, to hear how your brother has gone on!

Jos. Charles has been imprudent, sir, to be sure; but I hope no busy people have already

prejudiced Sir Oliver against him. He 450 may reform.

Sir Benj. To be sure, he may; for my part, I never believed him to be so utterly void of principle as people say; and though he has lost all his friends, I am told nobody is better 455 spoken of by the Jews.

Crab. That's true, egad, nephew. If the Old Jewry[1] was a ward, I believe Charles would be an alderman. No man more popular there, 'fore Gad! I hear he pays as many an- 460 nuities as the Irish tontine;[2] and that whenever he is sick, they have prayers for the recovery of his health in all the synagogues.

Sir Benj. Yet no man lives in greater splendor. They tell me, when he entertains 465 his friend, she will sit down to dinner with a dozen of his own securities; have a score of tradesmen waiting in the antechamber, and an officer behind every guest's chair.

Jos. This may be entertainment to 470 you, gentlemen, but you pay very little regard to the feelings of a brother.

Maria (aside). Their malice is intolerable. — Lady Sneerwell, I must wish you a good morning: I'm not very well. (*Exit.* 475

Mrs. Can. Oh, dear! she changes color very much.

Lady Sneer. Do, Mrs. Candour, follow her: she may want assistance.

Mrs. Can. That I will, with all my 480 soul, ma'am. Poor dear girl, who knows what her situation may be! (*Exit.*

Lady Sneer. 'Twas nothing but that she could not bear to hear Charles reflected on, notwithstanding their difference. 485

Sir Benj. The young lady's *penchant*[3] is obvious.

Crab. But, Benjamin, you must not give up the pursuit for that: follow her, and put her into good humor. Repeat her some of 490 your own verses. Come, I'll assist you.

Sir Benj. Mr. Surface, I did not mean to

[1] A popular watering place thirty miles south of London.

[1] A quarter in the heart of London near the Bank of England, then inhabited by Jewish moneylenders.
[2] The Irish government in the 1770's secured revenue by selling annuities which ceased on the death of the subscriber: a scheme invented by an Italian banker, Lorenzo Tonti, and hence called the "tontine" plan.
[3] Preference.

hurt you; but depend on't your brother is utterly undone.

Crab. Oh, Lud, ay! undone as ever man 495 was. Can't raise a guinea!

Sir Benj. And everything sold, I'm told, that was movable.

Crab. I have seen one that was at his house. Not a thing left but some empty bottles 500 that were overlooked, and the family pictures, which I believe are framed in the wainscots.

Sir Benj. And I'm very sorry, also, to hear some bad stories against him.

Crab. Oh! he has done many mean 505 things, that's certain. (*Going.*

Sir Benj. But, however, as he's your brother —— (*Going.*

Crab. We'll tell you all another opportunity.
(*Exeunt* CRABTREE *and* SIR BENJAMIN.

Lady Sneer. Ha! ha! 'tis very hard for 510 them to leave a subject they have not quite run down.

Jos. And I believe the abuse was no more acceptable to your ladyship than to Maria.

Lady Sneer. I doubt[1] her affections are 515 farther engaged than we imagined. But the family are to be here this evening, so you may as well dine where you are, and we shall have an opportunity of observing farther; in the meantime, I'll go and plot mischief, and 520 you shall study sentiment. (*Exeunt.*

SCENE 2. SIR PETER'S *house.*

Enter SIR PETER

Sir Pet. When an old bachelor marries a young wife, what is he to expect? 'Tis now six months since Lady Teazle made me the happiest of men; and I have been the most miserable dog ever since! We tifted a little 5 going to church, and fairly quarreled before the bells had done ringing. I was more than once nearly choked with gall during the honeymoon, and had lost all comfort in life before my friends had done wishing me joy. Yet I chose 10 with caution — a girl bred wholly in the country, who never knew luxury beyond one silk gown, nor dissipation above the annual gala

[1] Believe.

of a race ball. Yet now she plays her part in all the extravagant fopperies of the fashion 15 and the town, with as ready a grace as if she had never seen a bush or a grass-plot out of Grosvenor Square! I am sneered at by all my acquaintance, and paragraphed in the newspapers. She dissipates my fortune, and 20 contradicts all my humors: yet the worst of it is, I doubt I love her, or I should never bear all this. However, I'll never be weak enough to own it.

Enter ROWLEY

Row. Oh! Sir Peter, your servant; how 25 is it with you, sir?

Sir Pet. Very bad, Master Rowley, very bad. I meet with nothing but crosses and vexations.

Row. What can have happened to 30 trouble you since yesterday?

Sir Pet. A good question to a married man!

Row. Nay, I'm sure your lady, Sir Peter, can't be the cause of your uneasiness.

Sir Pet. Why, has anybody told you she 35 was dead?

Row. Come, come, Sir Peter, you love her, notwithstanding your tempers don't exactly agree.

Sir Pet. But the fault is entirely hers, 40 Master Rowley. I am, myself, the sweetest tempered man alive, and hate a teasing temper; and so I tell her a hundred times a day.

Row. Indeed!

Sir Pet. Ay; and what is very extraor- 45 dinary, in all our disputes she is always in the wrong! But Lady Sneerwell, and the set she meets at her house, encourage the perverseness of her disposition. Then, to complete my vexation, Maria, my ward, whom I ought to 50 have the power over, is determined to turn rebel too, and absolutely refuses the man whom I have long resolved on for her husband; meaning, I suppose, to bestow herself on his profligate brother. 55

Row. You know, Sir Peter, I have always taken the liberty to differ with you on the subject of these two young gentlemen. I only wish you may not be deceived in your opinion

of the elder. For Charles, my life on't! 60
he will retrieve his errors yet. Their worthy
father, once my honored master, was, at his
years, nearly as wild a spark; yet, when he died,
he did not leave a more benevolent heart to
lament his loss. 65

Sir Pet. You are wrong, Master Rowley. On
their father's death, you know, I acted as a
kind of guardian to them both, till their uncle
Sir Oliver's liberality gave them an early independence: of course, no person could have 70
more opportunities of judging of their hearts,
and I was never mistaken in my life. Joseph
is indeed a model for the young men of the age.
He is a man of sentiment, and acts up to the
sentiments he professes; but for the other, 75
take my word for't, if he had any grain of virtue
by descent, he has dissipated it with the rest of
his inheritance. Ah! my old friend, Sir Oliver,
will be deeply mortified when he finds how
part of his bounty has been misapplied. 80

Row. I am sorry to find you so violent against
the young man, because this may be the most
critical period of his fortune. I came hither
with news that will surprise you.

Sir Pet. What! let me hear. 85

Row. Sir Oliver *is* arrived, and at this moment in town.

Sir Pet. How! you astonish me! I thought
you did not expect him this month.

Row. I did not; but his passage has been 90
remarkably quick.

Sir Pet. Egad, I shall rejoice to see my old
friend. 'Tis fifteen years since we met. We
have had many a day together; but does he still
enjoin us not to inform his nephews of his 95
arrival?

Row. Most strictly. He means, before it is
known, to make some trial of their dispositions.

Sir Pet. Ah! there needs no art to discover
their merits; however, he shall have his 100
way. But, pray, does he know I am married?

Row. Yes, and will soon wish you joy.

Sir Pet. What, as we drink health to a friend
in a consumption. Ah! Oliver will laugh at me.
We used to rail at matrimony together, 105
and he has been steady to his text. Well, he
must be soon at my house, though! I'll instantly give orders for his reception. But,

Master Rowley, don't drop a word that Lady
Teazle and I ever disagree. 110

Row. By no means.

Sir Pet. For I should never be able to stand
Noll's jokes; so I'd have him think, Lord forgive me! that we are a very happy couple.

Row. I understand you; but then you 115
must be very careful not to differ while he is in
the house with you.

Sir Pet. Egad, and so we must, and that's
impossible. Ah! Master Rowley, when an old
bachelor marries a young wife, he de- 120
serves — no — the crime carries its punishment along with it. (*Exeunt.*

ACT II

Scene i. Sir Peter's *house.*

Enter Sir Peter *and* Lady Teazle

Sir Pet. Lady Teazle, Lady Teazle, I'll
not bear it!

Lady T. Sir Peter, Sir Peter, you may bear
it or not, as you please; but I ought to have my
own way in everything, and what's more, 5
I will, too. What! though I was educated in
the country, I know very well that women of
fashion in London are accountable to nobody after they are married.

Sir Pet. Very well, ma'am, very well; 10
so a husband is to have no influence, no authority?

Lady T. Authority! No, to be sure, if you
wanted authority over me, you should have
adopted me, and not married me: I am 15
sure you were old enough.

Sir Pet. Old enough! ay, there it is. Well,
well, Lady Teazle, though my life may be made
unhappy by your temper, I'll not be ruined by
your extravagance. 20

Lady T. My extravagance! I'm sure I'm not
more extravagant than a woman of fashion
ought to be.

Sir Pet. No, no, madam, you shall throw
away no more sums on such unmeaning 25
luxury. 'Slife! to spend as much to furnish
your dressing-room with flowers in winter as
would suffice to turn the Pantheon [1] into a

[1] A fashionable concert hall, with tearooms, located
in Oxford Street and opened in 1770.

green-house, and give a *fête champêtre*[1] at Christmas.   30

Lady T. And am I to blame, Sir Peter, because flowers are dear in cold weather? You should find fault with the climate, and not with me. For my part, I'm sure, I wish it was spring all the year round, and that roses grew un- 35 der our feet.

Sir Pet. Oons! madam; if you had been born to this, I shouldn't wonder at your talking thus; but you forget what your situation was when I married you.   40

Lady T. No, no, I don't; 'twas a very disagreeable one, or I should never have married you.

Sir Pet. Yes, yes, madam; you were then in somewhat a humbler style: the daughter 45 of a plain country squire. Recollect, Lady Teazle, when I saw you first sitting at your tambor,[2] in a pretty figured linen gown, with a bunch of keys at your side; your hair combed smooth over a roll, and your apartment 50 hung round with fruits in worsted, of your own working.

Lady T. Oh, yes! I remember it very well, and a curious life I led — my daily occupation to inspect the dairy, superintend the poul- 55 try, make extracts from the family receipt book, and comb my aunt Deborah's lap-dog.

Sir Pet. Yes, yes, ma'am, 'twas so indeed.

Lady T. And then, you know, my evening amusements! To draw patterns for 60 ruffles, which I had not materials to make up; to play Pope Joan[3] with the curate; to read a sermon to my aunt; or to be stuck down to an old spinet to strum my father to sleep after a fox-chase.   65

Sir Pet. I am glad you have so good a memory. Yes, madam, these were the recreations I took you from; but now you must have your coach — *vis-à-vis*[4] — and three powdered footmen before your chair; and in the summer, 70 a pair of white cats[5] to draw you to Kensing-

ton Gardens.[1] No recollection, I suppose, when you were content to ride double, behind the butler, on a docked coach-horse?

Lady T. No; I swear I never did that. 75 I deny the butler and the coach-horse.

Sir Pet. This, madam, was your situation; and what have I done for you? I have made you a woman of fashion, of fortune, of rank; in short, I have made you my wife.   80

Lady T. Well, then, and there is but one thing more you can make me to add to the obligation, and that is ——

Sir Pet. My widow, I suppose?

Lady T. Hem! hem!   85

Sir Pet. I thank you, madam; but don't flatter yourself; for though your ill conduct may disturb my peace, it shall never break my heart, I promise you; however, I am equally obliged to you for the hint.   90

Lady T. Then why will you endeavor to make yourself so disagreeable to me, and thwart me in every little elegant expense?

Sir Pet. 'Slife, madam, I say, had you any of these little elegant expenses when you 95 married me?

Lady T. Lud, Sir Peter! would you have me be out of the fashion?

Sir Pet. The fashion, indeed! what had you to do with the fashion before you married 100 me?

Lady T. For my part, I should think you would like to have your wife thought a woman of taste.

Sir Pet. Ay, there again; taste! 105 Zounds! madam, you had no taste when you married me!

Lady T. That's very true indeed, Sir Peter; and after having married you, I should never pretend to taste again, I allow. But 110 now, Sir Peter, if we have finished our daily jangle, I presume I may go to my engagement at Lady Sneerwell's.

Sir Pet. Ah, there's another precious circumstance; a charming set of acquaint- 115 ance you have made there!

Lady T. Nay, Sir Peter, they are all people of rank and fortune, and remarkably tenacious of reputation.

[1] An open-air entertainment.
[2] Embroidery frame.
[3] An unfashionable and rather slow card game of the time.
[4] Face to face, i.e., the coach occupants sit facing one another.   [5] White ponies.

[1] A large London park toward the west.

Sir Pet. Yes, egad, they are tenacious   120 of reputation with a vengeance; for they don't choose anybody should have a character but themselves! Such a crew! Ah! many a wretch has rid on a hurdle [1] who has done less mischief than these utterers of forged tales, coiners   125 of scandal, and clippers of reputation.

Lady T. What! would you restrain the freedom of speech?

Sir Pet. Ah! they have made you just as bad as any one of the society.   130

Lady T. Why, I believe I do bear a part with a tolerable grace. But I vow I bear no malice against the people I abuse. When I say an ill-natured thing, 'tis out of pure good humor; and I take it for granted, they deal ex-   135 actly in the same manner with me. But, Sir Peter, you know you promised to come to Lady Sneerwell's too.

Sir Pet. Well, well, I'll call in just to look after my own character.   140

Lady T. Then indeed you must make haste after me, or you'll be too late. So, good-bye to ye.   (*Exit.*

Sir Pet. So, I have gained much by my intended expostulation; yet, with what a   145 charming air she contradicts everything I say, and how pleasingly she shows her contempt for my authority! Well, though I can't make her love me, there is great satisfaction in quarreling with her; and I think she never appears   150 to such advantage as when she is doing everything in her power to plague me.   (*Exit.*

SCENE 2. *At* LADY SNEERWELL'S.

Enter LADY SNEERWELL, MRS. CANDOUR, CRABTREE, SIR BENJAMIN BACKBITE, *and* JOSEPH SURFACE .

Lady Sneer. Nay, positively, we will hear it.

Jos. Yes, yes, the epigram, by all means.

Sir Benj. Oh, plague on't, uncle! 'tis mere nonsense.

Crab. No, no; 'fore Gad, very clever for   5 an extempore!

Sir Benj. But, ladies, you should be acquainted with the circumstances. You must know, that one day last week, as Lady Betty

[1] A rude wagon which bore criminals to the gallows.

Curricle was taking the dust in Hyde Park,[1]   10 in a sort of duodecimo [2] phaëton, she desired me to write some verses on her ponies, upon which I took out my pocket-book, and in one moment produced the following:
Sure never were seen two such beautiful po-
    nies;   15
Other horses are clowns, but these macaronies:
To give them this title I'm sure can't be wrong,
Their legs are so slim, and their tails are so long.

Crab. There, ladies, done in the smack of a whip, and on horseback too.   20

Jos. A very Phoebus mounted, indeed, Sir Benjamin.

Sir Benj. Oh, dear sir! trifles, trifles.

Enter LADY TEAZLE *and* MARIA

Mrs. Can. I must have a copy.

Lady Sneer. Lady Teazle, I hope we   25 shall see Sir Peter?

Lady T. I believe he'll wait on your ladyship presently.

Lady Sneer. Maria, my love, you look grave. Come, you shall sit down to piquet with   30 Mr. Surface.

Maria. I take very little pleasure in cards; however, I'll do as you please.

Lady T. (*aside*). I am surprised Mr. Surface should sit down with her; I thought he   35 would have embraced this opportunity of speaking to me, before Sir Peter came.

Mrs. Can. Now, I'll die, but you are so scandalous, I'll forswear your society.

Lady T. What's the matter, Mrs. Can-   40 dour?

Mrs. Can. They'll not allow our friend, Miss Vermilion, to be handsome.

Lady Sneer. Oh, surely she is a pretty woman.   45

Crab. I'm very glad you think so, ma'am.

Mrs. Can. She has a charming fresh color.

Lady T. Yes, when it is fresh put on.

Mrs. Can. Oh, fie! I'll swear her color is natural; I have seen it come and go.   50

Lady T. I dare swear you have, ma'am; it

[1] The park in which the most fashionable drive was located.

[2] Very small, like a book in duodecimo.

goes off at night, and comes again in the morning.

Sir Benj. True, ma'am, it not only comes and goes, but what's more, egad! her maid 55 can fetch and carry it.

Mrs. Can. Ha! ha! ha! how I hate to hear you talk so! But surely, now, her sister *is*, or *was*, very handsome.

Crab. Who? Mrs. Evergreen? Oh, 60 Lord! she's six and fifty if she's an hour.

Mrs. Can. Now positively you wrong her; fifty-two or fifty-three is the utmost; and I don't think she looks more.

Sir Benj. Ah! there's no judging by her 65 looks, unless one could see her face.

Lady Sneer. Well, well, if Mrs. Evergreen *does* take some pains to repair the ravages of time, you must allow she effects it with great ingenuity, and surely that's better than the 70 careless manner in which the widow Ochre chalks her wrinkles.

Sir Benj. Nay, now, Lady Sneerwell, you are severe upon the widow. Come, come, 'tis not that she paints so ill, but when she 75 has finished her face, she joins it so badly to her neck, that she looks like a mended statue, in which the connoisseur sees at once that the head's modern though the trunk's antique.

Crab. Ha! ha! ha! well said, nephew. 80

Mrs. Can. Ha! ha! ha! well, you make me laugh, but I vow I hate you for it. What do you think of Miss Simper?

Sir Benj. Why, she has very pretty teeth.

Lady T. Yes, and on that account, when 85 she is neither speaking nor laughing (which very seldom happens), she never absolutely shuts her mouth, but leaves it on a jar, as it were — thus ——   (*Shows her teeth.*

Mrs. Can. How can you be so ill- 90 natured?

Lady T. Nay, I allow even that's better than the pains Mrs. Prim takes to conceal her losses in front. She draws her mouth till it positively resembles the aperture of a poor's 95 box,[1] and all her words appear to slide out edgewise, as it were thus, *How do you do, madam? Yes, madam.*

[1] A box with a slit in the top, which is placed in church vestibules to receive offerings for charity.

Lady Sneer. Very well, Lady Teazle; I see you can be a little severe.   100

Lady T. In defense of a friend it is but justice. But here comes Sir Peter to spoil our pleasantry.

Enter SIR PETER TEAZLE

Sir Pet. Ladies, your most obedient. (*Aside*) Mercy on me! here is the whole set! a 105 character dead at every word, I suppose.

Mrs. Can. I am rejoiced you are come, Sir Peter. They have been *so* censorious; and Lady Teazle as bad as anyone.

Sir Pet. It must be very distressing to 110 *you*, Mrs. Candour, I dare swear.

Mrs. Can. Oh, they will allow good qualities to nobody; not even good nature to our friend Mrs. Pursy.

Lady T. What, the fat dowager who 115 was at Mrs. Quadrille's last night?

Mrs. Can. Nay, her bulk is her misfortune; and when she takes such pains to get rid of it, you ought not to reflect on her.

Lady Sneer. That's very true, indeed. 120

Lady T. Yes, I know she almost lives on acids and small whey; laces herself by pulleys; and often, in the hottest noon in summer, you may see her on a little squat pony, with her hair plaited up behind like a drummer's, 125 and puffing round the Ring [1] on a full trot.

Mrs. Can. I thank you, Lady Teazle, for defending her.

Sir Pet. Yes, a good defense, truly!

Mrs. Can. Truly, Lady Teazle is as 130 censorious as Miss Sallow.

Crab. Yes, and she is a curious being to pretend to be censorious — an awkward gawky, without any one good point under heaven.

Mrs. Can. Positively you shall not be 135 so very severe. Miss Sallow is a near relation of mine by marriage, and as for her person, great allowance is to be made; for, let me tell you, a woman labors under many disadvantages who tries to pass for a girl at six- 140 and-thirty.

Lady Sneer. Though, surely, she is handsome still; and for the weakness in her eyes, con-

[1] The fashionable circular drive in Hyde Park.

sidering how much she reads by candlelight, it is not to be wondered at.   145

Mrs. Can. True, and then as to her manner; upon my word I think it is particularly graceful, considering she never had the least education; for you know her mother was a Welsh milliner, and her father a sugar-baker at   150 Bristol.

Sir Benj. Ah! you are both of you too good natured!

Sir Pet. (*aside*). Yes, damned good natured! This their own relation! mercy on me!   155

Mrs. Can. For my part, I own I cannot bear to hear a friend ill spoken of.

Sir Pet. No, to be sure!

Sir Benj. Oh! you are of a moral turn. Mrs. Candour and I can sit for an hour and   160 hear Lady Stucco talk sentiment.

Lady T. Nay, I vow Lady Stucco is very well with the dessert after dinner; for she's just like the French fruits one cracks for mottoes[1] — made up of paint and proverb.   165

Mrs. Can. Well, I never will join in ridiculing a friend; and so I constantly tell my cousin Ogle, and you all know what pretensions she has to be critical on beauty.

Crab. Oh, to be sure! she has herself the   170 oddest countenance that ever was seen; 'tis a collection of features from all the different countries of the globe.

Sir Benj. So she has, indeed — an Irish front ——   175

Crab. Caledonian[2] locks ——

Sir Benj. Dutch nose ——

Crab. Austrian lips ——

Sir Benj. Complexion of a Spaniard ——

Crab. And teeth *à la Chinois*.[3]   180

Sir Benj. In short, her face resembles a *table d'hôte* at Spa,[4] where no two guests are of a nation ——

Crab. Or a congress at the close of a general war — wherein all the members, even to   185 her eyes, appear to have a different interest,

and her nose and chin are the only parties likely to join issue.

Mrs. Can. Ha! ha! ha!

Sir Pet. (*aside*). Mercy on my life! —   190 a person they dine with twice a week.

Lady Sneer. Go, go; you are a couple of provoking toads.

Mrs. Can. Nay, but I vow you shall not carry the laugh off so; for give me leave to   195 say that Mrs. Ogle ——

Sir Pet. Madam, madam, I beg your pardon; there's no stopping these good gentlemen's tongues. But when I tell you, Mrs. Candour, that the lady they are abusing is a partic-   200 ular friend of mine, I hope you'll not take her part.

Lady Sneer. Ha! ha! ha! Well said, Sir Peter! But you are a cruel creature — too phlegmatic yourself for a jest, and too   205 peevish to allow wit in others.

Sir Pet. Ah, madam, true wit is more nearly allied to good nature than your ladyship is aware of.

Lady T. True, Sir Peter. I believe   210 they are so near akin that they can never be united.

Sir Benj. Or rather, madam, suppose them to be man and wife, because one seldom sees them together.   215

Lady T. But Sir Peter is such an enemy to scandal, I believe he would have it put down by Parliament.

Sir Pet. 'Fore heaven, madam, if they were to consider the sporting with reputation   220 of as much importance as poaching on manors, and pass an Act for the Preservation of Fame, I believe there are many would thank them for the bill.

Lady Sneer. Oh, Lud! Sir Peter;   225 would you deprive us of our privileges?

Sir Pet. Ay, madam; and then no person should be permitted to kill characters or run down reputations, but qualified old maids and disappointed widows.   230

Lady Sneer. Go, you monster!

Mrs. Can. But, surely, you would not be quite so severe on those who only report what they hear?

Sir Pet. Yes, madam, I would have   235

[1] Artificial fruits containing sentiments on slips of paper, like the more modern "cracker" favors made of paper.
[2] Scottish.
[3] After the Chinese type.
[4] A fashionable watering place in Belgium.

law merchant [1] for them too; and in all cases of slander currency, whenever the drawer of the lie was not to be found, the injured parties should have a right to come on any of the indorsers. 240

Crab. Well, for my part, I believe there never was a scandalous tale without some foundation.

Sir Pet. Oh, nine out of ten of the malicious inventions are founded on some ridicu- 245 lous misrepresentation.

Lady Sneer. Come, ladies, shall we sit down to cards in the next room?

Enter a Servant, *who whispers to* SIR PETER

Sir Pet. I'll be with them directly. (*Exit* Servant. *Aside*) I'll get away unper- 250 ceived.

Lady Sneer. Sir Peter, you are not going to leave us?

Sir Pet. Your ladyship must excuse me; I'm called away by particular business. But 255 I leave my character behind me. (*Exit.*

Sir Benj. Well certainly, Lady Teazle, that lord of yours is a strange being; I could tell you some stories of him would make you laugh heartily if he were not your husband. 260

Lady T. Oh, pray don't mind that; come, do let's hear them.

(*Joins the rest of the company who are going into the next room.*

Jos. Maria, I see you have no satisfaction in this society.

Maria. How is it possible I should? 265 If to raise malicious smiles at the infirmities or misfortunes of those who have never injured us be the province of wit or humor, Heaven grant me a double portion of dullness!

Jos. Yet they appear more ill-natured 270 than they are; they have no malice at heart.

Maria. Then is their conduct still more contemptible; for, in my opinion, nothing could excuse the intemperance of their tongues, but a natural and uncontrollable bitterness 275 of mind.

Jos. Undoubtedly, madam; and it has al-

[1] Mercantile law, wherein the indorsers are liable for the debts if the principals fail to pay.

ways been a sentiment of mine, that to propagate a malicious truth wantonly is more despicable than to falsify from revenge. 280 But can you, Maria, feel thus for others, and be unkind to me alone? Is hope to be denied the tenderest passion?

Maria. Why will you distress me by renewing this subject? 285

Jos. Ah, Maria! you would not treat me thus, and oppose your guardian, Sir Peter's will, but that I see that profligate Charles is still a favored rival.

Maria. Ungenerously urged! But 290 whatever my sentiments are for that unfortunate young man, be assured I shall not feel more bound to give him up, because his distresses have lost him the regard even of a brother. 295

Jos. Nay, but Maria, do not leave me with a frown; by all that's honest, I swear (*kneels*) — —

Re-enter LADY TEAZLE, *behind*

(*Aside*) Gad's life, here's Lady Teazle (*Aloud to* MARIA) You must not — no, you shall not — for, though I have the greatest 300 regard for Lady Teazle ——

Maria. Lady Teazle!

Jos. Yet were Sir Peter to suspect ——

Lady T. (*coming forward*). What is this, pray? Do you take her for me? Child, 305 you are wanted in the next room. (*Exit* MARIA.) What is all this, pray?

Jos. Oh, the most unlucky circumstance in nature! Maria has somehow suspected the tender concern I have for your happiness, 310 and threatened to acquaint Sir Peter with her suspicions, and I was just endeavoring to reason with her when you came in.

Lady T. Indeed! but you seemed to adopt a very tender mode of reasoning. Do you 315 usually argue on your knees?

Jos. Oh, she's a child, and I thought a little bombast —— But, Lady Teazle, when are you to give me your judgment on my library, as you promised? 320

Lady T. No, no; I begin to think it would be imprudent, and you know I admit you as a lover no farther than fashion sanctions.

Jos. True, a mere platonic cicisbeo [1] —
what every wife is entitled to.   325

Lady T. Certainly, one must not be out of
fashion. However, I have so many of my
country prejudices left, that, though Sir Peter's
ill-humor may vex me ever so, it never shall
provoke me to ——   330

Jos. The only revenge in your power. Well,
I applaud your moderation.

Lady T. Go; you are an insinuating wretch.
But we shall be missed; let us join the company.   335

Jos. But we had best not return together.

Lady T. Well, don't stay; for Maria sha'n't
come to hear any more of your reasoning, I
promise you.   (*Exit.* 340

Jos. A curious dilemma my politics have
run me into! I wanted, at first, only to ingratiate myself with Lady Teazle, that she
might not be my enemy with Maria; and I
have, I don't know how, become her 345
serious lover. Sincerely I begin to wish I had
never made such a point of gaining so very
good a character, for it has led me into so many
cursed rogueries that I doubt I shall be exposed at last.   (*Exit.* 350

SCENE 3. SIR PETER TEAZLE'S *house.*

Enter ROWLEY *and* SIR OLIVER SURFACE

Sir Ol. Ha! ha! ha! So my old friend is
married, hey? — a young wife out of the country. Ha! ha! ha! that he should have stood
bluff [2] to old bachelor so long, and sink into a
husband at last!   5

Row. But you must not rally him on the
subject, Sir Oliver; 'tis a tender point, I assure
you, though he has been married only seven
months.

Sir Ol. Then he has been just half a year 10
on the stool of repentance! Poor Peter! But
you say he has entirely given up Charles —
never sees him, hey?

Row. His prejudice against him is astonishing, and I am sure greatly increased by 15
a jealousy of him with Lady Teazle, which he

[1] A gallant, usually the lover of a married woman.
[2] Firm.

has industriously been led into by a scandalous society in the neighborhood, who have
contributed not a little to Charles's ill name.
Whereas the truth is, I believe, if the lady 20
is partial to either of them, his brother is the
favorite.

Sir Ol. Ay, I know there is a set of malicious,
prating, prudent gossips, both male and
female, who murder characters to kill 25
time, and will rob a young fellow of his good
name before he has years to know the value
of it. But I am not to be prejudiced against
my nephew by such, I promise you. No, no; if
Charles has done nothing false or mean, 30
I shall compound for his extravagance.

Row. Then, my life on't, you will reclaim
him. Ah, sir! it gives me new life to find that
your heart is not turned against him; and that
the son of my good old master has one 35
friend, however, left.

Sir Ol. What! shall I forget, Master Rowley,
when I was at his years myself? Egad, my
brother and I were neither of us very prudent
youths; and yet, I believe, you have not 40
seen many better men than your old master
was.

Row. Sir, 'tis this reflection gives me assurance that Charles may yet be a credit to his
family. But here comes Sir Peter.   45

Sir Ol. Egad, so he does. Mercy on me! he's
greatly altered, and seems to have a settled
married look! One may read *husband* in his
face at this distance!

Enter SIR PETER TEAZLE

Sir Pet. Ha! Sir Oliver, my old friend! 50
Welcome to England a thousand times!

Sir Ol. Thank you — thank you, Sir Peter!
and i' faith I am glad to find you well, believe
me.

Sir Pet. Oh! 'tis a long time since we 55
met — fifteen years, I doubt, Sir Oliver, and
many a cross accident in the time.

Sir Ol. Ay, I have had my share. But
what! I find you are married, hey? Well,
well, it can't be helped; and so — I wish 60
you joy with all my heart.

Sir Pet. Thank you, thank you, Sir Oliver.

Yes, I have entered into — the happy state; but we'll not talk of that now.

Sir Ol. True, true, Sir Peter; old friends 65 should not begin on grievances at first meeting; no, no, no.

Row. Take care, pray, sir.

Sir Ol. Well, so one of my nephews is a wild fellow, hey? 70

Sir Pet. Wild! Ah! my old friend, I grieve for your disappointment there; he's a lost young man, indeed. However, his brother will make you amends. Joseph is, indeed, what a youth should be. Everybody in the world 75 speaks well of him.

Sir Ol. I am sorry to hear it; he has too good a character to be an honest fellow. Everybody speaks well of him! Pshaw! then he has bowed as low to knaves and fools as to the honest 80 dignity of genius and virtue.

Sir Pet. What, Sir Oliver! do you blame him for not making enemies?

Sir Ol. Yes, if he has merit enough to deserve them. 85

Sir Pet. Well, well; you'll be convinced when you know him. 'Tis edification to hear him converse; he professes the noblest sentiments.

Sir Ol. Oh! plague of his sentiments! If he salutes me with a scrap of morality in his 90 mouth, I shall be sick directly. But, however, don't mistake me, Sir Peter; I don't mean to defend Charles's errors — but before I form my judgment of either of them, I intend to make a trial of their hearts; and my friend Rowley 95 and I have planned something for the purpose.

Row. And Sir Peter shall own for once he has been mistaken.

Sir Pet. Oh! my life on Joseph's honor.

Sir Ol. Well — come, give us a bot- 100 tle of good wine, and we'll drink the lad's health, and tell you our scheme.

Sir Pet. Allons,[1] then!

Sir Ol. And don't, Sir Peter, be so severe against your old friend's son. Odds my 105 life! I am not sorry that he has run out of the course a little; for my part I hate to see prudence clinging to the green suckers of youth; 'tis like ivy round a sapling, and spoils the growth of the tree. (*Exeunt.* 110

[1] Let us go.

ACT III

SCENE I. SIR PETER TEAZLE's *house.*

Enter SIR PETER TEAZLE, SIR OLIVER SURFACE, *and* ROWLEY

Sir Pet. Well, then, we will see this fellow first, and have our wine afterwards; but how is this, Master Rowley? I don't see the jet[1] of your scheme.

Row. Why, sir, this Mr. Stanley, whom 5 I was speaking of, is nearly related to them by their mother. He was a merchant in Dublin, but has been ruined by a series of undeserved misfortunes. He has applied, by letter, to Mr. Surface and Charles; from the former he 10 has received nothing but evasive promises of future service, while Charles has done all that his extravagance has left him power to do, and he is, at this time, endeavoring to raise a sum of money, part of which, in the midst of 15 his own distresses, I know he intends for the service of poor Stanley.

Sir Ol. Ah! he is my brother's son.

Sir Pet. Well, but how is Sir Oliver personally to —— 20

Row. Why, sir, I will inform Charles and his brother that Stanley has obtained permission to apply personally to his friends, and as they have neither of them ever seen him, let Sir Oliver assume his character, and he will 25 have a fair opportunity of judging, at least, of the benevolence of their dispositions; and believe me, sir, you will find in the younger brother one who, in the midst of folly and dissipation, has still, as our immortal bard ex- 30 presses it, "a heart to pity, and a hand, open as day, for melting charity."[2]

Sir Pet. Pshaw! What signifies his having an open hand or purse either, when he has nothing left to give? Well, well, make the 35 trial, if you please. But where is the fellow whom you brought for Sir Oliver to examine, relative to Charles's affairs?

Row. Below, waiting his commands, and no one can give him better intelligence. This, 40

[1] Point.
[2] Shakespeare's phrase in *2 Henry IV*, Act IV, Scene 4, ll. 31–32, begins: "a tear for pity," etc.

Sir Oliver, is a friendly Jew, who, to do him justice, has done everything in his power to bring your nephew to a proper sense of his extravagance.

Sir Pet. Pray let us have him in. 45

Row. (*apart to* Servant). Desire Mr. Moses to walk upstairs.

Sir Pet. But, pray, why should you suppose he will speak the truth?

Row. Oh! I have convinced him that he 50 has no chance of recovering certain sums advanced to Charles, but through the bounty of Sir Oliver, who he knows is arrived, so that you may depend on his fidelity to his own interests. I have also another evidence in my power 55 — one Snake, whom I have detected in a matter little short of forgery, and shall speedily produce him to remove some of your prejudices.

Sir Pet. I have heard too much on that subject. 60

Row. Here comes the honest Israelite.

Enter MOSES

This is Sir Oliver.

Sir Ol. Sir, I understand you have lately had great dealings with my nephew, Charles.

Moses. Yes, Sir Oliver, I have done all I 65 could for him; but he was ruined before he came to me for assistance.

Sir Ol. That was unlucky, truly; for you have had no opportunity of showing your talents. 70

Moses. None at all; I hadn't the pleasure of knowing his distresses till he was some thousands worse than nothing.

Sir Ol. Unfortunate, indeed! But I suppose you have done all in your power for him, 75 honest Moses?

Moses. Yes, he knows that. This very evening I was to have brought him a gentleman from the city, who does not know him, and will, I believe, advance him some money. 80

Sir Pet. What! one Charles has never had money from before?

Moses. Yes; Mr. Premium, of Crutched Friars,[1] formerly a broker.

Sir Pet. Egad, Sir Oliver, a thought 85

[1] A street near the Tower of London.

strikes me! Charles, you say, does not know Mr. Premium?

Moses. Not at all.

Sir Pet. Now then, Sir Oliver, you may have a better opportunity of satisfying 90 yourself than by an old romancing tale of a poor relation. Go with my friend Moses, and represent Premium, and then, I'll answer for it, you'll see your nephew in all his glory.

Sir Ol. Egad, I like this idea better than 95 the other, and I may visit Joseph afterwards as Old Stanley.

Sir Pet. True, so you may.

Row. Well, this is taking Charles rather at a disadvantage, to be sure. However, 100 Moses, you understand Sir Peter, and will be faithful?

Moses. You may depend upon me. This is near the time I was to have gone.

Sir Ol. I'll accompany you as soon as 105 you please, Moses. But hold! I have forgot one thing — how the plague shall I be able to pass for a Jew?

Moses. There's no need — the principal is Christian. 110

Sir Ol. Is he? I'm very sorry to hear it. But then, again, a'n't I rather too smartly dressed to look like a money lender?

Sir Pet. Not at all; 'twould not be out of character if you went in your own carriage 115 — would it, Moses?

Moses. Not in the least.

Sir Ol. Well, but how must I talk? There's certainly some cant of usury and mode of treating that I ought to know. 120

Sir Pet. Oh! there's not much to learn. The great point, as I take it, is to be exorbitant enough in your demands — hey, Moses?

Moses. Yes, that's a very great point.

Sir Ol. I'll answer for't I'll not be want- 125 ing in that. I'll ask him eight or ten per cent on the loan, at least.

Moses. If you ask him no more than that, you'll be discovered immediately.

Sir Ol. Hey! what the plague! How 130 much, then?

Moses. That depends upon the circumstances. If he appears not very anxious for the supply, you should require only forty or

fifty per cent; but if you find him in great 135
distress, and want the moneys very bad, you
may ask double.

Sir Pet. A good honest trade you're learning,
Sir Oliver!

Sir Ol. Truly, I think so; and not un- 140
profitable.

Moses. Then, you know, you hav'n't the
moneys yourself, but are forced to borrow them
for him of an old friend.

Sir Ol. Oh! I borrow it of a friend, 145
do I?

Moses. And your friend is an unconscionable dog; but you can't help that.

Sir Ol. My friend is an unconscionable dog?

Moses. Yes, and he himself has not 150
the moneys by him, but is forced to sell stock
at a great loss.

Sir Ol. He is forced to sell stock at a great
loss, is he? Well, that's very kind of him.

Sir Pet. I' faith, Sir Oliver — Mr. 155
Premium, I mean — you'll soon be master of
the trade. But, Moses! would not you have
him run out a little against the Annuity Bill? [1]
That would be in character, I should think.

Moses. Very much. 160

Row. And lament that a young man now
must be at years of discretion before he is
suffered to ruin himself?

Moses. Ay, great pity!

Sir Pet. And abuse the public for al- 165
lowing merit to an Act, whose only object is to
snatch misfortune and imprudence from the
rapacious gripe of usury, and give the minor
a chance of inheriting his estate without being
undone by coming into possession. 170

Sir Ol. So, so; Moses shall give me further instructions as we go together.

Sir Pet. You will not have much time, for
your nephew lives hard by.

Sir Ol. Oh, never fear! My tutor ap- 175
pears so able, that though Charles lived in the
next street, it must be my own fault if I am not
a complete rogue before I turn the corner.

(*Exeunt* SIR OLIVER SURFACE *and*
MOSES.

[1] An act of Parliament, just passed in May, 1777, and
intended to protect minors against the sellers of annuities.

Sir Pet. So now, I think Sir Oliver will be
convinced. You are partial, Rowley, 180
and would have prepared Charles for the other
plot.

Row. No, upon my word, Sir Peter.

Sir Pet. Well, go bring me this Snake, and
I'll hear what he has to say presently. 185
I see Maria, and want to speak with her.
(*Exit* ROWLEY.) I should be glad to be convinced my suspicions of Lady Teazle and
Charles were unjust. I have never yet opened
my mind on this subject to my friend Jo- 190
seph. I am determined I will do it; he will
give me his opinion sincerely.

Enter MARIA

So, child, has Mr. Surface returned with you?

Maria. No, sir; he was engaged.

Sir Pet. Well, Maria, do you not reflect, 195
the more you converse with that amiable
young man, what return his partiality for you
deserves?

Maria. Indeed, Sir Peter, your frequent
importunity on this subject distresses me 200
extremely; you compel me to declare, that I
know no man who has ever paid me a particular
attention, whom I would not prefer to Mr.
Surface.

Sir Pet. So, here's perverseness! No, 205
no, Maria, 'tis Charles only whom you would
prefer. 'Tis evident his vices and follies have
won your heart.

Maria. This is unkind, sir. You know I
have obeyed you in neither seeing nor 210
corresponding with him. I have heard enough
to convince me that he is unworthy my regard.
Yet I cannot think it culpable, if, while my
understanding severely condemns his vices, my
heart suggests some pity for his distresses. 215

Sir Pet. Well, well, pity him as much as you
please; but give your heart and hand to a
worthier object.

Maria. Never to his brother!

Sir Pet. Go, perverse and obstinate! 220
But take care, madam; you have never yet
known what the authority of a guardian is.
Don't compel me to inform you of it.

Maria. I can only say, you shall not have

just reason. 'Tis true, by my father's will, 225
I am for a short period bound to regard you
as his substitute; but must cease to think you
so, when you would compel me to be miserable.
(Exit.

Sir Pet. Was ever man so crossed as I am?
Everything conspiring to fret me! I had 230
not been involved in matrimony a fortnight,
before her father, a hale and hearty man, died,
on purpose, I believe, for the pleasure of plaguing me with the care of his daughter. But
here comes my helpmate! She appears 235
in great good humor. How happy I should
be if I could tease her into loving me, though
but a little!

Enter LADY TEAZLE

Lady T. Lud! Sir Peter, I hope you hav'n't
been quarreling with Maria? It is not 240
using me well to be ill-humored when I am not
by.

Sir Pet. Ah! Lady Teazle, you might have
the power to make me good-humored at all
times. 245

Lady T. I am sure I wish I had; for I want
you to be in a charming sweet temper at this
moment. Do be good-humored now, and let
me have two hundred pounds, will you?

Sir Pet. Two hundred pounds! What, 250
a'n't I to be in a good humor without paying
for it? But speak to me thus, and i' faith
there's nothing I could refuse you. You shall
have it; but seal me a bond for the repayment.

Lady T. Oh no — there. My note of 255
hand will do as well.   *(Offering her hand.*

Sir Pet. And you shall no longer reproach
me with not giving you an independent settlement. I mean shortly to surprise you. But
shall we always live thus, hey? 260

Lady T. If you please. I'm sure I don't
care how soon we leave off quarreling, provided
you'll own you were tired first.

Sir Pet. Well, then let our future contest be,
who shall be most obliging. 265

Lady T. I assure you, Sir Peter, good nature
becomes you. You look now as you did before
we were married, when you used to walk with
me under the elms, and tell me stories of what a

gallant you were in your youth, and 270
chuck me under the chin, you would, and ask
me if I thought I could love an old fellow, who
would deny me nothing — didn't you?

Sir Pet. Yes, yes; and you were as kind and
attentive —— 275

Lady T. Ay, so I was, and would always take
your part, when my acquaintance used to
abuse you, and turn you into ridicule.

Sir Pet. Indeed!

Lady T. Ay, and when my cousin 280
Sophy has called you a stiff, peevish old
bachelor, and laughed at me for thinking of
marrying one who might be my father, I have
always defended you, and said, I didn't think
you so ugly by any means, and I dared 285
say you'd make a very good sort of a husband.

Sir Pet. And you prophesied right; and we
shall now be the happiest couple ——

Lady T. And never differ again?

Sir Pet. No, never! Though at the 290
same time, indeed, my dear Lady Teazle, you
must watch your temper very seriously; for in
all our little quarrels, my dear, if you recollect,
my love, you always began first.

Lady T. I beg your pardon, my dear 295
Sir Peter: indeed, you always gave the provocation.

Sir Pet. Now see, my angel! take care; con-
tradicting isn't the way to keep friends.

Lady T. Then don't you begin it, my 300
love!

Sir Pet. There, now! you — you are going
on. You don't perceive, my life, that you are
just doing the very thing which you know
always makes me angry. 305

Lady T. Nay, you know if you will be angry
without any reason, my dear ——

Sir Pet. There! now you want to quarrel
again.

Lady T. No, I am sure I don't; but if 310
you will be so peevish ——

Sir Pet. There now! who begins first?

Lady T. Why you, to be sure. I said nothing; but there's no bearing your temper.

Sir Pet. No, no, madam; the fault's in 315
your own temper.

Lady T. Ay, you are just what my cousin
Sophy said you would be.

Sir Pet. Your cousin Sophy is a forward, impertinent gipsy.   320

Lady T. You are a great bear, I'm sure, to abuse my relations.

Sir Pet. Now may all the plagues of marriage be doubled on me, if ever I try to be friends with you any more!   325

Lady T. So much the better.

Sir Pet. No, no, madam; 'tis evident you never cared a pin for me, and I was a madman to marry you — a pert, rural coquette, that had refused half the honest squires in the   330 neighborhood.

Lady T. And I am sure I was a fool to marry you — an old dangling bachelor, who was single at fifty, only because he never could meet with anyone who would have him.   335

Sir Pet. Ay, ay, madam; but you were pleased enough to listen to me; you never had such an offer before.

Lady T. No! didn't I refuse Sir Tivy Terrier, who everybody said would have been a   340 better match? for his estate is just as good as yours, and he has broke his neck since we have been married.

Sir Pet. I have done with you, madam! You are an unfeeling, ungrateful — but   345 there's an end to everything. I believe you capable of everything that is bad. Yes, madam, I now believe the reports relative to you and Charles, madam. Yes, madam, *you* and Charles are — not without grounds ——   350

Lady T. Take care, Sir Peter; you had better not insinuate any such thing! I'll not be suspected without cause, I promise you.

Sir Pet. Very well, madam! very well! A separate maintenance as soon as you   355 please. Yes, madam, or a divorce! I'll make an example of myself for the benefit of all old bachelors. Let us separate, madam.

Lady T. Agreed, agreed! And now, my dear Sir Peter, we are of a mind once   360 more, we may be the happiest couple, and never differ again, you know — ha! ha! ha! Well, you are going to be in a passion, I see, and I shall only interrupt you; so, bye — bye!
                   (*Exit.*

Sir Pet. Plagues and tortures! Can't   365 I make her angry either? Oh, I am the most

miserable fellow! But I'll not bear her presuming to keep her temper. No! she may break my heart, but she sha'n't keep her temper. (*Exit.*

SCENE 2. CHARLES SURFACE'S *house.*

Enter TRIP, MOSES, *and* SIR OLIVER SURFACE

Trip. Here, Master Moses! if you'll stay a moment, I'll try whether — what's the gentleman's name?

Sir Ol. (*aside*). Mr. Moses, what is my name?   5

Moses. Mr. Premium.

Trip. Premium — very well.
                (*Exit, taking snuff.*

Sir Ol. To judge by the servants, one wouldn't believe the master was ruined. But what! — sure, this was my brother's   10 house?

Moses. Yes, sir; Mr. Charles bought it of Mr. Joseph, with the furniture, pictures, &c., just as the old gentleman left it. Sir Peter thought it a piece of extravagance in him.   15

Sir Ol. In my mind, the other's economy in selling it to him was more reprehensible by half.

Enter TRIP

Trip. My master says you must wait, gentlemen; he has company, and can't speak with you yet.   20

Sir Ol. If he knew who it was wanted to see him, perhaps he would not send such a message?

Trip. Yes, yes, sir; he knows you are here. I did not forget little Premium; no, no, no.

Sir Ol. Very well; and I pray, sir, what   25 may be your name?

Trip. Trip, sir; my name is Trip, at your service.

Sir Ol. Well, then, Mr. Trip, you have a pleasant sort of place here, I guess?   30

Trip. Why, yes; here are three or four of us pass our time agreeably enough; but then our wages are sometimes a little in arrear — and not very great either — but fifty pounds a year, and find our own bags and bouquets.[1]   35

---

[1] Provide our own bag wigs and shoulder bouquets: these were fashionable adornments for footmen.

Sir Ol. (*aside*). Bags and bouquets! halters and bastinadoes!

Trip. And, *à propos*, Moses; have you been able to get me that little bill discounted?

Sir Ol. (*aside*). Wants to raise money 40 too! mercy on me! Has his distresses too, I warrant, like a lord, and affects creditors and duns.

Moses. 'Twas not to be done, indeed, Mr. Trip. 45

Trip. Good lack, you surprise me! My friend Brush has indorsed it, and I thought when he put his name on the back of a bill 'twas the same as cash.

Moses. No! 'twouldn't do. 50

Trip. A small sum; but twenty pounds. Hark'ee, Moses, do you think you couldn't get it me by way of annuity?

Sir Ol. (*aside*). An annuity! ha! ha! a footman raise money by way of annuity! Well 55 done, luxury, egad!

Moses. Well, but you must insure your place.

Trip. Oh, with all my heart! I'll insure my place, and my life, too, if you please.

Sir Ol. (*aside*). It is more than I would 60 your neck.

Moses. But is there nothing you could deposit?

Trip. Why, nothing capital of my master's wardrobe has dropped lately; but I 65 could give you a mortgage on some of his winter clothes, with equity of redemption before November; or you shall have the reversion of the French velvet, or a post-obit [1] on the blue and silver: [2] these, I should think, Moses, 70 with a few pair of point ruffles, [3] as a collateral security; hey, my little fellow?

Moses. Well, well.   (*Bell rings.*

Trip. Egad, I heard the bell! I believe, gentlemen, I can now introduce you. Don't 75 forget the annuity, little Moses! This way, gentlemen. I'll insure my place, you know.

Sir Ol. If the man be a shadow of the master, this is the temple of dissipation indeed!

                                 (*Exeunt.*

---

[1] A note given by an heir, which becomes payable on the death of the person whose property he expects to inherit.

[2] I.e., a suit of clothes.   [3] Shirt ruffles of lace.

SCENE 3. *Another room.*

CHARLES SURFACE, SIR HARRY BUMPER, CARELESS, *and others, discovered at a table with wine, &c.*

Char. 'Fore heaven, 'tis true! there's the great degeneracy of the age. Many of our acquaintance have taste, spirit, and politeness; but plague on't, they won't drink.

Care. It is so indeed, Charles! they give 5 in to all the substantial luxuries of the table, and abstain from nothing but wine and wit. Oh certainly society suffers by it intolerably; for now, instead of the social spirit of raillery that used to mantle over a glass of bright Bur- 10 gundy, their conversation is become just like the Spa-water they drink, which has all the pertness and flatulence of Champagne, without its spirit or flavor.

1st Gent. But what are they to do who 15 love play better than wine?

Care. True! there's Sir Harry diets himself for gaming, and is now under a hazard regimen.

Char. Then he'll have the worst of it. What! you wouldn't train a horse for the course 20 by keeping him from corn? [1] For my part, egad, I am never so successful as when I am a little merry; let me throw on a bottle of Champagne, and I never lose; at least, I never feel my losses, which is exactly the same thing. 25

2d Gent. Ay, that I believe.

Char. And then, what man can pretend to be a believer in love, who is an abjurer of wine? 'Tis the test by which the lover knows his own heart. Fill a dozen bumpers to a 30 dozen beauties, and she that floats atop is the maid that has bewitched you.

Care. Now then, Charles, be honest, and give us your real favorite.

Char. Why, I have withheld her only in 35 compassion to you. If I toast her, you must give a round of her peers, which is impossible — on earth.

Care. Oh! then we'll find some canonized vestals or heathen goddesses that will do, 40 I warrant!

Char. Here then, bumpers, you rogues! bumpers! Maria! Maria!   (*All drink.*

[1] Grain.

Sir Harry. Maria who?

Char. Oh, damn the surname! 'Tis too 45
formal to be registered in Love's calendar; but
now, Sir Harry, beware, we must have beauty
superlative.

Care. Nay, never study,[1] Sir Harry; we'll
stand to the toast, though your mistress 50
should want an eye, and you know you have a
song will excuse you.

Sir Harry. Egad, so I have! and I'll give him
the song instead of the lady.

SONG

Here's to the maiden of bashful fifteen; 55
　　Here's to the widow of fifty;
Here's to the flaunting extravagant quean,
　　And here's to the housewife that's thrifty.
Chorus.　　　Let the toast pass,
　　　　　　Drink to the lass, 60
I'll warrant she'll prove an excuse for the glass.

Here's to the charmer whose dimples we prize;
　　Now to the maid who has none, sir;
Here's to the girl with a pair of blue eyes, 64
　　And here's to the nymph with but *one*, sir.
Chorus.　　　Let the toast pass, &c.

Here's to the maid with a bosom of snow;
　　Now to her that's as brown as a berry;
Here's to the wife with a face full of woe,
　　And now to the girl that is merry. 70
Chorus.　　　Let the toast pass, &c.

For let 'em be clumsy, or let 'em be slim,
　　Young or ancient, I care not a feather;
So fill a pint bumper quite up to the brim,
　　And let us e'en toast them together. 75
Chorus.　　　Let the toast pass, &c.

All. Bravo! bravo!

Enter TRIP, *and whispers to* CHARLES SURFACE

Char. Gentlemen, you must excuse me a
little. Careless, take the chair, will you?

Care. Nay, pr'ythee, Charles, what now? 80
This is one of your peerless beauties, I suppose,
has dropt in by chance?

Char. No, faith! To tell you the truth, 'tis

[1] Never fear.

a Jew and a broker, who are come by appointment. 85

Care. Oh, damn it! let's have the Jew in.

1st Gent. Ay, and the broker too, by all
means.

2d Gent. Yes, yes, the Jew and the broker.

Char. Egad, with all my heart! — Trip, 90
bid the gentlemen walk in. (*Exit* TRIP.) —
Though there's one of them a stranger, I can
tell you.

Care. Charles, let us give them some generous Burgundy, and perhaps they'll grow 95
conscientious.

Char. Oh, hang 'em, no! wine does but draw
forth a man's natural qualities, and to make
them drink would only be to whet their
knavery. 100

Enter TRIP, SIR OLIVER SURFACE, *and* MOSES

Char. So, honest Moses, walk in; walk in,
pray, Mr. Premium — that's the gentleman's
name, isn't it, Moses?

Moses. Yes, sir.

Char. Set chairs, Trip — sit down, Mr. 105
Premium — glasses, Trip — sit down, Moses.
Come, Mr. Premium, I'll give you a sentiment;
here's *Success to usury!* Moses, fill the gentleman a bumper.

Moses. Success to usury!　　(*Drinks.* 110

Care. Right, Moses; usury is prudence and
industry, and deserves to succeed.

Sir Ol. Then here's *All the success it deserves!*
　　　　　　　　　　　　　　　(*Drinks.*

Care. No, no, that won't do! Mr. Premium, you have demurred at the toast, 115
and must drink it in a pint bumper.

1st Gent. A pint bumper, at least.

Moses. Oh, pray, sir, consider; Mr. Premium's a gentleman.

Care. And therefore loves good wine. 120

2d Gent. Give Moses a quart glass; this is
mutiny, and a high contempt for the chair.

Care. Here, now for't! I'll see justice done,
to the last drop of my bottle.

Sir Ol. Nay, pray, gentlemen; I did not 125
expect this usage.

Char. No, hang it, Careless, you sha'n't!
Mr. Premium's a stranger.

Sir Ol. (*aside*). Odd! I wish I was well out of this company.   130

Care. Plague on 'em, then! If they won't drink, we'll not sit down with them. Come, Harry, the dice are in the next room. Charles, you'll join us when you have finished your business with the gentlemen?   135

Char. I will! I will! (*Exeunt all the Gentlemen.*) Careless!

Care. (*returning*). Well!

Char. Perhaps I may want you.   139

Care. Oh, you know I am always ready: word, note, or bond, 'tis all the same to me. (*Exit.*

Moses. Sir, this is Mr. Premium, a gentleman of the strictest honor and secrecy; and always performs what he undertakes. Mr. Premium, this is ——   145

Char. Pshaw! have done. Sir, my friend Moses is a very honest fellow, but a little slow at expression: he'll be an hour giving us our titles. Mr. Premium, the plain state of the matter is this: I am an extravagant young   150 fellow who wants to borrow money; you I take to be a prudent old fellow, who has got money to lend. I am blockhead enough to give fifty per cent sooner than not have it; and you, I presume, are rogue enough to take a hun-   155 dred if you can get it. Now, sir, you see we are acquainted at once, and may proceed to business without further ceremony.

Sir Ol. Exceeding frank, upon my word. I see, sir, you are not a man of many com-   160 pliments.

Char. Oh, no, sir! plain dealing in business I always think best.

Sir Ol. Sir, I like you the better for it. However, you are mistaken in one thing: I   165 have no money to lend, but I believe I could procure some of a friend; but then he's an unconscionable dog, isn't he, Moses?

Moses. But you can't help that.

Sir Ol. And must sell stock to accom-   170 modate you — mustn't he, Moses?

Moses. Yes, indeed! You know I always speak the truth, and scorn to tell a lie!

Char. Right. People that speak truth generally do: but these are trifles, Mr. Pre-   175 mium. What! I know money isn't to be bought without paying for 't!

Sir Ol. Well, but what security could you give? You have no land, I suppose?

Char. Not a molehill, nor a twig, but   180 what's in the bough-pots [1] out of the window!

Sir Ol. Nor any stock, I presume?

Char. Nothing but live stock, and that's only a few pointers and ponies. But pray, Mr. Premium, are you acquainted at all with   185 any of my connections?

Sir Ol. Why, to say truth, I am.

Char. Then you must know that I have a a dev'lish rich uncle in the East Indies, Sir Oliver Surface, from whom I have the   190 greatest expectations.

Sir Ol. That you have a wealthy uncle I have heard; but how your expectations will turn out is more, I believe, than you can tell.

Char. Oh, no! there can be no doubt.   195 They tell me I'm a prodigious favorite, and that he talks of leaving me everything.

Sir Ol. Indeed! this is the first I've heard of it.

Char. Yes, yes, 'tis just so. Moses   200 knows 'tis true; don't you, Moses?

Moses. Oh, yes! I'll swear to 't.

Sir Ol. (*aside*). Egad, they'll persuade me presently I'm at Bengal.[2]

Char. Now, I propose, Mr. Premium,   205 if it's agreeable to you, a post-obit on Sir Oliver's life; though at the same time the old fellow has been so liberal to me, that I give you my word, I should be very sorry to hear that anything had happened to him.   210

Sir Ol. Not more than I should, I assure you. But the bond you mention happens to be just the worst security you could offer me, for I might live to a hundred, and never see the principal.   215

Char. Oh, yes, you would; the moment Sir Oliver dies, you know, you would come on me for the money.

Sir Ol. Then I believe I should be the most unwelcome dun you ever had in your life.   220

Char. What! I suppose you're afraid that Sir Oliver is too good a life?

Sir Ol. No, indeed, I am not; though I have heard he is as hale and healthy as any man of his years in Christendom.   225

[1] Flower-pots.   [2] A province of east central India.

Char. There again now you are misinformed. No, no, the climate has hurt him considerably, poor uncle Oliver! Yes, yes, he breaks apace, I'm told, and is so much altered lately, that his nearest relations don't know him.   230

Sir Ol. No! ha! ha! ha! so much altered lately, that his nearest relations don't know him! ha! ha! ha! ha! egad — ha! ha! ha!

Char. Ha! ha! you're glad to hear that, little Premium?   235

Sir Ol. No, no, I'm not.

Char. Yes, yes, you are — ha! ha! ha! You know that mends your chance.

Sir Ol. But I'm told Sir Oliver is coming over. Nay, some say he is actually ar-   240 rived.

Char. Pshaw! Sure I must know better than you whether he's come or not. No, no; rely on't, he's at this moment at Calcutta.[1] Isn't he, Moses?   245

Moses. Oh, yes, certainly.

Sir Ol. Very true, as you say, you must know better than I, though I have it from pretty good authority. Haven't I, Moses?

Moses. Yes, most undoubted!   250

Sir Ol. But, sir, as I understand you want a few hundreds immediately, is there nothing you could dispose of?

Char. How do you mean?

Sir Ol. For instance, now, I have heard   255 that your father left behind him a great quantity of massive old plate?

Char. Oh, Lud! that's gone long ago. Moses can tell you how better than I can.

Sir Ol. (*aside*). Good lack! all the fam-   260 ily race-cups and corporation-bowls![2] — Then it was also supposed that his library was one of the most valuable and compact ——

Char. Yes, yes, so it was — vastly too much so for a private gentleman. For   265 my part, I was always of a communicative disposition, so I thought it a shame to keep so much knowledge to myself.

Sir Ol. (*aside*). Mercy upon me! Learning that had run in the family like an heir-   270 loom! — Pray, what are become of the books?

[1] Capital of Bengal.
[2] Testimonials from the city corporation for distinguished services.

Char. You must enquire of the auctioneer, Master Premium, for I don't believe even Moses can direct you.

Moses. I know nothing of books.   275

Sir Ol. So, so, nothing of the family property left, I suppose?

Char. Not much, indeed; unless you have a mind to the family pictures. I have got a room full of ancestors above, and if you have a   280 taste for paintings, egad, you shall have 'em a bargain.

Sir Ol. Hey! what the devil! sure, you wouldn't sell your forefathers, would you?

Char. Every man of them to the best   285 bidder.

Sir Ol. What! your great uncles and aunts?

Char. Ay, and my great grandfathers and grandmothers too.

Sir Ol. (*aside*). Now I give him up. —   290 What the plague, have you no bowels for your own kindred? Odd's life, do you take me for Shylock in the play, that you would raise money of me on your own flesh and blood?

Char. Nay, my little broker, don't be   295 angry: what need *you* care if you have your money's worth?

Sir Ol. Well, I'll be the purchaser: I think I can dispose of the family canvas —— (*Aside*) Oh, I'll never forgive him this! never!   300

Enter CARELESS

Care. Come, Charles, what keeps you?

Char. I can't come yet: i' faith we are going to have a sale above stairs. Here's little Premium will buy all my ancestors.

Care. Oh, burn your ancestors!   305

Char. No, he may do that afterwards, if he pleases. Stay, Careless, we want you; egad, you shall be auctioneer; so come along with us.

Care. Oh, have with you, if that's the case. I can handle a hammer as well as a dice-   310 box!

Sir Ol. (*aside*). Oh, the profligates!

Char. Come, Moses, you shall be appraiser, if we want one. Gad's life, little Premium, you don't seem to like the business?   315

Sir Ol. Oh, yes, I do, vastly. Ha! ha! ha! yes, yes, I think it a rare joke to sell one's family by auction — ha! ha! — (*Aside*) Oh, the prodigal!

Char. To be sure! when a man wants 320 money, where the plague should he get assistance if he can't make free with his own relations?   (*Exeunt.*

ACT IV

SCENE I. *Picture room at* CHARLES SURFACE'S.

Enter CHARLES SURFACE, SIR OLIVER SURFACE, MOSES, *and* CARELESS

Char. Walk in, gentlemen; pray walk in. Here they are, the family of the Surfaces, up to the Conquest.

Sir Ol. And, in my opinion, a goodly collection.   5

Char. Ay, ay; these are done in the true spirit of portrait painting; no *volontière grace* [1] or expression. Not like the works of your modern Raphaels, who give you the strongest resemblance, yet contrive to make your 10 portrait independent of you; so that you may sink the original and not hurt the picture. No, no; the merit of these is the inveterate likeness — all stiff and awkward as the originals, and like nothing in human nature besides.   15

Sir Ol. Ah! we shall never see such figures of men again.

Char. I hope not. Well, you see, Master Premium, what a domestic character I am. Here I sit of an evening surrounded by my 20 family. But come, get to your pulpit, Mr. Auctioneer; here's an old gouty chair of my grandfather's will answer the purpose.

Care. Ay, ay, this will do. But, Charles, I hav'n't a hammer; and what's an auc- 25 tioneer without his hammer?

Char. Egad, that's true. What parchment have we here? (*Takes down a roll.*) Oh, our genealogy in full. Here, Careless, you shall have no common bit of mahogany; here's 30 the family tree for you, you rogue; this shall be your hammer, and now you may knock down my ancestors with their own pedigree.

Sir Ol. (*aside*). What an unnatural rogue! an *ex post facto* [2] parricide!   35

[1] Added charm.   [2] Retroactive.

Care. Yes, yes, here's a list of your generation indeed; faith, Charles, this is the most convenient thing you could have found for the business, for 'twill serve not only as a hammer, but a catalogue into the bargain. Come, 40 begin — A-going, a-going, a-going!

Char. Bravo, Careless! Well, here's my great uncle, Sir Richard Raveline, a marvelous good general in his day, I assure you. He served in all the Duke of Marlborough's 45 wars, and got that cut over his eye at the battle of Malplaquet.[1] What say you, Mr. Premium? Look at him; there's a hero, not cut out of his feathers, as your modern clipp'd captains are, but enveloped in wig and 50 regimentals, as a general should be. What do you bid?

Moses. Mr. Premium would have *you* speak.

Char. Why, then, he shall have him for ten pounds, and I'm sure that's not dear for a 55 staff-officer.

Sir Ol. (*aside*). Heaven deliver me! his famous uncle Richard for ten pounds! — Well, sir, I take him at that.

Char. Careless, knock down my uncle 60 Richard. Here, now, is a maiden sister of his, my great-aunt Deborah, done by Kneller,[2] thought to be in his best manner, and a very formidable likeness. There she is, you see, a shepherdess feeding her flock. You shall 65 have her for five pounds ten; the sheep are worth the money.

Sir Ol. (*aside*). Ah! poor Deborah! a woman who set such a value on herself! — Five pounds ten; she's mine.   70

Char. Knock down my aunt Deborah! Here, now, are two that were a sort of cousins of theirs. You see, Moses, these pictures were done sometime ago, when beaux wore wigs, and the ladies their own hair.   75

Sir Ol. Yes, truly, headdresses appear to have been a little lower in those days.

Char. Well, take that couple for the same.

Moses. 'Tis a good bargain.

Char. Careless! This, now, is a grand- 80 father of my mother, a learned judge, well

[1] An English victory over the French in 1709.
[2] Sir Godfrey Kneller (1648–1723), the most fashionable portrait painter of the early eighteenth century.

known on the Western Circuit. **What do you** rate him at, Moses?

Moses. Four guineas.

Char. Four guineas! Gad's life, you 85 don't bid me the price of his wig. Mr. Premium, you have more respect for the woolsack;[1] do let us knock his lordship down at fifteen.

Sir Ol. By all means. 90

Care. Gone!

Char. And there are two brothers of his, William and Walter Blunt, Esquires, both members of Parliament, and noted speakers, and what's very extraordinary, I believe, 95 this is the first time they were ever bought or sold.

Sir Ol. That is very extraordinary, indeed! I'll take them at your own price, for the honor of Parliament. 100

Care. Well said, little Premium! I'll knock them down at forty.

Char. Here's a jolly fellow; I don't know what relation, but he was mayor of Manchester. Take him at eight pounds. 105

Sir Ol. No, no; six will do for the mayor.

Char. Come, make it guineas,[2] and I'll throw you the two aldermen there into the bargain.

Sir Ol. They're mine.

Char. Careless, knock down the mayor 110 and aldermen. But, plague on't, we shall be all day retailing in this manner. Do let us deal wholesale; what say you, little Premium? Give us three hundred pounds for the rest of the family in the lump. 115

Care. Ay, ay, that will be the best way.

Sir Ol. Well, well, anything to accommodate you — they are mine. But there is one portrait which you have always passed over.

Care. What, that ill-looking little fel- 120 low over the settee?

Sir Ol. Yes, sir, I mean that; though I don't think him so ill-looking a little fellow, by any means.

Char. What, that? Oh! that's my 125 uncle Oliver; 'twas done before he went to India.

[1] The seat of the Lord Chancellor in the House of Lords; here, a term symbolic of the legal profession.
[2] A guinea is twenty-one shillings; a pound, twenty.

Care. Your uncle Oliver! Gad, then, you'll never be friends, Charles. That, now, to me, is as stern a looking rogue as ever I saw — 130 an unforgiving eye, and a damned disinheriting countenance! an inveterate knave, depend on't. Don't you think so, little Premium?

Sir Ol. Upon my soul, sir, I do not. I think it is as honest a looking face as any in the 135 room, dead or alive. But I suppose uncle Oliver goes with the rest of the lumber?

Char. No, hang it! I'll not part with poor Noll. The old fellow has been very good to me, and, egad, I'll keep his picture while 140 I've a room to put it in.

Sir Ol. (aside). The rogue's my nephew after all! — But, sir, I have somehow taken a fancy to that picture.

Char. I'm sorry for't, for you certainly 145 will not have it. Oons, haven't you got enough of them?

Sir Ol. (aside). I forgive him everything! — But, sir, when I take a whim in my head I don't value money. I'll give you as much for 150 that as for all the rest.

Char. Don't tease me, master broker. I tell you I'll not part with it, and there's an end of it.

Sir Ol. (aside). How like his father 155 the dog is! — Well, well, I have done. — (*Aside*) I did not perceive it before, but I think I never saw such a striking resemblance. — Here is a draft for your sum. 159

Char. Why, 'tis for eight hundred pounds.

Sir Ol. You will not let Sir Oliver go?

Char. Zounds! no! I tell you once more.

Sir Ol. Then never mind the difference, we'll balance that another time. But give me your hand on the bargain; you are an honest 165 fellow, Charles. I beg pardon, sir, for being so free. Come, Moses.

Char. Egad, this is a whimsical old fellow! But hark'ee, Premium, you'll prepare lodgings for these gentlemen? 170

Sir Ol. Yes, yes, I'll send for them in a day or two.

Char. But, hold; do now send a genteel conveyance for them, for, I assure you, they were most of them used to ride in their own 175 carriages.

Sir Ol. I will, I will; for all but Oliver.

Char. Ay, all but the little nabob.

Sir Ol. You're fixed on that?

Char. Peremptorily.   180

Sir Ol. (*aside*). A dear extravagant rogue! — Good day! Come, Moses. Let me hear now who dares call him profligate!

(*Exeunt* Sir Oliver Surface *and* Moses.

Care. Why, this is the oddest genius of the sort I ever saw!   185

Char. Egad! he's the prince of brokers, I think. I wonder how Moses got acquainted with so honest a fellow. Ha! here's Rowley. Do, Careless, say I'll join the company in a few moments.   190

Care. I will; but don't let that old blockhead persuade you to squander any of that money on old musty debts, or any such nonsense; for tradesmen, Charles, are the most exorbitant fellows.   195

Char. Very true, and paying them is only encouraging them.

Care. Nothing else.

Char. Ay, ay, never fear. (*Exit* Careless.) So! this was an odd old fellow,   200 indeed. Let me see; two-thirds of this is mine by right, five hundred and thirty odd pounds. 'Fore heaven! I find one's ancestors are more valuable relations than I took them for! Ladies and gentlemen, your most obedient and   205 very grateful servant. (*Bows.*

Enter Rowley

Ha! old Rowley! egad, you are just come in time to take leave of your old acquaintance.

Row. Yes, I heard they were a-going.   210 But I wonder you can have such spirits under so many distresses.

Char. Why, there's the point! my distresses are so many, that I can't afford to part with my spirits; but I shall be rich and sple-   215 netic, all in good time. However, I suppose you are surprised that I am not more sorrowful at parting with so many near relations. To be sure 'tis very affecting; but you see they never move a muscle, so why should I?   220

Row. There's no making you serious a moment.

Char. Yes, faith, I am so now. Here, my honest Rowley, here, get me this changed directly, and take a hundred pounds of it   225 immediately to old Stanley.

Row. A hundred pounds! Consider only —

Char. Gad's life, don't talk about it. Poor Stanley's wants are pressing, and if you don't make haste, we shall have someone call   230 that has a better right to the money.

Row. Ah! there's the point! I never will cease dunning you with the old proverb ——

Char. "Be just before you're generous." Why, so I would if I could; but Justice   235 is an old, lame, hobbling beldame, and I can't get her to keep pace with Generosity for the soul of me.

Row. Yet, Charles, believe me, one hour's reflection ——   240

Char. Ay, ay, it's all very true; but, hark'ee, Rowley, while I have, by heaven, I'll give! So damn your economy! And now for hazard!

(*Exeunt.*

Scene 2. *The parlor.*

Enter Sir Oliver Surface *and* Moses

Moses. Well, sir, I think, as Sir Peter said, you have seen Mr. Charles in high glory; 'tis great pity he's so extravagant.

Sir Ol. True, but he would not sell my picture.   5

Moses. And loves wine and women so much.

Sir Ol. But he would not sell my picture.

Moses. And games so deep.

Sir Ol. But he would not sell my picture. Oh, here's Rowley.   10

Enter Rowley

Row. So, Sir Oliver, I find you have made a purchase ——

Sir Ol. Yes, yes; our young rake has parted with his ancestors like old tapestry.

Row. And here has he commissioned me   15 to re-deliver you part of the purchase money. I mean, though, in your necessitous character of old Stanley.

Moses. Ah! there is the pity of it all; he is so damned charitable.   20

Row. And I left a hosier and two tailors in the hall, who, I'm sure, won't be paid, and this hundred would satisfy them.

Sir Ol. Well, well, I'll pay his debts, and his benevolence too. But now I am no more 25 a broker, and you shall introduce me to the elder brother as old Stanley.

Row. Not yet awhile; Sir Peter, I know, means to call there about this time.

Enter TRIP

Trip. Oh, gentlemen, I beg pardon for 30 not showing you out; this way. Moses, a word.
                       (*Exeunt* TRIP *and* MOSES.

Sir Ol. There's a fellow for you! Would you believe it, that puppy intercepted the Jew on our coming, and wanted to raise money before he got to his master.   35

Row. Indeed!

Sir Ol. Yes, they are now planning an annuity business. Ah, Master Rowley, in my days servants were content with the follies of their masters, when they were worn a 40 little threadbare; but now, they have their vices, like their birthday clothes,[1] with the gloss on.   (*Exeunt.*

SCENE 3. *A library in* JOSEPH SURFACE'S *house.*

Enter JOSEPH SURFACE *and a* Servant

Jos. No letter from Lady Teazle?

Serv. No, sir.

Jos. I am surprised she has not sent, if she is prevented from coming. Sir Peter certainly does not suspect me. Yet I wish I may not 5 lose the heiress, through the scrape I have drawn myself into with the wife. However, Charles's imprudence and bad character are great points in my favor.
             (*Knocking heard without.*

Serv. Sir, I believe that must be Lady 10 Teazle.

[1] Elegant costumes for the king's birthday, a time of celebration.

Jos. Hold! See whether it is or not before you go to the door: I have a particular message for you, if it should be my brother.

Serv. 'Tis her ladyship, sir; she always 15 leaves her chair at the milliner's in the next street.

Jos. Stay, stay; draw that screen before the window — that will do. My opposite neighbor is a maiden lady of so anxious a temper. 20 (*Servant draws the screen, and exit.*) I have a difficult hand to play in this affair. Lady Teazle has lately suspected my views on Maria; but she must by no means be let into that secret — at least, till I have her more in 25 my power.

Enter LADY TEAZLE

Lady T. What, sentiment in soliloquy now? Have you been very impatient? Oh, Lud! don't pretend to look grave. I vow I couldn't come before.   30

Jos. Oh, madam, punctuality is a species of constancy, a very unfashionable quality in a lady.

Lady T. Upon my word you ought to pity me. Do you know, Sir Peter is grown so ill- 35 natured to me of late, and so jealous of Charles too! That's the best of the story, isn't it?

Jos. (*aside*). I am glad my scandalous friends keep that up.

Lady T. I am sure I wish he would let 40 Maria marry him, and then perhaps he would be convinced. Don't you, Mr. Surface?

Jos. (*aside*). Indeed I do not. — Oh, certainly I do! for then my dear Lady Teazle would also be convinced how wrong her 45 suspicions were of my having any design on the silly girl.

Lady T. Well, well, I'm inclined to believe you. But isn't it provoking, to have the most ill-natured things said of one? And there's 50 my friend, Lady Sneerwell, has circulated I don't know how many scandalous tales of me, and all without any foundation too! That's what vexes me.

Jos. Ay, madam, to be sure, that is the 55 provoking circumstance — without foundation. Yes, yes, there's the mortification, indeed; for when a scandalous story is believed against one, there certainly is no comfort like the consciousness of having deserved it.   60

Lady T. No, to be sure, then I'd forgive their malice; but to attack me, who am really so innocent, and who never say an ill-natured thing of anybody — that is, of any friend; and then Sir Peter too, to have him so peevish, and   65 so suspicious, when I know the integrity of my own heart! Indeed 'tis monstrous!

Jos. But, my dear Lady Teazle, 'tis your own fault if you suffer it. When a husband entertains a groundless suspicion of his wife,   70 and withdraws his confidence from her, the original compact is broken, and she owes it to the honor of her sex to outwit him.

Lady T. Indeed! So that if he suspects me without cause, it follows that the best way   75 of curing his jealousy is to give him reason for't?

Jos. Undoubtedly; for your husband should never be deceived in you; and in that case it becomes you to be frail in compliment to his discernment.   80

Lady T. To be sure, what you say is very reasonable, and when the consciousness of my innocence ——

Jos. Ah! my dear madam, there is the great mistake: 'tis this very conscious innocence   85 that is of the greatest prejudice to you. What is it makes you negligent of forms, and careless of the world's opinion? Why, the consciousness of your own innocence. What makes you thoughtless in your conduct, and apt   90 to run into a thousand little imprudences? Why, the consciousness of your own innocence. What makes you impatient of Sir Peter's temper, and outrageous at his suspicions? Why, the consciousness of your own innocence.   95

Lady T. 'Tis very true!

Jos. Now, my dear Lady Teazle, if you would but once make a trifling *faux pas*,[1] you can't conceive how cautious you would grow, and how ready to humor and agree with   100 your husband.

Lady T. Do you think so?

Jos. Oh! I'm sure on't; and then you would find all scandal would cease at once; for, in short, your character at present is like a   105

[1] False step, mistake.

person in a plethora, absolutely dying from too much health.

Lady T. So, so; then I perceive your prescription is, that I must sin in my own defense, and part with my virtue to secure my   110 reputation?

Jos. Exactly so, upon my credit, ma'am.

Lady T. Well, certainly, this is the oddest doctrine and the newest receipt for avoiding calumny!   115

Jos. An infallible one, believe me. Prudence, like experience, must be paid for.

Lady T. Why, if my understanding were once convinced ——

Jos. Oh, certainly, madam, your under-   120 standing should be convinced. Yes, yes; heaven forbid I should persuade you to do anything you thought wrong. No, no, I have too much honor to desire it.

Lady T. Don't you think we may as   125 well leave *honor* out of the question?

Jos. Ah! the ill effects of your country education, I see, still remain with you.

Lady T. I doubt they do indeed; and I will fairly own to you, that if I could be per-   130 suaded to do wrong, it would be by Sir Peter's ill-usage sooner than your *honorable logic*, after all.

Jos. Then, by this hand, which he is unworthy of ——   (*Taking her hand.*   135

Enter Servant

'Sdeath, you blockhead! What do you want?

Serv. I beg your pardon, sir, but I thought you would not choose Sir Peter to come up without announcing him.

Jos. Sir Peter! Oons — the devil!   140

Lady T. Sir Peter! Oh, Lud, I'm ruined! I'm ruined!

Serv. Sir, 'twasn't I let him in.

Lady T. Oh, I'm quite undone! What will become of me? Now, Mr. Logic. Oh!   145 he's on the stairs. I'll get behind here; and if ever I'm so imprudent again ——

(*Goes behind the screen.*

Jos. Give me that book.

(*Sits down.* Servant *pretends to adjust his chair.*

Enter Sir Peter

Sir Pet. Ay, ever improving himself. Mr.
Surface! Mr. Surface! 150

Jos. Oh! my dear Sir Peter, I beg your pardon. (*Gaping, throws away the book.*) I have
been dozing over a stupid book. Well, I am
much obliged to you for this call. You haven't
been here, I believe, since I fitted up this 155
room. Books, you know, are the only things in
which I am a coxcomb.

Sir Pet. 'Tis very neat indeed. Well, well,
that's proper; and you can make even your
screen a source of knowledge — hung, I 160
perceive, with maps.

Jos. Oh, yes, I find great use in that screen.

Sir Pet. I dare say you must, certainly, when
you want to find anything in a hurry.

Jos. (*aside*). Ay, or to hide anything 165
in a hurry, either.

Sir Pet. Well, I have a little private business ——

Jos. (*to the* Servant). You need not stay.

Serv. No, sir. (*Exit.* 170

Jos. Here's a chair, Sir Peter. I beg ——

Sir Pet. Well, now we are alone, there is a
subject, my dear friend, on which I wish to unburden my mind to you — a point of the
greatest moment to my peace; in short, 175
my dear friend, Lady Teazle's conduct of late
has made me extremely unhappy.

Jos. Indeed! I am very sorry to hear it.

Sir Pet. Ay, 'tis too plain she has not the
least regard for me; but, what's worse, I 180
have pretty good authority to suppose she has
formed an attachment to another.

Jos. Indeed! you astonish me!

Sir Pet. Yes; and, between ourselves, I think
I've discovered the person. 185

Jos. How! you alarm me exceedingly.

Sir Pet. Ay, my dear friend, I knew you
would sympathize with me!

Jos. Yes, believe me, Sir Peter, such a discovery would hurt me just as much as it 190
would you.

Sir Pet. I am convinced of it. Ah! it is a
happiness to have a friend whom we can trust
even with one's family secrets. But have you
no guess who I mean? 195

Jos. I haven't the most distant idea. It can't
be Sir Benjamin Backbite!

Sir Pet. Oh, no! What say you to Charles?

Jos. My brother! impossible!

Sir Pet. Oh! my dear friend, the good- 200
ness of your own heart misleads you. You
judge of others by yourself.

Jos. Certainly, Sir Peter, the heart that is
conscious of its own integrity is ever slow to
credit another's treachery. 205

Sir Pet. True, but your brother has no sentiment; you never hear him talk so.

Jos. Yet I can't but think Lady Teazle herself has too much principle.

Sir Pet. Ay; but what is principle 210
against the flattery of a handsome, lively young
fellow?

Jos. That's very true.

Sir Pet. And there's, you know, the difference of our ages makes it very improbable 215
that she should have any very great affection
for me; and if she were to be frail, and I were
to make it public, why the town would only
laugh at me, the foolish old bachelor who had
married a girl. 220

Jos. That's true, to be sure; they would
laugh.

Sir Pet. Laugh — ay, and make ballads, and
paragraphs, and the devil knows what of me.

Jos. No, you must never make it 225
public.

Sir Pet. But then again — that the nephew
of my old friend, Sir Oliver, should be the person to attempt such a wrong, hurts me more
nearly. 230

Jos. Ay, there's the point. When ingratitude barbs the dart of injury, the wound has
double danger in it.

Sir Pet. Ay, I that was, in a manner, left
his guardian; in whose house he had been 235
so often entertained; who never in my life
denied him — my advice.

Jos. Oh, 'tis not to be credited. There may
be a man capable of such baseness, to be sure;
but, for my part, till you can give me posi- 240
tive proofs, I cannot but doubt it. However,
if it should be proved on him, he is no longer a
brother of mine. I disclaim kindred with him:
for the man who can break the laws of hospital-

ity, and tempt the wife of his friend, de-   245
serves to be branded as the pest of society.

Sir Pet. What a difference there is between
you! What noble sentiments!

Jos. Yet I cannot suspect Lady Teazle's
honor.   250

Sir Pet. I am sure I wish to think well of her,
and to remove all ground of quarrel between
us. She has lately reproached me more than
once with having made no settlement on her;
and, in our last quarrel, she almost hinted   255
that she should not break her heart if I was
dead. Now, as we seem to differ in our ideas of
expense, I have resolved she shall have her own
way, and be her own mistress in that respect
for the future; and if I were to die, she   260
will find I have not been inattentive to her interest while living. Here, my friend, are the
drafts of two deeds, which I wish to have
your opinion on. By one, she will enjoy eight
hundred a year independent while I live;   265
and, by the other, the bulk of my fortune at
my death.

Jos. This conduct, Sir Peter, is indeed truly
generous. — (*Aside*) I wish it may not corrupt my pupil.   270

Sir Pet. Yes, I am determined she shall have
no cause to complain, though I would not have
her acquainted with the latter instance of my
affection yet awhile.

Jos. (*aside*). Nor I, if I could help it.   275

Sir Pet. And now, my dear friend, if you
please, we will talk over the situation of your
hopes with Maria.

Jos. (*softly*). Oh, no, Sir Peter; another time,
if you please.   280

Sir Pet. I am sensibly chagrined at the little
progress you seem to make in her affections.

Jos. (*softly*). I beg you will not mention it.
What are my disappointments when your happiness is in debate! — (*Aside*) 'Sdeath, I   285
shall be ruined every way.

Sir Pet. And though you are so averse to my
acquainting Lady Teazle with your passion for
Maria, I'm sure she's not your enemy in the
affair.   290

Jos. Pray, Sir Peter, now, oblige me. I am
really too much affected by the subject we
have been speaking of, to bestow a thought on
my own concerns. The man who is intrusted
with his friend's distresses can never ——   295

Enter Servant

Well, sir?

Serv. Your brother, sir, is speaking to a
gentleman in the street, and says he knows you
are within.

Jos. 'Sdeath, blockhead, I'm not   300
within; I'm out for the day.

Sir Pet. Stay — hold — a thought has struck
me: you shall be at home.

Jos. Well, well, let him up. (*Exit* Servant.
(*Aside*) He'll interrupt Sir Peter, how-   305
ever.

Sir Pet. Now, my good friend, oblige me, I
entreat you. Before Charles comes, let me
conceal myself somewhere; then do you tax him
on the point we have been talking, and   310
his answer may satisfy me at once.

Jos. Oh, fie, Sir Peter! would you have me
join in so mean a trick? — to trepan my
brother, too?

Sir Pet. Nay, you tell me you are sure   315
he is innocent; if so, you do him the greatest
service by giving him an opportunity to clear
himself, and you will set my heart at rest.
Come, you shall not refuse me; here, behind
this screen will be —— Hey! what the   320
devil! there seems to be one listener here already. I'll swear I saw a petticoat!

Jos. Ha! ha! ha! Well, this is ridiculous
enough. I'll tell you, Sir Peter, though I hold
a man of intrigue to be a most despicable   325
character, yet, you know, it does not follow
that one is to be an absolute Joseph [1] either!
Hark'ee, 'tis a little French milliner — a silly
rogue that plagues me — and having some
character to lose, on your coming, sir, she   330
ran behind the screen.

Sir Pet. Ah! you rogue! But egad, she has
overheard all I have been saying of my wife.

Jos. Oh, 'twill never go any farther, you may
depend upon it.   335

Sir Pet. No? Then, faith, let her hear it out.
Here's a closet will do as well.

[1] Joseph utterly rejected the amorous advances of
Potiphar's wife (see *Genesis* XXXIX).

Jos. Well, go in there.

Sir Pet. Sly rogue! sly rogue!

(Going into the closet.

Jos. A narrow escape, indeed! and　340 a curious situation I'm in, to part man and wife in this manner.

Lady T. (*peeping*). Couldn't I steal off?

Jos. Keep close, my angel!

Sir Pet. (*peeping*). Joseph, tax him　345 home.

Jos. Back, my dear friend!

Lady T. (*peeping*). Couldn't you lock Sir Peter in?

Jos. Be still, my life!　350

Sir Pet. (*peeping*). You're sure the little milliner won't blab?

Jos. In, in, my good Sir Peter. (*Aside*) 'Fore Gad, I wish I had a key to the door.

Enter CHARLES SURFACE

Char. Holloa! brother, what has been　355 the matter? Your fellow would not let me up at first. What! have you had a Jew or a wench with you?

Jos. Neither, brother, I assure you.

Char. But what has made Sir Peter　360 steal off? I thought he had been with you.

Jos. He *was*, brother; but hearing you were coming, he did not choose to stay.

Char. What! was the old gentleman afraid I wanted to borrow money of him?　365

Jos. No, sir; but I am sorry to find, Charles, you have lately given that worthy man grounds for great uneasiness.

Char. Yes, they tell me I do that to a great many worthy men. But how so, pray?　370

Jos. To be plain with you, brother, he thinks you are endeavoring to gain Lady Teazle's affections from him.

Char. Who, I? Oh, Lud! not I, upon my word. Ha! ha! ha! ha! So the old fellow　375 has found out that he has got a young wife, has he? Or, what is worse, Lady Teazle has found out she has an old husband?

Jos. This is no subject to jest on, brother. He who can laugh ——　380

Char. True, true, as you were going to say — then, seriously, I never had the least idea of what you charge me with, upon my honor.

Jos. (*raising his voice*). Well, it will give Sir Peter great satisfaction to hear this.　385

Char. To be sure, I once thought the lady seemed to have taken a fancy to me; but, upon my soul, I never gave her the least encouragement. Besides, you know my attachment to Maria.　390

Jos. But sure, brother, even if Lady Teazle had betrayed the fondest partiality for you ——

Char. Why, look'ee, Joseph, I hope I shall never deliberately do a dishonorable action; but if a pretty woman was purposely to throw　395 herself in my way, and that pretty woman married to a man old enough to be her father ——

Jos. Well ——

Char. Why, I believe I should be obliged to borrow a little of your morality, that's　400 all. But, brother, do you know now that you surprise me exceedingly, by naming *me* with Lady Teazle? For, 'faith, I always understood you were her favorite.

Jos. Oh, for shame, Charles! This　405 retort is foolish.

Char. Nay, I swear I have seen you exchange such significant glances ——

Jos. Nay, nay, sir, this is no jest.

Char. Egad, I'm serious. Don't you　410 remember one day when I called here ——

Jos. Nay, prithee, Charles ——

Char. And found you together ——

Jos. Zounds, sir! I insist ——

Char. And another time when your　415 servant ——

Jos. Brother, brother, a word with you! —— (*Aside*) Gad, I must stop him.

Char. Informed, I say, that ——

Jos. Hush! I beg your pardon, but　420 Sir Peter has overheard all we have been saying. I knew you would clear yourself, or I should not have consented.

Char. How, Sir Peter! Where is he?

Jos. Softly; there! (*Points to the closet.*　425

Char. Oh, 'fore heaven, I'll have him out Sir Peter, come forth!

Jos. No, no ——

Char. I say, Sir Peter, come into court (*Pulls in* SIR PETER.) What! my old　430 guardian! What! turn inquisitor, and take evidence incog.?[1]

---

[1] Incognito, i.e., with identity concealed.

Sir Pet. Give me your hand, Charles. I believe I have suspected you wrongfully; but you mustn't be angry with Joseph. 'Twas my 435 plan!

Char. Indeed!

Sir Pet. But I acquit you. I promise you I don't think near so ill of you as I did. What I have heard has given me great satisfaction. 440

Char. Egad, then, 'twas lucky you didn't hear any more! (*Apart to* JOSEPH) Wasn't it, Joseph?

Sir Pet. Ah! you would have retorted on him.

Char. Ay, ay, that was a joke. 445

Sir Pet. Yes, yes, I know his honor too well.

Char. But you might as well have suspected *him* as *me* in this matter, for all that. (*Apart to* JOSEPH) Mightn't he, Joseph?

Sir Pet. Well, well, I believe you. 450

Jos. (*aside*). Would they were both out of the room!

Enter Servant, *and whispers to* JOSEPH SURFACE

Sir Pet. And in future perhaps we may not be such strangers. (*Exit* Servant.

Jos. Gentlemen, I beg pardon, I must 455 wait on you downstairs; here is a person come on particular business.

Char. Well, you can see him in another room. Sir Peter and I have not met a long time, and I have something to say to him. 460

Jos. (*aside*). They must not be left together. — I'll send this man away, and return directly. (*Apart to* SIR PETER) Sir Peter, not a word of the French milliner.

Sir Pet. (*apart to* JOSEPH). I! not for the 465 world! — (*Exit* JOSEPH.) Ah! Charles, if you associated more with your brother, one might indeed hope for your reformation. He is a man of sentiment. Well, there is nothing in the world so noble as a man of sentiment. 470

Char. Pshaw! he is too moral by half, and so apprehensive of his good name, as he calls it, that I suppose he would as soon let a priest into his house as a girl.

Sir Pet. No, no! come, come! you wrong 475 him. No, no! Joseph is no rake, but he is no such saint either in that respect. — (*Aside*) I

have a great mind to tell him; we should have a laugh at Joseph.

Char. Oh, hang him! He's a very an- 480 chorite, a young hermit.

Sir Pet. Hark'ee, you must not abuse him; he may chance to hear of it again, I promise you.

Char. Why, you won't tell him?

Sir Pet. No — but — this way. (*Aside*) 485 Egad, I'll tell him. — Hark'ee, have you a mind to have a good laugh at Joseph?

Char. I should like it of all things.

Sir Pet. Then, i'faith, we will; I'll be quit with him for discovering me. He had a 490 girl with him when I called.

Char. What! Joseph? You jest.

Sir Pet. Hush! a little French milliner, and the best of the jest is, she's in the room now.

Char. The devil she is! 495

Sir Pet. Hush! I tell you! (*Points.*

Char. Behind the screen! 'Slife, let's unveil her!

Sir Pet. No, no — he's coming — you sha'n't, indeed! 500

Char. Oh, egad, we'll have a peep at the little milliner!

Sir Pet. Not for the world; Joseph will never forgive me ——

Char. I'll stand by you —— 505

Sir Pet. Odds, here he is.

JOSEPH SURFACE *enters just as* CHARLES SURFACE *throws down the screen*

Char. Lady Teazle, by all that's wonderful!

Sir Pet. Lady Teazle, by all that's damnable!

Char. Sir Peter, this is one of the smartest French milliners I ever saw. Egad, you 510 seem all to have been diverting yourselves here at hide and seek, and I don't see who is out of the secret. Shall I beg your ladyship to inform me? Not a word! Brother, will you be pleased to explain this matter? 515 What! Is Morality dumb too? Sir Peter, though I found you in the dark, perhaps you are not so now! All mute! Well, though I can make nothing of the affair, I suppose you perfectly understand one another, so I'll 520 leave you to yourselves. (*Going*) Brother, I'm sorry to find you have given that worthy man

cause for so much uneasiness. Sir Peter! there's
nothing in the world so noble as a man of sentiment!   (*Exit* CHARLES. 525
    (*They stand for some time looking at
    each other.*)

Jos. Sir Peter — notwithstanding — I confess — that appearances are against me — if
you will afford me your patience — I make no
doubt — but I shall explain everything to your
satisfaction.   530

Sir Pet. If you please, sir.

Jos. The fact is, sir, that Lady Teazle, knowing my pretensions to your ward Maria — I
say, sir, Lady Teazle, being apprehensive of the
jealousy of your temper — and knowing   535
my friendship to the family —— she, sir, I say
— called here — in order that — I might explain these pretensions — but on your coming
— being apprehensive — as I said — of your
jealousy — she withdrew — and this, you   540
may depend on it, is the whole truth of the
matter.

Sir Pet. A very clear account, upon my word;
and I dare swear the lady will vouch for every
article of it.   545

Lady T. For not one word of it, Sir Peter!

Sir Pet. How! don't you think it worth while
to agree in the lie?

Lady T. There is not one syllable of truth in
what that gentleman has told you.   550

Sir Pet. I believe you, upon my soul, ma'am!

Jos. (*aside to* LADY TEAZLE). 'Sdeath,
madam, will you betray me?

Lady T. Good Mr. Hypocrite, by your leave,
I'll speak for myself.   555

Sir Pet. Ay, let her alone, sir; you'll find
she'll make out a better story than you, without
prompting.

Lady T. Hear me, Sir Peter! I came hither
on no matter relating to your ward, and   560
even ignorant of this gentleman's pretensions
to her. But I came seduced by his insidious
arguments, at least to listen to his pretended
passion, if not to sacrifice your honor to his
baseness.   565

Sir Pet. Now, I believe, the truth is coming
indeed!

Jos. The woman's mad!

Lady T. No, sir, she has recovered her senses,

and your own arts have furnished her with   570
the means. Sir Peter, I do not expect you to
credit me, but the tenderness you expressed for
me, when I am sure you could not think I was
a witness to it, has penetrated so to my heart,
that had I left the place without the   575
shame of this discovery, my future life should
have spoken the sincerity of my gratitude. As
for that smooth-tongued hypocrite, who would
have seduced the wife of his too credulous
friend, while he affected honorable ad-   580
dresses to his ward, I behold him now in a light
so truly despicable, that I shall never again respect myself for having listened to him.
                        (*Exit* LADY TEAZLE.

Jos. Notwithstanding all this, Sir Peter,
Heaven knows ——   585

Sir Pet. That you are a villain! and so I leave
you to your conscience.

Jos. You are too rash, Sir Peter; you shall
hear me. The man who shuts out conviction
by refusing to ——   590
    (*Exeunt,* JOSEPH SURFACE *following
    and speaking.*

ACT V

SCENE I. *The library in* JOSEPH SURFACE'S
house.

Enter JOSEPH SURFACE *and* Servant

Jos. Mr. Stanley! And why should you
think I would see him? You must know he
comes to ask something.

Serv. Sir, I should not have let him in, but
that Mr. Rowley came to the door with   5
him.

Jos. Pshaw! blockhead! to suppose that I
should now be in a temper to receive visits
from poor relations! Well, why don't you
show the fellow up?   10

Serv. I will, sir. Why, sir, it was not my
fault that Sir Peter discovered my lady ——

Jos. Go, fool! (*Exit* Servant.) Sure Fortune never played a man of my policy such a
trick before. My character with Sir Peter,   15
my hopes with Maria, destroyed in a moment!
I'm in a rare humor to listen to other people's
distresses! I sha'n't be able to bestow even a

benevolent sentiment on Stanley. So! here
he comes, and Rowley with him. I must 20
try to recover myself, and put a little charity
into my face, however.   (*Exit.*

Enter Sir Oliver Surface *and* Rowley

Sir Ol. What! does he avoid us? That was
he, was it not?

Row. It was, sir. But I doubt you are 25
come a little too abruptly. His nerves are so
weak, that the sight of a poor relation may be
too much for him. I should have gone first to
break it to him.

Sir Ol. Oh, plague of his nerves! Yet 30
this is he whom Sir Peter extols as a man of
the most benevolent way of thinking!

Row. As to his way of thinking, I cannot
pretend to decide; for, to do him justice, he
appears to have as much speculative be- 35
nevolence as any private gentleman in the
kingdom, though he is seldom so sensual as to
indulge himself in the exercise of it.

Sir Ol. Yet has a string of charitable sentiments at his fingers' ends.   40

Row. Or rather at his tongue's end, Sir
Oliver; for I believe there is no sentiment he
has such faith in, as that "Charity begins at
home."

Sir Ol. And his, I presume, is of that do- 45
mestic sort which never stirs abroad at all?

Row. I doubt you'll find it so — but he's
coming. I mustn't seem to interrupt you; and,
you know, immediately as you leave him, I
come in to announce your arrival in your 50
real character.

Sir Ol. True; and afterwards you'll meet me
at Sir Peter's.

Row. Without losing a moment.   (*Exit.*

Sir Ol. I don't like the complaisance of 55
his features.

Enter Joseph Surface

Jos. Sir, I beg you ten thousand pardons for
keeping you a moment waiting. Mr. Stanley, I
presume.

Sir Ol. At your service.   60

Jos. Sir, I beg you will do me the honor to
sit down. I entreat you, sir!

Sir Ol. Dear sir, there's no occasion. —
(*Aside*) Too civil by half!

Jos. I have not the pleasure of knowing 65
you, Mr. Stanley, but I am extremely happy
to see you look so well. You were nearly related to my mother, I think, Mr. Stanley?

Sir Ol. I was, sir; so nearly, that my present
poverty, I fear, may do discredit to her 70
wealthy children, else I should not have presumed to trouble you.

Jos. Dear sir, there needs no apology; he
that is in distress, though a stranger, has a
right to claim kindred with the wealthy. 75
I am sure I wish I was of that class, and had it
in my power to offer you even a small relief.

Sir Ol. If your uncle, Sir Oliver, were here,
I should have a friend.

Jos. I wish he was, sir, with all my 80
heart: you should not want an advocate with
him, believe me, sir.

Sir Ol. I should not need one — my distresses would recommend me. But I imagined his bounty would enable you to be- 85
come the agent of his charity.

Jos. My dear sir, you were strangely misinformed. Sir Oliver is a worthy man, a very
worthy man; but avarice, Mr. Stanley, is the
vice of age. I will tell you, my good sir, 90
in confidence, what he has done for me has
been a mere nothing; though people, I know,
have thought otherwise, and, for my part, I
never chose to contradict the report.

Sir Ol. What! has he never transmitted 95
you bullion — rupees [1] — pagodas? [2]

Jos. Oh, dear sir, nothing of the kind! No,
no; a few presents, now and then — china,
shawls, congou tea, [3] avadavats, [4] and Indian
crackers; [5] little more, believe me.   100

Sir Ol. (*aside*). Here's gratitude for twelve
thousand pounds! Avadavats and Indian
crackers!

Jos. Then, my dear sir, you have heard, I
doubt not, of the extravagance of my 105

---

[1] A silver coin of India, worth about fifty cents at the
time.
[2] A gold Indian coin, worth about two dollars.
[3] A black Chinese tea.
[4] Small Indian songbirds.
[5] Small firecrackers.

brother; there are very few would credit what I have done for that unfortunate young man.

Sir Ol. (*aside*). Not I, for one!

Jos. The sums I have lent him! Indeed I have been exceedingly to blame; it was an   110 amiable weakness. However, I don't pretend to defend it; and now I feel it doubly culpable, since it has deprived me of the pleasure of serving you, Mr. Stanley, as my heart dictates.

Sir Ol. (*aside*). Dissembler! — Then,   115 sir, you can't assist me?

Jos. At present, it grieves me to say, I cannot; but, whenever I have the ability, you may depend upon hearing from me.

Sir Ol. I am extremely sorry ——   120

Jos. Not more than I, believe me; to pity without the power to relieve, is still more painful than to ask and be denied.

Sir Ol. Kind sir, your most obedient humble servant.   125

Jos. You leave me deeply affected, Mr. Stanley. William, be ready to open the door.

Sir Ol. Oh, dear sir, no ceremony.

Jos. Your very obedient.

Sir Ol. Sir, your most obsequious.   130

Jos. You may depend upon hearing from me, whenever I can be of service.

Sir Ol. Sweet sir, you are too good!

Jos. In the mean time I wish you health and spirits.   135

Sir Ol. Your ever grateful and perpetual humble servant.

Jos. Sir, yours as sincerely.

Sir Ol. (*aside*). Charles, you are my heir!

(*Exit.*

Jos. This is one bad effect of a good   140 character; it invites application from the unfortunate, and there needs no small degree of address to gain the reputation of benevolence without incurring the expense. The silver ore of pure charity is an expensive article in   145 the catalogue of a man's good qualities; whereas the sentimental French plate I use instead of it, makes just as good a show, and pays no tax.

Enter ROWLEY

Row. Mr. Surface, your servant. I   150 was apprehensive of interrupting you, though my business demands immediate attention, as this note will inform you.

Jos. Always happy to see Mr. Rowley. (*Reads the letter.*) How! "Oliver Surface!"   155 My uncle arrived!

Row. He is, indeed; we have just parted — quite well, after a speedy voyage, and impatient to embrace his worthy nephew.

Jos. I am astonished! William! stop   160 Mr. Stanley, if he's not gone.

Row. Oh! he's out of reach, I believe.

Jos. Why did you not let me know this when you came in together?

Row. I thought you had particular   165 business; but I must be gone to inform your brother, and appoint him here to meet your uncle. He will be with you in a quarter of an hour.

Jos. So he says. Well, I am strangely   170 overjoyed at his coming. — (*Aside*) Never, to be sure, was anything so damned unlucky.

Row. You will be delighted to see how well he looks.

Jos. Ah! I'm rejoiced to hear it. ——   175 (*Aside*) Just at this time!

Row. I'll tell him how impatiently you expect him.

Jos. Do, do; pray give my best duty and affection. Indeed, I cannot express the   180 sensations I feel at the thought of seeing him. (*Exit* ROWLEY.) Certainly his coming just at this time is the cruelest piece of ill fortune!

(*Exit.*

SCENE 2.   SIR PETER TEAZLE'S *house.*

Enter MRS. CANDOUR *and* Maid

Maid. Indeed, ma'am, my lady will see nobody at present.

Mrs. Can. Did you tell her it was her friend Mrs. Candour?

Maid. Yes, ma'am; but she begs you will   5 excuse her.

Mrs. Can. Do go again; I shall be glad to see her, if it be only for a moment, for I am sure she must be in great distress. (*Exit* Maid.) Dear heart, how provoking! I'm   10 not mistress of half the circumstances! We shall have the whole affair in the newspapers, with the names of the parties at length, before I have dropped the story at a dozen houses. 15

Enter SIR BENJAMIN BACKBITE

Oh, Sir Benjamin, you have heard, I suppose ——

Sir Benj. Of Lady Teazle and Mr. Surface ——

Mrs. Can. And Sir Peter's discovery —— 20

Sir Benj. Oh! the strangest piece of business, to be sure!

Mrs. Can. Well, I never was so surprised in my life. I am so sorry for all parties, indeed.

Sir Benj. Now, I don't pity Sir Peter at 25 all; he was so extravagantly partial to Mr. Surface.

Mrs. Can. Mr. Surface! Why, 'twas with Charles Lady Teazle was detected.

Sir Benj. No, no, I tell you; Mr. Sur- 30 face is the gallant.

Mrs. Can. No such thing! Charles is the man. 'Twas Mr. Surface brought Sir Peter on purpose to discover them.

Sir Benj. I tell you I had it from one —— 35

Mrs. Can. And I have it from one ——

Sir Benj. Who had it from one, who had it ——

Mrs. Can. From one immediately — but here comes Lady Sneerwell; perhaps she 40 knows the whole affair.

Enter LADY SNEERWELL

Lady Sneer. So, my dear Mrs. Candour, here's a sad affair of our friend, Lady Teazle.

Mrs. Can. Ay, my dear friend, who would have thought —— 45

Lady Sneer. Well, there is no trusting appearances; though, indeed, she was always too lively for me.

Mrs. Can. To be sure, her manners were a little too free; but then she was so young! 50

Lady Sneer. And had, indeed, some good qualities.

Mrs. Can. So she had, indeed. But have you heard the particulars?

Lady Sneer. No; but everybody says 55 that Mr. Surface ——

Sir Benj. Ay, there; I told you Mr. Surface was the man.

Mrs. Can. No, no; indeed the assignation was with Charles. 60

Lady Sneer. With Charles! You alarm me, Mrs. Candour!

Mrs. Can. Yes, yes, he was the lover. Mr. Surface, to do him justice, was only the informer. 65

Sir Benj. Well, I'll not dispute with you, Mrs. Candour; but, be it which it may, I hope that Sir Peter's wound will not ——

Mrs. Can. Sir Peter's wound! Oh, mercy! I didn't hear a word of their fighting. 70

Lady Sneer. Nor I, a syllable.

Sir Benj. No! what, no mention of the duel?

Mrs. Can. Not a word.

Sir Benj. Oh, yes; they fought before they left the room. 75

Lady Sneer. Pray, let us hear.

Mrs. Can. Ay, do oblige us with the duel.

Sir Benj. "Sir," says Sir Peter, immediately after the discovery, "you are a most ungrateful fellow." 80

Mrs. Can. Ay, to Charles.

Sir Benj. No, no, to Mr. Surface — "a most ungrateful fellow; and, old as I am, sir," says he, "I insist on immediate satisfaction."

Mrs. Can. Ay, that must have been to 85 Charles; for 'tis very unlikely Mr. Surface should fight in his own house.

Sir Benj. Gad's life, ma'am, not at all. — "Giving me immediate satisfaction." On this, ma'am, Lady Teazle, seeing Sir Peter in 90 such danger, ran out of the room in strong hysterics, and Charles after her, calling out for hartshorn and water; then, madam, they began to fight with swords.

Enter CRABTREE

Crab. With pistols, nephew — pistols. 95 I have it from undoubted authority.

Mrs. Can. Oh, Mr. Crabtree, then it is all true!

Crab. Too true, indeed, madam, and Sir Peter is dangerously wounded —— 100

Sir Benj. By a thrust in *seconde* [1] quite through his left side ——

[1] A downward parry.

Crab. By a bullet lodged in the thorax.

Mrs. Can. Mercy on me! Poor Sir Peter!

Crab. Yes, madam; though Charles 105 would have avoided the matter, if he could.

Mrs. Can. I knew Charles was the person.

Sir Benj. My uncle, I see, knows nothing of the matter.

Crab. But Sir Peter taxed him with the 110 basest ingratitude.

Sir Benj. That I told you, you know —

Crab. Do, nephew, let me speak! and insisted on immediate ——

Sir Benj. Just as I said —— 115

Crab. Odds life, nephew, allow others to know something too! A pair of pistols lay on the bureau (for Mr. Surface, it seems, had come home the night before late from Salthill, where he had been to see the Montem [1] 120 with a friend, who has a son at Eton), so, unluckily, the pistols were left charged.

Sir Benj. I heard nothing of this.

Crab. Sir Peter forced Charles to take one, and they fired, it seems, pretty nearly to- 125 gether. Charles's shot took effect, as I tell you, and Sir Peter's missed; but what is very extraordinary, the ball struck against a little bronze Shakespeare that stood over the fireplace, grazed out of the window, at a right angle, 130 and wounded the postman, who was just coming to the door with a double letter [2] from Northamptonshire.

Sir Benj. My uncle's account is more circumstantial, I confess; but I believe mine 135 is the true one, for all that.

Lady Sneer. (*aside*). I am more interested in this affair than they imagine, and must have better information. (*Exit.*

Sir Benj. Ah! Lady Sneerwell's alarm 140 is very easily accounted for.

Crab. Yes, yes, they certainly do say; but that's neither here nor there.

Mrs. Can. But, pray, where is Sir Peter at present? 145

---

[1] The students of Eton College near Windsor used to go to the neighboring elevation of Salthill about June first of every third year for a festive ceremony called Montem from the Latin phrase, *processus ad montem*, i.e., the march to the hill.

[2] A heavy letter requiring double postage.

Crab. Oh! they brought him home, and he is now in the house, though the servants are ordered to deny him.

Mrs. Can. I believe so, and Lady Teazle, I suppose, attending him. 150

Crab. Yes, yes; and I saw one of the faculty [1] enter just before me.

Sir Benj. Hey, who comes here?

Crab. Oh, this is he: the physician, depend on't. 155

Mrs. Can. Oh, certainly: it must be the physician; and now we shall know.

Enter Sir Oliver Surface

Crab. Well, doctor, what hopes?

Mrs. Can. Ah, doctor, how's your patient?

Sir Benj. Now, doctor, isn't it a wound 160 with a small-sword?

Crab. A bullet lodged in the thorax, for a hundred!

Sir Ol. Doctor! a wound with a small-sword! and a bullet in the thorax! Oons! are 165 you mad, good people?

Sir Benj. Perhaps, sir, you are not a doctor?

Sir Ol. Truly, I am to thank you for my degree if I am.

Crab. Only a friend of Sir Peter's, then, 170 I presume. But, sir, you must have heard of his accident?

Sir Ol. Not a word!

Crab. Not of his being dangerously wounded?

Sir Ol. The devil he is! 175

Sir Benj. Run through the body ——

Crab. Shot in the breast ——

Sir Benj. By one Mr. Surface ——

Crab. Ay, the younger.

Sir Ol. Hey! what the plague! you 180 seem to differ strangely in your accounts; however, you agree that Sir Peter is dangerously wounded.

Sir Benj. Oh, yes, we agree there.

Crab. Yes, yes, I believe there can be 185 no doubt of that.

Sir Ol. Then, upon my word, for a person in that situation, he is the most imprudent man alive; for here he comes, walking as if nothing at all was the matter. 190

---

[1] Medical profession.

Enter SIR PETER TEAZLE

Odds heart, Sir Peter, you are come in good time, I promise you; for we had just given you over.

Sir Benj. Egad, uncle, this is the most sudden recovery! 195

Sir Ol. Why, man, what do you out of bed with a small-sword through your body, and a bullet lodged in your thorax?

Sir Pet. A small-sword, and a bullet!

Sir Ol. Ay, these gentlemen would 200 have killed you without law or physic, and wanted to dub me a doctor, to make me an accomplice.

Sir Pet. Why, what is all this?

Sir Benj. We rejoice, Sir Peter, that 205 the story of the duel is not true, and are sincerely sorry for your other misfortune.

Sir Pet. (*aside*). So, so; all over the town already.

Crab. Though, Sir Peter, you were 210 certainly vastly to blame to marry at your years.

Sir Pet. Sir, what business is that of yours?

Mrs. Can. Though, indeed, as Sir Peter made so good a husband, he's very much 215 to be pitied.

Sir Pet. Plague on your pity, ma'am! I desire none of it.

Sir Benj. However, Sir Peter, you must not mind the laughing and jests you will meet 220 with on this occasion.

Sir Pet. Sir, sir, I desire to be master in my own house.

Crab. 'Tis no uncommon case, that's one comfort. 225

Sir Pet. I insist on being left to myself; without ceremony. I insist on your leaving my house directly.

Mrs. Can. Well, well, we are going, and depend on't we'll make the best report of it 230 we can. (*Exit.*

Sir Pet. Leave my house!

Crab. And tell how hardly you've been treated. (*Exit.*

Sir Pet. Leave my house! 235

Sir Benj. And how patiently you bear it. (*Exit.*

Sir Pet. Fiends! vipers! furies! Oh! that their own venom would choke them!

Sir Ol. They are very provoking, indeed, Sir Peter. 240

Enter ROWLEY

Row. I heard high words. What has ruffled you, sir?

Sir Pet. Pshaw! what signifies asking? Do I ever pass a day without my vexations?

Row. Well, I'm not inquisitive. 245

Sir Ol. Well, Sir Peter, I have seen both my nephews in the manner we proposed.

Sir Pet. A precious couple they are!

Row. Yes, and Sir Oliver is convinced that your judgment was right, Sir Peter. 250

Sir Ol. Yes, I find Joseph is indeed the man, after all.

Row. Ay, as Sir Peter says, he is a man of sentiment.

Sir Ol. And acts up to the sentiments 255 he professes.

Row. It certainly is edification to hear him talk.

Sir Ol. Oh, he's a model for the young men of the age! But how's this, Sir Peter? 260 You don't join us in your friend Joseph's praise, as I expected.

Sir Pet. Sir Oliver, we live in a damned wicked world, and the fewer we praise the better.

Row. What! do you say so, Sir Peter, 265 who were never mistaken in your life?

Sir Pet. Pshaw! Plague on you both! I see by your sneering you have heard the whole affair. I shall go mad among you!

Row. Then, to fret you no longer, Sir 270 Peter, we are indeed acquainted with it all. I met Lady Teazle coming from Mr. Surface's so humbled that she deigned to request me to be her advocate with you.

Sir Pet. And does Sir Oliver know all 275 this?

Sir Ol. Every circumstance.

Sir Pet. What! of the closet and the screen, hey?

Sir Ol. Yes, yes, and the little French 280 milliner. Oh, I have been vastly diverted with the story! Ha! ha! ha!

Sir Pet. 'Twas very pleasant.

Sir Ol. I never laughed more in my life, I assure you. Ha! ha! ha!   285

Sir Pet. Oh, vastly diverting! Ha! ha! ha!

Row. To be sure, Joseph with his sentiments! ha! ha! ha!

Sir Pet. Yes, yes, his sentiments! Ha! ha! ha! Hypocritical villain!   290

Sir Ol. Ay, and that rogue Charles to pull Sir Peter out of the closet: ha! ha! ha!

Sir Pet. Ha! ha! 'twas devilish entertaining, to be sure!

Sir Ol. Ha! ha! ha! Egad, Sir Peter, I   295 should like to have seen your face when the screen was thrown down: ha! ha!

Sir Pet. Yes, yes, my face when the screen was thrown down: ha! ha! ha! Oh, I must never show my head again!   300

Sir Ol. But come, come, it isn't fair to laugh at you neither, my old friend; though, upon my soul, I can't help it.

Sir Pet. Oh, pray don't restrain your mirth on my account; it does not hurt me at all!   305 I laugh at the whole affair myself. Yes, yes, I think being a standing jest for all one's acquaintance a very happy situation. Oh, yes, and then of a morning to read the paragraphs about Mr. S——, Lady T——, and Sir   310 P—— will be so entertaining!

Row. Without affectation, Sir Peter, you may despise the ridicule of fools — but I see Lady Teazle going towards the next room. I am sure you must desire a reconciliation   315 as earnestly as she does.

Sir Ol. Perhaps my being here prevents her coming to you. Well, I'll leave honest Rowley to mediate between you; but he must bring you all presently to Mr. Surface's, where I am   320 now returning, if not to reclaim a libertine, at least to expose hypocrisy.

Sir Pet. Ah, I'll be present at your discovering yourself there with all my heart; though 'tis a vile unlucky place for discoveries!   325

Row. We'll follow.   (*Exit* SIR OLIVER.

Sir Pet. She is not coming here, you see, Rowley.

Row. No, but she has left the door of that room open, you perceive. See, she is in   330 tears.

Sir Pet. Certainly a little mortification appears very becoming in a wife. Don't you think it will do her good to let her pine a little?

Row. Oh, this is ungenerous in you!   335

Sir Pet. Well, I know not what to think. You remember the letter I found of hers, evidently intended for Charles?

Row. A mere forgery, Sir Peter, laid in your way on purpose. This is one of the points   340 which I intend Snake shall give you conviction of.

Sir Pet. I wish I were once satisfied of that. She looks this way. What a remarkably elegant turn of the head she has! Rowley,   345 I'll go to her.

Row. Certainly.

Sir Pet. Though when it is known that we are reconciled, people will laugh at me ten times more.   350

Row. Let them laugh, and retort their malice only by showing them you are happy in spite of it.

Sir Pet. I'faith, so I will! And if I'm not mistaken, we may yet be the happiest   355 couple in the country.

Row. Nay, Sir Peter, he who once lays aside suspicion ——

Sir Pet. Hold, Master Rowley! if you have any regard for me, let me never hear you   360 utter anything like a sentiment. I have had enough of them to serve me the rest of my life. (*Exeunt.*

SCENE 3. *The library in* JOSEPH SURFACE'S *house.*

Enter JOSEPH SURFACE *and* LADY SNEERWELL

Lady Sneer. Impossible! Will not Sir Peter immediately be reconciled to Charles, and, of course, no longer oppose his union with Maria? The thought is distraction to me.

Jos. Can passion furnish a remedy?   5

Lady Sneer. No, nor cunning neither. Oh! I was a fool, an idiot, to league with such a blunderer!

Jos. Sure, Lady Sneerwell, *I* am the greatest sufferer; yet you see I bear the accident   10 with calmness.

Lady Sneer. Because the disappointment doesn't reach your heart; your interest only attached you to Maria. Had you felt for her what I have for that ungrateful libertine, 15 neither your temper nor hypocrisy could prevent your showing the sharpness of your vexation.

Jos. But why should your reproaches fall on me for this disappointment? 20

Lady Sneer. Are you not the cause of it? Had you not a sufficient field for your roguery in imposing upon Sir Peter, and supplanting your brother, but you must endeavor to seduce his wife? I hate such an avarice of crimes; 25 'tis an unfair monopoly, and never prospers.

Jos. Well, I admit I have been to blame. I confess I deviated from the direct road of wrong, but I don't think we're so totally defeated neither. 30

Lady Sneer. No!

Jos. You tell me you have made a trial of Snake since we met, and that you still believe him faithful to us —

Lady Sneer. I do believe so. 35

Jos. And that he has undertaken, should it be necessary, to swear and prove that Charles is at this time contracted by vows and honor to your ladyship, which some of his former letters to you will serve to support? 40

Lady Sneer. This, indeed, might have assisted.

Jos. Come, come; it is not too late yet. (*Knocking at the door.*) But hark! this is probably my uncle, Sir Oliver. Retire to that 45 room; we'll consult farther when he is gone.

Lady Sneer. Well, but if *he* should find you out too?

Jos. Oh, I have no fear of that. Sir Peter will hold his tongue for his own credit's 50 sake; and you may depend on it I shall soon discover Sir Oliver's weak side!

Lady Sneer. I have no diffidence ¹ of your abilities! Only be constant to one roguery at a time. (*Exit.* 55

Jos. I will, I will. So! 'tis confounded hard, after such bad fortune, to be baited by one's confederate in evil. Well, at all events, my character is so much better than Charles's, that

¹ Doubt.

I certainly — hey! — what! — this is not 60 Sir Oliver, but old Stanley again. Plague on't that he should return to tease me just now! I shall have Sir Oliver come and find him here — and ——

Enter SIR OLIVER SURFACE

Gad's life, Mr. Stanley, why have you come 65 back to plague me at this time? You must not stay now, upon my word.

Sir Ol. Sir, I hear your uncle Oliver is expected here, and though he has been so penurious to you, I'll try what he'll do for me. 70

Jos. Sir, 'tis impossible for you to stay now, so I must beg — come any other time, and I promise you, you shall be assisted.

Sir Ol. No; Sir Oliver and I must be acquainted. 75

Jos. Zounds, sir! then I insist on your quitting the room directly.

Sir Ol. Nay, sir ——

Jos. Sir, I insist on't: here, William! show this gentleman out. Since you compel me, 80 sir, not one moment; this is such insolence!
             (*Going to push him out.*

Enter CHARLES SURFACE

Char. Hey day! what's the matter now! What the devil, have you got hold of my little broker here? Zounds, brother! don't hurt little Premium. What's the matter, my little 85 fellow?

Jos. So! he has been with you too, has he?

Char. To be sure he has. Why, he's as honest a little —— But sure, Joseph, you have not been borrowing money too, have you? 90

Jos. Borrowing! no! But, brother, you know we expect Sir Oliver here every ——

Char. Oh, Gad, that's true! Noll mustn't find the little broker here, to be sure.

Jos. Yet Mr. Stanley insists —— 95

Char. Stanley! why, his name's Premium.

Jos. No, sir, Stanley.

Char. No, no, Premium.

Jos. Well, no matter which — but ——

Char. Ay, ay, Stanley or Premium, 'tis 100 the same thing, as you say; for I suppose he

goes by half a hundred names, besides A.B. [1]
at the coffee-house.

                 (*Knocking.*

Jos. 'Sdeath, here's Sir Oliver at the door.
Now I beg, Mr. Stanley ——   105

Char. Ay, ay, and I beg, Mr. Premium ——

Sir Ol. Gentlemen ——

Jos. Sir, by heaven you shall go!

Char. Ay, out with him, certainly!

Sir Ol. This violence ——   110

Jos. Sir, 'tis your own fault.

Char. Out with him, to be sure.

      (*Both forcing* SIR OLIVER *out.*

Enter SIR PETER *and* LADY TEAZLE,
MARIA, *and* ROWLEY

Sir Pet. My old friend, Sir Oliver; hey!
What in the name of wonder! Here are dutiful
nephews! Assault their uncle at a first visit! 115

Lady T. Indeed, Sir Oliver, 'twas well we
came in to rescue you.

Row. Truly, it was; for I perceive, Sir Oliver,
the character of old Stanley was no protection
to you.   120

Sir Ol. Nor of Premium either: the necessities
of the former could not extort a shilling from
that benevolent gentleman; and now, egad, I
stood a chance of faring worse than my ancestors, and being knocked down without 125
being bid for.

Jos. Charles!

Char. Joseph!

Jos. 'Tis now complete!

Char. Very!   130

Sir Ol. Sir Peter, my friend, and Rowley
too — look on that elder nephew of mine.
You know what he has already received from
my bounty; and you also know how gladly I
would have regarded half my fortune as 135
held in trust for him. Judge then my disappointment in discovering him to be destitute of
faith, charity, and gratitude.

Sir Pet. Sir Oliver, I should be more surprised at this declaration, if I had not 140
myself found him to be mean, treacherous,
and hypocritical.

---

[1] A common pass name for secret meetings.

Lady T. And if the gentleman pleads not
guilty to these, pray let him call *me* to his character.   145

Sir Pet. Then, I believe, we need add no
more. If he knows himself, he will consider
it as the most perfect punishment, that he is
known to the world.

Char. (*aside*). If they talk this way to 150
honesty, what will they say to me, by and by?

Sir Ol. As for that prodigal, his brother,
there ——

Char. (*aside*). Ay, now comes my turn; the
damned family pictures will ruin me!   155

Jos. Sir Oliver — uncle, will you honor me
with a hearing?

Char. (*aside*). Now if Joseph would make
one of his long speeches, I might recollect myself a little.   160

Sir Pet. (*to* JOSEPH). I suppose you would
undertake to justify yourself entirely?

Jos. I trust I could.

Sir Ol. (*to* CHARLES). Well, sir! and you
could justify yourself too, I suppose?   165

Char. Not that I know of, Sir Oliver.

Sir Ol. What! Little Premium has been let
too much into the secret, I suppose?

Char. True, sir; but they were *family* secrets,
and should not be mentioned again, you 170
know.

Row. Come, Sir Oliver, I know you cannot
speak of Charles's follies with anger.

Sir Ol. Odd's heart, no more can I; nor with
gravity either. Sir Peter, do you know 175
the rogue bargained with me for all his ancestors; sold me judges and generals by the foot,
and maiden aunts as cheap as broken china!

Char. To be sure, Sir Oliver, I did make a
little free with the family canvas, that's 180
the truth on't. My ancestors may rise in
judgment against me, there's no denying it;
but believe me sincere when I tell you — and
upon my soul I would not say so if I was not —
that if I do not appear mortified at the ex- 185
posure of my follies, it is because I feel at this
moment the warmest satisfaction in seeing you,
my liberal benefactor.

Sir Ol. Charles, I believe you! Give me your
hand again; the ill-looking little fellow 190
over the settee has made your peace.

Char. Then, sir, my gratitude to the original is still increased.

Lady T. (*pointing to* MARIA). Yet I believe, Sir Oliver, here is one whom Charles is 195 still more anxious to be reconciled to.

Sir Ol. Oh, I have heard of his attachment there; and, with the young lady's pardon, if I construe right — that blush ——

Sir Pet. Well, child, speak your senti- 200 ments!

Maria. Sir, I have little to say, but that I shall rejoice to hear that he is happy; for me — whatever claim I had to his affection, I willingly resign to one who has a better title. 205

Char. How, Maria!

Sir Pet. Hey day! what's the mystery now? While he appeared an incorrigible rake, you would give your hand to no one else; and now that he is likely to reform, I'll warrant 210 you won't have him.

Maria. His own heart and Lady Sneerwell know the cause.

Char. Lady Sneerwell!

Jos. Brother, it is with great concern 215 I am obliged to speak on this point, but my regard to justice compels me, and Lady Sneerwell's injuries can no longer be concealed.

(*Opens the door.*

Enter LADY SNEERWELL

Sir Pet. So! another French milliner! Egad, he has one in every room of the house, 220 I suppose.

Lady Sneer. Ungrateful Charles! Well may you be surprised, and feel for the indelicate situation your perfidy has forced me into. 225

Char. Pray, uncle, is this another plot of yours? For, as I have life, I don't understand it.

Jos. I believe, sir, there is but the evidence of one person more necessary to make 230 it extremely clear.

Sir Pet. And that person, I imagine, is Mr. Snake. Rowley, you were perfectly right to bring him with us, and pray let him appear.

Row. Walk in, Mr. Snake. 235

Enter SNAKE

I thought his testimony might be wanted; however, it happens unluckily that he comes to confront Lady Sneerwell, not to support her.

Lady Sneer (*aside*). Villain! Treacherous to me at last! — Speak, fellow; have you too 240 conspired against me?

Snake. I beg your ladyship ten thousand pardons; you paid me extremely liberally for the lie in question; but I unfortunately have been offered double to speak the truth. 245

Sir Pet. Plot and counter-plot, egad!

Lady Sneer. The torments of shame and disappointment on you all!

Lady T. Hold, Lady Sneerwell! Before you go, let me thank you for the trouble you 250 and that gentleman have taken, in writing letters from me to Charles, and answering them yourself; and let me also request you to make my respects to the scandalous college, of which you are president, and inform them that 255 Lady Teazle, licentiate, begs leave to return the diploma they gave her, as she leaves off practice, and kills characters no longer.

Lady Sneer. You too, madam — provoking — insolent! May your husband live 260 these fifty years!

(*Exit.*

Sir Pet. Oons! what a fury!

Lady T. A malicious creature, indeed!

Sir Pet. Hey! Not for her last wish?

Lady T. Oh, no! 265

Sir Ol. Well, sir, and what have you to say now?

Jos. Sir, I am so confounded, to find that Lady Sneerwell could be guilty of suborning Mr. Snake in this manner, to impose on 270 us all, that I know not what to say. However, lest her revengeful spirit should prompt her to injure my brother, I had certainly better follow her directly. (*Exit.*

Sir Pet. Moral to the last drop! 275

Sir Ol. Ay, and marry her, Joseph, if you can. Oil and vinegar, egad! you'll do very well together.

Row. I believe we have no more occasion for Mr. Snake at present? 280

Snake. Before I go, I beg pardon once for

all, for whatever uneasiness I have been the humble instrument of causing to the parties present.

Sir Pet. Well, well, you have made 285 atonement by a good deed at last.

Snake. But I must request of the company that it shall never be known.

Sir Pet. Hey! What the plague! Are you ashamed of having done a right thing 290 once in your life?

Snake. Ah, sir! consider; I live by the badness of my character. I have nothing but my infamy to depend on! and if it were once known that I had been betrayed into an 295 honest action, I should lose every friend I have in the world.

Sir Ol. Well, well; we'll not traduce you by saying anything in your praise, never fear.

(*Exit* SNAKE.

Sir Pet. There's a precious rogue!   300

Lady T. See, Sir Oliver, there needs no persuasion now to reconcile your nephew and Maria.

Sir Ol. Ay, ay, that's as it should be, and egad we'll have the wedding tomorrow 305 morning.

Char. Thank you, dear uncle!

Sir Pet. What, you rogue! don't you ask the girl's consent first?

Char. Oh, I have done that a long 310 time — a minute ago — and she has looked *yes.*

Maria. For shame, Charles! I protest, Sir Peter, there has not been a word.

Sir Ol. Well, then, the fewer the better. May your love for each other never know 315 abatement!

Sir Pet. And may you live as happily together as Lady Teazle and I intend to do!

Char. Rowley, my old friend, I am sure you congratulate me; and I suspect that I owe 320 you much.

Sir Ol. You do indeed, Charles.

Row. If my efforts to serve you had not succeeded, you would have been in my debt for the attempt: but deserve to be happy, 325 and you overpay me.

Sir Pet. Ay, honest Rowley always said you would reform.

Char. Why, as to reforming, Sir Peter, I'll make no promises, and that I take to be a 330 proof that I intend to set about it; but here shall be my monitor — my gentle guide. Ah! can I leave the virtuous path those eyes illumine?

Though thou, dear maid, shouldst waive thy
     beauty's sway,   335
Thou still must rule, because I will obey:
An humble fugitive from Folly view,
No sanctuary near but Love and you.
(*To the audience*)
You can, indeed, each anxious fear remove,
For even Scandal dies if you approve.   340

EPILOGUE

BY MR. COLMAN [1]

Spoken by LADY TEAZLE

I, who was late so volatile and gay,
Like a trade wind must now blow all one way,
Bend all my cares, my studies, and my vows,
To one dull rusty weathercock — my spouse!
So wills our virtuous bard — the motley Bayes   5
Of crying epilogues and laughing plays!
Old bachelors, who marry smart young wives,
Learn from our play to regulate your lives:
Each bring his dear to town, all faults upon her,
London will prove the very source of honor.   10
Plunged fairly in, like a cold bath it serves,

---

[1] George Colman (1732–94), manager of the Haymarket Theatre and also playwright.

When principles relax, to brace the nerves.
Such is my case; and yet I must deplore
That the gay dream of dissipation's o'er.
And say, ye fair, was ever lively wife,   15
Born with a genius for the highest life,
Like me untimely blasted in her bloom,
Like me condemn'd to such a dismal doom?
Save money — when I just knew how to waste it!
Leave London — just as I began to taste it!   20
     Must I then watch the early crowing cock,
The melancholy ticking of a clock;
In a lone rustic hall for ever pounded,[1]
With dogs, cats, rats, and squalling brats surrounded?
With humble curate can I now retire   25
(While good Sir Peter boozes with the squire),
And at backgammon mortify my soul,
That pants for loo, or flutters at a vole?[2]
Seven's the main![3]   Dear sound that must expire,
Lost at hot cockles[4] round a Christmas fire!   30
The transient hour of fashion too soon spent,
Farewell the tranquil mind, farewell content![5]
Farewell the plumèd head, the cushioned tête
That takes the cushion from its proper seat!
The spirit-stirring drum[6] — card drums I mean!   35
Spadille[7] — odd trick — pam[8] — basto[9] — king and queen!
And you, ye knockers, that, with brazen throat,
The welcome visitors' approach denote!
Farewell all quality of high renown,
Pride, pomp, and circumstance of glorious town!   40
Farewell! your revels I partake no more,
And Lady Teazle's occupation's o'er!
All this I told our bard; he smiled, and said 'twas clear,
I ought to play deep tragedy next year.
Meanwhile he drew wise morals from his play,   45
And in these solemn periods stalk'd away: —
"Blest were the fair like you! her faults who stopp'd,
And closed her follies when the curtain dropp'd!
No more in vice or error to engage,
Or play the fool at large on life's great stage."   50

[1] Imprisoned.   [2] A "grand slam" in loo, the fashionable card game of the eighteenth century.
[3] The number which the caster of dice attempts to throw.
[4] An old game of striking on the back and guessing the offender.
[5] Ll. 32–42 are a parody on Othello's soliloquy, Act III, Scene 3, ll. 347–57.   [6] Smart party.
[7] The ace of spades.   [8] The jack of clubs.   [9] The ace of clubs.

INTRODUCTION TO

The Inspector-General

The Rise of the Russian Drama and Stage: Gogol and Realistic Comedy

THE RISE OF THE RUSSIAN DRAMA AND STAGE

THE earliest dramatic entertainments in Russia consisted of simple religious plays which were presented during the sixteenth and seventeenth centuries by folk groups. The backwardness of Russian culture prevented, however, any real flowering of a national drama before the nineteenth century.

The first professional playhouse in Russia, a wooden hall, was built at Moscow in 1672 by the Tsar Alexis who wanted to ape other European monarchs and be patron of a theater. He imported a German troupe who performed plays, mostly farces, in German before the Russian court. In 1682 the new Tsar, Peter the Great (*r.* 1676–1725), built another and better theater at Moscow for the performances of German plays, but the foreign atmosphere caused the eventual failure of this royal enterprise. Theatrical art in Russia continued to mark time with occasional alien productions until the Tsarina Elizabeth (*r.* 1741–62) patronized a Russian-managed theater in a slim repertory of Russian plays.

It was under the next monarch, Catherine the Great (*r.* 1762–96), that the Russian stage actually began to prosper. In 1765 the leading Russian director, Ivan Dmitrevsky, traveled to France and England to study theaters and procure plays. The large repertory of French drama which he brought back and produced set the style of the tentative Russian playwriting for a long time thereafter. Catherine the Great built splendid royal theaters at Moscow and St. Petersburg. She spared no expense to provide them with stage décor in imitation of the newest modes in the Italian theaters, at that time the most advanced in Europe. Foreign troupes, especially German, and Italian opera companies started to visit the Russian theaters regularly. The audiences were largely made up of the court aristocracy and the higher officials who copied the court taste. Since the atmosphere had little of the native or popular about it, Russian dramatists were not strongly inspired to depict distinctively national and contemporary material. Now and then a play, such as *The Brigadier-General* by Denis Fon-vízin (1744–92), exhibited genuine Russian life. This comedy of the Molière type satirizes the pretensions of the crude landed gentry to the refinements of French culture, and contains much rural color.

The reigns of Alexander I (*r.* 1801–25) and Nicholas I (*r.* 1825–55) found the stage under somewhat greater native influences. The theaters remained the playthings of the court and a limited intelligentsia. Foreign attractions still afforded a good deal of the entertainment. More Russian authors of talent, however, made efforts to contribute to the drama. Yet much of their dramatic composition was so affected by the extravagant romanticism from Germany that it did little to advance the cause of a national art. Alexander Pushkin (1799–1837), the chief poet of the day, wrote *Boris Godunov*, an historical tragedy of continued popularity on the Russian stage, but a drama full of imitative romantic elements. A play of more distinctive substance was a comedy, *Wit Comes to Woe* (1823), by Alexander Griboyédov (1795–1829). This Russian favorite in the Molière tradition takes off contemporary urban characters.

GOGOL AND REALISTIC COMEDY

The period of slow awakening to the Russian scene produced one figure of importance to world drama, Nikolái Vasílyevich Gógol-Yanovski, popularly known as Gogol (the Russian name for the golden-eyed duck). He was born on March 31, 1809, at the family estate near Poltava in the Ukraine. His father, one of the poor but more cultivated members of the landed gentry, attempted to be an amateur author and playwright. From 1821 to 1828 Gogol attended an academy near Kiev. There he pioneered a literary magazine, engaged in dramatics, and wrote a play, *The Robbers*. This small success at school led him in 1829 to seek his fortune as a writer in St. Petersburg (Leningrad).

Poverty soon stared him in the face. Then he took ship for America, but turned back before the boat had gone outside the Baltic Sea. During the next year the successful publication of a volume of sketches about Ukrainian peasant life secured him a position on the faculty of St. Petersburg University. He met in 1831 Madame Smirnova, a well-known patron of letters, and obtained entrée to various salons in the capital. About the same time a friendship with Pushkin spurred him to write more sketches and stories of Ukrainian life. Perhaps his increasing literary success made him weary of teaching, for in 1835 he gave up his university position. A year later the great triumph of his first play, *The Inspector-General*, stamped him as Russia's leading dramatist. The production nevertheless provoked many attacks from disgruntled officials. These quite upset his sensitive temperament. The Tsar, in consequence, awarded him a pension in order that he might go abroad and recover from his melancholia.

While residing in Italy, he started his famous novel, *Dead Souls*, partly published in 1842. It is a moving tale about the speculator Chichikov, who goes about Russia buying up "dead souls" (i.e., serfs dead since the last census), that he may pawn them to the unsuspecting government. Gogol sets down with devastating power the wretched influence of the serf-system. In 1842 also he brought out two more plays, *Marriage* and *The Gamblers*. The former is an amusing comedy of intrigue on the theme of a bridegroom's escape from marriage; the latter, a one-act, stark portrayal of a group of swindlers. Neither of these plays approached the dimensions of *The Inspector-General*, but they did further prove Gogol's insight into the Russian scene and his ability to dramatize it vividly.

Brooding too much over the subject of "dead souls" seems to have brought Gogol to hypochondria. He burned up the manuscript of the second part to his novel. He grew interested in mysticism, went on pilgrimage to the Holy Land in 1846, and returned to live out his last years unproductively. Death came as a blessed relief on March 3,

1852. With his dying breath Gogol repeated the old Russian saying, "And I shall laugh with a bitter laugh," and asked to have it placed on his tombstone. This epitaph stands as the soulful cry of a comic spirit finally broken by the evil of mankind.

Gogol intended *The Inspector-General* to be a satirical picture of Russian society with a moral undertone. He prefaced the comedy with an old proverb: "Don't blame the looking-glass when your own face is at fault." The saying reveals the serious purpose behind the play, a purpose best described in Gogol's own words: "I tried to gather in one heap all that was bad in Russia, as I then understood it: I wished to turn it all into ridicule. . . . Through the laughter that I have never laughed more loudly, the spectator may feel my bitterness and sorrow." Because he avoided, however, every trace of bitterness and sorrow, and of the reforming spirit, in his indictment of Russian society, *The Inspector-General* emerged as a masterpiece of comic realism.

"THE INSPECTOR-GENERAL"

Gogol's comedy originated in a conversation with Pushkin. The latter related how, while stopping once at Nijni-Novgorod (now Gorki), a provincial capital in central Russia, he had been taken for a government inspector and treated with amusing deference. Pushkin then went on to suggest that Gogol write a play based on this situation. The latter, delighted with the idea, began *The Inspector-General* in 1834 and finished it on December 4, 1835. His friend, Madame Smirnova, was so filled with enthusiasm that she showed the manuscript to the Tsar, Nicholas I. Roaring with laughter, he ordered that the comedy should be acted at the state theater. Certain government officials, hearing of the contents, opposed the production, but the Tsar insisted. The premiere took place on April 19, 1836, at the St. Petersburg Theater, in the presence of Nicholas and his court. Loud ovations greeted the performance. Soon *The Inspector-General* had established itself as the great Russian national comedy.

The Gogol drama early made its way into theatrical repertories all over the Continent, especially in Germany, but production in the English-speaking world was strangely delayed. The first recorded performance of an English version seems to have been the one by the Yale Dramatic Association in New York City on April 20, 1908. An adaptation, entitled *The Government Inspector*, received professional production at the Hudson Theater, New York City, on December 23, 1930. But, as yet, the English and American stages have not done justice to this popular European classic.

The Inspector-General in external form shows the influence of Molière and French classical comedy. Gogol preserves a strict unity of setting within the act by the classical method of scene-linking. The play as a whole also shows a tendency to unity of locale; only the second act transfers the action from the governor's house to the inn. The plot has all the simplicity and leisureliness of everyday life. The surprising twist given to the conclusion by the announcement of a *true* inspector brings the comedy to a superb climax. Gogol exhibited admirable dramatic restraint at this final moment. The *tableau vivant*, as he termed it, is the perfect theatrical ending.

The sprightliness of the comedy depends, however, more upon the characters than upon the action. They constitute an amusing cross-section of the black sheep in middle-class Russian society: the self-important governor; his socially ambitious wife; the grafting, incompetent officials; the trivially minded citizens; and the ordinary "sport"

turned deceiver, Khlestakóv. Gogol presents them with fidelity to local setting and in-
terests, but with emphasis upon the traits which give them a universal humanity.
Khlestakóv, as Gogol conceives him, "is not an intentional impostor, or a liar by pro-
fession; he forgets that he is telling falsehoods, and almost believes what he is saying.
His spirits rise as he finds he is a success — he becomes expansive, poetic, inspired. . . .
We all are, or have been, Khlestakóvs — only we don't care to admit it."

This little world of a Russian provincial city exhibits the absurd pettiness of common
men everywhere in all ages. Their mercurial behavior by reason of self-interest is dramatized with particular cleverness in the fifth act: first, the self-complacency of the governor and his wife because of their daughter's prospective marriage into high society; then,
the homage they receive from the officials and citizens in anticipation of that event;
next, the deflations and recriminations which arise after the revelation of the fraud; and
finally, the wonder, shock, and maliciousness which the approach of the actual inspector
calls forth. The same subtle medley of vanity and small mind runs through the entire
drama. That Gogol treats such human folly always with gay ridicule constitutes the
peculiar charm of his achievement. *The Inspector-General* is a brilliant specimen of high
comedy derived not from the drawing-room but from average community life.

[For a history of the early Russian theater, see Alexander Bakshy, *The Path of the Modern Russian Stage* (1916); for Gogol, see Boris Brasil, *The Mighty Three — Pushkin, Gogol, Dostoyevsky*
(1934).]

NIKOLAI V. GOGOL

The Inspector-General (*Revizór*)

[*Translated by* ARTHUR A. SYKES]

DRAMATIS PERSONAE

ANTÓN ANTÓNOVICH [1] SKVAZNÍK-DMUKHANÓV-SKI, *the governor of a Russian provincial town*

ÁNNA ANDRÉYEVNA, *his wife*

MÁRYA ANTÓNOVNA, *his daughter*

LUKÁ LUKÍCH KHLÓPOV, *the director of schools*

NÁSTYA, *his wife*

ÁMMOS FYÓDOROVICH LYÁPKIN-TYÁPKIN, *the judge of the county court*

ARTÉMI PHILÍPPOVICH ZEMLYANÍKA, *the charity commissioner and superintendent of the hospital*

IVÁN KUZMÍCH SHPYÓKIN, *the postmaster*

IVÁN ALEXÁNDROVICH KHLESTAKÓV, *a government clerk from the national capital*

OSIP, *his servant*

PETER IVÁNOVICH DOBCHÍNSKI } *gentlemen of independent means*
PYÓTR IVÁNOVICH BOBCHÍNSKI }

CHRÍSTIAN IVÁNOVICH HÜBNER, *the district doctor*

STEPÁN ÍLYICH UKHAVYÓRTOV, *superintendent of police*

SVISTUNÓV }
PÚGOVKIN } *police officers*
DERZHIMÓRDA }

LYÚLYUKOV }
RASTÁKOVSKI } *ex-officials*
KARÓBKIN }

ABDÚLIN, *a merchant*

MÍSHKA, *servant of the governor*

Locksmith's wife

Sergeant's wife

Waiter at the inn

Gentlemen and ladies, guests, merchants, citizens and petitioners

GOGOL'S "NOTES ON THE CHARACTERS AND COSTUMES"

THE GOVERNOR is a man who has grown old in the state service — in style and manner, a smart official. He wears an air of dignified respectability, but is by no means incorruptible. He speaks to the point, generally avoiding extremes, but sometimes launching into an argument. His features are harsh and stern, like those of a *chinóvnik* who has worked his way up from the lowest rank. His coarse and ill-educated nature causes him to pass with rapidity from fear to joy, and from servility to arrogance. He is dressed in uniform with loops and facings, and wears Hessian boots with spurs.

ÁNNA ANDRÉYEVNA, his wife, is still tolerably young, and a provincial coquette, brought up on novels and albums and household trivialities. She is very inquisitive, and displays now and then a vain disposition. Henpecks and ridicules her husband to a certain extent on minor points, when she can get the best of him in argument. Changes her dress four times in the course of the piece.

KHLESTAKÓV is a young man, about twenty-three years old, mean and insignificant

[1] The second of the three names which Russians possess is the patronymic. It is formed by adding to the father's *Christian* name "ovich" or "evich" (sometimes contracted to "ich") in the case of men, and "ovna" or "evna" in the case of women.

to look at. Not overburdened with common sense, being, as they say, "without a tsar in his head." He would be designated as "very frivolous" in the government offices. Speaks and acts without reflection, and lacks concentration. His style of address is abrupt, and his remarks are totally unexpected. (The actor should sustain this rôle with the greatest possible naïveté.) Dresses in the latest fashion.

OSIP, his servant, resembles other middle-aged persons of his class. Talks seriously, looks downwards, and is fond of arguing and lecturing his master. He scarcely varies the tone of his voice, addressing Khlestakóv bluntly and even rudely. He is the cleverer of the two, and sees through things quicker; is silent and uncommunicative, and a rogue. Wears a rather worn-out overcoat of a gray or blue color.

BOBCHÍNSKI and DOBCHÍNSKI are short, fat, inquisitive, and remarkably like each other. They both wear short waistcoats, and speak rapidly, with an excessive amount of gesticulation. Dobchínski is the taller and steadier, Bobchínski the more free and easy, of the pair.

LYÁPKIN-TYÁPKIN, the Judge, has read five or six books, and so is somewhat of a free-thinker. He is very fond of philosophic speculation, carefully weighing each word. (The player should be careful to preserve a judicial and consequential style.) Speaks with a bass voice and a prolonged drawl, clearing his throat beforehand, like an old-fashioned clock, which buzzes before it strikes.

ZEMLYANÍKA, the Charity Commissioner, is very fat, slow, and awkward; nevertheless an intriguing rascal, most obliging and officious.

The POSTMASTER is an artless simpleton.

The Scene is a Russian provincial town in the early nineteenth century.

ACT I

A room in the GOVERNOR'S *house.*

SCENE I

The GOVERNOR, *the* CHARITY COMMISSIONER, *the* DIRECTOR OF SCHOOLS, *the* JUDGE, *the* POLICE SUPERINTENDENT, *the* DOCTOR, *and two* POLICE-OFFICERS

Gov. I have called you together, gentlemen, to receive a very unpleasant piece of news: there's an inspector-general coming.

Judge and Char. Comm. What, a *revizór*?

Gov. Yes, an inspector from Petersburg,[1]   5 *incognito*. With secret instructions, too.

Judge. Well, I declare!

Char. Comm. We've escaped hitherto, so now it's *our* turn!

Luká. Good Lord! with secret in-   10 structions!

[1] St. Petersburg, the old capital of Russia, now called Leningrad.

Gov. I had a sort of presentiment of it: all last night I dreamt about a pair of monstrous rats. Upon my word, I never saw the like of 'em — so black and enormous. They   15 came and snuffed about — and vanished.... Here's a letter which I will read you from Andréi Ivánovich Chmíkov. *You* know him, Artémi Philíppovich[1] (*to the* CHARITY COMMISSIONER). This is what he says: "My   20 dear friend, my comrade and benefactor... (*He mutters over quickly the first few sentences.*) ... and to let you know" — Ah! that's it — "I hasten to let you know, amongst other things, that an official has been sent with instructions to inspect the whole province,   25 and your district especially. (*Lifts his finger significantly.*) That he *is* coming I know from very reliable sources, but he pretends to be a private person. So, as you have your little faults, you know, like everybody else   30

[1] In Russian it is polite to address every one by his or her paternal, as well as Christian, name.

(you're a sensible man, and don't let little perquisites slip through your fingers)..." (*Stopping*) H'm, that's after a manner of speaking
... "I advise you to take precautions, for he
may come any hour — if he has not al- 35
ready done so, and is staying somewhere *incognito*... Yesterday..." Oh, then come family
matters. "My cousin, Anna Kiríllovna, paid
us a visit, with her husband; Iván Kiríllovich
has got very fat, and is always playing the 40
fiddle..." etcetera, etcetera. Now, here's a
pretty business!

Judge. Yes, extraordinary, simply extraordinary. There must be some reason for 44
it.

Luká. But why, Antón Antónovich, why is
it? Why should *we* have an inspector?

Gov. (*sighing*). Oh, it's fate, I suppose! (*Sighs
again.*) Till now, thank goodness, they've
pried into other towns; but now our time 50
has come.

Judge. It's my opinion, Antón Antónovich,
that it's a deep political move, and it means —
let me see — that Russia... yes, that's it...
Russia wants to make war, and this Gov- 55
ernment has surreptitiously sent an official to
see if there's any disaffection anywhere.

Gov. Ah, you've got it! *you* know a thing or
two! The idea of treason in an inland town!
As if it lay on the frontier! Why, from 60
here you may gallop for three years before you
reach a foreign country.

Judge. No, I'll tell you how it is — you
don't understand — the Government looks
very closely into matters; it *may* be far 65
away, yet it observes everything ——

Gov. (*cutting him short*). It may or it may not
— anyhow, gentlemen, I have warned you. I
have made some arrangements on my own
behalf, and I advise you to do the same. 70
You especially, Artémi Philíppovich! (*To the*
CHARITY COMMISSIONER) Without doubt, this
chinóvnik [1] will want first of all to inspect your
hospital; and so you had better see that everything is in order; that the nightcaps are 75
clean, and that the sick persons don't go about
as they usually do — looking like black-
smiths.

[1] Official.

Char. Comm. Oh, that's all right. They
shall have clean nightcaps, if you like. 80

Gov. And you might write up over each bed,
in Latin or some other lingo — that's *your*
business, Chrístian Ivánovich (*to the* DOCTOR)
— the name of each complaint, when the patient got ill, the day of the week and 85
month... and I don't like your invalids smoking such strong tobacco; it makes you choke
when you come in. It would be better too if
there weren't so many of them; otherwise it
will be at once ascribed to bad supervision 90
or unskillful doctoring.

Char. Comm. Oh, Chrístian Ivánovich and
I have settled all about the *doctoring*; the nearer
we get to *nature* the better: we don't go in for
costly medicines. A man is a simple 95
affair — if he dies, he dies; if he gets well, why,
then he gets well. And it wouldn't be easy
for the sick people and Chrístian to understand
one another; he doesn't know a word of Russian. 100

(*The* DOCTOR *grunts unintelligibly.*)

Gov. Also I would recommend you, Ámmos
Fyódorovich (*to the* JUDGE) to turn your attention to the courthouse buildings. There's the
antechamber, where the petitioners usually
wait; you've let the attendants breed 105
geese there, and the goslings go poking their
beaks amongst people's legs. Of course, rearing geese is a laudable object, and there's no
reason why an usher should not do so; only,
you see, the County Court is not exactly 110
the place for it.... I intended to mention it
before, but it somehow escaped my memory.

Judge. Well, I'll tell them to take 'em all
into the kitchen today. Will you come to
dinner? 115

Gov. (*not noticing*). Besides that, it doesn't
do for the court chamber to get so full of rubbish of all sorts: why, there was a sporting
whip lying among the papers on your very
desk. I know you're fond of sport, but 120
there is a proper time and place for everything
— when the Inspector is gone you can put it
back again. Then your assessor... he's certainly a learned man, but he reeks of spirits,
as if he had just come out of a distillery; 125
that also is undesirable. I meant to tell you

of this some while ago, but something or other put it out of my head. There are ways of remedying it, if it is really, as he says, a natural failing: you can recommend him to 130 eat onions or garlic, or something of the sort. Chrístian Ivánovich can help him there with some of his nostrums.

(*The* DOCTOR *grunts as before.*

Judge. No, it's quite impossible to get rid of it; he says his nurse knocked him down 135 when he was a child, and ever since he has smelt of vodka.[1]

Gov. Well, I just reminded you of it. As regards the local administration, and what Andréi Ivánovich is pleased to call one's 140 "little faults" in his letter, I don't understand what he means. Why, of course, there isn't a man living who has not *some* peccadilloes to account for: Heaven made him so — let *free-thinkers* say what they like.   145

Judge. What do you mean by peccadilloes, Antón Antónovich? There are peccadilloes and peccadilloes. I tell everyone plainly that I take bribes, but what kind of bribes? Why, greyhound puppies. That's a totally 150 different matter.

Gov. H'm, whether they're puppies or anything else, they're all bribes alike.

Judge. No, indeed, Antón Antónovich. But suppose, for example, one receives a *cloak* 155 worth five hundred roubles,[2] or your good lady receives a *shawl* . . .

Gov. (*testily*). Yes; but what has that got to do with your being bribed with puppy greyhounds? Besides, you're an atheist; you 160 never go to church; while I, at least, am a firm believer, and attend service every Sunday. Whereas *you* — oh, I know *you;* when I hear you talking about the Creation my hair simply stands on end.   165

Judge. What of that? I have reasoned it all out with my own unaided intellect.

Gov. Anyhow, too much knowledge is worse than none at all. . . . However, I only made a remark about the County Court, and I 170 daresay nobody will ever look at it; there's an

[1] The national alcoholic beverage of Russia.

[2] At the time of this play the gold rouble was worth seventy-seven cents.

odor of sanctity about the place. But you, Luká Lukích, as Director of Educational Establishments, ought to have an eye on the teachers. They're very clever people, no 175 doubt, and are blessed with a college education; but they have very funny habits — inseparable from their profession, I suppose. One of them, for instance, the fat-faced man — I forget his name — can't get along with- 180 out screwing up his phiz like this — (*imitates him*) — when he's got into his chair; and then he sets to work clawing his necktie and scratching his chin. It doesn't matter, of course, if he makes a face at a pupil — perhaps it's 185 even necessary — I'm no judge of that; but you yourself will admit that if he grimaces at a visitor, it may leave a very bad impression. The honorable Inspector, or anyone else, might take it as meant for himself — and 190 then the deuce knows what might come of it.

Luká. What can I do with him, I ask? I have told him of it time after time. Only the other day, when our headmaster came into class, your friend made such a face at 195 him as I had never seen before. I daresay it was with the best intentions, but people come complaining to me about radical notions being instilled into the juvenile mind.

Gov. And then you should look to the 200 master of the history class. He has a learned head, that is evident, and has picked up any amount of knowledge; but he lectures with such ardor that he quite forgets himself. I once listened to him. As long as he was hold- 205 ing forth about the Assyrians and Babylonians, it was all right; but when he got on Alexander of Macedon, I can't describe his behavior. Good heavens, I thought, there's a fire! He jumped out of his chair, and 210 smashed a stool on the ground with all his might! Alexander of Macedon was a hero, we all know, but that's no reason for breaking the furniture; besides, the State has to pay for the damages.   215

Luká. Yes, he *is* fiery! I have spoken to him several times about it. He only says, "As you please, but in the cause of learning I will even sacrifice my life!"

Gov. Yes, it's a mysterious law of fate; 220

your clever man is either a drunkard, or he makes such frightful grimaces that you have to carry out the saints.[1]

Luká. Ah, Heaven save us from being schoolmasters! You're afraid of every- 225 thing; everybody meddles with you, and wants to show you that he's learned as you are.

Gov. Oh, all that's nothing; it's this cursed *incognito!* All of a sudden he'll look in: "Ah, so you're here, my friends! And who's 230 the judge here?" he'll say. "Lyápkin-Tyápkin." "Well, bring Lyápkin-Tyápkin here, then!" "And who is the Charity Commissioner?" "Zemlyaníka." "Call Zemlyaníka, too!" There'll be a pretty kettle of fish! 235

SCENE 2

Enter the POSTMASTER

Post. Tell me, gentlemen, who's coming? What sort of *chinóvnik?*

Gov. What, haven't you heard?

Post. I heard something from Bobchínski; he was just now with me at the post-office. 5

Gov. Well, what do you think about it?

Post. What do *I* think about it? Why, there'll be a war with the Turks.

Judge. Exactly; that's just what I thought!

Gov. Well, you're both wide of the mark. 10

Post. It'll be with the Turks, I'm sure. It's all the Frenchman's doing.[2]

Gov. Pooh! War with the Turks, indeed! it's *we* who are going to get into trouble, not the Turks. That's quite certain. I've a letter 15 to say so.

Post. Oh, then we shan't go to war with the Turks.

Gov. Well, how do *you* feel, Iván Kuzmích? (*to the* POSTMASTER).

Post. How do *I* feel? How do *you*, 20 Antón Antónovich?

Gov. I? Well, I'm no coward, but I *am* just a little uncomfortable. The shopkeepers and townspeople bother me. It seems I'm unpop-

ular with them; but, the Lord knows, if 25 I've blackmailed anybody, I've done it without a trace of ill-feeling. I even think — (*buttonholes him and takes him aside*) — I even think there must have been some sort of complaint drawn up against me... Why should we 30 have a *revizór* at all?... Look here, Iván Kuzmích, don't you think you could just slightly open every letter which comes in and goes out of your office, and read it (for the public benefit, you know), to see if it contains any 35 kind of information against me, or only ordinary correspondence? If it is all right, you can seal it up again; or simply deliver the letter opened.

Post. Oh, I know *that* game... Don't 40 teach me *that!* I do it from pure curiosity, not as a precaution; I'm death on knowing what's going on in the world. And they're very interesting to read, I can tell you! Now and then you come across a love letter, with bits of 45 beautiful language, and so edifying... much better than the *Moscow News!*

Gov. Tell me, then, have you read anything about any *chinóvnik* from Petersburg?

Post. No, nothing about anyone from 50 Petersburg, but plenty about the Kostromá [1] and Sarátov [2] people. It's a pity you don't read the letters. There's some very fine passages in them. For instance, not long ago a lieutenant writes to a friend, describing 55 a ball in first-rate style — splendid! "Dear friend," he says, "I live in Elysium; heaps of girls, music playing, flags flying,"... quite a glowing description, quite! I've kept it by me on purpose. Would you like to read it? 60

Gov. Thanks; there's no time now. But oblige me, Iván Kuzmích — if ever you chance upon a complaint or a denouncement, keep it back, without the slightest compunction.

Post. I will, with the greatest pleasure. 65

Judge (*who has overheard a little*). You had better mind; you'll get into trouble over that some time or other.

Post. (*innocently*). Eh? The saints forbid!

---

[1] To avoid shocking them. The picture of the patron saint used to be placed in the sacred corner of every house or shop in Russia before the First World War.

[2] The Russians and the French were bitter enemies in the early nineteenth century.

[1] A provincial capital, northeast of Moscow, on the Volga River in central Russia.

[2] Another provincial capital, also on the Volga River in southeastern Russia.

Gov. It was nothing — nothing. It would   70
be different if it concerned you or the public
— but it was a private affair, I assure you!

Judge. H'm, *some* mischief was brewing, *I*
know!... But I was going to say, Antón
Antónovich, that I had got a puppy to   75
make you a present of — own sister to the dog
you know about.   I daresay you've heard that
Chéptovich and Varkhovínski have gone to law
with one another; so now I live in clover — I
hunt hares first on one's estate, and then   80
on the other's.

Gov. I don't care about your hares now, my
good friend; I've got that cursed *incognito* on
the brain! I expect the door to be opened,
and all of a sudden...   85

SCENE 3

Enter BOBCHÍNSKI *and* DOBCHÍNSKI,
out of breath

Bob. What an extraordinary occurrence!
Dob. An unexpected piece of news!
All. What is it — what is it?
Dob. Something quite unforeseen; we go
into the inn ——   5
Bob. (*interrupting*). Yes, Pyótr Ivánovich
and I go into the inn ——
Dob. (*takes him up*). All right, Peter Iváno-
vich, let *me* tell it!
Bob. No, no, allow me — allow me....   10
You haven't got the knack.
Dob. Oh, but you'll get mixed up and forget
it all.
Bob. Oh, no, I shan't — good heavens, no!
There, don't interrupt me — *do* let me tell   15
the news — don't interrupt! Pray oblige me,
gentlemen, and tell Dobchínski not to interrupt.
Gov. Well, say on, for God's sake, what is it?
My heart is in my mouth! Sit down, sirs;   20
take seats! Pyótr Ivánovich, here's a chair
for you! (*They all sit round* BOBCHÍNSKI *and*
DOBCHÍNSKI.)   Well, now, what is it, what
is it?
Bob. Permit me — permit me; I can re-   25
late it properly.... H'm, as soon as I had the
pleasure of taking my leave after you were
good enough to be bothered with the letter

which you had received, sir — yes, then I ran
out — now please don't keep on taking me   30
up, Dobchínski; I know all about it, all, I tell
you, sir. — So, as you'll kindly take notice, I
ran out to see Karóbkin. But not finding
Karóbkin at home, I went off to Rastákovski,
and not seeing *him*, I went, you see, to Iván   35
Kuzmích, to tell him of the news you'd got; yes,
and going on from there I met Dobchínski ——
Dob. (*breaking in*). By the stall, where they
sell tartlets ——
Bob. — by the stall, where they sell   40
tartlets. Well, I meet Dobchínski and say to
him, "Have you heard the news that Antón
Antónovich has got? — the letter may be depended on!" But Peter Ivánovich had already
heard of it from your housekeeper, Av-   45
dótya, who, I don't know why, had been sent
to Philíp Antónovich Pachechúyev ——
Dob. (*interrupting*). To get a little cask for
some French brandy.
Bob. — yes, to get a little cask for some   50
French brandy. Then I went with Dobchínski
to Pachechúyev's — *will* you stop, Peter Ivánovich? — there, *do* have done with your interfering! — So off we go to Pachechúyev's, and
on our way Dobchínski says, "Let's go,"   55
says he, "to the inn. I've eaten nothing since
morning... there's such a rumbling in my
inner man"... Yes, sir, in Peter Ivánovich's
internals. "But they've got some fresh
salmon in the inn," he says; "so we can   60
have a snack." We hadn't come to the public-
house a moment when in comes a young
man ——
Dob. (*as before*). Rather good-looking and
well dressed.   65
Bob. — yes, rather good-looking and well
dressed — and walks into the room, with such
an expression on his face — such a physiognomy — and style — so distinguished a head-
piece (*moves his hand round his forehead*).   70
I had a kind of presentiment, and I say to Dobchínski, "There's something up here, sir!"
Yes — and Dobchínski beckoned, and called up
the landlord, Vlás, the innkeeper, you know —
three weeks ago his wife presented him   75
with a baby — such a fine, forward boy — he'll
grow up just like his father, and keep a public-

house. Well, we called up Vlás, and Dobchínski asks him quite privately, "Who," says
he, "is that young man?" And Vlás re- 80
plies, "That," says he — oh, don't interrupt
me so, Peter Ivánovich, please; good Lord! *you*
can't tell the story, you can't tell it — you
don't speak plainly, with only one tooth in your
head, and a lisp. — "That young man," 85
says he, "is a *chinóvnik*," — yes, sir — "who
is on his way from Petersburg, and his name,"
says he, "is Iván Alexándrovich Khlestakóv,
sir, and he's off," says he, "to the government
of Sarátov," says he, "and his goings-on 90
are very peculiar — he's stayed here over a
fortnight, he doesn't leave the house, he takes
everything on account, and doesn't pay a
kopék."[1] When he told me that, I felt illu-
minated from above, and I said to Peter 95
Ivánovich, "Hey!" ——

Dob. No, Pyótr Ivánovich, *I* said "Hey!"

Bob. Well, first *you* said it, and then *I* did.
"Hey!" said both of us, "and why does he stay
here, when he's bound for Sarátov?" 100
Yes, sir, that *chinóvnik* is HE!

Gov. Who — what *chinóvnik*?

Bob. Why, the *chinóvnik* of whom you were
pleased to get the notification — the *Revizór*.

Gov. (*in a panic*). Great God! *what* do 105
you say? It *can't* be he!

Dob. It *is*, though! Why, he pays no
money, and he doesn't go. Who else could it
be? And his *padarózhnaya*[2] is made out for
Sarátov. 110

Bob. It's he, it's he, good God, it's he!...
Why, he's so observant; he noticed everything.
He saw that Dobchínski and I were eating
salmon — all on account of Dobchínski's inside ... and he looked at our plates like 115
this (*imitates*). I was in an awful fright.

Gov. Lord, have mercy upon sinners like us!
Where is he staying now, then?

Dob. In room no. 5, first floor.

Bob. In the same room where the offi- 120

cers quarreled last year on their way through.

Gov. How long has he been here?

Dob. A fortnight or more. He came on Saint
Vasíli's Day.[1]

Gov. A fortnight! (*Aside*) Holy 125
Fathers and Saints, preserve me! In that fortnight the sergeant's wife was flogged! No provisions given to the prisoners! Dramshops
and dirt in the streets! Shameful — scandalous! (*Tears his hair.* 130

Char. Comm. What do you think, Antón Antónovich — had we better go to the inn in gala
uniform?

Judge. No, no! First send the mayor, then
the clergy and the tradespeople; it's all 135
in the book, *The Acts of John the Freema-
son.*[2] ...

Gov. No — no! Leave it to me! I've had
ticklish jobs before now, and I've managed
them all right, and even got thanks from 140
headquarters. Maybe the Lord will help us
out this time as well. (*Turns to* BOBCHÍNSKI.)
You say he's a *young* man?

Bob. Yes, about twenty-three or four at the
outside. 145

Gov. So much the better — it's easier to
ferret anything out. It's the devil if you've
got an old bird to deal with; but a young man's
all on the surface. You, gentlemen, had better
get all your departments in order, while 150
I'll go by myself, or with Dobchínski here, and
have a private stroll around, *to see that travelers
are treated with due consideration.* Here, Svistunóv! (*to one of the* POLICE-OFFICERS).

Svis. Sir? 155

Gov. Go at once to the Police Superintendent; or no — I shall want you. Tell somebody
to send him as quick as possible to me, and
then come back here.

(SVISTUNÓV *runs out at full speed.*

Char. Comm. Let us go, let us go, Ám- 160
mos Fyódorovich. Some mischief may happen,
I do believe.

[1] The *kopék* is the one-hundredth part of a rouble, and
hence worth at the period of the play about three-
fourths of a cent.

[2] An order for relays of post-horses. Travel by post-
horse was highly organized in the old Russian empire,
from Poland to eastern Siberia.

[1] Saint Vasíli of Egypt, whose day comes on February 28. The Russian lower classes used to reckon
largely by saints' days.

[2] The free-thinking Judge is alluding to a forbidden
book. The Freemasons used to be considered in Russia
a dangerous society, and, as such, were suppressed.

Judge. What's there for *you* to be afraid of? Give the sick clean nightcaps, and the thing's done!   165

Char. Comm. Nightcaps — bosh! The sick were ordered to have oatmeal porridge. Instead of that, there's such a smell of cabbages in all my corridors that you're obliged to hold your nose.   170

Judge. Well, *my* mind's at ease on *that* score. As to the County Court, who'll visit *that*? Supposing he *does* look at any of the papers, he'll wish he'd left it alone. Why, I've been sitting fifteen years on the bench — and do I   175 ever look at a charge-sheet? No, thank you! Solomon himself couldn't make head or tail of 'em!

(*The* JUDGE, CHARITY COMMISSIONER, SCHOOL DIRECTOR, *and* POSTMASTER *go out, and bump violently against the* POLICE-OFFICER *in the doorway as the latter returns.*)

SCENE 4

The GOVERNOR, BOBCHÍNSKI, DOBCHÍNSKI, *and the* POLICE-OFFICER, SVISTUNÓV

Gov. Well, is the droshky [1] ready?

Svis. Yes.

Gov. Go into the street ... or no, stop! ... go and bring ... Why, where are the others? How is it you are alone? Didn't I give   5 orders for Prókhorov to be here? Where's Prókhorov?

Svis. Prókhorov's in the police-office, and can't be employed on duty just now.

Gov. How's that?   10

Svis. Well — they brought him back this morning dead drunk. They've soused his head in water, but he's not got sober yet.

Gov. (*tearing his hair*). Oh, my God! my God! ... Go out into the street, quick —   15 or no! run to my room, sharp, d'ye hear? and fetch my new hat and sword. Now, Peter Ivánovich (*to* DOBCHÍNSKI), let us be off!

Bob. And me — me too! ... Let me come too, Antón Antónovich!   20

Gov. No, no, Bobchínski, it's impossible!

[1] A four-wheeled, open carriage.

Three's no company, you know, and we couldn't find room in the droshky either.

Bob. Oh, that doesn't matter; I'll manage it — I'll trot behind the droshky on foot —   25 on foot — on foot! I only just want to peep through a chink, *so,* to see what his ways are like ...

Gov. (*turning to the* POLICE-OFFICER *and taking the sword*). Run directly and get the constables together — let 'em each take a ...   30 there, see how this sword has got rusted! It's that dog of a trader, Abdúlin — he sees the Governor's sword's worn out, and he doesn't provide me with a new one! Oh, the scurvy set of tricksters! And I'll bet the   35 scoundrels have got their petitions against me ready under their coat-tails! ... Let each of 'em take hold of a street ... Damn! I don't mean a street — a broom ... and sweep the whole of the street that leads to the inn,   40 and sweep it clean, mind! ... Do you hear? And just look here — I know you, my friend; I know your little ways: you worm your way in there, and walk off with silver spoons in your boots — just you look out, I have a quick   45 ear ... What have you been up to with the merchant Chórnyaiev, eh? He gave you two yards of cloth for your uniform, and you stole the whole piece. Take care! Don't you rob more than your station warrants! Be off!   50

SCENE 5

Enter the POLICE SUPERINTENDENT

Gov. Hullo, Stepán Ílyich, where to goodness have you been hiding yourself? What kind of behavior do you call *that*?

Super. I was only beyond the door for a moment.   5

Gov. Well, listen, Stepán Ílyich! There's a *chinóvnik* come from Petersburg. What arrangements have you made?

Super. Exactly as you ordered. I have sent the *Kvartálni,* [1] Púgovitsin, with the con-   10 stables to clean up the streets.

Gov. But where's Derzhimórda?

Super. He's gone off with the fire-engine.

Gov. And Prókhorov's drunk?

[1] Ward inspector.

Super. Yes.   15

Gov. How is it you allowed that?

Super. The Lord only knows! Yesterday there was a row outside the town — he went there to stop it, and was brought back drunk.

Gov. Well, hear me, then — this is what 20 you are to do: the police lieutenant — he is tall, so he's to stand on the bridge — that will give a good effect. Then the old fence, near the bootmaker's, must be pulled down at once and scattered about, and a post stuck up with a 25 wisp of straw, so as to look like building operations. The more litter there is the more it will show the Governor's zeal and activity.... Good God! though, I forgot that about forty cartloads of rubbish have been shot behind 30 that fence. What a dirty town this is! No matter where you put a monument, or even a paling, they collect all kinds of rubbish from the devil knows where, and upset it there!... And if the newly come *chinóvnik* asks any 35 of the officials if they are contented, they're to say, "Perfectly, Your Honor"; and if anybody is not contented, I'll give him something afterwards to be discontented about.... (*Heaves a sigh.*) Ah-h-h! I'm a sinner — a terrible 40 sinner! (*Takes the hat-box instead of his hat.*) Heaven only grant that I may soon get quit of the matter, and then I'll give such a taper for a thank-offering as has never been given before! I'll levy three *puds* of wax from every 45 merchant for it! Oh, my God! my God! Let's be going, Peter Ivánovich!

     (*Tries to put the hat-box on his head instead of his hat.*

Super. Antón Antónovich, that's the hat-box, not your hat!

Gov. (*throwing the box down*). Damn it! 50 so it is!... And if he asks why the hospital chapel has not been built, for which the money was voted five years ago, they must mind and say that it began to be built, but got burnt down. Why, I drew up a report about it. 55 But of course some idiot is sure to forget it, and let out that the building was never begun.... And tell Derzhimórda that he's not to give such free play to his fists; guilty or innocent, he makes them all see stars, in the cause of 60 public order.... Come on, come on, Dobchín-

ski. (*Goes out and returns.*) And the soldiers are not to be allowed in the streets with next to nothing on: that scoundrelly garrison only put their tunics on over their shirts, with 65 nothing at all below.   (*All go out.*

SCENE 6

ÁNNA ANDRÉYEVNA *and* MÁRYA ANTÓNOVNA *rush on the scene*

Ánna. Where are they, where are they? Oh, my God!... (*Opening the door*) Husband! Antósha! Antón! (*Hurriedly, to* MÁRYA) And it's all your fault! — dawdling, and saying, "I want a pin — I want a handkerchief." 5 (*Runs up to the window and shouts.*) Antón, where are you, where are you? Has he come — eh? the Inspector? Has he got a moustache? What's it like?

Voice of Gov. Wait a bit, my dear, wait a 10 little!

Ánna. Wait? What an idea! *Wait*, forsooth!... Not a bit of it! I only want one word — is he a colonel, or what is he, eh? (*With disgust*) There, he's gone! I won't 15 forgive him for that!... And *you* kept saying, "Mamma, dear, do stop a moment while I pin back my scarf; I'll come directly." *Directly*, indeed, drat you! It's all through *you* we've missed the news! It's all your abominable 20 vanity. You heard the Postmaster was here, and so you must needs mince before the looking-glass and strike all sorts of attitudes. You fancy he's smitten with you; but I can tell you, miss, he simply makes a face at you as soon 25 as your back is turned.

Márya. But what's to be done then, mamma? It's all right; we shall know all about him in an hour or two.

Ánna. An hour or two, forsooth! Much 30 obliged to you, I'm sure! A pretty answer to give me! Why didn't you say — we shall know more in a *month*!... (*She leans out of the window.*) Here, Avdótya! I say!... Have you heard whether anybody's come, Av- 35 dótya?... No? you booby — *no*? Well, you should have *asked*! Oh, *you* can't find out anything with your head full of lovers and flimflams!... Eh, what? They went off in a hurry?

Well, you should have run after the 40
droshky! Be off at once, d'you hear? Run
and ask everybody where they are — ask nicely,
and find out what he's like — do you hear me?
Peep through the keyhole and find out all about
it — what sort of eyes he's got — see if 45
they're black or not, and be back here at once
this minute, d'you understand? Quick, quick,
quick!

(*She keeps on shouting, and they both
stand at the window until the curtain
drops.*)

ACT II

A small room in the inn.
(*Bed, table, portmanteau, empty bottle,
books, clothesbrush, etc.*)

SCENE I

Osip (*lying on his master's bed*). Devil take
it! I'm so hungry; there's a noise in my inside
like a whole troop of trumpeters. We shall
never get home at this rate! What are we to do,
I'd like to know? There's two months gone 5
since we left "Peter"![1] He's chucked away
all his cash on the journey, the gay young dog,
so now he's got to stick here, with his tail between his legs! We should have had plenty to
pay for the fare, but no, he must needs cut 10
a dash in every town in *this* style! (*Imitates
him.*) "Heah, Osip, go and engage me the best
room they've got, and order the very best dinner they can cook; I can't stand anything cheap
and nasty; I must have the best!" Any- 15
thing reasonable wouldn't have mattered, but
for an ordinary copyin'-clerk to go on like that!
Then he goes and makes friends on the road;
plays cards, and gets rooked, of course! Oh,
I'm sick of this sort of life! Reelly, it's 20
better in our village; there's not so much going
on, but there's less to worrit you; you lie the
whole while over the stove and eat tartlets. . . .
Still, there's nothing like life in "Peter," that's
a fack, and there's no denyin' of it. All 25
you want is money, and then you live like a
lord — theayters, dancing dogs, everythink.
And everybody talks so perlite — it's reelly

[1] St. Petersburg.

almost like bein' at Court; if you go to the
Shchukin Bazaar,[1] the shopkeepers call 30
you "my lord"; you sit with the *chinóvniks* in
the ferryboat; if you want company, you can go
into a shop, a gent will tell you there what's
going on in the army, and all about the stars
in the sky, just as if you had 'em all in your 35
'and. Then an old officer's wife will try and
flirt with you, or a pretty chambermaid will
give you such a look. Aha, you dog! (*Smirks
and wags his head.*) What doosid fine manners
they have too; you never hear any disre- 40
speckful langwidge; they always say *you*[2] to
you! If you're tired of walking, why you take
a droshky, and sit there like a nob; and if you
don't want to pay, why, you needn't; every
house has got a door open, and you can pop 45
in, and the devil himself couldn't catch you.
There's one objection, though: sometimes you
get a fust-class feed, and sometimes you're
starved — as we are now. It's all *his* fault!
What's to be done with him? The old man 50
sends him money — enough to rub along with
— and what for? . . . Why, he goes on the bust
with it; hires droshkies, says every day, "Go
and get a theayter ticket"; and then look at
him in a week — he has to pop his new 55
tail-coat! Another time he parts with everything to his last shirt, except p'raps an old coat
or a worn-out cape; s'help me, it's the truth!
Selling such beautiful English cloth! Every
dress-suit costs him a hundred and fifty 60
roubles, and he lets his uncle have it for twenty.
I won't speak of his breeches; they can't get a
buyer. And what's it all for? Why, because
he's never at his business; instead of attending
to his dooties, he gallivants along the 65
Proshpect,[3] and goes off card playing. Ah, if
the old man only knew it! He wouldn't stop to
think you're a *chinóvnik*, but he'd lift up your
little shirt-tail, and whip you so that you would
feel sore for a week. If you have dooties, 70
you ought to attend to 'em. Here's the land-

[1] A bazaar in Great Garden Street, St. Petersburg.
[2] Instead of the more familiar "thou." The Russian,
like the French and German, has the double form for
the second person singular pronoun.
[3] The *Nevski Prospékt* (New Avenue), the finest
avenue and promenade in St. Petersburg when it was
the Russian capital under the Tsars.

lord now, says he won't let you have anything
to eat unless you pay beforehand, and if we
don't pay? (*Sighs.*) Oh, good Lord! for a little
shchi![1] I'll bet everyone else has had a   75
square meal. Hullo! there's a knock; he's
coming!   (*Gets off the bed hastily.*

SCENE 2
Enter KHLESTAKÓV

Khles. Here, take these. (*Hands him his
cap and walking-stick.*) What, you've been
rolling on the bed again?

Osip. Me rolling on the bed! I haven't seen
any bed!   5

Khles. *That's* a lie; you *have* been. Look
here, it's all tumbled about!

Osip. Why blame *me* for it? *I* don't know
what a bed feels like. I've got legs, and I
stand. What do I want with your bed?   10

Khles. (*walks about the room*). Just see if
there's any tobacco left in the pouch there.

Osip. Tobacco, indeed! Why, you smoked
the last of it four days ago.

Khles. (*paces up and down, biting his lips;
then, loudly and peremptorily*). Here, Osip,   15
d'you hear?

Osip. What do you want?

Khles. (*less firmly*). Go down there.

Osip. Where?

Khles. (*in an almost supplicating tone*).
Downstairs to the buffet... and tell 'em   20
there... to give me something to eat.

Osip. No, indeed, that I will not!

Khles. What, you dare to refuse, you blockhead!

Osip. Yes, it's all the same, if I *do* go   25
— you won't get anything from there. The
landlord said he'll let you have nothing more.

Khles. How does he dare to say so? Bosh,
I say!

Osip. He even says, though: "I'll go to   30
the Governor — it's the third week your master
has not paid his bill. You and your master,"
he says, "are a pair of sharpers, and your
master's a scoundrel as well. We've had to do
with rogues and hangers-on like you be-   35
fore," says he.

[1] Cabbage soup.

Khles. And you, you beast, repeat it all to
me, and enjoy it.

Osip. "Yes," says he; "all that sort come
from there, and make theirselves at home,   40
run up a bill, and then you can't get rid of
them. I'm not joking," he said; "I'll go
straight and make a complaint, and have him
taken to the police-office, and then clapped
into jail."   45

Khles. Now, now, stop it, you fool. Do go
and speak to him! The ill-mannered brute!

Osip. I'd better call the landlord here himself.

Khles. What do *I* want him for? You   50
go and talk to him yourself.

Osip. But reelly, sir ——

Khles. Well, go to the devil, and call the
landlord here.   (OSIP *goes out.*

SCENE 3

Khles. (*alone*). How infernally hungry I am!
I took a little walk, thinking my appetite would
go — damn it, not a bit of it! I'm as ravenous
as ever. Yes, if I hadn't had that spree in
Penza,[1] I'd have had enough money to get   5
home with. That infantry captain cheated me
finely — the way the villain cut the cards was
astounding. He wasn't at it more than a quarter of an hour, and he cleaned me out entirely.
But, all the same, I'd give anything to have   10
another turn with him, only I shan't have the
chance!...

What a beastly little town! They'll give you
nothing on credit at the grocers' shops. It's
simply disgusting! (*Whistles an air from*   15
"*Robert the Devil*";[2] *then the tune of* "*The Red
Gown*";[3] *then variations of his own.*)... H'm,
nobody seems likely to come.

SCENE 4
Enter OSIP *and the* WAITER

Wait. The landlord wants to know what you
want.

[1] A provincial capital southeast of Moscow on the
way to Sarátov.
[2] A recent opera (1831) by the German composer,
Jakob Meyerbeer (1791–1864).
[3] A once popular folk song in Russia.

Khles. Ah, good day, my friend! And how are you?

Wait. Pretty well, thank you.   5

Khles. And how are you getting on in the inn? Business going on nicely?

Wait. Yes — thank the Lord — very nicely.

Khles. Plenty of visitors?

Wait. Yes, we've got enough.   10

Khles. Look here, my friend, I haven't had any dinner brought up yet — just hurry up with it, please, as soon as possible.... You see, I've got something particular to do directly after dinner.   15

Wait. But the landlord said they're not to send anything more. He was all but going to the Governor today to complain of you.

Khles. Complain of me! Why, consider for yourself, my good fellow — I must eat. If   20 this goes on, I shall become a skeleton. I really am very hungry, joking apart.

Wait. Quite so, sir. He said, "I'll give him no dinner till he pays for what he's had already." That was his answer.   25

Khles. But you reason with him — talk him over!

Wait. Yes, but what am I to say?

Khles. You speak to him seriously, and say I *must have something* to eat. As for the   30 money ... why, he seems to think that, because a muzhik [1] such as *he* is can go the whole day without food, anyone else can also. What an idea!   (*Exeunt* OSIP *and* WAITER.

SCENE 5

Khles. (*alone*). It will be *too* disgusting, though, if he flatly refuses to let me have anything. I never felt so ravenous as I do now.... Shall I try to raise anything on my *clothes?* Shall I pop my *trousers?* ... No, better   5 starve than not go home in Petersburg dress!... What a shame that Yokhím [2] wouldn't let me have a carriage on hire; it would have been damned fine to go home in a proper turnout, and drive up in style under some squire or   10 other's porch, with carriage-lamps alight, and Osip behind in livery. How they'd all flutter with excitement, I guess! "Who's that? What's that?" Then my footman goes up in a gold livery (*draws himself up and imitates*   15 *him*), and announces "Iván Alexándrovich Khlestakóv, of Petersburg; are they receiving?" Those bumpkins, though, don't know what that phrase means. If any boor of a farmer pays them a visit, he waddles in like   20 a bear, straight into the drawing-room.... And then you walk up to a pretty girl, and say, "How charmed I am, *Sudárinya*.[1] ..." (*Rubs his hands and makes a bow.*) ... Tfu! (*Spits.*) I feel quite sick, I'm so hungry.   25

SCENE 6

Enter OSIP, *and afterwards the* WAITER

Khles. Well, what is it?

Osip. They're bringing dinner.

Khles. (*claps his hands, and jumps up in his chair*). Aha! Dinner! dinner! dinner!

Wait. (*with plates and a napkin*). This is the last time the landlord will send you dinner.   5

Khles. Well, the landlord ... the landlord is a ... I *spit* on your landlord! What have you got there?

Wait. Soup and roast beef.

Khles. What, only two dishes?   10

Wait. That's all, sir.

Khles. What nonsense! I won't have it! Ask him what he means by it!... That's too little!

Wait. No, the landlord says it's a *good*   15 deal too much!

Khles. But isn't there any *sauce?*

Wait. No, there isn't any.

Khles. Pray, why not? I saw 'em myself getting a lot ready, as I went past the   20 kitchen. And at the public-house this morning two undersized little men were eating salmon and all sorts of good things.

Wait. Well, if you please, sir, there *is* some, and there isn't.   25

Khles. How not?

Wait. There *isn't* any, then.

---

[1] A peasant.

[2] A once celebrated horse- and carriage-dealer in St. Petersburg.

[1] "Madam." The Russian term is applied to married and unmarried ladies alike.

Khles. What, no salmon — no fish — no cutlets?

Wait. Only for the gentlemen as *pays*, 30 sir!

Khles. What a *fool* you are!

Wait. Yessir.

Khles. You beastly pig!... Why are *they* eating, while *I* mayn't? Why mayn't I 35 too, confound it? Ain't I a *bona-fide* traveler too, as good as they?

Wait. No, sir, not exactly, that's certain.

Khles. How's that, pray?

Wait. Well, the difference is pretty plain: 40 they *settles up!*

Khles. Oh, I won't argue with you, you booby! (*Pours out the soup and tastes it.*) What! Do you call *that* soup? Why, you've simply poured hot water into a cup; it's got 45 no taste, it only stinks! None of that for *me*, thank you. Bring me some other soup!

Wait. Very well, sir, I'll take it away. The boss said if you didn't like it, you could leave it.

Khles. (*holding on to his plate*). Well, 50 well... leave it alone, I say, you fool! You may be familiar with *others*, but I'm not that sort, my man! I advise you not to try it on with *me*.... (*Tastes it again.*) My God! what soup! (*Goes on eating it.*) I should think 55 no one in the world ever ate such soup. Here's some feathers floating about instead of butter! (*Comes across a piece of chicken.*) Well, I declare! *Ai, ai!* what a fowl!... Give me the roast beef! There's a little soup left, Osip; 60 take it yourself. (*Cuts the meat.*) What, is *that* what you call roast meat? *That's* not roast beef!

Wait. What is it, then?

Khles. Devil knows *what* it is — only it's 65 not roast beef. It's more like roast iron than meat! (*Eats it.*) Rogues and scoundrels! The stuff they give one! Why, my jaws ache with eating a single mouthful! (*Picks his teeth with his finger.*) Villains! it's as tough as 70 the bark of a tree; I can't get it out, anyhow. Such messes are enough to ruin one's teeth, curse the blackguards! (*Wipes his mouth with a napkin.*) Is there nothing more?

Wait. No.   75

Khles. Scoundrels, blacklegs, that they are!

There might have been some pastry! Rascals! It's only travelers that they fleece!

(*WAITER removes and carries the dishes out, accompanied by* OSIP.

SCENE 7

Khles. (*alone*). I swear it's just as if I'd eaten nothing at all: it has only whetted my appetite. If I *only* had a trifle to send to the market and buy a bun with!

Osip (*re-entering*). The Town Governor 5 has come for some reason or other; he has announced himself, and is asking for you.

Khles. (*in great alarm*). What do you say?... There, that brute of an innkeeper has gone and reported me!... Suppose he really hauls 10 me off to jail! How would it be if I went in aristocratic style?... No, no, I won't! There are the officers and the people strolling about the town, and I have regularly set the fashion, and ogled a merchant's daughter.... No, I 15 *can't*... and pray, who is *he*, that he has the audacity? Treating me as if I was actually a shopkeeper or a day-laborer! (*Puts on a courageous air and draws himself up.*) I'll just say straight out to him: "How *dare* you 20 to ——"

(*The door-handle is turned;* KHLESTA-KÓV *turns pale and collapses.*

SCENE 8

Enter the GOVERNOR *and* DOBCHÍNSKI. *The former advances a few steps and halts. They stare at each other in great trepidation for some moments.*

Gov. (*plucking up courage a little, and saluting deferentially*). I hope you are well, sir!

Khles. (*bows*). My respects to you, sir!

Gov. Excuse my intruding...

Khles. Pray don't mention it...

Gov. It is my duty, as chief magistrate of 5 this town, to take all due measures to prevent travelers and persons of rank from suffering any inconvenience....

Khles. (*hesitates a little at first, but towards the end adopts a loud and confident tone*). We-ell, what was to be done? It's no-ot my fault... 10

I really am . . . going to pay . . . they'll send me money from home. (BOBCHÍNSKI *peeps in at the door.*) *He's* to blame most: he sends me up beef as hard as a board; and the soup! the devil only knows *what* he'd mixed up with it: 15 I was obliged to pitch it out of the window. He starves me the whole day . . . and the tea's so peculiar — it smells of fish and nothing else! Why then should I . . . A *fine* idea, indeed!

Gov. (*nervously*). I assure you, it's not 20 my fault, really. I always get good beef from the market. The Kholmogóri [1] drovers bring it, and they are sober and well-principled people. I'm sure I don't know where he gets it from. But if anything's wrong . . . allow 25 me to suggest that you come with me and get other quarters.

Khles. No, that I will *not!* *I* know what "other quarters" means; it's another word for *jail.* And pray, what right have you — 30 how dare you . . .? Why, I . . . I'm a government official at Petersburg . . . (*Defiantly*) Yes, I . . . I . . . I . . .

Gov. (*aside*). Oh, my God! how angry he is! He knows all! Those cursed merchants 35 have told him all!

Khles. (*aggressively*). *That* for you and your gang together! I'll *not* go with you! I'll go straight to the Minister. (*Bangs his fist on the table.*) What do you mean, pray, what do 40 you mean?

Gov. (*starting and shaking all over*). Have pity on me! don't ruin me! I have a wife and small children! Don't make me a miserable man! 45

Khles. No, I'll *not* go with you! What's that got to do with me? Why am *I* to go to jail because you've a wife and small children? I like that — that's beautiful! (BOBCHÍNSKI *looks in through the door and disappears in terror.*) No, much obliged to you, sir, but 50 I'll not leave here!

Gov. (*quaking*). It was only my inexperience, I swear, only my inexperience! and insufficient means! Judge for yourself — the salary I get is not enough for sugar and tea. And if 55

I *have* taken any bribes, they were *very* little ones — something for the table, or a coat or two. . . . As for the sergeant's widow, who took to shopkeeping — whom they say I flogged [1] — it's a slander, I swear, it's a slander. 60 My enemies invented it — they're the kind of people who are ready to murder me in cold blood!

Khles. Yes, yes, but I've nothing to do with *them.* . . . (*Reflects.*) I don't see, though, 65 why you should dilate about your enemies to me, or talk about sergeants' widows. . . . A sergeant's *wife* would have been quite a different matter. . . . Don't you try to flog *me*, though — your arm's not long enough for *that!* . . . 70 Enough! Look you here! . . . I'll pay, I'll pay the bill all right, but at present I'm out of cash. That's just why I stay here, because I haven't a kopék left.

Gov. (*aside, recovering*). Oh, the cunning 75 rascal! That's a *nice* yarn! a pretty piece of mystification! You may believe as much of *that* as you please! . . . One doesn't know how to begin with him. Still, I've got to try — come of it what will, I must have a try some- 80 how! (*Aloud*) H'm, if you really are in want of funds, or anything else, I am ready to oblige you at once. It is — ahem! — my duty to assist travelers.

Khles. Lend me, then — lend me a 85 trifle! and then I'll settle up immediately with the landlord. I only want two hundred roubles, or even less.

Gov. (*getting out his pocketbook*). There's exactly two hundred roubles — don't trou- 90 ble to count them!

Khles. I'm very much obliged to you! I'll return it you directly I get home . . . it was a sudden case of impecuniosity. . . . I see you are a *gentleman. Now* the state of things is al- 95 tered.

Gov. (*aside*). Well, thank the Lord! he's taken my money. *Now* I guess we shall hit it off. I shoved four hundred instead of two into his hand. 100

Khles. Hi, Osip! (OSIP *enters.*) Call the waiter here! (*To the* GOVERNOR *and* DOBCHÍN-SKI) But why are you standing all the while?

---

[1] A town on the Dwina River near the Arctic port of Archangel. It was renowned for its fine breed of beef cattle.

[1] For engaging in trade without a license.

Pray oblige me, take a seat! (*To* Dobchínski) Please take a seat, I beg of you!　105
Gov. Oh no! We can stand very well.
Khles. But, please, please, be seated! I see
now completely the generosity and sincerity of
your character: at first I confess I thought you
had come with the object of putting me　110
in —— (*To* Dobchínski) Do take a chair!
(*The* Governor *and* Dobchínski *at
last sit down.*
(Bobchínski *looks in at the door and
listens.*
Gov. (*aside*). Now I must be a little bolder.
He wants his *incognito* kept up. Good, *we'll*
talk a little nonsense too — we'll pretend we
don't know in the least what he really is.　115
(*Aloud*) I was going my rounds in the performance of my duty with Peter Ivánovich Dobchínski here — he's a landed proprietor of this
place — and we came into the inn to ascertain
whether travelers are being well enter-　120
tained — because I am not like other governors,
who never attend to their business; no, out of
pure Christian philanthropy, apart from my
duty, I wish every mortal to be treated well
— and lo! as a reward for my pains, the　125
occasion has presented itself of making so agreeable an acquaintance.
Khles. I too am delighted. Without your
kind assistance I confess I should have had to
stay here for a *pretty* long while—I　130
hadn't the least idea how to pay my bill.
Gov. (*aside*). Oh yes, fib away. *Didn't know*
how to pay his bill! (*Aloud*) May I venture to
inquire into what locality you are pleased to
be going?　135
Khles. I am going to my own estate in the
Sarátov Government.
Gov. (*aside, with an ironical expression on his
face*). To the Sarátov Government! Oh, indeed! And he doesn't even *blush!* One must
keep a sharp lookout with *this* gentleman!　140
(*Aloud*) You have deigned, indeed, to engage
on a pleasant enterprise! It is quite true that
journeys are disagreeable, as they say, on account of the delays in posting; but, on the
other hand, they furnish an agreeable　145
diversion for the mind. You are traveling for
your own amusement, I suppose?

Khles. No, my father wants me. The old
man's angry because up till now I've made
no advance in the service in Petersburg.　150
He thinks that the moment you get there they
stick the Vladímir [1] in your buttonhole. No,
indeed, and I'd like to send *him* to knock about
a chancellor's office for a while!
Gov. (*aside*). Just observe, I ask you,　155
how he romances! and drags in his old father
too! (*Aloud*) And, may I ask, are you going
there for a long time?
Khles. Really I don't know. You see, my
father is stupid and obstinate, like a block　160
of wood — the old duffer! I shall tell him
straight out: "Do as you please, but I can't live
away from Petersburg." Why should I be condemned to rot away among rustics? That's
not my ideal — my soul craves for civi-　165
lization!
Gov. (*aside*). Well, he *is* a fine hand at spinning yarns, and no mistake! He lies, and lies,
but doesn't trip anywhere! Why, the ugly, insignificant little whippersnapper, I could　170
crush him with my fingernail! But stop, he'll
soon betray himself under *my* management!
I'll let him fib a little longer! (*To* Khlestakóv)
You condescended to observe, quite rightly
— what *can* one do in a dead-alive place?　175
Why, see what it's like here: you lie awake at
night, and toil for your country's good, you
spare no effort of exertion — and I should
like to know how much reward you get for
the pains! . . . (*He looks round the room.*)　180
Rather damp, this room, isn't it?
Khles. Yes, it's a dirty hole, and the *insects*
— well, I've never seen the like of 'em; they
bite like dogs!
Gov. You don't say so! An illustrious　185
visitor like you to be incommoded with — with
disgusting insects, that have no business to
exist! And I daresay it's dark in this room?
Khles. Dark? I should think so! The landlord has started the custom of not allow-　190
ing me any candles. Now and then I want to
do something, to read a bit, or the fancy strikes
me to compose a little — not a bit of it, it's
as dark as pitch!

[1] The St. Vladimir of the Fourth Class, the sixth
order of merit in the former Russian imperial service.

Gov. May I venture to ask you ... but 195 no, I am unworthy!

Khles. What do you mean?

Gov. No, no; I am unworthy, unworthy of the honor!

Khles. But what *do* you mean?   200

Gov. If I might be so bold ... I have a charming little room at home, light and comfortable. ... But no! I feel it is too great an honor. ... Don't be offended; God knows, I only meant well by the offer!   205

Khles. On the contrary, I accept it with pleasure. I should be much more comfortable in a private residence than in this pothouse.

Gov. I am only too delighted! How 210 glad my wife will be! It's a little habit I have; I always *was* hospitable from childhood, especially when my guest is distinguished and enlightened. Don't think I say this by way of flattery; no, I have not *that* vice. I 215 only speak from the fullness of my heart.

Khles. I am greatly obliged to you. I myself hate two-faced people. I'm very much struck with your open-heartedness and generosity; and, I assure you, I expect nothing 220 more than that people should treat me with consideration and esteem, ahem! esteem and consideration!

SCENE 9

Enter the WAITER, *escorted by* OSIP. BOBCHÍNSKI *peeps in again*

Wait. You were pleased to require —?

Khles. Yes, bring me the bill.

Wait. I gave you the second account not long ago.

Khles. Oh, I can't remember your stupid 5 accounts! Tell me what it comes to!

Wait. You were pleased to order dinner the first day, and the second day you only took salmon, and after that everything was put down on credit ——   10

Khles. You fool! you've begun to add it all up again! How much is it altogether?

Gov. Please don't let it bother you; he can very well wait. (*To the* WAITER) Get out of this; the money will be sent you.   15

Khles. Yes, of course; that will be the best. (*Pockets the notes.* *The* WAITER *goes out.* BOBCHÍNSKI *looks in again through the doorway.*)

SCENE 10

The GOVERNOR, KHLESTAKÓV, *and* DOBCHÍNSKI

Gov. Wouldn't you like now to inspect a few of the institutions in our town — say, the hospital and so on?

Khles. But what is there to see?

Gov. Well, you will see how we manage 5 matters — what excellent order there is. ...

Khles. Oh, with the greatest pleasure; I am ready.

(BOBCHÍNSKI *puts his head in at the door.*)

Gov. And then, if you wish, we can go on from there and inspect the district high 10 school, and see the good discipline with which our instruction is administered.

Khles. Oh, by all means!

Gov. Afterwards, if you like to visit the prison and the town jail, you will be able 15 to notice how carefully our criminals are kept.

Khles. Yes, yes; but why go to the *jail?* We had *very* much better look at the hospital.

Gov. As you please. Do you propose to ride in your own carriage, or go with me in a 20 droshky?

Khles. Well, I prefer to go with you in a droshky.

Gov. (*to* DOBCHÍNSKI). Now, Dobchínski, there will be no room for *you.*   25

Dob. Oh, it doesn't matter, I'll manage!

Gov. (*aside to* DOBCHÍNSKI). Listen: will you run, as fast as you can, and take a couple of notes — one to Zemlyaníka at the hospital, the other to my wife. (*To* KHLESTAKÓV) 30 May I take the liberty of asking you to permit me to write a line to my wife in your presence, to tell her to get ready to receive her honored guest?

Khles. But why all this ...? However, 35 there's the ink ... I don't know about *paper,* though ... Would that *bill* do?

Gov. Oh, yes! I'll write on that! (*Writes,*

talking to himself at the same time.) We'll see how business goes after *lunch*, and a pot- 40 bellied bottle or two! We have some native wine, not much to look at, but it will roll an elephant under the table. If I only knew what he really is, and how far I've got to be on my guard. 45

(*Finishes writing, and gives the note to* Dobchínski, *who is just going out, when the door suddenly flies off its hinges, and* Bobchínski, *who was listening on the other side, tumbles forward with it on the floor. All utter exclamations of surprise.* Bob-chínski *gradually picks himself up.*

Khles. What, have you hurt yourself anywhere?

Bob. Oh, nothing, nothing, sir, nothing to bother about, sir, only a little knock on the nose! I'll run over to Doctor Hübner's 50 — he has some splendid plaster — it'll soon get right.

Gov. (*making an angry gesture at* Bobchín-ski, *to* Khlestakóv). Oh, *that* doesn't matter, sir! With your kind permission we will go; but I'll tell your servant to take your port- 55 manteau across. (*Calls* Osip.) Here, my good fellow, take everything over to my house, the Governor's — anyone will show it you.... By your leave, sir! (*Makes way for* Khles-takóv, *and follows him; then turns, and severely addresses* Bobchínski.) *You* again! 60 Couldn't you find some *other* place to tumble in! and sprawling there, like the devil knows what! (*Goes out; after him,* Bobchínski.

Curtain falls.

ACT III

A room in the Governor's *house.*

Scene 1

Ánna Andréyevna *and* Márya Antónovna *standing at the window, in the same positions as at the end of Act I*

Ánna. There now, we've been waiting a whole hour, and it's all through your stupid vanity; you were quite ready dressed, but no!

you must still be dawdling!... Oh, dear! not a sound to be heard of her.... How vex- 5 atious it is!... There's not a soul to be seen, of course; it's just as if the whole place were dead.

Márya. There, mamma, *really* we shall know *all* about it in a minute or two. 10 Avdótya *must* come back soon. (*Looks out of the window and screams.*) Oh, *mámenka,*[1] mamma dear! someone *is* coming — away there at the end of the street!

Ánna. Who's coming? *Where?* You've 15 always got some fancy or other!... Ah, so there *is!* Who is it, now? He's short — in a dress-coat! Who can it be? Eh? How tiresome not to know! Who*ever* can it be?

Márya. It's Dobchínski, mamma. 20

Ánna. Dobchínski, indeed. One of your random guesses, miss! It's certainly *not* Dob-chínski. (*Waves her handkerchief.*) Hi! you come here! quick!

Márya. It's *really* Dobchínski, má- 25 menka!

Ánna. There now, you only want to contradict, of course. You're *told* it's *not* Dobchín-ski.

Márya. But look, mamma, look! You 30 see it *is* Dobchínski.

Ánna. Well, so it is.... I see now. Why do you want to *argue* about it? (*Shouts at the window.*) Hurry up, quick! How *slow* you walk!... Well, *where* are they — eh? 35 Tell me from where you are; it'll do just as well What, is he very severe? Eh? How about my husband — my *husband?* (*Moves away from the window a little, disgusted.*) How *stupid* he is! Not a single word will he utter till he's 40 got into the room!

Scene 2

Enter Dobchínski

Ánna. Now, if you please, tell me — aren't you *ashamed* of yourself? I used to think you were the only one of them who was a *gentleman* They all bolted off, and *you* after them! and here have *I* been all this while without a

[1] "Little mamma."

soul to tell me about it. Isn't it *disgraceful* of you? I stood godmother to your little Iván and Liza, and this is the way you treat me!

Dob. I vow, my dear lady, I ran so fast 10 to pay my respects to you, that I'm quite out of breath.... I have the honor to salute you, Márya Antónovna!

Márya. Good afternoon, Peter Ivánovich!

Ánna. Well, tell us now, what's going 15 on there?

Dob. Antón Antónovich has sent you this note.

Ánna. Yes, but what is he — a general?

Dob. No, not a general, but he's quite as 20 big a swell. Such manners — such dignified ways!

Ánna. Ah, it's the very same that was mentioned in the letter to my husband!

Dob. Precisely. Bobchínski and I were 25 the first to discover him.

Ánna. Good! Now tell me all about it!

Dob. I will. Thank the Lord, everything's all right now. At first he received Antón Antónovich rather roughly; I assure you, 30 ma'am, he got angry, and said that the inn was *most* uncomfortable, that he wouldn't come to the Governor's house, nor go to jail for him; but afterwards, when he found out Antón Antónovich's innocence, and had had a 35 short conversation with him, he changed his opinion directly, and then, thank heaven, all went well. They have now gone to inspect the hospital.... I confess, though, that Antón Antónovich quite thought that a secret 40 information would be lodged against him. I myself also was a little alarmed.

Ánna. Why should *you* be afraid? You're not an official, you know.

Dob. Yes, but you see, when a bigwig 45 speaks you can't help feeling a bit frightened.

Ánna. Well, well... all this is trifling, though; describe what he's like personally — is he young or old?

Dob. Young, quite young — about 50 twenty-three years old; but he talks quite like an old man. "Permit me," he says, "I will go *here*, and *there*" (*gesticulates*) — all in very distinguished style. "I am fond," says he, "of

writing and reading; it's a bore, though," 55 he says, "that it's rather dark in my room."

Ánna. But what's he like *to look at*, dark or fair?

Dob. No, auburn, rather, and his eyes flash like a wild beast's — they quite unnerve 60 you.

Ánna. H'm — let's see what's written in this note. (*Reads.*) "I hasten to let you know, my dear, that I was in a very critical predicament; but, relying on the mercy of 65 God, two pickled gherkins *à part* and a half portion of caviar — 1 rouble 25 kopeks..." (*Stops.*) What *ever* does he mean by pickled gherkins and caviar, there?

Dob. Oh, Antón Antónovich wrote on 70 a piece of paper that had been used before, to save time; there's some bill or other made out on it.

Ánna. Oh, I see exactly. (*Goes on reading.*) "But, relying on the mercy of God, I think 75 this all will come to a happy conclusion. Get a room ready quickly — the one with the gold wallpaper — for our distinguished guest; don't have anything extra for dinner, because we shall lunch at the hospital with 80 Artémi Philíppovich, but order in some more wine; tell Abdúlin to send some of his very best — otherwise I will wreck his whole cellar. I kiss your hand, my dear, and remain, thine, Antón Skvazník-Dmukhanóvski...." Oh, 85 my God! There's not a moment to lose! Hi, who's there? Míshka!

Dob. (*runs to the door and shouts*). Míshka! Míshka! Míshka!

Míshka *enters*

Ánna. Attend: run over to Abdúlin 90 the merchant.... Stop, I will give you a note. (*Sits at the table and writes, talking at the same time.*) Give that note to the coachman Sídor; he's to run to Abdúlin's with it, and bring back the wine. Then return here 95 directly, and get a room ready for the visitor. Put a bed, washstand, etcetera, there.

Dob. Well, I'll hurry off now, Ánna Andréyevna, and see how he does the inspecting!

Ánna. Go, then, go; I'll not detain you. 100

SCENE 3

Ánna. Now, Mashenka,[1] we must think about our toilet. He's a young dandy from town — the Lord forbid that he should laugh at us! You had better put on your blue dress with the little flounces.   5

Márya. Lor', mamma, the *blue* dress! I don't like it at all! The Lyápkin-Tyápkin goes about in blue, and Zemlyaníka's daughter in blue too. No, I'd much better put on my light pink gown.   10

Ánna. Your light pink gown!.... really, you only say that for the sake of contradiction! You will look much better in blue, because I wish to wear my favorite shade — straw color.

Márya. Oh, mamma, that doesn't suit   15 you at all!

Ánna. What! straw color doesn't suit me?

Márya. No. I'll bet anything you won't look well: your eyes ought to be quite dark to go with pale yellow.   20

Ánna. Oh, I *like* that! As if my eyes weren't dark! They're as dark as they can be! What rubbish you talk! How can they *help* being dark when I always draw the queen of *clubs*, if I tell my fortune by the cards?   25

Márya. Oh, *mámenka*, the queen of *hearts* is much more your style!

Ánna. Fiddlesticks! Nonsense! I never was a queen of hearts! (*Exit hastily with*   29 MÁRYA, *and speaks behind the scenes.*) *What* an idea—queen of hearts! Goodness gracious!

(*On their departure a door is opened, and* MÍSHKA *sweeps dust out.*

SCENE 4

OSIP *enters from another door, with a portmanteau on his head*

Osip. Where's this to go?

Mísh. Here, uncle, this way!

Osip. Stop! I must take breath first. Oh, what a miserable time I'm having! On an empty stomach any load seems heavy.   5

Mísh. Eh, uncle, will the general be here soon?

Osip. The general? — who?

[1] "Little Mary."

Mísh. Why, your noble master!

Osip. My "noble master"? *Him* a   10 general?

Mísh. Ain't he then a general?

Osip. Oh, yes, but in a different kind o' way.

Mísh. What is he, then? — higher or lower than a real general in rank?   15

Osip. Oh, *higher!*

Mísh. There, now! that's why there's all this to-do here.

Osip. Look here, young 'un! I see you're a smart chap — just get us something to eat!   20

Mísh. But for the likes of you, uncle, there's nothing good enough ready. You won't eat plain stuff — but they'll send you something, when your master sits down to table.

Osip. Well, but what "plain stuff" have   25 you got?

Mísh. Cabbage soup, and porridge, and pastry.

Osip. Let's have the cabbage soup, porridge, and pastry — it doesn't matter — I'll eat   30 it all. Now let's take the portmanteau! What, is there another door?

Mísh. Yes.

(*They both carry the portmanteau into the side chamber.*

SCENE 5

The POLICE-OFFICERS *throw both folding-doors open.* KHLESTAKÓV *enters; after him the* GOVERNOR, *then the* CHARITY COMMISSIONER, *the* DIRECTOR OF SCHOOLS, *and* BOBCHÍNSKI *with plaster on his nose. The* GOVERNOR *points out a piece of paper lying on the floor, to the* POLICE OFFICERS, *who rush breathlessly to pick it up, and butt against each other.*

Khles. Splendid institutions! I'm charmed with the way you have of showing strangers all that's to be seen in your town! In other places they showed me nothing.

Gov. In *other* towns, I venture to suggest,   5 the authorities and officials care most for their own advancement; but *here*, one may say, there is no other thought than how to win the recognition of the Government by good order and vigilance.   10

Khles. That lunch was excellent; I've quite overeaten myself. D'you then have a spread like that every day?

Gov. No; it was in honor of such an acceptable guest! 15

Khles. I'm fond of my dinner! What does one live for but to pluck the flowers of pleasure? What was that fish called?

Char. Comm. (*stepping forward*). Labardán,[1] sir! 20

Khles. It was exquisite! Where was it we lunched? In the infirmary, wasn't it?

Char. Comm. Precisely so, sir; in the hospital.

Khles. I remember, I remember — there 25 were beds there. But have the sick got well? There were not many of them, it seemed.

Char. Comm. Ten or so remain, not more; the rest have all recovered. The place is so well organized — there's such good dis- 30 cipline. It may seem incredible to you, perhaps, but ever since I've undertaken the management they all get well like flies.[2] The patient no sooner gets into the sick-ward than he's well again. It's not so much done by 35 the doctoring as by honesty and regularity.

Gov. And I venture to point out what a head-splitting business is the office of a town governor! How many multifarious matters are referred to him, concerning the clean- 40 ness of the town and repairs and alterations alone! ... In a word, the most competent of men might get into hopeless difficulties. God be thanked, though, everything progresses favorably here! Any *other* governor, to be 45 sure, would look after his own profit; but, believe me, that when I lie down to rest, my sole prayer is: "O Lord my God, grant that Government may see my zeal and be satisfied!" ... They may, or may not, reward me — that 50 is as they please, of course — but, at any rate, my conscience is clear. When there is order throughout the town, when the streets are swept clean, and the prisoners are well kept and locked up, when the number of drunk- 55 ards is small — what more do I want? Ah, I

[1] Salted or dried codfish.
[2] In allusion to the Russian saying, "The peasants *die* like flies."

long for no honors! They are, without doubt, alluring, but to the upright all dust and vanity!

Char. Comm. (*aside*). Ah, the villain, how he can spout! It's a gift of Heaven! 60

Khles. Quite true. I don't mind saying I also like to declaim now and then; sometimes it's in prose, and sometimes I throw off verses.

Bob. (*to* DOBCHÍNSKI). How well, how very well that was put, Pyótr Ivánovich! Such 65 an observation ... shows he's studied the liberal arts!

Khles. By the way, could you tell me if you have any amusements here, any places where you could get a game of *cards*, for instance? 70

Gov. (*aside*). Oho, my young friend, *I* know who you mean *that* for! (*Aloud*) God forbid! We've never even heard of such a thing as a card club here! I've not dealt a card in my life; I don't even know how cards are 75 played. I can't bear to *look* at 'em — if ever I happen to see a king of diamonds or such like, I'm so overcome with disgust that I just have to spit to relieve myself. It *did* once happen that, to please the children, I built a house 80 of cards, but I had a nightmare of the cursed things the night after! Lord forgive 'em — how *can* people waste precious time over card-playing? ...

Luká (*aside*). But, the rascal, he 85 rooked me to the tune of a hundred roubles at faro yesterday!

Gov. ... No, I think it better to employ my time for the Empire's benefit!

Khles. Well, I don't quite agree with 90 you, though. ... It all depends how you look at it. As long as you stop, say, after losing three-quarters of your cash, it's all right. ... No, don't say that cards are not good fun, now and then! 95

SCENE 6

Enter ÁNNA ANDRÉYEVNA *and* MÁRYA ANTÓNOVNA

Gov. May I take the liberty of introducing my family: my wife and my daughter!

Khles. (*bowing to each*). How fortunate I am, madam, in being permitted the pleasure of meeting you! 5

Ánna. It is far more agreeable to *us* to make the acquaintance of so distinguished a personage!

Khles. (*with an air of gallantry*). Pardon me, *Sudárinya*, it is quite the contrary; the 10 pleasure is on *my* side!

Ánna. Impossible, sir — you allow yourself to say that by way of compliment! I beg of you to take a seat.

Khles. To *stand* near you is happiness 15 enough; still, if you insist on it, I will sit. How favored I am, to sit at length by your side!

Ánna. Pardon me, but I cannot dare to take that as meant sincerely.... You have found the journey very disagreeable, I 20 should think, after life in the capital?

Khles. Excessively so! After being used, *comprenez-vous*,[1] to living in society — to find myself all at once on my travels — with dirty inns, in the depths of uncivilization!... 25 If it were not, I must say, for circumstances which ... (*looks meaningly at* ÁNNA, *showing off*) which recompense me for all the —

Ánna. Really, how unpleasant it must have been for you! 30

Khles. I find it quite the reverse, though, madam, at the present moment!

Ánna. Oh, how can you say so, sir! You do me too much honor. I do not deserve it.

Khles. Why *not*, indeed? *Sudárinya*, 35 you *do* deserve it!

Ánna. Oh, I live only in the country ...

Khles. Ah, but the country, all the same, has its charming hills and rivulets.... To be sure, who could compare it to St. Peters- 40 burg — what a life it is, indeed! I dare say you think I am only a copying-clerk; on the contrary, I'm on most friendly terms with the chief of our department. He slaps me on the back and says, "Come and dine, my boy!" 45 I only look in at my office for a couple of minutes or so, just to say, "This is to be done *so*, and that *so*." There's a rat of a clerk there, who scribbles away — tr-tr ... for dear life. They wanted even to make me a "College 50 Assessor."[2] I can guess pretty well why.

---

[1] "Do you understand?" He uses French, the courtly language, to show off.

[2] The eighth grade in the Russian civil service.

And the porter flies after me on the stairs with the blacking-brush: "Allow me, Iván Alexándrovich," says he, "to clean your boots for you!" (*To the* GOVERNOR) But why do 55 you *stand*, gentlemen? Pray be seated!

All Together {
Gov. Our rank is not high enough; we must stand!
Char. Comm. Oh, we had rather remain standing! 60
Luká. Don't allow yourself to bother about *us*!
}

Khles. No ceremony! I entreat you to take seats! (*The* GOVERNOR *and the rest sit down.*) I do not care to stand on my dignity; on 65 the contrary, I always try to slip away unobserved! But it's impossible to hide one's self. Quite impossible! No matter where I go, they cry at once: "There goes Iván Alexándrovich!" Once they even took me for the Com- 70 mander-in-Chief; the soldiers rushed out of the guardhouse and saluted. An officer, whom I knew very well, said to me afterwards, "Hullo, my boy, we completely mistook you for the Commander-in-Chief!" 75

Ánna. You don't say so!

Khles. I know nearly all the pretty actresses, and compose all sorts of vaudevilles. I frequently see literary men; I'm on a very friendly footing with Pushkin[1] — often 80 say to him: "Well, how-de-do, Pushkin, my boy!" "So-so, old man," he'd reply. "Things might be better...." A regular original, is Pushkin!

Ánna. So you *write* too? How delightful 85 it must be to be an author! And do you really write for the papers?

Khles. Yes, I write for the papers too. Besides that, there are a good many of my productions, such as "Figaro's Wedding," 90 "Robert the Devil," "Norma"[2] — I really forget some of their names. It all happened by chance. I didn't intend to write, but a theater-manager said, "*Do* turn me off something, old

---

[1] Alexándr Pushkin (1799–1837), the leading writer in Russia at the period of the play.

[2] Well-known operas by the Austrian, Wolfgang Mozart (1756–91); the German, Jakob Meyerbeer (1791–1864); and the Sicilian, Vincenzo Bellini (1802–35) respectively.

man." I consider a bit: "You may as 95
well, brother!" And so I knocked it off in one
evening, I daresay. I have a marvelous flow of
ideas, you know. All that came out under the
name of "Baron Brambeus,"[1] and "The
Frigate of Hope,"[2] and the *Moscow Tel-* 100
egraph[3] — all that was *my* composition!

Ánna. Is it possible; and so you were really
"Brambeus"?

Khles. Of course, and I correct all their
verses. Smirdin[4] gives me forty thou- 105
sand for that.

Ánna. And I daresay "Yúri Miloslávski"[5]
was composed by you.

Khles. Yes, that's by me.

Ánna. I thought so at once.   110

Márya. But, Mamma, dear, it says on the
title-page that Zagóskin was the author.

Ánna. There! of course: I *knew* you would
want to argue!

Khles. Ah, so it was; that's true, that 115
particular work *was* by Zagóskin; but there's
another "Yúri Miloslávski," and that was
written by *me*.

Ánna. Ah, to be sure! I read yours. How
beautifully it is written!   120

Khles. I must admit, I live by my pen. My
house is the first in Petersburg; it's well known
there as "Iván Alexándrovich's." (*Addresses
the company generally.*) Do me the favor, if
any of you are ever in Petersburg, to pay 125
me a visit — I beg, I beg of you! I give balls
too, you know.

Ánna. I can fancy with what good taste and
magnificence the balls are given!

Khles. It's a simple affair, not worth 130
talking about! On the table, for instance, is
a watermelon that costs seven hundred roubles.
The soup in the tureen comes straight from
Paris in a steamer: there's nothing in the
world to be compared with its flavor! I go 135

---

[1] The pen name of Josef Sienkowski, a popular journalist and critic of the time.
[2] A popular novel by A. Bestúzhev (1797–1837).
[3] A newspaper of the day, edited by N. Polevoí.
[4] A celebrated publisher in St. Petersburg of that
period.
[5] A well-known story laid in the "Time of Troubles,"
the Russian era just before the accession (1613) of
Michael, the first of the Romanoff Tsars.

to a ball every day. We have our whist-club
there too: the Foreign Minister, the French
Ambassador, the German Ambassador, and
myself. We regularly kill ourselves over
cards; there's nothing to be seen like it! 140
How I rush home, and clamber up four flights
of stairs, and just have strength to say to the
cook, "Here, Mavrúsha, take my greatcoat!"
... What do I say? I was forgetting that I
live on the first floor — Why, the staircase 145
alone cost me I don't know how much....
And it's a curious sight to see my antechamber:
counts and princes jostling and humming there
like bees; all you can hear is *buzz, buzz, buzz!*
Once there was a minister.... (*The* Gov- 150
ERNOR *and the rest start from their chairs in
alarm.*) They even write "Your Excellency"
in their letters to me.... On one occasion I
took charge of a Department. It was a funny
story: the Director went off somewhere — nobody knew where. So, naturally, people 155
began now to ask how his place was to be
taken. Who was to fill it? Any number of
generals coveted the post and tried it, but they
soon gave the thing up — too difficult for 'em!
It looked easy enough, but, on closer 160
inspection, it proved a devil of a business!
There was nothing to be done but come to *me*.
In a twinkling the streets were choke-full of
couriers, couriers after couriers. Just picture to yourselves thirty-five thousand 165
couriers! How's that for a situation, I ask
you? "Iván Alexándrovich, come and direct
the Department!" I own I was a little taken
aback. I went out in my dressing-gown and
wanted to refuse, but, thinks I, it'll get 170
to the Emperor's ears, and it wouldn't look
well on my record of service either ... so, "All
right," I say, "I'll undertake the job, I'll
undertake it! So be it!" I say, "I'll take
it; only remember, sharp's the word with 175
me — *sharp's the word*, mind!" And so it *was*;
I go through the Department like an earthquake; they all shake and tremble like an
aspen leaf. (*The* GOVERNOR *and others quake
with terror;* KHLESTAKÓV *proceeds with redoubled vehemence.*) Oh, it's no joke, I can 180
tell you. I gave them all a jobation! Even
the Council of the Empire is in awe of me.

And why not, indeed? I'm such a ... I don't spot anyone in particular. I address them all generally, and say, "*I* know my power; *I* know my business!" I'm every-where — everywhere! I go to Court every day. Why, tomorrow they're going to make me a field-marsh ——

(*Slips off his chair, and sprawls on the floor, but is respectfully helped up by the chinóvniks.*

Gov. (*approaches, trembling all over, and struggles to speak*). But, your E—e—ex ... 190

(*Gasps.*

Khles. (*sharply*). What's the matter?

Gov. Your E—e—ex ...

Khles. (*as before*). I can't make out a word you say; it's all nonsense.

Gov. Yo—ur E—e—xlncy, Excellency, 195 won't you be pleased to rest a little? ... Here is a room, and all you require.

Khles. Bosh! Rest a little?! ... Stay, I think I will! ... Your lunch, gentlemen, was excellent. ... I'm delighted, delighted! 200 (*Theatrically*) Labardán! Labardán!!

(*Exit into the side room, followed by the* GOVERNOR.

SCENE 7

The same, without KHLESTAKÓV *and the* GOVERNOR

Bob. There, Pyótr Ivánovich, there's a man for you! That's what I call a man! Never have I been before in the presence of such a swell — I nearly died of fright! What's his rank, do you think, Dobchínski? 5

Dob. I should think he's almost a general.

Bob. Well, *I* think that a general wouldn't do for the sole of his boots! Or if he is a general, then he must be the very Generalissimo himself! Did you hear how he bullies the 10 Council of State? Let's go quick, and tell Ámmos Fyódorovich and Karóbkin. Good afternoon, Ánna Andréyevna!

Dob. Good afternoon, *Kúmushka!*

(*Exit with* BOBCHÍNSKI.

Char. Comm. (*to* LUKÁ). It's a terrible 15 anxiety, and one doesn't know who's the culprit. We're not in uniform either! As soon

as he wakes he'll send a report about us to Petersburg!

(*Exit dejectedly with the* SCHOOL DIRECTOR, *both saying to* ÁNNA, *"Goodbye, Sudárinya!"*

SCENE 8

ÁNNA *and* MÁRYA

Ánna. Oh, what a charming young man!

Márya. *Akh,* how delightful he is!

Ánna. But what refinement of manners! You can see at once he's in society. His deportment and all ... *akh,* how fine! I'm 5 passionately fond of young men like that — I'm sure I charmed him exceedingly: I noticed — he kept looking at me all the time.

Márya. Oh, mamma, dear, he looked at *me!*

Ánna. Get along with your rubbish; 10 your remarks are quite out of place!

Márya. But, mamma, he *did*, really!

Ánna. There you are, *arguing* again! You're *not* to; that's flat! When did he look at you, pray? and why should he look at *you?* 15

Márya. Really, mamma dear, he *gazed* at me the whole time. When he began to talk about literature he looked at me, and when he described how he played whist with the ambassadors he kept his eyes on me. 20

Ánna. Well, perhaps he did once or twice, and that was only for the sake of appearances. He thought, "Oh, I suppose I had better give her a glance or two!"

SCENE 9

Gov. (*entering on tiptoe*). Sh — sh ——

Ánna. What?

Gov. I'm vexed that he has drunk so much. ... Now, supposing *half* of what he said was true! (*Reflects.*) And why shouldn't it be 5 so? When a man's tipsy he lets everything out: what's in his heart flies to his tongue. Of course he invented a little; but then no story is ever told without a little ornamentation. ... So he plays whist with Ministers, and goes 10 to Court. ... Upon my word, the more one thinks about it — the devil knows what to make of it — I feel as giddy as if I stood on the

top of a steeple, or they were going to hang
me.   15

Ánna. I don't feel the slightest nervousness;
I merely saw in him an educated, polished,
well-bred young man; but I don't bother myself about his rank.

Gov. Oh, that's just like you *women!*   20
That one word *woman* explains everything!
You women only care about fiddle-faddle, and
fire off remarks without rhyme or reason. *You*
may be let off with a flogging, but *your husband*
will never more be heard of. You treat   25
this gentleman, my dear, as familiarly as if he
was another Dobchínski.

Ánna. I recommend you not to trouble
about *that.* We shall see what we shall see....
          (*Glances significantly at her daughter.*

Gov. (*soliloquizing*). Oh, it's no good   30
talking to you! *What* a state of things this is!
I haven't yet been able to recover from my
fright. (*Opens the door, and calls off.*) Míshka,
call the police-officers Svistunóv and Derzhimórda; they are somewhere about near   35
the gate. (*After a short silence*) It's a very
queer world now. One *ought* to be able to
recognize such people by their distinguished
appearance; but *this* miserable stripling — how
is one to know *who* he is? A military   40
man reveals himself at once. When he puts on
civilian dress he looks like a fly with its wings
clipped.... But then he obstinately remained
at the inn, and just now gave vent to such
allegories and ambiguities that it would   45
take you an age to make head or tail of 'em.
However, he has surrendered at last. Yes, and
said a good deal more than he'd need to. It's
pretty plain he's *quite* young!

SCENE 10

Enter OSIP. *All rush to him, beckoning*

Ánna. Come here, my friend!
Gov. Hush!... Is he — is he asleep?
Osip. No, he's still stretching himself.
Ánna. Tell me — what's your name?
Osip. Osip, ma'am.   5
Gov. (*to his wife and daughter*). There, that's
enough, that'll do for *you.* (*To* OSIP) Well,
my friend, have you been well looked after?

Osip. Fustrate, sir, fustrate; and thank you
kindly.   10
Ánna. Tell me, now — a good many counts
and princes visit your master, don't they?
Osip (*aside*). What shall I say now? I
dessay, if I tell 'em *yes,* they'll feed me even
better still. (*Aloud*) Oh, yes, a lot of   15
counts come and see him.
Márya. Ah, my dear Osip, how handsome
your noble master is!
Ánna. But tell me, please, Osip, how does
he —?   20
Gov. Now, stop it, please! You only hinder
me with such foolish remarks. Well, now, my
friend ——
Ánna. But what is your master's rank?
Osip. Oh — the *usual* rank!   25
Gov. (*to* ÁNNA). Oh, my God! How you
keep on with your senseless questions! You
don't say a single word to the point! Now, my
man, what is your master *like* — eh? Strict?
Is he given to scolding you or not?   30
Osip. Yes, he likes orderliness. He must
have everything exact.
Gov. Well, I like your face, my friend. I'm
sure you're one of the right sort. Now
what ——   35
Ánna. Listen, Osip, what does your master
wear in town? Does he go about in uniform
or ——
Gov. Now, that'll do; really, what a magpie
you are! This is a serious business — a   40
matter of life and death.... (*To* OSIP) Yes,
I'm very pleased with you, my man; an extra
cup of tea on a journey is always acceptable;
it's a trifle cold now, so there's a couple of
silver roubles for tea.   45
Osip (*takes the money*). Oh, thank you
kindly, sir! The Lord give you very good
health! It's a great help to a poor man.
Gov. Certainly, certainly; and I'm very glad
to help you. Now, my friend, what ——   50
Ánna. Listen to me, Osip. What colored
eyes does your master like best —?
Márya. Osip, my life! what a charming little
nose your master has!
Gov. Have done! Let me speak. (*To*   55
OSIP) Just tell me, please, my good fellow,
what does your noble master pay most atten-

tion to — I mean, what pleases him most on his journeys?

Osip. Oh, he's fond of finding out all 60 about everything. Most of all, he likes being well received, being well entertained.

Gov. Well entertained?

Osip. Yes. As for me, I'm only a serf; but he sees that I'm well treated too. Lor' 65 bless us! One day we set off somewhere. He says, "Well, Osip, have they treated you well?" "Shabbily, your nobility," says I. "Oho," says he, "then he's no good as a host, Osip. You remind me of him when I come 70 along again!" "Ah!" thinks I to myself (*gesticulates*), "God help him! — and I'm a nobody."

Gov. Very good; you speak to the point. What I gave you was for tea — here's some- 75 thing extra for biscuits!

Osip. Oh, you're too liberal, your high nobility! (*Pockets the money.*) I'll make sure to spend it all in drinking your Honor's health!

Anna. Come to me, Osip, and you'll 80 get something more.

Márya. Osip, my life, kiss your master for me!

(KHLESTAKÓV *is heard to cough slightly in the next room.*

Gov. Sh! (*Walks on tiptoe; the rest of the scene is conducted in an undertone.*) Good 85 God! don't make a noise! Get out of the room! (*To* ÁNNA) We've had quite enough of you!

Ánna. Let us go, Mashenka; I'll tell you something I noticed about our guest that can only be said in *private*. 90

Gov. Oh, they're at it again! Just go and listen to them — you'll have to stop up your ears pretty quick! (*Turns to* OSIP.) Now, my friend ——

SCENE II

Enter SVISTUNÓV *and* DERZHIMÓRDA

Gov. Sh! Those bandy-legged bears — how they stump with their boots! They blunder about as if someone's throwing forty *puds* [1] out of a wagon. Where's the devil taking you to? 5

[1] A *pud* is 36 pounds.

Derz. (*loudly*). My orders were ——

Gov. Sh! (*Stops his mouth.*) You bark like a raven! (*Shakes him.*) *Your orders were* — were they indeed! Bellowing like a bull in a barrel! (*To* OSIP) Now, my man, you go 10 and get ready there — order anything that there is in the house! (OSIP *goes out.*) But *you* . . . stand on the landing, and don't stir from the spot! And let no stranger into the house, and above all, no merchants! And 15 just mind, if you let *one* even slip past you, then I'll . . . ! And just mind, if anyone comes with a petition, or even *without* one, if he looks like a person who would present a petition against me — then you kick him out head-foremost 20 — straight! So! (*Business.*) Do you understand? Sh! now, sh!

(*Exit on tiptoe with the* POLICE OFFICERS.

ACT IV

The same room in the GOVERNOR'S *house.*

SCENE I

Enter cautiously, almost on tiptoe, the JUDGE, *the* CHARITY COMMISSIONER, *the* POSTMASTER, *the* SCHOOL DIRECTOR, DOBCHÍNSKI, *and* BOBCHÍNSKI, *all in full gala uniform. The whole scene is played in an undertone*

Judge (*arranging them all in a semicircle*). For God's sake, gentlemen, form your circle quicker; let's have better order! Good heavens — he goes to Court, you know, and bullies the Council of State! Draw up in military order, absolutely in military order! Peter 5 Ivánovich, you must stand *there!*

(*Both* BOBCHÍNSKI *and* DOBCHÍNSKI *run on tiptoe to the place assigned.*

Char. Comm. It's as you please, Ámmos Fyódorovich; but we certainly *ought* to make the attempt.

Judge. What attempt? 10

Char. Comm. You know what I mean.

Judge. Palm-oil?

Char. Comm. Yes, try a little palm-oil.

Judge. It's risky — he'll storm at us; he's a State functionary, you know. Perhaps it 15 had better take the form of a *testimonial* from the nobility and gentry — some sort of souvenir.

Post. Or perhaps, say — there's some money being sent by post, and we don't know who 20 it's for.

Char. Comm. Mind he doesn't send *you* by post somewhere further than you care for. I tell you, these little matters are *not* so managed in a well-ordered State. Why is there a 25 whole squadron of us here? We ought to approach him one by one, and do ... what is needful in a private interview, so that nobody knows anything about it. *That's* how things are done in a well-managed community. So, Ámmos 30 Fyódorovich, you ought to begin first.

Judge. Much better *you;* the illustrious visitor broke bread in *your* hospital.

Char. Comm. No, no! Then Luká Lukích had better, as the enlightener of youth. 35

Luká. I can't, I can't, really, gentlemen! I confess I've been so brought up that, if any one a single degree above me in rank addresses me, I just lose my head, and my tongue's as if stuck in the mud. No, sirs, excuse me; really I 40 *must* beg to be let off!

Char. Comm. Then there's no one but you, Ámmos Fyódorovich. Why, every word you utter sounds like another Cicero talking!

Judge. What nonsense! *Cicero*, indeed! 45 *What* an idea! Just because one now and then spouts a little about house-dogs or bloodhounds!

All (surrounding him). No, not only about dogs — about the building of the *Tower of Babel* too.[1] ... No, Ámmos Fyódorovich, don't 50 desert us, Ámmos Fyódorovich!

Judge. Release me, gentlemen!

(*At this moment footsteps and expectorations are heard in* KHLESTAKÓV'S *room. All rush headlong to the door, jostling and struggling to get out. They squeeze and crush one another a good deal, and half-suppressed exclamations are heard.*

BOBCHÍNSKI'S VOICE. Ugh! Pyótr Ivánovich, you've trod on my toe!

ZEMLYANÍKA'S VOICE. I'm stifling, sti- 55 fling; give me room — only give me time to

[1] An allusion to the Judge's freethinking or skepticism.

repent! — you're squeezing the life out of me! (*Other ejaculations of "Ahh!" "Oohh!" etc. At last they all get through, and the room is left empty.*

SCENE 2

Khles. (*coming out alone, with the look of a man who has overslept himself*). I've had a proper snooze, it seems. Where did they get such mattresses and feather-beds from? I regularly perspired.... They must have plied me fairly well after lunch; my head aches yet.... 5 As far as I can see, I can pass the time here very comfortably. I like generosity and hospitality — all the more if I think they've not got a deep game to play.... And the Governor's daughter's not at all bad; while her mother, 10 well ... No, I don't know, but this sort of life just suits me to a T.

SCENE 3

Judge (enters and stops still, soliloquizing). Oh, Lord, Oh, Lord! grant me success! How my knees knock together! (*Aloud, drawing himself up and steadying himself with his sword*) I have the honor to present myself: County Court Judge of this district and College Assessor 5 Lyápkin-Tyápkin!

Khles. Pray take a seat! So you are the judge here?

Judge. I was elected judge for three years by the nobility and gentry in the year 10 1816, and have continued in the office ever since.

Khles. You find it profitable, I dare say, being a judge?

Judge. After three periods of the three years I was decorated with the Vladímir of the 15 Fourth Class, with commendation from the Government. (*Aside*) This money is regularly burning a hole through my hand!

Khles. Well, I like the Vladímir: it's better than the Anna of the Third Class, at any 20 rate.

Judge (thrusting his clenched fist somewhat forward, aside). Oh, Lord God! I don't know *where* I'm sitting! I feel as if I was on hot burning coals!

Khles. What have you got in your hand   25
there?

Judge (*loses his head, and drops the bank-notes
on the floor*). No—othing, sir!

Khles. Nothing? How's that? Why, I see
there's some money dropped!   29

Judge (*shaking all over*). I—impos—sible,
sir! (*Aside*) Oh, Lord, now *I'm* before the
judge! They've brought the cart to take me
to Siberia!

Khles. (*picks the notes up*). Yes, so it is; it's
money!   35

Judge. Now, all is over! I'm lost! I'm lost!

Khles. I say, *lend* me this!

Judge (*eagerly*). If you wish, sir, if you wish
— with the greatest of pleasure! (*Aside*)
Now, courage — courage! Aid me, Most   40
Holy Mother!

Khles. I spent all my money on the road,
you know, over one thing and another. However, as soon as I get home I'll return it you.

Judge. Don't mention it; it's quite unnec-   45
essary! The *honor* of lending it you is enough.
... Indeed, with my feeble powers but with all
zeal and loyalty to the Government.... I shall
endeavor to deserve ... (*Rises and stands erect,
hands down his sides.*) I will not ven-   50
ture to disturb you further with my presence.
... Will there be any injunction?

Khles. Injunction — what injunction?

Judge. I mean, will you not give any injunction to the judge of this district?   55

Khles. Why should I? I've no need of him
at present; no, thank you — thanks very
much!

Judge (*bowing and going out, aside*). Now
the town is ours!   60

Khles. (*alone*). H'm, the Judge is an excellent
fellow!

SCENE 4

Enter the POSTMASTER *in uniform, sword
in hand*

Post. I have the honor to present myself:
Postmaster and Court Councilor Shpyókin!

Khles. Ah, welcome! I'm very fond of
agreeable company! Take a seat! And so you
live here always?   5

Post. Yes, sir, just so.

Khles. Well, I like this little town of yours.
Cert'nly there are not many people in it, but
what of that? It's not the capital. That's true,
isn't it — it's *not* the capital?   10

Post. That's quite true, sir.

Khles. You see, it is only in the capital you
get *bon ton*,[1] and no country bumpkins. That's
your opinion, isn't it?

Post. Exactly so, sir! (*Aside*) Well, he's   15
not at all *haughty* — he talks about anything!

Khles. Still you admit you *can* live happily
in a small town?

Post. Precisely so, sir!   20

Khles. What does one want? In *my* opinion, all you want is that people should respect you, and sincerely like you — isn't that
so?

Post. Absolutely correct.   25

Khles. I must say I'm glad we are of the
same mind. I dare say I'm called eccentric,
but it's my nature. (*Catches the other's eye, and
speaks sotto voce.*) I may as well borrow a trifle
of this Postmaster too. (*Aloud*) A very   30
odd thing has happened to me: I've spent my
last coin on the way. Can you lend me three
hundred roubles?

Post. Of course! I shall count it a very great
happiness. Here it is — take it, sir,   35
please — delighted to oblige you!

Khles. Thanks, very much. You see, I've
a mortal hatred of stinting myself when
I'm traveling — why should I? Ain't I
right?   40

Post. Quite right, sir! (*Rises and draws himself up, with his hand on his sword.*) I will
not venture to disturb you further with my
presence.... Have you any observation to
make with reference to the postal admin-   45
istration?

Khles. No, nothing!

(*The* POSTMASTER *bows and exits.*

Khles. (*lighting a cigar*). The Postmaster,
it seems to me, is also a very good fellow —
at least, he's ready to oblige; that's the   50
sort of people I like.

---

[1] Good breeding. Khlestakov is showing off by using French terms.

SCENE 5

Enter LUKÁ, *the* SCHOOL DIRECTOR, *unceremoniously propelled from behind. A voice in the rear is heard saying, almost aloud, "Go on, what are you afraid of?"*

Luká (saluting nervously, with his hand on his sword). I have the honor of presenting myself: Director of Schools and Honorary Councilor Khlópov!

Khles. Ah, how d'ye do! Take a seat! Take a seat! Won't you have a weed? 5
(*Offers him one.*

Luká (aside, irresolutely). Good gracious, now! I never *thought* of that! Shall I take it or not?

Khles. Take it, take it; it's of an excellent brand. To be sure, it's not a Petersburg one. 10 I used to smoke cigars *there*, my good sir, that cost twenty-five roubles the hundred. Ah! you'd lick your fingers after smoking *them!* Here's a match — light up! (*Gives him a match.* LUKÁ *tries to smoke, shaking all over.*) There, don't put *that* end in your mouth! 15

Luká (throws the cigar down, spits, and gesticulates. Aside). Devil take it all; my cursed nervousness spoils everything!

Khles. I see you're not very fond of cigars, but I own they're one of *my* weaknesses. Not the only one, though — I'm rather sus- 20 ceptible to the charms of the fair sex too. What's *your* taste? Do you prefer brunettes, or blondes?

(LUKÁ *is completely dumbfounded.*

Khles. Now, out with it! — brunettes, or blondes? 25

Luká. I daren't give an opinion.

Khles. No, no; don't get out of it *that* way. I particularly want to know your taste.

Luká. I will venture to say then . . . (*Aside*) I don't know what I'm saying — my 30 head's in a whirl!

Khles. Aha! Aha! So you won't commit yourself! I'm sure you're smitten with some little brunette or other! Confess it now — you *are!* (LUKÁ *is speechless.*) Oho, you're 35 blushing. Look, look! Why won't you speak?

Luká. I'm too shy, Your Nob — Excell —

enity! (*Aside*) Confound my tongue, it's done for me, done for me! 40

Khles. Too shy — eh? Well, there's a certain something in my look which inspires that feeling; at least I know that not a woman can resist it — can they?

Luká. Certainly not, sir! 45

Khles. Now, there's a funny thing happened to me: I've spent all I possess in coming here. You couldn't lend me three hundred roubles, could you?

Luká (aside, grabbing at his purse). What 50 a case if I haven't got them! . . . Ah, I have, I have!

(*Takes some notes out, and hands them, trembling, to* KHLESTAKÓV.

Khles. I'm deeply indebted to you!

Luká. I will not venture to disturb you further with my presence. 55

Khles. Good-bye, then!

Luká (disappears hastily, remarking, aside). There! Thank Heaven! Perhaps he won't visit the schools now!

SCENE 6

Enter the CHARITY COMMISSIONER. *He draws himself up, like the others, in a military attitude of respectful attention, with his hand on his sword.*

Char. Comm. I have the honor to present myself: Charity Commissioner and Court-Councilor Zemlyaníka.

Khles. How do you do? Won't you take a seat? 5

Char. Comm. I had the honor of receiving and personally conducting you through the charitable institutions committed to my charge.

Khles. Ah, so you did, I remember. You gave me an excellent luncheon. 10

Char. Comm. I am glad to labor in the service of my Fatherland.

Khles. It's my weakness — I confess it — I'm fond of cookery. . . . But it seems as if you weren't so tall and erect yesterday, were 15 you?

Char. Comm. It's very possible. (*After a short silence*) I can only say that I spare no effort to perform my duty zealously. (*Draws his*

chair a little closer, and speaks in a lower tone.)
There's this Postmaster here does abso- 20
lutely nothing. Everything is in the greatest
state of neglect: letters and packages are kept
back ... pray investigate the matter yourself.
The Judge too, who was here just before me,
does nothing but hunt hares, and keep his 25
dogs in the County Court buildings; while his
general conduct, if I must unburden my mind
to you — certainly it's for my country's good
that I have to do it, though he's my friend and
connection — well, his conduct is most de- 30
plorable. There's a certain proprietor here,
Dobchínski by name — you have deigned to
meet him — and as soon as ever Dobchínski
goes away anywhere, his wife and the Judge
are having a tête-à-tête. I am ready to 35
swear to it ... and the children, down to the
youngest little girl, have a very strong likeness
to the Judge ——

Khles. Well, I declare! I never should have
thought it! 40

Char. Comm. Then there's the Director of
Schools. I can't think *how* the Government
could have appointed him. He's worse than
a Jacobin,[1] and he poisons the minds of the
young generation with revolutionary doc- 45
trines that simply baffle description. Hadn't
I better put all this down on paper?

Khles. Do, by all means; I shall be very glad
to have it! I like to read something amusing
when I'm bored.... By the way, what is 50
your name? I keep forgetting!

Char. Comm. Zemlyaníka.

Khles. Ah, of course — Zemlyaníka. And
tell me please, have you any children?

Char. Comm. To be sure I have, sir, five 55
of 'em; two are now grown up.

Khles. You don't say so; grown up! And,
now ... what are their —?

Char. Comm. I understand, you are pleased
to ask what their names are? 60

Khles. Yes, what are their names?

Char. Comm. Nikolaí, Iván, Yelizavéta,
Márya, and Perepetúya.

Khles. Good, good!

Char. Comm. As I will not venture to 65
disturb you further with my presence, or take

[1] A zealot of the French Revolution.

up the time which you consecrate to the performance of your duties ...

     (*Bows and prepares to leave.*

Khles. (*accompanying him out*). Oh, don't
mention it! All you've told me is very 70
amusing.... It's a great treat to me.... (*Turns
back and reopens the door, calling after him.*)
Hi, there! what are your ... I quite forget your
Christian and paternal names!

Char. Comm. Artémi Philíppovich.

Khles. Oh, I beg your pardon, Artémi 75
Philíppovich, but an odd thing happened to
me — I've cleaned myself out coming here.
You haven't got four hundred roubles to lend
me?

Char. Comm. Yes, I have. (*Gives it.* 80

Khles. Well, that *is* lucky! I thank you
most sincerely!

SCENE 7

Enter BOBCHÍNSKI *and* DOBCHÍNSKI

Bob. I have the honor to present myself:
Peter, son of Iván Bobchínski, citizen of this
town.

Dob. And I am Pyótr, son of Iván Dobchínski, landed proprietor. 5

Khles. Ah, but I've met you before! I think
you had a fall then? How is your nose now?

Bob. Glory to God! Quite well, thank you!
Please don't trouble about it — it's healed now,
quite healed up! 10

Khles. That's all right — I'm glad to hear
it.... (*Suddenly*) You haven't got any money
about you?

Dob. Money? What for?

Khles. Lend me a thousand! 15

Bob. Good God! I haven't got such a sum!
Haven't you, though, Pyótr Ivánovich?

Dob. No more have I, sir; because if you care
to know, all my money is deposited with the
Board of Guardians. 20

Khles. Well, then, if you haven't a thousand,
say a *hundred* roubles.

Bob. (*rummaging in his pockets*). Haven't
you got a hundred, Dobchínski? I have only
got forty in paper, altogether. 25

Dob. I've no more than twenty-five roubles.

Bob. Have another good look, then, Pyótr

IHvánovich! You've a hole in your right pocket, I know — I dare say there's some dropped through.   30

Dob. No, there's nothing in the hole, I'm positive.

Khles. Never mind, then — I'll do with that. Very well, let it be sixty-five roubles.... That's all right.   (*Takes the notes.* 35

Dob. I was going to presume to ask you a favor with reference to a very delicate question ——

Khles. Well, what is it?

Dob. It is a matter of a *very* delicate na-   40
ture, sir: my eldest son, will you condescend to observe, was born a little before my marriage ——

Khles. Hullo?

Dob. And so, if you please, I wish him   45
to be quite my — well, *legitimate* son now, sir, and to be called Dobchínski, like me, sir.

Khles. All right, that's quite possible: *let* him be called so.

Dob. I wouldn't trouble you, sir, only it   50
was a pity, with all his capabilities. The boy really gives me the greatest hopes: he repeats whole poems by heart; and if he finds a knife anywhere, he'll at once make a little toy droshky as neatly as a conjurer, sir.   55
Here's Bobchínski will testify to that.

Bob. Yes, he has wonderful talents!

Khles. Very good, very good! I'll do my best for him.... I'll speak about it.... I hope to ... that shall all be arranged — yes,   60
yes!... (*Turns to* BOBCHÍNSKI.) Haven't *you* something to ask me for?

Bob. Yes, I have a very humble request to make.

Khles. Well, then, what about?   65

Bob. I most respectfully beg of you, when you return to Petersburg, to tell all the different grandees there — the senators and admirals — that *here*, Your Serenity — I mean, Your Excellency — in this very town lives   70
Peter Ivánovich Bobchínski — merely to say that: Peter Ivánovich Bobchínski lives here.

Khles. Very good!

Bob. And if the Emperor should get to hear of it, then will you say to the Emperor   75
too: May it please Your Imperial Majesty, that

is the town where Peter Ivánovich Bobchínski lives.

Khles. Certainly!

Dob.⎱ Pardon us for troubling you so   80
Bob.⎰ with our presence.

Khles. Don't mention it, don't mention it! It's a great pleasure for me. (*Conducts them out.*

SCENE 8

Khles. (*solus*). There's a good many *chinóv-niks* here! It seems to me, though, they take me for a government official! I certainly drew the long bow yesterday.... What a set of flats they are! I must send an account of it all   5
to Tryapíchkin at Petersburg: he writes articles — he'll scribble off a fine description of them. Hi, Osip! bring me some ink and paper! (OSIP *looks in at the door and says, "Directly, sir!"*) But I must be careful with Trya-   10
píchkin — this may strike him as a good joke — he'll sell his own father for a jest, and he won't refuse a chance of making money. Besides, these officials are a good sort of people: their lending me money is a decided point in   15
their favor. I'll just see how much I've got.... There's three hundred from the Judge, and three hundred from the Postmaster.... Six, seven, eight hundred — what a greasy bit of paper — eight hundred, nine hundred....   20
Oho! it tots up to more than a thousand.... Now, then, my friend the captain, just let me catch you *now* — we'll see who'll be the winner!

SCENE 9

Enter OSIP, *with inkstand and paper*

Khles. Now, booby, you see how well they entertain me!   (*Begins to write.*

Osip. Yes, thank the Lord! Only, do you know, Iván Alexándrovich —?

Khles. Know *what*?   5

Osip. You ought to be starting! God knows, it's high time!

Khles. (*writing*). What nonsense! Why?

Osip. I mean it. The Lord be with 'em all! You've been going it here for two days —   10
reelly, it's quite enough! Why hobnob with 'em any longer? Spit on 'em! You don't

know what may happen next — somebody else may turn up.... God knows, Iván Alexándrovich! And there's splendid 'orses here — 15 they'd go like lightning!

Khles. (*writes*). No, I'd like to stay on here a little longer. Tomorrow will do.

Osip. Tomorrow! Lord love us! we *must* go, Iván Alexándrovich! If they make a lot 20 of you just now, it's all the better reason for starting at once. You see, they've been and mistook you for somebody else; and the old man will be angry at your loitering here.... Those 'orses would go famous, *I'll* under- 25 take — they'd give you real good 'uns here.

Khles. (*still writing*). Very well, then. Only take this letter first, please, and then get an order for post-horses — and mind you see that they're good ones. Tell the post-boys 30 I'll give them each a rouble for drink, if they drive like *feldjägers,*[1] and sing their loudest.... (*Continues writing.*) There, I fancy Tryapích-kin will die of laughing ——

Osip. I'll send it off, sir, by the man here. 35 I'd better be packing up, so's not to lose time.

Khles. Very good — bring me a light, though!

Osip (*goes out, and speaks behind the scene*). Hi, there, fellow! You take a letter to the post, and tell the Postmaster he's to frank it 40 — and order them to bring round their very best courier's *troika*[2] for my master at once; and say that the noble master don't pay any fare — he travels at the Government's expense, tell 'em. They're to look alive, or the 45 noble master will be furious. Stop, the letter ain't ready yet.

Khles. (*goes on with his letter*). I should like to know where's he living now — whether it's the *Pochtamskaya*[3] or the *Garokhavaya.*[4] 50 He likes to change his quarters pretty often — saves paying the rent. I'll make a shot at it, and address to the *Pochtamskaya.*

(*Folds the letter up and addresses it.*
Osip *brings the light.* KHLESTAKÓV

[1] Imperial couriers, who have precedence at the stations where horses are changed.

[2] A carriage for three horses.

[3] Post Office Street, a great thoroughfare in old St. Petersburg.

[4] Peas Street, another great thoroughfare.

seals the letter. At the same time DERZHIMÓRDA'S *voice is heard exclaiming:* "*Where are you coming to, old stick-in-the-mud? You've been told no one's to be let in.*"

Khles. (*gives* Osip *the letter*). There, take it out! 55

Merchants' Voices. Let us in, *batyushka* — you can't prevent us: we've come on business!

Derzhimórda's Voice. Be off! Be off! He's not receiving anyone! He's asleep.

(*The noise increases.*

Khles. What's up there, Osip? See what 60 the row's about!

Osip (*looks through the window*). Some tradesmen want to come in, and the police-officer won't let 'em. They're waving papers about — they want to see you, I'm sure. 65

Khles. (*going to the window*). Well, what do you want, my friends?

Merchants' Voices. We throw ourselves on your favor! Give orders that your lordship will receive our petition. 70

Khles. Let them in, let them in! Let them come! Osip, tell them they're to come in. (*Exit* Osip. KHLESTAKÓV *takes some petitions in through the window, turns them over, and reads.*) "To his High Well-born Illustrious Financial Lordship from the Merchant Abdúlin"... the devil knows what it's about; and what a 75 *title,* too!

SCENE 10

Enter the MERCHANTS, *with sugar-loaves and a basket of wine*

Khles. Now, my friends, what is it?

Merchants. We implore your favor!

Khles. Well, say what you want!

Merchants. Do not ruin us, your lordship! We are grievously and unjustly oppressed! 5

Khles. By whom?

One of the Merchants. It's all by the Governor of this town. There never was such a governor, sir! It is impossible to describe the outrages he commits. We're so ruined by 10 constant billeting that we may as well hang ourselves! He catches us by the beard, and says, "Ah, you dog of a Tartar!" My God!

if we don't pay him due respect ...! But we've always done our duty peaceably: we've 15 never refused anything that his lady or his daughter might want for dress. But no, you see, that is not enough for him; why, he comes into a shop, and anything he lights upon — he collars the lot: he'll see a piece of cloth and 20 say, "Ah, my friend, that's a nice little piece of stuff; just carry it to my house!" So we have to take it, and the piece will be fifty *arshins* ¹ or so in length.

Khles. Is it possible? *Akh*, what a 25 blackguard he is!

Merchants. Yes, by God! No one ever remembers such a governor. So we cover up everything in the shop when we see him coming along. And, let alone choice articles, he'll 30 take any sort of rubbish: some prunes had been lying in the barrel for seven years, too bad for my shop-boy to eat — he stuffs a whole handful of them into his pocket. He says his nameday is the feast of Saint Anthony,² and then 35 you have to bring him all kinds of things he doesn't even want — that's no matter, you've got to keep on bringing them; and more, he says Saint Humphrey's Day is another nameday of his, so there's nothing to be done 40 but come with your contributions on *that* day too.

Khles. Why, he's nothing more nor less than a brigand!

Merchants. That's true! But try to 45 thwart him, and he'll quarter a whole regiment of soldiers in your house. And if we have the doors barred in his face, he says, "I will not submit you to corporal punishment or torture, as that is forbidden by the law; but, my 50 dear, I will make you swallow red herrings." ³

Khles. What a thorough-paced villain! He ought to be sent straight to Siberia for that!

¹ Fifty *arshins* equal about forty yards.
² An orthodox Russian formerly did not celebrate his birthday, but the feast-day of his patron saint, on whose day, and after whom, he was christened. Hence he could be named only after one of the saints in the calendar of the Greek Catholic Church.
³ This form of torture, which produces excessive thirst, was employed by the secret police of the old Russian Empire.

Merchants. Yes, if you by your favor 55 will only remove him, all will be well, provided only he does not stay in our neighborhood. Do not, our father, despise our bread and salt; we pay our respects to you with this sugar-loaf and this basket of wine! 60

Khles. No, you don't imagine *that*; I never accept bribes. But if you offered me a *loan* of, say, three hundred roubles, that would be quite another matter. I *could* take that. 65

Merchants. Take it then, our father. (*They produce the money.*) But what is three hundred — better have five hundred; only help us!

Khles. If you wish it — it's a *loan* — I'll 70 not say a word! ... I'll take it!

Merchants (*offering the money on a silver tray*). Please accept the tray also!

Khles. Well, I may take the tray, perhaps.

Merchants (*bowing*). Then take the sugar-loaf as well! 75

Khles. Oh, no! I never accept any kind of *bribes* ——

Osip. Your High Nobility! why won't you have it! Take it — it will come in very useful on the journey! ... Give me the sugar- 80 loaves and the packing-case — it'll all do. What's that? Cord? Let's have the cord as well — the cord will be handy on the road: the carriage'll get damaged, or something or other — it'll do to tie it up with! 85

Merchants. Show us this favor then, your Excellency. If you refuse to aid us in our prayer, we don't know what will happen — we may as well go and hang ourselves!

Khles. Most undoubtedly I will, most 90 undoubtedly! I'll do my best!

(*The* MERCHANTS *take their leave. A woman's voice is heard without:* "No, you daren't stop me! I'll complain to him of you! Don't you push me so roughly!*"

Khles. Who's there? (*Goes to the window.*) Well, what's the matter, *matushka*?

Voices of Two Women. Take pity on us, father! Say that your worship will listen 95 to us!

Khles. (*at the window*). Let them come in.

SCENE II

Enter the LOCKSMITH'S WIFE *and the*
SERGEANT'S WIFE

Locksmith's Wife (*bowing to the ground*).
Have pity on me!

Sergeant's Wife. Have pity on me too!

Khles. Who are you, women?

Sergeant's Wife. I am the sergeant Ivánov's
wife.   5

Locksmith's Wife. I live here, my father;
I'm the locksmith's wife, Fevrónya Pyetróva
Pashlyópkina ——

Khles. Stop, *one* of you speak at a time —
what do *you* want?   10

Locksmith's Wife. Have mercy on me — I
beg for vengeance on the Governor. May the
Lord curse him with every kind of curse, so
that neither the villain himself, nor his children,
nor his uncles, nor his aunts, may ever   15
prosper in anything they undertake!

Khles. But why?

Locksmith's Wife. Why, wretch that he is!
he's ordered my husband to shave his forehead as a recruit, and the lot didn't fall   20
on us, and it's against the law, for he's married!

Khles. How then *could* he do it?

Locksmith's Wife. He *has* done it, though,
the villain; he's done it! May God blast   25
him in this world and the next! And his aunt,
if he has an aunt — may every sort of evil
blight *her* — may his father, if he's alive, may
he rot to death, the scoundrel, and may he
choke forever for his villainy! They ought   30
to have taken the tailor's drunken son,
but the parents gave him a big present; so he
sneaked off for the son of Panteléyeva the
merchant's wife, but Panteléyeva privately
sent Her Ladyship three pieces of linen,   35
so he pitches on *me.* "What do you want a
husband for?" he says; "he's no use to you."
Well, *I'm* the person to know whether he's
any use or not! "Then," he says, "your husband is a thief — if he hasn't stolen al-   40
ready, he *will* do so; it's all the same, and so
they shall take him next year for a soldier."
And how shall I do without my husband?

Blackguard! may none of your family ever
come to see the blessed light of God! may   45
your mother-in-law, if you *have* a mother-in-
law ——

Khles. There, there! that will do! (*Motions
the old woman out. To the other*) Now what
have you to say?   50

Locksmith's Wife (*going out*). Don't forget
me, my father!

Sergeant's Wife. I have come to beg for justice against the Governor!

Khles. Well, well, what is it? Cut it   55
short!

Sergeant's Wife. He has flogged me, little
father!

Khles. How?

Sergeant's Wife. By mistake, my father!   60
Our old women were quarreling in the market,
and the police came up and took and caught
and reported *me* — and I couldn't sit down
for two days after it!

Khles. What's to be done *now*, then?   65

Sergeant's Wife. To be sure, *that* can't be
altered. But command him to pay compensation for the mistake. I must bear my lot
without complaining — but a little money
would be very acceptable now!   70

Khles. Good, good! You can go now —
be off — I'll see to it. (*Hands with petitions
are thrust in through the window.*) What! any
more of 'em there? (*Goes to the window.*) No,
no, I can't attend you — it's impossible,   75
impossible! (*Going out*) What a nuisance
they are, devil take 'em! Don't let 'em in,
Osip!

Osip. (*calls out of the window*). Go away,
go away, there's no time today — come   80
tomorrow!

> (*The door opens, and a figure appears in
> a frieze greatcoat with unkempt
> beard, swollen lips, and head bound
> up; others are seen behind him in the
> background.*

Osip. Be off with you, be off! Where are
you a-coming to?

> (*He pushes his fists into the first man's
> stomach, shoves him into the passage,
> and goes out himself, shutting the
> door.*

SCENE 12

Enter MÁRYA ANTÓNOVNA

Márya. A-kh!

Khles. Why are you so frightened, *mademoiselle?*

Márya. Oh no! I was not frightened.

Khles. (*showing off*). Pardon me, *Su-* 5
dárinya, if I say that it is very agreeable to me
to think you have taken me for one who...
May I venture to inquire where you thought
of going?

Márya. Really, I was going nowhere.   10

Khles. Might I ask, then, why you were
going nowhere?

Márya. I wondered if mamma were
here ——

Khles. No; but I should really like to   15
know why you were *going nowhere?*

Márya. Oh, I'm disturbing you. You were
engaged on important business!

Khles. (*with a lady-killing air*). But a
glance from your eyes is better than any im-   20
portant business!... *You* could never disturb
me — that's quite impossible; on the contrary,
you afford me the very greatest pleasure!

Márya. Ah, you compliment as they do in
the capital!   25

Khles. A charming lady like you should only
be so addressed! May I dare to be so happy
as to offer you a chair? But no! you should
have a *throne*, not a chair!

Márya. Indeed, I do not know.... I   30
ought to be going.

(*Takes a seat.*

Khles. What a beautiful scarf you have!

Márya. You are making fun of me — you're
only laughing at countrified people!

Khles. How I should long, *mademoiselle*,   35
to be that scarf, so as to clasp your lily neck!

Márya. I don't in the least understand
what you mean.... What singular weather we
are having today!

Khles. Your little lips, though, *Sudá-*   40
rinya, are worth all the weather in the world!

Márya. You only say that because you...
I was going to ask you to write some verses in
my album as a souvenir. You know a good
many, of course.   45

Khles. For *you*, *mademoiselle*, I will do anything you wish. Say the word, what verses
will you have?

Márya. Oh, anything — so long as they're
good and new!   50

Khles. Let me see — verses! I know a lot
of them!

Márya. Well, will you tell me what you are
going to write?

Khles. Why should I repeat them? I   55
know them without that!

Márya. I'm *so* fond of poetry...

Khles. Yes, and I know a quantity of all
sorts. Would you like this, say, "Oh, thou
mortal man, who vainly in thine anguish   60
murmurest against God." [1]... Or there's others... I can't just remember 'em now —
they're all of no account. Instead I offer you
my *love*, which ever since your first glance...

(*Moves his chair closer.*

Márya. Love? I don't understand what   65
love is!... I've never known what love is
like....

(*Moves her chair away.*

Khles. But why do you move your chair
away? We had better sit close to each other!

Márya (*moves it still further*). Why *close?*   70
We're just as well apart!

Khles. (*moves his chair up*). Why *apart?*
We're just as well close together!

Márya. But why do you do that?

Khles. (*edging nearer*). I only *seem* near   75
you — *fancy* that I'm far away!

Márya (*looks out of the window*). Ah! what
was that, seemed to fly past? Was it a magpie,
or what?

Khles. (*kisses her on the shoulder, and looks
at the window*). Yes, that was a magpie!   80

Márya (*rises indignantly*). No, that's *too*
much.... What *rudeness!*

Khles. (*holding her back*). Forgive me,
mademoiselle — I did it for *love*, only for love
of you!   85

Márya. And so you think I'm a country
hoyden....

(*Struggles to free herself.*

---

[1] A hackneyed quotation from *An Ode on the Book of
Job* by Mikhail V. Lomonósov (1711–65), the earliest
Russian poet of prominence.

Khles. (still holding her).   It was for love,
really, for love!... I was only joking, Márya
Antónovna, don't be angry! I'm ready   90
to beg your pardon on my knees! *(Falls on
his knees.)   Do* forgive me, forgive me! You
see, you see, I'm on my knees!

SCENE 13

Enter ÁNNA ANDRÉYEVNA

Ánna (sees KHLESTAKÓV *kneeling).   Akh,*
what a situation!
Khles. (rising).   Oh, con-found it!
Ánna (to her daughter).   Well, miss, what's
the meaning of *this* behavior?   5
Márya.   Mamma dear, I——
Ánna.   Be off from here: d'you hear me, be
off, I say! and don't dare to show your face to
me again! (MÁRYA *goes out in tears.)*   Excuse
me, sir, but, I confess, I was so astonished   10
at these proceedings...
Khles. (aside).   But she isn't bad-looking,
either. *(Throws himself at her feet.)   Sudárinya,* you see, I burn with love!
Ánna.   What's this, you on your knees?   15
Oh, get up, sir, get up! The floor is quite dirty
here!
Khles.   No, on my knees — indeed, on my
knees, I wish to know my *fate* — life or death!
Ánna.   But allow me, sir; I don't quite   20
comprehend the meaning of your words. If
I am not mistaken, you were making a proposal to my daughter!
Khles.   No, I'm in love with *you!*   My life
hangs on a thread! If you will not crown   25
my constant love, then I am unfit for earthly
existence! With a flame at my heart, I ask for
your hand!
Ánna.   But permit me to mention that I am,
so to speak ... well, I am *married!*   30
Khles.   What matter?   Love knows no difference! Has not Karamzín said: "The *laws*
may condemn...."[1]   We will fly under the
canopy of heaven! Your hand — I crave your
hand——   35

[1] A quotation from the poetic romance, *Bornholm
Island,* by the great Russian historian, Nikolai M.
Karamzin (1766–1826).

SCENE 14

MÁRYA ANTÓNOVNA *suddenly runs in*

Márya.   Mamma dear, papa says, will you ...
(Sees KHLESTAKÓV *on his knees, and shrieks.)
Akh!*   What a situation!!
Ánna.   What is it, then?   What do you
want?   What have you come for?   What do
you mean by this flightiness?   Bursting in   5
all of a sudden, like a cat in a fit!... Well, what
have you seen that's so surprising?   What's
got into your head, then?   Why, really, you
act like a three-year-old child — *not* like, not
in the least like, what one would expect   10
from a girl of *eighteen!*   I wonder when you
will get more sensible, and behave as a well-
brought-up young lady *should,* and learn good
manners and steadiness of conduct!
Márya (through her tears).   Really,   15
mamma dear, I didn't know——
Ánna.   Oh, your head's always empty — you
copy Lyápkin-Tyápkin's daughters.   What do
you want to follow them for — you've no business to take them as your pattern.   You   20
have *other* examples, miss, before you — your
own mother!   That's the model you ought to
imitate!
Khles. (seizing MÁRYA'S *hand).*   Ánna Andréyevna, do not oppose our happiness,   25
but give your blessing to a constant love!
Ánna (astounded).   So it's *her* you're——
Khles.   Decide my fate!   Is it life or death?
Ánna (recovering, to MÁRYA*).*   There, *now*
you see, minx, now you see — it was all on   30
your account, you baggage, that our guest was
pleased to fall on his knees; and then you suddenly blunder in, as if you had taken leave of
your senses.   It would have served you *quite*
right if I had refused — you're not worthy   35
of such good fortune.
Márya.   I won't do it any more, mamma;
I'll never do so again——

SCENE 15

Enter the GOVERNOR, *breathlessly*

Gov.   I will never do so again, Your Excellency!   Don't ruin me — don't ruin me!
Khles.   Why, what's the matter?

Gov. The merchants have been here, complaining to Your Excellency. — I swear, on 5 my honor, not half of what they say is true. They cheat and rob the people themselves. The sergeant's wife lied when she told you I flogged her — it's false, God knows, it's false. Why, *she flogged herself!* 10

Khles. The sergeant's wife may go to the devil — I'm not going to bother about *her!*

Gov. Don't believe 'em — don't believe 'em! they're such liars... not a *child* will trust 'em even! The whole town knows they're 15 liars, and as for cheating, I'll go so far as to say the world has never bred such a gang!

Ánna. But do you know the honor Iván Alexándrovich has conferred on us? He has asked for our daughter's hand! 20

Gov. What? what?... You're *mad, matushka* ...Don't be offended, Your Excellency; but she's a little wrong in the head sometimes — she takes after her mother.

Khles. But I do really ask for her hand! 25 I'm deeply in love!

Gov. I can't believe it, Your Excellency —!

Ánna. Not when he *tells* you so?

Khles. I'm not joking... I'm madly in love with her! 30

Gov. I daren't believe it; I'm not worthy of such an honor!

Khles. If you refuse me Márya Antónovna's hand, the devil knows what I'm not ready for!

Gov. I *can't* believe you — you are 35 pleased to be jesting, Excellency!

Ánna. Oh, what a *blockhead* you are, to be sure! How many times are you to be told?

Gov. No, no — it's incredible!

Khles. Give me your consent, give me 40 your consent! I'm a desperate man — capable of anything! If I blow my brains out, you will be held responsible.

Gov. Oh, my God! I am innocent, body and soul! Don't take offence, I beg! Please 45 do what Your Honor thinks fit! My head's in such a whirl now... I can't realize what's going on.... I've become a regular tom-fool — such as I never was before!

Ánna. There, now, give them your bless- 50 ing! (KHLESTAKÓV *and* MÁRYA *approach him.*

Gov. May the Lord bless you — but I am innocent of it! (KHLESTAKÓV *kisses* MÁRYA. *The* GOVERNOR *stares at them, and at last realizes that it is not all a plot.*) *What?* what the devil! They're really...! (*Rubs his* 55 *eyes.*) *So* they are, they're kissing each other; they actually *are* — just as if they were engaged! Aha! Oho! What a stroke of luck! *Well*, I'm blest!!

SCENE 16

Enter OSIP

Osip. The horses are ready!

Khles. All right — I'll come directly!

Gov. Are you, then, going away?

Khles. Yes, I'm starting.

Gov. But just when — that is to say... 5 you condescended to hint at marriage, I thought!

Khles. I have to leave, though, at a minute's notice; but I'm only going for a day to see my uncle — he's a wealthy old boy — and I'll 10 be back tomorrow!

Gov. We won't venture to detain you then — we'll only hope for your safe return!

Khles. Thanks, thanks; I'll come back directly! (*To* MÁRYA) Good-bye, my love! 15 ...No, I can't bear to say it! Farewell, darling. (*Kisses her hand.*

Gov. Will you want anything for your journey? You were good enough, I think, to say you were short of funds? 20

Khles. Oh, no, it doesn't matter.... (*Reflects a little.*) Well... all the same... since you *are* so kind ——

Gov. How much do you want?

Khles. Well, you know, you have lent me 25 two hundred — that's to say, it wasn't *two* hundred, but *four* — I don't want to profit by your mistake — so, if you lend me as much again, that will make it a round sum, just eight hundred. 30

Gov. You shall have it at once! (*Takes the notes out of his purse.*) There, as if on purpose, there's some brand-new notes!

Khles. Ah, so they are! (*Takes the notes and examines them.*) That's fine! they 35 say new bank-notes mean good luck, don't they?

Gov. So they do, sir; exactly so!

Khles. Well, good-bye, Antón Antónovich! I'm deeply grateful to you for your hospi- 40 tality — I've never been so well treated as here. Good-bye, Ánna Andréyevna! Farewell, Márya Antónovna, my darling!

(*All go off, and their voices are heard behind the scenes.*

Khles. Farewell, Márya Antónovna, angel of my soul! 45

Gov. Oh, how's this? You're going to ride in a post-carriage?

Khles. Yes, it's a way I have. Springs give me a headache.

Driver. Tprr.... Whoa, there! 50

Gov. Have something then laid there; a rug, say. Won't you let me tell them to get you one?

Khles. Oh no, why? It's needless — still, if you like, let's have the rug!

Gov. Here, Avdotya, run to the cup- 55 board and get out the very best rug, the Persian one with the blue ground — make haste!

Driver. Tprr ——

Gov. How long are we to wait for your return? 60

Khles. Oh, tomorrow, or the next day!

Osip. Ah, is that the rug? Let's have it here — lay it *so!* And now put some hay this side!

Driver. Whoa, then, whoa ——

Osip. Here, on this side! this way! more 65 — that's right! that'll do famous! (*Pats the rug with his hand.*) Now you can take your seat, Your Honor!

Khles. Good-bye, Antón Antónovich!

Gov. Good-bye, Your Excellency! 70

Women's Voices. Good-bye, Iván Alexándrovich!

Khles. Good-bye, *mamenka!*

Driver. Gee-up, my beauties!

(*Bell tinkles; the curtain falls.*

ACT V

The same room in the GOVERNOR'S *house.*

SCENE I

The GOVERNOR, ÁNNA ANDRÉYEVNA, *and* MÁRYA ANTÓNOVNA

Gov. Well, Ánna Andréyevna — eh? Had you any idea of *that*, now? There's a prize, if you *like!* Now, confess it candidly — you never dreamt of such a thing! You were a simple town-governor's wife, and *now* see 5 who you've hooked for a son-in-law — a devil of a swell, confound you!

Ánna. Not at all — I knew it ages ago. It's *you* that's taken by surprise; you're only a commonplace person, and have never met 10 people of quality!

Gov. Why, madam, I'm one of the quality myself!... Just think, though, Ánna Andréyevna, what a fine pair of birds we've become — eh? Ánna Andréyevna! We can 15 fly pretty high now — devilish high!... Stop, won't I pepper up all the gentlemen who were so free with their petitions and complaints! Hi, who's there? (*A* POLICE-OFFICER *enters.*) Oh, that's you, Iván Kárpovich! Just 20 summon the merchants here, brother. Won't I let the blackguards have it! Informing about *me*, indeed! Wait a little, you cursed pack of Jews, you little turtle-doves! I chastised you before with whips, now I'll try the scor- 25 pions! Take note of all who came to protest against me, and especially the scribblers who concocted their petitions. And be sure to let 'em all know, from me, what an honor Heaven has sent the Governor; he's going to marry 30 his daughter, not to a nobody, but to a man whose equal the world's never seen, who can accomplish everything — everything! Make them all understand *that!* Shout it in everyone's ears, ring the bells — devil take it! 35 Now's my triumph, and triumph I *will!* (*The* POLICE-OFFICER *goes out.*) Now, Ánna Andréyevna, what d'you think — eh? Things being as they are, where shall we take up our abode — here, or in "Peter"? 40

Ánna. Oh, in Petersburg, of course. How could we remain here?

Gov. Very well, Petersburg be it, then! — only it's not bad here even. I fancy, though, the governorship can go to the devil — eh, 45 Ánna Andréyevna?

Ánna. Of course, what's a governorship indeed!

Gov. Now, don't you think, Ánna Andréyevna, we shall really get to the top of the 50 tree, as he's hail-fellow-well-met with all the

Ministers, and goes to Court; so he'll get me promoted, until in time I shall find myself among the generals? What do you think, Ánna Andréyevna, shall I *do* as a general? 55

Ánna. I should *say* so — beautifully!

Gov. Ah, confound it! It's splendid to be a general! They'll hang a ribbon across my shoulder! Which do you say's the best order to have — the red one or the blue? [1]   60

Ánna. Oh, decidedly the blue is the best.

Gov. Oh, that's what you aim at! The red one's pretty good, too. Why does one want to be a general? Why, because when you travel anywhere you have couriers and or- 65 derlies always galloping in front, shouting "horses!" and no one else can have 'em at the stations — everyone waits for you — all the councilors, captains, and town-governors — and you don't turn a hair! You dine 70 with the lord-lieutenant,[2] wherever it may be, and snub the town-governor! Ha, ha, ha! (*Laughs till the tears run down his cheeks.*) That's what I call tempting, damn it!

Ánna. Anything rude like that just pleases you. But you really must remember 75 that we shall have to live a quite different kind of life — it won't do for you to know any of your dog-fancier judges, whom you go hare-hunting with, or people like Zemlyaníka; on the contrary, your acquaintances will be 80 persons of distinction — counts and fashionables, all of them... only I'm anxious about you: you will go and let out some expression or other, which is never heard in polite society.

Gov. Well, what of that — a word 85 doesn't hurt!

Ánna. No, perhaps not, when you're only a town-governor; but *there*, you know, our circumstances will be totally altered.

Gov. Yes, indeed! You can get two 90 good sorts of fish, they say, there — the sea-eel and the smelt, and they make your mouth water when you begin to eat 'em.

Ánna. That's all he thinks about — *fish!* *I* shall wish our house to be the very 95

---

[1] The red ribbon is for the Order of St. Anne, first class; the blue for the White Eagle. They are of equal merit.

[2] I.e., the governor of a province.

first in the capital, and my boudoir to be full of such amber and perfume that you can't go in without shutting your eyes — *so!* (*Screws up her eyes and sniffs.*) A—h! how exquisite!

SCENE 2

Enter the MERCHANTS

Gov. Oh, good day, little falcons.

Merchants (*bowing*). We wish you health, little father.

Gov. Well, my little pigeons,[1] and how are you getting on? and how's business? 5 (*Changes his tone.*) And so you would report me, you tea-swillers, you peddling hucksters! You *would*, would you, you utter ruffians, you ringleaders of blackguardism, you sharks, you pirates you —! Eh? Complaining of 10 *blackmail?* Oh, you thought, here's a chance to clap him in prison!... May the seven fiends and a she-devil catch you! Do you *know* that —?

Ánna. Oh, my God! What *language* 15 you use, Antosha!

Gov. (*impatiently*). Oh, I can't be picking and choosing my words now! (*To the* MERCHANTS) Are you aware that the very same *chinóvnik* to whom you complained is now 20 engaged to my daughter? I'll pay you out!... Why, you fleece the whole nation!... You make a contract with the Government, and cheat it out of a hundred thousand with the rotten cloth you supply; and then, if you're 25 asked to give one a present of fifteen or twenty yards, you expect a consideration for it! Ay, if they only knew, they'd come down on you! And the *side* you put on! He's a *merchant* — don't you touch him! "We don't rank 30 after gentlefolks," say you — but gentlemen have had an education, you ape! I daresay they are flogged at school — otherwise they'd learn nothing. But what do *you* learn? Why, the A B C of swindling, for your master 35 beats you if you don't manage to rob properly. While you're still a small boy you don't know the Lord's Prayer, but you can *do* anybody; and *then*, don't you give yourselves airs when

---

[1] These phrases which the Governor uses were polite terms of address in old Russia.

you get bigger, and your purse gets fuller! 40
My! what a sight for sore eyes! Just because you blow out sixteen samovars [1] a day
you put a swagger on! I spit on your head
and your bumptiousness!

Merchants (bowing low). We are guilty, 45
Antón Antónovich!

Gov. You complained of me? But who was
it that winked at your robbery when you built
the bridge and charged twenty thousand for
less than a hundred roubles' worth of 50
wood? It was I, you goat's beard! Have you
forgotten *that?* If I had rounded on you, I
could have sent you to Siberia! What say
you to *that* — eh?

One of the Merchants. God knows, we are 55
guilty, Antón Antónovich — the devil tempted
us! We will never inform against you again!
Tell us what compensation you wish ... only
don't be angry!

Gov. Don't be angry! Oh, *now* you wal- 60
low at my feet — because I've got the upper
hand! But if I was in your position for a moment, you would roll me in the mud, you rabble, and club me on the head into the bargain!

Merchants (prostrating themselves). Spare 65
us, Antón Antónovich!

Gov. Spare you, indeed! It's "*spare us!*"
now, but what was it before — eh? I have a
good mind to ... but no! (*Waves his hands
condescendingly.*) There, may the Lord for- 70
give you! Enough — I bear no malice; only
beware, and mind your P's and Q's! for I'm
not giving my daughter to any ordinary gentleman; so see that the wedding presents are
... you understand? And don't flatter 75
yourselves you can put me off with your dried
fish or sugar-loaves.... There, now, you can
go, and the Lord be with you!

(*Exeunt* MERCHANTS.

SCENE 3

Enter the JUDGE, *the* CHARITY COMMISSIONER,
and afterwards RASTÁKOVSKI

Judge (almost before he has entered the room).
Are we to believe the report, Antón Antóno-

[1] A samovar is a Russian teapot. The allusion here
is to the excessive consumption of weak tea among the
traders while bargaining.

vich? Has an extraordinary piece of good
fortune befallen you?

Char. Comm. I have the honor to congratulate you on your extraordinary good for- 5
tune! I was heartily pleased when I heard
of it! (*Kisses* ÁNNA'S *hand.*) Ánna Andréyevna! (*Kisses* MÁRYA'S.) Márya Antónovna!

Rast. I congratulate Antón Antónovich! 10
May the Lord grant long life to you and the
bridal pair, and bless you with grandchildren
and great-grandchildren, and many descendants to succeed you! Ánna Andréyevna!
(*Kisses her hand.*) Márya Antónovna! 15
(*Kisses* MÁRYA'S *hand.*

SCENE 4

Enter KARÓBKIN *and his wife, and* LYÚLYUKOV

Kar. I have the honor to congratulate Antón Antónovich! Ánna Andréyevna! Márya
Antónovna!   (*Kissing their hands.*

Karóbkin's Wife. I sincerely congratulate
you, Antón Antónovich, on your good for- 5
tune!

Lyúl. I have the honor to congratulate you,
Ánna Andréyevna! (*Kisses her hand and turns
to the audience, smacking his lips with an air
of bravado.*) Márya Antónovna! I have the
honor! (*Goes through the same performance.* 10

SCENE 5

*Enter a number of visitors with overcoats and
in full dress; they first shake* ÁNNA'S
hand, and then MÁRYA'S, *saying, "Ánna
Andréyevna!" "Márya Antónovna!"
Enter also* BOBCHÍNSKI *and* DOBCHÍNSKI,
eagerly jostling each other

Bob. I have the honor to congratulate you ...
Dob. Antón Antónovich, I have the honor
to congratulate you!
Bob. ... On the happy occurrence!
Dob. Ánna Andréyevna! 5
Bob. Ánna Andréyevna!
(*They both approach at the same moment,
and knock their foreheads together.*
Dob. Márya Antónovna! (*Kisses her hand.*)
I have the honor of congratulating you! May
you enjoy the greatest, greatest happiness, and

walk about in cloth of gold, and eat all   10
sorts of choicely flavored soups, and always
pass your time very agreeably . . .

Bob. (*interrupting him*). Márya Antónovna!
I have the honor to congratulate you! May
God grant you wealth of every kind and   15
ducats and a baby boy, as *tiny*, yes, as tiny as
this! — (*Measures with his hand.*) — Small
enough to sit on the palm of your hand! yes,
and may the little darling cry all the time: *wah
— wah — wah!*   20

SCENE 6

Enter more visitors, who kiss hands; then LUKÁ
and his wife

Luká. I have the honor ——

Luká's Wife (*running forward*). I congratulate you, Ánna Andréyevna! (*They kiss each
other.*) But really I am *so* delighted! They
tell me Ánna Andréyevna has betrothed   5
her daughter. "Oh, thank the Lord!" thinks
I to myself, and I was so delighted that I say
to my husband, "Just listen, Lukánchik: what
a stroke of good luck for Ánna Andréyevna!"
"Yes, glory to God!" I say to myself, and   10
I tell him I'm so enchanted that I'm burning
with impatience to go and say so to Ánna Andréyevna myself . . . "Oh, thank the Lord!"
I think, "that's exactly what Ánna Andréyevna
has been looking out for — a match for her   15
daughter, and now there's a piece of good fortune — just what she wanted has happened!"
And I assure you I was *so* delighted that I
couldn't *speak* — I could only cry and cry; yes,
I regularly *sobbed!* Then Lukánchik says: 20
"What are you sobbing for, Nástenka?"
"Lukánchik," I say, "I don't know myself, but
see, the tears are streaming down in a torrent!"

Gov. Kindly sit down, gentlemen! Here,
Míshka, bring some more chairs.   25
(*The visitors take seats.*

SCENE 7

Enter the POLICE SUPERINTENDENT *and the*
POLICE-OFFICERS

Super. I have the honor to congratulate you,
Your High Nobility, and to wish you happiness
for many years!

Gov. Thanks — thanks! Please be seated,
gentlemen!   (*They sit down.*   5
Judge. Now tell us, please, Antón Antónovich, how it all came about — give us the
whole history of it!

Gov. It's an extraordinary story — he condescended to make the proposal himself in   10
person!

Ánna. In a *most* respectful and delicate way.
He said quite *too* nicely: "Ánna Andréyevna,
you have simply made a conquest of me!"
Such a handsome, well-bred young man;   15
such distinguished manners! "Believe me,
Ánna Andréyevna," he said, "I don't value
my life a kopék — it is only on account of your
rare and charming qualities that I . . ."

Márya. Oh, mamma, really that's what   20
he said to *me!*

Ánna. Be quiet! You know nothing about
it! Don't you meddle with what doesn't concern you! "I love to distraction, Ánna Andréyevna!" Such were his flattering   25
words . . . and when I began to say, "We dare
not hope for so high an honor!" down he went
on his knees in the most aristocratic manner.
"Ánna Andréyevna," he exclaimed, "don't
make me the most miserable of men!   30
Consent to respond to my passion, or with
death I will cut short my existence!"

Márya. But of course, mamma, he meant
that for *me*.

Ánna. Oh, no doubt, no doubt . . . he   35
meant it for you; I'm not denying that at all.

Gov. And how he frightened us, too: he said
he would blow his brains out. "I'll shoot myself; I'll shoot myself!" he cried.

Several of the Visitors. Good gracious,   40
you don't say so!

Judge. What a character!

Luká. In truth, this is the work of fate!

Char. Comm. Don't say it's *fate, bátyushka;*
fate's an old turkey-hen! The Governor's   45
public services have earned him this honor!
(*Aside*) They always cast pearls before swine,
like that!

Judge. If you like, Antón Antónovich, I'll
make you a present of the dog we were   50
bargaining about.

Gov. Oh, no! I can't bother about dogs now!

Judge. Oh, if you don't like *that* one, we'll arrange about another.

Karóbkin's Wife. Ah, Ánna André- 55 yevna, how glad I am at your good fortune! — you can't imagine!

Kar. May I ask where your distinguished guest is now? I heard he had left for some reason or other. 60

Gov. Yes, he has gone away for a day on very important business ——

Ánna. ... to see his uncle, and to ask for his blessing.

Gov. Yes, to ask for his blessing; but 65 tomorrow ... (*Sneezes; the rest simultaneously ejaculate "Bless you!"*) Many thanks! he'll be back again, I say, to-m —

(*Sneezes again; the ejaculations are repeated, and several of the company speak at the same time.*

Super. I wish you good health, Your High Nobility! 70

Bob. A sack of ducats and a hundred years!

Dob. May the Lord prolong them to a thousand!

Char. Comm. (*aside*). May you go to perdition! 75

Karóbkin's Wife (*aside*). May the devil fly away with you!

Gov. I thank you sincerely, and wish you all the same!

Ánna. We intend to live in Petersburg 80 now. *Here*, there's such an air, I must say ... it's really too rustic! ... *I* find it excessively disagreeable ... my husband too ... he will get general's rank there!

Gov. Yes, I own, gentlemen, I've a con- 85 suming ambition to be a general!

Luká. And may God grant it!

Rast. With man it is impossible, but with God all things are possible!

Judge. A great voyage befits a great 90 ship.[1]

Char. Comm. Your public services deserve the honor!

Judge (*aside*). And a *nice* blunder he'll make when he gets it! Why, a generalship will 95 suit him as well as a saddle does a cow! No, my friend, it's a far cry to *that*. There's plenty of

[1] A Russian proverb.

people cleverer than *you* who are not yet generals!

Char. Comm. (*aside*). *General*, indeed! 100 Confound him! It's not impossible, after all. He *may* get made one. With his bumptiousness, the devil wouldn't have him at any price! (*Turns to him.*) When you are a general, Antón Antónovich, don't forget *us!* 105

Judge. And if any business difficulty crops up, don't fail to help us out!

Kar. Next year I am going to take my son to the capital to serve his country; please be so kind as to take him under your protection 110 — be a father to the little orphan!

Gov. I'm quite ready, on my part — quite ready to help him!

Ánna. You're always free with your promises, Antosha! But, in the first place, 115 you'll not have time to think about that. How can you possibly burden yourself with such engagements?

Gov. Why not, my love? One can sometimes —— 120

Ánna. Of course! But you really cannot bother to be a friend and protector of all sorts of nobodies!

Karóbkin's Wife (*aside*). Do you hear how she treats us? 125

A Visitor. Oh, she was always like that — I know her. Seat her at table, and she'll put her feet on it.[1]

SCENE 8

Enter the POSTMASTER, *out of breath, with an opened letter in his hand*

Post. Here's an astounding thing happened, sirs! The *chinóvnik* we took to be the *Revizór* is *not* a *revizór!*

All. What? *not* a *revizór?*

Post. Not a *revizór* at all — I've found 5 that out from the letter.

Gov. What do you mean — what do you mean — from *what* letter?

Post. Why, from the letter he wrote *himself.* They bring me a letter to post. I look at 10 the address, and see "Post-Office Street" — I was regularly stunned. Well, I say to myself,

[1] Another common Russian saying.

he's without doubt found something wrong in the Postal Department, and he's reporting it to the authorities. So I took the letter 15 and — opened it.

Gov. How could you — ?

Post. I don't know — a supernatural force impelled me. I had already ordered a courier to take it by express, but such a feeling of 20 curiosity overpowered me as I had never known before. "I can't do it, I can't — I can't!" I hear myself saying; but I feel drawn, drawn to it! "Oh, don't open it, or you'll be utterly ruined!" that's what sounds in one ear; 25 and in the other, like a devil whispering, "Open it, open it, open it!" And so I broke the sealing-wax — my veins were on fire; but after I had done it they froze, by God, they froze. My hands shook, and everything whirled. 30

Gov. And so you *dared* to open the letter of so powerful a personage?

Post. That's where the joke is — he's neither a personage nor powerful!

Gov. What *is* he then, according to you? 35

Post. Neither the one nor the other; the devil knows *what* he is!

Gov. (*furiously*). What do you mean? How do you dare to call him neither the one nor the other, nor the devil knows what? I'll put 40 you under arrest — !

Post. Who? You?

Gov. Yes — *I* will!

Post. Pooh! That's beyond your power!

Gov. Are you aware that he is going to 45 marry my daughter? that I shall become a grandee? that I shall have power to send to *Siberia?*

Post. Eh, Antón Antónovich — *Siberia?* that's a long way off.... But I had better 50 read you the letter. Gentlemen, let me read it you!

All. Yes, read it, read it!

Post. (*reads*). "I hasten to let you know, my dear Tryapíchkin, all about my adven- 55 tures. On the way an infantry captain cleared me out completely, so that the innkeeper wanted to send me to jail; when all of a sudden, owing to my Petersburg get-up and appearance, the whole town took me for the 60 Governor-General. So now I am living at the

Governor's; I do just as I please; I flirt madly with his wife and daughter — but I can't settle which to begin with. Do you remember how hard-up we were, how we dined at 65 other folk's expense, and how the pastry cook once pitched me out neck-and-crop, because I had put some tarts I had eaten down to the account of the King of England? It is quite a different state of things now! They all 70 lend me as much money as ever I please. They are an awful set of originals — you would die of laughing if you saw them! You write articles, I know: bring these people in. First and foremost, there's the Governor — he's 75 as stupid as a mule...."

Gov. Impossible! it can't be there!

Post. (*showing him the letter*). Read it yourself!

Gov. (*reads*). "Stupid as a mule." It 80 can't be so — you've written it yourself!

Post. How *could* I have written it?

Char. Comm. Read!

Luká. Read on!

Post. (*resuming*). "The Governor — 85 he's as stupid as a mule..."

Gov. Oh, devil take it! Is it necessary to repeat *that?* As if it wasn't there without that!

Post. (*continues*). Hm... hm... hm... "as a mule. The Postmaster too is a good 90 fellow...." (*Stops.*) Well, he says something uncomplimentary about *me* too.

Gov. No — read it out!

Post. But what's the good?

Gov. No, no — confound it, if you read 95 *any* of it, read it all! Read it through!

Char. Comm. Allow me; I'll have a try! (*Puts on his spectacles, and reads.*) "The Postmaster is exactly like our office-beadle Mikhéyev, and a rascal into the bargain 100 — he drinks like a fish."

Post. (*to the company*). Well, the young blackguard ought to be flogged — that's all!

Char. Comm. (*continuing*). "The Charity Com... er... er..." (*Hesitates.* 105

Kar. But what are you stopping for?

Char. Comm. It's badly written... however, it's clearly something insulting.

Kar. Give it to me! my eyes are better, I fancy. (*Tries to take the letter.* 110

Char. Comm. (holding it back). No, we can leave that part out — further on it's plain enough.

Kar. But allow me — I can read!

Char. Comm. Why, so can *I* — further on, I tell you, it's quite easy to make out.   115

Post. No, read it all! It was all read before!

All. Give it up, Artémi Philíppovich; give the letter up! (*To* KARÓBKIN) You read it!

Char. Comm. Certainly! (*Hands the letter.*) There, if you please.... (*Covers the passage with his finger.*) *That's* where you begin.   120
(*All crowd round.*

Post. Read it, read it through; what nonsense! read it *all!*

Kar. (reading). "The Charity Commissioner, Zemlyaníka, is a regular pig in a skullcap."   125

Char. Comm. (to the rest). That's supposed to be *witty!* Pig in a skullcap! Who ever saw a pig in a skullcap?   130

Kar. (continues). "The School Director reeks of onions ——"

Luká (to the rest). Good God! and an onion has never crossed my lips!

Judge (aside). Thank goodness, there's nothing, at any rate, about *me!*   135

Kar. (reading). "The Judge ——"

Judge (aside). Now for it!... (*Aloud*) I think this letter is tedious. What the devil's the good of reading all that rubbish?   140

Luká. No!

Post. No, go on with it!

Char. Comm. No, read it through!

Kar. (resumes). "The Judge, Lyápkin-Tyápkin, is in the utmost degree *mové-   145
ton.*"[1] ... (*Stops.*) That must be a *French* word!

Judge. But the devil knows what's the meaning of it! It's bad enough if it's only — *swindler,* but it may be a good deal worse.

Kar. (goes on). "But, after all, the peo-   150
ple are hospitable and well-meaning. Farewell, my dear Tryapíchkin. I myself should like to follow your example and take up literature. It's a bore, my friend, to live as I do — one certainly wants food for the mind; one   155
must, I see, have some elevated pursuit. Write

[1] Phonetic spelling for the French phrase, *mauvais ton,* i.e., ill-bred.

to me at the village of Podkalitovka, Sarátov Government." (*He turns the letter over and reads the address.*) "To the Well-born and Gracious Mister Iván Vasiliyevich Try-   160
apíchkin, St. Petersburg, Post-Office Street, Number Ninety-Seven, within the Courtyard, Third Floor, on the Right."

One of the Ladies. What an unexpected rebuff!   165

Gov. He has as good as cut my throat! I'm crushed, crushed — regularly crushed! I can see nothing — only pigs' snouts instead of faces, nothing else ... Catch him, catch him!
(*Gesticulates wildly.*

Post. How can we catch him? Why, as   170
if on purpose, I told the manager to give him his very best *troika* — and the devil persuaded me to give him an order for horses in advance.

Karóbkin's Wife. Well, here's a pretty mess! the like of it has never happened!   175

Judge. Besides, sirs, confound it! he has borrowed three hundred roubles of me!

Char. Comm. And three hundred of *me* too!

Post. (groans). Ah! and three hundred of me as well!   180

Bob. Yes, and Dobchínski and I, sirs, gave him sixty-five, sirs, in bank-notes!

Judge (with a gesture of perplexity). How was it, gentlemen, that we came to make such a mistake?   185

Gov. (beats himself on the shoulders). How *could* I? There's not such another old blockhead as I am! I must be in my dotage, idiot of a mutton-head that I am.... Thirty years   190
have I been in the service; not a tradesman or contractor could cheat me; rogues after rogues have I overreached, sharpers and rascals I have hooked, that were ready to rob the whole universe! three governors-general I've duped!... Pooh! what are governors-gen-   195
eral? (*With a contemptuous wave of the hand*) They're not worth talking about!...

Ánna. But this can't be so, Antosha; he's engaged to Mashenka!...

Gov. (furiously). Engaged! Bosh! A   200
fig for your "engaged"! Confound your engagement! (*In desperation*) Look at me, look — all the world, all Christendom, all of you see how the Governor's fooled! Ass! booby! dotard

that I am! (*Shakes his fists at himself.*) 205 Ah, you fat-nose! Taking a brat, a rag, for a man of rank! And now he's rattling along the road with his bells, and telling the whole world the story! Not only do you get made a laughing stock of, but some quill-driver, some 210 paper-strainer will go and put you in a play! It's maddening! He'll spare neither your rank nor your calling, and all will grin and clap their hands. . . . Who are you laughing at? laugh at *yourselves!* . . . Ah! you . . . (*Stamps on the* 215 *ground ferociously.*) I would do for all the pack of scribblers! Ugh! the quill-splitters! damned liberals! devil's brood! I would scrag you all, I'd grind you to powder! You'd be a dish for the foul fiend, and the devil's cap 220 your resting-place! (*Shakes his fist and grinds his heel on the ground. Then after a short silence*) I can't collect myself yet. It's true, that if God will punish a man, he first drives him mad. To be sure, what was there like a *revizór* in that crack-brained trifler? Nothing at 225 all! Not the resemblance of half a little finger — and all of them shout at once: the *Revizór*, the *Revizór*! Who was it then who first gave out he was the *Revizór*? Answer me!

Char. Comm. (*shrugging his shoulders*). It all happened in such a way that I wouldn't 231 tell you, if you were to kill me. Our wits were befogged — it was the devil's doing!

Judge. Who started the idea? Why, there they are — those enterprising young bucks! 235 (*Points to* DOBCHÍNSKI *and* BOB-CHÍNSKI.

Bob. I swear it wasn't *me!* I never thought ——

Dob. I hadn't the *least* idea ——

Char. Comm. Undoubtedly it was *you!*

Luká. Why, certainly it was; they ran 240 like mad from the inn with the news — "He's here, he's come, he pays no money! . . ." A *fine* bird you discovered!

Gov. Of course, it was *you* — you gossiping busybodies, you damnable liars! 245

Char. Comm. I wish you had gone to the devil with your *Revizór* and your stories!

Gov. All you do is to run about the town and meddle with everybody, you confounded chatterboxes, you tittle-tattling scandal- 250 mongers, you short-tailed jackdaws!

Judge. You confounded bunglers!

Luká. You blockheads!

Char. Comm. You pot-bellied drivelers! (*All crowd up to them threateningly.*

Bob. God knows, it wasn't *me*, it was 255 Dobchínski!

Dob. No, Peter Ivánovich, you certainly were the first to ——

Bob. No, I did *not* — you began it.

SCENE 9

Enter a GENDARME

Gendarme. The Inspector-General sent by Imperial command has arrived, and requests your attendance at once. He awaits you in the inn.

(*All are thunderstruck at this announcement. The ladies utter simultaneous ejaculations of amazement; the whole group suddenly shift their positions and remain as if petrified.*

SCENE 10

(*without words*)

The GOVERNOR *is seen standing in the center, stiff as a post, with outstretched arms and head bent back. At his right are his wife and daughter, turning to him; beyond them the* POSTMASTER, *turning to the audience with a look of interrogation; behind him* LUKÁ LUKÍCH, *with an innocent expression; and farther, at the extreme edge of the scene, three ladies* (*visitors*), *who exchange satirical glances, sneering at the* GOVERNOR *and his family. To the* GOVERNOR'S *left is* ZEMLYANÍKA, *with his head slightly on one side, as if listening; behind him the* JUDGE, *shrugging his shoulders, bending low, and moving his lips, as if he were going to whistle or say: "Now we're in for it!" Next to him is* KARÓBKIN, *winking at the audience and making a contemptuous gesture at the* GOVERNOR; *and at the outside of the scene* BOBCHÍNSKI *and* DOBCHÍNSKI, *staring at each other open-mouthed. The others stay motionless as statues. The whole group retain the same positions for a minute or so, as if changed to stone; then the curtain falls.*

INTRODUCTION TO

Maria Magdalena

*The Rise of the Drama and Stage in Germany: The Romantic Movement
in German Drama: Hebbel and Middle-Class Tragedy*

THE RISE OF THE DRAMA AND STAGE IN GERMANY

GERMANY, like Russia, developed a national drama and stage very slowly. The existence of a large number of principalities, each concerned with propagating its own separate culture, delayed the growth of centers rich enough in intellectual and artistic interests to support a professional theater.

Folk production of the medieval miracle and saints' plays went on vigorously throughout Germany until the Protestant Reformation of the sixteenth century. In certain Catholic districts the Christmas and Easter, or Passion, plays were later revived. The revival of an old cycle at Oberammergau in 1662 started the world-famous Passion Play which has been given almost every ten years down to the present.

The bulk of the dramatic entertainment in Germany during the sixteenth and seventeenth centuries came from the English, French, and Italian actors who visited the larger towns and ducal courts. Late in the seventeenth century German troupes commenced to organize. Some wandered as far afield as Scandinavia and Russia, performing either German translations of English and French drama, or the new German farce which popularized the buffoonish character, Pickel-hering.

The eighteenth century witnessed the establishment of a really professional drama and theater. In 1727 a well-known actress-manager, Madame Caroline Neuber, settled with her troupe at Leipzig, then the leading seat of German culture. Her excellent productions of high-grade French and English plays in translation attracted the university students to the theater. One student, Gotthold Ephraim Lessing (1729–81), who as early as 1746 began to supply translations to her, brought forth in 1755 the first notable specimen of German drama, *Miss Sara Sampson*. George Lillo's *The London Merchant* (1731) inspired this prose tragedy about a middle-class German girl.

Lessing in 1767 had no more than issued his second play, *Minna von Barnhelm*, a comedy, when he was invited to serve as critic and adviser to the newly opened German National Theater at Hamburg, the first actual playhouse in Germany. Though that bold project toward a national tradition failed within a year, it afforded Lessing the occasion for an epoch-making series of critical essays on drama, collected under the title of *Hamburg Dramaturgy* (1768). This work attacked the long-honored French classical tradition of stifling art by a pedantic observance of rules such as the "unities." It set up Shakespeare as the supreme source of inspiration for the budding drama of Germany. Nevertheless Lessing's subsequent plays, *Emilia Galotti* (1772), another middle-class tragedy, and *Nathan the Wise* (1779), the first German tragedy in blank verse, lie nearer the classical than the Shakespearian model by reason of their compactness and restraint.

THE ROMANTIC MOVEMENT IN GERMAN DRAMA

Lessing's *Hamburg Dramaturgy*, however, laid the basis for the excessive romanticism, the so-called "Storm-and-Stress," which shortly burst forth in German drama and art. This movement glorified individuality, liberty, self-realization, and made feeling the measure of rightness. One of its earliest apostles was Johann Wolfgang Goethe (1749–1832), ultimately the greatest of German poets. In 1773, young Goethe, influenced by Lessing's advice, wrote in imitation of the Shakespearian chronicle history a prose drama, *Goetz von Berlichingen*, which depicts a medieval knight's battling for the cause of freedom. The composition, though noble in spirit, suffers from rhetoric, lyricism, and structural diffuseness. The same faults in greater or less degree characterize Goethe's later plays, *Egmont* (1787), *Iphigenia* (1787), *Tasso* (1790), *Faust* (Pt. I, 1808; Pt. II, 1832), and spoil their effectiveness as drama. *Faust*, his masterpiece, is really a vast philosophical poem on the medieval scholar who, for the sake of self-realization, puts himself in the Devil's hands.

Goethe became in 1791 the director of the court theater at Weimar, where a playhouse had existed as early as 1770. When in 1799 the Duke of Weimar completed a fine new theater, Goethe thought to eclipse his rivals, the Dresden Court Theater (1789) and the Berlin Court Theater (1796), and to make Weimar the most brilliant center of dramatic art in Germany. He obtained the help of the noted poet and playwright, Friedrich von Schiller (1759–1805), who had been connected with the first years of the Mannheim National Theater (1779). There Schiller had had produced his first two plays, *The Robbers* (1782), and *Intrigue and Love* (1784), typical Storm-and-Stress tragedies in which middle-class persons revolt against social tyranny. Schiller's new trilogy, *Wallenstein*, the tragedy of the Austrian commander in the Thirty Years' War, opened the Weimar Theater in 1799. Other pieces by him appeared on the same stage in rapid succession — *Maria Stuart* (1800), *Maid of Orleans* (1801), *Bride of Messina* (1803), *William Tell* (1804). All these plays, except *Bride of Messina*, combine the romantic features of historical subject, lofty sentiment, elevated speech in blank verse, and colorful incident, with the classical regard for unity of action, time, and place. Schiller's drama with its idealized characters in situations of large dimensions was intended to be acted in the grand manner. German taste, captivated at once, set him up as the nation's master dramatist. His pattern instituted the so-called "classical" tradition which dominated the German stage for the better part of the nineteenth century.

Outside of Schiller and Goethe the romantic movement in Germany yielded few playwrights of any lasting importance. The chief one, Heinrich von Kleist (1777–1811), showed a considerable talent in a few plays, notably *Prince Frederic of Homburg* (1811), a psychological study of discipline versus spirit, and *The Broken Pitcher* (1808), often praised as the finest German comedy. Yet the ultimate effect of romanticism was stultifying. Its adherents turned more and more to antiquarian, fantastic, and mystical subject matter. Their remoteness and exotic symbolism undermined the vitality of the serious drama in Germany until the 1880's.

HEBBEL AND MIDDLE-CLASS TRAGEDY

Before the middle of the nineteenth century, however, one German playwright, Christian Friedrich Hebbel, had awakened to the currents of modern thought, and come to grips with the contemporary age. He was born on March 18, 1813, at Wesselburen in the bleak lowlands of Holstein, a Danish duchy then, but now a province of north Germany. The bitterness of Hebbel's youth left an indelible impression on his mind. His father, a dour, upright, and pious stone-mason, was, according to the son, "a slave of marriage, bound with iron fetters to poverty." When Hebbel was six years old, the sale of the family cottage, forced by the failure of a disreputable friend, plunged the Hebbels to the bottom of the social scale and forever embittered the proud father. The latter discouraged all books in the house except the Bible and the hymnal, complained about the children's romping, condemned Friedrich's hobby of drawing, and generally hated joy. Outside the home Friedrich had to face ridicule, scorn, and hostility from the caste-bound youngsters of the village.

Hebbel at the age of twelve tried to learn the mason's trade upon the insistence of his father, but he demonstrated no aptitude whatsoever and finally refused to continue. His father thereafter considered him a ne'er-do-well who squandered his time on reading, drawing, and music. For eight years he acted as clerk to the local magistrate, Mohr. Though he suffered menial treatment from his employer, he had access to Mohr's library and read widely in the German poets and playwrights, Schiller and Kleist especially. He started among the young men of Wesselburen an amateur theater, of which he was the director. A few of his efforts at lyric poetry found their way into contemporary periodicals, including a Hamburg fashion magazine, *New Parisian Modes*. Then the editor, Dr. Amalie Schoppe, got interested in him, raised a fund on his behalf, and invited him to Hamburg for study in the spring of 1835.

Almost at once Hebbel struck up an intimacy with a seamstress and former schoolteacher, Elise Lensing, in whose stepfather's house he boarded temporarily. During the subsequent ten years she not only acted as his confidante and literary agent, but also bore him two sons. Yet he would not marry her for fear of hindering his art.

In the winter of 1839–40 Hebbel completed his first play, *Judith*, a psychological tragedy over which he had long brooded. It deals with the Apocryphal story of Judith the Jewess and her slaying of Holofernes, the Assyrian general. Hebbel's heroine, however, is an introspective modern woman who after the murder feels deep remorse rather than triumph. Dr. Schoppe helped to place *Judith* with the Berlin Court Theater where its premiere occurred in July, 1840. A favorable reception immediately caused the author's name to be known throughout the German literary world.

Since Hebbel's literary efforts were hardly paying him a subsistence, he went in 1842 to Copenhagen and eventually obtained, as a Danish subject, a traveling fellowship from King Christian VIII. When the King two years later refused to renew the fellowship, Hebbel, then in Italy, journeyed to Vienna. Two Austrian noblemen who admired his writings entertained him as their guest. He soon met the charming and noted Viennese actress, Christine Enghaus, speedily proposed, and married her in May, 1846.

Now, through his wife, Hebbel could be connected closely with the Vienna Burgtheater. He therefore returned to playwriting, and in 1848 finished *Herod and Mariamne*, another psychological tragedy on a Jewish situation. His heroine is the modern woman who expects her husband's recognition of her independent being. Christine Hebbel played Mariamne at the Vienna premiere in the next year, but even her superb acting did not bring about the success which *Judith* had experienced before the same audience a few months before.

Nothing daunted, Hebbel proceeded to write *Agnes Bernauer*, the tragedy of a barber's daughter beloved by a prince, but sacrificed finally to the welfare of his dynasty. The play enjoyed an enthusiastic premiere at Munich in 1852. During the next few years the management of the Vienna theater grew cool toward both Hebbel and his wife. His creative enthusiasm waned. Nevertheless he completed in 1860 his most elaborate drama, *The Nibelungs*, a tragic trilogy based on the great German folk epic. It enjoyed a gala production at Weimar in the summer with the author's wife playing the rôles of Brunhild and Kriemhild. During 1862 and 1863 Berlin and Vienna accorded *The Nibelungs* enthusiastic receptions. In November, 1863, it received the supreme dramatic award of the Berlin Schiller Prize. Hebbel at last had caught the admiration of Germany. Amid this triumph he quietly passed away on December 13.

Hebbel's career as a playwright discloses his inability to break away entirely from the Schiller tradition. He returned again and again to historical material, to romantic crises, and to verse. In *Maria Magdalena* alone he worked out a drama almost wholly independent of the "classical" form and content. This middle-class tragedy, as he called it, stemmed from the tradition which Lessing had instituted with *Miss Sara Sampson* almost a century before. The conventional plays of that German species stressed the opposition existing between the upper and middle classes, and the tragic results of the class feeling. *Maria Magdalena* substitutes a new theme, the tragic effect of middle-class environment on character.

The substitution of this entirely original theme sprang from Hebbel's philosophic turn of mind and his speculations on the relation between life and drama. "All life is struggle of the Individual with the Universe," he asserted. In that struggle the individual is sacrificed to the evolutionary life-process. Every act of self-assertion against environment, the individual's universe, brings on tragedy. That tragedy, however, does not have to depend upon any form of moral guilt, but only upon personal will exerted in some manner which conflicts with the will of environment.

In the evolutionary conflict between men and environment there are from time to time spiritual turning-points. These historical crises offer the most appropriate subjects for dramatic tragedy, because they illuminate more significantly the sacrifice of the individual for the development of a higher from a lower order of life. Such a crisis, according to Hebbel, existed right in his own age with the dawning of a new morality in respect to family and honor. *Maria Magdalena* embodies the contemporary crisis, where an ethics based on human necessity opposes the old formal morality. The tragic essence of *Maria Magdalena* is the inevitable personal sacrifice attendant upon the evolution of a better society from an outworn order. Hebbel's middle-class tragedy heralded the birth of a world-wide drama of sociology and ethics.

"MARIA MAGDALENA"

Maria Magdalena was begun at Copenhagen about March, 1843, and completed at Paris in December. The Berlin Theater, to which Hebbel first sent the play, refused performance on the ground that the subject was indelicate. The stage premiere finally occurred at Königsberg in March, 1846. Two years later the Vienna Burgtheater gave an impressive production with Christine Hebbel in the rôle of Klara. By the end of the century the tragedy had found its way into the standard repertoire of the German theaters and has been often revived.

At first Hebbel intended to entitle his tragedy after the heroine, Klara. The longer, however, his imagination brooded over this dishonored girl and her unselfish love, the more he was reminded of the New Testament fallen woman, Mary Magdalene, who "loved much" and gave her all to Jesus. He decided in the end to use the Biblical name for symbolic color.

Much personal experience lay behind the creation of *Maria Magdalena*. Hebbel's own home background colored its stern picture of family life. Master Anton, the carpenter, bears a strong resemblance to Hebbel's father, the stone-mason. The well and the pear tree in the garden recall the surroundings of the Wesselburen homestead. Childhood memories fused with later contacts and observations. Hebbel, soon after his arrival at Munich in 1836, had formed a liaison with the daughter of Anton Schwarz, a Catholic master-carpenter. Josepha Schwarz was a simple, affectionate, religious girl, the original of Klara in *Maria Magdalena*. Josepha too had had an unfortunate love affair, for which Hebbel, just as the Secretary in the play, had been inclined to blame the girl when he first heard of it. While he was living in the Schwarz house, the police arrested the spendthrift son for theft. According to Hebbel, "the whole respectable house was filled with gloom" by reason of the public disgrace. He incorporated the son, the arrest, and the family reaction in *Maria Magdalena*. The tragedy inherent in such an environment of oppressive respectability fixed itself even more deeply upon his consciousness when he saw his Hamburg mate, Élise Lensing, subjected to scandal and humiliation as an unwed mother.

The firm, austere pattern in which Hebbel cast *Maria Magdalena* mingles tradition and innovation. The few asides and soliloquies echo the technique of the Schiller drama, as do the linked scenes within the acts. On the other hand, Hebbel practises a new economy of structure by substituting for the prevailing mode of four or five acts a three-act division. Additional dramatic concentration is derived from the use of a single setting except in the first half of the final act. It is probable that even the earliest German productions of *Maria Magdalena* employed a "box-set," that is, a set with three walls and a ceiling to convey the illusion of a complete room. This important step in the direction of pictorial realism on the stage took place on the Continent a good while before it did in England, where the first instance of a box-set seems to date from 1841.

Hebbel's dramaturgy in *Maria Magdalena* shows the development of two devices to a degree of psychological subtlety far beyond any previous treatment in world drama. One of the devices is called "retrospective" or "analytic" exposition, a method of exposition which bit by bit discloses the molding of present characters and circumstances from vital factors out of the past. Master Anton's reminiscences to Leonhard about the harshness of his childhood, and about his sensitivity and awkwardness (Act I, Sc. 5, ll. 228–87) explain his now stern and touchy nature. Karl's soliloquy, in which he quotes bitterly his father's habitual injunctions (Act III, Sc. 7), reveals how the strict regimen of his home turned him into a rebellious youth. These and other detailed glimpses of the earlier life of the individual characters emphasize the inevitable conditioning of the present by the past.

The second of Hebbel's dramaturgical devices is more or less a complement to the first. He focused not only on concrete details from the past, but also on definite objects in the present which symbolize the inwardness of both character and situation. He insisted in reference to his characters that "all their utterances must relate to something external; only then does their inner nature come out vividly and expressively." Hence at the very opening of *Maria Magdalena* the mother in her wedding gown really betokens the mother in her shroud. Her spirit, aggravated by illness to pious morbidity, has already departed from the world. But there may well be another and more profound symbolism connected with the Mother and her dress. She cherishes it not merely from sentiment, but from the belief that it possesses a certain ageless style. Klara remarks, however, that *this time* the dress has *not fully* come back into fashion. That comment may be taken as Hebbel's judgment on the state of the society which his play sets forth. The mother typifies the complacency of the old middle-class order which thinks its principles never outmoded for good and all. In reality, it is clinging to a moral garment now finally antiquated beyond the redemption of the fashion cycle.

The milieu of antiquated morality exhibits a peculiar imperviousness to new values. There is almost no inclination to reason about or criticize class tradition, even when it operates with fatal effect. Each individual, however, tries to do right according to the narrow ethics which he has inherited. Therefore no one, in Hebbel's opinion, should be called guilty of the ensuing tragedy. The playwright declared: "The old man had become a giant, and Leonhard is merely a clown, no rascal; the son, the Secretary, all are blameless... and yet through the conflict of fundamentally opposed natures there results the most terrible tragedy." Master Anton, the inflexible father, whom Hebbel considered the chief character, is the passive victim, puzzled to the end by his lack of harmony with the world about him. He cannot imagine any higher point of view than his rigid code of honorableness. Klara, the active victim, is almost as much bound to that code. Love for her father and consequent loyalty to his standards of conduct transcend all personal convictions (Act III, Sc. 2, ll. 77–85). She sacrifices her life to prevent what would bring dishonor and death to him. Though the code of Klara and her father has largely disappeared, *Maria Magdalena* still endures as a provocative drama which points beyond its morally bankrupt society toward a day of more enlightened feeling.

[For the early German stage, see Karl Mantzius, *A History of Theatrical Art*, (6 vols., 1903–21); for the German romantic movement, Walter Silz, *Early German Romanticism* (1929); for later German drama, G. Wilkowski, *The German Drama of the Nineteenth Century* (2d ed., 1909); for Hebbel, Edna Purdie, *Friedrich Hebbel* (1932).]

FRIEDRICH HEBBEL

Maria Magdalena

A Tragedy of the Middle Class

[Translated by PAULA GREEN]

DRAMATIS PERSONAE

MASTER ANTON, *a carpenter*   KARL, *his son*   WOLFRAM, *a merchant*   A Boy

TERESA, *his wife*   LEONHARD   ADAM, *a bailiff*   A Servant Girl

KLARA, *his daughter*   A Secretary   Another bailiff

The Scene is a fair-sized town of Germany in the early nineteenth century.

ACT I

A room in ANTON'S *house.*

SCENE I

Enter KLARA *and her* MOTHER

Klara. Your wedding gown? Oh! How becoming! It looks as if it had been made just today!

Mother. That is true, child; you see, fashion runs ahead until it can run no further and 5 must turn back. This dress has been already ten times out of fashion, and each time it has come in again.

Klara. But not quite so this time, mother dear! The sleeves are too wide. You 10 must not be angry for my saying it.

Mother (*laughing*). If I were, I should only be *you.*

Klara. Well, then! Is that the way you looked? But you wore a wreath, I hope? 15

Mother. I should say so! Did I not nurse a little myrtle tree in a flowerpot for many years before my wedding?

Klara. I so often asked you to put on that dress, but you would never do it; you used 20 to say, "It is no longer my wedding gown, it is to be my shroud, and with such a thing we must not play." Finally I began to hate it, because hanging there in all its whiteness, it

reminded me of the day when the old 25 women will come and put it on you. What made you put it on today?

Mother. If people are as sick as I, and do not know whether they will ever get well again or not, then many a thought passes through 30 their minds, child. Death is more awful than we think. It is bitter! It darkens the world; it blows out all lights, one after another. All the lights that used to shimmer around us in such sparkling brightness! The friendly 35 eyes of a husband and the shimmering eyes of the children stop shining, and all grows black around us. But in our hearts a light is lit, there it will be bright, and then we see many things that we don't like to see. I don't remem- 40 ber of having done anything particularly wicked; I always observed the Lord's Commandments, have worked in the house all I could; I brought you up, you and your brother, in the fear of the Lord, and I saved all I could of 45 your father's earnings, and yet I always had a penny to spare for the poor. If now and then I refused to give, just because the man came at the wrong time, or because there were too many who came, it was not his loss, as I always 50 called him back and gave him more for it. But of what avail is all that! We tremble just the same when our last hour threatens to approach. We wriggle like a worm in the dust; we implore

God to grant us some more time, just 55
like a servant who implores his master to give
him another chance, so that he may not lose his
job.

Klara. Stop, mother dear, it tires you too
much!   60

Mother. No, my child, it does me good to
talk about it! I am all right now. The
Lord did not call me. He merely wanted to
warn me, to make me see that the festival garment is not quite clean and pure. He 65
made me turn back from the gate of the grave
and gave me a respite to prepare properly for
the heavenly wedding feast! He was not as
merciful as all that to the Seven Virgins in the
gospel, of whom you read to me last night. 70
That is why I wish to wear this gown today for
Communion. I wore it the day that I felt
most pious and made the best resolutions for
my life. It is to remind me of all the good resolutions which I did not keep. 75

Klara. Mother, you talk as you used to
when you were sick!

SCENE 2

Karl (*entering*). Good-morning, mother!
Well, Klara, what do you think of me?
Wouldn't you just fall in love with me, if I
were not your brother?

Klara. A gold chain? How did you get it? 5

Karl. What do I work for? Why do you
think that I stay two hours longer in the shop
than my comrades? You are impudent to ask
such questions, miss.

Mother. Quarreling on a Sunday morn- 10
ing! Shame on you, Karl!

Karl. Mother, have you no money you can
give me?

Mother. I have no money to spare. All I
have is household money. 15

Karl. Give me some of that! I'll not kick
if the pancakes are somewhat less rich. You
did it before, when you were saving for a white
dress for Klara. For months we had nothing
good on the table. I closed my eyes to it, 20
but I knew very well that something like a new
hat or dress was behind it. Let me, for once,
have a share in it, too!

Mother. You are impudent!

Karl. I have no time, or —— 25
(*He is about to leave.*

Mother. Where are you going?

Karl. I am not going to tell you, then you
need not blush when the old crank asks where
I am and you have to say that you don't
know. By the way, I don't need your 30
dollar, it is just as well! (*To himself*) Here
at home they think the worst of me, anyhow;
why should I not enjoy frightening them a little?
Why should I tell them that since I cannot get
the dollar, I'll have to go to church, unless 35
some friend comes along and helps me? (*Exit.*

SCENE 3

Klara. What does he mean?

Mother. Oh! He'll break my heart! Father
is right! These are the consequences! He
demands money now as defiantly as he used to
beg sweetly and irresistibly for a piece of 5
sugar when he was a little curly-headed boy.
I wonder whether he would ask for the dollar,
if I had refused him the sugar in those days?
That question often torments me now! And
I almost think he does not even love me. 10
Did you ever see him shed a tear while I was
sick?

Klara. I saw him very little, only at table.
He had a better appetite than I, to be sure!

Mother (*quickly*). That was but natural; 15
he had to do heavy work.

Klara. Of course! All men are that way.
They are more ashamed of tears than of their
worst sins! Ready at all times to show fight,
but never to show tears. Father is the 20
same. Didn't he cry like a child that day, when
they tried to bleed you and the blood would not
come? He was in his workshop and I felt so
sorry for him and caressed him; he said: "I
wonder whether you can get that splinter 25
out of my eye. There is so much to be done
and somehow or other always something like
that to interfere with my work."

Mother (*smiling*). Indeed! Well! Well! By
the way, what about Leonhard? I have 30
not seen him here for quite a while. How is
that?

Klara. Well, let him stay away, if he wants to!

Mother. I hope you do not meet him in 35 any other place than your home?

Klara. Do I stay so long when I go to the well in the evenings, that you are suspicious?

Mother. No, indeed! But I gave him 40 permission to see you here in our house so he wouldn't meet you secretly. That is the way my mother used to do.

Klara. I don't see him!

Mother. Did you have a falling out with 45 him? I rather like him. He is staid and settled! If he only had his position secured. In my time he would not have needed to wait so long. People were more than anxious for a good clerk, for they were very scarce. 50 Even small people like ourselves had use for such a man. They were given all kinds of clerking, such as writing a New Year's congratulation for a son to his father, and for the initial letter in gold and silver he 55 was paid enough money to buy a child's blanket. Then the next day the father asked him on the side to read that document to him, of course in secret, with all the doors locked, so that his ignorance would not be dis- 60 closed to his son. That meant double pay, of course. In those days the scribes played quite a part. But things have changed; now we old people who do not know how to read and write are laughed at by nine-year- 65 old youngsters. The world is getting too smart lately. Perhaps there will be a time when people have to be ashamed because they cannot dance on a rope.

Klara. There goes the bell! 70

Mother. Well, child, I pray for you. And as to Leonhard, love him as he loves God, no more, no less. These were the words my mother said to me, when she left this world and gave me her blessing. I kept that blessing 75 long enough and now I hand it on to you!

Klara (*giving her a bouquet*). Here!

Mother (*smiling*). From Karl, I suppose?

Klara (*nodding, then in an aside*). I wish it were! If anything is to give her pleasure 80 it must be from him.

Mother. He is good and loves me so dearly. (*Exit.*)

Klara (*looking after her through the window*). There she goes! Three times I saw her in her coffin, and now — oh, those terrible dreams! They clothe themselves in garments of 85 fear to frighten all our hopes. I will never believe in dreams again. I will not rejoice over a good one, so that I need not fear an evil one that may follow it. What a firm step she has. There she is already at the cemetery. I 90 wonder who will be the first one to meet her? I don't want it to mean anything, I only think —— (*Frightened*) The gravedigger! He just dug a grave and got out. She is greeting him and is looking into the dark hole; there 95 she throws the bouquet into it and enters the church. (*A hymn is heard being sung.*) They are singing. (*She folds her hands.*) Indeed, if mother had died I should never have been happy again, for —— (*with a glance toward* 100 *heaven*) But Thou art merciful! How I wish I were a Catholic, then I could make Thee a present. I would empty my whole bank and buy Thee a beautifully worked heart in gold and wind roses all around it. Our pastor 105 says that sacrifice is of no account to Thee, because all things are Thine, and we cannot give Thee what Thou already possessest. But all things in this house are my father's, too, and yet he likes me to buy him a handkerchief 110 and to embroider it for his birthday and put it at his place at table. Indeed! He even does me the honor to wear it only on high feast days, such as Christmas or Pentecost! Once I saw a tiny Catholic girl carrying cherries to the 115 altar. Oh! How pleased I was! They had been the first ones in that season and had been given her, and I noticed how eager she was for a taste of them. Yet she overcame her desire. She threw them away at the altar, quickly, 120 to end the temptation. The priest, who was just raising the chalice, looked angrily at her; she got frightened and ran off. But the Holy Virgin over the altar smiled down upon her, as if she wished to step out of her frame 125 and run after the child to kiss her. I did it in her place. Alas! Here is Leonhard!

Scene 4

Leon. (before the door). Are you dressed?

Klara. Since when are you so considerate? I am no princess.

Leon. (enters). I did not know that you were alone! While passing I thought I had 5 noticed Barbara from next door standing by the window.

Klara. Oh, is that the reason?

Leon. You are always in a bad humor. I may stay away for two whole weeks; rain 10 and sunshine may have come and gone ten times but there'll always be the same cloud in your face when I return.

Klara. There were times when things were very different. 15

Leon. Indeed! If you had always looked as you do now, I doubt that we ever would have become friends.

Klara. And what if we had not?

Leon. Do you feel yourself so free from 20 me? Well! I don't object, it is all the same to me. Then (*significantly*) your toothache the other day did not mean anything?

Klara. Leonhard, it was wrong of you!

Leon. Wrong! That I tied you, the 25 greatest of all my treasures, closer and firmer to me by the last bond? And at the very moment when I ran in danger of losing you? Do you think I did not see the furtive glances you exchanged with the secretary? Indeed, a 30 nice how-do-you-do! I take you to a dance, and ——

Klara. Stop insulting me! I looked at the secretary, why should I deny it? But only on account of his mustache, which he grew 35 while away at college, and which ——

(*She stops.*)

Leon. Is so becoming to him. That's what you wanted to say. Oh, you women! You are enchanted with such things as that, even in caricatures. The fool — I make no secret 40 of the fact that I hate him. He stood long enough in my way to you — he reminds me with his forest of hair, parted in the middle, of a rabbit hiding behind a bush.

Klara. I never praised him, so you need 45 not make fun of him.

Leon. You seem, nevertheless, warmly interested in him.

Klara. We used to play together as children, and afterward — you know it very well! 50

Leon. Do I know it? Indeed, I do! Just on that account.

Klara. Well, then, it was but natural that seeing him again after all those years, I should look at him, and marvel at his height and 55 how —— (*Interrupts herself.*

Leon. Why did you blush when he looked at you?

Klara. I thought he was looking at the wart on my left cheek, and I wondered whether 60 it had grown. You know, I always imagine *that* whenever anybody gazes at me, and I always blush. I feel as if that wart is growing each time anyone looks at it.

Leon. Well, anyway, I lost all control 65 and I thought: "This very night I shall test her. If she really wishes to marry me, then she knows that she risks nothing in giving herself to me completely. If she refuses, then ——"

Klara. Indeed! You said very wicked 70 words when I pushed you away from me and jumped up from the bench we were sitting on. The moon, which until then assisted me by shining gently into the arbor, suddenly drowned itself in the wet clouds. I 75 wanted to hurry away, but I felt myself detained. First, I thought it was you, but it was a rosebush which clung to my dress with its thorns. You outraged my feelings and I did not trust them any longer myself. You 80 stood before me like one who demands payment of a debt. I —— Oh, heavens!

Leon. I am not sorry for it. I know that otherwise you would never be mine, that it was the only way to keep you to myself. The 85 old love of your youth opened his eyes again and I could not close them quickly enough.

Klara. When I reached home I found my mother sick — sick unto death. Suddenly she had been stricken as if by some invisible 90 hand. Father wanted to send for me, but she would not have it, so as not to disturb my pleasure. You cannot imagine how I felt when I heard it. I kept away from her, I did not dare touch her, I trembled. She took it 95 for my anxiety for her and beckoned me to her. When I slowly approached, she drew me to her and kissed my desecrated lips. I nearly died. I felt like telling her all. I could have screamed and yelled out to her all I thought and 100 felt: "On my account you are lying here!" And I did so, but my tears and sobs stifled my words. She took my father's hand and pointing to me, she said, "What a loving heart!"

Leon. She is well now. I came to con- 105 gratulate her on her recovery, and — what do you think?

Klara. And?

Leon. To ask your father for your hand.

Klara. Oh! 110

Leon. Don't you want me to?

Klara. Want you to? It would be the death of me if I were not to become your wife, now. But you do not know my father! He does not know why we have to hurry — he cannot 115 know it — and we cannot tell him. A hundred times he declared that he would give his daughter only to a man who has, as he calls it, not only love in his heart, but also bread in the cupboard. He will say, "Wait a year 120 or two, my son." And what will you answer?

Leon. Little fool! That difficulty has been removed. I got the position, I am appointed cashier.

Klara. You are cashier? And what 125 about the other candidate for the place? The pastor's nephew?

Leon. He was drunk when he came for the examination. He bowed to the stove instead of to the mayor. When he sat down he 130 pushed three cups from the table. You know what a temper the old man has. "Sir!" he yelled, but as yet he controlled himself; he only bit his lips, and his eyes began to sparkle through his glasses like a pair of snakes 135 that are ready to jump, and every muscle in his face was tense. Then the examination in accounting began, and, ha, ha! my rival counted after a self-invented multiplication table which showed very original results. Well! "He 140 is miscalculating," the mayor said, and giving me a glance that assured me of my installation, shook hands with me, and, although they smelt of tobacco, I kissed them most humbly. Here

is the document, signed and sealed. 145

Klara. That is ——

Leon. Very unexpected, is it not? Well! It was not all mere chance. Do you know why I did not show up here for two whole weeks?

Klara. How do I know? I guess be- 150 cause we had a falling out the Sunday before!

Leon. That little quarrel I brought about myself on purpose, so that I could stay away without its being too conspicuous.

Klara. I don't understand you! 155

Leon. I believe you. I used that time to flirt with the mayor's little hunchback of a niece, who is the old man's pet and his right hand, just as the bailiff is his left. Now, understand me! I did not tell her anything nice 160 and agreeable myself, except a compliment about her hair, which is, as you know, red. I only told her a few things about you that she liked to hear.

Klara. About me? 165

Leon. Why should I keep it a secret from you? I did it with the best intention and for the best purpose. As if I never had cared for you seriously, as if —— Well! Let it go! I did it until I had this here in my hands. The 170 credulous little flirt will soon know how I meant it all — as soon as she hears the banns read in church.

Klara. Leonhard!

Leon. Child! Child! You may be 175 harmless as a dove; let me be wise as a serpent. Then we shall supplement each other, since husband and wife are one, at least according to the Bible. (*Laughs.*) It was not altogether mere chance that young Hermann was intoxi- 180 cated at the most important moment of his life. You never heard that the young fool has always been fond of drinking?

Klara. Never!

Leon. So much easier for my plans. It 185 needed only three glasses. A few of my boon companions had to take him in hand. "May we congratulate you?" "Not yet!" "Oh, but there can be not the slightest doubt about it! Your uncle ——" And then, "Drink! 190 Little brother, drink!" When I was on my way to you just now, he was standing on the bridge, leaning over the railing in a most melancholic attitude and looking into the water. I greeted him somewhat sarcastically and 195 asked if anything of his had fallen into the water. "Yes," he said, without looking up, "and, maybe, it would be better for me if I were to jump after it."

Klara. You wretch! Leave me! Get 200 out of my sight!

Leon. All right!

(*Moves as if he were to comply with her wish.*

Klara. Oh, Heavens! And I am tied to such a man!

Leon. Don't be childish! One more 205 word in confidence. Has your father still that mortgage of one thousand dollars on that drug-store?

Klara. I don't know anything about it.

Leon. Nothing about so important an 210 affair?

Klara. Father is coming.

Leon. Listen! I am asking because the drug-gist is said to be on the brink of bankruptcy.

Klara. I must be off to the kitchen. 215
(*Exit.*

Leon. (*alone*). Well! I declare! All that's lacking now would be if there were nothing for me to get here. But that cannot be. Master Anton is the kind who, if they were to put one letter more upon his tombstone than he 220 deserved, would go about as a spook until they had scratched it off. He would consider it dis-honest to own one letter more of the alphabet than is his due.

SCENE 5

Anton (*entering*). Good morning, Mr. Cashier. (*Takes off his hat and puts on a woolen cap.*) Will you allow an old man to cover his head?

Leon. Then you know already?

Anton. Since last night. I heard a few of your good friends call you by all kinds of 5 names when I went to the home of the dead miller to take the measure for his last house. Then I thought right away, "Well! Leonhard did not break his neck." In the house of the dead man I learned the details from the 10 sexton, who had come with me to comfort the widow and to get drunk.

Leon. And Klara had to learn it from me?

Anton. If you did not feel like giving that pleasure to her, why should I feel like 15 doing it? I do not light any candles in my house except my own. Then I know that no-body can come and extinguish them just at the very moment when we enjoy them most. 19

Leon. I hope you did not think of me ——

Anton. Think? Of you? Of anybody? I polish the boards with my plane to suit my mind, but not men to suit my thoughts. I gave that folly up long ago. If I see a tree turning green, then I think that it will soon blossom. 25 And if it blossoms, then I think, "Now it will soon bear fruit." In that I am not deceived, and for that reason I stick to my old habit. But as to men! I do not think at all of them, nothing at all; neither good nor evil. 30 Then I need not be disappointed if they excite my fear or deceive my hopes. All I do with re-gard to them is to make observations and draw conclusions from what I see. I do not think, but I see. As to you, I think I have had 35 my observations; now, however, that I see you here, it seems that my observation was but half a one, I must confess.

Leon. Master Anton, you are wrong. A tree depends upon wind and weather. Men 40 have rules and laws that they follow.

Anton. Do you think so? Indeed! We old people owe many thanks to death that it allows us to live so long among you young ones, and that the opportunity is given us to educate 45 and form ourselves. In former times this stupid world of ours thought that the father was here to educate his son. It is just the other way. It is the son's duty to give the last touches to his father's education, so that the poor old 50 simpleton need not be ashamed of the worms when he is in his grave. God be praised! I have an excellent teacher in my son Karl, who, regardless of my feelings, and without spoiling the old child, his father, knocks all preju- 55 dices out of him. Thus, for instance, he gave me two lessons just this morning, and in the most skillful manner, at that, without even ex-pressing it in words, without even seeing me, in fact — just on *that* account it was clever. 60 In the first place, he showed me that we need not keep our word; secondly, that it is wholly superfluous to go to church and to freshen up in our minds God's Commandments. Last night he made the promise to go to church. I 65 relied upon this promise, and I believed he would go to church. For I thought, "He will thank the good Lord for having restored his mother's health." But he did not go. It was very comfortable in my pew, which, to be 70 sure, feels very crowded with two people in it. I wonder how he would like it if I were to benefit by his lesson and were to break my word to him? I promised him a new suit of clothing for his birthday, and this would give me a 75 good opportunity to see his joy over my adaptability! But, then, I have still old-fashioned prejudices. Indeed, if it were not for those prejudices! That's why I shall not do it!

Leon. Maybe he was not well —— 80

Anton. Maybe. I need only ask my wife and I shall learn surely that he has been ill. She tells me the truth in all things except in what concerns the boy. And if not sick — that is another advantage that the young have 85 over us old ones — that they can find their edification in anything and everything. Therefore they can pray anywhere, while out hunting, walking, or even in the inn. "Our Father, Who art in Heaven!" — "Hello, Peter, are you 90 here too; going to dance tonight?" — "Hallowed be Thy name!" "Indeed, Catherine, it's easy for you to laugh at me, but we'll get even!" — "Thy will be done!" — "The dickens, I have not been shaved yet!" — And so on, and 95 as to the benediction, well! They can give *that* themselves, too, for they are men just as well as the preacher, and the power that is in the black gown is also in a blue coat. I don't object by any means, and if you wish to insert 100 between the seven supplications seven drinks, what does it matter? I cannot prove that beer and religion do not go together. And, maybe, it will become *the thing* to take Holy Communion that way. Old sinner that I am, of 105 course, I am not strong enough to keep step with Dame Fashion; I cannot catch devotion like a fly in the air. The chirping of the swallows and sparrows cannot take the place of the organ with me. If I am to have my 110

heart uplifted, then the heavy iron doors of the church have to close behind me and I must imagine that they are the gates of the world, and the gloomy high walls, with their narrow windows, which allow the bright daylight 115 to penetrate but scantily, must surround me, and in the distance I must be able to see the entrance to the cemetery with the death-head over the gate. Well — well! Maybe it's better that way. Who knows? 120

Leon. You are too exacting.

Anton. Perhaps so! Still, I must confess it is not always wholly true, what I said just now. In church today I was distracted; for the unoccupied seat next to mine made me 125 mad, and out in the garden under the pear tree devotion came back to me. You wonder why? Look here, I went home in sorrow, like a man whose harvest was destroyed by a hailstorm, for our children are the fields. We put 130 our good grain into them and only weeds shoot up. Beneath the pear tree, which has been eaten by caterpillars, I stopped. "Indeed," I thought, "my boy is like that tree here, empty and barren." Suddenly it came to me 135 that I was very thirsty, and that I simply had to go to the inn. I deceived myself, it was not for a glass of beer, it was only to look up the fellow and to give him a piece of my mind, and I knew I should have done so, if I had found 140 him. I was just about to go, when the old tree dropped a juicy pear at my feet, as if it wanted to say, "This is for your thirst, and also because you insulted me by comparing me to that scoundrel, your son." I came back to my 145 senses, bit into the fruit, and went into the house.

Leon. Do you know that the druggist is near bankruptcy?

Anton. What has that to do with me? 150

Leon. Nothing at all?

Anton. Oh! Well! I am a Christian, and the man has a lot of children.

Leon. And still more creditors. Children too, are creditors in a way. 15

Anton. Happy is he who has neither!

Leon. I thought you ——

Anton. Oh, that has been settled long ago.

Leon. You are a careful man. You mos

likely withdrew your money at once, when   160
you saw that things went against him.

Anton. So I did. I need no longer worry
about losing anything, since I lost all long ago.

Leon. You are joking!

Anton. No, indeed not!   165

Klara (*looking into the room through the open
door*). Did you call, father?

Anton. Are your ears ringing? We did not
talk about you.

Klara. The paper!   (*Exit.*

Leon. You are a philosopher.   170

Anton. What do you mean?

Leon. You know how to take things coolly.

Anton. Once in awhile I carry a millstone
around my neck just in place of a collar. Instead of going into the water with it —   175
well! It gives you a stiff backbone.

Leon. All who can would like to do the same,
I guess.

Anton. People who find such a companion as
you seem to be, ready to help carry the   180
burden, ought to be able even to dance beneath
it. You have become quite pale at this news
— well! That's what I call true sympathy.

Leon. I hope you'll not misjudge me.

Anton. Oh, no! By no means. (*Drum-*   185
ming upon a bureau) Too bad that wood is not
transparent. Don't you think so?

Leon. I don't understand you!

Anton. How stupid of our great-grandfather
to marry Eve, although she was naked   190
and did not even have a fig leaf for a dowry.
We, the two of us, would, no doubt, have
whipped her out of Paradise as a female tramp!
What do you think about it? Hm?

Leon. You are angry about your son. I   195
came to ask you about your daughter ——

Anton. Stop, perhaps I may consent, and
then ——

Leon. I hope you will. And I will tell you a
piece of my mind now. Even the ancient   200
Patriarchs did not scorn the treasures their
wives brought. Jacob loved Rachel and wooed
her for seven years, but he also liked the fat
sheep and rams he gained while in her father's
employ. I think it was no disgrace to   205
do so. I should have liked very much if
your daughter could have brought a few hun-

dred dollars into our household, and that is
but natural, for then I could have given her so
much more comfort. For if a girl brings   210
some wool along with which to line her nest, she
need not gather it. Well! It is not to be!
What does it matter? We'll make our week-
day food do for Sunday dinner, and the Sunday roast will be our Christmas dinner.   215
Things will go all right that way, too.

Anton (*shaking hands with him*). You speak
well! And God will approve of your words!
I'll forget that my daughter for the past two
weeks vainly placed a cup at the table   220
for you for tea at night. Now that you are
to become my son-in-law I'll tell you what
became of the thousand dollars.

Leon. (*to himself*). Gone after all! Well, then
I need not put up with all the whims and   225
caprices of the old fool when he is my father-in-
law.

Anton. In my youth I suffered much want.
I was no porcupine when I was born, any
more than you were, but the world made   230
one of me. First, all my quills were directed
inwards. Here they pressed and pinched my
smooth, yielding skin, and they rejoiced over
my suffering, because the points tore my heart.
I did not like that, I turned my skin   235
inside out, and now the points hurt them who
first laughed at my pains, and since then they
leave me in peace.

Leon. (*to himself*). Even the Devil himself
would leave him alone, I should think.   240

Anton. My father, because he did not take
any rest, night and day, worked himself to
death when only thirty years old. My mother
worked for me and made some money, as well
as she could by spinning. I grew up,   245
without learning anything. When I was bigger
and could not make any money, I should have
liked to get rid of the habit of eating, but, even
if at dinner I acted as if I were sick and pushed
back the plate, what did it matter? At   250
supper my stomach forced me to be well. My
greatest sorrow was that I was wholly un-
schooled, knew no trade. I used to get so
mad about it, as if it had been my fault. I
blushed when the sun shone on me. Right   255
after my confirmation Master Gebhard, the man

buried yesterday, came to us. He wrinkled his forehead and screwed up his face, as he always did when he had something good to tell. Then he said to mother, "Did you bring your 260 boy into the world that he should eat you out of house and home?" I was ashamed, and put the loaf, from which I was just about to cut off a slice, back into the cupboard. Mother was angry at the well-meant words; she stopped 265 the spinning-wheel and answered angrily that her son was a good boy. "Well! We'll see about that," the master answered; "if he wants to, he can, right now, just as he is, go with me to my shop. I don't ask any money 270 for his apprenticeship, I'll give him board and shall also look out for his clothes. And if he is willing to rise early and go to bed late he will not lack — once in a while — an extra penny for his old mother." Mother began to 275 cry and I danced around like one possessed. When I finally recovered speech, the master held his hands to his ears, walked out, and beckoned me to follow him. I did not take my hat, for I hadn't any. Without bidding 280 farewell to mother, I followed; and when on the following Sunday I was allowed to go and see her for an hour or so, he gave me half a ham for her. May God's blessing be with him in his grave. I am still hearing his half 285 grumbling and scolding words: "Tony, hide it, quick, beneath your coat, my wife is coming!"

Leon. I believe you are even crying over it now!

Anton (drying his tears). Yes. Each 290 time I think of it I must cry, however much I may be hardened in other ways. Well, never mind! (*With a sudden turn*) And what would you have done if, when calling on a man to whom you owed everything, in order to 295 smoke a pipe some Sunday afternoon in his company, you were to find that man all upset, a knife in his hand with which he had cut the bread for you many a time? If you were to see blood on his throat, and he were to pull 300 the kerchief close up to his chin ——

Leon. Old Gebhard always had his throat covered tight to the day of his death.

Anton. Yes, on account of the scar. And you were to come just in time, and you 305

could help save the man, not merely by tearing the knife away from him, and dressing the wound, but by giving him the miserable sum of one thousand dollars, which you had saved? And this had to be done on the quiet so 310 as not to excite the sick man, what would you have done in such a case?

Leon. Single as I am, with no wife and child to provide for, I should have sacrificed the money.

Anton. And if you had ten wives like 315 the Turks and as many children as were promised to Father Abraham, and you could have hesitated but for one moment, you'd be, you'd be — well! You are to be my son-in-law. Now you know where the money has gone. To- 320 day I can tell you about it, for my old master is buried. A month ago I would have kept it from everybody, even on my deathbed. The bond I put into the coffin with the dead body, before they closed the lid. I put it beneath his 325 head. If I had known how to write, I should have written beneath it: "Paid honestly." Ignorant as I am, I tore the paper lengthwise. Now, he can rest in peace, and I hope I can do so too, when I shall be put to rest 330 beside him.

SCENE 6

Mother (entering in haste). Do you remember?

Anton (pointing to the wedding gown). The frame indeed has kept well, but not the picture. Too many cobwebs have collected 5 upon it. Well! there has been time enough for them to collect.

Mother (to LEONHARD*).* Don't you think I have a very honest husband? But I need not praise him; honesty is the virtue of all 10 husbands.

Anton. Are you sorry that you were more gold-plated at twenty than you are at fifty?

Mother. No, of course not. If I hadn't been, I should have to be ashamed for you and 15 me.

Anton. Come, kiss me! I am shaved and tidier than usual.

Mother. I will, if only to find out whether you still know how to kiss. What in the 20 world made you think of it?

Anton. Good little wife. I'll not ask you to see me into my grave. It would be too hard on you. I'll perform this last act of charity on you and close your eyes; but you must 25 allow me time for it, do you hear? I'll be strong and must be prepared for the last act of love, so that I'll not blunder. As yet it would be too soon.

Mother. Thank the good Lord in heaven, 30 we'll stay together for a while yet.

Anton. I should hope so. Your cheeks are almost as ruddy as they used to be.

Mother. By the way, our new gravedigger is a funny kind of a man! He dug a grave 35 this morning. When I passed by I asked him for whom he was digging it. "For whomsoever God wishes it to be," he said. "Maybe for my own self; I may fare like my grandfather who dug a grave in advance, and 40 that very night, when returning from the inn, he fell and broke his neck."

Leon. (*who until now has been reading in the weekly paper*). The fellow is not from our town, so he can lie as much as he pleases. 44

Mother. I asked him why he did not wait until a grave is ordered to be dug. He answered that he was asked to a wedding today and that he knew he would not have a clear enough head tomorrow, and he was sure that somebody would be just mean enough to 50 die. Then he would have to get up early the following day without having a chance to rest after the spree.

Anton. Fool! Why did you not ask him, "And what if the grave were too small or 55 too large?"

Mother. That's exactly what I did ask. But you may shake questions out of your sleeve like the Devil the fleas, he would find an answer. "I took measure from 60 Weaver Veit," he said. "He is like King Saul, a head taller than anybody else. Now let come who will. He will not find his house too short. And if it is too long, it will hurt me only, since, as an honest man, I do not make 65 anybody pay for an inch more than the length of his coffin." I threw my flowers into the open space and said, "Now it is filled."

Anton. I think the fellow meant it for a joke,

and that is sinful. To prepare a grave in 70 advance is like setting a trap for death; the rascal who does such a thing ought to be bounced. (*To* LEONHARD, *who is still reading*) Anything new? Does some philanthropist seek a poor widow who needs a few hun- 75 dred dollars? Or does a poor widow want the philanthropist to give it to her?

Leon. The police publish a theft of jewels. Strange — that, in spite of the bad times, there should be people who own such things as 80 jewels.

Anton. A theft of jewelry? Where?

Leon. At Wolfram's.

Anton. At — impossible! Karl polished a desk in his house only a few days ago. 85

Leon. (*to* ANTON). Is that so? The jewelry was taken from a desk.

Mother. May God pardon you for such suspicion.

Anton. You are right. It was an out- 90 rageous thought.

Mother. Well, we know that wherever your son is concerned, you are acting like a stepfather. 94

Anton. Wife, don't let us discuss that today.

Mother. Because he differs from you, is it necessary that he is, on that account, a bad man?

Anton. Where is he, anyhow? The noon hour struck long ago. I bet you that 100 dinner is getting spoiled in the kitchen, because Klara has a secret order not to set the table until he shows up.

Mother. Where is he? Where else but 104 in some bowling alley, and he must take the one farthest away from home, so that you may not discover him. Of course, the return trip is a long one. I really don't know why you are so much against this innocent game.

Anton. Against the game? Not at all! 110 Fine gentlemen must have some sport. Without the king in the card game, the real king would often be bored to death. And if the bowling ball were not invented, who knows if princes and kings would not bowl with 115 our heads! But the worker can commit no greater sin than risk his hard-earned wages. Men must, or ought to, honor what they gain

with difficulty and with the sweat of their brow;
they ought to think highly of it, esteem   120
it, if they are not to lose themselves and think
their whole life's work contemptible. How is
it possible to do our best and keep ourselves
alert for the sake of a dollar that we intend to
throw away!   (*Door-bell rings.* 125
　Mother. Here he is now!

SCENE 7

ADAM *and another bailiff enter*

　Adam (*to* ANTON). Well! Now you may go
and pay your wager! People in red coats with
blue cuffs and collars (*the last three words he
accentuates*) are never to enter your house.
Wasn't that what you said, only the other   5
day? Now, here we are, two of us! (*To the
2d bailiff*) Why did you take your hat off?
Who is going to make so much ado with one's
equal?
　Anton. With one's equal, you rascal?   10
　Adam. You are right, we are not your equal!
Rascals and thieves are not our equals.
(*Points to the bureau.*) Open! And then
stand aside three steps from it! So that you
cannot smuggle anything from it.   15
　Anton. Wh — what? What?
　Klara (*entering with dishes*). Shall I ——
　　　　　　　　　　　　　　　　(*Stops.*
　Adam (*showing a paper*). Can you read
script?
　Anton. How can I know what my   20
schoolmaster did not even know?
　Adam. Then, listen! Your son stole jewels.
We have the thief. Now we are searching
your house.   24
　Mother. Good Lord! (*Falls down and dies.*
　Klara. Mother! Mother! Oh, look at her
eyes!
　Leon. I'll run for the doctor!
　Anton. Not necessary! That is the face of
a dead person. I have seen it a hundred   30
times. Good night, Teresa! You died when
they told you, and that fact ought to be put
on your tombstone.
　Leon. Perhaps —— (*Going away*) Horrible!
But well for myself!   (*Exit.* 35

　Anton (*drawing forth a bunch of keys and
throwing them away*). Here, open! One box
after another! Give me an axe! The key
for the trunk is lost. Oh! You rascals and
thieves! (*Turns his pockets out.*) There is
nothing in here!   40
　2d Bail. Master Anton, compose yourself,
calm down. Everybody knows that you are
the most honest man in town.
　Anton. Is that so? Do you think so?
(*Laughs.*) It seems that I used up all the   45
honesty in our family. The poor boy! Nothing
of it was left for him. She (*pointing to the
dead woman*) was much too honest, too. Who
knows whether or not her daughter —— (*Suddenly turning to* KLARA) What do you   50
think, my innocent little daughter?
　Klara. Father!
　2d Bail. (*to* ADAM). Have you no pity?
　Adam. No pity? Do I search the pockets of
that old fool? Do I force him to take off   55
his stockings? Or to turn his boots upside
down? I had had the intention of doing it, for I
hate him as much as I can hate a man, ever since
that day in the inn, when he took his glass and
—— Well! You know the story. And you,   60
too, ought to feel the same way if you had a
spark of honor in you. (*To* KLARA) Where
is your brother's room?
　Klara (*pointing to it*). In the back.   64
　　　　　　　　　　　(*Both bailiffs go out.*
　Klara. Father, he is innocent! He cannot
be guilty! He is your son! He is my brother!
　Anton. Innocent! And the murderer of his
mother.   (*Laughs.*
　A Servant Girl (*entering with a letter in her
hand*). From the cashier Leonhard.
　　　　　　　　　　　　　　　　(*Exit.*
　Anton. You need not read it. He is   70
breaking his engagement to you! Well done!
You rascal!   (*Beats his hands.*
　Klara (*having read the letter*). Yes! It is
so! Oh, my God!
　Anton. Let him go.   75
　Klara. Father! Father! I cannot! Oh,
my God!
　Anton. Cannot? You cannot? What
do you mean? Are you ——   79

Both bailiffs return

Adam (maliciously). Seek and you shall find.

2d Bail. (to ADAM*).* What nonsense! It does not apply to this case.

Adam. Shut up!   (*Both bailiffs go out.*

Anton. He is innocent and you — you ——

Klara. Father! Oh, you are horrible! 85

Anton (taking her hand, gently). My dear little daughter, Karl is only a blunderer. He killed his mother. And what is that after all! His father is still alive! Help him! Go to his aid! You cannot ask him to do the 90 whole job alone. Give me the last blow. It is true, the old tree looks strong, but it is already tottering. It will not cost much of an effort to strike it down. You need no axe, you have a pretty face, I never told you so before, 95 but today I may as well tell you, so that you may have courage and confidence in yourself. Your eyes, your nose, and your mouth will find, I am sure, many admirers — therefore you may become —— 100

Klara (half insane, falls at the feet of the dead woman, and calls out like a child). Mother! Mother!

Anton. Seize the hand of your dead mother and swear to me that you are what you ought to be! 105

Klara. I — swear — to you — that — I — shall — never — bring — disgrace — upon — you! Never!

Anton (taking his hat and putting it on). All right, then. Fine weather today. Let's 110 run the gauntlet up one street and down the next.   (*Exit.*

ACT II

A room in ANTON'S *house. A week later.*

SCENE I

ANTON *rises from the table.* KLARA *is about to clear it*

Anton. Again you have not eaten anything.

Klara. I have had enough.

Anton. Of nothing?

Klara. I ate some in the kitchen.

Anton. Only people with a bad con- 5 science don't eat. Well! We'll see. Time will show. Or was there any poison in the soup, as I dreamt last night? Some herb might, by chance, have come in with the vegetables? Then you did well! 10

Klara. Oh, heavens!

Anton. Pardon me, I — go to the dickens with your everlasting air of suffering, which you stole from the Mother of our Lord. You ought to have red cheeks, like all young 15 people have. Only one person has a right here to look that way, and he does not do so. Well! Praising one's self would be boasting, but what did I do when our neighbor was about to nail the lid on your mother's coffin? 20

Klara. You tore the hammer from his hands and did it yourself, and said, "This is to be my masterpiece." The deacon, who was just singing with the choir boys before the door, thought you had gone crazy. 25

Anton. Crazy? (*Laughs.*) Crazy! Indeed! He has a wise head upon his shoulders, and he will lose it some day. Mine is too firmly planted upon me, or — I was sitting comfortably in some part of the world and 30 thought that I had found a good shelter, when suddenly a light was put upon the table, and, behold! I was in a robber's den, and the attack came from all directions, but what does it matter? Fortunately I was given a heart 35 of stone.

Klara. Yes, father, so it is!

Anton. What do you know of it? Do you, perhaps, think you have a right to curse the world with me, just because your clerk has 40 abandoned you? Some other man will take you out for a Sunday walk; some other man will make you his wife, if you deserve it. But suppose for thirty long years you have borne all burdens that life brings, patiently and in 45 honor, never grumbling at them. Suppose you have borne it all — life, death, and every other misfortune in patience and with resignation, and then suddenly your son comes, he who was to be the prop of your old age, and brings 50 disgrace upon you; such disgrace that you want to implore the earth, "Devour me, if you are not overcome by disgust, for I am dirtier than you." Then you have a right to pro-

nounce all the curses that swell your heart. 55
Then you may tear out your hair and beat
your breast. I'll give you that privilege and
you shall have this advantage over me, for you
are a woman.

Klara. Oh, Karl! 60

Anton. I wonder what I'll do to him when I
have him again before me. Some evening, before the lights are brought in, he will enter the
room, his head shaved — for in jail they do not
allow fancy head-dressing — and he will 65
stammer out his "Good evening," his hand on
the doorknob. I'll do something for sure, but
cannot tell what it will be. (*Gnashing his teeth*)
And if they will keep him ten years, he'll find
me. And I'll live that long, I know I shall! 70
Mark my words, Death. Henceforth I am a
stone for your scythe; it will break rather than
move me from my place.

Klara (*taking his hand*). Father, you ought
to lie down for an hour or so. 75

Anton. In order to dream that you are to be
delivered of an illegitimate child? Then, that
I grab you, pack you off, and, coming to my
senses again, say, "Dear daughter, I did not
know what I was doing"? No! Thank 80
you! My slumber took a prophet into its services, who shows me the most horrible things
with his bloody fingers. And I don't know how
it is, but all things seem possible to me now.
Oh! I shudder when I think of the future. 85
I shrink from it as from a glass of water, seen
through a microscope — is that the word,
schoolmistress? You spelled the word for me
the other day. I looked through one once, in
Nuremberg,[1] at the fair, and could not 90
drink for the rest of the day. I saw "dear
Karl" last night with a pistol in his hand;
when I looked close at the hero, he fired it off.
I heard a scream, but could not see for the
smoke, and when the smoke vanished 95
gradually, I saw no broken skull, but my gentleman of a son had in the meanwhile become
a very rich man. He stood and counted gold
pieces from one hand into the other. His face
was — the devil take me, one could look 100
no calmer on closing up shop after a day's work!

[1] A large and picturesque city of Bavaria in southern
Germany.

Klara. Calm yourself, father!

Anton. Get well, you mean! Why am I sick?
Why not ask me that? Yes, physician, give
me medicine to make me well. Your 105
brother is a bad son, be a good daughter to me.
I must appear to the world like a miserable
bankrupt. I owed it a good strong man, who
could have taken the place of this old invalid,
and I deceived it by giving it such a 110
rascal and scamp. Be as good a woman as
your mother was, then people will say, "It was
not the parents' fault that the boy went wrong,
for the girl is straight and a model for all
women." (*With horrible coldness*) And 115
I'll do my share, I'll make matters easy for you.
The very moment that I notice people pointing
their fingers at you, I'll — I'll — (*with a motion
at his throat*) shave myself, and I swear to you,
I'll shave this whole head off. You may 120
spread the rumor that I did it by accident, in
sudden terror, because I saw a horse run away
in the streets, or the cat had overturned a chair
on the floor above, or a mouse ran across the
floor. The people who know me, it is 125
true, will shake their heads, for I am not nervous, as a rule, but what does it matter? I
could not live if people were to throw pitying
glances at me, or perhaps scorn me.

Klara. Oh, Almighty God, what am I 130
to do?

Anton. Nothing! Nothing! Dear child, I
know I am too harsh with you. Nothing!
Only be as you are now, then all will be well
and good. Heavens! I suffered such 135
great wrong that I have to do wrong, so that I
may not collapse. Look here! I just crossed
the street a short while ago, when Smallpox
Fritz passed by, that thief whom I a few years
ago had had arrested and convicted be- 140
cause he had robbed me three times. Ever
since then the scoundrel did not dare look at
me. This time he stretched out his hand to
shake mine. I was about to strike him down,
when suddenly I remembered that we 145
have been cousins for the past week, and relatives have to exchange greetings with one another. Our pastor, the kind man, called on me
yesterday. To be sure, he tried to tell me that
we are responsible only for our own mis- 150

deeds, not for those of others. He told me that it is arrogance on my part to feel responsible for my son's conduct: that, if this were the case, Adam himself would have to feel as badly as I. "Well, sir," I said, "I fully believe 155 that it will not disturb the peace of our first father in Paradise, if one of his distant descendants murders and steals, but did he not tear his hair over Cain?" No! No! I cannot stand it; it is too much. Once in a while I look 160 around for my shadow, just to see if it did not get darker. I can stand almost anything, I have given proof of that, but I cannot stand shame and disgrace. Put any burden you like upon my back, only do not cut the one 165 nerve which holds me together.

Klara. Father, as yet Karl did not confess anything, and they did not find the jewels with him.

Anton. What does that matter? I 170 went all over town and inquired about his debts in all the inns, and it was more than he could have made in my shop for the next three months, were he three times as industrious as he is. Now I also know the reason for his 175 working two hours overtime every day. But he saw all that could not have helped much, and therefore he took an easier road, and a quicker one, too, when opportunity presented itself. 180

Klara. You always believed the worst of Karl. You always did so. Don't you remember when ——

Anton. You talk like your mother, and I shall answer you as I would answer her — 185 by silence.

Klara. And what if Karl should be found innocent, after all? And what if the jewels were to be found?

Anton. Then I would hire a lawyer and 190 risk my last penny to see if the mayor has the right to have an honest man's son put into jail for nothing at all. And if so, then I have to submit, for what can happen to any man in the country may also happen to me, even if I 195 have to pay dearer for it than most other men. I'll accept it as my fate. I'll take it as a blow coming from God, and I'll fold my hands and say, "Lord, Thou knowest the reason for this

trial." But, if he has no right to do so, if 200 the man with the golden chain round his neck has been too hasty, thinking only that the man robbed is his brother-in-law, then I shall find out the why and wherefore. The king knows well that he owes justice to his subjects in 205 exchange for our loyalty and obedience to him. He does not like to own amends be made. — But all that is stuff and nonsense. The boy is as guilty as can be. He will as likely come forth innocent and guiltless from the trial — as 210 likely as your mother will ever come to life again in this world! I shall never derive comfort or joy from that scoundrel. Therefore, do not forget what you owe me. You keep to your oath, so that I need not keep mine. 215 (*He goes, but turns back again.*) I shall be home late tonight, as I have to go into the mountains to see the old lumber-dealer. He is the only man who is still greeting me, because he does not know of my disgrace. The man is deaf. 220 They can't tell him anything without screaming themselves hoarse over it, and even then he does not understand the story right — that's why he does not learn any news. (*Exit.*

SCENE 2

Klara (*alone*). Oh, Lord! My God! Have pity upon me! Have pity upon the old man! Take me! He cannot be helped in any other way! See, the sun shines so beautifully in the streets that the children try to grasp 5 it with their hands. The birds fly to and fro; flowers and herbs do not tire out and give up. Everything is alive and wishing to live. Thousands of sick people are trembling in fear of you, Death! Whoever cried for you last 10 night because he could no longer bear his pain, is satisfied now and thinks his bed soft and comfortable. But I cry to you for help! Spare him whose soul is most afraid of you, give him a respite until this beautiful world seems 15 again sad and barren to him, and take me in his stead. I shall not shudder when you are reaching out your cold hand for me. I shall grasp it courageously and follow you more joyfully than any human child has ever fol- 20 lowed you.

SCENE 3

Wolf. (entering). Good morning, Miss Klara! Your father at home?

Klara. He just left.

Wolf. I came — My jewels are found.

Klara. Oh, father! I wish you were here! 5 He forgot his glasses. How I wish he would miss them and come back for them! How? Where? With whom?

Wolf. My wife —— Tell me frankly, Miss Klara, did you never hear strange stories 10 about her?

Klara. Yes, I did.

Wolf. (breaking out in despair). Good Lord! All in vain! No servant who ever entered my house was allowed to go away, I gave them 15 double wages, and overlooked everything, only to buy their silence. And yet — those false, ungrateful creatures! My poor children! It was only for your sake that I tried to hide it all.

Klara. Do not blame your servants. 20 They are innocent. Since your neighbor's house burnt down — at the time when they saw your wife by the window laughing and clapping her hands, and trying to blow at the fire with full cheeks, as if she wanted it to 25 burn higher — since then it was only a question whether she was a devil or crazy. Hundreds of people saw her do it.

Wolf. It is the truth. Now that the whole town knows of my misfortune it would be 30 foolish if I were to ask you to promise silence. Well! Listen! The theft for which your brother is in jail was committed by an insane woman.

Klara. Your own wife! 35

Wolf. I have known for a long time that she, formerly the noblest and most charitable person in the world, had become malicious and took pleasure in seeing misfortune striking others. She is delighted when a servant 40 breaks a glass or cuts her finger. What I did not know, however, was that she takes all kinds of things — money and other things — and hides them from us. She takes paper, too, a thing I only learned today, at my ex- 45 pense. I was lying down, and was just about to fall asleep when I noticed her approaching me gently, examining me closely to see if I were asleep. I closed my eyes firmly. She took the key from the pocket of my vest (which 50 I had hung over my chair), opened my desk, took out a roll of money, locked it again, and put the key back. I was horror-struck, but controlled myself, so that I would not disturb her. She left the room, I glided after her 55 on tiptoes. She went to the attic, and there she threw the roll into an old chest, empty ever since grandfather's time. When she departed, I lit a candle, and searched the chest. Here I found my youngest daughter's doll, a pair 60 of slippers belonging to one of our maids, an account book, letters, and, worst of all, or rather fortunately, at the very bottom I found the jewels.

Klara. And my poor mother! It is hor- 65 rible!

Wolf. God knows that I would willingly lose the jewels could I thereby make reparation. But it is not my fault. If my suspicion fell upon your brother, in spite of my great 70 esteem for your father, it was but natural. He had polished the desk, and the jewels disappeared with him. I noticed the disappearance almost immediately, for I had to take some papers from the drawer in which they had 75 been. I did not think of taking any severe measures right away. All I did was to tell the bailiff, Adam, to investigate the matter discreetly. The bailiff, however, would not consent to keep the matter a secret. He 80 told me that he was in duty bound to report the case right away. Your brother, he said, is a drunkard and overwhelmed with debts. Unfortunately, the mayor thinks so much of Adam that the fellow can do as he pleases. 85 The man seems to have a deathly hatred against your father, I don't know why. It was an utter impossibility to pacify him. He would not listen to me, but in running out he cried, "If you were to make me a present of 90 the jewels it could not have made me happier than this!"

Klara. The bailiff once put his glass next to my father's when they were in the inn and nodded to my father, as if he wanted to 95 click glasses with him. My father withdrew his glass and said: "People in red coats with blue cuffs and collars had formerly to drink from glasses with a wooden base; they had also to stand modestly outside, and take their 100 hats off when the host offered them a drink. If they wanted to click glasses with anybody, they had to wait until the hangman came to them." Oh, God! My God! To think that my poor mother had to pay for all this 105 with her life!

Wolf. It is a dangerous thing to arouse anybody, especially bad people! Where is your father?

Klara. He went into the mountains to 110 see the lumber-dealer.

Wolf. I shall ride in that direction to meet him. I was at the mayor's before, but unfortunately he was not at home, or else your brother would be home by now. The sec- 115 retary sent a messenger after him. You'll see your brother before night, though.   (*Exit.*

SCENE 4

Klara (alone). Now I ought to feel happy. Oh, my God! My God! I can think of nothing else but "Now it is only you!" Yet certainly some idea will come to me which will make it all turn out right in the end.   5

SCENE 5

Secretary (entering). Good morning!

Klara (supporting herself by a chair to keep from falling). Oh, if he should not come home!

Sec'y. Your father not at home?

Klara. No.

Sec'y. I am bringing good tidings. Your 5 brother —— No, Klara, I cannot talk like that to you. It seems the tables, the chairs, all these old friends —— Good morning, then! (*Nodding at a clothes-press*) How are you? You have not changed one bit — you, around 10 which we children used to run and play. You will shake your old heads and laugh at the old fool, who does not talk in the old familiar way. — I must talk to you as I used to. If you don't like it, then think that I am dreaming 15 and that you can wake me. Then step before me, raise yourself to your full height, so that I

can see that you are no longer the little girl of our childhood days. See here, this was your height when you were eleven. (*He points* 20 *to a mark on the door.*) But you are a grown-up girl who can reach for the sugar now, even if it is put at the top of the closet. Do you remember? That was the fortress where it was safe from us, even if not locked away from 25 us. When it was out of our reach we used to pass away our time by chasing the flies which were flying around cheerfully, and, oh, how we begrudged them what we ourselves could not get! 30

Klara. I thought people forgot such things when they had gone through hundreds and thousands of books.

Sec'y. That is true! Oh, all the things we forget over Justinian[1] and Gaius![2] The 35 boys who object to studying their letters know very well why they do so. They know that they will never quarrel with the Bible if they have nothing to do with the Primer. But it is disgraceful, truly disgraceful. Show them 40 the picture of a red rooster in the back of the book with a basket of eggs, and then there is no stopping them, and they hurry down to the letter "Z" and so on, and so on, until finally they are in the very middle of the *Corpus* 45 *Juris.*[3] Then only do they notice with horror into what a wilderness those cursed twenty-four letters have carried them — those letters which first led a gay dance of all good things to eat and smell, combinations of such 50 words as "cherry" and "rose." These are the things that entice them first.

Klara. And what do they do afterwards?
    (*Absent-minded, without any interest.*

[1] Justinian I, or the Great, ruler of the Byzantine Empire (A.D. 527–65), who sponsored the final codification of the entire body of Roman law.

[2] A Roman jurist (A.D. c. 110–80), who wrote the *Institutes*, an introduction to Roman private law. His work has been a favorite legal handbook for centuries and provided the foundation for Justinian's compilation.

[3] *Corpus Juris Civilis* = the body of the Civil or Roman law, promulgated under Justinian, A.D. 528–34. It is the foundation for the study of jurisprudence throughout modern Europe.

   These allusions to law study are reminiscences of Hebbel's student days at Heidelberg University, 1836–37.

Sec'y. That depends upon different temperaments. Some work their way through 55 it all. These are the ones who, three or four years later, come back to daylight. They are, however, somewhat thin and pale, but we must not take offense at that! I belong to that class myself. Others lie down in the middle 60 of this big forest; they want only to rest, but they never get up again, or rarely. I myself have a friend who has been drinking his beer in the shade of his *Lex Julia* for the past three years. He chose that passage on account 65 of its name, which stirs pleasant memories in him. Again, some others become desperate, and turn back. Those are the most stupid of all, because, let loose from one desert, they run straight into another. And then there are 70 some who are even worse — they never end studying. (*To himself*) All the nonsense we talk, when we have something else upon our hearts and lack the courage to say it.

Klara. All seems so gay and cheerful to- 75 day; it must be on account of the fine weather we have.

Sec'y. Yes, in such weather the owls fall from their nests, the bats commit suicide because they have a feeling that the devil 80 created them. The mole digs his way so deep into the earth that he cannot find his way back to daylight, and he must choke miserably if he does not succeed in digging his way clear through to the other side of the earth 85 and saying how-do-you-do to America. On a day like this, each ear of wheat grows twice as quickly, and the poppies turn redder than ever before. Shall we human beings be put to shame by them? Shall we cheat God 90 of the only interest which His capital brings Him? A cheerful and happy face, which reflects all the glory of the world. Truly, when I see this grouchy fellow or that crank creeping out of his house early in the morning, 95 his forehead wrinkled up to his hair, and gazing at the sky, like a blotter, I then often think, "There'll be rain in a minute or two, God cannot help dropping the cloud curtain, if it were only to prevent Himself from getting 100 angry at that caricature of a face." Such fellows ought to be tried before a court-martial

for spoiling the weather for the harvest. How else can we give thanks for being alive, if not by living? Sing and be cheerful, bird, or 105 you do not deserve your throat.

Klara. Oh! How true! I could cry!

Sec'y. It is not meant for you. Knowing your old father, I can understand why you go around with such a sad face. But, thank 110 heaven, I can restore your cheerfulness. That's what I came here for. You will have your brother back before night. People will now point their fingers not at him, but at the people who had him arrested. Don't I 115 deserve a kiss for this good news? Only a sisterly kiss, if it cannot be otherwise. Or shall we play blindman's buff? If I cannot catch you within ten minutes then I shall have to go without one and get a box on the ear 120 into the bargain.

Klara (*to herself*). I feel as if I were a thousand years old, and as if time stood still. I cannot advance or retreat. Heavens! All this cheerfulness and this everlasting 125 sunshine around me.

Sec'y. You do not answer. Of course, I forgot, you are engaged to be married. Oh, Klara! Why did you do that? And yet — I have no right to complain about it. You 130 are good and sweet. Everything that is good and pure ought to have recalled you to my mind; and yet for years you did not exist for me. Therefore, you now have — Well! If it were at least a fellow of whose superiority 135 I could be convinced. But Leonhard——

Klara (*suddenly, at the mentioning of his name*). I must go to him. That's just it. I am no longer sister to a thief —— Oh, my God in heaven! What shall I do? Leonhard will not, and he must —— He cannot be a devil! 140 Then all will come out right. All will be as it was. (*Shuddering*) As it was! (*To the* SECRETARY) Don't take it amiss, Friedrich. Oh! Why do I suddenly feel so heavy?

Sec'y. You will —— 145

Klara. Go and see Leonhard. What else do you think! That is the only way left for me to take in this world.

Sec'y. Then you love him? Then——

Klara (*wildly*). Love him? Either 150

him or death! Should anyone wonder that I choose him? I would not do so if I were only thinking of myself.

Sec'y. Either him or death? Girl! Only despair can talk that way, or ——   155

Klara. Don't drive me crazy! Don't repeat those words! It is you, you I love. Now! Now! I told you, cried it out to you, as if already I were on the other side of the grave, where we don't blush any more, where 160 we all creep past each other, naked and chilled, because God's terrible and sacred nearness takes from us all thought of our neighbors!

Sec'y. You love me? Me! Still love me! Klara, I thought you did when I saw you 165 outside in the yard.

Klara. You did! Did you? So did the other one, too! (*Dully, as if alone*) And he came to me: "He or I!" Oh, my heart! My cursed heart! For his sake, in order to 170 prove to myself that it was not so, or — was it to stifle the feeling? Was that the reason that I did the thing which now —— (*Breaking into tears*) Oh, God, my God! *I* would have mercy if I were You! 175

Sec'y. Klara, be my wife! All I came for again was to look into your eyes in the old way. Had you not understood that glance, I should have left without speaking. Now I offer you all I am and all I have. It is little enough, 180 but it may become more as time goes on. I would have come long ago, had it not been for your mother's illness and her death.

(KLARA *laughs like one insane.*)

Sec'y. Calm yourself, my dear. The man has your word and that frightens and up- 185 sets you. To be sure it is —— How could you!

Klara. Oh! Don't ask! Heavens! All the things that come together to set me crazy. Nothing but scorn and contempt from all sides when you went off to the university and 190 did not write to me. "She is fool enough to think of him." "She thinks that such childish promises were meant seriously." "Does he write?" And then my mother: "Keep to your equals. Haughtiness and arrogance will 195 bring misery upon you. Leonhard is a good man. All wonder why you despise him." Then my own heart began to doubt. I wondered if

you had really forgotten me. It said: "Show him that you too ——" Oh, Lord! 200

Sec'y. It is my fault, I know it. Well, even if it should be a difficult matter, it is not on that account impossible! I shall ask him to release you. Perhaps ——

Klara. Oh, as to my word. — Here! 205
(*She throws* LEONHARD's *letter to him.*)

Sec'y. (*reading*). I, as the cashier — your brother — thief — very sorry — but on account of my position and office, I cannot —— (*To* KLARA) Did he write this the very day your mother died? He expresses at the same 210 time his sympathy for her sudden death.

Klara. I think so.

Sec'y. Well! I declare! I —— Oh, good Lord! The cats, snakes, and all the other monsters which slipped through Your fingers 215 at the creation must have stirred the Devil's joy and delight, and he imitated them. Only He improved on them greatly by putting them into a human skin. Now they are standing in rank and file with us and we can only find 220 them out when they sting and scratch us! (*To* KLARA) But well for us! That's just what we want. (*Starting to embrace her*) Come! Forever now! With this kiss ——

Klara (*falling on his shoulder*). No! 225 Not forever! But I must keep from falling to the floor. No kiss!

Sec'y. But, my dear! You don't love him. He gave you back his word ——

Klara (*dully, straightening herself*). And 230 yet I must go to him. I must throw myself at his feet and stammer, "Look at my father's white hair, and have pity upon me — take me!"

Sec'y. Oh, you unhappy girl! Do I 235 understand you aright?

Klara. Yes!

Sec'y. No man can overlook that! To have to blush and cast down one's eyes before a man who is fit to be spit at! (*Pressing* 240 KLARA *to his heart*) You poor girl! You poor girl!

Klara. Go now! Go!

Sec'y. (*to himself, brooding*). Or the dog who knows about it must be shot down! 245 Wish he would have the courage and accept a challenge! Or, maybe, I can force him to it. I am not afraid, as far as hitting him is concerned.

Klara. I beg you —— 250

Sec'y. (departing). When it will be dark! (*He turns around once more and takes* KLARA'S *hand.*) Girl! Klara! You stand before me —— (*Turning away again*) A thousand others would have been silent about it, 254 and would have whispered it into the ears of their husbands in the supreme hour of sweet forgetfulness. I know what I owe you.

(*Exit.*

SCENE 6

Klara (alone). Stop! Stop, my heart! Retire within me, so that not a drop of blood can escape which might be able to rekindle life in me. Something like hope offered itself to me. Now only do I realize it. (*Laughing*) No! 5 "No man can overlook such a thing!" And if —— Could I myself overlook it? Could I have the courage to seize a hand, which —— No! No! I would not have such an evil kind of courage. I have to shut myself in my 10 own hell, even if people were to open the door to me from without —— I am for all eternity — forever —— Oh! How I wish the pressure would stop! If it were only for a few minutes! A tormented person thinks to 15 have a rest, when his tormentor has to stop a moment to catch his breath. Relief comes over him as it does over the drowning man upon the waves, when the whirlpool that is dragging him down gives him up for an instant, only to 20 seize him again. Yet he does not gain anything by the respite except to have the struggle with death prolonged.

Well, Klara? Yes, father. I am going! Your daughter is not going to drive you to 25 suicide. I shall soon be the lawful wife of that man, or — Lord! I am not begging for any happiness, I am begging for misery, for utmost misery. You will grant me that misery! Away, now — where is the letter? (*She takes it.*) 30 I shall pass three wells on my way to him — I must not stop at any of them. As yet I have no right to do it. (*Exit.*

ACT III

A room in LEONHARD'S *house.*

SCENE 1

Leon. (at a table covered with legal papers, writing). Well! That's the sixth sheet since dinner. What a nice and important feeling when we do our duty. Let come who will, and if it were the king himself — I shall rise, to be sure, but I'd not be embarrassed one bit. 5 There is but one exception to it, and that is the old carpenter. But, what does he matter, after all? Poor Klara! I *am* sorry for her. I cannot think of her without some misgivings. Wish that one cursed night had not 10 been! To tell the truth, it was more from a feeling of jealousy, which was devouring me, than of love. I know she only yielded to prove that my reproaches were unfounded, for she was as cold as death. She will have to face 15 hard times now, and I, too, shall have many annoyances coming my way from the whole business. Well! Let each bear his own burden. Above all things, I must tie that little hunchback firmly to me so that she can- 20 not escape me when the storm will break loose! For then I shall have the mayor for me and need fear nothing.

SCENE 2

Klara (entering). Good evening, Leonhard!

Leon. Klara? (*To himself*) I did not expect her. (*Aloud*) Did you not get my note? But — maybe you are coming for your father — to pay the taxes. How much is it? (*Looking over some papers*) I ought to know by heart. 5

Klara. I came to return your letter! Here it is! Read it over once more.

Leon. (reading very earnestly). It is a very sensible letter. How can a man to whom 10 public money is entrusted marry into a family of — (*swallowing a word*) of which your brother is a member?

Klara. Leonhard!

Leon. Or do you think the whole town 15 is wrong? Is your brother not in jail? Did he never go to jail? Are you not the sister of a — of your brother?

Klara. I am here as my father's daughter. Not as the sister of a brother accused inno- 20 cently, who, moreover, has already been acquitted. He is only my brother. I did not come here as a girl trembling and fearing undeserved disgrace, for (*in a half whisper*) I am fearing you more. I am here as the daugh- 25 ter of the old man to whom I owe my life.

Leon. And what do you want?

Klara. Can you ask? I wish I could go and leave you. My father will cut his throat, if —— *Do* marry me. 30

Leon. Your father ——

Klara. He swore it. Marry me!

Leon. Our hands and throats are first cousins, they'll not harm each other. Don't worry about it! 35

Klara. He swore it — marry me, I shall commit suicide right after and I shall be grateful to you for both the marrying and the suicide.

Leon. Do you love me? Did you come because prompted by your heart? Am I 40 your all?

Klara. Answer that question yourself.

Leon. Can you swear that you love me? That you love me as a woman must love the man to whom she is tied forever and ever? 45

Klara. No, I cannot swear that. But this much I can: You'll never know whether I love you or not! I'll serve you! I'll slave for you! You need not support me, I'll do that myself. I shall do sewing and spinning at night, 50 and I'll go hungry if I cannot find work. I shall tear my own flesh rather than complain to my father. He'll not learn anything about it. If you whip me because your dog is not at hand, or because you did away with him, I shall 55 swallow my own tongue rather than betray you to the neighbors by my screams. I cannot promise that my skin will conceal the marks of your whip, for that does not depend upon me, but I shall lie to them. I'll tell them that 60 I fell and struck my head against the closet, or that I slipped on the floor; and I shall do so before anyone will have a chance to ask me any questions about my black marks. Marry me — I shall not live long. And should it last too 65 long, and should you regret the expenses of a divorce suit to get rid of me, well! then buy some poison in a drugstore, place it as if it were meant for the rats. I'll take it, and, dying, I'll let the neighbors know that I took it by 70 mistake.

Leon. If you expect me to do such things, you must not be astonished if I refuse to marry you.

Klara. Well! Then may God not judge 75 me too hard, if I go to Him before He calls me. Were it only for my own sake — I'd willingly bear the burden. I'd accept it as a well-deserved punishment, if people were to point their fingers at me instead of helping me. I 80 would love my child, even if it were to have the features of this wretch. I would shed so many tears in his presence that, when older and wiser, he would not despise nor curse his mother. But I am not the only one concerned. On the 85 Day of Judgment it will be easier to answer the Judge's question, "Why did you kill yourself?" than to answer, "Why did you drive your father to it?"

Leon. You talk as if you were the first 90 and the last one. Thousands met with the same fate before you, and thousands will meet with it after you, and they will all be resigned in the end. Are you any better than they? They, too, had fathers who invented all 95 kinds of new curses, when they first discovered their daughters' shame and disgrace. They, too, talked of murder and suicide. Afterwards they were ashamed of such talk; they sat down and rocked the cradle and shooed the flies off. 100

Klara. Oh, *you* wouldn't believe that anybody in the world would keep his word.

SCENE 3

A Boy (*entering*). Here are some flowers! I am not to tell from whom.

Leon. How lovely! (*Striking his forehead*) The dickens! How stupid of me! I ought to have sent some. How am I to get out of it 5 gracefully? The little hunchback is so exacting! She has nothing else to think of. (*Taking the flowers*) But I am not going to keep them all. (*To* KLARA) Did you not tell me once that these signify shame and repentance? 10

(KLARA *nods.*

Leon. (*to the boy*). Mind, my boy, these are for me, I pin them on me, right here, where my heart is. These, the dark red ones, which burn like fire, you'll take back. Do you understand me? By the way, don't forget to call when 15 my apples will be ripe.

Boy. That'll be a *long* time.   (*Exit.*

Scene 4

Leon. See here, Klara. You spoke about keeping one's promise. Just because I am a man of my word I had to answer you as I did. I gave you back your word a week ago. You cannot deny it, the letter is here. (*He gives* 5 *her the note; she takes it mechanically.*) Your brother — you say he is acquitted? I am glad. During that week I formed another alliance; I had the right to do so, since you did not object to my note. I was free to do so both in my 10 heart and before the law. Now you come to see me, but it is too late. I gave my word and received hers, in fact —— (*To himself*) How I wish it were true. — To tell you the truth, the other one is in the same condition as you. 15 I am sorry. (*He pushes her curls from her brow, and she allows him as if not noticing.*) But, you'll understand — there's no joking with the mayor.

Klara (*absent-minded*). No joking!   20

Leon. Well! Now you are getting sensible! And as to your father, you may tell him straight to his face that it is all his own fault. Don't look at me like that. Don't shake your head. It is so! Just tell him that. He'll under- 25 stand and be sorry, I'll vouch for it. (*To himself*) If he could give away his daughter's dowry he must not be astonished if his daughter is abandoned in the end. When I think of it I could — I could —— How I wish the old 30 fool were here to learn a lesson now. Why must I be so cruel? Only because he was a fool! He is responsible for whatever comes from it now. That's clear! (*To* Klara) Or do you want me to tell him? For your sake I'll 35 risk it. He'll be rude to me. He may hurl things at me, but he'll have to swallow the truth, no matter how painful, and will have to leave you in peace. Depend upon it. Is he home?   40

Klara (*straightening herself up to her full height*). I thank you.   (*She starts to depart.*

Leon. Shall I go with you? I have courage enough!

Klara. I thank you as much as I would thank a snake which had got hold of me and 45 now lets me go suddenly, because some other prey has come his way. I know that I am doomed by his bite, that he leaves me only because it is not worth his while to suck my life. Yet I *do* thank him, because now I shall 50 have a peaceful death. Yes, you scoundrel, I thank you. I felt when I first looked into your heart, that I saw the abyss of hell. Whatever my lot may be in that terrible eternity, one thing is sure, I'll have nothing in common 55 with you there, and that is *some* comfort. The unfortunate man who is bitten by a snake is not blamed for opening his veins that his poisoned life may flee quickly. So God's everlasting mercy will have pity upon me when He 60 looks at you and me and sees what you made of me. Only one more thing. My father does not know. He has no suspicion. I shall do away with myself this very day that he may never learn of my disgrace. If I were 65 to think you could —— (*She advances a step toward him, wildly.*) But that is folly! It can only be welcome to you when they will all stand around, shaking their heads and asking each other vainly: "How did it happen?"   70

Leon. There are such cases. What can be done? Klara!

Klara (*to herself*). Away, now! That monster can talk!   (*She starts to depart.*

Leon. Do you imagine I believe you?   75

Klara. No!

Leon. Fortunately, you cannot kill yourself without killing a child.

Klara. It is better to kill both than a father. I know well that one sin cannot be 80 atoned for by committing another. But what I am going to do now, I alone shall be responsible for. If I deliver the knife into my father's hands, it would hit both of us. It will hit me one way or another. That's what gives me 85 the courage and the strength in all my fear. You'll do well in the world.   (*Exit.*

SCENE 5

Leon. (alone). I must! I must marry her! Indeed! Why should I have to do it? She is about to do something crazy, in order to prevent her father from acting foolishly. Where is the necessity of it? Why should I pre- 5 vent her from committing a wild deed by doing a still wilder thing myself? I'll not do it! At least, not till I see before me a man who is ready to do a still madder thing, and should he think as I do, well! then there would be 10 no end of it. That sounds plausible and yet — I must go after her. Somebody is coming! Thank Heaven for it! Nothing is worse than to have to be at war with one's own thoughts.

SCENE 6

Sec'y. (entering). Good evening!

Leon. So it's the Secretary, is it? What gives me the pleasure of ——

Sec'y. You'll learn it soon enough!

Leon. To be sure, we were school- 5 mates ——

Sec'y. And maybe, we will be comrades in death! (*Drawing forth two pistols*) Do you know how to handle these?

Leon. I don't understand you! 10

Sec'y. (cocking one of the pistols). Look! That's the way. Then you take aim at me, the same as I now aim at you; and then you pull the trigger. This way!

Leon. What are you talking about? 15

Sec'y. One of us must die. Die! And that right away, this minute.

Leon. Die?

Sec'y. You know why!

Leon. By God in heaven, I don't! 20

Sec'y. That does not matter. You'll remember it when it comes to dying.

Leon. I have no idea ——

Sec'y. Remember! You had better do so! Or it might occur to me to take you for a 25 mad dog who bit the person I hold dearest in this world, unconsciously; and I might shoot you down like one, although I intended to treat you as my equal for the next half hour at least.

Leon. Don't talk so loud. If anybody 30 should hear ——

Sec'y. If there was anybody who could hear us you'd have called him long ago. Well?

Leon. If it is on account of the girl, well! I don't care, I may as well marry her as not. 35 I had almost made up my mind to do so when she was here just now.

Sec'y. She was here and left again? And you did not fall down at her feet in sorrow and repentance? Come now! Come! 40

Leon. I pray you —— You see a man before you who is ready to do anything you wish of him. I'll publish my engagement to her this very evening.

Sec'y. That will be my business, not 45 yours. You shall not touch even the hem of her garment, even if the salvation of the world depended upon it. Come! To the woods with us. But mind! I take you by your arm, and if, on our way, you utter but one cry, 50 I —— (*Raising the pistol*) You may believe me! But we had better take the back road behind the houses, past the yards, so that you may not be tempted.

Leon. One of these is for me — give me 55 this one.

Sec'y. Not yet! You might throw it away and force me to murder you, or to let you run away, is that it? Have patience till we are at the spot I have selected, then I'll share 60 it with you.

Leon. (going to the table and knocking his glass off by accident). Can I not first have another drink?

Sec'y. Courage, my boy! Maybe you'll fare well. It seems that God and the Devil 65 are constantly fighting for the possession of the world. Who knows who will have the upper hand and be the master?

(*He takes hold of* LEONHARD'S *arm; both go out.*)

SCENE 7

A room in ANTON'S *house. Evening.*

Karl (entering). Nobody home! If I did not know the rat hole beneath the door where they always hide the key, I couldn't have entered. Well! It would not have mattered much. I should like nothing better than to run 5 around the entire town. I can imagine no greater pleasure than making use of my legs. Let us have some light. (*He lights the lamp.*) The matches are in the same place as usual, I'll wager. Here in this house we have twenty 10 commandments, instead of ten. My hat goes on the third nail, not on the fourth. At half-past nine we must be tired. Before Saint Martin's Day [1] we must not be cold, and after it we must not perspire. All these command- 15 ments are on the same list with "Thou shalt love and fear the Lord thy God!" I am thirsty! (*He calls.*) Mother! The devil! I forgot that she is lying where even the inn-keeper's bartender cannot open his jaws 20 to let out his everlasting "Yes, sir!" I did not cry, when in my dark hole I heard the death-bell rung for her, but — Redcoat,[2] you did not allow me to make the last throw in the bowling alley, although I held the ball in 25 my hand, ready for throwing. I'll not allow you time for a last breath, when I meet you face to face. This may even happen tonight, for I know where you can be found around ten o'clock. After that, I'll take the first 30 boat. Where in the world is Klara? I am both hungry and thirsty. Today is Thursday. They have had veal soup. If it were winter there would have been cabbage; before Lent white cabbage, after Lent green cabbage. That's 35 as much a matter of fact as that Thursday must return after Wednesday, so that Thursday can't say to Friday, "Take my place; I have sore feet."

SCENE 8

KLARA *enters*

Karl. At last! You have no business to be kissing all the time. Wherever four red lips meet, a bridge is built for the Devil. What have you here?

Klara. Where? What? 5

Karl "Where? What?" In your hands, of course!

Klara. Nothing.

---

[1] November 11, the feast day for Martin, bishop of Tours, France, in the fourth century.

[2] I. e., Adam, the bailiff who arrested him.

Karl. Nothing? Is it a secret? (*Tearing* LEONHARD'S *letter from her hands*) Let me 10 see! If the father is not here the brother is the guardian.

Klara. I held it firmly in my hands, and yet the wind was so violent that it threw the tiles from the roof. When I went past the 15 church a tile flew down and I knocked my foot against it. "Oh God!" I prayed, "send another one!" and I stopped. That would have been too good to be true. They would have to bury me and they would say, "She met 20 with an accident!" I hoped in vain for another tile to come down.

Karl (*who, meanwhile, has read the letter*). Thunder and lightning! You scoundrel! The hand which wrote these lines shall be struck lame by me! Get me a bottle of wine! 25 Or is your savings bank empty?

Klara. There is another bottle in the house. I had bought it secretly for mother's birthday and put it aside. Tomorrow would have been the day. 30

Karl. Give it to me! (KLARA *brings wine.*

Karl (*drinking hastily*). Well! Now work can begin again! The eternal and everlasting planing, sawing, hammering; in between, eat-ing and drinking and sleeping, so that we 35 can go on planing, sawing, and hammering. On Sunday a prayer or two and a "I thank Thee, oh Lord, that Thou givest me the per-mission to plane, hammer, and saw!" (*Drinks again.*) Long life to every good dog who 40 does not bite when tied to the chain. (*Drinks again.*) Once more, "Long life to him!"

Klara. Karl, do not drink so much! Father says that the Devil is in wine!

Karl. And the priest says that God is 45 in it. (*Drinking*) We'll see who is right! The bailiff has been here in the house. How did he behave?

Klara. As if he were in a den of thieves and murderers. Mother fell down dead as soon 50 as he had opened his lips.

Karl. Very well! If tomorrow morning you should wake up and should hear that the scoun-drel has been found slain, do not curse the murderer. 55

Klara. Karl, I hope you will not ——

Karl. Am I his only enemy? Has he not often been attacked before? It will be hard to find the guilty one among all those who might have done it, provided the murderer 60 does not leave a cane or a hat behind him. (*Drinking*) Whoever may do it, "Here is to good success!"

Klara. Brother, you talk ——

Karl. Don't you like it? Well, it does 65 not matter! You'll not have to put up with me much longer.

Klara (*shuddering*). No!

Karl. No? Do you know already that I want to be a sailor? Are my thoughts 70 upon my forehead that you can read them? Or did the old crank, in his amiable manner, threaten to close his door to me? That would not mean much more than if the bailiff had sworn to me, "You shall no longer be here 75 in jail, I'll push you out into the open."

Klara. You don't understand me!

Karl (*singing*). The sails of yonder ship
The wind is swelling!

Ah, ha! Nothing can tie me any longer to 80 the workshop! Mother is dead. There is nobody here who would cease eating after each storm! And from my early youth it has been my desire. Away, then, with me! I shall never prosper here.   85

Klara. And you will leave father all alone?

Karl. Alone? Aren't you with him?

Klara. I?

Karl. You! His pet! What is going on in your brain that you ask such a silly thing? 90 I leave him his joy and rid him from his everlasting anger, namely, from my charming person! Why should I not do it? We don't get along together, that's a sure thing! He cannot have things narrow enough around him. 95 He would like to close his hand into a fist and creep into it. I should like to shed my skin just as I did the frock I wore when a little boy. If I only could!   (*Singing.*

The anchor is lifted,   100
The wheel is turned,
Now she flies away!

Tell me, did he doubt of my guilt for one instant? And was it not a comfort for him to be

able to say: "That's what I always ex- 105 pected! I always thought so! It could not end differently!" Oh, the over-wise fool! If it had been you, he'd have committed suicide! I'd like to see him! If you were to meet with the fate of some women, he'd feel as if it 110 were he himself who had to suffer it. And with the Devil into the bargain!

Klara (*to herself*). Oh! How it breaks my heart! — Yes, it is so! I must away!

Karl. What do you mean?   115

Klara. I must go to the kitchen — what else do you think? (*With her hand to her forehead*) Yes! That's it! That's what I returned home for!   (*Exit.* 119

Karl. She seems to me somewhat strange.
(*Singing.*

A fearless seagull
In welcome circles the mast.

Klara (*re-entering and talking to herself*). The last thing is done. Father's supper is on the stove. When I closed the kitchen door 125 and thought, "You'll never enter here again!" a shudder passed over my soul. That's the way I'll leave this room, this house, this world!

Karl (*singing as he walks back and forth, while* KLARA *remains in the background*).

The sun beats hotly down;
Many small fish, shiny and gay,   130
Frolic boldly round the guest.[1]

Klara (*to herself*). Why don't I do it? Shall I ever do it? Am I to postpone it from one day to another, as I do now from one minute to another? Until —— Away with me — 135 Away! Yet, I hesitate! Is it not as if something were to raise its little hands imploringly to me, as if eyes —— (*Sitting down on a chair*) What nonsense! Am I too weak? Then am I strong enough to see my father with cut 140 throat —— (*Rising*) No! No! Our Father, Who art in Heaven — Hallowed be Thy Kingdom — God! My God! My head is all wrong — all confused — my poor head — I cannot even pray. Brother! Brother! Help 145 me ——

Karl. What is the matter with you?

Klara. The Lord's Prayer! (*Coming to her senses*) I thought I was already in the

[1] I.e., the ship.

water, and was sinking, sinking, and had 150
forgotten to say my prayers!   I — (*suddenly*)
Forgive us our trespasses, as we forgive those
who trespass against us.   That's it!   Yes!
Yes! I forgive him!   To be sure, I do, I do!
I don't think of him any longer! —   Good- 155
night, Karl!

Karl. Are you going to bed so early?
Good-night!

Klara (*like a child who recites the Lord's
Prayer*). Forgive us ——

Karl. You could get me a glass of water 160
first, though, but let it be fresh!

Klara (*quickly*). I'll get it from the well —!

Karl. Well, if you want to, it is not so far.

Klara (*to herself*). Thanks! Thanks! That
was the last thing that troubled me.   The 165
deed itself would have given me away!   Now
they'll say, after all: "She met with an accident!
She fell into it!"

Karl. Be careful, the board is most likely
still loose!   170

Klara. The moon is bright!   Oh, my God!
I only go to You, because otherwise my father
would go!   Forgive me, as I — Have mercy
upon me — mercy ——   (*Exit.*)

SCENE 9

Karl (*singing*).

> How I wanted to plunge in,
> For out there is my realm!

Ha!   But before —— (*Looking at his watch*)
What time?   Nine!

> I'm still so young in years,   5
> I only care to travel.
> Whither, it matters not.

SCENE 10

Anton (*entering*). I have to ask your forgiveness, but if I pardon you for having incurred
debts secretly, if I pay them all for you, I may
spare myself asking your forgiveness.

Karl. The former is right and good, the 5
latter is not necessary.   If I sell my Sunday
clothes I can satisfy the people to whom I owe
a few dollars myself.   I'll do that tomorrow.

As a sailor — (*to himself*) now it's out — I
don't need them any more.   10

Anton. What nonsense are you talking
again!

Karl. It is not the first time you hear it.
You may say what you like this time, my decision is taken.   15

Anton. To be sure, you are of age.

Karl. Just because I am so, I don't stand
on my dignity about it.   But I think fish and
bird ought not to quarrel about whether it is
better to live in the water or in the air. 20
One more thing.   You'll either not see me
again, or, if you do, you'll pat my shoulder and
say, "You did well!"

Anton. We'll see.   I need not dismiss the
fellow I took in your place then.   That's 25
all.

Karl. I thank you.

Anton. Tell me, is it true that the bailiff,
instead of taking you the shortest way to the
Court House, took you all over town?   30

Karl. From one street into another, across
the market place, like an ox that is taken to
market.   But don't worry, I'll pay him for it,
too, before I leave here!

Anton. I don't blame you, but I forbid it! 35

Karl. Oh, I say!

Anton. I'll not let you out of my sight, and
I myself would assist the scoundrel if you were
to attack him.

Karl. I thought you loved my mother, 40
too!

Anton. And I'll prove it!

SCENE 11

Sec'y. (*entering pale and tottering, pressing a
kerchief against his chest*). Where is Klara?
(*Falling upon a chair*) Jesus! Good-evening!
Thank God that I got here!   Where is she?

Karl. She went to —— Where is she?   Her
talk — I begin to fear ——   (*Exit.* 5

Sec'y. She is avenged — the scoundrel fell —
but I, too, am —— Why this, my God?   Now
I cannot ——

Anton. What is the matter with you?

Sec'y. It does not matter about me!   10
Give me your word that you will not abandon

her — do you hear? Not abandon her when she ——

Anton. What queer talk! Why should I —— Oh! I understand! Is it possible that I 15 did do her no wrong, when I ——

Sec'y. Your word! Give me your hand!

Anton. No! (*Putting both hands into his pockets*) But I'll make room for her. She knows it, too. I told her I would! 20

Sec'y. (*horrified*). He told — her! (*To himself*) You poor girl! Only now do I understand you!

Karl (*rushing in*). Father! Father! Somebody is in the well! If only it is not —— 25

Anton. The big ladder! Hooks! Ropes! Hurry! Why are you so slow? And if it were only the bailiff; hurry!

Karl. All the things are there. The neighbors rushed to the spot at once. If it is 30 only not Klara!

Anton. Klara?   (*Grasps the table.*

Karl. She went for water, and they found her kerchief.

Sec'y. Scoundrel! Now I know why 35 your bullet hit. It is she!

Anton. Go and look, will you? (*Sitting down*) I can't! (KARL *exit.*) And yet! (*Rising*) If I understood you aright (*to the SEC-RETARY*), then all is well! 40

Karl (*returning*). Klara! Klara is dead! Dead! Her head horribly battered and smashed by the edge of the well, when she — Father, she did not fall in, she jumped in — a maid saw her. 45

Anton. She had better think it over before she talks. It is not light enough so that she could have distinguished clearly.

Sec'y. Do you doubt it? You would like to

do so, but you cannot! Only recall all you 50 told her! It is my fault that she did not come back. When you had a premonition of her misery, you thought only of the tongues that were going to whisper behind your back, you didn't think of the malice of the serpents 55 who own those tongues. You said words that drove her to despair. When she in her terrible fear opened her heart to me, I thought only of the scoundrel instead of taking her to my heart, and —— Well! I am paying it with 60 my life. Because I made myself dependent upon one who is worse than I. You, too, you, however firm you may seem, you, too, will say some day: "Daughter, I wish you had not saved me from the gossip of the Pharisees! 65 It is a greater sorrow to me that you will not be near me when I am on my death-bed, with nobody to do me the last service of love, with nobody to close my eyes for me."

Anton. She did not save me from any- 70 thing — they saw her!

Sec'y. She did all in her power. You were not worth it!

Anton. Or she was not!

(*Tumult outside.*

Karl. They are bringing her —— 75
(*He starts to leave.*

Anton (*firm to the end, calling after him*). Into the back room where her mother's coffin stood!

Sec'y. Let me go and see her! (*He wishes to rise, but falls back.*) Karl!
(KARL *helps him up, and accompanies him out.*

Anton. I don't understand this world 80 any more.

While he is deep in thought the curtain drops.

INTRODUCTION TO
Hedda Gabler

The Early Scandinavian Drama and Theater:
Ibsen and the Drama of Social Realism

THE EARLY SCANDINAVIAN DRAMA AND THEATER

DRAMATIC ART in Scandinavia developed no professional organization of importance until the eighteenth century, although a playhouse was built as early as 1660 at Stockholm, Sweden. In 1722 a "national theater" opened in Copenhagen, the capital of the Danish-Norwegian kingdom, and remained for a century and a half the leading Scandinavian playhouse. This new theater, having only translated foreign drama available for performance, invited Ludwig Holberg (1684–1754), professor of literature at the University, to contribute Danish plays. He proceeded to write numerous comedies in the pattern of Molière, but with native material. His best plays, like *Rasmus Montanus* (1731), are still revived in Scandinavia where he has long been honored as the father of its drama.

Norway, the birthplace of Holberg, secured her freedom from Denmark in 1814, but Danish culture continued to dominate Norwegian life for many years. At the middle of the nineteenth century, the Christiania (Oslo) Theater, the only important playhouse in Norway, produced mostly Danish plays with Danish actors. Nevertheless a strong movement for cultural and literary nationalism existed. One of its most earnest leaders was Ole Bull, the world-famous violinist and the idol of his countrymen. Desirous of seeing the old Norse spirit in the drama, he founded in 1850 a "national theater" at the ancient city of Bergen. On October 15, 1851, the Christiania students sponsored a concert in behalf of this theatrical venture. The evening's program commenced with a stirring prologue on the glorious future of Norway's art. Ole Bull was so much impressed with the prologue that he asked to meet its author. The latter turned out to be a twenty-three-year-old journalist, Henrik John Ibsen, who had had a one-act play, *The Warrior's Barrow*, produced at the Christiania Theater in the preceding year. Attracted by Ibsen's patriotic idealism and literary talent, Ole Bull in November, 1851, appointed him theater-poet and stage-manager of the Norwegian Theater at Bergen.

IBSEN AND THE DRAMA OF SOCIAL REALISM

This appointment marked the first important step toward fame for the serious-minded Ibsen, who as a small boy had determined to rise to greatness. Up until then circumstances had steadily conspired against his ambition. He had been born on March 20, 1828, into a well-to-do merchant family at Skien, a small seaport of southern Norway. When Henrik was eight years old, his father suddenly lost all financial resources in a trade depression, moved the family to a farm outside Skien, and relegated them to a meager, drab life. Relatives and friends among the gentry ostracized them. Young Ibsen resented the local snobbery, which forced him to attend an inferior "middle-class school." His imagination transformed Skien's square, with its ugly church, jail, pillory, and madhouse, into a symbol of the community's grimness His father's irresponsibility, his mother's pietism, and their mutual indifference to his love of painting further exasperated him. At the age of fifteen he cut himself loose forever from birthplace and family to become an apothecary's clerk in Grimstad, a shipbuilding town down the coast.

Grimstad proved as dour and provincial an environment as Skien. Its atmosphere of caste and respectability embittered Ibsen at his menial job. To offset drudgery and isolation he began studying for the entrance examinations at the University of Christiania, and reading widely in literature. Before long several free-thinking young men discovered in him a kindred spirit. Poetry, drama, satire, and pranks against local personages occupied this group of youthful rebels. By 1850 Ibsen found himself, so he stated later, "on a war footing with the little society of Grimstad."

In the spring of that year, therefore, he departed for Christiania with the idea of entering the medical course of the University. His failure, however, to pass all the examinations on the first trial delayed admission. He shortly abandoned medicine in favor of journalism. A new liberal weekly on public affairs took him on its staff, but it died within a year. Meanwhile he got mixed up with a revolutionary labor paper. When the government arrested and imprisoned the editor in the summer of 1851, Ibsen lost his enthusiasm for direct social agitation. He made up his mind henceforth to be content with the artist's indirect method "of rousing [his] countrymen from their lethargy and making them see the import of the great life problems." Soon after this decision the opportune meeting with Ole Bull took place.

Though Ibsen knew almost nothing about stage production, he carried out well his directorial responsibilities at the Bergen Theater during the winter of 1851–52. In the following spring he traveled to Copenhagen and Dresden for investigation of the repertories and stagecraft in the theaters there. The subsequent five years at Bergen made him an experienced man of the theater. His management proved so very successful that in 1857 the sponsors of a new "Norwegian" playhouse at Christiania selected him to take charge of the enterprise.

Ibsen's change of position was followed by important developments in his personal relationships. He married in June, 1858, Susannah Thoresen, the strong-minded daughter of a Bergen minister. For almost half a century she supported his genius with extraordinary loyalty, patience, and understanding. In 1859 he renewed acquaintance with the poet and dramatist, Björnstjerne Björnson (1832–1910). Together they founded a society to advance the Norwegian language, drama, and culture. Björnson stood godfather to Ibsen's only child, Sigurd, who eventually married his godfather's daughter. During the 1860's Björnson gave Ibsen indispensable financial aid and publicity. Antithetical temperaments and literary rivalries prevented, however, any long-continued intimacy between the two writers. Björnson's stage popularity in Norway equaled Ibsen's for many years, though the former did not reach the peak of his art until 1883 in *Beyond Human Power*, a strong drama on mystical religion.

The "Norwegian" theater project at Christiania, of which Ibsen gradually tired, ended with bankruptcy in 1862. He then applied to the government for a subsidy that would enable him to give his entire time to playwriting. When a traveling fellowship was awarded him a year later, he left in delight for Rome. Norway's spiritual bleakness, her provincialism, and, at the moment, her neutrality in the face of German aggression against Denmark, had irritated him beyond all patience. For twenty-seven years he lived abroad in either Italy or Germany, so that he did the most and the best of his writing outside of Norway. The first product of his exile was a stirring tragedy of Norwegian background and character, entitled *Brand*. Its publication in 1866 brought him immediate national acclaim. The Norwegian Parliament voted him a poet's pension for life. At last he saw his dream of greatness becoming reality.

Ibsen's playwriting during the next quarter-century extended his fame to all corners of the world, but at the same time it incited hostility in many quarters. Sometimes the dramatist himself publicly challenged intellectual and social conservatism. In 1879, for example, he proposed at the Scandinavian Club of Rome that women members be allowed to vote. Because the Club rejected his proposal, he appeared at its annual ball, halted the dancers with a blistering speech, and finally spread consternation by denouncing the women present as not only parasites, but also ignorant and immoral slaves. Still aroused, he proceeded to write *A Doll's House*, in which he exhibited one woman's emancipation. This play, performed before packed houses at Christiania in the season of 1879–80, stirred up tremendous agitation. Hostesses had to request in advance that their guests avoid discussion of *A Doll's House*. It caused a sensation in other countries too. England and America went so far as to taboo for at least two decades performances of the complete original version. Thus Ibsen shocked his age into disturbing thought.

In 1891 Norway welcomed her most widely known citizen home for good. His dumpy figure, attired in silk hat, white tie, frock coat and trousers of black broadcloth, became as distinctive a sight in Christiania as it had been in Rome and Munich. A chill and rather bristling presence discouraged popular idolizing. Yet Norway observed his seventieth birthday in 1898 with a round of public celebrations. At the magnificent state banquet, presided over by the King, Ibsen summed up the agony and the triumph of his career with a poet's touch: "My life has passed like a long, long Passion week, and as I stand here in the real Passion week, my life is transformed . . . into a summer night's dream."

Two years later the first of several paralytic strokes foreshadowed his life's close. The curtain did not actually fall until May 23, 1906. Mrs. Ibsen had only a miner's hammer carved on the granite monument over her husband's grave. In a favorite poem he had pictured himself a miner delving into the rock of error for the hidden truth, "hammer blow on hammer blow, till the lamp of life burns low."

Ibsen's mining represented half a century's unified effort to satisfy a Puritan sense of obligation and mission. "No man is ever free of responsibility for the society in which he belongs or without a share in its guilt," he declared. Social well-being depended, in his opinion, on the spiritual liberty and integrity of the individual citizens. Consequently the problem of the individual's relations to society engrossed his attention. All his plays in one guise or another argue for a free and rich personal life in opposition to any repressive convention. "The strongest man is he who stands most alone," he concluded, in *An Enemy of the People*.

Ibsen's treatment of the theme of individualism passed through three phases, the romantic, the realistic, and the symbolic. This sequence of change paralleled the evolution of European drama during the second half of the nineteenth century. The historical, or legendary, verse plays in the first phase were written under the influence of Goethe, Schiller, and the then fashionable Danish tragedian, Adam Oehlenschlager (1779–1850). Of Ibsen's poetic drama, *Brand* (1866) and *Peer Gynt* (1867) are easily the finest. *Brand* portrays a sturdy Norwegian priest, a rigid idealist, whose obsession for self-sacrifice leads him to disregard love and hence to be chastised by both his fellows and his God. *Peer Gynt*, a long, episodic fantasy, presents the very antithesis of Brand's tragedy in the picaresque career of its jaunty, boastful, dreaming, roguish, and yet lovable hero. Whereas Brand's failure results from an uncompromising spirit, Peer's lies in the adventurer's habit of perpetual compromise, which almost obliterates his soul. Ibsen's weaving of folklore and satire into many varicolored settings produces a brilliant poetic tapestry. The essentially untheatrical design, however, of both *Peer Gynt* and *Brand* has prevented more than an occasional stage performance.

As early as 1869 Ibsen indicated by his prose comedy, *The League of Youth*, a shifting of creative interest. He was beginning to be affected by the fashions which recent French playwrights had initiated. The "well-made plays" of Eugène Scribe (1791–1861), with their economy and finesse of structure, and their neat theatrical contrivances, had overrun the European stage. Ibsen during his Bergen directorate had acquired a thorough knowledge of Scribe by producing over twenty of the latter's plays. Another Frenchman, Alexandre Dumas *fils* (1824–95), had combined social and moral themes with the Scribe pattern to evolve the "thesis play." His famous piece, *The Lady of the Camellias* (1852), popularized a drama of social discussion.

Impelled by the currents which Scribe and Dumas had set in motion, Ibsen in 1877 embarked on an epoch-making series of social plays written in prose and expertly designed for acting. *The Pillars of Society* (1877) exposes the hypocrisy of a respected community leader who paid only lip-service to truth and freedom, the true pillars of society. *A Doll's House* (1879) depicts the intellectual awakening of an ingenuous young wife, "a doll," who walks out on her convention-bound husband. Ibsen shortly made an even more sensational attack on false conceptions of married life in *Ghosts* (1881), where a mother's enslavement by the "ghost" formulae of respectability dooms her son to congenital disease and mental disintegration. The frankness of this drama raised a furor of criticism. *An Enemy of the People* (1882) replied to this latest opposition by exhibiting a stalwart medical reformer whose attempt to cleanse the public baths is defeated by community selfishness. Yet Ibsen did not approve indiscriminate efforts at reform, as he soon made clear in *The Wild Duck* (1884). Herein a wrongheaded reformer, intent on truth-telling regardless of persons, brings confusion and death to a stupid injured family which, like a hurt wild duck, has been hiding in a marsh of harmless self-deception. *Rosmersholm* (1886) and *Hedda Gabler* (1890) return to the earlier theme of woman's individualism, but treat of the disasters which may come from her mistaken self-assertion. The heroine of *Rosmersholm*, an emancipated, self-centered woman who has murdered to win Pastor Rosmer, develops for him a self-denying love and in the end blindly commits suicide for his sake.

After *Hedda Gabler* Ibsen's playwriting entered upon its third and final phase. He no doubt sensed that reaction against realism and explicit social comment was in the air. The symbolism which hitherto had existed in his works as illuminating accompaniment to situation, now spread to embrace the whole dramatic action. The plays of this third period contain symbolic meanings behind seemingly ordinary scenes, meanings often so uncertain that they detract much from the artistry. The first and most successful of the species, *The Master Builder* (1892), deals with an egocentric architect, who saps his strength to keep younger rivals in subjection and then meets death in a fall from one of his own structures. In *John Gabriel Borkman* (1896) a financier jilts the woman he loves in order to get supposed wealth, gains nothing except imprisonment and loneliness, and ultimately dies aware of his spiritual folly. The repentance of a sculptor (perhaps Ibsen himself) for setting art ahead of life and love forms the theme of *When We Dead Awaken* (1899), Ibsen's valedictory to the stage.

These last plays by Ibsen encouraged the general Continental movement toward symbolistic drama in the 'nineties. Other leaders in this movement were the Swedish playwright, August Strindberg (1849–1912), and the Belgian, Maurice Maeterlinck (1862–   ). The latter's masterpiece, *Pelléas and Mélisande* (1893), contains a symbolism far more novel in its mystical, shadowy atmosphere than the symbolic art of his Norwegian contemporary.

It is the products of Ibsen's mid-career, however, which have contributed most to his renown. His seven realistic plays, from *Pillars of Society* to *Hedda Gabler*, inaugurated a new era in world drama. Their searching examination of the codes and ideals of modern society wedded in the popular consciousness the world of the theater to the world of affairs. Thus Ibsen established the stage as a leading agency for the modern man's intellectual and moral progress. Ibsen the poet-playwright rather than Ibsen the thinker accomplished this revolution in public attitude, for his ideas, though provocative, are neither original nor iconoclastic. Their embodiment in a powerfully dramatic form is what gives them enduring interest. Ibsen's representation of human life by no means equals the range of Shakespeare. Yet Ibsen within his narrower field created with as much, if not more, psychological intensity. Spiritual overtones, conveyed by abundant implications and symbols, fill his characterizations with unprecedented nuances. He attained this richer depiction of soul-states also by improving the current dramaturgy. The mechanics of exposition were simplified and refined; the external action more rigorously selected and compressed. Crispness of technique as well as of thought made Ibsen the most vital force in the world theater since the seventeenth century. He belongs for all time among the master builders of dramatic art.

"HEDDA GABLER"

Hedda Gabler represents Ibsen at the height of his power as a man of the theater. It is perhaps his most finished piece of dramatic art, and certainly his most objective. The first conceptions came to him at Munich during the winter of 1889–90; by summer they had fused into a design. He therefore gave up his usual holiday in the Tyrol mountains in order to work steadily upon the new play until its completion in November. The swift and unbroken course of its composition explains in part the superlative quality of the creation.

Munich witnessed the premiere of *Hedda Gabler* at the Residenz Theater on January

31, 1891. Many of the audience failed to grasp the character of Hedda and openly laughed at such pointed lines as her injunction to Lövborg to die "beautifully" (Act III, ll. 709–10). Other productions of the new Ibsen masterpiece followed rapidly. The Christiania Theater performed it in February; the Vaudeville Theater, London, in April; and the Vaudeville Theater, Paris, in December. *Hedda Gabler* soon gained an international popularity exceeding any other of its author's works. The title rôle has come to rank among the classic feminine parts on the twentieth-century stage. Noted actresses like Mrs. Patrick Campbell and Eleonora Duse in England, and Mrs. Fiske, Madame Nazimova, and Eva Le Gallienne in America, have immortalized Ibsen's heroine.

The heroine's maiden name, rather than her married one, graces the title of the play. What Ibsen wished to intimate by this particular titling appears in a note which he set down while drafting *Hedda Gabler:* "Hedda, as a personality, is to be regarded rather as her father's daughter than her husband's wife." It is plain that he considered Hedda's heritage and upbringing a point of critical significance. He once remarked about the education of upper-class women: "They are trained in idleness and longing for something uncertain. In the case of hopes unrealized, potentially useful personalities are crushed by their bitter disappointment." This comment outlines the exact situation dramatized in *Hedda Gabler*. The title helps to focus attention upon the heroine's family background and its connection with her fate.

Ibsen drew considerable important material for *Hedda Gabler* from persons whose actions had recently come to his notice. During the summer of 1889, while on holiday in the Tyrol mountains, he met a Viennese young lady who both charmed and repelled him. He found her sometimes a bored coquettish society girl of keen and cultivated mind, but, on other occasions, "a little daemonic wrecker, a bird of prey." This acquaintance in no small measure inspired the characterization of Hedda. Several of her acts Ibsen fashioned from real happenings of the day. The wife of the Norwegian composer Svendsen in a rage of jealousy burned the manuscript of a symphony which he had just completed. Likewise Hedda burns the manuscript belonging to her former admirer. Another Norwegian lady offered a further piece of devilish behavior. Her husband had conquered his addiction for liquor, but the whim seized her on his birthday to prove his self-control and her influence over him by placing a small keg of brandy in his study. Later she found him dead drunk on the floor. That occurrence suggested to Ibsen Hedda's testing of Lövborg. He borrowed much of Lövborg's character from a personal friend, a young Dane who was professor of Scandinavian languages at the University of Berlin. This brilliant scholar possessed an unbalanced personality and a shocking weakness for intoxicants. One day a railway porter stole his bag which contained the manuscript of a book by a fellow philologist. The episode formed the basis for Lövborg's losing the manuscript of his book. Thus, again and again, Ibsen appropriated from actual life those incidents in his plays which seem the most theatrical.

A consummate technique characterizes the dramatic pattern of *Hedda Gabler*. The more or less artificial expedients of the older stage — asides, soliloquies, obviously explanatory conversation — have disappeared. Ibsen relied for the disclosure of inward life upon a dialogue outwardly natural but directed with perfect economy to its objective. On a few occasions, to be sure, he revealed personality by a shrewd use of pantomime; for example, Hedda's pacing to and fro, at the opening of Act IV. The dramatic action, as in classical tragedy, opens not far from its culmination. Ibsen's "analytic" or "retrospective" method of character study, more subtly handled than in Hebbel's *Maria Magdalena*, swiftly weaves a complex set of relationships among five persons. Astute telescoping of events and human reactions reduces to a minimum the intervals between the various stages of the drama's development. Ibsen's superb craft enabled him without sacrificing psychological fidelity to compress a cycle of intricate action into thirty-six hours and one setting.

The elegant structure of *Hedda Gabler* reveals the influence of the "well-made play," but even more the strong architectural instinct of its author. No finer example of initial exposition can be found in all dramatic literature than this play's first act. It sets forth Hedda's essential maladjustments: contempt for her husband, dislike for his family, disillusionment over his professional prospects and her social position, disgust at approaching motherhood, and envy of a female rival. By the end of the act the storm clouds of frustration have gathered around her head. The act closes on the foreboding note of the pistols. The other acts finish on a similar note of dramatic intensity: the vision of Lövborg with vine leaves in his hair (Act II); the burning of Thea's and Lövborg's "child," the manuscript (Act III); the suicide (Act IV). Each act exhibits one step in Hedda's futile pursuit of self-realization.

The pistols and the vine leaves in the hair provide the symbolism which Ibsen's poetic vein urged him to incorporate in all his plays. These two symbols constitute important motifs, for they bring out the tragic antithesis in the heroine's personality. Her pseudo-classic image of the decorated reveler shows her hunger for that sense of life's beauty and exhilaration which she has never captured, at least partly because of the spell cast by the pistols. Hedda at a significant moment (Act I, ll. 1253–54) calls them General Gabler's pistols, stressing the fact that they are heirlooms. They symbolize the destructive nature of her paternal inheritance. It has left her cold and morbid with "no gift for anything but being bored," according to a note left by her creator. Her capacity for the joyous and lovely life which she imagined has been killed.

Yet Ibsen never interpolated the explicit idea of family or group responsibility in his analysis of Hedda's destiny. He presented her fate in an utterly detached character-drama. His study, rich in detail, creates a heroine of peculiar fascination, but one who does not warm the heart. The tragic effect of *Hedda Gabler*, therefore, depends more on the spectator's intellectual responsiveness to the general situation than on his sympathy with the protagonist, the usual bond in tragic drama. The spectacle of the destruction caused by Hedda's perverted and self-defeating individualism is intended to arouse pity and make the tragedy.

Ibsen did not let the curtain drop on this spectacle without a hint of its serious universality. He never spoke with more profound irony than in the play's last line where Judge Brack incredulously exclaims: "Good God! — people don't do such things." The sad truth, of course, is that everywhere in the world men and women with many of Hedda's attributes and inclinations are leading similarly ruinous careers. *Hedda Gabler* is a powerful tragedy on the human waste in modern society.

[For further study of Ibsen, see G. B. Shaw, *The Quintessence of Ibsenism* (revised edition, 1915); H. J. Weigand, *The Modern Ibsen* (1926); A. E. Zucker, *Ibsen, the Master Builder* (1929); M. C. Bradbrook, *Ibsen the Norwegian* (1946); P. F. D. Tennant, *Ibsen's Dramatic Technique* (1948).]

HENRIK IBSEN

Hedda Gabler

[*Translated by* EDMUND GOSSE *and* WILLIAM ARCHER]

DRAMATIS PERSONAE

GEORGE TESMAN
HEDDA TESMAN, *his wife*
MISS JULIANA TESMAN, *his aunt*
MRS. ELVSTED

JUDGE BRACK
EILERT LÖVBORG
BERTA, *servant at the* TESMANS'

The Scene is TESMAN'S *villa, in the west end of Christiania (Oslo), Norway*

ACT I

A spacious, handsome, and tastefully furnished drawing-room, decorated in dark colors. In the back, a wide doorway with curtains drawn back, leading into a smaller room decorated in the same style as the drawing-room. In the right-hand wall of the front room, a folding door leading out to the hall. In the opposite wall, on the left, a glass door, also with curtains drawn back. Through the panes can be seen part of a veranda outside, and trees covered with autumn foliage. An oval table, with a cover on it, and surrounded by chairs, stands well forward. In front, by the wall on the right, a wide stove of dark porcelain, a high-backed armchair, a cushioned foot-rest, and two footstools. A settee, with a small round table in front of it, fills the upper right-hand corner. In front, on the left, a little way from the wall, a sofa. Further back than the glass door, a piano. On either side of the doorway at the back a whatnot with terra-cotta and majolica ornaments. — Against the back wall of the inner room a sofa, with a table, and one or two chairs. Over the sofa hangs the portrait of a handsome elderly man in a General's uniform. Over the table a hanging lamp, with an opal glass shade. — A number of bouquets are arranged about the drawing-room, in vases and glasses. Others lie upon the tables. The floors in both rooms are covered with thick carpets. — Morning light. The sun shines in through the glass door.

MISS JULIANA TESMAN, *with her bonnet on and carrying a parasol, comes in from the hall, followed by* BERTA, *who carries a bouquet wrapped in paper.* MISS TESMAN *is a comely and pleasant-looking lady of about sixty-five. She is nicely but simply dressed in a gray walking-costume.* BERTA *is a middle-aged woman of plain and rather countrified appearance*

Miss Tes. (*stops close to the door, listens, and says softly*). Upon my word, I don't believe they are stirring yet!

Berta (*also softly*). I told you so, Miss. Remember how late the steamboat got in last 5 night. And then, when they got home! — good Lord, what a lot the young mistress had to unpack before she could get to bed.

Miss Tes. Well, well — let them have their sleep out. But let us see that they get a 10 good breath of the fresh morning air when they do appear. (*She goes to the glass door and throws it open.*

Berta (*beside the table, at a loss what to do*

with the bouquet in her hand). I declare there isn't a bit of room left. I think I'll put it 15 down here, Miss. (*She places it on the piano.*

Miss Tes. So you've got a new mistress now, my dear Berta. Heaven knows it was a wrench to me to part with you.

Berta (*on the point of weeping*). And do 20 you think it wasn't hard for me too, Miss? After all the blessed years I've been with you and Miss Rina.

Miss Tes. We must make the best of it, Berta. There was nothing else to be done. 25 George can't do without you, you see — he absolutely can't. He has had you to look after him ever since he was a little boy.

Berta. Ah, but, Miss Julia, I can't help thinking of Miss Rina lying helpless at 30 home there, poor thing. And with only that new girl, too! She'll never learn to take proper care of an invalid.

Miss Tes. Oh, I shall manage to train her. And of course, you know, I shall take most 35 of it upon myself. You needn't be uneasy about my poor sister, my dear Berta.

Berta. Well, but there's another thing, Miss. I'm so mortally afraid I shan't be able to suit the young mistress. 40

Miss Tes. Oh, well — just at first there may be one or two things ——

Berta. Most like she'll be terrible grand in her ways.

Miss Tes. Well you can't wonder at 45 that — General Gabler's [1] daughter! Think of the sort of life she was accustomed to in her father's time. Don't you remember how we used to see her riding down the road along with the General? In that long black habit — 50 and with feathers in her hat?

Berta. Yes, indeed — I remember well enough —! But good Lord, I should never have dreamt in those days that she and Master George would make a match of it. 55

Miss Tes. Nor I. — But, by the bye, Berta — while I think of it: in future you mustn't say Master George. You must say Doctor Tesman.

Berta. Yes, the young mistress spoke of 60

[1] The "a" in "Gabler" is pronounced like the "a" in "garden."

that too — last night — the moment they set foot in the house. Is it true then, Miss?

Miss Tes. Yes, indeed it is. Only think, Berta — some foreign university has made him a doctor — while he has been abroad, 65 you understand. I hadn't heard a word about it, until he told me himself upon the pier.

Berta. Well, well, he's clever enough for anything, he is. But I didn't think he'd have gone in for doctoring people too. 70

Miss Tes. No, no, it's not that sort of doctor he is. (*Nods significantly.*) But let me tell you, we may have to call him something still grander before long.

Berta. You don't say so! What can that 75 be, Miss?

Miss Tes. (*smiling*). H'm — wouldn't you like to know! (*With emotion*) Ah, dear, dear — if my poor brother could only look up from his grave now, and see what his little boy 80 has grown into! (*Looks around.*) But bless me, Berta — why have you done this? Taken the chintz covers off all the furniture?

Berta. The mistress told me to. She can't abide covers on the chairs, she says. 85

Miss Tes. Are they going to make this their everyday sitting-room then?

Berta. Yes, that's what I understood — from the mistress. Master George — the doctor — he said nothing. 90

GEORGE TESMAN *comes from the right into the inner room, humming to himself, and carrying an unstrapped empty portmanteau. He is a middle-sized, young-looking man of thirty-three, rather stout, with a round, open, cheerful face, fair hair, and beard. He wears spectacles, and is somewhat carelessly dressed in comfortable indoor clothes*

Miss Tes. Good morning, good morning, George.

Tes. (*in the doorway between the rooms*). Aunt Julia! Dear Aunt Julia! (*Goes up to her and shakes hands warmly.*) Come all this 95 way — so early! Eh?

Miss Tes. Why, of course I had to come and see how you were getting on.

Tes. In spite of your having had no proper night's rest? 100

Miss Tes. Oh, that makes no difference to me.

Tes. Well, I suppose you got home all right from the pier? Eh?

Miss Tes. Yes, quite safely, thank goodness. Judge Brack was good enough to 105 see me right to my door.

Tes. We were so sorry we couldn't give you a seat in the carriage. But you saw what a pile of boxes Hedda had to bring with her.

Miss Tes. Yes, she had certainly 110 plenty of boxes.

Berta (to TESMAN). Shall I go in and see if there's anything I can do for the mistress?

Tes. No, thank you, Berta — you needn't. She said she would ring if she wanted 115 anything.

Berta (going towards the right). Very well.

Tes. But look here — take this portmanteau with you.

Berta (taking it). I'll put it in the 120 attic.   (*She goes out by the hall door.*

Tes. Fancy, Auntie — I had the whole of that portmanteau chock full of copies of documents. You wouldn't believe how much I have picked up from all the archives I have been 125 examining — curious old details that no one has had any idea of ——

Miss Tes. Yes, you don't seem to have wasted your time on your wedding trip, George.

Tes. No, that I haven't. But do take 130 off your bonnet, Auntie. Look here! Let me untie the strings — eh?

Miss Tes. (while he does so). Well, well — this is just as if you were still at home with us.

Tes. (with the bonnet in his hand, looks at 135 *it from all sides).* Why, what a gorgeous bonnet you've been investing in!

Miss Tes. I bought it on Hedda's account.

Tes. On Hedda's account? Eh?

Miss Tes. Yes, so that Hedda needn't 140 be ashamed of me if we happened to go out together.

Tes. (patting her cheek). You always think of everything, Aunt Julia. (*Lays the bonnet on a chair beside the table.*) And now, look 145 here — suppose we sit comfortably on the sofa and have a little chat, till Hedda comes.

(*They seat themselves. She places her parasol in the corner of the sofa.*

Miss Tes. (takes both his hands and looks at him). What a delight it is to have you again, as large as life, before my very eyes, 150 George! My George — my poor brother's own boy!

Tes. And it's a delight for me, too, to see you again, Aunt Julia! You, who have been father and mother in one to me. 155

Miss Tes. Oh, yes, I know you will always keep a place in your heart for your old aunts.

Tes. And what about Aunt Rina? No improvement — eh?

Miss Tes. Oh, no — we can scarcely 160 look for any improvement in her case, poor thing. There she lies helpless, as she has lain for all these years. But heaven grant I may not lose her yet awhile! For if I did, I don't know what I should make of my life, 165 George — especially now that I haven't you to look after any more.

Tes. (patting her back). There, there, there —!

Miss Tes. (suddenly changing her tone). 170 And to think that here you are a married man, George! — And that you should be the one to carry off Hedda Gabler — the beautiful Hedda Gabler! Only think of it — she, that was so beset with admirers! 175

Tes. (hums a little and smiles complacently). Yes, I fancy I have several good friends about town who would like to stand in my shoes — eh?

Miss Tes. And then this fine long wedding-tour you have had! More than five — 180 nearly six months ——

Tes. Well, for me it has been a sort of tour of research as well. I have had to do so much grubbing among old records — and to read no end of books too, Auntie. 185

Miss Tes. Oh, yes, I suppose so. (*More confidentially, and lowering her voice a little*) But listen now, George — have you nothing — nothing special to tell me?

Tes. As to our journey? 190

Miss Tes. Yes.

Tes. No, I don't know of anything except what I have told you in my letters. I had a doctor's degree conferred on me — but that I told you yesterday. 195

Miss Tes. Yes, yes, you did. But what I

mean is — haven't you any — any — expectations —?

Tes. Expectations?

Miss Tes. Why, you know, George — 200 I'm your old auntie!

Tes. Why, of course I have expectations.

Miss Tes. Ah!

Tes. I have every expectation of being a professor one of these days.   205

Miss Tes. Oh, yes, a professor ——

Tes. Indeed, I may say I am certain of it. But my dear Auntie — you know all about that already?

Miss Tes. (*laughing to herself*). Yes, of 210 course I do. You are quite right there. (*Changing the subject*) But we were talking about your journey. It must have cost a great deal of money, George?

Tes. Well, you see — my handsome 215 traveling-scholarship went a good way.

Miss Tes. But I can't understand how you can have made it go far enough for two.

Tes. No, that's not so easy to understand — eh?   220

Miss Tes. And especially traveling with a lady — they tell me that makes it ever so much more expensive.

Tes. Yes, of course — it makes it a little more expensive. But Hedda had to have 225 this trip, Auntie! She really had to. Nothing else would have done.

Miss Tes. No, no, I suppose not. A wedding-tour seems to be quite indispensable nowadays. — But tell me now — have you 230 gone thoroughly over the house yet?

Tes. Yes, you may be sure I have. I have been afoot ever since daylight.

Miss Tes. And what do you think of it all?   235

Tes. I'm delighted! Quite delighted! Only I can't think what we are to do with the two empty rooms between this inner parlor and Hedda's bedroom.

Miss Tes. (*laughing*). Oh, my dear 240 George, I dare say you may find some use for them —in the course of time.

Tes. Why, of course you are quite right, Aunt Julia! You mean as my library increases — eh?   245

Miss Tes. Yes, quite so, my dear boy. It was your library I was thinking of.

Tes. I am specially pleased on Hedda's account. Often and often, before we were engaged, she said that she would never care 250 to live anywhere but in Secretary Falk's villa.[1]

Miss Tes. Yes, it was lucky that this very house should come into the market, just after you had started.

Tes. Yes, Aunt Julia, the luck was on 255 our side, wasn't it — eh?

Miss Tes. But the expense, my dear George! You will find it very expensive, all this.

Tes. (*looks at her, a little cast down*). Yes, I suppose I shall, Aunt!   260

Miss Tes. Oh, frightfully!

Tes. How much do you think? In round numbers? — Eh?

Miss Tes. Oh, I can't even guess until all the accounts come in.   265

Tes. Well, fortunately, Judge Brack has secured the most favorable terms for me — so he said in a letter to Hedda.

Miss Tes. Yes, don't be uneasy, my dear boy. — Besides, I have given security for 270 the furniture and all the carpets.

Tes. Security? You? My dear Aunt Julia — what sort of security could you give?

Miss Tes. I have given a mortgage on our annuity.   275

Tes. (*jumps up*). What! On your — and Aunt Rina's annuity!

Miss Tes. Yes, I knew of no other plan, you see.

Tes. (*placing himself before her*). Have 280 you gone out of your senses, Auntie! Your annuity — it's all that you and Aunt Rina have to live upon!

Miss Tes. Well, well, don't get so excited about it. It's only a matter of form, you 285 know — Judge Brack assured me of that. It was he that was kind enough to arrange the whole affair for me. A mere matter of form, he said.

Tes. Yes, that may be all very well. 290 But nevertheless ——

[1] In the Norwegian text, "*Statsradinde Falks villa*" — showing that it had belonged to the widow of a cabinet minister.

Miss Tes. You will have your own salary to depend upon now. And, good heavens, even if we did have to pay up a little —— ! To eke things out a bit at the start —— ! 295 Why, it would be nothing but a pleasure to us.

Tes. Oh, Auntie — will you never be tired of making sacrifices for me!

Miss Tes. (*rises and lays her hands on his shoulders*). Have I had any other happi- 300 ness in this world except to smooth your way for you, my dear boy? You, who have had neither father nor mother to depend on. And now we have reached the goal, George! Things have looked black enough for us, sometimes; 305 but, thank heaven, now you have nothing to fear.

Tes. Yes, it is really marvelous how everything has turned out for the best.

Miss Tes. And the people who opposed 310 you—who wanted to bar the way for you—now you have them at your feet. They have fallen, George. Your most dangerous rival — his fall was the worst. — And now he has to lie on the bed he has made for himself — poor mis- 315 guided creature.

Tes. Have you heard anything of Eilert? Since I went away, I mean.

Miss Tes. Only that he is said to have published a new book. 320

Tes. What! Eilert Lövborg! Recently — eh?

Miss Tes. Yes, so they say. Heaven knows whether it can be worth anything! Ah, when your new book appears — that will be an- 325 other story, George! What is it to be about?

Tes. It will deal with the domestic industries of Brabant [1] during the Middle Ages.

Miss Tes. Fancy — to be able to write on such a subject as that! 330

Tes. However, it may be some time before the book is ready. I have all these collections to arrange first, you see.

Miss Tes. Yes, collecting and arranging — no one can beat you at that. There you 335 are my poor brother's own son.

---

[1] A medieval duchy embracing what is now the northern part of Belgium and the southern part of the Netherlands. It was a district noted in the Middle Ages for its handicrafts, such as linen-weaving and jewelry.

Tes. I am looking forward eagerly to setting to work at it; especially now that I have my own delightful home to work in.

Miss Tes. And, most of all, now that 340 you have got the wife of your heart, my dear George.

Tes. (*embracing her*). Oh yes, yes, Aunt Julia. Hedda — she is the best part of it all! (*Looks towards the doorway.*) I believe I 345 hear her coming — eh?

HEDDA *enters from the left through the inner room. She is a woman of nine-and-twenty. Her face and figure show refinement and distinction. Her complexion is pale and opaque. Her steel-gray eyes express a cold, unruffled repose. Her hair is of an agreeable medium brown, but not particularly abundant. She is dressed in a tasteful, somewhat loose-fitting morning gown*

Miss Tes. (*going to meet* HEDDA). Good morning, my dear Hedda! Good morning, and a hearty welcome!

Hedda (*holds out her hand*). Good morn- 350 ing, dear Miss Tesman! So early a call! That is kind of you.

Miss Tes. (*with some embarrassment*). Well — has the bride slept well in her new home? 355

Hedda. Oh yes, thanks. Passably.

Tes. (*laughing*). Passably! Come, that's good, Hedda! You were sleeping like a stone when I got up.

Hedda. Fortunately. Of course one 360 has always to accustom one's self to new surroundings, Miss Tesman — little by little. (*Looking towards the left*) Oh — there the servant has gone and opened the veranda door, and let in a whole flood of sunshine. 365

Miss Tes. (*going towards the door*). Well, then we will shut it.

Hedda. No, no, not that! Tesman, please draw the curtains. That will give a softer light. 370

Tes. (*at the door*). All right — all right. — There now, Hedda, now you have both shade and fresh air.

Hedda. Yes, fresh air we certainly must

have, with all these stacks of flowers ——. 375
But — won't you sit down, Miss Tesman?

Miss Tes. No, thank you. Now that I have
seen that everything is all right here — thank
heaven! — I must be getting home again. My
sister is lying longing for me, poor thing. 380

Tes. Give her my very best love, Auntie;
and say I shall look in and see her later in the
day.

Miss Tes. Yes, yes, I'll be sure to tell her.
But by the bye, George (*feeling in her* 385
dress pocket) I had almost forgotten — I have
something for you here.

Tes. What is it, Auntie? Eh?

Miss Tes. (*produces a flat parcel wrapped in
newspaper and hands it to him*). Look 390
here, my dear boy.

Tes. (*opening the parcel*). Well, I declare! —
Have you really saved them for me, Aunt Julia!
Hedda! isn't this touching — eh?

Hedda (*beside the whatnot on the right*). 395
Well, what is it?

Tes. My old morning-shoes! My slippers.

Hedda. Indeed. I remember you often
spoke of them while we were abroad.

Tes. Yes, I missed them terribly. 400
(*Goes up to her.*) Now you shall see them,
Hedda!

Hedda (*going towards the stove*). Thanks, I
really don't care about it.

Tes. (*following her*). Only think — ill 405
as she was, Aunt Rina embroidered these for
me. Oh, you can't think how many associations cling to them!

Hedda (*at the table*). Scarcely for me.

Miss Tes. Of course not for Hedda, 410
George.

Tes. Well, but now that she belongs to the
family, I thought ——

Hedda (*interrupting*). We shall never get
on with this servant, Tesman. 415

Miss Tes. Not get on with Berta?

Tes. Why, dear, what puts that in your
head? Eh?

Hedda (*pointing*). Look there! She has left
her old bonnet lying about on a chair. 420

Tes. (*in consternation, drops the slippers on
the floor*). Why, Hedda ——

Hedda. Just fancy, if anyone should come
in and see it!

Tes. But Hedda — that's Aunt Julia's 425
bonnet.

Hedda. Is it!

Miss Tes. (*taking up the bonnet*). Yes, indeed
it's mine. And, what's more, it's not old,
Madam Hedda. 430

Hedda. I really did not look closely at it,
Miss Tesman.

Miss Tes. (*trying on the bonnet*). Let me tell
you it's the first time I have worn it — the very
first time. 435

Tes. And a very nice bonnet it is too — quite
a beauty!

Miss Tes. Oh, it's no such great thing,
George. (*Looks around her.*) My parasol
— ? Ah, here. (*Takes it.*) For this is 440
mine too — (*mutters*) — not Berta's.

Tes. A new bonnet and a new parasol!
Only think, Hedda!

Hedda. Very handsome indeed.

Tes. Yes, isn't it? Eh? But Auntie, 445
take a good look at Hedda before you go! See
how handsome she is!

Miss Tes. Oh, my dear boy, there's nothing
new in that. Hedda was always lovely.

(*She nods and goes towards the right.*

Tes. (*following*). Yes, but have you 450
noticed what splendid condition she is in?
How she has filled out on the journey?

Hedda (*crossing the room*). Oh, do be
quiet — !

Miss Tes. (*who has stopped and turned*). 455
Filled out?

Tes. Of course you don't notice it so much
now that she has that dress on. But I, who
can see ——

Hedda (*at the glass door, impatiently*). 460
Oh, you can't see anything.

Tes. It must be the mountain air in the
Tyrol ——

Hedda (*curtly, interrupting*). I am exactly
as I was when I started. 465

Tes. So you insist; but I'm quite certain you
are not. Don't you agree with me, Auntie?

Miss Tes. (*who has been gazing at her with
folded hands*). Hedda is lovely — lovely —
lovely. (*Goes up to her, takes her head* 470
*between both hands, draws it downwards, and
kisses her hair.*) God bless and preserve
Hedda Tesman — for George's sake.

Hedda (*gently freeing herself*). Oh! — Let me go.   475

Miss Tes. (*in quiet emotion*). I shall not let a day pass without coming to see you.

Tes. No, you won't, will you, Auntie? Eh?

Miss Tes. Good-bye — good-bye!

> (*She goes out by the hall door.* TES-MAN *accompanies her. The door remains half open.* TESMAN *can be heard repeating his message to Aunt Rina and his thanks for the slippers.*
>
> (*In the meantime,* HEDDA *walks about the room raising her arms and clenching her hands as if in desperation. Then she flings back the curtains from the glass door, and stands there looking out.*
>
> (*Presently* TESMAN *returns and closes the door behind him.*

Tes. (*picks up the slippers from the* 480 *floor*). What are you looking at, Hedda?

Hedda (*once more calm and mistress of herself*). I am only looking at the leaves. They are so yellow — so withered.

Tes. (*wraps up the slippers and lays them* 485 *on the table*). Well, you see, we are well into September now.

Hedda (*again restless*). Yes, to think of it! — Already in — in September.

Tes. Don't you think Aunt Julia's 490 manner was strange, dear? Almost solemn? Can you imagine what was the matter with her? Eh?

Hedda. I scarcely know her, you see. Is she often like that?   495

Tes. No, not as she was today.

Hedda (*leaving the glass door*). Do you think she was annoyed about the bonnet?

Tes. Oh, scarcely at all. Perhaps a little, just at the moment ——   500

Hedda. But what an idea, to pitch her bonnet about in the drawing-room! No one does that sort of thing.

Tes. Well, you may be sure Aunt Julia won't do it again.   505

Hedda. In any case, I shall manage to make my peace with her.

Tes. Yes, my dear, good Hedda, if you only would.

Hedda. When you call this afternoon, 510 you might invite her to spend the evening here.

Tes. Yes, that I will. And there's one thing more you could do that would delight her heart.

Hedda. What is it?   515

Tes. If you could only prevail on yourself to address her more familiarly. For my sake, Hedda? Eh?

Hedda. No, no, Tesman — you really mustn't ask that of me. I have told you so 520 already. I shall try to call her "Aunt"; and you must be satisfied with that.

Tes. Well, well. Only I think now that you belong to the family, you ——

Hedda. H'm — I can't in the least see 525 why ——

> (*She goes up towards the middle doorway.*

Tes. (*after a pause*). Is there anything the matter with you, Hedda? Eh?

Hedda. I'm only looking at my old piano. It doesn't go at all well with the other 530 things.

Tes. The first time I draw my salary we'll see about exchanging it.

Hedda. No, no — no exchanging. I don't want to part with it. Suppose we put it 535 there in the inner room and then get another here in its place. When it's convenient, I mean.

Tes. (*a little taken aback*). Yes — of course we could do that.   540

Hedda (*takes up the bouquet from the piano*). These flowers were not here last night when we arrived.

Tes. Aunt Julia must have brought them for you.   545

Hedda (*examining the bouquet*). A visiting card. (*Takes it out and reads.*) "Shall return later in the day." Can you guess whose card it is?

Tes. No. Whose? Eh?   550

Hedda. The name is "Mrs. Elvsted."

Tes. Is it really? Sheriff Elvsted's wife? Miss Rysing that was.

Hedda. Exactly. The girl with the irritating hair, that she was always showing off. 555 An old flame of yours, I've been told.

Tes. (*laughing*). Oh, that didn't last long; and it was before I knew you, Hedda. But fancy her being in town!

Hedda. It's odd that she should call 560 upon us. I have scarcely seen her since we left school.

Tes. I haven't seen her either for — heaven knows how long. I wonder how she can endure to live in such an out-of-the-way hole 565 — eh?

Hedda (*after a moment's thought, says suddenly*). Tell me, Tesman — isn't it somewhere near there that he — that — Eilert Lövborg is living? 570

Tes. Yes, he is somewhere in that part of the country.

BERTA *enters by the hall door*

Berta. That lady, ma'am, that brought some flowers a little while ago, is here again. (*Pointing*) The flowers you have in your hand, 575 ma'am.

Hedda. Ah, is she? Well, please show her in. (BERTA *opens the door for* MRS. ELVSTED, *and goes out herself.* — MRS. ELVSTED *is a woman of fragile figure, with pretty, soft features. Her eyes are light blue, large, round, and somewhat prominent, with a startled, inquiring expression. Her hair is remarkably light, almost flaxen, and unusually abundant and wavy. She is a couple of years younger than Hedda. She wears a dark visiting dress, tasteful, but not quite in the latest fashion.*)

Hedda (*receives her warmly*). How do you do, my dear Mrs. Elvsted? It's delightful to see you again. 580

Mrs. Elv. (*nervously, struggling for self-control*). Yes, it's a very long time since we met.

Tes. (*gives her his hand*). And we too — eh?

Hedda. Thanks for your lovely flow- 585 ers ——

Mrs. Elv. Oh, not at all — I would have come straight here yesterday afternoon; but I heard that you were away ——

Tes. Have you just come to town? 590 Eh?

Mrs. Elv. I arrived yesterday, about mid-day. Oh, I was quite in despair when I heard that you were not at home.

Hedda. In despair! How so? 595

Tes. Why, my dear Mrs. Rysing — I mean Mrs. Elvsted ——

Hedda. I hope that you are not in any trouble?

Mrs. Elv. Yes, I am. And I don't 600 know another living creature here that I can turn to.

Hedda (*laying the bouquet on the table*). Come — let us sit here on the sofa ——

Mrs. Elv. I am too restless to sit down. 605

Hedda. Oh no, you're not. Come here. (*She draws* MRS. ELVSTED *down upon the sofa and sits at her side.*)

Tes. Well? What is it, Mrs. Elvsted?

Hedda. Has anything particular happened to you at home?

Mrs. Elv. Yes — and no. Oh — I am 610 so anxious you should not misunderstand me ——

Hedda. Then your best plan is to tell us the whole story, Mrs. Elvsted.

Tes. I suppose that's what you have 615 come for — eh?

Mrs. Elv. Yes, yes — of course it is. Well then, I must tell you — if you don't already know — that Eilert Lövborg is in town, too.

Hedda. Lövborg ——! 620

Tes. What! Has Eilert Lövborg come back? Fancy that, Hedda!

Hedda. Well, well — I hear it.

Mrs. Elv. He has been here a week already. Just fancy — a whole week! In this ter- 625 rible town, alone! With so many temptations on all sides.

Hedda. But, my dear Mrs. Elvsted — how does he concern you so much?

Mrs. Elv. (*looks at her with a startled 630 air, and says rapidly*). He was the children's tutor.

Hedda. Your children's?

Mrs. Elv. My husband's. I have none.

Hedda. Your stepchildren's, then? 635

Mrs. Elv. Yes.

Tes. (*somewhat hesitatingly*). Then was he —
I don't know how to express it — was he —
regular enough in his habits to be fit for the
post? Eh?   640

Mrs. Elv. For the last two years his conduct
has been irreproachable.

Tes. Has it, indeed? Fancy that, Hedda!

Hedda. I hear it.

Mrs. Elv. Perfectly irreproachable, I   645
assure you! In every respect. But all the
same — now that I know he is here — in this
great town — and with a large sum of money
in his hands — I can't help being in mortal fear
for him.   650

Tes. Why did he not remain where he was?
With you and your husband? Eh?

Mrs. Elv. After his book was published he
was too restless and unsettled to remain with us.

Tes. Yes, by the bye, Aunt Julia told   655
me he had published a new book.

Mrs. Elv. Yes, a big book, dealing with the
march of civilization — in broad outline, as it
were. It came out about a fortnight ago.
And since it has sold so well, and been so   660
much read — and made such a sensation ——

Tes. Has it, indeed? It must be something
he has had lying by since his better days.

Mrs. Elv. Long ago, you mean?

Tes. Yes.   665

Mrs. Elv. No, he has written it all since he
has been with us — within the last year.

Tes. Isn't that good news, Hedda? Think
of that.

Mrs. Elv. Ah yes, if only it would last!   670

Hedda. Have you seen him here in town?

Mrs. Elv. No, not yet. I have had the
greatest difficulty in finding out his address.
But this morning I discovered it at last.

Hedda (*looks searchingly at her*). Do   675
you know, it seems to me a little odd of your
husband — h'm ——

Mrs. Elv. (*starting nervously*). Of my husband! What?

Hedda. That he should send you to   680
town on such an errand — that he does not
come himself and look after his friend.

Mrs. Elv. Oh, no, no — my husband has
no time. And besides, I — I had some shopping to do.   685

Hedda (*with a slight smile*). Ah, that is a different matter.

Mrs. Elv. (*rising quickly and uneasily*). And
now I beg and implore you, Mr. Tesman — receive Eilert Lövborg kindly if he comes to   690
you! And that he is sure to do. You see you
were such great friends in the old days. And
then you are interested in the same studies —
the same branch of science — so far as I can
understand.   695

Tes. We used to be, at any rate.

Mrs. Elv. That is why I beg so earnestly
that you — you too — will keep a sharp eye
upon him. Oh, you will promise me that, Mr.
Tesman — won't you?   700

Tes. With the greatest of pleasure, Mrs.
Rysing ——

Hedda. Elvsted.

Tes. I assure you I shall do all I possibly can
for Eilert. You may rely upon me.   705

Mrs. Elv. Oh, how very, very kind of you!
(*Presses his hands.*) Thanks, thanks, thanks!
(*Frightened*) You see, my husband is so very
fond of him!

Hedda (*rising*). You ought to write to   710
him, Tesman. Perhaps he may not care to
come to you of his own accord.

Tes. Well, perhaps it would be the right
thing to do, Hedda? Eh?

Hedda. And the sooner the better.   715
Why not at once?

Mrs. Elv. (*imploringly*). Oh, if you only
would!

Tes. I'll write this moment. Have you
his address, Mrs. — Mrs. Elvsted?   720

Mrs. Elv. Yes. (*Takes a slip of paper
from her pocket and hands it to him.*) Here it
is.

Tes. Good, good. Then I'll go in —— (*Looks
about him.*) By the bye — my slippers?   725
Oh, here. (*Takes the packet, and is about to go.*

Hedda. Be sure you write him a cordial,
friendly letter. And a good long one too.

Tes. Yes, I will.

Mrs. Elv. But please, please don't say   730
a word to show that I have suggested it.

Tes. No, how could you think I would? Eh?
(*He goes out to the right, through the
inner room.*

Hedda (*goes up to* Mrs. Elvsted, *smiles, and says in a low voice*). There! We have killed two birds with one stone.   735

Mrs. Elv. What do you mean?

Hedda. Could you not see that I wanted him to go?

Mrs. Elv. Yes, to write the letter ——

Hedda. And in order that I might 740 speak to you alone.

Mrs. Elv. (*confused*). About the same thing?

Hedda. Precisely.

Mrs. Elv. (*apprehensively*). But there is nothing more, Mrs. Tesman! Absolutely 745 nothing!

Hedda. Oh yes, but there is. There is a great deal more — I can see that. Sit here — and we'll have a cosy, confidential chat.

(*She forces* Mrs. Elvsted *to sit in the easy-chair beside the stove, and seats herself on one of the footstools.*

Mrs. Elv. (*anxiously, looking at her* 750 *watch*). But, my dear Mrs. Tesman — I was really on the point of going.

Hedda. Oh, you can't be in such a hurry. — Well? Now tell me something about your life at home.   755

Mrs. Elv. Oh, that is just what I care least to speak about.

Hedda. But to me, dear — ? Why, weren't we schoolfellows?

Mrs. Elv. Yes, but you were in the 760 class above me. Oh, how dreadfully afraid of you I was then!

Hedda. Afraid of me?

Mrs. Elv. Yes, dreadfully. For when we met on the stairs you used always to pull 765 my hair.

Hedda. Did I, really?

Mrs. Elv. Yes, and once you said you would burn it off my head.

Hedda. Oh, that was all nonsense, of 770 course.

Mrs. Elv. Yes, but I was so silly in those days. — And since then, too — we have drifted so far — far apart from each other. Our circles have been so entirely different.   775

Hedda. Well then, we must try to drift together again. Now listen! At school we said

du [1] to each other; and we called each other by our Christian names ——

Mrs. Elv. No, I am sure you must be 780 mistaken.

Hedda. No, not at all! I can remember quite distinctly. So now we are going to renew our old friendship. (*Draws the footstool closer to* Mrs. Elvsted.) There, now! (*Kisses* 785 *her cheek.*) You must say *du* to me and call me Hedda.

Mrs. Elv. (*presses and pats her hands*). Oh, how good and kind you are! I am not used to such kindness.   790

Hedda. There, there, there! And I shall say *du* to you, as in the old days, and call you my dear Thora. [2]

Mrs. Elv. My name is Thea. [3]

Hedda. Why, of course! I meant 795 Thea. (*Looks at her compassionately.*) So you are not accustomed to goodness and kindness, Thea? Not in your own home?

Mrs. Elv. Oh, if I only had a home? But I haven't any; I have never had a home.   800

Hedda (*looks at her for a moment*). I almost suspected as much.

Mrs. Elv. (*gazing helplessly before her*). Yes — yes — yes.

Hedda. I don't quite remember — was 805 it not as housekeeper that you first went to Mr. Elvsted's?

Mrs. Elv. I really went as governess. But his wife — his late wife — was an invalid — and rarely left her rooms. So 810 I had to look after the housekeeping as well.

Hedda. And then — at last — you became mistress of the house.

Mrs. Elv. (*sadly*). Yes, I did.   815

Hedda. Let me see — about how long ago was that?

Mrs. Elv. My marriage?

Hedda. Yes.

Mrs. Elv. Five years ago.   820

Hedda. To be sure; it must be that.

Mrs. Elv. Oh, those five years — ! Or at

---

[1] The familiar form of the second person pronoun in Norwegian.

[2] Pronounce *Tora.*

[3] Pronounce *Taya.*

all events the last two or three years of them! Oh, if you [1] could only imagine ——

Hedda (*giving her a little slap on the hand*). De? Fie, Thea!   825

Mrs. Elv. Yes, yes, I will try —— Well, if — you could only imagine and understand ——

Hedda (*lightly*). Eilert Lövborg has been in your neighborhood about three years, 830 hasn't he?

Mrs. Elv. (*looks at her doubtfully*). Eilert Lövborg? Yes — he has.

Hedda. Had you known him before, in town here?   835

Mrs. Elv. Scarcely at all. I mean — I knew him by name of course.

Hedda. But you saw a good deal of him in the country?

Mrs. Elv. Yes, he came to us every day. 840 You see, he gave the children lessons; for in the long run I couldn't manage it all myself.

Hedda. No, that's clear. — And your husband — ? I suppose he is often away from home?   845

Mrs. Elv. Yes. Being sheriff, you know, he has to travel about a good deal in his district.

Hedda (*leaning against the arm of the chair*). Thea — my poor, sweet Thea — now you must tell me everything — exactly as it stands. 850

Mrs. Elv. Well then, you must question me.

Hedda. What sort of a man is your husband, Thea? I mean — you know — in everyday life. Is he kind to you?

Mrs. Elv. (*evasively*). I am sure he 855 means well in everything.

Hedda. I should think he must be altogether too old for you. There is at least twenty years' difference between you, is there not?

Mrs. Elv. (*irritably*). Yes, that is true, 860 too. Everything about him is repellent to me! We have not a thought in common. We have no single point of sympathy — he and I.

Hedda. But is he not fond of you all the same? In his own way?   865

Mrs. Elv. Oh, I really don't know. I think

[1] Mrs. Elvsted in the Norwegian text uses the formal pronoun *De*, whereupon Hedda rebukes her. In her next speech Mrs. Elvsted says *du*.

he regards me simply as a useful property. And then it doesn't cost much to keep me. I am not expensive.

Hedda. That is stupid of you.   870

Mrs. Elv. (*shakes her head*). It cannot be otherwise — not with him. I don't think he really cares for anyone but himself — and perhaps a little for the children.

Hedda. And for Eilert Lövborg, Thea. 875

Mrs. Elv. (*looking at her*). For Eilert Lövborg? What puts that into your head?

Hedda. Well, my dear — I should say, when he sends you after him all the way to town — (*Smiling almost imperceptibly*) And be- 880 sides, you said so yourself, to Tesman.

Mrs. Elv. (*with a little nervous twitch*). Did I? Yes, I suppose I did. (*Vehemently, but not loudly*) No — I may just as well make a clean breast of it at once! For it must all come 885 out in any case.

Hedda. Why, my dear Thea — ?

Mrs. Elv. Well, to make a long story short: my husband did not know I was coming.

Hedda. What! Your husband didn't 890 know it!

Mrs. Elv. No, of course not! For that matter, he was away from home himself — he was traveling. Oh, I could bear it no longer, Hedda! I couldn't indeed — so utterly 895 alone as I should have been in the future.

Hedda. Well? And then?

Mrs. Elv. So I put together some of my things — what I needed most — as quietly as possible. And then I left the house.   900

Hedda. Without a word?

Mrs. Elv. Yes — and took the train straight to town.

Hedda. Why, my dear, good Thea — to think of you daring to do it!   905

Mrs. Elv. (*rises and moves about the room*). What else could I possibly do?

Hedda. But what do you think your husband will say when you go home again?

Mrs. Elv. (*at the table, looks at her*). Back to him?   910

Hedda. Of course.

Mrs. Elv. I shall never go back to him again.

Hedda (*rising and going towards her*). Then

you have left your home — for good and 915 all?

Mrs. Elv. Yes. There was nothing else to be done.

Hedda. But then — to take flight so openly.

Mrs. Elv. Oh, it's impossible to keep 920 things of that sort secret.

Hedda. But what do you think people will say of you, Thea?

Mrs. Elv. They may say what they like, for all *I* care. (*Seats herself wearily and* 925 *sadly on the sofa.*) I have done nothing but what I had to do.

Hedda (*after a short silence*). And what are your plans now? What do you think of doing?

Mrs. Elv. I don't know yet. I only 930 know this, that I must live here, where Eilert Lövborg is — if I am to live at all.

Hedda (*takes a chair from the table, seats herself beside her, and strokes her hands*). My dear Thea — how did this — this friendship 935 — between you and Eilert Lövborg come about?

Mrs. Elv. Oh, it grew up gradually. I gained a sort of influence over him.

Hedda. Indeed?
940

Mrs. Elv. He gave up his old habits. Not because I asked him to, for I never dared do that. But of course he saw how repulsive they were to me; and so he dropped them.

Hedda (*concealing an involuntary smile* 945 *of scorn*). Then you have reclaimed him — as the saying goes — my little Thea.

Mrs. Elv. So he says himself, at any rate. And he, on his side, has made a real human being of me — taught me to think, and 950 to understand so many things.

Hedda. Did he give you lessons too, then?

Mrs. Elv. No, not exactly lessons. But he talked to me — talked about such an infinity of things. And then came the lovely, 955 happy time when I began to share in his work — when he allowed me to help him!

Hedda. Oh, he did, did he?

Mrs. Elv. Yes! He never wrote anything without my assistance.
960

Hedda. You were two good comrades, in fact?

Mrs. Elv. (*eagerly*). Comrades! Yes, fancy,

Hedda — that is the very word he used! — Oh, I ought to feel perfectly happy, and yet 965 I cannot; for I don't know how long it will last.

Hedda. Are you no surer of him than that?

Mrs. Elv. (*gloomily*). A woman's shadow stands between Eilert Lövborg and me.

Hedda (*looks at her anxiously*). Who 970 can that be?

Mrs. Elv. I don't know. Someone he knew in his — in his past. Someone he has never been able wholly to forget.

Hedda. What has he told you — about 975 this?

Mrs. Elv. He has only once — quite vaguely — alluded to it.

Hedda. Well! And what did he say?

Mrs. Elv. He said that when they 980 parted, she threatened to shoot him with a pistol.

Hedda (*with cold composure*). Oh, nonsense! No one does that sort of thing here.

Mrs. Elv. No. And that is why I 985 think it must have been that red-haired singing-woman whom he once ——

Hedda. Yes, very likely.

Mrs. Elv. For I remember they used to say of her that she carried loaded firearms. 990

Hedda. Oh — then of course it must have been she.

Mrs. Elv. (*wringing her hands*). And now just fancy, Hedda — I hear that this singing-woman — that she is in town again! Oh, 995 I don't know what to do ——

Hedda (*glancing towards the inner room*). Hush! Here comes Tesman. (*Rises and whispers.*) Thea — all this must remain between you and me.
1000

Mrs. Elv. (*springing up*). Oh yes — yes! For heaven's sake — !

GEORGE TESMAN, *with a letter in his hand, comes from the right through the inner room*

Tes. There now — the epistle is finished.

Hedda. That's right. And now Mrs. Elvsted is just going. Wait a moment — 1005 I'll go with you to the garden gate.

Tes. Do you think Berta could post the letter, Hedda dear?

Hedda (*takes it*). I will tell her to.

BERTA *enters from the hall*

Berta. Judge Brack wishes to know if   1010
Mrs. Tesman will receive him.

Hedda. Yes, ask Judge Brack to come in.
And look here — put this letter in the post.

Berta (taking the letter). Yes, ma'am.

(*She opens the door for* JUDGE BRACK
and goes out herself. BRACK *is a
man of forty-five; thick-set, but well-
built and elastic in his movements.
His face is roundish with an aristocratic profile. His hair is short,
still almost black, and carefully
dressed. His eyes are lively and
sparkling. His eyebrows thick.
His moustaches are also thick, with
short-cut ends. He wears a well-cut
walking-suit, a little too youthful for
his age. He uses an eyeglass, which
he now and then lets drop.*

Brack (with his hat in his hand, bow-   1015
ing). May one venture to call so early in the
day?

Hedda. Of course one may.

Tes. (presses his hand). You are welcome
at any time. (*Introducing him*) Judge   1020
Brack — Miss Rysing ——

Hedda. Oh — !

Brack (bowing). Ah — delighted ——

Hedda (looks at him and laughs). It's nice to
have a look at you by daylight, Judge!   1025

Brack. Do you find me — altered?

Hedda. A little younger, I think.

Brack. Thank you so much.

Tes. But what do you think of Hedda —
eh? Doesn't she look flourishing? She   1030
has actually ——

Hedda. Oh, do leave me alone. You haven't
thanked Judge Brack for all the trouble he has
taken ——

Brack. Oh, nonsense — it was a pleas-   1035
ure to me ——

Hedda. Yes, you are a friend indeed. But
here stands Thea all impatience to be off — so
au revoir, Judge. I shall be back again presently.   1040

(*Mutual salutations.* MRS. ELVSTED
and HEDDA *go out by the hall door.*

Brack. Well, — is your wife tolerably satisfied ——

Tes. Yes, we can't thank you sufficiently.
Of course she talks of a little rearrangement
here and there; and one or two things   1045
are still wanting. We shall have to buy some
additional trifles.

Brack. Indeed!

Tes. But we won't trouble you about these
things. Hedda says she herself will look   1050
after what is wanting. — Shan't we sit down?
Eh?

Brack. Thanks, for a moment. (*Seats himself
beside the table.*) There is something I wanted
to speak to you about, my dear Tesman.   1055

Tes. Indeed? Ah, I understand! (*Seating
himself*) I suppose it's the serious part of the
frolic that is coming now. Eh?

Brack. Oh, the money question is not so very
pressing; though, for that matter, I wish   1060
we had gone a little more economically to work.

Tes. But that would never have done, you
know! Think of Hedda, my dear fellow! You,
who know her so well —— I couldn't possibly
ask her to put up with a shabby style of   1065
living!

Brack. No, no — that is just the difficulty.

Tes. And then — fortunately — it can't be
long before I receive my appointment.

Brack. Well, you see — such things   1070
are often apt to hang fire for a time.

Tes. Have you heard anything definite? Eh?

Brack. Nothing exactly definite —— (*Interrupting himself*) But, by the bye — I have
one piece of news for you.   1075

Tes. Well?

Brack. Your old friend, Eilert Lövborg, has
returned to town.

Tes. I know that already.

Brack. Indeed! How did you learn   1080
it?

Tes. From that lady who went out with
Hedda.

Brack. Really? What was her name? I
didn't quite catch it.   1085

Tes. Mrs. Elvsted.

Brack. Aha — Sheriff Elvsted's wife? Of
course — he has been living up in their regions.

Tes. And fancy — I'm delighted to   1090
hear that he is quite a reformed character!

Brack. So they say.

Tes. And then he has published a new book
— eh?

Brack. Yes, indeed he has.   1095

Tes. And I hear it has made some sensation!

Brack. Quite an unusual sensation.

Tes. Fancy — isn't that good news! A man
of such extraordinary talents —— I felt so
grieved to think that he had gone irre-   1100
trievably to ruin.

Brack. That was what everybody thought.

Tes. But I cannot imagine what he will take
to now! How in the world will he be able to
make his living? Eh?   1105

> (*During the last words,* HEDDA *has
> entered by the hall door.*

Hedda (*to* BRACK, *laughing with a touch of
scorn*). Tesman is forever worrying about how
people are to make their living.

Tes. Well, you see, dear — we were talking
about poor Eilert Lövborg.   1110

Hedda (*glancing at him rapidly*). Oh, indeed?
(*Seats herself in the armchair beside the stove
and asks indifferently.*) What is the matter with
him?

Tes. Well — no doubt he has run   1115
through all his property long ago; and he can
scarcely write a new book every year — eh? So
I really can't see what is to become of him.

Brack. Perhaps I can give you some information on that point.   1120

Tes. Indeed!

Brack. You must remember that his relations have a good deal of influence.

Tes. Oh, his relations, unfortunately, have
entirely washed their hands of him.   1125

Brack. At one time they called him the hope
of the family.

Tes. At one time, yes! But he has put an
end to all that.

Hedda. Who knows? (*With a slight*   1130
smile) I hear they have reclaimed him up at
Sheriff Elvsted's ——

Brack. And then this book that he has published ——

Tes. Well, well, I hope to goodness   1135
they may find something for him to do. I have

just written to him. I asked him to come and
see us this evening, Hedda dear.

Brack. But, my dear fellow, you are booked
for my bachelors' party this evening.   1140
You promised on the pier last night.

Hedda. Had you forgotten, Tesman?

Tes. Yes, I had utterly forgotten.

Brack. But it doesn't matter, for you may be
sure he won't come.   1145

Tes. What makes you think that? Eh?

Brack (*with a little hesitation, rising and resting his hands on the back of his chair*). My dear
Tesman — and you too, Mrs. Tesman — I
think I ought not to keep you in the dark   1150
about something that — that ——

Tes. That concerns Eilert — ?

Brack. Both you and him.

Tes. Well, my dear Judge, out with it.

Brack. You must be prepared to find   1155
your appointment deferred longer than you
desired or expected.

Tes. (*jumping up uneasily*). Is there some
hitch about it? Eh?

Brack. The nomination may perhaps   1160
be made conditional on the result of a competition ——

Tes. Competition! Think of that, Hedda!

Hedda (*leans further back in the chair*). Aha
— aha!   1165

Tes. But who can my competitor be?
Surely not — ?

Brack. Yes, precisely — Eilert Lövborg.

Tes. (*clasping his hands*). No, no — it's
quite inconceivable! Quite impossible!   1170
Eh?

Brack. H'm — that is what it may come to,
all the same.

Tes. Well, but, Judge Brack — it would show
the most incredible lack of considera-   1175
tion for me. (*Gesticulates with his arms.*) For
— just think — I'm a married man! We have
married on the strength of these prospects,
Hedda and I, and run deep into debt; and borrowed money from Aunt Julia too.   1180
Good heavens, they had as good as promised
me the appointment. Eh?

Brack. Well, well, well — no doubt you will
get it in the end; only after a contest.

Hedda (*immovable in her armchair*).   1185

Fancy, Tesman, there will be a sort of sporting interest in that.

Tes. Why, my dearest Hedda, how can you be so indifferent about it?

Hedda (*as before*). I am not at all in- 1190 different. I am most eager to see who wins.

Brack. In any case, Mrs. Tesman, it is best that you should know how matters stand. I mean — before you set about the little purchases I hear you are threatening. 1195

Hedda. This can make no difference.

Brack. Indeed! Then I have no more to say. Good-bye! (*To* TESMAN) I shall look in on my way back from my afternoon walk, and take you home with me. 1200

Tes. Oh yes, yes — your news has quite upset me.

Hedda (*reclining, holds out her hand*). Goodbye, Judge; and be sure you call in the afternoon. 1205

Brack. Many thanks. Good-bye, goodbye!

Tes. (*accompanying him to the door*). Goodbye, my dear Judge! You must really excuse me —— 1210

(JUDGE BRACK *goes out by the hall door.*

Tes. (*crosses the room*). Oh, Hedda — one should never rush into adventures. Eh?

Hedda (*looks at him, smiling*). Do you do that?

Tes. Yes, dear — there is no denying 1215 — it was adventurous to go and marry and set up house upon mere expectations.

Hedda. Perhaps you are right there.

Tes. Well — at all events, we have our delightful home, Hedda! Fancy, the 1220 home we both dreamed of — the home we were in love with, I may almost say. Eh?

Hedda (*rising slowly and wearily*). It was part of our compact that we were to go into society — to keep open house. 1225

Tes. Yes, if you only knew how I had been looking forward to it! Fancy — to see you as hostess — in a select circle! Eh? Well, well, well — for the present we shall have to get on without society, Hedda — only to in- 1230 vite Aunt Julia now and then. — Oh, I intended you to lead such an utterly different life, dear — !

Hedda. Of course I cannot have my man in livery just yet. 1235

Tes. Oh no, unfortunately. It would be out of the question for us to keep a footman, you know.

Hedda. And the saddle-horse I was to have had —— 1240

Tes. (*aghast*). The saddle-horse!

Hedda. — I suppose I must not think of that now.

Tes. Good heavens, no! — that's as clear as daylight. 1245

Hedda (*goes up the room*). Well, I shall have one thing at least to kill time with in the meanwhile.

Tes. (*beaming*). Oh, thank heaven for that! What is it, Hedda? Eh? 1250

Hedda (*in the middle doorway, looks at him with covert scorn*). My pistols, George.

Tes. (*in alarm*). Your pistols!

Hedda (*with cold eyes*). General Gabler's pistols. (*She goes out through the inner room, to the left.*

Tes. (*rushes up to the middle doorway and calls after her*). No, for heaven's sake, 1255 Hedda darling — don't touch those dangerous things! For my sake, Hedda! Eh?

Curtain

ACT II

The room at the TESMANS' *as in the first act, except that the piano has been removed, and an elegant little writing-table with bookshelves put in its place. A smaller table stands near the sofa on the left. Most of the bouquets have been taken away.* MRS. ELVSTED'S *bouquet is upon the large table in front. — It is afternoon.*

HEDDA, *dressed to receive callers, is alone in the room. She stands by the open glass door, loading a revolver. The fellow to it lies in an open pistol-case on the writing-table*

Hedda (*looks down the garden, and calls*). So you are here again, Judge!

Brack (*is heard calling from a distance*). As you see, Mrs. Tesman!

Hedda (*raises the pistol and points*). Now 5
I'll shoot you, Judge Brack!

Brack (*calling unseen*). No, no, no! Don't
stand aiming at me!

Hedda. This is what comes of sneaking in by
the back way. (*She fires into the air.* 10

Brack (*nearer*). Are you out of your
senses ——!

Hedda. Dear me — did I happen to hit you?

Brack (*still outside*). I wish you would let
these pranks alone! 15

Hedda. Come in, then, Judge.

JUDGE BRACK, *dressed as though for a men's
party, enters by the glass door. He carries
a light overcoat over his arm*

Brack. What the deuce — haven't you tired
of that sport yet? What are you shooting at?

Hedda. Oh, I am only firing into the air.

Brack (*gently takes the pistol out of her* 20
hand). Allow me, madam! (*Looks at it.*) Ah
— I know this pistol well! (*Looks around.*)
Where is the case? Ah, here it is. (*Lays the
pistol in it, and shuts it.*) Now we won't play at
that game any more today. 25

Hedda. Then what in heaven's name would
you have me do with myself?

Brack. Have you had no visitors?

Hedda (*closing the glass door*). Not one. I
suppose all our set are still out of town. 30

Brack. And is Tesman not at home either?

Hedda (*at the writing-table, putting the pistol-
case in a drawer which she shuts*). No. He
rushed off to his aunt's directly after luncheon;
he didn't expect you so early. 35

Brack. H'm — how stupid of me not to have
thought of that!

Hedda (*turning her head to look at him*). Why
stupid?

Brack. Because if I had thought of it I 40
should have come a little — earlier.

Hedda (*crossing the room*). Then you would
have found no one to receive you; for I have
been in my room changing my dress ever since
lunch. 45

Brack. And is there no sort of little chink
that we could hold a parley through?

Hedda. You have forgotten to arrange one.

Brack. That was another piece of stupidity.

Hedda. Well, we must just settle down 50
here — and wait. Tesman is not likely to be
back for some time yet.

Brack. Never mind; I shall not be impatient.

(HEDDA *seats herself in the corner of the
sofa.* BRACK *lays his overcoat over
the back of the nearest chair, and sits
down, but keeps his hat in his hand.
A short silence. They look at each
other.*

Hedda. Well?

Brack (*in the same tone*). Well? 55

Hedda. I spoke first.

Brack (*bending a little forward*). Come, let us
have a cosy little chat, Mrs. Hedda.

Hedda (*leaning further back in the sofa*).
Does it not seem like a whole eternity since 60
our last talk? Of course I don't count those
few words yesterday evening and this morning.

Brack. You mean since our last confidential
talk? Our last *tête-à-tête*?

Hedda. Well, yes — since you put it so. 65

Brack. Not a day has passed but I have
wished that you were home again.

Hedda. And I have done nothing but wish
the same thing.

Brack. You? Really, Mrs. Hedda? 70
And I thought you had been enjoying your
tour so much!

Hedda. Oh, yes, you may be sure of that!

Brack. But Tesman's letters spoke of nothing but happiness. 75

Hedda. Oh, Tesman! You see, he thinks
nothing so delightful as grubbing in libraries
and making copies of old parchments, or whatever you call them.

Brack (*with a spice of malice*). Well, that 80
is his vocation in life — or part of it, at any
rate.

Hedda. Yes, of course; and no doubt when
it's your vocation ——. But *I!* Oh, my dear
Mr. Brack, how mortally bored I have 85
been.

Brack (*sympathetically*). Do you really say
so? In downright earnest?

Hedda. Yes, you can surely understand
it ——! To go for six whole months with- 90
out meeting a soul that knew anything of our

circle, or could talk about the things we are interested in.

Brack. Yes, yes — I, too, should feel that a
deprivation.   95

Hedda. And then, what I found most intolerable of all ——

Brack. Well?

Hedda. — was being everlastingly in the
company of — one and the same per-   100
son ——

Brack (with a nod of assent). Morning, noon,
and night, yes — at all possible times and
seasons.

Hedda. I said "everlastingly."   105

Brack. Just so. But I should have thought,
with our excellent Tesman, one could ——

Hedda. Tesman is — a specialist, my dear
Judge.

Brack. Undeniably.   110

Hedda. And specialists are not at all amusing to travel with. Not in the long run, at any
rate.

Brack. Not even — the specialist one hap-
pens to love?   115

Hedda. Faugh — don't use that sickening
word!

Brack (taken aback). What do you say, Mrs.
Hedda?

Hedda (half laughing, half irritated).   120
You should just try it! To hear of nothing but
the history of civilization, morning, noon, and
night ——

Brack. Everlastingly.

Hedda. Yes, yes, yes! And then all   125
this about the domestic industry of the middle
ages ——! That's the most disgusting part of it!

Brack (looks searchingly at her). But tell me
— in that case, how am I to understand your
——? H'm ——   130

Hedda. My accepting George Tesman, you
mean?

Brack. Well, let us put it so.

Hedda. Good heavens, do you see anything
so wonderful in that?   135

Brack. Yes and no — Mrs. Hedda.

Hedda. I had positively danced myself
tired, my dear Judge. My day was done ——
(With a slight shudder) Oh no — I won't say
that; nor think it either!   140

Brack. You have assuredly no reason to.

Hedda. Oh, reasons —— *(Watching him
closely)* And George Tesman — after all, you
must admit that he is correctness itself.

Brack. His correctness and respect-   145
ability are beyond all question.

Hedda. And I don't see anything absolutely
ridiculous about him. — Do you?

Brack. Ridiculous? N — no — I shouldn't
exactly say so ——   150

Hedda. Well — and his powers of research,
at all events, are untiring. — I see no reason
why he should not one day come to the front,
after all.

Brack (looks at her hesitatingly). I   155
thought that you, like everyone else, expected
him to attain the highest distinction.

Hedda (with an expression of fatigue). Yes,
so I did. — And then, since he was bent, at all
hazards, on being allowed to provide for   160
me — I really don't know why I should not
have accepted his offer?

Brack. No — if you look at it in that
light ——

Hedda. It was more than my other   165
adorers were prepared to do for me, my dear
Judge.

Brack (laughing). Well, I can't answer for all
the rest; but as for myself, you know quite well
that I have always entertained a — a cer-   170
tain respect for the marriage tie — for marriage
as an institution, Mrs. Hedda.

Hedda (jestingly). Oh, I assure you I have
never cherished any hopes with respect to
you.   175

Brack. All I require is a pleasant and intimate interior, where I can make myself useful in every way, and am free to come and go
as — as a trusted friend ——

Hedda. Of the master of the house,   180
do you mean?

Brack (bowing). Frankly — of the mistress
first of all; but of course of the master, too, in
the second place. Such a triangular friendship
— if I may call it so — is really a great   185
convenience for all parties, let me tell you.

Hedda. Yes, I have many a time longed for
someone to make a third on our travels. Oh
— those railway-carriage *tête-à-têtes* ——!

Brack. Fortunately your wedding jour- 190 ney is over now.

Hedda (*shaking her head*). Not by a long — long way. I have only arrived at a station on the line.

Brack. Well, then the passengers jump 195 out and move about a little, Mrs. Hedda.

Hedda. I never jump out.

Brack. Really?

Hedda. No — because there is always some-one standing by to —— 200

Brack (*laughing*). To look at your ankles, do you mean?

Hedda. Precisely.

Brack. Well, but, dear me ——

Hedda (*with a gesture of repulsion*). I 205 won't have it. I would rather keep my seat where I happen to be — and continue the *tête-à-tête.*

Brack. But suppose a third person were to jump in and join the couple. 210

Hedda. Ah — that is quite another matter!

Brack. A trusted, sympathetic friend ——

Hedda. — with a fund of conversation on all sorts of lively topics ——

Brack. — and not the least bit of a 215 specialist!

Hedda (*with an audible sigh*). Yes, that would be a relief, indeed.

Brack (*hears the front door open, and glances in that direction*). The triangle is com- 220 pleted.

Hedda (*half aloud*). And on goes the train.

GEORGE TESMAN, *in a gray walking-suit, with a soft felt hat, enters from the hall. He has a number of unbound books under his arm and in his pockets*

Tes. (*goes up to the table beside the corner settee*). Ouf — what a load for a warm day — all these books. (*Lays them on the table.*) 225 I'm positively perspiring, Hedda. Hallo — are you there already, my dear Judge? Eh? Berta didn't tell me.

Brack (*rising*). I came in through the garden.

Hedda. What books have you got 230 there?

Tes. (*stands looking them through*). Some new books on my special subjects — quite in-dispensable to me.

Hedda. Your special subjects? 235

Brack. Yes, books on his special subjects, Mrs. Tesman.

(BRACK *and* HEDDA *exchange a confidential smile.*)

Hedda. Do you need still more books on your special subjects?

Tes. Yes, my dear Hedda, one can 240 never have too many of them. Of course, one must keep up with all that is written and published.

Hedda. Yes, I suppose one must.

Tes. (*searching among his books*). And 245 look here — I have got hold of Eilert Lövborg's new book, too. (*Offering it to her*) Perhaps you would like to glance through it, Hedda? Eh?

Hedda. No, thank you. Or rather — 250 afterwards perhaps.

Tes. I looked into it a little on the way home.

Brack. Well, what do you think of it — as a specialist?

Tes. I think it shows quite remarkable 255 soundness of judgment. He never wrote like that before. (*Putting the books together*) Now I shall take all these into my study. I'm longing to cut the leaves —! And then I must change my clothes. (*To* BRACK) I sup- 260 pose we needn't start just yet? Eh?

Brack. Oh, dear, no — there is not the slightest hurry.

Tes. Well, then, I will take my time. (*Is going with his books, but stops in the door- 265 way and turns.*) By the bye, Hedda — Aunt Julia is not coming this evening.

Hedda. Not coming? Is it that affair of the bonnet that keeps her away?

Tes. Oh, not at all. How could you 270 think such a thing of Aunt Julia? Just fancy ——! The fact is, Aunt Rina is very ill.

Hedda. She always is.

Tes. Yes, but today she is much worse than usual, poor dear. 275

Hedda. Oh, then it's only natural that her sister should remain with her. I must bear my disappointment.

Tes. And you can't imagine, dear, how

delighted Aunt Julia seemed to be — be- 280
cause you had come home looking so flourishing!

Hedda (half aloud, rising). Oh, those everlasting aunts!

Tes. What? 285

Hedda (going to the glass door). Nothing.

Tes. Oh, all right.

> *(He goes through the inner room, out to*
> *the right.*

Brack. What bonnet were you talking about?

Hedda. Oh, it was a little episode with Miss
Tesman this morning. She had laid 290
down her bonnet on the chair there — *(Looks
at him and smiles.)* And I pretended to think
it was the servant's.

Brack (shaking his head). Now my dear Mrs.
Hedda, how could you do such a thing? 295
To that excellent old lady, too!

Hedda (nervously crossing the room). Well,
you see — these impulses come over me all of
a sudden; and I cannot resist them. *(Throws
herself down in the easy-chair by the stove.)* 300
Oh, I don't know how to explain it.

Brack (behind the easy-chair). You are not
really happy — that is at the bottom of it.

Hedda (looking straight before her). I know
of no reason why I should be — happy. 305
Perhaps you can give me one?

Brack. Well — amongst other things, because you have got exactly the home you had
set your heart on.

Hedda (looks up at him and laughs). Do 310
you too believe in that legend?

Brack. Is there nothing in it, then?

Hedda. Oh, yes, there is something in it.

Brack. Well?

Hedda. There is this in it, that I made 315
use of Tesman to see me home from evening
parties last summer ——

Brack. I, unfortunately, had to go quite a
different way.

Hedda. That's true. I know you were 320
going a different way last summer.

Brack (laughing). Oh, fie, Mrs. Hedda!
Well, then — you and Tesman ——?

Hedda. Well, we happened to pass here one
evening. Tesman, poor fellow, was writh- 325
ing in the agony of having to find conversation;
so I took pity on the learned man ——

Brack (smiles doubtfully). You took pity?
H'm ——

Hedda. Yes, I really did. And so — to 330
help him out of his torment — I happened to
say, in pure thoughtlessness, that I should like
to live in this villa.

Brack. No more than that?

Hedda. Not that evening. 335

Brack. But afterwards?

Hedda. Yes, my thoughtlessness had consequences, my dear Judge.

Brack. Unfortunately that too often happens, Mrs. Hedda. 340

Hedda. Thanks! So you see it was this
enthusiasm for Secretary Falk's villa that first
constituted a bond of sympathy between
George Tesman and me. From that came our
engagement and our marriage, and our 345
wedding journey, and all the rest of it. Well,
well, my dear Judge — as you make your bed,
so you must lie, I could almost say.

Brack. This is exquisite! And you really
cared not a rap about it all the time. 350

Hedda. No, heaven knows I didn't.

Brack. But now? Now that we have made
it so homelike for you?

Hedda. Uh — the rooms all seem to smell of
lavender and dried rose-leaves. — But 355
perhaps it's Aunt Julia that has brought that
scent with her.

Brack (laughing). No, I think it must be a
legacy from the late Mrs. Secretary Falk.

Hedda. Yes, there is an odor of mor- 360
tality about it. It reminds me of a bouquet —
the day after the ball. *(Clasps her hands behind her head, leans back in her chair, and looks
at him.)* Oh, my dear Judge — you cannot
imagine how horribly I shall bore myself 365
here.

Brack. Why should not you, too, find some
sort of vocation in life, Mrs. Hedda?

Hedda. A vocation — that should attract
me? 370

Brack. If possible, of course.

Hedda. Heaven knows what sort of a vocation that could be. I often wonder whether
—— *(Breaking off)* But that would never do,
either. 375

Brack. Who can tell? Let me hear what it
is.

Hedda. Whether I might not get Tesman to go into politics, I mean.

Brack (laughing). Tesman? No, really 380 now, political life is not the thing for him — not at all in his line.

Hedda. No, I daresay not. — But if I could get him into it all the same?

Brack. Why — what satisfaction could 385 you find in that? If he is not fitted for that sort of thing, why should you want to drive him into it?

Hedda. Because I am bored, I tell you! (*After a pause*) So you think it quite out 390 of the question that Tesman should ever get into the ministry?

Brack. H'm — you see, my dear Mrs. Hedda — to get into the ministry, he would have to be a tolerably rich man. 395

Hedda (rising impatiently). Yes, there we have it! It is this genteel poverty I have managed to drop into ——! (*Crosses the room.*) That is what makes life so pitiable! So utterly ludicrous! — For that's what it is. 400

Brack. Now *I* should say the fault lay elsewhere.

Hedda. Where, then?

Brack. You have never gone through any really stimulating experience. 405

Hedda. Anything serious, you mean?

Brack. Yes, you may call it so. But now you may perhaps have one in store.

Hedda (tossing her head). Oh, you're thinking of the annoyances about this wretched 410 professorship! But that must be Tesman's own affair. I assure you I shall not waste a thought upon it.

Brack. No, no, I daresay not. But suppose now that what people call — in elegant 415 language — a solemn responsibility were to come upon you? (*Smiling*) A new responsibility, Mrs. Hedda?

Hedda (angrily). Be quiet! Nothing of that sort will ever happen! 420

Brack (warily). We will speak of this again a year hence — at the very outside.

Hedda (curtly). I have no turn for anything of the sort, Judge Brack. No responsibilities for me! 425

Brack. Are you so unlike the generality of women as to have no turn for duties which ——

Hedda (beside the glass door). Oh, be quiet, I tell you! — I often think there is only one thing in the world I have any turn for. 430

Brack (drawing near to her). And what is that, if I may ask?

Hedda (stands looking out). Boring myself to death. Now you know it. (*Turns, looks towards the inner room, and laughs.*) Yes, 435 as I thought! Here comes the Professor.

Brack (softly, in a tone of warning). Come, come, come, Mrs. Hedda!

GEORGE TESMAN, *dressed for the party, with his gloves and hat in his hand, enters from the right through the inner room*

Tes. Hedda, has no message come from Eilert Lövborg? Eh? 440

Hedda. No.

Tes. Then, you'll see, he'll be here presently.

Brack. Do you really think he will come?

Tes. Yes, I am almost sure of it. For what you were telling us this morning must 445 have been a mere floating rumor.

Brack. You think so?

Tes. At any rate, Aunt Julia said she did not believe for a moment that he would ever stand in my way again. Fancy that! 450

Brack. Well, then, that's all right.

Tes. (placing his hat and gloves on a chair on the right). Yes, but you must really let me wait for him as long as possible.

Brack. We have plenty of time yet. 455 None of my guests will arrive before seven or half-past.

Tes. Then meanwhile we can keep Hedda company, and see what happens. Eh?

Hedda (placing BRACK'S *hat and over-* 460 *coat upon the corner settee).* And at the worst Mr. Lövborg can remain here with me.

Brack (offering to take his things). Oh, allow me, Mrs. Tesman! — What do you mean by "At the worst"? 465

Hedda. If he won't go with you and Tesman.

Tes. (looks dubiously at her). But, Hedda dear — do you think it would quite do for him to remain with you? Eh? Remember, Aunt Julia can't come. 470

Hedda. No, but Mrs. Elvsted is coming. We three can have a cup of tea together.

Tes. Oh, yes, that will be all right.

Brack (smiling). And that would perhaps be the safest plan for him.   475

Hedda. Why so?

Brack. Well, you know, Mrs. Tesman, how you used to gird at my little bachelor parties. You declared they were adapted only for men of the strictest principles.   480

Hedda. But no doubt Mr. Lövborg's principles are strict enough now. A converted sinner ——

BERTA *appears at the hall door.*

Berta. There's a gentleman asking if you are at home, ma'am ——   485

Hedda. Well, show him in.

Tes. (softly). I'm sure it is he! Fancy that!

EILERT LÖVBORG *enters from the hall. He is slim and lean; of the same age as* TESMAN, *but looks older and somewhat worn-out. His hair and beard are of a blackish brown, his face long and pale, but with patches of color on the cheek-bones. He is dressed in a well-cut black visiting suit, quite new. He has dark gloves and a silk hat. He stops near the door, and makes a rapid bow, seeming somewhat embarrassed*

Tes. (goes up to him and shakes him warmly by the hand). Well, my dear Eilert — so at last we meet again!   590

Löv. (speaks in a subdued voice). Thanks for your letter, Tesman. *(Approaching* HEDDA*)* Will you too shake hands with me, Mrs. Tesman?

Hedda (taking his hand). I am glad to   495 see you, Mr. Lövborg. *(With a motion of her hand)* I don't know whether you two gentlemen —?

Löv. (bowing slightly). Judge Brack, I think.

Brack (doing likewise). Oh, yes — in   500 the old days ——

Tes. (to LÖVBORG, *with his hands on his shoulders).* And now you must make yourself entirely at home, Eilert! Mustn't he, Hedda? — For I hear you are going to settle in   505 town again? Eh?

Löv. Yes, I am.

Tes. Quite right, quite right. Let me tell you, I have got hold of your new book; but I haven't had time to read it yet.   510

Löv. You may spare yourself the trouble.

Tes. Why so?

Löv. Because there is very little in it.

Tes. Just fancy — how can you say so?

Brack. But it has been very much   515 praised, I hear.

Löv. That was what I wanted; so I put nothing into the book but what everyone would agree with.

Brack. Very wise of you.   520

Tes. Well, but, my dear Eilert —!

Löv. For now I mean to win myself a position again — to make a fresh start.

Tes. (a little embarrassed). Ah, that is what you wish to do? Eh?   525

Löv. (smiling, lays down his hat, and draws a packet, wrapped in paper, from his coat pocket). When this one appears, George Tesman, you will have to read it. For this is the real book — the book I have put my true self into.   530

Tes. Indeed? And what is it?

Löv. It is the continuation.

Tes. The continuation? Of what?

Löv. Of the book.

Tes. Of the new book?   535

Löv. Of course.

Tes. Why, my dear Eilert — does it not come down to our own days?

Löv. Yes, it does, and this one deals with the future.   540

Tes. With the future! Good heavens, we know nothing of the future!

Löv. No; but there is a thing or two to be said about it all the same. *(Opens the packet.)* Look here ——   545

Tes. Why, that's not your handwriting.

Löv. I dictated it. *(Turning over the pages)* It falls into two sections. The first deals with the civilizing forces of the future. And here is the second *(running through the pages to-*   550 *wards the end)* — forecasting the probable line of development.

Tes. How odd now! I should never have thought of writing anything of that sort.

Hedda (*at the glass door, drumming on* 555 *the pane*). H'm — I daresay not.

Löv. (*replacing the manuscript in its paper and laying the packet on the table*). I brought it, thinking I might read you a little of it this evening. 560

Tes. That was very good of you, Eilert. But this evening —? (*Looking at* BRACK) I don't quite see how we can manage it ——

Löv. Well, then, some other time. There is no hurry. 565

Brack. I must tell you, Mr. Lövborg — there is a little gathering at my house this evening — mainly in honor of Tesman, you know ——

Löv. (*looking for his hat*). Oh — then I won't detain you —— 570

Brack. No, but listen — will you not do me the favor of joining us?

Löv. (*curtly and decidedly*). No, I can't — thank you very much.

Brack. Oh, nonsense — do! We shall 575 be quite a select little circle. And I assure you we shall have a "lively time," as Mrs. Hed — as Mrs. Tesman says.

Löv. I have no doubt of it. But nevertheless —— 580

Brack. And then you might bring your manuscript with you, and read it to Tesman at my house. I could give you a room to yourselves.

Tes. Yes, think of that, Eilert — 585 why shouldn't you? Eh?

Hedda (*interposing*). But, Tesman, if Mr. Lövborg would really rather not! I am sure Mr. Lövborg is much more inclined to remain here and have supper with me. 590

Löv. (*looking at her*). With you, Mrs. Tesman?

Hedda. And with Mrs. Elvsted.

Löv. Ah —— (*Lightly*) I saw her for a moment this morning. 595

Hedda. Did you? Well, she is coming this evening. So you see you are almost bound to remain, Mr. Lövborg, or she will have no one to see her home.

Löv. That's true. Many thanks, Mrs. 600 Tesman — in that case I will remain.

Hedda. Then I have one or two orders to give the servant ——

(*She goes to the hall door and rings. BERTA enters. HEDDA talks to her in a whisper, and points towards the inner room. BERTA nods and goes out again.*)

Tes. (*at the same time, to* LÖVBORG). Tell me, Eilert — is it this new subject — 605 the future — that you are going to lecture about?

Löv. Yes.

Tes. They told me at the bookseller's that you are going to deliver a course of lec- 610 tures this autumn.

Löv. That is my intention. I hope you won't take it ill, Tesman.

Tes. Oh no, not in the least! But —?

Löv. I can quite understand that it 615 must be disagreeable to you.

Tes. (*cast down*). Oh, I can't expect you, out of consideration for me, to ——

Löv. But I shall wait till you have received your appointment. 620

Tes. Will you wait? Yes, but — yes, but — are you not going to compete with me? Eh?

Löv. No; it is only the moral victory I care for. 625

Tes. Why, bless me — then Aunt Julia was right after all! Oh, yes — I knew it! Hedda! Just fancy — Eilert Lövborg is not going to stand in our way!

Hedda (*curtly*). Our way? Pray leave 630 me out of the question.

(*She goes up towards the inner room, where BERTA is placing a tray with decanters and glasses on the table. HEDDA nods approval, and comes forward again. BERTA goes out.*)

Tes. (*at the same time*). And you, Judge Brack — what do you say to this? Eh?

Brack. Well, I say that a moral victory — h'm — may be all very fine ——

Tes. Yes, certainly. But all the 636 same ——

Hedda (*looking at* TESMAN *with a cold smile*). You stand there looking as if you were thunderstruck —— 640

Tes. Yes — so I am — I almost think ——

Brack. Don't you see, Mrs. Tesman, a thunderstorm has just passed over?

Hedda (pointing towards the inner room). Will you not take a glass of cold punch, 645 gentlemen?

Brack (looking at his watch). A stirrup-cup? Yes, it wouldn't come amiss.

Tes. A capital idea, Hedda! Just the thing! Now that the weight has been taken off 650 my mind ——

Hedda. Will you not join them, Mr. Lövborg?

Löv. (with a gesture of refusal). No, thank you. Nothing for me. 655

Brack. Why, bless me — cold punch is surely not poison.

Löv. Perhaps not for everyone.

Hedda. I will keep Mr. Lövborg company in the meantime. 660

Tes. Yes, yes, Hedda dear, do.

> (*He and* BRACK *go into the inner room, seat themselves, drink punch, smoke cigarettes, and carry on a lively conversation during what follows.* EILERT LÖVBORG *remains standing beside the stove.* HEDDA *goes to the writing-table.*

Hedda (raising her voice a little). Do you care to look at some photographs, Mr. Lövborg? You know Tesman and I made a tour in the Tyrol on our way home? 665

> (*She takes up an album, and places it on the table beside the sofa, in the further corner of which she seats herself.* EILERT LÖVBORG *approaches, stops, and looks at her. Then he takes a chair and seats himself to her left, with his back towards the inner room.*

Hedda (opening the album). Do you see this range of mountains, Mr. Lövborg? It's the Ortler group. Tesman has written the name underneath. Here it is: "The Ortler group near Meran." [1] 670

Löv. (who has never taken his eyes off her, says softly and slowly). Hedda — Gabler!

---

[1] Meran is now Merano in the northwestern part of the Italian Tyrol near the Swiss and German borders.

Hedda (glancing hastily at him). Ah! Hush!

Löv. (repeats softly). Hedda Gabler!

Hedda (looking at the album). That 675 was my name in the old days — when we two knew each other.

Löv. And I must teach myself never to say Hedda Gabler again — never, as long as I live. 680

Hedda (still turning over the pages). Yes, you must. And I think you ought to practise in time. The sooner the better, I should say.

Löv. (in a tone of indignation). Hedda Gabler married? And married to — George 685 Tesman!

Hedda. Yes — so the world goes.

Löv. Oh, Hedda, Hedda — how could you [1] throw yourself away!

Hedda (looks sharply at him). What? 690 I can't allow this!

Löv. What do you mean?

> TESMAN *comes into the room and goes towards the sofa*

Hedda (hears him coming and says in an indifferent tone). And this is a view from the Val d'Ampezzo, Mr. Lövborg. Just look 695 at these peaks! (*Looks affectionately up at* TESMAN.) What's the name of these curious peaks, dear?

Tes. Let me see. Oh, those are the Dolomites. [2] 700

Hedda. Yes, that's it! — Those are the Dolomites, Mr. Lövborg.

Tes. Hedda, dear, — I only wanted to ask whether I shouldn't bring you a little punch after all? For yourself, at any rate 705 — eh?

Hedda. Yes, do, please; and perhaps a few biscuits.

Tes. No cigarettes?

Hedda. No. 710

Tes. Very well.

> (*He goes into the inner room and out to the right.* BRACK *sits in the inner room, and keeps an eye from time to time on* HEDDA *and* LÖVBORG.

---

[1] He uses the familiar *du* in the Norwegian text.

[2] A famous mountain range in the Tyrol district of north central Italy.

Löv. (*softly, as before*). Answer me, Hedda — how could you go and do this?

Hedda (*apparently absorbed in the album*). If you continue to say *du* to me, I won't 715 talk to you.

Löv. May I not say *du* even when we are alone?

Hedda. No. You may think it; but you mustn't say it. 720

Löv. Ah, I understand. It is an offense against George Tesman, whom you [1] — love.

Hedda (*glances at him and smiles*). Love? What an idea?

Löv. You don't love him, then! 725

Hedda. But I won't hear of any sort of unfaithfulness! Remember that.

Löv. Hedda — answer me one thing ——

Hedda. Hush!

TESMAN *enters with a small tray from the inner room*

Tes. Here you are! Isn't this tempt- 730 ing?

(*He puts the tray on the table.*)

Hedda. Why do you bring it yourself?

Tes. (*filling the glasses*). Because I think it's such fun to wait upon you, Hedda.

Hedda. But you have poured out two 735 glasses. Mr. Lövborg said he wouldn't have any ——

Tes. No, but Mrs. Elvsted will soon be here, won't she?

Hedda. Yes, by the bye — Mrs. Elv- 740 sted ——

Tes. Had you forgotten her? Eh?

Hedda. We were so absorbed in these photographs. (*Shows him a picture.*) Do you remember this little village? 745

Tes. Oh, it's that one just below the Brenner Pass.[2] It was there we passed the night ——

Hedda. — and met that lively party of tourists.

Tes. Yes, that was the place. Fancy 750

---

[1] From this point on he uses the formal *De* in the Norwegian text.
[2] Gossensass in the Italian Tyrol, the favorite summer resort of Ibsen.

— if we could only have had you with us, Eilert! Eh?

(*He returns to the inner room and sits beside* BRACK.

Löv. Answer me this one thing, Hedda ——

Hedda. Well?

Löv. Was there no love in your friend- 755 ship for me either? Not a spark — not a tinge of love in it?

Hedda. I wonder if there was? To me it seems as though we were two good comrades — two thoroughly intimate friends. (*Smil-* 760 *ingly*) You especially were frankness itself.

Löv. It was you that made me so.

Hedda. As I look back upon it all, I think there was really something beautiful, something fascinating — something daring — in — 765 — in that secret intimacy — that comradeship which no living creature so much as dreamed of.

Löv. Yes, yes, Hedda! Was there not? — When I used to come to your father's in the afternoon — and the General sat over at 770 the window reading his papers — with his back towards us ——

Hedda. And we two on the corner sofa ——

Löv. Always with the same illustrated paper before us —— 775

Hedda. For want of an album, yes.

Löv. Yes, Hedda, and when I made my confessions to you — told you about myself, things that at that time no one else knew! There I would sit and tell you of my escapades 780 — my days and nights of devilment. Oh, Hedda — what was the power in you that forced me to confess these things?

Hedda. Do you think it was any power in me? 785

Löv. How else can I explain it? And all those — those roundabout questions you used to put to me ——

Hedda. Which you understood so particularly well —— 790

Löv. How could you sit and question me like that? Question me quite frankly ——

Hedda. In roundabout terms, please observe.

Löv. Yes, but frankly, nevertheless. 795 Cross-question me about — all that sort of thing?

Hedda. And how could you answer, Mr. Lövborg?

Löv. Yes, that is just what I can't un- 800 derstand — in looking back upon it. But tell me now, Hedda — was there not love at the bottom of our friendship? On your side, did you not feel as though you might purge my stains away — if I made you my confessor? Was it not so?

Hedda. No, not quite. 806

Löv. What was your motive, then?

Hedda. Do you think it quite incomprehensible that a young girl — when it can be done — without anyone knowing —— 810

Löv. Well?

Hedda. — should be glad to have a peep, now and then, into a world which —

Löv. Which —?

Hedda. — which she is forbidden to 815 know anything about?

Löv. So that was it?

Hedda. Partly. Partly — I almost think.

Löv. Comradeship in the thirst for life. But why should not that, at any rate, have 820 continued?

Hedda. The fault was yours.

Löv. It was you that broke with me.

Hedda. Yes, when our friendship threatened to develop into something more serious. 825 Shame upon you, Eilert Lövborg! How could you think of wronging your — your frank comrade?

Löv. (*clenching his hands*). Oh, why did you not carry out your threat? Why did 830 you not shoot me down?

Hedda. Because I have such a dread of scandal.

Löv. Yes, Hedda, you are a coward at heart.

Hedda. A terrible coward. (*Changing* 835 *her tone*) But it was a lucky thing for you. And now you have found ample consolation at the Elvsteds'.

Löv. I know what Thea has confided to you.

Hedda. And perhaps you have con- 840 fided to her something about us?

Löv. Not a word. She is too stupid to understand anything of that sort.

Hedda. Stupid?

Löv. She is stupid about matters of 845 that sort.

Hedda. And I am cowardly. (*Bends over towards him, without looking him in the face, and says more softly*) But now I will confide something to you. 850

Löv. (*eagerly*). Well?

Hedda. The fact that I dared not shoot you down ——

Löv. Yes!

Hedda. — that was not my most 855 arrant cowardice — that evening.

Löv. (*looks at her a moment, understands, and whispers passionately*). Oh, Hedda! Hedda Gabler! Now I begin to see a hidden reason beneath our comradeship! You [1] 860 and I —! After all, then, it was your craving for life ——

Hedda (*softly, with a sharp glance*). Take care! Believe nothing of the sort!

(*Twilight has begun to fall. The hall door is opened from without by* BERTA.

Hedda (*closes the album with a bang and* 865 *calls smilingly*). Ah, at last! My darling Thea — come along!

MRS. ELVSTED *enters from the hall. She is in evening dress. The door is closed behind her*

Hedda (*on the sofa, stretches out her arms towards her*). My sweet Thea — you can't think how I have been longing for you! 870

(MRS. ELVSTED, *in passing, exchanges slight salutations with the gentlemen in the inner room, then goes up to the table and gives* HEDDA *her hands. EILERT LÖVBORG has risen. He and* MRS. ELVSTED *greet each other with a silent nod.*

Mrs. Elv. Ought I to go in and talk to your husband for a moment?

Hedda. Oh, not at all. Leave those two alone. They will soon be going.

Mrs. Elv. Are they going out? 875

Hedda. Yes, to a supper-party.

Mrs. Elv. (*quickly to* LÖVBORG). Not you?

Löv. No.

Hedda. Mr. Lövborg remains with us.

---

[1] He makes a momentary slip and here uses the familiar *du* in the Norwegian text.

Mrs. Elv. (*takes a chair and is about*   880
to seat herself at his side). Oh, how nice it is
here!

Hedda. No, thank you, my little Thea! Not
there! You'll be good enough to come over
here to me. I will sit between you.   885

Mrs. Elv. Yes, just as you please.

> (*She goes round the table and seats her-*
> *self on the sofa on* HEDDA'S *right.*
> LÖVBORG *reseats himself on his chair.*

Löv. (*after a short pause, to* HEDDA). Is not
she lovely to look at?

Hedda (*lightly stroking her hair*). Only to
look at?   890

Löv. Yes. For we two — she and I — we
are two real comrades. We have absolute
faith in each other; so we can sit and talk with
perfect frankness ——

Hedda. Not round about, Mr. Lövborg?   895

Löv. Well ——

Mrs. Elv. (*softly clinging close to* HEDDA). Oh,
how happy I am, Hedda; for, only think, he
says I have inspired him too.

Hedda (*looks at her with a smile*). Ah!   900
Does he say that, dear?

Löv. And then she is so brave, Mrs. Tesman!

Mrs. Elv. Good heavens — am I brave?

Löv. Exceedingly — where your comrade is
concerned.   905

Hedda. Ah yes — courage! If one only
had that!

Löv. What then? What do you mean?

Hedda. Then life would perhaps be livable,
after all. (*With a sudden change of tone*)   910
But now, my dearest Thea, you really must
have a glass of cold punch.

Mrs. Elv. No, thanks — I never take anything of that kind.

Hedda. Well then, you, Mr. Lövborg?   915

Löv. Nor I, thank you.

Mrs. Elv. No, he doesn't either.

Hedda (*looks fixedly at him*). But if *I* say
you shall?

Löv. It would be no use.   920

Hedda (*laughing*). Then I, poor creature,
have no sort of power over you?

Löv. Not in that respect.

Hedda. But seriously, I think you ought to
— for your own sake.   925

Mrs. Elv. Why, Hedda ——!

Löv. How so?

Hedda. Or rather on account of other people.

Löv. Indeed?

Hedda. Otherwise people might be apt   930
to suspect that — in your heart of hearts —
you did not feel quite secure — quite confident
of yourself.

Mrs. Elv. (*softly*). Oh, please, Hedda ——

Löv. People may suspect what they   935
like — for the present.

Mrs. Elv. (*joyfully*). Yes, let them!

Hedda. I saw it plainly in Judge Brack's
face a moment ago.

Löv. What did you see?   940

Hedda. His contemptuous smile, when you
dared not go with them into the inner room.

Löv. Dared not? Of course I preferred to
stop here and talk to you.

Mrs. Elv. What could be more natural,   945
Hedda?

Hedda. But the Judge could not guess that.
And I saw, too, the way he smiled and glanced
at Tesman when you dared not accept his invitation to this wretched little supper-party   950
of his.

Löv. Dared not! Do you say I dared not?

Hedda. *I* don't say so. But that was how
Judge Brack understood it.

Löv. Well, let him.   955

Hedda. Then you are not going with them?

Löv. I will stay here with you and Thea.

Mrs. Elv. Yes, Hedda — how can you doubt
that?

Hedda (*smiles and nods approvingly to*   960
LÖVBORG). Firm as a rock! Faithful to your
principles, now and forever! Ah, that is how
a man should be! (*Turns to* MRS. ELVSTED
and caresses her.) Well, now, what did I tell
you, when you came to us this morning   965
in such a state of distraction ——

Löv. (*surprised*). Distraction!

Mrs. Elv. (*terrified*). Hedda — oh, Hedda —!

Hed. You can see for yourself! You haven't
the slightest reason to be in such mor-   970
tal terror —— (*Interrupting herself*) There!
Now we can all three enjoy ourselves!

Löv. (*who has given a start*). Ah — what
is all this, Mrs. Tesman?

Mrs. Elv. Oh, my God, Hedda! What 975 are you saying? What are you doing?

Hedda. Don't get excited! That horrid Judge Brack is sitting watching you.

Löv. So she was in mortal terror! On my account! 980

Mrs. Elv. (softly and piteously). Oh, Hedda — now you have ruined everything!

Löv. (looks fixedly at her for a moment. His face is distorted). So that was my comrade's frank confidence in me? 985

Mrs. Elv. (imploringly). Oh, my dearest friend — only let me tell you ——

Löv. (takes one of the glasses of punch, raises it to his lips, and says in a low, husky voice). Your health, Thea! 990

> (*He empties the glass, puts it down, and takes the second.*

Mrs. Elv. (softly). Oh, Hedda, Hedda — how could you do this?

Hedda. I do it? I? Are you crazy?

Löv. Here's to your health, too, Mrs. Tesman. Thanks for the truth. Hurrah for 995 the truth!

> (*He empties the glass and is about to refill it.*

Hedda (lays her hand on his arm). Come, come — no more for the present. Remember you are going out to supper.

Mrs. Elv. No, no, no! 1000

Hedda. Hush! They are sitting watching you.

Löv. (putting down the glass). Now, Thea — tell me the truth ——

Mrs. Elv. Yes. 1005

Löv. Did your husband know that you had come after me?

Mrs. Elv. (wringing her hands). Oh, Hedda — do you hear what he is asking?

Löv. Was it arranged between you 1010 and him that you were to come to town and look after me? Perhaps it was the Sheriff himself that urged you to come? Aha, my dear — no doubt he wanted my help in his office! Or was it at the cardtable that 1015 he missed me?

Mrs. Elv. (softly, in agony). Oh, Lövborg, Lövborg ——!

Löv. (seizes a glass and is on the point of filling it). Here's a glass for the old Sher- 1020 iff too!

Hedda (preventing him). No more just now. Remember you have to read your manuscript to Tesman.

Löv. (calmly, putting down the glass). 1025 It was stupid of me, all this, Thea — to take it in this way, I mean. Don't be angry with me, my dear, dear comrade. You shall see — both you and the others — that if I was fallen once — now I have risen again! Thanks 1030 to you, Thea.

Mrs. Elv. (radiant with joy). Oh, heaven be praised —!

> (BRACK *has in the meantime looked at his watch. He and* TESMAN *rise and come into the drawing-room.*

Brack (takes his hat and overcoat). Well, Mrs. Tesman, our time has come. 1035

Hedda. I suppose it has.

Löv. (rising). Mine too, Judge Brack.

Mrs. Elv. (softly and imploringly). Oh, Lövborg, don't do it!

Hedda (pinching her arm). They can 1040 hear you!

Mrs. Elv. (with a suppressed shriek). Ow!

Löv. (to BRACK*).* You were good enough to invite me.

Brack. Well, are you coming after all? 1045

Löv. Yes, many thanks.

Brack. I'm delighted ——

Löv. (to TESMAN, *putting the parcel of MS. in his pocket).* I should like to show you one or two things before I send it to the printers. 1050

Tes. Fancy — that will be delightful. But, Hedda dear, how is Mrs. Elvsted to get home? Eh?

Hedda. Oh, that can be managed somehow.

Löv. (looking towards the ladies). Mrs. 1055 Elvsted? Of course, I'll come again and fetch her. (*Approaching*) At ten or thereabouts, Mrs. Tesman? Will that do?

Hedda. Certainly. That will do capitally.

Tes. Well, then, that's all right. But 1060 you must not expect me so early, Hedda.

Hedda. Oh, you may stop as long — as long as ever you please.

Mrs. Elv. (trying to conceal her anxiety). Well,

then, Mr. Lövborg — I shall remain here　1065
until you come.

Löv. (*with his hat in his hand*).　Pray do, Mrs.
Elvsted.

Brack. And now off goes the excursion
train, gentlemen!　I hope we shall have　1070
a lively time, as a certain fair lady puts it.

Hedda. Ah, if only the fair lady could be
present unseen —!

Brack. Why unseen?

Hedda. In order to hear a little of your　1075
liveliness at first hand, Judge Brack.

Brack (*laughing*).　I should not advise the
fair lady to try it.

Tes. (*also laughing*).　Come, you're a nice
one, Hedda!　Fancy that!　　　　　1080

Brack. Well, good-bye, good-bye, ladies.

Löv. (*bowing*).　About ten o'clock, then.

(BRACK, LÖVBORG, *and* TESMAN *go
out by the hall door.　At the same
time* BERTA *enters from the inner
room with a lighted lamp, which she
places on the dining-room table; she
goes out by the way she came.*

Mrs. Elv. (*who has risen and is wandering
restlessly about the room*).　Hedda — Hedda —
what will come of all this?　　　　1085

Hedda. At ten o'clock — he will be here.　I
can see him already — with vine-leaves in his
hair — flushed and fearless ——

Mrs. Elv. Oh, I hope he may.

Hedda. And then, you see — then he　1090
will have regained control over himself.　Then
he will be a free man for all his days.

Mrs. Elv. Oh, God! — if he would only come
as you see him now!

Hedda. He will come as I see him —　1095
so, and not otherwise!　(*Rises and approaches*
THEA.)　You may doubt him as long as you
please; *I* believe in him.　And now we will
try ——

Mrs. Elv. You have some hidden mo-　1100
tive in this, Hedda!

Hedda. Yes, I have.　I want for once in my
life to have power to mould a human destiny.

Mrs. Elv. Have you not the power?

Hedda. I have not — and have never　1105
had it.

Mrs. Elv. Not your husband's?

Hedda. Do you think that is worth the
trouble?　Oh, if you could only understand
how poor I am.　And fate has made　1110
you so rich!　(*Clasps her passionately in her
arms.*)　I think I must burn your hair off, after
all.

Mrs. Elv. Let me go!　Let me go!　I am
afraid of you, Hedda!　　　　　1115

Berta (*in the middle doorway*).　Tea is laid
in the dining-room, ma'am.

Hedda. Very well.　We are coming.

Mrs. Elv. No, no, no!　I would rather go
home alone!　At once!　　　　　1120

Hedda. Nonsense!　First you shall have a
cup of tea, you little stupid.　And then — at
ten o'clock — Eilert Lövborg will be here —
with vine-leaves in his hair.

(*She drags* MRS. ELVSTED *almost by
force towards the middle doorway.*

Curtain

ACT III

The room at the TESMANS'.　*The curtains are
drawn over the middle doorway, and also over
the glass door.　The lamp, half turned
down, and with a shade over it, is burning on
the table.　In the stove, the door of which
stands open, there has been a fire, which is
now nearly burnt out.*

MRS. ELVSTED, *wrapped in a large shawl, and
with her feet upon a foot-rest, sits close to the
stove, sunk back in the armchair.*　HEDDA,
*fully dressed, lies sleeping upon the sofa,
with a sofa-blanket over her*

Mrs. Elv. (*after a pause, suddenly sits up in
her chair, and listens eagerly.　Then she sinks
back again wearily, moaning to herself*).　Not
yet! — Oh God — oh God — not yet!

BERTA *slips cautiously in by the hall door.
She has a letter in her hand*

Mrs. Elv. (*turns and whispers eagerly*).　5
Well — has anyone come?

Berta (*softly*).　Yes, a girl has just brought
this letter.

Mrs. Elv. (*quickly, holding out her hand*).　A
letter!　Give it to me!　　　　　1o

Berta. No, it's for Doctor Tesman, ma'am.

Mrs. Elv. Oh, indeed.

Berta. It was Miss Tesman's servant that brought it. I'll lay it here on the table.

Mrs. Elv. Yes, do.   15

Berta (laying down the letter). I think I had better put out the lamp. It's smoking.

Mrs. Elv. Yes, put it out. It must soon be daylight now.

Berta (putting out the lamp). It is day-   20 light already, ma'am.

Mrs. Elv. Yes, broad day! And no one come back yet ——— !

Berta. Lord bless you, ma'am — I guessed how it would be.   25

Mrs. Elv. You guessed?

Berta. Yes, when I saw that a certain person had come back to town — and that he went off with them. For we've heard enough about that gentleman before now.   30

Mrs. Elv. Don't speak so loud. You will waken Mrs. Tesman.

Berta (looks towards the sofa and sighs). No, no — let her sleep, poor thing. Shan't I put some wood on the fire?   35

Mrs. Elv. Thanks, not for me.

Berta. Oh, very well.

      (She goes softly out by the hall door.
Hedda (is awakened by the shutting of the door, and looks up). What's that — ?

Mrs. Elv. It was only the servant ———   40

Hedda (looking about her). Oh, we're here — ! Yes, now I remember. *(Sits erect upon the sofa, stretches herself, and rubs her eyes.)* What o'clock is it, Thea?

Mrs. Elv. (looks at her watch). It's past   45 seven.

Hedda. When did Tesman come home?

Mrs. Elv. He has not come.

Hedda. Not come home yet?

Mrs. Elv. (rising). No one has come.   50

Hedda. Think of our watching and waiting here till four in the morning ———

Mrs. Elv. (wringing her hands). And how I watched and waited for him!

Hedda (yawns, and says with her hand   55 *before her mouth).* Well, well — we might have spared ourselves the trouble.

Mrs. Elv. Did you get a little sleep?

Hedda. Oh yes; I believe I have slept pretty well. Have you not?   60

Mrs. Elv. Not for a moment. I couldn't, Hedda! — not to save my life.

Hedda (rises and goes towards her). There, there, there! There's nothing to be so alarmed about. I understand quite well what has   65 happened.

Mrs. Elv. Well, what do you think? Won't you tell me?

Hedda. Why, of course it has been a very late affair at Judge Brack's ———   70

Mrs. Elv. Yes, yes, that is clear enough. But all the same ———

Hedda. And then, you see, Tesman hasn't cared to come home and get us up in the middle of the night. *(Laughing)* Perhaps   75 he wasn't inclined to show himself either — immediately after a jollification.

Mrs. Elv. But in that case — where can he have gone?

Hedda. Of course he has gone to his   80 aunts' and slept there. They have his old room ready for him.

Mrs. Elv. No, he can't be with them; for a letter has just come for him from Miss Tesman. There it lies.   85

Hedda. Indeed? *(Looks at the address.)* Why, yes, it's addressed in Aunt Julia's own hand. Well then, he has remained at Judge Brack's. And as for Eilert Lövborg — he is sitting, with vine-leaves in his hair, reading   90 his manuscript.

Mrs. Elv. Oh Hedda, you are just saying things you don't believe a bit.

Hedda. You really are a little blockhead, Thea.   95

Mrs. Elv. Oh yes, I suppose I am.

Hedda. And how mortally tired you look.

Mrs. Elv. Yes, I am mortally tired.

Hedda. Well then, you must do as I tell you. You must go into my room and lie down   100 for a little while.

Mrs. Elv. Oh no, no — I shouldn't be able to sleep.

Hedda. I am sure you would.

Mrs. Elv. Well, but your husband is   105 certain to come soon now; and then I want to know at once ———

Hedda. I shall take care to let you know when he comes.

Mrs. Elv. Do you promise me, Hedda? 110

Hedda. Yes, rely upon me. Just you go in and have a sleep in the meantime.

Mrs. Elv. Thanks; then I'll try to.

(*She goes off through the inner room. HEDDA goes up to the glass door and draws back the curtains. The broad daylight streams into the room. Then she takes a little hand-glass from the writing-table, looks at herself in it, and arranges her hair. Next she goes to the hall door and presses the bell-button.*

BERTA *presently appears at the hall door*

Berta. Did you want anything, ma'am?

Hedda. Yes; you must put some more 115 wood in the stove. I am shivering.

Berta. Bless me — I'll make up the fire at once. (*She rakes the embers together and lays a piece of wood upon them; then stops and listens.*) That was a ring at the front door, ma'am. 120

Hedda. Then go to the door. I will look after the fire.

Berta. It'll soon burn up.

(*She goes out by the hall door. HEDDA kneels on the foot-rest and lays some more pieces of wood in the stove.*

After a short pause, GEORGE TESMAN enters from the hall. He looks tired and rather serious. He steals on tiptoe towards the middle doorway and is about to slip through the curtains

Hedda (*at the stove, without looking up*). Good morning. 125

Tes. (*turns*). Hedda! (*Approaching her*) Good heavens — are you up so early? Eh?

Hedda. Yes, I am up very early this morning.

Tes. And I never doubted you were 130 still sound asleep! Fancy that, Hedda!

Hedda. Don't speak so loud. Mrs. Elvsted is resting in my room.

Tes. Has Mrs. Elvsted been here all night?

Hedda. Yes, since no one came to fetch 135 her.

Tes. Ah, to be sure.

Hedda (*closes the door of the stove and rises*). Well, did you enjoy yourselves at Judge Brack's? 140

Tes. Have you been anxious about me? Eh?

Hedda. No, I should never think of being anxious. But I asked if you had enjoyed yourself.

Tes. Oh, yes — for once, in a way. 145 Especially the beginning of the evening; for then Eilert read me part of his book. We arrived more than an hour too early — fancy that! And Brack had all sorts of arrangements to make — so Eilert read to me. 150

Hedda (*seating herself by the table on the right*). Well? Tell me, then ——

Tes. (*sitting on a footstool near the stove*). Oh, Hedda, you can't conceive what a book that is going to be! I believe it is one of the most 155 remarkable things that have ever been written. Fancy that!

Hedda. Yes, yes; I don't care about that——

Tes. I must make a confession to you, Hedda. When he had finished reading — 160 a horrid feeling came over me.

Hedda. A horrid feeling?

Tes. I felt jealous of Eilert for having had it in him to write such a book. Only think, Hedda! 165

Hedda. Yes, yes, I am thinking!

Tes. And then how pitiful to think that he — with all his gifts — should be irreclaimable, after all.

Hedda. I suppose you mean that he has 170 more courage than the rest?

Tes. No, not at all — I mean that he is incapable of taking his pleasures in moderation

Hedda. And what came of it all — in the end? 175

Tes. Well, to tell the truth, I think it migh' best be described as an orgy, Hedda.

Hedda. Had he vine-leaves in his hair?

Tes. Vine-leaves? No, I saw nothing of the sort. But he made a long, rambling 18 speech in honor of the woman who had in spired him in his work — that was the phras' he used.

Hedda. Did he name her?

Tes. No, he didn't; but I can't help 185
thinking he meant Mrs. Elvsted. You may be
sure he did.

Hedda. Well — where did you part from
him?

Tes. On the way to town. We broke 190
up — the last of us at any rate — all together;
and Brack came with us to get a breath of
fresh air. And then, you see, we agreed to
take Eilert home; for he had had far more than
was good for him. 195

Hedda. I daresay.

Tes. But now comes the strange part of it,
Hedda; or, I should rather say, the melancholy
part of it. I declare I am almost ashamed —
on Eilert's account — to tell you —— 200

Hedda. Oh, go on ——

Tes. Well, as we were getting near town, you
see, I happened to drop a little behind the
others. Only for a minute or two — fancy
that! 205

Hedda. Yes, yes, yes, but — ?

Tes. And then, as I hurried after them —
what do you think I found by the wayside?
Eh?

Hedda. Oh, how should I know! 210

Tes. You mustn't speak of it to a soul,
Hedda! Do you hear! Promise me, for
Eilert's sake. (*Draws a parcel, wrapped in
paper, from his coat pocket.*) Fancy, dear — I
found this. 215

Hedda. Is not that the parcel he had with
him yesterday?

Tes. Yes, it is the whole of his precious,
irreplaceable manuscript! And he had gone
and lost it, and knew nothing about it. 220
Only fancy, Hedda! So deplorably ——

Hedda. But why did you not give him back
the parcel at once?

Tes. I didn't dare to — in the state he was
then in —— 225

Hedda. Did you not tell any of the others
that you had found it?

Tes. Oh, far from it! You can surely understand that, for Eilert's sake, I wouldn't do
that. 230

Hedda. So no one knows that Eilert Lövborg's manuscript is in your possession?

Tes. No. And no one must know it.

Hedda. Then what did you say to him afterwards? 235

Tes. I didn't talk to him again at all; for
when we got in among the streets, he and two
or three of the others gave us the slip and disappeared. Fancy that!

Hedda. Indeed! They must have 240
taken him home then.

Tes. Yes, so it would appear. And Brack,
too, left us.

Hedda. And what have you been doing with
yourself since? 245

Tes. Well, I and some of the others went
home with one of the party, a jolly fellow, and
took our morning coffee with him; or perhaps
I should rather call it our night coffee — eh?
But now, when I have rested a little, and 250
given Eilert, poor fellow, time to have his sleep
out, I must take this back to him.

Hedda (*holds out her hand for the packet*). No
— don't give it to him! Not in such a hurry,
I mean. Let me read it first. 255

Tes. No, my dearest Hedda, I mustn't, I
really mustn't.

Hedda. You must not?

Tes. No — for you can imagine what a state
of despair he will be in when he awakens 260
and misses the manuscript. He has no copy
of it, you must know! He told me so.

Hedda (*looking searchingly at him*). Can such
a thing not be reproduced? Written over again?

Tes. No, I don't think that would be 265
possible. For the inspiration, you see —

Hedda. Yes, yes — I suppose it depends on
that. (*Lightly*) But, by the bye — here is a
letter for you.

Tes. Fancy —— ! 270

Hedda (*handing it to him*). It came early this
morning.

Tes. It's from Aunt Julia! What can it be?
(*He lays the packet on the other footstool, opens
the letter, runs his eye through it, and 275
jumps up.*) Oh, Hedda — she says that poor
Aunt Rina is dying!

Hedda. Well, we were prepared for that.

Tes. And that if I want to see her again,
I must make haste. I'll run in to them 280
at once.

Hedda (*suppressing a smile*). Will you run?

Tes. Oh, dearest Hedda — if you could only make up your mind to come with me! Just think!   285

Hedda (*rises and says wearily, repelling the idea*). No, no, don't ask me. I will not look upon sickness and death. I loathe all sorts of ugliness.

Tes. Well, well, then——! (*Bustling*   290 *around*) My hat——? My overcoat——? Oh, in the hall — I do hope I mayn't come too late, Hedda! Eh?

Hedda. Oh, if you run——

BERTA *appears at the hall door*

Berta. Judge Brack is at the door, and   295 wishes to know if he may come in.

Tes. At this time! No, I can't possibly see him.

Hedda. But I can. (*To* BERTA) Ask Judge Brack to come in.   300
          (BERTA *goes out.*

Hedda (*quickly, whispering*). The parcel, Tesman! (*She snatches it up from the stool.*

Tes. Yes, give it to me!

Hedda. No, no, I will keep it till you come back.   305
          (*She goes to the writing-table and places it in the bookcase.* TESMAN *stands in a flurry of haste, and cannot get his gloves on.*

JUDGE BRACK *enters from the hall*

Hedda (*nodding to him*). You are an early bird, I must say.

Brack. Yes, don't you think so? (*To* TESMAN) Are you on the move, too?

Tes. Yes, I must rush off to my   310 aunt's. Fancy — the invalid one is lying at death's door, poor creature.

Brack. Dear me, is she indeed? Then on no account let me detain you. At such a critical moment ——   315

Tes. Yes, I must really rush —— Good-bye! Good-bye! (*He hastens out by the hall door.*

Hedda (*approaching*). You seem to have made a particularly lively night of it at your rooms, Judge Brack.   320

Brack. I assure you I have not had my clothes off, Mrs. Hedda.

Hedda. Not you, either?

Brack. No, as you may see. But what has Tesman been telling you of the night's   325 adventures?

Hedda. Oh, some tiresome story. Only that they went and had coffee somewhere or other.

Brack. I have heard about that coffee-   330 party already. Eilert Lövborg was not with them, I fancy?

Hedda. No, they had taken him home before that.

Brack. Tesman too?   335

Hedda. No, but some of the others, he said.

Brack (*smiling*). George Tesman is really an ingenuous creature, Mrs. Hedda.

Hedda. Yes, heaven knows he is. Then is there something behind all this?   340

Brack. Yes, perhaps there may be.

Hedda. Well then, sit down, my dear Judge, and tell your story in comfort.
          (*She seats herself to the left of the table.* BRACK *sits near her, at the long side of the table.*

Hedda. Now then?

Brack. I had special reasons for keep-   345 ing track of my guests — or rather of some of my guests — last night.

Hedda. Of Eilert Lövborg among the rest, perhaps?

Brack. Frankly, yes.   350

Hedda. Now you make me really curious ——

Brack. Do you know where he and one or two of the others finished the night, Mrs. Hedda?   355

Hedda. If it is not quite unmentionable, tell me.

Brack. Oh no, it's not at all unmentionable. Well, they put in an appearance at a particularly animated *soirée*.   360

Hedda. Of the lively kind?

Brack. Of the very liveliest ——

Hedda. Tell me more of this, Judge Brack ——

Brack. Lövborg, as well as the others,   365 had been invited in advance. I knew all about it. But he had declined the invitation; for now, as you know, he has become a new man.

Hedda. Up at the Elvsteds', yes. But he went after all, then?   370

Brack. Well, you see, Mrs. Hedda — unhappily the spirit moved him at my rooms last evening ——

Hedda. Yes, I hear he found inspiration.

Brack. Pretty violent inspiration.   375 Well, I fancy that altered his purpose; for we men folk are unfortunately not always so firm in our principles as we ought to be.

Hedda. Oh, I am sure you are an exception, Judge Brack. But as to Lövborg — ?   380

Brack. To make a long story short — he landed at last in Mademoiselle Diana's rooms.

Hedda. Mademoiselle Diana's?

Brack. It was Mademoiselle Diana that was giving the *soirée*, to a select circle of her   385 admirers and her lady friends.

Hedda. Is she a red-haired woman?

Brack. Precisely.

Hedda. A sort of a — singer?

Brack. Oh yes — in her leisure mo-   390 ments. And moreover a mighty huntress — of men — Mrs. Hedda. You have no doubt heard of her. Eilert Lövborg was one of her most enthusiastic protectors — in the days of his glory.   395

Hedda. And how did all this end?

Brack. Far from amicably, it appears. After a most tender meeting, they seem to have come to blows ——

Hedda. Lövborg and she?   400

Brack. Yes. He accused her or her friends of having robbed him. He declared that his pocket-book had disappeared — and other things as well. In short, he seems to have made a furious disturbance.   405

Hedda. And what came of it all?

Brack. It came to a general scrimmage, in which the ladies as well as the gentlemen took part. Fortunately, the police at last appeared on the scene.   410

Hedda. The police too?

Brack. Yes. I fancy it will prove a costly frolic for Eilert Lövborg, crazy being that he is.

Hedda. How so?

Brack. He seems to have made a vio-   415

lent resistance — to have hit one of the constables on the head and torn the coat off his back. So they had to march him off to the police-station with the rest.

Hedda. How have you learnt all this?   420

Brack. From the police themselves.

Hedda (*gazing straight before her*). So that is what happened. Then he had no vine-leaves in his hair.

Brack. Vine-leaves, Mrs. Hedda?   425

Hedda (*changing her tone*). But tell me now, Judge — what is your real reason for tracking out Eilert Lövborg's movements so carefully?

Brack. In the first place, it could not be entirely indifferent to me if it should appear   430 in the police-court that he came straight from my house.

Hedda. Will the matter come into court then?

Brack. Of course. However, I should   435 scarcely have troubled so much about that. But I thought that, as a friend of the family, it was my duty to supply you and Tesman with a full account of his nocturnal exploits.

Hedda. Why so, Judge Brack?   440

Brack. Why, because I have a shrewd suspicion that he intends to use you as a sort of blind.

Hedda. Oh, how can you think such a thing!

Brack. Good heavens, Mrs. Hedda —   445 we have eyes in our head. Mark my words! This Mrs. Elvsted will be in no hurry to leave town again.

Hedda. Well, even if there should be anything between them, I suppose there are   450 plenty of other places where they could meet.

Brack. Not a single home. Henceforth, as before, every respectable house will be closed against Eilert Lövborg.

Hedda. And so ought mine to be, you   455 mean?

Brack. Yes, I confess it would be more than painful to me if this personage were to be made free of your house. How superfluous, how intrusive he would be, if he were to force   460 his way into ——

Hedda. — into the triangle?

Brack. Precisely. It would simply mean that I should find myself homeless.

Hedda (*looks at him with a smile*). So 465
you want to be the one cock in the basket [1] —
that is your aim.

Brack (*nods slowly and lowers his voice*). Yes,
that is my aim. And for that I will fight —
with every weapon I can command. 470

Hedda (*her smile vanishing*). I see you are
a dangerous person — when it comes to the
point.

Brack. Do you think so?

Hedda. I am beginning to think so. 475
And I am exceedingly glad to think — that
you have no sort of hold over me.

Brack (*laughing equivocally*). Well, well,
Mrs. Hedda — perhaps you are right there.
If I had, who knows what I might be 480
capable of?

Hedda. Come, come now, Judge Brack!
That sounds almost like a threat.

Brack (*rising*). Oh, not at all! The triangle, you know, ought, if possible, to be 485
spontaneously constructed.

Hedda. There I agree with you.

Brack. Well, now I have said all I had to
say; and I had better be getting back to town.
Good-bye, Mrs. Hedda. 490

　　　　　(*He goes towards the glass door.*

Hedda (*rising*). Are you going through the
garden?

Brack. Yes, it's a short cut for me.

Hedda. And then it is a back way, too.

Brack. Quite so. I have no objection 495
to back ways. They may be piquant enough
at times.

Hedda. When there is ball practice going on,
you mean?

Brack (*in the doorway, laughing to her*). 500
Oh, people don't shoot their tame poultry, I
fancy.

Hedda (*also laughing*). Oh no, when there
is only one cock in the basket ——

　　　　　(*They exchange laughing nods of fare-
　　　　　well. He goes. She closes the door
　　　　　behind him.*

　　　　　(*HEDDA, who has become quite serious,
　　　　　stands for a moment looking out.
　　　　　Presently she goes and peeps through
　　　　　the curtain over the middle doorway.*

---

[1] A Norwegian proverbial saying.

*Then she goes to the writing-table,
takes* LÖVBORG'S *packet out of the
bookcase, and is on the point of
looking through its contents.* BERTA
is heard speaking loudly in the hall.
HEDDA *turns and listens. Then she
hastily locks up the packet in the
drawer, and lays the key on the inkstand.*

EILERT LÖVBORG, *with his great coat on and
his hat in his hand, tears open the hall
door. He looks somewhat confused and
irritated*

Löv. (*looking towards the hall*). And I 505
tell you I must and will come in!   There!

　　　　　(*He closes the door, turns and sees
　　　　　HEDDA, at once regains his self-con-
　　　　　trol, and bows.*

Hedda (*at the writing-table*). Well, Mr. Lövborg, this is rather a late hour to call for Thea.

Löv. You mean rather an early hour to call
on you.   Pray pardon me. 510

Hedda. How do you know that she is still
here?

Löv. They told me at her lodgings that she
had been out all night.

Hedda (*going to the oval table*). Did you 515
notice anything about the people of the house
when they said that?

Löv. (*looks inquiringly at her*). Notice anything about them?

Hedda. I mean, did they seem to think 520
it odd?

Löv. (*suddenly understanding*). Oh yes, of
course! I am dragging her down with me!
However, I didn't notice anything — I suppose Tesman is not up yet? 25

Hedda. No — I think not ——

Löv. When did he come home?

Hedda. Very late.

Löv. Did he tell you anything?

Hedda. Yes, I gathered that you had 530
had an exceedingly jolly evening at Judge
Brack's.

Löv. Nothing more?

Hedda. I don't think so. However, I was
so dreadfully sleepy —— 535

MRS. ELVSTED *enters through the curtains of the middle doorway*

Mrs. Elv. (*going towards him*). Ah, Lövborg! At last — !

Löv. Yes, at last. And too late!

Mrs. Elv. (*looks anxiously at him*). What is too late?   540

Löv. Everything is too late now. It is all over with me.

Mrs. Elv. Oh, no, no — don't say that!

Löv. You will say the same when you hear ——   545

Mrs. Elv. I won't hear anything!

Hedda. Perhaps you would prefer to talk to her alone! If so, I will leave you.

Löv. No, stay — you too. I beg you to stay.   550

Mrs. Elv. Yes, but I won't hear anything, I tell you.

Löv. It is not last night's adventures that I want to talk about.

Mrs. Elv. What is it then —?   555

Löv. I want to say that now our ways must part.

Mrs. Elv. Part!

Hedda (*involuntarily*). I knew it!

Löv. You can be of no more service to 560 me, Thea.

Mrs. Elv. How can you stand there and say that! No more service to you! Am I not to help you now, as before? Are we not to go on working together?   565

Löv. Henceforward I shall do no work.

Mrs. Elv. (*despairingly*). Then what am I to do with my life?

Löv. You must try to live your life as if you had never known me.   570

Mrs. Elv. But you know I cannot do that!

Löv. Try if you cannot, Thea. You must go home again ——

Mrs. Elv. (*in vehement protest*). Never in this world! Where you are, there will I be 575 also! I will not let myself be driven away like this! I will remain here! I will be with you when the book appears.

Hedda (*half aloud, in suspense*). Ah yes — the book!   580

Löv. (*looks at her*). My book and Thea's; for that is what it is.

Mrs. Elv. Yes, I feel that it is. And that is why I have a right to be with you when it appears! I will see with my own eyes how 585 respect and honor pour in upon you afresh. And the happiness — the happiness — oh, I must share it with you!

Löv. Thea — our book will never appear.

Hedda. Ah!   590

Mrs. Elv. Never appear!

Löv. Can never appear.

Mrs. Elv. (*in agonized foreboding*). Lövborg — what have you done with the manuscript?   595

Hedda (*looks anxiously at him*). Yes, the manuscript — ?

Mrs. Elv. Where is it?

Löv. Oh Thea — don't ask me about it!

Mrs. Elv. Yes, yes, I will know. I 600 demand to be told at once.

Löv. The manuscript —— Well, then — I have torn the manuscript into a thousand pieces.

Mrs. Elv. (*shrieks*). Oh no, no — ! 605

Hedda (*involuntarily*). But that's not ——

Löv. (*looks at her*). Not true, you think?

Hedda (*collecting herself*). Oh well, of course — since you say so. But it sounded so improbable ——   610

Löv. It is true, all the same.

Mrs. Elv. (*wringing her hands*). Oh God — oh God, Hedda — torn his own work to pieces!

Löv. I have torn my own life to pieces. So why should I not tear my life-work 615 too — ?

Mrs. Elv. And you did this last night?

Löv. Yes, I tell you! Tore it into a thousand pieces — and scattered them on the fjord — far out. There there is cool sea-water at 620 any rate — let them drift upon it — drift with the current and the wind. And then presently they will sink — deeper and deeper — as I shall, Thea.

Mrs. Elv. Do you know, Lövborg, that 625 what you have done with the book — I shall think of it to my dying day as though you had killed a little child.

Löv. Yes, you are right. It is a sort of child-murder.   630

Mrs. Elv. How could you, then —— ! Did not the child belong to me too?

Hedda (*almost inaudibly*). Ah, the child ——

Mrs. Elv. (*breathing heavily*). It is all over, then. Well, well, now I will go, Hedda. 635

Hedda. But you are not going away from town?

Mrs. Elv. Oh, I don't know what I shall do. I see nothing but darkness before me.

(*She goes out by the hall door.*

Hedda (*stands waiting for a moment*). 640 So you are not going to see her home, Mr. Lövborg?

Löv. I? Through the streets? Would you have people see her walking with me?

Hedda. Of course I don't know what 645 else may have happened last night. But is it so utterly irretrievable?

Löv. It will not end with last night — I know that perfectly well. And the thing is that now I have no taste for that sort of 650 life either. I won't begin it anew. She has broken my courage and my power of braving it out.

Hedda (*looking straight before her*). So that pretty little fool has had her fingers in a 655 man's destiny. (*Looks at him.*) But all the same, how could you treat her so heartlessly?

Löv. Oh, don't say that it was heartless!

Hedda. To go and destroy what has 660 filled her whole soul for months and years! You do not call that heartless!

Löv. To you I can tell the truth, Hedda.

Hedda. The truth?

Löv. First promise me — give me 665 your word — that what I now confide to you Thea shall never know.

Hedda. I give you my word.

Löv. Good. Then let me tell you that what I said just now was untrue. 670

Hedda. About the manuscript?

Löv. Yes. I have not torn it to pieces — nor thrown it into the fjord.

Hedda. No, no — But — where is it then?

Löv. I have destroyed it none the less 675 — utterly destroyed it, Hedda!

Hedda. I don't understand.

Löv. Thea said that what I had done seemed to her like a child-murder.

Hedda. Yes, so she said. 680

Löv. But to kill his child — that is not the worst thing a father can do to it.

Hedda. Not the worst?

Löv. No. I wanted to spare Thea from hearing the worst. 685

Hedda. Then what is the worst?

Löv. Suppose now, Hedda, that a man — in the small hours of the morning — came home to his child's mother after a night of riot and debauchery, and said: "Listen — I have 690 been here and there — in this place and in that. And I have taken our child with me — to this place and to that. And I have lost the child — utterly lost it. The devil knows into what hands it may have fallen — who 695 may have had their clutches on it."

Hedda. Well — but when all is said and done, you know — that was only a book ——

Löv. Thea's pure soul was in that book.

Hedda. Yes, so I understand. 700

Löv. And you can understand, too, that for her and me together no future is possible.

Hedda. What path do you mean to take, then? 705

Löv. None. I will only try to make an end of it all — the sooner the better.

Hedda (*a step nearer to him*). Eilert Lövborg — listen to me. Will you not try to — to do it beautifully? 710

Löv. Beautifully? (*Smiling*) With vine-leaves in my hair, as you used to dream in the old days — ?

Hedda. No, no. I have lost my faith in the vine-leaves. But beautifully, neverthe- 715 less! For once in a way! — Good-bye! You must go now — and do not come here any more.

Löv. Good-bye, Mrs. Tesman. And give George Tesman my love. 720

(*He is on the point of going.*

Hedda. No, wait! I must give you a memento to take with you.

(*She goes to the writing-table and opens the drawer and the pistol-case; then returns to* LÖVBORG *with one of the pistols.*

Löv. (*looks at her*). This? Is this the memento?

Hedda (*nodding slowly*). Do you re- 725
cognize it? It was aimed at you once.

Löv. You should have used it then.

Hedda. Take it — and do you use it now.

Löv. (*puts the pistol in his breast pocket*).
Thanks! 730

Hedda. And beautifully, Eilert Lövborg.
Promise me that!

Löv. Good-bye, Hedda Gabler.

(*He goes out by the hall door.*
(HEDDA *listens for a moment at the door.
Then she goes up to the writing-table,
takes out the packet of manuscript,
peeps under the cover, draws a few of
the sheets half out, and looks at them.
Next she goes over and seats herself in
the armchair beside the stove, with the
packet in her lap. Presently she opens
the stove door, and then the packet.*

Hedda (*throws one of the quires into the fire
and whispers to herself*). Now I am burn- 735
ing your child, Thea! — Burning it, curly-
locks! (*Throwing one or two more quires into
the stove*) Your child and Eilert Lövborg's.
(*Throws the rest in.*) I am burning — I am
burning your child. 740

Curtain

ACT IV

The same rooms at the TESMANS'. *It is evening.
The drawing-room is in darkness. The
back room is lighted by the hanging lamp
over the table. The curtains over the glass
door are drawn close.*

HEDDA, *dressed in black, walks to and fro in the
dark room. Then she goes into the back
room and disappears for a moment to the
left. She is heard to strike a few chords on
the piano. Presently she comes in sight
again, and returns to the drawing-room.*

BERTA *enters from the right, through the inner
room, with a lighted lamp, which she places
on the table in front of the corner settee in the
drawing-room. Her eyes are red with weeping, and she has black ribbons in her cap.
She goes quietly and circumspectly out to
the right.* HEDDA *goes up to the glass door,
lifts the curtain a little aside, and looks out
into the darkness.*

Shortly afterwards, MISS TESMAN, *in mourning,
with a bonnet and veil on, comes in from the
hall.* HEDDA *goes towards her and holds out
her hand*

Miss Tes. Yes, Hedda, here I am, in mourning and forlorn; for now my poor sister has at
last found peace.

Hedda. I have heard the news already, as
you see. Tesman sent me a card. 5

Miss Tes. Yes, he promised me he would.
But nevertheless I thought that to Hedda —
here in the house of life — I ought myself to
bring the tidings of death.

Hedda. That was very kind of you. 10

Miss Tes. Ah, Rina ought not to have left
us just now. This is not the time for Hedda's
house to be a house of mourning.

Hedda (*changing the subject*). She died quite
peacefully, did she not, Miss Tesman? 15

Miss Tes. Oh, her end was so calm, so beautiful. And then she had the unspeakable happiness of seeing George once more — and bidding him good-bye. — Has he not come home
yet? 20

Hedda. No. He wrote that he might be detained. But won't you sit down?

Miss Tes. No, thank you, my dear, dear
Hedda. I should like to, but I have so much
to do. I must prepare my dear one for her 25
rest as well as I can. She shall go to her grave
looking her best.

Hedda. Can I not help you in any way?

Miss Tes. Oh, you must not think of it!
Hedda Tesman must have no hand in such 30
mournful work. Nor let her thoughts dwell
on it either — not at this time.

Hedda. One is not always mistress of one's
thoughts ——

Miss Tes. (*continuing*). Ah, yes, it is the 35
way of the world. At home we shall be sewing
a shroud; and here there will soon be sewing
too, I suppose — but of another sort, thank
God!

GEORGE TESMAN *enters by the hall door*

Hedda. Ah, you have come at last! 40

Tes. You here, Aunt Julia? With Hedda?
Fancy that!

Miss Tes. I was just going, my dear boy. Well, have you done all you promised?

Tes. No; I'm really afraid I have for- 45 gotten half of it. I must come to you again to-morrow. Today my brain is all in a whirl. I can't keep my thoughts together.

Miss Tes. Why, my dear George, you mustn't take it in this way. 50

Tes. Mustn't —? How do you mean?

Miss Tes. Even in your sorrow you must rejoice, as I do — rejoice that she is at rest.

Tes. Oh yes, yes — you are thinking of Aunt Rina. 55

Hedda. You will feel lonely now, Miss Tesman.

Miss Tes. Just at first, yes. But that will not last very long, I hope. I daresay I shall soon find an occupant for poor Rina's little 60 room.

Tes. Indeed? Who do you think will take it? Eh?

Miss Tes. Oh, there's always some poor in-valid or other in want of nursing, unfortu- 65 nately.

Hedda. Would you really take such a burden upon you again?

Miss Tes. A burden! Heaven forgive you, child — it has been no burden to me. 70

Hedda. But suppose you had a total stranger on your hands ——

Miss Tes. Oh, one soon makes friends with sick folk; and it's such an absolute necessity for me to have someone to live for. Well, 75 heaven be praised, there may soon be something in this house, too, to keep an old aunt busy.

Hedda. Oh, don't trouble about anything here.

Tes. Yes, just fancy what a nice time we 80 might have together, if —?

Hedda. If —?

Tes. (*uneasily*). Oh, nothing. It will all come right. Let us hope so — eh?

Miss Tes. Well, well, I daresay you two 85 want to talk to each other. (*Smiling*) And perhaps Hedda may have something to tell you too, George. Good-bye! I must go home to Rina. (*Turning at the door*) How strange it is to think that now Rina is with me and 90 with my poor brother as well!

Tes. Yes, fancy that, Aunt Julia! Eh?

(*Miss Tesman goes out by the hall door.*

Hedda (*follows Tesman coldly and searchingly with her eyes*). I almost believe your Aunt Rina's death affects you more than it does 95 your Aunt Julia.

Tes. Oh, it's not that alone. It's Eilert I am so terribly uneasy about.

Hedda (*quickly*). Is there anything new about him? 100

Tes. I looked in at his rooms this afternoon, intending to tell him the manuscript was in safe keeping.

Hedda. Well, did you not find him?

Tes. No. He wasn't at home. But 105 afterwards I met Mrs. Elvsted, and she told me that he had been here early this morning.

Hedda. Yes, directly after you had gone.

Tes. And he said that he had torn his man-uscript to pieces — eh? 110

Hedda. Yes, so he declared.

Tes. Why, good heavens, he must have been completely out of his mind! And I suppose you thought it best not to give it back to him, Hedda? 115

Hedda. No, he did not get it.

Tes. But of course you told him that we had it?

Hedda. No. (*Quickly*) Did you tell Mrs. Elvsted? 120

Tes. No; I thought I had better not. But you ought to have told him. Fancy, if, in desperation, he should go and do himself some injury! Let me have the manuscript, Hedda! I will take it to him at once. Where is it? 125

Hedda (*cold and immovable, leaning on the armchair*). I have not got it.

Tes. Have not got it? What in the world do you mean?

Hedda. I have burnt it — every line 130 of it.

Tes. (*with a violent movement of terror*). Burnt! Burnt Eilert's manuscript!

Hedda. Don't scream so. The servant might hear you. 135

Tes. Burnt! Why, good God —! No, no no! It's impossible!

Hedda. It is so, nevertheless.

Tes. Do you know what you have done

Hedda? It's unlawful appropriation of 140 lost property. Fancy that! Just ask Judge Brack, and he'll tell you what it is.

Hedda. I advise you not to speak of it — either to Judge Brack or to anyone else.

Tes. But how could you do anything 145 so unheard of? What put it into your head? What possessed you? Answer me that — eh?

Hedda (suppressing an almost imperceptible smile). I did it for your sake, George.

Tes. For my sake!   150

Hedda. This morning, when you told me about what he had read to you ——

Tes. Yes, yes — what then?

Hedda. You acknowledged that you envied him his work.   155

Tes. Oh, of course I didn't mean that literally.

Hedda. No matter — I could not bear the idea that anyone should throw you into the shade.   160

Tes. (in an outburst of mingled doubt and joy). Hedda! Oh, is this true? But — but — I never knew you to show your love like that before. Fancy that!

Hedda. Well, I may as well tell you 165 that — just at this time —— (*Impatiently, breaking off*) No, no; you can ask Aunt Julia. She will tell you, fast enough.

Tes. Oh, I almost think I understand you, Hedda! (*Clasps his hands together.*) 170 Great heavens! do you really mean it! Eh?

Hedda. Don't shout so. The servant might hear.

Tes. (laughing in irrepressible glee). The servant! Why, how absurd you are, 175 Hedda. It's only my old Berta! Why, I'll tell Berta myself.

Hedda (clenching her hands together in desperation). Oh, it is killing me — it is killing me, all this!   180

Tes. What is, Hedda? Eh?

Hedda (coldly, controlling herself). All this — absurdity — George.

Tes. Absurdity! Do you see anything absurd in my being overjoyed at the news! 185 But after all — perhaps I had better not say anything to Berta.

Hedda. Oh —— why not that too?

Tes. No, no, not yet! But I must certainly tell Aunt Julia. And then that you have 190 begun to call me George too! Fancy that! Oh, Aunt Julia will be so happy — so happy!

Hedda. When she hears that I have burnt Eilert Lövborg's manuscript — for your sake?

Tes. No, by the bye — that affair of 195 the manuscript — of course nobody must know about that. But that you love me so much, Hedda — Aunt Julia must really share my joy in that! I wonder, now, whether this sort of thing is usual in young wives? Eh?   200

Hedda. I think you had better ask Aunt Julia that question too.

Tes. I will indeed, sometime or other. (*Looks uneasy and downcast again.*) And yet the manuscript — the manuscript! Good 205 God! it is terrible to think what will become of poor Eilert now.

MRS. ELVSTED, *dressed as in the first act, with hat and cloak, enters by the hall door*

Mrs. Elv. (greets them hurriedly, and says in evident agitation). Oh, dear Hedda, forgive my coming again.   210

Hedda. What is the matter with you, Thea?

Tes. Something about Eilert Lövborg again — eh?

Mrs. Elv. Yes! I am dreadfully afraid some misfortune has happened to him.   215

Hedda (seizes her arm). Ah — do you think so?

Tes. Why, good Lord — what makes you think that, Mrs. Elvsted?

Mrs. Elv. I heard them talking of him 220 at my boarding-house — just as I came in. Oh, the most incredible rumors are afloat about him today.

Tes. Yes, fancy, so I heard too! And I can bear witness that he went straight home to 225 bed last night. Fancy that!

Hedda. Well, what did they say at the boarding-house?

Mrs. Elv. Oh, I couldn't make out anything clearly. Either they knew nothing defi- 230 nite, or else —— They stopped talking when they saw me; and I did not dare to ask.

Tes. (moving about uneasily). We must hope

— we must hope that you misunderstood them,
Mrs. Elvsted.   235

Mrs. Elv. No, no; I am sure it was of him
they were talking. And I heard something
about the hospital or ——

Tes. The hospital?

Hedda. No — surely that cannot be!   240

Mrs. Elv. Oh, I was in such mortal terror!
I went to his lodgings and asked for him there.

Hedda. You could make up your mind to
that, Thea!

Mrs. Elv. What else could I do? I   245
really could bear the suspense no longer.

Tes. But you didn't find him either — eh?

Mrs. Elv. No. And the people knew nothing
about him. He hadn't been home since yesterday afternoon, they said.   250

Tes. Yesterday! Fancy, how could they
say that?

Mrs. Elv. Oh, I am sure something terrible
must have happened to him.

Tes. Hedda dear — how would it be if   255
I were to go and make inquiries — ?

Hedda. No, no — don't you mix yourself up
in this affair.

JUDGE BRACK, *with his hat in his hand, enters
by the hall door, which* BERTA *opens, and
closes behind him. He looks grave and bows
in silence*

Tes. Oh, is that you, my dear Judge? Eh?

Brack. Yes. It was imperative I   260
should see you this evening.

Tes. I can see you have heard the news
about Aunt Rina.

Brack. Yes, that among other things.

Tes. Isn't it sad — eh?   265

Brack. Well, my dear Tesman, that depends
on how you look at it.

Tes. (*looks doubtfully at him*). Has anything
else happened?

Brack. Yes.   270

Hedda (*in suspense*). Anything sad, Judge
Brack?

Brack. That, too, depends on how you look
at it, Mrs. Tesman.

Mrs. Elv. (*unable to restrain her anxi-* 275
ety). Oh! it is something about Eilert Lövborg!

Brack (*with a glance at her*). What makes
you think that, madam? Perhaps you have
already heard something — ?   280

Mrs. Elv. (*in confusion*). No, nothing at all,
but ——

Tes. Oh, for heaven's sake, tell us!

Brack (*shrugging his shoulders*). Well, I
regret to say Eilert Lövborg has been   285
taken to the hospital. He is lying at the point
of death.

Mrs. Elv. (*shrieks*). Oh God! oh God —!

Tes. To the hospital! And at the point of
death!   290

Hedda (*involuntarily*). So soon, then ——

Mrs. Elv. (*wailing*). And we parted in anger,
Hedda!

Hedda (*whispers*). Thea — Thea — be careful!   295

Mrs. Elv. (*not heeding her*). I must go to him!
I must see him alive!

Brack. It is useless, Madam. No one will
be admitted.

Mrs. Elv. Oh, at least tell me what has   300
happened to him? What is it?

Tes. You don't mean to say that he has himself —— Eh?

Hedda. Yes, I am sure he has.

Tes. Hedda, how can you —?   305

Brack (*keeping his eyes fixed upon her*). Unfortunately you have guessed quite correctly,
Mrs. Tesman.

Mrs. Elv. Oh, how horrible!

Tes. Himself, then! Fancy that!   310

Hedda. Shot himself!

Brack. Rightly guessed again, Mrs. Tesman.

Mrs. Elv. (*with an effort at self-control*). When
did it happen, Mr. Brack?   315

Brack. This afternoon — between three and
four.

Tes. But, good Lord, where did he do it? Eh?

Brack (*with some hesitation*). Where? Well
— I suppose at his lodgings.   320

Mrs. Elv. No, that cannot be; for I was there
between six and seven.

Brack. Well, then, somewhere else. I don't
know exactly. I only know that he was
found —— He had shot himself — in the   325
breast.

Mrs. Elv. Oh, how terrible! That he should die like that!

Hedda (*to* BRACK). Was it in the breast?

Brack. Yes — as I told you.   330

Hedda. Not in the temple?

Brack. In the breast, Mrs. Tesman.

Hedda. Well, well — the breast is a good place, too.

Brack. How do you mean, Mrs. Tes-   335
man?

Hedda (*evasively*). Oh, nothing — nothing.

Tes. And the wound is dangerous, you say — eh?

Brack. Absolutely mortal. The end   340
has probably come by this time.

Mrs. Elv. Yes, yes, I feel it. The end! The end! Oh, Hedda —!

Tes. But tell me, how have you learnt all this?   345

Brack (*curtly*). Through one of the police. A man I had some business with.

Hedda (*in a clear voice*). At last a deed worth doing!

Tes. (*terrified*). Good heavens, Hedda!   350
what are you saying?

Hedda. I say there is beauty in this.

Brack. H'm, Mrs. Tesman ——

Tes. Beauty! Fancy that!

Mrs. Elv. Oh, Hedda, how can you talk   355
of beauty in such an act!

Hedda. Eilert Lövborg has himself made up his account with life. He has had the courage to do — the one right thing.

Mrs. Elv. No, you must never think   360
that was how it happened! It must have been in delirium that he did it.

Tes. In despair!

Hedda. That he did not. I am certain of that.   365

Mrs. Elv. Yes, yes! In delirium! Just as when he tore up our manuscript.

Brack (*starting*). The manuscript? Has he torn that up?

Mrs. Elv. Yes, last night.   370

Tes. (*whispers softly*). Oh, Hedda, we shall never get over this.

Brack. H'm, very extraordinary.

Tes. (*moving about the room*). To think of Eilert going out of the world in this way!   375

And not leaving behind him the book that would have immortalized his name ——

Mrs. Elv. Oh, if only it could be put together again!

Tes. Yes, if it only could! I don't   380
know what I would not give ——

Mrs. Elv. Perhaps it can, Mr. Tesman.

Tes. What do you mean?

Mrs. Elv. (*searches in the pocket of her dress*). Look here. I have kept all the loose   385
notes he used to dictate from.

Hedda (*a step forward*). Ah ——!

Tes. You have kept them, Mrs. Elvsted! Eh?

Mrs. Elv. Yes, I have them here. I   390
put them in my pocket when I left home. Here they still are ——

Tes. Oh, do let me see them!

Mrs. Elv. (*hands him a bundle of papers*). But they are in such disorder — all   395
mixed up.

Tes. Fancy, if we could make something out of them, after all! Perhaps if we two put our heads together ——

Mrs. Elv. Oh, yes, at least let us   400
try ——

Tes. We will manage it! We must! I will dedicate my life to this task.

Hedda. You, George? Your life?

Tes. Yes, or rather all the time I can   405
spare. My own collections must wait in the meantime. Hedda — you understand, eh? I owe this to Eilert's memory.

Hedda. Perhaps.

Tes. And so, my dear Mrs. Elvsted,   410
we will give our whole minds to it. There is no use in brooding over what can't be undone — eh? We must try to control our grief as much as possible, and ——

Mrs. Elv. Yes, yes, Mr. Tesman, I   415
will do the best I can.

Tes. Well then, come here. I can't rest until we have looked through the notes. Where shall we sit? Here? No, in there, in the back room. Excuse me, my dear Judge.   420
Come with me, Mrs. Elvsted.

Mrs. Elv. Oh, if only it were possible!

(TESMAN *and* MRS. ELVSTED *go into the back room. She takes off her hat and cloak. They both sit at the table under the hanging lamp, and are soon deep in an eager examination of the papers.* HEDDA *crosses to the stove and sits in the armchair. Presently* BRACK *goes up to her.*

Hedda (*in a low voice*). Oh, what sense of freedom it gives one, this act of Eilert Lövborg's.

Brack. Freedom, Mrs. Hedda? Well, 425 of course, it is a release for him ——

Hedda. I mean for me. It gives me a sense of freedom to know that a deed of deliberate courage is still possible in this world — a deed of spontaneous beauty.   430

Brack (*smiling*). H'm — my dear Mrs. Hedda ——

Hedda. Oh, I know what you are going to say. For you are a kind of a specialist too, like — you know!   435

Brack (*looking hard at her*). Eilert Lövborg was more to you than perhaps you are willing to admit to yourself. Am I wrong?

Hedda. I don't answer such questions. I only know that Eilert Lövborg has had the 440 courage to live his life after his own fashion. And then — the last great act, with its beauty! Ah! that he should have the will and the strength to turn away from the banquet of life — so early.   445

Brack. I am sorry, Mrs. Hedda — but I fear I must dispel an amiable illusion.

Hedda. Illusion?

Brack. Which could not have lasted long in any case.   450

Hedda. What do you mean?

Brack. Eilert Lövborg did not shoot himself — voluntarily.

Hedda. Not voluntarily?

Brack. No. The thing did not hap- 455 pen exactly as I told it.

Hedda (*in suspense*). Have you concealed something? What is it?

Brack. For poor Mrs. Elvsted's sake I idealized the facts a little.   460

Hedda. What are the facts?

Brack. First, that he is already dead.

Hedda. At the hospital?

Brack. Yes — without regaining consciousness.   465

Hedda. What more have you concealed?

Brack. This — the event did not happen at his lodgings.

Hedda. Oh, that can make no difference.

Brack. Perhaps it may. For I must 470 tell you — Eilert Lövborg was found shot in — in Mademoiselle Diana's boudoir.

Hedda (*makes a motion as if to rise, but sinks back again*). That is impossible, Judge Brack! He cannot have been there again 475 today.

Brack. He was there this afternoon. He went there, he said, to demand the return of something which they had taken from him. Talked wildly about a lost child ——   480

Hedda. Ah — so that was why ——

Brack. I thought probably he meant his manuscript; but now I hear he destroyed that himself. So I suppose it must have been his pocket-book.   485

Hedda. Yes, no doubt. And there — there he was found?

Brack. Yes, there. With a pistol in his breast-pocket, discharged. The ball had lodged in a vital part.   490

Hedda. In the breast — yes.

Brack. No — in the bowels.

Hedda (*looks up at him with an expression of loathing*). That, too! Oh, what curse is it that makes everything I touch turn ludicrous 495 and mean?

Brack. There is one point more, Mrs. Hedda — another disagreeable feature in the affair.

Hedda. And what is that?

Brack. The pistol he carried ——   500

Hedda (*breathless*). Well? What of it?

Brack. He must have stolen it.

Hedda (*leaps up*). Stolen it! That is not true! He did not steal it!

Brack. No other explanation is possi- 505 ble. He must have stolen it —— Hush!

TESMAN *and* MRS. ELVSTED *have risen from the table in the back room, and come into the drawing-room*

Tes. (*with the papers in both his hands*). Hedda dear, it is almost impossible to see under that lamp. Think of that!

Hedda. Yes, I am thinking. 510

Tes. Would you mind our sitting at your writing-table — eh?

Hedda. If you like. (*Quickly*) No, wait! Let me clear it first!

Tes. Oh, you needn't trouble, Hedda. 515 There is plenty of room.

Hedda. No, no; let me clear it, I say! I will take these things in and put them on the piano. There!

(*She has drawn out an object, covered with sheet music, from under the bookcase, places several other pieces of music upon it, and carries the whole into the inner room, to the left. TESMAN lays the scraps of paper on the writing-table, and moves the lamp there from the corner table. HEDDA returns.*)

Hedda (*behind* MRS. ELVSTED'S *chair*, 520 *gently ruffling her hair*). Well, my sweet Thea — how goes it with Eilert Lövborg's monument?

Mrs. Elv. (*looks dispiritedly up at her*). Oh, it will be terribly hard to put in order. 525

Tes. We must manage it. I am determined. And arranging other people's papers is just the work for me.

(HEDDA *goes over to the stove, and seats herself on one of the footstools.* BRACK *stands over her, leaning on the armchair.*)

Hedda (*whispers*). What did you say about the pistol? 530

Brack (*softly*). That he must have stolen it.

Hedda. Why stolen it?

Brack. Because every other explanation ought to be impossible, Mrs. Hedda.

Hedda. Indeed? 535

Brack (*glances at her*). Of course Eilert Lövborg was here this morning. Was he not?

Hedda. Yes.

Brack. Were you alone with him?

Hedda. Part of the time. 540

Brack. Did you not leave the room whilst he was here?

Hedda. No.

Brack. Try to recollect. Were you not out of the room a moment? 545

Hedda. Yes, perhaps just a moment — out in the hall.

Brack. And where was your pistol-case during that time?

Hedda. I had it locked up in —— 550

Brack. Well, Mrs. Hedda?

Hedda. The case stood there on the writing-table.

Brack. Have you looked since, to see whether both the pistols are there? 555

Hedda. No.

Brack. Well, you need not. I saw the pistol found in Lövborg's pocket, and I knew it at once as the one I had seen yesterday — and before, too. 560

Hedda. Have you it with you?

Brack. No; the police have it.

Hedda. What will the police do with it?

Brack. Search till they find the owner.

Hedda. Do you think they will succeed? 565

Brack (*bends over her and whispers*). No, Hedda Gabler — not so long as I say nothing.

Hedda (*looks frightened at him*). And if you do not say nothing — what then?

Brack (*shrugs his shoulders*). There is 570 always the possibility that the pistol was stolen.

Hedda (*firmly*). Death rather than that.

Brack (*smiling*). People say such things — but they don't do them.

Hedda (*without replying*). And sup- 575 posing the pistol was not stolen, and the owner is discovered? What then?

Brack. Well, Hedda — then comes the scandal.

Hedda. The scandal! 580

Brack. Yes, the scandal — of which you are mortally afraid. You will, of course, be brought before the court — both you and Mademoiselle Diana. She will have to explain how the thing happened — whether it was 585 an accidental shot or murder. Did the pistol go off as he was trying to take it out of his pocket, to threaten her with? Or did she tear the pistol out of his hand, shoot him, and push it back into his pocket? That would be 590 quite like her; for she is an able-bodied young person, this same Mademoiselle Diana.

Hedda. But *I* have nothing to do with all this repulsive business.

Brack. No. But you will have to an- 595
swer the question: Why did you give Eilert
Lövborg the pistol? And what conclusions
will people draw from the fact that you did give
it to him?

Hedda (lets her head sink). That is true. 600
I did not think of that.

Brack. Well, fortunately, there is no danger,
so long as I say nothing.

Hedda (looks up at him). So I am in your
power, Judge Brack. You have me at 605
your beck and call, from this time forward.

Brack (whispers softly). Dearest Hedda —
believe me — I shall not abuse my advantage.

Hedda. I am in your power none the less.
Subject to your will and your demands. 610
A slave, a slave, then! (*Rises impetuously.*)
No, I cannot endure the thought of that!
Never!

Brack (looks half-mockingly at her). People
generally get used to the inevitable. 615

Hedda (returns his look). Yes, perhaps.
(*She crosses to the writing-table. Suppressing an
involuntary smile, she imitates* TESMAN's *intonations.*) Well? Are you getting on, George?
Eh? 620

Tes. Heaven knows, dear. In any case it
will be the work of months.

Hedda (as before). Fancy that! (*Passes her
hands softly through* MRS. ELVSTED's *hair.*)
Doesn't it seem strange to you, Thea? 625
Here you are sitting with Tesman — just as
you used to sit with Eilert Lövborg?

Mrs. Elv. Ah, if I could only inspire your
husband in the same way!

Hedda. Oh, that will come, too — in 630
time.

Tes. Yes, do you know, Hedda — I really
think I begin to feel something of the sort. But
won't you go and sit with Brack again?

Hedda. Is there nothing I can do to help 635
you two?

Tes. No, nothing in the world. (*Turning his
head*) I trust to you to keep Hedda company,
my dear Brack.

Brack (with a glance at HEDDA). With 640
the very greatest of pleasure.

Hedda. Thanks. But I am tired this evening.

I will go in and lie down a little on the sofa.

Tes. Yes, do dear — eh?

(HEDDA *goes into the back room and
draws the curtains. A short pause.
Suddenly she is heard playing a wild
dance on the piano.*

Mrs. Elv. (starts from her chair). Oh — 645
what is that?

Tes. (runs to the doorway). Why, my dearest
Hedda — don't play dance-music tonight!
Just think of Aunt Rina! And of Eilert,
too! 650

Hedda (puts her head out between the curtains).
And of Aunt Julia. And of all the rest of them
— After this, I will be quiet. (*Closes the cur-
tains again.*)

Tes. (at the writing-table). It's not 655
good for her to see us at this distressing work.
I'll tell you what, Mrs. Elvsted — you shall
take the empty room at Aunt Julia's, and
then I will come over in the evenings, and we
can sit and work there — eh? 660

Hedda (in the inner room). I hear what you
are saying, Tesman. But how am *I* to get
through the evenings out here?

Tes. (turning over the papers). Oh, I daresay Judge Brack will be so kind as to look 665
in now and then, even though I am out.

Brack (in the armchair, calls out gaily). Every
blessed evening, with all the pleasure in life,
Mrs. Tesman! We shall get on capitally together, we two! 670

Hedda (speaking loud and clear). Yes, don't
you flatter yourself we will, Judge Brack? Now
that you are the one cock in the basket ——

(*A shot is heard within.* TESMAN, MRS.
ELVSTED, *and* BRACK *leap to their feet.*

Tes. Oh, now she is playing with those pistols again. 675

(*He throws back the curtains and runs
in, followed by* MRS. ELVSTED.
HEDDA *lies stretched on the sofa, lifeless. Confusion and cries.* BERTA
enters in alarm from the right.

Tes. (shrieks to BRACK). Shot herself! Shot
herself in the temple! Fancy that!

Brack (half-fainting in the armchair). Good
God! — people don't do such things.

Curtain

INTRODUCTION TO

The Sea-Gull

Chekhov and Impressionistic Drama

DRAMATIC art gained so widespread a popularity in Russia subsequent to Gogol's time that in 1882 Alexander Ostrovsky (1823–86), the president of the Society of Dramatic Authors and Composers, persuaded the Tsar to abolish the government monopoly on public stage amusements. The end of that monopoly led to the opening of many theaters under private ownership. These latter in turn inspired a host of new playwrights, among them the already renowned novelist, Count Leo Tolstoy (1829–1910). Korsh's Theater, Moscow, produced in 1887 Tolstoy's maiden play, *The Power of Darkness*, a moving but grim masterpiece of rural life.

During the same year another novice, Anton Pavlovich Chekhov, also made his début at Korsh's Theater. In contrast to Tolstoy he came of peasant stock. His father's father had been a hard-working serf who finally had bought the freedom of his family and himself. Anton Chekhov was born on January 17, 1860, at Taganrog, an old port on the Black Sea. The severity of his father, a grocer, filled his boyhood with so much drudgery that he subsequently asserted: "I had no childhood." Almost every day after school Chekhov was obliged to tend shop until evening. Therefore, despite a weak chest, he had to study his lessons in the damp and cold of the grocery. Then to increase his misery, the father, an earnest choirmaster, insisted that Anton be a boy-chanter in the church. Many a night Anton was deprived of proper sleep by late choir practice or by the singing of masses before daybreak. These childhood rigors helped to develop a tubercular constitution, an unusual kindliness, and a skepticism toward religion.

Yet Chekhov's early life was by no means cheerless. With his brothers he often attended the Taganrog Theater. Afterwards at home he loved to imitate the actors; he especially delighted the family with his acting of the town governor from Gogol's *Inspector-General*. He frequently entertained with skits of his own, in which he changed make-up and voice so well that even relatives did not recognize him. Once, dressed as a beggar, he called at his uncle's door and procured alms without raising the slightest suspicion. All this youthful mimicry sharpened his dramatic instincts.

In 1879 Chekhov followed his parents to Moscow and entered the medical course of the university. He largely supported his family as well as himself by writing humorous fiction for newspapers and magazines. The year 1884 saw him secure his doctor's certificate and also publish his first volume. At about the same date he commenced to suffer from fits of tubercular coughing. Precarious health forced him gradually to shift his vocation from medicine to literature. While he was contentedly writing below stairs, friends used to swarm over his Moscow house. "I positively can't live without visitors," he often declared. In 1887 he composed by request of E. A. Korsh, a Moscow producer, his first serious play, *Ivanov*. This piece provoked more discussion than enthusiasm, but it definitely focused Chekhov's attention on the drama. A year later, once more by request, he tried his hand at another full-length play, *The Wood Spirit*. Its Moscow performance, however, won little approbation. Consequently, for the time being, he lost interest in playwriting. On the other hand, his tales in the same year won the Pushkin Prize. Thereafter he was recognized as Russia's foremost writer of the short-story.

In 1890 a sudden humanitarian impulse moved Chekhov to investigate the "place of unbearable sufferings," the Russian penal settlement on Saghalien Island off the Siberian coast. After his return he bought a run-down country estate of six hundred acres near Melikhovo, fifty miles southeast of Moscow. There he carried on scientific farming, directed local campaigns against famine and cholera, initiated the building of new roads and schools, participated in the district census, gave comfort to the neighborhood sick and distressed, kept open house for his numerous acquaintances, and all the while, despite more frequent hemorrhages, he continued his literary labors.

Chekhov's tubercular condition had grown so serious by 1898 that it forced him to abandon Melikhovo and settle in the milder climate of the Crimea at Yalta. His white stone cottage, surrounded by a garden of roses and cherry trees, stood on a promontory overlooking the Black Sea — an idyllic spot for the nature-loving owner. Here in succeeding years he enjoyed a veritable merry-go-round of visitors, including two young literary friends, Maxim Gorky (1868–1936) and Leonid Andreyev (1871–1919). Gorky's *The Lower Depths* (1902) and Andreyev's *He Who Gets Slapped* (1915) are among the outstanding specimens of twentieth century drama — the first, notable for its stark realism; the second, for its colorful symbolism.

In 1898, after Chekhov had gone south, his third long play, *The Sea-Gull*, met with a great success at the Moscow Art Theater. A year later the same troupe scored another triumph with his revision of *The Wood Spirit*, entitled *Uncle Vanya*. These stage "hits" led the Russian Academy of Sciences in January, 1900, to elect Chekhov an honorary member of their select body. During Eastertide in Yalta he viewed for the first time his own plays given by the "glorious Art Theater," as he called it. Fired with a new enthusiasm for the stage he completed by fall *The Three Sisters*, produced at Moscow in January, 1901. Thereafter his health grew steadily worse until he could carry on almost no literary effort. A feverish outburst of energy, however, in the autumn of 1903 brought forth his final and best known play, *The Cherry Orchard*. He insisted on traveling to Moscow and supervising the preparations for its performance, an altogether new procedure for him. The opening on the night of his forty-fourth birthday, January 17, 1904, turned into a celebration of homage with many speeches and flowers. Chekhov was so ill and exhausted that he could not stand to the end of the ceremonies. In desperate search for relief he journeyed to Badenweiler, a little spa in the Black Forest of Germany. There he died on July 2.

Chekhov in his playwriting exhibited a powerful and unique artistry, though one of somewhat limited range. His drama is concerned with the Russian bourgeoisie, both its intellectuals and its gentry. They constituted the circles in which he moved after the end of his medical course. More important, however, they deeply appealed to the bases of his temperament, namely, his wit and his compassion. The physician in him had early diagnosed as symptoms of decay the extreme excitability, indolence, boredom, and loneliness prevalent among the upper classes. His serious plays from first to last exposed these decadent traits with gentle irony. He realized amusedly that "while we educated people are rummaging among old rags and, according to the old Russian custom, biting one another, there is boiling up around us a life which we neither know nor notice." At the same time the decline of this pleasant genteel order of society aroused his compassion. He possessed the sensitivity of soul which he described as the ideal for all cultured persons: "They have sympathy not for beggars and cats alone. Their heart aches for what the eye does not see." Thus his almost morbid tenderness discovered a fascination in the invisible decline of the social group to which he felt bound. "Everything is crumbling and decrepit, but poetical, sad, and beautiful in the extreme," he observed.

To convey this paradoxical mood which the spectacle of Russian life engendered became the object of Chekhov's dramatic art. He invented an impressionistic method wherein he believed he was "abusing terribly the conventions of the stage." His plotting, casual only in appearance, depends upon "a thousand nothings which together make up something vitally important." It aims to play off one individual's sensibility against another, but to give to that emotional interplay a mosaic unity. Therefore Chekhov models the conversation of his characters on oblique or centrifugal lines. Much of the time they speak as if they were alone — in phrases, in unfinished speeches, which would imply a continuation of something already expressed. To achieve this curious style of dialogue Chekhov only had to imitate his own habits, so one friend testified: "Listening to a jolly story, or telling something himself, sitting with friends at a meal, talking to a woman, speaking to a dog, Chekhov always kept on thinking . . . he would at times suddenly cut himself short and stop on an unfinished phrase, or he would ask you a question which had nothing to do with the conversation." Sounds and silences, as well as talk, contribute to the markedly psychic atmosphere in Chekhov's drama. Indeed, as Andreyev so well said, "the dialogue never stops; it is transferred from human beings to objects, from objects to human beings, and from human beings to time, to stillness or noise, to the cricket or to voices round a fire. Everything is alive, has a soul and a voice."

"THE SEA-GULL"

The Sea-Gull first advertised to Russia and to the world Chekhov's greatness as a dramatist. Though its triumph took long in the making, none has been more important to the modern theater. During the summer of 1895 Chekhov set to writing a play at the "pretty lodge" in the garden of his Melikhovo estate. By November he had finished what he described as "a comedy . . . with a landscape (a view of a lake), much talk about literature, little action, and five tons of love." A production of the new script, entitled Chaïka (The Sea-Gull), was arranged at the Alexandrinsky Theater in St. Petersburg for the benefit of the popular comedienne Levkeyeva. The premiere on October 17, 1896, proved, to use Chekhov's words, "a huge failure." Stupid acting could not enlighten an audience which had come prepared for hilarity. Chekhov, "humiliated and vexed," fled to the country, cherishing The Sea-Gull as his "sick but favorite child" and vowing to write no more for the stage.

At least one spectator, however, the playwright Vladimir Nemirovich-Danchenko, had viewed *The Sea-Gull* with admiration. When he was awarded the prize for the best Russian play of 1896, he refused the honor on the ground that *The Sea-Gull* was "a new triumph of Russian playwriting." He resolved to found a theater where the intimacy, restraint, and symbolism of such drama as Chekhov's could and would be adequately presented. A year later he discovered in the actor Constantin Stanislavsky an ideal partner for the undertaking. These two men proceeded to organize the Moscow Art Theater. They persuaded Chekhov not only to be a shareholder, but to give to the repertoire *The Sea-Gull*. Stanislavsky directed its production with great intelligence, casting himself as the writer Trigorin, and Olga Knipper (who three years later married Chekhov) as the actress Madame Treplev. The opening performance on December 17, 1898, before a tense and overflowing audience called forth tremendous applause. Packed houses greeted every showing throughout the winter. A friend wrote to Chekhov that the city had "literally fallen in love with your play." This enthusiastic reception of *The Sea-Gull* vindicated Chekhov's dramatic genius; at the same time it assured prosperity to the Moscow Art Theater. Stanislavsky and his company within a decade became the finest acting organization of modern times. When in 1902 they opened their own specially designed playhouse, they called it the Chekhov Theater and adopted the sea-gull as their emblem to decorate the gray stage curtains.

Like all of Chekhov's plays *The Sea-Gull* made a tardy appearance on the English-speaking stage. The Scottish Repertory Company gave the first recorded performance at Glasgow in November, 1909. The tour of the Moscow Art Theater through the United States during 1923 introduced *The Sea-Gull* to American playgoers. Eva Le Gallienne in New York, 1929, and the Lunts in the same city, 1938, have offered perhaps the most notable presentations of this drama in English.

The scenes in *The Sea-Gull* reflect much of the milieu in which Chekhov was living at the time of its composition. From his Melikhovo lodge he could look through the trees to a large pond. This favorite vista doubtless suggested the distant view of a lake featured in the scenery of Acts I and II. Outdoor theatricals similar to those of Act I frequently occurred at the country manors in the vicinity of Melikhovo.

The use of a bird as a symbol which underlies and points up the whole dramatic action imitates Ibsen's design in *The Wild Duck* (1884) — a play which Chekhov knew well, for he read the great Norwegian's works with admiration. Certain experiences during his first years at Melikhovo suggested, however, the sea-gull and the development of its symbolism, even to specific situations. One April evening in 1892 he went out shooting with his guest, I. I. Levitan, a well-known painter. A snipe, shot in the wing by Levitan, fell into a pool and was picked up by Chekhov. Levitan, upset by the sight of the wounded snipe, begged Chekhov to hit the bird a mortal blow on the head. The latter completed the killing remorsefully and on the next day wrote: "There is one beautiful creature in love the less, while two fools went home and sat down to supper." In *The Sea-Gull* he depicts the sad irony of this very situation by bringing together the innocent, lovely Nina and the self-concerned, thoughtless Trigorin. This "man comes by chance, sees her, and having nothing better to do, destroys her . . ." (Act II, ll. 522–24).

A second episode connected with Levitan provided Chekhov with further ideas about bird symbol and plot. The painter was staying at a manor where he fell in love with a lady of the house. Rejected, he attempted to shoot himself. The bullet, however, only scratched his temple. The lady, knowing Chekhov a physician as well as a friend of Levitan, telegraphed for him to come post haste. After Chekhov's arrival Levitan took his gun, went to the near-by lake, and shot a sea-gull. He then brought the dead bird and threw it at the lady's feet. In *The Sea-Gull* the young writer Treplev lays a dead gull at Nina's feet with the remark, "I was so mean as to kill this bird today" (Act II, ll. 270–71). Not long afterward he tries, in a fit of despair, to shoot himself, but in the attempt he suffers only a minor head wound.

The Sea-Gull contains all the elements which are characteristic of Chekhov's dramatic pattern. There is the "sweet country boredom" with "no one ever doing anything, everyone airing their theories" (Act II, ll. 146–48); the group of intelligentsia who, like the middle-aged Sorin, cannot say much more for themselves than "I wanted to" (Act IV, ll. 128–40). Life treats their loves and ambitions with ironical perversity. Madame Treplev would imagine herself a great actress but a mediocre talent keeps her in the provinces; her son aspires to be a playwright but his "decadent rubbish" meets ridicule among family and friends; the young girl whom Treplev adores, Nina, feels love only for the mother's lover, Trigorin. Yet these characters, however indecisive or frustrated, pursue distinct inner lives, which are constantly revealed by the tangential dialogue peculiar to Chekhov. For example, during the lotto game of the fourth act, Madame Treplev chatters on about her stage triumphs; her son restlessly moves about with an occasional melancholy remark; Dorn and Trigorin engage in desultory and unfeeling comment on Treplev's work; Masha, absorbed in the game, calls off the card numbers; and Sorin in boredom falls asleep. By such discontinuous talk and action, punctuated variously with pauses, snatches of music, gusts of wind, and a watchman's tapping, Chekhov creates that delicate orchestration of emotions which is his unique dramatic attainment. The successive alterations of feeling are subtly blended into an almost dream-like lyrical movement.

The Sea-Gull adheres more strictly than Chekhov's later pieces to his artistic ideal of doing no more than "stating a problem correctly." The play throughout keeps implicit the sense of life's comi-tragedy. Tenderly and sadly Chekhov smiles at his unheroic figures: the vain and shallow actress, the infatuated young woman, the ultra-romantic young playwright, the jaded man of letters, the dull but conscientious schoolmaster. Immersed in their petty but (to them) urgent destinies, they rub against one another's sensibilities with the destructive casualness so common in human relationships. The sea-gull is, therefore, not merely a figurative counterpart to Nina; it is a leitmotif unifying the spiritual and the physical aspects of Chekhov's entire drama. By means of an unsurpassed impressionism *The Sea-Gull* presents the intricate quilting of joy and heartbreak beneath which life flows on ceaselessly.

[For the later Russian stage, see Leo Wiener, *The Contemporary Drama of Russia* (1924), and Constantin Stanislavsky, *My Life in Art* (1924); for Chekhov, S. S. Koteliansky, *Life and Letters of A. Tchekhov* (1925); Nina Toumanova, *Anton Chekhov* (1937); Walter H. Bruford, *Chekhov and His Russia* (1947); Matthew Josephson, *The Personal Papers of Anton Chekhov* (1948).]

ANTON CHEKHOV

The Sea-Gull

[*Translated by* CONSTANCE GARNETT]

DRAMATIS PERSONAE

IRÍNA NIKOLÁYEVNA ARKÁDIN (MADAME TRÉPLEV), *an actress*
KÓNSTANTIN GAVRÍLOVITCH TRÉPLEV, *her son, a young man*
PYÓTR NIKOLÁYEVITCH SÓRIN, *her brother*
NÍNA MIHAÍLOVNA ZARÉTCHNY, *a young girl, the daughter of a wealthy landowner*
ÍLYA AFANÁSYEVITCH SHAMRÁEV, *a retired lieutenant,* SÓRIN's *steward*
POLÍNA ANDRÉYEVNA, *his wife*
MÁRYA ILYINÍSHNA ("MÁSHA"), *his daughter*
BÓRIS ALEXÉYEVITCH TRIGÓRIN, *a literary man*
YEVGÉNY SERGÉYEVITCH DORN, *a doctor*
SEMYÓN SEMYÓNOVITCH MEDVÉDENKO, *a schoolmaster*
YÁKOV, *a laborer*
A Man Cook
A Housemaid

The Scene is SÓRIN's *country estate in Moscow province at the end of the nineteenth century*

ACT I

Part of the park on SÓRIN's *estate. A wide avenue leading away from the spectators into the depths of the park towards the lake is blocked up by a platform roughly put together for private theatricals, so that the lake is not visible. To right and left of the platform, bushes. A few chairs, a little table.*
The sun has just set. YÁKOV *and other laborers are at work on the platform behind the curtain; there is the sound of coughing and hammering.* MÁSHA *and* MEDVÉDENKO *enter on the left, returning from a walk*

Medv. Why do you always wear black?
Másha. I am in mourning for my life. I am unhappy.
Medv. Why? (*Pondering*) I don't understand... You are in good health; though 5 your father is not very well off, he has got enough. My life is much harder than yours. I only get twenty-three roubles[1] a month, and

[1] About $12.00.

from that they deduct something for the pension fund, and yet I don't wear mourning. 10
(*They sit down.*)
Másha. It isn't money that matters. A poor man may be happy.
Medv. Theoretically, yes; but in practice it's like this: there are my two sisters and my mother and my little brother and I, and 15 my salary is only twenty-three roubles. We must eat and drink, mustn't we? One must have tea and sugar. One must have tobacco. It's a tight fit.
Másha (*looking round at the platform*). 20 The play will soon begin.
Medv. Yes. Miss Zarétchny will act: it is Kónstantin Gavrílitch's play. They are in love with each other, and today their souls will be united in the effort to realize the same 25 artistic effect. But your soul and mine have not a common point of contact. I love you. I am so wretched I can't stay at home. Every day I walk four miles here and four miles back and I meet with nothing but indifference 30

from you. I can quite understand it. I am without means and have a big family to keep. ... Who would care to marry a man who hasn't a penny to bless himself with?

Másha. Oh, nonsense! (*Takes a pinch* 35 *of snuff.*) Your love touches me, but I can't reciprocate it — that's all. (*Holding out the snuff-box to him*) Help yourself.

Medv. I don't feel like it.   (*A pause.*

Másha. How stifling it is! There must 40 be a storm coming.... You're always discussing theories or talking about money. You think there is no greater misfortune than poverty, but to my mind it is a thousand times better to go in rags and be a beggar than ... But 45 you wouldn't understand that, though....

Sórin *and* Tréplev *enter on the right*

Sórin (*leaning on his walking-stick*). I am never quite myself in the country, my boy, and, naturally enough, I shall never get used to it. Last night I went to bed at ten and woke 50 up this morning at nine, feeling as though my brain were glued to my skull through sleeping so long. (*Laughs.*) And after dinner I accidentally dropped off again, and now I am utterly shattered and feel as though I were 55 in a nightmare, in fact....

Trêp. Yes, you really ought to live in town. (*Catches sight of* Másha *and* Medvédenko.) When the show begins, my friends, you will be summoned, but you mustn't be here now. 60 You must please go away.

Sórin (*to* Másha). Márya Ilyiníshna, will you be so good as to ask your papa to tell them to take the dog off the chain? — it howls. My sister could not sleep again last night. 65

Másha. Speak to my father yourself; I am not going to. Please don't ask me. (*To* Medvédenko) Come along!

Médv. (*to* Tréplev). So you will send and let us know before it begins? (*Both go out.* 70

Sórin. So I suppose the dog will be howling all night again. What a business it is! I have never done as I liked in the country. In old days I used to get leave for twenty-eight days and come here for a rest and so on, but they 75 worried me so with all sorts of trifles that before

I had been here two days I was longing to be off again. (*Laughs.*) I've always been glad to get away from here.... But now I am on the retired list, and I have nowhere else to go, 80 as a matter of fact. I've got to live here whether I like it or not....

Yákov (*to* Tréplev). We are going to have a bathe, Kónstantin Gavrílitch.

Trêp. Very well; but don't be more than 85 ten minutes. (*Looks at his watch.*) It will soon begin.

Yákov. Yes, sir.   (*Goes out.*

Trêp. (*looking round the stage*). Here is our theater. The curtain, then the first wing, 90 then the second, and beyond that — open space. No scenery of any sort. There is an open view of the lake and the horizon. We shall raise the curtain at exactly half-past eight, when the moon rises. 95

Sórin. Magnificent.

Trêp. If Nína is late it will spoil the whole effect. It is time she was here. Her father and her stepmother keep a sharp eye on her, and it is as hard for her to get out of the 100 house as to escape from prison. (*Puts his uncle's necktie straight.*) Your hair and your beard are very untidy. They want clipping or something.....

Sórin (*combing out his beard*). It's the 105 tragedy of my life. Even as a young man I looked as though I had been drinking for days or something of the sort. I was never a favorite with the ladies (*sitting down*). Why is your mother out of humor? 110

Trêp. Why? Because she is bored (*sitting down beside him*). She is jealous. She is set against me, and against the performance, and against my play because Nína is acting in it, and she is not. She does not know my 115 play, but she hates it.

Sórin (*laughs*). What an idea!

Trêp. She is annoyed to think that even on this little stage Nína will have a triumph and not she. (*Looks at his watch.*) My mother 120 is a psychological freak. Unmistakably talented, intelligent, capable of sobbing over a book, she will reel off all Nekrassov [1] by heart;

[1] Nikolai Nekrassov (1821–77), one of the earlier Russian humanitarian poets.

as a sick nurse she is an angel; but just try praising Duse [1] in her presence! O-ho! 125 You must praise no one but herself, you must write about her, make a fuss over her, be in raptures over her extraordinary acting in "La Dame aux Camélias" [2] or the "Ferment of Life"; [3] but she has none of this narcotic 130 in the country, she is bored and cross, and we are all her enemies — we are all in fault. Then she is superstitious — she is afraid of three candles,[4] of the number thirteen. She is stingy. She has got seventy thousand 135 roubles [5] in a bank at Odessa — I know that for a fact — but ask her to lend you some money, and she will burst into tears.

Sôrin. You imagine your mother does not like your play, and you are already upset 140 and all that. Don't worry; your mother adores you.

Trêp. (*pulling the petals off a flower*). Loves me, loves me not; loves me, loves me not; loves me, loves me not. (*Laughs.*) You see, 145 my mother does not love me. I should think not! She wants to live, to love, to wear light blouses; and I am twenty-five, and I am a continual reminder that she is no longer young. When I am not there she is only thirty- 150 two, but when I am there she is forty-three, and for that she hates me. She knows, too, that I have no belief in the theater. She loves the stage, she fancies she is working for humanity, for the holy cause of art, while to my 155 mind the modern theater is nothing but tradition and conventionality. When the curtain goes up, and by artificial light, in a room with three walls, these great geniuses, the devotees of holy art, represent how people eat, 160 drink, love, move about, and wear their jackets; when from these commonplace sentences and

[1] Eleonora Duse (1859–1924), great Italian actress whose art was admired all over Europe.

[2] A famous sentimental tragedy of a courtesan by the French novelist and playwright, Alexandre Dumas *fils* (1824–95), who dramatized in 1852 his novel by the same title.

[3] A then recent Russian stage success by B. Markévitch, produced as *Olga Rantseva* at St. Petersburg (Leningrad) in 1888.

[4] Omen of death, because in Russia three candles are put by a dead body, two at the head and one at the foot.

[5] About $35,000.

pictures they try to draw a moral — a petty moral, easy of comprehension and convenient for domestic use; when in a thousand vari- 165 ations I am offered the same thing over and over again — I run away as Maupassant [1] ran away from the Eiffel Tower which weighed upon his brain with its vulgarity.

Sôrin. You can't do without the stage. 170

Trêp. We need new forms of expression. We need new forms, and if we can't have them we had better have nothing. (*Looks at his watch.*) I love my mother — I love her very much — but she leads a senseless sort of life, always 175 taken up with this literary gentleman. Her name is always trotted out in the papers — and that wearies me. And sometimes the simple egoism of an ordinary mortal makes me feel sorry that my mother is a celebrated actress, 180 and I fancy that if she were an ordinary woman I should be happier. Uncle, what could be more hopeless and stupid than my position? She used to have visitors, all celebrities — artists and authors — and among them all 185 I was the only one who was nothing, and they only put up with me because I was her son. Who am I? What am I? I left the University in my third year — owing to circumstances "for which we accept no responsibility," 190 as the editors say; I have no talents, I haven't a penny of my own, and on my passport I am described as an artisan of Kiev.[2] You know my father was an artisan of Kiev, though he too was a well-known actor. So, when in 195 her drawing-room all these artists and authors graciously noticed me, I always fancied from their faces that they were taking the measure of my insignificance — I guessed their thoughts and suffered from the humiliation. . . . 200

Sôrin. And, by the way, can you tell me, please, what sort of man this literary gentleman is? There's no making him out. He never says anything.

Trêp. He is an intelligent man, good- 205 hearted and rather melancholy, you know. A

[1] Guy de Maupassant (1850–93), noted French writer of fiction, who hated the celebrated iron tower built at Paris in 1889.

[2] A large city in the Ukraine, the southwest section of European Russia.

very decent fellow. He is still a good distance off forty, but he is already celebrated and has enough and to spare of everything. As for his writings . . . what shall I say? They are 210 charming, full of talent, but . . . after Tolstoy [1] or Zola [2] you do not care to read Trigórin.

Sórin. Well, I am fond of authors, my boy. At one time I had a passionate desire for two things: I wanted to get married, and I 215 wanted to become an author; but I did not succeed in doing either. Yes, it is pleasant to be even a small author, as a matter of fact.

Trêp. (*listens*). I hear steps . . . (*Embraces his uncle.*) I cannot live without her. . . . 220 The very sound of her footsteps is lovely. . . . I am wildly happy. (*Goes quickly to meet* NÍNA ZARÉTCHNY *as she enters.*) My enchantress — my dream. . . .

Nína (*in agitation*). I am not late. . . . 225 Of course I am not late. . . .

Trêp. (*kissing her hands*). No, no, no!

Nína. I have been uneasy all day. I was so frightened. I was afraid father would not let me come. . . . But he has just gone out with 230 my stepmother. The sky is red, the moon is just rising, and I kept urging on the horse. (*Laughs.*) But I am glad.

(*Shakes* SÓRIN'S *hand warmly.*

Sórin (*laughs*). Your eyes look as though you have been crying. . . . Fie, fie! That's 235 not right!

Nína. Oh, it was nothing. . . . You see how out of breath I am. I have to go in half an hour. We must make haste. I can't stay, I can't! For God's sake don't keep me! 240 My father doesn't know I am here.

Trêp. It really is time to begin. We must go and call the others.

Sórin. I'll go this minute. (*Goes to the right, singing "To France Two Grena-* 245 *diers." Looks round.*) Once I sang like that, and a deputy prosecutor said to me, "You have a powerful voice, Your Excellency"; then he thought a little and added, "but not a pleasant one." (*Laughs and goes off.* 250

Nína. My father and his wife won't let me

[1] Count Leo Tolstoy (1828–1910), great Russian novelist.
[2] Émile Zola (1840–1902), French naturalistic novelist.

come here. They say it is so Bohemian here . . . they are afraid I shall go on the stage. . . . But I feel drawn to the lake here like a sea-gull. . . . My heart is full of you. (*Looks round.* 255

Trêp. We are alone.

Nína. I fancy there is someone there.

Trêp. There's nobody. (*They kiss.*

Nína. What tree is this?

Trêp. An elm. 260

Nína. Why is it so dark?

Trêp. It's evening; everything is getting dark. Don't go away early, I entreat you!

Nína. I must.

Trêp. And if I come to you, Nína, I'll 265 stand in the garden all night, watching your window.

Nína. You can't; the watchman would notice you. Trésor is not used to you, and he would bark. 270

Trêp. I love you!

Nína. Sh-h. . . .

Trêp. (*hearing footsteps*). Who is there? You, Yákov?

Yákov (*behind the stage*). Yes, sir. 275

Trêp. Take your places. It's time to begin. Is the moon rising?

Yákov. Yes, sir.

Trêp. Have you got the alcohol? Have you got the sulphur? When the red eyes ap- 280 pear there must be a smell of sulphur. (*To* NÍNA) Go, it's all ready. Are you nervous?

Nína. Yes, awfully! Your mother is all right — I am not afraid of her — but there's Trigórin . . . I feel frightened and ashamed 285 of acting before him . . . a celebrated author. . . . Is he young?

Trêp. Yes.

Nína. How wonderful his stories are.

Trêp. (*coldly*). I don't know. I haven't 290 read them.

Nína. It is difficult to act in your play. There are no living characters in it.

Trêp. Living characters! One must depict life not as it is, and not as it ought to be, 295 but as we see it in our dreams.

Nína. There is very little action in your play — nothing but speeches. And to my mind there ought to be love in a play.

(*Both go behind the stage.*

Enter POLÍNA ANDRÉYEVNA *and* DORN

Pol. It is getting damp. Go back and 300
put on your galoshes.

Dorn. I am hot.

Pol. You don't take care of yourself. It's
obstinacy. You are a doctor, and you know
perfectly well that damp air is bad for you, 305
but you want to make me miserable; you sat
out on the veranda all yesterday evening on
purpose....

Dorn (*hums*). "Do not say that youth is
ruined."   310

Pol. You were so absorbed in conversation
with Irína Nikoláyevna ... you did not notice
the cold. Own up ... you are attracted by her.

Dorn. I am fifty-five.

Pol. Nonsense! That's not old for a 315
man. You look very young for your age, and
are still attractive to women.

Dorn. Well, what would you have?

Pol. All you men are ready to fall down and
worship an actress, all of you!   320

Dorn (*hums*). "Before thee once again I
stand." If artists are liked in society and
treated differently from merchants, for example, that's only in the nature of things. It's
idealism.   325

Pol. Women have always fallen in love with
you and thrown themselves on your neck. Is
that idealism too?

Dorn (*shrugs his shoulders*). Well, in the attitude of women to me there has been a 330
great deal that was good. What they principally loved in me was a first-rate doctor. You
remember that ten or fifteen years ago I was the
only decent obstetrician in the district. Then,
too, I have always been an honest man. 335

Pol. (*seizes him by the hand*). Dearest!

Dorn. Sh-h! They are coming.

Enter MADAME ARKÁDIN *arm in arm with* SÓRIN,
TRIGÓRIN, SHAMRÁEV, MEDVÉDENKO, *and*
MÁSHA

Sham. In the year 1873 she acted marvel-
lously at the fair at Poltava.[1] It was a delight!
She acted exquisitely! Do you happen to 340

[1] Another important city in the Ukraine.

know, madam, where Pavel Semyonitch Tchadin, a comic actor, is now? His Raspluyev was
inimitable, even finer than Sadovsky's,[1] I assure you, honored lady. Where is he now?

Mad. Ark. You keep asking me about 345
antediluvians. How should I know? (*Sits down.*

Sham. (*with a sigh*). Pashka Tchadin! There
are no such actors now. The stage has gone
down, Irína Nikoláyevna! In old days there
were mighty oaks, but now we see nothing 350
but stumps.

Dorn. There are few actors of brilliant talents
nowadays, that's true; but the average level of
acting is far higher than it was.

Sham. I can't agree with you. But, of 355
course, it's a matter of taste. *De gustibus aut
bene aut nihil.*[2]

TRÉPLEV *comes out from behind the stage*

Mad. Ark. (*to her son*). My dear son, when is
it going to begin?

Trép. In a minute. I beg you to be 360
patient.

Mad. Ark. (*recites from "Hamlet"*).
"Oh Hamlet, speak no more!
Thou turn'st mine eyes into my very soul;
And there I see such black and grained spots
As will not leave their tint."[3]   366

Trép. (*from "Hamlet"*).
"And let me wring your heart, for so I shall,
If it be made of penetrable stuff."[4]

(*A horn is sounded behind the stage.*

Trép. Ladies and gentlemen, we begin! 370
I beg you to attend. (*A pause.*) I begin.
(*Taps with a stick and recites aloud.*) Oh, you
venerable old shadows that float at night-time
over this lake, lull us to sleep and let us dream
of what will be in two hundred thousand 375
years!

Sórin. There will be nothing in two hundred
thousand years.

[1] Sadovsky, a Moscow actor who starred as Raspluyev, a low-comedy character in *Kretchinsky's Wedding*
by Súkhovo-Kobýlin. He died in 1872.

[2] According to one's tastes it is either good or of no
account.

[3] The closet scene between Hamlet and his mother.
Act III, Sc. 4, ll. 88–91.

[4] Ll. 35–36 of the same scene.

Trép. Then let them present that nothing
to us.   380
Mad. Ark. Let them.   We are asleep.

(*The curtain rises; the view of the lake
is revealed; the moon is above the
horizon, its reflection in the water;*
NÍNA ZARÉTCHNY, *all in white, is
sitting on a big stone.*

Nína. Men, lions, eagles and partridges,
horned deer, geese, spiders, silent fish that dwell
in the water, starfishes and creatures which cannot be seen by the eye — all living things,   385
all living things, all living things, having completed their cycle of sorrow, are extinct. . . . For
thousands of years the earth has borne no living
creature on its surface, and this poor moon lights
its lamp in vain. On the meadow the cranes   390
no longer waken with a cry, and there is no sound
of the May beetles in the lime trees. It is cold,
cold, cold! Empty, empty, empty! Dreadful,
dreadful, dreadful! (*A pause.*) The bodies of living creatures have vanished into dust, and   395
eternal matter has transformed them into rocks,
into water, into clouds, while the souls of all have
melted into one. That world-soul I am — I. . . .
In me is the soul of Alexander the Great, of Caesar, of Shakespeare and of Napoleon, and   400
of the lowest leech. In me the consciousness of
men is blended with the instincts of the animals,
and I remember all, all, all! And I live through
every life over again in myself!

(*Will-of-the-wisps appear.*[1]

Mad. Ark. (*softly*). It's something deca-   405
dent.

Trép. (*in an imploring and reproachful voice*).
Mother!

Nína. I am alone. Once in a hundred years
I open my lips to speak, and my voice   410
echoes mournfully in the void, and no one
hears. . . . You too, pale lights, hear me not. . . .
The stagnant marsh begets you before daybreak and you wander until dawn, but without
thought, without will, without the tremor   415

[1] Tréplev's play is intended by Chekhov as a satiric
skit on the style and the content of the writings of the
French Decadents, who were quite fashionable reading
toward the end of the nineteenth century. These writers, such as Verlaine and Mallarmé, tended to be neurotic and artificial, emphasizing on the one hand the
morbid and, on the other, the mystically symbolic.

of life. For fear that life should spring up in
you the father of eternal matter, the Devil,
keeps the atoms in you, as in the stones and in
the water, in continual flux, and you are changing perpetually. For in all the universe   420
nothing remains permanent and unchanged but
the spirit. (*A pause.*) Like a prisoner cast
into a deep, empty well I know not where I am
and what awaits me. All is hidden from me
but that in the cruel, persistent struggle   425
with the Devil — the principle of the forces of
matter — I am destined to conquer, and, after
that, matter and spirit will be blended in glorious harmony and the Kingdom of the Cosmic
Will will come. But that will come only   430
little by little, through long, long thousands of
years when the moon and the bright Sirius [1] and
the earth are changed to dust. . . . Till then —
terror, terror . . . (*A pause; two red spots appear
upon the background of the lake.*) Here my   435
powerful foe, the Devil, is approaching. I see
his dreadful crimson eyes. . . .

Mad. Ark. There's a smell of sulphur. Is
that as it should be?

Trép. Yes.   440
Mad. Ark. (*laughs*). Oh, it's a stage effect!
Trép. Mother!
Nína. He is dreary without man ——
Pol. (*to* DORN). You have taken your hat off.
Put it on or you will catch cold.   445
Mad. Ark. The doctor has taken his hat off
to the Devil, the father of eternal matter.
Trép. (*flaring up, aloud*). The play is over!
Enough! Curtain!
Mad. Ark. What are you cross about?   450
Trép. Enough! The curtain! Let down
the curtain! (*Stamping*) Curtain! (*The cur-
tain falls.*) I am sorry! I lost sight of the fact
that only a few of the elect may write plays
and act in them. I have infringed the   455
monopoly. I . . . I . . .

(*Tries to say something more, but with
a wave of his hand goes out on left.*

Mad. Ark. What's the matter with him?
Sórin. Irína, you really must have more con-
sideration for youthful vanity, my dear.
Mad. Ark. What did I say to him?   460
Sórin. You hurt his feelings.

[1] The Dog-Star, the brightest one in the heavens.

Mad. Ark. He told us beforehand that it was a joke, and I regarded his play as a joke.

Sórin. All the same ...

Mad. Ark. Now it appears that he has 465 written a great work. What next! So he has got up this performance and smothered us with sulphur not as a joke but as a protest.... He wanted to show us how to write and what to act. This is getting tiresome! These con- 470 tinual sallies at my expense — these continual pin-pricks would put anyone out of patience, say what you like. He is a vain, whimsical boy!

Sórin. He meant to give you pleasure.

Mad. Ark. Really? He did not choose 475 an ordinary play, however, but made us listen to this decadent delirium. For the sake of a joke I am ready to listen to delirium, but here we have pretensions to new forms and a new view of art. To my thinking it's no ques- 480 tion of new forms at all, but simply bad temper.

Trig. Everyone writes as he likes and as he can.

Mad. Ark. Let him write as he likes and as he can, only let him leave me in peace. 485

Dorn. Jupiter! you are angry....

Mad. Ark. I am not Jupiter — I am a woman. (*Lights a cigarette.*) I am not angry — I am only vexed that a young man should spend his time so drearily. I did not mean to 490 hurt his feelings.

Medv. No one has any grounds to separate spirit from matter, seeing that spirit itself may be a combination of material atoms. (*With animation, to* TRIGÓRIN) But you know 495 someone ought to write a play on how we poor teachers live, and get it acted. We have a hard, hard life.

Mad. Ark. That's true, but don't let us talk either of plays or of atoms. It is such a 500 glorious evening! Do you hear? There is singing! (*Listens.*) How nice it is!

Pol. It's on the other side of the lake.
(*A pause.*

Mad. Ark. (*to* TRIGÓRIN). Sit down beside me. Ten or fifteen years ago there were 505 sounds of music and singing on that lake continually almost every night. There are six country houses on the shores of the lake. I remember laughter, noise, shooting, and love

affairs without end.... The *jeune premier*[1] 510 and the idol of all those six households was in those days our friend here, the doctor (*motions with her head towards* DORN), Yevgény Sergéitch. He is fascinating still, but in those days he was irresistible. But my con- 515 science is beginning to trouble me. Why did I hurt my poor boy's feelings? I feel worried. (*Aloud*) Kostya![2] Son! Kostya!

Másha. I'll go and look for him.

Mad. Ark. Please do, my dear. 520

Másha (*going to the left*). Aa-oo! Kónstantin Gavrílitch! Aa-oo! (*Goes off.*

Nína (*coming out from behind the stage*). Apparently there will be no going on, and I may come out. Good evening! 525
(*Kisses* MADAME ARKÁDIN *and* POLÍNA ANDRÉYEVNA.

Sórin. Bravo! Bravo!

Mad. Ark. Bravo! Bravo! We admired you. With such an appearance, with such a lovely voice, you really cannot stay in the country; it is a sin. You surely have talent. Do 530 you hear? It's your duty to go on the stage.

Nína. Oh, that's my dream! (*Sighing*) But it will never be realized.

Mad. Ark. Who knows? Here, let me introduce Bóris Alexéyevitch Trigórin. 535

Nína. Oh, I am so glad ... (*overcome with embarrassment*). I am always reading your ...

Mad. Ark. (*making her sit down beside them*). Don't be shy, my dear. He is a celebrity, but he has a simple heart. You see, he is shy 540 himself.

Dorn. I suppose we may raise the curtain; it's rather uncanny.

Sham. (*aloud*). Yákov, pull up the curtain, my lad. 545
(*The curtain goes up.*

Nína (*to* TRIGÓRIN). It is a queer play, isn't it?

Trig. I did not understand it at all. But I enjoyed it. You acted so genuinely. And the scenery was delightful. (*A pause.*) There 550 must be a lot of fish in that lake.

Nína. Yes.

Trig. I love angling. There is nothing I en-

[1] The dashing young lover.
[2] Kónstantin dear.

joy so much as sitting on the bank of a river in the evening and watching the float.[1]   555

Nína. But I should have thought that for anyone who has known the enjoyment of creation, no other enjoyment can exist.

Mad. Ark. (laughing). Don't talk like that. When people say nice things to him he is   560 utterly floored.

Sham. I remember one evening in the opera theater in Moscow the celebrated Silva took the lower *C!* As it happened, there was sitting in the gallery the bass of our church choir,   565 and all at once — imagine our intense astonishment — we heard from the gallery "Bravo, Silva!" a whole octave lower — like this: (*in a deep bass*) "Bravo, Silva!" The audience sat spellbound.   570
(*A pause.*

Dorn. The angel of silence has flown over us.

Nína. It's time for me to go.   Good-bye.

Mad. Ark. Where are you off to?   Why so early?   We won't let you go.

Nína. My father expects me.   575

Mad. Ark. What a man, really ... (*Kisses her.*) Well, there is no help for it.   I am sorry — I am sorry to let you go.

Nína. If you knew how grieved I am to go.

Mad. Ark. Someone ought to see you   580 home, my little dear.

Nína (frightened). Oh, no, no!

Sórin (to her, in an imploring voice). Do stay!

Nína. I can't, Pyótr Nikoláyevitch.

Sórin. Stay for an hour.   What is there   585 in that?

Nína (thinking a minute, tearfully). I can't!
(*Shakes hands and hurriedly goes off.*

Mad. Ark. Unfortunate girl she is, really. They say her mother left her father all her immense property — every farthing of it —   590 and now the girl has got nothing, as her father has already made a will leaving everything to his second wife.   It's monstrous!

Dorn. Yes, her father is a pretty thorough scoundrel, one must do him the justice   595 to say so.

Sórin (rubbing his cold hands). Let us go too, it's getting damp.   My legs ache.

Mad. Ark. They seem like wooden legs, you

[1] Fishing was Chekhov's favorite sport.

can hardly walk.   Let us go, unlucky old   600 man.
(*Takes his arm.*

Sham. (offering his arm to his wife). Madame?

Sórin. I hear that dog howling again.   (*To* SHAMRÁEV) Be so kind, Ílya Afanásyitch, as to tell them to let it off the chain.   605

Sham. It's impossible, Pyótr Nikoláyevitch, I am afraid of thieves getting into the barn. Our millet is there.   (*To* MEDVÉDENKO, *who is walking beside him*) Yes, a whole octave lower: "Bravo, Silva!"   And he not a   610 singer — simply a church chorister!

Medv. And what salary does a chorister get?
(*All go out except* DORN.

Dorn (alone). I don't know, perhaps I know nothing about it, or have gone off my head, but I liked the play.   There is something   615 in it.   When that girl talked about loneliness and afterwards when the Devil's eyes appeared, I was so excited that my hands trembled.   It is fresh, naïve... Here he comes, I believe.   I want to say all the nice things I can to him.   620

Enter TRÉPLEV

Trêp. They have all gone.

Dorn. I am here.

Trêp. Mashenka[1] is looking for me all over the park.   Insufferable creature she is!

Dorn. Kónstantin Gavrílitch, I liked   625 your play extremely.   It's a strange thing, and I haven't heard the end, and yet it made a strong impression!   You are a gifted man — you must persevere.
(TRÉPLEV *presses his hand warmly and embraces him impulsively.*

Dorn. Fie, what an hysterical fellow!   630 There are tears in his eyes!   What I mean is this.   You have taken a subject from the realm of abstract ideas.   So it should be, for a work of art ought to express a great idea.   A thing is only fine when it is serious.   How pale   635 you are!

Trêp. So you tell me to persevere?

Dorn. Yes.... But write only of what is important and eternal.   You know, I have had varied experiences of life, and have en-   640 joyed it; I am satisfied, but if it had been my

[1] Little Másha.

lot to know the spiritual heights which artists reach at the moment of creation, I should, I believe, have despised my bodily self and all that appertains to it and left all things 645 earthly as far behind as possible.

Trêp. Excuse me, where is Nína?

Dorn. And another thing. In a work of art there ought to be a clear, definite idea. You ought to know what is your aim in writ- 650 ing, for if you go along that picturesque route without a definite goal you will be lost and your talent will be your ruin.

Trêp (*impatiently*). Where is Nína?

Dorn. She has gone home.   655

Trêp. (*in despair*). What am I to do? I want to see her ... I must see her.... I must go....

Enter MÁSHA

Dorn (*to* TRÉPLEV). Calm yourself, my boy.

Trêp. But I am going all the same.   660 I must go.

Másha. Come indoors, Kónstantin Gavrí-litch. Your mother wants you. She is worried.

Trêp. Tell her that I have gone away. And I beg you — all of you — leave me in 665 peace! Let me alone! Don't follow me about!

Dorn. Come, come, come, dear boy.... You can't go on like that.... That's not the thing.

Trêp. (*in tears*). Good-bye, doctor. Thank you ...   670

(*Goes off.*

Dorn (*with a sigh*). Youth! youth!

Másha. When people have nothing better to say, they say, "Youth! youth!" ...

(*Takes a pinch of snuff.*

Dorn (*takes her snuff-box from her and flings it into the bushes*). That's disgusting!   675 (*A pause.*) I believe they are playing the piano indoors. We must go in.

Másha. Wait a little.

Dorn. What is it?

Másha. I want to tell you once more.   680 I have a longing to talk ... (*growing agitated*). I don't care for my father ... but I feel drawn to you. For some reason I feel with all my heart that you are very near me.... Help me. Help me, or I shall do something silly, I shall   685

make a mock of my life and ruin it.... I can't go on....

Dorn. What is it? Help you in what?

Másha. I am miserable. No one, no one knows how miserable I am! (*Laying her* 690 *head on his breast, softly*) I love Kónstantin!

Dorn. How hysterical they all are! How hysterical! And what a lot of love.... Oh, the sorcery of the lake! (*Tenderly*) But what can I do, my child? What? What?   695

Curtain

ACT II

A croquet lawn. The house with a big veranda in the background on the right; on the left is seen the lake with the blazing sun reflected in it.

Flower beds.   Midday.   Hot. MADAME ARKÁDIN, DORN, *and* MÁSHA *are sitting on a garden seat in the shade of an old lime tree on one side of the croquet lawn.* DORN *has an open book on his knee*

Mad. Ark. (*to* MÁSHA). Come, let us stand up. (*They both get up.*) Let us stand side by side. You are twenty-two and I am nearly twice as old. Yevgény Sergéitch, which of us looks the younger?   5

Dorn. You, of course.

Mad. Ark. There! And why is it? Because I work, I feel I am always on the go, while you stay always in the same place and have no life at all.... And it is my rule never to look 10 into the future. I never think about old age or death. What is to be, will be.

Másha. And I feel as though I had been born long, long ago; I trail my life along like an end-less train.... And often I have not the 15 slightest desire to go on living. (*Sits down.*) Of course, that's all nonsense. I must shake myself and throw it all off.

Dorn (*hums quietly*). "Tell her of love, oh my precious flowers."[1]   20

Mad. Ark. Then I am as particular as an Englishman. I keep myself in hand, as they say, my dear, and am always dressed and have

[1] From Siebel's song in the opera *Faust* by Charles Gounod, the French composer (1818–93).

my hair done *comme il faut.*[1] Do I allow myself to go out of the house even into the garden 25 in a dressing-gown, or without my hair being done? Never! What has preserved me is that I have never been a dowdy, I have never let myself go, as some women do... (*Walks about the lawn with her arms akimbo.*) 30 Here I am, as brisk as a bird. I could take the part of a girl of fifteen.

Dorn. Nevertheless, I shall go on. (*Takes up the book.*) We stopped at the corn merchant and the rats.... 35

Mad. Ark. And the rats. Read. (*Sits down.*) But give it to me, I'll read. It is my turn. (*Takes the book and looks in it.*) And rats.... Here it is.... (*Reads.*) "And of course for society people to spoil novelists 40 and to attract them to themselves is as dangerous as for a corn merchant to rear rats in his granaries. And yet they love them. And so when a woman has picked out an author whom she desires to captivate, she lays siege to 45 him by means of compliments, flattery, and favors..." Well, that may be so with the French, but there is nothing like that with us, we have no set rules. Among us, before a woman sets to work to captivate an author, 50 she is generally head over ears in love herself, if you please. To go no further, take Trigórin and me....

Enter Sórin, *leaning on his stick and with him* Nína; Medvédenko *wheels an empty bath-chair in after them*

Sórin (*in a caressing tone, as to a child*). Yes? We are delighted, aren't we? We are 55 happy today at last? (*To his sister*) We are delighted! Our father and stepmother have gone off to Tver,[2] and we are free now for three whole days.

Nína (*sits down beside* Madame Arká- 60 rin *and embraces her*). I am happy! Now I belong to you.

Sórin (*sits down in his bath-chair*). She looks quite a beauty today.

Mad. Ark. Nicely dressed and interest- 65

ing.... That's a good girl. (*Kisses* Nína.) But we mustn't praise you too much for fear of ill-luck. Where is Bóris Alexéyevitch?

Nína. He is in the bathing-house, fishing.

Mad. Ark. I wonder he doesn't get sick 70 of it! (*Is about to go on reading.*

Nína. What is that?

Mad. Ark. Maupassant's "Sur l'Eau," my dear. (*Reads a few lines to herself.*) Well, the rest isn't interesting or true. (*Shuts the 75 book.*) I feel uneasy. Tell me, what's wrong with my son? Why is he so depressed and ill-humored? He spends whole days on the lake and I hardly ever see him.

Másha. His heart is troubled. (*To 80 Nína, timidly*) Please, do read us something out of his play!

Nína (*shrugging her shoulders*). Would you like it? It's so uninteresting.

Másha (*restraining her enthusiasm*). 85 When he reads anything himself his eyes glow and his face turns pale. He has a fine mournful voice, and the gestures of a poet.

(*There is a sound of* Sórin *snoring.*

Dorn. Good night!

Mad. Ark. Petrusha![1] 90

Sórin. Ah?

Mad. Ark. Are you asleep?

Sórin. Not a bit of it. (*A pause.*

Mad. Ark. You do nothing for your health, brother, and that's not right. 95

Sórin. I should like to take something, but the doctor won't give me anything.

Dorn. Take medicine at sixty!

Sórin. Even at sixty one wants to live!

Dorn (*with vexation*). Oh, very well, 100 take valerian[2] drops!

Mad. Ark. It seems to me it would do him good to go to some mineral springs.

Dorn. Well, he might go. And he might not. 105

Mad. Ark. What is one to make of that?

Dorn. There's nothing to make of it. It's quite clear. (*A pause.*

Medv. Pyótr Nikoláyevitch ought to give up smoking. 110

Sórin. Nonsense!

---

[1] In the correct fashion.
[2] A city on the Volga River not far from Moscow.

[1] Peter dear.
[2] An herb drug used as a sedative.

Dorn. No, it's not nonsense. Wine and tobacco destroy the personality. After a cigar or a glass of vodka, you are not Pyótr Niko-láyevitch any more but Pyótr Nikoláye- 115 vitch plus somebody else; your ego is diffused and you feel towards yourself as to a third person.

Sórin (laughs). It's all very well for you to argue! You've lived your life, but what 120 about me? I have served in the Department of Justice for twenty-eight years, but I haven't lived yet, I've seen and done nothing, as a matter of fact, and very naturally I want to live very much. You've had enough and 125 you don't care, and so you are inclined to be philosophical, but I want to live, and so I drink sherry at dinner and smoke cigars and so on. That's all it comes to.

Dorn. One must look at life seriously, 130 but to go in for cures at sixty and to regret that one hasn't enjoyed oneself enough in one's youth is frivolous, if you will forgive my saying so.

Másha (gets up). It must be lunch-time. 135 (*Walks with a lazy, lagging step.*) My leg is gone to sleep. (*Goes off.*

Dorn. She will go and have a couple of glasses before lunch.

Sórin. She has no personal happiness, 140 poor thing.

Dorn. Nonsense, Your Excellency.

Sórin. You argue like a man who has had all he wants.

Mad. Ark. Oh, what can be more 145 boring than this sweet country boredom! Hot, still, no one ever doing anything, everyone airing their theories.... It's nice being with you, my friends, charming to listen to you, but ... to sit in a hotel room somewhere and 150 learn one's part is ever so much better.

Nina (enthusiastically). Delightful! I understand you.

Sórin. Of course, it's better in town. You sit in your study, the footman lets no one 155 in unannounced, there's a telephone ... in the streets there are cabs and everything....

Dorn (hums). "Tell her, oh my flowers."

ENTER SHAMRÁEV, *and after him* POLÍNA ANDRÉYEVNA

Sham. Here they are! Good morning! (*Kisses* MADAME ARKÁDIN'S *hand and* 160 *then* NÍNA'S.) Delighted to see you in good health. (*To* MADAME ARKÁDIN) My wife tells me that you are proposing to drive into town with her today. Is that so?

Mad. Ark. Yes, we are thinking of it. 165

Sham. Hm! that's splendid, but how are you going, honored lady? They are carting the rye today; all the men are at work. What horses are you to have, allow me to ask?

Mad. Ark. What horses? How should 170 I know what horses!

Sórin. We've got carriage horses.

Sham. (growing excited). Carriage horses! But where am I to get collars for them? Where am I to get collars? It's a strange thing! 175 It passes my understanding! Honored lady, forgive me, I am full of reverence for your talent. I would give ten years of my life for you, but I cannot let you have the horses!

Mad. Ark. But if I have to go! It's a 180 queer thing!

Sham. Honored lady! You don't know what farming means.

Mad. Ark. (flaring up). That's the old story! If that's so, I go back to Moscow today. 185 Give orders for horses to be hired for me at the village, or I'll walk to the station.

Sham. (flaring up). In that case I resign my position! You must look for another steward. (*Goes off*

Mad. Ark. It's like this every summer; 190 every summer I am insulted here! I won't set my foot in the place again.

(*Goes off at left where the bathing shed is supposed to be. A minute later she can be seen entering the house*. TRIGÓRIN *follows her, carrying fishing rods and tackle, and a pail.*

Sórin (flaring up). This is insolence! It's beyond everything. I am thoroughly sick of it. Send all the horses here this minute! 195

Nína (to POLÍNA ANDRÉYEVNA). To refuse Irína Nikoláyevna, the famous actress! Any wish of hers, any whim even, is of more conse quence than all your farming. It's positively incredible! 200

Pol. (*in despair*). What can I do? Put yourself in my position: what can I do?

Sórin (*to* NÍNA). Let us go to my sister. We will all entreat her not to go away. Won't we? (*Looking in the direction in which* 205 SHAMRÁEV *has gone*) Insufferable man! Despot!

Nína (*preventing him from getting up*). Sit still, sit still. We will wheel you in. (*She and* MEDVÉDENKO *push the bath-chair.*) Oh, how awful it is! 210

Sórin. Yes, yes, it's awful. But he won't leave, I'll speak to him directly.

(*They go out;* DORN *and* POLÍNA ANDRÉYEVNA *are left alone on the stage.*

Dorn. People are tiresome. Your husband ought to be simply kicked out, but it will end in that old woman Pyótr Nikoláyevitch 215 and his sister begging the man's pardon. You will see!

Pol. He has sent the carriage horses into the fields too! And there are misunderstandings like this every day. If you only knew 220 how it upsets me! It makes me ill; see how I am trembling.... I can't endure his rudeness. (*In an imploring voice*) Yevgény, dearest, light of my eyes, my darling, let me come to you.... Our time is passing, we 225 are no longer young, and if only we could lay aside concealment and lying for the rest of our lives anyway...   (*A pause.*

Dorn. I am fifty-five; it's too late to change my life. 230

Pol. I know you refuse me because there are other women too who are as near to you. You can't take them all to live with you. I understand. Forgive me, you are tired of me.

NÍNA *appears near the house; she is picking flowers*

Dorn. No, it's all right. 235

Pol. I am wretched from jealousy. Of course you are a doctor, you can't avoid women. I understand.

Dorn (*to* NÍNA, *who comes up to them*). How are things going? 240

Nína. Irína Nikoláyevna is crying and Pyótr Nikoláyevitch has an attack of asthma.

Dorn (*gets up*). I'd better go and give them both valerian drops.

Nína (*gives him the flowers*). Please 245 take these.

Dorn. Merci bien.[1] (*Goes towards the house.*

Pol. (*going with him*). What charming flowers! (*Near the house, in a smothered voice*) Give me those flowers! Give me those 250 flowers!

(*On receiving them, tears the flowers to pieces and throws them away. Both go into the house.*

Nína (*alone*). How strange it is to see a famous actress cry, and about such a trivial thing! And isn't it strange? A famous author, adored by the public, written 255 about in all the papers, his photographs for sale, his works translated into foreign languages — and he spends the whole day fishing and is delighted that he has caught two gudgeon. I thought famous people were proud, 260 unapproachable, that they despised the crowd, and by their fame and the glory of their name, as it were, revenged themselves on the vulgar herd for putting rank and wealth above everything. But here they cry and fish, play 265 cards, laugh and get cross like everyone else.

Enter TRÉPLEV, *hatless, with a gun and a dead sea-gull*

Trép. Are you alone here?

Nína. Yes.

(TRÉPLEV *lays the sea-gull at her feet.*

Nína. What does that mean?

Trép. I was so mean as to kill this bird 270 today. I lay it at your feet.

Nína. What is the matter with you?

(*Picks up the bird and looks at it.*

Trép. (*after a pause*). Soon I shall kill myself in the same way.

Nína. You have so changed, I hardly 275 know you.

Trép. Yes, ever since the day when I hardly knew you. You have changed to me, your eyes are cold, you feel me in the way.

[1] Thank you

Nina. You have become irritable of late, you express yourself so incomprehensibly, as it were in symbols. This bird is a symbol too, I suppose, but forgive me, I don't understand it. (*Lays the sea-gull on the seat.*) I am too simple to understand you. 285

Trép. This began from that evening when my play came to grief so stupidly. Women never forgive failure. I have burnt it all; every scrap of it. If only you knew how miserable I am! Your growing cold to me is awful, 290 incredible, as though I had woken up and found this lake had suddenly dried up or sunk into the earth. You have just said that you are too simple to understand me. Oh, what is there to understand? My play was not 295 liked, you despise my inspiration, you already consider me commonplace, insignificant, like so many others... (*stamping*). How well I understand it all, how I understand it! I feel as though I had a nail in my brain, 300 damnation take it, together with my vanity which is sucking away my life, sucking it like a snake... (*Sees* TRIGÓRIN, *who comes in reading a book.*) Here comes the real genius, walking like Hamlet and with a book too. 305 (*Mimics.*) "Words, words, words."... The sun has scarcely reached you and you are smiling already, your eyes are melting in its rays. I won't be in your way. (*Goes off quickly.*

Trig. (*making notes in his book*). Takes 310 snuff and drinks vodka. Always in black. The schoolmaster is in love with her....

Nina. Good morning, Bóris Alexéyevitch!

Trig. Good morning. Circumstances have turned out so unexpectedly that it seems 315 we are setting off today. We are hardly likely to meet again. I am sorry. I don't often have the chance of meeting young girls, youthful and charming; I have forgotten how one feels at eighteen or nineteen, and can't 320 picture it to myself, and so the young girls in my stories and novels are usually unreal. I should like to be in your shoes just for one hour to find out how you think, and altogether what sort of person you are. 325

Nina. And I should like to be in your shoes.

Trig. What for?

Nina. To know what it feels like to be a famous, gifted author. What does it feel like to be famous? How does it affect you, 330 being famous?

Trig. How? Nohow, I believe. I have never thought about it. (*After a moment's thought*) It's one of two things: either you exaggerate my fame, or it never is felt at all. 335

Nina. But if you read about yourself in the newspapers?

Trig. When they praise me I am pleased, and when they abuse me I feel out of humor for a day or two. 340

Nina. What a wonderful world! If only you knew how I envy you! How different people's lots in life are! Some can scarcely get through their dull, obscure existence, they are all just like one another, they are all un- 345 happy; while others — you, for instance — you are one out of a million, have an interesting life full of brightness and significance. You are happy.

Trig. I? (*Shrugging his shoulders*) Hm 350 ... You talk of fame and happiness, of bright, interesting life, but to me all those fine words, if you will forgive my saying so, are just like a sweetmeat which I never taste. You are very young and very naïve. 355

Nina. Your life is splendid!

Trig. What is there particularly nice in it? (*Looks at his watch.*) I must go and write directly. Excuse me, I mustn't stay... (*Laughs.*) You have stepped on my 360 favorite corn, as the saying is, and here I am beginning to get excited and a little cross. Let us talk though. We will talk about my splendid bright life.... Well, where shall we begin? (*After thinking a little*) There are such 365 things as fixed ideas, when a man thinks day and night, for instance, of nothing but the moon. And I have just such a moon. I am haunted day and night by one persistent thought: I ought to be writing, I ought to 370 be writing, I ought... I have scarcely finished one novel when, for some reason, I must begin writing another, then a third, after the third a fourth. I write incessantly, post haste, and I can't write in any other way. What is 375 there splendid and bright in that, I ask you? Oh, it's an absurd life! Here I am with you,

I am excited, yet every moment I remember that my unfinished novel is waiting for me. Here I see a cloud that looks like a grand 380 piano. I say to myself I must put into a story somewhere that a cloud sailed by that looked like a grand piano. There is a scent of helio-trope. I hurriedly make a note: a sickly smell, a widow's color, to be mentioned in the 385 description of a summer evening. I catch up myself and you at every sentence, every word, and make haste to put those sentences and words away into my literary treasure-house — it may come in useful! When I finish 390 work I race off to the theater or to fishing; if only I could rest in that and forget myself. But no, there's a new subject rolling about in my head like a heavy iron cannon ball, and I am drawn to my writing-table and must 395 make haste again to go on writing and writing. And it's always like that, always. And I have no rest from myself, and I feel that I am eating up my own life, and that for the sake of the honey I give to someone in space I am 400 stripping the pollen from my best flowers, tear-ing up the flowers themselves and trampling on their roots. Don't you think I am mad? Do my friends and acquaintances treat me as though I were sane? "What are you 405 writing at now? What are you going to give us?" It's the same thing again and again, and it seems to me as though my friends' notice, their praises, their enthusiasm — that it's all a sham, that they are deceiving me as an 410 invalid and I am somehow afraid that they will steal up to me from behind, snatch me and carry me off and put me in a mad-house. And in those years, the best years of my youth, when I was beginning, my writing was un- 415 mixed torture. A small writer, particularly when he is not successful, seems to himself clumsy, awkward, unnecessary; his nerves are strained and overwrought. He can't resist hanging about people connected with 420 literature and art, unrecognized and unnoticed by anyone, afraid to look anyone boldly in the face, like a passionate gambler without any money. I hadn't seen my reader, but for some reason I always imagined him hostile, and 425 mistrustful. I was afraid of the public, it

alarmed me, and when I had to produce my first play it always seemed to me that all the dark people felt hostile and all the fair ones were coldly indifferent. Oh, how awful 430 it was! What agony it was!

Nina. But surely inspiration and the very process of creation give you moments of ex-alted happiness?

Trig. Yes. While I am writing I enjoy 435 it. And I like reading my proofs, but... as soon as it is published I can't endure it, and I see that it is all wrong, a mistake, that it ought not to have been written at all, and I feel vexed and sick about it... (*laughing*). 440 And the public reads it and says: "Yes, charm-ing, clever. Charming, but very inferior to Tolstoy," or, "It's a fine thing, but Turgenev's 'Fathers and Sons' is finer." And it will be the same to my dying day, only charm- 445 ing and clever, charming and clever — and nothing more. And when I die my friends, passing by my tomb, will say: "Here lies Trigórin. He was a good writer, but inferior to Turgenev." [1] 450

Nina. Forgive me, but I refuse to under-stand you. You are simply spoiled by success.

Trig. What success? I have never liked myself; I dislike my own work. The worst of it is that I am in a sort of delirium, and 455 often don't understand what I am writing. I love this water here, the trees, the sky. I feel nature, it arouses in me a passionate, ir-resistible desire to write. But I am not simply a landscape painter; I am also a citizen. 460 I love my native country, my people; I feel that if I am a writer I am in duty bound to write of the people, of their sufferings, of their future, to talk about science and the rights of man and so on, and so on, and I write 465 about everything. I am hurried and flustered, and on all sides they whip me up and are angry with me; I dash about from side to side like a fox beset by hounds. I see life and science continually getting farther and farther 470 away while I fall farther and farther behind like a peasant too late for the train; and what

[1] Ivan Turgenev (1818–83), a Russian novelist who has exerted widespread influence on both European and American writers of fiction.

it comes to is that I feel I can only describe landscape and in everything else I am false to the marrow of my bones. 475

Nína. You are overworked and have not the leisure nor the desire to appreciate your own significance. You may be dissatisfied with yourself, but for others you are great and splendid! If I were a writer like you, I 480 should give up my whole life to the common herd, but I should know that there could be no greater happiness for them than to rise to my level, and they would harness themselves to my chariot. 485

Trig. My chariot, what next! Am I an Agamemnon, or what? (*Both smile.*

Nína. For such happiness as being a writer or an artist I would be ready to endure poverty, disappointment, the dislike of those 490 around me; I would live in a garret and eat nothing but rye bread, I would suffer from being dissatisfied with myself, from recognizing my own imperfections, but I should ask, in return, for fame . . . real, resounding fame. 495 . . . (*Covers her face with her hands.*) It makes me dizzy. . . . Ough!

(*The voice of* MADAME ARKÁDIN *from the house.*

Mad. Ark. Bóris Alexéyevitch!

Trig. They are calling for me. I suppose it's to pack. But I don't want to leave 500 here. (*Looks round at the lake.*) Just look how glorious it is! It's splendid!

Nína. Do you see the house and garden on the other side of the lake?

Trig. Yes. 505

Nína. That house was my dear mother's. I was born there. I have spent all my life beside this lake and I know every little islet on it.

Trig. It's very delightful here! (*Seeing the sea-gull*) And what's this? 510

Nína. A sea-gull. Kónstantin Gavrílitch shot it.

Trig. A beautiful bird. Really, I don't want to go away. Try and persuade Irína Nikoláyevna to stay. (*Makes a note in his book.*

Nína. What are you writing? 516

Trig. Oh, I am only making a note.[1] A

[1] Chekhov had notebooks filled with subjects for stories, rare names for characters, and the like.

subject struck me (*putting away the notebook*). A subject for a short story: a young girl, such as you, has lived all her life beside a lake; 520 she loves the lake like a sea-gull, and is as free and happy as a sea-gull. But a man comes by chance, sees her, and having nothing better to do, destroys her like that sea-gull here.

(*A pause.*

MADAME ARKÁDIN *appears at the window*

Mad. Ark. Bóris Alexéyevitch, where 525 are you?

Trig. I am coming. (*Goes and looks back at* NÍNA. *To* MADAME ARKÁDIN *at the window*) What is it?

Mad. Ark. We are staying. 530

(TRIGÓRIN *goes into the house.*

Nína (*advances to the footlights; after a few moments' meditation*). It's a dream!

Curtain

(*Between the Second and Third Acts there is an interval of a week.*)

ACT III

The dining-room in SÓRIN's *house. Doors on right and on left. A sideboard. A medicine cupboard. A table in the middle of the room. A portmanteau and hat-boxes; signs of preparation for departure.* TRIGÓRIN *is having lunch;* MÁSHA *stands by the table*

Másha. I tell all this to you as a writer. You may make use of it. I am telling you the truth: if he had hurt himself seriously I would not have gone on living another minute. But I have pluck enough all the same. I just 5 made up my mind that I would tear this love out of my heart, tear it out by the roots.

Trig. How are you going to do that?

Másha. I am going to be married. To Medvédenko.

Trig. That's the schoolmaster? 10

Másha. Yes.

Trig. I don't understand what's the object of it.

Másha. To love without hope, to spend   15 whole years waiting for something.... But when I marry, there will be no time left for love, new cares will smother all the old feelings. And, anyway, it will be a change, you know. Shall we have another?   20

Trig. Won't that be too much?

Másha. Oh, come! (*Fills two glasses.*) Don't look at me like that! Women drink much oftener than you imagine. Only a small proportion drink openly as I do, the major-   25 ity drink in secret. Yes. And it's always vodka or brandy. (*Clinks glasses.*) My best wishes! You are a good-hearted man; I am sorry to be parting from you. (*They drink.*)

Trig. I don't want to go myself.   30

Másha. You should beg her to stay.

Trig. No, she won't stay now. Her son is behaving very tactlessly. First, he shoots himself, and now they say he is going to challenge me to a duel. And whatever for?   35 He sulks, and snorts, and preaches new forms of art.... But there is room for all — new and old — why quarrel about it?

Másha. Well, there's jealousy too. But it is nothing to do with me.   40

  (*A pause.* YÁKOV *crosses from right to left with a portmanteau.* NÍNA *enters and stands by the window.*

Másha. My schoolmaster is not very brilliant, but he is a good, kind man, and poor, and he is very much in love with me. I am sorry for him. And I am sorry for his old mother. Well, let me wish you all happi-   45 ness. Don't remember evil against me. (*Shakes hands with him warmly.*) I am very grateful for your friendly interest. Send me your books and be sure to put in an inscription. Only don't write, "To my honored friend,"   50 but write simply, "To Márya who belongs nowhere and has no object in life." Good-bye! (*Goes out.*

Nína (*stretching out her arm towards* TRIGÓRIN, *with her fist clenched*). Odd or even?

Trig. Even.   55

Nína (*with a sigh*). Wrong. I had only one pea in my hand. I was trying my fortune whether to go on the stage or not. I wish someone would advise me.

Trig. It's impossible to advise in such   60 a matter. (*A pause.*

Nína. We are parting and... perhaps we shall never meet again. Won't you please take this little medallion as a parting gift? I had your initials engraved on one side of it...   65 and on the other the title of your book, "Days and Nights."

Trig. How exquisite! (*Kisses the medallion.*) A charming present!

Nína. Think of me sometimes.   70

Trig. I shall think of you. I shall think of you as you were on that sunny day — do you remember? — a week ago, when you were wearing a light-colored dress... we were talking together... there was a white sea-   75 gull lying on the seat.

Nína (*pensively*). Yes, a sea-gull... (*A pause.*) We can't talk any more, there's someone coming.... Let me have two minutes before you go, I entreat you...   80

  (*Goes out on the left.*

At the same instant MADAME ARKÁDIN, SÓRIN *in a dress coat with a star of some order on it, then* YÁKOV, *occupied with the luggage, enter on the right*

Mad. Ark. Stay at home, old man. With your rheumatism you ought not to go gadding about. (*To* TRIGÓRIN) Who was that went out? Nína?

Trig. Yes.   85

Mad. Ark. Pardon! We interrupted you. (*Sits down.*) I believe I have packed everything. I am worn out.

Trig. (*reads on the medallion*). "'Days and Nights,' page 121, lines 11 and 12."   90

Yákov (*clearing the table*). Am I to pack your fishing things too, sir?

Trig. Yes, I shall want them again. You can give away the hooks.

Yákov. Yes, sir.   95

Trig. (*to himself*). Page 121, lines 11 and 12. What is there in those lines? (*To* MADAME ARKÁDIN) Are there copies of my books in the house?

Mad. Ark. Yes, in my brother's study,   100 in the corner bookcase.

Trig. Page 121 ...   (*Goes out.*
Mad. Ark. Really, Petrusha, you had better stay at home.

Sórin. You are going away; it will be   105 dreary for me at home without you.

Mad. Ark. And what is there in town?

Sórin. Nothing particular, but still ... (*Laughs.*) There will be the laying of the foundation-stone of the Zemstvohall,[1] and all   110 that sort of thing. One longs to shake oneself free from this stagnant existence, if only for an hour or two. I've been too long on the shelf like some old cigarette-holder. I have ordered the horses for one o'clock; we'll set off at   115 the same time.

Mad. Ark. (*after a pause*). Come, stay here, don't be bored and don't catch cold. Look after my son. Take care of him. Give him good advice. (*A pause.*) Here I am go-   120 ing away and I shall never know why Kónstantin tried to shoot himself. I fancy jealousy was the chief cause, and the sooner I get Trigórin away from here, the better.

Sórin. What can I say? There were   125 other reasons too. It's easy to understand; he is young, intelligent, living in the country, in the wilds, with no money, no position and no future. He has nothing to do. He is ashamed of his idleness and afraid of it. I am   130 very fond of him indeed, and he is attached to me, yet in spite of it all he feels he is superfluous in the house, that he is a dependent, a poor relation. It's easy to understand, it's his vanity. ...   135

Mad. Ark. He is a great anxiety to me! (*Pondering*) He might go into the service, perhaps.

Sórin (*begins to whistle, then irresolutely*). I think that quite the best thing would be if   140 you were to ... let him have a little money. In the first place he ought to be able to be dressed like other people and all that. Just look at him. He's been going about in the same wretched jacket for the last three years and he has   145 no overcoat ... (*Laughs.*) It would do him no harm to have a little fun ... to go abroad or something. ... It wouldn't cost much.

Mad. Ark. But all the same ... I might
    [1] Council-hall.

manage the suit, perhaps, but as for going   150 abroad ... No, just at the moment I can't even manage the suit. (*Resolutely*) I have no money!   (Sórin *laughs.*

Mad. Ark. No!

Sórin (*begins to whistle*). Quite so. For-   155 give me, my dear, don't be cross. I believe you. ... You are a generous, noblehearted woman.

Mad. Ark. (*weeping*). I have no money.

Sórin. If I had money, of course I would   160 give him some myself, but I have nothing, not a half-penny. (*Laughs.*) My steward takes all my pension and spends it all on the land and the cattle and the bees, and my money is all wasted. The bees die, and the cows die,   165 they never let me have horses. ...

Mad. Ark. Yes, I have money, but you see I am an actress; my dresses alone are enough to ruin me.

Sórin. You are a kind, good creature   170 ... I respect you. ... Yes ... but there, I got a touch of it again ... (*Staggers.*) I feel dizzy. (*Clutches at the table.*) I feel ill and all that.

Mad. Ark. (*alarmed*). Petrusha! (*Trying to support him*) Petrusha, my dear! (*Call-*   175 *ing*) Help! help!

Enter Tréplev *with a bandage round his head and* Medvédenko

Mad. Ark. He feels faint!

Sórin. It's all right, it's all right! (*Smiles and drinks some water.*) It passed off ... and all that.   180

Trép. (*to his mother*). Don't be frightened, mother, it's not serious. Uncle often has these attacks now. (*To his uncle*) You must lie down, uncle.

Sórin. For a little while, yes. ... But   185 I am going to the town all the same. ... I'll lie down a little and then set off. ... It's quite natural.

(*Goes, leaning on his stick.*
Medv. (*gives him his arm*). There's a riddle in the morning on four legs, at noon on   190 two, in the evening on three. ...

Sórin (*laughs*). Just so. And at night on the back. Thank you, I can manage alone. ...

Medv. Oh come, why stand on ceremony! *(Goes out with* SÓRIN.

Mad. Ark. How he frightened me!   195

Trép. It is not good for him to live in the country. He gets depressed. If you would be generous for once, mother, and lend him fifteen hundred or two thousand roubles,[1] he could spend a whole year in town.   200

Mad. Ark. I have no money. I am an actress, not a banker.   *(A pause.*

Trép. Mother, change my bandage. You do it so well.

Mad. Ark. (takes out of the medicine 205 *cupboard some iodoform and a box with bandaging material).* The doctor is late.

Trép. He promised to be here at ten, and it is midday already.

Mad. Ark. Sit down. *(Takes the band-* 210 *age off his head.)* It's like a turban. Yesterday a stranger asked in the kitchen what nationality you were. But you have almost completely healed. There is the merest trifle left. *(Kisses him on the head.)* You won't do 215 any more click-clicking [2] while I am away, will you?

Trép. No, mother. It was a moment of mad despair when I could not control myself. It won't happen again. *(Kisses her hand.)* 220 You have such clever hands. I remember, long ago, when you were still acting at the Imperial Theater — I was little then — there was a fight in our yard and a washerwoman, one of the tenants, was badly beaten. Do you 225 remember? She was picked up senseless... you looked after her, took her remedies, and washed her children in a tub. Don't you remember?

Mad. Ark. No.   230

(Puts on a fresh bandage.

Trép. Two ballet dancers lived in the same house as we did at the time.... They used to come to you and have coffee....

Mad. Ark. I remember that.

Trép. They were very pious. *(A* 235 *pause.)* Just lately, these last days, I have loved you as tenderly and completely as when I was a child. I have no one left now but you.

[1] About $750 or $1000.

[2] Chekhov's onomatopoeia for pulling a pistol trigger.

Only why, why do you give yourself up to the influence of that man?   240

Mad. Ark. You don't understand him, Kónstantin. He is a very noble character....

Trép. And yet when he was told I was going to challenge him, the nobility of his character did not prevent him from funking it. He is 245 going away. Ignominious flight!

Mad. Ark. What nonsense! It is I who am asking him to go.

Trép. A very noble character! Here you and I are almost quarreling over him, and 250 at this very moment he is somewhere in the drawing-room or the garden laughing at us... developing Nína, trying to convince her finally that he is a genius.

Mad. Ark. You take a pleasure in say- 255 ing unpleasant things to me. I respect that man, and beg you not to speak ill of him before me.

Trép. And I don't respect him. You want me to think him a genius too, but forgive 260 me, I can't tell lies; his books make me sick.

Mad. Ark. That's envy. There's nothing left for people who have pretension without talent but to attack real talent. Much comfort in that, I must say!   265

Trép. (ironically). Real talent! *(Wrathfully)* I have more talent than all of you put together if it comes to that! *(Tears the bandage off his head.)* You, with your hackneyed conventions, have usurped the supremacy in art and 270 consider nothing real and legitimate but what you do yourselves; everything else you stifle and suppress. I don't believe in you! I don't believe in you or in him!

Mad. Ark. Decadent!   275

Trép. Get away to your charming theater and act there in your paltry, stupid plays!

Mad. Ark. I have never acted in such plays. Let me alone! You are not capable of writing even a wretched burlesque! You are 280 nothing but a Kiev shopman! living on other people!

Trép. You miser!

Mad. Ark. You ragged beggar!

*(*TRÉPLEV *sits down and weeps quietly.*

Mad. Ark. Nonentity! *(Walking up* 285 *and down in agitation)* Don't cry.... You mustn't cry. (*Weeps.*) Don't... (*Kisses him on the forehead, on the cheeks, and on the head.*) My dear child, forgive me.... Forgive your sinful mother. Forgive me, you know 290 I am wretched.

Trép. (*puts his arms around her*). If only you knew! I have lost everything! She does not love me, and now I cannot write... all my hopes are gone.   295

Mad. Ark. Don't despair... Everything will come right. He is going away directly; she will love you again. (*Wipes away his tears.*) Don't cry. We have made it up now.

Trép. (*kisses her hands*). Yes, mother. 300

Mad. Ark. (*tenderly*). Make it up with him too. You don't want a duel, do you?

Trép. Very well. Only, mother, do allow me not to meet him. It's painful to me — it's more than I can bear. (*Enter* TRIGÓRIN.) 305 Here he is... I am going... (*Rapidly puts away the dressings in the cupboard.*) The doctor will do the bandaging now.

Trig. (*looking in a book*). Page 121... lines 11 and 12. Here it is. (*Reads.*) "If ever 310 my life can be of use to you, come and take it."

(TRÉPLEV *picks up the bandage from the floor and goes out.*

Mad. Ark. (*looking at her watch*). The horses will soon be here.

Trig. (*to himself*). "If ever my life can be of use to you, come and take it."   315

Mad. Ark. I hope all your things are packed?

Trig. (*impatiently*). Yes, yes. (*Musing*) Why is it that I feel so much sorrow in that appeal from a pure soul, why does it wring my heart so painfully? "If ever my life can 320 be of use to you, come and take it." (*To* MADAME ARKÁDIN) Let us stay one day longer. (MADAME ARKÁDIN *shakes her head.*

Trig. Let us stay!

Mad. Ark. Darling, I know what keeps 325 you here. But have control over yourself. You are a little intoxicated; try to be sober.

Trig. You be sober too, be sensible and reasonable, I implore you; look at it all as 330 a true friend should. (*Presses her hand.*) You are capable of sacrifice. Be a friend to me, let me be free!

Mad. Ark. (*in violent agitation*). Are you so enthralled?   335

Trig. I am drawn to her! Perhaps it is just what I need.

Mad. Ark. The love of a provincial girl? Oh, how little you know yourself!

Trig. Sometimes people sleep as they 340 talk — that's how it is with me, I am talking to you and yet I am asleep and dreaming of her. ...I am possessed by sweet, marvelous dreams.... Let me be free....

Mad. Ark. (*trembling*). No, no! I am 345 an ordinary woman, you can't talk like that to me. Don't torture me, Bóris. It terrifies me.

Trig. If you cared to, you could be extraordinary. Love — youthful, charming, poetical, lifting one into a world of dreams — 350 that's the only thing in life that can give happiness! I have never yet known a love like that.... In my youth I never had time, I was always hanging about the editors' offices, struggling with want. Now it is here, 355 that love, it has come, it beckons to me. What sense is there in running away from it?

Mad. Ark. (*wrathfully*). You have gone mad!

Trig. Well, who cares?

Mad. Ark. You are all in a conspiracy 360 together to torment me today! (*Weeps.*

Trig. (*clutching at his heart*). She does not understand! She won't understand!

Mad. Ark. Am I so old and ugly that you don't mind talking of other women to me? 365 (*Puts her arms around him and kisses him.*) Oh, you are mad! My wonderful, splendid darling.... You are the last page of my life! (*Falls on her knees.*) My joy, my pride, my bliss!... (*Embraces his knees.*) If you 370 forsake me even for one hour I shall not survive it, I shall go mad, my marvelous, magnificent one, my master....

Trig. Someone may come in.

(*Helps her to get up.*

Mad. Ark. Let them; I am not 375 ashamed of my love for you. (*Kisses his hands.*) My treasure, you desperate boy, you want to be mad, but I won't have it, I won't let you... (*Laughs.*) You are mine... mine. ... This forehead is mine, and these eyes, 380 and this lovely silky hair is mine too... you are mine all over. You are so gifted, so clever, the best of all modern writers, you are the one hope of Russia.... You have so much truthfulness, simplicity, freshness, healthy humor.... 385 In one touch you can give all the essential characteristics of a person or a landscape, your characters are living. One can't read you without delight! You think this is exaggerated? That I am flattering you? But look into 390 my eyes... look.... Do I look like a liar? You see, I am the only one who can appreciate you; I am the only one who tells you the truth, my precious, wonderful darling.... Are you coming? Yes? You won't abandon 395 me?...

Trig. I have no will of my own... I have never had a will of my own.... Flabby, feeble, always submissive — how can a woman care for such a man? Take me, carry me off, 400 but don't let me move a step away from you....

Mad. Ark. (*to herself*). Now he is mine! (*In an easy tone, as though nothing had happened*) But, of course, if you like, you 405 can stay. I'll go by myself and you can come afterwards, a week later. After all, why should you be in a hurry?

Trig. No, we may as well go together.

Mad. Ark. As you please. Let us go 410 together, then.   (*A pause.*

                    (TRIGÓRIN *makes a note.*

Mad. Ark. What are you writing?

Trig. I heard a good name this morning, "The Maidens' Grove." It may be of use. (*Stretches.*)   So we are to go, then? 415 Again there will be railway carriages, stations, refreshment bars, mutton chops, conversations....

Enter SHAMRÁEV

Sham. I have the honor to announce, with regret, that the horses are ready. It's 420 time, honored lady, to set off for the station; the train comes in at five minutes past two. So please do me a favor, Irína Nikoláyevna, do not forget to inquire what has become of the actor Suzdáltsev. Is he alive and well? 425 We used to drink together at one time.... In

"The Plundered Mail" he used to play incomparably... I remember the tragedian Izmaïlov, also a remarkable personality, acted with him in Elisavetograd.[1]... Don't 430 be in a hurry, honored lady, you need not start for five minutes. Once they were acting conspirators in a melodrama, and when they were suddenly discovered, Izmaïlov had to say, "We are caught in a trap," but he said, 435 "We are caught in a tap!" (*Laughs.*) A tap!

        (*While he is speaking* YÁKOV *is busy looking after the luggage. The maid brings* MADAME ARKÁDIN *her hat, her coat, her umbrella, and her gloves; they all help* MADAME ARKÁDIN *to put on her things. The man-cook looks in at the door on left and after some hesitation comes in.*

Enter POLÍNA ANDRÉYEVNA, *then* SÓRIN *and* MEDVÉDENKO

Pol. (*with a basket*). Here are some plums for the journey.... Very sweet ones. You may be glad to have something nice....

Mad. Ark. You are very kind, Polína 440 Andréyevna.

Pol. Good-bye, my dear! If anything has not been to your liking, forgive it.   (*Weeps.*

Mad. Ark. (*embraces her*). Everything has been nice, everything! But you mustn't 445 cry.

Pol. The time flies so fast!

Mad. Ark. There's no help for it.

Sórin (*in a great-coat with a cape to it, with his hat on and a stick in his hand, enters* 450 *from door on left, crossing the stage*). Sister, it's time to start, or you may be too late after all. I am going to get into the carriage.

                    (*Goes out.*

Med. And I shall walk to the station... to see you off. I'll be there in no time... 455

                    (*Goes out.*

Mad. Ark. Good-bye, dear friends.... If we are all alive and well, we shall meet again next summer. (*The maid, the cook and* YÁKOV *kiss her hand.*) Don't forget me. (*Gives the*

[1] A city of the southern Ukraine between Kiev and Odessa.

cook a rouble.) Here's a rouble [1] for the three of you.

Cook. We humbly thank you, madam! Good journey to you! We are very grateful for your kindness!

Yákov. May God give you good luck!

Sham. You might rejoice our hearts with a letter! Good-bye, Bóris Alexéyevitch!

Mad. Ark. Where is Kónstantin? Tell him that I am starting; I must say good-bye. Well, don't remember evil against me. (*To Yákov*) I gave the cook a rouble. It's for the three of you.

> (*All go out on right. The stage is empty. Behind the scenes the noise that is usual when people are being seen off. The maid comes back to fetch the basket of plums from the table and goes out again.*

Trig. (*coming back*). I have forgotten my stick. I believe it is out there, on the veranda. (*Goes and, at door on left, meets* Nína, *who is coming in.*) Is that you? We are going....

Nína. I felt that we should see each other once more. (*Excitedly*) Bóris Alexéyevitch, I have come to a decision, the die is cast, I am going on the stage. I shall be gone from here tomorrow; I am leaving my father, I am abandoning everything, I am beginning a new life. Like you, I am going... to Moscow. We shall meet there.

Trig. (*looking round*). Stay at the "Slavyansky Bazaar"... Let me know at once... Molchanóvka, Grohólsky House.... I am in a hurry... (*A pause.*

Nína. One minute more....

Trig. (*in an undertone*). You are so lovely.... Oh, what happiness to think that we shall see each other soon! (*She sinks on his breast.*) I shall see again those wonderful eyes, that inexpressibly beautiful tender smile... those soft features, the expression of angelic purity.... My darling...

> (*A prolonged kiss.*

Curtain

(*Between the Third and Fourth Acts there is an interval of two years.*)

[1] This coin at the time was worth a half-dollar.

ACT IV

One of the drawing-rooms in Sórin's *house, which has been turned into a study for* Kónstantin Tréplev. *On the right and left, doors leading to inner apartments. In the middle, glass door leading on to the veranda. Besides the usual drawing-room furniture there is, in corner on right, a writing-table; near door on left, a sofa, a bookcase; and books in windows and on the chairs. Evening. There is a single lamp alight with a shade on it. It is half dark. There is the sound of the trees rustling, and the wind howling in the chimney. A watchman is tapping.*

Enter Medvédenko *and* Másha

Másha (*calling*). Kónstantin Gavrílitch! Kónstantin Gavrílitch! (*Looking round*) No, there is no one here. The old man keeps asking every minute, "Where is Kostya, where is Kostya?" He cannot live without him....

Med. He is afraid of being alone. (*Listening*) What awful weather! This is the second day of it.

Másha (*turns up the lamp*). There are waves on the lake. Great big ones.

Med. How dark it is in the garden! We ought to have told them to break up that stage in the garden. It stands as bare and ugly as a skeleton, and the curtain flaps in the wind. When I passed it yesterday evening, it seemed as though someone were crying in it.

Másha. What next?... (*A pause.*

Med. Let us go home, Másha.

Másha (*shakes her head*). I shall stay here for the night.

Med. (*in an imploring voice*). Másha, do come! Our baby must be hungry.

Másha. Nonsense. Matryóna will feed him. (*A pause.*

Med. I am sorry for him. He has been three nights now without his mother.

Másha. You are a bore. In the old days you used at least to discuss general subjects, but now it is only home, baby, home, baby — that's all one can get out of you.

Med. Come along, Másha!

Másha. Go by yourself.

Med. Your father won't let me have a horse.

Másha. Yes, he will.　You ask, and he will.

Med. Very well, I'll ask.　Then you will come tomorrow?　　　　　35

Másha (taking a pinch of snuff). Very well, tomorrow.　How you pester me!

Enter TRÉPLEV *and* POLÍNA ANDRÉYEVNA.
TRÉPLEV *brings in pillows and a quilt, and* POLÍNA ANDRÉYEVNA *sheets and pillow-cases; they lay them on the sofa.　Then* TRÉPLEV *goes to his table and sits down*

Másha. What's this for, mother?

Pol. Pyótr Nikoláyevitch asked us to make a bed for him in Kostya's room.　　40

Másha. Let me do it.　　　　(*Makes the bed.*

Pol. (sighing). Old people are like children.
(*Goes up to the writing-table, and leaning on her elbow, looks at the manuscript.　A pause.*

Med. Well, I am going, then.　Good-bye, Másha.　(*Kisses his wife's hand.*)　Good-bye, mother.　　　　45
(*Tries to kiss his mother-in-law's hand.*

Pol. (with vexation). Come, if you are going, go.

Med. Good-bye, Kónstantin Gavrílitch.
(*TRÉPLEV gives him his hand without speaking;* MEDVÉDENKO *goes out.*

Pol. (looking at the manuscript). No one would have guessed or thought that you　50 would have become a real author, Kostya. And now, thank God, they send you money from the magazines.　(*Passes her hand over his hair.*)　And you have grown good-looking too.
... Dear, good Kostya, do be a little　55 kinder to my Mashenka!

Másha (as she makes the bed). Leave him alone, mother.

Pol. (to TRÉPLEV).　She is a nice little thing. (*A pause.*)　A woman wants nothing, you　60 know, Kostya, so long as you give her a kind look.　I know from myself.
(*TRÉPLEV gets up from the table and walks away without speaking.*

Másha. Now you have made him angry. What induced you to pester him?

Pol. I feel so sorry for you, Mashenka.　65

Másha. Much use that is!

Pol. My heart aches for you.　I see it all, you know, I understand it all.

Másha. It's all foolishness.　There is no such thing as hopeless love except in　70 novels.　It's of no consequence.　The only thing is one mustn't let oneself go and keep expecting something, waiting for the tide to turn. ... When love gets into the heart there is nothing to be done but to clear it out.　75 Here they promised to transfer my husband to another district.　As soon as I am there, I shall forget it all. ... I shall tear it out of my heart.
(*Two rooms away a melancholy waltz is played.*

Pol. That's Kostya playing.　He must be depressed.　　　　80

Másha (noiselessly dances a few waltz steps). The great thing, mother, is not to have him before one's eyes.　If they only give my Semyon his transfer, trust me, I shall get over it in a month.　It's all nonsense.　　85

Door on left opens. DORN *and* MEDVÉDENKO *wheel in* SÓRIN *in his chair*

Med. I have six of them at home now.　And flour is two kopeks [1] per pound.

Dorn. You've got to look sharp to make both ends meet.

Med. It's all very well for you to laugh.　90 You've got more money than you know what to do with.

Dorn. Money?　After thirty years of practice, my boy, troublesome work during which I could not call my soul my own by day or　95 by night, I only succeeded in saving two thousand roubles,[2] and that I spent not long ago abroad.　I have nothing.

Másha (to her husband). You have not gone?

Med. (guiltily). Well, how can I when　100 they won't let me have a horse?

Másha (with bitter vexation, in an undertone). I can't bear the sight of you.
(*The wheel-chair remains in the left*

---

[1] About one cent, at that time.　One hundred kopeks = a rouble.

[2] About $1000.

half of the room; POLÍNA ANDRÉ-
YEVNA, MÁSHA, *and* DORN *sit
down beside it.* MEDVÉDENKO
moves mournfully to one side.

Dorn. What changes there have been here! 105
The drawing-room has been turned into
a study.

Másha. It is more convenient for Kónstantin Gavrílitch to work here. Whenever
he likes, he can walk out into the garden and
think there.   (*A watchman taps.* 110

Sórin. Where is my sister?

Dorn. She has gone to the station to meet
Trigórin. She will be back directly.

Sórin. Since you thought it necessary to
send for my sister, I must be dangerously 115
ill. (*After a silence*) It's a queer thing, I am
dangerously ill and here they don't give me
any medicines.

Dorn. Well, what would you like to have?
Valerian drops? Soda? Quinine? 120

Sórin. Ah, he is at his moralizing again!
What an infliction it is! (*With a motion of his
head towards the sofa*) Is that bed for me?

Pol. Yes, it's for you, Pyótr Nikoláyevitch.

Sórin. Thank you. 125

Dorn (*hums*). "The moon is floating in the
midnight sky."

Sórin. I want to give Kostya a subject for
a story. It ought to be called "The Man Who
Wanted To" — *L'homme qui a voulu.* In 130
my youth I wanted to become a literary man —
and didn't; I wanted to speak well — and I
spoke horribly badly, (*mimicking himself*)
"and all the rest of it, and all that, and so on,
and so forth" ... and I would go plod- 135
ding on and on, trying to sum up till I was in
a regular perspiration; I wanted to get married
— and I didn't; I always wanted to live in
town and here I am ending my life in the
country — and so on. 140

Dorn. You wanted to become an Actual
State Councilor [1] — and you have.

Sórin (*laughs*). *That* I had no hankerings
after. That happened of itself.

Dorn. To be expressing dissatisfaction 145

---

[1] Fourth highest grade in the civil service of the old
monarchial régime, a rank equal to major-general and
rear-admiral.

with life at sixty-two is really ungracious, you
know.

Sórin. What a pig-headed fellow you are!
You might understand that one wants to live!

Dorn. That's just frivolity. It's the 150
law of nature that every life must have an end.

Sórin. You argue like a man who has had
enough. You are satisfied and so you are indifferent to life, nothing matters to you. But
even you will be afraid to die. 155

Dorn. The dread of death is an animal fear.
One must overcome it. A rational fear of
death is only possible for those who believe in
eternal life and are conscious of their sins.
And you, in the first place, don't believe, 160
and, in the second, what sins have you to worry
about? You have served in the courts of
justice for twenty-five years — that's all.

Sórin (*laughs*). Twenty-eight....

TRÉPLEV *comes in and sits down on a stool at
SÓRIN's feet.* MÁSHA *never takes her eyes
off him*

Dorn. We are hindering Kónstantin 165
Gavrílitch from working.

Trép. Oh no, it doesn't matter. (*A pause.*

Med. Allow me to ask you, doctor, what
town did you like best abroad?

Dorn. Genoa. 170

Trép. Why Genoa?

Dorn. The life in the streets is so wonderful
there. When you go out of the hotel in the
evening, the whole street is packed with people.
You wander aimlessly, zigzagging about 175
among the crowd, backwards and forwards;
you live with it, are psychologically at one with
it, and begin almost to believe that a world-
soul is really possible, such as was acted by
Nína Zarétchny in your play. And, by 180
the way, where is she now? How is she getting
on?

Trép. I expect she is quite well.

Dorn. I was told that she was leading a
rather peculiar life. How was that? 185

Trép. That's a long story, doctor.

Dorn. Well, tell it briefly. (*A pause.*

Trép. She ran away from home and had an
affair with Trigórin. You know that?

Dorn. I know. 190

Trép. She had a child. The child died. Trigórin got tired of her and went back to his old ties, as might have been expected; though, indeed, he had never abandoned them, but in his weak-willed way contrived to 195 keep both going. As far as I can make out from what I have heard, Nína's private life was a complete failure.

Dorn. And the stage?

Trép. I fancy that was worse still. 200 She made her début at some holiday place near Moscow, then went to the provinces. All that time I did not lose sight of her, and wherever she went I followed her. She always took big parts, but she acted crudely, without 205 taste, rantingly, with violent gestures. There were moments when she uttered a cry successfully or died successfully, but they were only moments.

Dorn. Then she really has some talent? 210

Trép. It was difficult to make it out. I suppose she has. I saw her but she would not see me, and the servants would not admit me at the hotel. I understood her state of mind and did not insist on seeing her. (*A* 215 *pause.*) What more can I tell you? Afterwards, when I was back at home, I had some letters from her — warm, intelligent, interesting letters. She did not complain, but I felt that she was profoundly unhappy; every 220 line betrayed sick overstrained nerves. And her imagination is a little unhinged. She signed herself "The Sea-Gull." In Pushkin's "Nixie"[1] the miller says that he is a raven, and in the same way in her letters she 225 kept repeating that she was a sea-gull. Now she is here.

Dorn. Here? How do you mean?

Trép. In the town, staying at an inn. She has been there for five days. I did go to 230 see her, and Márya Ilyiníshna[2] here went too, but she won't see anyone. Semyón Semyón-itch declares he saw her yesterday afternoon in the fields a mile and a half from here.

[1] A poem by Aleksandr Pushkin (1799–1837), the first great Russian poet. A "nixie" is a female water sprite.
[2] I.e., Másha.

Med. Yes, I saw her. She went in 235 that direction, towards the town. I bowed to her and asked her why she did not come to see us. She said she would come.

Trép. She won't come. (*A pause.*) Her father and step-mother refuse to recog- 240 nize her. They have put watchmen about so that she may not even go near the house. (*Walks away with the doctor towards the writing-table.*) How easy it is to be a philosopher on paper, doctor, and how difficult it is in 245 life!

Sórin. She was a charming girl.

Dorn. What?

Sórin. She was a charming girl, I say. Actual State Councilor Sórin was posi- 250 tively in love with her for a time.

Dorn. The old Lovelace![1]

(SHAMRÁEV'S *laugh is heard.*)

Pol. I fancy our people have come back from the station . . .

Trép. Yes, I hear mother. 255

Enter MADAME ARKÁDIN, TRIGÓRIN, *and with them* SHAMRÁEV

Sham. (*as he enters*). We all grow old and dilapidated under the influence of the elements, while you, honored lady, are still young . . . a light blouse, sprightliness, grace. . . .

Mad. Ark. You want to bring me ill- 260 luck again, you tiresome man!

Trig. How do you do, Pyótr Nikoláyevitch! So you are still poorly? That's bad! (*Seeing* MÁSHA, *joyfully*) Márya Ilyiníshna!

Másha. You know me, do you? 265
(*Shakes hands.*)

Trig. Married?

Másha. Long ago.

Trig. Are you happy? (*Bows to* DORN *and* MEDVÉDENKO, *then hesitatingly approaches* TRÉPLEV.) Irína Nikoláyevna[2] has 270 told me that you have forgotten the past and are no longer angry.

(TRÉPLEV *holds out his hand.*)

Mad. Ark. (*to her son*). Bóris Alexéyevitch

[1] Richard Lovelace (1618-58), an English Cavalier poet who wrote in a gracious and mildly gallant vein.
[2] Madame Arkádin.

has brought the magazine with your new story in it.   275

Trêp. (*taking the magazine, to* TRIGÓRIN). Thank you, you are very kind. (*They sit down.*

Trig. Your admirers send their greetings to you.... In Petersburg [1] and Moscow there is great interest in your work and I am con- 280 tinually being asked questions about you. People ask what you are like, how old you are, whether you are dark or fair. Everyone imagines, for some reason, that you are no longer young. And no one knows your real 285 name, as you always publish under a pseudonym. You are as mysterious as the Man in the Iron Mask.[2]

Trêp. Will you make us a long stay?

Trig. No, I think I shall go back to 290 Moscow tomorrow. I am obliged to. I am in a hurry to finish my novel, and besides, I have promised something for a collection of tales that is being published. It's the old story, in fact.   295

(*While they are talking* MADAME ARKÁDIN *and* POLÍNA ANDRÉYEVNA *put a card-table in the middle of the room and open it out.* SHAMRÁEV *lights candles and sets chairs. A game of lotto is brought out of the cupboard.*

Trig. The weather has not given me a friendly welcome. There is a cruel wind. If it has dropped by tomorrow morning I shall go to the lake to fish. And I must have a look at the garden and that place where — you 300 remember? — your play was acted. I've got a subject for a story, I only want to revive my recollections of the scene in which it is laid.

Másha (*to her father*). Father, let my husband have a horse! He must get home. 305

Sham. (*mimicking*). Must get home — a horse! (*Sternly*) You can see for yourself: they have just been to the station. I can't send them out again.

Másha. But there are other horses. 310

[1] The old Russian capital, now Leningrad.
[2] The famous prisoner of the Bastille, Paris, who always wore a mask of black velvet until his death in 1703, and thus caused much legend to grow up about him.

(*Seeing that her father says nothing, waves her hand.*) There's no doing anything with you.

Med. I can walk, Másha. Really....

Pol. (*with a sigh*). Walk in such weather! ... (*Sits down to the card-table.*) Come, 315 friends.

Med. It is only four miles. Good-bye. (*Kisses his wife's hand.*) Good-bye, mother. (*His mother-in-law reluctantly holds out her hand for him to kiss.*) I wouldn't trouble 320 anyone, but the baby... (*Bows to the company.*) Good-bye...   (*Goes out with a guilty step.*

Sham. He can walk right enough. He's not a general.

Pol. (*tapping on the table*). Come, 325 friends. Don't let us waste time, we shall soon be called to supper.

(SHAMRÁEV, MÁSHA, *and* DORN *sit down at the table.*

Mad. Ark. (*to* TRIGÓRIN). When the long autumn evenings come on, they play lotto here. Look, it's the same old lotto that we 330 had when our mother used to play with us, when we were children. Won't you have a game before supper? (*Sits down to the table with* TRIGÓRIN.) It's a dull game, but it is not so bad when you are used to it.   335

(*Deals three cards to everyone.*

Trêp. (*turning the pages of the magazine*). He has read his own story, but he has not even cut mine.

(*Puts the magazine down on the writing-table, then goes towards door on left. As he passes his mother, he kisses her on the head.*

Mad. Ark. And you, Kostya?

Trêp. Excuse me, I would rather not 340 ... I am going out.   (*Goes out.*

Mad. Ark. The stake is ten kopeks.[1] Put it down for me, doctor, will you?

Dorn. Right.

Másha. Has everyone put down their 345 stakes? I begin... Twenty-two.

Mad. Ark. Yes.

Másha. Three!

Dorn. Right!

Másha. Did you play three? Eight! 350 Eighty-one! Ten!

[1] Five cents.

Sham. Don't be in a hurry!

Mad. Ark. What a reception I had in Kharkov![1] My goodness! I feel dizzy with it still.   355

Másha. Thirty-four!

(*A melancholy waltz is played behind the scenes.*

Mad. Ark. The students gave me an ovation.... Three baskets of flowers ... two wreaths and this, see.

(*Unfastens a brooch on her throat and lays it on the table.*

Sham. Yes, that's the real thing....   360

Másha. Fifty!

Dorn. Exactly fifty?

Mad. Ark. I had a wonderful dress.... Whatever I don't know, I do know how to dress.   365

Pol. Kostya is playing the piano; he is depressed, poor fellow.

Sham. He is awfully abused in the newspapers.

Másha. Seventy-seven!   370

Mad. Ark. As though that mattered!

Trig. He never quite comes off. He has not yet hit upon his own medium. There is always something queer and vague, at times almost like delirium. Not a single living char- 375 acter.

Másha. Eleven!

Mad. Ark. (*looking round at* Sórin). Petrusha, are you bored? (*A pause.*) He is asleep.   380

Dorn. The Actual State Councilor is asleep.

Másha. Seven! Ninety!

Trig. If I lived in such a place, beside a lake, do you suppose I should write? I should overcome this passion and should do nothing 385 but fish.

Másha. Twenty-eight!

Trig. To catch a bass is so delightful![2]

Dorn. Well, I believe in Kónstantin Gavrílitch. There is something in him! 390 There is something in him! He thinks in images; his stories are vivid, full of color, and they affect me strongly. The only pity is that

[1] An important city in the eastern Ukraine.
[2] In one of his letters Chekhov wrote: "To catch a bass! It is nobler and sweeter than love."

he has not got definite aims. He produces an impression and that's all, but you 395 can't get far with nothing but an impression. Irína Nikoláyevna, are you glad that your son is a writer?

Mad. Ark. Only fancy, I have not read anything of his yet. I never have time.   400

Másha. Twenty-six!

Tréplev *comes in quietly and sits down at his table*

Sham. (*to* Trigórin). We have still got something here belonging to you, Bóris Alexéyevitch.

Trig. What's that?   405

Sham. Kónstantin Gavrílitch shot a sea-gull and you asked me to get it stuffed for you.

Trig. I don't remember. (*Pondering*) I don't remember.

Másha. Sixty-six! One!   410

Trép. (*flinging open the window, listens*). How dark it is! I don't know why I feel so uneasy.

Mad. Ark. Kostyá, shut the window, there's a draught.   415

(Tréplev *shuts the window.*

Másha. Eighty-eight!

Trig. The game is mine!

Mad. Ark. (*gaily*). Bravo, bravo!

Sham. Bravo!

Mad. Ark. That man always has luck in 420 everything. (*Gets up.*) And now let us go and have something to eat. Our great man has not dined today. We will go on again after supper. (*To her son*) Kostya, leave your manuscripts and come to supper.   425

Trép. I don't want any, mother, I am not hungry.

Mad. Ark. As you like. (*Wakes* Sórin.) Petrusha, supper! (*Takes* Shamráev's *arm.*) I'll tell you about my reception in 430 Kharkov.

(Polína Andréyevna *puts out the candles on the table. Then she and* Dorn *wheel the chair. All go out by door on left; only* Tréplev, *sitting at the writing-table, is left on the stage.*

Trép. (*settling himself to write; runs through*

what he has written already). I have talked so much about new forms, and now I feel that little by little I am falling into a conven- 435 tion myself. (*Reads.*) "The placard on the wall proclaimed. . . . Her pale face in its setting of dark hair."[1] Proclaimed, setting. That's stupid. (*Scratches out.*) I will begin where the hero is awakened by the patter of the 440 rain, and throw out all the rest. The description of the moonlight evening is long and over-elaborate. Trigórin has worked out methods for himself, it's easy for him now. . . . With him the broken bottle neck glitters on the 445 dam and the mill-wheel casts a black shadow — and there you have the moonlight night — while I have the tremulous light, and the soft twinkling of the stars, and the far-away strains of the piano dying away in the still fragrant air. 450 . . . It's agonizing. (*A pause.*) I come more and more to the conviction that it is not a question of new and old forms, but that what matters is that a man should write without thinking about forms at all, write because it 455 springs freely from his soul. (*There is a tap at the window nearest to the table.*) What is that? (*Looks out of window.*) There is nothing to be seen . . . (*Opens the glass door and looks out into the garden.*) Someone ran down the 460 steps. (*Calls.*) Who is there? (*Goes out and can be heard walking rapidly along the veranda; returns half a minute later with* NÍNA ZA-RÉTCHNY.) Nína, Nína!

(NÍNA *lays her head on his breast and weeps with subdued sobs.*

Trêp. (*moved*). Nína! Nína! It's you 465 . . . you. . . . It's as though I had foreseen it, all day long my heart has been aching and restless. (*Takes off her hat and cape.*) Oh, my sweet, my precious, she has come at last. Don't let us cry, don't let us! 470

Nína. There is someone here.

Trêp. No one.

Nína. Lock the doors, someone may come in.

Trêp. No one will come in.

[1] Almost in the same words which Tréplev uses, Chekhov wrote to a budding short-story writer, Zhirkevitch, and criticized his style: "It is only ladies who nowadays write, 'the placard proclaimed,' 'her face in its setting of hair.'"

Nína. I know Irína Nikoláyevna is 475 here. Lock the doors.

Trêp. (*locks the door on right, goes to door on left*). There is no lock on this one. I'll put a chair against it. (*Puts an armchair against the door.*) Don't be afraid, no one will 480 come.

Nína (*looking intently into his face*). Let me look at you. (*Looking round*) It's warm, it's nice. . . . In old days this was the drawing-room. Am I very much changed? 485

Trêp. Yes . . . You are thinner and your eyes are bigger. Nína, how strange it is that I should be seeing you. Why would not you let me see you? Why haven't you come all this time? I know you have been here almost 490 a week. . . . I have been to you several times every day; I stood under your window like a beggar.

Nína. I was afraid that you might hate me. I dream every night that you look at me 495 and don't know me. If only you knew! Ever since I came I have been walking here . . . by the lake. I have been near your house many times and could not bring myself to enter it. Let us sit down. (*They sit down.*) Let us 500 sit down and talk and talk. It's nice here, it's warm and snug. Do you hear the wind? There's a passage in Turgenev, "Well for the man on such a night who sits under the shelter of home, who has a warm corner in 505 safety." I am a sea-gull. . . . No, that's not it. (*Rubs her forehead.*) What was I saying? Yes . . . Turgenev . . . "And the Lord help all homeless wanderers!" . . . It doesn't matter.
                                        (*Sobs.*)

Trêp. Nína, you are crying again. . . . 510 Nína!

Nína. Never mind, it does me good . . . I haven't cried for two years. Yesterday, late in the evening, I came into the garden to see whether our stage was still there. It is 515 still standing. I cried for the first time after two years and it eased the weight on my heart and made it lighter. You see, I am not crying now. (*Takes him by the hand.*) And so now you are an author. . . . You are an author, I 520 am an actress. . . . We too have been drawn into the whirlpool. I used to be as happy as a child

— I woke up singing in the morning; I loved you and dreamed of fame — and now? Early tomorrow morning I must go to Yelets[1] 525 third-class... with peasants, and at Yelets the cultured tradesmen will pester me with attentions. Life is a coarse business!

Trép. Why to Yelets?

Nína. I have taken an engagement for 530 the whole winter. It is time to go.

Trép. Nína, I cursed you, I hated you, I tore up your letters and photographs, but I was conscious every minute that my soul is bound to yours for ever. It's not in my power 535 to leave off loving you, Nína. Ever since I lost you and began to get my work published, my life has been unbearable — I am wretched. ... My youth was, as it were, torn away all at once, and it seems to me as though 540 I have lived for ninety years already. I call upon you, I kiss the earth on which you have walked; wherever I look I see your face, that tender smile that lighted up the best days of my life.... 545

Nína (distractedly). Why does he talk like this, why does he talk like this?

Trép. I am alone in the world, warmed by no affection. I am as cold as though I were in a cellar, and everything I write is dry, hard, 550 and gloomy. Stay here, Nína, I entreat you, or let me go with you!

(Nína *rapidly puts on her hat and cape.*

Trép. Nína, why is this? For God's sake, Nína!

(*Looks at her as she puts her things on. A pause.*

Nína. My horses are waiting at the 555 gate. Don't see me off, I'll go alone.... (*Through her tears*) Give me some water....

Trép. (gives her some water). Where are you going now?

Nína. To the town. (*A pause.*) Is 560 Irína Nikoláyevna here?

Trép. Yes.... Uncle was taken worse on Thursday and we telegraphed for her.

Nína. Why do you say that you kissed the earth on which I walked? I ought to be 565

[1] A city in Orel Province, about 200 miles south of Moscow.

killed. (*Bends over table.*) I am so tired! If I could rest... if I could rest! (*Raising her head*) I am a sea-gull.... No, that's not it. I am an actress. Oh, well! (*Hearing* MADAME ARKÁDIN *and* TRIGÓRIN *laughing, she lis-* 570 *tens, then runs to door on left and looks through the keyhole.*) He is here too.... (*Turning back to* TRÉPLEV) Oh, well... it doesn't matter... no. ... He did not believe in the stage, he always laughed at my dreams, and little by little 575 I left off believing in it too, and lost heart.... And then I was fretted by love and jealousy, and continually anxious over my little one.... I grew petty and trivial, I acted stupidly.... I did not know what to do with my 580 arms, I did not know how to stand on the stage, could not control my voice. You can't understand what it feels like when one knows one is acting disgracefully. I am a sea-gull. No, that's not it.... Do you remember 585 you shot a sea-gull? A man came by chance, saw it and, just to pass the time, destroyed it. ... A subject for a short story.[1]... That's not it, though. (*Rubs her forehead.*) What was I saying?... I am talking of the stage. 590 Now I am not like that. I am a real actress, I act with enjoyment, with enthusiasm, I am intoxicated when I am on the stage and feel that I am splendid. And since I have been here, I keep walking about and thinking, think- 595 ing and feeling that my soul is getting stronger every day. Now I know, I understand, Kostya, that in our work — in acting or writing — what matters is not fame, not glory, not what I dreamed of, but knowing how to be 600 patient. To bear one's cross and have faith. I have faith, and it all doesn't hurt so much; and when I think of my vocation, I am not afraid of life.

Trép. (mournfully). You have found 605 your path, you know which way you are going, but I am still floating in a chaos of dreams and images, not knowing what use it is to anyone. I have no faith and don't know what my vocation is. 610

Nína (listening). 'Sh-sh... I am going. Good-bye. When I become a great actress, come and look at me. Will you promise? But

[1] Cf. Act II, ll. 517–24.

now ... (*presses his hand*) it's late. I can hardly stand on my feet.... I am worn 615 out and hungry. . . .

Trép. Stay, I'll give you some supper.

Nína. No, no. . . . Don't see me off, I will go by myself. My horses are close by. . . . So she brought him with her? Well, it doesn't 620 matter. When you see Trigórin, don't say anything to him. . . . I love him! I love him even more than before. . . . A subject for a short story . . . I love him, I love him passionately, I love him to despair. It was nice 625 in the old days, Kostya! Do you remember? How clear, warm, joyous, and pure life was, what feelings we had — feelings like tender, exquisite flowers. . . . Do you remember? (*Recites.*) "Men, lions, eagles, and 630 partridges, horned deer, geese, spiders, silent fish that dwell in the water, star-fishes, and creatures which cannot be seen by the eye — all living things, all living things, all living things, have completed their cycle of 635 sorrow, are extinct. . . . For thousands of years the earth has borne no living creature on its surface, and this poor moon lights its lamp in vain. On the meadow the cranes no longer waken with a cry and there is no sound 640 of the May beetles in the lime trees . . ." [1]

(*Impulsively embraces* TRÉPLEV *and runs out by the glass door.*)

Trép. (*after a pause*). It will be a pity if someone meets her in the garden and tells mother. It may upset mother. . . .

> (*He spends two minutes in tearing up all his manuscripts and throwing them under the table; then unlocks the door on right and goes out.*)

Dorn (*trying to open the door on left*). 645 Strange. The door seems to be locked . . . (*Comes in and puts the armchair in its place.*) An obstacle race.

---

[1] Nína's opening speech in Tréplev's play, which was performed in the early part of Act I. That had been her maiden appearance as an actress.

Enter MADAME ARKÁDIN *and* POLÍNA ANDRÉYEVNA, *behind them* YÁKOV *carrying a tray with bottles;* MÁSHA; *then* SHAMRÁEV *and* TRIGÓRIN

Mad. Ark. Put the claret and the beer for Bóris Alexéyevitch here on the table. 650 We will play as we drink it. Let us sit down, friends.

Pol. (*to* YÁKOV). Bring tea too at the same time.

> (*Lights the candles and sits down to the card-table.*)

Sham. (*leads* TRIGÓRIN *to the cupboard*). 655 Here's the thing I was speaking about just now. (*Takes the stuffed sea-gull from the cupboard.*) This is what you ordered.

Trig. (*looking at the sea-gull*). I don't remember it. (*Musing*) I don't remember. 660

> (*The sound of a shot coming from right of stage; everyone starts.*)

Mad. Ark. (*frightened*). What's that?

Dorn. That's nothing. It must be something in my medicine-chest that has gone off. Don't be anxious. (*Goes out at door on right, comes back in half a minute.*) That's 665 what it is. A bottle of ether has exploded. (*Hums.*) "I stand before thee enchanted again. . . ."

Mad. Ark. (*sitting down to the table*). Ough, how frightened I was. It reminded me 670 of how . . . (*Hides her face in her hands.*) It made me quite dizzy. . . .

Dorn (*turning over the leaves of the magazine; to* TRIGÓRIN). There was an article in this two months ago — a letter from America 675 — and I wanted to ask you, among other things (*puts his arm round* TRIGÓRIN'S *waist and leads him to the footlights*) as I am very much interested in the question. . . . (*In a lower tone, dropping his voice*) Get Iρίna Nikoláyevna 680 away somehow. The fact is, Kónstantin Gavrílitch has shot himself. . . .

Curtain

INTRODUCTION TO

The Admirable Crichton

The Decline and Rise of the English Drama in the Nineteenth Century:
Barrie and the Comedy of Fancy

THE DECLINE AND RISE OF THE ENGLISH DRAMA IN THE
NINETEENTH CENTURY

THE ENGLISH THEATER reached in the early nineteenth century its lowest ebb since Queen Elizabeth's accession. It gave up almost all pretension to art and catered to the indiscriminate tastes of a largely bourgeois audience. Up to 1843, when an act of Parliament abolished the monopoly, "legitimate" drama could be performed in London only at the huge Drury Lane and Covent Garden Theaters. Suburban playhouses like Sadler's Wells offered, however, during the summer regular plays in addition to their customary program of burlettas, tight-rope dancing, trick animals, and water-tank battles. With the abolition of the London theatrical monopoly dramatic entertainment at once rose in quantity, but not in quality. The only plays of the first half of the century which have survived in any modern professional repertoire are *The Lady of Lyons* (1838) and *Richelieu* (1839), melodramas in blank verse by the well-known novelist Edward Bulwer, Lord Lytton (1803–73).

During the later Victorian period English playwriting began to show a return of artistic vitality. T. W. Robertson (1829–71) created a lively though rather too wholesome "cup and saucer" comedy with *Society* (1865) and *Caste* (1867), pieces still occasionally acted. The famous light operas of W. S. Gilbert (1836–1911) and Arthur Sullivan (1842–1900), such as *H.M.S. Pinafore* (1878) and *The Mikado* (1885), introduced satire of contemporary institutions and paved the way for a more searching criticism of national life on the stage. Ibsen's influence at the opening of the 'nineties gave impetus to this trend. Arthur Pinero (1855–1934) proceeded to make fashionable a drama of serious social import, starting with *The Second Mrs. Tanqueray* (1893) and continuing with well-made but superficial plays like *The Notorious Mrs. Ebbsmith* (1895), *Iris* (1901), and *Mid-Channel* (1909). At the same time Oscar Wilde (1854–1900) applied technical craft to a lighter vein and resuscitated the English comedy of manners, which had lapsed since Sheridan. The sparkling dialogue of *Lady Windermere's Fan* (1892), *A Woman of No Importance* (1893), and *The Importance of Being Earnest* (1895) has sufficiently obscured their silly plots to keep them on the boards ever since.

It took an Irishman resident in London, George Bernard Shaw (1856–1950), to sweep out of the English theater the last vestiges of "the sweet-shop view," as he aptly termed it. By his dramatic criticism in the *Saturday Review*, 1895–98, and his early playwriting he drove public, critics, and producers alike to a concern for the intellectual dignity of the stage.   As a dramatist he got his first hearings through J. T. Grein's Independent Theater, dedicated to Ibsen and active in London and the provinces, 1891–97.   A "pleasant" satire on war, *Arms and the Man* (1894), was his initial success.   In 1898 he caused a sensation by issuing his maiden volumes of dramatic work with detailed stage directions, and with lengthy prefaces as "first aid to critics."   His unorthodox texts did much to re-establish drama as literature and to popularize the reading of plays.

For over half a century Shaw exposed the shams and lies of modern civilization in a prolific output of brilliantly argumentative drama which ranges through history, politics, science, religion, art, economics, and sociology.   The astonishing wit and the theatrical deftness of his more notable comedies, *Candida* (1895), *You Never Can Tell* (1896), *Caesar and Cleopatra* (1897), *Man and Superman* (1901), *Major Barbara* (1905), *The Doctor's Dilemma* (1906), *Pygmalion* (1912), revolutionized English taste.   They made theater-goers enjoy the blasting of cherished idols and illusions on the stage.   Though Shaw's temperament preferred intellect to emotion and dialectics to characterization, one of his finest and most serious achievements, *Saint Joan* (1923), reveals the imaginative sympathy associated with great dramatic genius.   He was the first English-speaking playwright to be honored with the Nobel Prize for Literature.   That award in 1926 came as a recognition of his pre-eminence among modern British dramatists.

BARRIE AND THE COMEDY OF FANCY

According to Shaw, however, "the final relegation of the nineteenth-century London theater to the dust-bin" resulted from the playwriting of a Scotsman, Sir James Matthew Barrie.   Born at Kirriemuir, Forfarshire, on May 7, 1860, he was one of ten children in a humble weaver's family.   His mother from the beginning encouraged his interest in books.   At thirteen he went to live with his brother Alexander, a teacher at Dumfries Academy.   During his five years as a schoolboy there he not only acted in the productions of the dramatics club, but wrote *Bandelero the Bandit* and several other plays for the academy stage.   From 1878 to 1882 he studied for an M.A. in literature at Edinburgh University.   While a collegian, he often attended the theater to review plays for *The Evening Courant*.   After the university he joined the staff of a Nottingham newspaper, and then in March, 1885, moved on to London as a free-lance journalist.   Within a few years his delightful sketches of Scottish weavers and village life, collected in *Auld Licht Idylls* (1888) and *A Window in Thrums* (1889), put him at the head of the then popular group of Scottish writers known as the "Kailyard School."

By the spring of 1891 the Ibsen cult in London had grown extremely zealous, much to the amusement of Barrie and certain theatrical folk.   After a production of *Hedda Gabler* in April, J. L. Toole, the city's leading comedian, persuaded Barrie to concoct a burlesque on Ibsen's work, entitled *Ibsen's Ghost, or Toole up-to-date: Hedda in one act*. It portrayed Thea Elvsted, married to Tesman after Hedda's suicide, killing herself with a toy popgun at the final curtain.   Barrie intended his uproarious satire as purely theatrical fun; he was expressing no personal reaction against Ibsen, whom he later praised as "the mightiest craftsman that ever wrote for our kind friends in front." The success of *Ibsen's Ghost* spurred Barrie to compose *Walker, London* (1892), and *The Professor's Love Story* (1892), stage "hits" but very thin art.   Now a famous man on both sides of the Atlantic, he visited the United States in the autumn of 1896 to meet the noted producer, Charles Frohman, and the latter's chief actress, Maude Adams. The trio soon formed an ideal partnership which lasted until Frohman's death in the *Lusitania* sinking twenty years afterward. Barrie's dramatization of his already popular novel, *The Little Minister*, enjoyed with Miss Adams' starring a tremendous success in New York during 1897–98. Thenceforth he devoted himself chiefly to the theater, but he felt inspired at such irregular intervals that he produced only a handful of memorable full-length plays: *Quality Street* (1901), a gentle comedy of the Napoleonic period; *The Admirable Crichton* (1902); *Peter Pan* (1904), a boy's fairy tale, revived annually in London as Christmas entertainment; *What Every Woman Knows* (1908), an amusing demonstration of woman's superior understanding; *Dear Brutus* (1917), a "Midsummer Night's Dream" on the theme of man's desire for a second chance.

Barrie's playwriting brought him high public esteem. He received a baronetcy in 1913, and the Order of Merit in 1922. Two of the Scottish universities elected him as their honorary head, St. Andrews making him its rector in 1922 and Edinburgh its chancellor in 1930. For a quarter-century he occupied an apartment in Adelphi Terrace on the Thames Embankment, London, just across the street from Bernard Shaw. The two literary notables lived on the most intimate terms with each other, often holding window conversations even in the dead of night. Once, when the Shaws were giving a dinner party, Barrie in boyish sport tossed a piece of bread through their open dining-room window. Shaw, holding the bread up to view, called out to Barrie and asked him if it were manna from Heaven!

Barrie's career ended on a rather sad note of anticlimax. Utterly charmed by Elisabeth Bergner on first sight of her acting in 1934, he asked to write a play for her. She suggested that he fashion a play out of the Biblical narrative of King David's youth. The resulting creation entitled *The Boy David* aroused, despite the brilliant Miss Bergner as the hero, only mild applause during a very short London run in December, 1936. Six months later, on June 19, 1937, Barrie, broken by the disappointment, died. He left behind an estate of $865,000 to prove him as canny as the proverbial Scotsman.

The plays of Barrie occupy an altogether unique place in world drama, though at moments they suggest the magic and romance of such Elizabethan comedy as Greene's *James IV* and Shakespeare's *The Tempest*. Barrie shared with these distant predecessors the gift for humorous fantasy. It was, so he said, "the fanciful half" of him, called M'Connachie, who did the playwriting. For M'Connachie "beauty boils over and then spirits are abroad." His elfin temperament imparted to the Barrie drama a distinctive airy levity. The pervading fancy, however, did not spring from the genius of a mere Peter Pan, "the boy who would not grow up." It is colored at every turn by a tender and mildly satirical attitude which only mature insight into life can produce. Barrie found mankind in essence lovable, but in particulars amusing. Sometimes, to be sure, he treated men and women with too much delicacy, indeed, with sentimentality. Yet the keen understanding of human nature and the gay, innocent, fantastic humor give to Barrie's comedy at its best a charm that cannot be surpassed.

"THE ADMIRABLE CRICHTON"

The Admirable Crichton Barrie for many years thought his masterpiece. It had its premiere at the Duke of York's Theater, London, on November 4, 1902, with the

English stars, Henry Irving, Gerald du Maurier, and Irene Vanburgh, in the rôles of Crichton the butler, The Hon. Ernest Woolley, and Lady Mary. London welcomed the "fantasy" (the programme's description) with such acclaim that it ran until the following September. Then there ensued a long engagement in New York and around the United States with the famous William Gillette as Crichton. Barrie delayed publication of the play until 1914, when, following Shaw's example, he printed it with lavish stage directions. Their incomparable humor gives to the printed text a flavor which performance can never supply. No other playwright has equaled Barrie in the felicity of his running comment.

The plot of *The Admirable Crichton,* according to Sir Arthur Conan Doyle, developed from his suggestion to Barrie of a story about a master and his man cast away on a desert island where the man would become master. The opening scene, wherein Lord Loam holds one of his monthly teas for the domestics, grew out of Barrie's hearing in 1899 that the radical Countess of Carlisle, sister to the Earl of Airlie who was the Kirriemuir "laird," entertained her servants in the drawing-room. A typical flash of whimsy inspired Barrie to name both his comedy and its hero, the "perfect butler," after one of his favorite Scottish figures, James Crichton (1560–85?), who was born in Barrie's countryside and later surnamed "The Admirable" for remarkable learning.

The most colorful portions of *The Admirable Crichton* are, of course, the scenes on the desert island in the Pacific. These constituted Barrie's first experiment with the device of "slipping in an island," as he phrased it, a device which he afterward used again and again. He confessed in his rectoral address to the St. Andrews undergraduates that he had a real "greed for islands." "I should feel as if I had left off my clothing, if I were to write without an island," he remarked on another occasion. Island settings permitted him to indulge his love for testing out life and man in fancy's laboratory where no restrictions upon circumstance exist. The contrasting environments of Mayfair and the island in *The Admirable Crichton* make possible a delightful exposure of the more essential and dramatic relations which always exist beneath society's veneer.

Though Barrie built *The Admirable Crichton* around the theme of human equality and pointedly demonstrated the absence of equality either in society or in Nature, he was not too much concerned with this intellectual framework. Light-hearted satire of human nature rather than social criticism is the dominant note. *The Admirable Crichton* differs from perhaps all other Barrie plays in that it contains no touches of sentimentalism or pathos. It concentrates throughout upon depicting of what humorous stuff we mortals are composed with our vanities, our cares, and above all, our repetitious patterns of emotion. The superb pantomime of the pot scene at the end of Act II displays the universal and absurd behavior of humanity in the grip of hunger. The courting scene between Crichton and Lady Mary in the third act throws into high relief the ridiculous sameness of every mating between civilized man and woman. Barrie's ridicule holds no trace of condemnation, but on the contrary, a gleeful chuckle that men can be such jolly entertainment for their fellows. It is this tone of impish playfulness which gives a peculiar distinction to the comedy of *The Admirable Crichton.*

[For further study, see J. M. Barrie, *The Greenwood Hat* (1934); Sir John Hammerton, *Barrie, The Story of a Genius* (1928); W. A. Darlington, *J. M. Barrie* (1938); Denis Mackail, *Barrie, The Story of J.M.B.* (1941).]

J. M. BARRIE

The Admirable Crichton

A Comedy

DRAMATIS PERSONAE

(In the order of their appearance)

HON. ERNEST WOOLLEY, *nephew of the*
  EARL OF LOAM
CRICHTON, *the* EARL OF LOAM'S *butler*
LADY AGATHA LASENBY ⎱ *daughters of*
LADY CATHERINE LASENBY ⎰ *the* EARL
LADY MARY LASENBY ⎰ OF LOAM
REV. JOHN TREHERNE
THE EARL OF LOAM
LORD BROCKLEHURST
MRS. PERKINS, *the* EARL OF LOAM'S *house-*
  keeper
FLEURY, *the chef*
ROLLESTON, *the valet*
TOMPSETT, *the coachman*

FISHER, LADY MARY'S *maid*
SIMMONS, *a maid*
JEANNE, *a maid*
THOMAS, *the first footman*
JOHN, *the second footman*
JANE, *a parlor maid*
GLADYS, *another parlor maid*
"TWEENY," *a kitchen maid*
A Stable-Boy
A Page
A Naval Officer
THE COUNTESS OF BROCKLEHURST, *mother*
  of LORD BROCKLEHURST

ACT I

AT LOAM HOUSE, MAYFAIR [1]

A moment before the curtain rises, the Honorable Ernest Woolley drives up to the door of Loam House in Mayfair. There is a happy smile on his pleasant, insignificant face, and this presumably means that he is thinking of himself. He is too busy over nothing, this man about town, to be always thinking of himself, but, on the other hand, he almost never thinks of any other person. Probably Ernest's great moment is when he wakes of a morning and realizes that he really is Ernest, for we must all wish to be that which is our ideal. We can conceive him springing out of bed light-heartedly and waiting for his man to do the rest. He is dressed in excellent taste, with just the little bit more which shows that he is not without a sense of humor: the dandiacal are often saved by carrying a smile at the whole thing in their spats, let us say. Ernest left Cambridge the other day, a member of the Athenaeum (which he would be sorry to have you confound with a club in London of the same name). He is a bachelor, but not of arts, no mean epigrammatist (as you shall see), and a favorite of the ladies. He is almost a celebrity in restaurants, where he dines frequently, returning to sup; and during this last year he has proba-

[1] London's fashionable residential district east of Hyde Park; so called from a fair held there in May of each year prior to the early eighteenth century.

bly paid as much in them for the privilege of handing his hat to an attendant as the rent of a workingman's flat. He complains brightly that he is hard up, and that if somebody or other at Westminster [1] does not look out, the country will go to the dogs. He is no fool. He has the shrewdness to float with the current because it is a labor-saving process, but he has sufficient pluck to fight, if fight he must (a brief contest, for he would soon be toppled over). He has a light nature, which would enable him to bob up cheerily in new conditions and return unaltered to the old ones. His selfishness is his most endearing quality. If he has his way he will spend his life like a cat in pushing his betters out of the soft places, and until he is old he will be fondled in the process.

He gives his hat to one footman and his cane to another, and mounts the great staircase unassisted and undirected. As a nephew of the house he need show no credentials even to Crichton, who is guarding a door above.

It would not be good taste to describe Crichton, who is only a servant; if to the scandal of all good houses he is to stand out as a figure in the play, he must do it on his own, as they say in the pantry and the boudoir. We are not going to help him. We have had misgivings ever since we found his name in the title, and we shall keep him out of his rights as long as we can. Even though we softened to him he would not be a hero in these clothes of servitude; and he loves his clothes. How to get him out of them? It would require a cataclysm. To be an indoor servant at all is to Crichton a badge of honor; to be a butler at thirty is the realization of his proudest ambitions. He is devotedly attached to his master, who, in his opinion, has but one fault, he is not sufficiently contemptuous of his inferiors. We are immediately to be introduced to this solitary failing of a great English peer.

This perfect butler, then, opens a door, and ushers Ernest into a certain room. At the same moment the curtain rises on this room, and the play begins.

It is one of several reception-rooms in Loam House, not the most magnificent but quite the softest; and of a warm afternoon all that those who are anybody crave for is the softest. The larger rooms are magnificent and bare, carpetless, so that it is an accomplishment to keep one's feet on them; they are sometimes lent for charitable purposes; they are also all in use on the night of a dinner-party, when you may find yourself alone in one, having taken a wrong turning; or alone, save for two others who are within hailing distance. This room, however, is comparatively small and very soft. There are so many cushions in it that you wonder why, if you are an outsider and don't know that it needs six cushions to make one fair head comfy. The couches themselves are cushions as large as beds, and there is an art of sinking into them and of waiting to be helped out of them. There are several famous paintings on the walls, of which you may say "Jolly thing that," without losing caste as knowing too much; and in cases there are glorious miniatures, but the daughters of the house cannot tell you of whom; "there is a catalogue somewhere." There are a thousand or so of roses in basins, several library novels, and a row of weekly illustrated newspapers lying against each other like fallen soldiers. If anyone disturbs this row Crichton seems to know of it from afar and appears noiselessly and replaces the wanderer. One thing unexpected in such a room is a great array of tea things. Ernest spots them with a twinkle, and has his epigram at once unsheathed. He dallies, however, before delivering the thrust.

[1] Houses of Parliament in the Borough of Westminster, London.

Ern. I perceive, from the tea cups, Crichton, that the great function is to take place here.

Crich. (*with a respectful sigh*). Yes, sir.

Ern. (*chuckling heartlessly*). The serv- 5 ants' hall coming up to have tea in the drawing-room! (*With terrible sarcasm*) No wonder you look happy, Crichton.

Crich. (*under the knife*). No, sir.

Ern. Do you know, Crichton, I think 10 that with an effort you might look even happier. (CRICHTON *smiles wanly.*) You don't approve of his lordship's compelling his servants to be his equals — once a month?

Crich. It is not for me, sir, to disap- 15 prove of his lordship's Radical views.

Ern. Certainly not. And, after all, it is only once a month that he is affable to you.

Crich. On all other days of the month, sir, his lordship's treatment of us is everything 20 that could be desired.

Ern. (*This is the epigram.*) Tea cups! Life, Crichton, is like a cup of tea; the more heartily we drink, the sooner we reach the dregs. 25

Crich. (*obediently*). Thank you, sir.

Ern. (*becoming confidential, as we do when we have need of an ally*). Crichton, in case I should be asked to say a few words to the servants, I have strung together a little speech. (*His hand strays to his pocket.*) I was 30 wondering where I should stand.

> (*He tries various places and postures, and comes to rest leaning over a high chair, whence, in dumb show, he addresses a gathering.* CRICHTON, *with the best intentions, gives him a footstool to stand on, and departs, happily unconscious that* ERNEST *in some dudgeon has kicked the footstool across the room.*)

Ern. (*addressing an imaginary audience, and desirous of startling them at once*). Suppose you were all little fishes at the bottom of the sea ——

> (*He is not quite satisfied with his position, though sure that the fault must lie with the chair for being too high, not with him for being too short.*

CRICHTON'S *suggestion was not perhaps a bad one after all. He lifts the stool, but hastily conceals it behind him on the entrance of the* LADIES CATHERINE *and* AGATHA, *two daughters of the house.* CATHERINE *is twenty, and* AGATHA *two years younger. They are very fashionable young women indeed, who might wake up for a dance, but they are very lazy,* CATHERINE *being two years lazier than* AGATHA.

Ern. (*uneasily jocular, because he is concealing the footstool*). And how are my little 35 friends today?

Aga. (*contriving to reach a settee*). Don't be silly, Ernest. If you want to know how we are, we are dead. Even to think of entertaining the servants is so exhausting. 40

Cath. (*subsiding nearer the door*). Besides which, we have had to decide what frocks to take with us on the yacht, and that is such a mental strain.

Ern. You poor overworked things. 45 (*Evidently* AGATHA *is his favorite, for he helps her to put her feet on the settee, while* CATHERINE *has to dispose of her own feet.*) Rest your weary limbs.

Cath. (*perhaps in revenge*). But why have you a footstool in your hand?

Aga. Yes? 50

Ern. Why? (*Brilliantly; but to be sure he has had time to think it out*) You see, as the servants are to be the guests I must be butler. I was practicing. This is a tray, observe.

> (*Holding the footstool as a tray, he minces across the room like an accomplished footman. The gods favor him, for just here* LADY MARY *enters, and he holds out the footstool to her.*)

Tea, my lady? 55

LADY MARY *is a beautiful creature of twenty-two, and is of a natural hauteur which is at once the fury and the envy of her sisters. If she chooses she can make you seem so insignificant that you feel you might be swept away with the crumb-brush. She seldom chooses, because of the trouble of preening* herself as she does it; she is usually content to show that you merely tire her eyes. She often seems to be about to go to sleep in the middle of a remark: there is quite a long and anxious pause, and then she continues, like a clock that hesitates, bored in the middle of its strike.

Lady Mary (arching her brows). It is only you, Ernest; I thought there was someone here (*and she also bestows herself on cushions*).

Ern. (a little piqued, and deserting the footstool). Had a very tiring day also, Mary?

Lady Mary (yawning). Dreadfully. Been trying on engagement-rings all the morning. 60

Ern. (who is as fond of gossip as the oldest club member). What's that? (*To* AGATHA) Is it Brocklehurst? (*The energetic* AGATHA *nods.*) You have given your warm young heart to Brocky? (LADY MARY *is impervious to his humor, but he continues bravely.*) I don't 65 wish to fatigue you, Mary, by insisting on a verbal answer, but if, without straining yourself, you can signify Yes or No, won't you make the effort? (*She indolently flashes a ring on her most important finger, and he starts back melodramatically.*) The ring! Then I am too 70 late, too late! (*Fixing* LADY MARY *sternly, like a prosecuting counsel*) May I ask, Mary, does Brocky know? Of course, it was that terrible mother of his who pulled this through. Mother does everything for Brocky. Still, in the 75 eyes of the law you will be, not her wife, but his, and, therefore, I hold that Brocky ought to be informed. Now —— (*He discovers that their languorous eyes have closed.*) If you girls are shamming sleep in the expectation 80 that I shall awaken you in the manner beloved of ladies, abandon all such hopes.

(CATHERINE *and* AGATHA *look up without speaking.*)

Lady Mary (speaking without looking up). You impertinent boy.

Ern. (eagerly plucking another epigram from his quiver). I knew that was it, though I don't know everything. Agatha, I'm not 85 young enough to know everything.

(*He looks hopefully from one to another, but though they try to grasp this, his brilliance baffles them.*

Aga. (his secret admirer). Young enough?

Ern. (encouragingly). Don't you see? I'm not young enough to know everything.

Aga. I'm sure it's awfully clever, but 90 it's so puzzling.

Here CRICHTON *ushers in an athletic, pleasant-faced young clergyman,* MR. TREHERNE, *who greets the company*

Cath. Ernest, say it to Mr. Treherne.

Ern. Look here, Treherne, I'm not young enough to know everything.

Tre. How do you mean, Ernest? 95

Ern. (a little nettled). I mean what I say.

Lady Mary. Say it again; say it more slowly.

Ern. I'm — not — young — enough — to — know — everything.

Tre. I see. What you really mean, my 100 boy, is that you are not old enough to know everything.

Ern. No, I don't.

Tre. I assure you that's it.

Lady Mary. Of course it is. 105

Cath. Yes, Ernest, that's it.

(ERNEST, *in desperation, appeals to* CRICHTON.

Ern. I am not young enough, Crichton, to know everything.

(*It is an anxious moment, but a smile is at length extorted from* CRICHTON *as with a corkscrew.*

Crich. Thank you, sir. (*He goes.*

Ern. (relieved). Ah, if you had that 110 fellow's head, Treherne, you would find something better to do with it than play cricket. I hear you bowl with your head.

Tre. (with proper humility). I'm afraid cricket is all I'm good for, Ernest. 115

Cath. (who thinks he has a heavenly nose). Indeed, it isn't. You are sure to get on, Mr. Treherne.

Tre. Thank you, Lady Catherine.

Cath. But it was the bishop who told me so. He said a clergyman who breaks both 120 ways is sure to get on in England.

Tre. I'm jolly glad.

The master of the house comes in, accompanied by LORD BROCKLEHURST. *The* EARL OF LOAM *is a widower, a philanthropist, and a peer of advanced ideas. As a widower he is at least able to interfere in the domestic concerns of his house — to rummage in the drawers, so to speak, for which he has felt an itching all his blameless life; his philanthropy has opened quite a number of other drawers to him; and his advanced ideas have blown out his figure. He takes in all the weightiest monthly reviews, and prefers those that are uncut, because he perhaps never looks better than when cutting them; but he does not read them, and save for the cutting it would suit him as well merely to take in the covers. He writes letters to the papers, which are printed in a type to scale with himself, and he is very jealous of those other correspondents who get his type. Let laws and learning, art and commerce die, but leave the big type to an intellectual aristocracy. He is really the reformed House of Lords which will come some day.*

Young LORD BROCKLEHURST is nothing save for his rank. You could pick him up by the handful any day in Piccadilly or Holborn, buying socks — or selling them.

Lord Loam (*expansively*). You are here, Ernest. Feeling fit for the voyage, Treherne?

Tre. Looking forward to it enormously. 125

Lord Loam. That's right. (*He chases his children about as if they were chickens.*) Now then, Mary, up and doing, up and doing. Time we had the servants in. They enjoy it so much. 130

Lady Mary. They hate it.

Lord Loam. Mary, to your duties.

(*And he points severely to the tea-table.*

Ern. (*twinkling*). Congratulations, Brocky.

Lord Brock. (*who detests humor*). Thanks.

Ern. Mother pleased? 135

Lord Brock. (*with dignity*). Mother is very pleased.

Ern. That's good. Do you go on the yacht with us?

Lord Brock. Sorry I can't. And look 140 here, Ernest, I will *not* be called Brocky.

Ern. Mother don't like it?

Lord Brock. She does not.

(*He leaves ERNEST, who forgives him and begins to think about his speech.*

CRICHTON *enters*

Lord Loam (*speaking as one man to another*). We are quite ready, Crichton.

(CRICHTON *is distressed.*

Lady Mary (*sarcastically*). How Crich- 145 ton enjoys it!

Lord Loam (*frowning*). He is the only one who doesn't; pitiful creature.

Crich. (*shuddering under his lord's displeasure*). I can't help being a Conservative, my lord. 150

Lord Loam. Be a man, Crichton. You are the same flesh and blood as myself.

Crich. (*in pain*). Oh, my lord!

Lord Loam (*sharply*). Show them in; and, by the way, they were not all here last 155 time.

Crich. All, my lord, except the merest trifles.

Lord Loam. It must be everyone. (*Lowering*) And remember this, Crichton, for the time being you are my equal. (*Testily*) 160 I shall soon show you whether you are not my equal. Do as you are told. (*Crichton departs to obey, and his lordship is now a general. He has no pity for his daughters, and uses a terrible threat.*) And girls, remember, no condescension. The first who condescends recites. (*This sends them scurrying to their labors.*) By 165 the way, Brocklehurst, can you do anything?

Lord Brock. How do you mean?

Lord Loam. Can you do anything — with a penny or a handkerchief, make them disappear, for instance? 170

Lord Brock. Good heavens, no.

Lord Loam. It's a pity. Everyone in our position ought to be able to do something. Ernest, I shall probably ask you to say a few words; something bright and sparkling. 175

Ern. But, my dear uncle, I have prepared nothing.

Lord Loam. Anything impromptu will do.

Ern. Oh — well — if anything strikes me on the spur of the moment. 180

(*He unostentatiously gets the footstool into position behind the chair. CRICHTON reappears to announce the guests, of whom the first is the housekeeper*

Crich. (*reluctantly*). Mrs. Perkins.

Lord Loam (*shaking hands*). Very delighted, Mrs. Perkins. Mary, our friend, Mrs. Perkins.

Lady Mary. How do you do, Mrs. 185 Perkins? Won't you sit here?

Lord Loam (*threateningly*). Agatha!

Aga. (*hastily*). How do you do? Won't you sit down?   189

Lord Loam (*introducing*). Lord Brocklehurst — my valued friend, Mrs. Perkins.

> (LORD BROCKLEHURST *bows and escapes.* *He has to fall back on* ERNEST.

Lord Brock. For heaven's sake, Ernest, don't leave me for a moment; this sort of thing is utterly opposed to all my principles.

Ern. (*airily*). You stick to me, Brocky, 195 and I'll pull you through.

Crich. Monsieur Fleury.

Ern. The chef.

Lord Loam (*shaking hands with the chef*). Very charmed to see you, Monsieur Fleury.

Fleu. Thank you very much.   200

> (FLEURY *bows to* AGATHA, *who is not effusive.*

Lord Loam (*warningly*). Agatha — recitation!

> (*She tosses her head, but immediately finds a seat and tea for* M. FLEURY. TREHERNE *and* ERNEST *move about, making themselves amiable.* LADY MARY *is presiding at the tea-tray.*

Crich. Mr. Rolleston.

Lord Loam (*shaking hands with his valet*). How do you do, Rolleston?

> (CATHERINE *looks after the wants of* ROLLESTON.

Crich. Mr. Tompsett.   205

> (TOMPSETT, *the coachman, is received with honors, from which he shrinks.*

Crich. Miss Fisher.

> (*This superb creature is no less than* LADY MARY'S *maid, and even* LORD LOAM *is a little nervous.*

Lord Loam. This is a pleasure, Miss Fisher.

Ern. (*unabashed*). If I might venture, Miss Fisher (*and he takes her unto himself*).

Crich. Miss Simmons.   210

Lord Loam (*to* CATHERINE'S *maid*). You are always welcome, Miss Simmons.

Ern. (*perhaps to kindle jealousy in* MISS FISHER). At last we meet. Won't you sit down?

Crich. Mademoiselle Jeanne.   215

Lord Loam. Charmed to see you, Mademoiselle Jeanne.

> (*A place is found for* AGATHA'S *maid, and the scene is now an animated one; but still our host thinks his girls are not sufficiently sociable.* *He frowns on* LADY MARY.

Lady Mary (*in alarm*). Mr. Treherne, this is Fisher, my maid.

Lord Loam (*sharply*). Your what, Mary?

Lady Mary. My friend.   221

Crich. Thomas.

Lord Loam. How do you do, Thomas?

> (*The first footman gives him a reluctant hand.*

Crich. John.

Lord Loam. How do you do, John?   225

> (ERNEST *signs to* LORD BROCKLEHURST, *who hastens to him.*

Ern. (*introducing*). Brocklehurst, this is John. I think you have already met on the doorstep.

Crich. Jane.

> (*She comes, wrapping her hands miserably in her apron.*

Lord Loam (*doggedly*). Give me your 230 hand, Jane.

Crich. Gladys.

Ern. How do you do, Gladys. You know my uncle?

Lord Loam. Your hand, Gladys.   235

> (*He bestows her on* AGATHA.

Crich. Tweeny.

> (*She is a very humble and frightened kitchenmaid, of whom we are to see more.*

Lord Loam. So happy to see you.

Fish. John, I saw you talking to Lord Brocklehurst just now; introduce me.

Lord Brock. (*at the same moment to* ERNEST). That's an uncommon pretty girl; if I 240 must feed one of them, Ernest, that's the one.

> (*But* ERNEST *tries to part him and*

FISHER *as they are about to shake hands.*

Ern. No you don't, it won't do, Brocky. (*To* MISS FISHER) You are too pretty, my dear. Mother wouldn't like it. (*Discovering* TWEENY) Here's something safer. Charming girl, Brocky, dying to know you; let me introduce you. Tweeny, Lord Brocklehurst — Lord Brocklehurst, Tweeny.

(BROCKLEHURST *accepts his fate; but he still has an eye for* FISHER, *and something may come of this.*)

Lord Loam (*severely*). They are not all here, Crichton.   250

Crich. (*with a sigh*). Odds and ends.

A STABLE-BOY *and a* PAGE *are shown in, and for a moment no daughter of the house advances to them*

Lord Loam (*with a roving eye on his children*). Which is to recite?

(*The last of the company are, so to say, embraced.*)

Lord Loam (*to* TOMPSETT, *as they partake of tea together*). And how are all at home?

Tomp. Fairish, my lord, if 'tis the horses you are inquiring for?   255

Lord Loam. No, no, the family. How's the baby?

Tomp. Blooming, your lordship.

Lord Loam. A very fine boy. I remember saying so when I saw him; nice little fellow.   260

Tomp. (*not quite knowing whether to let it pass*). Beg pardon, my lord, it's a girl.

Lord Loam. A girl? Aha! ha! ha! exactly what I said. I distinctly remember saying, If it's spared it will be a girl.

(CRICHTON *now comes down.*)

Lord Loam. Very delighted to see you,   265 Crichton. (CRICHTON *has to shake hands.*) Mary, you know Mr. Crichton?

(*He wanders off in search of other prey.*)

Lady Mary. Milk and sugar, Crichton?

Crich. I'm ashamed to be seen talking to you, my lady.   270

Lady Mary. To such a perfect servant as you all this must be most distasteful. (CRICHTON *is too respectful to answer.*) Oh,

please to speak, or I shall have to recite. You do hate it, don't you?   275

Crich. It pains me, your ladyship. It disturbs the etiquette of the servants' hall. After last month's meeting the page-boy, in a burst of equality, called me Crichton. He was dismissed.   280

Lady Mary. I wonder — I really do — how you can remain with us.

Crich. I should have felt compelled to give notice, my lady, if the master had not had a seat in the Upper House. I cling to that.   285

Lady Mary. Do go on speaking. Tell me, what did Mr. Ernest mean by saying he was not young enough to know everything?

Crich. I have no idea, my lady.

Lady Mary. But you laughed.   290

Crich. My lady, he is the second son of a peer.

Lady Mary. Very proper sentiments. You are a good soul, Crichton.

Lord Brock. (*desperately to* TWEENY). And now tell me, have you been to the Opera?   296 What sort of weather have you been having in the kitchen? (TWEENY *gurgles.*) For heaven's sake, woman, be articulate.

Crich. (*still talking to* LADY MARY). No, my lady; his lordship may compel us to be   301 equal upstairs, but there will never be equality in the servants' hall.

Lord Loam (*overhearing this*). What's that? No equality? Can't you see, Crichton,   305 that our divisions into classes are artificial, that if we were to return to Nature, which is the aspiration of my life, all would be equal?

Crich. If I may make so bold as to contradict your lordship ——   310

Lord Loam (*with an effort*). Go on.

Crich. The divisions into classes, my lord, are not artificial. They are the natural outcome of a civilized society. (*To* LADY MARY) There must always be a master and   315 servants in all civilized communities, my lady, for it is natural, and whatever is natural is right.

Lord Loam (*wincing*). It is very unnatural for me to stand here and allow you to   320 talk such nonsense.

Crich. (*eagerly*). Yes, my lord, it is. That

is what I have been striving to point out to your lordship.

Aga. (*to* CATHERINE). What is the matter with Fisher? She is looking daggers.

Cath. The tedious creature; some question of etiquette, I suppose.

(*She sails across to* FISHER. How are you, Fisher?

Fisher (*with a toss of her head*). I am nothing, my lady, I am nothing at all.

Aga. Oh, dear, who says so?

Fisher (*affronted*). His lordship has asked that kitchen wench to have a second cup of tea.

Cath. But why not?

Fisher. If it pleases his lordship to offer it to *her* before offering it to *me* ——

Aga. So that is it. Do you want another cup of tea, Fisher?

Fisher. No, my lady — but my position — I should have been asked first.

Aga. Oh dear.

(*All this has taken some time, and by now the feeble appetites of the uncomfortable guests have been satiated. But they know there is still another ordeal to face — his lordship's monthly speech. Everyone awaits it with misgiving — the servants lest they should applaud, as last time, in the wrong place, and the daughters because he may be personal about them, as the time before.* ERNEST *is annoyed that there should be this speech at all when there is such a much better one coming, and* BROCKLEHURST *foresees the degradation of the peerage. All are thinking of themselves alone save* CRICHTON, *who knows his master's weakness, and fears he may stick in the middle.* LORD LOAM, *however, advances cheerfully to his doom. He sees* ERNEST'S *stool, and artfully stands on it, to his nephew's natural indignation. The three ladies knit their lips, the servants look down their noses, and the address begins.*

Lord Loam. My friends, I am glad to see you all looking so happy. It used to be predicted by the scoffer that these meetings would prove distasteful to you. Are they distasteful? I hear you laughing at the question. (*He has not heard them, but he hears them now, the watchful* CRICHTON *giving them a lead.*) No harm in saying that among us today is one who was formerly hostile to the movement, but who today has been won over. I refer to Lord Brocklehurst, who, I am sure, will presently say to me that if the charming lady now by his side has derived as much pleasure from his company as he has derived from hers, he will be more than satisfied. (*All look at* TWEENY, *who trembles.*) For the time being the artificial and unnatural — I say unnatural (*glaring at* CRICHTON, *who bows slightly*) — barriers of society are swept away. Would that they could be swept away forever. (*The* PAGE-BOY *cheers, and has the one moment of prominence in his life. He grows up, marries, and has children, but is never really heard of again.*) But that is entirely and utterly out of the question. And now for a few months we are to be separated. As you know, my daughters and Mr. Ernest and Mr. Treherne are to accompany me on my yacht, on a voyage to distant parts of the earth. In less than forty-eight hours we shall be under weigh. (*But for* CRICHTON'S *eye the reckless* PAGE-BOY *would repeat his success.*) Do not think our life on the yacht is to be one long idle holiday. My views on the excessive luxury of the day are well known, and what I preach I am resolved to practice. I have therefore decided that my daughters, instead of having one maid each as at present, shall on this voyage have but one maid between them.

(*Three maids rise; also three mistresses.*

Crich. My lord!

Lord Loam. My mind is made up.

Ern. I cordially agree.

Lord Loam. And now, my friends, I should like to think that there is some piece of advice I might give you, some thought, some noble saying over which you might ponder in my absence. In this connection I remember a proverb, which has had a great effect on my own life. I first heard it many years ago. I have never forgotten it. It constantly cheers and guides me. That proverb is — that proverb was — the proverb I speak of ——

(*He grows pale and taps his forehead.*

Lady Mary. Oh dear, I believe he has 390 forgotten it.

Lord Loam (*desperately*). The proverb — that proverb to which I refer —— (*Alas, it has gone. The distress is general. He has not even the sense to sit down. He gropes for the proverb in the air. They try applause, but it is no help.*) I have it now — (*not he*).

Lady Mary (*with confidence*). Crichton. 395

(*He does not fail her. As quietly as if he were in galoshes, mind as well as feet, he dismisses the domestics; they go according to precedence as they entered, yet, in a moment, they are gone. Then he signs to* MR. TRE-HERNE, *and they conduct* LORD LOAM *with dignity from the room. His hands are still catching flies; he still mutters, "The proverb — that proverb"; but he continues, owing to* CRICHTON'S *skillful treatment, to look every inch a peer. The ladies have now an opportunity to air their indignation.*

Lady Mary. One maid among three grown women!

Lord Brock. Mary, I think I had better go. That dreadful kitchenmaid ——

Lady Mary. I can't blame you, George. 400

(*He salutes her.*

Lord Brock. Your father's views are shocking to me, and I am glad I am not to be one of the party on the yacht. My respect for myself, Mary, my natural anxiety as to what mother will say. I shall see you, darling, 405 before you sail. (*He bows to the others and goes.*

Ern. Selfish brute, only thinking of himself. What about my speech?

Lady Mary. One maid among three of us. What's to be done? 410

Ern. Pooh! You must do for yourselves, that's all.

Lady Mary. Do for ourselves. How can we know where our things are kept?

Aga. Are you aware that dresses but- 415 ton up the back?

Cath. How are we to get into our shoes and be prepared for the carriage?

Lady Mary. Who is to put us to bed, and who is to get us up, and how shall we 420 ever know it's morning if there is no one to pull up the blinds?

(CRICHTON *crosses on his way out.*

Ern. How is his lordship now?

Crich. A little easier, sir.

Lady Mary. Crichton, send Fisher to me. 425

(*He goes.*

Ern. I have no pity for you girls, I ——

Lady Mary. Ernest, go away, and don't insult the broken-hearted.

Ern. And uncommon glad I am to go. Ta-ta, all of you. He asked me to say 430 a few words. I came here to say a few words, and I'm not at all sure that I couldn't bring an action against him.

(*He departs, feeling that he has left a dart behind him. The girls are alone with their tragic thoughts.*

Lady Mary (*become a mother to the younger ones at last*). My poor sisters, come here. (*They go to her doubtfully.*) We must 435 make this draw us closer together. I shall do my best to help you in every way. Just now I cannot think of myself at all.

Aga. But how unlike you, Mary.

Lady Mary. It is my duty to protect 440 my sisters.

Cath. I never knew her so sweet before, Agatha. (*Cautiously*) What do you propose to do, Mary?

Lady Mary. I propose when we are on 445 the yacht to lend Fisher to you when I don't need her myself.

Aga. Fisher?

Lady Mary (*who has the most character of the three*). Of course, as the eldest, I have decided that it is *my* maid we shall take with us. 450

Cath. (*speaking also for* AGATHA). Mary, you toad.

Aga. Nothing on earth would induce Fisher to lift her hand for either me or Catherine.

Lady Mary. I was afraid of it, Agatha. 455 That is why I am so sorry for you.

*The further exchange of pleasantries is
interrupted by the arrival of* FISHER

Lady Mary. Fisher, you heard what his
lordship said?

Fisher. Yes, my lady.

Lady Mary (*coldly, though the others would
have tried blandishment*). You have given 460
me some satisfaction of late, Fisher, and to
mark my approval I have decided that you
shall be the maid who accompanies us.

Fisher (*acidly*). I thank you, my lady.

Lady Mary. That is all; you may go. 465

Fisher (*rapping it out*). If you please, my
lady, I wish to give notice.

(CATHERINE *and* AGATHA *gleam, but*
LADY MARY *is of sterner stuff.*

Lady Mary (*taking up a book*). Oh, certainly
— you may go.

Cath. But why, Fisher?   470

Fisher. I could not undertake, my lady, to
wait upon three. *We* don't do it. (*In an indignant outburst to* LADY MARY) Oh, my lady,
to think that this affront ——

Lady Mary (*looking up*). I thought I 475
told you to go, Fisher.

(FISHER *stands for a moment irresolute; then goes. As soon as she has
gone* LADY MARY *puts down her
book and weeps. She is a pretty
woman, but this is the only pretty
thing we have seen her do yet.*

Aga. (*succinctly*). Serves you right.

(CRICHTON *comes.*

Cath. It will be Simmons after all. Send
Simmons to me.

Crich. (*after hesitating*). My lady, 480
might I venture to speak?

Cath. What is it?

Crich. I happen to know, your ladyship,
that Simmons desires to give notice for the
same reason as Fisher.   485

Cath. Oh!

Aga. (*triumphant*). Then, Catherine, we
take Jeanne.

Crich. And Jeanne also, my lady.

(LADY MARY *is reading, indifferent
though the heavens fall, but her
sisters are not ashamed to show their
despair to* CRICHTON.

Aga. We can't blame them. Could 490
any maid who respected herself be got to wait
upon three?

Lady Mary (*with languid interest*). I suppose
there are such persons, Crichton?

Crich. (*guardedly*). I have heard, my 495
lady, that there are such.

Lady Mary (*a little desperate*). Crichton,
what's to be done? We sail in two days; could
one be discovered in the time?

Aga. (*frankly a supplicant*). Surely 500
you can think of someone?

Crich. (*after hesitating*). There is in this
establishment, your ladyship, a young woman ——

Lady Mary. Yes?   505

Crich. A young woman, on whom I have for
some time cast an eye.

Cath. (*eagerly*). Do you mean as a possible
lady's-maid?

Crich. I had thought of her, my lady, 510
in another connection.

Lady Mary. Ah!

Crich. But I believe she is quite the young
person you require. Perhaps if you could see
her, my lady ——   515

Lady Mary. I shall certainly see her. Bring
her to me. (*He goes.*) You two needn't
wait.

Cath. Needn't we? We see your little game,
Mary.   520

Aga. We shall certainly remain and have our
two-thirds of her.

(*They sit there doggedly until* CRICH-
TON *returns with* TWEENY, *who
looks scared.*

Crich. This, my lady, is the young person.

Cath. (*frankly*). Oh dear!   524

(*It is evident that all three consider her
quite unsuitable.*

Lady Mary. Come here, girl. Don't be afraid.

(TWEENY *looks imploringly at her idol.*

Crich. Her appearance, my lady, is homely,
and her manners, as you may have observed,
deplorable, but she has a heart of gold.

Lady Mary. What is your position downstairs?   530

Twee. (*bobbing*). I'm a tweeny, your ladyship.

Cath. A what?

Crich. A tweeny; that is to say, my lady, she is not at present, strictly speaking, anything; a *between* maid; she helps the vegetable maid. It is she, my lady, who conveys the dishes from the one end of the kitchen table, where they are placed by the cook, to the other end, where they enter into the charge of Thomas and John.

Lady Mary. I see. And you and Crichton are — ah — keeping company?

(CRICHTON draws himself up.

Twee. (aghast). A butler don't keep company, my lady.

Lady Mary (indifferently). Does he not?

Crich. No, your ladyship, we butlers may — *(he makes a gesture with his arms)* — but we do not keep company.

Aga. I know what it is; you are engaged?

(TWEENY looks longingly at CRICHTON.

Crich. Certainly not, my lady. The utmost I can say at present is that I have cast a favorable eye.

(Even this is much to TWEENY.

Lady Mary. As you choose. But I am afraid, Crichton, she will not suit us.

Crich. My lady, beneath this simple exterior are concealed a very sweet nature and rare womanly gifts.

Aga. Unfortunately, that is not what we want.

Crich. And it is she, my lady, who dresses the hair of the ladies'-maids for our evening meals.

(The ladies are interested at last.

Lady Mary. She dresses Fisher's hair?

Twee. Yes, my lady, and I does them up when they goes to parties.

Crich. (pained, but not scolding). Does!

Twee. Doos. And it's me what alters your gowns to fit them.

Crich. What alters!

Twee. Which alters.

Aga. Mary?

Lady Mary. I shall certainly have her.

Cath. We shall certainly have her. Tweeny, we have decided to make a lady's-maid of you.

Twee. Oh lawks!

Aga. We are doing this for you so that your position socially may be more nearly akin to that of Crichton.

Crich. (gravely). It will undoubtedly increase the young person's chances.

Lady Mary. Then if I get a good character for you from Mrs. Perkins, she will make the necessary arrangements.

(She resumes reading.

Twee. (elated). My lady!

Lady Mary. By the way, I hope you are a good sailor.

Twee. (startled). You don't mean, my lady, I'm to go on the ship?

Lady Mary. Certainly.

Twee. But —— *(To CRICHTON)* You ain't going, sir?

Crich. No.

Twee. (firm at last). Then neither ain't I.

Aga. You must.

Twee. Leave him! Not me.

Lady Mary. Girl, don't be silly. Crichton will be — considered in your wages.

Twee. I ain't going.

Crich. I feared this, my lady.

Twee. Nothing'll budge me.

Lady Mary. Leave the room.

(CRICHTON shows TWEENY out with marked politeness.

Aga. Crichton, I think you might have shown more displeasure with her.

Crich. (contrite). I was touched, my lady. I see, my lady, that to part from her would be a wrench to me, though I could not well say so in her presence, not having yet decided how far I shall go with her.

He is about to go when LORD LOAM *returns, fuming*

Lord Loam. The ingrate! The smug! The fop!

Cath. What is it now, father?

Lord Loam. That man of mine, Rolleston, refuses to accompany us because you are to have but one maid.

Aga. Hurrah!

Lady Mary (in better taste). Darling father,

rather than you should lose Rolleston, we will consent to take all the three of them.   620

Lord Loam. Pooh, nonsense! Crichton, find me a valet who can do without three maids.

Crich. Yes, my lord. (*Troubled*) In the time — the more suitable the party, my lord, 625 the less willing will he be to come without the — the usual perquisites.

Lord Loam. Anyone will do.

Crich. (*shocked*). My lord!

Lord Loam. The ingrate! The puppy! 630
        (AGATHA *has an idea, and whispers to* LADY MARY.

Lady Mary. I ask a favor of a servant? — never!

Aga. Then I will. Crichton, would it not be very distressing to you to let his lordship go, attended by a valet who might prove 635 unworthy? It is only for three months; don't you think that you — you yourself — you —— (*As* CRICHTON *sees what she wants he pulls himself up with noble, offended dignity, and she is appalled.*) I beg your pardon.
                        (*He bows stiffly.*

Cath. (*to* CRICHTON). But think of the joy to Tweeny.   640
        (CRICHTON *is moved, but he shakes his head.*

Lady Mary (*so much the cleverest*). Crichton, do you think it safe to let the master you love go so far away without you while he has these dangerous views about equality?
        (CRICHTON *is profoundly stirred. After a struggle he goes to his master, who has been pacing the room.*

Crich. My lord, I have found a man.   645

Lord Loam. Already? Who is he? (CRICHTON *presents himself with a gesture.*) Yourself?

Cath. Father, how good of him.

Lord Loam (*pleased, but thinking it a small thing*). Uncommon good. Thank you, 650 Crichton. This helps me nicely out of a hole; and how it will annoy Rolleston! Come with me, and we shall tell him. Not that I think you have lowered yourself in any way. Come along.   655
        (*He goes, and* CRICHTON *is to fol-

low him, but is stopped by* AGATHA *impulsively offering him her hand.*

Crich. (*who is much shaken*). My lady — a valet's hand!

Aga. I had no idea you would feel it so deeply; why did you do it?
        (CRICHTON *is too respectful to reply.*

Lady Mary (*regarding him*). Crichton, 660 I am curious. I insist upon an answer.

Crich. My lady, I am the son of a butler and a lady's-maid — perhaps the happiest of all combinations, and to me the most beautiful thing in the world is a haughty, aristo- 665 cratic English house, with everyone kept in his place. Though I were equal to your ladyship, where would be the pleasure to me? It would be counterbalanced by the pain of feeling that Thomas and John were equal to 670 me.

Cath. But father says if we were to return to Nature ——

Crich. If we did, my lady, the first thing we should do would be to elect a head. 675 Circumstances might alter cases; the same person might not be master; the same persons might not be servants. I can't say as to that, nor should we have the deciding of it. Nature would decide for us.   680

Lady Mary. You seem to have thought it all out carefully, Crichton.

Crich. Yes, my lady.

Cath. And you have done this for us, Crichton, because you thought that — that 685 father needed to be kept in his place?

Crich. I should prefer you to say, my lady, that I have done it for the house.

Aga. Thank you, Crichton. Mary, be nicer to him. (*But* LADY MARY *has begun to* 690 *read again.*) If there was any way in which we could show our gratitude.

Crich. If I might venture, my lady, would you kindly show it by becoming more like Lady Mary. That disdain is what we like 695 from our superiors. Even so do we, the upper servants, disdain the lower servants, while they take it out of the odds and ends.
        (*He goes, and they bury themselves in cushions.*

Aga. Oh dear, what a tiring day.

Cath. I feel dead. Tuck in your feet, 700 you selfish thing.

> (LADY MARY *is lying reading on another couch.*

Lady Mary. I wonder what he meant by circumstances might alter cases.

Aga. (*yawning*). Don't talk, Mary, I was nearly asleep. 705

Lady Mary. I wonder what he meant by the same person might not be master, and the same persons might not be servants.

Cath. Do be quiet, Mary, and leave it to Nature; he said Nature would decide. 710

Lady Mary. I wonder ——

> (*But she does not wonder very much. She would wonder more if she knew what was coming. Her book slips unregarded to the floor. The ladies are at rest until it is time to dress.*

END OF ACT I

ACT II

THE ISLAND

Two months have elapsed, and the scene is a desert island in the Pacific, on which our adventurers have been wrecked.

The curtain rises on a sea of bamboo, which shuts out all view save the foliage of palm trees and some gaunt rocks. Occasionally Crichton and Treherne come momentarily into sight, hacking and hewing the bamboo, through which they are making a clearing between the ladies and the shore; and by and by, owing to their efforts, we shall have an unrestricted outlook on to a sullen sea that is at present hidden. Then we shall also be able to note a mast standing out of the water — all that is left, saving floating wreckage, of the ill-fated yacht the *Bluebell*. The beginnings of a hut will also be seen, with Crichton driving its walls into the ground or astride its roof of saplings, for at present he is doing more than one thing at a time. In a red shirt, with the ends of his sailor's breeches thrust into wading-boots, he looks a man for the moment; we suddenly remember someone's saying — perhaps it was ourselves — that a cataclysm would be needed to get him out of his servant's clothes, and apparently it has been forthcoming. It is no longer beneath our dignity to cast an inquiring eye on his appearance. His features are not distinguished, but he has a strong jaw and green eyes, in which a yellow light burns that we have not seen before. His dark hair, hitherto so decorously sleek, has been ruffled this way and that by wind and weather, as if they were part of the cataclysm and wanted to help his chance. His muscles must be soft and flabby still, but though they shriek aloud to him to desist, he rains lusty blows with his axe, like one who has come upon the open for the first time in his life, and likes it. He is as yet far from being an expert woodsman — mark the blood on his hands at places where he has hit them instead of the tree; but note also that he does not waste time in bandaging them — he rubs them in the earth and goes on. His face is still of the discreet pallor that befits a butler, and he carries the smaller logs as if they were a salver; not in a day or a month will he shake off the badge of servitude, but without knowing it he has begun.

But for the hatchets at work, and an occasional something horrible falling from a tree into the ladies' laps, they hear nothing save the mournful surf breaking on a coral shore.

They sit or recline huddled together against a rock, and they are farther from home, in every sense of the word, than ever before. Thirty-six hours ago, they were given three minutes in which to dress, without a maid, and reach the boats, and they have not made the best of that valuable time. None of them has boots, and had they known this prickly island they would have thought first of boots. They have a sufficiency of garments, but some of them were gifts dropped into the boat — Lady Mary's tarpaulin coat and hat, for instance, and Catherine's blue jersey and red cap, which certify that the two ladies were lately before the mast. Agatha is too gay in Ernest's dressing-gown, and clutches it to her person with both hands as if afraid that it may be claimed by its rightful owner. There are two pairs of bath slippers between the three of them, and their hair cries aloud and in vain for hairpins.

By their side, on an inverted bucket, sits Ernest, clothed neatly in the garments of day and night, but, alas, barefooted. He is the only cheerful member of this company of four, but his brightness is due less to a manly desire to succor the helpless than to his having been lately in the throes of composition, and to his modest satisfaction with the result. He reads to the ladies, and they listen, each with one scared eye to the things that fall from trees.

Ern. (*who has written on the fly-leaf of the only book saved from the wreck*). This is what I have written. "Wrecked, wrecked, wrecked! on an island in the Tropics, the following: the Hon. Ernest Woolley, the Rev. John Treherne, the Ladies Mary, Catherine, and 5 Agatha Lasenby, with two servants. We are the sole survivors of Lord Loam's steam yacht *Bluebell*, which encountered a fearful gale in these seas, and soon became a total wreck. The crew behaved gallantly, putting us all into 10 the first boat. What became of them I cannot tell, but we, after dreadful sufferings, and insufficiently clad, in whatever garments we could lay hold of in the dark" ——

Lady Mary. Please don't describe our 15 garments.

Ern. — "succeeded in reaching this island, with the loss of only one of our party, namely, Lord Loam, who flung away his life in a gallant attempt to save a servant who had 20 fallen overboard."

(*The ladies have wept long and sore for their father, but there is something in this last utterance that makes them look up.*)

Aga. But, Ernest, it was Crichton who jumped overboard trying to save father.

Ern. (*with the candor that is one of his most engaging qualities*). Well, you know, it was

rather silly of uncle to fling away his life 25 by trying to get into the boat first; and as this document may be printed in the English papers, it struck me, an English peer, you know ——

Lady Mary (*every inch an English peer's daughter*). Ernest, that is very thoughtful 30 of you.

Ern. (*continuing, well pleased*). —"By night the cries of wildcats and the hissing of snakes terrify us extremely" — (*this does not satisfy him so well, and he makes a correction*) — "terrify the ladies extremely. Against 35 these we have no weapons except one cutlass and a hatchet. A bucket washed ashore is at present our only comfortable seat" ——

Lady Mary (*with some spirit*). And Ernest is sitting on it. 40

Ern. H'sh! Oh, do be quiet. —"To add to our horrors, night falls suddenly in these parts, and it is then that savage animals begin to prowl and roar."

Lady Mary. Have you said that vam- 45 pire bats suck the blood from our toes as we sleep?

Ern. No, that's all. I end up, "Rescue us or we perish. Rich reward. Signed Ernest Woolley, in command of our little party." 50 This is written on a leaf taken out of a book of poems that Crichton found in his pocket.

Fancy Crichton being a reader of poetry. Now I shall put it into the bottle and fling it into the sea. (*He pushes the precious document* 55 *into a soda-water bottle, and rams the cork home. At the same moment, and without effort, he gives birth to one of his most characteristic epigrams.*) The tide is going out, we mustn't miss the post.

(*They are so unhappy that they fail to grasp it, and a little petulantly he calls for* CRICHTON, *ever his stand-by in the hour of epigram.* CRICHTON *breaks through the undergrowth quickly, thinking the ladies are in danger.*

Crich. Anything wrong, sir?

Ern. (*with fine confidence*). The tide, Crichton, is a postman who calls at our island twice a day for letters.   60

Crich. (*after a pause*). Thank you, sir.

(*He returns to his labors, however, without giving the smile which is the epigrammatist's right, and* ERNEST *is a little disappointed in him.*

Ern. Poor Crichton! I sometimes think he is losing his sense of humor. Come along, Agatha.

(*He helps his favorite up the rocks, and they disappear gingerly from view.*

Cath. How horribly still it is.   65

Lady Mary (*remembering some recent sounds*). It is best when it is still.

Cath. (*drawing closer to her*). Mary, I have heard that they are always very still just before they jump.

Lady Mary. Don't.   70

(*A distant chopping is heard, and they are startled.*

Lady Mary (*controlling herself*). It is only Crichton knocking down trees.

Cath. (*almost imploringly*). Mary, let us go and stand beside him.

Lady Mary (*coldly*). Let a servant see 75 that I am afraid!

Cath. Don't, then; but remember this, dear, they often drop on one from above.

(*She moves away, nearer to the friendly sound of the axe, and* LADY MARY *is left alone. She is the most courageous of them as well as the haughtiest, but when something she had thought*

to be a stick glides toward her, she forgets her dignity and screams.

Lady Mary (*calling*). Crichton, Crichton!

(*It must have been* TREHERNE *who was tree-felling, for* CRICHTON *comes to her from the hut, drawing his cutlass.*

Crich. (*anxious*). Did you call, my lady? 80

Lady Mary (*herself again, now that he is there*). I! Why should I?

Crich. I made a mistake, your ladyship. (*Hesitating*) If you are afraid of being alone, my lady ——

Lady Mary. Afraid! Certainly not. 85 (*Doggedly*) You may go.

(*But she does not complain when he remains within eyesight cutting the bamboo. It is heavy work, and she watches him silently.*

Lady Mary. I wish, Crichton, you could work without getting so hot.

Crich. (*mopping his face*). I wish I could, my lady.   (*He continues his labors.* 90

Lady Mary (*taking off her oilskins*). It makes me hot to look at you.

Crich. It almost makes me cool to look at your ladyship.

Lady Mary (*who perhaps thinks he is presuming*). Anything I can do for you in that 95 way, Crichton, I shall do with pleasure.

Crich. (*quite humbly*). Thank you, my lady.

(*By this time most of the bamboo has been cut, and the shore and sea are visible, except where they are hidden by the half-completed hut. The mast rising solitary from the water adds to the desolation of the scene, and at last tears run down* LADY MARY'S *face.*

Crich. Don't give way, my lady, things might be worse.

Lady Mary. My poor father.   100

Crich. If I could have given my life for his.

Lady Mary. You did all a man could do. Indeed I thank you, Crichton. (*With some admiration and more wonder*) You are a man.

Crich. Thank you, my lady.   105

Lady Mary. But it is all so awful. Crichton, is there any hope of a ship coming?

Crich. (*after hesitation*). Of course there is, my lady.

Lady Mary (*facing him bravely*). Don't 110 treat me as a child. I have got to know the worst, and to face it. Crichton, the truth.

Crich. (*reluctantly*). We were driven out of our course, my lady; I fear far from the track of commerce. 115

Lady Mary. Thank you; I understand.

> (*For a moment, however, she breaks down. Then she clenches her hands and stands erect.*

Crich. (*watching her, and forgetting perhaps for the moment that they are not just a man and woman*). You're a good pluckt 'un,[1] my lady.

Lady Mary (*falling into the same error*). I shall try to be. (*Extricating herself*) Crichton, how dare you? 120

Crich. I beg your ladyship's pardon: but you are. (*She smiles, as if it were a comfort to be told this, even by* CRICHTON.) And until a ship comes we are three men who are going to do our best for you ladies. 125

Lady Mary (*with a curl of the lip*). Mr. Ernest does no work.

Crich. (*cheerily*). But he will, my lady.

Lady Mary. I doubt it.

Crich. (*confidently, but perhaps thoughtlessly*). No work — no dinner — will make a 130 great change in Mr. Ernest.

Lady Mary. No work — no dinner. When did you invent that rule, Crichton?

Crich. (*loaded with bamboo*). I didn't invent it, my lady. I seem to see it growing all 135 over the island.

Lady Mary (*disquieted*). Crichton, your manner strikes me as curious.

Crich. (*pained*). I hope not, your ladyship.

Lady Mary (*determined to have it out with him*). You are not implying anything so 140 unnatural, I presume, as that if I and my sisters don't work there will be no dinner for *us*?

Crich. (*brightly*). If it is unnatural, my lady, that is the end of it.

Lady Mary. If? Now I understand. 145 The perfect servant at home holds that we are all equal now. I see.

Crich. (*wounded to the quick*). My lady, can you think me so inconsistent?

[1] A good-plucked one, i.e., a plucky person.

Lady Mary. That is it. 150

Crich. (*earnestly*). My lady, I disbelieved in equality at home because it was against Nature, and for that same reason I as utterly disbelieve in it on an island.

Lady Mary (*relieved by his obvious sincerity*). I apologize. 155

Crich. (*continuing unfortunately*). There must always, my lady, be one to command and others to obey.

Lady Mary (*satisfied*). One to command, others to obey. Yes. (*Then suddenly she* 160 *realizes that there may be a dire meaning in his confident words.*) Crichton!

Crich. (*who has intended no dire meaning*). What is it, my lady?

> (*But she only stares into his face and then hurries from him. Left alone he is puzzled, but being a practical man he busies himself gathering firewood, until* TWEENY *appears excitedly carrying coconuts in her skirt. She has made better use than the ladies of her three minutes' grace for dressing.*

Twee. (*who can be happy even on an island if* CRICHTON *is with her*). Look what I found.

Crich. Coconuts. Bravo!

Twee. They grows on trees. 165

Crich. Where did you think they grew?

Twee. I thought as how they grew in rows on top of little sticks.

Crich. (*wrinkling his brows*). Oh, Tweeny, Tweeny! 170

Twee. (*anxiously*). Have I offended of your feelings again, sir?

Crich. A little.

Twee. (*in a despairing outburst*). I'm full o' vulgar words and ways; and though I may 175 keep them in their holes when you are by, as soon as I'm by myself out they comes in a rush like beetles when the house is dark. I says them gloating-like, in my head — "Blooming," I says, and "All my eye," and "Ginger," 180 and "Nothink"; and all the time we was being wrecked I was praying to myself, "Please the Lord it may be an island as it's natural to be vulgar on." (*A shudder passes through* CRICHTON, *and she is abject.*) That's the kind 185

I am, sir. I'm 'opeless. You'd better give me up.

> (*She is a pathetic, forlorn creature, and his manhood is stirred.*

Crich. (*wondering a little at himself for saying it*). I won't give you up. It is strange that one so common should attract one so fastidious; but so it is. (*Thoughtfully*) There 190 is something about you, Tweeny, there is a *je ne sais quoi*[1] about you.

Twee. (*knowing only that he has found something in her to commend*). Is there, is there? Oh, I am glad.

Crich. (*putting his hand on her shoulder like a protector*). We shall fight your vulgarity 195 together. (*All this time he has been arranging sticks for his fire.*) Now get some dry grass.

> (*She brings him grass, and he puts it under the sticks. He produces an odd lens from his pocket, and tries to focus the sun's rays.*

Twee. Why, what's that?

Crich. (*the ingenious creature*). That's the glass from my watch and one from Mr. 200 Treherne's, with a little water between them. I'm hoping to kindle a fire with it.

Twee. (*properly impressed*). Oh sir!

> (*After one failure the grass takes fire, and they are blowing on it when excited cries near by bring them sharply to their feet.* AGATHA *runs to them, white of face, followed by* ERNEST.

Ern. Danger! Crichton, a tiger-cat!

Crich. (*getting his cutlass*). Where? 205

Aga. It is at our heels.

Ern. Look out, Crichton.

Crich. H'sh!

> (TREHERNE *comes to his assistance, while* LADY MARY *and* CATHERINE *join* AGATHA *in the hut.*

Ern. It will be on us in a moment.

> (*He seizes the hatchet and guards the hut. It is pleasing to see that* ERNEST *is no coward.*

Tre. Listen! 210

Ern. The grass is moving. It's coming.

---

[1] An "I know not what"; an inexpressible something.

It comes. But it is no tiger-cat; it is LORD LOAM *crawling on his hands and knees, a very exhausted and disheveled peer, wondrously attired in rags. The girls see him, and with glad cries rush into his arms*

Lady Mary. Father.

Lord Loam. Mary — Catherine — Agatha. Oh dear, my dears, my dears, oh dear!

Lady Mary. Darling. 215

Aga. Sweetest.

Cath. Love.

Tre. Glad to see you, sir.

Ern. Uncle, uncle, dear old uncle. 219

> (*For a time such happy cries fill the air, but presently* TREHERNE *is thoughtless.*

Tre. Ernest thought you were a tiger-cat.

Lord Loam (*stung somehow to the quick*). Oh, did you? I knew you at once, Ernest; I knew you by the way you ran.

> (ERNEST *smiles forgivingly.*

Crich. (*venturing forward at last*). My lord, I am glad. 225

Ern. (*with upraised finger*). But you are also idling, Crichton. (*Making himself comfortable on the ground*) We mustn't waste time. To work, to work.

Crich. (*after contemplating him without rancor*). Yes, sir. 230

> (*He gets a pot from the hut and hangs it on a tripod over the fire, which is now burning brightly.*

Tre. Ernest, you be a little more civil. Crichton, let me help.

> (*He is soon busy helping* CRICHTON *to add to the strength of the hut.*

Lord Loam (*gazing at the pot as ladies are said to gaze on precious stones*). Is that — but I suppose I'm dreaming again. (*Timidly*) It isn't by any chance a pot on top of a fire, is it? 235

Lady Mary. Indeed, it is, dearest. It is our supper.

Lord Loam. I have been dreaming of a pot on a fire for two days. (*Quivering*) There's nothing in it, is there? 240

Ern. Sniff, uncle. (LORD LOAM *sniffs.*

Lord Loam (*reverently*). It smells of onions!

> (*There is a sudden diversion.*

Cath. Father, you have boots!

Lady Mary. So he has.

Lord Loam. Of course I have.   245

Ern. (*with greedy cunning*). You are actually wearing boots, uncle. It's very unsafe, you know, in this climate.

Lord Loam. Is it?

Ern. We have all abandoned them, 250 you observe. The blood, the arteries, you know.

Lord Loam. I hadn't a notion.

     (*He holds out his feet, and* ERNEST *kneels.*

Ern. Oh Lord, yes.

     (*In another moment those boots will be his.*

Lady Mary (*quickly*). Father, he is try- 255 ing to get your boots from you. There is nothing in the world we wouldn't give for boots.

Ern. (*rising haughtily, a proud spirit misunderstood*). I only wanted the loan of them.

Aga. (*running her fingers along them lovingly*). If you lend them to anyone, it will be to us, won't it, father?   260

Lord Loam. Certainly, my child.

Ern. Oh, very well. (*He is leaving these selfish ones.*) I don't want your old boots. (*He gives his uncle a last chance.*) You don't think you could spare me *one* boot?   265

Lord Loam (*tartly*). I do not.

Ern. Quite so. Well, all I can say is I'm sorry for you. (*He departs to recline elsewhere.*

Lady Mary. Father, we thought we should never see you again.   270

Lord Loam. I was washed ashore, my dear, clinging to a hencoop. How awful that first night was.

Lady Mary. Poor father.

Lord Loam. When I woke, I wept. 275 Then I began to feel extremely hungry. There was a large turtle on the beach. I remembered from the *Swiss Family Robinson* that if you turn a turtle over he is helpless. My dears, I crawled towards him, I flung myself 280 upon him — (*here he pauses to rub his leg*) — the nasty, spiteful brute.

Lady Mary. You didn't turn him over?

Lord Loam (*vindictively, though he is a kindly man*). Mary, the senseless thing wouldn't wait; I found that none of them would 385 wait.

Cath. We should have been as badly off if Crichton hadn't ——

Lady Mary (*quickly*). Don't praise Crichton.   290

Lord Loam. And then those beastly monkeys. I always understood that if you flung stones at them they would retaliate by flinging coconuts at you. Would you believe it, I flung a hundred stones, and not one monkey 295 had sufficient intelligence to grasp my meaning. How I longed for Crichton.

Lady Mary (*wincing*). For us also, father?

Lord Loam. For you also. I tried for hours to make a fire. The authors say that 300 when wrecked on an island you can obtain a light by rubbing two pieces of stick together. (*With feeling*) The liars!

Lady Mary. And all this time you thought there was no one on the island but your- 305 self?

Lord Loam. I thought so until this morning. I was searching the pools for little fishes, which I caught in my hat, when suddenly I saw before me — on the sand —— 310

Cath. What?

Lord Loam. A hairpin.

Lady Mary. A hairpin! It must be one of ours. Give it me, father.

Aga. No, it's mine.   315

Lord Loam. I didn't keep it.

Lady Mary (*speaking for all three*). Didn't keep it? Found a hairpin on an island, and didn't keep it?

Lord Loam (*humbly*). My dears.   320

Aga. (*scarcely to be placated*). Oh, father, we have returned to Nature more than you bargained for.

Lady Mary. For shame, Agatha. (*She has something on her mind.*) Father, there is 325 something I want you to do at once — I mean to assert your position as the chief person on the island.   (*They are all surprised.*

Lord Loam. But who would presume to question it?   330

Cath. She must mean Ernest.

Lady Mary. Must I?

Aga. It's cruel to say anything against Ernest.

Lord Loam (*firmly*). If anyone pre- 335

sumes to challenge my position, I shall make short work of him.

Aga. Here comes Ernest; now see if you can say these horrid things to his face.

Lord Loam. I shall teach him his place 340 at once.

Lady Mary (anxiously). But how?

Lord Loam (chuckling). I have just thought of an extremely amusing way of doing it. (*As* ERNEST *approaches*) Ernest. 345

Ern. (loftily). Excuse me, uncle, I'm thinking. I'm planning out the building of this hut.

Lord Loam. I also have been thinking.

Ern. That don't matter.

Lord Loam. Eh? 350

Ern. Please, please, this is important.

Lord Loam. I have been thinking that I ought to give you my boots.

Ern. What!

Lady Mary. Father. 355

Lord Loam (genially). Take them, my boy. (*With a rapidity we had not thought him capable of,* ERNEST *becomes the wearer of the boots.*) And now I dare say you want to know why I give them to you, Ernest?

Ern. (moving up and down in them deliciously). Not at all. The great thing is, "I've got 'em, I've got 'em." 360

Lord Loam (majestically, but with a knowing look at his daughters). My reason is that, as head of our little party, you, Ernest, shall be our hunter, you shall clear the forests of those savage beasts that make them so dangerous. (*Pleasantly*) And now you 365 know, my dear nephew, why I have given you my boots.

Ern. This is my answer.

(*He kicks off the boots.*

Lady Mary (still anxious). Father, assert yourself. 370

Lord Loam. I shall now assert myself. (*But how to do it? He has a happy thought.*) Call Crichton.

Lady Mary. Oh father.

CRICHTON *comes in answer to a summons, and is followed by* TREHERNE

Ern. (wondering a little at LADY MARY'S *grave face).* Crichton, look here. 375

Lord Loam (sturdily). Silence! Crichton, I want your advice as to what I ought to do with Mr. Ernest. He has defied me.

Ern. Pooh!

Crich. (after considering). May I speak 380 openly, my lord?

Lady Mary (keeping her eyes fixed on him). That is what we desire.

Crich. (quite humbly). Then I may say, your lordship, that I have been considering Mr. Ernest's case at odd moments ever since 385 we were wrecked.

Ern. My case?

Lord Loam (sternly). Hush.

Crich. Since we landed on the island, my lord, it seems to me that Mr. Ernest's 390 epigrams have been particularly brilliant.

Ern. (gratified). Thank you, Crichton.

Crich. But I find — I seem to find it growing wild, my lord, in the woods, that sayings which would be justly admired in Eng- 395 land are not much use on an island. I would therefore most respectfully propose that henceforth every time Mr. Ernest favors us with an epigram his head should be immersed in a bucket of cold spring water. 400

(*There is a terrible silence.*

Lord Loam (uneasily). Serve him right.

Ern. I should like to see you try to do it, uncle.

Crich. (ever ready to come to the succor of his lordship). My feeling, my lord, is that at the next offence I should convey him to a 405 retired spot, where I shall carry out the undertaking in as respectful a manner as is consistent with a thorough immersion.

(*Though his manner is most respectful, he is firm; he evidently means what he says.*

Lady Mary (a ramrod). Father, you must not permit this; Ernest is your nephew. 410

Lord Loam (with his hand to his brow). After all, he is my nephew, Crichton; and, as I am sure, he now sees that I am a strong man ——

Ern. (foolishly in the circumstances). A strong man. You mean a stout man. You are 415 one of mind to two of matter.

(*He looks round in the old way for approval. No one has smiled, and to*

his consternation he sees that CRICH-
TON *is quietly turning up his sleeves.*
ERNEST *makes an appealing gesture
to his uncle; then he turns defiantly
to* CRICHTON.

Crich. Is it to be before the ladies, Mr.
Ernest, or in the privacy of the wood? (*He
fixes* ERNEST *with his eye.* ERNEST *is cowed.*)
Come.

Ern. (*affecting bravado*). Oh, all right.   420

Crich. (*succinctly*). Bring the bucket.

  (ERNEST *hesitates. He then lifts the
  bucket and follows* CRICHTON *to the
  nearest spring.*

Lord Loam (*rather white*). I'm sorry for him,
but I had to be firm.

Lady Mary. Oh father, it wasn't you who
was firm. Crichton did it himself.   425

Lord Loam. Bless me, so he did.

Lady Mary. Father, be strong.

Lord Loam (*bewildered*). You can't mean
that my faithful Crichton ——

Lady Mary. Yes, I do.   430

Tre. Lady Mary, I stake my word that
Crichton is incapable of acting dishonorably.

Lady Mary. I know that; I know it as well as
you. Don't you see that that is what makes
him so dangerous?   435

Tre. By Jove, I — I believe I catch your
meaning.

Cath. He is coming back.

Lord Loam (*who has always known himself
to be a man of ideas*). Let us all go into the
hut, just to show him at once that it is *our*   440
hut.

Lady Mary (*as they go*). Father, I implore
you, assert yourself now and for ever.

Lord Loam. I will.

Lady Mary. And, please, don't ask him   445
how you are to do it.

  (CRICHTON *returns with sticks to mend
  the fire.*

Lord Loam (*loftily, from the door of the hut*).
Have you carried out my instructions, Crichton?

Crich. (*deferentially*). Yes, my lord.

  (ERNEST *appears, mopping his hair,
  which has become very wet since we
  last saw him. He is not bearing*

malice, he is too busy drying, but
AGATHA *is specially his champion.*

Aga. It's infamous, infamous.   450

Lord Loam (*strongly*). *My* orders, Agatha.

Lady Mary. Now, father, please.

Lord Loam (*striking an attitude*). Before I
give you any further orders, Crichton ——

Crich. Yes, my lord.   455

Lord Loam (*delighted*). Pooh! It's all right.

Lady Mary. No. Please go on.

Lord Loam. Well, well. This question
of the leadership; what do you think now,
Crichton?   460

Crich. My lord, I feel it is a matter with
which *I* have nothing to do.

Lord Loam. Excellent. Ha, Mary? That
settles it, I think.

Lady Mary. It seems to, but — I'm not   465
sure.

Crich. It will settle itself naturally, my lord,
without any interference from us.

  (*This reference to Nature gives general
  dissatisfaction.*

Lady Mary. Father.

Lord Loam (*a little severely*). It settled   470
itself long ago, Crichton, when I was born a peer,
and you, for instance, were born a servant.

Crich. (*acquiescing*). Yes, my lord, that was
how it all came about quite naturally in England. We had nothing to do with it there,   475
and we shall have as little to do with it here.

Tre. (*relieved*). That's all right.

Lady Mary (*determined to clinch the matter*).
One moment. In short, Crichton, his lordship will continue to be our natural head.

Crich. I dare say, my lady, I dare say.   480

Cath. But you must *know.*

Crich. Asking your pardon, my lady, one
can't be sure — on an island.

  (*They look at each other uneasily.*

Lord Loam (*warningly*). Crichton, I don't
like this.   485

Crich. (*harassed*). The more I think of it,
your lordship, the more uneasy I become myself. When I heard, my lord, that you had
left that hairpin behind ——

  (*He is pained.*

Lord Loam (*feebly*). One hairpin among   490
so many would only have caused dissension.

Crich. (very sorry to have to contradict him). Not so, my lord. From that hairpin we could have made a needle; with that needle we could, out of skins, have sewn trousers — of which your lordship is in need; indeed, we are 495 all in need of them.

Lady Mary (suddenly self-conscious). All?

Crich. On an island, my lady.

Lady Mary. Father.

Crich. (really more distressed by the prospect than she). My lady, if Nature does not 500 think them necessary, you may be sure she will not ask you to wear them. *(Shaking his head)* But among all this undergrowth ——

Lady Mary. Now you see this man in his true colors. 505

Lord Loam (violently). Crichton, you will either this moment say, "Down with Nature," or ——

Crich. (scandalized). My lord!

Lord Loam (loftily). Then this is my 510 last word to you; take a month's notice.

> *(If the hut had a door he would now shut it to indicate that the interview is closed.*

Crich. (in great distress). Your lordship, the *disgrace* ——

Lord Loam (swelling). Not another word: you may go. 515

Lady Mary (adamant). And don't come to me, Crichton, for a character.

Ern. (whose immersion has cleared his brain). Aren't you all forgetting that this is an island?

> *(This brings them to earth with a bump.* LORD LOAM *looks to his eldest daughter for the fitting response.*

Lady Mary (equal to the occasion). It makes only this difference — that you may go 520 at once, Crichton, to some other part of the island.

> *(The faithful servant has been true to his superiors ever since he was created, and never more true than at this moment; but his fidelity is founded on trust in Nature, and to be untrue to it would be to be untrue to them. He lets the wood he has been gathering slip to the ground, and bows his sorrowful head. He turns*

to obey. Then affection for these great ones wells up in him.

Crich. My lady, let me work for you.

Lady Mary. Go.

Crich. You need me so sorely; I can't 525 desert you; I won't.

Lady Mary (in alarm, lest the others may yield). Then, father, there is but one alternative, *we* must leave him.

> *(LORD LOAM is looking yearningly at CRICHTON.*

Tre. It seems a pity.

Cath. (forlornly). You will work for us? 530

Tre. Most willingly. But I must warn you all that, so far, Crichton has done nine-tenths of the scoring.

Lady Mary. The question is, are we to leave this man? 535

Lord Loam (wrapping himself in his dignity). Come, my dears.

Crich. My lord!

Lord Loam. Treherne — Ernest — get our things.

Ern. We don't have any, uncle. They 540 all belong to Crichton.

Tre. Everything we have he brought from the wreck — he went back to it before it sank. He risked his life.

Crich. My lord, anything you would 545 care to take is yours.

Lady Mary (quickly). Nothing.

Ern. Rot! If I could have your socks, Crichton ——

Lady Mary. Come, father; we are 550 ready.

> *(Followed by the others, she and LORD LOAM pick their way up the rocks. In their indignation they scarcely notice that daylight is coming to a sudden end.*

Crich. My lord, I implore you — *I* am not desirous of being head. Do you have a try at it, my lord.

Lord Loam (outraged). A try at it! 555

Crich. (eagerly). It may be that you will prove to be the best man.

Lord Loam. May be! My children, come.

> *(They disappear proudly in a single file.*

Tre. Crichton, I'm sorry; but of course I must go with them.   560

Crich. Certainly, sir. (*He calls to* TWEENY, *and she comes from behind the hut, where she has been watching breathlessly.*) Will you be so kind, sir, as to take her to the others?

Tre. Assuredly.

Twee. But what do it all mean?   565

Crich. Does, Tweeny, does. (*He passes her up the rocks to* TREHERNE.) We shall meet again soon, Tweeny. Good night, sir.

Tre. Good night. I dare say they are not far away.   570

Crich. (*thoughtfully*). They went westward, sir, and the wind is blowing in that direction. That may mean, sir, that Nature is already taking the matter into her own hands. They are all hungry, sir, and the pot has come   575 a-boil. (*He takes off the lid.*) The smell will be borne westward. That pot is full of Nature, Mr. Treherne. Good night, sir.

Tre. Good night.

          (*He mounts the rocks with* TWEENY, *and they are heard for a little time after their figures are swallowed up in the fast-growing darkness.* CRICHTON *stands motionless, the lid in his hand, though he has forgotten it, and his reason for taking it off the pot. He is deeply stirred, but presently is ashamed of his dejection, for it is as if he doubted his principles. Bravely true to his faith that Nature will decide now as ever before, he proceeds manfully with his preparations for the night. He lights a ship's*

lantern, one of several treasures he has brought ashore, and is filling his pipe with crumbs of tobacco from various pockets, when the stealthy movements of some animal in the grass startle him. With the lantern in one hand and his cutlass in the other, he searches the ground around the hut. He returns, lights his pipe, and sits down by the fire, which casts weird moving shadows. There is a red gleam on his face; in the darkness he is a strong and perhaps rather sinister figure. In the great stillness that has fallen over the land, the wash of the surf seems to have increased in volume. The sound is indescribably mournful. Except where the fire is, desolation has fallen on the island like a pall.

Once or twice, as Nature dictates, CRICHTON leans forward to stir the pot, and the smell is borne westward. He then resumes his silent vigil.

Shadows other than those cast by the fire begin to descend the rocks. They are the adventurers returning. One by one they steal nearer to the pot until they are squatted round it, with their hands out to the blaze. LADY MARY only is absent. Presently she comes within sight of the others, then stands against a tree with her teeth clenched. One wonders, perhaps, what Nature is to make of her.*)

END OF ACT II

ACT III

THE HAPPY HOME

The scene is the hall of their island home two years later. This sturdy log-house is no mere extension of the hut we have seen in process of erection, but has been built a mile or less to the west of it, on higher ground and near a stream. When the master chose this site, the others thought that all he expected from the stream was a sufficiency of drinking water. They know better now every time they go down to the mill or turn on the electric light.

This hall is the living-room of the house, and walls and roof are of stout logs. Across the joists supporting the roof are laid many home-made implements, such as spades, saws, fishing-rods, and from hooks in the joists are suspended cured foods, of which hams are specially in evidence. Deep recesses halfway up the walls contain various provender in barrels and sacks. There are some skins, trophies of the chase, on the floor, which is otherwise bare. The chairs and tables are in some cases hewn out of the solid wood, and in others the result of rough but efficient carpentering. Various pieces of wreckage from the yacht have been turned to novel uses: thus the steering-wheel now hangs from the center of the roof, with electric lights attached to it encased in bladders. A lifebuoy has become the back of a chair. Two barrels have been halved and turn coyly from each other as a settee.

The farther end of the room is more strictly the kitchen, and is a great recess, which can be shut off from the hall by folding doors. There is a large open fire in it. The chimney is half of one of the boats of the yacht. On the walls of the kitchen proper are many plate-racks, containing shells; there are rows of these of one size and shape, which mark them off as dinner plates or bowls; others are as obviously tureens. They are arranged primly as in a well-conducted kitchen; indeed, neatness and cleanliness are the note struck everywhere, yet the effect of the whole is romantic and barbaric.

The outer door into this hall is a little peculiar on an island. It is covered with skins and is in four leaves, like the swing doors of fashionable restaurants, which allow you to enter without allowing the hot air to escape. During the winter season our castaways have found the contrivance useful, but Crichton's brain was perhaps a little lordly when he conceived it. Another door leads by a passage to the sleeping-rooms of the house, which are all on the ground-floor, and to Crichton's work-room, where he is at this moment, and whither we should like to follow him, but in a play we may not, as it is out of sight. There is a large window space without a window, which, however, can be shuttered, and through this we have a view of cattle-sheds, fowl-pens, and a field of grain. It is a fine summer evening.

Tweeny is sitting there, very busy plucking the feathers off a bird and dropping them on a sheet placed for that purpose on the floor. She is trilling to herself in the lightness of her heart. We may remember that Tweeny, alone among the women, had dressed wisely for an island when they fled the yacht, and her going-away gown still adheres to her, though in fragments. A score of pieces have been added here and there as necessity compelled, and these have been patched and repatched in incongruous colors; but, when all is said and done, it can still be maintained that Tweeny wears a skirt. She is deservedly proud of her skirt, and sometimes lends it on important occasions when approached in the proper spirit.

Someone outside has been whistling to Tweeny; the guarded whistle which, on a less savage island, is sometimes assumed to be an indication to cook that the constable is willing, if the coast be clear. Tweeny, however, is engrossed, or perhaps she is not in the mood for a follower, so he climbs in at the window undaunted, to take her willy nilly. He is a jolly-looking laboring man, who answers to the name of Daddy, and —— But though that may be his island name, we recognize him at once. He is Lord Loam, settled down to the new conditions, and enjoying life heartily as handy-man about the happy home. He is comfortably attired in skins. He is still stout, but all the flabbiness has dropped from him; gone too is his pomposity; his eye is clear, brown his skin; he could leap a gate.

In his hands he carries an island-made concertina, and such is the exuberance of his spirits that, as he lights on the floor, he bursts into music and song, something about his being a chickety chickety chick chick, and will Tweeny please to tell him whose chickety chick is she. Retribution follows sharp. We hear a whir, as if from insufficiently oiled machinery, and over the passage door appears a placard showing the one word "Silence." His lordship stops, and steals to Tweeny on his tiptoes.

Lord Loam. I thought the Gov. was out.

Twee. Well, you see he ain't. And if he were to catch you here idling ——

(LORD LOAM *pales. He lays aside his musical instrument and hurriedly dons an apron.* TWEENY *gives him the bird to pluck, and busies herself laying the table for dinner.*

Lord Loam (*softly*). What is he doing now?

Twee. I think he's working out that plan 5 for laying on hot and cold.

Lord Loam (*proud of his master*). And he'll manage it too. The man who could build a blacksmith's forge without tools ——

Twee. (*not less proud*). He made the 10 tools.

Lord Loam. Out of half a dozen rusty nails. The sawmill, Tweeny; the speaking-tube; the electric lighting; and look at the use he has made of the bits of the yacht that were 15 washed ashore. And all in two years. He's a master I'm proud to pluck for.

(*He chirps happily at his work, and she regards him curiously.*

Twee. Daddy, you're of little use, but you're a bright, cheerful creature to have about the house. (*He beams at this commendation.*) 20 Do you ever think of old times now? We was a bit different.

Lord Loam (*pausing*). Circumstances alter cases. (*He resumes his plucking contentedly.*

Twee. But, Daddy, if the chance was to 25 come of getting back?

Lord Loam. I have given up bothering about it.

Twee. You bothered that day long ago when we saw a ship passing the island. How 30 we all ran like crazy folk into the water, Daddy, and screamed and held out our arms. (*They

are both a little agitated.) But it sailed away, and we've never seen another.

Lord Loam. If we had had the electrical 35 contrivance we have now we could have attracted that ship's notice. (*Their eyes rest on a mysterious apparatus that fills a corner of the hall.*) A touch on that lever, Tweeny, and in a few moments bonfires would be blazing all round the shore. 40

Twee. (*backing from the lever as if it might spring at her*). It's the most wonderful thing he has done.

Lord Loam (*in a reverie*). And then — England — home!

Twee. (*also seeing visions*). London of a 45 Saturday night!

Lord Loam. My lords, in rising once more to address this historic chamber ——

Twee. There was a little ham and beef shop off the Edgware Road —— 50

(*The visions fade; they return to the practical.*

Lord Loam. Tweeny, do you think I could have an egg to my tea?

At this moment a wiry, athletic figure in skins darkens the window. He is carrying two pails, which are suspended from a pole on his shoulder, and he is ERNEST. *We should say that he is* ERNEST *completely changed if we were of those who hold that people change. As he enters by the window he has heard Lord Loam's appeal, and is perhaps justifiably indignant*

Ern. What is that about an egg? Why should you have an egg?

Lord Loam (*with hauteur*). That is my 55 affair, sir. (*With a Parthian shot as he with-*

draws stiffly from the room) The Gov. has never put *my* head in a bucket.

Ern. (*coming to rest on one of his buckets, and speaking with excusable pride. To* TWEENY). Nor mine for nearly three months. It was only last week, Tweeny, that he said to me, "Er- 60 nest, the water cure has worked marvels in you, and I question whether I shall require to dip you any more." (*Complacently*) Of course that sort of thing encourages a fellow.

Twee. (*who has now arranged the dinner table to her satisfaction*). I will say, Erny, I 65 never seen a young chap more improved.

Ern. (*gratified*). Thank you, Tweeny, that's very precious to me. (*She retires to the fire to work the great bellows with her foot, and* ERNEST *turns to* TREHERNE, *who has come in looking more like a cowboy than a clergyman. He has a small box in his hand which he tries to conceal.*) What have you got there, John?

Tre. Don't tell anybody. It is a little 70 present for the Gov.; a set of razors. One for each day in the week.

Ern. (*opening the box and examining its contents*). Shells! He'll like that. He likes sets of things.

Tre. (*in a guarded voice*). Have you 75 noticed that?

Ern. Rather.

Tre. He's becoming a bit magnificent in his ideas.

Ern. (*huskily*). John, it sometimes gives 80 me the creeps.

Tre. (*making sure that* TWEENY *is out of hearing*). What do you think of that brilliant robe he got the girls to make for him?

Ern. (*uncomfortably*). I think he looks too regal in it.   85

Tre. Regal! I sometimes fancy that that's why he's so fond of wearing it. (*Practically*) Well, I must take these down to the grindstone and put an edge on them.

Ern. (*buttonholing him*). I say, John, I 90 want a word with you.

Tre. Well?

Ern. (*become suddenly diffident*). Dash it all, you know, you're a clergyman.

Tre. One of the best things the Gov. 95 has done is to insist that none of you forget it.

Ern. (*taking his courage in his hands*). Then — would you, John?

Tre. What?

Ern. (*wistfully*). Officiate at a marriage 100 ceremony, John?

Tre. (*slowly*). Now, that's really odd.

Ern. Odd? Seems to me it's natural. And whatever is natural, John, is right.

Tre. I mean that same question has 105 been put to me today already.

Ern. (*eagerly*). By one of the women?

Tre. Oh, no; they all put it to me long ago. This was by the Gov. himself.

Ern. By Jove! (*Admiringly*) I say, 110 John, what an observant beggar he is.

Tre. Ah! You fancy he was thinking of you?

Ern. I do not hesitate to affirm, John, that he has seen the love-light in my eyes. 115 You answered ——

Tre. I said, Yes, I thought it would be my duty to officiate if called upon.

Ern. You're a brick.

Tre. (*still pondering*). But I wonder 120 whether he *was* thinking of you?

Ern. Make your mind easy about that.

Tre. Well, my best wishes. Agatha is a very fine girl.

Ern. Agatha? What made you think it 125 was Agatha?

Tre. Man alive, you told me all about it soon after we were wrecked.

Ern. Pooh! Agatha's all very well in her way, John, but I'm flying at bigger game. 130

Tre. Ernest, which is it?

Ern. Tweeny, of course.

Tre. Tweeny? (*Reprovingly*) Ernest, I hope her cooking has nothing to do with this.

Ern. (*with dignity*). Her cooking has 135 very little to do with it.

Tre. But does she return your affection?

Ern. (*simply*). Yes, John, I believe I may say so. I am unworthy of her, but I think I have touched her heart.   140

Tre. (*with a sigh*). Some people seem to have all the luck. As you know, Catherine won't look at me.

Ern. I'm sorry, John.

Tre. It's my deserts; I'm a second- 145

eleven sort [1] of chap. Well, my heartiest good wishes, Ernest.

Ern. Thank you, John. How's the little black pig today?　　　　149

Tre. (*departing*). He has begun to eat again.
　　　(*After a moment's reflection* ERNEST calls to TWEENY.

Ern. Are you very busy, Tweeny?

Twee. (*coming to him good-naturedly*). There's always work to do; but if you want me, Ernest ——

Ern. There's something I should like 155 to say to you if you could spare me a moment.

Twee. Willingly. What is it?

Ern. What an ass I used to be, Tweeny.

Twee. (*tolerantly*). Oh, let bygones be bygones.　　　　160

Ern. (*sincerely, and at his very best*). I'm no great shakes even now. But listen to this, Tweeny; I have known many women, but until I knew you I never knew any woman.

Twee. (*to whose uneducated ears this sounds dangerously like an epigram*). Take care 165 — the bucket.

Ern. (*hurriedly*). I didn't mean it in that way. (*He goes chivalrously on his knees.*) Ah, Tweeny, I don't undervalue the bucket, but what I want to say now is that the sweet 170 refinement of a dear girl has done more for me than any bucket could do.

Twee. (*with large eyes*). Are you offering to walk out with me, Erny?

Ern. (*passionately*). More than that. I 175 want to build a little house for you — in the sunny glade down by Porcupine Creek. I want to make chairs for you and tables; and knives and forks, and a sideboard for you.

Twee. (*who is fond of language*). I like 180 to hear you. (*Eyeing him*) Would there be anyone in the house except myself, Ernest?

Ern. (*humbly*). Not often; but just occasionally there would be your adoring husband.　　　　185

Twee. (*decisively*). It won't do, Ernest.

Ern. (*pleading*). It isn't as if I should be much there.

Twee. I know, I know; but I don't love you, Ernest. I'm that sorry.　　　　190

[1] Second-rate sort; not first eleven or varsity material.

Ern. (*putting his case cleverly*). Twice a week I should be away altogether — at the dam. On the other days you would never see me from breakfast time to supper. (*With the self-abnegation of the true lover*) If you like 195 I'll even go fishing on Sundays.

Twee. It's no use, Erny.

Ern. (*rising manfully*). Thank you, Tweeny; it can't be helped. (*Then he remembers.*) Tweeny, we shall be disappointing the 200 Gov.

Twee. (*with a sinking*). What's that?

Ern. He wanted us to marry.

Twee. (*blankly*). You and me? the Gov.! (*Her head droops woefully. From without is heard the whistling of a happier spirit, and* TWEENY *draws herself up fiercely.*) That's 205 her; that's the thing what has stole his heart from me.

A stalwart youth appears at the window, so handsome and tingling with vitality that, glad to depose CRICHTON, *we cry thankfully, "The hero at last." But it is not the hero; it is the heroine. This splendid boy, clad in skins, is what Nature has done for* LADY MARY. *She carries bow and arrows and a blow-pipe, and over her shoulder is a fat buck, which she drops with a cry of triumph. Forgetting to enter demurely, she leaps through the window*

Twee. (*sourly*). Drat you, Polly, why don't you wipe your feet?

Lady Mary (*good-naturedly*). Come, 210 Tweeny, be nice to me. It's a splendid buck.
　　　(*But* TWEENY *shakes her off, and retires to the kitchen fire.*

Ern. Where did you get it?

Lady Mary (*gaily*). I sighted a herd near Penguin's Creek, but had to creep round Silver Lake to get to windward of them. How- 215 ever, they spotted me and then the fun began. There was nothing for it but to try and run them down, so I singled out a fat buck and away we went down the shore of the lake, up the valley of rolling stones; he doubled 220 into Brawling River and took to the water, but I swam after him; the river is only half a mile broad there, but it runs strong. He went spinning down the rapids, down I went in pursuit; he clambered ashore, I clambered 225 ashore; away we tore helter-skelter up the hill and down again. I lost him in the marshes, got on his track again near Bread Fruit Wood, and brought him down with an arrow in Firefly Grove. 230

Twee. (staring at her). Aren't you tired?

Lady Mary. Tired! It was gorgeous.

    (She runs up a ladder and deposits her weapons on the joists. She is whistling again.

Twee. (snapping). I can't abide a woman whistling.

Lady Mary (indifferently). I like it. 235

Twee. (stamping her foot). Drop it, Polly, I tell you.

Lady Mary (stung). I won't. I'm as good as you are.

    (They are facing each other defiantly.

Ern. (shocked). Is this necessary? 240 Think how it would pain *him.*

    *(*LADY MARY's *eyes take a new expression. We see them soft for the first time.*

Lady Mary (contritely). Tweeny, I beg your pardon. If my whistling annoys you, I shall try to cure myself of it. *(Instead of calming* TWEENY, *this floods her face in tears.)* Why, how can that hurt you, Tweeny dear? 245

Twee. Because I can't make you lose your temper.

Lady Mary (divinely). Indeed, I often do. Would that I were nicer to everybody.

Twee. There you are again. *(Wist-* 250 *fully)* What makes you want to be so nice, Polly?

Lady Mary (with fervor). Only thankfulness, Tweeny. *(She exults.)* It is such fun to be alive. 255

    (So also seem to think CATHERINE *and* AGATHA, *who bounce in with fishing-rods and creel. They, too, are in manly attire.*

Cath. We've got some ripping fish for the Gov.'s dinner. Are we in time? We ran all the way.

Twee. (tartly). You'll please to cook them yourself, Kitty, and look sharp about it. 260

    (She retires to her hearth, where AGATHA *follows her.*

Aga. (yearning). Has the Gov. decided who is to wait upon him today?

Cath. (who is cleaning her fish). It's my turn.

Aga. (hotly). I don't see that.

Twee. (with bitterness). It's to be 265 neither of you, Aggy; he wants Polly again.

    *(*LADY MARY *is unable to resist a joyous whistle.*

Aga. (jealously). Polly, you toad.

    (But they cannot make LADY MARY *angry.*

Twee. (storming). How dare you look so happy?

Lady Mary (willing to embrace her). I 270 wish, Tweeny, there was anything I could do to make you happy also.

Twee. Me! Oh, I'm happy. *(She remembers* ERNEST, *whom it is easy to forget on an island.)* I've just had a proposal, I tell you.

    *(*LADY MARY *is shaken at last, and her sisters with her.*

Aga. A proposal? 275

Cath. (going white). Not — not ——

    (She dare not say his name.

Ern. (with singular modesty). You needn't be alarmed; it's only me.

Lady Mary (relieved). Oh, you!

Aga. (happy again). Ernest, you dear, 280 I got such a shock.

Cath. It was only Ernest. *(Showing him her fish in thankfulness)* They are beautifully fresh; come and help me to cook them.

Ern. (with simple dignity). Do you 285 mind if I don't cook fish tonight? *(She does not mind in the least. They have all forgotten him. A lark is singing in three hearts.)* I think you might all be a little sorry for a chap. *(But they are not even sorry, and he addresses* AGATHA *in these winged words:)* I'm particularly disappointed in you, Aggy; seeing that I 290 was half engaged to you, I think you might have had the good feeling to be a little more hurt.

Aga. Oh, bother.

Ern. (summing up the situation in so far as it

affects himself). I shall now go and lie 295
down for a bit.

> (*He retires coldly but unregretted.* LADY
> MARY *approaches* TWEENY *with her
> most insinuating smile.*

Lady Mary. Tweeny, as the Gov. has chosen
me to wait on him, please may I have the loan
of *it* again?

> (*The reference made with such charm-
> ing delicacy is evidently to* TWEENY'S
> *skirt.*

Twee. (*doggedly*). No, you mayn't. 300
Aga. (*supporting* TWEENY). Don't you give
it to her.

Lady Mary (*still trying sweet persuasion*).
You know quite well that he prefers to be
waited on in a skirt.

Twee. I don't care. Get one for your- 305
self.

Lady Mary. It is the only one on the island.

Twee. And it's mine.

Lady Mary (*an aristocrat after all*). Tweeny,
give me that skirt directly. 310

Cath. Don't.

Twee. I won't.

Lady Mary (*clearing for action*). I shall make
you.

Twee. I should like to see you try. 315

> (*An unseemly fracas appears to be in-
> evitable, but something happens.
> The whir is again heard, and the
> notice is displayed "Dogs delight to
> bark and bite." Its effect is instan-
> taneous and cheering. The ladies
> look at each other guiltily and im-
> mediately proceed on tiptoe to their
> duties. These are all concerned with
> the master's dinner.* CATHERINE
> *attends to his fish.* AGATHA *fills a
> quaint toast-rack and brings the
> menu, which is written on a shell.*
> LADY MARY *twists a wreath of green
> leaves around her head, and places a
> flower beside the master's plate.*
> TWEENY *signs that all is ready, and
> she and the younger sisters retire
> into the kitchen, drawing the screen
> that separates it from the rest of the
> room.* LADY MARY *beats a tom-*

*tom, which is the dinner bell. She
then gently works a punkah,[1] which
we have not hitherto observed, and
stands at attention. No doubt she is
in hopes that the Gov. will enter into
conversation with her, but she is too
good a parlor-maid to let her hopes
appear in her face. We may watch
her manner with complete approval.
There is not one of us who would not
give her £26 a year.*

*The master comes in quietly, a book in
his hand, still the only book on the
island, for he has not thought it
worth while to build a printing-press.
His dress is not noticeably different
from that of the others; the skins are
similar, but perhaps these are a trifle
more carefully cut or he carries them
better. One sees somehow that he has
changed for his evening meal. There
is an odd suggestion of a dinner
jacket about his doeskin coat. It is,
perhaps, too grave a face for a man of
thirty-two, as if he were overmuch
immersed in affairs, yet there is a
sunny smile left to lighten it at times
and bring back its youth; perhaps
too intellectual a face to pass as
strictly handsome, not sufficiently
suggestive of oats. His tall figure
is very straight, slight rather than
thick-set, but nobly muscular. His
big hands, firm and hard with labor
though they be, are finely shaped —
note the fingers so much more tapered,
the nails better tended than those of
his domestics; they are one of many
indications that he is of a superior
breed. Such signs, as has often been
pointed out, are infallible. A romantic figure, too. One can easily
see why the women-folks of this strong
man's house both adore and fear him.*

---

[1] A machine for fanning a room; usually a framework
covered with cloth and suspended from the ceiling.
By means of a rope attachment the frame can be pulled
back and forth by hand. The contraption originated in
India.

He does not seem to notice who is waiting on him tonight, but inclines his head slightly to whoever it is, as she takes her place at the back of his chair. LADY MARY *respectfully places the menu-shell before him, and he glances at it.*

Crich. Clear, please.

(LADY MARY *knocks on the screen, and a serving hatch in it opens, through which* TWEENY *offers two soup plates.* LADY MARY *selects the clear, and the aperture is closed. She works the punkah while the master partakes of the soup.*

Crich. (who always gives praise where it is due). An excellent soup, Polly, but still a trifle too rich.

Lady Mary. Thank you.

(*The next course is the fish, and while it is being passed through the hatch we have a glimpse of three jealous women.* LADY MARY'S *movements are so deft and noiseless that any observant spectator can see that she was born to wait at table.*

Crich. (unbending as he eats). Polly, 320 you are a very smart girl.

Lady Mary (bridling, but naturally gratified). La!

Crich. (smiling). And I'm not the first you've heard it from, I'll swear.

Lady Mary (wriggling). Oh, Gov.!   325

Crich. Got any followers on the island, Polly?

Lady Mary (tossing her head). Certainly not.

Crich. I thought that perhaps John or   330 Ernest ——

Lady Mary (tilting her nose). I don't say that it's for want of asking.

Crich. (emphatically). I'm sure it isn't. (*Perhaps he thinks he has gone too far.*) You may clear.   335

(*Flushed with pleasure, she puts before him a bird and vegetables, sees that his beaker is filled with wine, and returns to the punkah. She would love to continue their conversation,*

but it is for him to decide. For a time he seems to have forgotten her.

Crich. Did you lose any arrows today?

Lady Mary. Only one in Firefly Grove.

Crich. You were as far as that? How did you get across the Black Gorge?

Lady Mary. I went across on the rope. 340

Crich. Hand over hand?

Lady Mary (swelling at the implied praise). I wasn't in the least dizzy.

Crich. (moved). You brave girl! (*He sits back in his chair a little agitated.*) But never do that again.   345

Lady Mary (pouting). It is such fun, Gov.

Crich. (decisively). I forbid it.

Lady Mary (the little rebel). I shall.

Crich. (surprised). Polly! (*He signs to her sharply to step forward, but for a moment she holds back petulantly, and even when she does come it is less obediently than like a naughty, sulky child. Nevertheless, with the forbearance that is characteristic of the man, he addresses her with grave gentleness rather than severely.*) You must do as I tell you, you know.   350

Lady Mary (strangely passionate). I shan't.

Crich. (smiling at her fury). We shall see Frown at me, Polly; there, you do it at once. Clench your little fists, stamp your feet, bite your ribbons —— (*A student of women, or*   355 *at least of this woman, he knows that she is about to do those things, and thus she seems to do them to order.* LADY MARY *screws up her face like a baby and cries. He is immediately kind.*) You child of Nature; was it cruel of me to wish to save you from harm?

Lady Mary (drying her eyes). I'm an ungracious wretch. Oh, Gov., I don't try   360 half hard enough to please you. I'm even wearing — (*she looks down sadly*) — when I know you prefer *it.*

Crich. (thoughtfully). I admit I do prefer *it.* Perhaps I am a little old-fashioned in   365 these matters. (*Her tears again threaten.*) Ah, don't, Polly; that's nothing.

Lady Mary. If I could only please you, Gov.

Crich. (slowly). You do please me, child, very much — (*he half rises*) — very much   370 indeed. (*If he meant to say more he checks himself. He looks at his plate.*) No more, thank you.

(*The simple island meal is ended, save for the walnuts and the wine, and* CRICHTON *is too busy a man to linger long over them. But he is a stickler for etiquette, and the table is cleared charmingly, though with dispatch, before they are placed before him.* LADY MARY *is an artist with the crumb-brush, and there are few arts more delightful to watch. Dusk has come sharply, and she turns on the electric light. It awakens* CRICHTON *from a reverie in which he has been regarding her.*)

Crich. Polly, there is only one thing about you that I don't quite like. (*She looks up,* 375 *making a moue,*[1] *if that can be said of one who so well knows her place. He explains.*) That action of the hands.

Lady Mary. What do I do?

Crich. So — like one washing them. I have noticed that the others tend to do it also. 380 It seems odd.

Lady Mary (*archly*). Oh, Gov., have you forgotten?

Crich. What?

Lady Mary. That once upon a time a 385 certain other person did that.

Crich. (*groping*). You mean myself? (*She nods, and he shudders.*) Horrible!

Lady Mary (*afraid she has hurt him*). You haven't for a very long time. Perhaps it 390 is natural to servants.

Crich. That must be it. (*He rises.*) Polly! (*She looks up expectantly, but he only sighs and turns away.*)

Lady Mary (*gently*). You sighed, Gov.

Crich. Did I? I was thinking. (*He paces the room and then turns to her agitatedly, yet with control over his agitation. There is some mournfulness in his voice.*) I have always tried 395 to do the right thing on this island. Above all, Polly, I want to do the right thing by you.

Lady Mary (*with shining eyes*). How we all trust you. That is your reward, Gov.

Crich. (*who is having a fight with himself*).

[1] A pout.

And now I want a greater reward. Is 400 it fair to you? Am I playing the game? Bill Crichton would like always to play the game. If we were in England ——

(*He pauses so long that she breaks in softly.*)

Lady Mary. We know now that we shall never see England again. 405

Crich. I am thinking of two people whom neither of us has seen for a long time — Lady Mary Lasenby, and one Crichton, a butler.

(*He says the last word bravely, a word he once loved, though it is the most horrible of all words to him now.*)

Lady Mary. That cold, haughty, insolent girl. Gov., look around you and forget 410 them both.

Crich. I had nigh forgotten them. He has had a chance, Polly — that butler — in these two years of becoming a man, and he has tried to take it. There have been many fail- 415 ures, but there has been some success, and with it I have let the past drop off me, and turned my back on it. That butler seems a far-away figure to me now, and not myself. I hail him, but we scarce know each other. If I am 420 to bring him back it can only be done by force, for in my soul he is now abhorrent to me. But if I thought it best for you I'd haul him back; I swear as an honest man, I would bring him back with all his obsequious ways and 425 deferential airs, and let you see the man you call your Gov. melt forever into him who was your servant.

Lady Mary (*shivering*). You hurt me. You say these things, but you say them like a 430 king. To me it is the past that was not real.

Crich. (*too grandly*). A king! I sometimes feel —— (*For a moment the yellow light gleams in his green eyes. We remember suddenly what* TREHERNE *and* ERNEST *said about his regal look. He checks himself.*) I say it harshly, it is so hard to say, and all the 435 time there is another voice within me crying —— (*He stops.*)

Lady Mary (*trembling but not afraid*). If it is the voice of Nature ——

Crich. (*strongly*). I know it to be the 440 voice of Nature.

Lady Mary (*in a whisper*). Then, if you want to say it very much, Gov., please say it to Polly Lasenby.

Crich. (*again in the grip of an idea*). A 445
king! Polly, some people hold that the soul but leaves one human tenement for another, and so lives on through all the ages. I have occasionally thought of late that, in some past existence, I may have been a king. It has all 450
come to me so naturally, not as if I had had to work it out, but — as — if — I — remembered.

"Or ever the knightly years were gone,
 With the old world to the grave,
 I was a *king* in Babylon,   455
 And you were a Christian slave." [1]

It may have been; you hear me, it may have been.

Lady Mary (*who is as one fascinated*). It may have been.   460

Crich. I am lord over all. They are but hewers of wood and drawers of water for me. These shores are mine. Why should I hesitate; I have no longer any doubt. I do believe I am doing the right thing. Dear Polly, 465
I have grown to love you; are you afraid to mate with me? (*She rocks her arms; no words will come from her.*)

"I was a king in Babylon,
 And you were a Christian slave."

Lady Mary (*bewitched*). You are the 470
most wonderful man I have ever known, and I am not afraid. (*He takes her to him reverently. Presently he is seated, and she is at his feet looking up adoringly in his face. As the tension relaxes she speaks with a smile.*) I want you to tell me — every woman likes to know — when was the first time you thought 475
me nicer than the others?

Crich. (*who, like all big men, is simple*). I think a year ago. We were chasing goats on the Big Slopes, and you outdistanced us all;

---

[1] The opening stanza of a once celebrated poem by William Ernest Henley (1849–1903). (See "Echoes," no. xxxvii, in Henley's *Poems*.) The insertion of this quatrain was one of Barrie's little jokes on his warm friend Henley, who, he knew, would be in the audience at the London premiere of this play. Note the sly dig at Henley during the conversation between Crichton and the Brocklehursts in Act IV, ll. 352–56.

you were the first of our party to run a 480
goat down; I was proud of you that day.

Lady Mary (*blushing with pleasure*). Oh Gov., I only did it to please you. Everything I have done has been out of the desire to please you. (*Suddenly anxious*) If I thought 485
that in taking a wife from among us you were imperiling your dignity ——

Crich. (*perhaps a little masterful*). Have no fear of that, dear. I have thought it all out. The wife, Polly, always takes the same 490
position as the husband.

Lady Mary. But I am so unworthy. It was sufficient to me that I should be allowed to wait on you at that table.

Crich. You shall wait on me no longer. 495
At whatever table I sit, Polly, you shall soon sit there also. (*Boyishly*) Come, let us try what it will be like.

Lady Mary. As your servant at your feet.

Crich. No, as my consort by my side. 500
        (*They are sitting thus when the hatch
        is again opened and coffee offered.
        But* LADY MARY *is no longer there to
        receive it. Her sisters peep through
        in consternation. In vain they rattle
        the cup and saucer.* AGATHA
        brings the coffee to CRICHTON.

Crich. (*forgetting for the moment that it is not a month hence*). Help your mistress first, girl. (*Three women are bereft of speech, but he does not notice it. He addresses* CATHERINE *vaguely.*) Are you a good girl, Kitty?

Cath. (*when she finds her tongue*). I try to be, Gov.

Crich. (*still more vaguely*). That's right. 505
        (*He takes command of himself again,
        and signs to them to sit down.
        ERNEST comes in cheerily, but finding* CRICHTON *here is suddenly weak.
        He subsides on a chair, wondering
        what has happened.*

Crich. (*surveying him*). Ernest. (ERNEST *rises.*) You are becoming a little slovenly in your dress, Ernest; I don't like it.

Ern. (*respectfully*). Thank you.

        (ERNEST *sits again.* DADDY *and* TREHERNE *arrive.*

Crich. Daddy, I want you.   510

Lord Loam (*with a sinking*). Is it because I forgot to clean out the dam?

Crich. (*encouragingly*). No, no. (*He pours some wine into a goblet.*) A glass of wine with you, Daddy.   515

Lord Loam (*hastily*). Your health, Gov.

(*He is about to drink, but the master checks him.*

Crich. And hers. Daddy, this lady has done me the honor to promise to be my wife.

Lord Loam (*astounded*). Polly!

Crich. (*a little perturbed*). I ought first   520 to have asked your consent. I deeply regret — but Nature; may I hope I have your approval?

Lord Loam. May you, Gov.? (*Delighted*) Rather! Polly!   525

(*He puts his proud arms round her.*

Tre. We all congratulate you, Gov., most heartily.

Ern. Long life to you both, sir.

(*There is much shaking of hands, all of which is sincere.*

Tre. When will it be, Gov.?

Crich. (*after turning to* LADY MARY, *who whispers to him*). As soon as the bridal   530 skirt can be prepared. (*His manner has been most indulgent, and without the slightest suggestion of patronage. But he knows it is best for all that he should keep his place, and that his presence hampers them.*) My friends, I thank you for your good wishes, I thank you all. And now, perhaps you would like me to leave you to yourselves. Be joyous. Let there be   535 song and dance tonight. Polly, I shall take my coffee in the parlor — you understand.

(*He retires with pleasant dignity. Immediately there is a rush of two girls at* LADY MARY.

Lady Mary. Oh, oh! Father, they are pinching me.

Lord Loam (*taking her under his protection*). Agatha, Catherine, never presume to   540 pinch your sister again. On the other hand, she may pinch you henceforth as much as ever she chooses.

(*In the meantime* TWEENY *is weeping softly, and the two are not above using her as a weapon.*

Cath. Poor Tweeny, it's a shame.

Aga. After he had almost promised *you*.   545

Twee. (*loyally turning on them*). No, he never did. He was always honorable as could be. 'Twas me as was too vulgar. Don't you dare say a word agin that man.

Ern. (*to* LORD LOAM). You'll get a lot   550 of titbits out of this, Daddy.

Lord Loam. That's what I was thinking.

Ern. (*plunged in thought*). I dare say *I* shall have to clean out the dam now.

Lord Loam (*heartlessly*). I dare say.   555

(*His gay old heart makes him again proclaim that he is a chickety chick. He seizes the concertina.*

Tre. (*eagerly*). That's the proper spirit.

(*He puts his arm round* CATHERINE, *and in another moment they are all dancing to Daddy's music. Never were people happier on an island. A moment's pause is presently created by the return of* CRICHTON, *wearing the wonderful robe of which we have already had dark mention. Never has he looked more regal, never perhaps felt so regal. We need not grudge him the one foible of his rule, for it is all coming to an end.*

Crich. (*graciously, seeing them hesitate*). No, no; I am delighted to see you all so happy. Go on.

Tre. We don't like to before you, Gov.   560

Crich. (*his last order*). It is my wish.

(*The merrymaking is resumed, and soon* CRICHTON *himself joins in the dance. It is when the fun is at its fastest and most furious that all stop abruptly as if turned to stone. They have heard the boom of a gun. Presently they are alive again.* ERNEST *leaps to the window.*

Tre. (*huskily*). It was a ship's gun. (*They turn to* CRICHTON *for confirmation; even in that hour they turn to* CRICHTON.) Gov.?

Crich. Yes.

(*In another moment* LADY MARY *and* LORD LOAM *are alone.*

Lady Mary (*seeing that her father is unconcerned*). Father, you heard.   565

Lord Loam (placidly). Yes, my child.

Lady Mary (alarmed by his unnatural calmness). But it was a gun, father.

Lord Loam (looking an old man now, and shuddering a little). Yes — a gun — I have often heard it. It's only a dream, you know; why don't we go on dancing?   570

> (*She takes his hands, which have gone cold.*

Lady Mary. Father. Don't you see, they have all rushed down to the beach? Come.

Lord Loam. Rushed down to the beach; yes, always that — I often dream it.

Lady Mary. Come, father, come.   575

Lord Loam. Only a dream, my poor girl.

> (CRICHTON *returns. He is pale but firm.*

Crich. We can see lights within a mile of the shore — a great ship.

Lord Loam. A ship — always a ship.

Lady Mary. Father, this is no dream.   580

Lord Loam (looking timidly at CRICHTON). It's a dream, isn't it? There's no ship?

Crich. (soothing him with a touch). You are awake, Daddy, and there is a ship.

Lord Loam (clutching him). You are not deceiving me?   585

Crich. It is the truth.

Lord Loam (reeling). True? — a ship — at last!   (*He goes after the others pitifully.*

Crich. (quietly). There is a small boat between it and the island; they must have   590 sent it ashore for water.

Lady Mary. Coming in?

Crich. No. That gun must have been a signal to recall it. It is going back. They can't hear our cries.   595

Lady Mary (pressing her temples). Going away. So near — so near. (*Almost to herself*) I think I'm glad.

Crich. (cheerily). Have no fear. I shall bring them back.   600

> (*He goes towards the table on which is the electrical apparatus.*

Lady Mary (standing on guard as it were between him and the table). What are you going to do?

Crich. To fire the beacons.

Lady Mary. Stop! (*She faces him.*) Don't you see what it means?   605

Crich. (firmly). It means that our life on the island has come to a natural end.

Lady Mary (huskily). Gov., let the ship go.

Crich. The old man — you saw what it means to him.   610

Lady Mary. But I am afraid.

Crich. (adoringly). Dear Polly.

Lady Mary. Gov., let the ship go.

Crich. (she clings to him, but though it is his death sentence he loosens her hold). Bill Crichton has got to play the game.   615

> (*He pulls the levers. Soon through the window one of the beacons is seen flaring red. There is a long pause. Shouting is heard.* ERNEST *is the first to arrive.*

Ern. Polly, Gov., the boat has turned back. They are English sailors; they have landed! We are rescued, I tell you, rescued!

Lady Mary (wanly). Is it anything to make so great a to-do about?   620

Ern. (staring). Eh?

Lady Mary. Have we not been happy here?

Ern. Happy? Lord, yes.

Lady Mary (catching hold of his sleeve). Ernest, we must never forget all that the   625 Gov. has done for us.

Ern. (stoutly). Forget it? The man who could forget it would be a selfish wretch and a —— But I say, this makes a difference!

Lady Mary (quickly). No, it doesn't.   630

Ern. (his mind tottering). A mighty difference!

The others come running in, some weeping with joy, others boisterous. We see blue-jackets gazing through the window at the curious scene. LORD LOAM *comes accompanied by a naval officer, whom he is continually shaking by the hand*

Lord Loam. And here, sir, is our little home. Let me thank you in the name of us all, again and again and again.   635

Off. Very proud, my lord. It is indeed an honor to have been able to assist so distinguished a gentleman as Lord Loam.

Lord Loam. A glorious, glorious day. I shall

show you our other rooms. Come, my 640
pets. Come, Crichton.
> (*He has not meant to be cruel. He does
> not know he has said it. It is the old
> life that has come back to him. They
> all go. All leave* CRICHTON *except*
> LADY MARY.

Lady Mary (*stretching out her arms to him*).
Dear Gov., I will never give you up.
> (*There is a salt smile on his face as he
> shakes his head to her. He lets the*

cloak slip to the ground. *She will
not take this for an answer; again her
arms go out to him. Then comes the
great renunciation. By an effort of
will he ceases to be an erect figure; he
has the humble bearing of a servant.
His hands come together as if he were
washing them.*

Crich. (*it is the speech of his life*). My lady.
> (*She goes away. There is none to
> salute him now, unless we do it.*

END OF ACT III

ACT IV

THE OTHER ISLAND

Some months have elapsed, and we have again the honor of waiting upon Lord Loam in
his London home. It is the room of the first act, but with a new scheme of decoration,
for on the walls are exhibited many interesting trophies from the island, such as skins,
stuffed birds, and weapons of the chase, labeled "Shot by Lord Loam," "Hon. Ernest
Woolley's Blowpipe," etc. There are also two large glass cases containing other odds
and ends, including, curiously enough, the bucket in which Ernest was first dipped, but
there is no label calling attention to the incident.

It is not yet time to dress for dinner, and his lordship is on a couch, hastily yet furtively cutting the pages of a new book. With him are his two younger daughters and
his nephew, and they also are engaged in literary pursuits; that is to say, the ladies are
eagerly but furtively reading the evening papers, of which Ernest is sitting complacently but furtively on an endless number, and doling them out as called for. Note the
frequent use of the word "furtive." It implies that they do not wish to be discovered
by their butler, say, at their otherwise delightful task.

Aga. (*reading aloud, with emphasis on the
wrong words*). "In conclusion, we most heartily
congratulate the Hon. Ernest Woolley. This
book of his, regarding the adventures of himself and his brave companions on a desert isle,
stirs the heart like a trumpet."   5
> (*Evidently the book referred to is the one
> in* LORD LOAM'S *hands.*

Ern. (*handing her a pink paper*). Here is
another.

Cath. (*reading*). "From the first to the last of
Mr. Woolley's engrossing pages it is evident
that he was an ideal man to be wrecked 10
with, and a true hero." (*Large-eyed*) Ernest!

Ern. (*calmly*). That's how it strikes *them*,
you know. Here's another one.

Aga. (*reading*). "There are many kindly
references to the two servants who were 15
wrecked with the family, and Mr. Woolley pays
the butler a glowing tribute in a footnote."
> (*Someone coughs uncomfortably.*

Lord Loam (*who has been searching the index
for the letter L*). Excellent, excellent. At the
same time I must say, Ernest, that the whole
book is about yourself.   20

Ern. (*genially*). As the author ——

Lord Loam. Certainly, certainly. Still, you
know, as a peer of the realm — (*with dignity*)

— I think, Ernest, you might have given me one of your adventures.   25

Ern. I say it was you who taught us how to obtain a fire by rubbing two pieces of stick together.

Lord Loam (beaming). Do you, do you? I call that very handsome. What page?   30

Here the door opens, and the well-bred CRICHTON *enters with the evening papers as subscribed for by the house. Those we have already seen have perhaps been introduced by* ERNEST *up his waistcoat. Everyone except the intruder is immediately self-conscious, and when he withdraws there is a general sigh of relief. They pounce on the new papers.* ERNEST *evidently gets a shock from one, which he casts contemptuously on the floor.*

Aga. (more fortunate). Father, see page 81. "It was a tiger-cat," says Mr. Woolley, "of the largest size. Death stared Lord Loam in the face, but he never flinched."

Lord Loam (searching his book eagerly). Page 81.   35

Aga. "With presence of mind only equaled by his courage, he fixed an arrow in his bow."

Lord Loam. Thank you, Ernest; thank you, my boy.

Aga. "Unfortunately he missed."   40

Lord Loam. Eh?

Aga. "But by great good luck I heard his cries" ——

Lord Loam. My cries?

Aga. — "and rushing forward with drawn   45 knife, I stabbed the monster to the heart."

(LORD LOAM *shuts his book with a pettish slam. There might be a scene here were it not that* CRICHTON *reappears and goes to one of the glass cases. All are at once on the alert, and his lordship is particularly sly.*

Lord Loam. Anything in the papers, Catherine?

Cath. No, father, nothing — nothing at all.

Ern. (it pops out as of yore). The pa-   50

pers! The papers are guides that tell us what we ought to do, and then we don't do it.

(CRICHTON *having opened the glass case has taken out the bucket, and* ERNEST, *looking round for applause, sees him carrying it off and is undone. For a moment of time he forgets that he is no longer on the island, and with a sigh he is about to follow* CRICHTON *and the bucket to a retired spot. The door closes, and* ERNEST *comes to himself.*

Lord Loam (uncomfortably). I told him to take it away.

Ern. I thought — (*he wipes his brow*)   55 — I shall go and dress.   (*He goes.*

Cath. Father, it's awful having Crichton here. It's like living on tiptoe.

Lord Loam (gloomily). While he is here we are sitting on a volcano.   60

Aga. How mean of you! I am sure he has only stayed on with us to — to help us through. It would have looked so suspicious if he had gone at once.

Cath. (reveling in the worst). But sup-   65 pose Lady Brocklehurst were to get at him and pump him. She's the most terrifying, suspicious old creature in England; and Crichton simply can't tell a lie.

Lord Loam. My dear, that is the vol-   70 cano to which I was referring. (*He has evidently something to communicate.*) It's all Mary's fault. She said to me yesterday that she would break her engagement with Brocklehurst unless I told him about — you know what.   75

(*All conjure up the vision of* CRICHTON.

Aga. Is she mad?

Lord Loam. She calls it common honesty.

Cath. Father, have you told him?

Lord Loam (heavily). She thinks I have, but I couldn't. She's sure to find out tonight.   80

(*Unconsciously he leans on the island concertina, which he has perhaps been lately showing to an interviewer as something he made for* TWEENY. *It squeaks, and they all jump.*

Cath. It's like a bird of ill-omen.

Lord Loam (vindictively). I must have it taken away; it has done that twice.

LADY MARY *comes in. She is in evening dress. Undoubtedly she meant to sail in, but she forgets, and despite her garments it is a manly entrance. She is properly ashamed of herself. She tries again, and has an encouraging success. She indicates to her sisters that she wishes to be alone with papa*

Aga. All right, but we know what it's about. Come along, Kit.   85

         (*They go.* LADY MARY *thoughtlessly sits like a boy, and again corrects herself. She addresses her father, but he is in a brown study, and she seeks to draw his attention by whistling. This troubles them both.*

Lady Mary. How horrid of me!

Lord Loam (*depressed*). If you would try to remember ——

Lady Mary (*sighing*). I do; but there are so many things to remember.   90

Lord Loam (*sympathetically*). There are — (*In a whisper*) Do you know, Mary, I constantly find myself secreting hairpins.

Lady Mary. I find it so difficult to go up steps one at a time.   95

Lord Loam. I was dining with half a dozen members of our party last Thursday, Mary, and they were so eloquent that I couldn't help wondering all the time how many of their heads *he* would have put in the bucket.   100

Lady Mary. I use so many of his phrases. And my appetite is so scandalous. Father, I usually have a chop before we sit down to dinner.

Lord Loam. As for my clothes — (*wrig-* 105 *gling*). My dear, you can't think how irksome collars are to me nowadays.

Lady Mary. They can't be half such an annoyance, father, as ——

         (*She looks dolefully at her skirt.*

Lord Loam (*hurriedly*). Quite so — quite 110 so. You have dressed early tonight, Mary.

Lady Mary. That reminds me; I had a note from Brocklehurst saying that he would come a few minutes before his mother as — as he wanted to have a talk with me. He 115 didn't say what about, but of course we know. (*His lordship fidgets.*) (*With feeling*) It was good of you to tell him, father. Oh, it is hor-

rible to me — (*covering her face*). It seemed so natural at the time.   120

Lord Loam (*petulantly*). Never again make use of that word in this house, Mary.

Lady Mary (*with an effort*). Father, Brocklehurst has been so loyal to me for these two years that I should despise myself were 125 I to keep my — my extraordinary lapse from him. Had Brocklehurst been a little less good, then you need not have told him my strange little secret.

Lord Loam (*weakly*). Polly — I mean 130 Mary — it was all Crichton's fault; he ——

Lady Mary (*with decision*). No, father, no; not a word against him, though I haven't the pluck to go on with it; I can't even understand how it ever was. Father, do you not still 135 hear the surf? Do you see the curve of the beach?

Lord Loam. I have begun to forget — (*In a low voice*) But they were happy days; there was something magical about them.   140

Lady Mary. It was glamor. Father, I have lived Arabian nights. I have sat out a dance with the evening star. But it was all in a past existence, in the days of Babylon, and I am myself again. But he has been chiv- 145 alrous always. If the slothful, indolent creature I used to be has improved in any way, I owe it all to him. I am slipping back in many ways, but I am determined not to slip back altogether — in memory of him and his island. 150 That is why I insisted on your telling Brocklehurst. He can break our engagement if he chooses. (*Proudly*) Mary Lasenby is going to play the game.

Lord Loam. But my dear ——   155

      LORD BROCKLEHURST *is announced*

Lady Mary (*meaningly*). Father, dear, oughtn't you to be dressing?

Lord Loam (*very unhappy*). The fact is — before I go — I want to say ——

Lord Brock. Loam, if you don't mind, 160 I wish very specially to have a word with Mary before dinner.

Lord Loam. But ——

Lady Mary. Yes, father. (*She induces*

him to go, and thus courageously faces LORD
BROCKLEHURST *to hear her fate.*) I am 165
ready, George.

Lord Brock. (*who is so agitated that she ought
to see he is thinking not of her but of himself*).
It is a painful matter — I wish I could have
spared you this, Mary.

Lady Mary. Please go on.

Lord Brock. In common fairness, of 170
course, this should be remembered, that two
years had elapsed. You and I had no reason to
believe that we should ever meet again.

(*This is more considerate than she had
expected.*

Lady Mary (*softening*). I was so lost to the
world, George. 175

Lord Brock. (*with a groan*). At the same time,
the thing is utterly and absolutely inexcus-
able ——

Lady Mary (*recovering her hauteur*). Oh!

Lord Brock. And so I have already said 180
to mother.

Lady Mary (*disdaining him*). You have told
her?

Lord Brock. Certainly, Mary, certainly; I
tell mother everything. 185

Lady Mary (*curling her lip*). And what did
she say?

Lord Brock. To tell the truth, mother rather
pooh-poohed the whole affair.

Lady Mary (*incredulous*). Lady Brockle- 190
hurst pooh-poohed the whole affair!

Lord Brock. She said, "Mary and I will have
a good laugh over this."

Lady Mary (*outraged*). George, your mother
is a hateful, depraved old woman. 195

Lord Brock. Mary!

Lady Mary (*turning away*). Laugh, indeed,
when it will always be such a pain to me.

Lord Brock. (*with strange humility*). If only
you would let me bear all the pain, Mary. 200

Lady Mary (*who is taken aback*). George,
think you are the noblest man ——

(*She is touched, and gives him both her
hands. Unfortunately he simpers.*

Lord Brock. She was a pretty little thing.
She stares, but he marches to his doom.) Ah, not
beautiful like you. I assure you it was 205
the merest flirtation; there were a few letters,

but we have got them back. It was all owing
to the boat being so late at Calais. You see
she had such large, helpless eyes.

Lady Mary (*fixing him*). George, when 210
you lunched with father today at the club ——

Lord Brock. I didn't. He wired me that he
couldn't come.

Lady Mary (*with a tremor*). But he wrote
you? 215

Lord Brock. No.

Lady Mary (*a bird singing in her breast*). You
haven't seen him since?

Lord Brock. No.

(*She is saved. Is he to be let off also?
Not at all. She bears down on him
like a ship of war.*

Lady Mary. George, who and what is 220
this woman?

Lord Brock. (*cowering*). She was — she is —
the shame of it — a lady's-maid.

Lady Mary (*properly horrified*). A what?

Lord Brock. A lady's-maid. A mere 225
servant, Mary. (LADY MARY *whirls round so
that he shall not see her face.*) I first met her
at this house when you were entertaining the
servants; so you see it was largely your father's
fault. 230

Lady Mary (*looking him up and down*). A
lady's-maid?

Lord Brock. (*degraded*). Her name was
Fisher.

Lady Mary. My maid! 235

Lord Brock. (*with open hands*). Can you
forgive me, Mary?

Lady Mary. Oh George, George!

Lord Brock. Mother urged me not to tell you
anything about it; but —— 240

Lady Mary (*from her heart*). I am so glad you
told me.

Lord Brock. You see there was nothing wrong
in it.

Lady Mary (*thinking perhaps of another
incident*). No, indeed. 245

Lord Brock. (*inclined to simper again*). And
she behaved awfully well. She quite saw that
it was because the boat was late. I suppose
the glamor to a girl in service of a man in high
position —— 250

Lady Mary. Glamor! — yes, yes, that was it.

Lord Brock. Mother says that a girl in such circumstances is to be excused if she loses her head.

Lady Mary (impulsively). George, I 255 am so sorry if I said anything against your mother. I am sure she is the dearest old thing.

Lord Brock. (in calm waters at last). Of course for women of our class she has a very different standard. 260

Lady Mary (grown tiny). Of course.

Lord Brock. You see, knowing how good a woman she is herself, she was naturally anxious that I should marry someone like her. That is what has made her watch your 265 conduct so jealously, Mary.

Lady Mary (hurriedly thinking things out). I know. I — I think, George, that before your mother comes I should like to say a word to father.

Lord Brock. (nervously). About this? 270

Lady Mary. Oh, no; I shan't tell him of this. About something else.

Lord Brock. And you do forgive me, Mary?

Lady Mary (smiling on him). Yes, yes. I — I am sure the boat was *very* late, George. 275

Lord Brock. (earnestly). It really was.

Lady Mary. I am even relieved to know that you are not quite perfect, dear. (*She rests her hands on his shoulders. She has a moment of contrition.*) George, when we are married, we shall try to be not an entirely frivolous 280 couple, won't we? We must endeavor to be of some little use, dear.

Lord Brock. (the ass). Noblesse oblige.[1]

Lady Mary (haunted by the phrases of a better man). Mary Lasenby is determined to play the game, George. 285

(*Perhaps she adds to herself, "Except just this once." A kiss closes this episode of the two lovers; and soon after the departure of* LADY MARY *the* COUNTESS OF BROCKLEHURST *is announced. She is a very formidable old lady.*)

Lady Brock. Alone, George?

Lord Brock. Mother, I told her all; she has behaved magnificently.

[1] Nobility requires it; it is the obligation of high rank.

Lady Brock. (who has not shared his fears). Silly boy. (*She casts a supercilious eye on the island trophies.*) So these are the wonders 290 they brought back with them. Gone away to dry her eyes, I suppose?

Lord Brock. (proud of his mate). She didn't cry, mother.

Lady Brock. No? (*She reflects.*) 295 You're quite right. I wouldn't have cried. Cold, icy. Yes, that was it.

Lord Brock. (who has not often contradicted her). I assure you, mother, that wasn't it at all. She forgave me at once.

Lady Brock. (opening her eyes sharply to the full). Oh! 300

Lord Brock. She was awfully nice about the boat being late; she even said she was relieved to find that I wasn't quite perfect.

Lady Brock. (pouncing). She said that?

Lord Brock. She really did. 305

Lady Brock. I mean *I* wouldn't. Now if *I* had said that, what would have made me say it? (*Suspiciously*) George, is Mary all we think her?

Lord Brock. (with unexpected spirit). If 310 she wasn't, mother, you would know it.

Lady Brock. Hold your tongue, boy. We don't really know what happened on that island.

Lord Brock. You were reading the book 315 all the morning.

Lady Brock. How can I be sure that the book is true?

Lord Brock. They all talk of it as true.

Lady Brock. How do I know that they 320 are not lying?

Lord Brock. Why should they lie?

Lady Brock. Why shouldn't they? (*She reflects again.*) If I had been wrecked on a island, I think it highly probable that I 32 should have lied when I came back. Weren' some servants with them?

Lord Brock. Crichton, the butler. (*He i surprised to see her ring the bell.*) Why, mother you are not going to —— 33

Lady Brock. Yes, I am. (*Pointedly*) George watch whether Crichton begins any of his an swers to my questions with "The fact is."

Lord Brock. Why?

Lady Brock. Because that is usually 335 the beginning of a lie.

Lord Brock. (*as* CRICHTON *opens the door*). Mother, you can't do these things in other people's houses.

Lady Brock. (*coolly, to* CRICHTON). It was I who rang. (*Surveying him through her* 340 *eyeglass*) So you were one of the castaways, Crichton?

Crich. Yes, my lady.

Lady Brock. Delightful book Mr. Woolley has written about your adventures. 345 (CRICHTON *bows.*) Don't you think so?

Crich. I have not read it, my lady.

Lady Brock. Odd that they should not have presented you with a copy.

Lord Brock. Presumably Crichton is 350 no reader.

Lady Brock. By the way, Crichton, were there any books on the island?

Crich. I had one, my lady — Henley's poems.   355

Lord Brock. Never heard of him.

(CRICHTON *again bows.*

Lady Brock. (*who has not heard of him either*). I think you were not the only servant wrecked?

Crich. There was a young woman, my lady.

Lady Brock. I want to see her. (CRICHTON *bows, but remains.*) Fetch her up. (*He goes.* 360

Lord Brock. (*almost standing up to his mother*). This is scandalous.

Lady Brock. (*defining her position*). I am a mother. (CATHERINE *and* AGATHA *enter in dazzling confections, and quake in secret to find themselves practically alone with* LADY BROCKLE- HURST. *Even as she greets them*) How d'you do, Catherine — Agatha? You didn't 365 dress like this on the island, I expect! By the way, how did you dress?

(*They have thought themselves prepared, but* ——

Aga. Not — not so well, of course, but quite the same idea.

They are relieved by the arrival of TREHERNE, *who is in clerical dress*

Lady Brock. How do you do, Mr. Tre- 370 herne? There is not so much of you in the book as I had hoped.

Tre. (*modestly*). There wasn't very much of me on the island, Lady Brocklehurst.

Lady Brock. How d'ye mean?   375

(*He shrugs his honest shoulders.*

Lord Brock. I hear you have got a living, Treherne. Congratulations.

Tre. Thanks.

Lord Brock. Is it a good one?

Tre. So-so. They are rather weak in 380 bowling, but it's a good bit of turf.

Confidence is restored by the entrance of ERNEST, *who takes in the situation promptly, and, of course, knows he is a match for any old lady*

Ern. (*with ease*). How do you do, Lady Brocklehurst.

Lady Brock. Our brilliant author!

Ern. (*impervious to satire*). Oh, I don't 385 know.

Lady Brock. It is as engrossing, Mr. Woolley, as if it were a work of fiction.

Ern. (*suddenly uncomfortable*). Thanks, awfully. (*Recovering*) The fact is —— 390

(*He is puzzled by seeing the Brockle- hurst family exchange meaning looks.*

Cath. (*to the rescue*). Lady Brocklehurst, Mr. Treherne and I — we are engaged.

Aga. And Ernest and I.

Lady Brock. (*grimly*). I see, my dears; thought it wise to keep the island in the 395 family.

An awkward moment this for the entrance of LORD LOAM *and* LADY MARY, *who, after a private talk upstairs, are feeling happy and secure*

Lord Loam (*with two hands for his distin- guished guest*). Aha! ha, ha! younger than any of them, Emily.

Lady Brock. Flatterer. (*To* LADY MARY) You seem in high spirits, Mary.   400

Lady Mary (*gaily*). I am.

Lady Brock. (*with a significant glance at* LORD BROCKLEHURST). After ——

Lady Mary. I — I mean. The fact is ——

(*Again that disconcerting glance be- tween the Countess and her son.*

Lord Loam (*humorously*). She hears wedding bells, Emily, ha, ha!   405

Lady Brock. (*coldly*). Do you, Mary? Can't say I do; but I'm hard of hearing.

Lady Mary (*instantly her match*). If you don't, Lady Brocklehurst, I'm sure I don't.

Lord Loam (*nervously*). Tut, tut. Seen   410 our curios from the island, Emily? I should like you to examine them.

Lady Brock. Thank you, Henry. I am glad you say that, for I have just taken the liberty of asking two of them to step upstairs.   415

There is an uncomfortable silence, which the entrance of CRICHTON *with* TWEENY *does not seem to dissipate.* CRICHTON *is impenetrable, but* TWEENY *hangs back in fear*

Lord Brock. (*stoutly*). Loam, I have no hand in this.

Lady Brock. (*undisturbed*). Pooh, what have I done? You always begged me to speak to the servants, Henry, and I merely wanted   420 to discover whether the views you used to hold about equality were adopted on the island; it seemed a splendid opportunity, but Mr. Woolley has not a word on the subject.

                    (*All eyes turn to* ERNEST.

Ern. (*with confidence*). The fact is —   425
                    (*The fatal words again.*

Lord Loam (*not quite certain what he is to assure her of*). I assure you, Emily —

Lady Mary (*as cold as steel*). Father, nothing whatever happened on the island of which I, for one, am ashamed, and I hope Crichton will be allowed to answer Lady Brocklehurst's   430 questions.

Lady Brock. To be sure. There's nothing to make a fuss about, and we're a family party. (*To* CRICHTON) Now, truthfully, my man.

Crich. (*calmly*). I promise that, my   435 lady.

          (*Some hearts sink, the hearts that could never understand a* CRICHTON.

Lady Brock. (*sharply*). Well, were you all equal on the island?

Crich. No, my lady. I think I may say there was as little equality there as else-   440 where.

Lady Brock. All the social distinctions were preserved?

Crich. As at home, my lady.

Lady Brock. The servants?   445

Crich. They had to keep their place.

Lady Brock. Wonderful. How was it managed? (*With an inspiration*) You, girl, tell me that.

          (*Can there be a more critical moment?*

Twee. (*in agony*). If you please, my   450 lady, it was all the Gov.'s doing.

          (*They give themselves up for lost.*
          LORD LOAM *tries to sink out of sight.*

Crich. In the regrettable slang of the servants' hall, my lady, the master is usually referred to as the Gov.

Lady Brock. I see. (*She turns to* LORD   455 LOAM.) You —

Lord Loam (*reappearing*). Yes, I understand that is what they call me.

Lady Brock. (*to* CRICHTON). You didn't even take your meals with the family?   460

Crich. No, my lady, I dined apart.

          (*Is all safe?*

Lady Brock. (*alas*). You, girl, also? Did you dine with Crichton?

Twee. (*scared*). No, your ladyship.

Lady Brock. (*fastening on her*). With   465 whom?

Twee. I took my bit of supper with — with Daddy and Polly and the rest.   (*Væ victis.*[1]

Ern. (*leaping into the breach*). Dear old Daddy — he was our monkey. You re-   470 member our monkey, Agatha?

Aga. Rather! What a funny old darling he was.

Cath. (*thus encouraged*). And don't you think Polly was the sweetest little parrot,   475 Mary?

Lady Brock. Ah! I understand; animals you had domesticated?

Lord Loam (*heavily*). Quite so — quite so.

Lady Brock. The servants' teas that   480 used to take place here once a month —

Crich. They did not seem natural on the island, my lady, and were discontinued by the Gov.'s orders.

[1] Woe to the vanquished.

Lord Brock. A clear proof, Loam, that 485 they were a mistake here.

Lord Loam (*seeing the opportunity for a diversion*). I admit it frankly. I abandon them. Emily, as the result of our experiences on the island, I think of going over to the Tories. 490

Lady Brock. I am delighted to hear it.

Lord Loam (*expanding*). Thank you, Crichton, thank you; that is all.

(*He motions to them to go, but the time is not yet.*

Lady Brock. One moment. (*There is a universal but stifled groan.*) Young people, 495 Crichton, will be young people, even on an island; now, I suppose there was a certain amount of — shall we say sentimentalizing, going on?

Crich. Yes, my lady, there was. 500

Lord Brock. (*ashamed*). Mother!

Lady Brock. (*disregarding him*). Which gentleman? (*To* Tweeny) You, girl, tell me.

Twee. (*confused*). If you please, my lady ——

Ern. (*hurriedly*). The fact is —— 505

(*He is checked as before, and probably says "Damn" to himself, but he has saved the situation.*

Twee. (*gasping*). It was him — Mr. Ernest, your ladyship.

Lady Brock. (*counsel for the prosecution*). With which lady?

Aga. I have already told you, Lady Brocklehurst, that Ernest and I —— 510

Lady Brock. Yes, *now;* but you were two years on the island. (*Looking at* Lady Mary) Was it this lady?

Twee. No, your ladyship.

Lady Brock. Then I don't care which 515 of the others it was. (Tweeny *gurgles.*) Well, I suppose that will do.

Lord Brock. Do! I hope you are ashamed of yourself, mother. (*To* Crichton, *who is going*) You are an excellent fellow, 520 Crichton; and if, after we are married, you ever wish to change your place, come to us.

Lady Mary (*losing her head for the only time*). Oh, no, impossible.

Lady Brock. (*at once suspicious*). Why impossible? (Lady Mary *cannot answer,* 525

or perhaps she is too proud.) Do you see why it should be impossible, my man?

(*He can make or mar his unworthy* Mary now. Have you any doubt of him?

Crich. Yes, my lady. I had not told you, my lord, but as soon as your lordship is suited I wish to leave service. 530

(*They are all immensely relieved, except poor* Tweeny.

Tre. (*the only curious one*). What will you do, Crichton?

(Crichton *shrugs his shoulders; "God knows," it may mean.*

Crich. Shall I withdraw, my lord?

(*He withdraws without a tremor,* Tweeny *accompanying him. They can all breathe again; the thunderstorm is over.*

Lady Brock. (*thankful to have made herself unpleasant*). Horrid of me, wasn't it? But if one wasn't disagreeable now and again, it 535 would be horribly tedious to be an old woman. He will soon be yours, Mary, and then — think of the opportunities you will have of being disagreeable to me. On that understanding, my dear, don't you think we 540 might —? (*Their cold lips meet.*

Lord Loam (*vaguely*). Quite so — quite so.

(Crichton *announces dinner, and they file out.* Lady Mary *stays behind a moment and impulsively holds out her hand.*

Lady Mary. To wish you every dear happiness.

Crich. (*an enigma to the last*). The 545 same to you, my lady.

Lady Mary. Do you despise me, Crichton? (*The man who could never tell a lie makes no answer.*) You are the best man among us.

Crich. On an island, my lady, perhaps; but in England, no. 550

Lady Mary. Then there's something wrong with England.

Crich. My lady, not even from you can I listen to a word against England.

Lady Mary. Tell me one thing: you 555 have not lost your courage?

Crich. No, my lady.

(*She goes. He turns out the lights.*

THE END

INTRODUCTION TO
The Silver Box

The Rise of the "Art Theater": Galsworthy and the "Problem Play"

THE RISE OF THE "ART THEATER"

THE world's first "art theater" or "little theater" started at Paris in 1887 under the leadership of an amateur producer, André Antoine. The success of Antoine's Free Theater led Otto Brahm and Paul Schlenther to found the Free Theater of Berlin two years later. These playhouses welcomed any drama of literary merit, however experimental, but in the main they encouraged a style of playwriting, production, and acting as nearly like real life as possible. In close imitation of the Paris and Berlin Free Theaters, J. E. Vedrenne and Harley Granville-Barker, a talented playwright as well as stage director, opened England's first full-fledged "art theater" in 1904. This successful venture prompted the establishment of the influential "repertory theaters" at Manchester (1907) and Birmingham. Vedrenne and Granville-Barker produced during their three seasons (1904–07) at the Court Theater, London, the works of such well-known dramatists as Ibsen, Gorky, Maeterlinck, Hauptmann, and Shaw; they also discovered several native writers of promise. The most important of their discoveries was John Galsworthy; he, Shaw, and Barrie constituted the "Big Three" of English drama in the first half of the twentieth century.

GALSWORTHY AND THE "PROBLEM PLAY"

Galsworthy, born on August 14, 1867, at Coombe, Surrey, came from an old and superior Devon family. His background and education typified those of the English gentleman of property a half-century ago. He attended the fashionable Harrow School where he excelled both in scholarship and in extra-curricular activities, especially madrigal singing, football, and track. Then, electing his father's profession, he took the law course at New College, Oxford, achieved an honor degree, and was admitted to the London bar in 1890. His interest in a legal career soon waned; travel to Australia, Africa, and other far corners of the globe followed. In 1895 he commenced writing at the instigation of his cousin's wife, Ada, whom he himself married a decade later.

The year 1906 saw Galsworthy under the inspiration of this very happy marriage advance overnight to the front rank of both English novelists and dramatists. His maiden play, *The Silver Box*, and the initial volume of his now famous *Forsyte Saga, The Man of Property*, aroused lavish praise almost simultaneously. The popularity of both his fiction and his drama gradually spread around the world. In 1929 he was awarded the Order of Merit, and in 1932 the Nobel Prize for Literature. After the first World

War, except for occasional sojourns in Arizona, he carried on the retired life of a man of letters at Holly Brush Hill, Hampstead, a favorite suburb with London writers and artists. There, on January 31, 1933, he died, beloved by all sorts of persons for his charity and admired for being, in Barrie's words, "a bar of gold."

Galsworthy's drama reflected what he described as "an awakened humanity in the conscience of [his] age." All his more significant plays expound an obvious sociological message. *The Silver Box* (1906) deals with the law's injustice, a theme to other aspects of which Galsworthy returned in *Justice* (1910) and *Escape* (1926). *Strife* (1909) sets forth the conflict between capital and labor; *The Skin Game* (1920), the conflict between classes; *Loyalties* (1922), the conflict between races. *The Pigeon* (1912), a "nightmarish" piece about the treatment of social waifs and misfits, depicts its author in the person of the tenderminded artist, Wellwyn. This self-portrait reveals Galsworthy's belief in the supremacy of compassion among human attributes. It was his profound sympathy for the weak, the unfortunate, the persecuted — in fact, for the underdog in any situation — which gave rise to the social consciousness so predominant in his writing for the theater.

Galsworthy ventured into the theater with an unusual comprehension of his objectives and with an equally unusual capacity for their immediate attainment. He wrote in retrospect: "My dramatic invasion, and the form of it, was dictated by revolt at the artificial nature of the English play of the period, and by a resolute intention to present real life on the stage. I had never seen an Ibsen play . . . I never had any apprentice years." His pioneer effort for the stage so successfully conveyed the illusion of complete realism over against the background of a social problem that thenceforth he attempted little more than minor variations in his dramatic pattern. Behind this pattern lay his basic conviction that "the perfect dramatist rounds up his characters and facts within the ring-fence of a dominant idea." Hence "a drama must be shaped so as to have a spire of meaning. Every grouping of life and character has its inherent moral, and the business of the dramatist is so to pose the group as to bring that moral poignantly to the light of day." In his posing Galsworthy tried to express the "just, gentle, restrained" temper of his ideal playwright and "to set before the public the phenomena of life and character, selected and combined, but not distorted, by the dramatist's outlook, . . . leaving the public to put down such poor moral as nature may afford."

"Within the enclosing atmosphere of an idea," therefore, Galsworthy constructed his plot out of the interplay between temperament and circumstance, but always aimed to hang the plot to the characters. Nevertheless, in characterization, he admitted, the stage inclined him to "the fashioning of types rather than of individuals." Few well-rounded figures, like Roberts the labor leader in *Strife* and Calder the law-clerk in *Justice*, appear in his plays. His dramatic art derives its chief power from the skillful proportioning of action, dialogue, and character. He displayed superb command of what he termed "the most exacting and difficult of all techniques," the "naturalistic." It seeks, so he explained, "to *produce* the perfectly natural conversation and movements" of persons in a given locale, so that "each natural phrase spoken and each natural movement made has not only to contribute toward the growth and perfection of a drama's soul, but also to be revelation, phrase by phrase, movement by movement, of essential traits of character."

Galsworthy's "naturalism" presents human conflict not only with sympathy, balance, and rigorous actuality, but with a detachment which induces a sense of the ultimate irony in modern civilization. He saw the codes set up by mankind for mutual justice and protection now so institutionalized and inflexible that they wreak injustice or destruction on countless individuals. Thus men have become the victims of their own social systems. The numerous facets of this fundamental and ironic problem steadily furnished Galsworthy with "spires of meaning" for his theatrical works. Intellectual penetration, backed by masterful craftsmanship, qualifies his social problem plays for a permanent and notable place in world drama.

"THE SILVER BOX"

No play ever established its author's eminence more suddenly and at the same time more justifiably than *The Silver Box*. In the autumn of 1905 Edward Garnett, well-known London critic, recommended to Galsworthy that he turn aside from fiction for a moment and try his hand at a play for the select Granville-Barker "repertory theater." Galsworthy, after some months of deliberation on a subject, began in February, 1906, and by April completed a play which he first entitled *The Cigarette Box*. Subsequently he changed the name to *The Silver Box*, a title more suggestive of the wealth which is the crucial factor of the plot. Granville-Barker and his literary adviser, Bernard Shaw, at once approved the Galsworthy manuscript for performance. A distinguished cast gave *The Silver Box* its premiere on Tuesday, September 25, 1906, at the Court Theater. James Hearn acted Barthwick; Frances Ivor, Mrs. Barthwick; A. E. Matthews, Jack Barthwick; Norman McKinnel, Jones; Irene Rooke, Mrs. Jones. The original run consisted of eight matinées, but the play created such "a strong and immediate sensation" that it became an outstanding piece in Granville-Barker's repertoire both at the Court Theater and later at the Duke of York's Theater, London. The original American production at the Empire Theater, New York, in 1907 afforded Ethel Barrymore a fine opportunity to add to her early reputation by starring as Mrs. Jones.

The Silver Box exemplifies the primary rule of Galsworthy's dramaturgy that a play should be shaped around "a dominant idea." In this case the theme is, according to the author, that "the mechanical wide-branching power of money makes 'one law for the rich, another for the poor.'" Jack Barthwick, the good-for-nothing son of a wealthy Liberal member of Parliament, through family influence escapes any legal penalty for his petty theft, but Jones, the unemployed husband of the Barthwicks' charwoman, gets a prison sentence for the identical misdemeanor. Furthermore, the judge denounces Jones in open court as "a nuisance to the community" (Act III, l. 614), exactly what Barthwick had called his son in private. Galsworthy worked out his drama to the perfect climax in which to voice a protest at discrimination against the poorer classes. In the person of the sentenced Jones he reminds a world audience about young Barthwick with a bitter shout, "It's *'is money* got *'im* off — *Justice!*" (Act III, ll. 625–26).

Galsworthy assembled for his exhibit of the machinery of justice a group of characters with representative attitudes toward the issue involved. His instructions to Granville-Barker stated that Mrs. Barthwick, "the hard-mouthed woman," seen "by the dozen in Harrods Stores" (a high-class London department store with many branches), is to show "want of imagination"; Mr. Barthwick, "want of courage"; Jack Barthwick, "want of principle"; Mr. Jones, "smoldering revolt"; Mrs. Jones, "passivity." These typical strains of temperament clash in a neat, pyramid-like pattern of situations which reaches its apex with the final courtroom scene. The meeting between the Barthwicks and Mrs. Jones (Act I, ll. 421–610) excellently illustrates how Galsworthy's simple, accurate diction and careful economy of movement effect unusual dramatic intensity. The restraint of his technique and character-drawing preserves *The Silver Box* from what easily might become melodrama and turns it into a strong, deeply ironic comedy on a form of human injustice as prevalent in modern as in ancient society.

[For further study of the English theater since 1900, see E. R. Reynolds, *Modern English Drama* (1949); for Galsworthy, Robert H. Coats, *John Galsworthy as a Dramatic Artist* (1926); H. V. Marrott, *The Life and Letters of John Galsworthy* (1936); John Galsworthy, *Some Platitudes Concerning Drama* in *The Inn of Tranquillity* (1912).]

JOHN GALSWORTHY
The Silver Box

DRAMATIS PERSONAE

JOHN BARTHWICK, M.P., *a wealthy Liberal*
MRS. BARTHWICK, *his wife*
JACK BARTHWICK, *their son*
ROPER, *their solicitor*
MRS. JONES, *their charwoman*
MARLOW, *their manservant*
WHEELER, *their maidservant*
JONES, *the stranger within their gates*
MRS. SEDDON, *a landlady*

SNOW, *a detective*
A POLICE MAGISTRATE
AN UNKNOWN LADY, *from beyond*
TWO LITTLE GIRLS, *homeless*
LIVENS, *their father*
A RELIEVING OFFICER
A MAGISTRATE'S CLERK
AN USHER
Policemen, Clerks, and Others

TIME: *The present. The action of the first two acts takes place on Easter Tuesday; the action of the third on Easter Wednesday week.*

Act I, Scene 1: *Rockingham Gate, London. John Barthwick's dining-room.*
  Scene 2: *The same.*
  Scene 3: *The same.*
Act II, Scene 1: *The Jones's lodgings, Merthyr Street, London.*
  Scene 2: *John Barthwick's dining-room.*
Act III: *A London police court.*

ACT I

SCENE I

The curtain rises on the BARTHWICKS' *dining-room, large, modern, and well furnished; the window curtains drawn. Electric light is burning. On the large round dining-table is set out a tray with whisky, a syphon, and a silver cigarette-box. It is past midnight.*

A fumbling is heard outside the door. It is opened suddenly; JACK BARTHWICK *seems to fall into the room. He stands holding by the doorknob, staring before him, with a beatific smile. He is in evening dress and opera hat, and carries in his hand a sky-blue velvet lady's reticule. His boyish face is freshly colored and clean-shaven. An overcoat is hanging on his arm*

Jack. Hello! I've got home all ri' ——

(*Defiantly*) Who says I sh'd never've opened th' door without 'sistance? (*He staggers in, fumbling with the reticule. A lady's handkerchief and purse of crimson silk fall out.*) 5 Serve her joll' well right — everything droppin' out. Th' cat. I've scored her off — I've got her bag. (*He swings the reticule.*) Serves her joll' well right. (*He takes a cigarette out of the silver box and puts it in his mouth.*) Never 10 gave tha' fellow anything! (*He hunts through all his pockets and pulls a shilling out; it drops and rolls away. He looks for it.*) Beastly shilling! (*He looks again.*) Base ingratitude! Absolutely nothing. (*He laughs.*) Mus' 15 tell him I've got absolutely nothing.

He lurches through the door and down a corridor, and presently returns, followed by JONES, *who is advanced in liquor.* JONES, *about thirty years of age, has hollow cheeks, black circles round his eyes, and rusty clothes. He looks as though he might be unemployed, and enters in a hang-dog manner*

Jack. Sh! sh! sh! Don't you make a noise, whatever you do. Shu' the door, an' have a drink. (*Very solemnly*) You helped me to open the door — I've got nothin' for you. 20 This is my house. My father's name's Barthwick; he's Member of Parliament — Liberal Member of Parliament: I've told you that before. Have a drink! (*He pours out whisky and drinks it up.*) I'm not drunk —— 25 (*Subsiding on a sofa*) Tha's all right. Wha's your name? My name's Barthwick, so's my father's; *I'm a Liberal too — wha're you?*

Jones (*in a thick sardonic voice*). I'm a bloomin' Conser*vative.* My name's Jones! 30 My wife works 'ere; she's the char; she works 'ere.

Jack. Jones? (*He laughs.*) There's 'nother Jones at College with me. I'm not a Socialist myself; I'm a Liberal — there's ve-lill 35 difference, because of the principles of the Lib — Liberal Party. We're all equal before the law — tha's rot, tha's silly. (*Laughs.*) Wha' was I about to say? Give me some whisky. (*JONES gives him the whisky he desires, to-* 40 *gether with a squirt of syphon.*) Wha' I was goin' tell you was — I've had a row with her. (*He waves the reticule.*) Have a drink, Jones — sh'd never have got in without you — tha's why I'm giving you a drink. Don' care 45 who knows I've scored her off. Th' cat! (*He throws his feet up on the sofa.*) Don' you make a noise, whatever you do. You pour out a drink — you make yourself good long, long drink — you take cigarette — you take 50 anything you like. Sh'd never have got in without you. (*Closing his eyes*) You're a Tory — you're a Tory Socialist. I'm Liberal myself — have a drink — I'm an excel'nt chap.

(*His head drops back. He, smiling, falls asleep, and JONES stands looking at him; then, snatching up JACK'S glass, he drinks it off. He picks the reticule from off JACK'S shirt-front, holds it to the light, and smells at it.*)

Jones. Been on the tiles and brought 55 'ome some of yer cat's fur.

(*He stuffs it into JACK'S breast pocket.*
Jack (*murmuring*). I've scored you off! You cat!

(*JONES looks around him furtively; he pours out whisky and drinks it. From the silver box he takes a cigarette, puffs at it, and drinks more whisky. There is no sobriety left in him.*

Jones. Fat lot o' things they've got 'ere! (*He sees the crimson purse lying on the* 60 *floor.*) More cat's fur. Puss, puss! (*He fingers it, drops it on the tray, and looks at* JACK.) Calf! Fat calf! (*He sees his own presentment in a mirror. Lifting his hands, with fingers spread, he stares at it; then looks again at* 65 JACK, *clenching his fist as if to batter in his sleeping, smiling face. Suddenly he tilts the rest of the whisky into the glass and drinks it. With cunning glee he takes the silver box and purse and pockets them.*) I'll score *you* off too, that's 70 wot I'll do!

(*He gives a little snarling laugh and lurches to the door. His shoulder rubs against the switch; the light goes out. There is a sound as of a closing outer door.*

The curtain falls.
The curtain rises again at once.

SCENE 2

In the BARTHWICKS' *dining-room.* JACK *is still asleep; the morning light is coming through the curtains. The time is half-past eight.* WHEELER, *brisk person, enters with a dustpan, and* MRS. JONES *more slowly with a scuttle*

Wheel. (*drawing the curtains*). That precious husband of yours was round for you after you'd gone yesterday, Mrs. Jones. Wanted your money for drink, I suppose. He hangs about the corner here half the time. I saw him 5 outside the "Goat and Bells" when I went to the post last night. If I were you I wouldn't live with him. I wouldn't live with a man that raised his hand to me. I wouldn't put up with it. Why don't you take your children and 10 leave him? If you put up with 'im it'll only make him worse. I never can see why, because a man's married you, he should knock you about.

Mrs. Jones (slim, dark-eyed, and dark- 15 *haired; oval-faced, and with a smooth, soft, even voice; her manner patient, her way of talking quite impersonal; she wears a blue linen dress, and boots with holes).* It was nearly two last night before he come home, and he wasn't him- 20 self. He made me get up, and he knocked me about; he didn't seem to know *what* he was saying or doing. Of course I *would* leave him, but I'm really afraid of what he'd do to me. He's such a violent man when he's not him- 25 self.

Wheel. Why don't you get him locked up? You'll never have any peace until you get him locked up. If I were you I'd go to the police court tomorrow. That's what I would do. 30

Mrs. Jones. Of course I ought to go, because he does treat me so badly when he's not him-self. But you see, Bettina, he has a very hard time — he's been out of work two months, and it preys upon his mind. When he's in 35 work he behaves himself much better. It's when he's out of work that he's so violent.

Wheel. Well, if you won't take any steps you'll never get rid of him.

Mrs. Jones. Of course it's very wearing 40 to me; I don't get my sleep at nights. And it's not as if I were getting help from him, because I have to do for the children and all of us. And he throws such dreadful things up at me, talks of my having men to follow me about. 45 Such a thing never happens; no man ever speaks to me. And of course it's just the other way. It's what he does that's wrong and makes me so unhappy. And then he's always threatenin' to cut my throat if I leave him. 50 It's all the drink, and things preying on his mind; he's not a bad man really. Sometimes he'll speak quite kind to me, but I've stood so much from him, I don't feel it in me to speak kind back, but just keep myself to myself. 55 And he's all right with the children too, except when he's not himself.

Wheel. You mean when he's drunk, the beauty.

Mrs. Jones. Yes. *(Without change of* 60 *voice)* There's the young gentleman asleep on the sofa. *(They both look silently at* JACK.

Mrs. Jones (at last, in her soft voice). He doesn't look quite himself.

Wheel. He's a young limb, that's what 65 he is. It's my belief he was tipsy last night, like your husband. It's another kind of bein' out of work that sets *him* to drink. I'll go and tell Marlow. This is his job. *(She goes.*

*(*MRS. JONES, *upon her knees, begins a gentle sweeping.*

Jack (waking). Who's there? What is 70 it?

Mrs. Jones. It's me, sir, Mrs. Jones.

Jack (sitting up and looking round). Where is it — what — what time is it?

Mrs. Jones. It's getting on for nine 75 o'clock, sir.

Jack. For nine! Why — what! *(Rising, and loosening his tongue; putting hand to his head, and staring hard at Mrs. Jones)* Look here, you, Mrs. — Mrs. Jones — don't you 80 say you caught me asleep here.

Mrs. Jones. No, sir, of course I won't, sir.

Jack. It's quite an accident; I don't know how it happened. I must have forgotten to go to bed. It's a queer thing. I've got a 85 most beastly headache. Mind you don't say anything, Mrs. Jones.

Goes out and passes MARLOW *in the doorway.* MARLOW *is young and quiet; he is clean-shaven, and his hair is brushed high from his forehead in a coxcomb. Incidentally a butler, he is first a man. He looks at* MRS. JONES, *and smiles a private smile*

Mar. Not the first time, and won't be the last. Looked a bit dicky, eh, Mrs. Jones?

Mrs. Jones. He didn't look quite him- 90 self. Of course I didn't take notice.

Mar. You're used to them. How's your old man?

Mrs. Jones (softly, as throughout). Well, he was very bad last night; he didn't seem to 95 know what he was about. He was very late, and he was most abusive. But now, of course, he's asleep.

Mar. That's his way of finding a job, eh?

Mrs. Jones. As a rule, Mr. Marlow, he 100 goes out early every morning looking for work, and sometimes he comes in fit to drop — and of course I can't say he doesn't try to get it, because he does. Trade's very bad. (*She stands quite still, her pan and brush before her, at* 105 *the beginning and the end of long vistas of experience, traversing them with her impersonal eye.*) But he's not a good husband to me — last night he hit me, and he was so dreadfully abusive.

Mar. Bank 'oliday, eh! He's too fond 110 of the "Goat and Bells," that's what's the matter with him. I see him at the corner late every night. He hangs about.

Mrs. Jones. He gets to feeling very low walking about all day after work, and being re- 115 fused so often, and then when he gets a drop in him it goes to his head. But he shouldn't treat his wife as he treats me. Sometimes I've had to go and walk about at night, when he wouldn't let me stay in the room; but he's 120 sorry for it afterwards. And he hangs about after me, he waits for me in the street; and I don't think he ought to, because I've always been a good wife to him. And I tell him Mrs. Barthwick wouldn't like him coming 125 about the place. But that only makes him angry, and he says dreadful things about the gentry. Of course it was through me that he first lost his place, through his not treating me right; and that's made him bitter against 130 the gentry. He had a very good place as groom in the country; but it made such a stir, because of course he didn't treat me right.

Mar. Got the sack?

Mrs. Jones. Yes; his employer said he 135 couldn't keep him, because there was a great deal of talk; and he said it was such a bad example. But it's very important for me to keep my work here; I have the three children, and I don't want him to come about after 140 me in the streets, and make a disturbance as he sometimes does.

Mar. (*holding up the empty decanter*). Not a drain! Next time he hits you get a witness and go down to the court —— 145

Mrs. Jones. Yes, I think I've made up my mind. I think I ought to.

Mar. That's right. Where's the ciga—? (*He searches for the silver box; he looks at* MRS. JONES, *who is sweeping on her hands and* 150 *knees; he checks himself and stands reflecting. From the tray he picks two half-smoked cigarettes, and reads the name on them.*) Nestor — where the deuce —?

(*With a meditative air he looks again at* MRS. JONES, *and, taking up* JACK'S *overcoat, he searches in the pockets.*

WHEELER, *with a tray of breakfast things, comes in*

Mar. (*aside to* WHEELER). Have you 155 seen the cigarette-box?

Wheel. No.

Mar. Well, it's gone. I put it on the tray last night. And he's been smoking (*showing her the ends of cigarettes*). It's not in these 160 pockets. He can't have taken it upstairs this morning! Have a good look in his room when he comes down. Who's been in here?

Wheel. Only me and Mrs. Jones.

Mrs. Jones. I've finished here; shall I 165 do the drawing-room now?

Wheel. (*looking at her doubtfully*). Have you seen —— Better do the boudwower first.

(MRS. JONES *goes out with pan and brush.* MARLOW *and* WHEELER *look each other in the face.*

Mar. It'll turn up.

Wheel. (*hesitating*). You don't think 170 she —— (*Nodding at the door.*

Mar. (*stoutly*). I don't — I never believes anything of anybody.

Wheel. But the master'll have to be told.

Mar. You wait a bit, and see if it don't 175 turn up. Suspicion's no business of ours. I set my mind against it.

The curtain falls.

The curtain rises again at once.

SCENE 3

BARTHWICK *and* MRS. BARTHWICK *are seated at the breakfast table. He is a man between fifty and sixty; quietly important, with a bald forehead, and pince-nez, and the*

"Times" in his hand. She is a lady of nearly fifty, well dressed, with grayish hair, good features, and a decided manner. They face each other

Barth. (*from behind his paper*). The Labor man has got in at the by-election for Barnside, my dear.

Mrs. Barth. Another Labor? I can't think what on earth the country is about. 5

Barth. I predicted it. It's not a matter of vast importance.

Mrs. Barth. Not? How can you take it so calmly, John? To me it's simply outrageous. And there you sit, you Liberals, and pre- 10 tend to encourage these people!

Barth. (*frowning*). The representation of all parties is necessary for any proper reform, for any proper social policy.

Mrs. Barth. I've no patience with your 15 talk of reform — all that nonsense about social policy. We know perfectly well what it is they want; they want things for themselves. Those Socialists and Labor men are an absolutely selfish set of people. They have no sense 20 of patriotism, like the upper classes; *they simply want what we've got.*

Barth. Want what we've got! (*He stares into space.*) My dear, what are you talking about? (*With a contortion*) I'm no alarm- 25 ist.

Mrs. Barth. Cream? Quite uneducated men! Wait until they begin to tax our invest-ments. I'm convinced that when they once get a chance they will tax everything — 30 they've no feeling for the country. You Liberals and Conservatives, you're all alike; you don't see an inch before your noses. You've no imagination, not a scrap of imagina-tion between you. You ought to join 35 hands and nip it in the bud.

Barth. You're talking nonsense! How is it possible for Liberals and Conservatives to join hands, as you call it? That shows how absurd it is for women —— Why, the very es- 40 sence of a Liberal is to trust in the people!

Mrs. Barth. Now, John, eat your breakfast. As if there were any real difference between you and the Conservatives! All the upper classes have the same interests to protect, 45

and the same principles. (*Calmly*) Oh! you're sitting upon a volcano, John.

Barth. What!

Mrs. Barth. I read a letter in the paper yes-terday. I forget the man's name, but it 50 made the whole thing perfectly clear. You don't look things in the face.

Barth. Indeed! (*Heavily*) I am a Liberal! Drop the subject, please!

Mrs. Barth. Toast? I quite agree with 55 what this man says: Education is simply ruin-ing the lower classes. It unsettles them, and that's the worst thing for us all. I see an enormous difference in the manner of servants.

Barth. (*with suspicious emphasis*). I 60 welcome any change that will lead to some-thing better. (*He opens a letter.*) H'm! This is that affair of Master Jack's again. "High Street, Oxford. Sir, We have received Mr. John Barthwick, Senior's, draft for forty 65 pounds." Oh! the letter's to him! "We now enclose the check you cashed with us, which, as we stated in our previous letter, was not met on presentation at your bank. We are, sir, yours obediently, Moss and Sons, Tailors." 70 H'm! (*Staring at the check*) A pretty business altogether! The boy might have been pro-secuted.

Mrs. Barth. Come, John, you know Jack didn't mean anything; he only thought 75 he was overdrawing. I still think his bank ought to have cashed that check. They must know your position.

Barth. (*replacing in the envelope the letter and the check*). Much good that would have 80 done him in a court of law.

He stops as JACK *comes in, fastening his waist-coat and staunching a razor cut upon his chin*

Jack (*sitting down between them, and speaking with an artificial joviality*). Sorry I'm late. (*He looks lugubriously at the dishes.*) Tea, please, mother. Any letters for me? (BARTH- 85 WICK *hands the letter to him.*) But look here, I say, this has been opened! I do wish you wouldn't ——

Barth. (*touching the envelope*). I suppose I'm entitled to this name. 90

Jack (*sulkily*). Well, I can't help having your name, father! (*He reads the letter, and mutters.*) Brutes!

Barth. (*eyeing him*). You don't deserve to be so well out of that. 95

Jack. Haven't you ragged me enough, dad?

Mrs. Barth. Yes, John, let Jack have his breakfast.

Barth. If you hadn't had me to come to, where would you have been? It's the 100 merest accident — suppose you had been the son of a poor man or a clerk. Obtaining money with a check you knew your bank could not meet. It might have ruined you for life. I can't see what's to become of you if these 105 are your principles. I never did anything of the sort myself.

Jack. I expect you always had lots of money. If you've got plenty of money, of course ——

Barth. On the contrary, I had not your 110 advantages. My father kept me very short of money.

Jack. How much had you, dad?

Barth. It's not material. The question is, do you feel the gravity of what you did? 115

Jack. I don't know about the gravity. Of course, I'm very sorry if you think it was wrong. Haven't I said so! I should never have done it at all if I hadn't been so jolly hard up. 120

Barth. How much of that forty pounds have you got left, Jack?

Jack (*hesitating*). I don't know — not much.

Barth. How much?

Jack (*desperately*). I haven't got any. 125

Barth. What?

Jack. I know I've got the most beastly headache. (*He leans his head on his hand.*)

Mrs. Barth. Headache? My dear boy! Can't you eat any breakfast? 130

Jack (*drawing in his breath*). Too jolly bad!

Mrs. Barth. I'm so sorry. Come with me, dear; I'll give you something that will take it away at once.

They leave the room; and BARTHWICK, *tearing up the letter, goes to the fireplace and puts the pieces in the fire. While he is doing this*

MARLOW *comes in, and looking round him, is about quietly to withdraw*

Barth. What's that? What d'you 135 want?

Mar. I was looking for Mr. John, sir.

Barth. What d'you want Mr. John for?

Mar. (*with hesitation*). I thought I should find him here, sir. 140

Barth. (*suspiciously*). Yes, but what do you want him for?

Mar. (*offhandedly*). There's a lady called — asked to speak to him for a minute, sir.

Barth. A lady, at this time in the morn- 145 ing. What sort of a lady?

Mar. (*without expression in his voice*). I can't tell, sir; no particular sort. She might be after charity. She might be a Sister of Mercy, I should think, sir. 150

Barth. Is she dressed like one?

Mar. No, sir, she's in plain clothes, sir.

Barth. Didn't she say what she wanted?

Mar. No, sir.

Barth. Where did you leave her? 155

Mar. In the hall, sir.

Barth. In the hall? How do you know she's not a thief — not got designs on the house?

Mar. No, sir, I don't fancy so, sir.

Barth. Well, show her in here; I'll see 160 her myself.

MARLOW *goes out with a private gesture of dismay. He soon returns, ushering in a young pale lady with dark eyes and pretty figure, in a modish, black, but rather shabby dress, a black-and-white trimmed hat with a bunch of Parma violets wrongly placed, and fuzzy-spotted veil. At the sight of* MR. BARTH-WICK *she exhibits every sign of nervousness.* MARLOW *goes out*

Unknown Lady. Oh! but — I beg pardon — there's some mistake — I ——

                (*She turns to fly.*

Barth. Whom did you want to see, madam?

Unknown (*stopping and looking back*). 165 It was Mr. *John* Barthwick I wanted to see.

Barth. I am John Barthwick, madam. What can I have the pleasure of doing for you?

Unknown. Oh! I — I don't ——

(*She drops her eyes.* Barthwick *scrutinizes her, and purses his lips.*

Barth. It was my son, perhaps, you 170 wished to see?

Unknown (*quickly*). Yes, of course, it's your son.

Barth. May I ask whom I have the pleasure of speaking to? 175

Unknown (*appeal and hardiness upon her face*). My name is — oh! it doesn't matter — I don't want to make any fuss. I just want to see your son for a minute. (*Boldly*) In fact, I *must* see him. 180

Barth. (*controlling his uneasiness*). My son is not very well. If necessary, no doubt I could attend to the matter; be so kind as to let me know ——

Unknown. Oh! but I *must* see him — 185 I've come on purpose — (*She bursts out nervously.*) I don't want to make any fuss, but the fact is, last — last night your son took away — he took away my —— (*She stops.*

Barth. (*severely*). Yes, madam, what? 190

Unknown. He took away my — my reticule.

Barth. Your reti —?

Unknown. I don't care about the reticule; it's not *that* I want — I'm sure I don't want to make any fuss — (*her face is quivering*) 195 — but — but — all my money was in it!

Barth. In what — in what?

Unknown. In my purse, in the reticule. It was a crimson silk purse. Really, I wouldn't have come — I don't want to make any 200 fuss. But I must get my money back — mustn't I?

Barth. Do you tell me that my son —?

Unknown. Oh! well, you see, he wasn't quite — I mean he was —— 205

(*She smiles mesmerically.*[1]

Barth. I beg your pardon.

Unknown (*stamping her foot*). Oh! don't you see — tipsy! We had a quarrel.

Barth. (*scandalized*). How? Where?

Unknown (*defiantly*). At my place. 210 We'd had supper at the —— and your son ——

Barth. (*pressing the bell*). May I ask how you

[1] Fascinatingly.

knew this house? Did he give you his name and address?

Unknown (*glancing sidelong*). I got it 215 out of his overcoat.

Barth. (*sardonically*). Oh! you got it out of his overcoat. And may I ask if my son will know you by daylight?

Unknown. Know me? I should jolly 220 — I mean, of course he will!

(Marlow *comes in.*

Barth. Ask Mr. John to come down. (Marlow *goes out, and* Barthwick *walks uneasily about.*) And how long have you enjoyed his acquaintanceship? 225

Unknown. Only since — only since Good Friday.

Barth. I am at a loss — I repeat I am at a loss ——

He glances at this unknown lady, who stands with eyes cast down, twisting her hands. And suddenly Jack *appears. He stops on seeing who is here, and the unknown lady hysterically giggles. There is a silence*

Barth. (*portentously*). This young — 230 er — lady says that last night — I think you said last night, madam — you took away ——

Unknown (*impulsively*). My reticule, and all my money was in a crimson silk purse.

Jack. Reticule. (*Looking round for 235 any chance to get away*) I don't know anything about it.

Barth. (*sharply*). Come, do you deny seeing this young lady last night?

Jack. Deny? No, of course. (*Whis- 240 pering*) Why did you give me away like this? What on earth did you come here for?

Unknown (*tearfully*). I'm sure I didn't want to — it's not likely, is it? You snatched it out of my hand — you know you did — and 245 the purse had all my money in it. I didn't follow you last night because I didn't want to make a fuss and it was so late, and you were so ——

Barth. Come, sir, don't turn your back 250 on me — explain!

Jack (*desperately*). I don't remember anything about it. (*In a low voice to his friend*) Why on earth couldn't you have written?

Unknown (*sullenly*). I want it now; I   255
must have it — I've got to pay my rent today.
(*She looks at* BARTHWICK.) They're only too
glad to jump on people who are not — not
well off.

Jack. I don't remember anything   260
about it, really. I don't remember anything
about last night at all. (*He puts his hand up
to his head.*) It's all — cloudy, and I've got
such a beastly headache.

Unknown. But you *took* it; you know   265
you did. You said you'd score me off.

Jack. Well, then, it must be here. I remember now — I remember something. Why
did I take the beastly thing?

Barth. Yes, why did you take the   270
beastly —— (*He turns abruptly to the window.*

Unknown (*with her mesmeric smile*). You
weren't quite —— were you?

Jack (*smiling pallidly*). I'm *awfully* sorry.
If there's anything I can do ——   275

Barth. Do? You can restore this property,
I suppose.

Jack. I'll go and have a look, but I really
don't think I've got it.

He goes out hurriedly. And BARTHWICK, *placing a chair, motions to the visitor to sit;
then, with pursed lips, he stands and eyes
her fixedly. She sits, and steals a look at
him; then turns away, and, drawing up her
veil, stealthily wipes her eyes. And* JACK
comes back

Jack (*ruefully holding out the empty*   280
reticule). Is that the thing? I've looked all
over — I can't find the purse anywhere. Are
you sure it was there?

Unknown (*tearfully*). Sure? Of course I'm
sure. A crimson silk purse. It was all   285
the money I had.

Jack. I really am awfully sorry — my head's
so jolly bad. I've asked the butler, but he
hasn't seen it.

Unknown. I *must* have my money ——   290

Jack. Oh! Of course — that'll be all right;
I'll see that that's all right. How much?

Unknown (*sullenly*). Seven pounds — twelve
— it's all I've got in the world.

Jack. That'll be all right; I'll — send   295
you a — check.

Unknown (*eagerly*). No; now, please. Give
me what was in my purse; I've got to pay my
rent this morning. They won't give me another day; I'm a fortnight behind already.   300

Jack (*blankly*). I'm awfully sorry; I really
haven't a penny in my pocket.

(*He glances stealthily at* BARTHWICK.

Unknown (*excitedly*). Come, I say, you
must — it's my money, and you took it. I'm
not going away without it. They'll turn   305
me out of my place.

Jack (*clasping his head*). But I can't give you
what I haven't got. Don't I tell you I haven't
a beastly cent?

Unknown (*tearing at her handkerchief*).   310
Oh! do give it me! (*She puts her hands together
in appeal; then, with sudden fierceness*) If you
don't I'll summons you. It's stealing, that's
what it is!

Barth. (*uneasily*). One moment, please.   315
As a matter of — er — principle, I shall settle
this claim. (*He produces money.*) Here is
eight pounds; the extra will cover the value of
the purse and your cab fares. I need make no
comment — no thanks are necessary.   320

(*Touching the bell, he holds the door ajar
in silence. The unknown lady stores
the money in her reticule, she looks
from* JACK *to* BARTHWICK, *and her
face is quivering faintly with a smile.
She hides it with her hand, and steals
away. Behind her* BARTHWICK
shuts the door.

Barth. (*with a solemnity*). H'm! This is a
nice thing to happen!

Jack (*impersonally*). What awful luck!

Barth. So this is the way that forty pounds
has gone! One thing after another!   325
Once more I should like to know where you'd
have been if it hadn't been for me! You don't
seem to have any principles. You — you're
one of those who are a nuisance to society; you
— you're dangerous! What your mother   330
would say I don't know. Your conduct, as
far as I can see, is absolutely unjustifiable.
It's — it's criminal. Why, a poor man who
behaved as you've done . . . d'you think he'd

have any mercy shown him? What you 335 want is a good lesson. You and your sort are — (*he speaks with feeling*) — a nuisance to the community. Don't ask me to help you next time. You're not fit to be helped.

Jack (*turning upon his sire, with un-* 340 *expected fierceness*). All right, I won't then, and see how you like it. You wouldn't have helped me this time, I know, if you hadn't been scared the thing would get into the papers. Where are the cigarettes? 345

Barth. (*regarding him uneasily*). Well — I'll say no more about it. (*He rings the bell.*) I'll pass it over for this once, but —— (MARLOW *comes in.*) You can clear away.

    (*He hides his face behind the "Times."*

Jack (*brightening*). I say, Marlow, 350 where are the cigarettes?

Mar. I put the box out with the whisky last night, sir, but this morning I can't find it any-where.

Jack. Did you look in my room? 355

Mar. Yes, sir; I've looked all over the house. I found two Nestor ends in the tray this morn-ing, so you must have been smokin' last night, sir. (*Hesitating*) I'm really afraid someone's purloined the box. 360

Jack (*uneasily*). Stolen it!

Barth. What's that? The cigarette-box! Is anything else missing?

Mar. No, sir; I've been through the plate.

Barth. Was the house all right this 365 morning? None of the windows open?

Mar. No, sir. (*Quietly to* JACK) You left your latchkey in the door last night, sir.

    (*He hands it back, unseen by* BARTH-
      WICK.

Jack. Tst!

Barth. Who's been in the room this 370 morning?

Mar. Me and Wheeler, and Mrs. Jones is all, sir, as far as I know.

Barth. Have you asked Mrs. Barthwick? (*To* JACK) Go and ask your mother if 375 she's had it; ask her to look and see if she's missed anything else. (JACK *goes upon this mission.*) Nothing is more disquieting than losing things like this.

Mar. No, sir. 380

Barth. Have you any suspicions?

Mar. No, sir.

Barth. This Mrs. Jones — how long has she been working here?

Mar. Only this last month, sir. 385

Barth. What sort of person?

Mar. I don't know much about her, sir; seems a very quiet, respectable woman.

Barth. Who did the room this morning?

Mar. Wheeler and Mrs. Jones, sir. 390

Barth. (*with his forefinger upraised*). Now, was this Mrs. Jones in the room alone at any time?

Mar. (*expressionless*). Yes, sir.

Barth. How do you know that? 395

Mar. (*reluctantly*). I found her here, sir.

Barth. And has Wheeler been in the room alone?

Mar. No, sir, she's not, sir. I should say, sir, that Mrs. Jones seems a very hon- 400 est ——

Barth. (*holding up his hand*). I want to know this: Has this Mrs. Jones been here the whole morning?

Mar. Yes, sir — no, sir — she stepped 405 over to the greengrocer's for cook.

Barth. H'm! Is she in the house now?

Mar. Yes, sir.

Barth. Very good. I shall make a point of clearing this up. On principle I shall 410 make a point of fixing the responsibility; it goes to the foundations of security. In all your interests ——

Mar. Yes, sir.

Barth. What sort of circumstances is 415 this Mrs. Jones in? Is her husband in work?

Mar. I believe not, sir.

Barth. Very well. Say nothing about it to anyone. Tell Wheeler not to speak of it, and ask Mrs. Jones to step up here. 420

Mar. Very good, sir.

MARLOW *goes out, his face concerned; and* BARTHWICK *stays, his face judicial and a little pleased, as befits a man conducting an inquiry.* MRS. BARTHWICK *and her son come in*

Barth. Well, my dear, you've not seen it, I suppose?

Mrs. Barth. No. But what an extraordinary thing, John! Marlow, of course, is 425 out of the question. I'm certain none of the maids —— as for cook!

Barth. Oh, cook!

Mrs. Barth. Of course! It's perfectly detestable to me to suspect anybody. 430

Barth. It is not a question of one's feelings. It's a question of justice. On principle ——

Mrs. Barth. I shouldn't be a bit surprised if the charwoman knew something about it. It was Laura who recommended her. 435

Barth. (*judicially*). I am going to have Mrs. Jones up. Leave it to me; and — er — remember that nobody is guilty until they're proved so. I shall be careful. I have no intention of frightening her; I shall give her 440 every chance. I hear she's in poor circumstances. If we are not able to do much for them we are bound to have the greatest sympathy with the poor. (MRS. JONES *comes in.*) (*Pleasantly*) Oh! good morning, Mrs. 445 Jones.

Mrs. Jones (*soft, and even, unemphatic*). Good morning, sir! Good morning, ma'am!

Barth. About your husband — he's not in work, I hear? 450

Mrs. Jones. No, sir; of course he's not in work just now.

Barth. Then I suppose he's earning nothing.

Mrs. Jones. No, sir, he's not earning anything just now, sir. 455

Barth. And how many children have you?

Mrs. Jones. Three children; but of course they don't eat very much, sir.

(*A little silence.*)

Barth. And how old is the eldest?

Mrs. Jones. Nine years old, sir. 460

Barth. Do they go to school?

Mrs. Jones. Yes, sir, they all three go to school every day.

Barth. (*severely*). And what about their food when you're out at work? 465

Mrs. Jones. Well, sir, I have to give them their dinner to take with them. Of course I'm not always able to give them anything; sometimes I have to send them without; but my husband is very good about the children 470 when he's in work. But when he's not in work of course he's a very difficult man.

Barth. He drinks, I suppose?

Mrs. Jones. Yes, sir. Of course I can't say he doesn't drink, because he does. 475

Barth. And I suppose he takes all your money?

Mrs. Jones. No, sir, he's very good about my money, except when he's not himself, and then, of course, he treats me very badly. 480

Barth. Now what is he — your husband?

Mrs. Jones. By profession, sir, of course he's a groom.

Barth. A groom! How came he to lose his place? 485

Mrs. Jones. He lost his place a long time ago, sir, and he's never had a very long job since; and now, of course, the motor-cars are against him.

Barth. When were you married to him, 490 Mrs. Jones?

Mrs. Jones. Eight years ago, sir — that was in ——

Mrs. Barth. (*sharply*). Eight? You said the eldest child was nine. 495

Mrs. Jones. Yes, ma'am; of course that was why he lost his place. He didn't treat me rightly, and of course his employer said he couldn't keep him because of the example.

Barth. You mean he — ahem —— 500

Mrs. Jones. Yes, sir; and of course after he lost his place he married me.

Mrs. Barth. You actually mean to say you — you were ——

Barth. My dear —— 505

Mrs. Barth. (*indignantly*). How disgraceful!

Barth. (*hurriedly*). And where are you living now, Mrs. Jones?

Mrs. Jones. We've not got a home, sir. Of course we've been obliged to put away 510 most of our things.

Barth. Put your things away! You mean to — to — er — to pawn them?

Mrs. Jones. Yes, sir, to put them away. We're living in Merthyr Street — that is 515 close by here, sir — at No. 34. We just have the one room.

Barth. And what do you pay a week?

Mrs. Jones. We pay six shillings a week, sir, for a furnished room. 520

Barth. And I suppose you're behind in the rent?

Mrs. Jones. Yes, sir, we're a little behind in the rent.

Barth. But *you're* in good work, aren't 525 you?

Mrs. Jones. Well, sir, I have a day in Stamford Place Thursdays. And Mondays and Wednesdays and Fridays I come here. But today, of course, is a half-day, because of 530 yesterday's Bank Holiday.

Barth. I see; four days a week, and you get half a crown [1] a day, is that it?

Mrs. Jones. Yes, sir, and my dinner; but sometimes it's only half a day, and that's 535 eighteenpence.

Barth. And when your husband earns anything he spends it in drink, I suppose?

Mrs. Jones. Sometimes he does, sir, and sometimes he gives it to me for the chil- 540 dren. Of course he would work if he could get it, sir, but it seems there are a great many people out of work.

Barth. Ah! Yes. We — er — won't go into that. (*Sympathetically*) And how 545 about your work here? Do you find it hard?

Mrs. Jones. Oh! no, sir, not very hard, sir; except of course, when I don't get my sleep at night.

Barth. Ah! And you help do all the 550 rooms? And sometimes, I suppose, you go out for cook?

Mrs. Jones. Yes, sir.

Barth. And you've been out this morning?

Mrs. Jones. Yes, sir, of course I had to 555 go to the greengrocer's.

Barth. Exactly. So your husband earns nothing? And he's a bad character.

Mrs. Jones. No, sir, I don't say that, sir. I think there's a great deal of good in 560 him; though he does treat me very bad sometimes. And of course I don't like to leave him, but I think I ought to, because really I hardly know how to stay with him. He often raises his hand to me. Not long ago he gave me 565 a blow here (*touches her breast*), and I can feel it now. So I think I ought to leave him, don't *you,* sir?

Barth. Ah! I can't help you there. It's

[1] Two shillings sixpence.

a very serious thing to leave your hus- 570 band. Very serious thing.

Mrs. Jones. Yes, sir, of course I'm afraid of what he might do to me if I were to leave him; he can be so very violent.

Barth. H'm! Well, *that* I can't pre- 575 tend to say anything about. It's the bad principle I'm speaking of ——

Mrs. Jones. Yes, sir; I know nobody can help me. I know I must decide for myself, and of course I know that he has a very hard 580 life. And he's fond of the children, and it's very hard for him to see them going without food.

Barth. (*hastily*). Well — er — thank you, I just wanted to hear about you. I don't think I need detain you any longer, Mrs. — 585 Jones.

Mrs. Jones. No, sir, thank you, sir.

Barth. Good morning, then.

Mrs. Jones. Good morning, sir; good morning, ma'am. 590

Barth. (*exchanging glances with his wife*). By the way, Mrs. Jones — I think it is only fair to tell you, a silver cigarette-box — er — is missing.

Mrs. Jones (*looking from one face to the* 595 *other*). I am very sorry, sir.

Barth. Yes; you have not seen it, I suppose?

Mrs. Jones (*realizing that suspicion is upon her; with an uneasy movement*). Where was it, sir, if you please, sir? 600

Barth. (*evasively*). Where did Marlow say? Er — in this room, yes, in *this* room.

Mrs. Jones. No, sir, I haven't seen it — of course if I'd seen it I should have noticed it.

Barth. (*giving her a rapid glance*). 605 You — you are sure of that?

Mrs. Jones (*impassively*). Yes, sir (*with a slow nodding of her head*). I have not seen it, and of course I *don't* know where it is.

(*She turns and goes quietly out.*

Barth. H'm! 610

(*The three* BARTHWICKS *avoid each other's glances.*

The curtain falls.

ACT II

SCENE I

The JONES'S *lodgings, Merthyr Street, at half-past two o'clock.*

The bare room, with tattered oilcloth and damp, distempered walls, has an air of tidy wretchedness. On the bed lies JONES, *half-dressed; his coat is thrown across his feet, and muddy boots are lying on the floor close by. He is asleep. The door is opened and* MRS. JONES *comes in, dressed in a pinched black jacket and old black sailor hat; she carries a parcel wrapped up in the "Times." She puts her parcel down, unwraps an apron, half a loaf, two onions, three potatoes, and a tiny piece of bacon. Taking a teapot from the cupboard, she rinses it, shakes into it some powdered tea out of a screw of paper, puts it on the hearth, and sitting in a wooden chair quietly begins to cry*

Jones (stirring and yawning). That you? What's the time?

Mrs. Jones (drying her eyes, and in her usual voice). Half-past two.

Jones. What you back so soon for?   5

Mrs. Jones. I only had the half day today, Jem.

Jones (on his back, and in a drowsy voice). Got anything for dinner?

Mrs. Jones. Mrs. Barthwick's cook   10 gave me a little bit of bacon. I'm going to make a stew. *(She prepares for cooking.)* There's fourteen shillings owing for rent, James, and of course I've only got two and fourpence. They'll be coming for it to-   15 day.

Jones (turning towards her on his elbow). Let 'em come and find my surprise packet. I've had enough o' this tryin' for work. Why should I go round and round after a job   20 like a bloomin' squirrel in a cage? "Give us a job, sir" — "Take a man on" — "Got a wife and three children." Sick of it I am! I'd sooner lie here and rot. "Jones, you come and join the demonstration; come and 'old a   25 flag, and listen to the ruddy orators, and go 'ome as empty as you came." There's some

that seems to like *that* — the sheep! When I go seekin' for a job now, and see the brutes lookin' me up an' down, it's like a thou-   30 sand serpents in me. I'm not arskin' for any treat. A man wants to sweat hisself silly and not allowed — that's a rum start, ain't it? A man wants to sweat his soul out to keep the breath in him and ain't allowed — that's   35 justice — that's freedom and all the rest of it! *(He turns his face towards the wall.)* You're so milky mild; you don't know what goes on inside o' me. I'm done with the silly game. If they want me, let 'em come for me! (MRS.   40 JONES *stops cooking and stands unmoving at the table.*) I've tried and done with it, I tell you. I've never been afraid of what's before *me.* You mark my words — if you think they've broke my spirit, you're mistook. I'll lie   45 and rot sooner than arsk 'em again. What makes you stand like that — you long-sufferin', Gawd-forsaken image — that's why I can't keep my hands off you. So now you know. Work! You can work, but you haven't   50 the spirit of a louse!

Mrs. Jones (quietly). You talk more wild sometimes when you're yourself, James, than when you're not. If you don't get work, how are we to go on? They won't let us stay   55 here; they're looking to their money today, I know.

Jones. I see this Barthwick o' yours every day goin' down to Pawlyment snug and comfortable to talk his silly soul out; an' I see   60 that young calf, his son, swellin' it about, and goin' on the razzle-dazzle. Wot 'ave they done that makes 'em any better than wot I am? They never did a day's work in their lives. I see 'em day after day ——   65

Mrs. Jones. And I wish you wouldn't come after me like that, and hang about the house. You don't seem able to keep away at all, and whatever you do it for I can't think, because of course they notice it.   70

Jones. I suppose I may go where I like. Where *may* I go? The other day I went to a place in the Edgeware Road. "Gov'nor," I says to the boss, "take me on," I says. "I 'aven't done a stroke o' work not these   75 two months; it takes the heart out of a man," I

says; "I'm one to work; I'm not afraid of anything you can give me!" "My good man," 'e
says, "I've had thirty of you here this morning.
I took the first two," he says, "and that's 80
all I want." "Thank you, then rot the world!"
I says. "Blasphemin'," he says, "is not the
way to get a job. Out you go, my lad!" (*He
laughs sardonically.*) Don't you raise your
voice because you're starvin'; don't yer 85
even think of it; take it lyin' down! Take it
like a sensible man, carn't you? And a little
way down the street a lady says to me (*pinching his voice*): "D'you want to earn a few pence,
my man?" and gives me her dog to 'old 90
outside a shop — fat as a butler 'e was — tons
o' meat had gone to the makin' of *him.* It did
'er good, it did, made 'er feel 'erself that *charitable,* but I see 'er lookin' at the copper standin'
alongside o' me, for fear I should make off 95
with 'er bloomin' fat dog. (*He sits on the edge
of the bed and puts a boot on. Then looking up*)
What's in that head o' yours? (*Almost pathetically*) Carn't you speak for once?

There is a knock, and MRS. SEDDON, *the landlady, appears, an anxious, harassed, shabby
woman in working clothes*

Mrs. Sed. I thought I 'eard you come 100
in, Mrs. Jones. I've spoke to me 'usband, but
he says he really can't afford to wait another
day.

Jones (*with scowling jocularity*). Never you
mind what your 'usband says, you go 105
your own way like a proper independent woman. Here, Jenny, chuck her that.
(*Producing a sovereign from his trousers pocket, he throws it to his wife,
who catches it in her apron with a
gasp.* JONES *resumes the lacing of
his boots.*)
Mrs. Jones (*rubbing the sovereign stealthily*).
I'm very sorry we're so late with it, and of
course it's fourteen shillings, so if you've 110
got six, that will be right.
(MRS. SEDDON *takes the sovereign and
fumbles for the change.*)
Jones (*with his eyes fixed on his boots*). Bit of
a surprise for yer, ain't it?

Mrs. Sed. Thank you, and I'm sure I'm very
much obliged. (*She does indeed appear* 115
surprised.) I'll bring you the change.
Jones (*mockingly*). Don't mention it.
Mrs. Sed. Thank you, and I'm sure I'm very
much obliged. (*She slides away.*)
(MRS. JONES *gazes at* JONES, *who is
still lacing up his boots.*
Jones. I've had a bit of luck. (*Pulling* 120
out the crimson purse and some loose coins)
Picked up a purse — seven pound and more.
Mrs. Jones. Oh, James!
Jones. Oh, James! What about Oh, James!
I picked it up I tell you. This is lost 125
property, this is!
Mrs. Jones. But isn't there a name in it, or
something?
Jones. Name? No, there ain't no name.
This don't belong to such as 'ave visitin' 130
cards. This belongs to a perfec' lidy. Tike
an' smell it. (*He pitches her the purse, which
she puts gently to her nose.*) Now, you tell me
what I ought to have done. You tell me that.
You can always tell me what I ought to 135
ha' done, can't yer?
Mrs. Jones (*laying down the purse*). I can't
say what you ought to have done, James. Of
course the money wasn't yours; you've taken
somebody else's money. 140
Jones. Finding's keeping. I'll take it as
wages for the time I've gone about the streets
asking for what's my rights. I'll take it for
what's *overdue,* d'ye hear? (*With strange triumph*) I've got money in my pocket, my 145
girl. (MRS. JONES *goes on again with the preparation of the meal,* JONES *looking at her furtively.*) Money in my pocket! And I'm not
goin' to waste it. With this 'ere money I'm
goin' to Canada. I'll let you have a 150
pound. (*A silence.*) You've often talked of
leavin' me. You've often told me I treat you
badly — well I 'ope you'll be glad when I'm
gone.
Mrs. Jones (*impassively*). You *have* 155
treated me very badly, James, and of course I
can't prevent your going; but I can't tell
whether I shall be glad when you're gone.
Jones. It'll change *my* luck. I've 'ad nothing but bad luck since I first took up with 160

you. (*More softly*) And you've 'ad no bloomin' picnic.

Mrs. Jones. Of course it would have been better for us if we had never met. We weren't meant for each other. But you're set 165 against me, that's what you are, and you *have* been for a long time. And you treat me so badly, James, going after that Rosie and all. You don't ever seem to think of the children that I've had to bring into the world, and 170 of all the trouble I've had to keep them, and what'll become of them when you're gone.

Jones (crossing the room gloomily). If you think I want to leave the little beggars you're bloomin' well mistaken. 175

Mrs. Jones. Of course I know you're fond of them.

Jones (fingering the purse, half angrily). Well, then, you stow it, old girl. The kids'll get along better with you than when I'm 180 here. If I'd ha' known as much as I do now, I'd never ha' had one o' them. What's the use o' bringin' 'em into a state o' things like this? It's a crime, that's what it is; but you find it out too late; that's what's the matter with 185 this 'ere world.

(*He puts the purse back in his pocket.*

Mrs. Jones. Of course it would have been better for them, poor little things; but they're your own children, and I wonder at you talkin' like that. I should miss them dreadfully 190 if I was to lose them.

Jones (sullenly). An' you ain't the only one. If I make money out there —— (*Looking up, he sees her shaking out his coat — in a changed voice*) Leave that coat alone! 195

(*The silver box drops from the pocket, scattering the cigarettes upon the bed. Taking up the box she stares at it; he rushes at her and snatches the box away.*

Mrs. Jones (cowering back against the bed). Oh, Jem! oh, Jem!

Jones (dropping the box on to the table). You mind what you're sayin'! When I go out I'll take and chuck it in the water along with 200 that there purse. I 'ad it when I was in liquor, and for what you do when you're in liquor you're not responsible — and that's Gawd's

truth, as you ought to know. I don't want the thing — I won't have it. I took it out o' 205 spite. I'm no thief, I tell you; and don't you call me one, or it'll be the worse for you.

Mrs. Jones (twisting her apron strings). It's Mr. Barthwick's! You've taken away my reputation. Oh, Jem, whatever made 210 you?

Jones. What d'you mean?

Mrs. Jones. It's been missed; they think it's me. Oh! whatever made you do it, Jem?

Jones. I tell you I was in liquor. I 215 don't want it; what's the good of it to me? If I were to pawn it they'd only nab me. I'm no thief. I'm no worse than wot that young Barthwick is; he brought 'ome that purse that I picked up — a lady's purse — 'ad it off 220 'er in a row, kept sayin' 'e'd scored 'er off. Well, I scored 'im off. Tight as an owl 'e was! And d'you think anything'll happen to him?

Mrs. Jones (as though speaking to herself). Oh, Jem! it's the bread out of our mouths! 225

Jones. Is it then? I'll make it hot for 'em yet. What about that purse? What about young Barthwick? (*Mrs. Jones comes forward to the table and tries to take the box; Jones prevents her.*) What do you want with 230 that? You drop it, I say!

Mrs. Jones. I'll take it back and tell them all about it.

(*She attempts to wrest the box from him.*

Jones. Ah, would yer?

He drops the box, and rushes on her with a snarl. She slips back past the bed. He follows; a chair is overturned. The door is opened; Snow comes in, a detective in plain clothes and bowler hat, with clipped moustaches. Jones drops his arms, Mrs. Jones stands by the window gasping; Snow, advancing swiftly to the table, puts his hand on the silver box

Snow. Doin' a bit o' skylarkin'? Fancy 235 this is what I'm after. J. B., the very same. (*He gets back to the door, scrutinizing the crest and cypher on the box.*) (*To Mrs. Jones*) I'm a police officer. Are you Mrs. Jones?

Mrs. Jones. Yes, sir. 240

Snow. My instructions are to take you on a charge of stealing this box from J. Barthwick, Esquire, M.P., of 6, Rockingham Gate. Anything you say may be used against you. Well, missis?   245

Mrs. Jones (*in her quiet voice, still out of breath, her hand upon her breast*). Of course I did *not* take it, sir. I never have taken anything that didn't belong to me; and of course I know nothing about it.   250

Snow. You were at the house this morning; you did the room in which the box was left; you were alone in the room. I find the box 'ere. You say you didn't take it?

Mrs. Jones. Yes, sir, of course I say I   255 did not take it, because I did *not*.

Snow. Then how does the box come to be here?

Mrs. Jones. I would rather not say anything about it.   260

Snow. Is this your husband?

Mrs. Jones. Yes, sir, this is my husband, sir.

Snow. Do you wish to say anything before I take her? (*Jones remains silent, with his head bent down.*) Well then, missis, I'll   265 just trouble you to come along with me quietly.

Mrs. Jones (*twisting her hands*). Of course I wouldn't say I hadn't taken it if I had — and I *didn't* take it, indeed I didn't. Of course I know appearances are against me, and I   270 can't tell you what really happened. But my children are at school, and they'll be coming home — and I don't know what they'll do without me!

Snow. Your 'usband'll see to them,   275 don't you worry.

(*He takes the woman gently by the arm.*

Jones. You drop it — she's all right! (*Sullenly*) I took the thing myself.

Snow (*eyeing him*). There, there, it does you credit. Come along, missis.   280

Jones (*passionately*). Drop it, I say, you blooming teck. She's my wife; she's a respectable woman. Take her if you dare!

Snow. Now, now. What's the good of this? Keep a civil tongue, and it'll be the better   285 for all of us.

(*He puts his whistle in his mouth and draws the woman to the door.*

Jones (*with a rush*). Drop her, and put up your 'ands, or I'll soon make yer. You leave her alone, will yer! Don't I tell yer, I took the thing myself!   290

Snow (*blowing his whistle*). Drop your hands, or I'll take you too. Ah, would you?

(*Jones, closing, deals him a blow. A policeman in uniform appears; there is a short struggle and Jones is overpowered. Mrs. Jones raises her hands and drops her face on them.*

The curtain falls.

SCENE 2

The Barthwicks' *dining-room the same evening. The* Barthwicks *are seated at dessert*

Mrs. Barth. John! (*A silence broken by the cracking of nuts.*) John!

Barth. I wish you'd speak about the nuts — they're uneatable. (*He puts one in his mouth.*)

Mrs. Barth. It's not the season for them.   5 I called on the Holyroods.

(*Barthwick fills his glass with port.*

Jack. Crackers, please, dad.

(*Barthwick passes the crackers. His demeanor is reflective.*

Mrs. Barth. Lady Holyrood has got very stout. I've noticed it coming for a long time.

Barth. (*gloomily*). Stout? (*He takes up*   10 *the crackers — with transparent airiness.*) The Holyroods had some trouble with their servants, hadn't they?

Jack. Crackers, please, dad.

Barth. (*passing the crackers*). It got into   15 the papers. The cook, wasn't it?

Mrs. Barth. No, the lady's maid. I was talking it over with Lady Holyrood. The girl used to have her young man to see her.

Barth. (*uneasily*). I'm not sure they   20 were wise.

Mrs. Barth. My dear John, what are you talking about? How could there be any alternative? Think of the effect on the other servants!   25

Barth. Of course in principle — I wasn't thinking of that.

Jack (maliciously). Crackers, please, dad.

(BARTHWICK *is compelled to pass the crackers.*

Mrs. Barth. Lady Holyrood told me: "I had her up," she said; "I said to her, 'You'll 30 leave my house at once; I think your conduct disgraceful. I can't tell, I don't know, and I don't wish to know, what you were doing. I send you away on principle; you need not come to me for a character.' And the girl said: 35 'If you don't give me my notice, my lady, I want a month's wages. I'm perfectly respectable. I've done nothing.'" — Done nothing!

Barth. H'm!

Mrs. Barth. Servants have too much 40 license. They hang together so terribly you never can tell what they're really thinking; it's as if they were all in a conspiracy to keep you in the dark. Even with Marlow, you feel that he never lets you know what's really in 45 his mind. I hate that secretiveness; it destroys all confidence. I feel sometimes I should like to shake him.

Jack. Marlow's a most decent chap. It's simply beastly everyone knowing your 50 affairs.

Barth. The less you say about that the better!

Mrs. Barth. It goes all through the lower classes. You can*not* tell when they are 55 speaking the truth. Today when I was shopping after leaving the Holyroods, one of these unemployed came up and spoke to me. I suppose I only had twenty yards or so to walk to the carriage, but he seemed to spring up 60 in the street.

Barth. Ah! You must be very careful whom you speak to in these days.

Mrs. Barth. I didn't answer him, of course. But I could see at once that he wasn't 65 telling the truth.

Barth. (cracking a nut). There's one very good rule — look at their eyes.

Jack. Crackers, please, dad.

Barth. (passing the crackers). If their 70 eyes are straightforward I sometimes give them sixpence. It's against my principles, but it's most difficult to refuse. If you see that they're desperate, and dull, and shifty-looking, as so

many of them are, it's certain to mean 75 drink, or crime, or something unsatisfactory.

Mrs. Barth. This man had dreadful eyes. He looked as if he could commit a murder. "I've 'ad nothing to eat today," he said. Just like that. 80

Barth. What was William about? He ought to have been waiting.

Jack (raising his wine-glass to his nose). Is this the '63, dad?

(BARTHWICK, *holding his wine-glass to his eye, lowers it and passes it before his nose.*

Mrs. Barth. I hate people that can't 85 speak the truth. *(Father and son exchange a look behind their port.)* It's just as easy to speak the truth as not. *I've* always found it easy enough. It makes it impossible to tell what is genuine; one feels as if one were 90 continually being taken in.

Barth. (sententiously). The lower classes are their own enemies. If they would only trust us, they would get on so much better.

Mrs. Barth. But even then it's so often 95 their own fault. Look at that Mrs. Jones this morning.

Barth. I only want to do what's right in that matter. I had occasion to see Roper this afternoon. I mentioned it to him. He's com- 100 ing in this evening. It all depends on what the detective says. I've had my doubts. I've been thinking it over.

Mrs. Barth. The woman impressed me most unfavorably. She seemed to have no 105 shame. That affair she was talking about — she and the man when they were young, so immoral! And before you and Jack! I could have put her out of the room!

Barth. Oh! I don't want to excuse 110 them, but in looking at these matters one must consider ——

Mrs. Barth. Perhaps you'll say the man's employer was wrong in dismissing him?

Barth. Of course not. It's not there 115 that I feel doubt. What I ask myself is ——

Jack. Port, please, dad.

Barth. (circulating the decanter in religious imitation of the rising and setting of the sun). I ask myself whether we are sufficiently 120 careful in making inquiries about people before we engage them, especially as regards moral conduct.

Jack. Pass the port, please, mother!

Mrs. Barth. (*passing it*). My dear boy, aren't you drinking too much? 125

(JACK *fills his glass.*

Mar. (*entering*). Detective Snow to see you, sir.

Barth. (*uneasily*). Ah! say I'll be with him in a minute. 130

Mrs. Barth. (*without turning*). Let him come in here, Marlow.

SNOW *enters in an overcoat, his bowler hat in hand*

Barth. (*half-rising*). Oh! Good evening!

Snow. Good evening, sir; good evening, ma'am. I've called round to report what 135 I've done; rather late, I'm afraid — another case took me away. (*He takes the silver box out of his pocket, causing a sensation in the* BARTH-WICK *family.*) This is the identical article, I believe. 140

Barth. Certainly, certainly.

Snow. Havin' your crest and cypher, as you described to me, sir, I'd no hesitation in the matter.

Barth. Excellent. Will you have a 145 glass of (*he glances at the waning port*) — er — sherry — (*pours out sherry*). Jack, just give Mr. Snow this.

(JACK *rises and gives the glass to* SNOW; *then, lolling in his chair, regards him indolently.*

Snow (*drinking off wine and putting down the glass*). After seeing you I went round to 150 this woman's lodgings, sir. It's a low neighborhood, and I thought it as well to place a constable below — and not without 'e was wanted, as things turned out.

Barth. Indeed! 155

Snow. Yes, sir, I 'ad some trouble. I asked her to account for the presence of the article. She could give me no answer, except to deny the theft; so I took her into custody; then her husband came for me, so I was obliged 160 to take him, too, for assault. He was very violent on the way to the station — very vio-lent — threatened you and your son, and alto-gether he was a handful, I can tell you.

Mrs. Barth. What a ruffian he must be! 165

Snow. Yes, ma'am, a rough customer.

Jack (*sipping his wine, bemused*). Punch the beggar's head.

Snow. Given to drink, as I understand, sir.

Mrs. Barth. It's to be hoped he will get 770 a severe punishment.

Snow. The odd thing is, sir, that he persists in sayin' he took the box himself.

Barth. Took the box himself! (*He smiles.*) What does he think to gain by that? 175

Snow. He says the young gentleman was in-toxicated last night — (JACK *stops the cracking of a nut, and looks at* SNOW. BARTHWICK, *los-ing his smile, has put his wine-glass down; there is a silence* — SNOW, *looking from face to* 180 *face, remarks.*) — took him into the house and gave him whisky; and under the influence of an empty stomach the man says he took the box.

Mrs. Barth. The impudent wretch! 185

Barth. D'you mean that he — er— intends to put this forward tomorrow ——

Snow. That'll be his line, sir; but whether he's endeavoring to shield his wife, or whether (*he looks at* JACK) there's something in it, 190 will be for the magistrate to say.

Mrs. Barth. (*haughtily*). Something in what? I don't understand you. As if my son would bring a man like that into the house!

Barth. (*from the fireplace, with an effort* 195 *to be calm*). My son can speak for himself, no doubt. — Well, Jack, what do you say?

Mrs. Barth. (*sharply*). What does he say? Why, of course, he says the whole story's stuff!

Jack (*embarrassed*). Well, of course, I 200 — of course, I don't know anything about it.

Mrs. Barth. I should think not, indeed! (*To* SNOW) The man is an audacious ruffian!

Barth. (*suppressing jumps*). But in view of my son's saying there's nothing in this — 205 this fable — will it be necessary to proceed against the man under the circumstances?

Snow. We shall have to charge him with the assault, sir. It would be as well for your son to come down to the Court. There'll be a 210 remand, no doubt. The queer thing is there was quite a sum of money found on him, and a crimson silk purse. (BARTHWICK *starts;* JACK *rises and sits down again.*) I suppose the lady hasn't missed her purse?   215

Barth. (*hastily*). Oh, no! Oh! No!

Jack. No!

Mrs. Barth. (*dreamily*). No! (*To* SNOW) I've been inquiring of the servants. This man *does* hang about the house. I shall feel   220 much safer if he gets a good long sentence; I do think we ought to be protected against such ruffians.

Barth. Yes, yes, of course, on principle — but in this case we have a number of   225 things to think of. (*To* SNOW) I suppose, as you say, the man *must* be charged, eh?

Snow. No question about that, sir.

Barth. (*staring gloomily at* JACK). This prosecution goes very much against the grain   230 with me. I have great sympathy with the poor. In my position I'm bound to recognize the distress there is amongst them. The condition of the people leaves much to be desired. D'you follow me? I wish I could see my   235 way to drop it.

Mrs. Barth. (*sharply*). John! it's simply not fair to other people. It's putting property at the mercy of anyone who likes to take it.

Barth. (*trying to make signs to her aside*).   240 I'm not defending him, not at all. I'm trying to look at the matter broadly.

Mrs. Barth. Nonsense, John, there's a time for everything.

Snow (*rather sardonically*). I might   245 point out, sir, that to withdraw the charge of stealing would not make much difference, because the facts must come out (*he looks significantly at* JACK) in reference to the assault; and as I said, that charge will have to go   250 forward.

Barth. (*hastily*). Yes, oh! exactly! It's entirely on the woman's account — entirely a matter of my own private feelings.

Snow. If I were you, sir, I should let   255 things take their course. It's not likely there'll be much difficulty. These things are very quick settled.

Barth. (*doubtfully*). You think so — you think so?   260

Jack (*rousing himself*). I say, what shall I have to swear to?

Snow. That's best known to yourself, sir. (*Retreating to the door*) Better employ a solicitor, sir, in case anything should arise.   265 We shall have the butler to prove the loss of the article. You'll excuse me going, I'm rather pressed tonight. The case may come on any time after eleven. Good evening, sir; good evening, ma'am. I shall have to pro-   270 duce the box in court tomorrow, so if you'll excuse me, sir, I may as well take it with me.

(*He takes the silver box and leaves them with a little bow.*)

(BARTHWICK *makes a move to follow him, then dashing his hands beneath his coat tails, speaks with desperation.*

Barth. I do wish you'd leave me to manage things myself. You *will* put your nose into matters you know nothing of. A pretty   275 mess you've made of this!

Mrs. Barth. (*coldly*). I don't in the least know what you're talking about. If you can't stand up for your rights, I can. I've no patience with your principles, it's such non-   280 sense.

Barth. Principles! Good heavens! What have principles to do with it, for goodness' sake? Don't you know that Jack was drunk last night!

Jack. Dad!   285

Mrs. Barth. (*in horror, rising*). Jack!

Jack. Look here, mother — I had supper. Everybody does. I mean to say — you know what I mean — it's absurd to call it   290 being drunk. At Oxford everybody gets a bit "on" sometimes ——

Mrs. Barth. Well, I think it's most dreadful! If that is really what you do at Oxford ——

Jack (*angrily*). Well, why did you send   295 me there? One must do as other fellows do. It's such nonsense, I mean, to call it being drunk. Of course I'm awfully sorry. I've had such a beastly headache all day.

Barth. Tcha! If you'd only had the   300 common decency to remember what happened when you came in. Then we should know what truth there was in what this fellow says — as it is, it's all the most confounded darkness. 305

Jack (staring as though at half-formed visions). I just get a — and then — it's gone ——

Mrs. Barth. Oh, Jack! do you mean to say you were so tipsy you can't even remember——

Jack. Look here, mother! Of course 310 I remember I came — I must have come ——

Barth. (unguardedly, and walking up and down). Tcha! — and that infernal purse! Good heavens! It'll get into the papers. Who on earth could have foreseen a thing like 315 this? Better to have lost a dozen cigarette-boxes, and said nothing about it. (*To his wife*) It's all your doing. I told you so from the first. I wish to goodness Roper would come!

Mrs. Barth. (sharply). I don't know 320 what you're talking about, John.

Barth. (turning on her). No, you — you — you don't know anything! (*Sharply*) Where the devil is Roper? If he can see a way out of this he's a better man than I take him for. 325 I defy *anyone* to see a way out of it. *I* can't.

Jack. Look here, don't excite, dad — I can simply say I was too beastly tired, and don't remember anything except that I came in and (*in a dying voice*) went to bed the 330 same as usual.

Barth. Went to bed? Who knows where you went — I've lost all confidence. For all I know you slept on the floor.

Jack (indignantly). I didn't, I slept 335 on the ——

Barth. (sitting on the sofa). Who cares where you slept; what does it matter if he mentions the — the — a perfect disgrace?

Mrs. Barth. What? (*A silence.*) I in- 340 *sist* on knowing.

Jack. Oh! nothing ——

Mrs. Barth. Nothing? What do you mean by nothing, Jack? There's your father in such a state about it —— 345

Jack. It's only my purse.

Mrs. Barth. Your purse! You know perfectly well you haven't got one.

Jack. Well, it was somebody else's — it was all a joke — I didn't want the 350 beastly thing ——

Mrs. Barth. Do you mean that you had

had another person's purse, and that this man took it too?

Barth. Tcha! Of course he took it 355 too! A man like that Jones will make the most of it. It'll get into the papers.

Mrs. Barth. I don't understand. What on earth is all the fuss about? (*Bending over* JACK, *and softly*) Jack, now, tell me, dear! 360 Don't be afraid. What is it? Come!

Jack. Oh, don't, mother!

Mrs. Barth. But don't what, dear?

Jack. It was pure sport. I don't know how I got the thing. Of course I'd had a bit 365 of a row — I didn't know what I was doing — I was — I was — well, you know — I suppose I must have pulled the bag out of her hand.

Mrs. Barth. Out of her hand? Whose 370 hand? What bag — whose bag?

Jack. Oh! I don't know — *her* bag — it belonged to — (*in a desperate and rising voice*) a woman.

Mrs. Barth. A woman? *Oh! Jack! No!* 375

Jack (jumping up). You *would* have it. I didn't want to tell you. It's not my fault.

The door opens and MARLOW *ushers in a man of middle age, inclined to corpulence, in evening dress. He has a ruddy, thin moustache, and dark, quick-moving little eyes. His eyebrows are Chinese*

Mar. Mr. Roper, sir. (*He leaves the room.*

Roper (with a quick look round). How do you do? 380

(*But neither* JACK *nor* MRS. BARTH-WICK *makes a sign.*

Barth. (hurrying). Thank goodness you've come, Roper. You remember what I told you this afternoon; we've just had the detective here.

Roper. Got the box? 385

Barth. Yes, yes, but look here — it wasn't the charwoman at all; her drunken loafer of a husband took the things — he says that fellow there (*he waves his hand at* JACK, *who with his shoulder raised seems trying to* 390 *ward off a blow*) let him into the house last night. Can you imagine such a thing?

(ROPER *laughs.*

Barth. (*with excited emphasis*). It's no laughing matter, Roper. I told you about that business of Jack's too — don't you see? — the 395 brute took both the things — took that infernal purse. It'll get into the papers.

Roper (*raising his eyebrows*). H'm! The purse! Depravity in high life! What does your son say? 400

Barth. He remembers nothing. D——n! Did you ever see such a mess? It'll get into the papers.

Mrs. Barth. (*with her hand across her eyes*). Oh! it's not that —— 405
    (BARTHWICK and ROPER *turn and look at her.*

Barth. It's the idea of that woman — she's just heard ——
    (ROPER *nods. And* MRS. BARTHWICK, *setting her lips, gives a slow look at* JACK, *and sits down at the table.*
What on earth's to be done, Roper? A ruffian like this Jones will make all the capital he can out of that purse. 410

Mrs. Barth. I don't believe that Jack took that purse.

Barth. What — when the woman came here for it this morning?

Mrs. Barth. Here? She had the impu- 415 dence? Why wasn't I told?
    (*She looks round from face to face — no one answers her, there is a pause.*

Barth. (*suddenly*). What's to be done, Roper?

Roper (*quietly to* JACK). I suppose you didn't leave your latchkey in the door? 420

Jack (*sullenly*). Yes, I did.

Barth. Good heavens! What next?

Mrs. Barth. I'm certain you never let that man into the house, Jack, it's a wild invention. I'm sure there's not a word of truth in it, 425 Mr. Roper.

Roper (*very suddenly*). Where did you sleep last night?

Jack (*promptly*). On the sofa, there — (*hesitating*) that is — I —— 430

Barth. On the sofa? D'you mean to say you didn't go to bed?

Jack (*sullenly*). No.

Barth. If you don't remember anything, how can you remember that? 435

Jack. Because I woke up there in the morning.

Mrs. Barth. Oh, Jack!

Barth. Good gracious!

Jack. And Mrs. Jones saw me. I wish 440 you wouldn't bait me so.

Roper. Do you remember giving anyone a drink?

Jack. By Jove, I do seem to remember a fellow with — a fellow with —— (*He* 445 *looks at* ROPER.) I say, d'you want me — ?

Roper (*quick as lightning*). With a dirty face?

Jack (*with illumination*). I do — I distinctly remember his —— 450
    (BARTHWICK *moves abruptly;* MRS. BARTHWICK *looks at* ROPER *angrily, and touches her son's arm.*

Mrs. Barth. You don't remember, it's ridiculous! I don't believe the man was ever here at all.

Barth. You must speak the truth, if it *is* the truth. But if you *do* remember such a 455 dirty business, I shall wash my hands of you altogether.

Jack (*glaring at them*). Well, what the devil ——

Mrs. Barth. Jack! 460

Jack. Well, mother, I — I don't know what you *do* want.

Mrs. Barth. We want you to speak the truth and say you never let this low man into the house. 465

Barth. Of course if you think that you really gave this man whisky in that disgraceful way, and let him see what you'd been doing, and were in such a disgusting condition that you don't remember a word of it —— 470

Roper (*quick*). I've no memory myself — never had.

Barth. (*desperately*). I don't know what you're to say.

Roper (*to* JACK). Say nothing at all! 475 Don't put yourself in a false position. The man stole the things or the woman stole the things; you had nothing to do with it. You were asleep on the sofa.

Mrs. Barth. Your leaving the latchkey 480 in the door was quite bad enough, there's no need to mention anything else. (*Touching his forehead softly*) My dear, how hot your head is!

Jack. But I want to know what I'm to do. (*Passionately*) I won't be badgered like 485 this.

(MRS. BARTHWICK *recoils from him.*
Roper (*very quickly*). You forget all about it. You were asleep.

Jack. Must I go down to the Court tomorrow? 490

Roper (*shaking his head*). No.

Barth. (*in a relieved voice*). Is that so?

Roper. Yes.

Barth. But *you'll* go, Roper.

Roper. Yes. 495

Jack (*with wan cheerfulness*). Thanks, awfully! So long as I don't have to go. (*Putting his hand up to his head*) I think if you'll excuse me — I've had a most beastly day.

(*He looks from his father to his mother.*
Mrs. Barth. (*turning quickly*). Good- 500 night, my boy.

Jack. Goodnight, mother.

(*He goes out.* MRS. BARTHWICK *heaves a sigh. There is a silence.*

Barth. He gets off too easily. But for my money that woman would have prosecuted him. 505

Roper. You find money useful.

Barth. I've my doubts whether we ought to hide the truth ——

Roper. There'll be a remand.

Barth. What! D'you mean he'll have 510 to *appear* on the remand?

Roper. Yes.

Barth. H'm, I thought you'd be able to —— Look here, Roper, you *must* keep that purse out of the papers. 515

(ROPER *fixes his little eyes on him and nods.*

Mrs. Barth. Mr. Roper, don't you think the magistrate ought to be told what sort of people these Joneses are; I mean about their immorality before they were married? I don't know if John told you. 520

Roper. Afraid it's not material.

Mrs. Barth. Not material?

Roper. Purely private life! May have happened to the magistrate.

Barth. (*with a movement as if to shift a* 525 *burden*). Then you'll take the thing into your hands?

Roper. If the gods are kind.

(*He holds his hand out.*
Barth. (*shaking it dubiously*). Kind — eh? What? You going? 530

Roper. Yes. I've another case, something like yours — most unexpected.

(*He bows to* MRS. BARTHWICK *and goes out, followed by* BARTHWICK, *talking to the last.* MRS. BARTHWICK *at the table bursts into smothered sobs.* BARTHWICK *returns.*

Barth. (*to himself*). There'll be a scandal.

Mrs. Barth. (*disguising her grief at once*). I simply can't imagine what Roper means 535 by making a joke of a thing like that!

Barth. (*staring strangely*). You! You can't imagine anything! You've no more imagination than a fly!

Mrs. Barth. (*angrily*). You dare to tell 540 me that I have no imagination.

Barth. (*flustered*). I — I'm upset. From beginning to end, the whole thing has been utterly against my principles.

Mrs. Barth. Rubbish! You haven't 545 any! Your principles are nothing in the world but sheer — fright!

Barth. (*walking to the window*). I've never been frightened in my life. You heard what Roper said. It's enough to upset one 550 when a thing like this happens. Everything one says and does seems to turn in one's mouth — it's — it's uncanny. It's not the sort of thing I've been accustomed to. (*As though stifling, he throws the window open. The* 555 *faint sobbing of a child comes in.*) What's that?

(*They listen.*
Mrs. Barth. (*sharply*). I can't stand that crying. I must send Marlow to stop it. My nerves are all on edge.

(*She rings the bell.*
Barth. I'll shut the window; you'll hear 560 nothing.

(*He shuts the window. There is silence.*
Mrs. Barth. (*sharply*). That's no good! It's

on my nerves. Nothing upsets me like a child's crying. (MARLOW *comes in.*) What's that noise of crying, Marlow? It sounds like 565 a child.

Barth. It is a child. I can see it against the railings.

Mar. (*opening the window, and looking out — quietly*). It's Mrs. Jones's little boy, 570 ma'am; he came here after his mother.

Mrs. Barth. (*moving quickly to the window*). Poor little chap! John, we oughtn't to go on with this!

Barth. (*sitting heavily in a chair*). Ah! 575 but it's out of our hands!

(MRS. BARTHWICK *turns her back to the window. There is an expression of distress on her face. She stands motionless, compressing her lips. The crying begins again.* BARTHWICK *covers his ears with his hands, and* MARLOW *shuts the window. The crying ceases.*

The curtain falls.

ACT III

Eight days have passed, and the scene is a London police court at one o'clock. A canopied seat of Justice is surmounted by the lion and unicorn. Before the fire a worn-looking MAGISTRATE *is warming his coat-tails, and staring at two little girls in faded blue and orange rags, who are placed before the dock. Close to the witness-box is a* RELIEVING OFFICER *in an overcoat, and a short brown beard. Beside the little girls stands a bald* POLICE CONSTABLE. *On the front bench are sitting* BARTHWICK *and* ROPER, *and behind them* JACK. *In the railed enclosure are seedy-looking men and women. Some prosperous constables sit or stand about*

Mag. (*in his paternal and ferocious voice, hissing his s's*). Now let us dispose of these young ladies.

Usher. Theresa Livens, Maud Livens. (*The bald* CONSTABLE *indicates the little girls, who* 5

remain silent, disillusioned, inattentive.) Relieving Officer!

(*The* RELIEVING OFFICER *steps into the witness-box.*

Usher. The evidence you give to the Court shall be the truth, the whole truth, and nothing but the truth, so help you God! Kiss the 10 book! (*The book is kissed.*

Rel. Off. (*in a monotone, pausing slightly at each sentence end, that his evidence may be inscribed*). About ten o'clock this morning, Your Worship, I found these two little girls in 15 Blue Street, Pulham, crying outside a public-house. Asked where their home was, they said they had no home. Mother had gone away. Asked about their father. Their father had no work. Asked where they slept last night. 20 At their aunt's. I've made inquiries, Your Worship. The wife has broken up the home and gone on the streets. The husband is out of work and living in common lodging-houses. The husband's sister has eight children of 25 her own, and says she can't afford to keep these little girls any longer.

Mag. (*returning to his seat beneath the canopy of Justice*). Now, let me see. You say the mother is on the streets; what evidence 30 have you of that?

Rel. Off. I have the husband here, Your Worship.

Mag. Very well; then let us see him. (*There are cries of* "Livens!" *The* MAGISTRATE 35 *leans forward, and stares with hard compassion at the little girls.* LIVENS *comes in. He is quiet, with grizzled hair, and a muffler for a collar. He stands beside the witness-box.*) And you are their father? Now, why don't you keep your 40 little girls at home? How is it you leave them to wander about the streets like this?

Liv. I've got no home, Your Worship. I'm living from 'and to mouth. I've got no work; and nothin' to keep them on. 45

Mag. How is that?

Liv. (*ashamedly*). My wife, she broke my 'ome up and pawned the things.

Mag. But what made you let her?

Liv. Your Worship, I'd no chance to 50 stop 'er; she did it when I was out lookin' for work.

Mag. Did you ill-treat her?

Liv. (*emphatically*). I never raised my 'and
to her in my life, Your Worship.   55

Mag. Then what was it — did she drink?

Liv. Yes, Your Worship.

Mag. Was she loose in her behavior?

Liv. (*in a low voice*). Yes, Your Worship.

Mag. And where is she now?   60

Liv. I don't know, Your Worship. She went
off with a man, and after that I——

Mag. Yes, yes. Who knows anything of her?
(*To the bald* CONSTABLE) Is she known here?

Rel. Off. Not in this district, Your Wor-   65
ship; but I have ascertained that she is well
known ——

Mag. Yes — yes; we'll stop at that. Now
(*to* LIVENS) you say that she has broken up
your home, and left these little girls. What   70
provision can you make for them? You look a
strong man.

Liv. So I am, Your Worship. I'm willin'
enough to work, but for the life of me I can't
get anything to do.   75

Mag. But have you tried?

Liv. I've tried everything, Your Worship —
I've tried my 'ardest.

Mag. Well, well —— (*There is a silence.*

Rel. Off. If Your Worship thinks it's a   80
case, my people are willing to take them.

Mag. Yes, yes, I know; but I've no evidence
that this man is not the proper guardian for his
children. (*He rises and goes back to the fire.*

Rel. Off. The mother, Your Worship, is   85
able to get access to them.

Mag. Yes, yes; the mother, of course, is an
improper person to have anything to do with
them. (*To* LIVENS) Well, now what do you
say?   90

Liv. Your Worship, I can only say that if I
could get work I should be only too willing to
provide for them. But what can I do, Your
Worship? Here I am obliged to live from 'and
to mouth in these 'ere common lodging-   95
houses. I'm a strong man — I'm willing to
work — I'm half as alive again as some of 'em—
but you see, Your Worship, my 'air's turned a
bit, owing to the fever — (*touches his hair*) —
and that's against me; and I don't seem to   100
get a chance anyhow.

Mag. Yes — yes. (*Slowly*) Well, I think
it's a case. (*Staring his hardest at the little girls*)
Now, are you willing that these little girls
should be sent to a home?   105

Liv. Yes, Your Worship, I should be very
willing.

Mag. Well, I'll remand them for a week.
Bring them again today week; if I see no reason
against it then, I'll make an order.   110

Rel. Off. Today week, Your Worship.

(*The bald* CONSTABLE *takes the little
girls out by the shoulders. The father
follows them. The* MAGISTRATE, *returning to his seat, bends over and
talks to his* CLERK *inaudibly.*

Barth. (*speaking behind his hand*). A painful
case, Roper; very distressing state of things.

Roper. Hundreds like this in the police courts.

Barth. Most distressing! The more I   115
see of it, the more important this question of
the condition of the people seems to become. I
shall certainly make a point of taking up the
cudgels in the House. I shall move ——

(*The* MAGISTRATE *ceases talking to his*
CLERK.

Clerk. Remands!   120

BARTHWICK *stops abruptly. There is a stir and*
MRS. JONES *comes in by the public door;*
JONES, *ushered by policemen, comes from the
prisoner's door. They file into the dock*

Clerk. James Jones, Jane Jones.

Usher. Jane Jones!

Barth. (*in a whisper*). The purse — the purse
must be kept out of it, Roper. Whatever happens you must keep that out of the papers.   125

(ROPER *nods.*

Bald Const. Hush!

(MRS. JONES, *dressed in her thin, black,
wispy dress, and black straw hat,
stands motionless with hands crossed
on the front rail of the dock.* JONES
*leans against the back rail of the dock,
and keeps half turning, glancing defiantly about him. He is haggard and
unshaven.*

Clerk (*consulting with his papers*). This is the
case remanded from last Wednesday, sir. Theft

of a silver cigarette-box and assault on the po- 130
lice; the two charges were taken together. 130
Jane Jones! James Jones!

Mag. (*staring*). Yes, yes; I remember.

Clerk. Jane Jones.

Mrs. Jones. Yes, sir.

Clerk. Do you admit stealing a silver 135
cigarette-box valued at five pounds, ten shillings, from the house of John Barthwick, M.P.,
between the hours of 11 P.M. on Easter Monday
and 8.45 A.M. on Easter Tuesday last? Yes
or no? 140

Mrs. Jones (*in a low voice*). No, sir, I do not,
sir.

Clerk. James Jones? Do you admit stealing
a silver cigarette-box valued at five pounds, ten
shillings, from the house of John Barth- 145
wick, M.P., between the hours of 11 P.M. on
Easter Monday and 8.45 A.M. on Easter Tuesday last? And further making an assault on the
police when in the execution of their duty at
3 P.M. on Easter Tuesday? Yes or no? 150

Jones (*sullenly*). Yes, but I've got a lot to say
about it.

Mag. (*to the* CLERK). Yes — yes. But how
comes it that these two people are charged with
the same offense? Are they husband and 155
wife?

Clerk. Yes, sir. You remember you ordered
a remand for further evidence as to the story of
the male prisoner.

Mag. Have they been in custody since? 160

Clerk. You released the woman on her own
recognizances, sir.

Mag. Yes, yes, this is the case of the silver
box; I remember now. Well?

Clerk. Thomas Marlow. 165

The cry of "THOMAS MARLOW" *is repeated.*
MARLOW *comes in, and steps into the witness box*

Usher. The evidence you give to the Court
shall be the truth, the whole truth, and nothing
but the truth, so help you God. Kiss the book.

    (*The book is kissed. The silver box is
    handed up, and placed on the rail.*

Clerk (*reading from his papers*). Your name is
Thomas Marlow? Are you butler to John 170

Barthwick, M.P., of 6, Rockingham Gate?

Mar. Yes, sir.

Clerk. Did you, between 10.45 and 11 o'clock
on the night of Easter Monday last, place a
silver cigarette-box on a tray on the 175
dining-room table at 6, Rockingham Gate?
Is that the box?

Mar. Yes, sir.

Clerk. And did you miss the same at 8.45 on
the following morning, on going to remove 180
the tray?

Mar. Yes, sir.

Clerk. Is the female prisoner known to you?
(MARLOW *nods.*) Is she the charwoman employed at 6, Rockingham Gate? (*Again* 185
MARLOW *nods.*) Did you at the time of your
missing the box find her in the room alone?

Mar. Yes, sir.

Clerk. Did you afterwards communicate the
loss to your employer, and did he send 190
you to the police station?

Mar. Yes, sir.

Clerk (*to* MRS. JONES). Have you anything
to ask him?

Mrs. Jones. No, sir, nothing, thank 195
you, sir.

Clerk (*to* JONES). James Jones, have you anything to ask this witness?

Jones. I don't know 'im.

Mag. Are you sure you put the box in 200
the place you say at the time you say?

Mar. Yes, Your Worship.

Mag. Very well; then now let us have the
officer.

    (MARLOW *leaves the box, and* SNOW
      goes into it.

Usher. The evidence you give to the 205
Court shall be the truth, the whole truth, and
nothing but the truth, so help you God.

                (*The book is kissed.*

Clerk (*reading from his papers*). Your name
is Robert Snow? You are a detective in the
X.B. division of the Metropolitan police 210
force? According to instructions received did
you on Easter Tuesday last proceed to the
prisoner's lodgings at 34, Merthyr Street, St.
Soames's? And did you on entering see the box
produced, lying on the table? 215

Snow. Yes, sir.

Clerk. Is that the box?

Snow (*fingering the box*). Yes, sir.

Clerk. And did you thereupon take posses- 220
sion of it, and charge the female prisoner
with theft of the box from 6, Rockingham Gate?
And did she deny the same?

Snow. Yes, sir.

Clerk. Did you take her into custody?

Snow. Yes, sir. 225

Mag. What was her behavior?

Snow. Perfectly quiet, Your Worship. She
persisted in the denial. That's all.

Mag. Do you know her?

Snow. No, Your Worship. 230

Mag. Is she known here?

Bald Const. No, Your Worship, they're
neither of them known, we've nothing against
them at all.

Clerk (*to* MRS. JONES). Have you any- 235
thing to ask the officer?

Mrs. Jones. No, sir, thank you, I've nothing
to ask him.

Mag. Very well then — go on.

Clerk (*reading from his papers*). And 240
while you were taking the female prisoner did
the male prisoner interpose, and endeavor to
hinder you in the execution of your duty, and
did he strike you a blow?

Snow. Yes, sir. 245

Clerk. And did he say, "You let her go, I
took the box myself"?

Snow. He did.

Clerk. And did you blow your whistle and
obtain the assistance of another constable, 250
and take him into custody?

Snow. I did.

Clerk. Was he violent on the way to the station, and did he use bad language, and did he
several times repeat that he had taken the 255
box himself? (SNOW *nods*.) Did you thereupon ask him in what manner he had stolen the
box? And did you understand him to say he
had entered the house at the invitation of young
Mr. Barthwick (BARTHWICK, *turning in* 260
his seat, frowns at ROPER) after midnight on
Easter Monday, and partaken of whisky, and
that under the influence of the whisky he had
taken the box?

Snow. I did, sir. 265

Clerk. And was his demeanor throughout
very violent?

Snow. It *was* very violent.

Jones (*breaking in*). Violent — of course it
was! You put your 'ands on my wife 270
when I kept tellin' you I took the thing myself.

Mag. (*hissing, with protruded neck*). Now —
you will have your chance of saying what you
want to say presently. Have you any- 275
thing to ask the officer?

Jones (*sullenly*). No.

Mag. Very well then. Now let us hear what
the female prisoner has to say first.

Mrs. Jones. Well, Your Worship, of 280
course I can only say what I've said all along,
that I didn't take the box.

Mag. Yes, but did you know that it was
taken?

Mrs. Jones. No, Your Worship. And, of 285
course, as to what my husband says, Your Worship, I can't speak of my own knowledge. Of
course, I know that he came home very late on
the Monday night. It was past one o'clock when
he came in, and he was not himself at all. 290

Mag. Had he been drinking?

Mrs. Jones. Yes, Your Worship.

Mag. And was he drunk?

Mrs. Jones. Yes, Your Worship, he was almost quite drunk. 295

Mag. And did he say anything to you?

Mrs. Jones. No, Your Worship, only to call
me names. And of course in the morning when
I got up and went to work he was asleep. And
I don't know anything more about it until 300
I came home again. Except that Mr. Barthwick — that's my employer, Your Worship —
told me the box was missing.

Mag. Yes, yes.

Mrs. Jones. But of course when I was 305
shaking out my husband's coat the cigarette-
box fell out and all the cigarettes were scattered
on the bed.

Mag. You say all the cigarettes were scattered on the bed? (*To* SNOW) Did you see 310
the cigarettes scattered on the bed?

Snow. No, Your Worship, I did not.

Mag. You see, he says he didn't see them.

Jones. Well, they were there, for all that.

Snow. I can't say, Your Worship, that I 315 had the opportunity of going round the room; I had all my work cut out with the male prisoner.

Mag. (*to* MRS. JONES). Well, what more have you to say? 320

Mrs. Jones. Of course when I saw the box, Your Worship, I was dreadfully upset, and I couldn't think why he had done such a thing; when the officer came we were having words about it, because it is ruin to me, Your 325 Worship, in my profession, and I have three little children dependent on me.

Mag. (*protruding his neck*). Yes—yes—but what did he say to you?

Mrs. Jones. I asked him whatever came 330 over him to do such a thing—and he said it was the drink. He said he had had too much to drink, and something came over him. And of course, Your Worship, he had had very little to eat all day, and the drink does go to the 335 head when you have not had enough to eat. Your Worship may not know, but it is the truth. And I would like to say that all through his married life I have never known him to do such a thing before, though we have 340 passed through great hardships and (*speaking with soft emphasis*) I am quite sure he would not have done it if he had been himself at the time.

Mag. Yes, yes. But don't you know that that is no excuse? 345

Mrs. Jones. Yes, Your Worship. I know that it is no excuse.

(*The* MAGISTRATE *leans over and parleys with his* CLERK.

Jack (*leaning over from his seat behind*). I say, dad——

Barth. Tsst! (*Sheltering his mouth, he* 350 *speaks to* ROPER.) Roper, you had better get up now and say that considering the circumstances and the poverty of the prisoners, we have no wish to proceed any further, and if the magistrate would deal with the case as one 355 of disorder only on the part of——

Bald Const. Hssshh! (ROPER *shakes his head.*

Mag. Now, supposing what you say and what your husband says is true, what I have to consider is—how did he obtain access to 360 this house, and were you in any way a party to

his obtaining access? You are the charwoman employed at the house?

Mrs. Jones. Yes, Your Worship, and of course if I had let him into the house it 365 would have been very wrong of me; and I have never done such a thing in any of the houses where I have been employed.

Mag. Well—so you say. Now let us hear what story the male prisoner makes of it. 370

Jones (*who leans with his arms on the dock behind, speaks in a slow, sullen voice*). Wot I say is wot my wife says. I've never been 'ad up in a police court before, an' I can prove I took it when in liquor. I told her, an' she can tell 375 you the same, that I was goin' to throw the thing into the water sooner than 'ave it on my mind.

Mag. But how did you get into the *house?*

Jones. I was passin'. I was goin' 'ome 380 from the "Goat and Bells."

Mag. The "Goat and Bells,"—what is that? A public-house?

Jones. Yes, at the corner. It was Bank 'oliday, an' I'd 'ad a drop to drink. I see 385 this young Mr. Barthwick tryin' to find the keyhole on the wrong side of the door.

Mag. Well?

Jones (*slowly and with many pauses*). Well —I 'elped 'im to find it—drunk as a lord 390 'e was. He goes on, an' comes back again, and says, "I've got nothin' for you," 'e says, "but come in an' 'ave a drink." So I went in just as you might 'ave done yourself. We 'ad a drink o' whisky just as you might have 'ad, 'nd 395 young Mr. Barthwick says to me, "Take a drink 'nd a smoke. Take anything you like," 'e says. And then he went to sleep on the sofa. I 'ad some more whisky—an' I 'ad a smoke—and I 'ad some more whisky—an' I carn't tell 400 yer what 'appened after that.

Mag. Do you mean to say that you were so drunk that you can remember nothing?

Jack (*softly to his father*). I say, that's exactly what—— 405

Barth. Tssh!

Jones. That's what I do mean.

Mag. And yet you say you stole the box?

Jones. I never stole the box. I took it.

Mag. (*hissing with protruded neck*). You 410

did not steal it — you took it. Did it belong to you — what is that but stealing?

Jones. I took it.

Mag. You took it — you took it away from their house and you took it to your **415** house ——

Jones (*sullenly breaking in*). I ain't got a house.

Mag. Very well, let us hear what this young man Mr. — Mr. Barthwick — has to say **420** to your story.

(SNOW *leaves the witness-box. The* BALD CONSTABLE *beckons* JACK, *who, clutching his hat, goes into the witness-box.* ROPER *moves to the table set apart for his profession.*

Usher. The evidence you give to the Court shall be the truth, the whole truth, and nothing but the truth, so help you God.   Kiss the book.
(*The book is kissed.*

Roper (*examining*). What is your name? **425**

Jack (*in a low voice*). John Barthwick, Junior.
(*The* CLERK *writes it down.*

Roper. Where do you live?

Jack. At 6, Rockingham Gate.
(*All his answers are recorded by the* CLERK.

Roper. You are the son of the owner?

Jack (*in a very low voice*). Yes.   **430**

Roper. Speak up, please. Do you know the prisoners?

Jack (*looking at the* JONESES, *in a low voice*). I've seen Mrs. Jones. I — (*in a loud voice*) don't know the man.   **435**

Jones. Well, I know you!

Bald Const. Hssh!

Roper. Now, did you come in late on the night of Easter Monday?

Jack. Yes.   **440**

Roper. And did you by mistake leave your latchkey in the door?

Jack. Yes.

Mag. Oh! You left your latchkey in the door?   **445**

Roper. And is that all you can remember about your coming in?

Jack (*in a loud voice*). Yes, it is.

Mag. Now, you have heard the male prisoner's story, what do you say to that? **450**

Jack (*turning to the* MAGISTRATE, *speaks suddenly in a confident, straightforward voice*). The fact of the matter is, sir, that I'd been out to the theater that night, and had supper afterwards, and I came in late.   **455**

Mag. Do you remember this man being outside when you came in?

Jack. No, sir. (*He hesitates.*) I don't think I do.

Mag. (*somewhat puzzled*). Well, did he **460** help you to open the door, as he says? Did anyone help you to open the door?

Jack. No, sir — I — don't think so, sir — I don't know.

Mag. You don't know? But you must **465** know. It isn't a usual thing for you to have the door opened for you, is it?

Jack (*with a shamefaced smile*). No.

Mag. Very well, then ——

Jack (*desperately*). The fact of the mat- **470** ter is, sir, I'm afraid I'd had too much champagne that night.

Mag. (*smiling*). Oh! you'd had too much champagne?

Jones. May I ask the gentleman a ques- **475** tion?

Mag. Yes — yes — you may ask him what questions you like.

Jones. Don't you remember you said you was a Liberal, same as your father, and **480** you asked me wot I was?

Jack (*with his hand against his brow*). I seem to remember ——

Jones. And I said to you, "I'm a bloomin' Conservative," I said; an' you said to me: **485** "You look more like one of these 'ere Socialists. Take wotever you like," you said.

Jack (*with sudden resolution*). No, I don't. I don't remember anything of the sort.

Jones. Well, I do, an' my word's as **490** good as yours. I've never been had up in a police court before. Look 'ere, don't you remember you had a sky-blue bag in your 'and ——

(BARTHWICK *jumps.*

Roper. I submit to Your Worship that **495** these questions are hardly to the point, the prisoner having admitted that he himself does not remember anything. (*There is a smile on the* *face of Justice.*)   It is a case of the blind leading the blind.   500

Jones (*violently*).   I've done no more than wot he 'as.   I'm a poor man; I've got no money an' no friends — he's a toff — he can do wot I can't.

Mag.   Now, now!   All this won't help you — you must be quiet.   You say you took   505 this box?   Now, what made you take it?   Were you pressed for money?

Jones.   I'm always pressed for money.

Mag.   Was that the reason you took it?

Jones.   No.   510

Mag. (*to* SNOW).   Was anything found on him?

Snow.   Yes, Your Worship.   There was six pounds twelve shillin's found on him, and this purse.   (*The red silk purse is handed to the*
              MAGISTRATE.   BARTHWICK *rises in*
              his seat, but hastily sits down again.

Mag. (*staring at the purse*).   Yes, yes —   515 let me see —— (*There is a silence.*)   No, no, I've nothing before me as to the purse.   How did you come by all that money?

Jones (*after a long pause, suddenly*).   I declines to say.   520

Mag.   But if you had all that money, what made you take this box?

Jones.   I took it out of spite.

Mag. (*hissing, with protruded neck*).   You took it out of spite?   Well now, that's   525 something!   But do you imagine you can go about the town taking things out of spite?

Jones.   If you had my life, if you'd been out of work ——

Mag.   Yes, yes; I know — because   530 you're out of work you think it's an excuse for everything.

Jones (*pointing at* JACK).   You ask 'im wot made 'im take the ——

Roper (*quietly*).   Does Your Worship re-   535 quire this witness in the box any longer?

Mag. (*ironically*).   I think not; he is hardly profitable.
              (JACK *leaves the witness-box, and, hang-*
              ing his head, resumes his seat.

Jones.   You ask 'im wot made 'im take the lady's ——   540
              (*But the* BALD CONSTABLE *catches him*
              by the sleeve.

Bald Const.   Sssh!

Mag. (*emphatically*).   Now listen to me. I've nothing to do with what he may or may not have taken.   Why did you resist the police in the execution of their duty?   545

Jones.   It warn't their duty to take my wife, a respectable woman, that 'adn't done nothing.

Mag.   But I say it was.   What made you strike the officer a blow?

Jones.   Any man would 'a' struck 'im a   550 blow.   I'd strike 'im again, I would.

Mag.   You are not making your case any better by violence.   How do you suppose we could get on if everybody behaved like you?

Jones (*leaning forward, earnestly*).   Well,   555 wot about 'er; who's to make up to 'er for this? Who's to give 'er back 'er good name?

Mrs. Jones.   Your Worship, it's the children that's preying on his mind, because of course I've lost my work.   And I've had to find   560 another room owing to the scandal.

Mag.   Yes, yes, I know — but if he hadn't acted like this nobody would have suffered.

Jones (*glaring round at* JACK).   I've done no worse than wot 'e 'as.   Wot I want to   565 know is wot's goin' to be done to *im.*'
              (*The* BALD CONSTABLE *again says*
              "*Hssh!*"

Roper.   Mr. Barthwick wishes it known, Your Worship, that considering the poverty of the prisoners he does not press the charge as to the box.   Perhaps Your Worship would deal   570 with the case as one of disorder.

Jones.   I don't want it smothered up, I want it all dealt with fair — I want my rights ——

Mag. (*rapping his desk*).   Now you have said all you have to say, and you will be quiet.   575 (*There is a silence; the* MAGISTRATE *bends over and parleys with his* CLERK.)   Yes, I think I may discharge the woman.   (*In a kindly voice he addresses* MRS. JONES, *who stands unmoving with her hands crossed on the rail.*)   It is   580 very unfortunate for you that this man has behaved as he has.   It is not the consequences to him but the consequences to you.   You have been brought here twice, you have lost your work — (*he glares at* JONES) and this is   585 what always happens.   Now you may go away, and I am very sorry it was necessary to bring you here at all.

Mrs. Jones (softly). Thank you very much, Your Worship.   590

(*She leaves the dock, and looking back at* JONES, *twists her fingers and is still.*

Mag. Yes, yes, but I can't pass it over. Go away, there's a good woman. (MRS. JONES *stands back. The* MAGISTRATE *leans his head on his hand: then raising it, he speaks to* JONES.) Now, listen to me. Do you wish the case   595 to be settled here, or do you wish it to go before a jury?

Jones (muttering). I don't want no jury.

Mag. Very well then, I will deal with it here. (*After a pause*) You have pleaded guilty   600 to stealing this box ——

Jones. Not to stealin' ——

Bald Const. Hssshh!

Mag. And to assaulting the police ——

Jones. Any man as was a man ——   605

Mag. Your conduct here has been most improper. You give the excuse that you were drunk when you stole the box. I tell you that is no excuse. If you choose to get drunk and break the law afterwards you must take   610 the consequences. And let me tell you that men like you, who get drunk and give way to your spite or whatever it is that's in you, are — are — a *nuisance to the community.*

Jack (leaning from his seat). Dad! that's   615 what you said to me!

Barth. Tsst!

(*There is a silence while the* MAGIS-TRATE *consults his* CLERK; JONES *leans forward, waiting.*

Mag. This is your first offense, and I am going to give you a light sentence. (*Speaking sharply, but without expression*) One   620 month with hard labor.

(*He bends, and parleys with his* CLERK. *The* BALD CONSTABLE *and another help* JONES *from the dock.*

Jones (stopping and twisting round). Call this justice? What about 'im? 'E got drunk! 'E took the purse — 'e took the purse but (*in a muffled shout*) it's 'is money got 'im off —   625 *Justice!*

(*The prisoner's door is shut on* JONES, *and from the seedy-looking men and women comes a hoarse and whispering groan.*

Mag. We will now adjourn for lunch!

(*He rises from his seat.*

(*The Court is in a stir.* ROPER *gets up and speaks to the reporter.* JACK, *throwing up his head, walks with a swagger to the corridor;* BARTHWICK *follows.*

Mrs. Jones (turning to him with a humble gesture). Oh! sir! ——

(BARTHWICK *hesitates; then, yielding to his nerves, he makes a shamefaced gesture of refusal, and hurries out of court.* MRS. JONES *stands looking after him.*

The curtain falls.

INTRODUCTION TO

The Playboy of the Western World

The Rise of the Irish Theater and Drama: Synge and Folk-Comedy

THE RISE OF THE IRISH THEATER AND DRAMA

AN OUTSTANDING development in the world theater of the twentieth century has been the birth of a flourishing national drama in Ireland. From the opening of the first playhouse at Dublin about 1637 English traditions dominated the evident theatrical genius of the Irish until the last years of the nineteenth century. Then the quickening struggle for Ireland's political freedom awakened interest in a renaissance of Celtic literature and art. The chief leader of this cultural movement was a young poet, William Butler Yeats (1865–1939), who started the Irish Literary Society in 1891. Three years later the Independent Theater of London performed his first drama, *The Land of Heart's Desire*, written in verse and filled with Irish folk-lore. Yeats now began to dream of a national theater in Ireland. One summer afternoon in 1898 at a country house on Galway Bay he shared his dream with a member of the local landed gentry, Lady Isabella Augusta Gregory (1859–1932), and won her instant enthusiasm. Together they set about organizing the Irish Literary Theater with this pronouncement: "We propose to have performed in Dublin, in the spring of every year, certain Celtic and Irish plays, which whatever be their degree of excellence will be written with a high ambition, and so to build up a Celtic and Irish school of dramatic literature. We hope to find in Ireland an uncorrupted and imaginative audience trained to listen by its passion for oratory, and believe that our desire to bring upon the stage the deeper thoughts and emotions of Ireland will ensure for us a tolerant welcome, and that freedom to experiment which is not found in theaters of England, and without which no new movement in art or literature can succeed."

The Irish Literary Theater got under way on May 8, 1899, with the production of a second verse play by Yeats, *The Countess Cathleen*, at the Ancient Concert Rooms in Brunswick (now Pearse) Street, Dublin. The actors were all English, recruited and rehearsed in London, because no competent Irish players could be secured. Opposition to *The Countess Cathleen* unexpectedly flared up. A pamphlet, *Souls for Gold*, distributed outside the door, condemned the play as both anti-Irish and anti-Catholic. Police had to line the hall to keep order, but despite their presence Catholic university students interrupted the performance with loud hoots from the gallery. That riotous beginning portended in what dead earnest Irishmen were to take their new national drama.

The Irish Literary Theater came to an end after sponsoring two more annual series of Irish plays with English casts. Its programs had shown that English actors, however excellent, could not impart the native atmosphere of the new Irish plays. Yeats and Lady Gregory therefore joined forces with the Irish National Dramatic Company, a group of Dublin amateurs, led by William Fay, a former professional comedian, and his brother, Frank, an electrician. This troupe, composed mostly of humble artisans, rehearsed evenings in a dismal room at the back of a shop off run-down Camden Street. On April 2, 1902, they presented in a crowded temperance hall *Cathleen ni Houlihan* by Yeats, and *Deirdre* by G. W. Russell (1867–1935), the first serious Irish plays to be written, directed, and acted entirely by Irishmen.

The following winter saw the formation of the Irish National Theater Society with Yeats as president, and William Fay as stage manager. The Camden Street troupe constituted the acting organization and carried on without pay. In May, 1903, the Irish National Theater Company undertook an epoch-making visit to London. The refreshing quality of their plays and their playing so charmed a wealthy devotee of the arts, Miss A. E. F. Horniman, that she promised to furnish in Dublin a playhouse suitable as a national theater and to provide an annual subsidy for maintenance. Thus it ironically came about that English generosity put the Irish dramatic movement on its feet.

Miss Horniman proceeded to acquire the Mechanics Institute Hall in Abbey Street, Dublin, along with the former city morgue adjoining, and to reconstruct and redecorate the interiors. The dressing rooms and the "green room" were located in the old morgue. The actors at first found the atmosphere there so eerie that they adjourned a rehearsal of *The Countess Cathleen* because one of their number felt himself grasped by an invisible hand. The drab hall was transformed into an attractive, partly wainscoted auditorium, seating rather less than six hundred persons. A proscenium bearing the arms of Ireland and of Dublin framed a stage, eighteen feet by twelve, too small for elaborate scenic effects. The first endowed playhouse in any English-speaking country, the Abbey Theater opened its doors to the public on December 27, 1904. Ever since, in spite of riots within and rebellions without, it has stood firm as the national home of Irish drama. From the beginning the prices of admission have remained fixed at twenty-five to seventy-five cents in order to forward Yeats' ideal of a "people's theater."

Yeats originally intended such a theater to be "poetic," offering a lyrical and imaginative re-creation of the ancient folk-culture. Really, however, he helped to establish a theater which in the main was realistic, because almost no one but himself would or could write romantic plays in verse. The early repertoire of the Abbey Theater consisted principally of folk-drama, that is, plays about contemporary villagers and peasants. William Fay, the stage manager, produced these plays of Irish country life with extraordinary accuracy of detail. The sets were facsimiles of existing scenes; the properties taken out of rural cottages. For instance, the cowskin sandals, or "pampooties," worn in Synge's *Riders to the Sea*, came direct from Aran; the turf baskets and panniers from the Kerry coast. Peasant tailors were hired to make the costumes exact reproductions of the folk dress. The players went out and studied the ways of the peasantry, so that they might imitate the latter's actual movements, gestures, and intonations. In consequence, the Abbey company developed an acting style all its own, unsurpassed for simplicity, restraint, artless stage groupings, and musical delivery.

By 1910 the Abbey Theater seemed to Miss Horniman to have come of age. Hence she withdrew her subsidy and turned over the property to the National Theater Society. Thereafter the Abbey's policy altered little, but its repertoire changed a good deal. Plays concerning Irish town life and the middle class, such as *The White Headed Boy* (1916), an excellent comedy by Lennox Robinson (1886–   ), gradually superseded the peasant drama. During the First World War and the subsequent civil war in Ireland the Abbey Theater faced lean years. Then in 1924 the new Irish Free State agreed to make it an annual grant of £1000. It thereby became the first government-subsidized theater of the English-speaking world. At the same time a Dublin laborer turned playwright, Sean O'Casey (1884–   ), brought a fresh popularity and a more proletarian audience through his *Juno and the Paycock* (1924) and *The Plough and the Stars* (1926). These "tragic farces" did for the Dublin tenement dwellers what the Abbey Theater pioneers had done for the peasants. The superb gusto of O'Casey's slum characters with their vivid, rhythmic dialect and naïve humor gained fame for his plays abroad as well as at home. His success again proved the unusual wealth of dramatic genius in twentieth-century Ireland. Though its entire population is not half that of metropolitan New York, this little country has done as much as any to enrich the international stage since 1900.

SYNGE AND FOLK-COMEDY

It was the dramatic art of John Millington Synge which first drew the attention of the world to the Irish theater. The youngest son of a Protestant barrister and landlord, Synge was born on April 16, 1871, at Newton Little near Rathfarnham, a Dublin suburb. He entered Trinity College, Dublin, in 1888; concentrated on languages (including Irish) and music; won in 1892 the Royal Irish Academy Prize for Harmony and Counterpoint; and finished his B.A. course during the next winter. Soon afterward he went to Germany in order to study piano and violin, but in a year or so he gave up his idea of a professional musical career because the Germans appeared to him "more innately gifted." By January, 1895, he had turned his attention to literature and come to Paris.

There at a hotel in the student quarter the poet Yeats made Synge's acquaintance during the autumn of 1896. This was a momentous meeting for the future Irish drama. Yeats found Synge living alone in a garret, reading the French Decadents, and writing morbid verse; he saw a "poor Irishman" wasting away talent in a depressing and arid environment. The sight recalled, in contrast, the fresh, heroic atmosphere of the Aran Islands, three rocky dots off the Atlantic coast of Ireland, which had fascinated Yeats just a few months earlier. "Go to the Aran Islands," he urged Synge, "live there as if you were one of the people themselves; express a life that has never found expression." Synge eventually followed this advice by crossing to Aran in the summer of 1898. For weeks he roamed over the storm-swept landscape, sat by the peat-fires of the fisher-folk, and entertained his simple-hearted hosts with flute, violin, and tricks of magic. Here on these bleak but lovely isles "the wonder and beauty of the world" overwhelmed him for the first time. Henceforth he lived under the spell of the primitive.

Paris for some years continued Synge's abode in winter. The summers, however, drew him back to Aran or to the lonely hills of Wicklow not far from his boyhood home. Then at the close of 1902 he deserted the French capital for London, where he became friendly with a group of young literary men, John Masefield in particular. Anxious for help in a new craft, he read aloud to this circle the first fruits of his Irish sojourning —

Riders to the Sea, an Aran tragedy in one act, and *In the Shadow of the Glen*, a Wicklow comedy also in one act. From the summer of 1903 onwards he stayed in Ireland, tramping often through the more remote Irish-speaking districts of both east and west coasts. His debut as a playwright occurred on October 8, 1903, when the Irish National Theater Company performed *In the Shadow of the Glen*. The Sinn Feiners (the extreme nationalists), crying out that the comedy ridiculed the sanctity of marriage as well as libeled Irish women, precipitated a near-riot. All the agitation served only to advertise to the entire country the arrival of an Irish dramatist of the first water.

The production of *Riders to the Sea* in February, 1904, confirmed for Yeats and Lady Gregory the genius of Synge. They invited him, upon the opening of the Abbey Theater, to act along with them as a director. Two months later his first full-length play, *The Well of the Saints*, reached the Abbey boards. Intermittent attacks of illness now began to hamper his writing. Two further comedies, *The Playboy of the Western World* and *The Tinker's Wedding*, appeared in 1907. Thereafter Synge's health failed steadily, so that he never completed *Deirdre of the Sorrows*, a tragedy on the poignant legend so dear to Irish poets. On March 24, 1909, from a private Dublin hospital, he took what in one of his poems he had called his "poor passage to the stall of Night."

Synge had, as an Irishman, one unique trait: he had no care at all for politics. Yeats got him to join the Young Ireland Society of Paris, but he resigned after a few months of boredom. He never felt much interest in ideologies and, for that reason, in the intellectual modern drama. According to his view, "the drama, like the symphony, does not teach or prove anything." He wrote as a pure artist, cherishing a scene not because it represented some point of doctrine, but because it contained vitality and color. Every detail in living which possessed richness stirred Synge's delight. He, like Pegeen Mike in *The Playboy of the Western World*, loved his shoes to have "brassy eyes." For him the serious mission of dramatic art was its nourishment of man's imagination. It should convey the joy to be found "in what is superb and wild in reality."

Hence the wildness of the Irish country people, which Synge termed "a thing that is priceless beyond words," altogether captivated him. His discovery that these people "have still a life, and a view of life, that are rich and genial and humorous" resulted in a generally zestful and comic tone to his plays. They reproduce the extravagant imagination, the unrestrained feeling, the racy, exuberant speech of the Irish folk. The language of Synge's drama is the language of the peasants in so far as it contains no words or imagery which the peasants did not really use. At the same time it is not the language of the peasants inasmuch as no Irish peasants ever talked with such consistent fancy and music as Synge's characters. The color, the lilt, the nutty flavor, the tender and haunting note, make his the most individual and beautiful dialogue on the modern English-speaking stage. Yet his pre-eminence finally proceeds from his superlative blending of poetry and realism. He was the first dramatist to set down truthfully the passion and the splendor in folk life.

"THE PLAYBOY OF THE WESTERN WORLD"

The Playboy of the Western World is the fullest, the most subtle of all Synge's plays and his undoubted masterpiece. For almost two years he worked over it, rewriting the last act thirteen times. Its turbulent premiere at the Abbey Theater on Saturday, January

26, 1907, has become one of the celebrated events in theatrical history. The audience, watching for reflections on Irish virtue, broke into an uproar before the end of the third act and would not listen the play out. On the following Monday, hoots, tin trumpets, and raw potatoes joined in the performance from the rise of the curtain. Lady Gregory therefore asked her nephew to bring a crowd of Trinity College athletes to help maintain order on Tuesday night. Their efforts only provoked the townsmen to noisier outbursts. In indignation John B. Yeats, father of the poet and a man of commanding presence, mounted the stage before the raging crowd. "Ireland is full of saints," he cried, and then, as the applause died out, "but they are all plaster." No further speech by actors or anyone else was heard that evening. The battle lasted through the week. Every night protesters raised a din; every night the police carried off a score of troublemakers to court. By the next Saturday the opposition had petered out and the Irish national theater had been preserved from mob censorship.

The bizarre plot of *The Playboy* is not wholly Synge's invention. The essential circumstances grew out of a true story told to him on Aranmor. A Connaught man "killed his father with the blow of a spade when he was in passion, and then fled to this island and threw himself on the mercy of some of the natives . . . They hid him in a hole . . . and kept him safe for weeks . . . After much trouble the man was safely shipped to America." Synge shifted the locale from Aranmor to County Mayo on the neighboring mainland. He revised the original situation by having the father only wounded and quite able to pursue his assailant; he then added a love element, though elsewhere he remarked that the Irish country people "are nearly as far from the romantic moods of love as they are from the impulsive life of the savage."

Synge, according to his own statement, "wrote *The Playboy* directly, as a piece of life." Nevertheless, as he too intimated, the play has several sides. It is, to begin with, extravagant comedy saturated with elemental fancy and high spirits, an artistic distillation of folk existence. The comedy, however, contains a measure of symbolism and satire on Ireland — her love of "heroes" and her tendency to confuse the fools with the heroes in her long struggle for freedom. Above all, *The Playboy* pictures "the truth about the world," to quote Bernard Shaw. People everywhere insist upon finding a "hero" among themselves, and then there is always a man ready to act that part. It is this theme of humanity's preference for the dream rather than the actual which infuses the comedy with universal meaning.

The theme is centered about a glamorous and unforgettable character. Synge's "hero," Christy Mahon, under the transforming power of imagination progresses from a peasant clod dazed by his own violence to "a likely gaffer in the end of all, the only Playboy of the Western World." Christy carries through his rise with "such poet's talking and such bravery of heart" as has no parallel in the modern theater. The love-scene between Pegeen Mike and the Playboy (Act III, ll. 324–426) is among the most delicate and enchanting in all literature. Thus Synge clothed man's inherent romancing with unique humor and beauty of speech to produce one of the world's great comedies.

[For the Irish drama and theater, see A. E. Malone, *The Irish Drama* (1929); Curtis Canfield, *Plays of Changing Ireland* (1936); for Synge, Maurice Bourgeois, *John Millington Synge and the Irish Theatre* (1913).]

J. M. SYNGE

The Playboy of the Western World

PREFACE

In writing *The Playboy* [1] *of the Western World,* [2] as in my other plays, I have used one or two words only that I have not heard among the country people of Ireland, or spoken in my own nursery before I could read the newspapers. A certain number of the phrases I employ I have heard also from herds [3] and fishermen along the coast from Kerry to Mayo, [4] or from beggar-women and ballad-singers nearer Dublin; and I am glad to acknowledge how much I owe to the folk-imagination of these fine people. Anyone who has lived in real intimacy with the Irish peasantry will know that the wildest sayings and ideas in this play are tame indeed, compared with the fancies one may hear in any little hillside cabin in Geesala, or Carraroe, or Dingle Bay. [5] All art is a collaboration; and there is little doubt that, in the happy ages of literature, striking and beautiful phrases were as ready to the story-teller's or the playwright's hand as the rich cloaks and dresses of his time. It is probable that when the Elizabethan dramatist took his ink-horn and sat down to his work he used many phrases that he had just heard, as he sat at dinner, from his mother or his children. In Ireland, those of us who know the people have the same privilege. When I was writing *The Shadow of the Glen,* some years ago, I got more aid than any learning could have given me from a chink in the floor of the old Wicklow [6] house where I was staying, that let me hear what was being said by the servant girls in the kitchen. This matter, I think, is of importance, for in countries where the imagination of the people, and the language they use, is rich and living, it is possible for a writer to be rich and copious in his words, and at the same time to give the reality, which is the root of all poetry, in a comprehensive and natural form. In the modern literature of towns, however, richness is found only in sonnets, or prose poems, or in one or two elaborate books that are far away from the profound and common interests of life. One has, on one side, Mallarmé [7] and Huysmans [8] producing this literature; and on the other, Ibsen and Zola [9] dealing with the reality of life in joyless and pallid words. On the stage one must have reality, and one must have joy; and that is why the intellectual modern drama has failed, and people have grown sick of the false joy of the musical comedy, that has been given them in place of the rich joy found only in what is superb and wild in reality. In a good play every speech should be as fully flavored as a nut or apple, and such speeches cannot be written by anyone who works among people who

[1] Originally a term used in the Irish sport of hurling (somewhat like hockey), meaning a boy or player of the game. Then in Irish slang the term came to signify a daredevilish fellow who was a hoaxer.
[2] Folk term for the west coast of Ireland.   [3] Herdsmen.
[4] Counties of the Irish west coast; Kerry at the south, Mayo at the north.
[5] Districts on the west coast. Dingle Bay is a famous scenic spot in Kerry.
[6] The county of the east coast just south of Dublin.
[7] Stéphane Mallarmé (1842–98), French symbolist poet.
[8] Joris Karl Huysmans (1848–1907), French novelist.
[9] Emile Zola (1840–1902), French naturalistic novelist.

have shut their lips on poetry. In Ireland, for a few years more, we have a popular imagination that is fiery and magnificent, and tender; so that those of us who wish to write start with a chance that is not given to writers in places where the springtime of the local life has been forgotten, and the harvest is a memory only, and the straw has been turned into bricks.

J. M. S.

January 21, 1907

DRAMATIS PERSONAE

CHRISTOPHER MAHON
OLD MAHON, *his father, a squatter*
MICHAEL JAMES FLAHERTY, called MICHAEL JAMES, *a publican*
MARGARET FLAHERTY, called PEGEEN MIKE, *his daughter*
WIDOW QUIN, *a woman of about thirty*
SHAWN KEOGH, *her cousin, a young farmer*
PHILLY CULLEN and JIMMY FARRELL, *small farmers*
SARA TANSEY, SUSAN BRADY, HONOR BLAKE, and NELLY, *village girls*
A Bellman
Some Peasants

The action takes place near a village, on a wild coast of Mayo. The first act passes on an evening of autumn, the other two acts on the following day.

ACT I

SCENE. *Country public-house or shebeen, very rough and untidy. There is a sort of counter on the right with shelves, holding many bottles and jugs, just seen above it. Empty barrels stand near the counter. At back, a little to left of counter, there is a door into the open air; then, more to the left, there is a settle with shelves above it, with more jugs, and a table beneath a window. At the left there is a large open fireplace, with turf fire, and a small door into inner room. PEGEEN, a wild-looking but fine girl, of about twenty, is writing at table. She is dressed in the usual peasant dress.*

Peg. (slowly as she writes). Six yards of stuff for to make a yellow gown. A pair of lace boots with lengthy heels on them and brassy eyes. A hat is suited for a wedding-day. A fine-tooth comb. To be sent with three 5 barrels of porter in Jimmy Farrell's creel cart on the evening of the coming Fair to Mister Michael James Flaherty. With the best compliments of this season. Margaret Flaherty.

SHAWN KEOGH, *a fat and fair young man, comes in as she signs, looks round awkwardly, when he sees she is alone*

Shawn. Where's himself?   10
Peg. (without looking at him). He's coming. (*She directs the letter.*) To Mister Sheamus Mulroy, Wine and Spirit Dealer, Castlebar.[1]
Shawn (uneasily). I didn't see him on the road.   15
Peg. How would you see him (*licks stamp and puts it on letter*) and it dark night this half hour gone by?
Shawn (turning towards the door again). I stood a while outside wondering would I 20 have a right to pass on or to walk in and see you, Pegeen Mike (*comes to fire*), and I could hear the cows breathing, and sighing in the stillness of the air, and not a step moving any place from this gate to the bridge.   25

[1] The county seat of Mayo.

Peg. (*putting letter in envelope*). It's above at the crossroads he is, meeting Philly Cullen; and a couple more are going along with him to Kate Cassidy's wake.

Shawn (*looking at her blankly*). And he's 30 going that length in the dark night?

Peg. (*impatiently*). He is surely, and leaving me lonesome on the scruff of the hill. (*She gets up and puts envelope on dresser, then winds clock.*) Isn't it long the nights are now, Shawn Keogh, to be leaving a poor girl with her own 35 self counting the hours to the dawn of day?

Shawn (*with awkward humor*). If it is, when we're wedded in a short while you'll have no call to complain, for I've little will to be walk-ing off to wakes or weddings in the dark- 40 ness of the night.

Peg. (*with rather scornful good-humor*). You're making mighty certain, Shaneen,[1] that I'll wed you now.

Shawn. Aren't we after making a good bar-gain, the way we're only waiting these 45 days on Father Reilly's dispensation from the bishops, or the Court of Rome?

Peg. (*looking at him teasingly, washing up at dresser*). It's a wonder, Shaneen, the Holy Father'd be taking notice of the likes of you; for if I was him I wouldn't bother with this 50 place where you'll meet none but Red Linahan has a squint in his eye, and Patcheen is lame in his heel, or the mad Mulrannies were driven from California and they lost in their wits. We're a queer lot these times to go troub- 55 ling the Holy Father on his sacred seat.

Shawn (*scandalized*). If we are, we're as good this place as another, maybe, and as good these times as we were forever.

Peg. (*with scorn*). As good, is it? 60 Where now will you meet the like of Daneen Sullivan knocked the eye from a peeler,[2] or Marcus Quin, God rest him, got six months for maiming ewes, and he a great warrant to tell stories of holy Ireland till he'd have the old 65

Shawn (*timidly*). If you don't, it's a good job, maybe; for (*with peculiar emphasis on the words*) Father Reilly has small conceit to 70 have that kind walking around and talking to the girls.

Peg. (*impatiently, throwing water from basin out of the door*). Stop tormenting me with Fa-ther Reilly (*imitating his voice*) when I'm ask-ing only what way I'll pass these twelve 75 hours of dark, and not take my death with the fear. (*Looking out of door.*)

Shawn (*timidly*). Would I fetch you the Widow Quin, maybe?

Peg. Is it the like of that murderer? 80 You'll not, surely.

Shawn (*going to her, soothingly*). Then I'm thinking himself will stop along with you when he sees you taking on, for it'll be a long night-time with great darkness, and I'm after 85 feeling a kind of fellow above in the furzy[1] ditch groaning wicked like a maddening dog, the way it's good cause you have, maybe, to be fearing now.

Peg. (*turning on him sharply*). What's 90 that? Is it a man you seen?

Shawn (*retreating*). I couldn't see him at all; but I heard him groaning out, and breaking his heart. It should have been a young man from his words speaking. 95

Peg. (*going after him*). And you never went near to see was he hurted or what ailed him at all?

Shawn. I did not, Pegeen Mike. It was a dark, lonesome place to be hearing the 100 like of him.

Peg. Well, you're a daring fellow, and if they find his corpse stretched above in the dews of dawn, what'll you say then to the peelers, or the Justice of the Peace? 105

Shawn (*thunderstruck*). I wasn't thinking of that. For the love of God, Pegeen Mike, don't let on I was speaking of him. Don't tell your father and the men is coming above; for if they heard that story, they'd have 110 great blabbing this night at the wake.

---

women shedding down tears about their feet? Where will you find the like of them, I'm saying?

[1] "Johnnie" < Shawn (John) + een. The Irish suffix "-een," originally diminutive, often connotes endear-ment or playfulness, just as the English "-ie."

[2] Irish slang term for a policeman; so called from the fact that the British police force was begun in 1814 by Sir Robert *Peel.*

[1] Furze, a spiny evergreen shrub, also called gorse.

Peg. I'll maybe tell them, and I'll maybe not.

Shawn. They are coming at the door. Will you whisht,[1] I'm saying?   115

Peg. Whisht yourself.

She goes behind counter. MICHAEL JAMES, *fat jovial publican, comes in, followed by* PHILLY CULLEN, *who is thin and mistrusting, and* JIMMY FARRELL, *who is fat and amorous, about forty-five*

Men (*together*). God bless you. The blessing of God on this place.

Peg. God bless you kindly.   119

Mich. (*to men, who go to the counter*). Sit down now, and take your rest. (*Crosses to* SHAWN *at the fire.*) And how is it you are, Shawn Keogh? Are you coming over the sands to Kate Cassidy's wake?

Shawn. I am not, Michael James. I'm   125 going home the short cut to my bed.

Peg. (*speaking across the counter*). He's right, too, and have you no shame, Michael James, to be quitting off for the whole night, and leaving myself lonesome in the shop?   130

Mich. (*good-humoredly*). Isn't it the same whether I go for the whole night or a part only? And I'm thinking it's a queer daughter you are if you'd have me crossing backward through the Stooks[2] of the Dead Women,   135 with a drop taken.

Peg. If I am a queer daughter, it's a queer father'd be leaving me lonesome these twelve hours of dark, and I piling the turf with the dogs barking, and the calves mooing, and   140 my own teeth rattling with the fear.

Jimmy (*flatteringly*). What is there to hurt you, and you a fine, hardy girl would knock the head of any two men in the place?

Peg. (*working herself up*). Isn't there   145 the harvest boys with their tongues red for drink, and the ten tinkers is camped in the east glen, and the thousand militia — bad cess[3] to them! — walking idle through the land? There's lots surely to hurt me, and I won't   150 stop alone in it, let himself do what he will.

Mich. If you're that afeard, let Shawn Keogh

[1] Hush.   [2] Stook = bundle of sheaves.   [3] Luck.

stop along with you. It's the will of God, I'm thinking, himself should be seeing to you now.   (*They all turn on* SHAWN.   155

Shawn (*in horrified confusion*). I would and welcome, Michael James, but I'm afeard of Father Reilly; and what at all would the Holy Father and the Cardinals of Rome be saying if they heard I did the like of that?   160

Mich. (*with contempt*). God help you! Can't you sit in by the hearth with the light lit and herself beyond in the room? You'll do that surely, for I've heard tell there's a queer fellow above, going mad or getting his   165 death, maybe, in the gripe[1] of the ditch, so she'd be safer this night with a person here.

Shawn (*with plaintive despair*). I'm afeard of Father Reilly, I'm saying. Let you not be tempting me, and we near married itself.   170

Philly (*with cold contempt*). Lock him in the west room. He'll stay then and have no sin to be telling to the priest.

Mich. (*to* SHAWN, *getting between him and the door*). Go up now.

Shawn (*at the top of his voice*). Don't   175 stop me, Michael James. Let me out of the door, I'm saying, for the love of the Almighty God. Let me out (*trying to dodge past him*). Let me out of it, and may God grant you His indulgence in the hour of need.   180

Mich. (*loudly*). Stop your noising, and sit down by the hearth.

(*Gives him a push and goes to counter laughing.*

Shawn (*turning back, wringing his hands*). Oh, Father Reilly and the saints of God, where will I hide myself today? Oh, Saint Joseph and Saint Patrick and Saint Brigid, and   185 Saint James, have mercy on me now!

(SHAWN *turns round, sees door clear, and makes a rush for it.*

Mich. (*catching him by the coat-tail*). You'd be going, is it?

Shawn (*screaming*). Leave me go, Michael James, leave me go, you old Pagan, leave   190 me go, or I'll get the curse of the priests on you, and of the scarlet-coated bishops of the courts of Rome.

(*With a sudden movement he pulls him-*

[1] Gutter.

self out of his coat, and disappears out of the door, leaving his coat in MICHAEL'S *hands.*

Mich. (turning round, and holding up coat). Well, there's the coat of a Christian man. Oh, there's sainted glory this day in the 195 lonesome west; and by the will of God I've got you a decent man, Pegeen, you'll have no call to be spying after if you've a score of young girls, maybe, weeding in your fields.

Peg. (taking up the defense of her property). What right have you to be making game 200 of a poor fellow for minding the priest, when it's your own the fault is, not paying a penny pot-boy to stand along with me and give me courage in the doing of my work?

       (She snaps the coat away from him, and goes behind counter with it.

Mich. (taken aback). Where would I 205 get a pot-boy? Would you have me send the bellman screaming in the streets of Castlebar?

Shawn (opening the door a chink and putting in his head, in a small voice). Michael James!

Mich. (imitating him). What ails you?

Shawn. The queer dying fellow's be- 210 yond looking over the ditch. He's come up, I'm thinking, stealing your hens. *(Looks over his shoulder.)* God help me, he's following me now *(he runs into room)*, and if he's heard what I said, he'll be having my life, and I going 215 home lonesome in the darkness of the night.

For a perceptible moment they watch the door with curiosity. Someone coughs outside. Then CHRISTY MAHON, *a slight young man, comes in very tired and frightened and dirty*

Chris. (in a small voice). God save all here!

Men. God save you kindly.

Chris. (going to the counter). I'd trouble you for a glass of porter, woman of the house. 220

       (He puts down coin.

Peg. (serving him). You're one of the tinkers, young fellow, is beyond camped in the glen?

Chris. I am not; but I'm destroyed walking.

Mich. (patronizingly). Let you come 225 up then to the fire. You're looking famished with the cold.

Chris. God reward you. *(He takes up his glass and goes a little way across to the left, then stops and looks about him.)* Is it often the police do be coming into this place, mas- 230 ter of the house?

Mich. If you'd come in better hours, you'd have seen "Licensed for the sale of Beer and Spirits, to be consumed on the premises," written in white letters above the door, and 235 what would the polis[1] want spying on me, and not a decent house within four miles, the way every living Christian is a bona fide,[2] saving one widow alone?

Chris. (with relief). It's a safe house, so. 240

       (He goes over to the fire, sighing and moaning. Then he sits down, putting his glass beside him, and begins gnawing a turnip, too miserable to feel the others staring at him with curiosity.

Mich. (going after him). Is it yourself is fearing the polis? You're wanting, maybe?

Chris. There's many wanting.

Mich. Many surely, with the broken harvest and the ended wars. *(He picks up some 245 stockings, etc., that are near the fire, and carries them away furtively.)* It should be larceny, I'm thinking?

Chris. (dolefully). I had it in my mind it was a different word and a bigger.

Peg. There's a queer lad. Were you 250 never slapped in school, young fellow, that you don't know the name of your deed?

Chris. (bashfully). I'm slow at learning, a middling scholar only.

Mich. If you're a dunce itself, you'd 255 have a right to know that larceny's robbing and stealing. Is it for the like of that you're wanting?

Chris. (with a flash of family pride). And I the son of a strong farmer, *(with a sudden 260 qualm)* God rest his soul, could have bought up the whole of your old house a while since, from the butt of his tail-pocket, and not have missed the weight of it gone.

Mich. (impressed). If it's not steal- 265 ing, it's maybe something big.

Chris. (flattered). Aye; it's maybe something big.

[1] The police.   [2] A person who acts in good faith.

Jimmy. He's a wicked-looking young fellow. Maybe he followed after a young 270 woman on a lonesome night.

Chris. (*shocked*). Oh, the saints forbid, mister; I was all times a decent lad.

Philly (*turning on* JIMMY). You're a silly man, Jimmy Farrell. He said his father 275 was a farmer a while since, and there's himself now in a poor state. Maybe the land was grabbed from him, and he did what any decent man would do.

Mich. (*to* CHRISTY, *mysteriously*). Was 280 it bailiffs?

Chris. The divil a one.

Mich. Agents?

Chris. The divil a one.

Mich. Landlords? 285

Chris. (*peevishly*). Ah, not at all, I'm saying. You'd see the like of them stories on any little paper of a Munster[1] town. But I'm not calling to mind any person, gentle, simple, judge or jury, did the like of me. 290

    (*They all draw nearer with delighted curiosity.*

Philly. Well, that lad's a puzzle-the-world.

Jimmy. He'd beat Dan Davies' circus, or the holy missioners[2] making sermons on the villainy of man. Try him again, Philly.

Philly. Did you strike golden guineas[3] 295 out of solder, young fellow, or shilling coins itself?

Chris. I did not, mister, not sixpence nor a farthing[4] coin.

Jimmy. Did you marry three wives 300 maybe? I'm told there's a sprinkling have done that among the holy Luthers of the preaching north.

Chris. (*shyly*). I never married with one, let alone with a couple or three. 305

Philly. Maybe he went fighting for the Boers,[5] the like of the man beyond, was judged to be hanged, quartered and drawn. Were you off east, young fellow, fighting bloody wars

for Kruger[1] and the freedom of the Boers? 310

Chris. I never left my own parish till Tuesday was a week.

Peg. (*coming from counter*). He's done nothing, so. (*To* CHRISTY) If you didn't commit murder or a bad, nasty thing, or false 315 coining, or robbery, or butchery, or the like of them, there isn't anything that would be worth your troubling for to run from now. You did nothing at all.

Chris. (*his feelings hurt*). That's an 320 unkindly thing to be saying to a poor orphaned traveler, has a prison behind him, and hanging before, and hell's gap gaping below.

Peg. (*with a sign to the men to be quiet*). You're only saying it. You did nothing at all. A soft lad the like of you wouldn't slit 325 the windpipe of a screeching sow.

Chris. (*offended*). You're not speaking the truth.

Peg. (*in mock rage*). Not speaking the truth, is it? Would you have me knock the 330 head of you with the butt of the broom?

Chris. (*twisting round on her with a sharp cry of horror*). Don't strike me. I killed my poor father, Tuesday was a week, for doing the like of that.

Peg. (*with blank amazement*). Is it 335 killed your father?

Chris. (*subsiding*). With the help of God I did surely, and that the Holy Immaculate Mother may intercede for his soul.

Philly (*retreating with* JIMMY). There's 340 a daring fellow.

Jimmy. Oh, glory be to God!

Mich. (*with great respect*). That was a hanging crime, mister honey. You should have had good reason for doing the like of that. 345

Chris. (*in a very reasonable tone*). He was a dirty man, God forgive him, and he getting old and crusty, the way I couldn't put up with him at all.

Peg. And you shot him dead? 350

Chris. (*shaking his head*). I never used weapons. I've no license, and I'm a law-fearing man.

---

[1] The southwestern of the four Irish provincial divisions under the former English rule.
[2] Clergy on preaching missions.
[3] An old British coin worth twenty-one shillings.
[4] A coin worth one-quarter of an English penny.
[5] The Dutch settlers in South Africa, conquered by the British in the Boer War, 1899–1902.

[1] Stephen John Paul Kruger (1825–1904), president of the South African Republic set up by the Boers in opposition to British rule.

Mich. It was with a hilted knife maybe?
I'm told, in the big world it's bloody 355
knives they use.

Chris. (*loudly, scandalized*). Do you take
me for a slaughter-boy?

Peg. You never hanged him, the way Jimmy
Farrell hanged his dog from the license, 360
and had it screeching and wriggling three
hours at the butt of a string, and himself
swearing it was a dead dog, and the peelers
swearing it had life?

Chris. I did not then. I just riz the 365
loy [1] and let fall the edge of it on the ridge of
his skull, and he went down at my feet like an
empty sack, and never let a grunt or groan from
him at all.

Mich. (*making a sign to* PEGEEN *to fill*
CHRISTY's *glass*). And what way weren't 370
you hanged, mister? Did you bury him then?

Chris. (*considering*). Aye. I buried him then.
Wasn't I digging spuds in the field?

Mich. And the peelers never followed after
you the eleven days that you're out? 375

Chris. (*shaking his head*). Never a one of
them, and I walking forward facing hog, dog,
or divil on the highway of the road.

Philly (*nodding wisely*). It's only with a
common week-day kind of a murderer 380
them lads would be trusting their carcass, and
that man should be a great terror when his
temper's roused.

Mich. He should then. (*To* CHRISTY)
And where was it, mister honey, that you 385
did the deed?

Chris. (*looking at him with suspicion*). Oh,
a distant place, master of the house, a windy
corner of high, distant hills.

Philly (*nodding with approval*). He's a 390
close man, and he's right, surely.

Peg. That'd be a lad with the sense of Solomon to have for a pot-boy, Michael James,
if it's the truth you're seeking one at all.

Philly. The peelers is fearing him, 395
and if you'd that lad in the house there isn't
one of them would come smelling around if the
dogs itself were lapping poteen [2] from the
dung-pit of the yard.

[1] An Irish type of small spade.
[2] Irish whiskey illicitly distilled.

Jimmy. Bravery's a treasure in a 400
lonesome place, and a lad would kill his father,
I'm thinking, would face a foxy divil with a
pitchpike on the flags of hell.

Peg. It's the truth they're saying, and if I'd
that lad in the house, I wouldn't be fear- 405
ing the looséd kharki [1] cut-throats, or the
walking dead.

Chris. (*swelling with surprise and triumph*).
Well, glory be to God!

Mich. (*with deference*). Would you think
well to stop here and be pot-boy, mister 410
honey, if we gave you good wages, and didn't
destroy you with the weight of work?

Shawn (*coming forward uneasily*). That'd be
a queer kind to bring into a decent quiet household with the like of Pegeen Mike. 415

Peg. (*very sharply*). Will you whisht?
Who's speaking to you?

Shawn (*retreating*). A bloody-handed murderer the like of . . .

Peg. (*snapping at him*). Whisht I am 420
saying; we'll take no fooling from your like at
all. (*To* CHRISTY *with a honeyed voice*) And
you, young fellow, you'd have a right to stop,
I'm thinking, for we'd do our all and utmost to
content your needs. 425

Chris. (*overcome with wonder*). And I'd be
safe in this place from the searching law?

Mich. You would, surely. If they're not
fearing you, itself, the peelers in this place is
decent droughty [2] poor fellows, wouldn't 430
touch a cur dog and not give warning in the
dead of night.

Peg. (*very kindly and persuasively*). Let you
stop a short while anyhow. Aren't you destroyed walking with your feet in bleed- 435
ing blisters, and your whole skin needing washing like a Wicklow sheep?

Chris. (*looking round with satisfaction*). It's
a nice room, and if it's not humbugging me
you are, I'm thinking that I'll surely stay. 440

Jimmy (*jumps up*). Now, by the grace of
God, herself will be safe this night, with a man
killed his father holding danger from the door,
and let you come on, Michael James, or they'll
have the best stuff drunk at the wake. 445

Mich. (*going to the door with men*). And

[1] Khaki. [2] Thirsty.

begging your pardon, mister, what name will we call you, for we'd like to know?

Chris. Christopher Mahon.

Mich. Well, God bless you, Christy, 450 and a good rest till we meet again when the sun'll be rising to the noon of day.

Chris. God bless you all.

Men. God bless you.

(*They go out except* SHAWN, *who lingers at door.*

Shawn (*to* PEGEEN). Are you want- 455 ing me to stop along with you and keep you from harm?

Peg. (*gruffly*). Didn't you say you were fearing Father Reilly?

Shawn. There'd be no harm staying 460 now, I'm thinking, and himself in it too.

Peg. You wouldn't stay when there was need for you, and let you step off nimble this time when there's none.

Shawn. Didn't I say it was Father Reilly...

Peg. Go on, then, to Father Reilly (*in* 466 *a jeering tone*), and let him put you in the holy brotherhoods, and leave that lad to me.

Shawn. If I meet the Widow Quin...

Peg. Go on, I'm saying, and don't be 470 waking this place with your noise. (*She hustles him out and bolts the door.*) That lad would wear the spirits from the saints of peace. (*Bustles about, then takes off her apron and pins it up in the window as a blind.* CHRISTY *watching her timidly.* Then she comes to him and speaks with bland good-humor.*) Let you stretch out now by the fire, young fellow. 475 You should be destroyed traveling.

Chris. (*shyly again, drawing off his boots*). I'm tired, surely, walking wild eleven days, and waking fearful in the night.

(*He holds up one of his feet, feeling his blisters, and looking at them with compassion.*)

Peg. (*standing beside him, watching him with delight*). You should have had great people in your family, I'm thinking, with the 480 little, small feet you have, and you with a kind of a quality name, the like of what you'd find on the great powers and potentates of France and Spain.

Chris. (*with pride*). We were great 485

surely, with wide and windy acres of rich Munster land.

Peg. Wasn't I telling you, and you a fine, handsome young fellow with a noble brow?

Chris. (*with a flash of delighted surprise*). Is it me? 491

Peg. Aye. Did you never hear that from the young girls where you come from in the west or south?

Chris. (*with venom*). I did not then. 495 Oh, they're bloody liars in the naked parish where I grew a man.

Peg. If they are itself, you've heard it these days, I'm thinking, and you walking the world telling out your story to young girls or old. 500

Chris. I've told my story no place till this night, Pegeen Mike, and it's foolish I was here, maybe, to be talking free, but you're decent people, I'm thinking, and yourself a kindly woman, the way I wasn't fearing you 505 at all.

Peg. (*filling a sack with straw*). You've said the like of that, maybe, in every cot and cabin where you've met a young girl on your way.

Chris. (*going over to her, gradually raising his voice*). I've said it nowhere till this night, 510 I'm telling you, for I've seen none the like of you the eleven long days I am walking the world, looking over a low ditch or a high ditch on my north or my south, into stony scattered fields, or scribes [1] of bog, where you'd see 515 young, limber girls, and fine, prancing women making laughter with the men.

Peg. If you weren't destroyed traveling, you'd have as much talk and streeleen,[2] I'm thinking, as Owen Roe O'Sullivan or the 520 poets of the Dingle Bay, and I've heard all times it's the poets are your like, fine fiery fellows with great rages when their temper's roused. 524

Chris. (*drawing a little nearer to her*). You've a power of rings, God bless you, and would there be any offense if I was asking are you single now?

Peg. What would I want wedding so young?

Chris. (*with relief*). We're alike, so. 530

Peg. (*putting sack on settle and beating it up*). I never killed my father. I'd be afeard to do

[1] Strips.   [2] Prating.

that, except I was the like of yourself with blind rages tearing me within, for I'm thinking you should have had great tussling when the end was come. 535

Chris. (*expanding with delight at the first confidential talk he has ever had with a woman*). We had not then. It was a hard woman was come over the hill, and if he was always a crusty kind when he'd a hard woman setting him on, not the divil himself or his four fathers [1] 540 could put up with him at all.

Peg. (*with curiosity*). And isn't it a great wonder that one wasn't fearing you?

Chris. (*very confidentially*). Up to the day I killed my father, there wasn't a person 545 in Ireland knew the kind I was, and I there drinking, waking, eating, sleeping, a quiet, simple poor fellow with no man giving me heed.

Peg. (*getting a quilt out of the cupboard and putting it on the sack*). It was the girls were giving you heed maybe, and I'm think- 550 ing it's most conceit you'd have to be gaming with their like.

Chris. (*shaking his head, with simplicity*). Not the girls itself, and I won't tell you a lie. There wasn't anyone heeding me in that place saving only the dumb beasts of the field. 555
           (*He sits down at fire.*

Peg. (*with disappointment*). And I thinking you should have been living the like of a king of Norway or the Eastern world.
       (*She comes and sits beside him after
         placing bread and mug of milk on
         the table.*

Chris. (*laughing piteously*). The like of a king, is it? And I after toiling, moiling,[2] 560 digging, dodging from the dawn till dusk with never a sight of joy or sport saving only when I'd be abroad in the dark night poaching rabbits on hills, for I was a devil to poach, God forgive me, (*very naïvely*) and I near got 565 six months for going with a dung fork and stabbing a fish.

Peg. And it's that you'd call sport, is it, to be abroad in the darkness with yourself alone?

Chris. I did, God help me, and there I'd 570 be as happy as the sunshine of Saint Martin's

Day,[1] watching the light passing the north or the patches of fog, till I'd hear a rabbit starting to screech and I'd go running in the furze. Then when I'd my full share I'd come 575 walking down where you'd see the ducks and geese stretched sleeping on the highway of the road, and before I'd pass the dunghill, I'd hear himself snoring out, a loud lonesome snore he'd be making all times, the while he was sleep- 580 ing, and he a man'd be raging all times, the while he was waking, like a gaudy officer you'd hear cursing and damning and swearing oaths.

Peg. Providence and Mercy, spare us all!

Chris. It's that you'd say surely if you 585 seen him and he after drinking for weeks, rising up in the red dawn, or before it maybe, and going out into the yard as naked as an ash tree in the moon of May, and shying clods against the visage of the stars till he'd put the fear 590 of death into the banbhs [2] and the screeching sows.

Peg. I'd be well-nigh afeard of that lad myself, I'm thinking. And there was no one in it but the two of you alone? 595

Chris. The divil a one, though he'd sons and daughters walking all great states and territories of the world, and not a one of them, to this day, but would say their seven curses on him, and they rousing up to let a cough 600 or sneeze, maybe, in the deadness of the night.

Peg. (*nodding her head*). Well, you should have been a queer lot. I never cursed my father the like of that, though I'm twenty 605 and more years of age.

Chris. Then you'd have cursed mine, I'm telling you, and he a man never gave peace to any, saving when he'd get two months or three, or be locked in the asylums for battering 610 peelers or assaulting men (*with depression*) the way it was a bitter life he led me till I did up a Tuesday and halve his skull.

Peg. (*putting her hand on his shoulder*). Well, you'll have peace in this place, Christy 615 Mahon, and none to trouble you, and it's near time a fine lad like you should have your good share of the earth.

---

[1] Forefathers.
[2] Drudging (in wet or dirt, usually).

[1] The feast day of St. Martin, bishop of Tours, France, observed on November 11.   [2] Old women.

Chris. It's time surely, and I a seemly fellow with great strength in me and bravery   620 of ...   (*Someone knocks.* (*Clinging to* PEGEEN) Oh, glory! it's late for knocking, and this last while I'm in terror of the peelers, and the walking dead.
    (*Knocking again.*

Peg. Who's there?   625
Voice (*outside*). Me.
Peg. Who's me?
Voice. The Widow Quin.
Peg. (*jumping up and giving him the bread and milk*). Go on now with your supper, and let on to be sleepy, for if she found you were   630 such a warrant to talk, she'd be stringing gabble till the dawn of day.
    (*He takes bread and sits shyly with his back to the door.*

Peg. (*opening door, with temper*). What ails you, or what is it you're wanting at this hour of the night?   635
Wid. Quin (*coming in a step and peering at* CHRISTY). I'm after meeting Shawn Keogh and Father Reilly below, who told me of your curiosity man,[1] and they fearing by this time he was maybe roaring, romping on your hands with drink.   640
Peg. (*pointing to* CHRISTY). Look now is he roaring, and he stretched away drowsy with his supper and his mug of milk. Walk down and tell that to Father Reilly and to Shaneen Keogh.   645
Wid. Quin (*coming forward*). I'll not see them again, for I've their word to lead that lad forward for to lodge with me.
Peg. (*in blank amazement*). This night, is it?
Wid. Quin (*going over*). This night.   650 "It isn't fitting," says the priesteen, "to have his likeness lodging with an orphaned girl." (*To* CHRISTY) God save you, mister!
Chris. (*shyly*). God save you kindly.
Wid. Quin (*looking at him with half-amazed curiosity*). Well, aren't you a little smil-   655 ing fellow? It should have been great and bitter torments did rouse your spirits to a deed of blood.
Chris. (*doubtfully*). It should, maybe.
Wid. Quin. It's more than "maybe"   660

[1] I.e., a man who excites curiosity.

I'm saying, and it'd soften my heart to see you sitting so simple with your cup and cake, and you fitter to be saying your catechism than slaying your da.[1]   664
Peg. (*at counter, washing glasses*). There's talking when any'd see he's fit to be holding his head high with the wonders of the world. Walk on from this, for I'll not have him tormented and he destroyed traveling since Tuesday was a week.   670
Wid. Quin (*peaceably*). We'll be walking surely when his supper's done, and you'll find we're great company, young fellow, when it's of the like of you and me you'd hear the penny poets singing in an August Fair.   675
Chris. (*innocently*). Did you kill your father?
Peg. (*contemptuously*). She did not. She hit himself with a worn pick, and the rusted poison did corrode his blood the way he never overed it, and died after. That was a   680 sneaky kind of murder did win small glory with the boys itself. (*She crosses to* CHRISTY'S *left.*
Wid. Quin (*with good-humor*). If it didn't, maybe all knows a widow woman has buried her children and destroyed her man is a   685 wiser comrade for a young lad than a girl, the like of you, who'd go helter-skeltering after any man would let you a wink upon the road.
Peg. (*breaking out into wild rage*). And you'll say that, Widow Quin, and you   690 gasping with the rage you had racing the hill beyond to look on his face.
Wid. Quin (*laughing derisively*). Me, is it? Well, Father Reilly has cuteness to divide you now. (*She pulls* CHRISTY *up.*) There's   695 great temptation in a man did slay his da, and we'd best be going, young fellow; so rise up and come with me.
Peg. (*seizing his arm*). He'll not stir. He's pot-boy in this place, and I'll not have   700 him stolen off and kidnabbed while himself's abroad.
Wid. Quin. It'd be a crazy pot-boy'd lodge him in the shebeen where he works by day, so you'd have a right to come on, young   705 fellow, till you see my little houseen, a perch off on the rising hill.
Peg. Wait till morning, Christy Mahon.

[1] Father.

Wait till you lay eyes on her leaky thatch is growing more pasture for her buck goat 710 than her square of fields, and she without a tramp itself to keep in order her place at all.

Wid. Quin. When you see me contriving in my little gardens, Christy Mahon, you'll swear the Lord God formed me to be living 715 lone, and that there isn't my match in Mayo for thatching, or mowing, or shearing a sheep.

Peg. (*with noisy scorn*). It's true the Lord God formed you to contrive indeed. Doesn't the world know you reared a black lamb 720 at your own breast, so that the Lord Bishop of Connaught felt the elements of a Christian, and he eating it after in a kidney stew? Doesn't the world know you've been seen shaving the foxy skipper from France 725 for a threepenny bit and a sop of grass tobacco would wring the liver from a mountain goat you'd meet leaping the hills?

Wid. Quin (*with amusement*). Do you hear her now, young fellow? Do you hear the 730 way she'll be rating at your own self when a week is by?

Peg. (*to* CHRISTY). Don't heed her. Tell her to go into her pigsty and not plague us here.

Wid. Quin. I'm going; but he'll come 735 with me.

Peg. (*shaking him*). Are you dumb, young fellow?

Chris. (*timidly, to* WIDOW QUIN). God increase you; but I'm pot-boy in this 740 place, and it's here I'd liefer stay.

Peg. (*triumphantly*). Now you have heard him, and go on from this.

Wid. Quin (*looking round the room*). It's lonesome this hour crossing the hill, and 745 if he won't come along with me, I'd have a right maybe to stop this night with yourselves. Let me stretch out on the settle, Pegeen Mike; and himself can lie by the hearth.

Peg. (*short and fiercely*). Faith, I 750 won't. Quit off or I will send you now.

Wid. Quin (*gathering her shawl up*). Well, it's a terror to be aged a score. (*To* CHRISTY) God bless you now, young fellow, and let you be wary, or there's right torment 755 will await you here if you go romancing with her like, and she waiting only, as they bade me say, on a sheepskin parchment to be wed with Shawn Keogh of Killakeen.

Chris. (*going to* PEGEEN *as she bolts the door*). What's that she's after saying? 760

Peg. Lies and blather, you've no call to mind. Well, isn't Shawn Keogh an impudent fellow to send up spying on me? Wait till I lay hands on him. Let him wait, I'm saying.

Chris. And you're not wedding him 765 at all?

Peg. I wouldn't wed him if a bishop came walking for to join us here.

Chris. That God in glory may be thanked for that. 770

Peg. There's your bed now. I've put a quilt upon you I'm after quilting a while since with my own two hands, and you'd best stretch out now for your sleep, and may God give you a good rest till I call you in the morning 775 when the cocks will crow.

Chris. (*as she goes to inner room*). May God and Mary and Saint Patrick bless you and reward you, for your kindly talk. (*She shuts the door behind her. He settles his bed slowly, feeling the quilt with immense satisfaction.*) Well, it's a clean bed and soft with it, and 780 it's great luck and company I've won me in the end of time — two fine women fighting for the likes of me — till I'm thinking this night wasn't I a foolish fellow not to kill my father in the years gone by. 785

Curtain

ACT II

SCENE, *as before. Brilliant morning light.* CHRISTY, *looking bright and cheerful, is cleaning a girl's boots.*

Chris. (*to himself, counting jugs on dresser*). Half a hundred beyond. Ten there. A score that's above. Eighty jugs. Six cups and a broken one. Two plates. A power of glasses. Bottles, a schoolmaster'd be hard set to count, and enough in them, I'm thinking, to 5 drunken all the wealth and wisdom of the County Clare.[1] (*He puts down the boot care-*

[1] The center county of the Irish west coast, between Galway and Limerick.

fully.) There's her boots now, nice and decent for her evening use, and isn't it grand brushes she has? (*He puts them down and goes by degrees to the looking-glass*.) Well, this'd be a fine place to be my whole life talking out with swearing Christians, in place of my old dogs and cat, and I stalking around, smoking my pipe and drinking my fill, and never a day's work but drawing a cork an odd time, or wiping a glass, or rinsing out a shiny tumbler for a decent man. (*He takes the looking-glass from the wall and puts it on the back of a chair; then sits down in front of it and begins washing his face*.) Didn't I know rightly I was handsome, though it was the divil's own mirror we had beyond, would twist a squint across an angel's brow; and I'll be growing fine from this day, the way I'll have a soft lovely skin on me and won't be the like of the clumsy young fellows do be ploughing all times in the earth and dung. (*He starts*.) Is she coming again? (*He looks out*.) Stranger girls. God help me, where'll I hide myself away and my long neck naked to the world? (*He looks out*.) I'd best go to the room maybe till I'm dressed again. (*He gathers up his coat and the looking-glass, and runs into the inner room. The door is pushed open, and* SUSAN BRADY *looks in, and knocks on door*.

Susan. There's nobody in it. (*Knocks again*.

Nelly (*pushing her in and following her, with* HONOR BLAKE *and* SARA TANSEY). It'd be early for them both to be out walking the hill.

Susan. I'm thinking Shawn Keogh was making game of us and there's no such man in it at all.

Honor (*pointing to straw and quilt*). Look at that. He's been sleeping there in the night. Well, it'll be a hard case if he's gone off now, the way we'll never set our eyes on a man killed his father, and we after rising early and destroying ourselves running fast on the hill.

Nelly. Are you thinking them's his boots?

Sara (*taking them up*). If they are, there should be his father's track on them. Did you never read in the papers the way murdered men do bleed and drip?

Susan. Is that blood there, Sara Tansey?

Sara (*smelling it*). That's bog water, I'm thinking, but it's his own they are surely, for I never seen the like of them for whity mud, and red mud, and turf on them, and the fine sands of the sea. That man's been walking, I'm telling you.

(*She goes down right, putting on one of his boots*.

Susan (*going to window*). Maybe he's stolen off to Belmullet [1] with the boots of Michael James, and you'd have a right so to follow after him, Sara Tansey, and you the one yoked the ass cart and drove ten miles to set your eyes on the man bit the yellow lady's nostril on the northern shore. (*She looks out*.

Sara (*running to window with one boot on*). Don't be talking, and we fooled today. (*Putting on other boot*) There's a pair do fit me well, and I'll be keeping them for walking to the priest, when you'd be ashamed this place, going up winter and summer with nothing worth while to confess at all.

Honor (*who has been listening at the door*). Whisht! there's someone inside the room. (*She pushes door a chink open*.) It's a man.

(SARA *kicks off boots and puts them where they were. They all stand in a line looking through chink*.

Sara. I'll call him. Mister! Mister! (*He puts in his head*.) Is Pegeen within?

Chris. (*coming in as meek as a mouse, with the looking-glass held behind his back*). She's above on the cnuceen, [2] seeking the nanny goats, the way she'd have a sup of goat's milk for to color my tea.

Sara. And asking your pardon, is it you's the man killed his father?

Chris. (*sidling toward the nail where the glass was hanging*). I am, God help me!

Sara (*taking eggs she has brought*). Then my thousand welcomes to you, and I've run up with a brace of duck's eggs for your food today. Pegeen's ducks is no use, but these are the real rich sort. Hold out your hand and you'll see it's no lie I'm telling you.

Chris. (*coming forward shyly, and holding out his left hand*). They're a great and weighty size.

[1] A coastal town in the northwest part of Mayo.
[2] Headland.

Susan. And I run up with a pat of butter, for it'd be a poor thing to have you eating your spuds dry, and you after running a great   90 way since you did destroy your da.

Chris. Thank you kindly.

Honor. And I brought you a little cut of cake, for you should have a thin stomach on you, and you that length walking the world.   95

Nelly. And I brought you a little laying pullet — boiled and all she is — was crushed at the fall of night by the curate's car. Feel the fat of that breast, mister.

Chris. It's bursting, surely.   100

(*He feels it with the back of his hand, in which he holds the presents.*

Sara. Will you pinch it? Is your right hand too sacred for to use at all? (*She slips round behind him.*) It's a glass he has. Well, I never seen to this day a man with a looking-glass held to his back. Them that kills   105 their fathers is a vain lot surely.

(*Girls giggle.*

Chris. (*smiling innocently and piling presents on glass*). I'm very thankful to you all to-day . . .

Wid. Quin (*coming in quickly, at door*). Sara Tansey, Susan Brady, Honor Blake!   110 What in glory has you here at this hour of day?

Girls (*giggling*). That's the man killed his father.

Wid. Quin (*coming to them*). I know well it's the man; and I'm after putting him down   115 in the sports below for racing, leaping, pitching, and the Lord knows what.

Sara (*exuberantly*). That's right, Widow Quin. I'll bet my dowry that he'll lick the world.   120

Wid. Quin. If you will, you'd have a right to have him fresh and nourished in place of nursing a feast. (*Taking presents*) Are you fasting or fed, young fellow?

Chris. Fasting, if you please.   125

Wid. Quin (*loudly*). Well, you're the lot. Stir up now and give him his breakfast. (*To* CHRISTY) Come here to me (*she puts him on bench beside her while the girls make tea and get his breakfast*) and let you tell us your story before Pegeen will come, in place of grin-   130 ning your ears off like the moon of May.

Chris. (*beginning to be pleased*). It's a long story; you'd be destroyed listening.

Wid. Quin. Don't be letting on to be shy, a fine, gamey, treacherous lad the like of   135 you. Was it in your house beyond you cracked his skull?

Chris. (*shy but flattered*). It was not. We were digging spuds in his cold, sloping, stony, divil's patch of a field.   140

Wid. Quin. And you went asking money of him, or making talk of getting a wife would drive him from his farm?

Chris. I did not, then; but there I was, dig-ging and digging, and "You squinting   145 idiot," says he, "let you walk down now and tell the priest you'll wed the Widow Casey in a score of days."

Wid. Quin. And what kind was she?

Chris. (*with horror*). A walking terror   150 from beyond the hills, and she twoscore and five years, and two hundredweights and five pounds in the weighing scales, with a limping leg on her, and a blinded eye, and she a woman of noted misbehavior with the old and young.   155

Girls (*clustering round him, serving him*). Glory be.

Wid. Quin. And what did he want driving you to wed with her?

(*She takes a bit of the chicken.*

Chris. (*eating with growing satisfaction*). He was letting on I was wanting a protector   160 from the harshness of the world, and he with-out a thought the whole while but how he'd have her hut to live in and her gold to drink.

Wid. Quin. There's maybe worse than a dry hearth and a widow woman and your   165 glass at night. So you hit him then?

Chris. (*getting almost excited*). I did not. "I won't wed her," says I, "when all know she did suckle me for six weeks when I came into the world, and she a hag this day with a   170 tongue on her has the crows and seabirds scat-tered, the way they wouldn't cast a shadow on her garden with the dread of her curse."

Wid. Quin (*teasingly*). That one should be right company.   175

Sara (*eagerly*). Don't mind her. Did you kill him then?

Chris. "She's too good for the like of you,"

says he, "and go on now or I'll flatten you
out like a crawling beast has passed under　180
a dray." "You will not if I can help it," says
I. "Go on," says he, "or I'll have the divil
making garters of your limbs tonight." "You
will not if I can help it," says I.

(*He sits up, brandishing his mug.*

Sara. You are right surely.　　　　185
Chris. (*impressively*). With that the sun
came out between the cloud and the hill, and
it shining green in my face. "God have mercy
on your soul," says he, lifting a scythe; "or on
your own," says I, raising the loy.　　　190
Susan. That's a grand story.
Honor. He tells it lovely.
Chris. (*flattered and confident, waving bone*).
He gave a drive with the scythe, and I gave
a lep to the east. Then I turned around with
my back to the north, and I hit a blow　195
on the ridge of his skull, laid him stretched
out, and he split to the knob of his gullet.

(*He raises the chicken bone to his
Adam's apple.*

Girls (*together*). Well, you're a marvel!
Oh, God bless you! You're the lad surely!
Susan. I'm thinking the Lord God　200
sent him this road to make a second husband
to the Widow Quin, and she with a great yearning to be wedded, though all dread her here.
Lift him on her knee, Sara Tansey.
Wid. Quin. Don't tease him.　　　205
Sara (*going over to dresser and counter very
quickly, and getting two glasses and porter*).
You're heroes surely, and let you drink a
supeen [1] with your arms linked like the outlandish lovers in the sailor's song. (*She links
their arms and gives them the glasses.*) There
now. Drink a health to the wonders of the　210
western world, the pirates, preachers, poteen-
makers, with [2] the jobbing jockies,[3] parching
peelers,[4] and the juries fill [5] their stomachs selling judgments of the English law.

(*Brandishing the bottle.*

Wid. Quin. That's a right toast, Sara　215
Tansey. Now Christy.

[1] Swallow.　　[2] I.e., against.
[3] Grafting traders; in this case, liquor dispensers.
[4] I.e., police who dry up the country by arrests for
liquor distilling, etc.　　　　[5] I.e., juries who fill.

*They drink with their arms linked, he drinking
with his left hand, she with her right. As
they are drinking,* PEGEEN MIKE *comes in
with a milk can and stands aghast. They all
spring away from* CHRISTY. *He goes down
left.* WIDOW QUIN *remains seated*

Peg. (*angrily, to* SARA). What is it you're
wanting?
Sara (*twisting her apron*). An ounce of tobacco.　　　　　　　　　　220
Peg. Have you tuppence? [1]
Sara. I've forgotten my purse.
Peg. Then you'd best be getting it and not
fooling us here. (*To the* WIDOW QUIN, *with
more elaborate scorn*) And what is it　225
you're wanting, Widow Quin?
Wid. Quin (*insolently*). A penn'orth [2] of
starch.
Peg. (*breaking out*). And you without a
white shift or a shirt in your whole family　230
since the drying of the flood! I've no starch
for the like of you, and let you walk on now to
Killamuck.
Wid. Quin (*turning to* CHRISTY, *as she goes
out with the girls*). Well, you're mighty huffy
this day, Pegeen Mike, and, you young　235
fellow, let you not forget the sports and racing
when the noon is by.　　　　(*They go out.*
Peg. (*imperiously*). Fling out that rubbish
and put them cups away. (CHRISTY *tidies
away in great haste.*) Shove in the bench　240
by the wall. (*He does so.*) And hang that glass
on the nail. What disturbed it at all?
Chris. (*very meekly*). I was making myself
decent only, and this a fine country for young
lovely girls.　　　　　　　245
Peg. (*sharply*). Whisht your talking of
girls.　　　　　　(*Goes to counter, right.*
Chris. Wouldn't any wish to be decent in a
place . . .
Peg. Whisht I'm saying.　　　250
Chris. (*looks at her face for a moment with
great misgivings, then as a last effort, takes up a
loy, and goes towards her, with feigned assurance*). It was with a loy the like of that I killed
my father.

[1] Two pence, pronounced as spelled above.
[2] A penny's worth.

Peg. (still sharply). You've told me that story six times since the dawn of day.

Chris. (reproachfully). It's a queer thing 255 you wouldn't care to be hearing it and them girls after walking four miles to be listening to me now.

Peg. (turning round astonished). Four miles!

Chris. (apologetically). Didn't himself 260 say there were only four bona fides living in the place?

Peg. It's bona fides by the road they are, but that lot came over the river, lepping the stones. It's not three perches ¹ when you 265 go like that, and I was down this morning looking on the papers the post-boy does have in his bag. *(With meaning and emphasis)* For there was great news this day, Christopher Mahon. 270

(She goes into room, left.)

Chris. (suspiciously). Is it news of my murder?

Peg. (inside). Murder, indeed.

Chris. (loudly). A murdered da?

Peg. (coming in again and crossing right). There was not, but a story filled half a 275 page of the hanging of a man. Ah, that should be a fearful end, young fellow, and it worst of all for a man who destroyed his da, for the like of him would get small mercies, and when it's dead he is, they'd put him in a narrow 280 grave, with cheap sacking wrapping him round, and pour down quicklime on his head, the way you'd see a woman pouring any frish-frash ² from a cup.

Chris. (very miserably). Oh, God help 285 me. Are you thinking I'm safe? You were saying at the fall of night, I was shut of jeopardy and I here with yourselves.

Peg. (severely). You'll be shut of jeopardy no place if you go talking with a pack of 290 wild girls the like of them do be walking abroad with the peelers, talking whispers at the fall of night.

Chris. (with terror). And you're thinking they'd tell? 295

Peg. (with mock sympathy). Who knows, God help you.

¹ A "perch" is also a "rod" and equals 5½ yards.
² Dregs.

Chris. (loudly). What joy would they have to bring hanging to the likes of me?

Peg. It's queer joys they have, and who 300 knows the thing they'd do, if it'd make the green stones cry itself to think of you swaying and swiggling ¹ at the butt of a rope, and you with a fine, stout neck, God bless you! the way you'd be a half an hour, in great anguish, 305 getting your death.

Chris. (getting his boots and putting them on). If there's that terror of them, it'd be best, maybe, I went on wandering like Esau, or Cain and Abel, on the sides of Neifin ² or the Erris plain.³ 310

Peg. (beginning to play with him). It would, maybe, for I've heard the Circuit Judges this place is a heartless crew.

Chris. (bitterly). It's more than Judges this place is a heartless crew. *(Looking up at 315 her)* And isn't it a poor thing to be starting again and I a lonesome fellow will be looking out on women and girls the way the needy fallen spirits do be looking on the Lord?

Peg. What call have you to be that 320 lonesome when there's poor girls walking Mayo in their thousands now?

Chris. (grimly). It's well you know what call I have. It's well you know it's a lonesome thing to be passing small towns with the 325 lights shining sideways when the night is down, or going in strange places with a dog noising before you and a dog noising behind, or drawn to the cities where you'd hear a voice kissing and talking deep love in every shadow of 330 the ditch, and you passing on with an empty, hungry stomach failing from your heart.

Peg. I'm thinking you're an odd man, Christy Mahon. The oddest walking fellow I ever set my eyes on to this hour today. 335

Chris. What would any be but odd men and they living lonesome in the world?

Peg. I'm not odd, and I'm my whole life with my father only.

Chris. (with infinite admiration). How 340

¹ Swinging.
² A mountain range running north and south across the northern peninsula of County Mayo.
³ The district to the northwest of the Neifin range toward the Belmullet isthmus.

would a lovely handsome woman the like of you be lonesome when all men should be thronging around to hear the sweetness of your voice, and the little infant children should be pestering your steps I'm thinking, and you 345 walking the roads.

Peg. I'm hard set to know what way a coaxing fellow the like of yourself should be lonesome either.

Chris. Coaxing?   350

Peg. Would you have me think a man never talked with the girls would have the words you've spoken today? It's only letting on you are to be lonesome, the way you'd get around me now.   355

Chris. I wish to God I was letting on; but I was lonesome all times, and born lonesome, I'm thinking, as the moon of dawn.

(*Going to door.*

Peg. (*puzzled by his talk*). Well, it's a story I'm not understanding at all why you'd 360 be worse than another, Christy Mahon, and you a fine lad with the great savagery to destroy your da.

Chris. It's little I'm understanding myself, saving only that my heart's scalded 365 this day, and I going off stretching out the earth between us, the way I'll not be waking near you another dawn of the year till the two of us do arise to hope or judgment with the saints of God, and now I'd best be going 370 with my wattle [1] in my hand, for hanging is a poor thing (*turning to go*), and it's little welcome only is left me in this house today.

Peg. (*sharply*). Christy! (*He turns round.*) Come here to me. (*He goes towards* 375 *her.*) Lay down that switch and throw some sods on the fire. You're pot-boy in this place, and I'll not have you mitch [2] off from us now.

Chris. You were saying I'd be hanged if I stay.   380

Peg. (*quite kindly at last*). I'm after going down and reading the fearful crimes of Ireland for two weeks or three, and there wasn't a word of your murder. (*Getting up and going over to the counter*) They've likely not found 385 the body. You're safe so with ourselves.

[1] Switch.
[2] Sneak.

Chris. (*astonished, slowly*). It's making game of me you were (*following her with fearful joy*), and I can stay so, working at your side, and I not lonesome from this mortal day. 390

Peg. What's to hinder you from staying, except the widow woman or the young girls would inveigle you off?

Chris. (*with rapture*). And I'll have your words from this day filling my ears, and 395 that look is come upon you meeting my two eyes, and I watching you loafing around in the warm sun, or rinsing your ankles when the night is come.   399

Peg. (*kindly, but a little embarrassed*). I'm thinking you'll be a loyal young lad to have working around, and if you vexed me a while since with your leaguing with the girls, I wouldn't give a thraneen [1] for a lad hadn't a mighty spirit in him and a gamey heart. 405

SHAWN KEOGH *runs in carrying a cleeve* [2] *on his back, followed by the* WIDOW QUIN

Shawn (*to* PEGEEN). I was passing below, and I seen your mountainy sheep eating cabbages in Jimmy's field. Run up or they'll be bursting surely.

Peg. Oh, God mend them!   410

(*She puts a shawl over her head and runs out.*

Chris. (*looking from one to the other. Still in high spirits*). I'd best go to her aid maybe. I'm handy with ewes.

Wid. Quin (*closing the door*). She can do that much, and there is Shaneen has long speeches for to tell you now.   415

(*She sits down with an amused smile.*

Shawn (*taking something from his pocket and offering it to* CHRISTY). Do you see that, mister?

Chris. (*looking at it*). The half of a ticket to the Western States!

Shawn (*trembling with anxiety*). I'll give 420 it to you and my new hat (*pulling it out of hamper*); and my breeches with the double seat (*pulling it off*); and my new coat is woven from the blackest shearings for three miles around (*giving him the coat*); I'll give you the whole 425

[1] A straw.
[2] Basket.

of them, and my blessing, and the blessing of
Father Reilly itself, maybe, if you'll quit from
this and leave us in the peace we had till last
night at the fall of dark.

Chris. (*with a new arrogance*). And for   430
what is it you're wanting to get shut of me?

Shawn (*looking to the* WIDOW *for help*). I'm
a poor scholar with middling faculties to coin
a lie, so I'll tell you the truth, Christy Mahon.
I'm wedding with Pegeen beyond, and   435
I don't think well of having a clever fearless
man the like of you dwelling in her house.

Chris. (*almost pugnaciously*). And you'd be
using bribery for to banish me?

Shawn (*in an imploring voice*). Let you   440
not take it badly, mister honey; isn't beyond
the best place for you where you'll have golden
chains and shiny coats and you riding upon
hunters with the ladies of the land?

(*He makes an eager sign to the* WIDOW
QUIN *to come to help him.*

Wid. Quin (*coming over*). It's true for   445
him, and you'd best quit off and not have that
poor girl setting her mind on you, for there's
Shaneen thinks she wouldn't suit you though
all is saying that she'll wed you now.

(CHRISTY *beams with delight.*

Shawn (*in terrified earnest*). She   450
wouldn't suit you, and she with the divil's own
temper the way you'd be strangling one another
in a score of days. (*He makes the movement of
strangling with his hands.*) It's the like of me
only that she's fit for, a quiet, simple   455
fellow wouldn't raise a hand upon her if she
scratched itself.

Wid. Quin (*putting* SHAWN'S *hat on* CHRISTY).
Fit them clothes on you anyhow, young fellow, and he'd maybe loan them to you for the
sports. (*Pushing him towards inner door*)   460
Fit them on and you can give your answer
when you have them tried.

Chris. (*beaming, delighted with the clothes*).
I will then. I'd like herself to see me in them
tweeds and hat.

(*He goes into room and shuts the door.*

Shawn (*in great anxiety*). He'd like her-   465
self to see them! He'll not leave us, Widow
Quin. He's a score of divils in him the way it's
well-nigh certain he will wed Pegeen.

Wid. Quin (*jeeringly*). It's true all girls are
fond of courage and do hate the like of you.   470

Shawn (*walking about in desperation*). Oh,
Widow Quin, what'll I be doing now? I'd
inform again him, but he'd burst from Kilmainham [1] and he'd be sure and certain to destroy me. If I wasn't so God-fearing, I'd   475
near have courage to come behind him and
run a pike into his side. Oh, it's a hard
case to be an orphan and not to have your
father that you're used to, and you'd easy kill
and make yourself a hero in the sight of   480
all. (*Coming up to her*) Oh, Widow Quin,
will you find me some contrivance when I've
promised you a ewe?

Wid. Quin. A ewe's a small thing, but what
would you give me if I did wed him and   485
did save you so?

Shawn (*with astonishment*). You?

Wid. Quin. Aye. Would you give me the
red cow you have and the mountainy ram, and
the right of way across your rye path, and   490
a load of dung at Michaelmas,[2] and turbary [3]
upon the western hill?

Shawn (*radiant with hope*). I would surely,
and I'd give you the wedding ring I have, and
the loan of a new suit, the way you'd have   495
him decent on the wedding day. I'd give you
two kids for your dinner, and a gallon of poteen,
and I'd call the piper on the long car to your
wedding from Crossmolina [4] or from Ballina.[4]
I'd give you...   500

Wid. Quin. That'll do so, and let you whisht,
for he's coming now again.

CHRISTY *comes in very natty in the new clothes.*
WIDOW QUIN *goes to him admiringly*

Wid. Quin. If you seen yourself now, I'm
thinking you'd be too proud to speak to us at
all, and it'd be a pity surely to have your   505
like sailing from Mayo to the Western World.

Chris. (*as proud as a peacock*). I'm not going.

[1] Kilmainham Jail near Dublin, where Charles Par-
nell (1846–91), the famous champion of Irish freedom,
was confined in 1881–82.
[2] September 29, the fall date for payment of rents.
[3] Lease ground for digging turf.
[4] Towns in northeastern Mayo.

If this is a poor place itself, I'll make myself contented to be lodging here.

(WIDOW QUIN *makes a sign to* SHAWN *to leave them.*

Shawn. Well, I'm going measuring the 510 race course while the tide is low, so I'll leave you the garments and my blessing for the sports today. God bless you!

(*He wriggles out.*

Wid. Quin (*admiring* CHRISTY). Well, you're mighty spruce, young fellow. Sit down 515 now while you're quiet till you talk with me.

Chris. (*swaggering*). I'm going abroad on the hillside for to seek Pegeen.

Wid. Quin. You'll have time and plenty for to seek Pegeen, and you heard me saying 520 at the fall of night the two of us should be great company.

Chris. From this out I'll have no want of company when all sorts is bringing me their food and clothing (*he swaggers to the door,* 525 *tightening his belt*), the way they'd set their eyes upon a gallant orphan cleft his father with one blow to the breeches belt. (*He opens door, then staggers back.*) Saints of glory! Holy angels from the throne of light! 530

Wid. Quin (*going over*). What ails you?

Chris. It's the walking spirit of my murdered da!

Wid. Quin (*looking out*). Is it that tramper?

Chris. (*wildly*). Where'll I hide my 535 poor body from that ghost of hell?

The door is pushed open, and old MAHON *appears on threshold.* CHRISTY *darts in behind door*

Wid. Quin (*in great amusement*). God save you, my poor man.

Mahon (*gruffly*). Did you see a young lad passing this way in the early morning or 540 the fall of night?

Wid. Quin. You're a queer kind to walk in not saluting at all.

Mahon. Did you see the young lad?

Wid. Quin (*stiffly*). What kind was he? 545

Mahon. An ugly young streeler[1] with a murderous gob[2] on him, and a little switch in

[1] Loiterer or tramp.
[2] Literally mouth; here, face.

his hand.   I met a tramper seen him coming this way at the fall of night.

Wid. Quin. There's harvest hundreds 550 do be passing these days for the Sligo[1] boat. For what is it you're wanting him, my poor man?

Mahon. I want to destroy him for breaking the head on me with the clout of a loy. (*He takes off a big hat, and shows his head in a mass of bandages and plaster, with some pride.*) It was he did that, and amn't I a great 555 wonder to think I've traced him ten days with that rent in my crown?

Wid. Quin (*taking his head in both hands and examining it with extreme delight*). That was a great blow. And who hit you? A robber maybe? 560

Mahon. It was my own son hit me, and he the divil a robber, or anything else, but a dirty, stuttering lout.

Wid. Quin (*letting go his skull and wiping her hands in her apron*). You'd best be wary of a mortified scalp, I think they call it, lep- 565 ping around with that wound in the splendor of the sun. It was a bad blow surely, and you should have vexed him fearful to make him strike that gash in his da.

Mahon. Is it me? 570

Wid. Quin (*amusing herself*). Aye. And isn't it a great shame when the old and hardened do torment the young?

Mahon (*raging*). Torment him is it? And I after holding out with the patience of a 575 martyred saint till there's nothing but destruction on, and I'm driven out in my old age with none to aid me.

Wid. Quin (*greatly amused*). It's a sacred wonder the way that wickedness will 580 spoil a man.

Mahon. My wickedness, is it? Amn't I after saying it is himself has me destroyed, and he a liar on walls, a talker of folly, a man you'd see stretched the half of the day in the 585 brown ferns with his belly to the sun.

Wid. Quin. Not working at all?

Mahon. The divil a work, or if he did itself, you'd see him raising up a haystack like the stalk of a rush, or driving our last cow 590

[1] The seat of the county adjoining Mayo on the northeast, a coast town.

till he broke her leg at the hip, and when he wasn't at that he'd be fooling over little birds he had — finches and felts — or making mugs [1] at his own self in the bit of a glass we had hung on the wall.   595

Wid. Quin (*looking at* CHRISTY). What way was he so foolish? It was running wild after the girls maybe?

Mahon (*with a shout of derision*). Running wild, is it? If he seen a red petticoat   600 coming swinging over the hill, he'd be off to hide in the sticks, and you'd see him shooting out his sheep's eyes between the little twigs and the leaves, and his two ears rising like a hare looking out through a gap. Girls, indeed!   605

Wid. Quin. It was drink maybe?

Mahon. And he a poor fellow would get drunk on the smell of a pint. He'd a queer rotten stomach, I'm telling you, and when I gave him three pulls from my pipe a   610 while since, he was taken with contortions till I had to send him in the ass cart to the females' nurse.

Wid. Quin (*clasping her hands*). Well, I never till this day heard tell of a man the   615 like of that!

Mahon. I'd take a mighty oath you didn't surely, and wasn't he the laughing joke of every female woman where four baronies [2] meet, the way the girls would stop their   620 weeding if they seen him coming the road to let a roar at him, and call him the looney [3] of Mahon's.

Wid. Quin. I'd give the world and all to see the like of him. What kind was he?   625

Mahon. A small low fellow.

Wid. Quin. And dark?

Mahon. Dark and dirty.

Wid. Quin (*considering*). I'm thinking I seen him.   630

Mahon (*eagerly*). An ugly young blackguard.

Wid. Quin. A hideous, fearful villain, and the spit of you.

Mahon. What way is he fled?

Wid. Quin. Gone over the hills to   635 catch a coasting steamer to the north or south.

[1] Faces.
[2] A barony is an Irish form of land sectioning.
[3] Lunatic.

Mahon. Could I pull up on him now?

Wid. Quin. If you'll cross the sands below where the tide is out, you'll be in it as soon as himself, for he had to go round ten   640 miles by the top of the bay. (*She points to the door.*) Strike down by the head beyond and then follow on the roadway to the north and east.   (*Mahon goes abruptly.*)

Wid. Quin (*shouting after him*). Let   645 you give him a good vengeance when you come up with him, but don't put yourself in the power of the law, for it'd be a poor thing to see a judge in his black cap reading out his sentence on a civil warrior the like of you.   650

(*She swings the door to and looks at* CHRISTY, *who is cowering in terror, for a moment; then she bursts into a laugh.*)

Wid. Quin. Well, you're the walking Playboy of the Western World, and that's the poor man you had divided to his breeches belt.

Chris. (*looking out: then, to her*). What'll Pegeen say when she hears that story?   655 What'll she be saying to me now?

Wid. Quin. She'll knock the head of you, I'm thinking, and drive you from the door. God help her to be taking you for a wonder, and you a little schemer making up the   660 story you destroyed your da.

Chris. (*turning to the door, nearly speechless with rage, half to himself*). To be letting on he was dead, and coming back to his life, and following after me like an old weasel tracing a rat, and coming in here laying desolation   665 between my own self and the fine women of Ireland, and he a kind of carcass that you'd fling upon the sea . . .

Wid. Quin (*more soberly*). There's talking for a man's one only son.   670

Chris. (*breaking out*). His one son, is it? May I meet him with one tooth and it aching, and one eye to be seeing seven and seventy divils in the twists of the road, and one old timber leg on him to limp into the scalding   675 grave. (*Looking out*) There he is now crossing the strands, and that the Lord God would send a high wave to wash him from the world.

Wid. Quin (*scandalized*). Have you no   680

shame? (*Putting her hand on his shoulder and turning him round*) What ails you? Near crying, is it?

Chris. (*in despair and grief*). Amn't I after seeing the love-light of the star of knowl-   685
edge shining from her brow, and hearing words would put you thinking on the holy Brigid speaking to the infant saints, and now she'll be turning again, and speaking hard words to me, like an old woman with a spav-   690
indy [1] ass she'd have, urging on a hill.

Wid. Quin. There's poetry talk for a girl you'd see itching and scratching, and she with a stale stink of poteen on her from selling in the shop.   695

Chris. (*impatiently*). It's her like is fitted to be handling merchandise in the heavens above, and what'll I be doing now, I ask you, and I a kind of wonder was jilted by the heavens when a day was by.   700

(*There is a distant noise of girls' voices.
WIDOW QUIN looks from window and comes to him hurriedly.*

Wid. Quin. You'll be doing like myself, I'm thinking, when I did destroy my man, for I'm above many's the day, odd times in great spirits, abroad in the sunshine, darning a stocking or stitching a shift; and odd times   705
again looking out on the schooners, hookers, trawlers is sailing the sea, and I thinking on the gallant hairy fellows are drifting beyond, and myself long years living alone.

Chris. (*interested*). You're like me, so.   710

Wid. Quin. I am your like, and it's for that I'm taking a fancy to you, and I with my little houseen above where there'd be myself to tend you, and none to ask were you a murderer or what at all.   715

Chris. And what would I be doing if I left Pegeen?

Wid. Quin. I've nice jobs you could be doing, gathering shells to make a whitewash for our hut within, building up a little goose-   720
house, or stretching a new skin on an old curragh [2] I have, and if my hut is far from all sides, it's there you'll meet the wisest old men, I tell you, at the corner of my wheel, and

[1] An ass afflicted with the spavin, a lameness in the leg muscles.   [2] A small boat.

it's there yourself and me will have great   725
times whispering and hugging. . . .

Voices (*outside, calling far away*). Christy! Christy Mahon! Christy!

Chris. Is it Pegeen Mike?   729

Wid. Quin. It's the young girls, I'm thinking, coming to bring you to the sports below, and what is it you'll have me to tell them now?

Chris. Aid me for to win Pegeen. It's herself only that I'm seeking now. (WIDOW QUIN *gets up and goes to window.*) Aid me for   735
to win her, and I'll be asking God to stretch a hand to you in the hour of death, and lead you short cuts through the Meadows of Ease, and up the floor of Heaven to the Foot-stool of the Virgin's Son.   740

Wid. Quin. There's praying.

Voices (*nearer*). Christy! Christy Mahon!

Chris. (*with agitation*). They're coming. Will you swear to aid and save me for the love of Christ?   745

Wid. Quin (*looks at him for a moment*). If I aid you, will you swear to give me a right of way I want, and a mountainy ram, and a load of dung at Michaelmas, the time that you'll be master here?   750

Chris. I will, by the elements and stars of night.

Wid. Quin. Then we'll not say a word of the old fellow, the way Pegeen won't know your story till the end of time.   755

Chris. And if he chances to return again?

Wid. Quin. We'll swear he's a maniac and not your da. I could take an oath I seen him raving on the sands today.

Girls run in

Susan. Come on to the sports be-   760
low. Pegeen says you're to come.

Sara. The lepping's beginning, and we've a jockey's suit to fit upon you for the mule race on the sands below.

Honor. Come on, will you?   765

Chris. I will then if Pegeen's beyond.

Sara. She's in the boreen [1] making game of Shaneen Keogh.

Chris. Then I'll be going to her now.

(*He runs out, followed by the girls.*

[1] Lane.

Wid. Quin. Well, if the worst comes in　770
the end of all, it'll be great game to see there's
none to pity him but a widow woman, the like
of me, has buried her children and destroyed
her man.　　　　　　　　　　*(She goes out.*

Curtain

ACT III

SCENE, *as before.　Later in the day.* JIMMY
comes in, slightly drunk

Jimmy (calls). Pegeen!　*(Crosses to inner
door.)* Pegeen Mike!　*(Comes back again into
the room.)* Pegeen!　*(*PHILLY *comes in in the
same state.)*　*(To* PHILLY*)* Did you see herself?　　　　　　　　　　　　　　　　5
Philly. I did not; but I sent Shawn Keogh
with the ass cart for to bear him home.　*(Trying cupboards which are locked)* Well, isn't he
a nasty man to get into such staggers at a
morning wake?　And isn't herself the divil's　10
daughter for locking, and she so fussy after
that young gaffer, you might take your death
with drought and none to heed you?
Jimmy. It's little wonder she'd be fussy,
and he after bringing bankrupt ruin on the　15
roulette man, and the trick-o'-the-loop man,
and breaking the nose of the cockshot-man,
and winning all in the sports below, racing,
lepping, dancing, and the Lord knows what!
He's right luck, I'm telling you.　　　20
Philly. If he has, he'll be rightly hobbled
yet, and he not able to say ten words without
making a brag of the way he killed his father,
and the great blow he hit with the loy.
Jimmy. A man can't hang by his own in-　25
forming, and his father should be rotten by
now.　　　*(Old* MAHON *passes window slowly.*
Philly. Supposing a man's digging spuds in
that field with a long spade, and supposing he
flings up the two halves of that skull,　30
what'll be said then in the papers and the
courts of law?
Jimmy. They'd say it was an old Dane,[1]
maybe, was drowned in the flood.　*(Old*

[1] The Danes, who came to Ireland in the ninth century A.D., were the earliest invaders of the island after
the Irish settlement.

MAHON *comes in and sits down near door, listening.)*　Did you never hear tell of the skulls　35
they have in the city of Dublin, ranged out like
blue jugs in a cabin of Connaught?[1]
Philly. And you believe that?
Jimmy (pugnaciously). Didn't a lad see them
and he after coming from harvesting in the　40
Liverpool boat?　"They have them there,"
says he, "making a show of the great people
there was one time walking the world.　White
skulls and black skulls and yellow skulls, and
some with full teeth, and some haven't　45
only but one."
Philly. It was no lie, maybe, for when I was
a young lad there was a graveyard beyond the
house with the remnants of a man who had
thighs as long as your arm.　He was a　50
horrid man, I'm telling you, and there was
many a fine Sunday I'd put him together for
fun, and he with shiny bones, you wouldn't
meet the like of these days in the cities of the
world.　　　　　　　　　　　　　55
Mahon (getting up). You wouldn't, is it?
Lay your eyes on that skull, and tell me where
and when there was another the like of it, is
splintered only from the blow of a loy.
Philly. Glory be to God!　And who hit　60
you at all?
Mahon (triumphantly). It was my own son
hit me.　Would you believe that?
Jimmy. Well, there's wonders hidden in the
heart of man!　　　　　　　　　　65
Philly (suspiciously). And what way was
it done?
Mahon (wandering about the room). I'm
after walking hundreds and long scores of miles,
winning clean beds and the fill of my belly　70
four times in the day, and I doing nothing but
telling stories of that naked truth.　*(He comes
to them a little aggressively.)* Give me a supeen
and I'll tell you now.

WIDOW QUIN *comes in and stands aghast behind
him.　He is facing* JIMMY *and* PHILLY*, who
are on the left*

Jimmy. Ask herself beyond.　She's the　75
stuff hidden in her shawl.

[1] The northwest one of the four old Irish provinces.
Mayo is one of the Connaught counties.

Wid. Quin (*coming to* MAHON *quickly*). You here, is it? You didn't go far at all?

Mahon. I seen the coasting steamer passing, and I got a drought upon me and a 80 cramping leg, so I said, "The divil go along with him," and turned again. (*Looking under her shawl*) And let you give me a supeen, for I'm destroyed traveling since Tuesday was a week.   85

Wid. Quin (*getting a glass, in a cajoling tone*). Sit down then by the fire and take your ease for a space. You've a right to be destroyed indeed, with your walking, and fighting, and facing the sun (*giving him poteen from a stone jar she has brought in*). There now is a 90 drink for you, and may it be to your happiness and length of life.

Mahon (*taking glass greedily and sitting down by fire*). God increase you!

Wid. Quin (*taking men to the right stealthily*). Do you know what? That man's raving from his wound today, for I met him a while 95 since telling a rambling tale of a tinker had him destroyed. Then he heard of Christy's deed, and he up and says it was his son had cracked his skull. Oh isn't madness a fright, for he'll go killing someone yet, and he thinking 100 it's the man has struck him so?

Jimmy (*entirely convinced*). It's a fright, surely. I knew a party was kicked in the head by a red mare, and he went killing horses a great while, till he eat the insides of a 105 clock and died after.

Philly (*with suspicion*). Did he see Christy?

Wid. Quin. He didn't. (*With a warning gesture*) Let you not be putting him in mind of him, or you'll be likely summoned if there's 110 murder done. (*Looking round at* MAHON) Whisht! He's listening. Wait now till you hear me taking him easy and unraveling all. (*She goes to* MAHON.) And what way are you feeling, mister? Are you in contentment 115 now?

Mahon (*slightly emotional from his drink*). I'm poorly only, for it's a hard story the way I'm left today, when it was I did tend him from his hour of birth, and he a dunce never reached his second book, the way he'd come from 120 school, many's the day, with his legs lamed

under him, and he blackened with his beatings like a tinker's ass. It's a hard story, I'm saying, the way some do have their next and nighest raising up a hand of murder on them, 125 and some is lonesome getting their death with lamentation in the dead of night.

Wid. Quin (*not knowing what to say*). To hear you talking so quiet, who'd know you were the same fellow we seen pass today? 130

Mahon. I'm the same surely. The wrack and ruin of threescore years; and it's a terror to live that length, I tell you, and to have your sons going to the dogs against you, and you wore out scolding them, and skelping 135 them, and God knows what.

Philly (*to* JIMMY). He's not raving. (*To* WIDOW QUIN) Will you ask him what kind was his son?

Wid. Quin (*to* MAHON, *with a peculiar look*). Was your son that hit you a lad of one 140 year and a score maybe, a great hand at racing and lepping and licking the world?

Mahon (*turning on her with a roar of rage*). Didn't you hear me say he was the fool of men, the way from this out he'll know the orphan's lot with old and young making game of 145 him and they swearing, raging, kicking at him like a mangy cur.

(*A great burst of cheering outside, some way off.*)

Mahon (*putting his hands to his ears*). What in the name of God do they want roaring below?   150

Wid. Quin (*with the shade of a smile*). They're cheering a young lad, the champion Playboy of the Western World.   (*More cheering.*)

Mahon (*going to window*). It'd split my heart to hear them, and I with pulses in 155 my brain-pan for a week gone by. Is it racing they are?

Jimmy (*looking from door*). It is then. They are mounting him for the mule race will be run upon the sands. That's the play- 160 boy on the winkered mule.[1]

Mahon (*puzzled*). That lad, is it? If you said it was a fool he was, I'd have laid a mighty oath he was the likeness of my wandering son (*uneasily, putting his hand to his head*).

[1] Mule wearing blinders.

Faith, I'm thinking I'll go walking for to 166 view the race.

Wid. Quin (*stopping him, sharply*). You will not. You'd best take the road to Belmullet, and not be dilly-dallying in this 170 place where there isn't a spot you could sleep.

Philly (*coming forward*). Don't mind her. Mount there on the bench and you'll have a view of the whole. They're hurrying before the tide will rise, and it'd be near over 175 if you went down the pathway through the crags below.

Mahon (*mounts on bench,* WIDOW QUIN *beside him*). That's a right view again the edge of the sea. They're coming now from the point. He's leading. Who is he at all? 180

Wid. Quin. He's the champion of the world, I tell you, and there isn't a hop'orth[1] isn't falling lucky to his hands today.

Philly (*looking out, interested in the race*). Look at that. They're pressing him now.

Jimmy. He'll win it yet. 185

Philly. Take your time, Jimmy Farrell. It's too soon to say.

Wid. Quin (*shouting*). Watch him taking the gate. There's riding.

Jimmy (*cheering*). More power to the 190 young lad!

Mahon. He's passing the third.

Jimmy. He'll lick them yet!

Wid. Quin. He'd lick them if he was running races with a score itself. 195

Mahon. Look at the mule he has, kicking the stars.

Wid. Quin. There was a lep! (*Catching hold of* MAHON *in her excitement*) He's fallen! He's mounted again! Faith, he's passing 200 them all!

Jimmy. Look at him skelping[2] her!

Philly. And the mountain girls hooshing[3] him on!

Jimmy. It's the last turn! The post's 205 cleared for them now!

Mahon. Look at the narrow place. He'll

be into the bogs! (*With a yell*) Good rider! He's through it again!

Jimmy. He neck and neck! 210

Mahon. Good boy to him! Flames, but he's in!

(*Great cheering, in which all join.*)

Mahon (*with hesitation*). What's that? They're raising him up. They're coming this way. (*With a roar of rage and as-* 215 *tonishment*) It's Christy! by the stars of God! I'd know his way of spitting and he astride the moon.

(*He jumps down and makes for the door, but* WIDOW QUIN *catches him and pulls him back.*

Wid. Quin. Stay quiet, will you. That's not your son. (*To* JIMMY) Stop him, or 220 you'll get a month for the abetting of manslaughter and be fined as well.

Jimmy. I'll hold him.

Mahon (*struggling*). Let me out! Let me out, the lot of you! till I have my 225 vengeance on his head today.

Wid. Quin (*shaking him, vehemently*). That's not your son. That's a man is going to make a marriage with the daughter of this house, a place with fine trade, with a license, 230 and with poteen too.

Mahon (*amazed*). That man marrying a decent and a moneyed girl! Is it mad yous are? Is it in a crazy-house for females that I'm landed now? 235

Wid. Quin. It's mad yourself is with the blow upon your head. That lad is the wonder of the Western World.

Mahon. I seen it's my son.

Wid. Quin. You seen that you're mad. 240 (*Cheering outside*) Do you hear them cheering him in the zigzags of the road? Aren't you after saying that your son's a fool, and how would they be cheering a true idiot born?

Mahon (*getting distressed*). It's maybe 245 out of reason that that man's himself. (*Cheering again*) There's none surely will go cheering him. Oh, I'm raving with a madness that would fright the world! (*He sits down with his hand to his head.*) There was one time 250 I seen ten scarlet divils letting on they'd cork my spirit in a gallon can; and one time I seen

---

[1] Hoopworth; i.e., the amount of a hoop, the space between two adjacent hoops on an old-fashioned, barrel-like quart pot.

[2] Beating.

[3] Cheering.

rats as big as badgers sucking the life blood from the butt of my lug;[1] but I never till this day confused that dribbling idiot 255 with a likely man. I'm destroyed surely.

Wid. Quin. And you'd wonder when it's your brain-pan that is gaping now?

Mahon. Then the blight of the sacred drought upon myself and him, for I never 260 went mad to this day, and I not three weeks with the Limerick [2] girls drinking myself silly, and parlatic [3] from the dusk to dawn. (*To* WIDOW QUIN, *suddenly*) Is my visage astray?

Wid. Quin. It is then. You're a snig- 265 gering maniac, a child could see.

Mahon (*getting up more cheerfully*). Then I'd best be going to the union [4] beyond, and there'll be a welcome before me, I tell you (*with great pride*), and I a terrible and fearful case, 270 the way that there I was one time, screeching in a straitened waistcoat, with seven doctors writing out my sayings in a printed book. Would you believe that?

Wid. Quin. If you're a wonder itself, 275 you'd best be hasty, for them lads caught a maniac one time and pelted the poor creature till he ran out, raving and foaming, and was drowned in the sea.

Mahon (*with philosophy*). It's true 280 mankind is the divil when your head's astray. Let me out now and I'll slip down the boreen, and not see them so.

Wid. Quin (*showing him out*). That's it. Run to the right, and not a one will see. 285
(*He runs off.*

Philly (*wisely*). You're at some gaming, Widow Quin; but I'll walk after him and give him his dinner and a time to rest, and I'll see then if he's raving or as sane as you.

Wid. Quin (*annoyed*). If you go near 290 that lad, let you be wary of your head, I'm saying. Didn't you hear him telling he was crazed at times?

Philly. I heard him telling a power; and I'm

---

[1] The lobe of my ear.
[2] A county of the west coast between Clare and Kerry.
[3] Paralytic.
[4] Asylum, — so called because it is maintained by a union of parish districts.

thinking we'll have right sport, before 295 night will fall.
(*He goes out.*

Jimmy. Well, Philly's a conceited and foolish man. How could that madman have his senses and his brain-pan slit? I'll go after them and see him turn on Philly now. 300
(*He goes;* WIDOW QUIN *hides poteen behind counter. Then hubbub outside.*

Voices. There you are! Good jumper! Grand lepper! Darlint boy! He's the racer! Bear him on, will you!

CHRISTY *comes in, in jockey's dress, with* PEGEEN MIKE, SARA, *and other girls, and men*

Peg. (*to crowd*). Go on now and don't destroy him and he drenching with sweat. 305 Go along, I'm saying, and have your tug-of-warring till he's dried his skin.

Crowd. Here's his prizes! A bagpipes! A fiddle was played by a poet in the years gone by! A flat and three-thorned blackthorn 310 would lick the scholars out of Dublin town!

Chris. (*taking prizes from the men*). Thank you kindly, the lot of you. But you'd say it was little only I did this day if you'd seen me a while since striking my one single blow. 315

Town Crier (*outside, ringing a bell*). Take notice, last event of this day! Tug-of-warring on the green below! Come on, the lot of you! Great achievements for all Mayo men!

Peg. Go on, and leave him for to rest 320 and dry. Go on, I tell you, for he'll do no more.
(*She hustles crowd out;* WIDOW QUIN *following them.*

Men (*going*). Come on then. Good luck for the while!

Peg. (*radiantly, wiping his face with her shawl*). Well, you're the lad, and you'll have great times from this out when you could 325 win that wealth of prizes, and you sweating in the heat of noon!

Chris. (*looking at her with delight*). I'll have great times if I win the crowning prize I'm seeking now, and that's your promise that 330 you'll wed me in a fortnight, when our banns is called.

Peg. (*backing away from him*). You've right

daring[1] to go ask me that, when all knows you'll be starting to some girl in your 335 own townland, when your father's rotten in four months, or five.

Chris. (indignantly). Starting from you, is it? (*He follows her.*) I will not, then, and when the airs is warming in four months, or 340 five, it's then yourself and me should be pacing Neifin in the dews of night, the times sweet smells do be rising, and you'd see a little shiny new moon, maybe, sinking on the hills.

Peg. (looking at him playfully). And 345 it's that kind of a poacher's love you'd make, Christy Mahon, on the sides of Neifin, when the night is down?

Chris. It's little you'll think if my love's a poacher's, or an earl's itself, when you'll 350 feel my two hands stretched around you, and I squeezing kisses on your puckered lips, till I'd feel a kind of pity for the Lord God is all ages sitting lonesome in his golden chair.

Peg. That'll be right fun, Christy 355 Mahon, and any girl would walk her heart out before she'd meet a young man was your like for eloquence, or talk, at all.

Chris. (encouraged). Let you wait, to hear me talking, till we're astray in Erris,[2] when 360 Good Friday's by, drinking a sup from a well, and making mighty kisses with our wetted mouths, or gaming in a gap or sunshine,[3] with yourself stretched back unto your necklace, in the flowers of the earth. 365

Peg. (in a lowered voice, moved by his tone). I'd be nice so, is it?

Chris. (with rapture). If the mitered bishops seen you that time, they'd be the like of the holy prophets, I'm thinking, do be straining the bars of Paradise to lay eyes on the Lady 370 Helen of Troy, and she abroad, pacing back and forward, with a nosegay in her golden shawl.

Peg. (with real tenderness). And what is it I have, Christy Mahon, to make me fitting entertainment for the like of you, that has 375 such poet's talking, and such bravery of heart?

Chris. (in a low voice). Isn't there the light of seven heavens in your heart alone, the way you'll be an angel's lamp to me from this out,

and I abroad in the darkness, spearing 380 salmons in the Owen,[1] or the Carrowmore?[2]

Peg. If I was your wife, I'd be along with you those nights, Christy Mahon, the way you'd see I was a great hand at coaxing bailiffs, or coining funny nicknames for the stars 385 of night.

Chris. You, is it? Taking your death in the hailstones, or in the fogs of dawn.

Peg. Yourself and me would shelter easy in a narrow bush, (*with a qualm of dread*) 390 but we're only talking, maybe, for this would be a poor, thatched place to hold a fine lad is the like of you.

Chris. (putting his arm round her). If I wasn't a good Christian, it's on my naked 395 knees I'd be saying my prayers and paters to every jackstraw you have roofing your head, and every stony pebble is paving the laneway to your door.

Peg. (radiantly). If that's the truth, I'll 400 be burning candles from this out to the miracles of God that have brought you from the south today, and I, with my gowns bought ready, the way that I can wed you, and not wait at all.

Chris. It's miracles, and that's the 405 truth. Me there toiling a long while, and walking a long while, not knowing at all I was drawing all times nearer to this holy day.

Peg. And myself, a girl, was tempted often to go sailing the seas till I'd marry a Jew- 410 man, with ten kegs of gold, and I not knowing at all there was the like of you drawing nearer, like the stars of God.

Chris. And to think I'm long years hearing women talking that talk, to all bloody 415 fools, and this the first time I've heard the like of your voice talking sweetly for my own delight.

Peg. And to think it's me is talking sweetly, Christy Mahon, and I the fright of seven townlands for my biting tongue. Well, 420 the heart's a wonder; and, I'm thinking, there won't be our like in Mayo, for gallant lovers, from this hour, today. (*Drunken singing is heard outside.*) There's my father coming

---

[1] Real presumption.   [2] See note to Act II, l. 310.
[3] In a ravine during sunshine.

[1] A river which runs off the Neifin range and empties into the sea on the west coast of Mayo.
[2] A lake of northwest Mayo, the waters of which run into the Owen.

from the wake, and when he's had his   425
sleep we'll tell him, for he's peaceful then.
            (*They separate.*)
Mich. (*singing outside*).
    The jailor and the turnkey,
      They quickly ran us down,
    And brought us back as prisoners
      Once more to Cavan town.[1]   430

He comes in supported by SHAWN

    There we lay bewailing
      All in a prison bound. . . .
    (*He sees* CHRISTY. *Goes and shakes
    him drunkenly by the hand, while*
    PEGEEN *and* SHAWN *talk on the left.*
Mich. (*to* CHRISTY). The blessing of God
and the holy angels on your head, young fellow. I hear tell you're after winning all   435
in the sports below; and wasn't it a shame I
didn't bear you along with me to Kate Cassidy's wake, a fine, stout lad, the like of you,
for you'd never see the match of it for flows
of drink, the way when we sunk her   440
bones at noonday in her narrow grave, there
were five men, aye, and six men, stretched
out retching speechless on the holy stones.
Chris. (*uneasily, watching* PEGEEN). Is that
the truth?   445
Mich. It is then, and aren't you a louty
schemer to go burying your poor father unbeknownst when you'd a right to throw him
on the crupper of a Kerry mule and drive him
westwards, like holy Joseph in the days   450
gone by, the way we could have given him a decent burial, and not have him rotting beyond,
and not a Christian drinking a smart drop to
the glory of his soul?
Chris. (*gruffly*). It's well enough he's   455
lying, for the likes of him.
Mich. (*slapping him on the back*). Well,
aren't you a hardened slayer? It'll be a poor
thing for the household man where you go sniffing for a female wife; and (*pointing to*   460
SHAWN) look beyond at that shy and decent
Christian I have chosen for my daughter's
hand, and I after getting the gilded dispensation this day for to wed them now.

[1] The seat of county Cavan in north central Ireland
on the Ulster border.

Chris. And you'll be wedding them   465
this day, is it?
Mich. (*drawing himself up*). Aye. Are you
thinking, if I'm drunk itself, I'd leave my
daughter living single with a little frisky rascal
is the like of you?   470
Peg. (*breaking away from* SHAWN). Is it the
truth the dispensation's come?
Mich. (*triumphantly*). Father Reilly's after
reading it in gallous[1] Latin, and "It's come
in the nick of time," says he; "so I'll wed   475
them in a hurry, dreading that young gaffer
who'd capsize the stars."
Peg. (*fiercely*). He's missed his nick of
time, for it's that lad, Christy Mahon, that
I'm wedding now.   480
Mich. (*loudly with horror*). You'd be making
him a son to me, and he wet and crusted with
his father's blood?
Peg. Aye. Wouldn't it be a bitter thing for
a girl to go marrying the like of Shaneen,   485
and he a middling kind of a scarecrow, with
no savagery or fine words in him at all?
Mich. (*gasping and sinking on a chair*). Oh,
aren't you a heathen daughter to go shaking
the fat of my heart, and I swamped and   490
drownded with the weight of drink? Would
you have them turning on me the way that I'd
be roaring to the dawn of day with the wind
upon my heart? Have you not a word to
aid me, Shaneen? Are you not jealous   495
at all?
Shan. (*in great misery*). I'd be afeard to be
jealous of a man did slay his da.
Peg. Well, it'd be a poor thing to go marrying your like. I'm seeing there's a world   500
of peril for an orphan girl, and isn't it a great
blessing I didn't wed you, before himself came
walking from the west or south?
Shawn. It's a queer story you'd go picking a
dirty tramp up from the highways of the   505
world.
Peg. (*playfully*). And you think you're a
likely beau to go straying along with, the
shiny Sundays of the opening year, when it's
sooner on a bullock's liver you'd put a   510
poor girl thinking than on the lily or the
rose?

[1] Bad.

Shawn. And have you no mind of my weight of passion, and the holy dispensation, and the drift [1] of heifers I am giving, and the   515 golden ring?

Peg. I'm thinking you're too fine for the like of me, Shawn Keogh of Killakeen, and let you go off till you'd find a radiant lady with droves of bullocks on the plains of Meath, [2]   520 and herself bedizened [3] in the diamond jewelries of Pharaoh's ma. That'd be your match, Shaneen. So God save you now!

(*She retreats behind* CHRISTY.

Shawn. Won't you hear me telling you . . . ?

Chris. (*with ferocity*). Take yourself   525 from this, young fellow, or I'll maybe add a murder to my deeds today.

Mich. (*springing up with a shriek*). Murder is it? Is it mad yous are? Would you go making murder in this place, and it piled with   530 poteen for our drink tonight? Go on to the foreshore if it's fighting you want, where the rising tide will wash all traces from the memory of man. (*Pushing* SHAWN *towards* CHRISTY.

Shawn (*shaking himself free, and getting behind* MICHAEL). I'll not fight him,   535 Michael James. I'd liefer live a bachelor, simmering in passions to the end of time, than face a lepping savage the like of him has descended from the Lord knows where. Strike him yourself, Michael James, or you'll lose my   540 drift of heifers and my blue bull from Sneem. [4]

Mich. Is it me fight him, when it's father-slaying he's bred to now? (*Pushing* SHAWN) Go on, you fool, and fight him now.

Shawn (*coming forward a little*). Will I   545 strike him with my hand?

Mich. Take the loy is on your western side.

Shawn. I'd be afeard of the gallows if I struck him with that.

Chris. (*taking up the loy*). Then I'll   550 make you face the gallows or quit off from this.

(SHAWN *flies out of the door.*

Chris. Well, fine weather be after him, (*going to* MICHAEL, *coaxingly*) and I'm thinking you wouldn't wish to have that quaking blackguard

in your house at all. Let you give us   555 your blessing and hear her swear her faith to me, for I'm mounted on the springtide of the stars of luck, the way it'll be good for any to have me in the house.   559

Peg. (*at the other side of* MICHAEL). Bless us now, for I swear to God I'll wed him, and I'll not renege.

Mich. (*standing up in the center, holding on to both of them*). It's the will of God, I'm thinking, that all should win an easy or a cruel end, and it's the will of God that all   565 should rear up lengthy families for the nurture of the earth. What's a single man, I ask you, eating a bit in one house and drinking a sup in another, and he with no place of his own, like an old braying jackass strayed upon the   570 rocks? [1] (*To* CHRISTY) It's many would be in dread to bring your like into their house for to end them, maybe, with a sudden end; but I'm a decent man of Ireland, and I liefer face the grave untimely and I seeing a score of   575 grandsons growing up little gallant swearers by the name of God, than go peopling my bed-side with puny weeds the like of what you'd breed, I'm thinking, out of Shaneen Keogh. (*He joins their hands.*) A daring fel-   580 low is the jewel of the world, and a man did split his father's middle with a single clout, should have the bravery of ten, so may God and Mary and Saint Patrick bless you, and increase you from this mortal day.   585

Chris. and Peg. Amen, O Lord!

(*Hubbub outside.*

Old MAHON *rushes in, followed by all the crowd, and* WIDOW QUIN. *He makes a rush at* CHRISTY, *knocks him down, and begins to beat him*

Peg. (*dragging back his arm*). Stop that will you! Who are you at all?

---

[1] Drove.
[2] The county adjoining Dublin on the northwest.
[3] Bedecked.
[4] A town on Kenmore Bay in southwest Kerry.

[1] This sentence well illustrates the collaboration of Synge's verbal art and Irish folk speech. In *The Aran Islands* he records the comment of an old islander Mourteen: "Listen to what I'm telling you: a man who is not married is no better than an old jackass. He goes into his sister's house, and into his brother's house; he eats a bit in this place and a bit in another place, but he has no home for himself; like an old jackass straying on the rocks."

Mahon. His father, God forgive me!

Peg. (*drawing back*). Is it rose from 590 the dead?

Mahon. Do you think I look so easy quenched with the tap of a loy?

(*Beats* CHRISTY *again.*

Peg. (*glaring at* CHRISTY). And it's lies you told, letting on you had him slitted, and 595 you nothing at all.

Chris. (*catching* MAHON's *stick*). He's not my father. He's a raving maniac would scare the world. (*Pointing to* WIDOW QUIN) Herself knows it is true. 600

Crowd. You're fooling Pegeen! The Widow Quin seen him this day, and you likely knew! You're a liar!

Chris. (*dumbfounded*). It's himself was a liar, lying stretched out with an open head 605 on him, letting on he was dead.

Mahon. Weren't you off racing the hills before I got my breath with the start I had seeing you turn on me at all?

Peg. And to think of the coaxing glory 610 we had given him, and he after doing nothing but hitting a soft blow and chasing northward in a sweat of fear. Quit off from this.

Chris. (*piteously*). You've seen my doings this day, and let you save me from the 615 old man; for why would you be in such a scorch of haste to spur me to destruction now?

Peg. It's there your treachery is spurring me, till I'm hard set to think you're the one I'm after lacing in my heart-strings half 620 an hour gone by. (*To* MAHON) Take him on from this, for I think bad the world should see me raging for a Munster liar, and the fool of men.

Mahon. Rise up now to retribution, 625 and come on with me.

Crowd (*jeeringly*). There's the playboy! There's the lad thought he'd rule the roost in Mayo. Slate him now, mister.

Chris. (*getting up in shy terror*). What 630 is it drives you to torment me here, when I'd asked the thunders of the might of God to blast me if I ever did hurt to any saving only that one single blow?

Mahon (*loudly*). If you didn't, you're a 635 poor good-for-nothing, and isn't it by the like of you the sins of the whole world are committed?

Chris. (*raising his hands*). In the name of the Almighty God ...

Mahon. Leave troubling the Lord God. 640 Would you have Him sending down droughts, and fevers, and the old hen and the cholera morbus?[1]

Chris. (*to* WIDOW QUIN). Will you come between us and protect me now? 645

Wid. Quin. I've tried a lot, God help me, and my share is done.

Chris. (*looking round in desperation*). And I must go back into my torment is it, or run off like a vagabond straying through the 650 Unions[2] with the dusts of August making mudstains in the gullet of my throat, or the winds of March blowing on me till I'd take an oath I felt them making whistles of my ribs within? 655

Sara. Ask Pegeen to aid you. Her like does often change.

Chris. I will not then, for there's torment in the splendor of her like, and she a girl any moon of midnight would take pride to 660 meet, facing southwards on the heaths of Keel.[3] But what did I want crawling forward to scorch my understanding at her flaming brow?

Peg. (*to* MAHON, *vehemently, fearing she will break into tears*). Take him on from this or I'll set the young lads to destroy him here. 665

Mahon (*going to him, shaking his stick*). Come on now if you wouldn't have the company to see you skelped.

Peg. (*half laughing, through her tears*). That's it, now the world will see him pandied,[4] 670 and he an ugly liar was playing off the hero, and the fright of men.

Chris. (*to* MAHON, *very sharply*). Leave me go!

Crowd. That's it. Now Christy. If 675 them two set fighting, it will lick the world.

Mahon (*making a grab at* CHRISTY). Come here to me.

[1] Disease.

[2] Workhouses, maintained by unions of parish districts.

[3] Keel Bay lies near Achill Head on the extreme west coast of Mayo.

[4] Struck (literally, struck on the hands).

Chris. (more threateningly). Leave me go, I'm saying.   680

Mahon. I will maybe, when your legs is limping, and your back is blue.

Crowd. Keep it up, the two of you. I'll back the old one. Now the playboy.

Chris. (in low and intense voice). Shut   685 your yelling, for if you're after making a mighty man of me this day by the power of a lie, you're setting me now to think if it's a poor thing to be lonesome, it's worse maybe to go mixing with the fools of earth.   690

(MAHON *makes a movement towards him.*)

Chris. (almost shouting). Keep off ... lest I do show a blow unto the lot of you would set the guardian angels winking in the clouds above.   694

(*He swings round with a sudden rapid movement and picks up a loy.*)

Crowd (half frightened, half amused). He's going mad! Mind yourselves! Run from the idiot!

Chris. If I am an idiot, I'm after hearing my voice this day saying words would raise the topknot on a poet in a merchant's   700 town. I've won your racing, and your lepping, and ...

Mahon. Shut your gullet and come on with me.   704

Chris. I'm going, but I'll stretch you first.

(*He runs at old* MAHON *with the loy, chases him out of the door, followed by crowd and* WIDOW QUIN. *There is a great noise outside, then a yell, and dead silence for a moment.* CHRISTY *comes in, half dazed, and goes to fire.*)

Wid. Quin (coming in, hurriedly, and going to him). They're turning again you. Come on, or you'll be hanged, indeed.

Chris. I'm thinking, from this out, Pegeen'll be giving me praises the same as in the hours gone by.   710

Wid. Quin (impatiently). Come by the back door. I'd think bad to have you stifled on the gallows tree.

Chris. (indignantly). I will not, then. What good'd be my lifetime, if I left Pegeen?   715

Wid. Quin. Come on, and you'll be no worse than you were last night; and you with a double murder this time to be telling to the girls.

Chris. I'll not leave Pegeen Mike.

Wid. Quin (impatiently). Isn't there   720 the match of her in every parish public, from Binghamstown[1] unto the plain of Meath? Come on, I tell you, and I'll find you finer sweethearts at each waning moon.

Chris. It's Pegeen I'm seeking only,   725 and what'd I care if you brought me a drift of chosen females, standing in their shifts itself, maybe, from this place to the Eastern World?

Sara (runs in, pulling off one of her petticoats). They're going to hang him. (*Holding out petticoat and shawl*) Fit these upon him, and   730 let him run off to the east.

Wid. Quin. He's raving now; but we'll fit them on him, and I'll take him, in the ferry, to the Achill boat.

Chris. (struggling feebly). Leave me go,   735 will you, when I'm thinking of my luck today, for she will wed me surely, and I a proven hero in the end of all.

(*They try to fasten petticoat round him.*)

Wid. Quin. Take his left hand, and we'll pull him now. Come on, young fellow.   740

Chris. (suddenly starting up). You'll be taking me from her? You're jealous, is it, of her wedding me? Go on from this.

(*He snatches up a stool, and threatens them with it.*)

Wid. Quin (going). It's in the mad-house they should put him, not in jail, at all.   745 We'll go by the back door, to call the doctor, and we'll save him so.

(*She goes out, with* SARA, *through inner room. Men crowd in the doorway.* CHRISTY *sits down again by the fire.*)

Mich. (in a terrified whisper). Is the old lad killed surely?

Philly. I'm after feeling the last gasps   750 quitting his heart. (*They peer in at* CHRISTY.)

Mich. (with a rope). Look at the way he is. Twist a hangman's knot on it, and slip it over his head, while he's not minding at all.

Philly. Let you take it, Shaneen.   755 You're the soberest of all that's here.

Shawn. Is it me to go near him, and he the

[1] A village in northwest Mayo.

wickedest and worst with me? Let you take it, Pegeen Mike.

Peg. Come on, so.   760
   (*She goes forward with the others, and they drop the double hitch over his head.*

Chris. What ails you?

Shawn (*triumphantly, as they pull the rope tight on his arms*). Come on to the peelers, till they stretch you now.

Chris. Me!

Mich. If we took pity on you, the 765 Lord God would, maybe, bring us ruin from the law today, so you'd best come easy, for hanging is an easy and a speedy end.

Chris. I'll not stir. (*To* PEGEEN) And what is it you'll say to me, and I after 770 doing it this time in the face of all?

Peg. I'll say, a strange man is a marvel, with his mighty talk; but what's a squabble in your backyard, and the blow of a loy, have taught me that there's a great gap 775 between a gallous story and a dirty deed. (*To Men*) Take him on from this, or the lot of us will be likely put on trial for his deed today.

Chris. (*with horror in his voice*). And 780 it's yourself will send me off, to have a horny-fingered hangman hitching his bloody slip-knots at the butt of my ear.

Men (*pulling rope*). Come on, will you? 784
   (*He is pulled down on the floor.*

Chris. (*twisting his legs round the table*). Cut the rope, Pegeen, and I'll quit the lot of you, and live from this out, like the madmen of Keel, eating muck and green weeds, on the faces of the cliffs.

Peg. And leave us to hang, is it, for a 790 saucy liar, the like of you? (*To Men*) Take him on, out from this.

Shawn. Pull a twist on his neck, and squeeze him so.

Philly. Twist yourself. Sure he can- 795 not hurt you, if you keep your distance from his teeth alone.

Shawn. I'm afeard of him. (*To* PEGEEN) Lift a lighted sod, will you, and scorch his leg.   800

Peg. (*blowing the fire with a bellows*). Leave go now, young fellow, or I'll scorch your shins.

Chris. You're blowing for to torture me. (*His voice rising and growing stronger*) That's your kind, is it? Then let the lot of you 806 be wary, for, if I've to face the gallows, I'll have a gay march down, I tell you, and shed the blood of some of you before I die.

Shawn (*in terror*). Keep a good hold, 810 Philly. Be wary, for the love of God. For I'm thinking he would liefest wreak his pains on me.

Chris. (*almost gaily*). If I do lay my hands on you, it's the way you'll be at the fall of night, hanging as a scarecrow for the 815 fowls of hell. Ah, you'll have a gallous jaunt I'm saying, coaching out through Limbo with my father's ghost.

Shawn (*to* PEGEEN). Make haste, will you? Oh, isn't he a holy terror, and isn't it true 820 for Father Reilly, that all drink's a curse that has the lot of you so shaky and uncertain now?

Chris. If I can wring a neck among you, I'll have a royal judgment looking on the trembling jury in the courts of law. And 825 won't there be crying out in Mayo the day I'm stretched upon the rope with ladies in their silks and satins sniveling in their lacy ker-chiefs, and they rhyming songs and ballads on the terror of my fate?   830
   (*He squirms round on the floor and bites* SHAWN'S *leg.*

Shawn (*shrieking*). My leg's bit on me. He's the like of a mad dog, I'm thinking, the way that I will surely die.

Chris. (*delighted with himself*). You will then, the way you can shake out hell's 835 flags of welcome for my coming in two weeks or three, for I'm thinking Satan hasn't many have killed their da in Kerry, and in Mayo too.

Old MAHON *comes in behind on all fours and looks on unnoticed*

Men (*to* PEGEEN). Bring the sod, will you?

Peg. (*coming over*). God help him so. 840
   (*Burns his leg.*

Chris. (*kicking and screaming*). Oh, glory be to God!
   (*He kicks loose from the table, and they all drag him towards the door.*

Jimmy (*seeing old* MAHON). Will you look what's come in?

(*They all drop* CHRISTY *and run, left.*

Chris. (*scrambling on his knees face to face with old* MAHON). Are you coming to be 845 killed a third time, or what ails you now?

Mahon. For what is it they have you tied?

Chris. They're taking me to the peelers to have me hanged for slaying you.

Mich. (*apologetically*). It is the will of 850 God that all should guard their little cabins from the treachery of law, and what would my daughter be doing if I was ruined or was hanged itself? 854

Mahon (*grimly, loosening* CHRISTY). It's little I care if you put a bag on her back, and went picking cockles till the hour of death; but my son and myself will be going our own way, and we'll have great times from this out telling stories of the villainy of Mayo, and the 860 fools is here. (*To* CHRISTY, *who is freed*) Come on now.

Chris. Go with you, is it? I will then, like a gallant captain with his heathen slave. Go on now and I'll see you from this day stew- 865 ing my oatmeal and washing my spuds, for

I'm master of all fights from now. (*Pushing* MAHON) Go on, I'm saying.

Mahon. Is it me?

Chris. Not a word out of you. Go on 870 from this.

Mahon (*walking out and looking back at* CHRISTY *over his shoulder*). Glory be to God! (*With a broad smile*) I am crazy again! (*Goes.*

Chris. Ten thousand blessings upon all that's here, for you've turned me a likely 875 gaffer in the end of all, the way I'll go rómancing through a romping lifetime from this hour to the dawning of the judgment day.

(*He goes out.*

Mich. By the will of God, we'll have peace now for our drinks. Will you draw the 880 porter, Pegeen?

Shawn (*going up to her*). It's a miracle Father Reilly can wed us in the end of all, and we'll have none to trouble us when his vicious bite is healed. 885

Peg. (*hitting him a box on the ear*). Quit my sight. (*Putting her shawl over her head and breaking out into wild lamentations*) Oh, my grief, I've lost him surely. I've lost the only Playboy of the Western World. 890

Curtain.

INTRODUCTION TO

The Life of the Insects

Experimentation in the European Theater after World War I:
The Čapek Brothers and Philosophic Fantasy

EXPERIMENTATION IN THE EUROPEAN THEATER AFTER WORLD WAR I

THE FIRST WORLD WAR complicated the theatrical art of Europe no less than its geography. At the opening of the twentieth century, the vogue of realism, initiated by Ibsen, had been established throughout the Continent by such outstanding playwrights and plays as the following: in Germany, Gerhart Hauptmann (1862–1946), *The Weavers* (1892); in Austria, Arthur Schnitzler (1862–1931), *Light-O'-Love* (1894); in Russia, Anton Chekhov (1860–1904), *The Sea-Gull* (1896); in Holland, Herman Heijermans (1864–1924), *The Good Hope* (1900); in France, Eugène Brieux (1858–1932), *The Red Robe* (1900); in Spain, Benito Galdós (1845–1921), *Electra* (1901). Despite excursions into symbolic fantasy on the part of Strindberg (1849–1912), Andreyev (1871–1919), Wedekind (1864–1918), and a few others, during the early 1900's, the realistic mode continued dominant until the war years of 1914–18. Then realism gave way rapidly to a new imaginativeness, sometimes delicate, sometimes grotesque. Hence with the coming of peace, widespread experimentation set in, affecting the production as well as the writing of plays. The revolutionary ideas of the Swiss designer, Adolphe Appia (1862–1928), and of the English stage artist, E. Gordon Craig (1872–   ), began to exert a marked influence upon playhouse architecture and scenery. Stages without a proscenium and front curtain, or without any scenic devices except hangings and lights, came into use. Pure emotional suggestion contended with imitation of reality as the object of stage décor. Abstract modern art — cubism with its geometrical lines and shapes, and constructivism with its levels and mechanical forms — encouraged settings of an expressive and fantastic, rather than representational, character. Thus novel and unconventional impulses abounded in the post-war theater of Europe.

THE ČAPEK BROTHERS AND PHILOSOPHIC FANTASY

One of the most vigorous and important centers of theatrical activity developed in Prague, the capital of Czechoslovakia. The Czech republic, established in the autumn of 1918, enjoyed during the 1920's a renaissance in art and letters similar to that of Ireland a decade or two earlier. Leading spirits in this Czech cultural movement were Josef and Karel Čapek, sons of a physician in Malé Svatonvice, a mountain village of northeastern Bohemia. Josef, born in 1887, attended the School of Arts and Crafts, Prague, and afterward studied art in Paris. On his return home he attracted attention not only as a painter of the modernistic school, but also as a critic whose writings stimulated concern for the native folk art. Karel, born in 1890, had a literary and reflective turn of mind which inspired him to publish poems and sketches when still in his teens. He pursued courses in literature and philosophy at the universities of Prague, Berlin, and finally Paris, where he took a Ph.D. degree. The First World War diverted him from an academic career into journalism. Exempt from military service on account of ill health, he wrote fiction and essays for various Czech newspapers. His newspaper work broadened in scope after the coming of peace. From 1923 till his death he occupied an important editorial post on the Lidove Noviny, the chief liberal daily in Prague.

The two Čapeks focused their interest on dramatic art as soon as Czech independence had given the National Art Theater of Prague the chance to become at last a really national institution. For that theater Josef Čapek undertook scene designing; Karel, playwriting. The latter's *R. U. R. (Rossum's Universal Robots)*, first presented in January, 1921, traveled rapidly abroad to bring its author and the Czech stage into the international limelight. Meanwhile Karel Čapek was appointed art director of the National Theater. He did not long remain in this office, for during 1922 his brother and he opened an experimental playhouse, the Vinohrady Theater. Here, in addition to their own works and those of promising Czech writers, they put on the masterpieces of Shakespeare, Molière, Ibsen, Hauptmann, and other moderns. Their productions with Josef's bold and impressive stage décor excited world-wide notice.

By the late 1920's Karel Čapek, more brilliant and versatile than his older brother, was universally recognized as Czechoslovakia's foremost man of letters. He had married a distinguished actress, Olga Scheinpflugowa; he had published voluminously — short stories, novels, sketches, as well as plays; and he had filled the rôle of cultural ambassador to England and other European countries. During the next decade Czech intellectuals made his attractive Prague villa their rendezvous. His warm friendship with President Thomas Masaryk and with the latter's successor, Eduard Beneš, led him more and more into the councils of state. When relations with the Sudeten Germans were approaching a crisis in 1937 and 1938, he took an important part in the efforts at conciliation. On June 22, 1938, he voiced to the Sudeten Germans over the Prague radio his heartfelt conviction that "if we could in one way or another collect all the good that is, after all, in each one of us sinful human creatures, I believe that on it could be built a world that would be surely far kinder than the present one." The Munich pact of September, 1938, which spelled the doom of Czechoslovakia, shattered Karel Čapek's spirit. "For me the world is dead," he remarked to his friends. Then this man of good will caught pneumonia and died on Christmas Day of the same year. At least he escaped the Nazi hate which threw his brother Josef into a concentration camp in the fateful spring of 1939 and finally brought about the latter's death there in 1945.

The Čapek brothers found in the drama an outlet for the whimsical imagination and the social philosophy which they possessed in common. Zealous for the betterment of human living, they were perturbed at the divisiveness and materialism born out of the First World War. As a result their plays center upon the problem of man's destiny, especially in the face of a mechanistic and greedy civilization. The problem is always projected by means of parable and symbol against a colorful background of Nowhere. And always too the humane wit of the Čapeks notes in that problem the multifarious irony and discloses it with good-natured satire.

Karel Čapek's *R. U. R.* (1921) depicts the danger of mechanization to human values. A professor's ingenuity effects the birth of a race of machine-like people, the Robots. These Robots finally kill off their human masters, but at the same time lose the secret of their manufacture. In the epilogue two super Robots, a male and a female, suddenly evolve souls and sentiments of love, the requisites for any new race of beings. Josef Čapek's *The Land of Many Names* (1923) describes the vanity of human Utopias. The report that a new continent has arisen from the sea stirs a whole city to plan exploitation; each citizen envisions there the land of his desire. Two rival capitalists incite a war over the continent's possession. Soon the Land of the New Life, as one of them calls it, is transformed into the Land of Dead Armies. Then it abruptly disappears beneath the sea. *Adam the Creator* (1927), by both Josef and Karel Čapek, satirizes the yearning to remake the world and human nature. Adam in a moment of petulance destroys the Earth, but God requires him to recreate it. He bungles the job by producing, among other creatures, fleas, a coquette Lilith, a superwoman Eve, a warlike superman, and Oddly-Come-Short, a poverty-stricken figure with six filthy children. Adam, thoroughly disgusted at his creation, would like to annihilate it. God and he, however, agree to tolerate the new world, imperfect though it is. Karel Čapek's *The White Plague* (1937), also called *Power and Glory*, sets forth the ironic effects of the Nazi and Fascist philosophy of war. A Doctor Galen has the only remedy for a strange disease, akin to leprosy, which is killing the citizens over forty-five in a certain European nation. The doctor refuses, however, to use his remedy until the head of the state bans all warfare. The Marshal, attacked by the disease, calls off the war on a small neighboring country in order to benefit by Doctor Galen's cure. The Marshal's move so infuriates the young citizens, who are enthusiastic over the war and glad to be rid of the older people, that they fatally injure the doctor and thus seal the death of the Marshal. These striking philosophic fantasies, filled with original scenic effects, rank the Čapek drama among the few distinctive contributions of Europe to the world theater since World War I.

"THE LIFE OF THE INSECTS"

The Life of the Insects, the most sensational and profound of the Čapek plays, was the first of the two collaborations between Josef and Karel. The famous Czech director, M. Hilar, produced it in 1921 at the National Art Theater of Prague with stage sets by Josef Čapek. Its great success induced William Brady to bring it out on October 31, 1922, at the Jolsen Theater, New York, in an English version by Owen Davis, entitled *The World We Live In*. Sir Nigel Playfair directed in May, 1923, a London performance of another version, named *The Insect Play*.

The picture of the insect world which forms the basis of this Čapek drama derived in part from the authors' personal experiences. They had collected butterflies and beetles from childhood. Their hobby little by little impressed upon them the parallelisms between insect and human habits. Then in 1919 they read *Social Life of the Insects* and *Entomological Memories* by Henri Jules Fabre, the noted French scientist. They now fully realized how clear a mirror of human morality insect behavior afforded.

Two years later the Čapek brothers brought forth *The Life of the Insects*, a highly ingenious drama cast in the play-within-a-play mold. The Prelude introduces the authors' mouthpiece, a poetic and philosophic Vagrant. In their opinion such a tramp is the ideal observer of life. He does not hold property; he possesses no family; he has seen much of nature and of men. His non-participation in the world's affairs leaves him free to reflect on the meaning of human existence. The dream of this ideal critic, who falls asleep at the close of the Prelude, comprises the drama proper.

The Vagrant in his dream watches three insect realms which respectively exhibit three leading phases of the human world. The butterflies of Act I portray man's sex life, the fascinating pursuit of love. Their behavior points especially at the smart set's dalliance and philandering, cloaked in suggestive aestheticism. The beetles, crickets, and flies of Act II display the predatory tactics which characterize man's acquisitiveness and business enterprise. The Ichneumon Fly is the counterpart of the "robber baron" capitalist. "My good sir, if you want to keep alive, you've got to fight your way.... A strong personality is bound to assert itself," says the Fly (Act II, ll. 667–72). The ant realm of Act III presents man's industrial and nationalistic society with its attendant evils of mechanization, competition, and war.

In the Epilogue the Vagrant's dream comes to a close. A Chrysalis for two acts has been proclaiming its momentary birth with the silly presumption of the insignificant human individual. Now its transformation into moth and its almost immediate death illustrate the "unending moth-gift of life" (ll. 98–99). Then the death of the awakened Vagrant and the appearance of the baby reinforce the idea of life's unbroken cycle. "One is born, and another dies," says the Woodcutter (l. 249), as he looks from the child to the corpse. The Vagrant, however, did not die before glimpsing the meaning to this cycle: "Tiny self, there is something above you, call it nation, mankind, or state, call it how you will, if only you serve it: You are naught. The greatest worth of living is to sacrifice one's life" (Act III, ll. 35–39).

The Čapeks, who through the Vagrant shout in joy, "Life, life, you have cast a spell upon us" (Epilogue, ll. 106–07), press the theme of service and coöperation with perhaps too obvious didacticism. Still this tendency never really obstructs their diverting tragi-comic fable. The third act of *The Life of the Insects* contains brilliant historical prophecy. The industrial and military mobilization of the Ant-Realm, and the ruthless conduct of the war by the Ant Dictator are identical with the methods of Hitler and the German Nazis for Europe's "New Order." The staccato, chantlike tone of the stylized dialogue emphasizes to perfection that men become mere automatons in the totalitarian state. The spectacle of the ants is the most startling piece of sociological fantasy in the modern theater. Yet the contemporaneity of these particular scenes must not obscure the deep poetic wisdom behind the entire play. *The Life of the Insects* gains lasting importance as dramatic art from its graphic and unique satire of man's ridiculously Lilliputian world.

[For the Čapeks and other modern European dramatists, see F. W. Chandler, *Modern Continental Playwrights* (1931); T. H. Dickinson, *The Theater in a Changing Europe* (1933); Eric Bentley, *The Playwright as Thinker* (1946); B. H. Clark and George Freedley, *A History of Modern Drama* (1947); for twentieth-century stagecraft, Sheldon Cheney, *Stage Decoration* (1928) and Lee Simonson, *The Stage Is Set* (1946).]

JOSEF AND KAREL ČAPEK

The Life of the Insects[1]

A Comedy in Three Acts

with

Prelude and Epilogue

[*Translated by* PAUL SELVER]

DRAMATIS PERSONAE

Prelude

VAGRANT
PEDANT

Act I

The Butterflies

APATURA IRIS
APATURA CLYTHIA ("CLYTHIE")
FELIX
VICTOR } *Male Butterflies*
OTAKAR

Act II

The Marauders

CHRYSALIS
MALE BEETLE
FEMALE BEETLE
ANOTHER MALE BEETLE
ICHNEUMON FLY
ITS LARVA
MALE CRICKET
FEMALE CRICKET
PARASITE
BAND OF PILLAGERS

Act III

The Ants

FIRST ENGINEER, *Dictator*
SECOND ENGINEER, *Head of the General Staff*

BLIND ANT
INVENTOR
MESSENGER
QUARTERMASTER-GENERAL
JOURNALIST
PHILANTHROPIST
TELEGRAPHIST
COMMANDER-IN-CHIEF OF THE YELLOWS
ANT WORKERS AND SOLDIERS, OFFICIALS, MESSENGERS,
OFFICERS, STRETCHER-BEARERS, WOUNDED, *etc.*
ARMY OF THE YELLOWS

Epilogue

Life and Death

FIRST MOTH
SECOND MOTH
THIRD MOTH
CHORUS OF MOTH-DANCERS
FIRST SNAIL
SECOND SNAIL
A WOODCUTTER
AN AUNT
A SCHOOLGIRL
A WANDERER

The insects wear human clothing. The BUTTERFLIES have drawing-room attire; the MARAUDERS are dressed as citizens; the ANTS are dressed in black or yellow close-fitting workmen's garb with belts, the MOTHS in gauze veils. The insect characteristics are expressed chiefly by pantomimic gestures.

PRELUDE

A green forest-glade

Vagrant [1] (*staggers on from the side of the stage, stumbles and falls*). Ha, ha, ha. What fun, eh? Never mind. You needn't laugh. I haven't hurt myself. (*Props himself on his elbow.*) You — you — you think I'm drunk? Oh no. I'm resting quite firmly, you know. You saw how steadily I fell. Like a tree. Like a hero. I was performing — the fall — of man. What a spectacle. (*Sits up.*) Why, I'm not staggering. 5 Not me, but everything else is drunk, everything's staggering about, whirling around — round and round the whole time in a circle. Ha, ha, that's enough, it makes me feel bad. (*Looks round.*) What's that? Everything's whirling round me. The whole earth. The whole universe. Doing me too great an honor. (*Smooths his clothing.*)

[1] The Vagrant is to be imagined *not* as a tramp, but as a vagabond poet and philosopher, a whimsical spectator of the phenomena of Life.

Excuse me, I'm not dressed for the part of acting as center of the harmony of the   10
spheres. (*Throws his cap to the ground.*) There's the center. Whirl around my cap, it
won't come to any harm. Let's see, where did I leave off?

Oh yes, I know. I fell down beneath my load. And you, blossom, thought I was
drunk? Speedwell, veronica, don't get so puffed up with your sobriety. They put your
leaves, veronica, on wounds; wait, speedwell, I'll lay my heart on you. I don't say   15
I'm not drunk; if I had roots like you, I wouldn't wander all over the world like a vagabond. That's how it is. Why, I was in the great war; I knew Latin too, and now I can
do all sorts of things. Clear manure, sweep the streets, mount guard, draw beer and
what not. Everything that another man wouldn't like to do. Now you see who I am.
Let's see, where did I leave off?   20

Ah, I know. Yes, that's me. They know me everywhere. I'm a man. Nobody
calls me anything else. They say to me: "Man, I'll have you arrested," or "Man, tidy
up, do this for me, bring that to me," or "Clear off, man." And I'm not offended at
being a man. If I were to say to somebody: "Man, give me sixpence," he'd be offended.
If he doesn't like it, well and good. I'll regard him as a butterfly, or a beetle, or an   25
ant, just as he prefers. It's all the same to me, man or insect, I don't want to put anyone right. Neither insect nor man. I just look on.

I just look on. If I had roots or a bulb in the earth, I'd look at the sky. (*Rises to his
knees.*) At the skies. To my dying day I'd look straight at the sky. (*Stands up.*)
But I'm a man, I must look at people. (*Looks round.*) And I see them.   30

Pedant (*running in with a net*). Ha, ha. Oh, oh, oh. What fine specimens. Apatura
Iris. Apatura Clythia. The painted lady and the light blue butterfly. Ha, ha, what
magnificent creatures. Oh, just you wait, I'll have you. Ha, ha, they're off again.
Ha, ha, cautiously, careful, hush, softly, softly, ah, ah, gently, gently — aha, ho, careful,
careful, ah, oho, oho ——   35

Vagrant. Hi, what are you catching butterflies for? Good day to you, kind sir.

Pedant. Softly, softly, careful. Don't move. They've settled on you. Butterflies.
Nymphalidae. Careful, keep still. They settle on everything that smells. On mud.
On offal. On garbage. Careful, they've settled on you. Oho, oho.

Vagrant. Let them be. They're playing.   40

Pedant. What, playing? Their play is only the overture to pairing. The male
pursues the female. The bride slips away, allures. The pursuer tickles her with his
feelers, sinks down exhausted. The female flits off. A new, stronger, sturdier male
will come. The female slips away, entices the lover after her, aha, aha. Do you catch
my meaning? That's the way of nature. The eternal contest of love. The eternal   45
mating. The eternal round of sex. Hush, softly.

Vagrant. And what will you do with them when you catch them?

Pedant. What will I do? Well, the butterfly must be identified, recorded, and
assigned a place in my collection. But the pollen mustn't be rubbed off. The net
should be of delicate texture. The butterfly should be carefully killed by crushing   50
its breast. And then impaled on a pin. And fastened down with paper strips. And
placed in the collection when it's properly dried. It should be protected against dust
and moth. Put a small sponge of cyanide into the case.

Vagrant. And what's all that for?

Pedant. Love of nature. Man alive, you've no love of nature. Aha, there they 55
are again. Ha, ha, careful, careful, softly. You won't escape me, ha, ha. (*Runs off.*

Vagrant. Eternal mating, love's eternal contest,
'Tis even so; 'tis ever pairing-time,
As said the pedant. Kindly pardon me
For being drunk. Why, I can see quite well. 60
Everything's twofold, everything's in pairs,
Here, there, and here again, and everywhere,
All things in pairs. Clouds, gnats and trees,
All things embrace and fondle, dally, provoke and pursue.
Birds in the tree-tops, I see you, I see you, 65
I see all. And you two, yonder in the shadow,
I see you linking your fingers, struggling hotly and softly.
Let none of you think I don't see you from here.
That's eternal mating. Kindly pardon me.
I'm drunk, but honest. (*Covers his eyes.*) I see nothing. 70
Do what you will. I'll shout before I uncover my eyes. (*Darkness.*
All strive to pair. Only you, standing here in the darkness,
Alone, alone, alone you wander your crooked way,
Vainly, vainly, vainly would you lift your hands
In love's hide-and-seek. Enough. But ye shall take joy of each other. 75
For that I praise you, that's a goodly thing
And nature's wise order, as the pedant said.
All strives to pair. — Now do I behold (*The back curtain rises.*
The blissful garden of love bedecked with flowers,
Wherein young pairs, beauteous twin beings, 80
Butterflies swept along by the gust of love,
In rapturous flight, as though they were at play,
Unendingly they bear eternal matings,
For all doth strive to pair. (*He uncovers his eyes. The scene is lit up.*
Where am I? 85

ACT I

The Butterflies

A radiant, azure space, bedecked with flowers and cushions; mirrors, a small table with colored glasses containing cold drinks and straws. High seats, as in a bar

Vagrant (rubbing his eyes and looking around). Hallo, how lovely and beautiful. Why, it's just like — like being in paradise. A painter couldn't have made a better picture. And what a delightful fragrance.

CLYTHIE *runs in laughing*

Otakar (running after her). I love you, 5
Clythie. (CLYTHIE *runs off laughing,* OTAKAR *after her.*

Vagrant. Butterflies. Aha, butterflies. They're playing. I'd have a look at 'em, if I wasn't so — (*Brushes his clothes.*) Oh, let 'em kick me out. I'll lie down here. (*Ar-* 10 *ranges the cushions.*) I'll lie down. Upon my soul I will. (*Arranges a bed in the proscenium.*) And if we don't like it, we'll close our eyes and have forty winks. (*Lies down.*) That's the way. 15

Enter FELIX

Felix. Where is Iris? I saw her quaff the scent of the flowers — Iris. Iris. If I could at least find a rhyme to you. (*Sits down among the cushions.*) "Beauteous Iris, who as pure as fire is" — No. Something else "— a 20 diamond buckler my love's attire is, and has filled me with angel-strength — Iris, Iris, Iris." That would do. But where is Iris? How can she always be with that fellow Victor? Oh dear. "Upon thy lips divine, grows not 25 oft bitter, Iris, thy smile of victory, when sorrow's gesture dire is —" I'll make an elegy of this, in regular alexandrines [1] when she disappoints me. Ah, 'tis a poet's lot to suffer. (*Laughter behind the scene.*) That's Iris. 30

(*Behind, by the entrance, a picture of delicate grief, he props his head in his hands.*)

IRIS *enters,* VICTOR *after her*

Iris. Felix, is that you there by yourself? And so interestingly sad?

Felix (*turning round*). You, Iris? Ah, I didn't imagine ——

Iris. Why aren't you playing outside? 35 Such lots of girls are there.

Felix (*jumping up*). You know, Iris, that — that they don't interest me.

Iris. Oh, poor fellow. Why not?

Victor. Not yet? 40

Felix. No longer.

Iris (*sitting down among the pillows*). Do you hear that, Victor? And he says that right to my face. Come here, you impolite man. Sit down here, nearer, still nearer. Tell 45 me, darling, don't women interest you any longer?

Felix. No. I'm tired of them.

Iris (*with a huge sigh*). Oh, you men. What cynics you are. You just have your en- 50 joyment, as much enjoyment as you can, and then you all say: "I'm tired of them." How terrible it is to be a woman.

Victor. Why?

Iris. We are never tired. What sort 55

[1] Rimed couplets with six stresses to each line.

of a past have you had, Felix? When did you love for the first time?

Felix. I don't know now. It's too long ago. And even then it wasn't for the first time. I was a school-boy —— 60

Victor. Ah, you were still a caterpillar. A green caterpillar, devouring the leaves.

Iris. Felix, was she dark? Was she beautiful?

Felix. Beautiful as the day, as the azure, 65 as ——

Iris. — as what? Quickly.

Felix. As beautiful as you.

Iris. Felix, dearest, did she love you?

Felix. I don't know. I never spoke to 70 her.

Iris. Good heavens, what did you do to her then?

Felix. I looked at her from afar ——

Victor. — sitting on a green leaf —— 75

Felix. — and wrote poems; letters; my first novel ——

Victor. It's appalling the number of leaves such a caterpillar uses up.

Iris. You're horrid, Victor. Look, Fe- 80 lix has his eyes full of tears. Isn't that nice?

Victor. Tears? Why ——

Felix. It isn't true. I haven't got tears in my eyes. On my honor I haven't. 84

Iris. Let's see. Look into my eyes, quickly.

Victor. One, two, three, four — I knew he wouldn't hold out any longer.

Iris (*laughing*). Now then, Felix, tell me at once what sort of eyes I have.

Felix. Azure blue. 90

Iris. You are kind. Yours are brown. Ah, someone told me that they are golden. I don't care for blue eyes. They're so cold, so devoid of passion. Poor Clythie has blue eyes, hasn't she? Do you like her eyes, Felix? 95

Felix. Clythie's? I don't know. Yes, she has beautiful eyes.

Iris. Get along with you, she has such thin legs. Oh, you're such bad judges of women, you poets. 100

Victor. Have you read the last poem that Felix wrote? (*Taking a book out of his pocket*) It came out in the Spring Almanac.

Iris. Quick, read it to me.

Felix. No, I won't let you read it to   105
her. (*Trying to stand up*) It's bad. It's old.
I've long since got past that stage.

Iris (*holding him back*). Sit down quietly,
Felix.

Victor. It's called "Eternal Downfall."   110

Felix (*putting his hands over his ears*). But
I don't want you to read it to her.

Victor (*reading with emphasis*).
"Downwards, downwards, swift and fleet
    The pace at which we fly.
The world desires deceit, deceit —   115
    Woman desires to lie."

Iris. That's witty, isn't it, Victor? Felix,
where did you get it from?

Victor. "The dream be not frustrated —
    Let love be consummated.   120
    All ever falls pell-mell;
    Maiden, we'll fall as well."

Iris. Fall, I understand that; but what is
"consummated"?

Victor. That is love which, hm, has   125
achieved its aim.

Iris. What aim?

Victor. Well, its usual one.

Iris. Oh, how shocking. Felix, did you write
such a thing? I'm afraid of you. How   130
depraved you are. Is Latin always so immoral?

Felix. Have pity, Iris. It's such a bad
poem.

Iris. Why bad?   135

Felix. It hasn't got the — the — real thing
in it.

Iris. Aha. Victor, you'll find my fan in the
garden.

Victor. Oh, don't let me disturb you.   140
                                    (*Exit.*

Iris. Quick, Felix. Tell me the truth. You
can tell me everything.

Felix. Iris, Iris, how can you bear him about
you? Such an old fop. Such a back number. Such a thorough paste satyr.   145

Iris. Victor?

Felix. How basely he looks upon you, upon
love, upon everything. How shamefully.
How... how... how uncouthly. How can
you put up with it?   150

Iris. Poor Victor. He's so soothing. No,

Felix, talk about poetry. I'm so fond of
poetry. "The dream be not frustrated..."
(*Sits down among the pillows.*) Felix, you're
awfully talented. "Maiden, we'll fall   155
as well." Heavens, how passionately it's expressed. Tell me, Felix, poets are fearfully,
fearfully passionate, aren't they?

Felix. Oh Iris, I've long since got past what's
in that poem.   160

Iris. If only the Latin wasn't so coarse. I
can put up with anything, anything, but it
mustn't have a horrid name. Felix, we must
be delicate towards women. If you were to
kiss me now, would you give that a horrid   165
name too?

Felix. Iris, how could I dare to kiss you?

Iris. Come, come, you men are capable of
anything. Felix, bend down towards me.
To whom did you write that poem? To   170
Clythie?

Felix. No, I assure you ——

Iris. To whom then?

Felix. To nobody, upon my honor, to nobody. Or rather, to all the women in the   175
world.

Iris (*leaning on her elbow*). Good gracious,
have you con... con... what do you call it?

Felix. Iris, I swear to you ——   179

Iris (*sinking down among the pillows*). Felix,
you're a terrible seducer. Tell me, who was
your mistress?

Felix. Iris, you won't tell anybody? You
really won't?

Iris. No.   185

Felix. Well then — I haven't got one.

Iris. What?

Felix. Not yet. Upon my honor.

Iris. Oh what a fib. How many women
have you told that to, you innocent   190
creature? Felix, Felix, I see through you.
What a dangerous man you are.

Felix. Iris, you mustn't laugh at me. I've
had terrible experiences in my imagination.
Awful disappointments. Loves without   195
number, but only in my dreams. Dreams are
the poet's life. I know all women, and haven't
known one. Upon my honor, Iris.

Iris (*leaning on her elbow*). Then why do
you say that you are tired of women?   200

Felix. Oh Iris, everyone disparages the thing he loves the most.

Iris. Brunettes?

Felix. No, dreams. Eternal dreams.

Iris. "The dream be not frustrated." 205 You have such passionate eyes. You're fearfully talented, Felix. (*Sinks down among the pillows.*) What are you thinking of now?

Felix. Of you. Woman is a riddle.

Iris. Solve her then. But gentle, Felix, 210 please.

Felix. I cannot see into the depths of your eyes.

Iris. Then begin elsewhere.

Felix. I ... Iris ... really ... 215

Iris. Felix, I'm in such a queer mood today. How stupid it is to be a woman. Today I should like to be a man, to conquer, to allure, to embrace ... Felix, I should be such a fearfully passionate man. I should ... I ... 220 I should snatch everyone away wildly, savagely ... what a pity that you aren't a girl. Let's pretend, shall we? You will be Iris and I will be your Felix.

Felix. No, Iris. It's too venturesome 225 to be Felix. That means desiring, desiring something ...

Iris (*in a faint voice*). Oh Felix, everything.

Felix. There is something greater than to desire everything. 230

Iris. And that is ...

Felix. To desire something impossible.

Iris (*disappointedly*). You're right. You're always right, poor Felix. (*Stands up.*) What can be keeping Victor so long? Would 235 you mind calling him?

Felix (*jumping up*). Iris, how have I offended you? Oh, I said too much.

Iris (*turning round in front of the mirror*). Oh, I wouldn't call it too much.

Felix. To desire the unattainable. 240 Iris, I was mad to talk to you like that.

Iris. Or, at least, impolite. Really, you know, it's appalling the trouble I'm taking with you. When we're in the company of ladies, we mustn't behave as if we were 245 longing for something which isn't there.

Felix. The unattainable is there.

Iris (*looking round*). Where?

Felix (*pointing to the mirror*). Your image, Iris. 250

Iris (*laughing*). My image? Have you fallen in love with my image? (*Stretching out her hands towards the mirror*) Look, my image has heard you. Embrace it. Kiss it, quickly. 255

Felix. It is as unapproachable as you.

Iris (*turning to him*). I am unapproachable? How do you know?

Felix. If I did not know, I should not love you. 260

Iris. Felix, what a pity that I am so unapproachable.

Felix. Ah Iris, there is no true love except in the unapproachable.

Iris. Do you think so? (*Pulls him by* 265 *the hair and sings.*) "Maiden, we'll fall as well."

Felix. Don't repeat that poem.

Iris. Make one for me, quickly. Something passionate. 269

Felix. "When in the final moment I cried: Death, hark to a mournful lover, Lay your hand where my heart once was, And a single wound you'll discover — I am filled with angel-strength, for A diamond buckler my love's attire is. 275 I am filled with angel-strength, by Iris, Iris, Iris."

Iris. Iris — attire is. How beautiful it is.

Clythie (*behind the scene*). Iris, Iris.

Iris. There she is again. And with 280 that horrible husband of hers. Just as we ...

Clythie (*running in laughing*). Just fancy, Iris, Otakar says ... ah, you've got Felix here. How are you, Felix? Iris, you've been teasing him, haven't you? He's quite red. 285

Otakar (*running in*). I've got you now, Clythie ... Oh, I beg your pardon. Good day, Iris. How are you, my boy?

Felix (*sitting down among the pillows*). Whew.

Iris. How hot you are, Clythie! 290

Clythie.} Otakar chased me.

Otakar.} Clythie flew away, and I had to follow her.

Victor (*entering*). Hallo, there's quite a company here. (*Greets* CLYTHIE. 295

Clythie. Oh, I'm so thirsty.

(*Drinks from a glass through a straw.*

Iris. Take care of yourself, dearest. Victor, see how thin she's got again. You look terrible.

Clythie. Thanks, darling, you're so 300 motherly.

Victor. Were you at the garden-party yesterday?

Clythie. Pooh, yesterday. That's ancient history. 305

Victor. Marvellous weather.

Iris (to CLYTHIE). Just a moment, dearest. (*Arranges her bodice.*) What have you been doing? Your bodice is torn.

Clythie. Perhaps Otakar trod on me. 310

Iris. Trod on you? Up to your throat?

Clythie. Look at him, he's all foot. Aren't you, foot?

Otakar. Eh?

Victor. And what am I? 315

Clythie. You're all tongue.

Iris. Oh, Clythie. And what is Felix?

Clythie. Poor fellow, he's so sad. (*Kneels down to him.*) What is the matter with you, prince? 320

Felix. I'm thinking.

Clythie. Go on. What do you keep thinking about?

Felix. Men's minds were given them to use.

Clythie. And women? 325

Felix. To misuse.

Iris. Oh, very good, Felix.

Clythie (*standing up*). The horrid creature hates me.

Victor. Be careful, Clythie, that's the 330 first step towards love.

Otakar. Eh?

Iris. Felix and love? The idea. Why, he wrote something about women — wait ... 335

Felix. Iris, I implore you.

Iris. "Downwards, downwards, swift and fleet
The pace at which we fly.
The world desires deceit, deceit —
Woman desires to lie." 340

Clythie. Desires what?

Iris. To lie.

Victor. Felix, you rascal, how many women have you already caused to lie?

Otakar. Ha, ha, ha. To lie. I see, of 345 course. To lie. Ha, ha, ha.

Iris (*going on reciting*). "The dream be not frustrated."

Clythie. Wait, Otakar is going to laugh again.

Otakar. Ha, ha, ha. 350

Felix. I won't allow you to read it out. I've got past that stage.

Iris. Felix is frightfully talented. None of you could find a rhyme to "Iris."

Clythie. "Iris, than whom none slyer 355 is."

Felix. Oh ye gods, do stop it.

Otakar. Ha, ha, ha, that's splendid. Iris — slyer is.

Iris (*keeping her temper*). Darling, you 360 have such strange ideas of poetry. But you'd never believe what a beautiful rhyme Felix made to my name. Guess.

Victor. I give it up.

Clythie. Oh tell us, Iris. 365

Iris (*triumphantly*). "A diamond buckler my love's attire is."

Victor. What?

Iris. " ... my love's attire is."

Otakar. Ha, ha, ha. Attire is. What 370 fun.

Iris. Oh, you're horrid. You've no sense of art. I've got no patience with you.

Victor. Felix O, he kicks so.

Iris (*clapping her hands*). Splendid, 375 Victor. You're frightfully witty.

Clythie. Good heavens, Victor's managed to produce a rhyme.

Otakar. Ha, ha, ha. Felix O, he kicks so. That's good. 380

Victor. Pooh, poetry, what is it? Lying or fooling.

Iris. Oh no. It stirs the feelings. I'm fearfully fond of it.

Otakar. Guitar. 385

Clythie. What guitar?

Otakar. Rhymes with Otakar, ha, ha, ha. Good, eh?

Iris. You're fearfully talented, Otakar. Why don't you write poems? 390

Otakar. Me? Hm. What about?

Iris. About love. I adore poetry.

Otakar. Lovely star.

Iris. What lovely star? Whom do you mean?

Otakar. Ha, ha, ha. That's a rhyme.   395

Iris. Otakar, you have such a fearfully poetic soul.

Clythie (yawning). Do stop talking about literature. I'm so heartily sick of it.

Victor. Heartily? Fancy, poor Clythie 400 imagines she's got a heart somewhere.

Iris. Ha, ha, ha. Victor, you're awfully good company. I could give you a kiss. I do so admire witty people. See if you can catch me. *(Runs out.* VICTOR *runs after her.* 405

Clythie. Oh, what a silly creature. What a perfect fright. What an awful figure. Felix?

Felix (jumping up). Yes?

Clythie. How ever could you fall in love with her?   410

Felix. With whom?

Clythie. With that old frump.

Felix. Whom do you mean?

Clythie. Iris, of course.

Felix. I? What can you be thinking 415 of! That's all done with, long ago.

Clythie. I understand. Iris is so fearfully ignorant. Such awful feet. Oh Felix, at your age we still have so many illusions about women. *(Sits down among the pillows.* 420

Felix. I? I assure you, Clythie — upon my honor, I've long since got past that stage.

Clythie. No, Felix, you don't know women. Sit down beside me, will you? You've no idea of what they're like. Their opinions. 425 Their minds. And their bodies. Ugh. You are so young ...

Felix. Oh no. I'm not young, no. I've had so much experience.

Clythie. You must be thoroughly 430 young. That's the fashion now. To be young, to be a butterfly, to be a poet. Is there anything more beautiful in the whole world?

Felix. No, Clythie. The lot of youth is to suffer. And the lot of a poet is to suffer 435 a hundredfold. Upon my honor.

Clythie. The lot of a poet is to be frightfully happy. To enjoy life. Ah Felix, you remind me of my first love.

Felix. Who was that?   440

Clythie. Nobody. None of my loves was the first. Ugh, that Victor. I do hate men so.

Let's be friends, Felix, like two women together.

Felix. Like two women?

Clythie. Love means nothing to you. 445 Love is so common. Ah, I'd like something quite special and pure. Something out of the ordinary. Something new.

Felix. A poem?

Clythie. Yes, that would do. You see 450 how I like you.

Felix. Wait.   *(Jumps up excitedly.*
"Into my heart took flight
As into the eye of a child
A ray of light.   455
When I met her, as a poppy she glowed,
A bloom to the sight,
And her shyness upon me she bestowed."

Clythie (standing up). What's that?

Felix. A poem. The beginning.   460

Clythie. And how does it go on?

Felix. I'll bring you the end in a moment. Now I've got past the stage of everything I've written till now.

                    (Flies off.

Clythie. Bah. *(Turns to* OTAKAR *who,* 465 *in the meanwhile, has been twirling his moustache in huge annoyance.)* Now then, can't you leave those whiskers alone?

Otakar. Be mine. Be mine now.

Clythie. Don't! Ouch!

Otakar. Be mine. We are betrothed. 470 I ... I ...

Clythie. Otakar, you are so handsome.

Otakar. I love you madly.

Clythie. I know. It's delightful the way your heart is beating. Say "ha." 475

Otakar. Ha.

Clythie. Again.

Otakar. Hm. Ha.

Clythie. How that rumbles in your chest. Like thunder. Otakar, you're fearfully 480 strong, aren't you?

Otakar. Cly ... Cly ... Cly ...

Clythie. What is it now?

Otakar. Be mine.

Clythie. Don't be tiresome, please.   485

Otakar. I ... I ...

Clythie. So do I ...

Otakar (catching hold of her). Be mine. I adore you.

Clythie (*running away*). Not a bit of   490
it. I should only spoil my figure. ——
Otakar (*pursuing her*). I . . . I . . . I want . . .
Clythie (*laughing and flying off*). Wait, only
wait. You mustn't be impatient.
Otakar (*flying after her*). Clythie, be   495
mine.   (*Exeunt.*
Vagrant (*standing up*). Whew. Off they go,
    love's motley crew.
How they ogled, how they dallied and dallied;
Ha, ha, the hunted female. Ha, ha, the in-
    sect legs,
Ha, ha, the greedy body behind the silken
    wings.   500
Leave me in peace, I know it. I'll warrant you:
That's — what — they — call — love.

CLYTHIE *flies in from the other side, puts on
    make-up and powders herself by the mirror*

Clythie. Whew! I managed to get away
from him. Ha, ha.
Vagrant. Ha, ha, drawing-room society
    Ha, ha, ha, poetry.   505
Sipping at life's enjoyments through the
    thinnest of straws,
These low-neck delights, these thrills and soft
    ticklings,
Eternal lie of eternal lovers eternally unap-
    peased,
What insects they are!
Clythie (*flying up to him*). Are you a   510
butterfly? (*The Vagrant throws his cap at her.*
Clythie (*flying away*). Aren't you a butterfly?
Vagrant. I am a man.
Clythie. What is that? Is it alive?
Vagrant. Yes.   515
Clythie (*flying up*). Does it love?
Vagrant. Yes. It's a butterfly.
Clythie. How interesting you are. Why do
you wear a black down?
Vagrant. That's dirt.   520
Clythie. Oh, how nice you smell.
Vagrant. That's sweat and dust.
Clythie. Your fragrance intoxicates me. It
is so new.
Vagrant (*throwing his cap at her*). Shoo,   525
you hussy.
Clythie (*flying away*). Catch me. Catch me.

Vagrant. Flighty jade, worthless bag-
bage ——
Clythie (*approaching him*). Let me just   530
smell. Let me just taste. You are so unusual.
Vagrant. I've met the likes of you before,
you minx. Why did I love her? (*Catches hold
of* CLYTHIE.) I caught hold of her insect hands
like that, and begged her to smile at me,   535
and then I let her go. Oh, if I had only killed
her. (*Lets her go.*) Fly away, you wench, I
don't want you.
Clythie (*flying away*). Ugh, how strange you
are!   (*Powders herself in front of the mirror.*
Vagrant. Scented wanton, strumpet,   541
skinny troll, skeleton ——
Clythie (*coming close to him*). Again, again.
It's so lovely, so coarse, so violent.
Vagrant. What, you pest, isn't that   545
enough for you, you white-faced harridan?
Clythie. I love you. Oh, I adore you.
Vagrant (*drawing back from her*). Go, go, go.
You're loathsome.
Clythie. How tiresome you are. Wretch.
                (*Combs her hair by the mirror.*
Iris (*returning beaten*). Something to   551
drink, quick.
Clythie. Where have you been?
Iris (*drinking through a straw*). Outside.
Oh, it's so hot.   555
Clythie. Where did you leave Victor?
Iris. Victor? Which Victor?
Clythie. Why, you went with him ——
Iris. With Victor. Oh no. Aha, I see.
(*Laughs.*) No, that was only fun.   560
Clythie. With Victor?
Iris. Of course. Wait, it'll make you laugh.
He kept running after me, ha, ha, ha.
Clythie. Where did you leave him?
Iris. I'm telling you. He kept running   565
after me like mad, and suddenly, ha, ha, ha, a
bird flew along and ate him up.
Clythie. Never.
Iris. As true as I'm standing here. Oh, it
did make me laugh.   570
        (*Throws herself down among the pillows
            and hides her face.*
Clythie. What's the matter with you?
Iris. Ha, ha, ha. Oh, these men.
Clythie. Do you mean Victor?

Iris. No, Otakar. Victor was eaten by a bird. Just fancy. Immediately after- 575 wards, your Otakar came flying up, oh, the look in his eyes, all on fire, and then, ha, ha, ha ——

Clythie. What then?

Iris. He came right after me. Be mine. I love you madly, ha, ha, ha. 580

Clythie. Iris, what did you do?

Iris. Ha, ha, ha. I lo — lo — love you fearfully. You mu — mu — must be mi — mi — mine.

Felix (*flying up with a poem in his hands*). Clythie, here it is. Listen. (*Reads* 585 *with boundless emotion.*)

"Into my heart took flight
    As into the eye of a child
    A ray of light."

Iris (*with her head among the pillows, laughing hysterically*). Ha, ha, ha.

Felix (*stopping reading*). What is it? 590

Iris (*sobbing*). What a coarse fellow. Fie, for shame. I would have strangled him.

Clythie. Otakar?

Felix. Listen, Clythie. This is quite a new style: 595

"When I met her, as a poppy she glowed,
A bloom to the sight,
And her shyness upon me she bestowed.
''Tis I,' she said, 'you know me not.
What I am, I myself cannot tell, 600
I'm a child and I blossom, I'm life and I swell,
I'm a woman and lure, so bewildered am
    I ——'"

Iris (*standing up*). Is my hair fearfully untidy?

Clythie. Fearfully. Wait, dearest. 605 (*Puts her hair straight, then aside.*) Beast.

Iris. You're angry, aren't you? Ha, ha, ha, Otakar loves wond-er-ful-ly. (*Flies off.*

Felix. Now, Clythie, this is the best part: "I'm a child and I blossom, I'm life and I swell, I'm a woman and lure, so bewildered am I ——" 611

Clythie. Leave off. (*Aside*) The beast! (*Flies away.*) Where is somebody new?

Felix (*after her*). Wait, wait. This is just where love comes in. 615

Vagrant. Fool!

Felix. What's that? Ah, here's somebody. That's good. I'll read you the end. "I'm a woman and lure, so bewildered am I, Great world, what does it signify ...?" 620

Vagrant (*throwing his cap at him*). Shoo.

Felix (*flying about*).

" ... What does it signify,
That today my blood is all aglow?
I'm a woman, I love. I am life and I bloom.
I'm a child, and love for the first time I know."
Do you understand? That is Clythie, 626 Clythie, Clythie. (*Flies off.*

Vagrant (*stretching out his hands to the auditorium*). Ha, ha, ha, butterflies.

Curtain

ACT II

The Marauders

The scene represents a sandy hillock, with a scanty growth of grass, the size of a tree-trunk. On the left side, the lair of the ICHNEUMON FLY; [1] *on the right side, the deserted cavity of a cricket. The* VAGRANT *lies asleep in the proscenium. A* CHRYS-ALIS *is fastened to a blade of grass. The* CHRYSALIS *is attacked by a gang of rapacious insects. From the left, a small* BEETLE *runs in, and unfastens it from the blade of grass. From the right, a second one runs out, chases the first one off, and tries to snatch the* CHRYSALIS *away. From the prompt-box, a third leaps forth, chases the second one away and drags the* CHRYSALIS *off*

Chrysalis. I...I...I... (*The third rapacious* BEETLE *plunges headlong into the prompt-box. From the left, the first, and from the right, the second* BEETLES *run in and wrangle about the* CHRYSALIS. *The third darts out of the box and chases them both away, whereupon it takes the* CHRYSALIS *itself.*) The whole earth is bursting. I am being born.

[1] A genus of small four-winged insects similar to saw-flies and noted for their habit of preying upon other insects.

Vagrant (raising his head). What's that?

    (*The third* BEETLE *rushes into the box.*

Chrysalis. Something great is at hand. 5

Vagrant. That's good. (*Lays his head down.*)

A pause

A Man's Voice (behind the scenes). What
are you up to?

A Woman's Voice. I?

1st Voice. You.   10

2d Voice. I?

1st Voice. You.

2d Voice. I?

1st Voice. You. Clumsy slattern.

2d Voice. You wretch.   15

1st Voice. Fathead.

2d Voice. Dolt.

1st Voice. Slut. Frump.

2d Voice. Muck-rake.

1st Voice. Take care. Look out.   20

2d Voice. Slowly.

1st Voice. Lo . . . lo . . . ook out.

*A large ball of manure rolls on to the stage,
pushed by a pair of* BEETLES

Male Beetle. Nothing's happened to it?

Female Beetle. Oh dear, I do hope not. I'm
all of a tremble.   25

Male Beetle. Ha, ha, that's our capital. Our
nest-egg. Our stock-in-trade. Our all.

Female Beetle. Oh, what a lovely little pile,
what a treasure, what a beautiful little ball,
what a precious little fortune.   30

Male Beetle. It's our only joy. To think
how we've saved and scraped, toiled and
moiled, denied ourselves, gone without this,
stinted ourselves that ——

Female Beetle. — and worked our legs off 35
and drudged and plodded to get it together
and ——

Male Beetle. — and seen it grow and added
to it, bit by bit. Oh, what a boon it is.

Female Beetle. Our very own.   40

Male Beetle. Our life.

Female Beetle. All our own work.

Male Beetle. Just sniff at it, old girl. Oh,
how lovely. Just feel the weight of it. And
it's ours.   45

Female Beetle. What a godsend!

Male Beetle. What a blessing!

Chrysalis. The fetters of the world are
rended,
Now another life is blended.
I am born. (*The Vagrant raises his head.*) 50

Female Beetle. Husband.

Male Beetle. What is it?

Female Beetle. Ha, ha, ha, ha.

Male Beetle. Ha, ha. Ha, ha. Wife.

Female Beetle. What is it?   55

Male Beetle. Ha, ha, ha, it's fine to own
something. Your property. The dream of
your life. The fruit of your labors.

Female Beetle. Ha, ha, ha.

Male Beetle. I'm going off my head with 60
joy. I'm . . . I'm . . . I'm . . . going off my head
with sheer worry. Upon my soul, I'm going
off my head.

Female Beetle. Why?

Male Beetle. With worry. Now we've 65
got our little pile. I've been so much looking
forward to it, and now we've got it, we'll have
to make another one. Nothing but work,
work, work.

Female Beetle. Why another one?   70

Male Beetle. You stupid creature, so that we
can have two, of course.

Female Beetle. Ah, two. Quite right.

Male Beetle. Ah, just fancy, two of them.
At least two. Let's say even three. You 75
know, everyone who's made one pile has to
make another.

Female Beetle. So that he can have two.

Male Beetle. Or even three.

Female Beetle. Husband.   80

Male Beetle. Well, what is it?

Female Beetle. I'm scared. Suppose someone was to steal it from us.

Male Beetle. What?

Female Beetle. Our little pile. Our joy. 85
Our all.

Male Beetle. Our pi . . . pile? My goodness,
don't frighten me.

Female Beetle. We . . . we . . . we can't roll it
about with us, till we've made another one. 90

Male Beetle. I tell you what, we'll invest it.
In-vest it. We'll store it up. We'll bury it
nicely. Wait a bit, in some hole, in some

cranny. Out of harm's way, you know. It
must be put aside.   95

Female Beetle. I only hope nobody'll find it.

Male Beetle. Eh? Not likely. What, steal it
from us? Our little pile. Our treasure. Our
little round nest-egg.

Female Beetle. Our precious little store.   100
Our life. Our whole concern.

Male Beetle. Wait, stay here and watch —
watch it. Keep an eye on it.   (*Runs off.*)

Female Beetle. Where are you off to now?

Male Beetle. To look for a hole...a   105
little hole...a deep hole...to bury it in. Our
precious gold...out of harm's way. Be
care...ful.   (*Exit.*

Female Beetle. Husband, husband, come
here...Wait a bit...There's...Hus-   110
band...He can't hear me. And I've found
such a nice hole. Husband. He's gone.
And I've found such a beautiful little hole.
What a stupid he is. The booby. The fool.
If only I could just have a look at it. No,   115
I mustn't leave you, little pile. If I could...
only...peep. Little pile, dear little pile, wait
a moment, I'll be back at once. I'll only have
just a peep, and I'll be back again. (*Runs to
the back and turns round.*) Little pile,   120
you'll be good and wait for me, won't you?
I'll be back at once, little pile —

(*Enters the lair of the* ICHNEUMON FLY.
Chrysalis. Oh, to be born, to be born. The
new world.   (*The* VAGRANT *stands up.*

A Strange Beetle (*running in from the wings,
where he has been lurking*). They've gone.   125
Now's my chance.   (*Rolls the pile away.*

Vagrant. Here, don't knock me over.

Strange Beetle. Out of the way, citizen.

Vagrant. What's that you're rolling
along?   130

Strange Beetle. Ha, ha, ha. That's my pile.
Capital. Gold.

Vagrant (*drawing back*). That gold of yours
smells.

Strange Beetle. Gold doesn't smell.   135
Roll along, pile, off you go. Bestir yourself.
Come on. Possession's nine points of the law.
Ha, ha, ha, my boy.

Vagrant. What's that?

Strange Beetle. Ah, it's nice to own   140

something. (*Rolls the pile to the left.*) My
treasure. You lovely nest-egg. My jewel. My
all. What a thing to possess. A little fortune
to invest. To bury carefully. Lo-ok out. (*Exit.*

Vagrant. To possess? Why not.   145
Everyone likes something of his own.

Female Beetle (*returning*). Oh dear, oh dear.
Someone's living there. A little chrysalis.
We can't put you there, pile. Where is the
pile? Oh, where has my pile gone to?   150
Where is our dear little pile?

Vagrant. Why, just this minute...

Female Beetle (*rushing upon him*). Thief,
thief. What have you done with my pile?

Vagrant. I'm telling you, just this min-   155
ute...

Female Beetle. You villain, give it here.
Hand it back.

Vagrant. Just this minute some gentleman
rolled it over there.   160

Female Beetle. What gentleman? Who?

Vagrant. A pot-bellied fellow, a fat, round
man...

Female Beetle. My husband.

Vagrant. A surly chap with crooked   165
feet, a vulgar, conceited person.

Female Beetle. That's my husband.

Vagrant. And he said it was nice to own
something and to bury something.

Female Beetle. That's him. He must   170
have found another hole. (*Calls out.*) Husband, wait a bit. Husband. Darling. Where
is the stupid creature?

Vagrant. That's where he rolled it to.

Female Beetle. The booby. Couldn't he   175
have called me? (*Rushes to the left.*) Husband,
wait a bit. The pile. The pi-i-i-ile.   (*Exit.*

Vagrant. This is a different one, that's clear
        straightway.
This one belongs to the steadier classes.
Allow me, I was a little drunk.   180
I quite thought they were all butterflies,
Beautiful butterflies, a little bit crazed,
Cream of the world, always pairing.
You interesting ladies and their wooers,
Ha, ha, these insects panting after a morsel of
        bliss,   185
Leave me in peace with such gentry.
These others at least smell of honest labor.

They don't want to enjoy, they only want to
    possess something.
They aren't gallant, but then they are human.
Wisely earth behaves, trusting only in what
    lasts,   190
Humbly building its happiness, even if it were
    of manure;
If work is not fragrant, fragrant is the gain.
You love for yourself, you build for all,
You labor for others, and if you're stingy,
Well, stinginess is a virtue, when it's for the
    family.   195
The family has its rights, the family sanctifies
    everything,
Even theft, if need be, for, after all, there are
    children.
That's how it is, I tell you, and that's the whole
    point:
A man will do anything to preserve his kin-
    dred.
    Chrysalis (shouting). Upon the world pre-
    pare more space;   200
Something huge will now take place.
    Vagrant (turning to it). What's that?
    Chrysalis. I'm being born.
    Vagrant. That's good. And what are you
going to be?   205
    Chrysalis. I don't know. I don't know.
Something great.
    Vagrant. Aha!
        (*Lifts it up and fastens it on to a blade
        of grass.*
    Chrysalis. I'll do something amazing.
    Vagrant. What's that?   210
    Chrysalis. I'm being born.
    Vagrant. I praise you, chrysalis, for that. In
    fervid urge
All things in the world are toiling for their
    birth,
Desiring to be, desiring to live, desiring to
    last,
And let them feel what they will,   215
'Tis only one thing: the dire bliss of being.
    Chrysalis. Let the whole world give ear;
        The mighty moment is here,
          When I ... when I ...
    Vagrant. What?   220
    Chrysalis. Nothing. I don't know yet. I
desire to do something great.

    Vagrant. Great? Something great? Good,
    make yourself drunk with that:
These good folk with their pile won't under-
    stand you.
Small and full is the pile, great and empty are
    promises ...   225
    Chrysalis. Something unbounded.
    Vagrant. And yet, chrysalis, this somehow
    pleases me in you.
Something great, happen. Only it must be
    great.
What will crawl from you, chrysalis? Why
    don't you bestir yourself?
    Chrysalis. The whole world will be   230
astounded when I am born.
    Vagrant. Do it then. I'll wait. (*Sits down.*
    *Ichneumon Fly (from behind, with long quiet
strides, dragging the corpse of a cricket to its lair).*
Look, larva. Daddy's bringing you some-
thing nice.   (*Enters the hole.*
    Chrysalis (shouting). What pain. The pangs
    of birth   235
        Now bursts the mighty earth
        That it may set me free.
    Vagrant. Be born.
    Ichneumon Fly (returning from the hole).
No, no, daughter, you must eat. You mustn't
come out, it wouldn't do at all. Daddy'll 240
soon be here and he'll bring you something
nice, eh? What would you like, you greedy
little girl?
    Larva (in front of the hole). Daddy, I feel
bored here.   245
    Ichneumon Fly. Ha, ha, that's a nice thing.
Come and give me a kiss. Papa'll bring you
something tasty. What, you want another
cricket? Ha, ha, not at all a bad idea of yours.
    Larva. I should like ... I don't know. 250
    Ichneumon Fly. Good heavens, how clever
of you, larva. I must give you something
for that. Tata, my child, daddy must go to
work now, and get something for his darling,
for his pretty little baby. Go in now, 255
my pet. Have a nice feed.   (*Exit larva.*
    Ichneumon Fly (approaching the VAGRANT
with long strides). Who are you?
    Vagrant (jumps up and retreats). I.
    Ichneumon Fly. Are you eatable?
    Vagrant. No — I don't think so. 260

Ichneumon Fly (*sniffing at him*). You're not fresh enough. Who are you?

Vagrant. A vagabond.

Ichneumon Fly (*bowing slightly*). Have you any children?   265

Vagrant. No, I don't think so.

Ichneumon Fly. Ah, did you see her?

Vagrant. Whom?

Ichneumon Fly. My larva. Charming, eh? A smart child. And how she grows. 270 What an appetite she has, ha, ha. Children are a great joy, aren't they?

Vagrant. Everyone says so.

Ichneumon Fly. Aren't they? When you have them, you do at least know whom 275 you're working for. If you have a child, then you must strive, work, struggle. That's real life, eh? Children want to grow, to eat, to feast, to play, don't they? Aren't I right?

Vagrant. Children want a lot.   280

Ichneumon Fly. Would you believe that I take her two or three crickets every day?

Vagrant. To whom?

Ichneumon Fly. To my child. Charming, eh? And so clever. Do you think she eats 285 them all up? No, only the softest bits, while they're still alive, ha, ha. A splendid child, eh?

Vagrant. I should think so.

Ichneumon Fly. I'm proud of her. 289 Really proud. Just like her daddy, eh? She takes after me, you know. Ha, ha, and I'm gossiping here, instead of getting to work. Oh, the fuss and running about. But as long as we do it for somebody, what does it matter? Aren't I right?   295

Vagrant. I suppose you are.

Ichneumon Fly. A pity you aren't eatable. Really it's a pity, you know. I must take her something, mustn't I? (*Fingering the* CHRYSALIS) What's this?   300

Chrysalis (*shouting*). I proclaim the rebirth of the world.

Ichneumon Fly. You aren't ripe yet. No good, is it?

Chrysalis. I'll create something.   305

Ichneumon Fly. It's a worry to bring up children. A great worry, isn't it? To rear a family, just imagine. To feed those poor little mites. To provide for them, to secure

their future, eh? It's no trifle, is it? 310 Well, I must be off now. Good day to you. Pleased to have met you, sir. (*Runs off.*) Tata, baby, I'll be back soon.   (*Exit.*

Vagrant. To provide for them. To feed these hungry little mouths.

That's the demands of a family. And to take live crickets to them.   315

And yet even a cricket wants to live, and kills nobody.

The good creature, he extols life with his humble melody.

I can't make this out.

Larva (*crawling out of the hole*). Daddy, daddy.   320

Vagrant. So you're the larva? Let's have a look at you.

Larva. How ugly you are.

Vagrant. Why?

Larva. I don't know. Oh, how bored 325 I am! I should like . . . I should like . . .

Vagrant. What else?

Larva. I don't know. To tear something up, something alive . . . Ah, it makes me writhe.

Vagrant. What's the matter with you? 330

Larva. Ugly, ugly, ugly.   (*Crawls away.*

Vagrant. Feeding a family like that. I can't make it out.

This is a thing about insects that a man can't help condemning.

Enter the MALE BEETLE

Male Beetle. Come along, old girl, I've found a hole. Where are you? Where's my 335 pile? Where's my wife?

Vagrant. Your wife? Do you mean that old harridan? That fat, ugly chatter-box ——

Male Beetle. That's her. Where's my pile?

Vagrant. —— that bad-tempered, 340 dirty rag-bag.

Male Beetle. That's her, that's her. She had my pile. What has she done with my pile?

Vagrant. Why, your better half went to look for you.   345

Male Beetle. And where is my pile?

Vagrant. That large stinking ball?

Male Beetle. Yes, yes, my nest-egg. My

capital. My savings. Where is my beautiful pile? I left my wife with it. 350

Vagrant. There was some gentleman who rolled it away yonder. It looked as if it was his.

Male Beetle. I don't care what he did with my wife. But where is my pile?

Vagrant. I keep telling you. The 355 gentleman rolled it away. Your wife wasn't here at the time.

Male Beetle. Where was she? Where is she?

Vagrant. She went after him. She thought it was you. She was shouting for you. 360

Male Beetle. My pile?

Vagrant. No, your wife.

Male Beetle. I'm not asking about her. Where is my pile, I say?

Vagrant. The gentleman rolled it away. 365

Male Beetle. What, rolled it away? My pile? God in heaven! Catch him. Catch him. Thief. Murder. (*Flings himself to the ground.*) My hard-earned fortune. They've killed me. I'd rather give up my life 370 than that ball of golden manure. (*Jumps up.*) Help. Catch him. Mur-der.

(*Dashes off to the left.*

Vagrant. Ha, ha, ha! Murder. Crime.

Burst, O ye clouds,

For the stolen pile. In such appalling grief

There is only one solace: That the beetle's pile

Will never belong to anyone but another muck-

rake. (*Sits down on one side.* 376

Male Voice (*behind the scenes*). Look out, woman, take care you don't stumble. Here we are, here we are. This is where we live, this is our new little home. Oh, look out, you 380 haven't hurt yourself, have you?

Female Voice. No, Cricket, don't be absurd.

Male Voice. But darling, you must be careful. When you're expecting ——

Enter a MALE CRICKET *with a pregnant* FEMALE CRICKET

Male Cricket. And now open the peep- 385 hole. There. How do you like it?

Female Cricket. Oh, Cricket, how tired I am.

Male Cricket. Sit down, sit down, darling, sit down. Take great care of yourself now.

Female Cricket (*sitting down*). What a 390

long way. And all that moving, too. No, Cricket, really it's not right of you.

Male Cricket. Oh, darling, come, come. Look, darling, look.

Female Cricket. Now don't get angry, 395 you horrid man.

Male Cricket. I won't say another word, really I won't. Fancy, Mrs. Cricket won't take care of herself, and in her state, too. What do you think of her? 400

Female Cricket (*tearfully*). You naughty man, how can you joke about it?

Male Cricket. But darling, when I'm so happy. Just fancy, all those little crickets, the noise, the chirping, ha, ha, ha. Darling, 405 I'm mad with joy.

Female Cricket. You ... you ... silly boy. Look, daddy, ha, ha.

Male Cricket. Ha, ha, ha. And how do you like it? 410

Female Cricket. It's nice. Is this our new house?

Male Cricket. Our little nest, our villa, our little show, our, ha, ha, our residence.

Female Cricket. Will it be dry? Who 415 built it?

Male Cricket. Why, goodness me, another cricket has been living here.

Female Cricket. Fancy. And why has he moved? 420

Male Cricket. Ha, ha, ha, he moved away. He moved away. Don't you know where to? Have a guess.

Female Cricket. I don't know. Oh dear, what a long time you are before you say 425 anything. Do tell me, Cricket, quickly.

Male Cricket. Well then — yesterday a bird came and fastened him on to a thorn. Upon my soul, darling, from end to end. Just imagine. His feet were wriggling there, 430 ha, ha, he was still alive. So when I came along, I at once saw that it would suit us. So we're moving into his house. By Jove, what a slice of luck. Ha, ha, what do you think of it? 435

Female Cricket. And he's still alive? Ugh, how horrible.

Male Cricket. Eh? Oh, what a godsend for us. Tralala, tratra, tralala tra. Wait a bit,

we'll hang up our door-plate. (*From a*
bag he takes out a plate with the inscription
"CRICKET, MUSIC DEALER.") Where
shall we hang it? Up there? More to the
right? More to the left?

Female Cricket. A little high. And you say
that his feet are still wriggling?   445

Male Cricket (kneeling and pointing). I'm
telling you: like that.

Female Cricket. Brr. Where is he?

Male Cricket. Would you like to see it?

Female Cricket. Yes, I would. No, I   450
wouldn't. Is it horrible?

Male Cricket. Ha, ha, ha, I should think so.
Is it hanging properly?

Female Cricket. Yes. Cricket, I have such
a queer feeling ——   455

Male Cricket (running up to her). Good
heavens, perhaps it's . . . it's already . . .

Female Cricket. Oh dear, I'm so frightened.

Male Cricket. But darling, why be frightened? Every lady ——   460

Female Cricket. It's all very well for you to
talk. (*Bursts into tears.*) Cricket, will you
always love me?

Male Cricket. Of course, darling. Dear me,
don't cry. Come, come.   465

Female Cricket (sobbing). Show me how his
feet wriggled.

Male Cricket. Like this.

Female Cricket. Ha, ha, how funny that
must be.   470

Male Cricket. Well, well, you see there's
nothing to cry about. (*Sits down beside her.*)
We'll furnish this place beautifully. And as
soon as we can manage it, we'll put up
some . . .   475

Female Cricket. Curtains.

Male Cricket. Curtains as well. Ha, ha, ha,
curtains, of course. How clever of you to
think of it. Give me a kiss.

Female Cricket. Never mind that now.   480
Go on, you're so silly.

Male Cricket. Of course I am. (*Jumps up.*)
Guess what I've bought.

Female Cricket. Curtains.

Male Cricket. No, something smaller.   485
(*Searches in his pockets.*) Where did I . . .

Female Cricket. Quick, quick, let me see.
  (*The* MALE CRICKET *from his pocket
  takes a child's rattle and shakes it
  with both hands.*

Female Cricket. Oh, how sweet. Cricket,
give it to me.

Male Cricket (shaking it and singing).

There was born a little   490
Cricket, Cricket, Cricket.
By his little bed there stood
Mama, mama, daddy.
Their two heads together
They banged, banged, banged ——   495
Prettily his lullaby they
Twanged, twanged, twanged.
                    Ha, ha, ha.

Female Cricket. Lend it to me, quickly. Oh,
daddy, I'm so pleased.   500

Male Cricket. Listen then, darling . . .

Female Cricket (shaking it and singing).
Cricket, Cricket, Cricket.

Male Cricket. Now I must run round a little.
Let people know I'm here. Knock at the
doors.   505

Female Cricket (shaking it and singing).
They banged, banged, banged.

Male Cricket. I must get some introductions,
fix up orders, have a look round. Give me
the rattle, I'll use it on my way.

Female Cricket. And what about me?   510
(*Tearfully*) You won't leave me?

Male Cricket. Rattle for me. And I expect
a neighbor will be coming along. You must
have a little chat with him, ask about the children, and all that, you know. And we will   515
wait for the thingumabob. Till I come back.

Female Cricket. You bad boy.

Male Cricket. Ha, ha, ha. Now, darling,
be careful. It won't be long now, my pet.
                    (*Runs off.*

Female Cricket (shaking the rattle, the MALE
CRICKET *answering in the distance*). There   520
was born a little . . . Cricket . . . I feel so frightened.

Vagrant (standing up). Don't be frightened.
Small things are born easily.

Female Cricket. Who's there? Ugh, a   525
beetle. You don't bite?

Vagrant. No.

Female Cricket. And how are the children?

Vagrant. I have none. I have none. Never
　have I in wedlock

Hatched the tender love of a family, 530

Nor have I known the joy of my own roof
　above me,

Nor even the warm delight at another's ill-
　success.

Female Cricket. Oh dear, haven't you any
children? That's a pity. (*Shakes the rattle.*)
Cricket. Cricket. Oh, he doesn't answer. 535
And why did you never marry, beetle?

Vagrant. Selfishness, dear madam, selfish-
　ness. I ought to be ashamed of it.

The egoist seeks comfort in his solitude.

He need not love so much, or hate so
　much,

Or grudge others their small share of space.

Female Cricket. Yes, yes, these men. 541
(*Rattles.*) Cricket, Cricket, Cricket.

Chrysalis (*shouting*). Within me I bear the
future. I ... I ...

Vagrant (*approaching*). Be born. 545

Chrysalis. I will achieve something illustrious.

Female Beetle (*running in*). Isn't my husband
there? Where is the stupid man? Where is
our pile? 550

Female Cricket. Oh, madam, can you play
with it? Do let me see it.

Female Beetle. It's not to play with, it's our
future, our nest-egg, our all. My husband, the
clumsy creature, has gone off with it. 555

Female Cricket. Oh dear, perhaps he's run
away from you.

Female Beetle. And where is yours?

Female Cricket. He's away on business.
(*Rattles.*) Cricket. Cricket. 560

Female Beetle. Fancy him leaving you all
alone like that, poor thing. And you're expecting ...

Female Cricket. Oh dear!

Female Beetle. So young, too. And 565
aren't you making a pile?

Female Cricket. What for?

Female Beetle. A pile, that's for the family.
That's the future. That's your whole life.

Female Cricket. Oh no. My whole life 570

is to have my own little house, my nest, a little
place of my own. And curtains. And children. And to have my Cricket. My own
home. That's all.

Female Beetle. How can you live with- 575
out a pile?

Female Cricket. What would we do with
it?

Female Beetle. Roll it about with you everywhere. I tell you, there's nothing like 580
a pile for holding a man.

Female Cricket. Oh no, a little house.

Female Beetle. A pile, I tell you.

Female Cricket. A little house.

Female Beetle. Dear me, I should so 585
much like to have a chat with you. You're so
nice ...

Female Cricket. And what about your children?

Female Beetle. If only I had my pile. 590
Pi-pi-pi-le. Pi-pi —— (*Exit.*

Female Cricket. Ugh, what a frump. And
her husband's run away from her, ha, ha, ha.
They twanged, twanged, twanged. I — I —
have such a queer ... (*Clearing up by the* 595
door) Ha, ha, ha, how his feet wriggle.

Ichneumon Fly (*running in from the wings*).
Aha. (*Approaches her with long, quiet strides,
takes a dagger from his coat-tails, pierces the*
FEMALE CRICKET *with a great lunge and drags
her to his lair.*) Out of it.

Vagrant (*drawing back*). Oh ... oh. Murder. 600

Ichneumon Fly (*in the entrance to his lair*).
Look, daughter. Come quick and have a look
at what daddy's bringing you.

Vagrant. He's killed her. And I ... I stood
there like a log. Good heavens, she didn't
even utter a sound. And nobody 605
shouted with horror. Nobody ran to help her.

Parasite (*entering from the back*). Bravo,
comrade, that's just my opinion too.

Vagrant. To perish so defenseless.

Parasite. That's just what I say. I've 610
been looking on for quite a while, but I could-
n't do a thing like that. No, I couldn't.
Everyone wants to live, don't they?

Vagrant. Who are you?

Parasite. I? Oh, nothing really. I'm 615

a poor man. An orphan. They call me a parasite.

Vagrant. How can anyone dare to kill like that?

Parasite. That's exactly what I say. 620 Do you think he needs it? Do you think he's hungry, like me? Not a bit of it. He kills to add to his store. He collects things. It's a scandal, isn't it? Isn't this a piece of injustice? Why has one got a store while an- 625 other starves? Why has he got a dagger while I've only got these bare hands? Aren't I right?

Vagrant. I should say so.

Parasite. That's what I say. There's 630 no equality. For instance, I don't kill anyone. My jaws are too tender. I haven't got the necessary attupt — appart — appurtenances. I'm merely hungry. Is that right?

Vagrant. Killing shouldn't be allowed. 635

Parasite. My very words, comrade. Or, at any rate, collecting things shouldn't be allowed. You eat your fill and you've got enough. Collecting things is robbing them who can't collect things. Eat your fill 640 and have done with it. Then there'd be enough for all, wouldn't there now?

Vagrant. I don't know.

Parasite. But I'm telling you.

Ichneumon Fly (returning from his lair). Eat it up, baby, eat it up. Choose 645 what you like. Haven't you a nice daddy, eh?

Parasite. Good day to you, sir.

Ichneumon Fly. How are you? How are you? Eatable?   *(Sniffs at him.*

Parasite. Ha, ha, you're joking, sir. 650 Why me?

Ichneumon Fly. Get out, you filthy creature. You scamp. What do you want here? Clear off.

Parasite. Ha, ha, that's what I say, 655 sir.   *(Cowers.*

Ichneumon Fly (to the Vagrant). Good day, sir — Well, did you see that?

Vagrant. Yes.

Ichneumon Fly. A fine piece of work, 660 eh? Ha, ha, it's not everyone who could do that. Ah, my boy, for that you want *(taps his forehead)* expert knowledge. Enterprise. I-ni-

tiative. And foresight. And love for work, let me tell you. 665

Parasite (approaching). Just what I say.

Ichneumon Fly. My good sir, if you want to keep alive, you've got to fight your way. There's your future. There's your family. And then, you know, there's a certain 670 amount of ambition. A strong personality is bound to assert itself. Aren't I right?

Parasite. That's what I say, sir.

Ichneumon Fly. Of course, of course. Make your way in the world, use the talent 675 that's in you, that's what I call a useful life.

Parasite. Absolutely, sir.

Ichneumon Fly. Hold your tongue, you disgusting object, I'm not talking to you.

Parasite. Just what I say, sir. 680

Ichneumon Fly. And how it cheers you up, when you fulfil your duty like that. When you perform your job. When you feel that you're not living in vain. It's so elevating, isn't it? Well, good day to you, sir. I must be off 685 again. My best respects. *(Runs off.)* Larva, au revoir.   *(Exit.*

Parasite. The old murderer. Believe me, it was all I could do not to fly at his throat. Yes, sir, I'd work too, if need be. But why 690 should I work when someone else has more than he can consume? I've got initiative too, ha, ha, but here *(pats his stomach)* I'm hungry, that's what I am, hungry, I tell you. A fine state of things, eh? 695

Vagrant. Anything for a piece of meat.

Parasite. That's just what I say. Anything for a piece of meat, and a poor man's got nothing. It's against nature. Everyone should have what he can eat, eh? 700

Vagrant (picking up the rattle and shaking it). Poor creature, poor creature, poor creature.

Parasite. That's it. Everyone wants to live.

    (Behind the scenes there is a chirping in reply.

Male Cricket (running in shaking a rattle). Here I am, my pet, here, here, here. Where are you, darling? Guess what hubby's bought you. 705

Ichneumon Fly (appearing behind him). Aha.

Vagrant. Look out. Look out.

Parasite (stopping him). Don't interfere,

mate. Don't get mixed up in it. What must be, must be.   710

Male Cricket. But mummy?

Ichneumon Fly (with a great lunge piercing him and carrying him toward his lair). Daughter. Larva, what's your kind daddy bringing you now, eh?   (*Enters his lair.*

Vagrant (raising his fist). Oh, Almighty God, how can You allow it?   715

Parasite. Just what I say. That's the third cricket he's had already, and me nothing. And that's what the likes of us are expected to put up with.

Ichneumon Fly (running out from his lair). No, no, baby, I've got no time. Daddy   720 must go back to work. Eat, eat, eat. Be quiet now, I'll be back in an hour. (*Runs off.*

Parasite. I'm simply boiling over. The old scoundrel. (*Approaching the lair*) What injustice. What a disgrace. I'll show him,   725 that I will. Just you wait! Has he gone? I must have a look.   (*Enters the lair.*

Vagrant. Murder and again murder. Heart, cease your beating.
They are only insects, they are only beetles.
It is only a tiny drama between blades of grass,   730
Nothing but insect-war, nothing but beetle-doings;
Insects live one way, human beings another.
Ah, to be among human beings again. Then a man can at least see
That there is, after all, something better than this insect crew.
Man does not crave merely to devour, he craves to create and build,   735
He indeed has some aim, and raises his pile —
No, that's the beetles again, ugh. I can't get it out of my head —
A pile for the beetles, but for human beings there are more humane ideals.
Peaceable man extols life by his whole life.
So little suffices for happiness. To have a home, however small,   740
To harm nobody, to have few worries and to beget children,
For indeed life desires only life, and sweet it is to regard
How you are living, and how your neighbor's ... feet ... are wriggling —

No, that's the crickets again. Why do I keep getting muddled?
I'm confusing him with the beetles. The narrow, paltry existence,   745
The ludicrous joy of crickets would not satisfy man.
Man desires something more than just to eat his fill
And gratefully, contentedly to munch a morsel of happiness.
Life calls for men, life calls for heroes, life calls for struggle.
If you would overcome life, seize it with a strong grip;   750
If you would be fully a man, you dare not be puny and weak;
If you would live, then rule; if you would eat, then ... kill —
No, that's the ichneumon fly. Silence. Do you not hear
How throughout the world feverish jowls are working?
Chew-chew-chew, the blood-stained, sated smacking of lips   755
Over the still living morsel. Life is the prey of life.

Chrysalis (tossing to and fro). I feel something great. Something great.

Vagrant. What is great?

Chrysalis. To be born. To live.   760

Vagrant. Chrysalis, Chrysalis, I will not desert you.

Parasite (rolling out of the lair, enormously fat, and hiccoughing). Ha, ha, ha. Ha, ha, ha, hup, ha, ha, ha. Ha, ha, ha. Hup, that's — ha, ha, ha, hup, the old miser, he —   765 hup — had stores — hup — for that white-faced — hup — daughter of his. Hup, ha, ha, ha. Ha, ha, ha, hup. I feel quite — hup. I'm going to burst. (*Hiccoughs.*) Why, what a — hup — confounded fit of the hic-   770 coughs. Sir, I'm some — somebody, too. It's not everyone who could, eh — hup — eh? Eat as much as that, eh?

Vagrant. And what about the Larva?

Parasite. Ha, ha, ha, hup, ha, ha, ha.   775 Ha, ha, ha, I, hup — , I gobbled her up, too. The table of nature is spread for all. Hup, hup, hup.

Curtain

ACT III

The Ants

A green forest-glade

Vagrant (seated, in thought).
Enough, enough you have seen. You have
    seen all creatures
Sucking like lice at the great body of creation
In a fearful craving to increase their share
By depriving others. You have seen enough.
                      (Pause.
And am I myself any different from the insects?
I am a cockroach, and from the dust I gather
    crumbs   6
That others have left. That is your life,
Fit for nothing, for nothing, not even fit
To be devoured by somebody.   9
    Chrysalis (shouting).
Make room. Make room. I'm being born.
From my prison I'll set the whole world free.
What a gigantic thought!
    Vagrant. This eternal wrangling about one's
    tiny self,
This greedy bustle, this insect desire
To perpetuate one's own insignificance in one's
    own species —   15
I will not, I will not. Accursed magic,
I long to tread human paths again,
Ah, human paths. After my wandering,
When will ye greet me again, ye sign-boards
Which in human speech betoken   20
Parish and district, province and state?
Brain, tarry a while. First the parish,
Then the district, then the land, the nation
And native country and mankind; and all this
    is greater
Than any self. Yes, this is the whole gist of
    it —   25
That insect selfishness knows only itself
And comprehends not that there is anything
    more,
Parish and district, the whole community.
    Chrysalis. O pangs of creation,
The tormenting thirst   30
For a great deed.
    Vagrant (jumping up).
The whole community. Now I have found
    you,

Notion of humanity. We are only corn-grains
Of a great harvest which belongs to all.
Tiny self, there is something above you,   35
Call it nation, mankind or state,
Call it how you will, if only you serve it:
You are naught. The greatest worth of living
Is to sacrifice one's life.   *(Sits down.*
    Chrysalis. The hour of salvation draws nigh.
Great tokens and great words   41
Herald my advent.
    Vagrant. Great is man by his great indebted-
    ness.
He is only whole where he is part of a whole,
And lives humanly if he gives his life   45
For something greater than himself. Call it
    how you will
If only you serve for this.
    Chrysalis (tossing about).
See what wings I have,
What boundless wings.
    Vagrant. If only I knew the way to the   50
nearest parish. What's that biting me? Is
that you, ant? And there's another. And a
third. Why, good heavens. I've sat on an
ant-heap. *(Stands up.)* Fools, what are you
crawling on to me for? Look at them   55
running after me, look — one, two, three, four.
And here's another one, two, three ...
    *(In the meanwhile the back curtain rises
    and displays the entrance to an ant-
    heap, a red building of several stories.
    By the entrance sits a blind ant who
    counts continuously. Ants with
    sacks, beams, shovels, etc., enter and
    run across the stories of the building
    in time to the blind ant's counting.*
    Blind Ant (continuously). One two three
four, one two three four.
    Vagrant. What's that? What are you   60
counting, old boy?
    Blind Ant. One two three four ...
    Vagrant. What's this here? A warehouse or
a factory, isn't it? Hi, what's this factory for?
    Blind Ant. One two three four ...   65
    Vagrant. What's this factory for, I'm asking.
Why is this blind creature counting? Ah, he's
giving them the time. They all move in time
as he counts. One two three four. Like machines. Bah, it makes my head swim.   70

Blind Ant. One two three four . . .

1st Engineer (running in). Quicker, quicker. One two three four.

Blind Ant (more quickly). One two three four, one two three four.   75
(*They all move more quickly.*

Vagrant. What's that? I'm asking, sir, what that factory's for?

1st Engineer. Who's here?

Vagrant. Myself.

1st Engineer. From which of the ants?   80

Vagrant. From the humans.

1st Engineer. This is the Ant-Realm. What do you want here?

Vagrant. I'm having a look.

1st Engineer. Are you trying to find   85 work?

Vagrant. I don't mind.

2d Engineer (running in). A discovery. A discovery.

1st Engineer. What is it?   90

2d Engineer. A new method of speeding up. Don't count one two three four. Count blank two three four. That's shorter. Saves time. Blank two three four. Blind fellow, hallo.

Blind Ant. One two three four.   95

2d Engineer. Wrong. Blank two three four.

Blind Ant. Blank two three four. Blank two three four.   (*They all move more quickly.*

Vagrant. Not so quickly. It makes me feel giddy.   100

2d Engineer. Who are you?

Vagrant. A stranger.

2d Engineer. Where from?

1st Engineer. From the humans. Where is the humans' ant-heap?   105

Vagrant. What?

1st Engineer. Where is the humans' ant-heap?

Vagrant. Oh, yonder. And yonder again. Everywhere.

2d Engineer (yelping). Ha, ha. Every-   110 where. Fool.

1st Engineer. Are there many humans?

Vagrant. Yes. They're called the masters of the world.

2d Engineer. Ha, ha. Masters of the   115 world.

1st Engineer. We're the masters of the world.

2d Engineer. The Ant-Realm.

1st Engineer. The largest ant-state.

2d Engineer. A world power.   120

1st Engineer. The largest democracy.

Vagrant. What's that?

1st Engineer. All must obey.

2d Engineer. All have to work. All for Him.

1st Engineer. As He orders.   125

Vagrant. Who?

1st Engineer. The Whole. The State. The Nation.

Vagrant. Why, that's just like us. For instance, we have M.P.'s.[1] An M.P., that's   130 democracy. Have you got M.P.'s too?

1st Engineer. No. We have the Whole.

Vagrant. And who speaks for the Whole?

2d Engineer. Ha, ha. He knows nothing.

1st Engineer. The one who orders. The   135 Whole only issues commands.

2d Engineer. He abides in the laws. He is nowhere else.

Vagrant. And who rules you?

1st Engineer. Reason.   140

2d Engineer. Law.

1st Engineer. The interests of the State.

2d Engineer. That's it, that's it.

Vagrant. I like that. I say, all for the Whole.   145

1st Engineer. For its greatness.

2d Engineer. And against the enemies.

Vagrant. What's that? Against whom?

1st Engineer. Against all.

2d Engineer. We are surrounded by   150 enemies.

1st Engineer. We defeated the Black Ants.

2d Engineer. And starved out the Russets.

1st Engineer. And subjugated the Grays. Only the Yellows are left. We must   155 starve out the Yellows.

2d Engineer. We must starve out all.

Vagrant. Why?

1st Engineer. In the interests of the Whole.

2d Engineer. The interests of the whole   160 are the highest.

1st Engineer. Interests of race.

2d Engineer. Industrial interests.

1st Engineer. Colonial interests.

[1] A term of abbreviation for Members of Parliament, who are the English equivalents of the American Congressmen.

2d Engineer. World interests.   165

1st Engineer. Interests of the Whole.

2d Engineer. Yes, yes, that's it.

1st Engineer. The Whole has nothing but interests.

2d Engineer. Nobody may have as   170 many interests as the Whole.

1st Engineer. Interests preserve the Whole.

2d Engineer. And wars nourish it.

Vagrant. Aha, you're — you're the war-like ants.   175

2d Engineer. Tut, tut. He knows nothing.

1st Engineer. Our ants are the most peaceful ants.

2d Engineer. A nation of peace.

1st Engineer. A labor state.   180

2d Engineer. They only wish for world-power ——

1st Engineer. Because they wish for world-peace ——

2d Engineer. In the interests of their   185 peaceable labor ——

1st Engineer. And in the interests of progress.

2d Engineer. In the interests of their interests. When we rule over the world ——

1st Engineer. We shall conquer time.   190 We wish to rule over time.

Vagrant. Over what?

1st Engineer. Time. Time is greater than space.

2d Engineer. Time has found no mas-   195 ter yet.

1st Engineer. The master of time will be master of all.

Vagrant. Slowly, for heaven's sake, slowly. Let me think.   200

1st Engineer. Speed is the master of time.

2d Engineer. The taming of time.

1st Engineer. He who commands speed will be ruler of time.

2d Engineer. Blank two three four.   205 Blank two three four.

Blind Ant (more quickly). Blank two three four. Blank two.... (*All move more quickly.*

1st Engineer. We must quicken the pace.

2d Engineer. The pace of output.   210

1st Engineer. The pace of life.

2d Engineer. Every movement must be quickened.

1st Engineer. Shortened.

2d Engineer. Reckoned out.   215

1st Engineer. To an instant.

2d Engineer. To a hundredth of an instant.

1st Engineer. So as to save time.

2d Engineer. So as to increase output.

1st Engineer. Work has been proceed-   220 ing too slowly. Too ponderously. The ants were decaying with fatigue.

2d Engineer. Unsparingly.

1st Engineer. Inhumanely. Now they're decaying without speed.   225

Vagrant. And what are they hurrying after like that?

1st Engineer. The interests of the Whole.

2d Engineer. A question of output. A question of power.   230

1st Engineer. There is peace. Peace is rivalry.

2d Engineer. We are waging the battle of peace.

Blind Ant. Blank two three four.   235

An ant-official approaches the two engineers and reports something to them

Vagrant. Blank two three four. Quicker still. Blank —
Flog this old slow time with the ship of speed,
Lash and hound it, make it soar forward more
    speedily,
For speed is progress. The world desires to
    rush more hastily onwards,
Desires to soar to its goal, even if it soared to
    ruin,   240
If only it be more quickly. Blind creature,
    count: Blank.

Blind Ant. Two three four ...

1st Engineer. Quicker, quicker.

An Ant (collapsing beneath his load). Oh!

2d Engineer. Tut, tut. What's that?   245 Get up.

Another Ant (bending over the one who has collapsed). Dead.

1st Engineer. One two carry him away. Quickly!   (*Two ants lift up the corpse.*

2d Engineer. What an honor. He fell   250 on the field of speed.

1st Engineer. How are you lifting him? Too

slowly. You're wasting time. Drop him. (*The two ants drop the corpse.*) Now, head and feet together. Blank two three. Wrong. 255 Drop him. (*The two ants drop the corpse.*) Head and feet blank two three four. Take him away, quick march. Blank two, blank two, blank . . .

2d Engineer. Two three four. Quicker. 260

Vagrant. Anyhow, he died quick enough.

1st Engineer. To work, to work. He who has more must work more.

2d Engineer. He requires more.

1st Engineer. He has more to defend. 265

2d Engineer. And more to gain.

1st Engineer. We are a nation of peace. Peace means work.

2d Engineer. And work, strength.

1st Engineer. And strength, war. 270

2d Engineer. Yes, yes.

A Voice. Look out, look out. Step aside.

Enter an Inventor, groping

2d Engineer. Hallo, our Inventor.

Inventor. Take care, take care. Don't knock against my head. It is huge, it is is of 275 glass, it is fragile. It is greater than I am. Keep out of the way, it would burst, it would be smashed — bang. Look out, I'm carrying a head. Don't knock it. Step aside.

2d Engineer. Hallo, how goes it? 280

Inventor. It's hurting, it's bursting. It's knocking against the walls — bang. No, no, I can't get my two hands round it. No, no, I can't even carry it now. Look out, do you hear? Whew, whew, whew. 285

1st Engineer. What is it?

Inventor. A machine, a new machine. In my head. Do you hear it working? It's smashing my head. Oh, oh — a huge machine. Out of the way. Out of the way. I'm 290 carrying a machine.

1st Engineer. What sort of machine?

Inventor. A war-machine. An enormous one. The swiftest, most effective crusher of lives. The greatest progress. The acme of 295 science. Whew, whew, whew, do you hear it? Ten thousand, a hundred thousand dead. Whew, whew. It keeps on working. Two

hundred thousand dead. Whew, whew, whew, whew. 300

1st Engineer. A genius, eh?

Inventor. Oh, oh. What pain. My head's splitting. Out of the way, out of the way. Take care I don't knock against you. Whew, whew, whew —— (*Exit.* 305

1st Engineer. A great intellect. The greatest of scientists.

2d Engineer. Nothing serves the state so much as science.

1st Engineer. Science is a great thing. 310 There will be war.

Vagrant. Why war?

1st Engineer. Because we shall have a new war-machine.

2d Engineer. Because we still need a 315 new bit of the world.

1st Engineer. A bit of the world from the birch-tree to the pine-tree.

2d Engineer. And a road between two blades of grass. 320

1st Engineer. The only open road to the south.

2d Engineer. A question of prestige.

1st Engineer. And trade.

2d Engineer. The greatest national 325 idea.

1st Engineer. Either us or the Yellows.

2d Engineer. Never was war more honorable or more urgent ——

1st Engineer. Than the one we must 330 wage.

2d Engineer. We are prepared.

1st Engineer. We must only have a cause.

Blind Ant. Blank two three four. (*A gong*

1st Engineer. What's that? 335

Voices. A messenger. A messenger.

Messenger (*running in*). I beg to announce myself. I am the guard of the southern army

1st Engineer. Good.

Messenger. In accordance with orders 340 we crossed the frontier of the Yellows.

1st Engineer. What then?

Messenger. The Yellows captured me and took me to their commander.

1st Engineer. And? 34

Messenger. Here is the commander's letter.

1st Engineer. Show it me. (*Takes the pape*

and reads.) "The Government of the Yellow Ants calls upon the Ant-Realm within three minutes to withdraw his army lying be- 350 tween the birch-tree and the pine-tree on the road between two blades of grass."

2d Engineer. Listen, listen.

1st Engineer. "This territory comprises the historical, vital, industrial, sacred and 355 military interests of our State, so that it rightfully belongs to us."

2d Engineer. An insult. We shall not tolerate it.

1st Engineer. "At the same time we 360 are instructing our regiments to start advancing." (*Drops the paper.*) War. War at last.

2d Engineer. At last a war that is forced upon us.

1st Engineer. To arms.   365

New Messenger (*running in*). The Yellows are marching across our frontiers.

1st Engineer (*running into the ant-heap*). To arms. To arms.

2d Engineer (*in another passage of the ant-heap*). Mobilization. To arms.   370

Both Messengers (*in various passages*). To arms, to arms.

    (*Alarm sirens. From all sides the ants scramble into the ant-heap.*

Blind Ant. Blank two three four. Blank two three four.

    (*An increasing din within.*

Vagrant. To arms, to arms. The road between the blades of grass   375 Is threatened. Do you hear? The cranny from blade to blade, A span of earth from grass to grass, your sacred rights, The greatest interests of the State, the greatest problem in the world, All is at stake. Ants, to arms! How could you live, if another possessed 380 The world between two husks? If another carried Ant-baggage into a strange ant-heap? A hundred thousand lives for these two blades of grass Are too few. I was in the war. Oh, That's a handiwork for insects, indeed. Dig trenches,   385

Root yourself in clay. Hurra, an attack in extended order, At the double over stacks of corpses. Fix bayonets! Fifty thousand dead, to capture Twenty paces of latrines. Hurra, to arms! The interest of the whole is concerned, the heritage of your history is concerned, 390 Nay more, the freedom of your native-land, nay more, world-power, Nay more, two blades of grass. Such a mighty cause Can be settled only by the dead. To arms! to arms!

Chrysalis. The whole earth is quivering, Something mighty it is delivering, 395 I am being born.

To the beating of a drum the troops of the Ants advance with rifles, bayonets and machine-guns, with metal helmets on their heads, and line up in ranks. Enter the FIRST ENGINEER *with the badge of a commander-in-chief, his staff, the* SECOND ENGINEER *as head of the general staff, and a retinue of officers*

Vagrant (*passing along the ranks*). See what good training does. Attention. Sound the roll-call. Soldiers, your country is sending you to war, That you may fall. Two blades of grass Are watching you.   400

1st Engineer (*on an elevation*). Soldiers, we find ourselves compelled to call you to the colors. A wicked enemy has treacherously attacked us, for the purpose of outwitting our pacific preparations. At this grave hour 405 I am appointed dictator.

2d Engineer. Three cheers for the dictator. Shout, boys, or ...

Soldiers. Three cheers for the dictator. 409

1st Engineer Dictator (*saluting*). Thank you. You have realized the demand of the moment. Soldiers, we are fighting for liberty and right ...

2d Engineer. And for the greatness of the State ...   415

Dictator. And for the greatness of the

State. We shall wage war for civilization and military honor. Soldiers, I am with you to the last drop of blood.

2d Engineer. Long live our beloved 420 commander-in-chief.

Soldiers. Long may he live.

Dictator. I know my soldiers. They will fight until the final victory. Long live our gallant men, hurra. 425

Soldiers. Hurra, hurra.

Dictator (*to the* SECOND ENGINEER). First and second divisions attack. Fourth division surround the pine-wood and break into the ant-heap of the Yellows. Women and 430 embryos to be slaughtered. Third division reserve. No quarter.

(SECOND ENGINEER *as head of the general staff, salutes.*

Dictator. May God assist us in this. Soldiers, right turn, quick march.

(*Beating of drums.*

Head of the General Staff. One two. 435 War forced upon us. One two, one two. In the name of justice. Give no quarter. For your hearths and homes. One two. One two. We are only defending ourselves. War for the world. For a greater native-land. One 440 two. An inveterate enemy. Will of the nation. To battle, strike hard. Historical claim. Brilliant spirit of the army. One two. One two.

Fresh troops continue to march past to the beating of drums

Dictator. Good luck, soldiers. I shall be behind you. Fifth regiment, bravo. The 445 conqueror of the pine-cones. A mighty epoch. To victory. Conquer the world. Magnificent daring. One two. One two. Seventh regiment, hurra. Beat them, soldiers. The Yellows are cowards. Burn and 450 hack, heroes.

Messenger (*running in*). The Yellows have invaded the stretch of country between the roots of the pine-tree and the stone. 454

Dictator. Entirely according to plan. Faster, soldiers. One two. War forced upon us for honor and glory needs of the State nobody's conception of justice soldiers show your brav-

ery victory is ours greatest moment in history quick march quick march quick march. 460

In the distance dull shots: bang, bang

Dictator. The battle is beginning. Second levy. (*Inspects the battlefield through a folding telescope.*

Blind Ant. Blank two three four, blank two...

An increasing din

Chrysalis (*shouting*). The earth is bursting. Hearken to my sign. 465
The depths of the world
Are toiling in pain for the birth that is mine.

Dictator. Second levy. Third levy. To arms. To arms. (*To the* QUARTERMASTER-GENERAL) Issue a report. 470

Quartermaster-general (*in a low voice*). The battle has begun at last amid favorable weather conditions. Our heroic men are fighting in magnificent spirits.

New troops march past to the beating of drums from the ant-heap

Dictator. Right turn, quick march. 475 One two, one two. Faster, boys.

Messenger (*running in*). Our right wing is retreating. The fifth regiment is completely destroyed.

Dictator. According to plan. Sixth 480 regiment replace them. (*Messenger runs off.*

Vagrant. Ha, ha, according to plan. So it's all right,
When death himself serves on the staff as a general
And carries out orders: I beg to report
The fifth regiment is destroyed, according to plan. 485
Oh, I know all about this, and I've seen it before;
I've seen broad fields bestrewn with corpses,
Slaughtered human flesh frozen in the snow;
I've seen the Supreme Staff, and Death himself with falloons,
With a breast full of medals, with a fluttering plume, 490

Survey the fallen, to see whether they are
    heaped according to plan
On the chart of the dead.

Stretcher-bearers run in with wounded

A Wounded Man (screaming). The fifth
regiment. Our regiment. We're all killed.
Stop, stop.   495

The telegraph instrument clatters

Telegraph Officer (reading dispatch). Fifth
regiment destroyed. We await orders.

Dictator. Sixth take their places. (*To
the* QUARTERMASTER-GENERAL) Issue a report.

Quartermaster-general (in a loud voice). The
battle is developing successfully. The   501
fifth regiment specially distinguished itself,
heroically repelling all attacks, whereupon it
was relieved by the sixth.

Dictator. Bravo. I will decorate you   505
with the great order of merit.

Quartermaster-general. Thank you. I am
only doing my duty.

*Lame Journalist (approaching with a note-
book).* I am a journalist. Sha — sha — sha
— shall we announce a vi — vi — vi —   510
victory?

Dictator. Yes. Successful operations.
Thanks to our plans prepared long ago. The
admirable spirit of our forces. Irresistible
advance. The enemy demoralized.   515

Lame Journalist. W-w-we . . . w-w-we . . . we,
we, we . . . w-w-we . . .

Dictator. Eh?

Lame Journalist. We will print everything.

Dictator. Good. We rely upon the co-   520
operation of the press. Don't forget the admirable spirit.

Lame Journalist. The press is per-per-per-
forming its du-du-duty.   (*Runs off.*   524

Philanthropist (with collecting-box). Help
the wounded. All for the wounded. Gifts for
the wounded. Give to the wounded. Help for
the cripples. All for the cripples. Aid the
cripples.

Dictator. Second division attack. It   530
must break through. Whatever the sacrifice.

Philanthropist. For our heroes. Help your
brothers. Help for the wounded.

Vagrant. All for the wounded. War for the
wounded. All for their wounds.   535

Philanthropist. Help for the cripples. Give
to the wounded.

*Vagrant (tearing off a button and putting it into
the collecting-box).* All for the wounded. My
last button for the war.

*Another Wounded Man (groaning in the
ambulance).* Oh, oh, oh, put me out of   540
my misery. Oh, oh, oh.

Philanthropist (going out). Aid the
wounded . . .

The telegraph instrument rattles

Telegraphist. The right wing of the Yellows
is retreating.   545

Dictator. Pursue them. Finish them off.
Don't be bothered with prisoners.

Quartermaster-general (in a loud voice). The
enemy retiring in confusion. Our regiments,
in defiance of death, dogging his foot-   550
steps with splendid daring.

Dictator. Fourth levy.

      (QUARTERMASTER-GENERAL *runs into
         the ant-heap.*

Telegraphist. Sixth regiment destroyed to
the last man.

Dictator. According to plan. Tenth   555
take their place. Fourth levy.

*New detachments of armed troops
march up*

Dictator. At the double.

      (*Ants advance to the battlefield at the
         double.*

Telegraphist. The fourth division has invested the pine-tree and made a rear attack
on the ant-heap of the Yellows. The gar-   560
rison is slaughtered.

Dictator. Raze it to the ground. Kill the
women and embryos.

Telegraphist. The enemy is overwhelmed.
They have evacuated a foot of the reed-   565
patch.

Dictator. Victory is ours. (*Falls down on his
knees and removes his helmet.*) Great God of the
ants, thou hast granted victory unto justice.
I appoint thee colonel.   (*Jumps up.*)   570

Third division forward against the enemy. All reserves forward against them. Spare nobody. No prisoners. Forward. (*Flings himself down on his knees.*) Righteous God of strength, thou knowest that our holy cause —— (*Jumps* 575 *up.*) After them, after them. Attack them. Hunt them down. Slaughter all. The rule of the world is settled. (*Kneels.*) God of the ants, in this significant hour ... 579
(*Prays softly.*

Vagrant (*bending over him, softly*). Rule of the world? Wretched ant, you call this bit of clay and grass the world, do you? This miserable, dirty span of earth? Trample down all this ant-heap of yours, and you with it, and not a tree-top will rustle above you, fool 585 that you are.

Dictator. Who are you?

Vagrant. Now only a voice; yesterday perhaps a soldier in another ant-heap. What do you think of yourself, conqueror of the 590 world? Do you feel great enough? Doesn't it seem to you that this heap of corpses is too small, upon which your glory is established, you poor wretch?

Dictator (*rising*). It does not matter. 595 I proclaim myself emperor.

The telegraph instrument clatters

Telegraphist. The second division is asking for reinforcements. Our troops fell exhausted.

Dictator. What? They must hold out. Drive them with whips. 600

Telegraphist. The third division has been thrown into confusion.

An Ant (*escaping across the stage*). We're running away.

Dictator. Fifth levy. All to arms. 605

A Shout (*behind the scenes*). Stop. No, no. Back.

A Piercing Outcry. Save yourselves.

Dictator. Fifth Levy. The unfit to the front. All to the front. 610

A Soldier (*fleeing from the left*). They're beating us. Run.

Two Soldiers (*running from the right*). They've surrounded us. Escape.

A Soldier (*from the left*). To the west. Escape to the west. 615

Soldiers (*from the right*). They've surrounded us from the west. Run to the east.

Dictator (*yelling*). Back. To your places. To the front.

A Squad (*from the right in a mad stampede*). Out of it. The flames are spurting. 620

A Squad (*from the left*). To the west. Save yourselves. Out of the way.

A Throng (*from the right*). Escape, they're hunting us down. To the east.

A Throng (*from the left*). To the west. 625 Out of the way. They're here.
(*The two streams begin to scuffle and fight in a panic.*

Dictator (*jumping upon them and striking at them*). Back. Cowards. You cattle, I am your emperor.

A Soldier. Lie down. (*Runs him through.*) Escape. 630

2d Engineer (*running in wounded and jumping on to the elevation*). They've taken the city. Put out the lights.

The Yellows (*entering from both sides*). Hurra, hurra. The ant-heap is ours.
(*The lights go out. Darkness, turmoil, confusion.*

Voice of the 2d Engineer. Fight, fight. 635 Ah-h-h.

Voice of the Yellow Leader. Into the passages after them. Spare nobody. Slaughter all the men.

Shout of the Slaughtered Men. Ah-h-h. 640

Blind Ant. Blank two. Blank two. Blank two.

The Yellow Leader. Slaughter the women and embryos.

Shout of the Women. O-o-o-o-o. 645

Blind Ant. Blank two. Blank two. Blank two.

The Yellow Leader. After them. Murder. Murder them all.
(*The din becomes more remote.*

Blind Ant. Blank two. Blank two. 650 Blank o-o-o.

The Yellow Leader. Light.
(*The lights are lit. The foreground is empty. The Yellows are penetrating into the passages of the ant-heap and flinging Ants down from the top*

stories. *Corpses heaped up on all
sides.*

The Yellow Leader. Excellent, Yellows. All
are slaughtered.

*Vagrant (reeling amongst the heaped-up
corpses).* Enough, general.   655

The Yellow Leader. The victory of the Yellows. The victory of justice and progress.
Ours is the path between two blades of grass.
The world belongs to us Yellows. I proclaim myself ruler of the universe.   660

(*The din becomes very remote amid the
passages.*

Chrysalis (tossing about). I...I...I...

*The Yellow Leader (falling down on his knees
and removing his helmet).* Most righteous God,
thou knowest that we fight only for justice.
Our history, our national honor, our commercial interests...   665

Vagrant (rushing out and kicking THE YEL-
LOW LEADER *over, then trampling and grinding
him to pieces with his boot).* Bah, you insect.
You stupid insect.

Curtain

EPILOGUE

Life and Death

The interior of a forest. Pitch-black night. The
VAGRANT *sleeping in the foreground*

Vagrant (dreaming and talking in his sleep).
Enough, general. (*Wakes up.*) What, have
I been sleeping? Where am I? This awful
darkness. I can't — can't — I can't see my
hand before my eyes. (*Stands up.*) Why is
it so dark? I can't see a step before me. 5
Who's speaking? Who's there? (*Shouts.*)
Who's there? (*Gropes about him.*) Nothing...
nothing...nothing... (*Shouts.*) Is anything
there? Is anything there at all? An abyss,
everywhere this awful abyss. On which 10
side does it begin to fall? If I had something
to hold on to. There's nothing. There's nothing. O God, I'm frightened. Where's the sky

got to? If at least the sky were left. Or a
single will-o'-the-wisp. A single human 15
glimmer. If — at least — some direction were
left. Where am I? (*Kneels.*) I'm frightened.
Light. If only there were light.

Voice (from the darkness). There is light.
Light enough.   20

Vagrant (lying on the ground). A single
human glimmer. Only one ray.

Another Voice. This hunger. This thirst.

Another Voice. I'm calling you. Come. I'm
seeking you. I'm calling. Come.   25

A Thin Voice. A drink, a drink, a drink.

Vagrant. For God's sake. Only a tiny spark
of light. What's that? Where am I?

Voice of the Male Beetle (far off). My little
pile. Where is my little pile?   30

Vagrant. Light.

A Voice. This hunger. This thirst.

A Dying Voice. Put me out of my misery.

Another Voice. Be mine.

Another Voice. Aha, aha, I've got him.   35

Vagrant. Light. What's here? Ah, a stone.

A Voice. This thirst. This thirst.

Another Voice. Mercy.

Vagrant. If I can only strike a small spark
out of it. (*Beats a stone against the stone.*) 40
A single spark of light. The last tiny spark.
(*Sparks burst from the stone. The interior of the
forest is lit up with a spectral radiance. The*
VAGRANT *stands up.*) Light.

Voices (vanishing). Escape, light. Flee.

Vagrant. Aha, what beauty.

Voices (approaching from behind the scenes).
Light. Light.   45

Chrysalis. Who is calling me?

Vagrant. Light, praise God.

(*An increasing glow with soft music.*

Chrysalis. Upon your knees. Upon your
knees.

I — I — I, the chosen one,
Am entering the world.   50

Voices (approaching). Behold, light.

Chrysalis. In travail of birth
     Bursts my prison's girth.
     Seen, heard by none,
     A deed is done.   55
     I shall be.

A bevy of MOTHS *fly into the midst of the radiance and dance*

Vagrant. Where are you from with your transparent wings?

1st Moth (flying from the center of the others and whirling round).

O — o — o.　　　　　　　(*Stands still.*
Like a ray from the gloom　　　　　60
Has burst forth the radiant, eternal,
Mighty life of the moths.
Dance, my sisters.　O — o — o —
　　　　　　　　　　　(*Whirls round.*
Chorus of Moths. Life we encircle.
　　　　　Life we dance through. 65
　　　　　We are life itself.
　　　　　Life.　Life.
1st Moth (standing still). From chiming of rays our wings are woven;
From star unto star, from glittering threads
An age-old divine weaver wove them.　We
　　　　　dance through the universe,　70
We, the spirit of life, borne from light,
Images of God, who —　(*Sinks down dead.*
2d Moth (coming forward and whirling round).
　—— who in us beholds himself.
　　O — o — o.　Eternal, eternal is life.
Vagrant (reeling towards her). How...　75
how then, is it eternal?
2d Moth. To live, to encircle, to whirl.
　　From the depths of the universe
Responds to us the creative, unbounded
Whirling of moth-wings.　To us is given
The mysterious task of eternally whirling;　80
From our wings is showered the harmony of
　　the spheres.
O what a duty and what creative joy
To be a moth.　To live is to rotate.
O — o — o.
　　　　　　　　　　　(*Whirls round.*
Chorus of Moths. Eternal, eternal is life.　85
Vagrant (amongst them). O what a duty and
　　what creative joy ——
Chorus of Moths. —— to rotate.　Sisters,
　　round we dance.
2d Moth (standing still). Unravel life.　What
　　are we else,
We, woven from daintiest fabrics,
But thought and soul of creation?　　　90

We are transparent.　We are without weight
　　or havoc.
We are life itself.　Like sparks from God's
　　furnace
Have we burst forth and we glorify ——
　　　　　　　　　　　(*Falls dead.*
Vagrant. See, she is dead.
3d Moth (coming forward and whirling).
O — o — o.　　　　　(*Stands still.* 95
With us the whole world circles, its thanks and
　　praises blending.
It glorifies, leaps and rotates
Before thee, mighty, lovely, unending
Moth-gift of life.
Breathless delight, eternal ecstasy,　　　100
Hail to thee, life's roundelay,
Fiery dance, to which no end can be.
All...　　　　　　　　　(*Falls dead.*
Vagrant (raising his hands and turning).
O — o — o —
Chorus of Moths. All hail.　All hail.　105
Vagrant. Life, life, you have cast a spell upon
us.　For even I, old, battered moth that I am,
circle and shout, O life...
Chorus of Moths. All hail, all hail.
Vagrant. Let us live, all of us.　Look,　110
each one desires to live.　Each one defends him-
self, and each one fights on his own.　See, if we
once were to try it thus together.　If you yourself were to lead us against — against destruction, against death.　　　　　　115
Chorus of Moths. All hail, be glorified.
　　　　　(*Moth after moth falls dead.*
Vagrant. We all would follow you.　All
moths and all mortals, and thoughts, and
works, and the creatures in the water, and ants,
and grass, all unite with you.　But first　120
we ourselves must unite, all of us who live, into
one regiment.　And you will lead us, O
omnipotent life...
Chorus of Moths. All hail to life.
Chrysalis (in a piercing shriek). Make　125
room! (*Rends its husk and leaps forth as a moth.*)
Here I am!
Vagrant (staggering towards it). You, chrysalis?　You?　Show yourself.　At last you
have been born.　　　　　　130
Chrysalis-moth (whirling).
O — o — o.　(*Standing still*) I

Proclaim sway over life.   I
Enjoin creation: live, for the empery
Of life has come.   (*Whirling*) O — o — o.
A Few of the Last Moths. Eternal, 135
eternal is life.   (*They fall dead.*
Chrysalis-moth (*standing still*).   The whole
of life surged up to bring me forth,
And it burst in its throes.   Hearken, O hearken.
I bear a mighty mission; I proclaim
Immense tidings.   Silence, silence.   140
I will utter great words.   (*Falls dead.*
Vagrant (*kneeling down*).   Rise up, moth.
Why have you fallen?   (*Lifts it up.*)   It is
dead.   Alas, delightful countenance, alas, clear
and serene eyes.   Dead.   Do you hear, 145
chrysalis?   What did you desire to say?
Speak yet.   (*Carries it in his arms.*)   Dead.
How light it is, O God, how beautiful.   Why
had it to die?   Wherefore this fearful lack of
meaning?   Moth.   (*Lays it on the ground.*)   150
Dead.   (*Creeps along the ground and examines
the dead moths, lifting their heads.*)   And you too
are dead, you who danced?   And you who
sang?   And you, who were so young?   Ah,
these lips will utter no more sound.   155
Dead.   Do you hear, green moth?   If only it
opened its eyes.   Look, it is so good to live.
Awake, live.   All — hail — to — life.   (*Crawls
forward on his hands and knees.*)   All hail.   Ugh.
Who clutched at me?   Away with you.   160
(*The light goes out, only a sharp ray falls on the
VAGRANT.*)   Who is here?   Ugh, stop, I feel
a chill ... Who are you?   (*Brandishes his hands
in the void.*)   Away with you, cold hand.   I desire not ... (*Stands up.*)   Don't touch.   Who
are you?   (*Defends himself.*)   But stop,   165
why are you strangling me?   Ha, ha, wait, I
know who you are.   You are ... you are
Death.   So many times have I seen you today.
But I — will — not.   Stop, skeleton, eyeless
and loathsome.   (*Struggles in the void.*)   170
Cease.

From the right two SNAILS *crawl in*

1st Snail. Stop.   Someone's making a noise.[1]
2d Snail. You ass, come back.
Vagrant (*struggling*).   That's for you, rat-
tlebones.   Ha, ha, ha, you felt that, eh.   175

[1] In the Czech original the Snails are made to lisp.

(*Thrust to his knees.*)   Leave me alone.   Don't
smother so.   Come now, I only want to live.   Is
that so much?   (*Rises and waves his hands.*)   I
won't give you my life, you old death's-head,
I won't.   That's for you.   (*Falls.*)   Oh,   180
you're putting out your foot, too.
1st Snail. I say, snail.
2d Snail. What?
1st Snail. He's struggling with death.
2d Snail. We'll have a look, eh?   185
Vagrant (*rising*).   Let me live.   What will it
matter to you?   Only this time.   At least
till tomorrow.   Let ... only ... breathe ...
(*Struggles.*)   Stop, don't strangle.   I don't
want to die.   I've had so little enjoyment   190
of life.   (*Shouts.*)   Ah!   (*Falls on his face.*
1st Snail. What fun, eh?
2d Snail. I say, snail.
1st Snail. What?
2d Snail. He's already done for.   195
Vagrant (*rising to his knees*).   You strangle
a man when he's down, do you, coward?   Stop
now, let me tell — all — I want — another
moment.   (*Rises and staggers.*)   Let me —
live.   Only live.   (*Shrieks.*)   No!   Go   200
away!   There's still so much for me to say.
(*Sinks on to his knees.*)   Now — I know —
how to live.   (*Falls on his back.*
1st Snail (*crawls slowly forward*).   Well, it's
all up with him.   205
2d Snail. Jesus, Jesus, what a blow.   Oh
dear, oh dear.   What misfortune.   Why have
you deserted us?
1st Snail. What are you complaining about?
It's nothing to do with us.   210
2d Snail. But you know that's what people
say when someone dies.
1st Snail. Oh yes.   Well, we'll keep still.
2d Snail. Oh yes.   That's the way of the
world.   215
1st Snail. It's a pity there aren't fewer snails
and more cauliflower.
2d Snail. Hi, snail, look.
1st Snail. What?
2d Snail. What a lot of dead moths   220
here.
1st Snail. It's a pity they can't be eaten.
2d Snail. Oh yes.   Well, we'll keep still,
eh?

1st Snail. As long as we're alive. 225
2d Snail. That's about it. I say, snail...
1st Snail. What?
2d Snail. Life's pleasant.
1st Snail. Rather. Nothing like life, you know. 230
2d Snail. Then we'll keep still.
　　　　　　　　　(*They enter the wings.*
1st Snail. That was a joke, eh?
2d Snail. Rather. As long as — we're — alive. (*Exeunt.*
　　(*Pause. It becomes light. Birds awaken.*

A WOODCUTTER *enters from the back with his axe on his shoulder, sees the* VAGRANT'S *corpse behind a bush, and bends down to it*

Woodcutter. What's that? Do you hear, 235 old man? Come on, old fellow, wake up. What's the matter with you? (*Stands up, takes off his cap and crosses himself.*) He's dead. Poor old man. (*Pause*) Anyhow — he's finished with everything. 240
Aunt (*entering from the left and carrying a newly born child to be baptized*). Good day to you. What have you there, uncle?
Woodcutter. Good day, aunt. Someone's died here. It's a tramp. (*Pause.*

Aunt. Poor man. 245
Woodcutter. And what about you, aunt? To a baptism? To a baptism?
Aunt. That's my sister's baby.
Woodcutter. One is born and another dies.
Aunt. And there are always people 250 enough.
Woodcutter (*tickling the baby under the chin*). Ks, ks, laddie. Wait till you grow up.
Aunt. If only he's better off than we are, uncle.
Woodcutter. Why, as long as a man's 255 got something to do the whole time.
Schoolgirl (*entering from the right with a bag on her back*). Praised be the Lord...
Aunt. Forever and ever.
Woodcutter. Forever and ever. (*The* SCHOOLGIRL *passes out.*) It's fine today, aunt, 260 eh? More than words can tell.
Schoolgirl's Voice. Praised be the Lord...
A Man's Voice (*behind the scenes*). Forever and ever.
Aunt. Yes, it's a fine day we're having. 265
Wanderer (*entering from the left*). Good day.
Aunt. Good day.
Woodcutter. A happy good day to you.

Curtain

INTRODUCTION TO

Naked

The Rise of Italian Drama: Pirandello and the Drama of Mental Analysis

THE RISE OF ITALIAN DRAMA

UP TO THE twentieth century theatrical art in Italy quite overshadowed dramatic literature. It was the aristocrats of the Italian Renaissance who originated in their palace theaters the "picture stage," and scenery in the form of movable, painted flats. The plays which these wealthy patrons staged with a lavish display then unknown in other countries were, however, only sterile imitations of Roman drama, and pastorals. Toward the close of the sixteenth century Italian players invented the *commedia dell'arte* and proceeded to perform it all over Europe during the next two hundred years. Yet the *commedia dell'arte*, a fantastic masked comedy with improvised dialogue, was essentially a theatrical vehicle, dependent upon the actors' wit and "business." A literary drama rooted in Italian life did not get well established until Carlo Goldoni (1707–93), an admirer of Molière, wrote scores of light but telling comedies like *The Mistress of the Inn* (1753). More than another hundred years passed before Gabriele d'Annunzio (1863–1938), swashbuckling lover, patriot, novelist, and poet, created serious Italian drama of outstanding merit. Eleonora Duse, the world's greatest actress at the turn of the last century, inspired him to two notable lyrical tragedies, *La Gioconda* (1898) and *Francesca da Rimini* (1902).

D'Annunzio's florid romanticism dominated the theater of Italy in the early 1900's, though there existed some would-be realists, or Verists as they called themselves, of whom Roberto Bracco (1862–1943) was the most important. Then a reaction began against the existing Italian drama, whether romantic or realistic. In 1909 Filippo Marinetti (1876–1944) issued a manifesto for one group of rebels, the Futurists. They scorned religion, sex, romance, and the conventional technique of the well-made play; they exalted the speed, brevity, and abandon of contemporary human experience. Their cynical extravaganzas, often composed of scenes without sequence, sought to create, according to one Futurist, a "synthetic experience of cerebral energy." A second line of revolt reached its climax in Luigi Chiarelli (b. 1884), who wrote *The Mask and the Face* (1914), the bizarre struggle of a man to maintain his identity ("face") against society's repeated masking of it. Chiarelli and his followers in the Grotesque drama utilized strange unpleasant plots to emphasize a topsy-turvydom in men's thinking, an endless conflict of reality and illusion. The Futurist and Grotesque schools introduced a new spiritual atmosphere into the Italian theater. Both schools cultivated a growing awareness of the human mind as an inextricable maze. They paved the way for the thorough exploration of that maze by Italy's greatest dramatist, Luigi Pirandello.

PIRANDELLO AND THE DRAMA OF MENTAL ANALYSIS

Pirandello, son of an affluent sulphur-mine owner, was born on June 28, 1867, in Grigenti (or Agrigentum), a picturesque and historic town of the south coast of Sicily. After studying at Palermo and Rome, he entered the University of Bonn, Germany, in 1891 and secured his doctor's degree in philology. On his return to Italy in 1894 his father made him marry a girl whom he had never known, a daughter of the father's business partner. The young couple settled at Rome, where Pirandello started a literary career. About 1897 floods in Sicily ruined his family's mines and fortune. He therefore accepted a professorship of Italian literature at the Normal College for Women in Rome, a position which he held for a quarter-century.

In 1904 Pirandello's best-known novel, *The Late Mattia Pascal*, came out. This intricate narrative of a weak, tormented man, who twice pretends suicide and consequently has to assume three distinct characters, points toward the psychological complexity of its author's later dramatic art. At about this same time Pirandello's wife grew unsettled in mind. Her insanity, taking the shape of unreasoning jealousy, increased gradually in violence until it drove her husband almost to despair before her death in 1918. Yet, even when the wife's persecution of their daughter caused the latter to attempt suicide, he would not, out of kindness, commit his wife to an asylum. It is no wonder that the imposed seclusion of fifteen years with a mad woman developed in him a lasting obsession for analyzing man's psychic life, because, to quote a Pirandellian aphorism, "man never reasons so much and becomes so introspective as when he suffers."

Early in the First World War an actor friend called on Pirandello for some short comedies to entertain the soldiers. Up till then his dramatic efforts had been few and tentative. He was soon happily engrossed in playwriting, but he did not attain popularity until 1921 when his fantasy on real life versus life in art, *Six Characters in Search of an Author*, aroused a tremendous excitement at Rome. Six characters, born of a playwright's imagination but then sidetracked, come upon a stage where a group of actors are in rehearsal. The Six Characters proceed to enact the unhappy drama for which they were conceived, and insist that the company rehearse it after them. The actors endeavor unsuccessfully to play the Six Characters until the unexpected suicide of one of the Characters stops the rehearsal. Within a year this novel play, repeating its success in New York, London, and various Continental capitals, had set up its creator as a leading figure in the drama of the day. In 1922 he resigned his professorship to devote his whole life to the theater.

Italy during the early 'twenties seethed with controversy over Pirandello as well as Mussolini. Audiences divided into two camps — the Pirandellians and the anti-Pirandellians — and argued excitedly during the intermissions. The master went up and down the land, expounding his theories. Finally in 1925 he opened at Rome an art theater in the Odescalchi Palace. Here he trained his own company in a new acting technique stylized to fit his plays. During the summer of 1925 the Pirandello troupe aroused widespread acclaim by a tour of England, France, and Germany. The Odescalchi Art

Theater established itself as a brilliant artistic success. Rome with Pirandello seemed in a fair way to become a vital center of dramatic experimentation.

Then this rosy prospect faded. After a couple of years Pirandello's Art Theater had to close for financial reasons. Disappointed and disillusioned, he took to the road in order to supervise performances of his plays in Milan, Berlin, Paris, New York, etc. "Henceforth I live in the vast world," he said, but the will to live ebbed fast despite the award to him of the Nobel Prize for Literature in 1934. He died on December 10, 1936, of pneumonia. No religious rites celebrated his departure. The funeral, in accordance with his instructions, consisted of "the hearse, the horse, the driver — nothing more."

The Pirandellian drama is a drama of analysis and interrogation. It represents the quest of an extremely speculative and skeptical temperament which came under the sway of the anti-logical and anti-rational ideas in certain modern philosophers. Pirandello haunted himself with the question: "Who can say with surety . . . what is illusion, and what is reality?" His chief plays are symphonic variations on this theme of illusion versus reality. The earliest, *Right You Are, If You Think You Are* (1916), is a demonstration of his conclusion that "truth is the representation that each of us makes of it." An investigation occurs in a small Italian town as to the identity of Signora Ponza. Her husband claims that she is his second wife; that his first wife, the daughter of Signora Frola, died in an earthquake. Signora Frola, on the contrary, asserts that Ponza went insane after the earthquake and that later she allowed him to marry her daughter, his first wife, over again. Then Signora Ponza is brought to testify, but she concludes: "I am nobody . . . I am . . . whomever you choose to have me."

As You Desire Me (1930), which Hollywood filmed in 1932 with Greta Garbo as the star, approaches the relative nature of truth from a slightly different angle. Bruno Pieri's wife, Cia, supposedly lost in the Austrian invasion of the First World War, returns to her husband after ten years as a dancer in Germany. Called The Strange Lady, she cannot convince him, his relatives and friends, to accept her new identity permanently. Another woman is brought to Bruno with plausible evidence that she is the actual Cia. He now thinks The Strange Lady an impostor. The latter in angry despair gives up her rôle of Cia and departs. Belief for a time created reality; doubt finally destroyed it. No one can avoid these consequences of the inexorable law that the true reality is whatever a man happens to believe at the moment.

Pirandello's concept of the relativity of truth involves the all-important corollary that personality is also fluid and relative. The individual has no "fixed" character; he is a multiple personality, constantly exchanging one self for another. "This *you* as you feel it today — all this present reality of yours — is fated to seem a mere illusion to you tomorrow," says Pirandello. Hence "our personality is a fiction . . . which we build up about our real life, or which others build up about us." A man's sanity or insanity, therefore, depends upon illusion and nothing more, as *Henry IV* (1922) seeks to prove. A severe accident to a young Roman nobleman, while masked as the Emperor Henry IV of Germany, causes him to go mad and to believe himself the Emperor, a fiction which his friends keep up. After twelve years, he suddenly becomes sane, but continues to feign madness and live the untroubled life of his illusion. After eight more years his unsuspecting friends, including Belcredi, who was responsible for the accident, decide to shock him into sanity, if possible. At the height of their test "Henry IV" stops his feigning and stabs Belcredi. This murder at once forces "Henry IV," out of self-protection, to return forever to his pose of madness. Thus sanity becomes insanity, and vice-versa.

These plays illustrate Pirandello's impish spirit which takes delight in tearing human beings apart to reveal how they function. He shows them habitually striving to fix the flux of personality and of life in mental images which are false almost as soon as made. Both the individual and society always operate by these false images, or illusions. Even though men act logically, so they believe, their behavior is inconsistent with reality. In the face of their conceit their necessary dependence upon illusions forms a ridiculous antithesis for Pirandello's dissecting mind. Hence he terms his plays, focusing as they do upon this antithesis, "comedies," however grim the situations.

Yet Pirandello's understanding, even if sardonic, humor also perceives that this most unstable of worlds, ruled not by logic but by accident, is "a labyrinth where our soul wanders through countless, conflicting paths, without ever finding a way out." Even a man's personality must ever remain a puzzle to himself. With such jarring complexities "life is a very sad piece of buffoonery." It possesses a grotesque, two-faced quality, laughing "with one face at the other face's weeping." Therefore, though ruthlessly exposing human illusions, Pirandello's art is, as he asserts, "full of bitter compassion." He would claim for his plays an humanitarian effect: "If I destroy conventional standards it is to reveal the tragedy and despair they may conceal. Does not the fundamental philosophy underlying my plays make for a deeper sympathy and understanding of humanity?"

Pirandello did not intend that his psychological dialectics in the form of drama should produce a complete semblance of life. He conceived his plays as laboratory demonstrations of man's mental world. As such, they demanded a peculiar technique. Pirandello cleverly realized how suitable to his purpose were the elements of the beloved Italian *commedia dell'arte*. It utilized fantastic plots, embroiled odd and puppet-like characters in amazing situations, and carried out a seemingly impossible unraveling of complications to effect a surprising conclusion. Pirandello proceeded to apply much of the *commedia dell'arte's* formula to his subjective theater. His plots tend to the sensational and violent. Thus they epitomize forcefully the incongruities and cruelties of life. As a rule the plots develop fitfully with many surprising turns and a strong "curtain." The stage action usually covers just the climactic period of the whole drama. For this reason Pirandello, to an even greater extent than Ibsen and Chekhov, has to employ retrospective exposition in order to make clear his characters' intricate mental problems. Some of his characters are mere reasoning marionettes; more of them are abnormal or eccentric creatures, highly introspective and articulate. In general they appear "grotesque," so to speak, because he conceives of every man as not a homogeneous individual but an individual who is merely that one personality, out of an indefinite number of personalities, which for the moment dominates over the others.

Pirandello's plays demonstrating this theory of multiple personality mark a new departure in dramatic art. He was the first to fashion an effective dramatization of metaphysical argument. The innovator afterward described the significance of that achievement most aptly: "The new drama possesses a distinct character from the old; whereas the latter had as its basis passion, the former is an expression of the intellect. One of the novelties that I have given to modern drama consists in converting the intellect into passion." Thus Pirandello has made the conflict between mere states of mind really exciting. His drama opens up a fascinating looking-glass world which so transforms men's shapes that we become uncertain of our own images. It is a world of fantasy the like of which the theater has never seen before.

"NAKED"

Naked, one of the most lucid and moving examples of Pirandellian drama, was produced originally at Rome in 1922 and then, on November 3, 1926, at the Princess Theater, New York. The lovely and versatile Marta Abba, whose acting first gained American recognition in *Tovarich* (1936), played the heroine, Ersilia Drei, at the Rome premiere. Her personality and talent so greatly attracted Pirandello on this occasion that she became the key figure of his Art Theater troupe and the Muse of his later dramatic work.

Pirandello stresses in *Naked* one of his favorite variations on the theme of illusion versus reality. The play's Italian title, *Vestire gl'Ignudi (To Clothe the Naked)*, suggests the motivating principle which Pirandello finds in all human conduct and which he uses as a precipitant of the conflict. People constantly hide behind illusions to avoid unpleasant reality. The leading figures in *Naked*, Ersilia, Laspiga, and the Consul, try to cloak with lies the naked truths about both their actions and their characters. "The truth — we cannot tell! It is too ugly, too horrible!", Ersilia pleads (Act II, ll. 1024–25). In the final curtain speech she lays bare her motives for inventing the romantic story about her attempted suicide: "We all of us want to make a good impression! . . . Never in my whole life . . . had I been able to make a good appearance . . . But I wanted a good dress to die in . . . the one I had dreamed of. . . ."

The stage action in *Naked* follows Pirandello's usual formula and includes only the last crisis in Ersilia's struggle to clothe her sordid existence. To bring on that crisis he arranges a situation which must awaken Ersilia to torturing self-awareness. This device Pirandello has described as characteristic of his dramaturgy: "When a man lives, he lives and does not see himself. Well, put a mirror before him and make him see himself in the act of living, under the sway of his passions: . . . In a word, there arises a crisis, and that crisis is my theater." While the crisis is coming to a head, skillful retrospective exposition unveils bit by bit Ersilia's mean, drab past and her futile relationships with Laspiga and the Consul.

The two men are typical Pirandellian puppets, but Ersilia, "a little stray dog lost on the streets" (Act II, ll. 97–98), gives constant evidence of blood and heart. Though rather too facile in psychological argument, an inevitable weakness of all Pirandello's characterizations, she reacts to her experience with convincing human passion. She has striven to create an imagined life of her own, but the world keeps interfering with her dreams, just as the noises and people in the street keep intruding during the whole play upon the quiet of Ludovico's study. The world's merciless pursuit, like the hubbub outside, harasses her until she cries out in torment at the close of Act I, "The street! the street!" The fictional character which she has given herself is soon torn from her by the world. The death of the poor old man in the street traffic (Act I, l. 497) foreshadows the world's destruction of this last precious illusion and of herself with it.

Pirandello through his stage counterpart, the cold intellectual Ludovico, sees the grotesque irony in the exposure of Ersilia and calls it "this comedy of a lie discovered" (Act III, ll. 491–92). Keenly conscious, however, of a tormented mankind in need of falsehood, he goes on to finish his grim "comedy" with Ersilia on the brink of death. She had wanted to be "somebody" instead of "nobody." Stripped of her beautiful lie, she will die as "nobody." She has to face the most harrowing of all conclusions to human existence: "I must die discovered . . . despised . . . humiliated . . . naked!" (Act III, ll. 842–46). Thus Pirandello turns *Naked* into an extraordinary and provocative tragic satire of life, where men cannot live as they forever dream of living, and where they must end as "naked masks."

[For the recent Italian drama, see Lander MacClintock, *The Contemporary Drama of Italy* (1920); for Pirandello, Walter Starkie, *Luigi Pirandello* (2d ed., 1937).]

LUIGI PIRANDELLO

Naked

(*Vestire gl'Ignudi*) [1]

[*Translated by* ARTHUR LIVINGSTON]

DRAMATIS PERSONAE

ERSILIA DREI
FRANCO LASPIGA, *ensign in the Italian navy*
GROTTI, *Italian consul of Smyrna*
LUDOVICO NOTA, *a novelist*
ALFREDO CANTAVALLE, *a newspaper man*
SIGNORA ONORIA, *a landlady*
EMMA, *the maid*

The Scene is laid in Rome in the twentieth century

ACT I

The study of Ludovico Nota, a novelist. It is one of two "furnished rooms" rented by the author in the lodging house of Signora Onoria. Odd pieces of antique furniture belonging to the novelist are in strong contrast with the standard second-hand articles supplied by the house mistress. In the back set two bookcases with numerous shelves stand one beside the other. The books have been carefully bound in uniform bindings of imitation parchment, the titles printed in red letters on the backs. On the right, between two windows with cheap curtains, a tall writing desk high enough for a person standing to write on. The shelf connecting the two pairs of legs is loaded with heavy dictionaries. In front of each window a large bird cage on a tall wooden rest. One cage is full of canaries, the other of thrushes and goldfinches. To the left, an old sofa upholstered in a figured damask of a light color, but covered with white lace tidies, probably to disguise the pitiable state of the ancient divan. In front of it a Turkish or Persian rug, faded and much the worse for wear. Easy chairs; wooden chairs with upholstered backs and seats; a stand with various articles. On this wall (to the left, that is) and well toward the front of the stage, is the general entrance. In back, to one side of the bookcase, is a door hidden by a portière, and leading into the novelist's bedroom. In the middle of the room an oval-shaped table with books, magazines, newspapers, vases with flowers, ash trays, and a statuette or two. The walls to the left and right are overdecorated with paintings, etchings, water colors, charcoal drawings, of scant artistic worth — the gifts of artists whom the novelist knows.

Despite its two windows, the room is rather dark because the walls of adjoining houses

[1] "To clothe the naked," the title of the play in the Italian text.

cut off the light. The truth is that Signor Nota's apartment is on a narrow alley, branching from a busy, noisy thoroughfare. In fact, during pauses in the action on the stage, sounds from the bustling street outside will reach the stage: the rumbling of a truck; the shouts of a hawker; the exhaust of a motor-cycle; the starting of an automobile; the cries of a newsboy; the laughter of young people.

As the curtain rises the stage is empty. Through the two windows, which are open, come the noises from the street. The door to the left (the general entrance) opens and Ersilia Drei appears.

Twenty-four or twenty-five years old, she is a beautiful girl, but her face is pale and her eyes are sunken deep in their sockets. (Why not? She has just been recalled from the very brink of the grave!) Her dress is plain, black, neat but threadbare — such as a school-teacher or a governess, in poor circumstances, might wear. Her hat is in keeping with the rest of her costume.

Advancing a step or two from the doorway, she stops in hesitation, as though not quite sure of herself, and looks about the room. She does not take a chair, but remains standing, apparently waiting for someone who is still to come. Her eyes survey the furnishings, and she smiles, faintly, at the confusion she sees.

A burst of noise from the busy street. She frowns thoughtfully.

Through the general entrance at last comes Ludovico Nota, returning his purse to the inside pocket of his coat as he passes through the door. He is almost bald on the top of his head. What hair he has is prematurely gray. Inclined to stoutness, he has a clean-shaven, florid, ruddy face with lively blue eyes. His white mustache is soiled from cigarette smoke. Around his lips, still fresh and sensuous, an almost youthful smile plays. Cold, intellectual, without any of the qualities which inspire sympathy and confidence out of hand, and at the same time unable to affect an emotionality he does not feel, Nota makes an effort to seem affable, jovial, at least; but this amiability, never quite spontaneous, fails to put people at their ease, and at times is actually embarrassing, not to say disconcerting.

Lud. Ah, here we are! Have a chair! Make yourself comfortable! My! My! The windows are open! What a noise! The plague of my life! But if I don't keep them open it gets so close in here, you know! (*Takes out a* 5 *cigarette and starts to light it.*) Do you object, Signorina? (*He walks nervously about the room, uneasy in tone and gesture.*) But do take off your hat! Make yourself quite at home! (Ersilia *removes her hat.*) Awfully close! 10 I don't know ... perhaps on account of that sofa ... those chairs ... a lot of old junk, corpses from my past, you might say. Or perhaps because the landlady insists on washing the floor with water every morning — and she al- 15 ways leaves it damp. Anyhow, stuffy... smelly, awfully close! Well, old houses like these!

Through the door at the rear enters Signora Onoria, *a broom in one hand, and, under the other arm, a roll of sheets and pillowcases which she is about to send to the wash.* Signora Onoria *is about forty years old, short, stout, talkative, her hair dyed, a trace of rouge on her cheeks*

Ono. Will you excuse me?

Lud. (*embarrassed by her sudden appearance*). Oh, you were in the other room? 20

Ono. (*spitefully*). I have put fresh sheets on your bed, as you asked me to do in the note you left on the hall table this morning.

Lud. Oh, yes!

Ono. (*turning and surveying* Ersilia *from head to foot*). But of course if it's for... 25 (*She breaks off.*) Look, Signor Nota, we two had better understand each other clearly. I'll just go and leave these things downstairs . . .

Lud. (*in some embarrassment and smiling in an effort to conceal it*). Yes, I would get rid of them, if I were you! Dirty clothes!   30

Ono. (*turning on him angrily*). Oh, you would, would you? And dirty, eh?

Lud. Oh, just an impression I had! I thought you were of the same opinion. I was merely agreeing with you.   35

Ono. Yes, but there are other things I should like to be rid of!

Lud. That's interesting! What, for instance?

Ono. Why, here I find you bringing a   40 young lady into the house! You think that's as clean as it might be?

Lud. That's a bit too much! You will please speak with respect of my guests or! . . .

Ono. Or what? I am speaking my mind   45 and I intend to tell you just what I think! I'll leave these things downstairs and then I'll be back!

(*She flutters away through the general entrance.*

Lud. (*mastering an impulse to follow her*). Silly old gossip!

Ers. (*trying to restrain him*). Oh, no,   50 please let me go away!

Lud. Nothing of the kind! I pay the rent for these rooms! This is my house and I'll have anyone I want here! You just sit down!

Ono. (*sweeping back through the door pugnaciously*). Signor Nota, I have rented you   55 a study and a bedroom in my house, but I must remind you that this is the house of a respectable lady!

Lud. A lady? You? Your actions show it!

Ono. A lady! Exactly! I refuse to per-   60 mit you to keep a girl in these rooms!

Lud. I consider what you say insulting in the extreme! You're a boardinghouse-keeper! You're not a lady!

Ono. You ought to be ashamed, a man   65 your age! And be careful what language you use toward me!

Lud. You are not a real lady! You have no tact! You don't seem able to distinguish one sort of person from another!   70

Ers. I've been ill! I'm just out of the hospital!

Lud. Don't bother to explain anything to this woman!

Ono. Oh, if you're sick . . .   75

(*The windows rattle, a truck crashes along the street.*

Lud. So we'll drop the subject, eh? You can't prevent me from lending my quarters for a few days!

Ono. Yes, I can! Yes, I can! These are my rooms! I choose the people to whom I   80 rent them!

Lud. But if one of my sisters . . . a cousin . . . an aunt of mine comes to town . . .

Ono. They can find plenty of hotels!

Lud. Oh, really? And I can't put them   85 up for a night or two here?

Ono. But this girl . . . is she your sister or your cousin or your aunt? Do you see anything green in my eyes?

Lud. But what do you care? What   90 business is it of yours? Supposing I'm the one who goes to the hotel?

Ono. In that case you ought to ask me in advance, politely, as a gentleman should, whether I am willing to entertain a young lady!   95

Lud. Ask you to invite her, eh?

Ono. Precisely! And ask me politely, too, because I am a lady — a respectable lady, though misfortunes have compelled me to earn my living by renting rooms, and doing   100 menial service for men like you!

Lud. Men like me?

Ono. Yes, you are always complaining! If I mop the floor every morning, it's to keep the dirt out of the room. And all those birds!   105 What do you think this is, a hen coop? They sing, eh? But that's not all they do! That's not all they do! Sometimes it takes me half a day to clean! So if the house smells . . .

Lud. The birds do all that? No,   110 madam! The house itself is dirty! You shut the windows and . . . well . . . can't you smell it yourself? Now I have to work in here, and if I don't keep the windows closed the noise from the street drives me crazy!   115

Ono. Crazy? Drives you crazy? I like that! It is not my street that drives you crazy, my dear sir! You were crazy before you ever came here!

Lud. (*laughing good-naturedly in spite of him-self*). That's a good one!　　120

Ono. Just as I say! Crazy! Anyhow, if you don't like it, why don't you go away? I wish you would! I wish you would!

Lud. Well, I'll move! Right away! Meantime, would you mind going about your　125 business?

Onc. Are you giving up your rooms?

Lud. Yes, in a few days! At the end of the month!

Ono. Very well! In that case, I have　130 nothing more to say!

Lud. Meantime, you were going downstairs!

Ono. I'm going! I'm going! Don't worry! I have had my say!

Lud. What a woman! What a　135 woman! (*Now that the windows are closed the noise comes somewhat more softly from the street.*) I am so sorry, Signorina! Your first minute here ... and a scene like that!

Ers. Oh, that's all right! What troubles me is that it should be on my account! ...　140

Lud. No, no! I have a set-to with that old witch every day! But I am tied to her! I can't get away! This ramshackle place! All this cheap, vulgar, common stuff! Look at those curtains! But such are the delightful re-　145 wards this age of business men gives to the poor fools who take up literature, especially when they are fools as impractical as I am. You perhaps thought ... well ... the home of a writer ... of an artist! ...　　　　　150

Ers. Oh, no! I don't mind for myself; but it's too bad that a man like you, a man so famous ...

(*Another burst of noise from the street.*

Lud. You hear my orchestra? Famous, did you say? You have seen one of my　155 books?

Ers. One of them? I have read many of them!

Lud. Did you like them?

Ers. Oh, yes! Very much!　　　160

Lud. Fame! Reputation! ... Well ... you know how it is with us? You know the milk-weed, don't you? — those little seeds hung on

parachutes, the lightest breeze carrying them all around, here and there? That's the　165 way it is with us! That's the way! Fad ... fashion gets hold of a writer and spreads his name to the four winds; but finally it lets him down in some dark corner of forgetfulness! Writing is a game! It is something like　170 playing the market where the stocks go up and go down! Yesterday my name was worth a hundred; today it is way below par, almost approaching zero!

Ers. Oh, I don't believe that!　　175

Lud. Zero, or virtually zero! But that doesn't bother me! Tomorrow a hundred again, or perhaps a thousand! Let's hope so, eh? I've just put something big across, you know! Two big contracts! One with a　180 newspaper syndicate, and the other with a pub-lisher! There'll be quite an advance, so that at the end of the month we'll go and get a nice little apartment, eh? In one of those new modern buildings on the park! What do　185 you say? Tomorrow we'll go house hunting to-gether! And we'll go looking for furniture — together! You will do the choosing. You must build your nest with your own hands!

Ers. Oh, but all on my account?　　190

Lud. No! No! No! I had to get out any-how! Couldn't stand it any longer here! Im-possible! They say a writer is a sedentary per-son, but look at my desk! I do all my writing on my feet! I refuse to have anything　195 to do with tradition! However, I can see the necessity of having a house of my own at last ... even if it's just a little three-room apartment! But with my own things! Oh, perhaps I won't live there myself! You see I'm like ...　200 well ... I'm a person who is always beginning over again! But you can't imagine how happy I am that I had that inspiration — the idea of writing to you — of beginning over again, this time, with you, sharing with you this　205 little stroke of good luck that has come to me! A mud-hole ... flies ... mosquitoes ... the stench of stagnant water; and then suddenly — oof! What has happened? Nothing! A breath of air! The wind has risen! That's　210 the way I am! And we'll buy everything brand new, eh? Even ... yes, eh? — a set of dishes ... things for the kitchen! Ha ha ha! How funny it is! Things for the kitchen! Who could imagine I would ever own a frying 215 pan, an iron kettle, a dish rag! Ha ha ha! But it's great, isn't it? A house of my own, and a woman to look after it ... a beautiful little creature like you! Oh, you'll see ... you'll see!

Ers. Yes, I can take care of an apart- 220 ment! I am a good housekeeper! How can I ever thank you? How can I ever thank you?

Lud. I can do without the thanks! Or rather I'm sure I should thank you for having accepted the little that I ... 225

Ers. Oh, it is not a little — don't say that! It is so much ... so much ... for me!

Lud. It will be much, perhaps, in the end, because of what you make it; but now it's very, very little! 230

Ers. Don't say that! Of the ten offers or more that came to me while I was in the hospital ...

Lud. (*in surprise*). Ten or more? Offers from whom? 235

Ers. From various people! I have them in my handbag, here! All their names and addresses, and some of them well-known names!

Lud. Well! Well! Who, for example? Let me look at them! 240

Ers. No! Perhaps later on ... or wouldn't it be better to tear them up? You see, of them all I chose yours!

Lud. (*taking her hand and kissing it*). Thank you! (*Then bringing himself to order* 245 *again*) And yet ... ah ... well, I wonder! Ah, you little rogue! I can see it in your eyes!

Ers. What?

Lud. Something not very complimentary to me! See if I haven't guessed it: of the 250 ten offers you received — honest now! — you chose mine because I said in my letter "if you would deign to accept, Signorina, the companionship of an old writer" ...

Ers. But there was no signature except 255 your first name: "Faust."

Lud. Worse luck! In that case, I can see it was the word "old" that got you, and not the name! But you might have thought that an old man who signed himself "Faust" could 260 easily prove dangerous!

Ers. Dangerous? Why?

Lud. Why, an old man named "Faust" might sell his soul to the Devil, for instance, to get back his youth again! 265

Ers. Oh, if you only knew — I am so mortified!

Lud. Mortified? Why?

Ers. Because of this great good fortune!

Lud. Why good fortune? Because I'm 270 a writer — as you say, a famous writer?

Ers. Because the story of my troubles printed in the papers — the story of the desperate attempt I made — was able to win the attention, the respect, the pity! ... 275

Lud. Why don't you say selfishness ... was able to stir the selfish interest? ...

Ers. ... of a man like ... like you!

Lud. Well, you see ... fact is ... I felt — how shall I say it — I felt all stirred up, 280 there! ... all stirred up; when I read your story in the papers! It was something like ... well, you know ... we novelists ... well, sometimes a fact, a situation comes to our attention, quite casually, and we experience inside us — 285 oh, I don't know — a shock, let us call it — a sudden wave of sympathy that sweeps over us, the conviction in short, that we have found, without effort on our part, without our trying to find it, the nucleus, the starting point, 290 the germ, of a story, of a novel ...

Ers. So you thought that ... I mean to say ... you thought you could put me into a book?

Lud. No! Please don't misunderstand! 295 Please don't imagine I have been trying to use you as mere material for my writing! I drew the parallel to make you see more clearly how I felt, how your case caught me, took possession of me all over! 300

Ers. But I shouldn't mind even if it were that!

Lud. Please believe what I say!

Ers. I do! But if my poor life, all my sorrows and misfortunes, can serve at least 305 for such a purpose! ...

Lud. For one of my books?

Ers. Why not? I would be happy, proud, oh so proud, really!

Lud. I throw up my hands! 310

Ers. Why?

Lud. Because you again remind me that I am an old, old man!

Ers. I do? Why? I don't mean that! I mean ...   315

Lud. A novel, my dear child, can be written, but it can also be lived! I said that I felt you taking entire possession of me; but it wasn't to write a novel — it was to live one! I hold out my arms to you — but you, instead of offer- 320 ing me — what shall I say — your lips, for instance — hand me pen and paper to write your story!

Ers. (*embarrassed, bowing her head*). But we hardly know each other! It is too soon!   325

Lud. Too soon for your lips, I grant you that; but — later on perhaps?

Ers. (*sorrowfully*). No!

Lud. Just notice how differently you and I are feeling toward the present situation. 330 I was hurt a little because you might have thought my interest in your case merely the curiosity of a writer; and you on the other hand are hurt (or at least you are not very much pleased), if I tell you that the writer, as a writer 335 pure and simple — clever I mean to say, and not just old — did not need to make you any such offer as I have made, nor to go and get you at the very door of the hospital; because the novel ... well ... as I read about you in the 340 papers ... the novel came into my head full-grown — the plot, the characters, the episodes, everything!

Ers. Really? All of a sudden? Just like that?   345

Lud. All of a sudden! It just flashed through my mind! I could see it almost paragraph by paragraph, with all its wealth of situation and detail! Oh, magnificent! The East ... the Levant [1] ... a villa on the seashore ... a 350 house with a flat roof! You there, a governess! And the baby falls from the roof, and you are sent away. Then a ship at sea! Then here you are home again, and you discover how terrible ... oh, I could see it all ... the whole thing 355 — even before I knew what you looked like, before I was acquainted with you at all!

[1] The Near East, but more specifically Turkey and adjoining Mediterranean islands.

Ers. In your imagination, that is! (*Piqued with curiosity*) So you imagined me? How did you think of me? What was I like? This 360 way? As I really am?

Lud. No!

(*With a negative gesture, and smiling.*

Ers. (*insisting*). How did you think of me? Please tell me!

Lud. Why are you so anxious to find 365 out?

Ers. Because I should like to be just as you thought of me!

Lud. Oh, no! Because I like you very much as you are! In fact, I like you better this 370 way — for myself, that is — not for the novel, necessarily!

Ers. But in that case, the novel that was mine, my story, you made it up around another woman!   375

Lud. Of course! Of course! Around the woman I had imagined!

Ers. Was she very different from me?

Lud. She was another woman!

Ers. Oh, dear, dear! In that case ... 380 well ... I don't understand ... I don't understand!

Lud. What don't you understand?

Ers. Why are you interested in me! Why me?

Lud. Whom should I be interested in if 385 not in you?

Ers. But I am not the woman in your story! If my experience, my misfortunes, everything in short that interested you when you read about it in the papers ... I mean ... if it 390 interested you not on my account, but in connection with another woman who is not like me ...   (*She breaks off in bewilderment.*

Lud. What were you going to say, little girl?

Ers. ... then I can go away!   395

Lud. (*catching her, and resting an arm delicately around her waist*). But not at all, not at all, my dear child! The idea! We'll let the woman in the novel go away! But she isn't you, she isn't you!

Ers. (*hurt, suspiciously*). She and I 400 are different people? (*Almost in terror*) You don't believe, then ...

Lud. (*smiling*). Of course, I believe! Of course! But I should prefer not to think of you

any longer in connection with the novel 405
which may have been yours, to be sure...
which is yours, in fact...yes! However, I
don't think of you in that connection any
longer; because, you understand, as I thought
of you for my book you were different; 410
you were another person! Now I should like to
think of you in your new life, such as it is to be,
as it is going to be from now on, that is, with
me! And I hope that you, too, will think of
yourself only in this new life, forgetting 415
all about the terrible things that have happened to you!

Ers. (*with infinite sadness, but with a smile
nevertheless*). But in that case, I shall be not
the woman I was, nor the woman I am, but
still another! 420

Lud. Another? Yes! The woman you are
going to be!

Ers. (*looks at him in amazement*). I? (*With
a slight gesture of her two hands, which have
hitherto been limply folded on her knees*) I
have never been anything! I have never 425
been anybody!

Lud. Oh, now — wait! You've never been
anybody?

Ers. Nobody — ever!

Lud. But you are yourself! 430

Ers. Who am I? What am I?

Lud. First of all, you're a sweet, charming,
beautiful, little girl!

Ers. (*shrugging her shoulders*). Good-looking? I doubt that! But even if I were, 435
I've never been able to profit by it.

Lud. That's important, it's true. In fact,
it may even occur to a girl...in sheer despair
...to make an extreme resolution at last, let
herself go, throw herself haphazard upon 440
life!

Ers. (*looking at him fearfully*). Oh, how
can you say that?

Lud. No, I wasn't referring to you! It came
into my mind, I suppose, because I had 445
thought of her, the girl in the novel, in that way!
(*Speaking as though he could see the character before his eyes and improvising*) Despair! Not
knowing what to do! Evening! The hall bedroom of a hotel! Then she looks into the mirror
and — a sudden decision! A mad reso- 450

lution! Her bill from the landlord! In her
purse a penny or two! And the clerk is insisting
on his money!

Ers. (*starting in great terror*). Did they put
that in the papers? 455

Lud. No! I invented it! (*Looking at her in
delight*) Do you mean that this was actually
the case with you?

Ers. (*hardly able to utter the word*). Yes!

Lud. (*beaming with pleasure*). Well! 460
Well! Well! So I guessed it right! You went
down into the street that night?

Ers. (*faintly*). Yes! Yes!

Lud. ...and — it was like this: a man came
along the street...a man...any one at 465
all! Wasn't that it?

Ers. (*covering her face, with a shudder of horror*). ...and not knowing how to go about
it...

Lud. How to ask him? 469

Ers. (*nodding, with her face still covered*). Yes!

Lud. (*as though he understood the situation perfectly*). And he refused, eh?

Ers. (*looking at him wildly, her lips apart. She
nods in the affirmative*). Yes!

Lud. (*beaming with pleasure again*). So I got
even the details, even the details — to perfection! And then — disgust! Repentance! 475
Loathing for that ugly and fruitless effort!
To perfection! To perfection! (ERSILIA *bursts
into sobs, and the novelist, quickly*) But no,
why do you feel so bad about it? It's all over
now! No! No! Please don't cry! 480

(*He stoops and tries to put his arm re-
assuringly about her shoulders.*

Ers. Don't touch me! Let me go! I want
to go away!

Lud. But why? Why go away?

Ers. Now that you know this!

Lud. But I knew it already! I knew 485
it already!

Ers. How did you know it already?

Lud. Because I imagined it that way — in
the novel! Don't you see? I was right! That's
the way it happened! Exactly as it hap- 490
pened!

Ers. But I am so ashamed!

(*At this moment an unusually violent
burst of noise comes from down the*

street, apparently because of some collision or other: a crash of vehicles, screams, cries, oaths, hoots, threats.

Lud. Ashamed? Why? Don't say that! ... (*He breaks off and turns toward the window.*) But what the devil has happened?

Ers. They're shouting! There's been 495 an accident or something!

The uproar increases. Cries of "Help! Help!" The door to the left opens and SIGNORA ONORIA *rushes headlong into the room*

Ono. They've run over a poor old man! I guess he's killed! Right here in front of the house! (*She runs to one of the windows while* LUDOVICO *and* ERSILIA *hurry toward the other. With the window open, the noise in the street holds the stage for some time. An automobile has collided with a wagon. In trying to avoid the wagon, the chauffeur turned his car across a sidewalk, running over an old man who was not quick enough to get out of the way. The victim is dying, or perhaps dead. People are standing about him. The ambulance comes clanging up in the midst of the shouting and confusion, and hurries away again. What is going on is made clear by the various sounds, exclamations, words that are distinguishable in the general clamor.*

Voices in Street. Oh, oh! Poor fellow! 500 Help! Help! Ran across his chest! Give him air! Arrest him! Arrest him! He's dead! Poor old man! Hurry! Hurry! Don't let him get away! Back broken! Dead! He made a sharp turn! He had the right of way! No, 505 no! It isn't true! Hang him! Hang him! He ought to be in jail! These speeders! Give him air! No! He's dead! Poor fellow! Hurry! Hurry! The police station! No, the hospital! Here's his hat! Here's his hat! The mur- 510 derer! They ought to hang him!

(*The agitation on the sidewalk is reflected in the gestures and exclamations of the three people at the windows.*

Ono. He's dead! He's dead! Poor old man!

Oh, don't let him get away! He was trying to get away! He looks like a murderer! He's trying to excuse himself! Flattened him 515 out like a toad!

Ers. (*springing back from the window horrified*). Oh, how terrible! How terrible!

Lud. (*stepping back also and closing the window*). Poor devil! Probably he has a family! (*Irritated by the noise*) Please, Signora, close the window! 520

Ono. They've carried him away! (*Shutting the window*) But he's dead by this time!

Lud. If he's not dead already, he will be by the time they get him to the hospital!

Ono. I'm going downstairs to find out 525 about it! How terrible! How terrible!

(*She ambles, in her usual fussy manner, out of the room. The noises in the street gradually die down.*

Lud. Filthy street this is! They never clean it up! And when it rains you can hardly paddle your way through the mud! And just one jam of traffic: carts, trucks, automobiles, 530 everything! And they permit pushcarts there into the bargain! Just imagine! Pushcarts!

Ers. (*after a pause, staring horror-stricken into space in front of her*). The street! The street! How terrible!

Lud. What a school for a man who 535 writes! For a man like myself! Oh, you can free yourself from all common, vulgar concerns! Your imagination lifts you above all this! You soar to the clouds! But down there is the street with its people going to and fro! All the 540 noises of life, the life of other people, foreign to you, but still present before your mind, ringing in your ears; intruding on your thoughts; interrupting; deforming everything ... But we are going to be together, aren't we? We're go- 545 ing to work out a pretty story together, aren't we? Yes! Just imagine; supposing I were the old man who was just run over down in the street there! What would you be doing here in such circumstances? But you had your 550 life broken into once by something like that, didn't you? An accident! A child falling from the roof!

Ers. Oh!

Lud. You think of something, and a 555

hawker barks, out in the street, or a newsboy comes along — and your ideas . . . good-by! It's as though two fingers were stretched out into space to catch the lark by the tail just as it is soaring to the sky to greet the sunshine   560 in its joy . . . and pull it back to earth again!

Ers. You are a servant in a house, obedient to other people! — yourself? Nobody! Nothing! How terrible! To feel one's self just nobody! Alone in the world!   No one even   565 thinking of you as a person! And to me — the street . . . I saw my life as though it had no real existence! As though it were a dream . . . just things about me! A few people in the garden at noon! Trees! A settee! Chairs! And I   570 refused to be just nobody — to be just nothing!

Lud. Ah, as for that, now!   No, that isn't true!

Ers. It isn't true?   I made up my mind to kill myself!   575

Lud. Yes, but making a good story out of it!

Ers. (*fearful again*). What do you mean — a good story? Do you think I was inventing it all?

Lud. No! No! I was thinking of my-   580 self! You made a good story for me by just telling of your experiences!

Ers. When they picked me up in the garden there?

Lud. Yes! And later on at the hos-   585 pital! How can you have been nobody if your story aroused so much pity in everyone? You can't imagine the impression you made in the town when the newspapers came out with it! The interest you aroused! You have a   590 proof of it in me and in those letters in your handbag, in all the offers you received! Ten! Ten or more!

Ers. Have you kept them?

Lud. Kept what?   595

Ers. The newspapers! I would like to read the story myself, with my own eyes! Have you kept them?

Lud. Why, perhaps! I imagine I could find one!   600

Ers. Please look for it! Please hunt it up! I would like to see it!

Lud. But no, why should you bother with all that now?

Ers. I want to see what the papers   605 said! Please! I must read it for myself!

Lud. I imagine they printed just what you told them.

Ers. But I don't remember what I said at such a time! I should like to see it! I   610 should like to read about it! Please try to find the paper!

Lud. I wonder where it could be . . . all this rubbish here . . . I never was very neat! What do you say — let's wait a while! We'll   615 come across it later on!

Ers. It gave the whole story? Was it very long?

Lud. At least three columns on the front page! Summertime . . . not much doing!   620 When the reporters get hold of a story like yours, they eat it up!

Ers. But him . . . what did they say of him?

Lud. Why, that he had jilted you!   625

Ers. No, not him! I mean . . . I mean . . . the other! The other one!

Lud. The consul?

Ers. (*greatly shocked*). Did they say he was a consul?   630

Lud. Yes, our consul at Smyrna! [1]

Ers. (*still in great alarm*). Oh, dear, dear! They even told where it happened! They promised me they wouldn't!

Lud. Oh, yes . . . but these reporters! . . .   635

Ers. But they didn't need to, did they? The story was just as good even if it didn't tell where it happened or who was concerned. Well, what did they say?

Lud. They said that when the baby fell   640 from the roof! . . .

Ers. (*covering her face with her hands*). Oh, poor little thing! Poor little thing!

Lud. After the baby fell from the roof, the consul was fearfully cruel toward you!   645

Ers. Oh, no, he wasn't. It was his wife! It was his wife!

Lud. They said he was too!

Ers. Oh, no, not he! His wife! Oh, dear, dear me!   650

---

[1] Smyrna is the largest Turkish seaport on the Mediterranean, situated about midway of the western shore of Asia Minor.

Lud. Because his wife was jealous of you! Oh, I can imagine her, strapping big woman, a regular grenadier. . . .

Ers. Oh, no, she wasn't! Not at all! She was a tiny little thing! Slender, all shriveled up, yellow! She was a lemon!   656

Lud. Oh, now, wait, now! Why, you know, I can just see her! She's this way! Tall, dark-haired, her eyebrows joining over her nose! I could paint her picture!   660

Ers. But she wasn't that kind of woman at all! Who knows how you must have imagined me! No, no! She's just as I said!

Lud. Yes, but that doesn't matter! For my purposes I needed a big woman, while the   665 baby was small and slight . . . a tiny thing . . . emaciated!

Ers. Emaciated? Tiny? My Mimetta? Oh, dear me!

Lud. I called it Titì!   670

Ers. Not Titì! Mimetta . . . and a beautiful child! Fat as butter! She would toddle around on her little fat legs, her rosy cheeks, and her golden curls shaking all over her head! And she was so fond of me! I was the   675 only one she liked!

Lud. So naturally the mother was jealous of you on that account as well!

Ers. Oh, yes, I should say so, especially on the baby's account! And it was her   680 fault, you know! For when that other man came, on the cruiser . . .

Lud. The ensign in the navy?

Ers. Yes . . . that night she put me, on purpose, in a situation where I would be   685 very likely to succumb! Alone there! In that garden! Palm trees all around me! And the fragrance of the flowers! How sweet! How wonderful! Drugged with perfume!

Lud. Oh, a magnificent story! Mag-   690 nificent! Full of color, you see! The sea; sunshine; fragrance; night in the Levant!

Ers. If it had not been so terrible for me! . . .

Lud. With that hellhound of a woman!   695 . . . I can just imagine her! Treachery, you see — the treachery of a person who has never known what love is, and who understands that the joy she prepares for another woman will

soon be destroyed in a most terrible mis-   700 fortune! Magnificent!

Ers. I wish you could have seen her! As kind toward me as my own mother! He had asked for my hand quite formally, applying to her and to the consul! They were my   705 guardians, you see! Oh, my own way in everything! But then when he went away! (*Horrified*) How can a person change so suddenly! An irritation you can't understand! Nothing suited her any more! Just one humilia-   710 tion after another for me! And then at last — I was blamed for the accident!

Lud. While it was she who sent you out of the house on some errand or other! . . .

Ers. (*turning on him suddenly, deeply impressed, and in some alarm*). Who said that?

Lud. It was in the papers!   716

Ers. That too?

Lud. You must have said so yourself!

Ers. No, I don't remember saying that! I don't believe I said it!   720

Lud. Do you think I imagined it, then? Probably some newspaper man invented it to color up the cruelty of your dismissal a bit! . . . For you were sent away, and they didn't even give you money for your ticket home!   725 That much is true?

Ers. Yes, that's true! That's true!

Lud. Almost as though you could be made to pay in money for the death of the child!

Ers. And she threatened me with that,   730 you know! Yes, she did! She did! And she would have had me arrested for it if she hadn't been afraid that certain things might be found out!

Lud. Certain things about her? Ah,   735 so it's true, then!

Ers. (*embarrassed*). No! I don't mean . . . anyhow I'm sorry the papers said that she sent me away! I would like to forget all about what happened out there! I'm thinking of the   740 journey home! Oh, how I suffered! I'm sure that that poor baby, buried in her grave, came away on the steamer with me just the same so as not to be left there with those cruel parents! And I felt this way . . . it   745 seemed as though I lost her when I went down into the street from my hotel that night!

Lud. But when you got here, if I may ask, you didn't look him up?

Ers. How could I look him up? I 750 didn't know his address! I wrote him in care of General Delivery! Then I went to the Navy Building!

Lud. Well?

Ers. They told me he had resigned 755 his commission!

Lud. But you should have followed him up, to make him atone for the crime, the downright crime, he committed against you!

Ers. I never was good at asserting my rights!

Lud. He had promised to marry you! 761

Ers. I was crushed! When they told me that he was to be married the next day, the sense of his betrayal, which was so cruel and so unexpected, came over me so strongly 765 that I was crushed! I had only a little money left! And the thought of actually having to beg!... In the garden there with that poison in my hand I thought of the little child, and I gathered courage from the feeling that 770 having lost her the evening before I would then be going to find her again!

Lud. Oh, come, come! Let's not think of those things now! Try to cheer up, little girl! 775

Ers. (*after a pause and with a smile of deepest sadness*). Yes, but at least, let me be that woman ...

Lud. That woman! What woman?

Ers. The woman you imagined! Dear me! If I amounted to something at least once 780 in my life, as you have said, I want to be in your novel, myself, but I, you understand, I, the woman I am! It seems quite unfair that you should see another woman in me!

Lud. (*laughing*). That's a great idea! 785 It's as though she were robbing you, eh?

Ers. Why, yes! You are stealing things that happened to me; you are stealing my life, the life that I had decided to do away with! I lived that life to the very depths of de- 790 spair and it seems that now, if you don't mind, I have a right to be in the story you make of it ... a beautiful story, like a novel I read of yours. It is called — wait — what did you call it? *The Outcast* — yes, *The Outcast*. 795

Lud. The Outcast? Oh, no, you're mistaken! *The Outcast* was not written by me!

Ers. (*surprised*). Wasn't that one of your novels?

Lud. No! 800

Ers. How strange! I thought ...

Lud. In fact, it's by a writer whom I cordially detest!

Ers. (*mortified, covering her face with her hands*). Dear me! Dear me!

Lud. Now, now, what does that all mat- 805 ter? You are mixing it up with some other book. (*ERSILIA begins to weep, still covering her face with her hands.*) But you're not really hurt, are you? My dear, what are you crying for? Why should I care about a little mistake like that? It's a bad novel, all right; but I'm not 810 insulted just because you thought I wrote it!

Ers. No, you see that's the way it always is with me! Nothing ever, ever comes out right! (*There is a knock at the door to the left.*

Lud. Yes! Come in! Come right in! 815

It is SIGNORA ONORIA, *now all smiles, all honey, and absurdly sentimental over what she has learned*

Ono. May I come in? (*She looks about the room for* ERSILIA.) Where is the poor little thing? (*She stops and joins her hands in a gesture of pity as she sees* ERSILIA *weeping.*) Oh, the poor little thing — in tears? 820

Lud. (*in astonishment, unable to understand the sudden change in the woman's manner*). Why, what's the matter?

Ono. You might have told me she was the girl the newspapers were talking about! Signorina Drei, isn't it? Ersilia Drei! Poor 825 child! You poor thing! I am so glad you are well again and out of the hospital! I'm delighted to have you here!

Lud. But how did you find out that it was she? 830

Ono. A great question! Don't you suppose I read the papers?

Lud. Yes, but how did you know that she was the girl?

Ono. Why, because ... well ... look at 835 this! (*She hands him a visiting card.*) There's a reporter downstairs, and he told me the whole story!

Lud. A reporter . . . here?

Ers. A reporter?   840

Lud. What does he want?

Ono. He says there are a number of important things which the young lady must explain!

Ers. Things to explain?

Lud. This is too much, upon my word!   845

Ers. What does he want me to explain?

Lud. And who told him that the young lady was here?

Ono. I don't know!

Ers. Neither do I!   When he inter-   850 viewed me I never even dreamed that I would come here to your house!

Lud. (*almost to himself*). I see!   I see!   Talking, as usual!   (*With a nod in* ONORIA's *direction.   Then turning to* ERSILIA) Well,   855 what do you say?   Shall we have him come in?

Ers. No . . . I . . . no . . . no!   I don't know! What shall I say to him?   What does he want me to explain?   859

Lud. I'm going to have a talk with the fellow!
> (*He goes out through the door to the left.*

Ono. Oh, you poor child!   If you only knew how I cried when I read your story in the papers . . . such a terrible story!

Ers. But what do they want of me now?

Ono. Perhaps . . . well . . . you know!   865

Ers. Oh, dear me!   Dear me!   I can't endure another ordeal!   More trouble would quite kill me!

Ono. You're not well?

Ers. Oh, I'm all right, I think!   But   870 here . . . (*She puts a hand to her breast.*) I don't know . . . it's hard for me to breathe, somehow! They say I am well; but perhaps there is still something wrong, here!   It hurts when I press with my hand, here, and then here, and in   875 my back!   Oh, a terrible pain!   It seems to run all over me!   (*She weeps and groans.*) Dear me!   Dear me!
> (*From the street comes a sudden burst of music from a hurdy-gurdy, playing a popular song.*

Ono. Unbutton your waist!   Let me see!

Ers. No!   No!   (*Irritated by the music*   880

from the hurdy-gurdy) Oh, please send that man away!   I can't bear it.

Ono. Yes, with pleasure . . . right away!   (*She takes a purse from the pocket of her apron.*) With pleasure!   (*She goes to the window, opens*   885 *the lower sash, and calls to the organ grinder below, motioning to him to go away.   The music continues.* ONORIA *opens her pocketbook, takes out some coins, and tosses them down from the window.*)   There are sick people in the house! (*Again she motions the man away.   The hurdy-gurdy breaks off suddenly in the middle of a tune.* ONORIA *closes the window and hurries back to* ERSILIA's *side.*)   So there you are!   We have sent him away!   Now listen to me!   You just unbutton your clothes . . .

Ers. No, I can't do that!   I must be   890 ready!   I'm afraid that not even this can last!

Ono. What?   What can last?

Ers. Oh, if you only knew!   I am so unhappy, so unhappy!   I can't endure it!   This sash . . . oh!   (*She loosens her sash.*) I can't endure   895 it . . . it's too tight . . . it's too tight!   I can't bear it!
> (*Through the door to the left the sound of talking is heard.   It is* LUDOVICO *inviting someone to come in.*

Lud. No!   No!   Go right along!   After you, please!

ALFREDO CANTAVALLE, *a newspaper man, enters, followed by the novelist.* CANTAVALLE *is a handsome young Neapolitan, pretentious, elegant, and fashionable.   He even wears a monocle, but he has the greatest difficulty in keeping it in place.   He is a jolly, good-natured, talkative fellow.   His hair, parted in the middle like a schoolboy's, falls thick over his forehead.   He has a long, fat, ruddy face. His fat legs show almost feminine lines through tight-fitting trousers*

Cant. Sorry to trouble you, ladies!   900 Oh, my dear Signorina, you remember me, I am sure!

Lud. (*introducing*). Signor Alfredo Cantavalle, of the press!

Ers. Yes, I remember you!   905

Cant. I thought you would!   (*And noting*

Signora Onoria) Oh, Signora, you are a
relative of this young lady?

Lud. No, she is the mistress of the house!

Cant. Oh! Delighted! (*He makes a* 910
slight bow.) I remember in fact that the young
lady has no relatives! You just had a serious
accident out in front here, I understand.

Lud. Yes, a poor old man!

Ono. How frightened I was!   915

Cant. He's dead!

Ono. Dead? He's dead?

Cant. Yes, died in the ambulance on the way
to the hospital!

Ono. Who was he?   920

Cant. He hasn't been identified yet. (*Turning to* Ersilia) My dear Signorina, I hope
you will allow me not only to congratulate you
on your recovery, but to congratulate myself!
Yes, it was a great piece of luck, and it 925
turned out all in your favor! The article I
wrote about your experiences has had the singular good fortune to be noted by a famous author.
(*He bows to* Ludovico.) But it's all nonsense,
Signor Nota, what that friend of yours 930
says.... This is the noblest thing you have done
in your whole life! (*Again turning to* Ersilia)
You can imagine how pleased I am at hearing it!

Ers. Yes, it was wonderful good fortune for
me!   935

Lud. Oh, please! What are you talking
about?

Cant. No, Signor Nota, she is right! And
for other reasons, also! Now we can have the
advantage of your co-operation and sup- 940
port — and we need it, I assure you! Shall I
explain?... If I may venture to speak in the
presence of this lady here...

(*He nods in* Onoria's *direction.*

Ono. I'm going right away... but the Signorina was not feeling very well!   945

Lud. Not feeling very well?

Ono. In fact, she was in the greatest distress!

Lud. What's the matter?

Ers. I don't know... I don't know! I have
a chill, I guess... my nerves!   950

Ono. Now you just listen to me! Come into
the other room!

(*She points to the door at the rear.*

Ers. No! No!

Ono. Yes, you'd better... and just get into
bed!   955

Lud. Do so, please, if you're not well!

Ono. Once she gets her clothes off and goes to
bed...

Ers. No, thank you! I shall be all right!
I can stay here!   960

Cant. The effects of the poison, I suppose!
But you'll see... with a little care...

Lud. ... and a quiet environment!...

Ono. I am always right here, my dear child!
If you need anything, call me! I shall be 965
only too glad!...

Ers. Yes, thank you... thank you, Signora!

Cant. In that case I shall be going! Good
afternoon, Signorina!

Ono. (*approaching* Ludovico *and in a whisper*). Don't disturb her now. A little 970
common sense! Can't you see how the poor
thing is suffering?

(*She withdraws through the door to the
left, which* Ludovico *closes behind
her.*

Cant. I am so sorry if my coming here...

Lud. (*with some annoyance*). Oh, it's all right,
Cantavalle, but get through as soon as you can!

Cant. I can find out what I want to 976
know in two minutes, Signor Nota! Give me
just two minutes!

Lud. Well, let's come to the point! What is
it precisely that that fool consul of yours...

Ers. (*starting in terror*). The consul? 981

Lud. The consul, precisely! (*Speaking to*
Cantavalle) We must put that fellow in his
place!

Ers. (*in great alarm*). What do you 985
mean? The consul is here... in town?

Cant. He came down to our office yesterday
and raised a terrible rumpus, Signorina!

Ers. (*moaning in despair*). Oh, dear! Oh,
dear! Oh, dear!   990

Lud. And you say he insists on a retraction?

Cant. Yes... of everything, he says, of
everything.

Ers. (*to* Cantavalle). Now you can 995
see all the harm you have done! You said
things I didn't want you to say, and you
promised me you wouldn't.

Cant. I? What harm have I done?

Ers. Yes, you! You shouldn't have 1000 mentioned the name of the city! You shouldn't have said who the people were!

Lud. A general retraction he wants? What do you mean?

Cant. Why, he wants us to deny the 1005 whole story, which, he says, is a tissue of false-hoods! One moment, Signor Nota... I must answer the young lady! His name, you see, I was careful not to mention!

Lud. You did very well to show up a 1010 rascal like that!

Cant. No, all I said was "the Italian con-sul in Smyrna!" Who the devil cares who the consul in Smyrna is! Who is ever going to know? I didn't even know myself! And 1015 I don't know even now! Anyhow, the last thing in the world I should ever have expected was that he would come tearing into our office yesterday like a bull in a crockery shop!

Ers. (*again moaning in despair*). Oh, 1020 dear! Oh, dear!

Lud. So he came to Rome, eh? All on ac-count of this?

Cant. Not on account of this exactly! He came on account of an accident that 1025 happened to his baby! That was in the story, to be sure! He came because his wife, as he says, is in a terrible state of mind! In short, an impossible situation, there, in Smyrna!

Ers. Yes, that woman! That woman! 1030

Cant. He came on home to ask for a transfer; but he has seen the newspapers! A pretty mess we are in, Signor Nota!

Lud. But why?

Cant. Why? Why, the man has an offi- 1035 cial position, you understand! He is certain to bring a suit against my paper... a suit for libel!

Lud. But what did the article have to say about him, after all?

Cant. Nothing but lies, as he claims... 1040 things very much to his discredit!

Lud. Lies? Were they lies?

Ers. I don't know! I haven't seen your arti-cle! I don't know what you may have said of him or of his wife or of the accident! 1045

Cant. I assure you, Signorina, that I reported exactly what you said! Nothing more, nothing

less! Oh, of course, I was very much affected by your story, and my style... well... but as regards matters of fact, I didn't change 1050 a thing! You can see for yourself, if you just look at the paper!

Lud. (*beginning to rummage around the room*). I am sure I had it here! It must be here some-where!

Cant. Never mind, I'll send you a 1055 copy! But as you can well see, Signorina, I have come here to find out from you what I am to do in the face of the complaint and the threat of this gentleman!

Ers. (*with a convulsive burst of anger, and al-most hissing as she speaks*). He has 1060 nothing to complain of, that man! And as for his threats!...

Cant. All the better in that case... all the better!

Ers. Oh, dear me! Oh, dear me! I 1065 am so tired! I don't feel well!

(*She begins to sob, shivering and shak-ing all over, her weeping soon rising to a shrill note that might be mistaken for laughter. Finally she falls back in a faint.*)

Lud. (*running to her anxiously and help-ing* CANTAVALLE *to hold her up and keep her from slipping to the floor*). Ersilia! Ersilia! Please!

Cant. Oh, Signorina! No! Please! Please! Don't worry, please! 1070

Lud. What's the matter? Oh, please don't! Everything is all right!

Cant. There's nothing to be afraid of, Si-gnorina!

Lud. She's gone! Fainted! Just call 1075 the lady, will you please?

Cant. (*running to the door, left*). Signora! Signora!

Lud. (*also calling*). Signora Onoria! 1079

Cant. Signora Onoria! Signora Onoria!

(*He goes out into the hall.*)

Lud. Oh, no! Ersilia dear! No! No! Be a good girl! Everything is all right!

CANTAVALLE *returns with* SIGNORA ONORIA. *She has a bottle of smelling salts in her hand*

Ono. Here I am! What's the matter? Oh,

poor child! There! There! Just hold her head up ... a little higher ... there we are! 1085 Poor child! (*She puts the bottle of smelling salts to* ERSILIA'S *nose.*) And I told you men not to trouble her! She is not in a condition to be disturbed!

Cant. Ah, she is coming to again!   1090

Lud. We must get her into the other room to bed!

Ono. Just a moment!

Lud. Ersilia!

Ono. There! There! Poor child! 1095 Now you're all right! Come, now ... brace up!

Lud. Yes! Yes! Poor little girl! Ersilia! Ersilia!

Cant. I'm so sorry, Signorina, but everything is all right! Everything is all right!   1100

Ers. (*almost laughing, in a tone of childish wonder*). Oh, dear me, did I fall?

Lud. No! Why? No, you didn't fall — but you scared us almost to death!

Ers. I didn't fall?   1104

Lud. Oh, no! What were you dreaming of?

Ono. And now, poor child, just see if you can stand on your feet!

Lud. Yes! Now, there! Gently, now ... careful!

Ers. Oh, I thought it was ... as if   1110 suddenly ... I don't know ... as though I were made of lead! (*She looks up and sees* CANTA-VALLE. *A nervous terror runs over her. She leaps to her feet.*) Oh, no! No!

      (*She staggers and is again about to fall.* LUDOVICO *and* ONORIA *catch her in their arms.*

Lud. No, Ersilia! What's the matter? What's the matter?   1115

Ers. Let me go! Let me go!

Ono. Yes! Yes! All right! But now we are going into the other room!

Lud. And you lie down on the bed! Yes! Now, then, there you are! See? We   1120 won't let you fall!

Ono. Careful, now ... careful! And I'll stay with you in there! You can lie down and be all cozy and comfortable!

Lud. You will rest up a little, and   1125 everything will be all right!

Ers. I can't endure it! I am all tired out! I can't endure it!

Ono. (*blocking* LUDOVICO *in the doorway, rear*). You stay in here! I'll attend to her!

      (*She helps* ERSILIA *into the bedroom.*

Lud. If you ask me, I'd say that   1130 they've tormented that poor girl long enough!

Cant. I hope you don't blame me! I am more sorry than I can tell you, Signor Nota; but unfortunately you don't know the worst of it yet! There's more trouble ahead for   1135 the young lady!

Lud. More trouble?

Cant. Yes! And I think you ought to know about it! The consul brought the matter up while he was in our office!   1140

Lud. You just tell that consul to go to the devil!

Cant. Now, not quite so fast! You know, Signor Nota — oh, my article had a perfectly marvelous effect! It seems that the girl   1145 who was going to marry the boy in the story is indignant at the trick he played on this young lady here, so she has called the wedding off! Understand?

Lud. Called the wedding off?   1150

Cant. My article was a corker, I can tell you! Not only that! When the story came out, the girl called off her marriage, as I said, but it seems her young man saw the light and he has repented too. What do you   1155 think of that? Oh, I got the right touch into my story of her suicide! That boy has lost his head completely.

Lud. You mean the ensign in the navy?

Cant. Yes! His name ... wait ... I   1160 think his name is Laspiga! Anyhow, he'd lost his head completely! So the consul said, at any rate!

Lud. And how did he find it out?

Cant. Why, it seems that the girl's   1165 father went and looked him up at the Foreign Office! It was the old man who told the consul!

Lud. Some mixup, I'll say!

Cant. Yes, especially from your point of view, since now you're involved yourself!   1170

Lud. Why?

Cant. And me, too, for that matter! Just imagine ... here I am with a libel suit, probably, on my hands!

Lud. But this old man — the father   1175 of the young lady?

Cant. He is raising the very devil! The girl at first, was angry, but later on, you understand... there she was about to be married... well... just what you might expect! 1180 Tears; convulsions; hysterics—a pretty mess! The consul, you see, became acquainted with Laspiga out there in Smyrna. Signorina Drei was a governess in the consul's house.

Lud. So the consul looked up Laspiga?

Cant. Yes! 1186

Lud. It's not hard to guess what the ensign told him! The consul blames Signorina Drei for the death of the baby!

At this point through the door on the left, which has been left open, FRANCO LASPIGA *rushes upon the stage, pale, trembling, in the greatest agitation, his face showing the livid pallor that comes from many sleepless nights.* LASPIGA *is twenty-seven years old, light-haired, tall, slender, fashionably dressed*

Las. I beg your pardon! May I 1190 come in? Ersilia... where is she? Is she here? Where is she?

Lud. (*in astonishment at this unexpected visit*). But, who are you?

Las. I am Franco Laspiga. Signorina Drei tried to kill herself on my account! 1195

Cant. Ah! Signor Laspiga! Ah!

Lud. You here too!

Las. I went to the hospital, but she had already left, so I hurried to the office of a newspaper where I found out... (*He stops* 1200 *and looks at* CANTAVALLE.) I beg your pardon ... you are Signor Ludovico Nota?

Cant. Why, no... there's Signor Nota!

Las. Oh, you are Signor Nota?

Lud. Yes... but how is this? So 1205 everybody knows, then?

Cant. But my dear Signor Nota, you forget who you are!

Lud. (*very much annoyed and raising his arms in helplessness*). I give up!

Cant. Your generous, your magnificent 1210 act has naturally made an impression in town!

Las. (*surprised*). Magnificent act! What have you done? Tell me! Isn't she here?

Lud. (*to* CANTAVALLE). I had no intention of seeking notoriety for myself, and 1215

much less, notoriety in connection with this young lady!

Cant. Oh, please, what do you mean?

Lud. I am disgusted with this sudden popularity of mine! (*To* LASPIGA) You will 1220 believe me when I say that the young lady has been here less than an hour!

Las. Oh, so she is here, then! Where is she? Where?

Lud. Why, I went to meet her at the 1225 hospital...

Las. You did? Well?

Lud. She had no place to go, so I offered her this apartment here! This evening, of course, I shall go to a hotel myself! 1230

Las. I am very grateful to you!

Lud. And why, pray? I suppose... because I'm not so young as I might be — that's why you're grateful to me! Well, never mind! Why did you come here? 1235

Las. Why? I came to make good, sir! Make good for the harm I have done... throw myself at her feet... compel her to forgive me!

Cant. That's the way to talk! Good 1240 for you! It's all a decent fellow could do!

Lud. But you might have thought of it a little sooner, it seems to me!

Las. You're right! Yes! I didn't realize! I had tried deliberately to forget her! I 1245 passed whole days... But where is she... in the other room? Let me see her!

Lud. At just this moment I should prefer...

Las. No, let me have a talk with her, please!

Cant. It might be better, perhaps, to 1250 let her know you are here...

Lud. She's in bed!

Cant. The joy of seeing you again might...

Las. Is she still sick? Is she still in danger?

Lud. She fainted, right here, a few 1255 moments ago!

Cant. Then — you understand — any more excitement might...

Las. (*in a frenzy*). I didn't realize... I couldn't imagine that my leaving her... 1260 oh, what an end! All of a sudden, right across my life... breaking everything to pieces... the newsboys shouting those headlines in the papers! It was as if someone had seized me and hurled me to the ground! Our names 1265 called out in the streets! My fiancée... her father... her mother... our neighbors in the house where we lived... so I went as fast as I could to the hospital! They wouldn't let me see her! Oh, how I have wronged her; 1270 how I have wronged everybody! The whole world seems to be full of the wrong that I have done! And I can't endure it! I must make up for it somehow! I must undo what I have done!

Cant. Splendid! Splendid! Just what 1275 is needed here! You couldn't beat that ending to the story! I am delighted, Signor Nota, delighted!

At this moment SIGNORA ONORIA *appears in the doorway at the rear, her two hands raised to suggest silence. She closes the door behind her and comes forward*

Ono. Not so loud! Not so loud, please! She heard everything you said! 1280

Las. She knows that I am here?

Ono. Yes! She does! And she is all worked up! She's in agony! She says she'll jump out of the window if you go in there!

Las. What? Why should she do that? 1285 Won't she forgive me?

Cant. (*speaking at the same time*). Why, the idea! On the contrary, she ought...

Ono. No, she's an angel! But she says she refuses! 1290

Lud. Refuses what?

Ono. (*to* LASPIGA). She says that you should go back to the girl you were to marry!

Las. (*speaking up quickly and raising his voice in determination*). No! That's all over, all over!

Ono. She doesn't want any harm to 1295 come to another girl through her!

Las. I refuse! What other girl? She is the girl I want to marry! She, and no one else!

Ono. No, never mind that! She re- 1300 fuses to consider such a proposition!

Las. But I came here to get her forgiveness, to make amends for all the harm that I have done her!

Ono. Please, please, not so loud! She 1305 can hear if you raise your voice like that!

Las. (*to* LUDOVICO). Won't you go in

and explain to her? Try to bring her to reason!

Lud. Why, yes! This, certainly, 1310 would be the best way out for her!

Cant. I should say so! It would settle everything!

Las. Tell her to forget all about what has happened! Tell her that I am here... 1315 that my first duty is toward her. Tell her not to spoil this chance we now have to settle everything in time! Please go in and see her! Please!

(LUDOVICO *withdraws through the door at the rear.*

Ono. She is doing it for the sake of that other girl! 1320

Las. But I have broken with her, absolutely! It's all over! Absolutely all over!

Ono. She refuses! She refuses!

Las. But how can that be? I've broken with the girl! It's all over, and that's all there 1325 is to it! I can't change again now! It's a question of myself... here... inside me! I can't, because now everything has come back to me!

Cant. Ah, yes... the past! You remember the past now? 1330

Las. Something that I had almost forgotten... something that... oh, I don't know how... had gotten to be so far, far away... more like a dream than anything else... so that I... it was as though I had never given 1335 the promise there, that night — a promise such as a person makes in those circumstances! Yes, because then you almost have to make them!

Cant. And then... later on... it all 1340 goes out of your mind, eh?

Las. (*continuing vehemently*). Why, I imagined there was no particular obligation! ... I supposed I was quite free! I kept getting letters from her. But I burned them — 1345 unable somehow to take them seriously! And yet, it's incredible! I don't understand how I was able to lie like that... lie to myself... do what I have done while, meantime, the promise I had given to her had, in fact, not been 1350 withdrawn! It was almost like a dream for me, you see! But there my promise stood! It was true... true... so true, indeed, that when she came here, my betrayal, my treachery toward her . . . oh, now I understand! For 1355 her it was the same as it was for me! Those newsboys calling in the street . . . and reality was suddenly there, before my eyes! And it struck me down! Crushed me! Annihilated me!

LUDOVICO *re-enters from the door at the rear. He is wearing a very long face. There is a note of perplexity, but still of determination, in his voice*

Lud. It's no use! For the moment 1360 it's impossible!

Las. What do you mean! How can that be?

Lud. She has promised to see you tomorrow!

Las. Tomorrow? That's ridiculous! 1365 I can't wait till tomorrow! I can't stand another night . . . no!

Lud. But you'll have to! For the moment there's nothing that can be done.

Las. But I haven't had a wink of sleep 1370 for days! Let me have just one word with her at least!

Lud. There's no use insisting! It would be worse for you, if you were to see her!

Las. But why? 1375

Lud. Let's give her a night to think it over! I talked to her! I told her what you . . .

Las. But why does she refuse? On account of that woman? But that's all off! I don't understand! If she tried to kill herself 1380 on my account, why does she refuse?

Lud. She'll come around all right! She'll probably do what you want in the end! But man alive, give her a chance to pull herself together! 1385

Cant. And you might calm down a bit, yourself!

Las. I can't! I can't!

Lud. Now you just listen to me! I'm quite sure that tomorrow everything will come 1390 out all right! We'll bring her around! (*Turning to* SIGNORA ONORIA) Meantime, you go in to her, please. We mustn't leave her alone!

Ono. Yes! Yes! Of course I will go right in! But you'd better turn the lights on, eh? 1395 It's getting dark!

(*She goes out through the door at the rear.* LUDOVICO *turns on the lights.*

Lud. Now we had better be going, don't you think?

Las. But can't I even see her?

Lud. You can see her tomorrow and 1400 have a talk with her. I'll come here with you myself. But now we'd better be going!

(*He picks up his hat and cane, and stands waiting for the others to precede him through the door.*

Cant. But she ought to see that this solution is the best one for her!

Lud. For the moment we've got to 1405 leave her alone! Let her quiet down a little! She's not well, poor thing! It's too much for her! Shall we go now?

Las. (*stopping in the doorway, left*). But I thought that on my coming here . . . 1410

Lud. (*pushing* CANTAVALLE *toward the door*). After you, Cantavalle!

Cant. Thank you, Signor Nota!

(*He goes to the door.*

Lud. (*to* LASPIGA). After you, sir! On the contrary, your coming here . . .

(*He follows* LASPIGA *out, closing the door behind him. The stage is left empty for a moment. The noises from the street continue.*

The door at the rear is thrown open and ERSILIA *appears. She is buttoning the last buttons on her waist.* SIGNORA ONORIA *follows close behind her*

Ers. No, I am going away! I am going 1415 away!

Ono. But where would you go?

Ers. I don't know, but I am going away!

Ono. That's a foolish thing to do!

Ers. Oh, I must drop out of sight, 1420 somewhere! I must disappear . . . down there, in the street! I don't know!

(*She starts to put on her hat.*

Ono. (*restraining her*). No! No! I won't let you do any such thing!

Ers. Let me go! Let me go! I re- 1425 fuse to stay here a moment longer!

Ono. But why?

Ers. I don't know — because I don't want to see anyone! I don't want to talk with anyone! 1430

Ono. Which means that you won't see him tomorrow?

Ers. No! No! I won't see anyone! Let me go!

Ono. You won't have to see anyone! 1435 I'll tell Signor Nota! Don't worry!

Ers. Was it my fault if they saved my life?

Ono. Your fault? Nonsense! Your fault!

Ers. But they're accusing me! They're accusing me! 1440

Ono. But who is accusing you?

Ers. They are all accusing me ... didn't you hear?

Ono. Not at all, child! He came to ask your forgiveness! 1445

Ers. Ah, forgiveness! I talked about him because I was going to die! But now ... I have had enough of it ...

Ono. Very well! Let it go at that! You can tell Signor Nota all about it tomorrow! 1450

Ers. I thought I could stay here in peace! ...

Ono. And why can't you stay here if you want to?

Ers. Because, you'll see! They'll keep after him ... they'll annoy him! They'll wear 1455 him out!

Ono. Signor Nota?

Ers. Signor Nota!

Ono. I don't believe it! He's a bit of a crank, Signor Nota is; but he's a good kind man 1460 at bottom! You'll see! He's a very good man!

Ers. But there's that other man!

Ono. What other man?

Ers. That other man! I didn't even mention his name! He's going to bring a suit 1465 against the paper!

Ono. The consul?

Ers. The consul! He will never let me alone! (*Again rising to her feet*) Oh! Oh! Let me go! Let me go! 1470

Ono. But no! Sit down! You just be quiet now! Signor Nota will see about that man! He will keep him in his place! Besides, how can he harm you after the way he's treated you? Don't you worry! You just sit down, 1475 here! Don't you see you're hardly fit to be up?

Ers. Yes! Yes! That's so! Oh, what can I do?

Ono. Supposing you go in and lie down

again ... that's a good girl! I will bring 1480 you a cup of broth to drink! You'll get a little rest, and then you'll feel better!

Ers. (*timidly, in a low voice, as one woman, confidingly, to another*). But you understand, don't you? I am just as you saw me and ...

Ono. And what? 1485

Ers. I haven't a thing, not a thing, with me! In the hotel there, I had a bag! I don't know what has become of it! They probably took it to the police station!

Ono. We'll get it back for you tomor- 1490 row! Don't worry about that! I'll send someone, or I'll go and get it myself!

Ers. Yes! But now, now, I haven't a thing! I am naked! I am naked ... naked!

Ono. (*affectionately, comfortingly*). But 1495 I'll see to that! I'll see to everything! You just go in to bed and I'll stay with you! Now I'll run downstairs and get something for you! You just lie down and I'll be right back! It won't take me a second! 1500

(*She goes out through the door at the left.*

ERSILIA *remains seated on the stage, looking in bewilderment around the room. Her head droops to one side as though she were desperately weary. She seems to have difficulty in breathing. She passes a hand across her cold brow. Apparently in fear of fainting again, she rises, walks to a window, and throws it open. It is evening now. The noises in the street have softened. They are less numerous and less varied. Finally they cease altogether. Silence. A company of young men comes down along the sidewalk, talking, laughing, joking. One of them starts a song, but his voice cracks. An uproar of hoots and guffaws.* ERSILIA *returns to her seat at the table. The footfalls of the mirthful company grow faint in the distance and finally are heard no more.* ERSILIA *looks about the room with staring eyes, and in a barely audible voice she murmurs:*

Ers. The street! The street!

Curtain

ACT II

The same scene as in Act I. The following morning. The curtain rises on an empty stage. After a time, the door at the left opens, and FRANCO LASPIGA *and* LUDOVICO NOTA, *followed by* EMMA, *the maid, enter.* LUDOVICO *has his hat on.* LASPIGA *sets his hat on the chair nearest the door. After a time* LUDOVICO *removes his hat*

Lud. (*to the maid*). Is Signora Onoria in?

Emma (*pointing to the door at the rear*). She's in the other room with the young lady.

Lud. Did Signorina Drei have a good night?

Emma. I don't think so. She was not 5 at all well. I don't believe she got a wink of sleep. Nor did the Signora either.

Las. If I had been able to say a word to her last evening ...

Lud. (*to the maid*). Won't you just go 10 in and tell Signora Onoria that I am here?

Emma. Very well, sir!

     (*She starts toward the door at the rear.*

Lud. Was there any mail?

Emma. Yes, sir! Yes, sir! There it is on your desk.   15

     (*She opens the door at the rear, very softly, and goes out.*

Lud. (*picking up his mail from the desk, and addressing* LASPIGA). Oh, please, have a chair, won't you? Please, have a chair!

Las. Thank you! I think I'd rather stand!

Lud. (*with a grunt of disgust*). My, how close it is in here!   20

     (*He goes and opens one of the windows, returning to his mail, which proves to be nothing but newspapers. It is market time in the street. The noises from the traffic are as loud as ever. At a certain point* LUDOVICO *loses patience and pulls the window down again. Then he steps over to* LAS-PIGA, *with a newspaper open in his hand, pointing with his finger to the headlines of an article.*

Lud. Here we are! Won't you just read this?   (*He hands the newspaper to* LASPIGA.

Las. (*after looking it over*). A correction? Deny the whole story?

Lud. Yes! It says they will publish it 25 tomorrow!

Through the door at the rear comes SIGNORA ONORIA, *followed by* EMMA, *who crosses the stage and goes out at the left*

Las. (*looking up as* ONORIA *enters, anxiously*). Ah! Here she is! Here she is!

Ono. (*gesticulating emphatically*). What a night! What a night!

Las. And what is she doing! Won't 30 she come in?

Ono. She will, if she can! She knows that you are here! She guessed it!

Las. But ... you see the state that I am in! Didn't you tell her?   35

Ono. Don't disturb her, please! She was getting a bit of sleep for the first time, just now.

Lud. How can a person sleep in this bedlam?

Ono. That wasn't it! The maid came in 40 and said you were here with another gentleman! That's what woke her up! I was afraid she would refuse, as she did yesterday.

Las. Oh, no! No!

Ono. Well, she didn't. She said she is 45 willing to see you!

Las. Ah! That's better! She is probably convinced. ...

Lud. Oh, of course! And if she isn't, we'll convince her!   50

Ono. I am not so sure of that! Yesterday, after you gentlemen left, she tried to run away!

Lud. Run away?

Las. And where? Why did she want to go?

Ono. Who knows? I had to do my very 55 best to keep her! But one thing I don't understand ... why did they ever let her out of the hospital? She isn't anywhere near well!

Lud. (*bored, and rather coldly*). But when she was with me yesterday! ...   60

Ono. Oh, I don't think so! She was doing her best to bear up, you see — trying to conceal her pain! She's so afraid you will be getting tired of all this!

Lud. I? Not at all! But ... now ... 65 it's rather. ... (*He nods in* LASPIGA's *direction.*

Las. Yes, I'll take care of her! I'll make her well again!

Ono. But now I think I'll go downstairs and lie down for a moment. I'm all worn out! 70 I have not had a wink of sleep! But of course, if there's any need of me!...

Lud. Yes, by all means!

Ono. ... you gentlemen can just call me! (*She starts toward the door, left, but stops and comes back, speaking to* LUDOVICO.) One 75 thing perhaps you don't know! The poor child hasn't a thing with her! They took her bag away, either the people in the hotel or the police! We've got to get it back for her!

Lud. Yes! Yes! I'll attend to that! 80

Ono. But right away, if you can! This morning! She says she is... (ONORIA *hesitates at the word "naked."*) A girl has got to dress these days, you know. You'll attend to it? 85

Las. I'll attend to it! I'll attend to it!

Ono. I think it would be better if you would, Signor Nota!

Lud. (*again with some annoyance*). Yes, don't worry! Don't worry! (*Then changing tone*) 90 Now, we're waiting for her to say whether....

Ono. Oh, please don't be harsh with her!

Lud. Ah, I like that! Yesterday you wanted to drive her out of the house, and now.... 95

Ono. But yesterday I didn't know... Oh, now she reminds me of a little stray dog lost on the streets, with all the other dogs after her! And the gentler she is, the more helpless she is, the more they worry her and torment 100 her. The poor child! She is crushed, discouraged! She hardly dares say her soul's her own!

Lud. (*angrily taking out his handkerchief and blowing his nose*). But now, you understand, things look a little different, even to me! 105

Ono. What? Anything about her?

(*She nods toward the door at the rear.*

Lud. Why, the whole story!... I thought everything was settled! And it is all so different from the way I had imagined it! Things couldn't be worse, really! In the first 110 place, that reporter with his newspaper! Then, there's this gentleman here! (*He points to* LASPIGA.) Then there's that consul tearing around and making a fuss! (*Putting his hand-*

kerchief back into his pocket, and addressing LASPIGA) Did you read what it said in 115 the paper there?

Las. But you mean that Grotti, the consul, is here in town?

Lud. (*angrily*). Where else? He's in town and so is everybody else! It seems that 120 the father of the young lady you were going to marry has had a talk with him!

Las. (*in surprise and with some alarm*). Had a talk with him? And why, please?

Lud. Oh, who knows? Probably to 125 find out all he can about the situation!

Las. (*angrily*). What do they want of me? They slammed the door in my face! But am I to infer that this man Grotti — the consul, that is — has turned against her? 130

(*With a nod toward the door at the rear.*

Ono. Oh, they're all against her!

Lud. It looks that way! In fact it's very certain! You understand, I live here, all taken up with my writing....

Las. (*angry, talking more to himself than to anybody else*). I should like to know why 135 that man Grotti....

Lud. He could probably tell you himself if you asked him! For my part, I'm just a writer... and I got interested in this affair because it seemed to me a curious situa- 140 tion — a "slice of life" — where things and people were — naturally — as I had imagined they were. Now, all this mixup... one thing after another... well, yes... I'll speak right out — it's getting on my nerves! It has 145 spoiled things for me! Spoiled things completely! But, fortunately, you are here!

Las. Yes, I am here! I am here!

Ono. Well, I'll be going, I think! But you gentlemen will just try... 150

(*She makes a gesture of warning "be careful!" — with her two hands and goes out through the door at the left.*

Las. (*energetically*). My idea is to take her away off somewhere! I can, you know... with my connections! Somewhere away off... far away!

Lud. But don't get too excited, eh? 155 You see what happens!

Las. Yes, but how about her?
(*With a nod toward the door at the rear.*

Lud. It seems to me she's the most unfortunate proof of the danger there is in losing your head! I mean that she is a victim of just 160 that very thing!

Las. Yes, a victim! But why? It was precisely to keep from losing my head, as you say, that I betrayed her . . . betraying myself first of all! I left the navy . . . I gave up the 165 sea, to drown here, in this way, in the slime of an ordinary humdrum scandal!

Lud. Whereas, my dear fellow, at a certain point. . . .

Las. (*with increasing intenseness*). No! 170 No! It's when we become convinced that we can't live as we had dreamed of living! It's when we realize that what seemed to us so easy in our dreams — so easy that we could almost lay our hands upon it — has become 175 difficult, impossible to attain! . . .

Lud. Yes! But because at certain moments our soul frees itself from all common trivialities. . . .

Las. Yes! Exactly! Exactly! 180

Lud. . . . soars above the petty obstacles of daily life, forgets all about the petty, insignificant needs we ordinarily feel, shakes from its shoulders all commonplace cares. . . .

Las. Exactly! And now free, un- 185 shackled, master of itself, it seems to breathe a fresher air . . . it tingles with life, ardor, enthusiasm . . . and the most difficult things, as I said, become easy. . . .

Lud. . . . and everything is possible! 190 Everything is fluid, liquid, smooth-running . . . a state of divine intoxication . . . yes, but this happens only at certain moments, my dear fellow, and those moments pass!

Las. (*violently*). Yes, because our souls 195 are not strong enough! They are unable to bear up under all that inspiration, that's why!

Lud. (*with a smile*). No, it isn't that! It's because you don't know all the tricks, all the surprises — pleasant and unpleasant — 200 that that soul of yours is playing on you as it breathes there in the airy sublimity of such moments — when it has shaken off all re-straints, abandoned all reflection, surrendered utterly to the glory of its dreams! You 205 don't notice those things, but some fine day — and it is an ugly day — you feel yourself pulled down to the solid earth again!

Las. Yes, that's it! But at such times we shouldn't give in — that's the point! We 210 should refuse to come down to the solid earth again! And that's why I tell you that I am going to go back out there, far away . . . take her back to the place where she lived, waiting for me, happy, joyous, confident in the 215 glory of that dream which to me — because my soul, my spirit, had been clouded somehow — had come to look like an attack of madness from which I had recovered — rejoicing even in my recovery, as though I had furnished 220 proof to myself that I was of a very wise and prudent self-control! But now I feel . . . I feel as if I had got back the exaltation which I lost! I have found the soul I had at that time! I have found myself again — and this I owe to 225 her!

Lud. But I advise you not to get too excited! Don't lose your head! You'll see how far she has fallen!

Las. But I'll set her on her feet again! 230 I'll make her what she was before! (*The door at the rear opens, and* ERSILIA *appears.*) Oh, here she is now! (*At sight of her his voice faints almost to a whisper.*) Oh!

(ERSILIA *is pale and wan, her hair falling disheveled over her shoulders. In desperate resolution, she goes straight to* LUDOVICO.

Ers. I can't! Signor Nota! I can't! 235 I should not have accepted even this much! Your proposal . . . no . . . it's impossible! I can't. I give it all up! I renounce everything!

Lud. But, my dear child, what in the world are you talking about! Don't you see 240 who's here (*pointing to* LASPIGA)?

Las. Ersilia! Ersilia!

Ers. You — why are you calling me! Don't you see who I am? Don't you see what I am? Oh, please! Don't! 245

Las. (*advancing toward her passionately*). I see how you are suffering! I see that you are ill! But you are still my Ersilia . . . my Ersilia

... and you will be the same Ersilia you have always been!   250

Ers. (*recoiling before him*). Don't touch me! Don't touch me! Let me alone!

Las. You talk that way to me? But you belong to me! You must be mine as you used to be!   255

Ers. Oh, this is horrible! I can't endure it! What can I say? How can I make you understand that for me everything was to have been all over — all over!

Las. All over? How can it be all over!   260 I am here with you again?

Ers. What you were for me out there you can never be again!

Las. But I can! I can! I am still the same! I am still the same!   265

Ers. No! But even if you were, I must tell you — you should be able to see for yourself! — that I am not and can never be the same!

Las. That isn't so! You tried to kill yourself, but for my sake, you said! Well,   270 then...

Ers. (*with desperate resolve*). Well then — it wasn't true!

Las. It wasn't true?

Ers. It wasn't true, I say! It was not   275 for your sake! It was not on your account! Why — I didn't even try to find you when I came here! I was lying!

Las. Lying?

Ers. Yes! I gave a reason — a reason   280 which at that particular moment happened to be true... but it isn't the reason any longer!

Las. Not the reason any longer? And why not?

Ers. Because I, unfortunately... I —   285 to my sorrow, am alive now! I am alive again!

Las. Fortunately, I should say! It seems to me the greatest of good fortunes!

Ers. No, thank you! Good fortune! You are trying to force me to be the woman   290 I tried to kill! No! No! Enough of that! Enough of her! For her it was on your account, as she said! Leave it that way! But it doesn't hold for me now... neither for me nor for you! That's all!   295

Lud. But why doesn't it hold, my dear child?

Las. That was why you tried to kill yourself!

Ers. Exactly! Exactly! That was a reason for dying... a reason for ending it all! But I didn't die, did I? It doesn't hold any   300 longer!

Las. But I can arrange everything, can't I! I can make everything right!

Ers. No! No!

Las. Why not? The reason you had   305 for dying should now be a reason for living, it seems to me!

Lud. Of course it should!

Las. That's why I came here!

Ers. (*with a cold determined voice, pronouncing the syllables one by one and stressing each with a gesture of her two hands, her forefinger crossed over her thumbs*). I doubt if I even know you!   310

Las. (*in surprise*). You don't know me?

(ERSILIA *makes a sudden gesture with her two hands wide opened, and falls into a chair — to the amazement of the two men, who stand there looking at her as though she were an entirely different person from the one they had supposed her to be. A pause.*

Ers. Don't torment me! (*Another pause, then resuming her former manner*) Don't you find it hard to recognize me?

Las. (*tenderly, in a voice that shows his inner anguish*). Why, no! Of course I don't!   315 Why do you think I should?

Ers. Do you know one thing? If I had seen you sooner, I really would not have been able to say...

Las. Say what?   320

Ers. That I tried to kill myself on your account! Besides, I didn't! But anyhow, your voice!... your eyes!... Not at all!... Is that the voice you talked to me with? Is that the way you looked at me? I thought of   325 you rather... well, who knows how I thought of you!

Las. (*suddenly chilled*). You are driving me away, Ersilia! You are making me doubt myself... and doubt you!   330

Ers. Because you can't understand! You can't. You can't understand what it means for a life to come back upon you like this... like... like a memory!... but a memory which, instead of rising from within you, comes   335 upon you unexpectedly from without — and so changed that you are scarcely able to recognize it! You can't fit it into your life somehow, because you too have changed! Nor can you adapt yourself to it — though you under- 340 stand all the while that it once was your life, an experience of yours, as you may have been once — though not for yourself, not as you really were ... the way you talked ... the way you looked ... the way you acted ... in 345 the memory of the other person — but not the way you really were!

Las. But I am the same person, Ersilia! I am going to be the same to you! I want to be the same to you! 350

Ers. But you can't! Don't you understand? You can't! Because as I look at you now, I am certain that you have never been the man I thought you were!

Las. What? 355

Ers. Why are you so surprised? I have noticed that you, too, right here ... right now, listening to me, seeing me, have been having quite the same impression!

Las. Yes, that's true, but only be- 360 cause you have been saying things ...

Ers. Things that are true! Well, why don't you profit by them? Everybody can, except me! I can't, to be sure! I'm the only one who can't! It's no fault of yours! 365

Las. But please, please, what's no fault of mine?

Ers. What you did to me!

Las. That was no fault of mine? But I am here precisely because I wronged you! 370

Ers. Oh, in life ... in life people do such things! They can, you know!

Las. But afterwards they feel sorry, as I do — and it's a sincere sorrow I feel! It isn't merely that I recognize my duty toward 375 you!

Ers. But supposing you then discover that I am not the woman you thought I was?

Las. (*in despair, as she persists in that way*). Oh, dear me! What in the world are you talking about? 380

Ers. And for you, too, Signor Nota ... quite a different person! But I assure you, for you I would have done my very best to be the woman you imagined! And for you ... yes, for you, I might have succeeded! It 385 would have been a question of living in the fiction you created ... But life! ... No! No! You see, life, the life I tried to escape from, refuses to let me go! It has sunk its teeth into me! It refuses to let me go! And now here 390 they all are upon me again! Where can I go?

Lud. (*to* LASPIGA). I told you so! The young lady needs a rest! Little by little she will get herself in hand again and ...

Ers. You too are trying to hurt me 395 now, Signor Nota?

Lud. Hurt you? No, quite the contrary!

Ers. But you must realize that it is no longer possible!

Lud. Why not, please? 400

Ers. You seemed to have understood it all so well! I suppose for you it can easily be ... just nothing ... or if anything, a pleasure! You were supposing many things of an image that existed only in your own mind, but 405 those things I suffered in my living flesh! I actually lived, actually endured the shame, the disgust, the horror of it all!

Lud. Oh, is that what you are thinking of?

Ers. Tell him! Tell him! Tell him 410 what I did! Then he'll go away!

Lud. Not at all! Not at all! No one can blame you for having done that!

Ers. Well, then, I'll tell him myself! Look! Out there! On the street! I offered 415 myself to the first man that came along!

Lud. (*breaking in, anxiously, as* LASPIGA *covers his face with his hands*). But in a moment of despair, the night before she tried to kill herself! Understand?

Las. Yes! Yes! Oh, Ersilia! 420

Lud. The next morning she took poison on a bench in the park because she didn't have enough money left even to pay her bill at the hotel! You understand?

Las. Yes! Yes! I understand! And 425 that makes my sorrow, and my remorse, and my responsibility all the greater! Oh, I must pay you back for all the harm that I have done you!

Ers. (*with a cry, exasperated*). No! 430 No! You! Oh!

Las. I, of course! Who else?

Ers. (*with utter bitterness*). So then you in-sist! You *will* make me tell it all! You *will* tear it out of me — things a woman 435 would never admit even to herself! (*She pauses a moment to master her emotions, then she says, firmly, decisively, gazing fixedly into space in front of her.*) I measured coldly, deliber-ately, dispassionately, the disgust I felt, to see whether I would be able to bear up under it! I rouged and powdered my cheeks before 440 going out of the hotel! I had a bottle in my purse . . . a bottle of poison! I was a nurse, you see — I had three of those bottles in my bag! I kept them with me all the time — it was a disinfectant! So I rouged my 445 cheeks and just as you imagined, Signor Nota, I looked at myself in the glass, there, on my dresser in the hotel! I did that not only be-fore I went out that first time! I did it also the second time — when I went out to 450 kill myself! But as I sat there on the bench in the park I did not know, I refused to admit, that I could ever do such a thing! And yet, it wasn't so hard, was it? I could have tried again if circumstances had been favor- 455 able! Supposing someone had come along who found me attractive or who was not repulsive to me? Well, in that case I wouldn't have killed myself, would I? I am not sure I would have! Notice — I had rouged my 460 cheeks again, and this time I had even painted my lips, and I had put on my newest dress — on purpose! (*She leaps to her feet.*) But if I am here now . . . well, what does it mean? It means that I overcame the loathing I felt 465 after having a chance to compare that with death! Otherwise I should not be here now with a man who, without even knowing me, wrote me a letter, offering me shelter, under his roof! 470

Las. (*with sudden decision*). Listen! I know! I know why you talk the way you are talking! I know why you enjoy tormenting yourself like this.

Ers. (*violently*). I? It is you who are 475 tormenting me!

Las. Ah, you see! You even say so your-self! You regard all this as a cruelty on the part of other people! Well, then, won't you let one of those other people make 480 amends for that cruelty, when his conscience has at last awakened?

Ers. Make amends? How? By torment-ing me still further?

Las. Why, no, of course not! 485

Ers. (*hammering on each word*). I tell you I was just pretending! I tell you that it isn't true! I tell you that I lied, and I repeat it! It wasn't anybody's fault! It wasn't your fault! It was life . . . just life! The life 490 I was tired of! The life I tried to escape from! The life that has found me again — oh, how horrible — without my ever having succeeded in getting my feet on the ground! What else need I tell you to drive you away? 495

(*There is a loud knock at the door on the left.*

Lud. What is it?

Emma (*entering*). Signor Grotti is here . . . the consul!

Ers. (*with a scream*). Ah, here he is! I knew he would come! 500

Lud. Does he want to see me?

Las. I am here too!

Emma. No, he wants to have a word with the Signorina!

Ers. Yes! Yes! Let him come in, 505 please! Let him come in! (*To* EMMA) Show him in! (EMMA *withdraws.*) It is just as well that I have a talk with him, and the sooner the better!

GROTTI, *the consul, enters. He is a man in his late thirties, dark-haired, solidly built. On his face and in his eyes, an expression of hard and almost cruel reserve. He is wear-ing a black suit*

Ers. Come in, Signor Grotti! (*Intro-* 510 *ducing him to* LUDOVICO) Signor Grotti, the Italian consul at Smyrna! (*Then to* GROTTI) Signor Ludovico Nota! . . .

Gro. (*with a bow*). A name familiar to me!

Ers. (*continuing*). Signor Nota was 515 kind enough to offer me hospitality here! (*With a gesture toward* LASPIGA) Signor Franco Laspiga, whom you already know!

Las. You knew me under far different circumstances ... but now I am here! 520

Ers. (*breaking in*). Please! Please!

Las. No! (*Turning to* GROTTI) Look! (*With a gesture toward* ERSILIA) Here is the woman whose hand I asked of you in marriage — out there! 525

Ers. (*in great anger*). Please! Please! No more of that!

Las. I will say no more! (*To* GROTTI) Her anger, the condition you find her in, will explain sufficiently why you see me here! 530

Ers. (*impatiently*). Never mind about my condition! I have told you repeatedly that there is no reason for your remaining here, and I am glad to repeat it now in the presence of Signor Grotti so that he may know that, 535 if I am angry, I am angry because you refuse to understand.

Las. Yes, you repeat it because you are aware that the father of the girl I was to marry has had a talk with him! 540

Ers. (*in surprise*). No! I didn't know that! (*She looks at* GROTTI, *in dismay, doing her best to control herself.*) Ah, and you ... you talked to him about me?

Gro. (*coolly, with perfect composure*). No, Signorina, but I promised him I would 545 come and have a talk with you!

Las. (*breaking in violently*). It won't do the slightest good, you know!

Ers. (*with a burst of imperious anger*). I should like to have a word alone with Si- 550 gnor Grotti! (*Turning to* LUDOVICO, *her voice softening*) Won't you let me, Signor Nota?

Lud. Why, as far as I am concerned ...

(*He starts to leave the room.*

Las. (*detaining him, resolutely*). No, wait a moment! (*Turning to* ERSILIA, *coldly*, 555 *on his dignity*) I shall not intrude, but I must say something here to Signor Grotti so that he may deliver the message to anybody interested! Now *that is all over*, all over! (*With a gesture toward* ERSILIA) That is a 560 point not for her but for me to decide! (*To* ERSILIA) And I insist on this, right here, before you! Hitherto I have begged you, beseeched you, to do as I say! I have consented to listen to the most cruel things from your lips. 565 But now I am through! It is my turn to speak

in another tone of voice! You can send me away; but that doesn't mean that I shall ever go back to a woman who, outraged, justly outraged, at the story printed in the 570 papers about you, closed her door in my face in an impulse of displeasure and shame, but now changes her mind, repents, and tries to fix things up in a roundabout way through you, here! 575

Gro. Oh, that isn't the point! I didn't come here on that account!

Ers. I have told you that anything you may have done was in no way responsible for my trying to kill myself! 580

Las. That's not so!

Ers. What? Signor Nota here can bear me witness!

Las. Yes, he can testify that you said such things! Very well! (*Turning to* GROTTI) 585 She said the most terrible things about herself, "things," as she said, "which a woman would never admit even to herself!" But I have my own sense of what is right and wrong, even if your conscience compels you to refuse 590 me because of a wrong you may have done to me! But my conduct cannot be modified by anything that he (*with a gesture toward* GROTTI) may say to you, or that you may say to him — in the interest of some third person for 595 whom you are both working together! There! That was what I wanted to say! (*To* LUDO- VICO) I am ready now, Signor Nota! And I know that you are on my side and that you agree with me! Good morning, Signor 600 Grotti, good morning!

(*He starts for the door at the left.*

Lud. (*to* ERSILIA, *in a low affectionate voice, trying to encourage and reassure her*). I'll just run out and see about that bag of yours! I hope I can have it here for you very shortly! 605

Ers. Yes, thank you! And you'll forgive me, won't you, Signor Nota?

Lud. But, my dear girl, there's nothing to forgive you for! Good morning, Signor Grotti! 610

Gro. Good morning!

(LUDOVICO *and* LASPIGA *withdraw through the door at the left. The moment the door closes,* ERSILIA *loses her composure. She seems to shrink in upon herself, all of a tremble, looking up fearfully at* GROTTI, *who stands there surveying her with a gaze of cold and hostile scorn. Unable to resist this stare,* ERSILIA *hides her face in her hands, raising one shoulder to cover her cheek, as though to protect herself from the hate he is darting upon her.*

Gro. (approaching her, his voice almost a hiss). You fool! You dunce! You idiot! Lying like that! Just plain stupid lying!

Ers. (terrified, without lowering her defense). But I wanted to die! I really tried to die!

Gro. (insisting, violently). And why? 615 And why all the lies after that? And why bring this final remorse upon yourself?

Ers. (quick to justify herself). No, it wasn't for my own sake! Don't you understand? And he says that I have nothing to do 620 with it, too! But I actually screamed it in his face! I told him that I had lied! I told him it wasn't true that I had tried to kill myself on his account!

Gro. (angrily, with a sneer). But he 625 thinks you did! Don't you know he thinks you did?

Ers. (aroused to her own defense, and now mistress of herself). How can I help that? It's his remorse! It's his remorse! He would be ready to believe me — if it weren't for 630 his own sense of guilt!

Gro. (contemptuously). How do you dare speak of the wrong other people have done? How dare you? You!

Ers. You think I have done more 635 wrong than the rest of you? You think that I have more reason to feel guilty than the rest of you! You're mistaken! I have less reason than anybody else! Yes! Yes! Oh, I understand... you won't admit that, because 640 it was I who had the courage to kill myself, and not you!

Gro. I? I should have killed myself?

Ers. Oh, don't worry about that! It wasn't from remorse that I tried to die! And 645 you — you needn't feel alarmed about anything you did! You have money! You don't

have to worry about your next day's living! But I... I was in the street! I was poor! I was naked! And in such circumstances, 650 you know, it's harder!... In my despair I thought of your little girl; and I had already experienced the last, the extreme humiliation a woman can suffer! All that together! That was why I was strong enough to do what I 655 did!

Gro. But you couldn't help lying even then, could you?

Ers. It wasn't because I meant to lie! You see — he had promised to marry me, 660 back there in Smyrna!

Gro. Yes, but it was a joke!

Ers. That isn't true! But even if it were — well, all the more dishonorable on his part! Because he didn't know about what hap- 665 pened there between you and me, after he went away! He got engaged to another girl here and was about to marry her!

Gro. But you! *You* knew what had happened between you and me, and — you 670 lied!

Ers. All the same, what he was doing was worse! Without knowing that I had been false to him, he was deserting me here, as calmly as you please! Actually marrying another 675 woman!

Gro. Just as I say, then! It was a joke! Any promise he made at Smyrna, he could not have meant seriously.

Ers. No! He really promised... but 680 in any case, he says he meant it, now, as you have just heard! But you are saying all this to make things easy for yourself! It eases your conscience! It gives you an excuse for what you did there — behind his back — 685 the moment he went away!

Gro. And you raised all this rumpus here just to prevent him from marrying another woman!

Ers. No! I didn't even dream of such 690 a thing! I said what I said when I thought I was going to die! I wasn't trying to stop anything, and I'm not trying to now! I refuse! I refuse!

Gro. But supposing he had remained 695 faithful to you... supposing you had found him here, quite free, and ready to make his promise good? . . .

Ers. (*shuddering*). No! No! Never! I would never have deceived him! I swear 700 to you by the soul of your little girl — I would never have deceived him! I didn't go near him! Ask him yourself! I didn't go near him! It was because he had betrayed me — and it was real treachery on his part — that I 705 was able to tell the lie I told, saying that I had tried to kill myself on his account!

Gro. You didn't look him up?

Ers. No!

Gro. How did you know about his en- 710 gagement, then?

Ers. Oh, yes, I did look him up, but I went there, to the Navy Building!

Gro. Yes! Trust you not to look him up!

Ers. (*with difficulty restraining the helpless rage within her, threateningly*). You 715 ought to be grateful to me!

Gro. What for? For your having gone to look him up?

Ers. No! They told me he had resigned his commission in the navy and that he 720 was soon going to be married! That took away from me every temptation of revenge! Hah! You think you have caught me? You think I had some design in going to the Navy Building? You don't understand the state of 725 mind I was in when I went there! Here I was, absolutely alone in the world, lost, driven out of the house by your wife after she surprised us there in that terrible moment — the people down in the street calling, shouting, be- 730 cause the baby had fallen from the roof! I was in utter despair! I was like a beggar, with nothing, nothing, to look forward to, except death — or the insane asylum! I was out of my mind, and I wanted to find him . . . 735 to tell him everything!

Gro. You were going to tell him about us two?

Ers. Not about me! About you! About you! After his departure you took ad- 740 vantage . . .

Gro. Only about me?

Ers. Yes! And about how you treated me! Look, I can tell everything now . . . everything

. . . things that no one would ever dare to 745 tell! I have reached bottom, the very bottom. I can scream the truth that only lunatics dare tell . . . the truth that a person tells when he thinks he can never get to his feet again . . . since the truth is all he has to hide his in- 750 nermost shame! You came to me there when my flesh was tingling with the passion which he had aroused . . . when I was unable to resist the slightest touch! Deny it if you dare! Deny that I beat you, that I scratched your 755 face, your neck, your hands, your arms!

Gro. Oh! You were leading me on!

Ers. You are lying! Not in the least! It was you!

Gro. At first . . . yes, but after that . . . 760

Ers. Never! Never!

Gro. You pinched my arm as I was standing near you!

Ers. I didn't.

Gro. You are lying! You even came 765 up behind me once and pricked me with a needle!

Ers. But because you didn't leave me alone!

Gro. Fine! Fine!

Ers. I was your servant! . . . 770

Gro. So I suppose you had to obey?

Ers. My flesh . . . yes! My flesh obeyed, but my heart . . . no, never . . . my heart never! I hated you!

Gro. But you wanted me! 775

Ers. No! No! It was hatred! I hated you — and all the more because I wanted you! After that I could have torn you to pieces like my shame itself! My heart was never yours! My heart was bleeding because I was 780 stealing that pleasure — like a thief — betraying my real heart! I looked at my naked arms and I bit them. I yielded to you — yes! I kept yielding! But I felt all the while inside me that my heart . . . no . . . my heart 785 never yielded! Oh, you fiend! It was you who robbed me of the only real joy I ever had in my life . . . a joy so great I could hardly believe it true — the joy of feeling that I was about to become a wife! 790

Gro. Meantime he was over here, getting himself another woman!

Ers. So you see? You are all like that!

You are all worthless! You are all dogs! And now you have the face to come and tell 795 me that it's my fault... my fault because I have never had the strength to be anything... no... not one thing, not even a doll that you might make with your hands out of wax or clay! And a doll... well, if you drop a 800 doll on the floor it breaks, doesn't it?... and the pieces tell you that at least it was a doll! But I... my life... just one day following the day before it!... No one whom I could ever call mine!... Pulled this way and that 805 by the things about me! Never a will of my own! Never able to feel myself on solid ground! Tormented, tortured, trodden under foot! Never the power to rise and say "Here am I!" (*Suddenly changing tone and* 810 *turning on him like an animal stung with a lash*) But tell me, what are you doing here? How is it you have dared to come into my presence again?

Gro. Because you've gone and blabbed... that's why! Because you've talked! You 815 have made a mess of things! You tried to kill yourself!

Ers. Oh, yes! I should have kept my mouth shut, I know! A hole in the ground and a stone on top... and good-by! 820

Gro. As for the stone... you've gone and thrown it into a puddle and you've splashed the mud all around on everybody! All of us are covered!

Ers. Yes, and the mud sticks, eh? 825

Gro. Yes, the mud sticks!

Ers. Whereas life...

Gro. The mud sticks! You have made a cesspool all around yourself!

Ers. But you want me to be the only 830 one to get drowned in it, don't you? You two want your lives to run along easily, as before! When he finds out about you and me, he will go back to his fiancée; and you will go back to your consulate in Smyrna! 835

Gro. And to all my life. A life that you, cursed woman, broke up for a moment, to my confusion! Do you think you know *me!* Do you think that bit of nonsense, that moment or two of play, was really me! And what 840 have you made it cost me? You have made it

cost me the unhappiness of my whole life: the death of my little girl!

Ers. It was you! It was you! I can see it all still! That chair, which I had carried 845 up to the roof for the baby, and you didn't give me time to take it down again!

Gro. But what were you doing on the roof? Your place was there, in the room where my wife was sleeping, sick! You should have 850 been ready to answer if she called! What were you doing on the roof?

Ers. I was working, and the baby was playing!

Gro. No! You went there on pur- 855 pose... knowing that I would follow you!

Ers. What a coward! You would have come to me even there, in that room, at your wife's bedside!

Gro. No! No! 860

Ers. Say no if you dare! As though you hadn't tried to many times before! And so — since I didn't feel safe even there...

Gro. But because you wanted me, too! Because you wanted me, too! 865

Ers. No, because — you should say — because in the end, after all your insistence, after all the temptation you put in my way, I *would* have wanted you! That is what you might say! I went up to the roof so she 870 couldn't hear... so your wife couldn't hear! Ah, but now I know! Something inside me kept warning me! I knew I shouldn't leave the chair just where I did! Because the baby was there with her toys, playing, on the 875 roof! She might get up on the chair and fall off! I knew that! My common sense kept telling me that! But I didn't listen... I didn't listen! Don't you remember? You came upon me from the stairway, like a wild 880 animal! And you insisted... you insisted! Oh! I dream of it, nights, still! It is always before my mind! I can see it there... the chair... near the railing! I see it in my dreams and in my dreams I try to move it 885 away... to move it away... and I can't... I can't! (*She bursts into a sob. A pause.*

Gro. (absorbed in his own thoughts and trying in his own mind to get a look at his life apart from all that horror. *Ersilia meantime continues sobbing convulsively*). I was busy with my work, I was always a hard worker! I lived outside myself, for other people, 890 wholly for other people!... My mind always on my work!... And a great emptiness in my life! ... The home I had dreamed of I had never had! The woman I had married — gloomy, sickly, unattractive! There I was, far 895 from home, and homesick! And the gratitude of our people there!... They kept coming to me and asking me to help them, and they were grateful for the attentions I gave them — for my courtesy, my kindness, my assist- 900 ance, ... and this cheered me, made me patient, good-natured, affectionate, even to my wife! And you came... how did I treat you at first when you came?

Ers. (*tenderly, through her tears*). You 905 were very kind to me!

Gro. Because the more depressed, the more unhappy I felt inside, the greater my need for doing good to others, for carrying all the burdens myself, that the lives of others might 910 be made easier! And because of this need I felt of making life pleasant for others — that my own life, after a fashion, might be more bearable — since I could never be really happy! ... And how I described you to him 915 when he came into the harbor there, on his warship! How I praised you... making you out the sweetest and most beautiful woman that ever lived! It was to do you a good turn, to make him fall in love with you! And dur- 920 ing those days I was kinder than ever toward my wife, for I wanted her to be well disposed toward you! I wanted her to help me carry out the little plan I had made for your life — and I made it just for the pleasure it would 925 give me to know that you would be owing all your good fortune to me! And when I saw that you were in love with each other... No, no! It wasn't because I knew that you had gone too far... that you had given your- 930 self to him!... That made my wife angry, but not me! It made her lose all respect for you!

Ers. But only with him! I had never loved anyone else before! He was going away, and the night before he left... I was mad! 935 I was mad!

Gro. I know! I understand! I never thought of blaming you! And I would never have profited by your weakness, if you...

Ers. I? 940

Gro. Not that you meant to... but I don't know... you looked at me once as we were getting up from the table... because, you see, you couldn't imagine!... I felt that you didn't believe I had been kind to you out 945 of a pure, unselfish desire to make you happy! That's the point! And because you didn't really understand, you spoiled everything! Because I needed that faith on your part more than ever — to keep going, to resist 950 temptation!

Ers. But not temptation from me... not from me!

Gro. No, the temptation within myself! But if you had understood how disinter- 955 ested my kindness was, how sincere and real it was, the beast would never have awakened in me all of a sudden as it did, with all its desperate fury! And even now, as I see you here before me, after you have laid an insur- 960 mountable obstacle — the dead body of our child — between me and that woman... (*He advances upon her threateningly, hatefully.*) No! ... understand?... no!

Ers. (*backing away in alarm*). What 965 do you want?

Gro. I want you to suffer... to suffer as I have suffered!... to suffer with me for the wrong that we have both done!

Ers. You want me to suffer more than 970 I have suffered?

Gro. All that is past! You took pains to come back to life again! You did!

Ers. No! No!

Gro. Taking advantage of the remorse 975 that you knew he would feel!

Ers. No! No! I have told you that I never thought of that! I have told you that I refuse to accept anything from him! And don't you see what I am? This is the house of a 980 man I don't even know! He offered me shelter as I was leaving the hospital, where I thought, I was sure, I was going to die! I had ceased to hope for anything, and here I am like a person called back from the grave, not knowing 985 what will become of me tomorrow! Let me alone!

Gro. But in the end you will do as he says!

Ers. No! Rather than that I will tell him everything! Do you want me to? I am 990 ready to tell him everything.

Gro. I refuse to be the only one to suffer punishment for the death of my little girl! I will not allow you now to go off and marry him as though that horrible thing had never 995 happened!

Ers. No! No! I will never marry him! You may be sure of that! I will stay here with the man who has taken me in.

Gro. But you won't be able to, don't 1000 you see? He already agrees with that other fellow! They both went away together! Nota is already bored with the whole business! He surely thinks you're crazy in not accepting the boy's repentance, and the reparation 1005 which he offers!

Ers. But I have told him that I refuse!

Gro. Yes, but they of course think you are just obstinate and unreasonable! Neither of them will accept your refusal as final! 1010 You have never told him the real reason why you refused!

Ers. Well, I will tell him if necessary.

Gro. But then he will be disgusted with what you have done! It will seem to 1015 him so ugly — the lie you told, the trouble you have made: a broken engagement; a public scandal; pity you have wrongfully aroused; public sympathy... 1019

Ers. (*crushed and hardly able to stand*). Yes, that's true! But I... I didn't intend all this! I told him just as I have told you — I told him that I lied because I thought that I was going to die! The truth — we cannot tell! It is too ugly, too horrible! We two 1025 have been able to speak honestly to each other because we both are smirched with a common shame! Why do you wish, how can you wish, the truth to be told?

Gro. I? That isn't the point! It's be- 1030 cause of the lie! If he doesn't know what happened between you and me, he will never go back to his fiancée — he told you so — even if you refuse to accept his reparation.

Ers. I must tell him the truth, then, 1035 so that he will return to her? Why didn't you tell the truth to her father?

Gro. I couldn't!

Ers. (*sarcastically*). No, you couldn't! You told him you would come and see me 1040 and force me to confess everything! Are you so anxious for the truth, then?

Gro. (*with passionate vehemence*). Why, no, no! Why should I be? I don't know those people! I was outraged at your lie 1045 ... and when the old man described all the trouble it had caused: the girl's indignation; the boy's remorse; his intention to offer marriage to you... I don't know how I restrained myself! I ran to the newspaper office to 1050 deny the story so far as it concerned me! You don't know how angry my wife got when she read it all in the papers! She insisted on going to see the young lady at once, to tell her everything... to tell her how you had been 1055 dismissed from our house, even how she had found you with me! I had to keep her quiet ... I had to promise her on my honor that the consequences of your falsehood would be remedied at least so far as a wholly innocent 1060 family is concerned.

Ers. (*sarcastically*). I understand! I understand! (*A pause. She sits looking straight ahead of her into space, her face dark and determined.*) Very well! I understand! (*She rises. Another pause. At last she says:*) Well, 1065 you go away now! Everything will be all right!

Gro. (*looking at her in dismay*). What are you going to do?

Ers. You said we must straighten 1070 everything out! I'll attend to that!

Gro. (*after a pause and still looking at her fixedly*). Ersilia! Ersilia! You poor child! You poor child! How terrible this has been for you! (*He runs toward her to take her in his arms.*) Ersilia! Ersilia! 1075

Ers. (*drawing up haughtily and holding aloof*). Ah, no! That is too much! Let me alone!

Gro. (*forcing himself upon her, trying frantically to embrace her*). No! No! Listen to me! Listen to me!

Ers. (*repelling him*). Let me alone, I tell you!

Gro. (*insisting*). Let's go away to- 1080
gether somewhere and live out our despair —
together!

Ers. (*tearing away from him with a scream*).
Mimetta! Mimetta!

Gro. (*drawing back, pressing his hands to his
face as though to shut out a horrible vision*). You
murdered her! (*A pause. He is trem-* 1085
bling convulsively.) I am mad! I am mad!
(*Again he rushes toward her.*) But I need you,
Ersilia! I need you! We are just two unhappy people! Let's go away . . . together!

Ers. (*running to one of the windows*). Go
away! Go away! . . . Or I will call! 1091

Gro. (*insisting*). No! Ersilia! Listen! Listen!

Ers. (*throwing the window open*). I'll call!
Are you going? 1095

(*The sound of a distant hurdy-gurdy
playing a gay popular song enters
through the open window.* ERSILIA
*points to the door with a gesture that
brooks no denial.*)

Curtain

ACT III

*The same set as in the preceding acts. Toward
evening of the same day.* SIGNORA ONORIA
*is standing at one of the windows, which is
open, allowing unimpeded entrance to the
usual noises from the street; but these are
softening with the end of the day.* SIGNORA
ONORIA *is talking with another woman, a
neighbor, who is, presumably, leaning out
of a window across the street.* EMMA, *the
maid, is busy with the final touches of her
dusting about the room*

Ono. What's that? Oh, yes, yes! I'll tell
you about that later. (*A pause.*) Till about
noon . . . but you know how it is — that's never
like sleeping at night! . . . (*A pause.*) What's
that? I couldn't hear! (*A pause.*) Ah, 5
yes, yes! She's gone out now with Signor
Nota. (*A pause.*) Yes, to get her bag!
They wouldn't give it to him.

Emma. And you'll see — they won't give
it to her either! 10

Ono. (*still talking through the window*). Oh,
they couldn't, any sooner!

Emma. I hope one thing . . . that it won't
be like this every day!

Ono. (*drawing her head in and talking to
EMMA*). What are you growling about? 15
You make so much noise I can't hear a thing!

Emma. I like to get my work done in the
morning! Making beds at this time of the
day! It's almost dark!

Ono. (*again with her head out of the window*).
Signor Nota was probably one of them! 20
What do you expect? (*She laughs.*) It seems
he's decided to keep her here! (*A pause.*) Not
at all! She won't have anything to do with that
man! He must have done the kissing! (*A
pause. Then excitedly*) No! No! That 25
can't be! You must be mistaken! It couldn't
have been! (*A pause. She waves her hand in
a gesture of farewell.*) However, I'll see you
later. Good-by! Good-by! (*She lowers
the window.*) What do you think of 30
that? She says she saw three men in here and
that they each kissed her!

Emma. Even that consul man?

Ono. That's ridiculous! She couldn't have
seen straight! That old baboon of a 35
Signor Nota . . . he may have, but the consul —
that's ridiculous!

Emma. But I heard them talking at the top
of their voices when they were in here alone!

Ono. And you didn't . . . I suppose you 40
don't know what they were talking about?

Emma. Oh, I'm not minding other people's
business! I happened to be going through the
room under this and I heard them talking very
loud — that's all! But she was talking 45
louder than he!

Ono. I'd like to know what he wants of the
poor girl; and what he was doing here, after he
went and made all that trouble with the newspaper, threatening to bring a suit! 50

Emma. He's probably trying to keep her
from making up with her man!

Ono. But what business is that of his? And
she won't hear of such a thing either! For my
part, I'm sorry! 55

Emma. I'd like to see myself turning down a perfectly good husband for an old fool like the one you have here!

Ono. And he's getting sick of the whole business! He's trying to get out of it! 60 And I guess he told her as much in so many words! Who knows what he must have thought ...as if the poor little thing were making believe! I can't see how she's done so very much that's bad! I can't understand these men 65 sometimes! Some men ... well ... I just can't understand them! You'd think they were old enough to know better! They get old in years, but in experience ...! Why, just imagine! ... He goes and gets her at the hospital 70 — picks her up at death's door, you might say, with her insides all burned out with that poison — hardly able to stand on her two feet! ... And yet, who knows what good times he was looking forward to! However, that young man 75 comes in and says he's sorry! Then there's that newspaper reporter, afraid of a lawsuit, and Nota, as nice as you please, gets scared and backs out!

Emma. It may be just as well for her in 80 the end! When she sees he won't keep her, she'll probably make up her mind to go with the young man!

Ono. Perhaps, but do you know how it is? She don't trust him! She don't trust him! 85 ...That's the point! You can fool a girl once, all right, but the second time ... well, she's more wary! Besides, what he did to her was going pretty strong! She comes here, and what is he up to? He's getting ready to marry 90 another girl, if you please! However, if I guess him right, he's really sorry for it now!

Emma. I thought so, too!

Ono. But, you see, she's worrying about that other girl who would be jilted on her 95 account!

Emma. I wouldn't worry, if I was her! Why, the poor thing almost died on account of that man!

Ono. Yes! Yes! But you mustn't 100 forget that he went away and left her in the lurch! They told all about that in the papers! Perhaps she hates him now! And she must have understood that, here, Signor Nota ... (*She*

makes a wry face.) ... I saw her when she 105 was going out with him ... well ... it seemed to me she had ... oh ... a sort of veil in front of her eyes. She stared at everything, but she seemed not to see a thing ... and she couldn't speak nor lift her hand! I asked 110 her how she was, but she just smiled, and that smile — it froze me! And then again ... her hands were as cold as ice! (*She stops suddenly and listens. Then, in a quite different tone of voice*) Why, there's a peddler going by now! Say, you just run down and get me that 115 ribbon — two yards and a half, as I said! I'll stop him from up here as he goes by!

> (EMMA *runs off stage through the door at the left.* SIGNORA ONORIA *hurries to a window, throws it open, and leans out, looking down into the street. She spies the peddler and waves to him to stop.*

At this point FRANCO LASPIGA *enters through the door to the left, his face tense and drawn*

Las. (*stopping in the doorway and calling twice, because he can hardly make his voice heard in the noise pouring through the open window*). May I come in? May I come in?

Ono. (*turning around at last and closing the window*). Oh, it's you, Signor Laspiga! Won't you have a chair? Signor Nota is out 120 somewhere with the young lady; but he'll be right back. (*Then in a low voice confidentially*) You just keep at her and she'll do as you say!

Las. (*looking up at her in surprise as though he had not quite understood. Then sarcastically, in repressed rage*). Yes! Yes! Don't you worry! I'll keep at her all right! 125

Ono. (*confidentially*). He told her what was what, I assure you! The consul I mean!

Las. (*between his teeth*). The miserable cur!

Ono. You're right! You're right! That poor child! 130

Las. (*losing control of himself*). Poor child be damned! ... Poor child! You know what that woman is? She's as bad as they make 'em!

Ono. (*as though someone had struck her in the*

face). Oh, dear me! Oh, dear me! 135
What do you mean?

At this moment Ludovico Nota *enters from the left, his hat still on his head*

Lud. (*catching sight of* Laspiga). Oh, you're here already? (*Then turning to* Onoria, *but alluding to* Ersilia) Hasn't she come in yet?

Ono. (*turns and looks at him in amazement, then without answering turns to* Laspiga). How can this be? 140

Lud. (*not understanding*). How can what be?

Las. (*drawing himself up with the greatest determination and speaking vigorously and with heat*). The fact is that the wife of this Grotti fellow has found out that he came here this morning for a meeting with his mistress!

Lud. (*with a start, in utter astonishment*). Who? What mistress? 145

Ono. She? The consul's mistress?

Las. That's what I said! Though I might have used a worse word! So Grotti's wife went to my fiancée's this morning and denounced the whole intrigue to her parents! 150

Lud. Intrigue! What intrigue? Signorina Drei — with her husband?

Ono. Signorina Drei ... the consul's mistress?

Las. Exactly! Yes, ma'am! Yes, 155 sir! What I don't know is whether this all happened *before* or *after* I asked her to marry me out there in Smyrna! That's what I want to find out now! I came here for that purpose!

Ono. Mercy on us! With that man! 160 So they were in cahoots out there, eh? Ah, now I understand! That's why that woman said ... (*She nods toward the window.*) Aha, so that's why she said what she said!

Las. What do you mean? 165

Ono. Why, the woman in the house across the way saw them, and she said he kissed her!

Lud. Here? Here in this room?

Ono. Yes, here in this room! That's 170 what the woman told me, and I wouldn't believe it! She saw him kissing her, through the window there!

Las. What did I tell you? (*To* Ludovico) Right here ... in your house! 175

Ono. Why! Why! Why! This is beyond me! Why! Why! I don't know which end I'm standing on!

Las. And do you know how, and do you know when, Grotti's wife caught them at 180 it? Their baby fell off the roof and was killed!

Ono. (*with a scream, covering her face with her hands*). Oh, dear me! Dear me!

Las. Yes, she caught them! They were together! And she drove this hussy out of the house, because, between the two of them, 185 they had left the baby alone on the roof!

Ono. Murder! Murder is no name for it! How do they ever dare look an honest person in the face again? Poor baby! So that was why! So that was why! And they 190 didn't pay her ticket home! I should say not! ... After all that! ...

Las. If it weren't partly his fault, too, jail would be the place for her! She ought to be in jail! 195

Ono. Jail would be too good for her! I should say so! You are quite right!

Las. And after all that, you understand ...

Ono. ... she had the brazen face ...

Las. ... to come and stir up trouble 200 for me!

Ono. And not only you — everybody! She's made trouble for everybody!

Las. But do you realize what she's done to me? 205

Lud. (*musingly, almost to himself*). I wonder! I wonder! ...

Ono. And posing around here as a martyr! My, what a fraud!

Las. Everything kicked sky high! My 210 name in the papers! A public scandal! The girl I was going to marry slamming the door in my face! I thought I was losing my head! How I managed not to, I'm sure I don't know!

Ono. So that's why ... that's why she 215 wanted to get away! The moment she saw you, the moment she found out that other man was here, too, ... (*She mimics* Ersilia's *voice.*) "I won't!" "I won't see anyone!" "I don't want to talk with anyone!" Ha! You 220 bet she didn't! The little fraud! She could see her game was going to be found out! (*Spitefully, changing her tone of voice*) I wish

I could get back a few of the tears I've wasted in sympathy for her! Poor, downtrodden little girl, trying to kill herself because she had been betrayed! (*Snapping at* LUDOVICO) Let me tell you one thing, Signor Nota; you get that girl out of this house this minute! I won't have her in here again! My doors are closed to her! This is a respectable house! I cannot afford to be mixed up in such a mess!

Lud. (*annoyed, but at a loss for something to say*). Let's not be in too big a hurry now! Suppose we wait!

Ono. Wait? I've waited long enough! You get her out of here at once! I won't have her! I won't have her!

Lud. But don't talk so much! I can't hear myself think! Just a moment now! (*To* LASPIGA) How does it happen that the con- sul ... (*He breaks off.*) You know, don't you, that the consul was the very first one to protest against the article in the papers?

Las. That's easy to understand!

Lud. It doesn't seem to me so easy to understand! They should have stuck to- gether, it seems to me — as lovers!

Las. Yes, but his wife was there with him! His wife ... and this girl had made the news- paper say atrocious things about his wife!

Lud. (*remembering*). Ah, yes! That's so! And in fact ... yes ... that's why she was so much embarrassed when she found out that the newspaper had said ...

Ono. ... that this poor woman had sent her up to the roof on an errand!

Las. His wife must have forced him to deny the story!

Lud. So, then, the whole thing is an im- posture!

Las. And a very low-down one! It's vile! It's rotten!

Lud. (*continuing*). She must have been lying when she said she tried to commit suicide on your account!

Ono. What I should like to know is how a girl could lie as brazenly as that!

Lud. (*thoughtfully, to himself*). Ah, yes! Of course! And that's why she refused so obsti- nately to accept any reparation from you!

Las. It would have been the last straw if she *had* accepted!

Ono. I should say so, you poor man!

Lud. (*irritated more and more by* ONO- RIA'S *chatter and led accordingly to disagree with* LASPIGA). No! Listen! You must admit that she had at least one scruple!

Las. And when, if you please? When she saw me here, ready to straighten out a mess I thought myself responsible for?

Lud. I understand that, but ...

Las. And this too, notice, only on the most favorable hypothesis — on the hypothe- sis, I mean, that she became his lover *after- wards!* If she was his lover first, I would be the victim — well ... imagine for yourself! The victim of the most cowardly deceit con- ceivable on the part of both of them!

Lud. Oh, no! Hardly that!

Las. I've come here this time to get that point clear!

Lud. What do you think you can do? Certainly you can't deny that you met the most decisive and violent opposition on her part!

Las. But I'm talking about what went on *before!* What went on before!

Lud. Ah, no! That's going too far! In the worst case you would never have suffered any wrong!

Las. I wouldn't? Why not? I ...

Lud. (*insisting*). No wrong whatever! Even if it did happen *before!* You were about to marry another woman here, remember!

Las. Not at all! Just a moment! ...

Lud. Let me finish! You were getting even by betraying her!

Las. But I admitted the wrong I was doing!

Lud. Even so, you would have been get- ting even in advance for a wrong you didn't as yet know they had done you!

Las. You mean that what I did ex- cuses them?

Lud. Certainly not! But it does prevent you from getting on your high horse! You are not in a position to blame them!

Las. (*violently*). I beg your pardon! I am in a position to do just that! And she will have to explain: because they went the full length: they played their whole trick on me, while I called my marriage off and came hurry- ing here!

Lud. But not until you heard that she had tried to kill herself!

Las. But it wasn't on my account! She has confessed that herself!

Lud. But you didn't know that! Here 325 you were, quietly arranging — in ignorance of their duplicity toward you — to marry another woman! You were planning to play your trick on her! It seems to me you're quits, to say the least! 330

Las. That's a great idea! You're blaming me for what I did as though anything I might have done could ever be regarded as treachery toward her!

Lud. No! No! Look! I'm not 335 blaming anybody! I'm simply trying to show you that you are right only in one respect . . . in the fact merely that she told a lie when she said — without having any right to say it — that she tried to kill herself on your account! 340 Now, that lie . . . that lie . . . well, it interests me! I can't understand why she should have told that lie! . . . and have told it there, on the very brink of the grave!

Las. Why? Because after she had 345 been dismissed on account of the baby's death, she came here with the intention of resuming her relations with me!

Lud. But no! The moment she found out that you were about to be married . . . 350

Ono. (*speaking up*). She took poison, eh?

Lud. (*to* LASPIGA). . . . without even trying to see you!

Ono. But are you sure it was real poison she took? 355

Lud. Oh, as for that! . . .

Ono. Well, let us say it was! Couldn't she have figured on their saving her, and in that case, on everybody's taking her side — a person like you, for example? . . . And come to 360 think of it . . . where did she go to take her poison? To a public park, where she couldn't help being found right away and carried to a hospital!

Lud. But she refused to accept Si- 365 gnor Laspiga as her husband right here in this room — and she was in earnest!

Las. Yes, that was when she saw all the harm her lie had done . . . and not to me only!

She had made trouble all around! I had 370 come back repentant and she felt she couldn't accept what I had to offer! Oh, you don't understand what went on inside me here! You don't know how I suffered all those days! Why, you yourself kept encouraging me 375 not to lose my grip on myself! Well, now, just consider how I must feel on discovering it was all a low and vile intrigue! I don't know what I ought to do!

Lud. I don't see that there's anything 380 to do! What is there to be done now that everything is clear?

Las. Ah, no! You people have been telling me that all I had to do was show my contempt for her . . . 385

Lud. The best you can do is go away and marry the girl you were going to marry!

Las. No! No! I have been humiliated disgracefully! I've been made a fool of!

Lud. But just remember this . . . after 390 all, whether it was remorse or poverty or what not, this poor girl tried to kill herself!

Las. I know what she's done to me!

Lud. You're right! But after all, not till after you had done her all the harm you 395 say, and not knowing that the truth, naked and raw as it is, would be discovered! Oh, really, you can't claim that she tried to deceive you!

Las. Why did she do it, then — if 400 not to trick me, if not to get even with me?

Lud. By killing herself? She wanted to prevent your marriage, eh? But why did she care about that when she would soon be dead? Unfortunately there on the street, she 405 didn't happen to find a man she really liked or who liked her! Oh, come now, Signor Laspiga, when a woman goes so far as to confess a thing like that, rest assured that she's not trying to get even with anybody! Surely she 410 didn't tell that lie to get even with you!

Las. So it wasn't to trick me, eh? And it wasn't to get even with me? Well, why was it, then?

Lud. Well, as I said, I don't know 415 why she told that lie! I can't understand it! Lies may be useful for a person intending to live, but hardly for a person intending to die!

She herself has recognized that the lie was
quite useless!   420
   Las. But those words are yours, not hers!
   Ono. You are simply refusing to take account of the facts!
   Lud. Ah, there we have it! You're right!
It is one of my faults! I never am able to   425
take account of the facts!
   Ono. Well, I'm glad to hear you admit as
much yourself! Now for the facts! You know
what they are? Fact number one: she didn't
die!   430
   Las. And the lie did prove to be useful to
her! Yes, I insist upon the word *useful!* If
the lie didn't win me back — thank heaven
for that!... it at least enabled her to find a
person like you...   435
   Ono. Just imagine... a novelist!
   Lud. Yes, a fool, you really mean.
   Las. (*speaking up quickly*). Oh, I don't say
that!
   Lud. You might as well!   440
   Ono. What's the harm, since he says so
himself?
   Las. Certainly she must have been flattered!
Hah! I should say so!... to see her lie picked
up from the gutter and glorified in the   445
realm of art... the romantic story of her suicide for love, written up, printed, published,
and this time not by a mere newspaperman,
but by a writer of your reputation!
   Lud. Yes, that's so! She did ask me to. 450
   Las. So you see!
   Lud. She was even disappointed that the
heroine I had thought of was not herself but
another, a different sort of woman.
   Ono. You two would have made a fine 455
team: she telling the lies and you writing them
down!
   Lud. Lies? Yes! But we call them stories
sometimes, don't we? But it's not the story's
fault if it isn't true! It's almost better 460
that it shouldn't be true, so long as it's beautiful! It's an ugly story for her, as she lived it,
but that won't prevent it's turning out very
well for me, as I write it! I can say more than
that: it's much more beautiful the way it 465
is! Ah, yes... much, much more beautiful...
and I'm glad that we have gone to the very

bottom of it! (*To* Laspiga, *pointing to*
Onoria) Here's this woman, for example! At
first she was as cross as could be because 470
I brought the Signorina here! Later on she
became all honey! And now look at her, if you
please,... the living picture of holy horror!
   Ono. (*rising in her wrath*). And why shouldn't
I be?   475
   Lud. (*approving*). Of course! You should
be! You're quite right! Quite right! But as
I was saying, for a story it's splendid... it
couldn't be better! (*Turning to* Laspiga) And
there you were: when you first came,   480
yesterday — quite out of your head!
   Las. (*reacting in his turn*). But I admitted
that, myself!
   Lud. (*again approving*). Yes! yes! Quite so!
Quite so! I wasn't blaming you! But for 485
that reason... beautiful for the story... beautiful! But may I ask you good people... you
think I'm playing the fool here? You do, don't
you? Very well! So I amuse myself by pointing out how beautiful it is, how ex- 490
quisite, how perfect, this comedy of a lie
discovered!
   Las. Beautiful... exquisite... you say?
   Lud. Precisely because it is so terrible to you
and because you have suffered so! It is 495
true, very true, that you have suffered and are
still suffering! Believe me, I understand...
I am keenly conscious of all that you are
suffering! You may be sure that I will draw
your feelings to the life, if I decide to put 500
you into a novel or a play!
   Ono. Aren't you going to give me a little
part in it, too?
   Lud. Perhaps, if I decide to make a farce out
of it!   505
   Ono. Well, don't you dare go putting me on
the stage!
   Lud. What would you do? I suppose you'd
make a noise and say it wasn't true?
   Ono. That I would! I would say it 510
wasn't true, and that you were an impostor to
match that girl!
   Lud. Why go to all that trouble? The critics would say that for you! So don't bother!
(*Changing his line of thought*) But why 515
isn't she here? It's getting late! She ought to

be back by this time! The only money she has is what I gave her ...

Ono. Ah, so you gave her money! I see! In that case you needn't worry! 520

Lud. I gave her just a little money to pay her bill at the hotel and get her baggage back!

Ono. If you gave her money, we'll never set eyes on her again! She'll never come back here! And good-by to your comedy! I 525 won't have to worry about what you say of me!

Lud. Ah, as for that, you can't be sure! There's always a way to put an ending on a comedy even if the story doesn't end in life!

Las. Are you really afraid she will never 530 come back?

Lud. Well, that depends! It's this way! If the purpose of the lie she told lay in the "facts," as you say, I'm afraid she won't come back again! She'll come back only in case 535 her purpose was, as it seems to me it must have been, above and beyond the facts! And in the latter case, I shall have my play ... though I'll write the play anyhow, even if she doesn't come back! 540

Las. Ignoring the facts, then!

Lud. Facts! Facts! You're always harping on the facts! My dear Laspiga, facts are what we assume them to be; and then, in their reality, they cease to be facts, and become 545 mere semblances of life which appears in this or in that or in some other way! Facts are the past, when the spirit yields — those were the words she used — and life goes out of them! That's why I don't believe in facts! 550

At this moment EMMA *appears in the door to the left and announces*

Emma. Signor Grotti, the consul, is calling! He wants to see the young lady, or at least you, Signor Nota!

Lud. Ah, he's the one who is coming, instead of her! 555

Las. (*drawing up in a haughty, threatening attitude and facing the door pugnaciously*). He's coming at the right moment!

Lud. (*going up to him and speaking calmly, but in earnest*). I must remind you ... this is my house! You will be careful, therefore,

not to make any trouble! And I repeat ... you have no right to demand any- 560 thing of anybody!

Las. I suppose I have the privilege of stepping outside?

Lud. No, you will be so kind as to remain here! I will attend to this gentleman! 565

GROTTI *appears in the doorway in great anxiety and agitation.* EMMA *withdraws*

Gro. Good afternoon ... good afternoon, sir! May I see Signorina Drei?

Ono. (*alarmed, irritated, but bubbling over with curiosity*). But she isn't here! She's gone away!

Las. And perhaps she'll never come 570 back again!

Gro. Oh, but you people don't know ... I should speak to you rather, Signor Nota!

Lud. You have forced your way into my house without being invited! 575

Gro. I must ask your pardon for that; but I must find out whether Signorina Drei is aware that my wife ...

Las. (*breaking in*). ... went to my fiancée's this morning and betrayed ... 580

Gro. (*breaking in violently*). ... her own lunacy!

Las. So you deny her story?

Gro. (*angrily and with contempt*). I have nothing to confirm or to deny — to you! 585

Las. You are mistaken, sir! You *are* called upon to answer *me!* ...

Gro. What would you have me answer? Tell you that my wife is crazy? I am ready to guarantee that any time you wish! 590

Las. I shall remember that, sir!

Gro. (*turning to* LUDOVICO). Signor Nota, I am anxious to find out whether Signorina Drei is aware of what my wife has done.

Lud. I hardly think so! 595

Gro. Thank heaven for that! Thank God! Thank God!

Lud. She was with me all the time! I left her because she had to go back to the hotel where she stayed ... 600

Gro. You didn't know, yourself?

Lud. No! I found Signor Laspiga here on my return, and he told me.

Gro. Good! I am glad of that! In the state of mind in which she is at present 605 this added blow . . .

Lud. The fact is that we have been waiting for her for some time; and she isn't back yet. . . .

Las. But if she doesn't know, it is more 610 than probable that she suspects. Signor Nota here gave her a little money . . . there's a chance that she's run away!

Gro. I wish that could be true, but unfortunately I fear . . . 615

Las. Ah, so you admit, then . . .

Gro. I admit nothing!

Las. Yes, that's the part of a gentleman!

Gro. But don't you understand that I don't care a damn what you think? You may 620 believe anything you wish, anything you please!

Las. Anything I please? No, thanks! I am after the truth! What I want is the truth, and not something I should like to believe!

Gro. And what then? Supposing I tell 625 you that my wife's story is not true? You refuse to admit that you were the one who got her into all this trouble?

Las. But if she was driven out of your house by your wife — innocent, without the 630 slightest responsibility for the death of your child! . . .

Gro. (*emphatically*). That is not true!

Las. It's a lie, then?

Gro. I went to the newspaper office to 635 clear up that point . . . to protest against that lie!

Las. But then you came here to fix up a story with her! 639

Gro. (*restraining himself with difficulty*). I came here because your fiancée's father asked me to come here; and I found that she — for that matter in your presence and in the presence of everybody here — was in despair because you . . . 645

Las. (*interrupting, forcing his point*). . . . because I wanted to make reparation for the wrong I had done! What I want to know now is this: why should she feel that way if the wrong I did her was really a wrong? 650

Gro. Why, because she doesn't want you and your reparation! That's evident! Because she doesn't want you . . . She doesn't want you! That's reason enough, isn't it? She told you so, and she repeated it! 655 Can't you get that through your head?

Las. But you can't suppose that that helps me very much! That's not the point! You are taking advantage of her state of mind to put me to one side here, so that you can play 660 your part more easily for the benefit of this gentleman (*pointing to* LUDOVICO), giving him to understand that there is nothing to your wife's story! But I am here not because I want to be, but because she — out of her own 665 mouth — publicly declared that she had tried to kill herself on my account!

Gro. But hasn't she already confessed that she was lying?

Las. (*violently*). A second lie, then! 670 Lie number two! Who was obliging her to lie? Was I?

Gro. Who knows? She may have said "no" for that very reason!

Las. So, then, it may actually be true 675 that she tried to kill herself on my account?

Gro. I don't know why she did it!

Las. If it's all as you say it is, she did it on my account, because I had betrayed her! I don't see any other reason for her do- 680 ing so!

Lud. Unless it was for the reason she gave me a little while ago!

Las. (*turning on him violently*). But no, excuse me! Just a moment ago you said 685 that you could think of no reason, yourself!

Lud. Well, I meant to say . . . it was such a disgrace, wasn't it? Out on the street there . . . in the gutter, like a beggar!

Las. (*ironically*). Yes, and she offered 690 herself that night to the first man who came along!

Gro. (*his face darkening*). She said that?

Las. (*coming forward, insisting, with fury*). Yes, she said that! Just that! And she said she would have done it, too — all on my 695 account, because I had betrayed her! Well, in such a case, you think I could help insisting, with all my soul and conscience, on her accepting my reparation! In any case, I am still ready to make the same offer and insist 700 upon it ... if you, for your part, will give me your word of honor that your wife told a lie in saying that this girl has been your mistress!

EMMA *dashes in through the door to the left, screaming in terror*

Emma. Signora! Signora! Oh! Oh! Signora!   705

Ono. What's the matter?

Lud. Is she here? Is it she?

Emma. Yes, sir! She has come back!

Ono. Where is she?

Emma. Oh, I opened the door ... and 710 she fell in ... with her bag ... in her hand!

Lud. Oh, that poison! In her bag! She had poison in her bag!

The stage is in great commotion as ERSILIA *appears in the doorway to the left. She is pale but calm. Her face is soft, sweet, almost smiling*

Ono. (*drawing back as do the others*). Oh, there she is!   715

Gro. (*with an outburst*). What have you done? Ersilia! Ersilia!

Las. (*instinctively, almost to himself*). Ah, they did! He betrayed himself!

Lud. (*running toward* ERSILIA *to keep her from falling*). Signorina! Signorina!   720

Ono. (*with a shudder, to herself*). Oh, again! Again!

Ers. It's nothing! Hush! (*She makes a gesture of silence, her forefinger across her two lips.*) This time — it's nothing!

Gro. (*with a cry*). No! No! We must do 725 something for her! Get her a doctor, at once!

Ono. (*frightened*). Yes, a doctor! A doctor! Get her to the hospital!

Lud. (*taking* ERSILIA'S *arm*). Yes! Yes! Come, Signorina, come!   730

Ers. (*drawing back*). No! I won't! Please don't! I won't!

Gro. (*advancing*). But yes! Come with me! I will take you!

Ers. (*as above*). I won't, I say!   735

Lud. Oh, please, Signorina, come, do as we wish! Don't say no! Come!

Ono. I will send for a carriage!

Ers. Oh, please! Don't torture me! It would do no good!   740

Gro. How can you be sure of that? Let's hurry! We mustn't lose any time!

Ers. It would do no good! There's no help possible now! But hush, please, all you people! Let me alone! If you, Signor Nota, and 745 the Signora here ... it won't be right away ... but ... I hope ... soon! ...

Lud. Yes! Yes! What do you want? What do you want?

Ers. Your bed!   750

Lud. Why, yes, right away ... come!

Ono. Come! Come!

Gro. (*again breaking in, with violent emotion*). What have you done? What have you done?

Ers. Never mind! Please go away! Let me alone!   755

Lud. You ought to have remembered, Signorina, that I was here! You could have stayed here with me!

Ers. But if I hadn't done this, no one would have believed me!   760

Las. (*desperately, in a paroxysm of agony*). But believe what ... believe what?

Ers. (*calmly*). That I didn't lie, just to gain something! That's all!

Las. But why did you tell the lie then?

Ers. It was just to die! There! Don't 765 you see? I told you ... I told you as loud as I could that when I told that lie I thought everything was over with me — and that was why I told it! You weren't willing to believe me, and you were right! I didn't really think 770 of you! No, not at all! You're right! And I didn't dream I would upset you so, make it hard for you ... but I had such a loathing for myself!

Las. But why? You accused me ...   775

Ers. No!

Las. How can you say that!

Ers. No! It's so hard to explain it, let alone believe it! But now I'll tell you! I had such contempt for myself! — could I suppose 780 I would cause you all this trouble? But now you can believe me! Look! I wanted first to earn this right to be believed, just so that I could tell you! I caused you all this trouble,

you and the girl you were to marry! And 785
all the time I realized I ought not to be doing it!
That I had no right to do it, because... (*She
looks toward* GROTTI, *then turns again to* LAS-
PIGA.) You found out about *that*, didn't you?
From his wife!

Las. (*hardly able to speak*). Yes!　　　790

Ers. I foresaw that! And he came here to
deny the story, didn't he?

Las. Yes!

Ers. So you see!... (*She looks at him and
makes a gesture of disconsolate pity, barely
opening her two hands, a gesture which explains
without words the reason why tormented humanity
feels the need of falsehood. Then she adds in
a very faint voice*) And you too lied!　　　795

Las. (*deeply moved, with an impulse of sincerity, understanding her accusation*). Yes! I,
too! I lied, too!

Ers. (*her face brightening with a smile*).
Lied? You put a dream of yours into words
... oh, things of beauty... that you dreamed
... and you came here to help make　　　800
things right! Yes — just as he did! (*Pointing
to* GROTTI) He came here to help make things
right — and he lied! (GROTTI *bursts into tears.*
ERSILIA *loses her composure and begs him
with a gesture to be still.*) No! No! Please
don't! We all of us want to make a　　　805
good impression! The worse we are, the uglier
we are — the more anxious we are to appear
good and beautiful,... that's it! (*She smiles.*)
Hah! Yes! That's it! But I was naked!
I had nothing beautiful to put on!...　　　810
Then I learned that you, too, yes... you had
taken off your uniform, your wonderful
sailor's uniform... And then I found myself...
I found myself in the street without anything
— and... (*Her face darkens at the memory　　815

of that evening on the street after she left the hotel.*)
Yes, just one more bit of mud upon me ...
one last touch to make me dirtier than before... one last touch of filth! Oh, how disgusting! How horrible! And then... well,
then I wanted at least to be buried in　　　820
decent clothes! Just a decent dress to die in!
There! That's why I lied! That's why I lied!
I assure you! Never in my whole life long had
I been able to make a good appearance in life!
Every dress I wore was torn off my body　　825
by dogs... yes... dogs... dogs who barked
at me and jumped out upon me from here,
from there, from everywhere! I was soiled
with all the lowest and vilest filth in the world!
But I wanted a good dress to die in, some-　　830
thing beautiful to be buried in... the most
beautiful dress in the world... the one I had
dreamed of, the one I had hoped for, out there,
as the realization of a dream, but which was
torn off my back like all the others: a　　　835
wedding dress, the dress of a bride... the dress
of a wife! But it was to die in! It was to die
in! A tear of sympathy from people... that
was all! But no... no... not even that have I
been allowed to keep! You have torn it　　　840
from me... even this one you have torn from
my back! No! No! I must die naked! I
must die discovered... despised... humiliated
... found out! So there! Are you satisfied?
Are you satisfied? Now go away and　　　845
let me alone! Let me die in silence — naked!
Go! Go! I can say it now! Can't I? I can
shout it at all of you, can't I? There's no one I
want to see! There's no one I want to talk to!
Let me alone! Let me alone! Go and　　　850
tell it to them all — you to your wife, and you
to your fiancée... that I am dead... yes, and
that I died naked!

Curtain

INTRODUCTION TO

The Hairy Ape

The Rise of American Drama: O'Neill and Expressionistic Tragedy

THE RISE OF AMERICAN DRAMA

TOURING ENGLISH ACTORS brought theatrical entertainment to colonial America about the middle of the eighteenth century. The works of Shakespeare and such other favorites of the period as Dryden, Rowe, and Farquhar composed the bills. The first stage play by an American came from the pen of Thomas Godfrey (1736–63), who did not live to see it acted at Philadelphia in 1767. His *Prince of Parthia*, an imitation of Beaumont and Fletcher, contains no American touches whatsoever. It therefore remained for Royall Tyler (1757–1826) to create in his Sheridan-like comedy, *The Contrast* (1787), the first drama with native color, notably in the character of Jonathan, the original "Stage Yankee."

Despite these hints of a coming American theater, England continued to furnish the United States with most of her plays and players until after 1850. Even to the end of the century, mediocre European drama flooded the American stage to the serious detriment of the home product. Native playwrights found it both fashionable and remunerative to copy the successful foreign models. Their most vigorous and polished effort went into romantic melodramas; for example, *Francesca da Rimini* (1855) by George H. Boker (1823–90), *The Octoroon* (1859) by Dion Boucicault (1820?–90), and *Shenandoah* (1888) by Bronson Howard (1842–1908). The inferiority of American dramatic literature during the nineteenth century may be attributed no more to a dearth of talent than to a national taste generally uninterested in the stage as a cultural enterprise.

The first two decades of the twentieth century were marked in the United States by an increasingly serious attitude toward the theater, an attitude largely inspired by the renaissance of dramatic art in Europe, England, and Ireland. The more prominent playwrights displayed a greater integrity in both content and form: Clyde Fitch (1865–1909) in his social comedy, *The Truth* (1906); William Vaughn Moody (1869–1910) in his religious folk-play, *The Faith Healer* (1909); Percy MacKaye (1875–   ) in his fantasy, *The Scarecrow* (1910); Edward Sheldon (1886–1946) in his realistic study, *The Boss* (1916). During this same period American colleges and universities began to devote attention to the drama, to playwriting, and even to stage production. Professor George P. Baker led off at Harvard University in 1905 with "English 47," a course in playwriting, supplemented in 1912 by the 47 Workshop, a stage laboratory. From that latter year onward "little theater" groups sprang up throughout this country in imitation of the Free Theater at Paris, the Moscow Art Theater, and the Abbey Theater of Dublin. The Neighborhood Playhouse and the Washington Square Players, both founded in New York during 1915, came to exert an elevating influence on Broadway. The Washington Square Players developed into The Theater Guild (1919), a producing organization which has done more than any other to raise the artistic standards of the commercial American stage. In 1915 also, a few Greenwich Village writers, led by Susan Glaspell, started a highly important venture when they opened on a wharf at Provincetown, Massachusetts, a summer playhouse devoted to untested American works. By 1920 these various academic and "little" theaters, in conjunction with a greater national interest in the arts, had brought about a climate favorable to a drama as mature as that of Europe.

O'NEILL AND EXPRESSIONISTIC TRAGEDY

The first major product of this new climate and the first American playwright of international reputation is Eugene O'Neill. The son of a well-known actor, James O'Neill, he began on October 16, 1888, in a New York hotel a life which has led him in and out of the theater ever since. For his first seven years he toured the country with his father. After attendance at various secondary schools his formal education ended in the spring of 1907 when as a freshman at Princeton he suffered expulsion for throwing a beer-bottle, so it is said, through a window of President Wilson's residence. From then until the winter of 1912–13 he sought the romance "beyond the horizon" in an extraordinary series of rôles: clerk in a New York mail-order house; husband and father; gold-prospector in Honduras; assistant manager of his father's traveling troupe; seaman on a Norwegian boat to the Argentine; clerk with three different American firms in Buenos Aires; habitué of the Sailor's Opera, a dive on the Buenos Aires docks; mule-tender on a cattle-ship to South Africa and back to Buenos Aires; seaman on a tramp steamer to New York; Bowery "bum" at Jimmy-the-Priest's, a waterfront "hell-house" where "one roommate of mine jumped out of the window to his death"; able seaman on a trans-Atlantic liner; actor in his father's road show, *The Count of Monte Cristo;* reporter on a New London, Connecticut, newspaper. These colorful years of wandering crammed his mind with scenes of a raw, discontented, lonely humanity, scenes of strange ugliness and passion at sea or ashore. They did much to nourish a somber imagination and philosophy.

O'Neill's wayward life as a vagabond finally took its toll in the shape of incipient tuberculosis. While convalescing from this illness in the spring of 1913, he decided to become a playwright. For well over a year he read intensively the Greek and English dramatists, Ibsen, and above all, Strindberg, whose psychoanalytic bent appealed to O'Neill's rather introspective temperament. Anxious for instruction in dramatic technique, he spent the academic year of 1914–15 at Harvard in Professor Baker's 47 Workshop. The following summer and winter saw him in Greenwich Village, hobnobbing with radicals, negroes, Italians, and derelicts. His vision of a restive mankind in a cruel world deepened.

During the summer of 1916 O'Neill witnessed the first staging of one of his plays. *Bound East for Cardiff,* a one-act tragedy of the sea, was given by the Provincetown Players with immense success. This performance initiated between the author and the producers an epoch-making association which lasted for a decade. In November the Provincetown Players opened their new Playwright's Theater on Macdougal Street, Greenwich Village. Thus O'Neill had available an ideal stage laboratory in the theatrical center of the country. No other American playwright ever enjoyed such a golden opportunity for the free expression of his genius. O'Neill did not fail to make the most of it. He passed three years in experimenting with short atmospheric studies, chiefly on sailor life. Then he undertook his first full-length play, *Beyond the Horizon*, a realistic tragedy, with a farm background, of man's hunger for romance. It won the Pulitzer Prize in 1920 and gave him national prominence.

During the next five seasons the Provincetown Players produced a succession of O'Neill works with amazingly varied subject matter and design: *The Emperor Jones* (1920), chiefly a dramatic monologue, depicting a fear-crazed negro in a tropical jungle; *Anna Christie* (1921), O'Neill's second Pulitzer Prize play, a realistic piece on waterfront love; *The Hairy Ape* (1922), a symbolic fantasy about a stoker's search for a place in society; *All God's Chillun Got Wings* (1924), a tragedy of marriage between a white woman and a negro, set in a city apartment; *Desire Under the Elms* (1924), a tragedy of avarice and sex on a New England farm. These original and searching plays revealed an imaginative genius of far greater power than any previously devoted to American drama. They not only confirmed O'Neill as the foremost of all native playwrights, but also provided the first American works deemed worthy of production abroad.

In 1927 O'Neill transferred his allegiance to the Theater Guild, because he desired the more pretentious Broadway production which his fame now justified. In 1928 *Marco Millions* and *Strange Interlude*, the Pulitzer Prize play for the year, appeared under the Guild's auspices. The former is a poetic satire on the American "Babbitt" surrounded by Oriental pageantry; the latter, a Freudian study of a neurotic woman's sex life, done in nine acts with constant asides. The magnitude of *Strange Interlude* only stimulated O'Neill to even greater magnitude in *Mourning Becomes Electra* (1931), a trilogy in thirteen acts. He attempts in his trilogy to invest the House of Atreus tragedy, so popular among classical dramatists, with what he believed a "modern psychological approximation of the Greek sense of fate." His version, based on an aristocratic, but decadent, New England family of the Civil-War period, offers Freudian interpretations of a tangled family conflict that eventuates in murder, incest, and suicide. This epic drama of enormous theatrical intensity earned for him in 1936 the Nobel Prize in Literature.

Mourning Becomes Electra exhausted neither O'Neill's energy nor his muse, though he obviously enjoyed an interlude in writing *Ah, Wilderness* (1933), a pleasant comedy of adolescence amid a small-town family. Thereafter, until bad health stopped all his writing in 1949, O'Neill busied himself on a herculean cycle of plays tentatively entitled *A Tale of Possessors Self-Dispossessed* and designed to be an American family saga of the past century. Occasionally he took time to finish off other unrelated plays. Of these only *The Iceman Cometh*, grim tragedy in a Bowery saloon, enjoyed a successful production in 1946.

With a rich diversity of material and technique, O'Neill's drama issues from a poetic brooding over the inner turmoils of man. For him the personal psychological conflicts quite overshadow in importance the social issues which have occasioned so much of modern playwriting. "Life is struggle, often, if not usually, unsuccessful struggle; for most of us have something within us which prevents us from accomplishing what we dream and desire. . . . I suppose that is one reason why I have come to feel so indifferent toward political and social movements of all kinds. . . . Life as a whole is changed very little, if at all, as a result of their course."

The *unsuccessful* struggle of men for freedom and meaning in life has particularly appealed to O'Neill's imagination. Moved in part by his youthful adventuring in the sad basements of humanity from Honduras to Greenwich Village, and, in part, by the fascination of Strindberg's gloomy and deterministic drama, O'Neill came to see man largely as the victim of cruel, relentless "Force." He symbolizes this view by the dark implacable sea in his first noteworthy work, *Bound East for Cardiff*. His subsequent plays reveal that the disruptive agencies lie for the most part within man himself. Fear destroyed the Emperor Jones; avarice and sex, Ephraim Cabot in *Desire Under the Elms*; sex, Nina Leeds in *Strange Interlude* and the Mannon family in *Mourning Becomes Electra*. These, however, and most of O'Neill's protagonists are, from the outset, brutish, stunted, or warped characters. They suffer not merely defeat, but a foregone inner defeat. Their end images spiritual failure, the degradation or disintegration of personality. Hence O'Neill's tragedy in general conveys a sense of man's littleness and of life's futility. Yet he admires the tragedy of the Greeks and the Elizabethans because "it roused them spiritually to a deeper understanding of life." Though he early expressed a desire to foster "exaltation, an intensified feeling of the significant worth of man's being and becoming," a confessed love for the stark and the ugly often perverts the emotional beauty of his tragedy. It rarely sounds the note of aspiration; it is seldom ennobling.

O'Neill's restless and creative spirit was not long satisfied with traditional realism as a medium for tragedy. Realism, in his opinion, is shallow and inadequate, for it offers nothing but "the banality of surfaces." The complexity of man's inner disturbance requires, he believes, a "behind-life" treatment that focuses upon the internal world of thought and impulse, and reveals both conscious and unconscious motives. "It is only by means of some form of 'supernaturalism' that we may express in the theater what we comprehend intuitively of that self-obsession which is the particular discount we moderns have to pay for the loan of life." He has found a form of "supernaturalism" suited to his purpose in that drama of symbolism and abstraction to which German writers of the *Sturm* school during the First World War applied the term "expressionism." At the close of the War it enjoyed a great vogue in Germany with Georg Kaiser (1878–1945) and Ernst Toller (1893–1939), its leading practitioners. Kaiser's *From Morn to Midnight* (1916) and *Gas* (Part 1, 1918; Part 2, 1920), along with Toller's *Masses and Man* (1919) and *Machine Wreckers* (1920), quickly enjoyed international performances. This movement of expressionism traces back to the symbolistic, dreamlike fantasies of Strindberg, such as *The Dream Play* (1902) and *The Spook Sonata* (1907). It is from Strindberg more than from the German dramatists that O'Neill claims to have drawn inspiration for his numerous experiments with expressionistic method.

Expressionism is so called because it casts aside representation of outer reality in order to give expression solely to inner significances. These subjective values, arising either from a state of mind in the playwright or in the human objects of his study, are made concrete by means of symbols especially adapted to the stage. The words and actions of external reality may still be used, but they no longer control the meaning. Usually the scenes and characters are stylized, or distorted in an arbitrarily fantastic manner. The settings present, not actual environment, but pictorial fabrications with emotional suggestion. The characters emerge as typed individuals or as composites symbolizing group habits, mentalities, and ideals. Often they bear generic names — the Son, the Official, the Billionaire — or symbolic proper names, as Mr. Zero. In a completely expressionistic drama the plot takes the form of a parable, communicating both the abstract ideas and the peculiar fancies of the author. The development of action is not closely integrated, but resembles the "movie" method of brief, disconnected "shots." The total effect approximates the weirdness and intensity of a phantasmagoria or a dream. Thus by its manifold imaginative devices expressionism may, in an incomparable fashion, dissect individual consciousness, mass psychology, or the nature of Life. The rich variety of its dissections, subject as they are to no conventions of material or design except those imposed by each artist's own temperament, has established expressionism as the most fickle but, at the same time, the most exciting pattern of dramatic art in the modern theater.

"THE HAIRY APE"

The Hairy Ape is one of the outstanding specimens of expressionism in world drama, as well as O'Neill's finest effort in that genre. Written in three weeks during the fall of 1921, the play had its premiere on March 9, 1922, at the Provincetown Playhouse in Greenwich Village. Later the Provincetown Players moved the production to Broadway for a long run at the Plymouth Theater. Louis Wolheim gave a magnificent performance as the stoker hero, Yank.

According to O'Neill, *The Hairy Ape* grew out of his life as a seaman on the transatlantic liner S.S. New York about 1911. At that time he got to know the slum-dwellers of the sea, the stokers, and the depressing holes below waterline where they lived out their days aboard ship. One of his stoker acquaintances, a Liverpool Irishman by the name of Driscoll, "came to a strange end. He committed suicide by jumping overboard in mid-ocean ... Why?" The why of Driscoll's suicide prompted disturbing but fruitful reflection.

Nevertheless, O'Neill's experiences at sea do not seem to have been the sole source of inspiration for *The Hairy Ape*. While he was enjoying the proletarian atmosphere of Greenwich Village in 1915, there appeared a novel by Ernest Poole (1880–   ) about conditions in New York harbor. Because *The Harbor* expressed what were then thought radical views about the social and economic order, it caused a considerable stir and evidently attracted O'Neill's attention. Book III of *The Harbor* turns the spotlight upon the "harbor of slaves driven into fierce revolt," and especially upon the crowded fermenting stokeholes, "mixing bowls for all the world." Chapter 5 of Book III recounts a visit to the stokers' quarters on a liner with the following significant details:

> The low chamber was crowded with rows of bunks, steel skeleton bunks three tiers high, the top tier just under the ceiling. ... Some [men] were almost naked, and the smells of their bodies filled the place. ... Half the crew were already well soused. Some moved restlessly about. *One huge bull of a creature with large, limpid, shining eyes stopped suddenly with a puzzled stare*, then leaned back on a bunk and laughed uproariously. ... Louder rose the singing. ... The singers kept pounding each other's backs or waving bottles over their heads. Two bottles smashed together and brought a still higher burst of glee. ...
> As we climbed ladder after ladder, fainter and fainter on our ears rose that yelling from

below. Suddenly we came out on deck and slammed an iron door behind us. *And I was where I belonged.* I was in dazzling sunshine and keen frosty Autumn air. . . . Dainty women brushed me by. . . . I saw their fresh immaculate clothes. . . . And I knew that deep below all this, down in the bottom of the ship, the stokers were still singing.

Poole's description not only offers an abbreviated sketch of the opening stokehole scene in *The Hairy Ape*, but it also suggests the contrasting promenade-deck world which is depicted in Scene 2 of that play. In connection with these two worlds, one deep below deck and one in the upper air, Poole projects the idea of "belonging." This same idea constitutes the intellectual motif of *The Hairy Ape*. And finally, O'Neill's perplexed giant-like hero is prefigured by the "huge bull of a creature . . . with a puzzled stare" in Poole's stokehole picture.

This series of important parallels would indicate that O'Neill almost certainly picked up scenic and ideological suggestions direct from *The Harbor*. These materials his imagination fused with his own dark retrospections on stokeholes and stokers, Driscoll in particular. Out of the fusion arose the conception of a play dealing with a stoker's fruitless attempt to fit into the social order. O'Neill did not intend his dramatic fable to describe primarily the plight of the laborer in the present economic structure; he rather intended to point beneath classes and systems at what he believed to be the general frustration of mankind in a scientific and industrialized world. The stoker symbolizes the type man of our era, the worker dependent on the machine. Thus Yank Smith with his generic American name is, according to his creator, "a symbol of man, who has lost his old harmony with nature, the harmony which he used to have as an animal and has not yet acquired in a spiritual way." The "punches" which Yank receives on ship, on Fifth Avenue, in the I.W.W. hall, in the city prison, and at the zoo, symbolize the rebuffs which the common man today suffers in a universe where he finds himself an alien. Hence the essential problem in *The Hairy Ape*, as always with O'Neill, is personal and psychological. The precise theme is, to quote the author, "man and his struggle with his own fate. The struggle used to be with the gods, but is now with himself . . . his attempt 'to belong.'" This age-long struggle of man the bitterly ironic subtitle to the play calls "a comedy of ancient and modern life."

To project the problem of "belonging," O'Neill decided the expressionistic method to be the most effective medium, for in his opinion the large mass of humanity, the common men, never become fully aware and never articulate their restive state of mind, compounded of disillusionment, loneliness, and mystification. The stylization and distortion apparent in every scene serve to bring out emotional values of which the protagonist, Yank, may not always be conscious. The lurid stokehole (Scene 3), for example, suggests the inhuman, dissonant, mechanized elements in modern life by the brutish postures, the tumult, the rhythmic motion of the stokers; but, of course, Yank does not have any such impression of the scene. On the other hand, he does recognize the grotesque impersonal behavior of the Fifth Avenue crowd in Scene 5. Even those scenes, such as the forecastle (Scenes 1, 4) and the I.W.W. hall (Scene 7), where realism predominates on the surface, are finally characterized by the expressionistic undertones. The nervous rhythms of language and the patterned movements of the characters induce various unnatural symbolic effects.

This mixture of symbolism and realism greatly enhances the characterization of Yank.

A fundamental weakness in expressionistic drama is the usually abstract nature of its characters, their "flat" personalities. In general they fail to arouse much sympathy in the spectator because he does not find himself intimate with any one individual. Yank, however, gathers fullness of character as the play progresses. The grandiose symbol of Man which O'Neill intended him to bear is gradually forgotten. He develops into a gripping figure whose individual frustration ends on a crescendo of emotion. O'Neill, at his verbal best in Yank's East-Side-of-New-York dialect, imparts a rhythmic beauty to the latter's racy, staccato speech. Brilliantly characteristic utterances flash again and again, such as the stoker's early boast, "Hell, sure, dat's my fav'rite climate! I eat it up! I get fat on it!" (Scene 1, ll. 290–92), and his bitter last confession, "I don't tick, see? I'm a busted Ingersoll, dat's what" (Scene 7, ll. 180–81). This crude eloquence clothes his undaunted, though puzzled, spirit with a genuine tragic dignity. Yet the fate of so primitive a character can hardly provoke the magnitude of feeling commensurate with the universal human tragedy which O'Neill thought to symbolize. Even so, the colorful, swift, intense drama in *The Hairy Ape* does express better than any other of O'Neill's plays what once he supremely valued, "the transforming nobility of tragedy in seemingly the most ignoble, debased lives."

[For a survey of American drama, see A. H. Quinn, *A History of the American Drama from the Civil War to the Present Day* (1936); for expressionism, Carl Dahlström, *Strindberg's Dramatic Expressionism* (1930), and Richard Samuel, *Expressionism in German Life, Literature, and the Theatre* (1939); for O'Neill, Barrett H. Clark, *Eugene O'Neill: The Man and His Work* (1947).]

EUGENE O'NEILL

The Hairy Ape
A Comedy of Ancient and Modern Life

DRAMATIS PERSONAE

ROBERT SMITH, "YANK"
PADDY
LONG
MILDRED DOUGLAS
HER AUNT

SECOND ENGINEER
A Guard
A Secretary of an Organization
Stokers, Ladies, Gentlemen, etc.

SCENES

Scene   I: The firemen's forecastle of an ocean liner — an hour after sailing from New York
Scene   II: Section of promenade deck, two days out — morning.
Scene   III: The stokehole. A few minutes later.
Scene   IV: Same as Scene I. Half an hour later.
Scene   V: Fifth Avenue, New York. Three weeks later.
Scene   VI: An island near New York. The next night.
Scene   VII: In New York. About a month later.
Scene VIII: In New York. Twilight of the next day.

Time: The Modern.

SCENE I

The firemen's forecastle of a transatlantic liner an hour after sailing from New York for the voyage across. Tiers of narrow steel bunks, three deep, on all sides. An entrance in rear. Benches on the floor before the bunks. The room is crowded with men, shouting, cursing, laughing, singing — a confused, inchoate uproar swelling into a sort of unity, a meaning — the bewildered, furious, baffled defiance of a beast in a cage. Nearly all the men are drunk. Many bottles are passed from hand to hand. All are dressed in dungaree pants, heavy ugly shoes. Some wear singlets, but the majority are stripped to the waist.

  The treatment of this scene, or of any other scene in the play, should by no means be naturalistic. The effect sought after is a cramped space in the bowels of a ship, imprisoned by white steel. The lines of bunks, the uprights supporting them, cross each other like the steel framework of a cage. The ceiling crushes down upon the men's heads. They cannot stand upright. This accentuates the natural stooping posture which shoveling coal and the resultant overdevelopment of back and shoulder muscles have given them. The men themselves should resemble those pictures in which the appearance of

Neanderthal Man [1] is guessed at. All are hairy-chested, with long arms of tremendous power, and low, receding brows above their small, fierce, resentful eyes. All the civilized white races are represented, but except for the slight differentiation in color of hair, skin, eyes, all these men are alike.

The curtain rises on a tumult of sound. YANK is seated in the foreground. He seems broader, fiercer, more truculent, more powerful, more sure of himself than the rest. They respect his superior strength — the grudging respect of fear. Then, too, he represents to them a self-expression, the very last word in what they are, their most highly developed individual.

Voices:

Gif me trink dere, you!
'Ave a wet!
Salute!
Gesundheit! [2]
Skoal! [3]   5
Drunk as a lord, God stiffen you!
Here's how!
Luck!
Pass back that bottle, damn you!
Pourin' it down his neck!   10
Ho, Froggy! [4] Where the devil have you been?
La Touraine.
I hit him smash in yaw, py Gott!
Jenkins — the First — he's a rotten swine —
And the coppers nabbed him — and I run —   15
I like peer better. It don't pig head gif you.
A slut, I'm sayin'! She robbed me aslape —
To hell with 'em all!
You're a bloody liar!
Say dot again!   20
        (*Commotion. Two men about to fight are pulled apart.*
No scrappin' now!
Tonight —
See who's the best man!
Bloody Dutchman!
Tonight on the for'ard square.   25
I'll bet on Dutchy.
He packa da wallop, I tella you!

Shut up, Wop! [1]
No fightin', maties. We're all chums, ain't we?
        (*A voice starts bawling a song.*
"Beer, beer, glorious beer!   30
Fill yourselves right up to here."
        Yank (*for the first time seeming to take notice of the uproar about him, turns around threateningly — in a tone of contemptuous authority*). Choke off dat noise! Where d'yuh get dat beer stuff? Beer, hell! Beer's for goils — and Dutchmen. Me for somep'n wit a kick to it! Gimme a drink, one of youse guys. (*Several bot- 35 tles are eagerly offered. He takes a tremendous gulp at one of them; then, keeping the bottle in his hand, glares belligerently at the owner, who hastens to acquiesce in this robbery by saying*) All righto, Yank. Keep it and have another.
        (*YANK contemptuously turns his back on the crowd again. For a second there is an embarrassed silence. Then* ——

Voices:

We must be passing the Hook. [2]
She's beginning to roll to it.
Six days in hell — and then Southampton. [3]   40
Py Yesus, I vish somepody take my first vatch for me!
Gittin' seasick, Square-head?
Drink up and forget it!
What's in your bottle?   45
Gin.
Dot's nigger trink.
Absinthe? It's doped. You'll go off your chump, Froggy!
Cochon! [4]   50
Whisky, that's the ticket!
Where's Paddy?
Going asleep.

---

[1] A prehistoric type of man supposed to have lived widely in Europe during the Early Stone Age.
[2] "To your health," a German toast or greeting.
[3] "Hail," a Scandinavian toast or salutation.
[4] A slang term for a Frenchman.

[1] A slang term for an Italian.
[2] Sandy Hook, New Jersey, the finger-like cape which projects into New York Bay and past which all ocean liners go.
[3] English Channel port.
[4] Pig.

Sing us that whisky song, Paddy.

> (*They all turn to an old, wizened Irish-man who is dozing, very drunk, on the benches forward. His face is extremely monkey-like with all the sad, patient pathos of that animal in his small eyes.*

Singa da song, Caruso Pat!   55
He's gettin' old. The drink is too much for him.
He's too drunk.

Paddy (blinking about him, starts to his feet resentfully, swaying, holding on to the edge of a bunk). I'm never too drunk to sing. 'Tis only when I'm dead to the world I'd be wishful 60
to sing at all. (*With a sort of sad contempt*) "Whisky Johnny," ye want? A chanty, ye want? Now that's a queer wish from the ugly like of you, God help you. But no matther.

> (*He starts to sing in a thin, nasal, dole-ful tone.*

Oh, whisky is the life of man!   65
Whisky! O Johnny!

> (*They all join in on this.*

Oh, whisky is the life of man!
Whisky for my Johnny!

> (*Again chorus.*

Oh, whisky drove my old man mad!
Whisky! O Johnny!   70
Oh, whisky drove my old man mad!
Whisky for my Johnny!

YANK (*again turning around scornfully*). Aw hell! Nix on dat old sailing ship stuff! All dat bull's dead, see? And you're dead, too, 75
yuh damned old Harp,[1] on'y yuh don't know it. Take it easy, see. Give us a rest. Nix on de loud noise. (*With a cynical grin*) Can't youse see I'm tryin' to tink?

All (repeating the word after him as one with the same cynical amused mockery). Think! 80

> (*The chorused word has a brazen metal-lic quality as if their throats were phonograph horns. It is followed by a general uproar of hard, barking laughter.*

Voices:
Don't be cracking your head wid ut, Yank.

[1] A slang term for an Irishman.

You gat headache, py yingo!
One thing about it — it rhymes with drink!
Ha, ha, ha!
Drink, don't think!   85
Drink, don't think!
Drink, don't think!

> (*A whole chorus of voices has taken up this refrain, stamping on the floor, pounding on the benches with fists.*

Yank (taking a gulp from his bottle — good-naturedly). Awright. Can de noise. I got yuh de foist time.

> (*The uproar subsides. A very drunken sentimental tenor begins to sing.*

"Far away in Canada,   90
Far across the sea,
There's a lass who fondly waits
Making a home for me ——"

Yank (fiercely contemptuous). Shut up, yuh lousy boob! Where d'yuh get dat tripe? 95
Home? Home, hell! I'll make a home for yuh! I'll knock yuh dead. Home. T'hell wit home! Where d'yuh get dat tripe? Dis is home, see? What d'yuh want wit home? (*Proudly*) I runned away from mine when 100
I was a kid. On'y too glad to beat it, dat was me. Home was lickings for me, dat's all. But yuh can bet your shoit no one ain't never licked me since! Wanter try it, any of youse? Huh! I guess not. (*In a more 105
placated but still contemptuous tone*) Goils waitin' for yuh, huh? Aw, hell! Dat's all tripe. Dey don't wait for no one. Dey'd doublecross yuh for a nickel. Dey're all tarts, get me? Treat 'em rough, dat's me. To hell wit 110
'em. Tarts, dat's what, de whole bunch of 'em.

Long (very drunk, jumps on a bench excit-edly, gesticulating with a bottle in his hand). Listen 'ere, Comrades! Yank 'ere is right. 'E says this 'ere stinkin' ship is our 'ome. And 'e says as 'ome is 'ell. And 'e's right! This is 'ell. We lives in 'ell, Comrades — and 115
right enough we'll die in it. (*Raging*) And who's ter blame, I arsks yer? We ain't. We wasn't born this rotten way. All men is born free and ekal. That's in the bleedin' Bible, maties. But what d'they care for the 120
Bible — them lazy, bloated swine what travels first cabin? Them's the ones. They dragged us

down 'til we're on'y wage slaves in the bowels of a bloody ship, sweatin', burnin' up, eatin' coal dust! Hit's them's ter blame — 125 the damned capitalist clarss!

> (*There had been a gradual murmur of contemptuous resentment rising among the men until now he is interrupted by a storm of catcalls, hisses, boos, hard laughter.*)

Voices:
Turn it off!
Shut up!
Sit down!
Closa da face!   130
Tamn fool! (*Etc.*)

Yank (*standing up and glaring at* LONG). Sit down before I knock yuh down! (LONG *makes haste to efface himself.* YANK *goes on contemptuously.*) De Bible, huh? De cap'tlist class, huh? Aw, nix on dat Salvation Army- 135 Socialist bull. Git a soapbox! Hire a hall! Come and be saved, huh? Jerk us to Jesus, huh? Aw g'wan! I've listened to lots of guys like you, see. Yuh're all wrong. Wanter know what I t'ink? Yuh ain't no good 140 for no one. Yuh're de bunk. Yuh ain't got no noive, get me? Yuh're yellow, dat's what. Yellow, dat's you. Say! What's dem slobs in de foist cabin got to do wit us? We're better men dan dey are, ain't we? Sure! One 145 of us guys could clean up de whole mob wit one mit. Put one of 'em down here for one watch in de stokehole, what'd happen? Dey'd carry him off on a stretcher. Dem boids don't amount to nothin'. Dey're just baggage. 150 Who makes dis old tub run? Ain't it us guys? Well, den, we belong, don't we? We belong and dey don't. Dat's all. (*A loud chorus of approval.* YANK *goes on.*) As for dis bein' hell — aw, nuts! Yuh lost your noive, 155 dat's what. Dis is a man's job, get me? It belongs. It runs dis tub. No stiffs need apply. But yuh're a stiff, see? Yuh're yellow, dat's you.

Voices (*with a great hard pride in them*):
Righto!   160
A man's job!
Talk is cheap, Long.
He never could hold up his end.

Divil take him!
Yank's right. We make it go.   165
Py Gott, Yank say right ting!
We don't need no one cryin' over us.
Makin' speeches.
Throw him out!
Yellow!   170
Chuck him overboard!
I'll break his jaw for him!

> (*They crowd around* LONG *threateningly.*)

Yank (*half good-natured again — contemptuously*). Aw, take it easy. Leave him alone. He ain't woith a punch. Drink up. Here's how, whoever owns dis.   175

> (*He takes a long swallow from his bottle. All drink with him. In a flash all is hilarious amiability again, back-slapping, loud talk, etc.*)

Paddy (*who has been sitting in a blinking, melancholy daze, suddenly cries out in a voice full of old sorrow*). We belong to this, you're saying? We make the ship to go, you're saying? Yerra, then, that Almighty God have pity on us! (*His voice runs into the wail of a keen, he rocks back and forth on his bench. The men stare at him, startled and impressed in spite of themselves.*) Oh, to be back in the fine 180 days of my youth, ochone![1] Oh, there was fine beautiful ships them days — clippers wid tall masts touching the sky — fine strong men in them — men that was sons of the sea as if 'twas the mother that bore them. Oh, 185 the clean skins of them, and the clear eyes, the straight backs and full chests of them! Brave men they was, and bold men surely! We'd be sailing out, bound down round the Horn[2] maybe. We'd be making sail in the dawn, 190 with a fair breeze, singing a chanty song wid no care to it. And astern the land would be sinking low and dying out, but we'd give it no heed but a laugh, and never a look behind. For the day that was, was enough, for we was free 195 men — and I'm thinking 'tis only slaves do be giving heed to the day that's gone or the day to come — until they're old like me. (*With a sort of religious exaltation*) Oh, to be scudding south again wid the power of the Trade 200

---

[1] "Alas!" — a Gaelic lament.
[2] Cape Horn at the southern tip of South America.

Wind driving her on steady through the nights and the days! Full sail on her! Nights and days! Nights when the foam of the wake would be flaming wid fire, when the sky'd be blazing and winking wid stars. Or the full 205 of the moon maybe. Then you'd see her driving through the gray night, her sails stretching aloft all silver and white, not a sound on the deck, the lot of us dreaming dreams, till you'd believe 'twas no real ship at all you was 210 on but a ghost ship like the Flying Dutchman [1] they say does be roaming the seas forevermore widout touching a port. And there was the days, too. A warm sun on the clean decks. Sun warming the blood of you, and wind over 215 the miles of shiny green ocean like strong drink to your lungs. Work — aye, hard work — but who'd mind that at all? Sure, you worked under the sky and 'twas work wid skill and daring to it. And wid the day done, in the 220 dog watch,[2] smoking me pipe at ease, the lookout would be raising land maybe, and we'd see the mountains of South Americy wid the red fire of the setting sun painting their white tops and the clouds floating by them! (*His* 225 *tone of exaltation ceases. He goes on mournfully.*) Yerra, what's the use of talking? 'Tis a dead man's whisper. (*To* YANK, *resentfully*) 'Twas them days men belonged to ships, not now. 'Twas them days a ship was part of the sea, and a man was part of a ship, and the 230 sea joined all together and made it one. (*Scornfully*) Is it one wid this you'd be, Yank — black smoke from the funnels smudging the sea, smudging the decks — the bloody engines pounding and throbbing and shaking — 235 wid divil a sight of sun or a breath of clean air — choking our lungs wid coal dust — breaking our backs and hearts in the hell of the stokehole — feeding the bloody furnace — feeding our lives along wid the coal, I'm think- 240 ing — caged in by steel from a sight of the sky like bloody apes in the Zoo! (*With a harsh laugh*) Ho-ho, divil mend you! Is it to belong

[1] The vessel of the legendary Dutch mariner who, angered by adverse winds, swore to round the Cape of Good Hope, South Africa, if it took till the Day of Judgment. God then condemned him to perform his oath.
[2] The watch from 4 to 6 P.M., or from 6 to 8 P.M.

to that you're wishing? Is it a flesh and blood wheel of the engines you'd be? 245
Yank (*who has been listening with a contemptuous sneer, barks out the answer*). Sure ting! Dat's me! What about it?
Paddy (*as if to himself — with great sorrow*). Me time is past due. That a great wave wid sun in the heart of it may sweep me over the side sometime I'd be dreaming of the 250 days that's gone!
Yank. Aw, yuh crazy Mick! (*He springs to his feet and advances on* PADDY *threateningly — then stops, fighting some queer struggle within himself — lets his hands fall to his sides — contemptuously.*) Aw, take it easy. Yuh're aw right, at dat. Yuh're bugs, dat's all — nutty as a cuckoo. All dat tripe yuh been 255 pullin' — Aw, dat's all right. On'y it's dead, get me? Yuh don't belong no more, see. Yuh don't get de stuff. Yuh're too old. (*Disgustedly*) But aw say, come up for air onct in a while, can't yuh? See what's happened 260 since yuh croaked. (*He suddenly bursts forth vehemently, growing more and more excited.*) Say! Sure! Sure I meant it! What de hell — Say, lemme talk! Hey! Hey, you old Harp! Hey, youse guys! Say, listen to me — wait a 265 moment — I gotter talk, see. I belong and he don't. He's dead but I'm livin'. Listen to me! Sure I'm part of de engines! Why de hell not! Dey move, don't dey? Dey're speed, ain't dey? Dey smash trou, don't dey? 270 Twenty-five knots a hour! Dat's goin' some! Dat's new stuff! Dat belongs! But him, he's too old. He gets dizzy. Say, listen. All dat crazy tripe about nights and days; all dat crazy tripe about stars and moons; all dat 275 crazy tripe about suns and winds, fresh air and de rest of it — Aw, hell, dat's all a dope dream! Hittin' de pipe of de past, dat's what he's doin'. He's old and don't belong no more. But me, I'm young! I'm in de pink! I 280 move wit it! It, get me! I mean de ting dat's de guts of all dis. It plows trou all de tripe he's been sayin'. It blows dat up! It knocks dat dead! It slams dat offen de face of de oith! It, get me! De engines and de coal and 285 de smoke and all de rest of it! He can't breathe and swallow coal dust, but I kin, see?

Dat's fresh air for me! Dat's food for me! I'm new, get me? Hell in de stokehole? Sure! It takes a man to work in hell. Hell, sure, 290 dat's my fav'rite climate. I eat it up! I git fat on it! It's me makes it hot! It's me makes it roar! It's me makes it move! Sure, on'y for me everyting stops. It all goes dead, get me? De noise and smoke and all de 295 engines movin' de woild, dey stop. Dere ain't nothin' no more! Dat's what I'm sayin'. Everyting else dat makes de woild move, somep'n makes it move. It can't move witout somep'n else, see? Den yuh get down to me. 300 I'm at de bottom, get me! Dere ain't nothin' foither. I'm de end. I'm de start! I start somep'n and de woild moves! It — dat's me! — de new dat's moiderin' de old! I'm de ting in coal dat makes it boin; I'm steam and 305 oil for de engines; I'm de ting in noise dat makes yuh hear it; I'm smoke and express trains and steamers and factory whistles; I'm de ting in gold dat makes it money! And I'm what makes iron into steel! Steel, dat 310 stands for de whole ting! And I'm steel — steel — steel! I'm de muscles in steel, de punch behind it! (*As he says this he pounds with his fist against the steel bunks. All the men, roused to a pitch of frenzied self-glorification by his speech, do likewise. There is a deafening metallic roar, through which* YANK's *voice can be heard bellowing.*) Slaves, hell! We run de whole woiks. All de rich guys dat tink 315 dey're somep'n, dey ain't nothin'! Dey don't belong. But us guys, we're in de move, we're at de bottom, de whole ting is us! (PADDY *from the start of* YANK's *speech has been taking one gulp after another from his bottle, at first frightenedly, as if he were afraid to listen, then desperately, as if to drown his senses, but finally has achieved complete indifferent, even amused, drunkenness.* YANK *sees his lips moving. He quells the uproar with a shout.*) Hey, youse guys, take it easy! Wait a mo-

ment! De nutty Harp is sayin' somep'n. 320 *Paddy (is heard now — throws his head back with a mocking burst of laughter).* Ho-ho-ho-ho-ho ——
Yank (drawing back his fist, with a snarl). Aw! Look out who yuh're givin' the bark!
Paddy (begins to sing the "Miller of Dee" with enormous good-nature).
"I care for nobody, no, not I,
　　And nobody cares for me." 325
Yank (good-natured himself in a flash, interrupts PADDY *with a slap on the bare back like a report).* Dat's de stuff! Now yuh're gettin' wise to somep'n. Care for nobody, dat's de dope! To hell wit 'em all! And nix on nobody else carin'. I kin care for myself, get me! (*Eight bells sound, muffled, vibrating through the steel walls as if some enormous brazen gong were imbedded in the heart of the ship. All the men jump up mechanically, file through the door silently, close upon each other's heels in what is very like a prisoners' lockstep.* YANK *slaps* PADDY *on the back.*) Our watch, yuh old 330 Harp! (*Mockingly*) Come on down in hell. Eat up de coal dust. Drink in de heat. It's it, see! Act like yuh liked it, yuh better — or croak yuhself.
Paddy (with jovial defiance). To the 335 divil wid it! I'll not report this watch. Let thim log me and be damned. I'm no slave the like of you. I'll be sittin' here at me ease, and drinking, and thinking, and dreaming dreams.
Yank (contemptuously). Tinkin' and 340 dreamin', what'll that get yuh? What's tinkin' got to do wit it? We move, don't we? Speed, ain't it? Fog, dat's all you stand for. But we drive trou dat, don't we? We split dat up and smash trou — twenty-five knots a 345 hour! (*Turns his back on* PADDY *scornfully.*) Aw, yuh make me sick! Yuh don't belong!
(*He strides out the door in rear.* PADDY *hums to himself, blinking drowsily.*)

Curtain

SCENE 2

Two days out. A section of the promenade deck. Mildred Douglas and her aunt are discovered reclining in deck chairs. The former is a girl of twenty, slender, delicate, with a pale, pretty face marred by a self-conscious expression of disdainful superiority. She looks fretful, nervous, and discontented, bored by her own anemia. Her aunt is a pompous and proud — and fat — old lady. She is a type even to the point of a double chin and lorgnette. She is dressed pretentiously, as if afraid her face alone would never indicate her position in life. Mildred is dressed all in white.

The impression to be conveyed by this scene is one of the beautiful, vivid life of the sea all about — sunshine on the deck in a great flood, the fresh sea wind blowing across it. In the midst of this, these two incongruous, artificial figures, inert and disharmonious, the elder like a gray lump of dough touched up with rouge, the younger looking as if the vitality of her stock had been sapped before she was conceived, so that she is the expression not of its life energy but merely of the artificialities that energy had won for itself in the spending.

Mil. (looking up with affected dreaminess). How the black smoke swirls back against the sky! Is it not beautiful?

Aunt (without looking up). I dislike smoke of any kind.

Mil. My great-grandmother smoked a 5 pipe — a clay pipe.

Aunt (ruffling). Vulgar!

Mil. She was too distant a relative to be vulgar. Time mellows pipes. 9

Aunt (pretending boredom, but irritated). Did the sociology you took up at college teach you that — to play the ghoul[1] on every possible occasion, excavating old bones? Why not let your great-grandmother rest in her grave?

Mil. (dreamily). With her pipe beside 15 her — puffing in Paradise.

Aunt (with spite). Yes, you are a natural-born ghoul. You are even getting to look like one, my dear.

Mil. (in a passionless tone). I detest 20 you, Aunt. *(Looking at her critically)* Do you know what you remind me of? Of a cold pork pudding against a background of linoleum tablecloth in the kitchen of a — but the possibilities are wearisome. 25

(She closes her eyes.

Aunt (with a bitter laugh). Merci[2] for your candor. But since I am and must be your chaperon — in appearance, at least — let us patch up some sort of armed truce. For my part you are quite free to indulge any pose 30 of eccentricity that beguiles you — as long as you observe the amenities ——

[1] An evil being supposed to rob graves.   [2] Thanks.

Mil. (drawling). The inanities?

Aunt (going on as if she hadn't heard). After exhausting the morbid thrills of social 35 service work on New York's East Side — how they must have hated you, by the way, the poor that you made so much poorer in their own eyes! — you are now bent on making your slumming international. Well, I hope 40 Whitechapel[1] will provide the needed nerve tonic. Do not ask me to chaperon you there, however. I told your father I would not. I loathe deformity. We will hire an army of detectives and you may investigate every- 45 thing — they allow you to see.

Mil. (protesting with a trace of genuine earnestness). Please do not mock at my attempts to discover how the other half lives. Give me credit for some sort of groping sincerity in that, at least. I would like to help them. I 50 would like to be some use in the world. Is it my fault I don't know how? I would like to be sincere, to touch life somewhere. *(With weary bitterness)* But I'm afraid I have neither the vitality nor integrity. All that was burnt 55 out in our stock before I was born. Grandfather's blast furnaces, flaming to the sky, melting steel, making millions — then father keeping those home fires burning, making more millions — and little me at the tail-end of it 60 all. I'm a waste product in the Bessemer process[2] — like the millions. Or rather, I inherit

[1] Notorious slum district of East London.

[2] A process of making steel from molten cast iron by blasting out the impurities with air; so called from the English inventor of the process, Sir Henry Bessemer.

the acquired trait of the by-product, wealth, but none of the energy, none of the strength of the steel that made it. I am sired by 65 gold and damned by it, as they say at the race track — damned in more ways than one.

(*She laughs mirthlessly.*

Aunt (*unimpressed — superciliously*). You seem to be going in for sincerity today. It isn't becoming to you, really — except as an 70 obvious pose. Be as artificial as you are, I advise. There's a sort of sincerity in that, you know. And, after all, you must confess you like that better.

Mil. (*again affected and bored*). Yes, I 75 suppose I do. Pardon me for my outburst. When a leopard complains of its spots, it must sound rather grotesque. (*In a mocking tone*) Purr, little leopard. Purr, scratch, tear, kill, gorge yourself and be happy — only stay 80 in the jungle where your spots are camouflage. In a cage they make you conspicuous.

Aunt. I don't know what you are talking about.

Mil. It would be rude to talk about 85 anything to you. Let's just talk. (*She looks at her wrist watch.*) Well, thank goodness, it's about time for them to come for me. That ought to give me a new thrill, Aunt.

Aunt (*affectedly troubled*). You don't 90 mean to say you're really going? The dirt — the heat must be frightful ——

Mil. Grandfather started as a puddler. I should have inherited an immunity to heat that would make a salamander shiver. 95 It will be fun to put it to the test.

Aunt. But don't you have to have the captain's — or someone's — permission to visit the stokehole?

Mil. (*with a triumphant smile*). I have 100 it — both his and the chief engineer's. Oh, they didn't want to at first, in spite of my social service credentials. They didn't seem a bit anxious that I should investigate how the other half lives and works on a ship. So I had to 105 tell them that my father, the president of Nazareth Steel, chairman of the board of directors of this line, had told me it would be all right.

Aunt. He didn't.

Mil. How naïve age makes one! But 110

I said he did, Aunt. I even said he had given me a letter to them — which I had lost. And they were afraid to take the chance that I might be lying. (*Excitedly*) So it's ho! for the stokehole. The second engineer is to escort 115 me. (*Looking at her watch again*) It's time. And here he comes, I think.

The SECOND ENGINEER *enters. He is a husky, fine-looking man of thirty-five or so. He stops before the two and tips his cap, visibly embarrassed and ill-at-ease*

Sec. Eng. Miss Douglas?

Mil. Yes. (*Throwing off her rugs and getting to her feet*) Are we all ready to start? 120

Sec. Eng. In just a second, ma'am. I'm waiting for the Fourth.[1] He's coming along.

Mil. (*with a scornful smile*). You don't care to shoulder this responsibility alone, is that it?

Sec. Eng. (*forcing a smile*). Two are 125 better than one. (*Disturbed by her eyes, glances out to sea — blurts out*) A fine day we're having.

Mil. Is it?

Sec. Eng. A nice warm breeze ——

Mil. It feels cold to me. 130

Sec. Eng. But it's hot enough in the sun ——

Mil. Not hot enough for me. I don't like Nature. I was never athletic.

Sec. Eng. (*forcing a smile*). Well, you'll 135 find it hot enough where you're going.

Mil. Do you mean hell?

Sec. Eng. (*flabbergasted, decides to laugh*). Ho-ho! No, I mean the stokehole.

Mil. My grandfather was a puddler. He played with boiling steel. 140

Sec. Eng. (*all at sea — uneasily*). Is that so? Hum, you'll excuse me, ma'am, but are you intending to wear that dress?

Mil. Why not?

Sec. Eng. You'll likely rub against oil 145 and dirt. It can't be helped.

Mil. It doesn't matter. I have lots of white dresses.

Sec. Eng. I have an old coat you might throw over —— 150

Mil. I have fifty dresses like this. I will throw this one into the sea when I come back.

[1] I.e., the Fourth Engineer.

That ought to wash it clean, don't you think?

Sec. Eng. (*doggedly*). There's ladders to climb down that are none too clean — and dark   155 alleyways ——

Mil. I will wear this very dress and none other.

Sec. Eng. No offense meant. It's none of my business. I was only warning you ——   160

Mil. Warning? That sounds thrilling.

Sec. Eng. (*looking down the deck — with a sigh of relief*). There's the Fourth now. He's waiting for us. If you'll come ——

Mil. Go on. I'll follow you. (*He goes.* MILDRED *turns a mocking smile on her aunt.*) An oaf — but a handsome, virile oaf.[1]   165

Aunt (*scornfully*). Poser!

[1] Simpleton.

Mil. Take care. He said there were dark alleyways —

Aunt (*in the same tone*). Poser!

Mil. (*biting her lips angrily*). You are   170 right. But would that my millions were not so anemically chaste!

Aunt. Yes, for a fresh pose I have no doubt you would drag the name of Douglas in the gutter!   175

Mil. From which it sprang. Good-by, Aunt. Don't pray too hard that I may fall into the fiery furnace.

Aunt. Poser!

Mil. (*viciously*). Old hag!   180

(*She slaps her aunt insultingly across the face and walks off, laughing gaily.*

Aunt (*screams after her*). I said poser!

Curtain

SCENE 3

The stokehole. In the rear, the dimly outlined bulks of the furnaces and boilers. High overhead one hanging electric bulb sheds just enough light through the murky air laden with coal dust to pile up masses of shadows everywhere. A line of men, stripped to the waist, is before the furnace doors. They bend over, looking neither to right nor left, handling their shovels as if they were part of their bodies, with a strange, awkward, swinging rhythm. They use the shovels to throw open the furnace doors. Then from these fiery round holes in the black a flood of terrific light and heat pours full upon the men who are outlined in silhouette in the crouching, inhuman attitudes of chained gorillas. The men shovel with a rhythmic motion, swinging as on a pivot from the coal which lies in heaps on the floor behind to hurl it into the flaming mouths before them. There is a tumult of noise — the brazen clang of the furnace doors as they are flung open or slammed shut, the grating, teeth-gritting grind of steel against steel, of crunching coal. This clash of sounds stuns one's ears with its rending dissonance. But there is order in it, rhythm, a mechanical regulated recurrence, a tempo. And rising above all, making the air hum with the quiver of liberated energy, the roar of leaping flames in the furnaces, the monotonous throbbing beat of the engines.

As the curtain rises, the furnace doors are shut. The men are taking a breathing spell. One or two are arranging the coal behind them, pulling it into more accessible heaps. The others can be dimly made out leaning on their shovels in relaxed attitudes of exhaustion

Paddy (*from somewhere in the line — plaintively*). Yerra, will this divil's own watch nivir end? Me back is broke. I'm destroyed entirely.

Yank (*from the center of the line — with exuberant scorn*). Aw, yuh make me sick! Lie down and croak, why don't yuh? Always   5 beefin', dat's you! Say, dis is a cinch! Dis was made for me! It's my meat, get me! (*A whistle is blown — a thin, shrill note from somewhere overhead in the darkness.* YANK *curses without resentment.*) Dere's de damn

engineer crackin' de whip. He tinks we're
loafin'.   10

Paddy (*vindictively*). God stiffen him!

Yank (*in an exultant tone of command*).
Come on, youse guys! Git into de game!
She's gittin' hungry! Pile some grub in her!
Trow it into her belly! Come on, now, all
of youse! Open her up!   15

(*At this last all the men, who have followed his movements of getting into
position, throw open their furnace
doors with a deafening clang. The
fiery light floods over their shoulders
as they bend round for the coal.
Rivulets of sooty sweat have traced
maps on their backs. The enlarged
muscles form bunches of high light
and shadow.*)

Yank (*chanting a count as he shovels without
seeming effort*). One — two — tree — (*His
voice rising exultantly in the joy of battle*) Dat's
de stuff! Let her have it! All togedder now!
Sling it into her! Let her ride! Shoot de piece
now! Call de toin on her! Drive her   20
into it! Feel her move! Watch her smoke!
Speed, dat's her middle name! Give her coal,
youse guys! Coal, dat's her booze! Drink it
up, baby! Let's see yuh sprint! Dig in and
gain a lap! Dere she go-o-es ——   25

(*This last in the chanting formula of
the gallery gods at the six-day bike
race. He slams his furnace door
shut. The others do likewise with as
much unison as their wearied bodies
will permit. The effect is of one fiery
eye after another being blotted out
with a series of accompanying bangs.*)

Paddy (*groaning*). Me back is broke. I'm
bate out — bate ——

(*There is a pause. Then the inexorable
whistle sounds again from the dim
regions above the electric light. There
is a growl of cursing rage from all
sides.*)

Yank (*shaking his fist upward — contemptuously*). Take it easy dere, you! Who d'yuh
tink's runnin' dis game, me or you? When
I git ready, we move. Not before!   30
When I git ready, get me!

Voices (*approvingly*):
That's the stuff!
Yank tal him, py golly!
Yank ain't affeerd.
Goot poy, Yank!   35
Give him hell!
Tell 'im 'e's a bloody swine!
Bloody slave-driver!

Yank (*contemptuously*). He ain't got no noive.
He's yellow, get me? All de engineers   40
is yellow. Dey got streaks a mile wide. Aw,
to hell wit him! Let's move, youse guys. We
had a rest. Come on, she needs it! Give
her pep! It ain't for him. Him and his whistle, dey don't belong. But we belong, see!   45
We gotter feed de baby! Come on!

(*He turns and flings his furnace door
open. They all follow his lead. At
this instant the SECOND and FOURTH
ENGINEERS enter from the darkness
on the left with MILDRED between
them. She starts, turns paler, her
pose is crumbling, she shivers with
fright in spite of the blazing heat, but
forces herself to leave the ENGINEERS
and take a few steps nearer the men.
She is right behind YANK. All this
happens quickly while the men have
their backs turned.*)

Yank. Come on, youse guys! (*He is turning to get coal when the whistle sounds again
in a peremptory, irritating note. This drives
YANK into a sudden fury. While the other men
have turned full around and stopped dumfounded
by the spectacle of MILDRED standing there in her
white dress, YANK does not turn far enough to
see her. Besides, his head is thrown back, he
blinks upward through the murk trying to find the
owner of the whistle, he brandishes his shovel
murderously over his head in one hand, pounding
on his chest, gorilla-like, with the other, shouting*)
Toin off dat whistle! Come down outa dere,
yuh yellow, brass-buttoned, Belfast [1] bum, yuh!
Come down and I'll knock yer brains   50
out! Yuh lousy, stinkin', yellow mutt of a
Catholic-moiderin' bastard! Come down and

[1] The capital of Northern Ireland, where feeling runs
high between the Protestant majority and the Catholic
minority.

I'll moider yuh! Pullin' dat whistle on me, huh? I'll show yuh! I'll crash yer skull in! I'll drive yer teet' down yer troat! I'll 55 slam yer nose trou de back of yer head! I'll cut yer guts out for a nickel, yuh lousy boob, yuh dirty, crummy, muck-eatin' son of a ——

(*Suddenly he becomes conscious of all the other men staring at something directly behind his back. He whirls defensively with a snarling, murderous growl, crouching to spring, his lips drawn back over his teeth, his small eyes gleaming ferociously. He sees* MILDRED, *like a white apparition in the full light from the open furnace doors. He glares into her eyes, turned to stone. As for her, during his speech she has listened, paralyzed with horror, terror, her whole personality crushed, beaten in, collapsed, by the terrific impact of this unknown, abysmal brutality, naked and shameless. As she looks at his gorilla face, as his eyes bore*

into hers, she utters a low, choking cry and shrinks away from him, putting both hands up before her eyes to shut out the sight of his face, to protect her own. This startles YANK *to a reaction. His mouth falls open, his eyes grow bewildered.*

MIL. (*about to faint — to the* ENGINEERS, *who now have her one by each arm — whimperingly*). Take me away! Oh, the filthy beast!

(*She faints. They carry her quickly back, disappearing in the darkness at the left, rear. An iron door clangs shut. Rage and bewildered fury rush back on* YANK. *He feels himself insulted in some unknown fashion in the very heart of his pride. He roars:* God damn yuh! *And hurls his shovel after them at the door which has just closed. It hits the steel bulkhead with a clang and falls clattering on the steel floor. From overhead the whistle sounds again in a long, angry, insistent command.*

Curtain

SCENE 4

The firemen's forecastle. Yank's watch has just come off duty and had dinner. Their faces and bodies shine from a soap and water scrubbing but around their eyes, where a hasty dousing does not touch, the coal dust sticks like black make-up, giving them a queer, sinister expression. Yank has not washed either face or body. He stands out in contrast to them, a blackened, brooding figure. He is seated forward on a bench in the exact attitude of Rodin's "The Thinker." [1] The others, most of them smoking pipes, are staring at Yank half-apprehensively, as if fearing an outburst; half-amusedly, as if they saw a joke somewhere that tickled them.

Voices:
He ain't ate nothin'.
Py golly, a fallar gat to gat grub in him.
Divil a lie.
Yank feeda da fire, no feeda da face.
Ha-ha.   5
He ain't even washed hisself.

He's forgot.
Hey, Yank, you forgot to wash.
Yank (*sullenly*). Forgot nothin'! To hell wit washin'.   10
Voices:
It'll stick to you.
It'll get under your skin.
Give yer the bleedin' itch, that's wot.
It makes spots on you — like a leopard.
Like a piebald [1] nigger, you mean.   15

[1] A famous statue of a seated man with head bent and chin resting on the back of his upraised right hand. It was done by the French sculptor, Auguste Rodin (1840–1917).

[1] Spotted.

Better wash up, Yank.
You sleep better.
Wash up, Yank.
Wash up! Wash up!

Yank (*resentfully*). Aw, say, youse guys. 20
Lemme alone. Can't youse see I'm tryin' to
tink?

All (*repeating the word after him, as one, with
cynical mockery*). Think!

> (*The word has a brazen, metallic quality
> as if their throats were phonograph
> horns. It is followed by a chorus of
> hard, barking laughter.*

Yank (*springing to his feet and glaring at
them belligerently*). Yes, tink! Tink, dat's
what I said! What about it?   25

> (*They are silent, puzzled by his sud-
> den resentment at what used to be
> one of his jokes. YANK sits down
> again in the same attitude of "The
> Thinker."*

Voices:
Leave him alone.
He's got a grouch on.
Why wouldn't he?

Paddy (*with a wink at the others*). Sure I know
what's the matther. 'Tis aisy to see. He's 30
fallen in love, I'm telling you.

All (*repeating the word after him, as one, with
cynical mockery*). Love!

> (*The word has a brazen, metallic quality
> as if their throats were phonograph
> horns. It is followed by a chorus of
> hard, barking laughter.*

Yank (*with a contemptuous snort*). Love, hell!
Hate, dat's what. I've fallen in hate, get me?

Paddy (*philosophically*). 'Twould take 35
a wise man to tell one from the other. (*With a
bitter, ironical scorn, increasing as he goes on*)
But I'm telling you it's love that's in it. Sure
what else but love for us poor bastes in the
stokehole would be bringing a fine lady, dressed
like a white quane, down a mile of ladders 40
and steps to be havin' a look at us?

> (*A growl of anger goes up from all sides.*

Long (*jumping on a bench — hectically*). Hinsultin' us! Hinsultin' us, the bloody cow!
And them bloody engineers! What right 'as
they got to be exhibitin' us 's if we was 45

bleedin' monkeys in a menagerie? Did we sign
for hinsults to our dignity as 'onest workers? Is
that in the ship's articles? You kin bloody well
bet it ain't! But I knows why they done it.
I arsked a deck steward 'o she was and 'e 50
told me. 'Er old man's a bleedin' millionaire,
a bloody capitalist! 'E's got enuf bloody gold
to sink this bleedin' ship! 'E makes arf the
bloody steel in the world! 'E owns this bloody
boat! And you and me, comrades, we're 55
'is slaves! And the skipper and mates and
engineers, they're 'is slaves! And she's 'is
bloody daughter and we're all 'er slaves, too!
And she gives 'er orders as 'ow she wants to see
the bloody animals below decks and down 60
they takes 'er!

> (*There is a roar of rage from all sides.*

Yank (*blinking at him bewilderedly*). Say!
Wait a moment! Is all dat straight goods?

Long. Straight as string! The bleedin'
steward as waits on 'em, 'e told me about 65
'er. And what're we goin' ter do, I arsks yer?
'Ave we got ter swaller 'er hinsults like dogs?
It ain't in the ship's articles. I tell yer we got
a case. We kin go ter law ——

Yank (*with abysmal contempt*). Hell! Law! 70

All (*repeating the word after him, as one, with
cynical mockery*). Law!

> (*The word has a brazen metallic quality
> as if their throats were phonograph
> horns. It is followed by a chorus of
> hard, barking laughter.*

Long (*feeling the ground slipping from under
his feet — desperately*). As voters and citizens
we kin force the bloody governments ——

Yank (*with abysmal contempt*). Hell! Governments!   75

All (*repeating the word after him, as one, with
cynical mockery*). Governments!

> (*The word has a brazen metallic quality
> as if their throats were phonograph
> horns. It is followed by a chorus of
> hard, barking laughter.*

Long (*hysterically*). We're free and equal in
the sight of God ——

Yank (*with abysmal contempt*). Hell! God!

All (*repeating the word after him, as one, with
cynical mockery*). God!   80

> (*The word has a brazen metallic quality

as if their throats were phonograph horns. It is followed by a chorus of hard, barking laughter.

Yank (witheringly). Aw, join de Salvation Army.

All. Sit down! Shut up! Damn fool! Sea-lawyer! (LONG *slinks back out of sight.*

Paddy (continuing the trend of his thoughts as if he had never been interrupted — bitterly). And there she was standing behind us, and the 86 Second pointing at us like a man you'd hear in a circus would be saying: In this cage is a queerer kind of baboon than ever you'd find in darkest Africy. We roast them in their 90 own sweat — and be damned if you won't hear some of thim saying they like it!

(*He glances scornfully at* YANK.

Yank (with a bewildered uncertain growl). Aw!

Paddy. And there was Yank roarin' curses and turning round wid his shovel to brain 95 her — and she looked at him, and him at her ——

Yank (slowly). She was all white. I tought she was a ghost. Sure. 99

Paddy (with heavy, biting sarcasm). 'Twas love at first sight, divil a doubt of it! If you'd seen the endearin' look on her pale mug when she shriveled away with her hands over her eyes to shut out the sight of him! Sure, 'twas as if she'd seen a great hairy ape 105 escaped from the Zoo!

Yank (stung — with a growl of rage). Aw!

Paddy. And the loving way Yank heaved his shovel at the skull of her, only she was out the door! (*A grin breaking over his face*) 110 'Twas touching, I'm telling you! It put the touch of home, swate home in the stokehole.

(*There is a roar of laughter from all.*

Yank (glaring at PADDY *menacingly).* Aw, choke dat off, see!

Paddy (not heeding him — to the others). And her grabbin' at the Second's arm for pro- 116 tection. (*With a grotesque imitation of a woman's voice*) Kiss me, Engineer dear, for it's dark down here and me old man's in Wall Street making money! Hug me tight, dar- 120 lin', for I'm afeerd in the dark and me mother's on deck makin' eyes at the skipper!

(*Another roar of laughter.*

Yank (threateningly). Say! What yuh tryin' to do, kid me, yuh old Harp?

Paddy. Divil a bit! Ain't I wishin' 125 myself you'd brained her?

Yank (fiercely). I'll brain her! I'll brain her yet, wait'n' see! (*Coming over to* PADDY — *slowly*) Say, is dat what she called me — a hairy ape? 130

Paddy. She looked it at you if she didn't say the word itself.

Yank (grinning horribly). Hairy ape, huh? Sure! Dat's de way she looked at me, aw right. Hairy ape! So dat's me, huh? (*Burst-* 135 *ing into rage — as if she were still in front of him*) Yuh skinny tart! Yuh white-faced bum, yuh! I'll show yuh who's a ape! (*Turning to the others, bewilderment seizing him again*) Say, youse guys. I was bawlin' him out for pullin' de whistle on us. You heard me. And den I seen youse lookin' at somep'n and 140 I tought he'd sneaked down to come up in back of me, and I hopped round to knock him dead wit de shovel. And dere she was wit de light on her! Christ, yuh coulda pushed me over with a finger! I was scared, get me? 145 Sure! I tought she was a ghost, see? She was all in white like dey wrap around stiffs. You seen her. Kin yuh blame me? She didn't be-long, dat's what. And den when I come to and seen it was a real skoit and seen de way 150 she was lookin' at me — like Paddy said — Christ, I was sore, get me? I don't stand for dat stuff from nobody. And I flung de shovel — on'y she'd beat it. (*Furiously*) I wished it'd banged her! I wished it'd knocked 155 her block off!

Long. And be 'anged for murder or 'lectro-cuted? She ain't bleedin' well worth it.

Yank. I don't give a damn what! I'd be square wit her, wouldn't I? Tink I wanter 160 let her put somep'n over on me? Tink I'm goin' to let her git away wit dat stuff? Yuh don't know me! No one ain't never put nothin' over on me and got away wit it, see! — not dat kind of stuff — no guy and no 165 skoit neither! I'll fix her! Maybe she'll come down again ——

Voice. No chance, Yank. You scared her out of a year's growth.

Yank. I scared her? Why de hell should 170 I scare her? Who de hell is she? Ain't she de same as me? Hairy ape, huh? (*With his old confident bravado*) I'll show her I'm better'n her, if she on'y knew it. I belong and she don't, see! I move and she's dead! Twenty- 175 five knots a hour, dat's me! Dat carries her, but I make dat. She's on'y baggage. Sure! (*Again bewilderedly*) But, Christ, she was funny lookin'! Did yuh pipe her hands? White and skinny. Yuh could see de bones trough 180 'em. And her mush, dat was dead white, too. And her eyes, dey was like dey'd seen a ghost. Me, dat was! Sure! Hairy ape! Ghost, huh? Look at dat arm! (*He extends his right arm, swelling out the great muscles.*) I coulda 185 took her wit dat, wit just my little finger even, and broke her in two. (*Again bewilderedly*) Say, who is dat skoit, huh? What is she? What's she come from? Who made her? Who give her de noive to look at me like dat? 190 Dis ting's got my goat right. I don't get her. She's new to me. What does a skoit like her mean, huh? She don't belong, get me! I can't see her. (*With growing anger*) But one ting I'm wise to, aw right, aw right! Youse 195 all kin bet your shoits I'll git even wit her. I'll show her if she tinks she — She grinds de organ and I'm on de string, huh? I'll fix her! Let her come down again and I'll fling her in de furnace! She'll move den! She won't 200 shiver at nothin', den! Speed, dat'll be her! She'll belong den! (*He grins horribly.*

Paddy. She'll never come. She's had her belly-full, I'm telling you. She'll be in bed now, I'm thinking, wid ten doctors and 205 nurses feedin' her salts to clean the fear out of her.

Yank (*enraged*). Yuh tink I made her sick, too, do yuh? Just lookin' at me, huh? Hairy ape, huh? (*In a frenzy of rage*) I'll 210 fix her! I'll tell her where to git off! She'll git down on her knees and take it back, or I'll bust de face offen her! (*Shaking one fist upward and beating on his chest with the other*) I'll find yuh! I'm comin', d'yuh hear? I'll 215 fix yuh, God damn yuh!

(*He makes a rush for the door.*

Voices:
Stop him!
He'll get shot!
He'll murder her!
Trip him up! 220
Hold him!
He's gone crazy!
Gott, he's strong!
Hold him down!
Look out for a kick! 225
Pin his arms!

(*They have all piled on him and, after a fierce struggle, by sheer weight of numbers have borne him to the floor just inside the door.*

Paddy (*who has remained detached*). Kape him down till he's cooled off. (*Scornfully*) Yerra, Yank, you're a great fool. Is it payin' attention at all you are to the like of 230 that skinny sow widout one drop of rale blood in her?

Yank (*frenziedly, from the bottom of the heap*). She done me doit! She done me doit, didn't she? I'll git square wit her! I'll get her some way! Git offen me, youse guys! 235 Lemme up! I'll show her who's a ape!

Curtain

SCENE 5

Three weeks later. A corner of Fifth Avenue, New York, in the Fifties on a fine Sunday morning. A general atmosphere of clean, well-tidied, wide street; a flood of mellow, tempered sunshine; gentle, genteel breezes. In the rear, the show windows of two shops, a jewelry establishment on the corner, a furrier's next to it. Here the adornments of extreme wealth are tantalizingly displayed. The jeweler's window is gaudy with glittering diamonds, emeralds, rubies, pearls, etc., fashioned in crude tiaras, crowns, necklaces, collars, etc. From each piece hangs an enormous tag from which a dollar sign and numerals in intermittent electric lights wink out the incredible prices. The same in the furrier's. Rich furs of all varieties hang there bathed in a downpour of artificial light. The general effect is of a background of magnificence cheapened and made grotesque by commercialism, a background in tawdry disharmony with the clear light and sunshine on the street itself.

Up the side street YANK *and* LONG *come swaggering.* LONG *is dressed in shore clothes, wears a black Windsor tie, cloth cap.* YANK *is in his dirty dungarees. A fireman's cap with black peak is cocked defiantly on the side of his head. He has not shaved for days and around his fierce, resentful eyes — as around those of* LONG *to a lesser degree — the black smudge of coal dust still sticks like make-up. They hesitate and stand together at the corner, swaggering, looking about them with a forced, defiant contempt*

Long (*indicating it all with an oratorical gesture*). Well, 'ere we are. Fif' Avenoo. This 'ere's their bleedin' private lane, as yer might say. (*Bitterly*) We're trespassers 'ere. Proletarians keep orf the grass!

Yank (*dully*). I don't see no grass, yuh 5 boob. (*Staring at the sidewalk*) Clean, ain't it? Yuh could eat a fried egg offen it. The white wings [1] got some job sweepin' dis up. (*Looking up and down the avenue — surlily*) Where's all de white-collar stiffs yuh said was here 10 — and de skoits — *her* kind?

Long. In church, blarst 'em! Arskin' Jesus to give 'em more money.

Yank. Choich, huh? I useter go to choich onct — sure — when I was a kid. Me 15 old man and woman, dey made me. Dey never went demselves, dough. Always got too big a head on Sunday mornin', dat was dem. (*With a grin*) Dey was scrappers for fair, bot' of dem. On Satiday nights when dey bot' got a 20 skinful dey could put up a bout oughter been staged at de Garden.[2] When dey got trough dere wasn't a chair or table wit a leg under it. Or else dey bot' jumped on me for somep'n. Dat was where I loined to take punishment. 25

---

[1] The street-cleaners, so called from their white uniforms.

[2] Madison Square Garden in New York City, a huge indoor amphitheater.

(*With a grin and a swagger*) I'm a chip offen de old block, get me?

Long. Did yer old man follow the sea?

Yank. Naw. Worked along shore. I runned away when me old lady croaked wit de 30 tremens.[1] I helped at truckin' and in de market. Den I shipped in de stokehole. Sure. Dat belongs. De rest was nothin'. (*Looking around him*) I ain't never seen dis before. De Brooklyn waterfront, dat was where I was 35 dragged up. (*Taking a deep breath*) Dis ain't so bad at dat, huh?

Long. Not bad? Well, we pays for it wiv our bloody sweat, if yer wants to know!

Yank (*with sudden angry disgust*). Aw, 40 hell! I don't see no one, see — like her. All dis gives me a pain. It don't belong. Say, ain't dere a back room around dis dump? Let's go shoot a ball. All dis is too clean and quiet and dolled-up, get me! It gives me a pain. 45

Long. Wait and yer'll bloody well see ——

Yank. I don't wait for no one. I keep on de move. Say, what yuh drag me up here for, anyway? Tryin' to kid me, yuh simp, yuh? 50

Long. Yer wants to get back at her, don't yer? That's what yer been sayin' every bloomin' 'our since she hinsulted yer.

Yank (*vehemently*). Sure ting I do! Didn't I try to git even wit her in Southamp- 55 ton? Didn't I sneak on de dock and wait for her by de gangplank? I was goin' to spit in her pale mug, see! Sure, right in her pop-eyes! Dat woulda made me even, see? But no chanct. Dere was a whole army of plain 60 clothes bulls [2] around. Dey spotted me and gimme de bum's rush. I never seen her. But I'll git square wit her yet, you watch! (*Furiously*) De lousy tart! She tinks she kin get

---

[1] I.e., delirium tremens, a violent and mortal form of insanity due to excessive intoxication.

[2] Policemen.

away wit moider — but not wit me! I'll fix 65
her! I'll tink of a way!

Long (as disgusted as he dares to be). Ain't
that why I brought yer up 'ere — to show yer?
Yer been lookin' at this 'ere 'ole affair wrong.
Yer been actin' an' talkin' 's if it was 70
all a bleedin' personal matter between yer and
that bloody cow. I wants to convince yer she
was on'y a representative of 'er clarss. I wants
to awaken yer bloody clarss consciousness.
Then yer'll see it's 'er clarss yer've got 75
to fight, not 'er alone. There's a 'ole mob of
'em like 'er, Gawd blind 'em!

Yank (spitting on his hands — belligerently).
De more de merrier when I gits started. Bring
on de gang!

Long. Yer'll see 'em in arf a mo', when 80
that church lets out. (*He turns and sees the
window display in the two stores for the first
time.*) Blimey! Look at that, will yer? (*They
both walk back and stand looking in the jeweler's.
*Long *flies into a fury.*) Just look at this 'ere
bloomin' mess! Just look at it! Look at the
bleedin' prices on 'em — more'n our 'ole 85
bloody stockhole makes in ten voyages sweatin'
in 'ell! And they — her and her bloody clarss
— buys 'em for toys to dangle on 'em! One
of these 'ere would buy scoff¹ for a starvin'
family for a year! 90

Yank. Aw, cut de sob stuff! T' hell wit
de starvin' family! Yuh'll be passin' de hat to
me next. (*With naïve admiration*) Say, dem
tings is pretty, huh? Bet yuh dey'd hock for
a piece of change aw right. (*Then turn-* 95
ing away, bored) But, aw hell, what good are
dey? Let her have 'em. Dey don't belong no
more'n she does. (*With a gesture of sweeping
the jeweler's into oblivion*) All dat don't count,
get me? 100

*Long (who has moved to the furrier's — in-
dignantly).* And I s'pose this 'ere don't count
neither — skins of poor, 'armless animals
slaughtered so as 'er and 'ers can keep their
bleedin' noses warm!

*Yank (who has been staring at something
inside — with queer excitement).* Take a 105
slant at dat! Give it de once-over! Monkey
fur — two t'ousand bucks! (*Bewilderedly*) Is

¹ Provisions.

dat straight goods — monkey fur? What de
hell — ?

Long (bitterly). It's straight enuf. 110
(*With grim humor*) They wouldn't bloody well
pay that for a 'airy ape's skin — no, nor for the
'ole livin' ape with all 'is 'ead, and body, and
soul thrown in!

*Yank (clenching his fists, his face growing pale
with rage as if the skin in the window were a personal insult).* Trowin' it up in my face! 115
Christ! I'll fix her!

Long (excitedly). Church is out. 'Ere they
come, the bleedin' swine. (*After a glance at
*Yank's *lowering face — uneasily*) Easy goes,
comrade. Keep yer bloomin' temper. 120
Remember force defeats itself. It ain't our
weapon. We must impress our demands
through peaceful means — the votes of the on-
marching proletarians of the bloody world!

Yank (with abysmal contempt). Votes, 125
hell! Votes is a joke, see. Votes for women!
Let dem do it!

Long (still more uneasily). Calm, now. Treat
'em wiv the proper contempt. Observe the
bleedin' parasites, but 'old yer 'orses. 130

Yank (angrily). Git away from me! Yuh're
yellow, dat's what. Force, dat's me! De
punch, dat's me every time, see!

*The crowd from church enter from the right,
sauntering slowly and affectedly, their heads
held stiffly up, looking neither to right nor
left, talking in toneless, simpering voices.
The women are rouged, calcimined, dyed,
overdressed to the nth degree. The men are
in Prince Alberts, high hats, spats, canes,
etc. A procession of gaudy marionettes, yet
with something of the relentless horror of
Frankensteins in their detached, mechanical
unawareness*

Voices:

Dear Doctor Caiaphas!¹ He is so sincere!
What was the sermon? I dozed off. 135
About the radicals, my dear — and the false
   doctrines that are being preached.
We must organize a hundred per cent Ameri-
   can bazaar.

¹ Caiaphas was the Jewish high priest who suggested
the crucifixion of Jesus.

And let everyone contribute one one-hun- 140
dredth per cent of their income tax.

What an original idea!

We can devote the proceeds to rehabilitating
the veil of the temple.

But that has been done so many times. 145

*Yank (glaring from one to the other of them
— with an insulting snort of scorn).* Huh! Huh!

> (*Without seeming to see him, they make
> wide detours to avoid the spot where
> he stands in the middle of the side-
> walk.*)

Long (frightenedly). Keep yer bloomin'
mouth shut, I tells yer.

Yank (viciously). G'wan! Tell it to
Sweeney! (*He swaggers away and delib-* 150
*erately lurches into a top-hatted gentleman, then
glares at him pugnaciously.*) Say, who d'yuh
tink yuh're bumpin'? Tink yuh own de oith?

Gent. (coldly and affectedly). I beg your pardon. 154

> (*He has not looked at* YANK *and passes
> on without a glance, leaving him be-
> wildered.*)

Long (rushing up and grabbing YANK'S *arm).*
'Ere! Come away! This wasn't what I meant.
Yer'll 'ave the bloody coppers down on us.

*Yank (savagely — giving him a push that
sends him sprawling).* G'wan!

Long (picks himself up — hysterically). I'll
pop orf, then. This ain't what I meant. And
whatever 'appens, yer can't blame me. 160

> (*He slinks off left.*)

Yank. T' hell wit youse! (*He approaches
a lady — with a vicious grin and a smirking wink.*) Hello, Kiddo. How's every
little ting? Got anyting on for tonight? I
know an old boiler down to de docks we kin
crawl into. (*The lady stalks by without a* 165
look, without a change of pace. YANK *turns to
others — insultingly.*) Holy smokes, what a
mug! Go hide yuhself before de horses shy at
yuh. Gee, pipe de heinie on dat one! Say,
youse, yuh look like de stoin of a ferry-boat.
Paint and powder! All dolled up to 170
kill! Yuh look like stiffs laid out for de bone-
yard! Aw, g'wan, de lot of youse! Yuh give
me de eye-ache. Yuh don't belong, get me!
Look at me, why don't youse dare? I be-

long, dat's me! (*Pointing to a skyscraper* 175
*across the street which is in process of construc-
tion — with bravado*) See dat building goin' up
dere? See de steel work? Steel, dat's me!
Youse guys live on it and tink yuh're somep'n.
But I'm *in* it, see! I'm de hoistin' engine dat
makes it go up! I'm it — de inside and 180
bottom of it! Sure! I'm steel and steam and
smoke and de rest of it! It moves — speed
— twenty-five stories up — and me at de top
and bottom — movin'! Youse simps don't
move. Yuh're on'y dolls I winds up to 185
see 'm spin. Yuh're de garbage, get me — de
leavins — de ashes we dump over de side! Now,
what 'a' yuh gotta say? (*But as they seem neither
to see nor hear him, he flies into a fury.*) Bums!
Pigs! Tarts! Bitches! (*He turns in a* 190
*rage on the men, bumping viciously into them
but not jarring them the least bit. Rather
it is he who recoils after each collision. He
keeps growling.*) Git off de oith! G'wan,
yuh bum! Look where yuh're goin', can't
yuh? Git outa here! Fight, why don't yuh?
Put up yer mitts! Don't be a dog! Fight
or I'll knock yuh dead! 195

> (*But, without seeming to see him, they
> all answer with mechanical affected
> politeness:* "I beg your pardon."
> *Then at a cry from one of the women,
> they all scurry to the furrier's window.*)

Woman (ecstatically, with a gasp of delight).
Monkey fur! (*The whole crowd of men and
women chorus after her in the same tone of affected delight.*) Monkey fur!

*Yank (with a jerk of his head back on his
shoulders, as if he had received a punch full in the
face — raging).* I see yuh, all in white! I see
yuh, yuh white-faced tart, yuh! Hairy ape,
huh? I'll hairy ape yuh! 200

*He bends down and grips at the street curbing as
if to pluck it out and hurl it. Foiled in this,
snarling with passion, he leaps to the lamp-
post on the corner and tries to pull it up for a
club. Just at that moment a bus is heard
rumbling up. A fat, high-hatted, spatted
gentleman runs out from the side street. He
calls out plaintively:* "Bus! Bus! Stop

there!" *and runs full tilt into the bending, straining* YANK, *who is bowled off his balance*

YANK (*seeing a fight — with a roar of joy as he springs to his feet*). At last! Bus, huh? I'll bust yuh!

(*He lets drive a terrific swing, his fist landing full on the fat gentleman's face. But the gentleman stands unmoved as if nothing had happened.*

GENT. I beg your pardon. (*Then irritably*) You have made me lose my bus.

Curtain

(*He clasps his hands and begins to scream:* "Officer! Officer!" *Many police whistles shrill out on the instant and a whole platoon of policemen rush in on* YANK *from all sides. He tries to fight, but is clubbed to the pavement and fallen upon. The crowd at the window have not moved or noticed this disturbance. The clanging gong of the patrol wagon approaches with a clamoring din.*

SCENE 6

Night of the following day. A row of cells in the prison on Blackwell's Island.[1] The cells extend back diagonally from right front to left rear. They do not stop, but disappear in the dark background as if they ran on, numberless, into infinity. One electric bulb from the low ceiling of the narrow corridor sheds its light through the heavy steel bars of the cell at the extreme front and reveals part of the interior. Yank can be seen within, crouched on the edge of his cot in the attitude of Rodin's "The Thinker." His face is spotted with black and blue bruises. A bloodstained bandage is wrapped around his head.

YANK (*suddenly starting as if awakening from a dream, reaches out and shakes the bars — aloud to himself, wonderingly*). Steel. Dis is de Zoo, huh?

(*A burst of hard, barking laughter comes from the unseen occupants of the cells, runs back down the tier, and abruptly ceases.*

VOICES (*mockingly*):
The Zoo? That's a new name for this coop — a damn good name!
Steel, eh? You said a mouthful. This is 5 the old iron house.
Who is that boob talkin'?
He's the bloke they brung in out of his head.
The bulls had beat him up fierce.
YANK (*dully*). I musta been dreamin'. 10 I tought I was in a cage at de Zoo — but de apes don't talk, do dey?

VOICES (*with mocking laughter*):
You're in a cage aw right.
A coop!
A pen!   15
A sty!
A kennel! (*Hard laughter — a pause.*
Say, guy! Who are you? No, never mind lying. What are you?
Yes, tell us your sad story. What's your 20 game?
What did they jug yuh for?
YANK (*dully*). I was a fireman — stokin' on de liners. (*Then with sudden rage, rattling his cell bars*) I'm a hairy ape, get me? And 25 I'll bust youse all in de jaw if yuh don't lay off kiddin' me.
VOICES:
Huh! You're a hard-boiled duck, ain't you!
When you spit, it bounces!
(*Laughter.*
Aw, can it. He's a regular guy. Ain't you? 30
What did he say he was — a ape?

[1] The New York City Prison, situated on Blackwell's Island in the East River between Manhattan and Queens County, Long Island.

Yank (*defiantly*). Sure ting! Ain't dat what youse all are — apes?

  (*A silence. Then a furious rattling of bars from down the corridor.*

A Voice (*thick with rage*). I'll show yuh who's a ape, yuh bum! 35

Voices:

Ssshh! Nix!

Can de noise!

Piano!

You'll have the guard down on us!

Yank (*scornfully*). De guard? Yuh 40 mean de keeper, don't yuh?

  (*Angry exclamations from all the cells.*

Voice (*placatingly*). Aw, don't pay no attention to him. He's off his nut from the beatin'-up he got. Say, you guy! We're waitin' to hear what they landed you for — or ain't 45 yuh tellin'?

Yank. Sure, I'll tell youse. Sure! Why de hell not? On'y — youse won't get me. Nobody gets me but me, see? I started to tell de Judge and all he says was: "Toity days 50 to tink it over." Tink it over! Christ, dat's all I been doin' for weeks! (*After a pause*) I was tryin' to git even wit someone, see? — someone dat done me doit.

Voices (*cynically*):

De old stuff, I bet. Your goil, huh? 55

Give yuh the double-cross, huh?

That's them every time!

Did yuh beat up de odder guy?

Yank (*disgustedly*). Aw, yuh're all wrong! Sure dere was a skoit in it — but not what 60 youse mean, not dat old tripe. Dis was a new kind of skoit. She was dolled up all in white — in de stokehole. I tought she was a ghost. Sure.

  (*A pause.*

Voices (*whispering*):

Gee, he's still nutty. 65

Let him rave. It's fun listenin'.

Yank (*unheeding — groping in his thoughts*). Her hands — dey was skinny and white like dey wasn't real but painted on somep'n. Dere was a million miles from me to her — twenty-five knots a hour. She was like some 70 dead ting de cat brung in. Sure, dat's what. She didn't belong. She belonged in de window of a toy store, or on de top of a garbage can, see!

Sure! (*He breaks out angrily.*) But would yuh believe it, she had de noive to do me 75 doit. She lamped me like she was seein' somep'n broke loose from de menagerie. Christ, yuh'd oughter seen her eyes! (*He rattles the bars of his cell furiously.*) But I'll get back at her yet, you watch! And if I can't find her 80 I'll take it out on de gang she runs wit. I'm wise to where dey hangs out now. I'll show her who belongs! I'll show her who's in de move and who ain't. You watch my smoke!

Voices (*serious and joking*):

Dat's de talkin'! 85

Take her for all she's got!

What was this dame, anyway? Who was she, eh?

Yank. I dunno. First-cabin stiff. Her old man's a millionaire, dey says — name 90 of Douglas.

Voices:

Douglas? That's the president of the Steel Trust, I bet.

Sure. I seen his mug in de papers.

He's filthy with dough. 95

Voice. Hey, feller, take a tip from me. If you want to get back at that dame, you better join the Wobblies. You'll get some action then.

Yank. Wobblies? What de hell's dat? 100

Voice. Ain't you ever heard of the I.W.W.?

Yank. Naw. What is it?

Voice. A gang of blokes — a tough gang. I been readin' about 'em today in the paper. The guard give me the *Sunday Times.* 105 There's a long spiel about 'em. It's from a speech made in the Senate by a guy named Senator Queen. (*He is in the cell next to* YANK'S. *There is a rustling of paper.*) Wait'll I see if I got light enough and I'll read you. 110 Listen. (*He reads.*) "There is a menace existing in this country today which threatens the vitals of our fair Republic — as foul a menace against the very life-blood of the American Eagle as was the foul conspiracy of 115 Catiline [1] against the eagles of ancient Rome!"

  [1] Lucius Sergius Catiline (108–62 B.C.), a Roman politician and grafter who conspired to kill the great orator Marcus Tullius Cicero (106–43 B.C.), but was himself slain finally by a Roman army.

Voice (*disgustedly*). Aw, hell! Tell him to salt de tail of dat eagle!

Voice (*reading*). "I refer to that devil's brew of rascals, jailbirds, murderers, and cut- 120 throats who libel all honest working men by calling themselves the Industrial Workers of the World;[1] but in the light of their nefarious plots, I call them the Industrious *Wreckers* of the World!" 125

Yank (*with vengeful satisfaction*). Wreckers, dat's de right dope! Dat belongs! Me for dem!

Voice. Ssshh! (*Reading*) "This fiendish organization is a foul ulcer on the fair body 130 of our Democracy ——"

Voice. Democracy, hell! Give him the boid, fellers — the raspberry! (*They do.*

Voice. Ssshh! (*Reading*) "Like Cato[2] I say to this Senate, the I.W.W. must be de- 135 stroyed! For they represent an everpresent dagger pointed at the heart of the greatest nation the world has ever known, where all men are born free and equal, with equal opportunities to all, where the Founding Fathers 140 have guaranteed to each one happiness, where Truth, Honor, Liberty, Justice, and the Brotherhood of Man are a religion absorbed with one's mother's milk, taught at our father's knee, sealed, signed, and stamped upon in 145 the glorious Constitution of these United States!"

(*A perfect storm of hisses, catcalls, boos, and hard laughter.*

Voices (*scornfully*):
Hurrah for de Fort' of July!
Pass de hat!
Liberty! 150
Justice!
Honor!
Opportunity!
Brotherhood!

All (*with abysmal scorn*). Aw, hell! 155

Voice. Give that Queen Senator guy the

---

[1] The I.W.W., a radical labor organization which sought for the workers' control of industry, flourished in the United States during the First World War and the years just succeeding.

[2] Marcus Porcius Cato the Elder (234–149 B.C.), a famous Roman orator who constantly asserted in reference to Rome's chief rival, "Carthage must be destroyed."

---

bark! All togedder now — one — two — tree — (*A terrific chorus of barking and yapping.*

Guard (*from a distance*). Quiet there, youse — or I'll git the hose. 160

(*The noise subsides.*

Yank (*with a growling rage*). I'd like to catch dat Senator guy alone for a second. I'd loin him some trute!

Voice. Ssshh! Here's where he gits down to cases on the Wobblies. (*Reads.*) "They 165 plot with fire in one hand and dynamite in the other. They stop not before murder to gain their ends, nor at the outraging of defenseless womanhood. They would tear down society, put the lowest scum in the seats of the 170 mighty, turn Almighty God's revealed plan for the world topsy-turvy, and make of our sweet and lovely civilization a shambles, a desolation where man, God's masterpiece, would soon degenerate back to the ape!" 175

Voice (*to* YANK). Hey, you guy. There's your ape stuff again.

Yank (*with a growl of fury*). I got him. So dey blow up tings, do dey? Dey turn tings round, do dey? Hey, lend me dat paper, 180 will yuh?

Voice. Sure. Give it to him. On'y keep it to yourself, see. We don't wanter listen to no more of that slop.

Voice. Here you are. Hide it under 185 your mattress.

Yank (*reaching out*). Tanks. I can't read much, but I kin manage. (*He sits, the paper in the hand at his side, in the attitude of Rodin's "The Thinker."* A pause. *Several snores from down the corridor. Suddenly* YANK *jumps to his feet with a furious groan as if some appalling thought had crashed on him — bewilderedly.*) Sure — her old man — president of de Steel Trust — makes half de steel in de world — 190 steel — where I tought I belonged — drivin' trou — movin' — in dat — to make *her* — and cage me in for her to spit on! Christ! (*He shakes the bars of his cell door till the whole tier trembles. Irritated, protesting exclamations from those awakened or trying to get to sleep.*) He made dis — dis cage! Steel! *It* don't belong, dat's what! Cages, cells, locks, 195

bolts, bars — dat's what it means! — holdin' me down wit him at de top! But I'll drive trou! Fire, dat melts it! I'll be fire — under de heap — fire dat never goes out — hot as hell — breakin' out in de night —   200
(*While he has been saying this last he has shaken his cell door to a clanging accompaniment. As he comes to the "breakin' out" he seizes one bar with both hands and, putting his two feet up against the others so that his position is parallel to the floor like a monkey's, he gives a great wrench backwards. The bar bends like a licorice stick under his tremendous strength. Just at this moment the* PRISON GUARD *rushes in, dragging a hose behind him.*)
Guard (*angrily*). I'll loin youse bums to wake

me up! (*Sees* YANK.) Hello, it's you, huh? Got the D.Ts.,[1] hey? Well, I'll cure 'em. I'll drown your snakes for yuh! (*Noticing the bar*) Hell, look at dat bar bended! On'y a bug[2]   205 is strong enough for dat!
Yank (*glaring at him*). Or a hairy ape, yuh big yellow bum! Look out! Here I come!
           (*He grabs another bar.*)
Guard (*scared now — yelling off left*). Toin de hose on, Ben! — full pressure! And   210 call de others — and a strait-jacket!
     (*The curtain is falling. As it hides* YANK *from view, there is a splattering smash as the stream of water hits the steel of* YANK'S *cell.*)

[1] Delirium tremens.
[2] Crazy person.

Curtain

SCENE 7

Nearly a month later. An I.W.W. local near the waterfront, showing the interior of a front room on the ground floor, and the street outside. Moonlight on the narrow street, buildings massed in black shadow. The interior of the room, which is general assembly room, office, and reading-room, resembles some dingy settlement boys' club. A desk and high stool are in one corner. A table with papers, stacks of pamphlets, chairs about it, is at center. The whole is decidedly cheap, banal, commonplace, and unmysterious as a room could well be. The Secretary is perched on the stool making entries in a large ledger. An eye shade casts his face into shadows. Eight or ten men, longshoremen, iron workers, and the like, are grouped about the table. Two are playing checkers. One is writing a letter. Most of them are smoking pipes. A big signboard is on the wall at the rear, "Industrial Workers of the World — Local No. 57."

YANK *comes down the street outside. He is dressed as in Scene Five. He moves cautiously, mysteriously. He comes to a point opposite the door; tiptoes softly up to it, listens, is impressed by the silence within, knocks carefully, as if he were guessing at the password to some secret rite. Listens. No answer. Knocks again a bit louder. No answer. Knocks impatiently, much louder*

Sec. (*turning around on his stool*). What the devil is that — someone knocking? (*Shouts.*) Come in, why don't you?

All the men in the room look up. YANK *opens the door slowly, gingerly, as if afraid of an*

ambush. He looks around for secret doors, mystery, is taken aback by the commonplaceness of the room and the men in it, thinks he may have gotten in the wrong place, then sees the signboard on the wall and is reassured

Yank (*blurts out*). Hello.
Men (*reservedly*). Hello.   5
Yank (*more easily*). I tought I'd bumped into de wrong dump.
Sec. (*scrutinizing him carefully*). Maybe you have. Are you a member?
Yank. Naw, not yet. Dat's what I come 10 for — to join.
Sec. That's easy. What's your job — longshore?

Yank. Naw. Fireman — stoker on de liners.   15

Sec. (with satisfaction). Welcome to our city. Glad to know you people are waking up at last. We haven't got many members in your line.

Yank. Naw. Dey're all dead to de woild.

Sec. Well, you can help to wake 'em.   20 What's your name? I'll make out your card.

Yank (confused). Name? Lemme tink.

Sec. (sharply). Don't you know your own name?

Yank. Sure; but I been just Yank for so   25 long — Bob, dat's it — Bob Smith.

Sec. (writing). Robert Smith. (*Fills out the rest of card.*) Here you are. Cost you half a dollar.

Yank. Is dat all — four bits? Dat's   30 easy.   (*Gives the* SECRETARY *the money.*)

Sec. (throwing it in drawer). Thanks. Well, make yourself at home. No introductions needed. There's literature on the table. Take some of those pamphlets with you to dis-   35 tribute aboard ship. They may bring results. Sow the seed, only go about it right. Don't get caught and fired. We got plenty out of work. What we need is men who can hold their jobs — and work for us at the same time.   40

Yank. Sure.

     (*But he still stands, embarrassed and uneasy.*

Sec. (looking at him — curiously). What did you knock for? Think we had a coon in uniform to open doors?

Yank. Naw. I tought it was locked —   45 and dat yuh'd wanter give me the onceover trou a peep-hole or somep'n to see if I was right.

Sec. (alert and suspicious, but with an easy laugh). Think we were running a crap game? That door is never locked. What put that in your nut?   50

Yank (with a knowing grin, convinced that this is all camouflage, a part of the secrecy). Dis burg is full of bulls, ain't it?

Sec. (sharply). What have the cops got to do with us? We're breaking no laws.

Yank (with a knowing wink). Sure. Youse   55 wouldn't for woilds. Sure. I'm wise to dat.

Sec. You seem to be wise to a lot of stuff none of us knows about.

Yank (with another wink). Aw, dat's awright, see. (*Then, made a bit resentful by*   60 *the suspicious glances from all sides*) Aw, can it! Youse needn't put me trou de toid degree. Can't youse see I belong? Sure! I'm reg'lar. I'll stick, get me? I'll shoot de woiks for youse. Dat's why I wanted to join in.   65

Sec. (breezily, feeling him out). That's the right spirit. Only are you sure you understand what you've joined? It's all plain and above board; still, some guys get a wrong slant on us. (*Sharply*) What's your notion of the pur-   70 pose of the I.W.W.?

Yank. Aw, I know all about it.

Sec. (sarcastically). Well, give us some of your valuable information.

Yank (cunningly). I know enough not   75 to speak outa my toin. (*Then, resentfully again*) Aw, say! I'm reg'lar. I'm wise to de game. I know yuh got to watch your step wit a stranger. For all youse know, I might be a plain-clothes dick,[1] or somep'n, dat's what   80 yuh're tinkin', huh? Aw, forget it! I belong, see? Ask any guy down to de docks if I don't.

Sec. Who said you didn't?

Yank. After I'm 'nitiated, I'll show yuh.

Sec. (astounded). Initiated? There's   85 no initiation.

Yank (disappointed). Ain't there no password — no grip nor nothin'?

Sec. What'd you think this is — the Elks — or the Black Hand?[2]   90

Yank. De Elks, hell! De Black Hand, dey're a lot of yellow backstickin' Ginees.[3] Naw. Dis is a man's gang, ain't it?

Sec. You said it! That's why we stand on our two feet in the open. We got no secrets.   95

Yank (surprised, but admiringly). Yuh mean to say yuh always run wide open — like dis?

Sec. Exactly.

Yank. Den yuh sure got your noive wit youse!   100

Sec. (sharply). Just what was it made you want to join us? Come out with that straight.

Yank. Yuh call me? Well, I got noive,

---

[1] Detective.

[2] A secret blackmailing society among Italians in the United States.

[3] Italians.

too! Here's my hand. Yuh wanter blow tings up, don't yuh? Well, dat's me! 105 I belong!

Sec. (*with pretended carelessness*). You mean change the unequal conditions of society by legitimate direct action — or with dynamite? 110

Yank. Dynamite! Blow it offen de oith — steel — all de cages — all de factories, steamers, buildings, jails — de Steel Trust and all dat makes it go.

Sec. So — that's your idea, eh? And 115 did you have any special job in that line you wanted to propose to us?

(*He makes a sign to the men, who get up cautiously one by one and group behind* YANK.

Yank (*boldly*). Sure, I'll come out wit it. I'll show youse I'm one of de gang. Dere's dat millionaire guy, Douglas —— 120

Sec. President of the Steel Trust, you mean? Do you want to assassinate him?

Yank. Naw, dat don't get yuh nothin'. I mean blow up de factory, de woiks, where he makes de steel. Dat's what I'm after — 125 to blow up de steel, knock all de steel in de woild up to de moon. Dat'll fix tings! (*Eagerly, with a touch of bravado*) I'll do it by me lonesome! I'll show yuh! Tell me where his woiks is, how to git there, all de dope. Gimme 130 de stuff, de old butter — and watch me do de rest! Watch de smoke and see it move! I don't give a damn if dey nab me — long as it's done! I'll soive life for it — and give 'em de laugh! (*Half to himself*) And I'll write 135 her a letter and tell her de hairy ape done it. Dat'll square tings.

Sec. (*stepping away from* YANK). Very interesting.

(*He gives a signal. The men, huskies all, throw themselves on* YANK, *and before he knows it they have his legs and arms pinioned. But he is too flabbergasted to make a struggle, anyway. They feel him over for weapons.*

Man. No gat, no knife. Shall we give 140 him what's what and put the boots to him?

Sec. No. He isn't worth the trouble we'd get into. He's too stupid. (*He comes closer and laughs mockingly in* YANK'S *face.*) Ho-ho! By God, this is the biggest joke they've put up on us yet. Hey, you 145 Joke! Who sent you — Burns or Pinkerton? [1] No, by God, you're such a bonehead I'll bet you're in the Secret Service! Well, you dirty spy, you rotten agent provocator, you can go back and tell whatever skunk is paying 150 you blood-money for betraying your brothers that he's wasting his coin. You couldn't catch a cold. And tell him that all he'll ever get on us, or ever has got, is just his own sneaking plots that he's framed up to put us in jail. 155 We are what our manifesto says we are, neither more nor less — and we'll give him a copy of that any time he calls. And as for you — (*He glares scornfully at* YANK, *who is sunk in an oblivious stupor.*) Oh, hell, what's the use of talking? You're a brainless ape. 160

Yank (*aroused by the word to fierce but futile struggles*). What's dat, yuh Sheeny [2] bum, yuh!

Sec. Throw him out, boys.

(*In spite of his struggles, this is done with gusto and éclat. Propelled by several parting kicks,* YANK *lands sprawling in the middle of the narrow cobbled street. With a growl he starts to get up and storm the closed door, but stops bewildered by the confusion in his brain, pathetically impotent. He sits there, brooding, in as near to the attitude of Rodin's "Thinker" as he can get in his position.*

Yank (*bitterly*). So dem boids don't tink I belong, neider. Aw, to hell wit 'em! 165 Dey're in de wrong pew — de same old bull — soapboxes and Salvation Army — no guts! Cut out an hour offen de job a day and make me happy! Gimme a dollar more a day and make me happy! Tree square a day, and 170 cauliflowers in de front yard — ekal rights — a woman and kids — a lousy vote — and I'm all fixed for Jesus, huh? Aw, hell! What does dat get yuh? Dis ting's in your inside, but it ain't your belly. Feedin' your face — 175 sinkers and coffee — dat don't touch it. It's way down — at de bottom. Yuh can't grab

[1] Well-known American detective agencies.   [2] Jew.

it, and yuh can't stop it. It moves, and every-ting moves. It stops and de whole woild stops. Dat's me now — I don't tick, see? 180 — I'm a busted Ingersoll,[1] dat's what. Steel was me, and I owned de woild. Now I ain't steel, and de woild owns me. Aw, hell! I can't see — it's all dark, get me? It's all wrong! (*He turns a bitter mocking face up* 185 *like an ape gibbering at the moon.*) Say, youse up dere, Man in de Moon, yuh look so wise, gimme de answer, huh? Slip me de inside dope, de information right from de stable — where do I get off at, huh? 190

A Policeman (*who has come up the street in time to hear this last — with grim humor*). You'll get off at the station, you boob, if you don't get up out of that and keep movin'.

[1] A cheap and widely distributed watch of American manufacture.

Yank (*looking up at him — with a hard, bitter laugh*). Sure! Lock me up! Put me in a cage! Dat's de on'y answer yuh know. G'wan, lock me up! 195

Pol. What you been doin'?

Yank. Enuf to gimme life for! I was born, see? Sure, dat's de charge. Write it in de blotter. I was born, get me!

Pol. (*jocosely*). God pity your old 200 woman! (*Then matter-of-fact*) But I've no time for kidding. You're soused. I'd run you in but it's too long a walk to the station. Come on, now, get up, or I'll fan your ears with this club. Beat it now! 205

(*He hauls* YANK *to his feet.*

Yank (*in a vague, mocking tone*). Say, where do I go from here?

Pol. (*giving him a push — with a grin, indifferently*). Go to hell.

Curtain

SCENE 8

Twilight of the next day. The monkey house at the Zoo. One spot of clear gray light falls on the front of one cage so that the interior can be seen. The other cages are vague, shrouded in shadow from which chatterings pitched in a conversational tone can be heard. On the one cage a sign from which the word "gorilla" stands out. The gigantic animal himself is seen squatting on his haunches on a bench in much the same attitude as Rodin's "Thinker."

YANK *enters from the left. Immediately a chorus of angry chattering and screeching breaks out. The gorilla turns his eyes, but makes no sound or move*

Yank (*with a hard, bitter laugh*). Welcome to your city, huh? Hail, hail, de gang's all here! (*At the sound of his voice the chattering dies away into an attentive silence.* YANK *walks up to the gorilla's cage and, leaning over the railing, stares in at its occupant, who stares back at him, silent and motionless. There is a pause of dead stillness. Then* YANK *begins to talk in a friendly confidential tone, half-mockingly, but with a deep undercurrent of sympathy.*) Say, yuh're some hard-lookin' guy, ain't yuh? I 5 seen lots of tough nuts dat de gang called goril-las, but yuh're de foist real one I ever seen. Some chest yuh got, and shoulders, and dem.

arms and mitts! I bet yuh got a punch in eider fist dat'd knock 'em all silly! (*This with* 10 *genuine admiration. The gorilla, as if he understood, stands upright, swelling out his chest and pounding on it with his fist.* YANK *grins sympathetically.*) Sure, I get yuh. Yuh challenge de whole woild, huh? Yuh got what I was sayin' even if yuh muffed de woids. (*Then bitterness creeping in*) And why wouldn't yuh get me? Ain't we both members of de 15 same club — de Hairy Apes! (*They stare at each other — a pause — then* YANK *goes on slowly and bitterly.*) So yuh're what she seen when she looked at me, de white-faced tart! I was you to her, get me? On'y outa de cage — broke out — free to moider her, see? Sure! Dat's 20 what she t'ought. She wasn't wise dat I was in a cage, too — worser'n yours — sure — a damn sight — 'cause you got some chanct to

bust loose — but me — (*He grows confused.*)
Aw, hell! It's all wrong, ain't it? (*A 25
pause.*) I s'pose yuh wanter know what I'm
doin' here, huh? I been warmin' a bench down
to de Battery [1] — ever since last night. Sure.
I seen de sun come up. Dat was pretty, too —
all red and pink and green. I was lookin' 30
at de skyscrapers — steel — and all de ships
comin' in, sailin' out, all over de oith — and
dey was steel, too. De sun was warm, dey
wasn't no clouds, and dere was a breeze
blowin'. Sure, it was great stuff. I got it 35
aw right — what Paddy said about dat bein'
de right dope — on'y I couldn't get *in* it, see?
I couldn't belong in dat. It was over my head.
And I kept tinkin' — and den I beat it up here
to see what youse was like. And I waited 40
till dey was all gone to git yuh alone. Say,
how d'yuh feel sittin' in dat pen all de time,
havin' to stand for 'em comin' and starin' at
yuh — de white-faced, skinny tarts and de
boobs what marry 'em — makin' fun of 45
yuh, laughin' at yuh, gittin' scared of yuh —
damn 'em! (*He pounds on the rail with his fist.
The gorilla rattles the bars of his cage and snarls.
All the other monkeys set up an angry chattering in the darkness. YANK goes on excitedly.*)
Sure! Dat's de way it hits me, too. On'y yuh're
lucky, see? Yuh don't belong wit 'em and
yuh know it. But me, I belong wit 'em — 50
but I don't, see? Dey don't belong wit me,
dat's what. Get me? Tinkin' is hard — (*He
passes one hand across his forehead with a
painful gesture. The gorilla growls impatiently.
YANK goes on gropingly.*) It's dis way, what
I'm drivin' at. Youse can sit and dope dream
in de past, green woods, de jungle, and de 55
rest of it. Den yuh belong and dey don't.
Den yuh kin laugh at 'em, see? Yuh're de
champ of de woild. But me — I ain't got no
past to tink in, nor nothin' dat's comin', on'y
what's now — and dat don't belong. Sure, 60
you're de best off! Yuh can't tink, can yuh?
Yuh can't talk neider. But I kin make a bluff
at talkin' and tinkin' — a'most git away wit it
— a'most! — and dat's where de joker comes
in. (*He laughs.*) I ain't on oith and I ain't 65

[1] Battery Park at the tip end of lower Manhattan
Island, New York City.

in heaven, get me? I'm in de middle tryin' to
separate 'em, takin' all de woist punches from
bot' of 'em. Maybe dat's what dey call hell,
huh? But you, yuh're at de bottom. You
belong! Sure! Yuh're de on'y one in de 70
woild dat does, yuh lucky stiff! (*The gorilla
growls proudly.*) And dat's why dey gotter
put yuh in a cage, see? (*The gorilla roars
angrily.*) Sure! Yuh get me. It beats it
when you try to tink it or talk it — it's way 75
down — deep — behind — you 'n' me we feel
it. Sure! Bot' members of dis club! (*He
laughs — then in a savage tone*) What de hell!
T' hell wit it! A little action, dat's our meat!
Dat belongs! Knock 'em down and keep 80
bustin' 'em till dey croaks yuh wit a gat — wit
steel! Sure! Are yuh game? Dey've looked
at youse, ain't dey — in a cage? Wanter git
even? Wanter wind up like a sport 'stead of
croakin' slow in dere? (*The gorilla roars 85
an emphatic affirmative. YANK goes on with a
sort of furious exaltation.*) Sure! Yuh're
reg'lar! Yuh'll stick to de finish! Me 'n' you,
huh? — bot' members of this club! We'll
put up one last star bout dat'll knock 'em offen
deir seats! Dey'll have to make de cages 90
stronger after we're trou! (*The gorilla is
straining at his bars, growling, hopping from one
foot to the other. YANK takes a jimmy from under his coat and forces the lock on the cage door.
He throws this open.*) Pardon from de governor! Step out and shake hands! I'll take
yuh for a walk down Fif' Avenoo. We'll
knock 'em offen de oith and croak wit de 95
band playin'. Come on, Brother. (*The gorilla
scrambles gingerly out of his cage. Goes to YANK
and stands looking at him. YANK keeps his
mocking tone — holds out his hand.*) Shake —
de secret grip of our order. (*Something, the
tone of mockery, perhaps, suddenly enrages
the animal. With a spring he wraps his huge
arms around YANK in a murderous hug. There
is a crackling snap of crushed ribs — a gasping
cry, still mocking, from YANK.*) Hey, I didn't
say, kiss me. (*The gorilla lets the crushed 100
body slip to the floor; stands over it uncertainly,
considering; then picks it up, throws it in the
cage, shuts the door, and shuffles off menacingly
into the darkness at left. A great uproar of*

frightened chattering and whimpering comes from the other cages. Then YANK *moves, groaning, opening his eyes, and there is silence. He mutters painfully.)* Say — dey oughter match him — wit Zybszko.[1] He got me, aw right. I'm trou. Even him didn't tink I belonged. (*Then, with sudden passionate despair*) Christ, where do I get off at? Where do I fit in? (*Checking himself as suddenly*) Aw, what de hell! No squawkin', see! No quittin',

[1] Stanislaus Zybszko, a Pole, who held the heavy-weight wrestling championship of the world for some time previous to 1920.

get me! Croak wit your boots on! (*He grabs hold of the bars of the cage and hauls himself painfully to his feet — looks around him bewilderedly — forces a mocking laugh.*) In de cage, huh? (*In the strident tones of a circus barker*) Ladies and gents, step forward and take a slant at de one and only — (*his voice weakening*) — one and original — Hairy Ape from de wilds of —

(*He slips in a heap on the floor and dies. The monkeys set up a chattering, whimpering wail. And, perhaps, the Hairy Ape at last belongs.*)

Curtain

INTRODUCTION TO
Roll Sweet Chariot

Paul Green and Symphonic Folk-Tragedy

THOUGH the literary exploration of American regional and folk life started in the last decades of the nineteenth century, it did not take the form of drama until after the First World War when the "little theater" movement began to supply local centers of production. As a result of the establishment of these provincial art theaters, particularly widespread in the South and Southwest, the folk-drama has grown into one of the most promising and significant phases of the American stage. The founder of the folk-theater in the United States was the late Frederick H. Koch, who came to the University of North Carolina at Chapel Hill in 1918, organized the Carolina Playmakers, and opened the Playmakers Theater as the first playhouse in America to be dedicated to the creation of a native drama. The subsequent influence of the Playmakers Theater has been similar to that of the Abbey Theater in Ireland. The Chapel Hill playhouse has not uncovered anything like as much dramatic genius, but it has inspired many picturesque and substantial plays concerning the Southern negroes and rural whites.

The most distinguished product of Professor Koch's enterprise and of the American folk-theater is Paul Green, a son of the Carolina soil. He was born March 17, 1894, on a farm near Lillington, North Carolina, where he continued to live until his twenties. As a boy he worked in the fields spring, summer, and fall, and went to school a few months each winter. He became champion cotton picker of the county, and an expert harvester. One of the negro field hands years later said of him admiringly, "Why, he useter could pull fodderland lak a whirlwind."

After graduating from Buie's Creek Academy in 1914 and teaching country school for two years, Green entered the University of North Carolina in 1916. A year later he joined the Army Engineer Corps and served with the A.E.F. in France during 1918. When he resumed his university course in 1919, he came under the influence of Professor Koch and joined the Carolina Playmakers. He wrote for them several plays of no peculiar merit, but the experience thoroughly aroused his enthusiasm for playwriting. Upon graduation in 1921, he studied philosophy, first at Chapel Hill and then at Cornell University. In 1923 his Alma Mater appointed him to a post on the philosophy faculty. Some years ago he shifted his academic duties at Chapel Hill from philosophy to dramatic art, and now holds a professorship in that department.

Green attracted national attention for the first time in 1925 when his one-act play, *The No 'Count Boy*, acted by the Little Theater of Dallas, Texas, won the Belasco Cup at the national "little theater" tournament in New York. As a result the Provincetown Players took his first full-length play, *In Abraham's Bosom*, for production at the end of 1926. Though soon withdrawn, it gained the Pulitzer Prize a few months later. Then it was revived by the Players and enjoyed a "hit." In 1928 Green was honored with a Guggenheim Fellowship to study and write in Europe for two years. His next success came in the autumn of 1931 with *The House of Connelly*. As the maiden production of the Group Theater, an offshoot from the Theater Guild, it turned into a Broadway box-office attraction. In 1936 the Group Theater performed Green's last New York play to date, a serio-comic war extravaganza entitled *Johnny Johnson*. His most recent undertakings have been Carolina historical pageants, *The Lost Colony* (1937) and *The Highland Call* (1940).

The background of Green's drama is what he knows and loves best — the South. As he sees it, the South is "mainly a rural region whose ideologies and ethics of living are derived from the fields, the sky, the trees, and the hills — a region of violent contradictions like nature itself, . . . of hate and love, of wealth and degraded poverty, of passion and sloth, of roaring ambition and empty death." Green chooses as his particular setting the east coastal plain of North Carolina, where his ancestral farm lies. Life in the fields there nurtured in him a profound awareness of the earth, and of human kinship without distinction of race. Of his early experience he writes: "My first memories are of negro ballads ringing out by moonlight, and the rich laughter of the resting blacks, down by the river bottom. I started out very close to life — in the elemental . . ." He has never lost an almost mystic sense of communion with the simple people of the soil who formed his first world: "Back with my own folks, and I mean black and white, I can't help feeling . . . at home as I'll never feel at home elsewhere. The smell of their sweaty bodies, the gusto of their indecent jokes, the knowledge of their twisted philosophies, the sight of their feet entangled among the pea vines and grass, their shouts, grunts, and belly-achings, the sun blistering down upon them and the rim of the sky enclosing them forever, all took me wholly, and I was one of them — neither black nor white, but one of them, children of the moist earth underfoot." This impassioned expression of unity with all the common humanity in the South points to the secret of Green's power as a dramatist. He possesses that intuitive understanding of his people which develops only in those who actively have shared the ethnic life.

Green designates his plays as "folk-plays," a term first officially used in the American theater on the 1919 bills of the Carolina Playmakers. The "folk" are to Green "the people whose manners, ethics, religious and philosophical ideals, are more nearly derived from and controlled by the ways of the outside physical world than by the ways and institutions of men in a specialized society." They stir Green's imagination to an exalted vision of their character. He sees them "live as it were with their feet in the earth and their heads bare to the storms; labor with their hands wresting from cryptic nature her goods; develop a wisdom of living . . . more real and beautiful than those who develop their values and ambitions from rubbing shoulders in a crowded city." This folk-wisdom he defines as a "consciousness of the great eternal Presence (good, bad, or impersonal) by which men live and move and are allowed their existence." It emerges as a motif, either major or minor, in almost all his works.

The best known of Green's long folk-plays treat of basic conflicts in the contemporary South. *In Abraham's Bosom* (1924), which he subtitles "the tragedy of a negro educator," presents in seven scenes the biography of Abe McCrannie, son of a white plantation-owner and a negro woman. Abe, eager for the uplift of his race, tries with a smattering of knowledge to be a schoolteacher and lead his fellow negroes toward the light. Their indifference, however, and the opposition of neighboring whites put an end to his project and then to his life. Abe's aspiration, unselfishness, and courage make his frustration and death a deeply moving tragedy. His ringing appeal to the colored people echoes on after the fall of the curtain: "We got to be free, freedom of the soul and of the mind. Ignorance means sin and sin means destruction." The play contains an evident undertone of protest, summed up in Abe's exclamation: "Color hadn't ought to count. It's the man, the man that lasts!"

The Field God (1925) deals with religious rather than racial conflict. Hardy Gilchrist, a white farmer, suffers the hostility of both wife and community because he does not hold to the narrow, repressive tenets of the traditional fire-and-brimstone faith. The fanaticism and ecstasy in the old folk-religion is powerfully depicted in the play's one memorable scene, in which a country preacher and some zealots of his flock come to the Gilchrist home to pray over the recalcitrant farmer and his new wife. The play reaches a melodramatic and inconclusive end in all three versions which Green has tried out.

The House of Connelly (1931) exhibits social conflict, a decadently genteel Old South versus a democratic, hard-working New South. Will Connelly, the weak heir of Connelly Hall, finally disregards family opposition in order to marry Patsy Tate, a vigorous, land-loving, farmer girl, and revive the decayed Connelly estate. Thus, as Patsy says, "the dead and the proud have to give way to us — to us the living."

These full-length plays reveal consistent technical and intellectual deficiencies. Green has confessed all too truly: "I haven't any dramatic technique. I merely tell the story episode by episode." Inattention to structure often leads in his development of plot to misplaced emphasis and hence to a lack of dramatic focus. His scenes on occasion display overelaboration and poor linking. Furthermore Green, like O'Neill, sometimes allows the thinker in him to override the dramatist. His characters then grow unconvincing in their reflections. They utter philosophical statements which sound affected and bombastic. For example, the religious convictions voiced by Gilchrist at the close of *The Field God* constitute mere bathos and spoil the climax.

Green's genius, however, for characterization and atmosphere more than offsets his weaknesses. He can illuminate the significant humanity in the Carolina farmers and negro poor. His drama pictures with a rare sensitivity their simple, emotional natures; like them, it moves easily from humor to pathos, from comedy to tragedy. Tragedy tends to predominate because Green does not long forget that man is "a part of an all-powerful and demanding universe . . . never funny nor playful." His dialogue catches to perfection the coarse and racy speech of the strongly earth-bound natives. Following the Synge tradition, he seeks to record the poetry and the music of their living. He would restore to the theater its ancient lyric heritage, the union of drama and song found in the stage representations of the Greeks. By the profuse insertion of singing and chant, and the weaving of these musical elements into the dramatic movement, he has striven to create a richer form of art which he calls the "symphonic play." This "symphonic" pattern represents a notably fresh amalgam of materials from native folk-life. Green thereby has suggested an important new horizon for the American drama of tomorrow.

"ROLL SWEET CHARIOT"

Roll Sweet Chariot, "a symphonic play of the negro people," discloses Green at his peak as folk poet and musician in the theater. The play was first published in 1931 under the title of *Potter's Field*, but had not then been acted on account of its difficulty of production. Finally on April 16, 1934, Margaret Hewes staged with an all-negro cast its world premiere at the Plymouth Theater, Boston. After the Boston performances, which had no intermission, Green divided the play into four scenes, improved the text at many points, and changed the title. The new version, *Roll Sweet Chariot*, opened at the Cort Theater, New York, on October 2, 1934, and excited admiration from the theatrical intelligentsia.

In *Roll Sweet Chariot* Green has laid bare with poetic veracity the troubled soul of the colored race. His drama, unlike Marc Connelly's Pulitzer prizewinner, *The Green Pastures* (1930), does not sacrifice harsh social truth to picturesqueness; it focuses upon how the negro imagination views the Kingdom on Earth rather than in Heaven. Uzzell the seer reveals Green's awareness of the secret tension and grief in the heart of the black folk: "Ignorant and blind! Under the tight pot I hear you calling." (Play headnote) The intensity of emotion in *Roll Sweet Chariot* springs from its author's indignation at the white man's complacency as expressed by the judge: "These everlasting niggers, always fighting, always killing. They've got no sense. They'll never have no sense." (Sc. 4, opening stage dir.) But Green's wise sympathy insists, "Something wrong. Wrong here." (Sc. 4, ll. 139–40) The road-blasting with its culmination in the fall of Quiviene's house symbolizes the root wrong — the disruptive oppression of the whites. That oppression is fully suggested by the final scene where the chain-gang digs the white man's road straight through the negro settlement of Potter's Field. The burly leader of the black convicts, "John Henry," a spiritual ever on his lips, epitomizes the sorrowful but unbroken spirit of his people.

The stylized, symbolic action which predominates in the chain-gang scene forms an effective contrast and climax to the play's earlier realism. Behind this blending of realism and symbolism *Roll Sweet Chariot* displays a steady ascent of feeling. Scene by scene tension among the Potter's Field negroes increases; scene by scene passion mounts. At the outset, though childishly restless and moody, they are more or less at peace, cavorting, joking, singing, romancing. The blasts of the road builders, however, intermittently disturb their peace. Then "John Henry" with his magic and his prophecies rouses uneasiness. Next, Bantam's return provokes fear and hatred. Finally violence in the shape of Bantam's murder confronts them with both Death and the Law. Under the lash of the Law sorrow turns to agony and despair. "God sits on high, his face from the Negro. The poor and needy cry in vain..." (Sc. 4, ll. 131–32) But piety and faith triumph when Uzzell bursts into his trumpet cry, "Dig on the road to heaven!" (Sc. 4, l. 150) All the negroes, convicts and residents alike, catch his vision and begin to sing their song of salvation in Jesus. Thus Potter's Field step by step rises from playful ease to spiritual exaltation. It is the ultimate note of aspiration, first uttered by Henry, "In the darkness of the valley. But the weary struggler must keep climbing" (Sc. 2, ll. 350–51), which elevates the racial weakness and defeat in *Roll Sweet Chariot* to the plane of high tragedy.

Green achieves superb progression of mood in part by his "symphonic" technique with its liberal use of vocal music to point up or to further action. After the death of Bantam, for example, the antiphonal preaching and chanting transform the negroes' confusion and excitement little by little into calm resignation (Sc. 3, ll. 100–215). Then all at once the loud voice of the Law strikes against the soft chant of the mourners to produce an abrupt finale. Green supplements his "symphonic" method by other audible devices. With all Chekhov's art he weaves noises and silences to bring out that perpetual ebb and flow of emotion which accompanies the passing of time in any inhabited place. As Quiviene's boarders sit listening in the twilight to the low strumming of a guitar, the Florida Limited passes with a whistle and a roar (Sc. 1, l. 388). The boarders jump up, shout delightedly, lapse again into silence, and then hear with disquiet a faraway blast. No sooner does stillness once more reign than a hullabaloo starts up nearby. This subtle orchestration of feeling and sound throughout *Roll Sweet Chariot* renders it a beautiful and unusual play that draws poetry out of the seeming commonplace, philosophy out of illiteracy, and a meaningful suffering world out of a dark patch in Carolina.

[For further study see Paul Green, *The Hawthorn Tree: Some Papers and Letters on Life and the Theater* (1943); Arthur H. Quinn, *A History of the American Drama* (1936); Barrett H. Clark, *Paul Green* (1928).]

PAUL GREEN [1]

Roll Sweet Chariot

A Symphonic Play of the Negro People

Seas—rivers of brick, mortar and iron—
Let it flow on—open the way.
JOHN HENRY

DRAMATIS PERSONAE

OLD QUIVIENE LOCKLEY, *an old boarding-house keeper*
WILLIE LOCKLEY, *her youngish and feeble-minded husband*
ZEB VANCE LOCKLEY, *her illegitimate son*
MILLY WILSON, *a boarder and cook for the white folks*
BANTAM WILSON, *her husband, a convict*
TOM STERLING, *a boarder and bricklayer,* MILLY'S *sweetheart*
ED UZZELL, *the seer*
LEVIN FARROW, *a laborer*
SEENY GRAY, *a dishwasher* } *Additional boarders with* OLD QUIVIENE
BAD-EYE SMITH, *a drayman*
"JOHN HENRY," *a stranger*
JIM PARR, *a barber and undertaker*
BELLE UTLEY, *a mulatto beauty*
SPORT WOMACK, *her sweetheart*
DODE WILSON, *a blind musician, father of* BANTAM *and* DOODLE
DOODLE WILSON, *a boy preacher*
SUDIE WILSON, DODE'S *wife*
FLOSSIE TUCKER, *a neighboring Negro girl*
First Guard
Second Guard
Chain Gang

The Scene is Potter's Field, a Negro village somewhere in the South

The Time is the present

Scene 1: The yard and front porch of Old Quiviene Lockley's boarding-house — late one Saturday afternoon in midsummer.

Scene 2: The yard, front porch, and interior of Old Quiviene's house — early evening of the same day.

Scene 3: Same as Scene II — night of the same day.

Scene 4: A blazing new road through Potter's Field — a few weeks later.

NOTE

In a sort of valley close by the white folks' town is a Negro settlement, formerly known as Potter's Field. It was so called after a wealthy planter named Potter who owned it before the Civil War. The field was always a waste place, cut with gulleys, full of briars, stones, and garbage, and in the parlance of that section fit only to help hold the world together. When the Negroes were freed from slavery, many of them squatted on this spot and gradually built up a kind of hog-dump colony of their owning. Later on, old Potter's nephew questioned their titles and brought them into court, and thereupon they began paying rent from their wash and hoe money. When at last it was generally understood what Potter's Field meant in the Bible,[1] many of the more respecting inhabitants got together and restyled the place Johnstown after one of their native sons, a designation not generally adopted to this day. This Johnson was a bound boy to a white man, and through poverty and discouragement got himself a college education and a sort of M.D. degree and returned home a middle-aged man to practice his calling in his native place. Battling the tide of poverty, dirt, and disease, he soon wore himself out in the struggle and died before he was old. Some of the homefolks then honored him by naming their little town after him, as aforesaid, at the same time trying to dispense with a term that was falling more and more into disfavor.

Many laborers have come recently into this place — from different parts of the state, some from neighboring states — for the building of new institutions up in the town — warehouses and college buildings. They herd together here, sleeping and eating as best they can. In the evenings you will find them laughing, singing, and sitting before the shacks with their girls, or walking out if the weather is fine towards the hilly fields that lie west of the town. Swarms of kinky-headed children shoot marbles or roll battered automobile tires along the crooked paths and roads called streets. At times they stop and look on in awe and innocence as Belle's sweetheart from Raleigh comes cadillacking along in his wire-wheeled Ford. The sport calls to a girl sitting in the yard with a man, and she rises and goes with him. Her companion left alone growls to himself and registers an oath on high that he too will ride like that some day, goddam he will. But he won't, for the crap-shooters know his soul.

On the porch of Old Quiviene Lockley's shack across the street sits Ed Uzzell, a man past fifty, with his head bent despondently in his hands. Bad Ed he had been called in the old Memphis days. Bootleg liquor, women, and cards have caved him in. He looks out towards the west where the sun is setting behind the smokestacks of the cotton mill and hums a song to himself about Brady, the rounder, who broke the hearts of the women in Gawgy. He too was like that once. And remembering the girl in Winston-Salem and the three kids that had been his, he hits the side of his chair and spits softly into the yard.

[1] A public burial-place, particularly for paupers and vagrants (see *Matthew* XXVII. 7).

Uzzell (*thinking*). After a life of fun and sweet momma from Louisville to Mobile, this swinging a pick in a ditch for two bucks a day and all the manhood gone out of you is a hell of a way to end. And then too, them white men stand round in their collars and tell you what to do — Jesus! — The big bugs come down from Durham and Raleigh and the Lord knows where, rolling around in their Packards and Franklins and Buicks. They walk about with the big boss and point with their canes. Great God A'mighty! And sometimes their women come with them, tripping over ditches and piled out earth with little trim feet, prattling in baby voices about the warehouses going up. They look with round possessive eyes at their men, captains of industry and the big wheel, their small heads rising out of smotherly furs like lovely dolls. And all the while Bad Ed is digging far below in the deep foundation ditch; like a mole he digs from seven to twelve, from one to six, twirling the iron-snouted pick above his head and driving it straight home.

Spitting again, Uzzell gets up, takes a step or two, and then reseats himself with his head in his hand, his mind black and turmoiling.

The sun goes down, other boarders come out of the house and join him on the porch. They light their pipes and cigarettes, they talk a bit now and then. Ever and anon the spurt of a match lights up a face, and the coal of a smoker glows and subsides like a dull intermittent firefly. Far down an alley a guitar goes thrumming, a man's muffled growl following along with something about how the Red River runs from his back door to Lord knows where; then presently nearer at hand the husky voice of a woman calling — "Oh, where is my loving Daddy gone?"

The sounds up and down the street grow softer, come less often, and quiet settles over the sort of town. The boarders on Old Quiviene's porch sit in long stretches of motionless silence. Each grows busy with his thoughts of tomorrow and yesterday and each withdraws into the sanctuary of himself. Soon they will get up one by one, "See you tomorrow," and mosey off to their bug-ridden beds in different parts of the valley.

Uzzell (*to himself*). Ignorant and blind! Under the tight pot I hear you calling.

Or if it is winter the Negroes in Potter's Field huddle indoors, breathing the close and suffocating air. The broken pane is stuffed with pillows and rags, and pasteboard nailed over the cracks in the walls. But rags and paper won't stop the wide leaks in the sagging roof. Sleets and rains seep through and wet the sleepers in their beds, and then pneumonia and galloping consumption rot out their lungs. The gasp of the dying child and the groan of the laborer struggling in his bed are too frequently heard, and Jim Parr's run-down hearse is seen rattling off to the graveyard many times too often.

Again things other than sickness break out among them as if an invisible and malignant devil were sicking them on to blood and murder. And some of them even believe there are wandering niggers much like the devil whose souls are given over to evil, and wherever they go trouble follows. Listen close at night, they say, and one can be heard passing along the road, singing to himself —

      "Done sold my soul to the Devil,
         And my heart's done turned into stone."

And it won't be long before somewhere somebody will pull out a knife or a pistol and put daylight through a man. Then a heavy tramp will sound on the porch, a loud whamming on the door, and the voice of the law will call out, "Heigh, I say, heigh there! —"

Uzzell (to himself). Oh Cap'n, Cap'n, take that body away!

SCENE I

It is a sultry Saturday afternoon in early summer, and a group of Negroes are sprawling around OLD QUIVIENE'S *front porch, dozing, laughing, singing in relaxation, and stringing one another with catches and drolleries after their week's work is done. The shack of a house, with a drunken chimney at the right, is set diagonally across a little yard; and beyond, a narrow alley runs at right angles to it. Tacked on a post near the steps at the center is a plank sign — "Lockley's Bording Hous." A thick cypress vine, lacy-leaved and with scarlet tubular flowers, overruns the left end of the porch and house and bangs down along a windowed shed room built in the side somewhat farther back. A smaller shack is a step away at the left — not much larger than a good-sized dog kennel but proclaiming in crooked letters on its front that it is "Parr's Shavin Parler." At the right a path leads in from the alley to the porch steps, and growing near it to the front is a small thick china tree. Along the path and here and there in the yard are borders and beds of purplish red petunias with zinnias and marigolds planted among them. The whole scene is florid with the mixture of colors from the flowers and cypress vine — yellow, orange, purple, and scarlet — which seems to increase the already intense heat of the summer day. Somewhere far off at the right an intermittent blasting in the earth goes on. Nearer, children are heard screaming at play, and now and then a sleepy inhabitant of the valley wanders aimlessly by in the alley at the right.* LEVIN FARROW, *a restless alert young fellow, and quick on the call, is standing by a low stake near the china tree with two horseshoes in his hand. He has been addressing one of his vulgar stories to the boarders on the porch, who for the moment are interrupting him with their laughter.*

Old Quiv. (a slatternly gray-haired woman about sixty years old sitting in a chair near the door that leads into the house). That ain't fitten for women-folks to hear, Levin.

    (*But still she looks interested and takes a large dip of snuff with her brush in anticipation.*

Seeny Gray (a bold-eyed girl of twenty who is sitting on the edge of the porch at the right dangling her feet down). Pshaw, women-folks know more'n men, Aunt Quivie.

    (*She smiles broadly at* FARROW, *revealing a row of pearly teeth set off by a gleaming gold one in the corner of her dimpled mouth.*

Far. Then uh — uh, one night when 5 they were feeling for Jesus with the lights blowed out, them two preachers got to working on her tin britches with can openers. Hah-hah-hah.

    (*The boarders on the porch laugh and slap each other, and even* UZZELL, *who is sitting at the right, bent over in his chair, lets out a twisting smile. The fun suddenly dies out of* FARROW'S *countenance and for an instant he raises his face to the sky and gives a high-calling Negro "holler" — oodle — oodle — oo! He listens a moment as if expecting a voice to answer him from the deep above, and then from the deep bowels of the earth far away the blasting does seem to reply to him.*

Uzz. (cryptically). And he puts a ques- 10 tion up to heaven! Wherefore? But the earth do answer him.

    (FARROW *and all the others listen intently a moment.*

Far. (with a touch of uncertainty in his voice). Dynamite on the big road, chillun, having a word with man.

Uzz. (as if warning them all). That blast- 15 ing coming nearer every day. (*Gazing morosely around him*) The road, I said — coming nearer every day.

Far. Yah, yah, old sour face. (*Letting fly his horseshoe, he slaps himself in triumph at the result.*) Hot damn, a ringer! 20

> (BAD-EYE SMITH, *who is sitting on a blacksmith's anvil near the china tree, bent under an old felt hat, shifts himself around and stares quietly at the stake.* FARROW *sets himself and throws the second shoe, which knocks down the first.*

Parr (*who is sitting in a chair before his barber shop and finishing some sandwiches from a greasy paper bag*). Yeh, you knocked it down. (*Choking with a piece of biscuit*) Harr — p!

> (PARR *is a squatty black fellow of middle age, dressed in a dirty barber's coat. The stems of his waxed and rolled mustache protrude on either side of his nose like a pair of steer horns, and he is ever petting and fingering them.* FARROW *moves over, gets the shoes and begins throwing them back to the first stake.*

Sterling (*a strong, handsome young mulatto of twenty-eight, sleepily and reminiscent as he lies on the porch at the right by* MILLY WILSON'S *side*). Knowed of a man in Mobile could ring 'em forty times in a row.

Far. Yeh, knowed of a man —— (*Turn-* 25 *ing and pushing* BAD-EYE *off his seat*) Wake up, gimme room, son o' man.

Bad-Eye (*turning up a gnarled face set with two crossed and bloodshot eyes*). 'Scuse me. (*Thinking*) Son? (*Defensively*) Better be son o' man. 30

> (*He crawls on his knees and hands over to the tree and lies down contentedly like a dog.* FARROW *goes on throwing his horseshoes.*

Far. (*half-singing into the air*). Onct I was broke in Charlotte. Got me an old clawhammer coat and held service — preaching on the children starving in the wilderness — third book of Ham, eleventh to twelveteenth 35 verse. Well, 'bout collection time somebody stood up in the congergation and said he knowed me — hah — hah — Rode out with a

window frame round my shoulders. Talk 'bout rainbows — Good Lord! (*Singing*) 40

"Everywhere I look, I look this mawning,
Looks like rain, Lord, look-a like rain.
I got a rainbow round my shoulder ——"
Jesus, show me my heavenly home!

Seeny (*to* UZZELL, *looking back over her shoulder with wide luminous eyes*). You know 45 heaps the ladies told you. Wise, wise man.

> (*She touches him gently on the knee, pulling her hand quickly and coquettishly away.*

Uzz. (*giving her a sharp and penetrating look*). Yeh, but it turns sour like milk in the heat.

> (*He gazes out to the west, his haggard face illumined by the sinking sun.*

Ster. (*boring his forefinger around in* MILLY WILSON'S *heavy hair*). Better go in and take your nap, honey.

> (MILLY *is a dark plump mulatto of twenty-five, with a wistful face and heavy-lidded eyes.*

Milly. Too hot in the house. 50

Quiv. Heard from your family lately, Ed?

Far. (*singing*).

"For they got another daddy on the Salt Lake Line."

Uzz. No. (*Sharply to* FARROW) That's right, you ain't singing to me.

> (*He pulls a newspaper from his pocket and begins reading it.*

Parr (*with an exclamation*). Push my face! 55 (*Looking up from an old magazine he is reading*) Says here Charlie Chaplin done spent a million dollars on his divorce. And ain't free yet. (*Listening to the roll of blasting now a bit louder*) Ah, that old road coming on down to our door — every day he slides a little bit nearer.

Far. (*with a high wild call in the direction of the blasting*). Sling yo' pick, Bantam, on that 60 long road! Milly ain't thinking of you now!

Ster. Heigh!

Far. How much your divo'ce gonna cost, Milly?

Seeny (*with a restless woman's touch of spite*). Jew price — dollar ninety-nine. 65

Milly (*softly*). Ten dollars the lawyer said.

> (*She bends her face shyly and full of love toward* STERLING.

Far. (singing again).
  "I axed her do she love-a me
  And she say she do."
  (*He flaps his arms like a chicken.*
  UZZELL *makes a restless movement
  in his chair, settles himself, and goes
  on reading.*

Ster. When that judge writes a little word
on a piece of paper, you gonna see the 70
procession.

Far. (stingingly). Better git the percession
over before convict Bantam come looking for
his wife.

Quiv. I got a frying pan I'll give the 75
bride.

Parr. And I'll shave up the groom for nothing.

Ster. And you'll haul us to the preacher on
your truck, won't you, Bad-Eye? 80

Far. Yeh! Haul you on the rims.

Bad-Eye. White man run into me this
mawning and busted the last good tiah off'n
my truck.

Far. Pay you? 85

Uzz. (loudly). No!

Far. Shush.

Bad-Eye. But anudder white man passing seen it. Gimme two dollars — said he felt
sorry. 90

*Ster. (turning himself around and laying his
head on* MILLY'S *lap).* Fan me, honey. Whew,
hot!

Far. (bursting into a loud laugh). That
woman's lap ain't gonna cool you none.

Milly (timidly). Get up, Tom. 95

Ster. Let the po' man lie.

  (*After a moment she begins to fan him,
  looking dreamily into his eyes.*

Seeny. Come here and fan me, Levin honey
boy.

Far. I don't wear no dress.

Seeny. Po' Ed needs a little fanning. 100

  (*She climbs up on the porch, takes
  UZZELL'S hat, and begins to fan him
  and smooth his head.*

Far. Heah now!

Parr. Oh-ho.

  (UZZELL *jerks his hat from her, and she
  wanders up and down the porch, now*

*and then sliding through a sort of
  waltz step.*

Seeny. Got to go back to the cafeteria in a
few minutes. Who'll take me a little walk?

Far. Gotta wait heah till Zeb Vance 105
come back with that watermelon.

Seeny (sitting down again). You and yo'
pardner — Ed?

Uzz. Heard a man say once a goose wouldn't
eat shucks. 110

Far. Hah-hah-hah, now, now!

Seeny. And him that thinks a watermelon
is sweeter than me — well, he can have the
melon. (*She flings herself on the porch in a
  careless attitude.* BAD-EYE *slowly
  crawls around under the tree and
  peers up at her.*

Parr (breaking into a laugh). Heigh, 115
Ed. Says here — (*reading from his magazine*)
Papa's silent partner, gland-glad extract, one
dollar, sent postpaid.

Far. Hah-hah-hah. Gland-glad extract!
Niggers in Potter's Field don't need that. 120

  (*His face is once more contorted with
  merriment and he wanders around
  the yard, bent over, his hands resting
  on his thighs. The others laugh, and
  even* BAD-EYE *rolls over on the
  ground.*

Uzz. (spitting). Hyack.

Far. Grinning goats. Let me try my old
anvil! (*He goes over to the anvil and begins
  struggling with it.*

Ster. You're foolish, Levin — I can't lift
that thing but a foot high myself. 125

Parr. I heahd of a man onct who could
muscle that thing out in bofe his two hands.

Far. (grunting). Heahd of a man — yeh.

Ster. Looks like a week's work'd be enough
for Levin and he'd rest on Saturday eve- 130
ning. (LEVIN *sits down on the anvil, fanning
  himself with his cap and staring
  fixedly at the ground. Pulling some
  bones from his pocket, he fits them
  between his fingers and begins knocking them.*

Seeny. Bad-Eye, you be 'shamed, looking up
a lady's dress lak that!

Far. (snapping at him). Quit it. (*Singing*)

"Oh, my Lawd, oh, my Lawd,   135
     What shall I do?"

Bad-Eye (*humbly*). I ain't doing nothing.

Far. (*making a half-serious pass at him with his fist and gazing at him as if he were some strange creature*). Whew, that face!

Milly. Aw, hush, Levin.

Bad-Eye. I can't help it.   140

Far. You couldn't a growed it thataway.

Ster. (*sitting up*). Bad-Eye, don't you worry no more 'bout your face. You was born thataway. (BAD-EYE'S *face smooths itself out and he smiles at* STERLING.) Go on, play your   145 Jew-harp.

> (BAD-EYE *pulls out his harp, sticks it to his tongue, and begins whinging away.* FARROW *pats his feet and hands and knocks his bones. Far down the alley a woman is heard singing —* "*You broke the heart of many a poor girl, you'll never break this heart of mine.*"

Far. (*singing*).
"When she wore her apern low,
When she wore her apern low,
When she wore her apern low,
The boys they hung about her do'."   150

Quiv. (*as a baby begins squealing inside the house*). Yo' babies crying, Milly.

> (MILLY *gets up and goes into the house.* FARROW *continues singing.*

Far. "Now she wears her apern high — (*finishing his song*) And the boys they pass on by." (*Through the window* MILLY *can be seen bending over the bed attending to her babies.*

Parr. Can't I cut some you folkses'   155 hair or shave you? — ten cents with hot towels.

Far. Hot dishrag and a hawg scraper. No, thanky.

Parr (*genially*). Quit th'owing off on my razor.   160

Far. (*singing*). Business dull. Nobody to bury, nobody to shave.

> (*The blasting sounds again. They all listen for an instant with the exception of* FARROW, *who is still knocking his bones.*

Ster. Levin, for cripe's sake, be still.

Far. (*springing up*). Oh Potter's Field, where be yo' sperit and yo' juice? (*Chanting*   165 *as he dances and knocks his bones, all in time to* BAD-EYE'S *whinging*) Took my gun early one morning. (*He makes the pantomime of shouldering a gun.*) Went down to the river bottom see could I kill me a little game. Lawd, it was mighty cold — hah-hah-   170 hah. (*He sticks the imaginary gun in the crook of his arm and blows on his fingers.*) Down in the marshes walking on ice. Seed a fox-squirrel setting on a limb. (*He aims the gun and some of the others, now growing interested, do likewise.*) Let him have it ker-bang   175 a-lang. Old muzzle-loader busted wide open. Piece to the east and swubbed down a deer. Piece to the west and cut down a tree — hah-hah-hah. Tree fell and killed a wildcat in the top — and squashed a grizzly bear lying   180 in the grass. Ramrod whanged 'way up in the sky and brung down a flock of wild geese passing. Honk, honk, they were saying, but they said it no mo'. (*The spirit of imagination and fun begins to rise among the boarders.*) Hammer flew off and killed a bull-buffalo   185 standing on the hill. Old gun kicked me so hard jammed me th'ough the ice and I fell in the river. Climbed out with my britches full o' yellow pyerch. Heavy big button flew off my britches and killed a turkey in the top   190 of a slash pine. (SEENY *suddenly springs up and begins to dance wildly with him in the yard. The others clap their hands — clap — clap — clap-a-clap.*) Took off my coat and th'owed it on the grass to dry, and smothered gang o' pa'tridges to death. Had enough game foh one day. But ain't seed that squirrel yet   195 — hee-hee — (*Eyeing them*) Yeh, still got life in Potter's Field. (*He turns a handspring and lies flat on his back staring up at the sky.*) Whoo — I wonder how far it is up to that sky?

Quiv. (*jubilantly*). Look at him in a heavy sweat. Mebbe he'll rest now.   200

FLOSSIE TUCKER, *a Negro girl of about eighteen, comes giggling and nodding into the yard at the right. She has an exquisite little head set on a wedge-shaped body that spreads down into two large hips, shapeless heavy legs and feet. She glances about the scene in search of someone. FARROW looks up*

Far. Heigh, Floss!
> (*Sliding along the ground, he tries to lift up her dress.*

Flos. (*dancing out of his way*). I seen you cutting up, Levin.
> (*Sticking her head to one side, she wanders out at the left.*

Seeny. Better shet Zeb Vance up, Aunt Quivie, Flossie's after yo' son. 205
> (*Far off there comes again a low rumble of thunder-like sound, and the windows rattle in their sockets.*

Quiv. (*sending a sudden angry call afar off*). Quit blasting out my window-panes!

WILLIE *comes hurriedly out of the house and down into the yard, carrying a small wired-over box in his hand. He is a slender Negro about thirty years old with a childish face and cloudy eyes. Going uneasily to the edge of the yard he looks off at the horizon*

Willie (*quavering*). I don't like dat loud pouncing way down dere.

Quiv. A mile away on that big road, honey.

Willie. I'm skeared o' dat dynamite, 210 Mis' Quivie.

Ster. It won't hurt you.
> (WILLIE *turns back into the yard and sits down on the ground. He begins pushing bread crumbs through the wire at his squirrel. They all sit watching him in silence. BAD-EYE has quit playing his Jew's-harp and is staring at the setting sun.*

Parr. Hear the landlord say maybe they carry the road around Potter's Field.

Ster. Heard him say we better keep 215 the peace, though.

Quiv. Whatever the white folks 'cide ain't gonna help us none, is it, Ed?

Uzz. (*staring before him*). Dig on, dig on to your heavenly home! 220

Quiv. Tchk!

Ster. Better quit fighting and cutting or

they're gonna rip through this hog dump like a new bull tongue.

Quiv. Go get me some stovewood, 225 Willie.

Far. (*as* WILLIE *continues playing with his squirrel*). Go get your mammy her wood.

Willie (*quickly*). She ain't my mammy, I tell you, she's my wife.

Far. (*to* UZZELL). The night Aunt 230 Quivie and Willie got married Willie was scared to death. Come bedtime he didn't know what to do. Said, "Levin, I give you a quarter to sleep with her." Hah-hah!

Seeny (*irritably*). Who wants to take 235 me for a little walk through Potter's Field?

Far. (*with his hands behind his head, singing*). "Walk and talk with Jesus, don't you want to go?"

Seeny (*sharply*). Wisht you'd do sump'n beside sing and cut up, Levin. 240

Far. (*musing*). Potter's Field — uhm — Potter's Field! Where'd it git such a name?

Quiv. They say it's named that 'cause a long time ago a' old man Potter lived here — (*Fearsomely*) And they say he was hanged for 245 killing somebody.

Uzz. Name's in the Bible — means where they bury dead dogs and worthless things.

Far. Bible sho' give us a bad repitation.

Parr. And we better keep the peace, 250 the peace.

Far. But old trouble allus poking about to fly out and grab you. Ain't no peace.

Seeny. How come?

Uzz. Nobody know how come! A 255 man's life is writ in the sky.

Bad-Eye (*croaking as he suddenly looks toward the west*). Heigh, old sun.

Willie (*murmuring as he shields his eyes with his hand*). Red, red, dat sun's red lak blood.
> (*He goes hastily over, taking his squirrel with him, and sits down like a little puppy by* QUIVIENE's *chair. She puts her hand on his head as if he were a small boy and rubs his hair lovingly around.*

Quiv. That's a good sun. It makes crops grow, makes everything smell sweet and 260 warm, makes my flowers grow.

MILLY *comes out of the house and resumes her seat by* STERLING. *The babies squeal after her. For a moment her face is strained and harassed*

Ster. Willie, go in there and play with the babies. Show 'em yo' squirrel.

Willie. Dey don't notice him.

(*He hesitates, then takes up his box and goes in.*

Bad-Eye (*in the gap of silence announcing a fact as if to the whole world*). Bet that 265 sun's big as dis house.

Far. (*pityingly*). Big, gre't big. Gimme your Joo-harp and I'll play to it, saying, go down, old sun, keep going on down.

(BAD-EYE *hands it over and* FARROW *lies back playing it.*

Parr (*strangely*). Say on while I bury 270 the dead.

Bad-Eye (*shyly and not yet crushed by* FARROW's *ego*). Look like a gre't big ortymobile wheel.

Uzz. Cannon-ball take a hundred years to reach that sun, traveling all the time. 275

Far. Ever see that milky road 'cross the sky at night, Bad-Eye? Has? God's big road where he drives in his chariot.

Bad-Eye. Chariot? — Go 'way! (*As* FARROW *nods conclusively*) Who built dat road? 280

Far. God done it with stars for paving stones. Big road on earth, big road in heaven.

Bad-Eye. Um-um. What hold it up, den?

Uzz. (*calling*). Will the chillun ride on that heavenly road? 285

Parr (*throwing down his paper*). Good God, hush yo' fuss, man! (ZEB VANCE *enters carrying a melon under his coat. He gestures slyly to* FARROW *to follow, and* FARROW *rises quick as a flash, but* PARR *spies him.*) Heigh you, Zeb Vance, bring that melon back!

Bad-Eye. Melon! 290

(STERLING *grabs* ZEB VANCE *as he and* FARROW *try to dart away at the left.*

Ster. Now let yo' mammy have some.

(ZEB VANCE *makes the best of the situation and starts to cut the melon as the others crowd around him.*

Quiv. (*wiping her hands on her apron in anticipation*). What kind is it, honey?

Zeb. Silver sugar-meat, he said. (*Eyeing it in perplexity*) Seem mighty tough.

(*He makes another effort at cutting it.*

Far. Git a' ax and bust it. 295

(ZEB VANCE *lifts it in his hands and flings it against the ground. It bounces along like a rubber ball.*

Zeb (*springing on it with a shout*). God-damned white man done sold me a citron! (*The Negroes look on in stupefied disappointment a moment and then roar with laughter.* ZEB VANCE *grabs the melon up in his arms and starts running off to the right. Then he stops in the alley and finally turns back, half-whining.*) Wisht that thing was busted on his haid.

He rolls the citron angrily under the house, then goes over and picks up the horseshoes. He and FARROW *begin throwing them.* BELLE UTLEY, *the queen of Potter's Field, comes in at the left. She is a beautiful yellow girl, showily dressed, with round apple-painted cheeks and thick bobbed hair*

Parr (*smirking and bowing*). Come right in the shop. Yes, ma'm — everything 300 just waiting foh you.

(ZEB VANCE *and* FARROW *stop their game a moment and stand looking at her admiringly.*

Belle (*in a studied teacherish voice*). You all sure look nice and comfortable sitting in the cool. Beau haven't kicked you, have he, Seeny? 305

(*Laughing she goes on into the barber shack,* PARR *following and looking down at her hips and legs.*

Zeb (*whistling*). De purtiest woman in dis world!

Far. Lawd, King Bantam, come home from dat road!

Belle (*in a silvery voice from within*). Look at this man pumping me up — ooh. 310

(PARR *is seen working the barber chair up to the right height, with* BELLE *sitting in it.*

Seeny (*enviously*). Let Belle keep proudin'!

Some day, hyack, little dogs bark at her skirt.

Far. (*astounded*). Hyah, you! Cut out that rough talk!

Seeny. Hush, old sappy bones!   315

> (*She starts angrily out of the yard at the right.*

Far. (*throwing down his horseshoes and following after her*). And when I slaps you —— (*He catches her by the arm and tries to pull her back.*) You come set down.

Quiv. Ain't gonna have no rowing 'round my house, heah me?

> (BAD-EYE *folds his hat under his head and lies down to sleep.* SEENY *suddenly bursts into tears.*

Zeb (*tapping his horseshoes aimlessly in his hands*). Never seed a woman wan't crazy   320 or sump'n.

> (FARROW *hovers over* SEENY *and in a flutter of love and warmth pets her up and hugs her to him.*

Far. Sugar-babe, sugar-babe! Darling woman.

> (*He kisses her and smooths back her hair.* UZZELL *slowly lets his paper fall to the floor and lowers his head into his hands.*

Seeny (*smiling and wiping her nose with her handkerchief*). I'm all right. (*Her chin quivering*) But you won't talk to me, Levin.   325

Zeb (*sniffling, smelling the air, his upper lip wrinkled back*). Little turkle doves!

Far. (*whispering something in her ear*). And git back befo' eight-thirty, honey.

Seeny (*rubbing his cheeks tightly between her hands*). I will, ah — sugar-pie.

> (*She looks deeply into his face and then as if half-ashamed runs off up the alley.*

Quiv. Levin, you 'bout worry that gal   330 to death. Why don't you marry her?

Far. (*Lying down on the porch and mocking the woman's voice which is still singing down the alley*).

"She broke the heart of many a po' man,
    She'll never break this heart of mine."

Uzz. (*explosively*). Got no heart to break!

> (*He mutters something to himself.*

Far. (*changing his tune*).

"O sing, sing, sing of Lydia Pinkham   335
And of her friendship for the female race.
She invented her vegetable compound,
And now the papers all publish her face."

Ster. Oh, me, me, could lie right here and sleep — sleep. (*Stretching his arms*)   340 Oooh-ooh—— (*Whispering to* MILLY *and kissing her*) Honey, honey.

Milly (*staring at him, her soul in her eyes*). Ah — ah ——

Zeb. You marry Seeny, Mr. Uzzell.

Far. (*stingingly*). And him with three   345 or four wives already. No 'count work mule.

Uzz. (*with a sort of agony*). Heigh!

Far. Be quiet and leave me lay where Jesus flang me. (*The blasting goes off again in the distance.*) Blow a hole in the great world   350 and lemme ride through on a dream. Blow — blow — blow! Blow Bantam home again! (*Turning and staring at* STERLING *and* MILLY) Uh-uh!

Belle (*with a high silvery laugh from the barber shack*). Lord, you smell me all up! Child, child!

Far. Belle getting ready to chloroform   355 that Sport Womack.

Parr (*to* BELLE *as he squirts perfume on her*). Make old Sport lose his senses — hah-hah!

Belle (*with another high laugh*). Now don't lose yours, black man.

WILLIE *comes out of the house and looks uneasily about the world, then sits down close to* OLD QUIVIENE *again*

Willie. What make 'em do dat?   360

Ster. (*chuckling indulgently*). Call to the white men, Willie, and tell 'em to quit.

Willie (*after a moment, calling in his high voice as he looks away toward the horizon*). Please suh, white folks, don't do dat blasting no mo'!

> (*They roar with laughter at him, and he sits down near his squirrel saddened and perplexed.*

Quiv. Smile, Milly, smile. Much her   365 up, Tom.

Milly (*sighing*). Seem like when Saddy evening come I'm always so tired I want-a just spread out like molasses or sump'n.

Ster. (*pulling her back across his chest*). Rest on this pillow, darly babe.   371

Willie (*in his thin piping voice*). Milly wuk too hard.   (*The others nod their confirmation.*

Milly. Woman with two babies can't rest in no plush rocking-chair.   375

Willie. Li'l Sonny gwine die somebody don't do sump'n.

Milly. Oh! Willie! Oh, he keeps saying it.

Quiv. (*giving him a smart slap*). Shet yo' mouth!   380

Willie (*whimpering*). My squirrel gwine die too.

Quiv. Well, let him. A squirrel ain't a human being.

    (*WILLIE stretches himself out on the floor, whining softly to himself.*

Zeb. Hush, Willie, I'll bring you a 385 Barlow knife from work a-Monday.

    (*He leaves the anvil and lies down in the yard fanning himself.*

Quiv. Hush now, and go build me up a fiah in the stove. Getting suppertime.

    (*WILLIE gets up and goes in. A guitar begins playing in a shack across the alley at the right. They all sit listening, saying nothing. After a moment the whistle and roar of the Florida Limited are heard across the valley. Some of them move from their places and stand in the yard looking off up the alley like eager expectant children. The train comes on like a rising storm, its melodious whistle splitting the sky.*

Milly (*waking and staring up in STERLING's face as she listens*). Oh, honey, if we could just get on that train and ride — ride forever 390 and never think of trouble.

Ster. (*laughing softly and happily by her face*). Trouble — trouble. You ain't gonna have no mo' trouble now.

Milly (*searching his face and then smiling*). Yeh — oh yeh.

Zeb. Dere she come!   395

    (*Along the side of the bluff that shows above the shacks in the distance a train dashes with a shower of sparks and smoke, the low-running locomotive seeming to stretch its neck forward like a racing black stallion, and*

the lighted windows of the coaches flying behind with a tail of flame in the dusk. The Negroes stand gazing off, lost in a deep wonder and delight.

Far. (*with a long-drawn-out, throaty cry*). Ho — t — dawg!

    (*The others nod jubilantly at him and to themselves and gradually return to their places without a word, a few of them cutting steps, or gesturing with their hands, expressive of the longing each one feels. The blasting sounds again, and the romance and wonder die from their faces.*

Zeb. Feel de ground shake.

A moment passes, and then across the alley at the right a hullabaloo sets up, and a woman flies out of a shack. She stops in the alley, looking back, waving her hands about and crying to the silent houses. FARROW and ZEB VANCE go lazily over to the edge of the yard and look out

Quiv. Quit that fussing over there!

Far. The law! the law! (*To PARR*) You gonna have to bury that Sude some these 400 days.

A big black man of middle age reels down the steps of the shack across the street, brandishing a guitar in his hand. A little boy of seven or eight comes out on the porch behind him and stands laughing

Dode Wilson (*wandering around in his yard*). Whah's dat 'oman. I'll wring her chicken neck, God damn her! (*To the boy*) Whah she, Doodle?

Quiv. (*as if speaking to the air*). Po' 405 Dode, his mind's failing away.

Doo. (*laughing*). Hunt foh her, Pappy. Hunt foh her.

Sudie (*wailing*). Doodle!

Dode. I heah her.   410

    (*He stumbles across the yard toward the alley. FARROW signals to SUDIE, and she runs weeping into OLD QUIVIENE's yard. She is a little pasty-faced woman of forty, snaggle-*

toothed and thin. Her hard rounded breast-bone shows above her torn dress like a piece of wood.

Milly (waking up). What's the matter, Sude?

Dode (now in the alley). Is she over dere, Quivie?

Quiv. (calling). No, she's gone on up the street! *(Softly)* Hush, Sude.   415

(The little boy on the porch bows up and down with laughter like a Punch and Judy figure.

Dode. Doodle, come heah.

(DOODLE comes down into the alley, takes his father by the hand, and leads him away.

Sudie. He gwine kill me some day.

(She puts the sickly whitish palms of her hands against her face.

Far. (coming over to her). Quit pecking on him and he won't. Hyuh. *(He pulls a pin from his shirt and fastens her dress up over her breast.)* Nuff trouble in Potter's Field with-   420 out you bringing the law with yo' screeching!

Sudie. He stays mad all de time.

(She falls to weeping again. BAD-EYE sits in the yard looking at her, his gnarled face full of infinite pity.

Far. (wiping her bruised mouth with his shirt-sleeve). Stop crying.

WILLIE *comes out of the house again and stands watching* SUDIE. DODE *comes along at the right, with* DOODLE *holding to his belt trying to pull him back. He is using his guitar like a walking-stick to feel his way*

Doo. She ain't in dere, Pappy.

(For awhile DODE stands listening.

Dode. I heah her.   425

(As he turns into QUIVIENE's yard, SUDIE shrinks away and stands behind STERLING, who catches DODE by the arm.

Ster. (kindly). This Tom got you, Dode. Now you rest easy.

Dode. Yeh, you over heah courtin' po' Bantam's wife. *(Crying out)* But what kin I do — do in dis darkness!   430

(STERLING leads him to the steps, where he sits down. He raises his sightless

face and begins singing in a hoarse voice.

"I ain't nothing but a broke down man,
Lying in the pa'm of God's great han',
And all my strength been taken away,
    Taken away.

"I heah'd God say he's bigger'n me,   435
Made de high mountains, dug de deep sea,
And all my strength been taken away,
    Taken away."

(DOODLE has motioned to WILLIE, who comes out into the yard. They draw a ring on the ground and shoot marbles while DODE is singing.

Sudie (sniffling). He sets and makes dem songs ag'in God.   440

Dode. Hush now, Sude, I ain't gwine bother you.

Doo. You got my taw. Dat glass un's mine.

(A low rumble of blasting is heard again.

Dode. Dere he go wid his blasting. *(Laughing)* His voice do tickle me and make me   445 laugh. Hah-hah! *(Opening upward the mouth of a tow sack he carries tucked behind his belt)* Yea, po' me down a blessing. Let a hambone fall down out o' heaben foh dis po' dog to gnaw on.

(The boarders look at him in half fear.

Belle (sitting in the barber chair and singing as PARR gives her the finishing touches with the curling irons).

"When you wore a tulip, a sweet yellow tulip,   450
And I wore a big red rose."
Don't burn me, big boy.

(The notes of her silvery laugh sprinkle and scatter over the scene.

Dode. Sweet Belle Utley and Sport Womack. — Love — love. *(Calling)* How you, Belle?

Belle (from the barber shack). Fine.   455 How you come on, Dode!

Dode (strumming his guitar in a halting accompaniment as he talks). Dis heah Dode Wilson down in de valley, Lawd. De man useter lay his thousand brick and plaster his fo' rooms a day. *(In a low mad-   460 dened hum)* All my strength been taken —— *(With a shout)* Heah me up dere!

Belle (*coming out of the barber shop*). Charge that till next time, Jimmie. (*Looking about her*) Good-bye — everybody. 465

Dode (*softly*). Bye, Belle.

　　　　　　(*She skips off at the left.*

Far. (*as* PARR *resumes his magazine and chair*). Done horned her wid dat old mustache — kerr — foo. Charge it!

　　　　(PARR *twists his mustache most man-nishly and settles himself in his chair.*

Far. Don't mind Sport'll bite it off for him.

　　　　(*He scampers around the yard, then falls down on his knees watching* DOODLE *and* WILLIE *at their mar-bles.* PARR *continues to twist his mustache like a cocky vaudeville villain and smile knowingly to him-self.*

Doo. (*angrily*). Venture dubbs. 470

Willie (*piteously*). I knocked two out.

Far. (*to* DOODLE). Hyuh, give Willie back his marbles.

　　　　(SUDIE *gets up and slips away home at the left, and* MILLY *goes back and sits with* STERLING, *lost instantly in her love.* QUIVIENE *rises and goes into the house.*

Dode. Tell 'em 'bout de po' man you read me last night, Doodle. 475

　　　　(*He sits with his head bowed over, his own misery filling the world for him.*

Uzz. Rest, Dode.

Dode. Dat you, Ed? Tell 'em, Doodle.

　　　　(DOODLE *reluctantly leaves his marbles and stands before them twisting his cap about.*

Doo. Will speak you a little bit 'bout de man God treated wrong. (*Reciting*) Dere was a man in de land of Ooz, a righteous and a up- 480 right man. And he was afraid of God and done good.

Dode (*whispering*). Yeh, said he done good.

Doo. And he had a gre't big farm wid cattle and thousand of sheep, and was plenty 485 good things to eat in dat big house. Den God looked over heaven's battlements and seen dat he was a big man, plenty money. And God said he gitting 'bout big and pow'ful lak

me, must do sump'n to weaken him down 490 —— (*As he goes on he begins to act like a Negro preacher in the pulpit, waving his arms and now and then letting out a throaty "hanh — hanh."*) Den God called de devil up on de phom and said, See dat man Job 'way down dere? You slip down dere and try him — yes — hanh — try him, see kin you break his speerit.

HENRY, *a stranger, comes into the yard from the right and stands near* DOODLE. *He is a well-dressed heavy man with a bluish sooty black face — wearing a derby hat, yellow gloves, a silk handkerchief protruding from his outer breast pocket, and a large rose in his lapel. He carries a small satchel in his hand. The boarders look at him in astonish-ment*

Doo. And de devil kicked up sand com- 495 ing to Job's house — and so fast he come sparks flewed out'n his heels and de grass burnt up and de trees wuh scorched and — and —— (*He stops as he sees* HENRY.) Dat's all I'll preach you dis time. 500

Henry (*smiling and showing a set of stout gold teeth*). And the people of the world saw the devil and thought it was a shooting star falling thoo that lonesome night.

Doo. (*in hushed delight*). Yeh, yeh, dey did.

Far. (*as they all watch the newcomer*). Good evening, suh. 505

　　　　(STERLING *raises himself up, looks out, and then lies suddenly back on the floor by* MILLY.

Henry (*winking at them all and singing in a low bass voice*).

"A black evil spirit, hanh?
One hundred years he slept in the hill,
Couldn't turn over,
Couldn't lie still.
They thought he was a rock deep under-
　　　ground, 510
And they blasted him out with the earthquake
　　　sound."

Far. Name of my soul!

Zeb (*satirically*). Eels and barking fishes!

Far. Shooting off his mouth in poetry.

Willie (*sitting down on his haunches near the*

door and eyeing the stranger fearfully). What's
his name?   516

Henry (laughing). My name is John Henry.[1]

*Far. (skipping up before him and peering at
him).* Why — why —

(Finally singing with weak braggadocio)

"This heah (the) hammer killed John Henry,
Killed him dead, boys,   520
Killed him dead.
Busted the brains all out'n my pardner,
In the head, boys, in the head."

Henry (singing impassively).

"Heard mighty rumbling, heard mighty rum-
bling,
Heard mighty rumbling under the ground. 525
Must be John Henry turning round.
Nine pound hammer, nine pound hammer,
Can't kill me, well, it can't kill me.
Nine pound hammer couldn't kill me.

(As if listening)

Up on the mountains I hear John Henry crying ——"   530

*(The blasting sounds again on the dis-
tant road.*

Willie (whimpering). Make him stop it.

Far. For Christ's sake!

*(Uzzell watches him with growing in-
terest. His face, before sagged and
dead, now seems alive. The others
look on not knowing what to say.*

*Henry (pulling a sheaf of papers from his
breast pocket and selecting one).* The Reverend
John Henry shall have power to ordain others
into the ministry of the Lord Jesus 535
Christ wherever and whenever found full of
grace and good works. Signed. *(Suddenly
arching his back over and staring* DOODLE *in the
face)* This young man is full of grace and
power. What's your full name?

Doo. Roosevelt Wilson. Call me Doo- 540
dle 'cause I used to ketch so many doodles.[2]

*(Chanting with his eyes closed and boring
downward in the air with his forefinger like an
auger bit)*

"Doodle-doodle, yo' house burning up,

---

[1] The name of a fabulous negro who lived in Louis-
iana, did feats of gigantic strength, and spoke in picturesque rhetoric or poetry.

[2] Doodle-bugs, larvae of the ant lion.

Doodle-doodle, yo' house burning up."

Henry. Thou shalt be consecrated.

Ster. Pshaw, he's a little boy.   545

Henry (staring close at STERLING *where he lies
on the porch).* This ain't — well, oh — pardon
me, pardon me.

Ster. (steadily). My name's Tom Sterling.

Henry. Can see you a mighty man of valor
like Uriah[1] of old, Mr. ah-Sterling.   550

Ster. Thank you.

*(Henry turns calmly, picks up the
anvil, and raises it above his head and
lowers it three times. The boarders
burst out into exclamations of amazement.*

Henry. Take not His name in vain.

Parr (still eyeing Henry). Why, the strongest man I knowed in ——

Quiv. (appearing at the door). Come 555
help me with supper, Milly.

Far. This is the Reverend John Henry — a
preacher.

Henry. Could I get board here?

Quiv. No bed — but can feed you. 560
How long, suh?

Henry (his eye cutting by the group). 'Bout a
week, I suppose.

Quiv. Want supper?

Henry. If you please.   565

Quiv. It'll be ready soon. Make yourself
at home — Come on, Milly.

(She and MILLY *return into the house.*
HENRY *opens his satchel and takes
out a little black packet wrapped
tightly in a string.*

Henry (in a honeyed rolling voice). Little
dark secret wrapped in yellow gal's hair that
walks among flowers sucking their sweet- 570
ness. Told me in a dream while I slept high
up in the mountain.

Uzz. (whispering). Now — conjure balls.
Same old mess to fool the niggers.

Henry (smiling at them sweetly). Makes 575
me strong. *(Pulling another packet from his
pocket)* See. *(He lays them both down and tries*

---

[1] Uriah the Hittite, whose wife, Bathsheba, King
David loved. David therefore had him placed in the
front line of warriors at the siege of Rabbah, so that
Uriah might be killed (see *II Samuel*: 11).

to lift the anvil.) Can't do it. (*He puts the packet back in his pocket.*) Now I do it easy. (*He raises the anvil with one hand. The boarders are dumb with amazement.*) Can read 580 your names in it. Bad-Eye — Farrow — Zeb Vance, anxious to be married — I'm the preacher — Dode Wilson, father of Bantam and Doodle — Uzzell — Sterling, oh, — maybe — in love with another man's lady — 585 Parr, barber and undertaker. (*The boarders look at him with open mouths.* HENRY *stares down at the packet on the ground.*) Look at it — got life in it. See it move.

 (*He picks up a twig, touches it, and causes it to move along toward* BAD-EYE, *who springs out of the way terrified and trots across the yard on all fours. He crawls under the edge of the porch and catches hold of one of* STERLING'S *hanging feet.*)

Bad-Eye (*with a blubbering whicker*). Don't you set dat thing on me! 590

Henry. Some buy insurance, some pay the undertaker, some pay the doctor — dollars and dollars, and pore man never any better off. Ain't it so, Dode?

Dode. Dis mawnin' I went to de doctor. 595 Charged me five dollars to tell me I gwine stay blind. Sump'n working in my head lak gnats.

Bad-Eye (*upset as he watches the conjure packet*). Uh-uh!

Dode. What do it look like, Bad-Eye?

Bad-Eye (*sticking his head from under the porch*). Little black hairy thing big as a 600 dollar.

Henry. Never try to see what's in it — evaporates away like the morning dew — (*Surveying them*) Little packet for the men is called Emma — them for the women called Joe. 605 How come I got money, dressed so well, know so much, happy? My little package. How come you all so tired, miserable, weak, hungry, quarreling, fighting, ignorant? Got no little packet. (*He stops and eyes them.* 610

Zeb (*laughing*). Sell me one on a credick. Then I pay you with the good luck money I makes ——

Far. Now — now ——

Henry (*stopping and thinking*). Can give 615

somebody one — you — you — you? (*They all shake their heads.*) Now you watch and see him have good luck. (*He quickly sticks a packet into* ZEB VANCE'S *pocket.* DOODLE *follows his movements as if hypnotized.* ZEB VANCE *starts to take the packet out of his pocket.*) Nanh — Nanh — let it stay there and get to work. Maybe two hours — maybe 620 sooner — you begin to have good luck.

Far. Zeb, that thing sets you britches on fire.   (PARR *laughs.*

Henry. Maybe it don't like the smell of your body — soon get 'climated. 625

Zeb (*slapping himself*). Quit tickling me, Emma.

Henry (*to the others*). Have one and receive light to heavenly truth? (*Singing*) "Heaven, heaven, everybody talking 'bout" —— 630 Heah, son? (*He catches the waiting* DOODLE *by the shoulders and moves him into the ring drawn off for marble-shooting.*) Down on your knees. (DOODLE *kneels down with his hands crossed on his breast, his eyes lowered.* HENRY *takes a small Bible from his satchel and opens it.* OLD QUIVIENE *and* MILLY *come to the door and look out, a distrustful interest on* QUIVIENE'S *face.* HENRY *lifts up his hand and reads.*) "But some of them said, he casteth out devils through Beelzebub the chief of the devils. And 635 others, tempting him, sought out a sign from heaven. But he, knowing their thoughts, said unto them, Every kingdom divided against itself is brought to desolation; and a house divided against a house falleth." So 640 readeth the gospel according to Saint Luke. Lead us in a word of prayer, son.

 (*Henry gets down on his knees in the yard, motioning to the others to bow down likewise. But only* WILLIE *and* DOODLE *kneel, the others inclining their heads a bit forward.* BAD-EYE, *who has got over his fright, comes out and sits down on the steps, and leans his head over in his hands.* DODE *sits upright, and* UZZELL, *again in his chair, stares out towards the west, from which the light has all but died.*

Doo. (*his childish voice babbling in the falling*

gloom). Oh, Lawd, dis is Doodle, Lawd, and I wanter do dy will and preach de gospel to de sinners. I'se twelve yeah old, and I   645 wanter serve and I want you to make my pappy so he kin see ag'in. His name's Dode and he live down heah in Potter's Field. And take trouble from my mammy. Huh name's Sude. And I ain't much size yit, Lawd.   650

     (HENRY *stands up, and taking* DOODLE *by the shoulders dips him into an imaginary pool of water.*

Henry. I baptizes and ordains you in the name of the Father and the Son and the Holy Ghost.

     Zeb (*spontaneously*). Amen.   654

     Quiv. (*sharply*). You! Le's set the table.

     (*She and* MILLY *go back into the house.* HENRY *lifts* DOODLE *up and wipes his face and eyes with his flowing silk handkerchief as if drying away water.*

Henry. I give you yo' papers.

     (*He pulls out a paper like the former one, unstops his fountain pen, and writes.*

Doo. (*in a small voice to his audience as he jumps up and down*). Feel saved. Glory! Feel happy. Hallelujah! Jesus! (*Watching* HENRY *write, he makes a snuggling sound through his nose like a young pig sucking.*) Dat mine?   660

Henry (*folding the paper and handing it to* DOODLE). You are now ordained the Reverend Doodle Wilson, and go preach ye unto every name and nation. (*Lifting up his voice*) I let my power come unto you. Travel the paved street or miry road, the banks and   665 the hollows, seeing through the houses and walls to people's souls. And some will call you prophet and some will call you devil. And what you know, like me you will know. Amen.

     (WILLIE *turns over on his face and begins to whimper again.*

Zeb (*running up to* DOODLE *to look at the paper*). You's a real preacher now?   670

Doo. (*pushing him off with his elbow*). Hyuh.

     (BAD-EYE *gradually bends over from the steps and rests his knuckles on the ground like a huge ape, his face caught in a study over some problem.*

Sudie (*coming out on the porch across the street and calling*). Come on home, Dode!

Dode. I had gre't trouble wid my fust son, suh. Allus wildish sort in trouble and de law tuk him and put him away. Bantam   675 was his name — (*With sudden and pathetic eagerness*) Maybe, suh, you could —— (*with a half-outstretched hand*) My eyes, I mean ——

Henry (*staring at* DODE'S *face searchingly — then kindly*). Where God puts his mark, Dode, no man can rub it out.   680

Dode (*sadly*). Yeh — (*to* DOODLE) Son!

     (*Led by* DOODLE, *he goes out at the right, singing in his hoarse voice.*

"I ain't nothing but a broke-down man
Laying in the palm of God's great hand,
And all my strength been taken away,
     Taken away."   685

     (HENRY *sits down in his chair and bows his head over. The others look at him in silence and stir restlessly about in the yard. The waning moon has come out in the middle of the sky and mixed a faint light with the gloom rolling in from the east. The figures on the porch and in the yard have lost their distinctness of outline and merged into the pallid twilight, appearing as if seen through a gauze or slightly moist glass. In the gap of silence* UZZELL *relights his pipe, and some of the others light cigarettes.*

Quiv. (*her voice calling as it does every day in the year*). Sup-per!

     (*At the same instant other women's voices in Potter's Field begin calling — "Supper — supper!"*

Far. Supper! Hot ziggity! (*He steps waveringly by* HENRY *and goes up into the house, singing with forced bravado as he goes.*) "Soupy — soupy — soupy."

     (BAD-EYE *follows after him, and* UZZELL, *rising, knocks the fire out of his pipe and goes in. As* ZEB VANCE *starts across the yard toward the steps,* FLOSSIE TUCKER *is heard calling off at the left.*

Flos. Yo-ho — Zeb!   690

> (ZEB *listens an instant, then turns and darts away. PARR gets up and locks his barber shop with a big barn lock. Then he starts sauntering off.*

Parr (*stopping by* HENRY). Brother Henry, how about filling our pulpit tomorrow?

Henry. So — so? Well, now I'll consider it, deacon.

Parr. Eleven o'clock sharp tomorrow   695 — the sabbath.

Henry. Good night. Sure, sure, I'll do it.

Parr. Good night.

> (*He chuckles softly to himself and goes away at the right.* HENRY *stares after him a moment, then picks up his satchel and goes toward the house.* STERLING *moves forward and bars his way.*

Ster. (*in a low voice*). I didn't know you at first. But now I do — when you lifted   700 that anvil.

Henry. I've done told you my name.

Ster. You changed your color.

Henry (*with mock courtesy*). A little chemical mixtry, suh.   705

Ster. I've met you —

Henry. 'Way down in Gawgy on a hog? I know you too, brother.

Ster. (*levelly*). And you know nothing but good about me.   710

Henry (*chuckling*). Sure, sure. And I'll hold my peace.

Ster. (*with sudden and low vehemence*). Since I come here to work I'm living straight! I'm gonna marry and do right. All the past   715 is past.

Henry. Ain't the good life my specialty? I congratulate you, brother.

Ster. Stop it.

Henry (*huskily*). Who tells Henry to   720 stop what?

Ster. All right — all right. But remember — if anything happens you're to blame.

Henry (*amiably*). So-so. Stay quiet, brother, and I stay quiet.   725

> (HENRY *lays his hand gently on* STER-LING'S *shoulder, but he shakes it off.* STERLING *turns and goes up into the*

house. HENRY *waits a moment and then puts a little green packet at the foot of the china tree. The blasting sounds in the distance, louder, more ominous. He straightens up listening.*

Quiv. (*calling inside the house*). Supper — supper —

> (HENRY *adjusts his tie and goes up on the porch, clearing his throat in announcement as he approaches the door.*

Curtain

SCENE 2

A few minutes later. The front wall of OLD QUIVIENE'S *boarding shack has been removed and we can see the interior of the house, lighted by an oil lamp. There is a sort of lean-to at the back where the cookstove is. A bed is in the left rear corner of the main room, and farther front to the left a door which leads into the little shed. In the center is the eating table, around which the boarders are crowded eating away. At the right front is a smaller table where* HENRY *sits alone, eating his supper in great mouthfuls. More than once he rakes out a dish which* AUNT QUIVIENE *politely passes on to him — much to* FARROW'S *sorrowful astonishment. A huge white handkerchief, large as a small table cloth, is tucked under his chin.* STERLING *is standing on the little porch outside leaning against the corner of the house.* MILLY, *who has been waiting on her babies in the shed room at the left, notices his absence from the table and comes out to him. He moves restlessly from the porch and steps down into the yard, she following.*

Milly (*clutching his hand*). What's the matter?

Ster. Nothing.

Milly. Yes, they is.

Ster. Nothing.   5

Milly. Everything'll be all right some day.

Ster. Some day — yeh, yeh.

> (*He wanders over to the left.*

Milly (*putting her arms around him*). I do love you so.

Ster. (*suddenly drawing her to him and kissing her*). And me you — me you. And 10 you'll always love me no matter what happens?

Milly. I will — always. (*He pulls her tightly to him and stares hungrily down in her face.*) What makes you get to thinking like this, honey?

Ster. (*almost harshly*). Ne' mind.   15

Milly (*childishly*). Something upset you?

Ster. No, no.

Milly. Three mo' weeks we'll have a little house all to ourselves. Think of that, honey, we will!   20

Ster. (*softly*). I do. Go back now — I wanter think.

> (*She gives him a long kiss and returns to helping* QUIVIENE. *After a moment he hits the side of the post with his knuckles and goes up on the porch again.*)

Far. (*as* STERLING *enters*). Po' Tom's got the fo' day blues coming on. What that preacher, suh, mean — seem to think you 25 somebody else?

Ster. (*sitting down at the table*). You keep begging for trouble, Levin.

Quiv. (*from the lean-to at the back where she is working at the stove*). Yo' babies crying again, Milly.   30

Milly (*wearily*). They're hungry — but they won't eat.

> (*She goes into the shed room.* STERLING *rises from the table and follows her.*

Henry. Them twins in there belong to Milly Wilson and their daddy's named Bantam Wilson, and he's on that long road, anh? 35 Ta — room go the blasting — dig — dig — dig —anh!

> (*He pulls a pair of beribboned glasses from his pocket — fastens them carefully on his nose, then looks genially around him and falls to eating again.*)

Uzz. (*muttering laconically*). Dig — dig!

Henry. Yes, my good man.

A car is heard coming down the alley, its horn honking pridefully as it draws up by the

house. FARROW *rises and comes down the porch as* SPORT WOMACK *enters the yard*

Sport (*in a drawling voice*). Hy.   40

Far. Hello, Raleigh Sport — old frazzle tail.

> (SPORT *is a small slender Negro of twenty-five dressed in a gray suit, a gray felt hat, shining black oxfords, and withal the despair of fashion. A diamond pin sparkles in his silk cravat.*)

Sport. Thought mebbe could take you and Seeny foh a little drive in the rumble seat.

Far. (*forlornly*). I swear! But she's up at the Cafeteria. Be back adder while though. 45

Sport. Well — we'll drive around and come back later — say so?

Far. Right as rain.

Belle (*from the car*). Yoo-hoo, Levin!

Levin. Yoo-hoo, Belle!   50

Sport. Heah baby calling? (*He digs* FARROW *in the side.*) Purty moonlight, boy.

Far. (*slapping him in turn*). Um-um, ain't it?

Sport. Two haystacks in a big field by the woods. A little road leads that way.   55

Belle. Yoo-hoo!

Far. Yoo-hoo. Loving Momma honing foh sweet clover grass. (*Bending double in his gale of laughter, his face bursting with merriment*) Now — now — done said.

Sport. Yeh, done said. — bye, old beau- 60 hunkus — see you after supper.

> (*He goes away.* FARROW *stands staring after him, then turns back on the porch as the car is heard driving off.*)

Far. (*listening to the music of the motor*). I'm gonna ride like that someday, Goddamn I am!

Henry (*from inside the house, with a chuckle*). No, you won't, for the crap-shooters know your soul. Roll, Little Phoebe, lie still, Little 65 Dick! (FARROW *goes sharply into the house and slinks by* HENRY *to his seat. Foolishly he picks up an empty dish and scrapes it wrathfully out.* SEENY *comes tripping into the lean-to at the rear. She begins washing her face and dolling herself up before a mirror that hangs on the wall.*

Far. Oh, there you is, light of the summer's eve! (*He gets up and goes into the rear shed and is seen telling* SEENY *about* SPORT'S *invitation. She seems tickled at it and gives* FARROW *a pecking slap on the cheek.* UZZELL *raises his head and stares around at the two.*

Seeny (*with a round resonant voice as she comes down to the table*). How you all come on now? (*To* HENRY, *who rises somewhat mockingly courteous*) Good evening, suh. 70

Henry (*displaying his gold-chained vest as well as his gold front teeth*). And how do you do?

Far. Miss Gray, meet Mr. John Henry — Reverend John Henry. Maybe the great steel-driving man, maybe not-new preacher — 75 (*whistling*) — and we don't know what he is.

Seeny (*stretching out a quick impetuous palm*). Glad to meet you.

Henry (*bowing over it unduly long*). The pleasure's mine, all mine.

Seeny. Where'd you come from, Rev- 80 erend Henry?

Henry (*winking broadly at* FARROW, *who looks back at him with a puzzled face*). Mebbe out of the great darkness. (*Pulling out his watch again*) Now reading eight-twenty and a half, railroad time. (*Singing*) 85
"Tumbled me out with the thunder's howl,
Little dogs whistle, the bad boys growl."

Far. Said they blasted him out'n a hill.

Seeny (*archly*). Really?

Willie (*with a squeal*). I heah dat old 90 blasting again.

Quiv. (*listening*). Why — pshaw — they ain't no blasting.

Suddenly there is a great scamper in the yard outside and ZEB VANCE *comes running in, opening a suit box as he enters*

Zeb (*going up into the house and singing*). "Come all you rounders if you want to see What the U.S. mail done brung to me." 95
(*He hurries up to the table, opens the box, and pulls out a new suit of clothes.*

Far. (*crowding forward*). He's got sump'n — sho' 'nough.

(ZEB VANCE *begins trying on the coat.*

Zeb. Sweet spirits of nitre! How do she fit, folkses? (*He pirouettes around the floor.*

Bad-Eye (*enviously*). Look lak it growed 100 on you.

Far. (*as he fumbles in the box*). I swear to — Hyuh's a letter.

STERLING *and* MILLY *come in from the shed room and stand looking on*

Zeb (*opening the letter — with a shout*). Pole- cats and buzzards — a nice strip of green- 105 back! (*He crams it into his pocket.* HENRY *stands watching him blandly, his thumbs in the armholes of his vest.*

Far. (*turning excitedly around*). They's sump'n to it — they is!

Zeb (*cake-walking about and singing*).
"Well, she said unto her momma —
Momma, what you think of this? 110
A sporting guy with a new suit on
Gimme a loving kiss —
    He'll be my man —
    He'll be my man."
(*With a whoop*) Shake hands, everybody. 115
I'm free and twenty-one. Going in here and try on the britches.
(*With the gesture of a girl he wriggles off into the shed room with his box.*

Seeny. Zeb'll be in devilment now. Go wake Flossie Tucker out of bed.

Far. (*singing*).
    "Get him Momma mad, 120
    Make his soul glad" ——

Zeb (*suddenly reappearing in the door at the left*). Land o' Goshen! One o' them Emmas was in my pocket.

Henry. I told him he'd have good luck, Mrs. Lockley. 125

Quiv. Had good luck befo' you come, suh.

Seeny. Bet you an interusting preacher, Reverend Henry.
(*The blasting sounds suddenly through the night.* HENRY *grabs up a cup from the table.*

Henry (*peering into the cup*). Believers, on-believers! Peoples in the valley. (*Lift- 130 ing up his voice*) Peoples on the mountain, listen to the word!
(FARROW *throws up his hands in joyful yet uncertain scorn.*

Seeny. Look out, Levin. That man maybe

got power. *(Softly)* Yeh, he got power, strange power.   135

Henry (passing his hand back and forth before his eyes). I see sorrow and I see pleasure. Both pleasure and sorrow I see.

Uzz. (reaching his fork for a biscuit). And where do you see 'em, brother?

Henry. I sees the face of Levin Farrow.   140 And it looks mighty sad.

    (SEENY *cackles out loud, and* FARROW *moves his chair around in discomfiture.* WILLIE *backs away from the table, goes over to the corner at the right rear near the lean-to and stands looking on in fear.* BAD-EYE, *now full of food and nodding in spite of himself, has laid his head over on the table.*

Far. (suddenly afraid). Cut out that prosticating!

Henry. In the first place I see you about to lose your gal.   145

    (FARROW *turns quickly and looks at* SEENY.

Seeny (tossing her head as FARROW *eyes her).* Ooh — say on.

Henry (impressively). In the second place I see pleasure.

Far. That makes it equal, then — first sorrow — then pleasure.   150

    (*He beams unsteadily around at the others, who with the exception of* BAD-EYE *watch* HENRY *with growing interest. Even* UZZELL *turns his chair around, waiting to see what will happen.*

Henry (bending low over the cup). What do I see? *(Suddenly shouting)* Bad-Eye, Bad-Eye!

Bad-Eye (starting up with a clatter). Who dat call my name so loud?

Willie (quavering). He done see sump'n   155 in dat cup 'bout you. Keep away f'om it.

Bad-Eye. Dat bizness? *(Looking around for his hat)* Great Lawd — spell bizness!

Henry. I see money waiting for you here and yonder.   160

Uzz. Yeah, waiting for him to dig it out'n a ditch.

Henry (staring more intently in the cup). See it on top o' the ground. There's a stump —

there the jamb of a fence, a tin can under   165 a sill, and look, look, there's a little tree with something at the foot of it. Now the little tree comes plainer, look like a chaney tree — see a' anvil close by — see a little something green lying there, waiting for Bad-Eye to pick   170 it up. *(They all look at him mystified, and some of them cut their eyes around toward the yard.*

Zeb. I'll go see, Bad-Eye.

    (*But* BAD-EYE *suddenly springs from his seat and comes tearing down the porch into the yard. He strikes a match and crawls around under the china tree looking at the ground. Some of the others in the house rise from the table and stand looking out through the door.* BAD-EYE *grabs a packet up out of the dirt and stares at it stupefied.*

Bad-Eye (murmuring). Ain't nothing but a fixment o' some kind.

    (*The burning match dies down into a coal against his fingers.*

Zeb (from the porch). What you got   175 there?

Bad-Eye (sticking what he found into his pocket and returning to the table). Nothing.

    (ZEB VANCE *goes in after him.*

Henry. Look, he found it.

Far. (walking excitedly about the room, a greedy anxiety written on his face). Did you find sump'n, Bad-Eye?   180

Henry. Tell 'em, Bad-Eye. Plenty more waiting when you git a little Emma in your pocket.

Bad-Eye (pulling out three one-dollar bills). Found dat.

Far. Jerking Jesus — greenbacks! —   185 Three dollars!

    (*He pulls* ZEB VANCE *out on the porch at the left and whispers to him.*

Bad-Eye (his crossed eyes gleaming). Whah's some mo'?

Henry (shrugging his shoulders). Put a little Emma in your pocket, soon it'll come   190 to you in a dream.

Bad-Eye (muttering). Gimme one dem things quick.

Henry. And the little price is five.

Bad-Eye (*throwing the three dollars on the table and adding two dollars to it from his breast pocket*). Heah she is. 195

 (HENRY *gets a packet from his satchel and slips it into* BAD-EYE'S *hand.*

Quiv. (*draining down a cup of coffee*). The mischief!

Far. Lend me five dollars. Come on, Buddy, he'll change that bill.

 (ZEB VANCE *hands him the ten-dollar bill, and they turn back into the room.*

Henry. Any more want to know the fu- 200 ture?

Far. Don't believe nothin' in it, but gimme one.

Henry. Nunh-unh, must believe first.

Far. All right, I believes. 205

 (HENRY *gets another packet from his satchel and gives it to* FARROW *for the ten dollars and returns him the change.*

Henry. Bad luck working ag'in you. Mebbe about two days your luck'll turn.

Far. Sho' damn better turn soon or they'll be a ruckus.

Quiv. (*starting up*). Ain't that Zeb 210 Vance's ten dollars?

Zeb (*who has got the five dollars change back from* FARROW). Just lending him a little.

Quiv. Don't want no more of that, Reverend Henry, in my house, nary another bit of it. You give my son back his money. 215

 (*She eyes* HENRY *unflinchingly.*

Henry. Yes, ma'am — and if I don't ——

Quiv. Then I orders you out of my house, and furdermore ——

Henry (*with comic malevolence*). Want me to tell something 'bout the white college 220 students used to come out here and raise fun with you and the other gals? Power of my God, I hear you!

Quiv. (*her snuff brush working up and down in anger*). Shet up that fuss, please, suh.

Henry. Want me to prophesy 'bout the 225 big white man now going round with the governor? The great white man that stand high — way up yonder like the sun? ——

Quiv. (*flurriedly stacking up the dishes*). Hush, hush, it's all done past.

Henry (*looking in his cup*). See he's the 230 same man sent po' Bantam Wilson to the roads. A judge! A judge! Oh, yus, oh, yus, come into court! Call yo' daddy's name, Mr. Vance! — way down here in the valley — see do he answer you. Hah — hah — he the 235 man sent you that ten dollars and suit of clothes on yo' birthday.

Quiv. (*shrilly*). I don't want you for a boarder no more! Go away from here, if you please, suh. 240

Milly (*uneasily*). We better put the babies to bed, Tom. (*They start towards the shed.*

Henry (*looking towards the door and eyeing them*). Fixing for a wedding? Better watch clost. I'm your spiritual friend. (*Looking in the cup again and letting out a great long-drawn "Ooh-ooh"*) Seem like I see Bantam 245 Wilson coming home from the road! (*Throwing the cup against the floor and breaking it to pieces*) And that's the end of my say tonight. (*He pulls a coin out of his pocket and goes over to* OLD QUIVIENE.) Bad luck not to break the cup, and here's a quarter to buy you five more. Sorry, but the spirit moves in me tur'ble 250 strong.

Quiv. Lord have mercy, keep it back from me! (*He throws the coin on the table and sits down silent by the stove. Putting his gold-rimmed glasses on his nose again, he begins reading his Bible.* QUIVIENE *bears a stack of dishes hurriedly into the kitchen.*

Bad-Eye (*talking to himself in amazement*). Seem like my mind see a ol' shack in a field.

Henry (*softly*). Emma working. 255

ZEB VANCE *sits hunched over on his seat at the table.* SPORT *and* BELLE *come into the yard at the right — snuggled up lovingly*

Belle. You an' me could do well enough alone. (*Kissing him*) Ah, Sport — Sport.

Sport (*chuckling*). Company make a sweet little picnic, baby, under this harvest moon.

 (*He kisses her.*

Zeb (*going up to* HENRY). Could I have 260

a little business in de alley with you — say in about ten minutes ——

Henry. I'll be right there, Mr. Vance.

Zeb. Thanks. Five dollars foh the job, suh?

Henry. Satisfied.   265

Sport (*releasing* BELLE *and calling*). Heigh, Levin!

Far. (*jumping up*). Ready, Seeny?

Seeny. Aunt Quivie wants me to help with the dishes.   270

Far. Willie's going to help her.

> (*But she gets up and busies herself about the table.*

Far. (*calling at the front door*). In a minute, Sport!

Sport (*with* BELLE *snuggled up against him again*). Take yo' time!

> (FARROW *turns and watches* SEENY *in perplexity as she carries an armful of dishes into the rear shed. A low chuckle breaks from* HENRY.

Far. Come on, gitting late.   275

Henry (*singing to himself*).

"When I get 'bout forty more dollars
Take my hammer to the Captain,
Tell him I'm gone, boys,
Tell him I'm gone."

Seeny (*coming in again*). I can't go   280 tonight, Levin.

Far. (*licking his lips*). Scabby Barnabus! (*Turning about the room and sputtering with helpless anger*) Don't let him come here and break things up like that!

Henry. Me? Don't try to hurry Emma   285 too fast.

Far. Emma, hell!

Zeb. Turn yo' year dis way.

> (*He comes up to* FARROW *and whispers something to him.* FARROW *nods a sullen agreement. They get their caps.*

Far. (*to* SEENY). Next time you call me, I won't answer.   290

> (*He and* ZEB VANCE *come out of the house and go into the alley at the right.*

Sport. Ready? Horse done pawing up the ground.

Far. Take your momma and ride on.

Madame Hootchie-Kootchy ain't going to-night.   295

Sport. Oo-la-la.

Belle. Don't get to grieving, Levin. Come, see me tomorrow, I'll rub your head.

Sport. Hah-hah-hah.

> (*But* FARROW *makes no answer as he and* ZEB VANCE *go up the alley.* SPORT *and* BELLE *go out at the right. In the shed room at the left,* TOM STERLING *sits down on the edge of the bed and takes* MILLY *into his lap.*

Ster. Honey child.   300

Milly. Yeh, sweet — ah ——

Ster. Want to ask you something.

Milly (*sitting up in alarm*). What is it, Tom?

Ster. — Want to ask you let's move away from Potter's Field.   305

Milly. We are, honey, in three more weeks.

Ster. Tomorrow.

Milly. Tomorrow?

Ster. Soon, honey, soon.

Milly. What's wrong?   310

Ster. Nothing.

Milly. We can't tomorrow. We can't go away together till — till — we're married.

Ster. But soon?

Milly. We will, honey. What is it?   315

Ster. We'll go to a better town. Won't we?

Milly. Yes, honey.

Ster. I love you. — (*Brokenly*) Ain't no woman like you — I love you so.

Milly (*kissing him passionately*). And   320 I do you.   (*He rocks her in his arms.*

Quiv. (*from the kitchen*). Help me with these dishes, Willie.

> (WILLIE, *who has been trying to feed his squirrel in its cage by the back wall, sighs and goes into the kitchen.*

Bad-Eye (*who has been sitting at the table in a study*). See dat old house shining in de moon-light.   325

Henry. Right, right. Go get your money, keep searching.

Bad-Eye. Sho' 'nough? Yeh, yeh.

> (*He hurries down out of the house and goes off by the barber shack.*

Uzz. (*hoarsely*). What time by your squash?

Henry (*whistling*). Once I saw an old   330

bird setting on a winter nest. Squash? No, mine's a love melon — exactly.

Uzz. I'm too old to play with.

Henry. Oh, I understand you. And you me? 335

Uzz. And me you.

Henry. Hah-hah-hah.

Uzz. (*wryly*). Hah-hah-hah.

Quiv. (*from the rear*). Come dry the dishes, Willie. 340

SEENY *comes in with a wet cloth and begins scrubbing off the table.* UZZELL, *who has stood up to go, moves over and stops by her*

Uzz. A little drink of water.

Seeny (*looking at him out of the depths of her smiling eyes*). Cool drink of water.

Henry (*singing, as he thumbs his Bible*). "Cool drink of water 'fore he dies."

> (SEENY *takes a dipper of water from a bucket in a chair near* WILLIE'S *squirrel cage and sticks it out toward* UZZELL. *He takes the dipper with one hand and with the other catches* SEENY'S *outstretched palm.*

Seeny (*softly, as she looks at* HENRY'S *bowed back*). Ed, Bad Ed, you used to be.

Uzz. (*with a wretched sigh*). Seeny 345 girl, don't do it.

> (*He glances slowly behind him and then looks hungrily at her.*

Seeny (*with quiet hardness*). Old hawks and young pullets, you've said so much.

Uzz. (*his writhing smile playing about his lips — whispering*). I like you, Seeny.

> (SEENY *pulls her hand from his and goes back into the kitchen.* UZZELL *returns the dipper to the bucket and stands thinking, his hands shoved deep into his pockets.*

Henry. In the darkness of the valley. 350 But the weary struggler must keep climbing.

Uzz. Up the mountain that never ends.

> (HENRY *says no more.* SEENY *comes to the back shed door.*

Seeny (*petulantly*). Now why has Aunt Quiviene gone to crying?

Willie (*in the kitchen*). Stop, Mis' 355 Quivie child, you make me cry.

Uzz. (*jocularly*). Eigh, sister! (*As near to a chant as he ever gets*) "Let the tears come twinkling down like rain."

Henry (*singing*). "Let the tears come 360 twinkling down like rain."

Uzz. (*coming out on the porch*). Good night, everybody. See you in the morning, let us hope. 364

He stands whistling a moment to himself and then goes off across the yard to the left. In the shed at the left MILLY *has gone to sleep in* STERLING'S *arms. Presently he lifts her up and sits down in a rocking-chair and begins rocking her. With one hand, he reaches over and turns down the lamp to a faint flame. The blasting sounds again. By the barber shack a* NEGRO *creeps up and stands in the moonlight as if listening. He is an ebony-black little fellow, squat, agile, and ape-like, with slender legs and powerful shoulders. His massive hands hang down below his knees. Peeping around the edge of the shack, he sees the bent figure of* HENRY *through the door. He starts with a low exclamation of surprise and then gives a low sly whistle.* HENRY *raises his head up and listens*

Henry (*after a moment, calling to* SEENY). So hot I'll take a little fresh air in the yard till you're ready, Miss Gray.

Seeny. In a moment, Reverend Henry.

> (HENRY *comes down into the yard. The* NEGRO *by the shack whistles softly again.*

Henry (*moving indirectly toward the shack and chanting his information as if to himself*).

"Some fair weather and right much cloud,
    Better sit easy and not crow loud." 370
(*He turns suddenly and grabs the little* NEGRO *by the collar.*) You the biggest fool that ever walked!

Little Negro (*standing still and docile*). Easy, big Sampson, and don't scrush my neckbone.

Henry (*dropping his hands*). What you 375 doing here?

Little Negro. Thought I'd take a little fresh air too.

Henry. Them officers'll be here in an hour after you.   380

Little Negro. Not hardly. I went to bed early — sick. A wad of guano [1] sacks is sleeping in my bed.

Henry. You're a big fool for a little man.

Little Negro. Yah, but you and me 385 gonna leave here 'fore sun-up. Get Sport to take us away. Two days and I be sleeping in de nests of Harlem.

Henry. How come and these sheep need a shepherd?   390

Little Negro. Den I waits foh you some-whah, till you's gathered yo' wool. (*Gleefully*) Git a lot foh our pillow, my head wants a long rest. (*Threateningly*) Look heah, bo, I ain't run away from no roads — git it? 395 (HENRY *grows suddenly thoughtful.*) Talk up, I don't lak you when you gits dat silent way.

Henry (*pulling a paper from his pocket and handing it to the* NEGRO). Course you ain't 'scaped from no chain-gang, for here's your pardon. Just remember you been pardoned, 400 and show one of the Reverend's papers.

Little Negro. I declah, I declah, you use yo' head foh sump'n besides a knot at de end o' yo' spine. (*Looking at him*) You — you — what kind o' man is you?   405

Henry. Hah-hah.

Little Negro. Maybe sump'n ain't right about you. (*With a low musical laugh*) Would lak to see dat gyard's face. Dere he sot dis evening and heard you preach Jesus 410 to de convicts and you passing me out a song-book wid a file in it.

Henry. And I didn't mean you to go using it so quick either.

Little Negro. Hunh, done gone to work 415 here? I ain't gwine break it up. Fool — he didn't know you de same man was digging on that road wid me fo' months ago. Hee, hee, you was a yellow man der.

Henry (*feeling the little* NEGRO's *shoulder*). And you found the clothes under the 420 bushes.

Little Negro. Did, and de gat. (*Sharply*) How you fixed foh cash?

Henry. Freshet already beginning to rise.

[1] A fertilizer composed of bird dung.

Two more days and I'll break the dam. 425

Little Negro (*stretching out his hand*). Some foh de early mawning journey — mebbe?

Henry. Oh, so quick, little creeper.

(*He takes out a folder, extracts a bill, and hands it to him.*)

Little Negro. What you mean by right much cloud?   430

Henry. Ain't so fair for you in this hollow.

Little Negro. None de niggers ever tell on Bantam.

Henry. Better keep right on traveling, yes, right on traveling.   435

Ban. (*stirring uneasily*). Knows you mighty wise, but cain't go on right now. Gonna have a little sleeping wid my 'oman if hell freeze over. (*Intensely*) Ain't you see how sweet she is? (*Looking down at the ground*) And dem 440 chillun, I'd lak to see 'em.

Henry. 'Spose another man been muddying your spring.

Ban. Do and I kill him.

(*He puts his hand on his hip pocket.*)

Henry. Oh, but high-class love.   445

Ban. All right, den. After I'm through with her tonight he kin have her. Slip in and tell 'em a friend out heah.

Henry (*chuckling*). Have it your way, little man.   450

Seeny (*within*). I'm ready, Reverend Henry.

Ban. Henry?

Henry. Not Broadhurst or Jenkins or Bolis. (*Calling*) A moment, Miss Gray.

Ban. Woman a'ready?   455

Henry. Feeling out the land. (*Softly*) Never seen such grapes — such milk and honey.

(*He goes in.* QUIVIENE *has finished cleaning up and is sitting in a chair dipping snuff, every now and then lifting the lid of the stove to spit.* WILLIE *is lying on the floor looking at his squirrel.*)

Henry (*to* QUIVIENE). Sorry, but they's a friend of the family would like to see you all.   460

Quiv. Who is it?

Henry. Seems like he said his name Wilson — or something like that. Ain't a blind man, either.

Quiv. (starting up). Lord a-mercy!   465

Ban. (going up on the porch). Hy, Seeny.

Seeny (half afraid). My land o' living, look what the cat's brung in!

Ban. (going in). Nobody but me, Aunt Quivie. How you come on?   470

Quiv. How'd you get here?

Henry (interposing as BANTAM *hesitates).* He's been pardoned.

Ban. Yessuh. (*He pulls the paper out and waves it in his hand.*) Pardoned slam and in de full. Good behavior. But needn't say   475 nothing 'bout it till tomorrow. Wants to rest quiet at home tonight. Ain't dressed up much. (*With bland impersonality*) De goddamed white folks turn't me loose in these heah old clothes. Hell of a price foh a yeah's   480 work.

Quiv. (staring at him). Is you really free?

Ban. Is dat. And how is everybody? You too, Willie. I ain't gwine hurt you.

(*Debonairly he goes around, shaking their limp hands.*

Seeny (laughing). Same old Bantam.   485 I'll declare, seem good to have you back.

Quiv. Ain't gonna seem good to some folks.

STERLING *opens the door at the left and stands looking in.* MILLY *has thrown herself down across the bed in the shed room*

Henry (punctiliously). I want you gentlemen to meet one another and be friends for a short while. Mr. Sterling, this is Mr.   490 Wilson.

Ban. (sticking out a huge paw). Glad to meet you, suh.

(STERLING *stares blankly from him to* HENRY, *his face gradually setting into a sullen wrath.*

Henry (grinning). Just turned loose from the roads and mighty 'fectionate this evening.   495

Ban. (still holding his hand out). Bantam Wilson, suh, high stepper, Lawd, I'm gwine be free. (STERLING *continues gazing at him, saying nothing.*) Damn, don't seem so happy over sump'n. (*Turning and slapping* SEENY   500 *affectionately on the back*) And how's the old gal? Any yo' tail fedders missing?

Seeny. Ain't shedding time.

Ban. (his gaze sweeping by HENRY*).* Coming close to it.   505

Quiv. (stirring herself). Had your supper?

Ban. Could eat a little bit mo'!

Quiv. (with a glance by HENRY*).* Everything been cleaned out here. (*With forced gaiety*) Now you'll rest easy. Plenty good   510 work up at the college — and new warehouses going up in town — need men.

Ban. (lighting a cigarette). Sweating like a ball of tallow in de ditch — nunh-unh, not me. I sweated enough de last yeah.   515

Quiv. Got to live.

Ban. (nodding). Milly boa'd heah still? (*Nobody says anything.*) I say do Milly boa'd heah?

Quiv. Well, now — oh, she's round   520 and about.

Ban. (archly). Outdoors?

Quiv. Oh, mebbe not.

Ban. (smiling). Built to yo' house de last yeah?   525

Quiv. Built nothing.

Ban. (laughing). Den she cain't be in de house. (*He glances at* STERLING *as he blows rings of smoke into the air.*) You got only three rooms. De kitchen, dis room, and de   530 shed room dere. She ain't in de kitchen, she ain't in dis room, and she cain't be in dere. . . .

Henry (softly, a brief flash in his eye as he glances at STERLING*).* How come, Brother?

Ban. 'Cause dat's Mr. Sterling's room.

Quiv. Ain't Mr. Sterling's room.   535

Ban. Oh-ho, den goddam it what he doing in dat room wid her and de do' closed? (*Listening*) Seem lak I heah somebody a-crying in dere. (*Chuckling*) How de babies come on?   540

Quiv. 'Bout like when you left.

Ban. Sonny's feet turnt 'round yit?

Quiv. And they won't till a doctor straightens 'em 'round.

Ban. Damn de doctors. All dey do is   545 turn yo' pocketbook round. (*Listening*) Who dat crying? (*Calling*) Don't cry, Momma, yo' poppa done come home!

Ster. (controlling himself). My eyes don't tell me that.   550

Ban. (*bouncing around*). Who's talking so loud to King Bantam?

Henry (*singing slowly and deliberately*).
"There was a bad man Murdock
And he wore the ball and chain . . ."

Ster. Hush! Hush!   555
(MILLY *is heard sobbing loudly in the shed at the left.*

Ban. Hanh, ne' mind. (*Calling again*) Don't grieve, Momma, de comforter have come!

Ster. (*over his shoulder, keeping his eyes alertly on* BANTAM). Stop, Milly, I'll see to him.

Ban. (*his eyes shining, but his face never losing its smile*). Dat man ain't bad, he   560
just smell bad.

Quiv. (*quavering somewhat like* WILLIE *now*). Bantam'll kill you, Tom.

Ster. (*appearing more at ease*). Pardoned? He's broke loose from the roads. And this devil of a preacher mixed up in it.   565

Ban. Dat hardly relative to de case in hand, as de judge said. Wanter see my pardon?

Seeny (*coming up to* STERLING). Be easy with him, Tom.

Ban. (*guffawing in sudden fun*). Easy   570
wid me? He don't know I'm de baddest man in de hollow. Better tell him, folkses. Whup my weight in wildcats and cold steel. Onct I fou't a circular saw and broke out a handful of his teeth — haw-haw-haw.   575

Ster. Don't care how bad he is. If he lays hands on her, I'll fold 'em for him in his grave.

Ban. Dat sounds lak real talk, bo. (*With sudden pleasantness*) Well, you sho'   580
gyards dat do'. Reckon you wins, big boy.
(*Gradually* STERLING *somewhat relaxes his watchful attitude.*

Ster. You let her alone, I let you alone — that's all.

Ban. (*a piteous look spreading over his face*). Why you come stepping in 'twixt me and my 'oman? Twelve months breaking   585
dem rocks. Let her rain, let her shine, de old hammer swinging all de time. (*Spreading out his huge calloused palms*) Look-a-dere, dem horny hands. I broke enough rocks and drove enough steel down ——   590

Henry (*softly*). Steel driving.

Ban. And drove enough steel down — amm — from de end of Kayntucky to Alabam. (*Vehemently*) Twelve months and all de time no word from my 'oman. (*In a worker's   595
sing-song*)
"Let he up — hunh — let her down,
Muscle dat make — hunh — de world go 'round."
(*As* BANTAM *repeats his song,* HENRY *begins to sing and dig in pantomime. Suddenly he realizes what he is doing and stops before* SEENY'S *questioning eyes.* BANTAM *begins walking back and forth across the room by* STERLING *as he tells his woes.*

Ban. Dat sun and dat rain, and in de winter freeze. No wimmen and no wimmen to smoove de weary brow. Dey all skeahed.   600
(*Weaving his head from side to side*) And de white folks pass in deir cyars and de colored folks pass in deirn — on dat long, long road built wid our sweat and muscle power and bone — and dey look at you lak sump'n   605
quare. (*Savagely to all around him*) What you know 'bout it? (*To* STERLING *as he passes*) Wait till dey beat you and de blood run all over de barrel, yea, de barrel, same lak it was made to ketch it in. Talk 'bout de blood of   610
Jesus. (*Shaking his head, he reaches over and gives* SEENY'S *cheek a playful pinch.*) And den, honey, dem yaller gals come out in July wid deir sunbonnets on, picking blackberries by de way. And dey laugh, and deir laugh   615
sound cool, but dey stand way off. Skeahed of dem gyards, skeahed of de po' convicts. (*Fiercely*) And all de time my 'oman heah messing up wid him.
(STERLING *stands looking down at the floor.*

Henry. Yeah, him dat walks in freedom   620
while you wear the ball and chain.
(BANTAM *suddenly sticks his foot before* STERLING *and throwing his arm around his neck sends him sprawling across the floor. At the same time he whips out a pistol and stands in the door guarding it. With a loud laugh he continues his speech.*

Ban. But King Bantam Rooster never say

die. One night he come home and find a creeper fooling wid his bed — what he do? Why, mebbe lak I onct took a rock and 625 mashed a moccasin's head tried to bite me.

> (*He smiles quietly at* STERLING. *The blasting sounds again in the distance.*

Ster. (*gasping as he climbs to his feet*). I kill you! I kill you!

> (MILLY *is seen rising from the bed and going to the window.*

Quiv. (*moaning*). Go away, Tom, go away from here. 630

Seeny (*clinging to* STERLING). He'll shoot you!

> (WILLIE *suddenly seizes his squirrel cage and tears out through the shed at the rear.*

Ster. Get — get! I'll —

> (*He chokes with fury, staring at the pistol.*

Henry (*stepping before him*). Here, Mr. Sterling. It's his wife. In a little while 635 she'll be yours maybe.

Seeny. He knows, Tom, he knows.

> (STERLING *whirls upon him and strikes at him, but* HENRY *knocks the blow off with his arm. In the shed,* MILLY *raises the window and tries to jump out, but* BANTAM *runs in, seizes her, and drags her back.*

Ban. Ho, little Birdie, don't fly away! Dere, dere, honey. Gi' us a kiss. (*With a loud smack*) Dat's it, several of 'em, a whole 640 armful.

Milly. Tom, Tom!

Ster. I kill that Wilson!

Ban. (*cocking his pistol*). Nunh — unh, you won't. (OLD QUIVIENE *moans and rocks* 645 *in her chair.* BANTAM *stands in the door with one arm around the sobbing* MILLY, *the other grasping his gun. He coos over her.*) Momma, momma, pritty baby. (*Kissing the back of her neck*) 'Stress and grief make a 'oman so loving.

Seeny (*turning from* STERLING *and pulling at* HENRY'S *arm*). Come on! Come on!

Ster. (*quietly*). Let me loose. 650

> (HENRY *gradually releases him, and he stands bent over on the floor.*

Seeny (*laying her face against* HENRY'S).

Come on, come on. Take me 'way from here.

> (HENRY *waits a moment and then takes her arm.*

Henry (*giving* STERLING *a long look which gradually changes into a smile*). You ain't bad, and let everything rest. I'm your spiritual friend.

Quiv. (*rousing herself*). For God's sake, 655 Tom, git away and don't bring trouble on me!

> (*She pulls at* STERLING *in a frenzy of hen-like activity.*

Ban. I gi' you one minute and den trot. (MILLY *tries to claw at his face, but* BANTAM *holds her suffocatingly against him.* STERLING *stares at him blankly.*) Don't git wild, honey. — Heah me? I said one minute. De master's voice. 660

Quiv. Ain't nothing you can do, Tom.

> (*She sits down in her chair weeping.* STERLING *stares at* MILLY.

Ster. (*wetting his lips*). Plenty I can do. I done told him what if he lays hands on her.

Milly (*wailing*). Nothing — nothing! Go on, Tom. 665

> (STERLING *turns and comes out of the house, walks around in a circle a moment, and then as if deciding on something, runs suddenly away at the left.*

Ster. (*muttering as he runs*). I come back. I come back. (*Wagging his head*) Jesus, Jesus!

Ban. (*lowering his pistol and kissing his hand after him*). Good-bye, good-bye fohever. (*Turning back with* MILLY *into the shed room, his huge hands spread fan-like over her breast, as he pushes her before him*) Honey babe, you's a soft bunch of flowers. Nunh-unh, sweet. 670

> (*He closes the door behind them and is seen pulling her down to him. After a moment he bends far over and blows out the lamp.*

Henry. Come on, my lady.

> (*He picks up his satchel and derby from the cot, and taking* SEENY'S *arm, comes down out of the house.*

Seeny. Something gonna happen. Oh, it is!

Henry. The world keeps turning, things bound to happen. (*Pointing*) A big star by the moon. 675

Seeny (shivering). Sell me one them little balls.

Henry. Don't you worry, you don't need it.

Seeny (clinging to him). Never any man like you, Reverend Henry. *(Dreamily as she 680 leans against him)* Yes, look at that purty little star and the moon. Let's take a little walk. I'm not afraid, not with you.

Henry (chuckling and bending over her as they go across the yard). I'll be your shepherd, sister.

Seeny. And I yo' little lamb. 685

    (They go away up the alley at the right.

Quiv. (crawling up and making her way to the door at the rear). Willie, come back, honey! Ain't nothing to hurt you now!

    (She turns around, and goes heavily to the bed. Sitting down, she rocks her head back and forth in her hands. Presently she pulls off her shoes, drops her skirt, turns down the cover, and wraps herself up in the sheet. WILLIE comes cautiously in at the rear.

Willie. Whah is he?

Quiv. (her shoulders jerking with suppressed sobs). Shet the do' and git to bed, son.

    (WILLIE shuts the door at the front, blows out the light, takes off his shoes and trousers and crawls into bed with her. The room is dark, save for a dim trickle of moonlight that comes in from under the eaves of the porch. BAN- TAM'S caressing voice, broken by MILLY'S low sobs, is heard from the shed room as the convict goes to his long awaited rest. MILLY'S sobs gradually die away to low moans, and presently BANTAM is heard snicker- ing, even giggling. MILLY'S moans also gradually take on a different tone.

Willie. Fohgot my prayers. 690

Quiv. Yeh, better say 'em, honey.

    (WILLIE climbs out of bed, and crouch- ing on his knees, begins to mumble.

Willie. Our Father who art ——

Quiv. (joining in fervently as he mumbles in forgetfulness). — Thy kingdom come, thy will be done on earth as it is in heaven.

Willie and Quiv. Fohgive us our trus- 695 passes as we fohgive those who truspass against us ——

Willie (starting). Won't the p'lice come git Bantam?

Quiv. Hush! Won't bother him —— 700 Lead us not into temptation ——

Willie. Will they bother me?

Quiv. They won't bother you, baby —— And deliver us from evil.

Quiv. and Willie. For thine is the king- 705 dom, the power, and the glory, forever and ever. Amen.

            Curtain

SCENE 3

An hour or two later. The curtain rises revealing the shadowy lump of QUIVIENE'S boarding house bathed in the silvery radiance of the moonlight. Somewhere in the night a mock- ing bird is chirping out his light but melan- choly note. A moment passes and then BAD-EYE comes wandering in from the left thrumming his Jew's-harp. He stops and stands eyeing the house

Bad-Eye (calling to the house as if it were a man). Heigh! *(He listens a moment.)* Heigh! *(Plucking his harp)* Whah dat preacher man? *(Calling)* Which way he go, Aunt Quivie?

Quiv. (within). Don't know, don't care! Mebbe towards hell! 5

Bad-Eye (going over and staring at the foot of the china tree). Dat man sho' put dat money dere. Ain't I a fool? Hot weather mess my haid up.

    (Spitting, he eyes the moon a moment, then with his Jew's-harp going, wanders mournfully along the alley at the rear. Now and then he is heard giving a cold calling whistle that echoes over the valley and among the houses. The blasting is heard in the distance again.

Willie (inside the house — throwing the cover from his head). Ooh, dat old blasting!

Quiv. (pulling him back). I take care of 10 you, honey.

*They lie wrapped in each other's embrace under
the sheet. The sounds in the house die
away. Presently* FARROW *comes stepping
into the yard from the right. He beckons
behind him, and* ZEB VANCE *and* FLOSSIE
TUCKER *come in, holding each other by the
hand,* FLOSSIE *now and then giving her high
suppressed giggle.* FARROW *goes up on the
porch and knocks at the door.* WILLIE *is
heard whining in fright*

Far. Nobody but Levin, Aunt Quivie!

    (QUIVIENE *is heard muttering and
grumbling as she gets up, lights the
lamp, and opens the door, her gray
hair sticking out in a flare around
her face.*

Quiv. What the name o' God you want?

Far. (going in — ZEB VANCE *and* FLOSSIE
following him). Brung you a new daughter.

Quiv. (throwing up her hands). Oh, you 15
— you — fool!

Willie (poking his head out from the cover).
What's de matter — police?

Quiv. (ejaculating). S-sh! This mush-
headed Zeb Vance done got married!

    (*She puts the lamp back on the table
and sits down on the edge of the
bed.*

Zeb (placatingly). Now, Mammy —— 20

Quiv. (snapping). Yeh, call on Mammy the
first thing. Now two of you to be calling.

Zeb. Flossie can help wid de cooking.

Quiv. And the eating. (*Bitterly*) And first
thing you know be a baby, then another 25
— yeh, mammy — mammy — (*She makes an
angry guttural noise in her throat.*) Haruck!
(*Getting into bed again*) Dunno where you'll
sleep. Make you a pallet, and it ain't gonna
be in here. This mine and Willie's room. 30

    (FLOSSIE *stands in the middle of the
floor, her eyes cast down.*

Zeb. Help me move dat cot, Levin.

    (*He and* FARROW *take the cot into the
kitchen shed.*

Quiv. (settling her head on her pillow). Ain't
you two a pair in this world! Who married
you?

Flos. Dat new preacher. 35

Far. (from the kitchen). Me'n Seeny witnessed.

*Quiv. (beating her pillow angrily and fitting
her head to it again).* Ain't no preacher. He's
a plumb devil wearing black. Well, make de
best of it. Ain't gonna worry no more if the 40
world blow up. Didn't have no license, did
you?

Zeb (as he and FARROW *come in again).*
Preacher give us a paper.

Quiv. Reckon it'll hold long enough anyhow.

Far. (mournfully). Somebody's gonna 45
be weak wid de pick on Monday. Good night,
everybody, and take yo' rest.

    (*He comes out of the house and goes into
the alley. Pacing up and down a moment undecidedly, he raises his voice
in his lonely "holler" and goes away
in the direction he came.* ZEB
VANCE *walks around the room, waiting for somebody to say something.*

Quiv. For Jesus' sake quit that walking.
Bofe of you fools, go on to bed. Know what's
in your minds. 50

    (FLOSSIE *gives her foolish giggle and
*ZEB VANCE *takes up the lamp. He
latches the door, and he and* FLOSSIE
*go into the shed at the rear. The
light streams in partially illuminating* OLD QUIVIENE'S *room. The
bride and groom begin to undress in
embarrassment.* FLOSSIE *continues
to give her foolish giggle. Presently
*ZEB VANCE *blows out the light and
pulls* FLOSSIE *down to him. A moment passes, and* TOM STERLING
*slides in by the barber shack with his
hand in his shirt. He tiptoes over
and stands by the window to* MILLY'S
*room, pressing himself flat against
the wall and listening. He wags his
head in pain and after a while moves
his hand along the sill and pushes the
window around on its hinges. The
moonlight shines into the room.*

Milly (within). Must be the wind.

    (*But there is no answer from* BANTAM.
STERLING *stands still as a statue as
he waits, looking like a dark bronze*

bas-relief against the house. The round gleaming barrel of a pistol is gradually pushed out over the window sill from within. It stops as if surveying the scene with its round hole of an eye. Then in the shadow of the room behind it the dim outline of BANTAM'S *head and shoulders rises, stopping and then rising a bit more.*

Ban. (*with a low chuckle*). Yeh, a little breeze.

    (*He reaches up cautiously to close the window, when* STERLING *suddenly sticks his hand out with a pistol in it and shoots him twice.* MILLY *lets out a loud scream, and* BANTAM *is heard struggling and cursing around the room. He breaks through the door into* QUIVIENE'S *room, where she is hugging the moaning* WILLIE *in her arms. There he clings to the lintel of the front door, his knees sagging under him, moaning and cursing.*

Ban. Goddamn him — de goddamn snake he killed me — ooh — killed me!   55

    (ZEB VANCE *rushes in from the shed, half-dressed and carrying a lamp. The light pours out over* BANTAM'S *body twisting in agony.*

Quiv. (*with a loud cry*). Help, help!

Ban. (*gasping for breath, his voice already gurgling in a death choke*). Whah is he? (*Crawling along the porch*) Jesus, gimme a chanct at him! I shoot — I kill — Ooh ——

    (*He catches sight of* STERLING *and tries to lift his pistol, but it gradually falls with his weakening hand, and then suddenly he turns over and rolls halfway down the steps and lies still, his body only half-covered in a single shirt.* MILLY, *in a loose skirt wrapped hastily around her, runs through the room and out onto the porch. She holds* BANTAM'S *head upon her lap and moans over him. Her wrap falls unnoticed to the ground.*

Milly (*presently springing away from him*).

They's blood all over him! (*Screaming*)   60 Git a doctor! Git a doctor!

Ster. (*throwing down his pistol and coming mechanically up to her*). Don't need no doctor — Milly! (*Now the vengeful blasting goes off near at hand, jarring the earth.* STERLING *listens aghast.*) Listen there!

Milly (*clinging to him, forgetful of her nakedness*). Somebody shot Bantam — oh some-   65 body did — (*She clings to him, weeping wildly.*

Ster. (*calling to the others in the house*). Hush now! Nobody gonna git hurt.

Milly (*running back up on the porch and fluttering her hands helplessly*). He was all right — Bantam was good. (*Childishly*) I didn't   70 want you to do it.

Ster. Told him you was my woman.

Milly. Ain't, ain't. (*Shaking her head*) Nobody's woman. (*Naked, she runs back into the house and flings herself on the bed with* QUIVIENE *and* WILLIE. STERLING *looks at* BANTAM *and then gently lays his head up on the porch.*)

Quiv. (*climbing out of bed*). Go git Sport   75 Womack, somebody. He'll take Tom away.

    (*She fastens a sheet around* MILLY.

Ster. (*sitting on the edge of the porch*). You all go away — leave. I stay heah.

    (MILLY *runs back on the porch and hugs* STERLING *to her.*

Milly. I am yo'n, too. And you's mine, honey. I won't let 'em take you away.   80

    (*The babies set up a squeal in the shed.*

Ster. (*calling to the terrified group in the house*). Take the babies and all you go to Sude's and Dode's. (*Bitterly*) Say somebody in the hollow killing cats.

He begins walking helplessly back and forth in the yard. JIM PARR *runs in at the left*

Parr. What's happened —? (*With a shout*) Oh, Good God A'mighty! (*Going over*   85 *and feeling* BANTAM'S *body*) Dead as a rock.

    (*There is a hurried scrambling and grabbing up of clothes by the four in the house,* QUIVIENE *constantly pushing* WILLIE'S *clinging arms from her.*

Quiv. (*moaning over and over*). Oh, Lawd! Oh, Lawd!

Parr. How come he heah?

Quiv. Say he been pardoned.   90

Parr (thinking a moment). You all keep quiet as you can. I'll be right back. Don't say a word. Don't, I tell you.

      (*He hurries out the way he came. Excited shouts and halloos sound around the house, and several figures come running up the alley and stand in the edge of the yard, looking on, whispering and gesticulating, appearing in the half light like grotesque life-sized puppets. Some of them are half-dressed and some are busy pulling on their shirts and coats.* QUIVIENE *and the others go out of the house at the rear and then into the alley. After a moment they come around and join the group at the end of the porch.*

Quiv. Somebody killed Bantam, there he lie on the porch!   95

      (*She hugs* WILLIE *to her, and the others stare at the stretched-out figure in horrified silence.*

Milly (following STERLING *up and down the yard).* Go find Sport.

Ster. (turning upon the group at the right). Go on away, you'll all be slammed in jail.

      (*A lamp is lighted in* DODE'S *house across the alley, and* DODE *comes out on the porch, calling in his heavy voice.*

Dode. What's happened over dere?

No one answers. The men and women begin to moan and growl mournfully to themselves. HENRY *and* SEENY *come up the alley and stop at the edge of the yard.* STERLING *sits down on the anvil, and* MILLY *drops on her knees beside him, laying her head in his lap, her arms around him.* FARROW *bounds into the yard from the left and stops thunderstruck*

Quiv. (setting up a sort of low frightened keen). Bantam's gone from here.   100

Others (from the group in a rasping whisper). Bantam's gone.

DODE WILSON *comes blundering in, led by* DOODLE, *with* SUDIE *blubbering behind*

Seeny (with a gasp). Po' Bantam Wilson.

      (*She jerks loose from* HENRY'S *arm and flies across the yard to* FARROW. BAD-EYE *comes up in the crowd and stands looking on, swaying his shoulders from side to side like a restless ape.*

Dode (dully). Bantam? Bantam on de road, on de big road.

Sudie (with a cry as she stares at the body). My boy!   105

      (*She turns and holds tightly to* DODE, *who stands still as a post.*

Henry (stepping before them with a Bible in his hands, raising his voice rhythmically above the chant which has been started among the NEGROES *around* QUIVIENE). Brother done gone to his long home. He done gone. They called his name — hush — hush ——

Others (chanting). "Hush, hush, somebody called his name."   110

Ster. (going on quietly). Now everybody get away from here. Go back to your beds, I'll talk to the Law.

      (*The chant dies down a moment, but still no one makes a move to go.*

Dode (swinging his arms). Who shot my boy? Where is de God-damned dawg?   115

Henry (with quiet oily persuasion). Nobody knows, nobody knows — haven't heard nothing. (*Giving the cue again*) Hush — hush.

JIM PARR *and* UZZELL *come in at the left with a long splint-woven basket. They put it down and lift* BANTAM *into it. The chant of the* NEGROES *suddenly breaks out again*

Negroes.

"Hush, hush, somebody call-a his name,

Hush, hush, somebody call-a his name,   120

Hush, hush, somebody call-a his name.

Oh, my Lawd, oh my Lawd, what shall I do!"

      (*Putting his Bible into his satchel,* HENRY *goes over and looks down into the basket.* DOODLE *moves up and stands behind him.* HENRY *reaches out and puts his hand on* DOODLE'S *shoulder.*

Parr. Let's get him away quick.

Ster. (*jumping up and throwing* MILLY *from him — yelling*). Don't you move him! Let the Law come.   125

   (*He begins walking up and down in the yard again.* PARR *and* UZZELL *set the basket down and stand undecided. The wailing* NEGROES *gradually creep into the yard and surround the basket as if fascinated. After a moment,* HENRY *lifts* DOODLE *up and places him on the porch.*

Uzz. Have nothing more to do with it. (*Throwing up his hands and wiggling them despairingly over his head*) Fools! Fools!

   (*He turns abruptly and goes off by the barber shack.*

Henry (*to* DOODLE). Po' sinner man come home one night. Death was waiting at his door. Preach it, Brother.   130

Doo. (*crying out, his eyes flashing as he begins to preach*). Soon one mawning Death come creeping at yo' do'.

Henry (*chanting*). Soon one morning! —

   (*The* NEGROES *catch up the words.*

Negroes.

"Soon one mawning Death come creeping at yo' do',

Soon one mawning Death come creeping at yo' do',   135

Soon one mawning Death come creeping at yo' do',

Oh, my Lawd, oh, my Lawd, what shall I do!"

   (*The chant goes on, and* DOODLE'S *voice rises above it.*

Doo. Why don't he say sump'n now? What makes him so still in dat basket? Why don't he move dat hand a little bit? Cain't,   140 cain't, Death done struck him down.

Henry. Death, oh death ——

   (*The* NEGROES *stare down into the basket as if mesmerized.* OLD QUIVIENE *leads the chant into another tune.*

Quiv.

"Death, O Death, Death, O Death, Death, O Death,

Spare me over another day."

   (*The other* NEGROES *join her.* DOODLE *goes on preaching.*

Doo. Bantam gone — gone — gone —   145 Bantam gone to come no mo'. Us gonna miss him, us gonna mo'n. Us gonna miss him now he's gone.

Henry (*with a loud shout*). Amen!

   (*He begins singing with the* NEGROES. MILLY *follows* STERLING *around in the yard, wringing her hands.*

Henry. We gonna miss him ——   150

Negroes (*changing back into the former chant*).

"We gonna miss him — miss him now he's gone,

We gonna miss him — miss him now he's gone,

We gonna miss him — miss him now he's gone,

Oh, my Lawd, oh, my Lawd, what shall I do?"

Doo. Bantam, whah is you now tonight?   155 Us in Potter's Field axes you what is you at now? Is he in heaben, is he in hell? I look to de east, I look to de west. — (*He turns and does so.*) — I sees de angel rise up wid a cap on lak a snowy cloud. Dere he stand on de edge   160 o' de world and de wind blows loud on him ruffling his feathers. (*Crying out*) Tell us whah my brudder gone. (*Listening as the mourning song goes on*) He don't answer me — hanh. Up in heaben or down in hell?   165 (*Shuddering and hiding his face in his hands*) Look down in dat deep hole, see de gre't flames burning and br'iling. Mercy, mercy, I sees Old Satan, setting on his red-hot rock, Lawd, setting in de fiery furnace wid his feet in de hot ashes. Look, he spet on de rock and   170 gre't steam bile up. (*As if addressing him*) Whah my brudder? (*Listening*) Hanh, he pop his tail, he shake his hawns, he make no answer. He scrape de ground wid his iron hoofs.   175

Henry. God gonna raise him! —

Negroes.

"God gonna raise him out'n that fiery flame,

God gonna raise him out'n that fiery flame,

God gonna raise him out'n that fiery flame,

Oh, my Lawd, oh, my Lawd, what shall I do?"   180

Doo. Look up dere behind dat moon all pale like flour on its face — pale like a sick man. See my Lawd and Savior. (*Sending a high call up to Him*) Whah is po' Bantam now? See how de Lawd's tears fall down. He so 185 sorry dey lay de po' body down. (*With a high cry*) What dat sweeping and winking thoo them stars, looking lak a rainbow and burning cloud? (*Babbling*) Dat's de mighty God of Jacob and Job wid his beard lak a burning 190 bresh, coming to give Doodle answer. (*Calling through his cupped hands*) Is Bantam up dere wid you, God? (*He listens and then ecstatically answers himself in a faraway voice.*) Bantam done got home to his rest, Bantam sleeping 195 in his Father's breast. And don't you weep and don't you mo'n any more.

    (*A moaning cry of gladness runs among the people.*

Sudie (*falling on the ground and bobbing her head up and down*). Yeh, he is, yeh, he is! He's in heaben. Po' Bantam.

Dode (*shouting out*). And he gonna rise 200 — rise!   (*He waves his guitar, beating time.*

Henry. Rise!

Negroes (*breaking into a happier refrain*).

"He gonna rise like dew wid de mawning sun,
He gonna rise like dew wid de mawning sun,
He gonna rise like dew wid de mawning sun,
Oh, my Lawd, oh, my Lawd, what shall I do?" 206

Ster. (*falling on his knees by the basket*). I killed po' Bantam, I killed him! (*Stretching out his hands*) Folks, folks, I didn't mean to do it — sump'n made me mad, I lost my 210 senses! — Jesus! Jesus! — Bantam! — Bantam!   (*Several of the mourners draw away from him in fear.*

Henry. Death couldn't spare him —

Quiv. (*leading back into the second chant*).

"Death, O Death, Death, O Death, Death, O Death,
Spare me over another day." 215

    (*From somewhere in the distance a huge rasping voice calls — a voice so loud that like the blasting it jars the ground. It is the Law.*

Voice. Heigh! I say heigh, there!

    (*Immediately the group of mourners are transformed as if by an electric shock. They scatter right and left, running low in the shadows with hushed and excited cries.*

Mourners (*as they flee*). The Law, the Law! —

Others. Police! Police!

    (DOODLE *is left standing on the porch with* HENRY *near and* STERLING *and* MILLY *in the yard.*

Milly (*moaning*). Run, Tom, run! Oh, 220 do, do!

    (*She tries to pull him away, but he still rests on his knees as if waiting for something.* HENRY *starts casually away at the left.* STERLING *grabs up his pistol from the ground and springs before him.*

Ster. (*half-sobbing*). Get right back. Yeh, you caused all this!

Henry (*starting*). Hunh?

Ster. You move out of this yard and I 225 kill another man.

Henry. Stop fooling, I'm in a hurry.

Ster. Yeh, and I know the law wants you. We'll go together.

Henry (*snarling*). Get out of my way! 230

Ster. (*raising the pistol*). Make another move at me and I kill you sho's your name's Bad Man Bolis.

Henry (*smiling*). Bolis? Bolis? (*Watching him*) If you gonna keep me here don't 235 mind I light a cigarette, do you?

Ster. Put that hand in yo' pocket and you'll never take it out.

Henry (*throwing back his shoulders*). All right, I'll explain to the judge. 240

Doo. Oh! Oh!

    (*He runs away at the right weeping. The high purposeless wailing of the babies sets up in the house.*

Voice (*as before*). Heigh!

Ster. (*with the pistol stuck against* HENRY'S *back*). This is Bad Man Bolis and Red Murdock, Cap'n. Take us.

    (*With a cry* MILLY *runs out of the yard at the left.* HENRY *throws up his head with a half snarl, and* STERLING *marches him to the right as if to meet* their doom. And now with a low sardonic chuckle as if releasing the evil of his whole inner nature, HENRY moves ahead of him. A great wind begins to blow through Potter's Field, the china tree is twisted in its grip, the houses shake, sag, and sway, and with the whistle of an oncoming shell a terrific blast goes off in the center of the scene. The pallid light of the moon mixes in with the turmoil as QUIVIENE'S house totters and falls. Then the light goes out. The moon drops down the sky like a shot, and we see a few of the terrified inhabitants of the valley flying across the scene like stray autumn leaves in a storm.

Curtain

SCENE 4

The light comes up again into the bright glare of a day in August. It is a few weeks later. Eight or ten striped convicts in the right background are digging on the blazing new road that runs through Potter's Field — one stouter and more lusty-hearted digging ahead, all swinging their picks aloft and bringing them down together. BAD-EYE'S truck is drawn up in the alley back of the wrecked boarding-house, and QUIVIENE, WILLIE, and MILLY are loading their household goods in it preparatory to moving away. The white dust is thick as a haze in the air, resting like a cement dew on the ruined zinnia and marigold beds. The heat of August shimmers across the land as far as the eye can see. Lazy Lawrence dances his fiendish monkey dance. The sweat pours down, the only dampness in the world for the ten mourners on the road. On a stump to the left a GUARD squats, drowsy, vapid, like a toad. The rifle in the crook of his arm keeps alert, its muzzle warns like an eye, it threatens. On the bankside to the right another GUARD sits. He also is sleepy, drowsy. His rifle also keeps alert and watches, its muzzle threatens. The convicts dig with their backs to the GUARDS, their faces set down the in-

finite stretch of road. Like soulless puppets, they lift their hands towards the sky and bring them down, never any slower, never any faster. And as the picks come down against the earth with a thud, a husky desperate groan bursts from their baked lips. As rhythmic as the beating of their hearts the "hanh!" accompanies the falling of the picks, carrying over long maddening hours of pain until the sun sinks cooling in the west and the GUARD stirs and says, "Call it a day." At times their voices are raised in a chant, level, patient, as eternal and tough as the earth in which they dig. Sometimes they talk as they work, but not so often, for the staccato of conversation breaks up the rhythmic routine of labor and that's what they're here for — labor, labor, working on the roads. "Ten years on the roads, TOM STERLING, alias RED MURDOCK, and twenty years for you, JACK BOLIS, alias the REVEREND JOHN HENRY." The judge dropped his tobacco by his foot, rose, addressed the jury, and gave sentence. "These niggers, these everlasting niggers, always fighting, always shooting, always killing. They've got no sense. They'll never have no sense. Peace — peace, I say. The law — the law! For this is the Republic, these the institooshuns."

HENRY'S *spirit still walks unbroken.* STERLING'S *has gone under. The feel of iron and abuse of tongues have broken him. His great shoulders are bent, his legs hardly sustain his weight, and his arms fling up the pick and let it fall hour after hour, day after day, with slowly decreasing power. And all the while his lightless face stares at the earth beneath*

Henry (*driving in his pick, the monosyllables dropping at slow intervals from his lips, as if they had no meaning other than their sound*). Dig-dig-dig-hanh — dig-dig-hanh ——

    (*The* GUARD *at the right stirs in his sleepiness and beats at the flies with his hat.*

1st Guard. Rain or shine, the old dog-flies stay with you.

2d Guard (*lighting a cigarette and throwing the package across to the first*). And the damn muskeeters allus drilling for blood.   5

Henry. Dig-dig-dig-hanh — dig-dig-dig-hanh.

1st Guard (*to the* CONVICTS). Stir up, there — ketch the preacher!

2d Guard. Heigh, you, Sterling, raise up that pick and let her come down. 10

(*The* CONVICTS *dig on, accompanying every blow with their everlasting "hanh-hanh," saying never a word, except* HENRY *with his "dig-dig-dig."*

1st Guard. Hear me? Put some pep in that digging! Hell freeze over 'fore you git this little digging done.

(*They lapse into silence again. The* 2D GUARD *stretches his arms in a yawn.*

2d Guard. Lord, I'm sleepy — sleepy. 15

1st Guard. Better leave her off a few nights.

(*There is a snickering among the* CONVICTS.

2d Guard (*brutally, his voice sharp with hate*). Somebody begging for the little rawhide!

(*The* CONVICTS, *terrified, drive their picks deeper into the earth but never any slower, never any faster.* MILLY *with the one remaining baby in her arms comes around from behind* OLD QUIVIENE'S *house and stands on the edge of the road-cut.* BAD-EYE *is with her, his face full of sorrow. He stands swaying his body from side to side in a restless ape-like motion.*

Bad-Eye (*softly*). Tom, Tom.

(*But* STERLING *pays no attention to him, nor do any of the other* CONVICTS, *carrying on their digging, and carrying it on.*

Milly. Tom, Tom, please look up. This is Milly. 20

1st Guard. Ain't visiting time till Sunday.

Milly (*holding out a bottle*). Brung him some medicine. He needs it, he needs it bad.

2d Guard (*not unkindly, his little burst of anger over*). We got doctors. Go on, now.

1st Guard (*hurrying her*). Heigh, heigh. 25

(MILLY *turns and goes despairingly off the way she came, helped along by* BAD-EYE.

2d Guard. Water! I want some water.

1st Guard. Goddamned water boy's fell in and drownded. (*Standing up and calling*) Water boy, water jack! Could a-been there and halfway back. 30

(*The* CONVICTS *begin a wordless hum that rises like a dry gusty breathing from their mouths, pitiful and pleading.*

Henry (*in a wooden voice*). Mercy, mercy, it calls, water, water! Give them water!

(*The hum of the* CONVICTS *faintly increases its volume.*

1st Guard. Go to it, preacher, get this road built. Wheels got to turn.

2d Guard. Traffic got to move. 35

Henry (*chanting*). Seas — rivers of bricks, mortar and iron — let it flow on — open the way ——

1st Guard. That's right, Preacher. Sing him up. Water boy! Sing him out'n them bushes. 40

2d Guard. Bear down on them picks. Drive 'em to the eye! — Jesus Christ!

(STERLING *suddenly tumbles over and falls with his face flat in the dirt. A convulsive shudder runs through the other* CONVICTS, *save* HENRY. *All keep to their digging, never any faster, never any slower, their faces set down the infinite stretch of road before them. Only their humming increases in volume, full of begging, full of pain. With a cry* MILLY *runs in.* QUIVIENE *with her arms around the frightened* WILLIE *is seen behind her. Still clasping her baby,* MILLY *tries to make her way over to* STERLING, *but the* 1ST GUARD *pushes her back with his rifle, and she stands among the loose clods, an anguished moaning coming from her throat.*

Henry. Dig-dig-dig-hanh!

2d Guard (*marching up to the prostrate body*). Get that mouth out'n the dirt. (*Whirling on the* CONVICTS) Dig! Dig! Who wants the little cat-tails? 45

Henry (*as his companions' hum takes on a moaning wail*). Mourners on the road they whisper Jesus!

1st Guard. Snap out'n it, Sterling. 50

2d Guard (*getting a leather thong from his coat*). Put a fire coal on his tail and rise him.

Milly (*moaning*). Mister! Mister!

2d Guard. Stand back! Great God! Great God!

1st Guard. Gonna step to it, Sterling?   55 (*But* STERLING *makes no answer.*) He's a stall boy. Hell, he's stalling.

2d Guard. This ain't no party.

1st Guard. Hell, it ain't no party.

> (*The* 2d GUARD *smoothes the thong with his hand and looks at the* 1ST GUARD.

WILLIE (*shuddering in* QUIVIENE'S *arms*). Mis' Quivie! Mis' Quivie!   61

Henry. Dig-dig-hanh — work-work-work-hanh!

1st Guard. Make 'em work, that's right.

2d Guard. Work — work — that's what   65 he's here for — work.

1st Guard. Work — work — let him taste it.

2d Guard (*raising the strap above his head*). Thirty-nine, thirty-nine. (*His voice comes out stronger now, more sharply, strengthened by the strap in hand.*) The law, the law!

> (*But still he holds the leather poised without bringing it down. The humming of the* CONVICTS *rises higher and louder with sorrow — full of hate also, full of its deep begging, but helpless withal.*

Henry (*suddenly beginning to sing as he wags his head and drives his pick deep into the earth*).

> "They call their sister — hanh —   70
> They say their sister — hanh —
> They mean their sister — hanh —
> Eigh Lord."

1st Guard. Hold 'er a minute, we'll see, we'll see.   (*He goes up to* STERLING *and pokes*   75 *him gently in the ribs with the muzzle of his rifle, but only the twitching back makes answer.* SPORT WOMACK, BELLE UTLEY, FARROW, *and* SEENY *come down the alley. They stop terrified at what they see before them.*

2d Guard. Try him in the collar. (*He cuffs him gently in the collar, then with more insistence, at last with vehement roughness. A low whine, different from the* CONVICT *hum, is heard.*

1st Guard (*bending down*). Goddamn it, we'll see.

2d Guard. And what song is he singing now?

1st Guard. Don't say nothing. Grunts   80 and slobbers like an old steer. He don't say nothing.

Milly (*horror pouring from her breaking heart*). Jesus! Jesus!

2d Guard. By God, we'll see! — Oh yes, he'll talk. He'll tell us a mouthful.   85

> (*The humming grows fuller, deeper-toned, and the rhythm begins to shape the picks, to hold the rising and the falling arms to their labor.* UZZELL *comes up in the background and stands by the corner of the house looking on. His face is sombre and brooding.* BAD-EYE *is with him.*

Henry (*with a high call*). Air, air, under this tight pot! (*Singing*)

> "They call their brother — hanh —
> They say their brother — hanh —
> They mean their brother — hanh —   90
> Eigh Lord."

Uzz. (*joining in for an instant, his voice hoarse and tuneless*). Eigh Lord.

1st Guard (*shouting*). Let him have it!

> (*The* 2D GUARD *hands his rifle to the first and then looking around the world as if for a witness of justification, begins to beat the prostrate figure. The humming of the* CONVICTS *now is a shuddering groan. They drive their picks deeper into the ground, but never any faster, never any slower.*

Henry (*singing*).

> "They call their mother — hanh —
> They say their mother — hanh —"   95

2d Guard. Six-seven-eight — nine-ten ——

1st Guard. And now you'll work — and I reckon you'll work.

2d Guard. Eleven — twelve — thirteen — fourteen ——   100

Milly (*falling on her knees and lifting her baby towards heaven*). Mercy! Mercy! Blessed Jesus.

Henry.

> "They mean their mother — hanh —
> Eigh Lord."

And the watchers in the sky cry blood — blood. Hanh — cry — blood. Earth, earth, sweet 105 earth receive it — hanh. Keep it, save it till the next harvest — hanh.

1st Guard. Oh, yes, he'll work, and I reckon he'll work!

(DOODLE, *the water boy, bursts through the hedge of dead trumpet vines at the left, stands a moment terror-stricken, and then dropping his bucket with a clatter, tears down the road. The* NEGROES *of the settlement stand huddled behind the house and in the alley. Their mourning song, much like the hum of the* CONVICTS, *is faintly heard coming from their throats.*

Henry. Grave, grave, swallow them up, 110 hide them away, till the next harvest, keep them. — Dig — dig — dig — dig — hanh ——

2d Guard. Fifteen — sixteen — seventeen — eighteen ——

(*In a last burst of life* STERLING *staggers to his feet.*

1st Guard. Go to work — look out! 115
(*The* 2D GUARD *turns to grab his rifle, but* STERLING *is upon him. The* CONVICTS' *hum grows louder.*

Henry. Beat him to the earth — hanh — mash down the flowers. The goldenrod is trampled down — hanh — the lady fingers broken and torn — (*Singing — and some of the* CONVICTS *suddenly begin to sing with him*)
"They call their father — hanh —" 120
Ster. (*his voice coming out in a great animal scream*). Hah-hah-hah!
(*He beats the* GUARD's *upturned face with his fists.*

2d Guard. Kill him! Kill him!
(*The hum grows still louder, a fresher triumphant note creeping into it.*

Henry (*interpreting it*). Revenge. Revenge. Hope is not perished from them. Their arms are still strong. (*Singing — several of the* 125 CONVICTS *now joining in with their choking voices*)
"They say their father — hanh —
They mean their father — hanh —
Eigh Lord."
2d Guard. Kill him! Kill him!

(*The* 1ST GUARD *stands stupefied. Then as if suddenly awakening, he steps back, raises his rifle, and shoots* STERLING *through the back. He rolls over and lies with his face upturned in the burning sun.* MILLY *suddenly lets her arms with the crying baby drop to her lap and sits cold and still. Down the alleys the* NEGROES *are seen on their knees crushed and stupefied, their arms wrapped across their breasts, their heads bent down. The* 1ST GUARD *stands looking foolishly down at the dead Negro.*

Henry. Sing on — sing on — beaten — 130 darkness — night — God sits on high, his face from the Negro. The poor and needy cry in vain, the iron palings hold them — hanh! The steel and the iron divide them — hanh!

1st Guard. The God-damned fool, he's 135 dead, dead!

2d Guard (*sitting up with a high laugh as he wipes the blood from his face*). Had to kill him, we had to kill him! (*Peering forward*) Dead as a fly. (*Moaning*) Something wrong. Wrong here. 140

1st Guard. Sing, you bastards! Dig, you sons of bitches!

Henry (*chanting*). Moonlight, starlight all the singing, lay the po' body down. Hear the fly say zoom. The buzzard roosting on the 145 throne of God. And they sing, and they sing. Earth give answer! Jesus hear them! (*Shaking his great head savagely, sweeping his pick over the scene and driving it to the eye*) Dig-dig-dig-hanh!

(*He steps boldly forward on the road, digging as he goes. By this time the* CONVICTS *have dug along the road halfway across the scene,* HENRY *always several steps ahead. The sinking sun illuminates their faces, faces set down the road and toward the sun as if it were a goal calling them on. The pleaders in the alley still bow on their knees, their hands beating the air, their faces, too, shining in the evening light. Their lips move, but now no sound is heard coming from them.*

Suddenly the 2D GUARD *bursts into loud sobs and flings himself down on his face in the grass.* MILLY *with her wailing baby in her arms drags her broken form over to* STERLING'S *body and lays herself across it, pressing her silent lips against his face.* UZZELL *suddenly springs down into the road, seizes* STERLING'S *pick, and takes his place next to* HENRY.

Uzz. (his voice bursting from his lips in a trumpet cry). Dig on the road to heaven! 150 Digging towards the sun!

Bad-Eye (bowed on his knees, his face lighted by the sinking light, the words croaking from his rusty throat). Dig on, dig on!

     (*The people in the valley take up his cry, and as* HENRY *leads the pleading* CONVICTS *into song again, they begin joining in.*

Henry and the Convicts (singing).
     "They call their Jesus — hanh —
     They say their Jesus — hanh —"

     (*The lost and forlorn Potter's Field people now begin coming out from behind the wreck of their houses and onto the road.*

Potter's Field People (some of them joining in the song).
     "They mean their Jesus, hanh — 155
     Eigh Lord!"

Henry (all the woodenness dropping from him as he moves before them swinging his pick). The merciful Jesus! (*Leading the swelling chorus*)
     "They call King Jesus — hanh —"

     (*And now the pleaders of the valley begin falling in behind the* CONVICTS, *and* HENRY *moves ahead as he digs and he digs, as if leading them on — down the infinite stretch of road ahead.*

People of the Valley (more loudly still, with their rising song).
     "They say King Jesus — hanh." 160

     (*The* 2D GUARD *springs out into the road before them. Flinging up his arms, he screams.*

2d Guard. Stop it! stop it!

     (*But the* CONVICTS *dig impassively on and on, never any slower, never any faster. And they sing and they sing.*

Convicts and People (ever more loudly).
     "They mean King Jesus, hanh —
     Eigh Lord!"

     (*A radiant light from the setting sun begins to spread over Potter's Field, illuminating everything, even the flat senseless body of* MILLY *lying upon her love. And the* CONVICTS *dig impassively on, never any slower, never any faster, their faces set toward the beckoning goal.*

Curtain

INTRODUCTION TO
Mary of Scotland

The Rebirth of Poetic Drama: Maxwell Anderson and Poetic Tragedy

THE REBIRTH OF POETIC DRAMA

THE DRAMA of the Western World was born at Athens in poetry. The great revivals of dramatic art in Europe between the sixteenth and the nineteenth centuries were dominated by a poetic intention. They sought to mirror not what man does say, but what he would say if he should express himself with beauty and nobility. They sought to present not what man is, but what he dreams of being. The first years of the twentieth century, however, witnessed in playwriting all over the world the substitution of a social for a poetic purpose. This revolutionary change, upon which Ibsen had placed the final seal of authority, effected a monopoly for realistic prose drama, even in Ireland where the distinguished pioneers of her stage, Yeats and Synge, tried to plant a poetic tradition. In 1911 John Masefield sadly concluded: "The poetic impulse of the Renaissance is now spent. The poetic drama, the fruit of that impulse, is now dead."

Nevertheless the modern theater has not so completely abandoned its ancient heritage as Masefield believed. Since the First World War playwrights on both sides of the Atlantic have fostered a slow but persistent growth of interest in poetic drama. As early as 1920 the Provincetown Players in New York acted an important example of the species, *Aria da Capo*, an ironic fantasy on war by Edna St. Vincent Millay (1892–1950). T. S. Eliot (b. 1888) stirred England and then New York with *Murder in the Cathedral* (1935), a religious play suggestive of the Greek drama in its choral passages and of the medieval in its allegorical devices, but strikingly original in its varied cadences of speech. He again excited attention with *The Cocktail Party* (1949), a psychiatrical comedy applauded for its urbane yet natural verse. In the same year Christopher Fry (b. 1907) became the talk of London and New York by reason of his comedy, *The Lady's Not For Burning*, rich in imagery and verbal melodies.

MAXWELL ANDERSON AND POETIC TRAGEDY

Though these and other professional poets have been influential in promoting a contemporary poetic drama, by far the leading figure in the movement is a former teacher and journalist, Maxwell Anderson. He started life on December 15, 1888, as the son of a Baptist minister in a small town of northwestern Pennsylvania, Atlantic. His home moved by stages westward as far as North Dakota on account of his father's changing pastorates. In 1911 he graduated from the University of North Dakota where, as a charter member of the Dakota Playmakers, he participated in dramatics under Professor F. H. Koch, later the famous director of the Carolina Playmakers. After two years of teaching in South Dakota Anderson traveled to California and took an M.A.

degree in English from Stanford University in 1914. A brief and disillusioning experience with war-time academic freedom as a professor at Whittier College led him to take up newspaper work in San Francisco. In 1918 he drifted to New York, reported for several metropolitan journals, and at length obtained a staff position on the World. Meanwhile poetry had become his avocation. "Weary of plays in prose that never lifted from the ground," he eventually turned to playwriting in verse. His maiden piece, a tragedy of the North Dakota prairie entitled *White Desert*, secured a well-known Broadway producer, Brock Pemberton, but not the Broadway public. It ran for only two weeks in October, 1923.

Despite this inauspicious beginning Anderson's ambition to write successful poetic drama did not abate. His next venture, however, was of a very opposite character. He collaborated with a newspaper colleague, Laurence Stallings, on a vigorous, baldly realistic play, *What Price Glory?*, which depicts the A.E.F. in France during the First World War. The tremendous popularity of *What Price Glory?* in the New York season of 1924–25 enabled Anderson to relinquish journalism in favor of the theater. His ensuing years of experiment came to an end with the Broadway "hit" of 1930, *Elizabeth the Queen*. It enjoyed a magnificent production by the Theater Guild and their star actors, Lynn Fontanne and Alfred Lunt. This verse tragedy upon the romance of Queen Elizabeth and Lord Essex established Anderson's eminence in the American theater as well as furnished him the successful model that his genius had long desired. During the subsequent decade he brought forth a distinctive series of plays more or less historical in subject, and poetic in form: *Night over Taos* (1932), the American-Spanish troubles in New Mexico of 1847; *Mary of Scotland* (1933); *Valley Forge* (1934), the American Revolution in the winter of 1777–78; *Winterset* (1935), the famous Sacco-Vanzetti case of the 1920's; *The Wingless Victory* (1936), Salem (Massachusetts) and the Far East trade of the early nineteenth century; *High Tor* (1937), the legends of Catskill country about the Dutch explorer Hudson and the Indians; *The Masque of Kings* (1938), the suicide of Crown Prince Rudolph of Austria in 1889; *Key Largo* (1939), the Spanish Civil War of 1936–39; *Journey to Jerusalem* (1940), Jesus' youthful pilgrimage to Jerusalem in 8 A.D.

Beginning in 1941 with *Candle in the Wind*, a contemporary war play, Anderson abandoned the exclusive use of verse, but employed it at heightened moments in *Joan of Lorraine* (1946) and *Anne of the Thousand Days* (1948). This change in dramatic style meant, however, no shift in his idealistic attitude toward his art. His preface to *Candle in the Wind* describes the theater as "a religious institution devoted entirely to the exaltation of the spirit of man." It aims to "find, and hold up to our regard, what is admirable in the human race." Anderson condemns the prevailing view of the 1920's, which O'Neill's drama well epitomizes. That view, he believes, implied "a low opinion of the race of men" and "rejected the war between good and evil," whereas the theater should affirm that "man has a dignity and a destiny"; that "the good and evil in men are the good and evil of evolution"; and, finally, that "man is not perfect, but seeks perfection."

It is these lofty aspirations which have moved Anderson to reach so steadily into "the upper air of poetic tragedy." He considers the best prose in the world as inferior on the stage to the best poetry, for poetry is not only *the* language of emotion but also "a way of using language that impels the user toward whatever vision he may be able to formulate of human destiny." "Dramatic poetry is man's greatest achievement on his earth so far. . . . Without at least one [great poet] we shall never have a great theater in this country." Anderson has never thought himself the great poet in question; he has hoped only to modify "our starvation diet of prose." His poetry lacks the innovational qualities of MacLeish's free verse and of Eliot's subtly diversified rhythms. It reveals in both diction and music a Shakespearean descent, but the iambic pentameter by reason of frequent short or irregular cadences is less sonorous than Shakespeare's blank verse. Anderson also imitates Shakespearean practice in using prose for passages with much exposition or wit, and in heightening the language to verse when emotion deepens. His dialogue often displays the Elizabethan tendency to wordiness and rhetoric. At such moments the pretentious verbal machinery obstructs the drama, as in the closing scene of *Winterset*. Mio, the youthful protagonist, though aware of gunmen waiting near-by to kill him, stands outside a tenement door in the cold rain of a winter night and expounds his views upon men, love, and destiny until it is a relief when he walks off into the darkness to be shot down. Anderson's failures to discipline his poetry do not overshadow, however, the situations in which he has developed richness and depth of feeling through elevated speech. His best playwriting makes poetry, just as it was in Greece and Renaissance Europe, an organic rather than decorative element of tragedy.

Anderson's formula for tragedy follows the classic one of Aristotle and Shakespeare. Tragedy for him as for them centers about the struggle of an outstanding but not flawless character: "The protagonist must be an exceptional person. The man in the street simply will not do as the hero. The hero must not be a perfect man. . . . He must learn through suffering. . . . He suffers death as a consequence of his fault or his attempt to correct it, but before he dies he has become a nobler person. . . ." Hence the theme of Anderson's tragedy is the very antithesis of O'Neill's. The latter shows that man falls, cheated by himself and the universe; the former shows that man falls, but that man attains victory in defeat, a conquest of himself in the face of annihilation.

Anderson, then, intends his tragedies as exaltations of the human spirit, but he does not always achieve such an effect. His heart too easily clouds his mind. He connects the lives and loves of his main characters with conflicts of world significance, such as race prejudice in *The Wingless Victory*, and autocracy versus democracy in *The Masque of Kings*. Thus he tries to blend the romantic strain of older tragedy with the social motif of the modern. Not uncommonly, however, the love situation blurs the intellectual issues. In *Winterset*, for example, the Romeo-Juliet romance of Mio and Miriamne gradually obscures Mio's quest for justice until at the last the social implications of his tragedy are lost sight of. Again Anderson sometimes confuses the quality of the issue at stake and produces melodrama instead of tragedy, as in *Key Largo* where he arranges for King McCloud, the escaped war-veteran, to regain his honor and demonstrate man's unselfishness by a sophomoric finale of murder-suicide. Yet these instances of sentimental or superficial idealism are more than offset by scenes which contain a refreshing splendor in both action and language. Insistent upon "the glory of earth-born men and women," Anderson has restored to tragedy the heroic pattern so sadly missing since the advent of Ibsen. He more than any other modern has popularized poetic tragedy and returned this loftiest form of drama to a place of importance in the world theater.

"MARY OF SCOTLAND"

Anderson's most effective poetic tragedy on the stage is *Mary of Scotland*. The Theater Guild gave it a brilliant premiere at the Alvin Theater, New York, on November 27, 1933. Helen Hayes played Queen Mary; Helen Menken, Queen Elizabeth; and Philip Merivale, Lord Bothwell. After a winter and spring on Broadway *Mary of Scotland* went on tour and drew capacity houses throughout the United States. It is now an established piece of "little theater" repertory.

The exciting career of Mary, Queen of Scots, has been during the past three centuries a favorite subject for the theater. The last important production prior to *Mary of Scotland* was *Mary Stuart* (1922), a careful biographical drama by the well-known English playwright, John Drinkwater (1882–1937). Anderson, however, does not attempt a directly historical study. He treats history after the romantic method of Marlowe and Shakespeare. All the scenes are freely adapted or invented to fit the plot design. The conflict of religious, political, and social groups is simplified into one of opposing personalities. The characterizations take shape not so much according to documentary evidence as according to the dramatist's objective. Anderson chooses to imagine his situation, though historically it was far otherwise, as a clearcut battle between good and evil. He neatly balances the antagonists and paints them with only a few broad strokes: on the one side, Mary, the generous kind sovereign, and Bothwell, the impetuous honest soldier-lover; on the other, Elizabeth, the shrewd power-loving ruler, and John Knox, the dour religious fanatic. *Mary of Scotland* becomes the tragedy of a lovable, idealistic but misguided woman, set by Anderson amid the trappings of sixteenth-century history in consequence of his belief that poetic tragedy had "never been successfully written about its own place and time."

The development of Mary's tragedy conforms to the pattern which Anderson has laid down as the ideal: "A play should lead up to and away from a central crisis, and this crisis should consist in a discovery by the leading character which has an indelible effect on his thought and emotion, and completely alters his course of action." The central crisis of *Mary of Scotland* occurs in Act II, Scene 1, where Mary, after Rizzio's murder, realizes that her marriage to Darnley has been a dire error. She turns about and forms an alliance with Bothwell whose counsel and love she has previously rejected. She recognizes the "tragic guilt" which has sealed her fate:

> "I was wrong! I loved you all the time and denied you!
> Forgive me — even too late!" (Act II, Sc. 1, ll. 809–10)

Her original rejection of Bothwell Anderson conceives as the tragic fault which according to the Aristotle-Shakespeare formula causes the protagonist's downfall and forms the basis of the inner tragedy. The Greek and Shakespearean tragic heroes exhibit, however, a definite flaw in temperament or morals. Mary's fault consists of no such weakness in character; it lies in mistaken policy. Her downfall therefore has about it little of the spiritual inevitability that constitutes the most profound force in classic tragedy.

Anderson weaves into Mary's fate the unending clash between selfish and unselfish ideals of government. She envisions a kingdom with complete liberty of thought and religion: "But it's my thought that in Scotland, though it be the first time in the world, we shall all believe as we please and worship as we list" (Act II, Sc. 1, ll. 382–84). Such idealism provokes the common hatred of Queen Elizabeth, Knox, and the Scottish lords. Their principle of self-interest cannot tolerate Mary's faith that "those thrones will fall that are built on blood and craft" (Act I, Sc. 3, ll. 241–42) and that "to rule gently is to rule wisely" (Act I, Sc. 3, ll. 217–18). This struggle of political creeds increases the meaning and appeal of Mary's tragic situation. Anderson, to be sure, allows the love story of Bothwell and the queen to occupy the center of the stage now and again, but for once he keeps romance out of the climax and focuses upon larger issues of mind and conscience.

The climactic meeting between Mary and Elizabeth is a superb close to a play which opens vividly with Mary's landing in Scotland and then compresses into several well-chosen scenes her seven years of growing misfortune. The somewhat archaic diction and imagery in the dialogue suggest the age to perfection. Indeed Anderson's inclination to embroidered language suits *Mary of Scotland* as it does few other of his works. He rises to the height of his capacity as a poetic playwright in the final colloquy of the two queens. Here the union of feeling and imagination results in drama of unusual beauty. The rich color and rhythm of the verse conceal the occasional failure of the poetry to unfold the deeper shadings of character. Mary's refusal to save her life by abdication broadens into an affirmation of the human dream that virtue and honor ultimately conquer. "I'll win men's hearts in the end," she says exultantly (Act III, l. 652). Thus *Mary of Scotland* with its portrayal of heroic personality triumphant in defeat stands as a notable attempt to revive those spiritual as well as literary concepts of tragedy which Aeschylus and his successors at Athens introduced to the drama of the Western World.

[For further study, see Maxwell Anderson, *The Essence of Tragedy* (1939), *Off Broadway: Essays about the Theatre* (1947); Barrett H. Clark, *Maxwell Anderson: The Man and His Plays* (1933); J. W. Krutch, *American Drama Since 1918* (1939).]

MAXWELL ANDERSON

Mary of Scotland

DRAMATIS PERSONAE

(In the order of their appearance)

First Guard, JAMIE
Second Guard
Third Guard
JOHN KNOX
JAMES HEPBURN, *Earl of Bothwell*
CHÂTELARD
MARY STUART
DUC DE CHÂTELHERAULT
MARY BEATON
MARY SETON
MARY LIVINGSTONE
MARY FLEMING
ELIZABETH TUDOR
LORD BURGHLEY
HENRY, LORD DARNLEY
LORD GORDON

LORD DOUGLAS
DAVID RIZZIO
JAMES STUART, *Earl of Moray*
MAITLAND *of Lethington*
LORD HUNTLEY
LORD MORTON
LORD ERSKINE
LORD THROGMORTON
A Porter
LORD RUTHVEN
YOUNG RUTHVEN
First Sentinel
Second Sentinel
GRAEME, *a Sergeant*
A Warden
Soldiers and others

ACT I

SCENE I

SCENE: *A half-sheltered corner of the pier at Leith.[1] It is a sleety, windy night, and the tall piles of the background and the planks underfoot shine black and icy with their coating of freezing rain. Long cables stretch away into the dark. The only light comes from the lantern of two iron-capped* GUARDS *who are playing cards morosely on the head of a fish-tub in the lee of a great coil of rope.*

1st *Guard.* Na, na, put them away. I'm fair clabbered with the cold.

2d *Guard.* Aye, you'd say that, wi' ma siller-piece laced in your brogues!

[1] The port of entry for Edinburgh, the Scottish capital.

Enter JOHN KNOX [1] L., *a tall, bearded figure, muffled in a cloak*

1st *Guard.* Gie me the hand, then. But 5 man, it's an unco bitter nicht for indoor pleasures.

2d *Guard (throwing out cards).* It's a blastit wonner ——

1st *Guard.* Put out, put out! 10

2st *Guard (laying down a coin).* Aye.

1st *Guard.* And we'll just stop now, forbye to go on 'ud strain your two-year credit.

(He shows his hand.)

Knox. Aye, dicing, gaming, cards, drinking, dancing, whoring, and all the papistical 15

[1] Celebrated religious reformer and preacher (1505–72), who led the Protestant movement in Scotland and brought about the establishment of Presbyterianism as the faith of his country. He first began to preach virulently against the French and the Catholic influences in Scotland about 1555–56.

uses of the flesh — they run before her like a foul air ——

2d Guard (rising). It's the Master — wheest — put them awa'.

1st Guard. An' what of it? I'm na mem- 20 ber of his congregation.

     A 3D GUARD *runs in* R.; *stops* R.C.

3d Guard. I was right, Jamie! 'Tis the Queen's ship![1]

1st Guard. The Queen's ship, you goik! How could it be the Queen's ship? 25 She's to come in a galley, and she's none due this month yet.

3d Guard. My word on it, Tod, I rid out wi' the fishermen, and she's a galley wi' oars, and by God she carries the oriflamme![2]   30

2d Guard. Would the Queen's ship dock without notice to the lords, and no retinue at the pier?

3d Guard. There it lies — yon wi' the lights!

     (2D GUARD *stands on the pier and looks off* R.

1st Guard. She's lights aplenty, afore 35 God. Aweel, we've no orders aboot it.

3d Guard. But we can do no less than give her what escort we can ——

1st Guard. We're set to guard the pier, and for nowt else — And why are you so hot 40 for a Romish sovereign to set foot on Scottish soil, do you mind if I ask? It runs in my head we've had enough of the Guises and their Holy Father.[3] Let them stick to their warm climates where they're welcome — and may they 45 come to a hotter place before they set up another standard here!

     (*Crossing down* R. *and putting lantern on fish tub.*

Knox. Ye may be na member of the congre-

---

[1] Mary Stuart, Queen of Scots, returned from France to Scotland in 1561. This scene depicts that homecoming.

[2] The red ensign of the early French monarchs. Mary was now the widow of Francis II of France, whom she had married in 1558, and who had died in 1560.

[3] During the sixteenth century the Guises, who were originally dukes of Lorraine, were one of the most powerful houses in the French nobility, and also strong supporters of the Papal faith in its struggle against Protestantism. Mary Stuart's mother was Mary of Guise, sister of Francis, the second duke of that title.

gation, friend, but you will be if you keep in that opinion. For her or against her it's 50 to be in this land, and no halfway to stand on. The kirk of Christ or the huzzy of Rome, drowned in wine, bestial with fornication, corrupt with all diseases of mind and blood ——

2d Guard (taking a step toward KNOX). Is it the Queen's galley, Master?   55

Knox. Aye, it is.

1st Guard. For there's been no herald of it, nor anyone told ——

Knox. I have ways of knowing. And hearing of it, I came myself to see the white face 60 they speak of, and these taking graces, and to tell her to that white face of hers and despite her enchantments that we want and will have none of her here. For whatever beauty she may possess, or whatever winning airs, 65 they are given her of the devil to cozen us, they are born solely of the concupiscence of hell and set upon her like a sign. They say when she speaks she drips honey and she smells sweet with boughten perfumes, but I say the 70 man who tastes of her or the people who trust in her will chew on dry ashes in the last day and find no remedy for that thirst! I say she comes with a milk-white body and a tongue of music, but beware her, for she will be to you a 75 walking curse and a walking death!

2d Guard. You will say this to the Queen?

Knox. I will say this to her whey face!

BOTHWELL *enters* R. *with* SOLDIERS; *goes* C.

Both. Leg it over to the inn, one of you lads, and fetch a chair ——   80

*1st Guard (*R. *of* BOTHWELL). We're on guard here, my lord.

Both. Damn your guard duty! The Queen of Scotland's stepping out of a boat in velvet shoes ——   85

*2d Guard (*L. *of* BOTHWELL). I doubt there's a chair nearer than Edinburgh town ——

Both. There's one at the Leith Inn, as ye well know ——

1st Guard. We'd need the silver for that, 90 in any case ——

Both. My mannie, if I was to lay a fist to the side of that iron pot of yours I doubt the dent would come out in a hurry — What the devil

do ye mean bauchling [1] over a dirty chair? 95
Seize it! Seize it in the Queen's name!

2d Guard. I'll fetch it, sir. (*He exits* L.

Both. And do you go with him. I suspect ye
of being a psalm-singer with that face. (*The*
1ST GUARD *goes with the* 2D.) A verra 100
braw [2] evening to you, Master Knox.

Knox. And to you, my lord.

Both. It seems some here heard of her coming, though not perhaps those she'd have chosen. You're not here, by chance, to greet 105
the daughter of Mary of Guise? [3]

Knox. If I have aught to say to her, it will
be for her own ears.

Both. No doubt, no doubt. And I have a
little observe to make to you about that, 110
too, sir. Whatever it is you have to say to her
you won't say it.

Knox. And why not? Are the Papists [4] muz-
zling the ministers of God?

Both. I'm no Papist, as ye're aware, 115
Master Knox, and if I were I'm no such fool as
to try to muzzle a minister. Nevertheless,
whatever it was you were going to say, you
won't say it, that's my observe to you ——

Knox (*crossing down* R.). I shall say 120
what I have come to say.

(BOTHWELL *follows the* SOLDIERS *off* L.
*A man's voice, speaking French in a
light tenor, comes in from the* R.

Châtelard (*outside*). Que votre Majeste daigne
reconnaître une insigne d'honneur! [5]

Mary (*outside*). Veillez, pourtant, quand
vous voudrez encore poser votre cape dans 125
la boue, qu'aucun temoin n'en puisse faire la
rapport. [6]

Châtelard. On vous saurait reine, Madame,
s'il ne restait plus un seul sujet au monde. Les
arbres mêmes et les montagnes glacées se 130
baisseraient jusqu' à vos pieds. [7]

---

[1] Bungling. [2] A very fine.
[3] I.e., Mary, Queen of Scots. [4] The Roman Catholics.
[5] May Your Majesty deign to recognize a badge of
honor!
[6] Take care, however, when next you wish to toss
your cape in the mud, that some witness can report it.
[7] That you are queen would be known, Madame, even
if there no longer remained in the world a single subject.
The very trees and icy mountains would kneel at your
feet.

Mary. Oui, oui, je peut bien le figurer! [1]

(MARY THE QUEEN *enters* R. *with* PAGE, CHÂTE-
LARD, CHÂTELHERAULT, *and the* FOUR MARYS-
IN-WAITING.) Body o' me, I could wish the
clouds would stoop less to their queen in my
native land. 135

Châtelherault. [2] One forgets how damn dismal
this Scotland can be.

Mary. Dismal? Traitor, have you never
plucked a gowan [3] in spring — a fairy fresh
gowan —? 140

Châtelherault. Late — it comes late here ——

Mary. Or gorged with bright thorn-apples in
mid-August?

Châtelherault. Is there an August in this
heathenish climate? God, I can't remem- 145
ber it!

Mary. They are sweeter here than in France,
as I recall — (*Crosses a little* L. *All follow*) —
and all fruits are sweeter here, of those that
grow — and the summer's sweeter —— 150

Knox. And when they come they will bring
excellent devices of masks and ornament to deceive the eye, and soft words and stenches to
cumber the senses of mankind. Adulterers, jig-
masters and the like will come in author- 155
ity, and their counsel will be whoring and
carousing, the flowers and fruits of evil, of that
great sin, that sin that eats at the heart of the
world, the church of abominations, the church
of Rome! 160

(*He pauses. Mary stops to look back
at him.*

Mary. Châtelherault, I have been long away,
and the speech of Scotland falls strangely on
my ears, but is this talk usual among my people?

Knox. Yet is there a place reserved for 165
them, where the fire is unending and abates not,
even as their desires abate not, where their tender flesh shall be torn from them with white-hot
pincers, nor shall rank or station avail them,
whether they be queens or kings or the 170
lemans of queens and kings — !

Mary (*crossing* C., *tremulous*). Surely this is

---

[1] Yes, yes, I can well imagine it!
[2] Lord Boyd, Earl of Arran, who had been created
Duc de Châtelherault on his visit to the French court in
1560. [3] A daisy.

some jest, sir. Surely this is not said in welcome to me.

Knox. And what other welcome shall 175
we give the whore of Babylon — the leprous
and cankerous evangel of the beast!

(BOTHWELL *returns from* L.; *goes to* L.
of QUEEN MARY.

Both. Your Majesty, they are preparing a
room at the inn, and the chair will be here at
once. If you would deign to take my 180
cloak for your shoulders ——

Mary. No, thank you. I wish to speak to
this gentleman ——

Both. This is Master John Knox, of whom
Your Grace may have heard.   185

Mary (*crossing a little nearer* KNOX). Nay,
then I have heard of him, and I wish to speak to
him. Master Knox, it is true that I am Mary
Stuart, and your queen, and I have come back
from France after many years away, to 190
take up my rule in this country. It is true, too,
that I am sad to leave the south and the sun,
and I come here knowing that I shall meet with
difficulties that would daunt many older and
wiser than I am — for I am young and 195
inexperienced and perhaps none too adept in
statecraft. Yet this is my native place, Master
Knox, and I loved it as a child and still love it —
and whatever I may lack in experience, whatever I may have too much of youth, I shall 200
try to make up for, if my people will help me, in
tolerance, and mercy, and a quick eye for
wrongs and a quick hand to right them ——

Knox. Aye, they told me you spoke
honey ——   205

Mary. And cannot you also — you and your
people and those you know — cannot you too
be tolerant toward me a little space while I
find my way? For it will be hard enough at the
friendliest.   210

Knox. Woman, I remember whose daughter
and whose voice you are ——

Mary. If I were your daughter, Master
Knox, and this task before me, would you think
it fitting to lay such hard terms on me, 215
beast and whore and I know not what? For I
am not a whore, I can say truly, but the daughter of a prince, softly nurtured and loving honor
and truth. Neither is my body corrupt, nor

my mind. Nay, I am near to tears that 220
you should think so, and I was not far from
tears before, finding myself unexpected on this
coast, and no preparation to receive me. What
you have said comes as very cold comfort now
when I need greeting and reassurance. 225

Both. Your Majesty, if the old goat has said
anything that needs retracting ——

Mary (*facing* BOTHWELL). Nay. He shall
retract nothing in fear! I would have all men
my friends in Scotland!   230

Both. I'm afraid that's past praying for.

Mary (*facing* KNOX). Look on me, sir — and
judge my face and my words. In all fairness,
am I the evangel of the beast? Can we not be
friends?   235

Knox. I fear not, madam.

Mary. I strongly desire it. I have no wish
for any enemy of mine except that he become
my friend. You most of all, for I have met you
first, and it is an augury.   240

Knox. Your Majesty, I have said what I
came to say.

Mary. But you no longer mean it! See — I
give you my hand, Master Knox — it is a
queen's hand, and fair — and I look at 245
you out of honest eyes — and I mean well and
fairly — you cannot refuse me! Do you still
hesitate? It is clean. (*She smiles. He bows
stiffly over her hand.*) And will you come to see
me at Holyroodhouse,[1] and give me coun- 250
sel? For God knows I shall need counsel —
and I shall listen, that I promise.

Knox. Your Majesty, I should be untrue to
myself and my calling if I refused counsel where
it is asked.   255

Mary. You will come?

Knox. I will come.

Mary. I will send for you, and soon.

(*Her words are a kindly dismissal.*

Knox. Good night, Your Majesty ——

Mary. Good night, Master Knox. 260
(KNOX *goes out* L.) Now I wonder will he
hate me more or less?

Both. More, probably. However, it's just
as well to have him where you can watch him.

Mary. You're an outspoken man your- 265
self, Captain.

---

[1] The royal residence in Edinburgh.

Both. I am.

Mary. You will forgive me, but so far I have not heard your name.

Châtelherault (*crossing, a little* C.). The 270 captain is James Hepburn, madame — the Earl of Bothwell.

Mary. Why, then you are a friend! You fought ably for my mother.[1]

Both. I have been of some slight serv- 275 ice here and there.

Mary. You have indeed! Will you give me your hand, sir, and your welcome? (*He kneels and kisses her hand.*) Tell me, my lord of Both- well, have I done well so far? Shall I not 280 make this Scotland mine?

Both. Madame, it is a cold, dour, sour, bas- tardly, villainous country, and the folk on it are a cold, dour, sour, bastardly lot of close-shav- ing, psalm-retching villains, and I can only 285 hope no harm will come here to that bonny face of yours, and no misery to the spirit you bring.

Mary. Now here's a new kind of courtesy!

Both. You'll hear far and wide I'm no cour- tier, madame — but I have eyes, and I can 290 see that the new sovereign is a sonsie[2] lass and a keen one, and I was for her from the first I saw her face — but from my heart I could wish her a better country to rule over ——

Mary. Now, will no one speak well of 295 this poor Scotland of mine —?

Both. Your Majesty, shall I praise it for you — as high as it deserves —?

Mary. Say whatever good you can!

Both. Then this is Scotland, my lady: 300 To the north a few beggarly thousands of High- land Catholics who have not yet learned the trick of wearing britches, and to the south a few beggarly thousands of Lowland Protestants whose britches have no pockets to them. 305 Their pleasures are drinking and fighting, both of which they do badly, and what they fight about is that half of them are willing to sell their souls for a florin, whereas the other half

---

[1] Bothwell, who became Lord High Admiral of Scot- land in 1556, served Mary of Guise both as a warrior and statesman in the succeeding five years. He went on several diplomatic missions to England and France in her behalf.
[2] Comely.

have no expectation of getting so much. 310 What business they have is buying cheap and selling dear, but since none of them will sell cheap, and none will pay dear, the upshot is there's no business done ——

Mary. Enough, enough! — Solemnly 315 and truly, sir — it may be they are not a happy race, but they have beliefs — and what they believe they believe from the heart! Even this Master Knox ——

Both. He? He believes whatever's to 320 his own advantage, and prophesies whatever will line his nest if it comes to pass. He makes his living yelling nonsense into the lugs of these poor, benighted, superstitious savages — he's split the country wide open over your 325 coming and leads the pack against you, brawl- ing from his dunghill! We'll have bloodshed over it yet.

Mary. Bloodshed?

Both. And plenty. 330

Mary. No. If I thought that, I should turn now and bid the mariners hoist sail and put back for France. I shall win, but I shall win in a woman's way, not by the sword.

Both. Let us hope so. 335

Mary. Hope so! But I shall!

Both. I am no courtier, madame. I say, let us hope so. (1ST GUARD *enters* L., *followed by* 2D GUARD.) The chair has come, madame.

Mary. Yes, and in time. We're 340 chilled to the heart here. Come.

(*She goes out with* BOTHWELL L., *the others following.*

1st Guard. Did the old man spit his venom?

3d Guard (*up* C., *where he has been standing all through scene*). You'll not believe it. He kissed her hand.

2d Guard. She's a witch, then. 345

3d Guard. Aye, is she. The kind a man wouldna mind being bewitched by.

2d Guard. No.

3d Guard. I tell you she fair wenched him. The old man doddert a bit and then bent 350 over like a popinjay.

1st Guard. She's tha' kind, then?

3d Guard. Aye. She's tha' kind.

Curtain

SCENE 2

SCENE: *A corner of* QUEEN ELIZABETH'S *study at Whitehall.*[1] *It is morning, but the sun has not yet risen. She is up early to go over plans with* LORD BURGHLEY,[2] *who sits opposite her at a small table on which an hourglass stands like a paperweight on their notes. She is a young woman, still beautiful, with a crafty face. Tall candles burn behind them in a sconce. Outside the circle of light the scene is indefinite.*

Eliz. (*seated* R. *of table* C.). It still lacks something of dawn. We have one more hour before the palace will be stirring. You said, I believe, that you had made memoranda in regard to Mary Stuart? 5

Burgh. (*seated* L. *of table*). I have set down the facts as we must face them, and alternative policies.

Eliz. Read them, if you will. And turn the glass. It's run out. 10

Burgh. (*turning the glass and taking up a paper*). They are not in order, but the main points are covered. First, Mary Stuart has crossed from France to Scotland against your advice and without your safe-conduct. This is itself a slight to Your Majesty, and 15 almost a challenge, though not one of which you can take public cognizance.

Eliz. Yes.

Burgh. Second, she has been crowned queen of Scotland, this also against your wish 20 and in defiance of your policy. This may be construed as an open breach of friendship, or may be overlooked, as Your Majesty may desire — and as it may seem best.

Eliz. Yes. 25

Burgh. Third, she is a Catholic and related by blood to the most powerful Catholic house in France, which constitutes her a public danger to Protestant England. Fourth, she is next heir after Your Majesty to the throne of 30

[1] The royal palace in London.
[2] William Cecil, Baron Burghley (1521–98), private secretary of state to Queen Elizabeth from her accession in 1558; her principal adviser on matters of policy for forty years; and from 1572 until his death Lord High Treasurer of England.

England, and is held by Catholic Europe to be the rightful queen of England at the present time, Your Majesty being regarded by all Catholics as a pretender, unjustly seated on your throne. 35

Eliz. True. Proceed. You have more on that point. They believe me a bastard and say so. Very well, let us face that fact too.

Burgh. Fifth, then — you are held by Catholic Europe to be the illegitimate daughter 40 of Henry the Eighth, the divorce of Henry from Catherine of Aragon being unrecognized by the Church of Rome and his marriage to your mother, Anne Boleyn, being deemed invalid. Sixth, these things being true, Your Maj- 45 esty must not allow Marie Stuart to succeed as Queen of Scotland. For insofar as she is secure in Scotland you are insecure in England. Your Majesty will forgive my bad habit of setting down in writing what is so ob- 50 vious, but it is only by looking hard at these premises that I am able to discover what must be done.

Eliz. Out with it, then. What must be done? 55

Burgh. She must be defeated.

Eliz. How?

Burgh. Is there more than one way? We must pick our quarrel and send an army into Scotland. 60

Eliz. Declare war?

Burgh. Perhaps not openly — but we have an excuse for it.

Eliz. And reason?

Burgh. She must be defeated. 65

Eliz. Truly, but not so quick, not so quick with wars and troops and expenses. Have you no better counsel?

Burgh. In all my reading I have found no case of a sovereign deposed without vio- 70 lence.

Eliz. And in all those voluminous notes of yours you have set down no other method save warfare? The last resort, the most difficult, costly and hazardous of all? 75

Burgh. It is the only sure method, and you cannot afford to fail.

Eliz. My dear Burghley, in any project which affects England and our own person so

nearly we have no intention of failing. But　80
you have overlooked in your summary two considerations which simplify the problem.　One is
the internal dissension in Scotland, half Protestant, half Catholic, and divided in a mortal
enmity——　　　　　　　　　　　　　85
Burgh.　Overlook it!　Madame, it is the
main argument for an immediate declaration
of war — Edinburgh would rally to your arms
overnight!　This is our opportunity to unite
England and Scotland!　　　　　　　90
Eliz.　A war would unite Scotland against us
— unite Scotland under Mary.　No — it is
necessary first to undermine her with her own
subjects.
Burgh.　And how would that be accom-　95
plished?
Eliz.　This brings me to the second consideration which you overlook — the conduct and
reputation of Mary herself.
Burgh.　Would that affect our policy?　100
Eliz.　It will make it.　Merely to remind us,
will you read over again the report of Mary's
character in Randolph's latest budget of news?
Burgh.　This?　"As for the person of Marie,
our new queen, I must say in truth that　105
she is of high carriage, beautiful in a grave
way——"
Eliz.　So — go on.
Burgh.　"—— beautiful, in a grave way,
somewhat gamesome and given to light-　110
ness of manner, very quick-witted to answer
back, and addicted to mirth and dancing."
Eliz.　You see, she is a Stuart.
Burgh.　"Moreover, she hath allowed herself to be seen much in the company of　115
certain men, among them the Earl of Bothwell,
and hath borne herself among these men, they
being known of somewhat loose report, in such
fashion as to give scandal to the stricter sort
here, she not scanting to lend her eyes or　120
hands or tongue to a kind of nimble and facile
exchange of smiles and greetings which might
better become the hostess of an ale-house, seeking to win custom."
Eliz.　Yes, a Stuart.　　　　　　125
Burgh.　"Nevertheless she is liked, and
greatly liked, by those on whom she hath
smiled closely, they being won not as a wise

sovereign wins subjects, but as a woman wins
men."　　　　　　　　　　　　130
Eliz.　She has won our Randolph among
others.　He shall go north no more.
Burgh.　"Yet to be true again I must say also
that she is of noble mind, greatly religious in
her way, and the whispers against her　135
name not justified by what she is in herself, but
only by her manners, which she hath from
France.　And in addition she hath borne her
power thus far with so discreet and tolerant a
justness, impartial to north and south, to　140
Catholic and Protestant alike, that if she persevere in this fashion she is like to reconcile the
factions and establish herself firmly on the
throne of Scotland.　For vast numbers who
thought to curse her now remain her fast　145
friends."
Eliz.　Have you yet seen what we must do?
Burgh.　I find in this only a graver and more
malicious danger.
Eliz.　And you would still make war?　150
Burgh.　Your Majesty, it will be war whether
we like it or not — and there is imminent danger, danger to your throne and life.　The more
suddenly you act the less effort will be needed.
Eliz.　My lord, my lord, it is not easy to　155
thrust a queen from her throne, but suppose
a queen were led to destroy herself, led carefully
from one step to another in a long descent until
at last she stood condemned among her own
subjects, barren of royalty, stripped of　160
force, and the people of Scotland were to deal
with her for us?
Burgh.　She would crush a rebellion.
Eliz.　She would now, but wait.　She is a
Catholic, and for that half her people dis-　165
trust her.　She has a name for coquetry and
easy smiling, and we shall build that up into a
name for wantonness and loose behavior.　She
is seen to have French manners; we shall make
it appear that these manners indicate a　170
false heart and hollow faith.
Burgh.　Can this be done?
Eliz.　She is a woman, remember, and open
to attack as a woman.　We shall set tongues
wagging about her.　And since it may be　175
true that she is of a keen and noble mind, let us
take care of that too.　Let us marry her to a

weakling and a fool. A woman's mind and spirit are no better than those of the man she lies under in the night.   180

Burgh. She will hardly marry to our convenience, madame.

Eliz. Not if she were aware of it. But she is next heir to my throne; she will hope for children to sit on it, and she will therefore 185 wish to marry a man acceptable as the father of kings. We can make use of that.

Burgh. Only perhaps.

Eliz. No, certainly. She is a woman and already jealous for the children she may 190 bear. To my mind the man she marries must be of good appearance, in order that she may want him, but a fool, in order that he may ruin her, and a Catholic, in order to set half her people against her.   195

Burgh. We know that she is seen much with Bothwell.

Eliz. And he is a Protestant.

Burgh. He is a Protestant. Now suddenly it occurs to me. If she were to marry a 200 Protestant and turn Protestant herself, would she not make an acceptable ally? ——

Eliz. I do not wish her for an ally! Have you not yet understood? I wish her a Catholic and an enemy, that I may see her blood 205 run at my feet, lest mine run at hers! Since Bothwell is a Protestant, the more reason for dangling some handsome youngster instantly in the north, as if by accident, nay, as if against my will; some youngster with courtly 210 manners, lacking in brain, a Catholic, and of a blood-strain that would strengthen pretensions to the throne of England.

Burgh. You have thought of someone?

Eliz. I have thought of several. I shall 215 even let it be rumored that I oppose such a marriage. I shall let it go abroad that I favor someone else.

Burgh. Who is the man?

Eliz. I have thought of Darnley.[1]   220

[1] Henry Stuart, Lord Darnley, was son of Margaret Douglas, half-sister to James V of Scotland, while Mary Stuart was the daughter of James V. Mary and Darnley, therefore, were cousins and both in the line of succession to the English crown since they were grandchildren of Margaret Tudor, sister of Henry VIII and wife of James IV of Scotland.

Burgh. But after herself Darnley is next heir to the English throne. An alliance with him would actually strengthen her claim to succeed to your place.

Eliz. The better, the better. He is 225 handsome, and of good bearing?

Burgh. Yes.

Eliz. And a fool?

Burgh. A boasting, drunken boy.

Eliz. And a Catholic.   230

Burgh. As you know.

Eliz. If I give out that I am determined against it, she will marry him, and he will drag her down, awaken her senses to become his slave, turn her people against her, make 235 her a fool in council, curb this pretty strumpetry that gains her friends, haul her by the hair for jealousy, get her big with child, too, and spoil her beauty. I tell you, Burghley, a queen who marries is no queen, a woman who 240 marries is a puppet — and she will marry — she must marry to staunch that Stuart blood.

Burgh. This will take time.

Eliz. It may take many years. I can wait.

Burgh. And we shall need many de- 245 vices.

Eliz. You shall not find me lacking in devices, in the word to drop here, the rumor started there. We must have constant knowledge of her, and agents about her contin- 250 ually, so that her acts and sayings may be misconstrued and a net of half-lies woven about her.

Burgh. But, Your Majesty ——

Eliz. Yes, till her people believe her 255 a voluptuary, a scavenger of dirty loves, a bedder with grooms.

Burgh. But that — to accomplish that ——

Eliz. There is a man called Knox who can be used in this ——   260

Burgh. But to make of her what she is not —!

Eliz. We live in a world of shadows, my lord; we are not what we are, but what is said of us and what we read in others' eyes. 265 More especially is this true of queens and kings. It will grow up about her in whispers that she is tainted in blood, given over to lechery and infamous pleasures. She will be

known as double-tongued, a demon with 270
an angel's face, insatiable in desire, an emissary
of Rome, a prophetess of evil addicted to lascivious rites and poisonous revenges. And
before all this her own mind will pause in
doubt and terror of what she may be 275
that these things should be said of her — she
will lie awake in torment in the dark — and
she will lie broken, nerveless there in the dark.
Her own people will rise and take her scepter
from her. 280

Burgh. But, Your Majesty — you ——

Eliz. However, I am not to appear in this.
Always, and above all, I am to seem her friend.
— You would say that I am in myself more
nearly what will be said of her. 285

Burgh. No, no ——

Eliz. Why, perhaps. But that is not what is
said of me. Whatever I may be, it shall be
said only that I am queen of England, and
that I rule well. 290

Curtain

SCENE 3

SCENE: *A great hall in Mary Stuart's apartments,
Holyroodhouse. The room is rectangular,
with wide fireplaces glowing to the left and
right, with benches and stools in front of
them. An entrance door up right and two
doors at left lead, one to* MARY'S *study and
the other to her bedroom. The stone of the
walls is largely covered with stamped leather
hangings. A chair, slightly elevated, stands
in the middle of the rear wall, the royal arms
of Scotland draped above it. The floor is
stone with a few Eastern rugs. There are
two high, heavily draped windows at the
rear, on either side of the Queen's chair.
There is a chair and hassock right center.*
MARY BEATON, MARY SETON *and* MARY LIV-
INGSTONE *are concerning themselves with the
hangings of the ensign behind the dais chair,
and* LIVINGSTONE *has stepped upon a stool
to reach a fold of it.* LORD DARNLEY, LORD
GORDON *and* LORD DOUGLAS *are warming
themselves at the fire right, having just come
in.*

Beat. (*to the* MEN). It's to hang there because she wants it there. Isn't that enough?

Doug. (*sitting on stool below bench* R.). I've
heard my father say the kings of Scotland were
always plain folk, but queens are a fancy 5
breed, and their ways are fancy.

Darn. (*lounging on bench by fireplace* R.). A
thought higher with that fold, my dear — just a
thought higher.

Liv. (*standing on a stool by throne* C. *Turning*). And why? 10

Darn. Dod, lady, it's a neat turn of ankle
you show when you reach up. Reach a bit
higher.

Liv. (*back to her work*). Look your eyes full
if it does you any good, my Lord Darnley. 15

Darn. Man, man, but that's a pretty foot!

Doug. Aye.

Darn. Ye have heard it said, no doubt, what
they say about a woman's foot?

Doug. Aye. 20

Seton. What do they say?

Darn. About a woman's foot? Only that
it's, in a sort, a measure of her capacities.

Beat. (C.). Oh, is it, indeed? I've heard the
same in respect to a man's nose, and I can 25
only say, if it's true, your nose is no great ad-
vertisement for you.

Darn. (*crossing to* BEATON, C.). The nose
is a fallible signal, my lady, as I'll prove to you
— you naming your own place and time. 30

Beat. I to name the place?

Darn. It is your privilege.

Beat. Your own bedchamber, then.

Liv. Beaton!

Darn. Accepted! Accepted! My own 35
bedchamber! And the time?

Beat. The night of your wedding, by God!

Darn. My dear lady ——

Doug. She has you there, Darnley.

MARY FLEMING *enters* R.

Darn. Mistress Fleming, is it true our 40
sovereign is inaccessible this day?

Flem. Quite true, I fear.

Darn. God help the man who tries to woo a
queen.

Flem. And so He might if your lord- 45
ship prayed to Him with any serious intent.

Gor. Will ye come, man? Ye'll have no sight of the Queen today, and these trollops have no time for plain Scotchmen.

Darn. Aye.   50

Flem. Lord Darnley is to remain within call. It is Her Majesty's pleasure.

Darn. Ah, well, that's something.

Gor. It's dangling, to give it a plain name.   55

BOTHWELL *enters* L.

Liv. Oh, my Lord Bothwell.

Both. By God, my name's remembered, and that's a triumph. Tell the sweet Queen Lord Bothwell would see her alone.

Liv. Sir, she is closeted with her secretary —   60
We are not free to speak with her.

Both. (*by fireplace* L.). Closeted? So?
I like not that word closeted. Who is there here
Who can speak with her and tell her?

Flem. (*crossing* L.). My Lord, she has spaced   65
This day off into hours, so many to each,
And I fear your name is not scheduled.

Both. Distrust your schedule,
Then, my prim, for I'll see her.

Flem. The ambassador   70
From England arrives today, for his audience,
And before that Her Majesty plans to hold
A conclave with the Lords.

Darn. (*crossing* L.). We've been sloughed off
Much the same way, my lord.   75

Both. Run along, then, and practice
Wearing that tin sword you've got hung on you,
Before it trips you.

Darn. Trips me?

Both. (*crossing to* C.). Aye, run and play!   80
This one's been used. The nicks along the edges
Were made on tougher than you. Tell my lady queen
I wish to see her now.

Flem. I cannot myself.
I might speak to Master Rizzio.[1]   85

[1] David Rizzio, whom Mary brought with her from **France** as her secretary.

Both. Then do that. Is Scotland grown so formal
That a man's received like a money-lender?
           (FLEMING *goes out* R.

Beat. No,
But these matters must be arranged.
           (DARNLEY *laughs.*

Both. (*to* DARNLEY). Are you still here?

Darn. Still here.   91

Both. I knew a pimp in Paris had much your look,
But the women he brought me were foul.

Darn. But good enough,
I daresay.   95

Both. *You* might have thought so ——

RIZZIO *enters* R., FLEMING *following* R.

Riz. Oh, my Lord Bothwell.
There's such great pressure on our time today —
Matters that must be seen to; if you could come
Tomorrow ——   100

Both. (*crossing to fireplace* R.). Well, I cannot come tomorrow.
Tomorrow will not do. I am here today.
And will not be here tomorrow. Is that understood?
           (RIZZIO *pauses.*

Darn. Let him run his suit into the ground.

Gor. Aye, and himself.   105
      (DARNLEY, GORDON *and* DOUGLAS go out L. *All* MARYS *talk in a group* C.

Rizzio. My orders are strict, my lord. Her Majesty
Has great problems of state ——

Both. And they concern me
More than some others. (*Crossing* L. *and back to* R.C., *scattering* MARYS)
Now, before Christ, I've argued   110
Enough with women and women-faced men!
A room's a room
And a door's a door! Shall I enter without warning
Or will you announce me to her? Great pressure on
Our time! Our time, he says! My fine Italian ——

QUEEN MARY *enters* R.   *There is sudden quiet*

Mary. I will speak with my lord alone.   115
(*One by one, and silently,* RIZZIO *and*
    FLEMING *and* SETON *exit* R., LIV-
    INGSTONE *and* BEATON L.
Do I find you angry?

Both. At these pests and midges.

Mary. You saw me yesterday.

Both. I have been standing since this early
    morning —
I and some hundred crows, out in the cop-
    pice   120
On the cliff's edge, waiting for the smoke to rise
From your breakfast chimney. And by the
    Lord these crows
Are a funny company. I've had four full hours
To study them.

Mary (*crossing to* L.C.). You come to tell me
    this?   125

Both. (R. *of* MARY). I come to tell you
I've never shown such patience for a woman,
Not in my life before.

Mary. Did you call it patience
On a time when I could not see you, to wreck
    an inn,   130
Leave mine host in the road with a broken head
And lie with his daughter?

Both. That was not true.   Or at least
I had her good will for it.

Mary. And another time   135
To besiege the Governor's house with your
    border knaves
And rouse all Edinburgh? Are you a man
Or a storm at sea, not to be brought indoors?

Both. (*crossing to* MARY). When I would see
    my girl, why, I must see her
Or I am a storm, and indoors, too.   140

Mary. Your girl? Give me leave,
Since I am a queen, with a kingdom to reign
    over,
To queen it once in a while. (*Crossing a little* L.

Both. I tell you truly
I've the manners of a rook, for we're all crows
    here,   145
And that's what's understood in this town,
    (*coming close to* MARY) but I could
Be tame and split my tongue with courtly
    speeches

If I could be sure of you — if I could know from
    one day
To another what to make of your ways. You
    shut yourself up
With secretaries and ministers, harking for
    weeks   150
On end to their cackle — while I perch me on
    the rocks
And look my eyes out.

Mary. When I was but thirteen
A pretty lad fell in love with me; he'd come,
Oh, afternoon, late midnight, early dawn, 155
Sopping with dew-fall; he'd stand there, wait-
    ing for a glance —
I've never had such tribute.

Both. This is no boy,
This is a man comes beating your door in
    now.
It may be you're too young to know the dif-
    ference,   160
But it's time you learned.

Mary. You've had your way, my lord!
We've spoken together, though I had no time
    to give,
And now, with your pardon ——

Both. You'll go about the business   165
Of marrying someone else. That's what this
    mangy
Meeting of councilors means, and that's what
    portends
From Elizabeth's ambassador! I warn you,
Make no decisions without me!

Mary. I cannot marry you.   170
I beg you, ask it not; speak not of it. Our day
Has come between us. Let me go now. (*Cross-
    ing to* C.

Both. My lady,
I will speak softly. Have no fear of me
Or what I intend. (MARY *faces him.*)   175
But there have been days I remember
When you had less care what hostages you gave
The world. I think you showed more royally
    then
Than now, for you loved then and spoke your
    love, and I
Moved more than mortal for that while.   180

Mary. I fear I've been but too mortal where
    you're concerned.

Both. Oh, girl,

If we would be as the high gods, we must live
From within outward!   Let the heavens rain fire
Or the earth mud.   This is a muddy race 185
That breeds around us.   Will you walk in fear
    of mud-slingers,
Or walk proudly, and take my hand?
    Mary. I am a queen.
    Both. They've made a slave of you,
This bastard half-brother of yours,[1] this fox of
    a Maitland,   190
This doddering Châtelherault! They'll frighten
    you
With consequences.   They're afraid of men's
    tongues
And they've made you afraid.   But what they
    truly fear
Is that you'll win the country, be queen here
    truly
And they'll be out of it.   What they'd like
    best of all   195
Is to wreck you, break you completely, rule the
    country themselves,
And why they fear me is because I'm your man
    alone,
And man enough to stop them.
    Mary. Yes.   You are man enough.
It's dangerous to be honest with you, my Both-
    well,   200
But honest I'll be.   Since I've been woman
    grown
There's been no man save you but I could take
His hand steadily in mine, and look in his eyes
Steadily, too, and feel in myself more power
Than I felt in him.   All but yourself.   There is
    aching   205
Fire between us, fire that could take deep hold
And burn down all the marches of the west
And make us great or slay us.   Yet it's not to
    be trusted.
Our minds are not the same.   If I gave my
    hand
To you, I should be pledged to rule by wrath 210
And violence, to take without denial,
And mount on others' ruin.   That's your way
And it's not mine.

---

[1] James Stuart (?1531–70), Earl of Moray, who was
the natural son of King James V of Scotland by Lady
Margaret Erskine and therefore half-brother to Queen
Mary.

    Both. You'll find no better way.
There's no other way for this nation of churls
    and cravens.   215
    Mary. I have been queen of France — a
    child-queen and foolish —
But one thing I did learn, that to rule gently
Is to rule wisely.   The knives you turn on your
    people
You must sometime take in your breast.
    Both. You know not Scotland.   220
Here you strike first or die.   Your brother
    Moray[1]
Seeks your death, Elizabeth of England
Seeks your death, and they work together.
    Mary. Nay ——
You mistrust too much — and even if this were
    true   225
A sovereign lives always with death before and
    after,
And many have tried to murder their way to
    safety ——
But there's no safety there.   For each enemy
You kill you make ten thousand, for each one
You spare, you make one friend.   230
    Both. Friends?   Friends?   Oh, lass,
Thou'lt nurse these adders and they'll fang
    thee! Thou'rt
Too tender and too just.   My heart cries for
    thee ——
Take my help, take my hands!
                    (*Offers his hands.*
    Mary. I would I could take both.   235
God knows how I wish it.   But as I am queen
My heart shall not betray me, what I believe
And my faith.   This is my faith, dear my lord,
    that all men
Love better good than evil, cling rather to truth
Than falseness; answer fair dealing with fair
    return;   240
And this, too: those thrones will fall that are
    built on blood
And craft, that as you'd rule long, you must
    rule well. ——
This has been true, and is true.
    Both. God help thee, child.

---

[1] An ardent Calvinist and follower of Knox, he had
always been opposed to Mary's Catholicism and consequently sought Queen Elizabeth's support for the
Protestant party in Scotland.

Mary. Be staunch to me. You have been the
     staunchest of all.   245
Let me not lose your arm. No, nor your
     love ——
You know how much you have of mine. I'm
     here
Alone, made queen in a set, hard, bitter time.
Aid me, and not hinder.
     Both. So it shall be.   250
     Mary. And give me the help I'd have.
     Both. That I can't promise.
I'll help thee and defend thee. Lady dear,
Do you use guile on me?
     Mary. No, sweet, I love thee,   255
And I could love thee well.
     (*She goes to him. He kisses her hand
     and then her lips.*
Go now, and leave me.
We've been seen too much together.
     Both. You must lay this hand
In no one's else. It's mine.   260
     Mary. I have but lease on it,
Myself. It's not my own. But it would be
     yours
If it were mine to give.

MARY LIVINGSTONE *comes to the* L. *door*

     Liv. Your Majesty,
The Lords of the council are here.   265
     Mary (*crossing a little* R.). Let them be ad-
     mitted.   (LIVINGSTONE *goes out* L.
     Both. Has Your Majesty forgotten
That I am of the council, under your seal?
     Mary. I could wish you were elsewhere.
     These are the men I least
Have wanted to find us alone.   270
     (*Sits on throne chair.*

LORD JAMES STUART, Earl of Moray, MAIT-
LAND of Lethington, *the* DUC DE CHÂTEL-
HERAULT, HUNTLEY, MORTON *and* ER-
SKINE *enter* L.

     Mait. (L.C. *by throne chair*). We have not in-
     terrupted Your Majesty?
     Mary. No. The Earl of Bothwell is of the
     council.
I have asked him to take part.
     Mait. There was some agreement,

That since the Earl's name might come up, it
     would be as well   275
If he were not here.
     Both. (R. *by fireplace*). And then, again, since
     my name
May be mentioned, and there's none so able
     as I
To defend it, it may be as well that I'm here.
     Mait. My lord,   280
There was small thought to attack you.
     Both. Less now, perhaps.
     Mary. Lord Bothwell will remain.
     Moray. Sister, it may be that Bothwell will
     be offended
By something said.   285
     Mary. You are courtier enough
To couch it not to offend, my brother.
     Mait. (L. *of* MARY). Nay, then,
What we have come to say must be softly
     said,
But meant no less strictly. The question of
     our queen's marriage,   290
Of which everyone has spoken, let me add,
But which we have avoided here, must now
     come up
Whether or no we like it.
     Mary. Be not so tender
With me, dear Maitland. I have been mar-
     ried. I am   295
A widow, and free to marry again.
     Hunt. That's the lass!
They say widows are always ready.
     Mary. Do they say that?
Do they not say ready but — wary?   300
     Hunt. Aye, that too.
     Mary. But the truth is I should prefer my
     own time for wedding.
I know of no prince or king whose hand is
     offered,
And whose hand I'd take.
     Mait. It's not to be treated lightly,   305
I'm much afraid. The thrones of all the world
Are shaken with broils even as we stand here.
     The throne
On which you sit, our sovereign, is shaken too,
Though Your Majesty has done more than I'd
     dreamed
Could be done to still the factions. It's our
     belief   310

That a marriage, if the right one, would seat
   you more firmly,
Put an end to many questions.
   Mary. There's more of this?
   Mait. That's all we wish — to see you safe
   on your throne
So that we may be safe in our houses.   Until
   men know   315
What alliance we're to make, what hangs over
   us
In the way of foreign treaties, the clans will
   sleep
With dirks in their brogans,[1] and a weather eye
   still open
For fire in the thatch.   And yet to choose the
   man —
That's a point we can't agree on.   320
   Mary. I'm with you there.
For you see, I'm hard to please.
   Mait. And more than that,
Of princes that offer, or have been suggested,
   each one
Commits us to some alliance of church or
   state   325
We'd find embarrassing.   Philip of Spain, the
   Duke
Of Anjou — these are Catholic ——
   Both. Has it crossed your minds that there
   are lords in Scotland?
   Mait. And there, too —
If the choice were to fall on a Scottish earl,
   the houses   330
Passed over would take it ill — and it might
   well lead
To a breach of our peace ——
   Both. Yes?
   Mait. Nay, even to civil war.
   Mary. I cannot give myself out   335
As a virgin queen, yet our cousin Elizabeth's
   plan
Has virtues.   Must I marry at all?
   Mort. (*crossing toward throne*).   Your Maj-
   esty,
We have not yet said what we came to say,
And it needs saying bluntly.   The people of
   Scotland   340
Are given to morals almost as much as to
   drink.

   [1] Hose.

I'll not say they're moral themselves, but they'll
   insist
On morals in high places.   And they've got in
   their heads
That you're a light woman.   (MARY *rises.*
I don't know how it got there,   345
And I daresay it's not true ——
   Mary. Thank you.   For your daresay.
      (MORTON *crosses back to* L. *and stands
      with back to fireplace.*
   Mait. I could have wished to speak more
   delicately
Of this, but it's before us, and can't be de-
   nied.
Your Majesty, when you came to us from
   France   350
And I saw you first, I said to myself in my
   heart,
All will be well in Scotland.   What I thought
   then
I can say now, for you are wiser even
Than I had supposed, and you have dealt more
   justly
Than any could have hoped, yet still it's
   true   355
Some spreading evil has gone out against you,
A crawling fog of whispers.
   Mary. Who believes them?
           (*Sits on throne chair.*
   Mait. I'll not say they're believed.   I'm not
   sure they are.
But there was the episode of the boy who was
   hidden   360
In your bedchamber —
   Ersk. Châtelard.
   Mait. Aye, he, and
That may have begun it.   I believed at first it
   stemmed
From John Knox's preaching, for he holds all
   Catholics   365
To be the Devil's own, but there's more than
   that ——
A much more seeded, intentional crop of lyings
Planted here, till I've wondered if Châte-
   lard
May not have been an agent, or one of many.
   Mary. Planted by whom?   370
   Hunt. Why, by Elizabeth.
Who else?

Mait. But that's not certain either.
Châtelard came from France, and in all this
    scurrile [1]
I've traced no word to London.   375
    Mary. It's what they say,
Not what they believe.
    Hunt. You've lent them some color for
    it,
Your Majesty. You've been no statue.
    Mary. No,   380
Nor wish to be. My Lord of Lethington,
What you have said of me, how I was when you
    saw me,
How I seem to you now, I swear to you, you
    were not wrong.
I have not betrayed myself as woman or
    queen.
    Mait. I would swear that, too.   385
    Mary. And since I know that is true,
I have thought very little of whispers. For
    there is judgment
Somehow in the air; what I am will be known,
    what's false
Will wash out in the rains.
               (MORTON *moves restlessly.*
    Mait. My sovereign, you are yet young.   390
I once believed that. But I have lived long
    enough
To see error grow up and prosper, and send its
    roots
A century deep. There's force enough in these
    winds
Of malice to blow us all down ——
    Mary. I'll try to be serious,   395
For I see you are. It's your thought, then,
    that a marriage
Would end the rumors?
    Mait. Aye.
    Mary. But as to whom I'll marry —
Happily, that's not decided for me yet.   400
    Mort. By God,
If it was we'd see you to bed with him tonight.
    Mary. Has the woman no voice in such
    matters?
    Mort. Not in such cases.
    Mary. And what is my case, may I ask?   405
    Mort. (*crossing a little* c.). Why, we've said
    nothing

[1] Scurrilous talk.

About my Lord Bothwell. It's his name's
    coupled with yours,
His and young Rizzio's.
    Both. (*crossing a little* c.). I've thought often,
    Morton,
One of us would die before the other. Now   410
I'm sure of it. And soon.
    Mort. I have you.[1]
    Mary. My lords,
Will you quarrel in council over your queen's
    virtue?
Let me defend my own honor, and let you   415
Defend your own.
           (MORTON *and* BOTHWELL *give ground,*
           MORTON L., BOTHWELL R.
Do I understand that I
Am accused with Bothwell or Rizzio? Or
    both?
    Mait. You are accused of nothing.
    Mort. You are not accused,   420
Your Majesty. Moreover, you are queen
Of Scotland, and therefore no man here would
    dare
Accuse you ——
    Mary. Oh, speak out, man! Are you afraid?
When have I punished plain dealing?   425
    Mort. Why, then, you are queen,
And may set your own customs, but if my wife
    were seen
Abroad as you are, and half so free of contact
With young and old as you are, I'd not answer
For what was said about her!   430
    Mary. I'm no man's wife.
    Mort. No. And the sense of this council
Is that it might better if you were,
Better for your good name and better for Scot-
    land.
    Mary. I will answer these things: as for
    Rizzio,   435
He is my secretary; if I spend time
In private with him, that is the reason. If I
Had not liked him, he would not be my sec-
    retary.
As for Lord Bothwell, he has put more strength
Behind what I wished to do than any among
    you,   440
And at times when I had despaired. He is my
    good friend.

[1] I understand you.

We were here alone before this conference
And we differed in opinion. To wipe that
    out
I went to him of myself and kissed his lips.
  Mort. Aye!   445
  Mary. We had kissed but once before, may
    not kiss again,
But that's at my option, not yours.
        (MORTON *moves down stage a little.*
  Hunt. Lassie, ye've been
Too honest for your own good.
  Mary. Why, if so much weight   450
Is placed on a kiss in Scotland, come now, each
    one,
And take your kiss — or if that's no recom-
    pense
Come to me then in private, and you shall
    have,
Each one, one kiss.
  Mort. And after that, there are kisses 455
Elsewhere — and when you've finished,
    whether you'll marry
Or not may not be the question, but whether
    we can find
A prince who'll have you.
  Mary (*rising and taking a step down*). And
    having heard that word —
My lords, when you wish to talk with me
    again   460
As civilized men, and not barbarians,
You shall have audience. This Scottish kirk
    of yours
Has misled you as to the meaning of kisses. I
    am
Unsullied and young, and have my own faith to
    plight
And more to think of than these maunder-
    ings[1]   465
Over pantry gossip. I shall not marry till
I find it wise, nor until I have made quite sure
What effect it will have on my inheritance
Of the throne of England. You come here in
    high conclave
And spend three farthings' worth of wit to
    chaffer   470
Over a kiss in my audience-chamber! The
    question
Is not to save my name, I hope, nor my throne,
    [1] Grumblings.

But how best to meet the destiny that has
    made me
Fall heir to all this island. — Scotland is mine,
And England will come to me or to the
    child   475
I hope to have. It's this that makes my mar-
    riage
A matter of moment. — And this — with your
    good pardon —
Will be the last for today.   (*She goes out* R.
  Moray. Morton, I warned you
To leave all speech to Lethington.   480
  Mort. She sits on that throne
Only so long as we want her there, no longer.
  Both. (*crossing to* MORTON). If my Lord of
    Morton
Would care to lose those black feathers from
    his crest
I await his pleasure.   (*He goes out* L. 485
  Moray. I'm for that, too. Settle it between
    you,
And may you both win. We'll all be the better
    for it.

    LIVINGSTONE *enters* L.

  Liv. Lord Throgmorton is here from Eng-
    land
With embassies for the Queen.
  Mait. She's gone to her study.   490
She'll wish to admit him.
  Liv. Yes.   (*She goes out* R.
  Mait. We get no further
Today, then.   (*He goes to the door* L.
  Hunt. No. Erskine, a word with you. 495
    (ERSKINE *and* HUNTLEY *go out* L.
    THROGMORTON *enters* L.
  Mait. Come in, Lord Throgmorton. You've
    been announced within.
  Throg. Greetings, my lord, fair greetings.
  Mait. We can have speech later.
  Throg. We shall.
    (MAITLAND *and* MORTON *go out* L.
    THROGMORTON *and* MORAY *are alone.*
Greetings also to my Lord James Stuart, 500
In fine, the best of greetings.
  Moray (C.). From Elizabeth?
  Throg. (L. of MORAY). I'm burdened with
    them — and more to you than any.

Moray. May I know the drift?

Throg. This is hardly the place for that ——

But this much for now: Elizabeth has determined   506

That you are to reign in Scotland, if not as king,

Then as regent again.

Moray. Well, that's news.

Throg. She bids me tell you   510

As if from herself, you are not to be disturbed

If her policy seems at variance with her mind.

It's a wide arc of intrigue, but she carries

These schemes in her head like a gambit,[1] and
she means

To play it to the end.   Your sister Mary   515

Is not acceptable to her.

Moray. But this scheme of hers?

Throg. Sh, later, later.   You're a silent
man, I know.

No word.

Moray. None.   520

Queen Mary *enters* R.

Mary. Lord Throgmorton?

Throg. Your Majesty.

      (*He kneels.   She comes to him and
      gives him her hand to kiss.*)

From one great queen to another, happiness.

Mary. A courtier in the grand style.

Throg. Nay, Majesty,   525

A plain man of business.

      (Moray *crosses to fireplace* L.

Mary. Let us to business, then.

      (*She motions him to rise, and he does
      so, and crosses to fireplace* R.   Mary
      crosses to throne.)

My brother, did you wish further word with
me?

Moray. No, madame, only that I may see
you tomorrow.

Mary (*sits in her chair*). At your own time.

      (Moray *bows low and goes out* L.

You had more to say?   531

Throg. (R. *by fireplace*). Much more.   My
poor brain's taxed with remembering.

But to begin, Queen Elizabeth sends her love

[1] In the game of chess, an opening where one player
voluntarily gives up one or several pieces for an ultimate advantage in position.

To her cousin of Scotland, wishes her well, and
a reign

Both long and easy, and proffers to that end

Whatever friendship and amity between
thrones   536

Your Majesty will accept.

Mary. Tell Elizabeth

She will not find me niggard of friendship or
love.

Throg. I shall report Your Majesty so.   Then,
further,   540

I'm bid to say, what Elizabeth most desires

Is that all briars of discord that have grown

Between this city and England, be wed
away,

And leave a path for peace.

Mary. I desire that, too.   545

Does she put a name to these briars?

Throg. Your Majesty, I am

Permitted to speak quite frankly?

Mary. I beg you to.

Throg. You are next heir to the throne of
England, and you   550

Are a Catholic.   This is a danger to you

As well as Elizabeth.   Were you to turn
Protestant

Elizabeth would at once recognize in you

Next heir to her succession.

Mary. I should think she might,   555

Since I am next heir.

Throg. If this seems difficult, I am but to
remind you

That Elizabeth was a Catholic, but became

A Protestant for political reasons.

Mary. That   560

I could never do.   Nor do I see that one's faith

Should be touched by politics.

Throg. (*walking* R. *and back*).   Nay, not politics,

My gracious queen!   God forbid me that I
should bring

That word into such a context!   We know,
however,   565

How one clings, shall we say for sentimental
reasons,

To the rituals of his youth!   Aye, and even a
prince,

We admit, would rather say his pater nosters [1]

[1] Prayers; literally, "our fathers."

The way he learned them when he was a child.
    And yet
Must we take these childish things so gravely
    now,   570
When war or peace hangs on them?   There are
    Catholics
In England still.   They still plot against our
    queen.
Were she struck down by one of them you'd
    take
Her throne and rule us.   It follows that your
    faith
Is a challenge to her — yes, if Your Grace will
    pardon   575
The word — a defiance.
    Mary.   Your manner
Is packed with the most magniloquent impu-
    dence
That's come my way.   Do you or your queenly
    mistress
Deem me an inferior, to be given orders
    blithely,   580
With a high hand?
    Throg.   No, madame.
    Mary.   Say three words more
In this cavalier offensive style of yours
And you'll find yourself in the courtyard.   585
    Throg.   Madame, I ——
    Mary.   Come down to earth, and speak with-
    out swaggering.
    Throg.   I've been in the wrong.
    Mary.   That's better.
    Throg.   It's true that I'd   590
Rehearsed my song and dance.   Your wit is
    quicker
Than's been supposed in London.
    Mary.   Quick enough
To perceive an insult, I hope.
    Throg.   Your Majesty,   595
There was none intended, but I might have
    spoken more wisely
Had I known your mettle.   Elizabeth is con-
    cerned,
As I have said, with the differences that are
    certain
To arise over your religion.   Further than
    that,
What arrangements may be made to avert a
    breach   600

In the present concord, if we may discuss these
    things
Frankly, and you will make frank replies, I
    have
No other mission.
    Mary.   Now you talk sense.   And frankly,
I will not change my faith.   605
    Throg.   And, frankly again,
There was little hope that you would.   There
    is some hope,
However, that when Your Majesty seeks a
    consort
You will not do so to bolster up your claim
To the English crown, which is strong enough
    already   610
To cause us uneasiness in London.
    Mary.   That
Had not occurred to me.
    Throg.   But surely your choice in marriage
Will imply your attitude?   615
    Mary.   I have no intention
Of plighting my troth at once, but if I had
I've received advice already on that point,
A mort [1] of it — and I'm tender.
    Throg.   Say no more,   620
Madame, and I'll say no more.
    Mary.   Oh, out with it now.
Give the advice.   I won't take it.
    Throg.   Why, it's only this:
If Your Majesty were to marry a Protestant
    lord   625
Of no royal pretensions, it would indicate
That you meant no danger to our Elizabeth.
    Mary.   She has chosen for me, I daresay?
    She has some lord
Of the sort in mind?
    Throg.   You embarrass me to go on.   630
She mentioned a name.
    Mary.   Yes?
    Throg.   Madame, the Earl of Leicester.
    Mary.   I hope her ears burn now.   Leicester?
    Her cast-off —
Her favorite — the one she's dangled?   This
    is an affront —   635
She named Lord Leicester?
    Throg.   Nay, nay — only to show you
What it was she had in mind.   The kind of
    match.

    [1] An abundance.

Mary. I would hope so.

Throg. For, you see, Your Majesty,   640
She had a fear of this — the young Lord
     Darnley
Has come north against her will. Why he's
     here we don't know.
Nor whether by invitation, nor what your
     plans
Might be concerning him.

Mary. I have none.   645

Throg. Then, if you will,
Forget what I've said. It was only that this
     Darnley
Combines to exactness what Elizabeth dreads
In case you marry. After you he's next to her
     throne,
And he's a Catholic. Should you marry Lord
     Darnley   650
And call up Catholic Europe to your back —
Well, we'd be ringed in steel.

Mary. I have offered your queen
My friendship and love. I meant that offer.

Throg. But even   655
If there were no quarrel, and you should marry
     Darnley
And have a son by him — he'd be heir to Eng-
     land —
And I think the plain fact is that Elizabeth
Would rather choose her own heir.

Mary. Now God forgive me! —   660
I am heir to the throne of England, and after me
Whatever children I have — unless by some
     chance
The virgin queen should bear sons! Is it part
     of her love
To cut me off from my rights?

Throg. It must be remembered   665
That England is Protestant, and it might come
     hard
To accept a Romish sovereign. In brief, my
     queen
Has wished that you might choose Bothwell,
     or perhaps some other
Of Protestant persuasion!

Mary (rising). And that's the message.   670
We're down to it at last. My Lord Throg-
     morton,
I marry where I please — whether now or
     later,

And I abate not one jot of my good blood's lien
On the English throne. Nay, knowing now
     the gist
Of Elizabeth's policy toward that claim, I shall
     rather   675
Strengthen it if I can. The least worthy sov-
     ereign
Has a duty toward his blood, not to weaken it
Nor let it decline in place.

Throg. This will hardly please.

Mary. I could hardly expect it would. But
     I too am a power,   680
And it matters what pleases me. This was all?

Throg. This was all
I was commissioned with.

Mary. I shall see to your safe-conduct.

Throg. I thank Your Majesty.   685
     (*He goes out* L. MARY *is alone a mo-*
     ment, brooding. Then sits in throne
     chair.

RIZZIO *enters* R. *and goes to* R. *of* QUEEN

Mary. Oh, Rizzio, Rizzio.
They make mock of me! It was as you pre-
     dicted
To the utter syllable.

Riz. A warning, then.

Mary. We'll expect no friendship from Eng-
     land.   690
She cuts me off, me and my line.

Riz. May I say that this
Is only her wish, not to be accomplished?

Mary. Aye, and not to be.
I'd have stood her friend, Rizzio, meant to be
     her friend,   695
But now — this is not to be borne! Go and
     find Lord Darnley.   (*Rises.*

Riz. Your Majesty — you have made a
     decision?

Mary. Yes.

Riz. Now I thank you. Now, God helping
     us, we'll win.
She'll not stamp you out.   700

Mary. So I think. And now find him.

Riz. Yes.   (*Exits* L.

MARY BEATON *comes to the door* L.

Beat. Will Your Majesty see a gentleman
     calling himself Lord Bothwell?

BOTHWELL *comes to the door* L.

Mary. He's in again?

Beat. There's no keeping him out.   705

Both. (*entering*). The doxy invited me in herself. She's a slut, This Beaton of yours.

Mary. Oh, I know.

Beat. May I put in a word For this gentleman, madame? Of all who come calling on you   710 He's the most ill-favored. It may be that he's honest, I hope so, to go with that face. You're not afraid To be left alone with him?

Mary. You may go, Beaton.

Beat. Yes, Majesty.   715

(*She curtseys hurriedly, and goes out* L.

Both. Now, what an inexperienced queen you are To surround yourself with such taking bitches!

Mary. My lord, I have heard from England.

Both. (L. *of throne*). Mary, my queen, what you heard   720 I could have guessed. She's your demon. She bodes you ill.

Mary. I believe it now.

Both. And moreover, between the two, This cormorant brother of yours, and that English harpy, They'll have the heart out of you, and share it. Trust   725 Not one word they say to you, trust not even the anger Their words rouse in you. They calculate effects.

Mary. Where is Lord Morton?

Both. Lord Morton is not well.

(*He is very serious.*

A sudden indisposition.   730

Mary. Bothwell, Bothwell——— You've fought with him!

Both. A mere puncture. What men think I cannot punish, nor what they say elsewhere, but when I hear them, by Christ, they'll learn manners.

Mary. I forbade it.   736

Both. Forbade it? My dear, not God nor the holy angels Forbid me when I'm angry.

Mary. I say I forbade it. It's I who's responsible for my kingdom — not you —   740 You were bound to keep the peace!

Both. (*a step up on throne platform*). When my lady's slandered? I'll teach them to hold their peace where you're concerned Or find their sweet peace in heaven.

Mary. Would God I'd been born   745 Deep somewhere in the Highlands, and there met you — A maid in your path, and you but a Highland bowman Who needed me.

Both. Why, if you love me, Marie, You're my maid and I your soldier.   750

Mary (*rising and crossing* L.). And it won't be.

Both. Aye, it will be.

Mary (*walking up and down* L.). For, hear me, my lord of Bothwell. I too have a will — a will as strong as your own, And enemies of my own, and my long revenges   755 To carry through. I will have my way in time Though it burn my heart out and yours. The gods set us tasks, My lord, what we must do.

Both. (R. *of* MARY). Let me understand you. The gods, supposing there are such, have thrown us together   760 Somewhat, of late.

Mary. Look, Bothwell. I am a sovereign, And you obey no one. Were I married to you I'd be Your woman to sleep with. You'd be king here in Edinburgh, And I have no mind to your ruling.   765

Both. (*taking a step toward* MARY). They'll beat you alone. Together we could cope them.

Mary. Love you I may — Love you I have — but not now, and no more. It's for me To rule, not you. I'll deliver up no land   770

To such a hot-head. If you'd been born to
    the blood
I'd say, aye, take it, the heavens had a meaning
    in this,
But the royal blood's in me. — It's to me they
    turn
To keep the peace, patch up old quarrels, bring
    home
Old exiles, make a truce to anarchy. Escape it
    I cannot.   775
Delegate it I cannot. The blame's my own
For whatever's done in my name. — I will have
    no master.
        (BOTHWELL *is silent when she pauses.*
        MARY *crosses to* C. BOTHWELL *goes*
        up L.
Nay, I am jealous of this my Stuart blood.
Jealous of what it has meant in Scotland, jeal-
    ous
Of what it may mean. They've attacked that
    blood, and I'm angry.   780
They'll meet more anger than they know.
    Both. And who
Has angered you? Not I?
    Mary. Elizabeth.
    Both. I thought so.   785
She's afraid, if I'm half a prophet,
That you'll marry me.
    Mary (*crossing* R.). Her fears run the other
    way.
She's afraid I'll marry a Catholic and threaten
    her throne!
She threatens disinheritance! Offers me
    Leicester!   790
Her leavings!
    Both. (*coming down* C.). Yes, by God, that's
    a cold potato.
    Mary. And means to choose another heir
    for her throne!
I may never sit on it, but the Stuart line
Shall not suffer by me!   795
    Both. Will you tell me what that means?
    Mary. I mean if I have a son he'll govern
    England.
    Both. And so he might, if he were mine,
    too.
    Mary. Nay, might —
But it must be!   800
She dares to threaten my heritage!

    Both. Does that mean Lord Darnley?
        (*She is silent.* BOTHWELL *crosses* R. *to*
        MARY.
Aye, lady, will you stoop so low to choose
A weapon? This is not worthy of the girl
I've known. Am I to be ousted by a papejay [1]
Who drinks in the morning and cannot carry
    his drink?   806
An end of mouldy string? You take too much
On yourself of the future. Think of us, and the
    hours
Close on us here we might have together.
    Leave something
To the gods in heaven! They look after lovers!
    Mary (*with back to* BOTHWELL). Oh, what's
    a little love, a trick of the eyes,   811
A liking, to be set beside the name
You'll have forever, or your son will have?
    Both. Well, it's been nibbling at you this
    long while,
And now it's got you, the blight of Charle-
    magne —   815
The itch to conquer.
    Mary (*facing* BOTHWELL). I have an itch to
    conquer?
    Both. It goes deep, too, that itch. It eats
    out the brain.
    Mary. Well, and my love for you, how wor-
    thy is that?
It's my body wants you. Something I've
    fought against   820
Comes out in me when you're near. You've
    not held it sacred,
You've taken others. I've known. And then
    come wooing.
It would happen again.
    Both. It's a man's way. I've loved you
None the less.   825
    Mary. You don't offer enough, Lord Both-
    well.
You're not true in it, and I'm not true to my-
    self
In what I feel for you.
    Both. I'm no lute-player,
To languish and write sonnets when my lady
Says me nay. Faith, I've lived rough on the
    border,   831

    [1] Lit., a popinjay or a parrot; *i.e.,* a talkative cox-
comb.

And cut some throats I don't forgive my-
    self
Too easily, when I look back, but I tell you
If I give my pledge to you it's an honest pledge,
And I'll keep it. Yes, and when the tug begins
Around your throne, you'll be lost without me.
    Try   836
No threats toward England. — It will tax a
    hardy man
All his time to hold what you have.
    Mary. We differ there, too.
What I have I'll defend for myself.   840
    Both. If you marry this Darnley
I take away my hand.
    Mary. Before God, he believes
He's held me up so far, and I'd fall without
    him!   (*Crossing to* c.
    Both. I believe it, and it's true; Darnley,
    sweet Christ!   845
No miracle could make him a king! He's a
    punk,
And he'll rule like a punk!
    Mary. We shall see, Lord Bothwell.
    Both. Well, I'm sped. My suit's cold. But,
    dod, lady — Darnley —
He sticks in my craw — I can't go him. You'll
    find few that can.   850
Think twice about that. Let him not cross my
    way,
Or he'll lose his plumes like Morton!
    Mary. Will you learn, Lord Bothwell,
That this is not your palace, but mine? Or
    must you
Be taught that lesson?   855
    Both. There's been a bond between us
We'll find it hard to forget.
    Mary. You may. Not I.
I've set my face where I'm going.

RIZZIO *enters* L.

    Riz. Lord Darnley is here,   860
Your Majesty.
    Mary. Let him enter.
    Both. Lass, lass, God fend thee.
            (*Crossing to door up* L.
You've seen the last of me.
    Mary. I've given no leave   865
For departure, Lord Bothwell.

    Both. I need no leave, nor leave-taking.
You see no more of me.
        (*He goes out* L. RIZZIO *bows and follows
    him.* DARNLEY *enters* L. MARY
    crosses the room away from* DARN-
    LEY *and looks for a moment in the
    fire* R. *Then she turns to him.*
    Mary. I have sent for you,
Lord Darnley, to tell you your suit has pros-
    pered. You've asked   870
My hand in marriage, and I grant it.
    Darn. Your Majesty —
I hardly hoped — I haven't dared — this is
    fortune
To take one's breath! (*He comes forward and
    falls to one knee.*)
I shall love you, keep you, defend you!   875
    Mary. We shall face troubled times.
    Darn. We'll meet them bravely.
This is some dream — or a jest. It can't be.
    Mary. Aye. I feel that.
And yet it's true.   880
    Darn. I'm to hold you in my arms!
    Mary. Not yet. And yet, if you like, come,
    kiss me.
    Darn. They say
A kiss seals the bargain!
        (*He rises, staggering slightly.*
    Mary. I've heard so.   885
        (*He crosses to her.*
You've drunk too much.
    Darn. Nay, only a morning cup. Oh, lady,
    lady —
When you're kind the whole world's kind!
    Mary (*faces him, then draws back a step in re-
    pulsion*). You're a boy, a child.
    Darn. Older than you, though.   890
It's a bargain, then?
    Mary. Yes. (*He puts his arms around her.
    She pushes him off.*)
Let the kissing go. Let it go till the bond's
    sealed.
    Darn. Aye, madame.
        (*He drops his arms. They stand look-
    ing at each other.*[1]

Curtain

[1] Mary and Darnley were married in 1565, so that the
scenes of Act I cover events of some four years.

ACT II

SCENE I

SCENE: *The great hall at Holyroodhouse. Evening.*
MARY *and the* FOUR MARYS-IN-WAITING
are sitting near the fire, listening as RIZZIO
sings to his lute.

Riz. (*on hassock* L. *of* MARY'S *chair* R.**.**).
    My heart's in the north,
    And my life's in the south,
    False I've pledged with my hand,
    False I've kissed with my mouth.

    Oh, would we might lie   5
    Where we lay by the firth,
    With one cloak about us
    To keep us from earth,

    With hand caught to hand
    And the rain driving blind,   10
    As the new years have driven
    Old love out of mind.

Mary (*seated in chair by fireplace* R.). What
is the line, "False I've pledged with my hand"?
Riz.
    False I've pledged with my hand,   15
    False I've kissed with my mouth.
Mary. Where did you come by the song?
Riz. It's one I made.
Mary. I thought so. Well, it's too true —
and past time for crying.   20
Beat. (*seated on bench by fireplace* R.). These
poets make much of false pledges and false
kisses — but they often turn out quite as well.
Mary. Nay, they turn out badly. If you
should love, Beaton, give yourself where   25
you love.
Beat. There's one of these silly hackbuteers [1]
I could have a mind to, but I gather he has his
penny a day and no more.
Mary. Then if I were you I'd take him.   30
Liv. (*seated on stool just above* MARY). And
live on a penny a day?
Mary. Or anything.
Riz. My lady, I shall never forgive myself.
Mary. It was my own doing.   35

---

[1] Soldiers armed with hackbuts or heavy muskets
with hooked butts.

Riz. My counsel weighed with you. I fa-
vored Darnley because he was of my faith. And
he's our weakness, not our strength.
Mary. None could have known that.
Riz. I should have known. Bothwell   40
would have been better.
Liv. Bothwell!
Riz. Aye, Bothwell. He'd have held them
off. There's no trifling with him.
Liv. We do well enough without him.   45
Riz. Well enough, perhaps.
Mary. Let's have no talk of Bothwell.
Liv. He's better away. The country's been
much quieter since he left it. Hasn't it,
madame?   50
Mary. Much quieter.
Flem. You will have a child, Your Majesty.
You will have an heir, and then you will be hap-
pier.
Mary. With Darnley's child?   55
Flem. He will change, too. The man changes
when there are children.
Mary. We must hope so.
Seton. His Majesty will return tomorrow?
     (RIZZIO *rises.*)
Mary. He was to have returned three   60
days since. But the hunting may have been
delayed.
Beat. The hunting! He does his hunting o'
nights.
Mary. Nay, Beaton!   65
Beat. Nor do I take much joy in hearing him
called His Majesty.
Seton. But it's the correct address. Lord
Darnley has been crowned.
Beat. Is that a reason for giving him   70
any deference among ourselves? He's a baby,
and a spoilt one, and it would give me small
pain if I never saw his foolish face again.
Seton. I think that's very treacherous talk!
Mary. It is, too.   75
Beat. I'm true to my queen, and I'll be true
to none else.
Mary. Not even your hackbuteer?
Beat. Not even him.
Riz. Your Majesty, I have a request   80
which you have denied before, but which I
must make again. It is necessary for me to
leave Scotland.

Mary. David, David!

Riz. I grow lonely for Italy.   85

Mary. And who will write my letters?

Riz. There are many who could write your letters.

Mary. Can you name one — both efficient and to be trusted?   90

Riz. Maitland.

Mary. Would *you* trust him?

Riz. I think I should go, Your Majesty.

Mary. We know why, David, and I won't have it. I won't have my friends driven   95 from me.

Riz. I think it's best.

Mary. Has His Majesty spoken to you?

Riz. Only by the way. — I'm not wanted here — you know that.   100

Mary. The King is full of these whims and fancies, my dear Rizzio. If I gave way to one I should have to humor him in all. You and I know that I am quite innocent with you, and you with me. And I can't spare you.   105

Riz. God knows you are innocent, madame, and I too, unless it be a crime to love you. I do love you. I can't deny that.   (*Kneels.*

Mary. Nor do I hold it a crime.

Riz. Majesty, I tell you honestly it's   110 torture to speak of going away — and yet — oh, I want no harm to come to you through me!

Mary. And none will. The King is jealous, of everyone, my Rizzio, everyone I see or have seen. It's a brain-sick notion. I know   115 that he has acted and spoken foolishly in many such matters. But as for danger, there is none.

Riz. I hope there is none.

(*There is a clatter of armor in the hall to the right.*

Mary. Say no more of going.

Riz. My queen, I am too easy to con-   120 vince in this! Too much of me cries out to stay — and yet — say no more and let me go!

Mary. Why, very well.

Riz. But not angrily — not in anger.

Mary. Not in anger.   125

Riz. I thank Your Majesty.

A PORTER *comes to the door* L.

Por. Master Rizzio?

Riz. (*rises*). Yes?

Por. Lord Maitland of Lethington and Master John Knox are here.   130

Mary. They are to come in.

(RIZZIO *makes a gesture to the* PORTER, *who goes out. The Queen rises.* RIZZIO *goes to the door and ushers in* MAITLAND *and* KNOX, *then goes out.* KNOX *stands at the door.*

Mait. Ah, Your Majesty — I was to bring Master Knox.

Mary. Yes, I remember.

Mait. (*looking about*). I gather that he   135 wishes to speak with you in private.

Mary. I doubt that we shall find the subject makes it necessary. — Master Knox, will you come closer to the fire?

Knox. I am very well here, I thank   140 Your Majesty.

Mary. You come — was it the word? — to make a protest?

Knox. Would it be convenient that I speak with you alone?   145

Mary. When we last spoke alone, sir, there was some talk to the effect that I had used arts on you. I could wish to avoid a repetition of that.

Knox. Why, then, I have but one thing   150 to say and I shall make shift to say it quickly. You are a Catholic queen in a Protestant land, Your Majesty.

Mary. Only in part Protestant.

Knox. Protestant in great majority——   155

Mary. Yes.

Knox. You have taken a Catholic husband and set him on the throne beside you, giving him what is called in the courts of this world the crown matrimonial. You have also set   160 up an altar in this your palace, where the Mass and other idolatrous rites are said for you. In these ways you encourage Lord Huntley and the Highland Catholics of the north in their heathenish practices, and in so doing bring   165 grave dissension among your people. I come to warn you.

Mary. To warn me of what, Master Knox?

Knox. That the forms and appurtenances of the Romish faith cannot be thrust upon   170 us. That this will not be borne by the defenders of the Lord's word and church.

Mary. I ask no one to subscribe to my faith, sir. But it has been mine from a child, and I keep it.   175

Knox. You seek to gain it a foothold here, and build it up about you. I wish no evil to you nor to this kingdom and I say the celebration of the Mass must cease, for there are those among us to whom it is abhorrent. 180 (*Crosses to* C. MAITLAND *comes down* L.) And though it cost civil war and the slaughter of brother by brother it will not be borne.

Mary. And are you among those who will not bear it?   185

Knox. I am.

Mary. Do you find it written that all men must worship in one fashion?

Knox. There is but one true faith and one true fashion of worship.   190

Mary. And you would enforce it with the sword?

Knox. There is no tolerance for the idolator nor the adulterer. They are to be weeded out — and even now — before they come 195 to the great pit and are given over to His un-ending fire — a fire not to be quenched nor remedied nor appeased.

Mary. I understand your attitude toward the idolator, Master Knox, but do you 200 consider it apposite to bring adulterers also into this conversation?

Knox. The idolator, the adulterer, the priests of Baal, they shall be uprooted, seed and seed-ling, and cast into the burning —— 205

Mary. But Master Knox, Master Knox, let us have a meeting of minds! An idolator is not the same as an adulterer. Confine yourself to some meaning.

Knox (*crossing a little* R.). They come 210 among us in one person — the priests of the flesh and the worshippers of the flesh ——

Mary (*rising, and* ALL MARYS *rise*). If you would but leave off prophesying for a moment and speak sense! Who is the idolator here? 215

Knox. Have you not set up an altar?

Mary. A very little one, sir. Nothing to what I could wish. And does that make me an idolator?

Knox. Will you deny it?   220

Mary (*crossing a little* C.). I do deny it. And now tell me who is the adulterer?

Knox. Let them search in their hearts who came from France.

Mary. I have searched in mine, and find 225 no adultery there. And shall not those who live in Scotland search in their hearts also?

Mait. Your Majesty, I have brought Master Knox here only because I am convinced that he voices an attitude which must be seriously 230 considered.

Mary. But I try to take him seriously and he speaks in parables. I ask him to define his words and he talks of a great fire. To him, a priest is a priest of Baal, an idolator is 235 the same as an adulterer, and those who come from France run especial danger of damnation. What can one say to such a man? (*Sits again.* ALL MARYS *sit.*) Master Knox, I believe you mean well, but can you not see that I also 240 mean well, and that there might be more than one opinion concerning the worship of Our Lord?

Knox. There will be but one opinion held in that last day — when He comes with His 245 armies, and driveth before Him those who are not His children!

Mary. Look, what can one say to him? You ask him a question — and he threatens you with the Last Judgment! You see, Mas- 250 ter Knox, you are not the judge who will sit over us in the Last Judgment. You are instead an elderly gentleman of provincial learning and fanatical beliefs, lately married to a niece of your own some forty years your junior, 255 and one who conducts his conversations almost exclusively in quotations from the Old Testa-ment. If you will talk sensibly with me I shall talk sensibly with you, but if you come here to frighten me I shall regard you as a most 260 ridiculous antediluvian figure, and find you very funny. Which shall it be?

Knox. Well I know you hold the Lord God as a jest and a mockery!

Mary. Do not confuse yourself with 265 Lord God again! There's a difference!

Knox. I am His spokesman.

RIZZIO *comes to the door*

Mary. Indeed. Will you show me your commission?

Knox. I call ruin to fall on this house,   270 the shelter of the great beast — !

Mary. And there again! Maitland, can you, by any stretch of the imagination, look upon me as the great beast?

Riz. Your Majesty, Lord Huntley is   275 here.

Mary. Come in, Lord Huntley! (HUNTLEY *enters* L., *crosses to* MARY *and stands* R. *of her.*) Sir, I have just heard myself likened to the great beast of Revelations. Can you see any similarity there?   280

Hunt. Why, lass, I'd say at the least it's an exaggeration!

Mait. If Your Majesty wishes to give audience to Lord Huntley ——

(*He starts to withdraw.*)

Mary. Nay, why should you go? And   285 why should John Knox and Lord Huntley not meet face to face in one room? I am aware that Master Knox is a Protestant and that Huntley is a Catholic, but they dwell in the same small kingdom, and it would be well if they   290 understood each other.

Knox. I am loathe to say it, but I am of a mind that there can be no understanding between him and me, no, nor between myself and Your Majesty, lest I betray my   295 Lord.

Hunt. Madame, it's my opinion we understand each other dom well. Too dom well.

Mary. But since you must both live in this kingdom and one must be Catholic and   300 one Protestant, surely it were wiser to be amiable over small matters, Maitland?

Mait. Aye, it would be wiser.

Knox. Not for what you have said to me or of my person, for that unto seventy times   305 seven those who follow Him forgive, but because the air of this house is offensive in His nostrils, I call ruin on it! Nor will I commune in it further, neither with those who make their beds here nor with those who come here   310 for counsel! Yea, if there are any here who would avoid the wrath, let them turn now, for it is upon you and your servants!

Mary. Well — it would seem there's little to be done about that. You are dismissed if   315 you wish to go.

Mait. I offer my apologies, Your Majesty.

Mary. Oh, surely.

Knox (*crossing to door up* L.). Yea, those who breed and take their ease in the places of   320 the anointed, turn now, before the axe fall quickly and be followed by silence! For now it is not too late, but no man knows when he cometh, nor on the wings of what morning!

(MAITLAND *and* KNOX *go out* L.
RIZZIO *rejoins the group at the fire.*)

Mary. You are duly impressed by this   325 talk, sir?

Beat. Why, the solemn ass! He should have been booted!

Hunt. My dear, you've been too easy with him, and if you continue to be easy we'll   330 pay for it.

Mary. And in what way, sir?

Hunt. You and I are alone here, Your Majesty, so far as Catholicism's concerned. My Highlanders are Catholics, it's true, and   335 there's plenty of them, and they're tough, but the rest are all against us, every noble and man of note. They're John Knox's men, and you heard yourself what he said.

Beat. He with the persimmon-colored   340 whiskers?

Hunt. Aye, he. And he means it.

Mary. What does he mean?

Hunt. Ruin to this house.

Mary. Is this a house to be blown down   345 with windy talk?

Hunt. My birdie — oh, I canna call you Ye're Majesty and all that.

Mary. You need not.

Hunt. Then, my bird, they draw their   350 nets tight about us. I told you before, and it's coming.

Mary. And who draws the net?

Hunt. (*looking at the others*). Lady ——

Mary. These five know my secret   355 heart. They'll say nothing.

Hunt. Lady, there's only one defense. Attack them first. And there's but one proper place for John Knox. He should be in Edinburgh Castle — and all those with him   360 who are of his mind.

Mary. You'd imprison him?

Hunt. He and some twenty others.

Mary. And then?

Hunt. Then you can go to work. 365
You're not safe here and I'm not safe here
while a sect of Protestant lords divide your do-
minion with you. You rule by sufferance only.

Mary. They are here by my sufferance,
Huntley. 370

Hunt. You have heard of the sheep that
nursed the wolf-pups till they tore her to pieces.

Mary. But we're not sheep and wolves, my
lord. There's room for all of us here, and for
whatever faiths we may choose to have. 375

Hunt. Never think it, my bird, never believe
it! It's never yet happened that a state survived with two religions in it. Never. Elizabeth knows that. She's behind this Knox.
He'd never dare be so bold if she weren't 380
behind him.

Mary. But it's my thought that in Scotland,
though it be the first time in the world, we shall
all believe as we please and worship as we list.
And Elizabeth may take it as she sees fit. 385

Hunt. She uses it against you, my dear, and
uses John Knox against you. Ladybird, I'm
willing to beg it of you, take heed of me now
or we're both done!

Mary. Rizzio? 390

Riz. You know my mind. I'm with Lord
Huntley in this.

Mary. But how can I bring myself to imprison men for no wrong they've done, on suspicion only, imprison them for their faith —? 395

Hunt. It's more than faith. It's works. You
heard John Knox!

Mary. It cuts athwart every right instinct
I have, my lord! Every fine fiber of me
that's royal shrinks at such penny-wise 400
petty doings! And John Knox — a doddering
imbecile, drooling prophecy!

Riz. He threatened you, lady.

Mary. No, no, I can't. Even if it were wisdom to do it, and it's not. (*The* L. *door* 405
opens suddenly and DARNLEY *stands in it.*
MARY *turns toward him.*) My lord!

Darn. (*walks slowly to the middle of the room*).
I'm unexpected, perhaps? Too early? A
thought
Too early? I'll retire. Come when I'm wanted.

Mary. No,

My lord, you've been long expected, and more
than welcome. 410

Darn. Why, a pretty wife, a housewife with
her maids;
A pretty sight, and maybe a cavalier
Or two, for the maids' company. Dod, sit
down, all!
Damn me if I'll intrude! 414

Mary. Will you speak to Lord Huntley?

Darn. (*focusing on* HUNTLEY). Right. That's
right. Lord Huntley, give me your
hand. (HUNTLEY *crosses to him.*
I thank you for watching over the pretty wife
here.
I've been away.

Hunt. Your Majesty, you've a wife 419
Such as I wish I'd had when I was young.

Darn. Right — you are right. They all say
that. I'd say it myself (*facing upstage*
R. *of* HUNTLEY),
Only I know her better.
I know her too well,
And not well enough. She wouldn't care to
hear it.
Not from me. 425

Mary. Darnley.

Darn. She sleeps alone.
At least as far as I know.

Hunt. I'll take my leave,
My Lady. 430

Mary. Yes.

Darn. Stay, stay. I'm going. I only
Tell you she sleeps alone as far as I know.
A pretty wife. These women — they get with
child,
You never know how — and then they won't
sleep with you. 435
(HUNTLEY *bows to* MARY, *turns delib-
erately, and goes out the door to the* L.,
closing it.
What's the matter with him? He's an old
married man.
He knows these things.

Mary. You're tired, my lord. Will you wish
Some service, something to eat and drink?

Darn. She sends me 440
Off to bed, you note. You note it, Rizzio?
There's a service she could do me, but I
doubt

She'll offer it.   And I'm a king, by God, a king.
And you're a clerk by office!

    Mary. My lord, I hoped   445
You'd have some other word for me when you
Returned.

    Darn. My pink, if I gave you the word
      you've earned
The room would smell.   I've been at the
      hunting.   We had   449
Something to drink.   Alban![1] Alban! Allons!

    Mary. You call someone?

    Darn. Alban!   God's right!   Saint Andrew!
    Alban!
I'm drunk, you see.

    Mary. I think not.   454

    Darn. (*crossing to door* L.). Yes, but I am.
Alban!   Christ his sonties,[2] am I left
Alone here!   God and Saint Andrew!

      (*The* L. *door opens and* RUTHVEN *enters*
        in full armor.

    Mary. What is this?
(*To* RUTHVEN) You will retire, sir.   Who are
    you?

    Darn. My good friend Ruthven.   460

    Mary. Is this a place for armor?   I will
    receive
Lord Ruthven another time.

    Darn. The callant's[3] there,
Ruthven.

    Ruth. (*down* L.). Aye.   465

    Mary. I had heard that Lord Ruthven was
    ill,
And thought to go to him, not to see him
here.

    Ruth. I am ill, and it's mortal, but I've
    sworn to be mortal
To another first.

    Mary. This is my apartment, sir,   470
And I ask you to go.

        DOUGLAS *enters* L.

I demand little courtesy,
But that little I must have — are these your
    friends?
If so, take them elsewhere.

    Darn. Aye, I'm to have my friends   475
In my apartment — and you're to have yours
    here.
I say no — they're to mingle ——
(*He points to* RIZZIO.) You see that grig[1]
With the kinked hair there?   He with the lady's
    hands
And feet?   Where does he sleep nights?   That's
    he, that's the one   480
We have in question!

    Mary. My lord, when you've been drinking
I have little taste for your company, and to-
    night
Less, perhaps, than ever.

    Darn. He, he, I tell you!   485
That Italian spawn!

      (RIZZIO, *trembling, steps back toward*
      up R. MORTON *enters* L.; *goes to* C.

    Mary (*stepping in front of* RIZZIO). Go into
    my study.
Lord Morton,
Whatever you have in hand here, put no faith
In this king I've crowned and set beside me!
    His word   490
Is a paper shield.

    Darn. I'm king in this country, mistress —
And I know my rights.

    Mary. Beaton, why were these men
Not stopped at my door?   495

    Darn. They came with me.

    Beat. (*facing* MORTON). Will you tell me
What you want with the Queen?

    Mort. (*his dagger drawn*). Damme, do you
    want this bodkin
Through that bodice of yours?   500

      (*She shrinks back.* RIZZIO, *having*
      reached the R. *door step by step, opens*
      it and reveals a GUARD, *a drawn*
      claymore[2] *in his hand.*

    Riz. Let me pass!

    The Guard. Nay, lad.

    Flem. Your Majesty,
They've broken into your rooms.

        (MARY *turns and sees the* GUARD.

    Mary. Lord Darnley, was that   505
By your order?

---

[1] Saint Alban, the first Christian martyr in Britain.
[2] Christ's sanctities — a common Elizabethan oath.
[3] Lad

[1] Dwarf.
[2] A large two-edged, sometimes two-handed, sword
peculiar to the Scottish Highlanders.

Riz. (*hardly able to speak for fear*). Save me, my Queen, save me!

Mary. Aye, Rizzio.

Mort. Look to thy women folk, Darnley. We'll care for him.

(DARNLEY *crosses* R. *and holds* MARY'S *arms.* RIZZIO *turns suddenly and leaps behind the heavy drapes of the high window* R.C. MORTON, DOUGLAS, *and* RUTHVEN *follow him,* DOUGLAS *with his dagger raised.*

Mary. Douglas, I'll remember this!   510

(*A fall is heard behind the curtains.* MARY *runs toward the window, but is met by* RUTHVEN, *sheathing his dagger.*

You've murdered him!
You pack of filthy cowards![1]

Ruth. (R. *of throne*). Yea, and done well.

Mary. Done well! Oh, fools and cowards!

(*She runs to the curtain and with* MARY BEATON *pulls it back from* RIZZIO, *then bends over him and draws back again in terror.*

Oh, David, David!   515
It was I wouldn't let you go!

Darn. (*down* R. *looking away*). You might cover that sight.

Mary. Is he dead, Beaton?

Beat. Yes, madame.

Mary. Oh, you do well, you do well,   520
All of you!

(*She conquers her repulsion, and tries to loosen* RIZZIO'S *ruff.* FLEMING *comes to help her.*

We'll help him if we can,
Fleming.

Flem. Yes.

Mary. You were too gentle for them,   525
David. They couldn't bear it — these boors and swine —
Your kerchief, Fleming! — He bleeds so!

Flem. It's useless, madame.

Mary (*rising*). Yes.
(*To the* LORDS) To take him unarmed, and poniard him —   530
One who had never hurt you!

---

[1] Rizzio was murdered in March, 1566.

Ruth. (*sinking into a chair* R. *of throne*). Well, the work's done,
And my queen's wiped clear of him.

Mary. Wiped clear! You believed
I was guilty with him!   535

Ruth. Were you not?

Mary. No!

Ruth. I'd be sorry
If you were not. I struck him down for that.

Mary. I was not guilty. But will you tell me now   540
Who'll believe me innocent? You've branded me deep
With this murder, and you've killed a guiltless man!
Why do you sit in my presence?

Ruth. Because I'm ill   544
And dying. I should be sorry if this thing
I've done were in error — for it's the last I'll do.

Mary. You'll stand in my presence!

(RUTHVEN *rises with difficulty.*

Whose order was it?

Ruth. Why, ask His Majesty that —
And Morton there, and Moray.   550

Mary. Moray too?

Ruth. Yes, your brother. For me — let me go home.

Mary. Go. Morton and Douglas, I give you three days
To leave this kingdom.

Mort. (*down* L.). And the King? I have the King's seal   555
For what I've done.

Mary (*crossing to* DARNLEY). Is that true?

Darn. Aye.

Mary. The worse for you.
The worse for you all.   560

Darn. My lady, this long while past
You've denied me your chamber, and when I've seen you, there's been
This Rizzio with you.

Mary. Never again while I live   564
Will you see me alone. I bear your child in me
Or you'd answer for this!

Darn. There'll be no answering!
We know what we know about you!

Mary. I would I knew
In what strange dark chamber of your oafish brain   570

You found reasons for Rizzio's death. If I saw
    you seldom
Remember how often you drank yourself
    imbecile
Before you came to me. You've slain your
    last friend, sir.
It was Rizzio's counsel put you where you are
And kept you there. These are not your
    friends, these three,   575
Nor Moray. They wanted Rizzio out of the
    way,
And they wanted to drag you down, and drag
    me down,
And you play into their hands. I've never been
Unfaithful to you, but we're at an end, we two.
From this time forward if I touch your hand
May God blight me and my child!   581
      (*Crossing to* R. *of* DARNLEY.
  Darn. I wanted you!
You kept away from me, and it drove me mad!
  Mary. You won't mend it now. Look,
    young Rizzio's dead;
You've blackened me, blackened yourself,
    thrown a black doubt   585
On the child who'll be your heir. The lords
    look on
And smile, knowing they've trapped you.
    You'll never climb
From the pit where you've fallen, and I may
    fall with you. Lord Moray
Weaves his web round us. You've helped him.
  Darn. God knows I wanted   590
Only my right.
  Mary. You pitiful dolt! To think
Such a calf should rule, and at my choosing!
    God
May forgive you — not I. Nor forgive my-
    self —— And Rizzio ——
Take yourselves out!   595
      (*Forcing* DARNLEY *to up* L.
You pollute the dead to stand there!
He wanted to go to Italy.
  Flem. Yes.
  Mary. Will you go?
      (MORTON *beckons the* GUARDS, *and*
      they go out R. MORTON *then exits* L.
  Ruth. (*at the door*). You'll want some help,
    mayhap.   600
  Mary. None of yours. I've noticed

It's men that kill, but women that wash the
    corpse
And weep for it. May none ever weep for you.
  Ruth. None will. I've been in the wrong.
  Mary. I'm sorry, Lord Ruthven.   605
It's an ill thing to have on your heart when
    you die.
  Ruth. Aye, it is.
      (*He goes out* L., *and* DARNLEY *and*
      DOUGLAS *follow him.* DARNLEY
      looks back as if he wished to speak to
      MARY, *but goes out silently.*
  Mary. And now we're alone. The lords
    have shown their hand.
Rizzio's gone — and Darnley, what there was
    to go.
We've been not long in Scotland, but time
    enough   610
To show I can lose it, have lost it in their minds
Already. We must lay the poor lad somewhere.
Could we lift him together?
  Seton. Oh, madame, I'm afraid!
  Mary. Of what?   615
  Seton. I've never seen one dead before.
I've not known it was like this.
  Mary. It's poor Rizzio.
No one to hurt us. And you and I will lie
Sometime like this, and folk will be afraid
Because we lie so still. How strange it is 621
That he should frighten us who wished us well,
And would still if he lived. We must take
    him up
And lay him on my bed. I'll sleep with Beaton
Tonight. (*She takes a step toward* RIZZIO. 625
  Beat. Madame, the blood will stain your
    dress.
  Mary. If that were all. This will bring
    more blood after.
Now I see it. Before I reign here clearly
There will be many men lie so for me,   629
Slain in needless quarrel. Slain, and each one
With blood to spill but once, like his. And yet
One steps on into it — steps from life to life
Till there are thousands dead, and goes on still
Till the heart faints and sickens, and still
    goes on
And must go on.   635
      (*An iron gate clangs outside.* BEATON
      parts the curtains to look out.

I tell you, Fleming, my soul
Is aghast at this blood spilled for me, and yet
It hardens me, too. These are their manners, this
Is the way they go to work. I shall work on them,
And not too lightly. They think of me as a girl,
Afraid of them. They shall see. — And yet
    my mind   641
Believes nothing of what I say; I'm weak as grief,
Stripped and wept out before them. They press me close,
And I have no one to send.
    (*There is a rattle of staves in the court-yard.*
    Beat. (*turning back*). It's the Provost, madame,   645
I heard them call his name.
    Mary. He's not to enter.
Let no one enter.   (BEATON *goes out* L.
No one. In all this kingdom
I can trust only five, and one's myself.   650
And we're women, all of us. — If they go scot-free
After this indignity, I'm no queen! For Ruthven,
He'll pay his own score. He's dying. Morton and Douglas
Must die too.
    Flem. They were under Lord Darnley's orders.   655
    Mary. He was under theirs. It won't save them.
    Flem. Your Majesty,
They've left the city by now. They should have been taken
While they were in your hands.
    Mary. I know. It's true.   660
They've fled to raise troops. When next we find them they'll meet us
With culverins.[1]

        BEATON *enters* L.

He's gone?
    Beat. (*crossing to* MARY; *she carries a feather*).
Yes. But there's one
   [1] Long cannon with serpent-shaped handles.

Below from France — says he has news.   665
    Mary (*down* R.). From France?
Tomorrow, though. I wish I were still in France
And had never seen these stone walls.
    Liv. And so do I.
    Mary. What is his name?   670
    Beat. He gave me
This token for you, no name. It's a crow's feather.
    Mary (*takes the feather, then pauses*). Tell my Lord Bothwell I have no wish to see him
Now or later.
    Beat. Madame, you'll see him? I brought him   675
Along with me.
    Mary. No. Not now. Not ever.
There's nothing to say between us now.
    Beat. He came
From France to see you.   680
    Mary. Tell him.

LORD BOTHWELL *is seen standing in the* L. *doorway*

    Both. (*crossing* C.). Your Majesty,
You've had unwelcome company this hour,
If I've heard aright, and I care not to be another,
But I come to make an offer I made before —
To be your soldier.   686
    Mary. I have no time to talk,
Lord Bothwell. Nor do I wish to see you. The time's
Gone by.
    Both. My queen, my queen, turn not away   690
Your friends. You've few enough, too few it seems
To prevent what's happened.
    Mary. Go.
    Both. Does he still lie here?
I'll lay the poor boy away for you at least,
And then I'll go, since you wish it.   696
    (*He crosses to* RIZZIO.
Aye, they made sure,
Lad — and their dirks were sharp. Shall I place him within?

Mary. Yes.

(BOTHWELL *picks up* RIZZIO *and carries him out* R. MARY *turns to* BEATON.

Must you betray me too?   700

Beat. I wished only ——

If you'd but follow your heart!

Mary. We two must twain,[1]

My Beaton. You take too much on you. Lord Bothwell

May be your friend, not mine.   705

Beat. Forgive me.

Mary. What warrant

Have you been given to vouch for my heart, or judge

Whether I should follow it?

Beat. None.   710

Mary. Oh, God, this vice

Of women, crying and tears! To weep, weep now

When I need my anger! Say my farewells for me,

I've gone to my study.   (*She turns to go.*

BOTHWELL *enters* R.

Both. Good night, my queen.   715

Mary. Good night.

I'm not unkind. But I'm cut off from you.

You know that.

Both. Yes. There's no need to hide your weeping.

He was over-young to die.   720

Mary. It's not for him.

No, it's for all I wanted my life to be,

And is not.

Both. Majesty, you have a fortunate star.

It will come well yet.   725

Mary. If I have a star at all

It's an evil one. To violate my room,

Kill my servant before my eyes —— How I must be hated!

Both. They'll pay for that.

Mary. Perhaps.   730

Both. I've taken an oath

They'll pay for it. Your Majesty, I wearied

Of France and exile, wearied of sun and wine,

[1] Part.

And looked north over the water, longing for fog

And heather and my own country. Further, the news   735

Was none too happy from Scotland. They want your throne

And plan to have it. But I mean to live in this land

And mean you to be queen of it. The Earl of Bothwell

Is home, and spoiling for a fight. Before

Day dawns they'll hear from me.   740

Mary. My lord, I thank you ——

Both. Give me no thanks. I like a fight too well

To pretend it's a virtue. Moreover, if I'm to live here

I'd rather you were my liege than Moray. I'm none

So fond of your half-brother. This night's work

Should show you he's what I knew him, half-bred, half-faced   746

And double-tongued.

Mary. You have no army.

Both. (*crossing to* MARY). I have

My border men. Lord Huntley's joined with me   750

With his Highland Kilties. If you'd call your clans

We could drive them to the wall.

Mary. It's a war, then.

Both. It's war,

Already. They've turned your Darnley against you. They'll use him   755

As long as they need his seal. Once they've got you out

They'll set Moray up as regent. They fear one chance:

That you and I should league together and balk them.

I've come back in time, not too soon.

Mary. I think you have.   760

My Lord, I had no heart to face you. The fault

Was mine when we parted.

Both. It's not too late.

Mary. It is too late ——

For you and me. These faults we commit have lives   765

Of their own, and bind us to them.

Both. (*pointing out* R.). Yon was Darnley's
     work.
Are you still his?
    Mary. Am I not?
         (BEATON *gathers up the three other*
         MARYS *with a look and goes out* R.
         with them silently.
I'm to bear his child.   770
I cannot hate my child.
    Both. It's in the wind
This Darnley's not to live long.
    Mary. I'd have no hand
In that — nor you!   775
    Both. It happens he's a pawn
In the game the lords are playing. They'll
     sacrifice him
When the time comes. It's no plot of mine.
    Mary. But he lives
And I'm his wife, and my babe is his. I must
     drink   780
My cup down to the rinse. It was I that
     filled it,
And if there's grief at the bottom, it's mine.
     I'll name you
My officer, but only if you can pledge
No harm will come through you to Darnley.
    Both. Lady,   785
I need you, and you need me, but I'll be damned
If Darnley's needed on this earth. I have
No project against him, but I'll give no pledge
To block me if I should have. There be men
Who wear their welcome out in this world early,
And Darnley's one of them.   791
    Mary. You have never yet
Learned how to take an order.
    Both. And never will —
From man or woman living, sovereign or knave,
Judge or vicegerent.[1] I have not been con-
     quered   796
And will not be. But I offer you my fealty,
And it's worth the more for that.
    Mary. You must make your own terms —
I'm but a beggar here.   800
    Both. Nay, nay, it's I
That sue, a beggar for what's impossible,
With this Darnley standing between us.
              (MARY *pauses again.*
    Mary. You shall be
   [1] Regent.

My Lord Admiral, and act for me. Yes, and to
     that   805
Let me add how my breath caught when I
     knew you here,
Hoping I know not what, things not to be,
Hopes that I must strangle down. Oh, Both-
     well, Bothwell!
I was wrong! I loved you all the time, and
     denied you!
Forgive me — even too late!   810
    Both. I tell you we
Shall be happy yet.
    Mary. No, for I think I've been
At the top of what I'll have, and all the rest
Is going down. It's as if a queen should
     stand   815
High up, at the head of a stair — I see this now
As in a dream — and she in her dream should
     step
From level to level downward, all this while
     knowing
She should mount and not descend — till at
     last she walks
An outcast in the courtyard — bayed at by
     dogs   820
That were her hunters — walks there in harsh
     morning
And the dream's done.
    Both. (*stepping toward her*). You're weary.
     You've borne too much.
They shall pay for this.
    Mary. Come no nearer, my lord. It's not
     ours   825
To have. Go now.
    Both. Yes, Your Majesty.   (*He turns.*
Yet
I tell you we shall be happy. And there will
     be nothing
Not ours to have.   (*He goes out* L. 830

            Curtain

          SCENE 2

SCENE: *Queen Elizabeth's study at Whitehall.*
    BURGHLEY *and* ELIZABETH *are seated*
    across a table. THROGMORTON *approaches*
    from the side R.

    Burgh. (*seated* L. *of table* C.). This will be Lord
     Throgmorton.

Eliz. (*seated* R. *of table* C.). You're early, sir.

Throg. Madame,
I rode all night. — I've news from the north.
Darnley's been murdered.[1]   5

   Eliz. How?

   Throg. Kirk o' Field was blown up.
The castle's in ruins.

   Eliz. Now that was a waste of powder —
And of castles too. But he's dead ——   10

   Throg. Yes, madame — they found him.
It was no accident. He'd been strangled.

   Eliz. So there's no more king in Scotland.
Who took this trouble?

   Throg. Moray, and Morton, no doubt —
perhaps Maitland ——   15

   Eliz. Not Bothwell? ——

   Throg. No — though he must have known
of it ——

   Eliz. And the Queen —
The Queen weeps for her Darnley?

   Throg. Madame ——   20

   Eliz. Ah, yes —
She'll weep and wear black — it becomes her.
A second time
She's a widow now. And she's borne a child.
She begins
To wear a little, no doubt? She must ponder
now
What costumes may become her?   25

   Throg. Nay, truly, Your Grace,
I'd say she charms as ever.

   Eliz. Would you say so?
But she weeps and puts on mourning?

   Throg. No, Madame. Bothwell   30
And the Queen are friends again — or more
than that.
They'd be married already, I think, only
Moray's against it
And the earls behind him.

   Eliz. Now in my day and time
I have known fools and blockheads, but never,
I swear,   35
In such numbers as among these Scotch earls.
Moray's against it?
Against the Queen's marriage with Bothwell?

   Burgh. Your Majesty —
If she were to marry Bothwell — we've opposed that, too,

[1] The murder occurred in February, 1567.

And even prevented it.   40

   Eliz. Aye, times have changed,
And we change along with them. She loves
this Bothwell?
It's a great love — a queen's love?

   Throg. It is indeed.
A madness, almost.   45

   Eliz. Yes, yes — and it's well sometimes
To be mad with love, and let the world burn
down
In your own white flame. One reads this in
romances —
Such a love smokes with incense; oh, and it's
grateful
In the nostrils of the gods! Now who would
part them   50
For considerations of earth? Let them have
this love
This little while — let them bed and board to-
gether —
Drink it deep, be happy — aye ——

   Burgh. Madame, this Bothwell's
No man to play with. If they marry she'll
crown him king ——   55

   Eliz. You did well to ride fast, Throgmor-
ton! Turn now
And ride as fast back again; you can sleep later
When we're old and the years are empty. —
And tell my Lord Moray
If he'd keep me a friend, let his sister marry
Bothwell —
Tell him to favor it — hurry it.   60

   Burgh. And with Bothwell king
Do you think to conquer Mary?

   Eliz. Send next to John Knox,
But do this cleverly, giving Knox evidence
That Bothwell slew Darnley with the Queen's
connivance   65
And they bed together in blood. Have you
wit enough
To see this well done?

   Throg. I think so, Majesty.

   Eliz. See to it.
Who will deny that Bothwell murdered Darn-
ley   70
When he lives with the Queen, and enjoys the
fruits? Or who
Will credit Bothwell's denial? Your brain, my
Burghley!

Where do you wear it, or what has it hardened
    into
That you're so easily gulled? [1]
   Burgh. But is it wise   75
To make a false accusation?   This project
    hangs
By a thread.   Make but one error and we shall
    lose
Whatever we've gained.
   Eliz. Go and do these things —
They are to marry — we sanction it — let none
    oppose it —   80
She refused him before when he could have
    saved her —
She'll take him now when it's fatal — let her
    have this love
This little while — we grant her that — then
    raise
The winds against them — rouse the clans, cry
    vengeance
On their guilty sleep and love —— I say within
This year at the very farthest, there's no more
    queen   86
Than king in Scotland!

Curtain

SCENE 3

SCENE: *A hall in Dunbar Castle.* A SENTINEL
is at his post near the outer gate R., *another
at the guardroom door* L. *There is a step on
the cobbles outside. The first* SENTINEL
swings round to the gate.

   Jamie (*outside*). Drop your point, man. Ye
ken me.
   1st Sent. Eh, Jamie.   What is it?

JAMIE *enters* R.

   Jamie. I'm late.   It was tough getting
through. The Queen's taken prisoner. Her   5
army's gone.
   1st Sent. Nay! And Bothwell?
   Jamie. Bothwell's free yet. Free and able
to fight. We're to put the castle in posture of
defense. Where's the sergeant?   10
   1st Sent. (*to* 2D SENT.). Call Graeme.

   [1] Misled.

   2d Sent. (*crossing to door* L.). Graeme! — I
told you this was no lucky battle to be in.
   1st Sent. Says John Knox!

GRAEME *enters* L.

   Jamie. I've orders for the guard. We're   15
to man the walls and be ready on the gates.
   Graeme. It goes that way?

BEATON *enters from the stair* L.

   Jamie. That way and worse.
          (*They turn toward the gate* R.)
   Beat. Jamie, what brings you?
   Jamie. Orders, lass.   20
   Beat. Quick, tell me!
   Jamie. It goes badly with us, lass.

LORD HUNTLEY *enters* R.

   Beat. My lord —
   Hunt. There's to be a parley here.   Make
ready for it.   25
   Jamie. Watch that outer post.
          (*The* SENTINELS *go out* R.)
   Beat. A parley — the battle's over?
   Hunt. Aye, over and done.   This is Moray's
kingdom now.
   Beat. And the Queen?   30
   Hunt. The Queen's a prisoner, lass.   My
men have deserted, her own men have turned
against her.
   Beat. My lord, you'll forgive me, but how
could that be?   35
   Hunt. This was John Knox's battle, lady.
The auld limmer took a stance [1] on a hill some
half-mile to windward, and there he stood ha-
ranguing like the angel Gabriel, swearing
Bothwell killed Darnley to have the   40
Queen. And the Queen's men listened to him,
the psalm-singing red-beards, and then turned
and made her prisoner and delivered her up to
Lord Moray.
   Graeme. Lord Bothwell's returning.   45
   Jamie. Upstairs with you, lass.
          (BEATON *goes up the stairs.*)
   Graeme. Shall I set the guard?
   Hunt. Wait a moment.

   [1] The old rascal took up a station.

BOTHWELL *enters* R.

Both. (*crossing* C. *to* HUNTLEY). We're not
through yet, my lord. You'll stand by me? 50

Hunt. Aye,
If it's any use. One may rally an army flying,
But one that flies toward the enemy and makes
　　friends ——

Both. (*crossing* L.). Who spoke of rallying?
　　They won by treachery,
And we'll treat them to some of the same! 55
(*To* JAMIE) There were ninety men
Left to guard the castle! They're here still?

Jamie. Aye, sir.

Both. They're under Lord Huntley's orders
　　while this parley's on.
Tell them to be ready. He'll join you. 60

Jamie. Aye. (*He goes into the guard-room* L.

Both. Sergeant, take the men you need and
　　guard that arch —
Let no one enter but the lords themselves.

Graeme. Aye, my lord. (*He goes out* R.

Both. I'll talk with these lords, and if they
　　listen to reason 65
They may keep their mangy lives, but if they
　　refuse
To release the Queen and give her back her
　　kingdom
Then Hell's their home! Watch my arm, and
　　hark
For my sword on steel. They're outnumbered
　　three to one
In this court. 70

Hunt. Kill them?

Both. Cut their throats
If you like that better.

Hunt. That's plain murder.

Both. Right, 75
And if they say no, they've earned it.

Hunt. And we'd die, too.

Both. Why, it might be we would. But I'd
　　stake more
On our living long with them dead. If the
　　Queen's deposed
Then I've lived long enough, and so have you.
Will you gamble with me? 81

Hunt. I will.
(*They shake hands. A trumpet sounds
　　outside.*

Both. Wait for the signal,
My sword on steel.
(HUNTLEY *goes into the guard-room* L.
　　*The voices of the lords are heard out-
　　side* R.

Mort. (*outside*). Go carefully now. Not too
　　fast. 85

Moray. Aye, you're the man to say that.

Mort. Let Maitland speak.

The lords enter R. *One or two bow ironically,
　　led by* MORTON *and* MORAY

Both. (L.C.). You may drop these scrapings.
　　We know what we think of each other!

Mort. (*up* C.). And that's true, too!

Moray. (R.C.). We have little to gain, Lord
　　Bothwell, 90
By a conference with you. The battle is ours.
　　The Queen
Is prisoner to us. But to spare ourselves fur-
　　ther bloodshed
And spare you bloodshed, we grant this re-
　　spite, and ask
That you surrender without conditions.

Both. No. 95
No, I thank you. Moreover if your tongue's
To be foremost in this council, we'll stop now
And argue the matter outside.

Mait. (R.C.). Be patient, Lord Moray.
We're here to make terms, as you are, Both-
　　well. The Queen 100
And you have been defeated. We made war
　　on you
Because you two were married,[1] and because
　　she planned
To make you king.

Both. You make war on us
Like the pack of lying hounds you are, by
　　swearing 105
In public and in court that we killed Darnley
So that we might marry! You know where
　　that guilt lies.

Moray. Who killed Darnley
We care not. Let the courts decide it.

Both. It was you that killed him! 110
And you fight us bearing false witness.

[1] Mary had married Bothwell in May, 1567, about
a month before this imagined scene.

Moray. You wanted him dead.

Both. I grant it. I wanted him dead. You
    killed him and managed
To shift the weight on me. You've won with
    that lie,
May your mouths rot out with it! And now
    what do you want —   115
What do you ask of us?

Mait. First, that you leave Scotland.

Both. That's easily said:
What next?

Mait. Why, next, that the Queen should
    delegate   120
Her powers to the Lords of the Council, those
    you see
Before you ——

Both. Aye, I see them.

Mait. And bind herself
To act with our consent only.   125

Both. No more?

Mait. No more.

Both. Then here are my conditions: I will
    leave,
And trouble you no more, if you pledge your
    word
That the Queen's to keep her throne and her
    power intact,   130
Without prejudice to her rights. But if you
    dare
Encroach one inch on her sovereignty, guard
    your gates,
For I'll be at them!

Mort. Aye, you make your terms!

Both. Aye, I make mine; defeated, I still
    make mine —   135
And you'll do well to heed them. I shall want
    leave also
To see the Queen for a moment.

Moray. You know our answer.

Both. Then look to yourselves!
              (*He lays a hand on his sword.*

Mait. Look, now, Bothwell.   140
It's you I rebel against. I'd lend no hand
In this company if the Queen were to rule
    alone,
And I've said as much to Lord Moray.

Mort. I speak for myself,
And say no to it.   145

Moray. And I.

Both. You've wanted my earldom,

Lord Moray. Well, you may have it. I'll
    make it over.
You shall choose a new Earl of Bothwell. I'll
    disband my army,
And threaten you no more. But on condi-
    tion   150
The Queen reigns here as before.

Moray. We'll make our conditions —
We have no time for yours.

Both. My lines are not broken.
I'll try conclusions yet, and you'll not sleep
    easy   155
While I'm within these borders!

Mait. Take his terms,
My Moray.

Moray. Are we to fight a war and win
And toss the spoils away?   160

Both. Find some agreement,
For I'm in haste, and if you say no to me
I've other plans!

Ers. Bothwell's been our one weapon
Against the Queen, Lord Moray. I believe it's
    wisdom   165
To banish him, but remember the Queen's a
    queen
And it's dangerous to touch her. When he's
    gone
You'll have no cause against her.

Moray. Why, damn you all!

Mort. Let him go, and leave her the throne.

Moray. And even Morton.   171

Mort. Gad, I want no long wars.
I'm a married man. Send him on his way!
He leaves his earldom.   (*Crossing* R.

Both. Then this sword stays in the scab-
    bard   175
And lucky for all of you. Do you give your
    pledge?

Mait. I give my pledge, Lord Bothwell, for
    all here present.
We have not rebelled against the Queen, and
    will not
If you are banished.

Both. Then give me leave to speak   180
Alone with her.

Mait. With the Queen?

Both. Aye, for a moment.

Moray. No.

Mait. There's no harm in that, Moray.   185
Ers. We'll wait in the courtyard.
It's day and we have orders to give.
   Mort. Gordon and Douglas,
You won't be needed.   Intercept Lord Hunt-
   ley's men
While there's yet time.   190
   Mait. The Queen is here, Lord Bothwell,
And will be free to see you.
       (BOTHWELL *puts his helmet on bench* L.C.

The Lords go out R.   *After a moment's pause,*
QUEEN MARY *comes to the door* R., *a soldier*
on either side.   *The guards retire* R., *leaving*
MARY *and* BOTHWELL *alone*

Mary (*meeting* BOTHWELL C.).   Thank God
   you're safe!
   Both. And you are safe, my Queen, safe and
   set free
And may keep your kingdom.   195
   Mary. At what price?
   Both. I've made a bargain with them.   God
   knows whether they'll keep it.
But I think they will, for Maitland gave me his
   word,
And he's been honest.
   Mary. What bargain?   (BOTHWELL *faces*
front.)   You've sacrificed   200
Yourself for this.   What have you offered?
   Both. Nothing
To weigh against what you'll keep.   I've given
   my earldom —
That's a trifle to what we save.
   Mary. You shall have it back,   205
And more to put with it.
   Both. No.   I've accepted exile.
I'm to leave the kingdom.
   Mary. Why, then, I'm exiled too.
I'm your wife and I love you, Bothwell.   210
   Both. The bargain's made.
You may keep your crown without me but not
   with me.
Do you abdicate your throne?   What's left?
              (*Sits on bench* L.C.
Mary (*crossing* L. *above bench*).   Call in
The men of your guard, cut our way through
   and ride!   215
They'll never head us!   (*Sits* L. *of* BOTHWELL

on bench, facing up stage.)   We can rouse
   the north,
Ask help from France and England, return with
   an army
They dare not meet!
   Both. You'd raise no army, Marie.
You forget what a drag I am on you.   The
   north   220
Is sullen as the south toward you and me.
What's left we must do apart.
   Mary. What if we lost?
At the worst we'd have each other.
   Both. And do you vision the end of that?   225
A woman who was a queen, a man who was
The earl, her husband, but fugitives, put to it
To ask for food and lodging, enemies
On every road; they weary, heartsick, turning
At last on each other with reproaches, she say-
   ing: 230
I was a queen, would be one now but for you;
And he: I have lost my earldom.
   Mary. I betrayed you once
And betrayed my love, but I learned by that; I
   swear
Though it cost my kingdom, not again!   235
   Both. If you wish
To thrive, break that oath, betray me, betray
   your love,
Give me up forever — for you know as I know
We lose together.   God knows what we'll ever
   win
Apart.   240
   Mary. Nothing.   Oh, Bothwell, the earth
   goes empty!
What worse could happen than parting?
   Both. Can I stay?   (*Rises; goes up* C.
This once for the last time I can save you from
   yourself,
And me.   There's something wills it.   I go
   alone.   245
This is your kingdom.   Rule it.
   Mary. We must say good-bye?
   Both. Aye, girl, we've spent what time we
   had,
And I know not when I'll see you.   Let's have
   no pretense
Unworthy of us.   It's likely we'll not meet
   again   250
On this same star.

Mary. God help me and all women
Here in this world, and all men. Fair fall all
    chances
The heart can long for — and let all women and
    men
Drink deep while they can their happiness. It
    goes fast   255
And never comes again. (*Rises; goes to* BOTH-
    WELL.) Mine goes with you,
Youth, and the fund of dreams, and to lie a
    while
Trusted, in arms you trust. We're alone, alone,
Alone — even while we lie there we're alone,
For it's false. It will end. Each one dies
    alone.   260
    Both. I'll come
If I can. We've loved well, lass, could love
    better.
We've had but the broken fragment of a year,
And whenever I've touched you, something
    that broods above us
Has made that touch disaster. This is not my
    choice.   265
Lest I bring you utter ruin we must wait,
Wait better times and luck. I'll come again
If I can.
    Mary. Yes, if you can. Aye, among all tides
And driftings of air and water it may be   270
Some dust that once was mine will touch again
Dust that was yours. I'll not bear it! Oh,
    God, I'll not bear it!
Take me with you! Let us be slaves and pick
Our keep from kitchen middens [1] and leavings!
    Let us
Quarrel over clouts and fragments, but not
    apart ——   275
Bothwell, that much we could have!
    Both. Is there refuge in this world for you
And me together? Go far as we could, is there
    one
Turfed roof where we'd not be reminded of
    good days
And end in bitterness? Face these lords like
    a queen   280
And rule like a queen. I'd help you if I could
But I'm no help. You must meet them
    now.
    Mary. Yes. I'll meet them.

[1] Refuse.

But you must not surrender,
They'll serve you as they served Darnley.   285
    Both. I'll not surrender.
I'll see to my own banishment, find my guard,
Force my way out, and go.
    Mary. Can you break through? They're
    watching.
    Both. It's a chance.   290
        (*Picks up helmet and crosses to door* L.
Huntley! Huntley!
    Hunt. (*outside* L.). I'm here.
    Both. We ride at once
For Stirling. Be ready for a fight.
    Hunt. We're ready.   295
    Both. I must take my moment.
    Mary. I know.
    Both. (*crossing to* MARY C.). Good-bye,
    sweet, but if they wrong you — if you
    ever need me,
Look for me back.
        (*He kisses her, and goes out* L.
    Mary. Good-bye. To our two worlds.   300

There is a cry beyond the guard-room: "Both-
    well, it's Bothwell!" The alarm is taken up
    by the men at the gate, who call: "On guard,
    there! Pistol him! Mount and after him!
    Ride, you devils! On guard! Drop the
    portcullis! He's gone!" There is a sound of
    running feet from the gate to the other side of
    the stage. MARY *stands facing the guard-*
    room door L. GORDON *and* DOUGLAS *run*
    in R.

    Doug. Through the guard-room!
    Gord. He'll be over the wall —
    Doug. (*crossing up* L. *to* MARY). Out of the
    way, madame ——
    Gord. Nay, it's the Queen —
    Doug. Will you let us pass?   305
    Mary. I guard this door, Lord Douglas.
You'll go the long way round!
    Gord. Your pardon, Your Majesty.
        (*He bows.* BEATON *appears on the*
        stairway L. MORTON, MORAY *and*
        MAITLAND *enter* R.
    Mort. This was hardly well done, Your
    Majesty.
    Mary. Take care whom you question, sir.

Moray. You've sent Bothwell off!   311
That was your ruse!
Mary. Lord Bothwell will leave Scotland.
That was what you wanted.

Enter ERSKINE R.

Moray. He's gone?   315
Ers. (R.C.). Clean away!
Mait. (C.). Madame, there was some under-
standing
You two would remain here.
Mary. None that I know of.
Mort. Eh, God, he'll wish he had.   320

KNOX *appears in the archway* R.

Mary. Remove that man from my presence!
Is every stranger
Free to enter my courts?
Knox (*crossing to* R.C.). Though you be a
queen
And have faith in gods and idols, yet in this day
It will not staunch nor avail! Bid the sea re-
move   325
From the castle front, and gnaw it no more, as
soon
Will it obey thee. Pluck down the whore!
Pluck her down,
This contamination of men!
Mary. Maitland, if there's to be counsel
here, send out
This preacher and his ravings!   330
Mait. He may stay, for me.
Moray. Madame, collect what necessities
you require.
You will change your residence.
Mary. That is at my will, I think.
Mort. Do you think so?   335
Mait. You are to be lodged
In Holyroodhouse for the time.
Mary. I am to be lodged —
And your faith? You pledged your faith and
word, — all of you —
To leave my power untouched, leave me my
throne   340
If Bothwell and I were parted.
Mait. We'll keep it
When Lord Bothwell's surrendered to us.

Mary. Go out and take him!
Take him if you can! But for your queen,
I warn you, never since there were kings and
queens   346
In Scotland, has a liegeman laid his hand
On my line without regret!
Mort. We'll take care of that.
Mary. My lords, if I go with you, expect no
pardon,   350
No clemency: I have friends, this farce will
end.
Once more, then, leave me in peace.
I have used you royally. Use me so.
Mait. What you need,
Gather it quickly.   355
Mary. This is betrayal at once
Of your word and sovereign.
Mort. We know that.   (*A pause.*)
Mary. I need nothing.
I am a prisoner, Beaton. Come after me   360
To Holyroodhouse. I may have my own rooms
there, perhaps?
Mait. Yes, madame.
Mary. You show great courtesy, for a liar
and traitor.
You lied to us, a black and level lie!
Blackest and craftiest! It was you we believed.
Moray. Aye, sister. It was *that* we counted
on.   366
Mary. Aye, brother.
(MARY *turns from* MAITLAND *to*
MORAY, *then walks to the archway
and goes out* R.

Curtain

ACT III

SCENE: *A room in Carlisle Castle, in England.*[1]
*There are two windows at the right, both
barred, a window at the center rear and the
hall-door, at the left. It is a prison room,
but furnished scantily now for the Queen's
habitation. It is evening, but still light.*
MARY *sits at one of the windows* R., *leaning her
head against the bars.* BEATON *is leaning*

[1] Mary, Queen of Scots, in May, 1568, fled with a
small retinue to Carlisle, the principal town in Cumberland, the northwesternmost county of England.

over a table, R.C., *where* FLEMING *has un-rolled a map.*

Flem. We came this way, through Cocker-mouth,[1] and then took hired horses.

Beat. If I had a thousand maps I couldna tell you how I came. Jamie's acquent wi' the drovers and all the back ways. Seton and   5 Livingstone, poor things, they're pining away back in Edinburgh Town.

Flem. We might be as well off in Edinburgh ourselves, as it turns out. We'd looked for-ward to England for a free country and   10 strained toward it till our shoulders ached, trying to help the boat through the water. And here we are, and there's bars on the win-dows.

Beat. But whose prisoners are we,   15 Fleming?

Flem. I would I knew. It's been a month now, and all I can tell you is we're prisoners, for we cannot leave.

Beat. There's some mistake, Fleming.   20

Flem. Aye, if it was a mistake, like, would it last a month? It's heartbreaking to escape one jailer and walk into the arms of another.

Mary. When does the guard change, Flem-ing?   25

Flem. At ten, madame.

Mary. You're certain Jamie will come?

Beat. Unless he's taken or dead, Your Majesty. He's true as one can have in a lad.

Mary. But they may unmask him.   30

Beat. It's true they may.

Flem. Ye've more friends than a few in this castle, madame. They'd let us know if sum-mat went wrong.

Mary. What friends?   35

Flem. The two guards that go on for evening watch.

Mary. I fear they can't help much.

Flem. They can always bring us news.

Beat. And you've more friends than   40 that, Your Majesty. Here and everywhere. As I came through the back roads I heard talk of you everywhere. I think they love their queen better now than before, now that she's shut away unjustly.   45

---

[1] A town in Cumberland to the southwest of Carlisle.

Mary. Do you think so?

Beat. From what I heard I'd say the lords had worked their own ruin when they first be-trayed you. If they could hear the buzzing against them they'd sleep badly these   50 nights. And who rules Scotland now? Moray has no right to it, and nobody can give him the right save your own self.

Mary. Aye, that's so. He'll come begging yet.   55

Beat. And for what he'll never have.

Mary. They've taken my son from me, though. If I have friends I would they'd hurry. (*She turns toward the* C. *window.*) God knows what Elizabeth means.   60

Flem. You'll hear from Bothwell tonight, madame, or hear of him. I'm certain of it.

Watchman (*calls outside* L.). Ten o' the clock, and all well. All well.

Beat. Ten o'clock and still light.   65

Flem. The days grow longer and longer.

Mary. They've grown so long that each is the whole time between a birth and a death — and yet they go so fast, too, that I catch at them with my hands. So fast that I watch   70 the evening light jealously, like a last candle burning. This is life, too, Fleming, here in this prison, and it goes from us quite as much as though we were free. We shall never see these same days again.   75

Flem. And little will I want to.

Mary. But suppose you were to spend all your life in prisons? Might not one grow to love even prison days — as better than none?

Beat. We shall have better, though.   80 These are the worst we shall have, and I think the last of them. (*There is a rasping at the door* L.) You hear? — the signal —
(*There is silence.*)

Flem. (*crossing to door* L. *and listening*). Nay, not yet.   (*Another pause.*)   85

Beat. (*crossing to door* L.). It's ten, and more.

Flem. If we must wait again, then we must wait. He'll come, at the latest, tomorrow.

Mary. But what could Elizabeth mean? What could she mean? Over and over she   90 writes she is my friend, I am her dear cousin, her sister sovereign, that she suffers when I suffer, that she would confine me on no pretext if it were not to secure me against my own enemies! Enemies! What enemies have 95 I in her kingdom? What right has she to imprison a sovereign who takes sanctuary in England?

Flem. Has anyone ever known Elizabeth's mind on any subject?   100

Mary. Writes, too, that she will come to see me, writes again to put it off, writes to say she cannot bear the week to pass without reassuring me of her good love.

Beat. And yet I believe if all else fails 105 Elizabeth will be found a friend and a good one at the end. If only for her own interest.

Mary. It may still be that she goes, in her own muddled and devious way, about the business of aiding me. It still may be.   110

(*There is a rasping at the door again.*

Beat. Yes?

(*The door opens a crack, a chain clanging.*

Jamie (*outside*). I may enter?

Beat. Aye, come in.

Jamie (*steps in* L., *closing the door. Down* L., *bonnet in hand*). Your Majesty!

Mary (L. *of table*). Good-evening, Ja- 115 mie.

Jamie. Ye'll forgive me. I was not sure I could jouk [1] in, for the Captain loitered about. However, the lad Mark keeps a lookout, and warns me if there's footsteps.   120

Beat. Was there a messenger through, Jamie?

Jamie. Aye, I'll be quick, for I must, though a man hates to be quick wi' ill news. There's been a messenger, true enough, coming 125 down wi' the drovers, as we cam' — and his tale is there was a battle at the Little Minch. Ma'am, it went badly for Bothwell, if the man says sooth, for he was defeated and taken.

Mary. Bothwell taken?   130

Jamie. Aye, madame. Aye, but there's some good, too. Kirkaldy of Grange [2] has come over to Your Majesty's side and makes his threats against Moray.

Mary. But Bothwell, Bothwell was 135 taken? How?

Jamie. That's the bare sum of it, madame.

[1] Duck.   [2] Sir William Kirkaldy (?-1573).

Just that he was prisoner to the lords. Only Kirkaldy has said Bothwell should be freed, and that he will see to it.   140

Mary. It's little comfort.

Jamie. Aye, so I feared. Though Kirkaldy was their best general, and they'll miss him.

Mary. I could have used him once.

Jamie. And now, if you'll pardon me, 145 I must go. I had little liking to come. It's sore bad manners to leave folk wi' heavy hearts ——

Mary (*sits* L. *of table*). Nay, run no risk — only come again if there's any tidings.   150

Jamie. Yes, Your Majesty, and I pray God they be better. (*There is a rap at the door.*) It's for me. Keep thee, and all here.

(*He opens the door and goes out* L., *closing it softly. The chain clanks. There is silence.*

Mary. It's this that drives one mad, Fleming, to know

That on one certain day, at a certain hour,

If I had but chosen well, he'd have stood beside me   156

In a land all mine and his. Choosing wrong, I bring him

To fight a long war for me, and lose, bow his shoulders

To a castle keep.[1]

Flem. They'll not hold him long.   160

Mary. Aye — aye, that's to remember! He's not a man to hold

Easily, no, nor hold at all. I've seen him

When they thought him trapped, and well caught. His face goes cold,

Stern, and morgue [2] under his morion.[3] While he lives

And I live, they'll not jail us two apart.   165

Nor keep our due from us. Aye, it's something to love,

Even late, even bitterly, where it's deserved. Kirkaldy

Throws his weight on our side. There'll be others too. Oh, Bothwell,

You've been my one hope! Bring me back to mind,

Now, as I bring you back!   170

(*Rises and goes* R. *The chains of the*

[1] Dungeon.   [2] Impassive.   [3] Vizorless helmet.

door are undone, and the door L.
opens. A GUARD *steps in*

Guard. Your Majesty,
Lord Ruthven desires to see you.
    Mary. Lord Ruthven's in Scotland.
    Guard. No, madame, he's here.
    Mary (R.). Why, I will see Lord Ruthven.
Yes, let him come in.   176

The door swings wider and RUTHVEN *enters* L.
He bows

Sir, there've been days,
Not so far back when I'd have shifted somehow
To do without your face, or any visage
Among a certain congeries of lords   180
Of which you're one. Perhaps I'm tamed a
    trace
Sitting mewed at my window, for I'd accept
Any visitor from Scotland, bailiffs and hang-
    men
Not excluded, I'm that lonely.
    Ruth. Madame,   185
You hold against me much that was not my
    own.
I'm of a party, and one must swim or go down
With those of his interest.
    Mary. Do you come now to see me
In your own person, then, or as representing
Those sharks you swam with last?   191
    Ruth. Why, Your Majesty,
It may be we're sharks. My mind's not made
    up. But I've come,
If you'll pardon me — and this is more truth, I
    think,   194
Than I'm supposed to say — because the lords
Who now hold Scotland had more hope
    you'd see me
Than any the others.
    Mary. That's frank.
    Ruth. And I lend myself
To the embassy because, as things drift at
    home,   200
We verge on the rocks there. You are still queen
    of Scotland,
Yet you don't rule, and can't rule, being here,
A prisoner — and the upshot is we're not ruled.
There's anarchy in the air. It's necessary
That some approach be made between you and
    your brother   205

Before there's anarchy in the streets.
    Beat. We were saying
That he'd come begging.
    Mary. What does my brother ask —
This good brother of mine?   210
    Ruth. That goes beyond
My mission. To be frank still, I'm sent before
To ask whether you will see him.
    Mary. Let him ask my jailers
Whether I may be seen.   215
    Ruth. He has asked already, madame.
The request is granted.
    Mary. Lord Moray is with you?
    Ruth. He is waiting.
    Mary. Why, this is an honor. And others
    too, no doubt?   220
A shoal of them?
    Ruth. Madame, as you have supposed,
They are all here.
    Mary. It will please me vastly to view them,
If only to know from them who gave permis-
    sion   225
To see me. For I swear, I guess not so far
Whose prisoner I am, or who keeps my jail.
    I've moithered [1]
Over this a good deal.
    Ruth. I may call them?
    Mary. If you'll be so good.   230
        (RUTHVEN *bows and goes out past the*
        GUARD.
Is it you, sir, who chain my door
So assiduously at night?
    Guard. No, madame, the turnkey
Goes the rounds at twelve.
    Mary. Will you ask him, then,   235
To make a thought less jangling if he can?
We try to sleep, you see, and these chimes at
    midnight
Are not conducive to slumber.
    Guard. He shall be told;
I'm very sorry, Your Majesty.   240
    Mary. Thank you.

MORTON *and* MORAY *come in, and behind them*
    MAITLAND *and* DOUGLAS. RUTHVEN *re-*
    enters with THROGMORTON

Gentlemen,
I greet you. You are all here, I see, the whole
   [1] Pondered.

Bloodthirsty race.   But we lack John Knox.
     Now, surely,
John Knox should be with you.   245
     Moray (*up* L.). Have your jest, my sister.
     For us,
We're not here for jesting.
               (*The* TWO MARYS *are over* R. *behind
                 the* QUEEN.
     Mary. Oh, I'd have sworn you weren't.
You're no harbinger of merriment, my brother,
Nor of good fortune.   The corbies of the
     wood   250
Presage more of that.   And here's the Lord
     Throgmorton
Presses in among you!   It should be a good day
When I'm crossed by this constellation!
     Throg. (*crossing to* L. *of* MARY). We pray
     it will,
Your Majesty, and that the things may be
     ironed out clean   255
That have grieved us all.
     Mary. Oh, do you know of grief,
You who take your meals in your own wide
     halls
And walk in the rainy air?   I had thought that
     grieving
Was something found behind bars.   260
     Mait. This has lasted too long,
This imprisonment, Your Majesty, and was
     never
To any purpose.   We come to offer you
Release, and speedily.
     Mary. The diplomat always, Maitland. 265
Always the secret thought glancing behind
The quick-silver tongue.   You come to ask for
     much
And give little for it, as ever.
     Moray (*crossing a little to* MARY). We come
     to ask
For what we have.   270
     Mary. There, now it's brutally said,
In my brother's plain Scotch way, spoken
     plainly out of
His plain Scotch face.   He comes to ask, he
     says,
For what he has, and he makes no doubt he'll
     get it.
What is it you have, dear brother, and if you
     have it,   275

Why ask for it?
     Mait. Will Your Majesty give me leave
To rehearse a brief history that may weary you
Since you know it?
     Mary. It will weary me, but go on.   280
     Mait. Forgive me: Your Majesty broke from
     prison in Scotland
And fled to England.   This action was tanta-
     mount
To abandoning your throne.
     Mary. Indeed it was not.
I came here for aid against you.   285
     Mait. We will pass that point.
     Mary. Do.   There is nothing gives me more
     pleasure, Lord Maitland,
Than passing a point.
     Mait. Then I am delighted to render
Your Majesty pleasure.   Your wit is sharper
     than mine.   290
But to proceed: You were taken prisoner in
     England ——
     Mary. By whom, Lord Maitland — will you
     tell me that?
Who holds me here?
     Mait. That I'm not free to answer.
It remains that you're a prisoner, and that your
     realm   295
Is governed only by makeshift.   Your son, the
     Prince James ——
     Mary. Aye, what of him?   My lords, I beg
     of you,
Whatever you must do, or think you must do,
To secure yourselves, he's but a babe, remem-
     ber.
I can stand up and fight you for myself,   300
But use my child more kindly.
     Mait. The Prince James
Is well, and well cared for, and will be.   The
     succession
Depends on him.   We plan to make him king.
Your absence makes this necessary.   305
     Mary. My absence
Is not permanent, I hope.   I am queen of Scot-
     land
And have not abdicated, nor do I intend
To abdicate.
     Mort. (*taking a step forward*). Will you tell
     us what you think   310
To find, should you return?

Mary (*crossing a little* R.). If I return
As I intend, I shall not find you there,
Lord Morton, if you're wise. The country's
    fickle
For you, as it was for me. Now they've pushed
    their queen   315
Aside, they begin to wonder if they were not
    wrong,
And wonder too if they profit by the exchange,
And give you sidelong looks.
    Mait. (*crossing a little* R.). If it's still in your
    mind
That you might win your throne back, ponder
    on this: 320
The Lord of the Isles has given you up, the
    north
Is solidly with us, Bothwell has broken
    faith ——
    Mary. Aye?
    Mait. For the good of the kingdom, to secure
    your son
His right to the throne, we ask you tonight to
    sign   325
Your abdication, let us take it back with us.
    Mary. Yes,
But I catch you in two lies. Kirkaldy of
    Grange
Has come over to me; you have taken Bothwell
    prisoner,
But before he fights on your side you'll rot in
    the damp   330
Under Edinburgh Castle, and he'll see you do
    it!
    Mait. Madame,
You've been misinformed.
    Mary. I've been lied to and by you
Specifically! Let me rehearse for you   335
A history you may recall, you that stand be-
    fore me:
It was you killed Rizzio, and made capital of it
To throw discredit on me. It was you
Killed Darnley, and then threw the weight of
    that
On Bothwell, saying through John Knox that
    I lived   340
With my husband's murderer. It was you
    promised
To give me fealty if Bothwell and I were
    parted,

And then cast me into prison! I escaped,
As the truth will escape about you, and when
    it's known,
My people will drive you out. What you ask
    of me   345
I refuse it, finally! I will not abdicate,
Not to this off-scum that's boiled up around
My throne to dirty me! Not now and not ever!
    (*The lords are silent for a moment, and
        then* MORAY *nods an assent to* MAIT-
        LAND.
    Mait. Your Majesty, you asked me a mo-
    ment since
Who held you prisoner here. I cannot an-
    swer   350
Still, but say there's another and higher judge
Must pass on these charges of yours.
    Mary. Nay, I know that.
    Mait. Oh, an earthly judge, Your Majesty,
    and yet
High enough, I think. We wish you good
    night.   355
    Mary. Good night.
    (*The Lords go out* L. MARY *stands un-
        moving, watching the door. After a
        pause the* GUARD *pushes the door
        back and withdraws.*

ELIZABETH *appears in the doorway* L. MARY
    looks at her questioningly

    Mary. I have seen but a poor likeness, and
    yet I believe
This is Elizabeth.
    Eliz. I am Elizabeth.
May we be alone together?   360
    (*At a sign from* MARY *the* MAIDS *go out
        R. ELIZABETH *enters and the hall-
        door swings to behind her.*
    Mary (R.). I had hoped to see you.
When last you wrote, you were not sure.
    Eliz. (L.C.). If I've come
So doubtfully and tardigrade, my dear,
And break thus in upon you, it's not for lack
Of thinking of you. Rather because I've
    thought   366
Too long, perhaps, and carefully. Then at last
It seemed if I saw you near, and we talked as
    sisters

Over these poor realms of ours, some light
    might break
That we'd never see apart.   370
   Mary. Have I been so much
A problem?
    Eliz. Have you not? When the winds blow
    down
The houses, and there's a running and arming
    of men,
And a great cry of praise and blame, and the
    center   375
Of all this storm's a queen, she beautiful —
As I see you are ——
   Mary. Nay ——
   Eliz. Aye, with the Stuart mouth
And the high forehead and French ways and
    thoughts ——   380
Well, we must look to it. — Not since that
    Helen
We read of in dead Troy, has a woman's face
Stirred such a confluence of air and waters
To beat against the bastions. I'd thought you
    taller (*takes a step* R.),
But truly, since that Helen, I think there's
    been   385
No queen so fair to look on.
   Mary. You flatter me.
   Eliz. It's more like envy. You see this line
Drawn down between my brows? No wash or
    ointments
Nor wearing of straight plasters in the night
Will take that line away. Yet I'm not much
    older   391
Than you, and had looks, too, once.
   Mary. I had wished myself
For a more regal beauty such as yours,
More fitting for a queen.   395
   Eliz. Were there not two verses
In a play I remember:
"Brightness falls from the air;
   Queens have died young and fair" —?
They must die young if they'd die fair, my
    cousin.   400
Brightness falls from them but not from you
    yet, believe me,
It's envy, not flattery.
   Mary. Can it be — as I've hoped —
Can it be that you come to me as a friend —
Wishing me well?   405

   Eliz. Would you have me an enemy?
   Mary. I have plenty to choose among as
    enemies —
And sometimes, as your word reached out to me
Through embassies, entangled with men's
    tongues,
It has seemed you judged me harshly, even
    denying   410
My right to a place beside you. But now you
    are here,
And a woman like myself, fearing as I do,
With the little dark fears of a woman, the creep-
    ing of age
On a young face, I see truer — I think I see
    truer,
And that this may be someone to whom I can
    reach a hand   415
And feel a clasp, and trust it. A woman's hand,
Stronger than mine in this hour, willing to help.
If that were so ——
   Eliz. Aye?
   Mary. Oh, if that were so,   420
I have great power to love! Let them buzz
    forever
Between us, these men with messages and lies,
You'll find me still there, and smiling, and
    open-hearted,
Unchanging while the cusped [1] hills wear down!
   Eliz. (*smiling*). Nay, pledge   425
Not too much, my dear, for in these uncertain
    times
It's slippery going for all of us. I, who seem
    now
So firm in my footing, well I know one misstep
Could make me a most unchancy friend. If
    you'd keep
Your place on this rolling ball, let the moun-
    tains slide   430
And slip to the valleys. Put no hand to them
Or they'll pull you after.
   Mary. But does this mean you can lend
No hand to me, or I'll pull you down?
   Eliz. I say it   435
Recalling how I came to my throne as you did,
Some five or six years before, beset as you were
With angry factions — and came there young,
    loving truth,
As you did. This was many centuries since,

   [1] Peaked.

Or seems so to me, I'm so old by now   440
In shuffling tricks and the huckstering of souls
For lands and pensions. I learned to play it
    young,
Must learn it or die. — It's thus if you would
    rule;
Give up good faith, the word that goes with
    the heart,
The heart that clings where it loves. Give
    these up, and love   445
Where your interest lies, and should your in-
    terest change
Let your love follow it quickly. This is
    queen's porridge,
And however little stomach she has for it
A queen must eat it.
    Mary. I, too, Elizabeth,   450
Have read my Machiavelli.[1] His is a text-
    book
Much studied in the French court. Are you
    serious
To rede [2] me this lesson?
    Eliz. You have too loving a heart,
I fear, and too bright a face to be a queen. 455
    Mary. That's not what's charged against me.
    When I've lost
So far, it's been because my people believed
I was more crafty than I am. I've been
Traduced as a murderess and adulteress
And nothing I could have said, and nothing
    done   460
Would have warded the blow. What I seek
    now is only
My freedom, so that I may return and prove
In open court, and before my witnesses,
That I am guiltless. You are the queen of
    England,
And I am held prisoner in England. Why am I
    held,   465
And who is it holds me?
    Eliz. It was to my interest, child,
To protect you, lest violence be offered to a
    princess

[1] Niccolo di Bernardo Machiavelli (1469–1527), a noted statesman of Florence, Italy, whose book on statecraft and politics, *The Prince*, was widely read throughout Europe during the sixteenth and seventeenth centuries.
    [2] Counsel.

And set a precedent. Is there anyone in Eng-
    land
Who could hold you against my will?   470
    Mary. Then I ask as a sovereign,
Speaking to you as an equal, that I be allowed
To go, and fight my own battles.
    Eliz. It would be madness.
    Mary. May I not judge of that?   475
    Eliz. See, here is our love!
    Mary. If you wish my love and good-will you
    shall have it freely
When I am free.
    Eliz. You will never govern, Mary. If I let
    you go
There will be long broils again in Scotland,
    dangers,   48c
And ripe ones, to my peace at home. To be
    fair
To my own people, this must not be.
    Mary. Now speak once
What your will is, and what behind it! You
    wish me here,
You wish me in prison — have we come to
    that?   485
    Eliz. It's safer.
    Mary. Who do you wish to rule in Scotland,
If not my Stuart line?
    Eliz. Have I said, my dear,
That I'd bar the Stuarts from Scotland, or bar
    your reign   490
If you were there, and reigned there? I say
    only
You went the left way about it, and since it's so
And has fallen out so, it were better for both
    our kingdoms
If you remained my guest.
    Mary. For how long?   495
    Eliz. Until
The world is quieter.
    Mary. And who will rule in my place?
    Eliz. Why, who rules now? Your brother.
    Mary. He rules by stealth!   500
    Eliz. But all this could be arranged,
Or so I'm told, if your son were to be crowned
    king,
And Moray made regent.
    Mary. My son in Moray's hands —
Moray in power ——   505
    Eliz. Is there any other way?   (*A pause.*

Mary. Elizabeth — I have been here a long
    time
Already — it seems so. If it's your policy
To keep me — shut me up — I can argue no
    more —
No — I beg now. There's one I love in the
    north,   510
You know that — and my life's there, my
    throne's there, my name
To be defended — and I must lie here darkened
From news and from the sun — lie here impaled
On a brain's agony — wondering even some-
    times
If I were what they said me — a carrion thing
In my desires — can you understand this? —
    I speak it   516
Too brokenly to be understood, but I beg you
As you are a woman and I am — and our bright-
    ness falls
Soon enough at best — let me go, let me have
    my life
Once more — and my dear health of mind
    again —   520
For I rot away here in my mind — in what
I think of myself — some death-tinge falls over
    one
In prisons ——
    Eliz. It will grow worse, not better. I've
    known
Strong men shut up alone for years — it's not
Their hair turns white only; they sicken
    within   526
And scourge themselves. If you would think
    like a queen
This is no place for you. The brain taints here
Till all desires are alike. Be advised and sign
The abdication.   530
    Mary. Stay now a moment. I begin to
    glimpse
Behind this basilisk [1] mask of yours. It was
    this
You've wanted from the first.
    Eliz. This that I wanted?
    Mary. It was you sent Lord Throgmorton
    long ago   535
When first I'd have married Bothwell. All this
    while
Some evil's touched my life at every turn,

    [1] A fabulous serpent or dragon whose look was fatal.

To cripple what I'd do. And now — why,
    now —
Looking on you — I see it incarnate before
    me —
It was your hand that touched me. Reaching
    out   540
In little ways — here a word, there an action
    — this
Was what you wanted. I thought perhaps a
    star —
Wildly I thought it — perhaps a star might
    ride
Astray — or a crone that burned an image
    down
In wax — filling the air with curses on me   545
And slander; the murder of Rizzio, Moray in
    that
And you behind Moray — the murder of Darn-
    ley, Throgmorton
Behind that too, you with them — and that
    winged scandal
You threw at us when we were married. Proof
    I have none
But I've felt it — would know it anywhere —
    in your eyes —   550
There — before me.
    Eliz. What may become a queen
Is to rule her kingdom. Had you ruled yours
    I'd say
She has her ways, I mine. Live and let live
And a merry world for those who have it. But
    now   555
I must think this over — sadness has touched
    your brain.
I'm no witch to charm you, make no incanta-
    tions:
You came here by your own road.
    Mary. I see how I came.
Back, back, each step the wrong way, and each
    sign followed   560
As you'd have me go, till the skein picks up and
    we stand
Face to face here. It was you forced Bothwell
    from me —
You there, and always. Oh, I'm to blame in
    this, too!
I should have seen your hand!
    Eliz. It has not been my use   565
To speak much or spend my time ——

Mary. How could I have been
Mistaken in you for an instant?
    Eliz. You were not mistaken.
I am all women I must be. One's a young
      girl,   570
Young and harrowed as you are — one who
      could weep
To see you here — and one's a bitterness
At what I've lost and can never have, and one's
The basilisk you saw. This last stands guard
And I obey it. Lady, you came to Scot-
      land   575
A fixed and subtle enemy, more dangerous
To me than you've ever known. This could
      not be borne
And I set myself to cull [1] you out and down,
And down you are.
    Mary. When was I your enemy?   580
    Eliz. Your life was a threat to mine, your
      throne to my throne,
Your policy a threat.
    Mary. How? Why?
    Eliz. It was you
Or I. Do you know that? The one of us must
      win   585
And I must always win. Suppose one lad
With a knife in his hand, a Romish [2] lad who
      planted
That knife between my shoulders — my king-
      dom was yours.
It was too easy. You might not have wished
      it,
But you'd take it if it came.   590
    Mary. And you'd take my life
And love to avoid this threat?
    Eliz. Nay, keep your life
And your love too. The lords have brought a
      parchment
For you to sign. Sign it and live.   595
    Mary. If I sign it
Do I live where I please? Go free?
    Eliz. Nay, I would you might,
But you'd go to Bothwell, and between you
      two
You might be too much for Moray. You'll
      live with me   600
In London. There are other loves, my dear.

---

    [1] Pluck.   [2] Roman Catholic.

You'll find amusement there in the court. I
      assure you
It's better than a cell.
    Mary. And if I will not sign
This abdication?   605
    Eliz. You've tasted prison. **Try**
A diet of it.
    Mary. And so I will.
    Eliz. I can wait.
    Mary. And I can wait. I can wait better
      than you.   610
Bothwell will fight free again. Kirkaldy
Will fight beside him, and others will spring up
From these dragon's teeth you've sown. Each
      week that passes
I'll be stronger, and Moray weaker.
    Eliz. And do you fancy   615
They'll rescue you from an English prison?
      Why,
Let them try it.
    Mary. Even that they may do. I wait for
      Bothwell —
And wait for him here.
    Eliz. Where you will wait, bear in mind,
Is for me to say. Give up Bothwell, give up
      your throne   621
If you'd have a life worth living.
    Mary. I will not.
    Eliz. I can wait.
    Mary. And will not because you play to lose.
      This trespass   625
Against God's right will be known. The na-
      tions will know it,
Mine and yours. They will see you as I see you
And pull you down.
    Eliz. Child, child, I've studied this gambit [1]
Before I play it. I will send each year   630
This paper to you. Not signing, you will step
From one cell to another, step lower always,
Till you reach the last, forgotten, forgotten of
      men,
Forgotten among causes, a wraith that cries
To fallen gods in another generation   635
That's lost your name. Wait then for Both-
      well's rescue.
It will never come.
    Mary. I may never see him?

---

    [1] See note to Act I, Sc. 3, l. 514.

Eliz. Never.
It would not be wise.   640
   Mary (*sitting* R. *of table*). And suppose indeed you won
Within our lifetime; still, looking down from
   the heavens
And up from men around us, God's spies that
   watch
The fall of the great and little, they will find
   you out ——
I will wait for that, wait longer than a life,   645
Till men and the times unscroll you, study the
   tricks
You play, and laugh, as I shall laugh, being
   known
Your better, haunted by your demon, driven
To death or exile by you, unjustly. Why,
When all's done, it's my name I care for, my
   name and heart,   650
To keep them clean. (*Rising*) Win now, take
   your triumph now,
For I'll win men's hearts in the end — though
   the sifting takes
This hundred years — or a thousand.
   Eliz. Child, child, are you gulled   654
By what men write in histories, this or
   that,
And never true? I am careful of my name
As you are, for this day and longer. It's not
   what happens
That matters, no, not even what happens that's
   true,
But what men believe to have happened. They
   will believe
The worst of you, the best of me, and that   660
Will be true of you and me. I have seen to
   this.
What will be said about us in after-years
By men to come, I control that, being who I
   am.
It will be said of me that I governed well,
And wisely, but of you, cousin, that your
   life,   665
Shot through with ill-loves, battened on lechery, made you
An ensign of evil, that men tore down and
   trampled.
Shall I call for the lords' parchment?
   Mary. This will be said — ?

But who will say it? It's a lie — will be known
   as a lie!   670
   Eliz. You lived with Bothwell before Darnley died,
You and Bothwell murdered Darnley.
   Mary. And that's a lie!
   Eliz. Your letters, my dear. Your letters
   to Bothwell prove it.
We have those letters.   675
   Mary. Then they're forged and false!
For I never wrote them!
   Eliz. It may be they were forged.
But will that matter, Mary, if they're believed?
All history is forged.   680
   Mary. You would do this?
   Eliz. It is already done.
   Mary. And still I win.
A demon has no children, and you have none,
Will have none, can have none, perhaps. This
   crooked track   685
You've drawn me on, cover it, let it not be believed
That a woman was a fiend. Yes, cover it deep,
And heap my infamy over it, lest men peer
And catch sight of you as you were and are.
   In myself
I know you to be an eater of dust. Leave me
   here   690
And set me lower thus year by year, as you
   promise,
Till the last is an oubliette,[1] and my name inscribed
On the four winds. Still, still I win! I have
   been
A woman, and I have loved as a woman loves,
Lost as a woman loses. I have borne a son,
And he will rule Scotland — and England.
   You have no heir!   696
A devil has no children.
   Eliz. By God, you shall suffer
For this, but slowly.
   Mary. And that I can do. A woman   700
Can do that. Come, turn the key. I have a hell
For you in my mind, where you will burn and
   feel it,
Live where you like, and softly.
   Eliz. Once more I ask you,

---

[1] A dungeon with an opening only at the top.

And patiently.   Give up your throne.   705
   Mary. No, devil.
My pride is stronger than yours, and my heart
   beats blood
Such as yours has never known.   And in this
   dungeon,
I win here, alone.
   Eliz. (*turning*). Good-night, then.   710
   Mary. Aye, good-night.
      (ELIZABETH *goes to the* L. *door.   She
      goes out slowly.   As the door begins
      to close upon her* MARY *calls:*
Beaton!

Eliz. (*turning*). You will not see your maids
   again,
I think.   It's said they bring you news from
   the north.
   Mary. I thank you for all kindness.   715
      (ELIZABETH *goes out.   MARY stands
      for a moment in thought, then walks
      to the wall and lays her hand against
      the stone, pushing outward.   The
      stone is cold, and she shudders.   Go-
      ing to the window, she sits again in
      her old place and looks out into the
      darkness.*

Curtain

MNOPQR—R—73210/698765

Notes on the Play Texts

The present editor has supplied the footnotes to all the plays except *The Pot of Gold*, where he is largely indebted to the translator.

Prometheus Bound, Electra, Alcestis: The present editor has composed and inserted the "Argument" before each play, and has emended a few stage directions.

The Birds: A few stage directions have been emended.

The Second Shepherds' Play: This modernized version is by C. G. Child. A few stage directions, however, have been emended.

Nice Wanton: A few phrases, as well as the spelling, capitalization, and punctuation, have been modernized.

Edward II, The Shoemakers' Holiday, The Maid's Tragedy, Epicoene, The Man of Mode: The spelling, capitalization, and punctuation have been modernized, and some scene descriptions and stage directions have been supplied or revised. The text of *Edward II* is based upon the editions of W. D. Briggs (1914), H. B. Charlton and R. D. Waller (1933), and Hazelton Spencer (1933); *The Shoemakers' Holiday*, upon the editions of A. F. Lange (1914), and Hazelton Spencer (1933); *The Maid's Tragedy*, upon the editions of P. A. Daniel (the Variorum text, 1904), and Hazelton Spencer (1933); *Epicoene*, upon the editions of Ben Jonson (folio, 1616), and Aurelia Henry (1906); *The Man of Mode*, upon the editions of H. F. Brett-Smith (1927), and G. H. Nettleton and A. E. Case (1939).

The School for Scandal: The text is based upon the edition of John Murray (1821) as re-edited by H. H. Webster (1917), but a few revisions of phrasing and punctuation have been made on the authority of the famous Crewe Manuscript as printed by G. H. Nettleton and A. E. Case (1939).

Maria Magdalena, The Sea-Gull: A few words and phrases have been altered to secure a more literal translation of the original texts.

The Admirable Crichton: The text is that of the 1918 or first New York edition, which differs from, and, in the present editor's opinion, is superior to, both the 1914 or first London edition and the 1928 edition (London and New York). These two latter also differ from each other.

The Silver Box: The text is a collation of the first or 1909 edition, and of the Manaton (London, 1923) edition, which corrects as well as revises the former at a few points.

Mary of Scotland: The text is based largely on the 1934 edition, except for the stage directions, which follow the 1937 acting edition.

Index